P9-DDC-491

THE CONCISE CONCORDANCE

TO THE NEW REVISED STANDARD VERSION

THE CONCISE CONCORDANCE

TO THE

NEW REVISED STANDARD VERSION

JOHN R. KOHLENBERGER III, EDITOR

New York   Oxford

Oxford University Press

Oxford University Press

Oxford New York Toronto
Delhi Bombay Calcutta Madras Karachi
Kuala Lumpur Singapore Hong Kong Tokyo
Nairobi Dar es Salaam Cape Town
Melbourne Auckland Madrid

and associated companies in

Berlin Ibadan

Copyright © 1993 by Oxford University Press, Inc.

Published by Oxford University Press, Inc.
200 Madison Avenue, New York, New York, 10016

Oxford is a registered trademark of Oxford University Press

All rights reserved. No part of this publication
may be reproduced, stored in a retrieval system, or transmitted,
in any form or by any means, electronic, mechanical,
photocopying, recording, or otherwise, without the prior
permission of Oxford University Press.

The Scripture quotations contained herein are from
the New Revised Standard Version Bible, copyright © 1989 by
the Division of Christian Education of the National Council of
the Churches of Christ in the United States of America,
and are used by permission. All rights reserved.

Printed in the United States of America

7 9 8 6

INTRODUCTION

A concordance is an index to a book. It is usually arranged in alphabetical order and shows the location of each word in the book. In addition, it often supplies several words of the context in which each word is found.

The Concise Concordance to the New Revised Standard Version (*CCNRSV*) is an selective concordance to the New Revised Standard Version. It covers all 84 books contained in the NRSV: the 66 (proto-)canonical books of the Old and New Testaments as well as 18 books received as apocryphal or deuterocanonical by the Roman Catholic and Eastern Orthodox Churches. However, it does not exhaustively index all 906,953 words of the NRSV. (For such an index see the author's *NRSV Concordance Unabridged* [Zondervan, 1991].) Rather, nearly 70,000 references to 7200 key words provide access to texts most significant to personal and professional Bible research.

FEATURES OF THE CONCISE CONCORDANCE TO THE NRSV

The *CCNRSV* indexes the Bible in three formats: (1) traditional concordance entries, (2) phrase indexes, and (3) capsule biographies.

CONCORDANCE ENTRIES

Below is a traditional concordance entry:

> **LOVE*** → BELOVED, BELOVED'S,
> LOVE-FEASTS, LOVE-SONG, LOVED,
> LOVER, LOVERS, LOVES, LOVING
>
> Ge 22: 2 your only son Isaac, whom you **l,**
>   24:12 steadfast **l** to my master Abraham.
>   24:14 have shown steadfast **l** to my master

Headings:

The heading consists of:

(1) the indexed word: **LOVE**;

(2) an asterisk (*) indicating that this word is indexed exhaustively;

(3) the list of related words following an arrow (→).

The NRSV contains a total of 906,953 words, with a vocabulary of 16,529 words. The *CCNRSV* indexes 7,173 words. 1,331 words are indexed exhaustively, including highly frequent but significant words like "grace," "love," and "salvation." Since contexts represent words spelled exactly as the entry headword, the key word is abbreviated and bold. If an indexed word occurs more than once in a context, it is abbreviated as many times as necessary within the context, as under the heading HOLY:

> Isa   6: 3 **"H, h, h** is the LORD of hosts;
> Rev 4: 8 **H, h, h,** the Lord God the Almighty

Related words point to other spellings of the headword (LOVED, LOVING) as well as cognate terms (BELOVED) and compounds (LOVE-FEASTS, LOVE-SONGS). Rather than listing all related words after each headword, the editor chose one indexed word to act as the "group heading." All related words are listed after the group heading, and each of the related word headings points back to the group heading. In the example above, LOVE serves as the group heading for nine related words.

Context Lines:

The context lines consist of:

(1) the book-chapter-verse reference;

(2) the context for the indexed word.

50,417 context lines represent 51,508 occurrences of the 7,173 headwords. Books of the Bible are abbreviated according to the table on page viii. As in the example above, the book abbreviation is listed only once in each entry. This allows for easier scanning, especially of longer articles. Context lines are listed in canonical order: Old Testament, New Testament, and Apocrypha.

Taken by themselves, context lines can and do misrepresent the teaching of Scripture by taking statements out of the larger context. "There is no God" is a context taken straight from Psalm 14:1. Of course the Bible does not teach this; it is what "Fools say in their hearts"! Similarly, a context for Leviticus 24:16 might read, "the LORD shall be put to death" while the text actually says, "One who blasphemes the name of the LORD shall be put to death."

Great care has been taken by the editor and programmer of the *CCNRSV* to create contexts that are informative and accurate. But the reader should always check word contexts by looking them up in the NRSV itself. "The Wicked Bible," a KJV edition of 1631, accidentally omitted the word "not" from the seventh commandment, for which the printers were fined 300 pounds sterling! Though there are no longer such fines for misleading contexts, the editor and publisher are still deeply concerned that the *CCNRSV* be used discerningly.

PHRASE-INDEX SUBHEADINGS

The *CCNRSV* also indexes 653 important phrases involving 280 key words, for example:

LOVE OF *GOD Ps 52:8; Lk 11:42; Jn 5:42; Ro 8:39; 2Co 13:13; 2Th 3:5; 1Jn 2:5; 5:3; Jude 1:21

LOVE ONE ANOTHER Jn 13:34, 34; 15:12, 17; Ro 12:10; 13:8; 1Th 4:9; 1Pe 1:22; 1Jn 3:11, 14, 23; 4:7, 11, 12; 2Jn 1:5

The key words were selected from the 828 words that occur more than 100 times in the NRSV. The key words were then analyzed in their contexts to determine important phrases and combinations in which they appear. These entries index more than 16,000 biblical texts.

CAPSULE BIOGRAPHIES

435 prominent personalities are given capsule biographies:

SIMON → =PETER, =SIMEON

1. See Peter.
2. Apostle, called the Zealot (Mt 10:4; Mk 3:18; Lk 6:15; Ac 1:13).
3. Samaritan sorcerer (Ac 8:9-24).

It is easier to represent and to locate key events in an individual's life in such an entry rather than by using context lines—especially in the entry on Jesus. As in the example above, different individuals of the same name are distinguished by separately numbered biographies. These entries index over 2,100 biblical texts.

SPECIAL SYMBOLS AND TYPOGRAPHY

When a person or place is known by more than one name in the biblical text, the cross-reference indicates this by using the equal sign (=):

SIMON → =PETER, =SIMEON

The equal sign does *not* mean that Peter is always the same individual as Simon, for there are twelve men named Simon in the NRSV.

Special typefaces. There are two headings apiece for GOD, LORD, and LORD'S. †LORD and †LORD'S represent the proper name of God, *Yahweh*, which is typeset in the NRSV as "Lᴏʀᴅ" and "Lᴏʀᴅ's." This distinguishes "Lᴏʀᴅ" from "Lord" and "lord," which are indexed under the heading *LORD, and "Lᴏʀᴅ's" from "Lord's" and "lord's," indexed under *LORD'S. In contexts where the Hebrew words for "Lord" (*Adonay*) and "Lᴏʀᴅ" (*Yahweh*) appear as a compound name, the NRSV translates Lord Gᴏᴅ. Therefore the heading †GOD is used for "Gᴏᴅ" and *GOD for "God" and "god."

Some words and verses are set in italic type in the NRSV. These include *Selah* and *Higgaion* throughout the Psalms and Habakkuk 3, the titles to the Psalms, and two added sections in Sirach, 26:19-27 and 51:12b. In addition to Gᴏᴅ and Lᴏʀᴅ, the NRSV uses small caps for words in Exodus 3:14; Daniel 5:25-28; and Sirach 18:30; 20:27; 23:7; 24:1; 30:1, 18; 44:1; 51:1. These typefaces are reflected in the context lines, as under the headings PIOUS and PRAYER:

Sir   26:23   *but a **p** wife is given to the man who*
Sir   51: 1   ᴘ ᴏꜰ ᴊᴇꜱᴜꜱ ꜱᴏɴ ᴏꜰ ꜱɪʀᴀᴄʜ

Double Brackets. Five passages of the New Testament are enclosed in double brackets (⟦ ⟧) to point out that most ancient authorities lack these verses. They are the traditional "longer ending" of Mark (16:9-20), the "shorter ending" of Mark (designated as 16:S in the *CCNRSV*), Luke 22:43-44; 23:34a; and John 7:53-8:11. All contexts from these verses are enclosed in single brackets to reflect the NRSV, as under the heading SALVATION:

Mk   16: S   [proclamation of eternal **s.**]

Books of One Chapter. Five canonical books have only one chapter: Obadiah, Philemon, 2 John, 3 John, and Jude. Therefore some reference books refer only to the verse number (e.g., Jude 1). In the *CCNRSV* all contexts from these books refer to chapter 1 in addition to the verse number (e.g., Jude 1:1).

Six deuterocanonical books have one chapter: The Letter of Jeremiah, The Prayer of Azariah, Susanna, Bel and the Dragon, The Prayer of Manasseh, and Psalm 151.

The Prayer of Azariah and The Prayer of Manasseh are both indexed by chapter 1 in the *CCNRSV*. The Letter of Jeremiah is also chapter 6 of Baruch. The *CCNRSV* reflects the NRSV by using 6 as its chapter number. Susanna is chapter 13 of the Greek version of Daniel, but its chapter number is 1 in the NRSV and therefore also in the *CCNRSV*. Bel and the Dragon is chapter 14 of the Greek version of Daniel, but its chapter number is 1 in the NRSV and therefore also in the *CCNRSV*. Psalm 151 is not a canonical Psalm, so its book abbreviation differs from that of the Psalms (Pm versus Ps), while 151 is used as its chapter number.

Prologues, Superscripts, and Titles. Of the canonical Psalms, 116 have superscripts or titles that are not numbered as verses in the NRSV, as does Psalm 151. The letter "T" is used as the verse designation for these titles.

The book of Sirach (or Ecclesiasticus) has a three-paragraph prologue preceding chapter 1. The abbreviation "Pr" is used as the "chapter" number of the prologue; the numbers 1, 2, and 3 are used as "verse" designations for the three paragraphs.

The Shorter Ending of Mark. The NRSV is one of the few translations to include the "shorter ending" of Mark. However, it places this ending in the text between Mark 16:8 and the traditional "longer ending," verses 9 to 20. Rather than index this passage as part of verse 8, the letter "S" is used as the verse designation for the "shorter ending."

TABLE OF ABBREVIATIONS

CANONICAL BOOKS

1Ch . . . . .1 Chronicles	Ecc . . . . .Ecclesiastes	La . . . . Lamentations
1Co . . . . 1 Corinthians	Eph . . . . Ephesians	Lev . . . . Leviticus
1Jn . . . . .1 John	Est . . . . Esther	Lk . . . . .Luke
1Ki . . . . .1 Kings	Ex . . . . Exodus	Mal . . . . Malachi
1Pe . . . . 1 Peter	Eze . . . . Ezekiel	Mic . . . . .Micah
1Sa . . . . 1 Samuel	Ezr . . . . .Ezra	Mk . . . . Mark
1Th . . . . 1 Thessalonians	Gal . . . . .Galatians	Mt . . . . .Matthew
1Ti . . . . 1 Timothy	Ge . . . . Genesis	Na . . . . .Nahum
2Ch . . . . .2 Chronicles	Hab . . . . Habakkuk	Ne . . . . Nehemiah
2Co . . . . 2 Corinthians	Hag . . . . Haggai	Nu . . . . Numbers
2Jn . . . . .2 John	Heb . . . . Hebrews	Ob . . . . Obadiah
2Ki . . . . .2 Kings	Hos . . . . Hosea	Phm . . . . Philemon
2Pe . . . . 2 Peter	Isa . . . . .Isaiah	Php . . . . .Philippians
2Sa . . . . 2 Samuel	Jas . . . . James	Pr . . . . .Proverbs
2Th . . . . 2 Thessalonians	Jdg . . . . .Judges	Ps . . . . Psalms
2Ti . . . . 2 Timothy	Jer . . . . Jeremiah	Rev . . . . Revelation
3Jn . . . . .3 John	Jn . . . . John	Ro . . . . Romans
Ac . . . . Acts	Jnh . . . . .Jonah	Ru . . . . .Ruth
Am . . . . Amos	Job . . . . .Job	SS . . . . Song of Songs
Col . . . . Colossians	Joel . . . . Joel	Tit . . . . .Titus
Da . . . . Daniel	Jos . . . . .Joshua	Zec . . . . .Zechariah
Dt . . . . .Deuteronomy	Jude . . . . .Jude	Zep . . . . Zephaniah

APOCRYPHA

1Es . . . . 1 Esdras	AdE . . . . .Additions to Esther	Man . . . . .Prayer of Manasseh
1Mc . . . . 1 Maccabees	Aza . . . . Prayer of Azariah	Pm . . . . Psalm 151
2Es . . . . 2 Esdras	Bar . . . . Baruch	Sir . . . . .Sirach
2Mc . . . . 2 Maccabees	Bel . . . . .Bel and the Dragon	Sus . . . . Susanna
3Mc . . . . 3 Maccabees	Jdt . . . . Judith	Tob . . . . Tobit
4Mc . . . . 4 Maccabees	LtJ . . . . .Letter of Jeremiah	Wis . . . . Wisdom

OTHER

S . . . . . . .Shorter Ending of Mark	T . . . . Psalm Titles	Pr: . . . . Sirach Prologue

THE CONCISE CONCORDANCE

TO THE NEW REVISED STANDARD VERSION

THE CONCISE CONCORDANCE

TO THE

NEW REVISED STANDARD VERSION

A

AARON

Genealogy of (Ex 6:16-20; Jos 21:4, 10; 1Ch 6:3-15).

Priesthood of (Ex 28:1; Nu 17; Heb 5:1-4; 7), vestments of (Ex 28; 39), consecration of (Ex 29), ordination of (Lev 8).

Spokesman for Moses (Ex 4:14-16, 27-31; 7:1-2). Supported Moses' hands in battle (Ex 17:8-13). Built golden calf (Ex 32; Dt 9:20). Spoke against Moses (Nu 12). Priesthood opposed (Nu 16); staff budded (Nu 17). Forbidden to enter the promised land (Nu 20:1-12). Death of (Nu 20:22-29; 33:38-39). Praise of (Sir 45:6-22).

AARON THE PRIEST Lev 7:34; 13:2; 21:21; Nu 3:6, 32; 4:16, 28, 33; 7:8; 16:37; 25:7, 11; 26:1, 64; 33:38; Jos 21:4, 13

DESCENDANT[S] OF AARON Lev 6:18; 21:21; Nu 16:40; Jos 21:4, 10, 13, 19; 1Ch 15:4; 23:28, 32; 24:1, 31; 2Ch 13:9, 10; 26:18; 29:21; 31:19; 35:14, 14; Ne 10:38; 12:47; Lk 1:5; 4Mc 7:12

SON OF AARON Nu 3:32; 4:16, 28, 33; 7:8; 16:37; 25:7, 11; 26:1; Jos 24:33; Jdg 20:28; 1Es 5:5; 8:2; 2Es 1:3

SONS OF AARON Lev 3:13; 6:14; 7:10, 33; 9:9; 16:1; 21:1; Nu 3:2, 3; 10:8; 1Ch 6:3, 50, 54, 57; 24:1; Tob 1:7; Sir 50:13, 16; 1Es 1:13, 14

ABADDON → =APOLLYON

Job 28:22 A and Death say, 'We have heard a
Ps 88:11 or your faithfulness in A?
Pr 15:11 and A lie open before the LORD,
27:20 Sheol and A are never satisfied,
Rev 9:11 his name in Hebrew is A,

ABANDON → ABANDONED

Nu 32:15 will again a them in the wilderness;
Dt 4:31 will neither a you nor destroy you;
Jos 10: 6 saying, "Do not a your servants;
1Ch 28: 9 forsake him, he will a you forever.
2Ch 15: 2 but if you a him, he will a you.
Ps 94:14 he will not a his heritage;
Mk 7: 8 You a the commandment of God
Ac 2:27 For you will not a my soul to Hades
Heb 10:35 Do not, therefore, a that confidence
Tob 4: 3 Honor your mother and do not a her
Sir 9:10 Do not a old friends, for new ones

ABANDONED → ABANDON

Dt 29:25 they a the covenant of the LORD,

32:15 He a God who made him,
Jdg 2:13 a the LORD, and worshiped Baal
2Ch 12: 5 You a me, so I have a you
Isa 54: 7 For a brief moment I a you,
Ac 2:31 'He was not a to Hades,
Rev 2: 4 you have a the love you had at first.
Sir 49: 4 for they a the law of the Most High;

ABATE → ABATED

Ge 8: 5 waters continued to a until the tenth

ABATED → ABATE

Nu 11: 2 prayed to the LORD, and the fire a.
Dt 34: 7 unimpaired and his vigor had not a.

ABBA*

Mk 14:36 "A, Father, for you all things are possible;
Ro 8:15 When we cry, "A! Father!"
Gal 4: 6 into our hearts, crying, "A! Father!"

ABDON

A judge of Israel (Jdg 12:13-15).

ABEDNEGO* → =AZARIAH

Deported to Babylon with Daniel (Da 1:1-6). Name changed from Azariah (Da 1:7). Refused defilement by food (Da 1:8-20). Refused idol worship (Da 3:1-12); saved from furnace (Da 3:13-30).

ABEL

Second son of Adam (Ge 4:2). Offered acceptable sacrifice (Ge 4:4; Heb 11:4; 12:24). Murdered by Cain (Ge 4:8; Mt 23:35; Lk 11:51; 1Jn 3:12).

ABHOR → ABHORRED, ABHORRENT, ABHORS

Lev 26:11 and I shall not a you.
Dt 7:26 You must utterly detest and a it,
23: 7 You shall not a any of the Edomites,
23: 7 You shall not a any of the Egyptians
Job 19:19 All my intimate friends a me,
Ps 119:163 a falsehood, but I love your law.
Am 5:10 they a the one who speaks the truth.
6: 8 I a the pride of Jacob and hate his
Mic 3: 9 who a justice and pervert all equity,
Ro 2:22 that a idols, do you rob temples?
2Es 16:50 so righteousness shall a iniquity,

ABHORRED → ABHOR

Lev 20:23 they did all these things, I a them.
Ps 106:40 his people, and he a his heritage;
Isa 49: 7 deeply despised, a by the nations,

ABHORRENT → ABHOR

Dt 14: 3 You shall not eat any a thing.
18: 9 not learn to imitate the a practices

ABHORS → ABHOR

Ps 5: 6 the LORD a the bloodthirsty and
Sir 17:26 and hate intensely what he a.

ABIATHAR

High priest in days of Saul and David (1Sa 22; 2Sa 15; 1Ki 1-2; Mk 2:26). Escaped Saul's slaughter of priests (1Sa 22:18-23). Supported David in Absalom's revolt (2Sa 15:24-29). Supported Adonijah (1Ki 1:7-42); deposed by Solomon (1Ki 2:22-35; cf. 1Sa 2:31-35).

ABIB*

The month of the Exodus and Passover (Ex 13:4; 23:15; 34:18; Dt 16:1).

ABIDE → ABIDES, ABODE

Ge 6: 3 "My spirit shall not a in mortals forever,
Ps 15: 1 O LORD, who may a in your tent?
37:27 and do good; so you shall a forever.
91: 1 a in the shadow of the Almighty,
Pr 2:21 For the upright will a in the land,
Jn 6:56 eat my flesh and drink my blood a
15: 4 A in me as I a in you.
15: 7 If you a in me, and my words a in
1Co 13:13 faith, hope, and love a, these three;
1Jn 2:28 And now, little children, a in him,
3:24 obey his commandments a in him,
4:16 and those who a in love a in God,
2Jn 1: 9 who does not a in the teaching
Wis 3: 9 the faithful will a with him in love,

ABIDES → ABIDE

Ps 26: 8 and the place where your glory a.
125: 1 cannot be moved, but a forever.
Hag 2: 5 My spirit a among you; do not fear.
Jn 15: 4 cannot bear fruit by itself unless it a
1Jn 3: 6 No one who a in him sins;
3:14 Whoever does not love a in death.

ABIGAIL

1. Sister of David (1Ch 2:16-17).
2. Wife of Nabal (1Sa 25:30); pled for his life with David (1Sa 25:14-35). Became David's wife after Nabal's death (1Sa 25:36-42); bore him Kileab (2Sa 3:3) also known as Daniel (1Ch 3:1).

ABIHU

Son of Aaron (Ex 6:23; 24:1, 9); killed for offering illicit fire (Lev 10; Nu 3:2-4; 1Ch 24:1-2).

ABIJAH → =ABIJAM

1. Second son of Samuel (1Ch 6:28); a corrupt judge (1Sa 8:1-5).
2. An Aaronic priest (1Ch 24:10; Lk 1:5).
3. Son of Jeroboam I of Israel; died as prophesied by Ahijah (1Ki 14:1-18).
4. Son of Rehoboam, also called Abijam; king

of Judah who fought Jeroboam I attempting to reunite the kingdom (1Ki 14:31-15:8; 2Ch 12:16-14:1; Mt 1:7).

ABIJAM → ABIJAH, 4.

ABILITY → ABLE
Ex 31: 3 filled him with divine spirit, with **a**,
Mt 25:15 to each according to his **a**.
Ac 2: 4 as the Spirit gave them **a**.
11:29 determined that according to their **a**,
Sir 29:20 Assist your neighbor to the best of your **a**,

ABIMELECH
1. King of Gerar who took Abraham's wife Sarah, believing her to be his sister (Ge 20). Later made a covenant with Abraham (Ge 21:22-33).
2. King of Gerar who took Isaac's wife Rebekah, believing her to be his sister (Ge 26:1-11). Later made a covenant with Isaac (Ge 26:12-31).
3. Son of Gideon (Jdg 8:31). Attempted to make himself king (Jdg 9).

ABIRAM
Sided with Dathan in rebellion against Moses and Aaron (Nu 16; 26:9; Dt 11:6; Sir 45:18).

ABISHAG*
Shunammite virgin; attendant of David in his old age (1Ki 1:1-15; 2:17-22).

ABISHAI
Son of Zeruiah, David's sister (1Sa 26:6; 1Ch 2:16). One of David's chief warriors (1Ch 11:15-21): against Edom (1Ch 18:12-13), Ammon (2Sa 10), Absalom (2Sa 18), Sheba (2Sa 20). Wanted to kill Saul (1Sa 26), killed Abner (2Sa 2:18-27; 3:22-39), wanted to kill Shimei (2Sa 16:5-13; 19:16-23).

ABLAZE
Dt 9:15 while the mountain was **a**;
Jas 3: 5 great a forest is set **a** by a small fire!
2Pe 3:12 heavens will be set **a** and dissolved,

ABLE → ABILITY, ENABLE, ENABLED, ENABLES
Ge 15: 5 if you are **a** to count them."
Ex 18:25 Moses chose **a** men from all Israel
Nu 1: 3 everyone in Israel **a** to go to war.
11:14 not **a** to carry all this people alone,
13:31 "We are not **a** to go up against this
14:16 the LORD was not **a** to bring this people into the land
Dt 7:24 no one will be **a** to stand against you
Jos 1: 5 No one shall be **a** to stand against
23: 9 no one has been **a** to withstand you
1Sa 17:33 not **a** to go against this Philistine
1Ki 3: 9 **a** to discern between good and evil;
1Ch 29:14 be **a** to make this freewill offering?
2Ch 2: 6 But who is **a** to build him a house,
25: 9 LORD is **a** to give you much more
32:15 nation or kingdom has been **a**
Pr 27: 4 who is **a** to stand before jealousy?
Isa 36:14 for he will not be **a** to deliver you.
Da 2:26 "Are you **a** to tell me the dream
3:17 God whom we serve is **a** to deliver
4:37 he is **a** to bring low those who walk
5:16 Now if you are **a** to read the writing
6:20 whom you faithfully serve been **a**
Hos 5:13 But he is not **a** to cure you or heal
Mt 9:28 "Do you believe that I am **a** to do
26:61 'I am **a** to destroy the temple of God
Mk 10:38 you **a** to drink the cup that I drink,
Lk 13:24 will try to enter and will not be **a**.
14:30 fellow began to build and was not **a**
21:15 none of your opponents will be **a**
Ac 5:39 you will not be **a** to overthrow them
15:10 our ancestors nor we have been **a**
Ro 4:21 that God was **a** to do what he had
8:39 will be **a** to separate us from the love of God
14: 4 the Lord is **a** to make them stand.

16:25 to God who is **a** to strengthen you
2Co 1: 4 be **a** to console those who are in any
5:12 be **a** to answer those who boast
9: 8 God is **a** to provide you with every
Eph 3:20 the power at work within us is **a**
6:11 **a** to stand against the wiles of the devil.
2Ti 1:12 he is **a** to guard until that day
2: 2 will be **a** to teach others as well.
3:15 sacred writings that are **a** to instruct
Heb 2:18 **a** to help those who are being tested.
4:12 it is **a** to judge the thoughts and
5: 2 is **a** to deal gently with the ignorant
7:25 he is **a** for all time to save
11:19 God is **a** even to raise someone from the dead—
Jas 3: 2 **a** to keep the whole body in check
4:12 who is **a** to save and to destroy.
2Pe 1:15 you may be **a** at any time to recall
Jude 1:24 who is **a** to keep you from falling,
Rev 5: 3 **a** to open the scroll or to look into it.
6:17 and who is **a** to stand?"
Jdt 11:18 of them will be **a** to withstand you.
1Mc 3:53 How will we be **a** to withstand them

ABNER
Cousin of Saul and commander of his army (1Sa 14:50; 17:55-57; 26). Made Ish-Bosheth king after Saul (2Sa 2:8-10), but later defected to David (2Sa 3:6-21). Killed Asahel (2Sa 2:18-32), for which he was killed by Joab and Abishai (2Sa 3:22-39).

ABODE → ABIDE
Ex 15:17 that you made your **a**, the sanctuary.
Ps 68:16 mount that God desired for his **a**,
Pr 3:33 but he blesses the **a** of the righteous.
Jer 31:23 bless you, O **a** of righteousness,

ABOLISH → ABOLISHED, ABOLISHES
Da 11:31 shall **a** the regular burnt offering
Hos 2:18 and I will **a** the bow, the sword,
Mt 5:17 think that I have come to **a** the law
5:17 I have come not to **a** but to fulfill.

ABOLISHED* → ABOLISH
La 2: 6 the LORD has **a** in Zion festival
Eph 2:15 **a** the law with its commandments
2Ti 1:10 who **a** death and brought life
1Mc 6:59 on account of their laws that we **a**
2Mc 2:22 the laws that were about to be **a**,
4Mc 4:20 but also the temple service was **a**.

ABOLISHES* → ABOLISH
Heb 10: 9 He **a** the first in order to establish

ABOMINABLE → ABOMINATION
1Ki 15:13 had made an **a** image for Asherah;
2Ch 28: 3 the **a** practices of the nations
33: 2 the **a** practices of the nations
Ps 14: 1 They are corrupt, they do **a** deeds;
Eze 7:20 they made their **a** images,
1Mc 1:48 to make themselves **a** by everything
2Mc 5: 2 altar was covered with **a** offerings

ABOMINATION → ABOMINABLE, ABOMINATIONS
Ge 43:32 for that is an **a** to the Egyptians.
Lev 18:22 a male as with a woman; it is an **a**.
20:13 both of them have committed an **a**;
Pr 6:16 seven that are an **a** to him:
11: 1 A false balance is an **a** to the LORD,
11:20 Crooked minds are an **a** to the LORD
12:22 Lying lips are an **a** to the LORD,
24: 9 and the scoffer is an **a** to all.
Da 9:27 shall be an **a** that desolates,
11:31 set up the **a** that makes desolate.
12:11 the **a** that desolates is set up,
Lk 16:15 prized by human beings is an **a**
Rev 21:27 anyone who practices **a** or falsehood
Sir 1:25 but godliness is an **a** to a sinner.
13:20 Humility is an **a** to the proud;
13:20 the poor are an **a** to the rich.

1Mc 6: 7 that they had torn down the **a** that

ABOMINATIONS → ABOMINATION
Lev 18:27 committed all of these **a**,
1Ki 14:24 all the **a** of the nations that the LORD
Ezr 9: 1 the peoples of the lands with their **a**,
Pr 26:25 there are seven **a** concealed within;
Isa 66: 3 and in their **a** they take delight;
Jer 4: 1 if you remove your **a** from my
13:27 I have seen your **a**, your adulteries
32:34 in the house that bears my name,
Eze 7: 3 I will punish you for all your **a**.
8: 6 Yet you will see still greater **a**."
16:51 you have committed more **a** than
44: 7 broken my covenant with all your **a**.
Rev 17: 5 mother of whores and of earth's **a**."
Sir 15:13 The Lord hates all **a**;

ABOUND → ABOUNDED, ABOUNDING
Dt 28:11 LORD will make you **a** in prosperity,
Ps 72: 7 righteousness flourish and peace **a**,
Pr 28:20 The faithful will **a** with blessings,
Ro 6: 1 in sin in order that grace may **a**?
15:13 so that you may **a** in hope
2Co 3: 9 ministry of justification **a** in glory!
1Th 3:12 **a** in love for one another and for all,

ABOUNDED* → ABOUND
Ro 5:15 Jesus Christ, **a** for the many.
5:20 sin increased, grace **a** all the more,

ABOUNDING* → ABOUND
Ex 34: 6 **a** in steadfast love and faithfulness,
Nu 14:18 and **a** in steadfast love, forgiving
Ne 9:17 slow to anger and **a** in steadfast love
Ps 86: 5 **a** in steadfast love to all who call on
86:15 **a** in steadfast love and faithfulness.
103: 8 slow to anger and **a** in steadfast love
145: 8 slow to anger and **a** in steadfast love
Pr 8:24 there were no springs **a** with water.
Joel 2:13 to anger, and **a** in steadfast love,
Jnh 4: 2 to anger, and **a** in steadfast love,
Col 2: 7 you were taught, **a** in thanksgiving.

ABOVE
Dt 4:39 the LORD is God in heaven **a** and on
Ps 8: 1 have set your glory **a** the heavens.
18:48 you exalted me **a** my adversaries;
57: 5 Be exalted, O God, **a** the heavens.
95: 3 and a great King **a** all gods.
103:11 as the heavens are high **a** the earth,
Isa 6: 2 Seraphs were in attendance **a** him;
37:16 who are enthroned **a** the cherubim,
40:22 who sits **a** the circle of the earth,
Eze 1:26 seated a the likeness of a throne
10:19 the glory of the God of Israel was **a**
11:22 the glory of the God of Israel was **a**
Mt 10:24 "A disciple is not **a** the teacher,
Jn 3: 7 'You must be born from **a**.'
3:31 The one who comes from **a** is **a** all;
8:23 "You are from below, I am from **a**;
Eph 1:21 and **a** every name that is named,
4:10 who ascended far **a** all the heavens,
Php 2: 9 the name that is **a** every name,
Col 3: 2 Set your minds on things that are **a**,
2Th 2: 4 exalts himself **a** every so-called god
1Ti 3: 2 Now a bishop must be **a** reproach,
5: 7 so that they may be **a** reproach.
Heb 7:26 and exalted **a** the heavens.
Jas 1:17 with every perfect gift, is from **a**,
3:17 But the wisdom from **a** is first pure,
1Pe 4: 8 **A** all, maintain constant love for one
Jdt 13:18 **a** all other women on earth;
Sir 32:13 But **a** all bless your Maker,

ABRAHAM → =ABRAM
Abram, son of Terah (Ge 11:26-27), husband of Sarah (Ge 11:29).
Covenant relation with the LORD (Ge 12:1-3; 13:14-17; 15; 17; 22:15-18; Ex 2:24; Ne 9:8; Ps 105; Mic 7:20; Lk 1:68-75; Ro 4; Heb 6:13-15).
Called from Ur, via Haran, to Canaan (Ge 12:1; Ac 7:2-4; Heb 11:8-10). Moved to Egypt, nearly

lost Sarah to Pharoah (Ge 12:10-20). Divided the land with Lot; settled in Hebron (Ge 13). Saved Lot from four kings (Ge 14:1-16); blessed by Melchizedek (Ge 14:17-20; Heb 7:1-20). Declared righteous by faith (Ge 15:6; Ro 4:3; Gal 3:6-9; 1Mc 2:52). Fathered Ishmael by Hagar (Ge 16).

Name changed from Abram (Ge 17:5; Ne 9:7). Circumcised (Ge 17; Ro 4:9-12). Entertained three visitors (Ge 18); promised a son by Sarah (Ge 18:9-15; 17:16). Questioned destruction of Sodom and Gomorrah (Ge 18:16-33). Moved to Gerar; nearly lost Sarah to Abimelech (Ge 20). Fathered Isaac by Sarah (Ge 21:1-7; Ac 7:8; Heb 11:11-12); sent away Hagar and Ishmael (Ge 21:8-21; Gal 4:22-30). Covenant with Abimelech (Ge 21:22-32). Tested by offering Isaac (Ge 22; Heb 11:17-19; Jas 2:21-24). Sarah died; bought field of Ephron for burial (Ge 23). Secured wife for Isaac (Ge 24). Fathered children by Keturah (Ge 25:1-6; 1Ch 1:32-33). Death (Ge 25:7-11).

Called servant of God (Ge 26:24), friend of God (2Ch 20:7; Isa 41:8; Jas 2:23), prophet (Ge 20:7), father of Israel (Ex 3:15; Isa 51:2; Mt 3:9; Jn 8:39-58). Praised (Sir 44:19-45:1).

ANCESTOR ABRAHAM Lk 1:73; Jn 8:56; Ac 7:2; Ro 4:12; Jas 2:21

DESCENDANT[S] OF ABRAHAM Jn 8:33, 37; Ro 11:1; 2Co 11:22; Gal 3:7; Heb 2:16; 3Mc 6:3

FATHER ABRAHAM Ge 22:7; 26:3, 15, 18, 24; 32:9; Jos 24:3; Lk 16:24, 30; Jn 8:53; Sir 44:22; 4Mc 16:20; 17:6

GOD OF ABRAHAM Ge 28:13; 31:42, 53; Ex 3:6, 15, 16; 4:5; 1Ki 18:36; 1Ch 29:18; 2Ch 30:6; Ps 47:9; Mt 22:32; Mk 12:26; Lk 20:37; Ac 3:13; 7:32; AdE 13:15; 14:18

SON OF ABRAHAM Mt 1:1; Lk 3:34; 19:9

ABRAM → =ABRAHAM

Ge 17: 5 No longer shall your name be **A,**

ABSALOM

Son of David by Maacah (2Sa 3:3; 1Ch 3:2). Killed Amnon for rape of his sister Tamar; banished by David (2Sa 13). Returned to Jerusalem; received by David (2Sa 14). Rebelled against David (2Sa 15-17). Killed (2Sa 18).

ABSENT

1Co 5: 3 **a** in body, I am present in spirit;
Col 2: 5 For though I am **a** in body,

ABSOLUTE·

1Ti 5: 2 women as sisters—with **a** purity.

ABSTAIN → ABSTINENCE

Ac 15:20 **a** only from things polluted by idols
     15:29 **a** from what has been sacrificed to
     21:25 **a** from what has been sacrificed to
Ro 14: 3 eat must not despise those who **a,**
1Th 4: 3 that you **a** from fornication;
     5:22 **a** from every form of evil.
1Pe 2:11 to **a** from the desires of the flesh

ABSTINENCE → ABSTAIN

1Ti 4: 3 and demand **a** from foods,

ABUNDANCE → ABUNDANT, ABUNDANTLY

Dt 33:15 the **a** of the everlasting hills;
Job 36:31 governs peoples; he gives food in **a.**
Ps 36: 8 They feast on the **a** of your house,
     37:16 than the **a** of many wicked.
Pr 11:14 in an **a** of counselors there is safety.
     24: 6 in **a** of counselors there is victory.
Isa 33: 6 **a** of salvation, wisdom, and
La 3:32 to the **a** of his steadfast love;
Mt 13:12 be given, and they will have an **a;**
     25:29 be given, and they will have an **a;**
Lk 6:45 **a** of the heart that the mouth speaks.
     12:15 one's life does not consist in the **a**

21: 4 have contributed out of their **a,**
2Co 8:14 your present **a** and their need,
     9: 8 provide you with every blessing in **a.**
1Pe 1: 2 May grace and peace be yours in **a.**
2Pe 1: 2 May grace and peace be yours in **a**
Jude 1: 2 peace, and love be yours in **a.**

ABUNDANT → ABUNDANCE

Ps 31:19 O how **a** is your goodness
     51: 1 according to your **a** mercy blot out
     145: 7 the fame of your **a** goodness,
     147: 5 Great is our Lord, and **a** in power;
Eze 17: 5 A plant by **a** waters, he set it like **a**
     31: 7 for its roots went down to **a** water.
Joel 2:23 he has poured down for you **a** rain,
2Co 1: 5 our consolation is **a** through Christ.

ABUNDANTLY → ABUNDANCE

Isa 55: 7 our God, for he will **a** pardon.
Jn 10:10 I came that they may have life, and have it **a.**
Eph 3:20 to accomplish **a** far more than all

ABUSE → ABUSED, ABUSIVE

Ex 22:22 shall not **a** any widow or orphan.
Pr 9: 7 Whoever corrects a scoffer wins **a;**
Lk 6:28 pray for those who **a** you.
Heb 10:33 being publicly exposed to **a**
     11:26 considered **a** suffered for the Christ
1Pe 2:23 he was abused, he did not return **a;**
     3: 9 Do not repay evil for evil or **a** for **a;**

ABUSED → ABUSE

Dt 28:29 shall be continually **a** and robbed,
Jdg 19:25 and **a** her all through the night

ABUSIVE → ABUSE

Col 3: 8 and **a** language from your mouth.
2Ti 3: 2 **a,** disobedient to their parents,
Sir 23:15 are accustomed to using **a** language

ABYSS

Lk 8:31 to order them to go back into the **a.**
Ro 10: 7 'Who will descend into the **a?**'"
Sir 1: 3 the **a,** and wisdom—who can search them out?
     24:29 her counsel deeper than the great **a.**
2Es 16:57 He searches the **a** and its treasures;

ACACIA

Ex 25:10 They shall make an ark of **a** wood;
     25:23 You shall make a table of **a** wood,
     26:15 make upright frames of **a** wood
     27: 1 You shall make the altar of **a** wood,

ACCENT·

Mt 26:73 one of them, for your **a** betrays you.

ACCEPT → ACCEPTABLE, ACCEPTANCE, ACCEPTED, ACCEPTING, ACCEPTS

Dt 16:19 and you must not **a** bribes,
Job 42: 8 I will **a** his prayer not to deal with
Ps 119:108 A my offerings of praise, O LORD,
Pr 4:10 Hear, my child, and **a** my words,
     19:20 Listen to advice and **a** instruction,
Jer 14:10 therefore the LORD does not **a** them,
     32:33 would not listen and **a** correction.
Eze 20:40 there I will **a** them,
     43:27 I will **a** you, says the Lord GOD.
Zep 3: 7 will fear me, it will **a** correction;
Mal 1:10 I will not **a** an offering from your
Mt 11:14 if you are willing to **a** it,
     19:11 "Not everyone can **a** this teaching,
Jn 1:11 his own people did not **a** him.
     5:41 I do not **a** glory from human beings.
     5:43 and you do not **a** me;
     6:60 teaching is difficult; who can **a** it?"
Ac 22:18 will not **a** your testimony about me.'

ACCEPTABLE → ACCEPT

Lev 1: 4 it shall be **a** in your behalf
     22:21 to be **a** it must be perfect;
Ps 19:14 meditation of my heart be **a** to you,
     51:17 sacrifice **a** to God is a broken spirit;

Pr 21: 3 righteousness and justice is more **a**
Isa 58: 5 call this a fast, a day **a** to the LORD?
Jer 6:20 Your burnt offerings are not **a,**
Ro 12: 1 a living sacrifice, holy and **a** to God,
     14:18 who thus serves Christ is **a** to God
2Co 6: 2 See, now is the **a** time;
Php 4:18 a sacrifice **a** and pleasing to God.
Col 3:20 for this is your **a** duty in the Lord.
1Pe 2: 5 to offer spiritual sacrifices **a** to God

ACCEPTANCE → ACCEPT

Ro 11:15 their **a** be but life from the dead!
1Ti 1:15 saying is sure and worthy of full **a,**
     4: 9 saying is sure and worthy of full **a.**

ACCEPTED → ACCEPT

Ge 4: 7 If you do well, will you not be **a?**
Job 42: 9 the LORD **a** Job's prayer.
Jer 2:30 they **a** no correction.
Zep 3: 2 it has **a** no correction.
Lk 4:24 no prophet is **a** in the prophet's hometown.
2Co 11: 4 different gospel from the one you **a,**
1Th 2:13 you **a** it not as a human word

ACCEPTING → ACCEPT

3Jn 1: 7 **a** no support from non-believers.

ACCEPTS → ACCEPT

Ps 6: 9 the LORD **a** my prayer.
Jn 3:32 yet no one **a** his testimony.
Heb 12: 6 chastises every child whom he **a.**"

ACCESS

Est 1:14 who had **a** to the king,
Ro 5: 2 we have obtained **a** to this grace
Eph 2:18 have **a** in one Spirit to the Father.
     3:12 we have **a** to God in boldness

ACCOMPLISH → ACCOMPLISHED, ACCOMPLISHES

Isa 55:11 but it shall **a** that which I purpose,
     60:22 in its time I will **a** it quickly.
Eze 17:24 I the LORD have spoken; I will **a** it.
Eph 3:20 to **a** abundantly far more than all we

ACCOMPLISHED → ACCOMPLISH

Mt 5:18 will pass from the law until all is **a.**
Mk 13: 4 the sign that all these things are about to be **a?**"
Lk 18:31 by the prophets will be **a.**
Ro 15:18 except what Christ has **a** through me

ACCOMPLISHES → ACCOMPLISH

Eph 1:11 **a** all things according to his counsel

ACCORD → ACCORDANCE, ACCORDING

Jn 10:18 but I lay it down of my own **a.**
Ac 12:10 It opened for them of its own **a,**
Php 2: 2 being in full **a** and of one mind.

ACCORDANCE → ACCORD

Dt 29:21 **a** with all the curses of the covenant
Jos 1: 7 careful to act in **a** with all the law
Mk 12:14 the way of God in **a** with truth.
1Co 15: 3 Christ died for our sins in **a** with the scriptures,
     15: 4 raised on the third day in **a** with the scriptures,

ACCORDING → ACCORD

Ge 1:26 in our image, **a** to our likeness;
Ex 26:30 erect the tabernacle **a** to the plan
2Ch 6:30 heart you know, **a** to all their ways,
Ps 7: 8 judge me, O LORD, **a** to my righteousness and **a** to the integrity
     18:24 **a** to the cleanness of my hands in
     28: 4 Repay them **a** to their work,
     109:26 Save me **a** to your steadfast love.
     119: 9 By guarding it **a** to your word.
     119:25 revive me **a** to your word.
     119:28 strengthen me **a** to your word.
Pr 26: 4 Do not answer fools **a** to their folly,
     26: 5 Answer fools **a** to their folly,

Isa 59:18 **A** to their deeds, so will he repay;
Eze 7: 3 I will judge you **a** to your ways,
Hos 12: 2 and repay him **a** to his deeds.
Mt 9:29 "**A** to your faith let it be done to you
Jn 19: 7 and **a** to that law he ought to die
Ac 2:23 **a** to the definite plan and
Ro 2: 6 he will repay **a** to each one's deeds.
8: 4 who walk not **a** to the flesh but **a** to the Spirit.
8:13 you live **a** to the flesh, you will die;
Eph 1: 5 **a** to the good pleasure of his will,
2Ti 1: 9 not **a** to our works but **a** to his own purpose and grace.
2: 5 crowned without competing **a** to
Heb 2: 4 Holy Spirit, distributed **a** to his will.
5: 6 **a** to the order of Melchizedek."
Jas 2: 8 the royal law **a** to the scripture,
1Jn 5:14 that if we ask anything **a** to his will,
2Jn 1: 6 we walk **a** to his commandments;
Rev 20:12 dead were judged **a** to their works,
22:12 to repay **a** to everyone's work.
Sir 16:12 he judges a person **a** to one's deeds.
50:22 and deals with us **a** to his mercy.

ACCOUNT → ACCOUNTABLE, ACCOUNTED, ACCOUNTING
Mt 12:36 judgment you will have to give an **a**
Lk 1: 1 I set down an orderly **a** of the events
Col 3: 6 On **a** of these the wrath of God
Heb 4:13 to whom we must render an **a.**
1Jn 2:12 sins are forgiven on **a** of his name.

ACCOUNTABLE → ACCOUNT
Ro 3:19 whole world may be held **a** to God.
14:12 each of us will be **a** to God.

ACCOUNTED → ACCOUNT
Isa 53: 4 **a** him stricken, struck down by God,

ACCOUNTING → ACCOUNT
1Pe 3:15 an **a** for the hope that is in you;
4: 5 **a** to him who stands ready to judge

ACCURATE → ACCURATELY
Pr 11: 1 but an **a** weight is his delight.

ACCURATELY → ACCURATE
Ac 18:25 taught **a** the things concerning Jesus

ACCURSED → CURSE
Mt 25:41 at his left hand, 'You that are **a,**
Ro 9: 3 I could wish that I myself were **a**
1Co 16:22 a who has no love for the Lord.
Gal 1: 8 let that one be **a!**
2Pe 2:14 hearts trained in greed. A children!
Rev 22: 3 Nothing **a** will be found there any
Wis 14: 8 But the idol made with hands is **a,**

ACCUSATION → ACCUSE
Lk 23: 4 no basis for an **a** against this man."
1Ti 5:19 Never accept any **a** against an elder except

ACCUSATIONS → ACCUSE
Mt 27:13 many **a** they make against you?"
Ac 26: 2 my defense today against all the **a**

ACCUSE → ACCUSATION, ACCUSATIONS, ACCUSED, ACCUSER, ACCUSERS, ACCUSES
Dt 19:16 witness comes forward to **a**
Ps 103: 9 He will not always **a,**
Zec 3: 1 Satan standing at his right hand to **a**
Mt 12:10 so that they might **a** him.
Lk 23: 2 They began to **a** him, saying,
Ro 2:15 and their conflicting thoughts will **a**

ACCUSED → ACCUSE
Mk 15: 3 chief priests **a** him of many things.
Ac 22:30 Paul was being **a** of by the Jews,
Tit 1: 6 not **a** of debauchery and not

ACCUSER → ACCUSE
Job 9:15 I must appeal for mercy to my **a.**

Ps 109: 6 let an **a** stand on his right.
Mt 5:25 Come to terms quickly with your **a**
Jn 5:45 your **a** is Moses,
Rev 12:10 the **a** of our comrades has been thrown down,

ACCUSERS → ACCUSE
Ps 109:20 the reward of my **a** from the LORD,

ACCUSES → ACCUSE
Rev 12:10 who **a** them day and night before

ACCUSTOMED → CUSTOM
Jer 13:23 can do good who are **a** to do evil.
Mt 27:15 governor was **a** to release a prisoner

ACHAN
Sin at Jericho caused defeat at Ai; stoned (Jos 7; 22:20; 1Ch 2:7).

ACHIEVE
Job 5:12 so that their hands **a** no success.

ACHIOR
Ammonite mercenary (Jdt 5:5-6:20); converted to Judaism after Judith's victory (Jdt 14:5-10).

ACHISH
King of Gath before whom David feigned insanity (1Sa 21:10-15). Later "ally" of David (2Sa 27-29).

ACHOR
Jos 7:26 to this day is called the Valley of **A.**
Hos 2:15 the Valley of **A** a door of hope.

ACKNOWLEDGE → ACKNOWLEDGED, ACKNOWLEDGES
Dt 4:35 you would **a** that the LORD is God;
Pr 3: 6 In all your ways **a** him,
Isa 26:13 but we **a** your name alone.
Jer 3:13 **a** your guilt, that you have rebelled
Hos 5:15 they **a** their guilt and seek my face.
Mt 10:32 I also will **a** before my Father in
Lk 12: 8 Son of Man also will **a** before the
Ro 1:28 since they did not see fit to **a** God,
3Jn 1: 9 does not **a** our authority.
Tob 12: 6 Do not be slow to **a** him.

ACKNOWLEDGED → ACKNOWLEDGE
Ps 32: 5 Then I **a** my sin to you,
Lk 7:29 **a** the justice of God,

ACKNOWLEDGES* → ACKNOWLEDGE
Mt 10:32 therefore who **a** me before others,
Lk 12: 8 everyone who **a** me before others,

ACQUAINTED
Ps 139: 3 and are **a** with all my ways.
Isa 53: 3 a man of suffering and **a** with infirmity;

ACQUIRE → ACQUIRED, ACQUIRES
Dt 17:17 And he must not **a** many wives
Pr 1: 5 and the discerning **a** skill,
8: 5 **a** intelligence, you who lack it.
Sir 51:25 **A** wisdom for yourselves without

ACQUIRED → ACQUIRE
Ru 4:10 I have also **a** Ruth the Moabite,
Pr 20:21 An estate quickly **a** in the beginning

ACQUIRES → ACQUIRE
Pr 18:15 An intelligent mind **a** knowledge,

ACQUIT
Ex 20: 7 not **a** anyone who misuses his name.
23: 7 for I will not **a** the guilty.

ACT → ACTED, ACTION, ACTIONS, ACTIVE, ACTIVITIES, ACTS
Ge 19: 7 my brothers, do not **a** so wickedly.
Ex 21:13 came about by an **a** of God,
Nu 31:16 made the Israelites **a** treacherously
Jos 1: 8 to **a** in accordance with all that is written

Jdg 19:23 my brothers, do not **a** so wickedly.
1Ki 8:32 and **a,** and judge your servants,
8:39 **a,** and render to all whose hearts
Ps 37: 5 trust in him, and he will **a.**
119:126 It is time for the LORD to **a,**
Ecc 7:16 too righteous, and do not **a** too wise;
Jer 9:24 I **a** with steadfast love, justice,
Eze 24:14 the time is coming, I will **a.**
Da 9:19 Lord, listen and **a** and do not delay!
Jn 8: 4 the very **a** of committing adultery.
Ro 14:23 because they do not **a** from faith;
Jas 1:25 hearers who forget but doers who **a**
Sir 32:23 Guard yourself in every **a,**

ACTED → ACT
Dt 9:12 from Egypt have **a** corruptly.
Jos 7:11 have stolen, they have **a** deceitfully,
2Ch 6:37 done wrong; we have **a** wickedly';
Ne 9:29 Yet they **a** presumptuously
Eze 20: 9 But I **a** for the sake of my name,
Mic 3: 4 because they have **a** wickedly.
Ac 3:17 I know that you **a** in ignorance,
1Ti 1:13 mercy because I had **a** ignorantly
2Es 8:35 born who has not **a** wickedly;

ACTION → ACT
Da 11:32 shall stand firm and take **a.**
Lk 12:35 "Be dressed for **a**
1Pe 1:13 Therefore prepare your minds for **a;**
1Jn 3:18 word or speech, but in truth and **a.**

ACTIONS → ACT
1Sa 2: 3 and by him **a** are weighed.
Isa 65: 7 their laps full payment for their **a.**
Ro 7:15 I do not understand my own **a.**
Tit 1:16 but they deny him by their **a.**

ACTIVE → ACT
Heb 4:12 the word of God is living and **a,**
Jas 2:22 faith was **a** along with his works,

ACTIVITIES → ACT
1Co 12: 6 and there are varieties of **a,**

ACTS → ACT
Ex 6: 6 outstretched arm and with mighty **a**
7: 4 of Egypt by great **a** of judgment.
Dt 3:24 can perform deeds and mighty **a**
Job 40:19 "It is the first of the great **a** of God
Ps 31:23 repays the one who **a** haughtily.
71:15 mouth will tell of your righteous **a,**
145: 4 and shall declare your mighty **a.**
Pr 8:22 the first of his **a** of long ago.
14:35 falls on one who **a** shamefully.
Eze 14:21 my four deadly **a** of judgment,
Mic 6: 5 know the saving **a** of the LORD."
Mt 7:24 hears these words of mine and **a**
Ro 1:27 Men committed shameless **a** with
Tob 1: 3 I performed many **a** of charity

ADAM
1. First man (Ge 1:26-2:25; Ro 5:14; 1Ti 2:13; Tob 8:6). Sin of (Ge 3; Hos 6:7 [note]; Ro 5:12-21; 2Es 3:21; 7:70-140). Children of (Ge 4:1-5:5). Death of (Ge 5:5; Ro 5:12-21; 1Co 15:22).
2. Town (Jos 3:16).

ADAR
Month in which temple was rebuilt (Ezr 6:15); celebration of Purim (Est 3:7; 9:1-21); of victory over Nicanor (1Mc 7:43-49).

ADD → ADDED, ADDING, ADDS
Dt 4: 2 You must neither **a** anything
12:32 not **a** to it or take anything from it.
1Ki 12:11 I will **a** to your yoke.
2Ki 20: 6 I will **a** fifteen years to your life.
Pr 30: 6 Do not **a** to his words, or else
Mt 6:27 by worrying **a** a single hour to your
Lk 12:25 by worrying **a** a single hour to your
Rev 22:18 God will **a** to that person the plagues

ADDED → ADD
Pr   9:11 and years will be **a** to your life.
Ecc 3:14 nothing can be **a** to it, nor anything
Ac   1:26 he was **a** to the eleven apostles.
      2:41 three thousand persons were **a.**
      2:47 the Lord **a** to their number
      5:14 believers were **a** to the Lord,
Gal 3:19 It was **a** because of transgressions,
Sir 42:21 Nothing can be **a** or taken away,

ADDER → ADDER'S
Ps 91:13 You will tread on the lion and the **a,**
Pr 23:32 like a serpent, and stings like an **a.**

ADDER'S* → ADDER
Isa 11:8 child shall put its hand on the **a** den.

ADDICTED*
Tit 1:7 or quick-tempered or **a** to wine

ADDING → ADD
Nu 5:7 for the wrong, **a** one fifth to it,
Ecc 7:27 **a** one thing to another to find the sum,

ADDRESSED → ADDRESSES
Dt 32:48 On that very day the LORD **a** Moses
Lk 23:20 Pilate, wanting to release Jesus, **a**
Ac 21:40 he **a** them in the Hebrew language,

ADDRESSES* → ADDRESSED
Heb 12:5 exhortation that **a** you as children—

ADDS → ADD
Gal 3:15 no one **a** to it or annuls it.
Rev 22:18 if anyone **a** to them, God will add
Sir 3:27 and the sinner **a** sin to sins.
   26:15 A modest wife **a** charm to charm,

ADJURE
SS 5:8 I **a** you, O daughters of Jerusalem,
Mk 5:7 I **a** you by God, do not torment me."
Ac 19:13 "I **a** you by the Jesus whom Paul

ADMAH
Dt 29:23 of Sodom and Gomorrah, **A**
Hos 11:8 How can I make you like **A?**

ADMINISTERED* → ADMINISTERING
1Sa 7:17 he **a** justice there to Israel,
2Sa 8:15 David **a** justice and equity to all his
1Ch 18:14 he **a** justice and equity to all his
Heb 11:33 **a** justice, obtained promises,

ADMINISTERING → ADMINISTERED
2Co 8:20 this generous gift that we are **a,**

ADMIRED
Est 2:15 Esther was **a** by all who saw her.
Jdt 10:19 They marveled at her beauty and **a**
Wis 8:11 and in the sight of rulers I shall be **a.**
Sir 38:3 the presence of the great they are **a.**

ADMITS*
Sir 20:3 **a** his fault will be kept from failure.

ADMONISH → ADMONITION
1Co 4:14 but to **a** you as my beloved children.
Col 3:16 and **a** one another in all wisdom;
1Th 5:12 charge of you in the Lord and **a** you;
Jdt 8:27 close to him in order to **a** them."

ADMONITION → ADMONISH
Pr 15:5 one who heeds **a** is prudent.
Tit 3:10 After a first and second **a,**

ADONIJAH
  1. Son of David by Haggith (2Sa 3:4; 1Ch 3:2). Attempted to be king after David; killed at Solomon's order (1Ki 1-2).
  2. Levite; teacher of the Law (2Ch 17:8).

ADOPT → ADOPTED, ADOPTING, ADOPTION
Isa 44:5 and **a** the name of Israel.
Ac 16:21 not lawful for us as Romans to **a** or

ADOPTED → ADOPT
2Ch 7:22 they **a** other gods, and worshiped
Est 2:7 Mordecai **a** her as his own daughter.
Ac 7:21 Pharaoh's daughter **a** him and
1Mc 1:43 from Israel gladly **a** his religion;

ADOPTING* → ADOPT
4Mc 8:8 Enjoy your youth by **a** the Greek

ADOPTION → ADOPT
Ro 8:23 groan inwardly while we wait for **a,**
     9:4 Israelites, and to them belong the **a,**
Gal 4:5 that we might receive **a** as children.
Eph 1:5 for **a** as his children through Jesus

ADORN → ADORNED, ADORNMENT, ADORNS
1Pe 3:3 Do not **a** yourselves outwardly

ADORNED → ADORN
2Ki 9:30 painted her eyes, and **a** her head,
Eze 16:11 I **a** you with ornaments:
Lk 21:5 how it was **a** with beautiful stones
Rev 17:4 **a** with gold and jewels and pearls,
   21:2 as a bride **a** for her husband.

ADORNMENT → ADORN
Ex 28:2 glorious **a** of your brother Aaron.
Pr 3:22 for your soul and **a** for your neck.
1Pe 3:4 let your **a** be the inner self with the

ADORNS* → ADORN
Ps 149:4 he **a** the humble with victory.
Isa 61:10 as a bride **a** herself with her jewels.

ADRAMMELECH
2Ki 17:31 burned their children in the fire to **A**

ADULLAM
1Sa 22:1 and escaped to the cave of **A;**
1Ch 11:15 to David at the cave of **A,**
Mic 1:15 the glory of Israel shall come to **A.**

ADULT* → ADULTS
1Co 13:11 an **a,** I put an end to childish ways.

ADULTERER → ADULTERY
Job 24:15 of the **a** also waits for the twilight,

ADULTERERS → ADULTERY
Jer 23:10 For the land is full of **a;**
Hos 7:4 They are all **a;** they are like a
Mal 3:5 against the **a,** against those who
Lk 18:11 **a,** or even like this tax collector.
1Co 6:9 idolaters, **a,** male prostitutes,
Heb 13:4 God will judge fornicators and **a.**

ADULTERESS → ADULTERY
Lev 20:10 the **a** shall be put to death.
Pr 2:16 from the **a** with her smooth words,
  23:27 an **a** is a narrow well.
Hos 3:1 woman who has a lover and is an **a,**
Ro 7:3 an **a** if she lives with another man

ADULTERIES → ADULTERY
Jer 3:8 for all the **a** of that faithless one,
Eze 23:43 Ah, she is worn out with **a,**

ADULTEROUS → ADULTERY
Mt 16:4 evil and **a** generation asks for a sign,
Mk 8:38 in this **a** and sinful generation,

ADULTERY → ADULTERER, ADULTERERS, ADULTERESS, ADULTERIES, ADULTEROUS
Ex 20:14 You shall not commit **a.**
Dt 5:18 Neither shall you commit **a.**
Pr 6:32 who commits **a** has no sense;
Jer 3:9 committing **a** with stone and tree.
Eze 23:37 their idols they have committed **a;**
Hos 2:2 and her **a** from between her breasts,
Mt 5:27 'You shall not commit **a.'**
   5:28 committed **a** with her in his heart.
   5:32 causes her to commit **a;**

   5:32 marries a divorced woman commits **a.**
  15:19 come evil intentions, murder, **a,**
  19:9 and marries another commits **a."**
  19:18 You shall not commit **a;**
Mk 7:22 **a,** avarice, wickedness, deceit,
  10:11 marries another commits **a** against her;
  10:12 marries another, she commits **a."**
  10:19 You shall not commit **a;**
Lk 16:18 and marries another commits **a,**
  16:18 from her husband commits **a.**
  18:20 'You shall not commit **a;**
Jn 8:3 a woman who had been caught in **a;**
Ro 2:22 that forbid **a,** do you commit **a?**
  13:9 "You shall not commit **a;**
Jas 2:11 said, "You shall not commit **a,"**
   2:11 Now if you do not commit **a** but if
2Pe 2:14 They have eyes full of **a,**
Sir 25:2 and an old fool who commits **a.**

ADULTS* → ADULT
1Co 14:20 infants in evil, but in thinking be **a.**

ADVANCE → ADVANCED
Lev 25:36 Do not take interest in **a**
Eze 18:17 takes no **a** or accrued interest,
Ac 12:24 word of God continued to **a**
1Pe 1:11 testified in **a** to the sufferings destined for Christ

ADVANCED → ADVANCE
Ge 18:11 and Sarah were old, **a** in age;
2Ki 20:9 the shadow has now **a** ten intervals;
Gal 1:14 I **a** in Judaism beyond many among

ADVANTAGE
Ecc 3:19 humans have no **a** over the animals;
   6:8 what **a** have the wise over fools?
   7:12 the **a** of knowledge is that wisdom gives life
Jn 16:7 it is to your **a** that I go away,
Ro 3:1 Then what **a** has the Jew?
   6:22 the **a** you get is sanctification.
1Co 10:24 Do not seek your own **a,** but that of
2Co 11:20 preys upon you, or takes **a** of you,
Jude 1:16 flattering people to their own **a.**

ADVERSARIES → ADVERSARY
Dt 32:41 I will take vengeance on my **a,**
Jos 5:13 you one of us, or one of our **a?"**
2Sa 22:49 you exalted me above my **a,**
Ps 38:20 my **a** because I follow after good.
  55:12 not **a** who deal insolently with me—
Isa 9:11 So the LORD raised **a** against them,
Na 1:2 the LORD takes vengeance on his **a**
Heb 10:27 fury of fire that will consume the **a.**

ADVERSARY → ADVERSARIES
Nu 22:22 took his stand in the road as his **a.**
1Ki 11:14 raised up an **a** against Solomon,
1Ti 5:14 give the **a** no occasion to revile us.
1Pe 5:8 roaring lion your **a** the devil prowls

ADVERSITY → ADVERSARY
Dt 30:15 life and prosperity, death and **a.**
Pr 17:17 and kinsfolk are born to share **a.**
Ecc 7:14 and in the day of **a** consider;
Isa 30:20 Lord may give you the bread of **a**
  48:10 I have tested you in the furnace of **a.**
Sir 20:9 good fortune for a person in **a,**

ADVICE → ADVISERS
Nu 31:16 These women here, on Balaam's **a,**
1Ki 12:14 according to the **a** of the young men
2Ch 10:13 rejected the **a** of the older men;
Ps 1:1 do not follow the **a** of the wicked;
Pr 8:14 I have good **a** and sound wisdom;
  12:5 the **a** of the wicked is treacherous.
  12:15 but the wise listen to **a.**
  19:20 Listen to **a** and accept instruction,
  20:18 Plans are established by taking **a;**
Tob 4:18 Seek **a** from every wise person
Sir 37:11 pay no attention to any **a** they give.

ADVISERS → ADVICE
Pr 15:22 but with many **a** they succeed.
Sir 6: 6 but let your **a** be one in a thousand.

ADVOCATE*
Jn 14:16 and he will give you another **A**,
14:26 But the **A**, the Holy Spirit,
15:26 the **A** comes, whom I will send
16: 7 the **A** will not come to you;
1Jn 2: 1 we have an **a** with the Father,
Wis 12:12 come before you to plead as an **a**

AENEAS
Paralytic healed by Peter (Ac 9:33-34).

AFFAIRS
2Ch 10:15 a turn of **a** brought about by God
Ps 112: 5 who conduct their **a** with justice.
1Co 7:32 anxious about the **a** of the Lord,
7:33 anxious about the **a** of the world,

AFFECTION
Ge 43:30 overcome with **a** for his brother,
Ro 12:10 love one another with mutual **a**;
2Pe 1: 7 and godliness with mutual **a**, and
mutual **a** with love.

AFFLICT → AFFLICTED, AFFLICTION, AFFLICTIONS, AFFLICTS
Dt 28:22 LORD will **a** you with consumption,
2Sa 7:10 evildoers shall **a** them no more,
La 3:33 for he does not willingly **a**
2Th 1: 6 repay with affliction those who **a**

AFFLICTED → AFFLICT
Ge 12:17 But the LORD **a** Pharaoh
Dt 26: 6 Egyptians treated us harshly and **a**
Job 36: 6 but gives the **a** their right.
Ps 9:12 he does not forget the cry of the **a**.
25:16 for I am lonely and **a**.
119:107 I am severely **a**; give me life,
Isa 53: 4 struck down by God, and **a**.
53: 7 He was oppressed, and he was **a**,
Na 1:12 Though I have **a** you, I will afflict
2Co 1: 6 being **a**, it is for your consolation
4: 8 are **a** in every way, but not crushed;
1Ti 5:10 washed the saints' feet, helped the **a**

AFFLICTION → AFFLICT
Ge 16:11 the LORD has given heed to your **a**.
29:32 the LORD has looked on my **a**;
31:42 God saw my **a** and the labor of my
Dt 16: 3 bread with it—the bread of **a**—
26: 7 LORD heard our voice and saw our **a**
28:61 Every other malady and **a**,
Job 36:15 He delivers the afflicted by their **a**,
Ps 25:18 Consider my **a** and my trouble,
44:24 Why do you forget our **a** and
Isa 30:20 of adversity and the water of **a**,
La 1: 9 "O LORD, look at my **a**,
2Co 1: 4 who consoles us in all our **a**,
4:17 this slight momentary **a** is preparing
7: 4 I am overjoyed in all our **a**.
Rev 2: 9 "I know your **a** and your poverty,

AFFLICTIONS → AFFLICT
Ps 34:19 Many are the **a** of the righteous,
Ac 7:10 and rescued him from all his **a**,
2Co 6: 4 through great endurance, in **a**,
Col 1:24 what is lacking in Christ's **a**
4Mc 18:15 'Many are the **a** of the righteous.'

AFFLICTS* → AFFLICT
Tob 13: 2 For he **a**, and he shows mercy;

AFFORD
Lev 5: 7 But if you cannot **a** a sheep,
5:11 if you cannot **a** two turtledoves
12: 8 If she cannot **a** a sheep,

AFFRONT*
Pr 17: 9 who forgives an **a** fosters friendship,

AFLAME → FLAME
1Co 7: 9 better to marry than to be **a** with passion.

AFRAID → FEAR
Ge 3:10 and I was **a**, because I was naked;
15: 1 not be **a**, Abram, I am your shield;
21:17 Do not be **a**; for God has heard
26:24 do not be **a**, for I am with you
50:19 Joseph said to them, "Do not be **a**!
Ex 2:14 Then Moses was **a** and thought,
3: 6 Moses hid his face, for he was **a** to look at God.
14:13 said to the people, "Do not be **a**,
20:20 said to the people, "Do not be **a**;
34:30 and they were **a** to come near him.
Lev 26: 6 and no one shall make you **a**;
Dt 2: 4 They will be **a** of you,
20: 3 Do not lose heart, or be **a**,
28:10 and they shall be **a** of you.
Jos 10:25 Joshua said to them, "Do not be **a**
Ru 3:11 my daughter, do not be **a**,
1Sa 3:15 Samuel was **a** to tell the vision to
18:12 Saul was **a** of David, because the
18:29 Saul was still more **a** of David.
1Ki 3: 1 Then he was **a**; he got up
1Ch 13:12 David was **a** of God that day;
21:30 he was **a** of the sword of the angel
Ezr 4: 4 and made them **a** to build,
Ne 2: 2 Then I was very much **a**.
6:16 all the nations around us were **a**
Ps 3: 6 I am not **a** of ten thousands
27: 1 of whom shall I be **a**?
56: 3 when I am **a**, I put my trust in you.
56: 4 I am not **a**; what can flesh do to me?
56:11 in God I trust; I am not **a**.
Pr 3:24 If you sit down, you will not be **a**;
Isa 12: 2 I will trust, and will not be **a**,
17: 2 and no one will make them **a**.
41:10 do not be **a**, for I am your God;
44: 8 Do not fear, or be **a**;
Jer 1: 8 Do not be **a** of them,
Eze 2: 6 do not be **a** of their words,
34:28 and no one shall make them **a**.
39:26 with no one to make them **a**,
Mic 4: 4 and no one shall make them **a**;
Zep 3:13 and no one shall make them **a**.
Mt 1:20 not be **a** to take Mary as your wife,
8:26 he said to them, "Why are you **a**,
10:31 So do not be **a**; you are of more
14:27 it is I; do not be **a**."
28: 5 said to the women, "Do not be **a**;
28:10 Jesus said to them, "Do not be **a**;
Mk 11:32 they were **a** of the crowd,
Lk 1:13 the angel said to him, "Do not be **a**,
1:30 said to her, "Do not be **a**, Mary,
2:10 angel said to them, "Do not be **a**;
12:32 "Do not be **a**, little flock,
Jn 14:27 and do not let them be **a**.
Ac 9:26 and they were all **a** of him,
27:24 and he said, 'Do not be **a**, Paul;
Ro 13: 4 do what is wrong, you should be **a**,
Heb 13: 6 Lord is my helper; I will not be **a**;
2Pe 2:10 not **a** to slander the glorious ones,

AFTERNOON → NOON
Mk 15:33 the whole land until three in the **a**.
Ac 3: 1 of prayer, at three o'clock in the **a**.
10: 3 One **a** at about three o'clock he had

AGABUS*
A Christian prophet (Ac 11:28; 21:10).

AGAG → AGAGITE
King of Amalekites; not killed by Saul (1Sa 15).

AGAGITE → AGAG
Est 8: 3 the evil design of Haman the **A**

AGAIN
Ge 8:21 "I will never **a** curse the ground
Dt 30: 9 the LORD will **a** take delight
2Ch 33: 8 I will never **a** remove the feet of

Job 14:14 If mortals die, will they live **a**?
Ps 42: 5 for I shall **a** praise him,
78:41 They tested God **a** and **a**,
85: 6 Will you not revive us **a**,
Ecc 3:20 and all turn to dust **a**.
Jer 12:15 I will **a** have compassion on them,
31: 4 **A** I will build you, and you shall be
Eze 37:22 Never **a** shall they be two nations,
Joel 2:26 shall never **a** be put to shame.
Zec 1:17 the LORD will **a** comfort Zion
Mt 26:29 I will never **a** drink of this fruit
27:63 'After three days I will rise **a**.'
Mk 8:31 and after three days rise **a**.
Jn 14: 3 I will come **a** and will take you to
Ro 6: 9 from the dead, will never die **a**;
11:23 has the power to graft them in **a**.
14: 9 to this end Christ died and lived **a**,
1Th 4:14 believe that Jesus died and rose **a**,
Heb 5:12 to teach you **a** the basic elements
6: 1 and not laying **a** the foundation:
6: 6 they are crucifying **a** the Son of God
9:25 Nor was it to offer himself **a** and **a**,

AGE → AGED, AGES
Ge 21: 2 bore Abraham a son in his old **a**,
37: 3 because he was the son of his old **a**;
Da 2:20 "Blessed be the name of God from **a** to **a**,
Mt 13:39 the harvest is the end of the **a**,
28:20 I am with you always, to the end of the **a**."
Lk 18:30 and in the **a** to come eternal life."
Gal 1: 4 to set us free from the present evil **a**,
1Ti 6:17 who in the present **a** are rich,
Tit 2:12 the present **a** to live lives that are self-controlled.

AGE TO COME Mt 12:32; Mk 10:30; Lk 18:30; Eph 1:21; Heb 6:5; 2Es 7:113; 8:52

END OF AGE Mt 13:39, 40, 49; 24:3; 28:20; Heb 9:26; 2Es 2:34; 6:9; 7:113

OLD AGE Ge 15:15; 21:2, 7; 25:8; 37:3; 44:20; Jdg 8:32; Ru 4:15; 1Sa 2:31, 32; 1Ki 15:23; 1Ch 29:28; Job 5:26; 21:7; Ps 71:9, 18; 92:14; Isa 46:4; Lk 1:36; Tob 3:10; 14:13; Wis 3:17; 4:8, 9, 16; Sir 3:12; 25:3; 30:24; 46:9; 2Mc 6:23, 25, 27; 3Mc 6:1; 2Es 5:50, 53; 14:17; 4Mc 5:12, 33, 36; 6:12, 18

THIS AGE Mt 12:32; Mk 10:30; Lk 16:8; 18:30; 20:34; 1Co 1:20; 2:6, 6, 8; 3:18; Eph 1:21; 2Es 2:36, 39; 4:27; 6:9; 7:113; 9:18

AGED → AGE
Lev 19:32 You shall rise before the **a**,
Job 12:12 Is wisdom with the **a**,
Ps 119:100 I understand more than the **a**,
Pr 17: 6 Grandchildren are the crown of the **a**,
20:29 the beauty of the **a** is their gray hair.
Sir 8: 9 Do not ignore the discourse of the **a**,
25: 5 How attractive is wisdom in the **a**,

AGES → AGE
Dt 4:32 For ask now about former **a**,
Ro 16:25 that was kept secret for long **a**
1Co 2: 7 decreed before the **a** for our glory.
Eph 2: 7 that in the **a** to come he might show
3: 9 the plan of the mystery hidden for **a**
Col 1:26 has been hidden throughout the **a**
1Ti 1:17 To the King of the **a**, immortal,
Tit 1: 2 promised before the **a** began—
Tob 13: 1 his kingdom lasts throughout all **a**.

AGONY
Isa 13: 8 Pangs and **a** will seize them;
Lk 16:24 for I am in **a** in these flames.'
Rev 12: 2 in the **a** of giving birth.
16:10 people gnawed their tongues in **a**,

AGREE → AGREEMENT
Job 22:21 "**A** with God, and be at peace;
Mt 18:19 if two of you **a** on earth about
Mk 14:56 and their testimony did not **a**.

Ro   7:16 I **a** that the law is good.
2Co 13:11 to my appeal, **a** with one another,
1Ti   6: 3 does not **a** with the sound words of
1Jn   5: 8 and the blood, and these three **a**.

AGREEMENT → AGREE

Dt   26:17 you have obtained the LORD's **a:**
Ne   9:38 Because of all this we make a firm **a**
Isa   28:15 and with Sheol we have an **a;**
1Co   7: 5 Do not deprive one another except
                 perhaps by **a**
2Co   6:16 **a** has the temple of God with idols?
Sir   41:19 ashamed of breaking an oath or **a,**

AGRIPPA
Descendant of Herod; king before whom Paul argued his case in Caesarea (Ac 25:13-26:32).

AGUR*
Pr   30: 1 The words of **A** son of Jakeh.

AHAB
1. Son of Omri; king of Israel (1Ki 16:28-22:40), husband of Jezebel (1Ki 16:31). Promoted Baal worship (1Ki 16:31-33); opposed by Elijah (1Ki 17:1; 18; 21), a prophet (1Ki 20:35-43), Micaiah (1Ki 22:1-28). Defeated Ben-Hadad (1Ki 20). Killed for failing to kill Ben-Hadad and for murder of Naboth (1Ki 20:35-21:40).
2. A false prophet (Jer 29:21-22).

AHASUERUS → =ARTAXERXES
King of Persia (Ezr 4:6), husband of Esther. Deposed Vashti; replaced her with Esther (Est 1-2). Sealed Haman's edict to annihilate the Jews (Est 3). Received Esther without having called her (Est 5:1-8). Honored Mordecai (Est 6). Hanged Haman (Est 7). Issued edict allowing Jews to defend themselves (Est 8). Promoted Mordecai (Est 8:1-2, 15; 9:4; 10). Called Artaxerxes in the Additions to Esther.

AHAZ
Son of Jotham; king of Judah, (2Ki 16; 2Ch 28; Mt 1:9). Idolatry of (2Ki 16:3-4, 10-18; 2Ch 28:1-4, 22-25). Defeated by Aram and Israel (2Ki 16:5-6; 2Ch 28:5-15). Sought help from Assyria rather than the LORD (2Ki 16:7-9; 2Ch 28:16-21; Isa 7).

AHAZIAH → =JEHOAHAZ
1. Son of Ahab; king of Israel (1Ki 22:51-2Ki 1:18; 2Ch 20:35-37). Made an unsuccessful alliance with Jehoshaphat (2Ch 20:35-37). Died for seeking Baal rather than the LORD (2Ki 1).
2. Son of Jehoram; king of Judah 8:25-29; 9:14-29), also called Jehoahaz (2Ch 21:17-22:9; 25:23). Killed by Jehu while visiting Joram (2Ki 9:14-29; 2Ch 22:1-9).

AHEAD
Ge   48:20 So he put Ephraim **a** of Manasseh.
Nu   22:26 Then the angel of the LORD went **a,**
Dt   1:22 send men **a** of us to explore the land
Jos   24:12 I sent the hornet **a** of you,
Eze   1: 9 each of them moved straight **a,**
Mt   2: 9 **a** of them, went the star that they
          11:10 sending my messenger **a** of you,
          26:32 I will go **a** of you to Galilee."
Jn   1:15 who comes after me ranks **a** of me
1Co 11:21 of you goes **a** with your own supper,
Php   3:13 straining forward to what lies **a,**
Heb 11:26 for he was looking **a** to the reward.

AHIJAH
1. Priest during Sauls reign (1Sa 14:3,18).
2. Prophet of Shiloh (1Ki 11:29-39; 14:1-18).

AHIKAM
Father of Gedaliah (2Ki 25:22), protector of Jeremiah (Jer 26:24).

AHIMAAZ
1. Father-in-law of Saul (1Sa 14:50).

2. Son of Zadok, the high priest, loyal to David (2Sa 15:27,36; 17:17-20; 18:19-33).

AHIMELECH
1. Priest who helped David in his flight from Saul (1Sa 21-22).
2. One of David's warriors (1Sa 26:6).

AHINOAM
1. Wife of Saul (1Sa 14:50).
2. Wife of David (1Sa 25:43; 30:5; 1Ch 3:1).

AHITHOPHEL
One of David's counselors who sided with Absalom (2Sa 15:12, 31-37; 1Ch 27:33-34); committed suicide when his advice was ignored (2Sa 16:15-17:23).

AI
Ge   12: 8 on the west and **A** on the east;
Jos   7: 4 and they fled before the men of **A.**
            8:26 destroyed all the inhabitants of **A.**

AID
Ps   22:19 O my help, come quickly to my **a!**

AIJALON
Jos   10:12 and Moon, in the valley of **A."**

AILMENT* → AILMENTS
Lk   13:12 you are set free from your **a."**

AILMENTS* → AILMENT
1Ti   5:23 your stomach and your frequent **a.**

AIM → AIMLESSLY
Ps   21:12 will **a** at their faces with your bows.
            64: 3 who **a** bitter words like arrows,
2Co   5: 9 we make it our **a** to please him.
1Ti   1: 5 the **a** of such instruction is love
2Ti   2: 4 soldier's **a** is to please the enlisting
            3:10 my conduct, my **a** in life, my faith,

AIMLESSLY → AIM
1Co   9:26 So I do not run **a,** nor do I box as

AIR
Ex   9: 8 and let Moses throw it in the **a**
Jer   14: 6 they pant for **a** like jackals;
Mt   6:26 Look at the birds of the **a;**
            8:20 and birds of the **a** have nests;
Mk   4:32 the birds of the **a** can make nests in
Lk   8: 5 and the birds of the **a** ate it up.
Ac   22:23 and tossing dust into the **a,**
1Co   9:26 nor do I box as though beating the **a**
          14: 9 For you will be speaking into the **a.**
Eph   2: 2 the ruler of the power of the **a,**
1Th   4:17 to meet the Lord in the **a;**
Rev 16:17 angel poured his bowl into the **a,**
Aza   1:58 Bless the Lord, all birds of the **a;**

ALABASTER*
SS   5:15 His legs are **a** columns,
Mt   26: 7 **a** woman came to him with an **a** jar
Mk   14: 3 an **a** jar of very costly ointment of
Lk   7:37 brought an **a** jar of ointment.

ALARM → ALARMED
Nu   10: 5 When you blow an **a,** the camps
Ps   31:22 I had said in my **a,**
Jer   4:19 sound of the trumpet, the **a** of war.
Joel   2: 1 sound the **a** on my holy mountain!
2Co   7:11 indignation, what **a,** what longing,
1Pe   3: 6 good and never let fears **a** you.

ALARMED → ALARM
Mk   13: 7 and rumors of wars, do not be **a;**
          16: 6 But he said to them, "Do not be **a;**
2Th   2: 2 to be quickly shaken in mind or **a,**

ALCIMUS*
A high priest in the time of the Maccabees (1Mc 7:5-25; 9; 2Mc 14).

ALERT
Jos   8: 4 from the city, but all of you stay **a.**

Mk   13:33 keep **a;** for you do not know when
Lk   12:37 slaves whom the master finds **a**
          21:36 Be **a** at all times, praying
1Co 16:13 Keep **a,** stand firm in your faith,
Eph   6:18 keep **a** and always persevere
Col   4: 2 keeping **a** in it with thanksgiving.
1Pe   5: 8 Discipline yourselves, keep **a.**

ALEXANDER
Ac   19:33 And **A** motioned for silence and
1Ti   1:20 among them are Hymenaeus and **A,**
2Ti   4:14 **A** the coppersmith did me great
                 harm;
1Mc   1: 1 **A** son of Philip, the Macedonian,
          10: 1 hundred sixtieth year **A** Epiphanes,

ALIEN → ALIENS
Ge   12:10 to Egypt to reside there as an **a,**
          20: 1 While residing in Gerar as an **a,**
          32: 4 'I have lived with Laban as an **a,**
Ex   2:22 an **a** residing in a foreign land."
          12:19 whether an **a** or a native of the land.
          22:21 not wrong or oppress a resident **a,**
Lev 19:34 you shall love the **a** as yourself,
          23:22 leave them for the poor and for the **a**
Dt   24:17 You shall not deprive a resident **a**

ALIENATE* → ALIENATED
Pr   17: 9 dwells on disputes will **a** a friend.
1Ti   5:11 sensual desires **a** them from Christ,

ALIENATED → ALIENATE
Eph   4:18 **a** from the life of God because of

ALIENS → ALIEN
Ge   15:13 your offspring shall be **a** in a land
Ex   23: 9 for you were **a** in the land of Egypt.
Ps 144:11 and deliver me from the hand of **a,**
Jer   51:51 for **a** have come into the holy places
La   5: 2 over to strangers, our homes to **a.**
Eph   2:19 you are no longer strangers and **a,**
1Pe   2:11 I urge you as **a** and exiles to abstain
1Mc   2: 7 the sanctuary given over to **a?**

ALIKE → LIKE
Nu   15:15 you and the alien shall be **a** before
Ps   14: 3 they are all **a** perverse;
          36: 6 you save humans and animals **a,**
Ecc   11: 6 or whether both **a** will be good.
Ro   14: 5 while others judge all days to be **a.**

ALIVE → LIVE
Ge   6:19 to keep them **a** with you;
          16:13 really seen God and remained **a**
Lev 16:10 presented **a** before the LORD to
                 make atonement
Nu   16:30 they go down **a** into Sheol,
Dt   5:26 as we have, and remained **a?**
            6:24 our lasting good, so as to keep us **a,**
          32:39 I kill and I make **a;** I wound and I
                 heal;
2Sa 12:18 "While the child was still **a,**
1Ki   3:23 'This is my son that is **a,** and your
Ps   55:15 let them go down **a** to Sheol;
Pr   1:12 like Sheol let us swallow them **a**
Zec 13: 8 and one-third shall be left **a.**
Lk   15:24 was dead and is **a** again;
          24:23 of angels who said that he was **a.**
Jn   4:51 and told him that his child was **a.**
Ac   1: 3 After his suffering he presented
                 himself **a**
            9:41 he showed her to be **a.**
Ro   6:11 dead to sin and **a** to God
            7: 9 I was once **a** apart from the law,
1Co 15:22 so all will be made **a** in Christ.
2Co   6: 9 as dying, and see—we are **a;**
Eph   2: 5 made us **a** together with Christ—
Col   2:13 God made you **a** together with him,
1Th   4:17 Then we who are **a,** who are left,
1Pe   3:18 but made **a** in the spirit,
Rev   1:18 I am a forever and ever;
            3: 1 you have a name of being **a,**
          19:20 were thrown **a** into the lake of fire

ALL

Ge 2: 3 on it God rested from **a** the work
3:20 she was the mother of **a** living.
6:13 to make an end of **a** flesh,
7:21 And **a** flesh died that moved on the
11: 6 and they have **a** one language;
12: 3 **a** the families of the earth shall be blessed."
13:15 **a** the land that you see I will give
45: 9 God has made me lord of **a** Egypt;
46: 6 Jacob and **a** his offspring with him,
Ex 3:15 and this my title for **a** generations.
11:10 **a** these wonders before Pharaoh;
12:12 on **a** the gods of Egypt I will execute judgments;
13:15 the LORD killed **a** the firstborn in
20: 1 Then God spoke **a** these words:
24: 4 Moses wrote down **a** the words of
24: 7 "**A** that the LORD has spoken we will do,
33:19 **a** my goodness pass before you,
Lev 20:22 You shall keep **a** my statutes
Nu 3:13 for **a** the firstborn are mine;
11:29 **a** the LORD's people were prophets,
27:16 the God of the spirits of **a** flesh,
Dt 6: 5 You shall love the LORD your God with **a** your heart, and with **a** your soul, and with **a** your might.
10:12 serve the LORD your God with **a** your heart
10:14 the earth with **a** that is in it,
11:13 serving him with **a** your heart
28: 2 **a** these blessings shall come
28:15 **a** these curses shall come upon you
Jos 8:34 he read **a** the words of the law,
21:44 not one of **a** their enemies had withstood them,
21:45 Not one of **a** the good promises that the LORD had made
1Sa 12:20 serve the LORD with **a** your heart;
2Sa 5: 1 **a** the tribes of Israel came to David
1Ki 4:30 wisdom surpassed the wisdom of **a**
16:25 more evil than **a** who were before
2Ki 17:16 They rejected **a** the commandments
23:25 turned to the LORD with **a** his heart,
Est 2:15 Esther was admired by **a** who saw
3: 6 Haman plotted to destroy **a** the Jews
4:13 any more than **a** the other Jews.
Job 1:22 In **a** this Job did not sin
2:10 In **a** this Job did not sin with his
Ps 1: 3 In **a** that they do, they prosper.
8: 1 majestic is your name in **a** the earth!
8: 6 have put **a** things under their feet,
34: 1 I will bless the LORD at **a** times;
34:20 He keeps **a** their bones;
47: 7 For God is the king of **a** the earth.
57: 5 Let your glory be over **a** the earth.
72:17 May **a** nations be blessed in him;
96: 5 **a** the gods of the peoples are idols,
100: 5 and his faithfulness to **a** generations.
135: 5 our Lord is above **a** gods.
145: 9 The LORD is good to **a**,
145:17 The LORD is just in **a** his ways,
Pr 3: 5 Trust in the LORD with **a** your heart,
3:17 and **a** her paths are peace.
8:36 **a** who hate me love death."
17:17 A friend loves at **a** times,
Ecc 1: 2 vanity of vanities! **A** is vanity.
3:20 **a** are from the dust, and **a** turn to dust again.
9: 2 since the same fate comes to **a**,
SS 8: 7 If one offered for love **a** the wealth
Isa 2: 2 **a** the nations shall stream to it.
25: 8 wipe away the tears from **a** faces,
44: 9 A who make idols are nothing,
53: 6 **A** we like sheep have gone astray;
Jer 3:17 and **a** nations shall gather to it,
10:16 he is the one who formed **a** things,
29:13 if you seek me with **a** your heart,
31:34 for they shall **a** know me,
Eze 36:33 I cleanse you from **a** your iniquities;
Joel 2:28 I will pour out my spirit on **a** flesh;

3: 2 I will gather **a** the nations
Zec 14: 9 will become king over **a** the earth;
Mt 6:29 even Solomon in **a** his glory
6:33 **a** these things will be given to you
12:15 and he cured **a** of them,
28:18 "**A** authority in heaven and on earth
Mk 7:19 (Thus he declared **a** foods clean.)
7:23 **A** these evil things come from
10:27 for God **a** things are possible."
14:36 "Abba, Father, for you **a** things are possible;
Lk 10:27 "You shall love the Lord your God with **a** your heart, and with **a** your soul, and with **a** your strength, and with **a** your mind;
Jn 1: 3 **A** things came into being through
1: 4 the life was the light of **a** people.
1: 7 so that **a** might believe through him.
1:12 But to **a** who received him,
1:16 From his fullness we have **a** received,
16:13 he will guide you into **a** the truth;
17:21 that they may **a** be one.
18: 4 Jesus, knowing **a** that was to happen
19:28 Jesus knew that **a** was now finished,
Ac 2: 4 **A** of them were filled with the Holy Spirit
2:17 will pour out my Spirit upon **a** flesh,
2:44 **A** who believed were together and had **a** things in common;
10:44 Holy Spirit fell upon **a** who heard
Ro 2:12 **a** who have sinned under the law
3:23 **a** have sinned and fall short of the glory of God;
5:12 so death spread to **a** because **a** have sinned—
6:10 he died to sin, once for **a**;
10:12 the same Lord is Lord of **a**
14:10 we will **a** stand before the judgment
1Co 6:12 "**A** things are lawful for me,"
9:22 I have become **a** things to **a** people,
10:23 "**A** things are lawful," but not **a** things are beneficial.
12:12 and **a** the members of the body,
12:29 Are **a** apostles? Are **a** prophets?
12:30 Do **a** speak in tongues?
14:26 Let **a** things be done for building up.
15:22 so **a** will be made alive in Christ.
15:28 When **a** things are subjected to him,
15:51 We will not **a** die, but we will **a** be changed,
2Co 5:14 convinced that one has died for **a**;
Eph 1:22 he has put **a** things under his feet
1:23 the fullness of him who fills **a** in **a**.
4: 6 one God and Father of **a**, who is above **a** and through **a** and in **a**.
Php 4: 7 peace of God, which surpasses **a** understanding,
4:13 I can do **a** things through him
Col 1:15 the firstborn of **a** creation;
1:16 **a** things have been created through
1:19 For in him **a** the fullness of God
2: 3 in whom are hidden **a** the treasures of wisdom
3:11 but Christ is **a** and in **a**!
1Th 5:18 give thanks in **a** circumstances;
1Ti 4:10 who is the Savior of **a** people,
6:10 For the love of money is a root of **a** kinds of evil,
2Ti 3:12 **a** who want to live a godly life
3:16 **A** scripture is inspired by God
Tit 1:15 To the pure **a** things are pure,
Heb 1: 2 whom he appointed heir of **a** things,
1: 3 sustains **a** things by his powerful
8:11 for they shall **a** know me,
9:26 appeared once for **a** at the end of
10:12 when Christ had offered for **a** time
1Pe 1:24 For "**A** flesh is like grass
3:18 For Christ also suffered for sins once for **a**,
5: 7 Cast **a** your anxiety on him,
2Pe 3: 9 but **a** to come to repentance.

1Jn 1: 9 cleanse us from **a** unrighteousness.
2:27 anointing teaches you about **a** things
Rev 4:11 for you created **a** things,
15: 4 **A** nations will come and worship
21: 5 "See, I am making **a** things new."
Tob 1:12 mindful of God with **a** my heart,
Wis 12:15 and you rule **a** things righteously,
16: 7 but by you, the Savior of **a**.
Sir 1: 1 **A** wisdom is from the Lord,
7:29 With **a** your soul fear the Lord,

ALL FLESH
Ge 6:12, 13, 17, 19; 7:15, 16, 21; 8:17; 9:11, 15, 15, 16, 17; Nu 16:22; 27:16; Dt 5:26; Job 34:15; Ps 65:2; 136:25; 145:21; Isa 49:26; 66:16, 23, 24; Jer 25:31; 32:27; 45:5; Eze 20:48; 21:4, 5; Joel 2:28; Lk 3:6; Ac 2:17; 1Co 15:39; 1Pe 1:24; Sir 41:4; 44:18

ALL GENERATIONS
Ge 9:12; Ex 3:15; 40:15; Ps 10:6; 33:11; 45:17; 49:11; 61:6; 71:18; 72:5; 85:5; 89:1, 4; 90:1; 100:5; 102:12, 24; 119:90; 145:13; 146:10; Pr 27:24; Isa 13:20; 51:8; Jer 50:39; La 5:19; Joel 3:20; Mt 1:17; Lk 1:48; Eph 3:21; Tob 1:4; 8:5; 13:10; Jdt 8:32; Sir 16:27; 24:33; 39:9; 44:16; 45:26

ALL ... HEART
Dt 4:29; 6:5; 10:12; 11:13; 13:3; 26:16; 30:2, 6, 10; Jos 22:5; 1Sa 7:3; 12:20, 24; 2Sa 3:21; 1Ki 2:4; 8:23, 48; 14:8; 2Ki 10:31; 23:3, 25; 2Ch 6:14, 30, 38; 15:12, 15; 22:9; 31:21; 34:31; Ps 119:58; Pr 3:5; Jer 29:13; 32:41; Joel 2:12; Zep 3:14; Mt 22:37; Mk 12:30, 33; Lk 10:27; Tob 1:12; 13:6; Sir 7:27; 39:35; 47:8; Aza 1:18; 2Mc 1:3

ALL ISRAEL
Ex 18:25; Nu 16:34; Dt 1:1; 5:1; 11:6; 13:11; 21:21; 27:9; 29:2; 31:1, 7, 11, 11; 32:45; 34:12; Jos 3:7, 17; 4:14; 7:24, 25; 8:15, 21, 24, 33; 10:15, 29, 31, 34, 36, 38, 43; 23:2; Jdg 8:27; 20:34; 1Sa 2:22; 3:20; 4:1, 5; 7:5; 11:2; 12:1; 13:4; 14:40; 17:11; 18:16; 19:5; 24:2; 25:1; 28:3, 4; 2Sa 2:9; 3:12, 21, 37; 4:1; 5:5; 8:15; 10:17; 11:1; 12:12; 14:25; 16:21, 22; 17:10, 11, 13; 19:11; 1Ki 1:20; 2:15; 3:28; 4:1, 7; 5:13; 8:62, 65; 11:16, 42; 12:1, 16, 18, 20, 20; 14:13, 18; 15:27, 33; 16:16, 17; 18:19, 20; 2Ki 3:6; 9:14; 10:21; 1Ch 9:1; 11:1, 4, 10; 12:38; 13:5, 6, 8; 14:8; 15:3, 28; 17:6; 18:14; 19:17; 21:4, 5; 28:4, 8; 29:21, 23, 25, 26; 2Ch 1:2, 2; 7:6, 8; 9:30; 10:1, 3, 16, 16; 11:3, 13; 12:1; 13:4, 15; 18:16; 24:5; 28:23; 29:24, 24; 30:1, 5, 6; 31:1; 35:3; Ezr 2:70; 6:17; 8:25, 35; 10:5; Ne 7:73; 12:47; 13:26; Da 9:7, 11; Mal 4:4; Ro 11:26; Tob 1:6; Jdt 15:14; AdE 13:18; 1Mc 2:70; 5:63; 9:20; 12:52; 13:26; 1Es 5:46; 7:8; 8:7, 55, 65, 96

ALL ... JEWS
Est 3:6, 13; 4:13, 16; 9:20, 24, 30; Mk 7:3; Jn 18:20; Ac 18:2; 21:21; 22:12; 24:5; 26:4; Ro 3:9; Tob 11:17; AdE 3:6; 4:13, 16; 8:13; 1Mc 10:29, 34; 1Es 4:49; 3Mc 2:28; 6:18

ALL JUDAH
1Ki 15:22; 2Ki 22:13; 2Ch 15:2, 9, 15; 16:6; 17:5, 19; 20:3, 13, 15, 18; 23:8; 25:5; 31:1, 20; 32:33; 34:9; 35:18, 24; Ne 13:12; Jer 13:19; 17:20; 20:4; 26:19; 44:11

ALL ... KINGDOMS
Dt 3:21; 28:25; Jos 11:10; 1Sa 10:18; 1Ki 4:21; 2Ki 19:15, 19; 1Ch 29:30; 2Ch 17:10; 20:6, 29; 36:23; Ezr 1:2; Ps 135:11; Isa 23:17; 37:16, 20; Jer 10:7; 15:4; 24:9; 25:26; 29:18; 34:1, 17; Da 2:44; 7:23; Mt 4:8; Lk 4:5; Bar 2:4; 2Es 12:13

ALL ... NATIONS
Ge 18:18; 22:18; 26:4; Dt 11:23; 17:14; 26:19; 28:1; 29:24; 30:1; Jos 23:3, 4; 2Sa 8:11; 1Ki 4:34; 1Ch 14:17; 18:11; 2Ch 32:23; Ne 6:16; Ps 9:17; 59:5, 8; 67:2; 72:11, 17; 82:8; 86:9; 113:4; 117:1; 118:10; Isa 2:2; 14:26; 25:7; 29:7, 8; 34:2; 37:18; 40:17; 43:9; 52:10; 61:11; 66:18, 20; Jer 3:17, 19; 9:26; 25:9, 13, 15, 17; 26:6; 27:7; 28:11, 14; 29:14, 18; 30:11; 33:9; 36:2; 43:5; 44:8; 46:28; Eze 25:8; 31:6; 39:21; Da 4:1; 5:19; 7:14; Joel 3:2, 11; Am 9:9, 12; Ob 1:15, 16; Hab 2:5; Hag 2:7, 7; Zec 7:14; 12:3, 9; 14:2,

19; Mal 3:12; Mt 24:9, 14; 25:32; 28:19; Mk 11:17; 13:10; Lk 21:24; 24:47; Ac 14:16; 17:26; Rev 12:5; 14:8; 15:4; 18:3, 23; Tob 3:4; 13:5; Jdt 3:8; AdE 13:4; 3:14; 4:11; 14:5; 10:10, 11; Sir 36:2; LtJ 6:51; 1Mc 2:19; 12:53; 13:6; 2Mc 8:9; 1Es 1:49; 3Mc 3:19, 20; 6:26; 7:4; 2Es 1:11; 13:33, 33

ALL ... PEOPLE Ge 19:4; 25:18; 26:11; 29:22; 35:6; 41:40; 42:6; Ex 1:22; 11:8; 18:14, 21, 23; 19:11, 16; 20:18; 23:27; 24:3; 32:3; 33:8, 10, 10; 34:10, 10; Lev 9:23, 24; 10:3; 16:33; 17:2; 21:24; 22:18; Nu 11:11, 12, 13, 14; 13:32; 21:23, 33, 34, 35; 32:15; Dt 2:32, 33; 3:1, 3; 13:9; 17:7, 13; 20:11; 27:1, 15, 16, 17, 18, 19, 20, 21, 22, 23, 24, 25, 26; Jos 1:2; 4:11; 5:5, 5; 6:5, 5; 7:3; 8:5, 14, 16, 25; 10:21; 11:14; 24:2, 27; Jdg 7:12; 9:49; 11:20, 21; 14:3; 16:30; 17:6; 20:2, 8; 21:25; Ru 4:9, 11; 1Sa 2:23; 10:24, 24, 24, 25; 11:4, 15; 12:18, 19; 13:7; 14:15, 20, 39; 15:6, 8; 18:5; 23:8; 30:6; 2Sa 2:28, 30; 3:31, 32, 34, 35, 36, 36, 37; 6:2, 19, 19; 7:7; 8:15; 12:29, 31; 15:17, 23, 23, 30; 16:6, 14; 17:2, 3, 3, 16, 22; 18:5; 19:9, 14, 39, 40, 41, 42; 20:2, 12, 13, 22; 1Ki 1:39, 40; 4:30; 8:2, 38, 63; 9:20; 12:12, 31; 13:33; 18:21, 24, 30, 30, 39; 20:8, 15; 2Ki 10:9, 18; 11:14, 18, 19, 20; 14:21; 16:15; 17:32; 23:2, 2, 3, 21; 25:26; 1Ch 13:4; 16:36, 43; 18:14; 20:3; 28:21; 2Ch 6:29; 7:3, 4, 5; 8:7; 10:12; 20:27; 23:5, 6, 10, 13, 16, 17, 20, 21; 24:10; 26:1; 29:36; 31:1; 32:9; 34:30, 30; 35:13; 36:23; Ezr 3:11; 7:25; 10:9, 9; Ne 8:1, 3, 5, 5, 5, 6, 9, 9, 11, 12, 13; 9:10, 32; Est 1:5; Job 1:3; 2:4; 36:25; Ps 36:7; 62:8; 106:48; 116:14, 18; 145:12; Ecc 4:16; Isa 8:12; 9:9; 40:5, 6; 64:9; Jer 7:2; 19:14; 25:1, 2, 19, 20; 26:7, 8, 8, 9, 11, 12, 16, 18; 27:16; 28:1, 5, 7, 11; 29:1, 16, 25; 34:8, 10, 19; 36:6, 9, 9, 10; 38:1, 4; 41:10, 13, 14; 42:1, 8, 17; 43:1, 4; 44:15, 20, 20, 24, 27; La 4:11; 3:14; Eze 39:13; 45:16, 22; Da 9:6; Am 9:1; Hag 2:4; Zec 2:13; 7:5; Mal 2:9; Mk 1:5; 6:39; Lk 2:10; 3:21; 7:29; 8:37, 47; 9:13; 18:43; 19:48; 20:6, 45; 21:38; 24:19; Jn 1:4; 2:24; 8:2; 12:32; 17:2; Ac 2:47; 3:9, 11; 4:10; 5:34; 10:41; 13:24; 17:30; 24:16; 1Co 9:22; 15:19, 29; 1Ti 4:10; Heb 9:19, 19; 1Pe 1:17; Jude 1:5; Tob 12:6; 13:8, 14; Jdt 1:6; 2:28; 4:3; 5:14, 22; 6:16; 7:13, 23; 8:29; 13:17, 20; 15:10, 11, 13, 14; AdE 13:2; Wis 12:13; 13:1; 16:12; Sir 44:22; 48:15; 50:17; Bar 1:3, 4, 7; Aza 1:60; Sus 1:47, 50; 1Mc 1:51; 4:55; 5:27; 6:19; 7:18; 10:7; 11:51; 12:44; 14:12, 46; 2Mc 1:26; 2:17; 3:34; 4:5; 11:6; 1Es 1:13; 4:10, 41; 5:62; 9:53; 3Mc 7:6, 8; 2Es 6:54; 8:62; 12:40; 13:36; 14:27; 15:57; 4Mc 1:11; 4:12

ALL ... PEOPLES Ex 19:5; Dt 4:19; 7:6, 7, 16, 19; 10:15; 14:2; 28:10, 37, 64; 30:3; Jos 4:24; 24:17, 18; 1Ki 8:43, 53, 60; 9:7; 1Ch 16:24; 2Ch 6:33; 7:20; 32:13; Est 1:16; 3:12, 14; 8:13; 9:2; Ps 47:1; 49:1; 67:3, 5; 96:3; 97:6; 99:2; 117:1; 148:11; Isa 25:6, 7; 56:7; Jer 34:1; La 1:18; Eze 31:12; Da 3:7, 7; 4:1; 5:19; 6:25; 7:14; Mic 4:5; Hab 2:5; Zep 3:20; Zec 11:10; 12:3; 14:12; Lk 2:31; Ac 15:17; Ro 15:11; 1Es 5:50

ALL ... SERVANTS Ge 20:8; 40:20; 41:37; 50:7; Dt 29:2; 34:11; 1Sa 18:22, 30; 19:1; 22:6, 14; 2Sa 11:9; 13:31, 36; 16:6, 11; 19:14; 1Ki 3:15; 2Ki 9:7; 17:23; Ne 5:16; 9:10; Ps 134:1; 135:9; Jer 7:25; 25:4; 35:15; 44:4; Rev 19:5; Jdt 10:20; 11:20; AdE 15:16

ALL THE ASSEMBLY Lev 16:17; Nu 14:5; Jos 8:35; Ru 3:11; 1Ki 8:14, 14, 22, 55; 12:3; 1Ch 29:10, 20; 2Ch 6:3, 3; 28:14; 30:2, 4; Ezr 10:12; Ne 5:13; 8:17; 1Mc 4:59

ALL THE CONGREGATION Ex 35:1, 4, 20; Lev 10:6; 19:2; Nu 13:26, 26; 14:1, 7, 36; 15:25, 26, 35; 16:3; 20:29; 27:2, 19, 20; 31:27; Jos 9:18, 19, 21; 22:20; 1Ki 8:5; 2Ch 5:6

ALL THE DAYS Ge 3:14, 17; 5:5, 8, 11, 14, 17, 20, 23, 27, 31; 9:29; Lev 15:25, 26; Nu

6:5, 6; Dt 4:9; 6:2; 12:1; 16:3; 17:19; Jos 1:5; 4:14; 24:31, 31; Jdg 2:7, 7, 18; 1Sa 7:13, 15; 14:52; 1Ki 4:21; 8:40; 11:25, 34; 15:5, 6; 2Ki 13:22; 23:22; 2Ch 6:31; 24:2, 14; 36:21; Job 14:14; Ps 23:6; 27:4; 128:5; 139:16; Pr 15:15; 31:12; Ecc 9:9; Isa 38:20; 63:9; Tob 1:3; 4:3, 5; 10:12, 12, 13; Jdt 8:6; 16:22; Sir 22:12; 1Mc 14:4; Man 1:15

ALL THE EARTH Ge 1:29; 7:3; 11:8, 9, 9; 18:25; Ex 9:14, 16; 34:10; Nu 14:21; Jos 3:11, 13; 23:14; 1Sa 17:46; 1Ki 2:2; 2Ki 5:15; 1Ch 16:14, 23, 30; Ps 8:1, 9; 19:4; 33:8; 45:16; 47:2, 7; 48:2; 57:5, 11; 66:1, 4; 83:18; 96:1, 9; 97:5, 9; 98:4; 100:1; 105:7; 108:5; Isa 10:14, 23; 12:5; 28:22; Jer 51:7, 49; La 2:15; Hab 2:20; Zep 3:8, 19; Zec 6:5; 14:9; Ro 9:17; 10:18; Rev 5:6; Tob 14:7; Jdt 11:1; Sir 24:6; 38:8; 48:15; Bar 2:15; 1Mc 15:9; 2Es 11:12, 40; 15:40

ALL THE FIRSTBORN Ex 11:5; 12:29, 29; 13:2, 12, 15; 34:20; Nu 3:12, 13, 13, 13, 40, 41, 41, 42, 43, 45; 8:17, 17, 18; Ps 78:51; 105:36

ALL THE INHABITANTS Ge 19:25; Ex 15:15; Nu 33:52; Jos 2:9, 24; 7:9; 8:24, 26; 9:11, 24; 13:6; Jdg 10:18; 11:8; 2Ki 23:2; 2Ch 15:5; Ps 33:8, 14; Jer 1:14; 13:13, 13; 17:20; 25:2, 29, 30; 35:17; 47:2; 51:24; Eze 27:35; 29:6; Da 4:35; Joel 1:14; 2:1; Zep 1:4, 18; Rev 13:8; Jdt 1:12; 5:15, 22

ALL THE ISRAELITES Ex 10:23; 12:42, 50; 16:6; 34:30, 32; Nu 8:16; 14:2, 10, 39; 17:9; 27:21; 32:18; Dt 27:14; Jos 3:1; 7:23; 10:24; 20:9; Jdg 2:4; 10:8; 19:30; 20:1; 20:26; 1Sa 2:14; 11:15; 13:20; 14:22; 17:24; 2Sa 16:15, 18; 18:17; 19:8; 1Ki 18:20; 2Ch 5:3; Tob 14:7; Sir 46:10; 1Mc 5:45

ALL THE KINGS Jos 5:1, 1; 9:1; 10:6; 2Sa 10:19; 1Ki 4:24, 34; 10:15, 23, 29; 16:33; 2Ki 18:5; 2Ch 1:17; 9:14, 22, 23, 26; Ps 102:15; 138:4; Isa 14:18; 62:2; Jer 25:20, 20, 22, 22, 24, 24, 25, 25, 25, 26; 2Es 15:20

ALL THE LAND Ge 13:15; 17:8; 19:28; 41:19, 29, 41, 43, 44, 46, 55, 56; 45:8, 20, 26; 47:13, 20; Ex 9:24, 25; 10:14, 15, 22; Lev 11:2; Dt 11:25; 19:8; 34:2; Jos 1:4; 2:24; 6:27; 9:24; 11:16; 13:4; 21:43; 24:3; Jdg 11:21; 1Sa 13:3, 19; 2Sa 9:7; 24:8; 1Ki 4:10; 9:19; 15:20; 2Ki 10:33; 15:29; 17:5; 1Ch 13:2; 2Ch 8:6; 15:8; 34:7; Job 42:15; Isa 7:24; Jer 44:26; Zec 5:6; Lk 4:25; Jdt 2:6

ALL THE MEN Ge 17:27; Dt 21:21; 29:10; Jdg 7:21, 24; 9:51; 12:4; 20:11; 1Sa 11:1; 17:19; 2Sa 1:11; 17:14, 24; 2Ki 24:16; 1Ch 10:7; Ezr 10:17; Jer 44:15; Jdt 7:12; 10:4; 15:13; 1Mc 11:70

ALL THE TRIBES Dt 29:21; Jos 24:1; Jdg 20:2, 10; 21:5; 1Sa 2:28; 10:20; 2Sa 5:1; 15:10; 19:9; 20:14; 24:2; 1Ki 11:32; 14:21; 2Ki 21:7; 1Ch 11:16; 12:13; 33:7; Jer 1:15; 25:9; Eze 48:19; Zec 9:1; Mt 24:30; Rev 1:7; Tob 1:4, 4; Sir 36:13

ALL THE/THESE WORDS Ge 45:27; Ex 4:28, 30; 19:7; 20:1; 24:3, 3, 4, 8; Nu 16:31; Dt 9:10; 12:28; 17:19; 27:3, 8; 28:58; 29:29; 31:1, 12; 32:44, 45, 46, 46; Jos 8:34; 24:27; Jdg 9:3; 1Sa 8:10, 21; 2Sa 7:17; 14:19; 2Ki 19:4; 22:16; 23:2; 1Ch 17:15; 2Ch 34:30; Pr 8:8; Isa 37:17; Jer 7:27; 11:6, 8; 16:10; 25:13, 30; 26:2, 12, 15; 30:2; 34:6; 36:2, 4, 11, 13, 16, 16, 17, 18, 20, 24, 28, 32; 43:1; 51:60, 61; Lk 2:19; Jdt 10:1; Bar 1:21

ALL THE WORK Ge 2:2, 3; Ex 36:7; 39:32, 43; Dt 14:29; Jos 24:31; Jdg 2:7; 1Ki 7:40, 51; 2Ki 22:17; 1Ch 6:49; 26:30; 28:13, 20, 21; 29:5; 2Ch 5:1; 8:16; Ne 10:33; Job 34:19; Ecc 8:17; Isa 64:8; Lk 10:40; 1Mc 4:51

ALL THE WORLD Ge 19:31; 41:57; Mk

16:15; Lk 2:1; Ac 11:28; 22:15; 1Pe 5:9; Aza 1:9, 14; 2Mc 5:15

ALL THESE THINGS Ge 20:8; 29:13; Lev 20:23; Dt 4:30; 30:1; Jdg 13:23; 1Sa 19:7; 2Sa 13:21; 1Ki 18:36; 1Ch 29:17; 2Ch 4:18; Job 33:29; Ecc 11:9; Isa 45:7; 66:2, 2; Jer 2:34; 5:19; 7:13; Eze 16:30, 43; 17:18; Da 12:7; Zec 8:12, 17; Mt 6:32, 32, 33; 13:34; 24:33, 34; 26:1; Mk 13:4, 30; Lk 1:65; 2:51; 7:18; 12:30; 18:34; 21:36; 24:14; Jn 15:21; Ac 7:50; Ro 8:37; 1Th 4:6; 2Pe 3:11; Tob 12:20; 14:4; Jdt 8:14; AdE 4:9; Sir 42:23; 1Mc 6:59; 11:29; 14:35; 2Es 6:33; 12:37

ALL THINGS Ge 24:1; Jos 1:17; 2Sa 14:20; 23:5; 2Ki 14:3; 1Ch 29:14; Job 42:2; Ps 8:6; 119:91; Pr 13:16; Ecc 1:8; 5:9; Isa 44:24; Jer 10:16; 51:19; Mt 11:27; 17:11; 19:26, 28; Mk 9:12, 23; 10:27; 14:36; Lk 10:22; 21:32; Jn 1:3; 3:35; 4:25; 13:3; 16:30; Ac 2:44; 17:25; Ro 8:28; 11:36; 1Co 2:15; 3:21; 4:13; 6:12, 12, 12; 8:6, 6; 9:22, 25; 10:23, 23, 23; 11:12; 13:7, 7, 7, 7; 14:26, 40; 15:27, 27, 28, 28; 2Co 11:6; Gal 3:22; Eph 1:10, 11, 22, 22; 3:9; 4:10; Php 2:14; 3:8, 21; 4:13; Col 1:16, 16, 17, 17, 20; 1Ti 3:11; 6:13; 2Ti 2:7; Tit 1:15; Heb 1:2, 3; 2:8, 8, 10; 3:4; 13:18; 1Pe 4:7, 11; 2Pe 3:4; 1Jn 2:27; Rev 4:11; 21:5; AdE 13:9; 12; 14:15; 16:18, 21; Wis 1:7, 10, 14; 7:22, 24, 27, 27; 8:1, 5; 9:1, 11; 10:2; 11:20, 23, 24, 26; 12:1, 15; 15:1; 16:17; 18:14, 16; Sir 18:26; 24:8; 42:24; 43:22, 26, 33; Bar 3:32; Sus 1:42; 2Mc 1:24; 7:23; 12:22; 15:2; 1Es 3:12; 4:35; 8:21; Man 1:4; 3Mc 2:3, 21; 5:28; 7:18; 2Es 8:44; 11:6; 16:62; 4Mc 11:5

AT ALL TIMES Ex 18:22, 26; Job 27:10; Ps 10:5; 34:1; 62:8; 106:3; 119:20; Pr 5:19; 17:17; Lk 21:36; Gal 4:18; Eph 5:20; 6:18; 2Th 3:16; Tob 4:19; 14:8; Wis 19:22; Sir 6:37; 22:6; 26:4; 1Mc 1:36

FOR ALL TIME Lev 25:34; Dt 4:40; 18:5; 1Sa 1:22; 1Ki 9:3; 2Ch 7:16; Ps 77:8; Jer 32:39; 33:18; 35:19; Eze 46:14; Heb 7:25; 10:12, 14; AdE 16:24; 9:28; Bar 3:32; 1Mc 10:30; 15:8; 3Mc 3:29

ALLEGORY*

Eze 17: 2 speak an **a** to the house of Israel.
    24: 3 utter an **a** to the rebellious house
Gal 4:24 an **a:** these women are two
    covenants.

ALLIANCE → ALLY

1Ki 3: 1 Solomon made a marriage **a** with
Isa 30: 1 who make an **a**, but against my will,

ALLOT → ALLOTMENT, ALLOTMENTS

Jos 13: 6 only **a** the land to Israel for an
Isa 53:12 I will **a** him a portion with the great,

ALLOTMENT → ALLOT

Dt 10: 9 Levi has no **a** or inheritance with
Eze 48:13 the Levites shall have an **a**

ALLOTMENTS → ALLOT

Jos 11:23 to Israel according to their tribal **a.**

ALLOW → ALLOWED

Lk 4:41 and would not **a** them to speak,
Ac 16: 7 the Spirit of Jesus did not **a** them;

ALLOWED → ALLOW

Ex 1:18 and **a** the boys to live?"
Ps 105:14 he **a** no one to oppress them;
Da 1: 9 Now God **a** Daniel to receive favor
Mt 19: 8 Moses **a** you to divorce your wives,
Ac 28:16 Paul was **a** to live by himself,

ALLURE*

Hos 2:14 Therefore, I will now **a** her,

ALLY → ALLIANCE

Pr 18:19 An **a** offended is stronger than a city
2Mc 8:24 With the Almighty as their **a,**

ALMIGHTY → MIGHT

Ge 17: 1 "I am God **A**; walk before me,
35:11 God said to him, "I am God **A**:
Ex 6: 3 Isaac, and Jacob as God **A**,
Nu 24: 4 who sees the vision of the **A**,
Ru 1:20 for the **A** has dealt bitterly with me.
Job 5:17 not despise the discipline of the **A**.
6: 4 For the arrows of the **A** are in me;
11: 7 Can you find out the limit of the **A**?
21:15 What is the **A**, that we should serve
33: 4 the breath of the **A** gives me life.
Ps 91: 1 who abide in the shadow of the **A**,
Isa 13: 6 come like destruction from the **A**!
Joel 1:15 as destruction from the **A** it comes.
Rev 1: 8 who was and who is to come, the **A**.
4: 8 the Lord God the **A**, who was and is
19: 6 For the Lord our God the **A** reigns.
21:22 its temple is the Lord God the **A**
Jdt 16: 5 Lord **A** has foiled them by the hand
Bar 3: 1 O Lord **A**, God of Israel,
Man 1: 1 O Lord **A**, God of our ancestors,

GOD ALMIGHTY Ge 17:1; 28:3; 35:11;
43:14; 48:3; Ex 6:3; Eze 10:5; Rev 11:17

LORD ALMIGHTY 2Co 6:18; Jdt 4:13;
8:13; 16:5, 17; Bar 3:1, 4; Man 1:1; 2Es 1:15,
22, 28, 33; 2:9, 31

ALMOND → ALMONDS

Ex 25:33 three cups shaped like **a** blossoms,
Jer 1:11 I said, "I see a branch of an **a** tree."

ALMONDS → ALMOND

Nu 17: 8 produced blossoms, and bore ripe **a**.

ALMOST

Ps 73: 2 my feet had **a** stumbled;

ALMS → ALMSGIVING

Mt 6: 2 "So whenever you give **a**,
Lk 12:33 Sell your possessions, and give **a**.
Ac 3: 2 that he could ask for **a** from those
Tob 4:16 Give all your surplus as **a**,
12: 8 better to give **a** than to lay up gold.
Sir 7:10 do not neglect to give **a**.

ALMSGIVING → ALMS

Tob 4:10 For **a** delivers from death
Sir 3:30 so **a** atones for sin.

ALONE → LONELY

Ge 2:18 not good that the man should be **a**;
Ex 18:18 heavy for you; you cannot do it **a**.
Dt 6: 4 The Lord is our God, the Lord **A**.
6:13 by his name you shall swear.
8: 3 that one does not live by bread **a**,
1Ki 19:10 I **a** am left, and they are seeking my
Ne 9:10 "You are the Lord, you **a**;
Ps 51: 4 Against you, you **a**, have I sinned,
62: 1 For God **a** my soul waits in silence;
136: 4 who **a** does great wonders,
148:13 for his name **a** is exalted;
Pr 16:33 but the decision is the Lord's **a**.
Ecc 4:11 but how can one keep warm **a**?
Isa 2:11 Lord **a** will be exalted in that day.
Mt 4: 4 'One does not live by bread **a**,
Mk 2: 7 Who can forgive sins but God **a**?"
10:18 No one is good but God **a**.
Jn 16:32 not **a** because the Father is with me.
Ro 11: 3 I **a** am left, and they are seeking my
Jas 2:24 justified by works and not by faith **a**
Rev 15: 4 For you **a** are holy.
Tob 8: 6 not good that the man should be **a**;
Sus 1:14 when they could find her **a**.

ALOUD → LOUD

Ezr 3:12 though many shouted **a** for joy,
Ps 27: 7 Hear, O Lord, when I cry **a**,
81: 1 Sing **a** to God our strength;
Rev 1: 3 reads **a** the words of the prophecy,

ALPHA*

Rev 1: 8 "I am the **A** and the Omega,"
21: 6 I am the **A** and the Omega,

22:13 I am the **A** and the Omega,

ALREADY

Mt 17:12 but I tell you that Elijah has **a** come,
Jn 3:18 do not believe are condemned **a**,
19:33 and saw that he was **a** dead,
Php 3:12 Not that I have **a** obtained this or
have **a** reached the goal;
2Th 2: 2 that the day of the Lord is **a** here.
2: 7 mystery of lawlessness is **a** at work,
2Ti 2:18 the resurrection has **a** taken place.
1Jn 2: 8 and the true light is **a** shining.

ALTAR → ALTARS

Ge 8:20 Then Noah built an **a** to the Lord,
12: 7 So he built there an **a** to the Lord,
13:18 and there he built an **a** to the Lord.
22: 9 Isaac, and laid him on the **a**,
26:25 So he built an **a** there,
33:20 an **a** and called it El-Elohe-Israel.
35: 1 Make an **a** there to the God
Ex 17:15 And Moses built an **a** and called it,
20:24 for me only an **a** of earth
24: 4 an **a** at the foot of the mountain,
27: 1 shall make the **a** of acacia wood,
30: 1 an **a** on which to offer incense;
32: 5 he built an **a** before it;
37:25 He made the **a** of incense of acacia
38: 1 the **a** of burnt offering also of acacia
Lev 8:11 anointed the **a** and all its utensils,
9:24 burnt offering and the fat on the **a**;
Dt 27: 5 an **a** there to the Lord your God,
Jos 8:30 Joshua built on Mount Ebal an **a** to
22:10 an **a** by the Jordan, an **a** of great size
Jdg 6:24 Gideon built an **a** there to the Lord,
13:20 went up toward heaven from the **a**,
21: 4 got up early, and built an **a** there,
1Sa 7:17 and built there an **a** to the Lord.
14:35 And Saul built an **a** to the Lord;
2Sa 24:25 David built there an **a** to the Lord,
1Ki 3: 4 a thousand burnt offerings on that **a**.
12:33 to the **a** that he had made in Bethel
13: 2 said, "O **a**, **a**, thus says the Lord:
16:32 He erected an **a** for Baal
18:30 **a** of the Lord that had been thrown
2Ki 16:10 he saw the **a** that was at Damascus.
1Ch 21:26 with fire from heaven on the **a** of
2Ch 4: 1 He made an **a** of bronze,
4:19 in the house of God: the golden **a**,
15: 8 He repaired the **a** of the Lord that
32:12 'Before one **a** you shall worship,
33:16 He also restored the **a** of the Lord
Ezr 3: 2 to build the **a** of the God of Israel,
Ne 10:34 on the **a** of the Lord our God,
Ps 43: 4 Then I will go to the **a** of God,
51:19 then bulls will be offered on your **a**.
118:27 up to the horns of the **a**.
Isa 6: 6 coal that had been taken from the **a**
60: 7 they shall be acceptable on my **a**,
La 2: 7 Lord has scorned his **a**,
Eze 8:16 between the porch and the **a**,
40:47 and the **a** was in front of the temple.
47: 1 of the temple, south of the **a**.
Joel 1:13 wail, you ministers of the **a**.
Am 2: 8 beside every **a** on garments taken in
9: 1 saw the Lord standing beside the **a**,
Mal 1: 7 By offering polluted food on my **a**.
Mt 5:24 leave your gift there before the **a**
23:18 swears by the **a** is bound by nothing,
Lk 11:51 who perished between the **a** and the
Ac 17:23 an **a** with the inscription,
1Co 10:18 eat the sacrifices partners in the **a**?
Heb 13:10 We have an **a** from which those
Jas 2:21 he offered his son Isaac on the **a**?
Rev 6: 9 I saw under the **a** the souls of those
8: 3 of all the saints on the golden **a**
11: 1 the temple of God and the **a**
Jdt 4:12 even draped the **a** with sackcloth
Sir 35: 8 of the righteous enriches the **a**.
1Mc 1:54 a desolating sacrilege on the **a** of
1:59 on the **a** that was on top of the **a**
2:24 he ran and killed him on the **a**.

4:45 So they tore down the **a**,
4:47 built a new **a** like the former one.
4:56 dedication of the **a** for eight days,
2Mc 1:19 took some of the fire of the **a**
1:32 the light from the **a** shone back,

ALTARS → ALTAR

Ex 34:13 You shall tear down their **a**,
Nu 3:31 the table, the lampstand, the **a**,
23: 1 said to Balak, "Build me seven **a**
Dt 7: 5 break down their **a**, smash their
Jdg 2: 2 of this land; tear down their **a**.'
2Ki 23:20 slaughtered on the **a** all the priests
2Ch 33: 3 and erected **a** to the Baals,
34: 4 they pulled down the **a** of the Baals
Isa 36: 7 and a Hezekiah has removed,
Eze 6: 5 scatter your bones around your **a**.
Hos 8:11 they became to him **a** for sinning,
1Mc 2:45 went around and tore down the **a**;

ALTER → ALTERED

Ps 89:34 or **a** the word that went forth from

ALTERED → ALTER

Est 1:19 so that it may not be **a**,

ALWAYS

Dt 5:29 to keep all my commandments **a**,
14:23 learn to fear the Lord your God **a**.
19: 9 and walking **a** in his ways—
Ps 16: 8 I keep the Lord **a** before me;
61: 8 I will **a** sing praises to your name,
103: 9 He will not **a** accuse,
Pr 5:19 be intoxicated **a** by her love.
6:21 Bind them upon your heart **a**;
23:17 **a** continue in the fear of the Lord.
Isa 57:16 nor will I **a** be angry;
Mt 26:11 For you **a** have the poor with you,
but you will not **a** have me.
28:20 And remember, I am with you **a**,
Lk 18: 1 to pray **a** and not to lose heart.
Jn 6:34 to him, "Sir, give us this bread **a**."
11:42 I knew that you **a** hear me,
Ac 2:25 'I saw the Lord **a** before me,
2Co 2:14 in Christ **a** leads us in triumphal
5: 6 So we are **a** confident;
6:10 sorrowful, yet **a** rejoicing;
Php 4: 4 Rejoice in the Lord **a**; again I will
1Th 5:15 but **a** seek to do good to one another
5:16 Rejoice **a**,
Phm 1: 4 in my prayers, I **a** thank my God
Heb 7:25 he **a** lives to make intercession for
1Pe 3:15 **A** be ready to make your defense

AMALEK → AMALEKITE, AMALEKITES

Ex 17: 8 Then **A** came and fought with Israel
17:14 blot out the remembrance of **A**
Nu 24:20 looked on **A**, and uttered his oracle,
Dt 25:17 Remember what **A** did to you
1Sa 15: 3 attack **A**, and utterly destroy all
28:18 carry out his fierce wrath against **A**,

AMALEKITE → AMALEK

2Sa 1: 8 I answered him, 'I am an **A**.'

AMALEKITES → AMALEK

Nu 14:43 **A** and the Canaanites will confront
1Sa 15: 8 He took King Agag of the **A** alive,

AMASA

Nephew of David (1Ch 2:17). Commander of
Absalom's forces (2Sa 17:24-27). Returned to
David (2Sa 19:13). Killed by Joab (2Sa 20:4-13).

AMASS*

Jer 17:11 so are all who **a** wealth unjustly;
Sir 31: 3 The rich person toils to **a** a fortune,

AMAZED → AMAZING

Mt 8:27 **a**, saying, "What sort of man is this,
9:33 and the crowds were **a** and said,
12:23 All the crowds were **a** and said,
15:31 so that the crowd was **a**
Mk 6: 6 And he was **a** at their unbelief.

15: 5 Jesus made no further reply, so that
       Pilate was **a.**
Ac   2: 7 **A** and astonished, they asked,
Rev 17: 8 will be **a** when they see the beast,

AMAZEMENT → AMAZING

Lk   5:26 **A** seized all of them, and they
       glorified God
Ac   3:10 they were filled with wonder and **a**
Rev 13: 3 In **a** the whole earth followed the
       beast.

AMAZIAH

1. Son of Joash; king of Judah (2Ki 14; 2Ch 25).
Defeated Edom (2Ki 14:7; 2Ch 25:5-13);
defeated by Israel for worshiping Edom's gods
(2Ki 14:8-14; 2Ch 25:14-24).
2. Idolatrous priest who opposed Amos (Am
7:10-17).

AMAZING → AMAZED, AMAZEMENT

Mk 12:11 and it is **a** in our eyes'?"
Rev 15: 3 "Great and **a** are your deeds,

AMBASSADOR* → AMBASSADORS

Eph   6:20 for which I am an **a** in chains.

AMBASSADORS → AMBASSADOR

2Co   5:20 So we are **a** for Christ,

AMBITION

Ro   15:20 my **a** to proclaim the good news,
Php   1:17 proclaim Christ out of selfish **a,**
      2: 3 Do nothing from selfish **a** or conceit
Jas   3:14 envy and selfish **a** in your hearts,
      3:16 where there is envy and selfish **a,**

AMBUSH

Jos   8: 2 Set an **a** against the city, behind it."
Jdg 20:29 So Israel stationed men in **a** around
2Ch 20:22 the LORD set an **a** against the
Pr   1:18 and set an **a**—for their own lives!
     12: 6 words of the wicked are a deadly **a,**
Ac 23:21 forty of their men are lying in **a**
     25: 3 an **a** to kill him along the way.

AMEN

Dt 27:15 people shall respond, saying, "**A!**"
1Ch 16:36 Then all the people said "**A!**"
Ne   5:13 And all the assembly said, "**A,**"
      8: 6 all the people answered, "**A, A,**"
Ps 89:52 Blessed be the LORD forever. **A** and
       A.
Ro   1:25 Creator, who is blessed forever! **A.**
      9: 5 over all, God blessed forever. **A.**
     11:36 To him be the glory forever. **A.**
1Co 14:16 say the "**A**" to your thanksgiving,
2Co   1:20 through him that we say the "**A,**"
Rev   3:14 The words of the **A,** the faithful and
      5:14 the four living creatures said, "**A!**"
     19: 4 seated on the throne, saying, "**A.**
     22:20 "Surely I am coming soon." **A.**
Tob   8: 8 And they both said, "**A, A.**"
Jdt 13:20 And all the people said, "**A. A.**"
1Es   9:47 and the multitude answered, "**A.**"

AMEND → AMENDS

Jer   7: 3 **A** your ways and your doings,

AMENDS → AMEND

Lev 26:41 and they make **a** for their iniquity,

AMMI*

Hos   2: 1 Say to your brother, **A,** and to your

AMMON → AMMONITE, AMMONITES

Ne 13:23 married women of Ashdod, **A,** and
Eze 25:10 **A** shall be remembered no more

AMMONITE → AMMON

Dt 23: 3 No **A** or Moabite shall be admitted
Ne   2:10 and Tobiah the **A** official heard this,
     13: 1 no **A** or Moabite should ever enter
Jdt   6: 5 Achior, you **A** mercenary,

AMMONITES → AMMON

Ge 19:38 the ancestor of the **A** to this day.
Dt   2:19 not give the land of the **A** to you as
Jdg 11: 4 the **A** made war against Israel.
1Sa 10:27 Now Nahash, king of the **A,**
2Sa 10: 1 the king of the **A** died,
1Ki 11: 5 Milcom the abomination of the **A.**
Jer 49: 6 I will restore the fortunes of the **A,**
Eze 21:28 the Lord GOD concerning the **A,**
     25: 2 the **A** and prophesy against them.
Zep   2: 9 Sodom and the **A** like Gomorrah,

AMNON

Firstborn of David (2Sa 3:2; 1Ch 3:1). Killed by
Absalom for raping his sister Tamar (2Sa 13).

AMON

1. Son of Manasseh; king of Judah (2Ki 21:18-
26; 1Ch 3:14; 2Ch 33:21-25).
2. Ruler of Samaria under Ahab (1Ki 22:26;
2Ch 18:25).

AMORITE → AMORITES

Ge 14:13 living by the oaks of Mamre the **A,**
Eze 16: 3 your father was an **A,** and your
Am   2: 9 Yet I destroyed the **A** before them,

AMORITES → AMORITE

Ge 15:16 iniquity of the **A** is not yet complete
Ex 34:11 I will drive out before you the **A,**
Nu 21:31 Israel settled in the land of the **A.**
Jdg   6:10 pay reverence to the gods of the **A,**
1Sa   7:14 peace also between Israel and the **A.**

AMOS

1. Prophet from Tekoa (Am 1:1; 7:10-17; Tob
2:6).
2. Ancestor of Jesus (Lk 3:25).

AMPLE

Lk 12:19 'Soul, you have **a** goods laid up for
Sir 31:19 **a** a little is for a well-disciplined

AMRAM

Ex   6:20 **A** married Jochebed his father's
1Ch   6: 3 The children of **A**: Aaron, Moses,

AMULETS*

Isa   3:20 the perfume boxes, and the **a**;

ANAK → ANAKIM

Nu 13:28 we saw the descendants of **A** there.
Jos 15:13 (Arba was the father of **A).**

ANAKIM → ANAK

Dt   1:28 saw there the offspring of the **A!**'"
Jos 11:22 None of the **A** was left in the land

ANANIAS

1. Husband of Sapphira; died for lying to God
(Ac 5:1-11).
2. Disciple who baptized Saul (Ac 9:10-19).
3. High priest at Paul's arrest (Ac 22:30-24:1).

ANATHOTH

Jer 32: 7 "Buy my field that is at **A,**

ANCESTOR → ANCESTORS

Ge 17: 4 be the **a** of a multitude of nations.
Dt 26: 5 "A wandering Aramean was my **a**;
Mt   3: 9 'We have Abraham as our **a**';
Ro   4: 1 our **a** according to the flesh?

ANCESTORS → ANCESTOR

Ex   3:13 'The God of your **a** has sent me to
Dt   1: 8 of the land that I swore to your **a,**
      4:31 not forget the covenant with your **a**
1Ki 19: 4 for I am no better than my **a.**"
Ps 22: 4 In you our **a** trusted; they trusted,
    106: 6 Both we and our **a** have sinned;
La   5: 7 Our **a** sinned; they are no more,
Am   2: 4 lies after which their **a** walked.
Zec   1: 4 Do not be like your **a,**
Lk 11:48 and approve of the deeds of your **a**;
Jn   4:20 Our **a** worshiped on this mountain,

6:31 Our **a** ate the manna in the
       wilderness;
Ac   5:30 The God of our **a** raised up Jesus,
Heb   1: 1 Long ago God spoke to our **a** in
     11: 2 by faith our **a** received approval.
Tob   8: 5 "Blessed are you, O God of our **a,**

GOD OF ... ANCESTORS Ex 3:13, 15, 16;

4:5; Dt 1:11, 21; 4:1; 6:3; 12:1; 26:7; 27:3;
29:25; Jos 18:3; Jdg 2:12; 2Ki 21:22; 1Ch
5:25; 12:17; 29:20; 2Ch 7:22; 11:16; 13:12,
18; 14:4; 15:12; 19:4; 20:6, 33; 21:10; 24:18,
24; 28:6, 9, 25; 29:5; 30:7, 19, 22; 33:12;
34:32, 33; 36:15; Ezr 7:27; 8:28; 10:11; Da
2:23; Ac 3:13; 5:30; 7:32; 22:14; 24:14; Tob
8:5; Jdt 10:8; Wis 9:1; Aza 1:3, 29; 1Es 1:50;
4:62; 9:8; Man 1:1; 3Mc 7:16; 4Mc 12:17

ANCHOR

Heb   6:19 a sure and steadfast **a** of the soul,

ANCIENT → ANCIENTS

Ps 24: 7 and be lifted up, O **a** doors!
     68:33 rider in the heavens, the **a** heavens;
Pr 22:28 Do not remove the **a** landmark
Isa 58:12 Your **a** ruins shall be rebuilt;
Jer   6:16 ask for the **a** paths, where the good
Da   7: 9 and an **A** One took his throne,
      7:13 And he came to the **A** One
      7:22 until the **A** One came;
Mic   5: 2 origin is from of old, from **a** days.
Rev 12: 9 was thrown down, that **a** serpent,
     20: 2 He seized the dragon, that **a** serpent,
Sir 16: 7 He did not forgive the **a** giants

ANCIENTS* → ANCIENT

Sir 39: 1 He seeks out the wisdom of all the **a**

ANDREW*

Apostle; brother of Simon Peter (Mt 4:18; 10:2;
Mk 1:16-18, 29; 3:18; 13:3; Lk 6:14; Jn 1:35-44;
6:8-9; 12:22; Ac 1:13).

ANEW* → NEW

1Pe   1:23 born **a,** not of perishable but
Wis 19: 6 in its nature was fashioned **a,**

ANGEL → ANGELS, ARCHANGEL,
   ARCHANGEL'S

Ge 16: 7 **a** of the LORD found her by a spring
     21:17 and the **a** of God called to Hagar
     22:11 the **a** of the LORD called to him
     24: 7 he will send his **a** before you,
     31:11 **a** of God said to me in the dream,
     48:16 the **a** who has redeemed me from all
Ex   3: 2 the **a** of the LORD appeared to him
     14:19 The **a** of God who was going before
     23:20 going to send an **a** in front of you,
     32:34 see, my **a** shall go in front of you.
     33: 2 I will send an **a** before you,
Nu 20:16 an **a** and brought us out of Egypt;
     22:22 the **a** of the LORD took his stand in
Jdg   2: 1 **a** of the LORD went up from Gilgal
      6:12 **a** of the LORD appeared to him and
      6:22 seen the **a** of the LORD face to face."
     13: 3 And the **a** of the LORD appeared to
1Sa 29: 9 in my sight as an **a** of God;
2Sa 14:17 the king is like the **a** of God,
     19:27 the king is like the **a** of God;
     24:16 the **a** stretched out his hand toward
1Ki 13:18 and an **a** spoke to me by the word
     19: 5 Suddenly an **a** touched him and said
2Ki   1: 3 the **a** of the LORD said to Elijah
      19:35 That very night the **a** of the LORD
1Ch 21:15 sent an **a** to Jerusalem to destroy it;
Job 33:23 should be for one of them an **a,**
Ps 34: 7 The **a** of the LORD encamps
     35: 5 the **a** of the LORD driving them on.
Isa 37:36 the **a** of the LORD set out and struck
     63: 9 or a but his presence that saved
Da   3:28 who has sent his **a** and delivered
      6:22 God sent his **a** and shut the lions'
Hos 12: 4 He strove with the **a** and prevailed,
Zec   1:11 they spoke to the **a** of the LORD

3: 1 standing before the **a** of the Lord,
Mt 1:20 an **a** of the Lord appeared to him in
2:13 an **a** of the Lord appeared to Joseph
28: 2 for an **a** of the Lord, descending
Lk 1:11 appeared to him an **a** of the Lord,
1:26 In the sixth month the **a** Gabriel
2: 9 Then an **a** of the Lord stood before
22:43 [an **a** from heaven appeared to him]
Jn 12:29 Others said, "An **a** has spoken to
Ac 5:19 during the night an **a** of the Lord
6:15 his face was like the face of an **a**.
7:30 **a** appeared to him in the wilderness
8:26 Then an **a** of the Lord said to Philip,
10: 3 in which he clearly saw an **a** of God
12: 7 an **a** of the Lord appeared and
23: 8 Sadducees say that there is no
resurrection, or **a**,
27:23 there stood by me an **a** of the God
2Co 11:14 Even Satan disguises himself as an
a of light.
Gal 1: 8 if we or an **a** from heaven should
4:14 but welcomed me as an **a** of God,
Rev 1: 1 by sending his **a** to his servant John,
2: 1 "To the **a** of the church in Ephesus
5: 2 a mighty **a** proclaiming with a loud
7: 2 I saw another **a** ascending from the
8: 3 Another **a** with a golden censer
9:11 the **a** of the bottomless pit;
14: 6 saw another **a** flying in midheaven,
16: 2 the first **a** went and poured his bowl
19:17 Then I saw an **a** standing in the sun,
22:16 "It is I, Jesus, who sent my **a** to you
Tob 5: 4 the **a** Raphael standing in front of
12:22 an **a** of God had appeared to them.
Sir 48:21 and his **a** wiped them out.
LtJ 6: 7 For my **a** is with you,
Aza 1:26 But the **a** of the Lord came down
Sus 1:59 **a** of God is waiting with his sword
Bel 1:34 the **a** of the Lord said to Habakkuk,
1Mc 7:41 your **a** went out and struck
2Mc 11: 6 to send a good **a** to save Israel.
2Es 2:44 Then I asked an **a**, "Who are these,
4: 1 Then the **a** that had been sent to me,
5:20 as the **a** Uriel had commanded me.

ANGEL OF GOD Ge 21:17; 31:11; Ex
14:19; Jdg 6:20; 13:6, 9; 1Sa 29:9; 2Sa 14:17,
20; 19:27; Ac 10:3; 27:23; Gal 4:14; Tob 5:4;
12:22; AdE 15:13; Sus 1:55, 59; Bel 1:39

ANGEL OF THE *LORD Mt 1:20, 24;
2:13, 19; 28:2; Lk 1:11; 2:9; Ac 5:19; 8:26;
12:7, 23; Aza 1:26; Bel 1:34, 36

ANGEL OF THE †LORD Ge 16:7, 9, 10,
11; 22:11, 15; Ex 3:2; Nu 22:22, 23, 24, 25,
26, 27, 31, 32, 34, 35; Jdg 2:1, 4; 5:23; 6:11,
12, 21, 21, 22, 22; 13:3, 13, 15, 16, 16, 17, 18,
20, 21, 21; 2Sa 24:16; 1Ki 19:7; 2Ki 1:3, 15;
19:35; 1Ch 21:12, 15, 16, 18, 30; Ps 34:7;
35:5, 6; Isa 37:36; Zec 1:11, 12; 3:1, 5, 6; 12:8

ANGELS → ANGEL
Ge 19: 1 The two **a** came to Sodom in the
28:12 **a** of God were ascending and
32: 1 and the **a** of God met him;
Job 4:18 and his **a** he charges with error;
Ps 78:25 Mortals ate of the bread of **a**;
91:11 command his **a** concerning you
103:20 Bless the Lord, O you his **a**,
148: 2 Praise him, all his **a**; praise him,
Mt 4: 6 command his **a** concerning you,'
4:11 suddenly **a** came and waited on him.
13:39 of the age, and the reapers are **a**.
16:27 Son of Man is to come with his **a**
18:10 in heaven their **a** continually see
24:36 neither the **a** of heaven, nor the Son,
25:41 fire prepared for the devil and his **a**;
26:53 more than twelve legions of **a**?
Mk 1:13 and the **a** waited on him.
8:38 glory of his Father with the holy **a**."
12:25 but are like **a** in heaven.
13:32 neither the **a** in heaven, nor the Son,
Lk 2:15 When the **a** had left them and gone

4:10 command his **a** concerning you,
12: 8 acknowledge before the **a** of God;
15:10 joy in the presence of the **a** of God
16:22 died and was carried away by the **a**
20:36 because they are like **a** and are
Jn 1:51 and the **a** of God ascending and
20:12 and she saw two **a** in white,
Ac 7:53 received the law as ordained by **a**,
Ro 8:38 that neither death, nor life, nor **a**,
1Co 4: 9 a spectacle to the world, to **a** and
6: 3 not know that we are to judge **a**—
11:10 on her head, because of the **a**.
13: 1 in the tongues of mortals and of **a**,
Gal 3:19 ordained through **a** by a mediator.
Col 2:18 on self-abasement and worship of **a**,
2Th 1: 7 from heaven with his mighty **a**
1Ti 5:21 seen by **a**, proclaimed among
5:21 of Christ Jesus and of the elect **a**,
Heb 1: 4 become as much superior to **a** as
1: 6 "Let all God's **a** worship him."
1: 7 Of the **a** he says, "He makes his **a**
winds,
1:14 not all **a** spirits in the divine service,
2: 2 declared through **a** was valid,
2: 7 for a little while lower than the **a**;
2: 9 while was made lower than the **a**,
12:22 to innumerable **a** in festal gathering,
13: 2 entertained **a** without knowing it.
1Pe 1:12 things into which **a** long to look!
3:22 with **a**, authorities, and powers
2Pe 2: 4 not spare the **a** when they sinned,
Jude 1: 6 the **a** who did not keep their own
Rev 1:20 the seven stars the **a** of the
seven churches,
3: 5 before my Father and before his **a**.
5:11 and I heard the voice of many **a**
7: 1 After this I saw four **a** standing at
8: 2 the seven **a** who stand before God,
9:14 "Release the four **a** who are bound
12: 7 Michael and his **a** fought against
15: 1 seven **a** with seven plagues,
21:12 and at the gates twelve **a**,
Tob 11:14 and blessed be all his holy **a**.
Wis 16:20 you gave your people food of **a**,
Aza 1:37 Bless the Lord, you **a** of the Lord;
2Es 1:19 you ate the bread of **a**.
6: 3 hosts of **a** were gathered together,
4Mc 4:10 **a** on horseback with lightning

ANGER → ANGERED, ANGRY
Ge 27:45 your brother's **a** against you turns
49: 7 Cursed be their **a**, for it is fierce,
Ex 4:14 **a** of the Lord was kindled against
Moses
32:19 the dancing, Moses' **a** burned hot,
34: 6 merciful and gracious, slow to **a**,
Nu 11: 1 heard it and his **a** was kindled.
11:33 **a** of the Lord was kindled against
12: 9 **a** of the Lord was kindled against
14:18 'The Lord is slow to **a**,
22:22 God's **a** was kindled because he
25: 3 the Lord's **a** was kindled against
32:10 Lord's **a** was kindled on that day
Dt 6:15 The **a** of the Lord your God would
9:19 I was afraid that the **a** that the Lord
29:28 uprooted them from their land in **a**,
32:22 For a fire is kindled by my **a**,
Jos 7: 1 the **a** of the Lord burned against
7:26 the Lord turned from his burning **a**.
23:16 the **a** of the Lord will be kindled
Jdg 2:12 and they provoked the Lord to **a**
14:19 In hot **a** he went back to his father's
1Sa 20:30 Then Saul's **a** was kindled against
2Sa 12: 5 David's **a** was greatly kindled
1Ki 14:15 provoking the Lord to **a**.
16:13 God of Israel to **a** with their idols.
Ne 9:17 slow to **a** and abounding in steadfast
Ps 6: 1 Lord, do not rebuke me in your **a**,
30: 5 For his **a** is but for a moment;
37: 8 Refrain from **a**, and forsake wrath.
78:38 often he restrained his **a**,
86:15 slow to **a** and abounding in steadfast

90: 7 For we are consumed by your **a**;
95:11 in my **a** I swore, "They shall not
103: 8 slow to **a** and abounding in steadfast
103: 9 nor will he keep his **a** forever.
145: 8 slow to **a** and abounding in steadfast
Pr 12:16 Fools show their **a** at once,
15: 1 but a harsh word stirs up **a**.
19:11 Those with good sense are slow to **a**
29:11 A fool gives full vent to **a**,
30:33 so pressing **a** produces strife.
Ecc 7: 9 Do not be quick to **a**,
Isa 5:25 For all this his **a** has not turned
48: 9 For my name's sake I defer my **a**,
63: 6 I trampled down peoples in my **a**,
Jer 3:12 will not look on you in **a**, for I am
La 4:11 he poured out his hot **a**,
Eze 43: 8 I have consumed them in my **a**.
Da 9:16 let your **a** and wrath, we pray,
Hos 11: 9 I will not execute my fierce **a**;
Joel 2:13 slow to **a**, and abounding in
Jnh 3: 9 he may turn from his fierce **a**,
4: 2 slow to **a**, and abounding in
Mic 7:18 He does not retain his **a** forever,
Na 1: 3 Lord is slow to **a** but great in power
Mk 3: 5 He looked around at them with **a**;
2Co 12:20 jealousy, **a**, selfishness, slander,
Gal 5:20 jealousy, **a**, quarrels, dissensions,
Eph 4:26 not let the sun go down on your **a**,
6: 4 do not provoke your children to **a**,
Col 3: 8 must get rid of all such things—**a**,
1Ti 2: 8 lifting up holy hands without **a** or
Heb 3:11 As in my **a** I swore, 'They will not
Jas 1:19 slow to speak, slow to **a**;
Rev 14:10 unmixed into the cup of his **a**,
Sir 5: 4 for the Lord is slow to **a**.
30:24 Jealousy and **a** shorten life,

ANGERED → ANGER
2Ki 24:20 Judah so **a** the Lord that he
Ezr 5:12 ancestors had **a** the God of heaven,

ANGRY → ANGER
Ge 4: 5 So Cain was very **a**, and his
18:30 not let the Lord be **a** if I speak.
Dt 4:21 The Lord was **a** with me because
1Ki 11: 9 the Lord was **a** with Solomon,
Ps 2:12 or he will be **a**, and you will perish
79: 5 Will you be **a** forever?
Pr 25:23 and a backbiting tongue, **a** looks.
Jer 3:12 I will not be **a** forever.
Jnh 4: 4 said, "Is it right for you to be **a?"**
Zec 1: 2 The Lord was very **a** with your
Mt 5:22 that if you are **a** with a brother or
20:24 they were **a** with the two brothers.
Lk 15:28 he became **a** and refused to go in.
Jn 7:23 are you **a** with me because I healed
Eph 4:26 Be **a** but do not sin;
Heb 3:17 with whom was he **a** forty years?
Rev 12:17 the dragon was **a** with the woman,

ANGUISH
Job 7:11 I will speak in the **a** of my spirit;
Ps 55: 4 My heart is in **a** within me,
Isa 9: 1 no gloom for those who were in **a**.
53:11 Out of his **a** he shall see light;
Jer 4:19 My **a**, my **a**! I writhe in pain!
Da 12: 1 There shall be a time of **a**,
Zep 1:15 a day of distress and **a**,
Lk 22:44 In his **a** he prayed more earnestly,
Jn 16:21 she no longer remembers the **a**
Ro 9: 2 sorrow and unceasing **a** in my heart.

ANIMAL → ANIMALS
Ge 2:19 God formed every **a** of the field
3: 1 the serpent was more crafty than
any other wild **a**
8:19 And every **a**, every creeping thing,
9: 2 dread of you shall rest on every **a** of
Ex 19:13 **a** or human being, they shall not live
22:19 lies with an **a** shall be put to death.
Lev 18:23 any woman give herself to an **a**
20:15 man has sexual relations with an **a**,
Dt 14: 6 Any **a** that divides the hoof and has

2Ch 25:18 but a wild **a** of Lebanon passed by
Ps 50:10 every wild **a** of the forest is mine,
    104:11 giving drink to every wild **a;**
Da 4:16 let the mind of an **a** be given to him.
Lk 10:34 Then he put him on his own **a,**
Heb 12:20 "If even an **a** touches the mountain,

ANIMALS → ANIMAL

Ge 1:25 God made the wild **a** of the earth of
    3:14 cursed are you among all **a**
    7: 2 with you seven pairs of all clean **a,**
Lev 26: 6 remove dangerous **a** from the land,
    26:22 I will let loose wild **a** against you,
Dt 14: 4 These are the **a** you may eat:
Job 12: 7 ask the **a,** and they will teach you;
Ps 36: 6 save humans and **a** alike, O LORD.
    147: 9 He gives to the **a** their food,
Ecc 3:19 humans and the fate of **a** is the same
Isa 30: 6 An oracle concerning the **a** of the
    40:16 its **a** enough for a burnt offering.
    43:20 The wild **a** will honor me,
Eze 14:21 famine, wild **a,** and pestilence,
    34: 5 they became food for all the wild **a.**
    34:28 nor shall the **a** of the land devour
Da 4:15 and let his lot be with the **a**
Joel 1:20 Even the wild **a** cry to you because
    2:22 Do not fear, you **a** of the field,
Hab 2:17 destruction of the **a** will terrify you
Mal 1: 8 you offer blind **a** in sacrifice, is that
Ac 11: 6 at it closely I saw four-footed **a,**
1Co 15:32 I fought with wild **a** at Ephesus,
Jude 1:10 irrational **a,** they know by instinct.
Wis 11:15 irrational **a,** serpents and worthless **a,**

ANNA

1. Prophetess who spoke about the child Jesus (Lk 2:36-38).
2. Wife of Tobit (Tob 1:20; 2:1, 11).

ANNALS

BOOK OF THE ANNALS 1Ki 14:19, 29;
    15:7, 23, 31; 16:5, 14, 20, 27; 22:39, 45; 2Ki
    1:18; 8:23; 10:34; 12:19; 13:8, 12; 14:15, 18,
    28; 15:6, 11, 15, 21, 26, 31, 36; 16:19; 20:20;
    21:17, 25; 23:28; 24:5; Ne 12:23; Est 2:23

ANNAS*

High priest A.D. 6-15 (Lk 3:2; Jn 18:13, 24; Ac 4:6).

ANNIHILATE*

Dt 20:17 You shall **a** them—the Hittites
Est 3:13 to destroy, to kill, and to **a** all Jews,
     8:11 to **a** any armed force of any people
AdE 13:15 eyes of our foes are upon us to **a** us,
1Mc 5:15 together against them "to **a** us."

ANNOUNCE → ANNOUNCED, ANNOUNCES, ANNOUNCING

Dt 17: 9 **a** to you the decision in the case.
Isa 21:10 the God of Israel, I **a** to you.

ANNOUNCED → ANNOUNCE

Isa 48: 5 before they came to pass I **a** them
Gal 4:13 that I first **a** the gospel to you;
1Pe 1:25 the good news that was **a** to you.
Rev 10: 7 as he **a** to his servants the prophets."

ANNOUNCES → ANNOUNCE

Isa 52: 7 feet of the messenger who **a** peace,

ANNOUNCING* → ANNOUNCE

Isa 63: 1 I, **a** vindication, mighty to save."
Ro 1: 9 serve with my spirit by **a** the gospel

ANNUAL*

2Ch 8:13 new moons, and the three **a** festivals

ANNUL → ANNULLED, ANNULLING

Isa 14:27 has planned, and who will **a** it?
Gal 3:17 does not **a** a covenant previously
Aza 1:11 and do not **a** your covenant.

ANNULLED* → ANNUL

Isa 28:18 your covenant with death will be **a,**
Zec 11:11 So it was **a** on that day,
Jn 10:35 and the scripture cannot be **a—**

ANNULLING → ANNUL

Zec 11:10 **a** the covenant that I had made with

ANOINT → ANOINTED, ANOINTING

Ex 28:41 and shall **a** them and ordain them
    30:26 you shall **a** the tent of meeting
    30:30 You shall **a** Aaron and his sons,
Dt 28:40 you shall not **a** yourself with the oil,
1Sa 9:16 you shall **a** him to be ruler over my
    15: 1 "The LORD sent me to **a** you king
1Ki 1:34 Nathan **a** him king over Israel;
    19:16 shall **a** Jehu son of Nimshi as king
    19:16 you shall **a** Elisha son of Shaphat
2Ki 9: 3 I **a** you king over Israel.'
Ps 23: 5 you **a** my head with oil; my cup
Da 9:24 and to **a** a most holy place.
Mk 16: 1 so that they might go and **a** him.
Lk 7:46 You did not **a** my head with oil,
Rev 3:18 salve to **a** your eyes so that you
Tob 6: 9 as for the gall, **a** a person's eyes

ANOINTED → ANOINT

Ge 31:13 you **a** a pillar and made a vow to me
Lev 4: 3 If it is the **a** priest who sins,
1Sa 2:10 and exalt the power of his **a."**
    10: 1 LORD has **a** you ruler over his
    16:13 and **a** him in the presence of his
    26: 9 raise his hand against the LORD's **a,**
2Sa 1:14 your hand to destroy the LORD's **a?**
    2: 4 there they **a** David king over the
    5: 3 and they **a** David king over Israel.
    19:21 because he cursed the LORD's **a?"**
1Ki 1:39 of oil from the tent and **a** Solomon.
1Ch 16:22 "Do not touch my **a** ones;
2Ch 6:42 LORD God, do not reject your **a** one.
Ps 2: 2 against the LORD and his **a,** saying,
    18:50 and shows steadfast love to his **a,**
    89:20 with my holy oil I have **a** him;
    105:15 "Do not touch my **a** ones;
Isa 61: 1 because the LORD has **a** me;
Eze 28:14 With an **a** cherub as guardian
Da 9:26 an **a** one shall be cut off and
Hab 3:13 to save your people, to save your **a.**
Zec 4:14 These are the two **a** ones who stand
Mk 6:13 **a** with oil many who were sick and
Lk 4:18 he has **a** me to bring good news to
    7:46 but she has **a** my feet with ointment.
Jn 1:41 Messiah" (which is translated **A**).
    12: 3 a Jesus' feet, and wiped them with
Ac 10:38 how God **a** Jesus of Nazareth with
2Co 1:21 with you in Christ and has **a** us,
Heb 1: 9 has **a** you with the oil of gladness
1Jn 2:20 you have been **a** by the Holy One,

†LORD'S ANOINTED 1Sa 16:6; 24:6, 6,
    10; 26:9, 11, 16, 23; 2Sa 1:14, 16; 19:21; La 4:20

ANOINTING → ANOINT

Ex 30:25 it shall be a holy **a** oil.
Jas 5:14 **a** them with oil in the name of the Lord.
1Jn 2:27 as his **a** teaches you about all things,

ANOTHER → ANOTHER'S

Ps 16: 4 choose **a** god multiply their sorrows
Pr 27: 2 Let **a** praise you, and not your own
    27:17 one person sharpens the wits of **a.**
Ecc 7:27 one thing to **a** to find the sum,
Isa 48:11 My glory I will not give to **a.**
Da 7: 5 A beast appeared, a second one,
Lk 19:44 leave within you one stone upon **a;**
Jn 4:37 holds true, 'One sows and **a** reaps.'
    5:43 if **a** comes in his own name,
    13:34 commandment, that you love one **a.**
    14:16 and he will give you **a** Advocate,
    18:15 Peter and **a** disciple followed Jesus.
Ro 12:10 love one **a** with mutual affection;

1Co 7: 5 Do not deprive one **a** except perhaps
    12: 9 to **a** faith by the same Spirit,
    16:20 Greet one **a** with a holy kiss.
Gal 1: 7 not that there is **a** gospel,
Eph 4: 2 patience, bearing with one **a** in love,
    4:25 for we are members of one **a.**
    4:32 tenderhearted, forgiving one **a,**
Col 3:16 and admonish one **a** in all wisdom;
1Th 4:18 encourage one **a** with these words.
Heb 3:13 But exhort one **a** every day,
    10:24 how to provoke one **a** to love
Jas 4:11 Whoever speaks evil against **a** or judges **a,**
1Pe 1:22 love one **a** deeply from the heart.
    4: 8 maintain constant love for one **a,**
1Jn 3:11 that we should love one **a.**
    3:23 his Son Jesus Christ and love one **a,**
Rev 20:12 **a** book was opened, the book of life.
Sir 9: 8 not gaze at beauty belonging to **a;**

LOVE ONE ANOTHER Jn 13:34, 34;
    15:12, 17; Ro 12:10; 13:8; 1Th 4:9; 1Pe 1:22;
    1Jn 3:11, 14, 23; 4:7, 11, 12; 2Jn 1:5

ONE ANOTHER Ge 11:3; 37:19; 42:1, 21,
    28; 43:33; Ex 10:23; 16:15; 26:3, 3, 5, 6;
    36:10, 10, 12; 37:9; Lev 19:11; 25:14, 17;
    26:37; Nu 14:4; Dt 25:11; Jdg 6:29; 10:18; 1Sa
    10:11; 18:7; 21:11; 29:5; 2Sa 14:6; 1Ki 20:29;
    2Ki 3:23; 7:3, 6, 9; 14:8, 11; 2Ch 20:23; 25:17,
    21; Ne 4:19; Est 9:19, 22; Isa 13:8; 41:6; Jer
    23:27, 30, 35; 31:34; 34:15; 36:16; Eze 1:9;
    3:13; 4:17; 24:23; 33:30; Da 2:43; 7:3; Joel
    2:8; Jnh 1:7; Zec 7:9, 10; 8:16, 17; 11:9; Mal
    2:10; 3:16; Mt 11:16; 16:7; 21:25; 24:10, 10;
    Mk 1:27; 4:41; 8:16; 9:34, 50; 10:26; 11:31;
    12:7, 28; 14:4; 16:3; Lk 2:15; 4:36; 6:11; 7:32;
    8:25; 12:1; 20:5; 22:23; Jn 4:33; 5:44; 7:35;
    11:56; 12:19; 13:22, 34, 34, 35; 15:12, 17;
    16:17; 19:24; Ac 2:12; 4:15; 19:38; 21:6;
    26:31; 28:4; Ro 1:27; 12:10, 10, 16; 13:8;
    14:13; 15:5, 7, 14; 16:16; 1Co 6:7; 7:5; 11:33;
    12:25; 16:20; 2Co 10:12, 12; 13:11, 12; Gal
    5:13, 15, 15, 26, 26; Eph 4:2, 25, 32, 32; 5:21;
    Col 3:9, 13, 16; 1Th 3:12; 4:9, 18; 5:11, 15;
    2Th 1:3; Tit 3:3; Heb 3:13; 8:11; 10:24, 25;
    Jas 4:11; 5:9, 16, 16; 1Pe 1:22; 3:8; 4:8, 9, 10;
    5:5, 14; 1Jn 1:7; 3:11, 14, 16, 23; 4:7, 11, 12;
    2Jn 1:5; Rev 6:4; Jdt 7:4; 10:19; 15:2; AdE
    9:19, 19; Wis 5:3; 14:24, 24; 18:23; 19:18; Sir
    16:28; 1Mc 3:43; 7:29; 10:54, 56; 11:6; 12:50;
    13:28; 2Mc 7:5; 14:26; 1Es 3:4; 4:4, 6, 33; 2Es
    5:9; 13:31, 33; 15:16, 35; 4Mc 13:8, 13, 23,
    24, 25

ANOTHER'S → ANOTHER

Pr 25: 9 and do not disclose **a** secret;
Jn 13:14 you also ought to wash one **a** feet.
Gal 6: 2 Bear one **a** burdens, and in this

ANSWER → ANSWERED, ANSWERING, ANSWERS

1Ki 18:26 crying, "O Baal, **a** us!"
    18:37 A me, O LORD, **a** me,
Job 30:20 I cry to you and you do not **a** me;
Ps 4: 1 A me when I call, O God of my
    20: 9 O LORD; **a** us when we call.
    38:15 you, O LORD my God, who will **a**
    65: 2 O you who **a** prayer!
Pr 15: 1 A soft **a** turns away wrath,
    18:13 gives **a** before hearing, it is folly
    24:26 who gives an honest **a** gives a kiss
    26: 5 A fools according to their folly,
Isa 46: 7 not **a** or save anyone from trouble.
    58: 9 you shall call, and the LORD will **a;**
    65:24 Before they call I will **a,**
Hos 14: 8 It is I who **a** and look after you.
Mt 22:46 No one was able to give him an **a,**
    27:14 He gave him no **a,**
Lk 23: 9 but Jesus gave him no **a,**

ANSWERED → ANSWER

1Ch 21:26 and he **a** him with fire from heaven
Ps 118:21 I thank you that you have **a** me

ANSWERING* → ANSWER

Sir 5:11 Be quick to hear, but deliberate in **a**.

ANSWERS → ANSWER

1Ki 18:24 god who **a** by fire is indeed God."

ANT* → ANTS

Pr 6: 6 Go to the **a**, you lazybones;

ANTICHRIST* → ANTICHRISTS

1Jn 2:18 As you have heard that **a** is coming,
    2:22 the **a**, the one who denies the Father
    4: 3 And this is the spirit of the **a**,
2Jn 1: 7 person is the deceiver and the **a**!

ANTICHRISTS* → ANTICHRIST

1Jn 2:18 so now many **a** have come.

ANTIOCH

Ac 11:26 in **A** that the disciples were first
         called "Christians."
    13: 1 the church at **A** there were prophets
Gal 2:11 But when Cephas came to **A**,

ANTIOCHUS

Antiochus IV Epiphanes, king of the Syrian Greeks B.C.E. 175-164 (1Mc 1:10-19). Plundered the temple in Jerusalem (1Mc 1:20-28). Attempted to force the Hellenization of the Jewish people (1Mc 1:41-53), including defiling the altar and holy place (1Mc 1:54-64). His policies sparked the Maccabean revolt.

ANTIPAS*

Rev 2:13 even in the days of **A** my witness,

ANTS* → ANT

Pr 30:25 the **a** are a people without strength,

ANXIETIES → ANXIETY

1Co 7:32 I want you to be free from **a**.

ANXIETY → ANXIETIES, ANXIOUS

Pr 12:25 **A** weighs down the human heart,
Ecc 11:10 Banish **a** from your mind,
1Pe 5: 7 Cast all your **a** on him, because he
         cares for you.

ANXIOUS → ANXIETY

1Co 7:32 is **a** about the affairs of the Lord,
Php 2:28 and that I may be less **a**.

ANYTHING

Ge 18:14 Is **a** too wonderful for the LORD?
Jer 32:27 is **a** too hard for me?
Mt 18:19 if two of you agree on earth about **a**
Mk 2:12 "We have never seen **a** like this!"
Jn 1:46 Can **a** good come out of Nazareth?
    14:14 If in my name you ask me for **a**,
    16:23 if you ask **a** of the Father in my
          name,
2Co 13: 8 For we cannot do **a** against the truth,
Gal 6:14 May I never boast of **a** except the
         cross

APART → PART

Ps 4: 3 that the LORD has set **a** the faithful
Jn 15: 5 **a** from me you can do nothing.
Ro 1: 1 set **a** for the gospel of God,
    3:21 **a** from law, the righteousness of
    7: 9 I was once alive **a** from the law,
Jas 2:20 that faith **a** from works is barren?

APOLLOS

Christian from Alexandria, learned in the Scriptures; instructed by Aquila and Priscilla (Ac 18:24-28). Ministered at Corinth (Ac 19:1; 1Co 1:12; 3; Tit 3:13).

APOLLYON* → =ABADDON

Rev 9:11 and in Greek he is called **A**.

APOSTASIES → APOSTASY

Jer 2:19 and your **a** will convict you.
Eze 37:23 I will save them from all the **a**

APOSTASY* → APOSTASIES

1Mc 2:15 officers who were enforcing the **a**

APOSTLE → APOSTLES, APOSTLES', APOSTLESHIP, SUPER-APOSTLES

Ro 1: 1 of Jesus Christ, called to be an **a**,
    11:13 as I am an **a** to the Gentiles,
1Co 1: 1 Paul, called to be an **a** of Christ
    9: 1 Am I not an **a**?
    15: 9 unfit to be called an **a**,
2Co 12:12 signs of a true **a** were performed
Gal 2: 8 making him an **a** to the circumcised
1Ti 2: 7 I was appointed a herald and an **a**
2Ti 1:11 I was appointed a herald and an **a**
Heb 3: 1 **a** and high priest of our confession,
1Pe 1: 1 Peter, an **a** of Jesus Christ,
2Pe 1: 1 Simeon Peter, a servant and **a** of
         Jesus Christ,

APOSTLES → APOSTLE

See also Andrew, Bartholomew, Barnabas, James, John, Judas, Matthew, Matthias, Nathanael, Paul, Peter, Philip, Simon, Thaddaeus, Thomas.

Mt 10: 2 the names of the twelve **a**:
Mk 3:14 twelve, whom he also named **a**,
Lk 6:13 of them, whom he also named **a**:
    11:49 'I will send them prophets and **a**,
Ac 1:26 and he was added to the eleven **a**.
    2:43 and signs were being done by the **a**.
    4:33 the **a** gave their testimony to the
         resurrection
    5:18 arrested the **a** and put them in the
    8: 1 and all except the **a** were scattered
    14:14 the **a** Barnabas and Paul heard of it,
Ro 16: 7 they are prominent among the **a**,
1Co 12:28 has appointed in the church first **a**,
    15: 9 For I am the least of the **a**,
2Co 11:13 For such boasters are false **a**,
Eph 2:20 foundation of the **a** and prophets,
    3: 5 revealed to his holy **a** and prophets
    4:11 he gave were that some would be **a**,
Jude 1:17 remember the predictions of the **a**
Rev 2: 2 tested those who claim to be **a** but
    21:14 are the twelve names of the twelve **a**

APOSTLES' → APOSTLE

Ac 2:42 themselves to the **a** teaching
    4:35 They laid it at the **a** feet,
    8:18 through the laying on of the **a** hands

APOSTLESHIP* → APOSTLE

Ac 1:25 **a** from which Judas turned aside to
Ro 1: 5 whom we have received grace and **a**
1Co 9: 2 you are the seal of my **a** in the Lord.

APPALLED → APPALLING

Ezr 9: 4 I sat **a** until the evening sacrifice.
Ps 40:15 those be **a** because of their shame
Jer 50:13 who passes by Babylon shall be **a**
Eze 19: 7 the land was **a**, and all in it,
    32:10 I will make many peoples **a** at you;

APPALLING* → APPALLED

Jer 5:30 **a** and horrible thing has happened
La 1: 9 her downfall was **a**, with none to

APPAREL

Dt 22: 5 A woman shall not wear a man's **a**,
Zec 3: 4 and I will clothe you with festal **a**."

APPARENT*

2Th 2: 9 is **a** in the working of Satan,

APPEAL → APPEALED

Mt 26:53 think that I cannot **a** to my Father,
Ac 25:11 I **a** to the emperor."
1Co 4:16 I **a** to you, then, be imitators of me.
2Co 5:20 God is making his **a** through us;
Phm 1: 9 rather **a** to you on the basis of love
1Pe 3:21 an **a** to God for a good conscience,
Jude 1: 3 and **a** to you to contend for the faith

APPEALED → APPEAL

2Co 12: 8 Three times I **a** to the Lord about

APPEAR → APPEARANCE, APPEARANCES, APPEARED, APPEARING, APPEARS

Ge 1: 9 and let the dry land **a**."
Ex 23:15 shall **a** before me empty-handed.
Lev 16: 2 I **a** in the cloud upon the mercy seat.
Ps 21: 9 like a fiery furnace when you **a**.
    102:16 build up Zion; he will **a** in his glory.
Mt 24:30 the sign of the Son of Man will **a** in
Mk 13:22 messiahs and false prophets will **a**
Lk 19:11 that the kingdom of God was to **a**
         immediately.
Ac 10:40 the third day and allowed him to **a**,
2Co 5:10 **a** before the judgment seat of Christ,
Heb 9:24 to **a** in the presence of God on our
    9:28 **a** a second time, not to deal with sin,
Sir 35: 6 not **a** before the Lord empty-handed

APPEARANCE → APPEAR

Ge 12:11 that you are a woman beautiful in **a**;
    26: 7 because she is attractive in **a**."
Ex 24:17 Now the **a** of the glory of the LORD
Nu 9:15 the tabernacle, having the **a** of fire.
1Sa 16: 7 not look on his **a** or on the height
Isa 52:14 at him—so marred was his **a**,
    53: 2 nothing in his **a** that we should
         desire him.
Eze 1: 5 their **a**: they were of human form.
    1:28 the **a** of the likeness of the glory of
    10:22 the same faces whose **a** I had seen
Da 3:25 and the fourth has the **a** of a god."
Joel 2: 4 They have the **a** of horses,
Mt 28: 3 His **a** was like lightning, and his
Mk 12:40 for the sake of **a** say long prayers.
Lk 12:56 know how to interpret the **a** of earth
2Co 5:12 those who boast in outward **a**
Col 2:23 an **a** of wisdom in promoting
         self-imposed piety,
Rev 9: 7 In **a** the locusts were like horses,
Jdt 8: 7 She was beautiful in **a**, and was
    11:23 You are not only beautiful in **a**,
AdE 2: 7 The girl was beautiful in **a**.
Sir 19:29 A person is known by his **a**,
Sus 1:31 great refinement and beautiful in **a**.

APPEARANCES → APPEAR

Jn 7:24 not judge by **a**, but judge with right

APPEARED → APPEAR

Ge 12: 7 Then the LORD **a** to Abram,
    17: 1 the LORD **a** to Abram, and said to
    18: 1 LORD **a** to Abraham by the oaks of
    26: 2 The LORD **a** to Isaac and said,
    35: 9 God **a** to Jacob again when he came
Ex 3: 2 the angel of the LORD **a** to him
    6: 3 I **a** to Abraham, Isaac, and Jacob
    16:10 the glory of the LORD **a** in the cloud.
Lev 9:23 and the glory of the LORD **a** to all
Nu 14:10 the glory of the LORD **a** at the tent
    16:19 glory of the LORD **a** to the whole
    20: 6 and the glory of the LORD **a** to them.
Jdg 6:12 angel of the LORD **a** to him and said
    13: 3 angel of the LORD **a** to the woman
1Ki 9: 2 the LORD **a** to Solomon a second
2Ch 1: 7 That night God **a** to Solomon,
Da 5: 5 the fingers of a human hand **a**
    7: 5 Another beast **a**, a second one,
    8: 1 a vision **a** to me, Daniel,
Mt 1:20 angel of the Lord **a** to him in a
    2:13 an angel of the Lord **a** to Joseph in
    2:19 an angel of the Lord suddenly **a** in
Mk 9: 4 there **a** to them Elijah with Moses,
Lk 1:11 there **a** to him an angel of the Lord,
    22:43 [an angel from heaven **a** to him]
    24:34 risen indeed, and he has **a** to Simon!
Jn 21:14 that Jesus **a** to the disciples after he
Ac 2: 3 tongues, as of fire, **a** among them,
    12: 7 Suddenly an angel of the Lord **a**
1Co 15: 5 he **a** to Cephas, then to the twelve.

Tit   2:11 For the grace of God has **a,**
Heb   9:26 **a** once for all at the end of the age
Rev 12: 1 A great portent **a** in heaven:
        15: 2 I saw what **a** to be a sea of glass
THE †LORD APPEARED Ge 12:7; 17:1;
18:1; 26:2, 24; Ex 3:2; 16:10; Lev 9:23; Nu
14:10; 19:41, 42; 20:6; Dt 31:15; Jdg 6:12;
13:3; 1Ki 3:5; 9:2; 2Ch 7:12; Jer 31:3

APPEARING → APPEAR
Hos   6: 3 his **a** is as sure as the dawn;
Ac   1: 3 **a** to them during forty days and
2Ti   1:10 through the **a** of our Savior Christ
        4: 8 to all who have longed for his **a.**

APPEARS → APPEAR
Mal   3: 2 and who can stand when he **a?**
Jas   4:14 For you are a mist that **a** for a little
1Pe   5: 4 And when the chief shepherd **a,**

APPETITE → APPETITES
Pr   6:30 who steal only to satisfy their **a**
       13: 4 The **a** of the lazy craves, and gets
       16:26 The **a** of workers works for them;
Ecc   6: 7 yet the **a** is not satisfied.
Isa   5:14 Therefore Sheol has enlarged its **a**

APPETITES → APPETITE
Ro   16:18 our Lord Christ, but their own **a,**
Sir   18:30 base desires, but restrain your **a.**
4Mc 1:33 reason is able to rule over **a?**

APPLE → APPLES
Dt   32:10 guarded him as the **a** of his eye.
Ps   17: 8 Guard me as the **a** of the eye;
Pr   7: 2 my teachings as the **a** of your eye;
SS   2: 3 As an **a** tree among the trees of the
        8: 5 Under the **a** tree I awakened you.
Zec   2: 8 touches you touches the **a** of my eye

APPLES* → APPLE
Pr   25:11 A word fitly spoken is like **a** of gold
SS   2: 5 with raisins, refresh me with **a;**
        7: 8 and the scent of your breath like **a,**

APPLIED → APPLY
Ecc   1:17 And I **a** my mind to know wisdom
        8:16 I **a** my mind to know wisdom,
1Co   4: 6 I have **a** all this to Apollos and
Tob 11:11 he **a** the medicine on his eyes,

APPLY → APPLIED
2Ki 20: 7 Let them take it and **a** it to the boil,
Pr   22:17 and **a** your mind to my teaching;
       23:12 **A** your mind to instruction and

APPOINT → APPOINTED, APPOINTS
1Sa   8: 5 **a** for us, then, a king to govern us,
Ps   61: 7 **a** steadfast love and faithfulness to
       75: 2 At the set time that I **a** I will judge
Isa 60:17 I will **a** Peace as your overseer
Hos   1:11 shall **a** for themselves one head;
1Co   6: 4 do you **a** as judges those who have
Tit   1: 5 and should **a** elders in every town,

APPOINTED → APPOINT
Ex   18:25 **a** them as heads over the people,
       31: 6 I have **a** with him Oholiab son of
Lev 23: 2 the **a** festivals of the LORD
1Sa 13:14 the LORD has **a** him to be ruler over
1Ki   1:35 I have **a** him to be ruler over Israel
1Ch 24: 3 according to the **a** duties
Ne   5:14 I was **a** to be their governor in the
        7: 1 singers, and the Levites had been **a,**
       10:33 the new moons, the **a** festivals,
Est   9:31 observed at their **a** seasons,
Job 14: 5 **a** the bounds that they cannot pass,
Ps   7: 6 O my God; you have **a** a judgment.
Ecc   3:17 for he has **a** a time for every matter,
Isa   1:14 and your **a** festivals my soul hates;
Jer 33:20 would not come at their **a** time,
Da   2:49 and he **a** Shadrach, Meshach,
        3:12 certain Jews whom you have **a** over
        8:19 for it refers to the **a** time of the end.

11:27 there remains an end at the time **a.**
Hab   2: 3 there is still a vision for the **a** time;
Mk   3:16 So he **a** the twelve: Simon (to whom
Lk   10: 1 the Lord **a** seventy others and sent
Jn   15:16 And I **a** you to go and bear fruit,
Ac   3:20 that he may send the Messiah **a** for
       15: 2 **a** to go up to Jerusalem to discuss
1Co 12:28 has **a** in the church first apostles,
1Ti   1:12 and **a** me to his service,
Heb   1: 2 whom he **a** heir of all things,
        9:27 just as it is **a** for mortals to die once,

APPOINTED FESTIVALS Lev 23:2, 2, 4,
37, 44; Nu 10:10; 15:3; 29:39; 1Ch 23:31; 2Ch
2:4; 31:3; Ne 10:33; Isa 1:14; 33:20; Eze
36:38; 44:24; 45:17; 46:9; Hos 2:11

APPOINTED TIME Ex 23:15; Nu 9:2, 3, 7,
13; 28:2; 1Sa 9:24; 2Sa 24:15; Job 34:23; Ps
102:13; Ecc 3:17; Jer 33:20; Eze 22:4; Da
8:19; Hab 2:3; 1Co 7:29; Sir 36:10; 39:16, 17,
34; 48:10

APPOINTED TIMES Ezr 10:14; Ne 10:34;
13:31; Tob 14:4; 2Es 4:27

TIME APPOINTED Ex 34:18; Lev 23:4; 1Sa
13:8; Est 9:27; Da 11:27, 29, 35; 1Es 9:12

APPOINTS → APPOINT
Heb   7:28 **a** a Son who has been made perfect

APPORTION → PORTION
Nu   33:54 You shall **a** the land by lot

APPORTIONED → PORTION
Dt   32: 8 When the Most High **a** the nations,
Jos 18:10 Joshua **a** the land to the Israelites,

APPROACH → APPROACHED,
APPROACHES, APPROACHING
Lev 18: 6 None of you shall **a** anyone near of
Nu   16: 5 will choose he will allow to **a** him.
Heb   4:16 **a** the throne of grace with boldness,
        7:25 save those who **a** God through him,
       11: 6 whoever would **a** him must believe
Sir   1:28 do not **a** him with a divided mind.
       21: 2 for if you **a** sin, it will bite you.

APPROACHED → APPROACH
Lk   22:47 He **a** Jesus to kiss him;

APPROACHES → APPROACH
Lev 20:16 If a woman **a** any animal and
Nu   17:13 Everyone who **a** the tabernacle

APPROACHING → APPROACH
Heb 10:25 all the more as you see the Day **a.**

APPROVAL → APPROVED
Gal   1:10 I now seeking human **a,** or God's **a?**
Heb 11: 2 by faith our ancestors received **a.**
1Pe   2:20 and suffer for it, you have God's **a.**
Sir 32:10 **a** goes before one who is modest.

APPROVED → APPROVAL
Ac   8: 1 And Saul **a** of their killing him.
Ro   16:10 Greet Apelles, who is **a** in Christ.
2Co 10:18 commend themselves that are **a,**
1Th   2: 4 but just as we have been **a** by God
2Ti   2:15 to present yourself to God as one **a**

APT*
Pr   15:23 To make an **a** answer is a joy to
1Ti   3: 2 hospitable, an **a** teacher,
2Ti   2:24 but kindly to everyone, an **a** teacher,
Sir 18:29 and pour forth **a** proverbs.

AQUILA*
  Husband of Priscilla; co-worker with Paul, instructor of Apollos (Ac 18; Ro 16:3; 1Co 16:19;
2Ti 4:19).

ARAB → ARABIA, ARABS
Ne   2:19 and Geshem the **A** heard of it,

ARABAH
Dt   3:17 the **A** also, with the Jordan and its

Jos 11:16 and the **A** and the hill country
Eze 47: 8 and goes down into the **A;**

ARABIA → ARAB
2Ch   9:14 all the kings of **A** and the governors
Gal   1:17 but I went away at once into **A,**
        4:25 Now Hagar is Mount Sinai in **A**

ARABS → ARAB
Ne   4: 7 and the **A** and the Ammonites
Isa 13:20 **A** will not pitch their tents there,
Ac   2:11 and **A**—in our own languages we
1Mc   5:39 also have hired **A** to help them,

ARAM → ARAMAIC, ARAMEAN, ARAMEANS
Ge   10:23 descendants of **A:** Uz, Hul, Gether,
Nu   23: 7 "Balak has brought me from **A,**
Jdg 10: 6 the gods of **A,** the gods of Sidon,
1Ki 19:15 anoint Hazael as king over **A.**
2Ki 13: 3 into the hand of King Hazael of **A,**
2Ch 16: 7 you relied on the king of **A,**

ARAM-NAHARAIM
Ge   24:10 and went to **A,** to the city of Nahor.
Jdg   3: 8 of King Cushan-rishathaim of **A;**

ARAMAIC* → ARAM
2Ki 18:26 to your servants in the **A** language,
Ezr   4: 7 the letter was written in **A** and
Isa 36:11 "Please speak to your servants in **A,**
Da   2: 4 Chaldeans said to the king (in **A),**
2Mc 15:36 is called Adar in the **A** language—

ARAMEAN → ARAM
Ge   31:20 And Jacob deceived Laban the **A,**
Dt   26: 5 "A wandering **A** was my ancestor;
2Ki   7: 6 the Lord had caused the **A** army to

ARAMEANS → ARAM
2Sa   8: 6 **A** became servants to David and
2Ki   8:28 where the **A** wounded Joram.

ARARAT
Ge   8: 4 the ark came to rest on the
                    mountains of **A.**
2Ki 19:37 and they escaped into the land of **A.**
Jer 51:27 against her the kingdoms, **A,** Minni,
Tob   1:21 and they fled to the mountains of **A,**

ARAUNAH → =ORNAN
2Sa 24:16 the threshing floor of **A** the Jebusite.

ARBA
Jos 14:15 **A** was the greatest man among the

ARBITRATE* → ARBITRATOR
Isa   2: 4 and shall **a** for many peoples;
Mic   4: 3 shall **a** between strong nations far

ARBITRATOR* → ARBITRATE
Lk   12:14 set me to be a judge or **a** over you?"

ARCHANGEL* → ANGEL
Jude 1: 9 **a** Michael contended with the devil
2Es   4:36 the **a** Jeremiel answered and said,

ARCHANGEL'S* → ANGEL
1Th   4:16 **a** call and with the sound of God's

ARCHELAUS*
Mt   2:22 heard that **A** was ruling over Judea

ARCHER → ARCHERS
Pr   26:10 an **a** who wounds everybody is one
Jer 51: 3 Let not the **a** bend his bow,

ARCHERS → ARCHER
Ge   49:23 The **a** fiercely attacked him;
1Sa 31: 3 the **a** found him, and he was badly
2Ch 35:23 **a** shot King Josiah;
Job 16:13 his **a** surround me. He slashes open
Jer 50:29 Summon **a** against Babylon.
Jdt   2:15 twelve thousand **a** on horseback,
1Mc   9:11 and the **a** went ahead of the army,

ARCHIPPUS*

Co-worker of Paul (Col 4:17; Phm 2).

ARCHITE

2Sa 16:16 When Hushai the **A**, David's friend,

ARCHITECT*

Heb 11:10 whose **a** and builder is God.

ARCHIVES

Ezr 5:17 a search made in the royal **a** there
1Mc 14:23 copy of their words in the public **a**,

ARDENT*

Ro 12:11 be **a** in spirit, serve the Lord.

ARENA*

2Mc 4:14 proceedings in the wrestling **a**
4Mc 11:20 to an **a** of sufferings for religion,

AREOPAGITE* → AREOPAGUS

Ac 17:34 including Dionysius the **A** and

AREOPAGUS* → AREOPAGITE

Ac 17:19 took him and brought him to the **A**
    17:22 Then Paul stood in front of the **A**

ARGUE → ARGUED, ARGUES, ARGUING, ARGUMENT, ARGUMENTS

Job 13: 3 and I desire to **a** my case with God.
Pr 25: 9 **A** your case with your neighbor
Isa 1:18 now, let us **a** it out, says the LORD:
     3:13 The LORD rises to **a** his case:
Mk   8:11 The Pharisees came and began to **a**
Ac 18: 4 Every sabbath he would **a** in the
Ro   9:20 a human being, to **a** with God?
Sir 8: 3 Do not **a** with the loud of mouth,
    11: 9 Do not **a** about a matter that does

ARGUED → ARGUE

Mk   9:34 the way they had **a** with one another
Ac   6: 9 stood up and **a** with Stephen.
     9:29 He spoke and **a** with the Hellenists;
    19: 9 and **a** daily in the lecture hall of

ARGUES* → ARGUE

Job 40: 2 who **a** with God must respond."

ARGUING → ARGUE

Mk   9:14 and some scribes **a** with them.
Php 2:14 all things without murmuring and **a**,

ARGUMENT → ARGUE

Lk   9:46 An **a** arose among them as to which
1Ti 2: 8 up holy hands without anger or **a**;

ARGUMENTS → ARGUE

Ac   2:40 with many other **a** and exhorted
2Co 10: 4 destroy strongholds. We destroy **a**
Col 2: 4 may deceive you with plausible **a**.

ARIEL

2Sa 23:20 struck down two sons of **A** of Moab.
Isa 29: 1 Ah, **A**, **A**, the city where David

ARIMATHEA

Jn 19:38 After these things, Joseph of **A**,

ARIOCH

Da   2:15 **A** then explained the matter to

ARISE → RISE

Nu 10:35 "**A**, O LORD, let your enemies be
1Ki 3:12 no one like you shall **a** after you.
2Ki 23:25 nor did any like him **a** after him.
SS   2:10 "**A**, my love, my fair one, and
Isa 60: 1 **A**, shine; for your light has come,
Da   7:17 four kings shall **a** out of the earth.
     7:24 of this kingdom ten kings shall **a**,
    12: 1 the protector of your people, shall **a**.
Mic 4:13 **A** and thresh, O daughter Zion,
Mt 24:11 false prophets will **a** and lead many
1Mc 14:41 until a trustworthy prophet should **a**,
2Es 12:32 will **a** from the offspring of David,

ARISEN → RISE

Dt 34:10 **a** a prophet in Israel like Moses,
Mt 11:11 has **a** greater than John the Baptist;
Lk   9: 8 one of the ancient prophets had **a**.

ARISTARCHUS*

Companion of Paul (Ac 19:29; 20:4; 27:2; Col 4:10; Phm 1:24).

ARK

Ge   6:14 Make yourself an **a** of cypress wood
     7: 1 LORD said to Noah, "Go into the **a**,
     8:16 "Go out of the **a**, you and your wife,
Ex 25:10 shall make an **a** of acacia wood;
    25:16 shall put into the **a** the covenant
    37: 1 Bezalel made the **a** of acacia wood;
    40:20 the covenant and put it into the **a**,
Nu   3:31 Their responsibility was to be the **a**,
    10:35 the **a** set out, Moses would say,
Dt 10: 5 the tablets in the **a** that I had made;
Jos 3: 3 When you see the **a** of the covenant
Jdg 20:27 (for the **a** of the covenant of God
1Sa 3: 3 where the **a** of God was.
     4:11 The **a** of God was captured;
     5: 2 Philistines took the **a** of God
     6: 3 "If you send away the **a** of the God
     7: 2 the **a** was lodged at Kiriath-jearim,
2Sa 6:17 They brought in the **a** of the LORD,
1Ki 8: 9 There was nothing in the **a** except
1Ch 13: 9 Uzzah put out his hand to hold the **a**
2Ch 35: 3 "Put the holy **a** in the house that
Ps 132: 8 you and the **a** of your might.
Jer 3:16 The **a** of the covenant of the LORD.
Lk 17:27 until the day Noah entered the **a**,
Heb 9: 4 the **a** of the covenant overlaid on all
    11: 7 and built an **a** to save his household;
1Pe 3:20 during the building of the **a**,
Rev 11:19 the **a** of his covenant was seen
2Mc 2: 4 that the tent and the **a** should follow
2Es 10:22 the **a** of our covenant has been

ARK OF ... COVENANT Ex 25:22; 26:33,

34; 30:6, 26; 31:7; 39:35; 40:3, 5, 21; Nu 4:5;
7:89; 10:33; 14:44; Dt 10:8; 31:9, 25, 26; Jos
3:3, 6, 8, 11, 14, 17; 4:7, 9, 16, 18; 6:6, 8;
8:33; Jdg 20:27; 1Sa 4:3, 4, 4, 5; 2Sa 15:24;
1Ki 3:15; 6:19; 8:1, 6; 1Ch 15:25, 26, 28, 29;
16:6, 37; 17:1; 22:19; 28:2, 18; 2Ch 5:2, 7; Jer
3:16; Heb 9:4; Rev 11:19; 2Es 10:22

ARK OF ... GOD 1Sa 3:3; 4:11, 13, 17, 18,

19, 21, 22; 5:1, 2, 7, 8, 8, 8, 10, 10, 10, 11; 6:3;
14:18, 18; 2Sa 6:2, 3, 4, 6, 7, 12, 12; 7:2;
15:24, 25, 29; 1Ch 13:3, 5, 6, 7, 12, 14; 15:1,
2, 15, 24; 16:1; 2Ch 1:4

ARK OF THE †LORD Jos 3:13; 4:5, 11;

6:6, 7, 11, 12, 13, 17; 7:6; 1Sa 4:6; 5:3, 4; 6:1,
2, 8, 11, 15, 18, 19, 21; 7:1, 1; 2Sa 6:9, 10, 11,
13, 15, 16, 17; 1Ki 8:4; 1Ch 13:6; 15:2, 3, 12,
14; 16:4; 2Ch 8:11

ARM → ARMED, ARMIES, ARMOR, ARMOR-BEARER, ARMS, ARMY

Ex   6: 6 redeem you with an outstretched **a**
Dt   4:34 mighty hand and an outstretched **a**,
     7:19 mighty hand and the outstretched **a**
1Ki 8:42 hand, and your outstretched **a**—
2Ch 32: 8 With him is an **a** of flesh;
Job 40: 9 Have you an **a** like God,
Ps 10:15 Break the **a** of the wicked and
    44: 3 did their own **a** give them victory;
    44: 3 but your right hand, and your **a**,
    89:13 You have a mighty **a**; strong is your
    98: 1 his holy **a** have gotten him victory.
SS   8: 6 as a seal upon your **a**;
Isa 33: 2 our **a** every morning, our salvation
    40:10 and his **a** rules for him;
    52:10 The LORD has bared his holy **a**
    53: 1 the **a** of the LORD been revealed?
Jer 27: 5 outstretched **a** have made the earth,
Zec 11:17 May the sword strike his **a** and his
Lk   1:51 He has shown strength with his **a**;
Jn 12:38 the **a** of the Lord been revealed?"

1Pe 4: 1 **a** yourselves also with the same

OUTSTRETCHED ARM Ex 6:6; Dt 4:34;

5:15; 7:19; 9:29; 11:2; 26:8; 1Ki 8:42; 2Ki
17:36; 2Ch 6:32; Ps 136:12; Jer 27:5; 32:17,
21; Eze 20:33, 34; Bar 2:11

ARMAGEDDON See HARMAGEDON

ARMED → ARM

Pr   6:11 and want, like an **a** warrior.
Lk 11:21 When a strong man, fully **a**, guards

ARMIES → ARM

1Sa 17:36 defied the **a** of the living God."
Job 25: 3 Is there any number to his **a**?
Ps 60:10 do not go out, O God, with our **a**.
Lk 21:20 you see Jerusalem surrounded by **a**,
Heb 11:34 in war, put foreign **a** to flight.
Rev 19:14 the **a** of heaven, wearing fine linen,

ARMOR → ARM

1Sa 17:38 Saul clothed David with his **a**;
    31: 9 cut off his head, stripped off his **a**,
1Ki 20:11 who puts on **a** should not brag like
    22:34 king of Israel between the scale **a**
1Ch 10:10 put his **a** in the temple of their gods,
Ro 13:12 and put on the **a** of light;
Eph 6:11 Put on the whole **a** of God,
     6:13 take up the whole **a** of God,
Wis 5:17 will take his zeal as his whole **a**,

ARMOR-BEARER → ARM, BEAR

1Sa 31: 4 Then Saul said to his **a**,

ARMS → ARM

Ge 49:24 his **a** were made agile by the hands
Jdg 15:14 ropes that were on his **a** became like
    16:12 he snapped the ropes off his **a** like a
2Sa 22:35 that my **a** can bend a bow of bronze.
Ps 37:17 the **a** of the wicked shall be broken,
Pr 31:17 and makes her **a** strong.
SS   5:14 His **a** are rounded gold, set with
Isa 40:11 he will gather the lambs in his **a**,
    51: 5 and my **a** will rule the peoples;
Da   2:32 its chest and **a** of silver,
    10: 6 his **a** and legs like the gleam of
Hos 11: 3 I took them up in my **a**;
Mk 10:16 And he took them up in his **a**,

ARMY → ARM

Ex 14:17 myself over Pharaoh and all his **a**,
    14:24 and threw the Egyptian **a** into panic.
    15: 4 and his **a** he cast into the sea;
Jos 5:14 as commander of the **a** of the LORD
Jdg 4:15 his chariots and all his **a** into a panic
     8:12 and threw all the **a** into a panic.
Ps 27: 3 Though an **a** encamp against me,
    33:16 A king is not saved by his great **a**;
Eze 38:15 a great horde, a mighty **a**;
Joel 2: 2 a great and powerful **a** comes;
     2:11 utters his voice at the head of his **a**;
2Ti 2: 4 in the **a** gets entangled in everyday
Rev 19:19 rider on the horse and against his **a**.

ARNON

Nu 21:13 for the **A** is the boundary of Moab.
Jos 12: 1 from the Wadi **A** to Mount Hermon,
Jer 48:20 by the **A**, that Moab is laid waste.

AROMA

2Co 2:15 For we are the **a** of Christ to God

AROSE → RISE

Jdg 5: 7 Deborah, **a** as a mother in Israel.
SS   5: 5 I **a** to open to my beloved,
2Pe 2: 1 But false prophets also **a** among the

AROUND

Jos 6: 4 march **a** the city seven times,
2Ki 17:15 followed the nations that were **a**
Ps   3: 3 O LORD, are a shield **a** me,
    18:11 made darkness his covering **a** him,
    34: 7 angel of the LORD encamps **a** those
    48:12 Walk about Zion, go all **a** it, count

Pr   3: 3 bind them **a** your neck,
Isa 11: 5 Righteousness shall be the belt **a**
Eze   1:18 of all four were full of eyes all **a.**
     10:12 were full of eyes all **a.**
Zec   2: 5 For I will be a wall of fire all **a** it,
Lk   2: 9 the glory of the Lord shone **a** them,
Jn   13: 4 and tied a towel **a** himself.
Eph   6:14 fasten the belt of truth **a** your waist,
1Pe   5: 8 your adversary the devil prowls **a,**
Rev   4: 3 and **a** the throne is a rainbow that
      7:11 all the angels stood **a** the throne

AROUSED → ROUSE

Isa 45:13 I have **a** Cyrus in righteousness,
Jer 32:31 This city has **a** my anger and wrath,
Eze 38:18 the Lord GOD, my wrath shall be **a.**
Ro   7: 5 our sinful passions, **a** by the law,
Jdt 12:16 and his passion was **a,**

AROUSES → ROUSE

Pr   6:34 For jealousy **a** a husband's fury,

ARPAD

Isa 36:19 the gods of Hamath and **A?**
Jer 49:23 Hamath and **A** are confounded,

ARPHAXAD

Jdt   1: 1 those days **A** ruled over the Medes

ARRANGED

1Co 12:18 God **a** the members in the body,

ARRAYED

Job   6: 4 the terrors of God are **a** against me.
Ps   55:18 for many are **a** against me.

ARREST → ARRESTED

Mt   21:46 wanted to **a** him, but they feared
Mk   14: 1 a way to **a** Jesus by stealth
Ac   12: 3 he proceeded to **a** Peter also.

ARRESTED → ARREST

Jer 37:14 and **a** Jeremiah and brought him to
Mt   14: 3 For Herod had **a** John, bound him,
     26:50 and laid hands on Jesus and **a** him.
Ac   5:18 **a** the apostles and put them in the
     28:17 yet I was **a** in Jerusalem and handed

ARROGANCE → ARROGANT, ARROGANTLY

1Sa   2: 3 let not **a** come from your mouth;
Pr   8:13 Pride and **a** and the way of evil
Isa   9: 9 but in pride and **a** of heart they said:
Jer 48:29 of his loftiness, his pride, and his **a,**
Eze   7:24 put an end to the **a** of the strong,
Jdt   9:10 their **a** by the hand of a woman.
Sir 10: 7 A is hateful to the Lord and to
1Mc   1:24 much blood, and spoke with great **a.**

ARROGANT → ARROGANCE

Ps   73: 3 For I was envious of the **a;**
    101: 5 and an **a** heart I will not tolerate.
    119:78 Let the **a** be put to shame,
Pr   21:24 named "Scoffer," acts with **a** pride.
Jer 50:32 The **a** one shall stumble and fall,
Da   7:11 **a** words that the horn was speaking.
Hab   2: 5 treacherous; the **a** do not endure.
Mal   3:15 Now we count the **a** happy;
1Co 13: 4 not coming to you, have become **a.**
     13: 4 love is not envious or boastful or **a**
2Ti   3: 2 boasters, **a,** abusive, disobedient to
Tit   1: 7 he must not be **a** or quick-tempered

ARROGANTLY → ARROGANCE

Ps   17:10 with their mouths they speak **a.**
Da   7: 8 this horn, and a mouth speaking **a.**
      8:11 the prince of the host it acted **a;**
1Mc   1:21 He **a** entered the sanctuary and took

ARROW → ARROWS

1Sa 20:36 As the boy ran, he shot an **a** beyond
2Ki   9:24 so that the **a** pierced his heart;
     13:17 he said, "The LORD's **a** of victory,
Ps   64: 7 But God will shoot his **a** at them;
     91: 5 or the **a** that flies by day,

Pr   25:18 a sharp **a** is one who bears false
Isa 49: 2 he made me a polished **a,**
Jer   9: 8 Their tongue is a deadly **a;**

ARROWS → ARROW

Ex   19:13 they shall be stoned or shot with **a;**
Dt   32:42 I will make my **a** drunk with blood,
1Sa 20:20 I will shoot three **a** to the side of it,
2Ki 13:15 said to him, "Take a bow and **a";**
Job   6: 4 For the **a** of the Almighty are in me;
Ps   38: 2 For your **a** have sunk into me,
     64: 3 who aim bitter words like **a,**
    127: 4 Like **a** in the hand of a warrior are
Pr   26:18 who shoots deadly firebrands and **a,**
La   3:13 He shot into my vitals the **a** of his
Hab   3:14 pierced with his own **a** the head
Eph   6:16 quench all the flaming **a** of the evil

ART → ARTISAN, ARTISANS, ARTS

2Ch 16:14 spices prepared by the perfumer's **a;**
Ac   17:29 an image formed by the **a** and

ARTAXERXES → =AHASUERUS

  1. King of Persia; allowed rebuilding of temple under Ezra (Ezr 4; 7), and of walls of Jerusalem under his cupbearer Nehemiah (Ne 2; 5:14; 13:6).
  2. See Ahasuerus.

ARTEMIS

Ac   19:27 the temple of the great goddess **A**

ARTISAN → ART

Ex   35:35 by any sort of **a** or skilled designer.
2Ch   2:13 dispatched Huram-abi, a skilled **a,**
Isa 40:20 a skilled **a** to set up an image that
Jer 10: 9 They are the work of the **a** and of
Hos   8: 6 an **a** made it; it is not God.

ARTISANS → ART

Hos 13: 2 all of them the work of **a.**
Ac   19:24 brought no little business to the **a.**
LtJ   6:45 can be nothing but what the **a** wish

ARTS → ART

Ex   7:11 did the same by their secret **a.**
      8:18 to produce gnats by their secret **a,**
Wis 18:13 everything because of their magic **a,**

ASA

  King of Judah (1Ki 15:8-24; 1Ch 3:10; 2Ch 14-16). Godly reformer (2Ch 15); in later years defeated Israel with help of Aram, not the LORD (1Ki 15:16-22; 2Ch 16).

ASAHEL

  1. Nephew of David, one of his warriors (2Sa 23:24; 1Ch 2:16; 11:26; 27:7). Killed by Abner (2Sa 2); avenged by Joab (2Sa 3:22-39).
  2. Levite; teacher (2Ch 17:8).

ASAPH

  1. Recorder to Hezekiah (2Ki 18:18, 37; Isa 36:3, 22).
  2. Levitical musician (1Ch 6:39; 15:17-19; 16:4-7, 37), seer (2Ch 29:30). Sons of (1Ch 25; 2Ch 5:12; 20:14; 29:13; 35:15; Ezr 2:41; 3:10; Ne 7:44; 11:17; 12:27-47). Psalms of (2Ch 29:30; Ps 50; 73-83).

ASCEND → ASCENDED, ASCENDING, ASCENTS

Ps   24: 3 Who shall **a** the hill of the LORD?
    139: 8 If I **a** to heaven, you are there;
Isa 14:13 in your heart, "I will **a** to heaven;
     14:14 I will **a** to the tops of the clouds,
Ac   2:34 David did not **a** into the heavens,
Ro   6: 'Who will **a** into heaven?'"
Rev 17: 8 is about to **a** from the bottomless pit
2Es   4: 8 neither did I ever **a** into heaven.'

ASCENDED → ASCEND

Jdg 13:20 angel of the LORD **a** in the flame of
2Ki   2:11 Elijah **a** in a whirlwind into heaven.
Ps   68:18 You **a** the high mount, leading
Pr   30: 4 has **a** to heaven and come down?

Eze 11:23 the glory of the LORD **a** from the
Jn   3:13 No one has **a** into heaven except
     20:17 I have not yet **a** to the Father.
Eph   4: 8 he **a** on high he made captivity

ASCENDING → ASCEND

Ge   28:12 the angels of God were **a** and
Jn   1:51 the angels of God **a** and descending
      6:62 if you were to see the Son of Man **a**
     20:17 I am **a** to my Father and your Father
Rev   7: 2 I saw another angel **a** from the
Tob 12:20 See, I am **a** to him who sent me.

ASCENTS → ASCEND

Songs of ascents (Ps 120-134).

ASCRIBE → ASCRIBED

Dt   32: 3 greatness to our God!
1Ch 16:29 **A** to the LORD the glory due his
Job 36: 3 and **a** righteousness to my Maker.
Ps   29: 1 **a** to the LORD glory and strength.
     68:34 **A** power to God,
     96: 7 **A** to the LORD, O families of the
Sir 39:15 **A** majesty to his name
Bar   2:17 not **a** glory or justice to the Lord;

ASCRIBED → ASCRIBE

1Sa 18: 8 They have **a** to David ten thousands
Pm 151: T This psalm is **a** to David as his own

ASH → ASHES

1Sa   2: 8 he lifts the needy from the **a** heap,
Ps   113: 7 and lifts the needy from the **a** heap,
La   4: 5 in purple cling to **a** heaps.

ASHAMED → SHAME

Ge   2:25 were both naked, and were not **a.**
Ezr   9: 6 I am too **a** and embarrassed to lift
Ps   6:10 All my enemies shall be **a** and
     34: 5 so your faces shall never be **a.**
Isa 24:23 moon will be abashed, and the sun **a**
     29:22 No longer shall Jacob be **a,**
Jer   3: 3 of a whore, you refuse to be **a.**
     48:13 Then Moab shall be **a** of Chemosh,
Eze 16:27 who were **a** of your lewd behavior.
     43:10 and let them be **a** of their iniquities.
Hos 10: 6 and Israel shall be **a** of his idol.
Zec 13: 4 On that day the prophets will be **a,**
Mk   8:38 who are **a** of me and of my words
Ro   1:16 For I am not **a** of the gospel;
      6:21 the things of which you now are **a?**
2Ti   1: 8 Do not be **a,** then, of the testimony
      2:15 a worker who has no need to be **a**
Heb   2:11 Jesus is not **a** to call them brothers
     11:16 God is not **a** to be called their God;

ASHDOD

Jos 13: 3 those of Gaza, **A,** Ashkelon, Gath,
1Sa   5: 1 they brought it from Ebenezer to **A;**
Ne   13:23 Jews who had married women of **A,**

ASHER

  Son of Jacob by Zilpah (Ge 30:13; 35:26; 46:17; Ex 1:4; 1Ch 2:2). Tribe of blessed (Ge 49:20; Dt 33:24-25), numbered (Nu 1:40-41; 26:44-47), allotted land (Jos 19:24-31; Eze 48:2), failed to fully possess (Jdg 1:31-32), failed to support Deborah (Jdg 5:17), supported Gideon (Jdg 6:35; 7:23) and David (1Ch 12:36), 12,000 from (Rev 7:6).

ASHERAH → ASHERAHS, ASTARTE

1Ki 18:19 and the four hundred prophets of **A,**
2Ch 15:16 made an abominable image for **A.**

ASHERAHS* → ASHERAH

Jdg   3: 7 and worshiping the Baals and the **A.**

ASHES → ASH

Ge   18:27 I who am but dust and **a.**
Lev   1:16 side of the altar, in the place for **a.**
1Ki 13: 5 and the **a** poured out from the altar,
Est   4: 1 and put on sackcloth and **a,**
Job 13:12 Your maxims are proverbs of **a,**

42: 6 and repent in dust and **a.**"
Ps 102: 9 For I eat **a** like bread,
Isa 44:20 He feeds on **a;** a deluded mind has
61: 3 to give them a garland instead of **a,**
Jer 6:26 put on sackcloth, and roll in **a;**
Da 9: 3 with fasting and sackcloth and **a.**
Jnh 3: 6 himself with sackcloth, and sat in **a.**
Mt 11:21 long ago in sackcloth and **a.**
Jdt 4:11 the temple and put **a** on their heads
Sir 17:32 but all human beings are dust and **a,**
Bel 1:14 ordered his servants to bring **a,**
1Mc 3:47 and sprinkled **a** on their heads,

ASHIMA·

2Ki 17:30 the people of Hamath made **A;**

ASHKELON

Jdg 1:18 **A** with its territory, and Ekron with
2Sa 1:20 proclaim it not in the streets of **A;**
Zec 9: 5 **A** shall see it and be afraid;

ASIA

Ac 2: 9 and Cappadocia, Pontus and **A,**
16: 6 Holy Spirit to speak the word in **A.**
Ro 16: 5 the first convert in **A** for Christ.
1Co 16:19 The churches of **A** send greetings.
Rev 1: 4 to the seven churches that are in **A:**

ASIDE → SIDE

Ex 32: 8 quick to turn **a** from the way that I
Dt 28:14 if you do not turn **a** from any of the
Jos 23: 6 turning **a** from it neither to the right
Jdg 2:17 They soon turned **a** from the way
2Sa 22:23 from his statutes I did not turn **a.**
Pr 7:25 Do not let your hearts turn **a** to her
Jer 5:23 they have turned **a** and gone away.
Da 9: 5 turning **a** from your commandments
Ro 3:12 All have turned **a,** together they
2Co 3:11 what was set **a** came through glory,
Col 2:14 He set this **a,** nailing it to the cross.
Heb 12: 1 also lay **a** every weight and the sin
1Mc 2:22 obey the king's words by turning **a**

ASK → ASKED, ASKING, ASKS

Ex 3:13 and they **a** me, 'What is his name?'
12:26 And when your children **a** you,
Dt 4:32 For a now about former ages,
32: 7 **a** your father, and he will inform
Jos 4: 6 When your children **a** in time to
Jdg 13:18 "Why do you **a** my name?
Ps 2: 8 **A** of me, and I will make the nations
Pr 30: 7 Two things I **a** of you;
Isa 7:11 **A** a sign of the LORD your God;
65: 1 sought out by those who did not **a,**
Jer 6:16 and **a** for the ancient paths,
Mt 6: 8 knows what you need before you **a**
7: 7 "**A,** and it will be given you;
Mk 6:23 swore to her, "Whatever you **a** me,
8:12 does this generation **a** for a sign?
11:24 whatever you **a** for in prayer,
Lk 11:13 the Holy Spirit to those who **a** him!"
Jn 14:14 If in my name you **a** me for
15: 7 **a** for whatever you wish,
16:24 **A** and you will receive,
Ro 10:20 myself to those who did not **a**
1Co 14:35 let them **a** their husbands at home.
Eph 3:20 far more than all we can **a**
Jas 1: 5 of you is lacking in wisdom, **a** God,
4: 3 You **a** and do not receive, because you **a** wrongly,
1Jn 3:22 we receive from him whatever we **a,**
5:14 we **a** anything according to his will,

ASKED → ASK

1Ki 3:10 the Lord that Solomon had **a** this.
1Ch 4:10 And God granted what he **a.**
Ps 21: 4 He **a** you for life; you gave it to him
27: 4 One thing I **a** of the LORD,
106:15 he gave them what they **a,**
Jn 16:24 have not **a** for anything in my name.
19:38 a Pilate to let him take away the body of Jesus.

ASKING → ASK

Mt 20:22 "You do not know what you are **a.**
Jn 17: 9 I am **a** on their behalf;

ASKS → ASK

Mt 12:39 adulterous generation **a** for a sign,
16: 4 adulterous generation **a** for a sign,
Lk 11:10 For everyone who **a** receives,
11:29 it **a** for a sign, but no sign will be

ASLEEP → SLEEP

Jnh 1: 5 had lain down, and was fast **a.**
Mt 8:24 by the waves; but he was **a.**
28:13 stole him away while we were **a.**'
Mk 14:37 he said to Peter, "Simon, are you **a?**
Jn 11:11 "Our friend Lazarus has fallen **a,**
1Th 5: 6 So then let us not fall **a** as others do,
2Pe 2: 3 and their destruction is not **a.**

ASP·

Isa 11: 8 shall play over the hole of the **a,**

ASS → ASSES

Ge 16:12 He shall be a wild **a** of a man,
Jer 2:24 a wild **a** at home in the wilderness,
Hos 8: 9 a wild **a** wandering alone;

ASSAIL → ASSAILANTS

Ps 62: 3 How long will you **a** a person,

ASSAILANTS → ASSAIL

2Sa 22:40 you made my **a** sink under me.
Ps 44: 5 your name we tread down our **a.**
109:28 Let my **a** be put to shame;

ASSASSINATE·

Est 2:21 and conspired to **a** King Ahasuerus.
6: 2 had conspired to **a** King Ahasuerus.

ASSAULT

Est 7: 8 "Will he even **a** the queen in my

ASSEMBLE → ASSEMBLED, ASSEMBLY

Nu 10: 3 the whole congregation shall **a**
1Ki 18:19 all Israel **a** for me at Mount Carmel,
Isa 48:14 **A,** all of you, and hear!
Joel 2:16 the congregation; **a** the aged;
Zep 3: 8 to gather nations, to **a** kingdoms,
Rev 16:14 to **a** them for battle on the great day

ASSEMBLED → ASSEMBLE

Nu 16:19 Korah **a** the whole congregation
1Ki 18:20 **a** the prophets at Mount Carmel.
1Co 5: 4 When you are **a,** and my spirit is
Rev 16:16 And they **a** them at the place

ASSEMBLY → ASSEMBLE

Ex 12:16 first day you shall hold a solemn **a,**
Lev 4:21 it is the sin offering for the **a.**
16:17 and for all the **a** of Israel.
Nu 16:33 perished from the midst of the **a.**
Dt 23: 1 be admitted to the **a** of the LORD.
2Ch 29:28 The whole **a** worshiped, the singers
Ne 8: 2 Ezra brought the law before the **a,**
Ps 149: 1 his praise in the **a** of the faithful.
Joel 1:14 Sanctify a fast, call a solemn **a.**
2:15 sanctify a fast; call a solemn **a.**
Lk 23: 1 a rose as a body and brought Jesus
Heb 12:23 the **a** of the firstborn who are
Jas 2: 2 in fine clothes comes into your **a,**

ALL THE ASSEMBLY Lev 16:17; Nu 14:5; Jos 8:35; Ru 3:11; 1Ki 8:14, 14, 22, 55; 12:3; 1Ch 29:10, 20; 2Ch 6:3, 3; 28:14; 30:2, 4; Ezr 10:12; Ne 5:13; 8:17; 1Mc 4:59

ASSEMBLY OF ISRAEL Lev 16:17; Dt 31:30; Jos 8:35; 1Ki 8:14, 14, 22, 55; 12:3; 1Ch 13:2; 2Ch 6:3, 3, 12, 13; Mic 4:59

ASSEMBLY OF THE †LORD Nu 16:3; 20:4; Dt 23:1, 2, 2, 3, 3, 8; 1Ch 28:8; Mic 2:5

SOLEMN ASSEMBLY Ex 12:16, 16; Lev 23:36; Nu 29:35; Dt 16:8; 2Ki 10:20; 2Ch 7:9; Ne 8:18; Joel 1:14; 2:15

WHOLE ASSEMBLY Ex 16:3; Dt 5:22;

31:30; Jos 22:12; 1Ch 13:2, 4; 29:1, 20; 2Ch 1:3; 6:12, 13; 23:3; 29:28; 30:23, 25, 25; Ezr 2:64; 10:14; Ne 7:66; Lk 1:10; Ac 15:12; Sus 1:60

ASSESSMENTS·

Lev 27:25 **a** shall be by the sanctuary shekel:

ASSHUR

Ge 10:22 **A,** Arpachshad, Lud, and Aram.

ASSIGN → ASSIGNED, ASSIGNING

Nu 4:19 and his sons shall go in and **a** each
Eze 4: 5 For I **a** to you a number of days,
47:23 you shall **a** them their inheritance,

ASSIGNED → ASSIGN

Pr 8:29 when he **a** to the sea its limit,
Ro 12: 3 the measure of faith that God has **a.**
1Co 3: 5 as the Lord **a** to each.
7:17 lead the life that the Lord has **a,**
2Co 10:13 within the field that God has **a** to us,

ASSIGNING· → ASSIGN

Nu 8:26 with the Levites in **a** their duties.

ASSIST → ASSISTANCE, ASSISTANT

Nu 8:26 may **a** their brothers in the tent of
Ac 13: 5 And they had John also to **a** them.
1Ti 5:16 it can **a** those who are real widows.
Sir 29:20 **A** your neighbor to the best of your

ASSISTANCE → ASSIST

1Co 12:28 then gifts of healing, forms of **a,**

ASSISTANT → ASSIST

Ex 24:13 So Moses set out with his **a** Joshua,
Nu 11:28 Joshua son of Nun, the **a** of Moses,
Jos 1: 1 to Joshua son of Nun, Moses' **a,**

ASSOCIATE → ASSOCIATED

Pr 20:19 therefore do not **a** with a babbler.
22:24 and do not **a** with hotheads,
Zec 13: 7 against the man who is my **a,**"
Ac 10:28 unlawful for a Jew to **a** with or to
Ro 12:16 haughty, but **a** with the lowly;
1Co 5: 9 not to **a** with sexually immoral
5:11 not to **a** with anyone who bears the
Wis 6:23 for envy does not **a** with wisdom.
Sir 37:12 But **a** with a godly person

ASSOCIATED → ASSOCIATE

Eph 5: 7 Therefore do not be **a** with them.

ASSURANCE → ASSURED

Dt 28:66 in dread, with no **a** of your life.
Heb 6:11 so as to realize the full **a** of hope
10:22 with a true heart in full **a** of faith,
11: 1 faith is the **a** of things hoped for,

ASSURED → ASSURANCE

Pr 11:21 Be **a,** the wicked will not go
Zec 3: 6 the angel of the LORD **a** Joshua,
Col 2: 2 all the riches of **a** understanding
4:12 you may stand mature and fully **a**

ASSYRIA → ASSYRIAN, ASSYRIANS

Ge 10:11 From that land he went into **A,**
2Ki 15:29 he carried the people captive to **A.**
18:11 king of **A** carried the Israelites away to **A,**
19:10 given into the hand of the king of **A.**
Isa 10: 5 Ah, **A,** the rod of my anger—
36: 1 Sennacherib of **A** came up against
37:37 Then King Sennacherib of **A** left,
Jer 50:18 as I punished the king of **A.**
Hos 14: 3 **A** shall not save us:
Na 3:18 shepherds are asleep, O king of **A;**
Zec 10:10 and gather them from **A;**
Tob 1:10 I was carried away captive to **A**

ASSYRIAN → ASSYRIA

Isa 31: 8 "Then the **A** shall fall by a sword,
Jdt 2:14 generals, and officers of the **A** army.
15: 6 fell upon the **A** camp and plundered

ASSYRIANS → ASSYRIA
Isa 10:24 do not be afraid of the A
Eze 23: 5 she lusted after her lovers the A,
Sir 48:21 Lord struck down the camp of the A

ASTARTE → ASHERAH, ASTARTES
1Sa 31:10 put his armor in the temple of A;
1Ki 11: 5 Solomon followed A the goddess

ASTARTES → ASTARTE
Jdg   2:13 and worshiped Baal and the A.
1Sa   7: 4 Israel put away the Baals and the A,
     12:10 have served the Baals and the A;

ASTONISHED
Isa 52:14 there were many who were a at him
Da   3:24 King Nebuchadnezzar was a and
Lk   2:48 his parents saw him they were a;
Jn   3: 7 Do not be a that I said to you,
      7:21 one work, and all of you are a.
Gal   1: 6 a that you are so quickly deserting

ASTOUNDED
Mt   7:28 the crowds were a at his teaching,
Lk   24:22 some women of our group a us.
Ac   10:45 a that the gift of the Holy Spirit

ASTRAY → STRAY
Nu   5:12 If any man's wife goes a and is
Dt   30:17 are led a to bow down to other gods
Ps   14: 3 They have all gone a, they are all
     58: 3 The wicked go a from the womb;
    119:67 Before I was humbled I went a,
   119:176 I have gone a like a lost sheep,
Pr   10:17 but one who rejects a rebuke goes a.
     20: 1 whoever is led a by it is not wise.
Isa   9:16 who led this people led them a,
     53: 6 All we like sheep have gone a;
Jer 23:13 by Baal and led my people Israel a.
     50: 6 their shepherds have led them a,
Eze 14:11 Israel may no longer go a from me,
Am   2: 4 have been led a by the same lies
Mt   18:12 go in search of the one that went a?
     24: 5 and they will lead many a.
Mk   13: 5 "Beware that no one leads you a.
1Co 12: 2 you were enticed and led a to idols
2Co 11: 3 your thoughts will be led a from a
1Pe   2:25 For you were going a like sheep,
2Pe   2:15 the straight road and have gone a,
Sir   3:24 For their conceit has led many a,
     31: 5 pursues money will be led a by it.

ASUNDER*
Ps   2: 3 "Let us burst their bonds a,
    107:14 and broke their bonds a.
Isa 24:19 is utterly broken, the earth is torn a,

ATE → EAT
Ge   3: 6 she took of its fruit and a;
      3:13 "The serpent tricked me, and I a."
     27:25 So he brought it to him, and he a;
     41: 4 The ugly and thin cows a up the
Ex   16:35 The Israelites a manna forty years,
     24:11 they beheld God, and they a and
     34:28 he neither a bread nor drank water.
Nu   25: 2 the people a and bowed down to
Ru   2:14 She a until she was satisfied,
2Sa   9:11 Mephibosheth a at David's table,
2Ki   6:29 So we cooked my son and a him.
Ps   41: 9 who a of my bread, has lifted
     78:25 Mortals a of the bread of angels;
Jer 15:16 words were found, and I a them,
Eze   3: 3 I a it; and in my mouth it was as
Da   4:33 a grass like oxen,
Ob   1: 7 who a your bread have set a trap
Mt   14:20 And all a and were filled;
     15:37 And all of them a and were filled;
Mk   6:42 And all a and were filled;
Lk   9:17 And all a and were filled.
Jn   6:58 not like that which your ancestors a,
1Co 10: 3 and all a the same spiritual food,
Rev 10:10 from the hand of the angel and a it;
Bel   1:27 The dragon a them, and burst open.

2Es   1:19 you a the bread of angels.

ATHALIAH
Granddaughter of Omri; wife of Jehoram and
mother of Ahaziah; encouraged their evil ways
(2Ki 8:18, 27; 2Ch 22:2). At death of Ahaziah she
made herself queen, killing all his sons but Joash
(2Ki 11:1-3; 2Ch 22:10-12); killed six years later
when Joash revealed (2Ki 11:4-16; 2Ch 23:1-15).

ATHENS
Ac   17:16 Paul was waiting for them in A,

ATHLETE → ATHLETES
2Ti   2: 5 And in the case of an a,

ATHLETES → ATHLETE
1Co   9:25 A exercise self-control in all things;

ATONE* → ATONEMENT
Da   4:27 a for your sins with righteousness,
      9:24 an end to sin, and to a for iniquity,
Sir   3: 3 who honor their father a for sins,
     20:28 who please the great a for injustice.

ATONED* → ATONEMENT
Pr   16: 6 and faithfulness iniquity is a for,

ATONEMENT → ATONE, ATONED, ATONES, ATONING
Ex   29:36 a bull as a sin offering for a.
     30:10 Aaron shall perform the rite of a
     32:30 perhaps I can make a for your sin."
Lev   4:31 priest shall make a on your behalf,
      5: 6 priest shall make a on your behalf
      5:18 priest shall make a on your behalf
      6: 7 priest shall make a on your behalf
     23:28 for it is a day of a,
Nu   8:21 Aaron made a for them to cleanse
     25:13 and made a for the Israelites.'"
1Ch   6:49 to make a for Israel, according to
Ne   10:33 sin offerings to make a for Israel,
Ro   3:25 God put forward as a sacrifice of a
Heb   2:17 to make a sacrifice of a for the sins
Sir 35: 5 to forsake unrighteousness is an a.

ATONES* → ATONEMENT
Sir   3:30 so almsgiving a for sin.

ATONING → ATONEMENT
1Jn   2: 2 and he is the a sacrifice for our sins,
      4:10 sent his Son to be the a sacrifice for
Sir 28: 5 will make an a sacrifice for his sins?

ATTACK → ATTACKED, ATTACKS
1Sa 15: 3 a Amalek, and utterly destroy all
     24: 7 and did not permit them to a Saul.
Ps 109: 3 and a me without cause.
Ac   18:12 the Jews made a united a on Paul
2Ti   4:18 will rescue me from every evil a
1Mc   2:41 comes to a us on the sabbath day;

ATTACKED → ATTACK
Ps 129: 1 "Often have they a me
1Mc   2:38 So they a them on the sabbath,

ATTACKS → ATTACK
Ex   21:14 But if someone willfully a and kills
Lk   11:22 one stronger than he a him and

ATTAIN → ATTAINABLE, ATTAINED
Ps 101: 2 When shall I a it?
    139: 6 it is so high that I cannot a it.
Pr   8:12 and I a knowledge and discretion.
Da   12:12 those who persevere and a
Php   3:11 a the resurrection from the dead.

ATTAINABLE* → ATTAIN
Heb   7:11 if perfection had been a through

ATTAINED → ATTAIN
Ro   9:30 not strive for righteousness, have a
Php   3:16 let us hold fast to what we have a.

ATTEMPTED
Dt   4:34 has any god ever a to go and take

Heb 11:29 the Egyptians a to do so they were
Bel   1:42 those who had a his destruction,

ATTEND → ATTENDANCE, ATTENDANT
Nu   3:10 they who shall a to the priesthood,
2Ch   9: 7 who continually a you and hear
Ps   17: 1 O LORD; a to my cry;
     55: 2 A to me, and answer me;

ATTENDANCE → ATTEND
Isa   6: 2 Seraphs were in a above him;

ATTENDANT → ATTEND
1Ki   1: 4 She became the king's a and served
Lk   4:20 the scroll, gave it back to the a,

ATTENTION → ATTENTIVE
Nu   16:15 "Pay no a to their offering.
Job 24:12 yet God pays no a to their prayer.
Lk   8:18 Then pay a to how you listen;
1Ti   4: 1 by paying a to deceitful spirits and
      4:13 a to the public reading of scripture,
Tit   1:14 not paying a to Jewish myths or
Heb   2: 1 greater a to what we have heard,
3Jn   1:10 I will call a to what he is doing
Sir   6:33 if you pay a you will become wise.

ATTENTIVE → ATTENTION
Ex   23:13 Be a to all that I have said to you.
2Ch   6:40 ears a to prayer from this place.
Ne   1:11 let your ear be a to the prayer of
Ps 130: 2 Let your ears be a to the voice of
Pr   2: 2 making your ear a to wisdom
      4:20 My child, be a to my words;
2Pe   1:19 be a to this as to a lamp shining in a

ATTESTED
Ac   2:22 a man a to you by God with deeds
Ro   3:21 and is a by the law and the prophets,
1Ti   2: 6 this was a at the right time.
      5:10 be well a for her good works,
Heb   2: 3 was a to us by those who heard him,
      7:17 a of him, "You are a priest forever,

ATTIRE
Jer   2:32 her ornaments, or a bride her a?
Jdt 10: 3 and dressed herself in the festive a
AdE 15: 1 and arrayed herself in splendid a.

ATTORNEY*
Ac   24: 1 and an a, a certain Tertullus,

ATTRACTIVE
Ge   26: 7 because she is a in appearance."
Sir 25: 5 How a is wisdom in the aged,

AUGUR* → AUGURY
Dt   18:10 a soothsayer, or an a, or a sorcerer,

AUGURY → AUGUR
Lev 19:26 shall not practice a or witchcraft.
2Ki 17:17 they used divination and a;

AUGUSTUS*
Lk   2: 1 a decree went out from Emperor A

AUTHOR*
Ac   3:15 and you killed the A of life,
Wis 13: 3 for the a of beauty created them.

AUTHORITIES → AUTHORITY
Lk   12:11 synagogues, the rulers, and the a,
Jn   7:26 the a really know that this is the Messiah?
     12:42 even of the a, believed in him.
Ac   16:19 into the marketplace before the a.
Ro   13: 1 be subject to the governing a;
     13: 6 for the a are God's servants,
Eph   3:10 made known to the rulers and a
      6:12 but against the rulers, against the a,
Col   2:15 He disarmed the rulers and a
Tit   3: 1 to be subject to rulers and a,
1Pe   3:22 a, and powers made subject to him.

AUTHORITY → AUTHORITIES
Ge   41:45 Thus Joseph gained a over the land

Pr   29: 2 When the righteous are in **a**,
     29:16 When the wicked are in **a**,
Isa   9: 6 **a** rests upon his shoulders;
Mt   7:29 for he taught them as one having **a**,
      9: 6 the Son of Man has **a** on earth to
            forgive sins"—
     28:18 "All **a** in heaven and on earth has
Mk   1:27 A new teaching—with **a**!
     11:28 "By what **a** are you doing these
Lk   4:32 because he spoke with **a**.
      5:24 the Son of Man has **a** on earth to
            forgive sins"—
      7: 8 For I also am a man set under **a**,
Jn   5:27 given him **a** to execute judgment,
Ac   1: 7 that the Father has set by his own **a**.
      5:29 "We must obey God rather than
            any human **a**.
Ro   13: 1 for there is no **a** except from God,
     13: 2 whoever resists **a** resists what God
1Co   7: 4 For the wife does not have **a** over
            her own body,
      7: 4 the husband does not have **a** over
            his own body,
     11:10 woman ought to have a symbol of **a**
     15:24 destroyed every ruler and every **a**
2Co 10: 8 if I boast a little too much of our **a**,
Eph   1:21 far above all rule and **a** and power
Col   2:10 who is the head of every ruler and **a**.
1Ti   2:12 I permit no woman to teach or to
            have **a** over
Tit   2:15 exhort and reprove with all **a**.
1Pe   2:13 the **a** of every human institution,
      3: 1 accept the **a** of your husbands,
      3: 5 adorn themselves by accepting the **a**
      5: 5 must accept the **a** of the elders.
2Pe   2:10 in depraved lust, and who despise **a**.
3Jn   1: 9 does not acknowledge our **a**.
Jude 1: 8 reject **a**, and slander the glorious
Rev   2:26 I will give **a** over the nations;
     11: 3 my two witnesses to prophesy
     12:10 and the **a** of his Messiah,
     13: 4 for he had given his **a** to the beast,
     20: 4 on them were given **a** to judge.
Sir 20: 8 and whoever pretends to **a** is hated.

AUTUMN*

Jer   5:24 the **a** rain and the spring rain,
Jude 1:12 **a** trees without fruit, twice dead,

AVAIL → AVAILS

Ps   39: 2 I held my peace to no **a**;
Pr   21:30 no counsel, can **a** against the LORD.
Jer   7: 8 trusting in deceptive words to no **a**.

AVAILS* → AVAIL

Ps   49: 7 Truly, no ransom **a** for one's life,

AVENGE → VENGEANCE

Nu   31: 2 "A the Israelites on the Midianites;
Dt   32:43 he will **a** the blood of his children,
1Sa 24:12 May the LORD **a** me on you;
2Ki   9: 7 I may **a** on Jezebel the blood of my
Joel 3:21 I will **a** their blood, and I will not
Ro   12:19 Beloved, never **a** yourselves,
Rev   6:10 and **a** our blood on the inhabitants
1Mc   2:67 **a** the wrong done to your people.

AVENGED → VENGEANCE

Ge   4:24 If Cain is **a** sevenfold, truly Lamech
Rev 19: 2 **a** on her the blood of his servants."

AVENGER → VENGEANCE

Nu   35:12 The cities shall be for you a refuge
            from the **a**,
Jos 20: 3 a refuge from the **a** of blood.
Ps   8: 2 to silence the enemy and the **a**.
1Th   4: 6 the Lord is an **a** in all these things,

AVENGES* → VENGEANCE

Ps   9:12 he who **a** blood is mindful of them;

AVENGING* → VENGEANCE

1Sa 25:33 and from **a** myself by my own hand!
Ps   79:10 Let the **a** of the outpoured blood of

Na   1: 2 A jealous and **a** God is the LORD,
            the LORD is **a** and wrathful;

AVERT → AVERTED

Jer 11:15 and sacrificial flesh **a** your doom?
Eze   7:22 I will **a** my face from them,
Sir   4: 5 Do not **a** your eye from the needy,

AVERTED → AVERT

2Sa 24:25 and the plague was **a** from Israel.
Ezr 10:14 of our God on this account is **a**
Jdt 13:20 and you **a** our ruin,

AVOID → AVOIDS

Pr   4:15 **A** it; do not go on it;
1Ti   6:20 **A** the profane chatter and
2Ti   2:16 **A** profane chatter, for it will lead
      3: 5 but denying its power. **A** them!
Tit   3: 2 to **a** quarreling, to be gentle,
      3: 9 But **a** stupid controversies,

AVOIDS → AVOID

Pr   16: 6 by the fear of the LORD one **a** evil.
     16:17 The highway of the upright **a** evil;

AWAKE → WAKE

Jdg   5:12 "A, **a**, Deborah! A, **a**, utter a song!
Ps   7: 6 **a**, O my God; you have appointed a
            judgment.
     44:23 **A**, do not cast us off forever!
     57: 8 **A**, my soul! **A**, O harp and lyre! I
            will **a** the dawn.
Pr   6:22 when you **a**, they will talk with you.
SS   5: 2 I slept, but my heart was **a**.
Isa 51: 9 **A**, **a**, put on strength, O arm of the
            LORD!
     52: 1 **A**, **a**, put on your strength, O Zion!
Da   12: 2 in the dust of the earth shall **a**,
Zec 13: 7 "A, O sword, against my shepherd,
Mt   24:42 Keep **a** therefore, for you do not
     26:38 remain here, and stay **a** with me."
Mk   14:37 Could you not keep **a** one hour?
Eph   5:14 "Sleeper, **a**! Rise from the dead,
1Th   5: 6 but let us keep **a** and be sober;
      5:10 so that whether we are **a** or asleep
Rev 16:15 Blessed is the one who stays **a** and

AWAKEN → WAKE

SS   8: 4 not stir up or **a** love until it is ready!
Jn   11:11 but I am going there to **a** him."

AWAKENED → WAKE

1Ki 18:27 perhaps he is asleep and must be **a**."
SS   8: 5 Under the apple tree I **a** you.

AWARE

Mt   22:18 But Jesus, **a** of their malice, said,
Mk   5:30 Immediately **a** that power had gone
Lk   9:47 But Jesus, **a** of their inner thoughts,
Jn   6:61 being **a** that his disciples were

AWAY

Ge   27:35 he has taken **a** your blessing."
     30:23 "God has taken **a** my reproach";
Ex   23:25 take sickness **a** from among you.
Nu   21: 7 to the LORD to take **a** the serpents
     22:33 turned **a** from me these three times.
Dt   7: 1 clears **a** many nations before you—
1Sa   7: 4 Israel put **a** the Baals and the
     28:15 and God has turned **a** from me
2Sa 12:13 "Now the LORD has put **a** your sin;
Ezr 10:19 themselves to send **a** their wives,
Job   1:21 the LORD gave, and the LORD has
            taken **a**;
Ps   1: 4 are like chaff that the wind drives **a**.
     22:19 But you, O LORD, do not be far **a**!
     51:11 not cast me **a** from your presence,
    119:51 but I do not turn **a** from your law.
Pr   3: 7 fear the LORD, and turn **a** from evil.
     15: 1 A soft answer turns **a** wrath,
Ecc   3: 6 time to keep, and a time to throw **a**;
SS   5:30 my love, my fair one, and come **a**;
Isa   9:12 all this his anger has not turned **a**;
Jnh   1: 3 **a** from the presence of the LORD.

Na   1:12 they will be cut off and pass **a**.
Zep   1: 2 I will utterly sweep **a** everything
      3:15 LORD has taken **a** the judgments
Hag   1: 9 you brought it home, I blew it **a**.
Mt   4:10 Jesus said to him, "A with you,
            Satan!
Mk   13:31 Heaven and earth will pass **a**, but
            my words will not pass **a**.
Lk   8:13 and in a time of testing fall **a**.
     24: 2 the stone rolled **a** from the tomb,
Jn   1:29 "Here is the Lamb of God who
            takes **a** the sin of the world!
      6:37 comes to me I will never drive **a**;
     14:28 say to you, 'I am going **a**,
1Co   7:31 form of this world is passing **a**.
2Co   5:17 everything old has passed **a**;
Heb   2: 1 so that we do not drift **a** from it.
      6: 6 and then have fallen **a**,
1Pe   1:19 turn **a** from evil and do good;
      5: 4 crown of glory that never fades **a**.
2Pe   3:10 the heavens will pass **a** with a loud
1Jn   2: 8 because the darkness is passing **a**
      2:17 world and its desire are passing **a**,
Rev   7:17 God will wipe **a** every tear from
     21: 1 and the first earth had passed **a**,

AWE → AWESOME

Jos   4:14 as they had stood in **a** of Moses,
1Ki   3:28 and they stood in **a** of the king,
Ps 119:161 my heart stands in **a** of your words.
Isa 29:23 will stand in **a** of the God of Israel.
Hos   3: 5 they shall come in **a** to the LORD
Hab   3: 2 of your renown, and I stand in **a**,
Mal   2: 5 and stood in **a** of my name.
Mt   9: 8 saw it, they were filled with **a**,
Lk   5:26 and were filled with **a**,
Ac   2:43 A came upon everyone, because
Ro   11:20 do not become proud, but stand in **a**.
Heb 12:28 worship with reverence and **a**;

AWESOME* → AWE

Ge   28:17 and said, "How **a** is this place!
Ex   15:11 majestic in holiness, in splendor,
     34:10 an **a** thing that I will do with you.
Dt   6:22 before our eyes great and **a** signs
      7:21 with you, is a great and **a** God.
     10:17 the great God, mighty and **a**,
     10:21 for you these great and **a** things
     28:58 fearing this glorious and **a** name,
2Sa   7:23 doing great and **a** things for them,
Ne   1: 5 and **a** God who keeps covenant
      4:14 the LORD, who is great and **a**,
      9:32 the great and mighty and **a** God,
Job 37:22 around God is **a** majesty.
Ps   47: 2 For the LORD, the Most High, is **a**,
     65: 5 By **a** deeds you answer us with
     66: 3 Say to God, "How **a** are your deeds!
     66: 5 he is **a** in his deeds among mortals.
     68:35 A is God in his sanctuary.
     76: 7 But you indeed are **a**!
     76:11 bring gifts to the one who is **a**,
     89: 7 and **a** above all that are around him?
     99: 3 praise your great and **a** name.
    106:22 and **a** deeds by the Red Sea.
    111: 9 Holy and **a** is his name.
    145: 6 of your **a** deeds shall be proclaimed,
Isa 64: 3 did **a** deeds that we did not expect,
Eze   1:18 There was **a** to them; and the
Da   9: 4 saying, "Ah, Lord, great and **a** God,
Sir 43:29 A is the Lord and very great,

AWL*

Ex   21: 6 shall pierce his ear with an **a**;
Dt   15:17 **a** and thrust it through his earlobe

AWOKE → WAKE

Ge   9:24 When Noah **a** from his wine
     41: 7 Pharaoh **a**, and it was a dream.
Jdg 16:20 When he **a** from his sleep,
1Ki   3:15 Solomon **a**; it had been a dream.
Ps   78:65 Then the Lord **a** as from sleep,
Mt   1:24 When Joseph **a** from sleep,

AX
2Ki   6: 5 his **a** head fell into the water;
Isa 10:15 the **a** vaunt itself over the one who
Mt   3:10 Even now the **a** is lying at the root

AZARIAH → =ABEDNEGO, =UZZIAH
1. King of Judah; see Uzziah (2Ki 15:1-7).
2. Prophet (2Ch 15:1-8).
3. Opponent of Jeremiah (Jer 43:2).
4. Jewish exile; see Abednego (Da 1:6-19).

AZAZEL
Lev 16: 8 for the LORD and the other lot for **A**.

AZEKAH
Jos 10:10 and struck them down as far as **A**

B

BAAL → BAALS
Nu   25: 3 Israel yoked itself to the **B** of Peor,
Dt   4: 3 did with regard to the **B** of Peor—
Jdg   2:13 and worshiped **B** and the Astartes.
        6:31 "Will you contend for **B**?
1Ki 16:32 an altar for **B** in the house of **B**,
      18:25 Elijah said to the prophets of **B**,
      19:18 the knees that have not bowed to **B**,
2Ki   3: 2 for he removed the pillar of **B**
      10:28 Thus Jehu wiped out **B** from Israel.
2Ch 23:17 they killed Mattan, the priest of **B**,
Ps 106:28 attached themselves to the **B** of Peor
Jer   2: 8 the prophets prophesied by **B**,
      19: 5 places of **B** to burn their children in
Hos   2:16 no longer will you call me, "My **B**."
      13: 1 incurred guilt through **B** and died.
Ro   11: 4 not bowed the knee to **B**."

BAAL-BERITH
Jdg   8:33 with the Baals, making **B** their god.

BAAL-ZEBUB
2Ki   1: 2 "Go, inquire of **B**, the god of Ekron,

BAALS → BAAL
Jdg   3: 7 worshiping the **B** and the Asherahs.
      10:10 and have worshiped the **B**."
1Sa   7: 4 So Israel put away the **B** and the
2Ch 17: 3 he did not seek the **B**,
      34: 4 pulled down the altars of the **B**;
Hos   2:17 I will remove the names of the **B**

BAASHA
King of Israel (1Ki 15:16-16:7; 2Ch 16:1-6).

BABBLER* → BABBLING
Pr   20:19 therefore do not associate with a **b**.
Ac   17:18 "What does this **b** want to say?"

BABBLING → BABBLER
Pr   10: 8 but a fool will come to ruin.

BABEL → BABYLON
Ge   11: 9 Therefore it was called **B**,

BABES* → BABIES
Ps   8: 2 Out of the mouths of **b** and infants
Isa   3: 4 and **b** shall rule over them.
La   2:11 infants and **b** faint in the streets of

BABIES → BABES
Mt   21:16 'Out of the mouths of infants and
            nursing **b**

BABYLON → BABEL, BABYLONIA,
   BABYLONIANS
2Ki 24:15 into captivity from Jerusalem to **B**.
1Ch   9: 1 taken into exile in **B** because of
2Ch 36:18 all these he brought to **B**.
      36:20 He took into exile in **B** those who
Ps 137: 1 By the rivers of **B**—there we sat
      137: 8 O daughter **B**, you devastator!

Isa 13: 1 The oracle concerning **B** that Isaiah
      14: 4 this taunt against the king of **B**:
      21: 9 he responded, "Fallen, fallen is **B**;
      47: 1 sit in the dust, virgin daughter **B**!
Jer 25:11 serve the king of **B** seventy years.
      50: 1 that the LORD spoke concerning **B**,
      51:37 and **B** shall become a heap of ruins,
      52:11 and the king of **B** took him to **B**,
Da   2:48 prefect over all the wise men of **B**.
        4:30 "Is this not magnificent **B**,
1Pe   5:13 Your sister church in **B**, chosen
Rev 14: 8 "Fallen, fallen is **B** the great!
      17: 5 "**B** the great, mother of whores and
      18: 2 "Fallen, fallen is **B** the great!
Bar   2:24 to serve the king of **B**;
LtJ   6: 1 who were to be taken to **B** as exiles
Bel   1:36 he set him down in **B**,

KING OF BABYLON 2Ki 20:18; 24:7, 12,
   12, 16, 17, 20; 25:6, 8, 8, 11, 20, 21, 23, 24;
   Isa 14:4; 39:7; Jer 20:4; 21:4, 10; 25:11, 12;
   27:8, 9, 11, 12, 13, 14, 17; 28:2, 4; 29:22;
   32:3, 4, 36; 34:2, 3, 7, 21; 36:29; 37:17, 19;
   38:3, 17, 18, 22, 23; 39:3, 3, 6, 6, 13; 40:5, 7,
   9, 11; 41:2, 18; 42:11; 50:18, 43; 51:31; 52:3,
   9, 10, 11, 12, 12, 15, 26, 27, 34; Eze 17:12;
   19:9; 21:19, 21; 24:2; 30:24, 25, 25; 32:11;
   Bar 2:21, 22, 24

DAUGHTER BABYLON Ps 137:8; Isa
   47:1; Jer 50:42; 51:33; Zec 2:7

BABYLONIA → BABYLON
Ezr   7: 6 this Ezra went up from **B**.

BABYLONIANS → BABYLON
Bel   1: 3 Now the **B** had an idol called Bel,

BACCHIDES
1Mc   7: 8 chose **B**, one of the king's Friends,
        9:11 Then the army of **B** marched out

BACK → BACKS, BACKSLIDING
Ge   8:11 dove came **b** to him in the evening,
      19:26 Lot's wife, behind him, looked **b**,
Ex   14:21 The LORD drove the sea **b**
Nu   14: 3 better for us to go **b** to Egypt?"
Ru   1: Naomi said, "Turn **b**, my daughters,
        2: 6 Moabite who came **b** with Naomi
2Sa 12:23 Can I bring him **b** again?
2Ki 20:11 he brought the shadow **b** the ten
1Ch 21:27 he put his sword **b** into its sheath.
Ps   90: 3 turn us **b** to dust, and say, "Turn **b**,
     114: 5 O Jordan, that you turn **b**?
     132:11 oath from which he will not turn **b**:
     137: 8 pay you **b** what you have done to us
Isa   38: 8 the sun turned **b** on the dial the ten
      38:17 have cast all my sins behind your **b**.
      49: 5 to bring Jacob **b** to him,
      55:12 go out in joy, and be led **b** in peace;
Jer   29:14 and I will bring you **b** to the place
La   3:64 Pay them **b** for their deeds, O LORD,
Eze   33:11 turn **b**, turn **b** from your evil ways;
Mt   27: 3 he repented and brought **b** the thirty
      28: 2 and rolled **b** the stone and sat on it.
Lk   9:62 puts a hand to the plow and looks **b**
Heb 10:39 are not among those who shrink **b**
      13:20 brought **b** from the dead our Lord
2Pe   2:22 "The dog turns **b** to its own vomit,"
Rev   5: 1 written on the inside and on the **b**,

BACKS → BACK
Ex   23:27 all your enemies turn their **b** to you.
Dt   33:29 and you shall tread on their **b**.
Ne   9:26 cast your law behind their **b**
Pr   19:29 and flogging for the **b** of fools.

BACKSLIDING* → BACK
Jer   8: 5 people turned away in perpetual **b**?

BAD → WORSE
Ge   37: 2 Joseph brought a **b** report of them
Pr   20:14 "**B**, **b**," says the buyer, then goes
Jer   24: 2 but the other basket had very **b** figs,
Mt   7:17 but the **b** tree bears **b** fruit.

      12:33 or make the tree **b**, and its fruit **b**;
1Co 15:33 "**B** company ruins good morals."

BAG → BAGGAGE
1Sa 17:49 David put his hand in his **b**,
Mic   6:11 and a **b** of dishonest weights?
Hag   1: 6 to put them into a **b** with holes.
Lk   10: 4 Carry no purse, no **b**, no sandals;

BAGGAGE → BAG
1Sa 10:22 has hidden himself among the **b**."
Eze 12: 7 out my **b** by day, as **b** for exile,

BAKE → BAKED, BAKER
Ex   16:23 **b** what you want to **b**

BAKED → BAKE
Ex   12:39 They **b** unleavened cakes of the
Lev   2: 4 a grain offering **b** in the oven,
Nu   11: 8 like the taste of cakes **b** with oil.
1Ch 23:29 unleavened bread, the **b** offering,

BAKER → BAKE
Ge   40: 1 his **b** offended their lord the king of

BALAAM
Prophet who attempted to curse Israel (Nu 22-
24; Dt 23:4-5; 2Pe 2:15; Jude 11; Rev 2:14).
Killed in Israel's vengeance on Midianites (Nu
31:8; Jos 13:22).

BALAK
Moabite king who hired Balaam to curse Israel
(Nu 22-24; Jos 24:9; Mic 6:5).

BALANCE → BALANCES
Job 31: 6 let me be weighed in a just **b**,
Isa   40:12 in scales and the hills in a **b**?
2Co   8:13 but it is a question of a fair **b**
Sir   6:15 no amount can **b** their worth.
2Mc   9: 8 weigh the high mountains in a **b**,

BALANCES → BALANCE
Lev   19:36 shall have honest **b**, honest weights,
Pr   16:11 Honest **b** and scales are the LORD's;
Eze 45:10 have honest **b**, an honest ephah,
Am   8: 5 and practice deceit with false **b**,
Sir   28:25 make **b** and scales for your words.

BALD → BALDHEAD
Eze 27:31 they make themselves **b** for you,
Mic   1:16 make yourselves as **b** as the eagle,

BALDHEAD* → BALD, HEAD
2Ki   2:23 saying, "Go away, **b**! Go away, **b**!"

BALL*
Isa   22:18 throw you like a **b** into a wide land;

BALM
Jer   8:22 Is there no **b** in Gilead?
      46:11 Go up to Gilead, and take **b**,

BALSAM
1Ch 14:15 marching in the tops of the **b** trees,

BAND → BANDS
Ex   28: 8 The decorated **b** on it shall be of
1Sa 10: 5 you will meet a **b** of prophets

BANDAGE → BANDAGED
1Ki 20:38 disguising himself with a **b** over his

BANDAGED* → BANDAGE
Lk   10:34 He went to him and **b** his wounds,
Sir   27:21 For a wound may be **b**,

BANDIT → BANDITS
Mt   26:55 to arrest me as though I were a **b**?
Jn   10: 1 in by another way is a thief and a **b**.
      18:40 Now Barabbas was a **b**.

BANDITS → BANDIT
Hos   7: 1 the thief breaks in, and the **b** raid
Mt   27:38 two **b** were crucified with him,
Jn   10: 8 came before me are thieves and **b**;
2Co 11:26 danger from **b**, danger from my own

BANDS → BAND

Hos 11: 4 of human kindness, with **b** of love.
Lk   2: 7 wrapped him in **b** of cloth, and laid
      2:12 find a child wrapped in **b** of cloth

BANISH

Ecc 11:10 **B** anxiety from your mind,
Jer 25:10 will **b** from them the sound of mirth
Eze 34:25 and **b** wild animals from the land,
Ro   11:26 he will **b** ungodliness from Jacob."

BANK → BANKERS, BANKS

Ex   2: 3 the reeds on the **b** of the river.
      7:15 stand by at the river **b** to meet him,
2Ki   2:13 and stood on the **b** of the Jordan.
Mk   5:13 down the steep **b** into the sea,

BANKERS* → BANK

Mt   25:27 have invested my money with the **b**,

BANKS → BANK

Ge   41:17 I was standing on the **b** of the Nile;
Jos   3:15 Now the Jordan overflows all its **b**
1Ch   3:15 when it was overflowing all its **b**,
Eze 47:12 On the **b**, on both sides of the river,

BANNER → BANNERS

Ex   17:15 and called it, The LORD is my **b**.
Ps   60: 4 set up a **b** for those who fear you,

BANNERS → BANNER

Ps   20: 5 in the name of our God set up our **b**.

BANQUET → BANQUETING, BANQUETS

Est   1: 3 he gave a **b** for all his officials and
      5: 5 the king and Haman came to the **b**
      6:14 to the **b** that Esther had prepared.
Mt   22: 2 a king who gave a wedding **b**
Lk   5:29 Then Levi gave a great **b** for him in
     14:13 when you give a **b**, invite the poor,
Jdt 12:10 the fourth day Holofernes held a **b**

BANQUETING → BANQUET

SS   2: 4 He brought me to the **b** house,

BANQUETS → BANQUET

Mk   12:39 and places of honor at **b!**

BAPTISM* → BAPTIZE

Mt   3: 7 and Sadducees coming for **b**,
     21:25 the **b** of John come from heaven,
Mk   1: 4 proclaiming a **b** of repentance for
     10:38 be baptized with the **b** that I am
     10:39 the **b** with which I am baptized,
     11:30 the **b** of John come from heaven,
Lk   3: 3 proclaiming a **b** of repentance for
      7:29 had been baptized with John's **b**.
     12:50 I have a **b** with which to be baptized
     20: 4 the **b** of John come from heaven,
Ac   1:22 the **b** of John until the day when he
     10:37 after the **b** that John announced:
     13:24 a **b** of repentance to all the people
     18:25 though he knew only the **b** of John.
     19: 3 They answered, "Into John's **b.**"
     19: 4 "John baptized with the **b** of
Ro   6: 4 buried with him by **b** into death,
1Co 15:29 receive **b** on behalf of the dead?
Eph   4: 5 one Lord, one faith, one **b**,
Col   2:12 with him in **b**,
1Pe   3:21 **b**, which this prefigured, now saves

BAPTISMS* → BAPTIZE

Heb   6: 2 about **b**, laying on of hands,
      9:10 with food and drink and various **b**,

BAPTIST → BAPTIZE

Mt   3: 1 In those days John the **B** appeared
     11:11 has arisen greater than John the **B**;
     14: 8 the head of John the **B** here on a
     16:14 they said, "Some say John the **B**,

BAPTIZE* → BAPTISM, BAPTISMS, BAPTIST, BAPTIZED, BAPTIZER, BAPTIZES, BAPTIZING

Mt   3:11 "I **b** you with water for repentance,
      3:11 He will **b** you with the Holy Spirit
Mk   1: 8 he will **b** you with the Holy Spirit."
Lk   3:16 by saying, "I **b** you with water;
      3:16 He will **b** you with the Holy Spirit
Jn   1:26 answered them, "I **b** with water.
      1:33 sent me to **b** with water said to me,
1Co   1:16 (I did **b** also the household of
      1:17 For Christ did not send me to **b** but

BAPTIZED* → BAPTIZE

Mt   3: 6 were **b** by him in the river Jordan,
      3:13 to John at the Jordan, to be **b**
      3:14 "I need to be **b** by you, and do you
      3:16 And when Jesus had been **b**,
Mk   1: 5 were **b** by him in the river Jordan,
      1: 8 I have **b** you with water;
      1: 9 was **b** by John in the Jordan.
     10:38 be **b** with the baptism that I am **b** with?"
     10:39 and with the baptism with which I am **b**, you will be **b**;
     16:16 who believes and is **b** will be saved;
Lk   3: 7 to the crowds that came out to be **b**
      3:12 Even tax collectors came to be **b**,
      3:21 Now when all the people were **b**,
      3:21 and when Jesus also had been **b** and
      7:29 had been **b** with John's baptism.
      7:30 But by refusing to be **b** by him,
     12:50 I have a baptism with which to be **b**,
Jn   3:22 some time there with them and **b**.
      3:23 kept coming and were being **b**
      4: 2 it was not Jesus himself but his disciples who **b**—
Ac   1: 5 John **b** with water, but you will be **b** with the Holy Spirit not many
      2:38 "Repent, and be **b** every one of you
      2:41 who welcomed his message were **b**,
      8:12 they were **b**, both men and women.
      8:13 After being **b**, he stayed constantly
      8:16 they had only been **b** in the name of
      8:36 is to prevent me from being **b**?"
      8:38 into the water, and Philip **b** him.
      9:18 Then he got up and was **b**,
     10:48 he ordered them to be **b** in the name
     11:16 'John **b** with water, but you will be **b** with the Holy Spirit.'
     16:15 she and her household were **b**,
     16:33 he and his entire family were **b**
     18: 8 became believers and were **b**.
     19: 3 said, "Into what then were you **b?**"
     19: 4 "John **b** with the baptism of
     19: 5 **b** in the name of the Lord Jesus.
     22:16 Get up, be **b**, and have your sins
Ro   6: 3 who have been **b** into Christ Jesus were **b** into his death?
1Co   1:13 Or were you **b** in the name of Paul?
      1:14 I thank God that I **b** none of you
      1:15 no one can say that you were **b** in
      1:16 not know whether I **b** anyone else.)
     10: 2 all were **b** into Moses in the cloud
     12:13 one Spirit we were all **b** into one
     12:13 are people **b** on their behalf?
Gal   3:27 aw were **b** into Christ have clothed

BAPTIZER → BAPTIZE

Mk   1: 4 John the **b** appeared in the
      6:24 replied, "The head of John the **b**."

BAPTIZES* → BAPTIZE

Jn   1:33 the one who **b** with the Holy Spirit.'

BAPTIZING* → BAPTIZE

Mt   28:19 **b** them in the name of the Father
Jn   1:25 "Why then are you **b** if you are
      1:28 across the Jordan where John was **b**.
      1:31 I came **b** with water for this reason,
      3:23 John also was **b** at Aenon near
      3:26 he is **b**, and all are going to him."

      4: 1 "Jesus is making and **b** more
     10:40 place where John had been **b** earlier,
Ac   10:47 withhold the water for **b** these

BAR → BARS

Jdg 16: 3 pulled them up, **b** and all, put them
Ne   7: 3 let them shut and **b** the doors,
Isa   9: 4 and the **b** across their shoulders,

BAR-JESUS* → =ELYMAS

Ac   13: 6 a Jewish false prophet, named **B**.

BARABBAS*

Prisoner released by Pilate instead of Jesus (Mt 27:16-26; Mk 15:7-15; Lk 23:18-19; Jn 18:40).

BARAK*

Judge who fought with Deborah against Canaanites (Jdg 4-5; 1Sa 12:11; Heb 11:32).

BARBARIAN* → BARBARIANS

Col   3:11 circumcised and uncircumcised, **b**,
2Mc   2:21 land and pursued the **b** hordes,

BARBARIANS* → BARBARIAN

Ro   1:14 am a debtor both to Greeks and to **b**,

BARBS*

Nu   33:55 let remain shall be as **b** in your eyes

BARE → BARED, BAREFOOT, BAREHANDED

Ps   18:15 were laid **b** at your rebuke,
Eze   4: 7 yet you were naked and **b**.
     23:29 and leave you naked and **b**,
Heb   4:13 all are naked and laid **b** to the eyes

BARED* → BARE

Isa 52:10 The LORD has **b** his holy arm
Eze   4: 7 with your arm **b** you shall prophesy

BAREFOOT → BARE, FOOT

Isa 20: 3 Isaiah has walked naked and **b**
Mic   1: 8 I will go **b** and naked;

BAREHANDED* → BARE, HAND

Jdg 14: 6 and he tore the lion apart **b** as one

BARGAIN → BARGAINED

Isa 57: 8 made a **b** for yourself with them,

BARGAINED* → BARGAIN

Hos   8: 9 Ephraim has **b** for lovers.

BARLEY

Ex   9:31 Now the flax and the **b** were ruined,
Ru   1:22 at the beginning of the **b** harvest.
2Ki   7: 1 and two measures of **b** for a shekel,
Jn   6: 9 a boy here who has five **b** loaves
Rev   6: 6 three quarts of **b** for a day's pay,
Jdt   8: 2 had died during the **b** harvest.

BARN* → BARNS

Hag   2:19 Is there any seed left in the **b?**
Mt   13:30 but gather the wheat into my **b**.'"
Lk   12:24 they have neither storehouse nor **b**,

BARNABAS* → =JOSEPH

Disciple, originally Joseph (Ac 4:36), prophet (Ac 13:1), apostle (Ac 14:14). Brought Paul to apostles (Ac 9:27), Antioch (Ac 11:22-29; Gal 2:1-13), on the first missionary journey (Ac 13-14). Together at Jerusalem Council, they separated over John Mark (Ac 15). Later co-workers (1Co 9:6; Col 4:10).

BARNS* → BARN

Dt   28: 8 the blessing upon you in your **b**,
Ps 144:13 May our **b** be filled, with produce
Pr   3:10 your **b** will be filled with plenty,
Mt   6:26 sow nor reap nor gather into **b**,
Lk   12:18 pull down my **b** and build larger

BARREN → BARRENNESS

Ge   11:30 Now Sarai was **b**; she had no child.
     25:21 for his wife, because she was **b**;

29:31 but Rachel was **b.**
Ex 23:26 No one shall miscarry or be **b** in
Jdg 13: 2 His wife was **b,** having borne no
1Sa 2: 5 The **b** has borne seven, but she who
Ps 113: 9 He gives the **b** woman a home,
Pr 30:16 the **b** womb, the earth ever thirsty
Isa 49:21 I was bereaved and **b,** exiled and
     54: 1 Sing, O **b** one who did not bear;
Lk   1: 7 because Elizabeth was **b,**
     23:29 they will say, 'Blessed are the **b,**
Heb 11:11 too old—and Sarah herself was **b—**
Jas 2:20 that faith apart from works is **b?**

BARRENNESS* → BARREN

Dt   7:14 neither sterility nor **b** among you
Ro   4:19 considered the **b** of Sarah's womb.

BARRIER

Jer 5:22 a perpetual **b** that it cannot pass;

BARS → BAR

Ex 26:26 You shall make **b** of acacia wood,
Nu   3:36 the **b,** the pillars, the bases,
Job 17:16 Will it go down to the **b** of Sheol?
Ps 147:13 he strengthens the **b** of your gates;
La   2: 9 he has ruined and broken her **b;**

BARSABBAS* → =JOSEPH, =JUDAS,
=JUSTUS

Ac   1:23 they proposed two, Joseph called **B,**
     15:22 They sent Judas called **B,** and Silas,

BARTHOLOMEW* → =NATHANAEL?

Apostle (Mt 10:3; Mk 3:18; Lk 6:14; Ac 1:13).
Possibly also called Nathanael (Jn 1:45-49; 21:2).

BARTIMAEUS*

Blind man healed by Jesus (Mk 10:46-52).

BARUCH*

Jeremiah's secretary (Jer 32:12-16; 36; 43:1-6;
45:1-2). Deuterocanonical book ascribed to him
(Bar 1:1, 3, 8).

BARZILLAI

1. Gileadite who aided David during Absalom's
revolt (2Sa 17:27; 19:31-39).
2. Son-in-law of 1. (Ezr 2:61; Ne 7:63).

BASE → BASED, BASES, BASIS

Ex 25:31 The **b** and the shaft of the lampstand
     29:12 pour out at the **b** of the altar.
2Ki 18:19 On what do you **b** this confidence
Ps 101: 3 before my eyes anything that is **b.**

BASED* → BASE

Ro   9:31 righteousness that is **b** on the law,
     9:32 but as if it were **b** on works.
Php 3: 9 righteousness from God **b** on faith.

BASES → BASE

Ex 26:19 and you shall make forty **b** of silver

BASHAN

Nu 21:33 King Og of **B** came out against
Jos 13:30 all **B,** the whole kingdom of King
     22: 7 Moses had given a possession in **B;**
Ps 22:12 strong bulls of **B** surround me;
Am   4: 1 you cows of **B** who are on Mount
Mic 7:14 let them feed in **B** and Gilead as in
Zec 11: 2 Wail, oaks of **B,** for the thick forest

BASIC

Heb 5:12 to teach you again the **b** elements
     6: 1 behind the **b** teaching about Christ,

BASIN → BASINS

Ex 30:18 You shall make a bronze **b** with a
1Ki 7:30 four corners were supports for a **b.**
Jn 13: 5 **b** and began to wash the disciples'

BASINS → BASIN

1Ki 7:38 He made ten **b** of bronze;
2Ch 4: 8 he made one hundred **b** of gold.

Ezr 1: 9 And this was the inventory: gold **b,**
              thirty; silver **b,** one thousand;

BASIS → BASE

Lk 23: 4 "I find no **b** for an accusation
Phm 1: 9 rather appeal to you on the **b** of love

BASKET → BASKETS

Ex   2: 3 she got a papyrus **b** for him,
Dt 28: 5 Blessed shall be your **b**
     28:17 Cursed shall be your **b**
Jer 24: 2 One **b** had very good figs, like
Am   8: 1 showed me—a **b** of summer fruit.
Zec 5: 6 He said, "This is a **b** coming out."
Mt   5:15 a lamp puts it under the bushel **b,**
Ac   9:25 in the wall, lowering him in a **b.**
2Co 11:33 let down in a **b** through a window in

BASKETS → BASKET

Mt 13:48 put the good into **b** but threw out
Mk   6:43 twelve **b** full of broken pieces and
      8: 8 broken pieces left over, seven **b?**
      8:19 many **b** full of broken pieces did

BATCH

Ro 11:16 then the whole **b** is holy;
1Co 5: 6 a little yeast leavens the whole **b** of
      5: 7 yeast so that you may be a new **b,**
Gal 5: 9 A little yeast leavens the whole **b** of

BATH

Eze 45:10 an honest ephah, and an honest **b.**

BATHE → BATHED, BATHING

Ex   2: 5 came down to **b** at the river,
Ps 58:10 they will **b** their feet in the blood of
Lk   7:38 began to **b** his feet with her tears
Sus 1:15 and wished to **b** in the garden,

BATHED → BATHE

SS   5: 3 I had **b** my feet; how could I soil
Eze 16: 9 Then I **b** you with water and
Jn 13:10 "One who has **b** does not need to

BATHING* → BATHE

2Sa 11: 2 he saw from the roof a woman **b;**
Jdt 12: 8 After **b,** she prayed the Lord God

BATHSHEBA*

Wife of Uriah who committed adultery with and
became wife of David (2Sa 11; Ps 51), mother of
Solomon (2Sa 12:24; 1Ki 1-2; 1Ch 3:5).

BATTLE → BATTLES

Ex 13:18 of the land of Egypt prepared for **b.**
Jos 4:13 to the plains of Jericho for **b.**
1Sa 17:47 the **b** is the LORD's and he will give
     31: 3 The **b** pressed hard upon Saul;
2Sa 1:25 How the mighty have fallen in the
              midst of the **b!**
     11: 1 the time when kings go out to **b,**
1Ki 22:30 I will disguise myself and go into **b,**
2Ch 20:15 for the **b** is not yours but God's.
Ps 24: 8 and mighty, the LORD, mighty in **b.**
     55:18 redeem me unharmed from the **b**
Ecc 9:11 nor the **b** to the strong, nor bread to
Eze 13: 5 stand in **b** on the day of the LORD.
1Co 14: 8 who will get ready for **b?**
Rev 16:14 them for **b** on the great day of God
     20: 8 Gog and Magog, in order to gather
              them for **b;**
1Mc 3:19 the army that victory in **b** depends,

BATTLES → BATTLE

1Sa 8:20 go out before us and fight our **b."**
     18:17 and fight the LORD's **b."**
     25:28 lord is fighting the **b** of the LORD;
2Ch 32: 8 to help us and to fight our **b."**

BEAM → BEAMS

Ezr 6:11 a **b** shall be pulled out of the house

BEAMS → BEAM

1Ki 6: 9 he roofed the house with **b** and
Ne   3: 3 they laid its **b** and set up its doors,

BEAR → ARMOR-BEARER, BEARING,
BEARS, BIRTH, BIRTHDAY, BIRTHRIGHT,
BORE, BORN, BORNE, CHILDBEARING,
CHILDBIRTH, CUPBEARER, FIRSTBORN,
NEWBORN, REBIRTH, STILLBORN

Ge   4:13 punishment is greater than I can **b!**
     17:19 your wife Sarah shall **b** you a son,
Ex 23: 2 when you **b** witness in a lawsuit,
     28:12 shall **b** their names before the LORD
Jdg 13: 3 you shall conceive and **b** a son.
Job 9: 9 who made the **B** and Orion,
Isa 7:14 is with child and shall **b** a son,
     11: 7 The cow and the **b** shall graze,
     53:11 and he shall **b** their iniquities.
Jer 30: 6 can a man **b** a child?
Eze 14:10 And they shall **b** their punishment—
     47:12 they will **b** fresh fruit every month,
Da   7: 5 a second one, that looked like a **b.**
Am   5:19 and was met by a **b;**
Mt   1:23 virgin shall conceive and **b** a son,
      3: 8 **B** fruit worthy of repentance.
      7:18 A good tree cannot **b** bad fruit,
Lk   1:13 wife Elizabeth will **b** you a son,
     11:46 load people with burdens hard to **b,**
Jn 15: 2 he prunes to make it **b** more fruit.
     15: 8 that you **b** much fruit and become
     15:16 I appointed you to go and **b** fruit,
Ac 15:10 nor we have been able to **b?**
Ro   7: 4 that we may **b** fruit for God.
1Co 15:49 **b** the image of the man of heaven.
Gal 6: 2 One another's burdens,
Col 1:10 as you **b** fruit in every good work
      3:13 **B** with one another and,
Heb 9:28 offered once to **b** the sins of many,
1Pe 4:16 glorify God because you **b** this
              name.
Rev 12: 4 woman who was about to **b** a child,

BEARD

2Sa 10: 4 shaved off half the **b** of each,
Ezr 9: 3 and pulled hair from my head and **b,**
Isa 50: 6 to those who pulled out the **b;**
Jer 48:37 head is shaved and every **b** cut off;

BEARING → BEAR

Ge   1:12 trees of every kind **b** fruit with the
Ro   8:16 very Spirit **b** witness with our spirit
Eph 4: 2 patience, **b** with one another in love,
Col 1: 6 as it is **b** fruit and growing in the

BEARS → BEAR

Ge 49:21 a doe let loose that **b** lovely fawns.
1Sa 17:36 servant has killed both lions and **b;**
Ps 68:19 Blessed be the Lord, who daily **b** us
Da   9:18 and the city that **b** your name.
Jn 12:24 but if it dies, it **b** much fruit.
1Co 13: 7 It **b** all things, believes all things,

BEAST → BEASTS

Isa 35: 9 nor shall any ravenous **b** come up
Da   7: 6 The **b** had four wings of a bird on
Rev 11: 7 **b** that comes up from the
              bottomless pit
     13: 1 a **b** rising out of the sea having ten
     13: 2 the **b** that I saw was like a leopard,
     13:11 another **b** that rose out of the earth;
     13:18 calculate the number of the **b,**
     16: 2 who had the mark of the **b**
     17: 3 a woman sitting on a scarlet **b**
     19:20 who had received the mark of the **b**
     20: 4 not worshiped the **b** or its image

BEASTS → BEAST

Da   7: 3 four great **b** came up out of the sea,
Mk   1:13 and he was with the wild **b;**

BEAT → BEATEN, BEATING, BEATINGS

Dt 24:20 you **b** your olive trees, do not strip
Ne 13:25 cursed them and **b** some of them
Pr 23:35 they **b** me, but I did not feel it.
SS   5: 7 they **b** me, they wounded me,
Isa 2: 4 shall **b** their swords into plowshares,

Joel	3:10 **B** your plowshares into swords,
Mic	4: 3 shall **b** their swords into plowshares,
Mt	7:25 the winds blew and **b** on that house,
Mk	14:65 also took him over and **b** him.
Lk	10:30 **b** him, and went away, leaving him
	22:63 began to mock him and **b** him;
Ac	22:19 and **b** those who believed in you.

BEATEN → BEAT

Ex	5:16 Look how your servants are **b**!
Ac	16:22 ordered them to be **b** with rods.
1Co	4:11 we are poorly clothed and **b** and
2Co	11:25 Three times I was **b** with rods.
1Pe	2:20 If you endure when you are **b** for

BEATING → BEAT

Ex	2:11 He saw an Egyptian **b** a Hebrew,
1Co	9:26 nor do I box as though **b** the air;

BEATINGS → BEAT

2Co	6: 5 **b**, imprisonments, riots, labors,

BEAUTIFUL* → BEAUTY

Ge	12:11 you are a woman **b** in appearance;
	12:14 saw that the woman was very **b**.
	29:17 and Rachel was graceful and **b**.
Dt	21:11 among the captives a **b** woman
Jos	7:21 I saw among the spoil a **b** mantle
1Sa	16:12 Now he was ruddy, and had **b** eyes,
	25: 3 The woman was clever and **b**,
2Sa	11: 2 bathing; the woman was very **b**.
	13: 1 a **b** sister whose name was Tamar;
	14:27 Tamar; she was a **b** woman.
1Ki	1: 3 for a **b** girl throughout all the
	1: 4 The girl was very **b**.
Est	2: 2 "Let **b** young virgins be sought out
	2: 3 to gather all the **b** young virgins
	2: 7 the girl was fair and **b**,
Job	42:15 no women so **b** as Job's daughters;
Ps	48: 2 **b** in elevation, is the joy of all
Pr	4: 9 she will bestow on you a **b** crown."
	11:22 a pig's snout is a **b** woman without
SS	1: 5 I am black and **b**, O daughters of
	1:15 you are **b**, my love; ah, you are **b**;
	1:16 you are **b**, my beloved, truly lovely.
	4: 1 How **b** you are, my love, how very
	b!
	4: 7 You are altogether **b**, my love;
	6: 4 You are **b** as Tirzah, my love,
Isa	2:16 and against all the **b** craft.
	4: 2 the branch of the LORD shall be **b**
	5: 9 **b** houses, without inhabitant.
	52: 1 your **b** garments, O Jerusalem,
	52: 7 How **b** upon the mountains are the
	64:11 Our holy and **b** house,
Jer	3:19 most **b** heritage of all the nations.
	13:18 for your **b** crown has come down
	13:20 that was given you, your **b** flock?
	46:20 A **b** heifer is Egypt—a gadfly from
Eze	7:20 their **b** ornament, in which they
	16:12 and a **b** crown upon your head.
	16:13 exceedingly **b**, fit to be a queen.
	16:17 You also took your **b** jewels of my
	16:39 and take your **b** objects and leave
	23:42 and **b** crowns upon their heads.
	31: 7 It was **b** in its greatness, in the
	31: 9 made it **b** with its mass of branches,
	33:32 a **b** voice and plays well on an
Da	4:12 Its foliage was **b**, its fruit abundant,
	4:21 foliage was **b** and its fruit abundant,
	8: 9 the east, and toward the **b** land.
	11:16 shall take a position in the **b** land,
	11:41 He shall come into the **b** land,
	11:45 the sea and the **b** holy mountain.
Am	8:13 In that day the **b** young women and
Mt	23:27 which on the outside look **b**,
Lk	21: 5 **b** stones and gifts dedicated to God,
Ac	3: 2 the temple called the **B** Gate so that
	3:10 for alms at the **B** Gate of the temple;
	7:20 and he was **b** before God.
Ro	10:15 **b** are the feet of those who bring
Heb	11:23 they saw that the child was **b**;
Tob	6:12 girl is sensible, brave, and very **b**,

Jdt	8: 7 She was **b** in appearance,
	10: 4 Thus she made herself very **b**,
	10:14 she was in their eyes marvelously **b**
	11:21 looks so **b** or speaks so wisely!"
	11:23 You are not only **b** in appearance,
AdE	1:11 for she was indeed a **b** woman.
	2: 2 "Let **b** and virtuous girls be sought
	2: 3 they shall select **b** young virgins to
	2: 7 The girl was **b** in appearance.
Wis	5:16 a glorious crown and a **b** diadem
	7:29 She is more **b** than the sun,
	13: 7 the things that are seen are **b**.
	14:19 the likeness to take more **b** form,
	15:19 they are not so **b** in appearance
Sir	25: 1 and they are **b** in the sight of God
	26:17 so is a **b** face on a stately figure.
	43:11 it is exceedingly **b** in its brightness.
	45:13 such **b** things did not exist.
Sus	1: 2 very **b** woman and one who feared
	1:31 refinement and **b** in appearance.
2Mc	3:26 gloriously **b** and splendidly dressed,
	10: 7 ivy-wreathed wands and **b** branches
1Es	4:18 gold and silver or any other **b** thing,
	4:19 gold or silver or any other **b** thing.
3Mc	3:17 magnificent and most **b** offerings,
2Es	6: 3 before the **b** flowers were seen,
4Mc	16:10 I who had so many and **b** children

BEAUTY* → BEAUTIFUL

2Sa	14:25 so much for his **b** as Absalom;
Est	1:11 the peoples and the officials her **b**;
Ps	27: 4 to behold the **b** of the LORD,
	45:11 and the king will desire your **b**.
	50: 2 Out of Zion, the perfection of **b**,
	96: 6 strength and **b** are in his sanctuary.
Pr	6:25 Do not desire her **b** in your heart,
	20:29 the **b** of the aged is their gray hair.
	31:30 Charm is deceitful, and **b** is vain,
Isa	3:24 of sackcloth; instead of **b**,
	28: 1 the fading flower of its glorious **b**,
	28: 4 the fading flower of its glorious **b**,
	28: 5 a diadem of **b**, to the remnant of his
	33:17 Your eyes will see the king in his **b**;
	44:13 in human form, with human **b**,
	62: 3 crown of **b** in the hand of the LORD,
La	2:15 that was called the perfection of **b**,
Eze	16:14 the nations on account of your **b**,
	16:15 But you trusted in your **b**,
	16:25 and prostituted your **b**,
	27: 3 you have said, "I am perfect in **b**."
	27: 4 your builders made perfect your **b**.
	27:11 they made perfect your **b**.
	28: 7 swords against the **b** of your
	28:12 full of wisdom and perfect in **b**.
	28:17 heart was proud because of your **b**;
	31: 8 the garden of God was like it in **b**.
	32:19 "Whom do you surpass in **b**?
Hos	14: 6 his **b** shall be like the olive tree,
Zec	9:17 For what goodness and **b** are his!
Jas	1:11 its flower falls, and its **b** perishes.
1Pe	3: 4 with the lasting **b** of a gentle
Jdt	10: 7 were very greatly astounded at her **b**
	10:19 They marveled at her **b** and admired
	10:23 all marveled at the **b** of her face.
	16: 6 the **b** of her countenance undid him.
	16: 9 her **b** captivated his mind,
AdE	1:11 and to have her display her **b** to all
	15: 5 She was radiant with perfect **b**,
Wis	7:10 I loved her more than health and **b**,
	8: 2 and became enamored of her **b**.
	13: 3 If through delight in the **b** of these
	13: 3 for the author of **b** created them.
	13: 5 from the greatness and **b** of created
Sir	9: 8 not gaze at **b** belonging to another;
	9: 8 have been seduced by a woman's **b**,
	25:21 Do not be ensnared by a woman's **b**,
	26:16 the **b** of a good wife in her
	36:27 woman's **b** lights up a man's face,
	40:22 The eye desires grace and **b**,
	42:12 Do not let her parade her **b** before
	43: 9 glory of the stars is the **b** of heaven,
	43:18 The eye is dazzled by the **b** of its

	47:10 He gave **b** to the festivals,
Bar	5: 1 the **b** of the glory from God.
LtJ	6:24 As for the gold that they wear for **b**
Sus	1:32 they might feast their eyes on her **b**.
	1:56 **b** has beguiled you and lust has
1Mc	1:26 the **b** of the women faded.
	2:12 And see, our holy place, our **b**,
1Es	4:18 woman lovely in appearance and **b**,
3Mc	1: 9 impressed by its excellence and its **b**
2Es	10:50 and the loveliness of her **b**.
4Mc	2: 1 for the enjoyment of **b** are rendered
	8: 5 and greatly respect the **b** and the

BECAME → BECOME

Ge	2: 7 and the man **b** a living being.
Ex	7:10 and his officials, and it **b** a snake.
	15:25 the water, and the water **b** sweet.
Lev	18:25 Thus the land **b** defiled;
Dt	26: 5 and there he **b** a great nation,
Jdg	8:27 and it **b** a snare to Gideon and to
2Ki	17:15 went after false idols and **b** false;
1Ch	11: 9 And David **b** greater and greater,
Da	2:35 the stone that struck the statue **b** a
	great mountain
Hos	9:10 and **b** detestable like the thing they
	loved.
Mt	17: 2 and his clothes **b** dazzling white.
Lk	6:16 and Judas Iscariot, who **b** a traitor.
Jn	1:14 And the Word **b** flesh and lived
	among us,
1Co	9:20 To the Jews I **b** as a Jew, in order to
2Co	8: 9 yet for your sakes he **b** poor,
Php	2: 8 and **b** obedient to the point of death
Heb	5: 9 he **b** the source of eternal salvation

BECOME → BECAME

Ge	2:24 to his wife, and they **b** one flesh.
	9:15 waters shall never again **b** a flood
Ex	15: 2 and he has **b** my salvation;
Jdg	16: 7 I shall **b** weak, and be like anyone
Ps	118:22 rejected has **b** the chief cornerstone.
	135:18 all who trust them shall **b** like them.
Isa	1:21 How the faithful city has **b** a whore!
Mt	19: 5 and the two shall **b** one flesh'?
Mk	12:10 rejected has **b** the cornerstone,
Lk	4: 3 this stone to **b** a loaf of bread."
Jn	1:12 he gave power to **b** children of God,
Ac	4:11 builders; it has **b** the cornerstone.'
1Co	9:22 I have **b** all things to all people,
Eph	5:31 and the two will **b** one flesh."
Heb	2:17 he had to **b** like his brothers and
	6:20 having **b** a high priest forever
	7:22 Jesus has also **b** the guarantee of a
1Pe	2: 7 has **b** the very head of the corner,"
Rev	11:15 has **b** the kingdom of our Lord and

BED → BEDS, SICKBED

Ge	47:31 bowed himself on the head of his **b**.
	48: 2 his strength and sat up in **b**.
1Ki	1:47 bowed in worship on the **b**
Ps	63: 6 when I think of you on my **b**,
	139: 8 if I make my **b** in Sheol, you are
Pr	26:14 so does a lazy person in **b**.
SS	3: 1 Upon my **b** at night I sought him
Isa	28:20 the **b** is too short to stretch oneself
Da	7: 1 visions of his head as he lay in **b**.
Mt	8:14 he saw his mother-in-law lying in **b**
	with a fever;
Lk	5:19 let him down with his **b** through the
	11: 7 and my children are with me in **b**;
	17:34 that night there will be two in one **b**;
Ac	9:34 get up and make your **b**!"
	28: 8 of Publius lay sick in **b** with fever
Heb	13: 4 let the marriage be kept undefiled;
Rev	2:22 Beware, I am throwing her on a **b**,
Jdt	13: 4 Then Judith, standing beside his **b**,
2Es	3: 1 I was troubled as I lay on my **b**,

BEDS → BED

Ps	4: 4 ponder it on your **b**, and be silent.
	36: 4 They plot mischief while on their **b**;
Mic	2: 1 and evil deeds on their **b**!

BEE* → BEES
Isa 7:18 the **b** that is in the land of Assyria.
Sir 11: 3 The **b** is small among flying

BEER-LAHAI-ROI
Ge 16:14 Therefore the well was called **B**;

BEER-SHEBA
Ge 21:31 Therefore that place was called **B**;
26:33 the name of the city is **B** to this day.
1Sa 3:20 And all Israel from Dan to **B** knew
2Sa 24:15 of the people died, from Dan to **B.**
1Ki 4:25 lived in safety, from Dan even to **B,**

BEES* → BEE
Dt 1:44 against you and chased you as **b** do.
Jdg 14: 8 a swarm of **b** in the body of the lion,
Ps 118:12 They surrounded me like **b**;
4Mc 14:19 since even **b** at the time

BEFALL → BEFALLEN, BEFALLS
Dt 31:29 In time to come trouble will **b** you,
Ps 91:10 no evil shall **b** you, no scourge
Am 3: 6 Does disaster **b** a city, unless the

BEFALLEN → BEFALL
Isa 51:19 These two things have **b** you
Jer 44:23 that this disaster has **b** you,

BEFALLS → BEFALL
Job 3:25 and what I dread **b** me.
Ecc 2:14 I perceived that the same fate **b** all
Sir 2: 4 Accept whatever **b** you,

BEFITS
Ps 33: 1 Praise **b** the upright.
93: 5 holiness **b** your house, O LORD,

BEFORE → BEFOREHAND
Ge 10: 9 He was a mighty hunter **b** the LORD;
17: 1 walk **b** me, and be blameless.
18:22 remained standing **b** the LORD.
24:15 **B** he had finished speaking, there
27: 4 so that I may bless you **b** I die."
45: 5 God sent me **b** you to preserve life.
Ex 4:21 perform **b** Pharaoh all the wonders
9:11 magicians could not stand **b** Moses
20: 3 you shall have no other gods **b** me.
23:15 shall appear **b** me empty-handed.
32: 1 gods for us, who shall go **b** us;
33: 2 I will send an angel **b** you,
Lev 10: 2 and they died **b** the LORD.
Nu 17: 7 Moses placed the staffs **b** the LORD
Dt 1:30 LORD your God, who goes **b** you,
7:22 God will clear away these nations **b**
11:26 I am setting **b** you today a blessing
30:15 See, I have set **b** you today life and
1Sa 4: 7 nothing like this has happened **b.**
Job 4:17 'Can mortals be righteous **b** God?
26: 6 Sheol is naked **b** God,
Ps 16: 8 I keep the LORD always **b** me;
37: 7 Be still **b** the LORD, and wait
97: 5 mountains melt like wax **b** the LORD
97: 7 all gods bow down **b** him.
139: 4 Even **b** a word is on my tongue,
Pr 8:23 **b** the beginning of the earth.
16:18 Pride goes **b** destruction,
18:12 but humility goes **b** honor.
18:13 gives answer **b** hearing, it is folly
Isa 43:10 **B** me no god was formed,
48: 5 **b** they came to pass I announced
49: 1 The LORD called me **b** I was born,
49:16 your walls are continually **b** me.
53: 7 like a sheep that **b** its shearers is
65:24 **B** they call I will answer,
Jer 1: 5 "**B** I formed you in the womb I
Zep 1: 7 Be silent **b** the Lord GOD!
Zec 2:13 Be silent, all people, **b** the LORD;
Mal 3: 1 my messenger to prepare the way **b**
4: 5 the prophet Elijah **b** the great and
Mt 5:16 let your light shine **b** others,
6: 8 Father knows what you need **b** you
7: 6 do not throw your pearls **b** swine,
11:10 who will prepare your way **b** you.'

24:38 For as in those days **b** the flood
Lk 12: 8 who acknowledges me **b** others,
22:61 "**B** the cock crows today,
Jn 1:15 ahead of me because he was **b** me.'
8:58 I tell you, **b** Abraham was, I am."
10: 8 All who came **b** me are thieves and
13:19 I tell you this now, **b** it occurs,
17: 5 your presence **b** the world existed.
Ac 2:25 'I saw the Lord always **b** me,
8:32 and like a lamb silent **b** its shearer,
Ro 4:10 not after, but **b** he was circumcised.
14:10 stand **b** the judgment seat of God.
Gal 1:15 who had set me apart **b** I was born
Col 1:17 He himself is **b** all things,
Tit 1: 2 who never lies, promised **b** the ages
Heb 12: 2 sake of the joy that was set **b** him
1Pe 1:20 He was destined **b** the foundation
Rev 7: 9 standing **b** the throne and **b** the Lamb,
Sir 1: 4 Wisdom was created **b** all other
18:19 **B** you speak, learn;

BEFOREHAND → BEFORE
Mk 13:11 worry **b** about what you are to say;
Ro 1: 2 he promised **b** through his prophets
9:23 which he has prepared **b** for glory—
Gal 3: 8 declared the gospel **b** to Abraham,

BEG → BEGGAR, BEGGED, BEGGING, BEGS
La 4: 4 the children **b** for food, but no one
Lk 16: 3 and I am ashamed to **b.**
Jn 9: 8 the man who used to sit and **b?**"

BEGAN → BEGIN
Ge 4:26 time people **b** to invoke the name of
Lk 3:23 thirty years old when he **b** his work.
14:30 fellow **b** to build and was not able

BEGGAR* → BEG
Mk 10:46 son of Timaeus, a blind **b,**
Jn 9: 8 who had seen him before as a **b**
Sir 18:33 a **b** by feasting with borrowed
40:28 My child, do not lead the life of a **b**;

BEGGED → BEG
Mt 8:31 demons **b** him, "If you cast us out,
Mk 6:56 **b** him that they might touch even

BEGGING → BEG
Ps 37:25 forsaken or their children **b** bread.
Mk 1:40 A leper came to him **b** him,

BEGIN → BEGAN, BEGINNING, BEGUN
1Pe 4:17 for judgment to **b** with the household of God;

BEGINNING → BEGIN
Ge 1: 1 In the **b** when God created the
Ps 111:10 fear of the LORD is the **b** of wisdom;
Pr 1: 7 The fear of the LORD is the **b** of knowledge;
4: 7 The **b** of wisdom is this:
8:22 The LORD created me at the **b** of his
9:10 fear of the LORD is the **b** of wisdom,
Ecc 3:11 what God has done from the **b** to
7: 8 Better is the end of a thing than its **b**
Isa 40:21 Has it not been told you from the **b?**
46:10 the **b** and from ancient times things
Mt 19: 8 but from the **b** it was not so.
24: 8 this is but the **b** of the birth pangs.
24:21 not been from the **b** of the world
Mk 1: 1 The **b** of the good news of Jesus
Lk 1: 2 who from the **b** were eyewitnesses
Jn 1: 1 In the **b** was the Word,
8:44 He was a murderer from the **b** and
15:27 you have been with me from the **b.**
Ac 1: 1 that Jesus did and taught from the **b**
1:22 **b** from the baptism of John until the
Col 1:18 is the **b**, the firstborn from the dead,
Heb 7: 3 neither **b** of days nor end of life,
1Jn 1: 1 declare to you what was from the **b,**
3: 8 devil has been sinning from the **b.**

2Jn 1: 6 as you have heard it from the **b—**
Rev 21: 6 and the Omega, the **b** and the end.
22:13 first and the last, the **b** and the end."
Wis 6:17 The **b** of wisdom is the most sincere
Sir 1:14 To fear the Lord is the **b** of wisdom;

BEGOTTEN
Ps 2: 7 You are my son; today I have **b** you.
Ac 13:33 are my Son; today I have **b** you.'
Heb 1: 5 are my Son; today I have **b** you"?
5: 5 are my Son, today I have **b** you";
2Es 6:58 have called your firstborn, only **b,**

BEGS* → BEG
Mt 5:42 Give to everyone who **b** from you,
Lk 6:30 Give to everyone who **b** from you;

BEGUILE → BEGUILED, BEGUILING
Jdt 16: 8 put on a linen gown to **b** him.

BEGUILED* → BEGUILE
Sus 1:56 beauty has **b** you

BEGUILING* → BEGUILE
Rev 2:20 teaching and **b** my servants

BEGUN → BEGIN
Nu 16:46 the plague has **b."**
Dt 3:24 have only **b** to show your servant your greatness
Rev 11:17 your great power and **b** to reign.

BEHALF
Lev 1: 3 in your **b** before the LORD.
4:26 priest shall make atonement on his **b**
5: 6 shall make atonement on your **b**
1Ki 2:18 I will speak to the king on your **b."**
Job 36: 2 yet something to say on God's **b.**
Ps 109:21 act on my **b** for your name's sake;
Jer 7:16 not raise a cry or prayer on their **b,**
Da 9:20 on **b** of the holy mountain of my God—
Jn 5:32 another who testifies on my **b,**
8:14 "Even if I testify on my own **b,**
16:26 that I will ask the Father on your **b**;
17: 9 I am asking on their **b**;
Heb 6:20 a forerunner on our **b**, has entered,
Rev 13:12 authority of the first beast on its **b,**

BEHAVE → BEHAVED, BEHAVING, BEHAVIOR
1Th 4:12 may **b** properly toward outsiders
1Ti 3:15 ought to **b** in the household of God,

BEHAVED → BEHAVE
Jer 16:12 have **b** worse than your ancestors,

BEHAVING → BEHAVE
1Co 7:36 is not **b** properly toward his fiancee,

BEHAVIOR → BEHAVE
Eze 16:27 who were ashamed of your lewd **b.**
Tit 2: 3 the older women to be reverent in **b,**

BEHEADED → HEAD
Lk 9: 9 Herod said, "John I **b**;
Rev 20: 4 the souls of those who had been **b**
Pm 151: 7 But I drew his own sword; I **b** him,

BEHELD → BEHOLD
Ex 24:11 they **b** God, and they ate and drank.
Nu 23:21 He has not **b** misfortune in Jacob;
Ps 139:16 eyes **b** my unformed substance.

BEHEMOTH*
Job 40:15 "Look at **B,** which I made just as I
2Es 6:49 the one you called **B** and the name
6:51 And you gave **B** one of the parts

BEHIND
Ps 50:17 and you cast my words **b** you.
139: 5 You hem me in, **b** and before,
Isa 38:17 have cast all my sins **b** your back.
Eze 3:12 I heard **b** me the sound of loud
Mt 16:23 said to Peter, "Get **b** me, Satan!

Lk 2:43 the boy Jesus stayed **b** in Jerusalem,
8:44 She came up **b** him and touched the
Php 3:13 forgetting what lies **b** and straining
Heb 6: 1 **b** the basic teaching about Christ,
Rev 1:10 I heard **b** me a loud voice like a
4: 6 full of eyes in front and **b:**

BEHOLD → BEHELD

Nu 23: 9 from the hills I **b** him;
24:17 I **b** him, but not near—
Job 19:27 my eyes shall **b,** and not another.
Ps 11: 7 the upright shall **b** his face.
17:15 I shall **b** your face in righteousness,
27: 4 to **b** the beauty of the LORD,
Hab 1:13 Your eyes are too pure to **b** evil,

BEING → BEINGS

Ge 2: 7 and the man became a living **b.**
Nu 23:19 God is not a human **b,**
1Sa 28:13 "I see a divine **b** coming up
Ps 51: 6 You desire truth in the inward **b;**
SS 5: 4 and my inmost **b** yearned for him.
Isa 61:10 my whole **b** shall exult in my God;
Eze 1:10 the four had the face of a human **b,**
8: 2 a figure that looked like a human **b;**
Da 7:13 one like a human **b** coming with the
Jn 1: 3 All things came into **b** through him,
1Co 15:45 Adam, became a living **b";**
Eph 3:16 strengthened in your inner **b** with
Heb 1: 3 the exact imprint of God's very **b,**

HUMAN BEING Ex 19:13; Lev 22:5; 24:17,
21; 27:2; Nu 19:11, 13; 23:19; Job 12:10; 25:6;
Isa 51:12; 66:3; Eze 1:10; 8:2; 10:14; 29:8; Da
7:4, 13; Jnh 3:7; Mt 12:12; Jn 10:33; 16:21; Ro
1:23; 3:20; 9:20; 1Co 2:11; 15:21, 21; Gal
1:16; Jas 5:17; Jdt 8:16; Wis 13:13; 14:15, 20;
15:16; 2Es 8:6; 16:27

LIVING BEING Ge 2:7; Dt 11:6; Da 2:30;
1Co 15:45; Tob 13:4; Jdt 11:7; Sir 49:16

BEINGS → BEING

Ge 6: 7 blot out from the earth the human **b**
Nu 18:15 of human **b** you shall redeem,
Job 4:17 **b** be pure before their Maker?
38: 7 all the heavenly **b** shouted for joy?
Ps 8: 4 what are human **b** that you are
89: 6 the heavenly **b** is like the LORD,
Mt 9: 8 given such authority to human **b.**
Lk 16:15 by human **b** is an abomination
Jn 5:41 I do not accept glory from human **b.**

HUMAN BEINGS Ge 6:7; 7:21, 23; 9:5; Ex
12:12; 13:2; Lev 27:29; Nu 18:15; Dt 4:32;
20:19; 2Sa 7:14; 2Ch 19:6; Job 4:17; 5:7; 7:1,
17; 35:8; Ps 8:4; 115:16; 135:8; 144:3; Ecc
1:13; 3:18; 6:10; 7:29; Jer 5:26; 7:20; 10:23;
21:6; 32:43; 33:10, 12; Eze 14:13, 17; 27:13; 36:11; 38:20; Da 2:38; 4:17;
Jnh 3:8; Hag 1:11; Mt 9:8; Lk 16:15; Jn 5:41;
1Co 15:39; 2Co 10:3; Heb 2:6; 6:16; Jdt 11:7;
AdE 16:24; Wis 7:20; 9:6; Sir 1:15; 10:18;
17:1; 17:30, 32; 18:7, 8, 13; 31:27; 33:10;
38:6; LtJ 6:11; 1Es 4:37; 3Mc 2:15; 2Es 13:41;
16:61; 4Mc 2:21; 14:14

BEL*

Babylonian deity (Isa 46:1; Jer 50:2; 51:44; LtJ
6:40; Bel 1:3-28).

BELIAR*

2Co 6:15 agreement does Christ have with **B?**

BELIEF* → BELIEVE

2Th 2:13 the Spirit and through **b** in the truth.
2Mc 15:11 of vision, which was worthy of **b.**

BELIEVE* → BELIEF, BELIEVED,
BELIEVER, BELIEVER'S, BELIEVERS,
BELIEVES, BELIEVING

Ge 45:26 stunned; he could not **b** them.
Ex 4: 1 "But suppose they do not **b** me or
4: 5 that they may **b** that the LORD,
4: 8 "If they will not **b** you or heed the

4: 8 they may **b** the second sign.
4: 9 they will not **b** even these two signs
Nu 14:11 long will they refuse to **b** in me,
1Ki 10: 7 but I did not **b** the reports until I
2Ki 17:14 did not **b** in the LORD their God.
2Ch 9: 6 but I did not **b** the reports until I
20:20 **B** in the LORD your God and you
32:15 in this fashion, and do not **b** him,
Job 9:16 I do not **b** that he would listen to
Ps 27:13 I **b** that I shall see the goodness of
78:32 they did not **b** in his wonders.
119:66 for I **b** in your commandments.
Pr 14:15 The simple **b** everything,
26:25 enemy speaks graciously, do not **b**
Isa 43:10 so that you may know and **b** me
Jer 12: 6 do not **b** them, though they speak
40:14 son of Ahikam would not **b** them.
La 4:12 The kings of the earth did not **b,**
Hab 1: 5 you would not **b** if you were told.
Mt 9:28 you **b** that I am able to do this?"
18: 6 one of these little ones who **b** in me,
21:25 'Why then did you not **b** him?'
21:32 and you did not **b** him,
21:32 not change your minds and **b** him.
24:23 or 'There he is!'—do not **b** it.
24:26 in the inner rooms,' do not **b** it.
27:42 from the cross now, and we will **b**
Mk 1:15 repent, and **b** in the good news."
5:36 "Do not fear, only **b.**"
9:24 "I **b;** help my unbelief!"
9:42 one of these little ones who **b** in me,
11:23 but **b** that what you say will come
11:24 **b** that you have received it, and it
11:31 Why then did you not **b** him?'
13:21 There he is!'—do not **b** it.
15:32 so that we may see and **b.**"
16:11 seen by her, they would not **b** it.
16:13 but they did not **b** them.
16:16 who does not **b** will be condemned.
16:17 signs will accompany those who **b:**
Lk 1:20 because you did not **b** my words,
8:12 so that they may not **b** and be saved.
8:13 they **b** only for a while and in a time
8:50 Only **b,** and she will be saved."
20: 5 Why did you not **b** him?'
22:67 "If I tell you, you will not **b;**
24:11 and they did not **b** them.
24:25 how slow of heart to **b** all that the
Jn 1: 7 so that all might **b** through him.
1:50 "Do you **b** because I told you that I
3:12 earthly things and you do not **b,**
3:12 you **b** if I tell you about heavenly
3:18 who **b** in him are not condemned;
3:18 do not **b** are condemned already,
4:21 Jesus said to her, "Woman, **b** me,
4:42 because of what you said that we **b,**
4:48 signs and wonders you will not **b.**"
5:38 you do not **b** whom he has sent.
5:44 How can you **b** when you accept
5:46 believed Moses, you would **b** me,
5:47 But if you do not **b** what he wrote,
5:47 how will you **b** what I say?"
6:29 you **b** in him whom he has sent."
6:30 so that we may see it and **b** you?
6:36 you have seen me and yet do not **b.**
6:40 and **b** in him may have eternal life;
6:64 there are some who do not **b.**"
6:64 who were the ones that did not **b,**
6:69 We have come to **b** and know that
8:24 will die in your sins unless you **b**
8:45 I tell the truth, you do not **b** me.
8:46 tell the truth, why do you not **b** me?
9:18 did not **b** that he had been blind
9:35 "Do you **b** in the Son of Man?"
9:36 Tell me, so that I may **b** in him."
9:38 He said, "Lord, I **b.**"
10:25 "I have told you, and you do not **b.**
10:26 do not **b,** because you do not belong
10:37 of my Father, then do not **b** me.
10:38 you do not **b** me, **b** the works,
11:15 not there, so that you may **b.**
11:25 who **b** in me, even though they die,

11:26 will never die. Do you **b** this?"
11:27 I **b** that you are the Messiah, the
11:42 that they may **b** that you sent me."
11:48 go on like this, everyone will **b**
12:36 you have the light, **b** in the light,
12:37 they did not **b** in him.
12:39 And so they could not **b,**
13:19 you may **b** that I am he.
14: 1 **B** in God, **b** also in me.
14:10 not **b** that I am in the Father
14:11 **B** me that I am in the Father and the
14:11 then **b** me because of the works
14:29 that when it does occur, you may **b.**
16: 9 because they do not **b** in me;
16:30 this we **b** that you came from God."
16:31 answered them, "Do you now **b?**
17:20 will **b** in me through their word,
17:21 world may **b** that you have sent me.
19:35 so that you also may **b.**
20:25 my hand in his side, I will not **b.**"
20:27 Do not doubt but **b.**"
20:29 not seen and yet have come to **b.**"
20:31 come to **b** that Jesus is the Messiah,
Ac 9:26 they did not **b** that he was a disciple.
13:41 a work that you will never **b.**
14:23 Lord in whom they had come to **b.**
15:11 we **b** that we will be saved through
16:31 answered, "**B** on the Lord Jesus,
19: 4 the people to **b** in the one who was
19: 9 When some stubbornly refused to **b**
26:27 Agrippa, do you **b** the prophets?
26:27 I know that you **b.**"
28:24 while others refused to **b.**
Ro 3:22 faith in Jesus Christ for all who **b.**
4:11 all who **b** without being circumcised
4:24 who **b** in him who raised Jesus our
6: 8 we **b** that we will also live with him.
10: 9 **b** in your heart that God raised him
10:14 **b** in one of whom they have never
14: 2 Some **b** in eating anything,
1Co 1:21 proclamation, to save those who **b.**
3: 5 through whom you came to **b,**
11:18 and to some extent I **b** it.
15: 2 unless you have come to **b** in vain.
15:11 and so you have come to **b.**
2Co 4:13 we also **b,** and so we speak,
Gal 2:16 we have come to **b** in Christ Jesus,
3: 7 **b** are the descendants of Abraham.
3: 9 this reason, those who **b** are blessed
3:22 might be given to those who **b.**
Eph 1:19 of his power for us who **b,**
1Th 4:14 For since we **b** that Jesus died and
2Th 2:11 leading them to **b** what is false,
1Ti 1:16 those who would come to **b** in him
4: 3 with thanksgiving by those who **b**
4:10 especially of those who **b.**
Tit 3: 8 **b** in God may be careful to devote
Heb 11: 6 would approach him must **b**
Jas 2: 1 with your acts of favoritism really **b**
2:19 You **b** that God is one; you do well.
2:19 Even the demons **b**—and shudder.
1Pe 1: 8 you do not see him now, you **b**
2: 7 To you then who **b,** he is precious;
2: 7 but for those who do not **b,**
1Jn 3:23 that we should **b** in the name
4: 1 Beloved, do not **b** every spirit,
4:16 So we have known and **b** the love
5:10 those who **b** in the Son of God
5:10 not **b** in God have made him a liar
5:13 I write these things to you who **b** in
Jude 1: 5 destroyed those who did not **b.**
Tob 2:14 But I did not **b** her,
10: 7 do not **b** that they will see me again.
14: 4 for I **b** the word of God that Nahum
14: 4 For I know and **b** that whatever
Sir 19:15 so do not **b** everything you hear.
1Mc 10:46 they did not **b** or accept them,
1Es 4:28 And now do you not **b** me?
2Es 1:35 without having heard me will **b.**
1:37 they will **b** the things I have said.
6:33 '**B** and do not be afraid!'
7130 they did not **b** him or the prophets

4Mc 5:25 since we **b** that the law was
       7:19 since they **b** that they, like our

BELIEVED* → BELIEVE

Ge   15: 6 And he **b** the LORD;
Ex   4:31 The people **b;** and when they heard
       14:31 **b** in the LORD and in his servant
Ps 106:12 Then they **b** his words; they sang
Isa 53: 1 Who has **b** what we have heard?
Jnh   3: 5 And the people of Nineveh **b** God;
Mt   21:32 collectors and the prostitutes **b** him;
Mk   16:14 not **b** those who saw him after he
Lk   1:45 And blessed is she who **b** that there
Jn   1:12 received him, who **b** in his name,
       2:11 and his disciples **b** in him.
       2:22 they **b** the scripture and the word
       2:23 many **b** in his name because they
       3:18 not **b** in the name of the only Son
       4:39 Many Samaritans from that city **b**
       4:41 many more **b** because of his word.
       4:50 The man **b** the word that Jesus
       4:53 So he himself **b,** along with his
       5:46 If you **b** Moses, you would believe
       7: 5 (For not even his brothers **b** in him.)
       7:31 Yet many in the crowd **b** in him
       7:48 or of the Pharisees **b** in him?
       8:30 saying these things, many **b** in him.
       8:31 Jesus said to the Jews who had **b** in
       10:42 And many **b** in him there.
       11:40 "Did I not tell you that if you **b,**
       11:45 had seen what Jesus did, **b** in him.
       12:38 "Lord, who has **b** our message,
       12:42 even of the authorities, **b** in him.
       16:27 you have loved me and have **b**
       17: 8 and they have **b** that you sent me.
       20: 8 also went in, and he saw and **b;**
       20:29 you **b** because you have seen me?
Ac   2:44 All who **b** were together and had all
       4: 4 of those who heard the word **b;**
       4:32 the whole group of those who **b**
       8:12 they **b** Philip, who was proclaiming
       8:13 Even Simon himself **b.**
       9:42 and many **b** in the Lord.
       11:17 gift that he gave us when we **b** in
       13:12 saw what had happened, he **b,**
       17:12 Many of them therefore **b,**
       22:19 and beat those who **b** in you.
Ro   4: 3 "Abraham **b** God, and it was
       4:17 presence of the God in whom he **b,**
       4:18 **b** that he would become "the father
       10:14 on one in whom they have not **b?**
       10:16 "Lord, who has **b** our message?"
2Co   4:13 "I **b,** and so I spoke"—
Gal   3: 6 Just as Abraham **"b** God,
       3: 9 are blessed with Abraham who **b.**
Eph   1:13 of your salvation, and had **b** in him,
2Th   1:10 on that day among all who have **b,**
       1:10 because our testimony to you was **b.**
       2:12 that all who have not **b** the truth but
1Ti   3:16 **b** in throughout the world, taken up
2Ti   3:14 what you have learned and firmly **b,**
Heb   4: 3 For we who have **b** enter that rest,
Jas   2:23 that says, "Abraham **b** God,
Jdt   14:10 had done, he **b** firmly in God.
Sus   1:41 **b** them and condemned her to death.
1Mc   1:30 words to them, and they **b** him;
       2:59 **b** and were saved from the flame.
3Mc   6:34 Those who had previously **b** that
2Es   3:32 so **b** the covenants as these tribes of
       5:29 on those who **b** your covenants.
       9: 7 the faith by which they have **b,**

BELIEVER* → BELIEVE

Ac   16: 1 of a Jewish woman who was a **b;**
       16:34 that he had become a **b** in God.
       18: 8 a **b** in the Lord, together with all his
1Co   6: 5 enough to decide between one **b**
       6: 6 but a **b** goes to court against a **b—**
       7:12 **b** has a wife who is an unbeliever,
2Co   6:15 Or what does a **b** share with an
Jas   1: 9 Let the **b** who is lowly boast in
1Jn   2:11 hates another **b** is in the darkness,

BELIEVER'S* → BELIEVE

Jn   7:38 'Out of the **b** heart shall flow rivers

BELIEVERS* → BELIEVE

Jn   7:39 which **b** in him were to receive;
Ac   1:15 the **b** (together the crowd numbered
       5:14 Yet more than ever **b** were added to
       9:30 When the **b** learned of it,
       9:32 went here and there among all the **b,**
       10:23 and some of the **b** from Joppa
       10:45 The circumcised **b** who had come
       11: 1 apostles and the **b** throughout
       11: 2 the circumcised **b** criticized him,
       11:21 a great number became **b** and
       11:29 send relief to the **b** living in Judea;
       12:17 "Tell this to James and to the **b.**"
       13:48 destined for eternal life became **b.**
       14: 1 of both Jews and Greeks became **b.**
       15: 3 and brought great joy to all the **b.**
       15: 5 some **b** who belonged to the sect of
       15: 7 of the good news and become **b.**
       15:23 to the **b** of Gentile origin in Antioch
       15:32 to encourage and strengthen the **b.**
       15:33 the **b** to those who had sent them.
       15:36 the **b** in every city where we
       15:40 the **b** commending him to the grace
       16: 2 He was well spoken of by the **b** in
       17: 6 some **b** before the city authorities,
       17:10 very night the **b** sent Paul and Silas
       17:14 the **b** immediately sent Paul away
       17:34 of them joined him and became **b,**
       18: 8 who heard Paul became **b**
       18:18 Paul said farewell to the **b** and
       18:27 the **b** encouraged him and wrote to
       18:27 through grace had become **b,**
       19: 2 Holy Spirit when you became **b?**"
       19:18 Also many of those who became **b**
       20: 2 given the **b** much encouragement,
       21: 7 we greeted the **b** and stayed with
       21:20 many thousands of **b** there are
       21:25 the Gentiles who have become **b,**
       28:14 There we found **b** and were invited
       28:15 The **b** from there, when they heard
Ro   13:11 to us now than when we became **b;**
1Co   8: 6 and defraud—and **b** at that.
       8:11 So by your knowledge those weak **b**
       14:22 a sign not for **b** but for unbelievers,
       14:22 is not for unbelievers but for **b.**
Gal   2: 4 because of false **b** secretly brought
1Th   1: 7 you became an example to all the **b**
       2:10 our conduct was toward you **b,**
       2:13 which is also at work in you **b.**
2Th   3: 6 keep away from **b** who are living in
       3:15 as enemies, but warn them as **b.**
1Ti   4:12 but set the **b** an example in speech
       6: 2 who benefit by their service are **b**
Tit   1: 6 only once, whose children are **b,**
1Pe   2:17 Love the family of **b.**

BELIEVES* → BELIEVE

Mk   9:23 can be done for the one who **b.**"
       16:16 The one who **b** and is baptized will
Jn   3:15 whoever **b** in him may have eternal
       3:16 who **b** in him may not perish
       3:36 Whoever **b** in the Son has eternal
       5:24 who **b** him who sent me has eternal life,
       6:35 **b** in me will never be thirsty.
       6:47 whoever **b** has eternal life.
       7:38 and let the one who **b** in me drink.
       11:26 everyone who lives and **b** in me
       12:44 "Whoever **b** in me **b** not in me but
                 in him who sent me.
       12:46 so that everyone who **b** in me
       14:12 who **b** in me will also do the works
Ac   10:43 who **b** in him receives forgiveness
       13:39 this Jesus everyone who **b** is set free
Ro   9:33 whoever **b** in him will not be put to
       10: 4 righteousness for everyone who **b.**
       10:10 **b** with the heart and so is justified,
       10:11 "No one who **b** in him will be put
1Co   13: 7 It bears all things, **b** all things,
1Pe   2: 6 whoever **b** in him will not be put to

1Jn   5: 1 Everyone who **b** that Jesus is
       5: 5 the one who **b** that Jesus is the Son
Sir   34: 2 so is anyone who **b** in dreams.

BELIEVING* → BELIEVE

Jn   12:11 the Jews were deserting and were **b**
       20:31 through **b** you may have life in his
Ac   24:14 **b** everything laid down according
Ro   15:13 fill you with all joy and peace in **b,**
1Co   9: 5 right to be accompanied by a **b** wife,
Gal   3: 2 of the law or by **b** what you heard?
       3: 5 or by your **b** what you heard?
Php   1:29 of **b** in Christ,
1Ti   5:16 any **b** woman has relatives who are
       6: 2 Those who have **b** masters must not
1Jn   5:10 have made him a liar by not **b**

BELITTLES*

Pr   11:12 Whoever **b** another lacks sense,

BELL → BELLS

Ex   28:34 a golden **b** and a pomegranate

BELLS → BELL

Zec 14:20 there shall be inscribed on the **b** of

BELLY

Ge   3:14 upon your **b** you shall go,
Lev 11:42 Whatever moves on its **b,**
Nu   25: 8 and the woman, through the **b.**
Jdg   3:21 and thrust it into Eglon's **b;**
2Sa 20:10 Joab struck him in the **b** so that
Pr   13:25 but the **b** of the wicked is empty.
Jnh   1:17 and Jonah was in the **b** of the fish
       2: 1 LORD his God from the **b** of the fish,
       2: 2 out of the **b** of Sheol I cried,
Mt   12:40 three days and three nights in the **b**
Php   3:19 is destruction; their god is the **b;**

BELONG → BELONGED, BELONGING, BELONGS

Ge   40: 8 "Do not interpretations **b** to God?
Dt   10:14 heaven of heavens **b** to the LORD
       29:29 The secret things **b** to the LORD our
                 God, but the revealed things **b** to us
Ps   47: 9 shields of the earth **b** to God;
       82: 8 for all the nations **b** to you!
Pr   16: 1 The plans of the mind **b** to mortals,
Da   9: 9 To the Lord our God **b** mercy and
Jn   10:16 sheep that do not **b** to this fold.
       15:19 Because you do not **b** to the world,
       17:14 just as I do not **b** to the world.
Ro   1: 6 yourselves who are called to **b**
       7: 4 so that you may **b** to another,
       8: 9 not have the Spirit of Christ does
                 not **b** to him.
       9: 6 not all Israelites truly **b** to Israel,
1Co   1:12 "I **b** to Paul," or "I **b** to Apollos,"
       3:23 you **b** to Christ, and Christ belongs
       12:15 I do not **b** to the body,"
       15:23 at his coming those who **b** to Christ.
2Co 10: 7 as you **b** to Christ, so also do we.
Gal   3:29 And if you **b** to Christ,
1Th   5: 8 we **b** to the day, let us be sober,
1Jn   2:19 out from us, but they did not **b** to us;

BELONGED → BELONG

1Ch   5: 2 yet the birthright **b** to Joseph.)
Jn   15:19 If you **b** to the world,
Ac   9: 2 if he found any who **b** to the Way,
       12: 1 upon some who **b** to the church.
Col   2:20 live as if you still **b** to the world?
1Jn   2:19 for if they had **b** to us,

BELONGING → BELONG

Ru   2: 3 to the part of the field **b** to Boaz,
1Co   7:22 slave is a freed person **b** to the Lord,
Sir   9: 8 do not gaze at beauty **b** to another;

BELONGS → BELONG

Ps   3: 8 Deliverance **b** to the LORD;
       22:28 For dominion **b** to the LORD,
       62:11 I heard this: that power **b** to God,
       68:20 GOD, the Lord, **b** escape from death.

89:18 For our shield **b** to the LORD,
Pr 21:31 but the victory **b** to the LORD.
Jnh 2: 9 Deliverance **b** to the LORD!"
Mt 19:14 that the kingdom of heaven **b."**
Jn 18:37 Everyone who **b** to the truth listens
1Co 3:23 to Christ, and Christ **b** to God.
2Co 4: 7 this extraordinary power **b** to God
Col 2:17 but the substance **b** to Christ.
Rev 7:10 "Salvation **b** to our God who is

BELOVED* → LOVE

Dt 33:12 The **b** of the LORD rests in safety—
    33:12 the **b** rests between his shoulders.
2Sa 1:23 Saul and Jonathan, **b** and lovely!
    1:26 greatly **b** were you to me;
Ne 13:26 and he was **b** by his God,
Ps 127: 2 for he gives sleep to his **b.**
SS 1:13 My **b** is to me a bag of myrrh that
    1:14 My **b** is to me a cluster of henna
    1:16 are beautiful, my **b,** truly lovely.
    2: 3 so is my **b** among young men.
    2: 8 The voice of my **b!**
    2: 9 My **b** is like a gazelle or a young
    2:10 My **b** speaks and says to me:
    2:16 My **b** is mine and I am his;
    2:17 turn, my **b,** be like a gazelle or
    4:16 Let my **b** come to his garden,
    5: 2 Listen! my **b** is knocking.
    5: 4 My **b** thrust his hand into the
    5: 5 I arose to open to my **b,**
    5: 6 I opened to my **b,** but my **b** had
    5: 8 of Jerusalem, if you find my **b,**
    5: 9 What is your **b** more than another **b,**
    5: 9 What is your **b** more than another **b,**
    5:10 My **b** is all radiant and ruddy,
    5:16 This is my **b** and this is my friend,
    6: 1 Where has your **b** gone, O fairest
    6: 1 Which way has your **b** turned,
    6: 2 My **b** has gone down to his garden,
    6: 3 am my beloved's and my **b** is mine;
    7:11 my **b,** let us go forth into the fields,
    7:13 I have laid up for you, O my **b.**
    8: 5 the wilderness, leaning upon her **b?**
    8:14 Make haste, my **b,** and be like a
Isa 5: 1 for my **b** my love-song concerning
    5: 1 My **b** had a vineyard on a very
    22: 4 for the destruction of my **b** people.
Jer 11:15 What right has my **b** in my house,
    12: 7 the **b** of my heart into the hands of
Da 9:23 to declare it, for you are greatly **b.**
    10:11 He said to me, "Daniel, greatly **b,**
    10:19 He said, "Do not fear, greatly **b,**
    11:37 or to the one **b** by women;
Mt 3:17 heaven said, "This is my Son, the **B,**
    12:18 my **b,** with whom my soul is well
    17: 5 "This is my Son, the **B;**
Mk 1:11 the **B;** with you I am well pleased."
    9: 7 my Son, the **B;** listen to him!"
    12: 6 He had still one other, a **b** son.
Lk 3:22 the **B;** with you I am well pleased."
    20:13 I will send my **b** son;
Ac 15:25 along with our **b** Barnabas and Paul,
Ro 1: 7 To all God's in Rome, who are
    9:25 her who was not **b** I will call '**b.**'"
    11:28 but as regards election they are **b,**
    12:19 **B,** never avenge yourselves,
    16: 5 Greet my **b** Epaenetus, who was the
    16: 8 Greet Ampliatus, my **b** in the Lord.
    16: 9 in Christ, and my **b** Stachys.
    16:12 Greet the **b** Persis, who has worked
1Co 4:14 to admonish you as my **b** children.
    4:17 my **b** and faithful child in the Lord,
    15:58 Therefore, my **b,** be steadfast,
2Co 7: 1 Since we have these promises, **b,**
    12:19 **b,** is for the sake of building you up.
Eph 1: 6 he freely bestowed on us in the **B.**
    5: 1 be imitators of God, as **b** children,
Php 1:12 to know, **b,** that what has happened
    2:12 **b,** just as you have always obeyed
    3:13 **B,** I do not consider that I have
    4: 1 firm in the Lord in this way, my **b.**
    4: 8 Finally, **b,** whatever is true,

Col 1: 7 Epaphras, our **b** fellow servant.
    1:13 us into the kingdom of his **b** Son,
    3:12 As God's chosen ones, holy and **b,**
    4: 7 he is a **b** brother, a faithful minister,
    4: 9 the faithful and **b** brother, who is
    4:14 Luke, the **b** physician, and Demas
1Th 1: 4 brothers and sisters **b** by God,
    4:10 But we urge you, **b,** to do so more
    5: 4 But you, **b,** are not in darkness,
    5:14 And we urge you, **b,** to admonish
    5:25 **B,** pray for us.
2Th 2:13 brothers and sisters **b** by the Lord,
    3: 6 Now we command you, **b,**
1Ti 6: 2 by their service are believers and **b.**
2Ti 1: 2 To Timothy, my **b** child: Grace,
Phm 1:16 but more than a slave, a **b** brother—
Heb 6: 9 though we speak in this way, **b,**
Jas 1:16 Do not be deceived, my **b.**
    1:19 You must understand this, my **b:**
    2: 5 Listen, my **b** brothers and sisters.
    5: 7 **b,** until the coming of the Lord.
    5: 9 **B,** do not grumble against one
    5:10 of suffering and patience, **b,**
    5:12 Above all, my **b,** do not swear,
1Pe 2:11 **B,** I urge you as aliens and exiles to
    4:12 **B,** do not be surprised at the fiery
2Pe 1:17 my **B,** with whom I am well pleased
    3: 1 **b,** the second letter I am writing to
    3: 8 But do not ignore this one fact, **b,**
    3:14 **b,** while you are waiting for these
    3:15 So also our **b** brother Paul wrote to
    3:17 **b,** since you are forewarned,
1Jn 2: 7 **B,** I am writing you no new
    3: 2 **B,** we are God's children now;
    3:21 **B,** if our hearts do not condemn us,
    4: 1 **b,** do not believe every spirit,
    4: 7 **B,** let us love one another,
    4:11 **B,** since God loved us so much,
3Jn 1: 1 The elder to the **b** Gaius, whom I
    1: 2 **B,** I pray that all may go well with
    1: 5 **B,** you do faithfully whatever you
    1:11 **B,** do not imitate what is evil
Jude 1: 1 who are **b** in God the Father and
    1: 3 **B,** while eagerly preparing to write
    1:17 **b,** must remember the predictions
    1:20 **b,** build yourselves up on your most
Rev 20: 9 camp of the saints and the **b** city.
Tob 3:10 'You had only one **b** daughter
    10:12 and Sarah is your **b** wife.
Jdt 9: 4 divided among your **b** children who
AdE 10: 3 of life was such as to make him **b**
    15: 5 as if **b,** but her heart was frozen
Sir 20:13 The wise make themselves **b**
    24:11 Thus in the **b** city he gave me a
    45: 1 and was **b** by God and people,
    46:13 Samuel was **b** by his Lord;
Bar 4:16 They led away the widow's **b** sons,
Aza 1:12 for the sake of Abraham your **b** and
1Mc 6:11 For I was kind and **b** in my power.'
3Mc 6:11 at the destruction of your **b** people,
4Mc 5:34 will I renounce you, **b** self-control.

BELOVED SON; SON, THE BELOVED

Mt 3:17; 17:5; Mk 1:11; 9:7; 12:6; Lk 3:22;
20:13; Col 1:13; 2Pe 1:17

MY BELOVED SS 1:13, 14, 16; 2:3, 8, 9, 10,
16, 17; 4:16; 5:2, 4, 5, 6, 6, 8, 10, 16; 6:2, 3;
7:11, 13; 8:14; Isa 5:1, 1; 22:4; Jer 11:15; Mt
12:18; Lk 20:13; Ro 16:5, 8, 9; 1Co 4:14, 17;
15:58; Php 2:12; 4:1; 2Ti 1:2; Jas 1:16, 19;
2:5; 5:12; 2Pe 1:17

YOUR BELOVED SS 5:9, 9; 6:1, 1; Tob
10:12; Jdt 9:4; Aza 1:12; 3Mc 6:11

BELOVED'S* → LOVE

SS 6: 3 I am my **b** and my beloved is mine;
    7:10 I am my **b,** and his desire is for me.

BELOW

Jos 2:11 in heaven above and on earth **b.**
Jn 8:23 He said to them, "You are from **b,**
Ac 2:19 above and signs on the earth **b,**

BELSHAZZAR*

King of Babylon in days of Daniel (Da 5; Bar
1:11-12).

BELT → BELTS

1Sa 18: 4 his sword and his bow and his **b.**
2Ki 1: 8 "A hairy man, with a leather **b**
Isa 11: 5 Righteousness shall be the **b** around
        his waist, and faithfulness the **b**
Da 10: 5 a **b** of gold from Uphaz around his
Mk 1: 6 with a leather **b** around his waist,
Jn 21:18 you used to fasten your own **b** and
Ac 21:11 He came to us and took Paul's **b,**
Eph 6:14 the **b** of truth around your waist,

BELTESHAZZAR → =DANIEL

Da 1: 7 other names: Daniel he called **B,**

BELTS → BELT

Mk 6: 8 no bag, no money in their **b;**

BEN-HADAD*

1. King of Syria in time of Asa (1Ki 15:18-20;
2Ch 16:2-4).
2. King of Syria in time of Ahab (1Ki 20; 2Ki
6:24; 8:7-15).
3. King of Syria in time of Jehoahaz (2Ki 13:3,
24-25; Jer 49:27; Am 1:4).

BEN-HINNOM* → HINNOM

2Ki 23:10 Topheth, which is in the valley of **B,**

BEN-ONI* → =BENJAMIN

Ge 35:18 (for she died), she named him **B;**

BENAIAH

A commander of Davids army (2Sa 8:18; 20:23;
23:20-30); loyal to Solomon (1Ki 1:8-2:46; 4:4).

BENCH*

Jn 19:13 sat on the judge's **b** at a place

BEND → BENT

2Sa 22:35 that my arms can **b** a bow of bronze.
Ps 11: 2 the wicked **b** the bow,
Jer 9: 3 They **b** their tongues like bows;
Php 2:10 name of Jesus every knee should **b,**
Man 1:11 And now I **b** the knee of my heart,

BENEATH

Dt 4:39 in heaven above and on the earth **b;**
    5: 8 or that is on the earth **b,**

BENEFACTOR* → BENEFACTORS

Ro 16: 2 she has been a **b** of many and of
AdE 16:13 our savior and perpetual **b,**
2Mc 4: 2 government the man who was the **b**
3Mc 6:24 me, your **b,** you are now attempting
4Mc 8: 6 I can be a **b** to those who obey me.

BENEFACTORS* → BENEFACTOR

Lk 22:25 in authority over them are called **b.**
AdE 16: 2 most generous kindness of their **b,**
    16: 3 to scheme against their own **b,**
Wis 19:14 slaves of guests who were their **b.**
3Mc 3:19 defiance of kings and their own **b,**

BENEFICIAL → BENEFIT

1Co 6:12 but not all things are **b.**
    10:23 lawful," but not all things are **b.**

BENEFIT → BENEFICIAL, BENEFITED, BENEFITS

Gal 5: 2 Christ will be of no **b** to you.
Phm 1:20 have this **b** from you in the Lord!
Heb 4: 2 message they heard did not **b** them,

BENEFITED → BENEFIT

Heb 13: 9 have not **b** those who observe them.

BENEFITS → BENEFIT

Ps 103: 2 and do not forget all his **b**—
1Co 9:11 if we reap your material **b?**

BENJAMIN → =BEN-ONI, BENJAMINITE

Twelfth son of Jacob by Rachel (Ge 35:16-24; 46:19-21; 1Ch 2:2). Jacob refused to send him to Egypt, but relented (Ge 42-45). Tribe of blessed (Ge 49:27; Dt 33:12), numbered (Nu 1:37; 26:41), allotted land (Jos 18:11-28; Eze 48:23), failed to fully possess (Jdg 1:21), nearly obliterated (Jdg 20-21), sided with Ish-Bosheth (2Sa 2), but turned to David (1Ch 12:2, 29). 12,000 from (Rev 7:8).

JUDAH AND BENJAMIN 1Ki 12:23; 2Ch 11:1, 3, 10, 12, 23; 15:2, 8, 9; 25:5; 31:1; 34:9; Ezr 1:5; 4:1; 10:9; 1Es 2:8; 5:66; 9:5

TRIBE OF BENJAMIN Nu 1:37; 2:22; 10:24; 13:9; 34:21; Jos 18:11, 20, 21, 28; 21:17; Jdg 20:12; 1Sa 9:21; 10:20, 21; 1Ki 12:21; 1Ch 6:60; Ac 13:21; Ro 11:1; Php 3:5; Rev 7:8; AdE 11:2; 2:5; 2Mc 3:4

BENJAMINITE → BENJAMIN

Jdg	3:15	the **B**, a left-handed man.
1Sa	9:21	Saul answered, "I am only a **B**,
2Sa	19:16	Shimei son of Gera, the **B**,
	20: 1	named Sheba son of Bichri, a **B**,
Est	2: 5	son of Shimei son of Kish, a **B**.

BENT → BEND

Hos	11: 4	I **b** down to them and fed them.
Lk	13:11	She was **b** over and was quite
Jn	8: 6	Jesus **b** down and wrote with his
	20: 5	He **b** down to look in and saw
Ro	11:10	and keep their backs forever **b**."

BEOR

Nu	22: 5	to Balaam son of **B** at Pethor,
	31: 8	they also killed Balaam son of **B**

BERACAH

2Ch 20:26 called the Valley of **B** to this day.

BEREA See BEROEA

BEREAVE → BEREAVED, BEREAVEMENT, BEREAVES, BEREFT

Lev	26:22	they shall **b** you of your children
Dt	32:25	In the street the sword shall **b**,
Eze	36:12	No longer shall you **b** them of
Hos	9:12	I will **b** them until no one is left.

BEREAVED → BEREAVE

Ge	43:14	if I am **b** of my children, I am **b**."
Isa	49:21	I was **b** and barren, exiled and put

BEREAVEMENT → BEREAVE

Isa 49:20 children born in the time of your **b**

BEREAVES* → BEREAVE

La 1:20 In the street the sword **b**;

BEREFT* → BEREAVE

La	3:17	my soul is **b** of peace;
1Ti	6: 5	depraved in mind and **b** of the truth,

BERNICE

Ac 25:13 Agrippa and **B** arrived at Caesarea

BEROEA

Ac 17:10 sent Paul and Silas off to **B**;

BERYL

Ex	28:20	and the fourth row a **b**, an onyx,
Eze	1:16	was like the gleaming of **b**;
Da	10: 6	His body was like **b**, his face like
Rev	21:20	the seventh chrysolite, the eighth **b**,

BESIDES

Dt	4:35	there is no other **b** him.
	32:39	there is no god **b** me.
1Sa	2: 2	no one **b** you; there is no Rock like
1Ch	17:20	there is no God **b** you,
Ps	18:31	And who is a rock **b** our God?—
Isa	45:21	There is no other god **b** me,
	47: 8	"I am, and there is no one **b** me;
	64: 4	no eye has seen any God **b** you,
Wis	12:13	For neither is there any god **b** you,

Bel 1:41 there is no other **b** you!"

BESIEGED → SIEGE

2Ki	17: 5	for three years he **b** it.
La	3: 5	he has **b** and enveloped me with
Da	1: 1	Babylon came to Jerusalem and **b** it.

BEST → GOOD

Ge	45:18	give you the **b** of the land of Egypt,
	47: 6	brothers in the **b** part of the land;
Ex	34:26	The **b** of the first fruits
Nu	18:29	the **b** of all of them is the part to be
Dt	33:21	He chose the **b** for himself,
SS	7: 9	your kisses like the **b** wine that
Mic	7: 4	The **b** of them is like a brier,
Mk	12:39	the **b** seats in the synagogues and
Php	1:10	to help you to determine what is **b**,
2Ti	2:15	your **b** to present yourself to God

BESTOW → BESTOWED, BESTOWER, BESTOWS

Pr 4: 9 will **b** on you a beautiful crown."

BESTOWED → BESTOW

1Ch	29:25	and **b** upon him such royal majesty
Est	6: 3	distinction has been **b** on Mordecai
Eph	1: 6	he freely **b** on us in the Beloved.

BESTOWER* → BESTOW

Isa 23: 8 the **b** of crowns, whose merchants

BESTOWS* → BESTOW

Ps 84:11 and shield; he **b** favor and honor.

BETH-SHAN

1Sa 31:10 fastened his body to the wall of **B**.

BETH-SHEMESH

1Sa 6:14 came into the field of Joshua of **B**,

BETHANY

Mt	26: 6	Jesus was at **B** in the house of
Mk	11:12	day, when they came from **B**,
Jn	1:28	in **B** across the Jordan where John
	11: 1	a certain man was ill, Lazarus of **B**,

BETHEL → =LUZ, EL-BETHEL

Ge	12: 8	the east of **B**, and pitched his tent,
	12: 8	**B** on the west and Ai on the east;
	28:19	He called that place **B**;
	31:13	I am the God of **B**,
	35: 8	was buried under an oak below **B**.
Jos	8: 9	lay between **B** and Ai, to the west
Jdg	20:18	Israelites proceeded to go up to **B**,
1Sa	7:16	a circuit year by year to **B**, Gilgal,
1Ki	12:29	He set one in **B**, and the other he
	13:11	Now there lived an old prophet in **B**.
2Ki	2: 2	So they went down to **B**.
	10:29	golden calves that were in **B** and in
	23:15	the altar at **B**, the high place erected
Am	4: 4	Come to **B**—and transgress;
	7:10	Then Amaziah, the priest of **B**,
Tob	2: 6	of Amos, how he said against **B**,

BETHLEHEM → BETHLEHEMITE, EPHRATH

Ge	35:19	on the way to Ephrath (that is, **B**),
Ru	1: 1	and a certain man of **B** in Judah
	1:19	went on until they came to **B**.
	1:19	When they came to **B**,
	4:11	and bestow a name in **B**;
1Sa	17:12	David was the son of an Ephrathite of **B**
2Sa	23:15	to drink from the well of **B** that is
Mic	5: 2	But you, O **B** of Ephrathah,
Mt	2: 1	after Jesus was born in **B** of Judea,
	2: 6	**B**, in the land of Judah, are by no
	2:16	around **B** who were two years old
Lk	2:15	"Let us go now to **B** and see this
Jn	7:42	from David and comes from **B**,

BETHLEHEMITE → BETHLEHEM

1Sa 16: 1 I will send you to Jesse the **B**,

BETHPHAGE

Mt 21: 1 near Jerusalem and had reached **B**,

BETHSAIDA

Mt	11:21	Chorazin! Woe to you, **B**!
Jn	1:44	Philip was from **B**, the city of

BETHUEL

Ge	22:23	**B** became the father of Rebekah.
	24:24	the daughter of **B** son of Milcah,

BETRAY → BETRAYED, BETRAYER, BETRAYING

Mt	10:21	Brother will **b** brother to death,
	24:10	and they will **b** one another and
	26:21	I tell you, one of you will **b** me."
Mk	14:11	to look for an opportunity to **b** him.
Jn	13:11	For he knew who was to **b** him;

BETRAYED → BETRAY

Lk	21:16	You will be **b** even by parents and
Jn	18: 2	Now Judas, who **b** him, also knew
1Co	11:23	Jesus on the night when he was **b**

BETRAYER → BETRAY

Isa	21: 2	the **b** betrays, and the destroyer
Mk	14:42	be going. See, my **b** is at hand."

BETRAYING → BETRAY

Lk 22:48 kiss that you are **b** the Son of Man?"

BETTER → GOOD

Nu	11:18	Surely it was **b** for us in Egypt.'
Ru	3:10	last instance of your loyalty is **b**
1Sa	15:22	Surely, to obey is **b** than sacrifice,
Ps	37:16	**B** is a little that the righteous
	63: 3	your steadfast love is **b** than life,
	118: 8	It is **b** to take refuge in the LORD
	119:72	The law of your mouth is **b** to me
Pr	3:14	for her income is **b** than silver,
	8:11	for wisdom is **b** than jewels,
	8:19	My fruit is **b** than gold, even fine
	12: 9	**B** to be despised and have a servant,
	15:16	**B** is a little with the fear of
	15:17	**B** is a dinner of vegetables where
	16: 8	**B** is a little with righteousness than
	16:16	much **b** to get wisdom than gold!
	16:19	It is **b** to be of a lowly spirit among
	16:32	One who is slow to anger is **b** than
	17: 1	**B** is a dry morsel with quiet than a
	17:12	**B** to meet a she-bear robbed of its
	19: 1	**B** the poor walking in integrity than
	19:22	and it is **b** to be poor than a liar.
	21: 9	It is **b** to live in a corner of the
	21:19	It is **b** to live in a desert land than
	22: 1	and favor is **b** than silver or gold.
	25:24	It is **b** to live in a corner of the
	27: 5	**B** is open rebuke than hidden love.
	27:10	**B** is a neighbor who is nearby than
	28: 6	**B** to be poor and walk in integrity
Ecc	2:24	There is nothing **b** for mortals than
	3:12	nothing **b** for them than to be happy
	3:22	So I saw that there is nothing **b** than
	4: 3	but **b** than both is the one who has
	4: 6	**B** is a handful with quiet than two
	4: 9	Two are **b** than one, because they
	4:13	**B** is a poor but wise youth than an
	5: 5	It is **b** that you should not vow than
	6: 3	I say that a stillborn child is **b** off
	6: 9	**B** is the sight of the eyes than the
	7: 1	A good name is **b** than precious
	7: 2	**b** to go to the house of mourning
	7: 3	Sorrow is **b** than laughter,
	7: 5	It is **b** to hear the rebuke of the wise
	7: 8	**B** is the end of a thing than its
	7: 8	the patient in spirit are **b** than the
	8:15	for there is nothing **b** for people
	9: 4	a living dog is **b** than a dead lion.
	9:16	So I said, "Wisdom is **b** than might;
	9:18	Wisdom is **b** than weapons of war,
SS	1: 2	For your love is **b** than wine,
	4:10	how much **b** is your love than wine,
Jer	10: 8	given by idols is no **b** than wood!

Da   1:20 he found them ten times **b** than all
Jnh   4: 3 for it is **b** for me to die than to live."
Mt   5:29 it is **b** for you to lose one of your
      18: 6 be **b** for you if a great millstone
      19:10 it is **b** not to marry."
      26:24 It would have been **b** for that one
Mk   14:21 It would have been **b** for that one
Lk   10:42 Mary has chosen the **b** part,
Jn   11:50 **b** for you to have one man die for
Ro   14: 5 Some judge one day to be **b** than
1Co   7: 9 it is **b** to marry than to be aflame
Php   1:23 and be with Christ, for that is far **b;**
      2: 3 in humility regard others as **b** than
Heb   6: 9 confident of **b** things in your case,
      7:19 the introduction of a **b** hope,
      7:22 the guarantee of a **b** covenant.
      8: 6 he is the mediator of a **b** covenant,
      8: 6 enacted through **b** promises.
      9:23 need **b** sacrifices than these.
     10:34 yourselves possessed something **b**
     11:16 But as it is, they desire a **b** country,
     11:35 in order to obtain a **b** resurrection.
     11:40 God had provided something **b** so
     12:24 sprinkled blood that speaks a **b**
1Pe   3:17 For it is **b** to suffer for doing good,
2Pe   2:21 For it would have been **b** for them
Tob   3: 6 For it is **b** for me to die than to live,
      12: 8 A little with righteousness is **b** than
Sir 16: 3 childless **b** than to have ungodly
     18:16 So a word is **b** than a gift.
     20:18 A slip on the pavement is **b** than a
     23:27 is **b** than the fear of the Lord,
     30:15 and fitness are **b** than any gold,
     40:20 the love of friends is **b** than either.
     40:23 but a sensible wife is **b** than either.
     40:26 the fear of the Lord is **b** than either.
     40:28 it is **b** to die than to beg.

BETWEEN

Ge   3:15 put enmity **b** you and the woman,
      9:13 a sign of the covenant **b** me and
     16: 5 the LORD judge **b** you and me!"
     17: 2 And I will make my covenant **b** me
     17:11 sign of the covenant **b** me and you.
     31:44 let it be a witness **b** you and me."
Ex   8:23 will make a distinction **b** my people
     31:17 a sign forever **b** me and the people
Jdg 11:10 "The LORD will be witness **b** us;
1Sa   7:12 Samuel took a stone and set it up **b**
Isa   2: 4 He shall judge **b** the nations,
      5: 3 judge **b** me and my vineyard.
Eze 20:12 as a sign **b** me and you,
     34:17 I shall judge **b** sheep and sheep, **b**
            rams and goats:
Mic   4: 3 He shall judge **b** many peoples,
Lk   11:51 who perished **b** the altar and the
Jn   19:18 on either side, with Jesus **b** them.
Ac   11:12 and not to make a distinction **b**
Ro   10:12 no distinction **b** Jew and Greek;
Eph   2:14 dividing wall, that is, the hostility **b**
Php   1:23 I am hard pressed **b** the two:
1Ti   2: 5 one mediator **b** God and humankind

BEWARE

Job 36:21 **B!** Do not turn to iniquity;
Ecc 12:12 anything beyond these, my child, **b.**
Jer   9: 4 **B** of your neighbors, and put no
Mt   6: 1 "**B** of practicing your piety before
      7:15 "**B** of false prophets, who come to
Mk   8:15 **b** of the yeast of the Pharisees and
     13: 5 "**B** that no one leads you astray.
Lk   20:46 "**B** of the scribes, who like to walk
Php   3: 2 **B** of the dogs, **b** of the evil workers,
Rev   2:10 **B,** the devil is about to throw some

BEWITCHED*

Gal   3: 1 foolish Galatians! who has **b** you?

BEYOND

Ge   31:52 I will not pass **b** this heap to you,
Nu   22:18 not go **b** the command of the LORD
Jos 24: 2 lived **b** the Euphrates and served
Ps 147: 5 his understanding is **b** measure.

Ecc 12:12 anything **b** these, my child, beware.
Isa 52:14 and his form **b** that of mortals—
La   5:22 and are angry with us **b** measure.
1Co   4: 6 "Nothing **b** what is written,"
     10:13 not let you be tested **b** your strength,
2Co   4:17 an eternal weight of glory **b** all
     10:16 the good news in lands **b** you,
2Jn   1: 9 but goes **b** it, does not have God;
Sir   3:23 not meddle in matters that are **b** you
      6:15 Faithful friends are **b** price;
      8:13 Do not give surety **b** your means;

BEZALEL

Judahite craftsman in charge of building the tabernacle (Ex 31:1-11; 35:30-39:31).

BIDDING

Ps 103:20 you mighty ones who do his **b,**

BIER

Lk   7:14 he came forward and touched the **b,**

BIG

Ex   29:20 and on the **b** toes of their right feet,
Lev   8:23 on the **b** toe of his right foot.
     14:14 and on the **b** toe of the right foot.

BILDAD*

One of Job's friends (Job 2:11; 8; 18; 25; 42:9).

BILHAH

Servant of Rachel, mother of Jacob's sons Dan and Naphtali (Ge 30:1-7; 35:25; 46:23-25).

BILL

Dt   24: 3 writes her a **b** of divorce, puts it in
Isa 50: 1 Where is your mother's **b** of divorce

BILLOWS

Ps   42: 7 and your **b** have gone over me.
Jnh   2: 3 and your **b** passed over me.

BIND → BINDERS, BINDING, BINDS, BOUND

Dt   6: 8 **B** them as a sign on your hand,
     11:18 shall **b** them as a sign on your hand,
Jdg 15:10 "We have come up to **b** Samson,
Pr   3: 3 **b** them around your neck,
      6:21 **B** them upon your heart always;
      7: 3 **b** them on your fingers, write them
Isa   8:16 **B** up the testimony, seal the
     61: 1 to **b** up the brokenhearted,
Eze 34:16 and I will **b** up the injured,
Mt   16:19 whatever you **b** on earth will be
     18:18 whatever you **b** on earth will be

BINDING → BIND

Ro   7: 1 the law is **b** on a person only during

BINDS → BIND

Job   5:18 For he wounds, but he **b** up;
Ps 147: 3 and **b** up their wounds.
Isa 30:26 the LORD **b** up the injuries of his
Col   3:14 **b** everything together in perfect

BIRD → BIRD'S, BIRDS

Ge   1:21 and every winged **b** of every kind,
      7:14 and every **b** of every kind—
Lev 20:25 the unclean **b** and the clean;
Dt   4:17 the likeness of any winged **b** that
Ps   11: 1 "Flee like a **b** to the mountains;
    124: 7 We have escaped like a **b** from the
Pr   7:23 He is like a **b** rushing into a snare,
     27: 8 a **b** that strays from its nest is one
Ecc 10:20 a **b** of the air may carry your voice,
Isa 46:11 calling a **b** of prey from the east,
Eze 17:23 Under it every kind of **b** will live;
Rev 18: 2 a haunt of every foul **b,**

BIRD'S* → BIRD

Dt   22: 6 If you come on a **b** nest,

BIRDS → BIRD

Ge   1:22 and let **b** multiply on the earth."
      7: 3 and seven pairs of the **b** of the air

Dt   14:11 You may eat any clean **b.**
Ps   50:11 I know all the **b** of the air,
Jer   7:33 be food for the **b** of the air, and for
Da   4:12 **b** of the air nested in its branches,
Hos 11:11 They shall come trembling like **b**
Mt   6:26 Look at the **b** of the air;
      8:20 holes, and **b** of the air have nests;
     13: 4 and the **b** came and ate them up.
Ac   10:12 and reptiles and **b** of the air.
Ro   1:23 human being or **b** or four-footed
Rev 19:21 the **b** were gorged with their flesh.

BIRTH → BEAR

Dt   32:18 you forgot the God who gave you **b.**
Jdg 13: 5 shall be a nazirite to God from **b.**
Job   3: 1 and cursed the day of his **b.**
Ps   22:10 On you I was cast from my **b,**
     58: 3 they err from their **b,** speaking lies.
     71: 6 Upon you I have leaned from my **b;**
Ecc   7: 1 the day of death, than the day of **b.**
Isa 26:18 but we gave **b** only to wind.
Jer   2:27 and to a stone, "You gave me **b."**
Mt   1:18 the **b** of Jesus the Messiah took
      24: 8 is but the beginning of the **b** pangs.
Lk   1:14 and many will rejoice at his **b,**
      1:57 time came for Elizabeth to give **b,**
Jn   9: 1 he saw a man blind from **b.**
Ac   3: 2 man lame from **b** was being carried
     14: 8 for he had been crippled from **b.**
1Co   1:26 not many were of noble **b.**
Eph   2:11 that at one time you Gentiles by **b,**
Jas   1:15 has conceived, it gives **b** to sin,
      1:18 he gave us **b** by the word of truth,
1Pe   1: 3 given us a new **b** into a living hope
Rev 12: 5 she gave **b** to a son, a male child,

BIRTHDAY → BEAR, DAY

Mt   14: 6 But when Herod's **b** came,

BIRTHRIGHT → BEAR, RIGHT

Ge   25:34 Thus Esau despised his **b.**
     27:36 He took away my **b;**
1Ch   5: 1 he defiled his father's bed his **b**
      5: 2 yet the **b** belonged to Joseph.)
Heb 12:16 who sold his **b** for a single meal.

BISHOP* → BISHOPS

1Ti   3: 1 whoever aspires to the office of **b**
      3: 2 Now a **b** must be above reproach,
Tit   1: 7 For a **b,** as God's steward, must be

BISHOPS* → BISHOP

Php   1: 1 who are in Philippi, with the **b**

BIT → BITE, BITS

Nu   21: 9 and whenever a serpent **b** someone,
2Ki 19:28 and my **b** in your mouth;
Ps   32: 9 temper must be curbed with **b** and

BITE* → BIT, BITES, BITTEN

Jer   8:17 and they shall **b** you, says the LORD.
Am   9: 3 the sea-serpent, and it shall **b** them.
Gal   5:15 If, however, you **b** and devour one
Sir 21: 2 if you approach sin, it will **b** you.

BITES → BITE

Pr   23:32 At the last it **b** like a serpent,

BITS → BIT

Jas   3: 3 we put **b** into the mouths of horses

BITTEN → BITE

Nu   21: 8 who is **b** shall look at it and live."

BITTER → BITTERLY, BITTERNESS

Ex   1:14 made their lives **b** with hard service
     12: 8 with unleavened bread and **b** herbs.
     15:23 water of Marah because it was **b.**
Nu   5:24 shall enter her and cause **b** pain.
Ru   1:13 it has been far more **b** for me than
Pr   5: 4 in the end she is **b** as wormwood,
     27: 7 to a ravenous appetite even the **b** is
Ecc   7:26 I found more **b** than death the
Isa   5:20 put **b** for sweet and sweet for **b!**

Zep 1:14 sound of the day of the LORD is **b**,
Rev 8:11 the water, because it was made **b**.
 10: 9 it will be **b** to your stomach,

BITTERLY → BITTER

Ru 1:20 the Almighty has dealt **b** with me.
Lk 22:62 And he went out and wept **b**.
Rev 5: 4 I began to weep **b** because no one

BITTERNESS → BITTER

Nu 5:18 the water of **b** that brings the curse.
Pr 14:10 The heart knows its own **b**,
 17:25 and **b** to her who bore them.
Ro 3:14 mouths are full of cursing and **b**."
Eph 4:31 Put away from you all **b** and wrath
Heb 12:15 that no root of **b** springs up and

BITUMEN*

Ge 11: 3 brick for stone, and **b** for mortar.
 14:10 Valley of Siddim was full of **b** pits;
Ex 2: 3 and plastered it with **b** and pitch;

BLACK → BLACKNESS

SS 1: 5 I am **b** and beautiful, O daughters
Jer 4:28 and the heavens above grow **b**;
Zec 6: 2 the second chariot **b** horses,
Mt 5:36 cannot make one hair white or **b**.
Rev 6: 5 I looked, and there was a **b** horse!
 6:12 the sun became **b** as sackcloth,

BLACKNESS* → BLACK

Job 3: 5 let the **b** of the day terrify it.
Isa 50: 3 I clothe the heavens with **b**,
Joel 2: 2 Like **b** spread upon the mountains

BLACKSMITHS*

Zec 1:20 Then the LORD showed me four **b**.

BLAME → BLAMELESS, BLAMELESSLY

Ge 43: 9 then let me bear the **b** forever.
1Ti 6:14 the commandment without spot or **b**

BLAMELESS* → BLAME

Ge 6: 9 Noah was a righteous man, **b** in his
 17: 1 walk before me, and be **b**.
1Sa 29: 9 as **b** in my sight as an angel
2Sa 22:24 I was **b** before him, and I kept
 22:26 with the **b** you show yourself **b**;
Job 1: 1 That man was **b** and upright,
 1: 8 a **b** and upright man who fears God
 2: 3 a **b** and upright man who fears God
 8:20 "See, God will not reject a **b** person,
 9:20 though I am **b**, he would prove me
 9:21 I am **b**; I do not know myself;
 9:22 destroys both the **b** and the wicked.
 12: 4 and **b** man, I am a laughingstock.
 22: 3 to him if you make your ways **b**?
Ps 18:23 I was **b** before him, and I kept
 18:25 with the **b** you show yourself **b**;
 19:13 Then I shall be **b**, and innocent of
 37:18 The LORD knows the days of the **b**,
 37:37 Mark the **b**, and behold the upright,
 51: 4 and **b** when you pass judgment.
 64: 4 shooting from ambush at the **b**;
 101: 2 I will study the way that is **b**.
 101: 6 whoever walks in the way that is **b**
 119: 1 Happy are those whose way is **b**,
 119:80 May my heart be **b** in your statutes,
Pr 11: 5 righteousness of the **b** keeps their
 11:20 but those of **b** ways are his delight.
 28:10 **b** will have a goodly inheritance.
 29:10 The bloodthirsty hate the **b**,
Eze 28:15 You were **b** in your ways from the
Da 6:22 because I was found **b** before him,
1Co 1: 8 be **b** on the day of our Lord Jesus
Eph 1: 4 holy and **b** before him in love.
Php 1:10 of Christ you may be pure and **b**,
 2:15 so that you may be **b** and innocent,
 3: 6 as to righteousness under the law, **b**.
Col 1:22 as to present you holy and **b** and
1Th 2:10 and **b** our conduct was toward you
 3:13 that you may be **b** before our God
 5:23 and **b** at the coming of our Lord
1Ti 3:10 then, if they prove themselves **b**,

Tit 1: 6 who is **b**, married only once,
 1: 7 bishop, as God's steward, must be **b**
Heb 7:26 **b**, undefiled, separated from sinners,
Rev 14: 5 mouth no lie was found; they are **b**.
AdE 16:13 Esther, the **b** partner of our kingdom
Wis 2:22 nor discerned the prize for **b** souls;
 4: 9 and a **b** life is ripe old age.
 10: 5 righteous man and preserved him **b**
 10:15 A holy people and **b** race wisdom
 18:21 For a **b** man was quick to act as
Sir 11:10 activities, you will not be held **b**.
 31: 8 the rich person who is found **b**,
 40:19 but a **b** wife is accounted better
1Mc 4:42 chose **b** priests devoted to the law,

BLAMELESSLY* → BLAME

Ps 15: 2 who walk **b**, and do what is right,
Pr 2: 7 he is a shield to those who walk **b**,
Lk 1: 6 living **b** according to all the

BLASPHEME* → BLASPHEMED, BLASPHEMER, BLASPHEMERS, BLASPHEMES, BLASPHEMIES, BLASPHEMING, BLASPHEMOUS, BLASPHEMY

Lev 24:16 when they **b** the Name,
Ac 26:11 I tried to force them to **b**;
1Ti 1:20 so that they may learn not to **b**.
Jas 2: 7 not they who **b** the excellent name
1Pe 4: 4 of dissipation, and so they **b**.

BLASPHEMED* → BLASPHEME

Lev 24:11 Israelite woman's son **b** the Name
Eze 20:27 In this again your ancestors **b** me,
Mt 26:65 tore his clothes and said, "He has **b**!
Ro 2:24 God is **b** among the Gentiles
1Ti 6: 1 God and the teaching may not be **b**.

BLASPHEMER → BLASPHEME

Lev 24:16 congregation shall stone the **b**.
1Ti 1:13 even though I was formerly a **b**,
Sir 3:16 forsakes a father is like a **b**,

BLASPHEMERS → BLASPHEME

Ac 19:37 robbers nor **b** of our goddess.

BLASPHEMES* → BLASPHEME

Lev 24:16 One who **b** the name of the LORD
Mk 3:29 whoever **b** against the Holy Spirit
Lk 12:10 whoever **b** against the Holy Spirit

BLASPHEMIES* → BLASPHEME

Ne 9:18 and had committed great **b**,
 9:26 and they committed great **b**.
Mk 3:28 their sins and whatever **b** they utter;
Lk 5:21 "Who is this who is speaking **b**?
Rev 13: 6 its mouth to utter **b** against God,
Tob 1:18 executed upon him because of his **b**.
1Mc 2: 6 He saw the **b** being committed in
 7:38 remember their **b**, and let them live
2Mc 8: 4 the **b** committed against his name;
 10:35 fired with anger because of the **b**,
2Es 1:23 I did not send fire on you for your **b**,

BLASPHEMING* → BLASPHEME

1Sa 3:13 because his sons were **b** God,
Mt 9: 3 said to themselves, "This man is **b**."
Jn 10:36 is **b** because I said,
Ac 13:45 **b**, they contradicted what was
Rev 13: 6 **b** his name and his dwelling, that is,
2Mc 10:34 kept **b** terribly and uttering wicked
 12:14 even **b** and saying unholy things.
2Es 1:22 thirsty and **b** my name,

BLASPHEMOUS* → BLASPHEME

Ac 6:11 "We have heard him speak **b** words
Rev 13: 1 and on its heads were **b** names.
 13: 5 uttering haughty and **b** words,
 17: 3 beast that was full of **b** names,
2Mc 10: 4 not be handed over to **b** and
 13:11 fall into the hands of the **b** Gentiles.

BLASPHEMY* → BLASPHEME

Da 3:29 nation, or language that utters **b**
Mt 12:31 will be forgiven for every sin and **b**,
 12:31 but **b** against the Spirit will not be
 26:65 You have now heard his **b**.
Mk 2: 7 fellow speak in this way? It is **b**!
 14:64 You have heard his **b**!
Jn 10:33 to stone you, but for **b**,
Bel 1: 9 he has spoken **b** against Bel."
1Mc 7:41 from the king spoke **b**,

BLAST → BLASTS

Ex 15: 8 At the **b** of your nostrils the waters
 19:13 When the trumpet sounds a long **b**,
 19:16 and a **b** of a trumpet so loud that all
Jos 6: 5 make a long **b** with the ram's horn,
2Sa 22:16 at the **b** of the breath of his nostrils.
Job 4: 9 **b** of his anger they are consumed.
Ps 18:15 O LORD, at the **b** of the breath of
Isa 27: 8 with his fierce **b** he removed them

BLASTS* → BLAST

Lev 23:24 commemorated with trumpet **b**.
Rev 8:13 at the **b** of the other trumpets that

BLAZING

Ex 3: 2 he looked, and the bush was **b**,
Dt 4:11 the mountain was **b** up to the very
Eze 20:47 the **b** flame shall not be quenched,
Da 3: 6 be thrown into a furnace of **b** fire."
Zec 12: 6 the clans of Judah like a **b** pot on a
Heb 12:18 a **b** fire, and darkness, and gloom,
Rev 8:10 a great star fell from heaven, **b** like

BLEACH*

Mk 9: 3 as no one on earth could **b** them.

BLEATING*

1Sa 15:14 "What then is this **b** of sheep in my

BLEMISH → BLEMISHED, BLEMISHES

Ex 12: 5 Your lamb shall be without **b**,
Lev 1: 3 you shall offer a male without **b**;
 21:18 no one who has a **b** shall draw near,
 22:20 not offer anything that has a **b**,
Nu 19: 2 in which there is no **b**
2Sa 14:25 of his head there was no **b** in him.
Eph 5:27 that she may be holy and without **b**.
Php 2:15 children of God without **b** in the
Heb 9:14 offered himself without **b** to God,
1Pe 1:19 that of a lamb without defect or **b**.
2Pe 3:14 at peace, without spot or **b**;
Jude 1:24 to make you stand without **b** in the

BLEMISHED* → BLEMISH

Mal 1:14 yet sacrifices to the Lord what is **b**;
Sir 34:21 ill-gotten goods, the offering is **b**;

BLEMISHES* → BLEMISH

2Pe 2:13 They are blots and **b**, reveling in
Jude 1:12 These are **b** on your love-feasts,

BLESS → BLESSED, BLESSEDNESS, BLESSES, BLESSING, BLESSINGS

Ge 12: 2 I will **b** you, and make your name
 12: 3 I will **b** those who **b** you,
 17:16 I will **b** her, and moreover I will
 17:20 I will **b** him and make him fruitful
 22:17 I will indeed **b** you, and I will make
 26: 3 I will be with you, and will **b** you;
 26:24 I am with you and will **b** you
 27: 4 so that I may **b** you before I die."
 27:34 his father, "**B** me, me also, father!"
 28: 3 May God Almighty **b** you and
 32:26 not let you go, unless you **b** me."
 48: 9 to me, please, that I may **b** them."
 49:25 the Almighty who will **b** you with
Ex 20:24 I will come to you and **b** you.
 23:25 I will **b** your bread and your water;
Nu 6:24 The LORD **b** you and keep you;
 22: 6 that whomever you **b** is blessed,
 23:20 See, I received a command to **b**;
 24: 1 that it pleased the LORD to **b** Israel,

Dt 1:11 a thousand times more and **b** you,
7:13 he will love you, **b** you, and
8:10 **b** the LORD your God for the good
14:29 the LORD your God may **b** you in
15: 4 the LORD is sure to **b** you in the land
16:15 for the LORD your God will **b** you
23:20 the LORD your God may **b** you
24:19 that the LORD your God may **b** you
26:15 and **b** your people Israel and the
28: 8 he will **b** you in the land that
30:16 the LORD your God will **b** you in
33:11 **B**, O LORD, his substance,
Jos 8:33 they should **b** the people of Israel.
Jdg 5: 2 themselves willingly—**b** the LORD!
Ru 2: 4 They answered, "The LORD **b** you."
1Sa 2:20 Eli would **b** Elkanah and his wife,
2Sa 7:29 may it please you to **b** the house
21: 3 may the heritage of the LORD?"
1Ch 4:10 "Oh that you would **b** me and
16:43 David went home to **b** his
29:20 "**B** the LORD your God."
Ne 9: 5 "Stand up and **b** the LORD your
Ps 5:12 For you **b** the righteous, O LORD;
16: 7 I **b** the LORD who gives me counsel;
26:12 congregation I will **b** the LORD.
28: 9 your people, and **b** your heritage;
29:11 the LORD **b** his people with peace!
34: 1 I will **b** the LORD at all times;
62: 4 they **b** with their mouths,
63: 4 So I will **b** you as long as I live;
66: 8 **B** our God, O peoples, let the sound
67: 1 God be gracious to us and **b** us and
68:26 "**B** God in the great congregation,
96: 2 Sing to the LORD, **b** his name;
100: 4 Give thanks to him, **b** his name.
103: 1 **B** the LORD, O my soul,
103: 2 **B** the LORD, O my soul,
103:20 **B** the LORD, O you his angels,
103:21 **B** the LORD, all his hosts,
103:22 **B** the LORD, all his works,
104: 1 **B** the LORD, O my soul.
104:35 **B** the LORD, O my soul.
109:28 Let them curse, but you will **b**.
115:12 mindful of us; he will **b** us;
115:18 we will **b** the LORD from this time
118:26 b you from the house of the LORD.
128: 5 The LORD **b** you from Zion.
129: 8 **b** you in the name of the LORD!"
132:15 I will abundantly **b** its provisions;
134: 1 **b** the LORD, all you servants of the
135:19 O house of Israel, **b** the LORD!
135:20 You that fear the LORD, **b** the LORD!
145: 2 Every day I will **b** you,
145:10 and all your faithful shall **b** you.
145:21 all flesh will **b** his holy name
Pr 30:11 and do not **b** their mothers.
Jer 31:23 "The LORD **b** you, O abode of
Eze 37:26 I will **b** them and multiply them,
Hag 2:19 From this day on I will **b** you.
Lk 6:28 **b** those who curse you, pray
Ac 3:26 to **b** you by turning each of you
Ro 12:14 **B** those who persecute you;
1Co 4:12 When reviled, we **b**;
10:16 The cup of blessing that we **b**,
Heb 6:14 "I will surely **b** you and multiply
Jas 3: 9 With it we **b** the Lord and Father,
Tob 4:19 At all times **b** the Lord God,
8:15 Let them **b** you forever.
12: 6 "**B** God and acknowledge him in
Sir 32:13 But above all **b** your Maker,
39:35 and **b** the name of the Lord.
Aza 1:35 "**B** the Lord, all you works of the

BLESS THE *LORD Jas 3:9; Tob 4:19;
13:6; Sir 39:14; 45:26; Aza 1:35, 36, 37, 38,
39, 40, 41, 42, 43, 44, 45, 46, 47, 48, 49, 50,
51, 52, 53, 54, 55, 56, 57, 58, 59, 60, 61, 62,
63, 64, 65, 66

BLESS THE †LORD Dt 8:10; Jdg 5:2, 9;
1Ch 21:20; Ne 9:5; Ps 16:7; 26:12; 34:1;
103:1, 2, 20, 21, 22, 22; 104:1, 35; 115:18;
134:1, 2; 135:19, 19, 20, 20

BLESS YOU Ge 12:2, 3; 22:17; 26:3, 24;
27:4, 7, 10, 25; 28:3; 49:25; Ex 20:24; Nu
6:24; Dt 1:11; 7:13; 14:29; 15:4, 10, 18; 16:15;
23:20; 24:13, 19; 28:8; 30:16; Ru 2:4; Ps 63:4;
118:26; 128:5; 129:8; 134:3; 145:2, 10; Jer
31:23; Hag 2:19; Ac 3:26; Heb 6:14; Tob 8:5,
15, 15; Jdt 15:10

BLESSED → BLESS

Ge 1:22 God **b** them, saying, "Be fruitful
2: 3 So God **b** the seventh day and
5: 2 and he **b** them and named them
9: 1 God **b** Noah and his sons, and said
9:26 "**B** by the LORD my God be Shem;
14:19 He **b** him and said, "**B** be Abram
18:18 of the earth shall be **b** in him?
24: 1 and the LORD had **b** Abraham in all
26:29 You are now the **b** of the LORD."
28:14 be **b** in you and in your offspring.
39: 5 LORD **b** the Egyptian's house for
47: 7 and Jacob **b** Pharaoh.
48:20 So he **b** them that day, saying,
Ex 20:11 the LORD **b** the sabbath day and
39:43 LORD had commanded, he **b** them.
Lev 9:22 toward the people and **b** them;
Nu 22: 6 know that whomever you bless is **b**,
24: 9 **B** is everyone who blesses you,
Dt 7:14 You shall be the most **b** of peoples,
12: 7 the LORD your God has **b** you.
28: 3 **B** shall you be in the city,
33:13 **B** by the LORD be his land,
Jos 22: 6 Joshua **b** them and sent them away,
Jdg 5:24 "Most **b** of women be Jael,
13:24 The boy grew, and the LORD **b** him.
Ru 2:19 **B** be the man who took notice of
1Sa 25:33 **B** be your good sense, and **b** be you,
26:25 Saul said to David, "**B** be you,
2Sa 22:47 **B** be my rock, and exalted be my
1Ki 1:48 '**B** be the LORD, the God of Israel,
2:45 But King Solomon shall be **b**,
1Ch 16: 2 he **b** the people in the name of the
17:27 O LORD, have **b** and are **b** forever."
2Ch 2:12 "**B** be the LORD God of Israel,
31:10 for the LORD has **b** his people,
Ne 9: 5 **B** be your glorious name,
Job 1:21 **b** be the name of the LORD."
42:12 The LORD **b** the latter days
Ps 18:46 **B** be my rock, and exalted be the
28: 6 **B** be the LORD, for he has heard the
31:21 **B** be the LORD, for he has
41:13 **B** be the LORD, the God of Israel,
66:20 **B** be God, because he has not
67: 6 God, our God, has **b** us.
68:19 **B** be the Lord, who daily bears us
72:17 May all nations be **b** in him;
72:19 **B** be his glorious name forever;
89:52 **B** be the LORD forever.
106:48 **B** be the LORD, the God of Israel,
113: 2 **B** be the name of the LORD from
118:26 **B** is the one who comes in the name
135:21 **B** be the LORD from Zion,
144: 1 **B** be the LORD, my rock,
Pr 5:18 Let your fountain be **b**, and rejoice
22: 9 Those who are generous are **b**,
Isa 30:18 **b** are all those who wait for him.
Jer 17: 7 **B** are those who trust in the LORD,
Da 2:20 "**B** be the name of God from age to
Mt 5: 3 "**B** are the poor in spirit,
5: 4 "**B** are those who mourn,
5: 5 "**B** are the meek, for they will
5: 6 "**B** are those who hunger and thirst
5: 7 "**B** are the merciful, for they will
5: 8 "**B** are the pure in heart, for they
5: 9 "**B** are the peacemakers, for they
5:10 "**B** are those who are persecuted
5:11 "**B** are you when people revile you
11: 6 **b** is anyone who takes no offense at
Mk 6:41 and **b** and broke the loaves,
10:16 laid his hands on them, and **b** them.
11: 9 **B** is the one who comes in the name
Lk 1:42 "**B** are you among women,
1:48 all generations will call me **b**;

6:20 "**B** are you who are poor,
6:21 "**B** are you who are hungry now,
6:21 "**B** are you who weep now, for you
6:22 "**B** are you when people hate you,
Jn 12:13 **B** is the one who comes in the name
13:17 you are **b** if you do them.
20:29 **B** are those who have not seen and
Ac 3:25 the families of the earth shall be **b**.'
20:35 It is more **b** to give than to receive.
Ro 1:25 the Creator, who is **b** forever!
4: 7 "**B** are those whose iniquities are
9: 5 who is over all, God **b** forever.
Gal 3: 8 "All the Gentiles shall be **b** in you."
Eph 1: 3 who has **b** us in Christ
1Ti 6:15 he who is the **b** and only Sovereign,
Tit 2:13 the **b** hope and the manifestation of
Heb 7: 7 the inferior is **b** by the superior.
Jas 1:12 **B** is anyone who endures temptation
5:11 call **b** those who showed endurance.
1Pe 3:14 for doing what is right, you are **b**,
4:14 for the name of Christ, you are **b**,
Rev 1: 3 **B** is the one who reads aloud the
1: 3 and **b** are those who hear
14:13 **B** are the dead who from now on
16:15 **B** is the one who stays awake and
19: 9 **B** are those who are invited to
20: 6 **B** and holy are those who share in
22: 7 **B** is the one who keeps the words of
22:14 **B** are those who wash their robes,
Tob 3:11 she prayed and said, "**B** are you,
8:15 So they **b** the God of heaven, and
Jdt 13:17 one accord, "**B** are you our God,
Aza 1: 3 "**B** are you, O Lord, God of our
Sus 1:60 raised a great shout and **b** God,

BLESSED [BE/BY] THE *LORD Ps
68:19; Lk 1:68; Tob 14:15; Jdt 13:18; Aza 1:3,
29; 2Mc 10:38; 15:34; 1Es 8:25; 9:46

BLESSED [BE/BY] THE †LORD Ge
9:26; 24:27, 31, 48; 26:29; Ex 18:10; Dt 33:13;
Jdg 17:2; Ru 3:10; 4:14; 1Sa 15:13; 23:21;
25:32, 39; 2Sa 2:5; 18:28; 1Ki 1:48; 5:7; 8:15,
56; 10:9; 1Ch 16:36; 29:10, 10, 20; 2Ch 2:12;
6:4; 9:8; 20:26; 31:8; Ezr 7:27; Ne 8:6; Ps
28:6; 31:21; 37:22; 41:13; 72:18; 89:52;
106:48; 115:15; 119:12; 124:6; 135:21; 144:1;
Isa 65:23; Zec 11:5

BLESSED ... GOD Ge 14:20; Jos 22:33; Ps
66:20; 68:35; Da 2:19; 3:28; 2Co 1:3; Eph 1:3;
1Ti 1:11; 1Pe 1:3; Tob 8:15; 9:6; 11:14; 13:1,
17; Aza 1:28; Sus 1:60; 1Es 4:40

GOD BLESSED Ge 1:22, 28; 2:3; 9:1;
25:11; Dt 33:1; 1Ch 26:5; Ro 9:5; 14:22

THE †LORD BLESSED Ge 26:12; 39:5;
Ex 20:11; Jdg 13:24; 2Sa 6:11; 1Ch 13:14; Job
42:12

BLESSEDNESS → BLESS
Ro 4: 6 So also David speaks of the **b** of

BLESSES → BLESS
Ge 27:29 blessed be everyone who **b** you!"
Nu 24: 9 Blessed is everyone who **b** you,
Ps 147:13 he **b** your children within you.
Pr 3:33 but he **b** the abode of the righteous.
27:14 Whoever **b** a neighbor with a loud

BLESSING → BLESS
Ge 12: 2 so that you will be a **b**.
22:18 the nations of the earth gain **b** for
26: 4 the nations of the earth shall gain **b**
27:36 now he has taken away my **b**."
49:28 **b** each one of them with a suitable
b.
Ex 12:32 And bring a **b** on me too!"
32:29 brought a **b** on yourselves this day."
Lev 25:21 order my **b** for you in the sixth year,
Dt 11:26 before you today a **b** and a curse:
23: 5 your God turned the curse into a **b**
27:12 Gerizim for the **b** of the people:
28: 8 LORD will command the **b** upon you
33: 1 This is the **b** with which Moses,

2Sa 7:29 **b** shall the house of your servant
Ne 13: 2 our God turned the curse into a **b**.
Ps   3: 8 may your **b** be on your people!
    24: 5 They will receive **b** from the LORD,
Pr 10:22 The **b** of the LORD makes rich,
Isa 44: 3 and my **b** on your offspring.
Eze 34:26 they shall be showers of **b**.
Joel 2:14 and leave a **b** behind him,
Zec 8:13 I will save you and you shall be a **b**.
Mal 3:10 for you an overflowing **b**.
Mk 14:22 of bread, and after **b** it he broke it,
Lk 24:51 While he was **b** them, he withdrew
Ro 15:29 in the fullness of the **b** of Christ.
1Co 10:16 The cup of **b** that we bless,
  14:16 if you say a **b** with the spirit,
Gal 3:14 in Christ Jesus the **b** of Abraham
Eph 1: 3 every spiritual **b** in the heavenly
Heb 6: 7 cultivated, receives a **b** from God.
  12:17 when he wanted to inherit the **b**,
Jas 3:10 same mouth come **b** and cursing.
1Pe 3: 9 but, on the contrary, repay with a **b**.
Rev 5:12 might and honor and glory and **b**!"
   7:12 **B** and glory and wisdom and
Tob 8:15 you, O God, with every pure **b**;
Sir 11:22 The **b** of the Lord is the reward of
  26: 3 A good wife is a great **b**;
  34:20 he gives health and life and **b**.
  40:27 The fear of the Lord is like a
      garden of **b**,
Aza 1: 1 hymns to God and **b** the Lord.

BLESSINGS → BLESS

Ge 48:20 "By you Israel will invoke **b**,
  49:26 The **b** of your father are stronger
Dt 21: 5 and to pronounce **b** in the name of
  28: 2 all these **b** shall come upon you
  30: 1 the **b** and the curses that I have set
Jos 8:34 the words of the law, **b** and curses,
1Ch 23:13 pronounce **b** in his name forever;
Ps 21: 6 You bestow on him **b** forever;
 144:15 Happy are the people to whom such
      b fall;
Pr 10: 6 **B** are on the head of the righteous,
  28:20 The faithful will abound with **b**,
Mal 2: 2 and I will curse your **b**;
Ro 15:27 come to share in their spiritual **b**,

BLEW → BLOW

Ex 15:10 You **b** with your wind, the sea
Jos 6: 9 while the trumpets **b** continually.
Jdg 7:22 they **b** the three hundred trumpets,
Hag 1: 9 you brought it home, I **b** it away.
Mt 7:25 the winds **b** and beat on that house,
Rev 8: 7 The first angel **b** his trumpet,
Tob 11:11 firmly, he **b** into his eyes,

BLIGHT → BLIGHTED

Dt 28:22 fiery heat and drought, and with **b**
1Ki 8:37 in the land, if there is plague, **b**,
Am 4: 9 I struck you with **b** and mildew;
Hag 2:17 the products of your toil with **b** and

BLIGHTED → BLIGHT

Ge 41: 6 seven ears, thin and **b** by the east

BLIND → BLINDED, BLINDFOLD, BLINDFOLDED, BLINDNESS, BLINDS

Ex 4:11 mute or deaf, seeing or **b**?
Lev 19:14 put a stumbling block before the **b**;
  21:18 one who is **b** or lame,
  22:22 Anything **b**, or injured, or maimed,
Dt 27:18 misleads a **b** person on the road."
2Sa 5: 8 and the lame shall not come into
Job 29:15 I was eyes to the **b**, and feet to the
Ps 146: 8 the LORD opens the eyes of the **b**.
Isa 35: 5 the eyes of the **b** shall be opened,
  42: 7 the eyes that are **b**,
  42:19 Who is **b** but my servant,
  56:10 Israel's sentinels are **b**, they are all
Mal 1: 8 you offer **b** animals in sacrifice,
Mt 9:27 two **b** men followed him, crying
  11: 5 **b** receive their sight, the lame walk,
  15:14 they are **b** guides of the **b**.

  23:16 "Woe to you, **b** guides, who say,
Mk 10:46 son of Timaeus, a **b** beggar,
Lk 6:39 "Can a **b** person guide a **b** person?
  14:13 the crippled, the lame, and the **b**.
Jn 9: 1 he saw a man **b** from birth.
  9:25 though I was **b**, now I see."
Ro 2:19 sure that you are a guide to the **b**,
2Pe 1: 9 **b**, and is forgetful of the cleansing
Rev 3:17 pitiable, poor, **b**, and naked.
Tob 2:10 until I became completely **b**.
LtJ 6:37 They cannot restore sight to the **b**;

BLINDED → BLIND

Zec 11:17 withered, his right eye utterly **b**!
Jn 12:40 "He has **b** their eyes and hardened
2Co 4: 4 has **b** the minds of the unbelievers,

BLINDFOLD* → BLIND

Mk 14:65 began to spit on him, to **b** him,

BLINDFOLDED* → BLIND

Lk 22:64 also **b** him and kept asking him,

BLINDNESS → BLIND

Ge 19:11 And they struck with **b** the men
Dt 28:28 will afflict you with madness, **b**,
2Ki 6:18 "Strike this people, please, with **b**."
Zec 12: 4 every horse of the peoples with **b**.
1Jn 2:11 the darkness has brought on **b**.

BLINDS* → BLIND

Ex 23: 8 for a bribe **b** the officials,
Dt 16:19 for a bribe **b** the eyes of the wise

BLOCK → BLOCKS

Lev 19:14 put a stumbling **b** before the blind;
Isa 44:19 I fall down before a **b** of wood?"
Eze 3:20 and I lay a stumbling **b** before them,
  14: 7 their iniquity as a stumbling **b**
Mt 16:23 You are a stumbling **b** to me;
Ro 11: 9 a stumbling **b** and a retribution for
  14:13 stumbling **b** or hindrance in the way
1Co 1:23 stumbling **b** to Jews and foolishness
  8: 9 become a stumbling **b** to the weak.
Rev 2:14 a stumbling **b** before the people of
Sir 31: 7 It is a stumbling **b** to those who are

BLOCKS → BLOCK

Jer 6:21 before this people stumbling **b**
Mt 18: 7 the world because of stumbling **b**!

BLOOD → BLOODGUILT, BLOODSHED, BLOODTHIRSTY, BLOODY

Ge 4:10 your brother's **b** is crying out to me
  9: 6 sheds the **b** of a human, by a human
      shall that person's **b** be shed;
Ex 4:25 you are a bridegroom of **b** to me!"
  7:17 and it shall be turned to **b**.
  12:13 when I see the **b**, I will pass over
  24: 8 the **b** of the covenant that the LORD
Lev 1: 5 the priests shall offer the **b**,
  3:17 you must not eat any fat or any **b**.
  17:11 it is the **b** that makes atonement.
  17:14 of every creature—its **b** is its life;
Nu 35:19 The avenger of **b** is the one who
  35:33 for **b** pollutes the land, and no
Dt 12:23 for the **b** is the life,
1Sa 14:32 and the troops ate them with the **b**.
1Ki 21:19 dogs will also lick up your **b**."
  22:38 the dogs licked up his **b**,
2Ki 9:33 some of her **b** spattered on the wall
Ps 9:12 who avenges **b** is mindful of them;
  50:13 or drink the **b** of goats?
  72:14 and precious is their **b** in his sight.
  78:44 He turned their rivers to **b**,
 106:38 and the land was polluted with **b**.
Pr 6:17 and hands that shed innocent **b**,
Isa 1:11 I do not delight in the **b** of bulls,
  9: 5 garments rolled in **b** shall be burned
  34: 6 LORD has a sword; it is sated with **b**,
  66: 3 like one who offers swine's **b**;
Eze 3:18 their **b** I will require at your hand.
  33: 4 **b** shall be upon their own heads.

Joel 2:30 **b** and fire and columns of smoke.
  2:31 to darkness, and the moon to **b**,
Zec 9:11 because of the **b** of my covenant
Mt 23:30 in shedding the **b** of the prophets.'
  26:28 for this is my **b** of the covenant,
  27: 6 since they are **b** money."
  27: 8 field has been called the Field of **B**
  27:24 "I am innocent of this man's **b**;
Mk 14:24 "This is my **b** of the covenant,
Lk 11:51 the **b** of Abel to the **b** of Zechariah,
  22:20 you is the new covenant in my **b**.
  22:44 sweat became like great drops of **b**
Jn 1:13 who were born, not of **b**
  6:53 of the Son of Man and drink his **b**,
  19:34 and at once **b** and water came out.
Ac 1:19 Hakeldama, that is, Field of **B**.)
  2:20 to darkness and the moon to **b**,
  15:20 has been strangled and from **b**.
  18: 6 "Your **b** be on your own heads!
  20:26 that I am not responsible for the **b**
Ro 3:25 as a sacrifice of atonement by his **b**,
  5: 9 that we have been justified by his **b**,
1Co 10:16 is it not a sharing in the **b** of Christ?
  11:25 cup is the new covenant in my **b**.
Eph 1: 7 we have redemption through his **b**,
  2:13 near by the **b** of Christ.
  6:12 not against enemies of **b** and flesh,
Col 1:20 peace through the **b** of his cross.
Heb 9: 7 without taking the **b** that he offers
  9:12 the **b** of goats and calves, but with
      his own **b**,
  9:20 "This is the **b** of the covenant that
  9:22 without the shedding of **b** there is
      no forgiveness
  10: 4 it is impossible for the **b** of bulls
  12: 4 to the point of shedding your **b**.
  12:24 to the sprinkled **b** that speaks a
      better word than the **b** of Abel.
  13:12 to sanctify the people by his own **b**.
  13:20 by the **b** of the eternal covenant,
1Pe 1:19 but with the precious **b** of Christ,
1Jn 1: 7 the **b** of Jesus his Son cleanses us
  5: 6 the one who came by water and **b**,
  5: 8 the Spirit and the water and the **b**,
Rev 1: 5 and freed us from our sins by his **b**,
  5: 9 by your **b** you ransomed for God
  6:10 and avenge our **b** on the inhabitants
  6:12 the full moon became like **b**,
  7:14 white in the **b** of the Lamb.
  8: 9 A third of the sea became **b**,
  11: 6 over the waters to turn them into **b**,
  12:11 conquered him by the **b** of the Lamb
  14:20 and **b** flowed from the wine press,
  16: 4 water, and they became **b**.
  16: 6 because they shed the **b** of saints
  17: 6 was drunk with the **b** of the saints
  18:24 in you was found the **b** of prophets
  19:13 He is clothed in a robe dipped in **b**,
Sir 28:11 and a hasty dispute sheds **b**.
  34:27 an employee of wages is to shed **b**.
1Mc 1:24 He shed much **b**, and spoke with

BLOODGUILT → BLOOD, GUILT

Dt 21: 8 Then they will be absolved of **b**.
1Sa 25:26 the LORD has restrained you from **b**

BLOODSHED → BLOOD, SHED

Lev 17: 4 he shall be held guilty of **b**;
Ps 51:14 Deliver me from **b**, O God,
Isa 5: 7 he expected justice, but saw **b**;
Jer 48:10 who keeps back the sword from **b**.
Eze 9: 9 the land is full of **b** and the city full
  35: 6 you did not hate **b**, **b** shall pursue
Hos 4: 2 and adultery break out; **b** follows **b**.
Hab 2: 8 because of human **b**, and violence
  2:12 Alas for you who build a town by **b**,
  2:17 because of human **b** and violence to

BLOODTHIRSTY → BLOOD

Ps 5: 6 the LORD abhors the **b** and deceitful.
  26: 9 nor my life with the **b**,
  55:23 the **b** and treacherous shall not live

59: 2 who work evil; from the **b** save me.
139:19 O God, and that that the **b** would depart
Pr 29:10 The **b** hate the blameless,

BLOODY → BLOOD

Eze 7:23 For the land is full of **b** crimes!
24: 9 Woe to the **b** city! I will even make

BLOSSOM → BLOSSOMS

Isa 27: 6 Israel shall **b** and put forth shoots,
35: 1 the desert shall rejoice and **b**;
Hos 14: 5 he shall **b** like the lily,
Hab 3:17 fig tree does not **b**, and no fruit is on

BLOSSOMS → BLOSSOM

Ex 25:33 three cups shaped like almond **b**,
Nu 17: 8 It put forth buds, produced **b**,

BLOT → BLOTS, BLOTTED

Ge 6: 7 "I will **b** out from the earth
Ex 17:14 **b** out the remembrance of Amalek
32:32 **b** me out of the book that you have
Dt 9:14 that I may destroy them and **b** out
Ps 51: 1 mercy **b** out my transgressions.
Jer 18:23 not **b** out their sins from your sight.
Rev 3: 5 not **b** your name out of the book of

BLOTS· → BLOT

Isa 43:25 He who **b** out your transgressions
2Pe 2:13 They are **b** and blemishes,

BLOTTED → BLOT

Ge 7:23 He **b** out every living thing that was
Dt 25: 6 his name may not be **b** out of Israel.
Jdg 21:17 a tribe may not be **b** out from Israel.
Ps 9: 5 you have **b** out their name forever
Isa 6: 7 has departed and your sin is **b** out."

BLOW → BLEW, BLOWING, BLOWN, BLOWS

Ge 8: 1 God made a wind **b** over the earth,
Nu 10: 5 When you **b** an alarm, the camps on
29: 1 It is a day for you to **b** the trumpets,
Ps 147:18 he makes his wind **b**,
SS 4:16 **B** upon my garden that its fragrance
Jer 14:17 is struck down with a crushing **b**,
Eze 33: 6 coming and does not **b** the trumpet,
Joel 2: 1 **B** the trumpet in Zion; sound the
Rev 7: 1 that no wind could **b** on earth or sea
8: 6 the seven trumpets made ready to **b**
Tob 6: 9 **b** upon them, upon the white films,

BLOWING → BLOW

Jos 6:13 **b** the trumpets continually.
2Ch 23:13 of the land rejoicing and **b** trumpets,
Lk 12:55 you see the south wind **b**, you say,

BLOWN → BLOW

Eph 4:14 **b** about by every wind of doctrine,

BLOWS → BLOW

2Sa 7:14 with **b** inflicted by human beings.
Ps 39:10 I am worn down by the **b** of your
Pr 20:30 **B** that wound cleanse away evil;
Isa 40: 7 the breath of the LORD **b** upon it;
Jn 3: 8 The wind **b** where it chooses,

BLUE

Ex 25: 4 **b**, purple, and crimson yarns
26:31 You shall make a curtain of **b**,
28:31 make the robe of the ephod all of **b**.
Nu 4: 6 and spread over that a cloth all of **b**,
2Ch 3:14 Solomon made the curtain of **b** and

BLUSH·

Isa 1:29 you shall **b** for the gardens that you
Jer 6:15 they did not know how to **b**.
8:12 they did not know how to **b**.

BOANERGES·

Mk 3:17 name **B**, that is, Sons of Thunder);

BOARD → BOARDS

Jnh 1: 3 so he paid his fare and went on **b**,

BOARDS → BOARD

Ex 27: 8 You shall make it hollow, with **b**.
1Ki 6:15 of the house on the inside with **b**
SS 8: 9 we will enclose her with **b** of cedar.

BOAST → BOASTED, BOASTERS, BOASTFUL, BOASTING, BOASTS

Ps 34: 2 My soul makes its **b** in the LORD;
52: 1 Why do you **b**, O mighty one,
75: 4 "Do not **b**," and to the wicked,
97: 7 who make their **b** in worthless idols;
Pr 27: 1 Do not **b** about tomorrow,
Jer 9:24 but let those who **b** **b** in this,
Ro 2:23 You that **b** in the law,
5: 3 but we also **b** in our sufferings,
11:18 do not **b** over the branches.
1Co 1:31 the one who boasts, **b** in the Lord."
4: 7 do you **b** as if it were not a gift?
13: 3 hand over my body so that I may **b**,
2Co 1:14 even as you are our **b**.
5:12 an opportunity to **b** about us,
10: 8 **b** a little too much of our authority,
10:17 the one who boasts, **b** in the Lord."
11:30 If I must **b**, I will **b** of the things
that show my weakness.
Gal 6:14 never **b** of anything except the cross
Eph 2: 9 of works, so that no one may **b**.
Php 2:16 that I can **b** on the day of Christ
Jas 1: 9 Let the believer who is lowly **b** in
Sir 25: 6 and their **b** is the fear of the Lord.

BOASTED → BOAST

Ps 44: 8 In God we have **b** continually,

BOASTERS· → BOAST

2Co 11:13 For such **b** are false apostles,
2Ti 3: 2 **b**, arrogant, abusive, disobedient to

BOASTFUL → BOAST

Ps 5: 5 The **b** will not stand before your
75: 4 I say to the **b**, "Do not boast,"
Ro 1:30 **b**, inventors of evil, rebellious
1Co 13: 4 love is not envious or **b** or arrogant
Jas 3:14 do not be **b** and false to the truth.

BOASTING → BOAST

1Co 5: 6 Your **b** is not a good thing.
1Th 2:19 or crown of **b** before our Lord Jesus
Jas 4:16 in your arrogance; all such **b** is evil.

BOASTS → BOAST

Pr 20:14 then goes away and **b**.
25:14 who **b** of a gift never given.
1Co 1:31 the one who **b**, boast in the Lord."
2Co 10:17 the one who **b**, boast in the Lord."
Jas 3: 5 yet it **b** of great exploits.

BOAT → BOATS

Mt 4:21 in the **b** with their father Zebedee,
8:23 he got into the **b**, his disciples
13: 2 around him that he got into a **b** and
14:13 he withdrew from there in a **b** to a
14:29 So Peter got out of the **b**,
Lk 5: 3 and taught the crowds from the **b**.
8:23 and the **b** was filling with water,
Jn 21: 6 the net to the right side of the **b**,
Sir 33: 2 is like a **b** in a storm.

BOATS → BOAT

Lk 5: 7 And they came and filled both **b**,

BOAZ

Wealthy Bethlehemite who showed favor to Ruth (Ru 2), married her (Ru 4). Ancestor of David (Ru 4:18-22; 1Ch 2:12-15), Jesus (Mt 1:5-16; Lk 3:23-32).

BODIES → BODY

Nu 14:29 your dead **b** shall fall in this very
1Ch 10:12 body of Saul and the **b** of his sons,
Isa 66:14 your **b** shall flourish like the grass;
Da 3:27 had not had any power over the **b**
Mt 27:52 many **b** of the saints who had fallen
Ro 1:24 to the degrading of their **b** among

8:23 adoption, the redemption of our **b**,
12: 1 present your **b** as a living sacrifice,
1Co 6:15 that your **b** are members of Christ?
Eph 5:28 as they do their own **b**.
Heb 3:17 whose **b** fell in the wilderness?
10:22 and our **b** washed with pure water.
Rev 11: 8 their dead **b** will lie in the street of

BODILY → BODY

Lk 3:22 upon him in **b** form like a dove.
Col 2: 9 in him the whole fullness of deity
dwells **b**,

BODY → BODIES, BODILY

2Sa 7:12 who shall come forth from your **b**,
Ps 16: 9 my **b** also rests secure.
132:11 of your **b** I will set on your throne.
Pr 15:30 and good news refreshes the **b**.
Eze 1:23 had two wings covering its **b**.
Mic 6: 7 fruit of my **b** for the sin of my soul?
Mt 6:22 "The eye is the lamp of the **b**.
10:28 Do not fear those who kill the **b** but
26:26 and said, "Take, eat; this is my **b**."
27:58 and asked for the **b** of Jesus;
Mk 14:22 and said, "Take; this is my **b**."
Lk 11:34 Your eye is the lamp of your **b**.
12: 4 do not fear those who kill the **b**,
12:23 and the **b** more than clothing.
22:19 my **b**, which is given for you.
24: 3 they did not find the **b**.
Jn 2:21 speaking of the temple of his **b**.
Ro 6: 6 that the **b** of sin might be destroyed,
7:24 will rescue me from this **b** of death?
8:10 though the **b** is dead because of sin,
12: 4 as in one **b** we have many members,
1Co 5: 3 absent in **b**, I am present in spirit;
6:13 **b** is meant not for fornication but
6:18 but the fornicator sins against the **b**
6:19 your **b** is a temple of the Holy Spirit
6:20 therefore glorify God in your **b**.
7: 4 the wife does not have authority
over her own **b**,
7: 4 husband does not have authority
over his own **b**,
9:27 but I punish my **b** and enslave it,
10:16 is it not a sharing in the **b** of Christ?
11:24 "This is my **b** that is for you.
12:12 though many, are one **b**,
12:13 we were all baptized into one **b**—
12:15 I do not belong to the **b**,"
15:44 It is sown a physical **b**, it is raised a
spiritual **b**.
2Co 4:10 carrying in the **b** the death of Jesus,
5: 8 be away from the **b** and at home
with the Lord.
12: 2 whether in the **b** or out of the **b** I do
not know;
Gal 6:17 the marks of Jesus branded on my **b**.
Eph 1:23 which is his **b**, the fullness of him
2:16 both groups to God in one **b**
4: 4 There is one **b** and one Spirit,
4:12 for building up the **b** of Christ,
5:30 because we are members of his **b**.
Php 1:20 be exalted now as always in my **b**,
3:21 transform the **b** of our humiliation
3:21 conformed to the **b** of his glory,
Col 1:18 He is the head of the **b**, the church;
1:24 afflictions for the sake of his **b**,
2: 5 for though I am absent in **b**,
1Th 4: 4 to control your own **b** in holiness
5:23 your spirit and soul and **b** be kept
Heb 10: 5 but a **b** you have prepared for me;
Jas 2:26 as the **b** without the spirit is dead,
1Pe 2:24 bore our sins in his **b** on the cross,
Jude 1: 9 and disputed about the **b** of Moses,

ONE BODY Jdg 20:1; Ro 12:4, 5; 1Co 6:16; 10:17; 12:12, 13, 20; Eph 2:16; 4:4; Col 3:15

WHOLE BODY Lev 15:16; Nu 8:7; Mt 5:29, 30; 6:22, 23; Lk 11:34, 36; Jn 7:23; Ac 5:21; 1Co 12:17, 17; Eph 4:16; Col 2:19; Jas 3:2, 6; 2Mc 15:12; 2Es 12:3

BOIL → BOILED, BOILING, BOILS

Ex 23:19 not **b** a kid in its mother's milk.
Isa 38:21 apply it to the **b**, so that he may

BOILED → BOIL

La   4:10 women have **b** their own children;

BOILING → BOIL

Jer   1:13 I said, "I see a **b** pot, tilted away

BOILS → BOIL

Ex   9: 9 shall cause festering **b** on humans
Dt 28:27 will afflict you with the **b** of Egypt,

BOLD → BOLDLY, BOLDNESS

Dt 31: 6 Be strong and **b;** have no fear
Pr 21:29 The wicked put on a **b** face,
     28: 1 but the righteous are as **b** as a lion.
2Co 10: 1 but **b** toward you when I am away!
Phm 1: 8 **b** enough in Christ to command you

BOLDLY → BOLD

Ex 14: 8 the Israelites, who were going out **b.**
Ac   9:28 speaking **b** in the name of the Lord.
     14: 3 speaking **b** for the Lord,

BOLDNESS → BOLD

Ac   4:13 they saw the **b** of Peter and John
     4:29 to speak your word with all **b,**
    28:31 the Lord Jesus Christ with all **b** and
Eph 3:12 whom we have access to God in **b**
Php 1:14 to speak the word with greater **b** and
Heb 4:16 approach the throne of grace with **b,**
1Jn 4:17 may have **b** on the day of judgment,

BOND → BONDAGE, BONDS

Eph 4: 3 unity of the Spirit in the **b** of peace.

BONDAGE → BOND

Ro   8:21 will be set free from its **b** to decay

BONDS → BOND

Ps   2: 3 "Let us burst their **b** asunder,
    107:14 and broke their **b** asunder.
    116:16 You have loosed my **b.**
Isa 52: 2 loose the **b** from your neck,
     58: 6 to loose the **b** of injustice,

BONE → BONES, JAWBONE

Ge   2:23 "This at last is **b** of my bones and
Eze 37: 7 the bones came together, **b** to its **b.**

BONES → BONE

Ge 50:25 you shall carry up my **b** from here."
Ex 12:46 and you shall not break any of its **b.**
     13:19 took with him the **b** of Joseph
Jos 24:32 **b** of Joseph, which the Israelites
2Ki 13:21 as the man touched the **b** of Elisha,
Ps 22:14 and all my **b** are out of joint;
     22:17 I can count all my **b.**
     34:20 He keeps all their **b;** not one of
Pr 14:30 but passion makes the **b** rot.
     25:15 and a soft tongue can break **b.**
Jer 20: 9 like a burning fire shut up in my **b;**
Eze 37: 4 O dry **b,** hear the word of the LORD.
Mt 23:27 inside they are full of the **b** of the
Jn 19:36 "None of his **b** shall be broken."
Sir 28:17 a blow of the tongue crushes the **b.**

BOOK → BOOKS

Ex 17:14 "Write this as a reminder in a **b** and
     24: 7 Then he took the **b** of the covenant,
     32:33 against me I will blot out of my **b.**
Dt 29:20 All the curses written in this **b** will
     31:24 writing down in a **b** the words of
Jos   1: 8 This **b** of the law shall not depart
     10:13 this not written in the **B** of Jashar?
     23: 6 and do all that is written in the **b** of
2Ki 22: 8 "I have found the **b** of the law in
Ne   8: 8 So they read from the **b,** from the
Ps 69:28 be blotted out of the **b** of the living;
Isa 34:16 and read from the **b** of the LORD:
Da 12: 1 who is found written in the **b.**
Mk 12:26 have you not read in the **b** of Moses,

Jn 20:30 which are not written in this **b.**
Ac   1: 1 In the first **b,** Theophilus,
Php 4: 3 whose names are in the **b** of life.
Heb 10: 7 scroll of the **b** it is written of me)."
Rev 1:11 "Write in a **b** what you see and
     3: 5 blot your name out of the **b** of life;
     13: 8 in the **b** of life of the Lamb that was
     17: 8 in the **b** of life from the foundation
     20:12 another **b** was opened, the **b** of life.
     20:15 not found written in the **b** of life
     21:27 who are written in the Lamb's **b**
     22: 7 words of the prophecy of this **b."**
     22:18 the words of the prophecy of this **b:**
1Mc 1:57 possessing the **b** of the covenant,
2Es 12:37 things that you have seen in a **b,**

BOOK OF LIFE Php 4:3; Rev 3:5; 13:8;
  17:8; 20:12, 15; 21:27

BOOK OF MOSES 2Ch 25:4; 35:12; Ezr
  6:18; Ne 13:1; Mk 12:26; Tob 6:13; 7:11, 12;
  1Es 1:11; 5:49; 7:6, 9

BOOK OF THE ANNALS 1Ki 14:19, 29;
  15:7, 23, 31; 16:5, 14, 20, 27; 22:39, 45; 2Ki
  1:18; 8:23; 10:34; 12:19; 13:8, 12; 14:15, 18,
  28; 15:6, 11, 15, 21, 26, 31, 36; 16:19; 20:20;
  21:17, 25; 23:28; 24:5; Ne 12:23; Est 2:23

BOOK OF THE COVENANT Ex 24:7;
  2Ki 23:2, 21; 2Ch 34:30; Sir 24:23; 1Mc 1:57

BOOK OF THE LAW Dt 28:61; 29:21;
  30:10; 31:26; Jos 1:8; 8:31, 34; 23:6; 24:26;
  2Ki 14:6; 22:8, 11; 2Ch 17:9; 34:14, 15; Ne
  8:1, 3, 18; 9:3; Gal 3:10; 1Mc 3:48; 1Es 9:45

BOOKS → BOOK

Ecc 12:12 Of making many **b** there is no end,
Da   7:10 in judgment, and the **b** were opened.
Jn 21:25 world itself could not contain the **b**
Rev 20:12 the throne, and **b** were opened.
1Mc 1:56 The **b** of the law that they found
2Es 14:44 ninety-four **b** were written.

BOOTH → BOOTHS

Am   9:11 I will raise up the **b** of David that is
Jnh 4: 5 and made a **b** for himself there.
Lk   5:27 named Levi, sitting at the tax **b;**

BOOTHS → BOOTH

Lev 23:34 the festival of **b** to the LORD.
Dt 16:13 the festival of **b** for seven days,
2Ch 8:13 of weeks, and the festival of **b.**
Ezr 3: 4 kept the festival of **b,** as prescribed,
Ne   8:14 Israel should live in **b** during
Zec 14:16 and to keep the festival of **b.**
Jn   7: 2 the Jewish festival of **B** was near.
1Mc 10:21 at the festival of **b,**
2Mc 1: 9 see that you keep the festival of **b** in

FESTIVAL OF BOOTHS Lev 23:34; Dt
  16:13, 16; 31:10; 2Ch 8:13; Ezr 3:4; Zec
  14:16, 18, 19; Jn 7:2; 1Mc 10:21; 2Mc 1:9, 18;
  10:6, 6; 1Es 5:51

BOOTY

Nu 14: 3 and our little ones will become **b;**
     14:31 who you said would become **b,**
Dt   1:39 you thought would become **b,**
Pr   1:13 we shall fill our houses with **b.**
Hab 2: 7 Then you will be **b** for them.

BORDER → BORDERS

Ex 16:35 until they came to the **b** of the land
2Ki 14:25 He restored the **b** of Israel from
2Ch 9:26 and to the **b** of Egypt.
     26: 8 fame spread even to the **b** of Egypt,
Eze 11:10 I will judge you at the **b** of Israel.

BORDERS → BORDER

Ex 23:31 I will set your **b** from the Red Sea
Ps 147:14 He grants peace within your **b;**
Mal 1: 5 "Great is the LORD beyond the **b** of

BORE → BEAR

Ge   6: 4 of humans, who **b** children to them.
     16: 1 Abram's wife, **b** him no children.

     16:15 Hagar **b** Abram a son;
Ex 19: 4 how I **b** you on eagles' wings and
Nu 17: 8 blossoms, and **b** ripe almonds.
Jos   3:17 who **b** the ark of the covenant of
Isa 53:12 yet he **b** the sin of many,
Eze 3:14 The spirit lifted me up and **b** me
Mt   8:17 our infirmities and **b** our diseases."
1Pe 2:24 He himself **b** our sins in his body

BORN → BEAR

Ge 17:17 "Can a child be **b** to a man who is a
Ex   1:22 "Every boy that is **b** to the Hebrews
Job 14: 1 **b** of woman, few of days and full of
Pr 17:17 kinsfolk are **b** to share adversity,
Ecc 3: 2 a time to be **b,** and a time to die;
Isa   9: 6 For a child has been **b** for us,
     49: 1 The LORD called me before I was **b,**
     66: 8 Shall a land be **b** in one day?
Jer   1: 5 before you were **b** I consecrated you
Mt   1:16 of whom Jesus was **b,** who is called
     2: 1 after Jesus was **b** in Bethlehem of
Mk 14:21 for that one not to have been **b."**
Lk   1:35 the child to be **b** will be holy;
     2:11 is **b** this day in the city of David
     7:28 I tell you, among those **b** of women
Jn   1:13 who were **b,** not of blood or of the
     3: 3 without being **b** from above."
     3: 5 without being **b** of water and Spirit.
     3: 7 'You must be **b** from above.'
     3: 8 everyone who is **b** of the Spirit."
     9: 3 he was **b** blind so that God's works
     18:37 For this I was **b,** and for this I came
Ro   9:11 Even before they had been **b**
1Co 15: 8 Last of all, as to one untimely **b,**
Gal 4: 4 **b** of a woman, **b** under the law,
Php 2: 7 being **b** in human likeness.
1Pe 1:23 You have been **b** anew,
1Jn 3: 9 who have been **b** of God do not sin,
     3: 9 because they have been **b** of God.
     4: 7 everyone who loves is **b** of God
     5: 1 is the Christ has been **b** of God,
     5: 4 is **b** of God conquers the world.
     5:18 those who are **b** of God do not sin,
     5:18 the one who was **b** of God protects
Rev 12: 4 devour her child as soon as it was **b.**

BORNE → BEAR

Ge 21: 7 I have **b** him a son in his old age."
Ps 69: 7 for your sake that I have **b** reproach,
Isa 53: 4 he has **b** our infirmities

BORROW* → BORROWER

Dt 15: 6 but you will not **b;**
     28:12 to many nations, but you will not **b.**
2Ki 4: 3 **b** vessels from all your neighbors,
Ne   5: 4 to **b** money on our fields and
Ps 37:21 The wicked **b,** and do not pay back,
Mt   5:42 anyone who wants to **b** from you.

BORROWER* → BORROW

Pr 22: 7 and the **b** is the slave of the lender.
Isa 24: 2 as with the lender, so with the **b;**
Sir 29: 6 the **b** has robbed the other of his

BOSOM

Ru   4:16 took the child and laid him in her **b,**
1Ki 1: 2 let her lie in your **b,**
Ps 41: 9 Even my **b** friend in whom I trusted,
Pr   6:27 Can fire be carried in the **b** without

BOTHER* → BOTHERED, BOTHERING

Ru   2: 9 ordered the young men not to **b** you.
Lk 11: 7 answers from within, 'Do not **b** me;

BOTHERED* → BOTHER

Ru   2:22 you might be **b** in another field."

BOTHERING* → BOTHER

Lk 18: 5 yet because this widow keeps **b** me,

BOTTLE*

Ps 33: 7 the waters of the sea as in a **b;**
     56: 8 put my tears in your **b.**

BOTTOM

Dt 28:13 be only at the top, and not at the **b**—
Am 9: 3 from my sight at the **b** of the sea,
Mk 15:38 was torn in two, from top to **b**.

BOTTOMLESS

Rev 9: 1 the key to the shaft of the **b** pit;
11: 7 beast that comes up from the **b** pit
17: 8 from the **b** pit and go to destruction.
20: 1 in his hand the key to the **b** pit and

BOUGEAN

AdE 9:10 the **B**, the enemy of the Jews—

BOUGH → BOUGHS

Ge 49:22 Joseph is a fruitful **b**, a fruitful **b** by

BOUGHS → BOUGH

Lev 23:40 **b** of leafy trees, and willows of the
Eze 31: 6 of the air made their nests in its **b**;

BOUGHT → BUY

Ge 33:19 he for one hundred pieces of
50:13 Abraham **b** as a burial site from
2Sa 24:24 So David **b** the threshing floor and
Ne 5: 8 we have **b** back our Jewish kindred
Mt 13:46 and sold all that he had and **b** it.
1Co 6:20 For you were **b** with a price;
7:23 You were **b** with a price;
2Pe 2: 1 even deny the Master who **b** them—

BOUND → BIND, BOUNDARY

Ge 22: 9 He **b** his son Isaac, and laid him on
Nu 30: 4 pledge by which she has **b** herself,
Jdg 16:21 and **b** him with bronze shackles;
1Sa 18: 1 Jonathan was **b** to the soul of David,
2Ki 25: 7 they **b** him in fetters and took him
Ps 122: 3 as a city that is **b** firmly together.
Pr 22:15 Folly is **b** up in the heart of a boy,
Jer 39: 7 and **b** him in fetters to take him to
40: 1 he took him **b** in fetters along with
Eze 34: 4 you have not **b** up the injured,
Da 3:21 So the men were **b**, still wearing
Mt 16:19 bind on earth will be **b** in heaven,
18:18 bind on earth will be **b** in heaven,
Mk 15: 1 They **b** Jesus, led him away,
Lk 13:16 daughter of Abraham whom Satan **b**
Ro 7: 2 a married woman is **b** by the law to
1Co 7:15 a case the brother or sister is not **b**.
7:39 is as long as her husband lives.
Rev 9:14 "Release the four angels who are **b**
20: 2 and **b** him for a thousand years,

BOUNDARIES → BOUNDARY

Nu 34:12 This shall be your land with its **b**
Dt 32: 8 he fixed the **b** of the peoples
Pr 15:25 but maintains the widow's **b**.
Eze 47:13 the **b** by which you shall divide

BOUNDARY → BOUND, BOUNDARIES, BOUNDLESS, BOUNDS

Nu 34: 3 Your southern **b** shall begin from
Dt 19:14 not move your neighbor's **b** marker,
Ps 16: 6 The **b** lines have fallen for me in
104: 9 You set a **b** that they may not pass,
Jer 5:22 I placed the sand as a **b** for the sea,
Eze 47:15 This shall be the **b** of the land:

BOUNDLESS → BOUNDARY

Eph 3: 8 the news of the **b** riches of Christ,

BOUNDS → BOUNDARY

Job 14: 5 the **b** that they cannot pass,
Ps 74:17 You have fixed all the **b** of the earth
148: 6 their **b**, which cannot be passed.

BOUNTIES* → BOUNTY

Ge 49:26 the **b** of the everlasting hills;

BOUNTIFULLY* → BOUNTY

Ps 13: 6 because he has dealt **b** with me.
116: 7 for the LORD has dealt **b** with you.
119:17 Deal **b** with your servant,
142: 7 for you will deal **b** with me.

2Co 9: 6 the one who sows **b** will also reap **b**.

BOUNTY* → BOUNTIES, BOUNTIFULLY

Dt 15:14 thus giving to him some of the **b**
26:11 shall celebrate with all the **b** that
1Ki 10:13 gave her out of Solomon's royal **b**.
Est 1: 7 was lavished according to the **b** of
Ps 65:11 You crown the year with your **b**;
116:12 to the LORD for all his **b** to me?
Jer 31:14 people shall be satisfied with my **b**,
Wis 16:25 it served your all-nourishing **b**,

BOW → BOWED, BOWS, BOWSTRING, BOWSTRINGS

Ge 9:13 I have set my **b** in the clouds,
27:29 and nations **b** down to you.
49: 8 your father's sons shall **b** down
Ex 20: 5 You shall not **b** down to them or
Dt 5: 9 You shall not **b** down to them or
26:10 **b** down before the LORD your God.
Jos 23: 7 or **b** yourselves down to them,
1Sa 18: 4 his sword and his **b** and his belt.
2Sa 1:18 that The Song of the **B** be taught to
22:35 my arms can bend a **b** of bronze.
1Ki 22:34 drew his **b** and unknowingly struck
2Ki 13:15 Elisha said to him, "Take a **b** and
Est 3: 2 But Mordecai did not **b** down or
Ps 7: 7 I will **b** down toward your holy
44: 6 not in my **b** do I trust, nor can my
95: 6 O come, let us worship and **b** down,
97: 7 all gods **b** down before him.
138: 2 I **b** down toward your holy temple
Isa 2: 8 **b** down to the work of their hands,
45:23 "To me every knee shall **b**,
Eze 1:28 Like the **b** in a cloud on a rainy day,
Hos 1: 7 I will not save them by **b**, or by
Zec 9:13 For I have bent Judah as my **b**;
Ro 14:11 every knee shall **b** to me,
Eph 3:14 I **b** my knees before the Father,
Rev 6: 2 Its rider had a **b**;

BOWED → BOW

Ge 18: 2 and **b** down to the ground.
37: 7 and **b** down to my sheaf."
42: 6 and **b** themselves before him with
47:31 Israel **b** himself on the head of his
Ex 12:27 the people **b** down and worshiped.
34: 8 Moses quickly **b** his head toward
Jdg 2:12 and **b** down to them;
1Ki 19:18 all the knees that have not **b** to Baal.
Ps 18: 9 He **b** the heavens, and came down;
35:14 **b** down and in mourning.
38: 6 I am utterly **b** down and prostrate;
145:14 and raises up all who are **b** down.
146: 8 The LORD lifts up those who are **b**
Mk 5: 6 he ran and **b** down before him;
7:25 she came and **b** down at his feet.
Jn 19:30 he **b** his head and gave up his spirit.
Ro 11: 4 who have not **b** the knee to Baal."
Jdt 10: 8 She **b** down to God.
13:17 They **b** down and worshiped God,

BOWELS

Nu 5:22 that brings the curse enter your **b**
2Ch 21:15 sickness with a disease of your **b**,
Ac 1:18 the middle and all his **b** gushed out.
2Mc 9: 5 a pain in his **b**, for which there was

BOWL → BOWLS

Dt 28: 5 your basket and your kneading **b**.
28:17 your basket and your kneading **b**.
Jdg 6:38 dew from the fleece to fill a **b** with
Ecc 12: 6 and the golden **b** is broken,
SS 7: 2 Your navel is a rounded **b** that
Mt 26:23 who has dipped his hand into the **b**
Rev 16: 2 first angel went and poured his **b** on

BOWLS → BOWL

1Ki 7:41 the two **b** of the capitals that were
Ezr 1:10 gold **b**, thirty; other silver **b**, four hundred ten;
Jer 52:19 the ladles, and the **b** for libation,
Rev 5: 8 a harp and golden **b** full of incense,

16: 1 the seven **b** of the wrath of God."
21: 9 seven angels who had the seven **b**

BOWS → BOW

1Sa 2: 4 The **b** of the mighty are broken,
Ps 37:15 and their **b** shall be broken.
Isa 44:15 carved image and **b** down before it.
46: 1 Bel **b** down, Nebo stoops,

BOWSTRING* → BOW

Job 30:11 God has loosed my **b** and humbled

BOWSTRINGS → BOW, STRING

Jdg 16: 7 "If they bind me with seven fresh **b**

BOX

1Co 9:26 nor do I **b** as though beating the air;

BOY → BOYS

Ge 21:17 And God heard the voice of the **b**;
22:12 "Do not lay your hand on the **b** or
44:22 'The **b** cannot leave his father,
Ex 1:22 "Every **b** that is born to
Jdg 13: 5 for the **b** shall be a nazirite to God
1Sa 2:11 **b** remained to minister to the LORD,
2:26 the **b** Samuel continued to grow
3: 8 that the LORD was calling the **b**.
17:33 for you are just a **b**,
1Ki 3:25 "Divide the living **b** in two;
Jer 1: 7 to me, "Do not say, 'I am only a **b**';
Mt 17:18 and the **b** was cured instantly.
Lk 2:43 **b** Jesus stayed behind in Jerusalem,
Jn 6: 9 a **b** here who has five barley loaves

BOYS → BOY

Ex 1:18 and allowed the **b** to live?"
2Ki 2:24 and mauled forty-two of the **b**.
Joel 3: 3 and traded **b** for prostitutes,
1Mc 2:46 circumcised all the uncircumcised **b**

BOZRAH

Isa 34: 6 For the LORD has a sacrifice in **B**,
Jer 49:13 **B** shall become an object of horror

BRACELETS

Ge 24:22 two **b** for her arms weighing ten
Isa 3:19 the pendants, the **b**, and the scarfs;
Eze 16:11 I put **b** on your arms, a chain on
Jdt 10: 4 **b**, rings, earrings, and all her other

BRAG*

1Ki 20:11 who puts on armor should not **b** like

BRAIDED*

1Ti 2: 9 not with their hair **b**, or with gold,

BRAMBLE → BRAMBLES

Jdg 9:14 So all the trees said to the **b**,
Lk 6:44 nor are grapes picked from a **b** bush.

BRAMBLES* → BRAMBLE

SS 2: 2 As a lily among **b**, so is my love

BRANCH → BRANCHES

Nu 13:23 from there a **b** with a single cluster
Isa 4: 2 On that day the **b** of the LORD shall
11: 1 and a **b** shall grow out of his roots.
Jer 1:11 And I said, "I see a **b** of an almond
23: 5 raise up for David a righteous **B**,
33:15 righteous **B** to spring up for David;
Da 11: 7 a **b** from her roots shall rise up in
Zec 3: 8 going to bring my servant the **B**.
6:12 Here is a man whose name is **B**:
6:12 for he shall **b** out in his place,
Mal 4: 1 it will leave them neither root nor **b**.
Jn 15: 2 every **b** in me that bears no fruit.
15: 4 as the **b** cannot bear fruit by itself
15:29 a sponge full of the wine on a **b** of
1Mc 13:37 the gold crown and the palm **b**

BRANCHES → BRANCH

Ge 2:10 there it divides and becomes four **b**.
40:10 and on the vine there were three **b**.
49:22 his **b** run over the wall.
Ex 25:32 shall be six **b** going out of its sides,

Lev 23:40 **b** of palm trees, boughs of leafy
2Sa 18: 9 the mule went under the thick **b** of
Ne 8:15 "Go out to the hills and bring **b** of
Ps 80:11 it sent out its **b** to the sea,
    118:27 Bind the festal procession with **b,**
Jer 48:32 Your **b** crossed over the sea,
Eze 17: 6 Its **b** turned toward him, its roots
    19:10 and full of **b** from abundant water.
    31: 3 a cedar of Lebanon, with fair **b** and
Da 4:12 the birds of the air nested in its **b,**
Zec 4:12 "What are these two **b** of the olive
Lk 13:19 birds of the air made nests in its **b."**
Jn 12:13 So they took **b** of palm trees and
    15: 5 I am the vine, you are the **b.**
Ro 11:21 if God did not spare the natural **b,**
Rev 7: 9 in white, with palm **b** in their hands.
Sir 1:20 and her **b** are long life.
1Mc 13:51 entered it with praise and palm **b,**

BRAND*
Am 4:11 were like a **b** snatched from the fire;
Zec 3: 2 this man a **b** plucked from the fire?"

BRANDED
Gal 6:17 the marks of Jesus **b** on my body.

BRASS
Isa 48: 4 an iron sinew and your forehead **b,**

BRAWLER*
Pr 20: 1 Wine is a mocker, strong drink a **b,**

BRAZEN*
Eze 16:30 the deeds of a **b** whore;

BREACH → BREACHED, BREACHES
Jos 22:22 or in **b** of faith toward the LORD,
Jdg 21:15 the LORD had made a **b** in the tribes
2Ki 25: 4 Then a **b** was made in the city wall;
Ps 106:23 stood in the **b** before him,
    144:14 May there be no **b** in the walls,
Eze 22:30 and stand in the **b** before me

BREACHED → BREACH
Pr 25:28 Like a city **b,** without walls,

BREACHES → BREACH
Eze 13: 5 You have not gone up into the **b,**
Am 9:11 repair its **b,** and raise up its ruins,

BREAD
Ge 3:19 sweat of your face you shall eat **b**
    14:18 of Salem brought out **b** and wine
Ex 12: 8 with unleavened **b** and bitter herbs.
    12:17 observe the festival of unleavened **b**
    16: 4 "I am going to rain **b** from heaven
    23:15 observe the festival of unleavened **b**
    23:15 you shall eat unleavened **b**
    25:30 set the **b** of the Presence on the table
    34:28 he neither ate **b** nor drank water.
Lev 7:13 offering with cakes of leavened **b.**
Dt 8: 3 that one does not live by **b** alone,
    16: 3 you shall eat unleavened **b** with
        it—the **b** of affliction—
    29: 6 you have not eaten **b,** and you have
Jdg 7:13 in it a cake of barley **b** tumbled into
1Sa 21: 4 "I have no ordinary **b** at hand, only
        holy **b**—
1Ki 17: 6 ravens brought him **b** and meat in
    22:27 on reduced rations of **b** and water
2Ch 4:19 the tables for the **b** of the Presence,
Ne 9:15 you gave them **b** from heaven,
Ps 37:25 or their children begging **b.**
    41: 9 who ate of my **b,** has lifted the heel
    53: 4 who eat up my people as they eat **b,**
    78:25 Mortals ate of the **b** of angels;
    80: 5 have fed them with the **b** of tears,
Pr 6:26 a prostitute's fee is only a loaf of **b,**
    9:17 and **b** eaten in secret is pleasant."
    20:17 **B** gained by deceit is sweet,
    23: 6 Do not eat the **b** of the stingy;
    31:27 and does not eat the **b** of idleness.
Ecc 9: 7 Go, eat your **b** with enjoyment,
    11: 1 Send out your **b** upon the waters,

Isa 55: 2 money for that which is not **b,**
La 2:12 mothers, "Where is **b** and wine?"
Eze 18: 7 gives his **b** to the hungry and
Am 8:11 not a famine of **b,** or a thirst for
Ob 1: 7 who ate your **b** have set a trap for
Mt 4: 3 these stones to become loaves of **b."**
    6:11 Give us this day our daily **b.**
    15:33 to get enough **b** in the desert to feed
    16: 5 they had forgotten to bring any **b.**
    26:26 were eating, Jesus took a loaf of **b,**
Mk 2:26 and ate the **b** of the Presence,
    14:20 one who is dipping **b** into the bowl
Lk 4: 4 'One does not live by **b** alone.'"
    11: 3 Give us each day our daily **b.**
    22:19 Then he took a loaf of **b,**
    24:35 to them in the breaking of the **b.**
Jn 6:33 the **b** of God is that which comes
    6:35 Jesus said to them, "I am the **b** of
        life.
    6:41 the **b** that came down from heaven."
    6:48 I am the **b** of life.
    6:51 I am the living **b** that came down
    13:27 After he received the piece of **b,**
    21:13 Jesus came and took the **b** and gave
Ac 2:42 to the breaking of **b** and the prayers.
1Co 5: 8 the unleavened **b** of sincerity and
    10:16 The **b** that we break, is it not a
    11:23 he was betrayed took a loaf of **b,**
    11:26 For as often as you eat this **b** and
Wis 16:20 from heaven with **b** ready to eat,
Sir 10:27 plenty than the boaster who lacks **b.**
    15: 3 will feed him with the **b** of learning,
    23:17 To a fornicator all **b** is sweet;
1Mc 1:22 the table for the **b** of the Presence,
    4:51 They placed the **b** on the table and
2Es 1:19 you ate the **b** of angels.

FESTIVAL OF UNLEAVENED BREAD
Ex 12:17; 23:15; 34:18; Lev 23:6; Dt 16:16;
2Ch 8:13; 30:13, 21; 35:17; Ezr 6:22; Mk
14:1; Lk 22:1; Ac 12:3; 1Es 1:19; 7:14

UNLEAVENED BREAD Ge 19:3; Ex 12:8,
15, 17, 18, 20; 13:6, 7; 23:15, 15; 29:2, 23;
34:18, 18; Lev 8:2, 26, 26; 23:6, 6; Nu 6:15,
17; 9:11; 28:17; Dt 16:3, 8, 16; 2Ki 23:9; 1Ch
23:29; 2Ch 8:13; 30:13, 21; 35:17; Ezr 6:22;
Eze 45:21; Mt 26:17; Mk 14:1, 12; Lk 22:1, 7;
Ac 12:3; 20:6; 1Co 5:8; 1Es 1:10, 19; 7:14

BREADTH → BROAD
Ge 13:17 walk through the length and the **b**
Eph 3:18 the **b** and length and height and

BREAK → BREAKING, BREAKS, BROKEN,
BROKENHEARTED, DAYBREAK
Ex 12:46 and you shall not **b** any of its bones.
    19:21 not to **b** through to the LORD to look
    34:20 not redeem it you shall **b** its neck.
Lev 26:44 them utterly and **b** my covenant
Nu 30: 2 he shall not **b** his word;
Dt 7: 5 **b** down their altars, smash their
Jdg 2: 1 I said, 'I will never **b** my covenant
Ezr 9:14 shall we **b** your commandments
Ps 2: 9 You shall **b** them with a rod of iron,
    3: 7 you **b** the teeth of the wicked.
    10:15 **B** the arm of the wicked and
Pr 25:15 and a soft tongue can **b** bones.
Ecc 3: 3 to **b** down, and a time to build up;
Isa 42: 3 a bruised reed he will not **b,**
Eze 17:15 he **b** the covenant and yet escape?
Mt 6:19 where thieves **b** in and steal;
    12:20 not **b** a bruised reed or quench a
    15: 3 why do you **b** the commandment of
Lk 5: 6 that their nets were beginning to **b.**
Jn 19:33 they did not **b** his legs.
Ac 20: 7 we met to **b** bread, Paul was holding
Ro 2:25 but if you **b** the law,
1Co 10:16 The bread that we **b,** is it not a
Rev 5: 2 to open the scroll and **b** its seals?"
Sir 10:19 Those who **b** the commandments.

BREAKFAST
Jn 21:12 Jesus said to them, "Come and have
        b."

BREAKING → BREAK
Ex 22: 2 If a thief is found **b** in, and is
Dt 31:20 despising me and **b** my covenant.
Eze 16:59 despised the oath, **b** the covenant;
Ac 2:42 to the **b** of bread and the prayers.
Ro 2:23 do you dishonor God by **b** the law?

BREAKS → BREAK
Ps 29: 5 The voice of the LORD **b** the cedars;
    46: 9 he **b** the bow, and shatters the spear;
Jer 23:29 a hammer that **b** a rock in pieces?
Mt 5:19 whoever **b** one of the least of these

BREAST → BREASTPIECE,
BREASTPLATE, BREASTPLATES, BREASTS
Ex 29:26 **b** of the ram of Aaron's ordination
Lev 7:30 you shall bring the fat with the **b,**
Nu 6:20 together with the **b** that is elevated
Ps 22: 9 you kept me safe on my mother's **b.**
    22:14 it is melted within my **b;**
Isa 66:11 be satisfied from her consoling **b;**
Lk 18:13 was beating his **b** and saying, 'God,

BREASTPIECE → BREAST, PIECE
Ex 28:15 You shall make a **b** of judgment,
    28:30 In the **b** of judgment you shall put
Lev 8: 8 and in the **b** he put the Urim and

BREASTPLATE → BREAST, PLATE
1Ki 22:34 between the scale armor and the **b;**
Isa 59:17 He put on righteousness like a **b,**
Eph 6:14 and put on the **b** of righteousness.
1Th 5: 8 and put on the **b** of faith and love,
Wis 5:18 he will put on righteousness as a **b,**

BREASTPLATES → BREAST, PLATE
Rev 9: 9 they had scales like iron **b,**
    9:17 the riders wore **b** the color of fire

BREASTS → BREAST
Ge 49:25 blessings of the **b** and of the womb.
Pr 5:19 May her **b** satisfy you at all times;
SS 4: 5 Your two **b** are like two fawns,
Isa 32:12 Beat your **b** for the pleasant fields,
Eze 23: 3 their **b** were caressed there,
Na 2: 7 like doves and beating their **b.**
Lk 11:27 and the **b** that nursed you!"
    23:29 and the **b** that never nursed.'

BREATH → BREATHED, BREATHES,
BREATHING
Ge 1:30 everything that has the **b** of life,
    2: 7 into his nostrils the **b** of life;
    6:17 all flesh in which is the **b** of life;
2Sa 22:16 at the blast of the **b** of his nostrils.
Job 7: 7 "Remember that my life is a **b;**
    27: 3 as long as my **b** is in me and the
Ps 39:11 surely everyone is a mere **b.**
    146: 4 When their **b** departs, they return to
Ecc 3:19 There all have the same **b,**
    12: 7 the **b** returns to God who gave it.
Isa 40: 7 the **b** of the LORD blows upon it;
Jer 10:14 images are false, and there is no **b**
La 4:20 LORD's anointed, the **b** of our life,
Eze 37: 9 he said to me, "Prophesy to the **b,**
Ac 17:25 gives to all mortals life and **b**
2Th 2: 8 will destroy with the **b** of his mouth,
Rev 11:11 the **b** of life from God entered them,
    13:15 was allowed to give **b** to the image
LtJ 6:25 but there is no **b** in them.
2Es 3: 5 you breathed into him the **b** of life,

BREATH OF LIFE Ge 1:30; 2:7; 6:17; 7:15,
22; La 4:20; Rev 11:11; 2Es 3:5

BREATHED → BREATH
Ge 2: 7 **b** into his nostrils the breath of life;
Mk 15:37 Jesus gave a loud cry and **b** his last.
Jn 20:22 he **b** on them and said to them,

BREATHES → BREATH

Ps 150: 6 everything that **b** praise the LORD!

BREATHING → BREATH

Ac 9: 1 Saul, still **b** threats and murder

BRIBE → BRIBES

Ex 23: 8 You shall take no **b**, for a **b** blinds
Dt 16:19 for a **b** blinds the eyes of the wise
      27:25 "Cursed be anyone who takes a **b** to
1Sa 12: 3 from whose hand have I taken a **b**
Pr 6:35 and refuses a **b** no matter how great.
Ecc 7: 7 and a **b** corrupts the heart.
Isa 5:23 who acquit the guilty for a **b**,
Mic 3:11 Its rulers give judgment for a **b**,

BRIBES → BRIBE

1Sa 8: 3 they took **b** and perverted justice.
Pr 15:27 but those who hate **b** will live.
Eze 22:12 In you, they take **b** to shed blood;

BRICK → BRICKS

Ge 11: 3 they had **b** for stone, and bitumen
Ex 1:14 hard service in mortar and **b** and in
Eze 4: 1 take a **b** and set it before you.

BRICKS → BRICK

Ge 11: 3 one another, "Come, let us make **b**,
Ex 5: 7 straw to make **b**, as before;

BRIDE → BRIDE-PRICE, BRIDEGROOM, BRIDESMAIDS

SS 4: 8 Come with me from Lebanon, my **b**
Isa 49:18 and like a **b** you shall bind them on.
      62: 5 the bridegroom rejoices over the **b**,
Jer 2: 2 of your youth, your love as a **b**,
Jn 3:29 He who has the **b** is the bridegroom.
Rev 19: 7 and his **b** has made herself ready;
      21: 2 as a **b** adorned for her husband.
      21: 9 the **b**, the wife of the Lamb."
      22:17 The Spirit and the **b** say, "Come."

BRIDE-PRICE* → BRIDE, PRICE

Ex 22:16 he shall give the **b** for her and make
      22:17 an amount equal to the **b** for virgins.

BRIDEGROOM → BRIDE

Ex 4:25 "Truly you are a **b** of blood to me!"
Ps 19: 5 like a **b** from his wedding canopy.
Jer 25:10 the voice of the **b** and the voice of
Mt 9:15 as long as the **b** is with them,
      25: 1 and went to meet the **b**.
Mk 2:20 days will come when the **b** is taken
Jn 3:29 He who has the bride is the **b**.
Rev 18:23 voice of **b** and bride will be heard
Bar 2:23 the voice of the **b** and the voice of

BRIDESMAIDS → BRIDE

Mt 25: 1 Ten **b** took their lamps and went to

BRIDLE

Ps 32: 9 must be curbed with bit and **b**,
Isa 30:28 peoples a **b** that leads them astray.
Jas 3: 2 the whole body in check with a **b**.
Rev 14:20 as high as a horse's **b**,

BRIEF → BRIEFLY

Ezr 9: 8 a **b** moment favor has been shown
Isa 54: 7 For a **b** moment I abandoned you,

BRIEFLY → BRIEF

2Co 7: 8 with that letter, though only **b**).
Heb 13:22 for I have written to you **b**.

BRIER → BRIERS

Isa 55:13 instead of the **b** shall come up the
Mic 7: 4 The best of them is like a **b**,

BRIERS → BRIER

Isa 7:24 for all the land will be **b** and thorns;
Eze 2: 6 though **b** and thorns surround you

BRIGHT → BRIGHTER, BRIGHTNESS

SS 6:10 **b** as the sun, terrible as an army
Mt 17: 5 suddenly a **b** cloud overshadowed

Rev 15: 6 robed in pure **b** linen,
      18: 1 earth was made **b** with his splendor.
      19: 8 with fine linen, **b** and pure"—
      22: 1 of the water of life, **b** as crystal,
      22:16 of David, the **b** morning star."

BRIGHTER → BRIGHT

Pr 4:18 which shines **b** and **b** until full day.
Ac 26:13 a light from heaven, **b** than the sun,

BRIGHTNESS → BRIGHT

Ps 18:12 Out of the **b** before him there broke
Isa 59: 9 and for **b**, but we walk in gloom.
      60: 3 and kings to the **b** of your dawn.
      60:19 nor for **b** shall the moon give light
Eze 1: 4 a great cloud with **b** around it
      10: 4 court was full of the **b** of the glory
Da 12: 3 wise shall shine like the **b** of the sky
Am 5:20 not light, and gloom with no **b** in it?
Ac 22:11 I could not see because of the **b** of

BRIM

1Ki 7:23 it was round, ten cubits from **b** to **b**,
Jn 2: 7 And they filled them up to the **b**.

BRING → BRINGING, BRINGS, BROUGHT

Ge 6:17 I am going to **b** a flood of waters on
      6:19 **b** two of every kind into the ark,
      28:15 and will **b** you back to this land;
Ex 3: 8 **b** them up out of that land to a good
      6:26 "**B** the Israelites out of the land of
      18:22 them **b** every important case to you,
      32:12 your mind and do not **b** disaster
Lev 1: 2 When any of you **b** an offering
Nu 20: 5 to **b** us to this wretched place?
Dt 24: 4 and you shall not **b** guilt on the land
      26:10 **b** the first of the fruit of the ground
2Sa 12:23 Can I **b** him back again?
1Ki 21:21 I will **b** disaster on you;
2Ki 22:16 I will indeed **b** disaster on this place
Ps 25:17 and **b** me out of my distress.
      50:23 Those who **b** thanksgiving
Pr 18: 6 A fool's lips **b** strife, and a fool's
      25: 8 do not hastily **b** into court;
Ecc 11: 9 God will **b** you into judgment.
      12:14 will **b** every deed into judgment,
Isa 42: 3 he will faithfully **b** forth justice.
      60:17 Instead of bronze I will **b** gold,
Jer 24: 6 and I will **b** them back to this land.
      26: 3 disaster that I intend to **b** on them
Eze 5:17 and I will **b** the sword upon you.
Da 9:24 to **b** in everlasting righteousness,
Zec 3: 8 going to **b** my servant the Branch.
      4: 7 he shall **b** out the top stone amid
Mt 10:34 not come to **b** peace, but a sword.
Mk 15: 4 many charges they **b** against you."
Lk 4:18 he has anointed me to **b** good news
      12:49 "I came to **b** fire to the earth,
Jn 10:16 I must **b** them also, and they will
Ro 8:33 **b** any charge against God's elect?
      10: 6 (that is, to **b** Christ down)
      10:15 the feet of those who **b** good news!"
1Co 8: 8 "Food will not **b** us close to God."
1Pe 3:18 in order to **b** you to God.
2Jn 1:10 to you and does not **b** this teaching;
Rev 21:24 kings of the earth will **b** their glory

BRINGING → BRING

Ex 36: 3 still kept **b** him freewill offerings
Nu 13: Why is the LORD **b** us into this land
Dt 8: 7 your God is **b** you into a good land,
Isa 1:13 **b** offerings is futile; incense is an
Lk 2:10 I am **b** you good news of great joy
      18:15 People were **b** even infants to him
Tit 2:11 has appeared, **b** salvation to all,
Heb 2:10 in **b** many children to glory,
2Pe 2: 1 **b** swift destruction on themselves.

BRINGS → BRING

1Sa 2: 6 The LORD kills and **b** to life;
Ps 34:21 Evil **b** death to the wicked,
Pr 12:18 but the tongue of the wise **b** healing.
      19: 4 Wealth **b** many friends,

Isa 52: 7 who **b** good news, who announces
Mt 12:35 good person **b** good things out of a
Lk 11:26 and **b** seven other spirits more evil
Ro 4:15 For the law **b** wrath;
2Co 7:10 leads to salvation and **b** no regret,
Heb 1: 6 he **b** the firstborn into the world,
Jas 5:20 that whoever **b** back a sinner
Sir 26: 2 A loyal wife **b** joy to her husband,

BRITTLE*

Da 2:42 shall be partly strong and partly **b**.

BROAD → BREADTH

2Sa 22:20 He brought me out into a **b** place;
Ps 31: 8 you have set my feet in a **b** place.
Isa 33:21 a place of **b** rivers and streams,
Mt 23: 5 for they make their phylacteries **b**

BROKE → BREAK

Ex 32:19 tablets from his hands and **b** them
      34: 1 on the former tablets, which you **b**.
Dt 32:51 both of you **b** faith with me among
Jos 7: 1 Israelites **b** faith in regard to the
2Ki 18: 4 He **b** in pieces the bronze serpent
      23:14 he **b** the pillars in pieces,
      25:13 the Chaldeans **b** in pieces,
2Ch 34: 4 He **b** down the sacred poles and the
      36:19 **b** down the wall of Jerusalem,
Ps 105:16 and **b** every staff of bread,
Jer 31:32 a covenant that they **b**, though I
Eze 17:19 and my covenant that he **b**
Zec 11:10 I took my staff Favor and **b** it,
Mt 14:19 and blessed and **b** the loaves,
      26:26 and after blessing it he **b** it
Mk 14:22 after blessing it he **b** it, gave it to
Ac 2:46 they **b** bread at home and ate thei
1Co 11:24 he **b** it and said, "This is my body
1Mc 3: 5 and pursued those who **b** the law;

BROKEN → BREAK

Ge 17:14 his people; he has **b** my covenant."
1Sa 4:18 and his neck was **b** and he died,
2Ki 18:21 on Egypt, that **b** reed of a staff,
Ezr 10: 2 "We have **b** faith with our God
Ne 1: 3 the wall of Jerusalem is **b** down,
Ps 34:20 not one of them will be **b**.
      51:17 acceptable to God is a **b** spirit;
Pr 18:14 but a **b** spirit—who can bear?
Ecc 4:12 A threefold cord is not quickly **b**.
      12: 6 and the golden bowl is **b**,
Jer 33:21 with my servant David be **b**,
Eze 44: 7 You have **b** my covenant
Da 8: 8 of its power, the great horn was **b**,
Hos 8: 1 because they have **b** my covenant,
Mt 14:20 what was left over of the **b** pieces,
      15:37 they took up the **b** pieces left over,
Lk 20:18 who falls on that stone will be **b**
Jn 7:23 that the law of Moses may not be **b**,
      19:36 "None of his bones shall be **b**."
Ro 11:20 were **b** off because of their unbelief,
Wis 4: 5 The branches will be **b** off before

BROKENHEARTED* → BREAK, HEART

Ps 34:18 The LORD is near to the **b**,
      109:16 and needy and the **b** to their death.
      147: 3 He heals the **b**, and binds up their
Isa 61: 1 the oppressed, to bind up the **b**,

BRONZE

Ge 4:22 made all kinds of **b** and iron tools.
Ex 26:11 You shall make fifty clasps of **b**,
      27: 2 and you shall overlay it with **b**.
      27:10 and their twenty bases shall be of **b**,
      30:18 make a **b** basin with a **b** stand for
Nu 16:39 Eleazar the priest took the **b** censers
      21: 9 look at the serpent of **b** and live.
Dt 28:23 The sky over your head shall be **b**,
1Sa 17: 5 He had a helmet of **b** on his head,
1Ki 7:15 He cast two pillars of **b**.
      7:27 He also made the ten stands of **b**;
2Ki 16:14 The **b** altar that was before
      25:13 and carried the **b** to Babylon.

Ps   18:34 that my arms can bend a bow of **b**.
Isa   60:17 Instead of **b** I will bring gold,
Eze   1: 7 and they sparkled like burnished **b**.
Da   2:32 its middle and thighs of **b**,
       7:19 with its teeth of iron and claws of **b**,
      10: 6 legs like the gleam of burnished **b**,
Zec   6: 1 two mountains—mountains of **b**.
Rev   1:15 his feet were like burnished **b**,
       2:18 and whose feet are like burnished **b**:
Bel   1: 7 is only clay inside and **b** outside,
1Mc 14:48 to inscribe this decree on **b** tablets,

BROOD

Nu   32:14 And now you, a **b** of sinners,
Job   30: 8 A senseless, disreputable **b**,
Mt   3: 7 he said to them, "You **b** of vipers!
      12:34 You **b** of vipers! How can you
      23:33 You snakes, you **b** of vipers!
Lk   13:34 a hen gathers her **b** under her wings,

BROOK → BROOKS

Jer   15:18 you are to me like a deceitful **b**,

BROOKS → BROOK

Jer   31: 9 I will let them walk by **b** of water,

BROOM

1Ki   19: 4 sat down under a solitary **b** tree.
Ps   120: 4 with glowing coals of the **b** tree!
Isa   14:23 sweep it with the **b** of destruction,

BROTH

Jdg   6:19 a basket, and the **b** he put in a pot,
Isa   65: 4 with **b** of abominable things in their

BROTHER → BROTHER'S,
BROTHER-IN-LAW, BROTHERS

Ge   4: 8 Cain rose up against his **b** Abel,
      20:13 say of me, He is my **b**.'"
      27:35 he said, "Your **b** came deceitfully,
      27:41 then I will kill my **b** Jacob."
      32:11 please, from the hand of my **b**,
      42:20 and bring your youngest **b** to me.
      43:30 overcome with affection for his **b**,
      45: 4 He said, "I am your **b**, Joseph,
Ex   7: 1 your **b** Aaron shall be your prophet.
Dt   13: 6 even if it is your **b**, your father's son
      25: 5 the duty of a husband's **b** to her,
2Sa 13:12 "No, my **b**, do not force me;
SS   8: 1 O that you were like a **b** to me,
Am   1:11 he pursued his **b** with the sword
Ob   1:10 and violence done to your **b** Jacob,
Mal   1: 2 Is not Esau Jacob's **b**?
Mt   5:22 if you are angry with a **b** or sister,
       5:24 first be reconciled to your **b** or
      10:21 **B** will betray **b** to death,
Mk   3:35 does the will of God is my **b** and
Lk   20:28 wrote for us that if a man's **b** dies,
Ro   14:15 your **b** or sister is being injured by
      14:21 that makes your **b** or sister stumble.
1Co   5:11 anyone who bears the name of **b**
Phm   1:16 a beloved **b**—especially to me
Jas   2:15 If a **b** or sister is naked and lacks
1Jn   2:10 loves a **b** or sister lives in the light,
       3:15 who hate a **b** or sister are murderers.
       3:17 and sees a **b** or sister in need
       4:20 not love a **b** or sister whom they
       5:16 you see your **b** or sister committing
Wis   10: 3 because in rage he killed his **b**.

BROTHER ... SISTER Nu 6:7; 2Sa 13:4;
Jer 22:18; Eze 44:25; Hos 2:1; Mt 5:22, 22, 23,
24; 12:50; 18:35; Mk 3:35; Ro 14:10, 10, 15,
21; 1Co 5:11; 7:15; 1Th 4:6; Jas 2:15; 1Jn 2:9,
10; 3:15, 17; 4:20; 5:16; Tob 7:11

BROTHER'S → BROTHER

Ge   4: 9 "I do not know; am I my **b** keeper?"
Lev   20:21 man takes his **b** wife, it is impurity;
Dt   25: 7 has no desire to marry his **b** widow,
Mk   6:18 lawful for you to have your **b** wife."

BROTHER-IN-LAW* → BROTHER

Ge   38: 8 and perform the duty of a **b** to her;

BROTHERS → BROTHER

Ge   9:25 lowest of slaves shall he be to his **b**.
      27:29 Be lord over your **b**,
      37:11 So his **b** were jealous of him,
      42:13 "We, your servants, are twelve **b**,
Lev   25:48 one of their **b** may redeem them,
Jdg   9: 5 killed his **b** the sons of Jerubbaal,
2Ch 21:13 because you also have killed your **b**,
Ps   22:22 I will tell of your name to my **b** and
Mt   5:47 if you greet only your **b** and sisters,
      12:49 "Here are my mother and my **b**!
      19:29 who has left houses or **b** or sisters
      20:24 they were angry with the two **b**.
Mk   3:33 "Who are my mother and my **b**?"
      12:20 There were seven **b**; the first
Lk   21:16 be betrayed even by parents and **b**,
      22:32 turned back, strengthen your **b**."
Jn   7: 5 (For not even his **b** believed in him.)
2Co 11:26 danger at sea, danger from false **b**
1Th   4:10 indeed you do love all the **b** and
       5:26 Greet all the **b** and sisters with a
1Ti   5: 1 as to a father, to younger men as **b**,
Heb   2:11 not ashamed to call them **b** and
       2:17 he had to become like his **b** and
1Jn   3:10 who do not love their **b** and sisters.
1Mc   3:25 Judas and his **b** began to be feared,
Pm 151: 1 I was small among my **b**,

BROTHERS ... SISTERS Jos 2:13; Job
42:11; Ps 22:22; Mt 5:47; 19:29; Mk 3:32;
10:29, 30; Lk 14:26; Ac 16:40; Ro 1:13; 7:1;
8:12; 10:1; 11:25; 12:1; 15:14, 30; 16:14, 17;
1Co 1:10, 11, 26; 2:1; 3:1; 4:6; 7:24, 29; 10:1;
11:33; 12:1; 14:6, 20; 15:1, 6, 31, 50; 16:15,
20; 2Co 1:8; 8:1; 11:26; 13:11; Gal 1:11; 3:15;
5:13; 6:18; Php 1:14; 3:1, 17; 4:1; Col 1:2;
4:15; 1Th 1:4; 2:1, 9, 14, 17; 3:7; 4:1, 9, 10,
13; 5:1, 12, 26; 2Th 1:3; 2:1, 13, 15; 3:1, 13;
1Ti 4:6; 2Ti 4:21; Heb 2:11, 12, 17; 3:1, 12;
13:22; Jas 1:2; 2:1, 5, 14; 3:1, 10, 12; 4:11;
5:19; 1Pe 5:9; 2Pe 1:10; 1Jn 3:10, 13; 4:20, 21;
Rev 6:11; Jdt 7:30; Sir 25:1; 2Mc 15:18

BROUGHT → BRING

Ge   2:19 and **b** them to the man
       2:22 into a woman and **b** her to the man.
      15: 7 **b** you from Ur of the Chaldeans,
      21: 6 Sarah said, "God has **b** laughter for
Ex   13: 9 the LORD **b** you out of Egypt.
      18:26 hard cases they **b** to Moses,
      32: 1 **b** us up out of the land of Egypt,
Nu   21: 5 you **b** us up out of Egypt to die in
Jdg   2: 1 "I **b** you up from Egypt, and **b** you
             into the land that I had promised
Ru   1:21 but the LORD has **b** me back empty;
2Ch 36:18 all these he **b** to Babylon.
Ezr   1: 7 Cyrus himself **b** out the vessels of
       6: 5 **b** back to the temple in Jerusalem,
Ne   9:15 you **b** water for them out of the rock
Est   2: 7 Mordecai had **b** up Hadassah, that is
Ps   18:19 He **b** me out into a broad place;
      30: 3 you **b** up my soul from Sheol,
     105:43 So he **b** his people out with joy,
     116: 6 when I was **b** low, he saved me.
Pr   8:25 before the hills, I was **b** forth—
Eze   11: 1 The spirit lifted me up and **b** me to
      37: 1 **b** me out by the spirit of the LORD
Da   5:13 Daniel was **b** in before the king.
Jnh   2: 6 yet you **b** up my life from the Pit,
Mt   4:24 and they **b** to him all the sick,
      22:19 And they **b** him a denarius.
Mk   6:28 **b** his head on a platter,
       8:22 Some people **b** a blind man to him
      15:22 **b** Jesus to the place called Golgotha
Lk   7:22 the poor have good news **b** to them.
Ro   6:13 who have been **b** from death to life,
Eph   2:13 once were far off have been **b** near
1Ti   6: 7 for we **b** nothing into the world,
Heb 13:20 who **b** back from the dead our Lord
Jas   5:19 from the truth and is **b** back by
1Mc   4:58 the disgrace **b** by the Gentiles was

BRUISED → BRUISES

Isa   42: 3 a **b** reed he will not break,
Mt   12:20 He will not break a **b** reed

BRUISES → BRUISED

Isa   53: 5 and by his **b** we are healed.

BRUTE* → BRUTES

Ps   73:22 I was like a **b** beast toward you.

BRUTES → BRUTE

Tit   1:12 "Cretans are always liars, vicious **b**,

BUCKET* → BUCKETS

Isa   40:15 the nations are like a drop from a **b**,
Jn   4:11 said to him, "Sir, you have no **b**,
2Es   6:56 their abundance to a drop from a **b**.

BUCKETS* → BUCKET

Nu   24: 7 Water shall flow from his **b**,

BUCKLER

Ps   35: 2 Take hold of shield and **b**,
      91: 4 his faithfulness is a shield and **b**.

BUDDED → BUDS

Ge   40:10 As soon as it **b**, its blossoms came
Eze   7:10 The rod has blossomed, pride has **b**.
Heb   9: 4 and Aaron's rod that **b**,

BUDS* → BUDDED

Nu   17: 8 It put forth **b**, produced blossoms,

BUGLE*

1Co   14: 8 if the **b** gives an indistinct sound,

BUILD → BUILDER, BUILDERS, BUILDING,
BUILDINGS, BUILDS, BUILT, REBUILD,
REBUILT

Ge   11: 4 "Come, let us **b** ourselves a city,
Ex   20:25 do not **b** it of hewn stones;
Nu   23: 1 Balaam said to Balak, "**B** me seven
Dt   6:10 fine, large cities that you did not **b**,
      27: 5 And you shall **b** an altar there to
2Sa   7: 5 Are you the one to **b** me a house to
1Ki   6: 1 began to **b** the house of the LORD.
Ps   102:16 For the LORD will **b** up Zion;
     127: 1 those who **b** it labor in vain.
Ecc   3: 3 to break down, and a time to **b** up;
Isa   57:14 said, "**B** up, **b** up, prepare the way,
      62:10 **b** up, **b** up the highway, clear it of
Jer   18: 9 a kingdom that I will **b** and plant it,
      31: 4 Again I will **b** you, and you shall be
Mic   3:10 who **b** Zion with blood and
Zep   1:13 Though they **b** houses, they shall
Hag   1: 8 and bring wood and **b** the house,
Zec   6:12 he shall **b** the temple of the LORD.
Mt   16:18 and on this rock I will **b** my church,
      23:29 For you **b** the tombs of the prophets
      27:40 destroy the temple and **b** it in three
Mk   14:58 and in three days I will **b** another,
Ac   20:32 a message that is able to **b** you up
1Co   3:10 must choose with care how to **b**
      10:23 are lawful," but not all things **b** up.
      14: 4 who prophesy **b** up the church.
1Th   5:11 encourage one another and **b** up
Jude   1:20 **b** yourselves up on your most holy

BUILDER → BUILD

1Co   3:10 skilled master **b** I laid a foundation,
       3:14 the **b** will receive a reward.
Heb   3: 3 as the **b** of a house has more honor
       3: 4 but the **b** of all things is God.)
      11:10 whose architect and **b** is God.

BUILDERS → BUILD

1Ki   5:18 So Solomon's **b** and Hiram's **b** and
Ezr   3:10 When the **b** laid the foundation of
Ne   4:18 And each of the **b** had his sword
Ps   118:22 The stone that the **b** rejected has
Mt   21:42 'The stone that the **b** rejected has
Mk   12:10 'The stone that the **b** rejected has
Lk   20:17 that the **b** rejected has become the
Ac   4:11 that was rejected by you, the **b**;

1Pe 2: 7 "The stone that the **b** rejected has
1Es 5:58 the **b** built the temple of the Lord.

BUILDING → BUILD

Jos 22:16 by **b** yourselves an altar today in
1Ki   6:12 this house that you are **b,**
      9: 1 When Solomon had finished the
Ezr   4: 1 the returned exiles were **b** a temple
Ne   2:18 Then they said, "Let us start **b!"**
      4:17 who were **b** the wall.
Mic   7:11 A day for the **b** of your walls!
Lk   6:48 That one is like a man **b** a house,
Ro 15: 2 good purpose of **b** up the neighbor.
1Co 3: 9 you are God's field, God's **b.**
    14:26 Let all things be done for **b** up.
2Co 5: 1 we have a **b** from God,
     10: 8 for **b** you up and not for tearing you
    12:19 is for the sake of **b** you up.
    13:10 that the Lord has given me for **b** up
Eph 4:12 for **b** up the body of Christ,
     4:29 but only what is useful for **b** up,

BUILDINGS → BUILD

Jer 51:30 her **b** are set on fire,
Mk 13: 1 large stones and what large **b!"**

BUILDS → BUILD

Ps 127: 1 Unless the Lord **b** the house,
    147: 2 The Lord **b** up Jerusalem;
Pr 14: 1 The wise woman **b** her house,
Jer 22:13 Woe to him who **b** his house by
1Co 3:12 Now if anyone **b** on the foundation
      8: 1 Knowledge puffs up, but love **b** up.
Sir 21: 8 Whoever **b** his house with other

BUILT → BUILD

Ge   8:20 Then Noah **b** an altar to the Lord,
     12: 7 So he **b** there an altar to the Lord,
     22: 9 Abraham **b** an altar there and laid
    26:25 So he **b** an altar there,
    35: 7 there he **b** an altar and called the
Ex 17:15 And Moses **b** an altar and called it,
    24: 4 and **b** an altar at the foot of the
    32: 5 When Aaron saw this, he **b** an altar
Jos   8:30 Joshua **b** on Mount Ebal an altar to
    22:11 the half-tribe of Manasseh had **b**
Jdg 6:24 Gideon **b** an altar there to the Lord.
1Sa 7:17 and **b** there an altar to the Lord.
    14:35 And Saul **b** an altar to the Lord:
2Sa 24:25 David **b** there an altar to the Lord.
1Ki 6:14 Solomon **b** the house, and finished
Ne   6: 1 of our enemies that I had **b** the wall
      7: 1 the wall had been **b** and I had set up
Ps 122: 3 **b** as a city that is bound firmly
Pr   9: 1 Wisdom has **b** her house,
    24: 3 By wisdom a house is **b,** and
Isa   5: 2 he **b** a watchtower in the midst of it,
Da   9:25 sixty-two weeks it shall be **b** again
Hos 10: 1 increased the more altars he **b;**
Mt   5:14 A city **b** on a hill cannot be hid.
      7:24 be like a wise man who **b** his house
Mk 12: 1 the wine press, and **b** a watchtower;
Lk   6:49 not act is like a man who **b** a house
1Co 3:14 If what has been **b** on the
    14:17 but the other person is not **b** up.
Eph 2:20 **b** upon the foundation of the
Col   2: 7 **b** up in him and established in the
Heb 11: 7 and **b** an ark to save his household;
1Pe 2: 5 be **b** into a spiritual house,
Rev 21:18 The wall is **b** of jasper,
Tob 13:16 Jerusalem will be **b** as his house for
Wis 14: 2 wisdom was the artisan who **b** it;
1Mc 4:47 **b** a new altar like the former one.

BULL → BULLS

Ex 29: 1 Take one young **b** and two rams,
Lev 1: 5 The **b** shall be slaughtered before
     4: 3 a **b** of the herd without blemish as a
Ps 50: 9 will not accept a **b** from your house,
    69:31 more than an ox or a **b** with horns

BULLS → BULL

Nu 23: 1 prepare seven **b** and seven rams for

    29:13 thirteen young **b,** two rams,
1Ch 29:21 a thousand **b,** a thousand rams,
Ezr 6:17 of this house of God one hundred **b,**
Ps 22:12 Many **b** encircle me, strong **b** of
          Bashan surround me;
    50:13 Do I eat the flesh of **b,**
    51:19 then **b** will be offered on your altar.
Isa 1:11 I do not delight in the blood of **b,**
Jer 52:20 the twelve bronze **b** that were under
Heb 10: 4 it is impossible for the blood of **b**

BULWARK*

Ps   8: 2 you have founded a **b**
1Ti 3:15 the pillar and **b** of the truth.
4Mc 13:13 use our bodies as a **b** for the law.

BURDEN → BURDENED, BURDENS, BURDENSOME

Ge 49:15 so he bowed his shoulder to the **b,**
Ex 18:22 and they will bear the **b** with you.
Nu 11:11 lay the **b** of all this people on me?
Ps 38: 4 weigh like a **b** too heavy for me.
    55:22 Cast your **b** on the Lord,
Isa 1:14 they have become a **b** to me,
    10:27 On that day his **b** will be removed
Jer 23:33 "What is the **b** of the Lord?"
Mt 11:30 my yoke is easy, and my **b** is light."
Ac 15:28 no further **b** than these essentials:
2Co 5: 4 in this tent, we groan under our **b,**
    11: 9 I did not **b** anyone,
    12:14 And I will not be a **b,**
2Th 3: 8 so that we might not **b** any of you.
Rev 2:24 I do not lay on you any other **b;**

BURDENED → BURDEN

Isa 43:24 But you have **b** me with your sins;
1Ti   5:16 let the church not be **b,**
2Es 3:21 the first Adam, **b** with an evil heart,

BURDENS → BURDEN

Ex   6: 6 free you from the **b** of the Egyptians
Lk 11:46 you load people with **b** hard to bear,
Gal 6: 2 Bear one another's **b,** and
Wis 9:15 and this earthy tent **b** the thoughtful

BURDENSOME → BURDEN

1Jn 5: 3 And his commandments are not **b,**

BURIAL → BURY

Ge 23: 6 in the choicest of our **b** places;
    49:30 from Ephron the Hittite as a **b** site.
Dt 34: 6 knows his **b** place to this day.
Mt 26:12 my body she has prepared me for **b.**

BURIED → BURY

Ge 15:15 you shall be **b** in a good old age.
Ru   1:17 I will die—there will I be **b.**
Ecc 8:10 Then I saw the wicked **b;**
Ac   2:29 that he both died and was **b,**
Ro   6: 4 have been **b** with him by baptism
1Co 15: 4 he was **b,** and that he was raised on
Col 2:12 you were **b** with him in baptism,

BURIES → BURY

Pr 19:24 lazy person **b** a hand in the dish,

BURN → BURNED, BURNING, BURNS, BURNT

Ex 21:25 **b** for **b,** wound for wound,
    32:10 my wrath may **b** hot against them
Dt   7: 5 and **b** their idols with fire.
Ps 79: 5 Will your jealous wrath **b** like fire?
    89:46 How long will your wrath **b** like
Jer   7:31 to **b** their sons and their daughters
    36:29 You have dared to **b** this scroll,
Mal 4: 1 the day that comes shall **b** them up,
Lk   3:17 but the chaff he will **b** with

BURNED → BURN

Ge 38:24 "Bring her out, and let her be **b."**
Ex   3: 3 and see why the bush is not **b** up."
    32:19 the dancing, Moses' anger **b** hot,
Lev 20:14 they shall be **b** to death,
    21: 9 she shall be **b** to death.

Nu 11: 3 the fire of the Lord **b** against them.
Dt   9:21 the calf, and **b** it with fire and
1Ki 13: 2 human bones shall be **b** on you.'"
2Ki 23:20 and **b** human bones on them.
2Ch 36:19 They **b** the house of God,
Isa   6:13 tenth part remain in it, it will be **b**
Mt 13:40 as the weeds are collected and **b** up
Jn 15: 6 thrown into the fire, and **b.**
1Co 3:15 If the work is **b** up, the builder will
Heb 6: 8 its end is to be **b** over.
Rev 8: 7 and a third of the earth was **b** up,
    18: 8 and she will be **b** with fire;
1Mc 1:31 He plundered the city, **b** it with fire,
     1:56 they tore to pieces and **b** with fire.
     4:38 the altar profaned, and the gates **b.**

BURNING → BURN

Lev 6: 9 the fire on the altar shall be kept **b.**
Ps 140:10 Let **b** coals fall on them!
Pr   6:27 the bosom without **b** one's clothes?
Eze 1:13 that looked like **b** coals of fire,
Da   7: 9 and its wheels were **b** fire.
Lk 24:32 "Were not our hearts **b** within us
Jn   5:35 He was a **b** and shining lamp,
Ac   7:30 in the flame of a **b** bush.
Ro 12:20 by doing this you will heap **b** coals
Rev 8: 8 like a great mountain, **b** with fire,
Aza 1:66 the midst of the **b** fiery furnace;

BURNISHED

1Ki 7:45 house of the Lord were of **b** bronze
Eze 1: 7 and they sparkled like **b** bronze.
Da 10: 6 and legs like the gleam of **b** bronze,
Rev 1:15 his feet were like **b** bronze,
     2:18 and whose feet are like **b** bronze:

BURNS → BURN

Dt 32:22 and **b** to the depths of Sheol;
Isa 44:16 Half of it he **b** in the fire;
Hos 8: 5 My anger **b** against them.
Rev 19:20 the lake of fire that **b** with sulfur.
    21: 8 their place will be in the lake that **b**
Sir 23:16 not be quenched until it **b** itself out;

BURNT → BURN

Ge   8:20 and offered **b** offerings on the altar.
    22: 2 and offer him there as a **b** offering
Ex 10:25 let us have sacrifices and **b** offerings
    18:12 brought a **b** offering and sacrifices
    40: 6 You shall set the altar of **b** offering
Lev 1: 3 If the offering is a **b** offering from
Dt 12: 6 bringing there your **b** offerings
Jos 8:31 on it **b** offerings to the Lord,
    22:26 build an altar, not for **b** offering,
Jdg 6:26 as a **b** offering with the wood of the
    13:16 if you want to prepare a **b** offering,
1Sa 15:22 Lord as great delight in **b** offerings
1Ki 3: 4 Solomon used to offer a thousand **b**
    10: 5 and his **b** offerings that he offered
Ezr 3: 2 to offer **b** offerings on it,
     8:35 this as a **b** offering to the Lord.
Job 1: 5 offer **b** offerings according to the
Ps 40: 6 **B** offering and sin offering you have
    51:16 if I were to give a **b** offering,
    66:15 I will offer to you **b** offerings of
Isa   1:11 I have had enough of **b** offerings of
    40:16 its animals enough for a **b** offering.
Jer 6:20 Your **b** offerings are not acceptable,
Eze 43:18 it is erected for offering **b** offerings
    46:13 for a **b** offering to the Lord daily;
Da   8:11 it took the regular **b** offering away
    11:31 shall abolish the regular **b** offering
    12:11 that the regular **b** offering is taken
Hos 6: 6 the knowledge of God rather than **b**
Mic 6: 6 Shall I come before him with **b**
Mk 12:33 more important than all whole **b**
Heb 10: 6 in **b** offerings and sin offerings you
Jdt 16:18 they offered their **b** offerings,
Wis 3: 6 a sacrificial **b** offering he accepted
1Mc 1:45 to forbid **b** offerings and sacrifices
     1:54 sacrilege on the altar of **b** offering.
     4:56 and joyfully offered **b** offerings;
4Mc 18:11 Isaac who was offered as a **b**

BURNT OFFERING Ge 22:2, 3, 6, 7, 8, 13;
Ex 18:12; 29:18, 25, 42; 30:9, 28; 31:9; 35:16;
38:1; 40:6, 10, 29, 29; Lev 1:3, 4, 6, 9, 10, 13,
14, 17; 3:5; 4:7, 10, 18, 24, 25, 25, 29, 30, 33,
34; 5:7; 10:6:9, 9, 10, 12, 25; 7:2, 8, 8, 37;
8:18, 21, 28; 9:2, 3, 7, 12, 13, 14, 16, 17, 22,
24; 10:19; 12:6, 8; 14:13, 19, 20, 22, 31;
15:15, 30; 16:3, 5, 24, 24; 17:8; 22:18; 23:12,
18; Nu 6:11, 14, 16; 7:15, 21, 27, 33, 39, 45,
51, 57, 63, 69, 75, 81, 87; 8:12; 15:3, 5, 8, 24;
28:6, 10, 10, 11, 13, 14, 15, 19, 23, 23, 24, 27,
31; 29:2, 6, 6, 8, 11, 13, 16, 19, 22, 25, 28, 31,
34, 36, 38; Dt 13:16; Jos 22:26, 29; Jdg 6:26;
11:31; 13:16, 23; 1Sa 6:14; 7:9, 10; 13:9, 9,
10, 12; 2Sa 24:22; 1Ki 18:33, 38; 2Ki 3:27;
5:17; 10:25; 16:13, 15, 15, 15, 15; 1Ch 6:49;
16:40; 21:26, 29; 22:1; 2Ch 4:6; 7:1, 7; 29:18,
24, 27, 27, 28, 32; Ezr 8:35; Ne 10:33; Job
42:8; Ps 40:6; 51:16; Isa 19:21; 40:16; Jer
14:12; Eze 40:38, 39, 42; 43:24; 44:11; 45:23;
46:2, 4, 12, 12, 13, 15; Da 8:11, 12, 13; 11:31;
12:11; Wis 3:6; Aza 1:15; 1Mc 1:54, 59; 4:44,
53; 7:33; 4Mc 18:11

BURNT OFFERINGS Ge 8:20; Ex 10:25;
20:24; 24:5; 32:6; Lev 23:37; Nu 10:10; 23:3,
6, 15, 17; 29:39; Dt 12:6, 11, 13, 14, 27; 27:6;
33:10; Jos 8:31; 22:23, 27, 28; Jdg 20:26;
21:4; 1Sa 6:15; 10:8; 15:22; 2Sa 6:17, 18;
24:24, 25; 1Ki 3:4, 15; 8:64, 64; 9:25; 10:5;
2Ki 10:24; 1Ch 16:1, 2, 40; 21:23, 24, 26;
23:31; 29:21; 2Ch 1:6; 2:4; 7:7; 8:12; 9:4;
13:11; 23:18; 24:14, 14; 29:7, 31, 32, 34, 35,
35; 30:15; 31:2, 3, 3, 3; 35:12, 14, 16; Ezr 3:2,
3, 4, 5, 6; 6:3, 9; 8:35; Job 1:5; Ps 50:8; 51:19,
19; 66:13, 15; Isa 1:11; 43:23; 56:7; Jer 6:20;
7:21, 22; 17:26; 19:5; 33:18; Eze 40:42; 43:18,
27; 45:15, 17, 17, 25; Hos 6:6; Am 5:22; Mic
6:6; Mk 12:33; Heb 10:6, 8; Jdt 4:14; 16:16,
18; Bar 1:10; Aza 1:17; 1Mc 1:45; 4:56; 5:54;
2Mc 2:10; 1Es 4:52; 5:49, 50

BURST → BURSTING
Ge   7:11 fountains of the great deep **b** forth,
2Sa   6: 8 angry because the LORD had **b** forth
Job   32:19 like new wineskins, it is ready to **b.**
Isa   54: 1 **b** into song and shout, you who
          55:12 hills before you shall **b** into song,
Jer   23:19 will **b** upon the head of the wicked.
Lk   5:37 the new wine will **b** the skins and
          6:48 river **b** against that house but could
Ac   1:18 headlong, he **b** open in the middle
Gal   4:27 bear no children, **b** into song and
Bel   1:27 The dragon ate them, and **b** open.

BURSTING → BURST
Pr   3:10 and your vats will be **b** with wine.

BURY → BURIAL, BURIED, BURIES
Ge   23: 4 I may **b** my dead out of my sight."
          47:29 Do not **b** me in Egypt.
          50: 7 So Joseph went up to **b** his father.
2Ki   9:10 and no one shall **b** her."
Mt   8:22 let the dead **b** their own dead."
Lk   9:60 "Let the dead **b** their own dead;

BUSH → ROSEBUSHES, THORNBUSH,
THORNBUSHES
Ex   3: 2 he looked, and the **b** was blazing,
Jnh   4: 6 The LORD God appointed a **b,**
Mk   12:26 in the story about the **b,** how God
Lk   20:37 in the story about the **b,**
Ac   7:35 angel who appeared to him in the **b.**
2Es   14: 1 suddenly a voice came out of a **b**

BUSHEL
Mt   5:15 lighting a lamp puts it under the **b**

BUSINESS → BUSY
Ecc   1:13 an unhappy **b** that God has given
          4: 8 also is vanity and an unhappy **b.**
Da   8:27 I arose and went about the king's **b.**
Ac   19:24 brought no little **b** to the artisans.
Jas   4:13 doing **b** and making money."

BUSY → BUSINESS, BUSYBODIES
1Ki   20:40 your servant was **b** here and there,
Sir   8: 8 but **b** yourself with their maxims;
          11:10 not **b** yourself with many matters;

BUSYBODIES· → BUSY
2Th   3:11 mere **b,** not doing any work.
1Ti   5:13 merely idle, but also gossips and **b,**

BUY → BOUGHT, BUYER, BUYING, BUYS
Ge   41:57 came to Joseph in Egypt to **b** grain,
Ex   21: 2 When you **b** a male Hebrew slave,
2Sa   24:21 "To **b** the threshing floor from you
Pr   23:23 **B** truth, and do not sell it;
Isa   55: 1 **b** wine and milk without money
Jer   13: 1 Go and **b** yourself a linen loincloth,
          19: 1 Go and **b** a potter's earthenware jug.
          32: 7 "**B** my field that is at Anathoth,
Mt   27: 7 used them to **b** the potter's field as
Jn   6: 5 are we to **b** bread for these people
Rev   3:18 to **b** from me gold refined by fire so
          13:17 no one can **b** or sell who does not

BUYER → BUY
Dt   28:68 slaves, but there will be no **b.**
Pr   20:14 "Bad, bad," says the **b,**

BUYING → BUY
Mt   21:12 drove out all who were selling and **b**
Lk   17:28 eating and drinking, **b** and selling,

BUYS → BUY
Pr   31:16 She considers a field and **b** it;
Mt   13:44 sells all that he has and **b** that field.
Rev   18:11 since no one **b** their cargo anymore.

BUZZARD → BUZZARDS
Dt   14:13 the **b,** the kite, of any kind;

BUZZARDS· → BUZZARD
Isa   34:15 there too the **b** shall gather,

BYWORD → WORD
Dt   28:37 and a **b** among all the peoples where
2Ch   7:20 proverb and a **b** among all peoples.
Job   17: 6 He has made me a **b** of the peoples,
Ps   44:14 made us a **b** among the nations,
Eze   23:10 and she became a **b** among women.
Joel   2:17 your heritage a mockery, a **b** among

C

CAESAREA
Mt   16:13 came into the district of C Philippi,
Ac   10: 1 C there was a man named Cornelius
          12:19 from Judea to C and stayed there.
          25: 4 that Paul was being kept at C,

CAIAPHAS·
High priest at trial of Jesus (Mt 26:3, 57; Lk 3:2;
Jn 11:49; 18:13-28); at trial of disciples (Ac 4:6).

CAIN·
Firstborn of Adam (Ge 4:1), murdered brother
Abel (Ge 4:1-25; Heb 11:4; 1Jn 3:12; Jude 11;
4Mc 18:11).

CAKE → CAKES
Ex   29:23 one **c** of bread made with oil, and
Jdg   7:13 in it a **c** of barley bread tumbled
1Ki   17:13 first make me a little **c** of it and
Hos   7: 8 Ephraim is a **c** not turned.

CAKES → CAKE
Ex   12:39 baked unleavened **c** of the dough
          29: 2 unleavened **c** mixed with oil,
Nu   11: 8 like the taste of **c** baked with oil.
Jdg   6:21 the meat and the unleavened **c;**
Jer   7:18 to make **c** for the queen of heaven;
          44:19 do you think that we made **c** for her,

Hos   3: 1 turn to other gods and love raisin **c."**
Jdt   10: 5 a bag with roasted grain, dried fig **c,**
Bel   1:27 boiled them together and made **c,**

CALAMITIES → CALAMITY
1Sa   10:19 who saves you from all your **c** and
2Co   6: 4 in afflictions, hardships, **c,**
          12:10 and **c** for the sake of Christ;

CALAMITY → CALAMITIES
Dt   32:35 because the day of their **c** is at hand,
Est   8: 6 For how can I bear to see the **c** that
Pr   1:26 I also will laugh at your **c;**
          22: 8 Whoever sows injustice will reap **c,**
          24:16 but the wicked are overthrown by **c.**
Da   9:13 all this **c** has come upon us.
Jnh   1: 8 "Tell us why this **c** has come upon
          3:10 God changed his mind about the **c**
Hab   3:16 wait quietly for the day of **c** to come

DAY OF ... CALAMITY Dt 32:35; 2Sa
22:19; Job 21:30; Ps 18:18; Pr 27:10; Jer
18:17; 46:21; Ob 1:13, 13, 13; Hab 3:16; Sir
5:8

CALCULATE
Rev   13:18 **c** the number of the beast,

CALEB
Judahite who spied out Canaan (Nu 13:6); allowed to enter land because of faith (Nu 13:30-
14:38; Dt 1:36; Sir 46:7-9; 1Mc 2:56). Given
Hebron (Jos 14:6-15:19).

CALF → CALVES
Ex   32: 4 and cast an image of a **c;**
Lev   9: 2 "Take a bull **c** for a sin offering and
Dt   9:16 for yourselves an image of a **c;**
Ne   9:18 when they had cast an image of a **c**
Isa   11: 6 the **c** and the lion and the fatling
Jer   31:18 I was like a **c** untrained.
Hos   8: 5 Your **c** is rejected, O Samaria.
Lk   15:23 And get the fatted **c** and kill it,
Ac   7:41 At that time they made a **c,**

CALL → CALLED, CALLING, CALLS,
SO-CALLED
Ge   2:19 man to see what he would **c** them;
          30:13 For the women will **c** me happy";
Dt   4:26 I **c** heaven and earth to witness
Ru   1:20 C me no longer Naomi, **c** me Mara,
1Sa   3: 5 But he said, "I did not **c;** lie down
2Sa   22: 4 I **c** upon the LORD, who is worthy to
1Ki   18:24 you **c** on the name of your god and
          I will **c** on the name of the LORD;
1Ch   16: 8 thanks to the LORD, **c** on his name,
Ps   4: 1 Answer me when I **c,** O God of my
          10:13 "You will not **c** us to account"?
          28: 1 To you, O LORD, I **c;** my rock,
          50:15 C on me in the day of trouble;
          61: 2 From the end of the earth I **c** to you,
          105: 1 thanks to the LORD, **c** on his name,
          116:13 and **c** on the name of the LORD,
          145:18 LORD is near to all who **c** on him,
          145:18 to all who **c** on him in truth.
Pr   1:28 they will **c** upon me, but I will not
          8: 1 Does not wisdom **c,** and does
          31:28 Her children rise up and **c** her happy
Isa   5:20 you who **c** evil good and good evil,
          12: 4 thanks to the LORD, **c** on his name;
          55: 6 **c** upon him while he is near;
          60:14 shall **c** you the City of the LORD,
          65:24 Before they **c** I will answer,
Jer   33: 3 C to me and I will answer you,
La   3:21 But this I **c** to mind, and therefore I
Hos   2:16 you will **c** me, "My husband,"
Jnh   1: 6 Get up, **c** on your god!
Zep   3: 9 may **c** on the name of the LORD
Zec   13: 9 **c** on my name, and I will answer
Mt   9:13 to **c** not the righteous but sinners."
          23: 9 And **c** no one your father on earth,
Mk   10:18 Jesus said to him, "Why do you **c**
          me good?"
Lk   6:46 "Why do you **c** me 'Lord, Lord,'

Jn	13:13	You c me Teacher and Lord—
	15:15	I do not c you servants any longer,
Ac	10:15	you must not c profane."
Ro	9:25	not beloved I will c 'beloved.'"
	10:12	and is generous to all who c on him.
1Co	1: 2	who in every place c on the name
	1:26	Consider your own c, brothers and
Php	3:14	goal for the prize of the heavenly c
1Th	4: 7	For God did not c us to impurity but
2Ti	2:22	who c on the Lord from a pure heart
Heb	2:11	not ashamed to c them brothers and
Jas	5:14	should c for the elders of the church
2Pe	1:10	the more eager to confirm your c
Rev	13:10	a c for the endurance and faith of
	14:12	a c for the endurance of the saints,
Jdt	16: 1	exalt him, and c upon his name.
Sir	42:15	c to mind the works of the Lord,
2Es	2:14	C, O c heaven and earth to witness:

CALLED → CALL

Ge	1: 5	God c the light Day, and the darkness he c Night.
	1: 8	God c the dome Sky.
	1:10	God c the dry land Earth,
	1:10	were gathered together he c Seas.
	2:19	whatever the man c every living
	2:23	this one shall be c Woman,
	3: 9	But the LORD God c to the man,
	13: 4	Abram c on the name of the LORD.
	21:17	and the angel of God c to Hagar
	21:33	c there on the name of the LORD,
	22:11	the angel of the LORD c to him from
	26:25	c on the name of the LORD,
	35:10	So he was c Israel.
Ex	3: 4	God c to him out of the bush,
	16:31	The house of Israel c it manna;
	19: 3	LORD c to him from the mountain,
1Sa	3: 4	Then the LORD c, "Samuel!
2Sa	22: 7	In my distress I c upon the LORD;
1Ki	18:26	c on the name of Baal from morning
1Ch	21:26	He c upon the LORD, and he
2Ch	7:14	if my people who are c by my name
Ps	116: 4	Then I c on the name of the LORD:
Pr	1:24	Because I have c and you refused,
SS	6: 9	maidens saw her and c her happy;
Isa	1:26	shall be c the city of righteousness,
	4: 1	just let us be c by your name;
	42: 6	I have c you in righteousness,
	43: 1	I have c you by name, you are mine.
	49: 1	The LORD c me before I was born,
	56: 7	house shall be c a house of prayer
	65:12	when I c, you did not answer,
Jer	7:10	which is c by my name, and say,
La	3:55	I c on your name, O LORD,
Da	1: 7	Daniel he c Belteshazzar,
Hos	11: 1	and out of Egypt I c my son.
Mt	1:16	of whom Jesus was born, who is c the Messiah.
	2:15	"Out of Egypt I have c my son."
	2:23	"He will be c a Nazorean."
	5: 9	for they will be c children of God.
	5:19	will be c least in the kingdom of
	21:13	house shall be c a house of prayer';
	23: 8	But you are not to be c rabbi,
Lk	1:32	will be c the Son of the Most High,
	1:35	he will be c Son of God.
	1:76	be c the prophet of the Most High;
	15:19	no longer worthy to be c your son;
Jn	10:35	word of God came were c 'gods'—
	15:15	but I have c you friends,
	19:17	which in Hebrew is c Golgotha.
Ro	1: 1	of Jesus Christ, c to be an apostle,
	1: 6	who are c to belong to Jesus Christ,
	1: 7	who are c to be saints:
	8:28	who are c according to his purpose.
	8:30	whom he predestined he also c; and those whom he c he also justified;
1Co	1: 9	c into the fellowship of his Son,
	1:24	but to those who are the c,
	7:15	It is to peace that God has c you.
	7:17	has assigned, to which God c you.
	7:24	In whatever condition you were c,

Gal	5:13	For you were c to freedom, brothers
Eph	1:18	the hope to which he has c you,
	4: 4	as you were c to the one hope of
Col	3:15	indeed you were c in the one body.
2Th	2:14	For this purpose he c you
1Ti	6:12	the eternal life, to which you were c
2Ti	1: 9	saved us and c us with a holy calling
Heb	9:15	so that those who are c may receive
	11:16	is not ashamed to be c their God;
Jas	2:23	and he was c the friend of God.
1Pe	1:15	Instead, as he who c you is holy,
	2: 9	of him who c you out of darkness
	3: 9	It is for this that you were c—
	5:10	c you to his eternal glory in Christ,
2Pe	1: 3	of him who c us by his own glory
1Jn	3: 1	that we should be c children of God;
Jude	1: 1	To those who are c,
Rev	12: 9	who is c the Devil and Satan,
	16:16	that in Hebrew is c Harmagedon.
	17:14	those with him are c and chosen
	19:11	Its rider is c Faithful and True,
	19:13	and his name is c The Word of God.

CALLING → CALL

1Sa	3: 8	Eli perceived that the LORD was c
Isa	40:26	numbers them, c them all by name;
Mt	27:47	they said, "This man is c for Elijah."
Mk	10:49	get up, he is c you."
Jn	5:18	but was also c God his own Father,
Ac	22:16	sins washed away, c on his name.'
Ro	11:29	and the c of God are irrevocable.
Eph	4: 1	lead a life worthy of the c to which
	4: 4	called to the one hope of your c,
2Ti	1: 9	saved us and called us with a holy c,
Heb	3: 1	holy partners in a heavenly c,

CALLS → CALL

Ps	42: 7	Deep c to deep at the thunder of
Pr	9: 3	she c from the highest places in the
Isa	64: 7	no one who c on your name,
Hos	7: 7	none of them c upon me.
Joel	2:32	Then everyone who c on the name
	2:32	shall be those whom the LORD c.
Mt	22:45	David thus c him Lord, how can he
Jn	10: 3	He c his own sheep by name and
Ac	2:21	Then everyone who c on the name
Ro	4:17	c into existence the things that do
	10:13	"Everyone who c on the name of
1Th	2:12	who c you into his own kingdom
	5:24	one who c you is faithful,
2Ti	2:19	"Let everyone who c on the name of
Rev	2:20	who c herself a prophet
	13:18	This c for wisdom: let anyone with
	17: 9	"This c for a mind that has wisdom:

CALM → CALMED, CALMNESS

Eze	16:42	I will be c, and will be angry no
Mk	4:39	ceased, and there was a dead c.
Sir	1:23	Those who are patient stay c until

CALMED* → CALM

Ps	131: 2	But I have c and quieted my soul,

CALMNESS* → CALM

Ecc	10: 4	for c will undo great offenses.

CALVES → CALF

1Ki	12:28	and made two c of gold.
2Ki	10:29	the golden c that were in Bethel and
Job	21:10	their cow c and never miscarries.
Hos	13: 2	People are kissing c!
Mic	6: 6	burnt offerings, with c a year old?
Mal	4: 2	go out leaping like c from the stall.
Heb	9:12	not with the blood of goats and c,

CAME → COME

Ge	7: 6	the flood of waters c on the earth.
	11: 5	The LORD c down to see the city
	15: 1	the word of the LORD c to Abram in
	20: 3	But God c to Abimelech in a dream
Ex	13: 3	day on which you c out of Egypt,
	32:24	into the fire, and out c this calf!"
Lev	9:24	Fire c out from the LORD and

Nu	11:25	LORD c down in the cloud and spoke
	12: 5	LORD c down in a pillar of cloud,
	16:35	And fire c out from the LORD and
	24: 2	Then the spirit of God c upon him,
Jdg	3:10	The spirit of the LORD c upon him,
	11:29	spirit of the LORD c upon Jephthah,
1Sa	3:10	Now the LORD c and stood there,
	11: 6	spirit of God c upon Saul in power
	16:13	the spirit of the LORD c mightily
	16:23	the evil spirit from God c upon Saul,
	19: 9	an evil spirit from the LORD c upon
	19:20	spirit of God c upon the messengers
	19:23	and the spirit of God c upon him.
2Ki	1:10	Then fire c down from heaven,
1Ch	12:18	Then the spirit c upon Amasai,
2Ch	15: 1	The spirit of God c upon Azariah
	20:14	spirit of the LORD c upon Jahaziel
Ps	18: 9	He bowed the heavens, and c down;
	68:17	the Lord c from Sinai into the holy
Ecc	5:16	just as they c, so shall they go;
Da	3:26	and Abednego c out from the fire.
Hab	3:13	You c forth to save your people,
Mt	2: 1	wise men from the East c to
	7:25	The rain fell, the floods c,
Mk	1:11	And a voice c from heaven, "You are my Son,
	10:45	the Son of Man c not to be served
Jn	1: 3	All things c into being through him,
	1:11	He c to what was his own,
	1:17	and truth c through Jesus Christ.
	6:41	"I am the bread that c down from
	6:51	I am the living bread that c down
	10:10	I c that they may have life,
	19:34	and at once blood and water c out.
Ac	19: 6	the Holy Spirit c upon them,
Ro	5:12	as sin c into the world through one
1Co	11:12	For just as woman c from man,
1Ti	1:15	Christ Jesus c into the world to save
1Jn	5: 6	the one who c by water and blood,
Rev	2: 8	who was dead and c to life:
	20: 4	c to life and reigned with Christ
	20: 9	fire c down from heaven and

THE WORD OF THE †LORD ... CAME

Ge 15:1, 4; 1Sa 15:10; 2Sa 7:4; 24:11; 1Ki
6:11; 13:20; 16:1, 7; 17:2, 8; 18:1, 31; 19:9;
21:17, 28; 2Ki 20:4; 1Ch 17:3; 22:8; 2Ch 11:2;
12:7; Isa 38:4; Jer 1:2, 4, 11, 13; 2:1; 13:3, 8;
14:1; 16:1; 18:5; 24:4; 26:1; 28:12; 29:30;
32:6, 26; 33:1, 19, 23; 34:12; 35:12; 36:27;
37:6; 39:15; 42:7; 43:8; 46:1; 47:1; 49:34; Eze
1:3; 3:16; 6:1; 7:1; 11:14; 12:1, 8, 17, 21, 26;
13:1; 14:2, 12; 15:1; 16:1; 17:1, 11; 18:1; 20:2,
45; 21:1, 8, 18; 22:1, 17, 23; 23:1; 24:1, 15,
20; 25:1; 26:1; 27:1; 28:1, 11, 20; 29:1, 17;
30:1, 20; 31:1; 32:1, 17; 33:1, 23; 34:1; 35:1;
36:16; 37:15; 38:1; Hos 1:1; Joel 1:1; Jnh 1:1;
3:1; Mic 1:1; Zep 1:1; Hag 1:1, 3; 2:1, 10, 20;
Zec 1:1, 7; 4:8; 6:9; 7:1, 8

CAMEL → CAMEL'S, CAMELS

Mt	19:24	c to go through the eye of a needle
	23:24	strain out a gnat but swallow a c!
Mk	10:25	c to go through the eye of a needle
Lk	18:25	c to go through the eye of a needle

CAMEL'S → CAMEL

Ge	31:34	gods and put them in the c saddle,
Mk	1: 6	Now John was clothed with c hair,

CAMELS → CAMEL

Ge	24:14	'Drink, and I will water your c'—

CAMP → CAMPED, CAMPING, ENCAMP, ENCAMPS

Ge	32: 2	he said, "This is God's c!"
Ex	16:13	quails came up and covered the c;
	16:13	a layer of dew around the c.
	33: 7	of meeting, which was outside the c.
Lev	24:14	Take the blasphemer outside the c;
Nu	9:17	there the Israelites would c.
	11:26	and so they prophesied in the c.
Dt	23:14	therefore your c must be holy,

1Sa 4: 7 said, "Gods have come into the **c**."
Heb 13:13 then go to him outside the **c** and
Jdt 16: 2 he sets up his **c** among his people;

CAMPED → CAMP
Ex 19: 2 **c** there in front of the mountain.
Nu 33:49 they **c** by the Jordan from
Jos 3: 1 They **c** there before crossing over.

CAMPING → CAMP
Nu 24: 2 Balaam looked up and saw Israel **c**

CAN → CANNOT
Ge   4:13 punishment is greater than I **c** bear!
    13:16 if one **c** count the dust of the earth,
    17:17 "**C** a child be born to a man who is
    41:15 there is no one who **c** interpret it.
Nu 23: 8 **c** I curse whom God has not cursed?
    23:10 Who **c** count the dust of Jacob,
    35:33 no expiation **c** be made for the land,
Dt 32:39 and no one **c** deliver from my hand.
1Sa 14: 6 **c** hinder the LORD from saving
Job 4:17 **C** mortals be righteous before God?
    11: 7 **C** you find out the limit of the
          Almighty?
    34:29 he hides his face, who **c** behold him,
    38:35 **C** you send forth lightnings,
    40: 9 **c** you thunder with a voice like his?
    42: 2 "I know that you **c** do all things,
Ps   6: 5 in Sheol who **c** give you praise?
    19:12 But who **c** detect their errors?
    22:17 I **c** count all my bones.
    49: 7 no price one **c** give to God for it.
    56: 4 what **c** flesh do to me?
   139: 7 Where **c** I go from your spirit?
Pr 20: 6 but who **c** find one worthy of trust?
    31:10 A capable wife who **c** find?
Ecc 3:14 nothing **c** be added to it, nor
     7:13 who **c** make straight what he has
Isa 43:13 I work and who **c** hinder it?
    44:10 or cast an image that **c** do no good?
Jer 18: 6 **C** I not do with you,
Eze 37: 3 "Mortal, **c** these bones live?"
Da   2: 9 you **c** give me its interpretation."
     5:16 heard that you **c** give interpretations
Hos 11: 8 How **c** I give you up, Ephraim?
Joel 2:11 terrible indeed—who **c** endure it?
Am   3: 8 has spoken; who **c** but prophesy?
Mal 3: 2 who **c** endure the day of his coming,
Mt   5:13 how **c** its saltiness be restored?
     6:24 "No one **c** serve two masters;
Mk   2: 7 Who **c** forgive sins but God alone?"
Lk 18:26 said, "Then who **c** be saved?"
Jn   3: 4 "How **c** anyone be born after
     3: 9 "How **c** these things be?"
     5:30 "I **c** do nothing on my own.
     6:44 No one **c** come to me unless drawn
    10:29 **c** snatch it out of the Father's hand.
    15: 5 apart from me you **c** do nothing.
Ro   9:19 For who **c** resist his will?"
Php 4:13 I **c** do all things through him who
Heb 2: 3 how **c** we escape if we neglect so
    13: 6 What **c** anyone do to me?"
Jas 2:14 not have works? **C** faith save you?
     3: 8 but no one **c** tame the tongue—
Rev 5: 5 he **c** open the scroll and its seven
    13: 4 and who **c** fight against it?"
    13:17 no one **c** buy or sell who does not
          have the mark,
Sir 15:15 you **c** keep the commandments,
Bar 3:35 no other **c** be compared to him.
LtJ 6:30 For how **c** they be called gods?

CANA
Jn   2: 1 there was a wedding in C

CANAAN → CANAANITE, CANAANITES
Ge   9:18 Ham was the father of C.
     9:25 "Cursed be the C; lowest of slaves
    13:12 Abram settled in the land of C,
    42: 5 famine had reached the land of C.
Ex   6: 4 to give them the land of C,
Nu 13: 2 "Send men to spy out the land of C,

    33:51 over the Jordan into the land of C,
    34: 2 of C, defined by its boundaries),
Dt 32:49 Jericho, and view the land of C,
Jdg 4: 2 into the hand of King Jabin of C,
1Ch 16:18 "To you I will give the land of C
Ps 106:38 they sacrificed to the idols of C;
Zep 2: 5 of the LORD is against you, O C,
Ac 13:19 seven nations in the land of C,
Sus 1:56 offspring of C and not of Judah,

LAND OF CANAAN Ge 11:31; 12:5, 5;
    13:12; 16:3; 17:8; 23:2, 19; 31:18; 33:18; 35:6;
    36:5, 6; 37:1; 42:5, 7, 13, 29, 32; 44:8; 45:17,
    25; 46:6, 12, 31; 47:1, 4, 13, 14, 15; 48:3, 7;
    49:30; 50:5, 13; Ex 6:4; 16:35; Lev 14:34;
    18:3; 25:38; Nu 13:2, 17; 26:19; 32:30, 32;
    33:40, 51; 34:2, 2, 29; 35:10, 14; Dt 32:49; Jos
    5:12; 14:1; 21:2; 22:9, 10, 11, 32; 24:3; Jdg
    21:12; 1Ch 16:18; Ps 105:11; Ac 13:19; Jdt
    5:9, 10

CANAANITE → CANAAN
Ge 28: 1 not marry one of the C women.
Mt 15:22 a C woman from that region came

CANAANITES → CANAAN
Ge 10:18 the families of the C spread abroad.
    12: 6 At that time the C were in the land.
    36: 2 Esau took his wives from the C:
Ex   3: 8 to the country of the C, the Hittites,
    33: 2 I will drive out the C, the Amorites,
Jos 16:10 so the C have lived within Ephraim
    17:12 the C continued to live in that land.
Jdg 1: 1 shall go up first for us against the C,
     1:27 the C continued to live in that land.
     3: 5 So the Israelites lived among the C,

CANCELED
Lk   7:42 he **c** the debts for both of them.

CANDACE*
Ac   8:27 of the C, queen of the Ethiopians,

CANNOT → CAN
Ex 33:20 But," he said, "you **c** see my face;
Nu 23: 8 he has blessed, and I **c** revoke it.
Jos 24:19 "You **c** serve the LORD, for he is a
2Sa 5: 6 thinking, "David **c** come in here."
1Ki 8:27 the highest heaven **c** contain you,
Job 23: 8 or backward, I **c** perceive him;
    37:23 The Almighty—we **c** find him;
Ecc 1:15 What is crooked **c** be made straight,
SS   8: 7 Many waters **c** quench love,
Isa 45:20 keep on praying to a god that **c** save.
Da   6: 8 so that it **c** be changed,
Mt   5:14 A city built on a hill **c** be hid.
    16: 3 **c** interpret the signs of the times.
    27:42 "He saved others; he **c** save himself.
Mk   3:24 against itself, that kingdom **c** stand.
Lk 16:13 You **c** serve God and wealth."
Jn   7:34 and where I am, you **c** come."
    13:33 'Where I am going, you **c** come.'
    15: 4 as the branch **c** bear fruit by itself
    16:12 but you **c** bear them now.
Ro   8: 8 who are in the flesh **c** please God.
1Co 10:21 You **c** drink the cup of the Lord and
    15:50 and blood **c** inherit the kingdom of
Jas 1:13 for God **c** be tempted by evil
Sir 9:10 for new ones **c** equal them.

CANOPY
2Sa 22:12 He made darkness around him a **c**,
Ps 18:11 his **c** thick clouds dark with water.
    19: 5 a bridegroom from his wedding **c**,
Isa 4: 5 over all the glory there will be a **c**.
Jer 43:10 he will spread his royal **c** over them.

CAPABLE
Pr 31:10 A **c** wife who can find?

CAPERNAUM
Mt   4:13 and made his home in C by the sea,
    11:23 C, will you be exalted to heaven?
Jn   4:46 royal official whose son lay ill in C.
     6:59 was teaching in the synagogue at C.

CAPITAL → CAPITALS
1Ki 7:16 height of the one **c** was five cubits,
Ne   1: 1 while I was in Susa the **c**,
Da   4:30 as a royal **c** by my mighty power
AdE 9:18 The Jews who were in Susa, the **c**,

CAPITALS → CAPITAL
Ex 36:38 He overlaid their **c** and their bases
1Ki 7:16 also made two **c** of molten bronze,
Am   9: 1 Strike the **c** until the thresholds

CAPTAIN → CAPTAINS
Ge 37:36 officials, the **c** of the guard.
2Ki 1: 9 king sent to him a **c** of fifty with his
Jnh 1: 6 The **c** came and said to him,

CAPTAINS → CAPTAIN
Jdg 7:25 They captured the two **c** of Midian,
Rev 19:18 flesh of **c**, the flesh of the mighty,

CAPTIVATE* → CAPTURE
2Ti 3: 6 into households and **c** silly women,

CAPTIVATED* → CAPTURE
Jdt 16: 9 her beauty **c** his mind,

CAPTIVE → CAPTURE
Ge 14:14 that his nephew had been taken **c**,
2Ki 15:29 he carried the people **c** to Assyria,
    24:16 king of Babylon brought **c** to
Ps 106:46 to be pitied by all who held them **c**.
SS   7: 5 a king is held **c** in the tresses.
Isa 52: 2 the dust, rise up, O **c** Jerusalem;
Jer 13:17 the LORD's flock has been taken **c**.
Ac 20:22 And now, as a **c** to the Spirit,
Ro   7:23 making me **c** to the law of sin
2Co 10: 5 take every thought **c** to obey Christ.
Eph 4: 8 he made captivity itself a **c**;
Col 2: 8 one takes you **c** through philosophy
2Ti 2:26 been held **c** by him to do his will.
Tob 1:10 I was carried away **c** to Assyria
1Mc 1:32 took **c** the women and children,

CAPTIVES → CAPTURE
Ps 68:18 leading **c** in your train and receiving
Isa 61: 1 to proclaim liberty to the **c**,
Lk   4:18 to proclaim release to the **c** and

CAPTIVITY → CAPTURE
Dt 28:41 for they shall go into **c**.
2Ch 6:38 heart and soul in the land of their **c**,
Ezr 3: 8 had come to Jerusalem from the **c**.
     8:35 those who had come from **c**,
Ne   1: 2 those who had escaped the **c**,
Jer 15: 2 and those destined for **c**, to **c**.
Eph 4: 8 on high he made **c** itself a captive;
Rev 13:10 into **c** you go;

CAPTORS → CAPTURE
1Ki 8:50 compassion in the sight of their **c**,
Ps 137: 3 For there our **c** asked us for songs,
Isa 14: 2 take captive those who were their **c**,

CAPTURE → CAPTIVATE, CAPTIVATED,
     CAPTIVE, CAPTIVITY, CAPTORS,
     CAPTURED, CAPTURES
1Sa 23:26 in on David and his men to **c** them.

CAPTURED → CAPTURE
1Sa 4:11 The ark of God was **c**;
2Ki 17: 6 the king of Assyria **c** Samaria;
Rev 19:20 And the beast was **c**, and with it
Jdt 1:14 **c** its towers, plundered its markets,

CARAVAN → CARAVANS
Ge 37:25 a **c** of Ishmaelites coming from

CARAVANS → CARAVAN
Jdg 5: 6 **c** ceased and travelers kept to the

CARCASS → CARCASSES
Lev 11:24 whoever touches the **c** of any of
Jdg 14: 9 the honey from the **c** of the lion.

CARCASSES → CARCASS
Ge 15:11 birds of prey came down on the **c**,
Lev 26:30 heap your **c** on the **c** of your idols.

CARCHEMISH
2Ch 35:20 Neco of Egypt went up to fight at C

CARE → CARED, CAREFUL, CAREFULLY, CARELESS, CARES, CARING
Ge 39:22 jailer committed to Joseph's **c** all
Dt   6:12 **c** that you do not forget the LORD,
Ps   8: 4 mortals that you **c** for them?
Mt 25:36 I was sick and you took **c** of me,
Lk 10:34 brought him to an inn, and took **c** of
1Co 12:25 have the same **c** for one another.
1Ti 3: 5 how can he take **c** of God's church?
Heb 2: 6 or mortals, that you **c** for them?
Jas 1:27 to **c** for orphans and widows in

CARED → CARE
Dt 32:10 he shielded him, **c** for him,

CAREFUL* → CARE
Ex 19:12 'Be **c** not to go up the mountain or
Dt   2: 4 of you, so, be very **c**
     4:23 So be **c** not to forget the covenant
     5:32 You must therefore be **c** to do as
    12:28 Be **c** to obey all these words
    15: 9 Be **c** that you do not entertain a
    24: 8 skin disease by being very **c**;
Jos 1: 7 being **c** to act in accordance with all
     1: 8 you may be **c** to act in accordance
    22: 3 but have been **c** to keep the charge
    23:11 Be very **c**, therefore, to love
Jdg 13: 4 **c** not to drink wine or strong drink,
2Ki 10:31 not **c** to follow the law of the LORD
    17:37 you shall always be **c** to observe.
    21: 8 if only they will be **c** to do
1Ch 22:13 if you are **c** to observe
2Ch 33: 8 **c** to do all that I have commanded
Eze 18: 9 and is **c** to observe my ordinances,
    18:19 been **c** to observe all my statutes,
    20:19 and be **c** to observe my ordinances,
    20:21 not **c** to observe my ordinances,
    36:27 you follow my statutes and be **c**
    37:24 shall follow my ordinances and be **c**
Eph 5:15 Be **c** then how you live,
Tit 3: 8 may be **c** to devote themselves
1Pe 1:10 made **c** search and inquiry,
Sir 13:13 Be on your guard and very **c**,
    29:20 but be **c** not to fall yourself.
    38:26 he is **c** about fodder for the heifers.
    38:27 and they are **c** to finish their work.
    38:28 he is **c** to complete its decoration.

CAREFULLY → CARE
Ex 15:26 "If you will listen **c** to the voice of
Lk   1: 3 investigating everything **c** from the

CARELESS* → CARE
Pr 14:16 the fool throws off restraint and is **c**.
Mt 12:36 to give an account for every **c** word

CARES* → CARE
Ps 94:19 When the **c** of my heart are many,
    142: 4 remains to me; no one **c** for me.
Ecc 5: 3 For dreams come with many **c**,
Jer 30:17 "It is Zion; no one **c** for her!"
Zec 10: 3 for the LORD of hosts **c** for his flock,
Mt 13:22 but the **c** of the world and the lure of
Mk   4:19 but the **c** of the world,
Lk   8:14 they are choked by the **c** and riches
Eph 5:29 he nourishes and tenderly **c** for it,
1Pe 5: 7 on him, because he **c** for you.
Wis 8: 9 and encouragement in **c** and grief.

CARGO
Jnh 1: 5 threw the **c** that was in the ship
Ac 27:18 to throw the **c** overboard,

CARING → CARE
1Th 2: 7 like a nurse tenderly **c** for her own

CARMEL
1Sa 25: 2 whose property was in C.
1Ki 18:20 assembled the prophets at Mount C.
Na   1: 4 Bashan and C wither, and the bloom

CARNELIAN
Ex 28:17 A row of **c**, chrysolite, and emerald
Rev 4: 3 seated there looks like jasper and **c**,
    21:20 the sixth **c**, the seventh chrysolite,

CAROUSING*
Gal 5:21 drunkenness, **c**, and things like these
1Pe 4: 3 drunkenness, revels, **c**, and lawless

CARPENTER* → CARPENTER'S, CARPENTERS
Isa 44:13 The **c** stretches a line, marks it out
Mk   6: 3 Is not this the **c**, the son of Mary
LtJ 6: 8 Their tongues are smoothed by the **c**

CARPENTER'S* → CARPENTER
Mt 13:55 Is not this the **c** son?

CARPENTERS → CARPENTER
1Ch 14: 1 and **c** to build a house for him.
2Ch 24:12 they hired masons and **c** to restore
Ezr 3: 7 money to the masons and the **c**,

CARRIED → CARRY
Ex   4:20 Moses **c** the staff of God in his hand
Nu 10:17 who **c** the tabernacle, set out.
Dt   1:31 saw how the LORD your God **c** you,
    31: 9 who **c** the ark of the covenant of the
2Sa 6: 3 They **c** the ark of God on a new cart,
2Ki 17: 6 he **c** the Israelites away to Assyria.
    24:14 He **c** away all Jerusalem, all the
Ezr 7: 7 that Nebuchadnezzar had **c** away
Est 2: 6 Nebuchadnezzar of Babylon had **c**
Pr   6:27 Can fire be **c** in the bosom without
Isa 53: 4 our infirmities and **c** our diseases;
    63: 9 he lifted them up and **c** them all the
Jer 10: 5 have to be **c**, for they cannot walk.
Lk 24:51 and was **c** up into heaven.
Jn 20:15 "Sir, if you have **c** him away,
Heb 13: 9 not be **c** away by all kinds of strange
2Pe 3:17 beware that you are not **c** away
Rev 17: 3 So he **c** me away in the spirit into a
    21:10 in the spirit he **c** me away to a great,

CARRIES → CARRY
Nu 11:12 as a nurse **c** a sucking child,'
Dt   1:31 just as one **c** a child,
Job 21:18 like chaff that the storm **c** away?
Isa 40:24 the tempest **c** them off like stubble.

CARRY → CARRIED, CARRIES, CARRYING
Ge 47:30 **c** me out of Egypt and bury me
    50:25 you shall **c** up my bones from here."
Ex 13:19 then you must **c** my bones with you
Nu   1:50 they are to **c** the tabernacle
Dt 10: 8 apart the tribe of Levi to **c** the ark
Jos 6: 6 have seven priests **c** seven trumpets
1Ch 15: 2 but the Levites were to **c** the ark
Ps 28: 9 their shepherd, and **c** them forever.
    49:17 when they die they will **c** nothing
Isa 40:11 and **c** them in his bosom,
    45:20 who **c** about their wooden idols,
    46: 4 when you turn gray I will **c** you.
    46: 4 I will **c** and will save.
Mt   3:11 I am not worthy to **c** his sandals.
    27:32 compelled this man to **c** his cross.
Lk 14:27 does not **c** the cross and follow me
Gal 6: 5 For all must **c** their own loads.
     6:17 I **c** the marks of Jesus branded on
2Ti 4: 5 **c** out your ministry fully.

CARRYING → CARRY
Ex 32:15 **c** the two tablets of the covenant in
1Sa 3: 3 of the LORD in Shiloh, **c** an ephod.
2Sa 15:24 **c** the ark of the covenant of God.
Mt 11:28 are weary and are **c** heavy burdens,
Lk   5:18 **c** a paralyzed man on a bed.
    22:10 man **c** a jar of water will meet you;

CART
1Sa 6:11 put the ark of the LORD on the **c**,
1Ch 13: 7 carried the ark of God on a new **c**,

CARVE* → CARVED, CARVINGS
Dt 10: 1 "C out two tablets of stone like the

CARVED → CARVE
Lev 26: 1 and erect no **c** images or pillars,
1Ki 6:29 He **c** the walls of the house all
2Ki 17:41 but also served their **c** images;
Ps 74: 6 they smashed all its **c** work.
Eze 41:19 They were **c** on the whole temple
1Mc 5:68 the **c** images of their gods he burned

CARVINGS → CARVE
1Ki 6:18 The cedar within the house had **c** of

CASE → CASES
Ex 18:22 bring every important **c** to you,
Jos 20: 4 explain the **c** to the elders of that
Job 13: 3 and I desire to argue my **c** with God.
    23: 4 I would lay my **c** before him,
Ps   5: 3 in the morning I plead my **c** to you,
Pr 18:17 one who first states a **c** seems right,
    25: 9 Argue your **c** with your neighbor
Isa 3:13 The LORD rises to argue his **c**;
    41:21 Set forth your **c**, says the LORD;
Jer 12: 1 but let me put my **c** to you.
Mic 6: 1 plead your **c** before the mountains,
Lk 12:58 make an effort to settle the **c**,
Jn 18:38 "I find no **c** against him.
    19: 6 I find no **c** against him."
Ac 25:14 Festus laid Paul's **c** before the king,
Sir 35:25 until he judges the **c** of his people

CASES → CASE
Ex 18:26 hard **c** they brought to Moses,
Nu   5:29 This is the law in **c** of jealousy,
1Co 6: 2 are you incompetent to try trivial **c**?

CAST → CASTING, CASTS, DOWNCAST
Ge 21:10 "C out this slave woman with her
Ex 32: 4 in a mold, and **c** an image of a calf;
    34:17 You shall not make **c** idols.
Lev 16: 8 Aaron shall **c** lots on the two goats,
Jos 18: 6 I will **c** lots for you here before
1Sa 14:42 "C the lot between me and my son
1Ki 7:15 He **c** two pillars of bronze.
2Ki 17:16 and made for themselves **c** images
Ne 10:34 have also **c** lots among the priests,
Est 3: 7 of King Ahasuerus, they **c** Pur—
     9:24 Jews to destroy them, and had **c** Pur
Ps 22:10 On you I was **c** from my birth,
    22:18 and for my clothing they **c** lots.
    42: 5 Why are you **c** down, O my soul,
    44:23 Awake, do not **c** us off forever!
    51:11 not **c** me away from your presence,
    55:22 C your burden on the LORD,
    71: 9 not **c** me off in the time of old age;
Pr 16:33 The lot is **c** into the lap,
Isa 38:17 all my sins behind your back.
Jer 7:15 And I will **c** you out of my sight,
Joel 3: 3 and **c** lots for my people,
Ob   1:11 his gates and **c** lots for Jerusalem,
Jnh 1: 7 they **c** lots, and the lot fell on Jonah.
Hab 2:18 a **c** image, a teacher of lies?
Mt   7:22 and **c** out demons in your name,
     8:16 and he **c** out the spirits with a word,
    12:27 If I **c** out demons by Beelzebul,
Mk   3:23 "How can Satan **c** out Satan?
Jn 19:24 and for my clothing they **c** lots."
    21: 6 "C the net to the right side of the
Ac   1:26 they **c** lots for them, and the lot fell
1Pe 5: 7 C all your anxiety on him,
Rev 4:10 **c** their crowns before the throne,

CASTING → CAST
Lev 18:24 the nations I am **c** out before you
Pr 18:18 C the lot puts an end to disputes
Mt   4:18 **c** a net into the sea—for they were

Jn 19:17 and **c** the cross by himself,
2Co 4:10 **c** in the body the death of Jesus,

27:35 among themselves by **c** lots;
Mk   1:16 and his brother Andrew **c** a net
   9:38 we saw someone **c** out demons in
AdE 3: 7 Haman came to a decision by **c** lots,

CASTLE*

Pr   18:19 quarreling is like the bars of a **c.**
Lk   11:21 man, fully armed, guards his **c,**

CASTRATE*

Gal   5:12 unsettle you would **c** themselves!

CASTS → CAST

Dt   18:11 one who **c** spells, or who consults
Ps 147: 6 he **c** the wicked to the ground.
Pr   21:12 he **c** the wicked down to ruin.
Isa 40:19 An idol? —A workman **c** it,
Lk   11:15 "He **c** out demons by Beelzebul,
1Jn   4:18 but perfect love **c** out fear;

CATAPULTS

1Mc   6:51 machines to shoot arrows, and **c.**

CATCH → CATCHES, CATCHING, CAUGHT

Nu   11:22 enough fish in the sea to **c** for them?
SS   2:15 **C** us the foxes, the little foxes,
Lk   5: 4 and let down your nets for a **c.**
   11:54 to **c** him in something he might say.
Tob   6: 4 "**C** hold of the fish and hang on to

CATCHES → CATCH

1Co   3:19 "He **c** the wise in their craftiness,"

CATCHING* → CATCH

Lk   5:10 from now on you will be **c** people."

CATERPILLAR

2Ch   6:28 plague, blight, mildew, locust, or **c;**
Ps   78:46 He gave their crops to the **c,**

CATTLE

Ge   1:25 and the **c** of every kind,
   2:20 The man gave names to all **c,**
Nu   32: 1 owned a very great number of **c.**
1Sa 15:14 and the lowing of **c** that I hear?"
Ps   50:10 the **c** on a thousand hills.
  104:14 cause the grass to grow for the **c,**
  144:14 and may our **c** be heavy with young.
Jn   temple he found people selling **c,**

CAUGHT → CATCH

Ge   22:13 **c** in a thicket by its horns.
   39:12 she **c** hold of his garment,
Ex   22: 7 the thief, if **c,** shall pay double.
   22:28 and they are **c** in the act,
   24: 7 If someone is **c** kidnaping another
1Sa 15:27 Saul **c** hold of the hem of his robe,
2Sa 18: 9 His head **c** fast in the oak,
Ps   10: 2 let them be **c** in the schemes
Pr   2: 2 by the words of your mouth.
Lk   5: 5 all night long but have **c** nothing.
Jn   8: 3 woman who had been **c** in adultery;
2Co 12: 2 was **c** up to the third heaven—
1Th   4:17 be **c** up in the clouds together with
Sir 27:26 whoever sets a snare will be **c** in it.

CAUSE → CAUSED, CAUSES

Jdg   6:31 Or will you defend his **c?**
1Ki   8:45 and their plea, and maintain their **c.**
Job   5: 8 and to God I would commit my **c.**
Ps   9: 4 For you have maintained my just **c;**
   17: 1 Hear a just **c,** O LORD;
   22: 8 "Commit your **c** to the LORD;
   35: 7 without **c** they hid their net for me;
   45: 4 victoriously for the **c** of truth and
   74:22 Rise up, O God, plead your **c;**
  109: 3 of hate, and attack me without **c.**
  119:86 I am persecuted without **c;**
  119:154 Plead my **c** and redeem me;
  140:12 LORD maintains the **c** of the needy,
Pr   24:28 against your neighbor without **c,**
Isa   1:23 the widow's **c** does not come before
   49: 4 yet surely my **c** is with the LORD,
Jer 11:20 for to you I have committed my **c.**
   51:36 I am going to defend your **c** and

La   3:59 done to me, O LORD; judge my **c.**
Eze 37: 5 I will **c** breath to enter you,
Lk   17: 2 the sea than for you to **c** one
Jn   15:25 'They hated me without a **c.'**
Ac   14:15 no **c** for a sentence of death,
Ro   14:15 Do not let what you eat **c** the ruin
   16:17 an eye on those who **c** dissensions
1Co   8:13 if food is a **c** of their falling,
1Jn   2:10 a person there is no **c** for stumbling.
Rev 13:15 and **c** those who would not worship

CAUSED → CAUSE

Ge   2:21 LORD God **c** a deep sleep to fall
   39: 3 LORD **c** all that he did to prosper in
1Ki 14:16 and which he **c** Israel to commit."
2Ki 23:15 son of Nebat, who **c** Israel to sin—
Ps 106:46 He **c** them to be pitied

CAUSES → CAUSE

Pr   10: 4 A slack hand **c** poverty,
La   3:32 he **c** grief, he will have compassion
Mt   5:29 If your right eye **c** you to sin,
   5:30 And if your right hand **c** you to sin,
   5:32 **c** her to commit adultery;
   18: 8 hand or your foot **c** you to stumble,

CAUTIOUS*

Pr   14:16 wise are **c** and turn away from evil,
   22: 5 the **c** will keep far from them.
Sir 18:27 One who is wise is **c** in everything;

CAVE → CAVES

Ge   19:30 lived in a **c** with his two daughters.
   23: 9 he may give me the **c** of Machpelah,
   25: 9 buried him in the **c** of Machpelah,
   49:29 in the **c** in the field of Ephron the
   50:13 and buried him in the **c** of the field
Jos 10:16 themselves in the **c** at Makkedah,
1Sa 22: 1 and escaped to the **c** of Adullam;
   24: 3 in the innermost parts of the **c.**
1Ki 18: 4 hid them fifty to a **c,**
   19: 9 At that place he came to a **c,**
Ps   57: T when he fled from Saul, in the **c.**
  142: T When he was in the **c.**
Jn   11:38 It was a **c,** and a stone was lying
Jdt 16:23 in the **c** of her husband Manasseh;

CAVERNS*

Isa   2:21 the **c** of the rocks and the clefts in

CAVES → CAVE

Jdg   6: 2 hiding places in the mountains, **c**
1Sa 13: 6 the people hid themselves in **c** and
Isa   2:19 Enter the **c** of the rocks and the
Heb 11:38 and in **c** and holes in the ground.
Rev   6:15 hid in the **c** and among the rocks of
2Mc   6:11 who had assembled in the **c** nearby,

CEASE → CEASED, CEASES

Ge   8:22 winter, day and night, shall not **c."**
Jos 22:25 our children **c** to worship the LORD.
Ps   46: 9 makes wars **c** to the end of the earth;
Pr   22:10 quarreling and abuse will **c.**
Jer 31:36 If this fixed order were ever to **c**
1Co 13: 8 as for tongues, they will **c;**
Heb   4:10 also **c** from their labors as God did

CEASED → CEASE

Ps   77: 8 Has his steadfast love **c** forever?
La   5:15 The joy of our hearts has **c;**
Jnh   1:15 and the sea **c** from its raging.
Mt   14:32 they got into the boat, the wind **c.**
1Mc   9:73 Thus the sword **c** from Israel.

CEASES → CEASE

La   3:22 steadfast love of the LORD never **c,**

CEDAR → CEDARS, CEDARWOOD

2Sa   7: 2 See now, I am living in a house of **c,**
1Ki   5:10 need for timber of **c** and cypress.
   7: 7 covered with **c** from floor to floor.
2Ch 25:18 thornbush on Lebanon sent to a **c**
Ezr   3: 7 the Tyrians to bring **c** trees from
Job 40:17 It makes its tail stiff like a **c;**

Ps   92:12 and grow like a **c** in Lebanon.
SS   8: 9 will enclose her with boards of **c.**
Isa 41:19 I will put in the wilderness the **c,**
Eze 17: 3 He took the top of the **c,**
   31: 3 Consider Assyria, a **c** of Lebanon,
Sir 24:13 "I grew tall like a **c** in Lebanon,

CEDARS → CEDAR

Jdg   9:15 and devour the **c** of Lebanon.'
Ps   29: 5 The voice of the LORD breaks the **c;**
Isa 37:24 I felled its tallest **c,** its choicest

CEDARWOOD → CEDAR, WOOD

Lev 14:49 with **c** and crimson yarn and hyssop,

CELEBRATE → CELEBRATED

Ex   5: 1 so that they may **c** a festival to me
   10: 9 we have the LORD's festival to **c."**
   12:14 shall **c** it as a festival to the LORD;
   12:47 congregation of Israel shall **c** it.
   12:48 with you wants to **c** the passover to
   12:48 then he may draw near to **c** it;
Lev 23: 4 you shall **c** at the time appointed
   23:37 shall **c** as times of holy convocation,
Nu   29:12 shall **c** a festival to the LORD seven
Dt   16:15 undertakings, and you shall surely **c.**
   26:11 shall **c** with all the bounty that
Ne   12:27 to Jerusalem to **c** the dedication
Ps 145: 7 They shall **c** the fame of your
Eze 45:21 shall **c** the festival of the passover
Na   1:15 **C** your festivals, O Judah, fulfill
Lk   15:23 calf and kill it, and let us eat and **c;**
   15:24 And they began to **c.**
   15:29 a young goat so that I might **c** with
   15:32 But we had to **c** and rejoice,
1Co   5: 8 Therefore, let us **c** the festival,
Rev 11:10 gloat over them and **c** and exchange

CELEBRATED → CELEBRATE

Ezr   6:16 **c** the dedication of this house of
Ps   45:17 I will cause your name to be **c** in all
AdE   9:18 They **c** the fifteenth with joy and
1Mc   4:56 they **c** the dedication of the altar for
   7:49 decreed that this day should be **c**

CELL* → CELLS

Ac   12: 7 appeared and a light shone in the **c.**
   16:24 in the innermost **c** and fastened

CELLAR*

Lk   11:33 after lighting a lamp puts it in a **c,**

CELLS* → CELL

Jer 37:16 in the **c,** and remained there many

CENSER → CENSERS

Lev 10: 1 Nadab and Abihu, each took his **c,**
Nu   16:18 So each man took his **c,**
2Ch 26:19 had a **c** in his hand to make offering,
Eze   8:11 Each had his **c** in his hand,
Rev   8: 3 Another angel with a golden **c** came

CENSERS → CENSER

Nu   16:38 the **c** of these sinners have become
1Mc   1:22 the bowls, the golden **c,** the curtain,

CENSUS

Ex   30:12 a **c** of the Israelites to register them,
Nu   1: 2 Take a **c** of the whole congregation
   26: 2 "Take a **c** of the whole congregation
2Sa 24: 2 and take a **c** of the people,

CENTER

Isa 19:19 be an altar to the LORD in the **c** of
Da   4:10 there was a tree at the **c** of the earth,
Rev   7:17 for the Lamb at the **c** of the throne

CENTURION → CENTURIONS

Mt   8: 5 he entered Capernaum, a **c** came to
   27:54 Now when the **c** and those with him,
Mk   15:39 when the **c,** who stood facing him,
Lk   23:47 the **c** saw what had taken place,
Ac   10: 1 a man named Cornelius, a **c**
   22:25 Paul said to the **c** who was standing
   27: 1 a **c** of the Augustan Cohort,

CENTURIONS → CENTURION
Ac 23:17 Paul called one of the c

CEPHAS* → =PETER
Name given to the apostle Peter (Jn 1:42; 1Co 1:12; 3:22; 9:5; 15:5; Gal 1:18; 2:9, 11, 14).

CEREMONIALLY*
Lev 12: 2 she shall be c unclean seven days;
13: 3 he shall pronounce him c unclean.
15: 2 his discharge makes him c unclean.

CERTIFICATE* → CERTIFIED
Dt 24: 1 and so he writes her a c of divorce,
Mt 5:31 let him give her a c of divorce.'
19: 7 give a c of dismissal and to divorce
Mk 10: 4 a man to write a c of dismissal

CERTIFIED* → CERTIFICATE
Jn 3:33 accepted his testimony has c this,
Sir 44:20 he c the covenant in his flesh,

CHAFF
Job 21:18 like c that the storm carries away?
Ps 1: 4 are like c that the wind drives away.
35: 5 Let them be like c before the wind,
Isa 33:11 You conceive c, you bring forth
Jer 13:24 I will scatter you like c driven by
Da 2:35 in pieces and became like the c
Hos 13: 3 like c that swirls from the threshing
Zep 2: 2 like the drifting c,
Mt 3:12 c he will burn with unquenchable
Lk 3:17 c he will burn with unquenchable

CHAIN → CHAINED, CHAINS
Ge 41:42 and put a gold c around his neck.
Da 5: 7 have a c of gold around his neck,
Mk 5: 3 him any more, even with a c;
Ac 28:20 that I am bound with this c."
Rev 20: 1 to the bottomless pit and a great c.

CHAINED* → CHAIN
2Ti 2: 9 the point of being c like a criminal.
But the word of God is not c.

CHAINS → CHAIN
Ex 28:14 two c of pure gold, twisted like
1Ki 6:21 then he drew c of gold across,
La 3: 7 he has put heavy c on me;
Mk 5: 4 but the c he wrenched apart,
Ac 8:23 bitterness and the c of wickedness."
12: 7 And the c fell off his wrists.
16:26 and everyone's c were unfastened.
Eph 6:20 for which I am an ambassador in c.
Col 4:18 Remember my c.
Heb 11:36 and even c and imprisonment.
2Pe 2: 4 them to c of deepest darkness
Jude 1: 6 in eternal c in deepest darkness for

CHALDEA → CHALDEAN, CHALDEANS
Isa 47: 5 and go into darkness, daughter C!
Jer 50:10 C shall be plundered; all who
Eze 23:16 and sent messengers to them in C.
Jdt 5: 7 of their ancestors who were in C.

CHALDEAN → CHALDEA
Ezr 5:12 the C, who destroyed this house
Da 5:30 Belshazzar, the C king, was killed.

CHALDEANS → CHALDEA
Ge 11:31 from Ur of the C to go into the land
15: 7 who brought you from Ur of the C,
2Ch 36:17 up against them the king of the C,
Ne 9: 7 brought him out of Ur of the C and
Jer 50:35 sword against the C, says the LORD,
Eze 1: 3 in the land of the C by the river
Da 1: 4 the literature and language of the C.
5:11 of the magicians, enchanters, C,
Hab 1: 6 For I am rousing the C,
Bar 1: 2 the C took Jerusalem and burned it

CHAMBER → CHAMBERS
Jdg 3:20 was sitting alone in his cool roof c,
2Sa 13:10 "Bring the food into the c,

1Ki 17:19 the upper c where he was lodging,
Job 37: 9 From its c comes the whirlwind,
Tob 6:14 and that they died in the bridal c.

CHAMBERS → CHAMBER
1Ch 9:26 in charge of the c and the treasures
23:28 the care of the courts and the c,
SS 1: 4 The king has brought me into his c.
Am 9: 6 builds his upper c in the heavens,

CHAMPION → CHAMPIONED
1Sa 17: 4 of the Philistines a c named Goliath,
17:51 saw that their c was dead, they fled.

CHAMPIONED* → CHAMPION
Job 29:16 and I c the cause of the stranger.

CHANCE
1Sa 6: 9 it happened to us by c."
Ecc 9:11 but time and c happen to them all.

CHANGE → CHANGED, CHANGERS, CHANGES
Ex 32:12 c your mind and do not bring
Nu 23:19 a mortal, that he should c his mind.
1Sa 15:29 will not recant or c his mind;
Ps 46: 2 not fear, though the earth should c,
110: 4 has sworn and will not c his mind,
Jer 13:23 Can Ethiopians c their skin
18: 8 I will c my mind about the disaster
26: 3 I may c my mind about the disaster
Jnh 3: 9 God may relent and c his mind;
Mal 3: 6 For I the LORD do not c;
Mt 18: 3 you c and become like children,
21:32 did not c your minds and believe
Heb 7:12 when there is a c in the priesthood,
7:21 has sworn and will not c his mind,
Jas 1:17 is no variation or shadow due to c.

CHANGED → CHANGE
Ge 31: 7 and c my wages ten times,
Ex 32:14 LORD c his mind about the disaster
Jer 2:11 Has a nation c its gods,
Da 4:16 his mind be c from that of a human,
6:15 that the king establishes can be c."
Jnh 3:10 God c his mind about the calamity
Lk 9:29 the appearance of his face c,
Jn 4:46 where he had c the water into wine.
1Co 15:51 will not all die, but we will all be c,
Heb 1:12 and like clothing they will be c.

CHANGERS* → CHANGE
Mt 21:12 overturned the tables of the money c
Mk 11:15 overturned the tables of the money c
Jn 2:14 the money c seated at their tables.
2:15 poured out the coins of the money c

CHANGES → CHANGE
Da 2:21 He c times and seasons, deposes
Sir 13:25 The heart c the countenance,

CHANNELS
Ps 18:15 Then the c of the sea were seen,
Isa 8: 7 above all its c and overflow all its
Eze 29: 3 sprawling in the midst of its c,

CHAOS
Job 10:22 the land of gloom and c,
Isa 45:18 he did not create it a c, he formed it
2Es 5: 8 shall be c also in many places,

CHARACTER → CHARACTERS
Ro 5: 4 and endurance produces c, and c produces hope,

CHARACTERS* → CHARACTER
Isa 8: 1 tablet and write on it in common c,
2Es 14:42 using c that they did not know.

CHARGE → CHARGED, CHARGES
Ge 39: 4 and put him in c of all that he had.
49:33 When Jacob ended his c to his sons,
Ex 23: 7 Keep far from a false c,
Nu 4:16 son of Aaron the priest shall have c
9:23 They kept the c of the LORD,

Dt 11: 1 his c, his decrees, his ordinances,
19:15 witnesses shall a c be sustained.
23:19 not c interest on loans to another
Job 1:22 not sin or c God with wrongdoing.
34:13 Who gave him c over the earth and
Ps 50:21 I rebuke you, and lay the c before
Mt 24:47 that one in c of all his possessions.
25:21 I will put you in c of many things;
27:14 no answer, not even to a single c,
Mk 15:26 The inscription of the c against him
Ro 8:33 will bring any c against God's elect?
1Co 9:18 I may make the gospel free of c,
2Co 11: 7 God's good news to you free of c?
13: 1 "Any c must be sustained by the
Phm 1:18 you anything, c that to my account.
1Pe 5: 3 Do not lord it over those in your c,

CHARGED → CHARGE
Ge 28: 6 and that as he blessed him he c him,
Nu 4:31 This is what they are c to carry,
Dt 27:11 The same day Moses c the people
33: 4 Moses c us with the law,
1Ki 2: 1 he c his son Solomon, saying:
Est 2:10 for Mordecai had c her not to tell.
Ac 23:29 was c with nothing deserving death
Sus 1:43 the wicked things that they have c

CHARGES → CHARGE
Job 4:18 and his angels he c with error;
Mk 15: 4 many c they bring against you."
Lk 23:14 this man guilty of any of your c
Ac 25: 7 bringing many serious c against him

CHARIOT → CHARIOTS
Ge 41:43 in the c of his second-in-command;
Ex 14:25 He clogged their c wheels so that
Jdg 4:15 Sisera got down from his c and fled
1Ki 7:33 wheels were made like a c wheel;
22:34 so he said to the driver of his c,
2Ki 2:11 a c of fire and horses of fire
1Ch 28:18 for the golden c of the cherubim
2Ch 1:17 a c for six hundred shekels of silver,
Ps 104: 3 you make the clouds your c,
SS 6:12 set me in a c beside my prince.
Zec 6: 2 The first c had red horses,
Ac 8:28 seated in his c, he was reading
Sir 48: 9 in a c with horses of fire.

CHARIOTS → CHARIOT
Ex 14:28 waters returned and covered the c
15:19 with his c and his chariot drivers
Jos 11: 4 with very many horses and c.
17:18 though they have c of iron,
Jdg 4: 3 for he had nine hundred c of iron,
2Sa 8: 4 but left enough for a hundred c.
1Ki 4:26 thousand stalls of horses for his c,
2Ki 6:17 and c of fire all around Elisha.
2Ch 1:14 Solomon gathered together c and
Ps 20: 7 Some take pride in c, and some in
Isa 36: 9 when you rely on Egypt for c and
Joel 2: 5 As with the rumbling of c,
Na 2: 3 metal on the c flashes on the day
Hag 2:22 and overthrow the c and their riders;
Zec 6: 1 and saw four c coming out from
Rev 9: 9 like the noise of many c with horses
Jdt 7:20 Assyrian army, their infantry, c,
1Mc 1:17 with c and elephants and cavalry

CHARITY
Ac 9:36 devoted to good works and acts of c.
Tob 1:16 many acts of c to my kindred,
Sir 31:11 assembly will proclaim his acts of c.

CHARM → CHARMED, CHARMER
Pr 31:30 C is deceitful, and beauty is vain,
Sir 7:19 for her c is worth more than gold.
26:15 A modest wife adds c to c,

CHARMED* → CHARM
Ecc 10:11 If the snake bites before it is c,
Jer 8:17 adders that cannot be c,

CHARMER → CHARM
Sir 12:13 pities a snake c when he is bitten,

CHASE → CHASED, CHASING
Lev 26: 7 You shall give **c** to your enemies,

CHASED → CHASE
Dt   1:44 against you and **c** you as bees do.
Ne 13:28 I **c** him away from me.
La   4:19 they **c** us on the mountains,

CHASING → CHASE
Ecc 1:14 all is vanity and a **c** after wind.
     2:11 all was vanity and a **c** after wind,
      6: 9 this also is vanity and a **c** after wind.

CHASM*
Lk 16:26 between you and us a great **c** has

CHASTE* → CHASTITY
2Co 11: 2 present you as a **c** virgin to Christ.
Tit   2: 5 **c**, good managers of the household,

CHASTENED* → CHASTISE
Job 33:19 are also **c** with pain upon their beds,

CHASTISE → CHASTENED,
  CHASTISEMENT, CHASTISES
Ps 39:11 **c** mortals in punishment for sin,
Jer 30:11 I will **c** you in just measure,

CHASTISEMENT → CHASTISE
La   4: 6 the **c** of my people has been greater
Sir 16:12 Great as his mercy, so also is his **c**;

CHASTISES* → CHASTISE
Heb 12: 6 and **c** every child whom he accepts.

CHASTITY* → CHASTE
Sir   7:24 Be concerned for their **c**,
     26:15 can weigh the value of her **c**.

CHATTER*
1Ti   6:20 Avoid the profane **c** and
2Ti   2:16 Avoid profane **c**, for it will lead
Sir 21:16 A fool's **c** is like a burden on a

CHEAT → CHEATED
Lev 19:35 shall not **c** in measuring length,
     25:14 you shall not **c** one another.
Mal   1:14 Cursed be the **c** who has a male in
Sir   4: 1 do not **c** the poor of their living,

CHEATED* → CHEAT
Ge 31: 7 yet your father has **c** me

CHEBAR
Eze   1: 1 was among the exiles by the river C,
     10:15 creatures that I saw by the river C.

CHEEK → CHEEKS
1Ki 22:24 slapped him on the **c**, and said,
Job 16:10 have struck me insolently on the **c**;
Ps   3: 7 you strike all my enemies on the **c**;
La   3:30 to give one's **c** to the smiter,
Mic 5: 1 strike the ruler of Israel upon the **c**.
Mt   5:39 if anyone strikes you on the right **c**,
Lk   6:29 strikes you on the **c**, offer the other

CHEEKS → CHEEK
SS   1:10 Your **c** are comely with ornaments,
      5:13 His **c** are like beds of spices,
Isa 50: 6 my **c** to those who pulled out the
La   1: 2 in the night, with tears on her **c**;
Hos 11: 4 like those who lift infants to their **c**.

CHEER → CHEERFUL, CHEERFULNESS,
  CHEERS
Ps 94:19 your consolations **c** my soul.
Ecc 2: 3 how to **c** my body with wine—

CHEERFUL → CHEER
Pr 15:13 A glad heart makes a **c** countenance,
   15:15 but a **c** heart has a continual feast.
   17:22 A **c** heart is a good medicine,
Zec 8:19 **c** festivals for the house of Judah:
2Co 9: 7 for God loves a **c** giver.
Jas 5:13 Are any **c**? They should sing songs

CHEERFULNESS* → CHEER
Ro 12: 8 diligence; the compassionate, in **c**.
Sir 1:23 and then **c** comes back to them.

CHEERS* → CHEER
Jdg 9:13 stop producing my wine that **c** gods
Pr 12:25 but a good word **c** it up.

CHEESE*
2Sa 17:29 sheep, and **c** from the herd,
Job 10:10 like milk and curdle me like **c**?

CHEMOSH
Nu 21:29 You are undone, O people of C!
1Ki 11: 7 Solomon built a high place for C
2Ki 23:13 for C the abomination of Moab,
Jer 48: 7 C shall go out into exile,

CHERETHITES
2Sa 15:18 passed by him; and all the C,
1Ki 1:38 and the C and the Pelethites,
Eze 25:16 cut off the C, and destroy the rest

CHERISH → CHERISHED
Job 36:13 "The godless in heart **c** anger;

CHERISHED* → CHERISH
Ps 66:18 If I had **c** iniquity in my heart,
Eze 35: 5 Because you **c** an ancient enmity,
Hos 9:16 I will kill the **c** offspring of their

CHERUB → CHERUBIM
Ex 25:19 Make one **c** at the one end,
1Ki 6:26 The height of one **c** was ten cubits,
2Ch 3:11 touched the wing of the other **c**;
Ps 18:10 He rode on a **c**, and flew;
Eze 10: 4 of the LORD rose up from the **c**
     10:14 the first face was that of the **c**,
     28:14 an anointed **c** as guardian I placed
     41:18 a palm tree between **c** and **c**.
     41:18 and cherub. Each **c** had two faces:

CHERUBIM → CHERUB
Ge   3:24 the garden of Eden he placed the **c**,
Ex 25:18 You shall make two **c** of gold;
     26: 1 you shall make them with **c**
Nu   7:89 covenant from between the two **c**;
1Sa 4: 4 who is enthroned on the **c**.
2Sa 6: 2 of hosts who is enthroned on the **c**.
1Ki 6:23 he made two **c** of olivewood,
2Ki 19:15 enthroned above the **c**, you are God,
1Ch 13: 6 LORD, who is enthroned on the **c**,
2Ch 3: 7 and he carved **c** on the walls.
Ps 80: 1 You who are enthroned upon the **c**,
     99: 1 He sits enthroned upon the **c**;
Isa 37:16 who are enthroned above the **c**,
Eze 10: 1 over the heads of the **c** there
     41:18 It was formed of **c** and palm trees,
Heb 9: 5 the **c** of glory overshadowing the
Sir 49: 8 him above the chariot of the **c**.

CHEST → CHESTS
2Ki 12: 9 Then the priest Jehoiada took a **c**,
Da   2:32 its **c** and arms of silver,
Zec 13: 6 "What are these wounds on your **c**?
Rev 1:13 and with a golden sash across his **c**.

CHESTS* → CHEST
Mt   2:11 Then, opening their treasure **c**,
Rev 15: 6 with golden sashes across their **c**.
1Es 1:54 the treasure of the Lord,

CHEW → CHEWS
Dt 14: 7 Yet of those that **c** the cud or

CHEWS → CHEW
Lev 11: 3 and **c** the cud—such you may eat.

CHIEF → CHIEFS
Ge 39:21 favor in the sight of the **c** jailer.
     40: 2 the **c** cupbearer and the **c** baker,
     41: 9 the **c** cupbearer said to Pharaoh,
1Sa 21: 7 the **c** of Saul's shepherds.
2Sa 3: 8 he was **c** of the Three;
     23:18 brother of Joab, was **c** of the Thirty.
Ezr 7: 5 Eleazar, son of the **c** priest Aaron—
Ps 118:22 has become the **c** cornerstone.
Da   5:11 made him **c** of the magicians,
     10:13 So Michael, one of the **c** princes,
Mt 20:18 will be handed over to the **c** priests
     27: 6 **c** priests, taking the pieces of silver,
Mk 15: 3 the **c** priests accused him of many
Jn   2: 8 and take it to the **c** steward."
Ac   9:14 he has authority from the **c** priests
     26:10 authority received from the **c** priests
1Pe 5: 4 And when the **c** shepherd appears,

CHIEF OFFICER 1Ch 9:11; 26:24; 27:4, 16;
  2Ch 31:12, 13; Jer 20:1

CHIEF OFFICERS 1Ki 9:23; 2Ch 8:10;
  35:8; Jer 39:13; 41:1; 1Es 1:8; 7:2

CHIEF PRIEST 2Ki 25:18; 2Ch 19:11;
  24:11; 26:20; 31:10; Ezr 7:5; Jer 52:24; 1Es
  9:39, 40, 49

CHIEF PRIESTS Ezr 8:29; Mt 2:4; 16:21;
  20:18; 21:15, 23, 45; 26:3, 14, 47, 59; 27:1, 3,
  6, 12, 20, 41, 62; 28:11; Mk 8:31; 10:33;
  11:18, 27; 14:1, 10, 43, 53, 55; 15:1, 3, 10, 11,
  31; Lk 9:22; 19:47; 20:1, 19; 22:2, 4, 52, 66;
  23:4, 10, 13; 24:20; Jn 7:32, 45; 11:47, 57;
  12:10; 18:3, 35; 19:6, 15, 21; Ac 4:23; 5:24;
  9:14, 21; 22:30; 23:14; 25:2, 15; 26:10, 12

CHIEFS → CHIEF
Jos 10:24 the **c** of the warriors who had gone
     22:14 with him ten **c**, one from each of
1Ch 11:10 these are the **c** of David's warriors,

CHILD → CHILD'S, CHILDBEARING,
  CHILDBIRTH, CHILDHOOD, CHILDISH,
  CHILDLESS, CHILDREN, CHILDREN'S,
  GRANDCHILDREN
Ge   4:25 God has appointed for me another **c**
     17:17 **c** be born to a man who is a hundred
     17:17 ninety years old, bear a **c**?"
Ex   2: 3 put the **c** in it and placed it among
Dt   1:31 just as one carries a **c**,
Jdg 11:34 She was his only **c**;
Ru   4:16 Naomi took the **c** and laid him in
1Sa 1:22 as the **c** is weaned, I will bring him,
      1:27 For this **c** I prayed; and the LORD
2Sa 12: 6 pleaded with God for the **c**,
1Ki 3: 7 although I am only a little **c**;
      17:22 life of the **c** came into him again,
Job 3:16 was I not buried like a stillborn **c**,
Ps 131: 2 like a weaned **c** with its mother;
Pr   1: 8 Hear, my **c**, your father's instruction
      2: 1 My **c**, if you accept my words and
      3: 1 My **c**, do not forget my teaching,
      4:10 Hear, my **c**, and accept my words,
      5: 1 My **c**, be attentive to my wisdom;
      7: 1 My **c**, keep my words and store
     10: 1 A wise **c** makes a glad father,
     13: 1 A wise **c** loves discipline,
     23:26 My **c**, give me your heart,
     29:15 is disgraced by a neglected **c**.
Ecc 6: 3 I say that a stillborn **c** is better off
Isa 7:14 is with **c** and shall bear a son,
      9: 6 For a **c** has been born for us, a son
     11: 6 and a little **c** shall lead them.
     49:15 Can a woman forget her nursing **c**,
     66:13 a mother comforts her **c**, so I will
Jer 4:31 as of one bringing forth her first **c**,
      6:26 make mourning as for an only **c**,
Eze 18:20 A **c** shall not suffer for the iniquity
Hos 11: 1 When Israel was a **c**, I loved him,
Zec 12:10 as one mourns for an only **c**,
Mt   1:18 with **c** from the Holy Spirit.
      2: 2 is the **c** who has been born king of
      2:11 saw the **c** with Mary his mother;
     18: 2 a **c**, whom he put among them,
Mk   5:39 The **c** is not dead but sleeping."
     10:15 the kingdom of God as a little **c**
Lk   1:41 the **c** leaped in her womb.

1:80 The **c** grew and became strong in
2:12 you will find a **c** wrapped in bands
2:21 it was time to circumcise the **c;**
2:40 **c** grew and became strong, filled
9:48 welcomes this **c** in my name
1Co 3:11 When I was a **c,** I spoke like a **c,**
Gal 4: 7 So you are no longer a slave but a **c,**
Heb 11:23 they saw that the **c** was beautiful;
12: 6 chastises every **c** whom he accepts."
1Jn 3: 8 who commits sin is a **c** of the devil;
5: 1 who loves the parent loves the **c.**
Rev 12: 4 that he might devour her **c** as soon
Tob 3:15 I am my father's only **c;**
Sir 6:18 My **c,** from your youth choose
10:28 My **c,** honor yourself with humility,
30: 9 Pamper a **c,** and he will terrorize

LITTLE CHILD 1Ki 3:7; Isa 11:6; Mk 9:36;
10:15; Lk 9:47; 18:17

MY CHILD Pr 1:8, 10, 15; 2:1; 3:1, 11, 21;
4:10, 20; 5:1, 7; 6:1, 3, 20; 7:1; 19:27; 23:15,
19, 26; 24:13, 21; 27:11; Ecc 12:12; 1Ti 1:18;
2Ti 2:1; Phm 1:10; Heb 12:5; Tob 2:2, 3; 4:19;
5:18; 7:7, 10, 11, 11; 8:21, 21; 10:4, 5, 7, 8,
11, 12, 12; 11:9; 12:1, 4; Sir 2:1; 3:12, 17; 4:1;
6:18, 23, 32; 10:28; 11:10; 14:11; 16:24;
18:15; 21:1; 31:22; 37:27; 38:9, 16; 40:28;
2Mc 7:28

ONLY CHILD Jdg 11:34; Jer 6:26; Zec
12:10; Lk 9:38; Tob 3:15

CHILD'S → CHILD

Ex 2: 8 girl went and called the **c** mother.
1Ki 17:21 let this **c** life come into him again."

CHILDBEARING* → CHILD, BEAR

Ge 3:16 greatly increase your pangs in **c;**
1Ti 2:15 Yet she will be saved through **c,**

CHILDBIRTH → CHILD, BEAR

Ge 35:16 Rachel was in **c,** and she had hard
Gal 4:19 the pain of **c** until Christ is formed

CHILDHOOD → CHILD

Pr 29:21 A slave pampered from **c** will come
2Ti 3:15 from **c** you have known the sacred

CHILDISH* → CHILD

1Co 13:11 an adult, I put an end to **c** ways.

CHILDLESS → CHILD

Ge 15: 2 will you give me, for I continue **c,**
1Sa 15:33 "As your sword has made women **c,**
Mt 22:24 Moses said, 'If a man dies **c,**
Gal 4:27 it is written, "Rejoice, you **c** one,
Sir 16: 3 to die **c** better than to have ungodly

CHILDREN → CHILD

Ge 3:16 in pain you shall bring forth **c,**
21: 7 Abraham that Sarah would nurse **c?**
30: 1 "Give me **c,** or I shall die!"
Ex 2: 6 must be one of the Hebrews' **c,"**
12:26 And when your **c** ask you,
20: 5 punishing **c** for the iniquity of
Dt 4: 9 make them known to your **c** and
your children's **c—**
6: 7 Recite them to your **c** and talk about
11:19 Teach them to your **c,** talking about
14: 1 You are **c** of the LORD your God.
24:16 shall not be put to death for their **c,**
29:29 belong to us and to our **c** forever,
32:46 give them as a command to your **c,**
Jos 4: 6 When your **c** ask in time to come,
1Sa 1: 2 Peninnah had **c,** but Hannah had no
c.
2: 5 but she who has many **c** is forlorn.
Ezr 10:44 they sent them away with their **c.**
Ne 13:24 half of their **c** spoke the language of
Job 1: 5 Job said, "It may be that my **c** have
Ps 34:11 O **c,** listen to me; I will teach you
37:25 forsaken or their **c** begging bread.
78: 5 our ancestors to teach to their **c;**
82: 6 "You are gods, **c** of the Most High,
103:13 a father has compassion for his **c.**

Pr 7:24 And now, my **c,** listen to me,
13:24 who spare the rod hate their **c,**
14:26 and one's **c** will have a refuge.
17: 6 and the glory of **c** is their parents.
19:18 Discipline your **c** while there is
20: 7 happy are the **c** who follow them!
22: 6 Train **c** in the right way, and when
23:13 not withhold discipline from your **c;**
31:28 Her **c** rise up and call her happy;
Ecc 6: 3 A man may beget a hundred **c,**
Isa 1: 4 who do evil, **c** who deal corruptly,
30: 1 Oh, rebellious **c,** says the LORD,
49:25 with you, and I will save your **c.**
54:13 your **c** shall be taught by the LORD,
Jer 4:22 they are stupid **c,** they have no
31:15 Rachel is weeping for her **c;**
La 1: 5 her **c** have gone away, captives
4: 4 the **c** beg for food, but no one gives
Eze 5:10 parents shall eat their **c** in your
midst, and **c** shall eat their parents;
23:37 offered up to them for food the **c**
Hos 1: 2 whoredom and have **c** of whoredom,
2: 4 Upon her **c** also I will have no pity,
Joel 1: 3 Tell your **c** of it, and let your **c** tell
their **c,**
Zec 10: 7 Their **c** shall see it and rejoice,
Mal 4: 6 turn the hearts of parents to their **c**
and the hearts of **c** to their parents,
Mt 2:18 Rachel weeping for her **c;**
3: 9 stones to raise up **c** to Abraham.
5: 9 for they will be called **c** of God.
7:11 how to give good gifts to your **c,**
13:38 the weeds are the **c** of the evil one,
18: 3 you change and become like **c,**
19:14 "Let the little **c** come to me;
27:25 "His blood be on us and on our **c!"**
Mk 10:14 "Let the little **c** come to me;
10:30 brothers and sisters, mothers and **c,**
13:12 and **c** will rise against parents and
Lk 18:16 "Let the little **c** come to me,
Jn 1:12 he gave power to become **c** of God,
8:39 to them, "If you were Abraham's **c,**
Ac 2:39 the promise is for you, for your **c,**
Ro 8:14 by the Spirit of God are **c** of God,
8:16 with our spirit that we are **c** of God,
9: 8 the **c** of the flesh who are the **c** of
God,
9: 8 the **c** of the promise are counted as
9:26 shall be called **c** of the living God."
1Co 14:20 sisters, do not be **c** in your thinking;
2Co 12:14 **c** ought not to lay up for their
parents, but parents for their **c.**
Gal 3:26 you are all **c** of God through faith.
4:28 are **c** of the promise, like Isaac.
Eph 2: 3 and we were by nature **c** of wrath,
5: 8 you are light. Live as **c** of light—
6: 1 **C,** obey your parents in the Lord,
6: 4 do not provoke your **c** to anger,
Php 2:15 **c** of God without blemish in the
Col 3:20 **C,** obey your parents in everything,
3:21 Fathers, do not provoke your **c,**
1Th 2: 7 nurse tenderly caring for her own **c.**
1Ti 3: 4 his **c** submissive and respectful
3:12 and let them manage their **c**
5:10 as one who has brought up **c,**
5:14 have younger widows marry, bear **c,**
Tit 1: 6 only once, whose **c** are believers,
2: 4 love their husbands, to love their **c,**
Heb 2:13 "Here am I and the **c** whom God has
12: 7 God is treating you as **c;**
1Pe 1:14 obedient **c,** do not be conformed to
1Jn 3: 1 that we should be called **c** of God;
3:10 The **c** of God and the **c** of the devil
5:19 We know that we are God's **c,**
2Jn 1: 1 The elder to the elect lady and her **c,**
3Jn 1: 4 that my **c** are walking in the truth.
Rev 21: 7 be their God and they will be my **c.**
Sir 4:11 Wisdom teaches her **c** and gives
7:23 Do you have **c?** Discipline them,
30: 1 **c** CONCERNING **c** He who loves his son
1Mc 1:60 who had their **c** circumcised,

CHILDREN OF GOD Mt 5:9; Lk 20:36; Jn

1:12; 11:52; Ro 8:14, 16, 19, 21; 9:8; Gal 3:26;
Php 2:15; 1Jn 3:1, 10; 5:2; Wis 5:5

CHILDREN'S CHILDREN Ge 45:10; Ex
34:7; Dt 4:9, 25; 6:2; 2Ki 17:41; Job 42:16; Ps
103:17; 128:6; Pr 13:22; Isa 59:21; Jer 2:9;
Eze 37:25; Sir 44:11; 2Es 1:5

LITTLE CHILDREN 2Ch 31:18; Eze 9:6;
Mt 19:13, 14; Mk 10:13, 14; Lk 18:16; Jn
13:33; Gal 4:19; 1Jn 2:1, 12, 28; 3:7, 18; 4:4;
5:21

WOMEN AND CHILDREN Ge 33:5; Ne
12:43; Est 3:13; Mt 14:21; 15:38; Jdt 7:32; Bel
1:20; 1Mc 1:32; 2Mc 12:21; 4Mc 4:9

CHILDREN'S → CHILD

Pr 13:22 an inheritance to their **c** children,
Jer 31:29 and the **c** teeth are set on edge."
Eze 18: 2 and the **c** teeth are set on edge"?
Mt 15:26 "It is not fair to take the **c** food and

CHISLEV

Ne 1: 1 In the month of **C,** in the twentieth
Zec 7: 1 of the ninth month, which is **C,**
1Mc 1:54 Now on the fifteenth day of **C,**
4:59 twenty-fifth day of the month of **C.**

CHOICE → CHOOSE

Dt 33:13 with the **c** gifts of heaven above,
1Ch 21:11 "Thus says the LORD, 'Take your **c;**
Pr 8:10 and knowledge rather than **c** gold;
10:20 tongue of the righteous is **c** silver;
Jer 2:21 I planted you as a **c** vine,

CHOKE → CHOKED

Mt 13:22 and the lure of wealth **c** the word,

CHOKED → CHOKE

Mk 4: 7 and the thorns grew up and **c** it,
Lk 8: 7 and the thorns grew with it and **c** it.
8:14 they are **c** by the cares and riches
2Es 16:77 Woe to those who are **c** by their sins

CHOOSE → CHOICE, CHOOSES, CHOSE, CHOSEN

Nu 14: 4 to one another, "Let us **c** a captain,
17: 5 of the man whom I **c** shall sprout;
Dt 12:14 at the place that the LORD will **c**
30:19 **C** life so that you and your
Jos 9:27 in the place that he should **c.**
24:15 **c** this day whom you will serve,
1Ki 18:25 "**C** for yourselves one bull and
Ps 65: 4 Happy are those whom you **c** and
Pr 1:29 did not **c** the fear of the LORD,
3:31 and do not **c** any of their ways;
Isa 7:15 to refuse the evil and **c** the good.
14: 1 will again **c** Israel, and will set them
58: 6 Is not this the fast that I **c:**
Zec 2:12 and will again **c** Jerusalem.
Mt 8: 2 if you **c,** you can make me clean."
Jn 6:70 Jesus answered them, "Did I not **c**
15:16 You did not **c** me but I chose you.
Sir 6:18 child, from your youth **c** discipline,
15:15 **c,** you can keep the commandments,

CHOOSES → CHOOSE

Nu 16: 7 whom the LORD **c** shall be the holy
Mt 11:27 anyone to whom the Son **c** to reveal
Lk 10:22 anyone to whom the Son **c** to reveal
Jn 3: 8 The wind blows where it **c,**
Ro 9:18 he has mercy on whomever he **c,**
1Co 12:11 one individually just as the Spirit **c.**

CHORAZIN*

Mt 11:21 "Woe to you, **C!** Woe to you,
Lk 10:13 "Woe to you, **C!** Woe to you,

CHOSE → CHOOSE

Ge 13:11 So Lot **c** for himself all the plain of
Dt 4:37 he **c** their descendants after them.
10:15 on your ancestors alone and **c** you,
1Sa 2:28 I **c** him out of all the tribes of Israel
17:40 **c** five smooth stones from the wadi,
Ne 9: 7 God who **c** Abram and brought him

Ps 47: 4 He **c** our heritage for us,
78:68 but he **c** the tribe of Judah,
78:70 He **c** his servant David, and took
Isa 65:12 and **c** what I did not delight in.
Eze 20: 5 On the day when I **c** Israel,
Mk 13:20 for the sake of the elect, whom he **c**,
Lk 6:13 he called his disciples and **c** twelve
Jn 15:16 You did not choose me but I **c** you.
Ac 6: 5 community, and they **c** Stephen,
15:40 But Paul **c** Silas and set out,
1Co 1:27 God **c** what is foolish in the world
Eph 1: 4 as he **c** us in Christ before the
2Th 2:13 because God **c** you as the first fruits

CHOSEN → CHOOSE

Ge 18:19 I have **c** him, that he may charge
Dt 7: 6 LORD your God has **c** you out of all
18: 5 the LORD your God has **c** Levi out
Jos 24:22 that you have **c** the LORD,
Jdg 10:14 cry to the gods whom you have **c**;
1Sa 8:18 whom you have **c** for yourselves;
12:13 here is the king whom you have **c**,
20:30 that you have **c** the son of Jesse
1Ki 8:44 toward the city that you have **c** and
Ne 1: 9 them to the place at which I have **c**
Ps 89: 3 made a covenant with my **c** one,
105: 6 children of Jacob, his **c** ones.
119:30 I have **c** the way of faithfulness;
Pr 22: 1 A good name is to be **c** rather than
Isa 41: 8 my servant, Jacob, whom I have **c**,
42: 1 my servant, whom I uphold, my **c**,
43:10 and my servant whom I have **c**,
Hag 2:23 have **c** you, says the LORD of hosts.
Zec 3: 2 LORD who has **c** Jerusalem rebuke
Mt 12:18 whom I have **c**, my beloved,
22:14 For many are called, but few are **c**."
Lk 9:35 my Son, my **C**; listen to him!"
10:42 Mary has **c** the better part,
23:35 if he is the Messiah of God, his **c**
Jn 15:19 but I have **c** you out of the world—
Ac 1: 2 to the apostles whom he had **c**.
9:15 an instrument whom I have **c** to
Ro 11: 5 there is a remnant, **c** by grace.
Col 3:12 As God's **c** ones, holy and beloved,
1Th 1: 4 beloved by God, that he has **c** you,
Jas 2: 5 God **c** the poor in the world to be
1Pe 2: 6 a cornerstone **c** and precious;
2: 9 you are a **c** race, a royal priesthood,
Rev 17:14 are called and **c** and faithful."
1Mc 2:19 have **c** to obey his commandments,

CHRIST → CHRIST'S, CHRISTIAN, CHRISTIANS, MESSIAH

Mk 1: 1 of the good news of Jesus **C**,
Jn 1:17 and truth came through Jesus **C**.
4:25 Messiah is coming" (who is called **C**).
Ac 3: 6 in the name of Jesus **C** of Nazareth,
4:10 good health by the name of Jesus **C**
9:34 to him, "Aeneas, Jesus **C** heals you;
Ro 1: 4 from the dead, Jesus **C** our Lord,
3:22 of God through faith in Jesus **C**
5: 1 peace with God through our Lord Jesus **C**,
5: 6 right time **C** died for the ungodly.
5: 8 while we still were sinners **C** died
5:11 in God through our Lord Jesus **C**,
5:17 life through the one man, Jesus **C**.
6: 4 just as **C** was raised from the dead
6:23 free gift of God is eternal life in **C**
7: 4 to the law through the body of **C**,
8: 1 for those who are in **C** Jesus.
8: 9 not have the Spirit of **C** does not
8:17 heirs of God and joint heirs with **C**
8:35 will separate us from the love of **C**?
10: 4 For **C** is the end of the law so that
12: 5 who are many, are one body in **C**,
13:14 Instead, put on the Lord Jesus **C**,
14: 9 For to this end **C** died and lived
15: 3 For **C** did not please himself;
15: 5 in accordance with **C** Jesus,
15: 7 just as **C** has welcomed you,
16:18 such people do not serve our Lord **C**
1Co 1: 2 those who are sanctified in **C** Jesus,
1: 2 on the name of our Lord Jesus **C**,
1: 7 the revealing of our Lord Jesus **C**.
1:13 Has **C** been divided? Was Paul
1:17 For **C** did not send me to baptize but
1:23 but we proclaim **C** crucified,
1:30 the source of your life in **C** Jesus,
2: 2 nothing among you except Jesus **C**,
2:16 But we have the mind of **C**.
3:11 that foundation is Jesus **C**.
5: 7 lamb, **C**, has been sacrificed.
6:15 that your bodies are members of **C**?
8: 6 and one Lord, Jesus **C**,
8:12 when it is weak, you sin against **C**.
10: 4 followed them, and the rock was **C**.
11: 1 Be imitators of me, as I am of **C**.
11: 3 that **C** is the head of every man,
12:27 the body of **C** and individually
15: 3 **C** died for our sins in accordance
15:14 and if **C** has not been raised,
15:22 so all will be made alive in **C**.
15:57 victory through our Lord Jesus **C**.
2Co 1: 5 consolation is abundant through **C**.
2:14 in **C** always leads us in triumphal
3: 3 you show that you are a letter of **C**,
3:14 since only in **C** is it set aside.
4: 4 light of the gospel of the glory of **C**,
4: 5 we proclaim Jesus **C** as Lord and
4: 6 glory of God in the face of Jesus **C**.
5:10 before the judgment seat of **C**,
5:14 For the love of **C** urges us on,
5:17 is in **C**, there is a new creation:
6:15 agreement does **C** have with Beliar?
10: 1 the meekness and gentleness of **C**—
11: 2 present you as a chaste virgin to **C**.
11:13 themselves as apostles of **C**.
Gal 1: 7 and want to pervert the gospel of **C**.
2:16 we might be justified by faith in **C**,
3:28 for all of you are one in **C** Jesus.
5: 1 For freedom **C** has set us free.
6: 2 way you will fulfill the law of **C**.
Eph 1: 3 who has blessed us in **C** with every
2: 5 made us alive together with **C**—
2:10 created in **C** Jesus for good works,
2:12 that time without **C**,
2:20 **C** Jesus himself as the cornerstone.
3: 8 news of the boundless riches of **C**,
3:17 **C** may dwell in your hearts through
4:13 the measure of the full stature of **C**.
4:15 into him who is the head, into **C**,
4:32 as God in **C** has forgiven you.
5: 2 as **C** loved us and gave himself up
5:21 one another out of reverence for **C**.
5:23 is the head of the wife just as **C** is
5:25 as **C** loved the church and gave
Php 1: 6 to completion by the day of Jesus **C**.
1:18 that **C** is proclaimed in every way,
1:21 to me, living is **C** and dying is gain.
1:23 desire is to depart and be with **C**,
1:27 a manner worthy of the gospel of **C**,
1:29 privilege not only of believing in **C**,
2: 5 same mind be in you that was in **C**
2:11 should confess that Jesus **C** is Lord,
3: 7 come to regard as loss because of **C**.
3:10 to know **C** and the power of his
3:18 live as enemies of the cross of **C**;
4:19 to his riches in glory in **C** Jesus.
Col 1: 4 heard of your faith in **C** Jesus and of
1:27 **C** in you, the hope of glory.
1:28 may present everyone mature in **C**.
2: 2 of God's mystery, that is, **C** himself,
2: 6 have received **C** Jesus the Lord,
2:17 but the substance belongs to **C**.
3: 1 So if you have been raised with **C**,
3: 3 your life is hidden with **C** in God.
3:15 the peace of **C** rule in your hearts,
3:16 the word of **C** dwell in you richly;
1Th 4:16 and the dead in **C** will rise first.
5: 9 salvation through our Lord Jesus **C**,
5:18 this is the will of God in **C** Jesus
2Th 2: 1 the coming of our Lord Jesus **C**
2:14 the glory of our Lord Jesus **C**.
1Ti 1:15 **C** Jesus came into the world to save
1:16 **C** might display the utmost patience
2: 5 one mediator between God and humankind, **C** Jesus,
4: 6 will be a good servant of **C** Jesus,
6:14 manifestation of our Lord Jesus **C**,
2Ti 1: 9 grace was given to us in **C** Jesus
1:10 the appearing of our Savior **C** Jesus,
2: 1 strong in the grace that is in **C** Jesus
2: 3 suffering like a good soldier of **C**
2: 8 Remember Jesus **C**, raised from the
2:10 the salvation that is in **C** Jesus,
3:12 to live a godly life in **C** Jesus will
3:15 salvation through faith in **C** Jesus.
Tit 2:13 our great God and Savior, Jesus **C**.
Phm 1: 6 the good that we may do for **C**.
1:20 Refresh my heart in **C**.
Heb 3: 6 **C**, however, was faithful over God's
3:14 For we have become partners of **C**,
5: 5 So also **C** did not glorify himself in
6: 1 behind the basic teaching about **C**,
9:11 when **C** came as a high priest of the
9:24 For **C** did not enter a sanctuary
9:28 so **C**, having been offered once to
10:10 offering of the body of Jesus **C** once
11:26 for the **C** to be greater wealth than
13: 8 Jesus **C** is the same yesterday and
1Pe 1: 2 to be obedient to Jesus **C** and to be
1: 3 through the resurrection of Jesus **C**
1:11 to the sufferings destined for **C** and
1:19 but with the precious blood of **C**,
2:21 because **C** also suffered for you,
3:15 in your hearts sanctify **C** as Lord.
3:18 For **C** also suffered for sins once
3:21 through the resurrection of Jesus **C**,
4: 1 Since therefore **C** suffered in the
4:14 If you are reviled for the name of **C**,
2Pe 1: 1 of our God and Savior Jesus **C**:
1:16 and coming of our Lord Jesus **C**,
3:18 of our Lord and Savior Jesus **C**.
1Jn 2: 1 advocate with the Father, Jesus **C**
2:22 one who denies that Jesus is the **C**?
3:23 in the name of his Son Jesus **C**
4: 2 spirit that confesses that Jesus **C**
5: 1 Jesus is the **C** has been born of God,
5: 6 came by water and blood, Jesus **C**,
5:20 him who is true, in his Son Jesus **C**.
2Jn 1: 7 who do not confess that Jesus **C** has
1: 9 the teaching of **C**, but goes beyond
Jude 1: 1 the Father and kept safe for Jesus **C**:
1: 4 our only Master and Lord, Jesus **C**.
1:17 of the apostles of our Lord Jesus **C**;
Rev 1: 1 The revelation of Jesus **C**,
1: 5 from Jesus **C**, the faithful witness,
20: 4 reigned with **C** a thousand years.
20: 6 they will be priests of God and of **C**,

CHRIST JESUS Ac 24:24; Ro 3:24; 6:3, 11, 23; 8:1, 2, 34, 39; 15:5, 16, 17; 16:3; 1Co 1:1, 2, 4, 30; 4:15, 17; 15:31; 16:24; 2Co 1:1; Gal 2:4, 16; 3:14, 26, 28; 4:14; 5:6, 24; Eph 1:1, 1; 2:6, 7, 10, 13, 20; 3:1, 6, 11, 21; Php 1:1, 1, 8, 26; 2:5; 3:3, 8, 12, 14; 4:7, 19, 21; Col 1:1, 4; 2:6; 4:12; 1Th 2:14; 5:18; 1Ti 1:1, 1, 2, 12, 14, 15; 2:5; 3:13; 4:6; 5:21; 6:13; 2Ti 1:1, 1, 2, 9, 10, 13; 2:1, 3, 10; 3:12, 15; 4:1; Tit 1:4; Phm 1:1, 9, 23

IN CHRIST Ac 24:24; Ro 3:24; 6:11, 23; 8:1, 2, 39; 9:1; 12:5; 15:17; 16:3, 7, 9, 10; 1Co 1:2, 4, 30; 3:1; 4:10, 15, 15, 17; 15:18, 19, 22, 31; 16:24; 2Co 1:21; 2:14, 17; 3:14; 5:17, 19; 12:2, 19; Gal 1:22; 2:4, 16, 16, 17; 3:14, 26, 28; 5:6; Eph 1:1, 3, 4, 9, 11, 20; 2:6, 7, 10, 13; 3:6, 11, 21; 4:32; Php 1:1, 26, 29; 2:1, 5; 3:3, 9, 14; 4:7, 19, 21; Col 1:2, 4, 28; 2:5; 1Th 2:14; 4:16; 5:18; 1Ti 1:14; 3:13; 2Ti 1:1, 9, 13; 2:1, 10; 3:12, 15; Phm 1:8, 20, 23; 1Pe 3:16; 5:10, 14

JESUS CHRIST Mk 1:1; Jn 1:17; 17:3; Ac 2:38; 3:6; 4:10; 8:12; 9:34; 10:36, 48; 11:17; 15:26; 16:18; 28:31; Ro 1:1, 4, 6, 7, 8; 2:16;

3:22; 5:1, 11, 15, 17, 21; 7:25; 13:14; 15:6, 30;
16:20, 25, 27; 1Co 1:2, 3, 7, 8, 9, 10; 2:2; 3:11;
6:11; 8:6; 15:57; 2Co 1:2, 3, 19; 4:5, 6; 8:9;
13:5, 13; Gal 1:1, 3, 12; 2:16; 3:1, 22; 6:14,
18; Eph 1:2, 3, 5, 17; 5:20; 6:23, 24; Php 1:2,
6, 11, 19; 2:11, 21; 3:20; 4:23; Col 1:3; 1Th
1:1, 3; 5:9, 23, 28; 2Th 1:1, 2, 12; 2:1, 14, 16;
3:6, 12, 18; 1Ti 1:16; 6:3, 14; 2Ti 2:8; Tit 1:1;
2:13; 3:6; Phm 1:3, 25; Heb 10:10; 13:8, 21;
Jas 1:1; 2:1; 1Pe 1:1, 2, 3, 3, 7, 13; 2:5; 3:21;
4:11; 2Pe 1:1, 1, 8, 11, 14, 16; 2:20; 3:18; 1Jn
1:3; 2:1; 3:23; 4:2; 5:6, 20; 2Jn 1:3, 7; Jude
1:1, 1, 4, 17, 21, 25; Rev 1:1, 2, 5

CHRIST'S* → CHRIST
1Co 9:21 God's law but am under C law)
Eph 4: 7 according to the measure of C gift.
Col 1:24 what is lacking in C afflictions
1Pe 4:13 as you are sharing C sufferings,

CHRISTIAN* → CHRIST
Ac 26:28 persuading me to become a C?"
1Pe 4:16 Yet if any of you suffers as a C,

CHRISTIANS* → CHRIST
Ac 11:26 the disciples were first called "C."

CHRYSOLITE
Ex 28:17 c, and emerald shall be the first row;
Eze 28:13 c, and moonstone, beryl, onyx, and
Rev 21:20 the seventh c, the eighth beryl,

CHURCH → CHURCHES
Mt 16:18 and on this rock I will build my c,
    18:17 to listen to them, tell it to the c;
Ac   5:11 And great fear seized the whole c
     8: 1 persecution began against the c
     8: 3 Saul was ravaging the c by entering
    12: 1 upon some who belonged to the c,
    14:23 appointed elders for them in each c,
    15: 4 they were welcomed by the c and
    20:28 to shepherd the c of God that he
Ro 16: 5 Greet also the c in their house.
1Co 4:17 I teach them everywhere in every c.
     6: 4 who have no standing in the c?
    10:32 to Jews or to Greeks or to the c
    11:18 when you come together as a c,
    12:28 has appointed in the c first apostles,
    14: 4 those who prophesy build up the c.
    14:12 excel in them for building up the c.
    14:35 shameful for a woman to speak in c.
    15: 9 because I persecuted the c of God.
Gal 1:13 violently persecuting the c of God
Eph 1:22 the head over all things for the c,
     3:10 the c the wisdom of God in its rich
     3:21 to him be glory in the c and in
     5:23 as Christ is the head of the c,
     5:25 as Christ loved the c and gave
Php 3: 6 as to zeal, a persecutor of the c;
Col 1:18 He is the head of the body, the c;
     1:24 the sake of his body, that is, the c.
1Ti 3: 5 how can he take care of God's c?
     3:15 which is the c of the living God,
Jas 5:14 elders of the c and have them pray
3Jn 1: 9 I have written something to the c;
Rev 2: 1 "To the angel of the c in Ephesus

CHURCHES → CHURCH
Ac 15:41 and Cilicia, strengthening the c.
    16: 5 the c were strengthened in the faith
1Co 7:17 This is my rule in all the c.
    11:16 no such custom, nor do the c of
    14:34 women should be silent in the c.
2Co 11: 8 robbed other c by accepting support
1Th 2:14 became imitators of the c of God in
2Th 1: 4 among the c of God for your
Rev 1: 4 John to the seven c that are in Asia:
     1:20 are the angels of the seven c,
     1:20 seven lampstands are the seven c.
     2: 7 to what the Spirit is saying to the c,
    22:16 to you with this testimony for the c.

CILICIA
Ac 15:41 He went through Syria and C,

21:39 "I am a Jew, from Tarsus in C,
Jdt 2:25 He also seized the territory of C,

CIRCLE → CIRCLING, ENCIRCLE
Job 26:10 a c on the face of the waters,
Pr   8:27 he drew a c on the face of the deep,
Isa 40:22 he who sits above the c of the earth,

CIRCLING → CIRCLE
Jos 6:11 went around the city, c it once;

CIRCUIT → CIRCUITS
1Sa 7:16 a c year by year to Bethel, Gilgal,
Ps 19: 6 and its c to the end of them;

CIRCUITS* → CIRCUIT
Ecc 1: 6 and on its c the wind returns.

CIRCUMCISE* → CIRCUMCISED,
CIRCUMCISION
Ge 17:11 shall c the flesh of your foreskins,
Dt 10:16 C, then, the foreskin of your heart,
    30: 6 LORD your God will c your heart
Jos 5: 2 flint knives and c the Israelites
Jer 4: 4 C yourselves to the LORD,
Lk 1:59 the eighth day they came to c the
    2:21 it was time to c the child;
Jn 7:22 and you c a man on the sabbath.
Ac 21:21 you tell them not to c their children

CIRCUMCISED → CIRCUMCISE
Ge 17:10 Every male among you shall be c.
    17:26 and his son Ishmael were c;
    21: 4 And Abraham c his son Isaac
    34:15 and every male among you be c.
Jos 5: 3 c the Israelites at Gibeath-haaraloth.
Ac 10:45 The c believers who had come
    11: 2 the c believers criticized him,
    15: 1 c according to the custom of Moses,
    16: 3 had him c because of the Jews who
Ro 3:30 justify the c on the ground of faith
    4: 9 then, pronounced only on the c,
1Co 7:18 at the time of his call already c?
Gal 2: 3 with me, was not compelled to be c,
     2: 7 entrusted with the gospel for the c
     6:13 c do not themselves obey the law,
Php 3: 5 c on the eighth day, a member of
Col 2:11 also you were c with a spiritual
     3:11 c and uncircumcised, barbarian,
Jdt 14:10 So he was c, and joined the house
AdE 8:17 many of the Gentiles were c and
1Mc 1:60 the women who had their children c,
     2:46 forcibly c all the uncircumcised
2Mc 6:10 brought in for having c their
4Mc 4:25 because they had c their sons,

CIRCUMCISION → CIRCUMCISE
Ex   4:26 "A bridegroom of blood by c."
Ac   7: 8 Then he gave him the covenant of c.
Ro   2:25 your c has become uncircumcision.
     2:29 and real c is a matter of the heart—
1Co 7:19 C is nothing, and uncircumcision is
Gal 5: 6 For in Christ Jesus neither c
Eph 2:11 a physical c made in the flesh by
Php 3: 3 For it is we who are the c,
Col 2:11 circumcised with a spiritual c,
Tit 1:10 especially those of the c;
1Mc 1:15 and removed the marks of c,

CIRCUMSTANCES
Php 4:12 and all c I have learned the secret
1Th 5:18 thanks in all c; for this is the will of

CISTERN → CISTERNS
2Ki 18:31 and drink water from your own c,
Pr   5:15 Drink water from your own c,
Jer 38: 6 Jeremiah and threw him into the c

CISTERNS → CISTERN
Dt   6:11 hewn c that you did not hew,
Ne   9:25 hewn c, vineyards, olive orchards,
Jer 2:13 cracked c that can hold no water.

CITADEL → CITADELS
Dt   2:36 there was no c too high for us.
Est 1: 2 on his royal throne in the c of Susa,
1Mc 1:33 strong towers, and it became their c.
     4:41 in the c until he had cleansed the

CITADELS* → CITADEL
Ps 48: 3 Within its c God has shown himself
    48:13 go through its c, that you may tell

CITIES → CITY
Ge 13:12 Lot settled among the c of the Plain
    19:25 and he overthrew those c,
Ex   1:11 built supply c, Pithom and Rameses,
Lev 25:32 As for the c of the Levites,
Nu 35:11 you shall select c to be c of refuge
Dt   6:10 fine, large c that you did not build,
Jos 20: 2 'Appoint the c of refuge,
Ps 69:35 Zion and rebuild the c of Judah;
Isa 6:11 Until c lie waste without inhabitant,
    64:10 holy c have become a wilderness,
Jer 4:16 they shout against the c of Judah.
Zec 1:17 My c shall again overflow with
Lk 19:17 small thing, take charge of ten c.'
2Pe 2: 6 and if by turning the c of Sodom
Jude 1: 7 Gomorrah and the surrounding c,
Rev 16:19 and the c of the nations fell.

CITIES OF JUDAH 2Sa 2:1; 2Ki 18:13;
23:5; 2Ch 10:17; 12:4; 14:5; 17:2, 7, 9, 13;
19:5; 24:5; 25:13; 31:1, 6; Ps 69:35; Isa 36:1;
40:9; 44:26; Jer 1:15; 4:16; 7:34; 10:22; 11:6,
12; 26:2; 32:44; 34:7, 7; Zec 1:12; 1Mc 1:29;
3:8

CITIES OF REFUGE Nu 35:6, 11, 13, 14;
Jos 20:2; 1Ch 6:57, 67

FORTIFIED CITIES Nu 32:36; Jos 14:12;
1Sa 6:18; 2Sa 20:6; 2Ki 18:13; 19:25; 2Ch
8:5; 11:10, 23; 12:4; 14:6; 17:2, 19; 19:5; 21:3;
32:1; 33:14; Isa 36:1; 37:26; Jer 4:5; 5:17;
8:14; 34:7; Hos 8:14; Zep 1:16; 1Mc 1:19

CITIZEN → CITIZENS, CITIZENSHIP
Lev 24:22 one law for the alien and for the c:
Ac 21:39 in Cilicia, a c of an important city;
    22:25 to flog a Roman c who is
    23:27 had learned that he was a Roman c,

CITIZENS → CITIZEN
Ac 16:38 they heard that they were Roman c;
Eph 2:19 but you are c with the saints and

CITIZENSHIP → CITIZEN
Ac 22:28 a large sum of money to get my c."
Php 3:20 But our c is in heaven,

CITY → CITIES, CITY'S
Ge   4:17 and he built a c, and named it Enoch
    11: 4 "Come, let us build ourselves a c,
    18:24 are fifty righteous within the c;
    19:14 the c is about to destroy the c."
Dt 28: 3 Blessed shall you be in the c,
    28:16 Cursed shall you be in the c,
Jos 6:16 For the LORD has given you the c.
Jdg 16: 3 took hold of the doors of the c gate
2Sa 5: 9 and named it the c of David.
1Ki 8:44 toward the c that you have chosen
1Ch 11: 7 it was called the c of David.
Ne 11: 1 to live in the holy c Jerusalem,
Ps 46: 4 streams make glad the c of God,
    48: 1 to be praised in the c of our God.
    60: 9 will bring me to the fortified c?
    122: 3 built as a c that is bound firmly
    127: 1 Unless the LORD guards the c,
Pr 11:10 with the righteous, the c rejoices;
    31:23 husband is known in the c gates,
    31:31 her works praise her in the c gates.
Isa 1:21 he faithful c has become a whore!
     1:26 Afterward you shall be called the c
           of righteousness, the faithful c.
    62:12 "Sought Out, A C Not Forsaken."
Jer 34: 2 I am going to give this c into the
    34:22 and will bring them back to this c;

La 1: 1 lonely sits the **c** that once was full
Eze 4: 1 On it portray a **c,** Jerusalem;
    11: 3 this **c** is the pot, and we are the meat
Da 9:24 for your people and your holy **c:**
Am 5: 3 The **c** that marched out a thousand
Jnh 1: 2 to Nineveh, that great **c,**
    3: 2 go to Nineveh, that great **c,**
    4:11 about Nineveh, that great **c,**
Na 3: 1 **C** of bloodshed, utterly deceitful,
Hab 2:12 and found a **c** on iniquity!"
Zep 2:15 this the exultant **c** that lived secure,
Zec 8: 3 shall be called the faithful **c,**
    14: 2 half the **c** shall go into exile,
Mt 4: 5 the devil took him to the holy **c** and
    5:14 A **c** built on a hill cannot be hid.
    23:37 the **c** that kills the prophets
Lk 2: 4 to the **c** of David called Bethlehem,
    19:41 and saw the **c,** he wept over it,
Ac 18: 10 many in this **c** who are my people."
Heb 11:10 forward to the **c** that has foundations
    12:22 Zion and to the **c** of the living God,
    13:12 Jesus also suffered outside the **c**
    13:14 For here we have no lasting **c,**
    13:14 are looking for the **c** that is to come.
Rev 3:12 and the name of the **c** of my God,
    11: 2 they will trample over the holy **c**
    16:19 great **c** was split into three parts,
    17:18 woman you saw is the great **c** that
    18:10 the great **c,** Babylon, the mighty **c!**
    20: 9 of the saints and the beloved **c.**
    21: 2 I saw the holy **c,** the new Jerusalem,
    21:22 I saw no temple in the **c,**
Tob 13: 9 O Jerusalem, the holy **c,** he afflicted
1Mc 1:31 He plundered the **c,** burned it with
    2:31 troops in Jerusalem the **c** of David,

CITY OF DAVID 2Sa 5:7, 9; 6:10, 12, 16;
1Ki 2:10; 3:1; 8:1; 9:24; 14:31; 15:8; 2Ki 8:24;
9:28; 12:21; 14:20; 15:7; 16:20; 1Ch 11:5,
7; 13:13; 15:1, 29; 2Ch 5:2; 8:11; 12:16; 14:1;
16:14; 21:1, 20; 24:16, 25; 25:28; 27:9; 32:5,
30; 33:14; Ne 3:15; 12:37; Isa 22:9; Lk 2:4,
11; 1Mc 1:33; 2:31; 7:32; 14:36

CITY OF REFUGE Nu 35:25, 26, 27, 28,
32; Jos 21:13, 21, 27, 32, 38

FORTIFIED CITY Jos 19:29; 2Ki 3:19; 10:2;
17:9; 18:8; Ps 60:9; 108:10; Isa 25:2; 27:10;
Jer 1:18

GREAT CITY Ge 10:12; Jer 22:8; Jnh 1:2;
3:2; 4:11; Rev 11:8; 16:19; 17:18; 18:10, 16,
18, 19, 21; Jdt 1:1

HOLY CITY Ne 11:1, 18; Isa 48:2; 52:1; Da
9:24; Mt 4:5; 27:53; Rev 11:2; 21:2, 10; 22:19;
Tob 13:9; Aza 1:5; 1Mc 2:7; 2Mc 1:12; 3:1;
9:14; 15:14; 3Mc 6:5

CLAIM → CLAIMED, CLAIMING, CLAIMS
Ne 2:20 or **c** or historic right in Jerusalem."
Jn 8:53 Who do you **c** to be?"
Ro 11:25 So that you may not **c** to be wiser
Rev 2: 2 tested those who **c** to be apostles

CLAIMED• → CLAIM
2Sa 18: 8 the forest **c** more victims that day
Jn 19: 7 he has **c** to be the Son of God."
Ac 4:32 no one **c** private ownership of any

CLAIMING• → CLAIM
Ac 5:36 **c** to be somebody, and a number of
Ro 1:22 **C** to be wise, they became fools;
2Ti 2:18 **c** that the resurrection has already

CLAIMS → CLAIM
Jn 19:12 Everyone who **c** to be a king sets
1Co 8: 2 Anyone who **c** to know something
    14:37 Anyone who **c** to be a prophet,

CLAN → CLANS
Nu 27: 4 be taken away from his **c** because
Isa 60:22 The least of them shall become a **c,**

CLANGING•
Ps 150: 5 Praise him with **c** cymbals;

1Co 13: 1 I am a noisy gong or a **c** cymbal.

CLANS → CLAN
Ge 36:15 These are the **c** of the sons of Esau.
Nu 1: 2 in their **c,** by ancestral houses,
    33:54 the land by lot according to your **c;**
Mic 5: 2 who are one of the little **c** of Judah,

CLAP → CLAPPED, CLAPS
Ps 47: 1 **C** your hands, all you peoples;
    98: 8 Let the floods **c** their hands;
Isa 55:12 all the trees of the field shall **c** their
La 2:15 All who pass along the way **c** their
Eze 6:11 **C** your hands and stamp your foot,
Na 3:19 All who hear the news about you **c**

CLAPPED• → CLAP
2Ki 11:12 they **c** their hands and shouted,
Eze 25: 6 Because you have **c** your hands

CLAPS• → CLAP
Job 27:23 It **c** its hands at them,
    34:37 he **c** hands among us,

CLASPS
Ex 26: 6 You shall make fifty **c** of gold,
    36:13 And he made fifty **c** of gold,

CLASSIFY•
2Co 10:12 not dare to **c** or compare ourselves

CLAUDIUS•
Ac 11:28 took place during the reign of **C.**
    18: 2 because **C** had ordered all Jews to
    23:26 "**C** Lysias to his Excellency the

CLAWS
Da 4:33 and his nails became like birds' **c.**
    7:19 its teeth of iron and **c** of bronze,

CLAY
Job 10: 9 that you fashioned me like **c;**
    33: 6 I too was formed from a piece of **c.**
Isa 29:16 the potter be regarded as the **c?**
    41:25 as on mortar, as the potter treads **c.**
    45: 9 Does the **c** say to the one who
    64: 8 we are the **c,** and you are our potter;
Jer 18: 6 Just like the **c** in the potter's hand,
Da 2:33 its feet partly of iron and partly of **c.**
Ro 9:21 Has the potter no right over the **c,**
2Co 4: 7 But we have this treasure in **c** jars,
2Ti 2:20 and silver but also of wood and **c,**
Wis 15: 7 the same **c** both the vessels that
Sir 33:13 Like **c** in the hand of the potter,
Bel 1: 7 thing is only **c** inside and bronze
2Es 7:52 will you add to them lead and **c?"**

CLEAN → CLEANNESS, CLEANSE,
CLEANSED, CLEANSES, CLEANSING
Ge 7: 2 seven pairs of all **c** animals,
Lev 10:10 and between the unclean and the **c;**
    20:25 the **c** animal and the unclean,
Dt 14:11 You may eat any **c** birds.
2Ki 5:10 be restored and you shall be **c."**
Job 15:14 mortals, that they can be **c?**
Ps 24: 4 who have **c** hands and pure hearts,
    51: 7 with hyssop, and I shall be **c;**
    73:13 All in vain I have kept my heart **c**
Pr 20: 9 say, "I have made my heart **c;**
Ecc 9: 2 the evil, to the **c** and the unclean,
Jer 4:14 wash your heart **c** of wickedness so
Eze 36:25 I will sprinkle **c** water upon you,
Zec 3: 5 So they put a **c** turban on his head
Mt 8: 2 if you choose, you can make me **c."**
    23:25 For you **c** the outside of the cup and
    27:59 and wrapped it in a **c** linen cloth
Mk 7:19 (Thus he declared all foods **c.**)
Lk 17:14 as they went, they were made **c.**
Jn 13:10 you are **c,** though not all of you."
Ac 10:15 "What God has made **c,**
Ro 14:20 Everything is indeed **c,** but it is
1Co 5: 7 **C** out the old yeast so that you may
Heb 10:22 with our hearts sprinkled **c** from
Wis 15: 7 both the vessels that serve **c** uses

CLEANNESS → CLEAN
2Sa 22:25 according to my **c** in his sight.
Am 4: 6 gave you **c** of teeth in all your cities,

CLEANSE → CLEAN
Dt 32:43 and **c** the land for his people.
2Ch 29:15 to **c** the house of the LORD.
Job 9:30 and my hands with lye,
Ps 51: 2 and **c** me from my sin.
Pr 20:30 Blows that wound **c** away evil;
Jer 33: 8 I will **c** them from all the guilt of
Eze 36:25 and from all your idols I will **c** you.
Zec 13: 1 to **c** them from sin and impurity.
Mt 10: 8 raise the dead, **c** the lepers,
2Co 7: 1 **c** ourselves from every defilement
2Ti 2:21 All who **c** themselves of the things
Jas 4: 8 **C** your hands, you sinners,
1Jn 1: 9 **c** us from all unrighteousness.
Sir 38:10 and **c** your heart from all sin.
1Mc 4:36 let us go up to **c** the sanctuary and

CLEANSED → CLEAN
Jos 22:17 even yet we have not **c** ourselves,
Ne 13:30 I **c** them from everything foreign,
Pr 30:12 yet are not **c** of their filthiness.
Eze 22:24 You are a land that is not **c,**
Da 11:35 they may be refined, purified, and **c,**
    12:10 Many shall be purified, **c,** and
Mt 8: 3 Immediately his leprosy was **c.**
    11: 5 the lepers are **c,** the deaf hear,
Lk 4:27 none of them was **c** except Naaman
Jn 15: 3 have already been **c** by the word
Heb 10: 2 since the worshipers, once for all,
1Mc 4:43 they **c** the sanctuary and removed

CLEANSES → CLEAN
1Jn 1: 7 of Jesus his Son **c** us from all sin.

CLEANSING → CLEAN
Mk 1:44 and offer for your **c** what Moses
Lk 5:14 make an offering for your **c,**
Eph 5:26 by **c** her with the washing of water
2Pe 1: 9 and is forgetful of the **c** of past sins.

CLEAR → CLEARED, CLEARING, CLEARLY
Lev 24:12 of the LORD should be made **c**
Nu 15:34 not **c** what should be done to him.
Ps 19: 8 the commandment of the LORD is **c,**
    19:12 **C** me from hidden faults.
Joel 3:21 and I will not **c** the guilty,
Na 1: 3 LORD will by no means **c** the guilty.
Mt 3:12 and he will **c** his threshing floor
Ac 23: 1 with a **c** conscience before God."
1Ti 3: 9 of the faith with a **c** conscience.
2Ti 1: 3 I worship with a **c** conscience,
Heb 13:18 sure that we have a **c** conscience,
1Pe 3:16 Keep your conscience **c,** so that,
Rev 21:11 rare jewel, like jasper, **c** as crystal.
    21:18 the city is pure gold, **c** as glass.

CLEARED → CLEAR
Ps 80: 9 You **c** the ground for it;
Isa 5: 2 He dug it and **c** it of stones,

CLEARING• → CLEAR
Ex 34: 7 yet by no means **c** the guilty,
Nu 14:18 but by no means **c** the guilty,

CLEARLY → CLEAR
Nu 12: 8 face to face—**c,** not in riddles;
Mk 8:25 and he saw everything **c.**
Lk 6:42 then you will see **c** to take the speck

CLEFT → CLEFTS
Ex 33:22 I will put you in a **c** of the rock,
Dt 14: 6 the hoof and has the hoof **c** in two,
Jer 13: 4 and hide it there in a **c** of the rock."

CLEFTS → CLEFT
SS 2:14 O my dove, in the **c** of the rock,
Isa 57: 5 valleys, under the **c** of the rocks?
Ob 1: 3 you that live in the **c** of the rock,

CLEVER → CLEVERLY, CLEVERNESS
1Sa 25: 3 The woman was **c** and beautiful,
Pr 13:16 The **c** do all things intelligently,
    14:15 but the **c** consider their steps.
Sir 6:32 apply yourself you will become **c**.

CLEVERLY → CLEVER
2Pe 1:16 we did not follow **c** devised myths

CLEVERNESS → CLEVER
Sir 19:23 There is a **c** that is detestable,
    32: 1 display your **c** at the wrong time.

CLIFF
Lk 4:29 that they might hurl him off the **c**.

CLIMB → CLIMBED
SS 7: 8 I say I will **c** the palm tree and lay
Am 9: 2 though they **c** up to heaven,

CLIMBED → CLIMB
Lk 19: 4 he ran ahead and **c** a sycamore tree

CLING → CLINGS, CLUNG
Ps 119:31 I **c** to your decrees, O LORD;
    137: 6 Let my tongue **c** to the roof of my
Rev 12:11 for they did not **c** to life even in the

CLINGS → CLING
Ge 2:24 and his mother and **c** to his wife,
Ps 63: 8 My soul **c** to you; your right hand
    119:25 My soul **c** to the dust;
Heb 12: 1 weight and the sin that **c** so closely,

CLOAK → CLOAKS
Ex 4: 6 "Put your hand inside your **c**."
    22:26 you take your neighbor's **c** in pawn,
Dt 22:12 tassels on the four corners of the **c**
Ru 3: 9 spread your **c** over your servant,
1Sa 24: 4 cut off a corner of Saul's **c**.
Eze 16: 8 I spread the edge of my **c** over you,
Mt 5:40 and take your coat, give your **c**
    9:21 touch his **c**, I will be made well."
Mk 15:17 And they clothed him in a purple **c**;
Heb 1:12 like a **c** you will roll them up,

CLOAKS → CLOAK
Ex 12:34 bowls wrapped up in their **c**
2Ki 9:13 Then hurriedly they all took their **c**
Mk 11: 8 people spread their **c** on the road,
Ac 22:23 were shouting, throwing off their **c**,

CLOSE → CLOSED, CLOSER, ENCLOSE
Ps 148:14 people of Israel who are **c** to him.
Pr 16:28 and a whisperer separates **c** friends.
Jn 1:18 who is **c** to the Father's heart,
1Co 8: 8 "Food will not bring us **c** to God."

CLOSED → CLOSE
Ge 2:21 he took one of his ribs and **c** up its
    20:18 the LORD had **c** fast all the wombs
1Sa 1: 5 though the LORD had **c** her womb.
Jer 6:10 their ears are **c**, they cannot listen.
Jnh 2: 5 The waters **c** in over me;
Lk 12: 3 what you have whispered behind **c**

CLOSER → CLOSE
Ex 3: 5 Then he said, "Come no **c!**
Pr 18:24 a true friend sticks **c** than one's

CLOTH → CLOTHS, SACKCLOTH
Nu 4: 6 and spread over that a **c** all of blue,
Dt 22:17 spread out the **c** before the elders
Isa 64: 6 righteous deeds are like a filthy **c**.
Mt 9:16 piece of unshrunk **c** on an old cloak,
    27:59 and wrapped it in a clean linen **c**
Mk 14:51 wearing nothing but a linen **c**.
Lk 2: 7 and wrapped him in bands of **c**,
Ac 16:14 of Thyatira and a dealer in purple **c**.

CLOTHE → CLOTHED, CLOTHES, CLOTHING
Ps 132:16 Its priests I will **c** with salvation,
    132:18 His enemies I will **c** with disgrace,

Hag 1: 6 **c** yourselves, but no one is warm;
Lk 12:28 how much more will he **c** you—
1Co 12:23 we think less honorable we **c** with
Eph 4:24 to **c** yourselves with the new self,
Col 3:14 Above all, **c** yourselves with love,
1Pe 5: 5 you must **c** yourselves with humility

CLOTHED → CLOTHE
Ge 3:21 man and for his wife, and **c** them.
Lev 8: 7 **c** him with the robe, and put the
1Sa 17:38 Saul **c** David with his armor;
2Ch 6:41 O LORD God, be **c** with salvation,
Ps 30:11 taken off my sackcloth and **c** me
    104: 1 You are **c** with honor and majesty,
    109:18 **c** himself with cursing as his coat,
    132: 9 your priests be **c** with righteousness,
Isa 61:10 **c** me with the garments of salvation,
Eze 9: 2 among them was a man **c** in linen,
Da 10: 5 looked up and saw a man **c** in linen,
Zec 3: 5 and **c** him with the apparel.
Lk 12:27 Solomon in all his glory was not **c**
    24:49 until you have been **c** with power
2Co 5: 2 longing to be **c** with our heavenly
Gal 3:27 have **c** yourselves with Christ.
Col 3:10 have **c** yourselves with the new self,
Rev 12: 1 a woman **c** with the sun,
    17: 4 woman was **c** in purple and scarlet,
    18:16 **c** in fine linen, in purple and scarlet,
    19:13 He is **c** in a robe dipped in blood,

CLOTHES → CLOTHE
Ge 37:29 was not in the pit, he tore his **c**.
    44:13 At this they tore their **c**.
Dt 8: 4 The **c** on your back did not wear out
    29: 5 on your back have not worn out,
2Sa 1:11 David took hold of his **c** and tore
1Ki 21:27 he tore his **c** and put sackcloth
2Ki 5: 7 he tore his **c** and said, "Am I God,
    11:14 Athaliah tore her **c** and cried,
Ne 9:21 their **c** did not wear out and their
Est 4: 1 Mordecai tore his **c** and put on
Ps 22:18 they divide my **c** among themselves,
Pr 6:27 the bosom without burning one's **c?**
Isa 37: 1 Hezekiah heard it, he tore his **c**,
Jer 52:33 So Jehoiachin put aside his prison **c**,
Zec 3: 3 Joshua was dressed with filthy **c** as
Mt 17: 2 and his **c** became dazzling white.
Mk 15:24 and divided his **c** among them,
Lk 8:44 and touched the fringe of his **c**,
Ac 10:30 suddenly a man in dazzling **c** stood
    14:14 they tore their **c** and rushed out into
    18: 6 protest he shook the dust from his **c**
1Ti 2: 9 or with gold, pearls, or expensive **c**,
Jas 2: 2 if a poor person in dirty **c** also
Rev 3: 4 who have not soiled their **c**;
Jdt 14:16 groaned and shouted, and tore his **c**.
1Mc 2:14 Mattathias and his sons tore their **c**,

CLOTHING → CLOTHE
Ex 3:22 and **c**, and you shall put them on
    12:35 jewelry of silver and gold, and for **c**,
    21:10 **c**, or marital rights of the first wife.
Ps 22:18 and for my **c** they cast lots.
    102:26 You change them like **c**, and they
Pr 31:25 Strength and dignity are her **c**,
Da 7: 9 his **c** was white as snow,
Joel 2:13 rend your hearts and not your **c**.
Mt 3: 4 Now John wore **c** of camel's hair
    7:15 sheep's **c** but inwardly are ravenous
    25:36 I was naked and you gave me **c**,
Jn 19:24 and for my **c** they cast lots."
1Ti 6: 8 but if we have food and **c**,
Heb 1:11 they will all wear out like **c**;
Sir 29:21 of life are water, bread, and **c**,

CLOTHS → CLOTH
Eze 16: 4 rubbed with salt, nor wrapped in **c**.
Lk 24:12 he saw the linen **c** by themselves;

CLOUD → CLOUDS
Ex 13:21 went in front of them in a pillar of **c**
    16:10 glory of the LORD appeared in the **c**.
    19: 9 going to come to you in a dense **c**,

    24:18 Moses entered the **c**, and went up on
    40:34 the **c** covered the tent of meeting,
Lev 16: 2 appear in the **c** upon the mercy seat.
Nu 9:15 the **c** covered the tabernacle,
Dt 1:33 in fire by night, and in the **c** by day,
1Ki 8:10 a **c** filled the house of the LORD,
    18:44 a little **c** no bigger than a person's
Ne 9:19 of **c** that led them in the way did
Ps 105:39 He spread a **c** for a covering,
Isa 19: 1 the LORD is riding on a swift **c** and
Eze 1: 4 a great **c** with brightness around it
    10: 4 the house was filled with the **c**,
Hos 6: 4 Your love is like a morning **c**,
Mk 9: 7 Then a **c** overshadowed them,
Lk 21:27 'the Son of Man coming in a **c**'
Ac 1: 9 and a **c** took him out of their sight.
1Co 10: 2 were baptized into Moses in the **c**
Heb 12: 1 by so great a **c** of witnesses,
Rev 10: 1 wrapped in a **c**, with a rainbow over
    11:12 And they went up to heaven in a **c**
    14:14 and seated on the **c** was one like the Son of Man,

PILLAR OF CLOUD Ex 13:21, 22; 14:19; 33:9, 10; Nu 12:5; 14:14; Dt 31:15, 15; Ne 9:12, 19; Ps 99:7; Sir 24:4

CLOUDS → CLOUD
Ge 9:13 I have set my bow in the **c**,
Jdg 5: 4 the **c** indeed poured water.
1Ki 18:45 the heavens grew black with **c** and
Job 38:37 has the wisdom to number the **c?**
Ps 36: 5 your faithfulness extends to the **c**.
    57:10 your faithfulness extends to the **c**.
    68: 4 song to him who rides upon the **c**—
    77:17 The **c** poured out water; the skies
    104: 3 you make the **c** your chariot,
Pr 25:14 Like **c** and wind without rain is one
Isa 14:14 I will ascend to the tops of the **c**,
Da 7:13 like a human being coming with the **c** of heaven.
Joel 2: 2 a day of **c** and thick darkness!
Na 1: 3 and the **c** are the dust of his feet.
Zep 1:15 a day of **c** and thick darkness,
Mt 24:30 'the Son of Man coming on the **c** of
    26:64 hand of Power and coming on the **c**
1Th 4:17 be caught up in the **c** together with
Jude 1:12 They are waterless **c** carried along
Rev 1: 7 He is coming with the **c**,
Aza 1:51 Bless the Lord, lightnings and **c**;
2Es 13: 3 this man flew with the **c** of heaven;

CLUB* → CLUBS
Pr 25:18 Like a war **c**, a sword,
Isa 10: 5 the **c** in their hands is my fury!
Jer 51:20 You are my war **c**, my weapon of
Bel 1:26 kill the dragon without sword or **c**."

CLUBS → CLUB
Mk 14:43 was a crowd with swords and **c**,

CLUNG → CLING
Ru 1:14 mother-in-law, but Ruth **c** to her.
1Ki 11: 2 Solomon **c** to these in love.
2Ki 3:11 to the sin of Jeroboam son of
Ac 3:11 While he **c** to Peter and John,

CLUSTER → CLUSTERS
Nu 13:23 from there a branch with a single **c**
Mic 7: 1 finds no **c** to eat;

CLUSTERS → CLUSTER
Rev 14:18 gather the **c** of the vine of the earth,

CO-WORKER → WORK
Ro 16:21 Timothy, my **c**, greets you;

CO-WORKERS → WORK
3Jn 1: 8 we may become **c** with the truth.

COAL → COALS
Isa 6: 6 a live **c** that had been taken from

COALS → COAL
Ps 11: 6 On the wicked he will rain **c** of fire

18: 8 glowing **c** flamed forth from him.
140:10 Let burning **c** fall on them!
Pr   6:28 one walk on hot **c** without scorching
       25:22 will heap **c** of fire on their heads,
Eze   1:13 that looked like burning **c** of fire,
       10: 2 fill your hands with burning **c** from
Ro   12:20 will heap burning **c** on their heads."

COAST → COASTLANDS

Nu   34: 6 shall have the Great Sea and its **c;**

COASTLANDS → COAST, LAND

Ps   97: 1 earth rejoice; let the many **c** be glad!
Isa   42: 4 and the **c** wait for his teaching.
       66:19 the **c** far away that have not heard

COAT → COATS

1Sa   17: 5 and he was armed with a **c** of mail;
Mt   5:40 wants to sue you and take your **c,**

COATS → COAT

Lk   3:11 "Whoever has two **c** must share
Ac   7:58 the witnesses laid their **c** at the feet
       22:20 keeping the **c** of those who killed

COCK

Jn   13:38 I tell you, before the **c** crows,
       18:27 and at that moment the **c** crowed.

CODE*

Ro   2:27 condemn you that have the written **c**
       7: 6 slaves not under the old written **c**

COFFIN*

Ge   50:26 and placed in a **c** in Egypt.

COHORT

Mk   15:16 they called together the whole **c.**
Ac   10: 1 a centurion of the Italian **C,**
       27: 1 to a centurion of the Augustan **C,**

COIN* → COINS

Mt   17:27 open its mouth, you will find a **c;**
       22:19 Show me the **c** used for the tax."
Lk   15: 9 I have found the **c** that I had lost.'

COINS → COIN

Lk   15: 8 what woman having ten silver **c,**
       21: 2 widow put in two small copper **c.**
Jn   2:15 the **c** of the money changers

COLD

Ge   8:22 **c** and heat, summer and winter
Ps   147:17 who can stand before his **c?**
Pr   25:25 Like **c** water to a thirsty soul,
Zec   14: 6 that day there shall not be either **c**
Mt   10:42 a cup of **c** water to one of these
       24:12 the love of many will grow **c.**
Rev   3:16 lukewarm, and neither **c** nor hot,

COLLECT → COLLECTED, COLLECTION, COLLECTOR, COLLECTORS

Ne   10:37 for it is the Levites who **c** the tithes
Mt   13:30 **C** the weeds first and bind them in
Mk   12: 2 the tenants to **c** from them his share

COLLECTED → COLLECT

Ecc   12:11 the **c** sayings that are given by one
Heb   7: 6 **c** tithes from Abraham

COLLECTION → COLLECT

Isa   57:13 let your **c** of idols deliver you!
1Co   16: 1 Now concerning the **c** for the saints:

COLLECTOR → COLLECT

Mt   10: 3 Thomas and Matthew the tax **c;**
Lk   5:27 and saw a tax **c** named Levi,
       18:10 one a Pharisee and the other a tax **c.**
       19: 2 he was a chief tax **c** and was rich.
1Mc   1:29 cities of Judah a chief **c** of tribute,

COLLECTORS → COLLECT

Mt   5:46 Do not even the tax **c** do the same?
       9:10 many tax **c** and sinners came and
       11:19 a friend of tax **c** and sinners!'
       17:24 the **c** of the temple tax came to Peter

21:32 tax **c** and the prostitutes believed

COLONY

Ac   16:12 of Macedonia and a Roman **c.**

COLT

Ge   49:11 his donkey's **c** to the choice vine,
Zec   9: 9 and riding on a donkey, on a **c,**
Mt   21: 5 mounted on a donkey, and on a **c,**
Jn   12:15 coming, sitting on a donkey's **c!"**

COME → CAME, COMES, COMING, OUTCOME

Ge   15:16 they shall **c** back here in the fourth
       38:16 and said, "**C,** let me **c** in to you,"
       50:24 but God will surely **c** to you,
Ex   3: 5 Then he said, "**C** no closer!
       19:11 the third day the LORD will **c** down
       24: 1 said to Moses, "**C** up to the LORD,
Nu   24:17 a star shall **c** out of Jacob,
Dt   28: 2 all these blessings shall **c** upon you
       28:45 All these curses shall **c** upon you,
1Sa   4: 7 "Gods have **c** into the camp."
2Sa   7:12 who shall **c** forth from your body,
Ps   14: 7 deliverance for Israel would **c** from
       17: 2 From you let my vindication **c;**
       24: 7 that the King of glory may **c** in.
       44:26 Rise up, **c** to our help.
       88: 2 let my prayer **c** before you;
       91:10 no scourge **c** near your tent.
      119:41 Let your steadfast love **c** to me,
      121: 1 from where will my help **c?**
      144: 5 your heavens, O LORD, and **c** down;
Pr   2: 6 from his mouth **c** knowledge and
       24:34 poverty will **c** upon you like a
SS   2:13 Arise, my love, my fair one, and **c**
Isa   1:18 **C** now, let us argue it out, says the
               LORD:
       13: 5 They **c** from a distant land,
       41:22 or declare to us the things to **c.**
       55: 1 who thirsts, **c** to the waters;
       59:20 And he will **c** to Zion as Redeemer,
Jer   51:45 **C** out of her, my people!
Eze   7: 6 An end has **c,** the end has **c.**
       36: 8 for they shall soon **c** home.
Hos   3: 5 they shall **c** in awe to the LORD and
Mic   6: 6 shall I **c** before the LORD,
Hab   2: 3 it will surely **c,** it will not delay.
Zec   10: 4 Out of them shall **c** the cornerstone,
       14: 5 Then the LORD my God will **c,**
Mt   2: 2 and have **c** to pay him homage."
       5:17 I have **c** not to abolish but to fulfill.
       6:10 Your kingdom **c.** Your will be done,
       10:34 not **c** to bring peace, but a sword.
       11:14 he is Elijah who is to **c.**
       12:28 the kingdom of God has **c** to you.
       15:19 out of the heart **c** evil intentions,
       17:12 I tell you that Elijah has already **c,**
       19:14 "Let the little children **c** to me,
       24: 5 many will **c** in my name, saying,
       27:40 Son of God, **c** down from the cross.
Mk   13:33 do not know when the time will **c.**
Lk   5:32 I have **c** to call not the righteous
       7:20 'Are you the one who is to **c,**
Jn   2: 4 My hour has not yet **c."**
       6:37 the Father gives me will **c** to me,
       12:23 hour has **c** for the Son of Man to be
       14: 3 I will **c** again and will take you to
Ac   1: 8 the Holy Spirit has **c** upon you;
       1:11 will **c** in the same way as you saw
1Co   16:22 Our Lord, **c!**
Gal   4: 4 But when the fullness of time had **c,**
Col   2:17 a shadow of what is to **c,**
Heb   10: 9 "See, I have **c** to do your will."
       12:22 But you have **c** to Mount Zion and
1Pe   2: 4 **C** to him, a living stone, though
2Pe   3: 9 but all to **c** to repentance.
1Jn   2:18 so now many antichrists have **c.**
       4: 2 that Jesus Christ has **c** in the flesh
Rev   1: 4 who is and who was and who is to **c,**
       3: 3 I will **c** like a thief,
       4: 1 said, "**C** up here,
       4: 8 who was and is and is to **c.**"

22:17 The Spirit and the bride say, "**C.**"
22:20 Amen. **C,** Lord Jesus!

AGE TO COME Mt 12:32; Mk 10:30; Lk
18:30; Eph 1:21; Heb 6:5; 2Es 7:113; 8:52

DAYS TO COME Ge 49:1; Nu 24:14; Ecc
2:16; Isa 2:2; 27:6; Mic 4:1

THINGS TO COME Isa 41:22; 44:7; Zec
3:8; Ro 8:38; Heb 10:1; Wis 8:8

TIME TO COME Dt 4:30; 6:20; 31:29; Jos
4:6, 21; 22:24, 27, 28; Pr 31:25; Isa 30:8; 42:23

COMES → COME

Ge   50:25 saying, "When God **c** to you,
Dt   8: 3 every word that **c** from the mouth
1Ch   16:33 for he **c** to judge the earth.
Job   3:25 Truly the thing that I fear **c** upon me
Ps   30: 5 but joy **c** with the morning.
       62: 1 from him **c** my salvation.
      112:10 desire of the wicked **c** to nothing.
      118:26 one who **c** in the name of the LORD.
      121: 2 My help **c** from the LORD,
Pr   11: 2 When pride **c,** then **c** disgrace;
       11:27 but evil **c** to the one who searches
Ecc   9: 2 since the same fate **c** to all,
Isa   40:10 See, the Lord GOD **c** with might,
Hos   14: 8 your faithfulness **c** from me.
Zec   9: 9 Lo, your king **c** to you; triumphant
Mt   4: 4 every word that **c** from the mouth
Mk   7:20 what **c** out of a person that defiles.
       11: 9 Blessed is the one who **c** in the
Lk   18: 8 the Son of Man **c,** will he find faith
       19:38 "Blessed is the king who **c** in the
Jn   3:31 The one who **c** from above is above
       4:35 months more, then **c** the harvest'?
       6:33 that which **c** down from heaven and
       10:10 the thief **c** only to steal and kill
       14: 6 No one **c** to the Father except
               through me.
       15:26 "When the Advocate **c,** whom I
       16:13 When the Spirit of truth **c,**
Ro   10:17 So faith **c** from what is heard,
1Co   11:12 so man **c** through woman;
Gal   2:21 for if justification **c** through the law,
       3:18 if the inheritance **c** from the law,
Php   3: 9 that **c** through faith in Christ,
1Jn   2:21 that no lie **c** from the truth.
2Jn   1:10 who **c** to you and does not bring
Rev   3:12 the new Jerusalem that **c** down
       11: 7 beast that **c** up from the bottomless
       19:15 From his mouth **c** a sharp sword
Sir   18:20 Before judgment **c,** examine

COMFORT* → COMFORTED, COMFORTER, COMFORTERS, COMFORTING, COMFORTS

Ge   37:35 all his daughters sought to **c** him;
1Ch   7:22 and his brothers came to **c** him.
Job   2:11 to go and console and to **c** him.
       7:13 When I say, 'My bed will **c** me,
       10:20 alone, that I may find a little **c**
       21:34 How then will you **c** me with empty
Ps   23: 4 your rod and your staff—they **c** me.
       71:21 my honor, and **c** me once again.
      119:50 This is my **c** in my distress,
      119:52 ordinances from of old, I take **c,**
      119:76 your steadfast love become my **c**
      119:82 I ask, "When will you **c** me?"
Ecc   4: 1 with no one to **c** them!
       4: 1 with no one to **c** them.
Isa   22: 4 not try to **c** me for the destruction
       40: 1 **C,** O **c** my people, says your God.
       51: 3 For the LORD will **c** Zion; he will **c**
               all her waste places,
       51:19 and sword—who will **c** you?
       57:18 lead them and repay them with **c,**
       61: 2 of our God; to **c** all who mourn;
       66:13 comforts her child, so I will **c** you;
Jer   16: 7 to offer **c** for the dead;
       31:13 mourning into joy, I will **c** them,
La   1: 2 her lovers she has no one to **c** her;
       1: 9 was appalling, with none to **c** her.

1:17 but there is no one to **c** her;
1:21 with no one to **c** me.
2:13 can I liken you, that I may **c** you,
Zec 1:17 the LORD will again **c** Zion
Ac   9:31 and in the **c** of the Holy Spirit,
2Co 7:13 In this we find **c**.
Col 4:11 and they have been a **c** to me.
2Th 2:16 and through grace gave us eternal **c**
2:17 **c** your hearts and strengthen them
AdE 15:16 and all his servants tried to **c** her.
Sir 30:23 Indulge yourself and take **c**,
Bar 4:30 the one who named you will **c** you.
2Es 12: 8 so that you may fully **c** my soul.
14:13 **c** the lowly among them,

COMFORTED* → COMFORT
Ge   24:67 Isaac was **c** after his mother's death.
37:35 but he refused to be **c**, and said,
Ru   2:13 you have **c** me and spoken kindly
Job 42:11 showed him sympathy and **c** him
Ps   77: 2 my soul refuses to be **c**.
86:17 LORD, have helped me and **c** me.
Isa 12: 1 anger turned away, and you **c** me.
49:13 For the LORD has **c** his people,
52: 9 for the LORD has **c** his people,
54:11 storm-tossed, and not **c**,
66:13 you shall be **c** in Jerusalem.
Jer 31:15 she refuses to be **c** for her children,
Mt   5: 4 those who mourn, for they will be **c**.
Lk   16:25 he is **c** here, and you are in agony.
Ac   20:12 alive and were not a little **c**.
AdE 15: 8 He **c** her with soothing words,
Sir 38:17 then be **c** for your grief.
38:23 and be **c** for him when his spirit has
48:24 and **c** the mourners in Zion.
49:10 for they **c** the people of Jacob

COMFORTER* → COMFORT
La   1:16 for a **c** is far from me,

COMFORTERS* → COMFORT
Job 16: 2 miserable **c** are you all.
Ps   69:20 and for **c**, but I found none.
Na   3: 7 Where shall I seek **c** for you?

COMFORTING* → COMFORT
Zec 1:13 replied with gracious and **c** words

COMFORTS* → COMFORT
Job 29:25 like one who **c** mourners.
Isa 51:12 I, I am he who **c** you;
66:13 As a mother **c** her child, so I will

COMING → COME
Ps   96:13 for he is **c** to judge the earth.
98: 9 for he is **c** to judge the earth.
Eze 43: 2 glory of the God of Israel was **c**
Da   7:13 like a human being **c** with the
clouds of heaven.
Joel 2: 1 the day of the LORD is **c**, it is near—
Mic 1: 3 lo, the LORD is **c** out of his place,
Zec 14: 1 See, a day is **c** for the LORD,
Mal 3: 2 But who can endure the day of his **c**,
4: 1 the day is **c**, burning like an oven,
Mt   21: 5 Look, your king is **c** to you, humble,
24:44 Son of Man is **c** at an unexpected
Mk   13:26 'the Son of Man **c** in clouds' with
Jn   1:27 the one who is **c** after me;
4:25 "I know that Messiah is **c**"
14:18 not leave you orphaned; I am **c** to
17:13 But now I am **c** to you,
1Th 1:10 rescues us from the wrath that is **c**.
4:15 who are left until the **c** of the Lord,
2Th 2: 1 As to the **c** of our Lord Jesus Christ
Heb 10:37 is **c** will **c** and will not delay;
Jas 5: 8 for the **c** of the Lord is near.
2Pe 1:16 and **c** of our Lord Jesus Christ,
3: 4 "Where is the promise of his **c**?
3:12 hastening the **c** of the day of God,
1Jn 2:18 you have heard that antichrist is **c**,
Jude 1:14 the Lord is **c** with ten thousands of
Rev 1: 7 He is **c** with the clouds;
3:11 I am **c** soon; hold fast to what

16:15 ("See, I am **c** like a thief!
21: 2 **c** down out of heaven from God,
21:10 the holy city Jerusalem **c** down out
22: 7 "See, I am **c** soon!
22:20 "Surely I am **c** soon."

DAYS ARE [SURELY] COMING 2Ki
20:17; Isa 39:6; Jer 7:32; 9:25; 16:14; 19:6;
23:5, 7; 30:3; 31:27, 31, 38; 33:14; 51:47; Lk
17:22; 23:29; Heb 8:8; 2Es 5:1; 6:18; 12:13;
13:29

TIME IS [SURELY] COMING 1Sa 2:31;
Jer 48:12; 49:2; 51:52; Eze 24:14; Am 4:2;
8:11; 9:13; 2Ti 4:3

COMMAND → COMMANDED, COMMANDER, COMMANDERS, COMMANDING, COMMANDMENT, COMMANDMENTS, COMMANDS
Ex   7: 2 You shall speak all that I **c** you,
34:11 Observe what I **c** you today.
Nu   9:18 At the **c** of the LORD the Israelites
14:41 do you continue to transgress the **c**
23:20 See, I received a **c** to bless;
Dt   1:26 rebelled against the **c** of the LORD
4: 2 neither add anything to what I **c**
8: 1 I **c** you today you must diligently
12:32 observe everything that I **c** you;
32:46 give them as a **c** to your children,
Jos 1: 9 I hereby **c** you: Be strong
Jdg 2: 2 But you have not obeyed my **c**.
Est 1:12 refused to come at the king's **c**
Ps   91:11 he will **c** his angels concerning you
Pr   8:29 waters might not transgress his **c**,
Ecc 8: 2 Keep the king's **c** because of your
Jer 1: 7 you shall speak whatever I **c** you,
1:17 tell them everything that I **c** you.
7:23 walk only in the way that I **c** you,
11: 4 to my voice, and do all that I **c** you.
26: 2 speak to them all the words that I **c**
Da   3:28 They disobeyed the king's **c**
Joel 2:11 are those who obey his **c**.
Zec 9:10 and he shall **c** peace to the nations;
Mt   4: 3 **c** these stones to become loaves of
4: 6 will **c** his angels concerning you,'
Lk   9:54 you want us to **c** fire to come down
Jn   10:18 received this **c** from my Father."
15:14 my friends if you do what I **c** you.
1Co 7: 6 I say by way of concession, not of **c**.
7:10 To the married I give this **c**—
7:25 virgins, I have no **c** of the Lord,
14:37 writing to you is a **c** of the Lord.
2Co 8: 8 I do not say this as a **c**,
1Ti 6:17 **c** them not to be haughty,
1Mc 2:31 who had rejected the king's **c**
2Mc 7:30 I will not obey the king's **c**,

COMMANDED → COMMAND
Ge   2:16 And the LORD God **c** the man,
3:11 tree of which I **c** you not to eat?"
7: 5 Noah did all that the LORD had **c**
Ex   7: 6 they did just as the LORD **c** them.
19: 7 words that the LORD had **c** him.
32: 8 turn aside from the way that I **c**
40:32 as the LORD had **c** Moses.
Lev 8:36 did all the things that the LORD **c**
10: 1 such as he had not **c** them.
Dt   6:24 us to observe all these statutes,
18:20 a word that I have not **c** the prophet
34: 9 doing as the LORD had **c** Moses.
Jos 1: 7 all the law that my servant Moses **c**
1:16 "All that you have **c** us we will do,
22: 2 obeyed me in all that I have **c** you;
2Sa 5:25 David did just as the LORD had **c**
2Ki 17:13 all the law that I **c** your ancestors
21: 8 according to all that I have **c** them,
2Ch 33: 8 careful to do all that I have **c** them,
Ezr 7:23 Whatever is **c** by the God of heaven,
Ps   33: 9 he **c**, and it stood firm.
78: 5 which he **c** our ancestors to teach
111: 9 he has **c** his covenant forever.
148: 5 for he **c** and they were created.

Isa 13: 3 myself have **c** my consecrated ones,
Am   2:12 and **c** the prophets, saying,
Mt   28:20 to obey everything that I have **c** you.
Lk   8:29 for Jesus had **c** the unclean spirit to
Jn   14:31 but I do as the Father has **c** me,
Ac   10:42 He **c** us to preach to the people
1Co 9:14 the Lord **c** that those who proclaim
1Jn 3:23 just as he has **c** us.
2Jn 1: 4 as we have been **c** by the Father.
Sir 15:20 He has not **c** anyone to be wicked,

COMMANDER → COMMAND
Jos 5:15 The **c** of the army of the LORD

COMMANDERS → COMMAND
Nu   31:14 **c** of thousands and the **c** of hundreds
Dt   1:15 **c** of thousands, **c** of hundreds,

COMMANDING → COMMAND
Dt   4:40 **c** you today for your own well-being
11:28 turn from the way that I am **c** you
30:11 **c** you today is not too hard for you,

COMMANDMENT → COMMAND
Dt   6: 1 Now this is the **c**—the statutes
7:11 Therefore, observe diligently the **c**
11:13 If you will only heed his every **c**
30:11 **c** that I am commanding you today
Jos 22: 5 to observe the **c** and instruction
1Sa 12:14 not rebel against the **c** of the LORD,
Ps   19: 8 **c** of the LORD is clear,
119:98 Your **c** makes me wiser than my
Pr   6:20 My child, keep your father's **c**,
19:16 Those who keep the **c** will live;
Mt   22:36 which **c** in the law is the greatest?"
22:38 This is the greatest and first **c**.
Mk   7: 8 You abandon the **c** of God and
12:31 no other **c** greater than these."
Lk   23:56 they rested according to the **c**.
Jn   13:34 I give you a new **c**, that you love
Ro   7: 8 sin, seizing an opportunity in the **c**,
7: 9 but when the **c** came, sin revived
7:10 the very **c** that promised life proved
7:11 sin, seizing an opportunity in the **c**,
7:12 and the **c** is holy and just and good.
13: 9 and any other **c**, are summed up
Gal 5:14 law is summed up in a single **c**,
Eph 6: 2 this is the first **c** with a promise:
1Ti 6:14 to keep the **c** without spot or blame
Heb 7:18 abrogation of an earlier **c** because
9:19 when every **c** had been told to all
1Jn 2: 7 I am writing you no new **c**,
3:23 this is his **c**, that we should believe
2Jn 1: 5 though I were writing you a new **c**,

COMMANDMENTS → COMMAND
Ge   26: 5 my **c**, my statutes, and my laws."
Ex   20: 6 those who love me and keep my **c**.
34:28 the words of the covenant, the ten **c**.
Lev 26: 3 keep my **c** and observe them
26:14 and do not observe all these **c**,
Dt   4:13 to observe, that is, the ten **c**;
5:10 those who love me and keep my **c**.
7: 9 those who love him and keep his **c**,
10: 4 the ten **c** that the LORD had spoken
11:27 the blessing, if you obey the **c**
28:13 if you obey the **c** of the LORD
30:16 If you obey the **c** of the LORD
Jdg 3: 4 whether Israel would obey the **c**
2Ki 17:16 They rejected all the **c** of the LORD
Ezr 9:10 For we have forsaken your **c**,
Ne   1: 5 those who love him and keep his **c**;
Ps   112: 1 who greatly delight in his **c**.
119:10 do not let me stray from your **c**.
119:66 for I believe in your **c**.
Pr   2: 1 treasure up my **c** within you,
10: 8 The wise of heart will heed **c**,
Ecc 12:13 Fear God, and keep his **c**;
Da   9: 4 those who love you and keep your **c**,
Mt   5:19 breaks one of the least of these **c**,
19:17 wish to enter into life, keep the **c**."
22:40 On these two **c** hang all the law and
Mk   10:19 know the **c**: 'You shall not murder;

Lk 1: 6 blamelessly according to all the **c**
   18:20 You know the **c**: 'You shall
Jn 14:15 If you love me, you will keep my **c.**
   15:10 If you keep my **c**, you will abide in
Ro 13: 9 The **c**, "You shall not commit
1Co 7:19 obeying the **c** of God is everything.
Eph 2:15 He has abolished the law with its **c**
1Jn 1: 3 that we know him, if we obey his **c.**
    5: 2 when we love God and obey his **c.**
    5: 3 And his **c** are not burdensome,
2Jn 1: 6 that we walk according to his **c;**
Rev 12:17 those who keep the **c** of God and
   14:12 those who keep the **c** of God and
Tob 3: 4 and disobeyed your **c.**
Sir 1:26 If you desire wisdom, keep the **c,**
   15:15 If you choose, you can keep the **c,**
1Mc 2:19 and have chosen to obey his **c,**

COMMANDS → COMMAND

Ex 25:22 I will deliver to you all my **c** for the
Ps 42: 8 the LORD **c** his steadfast love,
Zep 2: 3 humble of the land, who do his **c;**
Mk 1:27 He **c** even the unclean spirits,
Lk 8:25 he **c** even the winds and the water,
Ac 17:30 **c** all people everywhere to repent,
Col 2:22 are simply human **c** and teachings.
1Mc 2:34 nor will we do what the king **c**
    2:68 and obey the **c** of the law."

COMMEMORATED*
→ COMMEMORATION
Lev 23:24 a holy convocation **c** with trumpet

COMMEMORATION
→ COMMEMORATED
Est 9:28 nor should the **c** of these days cease

COMMEND → COMMENDABLE,
COMMENDATION, COMMENDED,
COMMENDS
Ecc 8:15 So I **c** enjoyment, for there is
Lk 23:46 into your hands I **c** my spirit."
1Co 11:17 instructions I do not **c** you,
2Co 3: 1 we beginning to **c** ourselves again?
    4: 2 statement of the truth we **c** ourselves
   10:12 some of those who **c** themselves.

COMMENDABLE* → COMMEND
Php 4: 8 whatever is pleasing, whatever is **c,**

COMMENDATION* → COMMEND
1Co 4: 5 each one will receive **c** from God.

COMMENDED → COMMEND
Job 29:11 When the ear heard, it **c** me,
Lk 16: 8 his master **c** the dishonest manager
2Co 6: 4 but as servants of God we have **c**
Heb 11:39 though they were **c** for their faith,

COMMENDS* → COMMEND
2Co 10:18 but those whom the Lord **c.**

COMMENTARY*
2Ch 24:27 in the **C** on the Book of the Kings.

COMMISSION
1Co 9:17 I am entrusted with a **c.**
Gal 1: 1 sent neither by human **c** nor from
Eph 3: 2 the **c** of God's grace that was given
Col 1:25 according to God's **c** that was given

COMMIT → COMMITS, COMMITTED,
COMMITTING
Ex 20:14 You shall not **c** adultery.
Dt 5:18 Neither shall you **c** adultery.
1Ki 14:16 and which he caused Israel to **c**."
2Ki 17:21 and made them **c** great sin.
Ps 22: 8 "**C** your cause to the LORD;
   31: 5 Into your hand I **c** my spirit;
   37: 5 **C** your way to the LORD;
Pr 16: 3 **C** your work to the LORD,
Jer 7: 9 Will you steal, murder, **c** adultery,
Mt 5:27 'You shall not **c** adultery.'

    5:32 causes her to **c** adultery;
   19:18 You shall not **c** adultery;
Mk 10:19 You shall not **c** adultery;
Lk 18:20 'You shall not **c** adultery;
Ro 2:22 forbid adultery, do you **c** adultery?
   13: 9 "You shall not **c** adultery;
Jas 2:11 Now if you do not **c** adultery but if
Rev 2:22 and those who **c** adultery with her

COMMITS → COMMIT
Lev 18:29 For whoever **c** any of these
2Sa 7:14 When he **c** iniquity, I will punish
Pr 6:32 But he who **c** adultery has no sense;
Eze 22:11 **c** abomination with his neighbor's
Mt 5:32 whoever marries a divorced woman
        c adultery.
   19: 9 and marries another **c** adultery."
Mk 10:11 marries another **c** adultery against
   10:12 marries another, she **c** adultery."
Lk 16:18 and marries another **c** adultery,
   16:18 whoever marries a woman divorced
        from her husband **c** adultery.
Jn 8:34 who **c** sin is a slave to sin.
1Co 6:18 Every sin that a person **c** is outside
Jas 4:17 to do and fails to do it, **c** sin.
1Jn 3: 4 who **c** sin is guilty of lawlessness;

COMMITTED → COMMIT
Nu 5: 7 confess the sin that has been **c.**
Jdg 20: 6 they have **c** a vile outrage in Israel.
1Sa 14:24 Saul a very rash act on that day.
2Ki 17:22 in all the sins that Jeroboam **c;**
   24: 3 Manasseh, for all that he had **c,**
Jer 2:13 for my people have **c** two evils:
   11:20 for to you I have **c** my cause.
   20:12 for to you I have **c** my cause.
Mt 5:28 with lust has already **c** adultery
Ro 1:27 Men **c** shameless acts with men
    3:25 passed over the sins previously **c;**
Jas 5:15 who has **c** sins will be forgiven.
1Pe 2:22 "He **c** no sin, and no deceit was
Rev 17: 2 of the earth have **c** fornication,
   18: 3 have **c** fornication with her,
1Mc 2: 6 He saw the blasphemies being **c**
Man 1: 9 For the sins I have **c** are more

COMMITTING → COMMIT
Jer 3: 9 **c** adultery with stone and tree.
Jn 8: 4 in the very act of **c** adultery.

COMMON
Lev 10:10 between the holy and the **c,**
2Ch 1:15 silver and gold as **c** in Jerusalem
    9:27 silver as **c** in Jerusalem as stone,
Pr 22: 2 The rich and the poor have this in **c:**
   29:13 and the oppressor have this in **c:**
Eze 22:26 between the holy and the **c,**
Ac 2:44 and had all things in **c;**
    4:32 they owned was held in **c.**
1Co 10:13 has overtaken you that is not **c**
   12: 7 of the Spirit for the **c** good.

COMMUNE* → COMMUNION
Ps 77: 6 I **c** with my heart in the night;

COMMUNION* → COMMUNE
2Co 13:13 the **c** of the Holy Spirit be with all

COMMUNITY
Dt 17:15 who is not of your own **c.**
Jn 21:23 So the rumor spread in the **c** that

COMPANIES → COMPANY
Ex 12:17 your **c** out of the land of Egypt:

COMPANION → COMPANIONS
Jdg 15: 2 so I gave her to your **c.**
Job 30:29 of jackals, and a **c** of ostriches.
Ps 55:13 But it is you, my equal, my **c,**
   55:20 My **c** laid hands on a friend
   119:63 I am a **c** of all who fear you,
Pr 13:20 but the **c** of fools suffers harm.
Mal 2:14 is your **c** and your wife by covenant.

COMPANIONS → COMPANION
Job 6:15 My **c** are treacherous like
Ps 38:11 My friends and **c** stand aloof
   45: 7 the oil of gladness beyond your **c;**
   88: 8 You have caused my **c** to shun me;
Da 2:13 they looked for Daniel and his **c,**
Ac 4:13 recognized them as **c** of Jesus.
Heb 1: 9 the oil of gladness beyond your **c.**"
Sir 9:16 Let the righteous be your dinner **c,**

COMPANY → COMPANIES
Ge 28: 3 that you may become a **c** of peoples.
   35:11 a **c** of nations shall come from you,
   48: 4 I will make of you a **c** of peoples,
Ex 6:26 out of the land of Egypt, **c** by **c.**"
   12:51 out of the land of Egypt, **c** by **c.**
Nu 1: 3 and Aaron shall enroll them, **c** by
   16: 5 Then he said to Korah and all his **c,**
2Ki 2: 7 Fifty men of the **c** of prophets also
    4:38 As the **c** of prophets was sitting
    4:38 some stew for the **c** of prophets."
Ps 14: 5 God is with the **c** of the righteous.
   26: 5 I hate the **c** of evildoers,
Jer 15:17 I did not sit in the **c** of merrymakers,
1Co 15:33 "Bad **c** ruins good morals."
Sir 45:18 their followers and the **c** of Korah,

COMPARE → COMPARED, COMPARING
Job 28:19 of Ethiopia cannot **c** with it,
Ps 40: 5 none can **c** with you.
Pr 3:15 nothing you desire can **c** with her.
    8:11 all that you may desire cannot **c**
Isa 40:18 or what likeness **c** with him?
   40:25 To whom then will you **c** me,
   46: 5 and **c** me, as though we were alike?
La 2:13 can I say for you, to what **c** you,
Eze 28: 2 **c** your mind with the mind of a god.
Da 1:13 then **c** our appearance with the
Mt 11:16 But to what will I **c** this generation?
Lk 7:31 I **c** the people of this generation,
   13:20 should I **c** the kingdom of God?
2Co 10:12 not dare to classify or **c** ourselves

COMPARED → COMPARE
Mt 13:24 "The kingdom of heaven may be **c**
   18:23 the kingdom of heaven may be **c** to
   22: 2 "The kingdom of heaven may be **c**
Bar 3:35 no other can be **c** to him.

COMPARING* → COMPARE
Ro 8:18 of this present time are not worth **c**

COMPASSION* → COMPASSIONATE,
COMPASSIONS
Dt 13: 8 Show them no pity or **c**
   13:17 his fierce anger and show you **c,**
   13:17 and in his **c** multiply you,
   30: 3 and have **c** on you,
   32:36 will vindicate his people, have **c**
Jdg 21: 6 the Israelites had **c** for Benjamin
   21:15 The people had **c** on Benjamin
1Sa 23:21 by the LORD for showing me **c!**
1Ki 3:26 because **c** for her son burned within
    8:50 grant them **c** in the sight of their
        captors, so that they may have **c** on
2Ki 13:23 gracious to them and had **c** on them;
2Ch 30: 9 will find **c** with their captors,
   36:15 he had **c** on his people and on his
   36:17 no **c** on young man or young
Ps 77: 9 Has he in anger shut up his **c?**"
   79: 8 let your **c** come speedily to meet us,
   90:13 Have **c** on your servants!
   102:13 You will rise up and have **c** on Zion,
   103:13 As a father has **c** for his children,
   103:13 LORD has **c** for those who fear him.
   106:45 showed **c** according to the
   135:14 and have **c** on his servants.
   145: 9 his **c** is over all that he has made.
Isa 9:17 or **c** on their orphans and widows;
   14: 1 the LORD will have **c** on Jacob
   27:11 made them will not have **c** on them,
   49:13 will have **c** on his suffering ones.

49:15 no **c** for the child of her womb?
54: 7 but with great **c** I will gather you.
54: 8 with everlasting love I will have **c**
54:10 says the LORD, who has **c** on you.
63:15 yearning of your heart and your **c?**
Jer 12:15 I will again have **c** on them,
13:14 or have **c** when I destroy them.
21: 7 pity them, or spare them, or have **c.**
30:18 and have **c** on his dwellings.
La 3:32 have **c** according to the abundance
Eze 16: 5 these things for you out of **c** for you;
Da 1: 9 Daniel to receive favor and **c**
Hos 11: 8 my **c** grows warm and tender.
13:14 **C** is hidden from my eyes.
Mic 7:19 He will again have **c** upon us;
Zec 1:16 I have returned to Jerusalem with **c;**
10: 6 back because I have **c** on them,
12:10 I will pour out a spirit of **c** and
Mt 9:36 saw the crowds, he had **c** for them,
14:14 had **c** for them and cured their sick.
15:32 "I have **c** for the crowd,
20:34 Moved with **c**, Jesus touched their
Mk 6:34 had **c** for them, because they were
8: 2 "I have **c** for the crowd,
Lk 7:13 Lord saw her, he had **c** for her
15:20 saw him and was filled with **c;**
Ro 9:15 I will have **c** on whom I have **c."**
Php 1: 8 for all of you with the **c** of Christ
2: 1 any sharing in the Spirit, any **c** and
Col 3:12 clothe yourselves with **c**, kindness,
Heb 10:34 had **c** for those who were in prison,
Tob 8:17 you had **c** on two only children.
Wis 10: 5 kept him strong in the face of his **c**
Sir 18:13 The **c** of human beings is for their
18:13 the **c** of the Lord is for every living
18:14 **c** on those who accept his discipline
Bar 2:27 kindness and in all your great **c**,
1Mc 3:44 and to pray and ask for mercy and **c.**
2Mc 7: 6 over us and in truth has **c** on us,
7: 6 he will have **c** on his servants."
Man 1: 7 of great **c**, long-suffering, and very
2Es 7:33 of judgment, and **c** shall pass away,
7:136 [66] and abundant in **c**,
4Mc 5:12 and have **c** on your old age
6:24 he had not been changed by their **c**,
8:10 have **c** for your youth and
8:20 and have **c** on our mother's age;
12: 2 he felt strong **c** for this child when
12: 6 to show **c** on her who had been

COMPASSIONATE* → COMPASSION
Ex 22:27 I will listen, for I am **c**.
Ps 78:38 he, being **c**, forgave their iniquity,
La 4:10 **c** women have boiled their own
Ro 12: 8 the leader, in diligence; the **c**,
Jas 5:11 how the Lord is **c** and merciful.
Sir 2:11 For the Lord is **c** and merciful;

COMPASSIONS* → COMPASSION
2Es 7136 because he makes his **c** abound

COMPEL → COMPELLED, COMPELS, COMPULSION
Lk 14:23 and **c** people to come in,
Gal 2:14 **c** the Gentiles to live like Jews?"
6:12 that try to **c** you to be circumcised—
2Mc 6: 1 to **c** the Jews to forsake the laws

COMPELLED → COMPEL
Ex 3:19 unless **c** by a mighty hand.
Mt 27:32 they **c** this man to carry his cross.
Gal 2: 3 was not **c** to be circumcised,

COMPELS* → COMPEL
Pr 7:21 with her smooth talk she **c** him.

COMPENSATE
Ex 21:26 a free person, to **c** for the eye.

COMPETE → COMPETENCE, COMPETENT, COMPETING, COMPETITION
Jer 12: 5 how will you **c** with horses?
1Co 9:24 that in a race the runners all **c**,

COMPETENCE* → COMPETE
2Co 3: 5 our **c** is from God,

COMPETENT → COMPETE
Da 1: 4 and **c** to serve in the king's palace;
2Co 3: 5 Not that we are **c** of ourselves to
3: 6 who has made us **c** to be ministers

COMPETING* → COMPETE
Gal 5:26 **c** against one another, envying one
2Ti 2: 5 is crowned without **c** according to

COMPETITION* → COMPETE
4Mc 17:13 of the seven sons entered the **c**,

COMPLACENCY* → COMPLACENT
Pr 1:32 and the **c** of fools destroys them;

COMPLACENT → COMPLACENCY, COMPLACENTLY
Dt 4:25 and become **c** in the land,
Isa 32: 9 **c** daughters, listen to my speech.

COMPLACENTLY* → COMPLACENT
Zep 1:12 I will punish the people who rest **c**

COMPLAIN → COMPLAINED, COMPLAINING, COMPLAINT, COMPLAINTS
Ex 16: 7 For what are we, that you **c** against
Nu 14:27 shall this wicked congregation **c**
Job 7:11 I will **c** in the bitterness of my soul.
Jer 2:29 Why do you **c** against me?
La 3:39 Why should any who draw breath **c**
Jn 6:43 "Do not **c** among yourselves.
1Co 10:10 And do not **c** as some of them did,

COMPLAINED → COMPLAIN
Ex 15:24 And the people **c** against Moses,
16: 2 the Israelites **c** against Moses and
17: 3 the people **c** against Moses and said,
Nu 11: 1 people **c** in the hearing of the LORD
14: 2 all the Israelites **c** against Moses and
Ac 6: 1 the Hellenists **c** against the Hebrews

COMPLAINING → COMPLAIN
Ex 16: 7 has heard your **c** against the LORD.
Pr 23:29 Who has strife? Who has **c?**
Jn 6:61 that his disciples were **c** about it,
1Pe 4: 9 hospitable to one another without **c**.

COMPLAINT → COMPLAIN
Job 10: 1 I will give free utterance to my **c;**
Ps 55: 2 I am troubled in my **c**.
64: 1 Hear my voice, O God, in my **c;**
142: 2 I pour out my **c** before him;
Da 6: 4 to find grounds for **c** against Daniel
Hab 2: 1 he will answer concerning my **c**.
Col 3:13 if anyone has a **c** against another,
Sir 35:17 the widow when she pours out her **c.**

COMPLAINTS → COMPLAIN
Nu 14:27 I have heard the **c** of the Israelites,
17: 5 put a stop to the **c** of the Israelites
Ne 5: 6 I heard their outcry and these **c.**

COMPLETE → COMPLETED, COMPLETELY, COMPLETING, COMPLETION
Ge 15:16 iniquity of the Amorites is not yet **c.**
Lev 16:31 It is a sabbath of **c** rest to you,
23: 3 seventh day is a sabbath of **c** rest,
25: 5 shall be a year of **c** rest for the land.
Zec 4: 9 his hands shall also **c** it.
Jn 4:34 him who sent me and to **c** his work.
15:11 and that your joy may be **c.**
16:24 so that your joy may be **c.**
17:13 they may have my joy made **c** in
1Co 13:10 but when the **c** comes, the partial
2Co 7:16 because I have **c** confidence in you.
10: 6 when your obedience is **c.**
Php 2: 2 make my joy **c;** be of the
Col 4:17 "See that you **c** the task that you
Tit 2:10 but to show **c** and perfect fidelity,
Heb 13:21 make you **c** in everything good so

Jas 1: 4 so that you may be mature and **c**,
1Jn 1: 4 so that our joy may be **c**.
2Jn 1:12 so that our joy may be **c.**
Rev 6:11 until the number would be **c**

COMPLETED → COMPLETE
1Ki 9:25 So he **c** the house.
Jer 25:12 Then after seventy years are **c**,
29:10 Babylon's seventy years are **c** will I
Da 11:36 until the period of wrath is **c**,
Lk 12:50 what stress I am under until it is **c!**

COMPLETELY → COMPLETE
Dt 18:13 You must remain **c** loyal to
1Ki 8:61 devote yourselves **c** to the LORD
11: 6 and did not **c** follow the LORD,
2Ch 12:12 so as not to destroy them **c;**
Pr 28: 5 who seek the LORD understand it **c.**
Jer 14:19 Have you **c** rejected Judah?
La 5:20 Why have you forgotten us **c?**
Jn 17:23 that they may become **c** one,

COMPLETING → COMPLETE
Col 1:24 in my flesh I am **c** what is lacking

COMPLETION → COMPLETE
Php 1: 6 work among you will bring it to **c**
Jas 2:22 faith was brought to **c** by the works.

COMPOSED → COMPOSITION
1Ki 4:32 He **c** three thousand proverbs,

COMPOSITION → COMPOSED
Pm 151: T is ascribed to David as his own **c**

COMPREHEND → COMPREHENDED, COMPREHENDS, COMPREHENSION
Isa 6:10 and **c** with their minds, and turn
33:19 an obscure speech that you cannot **c**,
Eph 3:18 that you may have the power to **c**,
Sir 16:20 and who can **c** his ways?

COMPREHENDED → COMPREHEND
Job 38:18 you **c** the expanse of the earth?
Col 1: 6 and truly **c** the grace of God.

COMPREHENDS* → COMPREHEND
1Co 2:11 no one **c** what is truly God's except

COMPREHENSION* → COMPREHEND
Sir 1:19 knowledge and discerning **c**,
2Es 8:21 and whose glory is beyond **c**,

COMPULSION → COMPEL
2Co 9: 7 not reluctantly or under **c**,
1Pe 5: 2 not under **c** but willingly,

COMRADES
Rev 12:10 the accuser of our **c** has been thrown
19:10 **c** who hold the testimony of Jesus.
22: 9 with you and your **c** the prophets,

CONCEAL → CONCEALED, CONCEALS
Ge 37:26 we kill our brother and **c** his blood?
Pr 25: 2 It is the glory of God to **c** things,

CONCEALED → CONCEAL
Ps 40:10 I have not **c** your steadfast love and
Pr 26:25 are seven abominations **c** within;
Jer 16:17 nor is their iniquity **c** from my sight.
Lk 9:45 its meaning was **c** from them,
Sir 11: 4 his works are **c** from humankind.

CONCEALS* → CONCEAL
Pr 10: 6 the mouth of the wicked **c** violence.
10:11 the mouth of the wicked **c** violence.
12:23 One who is clever **c** knowledge,
28:13 who **c** transgressions will prosper.

CONCEIT* → CONCEITED
Job 37:24 any who are wise in their own **c."**
2Co 12:20 selfishness, slander, gossip, **c**,
Php 2: 3 nothing from selfish ambition or **c**,
1Ti 3: 6 he may be puffed up with **c** and fall
2Ti 3: 4 reckless, swollen with **c**,

Sir 3:24 For their **c** has led many astray,

CONCEITED* → CONCEIT

Gal 5:26 Let us not become **c**, competing
1Ti 6: 4 is **c**, understanding nothing,

CONCEIVE → CONCEIVED

Nu 11:12 Did I **c** all this people?
Job 15:35 They **c** mischief and bring forth evil
Ps 7:14 they **c** evil, and are pregnant with
Isa 33:11 You **c** chaff, you bring forth stubble
Mt 1:23 the virgin shall **c** and bear a son,
Lk 1:31 you will **c** in your womb and bear a

CONCEIVED → CONCEIVE

Ge 21: 2 Sarah **c** and bore Abraham a son
1Sa 2:21 she **c** and bore three sons and two
Ps 51: 5 a sinner when my mother **c** me.
Isa 8: 3 and she **c** and bore a son.
Mt 1:20 **c** in her is from the Holy Spirit.
Lk 1:24 those days his wife Elizabeth **c**,
1Co 2: 9 ear heard, nor the human heart **c**,
Jas 1:15 desire has **c**, it gives birth to sin,

CONCERN → CONCERNED

Ge 39: 6 he had no **c** for anything but the
39: 8 my master has no **c** about anything
Eze 36:21 But I had **c** for my holy name,
Php 4:10 you have revived your **c** for me;
Heb 8: 9 I had no **c** for them, says the Lord.

CONCERNED → CONCERN

Jnh 4:10 said, "You are **c** about the bush,
1Co 9: 9 Is it for oxen that God is **c**?
Php 4:10 indeed, you were **c** for me,

CONCESSION*

1Co 7: 6 I say by way of **c**, not of command.

CONCUBINE → CONCUBINES

Ge 35:22 and lay with Bilhah his father's **c**;
Jdg 19:25 So the man seized his **c**,
2Sa 3: 7 have you gone in to my father's **c**?"

CONCUBINES → CONCUBINE

Ge 25: 6 to the sons of his **c** Abraham gave
2Sa 5:13 David took more **c** and wives;
16:21 "Go in to your father's **c**,
1Ki 11: 3 princesses and three hundred **c**;
Da 5: 3 wives, and his **c** drank from them.

CONDEMN → CONDEMNATION,
CONDEMNED, CONDEMNING, CONDEMNS,
SELF-CONDEMNED

Job 9:20 my own mouth would **c** me;
10: 2 I will say to God, Do not **c** me;
34:17 Will you **c** one who is righteous
34:29 When he is quiet, who can **c**?
40: 8 you **c** me that you may be justified?
Ps 94:21 and **c** the innocent to death.
109:31 save them from those who would **c**
141: 6 over to those who shall **c** them,
Mt 12:41 with this generation and **c** it,
12:42 with this generation and **c** it,
20:18 and they will **c** him to death;
Mk 10:33 and they will **c** him to death;
Lk 6:37 **c**, and you will not be condemned.
11:31 of this generation and **c** them,
11:32 with this generation and **c** it,
Jn 3:17 not send the Son into the world to **c**
8:11 And Jesus said, "Neither do I **c** you.
8:26 to say about you and much to **c**;
Ro 2: 1 judgment on another you **c** yourself,
2:27 the law will **c** you that have the
8:34 Who is to **c**?
14:22 no reason to **c** themselves because
2Co 7: 3 I do not say this to **c** you,
Col 2:16 anyone **c** you in matters of food and
1Jn 3:20 whenever our hearts **c** us;
3:21 Beloved, if our hearts do not **c** us,
Sir 14: 2 those whose hearts do not **c** them,
Sus 1:48 to **c** a daughter of Israel without

CONDEMNATION → CONDEMN

Pr 19:29 **C** is ready for scoffers, and flogging
Mk 12:40 They will receive the greater **c**."
Jn 5:29 done evil, to the resurrection of **c**.
Ro 3: 8 Their **c** is deserved!
5:16 following one trespass brought **c**,
5:18 one man's trespass led to **c** for all,
8: 1 no **c** for those who are in Christ
1Co 11:34 it will not be for your **c**.
2Co 3: 9 there was glory in the ministry of **c**,
1Ti 3: 6 fall into the **c** of the devil.
5:12 they incur **c** for having violated
Jas 5:12 so that you may not fall under **c**.
2Pe 2: 3 Their **c**, pronounced against them
Jude 1: 4 long ago were designated for this **c**
1: 9 not dare to bring a **c** of slander
Sir 5:14 and severe **c** to the double-tongued.

CONDEMNED* → CONDEMN

Job 9:29 I shall be **c**; why then do I labor in
Ps 34:21 who hate the righteous will be **c**.
34:22 who take refuge in him will be **c**.
37:33 let them be **c** when they are brought
Mt 12: 7 you would not have **c** the guiltless.
12:37 and by your words you will be **c**."
27: 3 his betrayer, saw that Jesus was **c**,
Mk 14:64 of them **c** him as deserving death.
16:16 one who does not believe will be **c**.
Lk 6:37 not condemn, and you will not be **c**.
23:41 And we indeed have been **c** justly,
24:20 handed him over to be **c** to death
Jn 3:18 Those who believe in him are not **c**;
3:18 who do not believe are **c** already,
8:10 Has no one **c** you?"
16:11 the ruler of this world has been **c**.
Ac 26:10 when they were being **c** to death.
Ro 3: 7 why am I still being **c** as a sinner?
8: 3 to deal with sin, he **c** sin in the flesh,
14:23 who have doubts are **c** if they eat,
1Co 11:32 disciplined so that we may not be **c**
2Th 2:12 in unrighteousness will be **c**.
Heb 11: 7 he **c** the world and became an heir
Jas 5: 6 have **c** and murdered the righteous
2Pe 2: 6 to ashes he **c** them to extinction
AdE 2: 1 and how he had **c** her.
Wis 17:11 **c** by its own testimony;
Sir 19: 5 rejoices in wickedness will be **c**,
Sus 1:41 assembly believed them and **c** her
1Mc 1:57 was **c** to death by decree of the king.
2Es 7:115 [45] on someone who has been **c** in

CONDEMNING* → CONDEMN

1Ki 8:32 **c** the guilty by bringing their
Ac 13:27 they fulfilled those words by **c** him.
Sus 1:53 **c** the innocent and acquitting the

CONDEMNS* → CONDEMN

Ex 22: 9 whom God **c** shall pay double to
Job 15: 6 Your own mouth **c** you, and not I;
Pr 12: 2 but those who devise evil he **c**.
17:15 wicked and one who **c** the righteous

CONDITION

1Co 7:20 in the **c** in which you were called.

CONDUCT

Ps 112: 5 who **c** their affairs with justice.
Pr 10:23 wise **c** is pleasure to a person of
21: 8 but the **c** of the pure is right.
Ecc 6: 8 to **c** themselves before the living?
8:14 according to the **c** of the wicked,
Eze 22:31 returned their **c** upon their heads,
Ro 13: 3 For rulers are not a terror to good **c**,
Col 4: 5 **C** yourselves wisely toward
1Pe 2:12 be holy yourselves in all your **c**;
3: 1 without a word by their wives' **c**,
Tob 4:14 and discipline yourself in all your **c**.
Sir 11:26 individuals according to their **c**.
37:17 The mind is the root of all **c**;

CONFESS → CONFESSED, CONFESSES,
CONFESSING, CONFESSION

Lev 5: 5 you shall **c** the sin that you have

16:21 **c** over it all the iniquities of the
26:40 But if they **c** their iniquity and the
Nu 5: 7 and shall **c** the sin that has been
1Ki 8:33 but turn again to you, **c** your name,
8:35 **c** your name, and turn from their sin
2Ch 6:24 but turn again to you, **c** your name,
6:26 **c** your name, and turn from their sin
Ps 32: 5 **c** my transgressions to the LORD,"
38:18 **c** my iniquity; I am sorry for my sin.
Jn 12:42 of the Pharisees they did not **c** it,
Ro 10: 9 **c** with your lips that Jesus is Lord
15: 9 I will **c** you among the Gentiles,
Php 2:11 should **c** that Jesus Christ is Lord,
Heb 13:15 the fruit of lips that **c** his name.
Jas 5:16 **c** your sins to one another,
1Jn 1: 9 If we **c** our sins, he who is faithful
4: 3 spirit that does not **c** Jesus is not
4:15 abides in those who **c** that Jesus
2Jn 1: 7 those who do not **c** that Jesus Christ
Rev 3: 5 will **c** your name before my Father
Sir 4:26 Do not be ashamed to **c** your sins,

CONFESSED → CONFESS

Ne 9: 2 and **c** their sins and the iniquities
Jn 1:20 He **c** and did not deny it, but
9:22 who **c** Jesus to be the Messiah
Ac 19:18 of those who became believers **c**
Heb 11:13 They **c** that they were strangers and

CONFESSES* → CONFESS

Pr 28:13 **c** and forsakes them will obtain
Ro 10:10 **c** with the mouth and so is saved.
1Jn 2:23 who **c** the Son has the Father also.
4: 2 every spirit that **c** that Jesus Christ

CONFESSING* → CONFESS

Ne 1: 6 **c** the sins of the people of Israel,
Da 9:20 **c** my sin and the sin of my people
Mt 3: 6 in the river Jordan, **c** their sins.
Mk 1: 5 in the river Jordan, **c** their sins.

CONFESSION* → CONFESS

Jos 7:19 God of Israel and make **c** to him.
Ezr 10: 1 While Ezra prayed and made **c**,
10:11 make **c** to the LORD the God of
Ne 9: 3 fourth they made **c** and worshiped
Da 9: 4 to the LORD my God and made **c**,
2Co 9:13 to the **c** of the gospel of Christ
1Ti 6:12 for which you made the good **c** in
6:13 made the good **c**,
Heb 3: 1 the apostle and high priest of our **c**,
4:14 let us hold fast to our **c**.
10:23 the **c** of our hope without wavering,
Bar 1:14 your **c** in the house of the Lord on
1Es 8:91 Ezra was praying and making his **c**,
9: 8 make **c** and give glory to the Lord

CONFIDENCE → CONFIDENT

Jdg 9:26 the lords of Shechem put **c** in him.
2Ki 18:19 what do you base this **c** of yours?
Job 4: 6 Is not your fear of God your **c**,
8:14 Their **c** is gossamer, a spider's
31:24 or called fine gold my **c**;
Ps 62:10 Put no **c** in extortion, and set no
118: 8 in the LORD than to put **c** in mortals.
Pr 3:26 for the LORD will be your **c**
3:32 but the upright are in his **c**.
11:13 is trustworthy in spirit keeps a **c**.
14:26 fear of the LORD one has strong **c**,
Isa 36: 4 what do you base this **c** of yours?
Mic 7: 5 in a friend, have no **c** in a loved one;
2Co 3: 4 the **c** that we have through Christ
7:16 because I have complete **c** in you.
8:22 because of his great **c**
Eph 3:12 in boldness and **c** through faith in
Php 3: 3 and have no **c** in the flesh—
3: 4 too, have reason for **c** in the flesh.
2Th 3: 4 we have **c** in the Lord concerning
Heb 3: 6 his house if we hold firm the **c** and
3:14 if only we hold our first **c** firm to
10:19 we have **c** to enter the sanctuary
10:35 not, therefore, abandon that **c** of
13: 6 say with **c**, "The Lord is my helper;

1Jn 2:28 when he is revealed we may have c
Sir 27:16 Whoever betrays secrets destroys c,

CONFIDENT → CONFIDENCE

Job 6:20 disappointed because they were c;
Ps 27: 3 rise up against me, yet I will be c.
2Co 5: 6 So we are always c;
    10: 7 are c that you belong to Christ,
Php 1: 6 I am c of this, that the one who
    3: 4 has reason to be c in the flesh,
Phm 1:21 C of your obedience, I am writing
Heb 6: 9 are c of better things in your case,
Sir 5: 5 not be so c of forgiveness that you

CONFINED

Ge 40: 3 in the prison where Joseph was c.
Jer 32: 2 the prophet Jeremiah was c in the
    33: 1 was still c in the court of the guard:
    39:15 came to Jeremiah while he was c

CONFIRM → CONFIRMATION, CONFIRMED, CONFIRMS

Dt   8:18 so that he may c his covenant
2Sa 7:25 c it forever; do as you have
Ps 119:38 C to your servant your promise,
Ro 15: 8 that he might c the promises given
2Pe 1:10 be all the more eager to c your call

CONFIRMATION* → CONFIRM

Php 1: 7 in the defense and c of the gospel.
Heb 6:16 and an oath given as c puts an end

CONFIRMED → CONFIRM

1Ki 8:26 O God of Israel, let your word be c,
1Ch 16:17 which he c to Jacob as a statute,
Ps 105:10 which he c to Jacob as a statute,
   119:106 I have sworn an oath and c it,
Mt 18:16 may be c by the evidence of two
Heb 7:20 This was c with an oath;
2Pe 1:19 the prophetic message more fully c.

CONFIRMS → CONFIRM

Isa 44:26 who c the word of his servant,
Ro   9: 1 conscience c it by the Holy Spirit—

CONFLICTING* → CONFLICTS

Ro   2:15 and their c thoughts will accuse

CONFLICTS* → CONFLICTING

Jas 4: 1 Those c and disputes among you,
    4: 2 so you engage in disputes and c.

CONFORMED* → CONFORMS

Ro   8:29 predestined to be c to the image of
    12: 2 Do not be c to this world,
Php 3:21 may be c to the body of his glory,
1Pe 1:14 do not be c to the desires that you

CONFORMS* → CONFORMED

1Ti 1:11 that c to the glorious gospel of the

CONFOUNDED

Ps 35: 4 and c who devise evil against me.
Isa 45:16 All of them are put to shame and c,
Ac   9:22 more powerful and c the Jews
1Mc 2: 6 all the evildoers were c;

CONFRONT → CONFRONTED, CONFRONTS

Dt 31:21 this song will c them as a witness,
Ps 17:13 Rise up, O LORD, c them, overthrow
Pr 17:12 than to c a fool immersed in folly.

CONFRONTED* → CONFRONT

Nu 16: 2 well-known men, and they c Moses.
2Sa 22: 6 the snares of death c me.
Ps 18: 5 the snares of death c me.
    18:18 They c me in the day of my
Ac   6:12 they suddenly c him, seized him,

CONFUSE* → CONFUSED, CONFUSING, CONFUSION

Ge 11: 7 go down, and c their language there,
Ps 55: 9 C, O Lord, confound their speech;
Isa 3:12 and c the course of your paths.

CONFUSED → CONFUSE

Ge 11: 9 there the LORD c the language of all
Isa 28: 7 they are c with wine, they stagger

CONFUSING* → CONFUSE

Gal 1: 7 but there are some who are c you
    5:10 that is c you will pay the penalty.

CONFUSION → CONFUSE

Ex 23:27 and will throw into c all the people
Dt 28:28 blindness, and c of mind;
1Sa 7:10 Philistines and threw them into c;
    14:20 so that there was very great c.
Ne   4: 8 against Jerusalem and to cause c in
Ps 44: 7 and have put to c those who hate us.
    70: 2 and c who seek my life.
Isa 45:16 the makers of idols go in c together.
Mic 7: 4 now their c is at hand.
Ac 19:29 The city was filled with the c;

CONFUTE* → CONFUTED

Isa 54:17 you shall c every tongue that rises

CONFUTED* → CONFUTE

Job 32:12 there was in fact no one that c Job,

CONGREGATION

Ex 12: 3 Tell the whole c of Israel that
Lev 4:13 c of Israel errs unintentionally
Nu   1: 2 a census of the whole c of Israelites,
Ps   1: 5 nor sinners in the c of the righteous,
    22:22 in the midst of the c I will praise
    26:12 in the great c I will bless the LORD.
    35:18 Then I will thank you in the great c;
    40: 9 news of deliverance in the great c;
    68:26 "Bless God in the great c,
Heb 2:12 the midst of the c I will praise you."
Sir 39:10 and the c will proclaim his praise.

ALL THE CONGREGATION Ex 35:1, 4,
20; Lev 10:6; 19:2; Nu 13:26, 26; 14:1, 7, 36;
15:25, 26, 35; 16:3; 20:29; 27:2, 19, 20; 31:27;
Jos 9:18, 19, 21; 22:20; 1Ki 8:5; 2Ch 5:6

CONGREGATION OF ISRAEL Ex 12:3,
6, 19, 47; Lev 4:13; Nu 16:9; 32:4; Jos 22:18,
20; 1Ki 8:5; 2Ch 5:6; 24:6; Sir 50:13

**CONGREGATION OF [THE]
ISRAELITES** Ex 16:1, 2, 9, 10; 17:1; 35:1, 4,
20; Nu 1:2, 53; 8:9, 20; 13:26; 14:5, 7; 15:25,
26; 16:41; 19:9; 25:6; 26:2; 27:20; 31:12; Jos
18:1; Sir 50:20

WHOLE CONGREGATION Ex 12:3, 47;
16:1, 2, 9, 10; 17:1; Lev 4:13; 8:3; 9:5; 24:14,
16; Nu 1:2, 18; 3:7; 8:9, 20; 10:3; 14:2, 10;
15:24, 33, 36; 16:19, 19, 22, 41; 20:1, 22, 27;
25:6; 26:2; 27:21, 22; Jos 18:1; 22:16, 18; Jdg
21:13; Sir 1:30; 50:13, 20

CONIAH → =JEHOIACHIN

Jer 22:28 Is this man C a despised broken pot,

CONJUGAL*

1Co 7: 3 give to his wife her c rights,

CONQUER → CONQUERED, CONQUERING, CONQUEROR, CONQUERORS, CONQUERS

Rev 3: 5 If you c, you will be clothed like
    3:12 If you c, I will make you a pillar in
    6: 2 he came out conquering and to c.
    11: 7 make war on them and c them and
    13: 7 war on the saints and to c them.
    17:14 and the Lamb will c them,
    21: 7 who c will inherit these things,

CONQUERED → CONQUER

Jn 16:33 take courage; I have c the world!"
Heb 11:33 who through faith c kingdoms,
1Jn 2:13 because you have c the evil one.
    4: 4 you are from God, and have c them;
Rev 3:21 as I myself c and sat down with my
    5: 5 the Root of David, has c,
    12:11 c him by the blood of the Lamb

    15: 2 who had c the beast and its image
1Mc 1: 2 fought many battles, c strongholds,

CONQUERING → CONQUER

Rev 6: 2 and he came out c and to conquer.

CONQUEROR* → CONQUER

Mic 1:15 I will again bring a c upon you,

CONQUERORS* → CONQUER

Jer 8:10 and their fields to c,
Ro   8:37 all these things we are more than c

CONQUERS → CONQUER

1Jn 5: 4 victory that c the world, our faith.
Rev 2: 7 To everyone who c, I will give
    2:11 Whoever c will not be harmed by
    2:17 To everyone who c I will give some
    2:26 To everyone who c and continues
    2:28 To the one who c I will also give
    3:21 To the one who c I will give a place

CONSCIENCE* → CONSCIENCES

1Sa 25:31 or pangs of c, for having shed blood
Ac 23: 1 I have lived my life with a clear c
    24:16 do my best always to have a clear c
Ro   2:15 their own c also bears witness;
    9: 1 my c confirms it by the Holy Spirit
    13: 5 of wrath but also because of c.
1Co 8: 7 and their c, being weak, is defiled.
    8:10 they not, since their c is weak,
    8:12 and wound their c when it is weak,
    10:25 any question on the ground of c,
    10:27 any question on the ground of c.
    10:28 and for the sake of c—
    10:29 I mean the other's c, not your own.
    10:29 the judgment of someone else's c?
2Co 1:12 our boast, the testimony of our c:
    4: 2 we commend ourselves to the c
1Ti 1: 5 a good c, and sincere faith.
    1:19 having faith and a good c.
    1:19 By rejecting c,
    3: 9 mystery of the faith with a clear c.
2Ti 1: 3 whom I worship with a clear c,
Heb 9: 9 perfect the c of the worshiper.
    9:14 purify our c from dead works to
    10:22 an evil c and our bodies washed
    13:18 we are sure that we have a clear c,
1Pe 3:16 Keep your c clear, so that,
    3:21 as an appeal to God for a good c,
Wis 17:11 distressed by c, it has always

CONSCIENCES* → CONSCIENCE

2Co 5:11 we are also well known to your c.
1Ti 4: 2 of liars whose c are seared
Tit 1:15 very minds and c are corrupted.
Sus 1: 9 They suppressed their c

CONSCIENTIOUS*

2Ch 29:34 Levites were more c than the priests

CONSCRIPTED

Nu 31: 5 a thousand from each tribe were c,
1Ki 5:13 King Solomon c forced labor out of

CONSECRATE → CONSECRATED

Ex 13: 2 C to me all the firstborn;
    19:10 and c them today and tomorrow.
    28:41 and ordain them and c them,
    40: 9 and c it and all its furniture,
Lev 8:12 head and anointed him, to c him.

CONSECRATED → CONSECRATE

Ex 20:11 blessed the sabbath day and c it.
    22:31 You shall be people c to me;
Lev 8:15 Thus he c it, to make atonement for
    8:30 Thus he c Aaron and his vestments,
1Ki 9: 3 I have c this house that you have
2Ch 7:16 now I have chosen and c this house
Ne   3: 1 They c it and set up its doors;
Jer 1: 5 and before you were born I c you;
1Mc 4:48 of the temple, and c the courts.

CONSENT → CONSENTED, CONSENTS

Pr   1:10 if sinners entice you, do not **c.**
Phm 1:14 to do nothing without your **c,**

CONSENTED → CONSENT

Mt   3:15 fulfill all righteousness." Then he **c.**
Lk   22: 6 So he **c** and began to look for an

CONSENTS* → CONSENT

1Co 7:12 and she **c** to live with him,
        7:13 and he **c** to live with her,

CONSEQUENCES*

Nu   9:13 one shall bear the **c** for the sin.
Eze 23:35 bear the **c** of your lewdness and
     44:13 **c** of the abominations that they
4Mc 1:21 both pleasure and pain have many **c.**

CONSIDER → CONSIDERATION, CONSIDERED, CONSIDERS

Ex   33:13 **C** too that this nation is your people.
Dt   32: 7 **c** the years long past;
1Sa 12:24 for **c** what great things he has done
2Ch 19: 6 "**C** what you are doing, for you
Job 37:14 and **c** the wondrous works of God.
Ps   13: 3 **C** and answer me, O LORD my God!
     41: 1 Happy are those who **c** the poor;
   107:43 and **c** the steadfast love of the LORD.
Pr   6: 6 the ant, you lazybones; **c** its ways,
     14:15 but the clever **c** their steps.
Ecc   2:12 I turned to **c** wisdom and madness
        7:13 **C** the work of God; who can make
Isa 43:18 or **c** the things of old.
La   2:20 Look, O LORD, and **c!**
Da   11:36 and **c** himself greater than any god,
Lk   12:24 **C** the ravens: they neither sow
     12:27 **C** the lilies, how they grow:
Ro   6:11 must **c** yourselves dead to sin
Heb 10:24 let us **c** how to provoke one another
     12: 3 **C** him who endured such hostility
Jas   1: 2 of any kind, **c** it nothing but joy,
1Pe   4:16 do not **c** it a disgrace,
Bar   2:16 from your holy dwelling, and **c.** us.

CONSIDERATION → CONSIDER

1Pe   3: 7 show **c** for your wives in your life

CONSIDERED → CONSIDER

Job   1: 8 "Have you **c** my servant Job?
        2: 3 "Have you **c** my servant Job?
Pr   17:28 fools who keep silent are **c** wise;
Lk   20:35 those who are **c** worthy of a place
Ac   5:41 were **c** worthy to suffer dishonor for
Heb 11:11 he **c** him faithful who had promised.

CONSIDERS → CONSIDER

Pr   31:16 She **c** a field and buys it;
Isa 44:19 No one **c,** nor is there knowledge

CONSIST

Lk   12:15 life does not **c** in the abundance
1Co 12:14 the body does not **c** of one member

CONSISTENT* → CONSISTENTLY

Ac   26:20 and do deeds **c** with repentance.
Tit   2: 1 teach what is **c** with sound doctrine.
Sir   5:10 and let your speech be **c.**

CONSISTENTLY* → CONSISTENT

Gal   2:14 not acting **c** with the truth of the

CONSOLATION → CONSOLE

Job   6:10 This would be my **c;**
     21: 2 and let this be your **c.**
Lk   2:25 looking forward to the **c** of Israel,
        6:24 for you have received your **c.**
1Co 14: 3 and encouragement and **c.**
2Co 1: 3 of mercies and the God of all **c,**
        1: 4 with the **c** with which we ourselves
        1: 6 it is for your **c** and salvation;
        7: 4 I am filled with **c;**
Php   2: 1 any **c** from love, any sharing in the

CONSOLATIONS* → CONSOLE

Job 15:11 Are the **c** of God too small for you,
Ps   94:19 your **c** cheer my soul.
Jer 31: 9 and with **c** I will lead them back,

CONSOLE → CONSOLATION, CONSOLATIONS, CONSOLED, CONSOLES

2Sa 10: 2 So David sent envoys to **c** him
2Co 1: 4 to **c** those who are in any affliction
        2: 7 you should forgive and **c** him,

CONSOLED → CONSOLE

Mt   2:18 she refused to be **c,** because they
2Co 1: 6 if we are being **c,** it is for your

CONSOLES* → CONSOLE

2Co 1: 4 who **c** us in all our affliction,
        7: 6 But God, who **c** the downcast,

CONSORT*

Ps   26: 4 nor do I **c** with hypocrites;

CONSPICUOUS

1Ti   5:24 The sins of some people are **c**

CONSPIRACY → CONSPIRE

2Sa 15:12 The **c** grew in strength,
Isa   8:12 not call **c** all that this people calls **c,**
Ac   23:12 the Jews joined in a **c**

CONSPIRATORS → CONSPIRE

Da   6:11 **c** came and found Daniel praying

CONSPIRE* → CONSPIRACY, CONSPIRATORS, CONSPIRED

Ps   2: 1 Why do the nations **c,**
     83: 5 They **c** with one accord;

CONSPIRED → CONSPIRE

1Sa 22:13 "Why have you **c** against me,
Da   6: 6 So the presidents and satraps **c**
Mt   26: 4 and they **c** to arrest Jesus by stealth

CONSTANT → CONSTANTLY

1Pe   4: 8 Above all, maintain **c** love for one

CONSTANTLY → CONSTANT

Ac   1:14 **c** devoting themselves to prayer,
     10: 2 and prayed **c** to God.

CONSTRUCTED → CONSTRUCTION

Heb 9: 2 For a tent was **c,** the first one,

CONSTRUCTION → CONSTRUCTED

Ex   38:24 in all the **c** of the sanctuary,
Ezr   5:16 until now it has been under **c,**
Ne   4:16 half of my servants worked on **c,**
Jn   2:20 "This temple has been under **c**

CONSULT → CONSULTED, CONSULTS

1Sa 28: 8 And he said, "**C** a spirit for me,
Ezr   2:63 a priest to **c** Urim and Thummim.
Ps   71:10 who watch for my life **c** together.
Isa   8:19 **C** the ghosts and the familiar spirits
     31: 1 Holy One of Israel or **c** the LORD!
     40:14 did he **c** for his enlightenment,
Eze 20: 3 Why are you coming? To **c** me?
Hos 4:12 My people **c** a piece of wood,
Sir   8:17 Do not **c** with fools, for they cannot
        9:14 your neighbors, and **c** with the wise.

CONSULTED → CONSULT

2Sa 16:23 as if one **c** the oracle of God;
1Ki 12: 8 and **c** with the young men who had
1Ch 10:13 had **c** a medium, seeking guidance,
Eze 20: 3 Lord GOD, I will not be **c** by you.

CONSULTS* → CONSULT

Dt   18:11 or who **c** ghosts or spirits,
Eze 21:21 he **c** the teraphim,

CONSUME → CONSUMED, CONSUMES, CONSUMING, CONSUMPTION

Ex   32:12 **c** them from the face of the earth'?
     33: 3 or I would **c** you on the way,

Nu   16:21 so that I may **c** them in a moment.
Dt   5:25 For this great fire will **c** us;
1Ki 21:21 I will **c** you, and will cut off
Ps   21: 9 up in his wrath, and fire will **c** them.
     59:13 **c** them in wrath; **c** them until they
Ecc 10:12 but the lips of fools **c** them.
Isa 26:11 Let the fire for your adversaries **c**
     43: 2 and the flame shall not **c** you.
Eze 15: 7 the fire shall still **c** them;
Mt   6:19 where moth and rust **c** and where
Jn   2:17 "Zeal for your house will **c** me."
Heb 10:27 of fire that will **c** the adversaries.

CONSUMED → CONSUME

Ge   19:15 else you will be **c** in the punishment
Ex   3: 2 bush was blazing, yet it was not **c.**
Lev   9:24 and **c** the burnt offering
Nu   11: 1 **c** some outlying parts of the camp.
     16:35 fire came out from the LORD and **c**
1Ki 18:38 fire of the LORD fell and **c** the burnt
2Ki 1:10 and **c** him and his fifty.
2Ch 7: 1 fire came down from heaven and **c**
Ps   69: 9 zeal for your house that has **c** me;
     90: 7 For we are **c** by your anger;
Isa   1:28 who forsake the LORD shall be **c.**
La   4:11 and kindled a fire in Zion that **c**
Zep   3: 8 all the earth shall be **c.**
Ro   1:27 were **c** with passion for one another.
Gal   5:15 that you are not **c** by one another.
Rev 20: 9 fire came down from heaven and **c**

CONSUMES → CONSUME

Ps 119:139 My zeal **c** me because my foes
Rev 11: 5 fire pours from their mouth and **c**

CONSUMING → CONSUME

Ps   39:11 **c** like a moth what is dear to them;
Heb 12:29 for indeed our God is a **c** fire.

CONSUMPTION* → CONSUME

Lev 26:16 **c** and fever that waste the eyes
Dt   28:22 The LORD will afflict you with **c,**
     32:24 burning **c,** bitter pestilence.

CONTAIN*

1Ki 8:27 the highest heaven cannot **c** you,
     18:32 enough to **c** two measures of seed.
2Ch 2: 6 even highest heaven, cannot **c** him?
        6:18 the highest heaven cannot **c** you,
Jn   21:25 world itself could not **c** the books

CONTEMPT → CONTEMPTIBLE

Ge   16: 5 she looked on me with **c.**
1Sa 2:17 the offerings of the LORD with **c.**
Est   1:17 to look with **c** on their husbands,
Ps 107:40 he pours **c** on princes and makes
     123: 3 we have had more than enough of **c.**
Pr   18: 3 When wickedness comes, **c** comes
Da   12: 2 some to shame and everlasting **c.**
Mk   9:12 sufferings and be treated with **c?**
1Co 11:22 you show **c** for the church of God
Heb 6: 6 and are holding him up to **c.**
1Mc 1:39 into a reproach, her honor into **c.**

CONTEMPTIBLE → CONTEMPT

Da   11:21 In his place shall arise a **c** person

CONTEND → CONTENDED, CONTENTIOUS

Jdg   6:31 "Will you **c** for Baal?
Job   9: 3 If one wished to **c** with him,
Ps   35: 1 **C,** O LORD, with those who **c** with
Isa 49:25 I will **c** with those who **c** with you,
Jude 1: 3 to **c** for the faith that was once for

CONTENDED → CONTEND

Dt   33: 8 you **c** at the waters of Meribah;
Ne   13:25 And I **c** with them and cursed them
Jude 1: 9 archangel Michael **c** with the devil

CONTENT → CONTENTMENT

Jos   7: 7 that we had been **c** to settle beyond
2Co 12:10 Therefore I am **c** with weaknesses,
Php   4:11 learned to be **c** with whatever I have

1Ti 6: 8 we will be **c** with these.
Heb 13: 5 and be **c** with what you have;
Sir 26: 4 Whether rich or poor, his heart is **c**,
     29:23 Be **c** with little or much,

CONTENTIOUS → CONTEND
Pr 21: 9 in a house shared with a **c** wife.
1Co 11:16 But if anyone is disposed to be **c**—

CONTENTMENT* → CONTENT
1Ti 6: 6 gain in godliness combined with **c;**

CONTEST
2Sa 2:14 men come forward and have a **c**
Job 9:19 a **c** of strength, he is the strong one!

CONTINUAL → CONTINUE
Ex 28:29 a **c** remembrance before the LORD.
Pr 15:15 but a cheerful heart has a **c** feast.
    27:15 A **c** dripping on a rainy day and

CONTINUALLY → CONTINUE
Ge 6: 5 of their hearts was only evil **c.**
1Ch 16:11 his strength, seek his presence **c.**
Ps 34: 1 his praise shall **c** be in my mouth.
    44: 8 In God we have boasted **c,**
    71:14 I will hope **c,** and will praise you
   119:44 I will keep your law **c,**
Isa 49:16 your walls are **c** before me.
Hos 12: 6 and wait **c** for your God.
Mt 18:10 angels **c** see the face of my Father
Lk 24:53 were **c** in the temple blessing God.
Heb 13:15 let us **c** offer a sacrifice of praise to
Tob 14: 2 giving alms and **c** blessing God
Sir 51:11 I will praise your name **c,**

CONTINUE → CONTINUAL,
CONTINUALLY, CONTINUED, CONTINUES
Lev 26:21 If you **c** hostile to me,
2Sa 7:29 so that it may **c** forever before you;
1Ch 17:27 that it may **c** forever before you.
Ps 36:10 O **c** your steadfast love to those
   89:36 His line shall **c** forever, and his
Isa 1: 5 Why do you **c** to rebel?
Jn 8:31 "If you **c** in my word,
Ac 13:43 urged them to **c** in the grace of God.
Ro 11:22 provided you **c** in his kindness;
2Co 1:10 so deadly a peril will **c** to rescue us;
Col 1:23 that you **c** securely established
    2: 6 **c** to live your lives in him,
1Th 3: 8 if you **c** to stand firm in the Lord.
1Ti 2:15 provided they **c** in faith and love
    4:16 **c** in these things, for in doing this
2Ti 3:14 **c** in what you have learned
Heb 8: 9 for they did not **c** in my covenant,
    13: 1 Let mutual love **c.**
1Mc 2:20 and my brothers will **c** to live by

CONTINUED → CONTINUE
Ge 7:17 The flood **c** forty days on the earth;
Jos 17:12 the Canaanites **c** to live in that land.
Jdg 1:27 the Canaanites **c** to live in that land.
2Ki 17:22 The people of Israel **c** in all the sins
Ac 6: 7 The word of God **c** to spread;
   12:24 word of God **c** to advance
   14: 7 they **c** proclaiming the good news.

CONTINUES → CONTINUE
Heb 7:24 because he **c** forever.
Rev 2:26 and **c** to do my works to the end,

CONTRADICT* → CONTRADICTED,
CONTRADICTIONS
Lk 21:15 be able to withstand or **c.**
Tit 1: 9 and to refute those who **c** it.

CONTRADICTED* → CONTRADICT
Ac 13:45 they **c** what was spoken by Paul.

CONTRADICTIONS* → CONTRADICT
1Ti 6:20 and **c** of what is falsely called
    knowledge;

CONTRARY
Ac 18:13 in ways that are **c** to the law."
Ro 3:31 On the **c,** we uphold the law.
   11:24 **c** to nature, into a cultivated olive
Gal 1: 8 a gospel **c** to what we proclaimed to
1Ti 1:10 else is **c** to the sound teaching

CONTRIBUTE* → CONTRIBUTED,
CONTRIBUTING, CONTRIBUTIONS
Ro 12:13 C to the needs of the saints;

CONTRIBUTED → CONTRIBUTE
Mk 12:44 have **c** out of their abundance;
Gal 2: 6 those leaders **c** nothing to me.

CONTRIBUTING* → CONTRIBUTE
Dt 16:10 **c** a freewill offering in proportion to
Mk 12:43 all those who are **c** to the treasury.

CONTRIBUTIONS → CONTRIBUTE
2Ch 31:12 Faithfully they brought in the **c,**

CONTRITE* → CONTRITION
Ps 51:17 broken and **c** heart, O God, you wil
Isa 57:15 who are **c** and humble in spirit,
   57:15 and to revive the heart of the **c.**
   66: 2 to the humble and **c** in spirit,
Aza 1:16 with a **c** heart and a humble spiri

CONTRITION* → CONTRITE
Jer 44:10 They have shown no **c** or fear to

CONTROL → CONTROLLED,
SELF-CONTROL, SELF-CONTROLLED
Ge 45: 1 Joseph could no longer **c** himself
1Co 7:37 but having his own desire under **c,**
1Th 4: 4 how to **c** your own body in holiness

CONTROLLED → CONTROL
Pr 16:32 and one whose temper is **c** than

CONTROVERSIES* → CONTROVERSY
Ac 18: 3 all the customs and **c** of the Jews;
2Ti 2:23 to do with stupid and senseless **c;**
Tit 3: 9 But avoid stupid **c,** genealogies,

CONTROVERSY → CONTROVERSIES
Mic 6: 2 the LORD has a **c** with his people,
1Ti 6: 4 and has a morbid craving for **c**

CONVERSATION
Sir 9:15 Let your **c** be with intelligent people
   19: 7 Never repeat a **c,** and you will lose

CONVERSION* → CONVERT
Ac 15: 3 they reported the **c** of the Gentiles,

CONVERT* → CONVERSION,
CONVERTED, CONVERTS
Mt 23:15 sea and land to make a single **c,**
   23:15 the new **c** twice as much a child
Ro 16: 5 was the first **c** in Asia for Christ.
1Ti 3: 6 He must not be a recent **c,**

CONVERTED* → CONVERT
Tob 14: 6 world will all be **c** and worship God
2Es 6:26 and **c** to a different spirit.

CONVERTS* → CONVERT
Ac 13:43 many Jews and devout **c** to Judaism
1Co 16:15 of Stephanas were the first **c**
Tob 1: 8 the **c** who had attached themselves

CONVICT → CONVICTED, CONVICTION,
CONVICTS
Dt 19:15 to **c** a person of any crime
Jer 2:19 and your apostasies will **c** you.
Jude 1:15 to **c** everyone of all the deeds of

CONVICTED* → CONVICT
Dt 21:22 When someone is **c** of a crime
Jas 2: 9 are **c** by the law as transgressors.
Sus 1:61 Daniel had **c** them of bearing false

CONVICTION* → CONVICT
Ro 14:22 have as your own **c** before God.
1Th 1: 5 in the Holy Spirit and with full **c;**
Heb 11: 1 the **c** of things not seen.

CONVICTS* → CONVICT
2Sa 14:13 this decision the king **c** himself,
Jn 8:46 Which of you **c** me of sin?

CONVINCE → CONVINCED,
CONVINCING
Ac 18: 4 would try to **c** Jews and Greeks.
   28:23 and trying to **c** them about Jesus
2Ti 4: 2 **c,** rebuke, and encourage,

CONVINCED → CONVINCE
Lk 16:31 neither will they be **c** even if
Ac 16:10 **c** that God had called us to proclaim
   26: 9 I myself was **c** that I ought to do
   28:24 Some were **c** by what he had said,
Ro 4:21 being fully **c** that God was able
   8:38 For I am **c** that neither death, nor
   14: 5 Let all be fully **c** in their own minds.
2Co 5:14 we are **c** that one has died for all;
Php 1:25 Since I am **c** of this,

CONVINCING* → CONVINCE
Ac 1: 3 to them by many **c** proofs,

CONVOCATION → CONVOCATIONS
Lev 23: 3 a sabbath of complete rest, a holy **c;**
Nu 28:18 the first day there shall be a holy **c.**
Isa 1:13 and sabbath and calling of **c**—

CONVOCATIONS → CONVOCATION
Lev 23: 2 that you shall proclaim as holy **c,**

COOKED
2Ki 6:29 So we **c** my son and ate him.

COOL
Jdg 3:20 sitting alone in his **c** roof chamber,
Lk 16:24 his finger in water and **c** my tongue;

COPIED* → COPY
Pr 25: 1 of King Hezekiah of Judah **c.**

COPPER
Lev 26:19 like iron and your earth like **c.**
Dt 8: 9 from whose hills you may mine **c.**
Mt 10: 9 Take no gold, or silver, or **c** in your
Mk 12:42 and put in two small **c** coins,

COPY → COPIED
Dt 17:18 he shall have a **c** of this law written
Jos 22:28 at this **c** of the altar of the LORD,
Heb 9:24 a mere **c** of the true one,

CORBAN*
Mk 7:11 is C' (that is, an offering to God)—

CORD → CORDS
Ge 38:18 replied, "Your signet and your **c,**
Ex 28:28 the rings of the ephod with a blue **c,**
Nu 15:38 and to put a blue **c** on the fringe
Jos 2:18 tie this crimson **c** in the window
Ecc 4:12 A threefold **c** is not quickly broken.
   12: 6 the silver **c** is snapped,

CORDS → CORD
2Sa 22: 6 the **c** of Sheol entangled me;
Ps 18: 4 The **c** of death encompassed me;
   129: 4 he has cut the **c** of the wicked.
Isa 54: 2 lengthen your **c** and strengthen your
Hos 11: 4 led them with **c** of human kindness,
Jn 2:15 of **c,** he drove all of them out of the

CORIANDER*
Ex 16:31 it was like **c** seed, white, and the
Nu 11: 7 Now the manna was like **c** seed,

CORINTH → CORINTHIANS
Ac 18: 1 Paul left Athens and went to C.
1Co 1: 2 To the church of God that is in C,
2Co 1: 1 To the church of God that is in C,

CORINTHIANS* → CORINTH

Ac 18: 8 **C** who heard Paul became believers
2Co 6:11 We have spoken frankly to you **C**;

CORNELIUS*

Roman to whom Peter preached; first Gentile Christian (Ac 10).

CORNER → CORNERS, CORNERSTONE

1Sa 24: 4 stealthily cut off a **c** of Saul's cloak.
Pr 1:21 At the busiest **c** she cries out;
7:12 and at every **c** she lies in wait.
21: 9 better to live in a **c** of the housetop
Ac 26:26 for this was not done in a **c**.
1Pe 7: 7 has become the very head of the **c**,"

CORNERS → CORNER

Dt 22:12 tassels on the four **c** of the cloak
Isa 41: 9 called from its farthest **c**,
Eze 7: 2 The end has come upon the four **c** of
Mt 6: 5 in the synagogues and at the street **c**,
Ac 10:11 lowered to the ground by its four **c**.
Rev 7: 1 standing at the four **c** of the earth,
20: 8 to deceive the nations at the four **c**

CORNERSTONE* → CORNER, STONE

Job 38: 6 its bases sunk, or who laid its **c**
Ps 118:22 rejected has become the chief **c**.
Isa 28:16 a tested stone, a precious **c**, a sure
Zec 10: 4 Out of them shall come the **c**,
Mt 21:42 builders rejected has become the **c**;
Mk 12:10 builders rejected has become the **c**;
Lk 20:17 builders rejected has become the **c**'?
Ac 4:11 the builders; it has become the **c**.'
Eph 2:20 with Christ Jesus himself as the **c**.
1Pe 2: 6 laying in Zion a stone, a **c** chosen

CORPSE

Lev 22: 4 anything made unclean by a **c**
Mt 24:28 the **c** is, there the vultures will

CORRECT → CORRECTING, CORRECTION, CORRECTOR, CORRECTS

Ps 141: 5 let the faithful **c** me.
Jer 10:24 **C** me, O LORD, but in just measure;
Sir 42: 8 Do not be ashamed to **c** the stupid

CORRECTING* → CORRECT

2Ti 2:25 **c** opponents with gentleness.

CORRECTION → CORRECT

Jer 2:30 your children; they accepted no **c**.
5: 3 but they refused to take **c**.
Zep 3: 2 to no voice; it has accepted no **c**.
3: 7 city will fear me, it will accept **c**;
2Ti 3:16 **c**, and for training in righteousness,

CORRECTOR → CORRECT

Ro 2:20 a **c** of the foolish, a teacher of

CORRECTS* → CORRECT

Pr 9: 7 Whoever **c** a scoffer wins abuse;

CORRESPONDING → CORRESPONDS

Ex 24: 4 **c** to the twelve tribes of Israel.
28:21 **c** to the names of the sons of Israel;

CORRESPONDS → CORRESPONDING

Gal 4:25 and **c** to the present Jerusalem,

CORRUPT → CORRUPTED, CORRUPTIBLE, CORRUPTION, CORRUPTLY, CORRUPTS

Ge 6:11 Now the earth was **c** in God's sight,
Ps 14: 1 They are **c**, they do abominable
Ac 2:40 yourselves from this **c** generation."
Eph 4:22 your old self, **c** and deluded

CORRUPTED → CORRUPT

Eze 28:17 you **c** your wisdom for the sake of
Mal 2: 8 you have **c** the covenant of Levi,
2Co 7: 2 wronged no one, we have **c** no one,
Tit 1:15 very minds and consciences are **c**.

Rev 19: 2 the great whore who **c** the earth

CORRUPTIBLE → CORRUPT

2Es 7:31 and that which is **c** shall perish.

CORRUPTION → CORRUPT

Da 6: 4 or any **c**, because he was faithful,
Ac 2:31 nor did his flesh experience **c**.'
13:35 not let your Holy One experience **c**.'
2Pe 1: 4 you may escape from the **c**

CORRUPTLY → CORRUPT

Dt 4:16 so that you do not act **c** by making
Isa 1: 4 children who deal **c**,
Jer 6:28 all of them act **c**.

CORRUPTS* → CORRUPT

Ecc 7: 7 and a bribe **c** the heart.

COSMIC*

Eph 6:12 **c** powers of this present darkness,

COST → COSTLY

Nu 16:38 become holy at the **c** of their lives.
Jos 6:26 the **c** of his firstborn he shall lay its
1Ki 16:34 at the **c** of Abiram his firstborn,
1Ch 21:24 burnt offerings that **c** me nothing."
Pr 7:23 knowing that it will **c** him his life.
Lk 14:28 not first sit down and estimate the **c**,

COSTLY → COST

1Ki 7: 9 All these were made of **c** stones,
Ps 49: 8 For the ransom of life is **c**,
Mt 26: 7 an alabaster jar of very **c** ointment,
Rev 18:12 all articles of **c** wood, bronze, iron,
1Mc 1:23 and the gold, and the **c** vessels;

COTS*

Ac 5:15 and laid them on **c** and mats,

COUCH → COUCHES

Est 7: 8 on the **c** where Esther was reclining;

COUCHES → COUCH

Am 6: 4 and lounge on their **c**,

COUNCIL → COUNCILS

Job 15: 8 Have you listened in the **c** of God?
Ps 82: 1 has taken his place in the divine **c**;
89: 7 God feared in the **c** of the holy ones,
Jer 23:18 who has stood in the **c** of the LORD
Mt 26:59 you will be liable to the **c**;
26:59 the whole **c** were looking for false
Mk 15:43 a respected member of the **c**,
Ac 5:34 a Pharisee in the **c** named Gamaliel,
23: 1 Paul was looking intently at the **c**

COUNCILS* → COUNCIL

Mt 10:17 for they will hand you over to **c**
Mk 13: 9 for they will hand you over to **c**;

COUNSEL → COUNSELOR, COUNSELORS, COUNSELS

2Sa 15:34 defeat for me the **c** of Ahithophel.
17:23 Ahithophel saw that his **c** was not
Job 12:13 he has **c** and understanding.
38: 2 that darkens **c** by words without
42: 3 that hides **c** without knowledge?'
Ps 2: 2 and the rulers take **c** together,
16: 7 I bless the LORD who gives me **c**;
33:11 The **c** of the LORD stands forever,
73:24 You guide me with your **c**,
107:11 and spurned the **c** of the Most High.
Pr 12:20 but those who **c** peace have joy.
15:22 Without **c**, plans go wrong,
Isa 11: 2 the spirit of **c** and might,
28:29 he is wonderful in **c**, and excellent
Rev 3:18 I **c** you to buy from me gold refined
Tob 4:18 and do not despise any useful **c**.
Wis 9:17 Who has learned your **c**,
Sir 25: 4 and for the aged to possess good **c**!

COUNSELOR → COUNSEL

Isa 9: 6 and he is named Wonderful **C**,
40:13 or as his **c** has instructed him?

Ro 11:34 Or who has been his **c**?"
Sir 42:21 and he needs no one to be his **c**.

COUNSELORS → COUNSEL

Job 12:17 He leads **c** away stripped,
Ps 119:24 are my delight, they are my **c**.
Pr 11:14 in an abundance of **c** there is safety.
24: 6 in abundance of **c** there is victory.
Sir 37: 7 All **c** praise the counsel they give,

COUNSELS → COUNSEL

Ps 5:10 let them fall by their own **c**;
81:12 to follow their own **c**.
Jer 7:24 they walked in their own **c**,
Na 1:11 against the LORD, who **c** wickedness

COUNT → COUNTED, COUNTING, COUNTS

Ge 13:16 if one can **c** the dust of the earth,
15: 5 Look toward heaven and **c** the stars,
Nu 23:10 Who can **c** the dust of Jacob,
Dt 16: 9 You shall **c** seven weeks;
1Ch 21: 1 incited David to **c** the people of
Ps 22:17 I can **c** all my bones.
48:12 go all around it, **c** its towers,
90:12 So teach us to **c** our days
139:18 I try to **c** them—they are more than
Rev 7: 9 great multitude that no one could **c**,

COUNTED → COUNT

Ge 13:16 your offspring also can be **c**.
1Ki 8: 5 they could not be **c** or numbered.
Job 18: 3 Why are we **c** as cattle?
Ps 40: 5 they would be more than can be **c**.
Ecc 1:15 and what is lacking cannot be **c**.
Mt 10:30 even the hairs of your head are all **c**.

COUNTENANCE

Ge 4: 6 and why has your **c** fallen?
Nu 6:26 the LORD lift up his **c** upon you,
Ps 44: 3 and the light of your **c**,
89:15 O LORD, in the light of your **c**;
Pr 15:13 A glad heart makes a cheerful **c**,
Jdt 16: 6 with the beauty of her **c** undid him.
Sir 13:25 heart changes the **c**, either for good

COUNTERFEIT*

2Ti 3: 8 of corrupt mind and **c** faith,
Wis 15: 9 a glorious thing to mold **c** gods.

COUNTING → COUNT

2Co 5:19 not **c** their trespasses against them,

COUNTRIES → COUNTRY

Isa 36:20 Who among all the gods of these **c**
Eze 11:16 I scattered them among the **c**,
20:34 and gather you out of the **c**

COUNTRY → COUNTRIES, COUNTRYSIDE

Ge 12: 1 "Go from your **c** and your kindred
Jos 9: 6 "We have come from a far **c**;
11:16 the hill of Israel and its lowland,
1Sa 6: 1 in the **c** of the Philistines seven
Jer 17: 3 on the mountains in the open **c**;
31:17 shall come back to their own **c**.
Eze 20:42 the **c** that I swore to give
Mal 1: 4 until they are called the wicked **c**,
Lk 15:13 and traveled to a distant **c**,
Jn 4:44 a prophet has no honor in the prophet's own **c**).
Heb 11:16 they desire a better **c**, that is,

HILL COUNTRY Ge 10:30; 12:8; 14:6, 10; 31:21, 23, 25, 25, 54; 36:8, 9; Nu 13:17, 29; 14:40, 44, 45; Dt 1:7, 7, 19, 20, 24, 41, 43, 44; 2:3, 37; 3:12, 25; Jos 2:16, 22, 23; 9:1; 10:6, 40; 11:2, 3, 16, 16, 21, 21; 12:8; 13:6; 14:12; 15:48; 16:1; 17:15, 16, 18; 18:12; 19:50; 20:7, 7, 7; 21:11, 21; 24:4, 30, 33; Jdg 1:9, 19, 34; 2:9; 3:27, 27; 4:5; 7:24; 10:1; 12:15; 17:1, 8; 18:2, 13; 19:1, 16, 18; 1Sa 1:1; 9:4; 13:2; 14:22, 23; 23:14; 2Sa 20:21; 1Ki 4:8; 5:15; 12:25; 2Ki 5:22; 1Ch 6:67; 2Ch 2:2,

18; 13:4; 15:8; 19:4; 21:11; 27:4; Jer 17:26;
31:6; 32:44; 33:13; Mal 1:3; Lk 1:39, 65; Jdt
1:6; 2:22; 5:3, 15, 19; 6:7, 11; 7:1, 18; 10:13;
11:2; 15:2, 5, 7; Sir 46:9; 1Mc 10:70

HILL COUNTRY OF EPHRAIM Jos
17:15; 19:50; 20:7; 21:21; 24:30, 33; Jdg 2:9;
3:27; 4:5; 7:24; 10:1; 17:1, 8; 18:2, 13; 19:1,
16, 18; 1Sa 1:1; 9:4; 14:22, 23; 2Sa 20:21; 1Ki
4:8; 12:25; 2Ki 5:22; 1Ch 6:67; 2Ch 13:4;
15:8; 19:4; Jer 31:6

COUNTRYSIDE → COUNTRY
Mk   1: 5 people from the whole Judean c

COUNTS → COUNT
Gal   5: 6 only thing that c is faith

COURAGE → COURAGEOUS
Jos   2:11 there was no c left in any of us
2Sa   4: 1 his c failed, and all Israel was
         7:27 therefore your servant has found c
1Ch 22:13 Be strong and of good c.
         28:20 "Be strong and of good c,
2Ch 15: 7 But you, take c! Do not let your
         15: 8 of Azariah son of Oded, he took c,
Ezr   7:28 I took c, for the hand of the LORD
Ps   107:26 c melted away in their calamity;
Eze 22:14 Can your c endure, or can your
Hag   2: 4 Yet now take c, O Zerubbabel,
Jn   16:33 But take c; I have conquered
Ac   23:11 near him and said, "Keep up your c!
         27:22 I urge you now to keep up your c,
         27:25 your c, men, for I have faith in God
Tob   5:10 But the young man said, "Take c;
         7:16 she said to her, "Take c,

COURAGEOUS → COURAGE
Jos   1: 6 Be strong and c; for you shall put
         1: 7 Only be strong and very c,
         1: 9 command you: Be strong and c;
         1:18 Only be strong and c."
         10:25 be strong and c;
2Sa 13:28 Be c and valiant."
2Ch 17: 6 heart was c in the ways of the LORD;
Da   10:19 Be strong and c!"
1Co 16:13 stand firm in your faith, be c,
1Mc   2:64 be c and grow strong in the law,

COURIERS
2Ch 30: 6 So c went throughout all Israel and
Est   3:15 The c went quickly by order of the
         8:10 and sent them by mounted c.

COURSE → WATERCOURSES
Ps   19: 5 like a strong man runs its c with joy.
Eph   2: 2 following the c of this world,
Sir   43: 5 at his orders it hurries on its c.

COURT → COURTS, COURTYARD
Ex   27: 9 shall make the c of the tabernacle.
Nu   3:26 the hangings of the c, the screen
1Ki   7: 8 in the other c back of the hall,
Pr   25: 8 do not hastily bring into c;
Eze 10: 3 and a cloud filled the inner c.
Da   7:10 c sat in judgment, and the books
Mt   5:25 while you are on the way to c
1Co   4: 3 judged by you or by any human c.
         6: 6 believer goes to c against a believer
Jas   2: 6 Is it not they who drag you into c?

COURTESIES* → COURTESY
Sir   6: 5 and a gracious tongue multiplies c.
         20:13 but the c of fools are wasted.

COURTESY* → COURTESIES
Tit   3: 2 and to show every c to everyone.

COURTS → COURT
1Ch 28: 6 who shall build my house and my c,
Ps   65: 4 and bring near to live in your c.
         84:10 in your c is better than a thousand
         96: 8 an offering, and come into his c.
         100: 4 thanksgiving, and his c with praise.
Isa   1:12 Trample my c no more;

COURTYARD → COURT
Mk   14:66 While Peter was below in the c,
AdE   2:11 every day Mordecai walked in the c
         6:12 Then Mordecai returned to the c,

COUSIN
Est   2: 7 his c, for she had neither father nor
Col   4:10 as does Mark the c of Barnabas,

COVENANT → COVENANTS
Ge   6:18 But I will establish my c with you;
         9: 9 I am establishing my c with you
         15:18 the LORD made a c with Abram,
         17: 2 And I will make my c between me
         21:27 and the two men made a c.
         31:44 let us make a c, you and I;
Ex   2:24 remembered his c with Abraham,
         6: 5 and I have remembered my c.
         19: 5 you obey my voice and keep my c,
         23:32 make no c with them and their gods.
         24: 7 Then he took the book of the c,
         34:28 on the tablets the words of the c,
         40: 3 put in it the ark of the c,
Lev 26:42 will I remember my c with Jacob;
Dt   4:13 He declared to you his c,
         29: 1 the c that the LORD commanded
Jos   3: 6 "Take up the ark of the c,
Jdg   2: 1 'I will never break my c with you.
1Sa 20:16 Thus Jonathan made a c with the
         23:18 of them made a c before the LORD;
1Ki   8: 1 bring up the ark of the c of the LORD
         8:21 in which is the c of the LORD that
         8:23 keeping c and steadfast love
2Ki 11:12 crown on him, and gave him the c;
         23: 2 all the words of the book of the c
1Ch 16:15 Remember his c forever,
2Ch 34:30 all the words of the book of the c
Ezr 10: 3 now let us make a c with our God
Ne   1: 5 and awesome God who keeps c
         9:32 keeping c and steadfast love—
Job 31: 1 "I have made a c with my eyes;
Ps   25:14 and he makes his c known to them.
         44:17 or been false to your c.
         78:37 they were not true to his c.
         89: 3 "I have made a c with my chosen
         105: 8 He is mindful of his c forever,
         111: 5 he is ever mindful of his c.
         132:12 If your sons keep my c and my
Pr   2:17 her youth and forgets her sacred c;
Isa 28:15 said, "We have made a c with death,
         42: 6 have given you as a c to the people,
         61: 8 I will make an everlasting c with
Jer 11: 2 Hear the words of this c,
         31:31 when I will make a new c with
         32:40 I will make an everlasting c with
Eze 16:60 establish with you an everlasting c.
         17:15 Can he break the c and yet escape?
         37:26 I will make a c of peace with them;
Da   9:27 a strong c with many for one week;
         11:28 heart shall be set against the holy c.
Hos   6: 7 at Adam they transgressed the c;
Mal   2: 4 that my c with Levi may hold,
         2:14 your companion and your wife by c.
         3: 1 The messenger of the c in whom
Mt   26:28 for this is my blood of the c,
Mk   14:24 to them, "This is my blood of the c,
Lk   1:72 and has remembered his holy c.
         22:20 is the new c in my blood.
Ac   7: 8 he gave him the c of circumcision.
Ro   11:27 "And this is my c with them,
1Co 11:25 "This cup is the new c in my blood.
2Co   3: 6 be ministers of a new c, not of letter
         3:14 they hear the reading of the old c,
Gal   3:17 not annul a c previously ratified by
Heb   7:22 become the guarantee of a better c.
         8: 8 establish a new c with the house
         9:15 reason he is the mediator of a new c,
         9:15 the transgressions under the first c.
         12:24 the mediator of a new c,
         13:20 by the blood of the eternal c,
Rev 11:19 the ark of his c was seen within his
Jdt   9:13 planned cruel things against your c,

Sir   28: 7 remember the c of the Most High,
         45: 7 He made an everlasting c with him,
1Mc   1:15 and abandoned the holy c.
         1:57 found possessing the book of the c,
         2:27 for the law and supports the c
2Es   2: 5 because they would not keep my c,
         3:15 You made an everlasting c with

ARK OF ... COVENANT Ex 25:22; 26:33,
34; 30:6, 26; 31:7; 39:35; 40:3, 5, 21; Nu 4:5;
7:89; 10:33; 14:44; Dt 10:8; 31:9, 25, 26; Jos
3:3, 6, 6, 8, 11, 14, 17; 4:7, 9, 16, 18; 6:6, 8;
8:33; Jdg 20:27; 1Sa 4:3, 4, 4, 5; 2Sa 15:24;
1Ki 3:15; 6:19; 8:1, 6; 1Ch 15:25, 26, 28, 29;
16:6, 37; 17:1; 22:19; 28:2, 18; 2Ch 5:2, 7; Jer
3:16; Heb 9:4; Rev 11:19; 2Es 10:22

BOOK OF THE COVENANT Ex 24:7;
2Ki 23:2, 21; 2Ch 34:30; Sir 24:23; 1Mc 1:57

COVENANT OF THE †LORD Nu 10:33;
14:44; Dt 10:8; 29:12, 25; 31:9, 25, 26; Jos
3:3, 17; 4:7, 18; 6:8; 7:15; 8:33; 23:16; 1Sa
4:3, 4, 5; 1Ki 3:15; 6:19; 8:1, 6, 21; 1Ch 15:25,
26, 28, 29; 16:37; 17:1; 22:19; 28:2, 18; 2Ch
5:2, 7; 6:11; Jer 3:16; 22:9

HIS COVENANT Ex 2:24; Dt 4:13; 8:18;
17:2; 2Ki 13:23; 17:15; 18:12; 1Ch 16:15; Ps
25:10, 14; 78:37; 103:18; 105:8; 106:45;
111:5, 9; Eze 17:14; Rev 11:19; Sir 42:2; 1Mc
4:10; 2Mc 1:2

MY COVENANT Ge 6:18; 9:9, 11, 15; 17:2,
4, 7, 9, 10, 13, 14, 19, 21; Ex 6:4, 5; 19:5; Lev
26:9, 15, 42, 42, 42, 44; Nu 25:12; Dt 31:16,
20; Jos 7:11; Jdg 2:1, 20; 1Ki 11:11; Ps 50:16;
89:28, 34; 132:12; Isa 54:10; 56:4, 6; 59:21;
Jer 33:20, 20, 21, 21, 25; 34:18; Eze 16:60, 61,
62; 17:19; 44:7; Hos 8:1; Zec 9:11; Mal 2:4, 5;
Ro 11:27; Heb 8:9; 2Es 2:5, 7

NEW COVENANT Jer 31:31; Lk 22:20; 1Co
11:25; 2Co 3:6; Heb 8:8, 13; 9:15; 12:24

YOUR COVENANT Dt 33:9; 2Sa 3:12; 1Ki
19:10, 14; Ps 44:17; 74:20; Isa 28:18; Jer
14:21; Jdt 9:13; Aza 1:11; 2Es 7:46

COVENANTS → COVENANT
Ro   9: 4 the adoption, the glory, the c,
Gal   4:24 an allegory: these women are two c.
Eph   2:12 and strangers to the c of promise,
Wis 12:21 oaths and c full of good promises!
Sir   44:12 Their descendants stand by the c;

COVER → COVERED, COVERING,
COVERINGS, COVERS
Ge   6:14 and c it inside and out with pitch.
Ex   33:22 I will c you with my hand
Nu   4: 5 and c the ark of the covenant with it;
Dt   27: 4 shall c them with plaster.
Ne   4: 5 Do not c their guilt, and do not let
Ps   5:12 c them with favor as with a shield.
         91: 4 he will c you with his pinions,
         139:11 "Surely the darkness shall c me,
Isa 11: 9 as the waters c the sea.
Hos 10: 8 shall say to the mountains, 'C us,
Hab   2:14 as the waters c the sea.
Mal   2:13 You c the LORD's altar with tears,
Lk   23:30 and to the hills, 'C us.'
Jas   5:20 and will c a multitude of sins.

COVERED → COVER
Ge   1: 2 darkness c the face of the deep,
         7:19 under the whole heaven were c;
Ex   14:28 waters returned and c the chariots
         16:13 quails came up and c the camp;
         24:15 and the cloud c the mountain.
         40:34 the cloud c the tent of meeting.
Nu   9:15 the cloud c the tabernacle.
Ps   32: 1 is forgiven, whose sin is c.
Isa   6: 2 with two they c their faces,
Jnh   3: 8 animals shall be c with sackcloth,
Mt   10:26 c up that will not be uncovered c;
Ro   4: 7 are forgiven, and whose sins are c;

COVERING → COVER

Ge 7:20 **c** them fifteen cubits deep.
Ex 35:11 its tent and its **c**, its clasps
Ps 18:11 He made darkness his **c** around him,
    105:39 He spread a cloud for a **c**,
Mal 2:16 and **c** one's garment with violence,
1Co 11:15 For her hair is given to her for a **c**.

COVERINGS → COVER

Pr 31:22 She makes herself **c**; her clothing is

COVERS → COVER

Pr 10:12 strife, but love **c** all offenses.
1Pe 4: 8 for love **c** a multitude of sins.

COVET → COVETED, COVETOUSNESS

Ex 20:17 shall not **c** your neighbor's house;
    34:24 no one shall **c** your land when you
Dt 5:21 shall you **c** your neighbor's wife.
    7:25 Do not **c** the silver or the gold that
Pr 21:26 All day long the wicked **c**,
Mic 2: 2 They **c** fields, and seize them;
Ro 7: 7 not have known what it is to **c** if the
        law had not said, "You shall not **c**."
    13: 9 not steal; You shall not **c**";
Jas 4: 2 you **c** something and cannot obtain
4Mc 2: 5 Thus the law says, "You shall not **c**

COVETED → COVET

Jos 7:21 then I **c** them and took them.
Ac 20:33 I **c** no one's silver or gold or

COVETOUSNESS → COVET

Ro 1:29 every kind of wickedness, evil, **c**,
    7: 8 produced in me all kinds of **c**.

COW → COW'S, COWS

Ex 34:19 the firstborn of **c** and sheep.
Isa 11: 7 The **c** and the bear shall graze,

COWARDICE → COWARDLY

2Ti 1: 7 for God did not give us a spirit of **c**,
1Mc 4:32 Fill them with **c**; melt the boldness

COWARDLY → COWARDICE

Rev 21: 8 But as for the **c**, the faithless, the

COWS → COW

Ge 41: 2 out of the Nile seven sleek and fat **c**,
1Sa 6: 7 and yoke the **c** to the cart,
Am 4: 1 you **c** of Bashan who are on Mount

CRACKED*

Jer 2:13 **c** cisterns that can hold no water.
    14: 4 because the ground is **c**.

CRAFT → CRAFTILY, CRAFTINESS, CRAFTY

Ex 31: 3 and knowledge in every kind of **c**,
Isa 2:16 and against all the beautiful **c**.

CRAFTILY* → CRAFT

Ps 105:25 to deal **c** with his servants.
Ac 7:19 He dealt **c** with our race

CRAFTINESS* → CRAFT

Job 5:13 He takes the wise in their own **c**;
Lk 20:23 But he perceived their **c** and said to
Ro 1:29 of envy, murder, strife, deceit, **c**,
1Co 3:19 "He catches the wise in their **c**,"
Eph 4:14 by their **c** in deceitful scheming.

CRAFTY* → CRAFT

Ge 3: 1 serpent was more **c** than any other
2Sa 13: 3 and Jonadab was a very **c** man.
Job 5:12 He frustrates the devices of the **c**,
    15: 5 and you choose the tongue of the **c**.
Ps 83: 3 They lay **c** plans against your people
2Co 12:16 (you say) since I was **c**, I took you
Sir 11:29 for many are the tricks of the **c**.

CRAGS

Nu 23: 9 For from the top of the **c** I see him,
Dt 32:13 nursed him with honey from the **c**,

CRAVED* → CRAVING

Ps 78:18 by demanding the food they **c**.
    78:29 for he gave them what they **c**.

CRAVES* → CRAVING

Pr 13: 4 of the lazy **c**, and gets nothing,

CRAVING* → CRAVED, CRAVES

Nu 11: 4 rabble among them had a strong **c**;
    11:34 buried the people who had the **c**.
Ps 78:30 But before they had satisfied their **c**,
    106:14 had a wanton **c** in the wilderness,
Pr 10: 3 but he thwarts the **c** of the wicked.
    21:25 The **c** of the lazy person is fatal,
Isa 32: 6 the **c** of the hungry unsatisfied,
1Ti 6: 4 a morbid **c** for controversy and for
4Mc 3:12 bitterly because of the king's **c**,

CRAWLING

Dt 32:24 with venom of things **c** in the dust.
Mic 7:17 like the **c** things of the earth;

CREATE* → CREATED, CREATES, CREATION, CREATOR

Ps 51:10 **C** in me a clean heart, O God,
Isa 4: 5 the Lord will **c** over the whole site
    45: 7 I form light and **c** darkness, I make
            weal and **c** woe;
    45:18 he did not **c** it a chaos, he formed it
    65:17 to **c** new heavens and a new earth;
    65:18 I am about to **c** Jerusalem as a joy,
Eph 2:15 **c** in himself one new humanity

CREATED → CREATE

Ge 1: 1 In the beginning when God **c** the
    1:21 So God **c** the great sea monsters
    1:27 So God **c** humankind in his image,
    1:27 in the image of God he **c** them;
    1:27 male and female he **c** them.
    2: 4 and the earth when they were **c**.
    5: 1 When God **c** humankind,
    5: 2 Male and female he **c** them,
    5: 2 "Humankind" when they were **c**.
    6: 7 the human beings I have **c**—
Dt 4:32 since the day that God **c** human
    32: 6 Is not he your father, who **c** you,
Ps 89:12 north and the south—you **c** them;
    89:47 what vanity you have **c** all mortals!
    104:30 send forth your spirit, they are **c**;
    148: 5 for he commanded and they were **c**.
Pr 8:22 The Lord **c** me at the beginning of
Isa 40:26 eyes on high and see: Who **c** these?
    41:20 the Holy One of Israel has **c** it.
    42: 5 who **c** the heavens and stretched
    43: 1 thus says the Lord, he who **c** you,
    43: 7 whom I **c** for my glory,
    45: 8 I the Lord have **c** it.
    45:12 I made the earth, and **c** humankind
    45:18 who **c** the heavens (he is God!),
    48: 7 They are **c** now, not long ago;
    54:16 See it is I who have **c** the smith
    54:16 I have also **c** the ravager to destroy.
Jer 31:22 For the Lord has **c** a new thing on
Eze 21:30 In the place where you were **c**,
    28:13 On the day that you were **c** they
    28:15 ways from the day that you were **c**,
Mal 2:10 Has not one God **c** us?
Mk 13:19 beginning of the creation that God **c**
1Co 11: 9 Neither was man **c** for the sake of
Eph 2:10 **c** in Christ Jesus for good works,
    3: 9 for ages in God who **c** all things;
    4:24 according to the likeness of God
Col 1:16 in heaven and on earth were **c**,
    1:16 all things have been **c** through him
1Ti 4: 3 **c** to be received with thanksgiving
    4: 4 For everything **c** by God is good,
Heb 1: 2 through whom he also **c** the worlds;
    12:27 what is shaken—that is, **c** things—
Rev 4:11 for you **c** all things, and by your
            will they existed and were **c**."
    10: 6 who **c** heaven and what is in it,
Jdt 13:18 who **c** the heavens and the earth,

CREATES* → CREATE

Nu 16:30 But if the Lord **c** something new,
Am 4:13 forms the mountains, **c** the wind,

CREATION → CREATE

Ge 2: 3 all the work that he had done in **c**.
Mk 10: 6 But from the beginning of **c**,
    13:19 not been from the beginning of the **c**
    16:15 the good news to the whole **c**.
Ro 1:20 since the **c** of the world his eternal
    8:19 the **c** waits with eager longing for
    8:20 for the **c** was subjected to futility,
    8:21 that the **c** itself will be set free from
    8:22 whole **c** has been groaning in labor
    8:39 nor depth, nor anything else in all **c**,
2Co 5:17 anyone is in Christ, there is a new **c**:
Col 1:15 invisible God, the firstborn of all **c**;
Heb 9:11 with hands, that is, not of this **c**),
2Pe 3: 4 they were from the beginning of **c**!"
Rev 3:14 true witness, the origin of God's **c**:
Tob 8: 5 and the whole **c** bless you forever.
Jdt 9:12 King of all your **c**,
Sir 16:17 for what am I in a boundless **c**?

CREATOR* → CREATE

Ecc 12: 1 Remember your **c** in the days of
Isa 40:28 the **C** of the ends of the earth.
    43:15 your Holy One, the **C** of Israel,
Ro 1:25 served the creature rather than the **C**
Col 3:10 according to the image of its **c**.
1Pe 4:19 to a faithful **C**,
Jdt 9:12 heaven and earth, **C** of the waters,
Wis 13: 5 corresponding perception of their **C**.
Sir 4: 6 their **C** will hear their prayer.
    24: 8 **C** of all things gave me a command,
    24: 8 my **C** chose the place for my tent.
2Mc 1:24 "O Lord, Lord God, **C** of all things,
    7:23 Therefore the **C** of the world,
    13:14 committing the decision to the **C** of
3Mc 2: 3 the **c** of all things and the governor
2Es 5:44 cannot move faster than the **C**,
4Mc 5:25 that in the nature of things the **C** of
    11: 5 we revere the **C** of all things

CREATURE → CREATURES

Ge 2:19 the man called every living **c**,
    9:10 with every living **c** that is with you,
Lev 11:43 yourselves detestable with any **c**
Ro 1:25 worshiped and served the **c** rather
Rev 4: 7 the first living **c** like a lion,
    5:13 Then I heard every **c** in heaven and

LIVING CREATURE Ge 1:21; 2:19; 8:21;
9:10, 12, 15, 16; Lev 11:46, 47; Eze 47:9;
Rev 4:7, 7, 7; 6:3, 5, 7

CREATURES → CREATURE

Ge 1:20 bring forth swarms of living **c**,
    1:24 earth bring forth living **c** of every
Lev 11: 2 these are the **c** that you may eat.
Ps 104:24 the earth is full of your **c**.
Eze 1: 5 was something like four living **c**.
    10:15 the living **c** that I saw by the river
Jas 1:18 a kind of first fruits of his **c**.
Rev 4: 6 are four living **c**, full of eyes
    5: 6 the throne and the four living **c** and
    8: 9 a third of the living **c** in the sea died,
    19: 4 elders and the four living **c** fell
Jdt 16:14 Let all your **c** serve you,
Wis 9: 2 dominion over the **c** you have made,
Sir 42:15 and all his **c** do his will.

LIVING CREATURES Ge 1:20, 24; Lev
11:10; Eze 1:5, 13, 13, 14, 15, 15, 19, 19, 20,
21, 22; 3:13; 10:15, 17, 20; Rev 4:6, 8, 9; 5:6,
8, 11, 14; 6:1, 6; 7:11; 8:9; 14:3; 15:7; 19:4;
Bel 1:5; 2Es 6:47, 48, 49

CREDIT → CREDITED, CREDITOR, CREDITORS

Lk   6:33 what c is that to you?
1Pe   2:20 for doing wrong, what c is that?

CREDITED* → CREDIT

Lev   7:18 nor shall it be c to the one who
Sir   3:14 will be c to you against your sins;

CREDITOR → CREDIT

Dt   15: 2 every c shall remit the claim that is
Ps 109:11 May the c seize all that he has;
Lk   7:41 "A certain c had two debtors;

CREDITORS* → CREDIT

Isa   50: 1 my c is it to whom I have sold you?
Hab   2: 7 Will not your own c suddenly rise,

CREEPING

Ge   1:24 cattle and c things and wild animals
Ps 148:10 c things and flying birds!
Eze   8:10 were all kinds of c things,

CRETANS* → CRETE

Ac   2:11 C and Arabs—in our own languages
Tit   1:12 "C are always liars, vicious brutes,

CRETE → CRETANS

Ac   27:12 It was a harbor of C,
Tit   1: 5 I left you behind in C for this

CRIED → CRY

Ex   2:23 under their slavery, and c out.
     14:10 fear the Israelites c out to the LORD.
Nu   20:16 when we c to the LORD, he heard
Jos   24: 7 When they c out to the LORD,
Jdg   3: 9 the Israelites c out to the LORD,
      4: 3 Israelites c out to the LORD for help;
      6: 6 Israelites c out to the LORD for help.
    10:12 you c to me, and I delivered you out
1Sa   7: 9 Samuel c out to the LORD for Israel,
     12: 8 then your ancestors c to the LORD
    28:12 woman saw Samuel, she c out with
Job 29:12 because I delivered the poor who c,
Ps   18: 6 to my God I c for help.
     22: 5 To you they c, and were saved;
     34: 6 This poor soul c, and was heard
   107:13 they c to the LORD in their trouble,
Jnh   1: 5 were afraid, and each c to his god.
     1:14 Then they c out to the LORD,
Mt   14:30 he c out, "Lord, save me!"
    27:46 Jesus c with a loud voice,
Jdt   7:19 The Israelites then c out to the Lord
Sus   1:24 Susanna c out with a loud voice,

CRIES → CRY

Ps   32: 7 with glad c of deliverance.
Pr   1:20 Wisdom c out in the street;
      8: 3 the entrance of the portals she c out:
Heb   5: 7 with loud c and tears,

CRIME → CRIMES, CRIMINAL, CRIMINALS

Ge   50:17 forgive the c of your brothers
Ps   56: 7 so repay them for their c;

CRIMES → CRIME

Ps   64: 6 Who can search out our c?
Eze   7:23 For the land is full of bloody c;

CRIMINAL → CRIME

Jn   18:30 "If this man were not a c,
2Ti   2: 9 the point of being chained like a c.
1Pe   4:15 suffer as a murderer, a thief, a c,

CRIMINALS → CRIME

Lk   23:32 Two others also, who were c,

CRIMSON

Ge   38:28 bound on his hand a c thread,
Ex   25: 4 purple, and c yarns and fine linen,
Lev   14: 4 cedarwood and c yarn and hyssop
Jos   2:21 she tied the c cord in the window.
Pr   31:21 all her household are clothed in c.
SS   4: 3 Your lips are like a c thread,

Isa   1:18 red like c, they shall become like
    63: 1 from Bozrah in garments stained c?

CRIPPLED

2Sa   9: 3 he is c in his feet."
Lk   14:13 a banquet, invite the poor, the c,
Ac   14: 8 for he had been c from birth.

CRISIS

1Co   7:26 that, in view of the impending c,

CRITICISM* → CRITICIZE

Sir   38:17 to avoid c; then be comforted for

CRITICIZE* → CRITICISM, CRITICIZED

Sir   11: 7 examine first, and then c.
    13:22 humble person slips, they even c

CRITICIZED* → CRITICIZE

Ac   11: 2 the circumcised believers c him,

CROCUS*

Isa   35: 1 rejoice and blossom; like the c

CROOKED

Dt   32: 5 a perverse and c generation.
2Sa 22:27 the c you show yourself perverse.
Ps   18:26 the c you show yourself perverse.
   125: 5 to their own c ways the LORD will
Pr   2:15 those whose paths are c, and who
      8: 8 there is nothing crooked or c in them.
    17:20 The c of mind do not prosper,
Ecc   1:15 What is c cannot be made straight,
     7:13 make straight what he has made c?
Isa   59: 8 Their roads they have made c;
La   3: 9 he has made my paths c.
Lk   3: 5 and the c shall be made straight,
Ac   13:10 not stop making c the straight paths
Php   2:15 in the midst of a c and perverse

CROP → CROPS

1Co   9:10 in hope of a share in the c.
Heb   6: 7 a c useful to those for whom it is
Jas   5: 7 farmer waits for the precious c

CROPS → CROP

2Ti   2: 6 to have the first share of the c.

CROSS → CROSSED, CROSSES, CROSSING, CROSSROADS

Nu   32: 5 do not make us c the Jordan."
Dt   4:22 but you are going to c over to take
    12:10 When you c over the Jordan and
    30:13 "Who will c to the other side of the
    31: 3 your God himself will c over before
    31: 3 Joshua also will c over before you,
Jos   3:14 from their tents to c over the Jordan,
Mt   10:38 not take up the c and follow me is
    16:24 deny themselves and take up their c
    27:32 compelled this man to carry his c.
Mk   15:30 and come down from the c!"
Lk   14:27 the c and follow me cannot be my
Jn   19:17 and carrying the c by himself,
    19:25 near the c of Jesus were his mother,
1Co   1:17 c of Christ might not be emptied of
     1:18 the c is foolishness to those who are
Gal   5:11 offense of the c has been removed.
     6:14 never boast of anything except the c
Eph   2:16 to God in one body through the c,
Php   2: 8 of death—even death on a c.
     3:18 many live as enemies of the c of
Col   1:20 peace through the blood of his c.
     2:14 He set this aside, nailing it to the c.
Heb 12: 2 was set before him endured the c,

CROSSED → CROSS

Jos   4: 7 When it c over the Jordan,
2Ki   2: 8 the two of them c on dry ground.

CROSSES → CROSS

Dt   9: 3 God is the one who c over before

CROSSING → CROSS

Ge   48:14 c his hands, for Manasseh was the
Dt   4:22 without c over the Jordan,

Jos   4: 1 had finished c over the Jordan,

CROSSROADS* → CROSS, ROAD

Pr   8: 2 at the c she takes her stand;
Jer   6:16 Stand at the c, and look, and ask for

CROW* → CROWED, CROWS

Lk   22:34 the cock will not c this day,

CROWD → CROWDS

Ex   12:38 A mixed c also went up with them,
Mt   14: 5 feared the c, because they regarded
    21: 8 A very large c spread their cloaks
Mk   8: 2 "I have compassion for the c,
    14:43 a c with swords and clubs,
Jn   7:31 many in the c believed in him

CROWDS → CROWD

Mt   4:25 great c followed him from Galilee,
     7:28 c were astounded at his teaching,
    12:23 All the c were amazed and said,
Lk   3: 7 John said to the c that came out
Ac   8: 6 The c with one accord listened
    14:19 and won over the c.
    17:13 to stir up and incite the c.

CROWED → CROW

Mt   26:74 At that moment the cock c.

CROWN → CROWNED, CROWNS

Lev   8: 9 the golden ornament, the holy c,
Job 19: 9 and taken the c from my head.
    31:36 I would bind it on me like a c;
Ps   21: 3 you set a c of fine gold on his head.
Pr   4: 9 will bestow on you a beautiful c."
    12: 4 A good wife is the c of her husband,
    14:24 The c of the wise is their wisdom,
    16:31 Gray hair is a c of glory;
    17: 6 Grandchildren are the c of the aged,
    27:24 nor a c for all generations.
Isa   62: 3 c of beauty in the hand of the LORD,
La   5:16 The c has fallen from our head;
Eze 16:12 and a beautiful c upon your head.
Zec   6:11 and gold and make a c,
     9:16 like the jewels of a c they shall
Mt   27:29 after twisting some thorns into a c,
Mk   15:17 twisting some thorns into a c, they
Jn   19: 2 soldiers wove a c of thorns and put
    19: 5 wearing the c of thorns and the
Php   4: 1 my joy and c, stand firm in the Lord
1Th   2:19 c of boasting before our Lord Jesus
2Ti   4: 8 there is reserved for me the c
Jas   1:12 the test and will receive the c
1Pe   5: 4 the c of glory that never fades away.
Rev   2:10 and I will give you the c of life.
     3:11 so that no one may seize your c.
     6: 2 Its rider had a bow; a c was given
    12: 1 and on her head a c of twelve stars.
    14:14 with a golden c on his head,
Sir   1:18 fear of the LORD is the c of wisdom,

CROWNED → CROWN

Ps   8: 5 and c them with glory and honor.
Pr   14:18 but the clever are c with knowledge.
SS   3:11 crown with which his mother c him
2Ti   2: 5 no one is c without competing
Heb   2: 7 you have c them with glory and
     2: 9 now c with glory and honor
Jdt   15:13 c themselves with olive wreaths.
Sir   45:26 Lord who has c you with glory.

CROWNS → CROWN

Ps 103: 4 who c you with steadfast love and
Isa   23: 8 against Tyre, the bestower of c,
Rev   4: 4 with golden c on their heads.
     4:10 they cast their c before the throne,
     9: 7 were what looked like c of gold;

CROWS → CROW

Jn   13:38 I tell you, before the cock c,

CRUCIFIED* → CRUCIFY

Mt   20:19 to be mocked and flogged and c;
    26: 2 will be handed over to be c."

27:22 All of them said, "Let him be **c!**"
27:23 all the more, "Let him be **c!**"
27:26 he handed him over to be **c.**
27:35 And when they had **c** him,
27:38 Then two bandits were **c** with him,
27:44 The bandits who were **c** with him
28: 5 are looking for Jesus who was **c.**
Mk 15:15 he handed him over to be **c.**
15:24 they **c** him, and divided his clothes
15:25 in the morning when they **c** him.
15:27 And with him they **c** two bandits,
15:32 who were **c** with him also taunted
16: 6 for Jesus of Nazareth, who was **c.**
Lk 23:23 loud shouts that he should be **c;**
23:33 they **c** Jesus there with the criminals
24: 7 **c,** and on the third day rise again."
24:20 condemned to death and **c** him.
Jn 19:16 he handed him over to them to be **c.**
19:18 they **c** him, and with him two others
19:20 the place where Jesus was **c**
19:23 When the soldiers had **c** Jesus,
19:31 the legs of the **c** men broken
19:32 and of the other who had been **c**
19:41 garden in the place where he was **c,**
Ac 2:23 you **c** and killed by the hands of
2:36 Messiah, this Jesus whom you **c.**"
4:10 whom you **c,** whom God raised
Ro 6: 6 We know that our old self was **c**
1Co 1:13 Was Paul **c** for you?
1:23 but we proclaim Christ **c,**
2: 2 except Jesus Christ, and him **c.**
2: 8 would not have **c** the Lord of glory.
2Co 13: 4 For he was **c** in weakness,
Gal 2:19 I have been **c** with Christ;
3: 1 Christ was publicly exhibited as **c!**
5:24 to Christ Jesus have **c** the flesh
6:14 which the world has been **c** to me,
Rev 11: 8 where also their Lord was **c.**

CRUCIFY* → CRUCIFIED, CRUCIFYING
Mt 23:34 some of whom you will kill and **c,**
27:31 Then they led him away to **c** him.
Mk 15:13 They shouted back, "**C** him!"
15:14 they shouted all the more, "**C** him!"
15:20 Then they led him out to **c** him.
Lk 23:21 they kept shouting, "**C, c** him!"
Jn 19: 6 they shouted, "**C** him! **C** him!"
19: 6 "Take him yourselves and **c** him;
19:10 to release you, and power to **c** you?"
19:15 Away with him! **C** him!"
19:15 asked them, "Shall I **c** your King?"

CRUCIFYING* → CRUCIFY
Heb 6: 6 they are **c** again the Son of God

CRUEL → CRUELTY
Ex 6: 9 broken spirit and their **c** slavery.
Pr 11:17 but the **c** do themselves harm.
12:10 but the mercy of the wicked is **c.**
27: 4 Wrath is **c,** anger is overwhelming,
Isa 13: 9 See, the day of the LORD comes, **c,**
Jdt 9:13 who have planned **c** things

CRUELTY → CRUEL
Na 3:19 has ever escaped your endless **c?**

CRUMBS*
Ps 147:17 He hurls down hail like **c—**
Mt 15:27 dogs eat the **c** that fall from their
Mk 7:28 under the table eat the children's **c.**"

CRUSH → CRUSHED, CRUSHES
Nu 24:17 it shall **c** the borderlands of Moab,
Job 6: 9 that it would please God to **c** me,
Ps 89:23 I will **c** his foes before him
Isa 53:10 it was the will of the LORD to **c** him
Da 2:40 it shall **c** and shatter all these.
Mt 21:44 it will **c** anyone on whom it falls."
Ro 16:20 will shortly **c** Satan under your feet.
Jdt 9:10 **c** their arrogance by the hand of a
woman.
1Mc 3:22 He himself will **c** them before us;

CRUSHED → CRUSH
Dt 9:21 burned it with fire and **c** it,
Jdg 5:26 struck Sisera a blow, she **c** his head,
9:53 Abimelech's head, and **c** his skull.
Ps 34:18 and saves the **c** in spirit.
51: 8 let the bones that you have **c** rejoice.
74:14 You **c** the heads of Leviathan;
89:10 You **c** Rahab like a carcass;
Isa 53: 5 **c** for our iniquities;
Da 2:45 and that it **c** the iron, the bronze,
2Co 4: 8 afflicted in every way, but not **c;**

CRUSHES → CRUSH
Jdt 16: 2 For the Lord is a God who **c** wars;
Sir 28:17 A blow of the tongue **c** the bones.

CRY → CRIED, CRIES, CRYING
Ex 2:23 Out of the slavery their **c** for help
3: 9 The **c** of the Israelites has now come
Jdg 10:14 and **c** to the gods whom you have
1Ki 18:27 Elijah mocked them, saying, "**C**
Ps 3: 4 I **c** aloud to the LORD,
5: 2 Listen to the sound of my **c,**
28: 2 as I **c** to you for help,
34:15 and his ears are open to their **c.**
40: 1 he inclined to me and heard my **c.**
88: 2 incline your ear to my **c.**
119:146 I **c** to you; save me,
130: 1 Out of the depths I **c** to you,
144:14 and no **c** of distress in our streets.
Pr 2: 3 if you indeed **c** out for insight,
21:13 close your ear to the **c** of the poor,
21:13 you will **c** out and not be heard.
Isa 3: 7 But the other will **c** out on that day,
40: 6 A voice says, "**C** out!"
Jer 4:31 I heard a **c** as of a woman in labor,
14:12 they fast, I do not hear their **c,**
La 2:18 **C** aloud to the Lord!
Hos 7:14 They do not **c** to me from the heart,
Hab 1: 2 how long shall I **c** for help,
2:11 very stones will **c** out from the wall,
Mk 15:37 Then Jesus gave a loud **c**
Ro 8:15 When we **c,** "Abba! Father!"
1Th 4:16 Lord himself, with a **c** of command,
Sus 1:44 The Lord heard her **c.**
1Mc 4:10 let us **c** to Heaven,

CRYING → CRY
Ge 4:10 your brother's blood is **c** out to me
Ps 69: 3 I am weary with my **c;**
Mt 3: 3 "The voice of one **c** out in the
Mk 1: 3 the voice of one **c** out in the
Gal 4: 6 into our hearts, **c,** "Abba! Father!"
Rev 12: 2 and was **c** out in birth pangs,
21: 4 **c** and pain will be no more,

CRYSTAL
Eze 1:22 shining like **c,** spread out above
Rev 4: 6 like a sea of glass, like **c.**
21:11 rare jewel, like jasper, clear as **c.**
22: 1 river of the water of life, bright as **c,**

CUBS
2Sa 17: 8 like a bear robbed of her **c** in the
Pr 17:12 to meet a she-bear robbed of its **c**
Hos 13: 8 like a bear robbed of her **c,**

CUCUMBER → CUCUMBERS
Isa 1: 8 like a shelter in a **c** field,

CUCUMBERS* → CUCUMBER
Nu 11: 5 the **c,** the melons, the leeks,

CUD
Lev 11: 3 is cleft-footed and chews the **c—**
Dt 14: 6 and chews the **c,** among the animals,

CULTIVATED
Ro 11:24 contrary to nature, into a **c** olive
Heb 6: 7 crop useful to those for whom it is **c**

CUM*
Mk 5:41 "Talitha **c,**" which means, "Little
girl, get up!"

CUMMIN
Isa 28:25 do they not scatter dill, sow **c,**
Mt 23:23 For you tithe mint, dill, and **c,**

CUNNING
Jos 9: 4 they on their part acted with **c:**
Ps 119:118 for their **c** is in vain.
2Co 4: 2 we refuse to practice **c** or to falsify
11: 3 as the serpent deceived Eve by its **c,**

CUP → CUPBEARER, CUPS
Ge 40:11 Pharaoh's **c** was in my hand;
44: 2 Put my **c,** the silver **c,** in the top
2Sa 12: 3 from his **c,** and lie in his bosom,
1Ki 7:26 brim was made like the brim of a **c,**
Ps 23: 5 my head with oil; my **c** overflows.
75: 8 there is a **c** with foaming wine,
Pr 23:31 it sparkles in the **c** and goes down
Isa 51:22 from your hand the **c** of staggering;
Jer 25:15 my hand this **c** of the wine of wrath,
La 4:21 but to you also the **c** shall pass;
Eze 23:31 I will give her **c** into your hand.
Hab 2:16 The **c** in the LORD's right hand will
Mt 10:42 gives even a **c** of cold water to one
20:22 Are you able to drink the **c** that I am
23:25 you clean the outside of the **c** and
23:26 First clean the inside of the **c,**
26:27 a **c,** and after giving thanks he gave
26:39 if it is possible, let this **c** pass from
Mk 9:41 a **c** of water to drink because you
10:38 you able to drink the **c** that I drink,
14:23 a **c,** and after giving thanks he gave
14:36 are possible; remove this **c** from me;
Lk 11:39 Pharisees clean the outside of the **c**
22:17 he took a **c,** and after giving thanks
22:20 "This **c** that is poured out for you is
22:42 are willing, remove this **c** from me;
Jn 18:11 not to drink the **c** that the Father
1Co 10:16 The **c** of blessing that we bless,
10:21 You cannot drink the **c** of the Lord
and the **c** of demons.
11:25 "This **c** is the new covenant in my
blood.
11:27 the **c** of the Lord in an unworthy
Rev 14:10 unmixed into the **c** of his anger,
17: 4 a golden **c** full of abominations and
18: 6 for her in the **c** she mixed.

CUPBEARER → BEAR, CUP
Ge 40: 1 the **c** of the king of Egypt
41: 9 Then the chief **c** said to Pharaoh,
Ne 1:11 At the time, I was **c** to the king.
Tob 1:22 Now Ahikar was chief **c,**

CUPS → CUP
Ex 25:33 three **c** shaped like almond
Mk 7: 4 the washing of **c,** pots, and bronze
1Mc 1:22 the **c** for drink offerings, the bowls,

CURDS
Ge 18: 8 Then he took **c** and milk and the calf
Dt 32:14 **c** from the herd, and milk from the
Isa 7:15 He shall eat **c** and honey by the time

CURE → CURED, CURING
2Ki 5: 3 He would **c** him of his leprosy."
Hos 5:13 But he is not able to **c** you or heal
Mt 8: 7 "I will come and **c** him."
Mk 3: 2 he would **c** him on the sabbath,
Lk 9: 1 over all demons and to **c** diseases,

CURED → CURE
Mt 8:16 and **c** all who were sick.
12:15 and he **c** all of them,
Lk 6:18 troubled with unclean spirits were **c.**
Ac 5:16 and they were all **c.**
28: 9 had diseases also came and were **c.**
Tob 12: 3 back to you safely, he **c** my wife,

CURING* → CURE
Mt 4:23 and **c** every disease
9:35 **c** every disease and every sickness,
Lk 9: 6 the good news and **c** diseases

CURSE → ACCURSED, CURSED, CURSES, CURSING

Ge	8:21	"I will never again **c** the ground
	12: 3	and the one who curses you I will **c**;
	27:13	mother said to him, "Let your **c** be
Ex	22:28	or **c** a leader of your people.
Nu	5:18	water of bitterness that brings the **c.**
	22: 6	Come now, **c** this people for me,
	22:12	not **c** the people, for they are blessed
Dt	11:26	before you today a blessing and a **c**:
	11:28	and the **c**, if you do not obey the
	21:23	hung on a tree is under God's **c.**
	23: 5	God turned the **c** into a blessing
Jos	24: 9	Balaam son of Beor to **c** you,
2Sa	16: 9	should this dead dog **c** my lord the
Ne	10:29	enter into a **c** and an oath to walk in
	13: 2	hired Balaam against them to **c** them
	13: 2	our God turned the **c** into a blessing.
Job	1:11	and he will **c** you to your face."
	2: 5	and he will **c** you to your face."
	2: 9	C God, and die."
Ps	62: 4	their mouths, but inwardly they **c.**
	109:28	Let them **c**, but you will bless.
Pr	3:33	**c** is on the house of the wicked,
	20:20	If you **c** father or mother,
	30:11	There are those who **c** their fathers
Isa	24: 6	Therefore a **c** devours the earth,
Jer	23:10	because of the **c** the land mourns,
La	3:65	your **c** be on them!
Mal	2: 2	then I will send the **c** on you and I will **c** your blessings;
	4: 6	come and strike the land with a **c.**
Mk	14:71	he began to **c**, and he swore an oath,
Lk	6:28	bless those who **c** you, pray
Ro	12:14	bless and do not **c** them.
Gal	3:10	the works of the law are under a **c**;
	3:13	Christ redeemed us from the **c** of the law by becoming a **c** for us—
Jas	3: 9	with it we **c** those who are made in
Sir	4: 5	and give no one reason to **c** you;
	28:13	C the gossips and the

CURSED → CURSE

Ge	3:14	**c** are you among all animals and
	3:17	**c** is the ground because of you;
	4:11	And now you are **c** from the ground,
	9:25	"C be Canaan; lowest of slaves
	27:29	C be everyone who curses you,
Nu	22: 6	and whomever your curse is **c.**"
	23: 8	can I curse whom God has not **c**?
	24: 9	and **c** is everyone who curses you."
Dt	27:15	"C be anyone who makes an idol or
	27:16	"C be anyone who dishonors father
	27:17	"C be anyone who moves
	27:18	"C be anyone who misleads a blind
	27:19	"C be anyone who deprives the
	27:20	"C be anyone who lies with his
	27:21	"C be anyone who lies with any
	27:22	"C be anyone who lies with his
	27:23	"C be anyone who lies with his
	27:24	"C be anyone who strikes down a
	27:25	"C be anyone who takes a bribe
	27:26	"C be anyone who does not uphold
	28:16	C shall you be in the city,
	28:16	and **c** shall you be in the field.
Jos	6:26	"C before the LORD be anyone who
1Sa	17:43	the Philistine **c** David by his gods.
2Sa	16: 7	Shimei shouted while he **c**, "Out!
	19:21	because he **c** the LORD's anointed?"
1Ki	21:13	"Naboth **c** God and the king.
2Ki	9:34	"See to that **c** woman and bury her;
Job	1: 5	and **c** God in their hearts."
	3: 1	Job opened his mouth and **c** the day
Jer	11: 3	C be anyone who does not heed the
	17: 5	C are those who trust in mere
Mal	1:14	C be the cheat who has a male in
Mk	11:21	fig tree that you **c** has withered."
1Co	12: 3	of God ever says "Let Jesus be **c!**"
Gal	3:10	"C is everyone who does not
	3:13	"C is everyone who hangs on a tree
Heb	6: 8	and on the verge of being **c**;

Rev	16: 9	but they **c** the name of God,
	16:11	and **c** the God of heaven because of
	16:21	**c** God for the plague of the hail,
Pm	151: 6	and he **c** me by his idols.

CURSES → CURSE

Ge	12: 3	and the one who **c** you I will curse;
	27:29	Cursed be everyone who **c** you,
Ex	21:17	Whoever **c** father or mother shall
Lev	24:15	who **c** God shall bear the sin.
Nu	5:23	priest shall put these **c** in writing,
	24: 9	and cursed is everyone who **c** you."
Dt	28:15	then all these **c** shall come upon you
	29:20	All the **c** written in this book will
	30: 1	blessings and the **c** that I have set
Jos	8:34	blessings and **c**,
2Ch	34:24	all the **c** that are written in the book
Sir	21:27	an ungodly person **c** an adversary, he **c** himself.

CURSING → CURSE

2Sa	16:10	If he is **c** because the LORD has said
Ps	10: 7	Their mouths are filled with **c**
	109:18	clothed himself with **c** as his coat,
Ro	3:14	"Their mouths are full of **c**
Jas	3:10	same mouth come blessing and **c.**

CURTAIN → CURTAINS

Ex	26:31	You shall make a **c** of blue, purple,
Lev	4:17	before the LORD, in front of the **c.**
2Ch	3:14	And Solomon made the **c** of blue
Isa	40:22	stretches out the heavens like a **c**,
Mt	27:51	the **c** of the temple was torn in two,
Mk	15:38	the **c** of the temple was torn in two,
Lk	23:45	the **c** of the temple was torn in two.
Heb	6:19	enters the inner shrine behind the **c**,
	9: 3	the second **c** was a tent called the
	10:20	that he opened for us through the **c**
1Mc	1:22	the bowls, the golden censers, the **c**,

CURTAINS → CURTAIN

Ex	26: 1	with ten **c** of fine twisted linen,
Nu	4:25	the **c** of the tabernacle,
1Mc	4:51	on the table and hung up the **c.**

CUSH → CUSHITE

Ge	2:13	flows around the whole land of C.
	10: 6	descendants of Ham: C, Egypt, Put,

CUSHITE → CUSH

Nu	12: 1	the C woman whom he had married
2Sa	18:21	Then Joab said to a C, "Go,

CUSTODY

Lev	24:12	and they put him in **c**,
Nu	15:34	They put him in **c**, because
Ac	4: 3	arrested them and put them in **c**
	24:23	the centurion to keep him in **c**,

CUSTOM → ACCUSTOMED, CUSTOMARY, CUSTOMS

Ru	4: 7	Now this was the **c** in former times
Est	9:23	Jews adopted as a **c**
Mk	10: 1	as was his **c**, he again taught them.
Lk	4:16	on the sabbath day, as was his **c.**
Jn	18:39	But you have a **c** that I release
	19:40	according to the burial **c** of the Jews
Ac	15: 1	circumcised according to the **c** of
	17: 2	And Paul went in, as was his **c**,
1Co	11:16	we have no such **c**, nor do
1Mc	1:14	in Jerusalem, according to Gentile **c**,

CUSTOMARY → CUSTOM

Da	3:19	seven times more than was **c**,

CUSTOMS → CUSTOM

2Ki	17: 8	the **c** of the nations whom the LORD
Jer	10: 3	For the **c** of the peoples are false:
Ac	16:21	advocating **c** that are not lawful for
1Mc	1:42	all should give up their particular **c.**

CUT → CUTS, CUTTING

Ge	9:11	never again shall all flesh be **c** off
	15:10	all these and **c** them in two,

	17:14	shall be **c** off from his people;
Ex	34:13	and **c** down their sacred poles
Dt	20:20	you may **c** them down for use
Jos	4: 7	the waters of the Jordan were **c** off.
Jdg	21: 6	"One tribe is **c** off from Israel this
1Sa	17:51	then he **c** off his head with it.
	24: 4	**c** off a corner of Saul's cloak.
2Sa	14:26	he **c** the hair of his head (for at the end of every year he used to **c** it;
	14:26	when it was heavy on him, he **c** it),
2Ch	15:16	Asa **c** down her image, crushed it,
Ps	37: 9	For the wicked shall be **c** off,
	118:10	the name of the LORD I **c** them off!
Pr	2:22	wicked will be **c** off from the land,
	10:31	the perverse tongue will be **c** off.
	23:18	and your hope will not be **c** off.
Isa	9:14	So the LORD **c** off from Israel head
	14:22	will **c** off from Babylon name and
	53: 8	**c** off from the land of the living,
Jer	34:18	like the calf when they **c** it in two
Eze	37:11	we are **c** off completely.'
Da	2:45	a stone was **c** from the mountain
	9:26	be **c** off and shall have nothing,
Mt	3:10	does not bear good fruit is **c** down
	24:22	if those days had not been **c** short,
Mk	9:43	hand causes you to stumble, **c** it off;
Jn	18:26	the man whose ear Peter had **c** off,
Ac	2:37	they were **c** to the heart and said to
Ro	11:22	otherwise you also will be **c** off.
1Co	11: 6	then she should **c** off her hair;
Gal	5: 4	have **c** yourselves off from Christ;
Jdt	13: 8	all her might, and **c** off his head.

CUTS → CUT

Ps	107:16	and **c** in two the bars of iron.

CUTTING → CUT

Pr	26: 6	like **c** off one's foot and drinking
Mt	26:51	slave of the high priest, **c** off his ear.

CYMBAL* → CYMBALS

1Co	13: 1	I am a noisy gong or a clanging **c.**

CYMBALS → CYMBAL

2Sa	6: 5	tambourines and castanets and **c.**
1Ch	15:16	on harps and lyres and **c**,
2Ch	5:12	fine linen, with **c**, harps, and lyres,
	29:25	in the house of the LORD with **c**,
Ezr	3:10	Levites, the sons of Asaph, with **c**,
Ne	12:27	and with singing, with **c**,
Ps	150: 5	Praise him with clanging **c**;
	150: 5	praise him with loud clashing **c!**

CYPRESS

Ge	6:14	Make yourself an ark of **c** wood;
1Ki	5: 8	in the matter of cedar and **c** timber.
Isa	55:13	of the thorn shall come up the **c**;
Hos	14: 8	I am like an evergreen **c**;

CYPRUS

Ac	4:36	a Levite, a native of C, Joseph,
	13: 4	and from there they sailed to C.

CYRENE

Mt	27:32	a man from C named Simon;

CYRUS

Persian king who allowed exiles to return (2Ch 36:22-Ezr 1:8), to rebuild temple (Ezr 5:13-6:14), as appointed by the LORD (Isa 44:28-45:13).

𝒟

DAGON

Jdg	16:23	a great sacrifice to their god **D**,
1Sa	5: 2	and brought it into the house of **D**
1Ch	10:10	fastened his head in the temple of **D.**

DAILY → DAY

Nu	28:24	In the same way you shall offer **d**,

Dt   24:15 You shall pay them their wages **d**
Ps   68:19 be the Lord, who **d** bears us up;
Mt   6:11 Give us this day our **d** bread.
Lk   9:23 take up their cross **d** and follow me.
      11: 3 Give us each day our **d** bread.
Jas   2:15 or sister is naked and lacks **d** food,

DAMASCUS

2Sa   8: 5 the Arameans of **D** came to help
2Ki   8: 7 Elisha went to **D** while King
      16:10 he saw the altar that was at **D.**
Isa   7: 8 For the head of Aram is **D,**
      17: 1 An oracle concerning **D.**
Jer   49:23 Concerning **D.** Hamath
Am   1: 3 For three transgressions of **D,** and
Ac   9: 3 was going along and approaching **D,**
      22: 6 was on my way and approaching **D,**

DAN

1. Son of Jacob by Bilhah (Ge 30:4-6; 35:25; 46:23). Tribe of blessed (Ge 49:16-17; Dt 33:22), numbered (Nu 1:39; 26:43), allotted land (Jos 19:40-48; Eze 48:1), failed to fully possess (Jdg 1:34-35), failed to support Deborah (Jdg 5:17), possessed Laish/Dan (Jdg 18).
2. Northernmost city in Israel (Ge 14:14; Jdg 18; 20:1).

DANCE → DANCED, DANCERS, DANCES, DANCING

Jdg   21:21 women of Shiloh come out to **d**
Ps   150: 4 Praise him with tambourine and **d;**
Ecc   3: 4 a time to mourn, and a time to **d;**
Jer   31: 4 forth in the **d** of the merrymakers.
      31:13 the young women rejoice in the **d,**
Mt   11:17 the flute for you, and you did not **d;**
Lk   7:32 the flute for you, and you did not **d;**
Jdt   15:12 of them performed a **d** in her honor.

DANCED* → DANCE

2Sa   6:14 David **d** before the LORD with all
       6:21 that I have **d** before the LORD.
Mt   14: 6 the daughter of Herodias **d** before
Mk   6:22 daughter Herodias came in and **d,**

DANCERS* → DANCE

Jdg   21:23 for each of them from the **d** whom
Ps   87: 7 Singers and **d** alike say, "All my

DANCES → DANCE

1Sa   21:11 not sing to one another of him in **d,**
      29: 5 whom they sing to one another in **d,**

DANCING → DANCE

Ex   15:20 with tambourines and with **d.**
      32:19 and saw the calf and the **d,**
Jdg   11:34 meet him with timbrels and with **d.**
1Sa   18: 6 singing and **d,** to meet King Saul,
2Sa   6:16 and saw King David leaping and **d**
1Ch   15:29 and saw King David leaping and **d;**
Ps   30:11 have turned my mourning into **d;**
      149: 3 Let them praise his name with **d,**
La   5:15 our **d** has been turned to mourning.
Lk   15:25 he heard music and **d.**

DANGER → DANGEROUS

1Sa   30: 6 David was in great **d;**
Pr   22: 3 The clever see **d** and hide;
      27:12 The clever see **d** and hide;
Lk   8:23 and they were in **d.**
Ac   19:40 in **d** of being charged with rioting
2Co   11:26 **d** from my own people, **d** from
                 Gentiles,
Sir   3:26 whoever loves **d** will perish in it.

DANGEROUS → DANGER

Lev   26: 6 remove **d** animals from the land,

DANIEL → =BELTESHAZZAR

1. Hebrew exile to Babylon, name changed to Belteshazzar (Da 1:6-7). Refused to eat unclean food (Da 1:8-21). Interpreted Nebuchadnezzar's dreams (Da 2; 4), writing on the wall (Da 5). Thrown into lion's den (Da 6). Visions of (Da

7-12). In deuterocanonical books of Bel and the Dragon, Susanna.
2. Son of David (1Ch 3:1).

DAPPLED

Zec   6: 3 fourth chariot **d** gray horses.

DARE → DARED

Mt   22:46 **d** to ask him any more questions.
Ac   7:32 to tremble and did not **d** to look.
      23: 4 you **d** to insult God's high priest?"
Ro   5: 7 someone might actually **d** to die.
1Co   6: 1 do you **d** to take it to court before

DARED → DARE

Lev   26:43 they **d** to spurn my ordinances,
Jer   36:29 You have **d** to burn this scroll,
Mk   12:34 After that no one **d** to ask him any
Jn   21:12 none of the disciples **d** to ask him,
Ac   5:13 None of the rest **d** to join them,

DARIUS

1. King of Persia (Ezr 4:5), allowed rebuilding of temple (Ezr 5-6).
2. Mede who conquered Babylon (Da 5:31).

DARK → DARKENED, DARKENS, DARKEST, DARKNESS

Ge   15:17 gone down and it was **d,**
Dt   4:11 very heavens, shrouded in **d** clouds.
Jos   2: 5 time to close the gate at **d,**
Ps   35: 6 Let their way be **d** and slippery,
      139:12 even the darkness is not **d** to you;
SS   1: 6 at me because I am **d,**
Lk   12: 3 whatever you have said in the **d** will
2Pe   1:19 as to a lamp shining in a **d** place,
Sir   45: 5 and led him into the **d** cloud,
2Es   12:42 and like a lamp in a **d** place,

DARKENED → DARK

Joel   2:10 The sun and the moon are **d,**
       3:15 The sun and the moon are **d,**
Mt   24:29 the sun will be **d,** and the moon will
Ro   1:21 and their senseless minds were **d.**
Eph   4:18 They are **d** in their understanding,
Rev   8:12 so that a third of their light was **d;**
       9: 2 and the sun and the air were **d**

DARKENS → DARK

Job   38: 2 that **d** counsel by words without
Am   5: 8 and **d** the day into night,

DARKEST* → DARK

Ps   23: 4 though I walk through the **d** valley,

DARKNESS → DARK

Ge   1: 2 the earth was a formless void and **d**
       1: 4 God separated the light from the **d.**
      15:12 a deep and terrifying **d** descended
Ex   10:22 was dense **d** in all the land of Egypt
      14:20 cloud was there with the **d,** and it lit
      20:21 near to the thick **d** where God was.
Dt   5:23 you heard the voice out of the **d,**
Jos   24: 7 **d** between you and the Egyptians,
2Sa   22:12 O LORD, the LORD lightens my **d.**
Job   12:22 and brings deep **d** to light.
Ps   18:11 He made **d** his covering around him,
      18:28 the LORD, my God, lights up my **d.**
      91: 6 or the pestilence that stalks in **d,**
      97: 2 Clouds and thick **d** are all around
      112: 4 They rise in the **d** as a light for the
      139:12 even the **d** is not dark to you;
      139:12 for **d** is as light to you.
Pr   4:19 way of the wicked is like deep **d;**
Ecc   2:13 excels folly as light excels **d.**
       5:17 Besides, all their days they eat in **d,**
Isa   5:20 put **d** for light and light for **d,**
       9: 2 walked in **d** have seen a great light;
      42:16 turn the **d** before them into light,
      45: 7 I form light and create **d,**
      58:10 then your light shall rise in the **d**
Jer   13:16 into gloom and makes it deep **d.**
Joel   2:31 The sun shall be turned to **d,**
Am   5:18 It is **d,** not light;

       5:20 the day of the LORD **d,** not light,
Na   1: 8 and will pursue his enemies into **d.**
Zep   1:15 a day of **d** and gloom,
Mt   4:16 who sat in **d** have seen a great light,
       6:23 light in you is **d,** how great is the **d!**
      22:13 and throw him into the outer **d,**
Lk   1:79 to give light to those who sit in **d**
      11:34 is not healthy, your body is full of **d.**
      23:44 and **d** came over the whole land
Jn   1: 5 The light shines in the **d,** and the **d**
                 did not overcome it.
       3:19 and people loved **d** rather than light
       8:12 follows me will never walk in **d**
      12:35 so that the **d** may not overtake you.
Ac   2:20 sun shall be turned to **d** and the
Ro   2:19 a light to those who are in **d,**
      13:12 Let us then lay aside the works of **d**
2Co   4: 6 who said, "Let light shine out of **d,"**
       6:14 is there between light and **d?**
Eph   5: 8 For once you were **d,** but now in
       5:11 no part in the unfruitful works of **d,**
Col   1:13 from the power of **d** and transferred
1Th   5: 5 we are not of the night or of **d.**
Heb   12:18 and **d** and gloom, and a tempest,
1Pe   2: 9 acts of him who called you out of **d**
2Pe   2:17 for them the deepest **d** has been
1Jn   1: 5 God is light and in him there is no **d**
       2: 8 because the **d** is passing away and
       2: 9 a brother or sister, is still in the **d.**
Jude   1: 6 in eternal chains in deepest **d** for
       1:13 the deepest **d** has been reserved
Rev   16:10 and its kingdom was plunged into **d;**
Tob   5:10 but I lie in **d** like the dead
Aza   1:48 Bless the Lord, light and **d;**

DASH → DASHED

2Ki   8:12 **d** in pieces their little ones,
Ps   2: 9 and **d** them in pieces like a potter's
      91:12 not **d** your foot against a stone.
Lk   4:11 not **d** your foot against a stone.'"
Jdt   16: 4 and **d** my infants to the ground,

DASHED → DASH

Isa   13:16 Their infants will be **d** to pieces
Hos   10:14 when mothers were **d** in pieces
Na   3:10 even her infants were **d** in pieces at
Lk   9:42 the demon **d** him to the ground

DATHAN*

Involved in Korah's rebellion against Moses and Aaron (Nu 16:1-27; 26:9; Dt 11:6; Ps 106:17; Sir 45:18; 4Mc 2:17).

DAUGHTER → DAUGHTER-IN-LAW, DAUGHTERS, DAUGHTERS-IN-LAW

Ge   24:24 "I am the **d** of Bethuel son of
      29:10 the **d** of his mother's brother Laban,
      34: 3 soul was drawn to Dinah **d** of Jacob;
      38: 2 There Judah saw the **d** of
Ex   2: 5 **d** of Pharaoh came down to bathe at
      21: 7 When a man sells his **d** as a slave,
Nu   27: 8 pass his inheritance on to his **d.**
Jdg   11:34 he had no son or **d** except her.
Ru   2: 2 She said to her, "Go, my **d."**
       3:10 you be blessed by the LORD, my **d;**
1Sa   18:20 Now Saul's **d** Michal loved David.
2Sa   6:16 Michal **d** of Saul looked out of the
1Ki   11: 1 along with the **d** of Pharaoh:
Est   2: 7 Mordecai adopted her as his own **d.**
Ps   9:14 and, in the gates of **d** Zion,
      137: 8 O **d** Babylon, you devastator!
Isa   47: 1 sit in the dust, virgin **d** Babylon!
      52: 2 from your neck, O captive **d** Zion!
      62:11 Say to **d** Zion, "See, your salvation
Jer   6: 2 likened **d** Zion to the loveliest
      46:11 and take balm, O virgin **d** Egypt!
La   2: 1 in his anger has humiliated **d** Zion!
Eze   16:45 you are your mother's **d,**
Mic   7: 6 the **d** rises up against her mother,
Zep   3:14 Sing aloud, O **d** Zion; shout,
       3:14 with all your heart, O **d** Jerusalem!
Zec   9: 9 Rejoice greatly, O **d** Zion!

Mal   9: 9 Shout aloud, O **d** Jerusalem!
Mal 2:11 has married the **d** of a foreign god.
Mt   9:18 saying, "My **d** has just died;
      14: 6 the **d** of Herodias danced before the
    15:28 And her **d** was healed instantly.
Mk 5:35 house to say, "Your **d** is dead.
     7:29 the demon has left your **d**."
Lk 12:53 against **d** and **d** against mother,
Heb 11:24 to be called a son of Pharaoh's **d**,
Jdt 10:12 replied, "I am a **d** of the Hebrews,

DAUGHTER BABYLON Ps 137:8; Isa
47:1; Jer 50:42; 51:33; Zec 2:7

DAUGHTER JERUSALEM 2Ki 19:21; Isa
37:22; La 2:13, 15; Mic 4:8; Zep 3:14; Zec 9:9

DAUGHTER OF PHARAOH;
PHARAOH'S DAUGHTER Ex 2:5, 7, 8, 9,
10; 1Ki 3:1; 7:8; 9:24; 11:1; 1Ch 4:17; 2Ch
8:11; Ac 7:21; Heb 11:24

DAUGHTER ZION 2Ki 19:21; Ps 9:14; Isa
1:8; 10:32; 16:1; 37:22; 52:2; 62:11; Jer 4:31;
6:2, 23; La 1:6; 2:1, 4, 8, 10, 13, 18; 4:22; Mic
1:13; 4:8, 10, 13; Zep 3:14; Zec 2:10; 9:9

DAUGHTER-IN-LAW → DAUGHTER
Ge 11:31 his **d** Sarai, his son Abram's wife,
    38:16 he did not know that she was his **d**.
Ru 1:22 Ruth the Moabite, her **d**,
    4:15 for your **d** who loves you,
1Ch 2: 4 His **d** Tamar also bore him Perez
Mic 7: 6 the **d** against her mother-in-law;
Mt 10:35 and a **d** against her mother-in-law;

DAUGHTERS → DAUGHTER
Ge 6: 4 of God went in to the **d** of humans,
  19:36 the **d** of Lot became pregnant by
        their father.
  29:16 Now Laban had two **d**; the name of
Ex 2:16 The priest of Midian had seven **d**.
Nu 27: 1 the **d** of Zelophehad came forward.
  27: 1 The names of his **d** were:
  36:10 The **d** of Zelophehad did as
Dt 7: 3 giving your **d** to their sons
   7: 3 or taking their **d** for your sons,
  12:31 even burn their sons and their **d** in
Ru 1:11 But Naomi said, "Turn back, my **d**,
Ezr 9:12 do not give your **d** to their sons,
Ne 5: 5 forcing our sons and **d** to be slaves,
Job 42:15 no women so beautiful as Job's **d**;
Ps 144:12 our **d** like corner pillars, cut for the
Pr 30:15 The leech has two **d**; "Give, give,"
SS 1: 5 and beautiful, O **d** of Jerusalem,
Eze 23: 2 two women, the **d** of one mother;
Joel 2:28 sons and your **d** shall prophesy,
Lk 23:28 to them and said, "**D** of Jerusalem,
Ac 2:17 sons and your **d** shall prophesy,
  21: 9 He had four unmarried **d** who had
2Co 6:18 and you shall be my sons and **d**,
1Pe 3: 6 You have become her **d** as long
Sir 7:24 Do you have **d**?

DAUGHTERS OF JERUSALEM SS 1:5;
2:7; 3:5, 10; 5:8, 16; 8:4; Lk 23:28

DAUGHTERS OF ZION SS 3:11; Isa 3:16,
17; 4:4

SONS ... DAUGHTERS Ge 5:4, 7, 10, 13,
16, 19, 22, 26, 30; 11:11, 13, 15, 17, 19, 21,
23, 25; 19:12; 31:28; 36:6; 37:35; 46:15; Ex
3:22; 10:9; 21:4; 32:2; 34:16; Lev 10:14; Nu
18:11, 19; 26:33; Dt 12:12, 31; 16:11, 14;
28:32, 41, 53; 32:19; Jos 7:24; 17:3; 1Sa 1:4;
2:21; 30:3, 6, 19; 2Sa 5:13; 19:5; 2Ki 17:17;
1Ch 23:4; 4:27; 14:3; 23:22; 25:5; 2Ch 11:21;
13:21; 24:3; 28:8; 29:9; 31:18; Ne 4:14; 5:2, 5;
10:28; Job 1:2, 13, 18; 42:13; Ps 106:38; Isa
56:5; Jer 3:24; 5:17; 7:31; 11:22; 14:16; 16:2,
3; 29:6, 6; 32:35; 35:8; Eze 14:16, 18, 22;
16:20; 23:4, 10, 25, 47; 24:21, 25; Joel 2:28;
3:8; Am 7:17; Ac 2:17; 2Co 6:18; Tob 4:13;
Wis 9:7; Bar 4:10, 14; 1Es 5:1

DAUGHTERS-IN-LAW → DAUGHTER
Ru 1: 8 But Naomi said to her two **d**,

DAVID
Son of Jesse (Ru 4:17-22; 1Ch 2:13-15), ancestor of Jesus (Mt 1:1-17; Lk 3:31). Wives and children (1Sa 18; 25:39-44; 2Sa 3:2-5; 5:13-16; 11:27; 1Ch 3:1-9).
Anointed king by Samuel (1Sa 16:1-13). Musician to Saul (1Sa 16:14-23; 18:10). Killed Goliath (1Sa 17). Relation with Jonathan (1Sa 18:1-4; 19-20; 23:16-18; 2Sa 1). Disfavor of Saul (1Sa 18:6-23:29). Spared Saul's life (1Sa 24; 26). Among Philistines (1Sa 21:10-14; 27-30). Lament for Saul and Jonathan (2Sa 1).
Anointed king of Judah (2Sa 2:1-11). Conflict with house of Saul (2Sa 2-4). Anointed king of Israel (2Sa 5:1-4; 1Ch 11:1-3). Conquered Jerusalem (2Sa 5:6-10; 1Ch 11;4-9). Brought ark to Jerusalem (2Sa 6; 1Ch 13; 15-16). The LORD promised eternal dynasty (2Sa 7; 1Ch 17; Ps 132). Showed kindness to Mephibosheth (2Sa 9). Adultery with Bathsheba, murder of Uriah (2Sa 11-12). Son Amnon raped daughter Tamar; killed by Absalom (2Sa 13). Absalom's revolt (2Sa 14-17); against David (2Sa 18). Sheba's revolt (2Sa 20). Victories: Philistines (2Sa 5:17-25; 21:15-22; 1Ch 14:8-17; 20:4-8), Ammonites (2Sa 10; 1Ch 19), various (2Sa 8; 1Ch 18). Mighty men (2Sa 23:8-39; 1Ch 11-12). Punished for numbering army (2Sa 24; 1Ch 21). Appointed Solomon king (1Ki 1:28-2:9). Prepared for building of temple (1Ch 22-29). Last words (2Sa 23:1-7). Death (1Ki 2:10-12; 1Ch 29:28).
Psalmist (Mt 22:43-45), musician (Am 6:5), prophet (2Sa 23:2-7; Ac 1:16; 2:30).
Psalms of: 2 (Ac 4:25), 3-32, 34-41, 51-65, 68-70, 86, 95 (Heb 4:7), 101, 103, 108-110, 122, 124, 131, 133, 138-145. Deuterocanonical Psalm 151 ascribed to.

CITY OF DAVID 2Sa 5:7, 9; 6:10, 12, 16;
1Ki 2:10; 3:1; 8:1; 9:24; 14:31; 15:8; 2Ki 8:24;
9:28; 12:21; 14:20; 15:7, 38; 16:20; 1Ch 11:5,
7; 13:13; 15:1, 29; 2Ch 5:2; 8:11; 12:16; 14:1;
16:14; 21:1, 20; 24:16, 25; 25:28; 27:9; 32:5,
30; 33:14; Ne 3:15; 12:37; Isa 22:9; Lk 2:4,
11; 1Mc 1:33; 2:31; 7:32; 14:36

FATHER DAVID 1Ki 2:12, 24, 26, 32, 44;
3:3, 6, 7, 14; 5:3, 5; 6:12; 7:51; 8:15, 17, 18,
20, 24, 25, 26; 9:5; 11:4, 6, 12, 27, 33, 43;
15:3, 11, 24; 22:50; 2Ki 22:2; 1Ch 29:23; 2Ch
1:8, 9; 2:3, 7, 14, 17; 3:1; 5:1; 6:4, 7, 8, 10, 15,
16; 7:17, 18; 8:14; 9:31; 21:12

HOUSE OF DAVID 1Sa 20:16; 2Sa 3:1, 6;
1Ki 12:19, 20, 26; 13:2; 14:8; 2Ki 17:21; 2Ch
10:19; 21:7; Ne 12:37; Ps 122:5; Isa 7:2, 13;
22:22; Jer 21:12; Zec 12:7, 8, 10, 12; 13:1; Lk
1:27; Tob 1:4; Sir 48:15; 1Es 5:5

KING DAVID 2Sa 3:31; 5:3, 6; 12, 16; 7:18;
8:8, 10, 11; 9:5; 13:21; 16:5, 6; 17:17, 21;
19:11, 16; 20:21; 1Ki 1:1, 13, 28, 31, 32, 37,
43, 47; 1Ch 15:29; 17:16; 18:10, 11; 21:24;
24:31; 26:26, 32; 27:24; 28:2; 29:1, 9, 24, 29;
2Ch 2:12; 7:6; 8:11; 29:27; 30:26; 35:4; Ezr
3:10; Mt 1:6; 1Es 1:5; 5:60

OF DAVID [in Psalm Titles] Ps 3:T; 4:T;
5:T; 6:T; 7:T; 8:T; 9:T; 11:T; 12:T; 13:T;
14:T; 15:T; 16:T; 17:T; 18:T; 19:T; 20:T;
21:T; 22:T; 23:T; 24:T; 25:T; 26:T; 27:T;
28:T; 29:T; 30:T; 31:T; 32:T; 34:T; 35:T;
36:T; 37:T; 38:T; 39:T; 40:T; 41:T; 51:T;
52:T; 53:T; 54:T; 55:T; 56:T; 57:T; 58:T;
59:T; 60:T; 61:T; 62:T; 63:T; 64:T; 65:T;
68:T; 69:T; 70:T; 72:20; 86:T; 101:T; 103:T;
108:T; 109:T; 110:T; 122:T; 124:T; 131:T;
138:T; 139:T; 140:T; 141:T; 142:T; 143:T;
144:T; 145:T

SERVANT DAVID 1Sa 19:4; 2Sa 3:18; 7:5,
8, 26; 1Ki 8:66; 11:13, 32, 34, 36; 14:8; 2Ki
8:19; 19:34; 1Ch 17:4, 7, 24; 2Ch 6:17, 42; Ps
78:70; 89:3, 20; 144:10; Isa 37:35; Jer 33:21,
22, 26; Eze 34:23, 24; 37:24, 25; Lk 1:69; 1Mc
4:30

SON OF DAVID 2Ch 1:1; 11:18; 13:6; 35:3;
Pr 1:1; Ecc 1:1; Mt 1:1, 20; 9:27; 12:23; 15:22;
20:30, 31; 21:9, 15; 22:42; Mk 10:47, 48;
12:35; Lk 3:31; 18:38, 39; 1Es 1:3

DAWN → DAWNED, DAWNS
Job 38:12 and caused the **d** to know its place,
Ps 57: 8 I will awake the **d**.
Pr 4:18 righteous is like the light of **d**,
SS 6:10 is this that looks forth like the **d**,
Isa 14:12 from heaven, O Day Star, son of **D**!
    58: 8 light shall break forth like the **d**,
    60: 3 kings to the brightness of your **d**.
    62: 1 her vindication shines out like the **d**,
Hos 6: 3 his appearing is as sure as the **d**;
Zep 3: 5 his judgment, each **d** without fail;
Sir 24:32 instruction shine forth like the **d**,

DAWNED → DAWN
Mt 4:16 and shadow of death light has **d**."

DAWNS → DAWN
Ps 97:11 Light **d** for the righteous,
2Pe 1:19 until the day **d** and the morning star

DAY → BIRTHDAY, DAILY, DAY'S,
DAYBREAK, DAYLIGHT, DAYS, DAYS'
Ge 1: 5 God called the light **D**, and
    1: 5 and there was morning, the first **d**.
    1: 8 there was morning, the second **d**.
   1:13 and there was morning, the third **d**.
   1:19 and there was morning, the fourth **d**.
   1:23 and there was morning, the fifth **d**.
   1:31 and there was morning, the sixth **d**.
   2: 2 the seventh **d** God finished the work
   2: 2 the seventh **d** from all the work
   8:22 **d** and night, shall not cease."
Ex 12:17 very **d** I brought your companies
  12:17 shall observe this **d** throughout your
  13:21 of them in a pillar of cloud by **d**,
  13:21 they might travel by **d** and by night.
  16:30 the people rested on the seventh **d**.
  20: 8 Remember the sabbath **d**, and keep
  40: 2 On the first **d** of the first month you
Nu 14:14 in a pillar of cloud by **d** and in
Dt 1:33 fire by night, and in the cloud by **d**,
  34: 6 knows his burial place to this **d**.
Jos 1: 8 you shall meditate on it **d** and night,
  10:14 no **d** like it before or since,
2Ki 7: 9 This is a **d** of good news;
  25:30 portion every **d**, as long as he lived.
1Ch 16:23 Tell of his salvation from **d** to **d**.
Ne 8:10 for this **d** is holy to our LORD;
   8:18 **d** by **d**, from the first **d** to the last **d**,
Ps 1: 2 his law they meditate **d** and night.
  19: 2 **D** to **d** pours forth speech,
  37:13 for he sees that their **d** is coming.
  50:15 Call on me in the **d** of trouble;
  84:10 For a **d** in your courts is better than
  96: 2 tell of his salvation from **d** to **d**.
 118:24 is the **d** that the LORD has made;
 119:97 It is my meditation all **d** long.
 119:164 a **d** I praise you for your righteous
Pr 11: 4 do not profit in the **d** of wrath,
  27: 1 do not know what a **d** may bring.
Ecc 7: 1 the **d** of death, than the **d** of birth.
Isa 2:12 has a **d** against all that is proud and
  13: 9 See, the **d** of the LORD comes, cruel,
  49: 8 on a **d** of salvation I have helped
  60:19 shall no longer be your light by **d**,
  66: 8 Shall a land be born in one **d**?
Jer 17:22 but keep the sabbath **d** holy,
  30: 7 that **d** is so great there is none like
  46:10 That **d** is the **d** of the Lord GOD of
       hosts, a **d** of retribution.
  50:31 for your **d** has come, the time when
Eze 4: 6 forty days I assign you, one **d** for
   7: 7 The time has come, the **d** is near—
  30: 2 Lord GOD: Wail, "Alas for the **d**!"
Da 6:13 saying his prayers three times a **d**."
Joel 1:15 Alas for the **d**! For the **d** of the
       LORD is near,

2:31 and terrible **d** of the LORD comes.
Am   3:14 On the **d** I punish Israel for its
      5:20 Is not the **d** of the LORD darkness,
Mic 7: 4 The **d** of their sentinels, of their
Hab 3:16 I wait quietly for the **d** of calamity
Zep 1:14 The great **d** of the LORD is near,
      1:14 sound of the **d** of the LORD is bitter,
Zec 2:11 to the LORD on that **d**,
     14: 1 See, a **d** is coming for the LORD,
     14: 7 And there shall be continuous **d**
Mal 3: 2 who can endure the **d** of his coming,
      4: 5 Elijah before the great and terrible **d**
Mt 10:15 of Sodom and Gomorrah on the **d**
     12:36 on the **d** of judgment you will have
     20:19 and on the third **d** he will be raised."
     24:38 until the **d** Noah entered the ark,
     25:13 you know neither the **d** nor the hour.
     28: 1 sabbath, as the first **d** of the week
Lk   1:59 eighth **d** they came to circumcise
     11: 3 Give us each **d** our daily bread.
     17:24 so will the Son of Man be in his **d**.
     24:46 to rise from the dead on the third **d**,
Jn   6:40 I will raise them up on the last **d**."
Ac   2: 1 When the **d** of Pentecost had come,
      2:20 of the Lord's great and glorious **d**.
      2:46 **D** by **d**, as they spent much time
      5:42 every **d** in the temple and at home
     17:11 and examined the scriptures every **d**
     17:31 a **d** on which he will have
Ro   2: 5 wrath for yourself on the **d** of wrath,
     14: 5 Some judge one **d** to be better than
1Co 5: 5 may be saved in the **d** of the Lord.
     15: 4 on the third **d** in accordance with
     15:31 I die every **d**! That is
2Co 4:16 our inner nature is being renewed **d**
           by **d**,
      6: 2 on a **d** of salvation I have helped
      6: 2 see, now is the **d** of salvation!
     11:25 a night and a **d** I was adrift at sea;
Eph 4:30 were marked with a seal for the **d**
      6:13 be able to withstand on that evil **d**,
Php 1: 6 will bring it to completion by the **d**
1Th 5: 2 very well that the **d** of the Lord
      5: 8 But since we belong to the **d**, let us
2Th 2: 2 that the **d** of the Lord is already
Heb 7:27 no need to offer sacrifices **d** after **d**,
2Pe 3: 8 that with the Lord one **d** is like a
           thousand years,
      3:10 **d** of the Lord will come like a thief,
1Jn 4:17 have boldness on the **d** of judgment,
Jude 1: 6 for the judgment of the great **D.**
Rev 1:10 I was in the spirit on the Lord's **d**,
      6:17 the great **d** of their wrath has come,
      8:12 third of the **d** was kept from shining,
     16:14 for battle on the great **d** of God
     20:10 they will be tormented **d** and night
     21:25 Its gates will never be shut by **d—**
Tob 12:18 Bless him each and every **d**;
Sir 5: 8 not benefit you on the **d** of calamity.
     39:28 on the **d** of reckoning they will
1Mc 4:54 **d** that the Gentiles had profaned it,
      7:48 celebrated that **d** as a **d** of great
2Mc 15:36 the **d** before Mordecai's **d**.

DAY AFTER DAY Ge 39:10; Jdg 16:16; 2Sa
13:37; 2Ch 21:15; 24:11; Est 3:4; Ps 61:8; Isa
58:2; Jer 7:25; Mt 26:55; Mk 14:49; Lk 22:53;
Heb 7:27; 10:11; 2Pe 2:8; AdE 3:4; Sus 1:12

DAY BY DAY 1Sa 18:10; 2Ch 30:21; Ezr
6:9; Ne 8:18; Ac 2:46, 47; 2Co 4:16; Tob 10:1

DAY OF CALAMITY Dt 32:35; 2Sa 22:19;
Job 21:30; Ps 18:18; Pr 27:10; Jer 18:17;
46:21; Ob 1:13, 13; Hab 3:16; Sir 5:8

DAY OF DEATH Ge 27:2; Jdg 13:7; 1Sa
1:11; 15:35; 2Sa 6:23; 20:3; 2Ki 15:5; 2Ch
26:21; Ecc 7:1; 8:8; Jer 52:11, 34; Jdt 12:14;
Sir 1:13; 11:26; 18:24; 40:2

DAY OF DISTRESS Ge 35:3; 2Ki 19:3; Ps
59:16; 102:2; Isa 37:3; Ob 1:12, 14; Zep 1:15;
Sir 3:15

DAY OF JUDGMENT Mt 10:15; 11:22, 24;

12:36; 2Pe 2:9; 3:7; 1Jn 4:17; Jdt 16:17; Wis
3:18; 2Es 7:38, 102, 104, 113; 12:34

DAY OF [THE/OUR] *LORD Jer 46:10;
1Co 1:8; 5:5; 2Co 1:14; 1Th 5:2; 2Th 2:2; 2Pe
3:10

DAY OF THE †LORD Isa 13:6, 9; 58:13;
Eze 13:5; 30:3; Joel 1:15; 2:1, 11, 31; 3:14;
Am 5:18, 18, 20; Ob 1:15; Zep 1:7, 14, 14;
Mal 4:5

DAY OF TROUBLE Ps 20:1; 27:5; 41:1;
50:15; 77:2; 86:7; Pr 16:4; Jer 16:19; 51:2; Na
1:7

DAY OF WRATH Job 20:28; 21:30; Ps
110:5; Pr 11:4; Eze 7:19; Zep 1:15, 18; 2:2, 3;
Ro 2:5; Rev 6:17

EACH DAY Ex 16:4; 29:38; Nu 7:11; 1Ki
8:59; 1Ch 16:37; 26:17, 17, 17; 2Ch 8:13, 14;
31:16; Ezr 3:4; Lk 11:3

EVERY DAY Ex 29:36; Nu 14:34; 1Sa
23:14; 2Ki 25:29, 30; Ne 11:23; Est 2:11; Ps
7:11; 88:9; 109:19; 145:2; Jer 52:33; Lk 16:19;
19:47; 21:37; Ac 5:42; 17:11, 17; 1Co 15:31;
Heb 3:13; Tob 10:7; 12:18; AdE 2:11; Sir
45:14; Sus 1:8; Bel 1:3, 4, 6, 32; 1Mc 8:15;
1Es 4:52; 5:51; 2Es 9:44

FIRST DAY Ge 1:5; 8:5, 13; Ex 12:15, 15,
16; 40:2, 17; Lev 23:7, 24, 35, 39, 40; Nu 1:1,
18; 7:12; 28:18; 29:1; 33:38; Dt 1:3; 16:4; Jdg
20:22; 2Ch 29:17; Ezr 3:6; 7:9, 9; 10:16, 17;
Ne 8:2, 18; Eze 26:1; 29:17; 31:1; 32:1; 45:18;
Da 10:12; Hag 1:1; Mt 26:17; 28:1; Mk 14:12;
16:2, 9; Lk 24:1; Jn 20:1, 19; Ac 20:7, 18; 1Co
16:2; Php 1:5; AdE 11:2; 2Es 6:38

LAST DAY Ne 8:18; Jn 6:39, 40, 44, 54;
7:37; 11:24; 12:48

ON THAT DAY Ge 7:11; 15:18; Ex 8:22;
12:41; 13:8; 19:1; 32:28; Lev 23:21; Nu 9:6, 6;
32:10; Dt 31:18; 32:48; Jos 4:14; 5:11; 6:15;
9:27; 10:28; 14:9, 12, 12; Jdg 4:23; 5:1; 6:32;
20:15, 21; 1Sa 3:12; 6:15; 14:24; 22:18, 22;
2Sa 5:8; 18:7; 1Ki 22:25; 1Ch 16:7; 29:22;
2Ch 15:11; 18:24; Ne 12:44; 13:1; Est 8:1, 13;
Ps 146:4; Isa 2:17, 20; 3:7; 4:2; 5:30; 7:18, 20,
21, 23; 10:20, 27; 11:10, 11; 17:4, 7, 9; 19:16,
18, 19, 21, 23, 24; 22:8, 20, 25; 24:21; 25:9;
26:1; 27:1, 2, 12, 13; 29:18; 30:23; 31:7; Jer
4:9; 25:33; 30:8; 39:16, 17; 48:41; 50:30; Eze
20:6; 24:26, 27; 29:21; 30:9; 38:10, 14, 18, 19;
39:11; 40:1; 45:22; Hos 1:5; 2:16, 18, 21; Am
8:9; 9:11; Ob 1:8; Mic 2:4; Zep 1:9, 10; 3:11,
16; Hag 2:23; Zec 2:11; 3:10; 9:16; 11:11;
12:3, 4, 6, 8, 9, 11; 13:1, 2, 4; 14:4, 6, 8, 9,
13, 20, 21; Mt 7:22; Mk 2:20; 4:35; Lk 10:12;
17:31; 24:13; Jn 14:20; 16:23, 26; 20:19; Eph
6:13; 2Th 1:10; 2Ti 1:18; 4:8; Tob 3:10;
11:17; Jdt 11:15; AdE 8:1; 16:20; 8:13; 9:2;
1Mc 5:67; 10:50; 11:47, 48; 2Es 7:105; 16:65;
4Mc 17:12

ONE DAY Ge 27:45; 33:13; 39:11; Ex 2:11;
Nu 11:19; 1Sa 14:1; 27:1; 1Ki 4:22; 20:29;
2Ki 4:8, 11, 18; 2Ch 28:6; Ezr 10:13; Ne 5:18;
6:10; Est 3:13; Job 1:6, 13; 2:1; Isa 9:14;
10:17; 47:9; 66:8; Eze 4:6; Lk 5:17; 8:22;
20:1; Ac 3:1; 16:16; 21:7; 28:13; Ro 14:5; 2Pe
3:8, 8; Tob 2:12; 9:4; Jdt 12:20; AdE 3:7; Sir
33:7; 38:17; 46:4; Sus 1:13; 1Mc 7:16; 1Es
4:34; 9:11

SEVENTH DAY Ge 2:2, 2, 3; Ex 12:15, 16;
13:6; 16:26, 27, 29, 30; 20:10, 11; 23:12;
24:16; 31:15, 17; 34:21; 35:2; Lev 13:5, 6, 27,
32, 34, 51; 14:9, 39; 23:3, 8; Nu 6:9; 7:48;
19:12, 12, 19, 19; 28:25; 29:32; 31:19, 24; Dt
5:14; 16:8; Jos 6:4, 15; Jdg 14:17, 18; 2Sa
12:18; 1Ki 20:29; 2Ki 25:8; Est 1:10; Eze
30:20; 45:20; Heb 4:4, 4; AdE 1:10; Bar 1:2;
Bel 1:40; 2Mc 6:11; 12:38; 15:4

THIRD DAY Ge 1:13; 22:4; 31:22; 34:25;
40:20; 42:18; Ex 19:11, 11, 15, 16; Lev 7:17,
18; 19:6, 7; Nu 7:24; 19:12, 12, 19; 29:20; Jos

9:17; Jdg *20:30; 1Sa 20:12; 30:1; 2Sa 1:2;
1Ki 3:18; 12:12, 12; 2Ki 20:5, 8; 2Ch 10:12,
12; Ezr 6:15; Est 5:1; Hos 6:2; Mt 16:21;
17:23; 20:19; 27:64; Lk 9:22; 13:32; 18:33;
24:7, 21, 46; Jn 2:1; Ac 10:40; 27:19; 1Co
15:4; AdE 15:1; 2Es 6:42, 44, 51; 14:1

DAY'S → DAY
Nu 11:31 about a **d** journey on this side
1Ki 19: 4 a **d** journey into the wilderness,
Jnh 3: 4 into the city, going a **d** walk.
Ac   1:12 a sabbath **d** journey away.
Rev 6: 6 "A quart of wheat for a **d** pay,
Sir 14:14 deprive yourself of a **d** enjoyment;

DAYBREAK → DAY, BREAK
Ge 32:24 a man wrestled with him until **d**.
Lk   4:42 At **d** he departed and went into a
Ac   5:21 the temple at **d** and went on with

DAYLIGHT → DAY, LIGHT
Am   8: 9 and darken the earth in broad **d**.
Jn 11: 9 "Are there not twelve hours of **d**?

DAYS → DAY
Ge   1:14 and for seasons and for **d** and years,
      3:14 dust you shall eat all the **d** of your
      3:17 in toil you shall eat of it all the **d** of
      7: 4 in seven **d** I will send rain on the
           earth for forty **d** and forty nights;
Ex 24:18 on the mountain for forty **d** and
     34:28 with the LORD forty **d** and forty
Nu 13:25 forty **d** they returned from spying
     14:34 forty **d**, for every day a year,
Dt 17:19 shall read in it all the **d** of his life,
     32: 7 the **d** of old, consider the years long
Jdg 17: 6 those **d** there was no king in Israel;
     18: 1 those **d** there was no king in Israel.
     21:25 those **d** there was no king in Israel;
1Sa 17:16 For forty **d** the Philistine came
1Ki 19: 8 that food forty **d** and forty nights
Ps 21: 4 length of **d** forever and ever.
     23: 6 mercy shall follow me all the **d** of
     34:12 and covets many **d** to enjoy good?
     39: 5 made my **d** a few handbreadths,
     90:10 The **d** of our life are seventy years,
     90:12 count our **d** that we may gain a wise
    103:15 for mortals, their **d** are like grass;
    128: 5 the prosperity of Jerusalem all the **d**
Pr   9:11 For by me your **d** will be multiplied,
     31:12 and not harm, all the **d** of her life.
Ecc 9: 9 all the **d** of your vain life that are
     12: 1 Remember your creator in the **d** of
Isa 53:10 and shall prolong his **d**;
Da 12:11 one thousand two hundred ninety **d**.
     12:12 thousand three hundred thirty-five **d**
Hos 3: 5 and to his goodness in the latter **d**.
Joel 2:29 male and female slaves, in those **d**,
Mt   4: 2 He fasted forty **d** and forty nights,
Mk   1:13 He was in the wilderness forty **d**,
     10:34 and after three **d** he will rise again."
Lk   4: 2 where for forty **d** he was tempted
      4: 2 He ate nothing at all during those **d**,
     19:43 Indeed, the **d** will come upon you,
Ac   1: 3 during forty **d** and speaking about
      2:17 'In the last **d** it will be,
Eph 5:16 of the time, because the **d** are evil.
2Ti 3: 1 in the last **d** distressing times will
Heb 1: 2 last **d** he has spoken to us by a Son,
2Pe 3: 3 that in the last **d** scoffers will come,
Rev 11: 3 one thousand two hundred sixty **d**,
     11:11 But after the three and a half **d**,
     12: 6 one thousand two hundred sixty **d**.
Tob 4: 5 Live uprightly all the **d** of your life,
Jdt 16:24 Israel mourned her for seven **d**.
Sir 22:12 Mourning for the dead lasts seven **d**,
1Mc 4:56 dedication of the altar for eight **d**,
2Es 14:42 They sat forty **d**; they wrote

ALL THE DAYS Ge 3:14, 17; 5:5, 8, 11, 14,
17, 20, 23, 27, 31; 9:29; Lev 15:25, 26; Nu
6:5, 6; Dt 4:9; 6:2; 12:1; 16:3; 17:19; Jos 1:5;
4:14; 24:31, 31; Jdg 2:7, 7, 18; 1Sa 7:13, 15;

14:52; 1Ki 4:21; 8:40; 11:25, 34; 15:5, 6; 2Ki
13:22; 23:22; 2Ch 6:31; 24:2, 14; 36:21; Job
14:14; Ps 23:6; 27:4; 128:5; 139:16; Pr 15:15;
31:12; Ecc 9:9; Isa 38:20; 63:9; Tob 1:3; 4:3,
5; 10:12, 12, 13; Jdt 8:6; 16:22; Sir 22:12; 1Mc
14:4; Man 1:15

DAYS ARE [SURELY] COMING 2Ki
20:17; Isa 39:6; Jer 7:32; 9:25; 16:14; 19:6;
23:5, 7; 30:3; 31:27, 31, 38; 33:14; 51:47; Lk
17:22; 23:29; Heb 8:8; 2Es 5:1; 6:18; 12:13;
13:29

DAYS OF ... LIFE Ge 3:14, 17; Dt 4:9; 6:2;
16:3; 17:19; Jos 1:5; 4:14; 1Sa 7:15; 1Ki 4:21;
11:34; 15:5, 6; Job 10:20; Ps 23:6; 27:4; 90:10;
128:5; Pr 31:12; Ecc 2:3; 5:18; 6:12; 8:15; 9:9;
Tob 1:3; 4:3, 5; 10:12, 13; Jdt 16:22; Sir
33:24; 37:25; 41:13; Man 1:15

DAYS OF OLD Dt 32:7; 2Ki 19:25; Ps 44:1;
77:5; 143:5; Isa 23:7; 37:26; 51:9; 63:9, 11; Jer
46:26; La 1:7; Am 9:11; Mic 7:14, 20; Mal
3:4; Sir 50:23

DAYS TO COME Ge 49:1; Nu 24:14; Ecc
2:16; Isa 2:2; 27:6; Mic 4:1

FORTY DAYS Ge 7:4, 12, 17; 8:6; 50:3; Ex
24:18; 34:28; Nu 13:25; 14:34; Dt 9:9, 11, 18,
25; 10:10; 1Sa 17:16; 1Ki 19:8; Eze 4:6; Jnh
3:4; Mt 4:2; Mk 1:13; Lk 4:2; Ac 1:3; Tob
1:21; 2Mc 5:2; 3Mc 4:15; 6:38; 2Es 14:23, 36,
42, 44, 45

LAST DAYS Ac 2:17; 2Ti 3:1; Heb 1:2; Jas
5:3; 2Pe 3:3; Sir 2:3; 2Es 7:84, 95; 10:59;
12:23, 28; 13:18, 20; 14:22

SEVEN DAYS Ge 7:4, 10; 8:10, 12; 31:23;
50:10; Ex 7:25; 12:15, 19; 13:6, 7; *22:30;
23:15; 29:30, 35, 37; 34:18; Lev 8:33, 33, 35;
12:2; 13:4, 5, 21, 26, 31, 33, 50, 54; 14:8, 38;
15:13, 19, 24, 28; 22:27; 23:6, 8, 34, 36, 39,
40, 41, 42; Nu 12:14, 14, 15; 19:11, 14, 16;
28:17, 24; 29:12; 31:19; Dt 16:3, 4, 13, 15; Jdg
14:12, 17; 1Sa 10:8; 13:8; 31:13; 1Ki 8:65;
16:15; 20:29; 2Ki 3:9; 1Ch 9:25; 10:12; 2Ch
7:8, 9, 9; 30:21, 22, 23, 23; 35:17; Ezr 6:22;
Ne 8:18; Est 1:5; Job 2:13; Isa 30:26; Eze
3:15, 16; 43:25, 26; 44:26; 45:21, 23, 23, 25;
Ac 20:6; 21:4, 27; 28:14; Heb 11:30; Tob
11:18; Jdt 16:24; AdE 2:18; Sir 22:12; 1Es
1:19; 4:63; 7:14; 3Mc 6:30; 7:17; 2Es 5:13, 19,
20, 21; 6:31, 35; 7:30, 31, 101, 101; 9:23, 27;
12:39, 40, 51; 13:1; 4Mc 14:7

SIX DAYS Ex 16:26; 20:9, 11; 23:12; 24:16;
31:15, 17; 34:21; 35:2; Lev 23:3; Dt 5:13;
16:8; Jos 6:3, 14; Mt 17:1; Mk 9:2; Lk 13:14;
Jn 12:1; AdE 1:5; Bel 1:31

THREE DAYS Ge 40:12, 13, 18, 19; 42:17;
Ex 10:22, 23; 15:22; Jos 1:11; 2:16, 22; 3:2;
9:16; Jdg 14:14; 19:4; 1Sa 9:20; 30:12, 13; 2Sa
20:4; 1Ki 12:5; 2Ki 2:17; 1Ch 12:39; 21:12;
2Ch 10:5; 20:25; Ezr 8:15, 32; 10:8, 9; Ne
2:11; Est 4:16; Am 4:4; Jnh 1:17; Mt 12:40,
40; 15:32; 26:61; 27:40, 63; Mk 8:2, 31; 9:31;
10:34; 14:58; 15:29; Lk 2:46; Jn 2:19, 20; Ac
9:9; 25:1; 28:7, 12, 17; Jdt 2:21; 12:7; AdE
4:16; 1Mc 10:34; 11:18; 2Mc 5:14; 13:12; 1Es
8:41, 62; 9:4, 5; 3Mc 6:38; 2Es 13:58

DAYS' → DAY

THREE DAYS' Ge 30:36; Ex 3:18; 5:3;
8:27; Nu 10:33, 33; 33:8; 2Sa 24:13; Jnh 3:3;
1Mc 5:24

DAZZLING
Mk   9: 3 and his clothes became **d** white,
Lk   24: 4 suddenly two men in **d** clothes
Ac 10:30 when suddenly a man in **d** clothes

DEACON* → DEACONS
Ro 16: 1 a **d** of the church at Cenchreae,

DEACONS* → DEACON
Php   1: 1 in Philippi, with the bishops and **d:**
1Ti   3: 8 **D** likewise must be serious, not

3:10 blameless, let them serve as **d.**
3:12 Let **d** be married only once,
3:13 for those who serve well as **d**

DEAD → DEADLY, DEATH, DIE, DIED, DIES,
DYING
Ex   12:30 not a house without someone **d.**
Nu   16:48 stood between the **d** and the living;
Dt   18:11 or who seeks oracles from the **d.**
Ru   4: 5 to maintain the **d** man's name on
1Ki   3:22 and the **d** son is yours."
Ps 115:17 The **d** do not praise the LORD,
Pr   9:18 do not know that the **d** are there,
Ecc   9: 4 a living dog is better than a **d** lion.
Isa   8:19 the **d** on behalf of the living,
       26:19 Your **d** shall live,
Mt   8:22 and let the **d** bury their own **d."**
        9:24 for the girl is not **d** but sleeping."
       10: 8 Cure the sick, raise the **d,** cleanse
       11: 5 the deaf hear, the **d** are raised,
       14: 2 he has been raised from the **d,**
       28: 7 'He has been raised from the **d,**
Mk   12:27 God not of the **d,** but of the living;
Lk   15:24 this son of mine was **d** and is alive
       16:31 even if someone rises from the **d.'"**
       20:37 that the **d** are raised Moses himself
       24: 5 look for the living among the **d?**
       24:46 is to suffer and to rise from the **d**
Jn   5:21 just as the Father raises the **d** and
       11:44 The **d** man came out, his hands and
       20: 9 that he must rise from the **d.**
       21:14 after he was raised from the **d.**
Ro   6: 4 just as Christ was raised from the **d**
        6:11 must consider yourselves **d** to sin
       14: 9 Lord of both the **d** and the living.
1Co 15:12 say there is no resurrection of the **d?**
       15:29 receive baptism on behalf of the **d?**
       15:29 If the **d** are not raised at all,
Eph   2: 1 You were **d** through the trespasses
        5:14 Rise from the **d,** and Christ will
Php   3:11 the resurrection from the **d.**
Col   1:18 the firstborn from the **d,**
        2:13 And when you were **d** in trespasses
1Th   4:16 and the **d** in Christ will rise first.
2Ti   4: 1 who is to judge the living and the **d,**
Heb 11:19 even to raise someone from the **d—**
Jas   2:26 so faith without works is also **d.**
1Pe   4: 5 ready to judge the living and the **d.**
Rev   1: 5 witness, the firstborn of the **d,**
        1:18 I was **d,** and see, I am alive
       11:18 and the time for judging the **d,**
       14:13 Blessed are the **d** who from now on
       20:12 And the **d** were judged according to

DEAD SEA Ge 14:3; Nu 34:3, 12; Dt 3:17;
Jos 3:16; 12:3; 15:2, 5; 18:19; 2Es 5:7

RAISED FROM THE DEAD Mt 14:2;
17:9; 27:64; 28:7; Mk 6:14; Lk 9:7; Jn 2:22;
12:1, 9; 21:14; Ac 3:15; 4:10; Ro 6:4, 9; 7:4;
1Co 15:12, 20; 1Th 1:10; 2Ti 2:8; 2Es 7:37

RESURRECTION OF THE DEAD Mt
22:31; Lk 20:35; Ac 4:2; 17:32; 23:6; 24:21;
Ro 1:4; 1Co 15:12, 13, 21, 42; Php 3:11; Heb
6:2

DEADLY → DEAD
Ex   9: 3 with a **d** pestilence your livestock
Ps   91: 3 and from the **d** pestilence;
Eze 14:21 my four **d** acts of judgment,

DEAF
Ex   4:11 Who makes them mute or **d,**
Lev 19:14 You shall not revile the **d**
Isa   29:18 On that day the **d** shall hear the
       35: 5 and the ears of the **d** unstopped;
       42:19 **d** like my messenger whom I send?
Mk   7:32 They brought to him a **d** man
Lk   7:22 the lepers are cleansed, the **d** hear,

DEAL → DEALING, DEALT
Ex   1:10 let us **d** shrewdly with them,
Lev 19:11 you shall not **d** falsely;
Jos 24:27 if you **d** falsely with your God."

Ps 119:124 **D** with your servant according
Eze 16:59 I will **d** with you as you have done,
Heb   5: 2 to **d** gently with the ignorant and
        9:28 second time, not to **d** with sin,

DEALING → DEAL
Pr   1: 3 for gaining instruction in wise **d,**

DEALT → DEAL
Ge   21: 1 The LORD **d** with Sarah as
Ex   1:20 God **d** well with the midwives;
Ru   1:21 the LORD has **d** harshly with me,
Ne   9:33 for you have **d** faithfully
Ps 116: 7 for the LORD has **d** bountifully
      147:20 not **d** thus with any other nation;
Hos   5: 7 **d** faithlessly with the LORD;
1Th   2:11 **d** with each one of you like a father

DEAR
Ps   39:11 consuming like a moth what is **d**
      102:14 For your servants hold its stones **d,**
Jer   31:20 Is Ephraim my **d** son?
1Co 10:14 my **d** friends, flee from the worship
Eph   6:21 a **d** brother and a faithful minister
1Th   2: 8 you have become very **d** to us.
Phm   1: 1 To Philemon our **d** friend and
2Jn   1: 5 But now, **d** lady, I ask you,
Sir   37: 2 a **d** friend turns into an enemy?

DEATH → DEAD
Ex   21:12 a person mortally shall be put to **d.**
       21:15 or mother shall be put to **d.**
       21:16 held in possession, shall be put to **d.**
       21:17 or mother shall be put to **d.**
       22:19 lies with an animal shall be put to **d.**
       31:14 profanes it shall be put to **d;**
       31:15 on the sabbath day shall be put to **d.**
Nu   23:10 Let me die the **d** of the upright,
       35:16 the murderer shall be put to **d.**
Dt   13: 5 divine by dreams shall be put to **d**
       17: 6 or three witnesses the **d** sentence
       30:19 that I have set before you life and **d,**
Ru   1:17 if even **d** parts me from you!"
2Ki   4:40 there is **d** in the pot!"
2Ch 23:15 and there they put her to **d.**
       25: 4 put to **d** for their own sins."
Job   3:21 who long for **d,** but it does not come
Ps   13: 3 or I will sleep the sleep of **d,**
       18: 4 The cords of **d** encompassed me;
       22:15 you lay me in the dust of **d.**
       49:14 **D** shall be their shepherd;
       89:48 Who can live and never see **d?**
      116:15 Precious in the sight of the LORD is
                   the **d** of his faithful ones.
Pr   5: 5 Her feet go down to **d;**
        8:36 all who hate me love **d."**
       10: 2 but righteousness delivers from **d.**
       14:12 but its end is the way to **d.**
       16:25 but in the end it is the way to **d.**
       18:21 **D** and life are in the power of the
Ecc   7: 1 the day of **d,** than the day of birth.
SS   8: 6 for love is strong as **d,**
Isa   25: 7 he will swallow up **d** forever.
       28:15 "We have made a covenant with **d,**
       53:12 because he poured out himself to **d,**
Jer   26:16 does not deserve the sentence of **d,**
Eze   18:23 pleasure in the **d** of the wicked,
       18:32 no pleasure in the **d** of anyone,
       33:11 no pleasure in the **d** of the wicked,
Hos   13:14 O **D,** where are your plagues?
Hab   2: 5 like **D** they never have enough.
Mt   10:21 Brother will betray brother to **d,**
       16:28 standing here who will not taste **d**
       26:66 They answered, "He deserves **d."**
Mk   10:33 and they will condemn him to **d;**
Lk   1:79 in darkness and in the shadow of **d,**
Jn   5:24 but has passed from **d** to life.
        8:51 keeps my word will never see **d."**
       11:13 had been speaking about his **d,**
Ac   2:24 him up, having freed him from **d,**
Ro   4:25 handed over to **d** for our trespasses
        5:12 and **d** came through sin,

5: 12 and so **d** spread to all because all
    have sinned—
6: 3 were baptized into his **d?**
6: 23 For the wages of sin is **d,**
7: 24 will rescue me from this body of **d?**
8: 13 by the Spirit you put to **d** the deeds
1Co 15: 21 For since **d** came through a human
15: 26 The last enemy to be destroyed is **d.**
15: 55 "Where, O **d,** is your victory?
2Co 2: 16 to the one a fragrance from **d** to **d,**
3: 7 Now if the ministry of **d,**
4: 10 carrying in the body the **d** of Jesus,
Php 2: 8 became obedient to the point of **d—**
Col 1: 22 reconciled in his fleshly body
    through **d,**
2Ti 1: 10 who abolished **d** and brought life
Heb 2: 14 that through **d** he might destroy the
    one who has the power of **d,**
Jas 5: 20 save the sinner's soul from **d** and
1Jn 3: 14 that we have passed from **d** to life
3: 14 Whoever does not love abides in **d.**
Rev 1: 18 I have the keys of **D** and of Hades.
2: 11 not be harmed by the second **d.**
6: 8 Its rider's name was **D,** and Hades
9: 6 they will long to die, but **d** will flee
20: 6 these the second **d** has no power,
20: 14 **D** and Hades were thrown into the
    lake of fire.
20: 14 This is the second **d,** the lake of fire;
21: 4 from their eyes. **D** will be no more;
21: 8 and sulfur, which is the second **d."**
Wis 1: 12 Do not invite by the error
Sir 4: 28 Fight to the **d** for truth,
8: 7 Do not rejoice over any one's **d;**
15: 17 Before each person are life and **d,**
LtJ 6: 36 They cannot save anyone from **d**
Aza 1: 66 saved us from the power of **d,**
Sus 1: 28 plot to have Susanna put to **d.**
1: 62 they put them to **d.**

DAY OF ... DEATH Ge 27:2; Jdg 13:7; 1Sa
1:11; 15:35; 2Sa 6:23; 20:3; 2Ki 15:5; 2Ch
26:21; Ecc 7:1; 8:8; Jer 52:11, 34; Jdt 12:14;
Sir 1:13; 11:26; 18:24; 40:2

LIFE ... DEATH Dt 30:15, 19; 1Sa 28:9; 2Sa
1:23; Jer 21:8; Ro 7:10; 1Co 3:22; Php 1:20;
Wis 16:13; Sir 11:14; 15:17; 33:14; 37:18; 2Es
7:92

DEBASED*

Ro 1: 28 God gave them up to a **d** mind

DEBATE* → DEBATED, DEBATER

Ac 15: 2 had no small dissension and **d**
15: 7 After there had been much **d,**

DEBATED* → DEBATE

Ac 17: 18 Stoic philosophers **d** with him.

DEBATER* → DEBATE

1Co 1: 20 Where is the **d** of this age?

DEBAUCHERIES → DEBAUCHERY

Na 3: 4 who enslaves nations through her **d,**

DEBAUCHERY* → DEBAUCHERIES

Ro 13: 13 not in **d** and licentiousness,
Eph 5: 18 drunk with wine, for that is **d;**
Tit 1: 6 not accused of **d** and not rebellious.
Wis 14: 26 in marriages, adultery, and **d.**
2Mc 6: 4 For the temple was filled with **d**

DEBIR

Jos 12: 13 the king of **D** one
Jdg 1: 11 of **D** was formerly Kiriath-sepher).

DEBORAH

1. Prophetess who led Israel to victory over
Canaanites (Jdg 4-5).
2. Rebekah's nurse (Ge 35:8).

DEBT* → DEBTOR, DEBTORS, DEBTS,
INDEBTED

Ex 21: 2 go out a free person, without **d.**

21: 11 she shall go out without **d,**
1Sa 22: 2 and everyone who was in **d,**
Ne 10: 31 and the exaction of every **d.**
Mt 18: 27 released him and forgave him the **d.**
18: 30 into prison until he would pay the **d.**
18: 32 I forgave you all that **d** because you
18: 34 until he would pay his entire **d.**
Lk 7: 43 whom he canceled the greater **d."**
1Mc 10: 43 owe money to the king or are in **d,**
15: 8 Every **d** you owe to the royal
1Es 3: 20 and forgets all sorrow and **d.**
4Mc 2: 8 and to cancel the **d** when the
    seventh year arrives.

DEBTOR* → DEBT

Isa 24: 2 as with the creditor, so with the **d.**
Eze 18: 7 but restores to the **d** his pledge,
Ro 1: 14 I am a **d** both to Greeks

DEBTORS* → DEBT

Mt 6: 12 as we also have forgiven our **d.**
Lk 7: 41 "A certain creditor had two **d;**
16: 5 summoning his master's **d** one by
Ro 8: 12 then, brothers and sisters, we are **d,**

DEBTS* → DEBT

Dt 15: 1 you shall grant a remission of **d.**
2Ki 4: 7 "Go sell the oil and pay your **d,**
Pr 22: 26 who become surety for **d.**
Mt 6: 12 And forgive us our **d,** as we
Lk 7: 42 he canceled the **d** for both of them.
1Mc 15: 8 any such future **d** shall be canceled

DECAPOLIS

Mt 4: 25 followed him from Galilee, the **D,**

DECAY → DECAYS

Ro 8: 21 set free from its bondage to **d**

DECAYS → DECAY

Sir 10: 9 Even in life the human body **d.**

DECEIT → DECEITFUL, DECEITFULLY,
DECEITFULNESS, DECEIVE, DECEIVED,
DECEIVER, DECEIVERS, DECEIVES,
DECEIVING, DECEPTION, DECEPTIVE

Dt 32: 4 A faithful God, without **d,**
Job 15: 35 and their heart prepares **d."**
27: 4 and my tongue will not utter **d.**
Ps 32: 2 and in whose spirit there is no **d.**
101: 7 No one who practices **d** shall remain
Pr 26: 24 speaking while harboring **d** within;
Isa 53: 9 and there was no **d** in his mouth.
Da 8: 25 his cunning he shall make **d** prosper
Mk 7: 22 wickedness, **d,** licentiousness, envy,
Jn 1: 47 Israelite in whom there is no **d!"**
Ac 13: 10 full of all **d** and villainy,
Ro 1: 29 Full of envy, murder, strife, **d,**
Col 2: 8 through philosophy and empty **d,**
1Th 2: 3 our appeal does not spring from **d**
1Pe 2: 22 and no **d** was found in his mouth."

DECEITFUL → DECEIT

Ps 35: 20 but they conceive **d** words
120: 2 lying lips, from a **d** tongue."
Na 3: 1 City of bloodshed, utterly **d,**
Zep 3: 13 nor shall a **d** tongue be found
2Co 11: 13 such boasters are false apostles, **d**
Eph 4: 14 by their craftiness in **d** scheming.
1Ti 4: 1 by paying attention to **d** spirits

DECEITFULLY → DECEIT

Ge 27: 35 But he said, "Your brother came **d,**
34: 13 Shechem and his father Hamor **d,**
Ps 24: 4 and do not swear **d.**
Pr 12: 17 but a false witness speaks **d.**
Da 11: 23 he shall act **d** and become strong
1Mc 1: 30 **D** he spoke peaceable words to them

DECEITFULNESS* → DECEIT

Heb 3: 13 hardened by the **d** of sin.

DECEIVE → DECEIT

Jos 9: 22 said to them, "Why did you **d** us,

2Ki 18: 29 'Do not let Hezekiah **d** you,
Job 13: 9 you **d** him, as one person deceives
Pr 24: 28 and do not **d** with your lips.
Jer 29: 8 diviners who are among you **d** you,
37: 9 says the LORD: Do not **d** yourselves,
Zec 13: 4 put on a hairy mantle in order to **d,**
Ro 16: 18 smooth talk and flattery they **d** the
1Co 3: 18 Do not **d** yourselves. If you think
Eph 5: 6 Let no one **d** you with empty words,
Col 2: 4 no one may **d** you with plausible
2Th 2: 3 Let no one **d** you in any way;
Jas 1: 22 merely hearers who **d** themselves.
1Jn 1: 8 that we have no sin, we **d** ourselves,
3: 7 Little children, let no one **d** you.
Rev 20: 8 to **d** the nations at the four corners

DECEIVED → DECEIT

Ge 31: 20 And Jacob **d** Laban the Aramean,
Nu 25: 18 they **d** you in the affair of Peor,
Ob 1: 3 Your proud heart has **d** you,
Jn 7: 47 "Surely you have not been **d** too,
Ro 7: 11 **d** me and through it killed me.
1Co 6: 9 the kingdom of God? Do not be **d!**
15: 33 Do not be **d:** "Bad company
2Co 11: 3 I am afraid that as the serpent **d** Eve
Gal 6: 7 Do not be **d;** God is not mocked,
1Ti 2: 14 was not **d,** but the woman was **d**
2Ti 3: 13 deceiving others and being **d.**
Jas 1: 16 Do not be **d,** my beloved.
Rev 18: 23 all nations were **d** by your sorcery.
20: 10 devil who had **d** them was thrown
Bel 1: 7 and said, "Do not be **d,**

DECEIVER → DECEIT

Job 12: 16 the deceived and the **d** are his.
2Jn 1: 7 person is the **d** and the antichrist!

DECEIVERS* → DECEIT

Tit 1: 10 rebellious people, idle talkers and **d,**
2Jn 1: 7 Many **d** have gone out into the

DECEIVES* → DECEIT

Job 13: 9 as one person **d** another?
Pr 26: 19 so is one who **d** a neighbor and
Rev 13: 14 it **d** the inhabitants of earth,

DECEIVING → DECEIT

Jn 7: 12 "No, he is **d** the crowd."
2Ti 3: 13 **d** others and being deceived.

DECENTLY*

1Co 14: 40 but all things should be done **d**
1Ti 2: 9 dress themselves modestly and **d**

DECEPTION → DECEIT

Mt 27: 64 the last **d** would be worse than the

DECEPTIVE* → DECEIT

Ex 5: 9 pay no attention to **d** words."
Pr 23: 3 delicacies, for they are **d** food.
Jer 7: 4 Do not trust in these **d** words:
7: 8 trusting in **d** words to no avail.
La 2: 14 seen for you false and **d** visions;
2Pe 2: 3 they will exploit you with **d** words.

DECIDE → DECIDED, DECISION

Ex 18: 16 I **d** between one person and another,
Isa 11: 3 or **d** by what his ears hear;
Eze 44: 24 it according to my judgments.
Ac 24: 22 tribune comes down, I will **d** your
1Co 6: 5 no one among you wise enough to **d**

DECIDED → DECIDE

Ex 18: 26 any minor case they **d** themselves.
Lk 1: 3 too **d,** after investigating everything

DECISION → DECIDE

Lev 24: 12 until the **d** of the LORD should be
Nu 27: 21 the **d** of the Urim before the LORD;
Pr 16: 33 but the **d** is the LORD's alone.
Joel 3: 14 multitudes, in the valley of **d!**
Zep 3: 8 For my **d** is to gather nations,
Mk 14: 64 his blasphemy! What is your **d?"**

DECLARE → DECLARED, DECLARES, DECLARING

Dt   5: 5 to **d** to you the words of the LORD;
1Ch 16:24 **D** his glory among the nations,
Job 38:18 **D**, if you know all this.
     40: 7 will question you, and you **d** to me.
     42: 4 will question you, and you **d** to me.'
Ps 50: 6 The heavens **d** his righteousness,
     96: 3 **D** his glory among the nations,
    145: 6 and I will **d** your greatness.
Isa 42: 9 and new things I now **d**;
     45:19 I **d** what is right.
     50: 9 who will **d** me guilty?
Jer 18: 7 At one moment I may **d**
Jn   8:38 I **d** what I have seen in the Father's
    16:14 what is mine and **d** it to you.
Col 4: 3 that we may **d** the mystery of Christ,
Tit 2:15 **D** these things; exhort
1Jn 1: 3 we **d** to you what we have seen
Sir 16:25 and **d** knowledge accurately.
     42:15 and will **d** what I have seen.

DECLARED → DECLARE

Dt   4:13 He **d** to you his covenant,
Ps 88:11 Is your steadfast love **d** in the grave,
Isa 41:26 Who **d** it from the beginning,
     48: 3 The former things I **d** long ago,
Mk   7:19 (Thus he **d** all foods clean.)
Ro   1: 4 and was **d** to be Son of God
Gal 3: 8 **d** the gospel beforehand to Abraham

DECLARES → DECLARE

Ps 19: 2 and night to night **d** knowledge.
    147:19 He **d** his word to Jacob,

DECLARING → DECLARE

2Th 2: 4 **d** himself to be God.

DECORATED

Ex 28: 8 The **d** band on it shall be of
1Mc 4:57 They **d** the front of the temple

DECORATION → DECORATE

1Mc 1:22 gold **d** on the front of the temple;

DECREASE·

Ps 107:38 and he does not let their cattle **d**.
Jer 29: 6 multiply there, and do not **d**.
Jn   3:30 He must increase, but I must **d**."

DECREE → DECREED, DECREES

Ezr 5: 3 "Who gave you a **d** to build
     6: 1 Then King Darius made a **d**,
Est 3: 9 a **d** be issued for their destruction,
Ps 122: 2 I will tell of the **d** of the LORD:
     81: 5 He made it a **d** in Joseph,
Jer 3: 8 sent her away with a **d** of divorce;
Da   2:13 The **d** was issued, and the wise men
     4:24 a **d** of the Most High that has come
Lk   2: 1 **d** went out from Emperor Augustus
Ro   1:32 They know God's **d**,
Sir 41: 3 This is the Lord's **d** for all flesh;
1Mc 1:57 to death by **d** of the king.

DECREED → DECREE

1Ki 22:23 the LORD has **d** disaster for you."
Ps 122: 4 as was **d** for Israel,
Isa 10:22 Destruction is **d**, overflowing with
Da   9:24 "Seventy weeks are **d** for your
1Co 2: 7 which God **d** before the ages

DECREES → DECREE

Dt   6: 2 and keep all his **d** and his
     11: 1 and keep his charge, his **d**, his
     30:16 observing his commandments, **d**,
2Ki 23: 3 keeping his commandments, his **d**,
Ps 19: 7 the **d** of the LORD are sure,
     25:10 who keep his covenant and his **d**.
    119: 2 Happy are those who keep his **d**,
    119:24 Your **d** are my delight,
    119:99 for your **d** are my meditation.
Isa 10: 1 Ah, you who make iniquitous **d**,
Ac 17: 7 They are all acting contrary to the **d**

Sir 17:12 and revealed to them his **d**.

DEDICATE → DEDICATED, DEDICATION

2Ch 2: 4 **d** it to him for offering fragrant
1Mc 4:36 cleanse the sanctuary and **d** it."

DEDICATED → DEDICATE

Nu 18: 6 now yours as a gift, **d** to the LORD,
2Sa 8:11 also King David **d** to the LORD,
1Ki 7:51 things that his father David had **d**,
     8:63 all the people of Israel **d** the house
Lk 21: 5 beautiful stones and gifts **d** to God,
1Mc 4:54 it was **d** with songs and harps and

DEDICATION → DEDICATE

Nu   7:10 offerings for the **d** of the altar
2Ch 7: 9 the **d** of the altar seven days and
Ezr 6:16 the **d** of this house of God with joy.
Ne 12:27 to celebrate the **d** with rejoicing,
Da   3: 2 to assemble and come to the **d**
Jn 10:22 the festival of the **D** took place in
1Mc 4:56 the **d** of the altar for eight days,

DEED → DO

Dt 11: 7 every great **d** that the LORD did.
Ecc 12:14 will bring every **d** into judgment,
Jer 32:10 I signed the **d**, sealed it,
Mt 19:16 good **d** must I do to have eternal life
Mk   6: 5 he could do no **d** of power there,
Lk 24:19 mighty in **d** and word before God
Col 3:17 And whatever you do, in word or **d**,
Sir 3: 8 Honor your father by word and **d**,

DEEDS → DO

Dt   3:24 in heaven or on earth can perform **d**
     34:12 the mighty **d** and all the terrifying
Ezr 9:13 has come upon us for our evil **d** and
Ps   9: 1 I will tell of all your wonderful **d**,
     26: 7 and telling all your wondrous **d**.
     28: 4 and according to the evil of their **d**;
     45: 4 your right hand teach you dread **d**.
     65: 5 By awesome **d** you answer us with
     66: 3 to God, "How awesome are your **d**!
     71:17 I still proclaim your wondrous **d**.
     75: 1 People tell of your wondrous **d**.
     77:11 will call to mind the **d** of the LORD;
     77:12 and muse on your mighty **d**.
     78: 4 the glorious **d** of the LORD,
    107:24 they saw the **d** of the LORD,
    141: 4 to busy myself with wicked **d** in
    145: 6 awesome **d** shall be proclaimed,
Ecc 1:14 the **d** that are done under the sun;
Isa 63: 7 the gracious **d** of the LORD,
Jer 50:29 Repay her according to her **d**;
La   3:64 Pay them back for their **d**, O LORD,
Hos 5: 4 Their **d** do not permit them to return
Ob   1:15 your **d** shall return on your own
Mt 13:58 did not do many **d** of power there,
Lk 10:13 For if the **d** of power done in you
     23:41 getting what we deserve for our **d**,
Jn   3:19 because their **d** were evil.
Ac   2:22 to you by God with **d** of power,
     26:20 and do **d** consistent with repentance.
Ro   2: 6 repay according to each one's **d**:
     8:13 you put to death the **d** of the body,
1Co 12:28 **d** of power, then gifts of healing,
Col 1:21 and hostile in mind, doing evil **d**,
2Ti 4:14 Lord will pay him back for his **d**.
Tit 2:14 who are zealous for good **d**.
Heb 10:24 one another to love and good **d**,
1Pe 1:17 impartially according to their **d**,
     2:12 see your honorable **d** and glorify
2Jn 1:11 is to participate in the evil **d**
Rev 14:13 from their labors, for their **d** follow
     15: 3 "Great and amazing are your **d**,
     18: 6 and repay her double for her **d**;
     19: 8 the righteous **d** of the saints.
Sir 12: 1 will be thanked for your good **d**.
     16:12 a person according to one's **d**.

DEEDS OF POWER Mt 7:22; 11:20, 21,
23; 13:54, 58; Mk 6:2; Lk 10:13; 19:37; Ac
2:11, 22; 1Co 12:28

DEEDS OF ... †LORD 1Sa 12:7; Ps 77:11;
78:4; 107:24; 118:17; Isa 5:12; 63:7

EVIL DEEDS Ezr 9:13; Ecc 4:3; Jer 11:18;
Mic 2:1; Zec 1:4; Col 1:21; 2Jn 1:11; 1Es
8:86; 2Es 1:5

GOOD DEEDS 2Ch 32:32; Ne 6:19; 13:14;
Tit 2:14; Heb 10:24; Sir 12:1; 18:15; 20:16;
3Mc 3:5

MIGHTY DEEDS Dt 34:12; Ps 71:16; 77:12;
145:12; 150:2; Sir 18:4; 36:10

REST OF THE DEEDS 2Ki 14:18; 15:11,
15, 21, 26; 20:20; 24:5; 2Ch 25:26

RIGHTEOUS DEEDS Ps 11:7; Isa 64:6;
Eze 3:20; 18:24; 33:13; Rev 19:8; Tob 2:14;
Sir 32:16; 44:10; Bar 2:19; 2Es 7:35

DEEP → DEEPEST, DEEPS, DEPTH, DEPTHS

Ge   1: 2 darkness covered the face of the **d**,
     2:21 So the LORD God caused a **d** sleep
     7:11 the fountains of the great **d** burst
     15:12 a **d** sleep fell upon Abram,
1Sa 26:12 a **d** sleep from the LORD had fallen
Job 11: 7 you find out the **d** things of God?
Ps 36: 6 your judgments are like the great **d**;
     42: 7 **D** calls to **d** at the thunder
     64: 6 For the human heart and mind are **d**.
     92: 5 Your thoughts are very **d**!
Pr   4:19 The way of the wicked is like **d**
     22:14 mouth of a loose woman is a **d** pit;
     23:27 For a prostitute is a **d** pit;
Isa 7:11 be **d** as Sheol or high as heaven.
     29:10 upon you a spirit of **d** sleep;
Eze 23:32 drink your sister's cup, **d** and wide;
Da   2:22 He reveals **d** and hidden things;
Jnh 2: 3 You cast me into the **d**, into the
Lk   5: 4 "Put out into the **d** water and let
Ac 20: 9 into a **d** sleep while Paul talked still
Ro   8:26 with sighs too **d** for words.
Rev 2:24 some call 'the **d** things of Satan,'

THE DEEP Ge 1:2; 8:2; 49:25; Dt 33:13; Job
11:7; 22:13; 28:14; 38:16, 30; 41:31, 32; Ps
69:14, 15; 78:15; 104:6; 106:9; 107:24; Pr
8:27, 28; Isa 44:27; Eze 26:19; 31:4, 15; Jnh
2:3, 5; Hab 3:10; Lk 5:4; Rev 2:24; Sir *43:23;
51:5; Man 1:3; 2Es 4:7, 8

DEEPEST → DEEP

2Pe 2: 4 them to chains of **d** darkness
Jude 1:13 the **d** darkness has been reserved
Tob 4:19 he casts down to **d** Hades.

DEEPS → DEEP

Ps 148: 7 you sea monsters and all **d**,
Pr   3:20 by his knowledge the **d** broke open,

DEER

2Sa 22:34 my feet like the feet of **d**,
Ps 42: 1 As a **d** longs for flowing streams,
Pr   5:19 a lovely **d**, a graceful doe.
Isa 35: 6 then the lame shall leap like a **d**,
Hab 3:19 my feet like the feet of a **d**,

DEFEAT → DEFEATED

Dt   7: 2 over to you and you **d** them,
Ro 11:12 if their **d** means riches for Gentiles,

DEFEATED → DEFEAT

Dt   1:42 you will be **d** by your enemies.'"
Jos 10:40 So Joshua the whole land,
     12: 1 whom the Israelites **d**,
Rev 12: 8 but they were **d**,
1Mc 5:43 All the Gentiles were **d** before him,

DEFECT·

Nu 19: 2 a red heifer without a **d**,
Dt 15:21 if it has any **d**—any serious **d**,
     17: 1 or a sheep that has a **d**,
Da   1: 4 without physical **d** and handsome,
1Pe 1:19 like that of a lamb without **d** or

DEFEND → DEFENSE, DEFENSELESS, DEFENSES

Jdg   6:31 Or will you **d** his cause?
Est   8:11 to assemble and **d** their lives,
      9:16 also gathered to **d** their lives,
Job 13:15 but I will **d** my ways to his face.
Ps   45: 4 and to **d** the right;
    72: 4 May he **d** the cause of the poor of
Pr   31: 9 **d** the rights of the poor and needy.
Isa   1:17 **d** the orphan, plead for the widow.
     1:23 They do not **d** the orphan,
Jer   5:28 do not **d** the rights of the needy.
  51:36 I am going to **d** your cause and take
Lk 12:11 about how you are to **d** yourselves
Ac   26: 1 and began to **d** himself:
Jdt   5:21 for their Lord and God will **d** them,
LtJ   6:15 but cannot **d** itself from war

DEFENSE → DEFEND

Ps 35:23 Bestir yourself for my **d,**
Lk 21:14 not to prepare your **d** in advance;
Ac   22: 1 listen to the **d** that I now make
    25: 8 Paul said in his **d,**
Php   1:16 put here for the **d** of the gospel;
1Pe 3:15 Always be ready to make your **d**

DEFENSELESS* → DEFEND

Ps 141: 8 I seek refuge; do not leave me **d.**

DEFENSES* → DEFEND

Job 13:12 your **d** are **d** of clay.
Ps 60: 1 you have rejected us, broken our **d;**

DEFERENCE → DEFERRED

Mt 22:16 and show **d** to no one;
Wis 6: 7 or show **d** to greatness;
Sir   4:22 or **d,** to your downfall.

DEFERRED* → DEFERENCE

Pr 13:12 Hope **d** makes the heart sick,

DEFIED → DEFY

1Sa 17:36 has **d** the armies of the living God."

DEFILE → DEFILED, DEFILES

Lev 11:43 you shall not **d** yourselves
Nu 35:34 You shall not **d** the land
Eze 20: 7 do not **d** yourselves with the idols
Da   1: 8 to allow him not to **d** himself.
Mt 15:20 unwashed hands does not **d."**
Mk   7:15 things that come out are what **d."**
Jude 1: 8 way these dreamers also **d** the flesh,
Jdt   9: 8 for they intend to **d** your sanctuary,
1Mc 1:46 to **d** the sanctuary and the priests,

DEFILED → DEFILE

Ge 34: 5 Shechem had **d** his daughter Dinah;
Nu   5:13 undetected though she has **d** herself,
Ps 79: 1 they have **d** your holy temple;
Eze 22: 4 **d** by the idols that you have made;
  23:13 And I saw that she was **d;**
Mk   7: 2 disciples were eating with **d** hands,
Rev 14: 4 these who have not **d** themselves
1Mc 1:37 they even **d** the sanctuary.
    4:43 removed the **d** stones to an unclean

DEFILES → DEFILE

Mt 15:11 comes out of the mouth that **d."**

DEFRAUD* → DEFRAUDED

Lev 19:13 You shall not **d** your neighbor;
Mk 10:19 You shall not **d;**
1Co 6: 8 you yourselves wrong and **d—**

DEFRAUDED → DEFRAUD

Lev 6: 2 or if you have **d** a neighbor,
1Co 6: 7 Why not rather be **d?**

DEFY → DEFIED

1Sa 17:10 "Today I **d** the ranks of Israel!

DEGENERATE*

Dt 32: 5 yet his **d** children have dealt falsely
Jer   2:21 How then did you turn **d**

DEGRADING

Ro   1:26 God gave them up to **d** passions.

DEITIES* → DEITY

Dt 32:17 to **d** they had never known,

DEITY* → DEITIES

Ac 17:29 not to think that the **d** is like gold,
Col   2: 9 whole fullness of **d** dwells bodily,

DELAY → DELAYED

Dt   7:10 He does not **d** but repays
Ps 40:17 my help and my deliverer; do not **d,**
    70: 5 my deliverer; O LORD, do not **d!**
Ecc 5: 4 a vow to God, do not **d** fulfilling it;
Da   9:19 O Lord, listen and act and do not **d!**
Hab 2: 3 it will surely come, it will not **d.**
Heb 10:37 will come and will not **d;**
Rev 10: 6 "There will be no more **d,**
Sir 35:22 Indeed, the Lord will not **d,**

DELAYED → DELAY

Mt 25: 5 As the bridegroom was **d,**
Lk 12:45 'My master is **d** in coming,'

DELIBERATE

Sir   5:11 quick to hear, but **d** in answering.

DELICACIES

Ge 49:20 and he shall provide royal **d.**
Ps 141: 4 do not let me eat of their **d.**
Pr 23: 3 Do not desire the ruler's **d,**
Jer 51:34 he has filled his belly with my **d,**
La   4: 5 Those who feasted on **d** perish in
Sir   3: 7 He will embarrass you with his **d,**

DELIGHT → DELIGHTED, DELIGHTING, DELIGHTS

Ge   3: 6 and that it was a **d** to the eyes,
Dt 28:63 took **d** in making you prosperous
    30: 9 will again take **d** in prospering you,
1Sa 15:22 "Has the LORD as great **d** in burnt
    19: 1 Jonathan took great **d** in David.
Ne   1:11 of your servants who **d** in revering
Job 22:26 you will **d** yourself in the Almighty,
    27:10 Will they take **d** in the Almighty?
Ps   1: 2 but their **d** is in the law of the LORD,
    16: 3 the noble, in whom is all my **d.**
    37: 4 Take **d** in the LORD, and he will
    40: 8 I **d** to do your will, O my God;
  51:16 For you have no **d** in sacrifice;
  51:19 then you will **d** in right sacrifices,
  68:30 scatter the peoples who **d** in war.
  111: 2 studied by all who **d** in them.
  112: 1 greatly **d** in his commandments.
  119:16 I will **d** in your statutes;
  119:24 Your decrees are my **d,** they are my
  119:35 of your commandments, for I **d** in it.
  119:47 I find my **d** in your commandments,
  119:70 but I **d** in your law.
  119:77 for your law is my **d.**
  119:92 If your law had not been my **d,**
 119:143 but your commandments are my **d.**
 119:174 O LORD, and your law is my **d.**
 147:10 His **d** is not in the strength of the
Pr   1:22 long will scoffers **d** in their scoffing
   2:14 and **d** in the perverseness of evil;
   8:30 I was daily his **d,** rejoicing before
  11: 1 but an accurate weight is his **d.**
  29:17 they will give **d** to your heart.
SS   2: 3 With great **d** I sat in his shadow,
Isa   1:11 I do not **d** in the blood of bulls,
  11: 3 **d** shall be in the fear of the LORD.
  13:17 no regard for silver and do not **d**
  55: 2 and **d** yourselves in rich food.
  58:13 a **d** and the holy day of the LORD
  62: 4 you shall be called My **D** Is in Her,
  65:18 as a joy, and its people as a **d.**
  65:19 in Jerusalem, and **d** in my people;
  66: 3 in their abominations they take **d;**
  66:11 that you may drink deeply with **d**
Jer   9:24 in these things I **d,** says the LORD.
  15:16 words became to me a joy and the **d**

DELIGHTED → DELIGHT

Dt 30: 9 he **d** in prospering your ancestors,
1Sa 18:22 'See, the king is **d** with you,
2Sa 22:20 delivered me, because he **d** in me.
2Ch 9: 8 **d** in you and set you on his throne
Ps 18:19 because he **d** in me.

DELIGHTING* → DELIGHT

Pr   8:31 and **d** in the human race.

DELIGHTS → DELIGHT

Ps   5: 4 not a God who **d** in wickedness;
   22: 8 him rescue the one in whom he **d!"**
  35:27 who **d** in the welfare of his servant."
   36: 8 them drink from the river of your **d.**
  37:23 when he **d** in our way;
Pr   3:12 as a father the son in whom he **d.**
Isa 42: 1 chosen, in whom my soul **d;**
Mic 7:18 he **d** in showing clemency.
Sir   1:12 The fear of the Lord the heart,
  26:13 A wife's charm **d** her husband,

DELILAH*

Philistine who betrayed Samson (Jdg 16:4-22).

DELIVER → DELIVERANCE, DELIVERED, DELIVERER, DELIVERS

Ex   3: 8 to **d** them from the Egyptians,
Dt 32:39 and no one can **d** from my hand.
Jdg 10:13 therefore I will **d** you no more.
Ps   6: 4 **d** me for the sake of your steadfast
  18:27 For you **d** a humble people,
  22: 8 your cause to the LORD; let him **d—**
  35:10 You **d** the weak from those
  50:15 I will **d** you, and you
 109:21 steadfast love is good, **d** me.
Ecc 8: 8 nor does wickedness **d** those who
Isa 50: 2 Or have I no power to **d?**
Jer   1: 8 for I am with you to **d** you,
Da   3:17 able to **d** us from the furnace
   6:20 able to **d** you from the lions?"
Mt 27:43 let God **d** him now,
Jdt   8:33 the Lord will **d** Israel by my hand.

DELIVERANCE → DELIVER

Ex 14:13 and see the **d** that the LORD will
Est   4:14 **d** will rise for the Jews from another
Ps   3: 8 **D** belongs to the LORD;
   32: 7 surround me with glad cries of **d.**
  53: 6 O that **d** for Israel would come
  72: 4 give **d** to the needy,
Jnh   2: 9 **D** belongs to the LORD!"
Php 1:19 this will turn out for my **d.**
Jdt   8:17 while we wait for his **d,**
1Mc 4:25 Thus Israel had a great **d** that day.

DELIVERED → DELIVER

Ex 18: 8 how the LORD had **d** them.
Jdg   2:16 raised up judges, who **d** them
Ps 18:48 you **d** me from the violent.
   22: 4 they trusted, and you **d** them.
  33:16 not **d** by his great strength.
   34: 4 and **d** me from all my fears.
 107: 6 and he **d** them from their distress;
 116: 8 For you have **d** my soul from death,
Isa 37:12 Have the gods of the nations **d**
   66: 8 Shall a nation be **d** in one moment?
Da 12: 1 at that time your people shall be **d,**
Aza 1:66 the midst of the fire he has **d** us.
1Mc 2:60 was **d** from the mouth of the lions.

DELIVERER* → DELIVER

Jdg   3: 9 LORD raised up a **d** for the Israelites,
   3:15 the LORD raised up for them a **d,**

18:28 There was no **d**, because it was far
1Sa 10:27 and would not grant Israel a **d**.
2Sa 22: 2 my rock, my fortress, and my **d**,
Ps   18: 2 my rock, my fortress, and my **d**,
      40:17 You are my help and my **d**;
      70: 5 You are my help and my **d**;
     140: 7 O LORD, my Lord, my strong **d**,
     144: 2 my stronghold and my **d**, my shield,
Ro   11:26 "Out of Zion will come the **D**;
3Mc 7:23 Blessed be the **D** of Israel

DELIVERS → DELIVER
Job 36:15 He **d** the afflicted by their affliction.
Ps   41: 1 LORD **d** them in the day of trouble.
      72:12 For he **d** the needy when they call,
     138: 7 and your right hand **d** me.
Pr   10: 2 but righteousness **d** from death.
      12: 6 the speech of the upright **d** them.
Da   6:27 He **d** and rescues, he works signs
Tob   4:10 for almsgiving **d** from death

DELUDED → DELUSION
Isa 44:20 a **d** mind has led him astray,
Eph   4:22 corrupt and **d** by its lusts,

DELUSION → DELUDED
Jer 10:15 They are worthless, a work of **d**;
2Th   2:11 God sends them a powerful **d**,

DEMAND → DEMANDED, DEMANDING
1Co 1:22 For Jews **d** signs and Greeks desire
1Ti   4: 3 and **d** abstinence from foods,

DEMANDED → DEMAND
Lk 12:20 This very night your life is being **d**
     12:48 been entrusted, even more will be **d**.
     22:31 Satan has **d** to sift all of you

DEMANDING → DEMAND
Ps 78:18 by **d** the food they craved.
Lk 11:16 kept **d** from him a sign from heaven.

DEMAS·
Associate of Paul (Col 4:14; 2Ti 4:10; Phm 24).

DEMETRIUS
Ac 19:24 A man named **D**, a silversmith
3Jn   1:12 has testified favorably about **D**,
1Mc 10: 2 When King **D** heard of it,

DEMOLISH → DEMOLISHED
Nu 33:52 and **d** all their high places.

DEMOLISHED → DEMOLISH
2Ki 10:27 Then they **d** the pillar of Baal,
2Ch 34: 4 he **d** the incense altars that stood

DEMON· → DEMONIAC, DEMONIACS,
DEMONIC, DEMONS, GOAT-DEMONS
Mt   9:33 And when the **d** had been cast out,
     11:18 and they say, 'He has a **d**';
     15:22 my daughter is tormented by a **d**."
     17:18 Jesus rebuked the **d**, and it came out
Mk   7:26 to cast the **d** out of her daughter.
      7:29 the **d** has left your daughter."
      7:30 lying on the bed, and the **d** gone.
Lk   4:33 who had the spirit of an unclean **d**,
      4:35 When the **d** had thrown him down
      7:33 and you say, 'He has a **d**';
      8:29 be driven by the **d** into the wilds.)
      9:42 the **d** dashed him to the ground in
     11:14 was casting out a **d** that was mute;
     11:14 when the **d** had gone out,
Jn   7:20 crowd answered, "You have a **d!**
      8:48 you are a Samaritan and have a **d**?"
      8:49 Jesus answered, "I do not have a **d**;
      8:52 "Now we know that you have a **d**.
     10:20 "He has a **d** and is out of his mind.
     10:21 not the words of one who has a **d**.
     10:21 Can a **d** open the eyes of the blind?"
Tob   3: 8 the wicked **d** Asmodeus had killed
      3:17 free from the wicked **d** Asmodeus.
      6: 8 of a man or woman afflicted by a **d**
      6:14 heard people saying that it was a **d**

6:16 and say no more about this **d**.
6:18 the **d** will smell it and flee,
8: 3 odor of the fish so repelled the **d**

DEMONIAC· → DEMON
Mt   9:32 a **d** who was mute was brought to
     12:22 brought to him a **d** who was blind
Mk   5:15 to Jesus and saw the **d** sitting there,
      5:16 seen what had happened to the **d**

DEMONIACS· → DEMON
Mt   4:24 **d**, epileptics, and paralytics, and he
      8:28 two **d** coming out of the tombs met
      8:33 about what had happened to the **d**.

DEMONIC· → DEMON
Rev 16:14 These are **d** spirits, performing signs

DEMONS· → DEMON
Dt 32:17 They sacrificed to **d**, not God,
Ps 106:37 and their daughters to the **d**;
Mt   7:22 and cast out **d** in your name,
      8:16 many who were possessed with **d**;
      8:31 The **d** begged him, "If you cast us
      9:34 "By the ruler of the **d** he casts out
              the **d**."
     10: 8 cleanse the lepers, cast out **d**.
     12:24 by Beelzebul, the ruler of the **d**,
              that this fellow casts out the **d**."
     12:27 If I cast out **d** by Beelzebul,
     12:28 the Spirit of God that I cast out **d**,
Mk   1:32 who were sick or possessed with **d**,
      1:34 diseases, and cast out many **d**;
      1:34 he would not permit the **d** to speak,
      1:39 their synagogues and casting out **d**.
      3:15 and to have authority to cast out **d**.
      3:22 by the ruler of the **d** he casts out **d**."
      5:18 by **d** begged him that he might be
      6:13 They cast out many **d**, and anointed
      9:38 casting out **d** in your name,
     16: 9 from whom he had cast out seven **d**.
     16:17 using my name they will cast out **d**;
Lk   4:41 **D** also came out of many, shouting,
      8: 2 from whom seven **d** had gone out,
      8:27 of the city who had **d** met him.
      8:30 "Legion"; for many **d** had entered
      8:32 the **d** begged Jesus to let them enter
      8:33 the **d** came out of the man and
      8:35 the man from whom the **d** had gone
      8:36 possessed by **d** had been healed.
      8:38 the **d** had gone begged that he
      9: 1 power and authority over all **d** and
      9:49 casting out **d** in your name,
     10:17 in your name even the **d** submit to
     11:15 "He casts out **d** by Beelzebul, the
              ruler of the **d**."
     11:18 that I cast out the **d** by Beelzebul.
     11:19 if I cast out the **d** by Beelzebul,
     11:20 finger of God that I cast out the **d**,
     13:32 I am casting out **d** and performing
1Co 10:20 they sacrifice to **d** and not to God.
     10:20 not want you to be partners with **d**.
     10:21 the cup of the Lord and the cup of **d**.
     10:21 table of the Lord and the table of **d**.
1Ti 4: 1 deceitful spirits and teachings of **d**,
Jas 2:19 Even the **d** believe—and shudder.
Rev 9:20 their hands or give up worshiping **d**
     18: 2 It has become a dwelling place of **d**,
Bar 4: 7 by sacrificing to **d** and not
      4:35 long time she will be inhabited by **d**.

DEMONSTRATE → DEMONSTRATION
Gal 2:18 then I **d** that I am a transgressor.

DEMONSTRATION → DEMONSTRATE
1Co 2: 4 with a **d** of the Spirit and of power,

DEN
Isa 11: 8 weaned child shall put its hand on
              the adder's **d**.
Jer 7:11 a **d** of robbers in your sight?
Da   6: 7 shall be thrown into a **d** of lions.
Na   2:11 What became of the lions' **d**,

Mt 21:13 you are making it a **d** of robbers."
Mk 11:17 you have made it a **d** of robbers."
Lk 19:46 you have made it a **d** of robbers."
Bel 1:31 They threw Daniel into the lions' **d**,
4Mc 18:13 praised Daniel in the **d** of the lions

DENARII → DENARIUS
Mt 18:28 slaves who owed him a hundred **d**;
Lk   7:41 one owed five hundred **d**, and the

DENARIUS· → DENARII
Mt 22:19 And they brought him a **d**.
Mk 12:15 Bring me a **d** and let me see it."
Lk 20:24 "Show me a **d**. Whose head

DENIED → DENY
Mt 26:70 But he **d** it before all of them,
Jn 18:25 He **d** it and said, "I am not."
Ac 19:36 Since these things cannot be **d**,
1Ti 5: 8 has **d** the faith and is worse than an
Rev 3: 8 my word and have not **d** my name.

DENIES· → DENY
Mt 10:33 but whoever **d** me before others,
Lk 12: 9 but whoever **d** me before others
1Jn 2:22 the liar but the one who **d** that Jesus
      2:22 one who **d** the Father and the Son.
      2:23 No one who **d** the Son has the
Sir 14: 4 What he **d** himself he collects for

DENOUNCE → DENOUNCED
Nu 23: 7 curse Jacob for me; Come, **d** Israel!'

DENOUNCED → DENOUNCE
Nu 23: 8 those whom the LORD has not **d**?
1Co 10:30 why should I be **d** because of that

DENY → DENIED, DENIES, DENYING,
SELF-DENIAL
Lev 16:29 you shall **d** yourselves,
     23:27 you shall **d** yourselves
Nu 29: 7 yourselves; you shall do no work.
Ezr 8:21 that we might **d** ourselves before
Mt 16:24 let them **d** themselves and take up
     26:34 you will **d** me three times."
Mk   8:34 let them **d** themselves and take up
Lk   9:23 let them **d** themselves and take
Ac   4:16 through the words of **d** this and
2Ti 2:12 if we **d** him, he will also **d** us;
      2:13 faithful—for he cannot **d** himself.
Tit 1:16 but they **d** him by their actions.
2Pe 2: 1 **d** the Master who bought them—
Jude 1: 4 and **d** our only Master
Rev 2:13 and you did not **d** your faith in me

DENYING· → DENY
Isa 59:13 and **d** the LORD, and turning away
2Ti 3: 5 form of godliness but **d** its power.

DEPART → DEPARTED, DEPARTURE
Ge 49:10 The scepter shall not **d** from Judah,
Jos 1: 8 law shall not **d** out of your mouth;
2Sa 12:10 the sword shall never **d** from your
Job 28:28 **d** from evil is understanding.'"
Ps 34:14 **D** from evil, and do good;
Pr   5: 7 not **d** from the words of my mouth.
Isa 52:11 **D**, **d**, go out from there!
Mt 25:41 **d** from me into the eternal fire
Jn 13: 1 hour had come to **d** from this world
Php 1:23 my desire is to **d** and be with Christ,

DEPARTED → DEPART
1Sa 4:21 "The glory has **d** from Israel,"
     16:14 the spirit of the LORD **d** from Saul,
La   1: 6 daughter Zion has **d** all her majesty.

DEPARTURE → DEPART
Lk   9:31 in glory and were speaking of his **d**,
2Ti 4: 6 and the time of my **d** has come.
2Pe 1:15 so that after my **d** you may be able

DEPEND → DEPENDS
Eze 33:26 You **d** on your swords,
Jdt 9:11 strength does not **d** on numbers,

Sir   5: 8 Do not **d** on dishonest wealth,

DEPENDS → DEPEND
Ro   4:16 For this reason it **d** on faith,
      9:16 So it **d** not on human will

DEPOSE → DEPOSES
LtJ   6:34 cannot set up a king or **d** one.

DEPOSES* → DEPOSE
Da   2:21 **d** kings and sets up kings;

DEPRAVED → DEPRAVITY
1Ti   6: 5 among those who are **d** in mind
2Pe   2:10 who indulge their flesh in **d** lust,

DEPRAVITY → DEPRAVED
Lev 20:14 that there may be no **d** among you.

DEPRIVE → DEPRIVED
Dt   24:17 not **d** a resident alien or an orphan
1Co   7: 5 not **d** one another except perhaps

DEPRIVED → DEPRIVE
Jer   5:25 and your sins have **d** you of good.

DEPTH → DEEP
Mt   13: 5 since they had no **d** of soil.
Ro   8:39 nor **d**, nor anything else in all
     11:33 O the **d** of the riches and wisdom
Eph   3:18 and length and height and **d,**

DEPTHS → DEEP
Ex   15: 5 went down into the **d** like a stone.
Ps   86:13 my soul from the **d** of Sheol.
     88: 6 put me in the **d** of the Pit,
   130: 1 Out of the **d** I cry to you, O LORD.
Pr   9:18 that her guests are in the **d** of Sheol.
1Co   2:10 even the **d** of God.

DERIDE → DERIDED, DERISION
Ps 119:51 The arrogant utterly **d** me,

DERIDED → DERIDE
Mk 15:29 Those who passed by **d** him,

DERISION → DERIDE
Ex   32:25 to the **d** of their enemies),
Ps   2: 4 the LORD has them in **d.**

DESCEND → DESCENDANT, DESCENDANTS, DESCENDED, DESCENDING
Ex   33: 9 the pillar of cloud would **d**
Dt   28:43 while you shall **d** lower and lower.
     29:20 the curses written in this book will **d**
Ro   10: 7 "or 'Who will **d** into the abyss?'"

DESCENDANT → DESCEND
Lev 21:21 No **d** of Aaron the priest who has
Ne   10:38 And the priest, the **d** of Aaron,
2Ti   2: 8 raised from the dead, a **d** of David
Rev 22:16 I am the root and the **d** of David,

DESCENDANTS → DESCEND
Ge   9: 9 with you and your **d** after you,
    15:18 saying, "To your **d** I give this land,
Ex   28:43 ordinance for him and for his **d**
Dt   4:37 he chose their **d** after them.
2Sa 22:51 to David and his **d** forever.
Ps   18:50 to David and his **d** forever.
   112: 2 Their **d** will be mighty in the land;
Isa   44: 3 I will pour my spirit upon your **d,**
Lk   1:55 to Abraham and to his **d** forever."
Ac   2:30 put one of his **d** on his throne.
Ro   9: 7 Abraham's children are his true **d;**
Gal   3: 7 who believe are the **d** of Abraham.

DESCENDANTS OF AARON Lev 6:18;
Nu 16:40; Jos 21:4, 10, 13, 19; 1Ch 15:4;
23:28, 32; 24:1, 31; 2Ch 13:9, 10; 26:18;
29:21; 31:19; 35:14, 14; Ne 12:47

DESCENDANTS OF ABRAHAM Jn
8:33, 37; 2Co 11:22; Gal 3:7; Heb 2:16; 3Mc
6:3; 4Mc 17:6

HIS DESCENDANTS Ex 28:43; 30:21; Lev
24:9; Nu 3:9, 10; 14:24; 25:13; Dt 1:36; 17:20;
2Sa 22:51; 1Ki 2:33, 33; 2Ki 8:19; 2Ch 21:7;
Ne 9:8; Est 10:3; Ps 18:50; Jer 29:32; 33:26;
35.14; Lk 1:55; Ac 2:30; 7:5, 6; Ro 4:13, 16;
Sir 44:23; 45:13, 15, 21, 24, 25; Bar 2:15; 1Es
8:47; 2Es 3:7, 15, 17, 26

THEIR DESCENDANTS Dt 1:8; 4:37;
10:15; 11:9; 23:2, 3; 31:21; 1Ki 9:21; 1Ch
9:23; 2Ch 8:8; Ne 9:23; Est 9:27, 28, 31; Ps
106:27; 112:2; Isa 61:9; 65:23; AdE 9:27, 28;
Sir 1:15; 4:16; 44:11, 12; Bar 3:21; Aza 1:13;
1Mc 1:9; 1Es 8:48, 70, 84; 3Mc 6:36; 4Mc
13:19

YOUR DESCENDANTS Ge 9:9; 15:5, 18;
26:3; Ex 32:13, 13; 33:1; Nu 9:10; 18:19; Dt
4:40; 28:46; 30:6, 19; 34:4; 1Sa 20:42; 2Ki
5:27; Job 5:25; Ps 89:4; Isa 44:3; 48:19; 54:3;
66:22; Ac 3:25; Ro 4:18; 2Mc 7:17; 1Es 8:84;
2Es 7:118

DESCENDED → DESCEND
Ex   19:18 the LORD had **d** upon it in fire;
     34: 5 LORD **d** in the cloud and stood
Lk   3:22 Holy Spirit **d** upon him in bodily
Jn   3:13 except the one who **d** from heaven,
     7:42 the Messiah is **d** from David
Ro   1: 3 was **d** from David according to the
Eph   4: 9 does it mean but that he had also **d**
Heb   7:14 that our Lord was **d** from Judah,

DESCENDING → DESCEND
Ge   28:12 angels of God were ascending and **d**
Mt   3:16 saw the Spirit of God **d** like a dove
Mk   1:10 and the Spirit **d** like a dove
Jn   1:32 the Spirit **d** from heaven like a dove,
     1:51 the angels of God ascending and **d**

DESERT → DESERTED, DESERTS
Dt   32:10 He sustained him in a **d** land,
Ps   78:17 against the Most High in the **d.**
   106:14 and put God to the test in the **d;**
Pr   21:19 It is better to live in a **d** land
Isa   35: 6 the wilderness, and streams in the **d;**
     40: 3 make straight in the **d** a highway
     51: 3 her **d** like the garden of the LORD;
Mk   8: 4 with bread here in the **d?"**

DESERTED → DESERT
Mt   26:56 all the disciples **d** him and fled.
2Ti   4:10 has **d** me and gone to Thessalonica;

DESERTS → DESERT
Zec 11:17 shepherd, who **d** the flock!
Heb 11:38 They wandered in **d** and mountains,

DESERVE → DESERVED, DESERVES, DESERVING
1Sa 26:16 As the LORD lives, you **d** to die,
1Ki   2:26 to your estate; for you **d** death.
Ps   94: 2 give to the proud what they **d!**
Pr   14:14 and the good, what their deeds **d.**
Jer   26:16 does not **d** the sentence of death,
     49:12 those who do not **d** to drink the cup
Lk   23:15 he has done nothing to **d** death.
     23:41 are getting what we **d** for our deeds,
Ac   26:31 man is doing nothing to **d** death
Ro   1:32 who practice such things **d** to die—
Rev   2:23 give to each of you as your works **d.**
     16: 6 It is what they **d!"**
Sir   8: 5 remember that we all **d** punishment.

DESERVED → DESERVE
Ezr   9:13 less than our iniquities **d**
Ro   3: 8 Their condemnation is **d!**

DESERVES → DESERVE
Dt   25: 2 If the one in the wrong **d** to be
2Sa 12: 5 the man who has done this **d** to die;
Mt   26:66 They answered, "He **d** death."
Lk   10: 7 for the laborer **d** to be paid.
1Ti   5:18 and, "The laborer **d** to be paid."

DESERVING → DESERVE
Mk 14:64 condemned him as **d** death.
Ac   23:29 nothing **d** death or imprisonment.
     25:25 that he had done nothing **d** death;

DESIGNATED
Heb   5:10 having been **d** by God a high priest

DESIGNS
Ex   31: 4 to devise artistic **d**, to work in gold,
2Co   2:11 for we are not ignorant of his **d.**

DESIRABLE → DESIRE
Pr   19:22 What is **d** in a person is loyalty,
SS   5:16 most sweet, and he is altogether **d.**

DESIRE → DESIRABLE, DESIRED, DESIRES, DESIRING
Ge   3:16 your **d** shall be for your husband,
     4: 7 its **d** is for you, but you
Dt   5:21 Neither shall you **d** your neighbor's
1Sa 19:20 And on whom is all Israel's **d** fixed,
2Sa 19:38 all that you **d** of me I will do for you
     23: 5 to prosper all my help and my **d?**
Job   13: 3 and I to argue my case with God.
     21:14 We do not **d** to know your ways.
Ps   10:17 you will hear the **d** of the meek;
     20: 4 May he grant you your heart's **d,**
     21: 2 You have given him his heart's **d,**
     40: 6 Sacrifice and offering you do not **d,**
     40:14 brought to dishonor who **d** my hurt.
     51: 6 You **d** truth in the inward being;
     70: 2 to dishonor who **d** to hurt me.
     73:25 on earth that I **d** other than you.
Pr   3:15 nothing you **d** can compare with her
     8:11 may **d** cannot compare with her.
     10:24 **d** of the righteous will be granted.
     11:23 **d** of the righteous ends only in good
     24: 1 the wicked, nor **d** to be with them;
Ecc 12: 5 drags itself along and **d** fails;
SS   7:10 my beloved's, and his **d** is for me.
Isa   26: 8 and your renown are the soul's **d.**
     53: 2 appearance that we should **d** him.
Hos   6: 6 I **d** steadfast love and not sacrifice,
Am   5:18 who **d** the day of the LORD!
Mic   7: 3 the powerful dictate what they **d;**
Mal   2:15 And what does the one God **d?**
Mt   9:13 learn what this means, 'I **d** mercy,
     12: 7 'I **d** mercy and not sacrifice,'
Ro   10: 1 my heart's **d** and prayer to God for
2Co   8:10 but even to **d** to do something—
Php   1:23 my **d** is to depart and be with Christ,
Heb 11:16 they **d** a better country, that is,
Jas   1:14 But one is tempted by one's own **d,**
     1:15 **d** has conceived, it gives birth to sin
1Pe   3:10 who **d** life and to see good days,
1Jn   2:16 the **d** of the flesh, the **d** of the eyes,
Sir   6:37 **d** for wisdom will be granted.

DESIRED → DESIRE
Ge   3: 6 was to be **d** to make one wise,
1Ki   9: 1 and all that Solomon **d** to build,
Ps   19:10 More to be **d** are they than gold,
     68:16 the mount that God **d** for his abode,
Ecc   2:10 my eyes **d** I did not keep from them;
Lk   22:15 I have eagerly **d** to eat this Passover
Tob   3:17 who had **d** to marry her.
Jdt 16:22 Many **d** to marry her,

DESIRES → DESIRE
Dt   12: 8 all of us according to our own **d,**
2Sa   3:21 reign over all that your heart **d."**
1Ki 11:37 shall reign over all that your soul **d;**
Job 17:11 are broken off, the **d** of my heart.
Ps   34:12 of you **d** life, and covets many days
     37: 4 he will give you the **d** of your heart.
   140: 8 O LORD, the **d** of the wicked;
Lk   5:39 after drinking old wine **d** new wine,
Jn   8:44 you choose to do your father's **d.**
Ro   13:14 for the flesh, to gratify its **d.**
Gal   5:16 do not gratify the **d** of the flesh.
Eph   2: 3 following the **d** of flesh and senses,
1Ti   2: 4 who **d** everyone to be saved

3: 1 aspires to the office of bishop **d**
5:11 sensual **d** alienate them from Christ,
6: 9 by many senseless and harmful **d**
2Ti 3: 6 sins and swayed by all kinds of **d,**
4: 3 teachers to suit their own **d,**
1Pe 1:14 not be conformed to the **d** that you
2:11 the **d** of the flesh that wage war
4: 2 earthly life no longer by human **d**
2Pe 2:18 and with licentious **d** of
Sir 18:30 Do not follow your base **d,**

DESIRING → DESIRE
Ro 9:22 What if God, **d** to show his wrath
Heb 13:18 **d** to act honorably in all things.

DESOLATE → DESOLATED,
DESOLATES, DESOLATING, DESOLATION,
DESOLATIONS, DESOLATOR
Ex 23:29 or the land would become **d** and
Isa 1: 7 it is **d,** as overthrown by foreigners.
54: 1 of the **d** woman will be more than
Eze 14:15 so that it is made **d,**
Da 8:13 the transgression that makes **d,**
11:31 the abomination that makes **d.**
Mt 23:38 See, your house is left to you, **d.**
Rev 17:16 they will make her **d** and naked;
1Mc 1:39 sanctuary became **d** like a desert;
4:38 There they saw the sanctuary **d,**
2Es 16:23 for the earth shall be left **d,**

DESOLATED → DESOLATE
Da 9:17 face shine upon your **d** sanctuary.

DESOLATES* → DESOLATE
Da 9:27 shall be an abomination that **d,**
12:11 and the abomination that **d** is set up,

DESOLATING* → DESOLATE
Mt 24:15 the **d** sacrilege standing in the holy
Mk 13:14 the **d** sacrilege set up where it ought
1Mc 1:54 erected a **d** sacrilege on the altar

DESOLATION → DESOLATE
Lev 26:33 your land shall be a **d,**
Isa 13: 9 to make the earth a **d,**
Jer 4:27 The whole land shall be a **d;**
Eze 12:20 and the land shall become a **d;**
Na 2:10 Devastation, **d,** and destruction!
Lk 21:20 then know that its **d** has come near.

DESOLATIONS* → DESOLATE
Ps 46: 8 what **d** he has brought on the earth.
Da 9:26 there shall be war. **D** are decreed.

DESOLATOR* → DESOLATE
Da 9:27 end is poured out upon the **d."**

DESPAIR → DESPAIRED
2Co 4: 8 perplexed, but not driven to **d;**

DESPAIRED* → DESPAIR
2Co 1: 8 crushed that we **d** of life itself.

DESPISE → DESPISED, DESPISES,
DESPISING
Nu 14:11 "How long will this people **d** me?
Job 5:17 not **d** the discipline of the Almighty.
36: 5 God is mighty and does not **d** any;
42: 6 I **d** myself, and repent in dust
Ps 51:17 contrite heart, O God, you will not **d**
102:17 and will not **d** their prayer.
Pr 1: 7 fools **d** wisdom and instruction.
3:11 do not **d** the LORD's discipline or
15:32 ignore instruction **d** themselves,
23:22 not **d** your mother when she is old.
Mt 6:24 devoted to the one and **d** the other.
Lk 16:13 devoted to the one and **d** the other.
Ro 2: 4 do you **d** the riches of his kindness
14:10 why do you **d** your brother or sister?
2Pe 2:10 depraved lust, and who **d** authority.

DESPISED → DESPISE
Ge 25:34 Thus Esau **d** his birthright.
2Sa 6: 16 and she **d** him in her heart.

Ps 22: 6 by others, and **d** by the people.
106:24 Then they **d** the pleasant land,
Pr 12: 8 but a perverse mind is **d,**
Ecc 9:16 yet the poor man's wisdom is **d,**
Isa 53: 3 He was **d** and rejected by others;
Mal 1: 6 "How have we **d** your name?"
1Co 1:28 God chose what is low and **d** in the

DESPISES → DESPISE
Pr 15: 5 A fool **d** a parent's instruction,

DESPISING → DESPISE
Dt 31:20 **d** me and breaking my covenant.
2Ch 36:16 **d** his words, and scoffing at his

DESTINE* → DESTINED, DESTINY
Isa 65:12 I will **d** you to the sword, and all

DESTINED → DESTINE
Jer 15: 2 those **d** for captivity, to captivity.
43:11 are **d** for the sword, to the sword.
Lk 2:34 "This child is **d** for the falling and
Jn 17:12 except the one **d** to be lost,
Ac 13:48 as had been **d** for eternal life
Eph 1: 5 He **d** us for adoption as his children
1:11 been **d** according to the purpose
1Th 3: 3 that this is what we are **d** for.
5: 9 For God has **d** us not for wrath but
2Th 2: 3 the one **d** for destruction.
1Pe 1: 2 chosen and **d** by God the Father
1:11 to the sufferings **d** for Christ
1:20 He was **d** before the foundation of
2: 8 as they were **d** to do.

DESTINY* → DESTINE
Isa 65:11 and fill cups of mixed wine for **D;**

DESTITUTE
Ps 102:17 He will regard the prayer of the **d,**
Pr 31: 8 for the rights of all the **d.**
Heb 11:37 about in skins of sheep and goats, **d,**

DESTROY → DESTROYED, DESTROYER,
DESTROYERS, DESTROYING, DESTROYS,
DESTRUCTION, DESTRUCTIVE
Ge 6:13 to **d** them along with the earth.
9:11 shall there be a flood to **d** the earth."
18:28 Will you **d** the whole city for lack
Dt 6:15 against you and he would **d** you
7: 2 then you must utterly **d** them.
1Sa 15: 9 and would not utterly **d** them;
2Ki 8:19 Yet the LORD would not **d** Judah,
13:23 and Jacob, and would not **d** them;
1Ch 21:15 sent an angel to Jerusalem to **d** it;
Est 3: 6 Haman plotted to **d** all the Jews,
Ps 145:20 but all the wicked he will **d.**
Isa 11: 9 hurt or **d** on all my holy mountain;
65: 8 "Do not **d** it, for there is a blessing
65:25 hurt or **d** on all my holy mountain,
Jer 1:10 to **d** and to overthrow, to build
Hos 11: 9 I will not again **d** Ephraim;
Mt 2:13 for the child, to **d** him."
10:28 rather fear him who can **d** both soul
Mk 14:58 'I will **d** this temple that is made
Lk 4:34 Have you come to **d** us?
Jn 10:10 comes only to steal and kill and **d.**
1Co 1:19 "I will **d** the wisdom of the wise,
3:17 destroys God's temple, God will **d**
Jas 4:12 who is able to save and to **d.**
1Jn 3: 8 to **d** the works of the devil.
Rev 11:18 destroying those who **d** the earth."

DESTROYED → DESTROY
Ge 19:29 when God **d** the cities of the Plain,
Dt 28:20 until you are **d** and perish quickly,
Jos 24: 8 their land, and I **d** them before you.
Est 7: 4 I and my people, to be **d,**
Job 19:26 and after my skin has been thus **d,**
Ps 37:38 transgressors shall be altogether **d;**
Da 2:44 a kingdom that shall never be **d,**
6:26 His kingdom shall never be **d,**
7:11 its body **d** and given over to be
Hos 4: 6 people are **d** for lack of knowledge;

Lk 17:27 the flood came and **d** all of them.
1Co 8:11 for whom Christ died are **d.**
15:24 after he has **d** every ruler and every
15:26 The last enemy to be **d** is death.
2Co 4: 9 struck down, but not **d;**
5: 1 if the earthly tent we live in is **d,**
2Pe 2:12 and when those creatures are **d,**
they also will be **d,**
Jude 1: 5 **d** those who did not believe.
Jdt 13:14 has **d** our enemies by my hand
Bel 1:28 he has **d** Bel, and killed the dragon,
1Mc 1:30 and **d** many people of Israel.
3: 8 he **d** the ungodly out of the land;

DESTROYER → DESTROY
Ex 12:23 not allow the **d** to enter your houses
Jer 6:26 suddenly the **d** will come upon us.
1Co 10:10 and were destroyed by the **d.**
Heb 11:28 that the **d** of the firstborn would not

DESTROYERS → DESTROY
Jer 15: 3 appoint over them four kinds of **d,**

DESTROYING → DESTROY
2Sa 24:17 the angel who was **d** the people,
Ps 106:23 to turn away his wrath from **d** them.
Rev 11:18 for **d** those who destroy the earth."

DESTROYS → DESTROY
Pr 1:32 complacency of fools **d** them;
6:32 he who does it **d** himself.
Ecc 9:18 but one bungler **d** much good.
Lk 12:33 no thief comes near and no moth **d.**
1Co 3:17 If anyone **d** God's temple,
Sir 22:20 reviles a friend **d** a friendship.
27:16 betrays secrets **d** confidence,

DESTRUCTION → DESTROY
Jos 6:17 shall be devoted to the LORD for **d.**
1Sa 15:21 the best of the things devoted to **d,**
Ps 107:20 and delivered them from **d.**
Pr 10:29 but **d** for evildoers.
16:18 Pride goes before **d,** and a haughty
Isa 10:22 **D** is decreed, overflowing with
13: 6 come like **d** from the Almighty!
14:23 sweep it with the broom of **d,**
Hos 13:14 O Sheol, where is your **d?**
Joel 1:15 as **d** from the Almighty it comes.
Hab 2:17 the **d** of the animals will terrify you
Mt 7:13 and the road is easy that leads to **d,**
Ro 9:22 objects of wrath that are made for **d;**
1Co 5: 5 to Satan for the **d** of the flesh,
Php 1:28 For them this is evidence of their **d,**
3:19 Their end is **d;** their god is the belly;
1Th 5: 3 then sudden **d** will come upon them,
2Th 1: 9 suffer the punishment of eternal **d,**
2: 3 is revealed, the one destined for **d.**
1Ti 6: 9 that plunge people into ruin and **d.**
2Pe 2: 1 bringing swift **d** on themselves.
2: 3 and their **d** is not asleep.
3: 7 of judgment and **d** of the godless.
3:16 and unstable twist to their own **d,**
Rev 17: 8 from the bottomless pit and go to **d.**
17:11 to the seven, and it goes to **d.**
Sir 36:11 who harm your people meet **d.**
51:12 for you saved me from **d**

DESTRUCTIVE → DESTROY
2Pe 2: 1 will secretly bring in **d** opinions.

DETAIL
Heb 9: 5 we cannot speak now in **d.**

DETERMINED → DETERMINES
Ge 6:13 to make an end of all flesh,
Ru 1:18 that she was **d** to go with her,
Job 14: 5 Since their days are **d,** and the
38: 5 Who **d** its measurements—surely
Jer 44:11 I am **d** to bring disaster on you,
Da 6:14 He was **d** to save Daniel,
11:36 for what is **d** shall be done.
1Mc 4:59 **d** that every year at that season

DETERMINES* → DETERMINED
Ps 147: 4 He **d** the number of the stars;

DETEST → DETESTABLE, DETESTED
Nu 21: 5 and we **d** this miserable food."
Dt 7:26 You must utterly **d** and abhor it,

DETESTABLE → DETEST
Lev 11:43 not make yourselves **d** with any
Hos 9:10 became **d** like the thing they loved.
Tit 1:16 **d**, disobedient, unfit for any good

DETESTED → DETEST
Zec 11: 8 with them, and they also **d** me.
Sir 20: 8 Whoever talks too much is **d**,

DEVASTATE → DEVASTATION
Lev 26:32 I will **d** the land,
Zec 11: 6 and they shall **d** the earth,

DEVASTATION → DEVASTATE
Dt 29:22 will see the **d** of that land
Na 2:10 **D**, desolation, and destruction!
Zep 1:15 a day of ruin and **d**,

DEVIATED*
1Ti 1: 6 Some people have **d** from these

DEVICES → DEVISE
Job 5:12 He frustrates the **d** of the crafty,
Ps 37: 7 over those who carry out evil **d**.

DEVIL* → DEVIL'S, DEVILISH
Mt 4: 1 wilderness to be tempted by the **d**.
     4: 5 the **d** took him to the holy city and
     4: 8 the **d** took him to a very high
     4:11 the **d** left him, and suddenly angels
    13:39 enemy who sowed them is the **d**;
    25:41 eternal fire prepared for the **d** and
Lk 4: 2 forty days he was tempted by the **d**.
     4: 3 The **d** said to him, "If you are the
     4: 5 the **d** led him up and showed him
     4: 6 the **d** said to him, "To you I will
     4: 9 Then the **d** took him to Jerusalem,
     4:13 When the **d** had finished every test,
     8:12 **d** comes and takes away the word
Jn 6:70 Yet one of you is a **d**."
     8:44 You are from your father the **d**,
    13: 2 **d** had already put it into the heart
Ac 10:38 all who were oppressed by the **d**,
    13:10 **d**, you enemy of all righteousness,
Eph 4:27 and do not make room for the **d**.
     6:11 to stand against the wiles of the **d**.
1Ti 3: 6 fall into the condemnation of the **d**.
     3: 7 into disgrace and the snare of the **d**,
2Ti 2:26 may escape from the snare of the **d**,
Heb 2:14 the power of death, that is, the **d**,
Jas 4: 7 Resist the **d**, and he will flee from
1Pe 5: 8 lion your adversary the **d** prowls
1Jn 3: 8 who commits sin is a child of the **d**;
     3: 8 the **d** has been sinning from the
     3: 8 to destroy the works of the **d**.
     3:10 the children of the **d** are revealed in
Jude 1: 9 Michael contended with the **d**
Rev 2:10 the **d** is about to throw some of you
    12: 9 who is called the **D** and Satan,
    12:12 the **d** has come down to you with
    20: 2 that ancient serpent, who is the **D**
    20:10 And the **d** who had deceived them

DEVIL'S* → DEVIL
Wis 2:24 through the **d** envy death entered

DEVILISH* → DEVIL
Jas 3:15 but is earthly, unspiritual, **d**.

DEVIOUS* → DEVISE
Pr 2:15 and who are **d** in their ways.
     4:24 and put **d** talk far from you.
    14: 2 who is **d** in conduct despises him.
Jer 17: 9 The heart is **d** above all else;

DEVISE → DEVICES, DEVIOUS, DEVISED, DEVISES, DEVISING
Ex 31: 4 to **d** artistic designs,
Pr 12: 2 but those who **d** evil he condemns.
    19:21 human mind may **d** many plans,
Sir 13:26 **d** proverbs requires painful thinking

DEVISED → DEVISE
Est 8: 5 to revoke the letters **d** by Haman
Ps 10: 2 caught in the schemes they have **d**.
Mt 28:12 they **d** a plan to give a large sum of
2Pe 1:16 we did not follow cleverly **d** myths

DEVISES* → DEVISE
Pr 6:18 a heart that **d** wicked plans,

DEVISING → DEVISE
Pr 6:14 with perverted mind **d** evil,
    24: 9 The **d** of folly is sin,
Jer 18:11 and **d** a plan against you.

DEVOID
Job 4:21 and they die **d** of wisdom.'
Jude 1:19 worldly people, **d** of the Spirit,

DEVOTE → DEVOTED, DEVOTING, DEVOTION
2Ch 31: 4 they might **d** themselves to the law
Mic 4:13 and shall **d** their gain to the LORD,
1Co 7: 5 to **d** yourselves to prayer,
Col 4: 2 **D** yourselves to prayer, keeping
Tit 3: 8 to **d** themselves to good works;
     3:14 to **d** themselves to good works in

DEVOTED → DEVOTE
Ex 22:20 shall be **d** to destruction.
Lev 27:28 **d** thing is most holy to the LORD.
Jos 6:18 from the things **d** to destruction,
     7: 1 broke faith in regard to the **d** things:
Ne 5:16 I **d** myself to the work on this wall,
Ps 86: 2 Preserve my life, for I am **d** to you;
Mt 6:24 **d** to the one and despise the other.
Ac 2:42 They **d** themselves to the apostles'
     9:36 She was **d** to good works and acts
1Co 16:15 have **d** themselves to the service of
1Mc 4:42 chose blameless priests **d** to the law,

DEVOTING → DEVOTE
Ac 1:14 constantly **d** themselves to prayer,

DEVOTION → DEVOTE
1Ch 29: 3 because of my **d** to the house of my
Est 2:17 the virgins she won his favor and **d**,
Jer 2: 2 I remember the **d** of your youth,
Ac 11:23 faithful to the Lord with steadfast **d**;
1Co 7:35 good order and unhindered **d** to
2Co 11: 3 astray from a sincere and pure **d** to
Jdt 8: 8 for she feared God with great **d**.

DEVOUR → DEVOURED, DEVOURING, DEVOURS
2Ch 7:13 or command the locust to **d** the land,
Jer 46:10 The sword shall **d** and be sated,
Hos 13: 8 there I will **d** them like a lion,
Mk 12:40 They **d** widows' houses and for the
Gal 5:15 you bite and **d** one another,
1Pe 5: 8 looking for someone to **d**.
Rev 12: 4 that he might **d** her child
Bel 1:32 so that they would **d** Daniel.

DEVOURED → DEVOUR
Ge 37:20 that a wild animal has **d** him,
Isa 1:20 you shall be **d** by the sword;
Jer 30:16 all who devour you shall be **d**,

DEVOURING → DEVOUR
Ex 24:17 glory of the LORD was like a **d** fire
Dt 9: 3 crosses over before you as a **d** fire;
Ps 18: 8 and **d** fire from his mouth;
    50: 3 before him is a **d** fire,
Isa 33:14 among us can live with the **d** fire?

DEVOURS → DEVOUR
2Sa 11:25 for the sword **d** now one

Pr 21:20 house of the wise, but the fool **d** it.

DEVOUT
Isa 57: 1 the **d** are taken away,
Lk 2:25 this man was righteous and **d**,
Ac 10: 2 a **d** man who feared God with all
    10: 7 two of his slaves and a **d** soldier
    13:43 **d** converts to Judaism followed Paul
    13:50 the Jews incited the **d** women of
    17: 4 the **d** Greeks and not a few of the
    17:17 with the Jews and the **d** persons,
    22:12 a **d** man according to the law and
Tit 1: 8 of goodness, prudent, upright, **d**,
Sir 12: 4 Give to the **d**, but do not help the

DEW → DEWS
Ge 27:28 God give you of the **d** of heaven,
Ex 16:13 there was a layer of **d** around
Dt 32: 2 my speech condense like the **d**;
Jdg 6:37 if there is **d** on the fleece alone,
2Sa 1:21 no **d** or rain upon you,
Job 38:28 or who has begotten the drops of **d**?
Pr 19:12 but his favor is like **d** on the grass.
Isa 26:19 For your **d** is a radiant **d**,
Da 4:15 bathed with the **d** of heaven.
Hos 6: 4 like the **d** that goes away early.
    14: 5 I will be like the **d** to Israel;
Hag 1:10 above you have withheld the **d**,
Zec 8:12 and the skies shall give their **d**;
Aza 1:42 "Bless the Lord, all rain and **d**;

DIADEM → DIADEMS
Ex 39:30 rosette of the holy **d** of pure gold,
Isa 62: 3 a royal **d** in the hand of your God.

DIADEMS* → DIADEM
Rev 12: 3 and seven **d** on his heads.
    13: 1 and on its horns were ten **d**,
    19:12 and on his head are many **d**;

DIAL
2Ki 20:11 sun had declined on the **d** of Ahaz.

DICTATED* → DICTATION
Jer 36:18 "He **d** all these words to me,
2Es 14:42 and by turns they wrote what was **d**,

DICTATION → DICTATED
Jer 36: 4 wrote on a scroll at Jeremiah's **d**
    45: 1 in a scroll at the **d** of Jeremiah,

DIDYMUS See TWIN

DIE → DEAD
Ge 2:17 eat of it you shall **d**."
     3: 3 touch it, or you shall **d**.'"
     3: 4 to the woman, "You will not **d**;
Ex 11: 5 firstborn in the land of Egypt shall **d**
    14:11 that you have taken us away to **d** in
Nu 23:10 Let me **d** the death of the upright,
Ru 1:17 Where you **d**, I will **d**—there will I
Job 2: 9 Curse God, and **d**."
    12: 2 and wisdom will **d** with you.
    14:14 If mortals **d**, will they live again?
Ps 118:17 I shall not **d**, but I shall live,
Pr 5:23 They **d** for lack of discipline,
    10:21 but fools **d** for lack of sense.
    15:10 but one who hates a rebuke will **d**.
    23:13 with a rod, they will not **d**.
Ecc 2:16 How can the wise **d** just like fools?
     3: 2 a time to be born, and a time to **d**;
Isa 22:13 eat and drink, for tomorrow we **d**."
    66:24 for their worm shall not **d**,
Jer 31:30 But all shall **d** for their own sins;
Eze 3:18 persons shall **d** for their iniquity;
    18: 4 the person who sins that shall **d**.
    18:31 Why will you **d**, O house of Israel?
    33: 8 the wicked shall **d** in their iniquity,
Jnh 4: 3 take away my life, for it is better for me to **d** than
     4: 8 "It is better for me to **d** than
Hab 1:12 my Holy One? You shall not **d**.
Mt 26:35 "Even though I must **d** with you,
Jn 6:50 so that one may eat of it and not **d**.
     8:21 but you will **d** in your sin.

11:26 and believes in me will never **d**.
11:50 to have one man **d** for the people
12:33 the kind of death he was to **d**.
18:14 it was better to have one person **d**
21:23 not say to him that he would not **d**,
Ro   5: 7 someone might actually dare to **d**.
       14: 8 if we **d**, we **d** to the Lord;
1Co 15:22 for as all **d** in Adam,
       15:31 I **d** every day!
       15:32 eat and drink, for tomorrow we **d**."
Heb   9:27 it is appointed for mortals to **d** once,
Rev   9: 6 will long to **d**, but death will flee
       14:13 are the dead who from now on **d** in
Tob   3: 6 For it is better for me to **d**
Sir   8: 7 remember that we must all **d**.
       40:28 it is better to **d** than to beg.

DIED → DEAD

Ge   7:21 And all flesh **d** that
Nu   14: 2 that we had **d** in the land of Egypt!
       16:49 Those who **d** by the plague were
2Sa 24:15 seventy thousand of the people **d**,
1Ki   3:19 this woman's son **d** in the night,
1Ch 10:13 So Saul **d** for his unfaithfulness;
Lk   16:22 The poor man **d** and was carried
       16:22 The rich man also **d** and was buried.
Jn   6:58 your ancestors ate, and they **d**.
Ro   5: 6 right time Christ **d** for the ungodly.
       5: 8 while we still were sinners Christ **d**
       6: 2 can we who **d** to sin go on living in
       6: 8 But if we have **d** with Christ,
       6:10 The death he **d**, he **d** to sin, once
       14: 9 to this end Christ **d** and lived again,
1Co   8:11 for whom Christ **d** are destroyed.
       15: 3 Christ **d** for our sins in accordance
2Co   5:15 And he **d** for all,
Gal   2:19 the law I **d** to the law,
Col   2:20 with Christ you **d** to the elemental
       3: 3 you have **d**, and your life is hidden
1Th   4:14 we believe that Jesus **d** and rose
       5:10 who **d** for us, so that whether we
2Ti   2:11 we have **d** with him, we will also
Heb 11:13 All of these **d** in faith without
Rev   8: 9 of the living creatures in the sea **d**,
       8:11 and many **d** from the water,
       16: 3 and every living thing in the sea **d**.

DIES → DEAD

Dt   14:21 not eat anything that **d** of itself;
       25: 5 and one of them **d** and has no son,
Ecc   3:19 as one **d**, so **d** the other.
Mt   22:24 Moses said, 'If a man **d** childless,
Mk   9:48 where their worm never **d**,
Jn   12:24 but if it **d**, it bears much fruit.
Ro   7: 2 if her husband **d**, she is discharged
1Co   7:39 But if the husband **d**, she is free
       15:36 does not come to life unless it **d**.
Sir 14:18 one **d** and another is born.

DIFFER → DIFFERENCE, DIFFERENT, DIFFERENTLY, DIFFERING, DIFFERS

Ro   12: 6 gifts that **d** according to the grace

DIFFERENCE → DIFFER

2Ch 12: 8 know the **d** between serving me
Eze 22:26 neither have they taught the **d**
       44:23 They shall teach my people the **d**

DIFFERENT → DIFFER

Lev 19:19 your animals breed with a **d** kind;
       19:19 a garment made of two **d** materials.
Nu   14:24 he has a **d** spirit and has followed
1Sa 10: 6 and be turned into a **d** person.
1Ki 18:21 go limping with two **d** opinions?
Est   3: 8 their laws are **d** from those of every
Da   7: 3 beasts came up out of the sea, **d**
       7: 7 It was **d** from all the beasts that
       7:19 which was **d** from all the rest,
       7:23 kingdom on earth that shall be **d**
       7:24 one shall be **d** from the former ones,
1Co   4: 7 For who sees anything **d** in you?
2Co 11: 4 or a **d** gospel from the one you
Gal   1: 6 and are turning to a **d** gospel—

1Ti   1: 3 not to teach any **d** doctrine,
Sir 38:34 How **d** the one who devotes himself

DIFFERENTLY → DIFFER

Php   3:15 and if you think **d** about anything,

DIFFERING* → DIFFER

Pr   20:23 **D** weights are an abomination to

DIFFERS* → DIFFER

1Co 15:41 indeed, star **d** from star in glory.

DIFFICULT

Dt   17: 8 If a judicial decision is too **d** for you
Eze   3: 5 of obscure speech and **d** language,
Da   2:11 thing that the king is asking is too **d**,
       4: 9 and that no mystery is too **d**
Jn   6:60 teaching is **d**; who can accept it?"
Sir   3:21 Neither seek what is too **d** for you,

DIG → DIGS, DUG

Job   3:21 and **d** for it more than for hidden
Eze   8: 8 **d** through the wall";
Am   9: 2 Though they **d** into Sheol,

DIGNITY

Est   4:14 royal **d** for just such a time as this."
Pr   31:25 Strength and **d** are her clothing,
1Ti   2: 2 peaceable life in all godliness and **d**.
AdE   6: 3 **d** did we bestow on Mordecai?"

DIGS* → DIG

Ex   21:33 or **d** a pit and does not cover it,
Pr   26:27 Whoever **d** a pit will fall into it,
Ecc 10: 8 Whoever **d** a pit will fall into it;
Sir 27:26 Whoever **d** a pit will fall into it,

DILIGENCE → DILIGENT

Ro   12: 8 the leader, in **d**;
Heb   6:11 each one of you to show the same **d**
Sir 11:18 rich through **d** and self-denial,

DILIGENT → DILIGENCE, DILIGENTLY

Pr   10: 4 but the hand of the **d** makes rich.
       12:24 The hand of the **d** will rule,
       12:27 but the **d** obtain precious wealth.
       13: 4 appetite of the **d** is richly supplied.
       21: 5 The plans of the **d** lead surely to

DILIGENTLY → DILIGENT

Dt   4: 6 You must observe them **d**,
       6: 3 O Israel, and observe them **d**,
       28:58 do not **d** observe all the words of
Pr   1:28 they will seek me **d**,
       8:17 and those who seek me **d** find me.
Zec   6:15 if you **d** obey the voice of the LORD
Mt   2: 8 "Go and search **d** for the child;

DIM → DIMLY

Ge   27: 1 eyes were **d** so that he could not see,
       48:10 the eyes of Israel were **d** with age,
1Sa   3: 2 whose eyesight had begun to grow **d**
1Ki 14: 4 his eyes were **d** because of his age.
Job 17: 7 My eye has grown **d** from grief,
La   5:17 our eyes have grown **d**:

DIMLY → DIM

1Co 13:12 For now we see in a mirror, **d**,

DINAH*

Only daughter of Jacob, by Leah (Ge 30:21; 46:15). Raped by Shechem; avenged by Simeon and Levi (Ge 34).

DINE → DINED, DINNER

Lk   11:37 Pharisee invited him to **d** with him;

DINED → DINE

2Ki 25:29 **d** regularly in the king's presence.

DINNER → DINE

Pr   15:17 Better is a **d** of vegetables where
Mk   2:15 And as he sat at **d** in Levi's house,
Lk   14:12 "When you give a luncheon or a **d**,
Sir   9:16 righteous be your **d** companions,

DIONYSIUS*

Ac   17:34 including **D** the Areopagite

DIONYSUS

2Mc   6: 7 when a festival of **D** was celebrated,
       14:33 build here a splendid temple to **D**."

DIOTREPHES*

3Jn   1: 9 but **D**, who likes to put himself first,

DIP → DIPPED

Ex   12:22 **d** it in the blood that is in the basin,
Lev   4: 6 priest shall **d** his finger in the blood
Lk   16:24 Lazarus to **d** the tip of his finger

DIPPED → DIP

Ge   37:31 and **d** the robe in the blood.
Mt   26:23 "The one who has **d** his hand into
Rev 19:13 He is clothed in a robe **d** in blood,

DIRECT → DIRECTED, DIRECTION, DIRECTIONS, DIRECTS

Job 11:13 "If you **d** your heart rightly,
Ps 119:128 I **d** my steps by all your precepts;
Jer 10:23 as they walk cannot **d** their steps.
2Th   3: 5 the Lord **d** your hearts to the love
Jdt 12: 8 the Lord God of Israel to **d** her way
Sir 37:15 Most High that he may **d** your way

DIRECTED → DIRECT

Isa 40:13 Who has **d** the spirit of the LORD,
Mt   26:19 So the disciples did as Jesus had **d**
Ac   7:44 as God **d** when he spoke to Moses,
Tit   1: 5 in every town, as I **d** you:
1Mc   1:44 he **d** them to follow customs strange

DIRECTION → DIRECT

Jos   9:14 and did not ask **d** from the LORD.
1Ch 28:19 in writing at the LORD's **d**,

DIRECTIONS → DIRECT

Eze   1:17 they moved in any of the four **d**
       10:11 they moved in any of the four **d**

DIRECTS* → DIRECT

Pr   16: 9 but the LORD **d** the steps.
Jas   3: 4 wherever the will of the pilot **d**.
1Mc   4:47 unhewn stones, as the law **d**,
       4:53 and offered sacrifice, as the law **d**,

DIRT → DIRTY

2Sa   1: 2 his clothes torn and **d** on his head.
1Pe   3:21 not as a removal of **d** from the body,

DIRTY → DIRT

Jas   2: 2 and if a poor person in **d** clothes

DISAGREEMENT

Ac   15:39 The **d** became so sharp that they

DISAPPEAR → DISAPPEARED

Heb   8:13 and growing old will soon **d**.
Jas   1:10 rich will **d** like a flower in the field.

DISAPPEARED → DISAPPEAR

Nu   32:13 evil in the sight of the LORD had **d**.
Ps   12: 1 the faithful have **d** from humankind.
Mic   7: 2 The faithful have **d** from the land,
Jn   5:13 for Jesus had **d** in the crowd

DISAPPOINT* → DISAPPOINTED

Ro   5: 5 and hope does not **d** us,

DISAPPOINTED → DISAPPOINT

Sir   2:10 trusted in the Lord and been **d**?
       51:18 and I shall never be **d**.

DISARMED*

Col   2:15 He **d** the rulers and authorities

DISASTER → DISASTERS

Ex   32:12 your mind and do not bring **d**
Dt   28:20 The LORD will send upon you **d**,
Ne   13:18 our God bring all this **d** on us
Jer   4:20 **D** overtakes **d**, the whole land is

17:17 you are my refuge in the day of **d**;
18: 8 I will change my mind about the **d**
26: 3 I may change my mind about the **d**
Eze 7: 5 Thus says the Lord GOD: **D** after **d!**
Am 3: 6 Does **d** befall a city, unless
Zep 3:15 you shall fear **d** no more.
Sir 29:12 and it will rescue you from every **d**;

DISASTERS → DISASTER
Dt 32:23 I will heap **d** upon them,

DISCERN → DISCERNED, DISCERNING, DISCERNMENT
Dt 32:29 would **d** what the end would be.
Job 6:30 Cannot my taste **d** calamity?

DISCERNED → DISCERN
1Co 2:14 because they are spiritually **d**.

DISCERNING· → DISCERN
Ge 41:33 a man who is **d** and wise,
41:39 there is no one so **d** and wise as you.
Dt 1:13 **d**, and reputable to be your leaders."
4: 6 nation is a wise and **d** people!"
2Sa 14:17 like the angel of God, **d** good and
1Ki 3:12 I give you a wise and **d** mind;
Pr 1: 5 in learning, and the **d** acquire skill,
17:10 A rebuke strikes deeper into a **d**
17:24 The **d** person looks to wisdom,
Isa 29:14 of the **d** shall be hidden.
Hos 14: 9 those who are **d** know them.
1Co 1:19 discernment of the **d** I will thwart."
11:29 eat and drink without **d** the body,
Sir 1:19 knowledge and **d** comprehension,

DISCERNMENT· → DISCERN
Dt 4: 6 this will show your wisdom and **d**
1Ki 4:29 Solomon very great wisdom, **d**,
Job 12:20 and takes away the **d** of the elders.
Isa 29:14 **d** of the discerning shall be hidden.
44:19 nor is there knowledge or **d** to say,
1Co 1:19 **d** of the discerning I will thwart."
12:10 prophecy, to another the **d** of spirits,

DISCIPLE → DISCIPLES, DISCIPLES'
Mt 10:24 "A **d** is not above the teacher,
10:42 little ones in the name of a **d**—
Lk 14:26 even life itself, cannot be my **d**.
14:27 and follow me cannot be my **d**.
14:33 none of you can become my **d** if
Jn 9:28 reviled him, saying, "You are his **d**,
19:26 the **d** whom he loved standing
19:38 Joseph of Arimathea, who was a **d**
20: 2 went to Simon Peter and the other **d**,
21: 7 That **d** whom Jesus loved said to
21:20 the **d** whom Jesus loved following
21:24 the **d** who is testifying to these
Ac 9:10 a **d** in Damascus named Ananias.
16: 1 there was a **d** named Timothy,

DISCIPLES → DISCIPLE
Isa 8:16 seal the teaching among my **d**.
Mt 9:10 and were sitting with him and his **d**.
10: 1 Then Jesus summoned his twelve **d**
12: 2 your **d** are doing what is not lawful
26:56 all the **d** deserted him and fled.
28:19 therefore and make **d** of all nations,
Mk 3: 7 Jesus departed with his **d** to the sea,
6:29 When his **d** heard about it,
7: 5 "Why do your **d** not live according
9:18 and I asked your **d** to cast it out,
14:14 I may eat the Passover with my **d**?'
Lk 6:13 he called his **d** and chose twelve of
11: 1 to pray, as John taught his **d**."
22:45 to the **d** and found them sleeping
Jn 2:11 and his **d** believed in him.
6:66 of his **d** turned back and no longer
8:31 in my word, you are truly my **d**;
9:28 but we are **d** of Moses.
12:16 His **d** did not understand these
13:35 will know that you are my **d**,
15: 8 bear much fruit and become my **d**.
18:17 one of this man's **d**, are you?"

20:20 **d** rejoiced when they saw the Lord.
20:30 signs in the presence of his **d**,
Ac 6: 1 the **d** were increasing in number,
9: 1 murder against the **d** of the Lord,
11:26 the **d** were first called "Christians."
13:52 **d** were filled with joy and with the
14:22 **d** and encouraged them to continue
18:23 and Phrygia, strengthening all the **d**.

DISCIPLES'· → DISCIPLE
Jn 13: 5 began to wash the **d** feet

DISCIPLINARIAN· → DISCIPLINE
Gal 3:24 the law was our **d** until Christ came,
3:25 we are no longer subject to a **d**,

DISCIPLINE → DISCIPLINARIAN, DISCIPLINED, DISCIPLINES, DISCIPLINING, SELF-DISCIPLINE
Dt 4:36 made you hear his voice to **d** you.
11: 2 seen the **d** of the LORD your God),
21:18 not heed them when they **d** him,
1Ki 12:11 but I will **d** you with scorpions.'"
Job 5:17 not despise the **d** of the Almighty.
Ps 6: 1 or **d** me in your wrath.
38: 1 or **d** me in your wrath.
94:12 Happy are those whom you **d**,
Pr 3:11 do not despise the LORD's **d** or
5:12 how I hated **d**, and my heart
5:23 They die for lack of **d**,
6:23 the reproofs of **d** are the way of life,
12: 1 Whoever loves **d** loves knowledge,
13: 1 A wise child loves **d**, but a scoffer
13:24 love them are diligent to **d** them.
15:10 severe **d** for one who forsakes the
19:18 **D** your children while there is hope;
22:15 but the rod of **d** drives it far away.
23:13 not withhold **d** from your children;
29:17 **D** your children, and they will give
Jer 7:28 their God, and did not accept **d**;
31:18 disciplined me, and I took the **d**;
Eze 21:10 have despised the rod, and all **d**.
Eph 6: 4 in the **d** and instruction of the Lord.
Heb 12: 5 not regard lightly the **d** of the Lord,
12: 7 Endure trials for the sake of **d**.
12: 7 is there whom a parent does not **d**?
12: 8 that **d** in which all children share,
12:11 **d** always seems painful rather than
1Pe 4: 7 be serious and **d** yourselves for the
5: 8 **D** yourselves, keep alert.
Rev 3:19 I reprove and **d** those whom I love.
Sir 1:27 fear of the Lord is wisdom and **d**,
6:18 from your youth choose **d**,
7:23 **D** them, and make them obedient
23: 7 **D** OF THE TONGUE Listen,

DISCIPLINED → DISCIPLINE
Pr 29:19 By mere words servants are not **d**,
Jer 31:18 "You **d** me, and I took the discipline
1Co 11:32 **d** so that we may not be condemned
Heb 12:10 they **d** us for a short time as seemed
Wis 3: 5 Having been **d** a little, they will
Sir 6:32 willing, my child, you can be **d**,

DISCIPLINES· → DISCIPLINE
Dt 8: 5 as a parent **d** a child so the LORD your God **d** you.
Ps 94:10 He who **d** the nations, he who
Heb 12: 6 for the Lord **d** those whom he loves,
12:10 but he **d** us for our good,
Sir 30: 2 He who **d** his son will profit by him,
2Mc 6:16 Although he **d** us with calamities,

DISCIPLINING· → DISCIPLINE
Sir 42: 5 and of frequent **d** of children,

DISCLOSE → DISCLOSED, DISCLOSES
Pr 25: 9 and do not **d** another's secret;
1Co 3:13 for the Day will **d** it,

DISCLOSED → DISCLOSE
Mk 4:22 nothing hidden, except to be **d**;
Ro 3:21 righteousness of God has been **d**,

1Co 14:25 of the unbeliever's heart are **d**,
Heb 9: 8 into the sanctuary has not yet been **d**
AdE 2:10 Now Esther had not **d** her people

DISCLOSES → DISCLOSE
Sir 27: 6 Its fruit **d** the cultivation of a tree;

DISCONTENTED·
1Sa 22: 2 who was **d** gathered to him;

DISCORD·
Pr 6:14 devising evil, continually sowing **d**;
6:19 and one who sows **d** in a family.
Sir 28: 9 **d** among those who are at peace.

DISCOURAGE· → DISCOURAGED
Nu 32: 7 Why will you **d** the hearts of the

DISCOURAGED· → DISCOURAGE
Nu 32: 9 they **d** the hearts of the Israelites
2Sa 17: 2 upon him while he is weary and **d**,
Ezr 4: 4 of the land **d** the people of Judah,
Isa 54: 4 do not be **d**, for you will not suffer
1Mc 4:27 he heard it, he was perplexed and **d**,

DISCOURSE·
Job 27: 1 Job again took up his **d** and said:
29: 1 Job again took up his **d** and said:
Sir 6:35 Be ready to listen to every godly **d**,
8: 8 Do not slight the **d** of the sages,
8: 9 Do not ignore the **d** of the aged,

DISCREDITED·
Tit 2: 5 that the word of God may not be **d**.

DISCREETLY· → DISCRETION
Pr 26:16 than seven who can answer **d**.

DISCRETION· → DISCREETLY
1Ch 22:12 may the LORD grant you **d** and
2Ch 2:12 endowed with **d** and understanding,
Ezr 8:18 they brought us a man of **d**,
Pr 8:12 and I attain knowledge and **d**.
Da 2:14 responded with prudence and **d**
Sir 17: 6 **D** and tongue and eyes, ears and
1Mc 8:30 they shall do so at their **d**,

DISCUSSED· → DISCUSSION
Lk 6:11 **d** with one another what they might
Ac 4:15 they **d** the matter with one another.

DISCUSSING· → DISCUSSION
Mk 2: 8 that they were **d** these questions
Lk 24:17 "What are you **d** with each other

DISCUSSION· → DISCUSSED, DISCUSSING
Jn 3:25 Now a **d** about purification arose
Ac 18:19 and had a **d** with the Jews.
20: 7 Paul was holding a **d** with them;

DISEASE → DISEASES
2Ch 16:12 in his **d** he did not seek the LORD,
21:15 a severe sickness with a **d** of your
26:19 leprous **d** broke out on his forehead,
Ps 106:15 but sent a wasting **d** among them.
Mt 4:23 of the kingdom and curing every **d**
9:35 curing every **d** and every sickness.
10: 1 to cure every **d** and every sickness.
Mk 5:29 that she was healed of her **d**.
5:34 in peace, and be healed of your **d**."

DISEASES → DISEASE
Ex 15:26 **d** that I brought upon the Egyptians;
Dt 7:15 all the dread **d** of Egypt that you
28:60 upon you all the **d** of Egypt,
Ps 103: 3 your iniquity, who heals all your **d**,
Isa 53: 4 our infirmities and carried our **d**;
Mt 4:24 who were afflicted with various **d**
8:17 took our infirmities and bore our **d**."
Mk 1:34 many who were sick with various **d**,
3:10 **d** pressed upon him to touch him.
Lk 4:40 kinds of **d** brought them to him;
5:15 hear him and to be cured of their **d**.
6:18 hear him and to be healed of their **d**;

7:21 just then cured many people of **d,**
9: 1 over all demons and to cure **d,**
9: 6 and curing **d** everywhere.
Ac 19:12 their **d** left them, and the evil spirits
28: 9 on the island who had **d** also came

DISFIGURE·
Mt   6:16 **d** their faces so as to show others

DISGRACE → DISGRACED,
DISGRACEFUL, DISGRACES
Jos 5: 9 I have rolled away from you the **d**
Ne   2:17 we may no longer suffer **d."**
Ps 44:15 All day long my **d** is before me,
78:66 he put them to everlasting **d.**
Pr   3:35 but stubborn fools, **d.**
6:33 and his **d** will not be wiped away.
11: 2 When pride comes, then comes **d;**
13:18 and **d** are for the one who ignores
18: 3 and with dishonor comes **d.**
Isa 4: 1 by your name; take away our **d."**
La   5: 1 has befallen us; look, and see our **d!**
Eze 16:52 ashamed, you also, and bear your **d,**
36:30 never again suffer the **d** of famine
Mt   1:19 unwilling to expose her to public **d,**
Lk   1:25 and took away the **d** I have endured
1Ti   3: 7 fall into **d** and the snare of the devil.
1Pe   4:16 do not consider it a **d,**
Jdt 14:18 One Hebrew woman has brought **d**
Sir   3:11 it is a **d** for children not to respect
20:26 A liar's way leads to **d,**
1Mc 4:58 the **d** brought by the Gentiles was
Pm 151: 7 took away **d** from the people of

DISGRACED → DISGRACE
Ps 71:24 have been put to shame, and **d.**
Pr 29:15 a mother is **d** by a neglected child.

DISGRACEFUL → DISGRACE
Dt 22:21 she committed a **d** act in Israel
1Co 11: 6 **d** for a woman to have her hair cut

DISGRACES· → DISGRACE
1Co 11: 4 something on his head **d** his head,
11: 5 with her head unveiled **d** her head—
Sir 22: 5 An impudent daughter **d** father and

DISGUISE → DISGUISED, DISGUISES,
DISGUISING
1Ki 14: 2 to his wife, "Go, **d** yourself,
2Ch 18:29 "I will **d** myself and go into battle,
2Co 11:15 also **d** themselves as ministers of

DISGUISED → DISGUISE
1Sa 28: 8 Saul **d** himself and put on other
2Ch 35:22 but **d** himself in order to fight with

DISGUISES → DISGUISE
2Co 11:14 Satan **d** himself as an angel of light.

DISGUISING· → DISGUISE
1Ki 20:38 **d** himself with a bandage over his
2Co 11:13 **d** themselves as apostles of Christ.

DISGUST
Ps 119:158 I look at the faithless with **d,**
Jer   6: 8 or I shall turn from you in **d,**
Eze 23:17 she turned from them in **d.**

DISH → DISHES
2Ki 21:13 wipe Jerusalem as one wipes a **d,**
Pr 19:24 lazy person buries a hand in the **d,**
Lk 11:39 the outside of the cup and of the **d,**
Jn 13:26 when I have dipped it in the **d."**

DISHEARTENED → HEART
Dt 20: 8 saying, "Is anyone afraid or **d?**
Eze 13:22 you have **d** the righteous falsely,

DISHES → DISH
Ex 25:29 make its plates and **d** for incense,

DISHONEST
Ex 18:21 are trustworthy, and hate **d** gain;
Jer 22:17 and heart are only on your **d** gain,

Eze 22:13 at the **d** gain you have made,
22:27 destroying lives to get **d** gain.
Mic 6:11 and a bag of **d** weights?
Lk 16: 8 master commended the **d** manager
16:10 and whoever is **d** in a very little is **d**
also in much.
Sir   5: 8 Do not depend on **d** wealth,

DISHONOR → DISHONORED,
DISHONORS
Ps 35: 4 Let them be put to shame and **d**
109:29 May my accusers be clothed with **d;**
Pr 18: 3 and with **d** comes disgrace.
Jer 14:21 do not **d** your glorious throne;
20:11 eternal **d** will never be forgotten.
La   2: 2 in **d** the kingdom and its rulers.
Jn   8:49 I honor my Father, and you **d** me.
Ac   5:41 considered worthy to suffer **d** for
Ro   2:23 do you **d** God by breaking the law?
1Co 15:43 It is sown in **d,** it is raised in glory.
2Co 6: 8 in honor and **d,** in ill repute
Sir   5:13 Honor and **d** come from speaking,
1Mc 1:40 now grew as great as her glory;

DISHONORED → DISHONOR
Dt 21:14 as a slave, since you have **d** her.
Jas   2: 6 But you have **d** the poor.

DISHONORS· → DISHONOR
Dt 27:16 "Cursed be anyone who **d** father or
Sir 26:26 *if she **d** him in her pride*

DISLIKED → DISLIKES
Dt 21:15 one of them loved and the other **d,**
Pr 14:20 poor are **d** even by their neighbors,
Sir 42: 9 or if married, for fear she may be **d;**

DISLIKES· → DISLIKED
Dt 22:13 after going in to her, he **d** her
22:16 in marriage to this man but he **d** her;
24: 3 Then suppose the second man **d** her,

DISLOYALTY·
Hos 14: 4 I will heal their **d;** I will love them

DISMAY → DISMAYED
Pr 21:15 to the righteous, but **d** to evildoers.

DISMAYED → DISMAY
Dt   1:21 do not fear or be **d."**
31: 8 Do not fear or be **d."**
Jos 1: 9 do not be frightened or **d,**
8: 1 said to Joshua, "Do not fear or be **d;**
1Sa 17:11 they were **d** and greatly afraid.
1Ch 22:13 Do not be afraid or **d.**
28:20 Do not be afraid or **d;**
Ps 30: 7 you hid your face; I was **d.**
Isa 8: 9 gird yourselves and be **d;**
Jer 17:18 them be **d,** but do not let me be **d;**

DISMISS → DISMISSAL
Mt   1:19 planned to **d** her quietly.
Sir   7:19 Do not **d** a wise and good wife,

DISMISSAL → DISMISS
Mt 19: 7 to give a certificate of **d** and to

DISOBEDIENCE → DISOBEY
Ro   5:19 **d** the many were made sinners,
11:30 received mercy because of their **d,**
11:32 For God has imprisoned all in **d** so
2Co 10: 6 We are ready to punish every **d**
Heb 2: 2 or **d** received a just penalty,
4: 6 news failed to enter because of **d,**
4:11 no one may fall through such **d** as

DISOBEDIENT· → DISOBEY
Ne   9:26 they were **d** and rebelled
Lk   1:17 **d** to the wisdom of the righteous,
Ac 26:19 I was not **d** to the heavenly vision,
Ro 10:21 I have held out my hands to a **d**
11:30 as you were once **d** to God but have
11:31 so they have now been **d** in order
Eph 2: 2 at work among those who are **d.**

5: 6 of God comes on those who are **d.**
Col   3: 6 is coming on those who are **d.**
1Ti   1: 9 innocent but for the lawless and **d,**
2Ti   3: 2 abusive, **d** to their parents,
Tit   1:16 detestable, **d,** unfit for any good
3: 3 ourselves were once foolish, **d,** led
Heb 3:18 if not to those who were **d?**
11:31 not perish with those who were **d,**
Sir 16: 6 and in a **d** nation wrath blazes up.
Bar   1:19 we have been **d** to the Lord our God
4Mc 9:10 as at those who are **d,**

DISOBEY → DISOBEDIENCE,
DISOBEDIENT, DISOBEYED, DISOBEYS
Lev 26:27 But if, despite this, you **d** me,
Est   3: 3 Why do you **d** the king's command?
1Pe   2: 8 stumble because they **d** the word,
Sir   1:28 Do not **d** the fear of the Lord;

DISOBEYED → DISOBEY
Da   9:14 for we have **d** his voice.
Lk 15:29 and I have never **d** your command;

DISOBEYS· → DISOBEY
Jos 1:18 your orders and **d** your words,
Jn   3:36 whoever **d** the Son will not see life,

DISORDER
1Co 14:33 God is a God not of **d** but of peace.
2Co 12:20 slander, gossip, conceit, and **d.**
Jas 3:16 be **d** and wickedness of every kind.

DISPERSE → DISPERSED, DISPERSION
Ps 106:27 would **d** their descendants among
Eze 12:15 when I **d** them among the nations

DISPERSED → DISPERSE
Isa 11:12 gather the **d** of Judah from the four
Jn 11:52 into one the **d** children of God.

DISPERSION· → DISPERSE
Jn   7:35 Does he intend to go to the **D**
Jas   1: 1 To the twelve tribes in the **D:**
1Pe   1: 1 To the exiles of the **D** in Pontus,

DISPLAY → DISPLAYED, DISPLAYS
Dt 26: 8 with a terrifying **d** of power,
Isa 61: 3 planting of the Lord, to **d** his glory.
Eze 36:23 through you I **d** my holiness before
39:21 I will **d** my glory among the nations
1Ti   1:16 Christ might **d** the utmost patience,
Sir 32: 4 not **d** your cleverness at the wrong

DISPLAYED → DISPLAY
Ps 78:43 when he **d** his signs in Egypt,

DISPLAYS → DISPLAY
Pr 13:16 but the fool **d** folly.

DISPLEASE → DISPLEASED,
DISPLEASING, DISPLEASURE
1Th 2:15 they **d** God and oppose everyone

DISPLEASED → DISPLEASE
Nu 11:10 very angry, and Moses was **d.**
2Sa 11:27 that David had done **d** the LORD.
Pr 24:18 else the LORD will see it and be **d,**
Isa 59:15 it **d** him that there was no justice.

DISPLEASING· → DISPLEASE
Ge 38:10 did was **d** in the sight of the LORD,
Nu 22:34 if it is **d** to you, I will return home."
Jnh 4: 1 very **d** to Jonah, and he became

DISPLEASURE· → DISPLEASE
Nu 14:34 years, and you shall know my **d."**

DISPOSSESS → DISPOSSESSED
Dt 11:23 and you will **d** nations larger
Jer 49: 2 shall **d** those who dispossessed him,

DISPOSSESSED → DISPOSSESS
Dt 12:29 when you have **d** them and live in
Ob   1:17 possession of those who **d** them.

DISPUTE → DISPUTED, DISPUTES

Ex 18:16 When they have a **d**, they come to
          24:14 whoever has a **d** may go to them."
Lk 22:24 A **d** also arose among them as to
Sir 28:11 and a hasty **d** sheds blood.

DISPUTED → DISPUTE

Jude 1: 9 and **d** about the body of Moses,

DISPUTES → DISPUTE

Dt   1:12 burden of your **d** all by myself?
Pr 18:18 Casting the lot puts an end to **d**
2Co 7: 5 **d** without and fears within.
Jas 4: 1 Those conflicts and **d** among you,

DISQUALIFIED* → DISQUALIFY

1Co 9:27 to others I myself should not be **d**.

DISQUALIFY* → DISQUALIFIED

Col 2:18 Do not let anyone **d** you,

DISREGARDED → DISREGARDING

Isa 40:27 and my right is **d** by my God"?
Eze 22:26 and they have **d** my sabbaths,

DISREGARDING → DISREGARDED

Heb 12: 2 endured the cross, **d** its shame,

DISREPUTE*

Ac 19:27 this trade of ours may come into **d**
1Co 4:10 You are held in honor, but we in **d**.

DISSENSION → DISSENSIONS

Ac   15: 2 Paul and Barnabas had no small **d**
          23: 7 a **d** began between the Pharisees and
1Co 12:25 there may be no **d** within the body,
1Ti   6: 4 From these come envy, **d**, slander,

DISSENSIONS* → DISSENSION

Ro   16:17 on those who cause **d** and offenses,
Gal   5:20 strife, jealousy, anger, quarrels, **d**,
Tit   3: 9 stupid controversies, genealogies, **d**,

DISSIPATION*

Lk 21:34 hearts are not weighed down with **d**
1Pe   4: 4 in the same excesses of **d**,
2Pe   2:13 reveling in their **d** while they feast

DISSOLVED

2Pe   3:10 and the elements will be **d** with fire,

DISTANCE → DISTANT

Ex   2: 4 His sister stood at a **d**,
          20:21 Then the people stood at a **d**,
Dt 32:52 you may view the land from a **d**,
Mk 14:54 Peter had followed him at a **d**,
          15:40 also women looking on from a **d**;
Heb 11:13 from a **d** they saw and greeted them.

DISTANT → DISTANCE

Jer   4:16 "Besiegers come from a **d** land;
          51:50 Remember the LORD in a **d** land,
Bar   4:15 For he brought a **d** nation against

DISTINCT → DISTINCTION, DISTINCTIONS

Ex 33:16 In this way, we shall be **d**,
1Co 14: 7 If they do not give **d** notes,

DISTINCTION → DISTINCT

Ex   8:23 I will make a **d** between my people
Lev 11:47 make a **d** between the unclean and
Eze 22:26 have made no **d** between the holy
Ac   15: 9 by faith he has made no **d** between
Ro   3:22 For there is no **d**,
          10:12 no **d** between Jew and Greek;

DISTINCTIONS* → DISTINCT

Jas   2: 4 you not made **d** among yourselves,

DISTINGUISH → DISTINGUISHED

Lev 10:10 You are to **d** between the holy and
Heb   5:14 by practice to **d** good from evil.

DISTINGUISHED → DISTINGUISH

Da   6: 3 Soon Daniel **d** himself above all
Lk 14: 8 in case someone more **d** than you

DISTORTING*

Ac 20:30 **d** the truth in order to entice

DISTRACTED

Lk 10:40 Martha was **d** by her many tasks;

DISTRESS → DISTRESSED, DISTRESSES, DISTRESSING

Dt   4:30 In your **d**, when all these things
Jdg   2:15 and they were in great **d**.
2Sa 22: 7 In my **d** I called upon the LORD;
2Ch 15: 4 in their **d** they turned to the LORD,
Ne   9:37 and we are in great **d**."
Ps 18: 6 In my **d** I called upon the LORD;
          25:17 and bring me out of my **d**.
          81: 7 In **d** you called, and I rescued you;
          107: 6 and he delivered them from their **d**;
          119:50 This is my comfort in my **d**,
          120: 1 In my **d** I cry to the LORD.
Pr   1:27 when **d** and anguish come upon you
Isa 25: 4 a refuge to the needy in their **d**,
          37: 3 This day is a day of **d**,
Jer 30: 7 it is a time of **d** for Jacob;
Ob   1:12 not have boasted on the day of **d**.
Jnh   2: 2 "I called to the LORD out of my **d**,
Lk 21:23 For there will be great **d** on the earth
Ro   2: 9 and **d** for everyone who does evil,
          8:35 Will hardship, or **d**, or persecution,
Jas   1:27 for orphans and widows in their **d**,
Rev   2:22 I am throwing into great **d**,
Sir   2:11 and saves in time of **d**.

DAY OF DISTRESS Ge 35:3; 2Ki 19:3; Ps
59:16; 102:2; Isa 37:3; Ob 1:12, 14; Zep 1:15;
Sir 3:15

GREAT DISTRESS Jdg 2:15; 1Sa 28:15;
2Sa 24:14; 1Ch 21:13; Ne 9:37; Lk 21:23; Rev
2:22; 1Mc 9:27; 2Es 10:7

TIME OF DISTRESS Jdg 10:14; 2Ch
28:22; Ps 32:6; Jer 15:11; 30:7; AdE 9:22; Sir
2:11; 22:23; 35:26; 1Mc 2:53; 13:5

DISTRESSED → DISTRESS

La   1:20 See, O LORD, how **d** I am;
Mk 14:33 and began to be **d** and agitated.
Ac 17:16 he was deeply **d** to see that the city
2Pe   2: 7 Lot, a righteous man greatly **d** by

DISTRESSES* → DISTRESS

1Sa 10:19 from all your calamities and your **d**;

DISTRESSING → DISTRESS

2Ti   3: 1 in the last days **d** times will come.

DISTRIBUTE → DISTRIBUTED, DISTRIBUTION

Mk   8: 6 and gave them to his disciples to **d**;
Lk 18:22 and **d** the money to the poor,
Ac   2:45 and goods and **d** the proceeds to all,

DISTRIBUTED → DISTRIBUTE

Jos 13:32 the inheritances that Moses **d**
Ps 112: 9 They have **d** freely,
Ac   4:35 it was **d** to each as any had need.
Heb   2: 4 gifts of the Holy Spirit, **d** according

DISTRIBUTION* → DISTRIBUTE

Ac   6: 1 neglected in the daily **d** of food.

DISTURB → DISTURBANCE, DISTURBED

Ac 15:24 have said things to **d** you

DISTURBANCE → DISTURB

Ac 19:23 **d** broke out concerning the Way.
          24:18 without any crowd or **d**.

DISTURBED → DISTURB

1Sa 28:15 you **d** me by bringing me up?"
2Sa   7:10 their own place, and be **d** no more;
Ps   4: 4 When you are **d**, do not sin;

Jn 11:33 he was greatly **d** in spirit and deeply

DIVERSE

Pr 20:10 **D** weights and **d** measures are both

DIVIDE → DIVIDED, DIVIDES, DIVIDING, DIVISION, DIVISIONS

Ex 14:16 your hand over the sea and **d** it,
1Ki   3:25 "**D** the living boy in two;
Ps 22:18 **d** my clothes among themselves,
Isa 53:12 he shall **d** the spoil with the strong;
Lk 12:13 brother to **d** the family inheritance
          22:17 this and **d** it among yourselves;
          23:34 And they cast lots to **d** his clothing.

DIVIDED → DIVIDE

Ge 10:25 for in his days the earth was **d**,
Ex 14:21 into dry land; and the waters were **d**.
Lev 11: 3 Any animal that has **d** hoofs
Dt 32: 8 when he **d** humankind,
Ne   9:11 And you **d** the sea before them,
Ps 136:13 who **d** the Red Sea in two,
Isa 63:12 who **d** the waters before them to
Da   2:41 it shall be a **d** kingdom;
          5:28 PERES, your kingdom is **d**
Mt 12:25 "Every kingdom **d** against itself is
Mk   6:41 he **d** the two fish among them all.
          15:24 and **d** his clothes among them,
Lk 11:18 If Satan also is **d** against himself,
Jn   9:16 And they were **d**.
          10:19 Again the Jews were **d** because
Ac   2: 3 **D** tongues, as of fire, appeared
1Co   1:13 Has Christ been **d**?
1Mc   1: 6 and **d** his kingdom among them

DIVIDES → DIVIDE

Heb   4:12 piercing until it **d** soul from spirit,

DIVIDING → DIVIDE

Jos 19:51 So they finished **d** the land.
Eph   2:14 and has broken down the **d** wall,

DIVINATION → DIVINE

Ge 44: 5 Does he not indeed use it for **d**?
Nu 23:23 against Jacob, no **d** against Israel;
Dt 18:10 who practices **d**, or is a soothsayer,
Jos 13:22 son of Beor, who practiced **d**.
1Sa 15:23 For rebellion is no less a sin than **d**,
2Ki 17:17 they used **d** and augury;
Eze 13:23 see false visions or practice **d**;
Ac 16:16 a slave-girl who had a spirit of **d**

DIVINATIONS* → DIVINE

Eze 13: 9 see false visions and utter lying **d**;
Sir 34: 5 **D** and omens and dreams are unreal,

DIVINE → DIVINATION, DIVINATIONS, DIVINER, DIVINERS, DIVINING, DIVINITIES

Ex 31: 3 and I have filled him with **d** spirit,
Dt 13: 1 who **d** by dreams appear among you
1Sa 28:13 "I see a **d** being coming up
Ps 82: 1 God has taken his place in the **d**
Mk   8:33 not on **d** things but on human things
Lk   2:52 and in **d** and human favor.
Ro   1:20 his eternal power and **d** nature,
2Co 10: 4 **d** power to destroy strongholds.
2Pe   1: 3 His **d** power has given us everything
          1: 4 become participants of the **d** nature.

DIVINER* → DIVINE

Isa   3: 2 judge and prophet, **d** and elder,

DIVINERS → DIVINE

1Sa   6: 2 called for the priests and the **d**
Isa   2: 6 they are full of **d** from the east and
          44:25 omens of liars, and makes fools of **d**
Jer 29: 8 the **d** who are among you deceive
Da   2:27 **d** can show to the king the mystery
Mic   3: 7 and the **d** put to shame;
Zec 10: 2 utter nonsense, and the **d** see lies;

DIVINING → DIVINE

Eze 21:29 false visions for you, **d** lies for you,

DIVINITIES* → DIVINE
Ac 17:18 to be a proclaimer of foreign **d**."

DIVISION → DIVIDE
2Ch 31: 2 **d** by **d**, everyone according to his
Lk 12:51 No, I tell you, but rather **d!**
Jn 7:43 a **d** in the crowd because of him.

DIVISIONS → DIVIDE
1Ch 23: 6 And David organized them in **d**
1Co 1:10 that there be no **d** among you,
11:18 I hear that there are **d** among you;
Tit 3:10 to do with anyone who causes **d**,
Jude 1:19 of the Spirit, who are causing **d.**

DIVORCE* → DIVORCED, DIVORCES
Dt 22:19 not be permitted to **d** her as long as
22:29 not be permitted to **d** her as long as
24: 1 so he writes her a certificate of **d**,
24: 3 writes her a bill of **d**, puts it in her
Isa 50: 1 Where is your mother's bill of **d**
Jer 3: 8 sent her away with a decree of **d**;
Mal 2:16 For I hate **d**, says the LORD,
Mt 5:31 let him give her a certificate of **d.'**
19: 3 a man to **d** his wife for any cause?"
19: 7 certificate of dismissal and to **d** her?
19: 8 Moses allowed you to **d** your wives,
Mk 10: 2 Is it lawful for a man to **d** his wife?"
10: 4 certificate of dismissal and to **d** her.
1Co 7:11 the husband should not **d** his wife.
7:12 live with him, he should not **d** her.
7:13 live with her, she should not **d** him.
Sir 7:26 Do not **d** her;

DIVORCED* → DIVORCE
Lev 21: 7 neither shall they marry a woman **d**
21:14 or a **d** woman, or a woman who has
22:13 a priest's daughter is widowed or **d**,
Nu 30: 9 vow of a widow or of a **d** woman,
Eze 44:22 not marry a widow, or a **d** woman,
Mt 5:32 whoever marries a **d** woman
Lk 16:18 a woman **d** from her husband

DIVORCES* → DIVORCE
Jer 3: 1 If a man **d** his wife and she goes
Mt 5:31 was also said, 'Whoever **d** his wife,
5:32 I say to you that anyone who **d** his
19: 9 I say to you, whoever **d** his wife,
Mk 10:11 to them, "Whoever **d** his wife
10:12 if she **d** her husband and marries
Lk 16:18 "Anyone who **d** his wife

DO → DEED, DEEDS, DID, DOER, DOERS,
DOES, DOING, DOINGS, DONE, EVILDOING,
EVILDOER, EVILDOERS, WRONGDOER,
WRONGDOERS, WRONGDOING
Ge 4: 7 **d** well, will you not be accepted?
18:25 Judge of all the earth **d** what is just?
Ex 19: 8 the LORD has spoken we will **d.**"
20:10 you shall not **d** any work—
2Ki 17:15 that they should not **d** as they did.
Ps 37: 3 Trust in the LORD, and **d** good;
143:10 Teach me to **d** your will,
Ecc 8:11 heart is fully set to **d** evil.
Jer 22: 3 **d** no wrong or violence to the alien,
Mt 23: 3 but **d** not **d** as they **d**,
Mk 3: 4 "Is it lawful to **d** good or to **d** harm
on the sabbath,
6: 5 he could not **d** deed of power there,
Lk 6:31 **D** to others as you would have them
d to you.
Jn 6:28 we **d** to perform the works of God?"
7:17 who resolves to **d** the will of God
Ac 16:30 "Sirs, what must I **d** to be saved?"
22:10 I asked, 'What am I to **d**, Lord?'
Ro 7:15 For I **d** not **d** what I want, but I **d**
the very thing I hate.
Col 3:17 **d** everything in the name of the
Lord Jesus,
1Pe 3:11 turn away from evil and **d** good;
Sir 12: 1 If you **d** good, know to whom you
d it,

14:13 **D** good to friends before you die,
15:11 for he does not **d** what he hates.
1Mc 1:15 and sold themselves to **d** evil.
2:34 nor will we **d** what the king

DOCTOR*
Lk 4:23 this proverb, '**D**, cure yourself!'

DOCTRINE* → DOCTRINES
Eph 4:14 blown about by every wind of **d**,
1Ti 1: 3 not to teach any different **d**,
2Ti 4: 3 people will not put up with sound **d**,
Tit 1: 9 able both to preach with sound **d**
2: 1 what is consistent with sound **d.**
2:10 they may be an ornament to the **d**

DOCTRINES* → DOCTRINE
Mt 15: 9 teaching human precepts as **d.'"**
Mk 7: 7 teaching human precepts as **d.'**

DOCUMENT
Ne 9:38 sealed **d** are inscribed the names
Est 3:14 A copy of the **d** was to be issued as
Isa 29:11 for you like the words of a sealed **d.**

DOE
Ge 49:21 Naphtali is a **d** let loose that bears
Pr 5:19 a lovely deer, a graceful **d.**

DOEG*
Edomite; Saul's chief shepherd; murdered 85
priests at Nob (1Sa 21:7; 22:6-23; Ps 52).

DOER → DO
Pr 21: 2 deeds are right in the sight of the **d**,
Jas 4:11 are not a **d** of the law but a judge.

DOERS → DO
Ro 2:13 **d** of the law who will be justified.
Jas 1:22 But be **d** of the word,
1:25 hearers who forget but **d** who act—

DOES → DO
Ps 135: 6 Whatever the LORD pleases he **d**,
Ecc 3:14 whatever God **d** endures forever;
Zep 3: 5 The LORD within it is righteous; he
d no wrong.
Mk 3:35 **d** the will of God is my brother
Jn 5:19 whatever the Father **d**, the Son **d**
Ro 10: 5 **d** these things will live by them."
3Jn 1:11 Whoever **d** good is from God;
Sir 34:31 and **d** the same things,

DOG → DOGS
Jdg 7: 5 as a **d** laps, you shall put to one side
1Sa 17:43 Philistine said to David, "Am I a **d**,
24:14 Whom do you pursue? A dead **d**?
Pr 26:11 Like a **d** that returns to its vomit
Ecc 9: 4 a living **d** is better than a dead lion.
2Pe 2:22 "The **d** turns back to its own vomit,"

DOGS → DOG
Ex 22:31 you shall throw it to the **d.**
1Ki 21:19 will also lick up your blood **d.**
2Ki 9:10 The **d** shall eat Jezebel in the
Ps 22:16 For **d** are all around me;
Isa 56:11 The **d** have a mighty appetite;
Mt 7: 6 "Do not give what is holy to **d**;
15:26 children's food and throw it to the **d**
Php 3: 2 Beware of the **d**, beware of the evil
Rev 22:15 Outside are the **d** and sorcerers

DOING → DO
Mk 11:28 "By what authority are you **d** these
1Pe 3:17 For it is better to suffer for **d** good,

DOINGS → DO
Ps 106: 2 utter the mighty **d** of the LORD,
145:17 and kind in all his **d.**

DOME
Ge 1: 6 "Let there be a **d** in the midst of the
Job 22:14 and he walks on the **d** of heaven.'
Eze 1:22 there was something like a **d**,
10: 1 and above the **d** that was over

DOMESTIC
Ge 7:14 and all **d** animals of every kind,

DOMINATED → DOMINION
1Co 6:12 but I will not be **d** by anything.

DOMINION → DOMINATED, DOMINIONS
Ge 1:26 and let them have **d** over
37: 8 Are you indeed to have **d** over us?"
Job 25: 2 "**D** and fear are with God;
Ps 8: 6 have given them **d** over the works
22:28 For **d** belongs to the LORD,
Da 7:14 His **d** is an everlasting **d** that shall
not pass away,
Zec 9:10 his **d** shall be from sea to sea,
Ro 5:17 death exercised **d** through that one,
6:14 For sin will have no **d** over you,
Eph 1:21 rule and authority and power and **d**,
1Ti 6:16 to him be honor and eternal **d.**
Rev 1: 6 to him be glory and **d** forever and
Sir 17: 4 gave them **d** over beasts and birds.

DOMINIONS* → DOMINION
Da 7:27 all **d** shall serve and obey them."
Col 1:16 whether thrones or **d** or rulers or

DONATION → DONATIONS
Lev 22:14 If a man eats of the sacred **d**
27:23 a sacred **d** to the LORD.
Nu 15:19 you shall present a **d** to the LORD.

DONATIONS → DONATION
Ex 28:38 consecrate as their sacred **d**;
Lev 22: 2 to deal carefully with the sacred **d**
Dt 12: 6 tithes and your **d**, your votive gifts,

DONE → DO
Ge 3:13 "What is this that you have **d**?"
4:10 the LORD said, "What have you **d**?
Ex 18: 9 all the good that the LORD had **d** to
Est 6: 6 "What shall be **d** for the man whom
Job 21:31 repays them for what they have **d**?
Ps 71:19 who have **d** great things, O God,
98: 1 for he has **d** marvelous things.
105: 5 the wonderful works he has **d**,
Ecc 1: 9 what has been **d** is what will be **d**;
Isa 3:11 what their hands have **d** shall be **d**
to them.
25: 1 for you have **d** wonderful things,
Jer 50:29 just as she has **d**, do to her—
Joel 2:21 for the LORD has **d** great things!
Ob 1:15 As you have **d**, it shall be **d** to you;
Mic 6: 3 my people, what have I **d** to you?
Mt 6:10 Your will be **d**, on earth as it is in
26:42 unless I drink it, your will be **d.**"
Lk 19:17 He said to him, 'Well **d**, good slave!
23:41 but this man has **d** nothing wrong."
Rev 16:17 from the throne, saying, "It is **d!**"
21: 6 Then he said to me, "It is **d!**

DONKEY
Nu 22:30 But the **d** said to Balaam, "Am I
not your **d**,
Dt 22:10 not plow with an ox and a **d** yoked
Jdg 15:15 he found a fresh jawbone of a **d**,
Zec 9: 9 humble and riding on a **d**,
Mt 21: 5 humble, and mounted on a **d**,
2Pe 2:16 a speechless **d** spoke with a human

DOOM → DOOMED
Dt 32:35 their **d** comes swiftly.
Ps 81:15 and their **d** would last forever.
Eze 30: 3 a time of **d** for the nations.

DOOMED → DOOM
Ps 79:11 preserve those **d** to die.
102:20 to set free those who were **d** to die;
Jer 8:14 LORD our God has **d** us to perish,
Zec 11: 4 shepherd of the flock **d** to slaughter.
14:11 again shall it be **d** to destruction;
1Co 2: 6 of this age, who are **d** to perish.

DOOR → DOORKEEPER, DOORKEEPERS, DOORPOST, DOORPOSTS, DOORS

Ge   4: 7 not do well, sin is lurking at the **d**;
      19: 9 came near the **d** to break it down.
Dt 15:17 through his earlobe into the **d**,
Jdg 19:22 and started pounding on the **d**.
Ps 141: 3 keep watch over the **d** of my lips.
Pr   5: 8 do not go near the **d** of her house;
      9:14 She sits at the **d** of her house,
   26:14 As a **d** turns on its hinges,
Mt   6: 6 shut the **d** and pray to your Father
    7: 7 knock, and the **d** will be opened for
Mk 15:46 a stone against the **d** of the tomb.
Lk 13:24 Strive to enter through the narrow **d**
Ac 14:27 opened a **d** of faith for the Gentiles.
1Co 16: 9 wide **d** for effective work has
2Co 2:12 a **d** was opened for me in the Lord;
Col   4: 3 God will open to us a **d** for the word
Rev 3: 8 I have set before you an open **d**,
    3:20 I am standing at the **d**, knocking;
    4: 1 and there in heaven a **d** stood open!
Sir 28:25 make a **d** and a bolt for your mouth.
Bel 1:11 and shut the **d** and seal it

DOORKEEPER → DOOR, KEEP

Ps 84:10 be a **d** in the house of my God

DOORKEEPERS* → DOOR, KEEP

Ezr 7:24 singers, the **d**, the temple servants,

DOORPOST → DOOR

Ex 21: 6 be brought to the door or the **d**;

DOORPOSTS → DOOR

Ex 12: 7 the blood and put it on the two **d**

DOORS → DOOR

Jdg 16: 3 the **d** of the city gate and the two
1Ki 6:31 sanctuary he made **d** of olivewood;
Ne   3: 1 They consecrated it and set up its **d**;
Ps 24: 7 and be lifted up, O ancient **d**!
Mal 1:10 among you would shut the temple **d**,
Jn 20:26 Although the **d** were shut,
Ac   5:19 of the Lord opened the prison **d**,
  16:26 immediately all the **d** were opened
Bel 1:21 They showed him the secret **d**

DORCAS* → =TABITHA

Disciple, also known as Tabitha, whom Peter raised from the dead (Ac 9:36-43).

DOUBLE → DOUBLE-MINDED, DOUBLE-TONGUED

Ex 22: 7 then the thief, if caught, shall pay **d**.
Dt 21:17 giving him a **d** portion of all that he
1Sa 1: 5 but to Hannah he gave a **d** portion,
2Ki 2: 9 me inherit a **d** share of your spirit."
Isa 40: 2 LORD's hand for all her sins.
    61: 7 they shall possess a **d** portion;
Hos 10:10 are punished for their **d** iniquity.
1Ti 5:17 be considered worthy of **d** honor,
Rev 18: 6 and repay her **d** for her deeds;
   18: 6 mix a **d** draught for her in the cup
Sir 20:10 and the gift to be paid back **d**.

DOUBLE-MINDED* → DOUBLE, MIND

Ps 119:113 I hate the **d**, but I love your law.
Jas 1: 7 being **d** and unstable in every way,
    4: 8 and purify your hearts, you **d**.

DOUBLE-TONGUED → DOUBLE, TONGUE

1Ti 3: 8 likewise must be serious, not **d**,
Sir 5:14 Do not be called **d** and do not
  28:13 Curse the gossips and the **d**,

DOUBT → DOUBTED, DOUBTER, DOUBTING, DOUBTS

Mt 14:31 of little faith, why did you **d**?"
  21:21 if you have faith and do not **d**,
Mk 11:23 and if you do not **d** in your heart,
Jn 20:27 Do not **d** but believe."

DOUBTED* → DOUBT

Mt 28:17 they worshiped him; but some **d**.

DOUBTER* → DOUBT

Jas 1: 7 the **d**, being double-minded and

DOUBTING* → DOUBT

Jas 1: 6 But ask in faith, never **d**,

DOUBTS* → DOUBT

Lk 24:38 and why do **d** arise in your hearts?
Ro 14:23 have **d** are condemned if they eat,
Jas 1: 6 one who **d** is like a wave of the sea,

DOUGH

Ex 12:39 **d** that they had brought out of Egypt
1Co 5: 6 yeast leavens the whole batch of **d**?
Gal 5: 9 yeast leavens the whole batch of **d**.

DOVE → DOVES

Ge   8: 8 Then he sent out the **d** from him,
Ps 55: 6 I say, "O that I had wings like a **d**!
SS   5: 2 to me, my sister, my love, my **d**,
Hos 7:11 Ephraim has become like a **d**,
Mk 1:10 Spirit descending like a **d** on him.

DOVES → DOVE

SS   4: 1 Your eyes are **d** behind your veil.
Isa 59:11 like **d** we moan mournfully.
Eze 7:16 the mountains like **d** of the valleys,
Mt 10:16 wise as serpents and innocent as **d**.
  21:12 and the seats of those who sold **d**.

DOWN → DOWNCAST, DOWNFALL, DOWNTRODDEN

Ge 11: 5 The LORD came **d** to see the city
  18:21 I must go **d** and see whether they
  46: 3 do not be afraid to go **d** to Egypt,
Ex   3: 8 and I have come **d** to deliver them
  19:11 the third day the LORD will come **d**
Nu 11:25 LORD came **d** in the cloud and spoke
2Sa 22:10 He bowed the heavens, and came **d**;
Ne   1: 3 the wall of Jerusalem is broken **d**,
    9:13 You came **d** also upon Mount Sinai,
Ps 18:16 He reached **d** from on high, he took
  23: 2 makes me lie **d** in green pastures;
 113: 6 who looks far **d** on the heavens and
Pr   5: 5 Her feet go **d** to death;
Ecc 3: 3 to break **d**, and a time to build up;
Da   8:10 threw **d** to the earth some of the host
Mk 6:40 So they sat **d** in groups of hundreds
  15:30 and come **d** from the cross!"
Lk   4: 9 throw yourself **d** from here,
Jn   6:41 the bread that came **d** from heaven."
  10:11 The good shepherd lays **d** his life
Heb 1: 3 at the right hand of the Majesty
  10:12 "he sat **d** at the right hand of God,"
1Jn 3:16 that he laid **d** his life for us—
Rev 3:12 new Jerusalem that comes **d** from
  12: 9 The great dragon was thrown **d**,
  21: 2 coming **d** out of heaven from God,
  21:10 the holy city Jerusalem coming **d**

DOWN FROM HEAVEN 2Ki 1:10, 10, 12, 12, 14; 2Ch 7:1; Ps 14:2; 33:13; 53:2; 80:14; Isa 55:10; 63:15; La 2:1; Da 4:13, 23; Lk 9:54; Jn 6:33, 38, 41, 42, 50, 51, 58; Ac 11:5; Rev 10:1; 13:13; 18:1; 20:1, 9; 2Mc 2:10

DOWN TO EGYPT Ge 12:10; 26:2; 37:25; 39:1; 43:15; 46:3; Nu 20:15; Dt 10:22; Jos 24:4; Isa 30:2; 31:1; Ac 7:15; Jdt 5:10

DOWNCAST → DOWN, CAST

Pr 17:22 but a **d** spirit dries up the bones.
2Co 7: 6 But God, who consoles the **d**,

DOWNFALL → DOWN, FALL

Est 6:13 before whom your **d** has begun,
Ps 140: 4 the violent who have planned my **d**.
Pr 29:16 the righteous will look upon their **d**.
Sir 25: 7 lives to see the **d** of his foes.

DOWNTRODDEN* → DOWN, TREAD

Ps 74:21 Do not let the **d** be put to shame;

 147: 6 The LORD lifts up the **d**;

DRAG → DRAGGED, DRAGGING

Ps   7: 2 they will **d** me away, with no one to
  28: 3 Do not **d** me away with the wicked,
Isa 5:18 you who **d** iniquity along with cords

DRAGGED* → DRAG

Mt 10:18 and you will be **d** before governors
Ac 14:19 Then they stoned Paul and **d** him

DRAGGING → DRAG

Jn 21: 8 **d** the net full of fish,
Ac   8: 3 **d** off both men and women,

DRAGON → DRAGONS

Job 7:12 Am I the Sea, or the **D**,
Isa 27: 1 and he will kill the **d** that
  51: 9 in pieces, who pierced the **d**?
Eze 29: 3 the great **d** sprawling in the midst
Rev 12: 3 a great red **d**, with seven heads and
  13: 2 **d** gave it his power and his throne
  16:13 coming from the mouth of the **d**,
  20: 2 seized the **d**, that ancient serpent,
Sir 25:16 rather live with a lion and a **d** than
Bel 1:23 in that place there was a great **d**,

DRAGONS → DRAGON

Ps 74:13 you broke the heads of the **d** in the
AdE 10: 7 The two **d** are Haman and myself.
2Es 15:29 The nations of the **d** of Arabia

DRANK → DRINK

Ge 9:21 He **d** some of the wine and became
Ex 24:11 beheld God, and they ate and **d**.
Dt   9: 9 I neither ate bread nor **d** water.
Jdg 15:19 When he **d**, his spirit returned,
Jer 51: 7 the nations **d** of her wine,
Da   5: 4 **d** the wine and praised the gods of
Mk 14:23 and all of them **d** from it.
1Co 10: 4 and all **d** the same spiritual drink.
Jdt 12:20 and **d** a great quantity of wine,
Bel 1: 7 and it never ate or **d** anything."
2Es 14:40 I took it and **d**;

DRAW → DRAWING, DREW

Ge 24:11 when women go out to **d** water.
Ex   2:16 They came to **d** water, and filled
1Sa 31: 4 "**D** your sword and thrust me
Isa 12: 3 With joy you will **d** water from the
  58: 2 they delight to **d** near to God.
Jn   2: 8 He said to them, "Now **d** some out,
    4: 7 Samaritan woman came to **d** water,
  12:32 will **d** all people to myself."
Jas 4: 8 **D** near to God, and he will **d** near

DRAWING → DRAW

Lk 21:28 your redemption is **d** near."

DREAD

Ge 9: 2 The fear and **d** of you shall rest
Ex 1:12 Egyptians came to **d** the Israelites.
Nu 22: 3 Moab was in great **d** of the people,
Dt 31: 6 have no fear or **d** of them,
Jos 2: 9 and that **d** of you has fallen on us,
1Sa 11: 7 Then the **d** of the LORD fell
Job 3:25 and what I **d** befalls me.
Pr   1:33 live at ease, without **d** of disaster."
  10:24 What the wicked **d** will come upon
Isa 8:13 and let him be your **d**.

DREAM → DREAMED, DREAMER, DREAMERS, DREAMS

Ge 20: 3 God came to Abimelech in a **d** by
  31:11 the angel of God said to me in the **d**,
  37: 5 Once Joseph had a **d**, and when he
  40: 5 each his own **d**, and each **d** with its own meaning.
Jdg 7:13 a man telling a **d** to his comrade;
1Ki 3: 5 LORD appeared to Solomon in a **d**
Jer 23:28 the prophet who has a **d** tell the **d**,
Da   2: 3 "I have had such a **d** that my spirit
    4: 5 I saw a **d** that frightened me;
    7: 1 Daniel had a **d** and visions of his

Joel	2:28	your old men shall **d** dreams,
Mt	1:20	of the Lord appeared to him in a **d**
	2:12	warned in a **d** not to return to Herod
	2:13	Lord appeared to Joseph in a **d**
	2:19	suddenly appeared in a **d** to Joseph
	2:22	And after being warned in a **d,**
	27:19	because of a **d** about him."
Ac	2:17	and your old men shall **d** dreams.
AdE	10: 5	for I remember the **d** that I had
2Es	10:59	will show you in those **d** visions
	11: 1	On the second night I had a **d:**
	12:35	This is the **d** that you saw,
	13: 1	After seven days I dreamed a **d** in

DREAMED → DREAM

Ge	28:12	he **d** that there was a ladder set up
	37: 6	them, "Listen to this dream that I **d.**
	41: 1	Pharaoh **d** that he was standing by
Da	2: 1	Nebuchadnezzar **d** such dreams
2Es	13: 1	After seven days I **d** a dream in the

DREAMER* → DREAM

Ge	37:19	to one another, "Here comes this **d.**

DREAMERS* → DREAM

Jer	27: 9	your **d,** your soothsayers, or your
Zec	10: 2	the **d** tell false dreams, and give
Jude	1: 8	in the same way these **d** also defile

DREAMS → DREAM

Nu	12: 6	I speak to them in **d.**
Dt	13: 1	or those who divine by **d** appear
1Sa	28: 6	LORD did not answer him, not by **d,**
Joel	2:28	your old men shall dream **d,**
Ac	2:17	and your old men shall dream **d.**
Sir	34: 7	For **d** have deceived many,

DREGS*

Ps	75: 8	earth shall drain it down to the **d.**
Isa	51:17	to the **d** the bowl of staggering.
Jer	48:11	settled like wine on its **d;**
Zep	1:12	who rest complacently on their **d,**
1Co	4:13	the **d** of all things, to this very day.

DRESS → DRESSED

1Ti	2: 9	should **d** themselves modestly
Jdt	12:15	**d** herself in all her woman's finery.

DRESSED → DRESS

Zec	3: 3	Joshua was **d** with filthy clothes as
Lk	7:25	Someone **d** in soft robes?
	12:35	Be **d** for action and have your lamps
Jn	19: 2	and they **d** him in a purple robe.
Rev	3: 4	they will walk with me, **d** in white,
	4: 4	twenty-four elders, **d** in white robes,
Jdt	8: 5	and **d** in widow's clothing.
	10: 7	in appearance and **d** differently,

DREW → DRAW

Ex	2:10	she said, "I **d** him out of the water."
Ps	18:16	he **d** me out of mighty waters.
	40: 2	He **d** me up from the desolate pit,
Jer	38:13	they **d** Jeremiah up by the ropes

DRIED → DRY

Ge	8:13	the waters were **d** up from the earth;
Jos	5: 1	had **d** up the waters of the Jordan
Ps	22:15	my mouth is **d** up like a potsherd,
Isa	51:10	Was it not you who **d** up the sea,
Rev	16:12	and its water was **d** up in order to

DRIES → DRY

Pr	17:22	but a downcast spirit **d** up the bones.
Isa	24: 4	The earth **d** up and withers,
Joel	1:10	grain is destroyed, the wine **d** up,
Am	1: 2	and the top of Carmel **d** up.
Na	1: 4	and he **d** up all the rivers;
2Es	8:23	whose look **d** up the depths

DRIFT*

Heb	2: 1	so that we do not **d** away from it.

DRINK → DRANK, DRINKING, DRINKS, DRUNK, DRUNKARD, DRUNKARDS, DRUNKENNESS

Ge	19:33	So they made their father **d** wine
	24:14	'D, and I will water your camels'—
	35:14	and he poured out a **d** offering on it,
Ex	15:23	not **d** the water of Marah because it
	17: 1	no water for the people to **d.**
	32: 6	the people sat down to eat and **d,**
	32:20	and made the Israelites **d** it.
Nu	4: 7	and the flagons for the **d** offering;
	6: 3	themselves from wine and strong **d;**
	20: 5	and there is no water to **d."**
Jdg	7: 5	all those who kneel down to **d,**
	13: 4	be careful not to **d** wine or strong **d,**
2Sa	23:15	to **d** from the well of Bethlehem
Ps	50:13	or **d** the blood of goats?
	60: 3	wine to **d** that made us reel.
	69:21	my thirst they gave me vinegar to **d.**
	80: 5	them tears to **d** in full measure.
Pr	5:15	**D** water from your own cistern,
	31: 7	let them **d** and forget their poverty,
Ecc	2:24	for mortals than to eat and **d,**
	9: 7	and **d** your wine with a merry heart;
Isa	22:13	eat and **d,** for tomorrow we die."
Jer	8:14	has given us poisoned water to **d,**
	25:15	the nations to whom I send you **d** it.
	35: 2	then offer them wine to **d.**
Eze	23:32	You shall **d** your sister's cup,
Da	1:12	vegetables to eat and water to **d.**
Am	2:12	But you made the nazirites **d** wine,
Hab	2:15	for you who make your neighbors **d,**
Mt	20:22	to **d** the cup that I am about to **d?"**
	26:27	saying, **"D** from it, all of you;
	27:34	wine to **d,** mixed with gall;
Lk	1:15	He must never **d** wine or strong **d;**
	12:19	for many years; relax, eat, **d,**
	22:18	I will not **d** of the fruit of the vine
Jn	4: 7	to her, "Give me a **d.**"
	6:54	and **d** my blood have eternal life,
	7:38	the one who believes in me **d,**
	18:11	not to **d** the cup that the Father has
Ro	14:17	kingdom of God is not food and **d**
1Co	10: 4	and all drank the same spiritual **d.**
	10:21	cannot **d** the cup of the Lord and
	12:13	we were all made to **d** of one Spirit.
	15:32	eat and **d,** for tomorrow we die."
Col	2:16	in matters of food and **d** or of
1Ti	5:23	No longer **d** only water,
Heb	9:10	deal only with food and **d** and
Rev	14: 8	has made all nations **d** of the wine
	14:10	also **d** the wine of God's wrath,
	16: 6	you have given them blood to **d.**
Tob	4:15	Do not **d** wine to excess
Jdt	12:17	"Have a **d** and be merry
Sir	15: 3	give him the water of wisdom to **d.**

DRINK OFFERING
Ge 35:14; Ex 29:40, 41; 30:9; Lev 23:13; Nu 4:7; 6:17; 15:5, 7, 10, 24; 28:7, 7, 8, 9, 10, 15, 24, 31; 29:16, 22, 25, 28, 34, 38; 2Ki 16:13, 15; Isa 57:6; Joel 1:9, 13; 2:14; Sir 50:15

DRINK OFFERINGS
Ex 25:29; 37:16; Lev 23:18, 37; Nu 6:15; 28:14; 29:6, 11, 18, 19, 21, 24, 27, 30, 31, 33, 37, 39; 2Ch 29:35; Ezr 7:17; Ps 16:4; Jer 7:18; Eze 20:28; 45:17; Hos 9:4; 1Mc 1:22, 45

STRONG DRINK
Lev 10:9; Nu 6:3; 28:7; Dt 14:26; 29:6; Jdg 13:4, 7, 14; 1Sa 1:15; Pr 20:1; 31:4, 6; Isa 5:11; 24:9; 28:7, 7, 7; 29:9; 56:12; Mic 2:11; Lk 1:15

DRINKING → DRINK

Est	5: 6	While they were **d** wine,
	7: 2	as they were **d** wine,
Job	1:13	**d** wine in the eldest brother's house,
Isa	5:22	you who are heroes in **d** wine
Mt	11:19	Son of Man came eating and **d,**
Lk	17:27	They were eating and **d,**

DRINKS → DRINK

Mt	24:49	and eats and **d** with drunkards,

Jn	4:13	"Everyone who **d** of this water will
1Co	11:27	the bread or **d** the cup of the Lord in

DRIP → DRIPPING, DRIPPINGS

Pr	5: 3	the lips of a loose woman **d** honey,
Joel	3:18	the mountains shall **d** sweet wine,
Am	9:13	the mountains shall **d** sweet wine,

DRIPPING* → DRIP

1Sa	14:26	honeycomb, the honey was **d** out;
Pr	19:13	quarreling is a continual **d** of rain.
	27:15	A continual **d** on a rainy day and

DRIPPINGS → DRIP

Ps	19:10	honey, and **d** of the honeycomb.

DRIVE → DRIVEN, DRIVES, DRIVING, DROVE

Ex	6: 1	by a mighty hand he will **d** them out
	23:30	Little by little I will **d** them out
Nu	33:52	you shall **d** out all the inhabitants of
Jos	13:13	Yet the Israelites did not **d** out the
	23:13	not continue to **d** out these nations
Jdg	1:19	but could not **d** out the inhabitants
Pr	22:10	**D** out a scoffer, and strife goes out;
Mk	11:15	to **d** out those who were selling
Jn	6:37	comes to me I will never **d** away;

DRIVEN → DRIVE

Ge	4:14	**d** me away from the soil,
Ex	12:39	**d** out of Egypt and could not wait,
Jos	23: 9	For the LORD has **d** out before you
Ps	31:22	I am **d** far from your sight."
Da	4:25	You shall be **d** away from human
Jnh	2: 4	said, 'I am **d** away from your sight;
Jn	12:31	the ruler of this world will be **d** out.
Jas	1: 6	and tossed by the wind;

DRIVES → DRIVE

Ps	1: 4	are like chaff that the wind **d** away.

DRIVING → DRIVE

Lev	20:23	practices of the nation that I am **d**
Jdg	2:23	not **d** them out at once,
Ps	35: 5	the angel of the LORD **d** them on.
Ac	26:24	Too much learning is **d** you insane!"

DROP → DROPPED, DROPPINGS, DROPS

Dt	28:40	for your olives shall **d** off.
	32: 2	May my teaching **d** like the rain,
	33:28	where the heavens **d** down dew.
Isa	40:15	nations are like a **d** from a bucket,

DROPPED → DROP

Lk	16:17	stroke of a letter in the law to be **d.**
Rev	16:21	**d** from heaven on people,

DROPPINGS* → DROP

Tob	2:10	their fresh **d** fell into my eyes

DROPS → DROP

Lk	22:44	sweat became like great **d** of blood

DROSS

Ps	119:119	wicked of the earth you count as **d;**
Pr	25: 4	Take away the **d** from the silver,
Isa	1:22	Your silver has become **d,**
	1:25	I will smelt away your **d** as with lye
Eze	22:18	house of Israel has become **d** to me;

DROUGHT

Dt	28:22	inflammation, with fiery heat and **d,**
1Ki	18: 1	in the third year of the **d,**
Jer	14: 1	came to Jeremiah concerning the **d:**
	17: 8	in the year of **d** it is not anxious,
Hag	1:11	I have called for a **d** on the land and
Sir	35:26	as clouds of rain in time of **d.**

DROVE → DRIVE

Ge	3:24	He **d** out the man;
Jos	24:18	the LORD **d** out before us all the
Ps	44: 2	your own hand **d** out the nations,
Mt	21:12	**d** out all who were selling and
Mk	1:12	Spirit immediately **d** him out into
1Mc	1:53	they **d** Israel into hiding

DROWN* → DROWNED

SS   8: 7 love, neither can floods **d** it.

DROWNED → DROWN

Mt   18: 6 neck and you were **d** in the depth of
Lk   8:33 steep bank into the lake and was **d.**
Heb 11:29 attempted to do so they were **d.**

DROWSINESS* → DROWSY

Pr   23:21 and **d** will clothe them with rags.

DROWSY → DROWSINESS

Mt   25: 5 all of them became **d** and slept.

DRUM

Da   3: 5 lyre, trigon, harp, **d,**

DRUNK → DRINK

Ge   9:21 some of the wine and became **d,**
Dt   32:42 I will make my arrows **d** with blood,
Ru   3: 7 When Boaz had eaten and **d,**
1Sa   1:13 therefore Eli thought she was **d.**
      25:36 within him, for he was very **d;**
2Sa 11:13 in his presence and made him **d;**
1Ki 16: 9 drinking himself **d** in the house
      20:16 drinking himself **d** in the booths,
SS   5: 1 drink, and be **d** with love.
Isa   29: 9 Be **d,** but not from wine;
Jn   2:10 after the guests have become **d.**
Ac   2:15 these are not **d,** as you suppose,
1Co 11:21 goes hungry and another becomes **d.**
Eph   5:18 Do not get **d** with wine,
1Th   5: 7 and those who are **d** get **d** at night.
Rev 17: 6 was **d** with the blood of the saints
      18: 3 have **d** of the wine of the wrath
Jdt   13: 2 on his bed, for he was dead **d.**
Sir   31:28 Wine **d** at the proper time

DRUNKARD → DRINK

Dt   21:20 He is a glutton and a **d."**
Pr   23:21 for the **d** and the glutton will come
Isa   19:14 as a **d** staggers around in vomit.
      24:20 The earth staggers like a **d,**
Mt   11:19 they say, 'Look, a glutton and a **d,**
1Co   5:11 is an idolater, reviler, **d,** or robber.
1Ti   3: 3 not a **d,** not violent but gentle,

DRUNKARDS → DRINK

Ps 107:27 they reeled and staggered like **d,**
Isa   28: 1 proud garland of the **d** of Ephraim,
Joel   1: 5 Wake up, you **d,** and weep;
Mt   24:49 and eats and drinks with **d,**
1Co   6:10 the greedy, **d,** revilers, robbers—

DRUNKENNESS* → DRINK

Ecc 10:17 for strength, and not for **d!**
Jer   13:13 inhabitants of Jerusalem—with **d.**
Eze 23:33 shall be filled with **d** and sorrow.
Lk   21:34 dissipation and **d** and the worries
Ro   13:13 in reveling and **d,** not in debauchery
Gal   5:21 **d,** carousing, and things like these.
1Pe   4: 3 living in licentiousness, passions, **d,**
Tob   4:15 to excess or let **d** go with you
Sir   31:30 **D** increases the anger of a fool

DRUSILLA*

Ac   24:24 when Felix came with his wife **D,**

DRY → DRIED, DRIES

Ge   1: 9 and let the **d** land appear."
       7:22 everything on **d** land in whose
Ex   14:16 may go into the sea on **d** ground,
Jos   3:17 were crossing over on **d** ground,
Jdg   6:37 and it is **d** on all the ground,
2Ki   2: 8 two of them crossed on **d** ground.
Ps   66: 6 He turned the sea into **d** land;
      95: 5 for he made it, and the **d** land,
Isa   53: 2 and like a root out of **d** ground;
Eze 17:24 I **d** up the green tree and make the
                d tree flourish.
      37: 4 **d** bones, hear the word of the LORD.
Jnh   2:10 it spewed Jonah out upon the **d** land.
Na   1: 4 He rebukes the sea and makes it **d,**
Lk   7:38 to **d** them with her hair.

Heb 11:29 the Red Sea as if it were **d** land,

DUE

Ge   18:10 return to you in **d** season,
Lev   6:18 as their perpetual **d** throughout
      10:13 it is your **d** and your sons' **d,**
1Sa   1:20 In **d** time Hannah conceived
1Ch 16:29 Ascribe to the LORD the glory **d** his
Ps   28: 4 render them their **d** reward.
      65: 1 Praise is **d** to you, O God, in Zion;
      90:11 as the fear that is **d** you.
Mal   1: 6 a father, where is the honor **d** me?
Ro   1:27 in their own persons the **d** penalty
      13: 7 Pay to all what is **d** them—
1Pe   5: 6 so that he may exalt you in **d** time.

DUG → DIG

Ps   57: 6 They **d** a pit in my path,
Isa   5: 2 He **d** it and cleared it of stones,
Jer   18:20 Yet they have **d** a pit for my life.
Mt   21:33 **d** a wine press in it,
Mk   2: 4 and after having **d** through it,

DULL

Isa   6:10 Make the mind of this people **d,**
      59: 1 nor his ear too **d** to hear.
Mt   13:15 For this people's heart has grown **d,**
Heb   5:11 have become **d** in understanding.

DUNG

Ex   29:14 and its skin, and its **d,**
Job   20: 7 will perish forever like their own **d;**
Mal   2: 3 and spread **d** on your faces,

DUNGEON

Ge   40:15 they should have put me into the **d."**
Isa   42: 7 bring out the prisoners from the **d,**

DUST

Ge   2: 7 LORD God formed man from the **d**
       3:14 and **d** you shall eat all the days of
       3:19 you are **d,** and to **d** you shall return.
      13:16 offspring like the **d** of the earth;
      28:14 offspring shall be like the **d** of the
Nu   23:10 Who can count the **d** of Jacob,
1Sa   2: 8 He raises up the poor from the **d;**
Job   42: 6 and repent in **d** and ashes."
Ps   22:15 you lay me in the **d** of death.
      72: 9 and his enemies lick the **d.**
      90: 3 You turn us back to **d,**
     103:14 he remembers that we are **d.**
Ecc   3:20 from the **d,** and all turn to **d** again.
Isa   65:25 but the serpent—its food shall be **d!**
Mic   7:17 they shall lick **d** like a snake,
Na   1: 3 and the clouds are the **d** of his feet.
Mt   10:14 shake off the **d** from your feet
Ac   13:51 shook the **d** off their feet in protest
      18: 6 he shook the **d** from his clothes
1Co 15:47 man was from the earth, a man of **d;**
Rev 18:19 And they threw **d** on their heads,
Sir   17:32 all human beings are **d** and ashes.
LtJ   6:13 faces are wiped because of the **d**

DUST OF THE EARTH Ge 13:16, 16;
28:14; Ex 8:16, 17, 17; 2Sa 22:43; 2Ch 1:9; Isa
40:12; Da 12:2; Am 2:7; Jdt 2:20; Sir 44:21

DUTIES → DUTY

Nu   3: 7 They shall perform **d** for him
       8:26 the Levites in assigning their **d.**
1Ch 25: 1 who did the work and of their **d**
Ne   13:30 I established the **d** of the priests and
Heb   9: 6 first tent to carry out their ritual **d;**

DUTY → DUTIES

Ge   38: 8 the **d** of a brother-in-law to her;
Dt   25: 5 the **d** of a husband's brother to her,
Col   3:20 your acceptable **d** in the Lord.

DWELL → DWELLING, DWELLINGS,
         DWELLS

Ex   25: 8 so that I may **d** among them.
1Ki   6:13 will **d** among the children of Israel,
       8:27 But will God indeed **d** on the earth?
Ps   23: 6 and I shall **d** in the house of

Isa   57:15 I **d** in the high and holy place,
Joel   3:17 the LORD your God, **d** in Zion,
Zec   2:11 and I will **d** in your midst.
Ac   7:48 the Most High does not **d** in houses
2Co 12: 9 the power of Christ may **d** in me.
Eph   3:17 that Christ may **d** in your hearts
Col   1:19 fullness of God was pleased to **d,**
       3:16 the word of Christ **d** in you richly;
Rev 12:12 heavens and those who **d** in them!
      21: 3 He will **d** with them as their God;

DWELLING → DWELL

Lev   26:11 I will place my **d** in your midst,
Dt   12:11 will choose as a **d** for his name:
1Ki   8:30 O hear in heaven your **d** place;
Ps   49:11 their **d** places to all generations,
      76: 2 his **d** place in Zion.
      90: 1 our **d** place in all generations.
Eze 37:27 My **d** place shall be with them;
Jn   14: 2 my Father's house there are many **d**
Ac   15:16 and I will rebuild the **d** of David,
2Co   5: 2 to be clothed with our heavenly **d**—
Eph   2:22 spiritually into a **d** place for God.
Rev 13: 6 blaspheming his name and his **d,**
1Mc   1:38 she became a **d** of strangers;

DWELLINGS → DWELL

Mt   17: 4 I will make three **d** here, one for

DWELLS → DWELL

Isa   8:18 from the LORD of hosts, who **d**
Joel   3:21 for the LORD **d** in Zion.
Jn   14:10 but the Father who **d** in me
Ro   7:17 but sin that **d** within me.
       8: 9 since the Spirit of God **d** in you.
1Co   3:16 and that God's Spirit **d** in you?
Col   2: 9 the whole fullness of deity **d** bodily,
1Ti   6:16 and **d** in unapproachable light,

DYING → DEAD

Jn   11:37 have kept this man from **d?"**
2Co   6: 9 as **d,** and see—we are alive;
Php   1:21 living is Christ and **d** is gain.

ℰ

EACH

Ge   49:28 blessing **e** one of them with a
Ex   12: 3 take a lamb for **e** family,
Nu   1: 4 A man from **e** tribe shall be with
      16:18 So **e** man took his censer,
      17: 2 one for **e** ancestral house,
Jos   4: 5 for **e** of the tribes of the Israelites,
Isa   6: 2 **e** had six wings:
Eze 10:14 **E** one had four faces:
Lk   11: 3 Give us **e** day our daily bread.
Ac   2: 6 **e** one heard them speaking in
Ro   2: 6 repay according to **e** one's deeds:
      14:12 **e** of us will be accountable to God.
1Co   7: 7 But **e** has a particular gift from God,
      12: 7 To **e** is given the manifestation of
1Pe   4:10 gift **e** of you has received.
Rev   2:23 **e** of you as your works deserve.
       4: 8 **e** of them with six wings,
       6:11 **e** given a white robe
      21:21 **e** of the gates is a single pearl,
      22: 2 producing its fruit **e** month;

EACH DAY Ex 16:4; 29:38; Nu 7:11; 1Ki
8:59; 1Ch 16:37; 26:17, 17, 17; 2Ch 8:13, 14;
31:16; Ezr 3:4; Lk 11:3

EACH OF THEM Ex 16:18; 33:8; Jdg 21:23;
1Sa 10:27; Ezr 10:16; Job 2:11; 42:11; Eze
1:6, 9; Zec 13:5; Mt 20:9, 10; Lk 4:40; Jn 6:7;
7:53; Ac 2:3; 21:26; Rev 4:8; Tob 3:8; Wis
15:7; Sir 17:14; 2Mc 7:21; 13:2; 15:11; 2Es
2:43; 4Mc 13:13; 15:7

EACH OF US Nu 31:50; 2Ki 6:2; Jer 18:12;

51:9; Ac 2:8; Ro 14:12; 15:2; Eph 4:7; Bar
2:8; 1Es 3:5

EACH OF YOU Ex 16:16, 29; 32:27, 27; Nu
25:5; Dt 3:20; Jos 4:5; Jdg 8:24; 21:21; Ru 1:8,
9; 1Sa 8:22; 2Ch 10:16; Jer 34:14, 16; 51:6,
45; Eze 33:26; Lk 13:15; Ac 3:26; 1Co 1:12;
7:17, 20; 11:21; 16:2; 2Co 9:7; Eph 5:33; Php
2:4; 1Pe 4:10; Rev 2:23; Jdt 14:2; 2Mc 7:22;
9:26; 1Es 2:6

EACH OTHER Ge 13:11; 1Sa 20:41, 41; 1Ki
7:4, 5; Job 41:17; Ps 12:2; 85:10; Isa 34:14;
Jer 31:34; Mic 7:2; Zec 3:10; Lk 23:12; 24:14,
17, 32; Ac 7:26; 28:25; Gal 5:17; Col 3:13;
1Th 5:11; Heb 8:11; Sus 1:10, 13, 13, 51, 52,
54, 58; 1Mc 10:71; 11:9; 1Es 1:26; 3Mc 5:49

EAGER → EAGERLY

Zep   3: 7 e to make all their deeds corrupt.
Ro   8:19 the creation waits with e longing
1Co 14:12 since you are e for spiritual gifts,
        14:39 So, my friends, be e to prophesy,
1Pe   3:13 Now who will harm you if you are e
2Pe   1:10 the more e to confirm your call and

EAGERLY → EAGER

Lk   22:15 e desired to eat this Passover with
Ac   8: 6 listened e to what was said
        16:14 Lord opened her heart to listen e
        17:11 welcomed the message very e

EAGLE → EAGLE'S, EAGLES, EAGLES'

Dt   14:12 the e, the vulture, the osprey,
        32:11 an e stirs up its nest,
Pr   30:19 the way of an e in the sky,
Jer   48:40 he shall swoop down like an e,
Eze   1:10 the left side, and the face of an e;
        17: 3 A great e, with great wings and long
Rev   4: 7 fourth living creature like a flying e.
        8:13 I heard an e crying with a loud voice
        12:14 given the two wings of the great e,
2Es 11: 1 an e that had twelve feathered wings
        12: 1 saying these words to the e,
        14:18 For the e that you saw in

EAGLE'S → EAGLE

Ps   103: 5 your youth is renewed like the e.
Jer   49:16 you make your nest as high as the e,

EAGLES → EAGLE

Isa   40:31 shall mount up with wings like e,

EAGLES' → EAGLE

Ex   19: 4 and how I bore you on e wings
Da   7: 4 like a lion and had e wings.

EAR → EARLOBE, EARRINGS, EARS

Ex   21: 6 shall pierce his e with an awl;
2Ki   19:16 Incline your e, O LORD, and hear;
Ne   1:11 let your e be attentive to the prayer
Job   12:11 not the e test words as the palate
Ps   5: 1 Give e to my words, O LORD;
        116: 2 Because he inclined his e to me,
Pr   2: 2 making your e attentive to wisdom
        25:12 is a wise rebuke to a listening e.
Ecc   1: 8 or the e filled with hearing.
Isa   59: 1 nor his e too dull to hear.
        64: 4 has heard, no e has perceived,
Da   9:18 Incline your e, O my God, and hear.
Mk   14:47 of the high priest, cutting off his e.
Lk   22:51 he touched his e and healed him.
1Co   2: 9 "What no eye has seen, nor e heard,
Rev   2: 7 Let anyone who has an e listen
        13: 9 Let anyone who has an e listen:
Sir   3:29 attentive e is the desire of the wise.
Bar   3: 9 give e, and learn wisdom!

EARLIER → EARLY

Heb   7:18 abrogation of an e commandment
        10:32 But recall those e days when,

EARLOBE* → EAR

Dt   15:17 thrust it through his e into the door,

EARLY → EARLIER

Dt   11:14 the e rain and the later rain,
Ps   127: 2 It is in vain that you rise up e and
Pr   27:14 loud voice, rising e in the morning,
Isa   5:11 who rise e in the morning in pursuit
Hos   6: 4 like the dew that goes away e.
Joel   2:23 the e and the later rain,
Lk   24:22 were at the tomb e this morning,
Jas   5: 7 receives the e and the late rains.
Sir   31:20 he rises e, and feels fit.

EARN

Pr   11:18 The wicked e no real gain,
Hag   1: 6 that e wages earn wages e wages to
                put them into a bag with holes.
2Th   3:12 quietly and to e their own living.

EARNEST → EARNESTLY,
EARNESTNESS

Rev   3:19 Be e, therefore, and repent.

EARNESTLY → EARNEST

Ps   78:34 they repented and sought God e.
Lk   22:44 In his anguish he prayed more e,
Ac   26: 7 as they e worship day and night.
Man   1:13 I e implore you, forgive me,

EARNESTNESS* → EARNEST

2Co   7:11 what e this godly grief has produced
        8: 8 of your love against the e of others.

EARRINGS → EAR, RING

Ex   35:22 brooches and e and signet rings
Eze   16:12 a ring on your nose, e in your ears,

EARS → EAR

Ge   41: 5 seven e of grain, plump and good,
Dt   29: 4 or eyes to see, or e to hear.
Ps   34:15 and his e are open to their cry.
        115: 6 They have e, but do not hear;
Pr   26:17 who takes a passing dog by the e
Isa   6:10 their eyes, and listen with their e,
        35: 5 and the e of the deaf unstopped;
Jer   6:10 their e are closed, they cannot listen.
Mt   11:15 Let anyone with e listen!
Mk   8:18 Do you have e, and fail to hear?
Ac   7:51 uncircumcised in heart and e,
        28:27 and their e are hard of hearing,
        28:27 their eyes, and listen with their e,
2Ti   4: 3 sound doctrine, but having itching e,
1Pe   3:12 and his e are open to their prayer.
Wis   15:15 nor e with which to hear,
Bar   2:31 that obeys and e that hear;

EARTH → EARTHEN, EARTHLY,
EARTHQUAKE, EARTHQUAKES

Ge   1: 1 God created the heavens and the e,
        1: 2 the e was a formless void and
        1:28 and fill the e and subdue it;
        4:12 a fugitive and a wanderer on the e."
        6:11 the e was corrupt in God's sight,
        6:17 to bring a flood of waters on the e,
        7:24 And the waters swelled on the e
        9:13 the covenant between me and the e.
        12: 3 families of the e shall be blessed."
        14:19 Most High, maker of heaven and e,
        18:25 Judge of all the e do what is just?"
        24: 3 the God of heaven and e,
        28:14 families of the e shall be blessed in
Ex   19: 5 Indeed, the whole e is mine,
Dt   5: 8 or that is on the e beneath,
Jos   3:13 the Lord of all the e,
1Ki   8:27 will God indeed dwell on the e?
1Ch   16:23 Sing to the LORD, all the e.
        16:30 tremble before him, all the e.
Job   26: 7 and hangs the e upon nothing.
Ps   8: 1 majestic is your name in all the e!
        24: 1 The e is the LORD's and all that is in
        46: 6 he utters his voice, the e melts.
        47: 2 a great king over all the e.
        73:25 on e that I desire other than you.
        90: 2 or ever you had formed the e and
        97: 1 Let the e rejoice; let the many

        102:25 ago you laid the foundation of the e,
        108: 5 and let your glory be over all the e.
Pr   8:26 he had not yet made e and fields,
Isa   6: 3 the whole e is full of his glory."
        24:20 e staggers like a drunkard, it sways
        37:16 you have made heaven and e.
        40:22 he who sits above the circle of the e,
        51: 6 the e will wear out like a garment,
        55: 9 as the heavens are higher than the e,
        65:17 to create new heavens and a new e;
        66: 1 my throne and the e is my footstool:
Jer   10:10 At his wrath the e quakes,
        23:24 Do I not fill heaven and e?
        33:25 and the ordinances of heaven and e,
Da   2:39 which shall rule over the whole e.
        12: 2 in the dust of the e shall awake,
Joel   2:30 portents in the heavens and on the e,
Am   9: 5 he who touches the e and it melts,
Hab   2:20 let all the e keep silence before him!
Hag   2: 6 I will shake the heavens and the e
        2:21 to shake the heavens and the e,
Zec   14: 9 will become king over all the e;
Mt   5: 5 the meek, for they will inherit the e.
        5:13 "You are the salt of the e;
        5:18 until heaven and e pass away,
        5:35 by the e, for it is his footstool,
        6:10 will be done, on e as it is in heaven.
        16:19 bind on e will be bound in heaven,
        24:35 Heaven and e will pass away,
        28:18 "All authority in heaven and on e
Lk   2:14 on e peace among those whom he
        5:24 has authority on e to forgive sins"—
Jn   12:32 I, when I am lifted up from the e,
Ac   2:19 and signs on the e below,
        4:24 made the heaven and the e, the sea,
        7:49 and the e is my footstool.
1Co 10:26 e and its fullness are the Lord's."
        15:47 The first man was from the e,
Eph   1:10 things in heaven and things on e.
        3:15 in heaven and on e takes its name.
Php   2:10 in heaven and on e and under the e,
Heb   1:10 beginning, Lord, you founded the e,
        12:26 I will shake not only the e but
2Pe   3:13 wait for new heavens and a new e,
Rev   5: 3 no one in heaven or on e or under
                the e was able to open the scroll
        6: 8 authority over a fourth of the e,
        8: 7 and a third of the e was burned up,
        12:12 But woe to the e and the sea,
        20:11 the e and the heaven fled from his
        21: 1 I saw a new heaven and a new e;
Jdt   2: 5 the lord of the whole e:
        13:18 who created the heavens and the e,
Sir   40:11 All that is of e returns to e,
Aza   1:52 "Let the e bless the Lord;

ALL THE EARTH Ge 1:29; 7:3; 11:8, 9, 9;
18:25; Ex 9:14, 16; 34:10; Nu 14:21; Jos 3:11,
13; 23:14; 1Sa 17:46; 1Ki 2:2; 2Ki 5:15; 1Ch
16:14, 23, 30; Ps 8:1; 33:8; 45:16;
47:2, 7; 48:2; 57:5, 11; 66:1, 4; 83:18; 96:1, 9;
97:5, 9; 98:4; 100:1; 105:7; 108:5; Isa 10:14,
23; 12:5; 25:8; Jer 51:7, 49; La 2:15; Hab
2:20; Zep 3:8, 19; Zec 6:5; 14:9; Ro 9:17;
10:18; Rev 5:6; Tob 14:7; Jdt 11:1; Sir 24:6;
38:8; 48:15; Bar 2:15; 1Mc 15:9; 2Es 11:12,
40; 15:40

DUST OF THE EARTH Ge 13:16, 16;
28:14; Ex 8:16, 17, 17; 2Sa 22:43; 2Ch 1:9; Isa
40:12; Da 12:2; Am 2:7; Jdt 2:20; Sir 44:21

EARTH ... HEAVEN 1Ki 8:27; 2Ki 19:15;
1Ch 21:16; 2Ch 6:18; Ps 148:13; Isa 37:16;
Eze 8:6:10; 16:19; 19:4; 33:8; 45:16; Mk
13:27; Col 1:20; Heb 12:26; Rev 20:11; 21:1;
1Es 4:34

END OF THE EARTH Dt 13:7; 28:49, 64;
Ps 46:9; 61:2; 135:7; Isa 42:10; 43:6; 48:20;
49:6; 62:11; Jer 25:33; Jdt 11:21; Wis 8:1

ENDS OF THE EARTH Dt 33:17; 1Sa
2:10; Job 28:24; Ps 2:8; 22:27; 48:10; 59:13;
65:5; 67:7; 72:8; 98:3; Pr 17:24; 30:4; Isa
5:26; 24:16; 40:28; 41:5, 9; 45:22; 52:10; Jer

10:13; 16:19; 25:31; 51:16; Da 4:22; Mic 5:4;
Zec 9:10; Mt 12:42; Mk 13:27; Lk 11:31; Ac
1:8; 13:47; Tob 13:11; Wis 6:1; Sir 44:21;
1Mc 1:3; 3:9; 8:4; 14:10

FOUNDATION[S] OF THE EARTH Job
38:4; Ps 82:5; 102:25; Pr 8:29; Isa 24:18;
40:21; 48:13; 51:13, 16; Jer 31:37; Mic 6:2;
Sir 10:16; 16:19; 2Es 6:15; 15:23; 16:15

HEAVEN ... EARTH Ge 14:19, 22; 24:3; Ex
20:11; 31:17; Dt 3:24; 4:26; 30:19; 31:28; 2Sa
18:9; 1Ki 8:23; 2Ki 19:15; 2Ch 2:12; 6:14; Ezr
5:11; Ps 69:34; 115:15; 121:2; 124:8; 134:3;
135:6; 146:6; Isa 24:21; 37:16; Jer 23:24;
33:25; La 2:1; Da 6:27; Mt 5:18; 11:25; 24:35;
28:18; Mk 13:31; Lk 21:14; 10:21; 16:17;
21:33; Ac 4:24; 14:15; 17:24; 1Co 8:5; Eph
3:15; Php 2:10; Col 1:16; Jas 5:12; Rev 5:3,
13; 9:1; 13:13; 14:7; 21:1; Tob 10:13; Jdt 7:28;
9:12; AdE 13:10; LtJ 6:55; Bel 1:5; 1Mc 2:37;
2Mc 7:28; 1Es 6:13; Man 1:2; 2Es 2:14; 6:38

HEAVENS ... EARTH Ge 1:1; 2:1, 4; Dt
11:21; 1Ch 29:11; Ps 78:69; 89:11; 113:6;
115:16; Isa 1:2; 49:13; 65:17; 66:22; Jer 10:11;
32:17; 51:48; Joel 2:30; 3:16; Hab 3:3; Hag
2:6, 21; Zec 12:1; 2Pe 3:7, 13; Jdt 13:18; 2Es
3:18

INHABITANTS OF THE EARTH Ps
33:14; Isa 24:6; 26:21; Jer 25:29, 30; Da 4:35,
35; Zep 1:18; Zec 11:6; Rev 3:10; 6:10; 8:13;
11:10, 10; 13:8; 17:2, 8; 2Es 3:35; 6:18

KINGDOMS OF THE EARTH Dt 28:25;
2Ki 19:15, 19; 1Ch 29:30; 2Ch 36:23; Ezr 1:2;
Ps 68:32; Isa 37:16, 20; Jer 15:4; 24:9; 29:18;
34:1, 17

KINGS OF THE EARTH 1Ki 4:34; 10:23;
2Ch 9:22, 23; Ps 2:2; 76:12; 89:27; 102:15;
138:4; 148:11; Isa 24:21; La 4:12; Eze 27:33;
Mt 17:25; Ac 4:26; Rev 1:5; 6:15; 17:2, 18;
18:3, 9; 19:19; 21:24; 1Mc 1:2; 1Es 8:77; 2Es
15:20

PEOPLES OF THE EARTH Dt 28:10; Jos
4:24; 1Ki 8:43, 53, 60; 2Ch 6:33; 32:19; Eze
31:12; Zep 3:20

WHOLE EARTH Ge 8:9; 9:19; 11:1, 4; Ex
19:5; 1Ki 10:24; Ps 72:19; Isa 6:3; 13:5; 14:7,
26; 54:5; Jer 50:23; 51:25, 41; Eze 32:4;
35:14; Da 2:35, 39; 4:11, 20; 7:23; 8:5; Mic
4:13; Zep 1:18; Zec 1:11; 4:10, 14; Lk 21:35;
Ac 17:26; Rev 13:3; Jdt 2:5, 9; 6:4; 11:7; Wis
5:23; 1Es 4:36; 3Mc 1:29; 2Es 11:2, 32, 46;
15:27

EARTHEN → EARTH
Isa 45: 9 e vessels with the potter!
La 4: 2 how they are reckoned as e pots,

EARTHLY → EARTH
Jn 3:12 If I have told you about e things
2Co 1:12 not by e wisdom but by the grace of
  5: 1 if the e tent we live in is destroyed,
Php 3:19 their minds are set on e things.
Col 3: 5 therefore, whatever in you is e:
Jas 3:15 but is e, unspiritual, devilish.

EARTHQUAKE → EARTH, QUAKE
1Ki 19:11 but the LORD was not in the e;
Isa 29: 6 with thunder and e and great noise,
Mt 28: 2 And suddenly there was a great e;
Ac 16:26 Suddenly there was an e,
Rev 6:12 I looked, and there came a great e;
  11:13 At that moment there was a great e,
  11:13 people were killed in the e,
  16:18 peals of thunder, and a violent e,
  16:18 upon the earth, so violent was that e.
AdE 11: 5 thunders and e, tumult on the earth!
2Es 3:19 four gates of fire and e and wind

EARTHQUAKES → EARTH, QUAKE
Mt 24: 7 be famines and e in various places:
2Es 9: 3 there shall appear in the world e,

EASE → EASIER, EASY
Pr 1:33 will be secure and will live at e,
Jer 30:10 shall return and have quiet and e,
Am 6: 1 Alas for those who are at e in Zion,
Lk 11:46 do not lift a finger to e them.

EASIER → EASE
Mt 9: 5 is e, to say, 'Your sins are forgiven,'
Lk 16:17 it is e for heaven and earth to pass
  18:25 e for a camel to go through the eye

EAST
Ge 2: 8 planted a garden in Eden, in the e;
Ex 14:21 the sea back by a strong e wind
Ps 103:12 as far as the e is from the west,
Eze 11:23 stopped on the mountain e of the
  43: 2 of Israel was coming from the e;
Hos 13:15 the e wind shall come, a blast from
Jnh 4: 8 God prepared a sultry e wind,
Zec 14: 4 shall be split in two from e to west
Mt 2: 1 wise men from the E came to
  8:11 come from e and west and will eat
Rev 16:12 the way for the kings from the e.

EAST SIDE Lev 1:16; Nu 2:3; 10:5; 34:11;
35:5; Dt 4:41, 49; Jdg 11:18; 1Ch 4:39; 6:78;
9:18; Eze 40:32; 42:16; 47:18, 18; 48:1, 2, 3,
4, 5, 6, 7, 8, 8, 16, 23, 24, 25, 26, 27, 32

EAST WIND Ge 41:6, 23, 27; Ex 10:13, 13;
14:21; Job 15:2; 27:21; 38:24; Ps 48:7; 78:26;
Isa 27:8; Eze 17:10; 19:12; 27:26; Hos 12:1;
13:15; Jnh 4:8; 2Es 15:39

PEOPLE OF THE EAST Ge 29:1; Jdg 6:3,
33; 7:12; 8:10; 1Ki 4:30; Job 1:3; Isa 11:14;
Jer 49:28; Eze 25:4, 10

EASY → EASE
Mt 7:13 road is e that leads to destruction,
  11:30 For my yoke is e, and my burden is

EAT → ATE, EATEN, EATER, EATING, EATS
Ge 2:16 freely e of every tree of the garden;
  2:17 of good and evil you shall not e,
  3:19 you shall e bread until you return to
  3:22 and e, and live forever"—
  9: 4 not e flesh with its life.
Ex 12:11 This is how you shall e it:
  12:20 You shall e nothing leavened;
  12:20 you shall e unleavened bread.
  16:12 them, 'At twilight you shall e meat,
  32: 6 the people sat down to e and drink,
Lev 3:17 not e any fat or any blood.
  11: 4 you shall not e the following:
Nu 11:13 to me and say, 'Give us meat to e!'
Dt 12:23 that you do not e the blood;
  14: 4 These are the animals you may e:
Jdg 14:14 of the eater came something to e.
2Sa 9: 7 yourself shall e at my table always."
2Ki 9:10 dogs shall e Jezebel
Ps 22:26 The poor shall e and be satisfied;
  50:13 Do I e the flesh of bulls,
Pr 31:27 and does not e the bread of idleness.
Ecc 2:24 nothing better for mortals than to e
  5:18 to e and drink and find enjoyment
Isa 7:15 He shall e curds and honey by the
  11: 7 the lion shall e straw like the ox.
  55: 1 have no money, come, buy and e!
  65:25 the lion shall e straw like the ox;
Jer 19: 9 make them e the flesh of their sons
  19: 9 shall e the flesh of their neighbors
La 2:20 Should women e their offspring,
Eze 3: 1 O mortal, e what is offered to you;
  3: 1 e this scroll, and go, speak to the
Da 1:12 be given vegetables to e and water
Hag 1: 6 you e, but you never have enough;
Mt 14:16 you give them something to e."
  15: 2 not wash their hands before they e."
  26:26 to the disciples, and said, "Take, e;
Mk 2:26 lawful for any but the priests to e,
  14:14 e the Passover with my disciples?'
Lk 10: 8 e what is set before you;
  12:19 relax, e, drink, be merry.'
  12:29 for what you are to e and what you

Jn 4:32 "I have food to e that you do not
  6:31 them bread from heaven to e.'"
  6:53 unless you e the flesh of the Son of
Ac 10:13 "Get up, Peter; kill and e."
Ro 14: 2 while the weak e only vegetables.
  14:15 is being injured by what you e,
  14:20 to make others fall by what you e;
1Co 5:11 Do not even e with such a one.
  8:13 I will never e meat, so that I may
  10:25 E whatever is sold in the meat
  10:31 whether you e or drink, or whatever
  11:26 For as often as you e this bread and
2Th 3:10 unwilling to work should not e.
Rev 2: 7 permission to e from the tree of life
  3:20 I will come in to you and e with you
  10: 9 and he said to me, "Take it, and e;
1Mc 1:62 not to e unclean food.

MAY EAT Ge 3:2; 27:25; Ex 12:44, 45;
23:11, 11; Lev 7:19; 10:14; 11:2, 3, 9, 9, 21,
22, 39; 19:25; 21:22; 22:4, 7, 11, 11, 13; 25:6;
Nu 11:21; 18:10, 11, 13, 31; Dt 2:6, 28; 8:9;
12:15, 20, 21, 22, 22, 27; 14:4, 6, 9, 9, 11, 20;
15:22; 18:1; 23:24; 26:12; 1Sa 2:36; 2Sa 13:6,
10; 1Ki 13:18; 17:12; 2Ki 6:22; Ne 5:2; Mk
14:14; Lk 17:8; 22:8, 11, 30; Jn 6:50

NOT EAT Ge 2:17; 3:1, 3, 17; 9:4; 24:33;
32:32; 43:32; Ex 12:9; 22:31; Lev 3:17; 7:24,
26; 10:17; 11:4, 8, 11, 42; 17:14; 19:26; 22:6,
8, 12; Dt 12:16, 23, 23, 24, 25; 14:3, 7, 8, 10,
12, 21; 15:23; 16:3; 28:31; Jdg 13:14, 16; 1Sa
1:7, 8; 9:13; 28:23; 1Ki 13:9, 17; 21:4, 5; 2Ki
4:40; 7:2, 19; Ezr 10:6; Pr 23:6; 31:27; Eze
18:6, 15; 44:31; Zec 7:6; Mk 7:3, 4; Lk 22:16;
1Co 8:8; 9:7; 10:28; 2Th 3:8, 10; Tob 12:19;
AdE 4:16; Sir 37:29; 1Es 9:2; 4Mc 5:25

SHALL EAT Ge 3:14, 17, 18, 19; Ex 12:8, 8,
11, 11, 15, 18, 20, 20, 43, 48; 13:6; 16:12;
23:15; 29:32, 33, 33; 34:18; Lev 6:16, 16, 18,
26, 29; 7:6, 23; 8:31; 10:13; 17:12; 22:10, 10,
13; 23:6, 14; 24:9; 25:12, 22; 26:5, 10, 16, 29,
29; Nu 6:4; 9:11; 11:18, 19, 19; 18:10; Dt
8:10; 12:7, 18; 14:23, 26; 15:20; 16:3; 28:33,
39; 1Sa 9:19; 2Sa 9:7; 1Ki 14:11, 11; 16:4, 4;
21:23, 24, 24; 2Ki 4:43; 9:10, 36; 19:29; Ps
22:26; 128:2; Pr 1:31; Isa 1:19; 3:10; 7:15, 22;
11:7; 62:9; 65:13, 25; Jer 5:17, 17, 17, 17;
19:9; Eze 4:9, 10, 12, 16; 5:10, 10; 12:19;
25:4; 39:17, 18, 19; 42:13; 44:29; Hos 4:10;
9:3; Joel 2:26; Mic 6:14; Tob 2:2; 2Es 15:58

EATEN → EAT
Ge 3:11 Have you e from the tree
Jer 31:29 "The parents have e sour grapes,
Eze 4:14 until now I have never e what died
Ac 10:14 never e anything that is profane
  12:23 and he was e by worms and died.
Rev 10:10 but when I had e it, my stomach
Bel 1:12 if you do not find that Bel has e

EATER → EAT
Jdg 14:14 "Out of the e came something to eat.
Isa 55:10 seed to the sower and bread to the e,
Na 3:12 they fall into the mouth of the e.

EATING → EAT
Lk 7:34 the Son of Man has come e and
Ro 14: 2 Some believe in e anything,
1Co 8: 4 as to the e of food offered to idols,
Tob 1:11 from e the food of the Gentiles.

EATS → EAT
Ex 12:15 for whoever e leavened bread
Lev 7:18 who e of it shall incur guilt.
1Sa 14:24 who e food before it is evening
Mt 24:49 and e and drinks with drunkards,
Lk 15: 2 welcomes sinners and e with them."
Jn 6:51 e of this bread will live forever;
1Co 11:27 e the bread or drinks the cup of the

EBAL
Dt 11:29 Gerizim and the curse on Mount E.
Jos 8:30 Joshua built on Mount E an altar to

EBED-MELECH·
An Ethiopian eunuch; saved Jeremiah from the cistern (Jer 38:1-13; 39:16).

EBENEZER·
1Sa 4: 1 they encamped at E,
    5: 1 they brought it from E to Ashdod;
    7:12 and named it E;

EBER
Ancestor of Abraham (Ge 11:14-17), of Jesus (Lk 3:35).

ECBATANA
Ezr 6: 2 in E, the capital in the province of
Tob 3: 7 On the same day, at E in Media,
Jdt 1: 1 Arphaxad ruled over the Medes in E

EDEN
Ge 2: 8 a garden in E, in the east;
Isa 51: 3 and will make her wilderness like E,
Eze 28:13 You were in E, the garden of God;
   31: 9 the envy of all the trees of E
Joel 2: 3 the land is like the garden of E,

EDGE → TWO-EDGED
Jos 3: 8 to the e of the waters of the Jordan,
Jer 31:29 the children's teeth are set on e."
Eze 16: 8 I spread the e of my cloak over you,
Heb 11:34 escaped the e of the sword,

EDICT
Ezr 1: 1 and also in a written e declared:
Heb 11:23 they were not afraid of the king's e.

EDOM → =ESAU, EDOMITE, EDOMITES
Ge 25:30 (Therefore he was called E.)
  36: 1 the descendants of Esau (that is, E).
Nu 20:18 But E said to him, "You shall not
1Ki 11:16 he had eliminated every male in E);
Ps 60: 8 my washbasin; on E I hurl my shoe;
Isa 63: 1 "Who is this that comes from E,
Jer 49: 7 Concerning E. Thus says the LORD
La 4:21 Rejoice and be glad, O daughter E,
Eze 25:12 Because E acted revengefully
Am 1:11 For three transgressions of E, and
Ob 1: 1 says the Lord GOD concerning E:
Mal 1: 4 If E says, "We are shattered but we

EDOMITE → EDOM
1Sa 22: 9 Doeg the E, who was in charge
Ps 52: T when Doeg the E came to Saul and

EDOMITES → EDOM
Dt 23: 7 You shall not abhor any of the E,
2Sa 8:13 he killed eighteen thousand E in the
1Ch 18:13 all the E became subject to David.
Ps 137: T the E the day of Jerusalem's fall,

EDUCATED· → EDUCATES, EDUCATION
Da 1: 5 They were to be e for three years,
Ac 22: 3 e strictly according to our ancestral
Sir 34: 9 An e person knows many things,
4Mc 13:24 they had been e by the same law

EDUCATES· → EDUCATED
Sir 10: 1 A wise magistrate e his people,

EDUCATION → EDUCATED
Sir 4:24 e through the words of the tongue.

EFFECT → EFFECTIVE
Isa 32:17 The e of righteousness will be peace
Ro 5:16 the free gift is not like the e of
Heb 9:17 For a will takes e only at death,
Jas 1: 4 and let endurance have its full e,

EFFECTIVE → EFFECT
Ro 3:25 by his blood, e through faith.
1Co 16: 9 a wide door for e work has opened
Phm 1: 6 sharing of your faith may become e
Jas 5:16 of the righteous is powerful and e.

EFFORT
Da 6:14 made every e to rescue him.

Gal 2:17 in our e to be justified in Christ,
Eph 4: 3 every e to maintain the unity of the
Heb 4:11 make every e to enter that rest,
2Pe 1: 5 make every e to support your faith
   1:15 I will make every e so that

EGG → EGGS
Lk 11:12 Or if the child asks for an e,

EGGS → EGG
Dt 22: 6 on the ground, with fledglings or e,
Isa 59: 5 whoever eats their e dies,

EGLAH·
A wife of David (2Sa 3:5; 1Ch 3:3).

EGLON
1. King of Moab killed by Ehud (Jdg 3:12-30).
2. City in Canaan (Jos 10).

EGYPT → EGYPTIAN, EGYPTIANS
Ge 12:10 So Abram went down to E to reside
  26: 2 "Do not go down to E;
  37:28 And they took Joseph to E.
  41:41 have set you over all the land of E."
  42: 3 down to buy grain in E.
  45: 9 God has made me lord of all E;
  45:20 best of all the land of E is yours.'"
  46: 6 into E, Jacob and all his offspring
  47:27 Thus Israel settled in the land of E,
Ex 1: 8 Now a new king arose over E,
  3:11 and bring the Israelites out of E?"
  7: 3 and wonders in the land of E.
  11: 5 firstborn in the land of E shall die,
  12:12 on all the gods of E I will execute
  12:40 in E was four hundred thirty years.
  12:41 went out from the land of E.
  32: 1 brought us up out of the land of E,
Nu 11:18 Surely it was better for us in E.'
  14: 4 choose a captain, and go back to E."
  24: 8 God who brings him out of E,
Dt 6:21 LORD brought us out of E with a
  16:12 that you were a slave in E,
Jos 15:47 to the Wadi of E, and the Great Sea
1Ki 4:30 and all the wisdom of E.
  10:28 import of horses was from E and
  11:40 but Jeroboam promptly fled to E,
  14:25 King Shishak of E came up against
2Ch 35:20 King Neco of E went up to fight at
  36: 3 king of E deposed him in Jerusalem
Ne 9:18 God who brought you up out of E,'
Ps 78:51 He struck all the firstborn in E,
  80: 8 You brought a vine out of E;
Isa 19: 1 An oracle concerning E.
Jer 42:19 O remnant of Judah, Do not go to E.
  44: 1 the Judeans living in the land of E,
  46: 2 Concerning E, about the army of
La 5: 6 We have made a pact with E and
Eze 29: 2 against him and against all E;
  30: 4 A sword shall come upon E,
Hos 11: 1 and out of E I called my son.
Mt 2:15 "Out of E I have called my son."
Heb 11:27 By faith he left E, unafraid of the
Rev 11: 8 prophetically called Sodom and E,

DOWN TO EGYPT Ge 12:10; 26:2; 37:25; 39:1; 43:15; 46:3; Nu 20:15; Dt 10:22; Jos 24:4; Isa 30:2; 31:1; Ac 7:15; Jdt 5:10

KING OF EGYPT Ge 40:1, 1, 5; 41:46; Ex 1:15, 17, 18; 2:23; 3:18, 19; 5:4; 6:11, 13, 27, 29; 14:5, 8; Dt 7:8; 11:3; 1Ki 3:1; 9:16; 11:18; 2Ki 17:7; 18:21; 23:29; 24:7, 7; 2Ch 36:3, 4; Isa 36:6; Jer 25:19; 44:30; 46:2, 17; Eze 29:2, 3; 30:21, 22; 31:2; 32:2; Ac 7:10; Jdt 5:11; 1Mc 10:51; 11:1; 1Es 1:25, 26, 35, 37

LAND OF EGYPT Ge 13:10; 21:21; 41:19, 29, 30, 33, 34, 36, 41, 43, 44, 45, 46, 48, 53, 54, 55, 56; 45:8, 18, 19, 20, 26; 46:20; 47:6, 11, 13, 14, 15, 20, 26, 27, 28; 48:5; 50:7; Ex 4:20; 5:12; 6:13, 26, 28; 7:3, 4, 19, 21; 8:5, 6, 7, 16, 17; 9:9, 9, 22, 22, 23, 24, 25; 10:12, 13, 14, 15, 21, 22; 11:3, 5, 6, 9; 12:1, 12, 12, 13, 17, 29, 41, 42, 51; 13:15, 18; 16:1, 3, 6, 32;

19:1; 20:2; 22:21; 23:9; 29:46; 32:1, 4, 7, 8, 11, 23; 33:1; Lev 11:45; 18:3; 19:34, 36; 22:33; 23:43; 25:38, 42, 55; 26:13, 45; Nu 1:1; 3:13; 8:17; 9:1; 14:2; 15:41; 26:4; 33:1, 38; Dt 1:27; 5:6, 15; 6:12; 8:14; 9:7; 10:19; 11:10; 13:5, 10; 15:15; 16:3, 3; 20:1; 24:22; 29:2, 16, 25; 34:11; Jos 24:17; Jdg 2:12; 19:30; 1Sa 12:6; 27:8; 1Ki 6:1; 8:9, 21; 9:9; 12:28; 2Ki 17:7, 36; 2Ch 6:5; 7:22; 20:10; Ps 78:12; 81:5, 10; Isa 11:16; 19:18, 19, 20; 27:13; Jer 2:6; 7:22, 25; 11:4, 7; 16:14; 23:7; 24:8; 31:32; 32:20, 21; 34:13; 42:14, 16; 43:7, 11, 12, 13; 44:1, 8, 12, 12, 13, 14, 15, 24, 26, 26, 27, 28, 28; 46:13; Eze 19:4; 20:5, 6, 8, 9, 10, 36; 23:19, 27; 29:9, 10, 12, 19, 20; 30:13, 13, 25; 32:15; Da 9:15; 11:42; Hos 2:15; 7:16; 11:5; 12:9; 13:4; Am 2:10; 3:1, 9; 9:7; Mic 6:4; 7:15; Zec 10:10; Ac 7:40; 13:17; Heb 8:9; Jude 1:5; Jdt 5:12; AdE 13:16; Bar 1:19, 20; 2:11; 1Mc 1:16, 19, 19; 2Es 1:7; 15:10

OUT OF EGYPT Ge 45:25; 47:30; Ex 3:10, 11, 12; 6:27; 12:39, 39; 13:3, 8, 9, 14, 16; 14:11; 17:3; 18:1; 23:15; Nu 20:5, 16; 21:5; 22:5, 11; 23:22; 24:8; 32:11; Dt 4:20, 37, 45; 6:21; 9:26; 16:1; 23:4; 24:9; 25:17; 26:8; Jos 2:10; 5:4, 4, 5, 6; 24:6; 1Sa 8:8; 10:18; 12:8; 15:2, 6; 1Ki 8:16, 51, 53; 2Ki 21:15; 2Ch 5:10; Ne 9:18; Ps 80:8; Jer 37:5; Hos 11:1; Hag 2:5; Mt 2:15; Jdt 6:5; 2Es 3:17; 14:4

WADI OF EGYPT Nu 34:5; Jos 15:4, 47; 1Ki 8:65; 2Ki 24:7; 2Ch 7:8; Isa 27:12; Eze 47:19; 48:28

EGYPTIAN → EGYPT
Ge 16: 1 E slave-girl whose name was Hagar,
Ex 1:19 Hebrew women are not like the E
  2:11 He saw an E beating a Hebrew,
  14:24 and threw the E army into panic.
Dt 11: 4 what he did to the E army,
Ac 7:24 avenged him by striking down the E

EGYPTIANS → EGYPT
Ex 1:12 the E came to dread the Israelites.
  3:22 and so you shall plunder the E."
  12:36 And so they plundered the E.
  14: 4 E shall know that I am the LORD.
  15:26 diseases that I brought upon the E;
Nu 14:13 "Then the E will hear of it,
Isa 19: 2 I will stir up E against E,
Eze 16:26 You played the whore with the E,
Ac 7:22 instructed in all the wisdom of the E
Heb 11:29 the E attempted to do so they were

EHUD
Left-handed judge who delivered Israel from Moabite king, Eglon (Jdg 3:12-30).

EIGHT → EIGHTH
Ge 17:12 circumcised when he is e days old,
  21: 4 when he was e days old,
2Ki 22: 1 Josiah was e years old when he
1Pe 3:20 e persons, were saved through water

EIGHTEEN
Lk 13:11 that had crippled her for e years.

EIGHTH → EIGHT
Lev 12: 3 On the e day the flesh of his
  23:39 and a complete rest on the e day.
  25:22 When you sow in the e year,
Lk 1:59 the e day they came to circumcise
Php 3: 5 the e day, a member of the people
Rev 17:11 it is an e but it belongs to the seven,
2Es 6:36 Then on the e night my heart

EIGHTY
Ex 7: 7 Moses was e years old and
2Sa 19:35 Today I am e years old;
Ps 90:10 life are seventy years, or perhaps e,

EIGHTY-FIVE
Jos 14:10 and here I am today, e years old.

EITHER
Lk 16:13 e hate the one and love the other,
Rev   3:15 I wish that you were e cold or hot.
Sir 40:18 but better than e is finding
     40:26 fear of the Lord is better than e.

EKRON
Jos 13: 3 Ashdod, Ashkelon, Gath, and E),
1Sa   5:10 But when the ark of God came to E,
      6:17 Ashkelon, one for Gath, one for E;
2Ki   1: 2 inquire of Baal-zebub, the god of E,
Am   1: 8 I will turn my hand against E,

EL-BERITH*
Jdg   9:46 the stronghold of the temple of E.

EL-BETHEL* → BETHEL
Ge   35: 7 and called the place E,

EL-ELOHE-ISRAEL* → ISRAEL
Ge 33:20 an altar and called it E.

ELAH
1. Son of Baasha; king of Israel (1Ki 16:6-14).
2. Valley in which David fought Goliath (1Sa 17:2, 19; 21:9).

ELAM
1Ch 1:17 E, Asshur, Arpachshad, Lud, Aram,
Jer 49:34 the prophet Jeremiah concerning E,

ELDAD
Nu 11:27 "E and Medad are prophesying

ELDER → ELDERS
Ge 25:23 the e shall serve the younger."
     29:16 the name of the e was Leah,
1Sa 18:17 "Here is my e daughter Merab;
Isa   3: 2 judge and prophet, diviner and e,
Eze 16:46 Your e sister is Samaria, who lived
Ro   9:12 "The e shall serve the younger."
1Ti   5:19 any accusation against an e except
1Pe   5: 1 as an e myself and a witness of the
2Jn   1: 1 The e to the elect lady and her
3Jn   1: 1 The e to the beloved Gaius, whom I
Sus 1:50 has given you the standing of an e."

ELDERS → ELDER
Ex   3:16 Go and assemble the e of Israel,
     24: 1 and seventy of the e of Israel,
Dt 25: 7 brother's widow shall go up to the e
Jos 24: 1 summoned the e, the heads, the
Jdg   2: 7 days of the e who outlived Joshua,
Ru   4: 2 Boaz took ten men of the e of the
Ps 105:22 and to teach his e wisdom.
Pr 31:23 taking his seat among the e
Isa   3:14 enters into judgment with the e
Eze   8:11 seventy of the e of the house of
Mt 15: 2 break the tradition of the e?
     27:12 accused by the chief priests and e,
Mk   7: 3 thus observing the tradition of the e;
Lk   9:22 be rejected by the e, chief priests,
Ac   4: 5 The next day their rulers, e,
    11:30 sending it to the e by Barnabas and
    14:23 appointed e for them in each church,
    15: 2 with the apostles and the e.
    15: 6 The apostles and the e met together
    15:23 brothers, both the apostles and the e,
    16: 4 by the apostles and e who were in
    20:17 asking the e of the church to meet
    21:18 and all the e were present.
    23:14 to the chief priests and e and said,
    24: 1 Ananias came down with some e
    25:15 and the e of the Jews informed me
1Ti   4:14 of hands by the council of e.
     5:17 the e who rule well be considered
Tit   1: 5 and should appoint e in every town,
Jas   5:14 e of the church and have them pray
1Pe   5: 1 I exhort the e
     5: 5 must accept the authority of the e.
Rev   4: 4 on the thrones are twenty-four e,
     4:10 the twenty-four e fall before
     5: 6 living creatures and among the e
     7:11 the e and the four living creatures,

    11:16 Then the twenty-four e who sit on
    14: 3 living creatures and before the e.
    19: 4 And the twenty-four e and
Sus   1: 8 Every day the two e used to see her,
     1:61 they took action against the two e,

ELDERS OF ISRAEL
Ex 3:16, 18; 12:21; 17:5, 6; 18:12; 24:1, 9; Lev 9:1; Nu 11:16, 30; 16:25; Dt 27:1; 31:9; Jos 7:6; 8:10; 1Sa 4:3; 8:4; 2Sa 3:17; 5:3; 17:4, 15; 1Ki 8:1, 3; 1Ch 11:3; 15:25; 2Ch 5:2, 4; Eze 14:1; 20:1, 3; Ac 5:21; 1Mc 11:23

ELDERS OF MY/THE PEOPLE
Ex 19:7; Nu 11:16, 24; Ru 4:4; 1Sa 15:30; Jer 19:1; Mt 21:23; 26:3, 47; 27:1; Lk 22:66; Sus 1:41; 1Mc 7:33; 12:35

ELDERS OF THE JEWS
Ezr 5:5; 6:7, 8, 14; Ac 25:15; 1Es 6:5, 8, 27; 7:2

ELEAZAR
1. Third son of Aaron (Ex 6:23-25). Succeeded Aaron as high priest (Nu 20:26; Dt 10:6). Allotted land to tribes (Jos 14:1). Death (Jos 24:33).
2. Father of the writer of Sirach (Sir 50:27).
3. Brother of Judas Maccabeus (1Mc 2:5; 6:43-46).

ELECT* → ELECTION
Mt 24:22 sake of the e those days will be cut
    24:24 lead astray, if possible, even the e.
    24:31 gather his e from the four winds,
Mk 13:20 the sake of the e, whom he chose,
    13:22 to lead astray, if possible, the e.
    13:27 gather his e from the four winds,
Ro   8:33 bring any charge against God's e?
    11: 7 The e obtained it, but the rest were
1Ti   5:21 of Christ Jesus and of the e angels,
2Ti   2:10 everything for the sake of the e,
Tit   1: 1 of God's e and the knowledge of
2Jn   1: 1 The elder to the e lady and her
     1:13 children of your e sister send you
Wis   3: 9 and he watches over his e.
     4:15 grace and mercy are with his e,
Sir 46: 1 a great savior of God's e,
2Es 15:21 as they have done to my e until this
    16:73 Then the tested quality of my e
    16:74 Listen, my e ones, says the Lord;

ELECTION* → ELECT
Ro   9:11 God's purpose of e might continue,
    11:28 but as regards e they are beloved,
2Pe   1:10 eager to confirm your call and e,

ELEMENTAL* → ELEMENTS
Gal   4: 3 enslaved to the e spirits of the world
     4: 9 to the weak and beggarly e spirits?
Col   2: 8 to the e spirits of the universe,
     2:20 with Christ you died to the e spirits

ELEMENTS → ELEMENTAL
Heb   5:12 the basic e of the oracles of God.
2Pe   3:10 and the e will be dissolved with fire,
     3:12 and the e will melt with fire?
Wis   7:17 the world and the activity of the e;

ELEPHANT → ELEPHANTS
1Mc 6:46 He got under the e, stabbed it from

ELEPHANTS → ELEPHANT
1Mc 1:17 with chariots and e and cavalry and

ELEVATION
Ex 29:24 as an e offering before the LORD.
Lev   7:30 as an e offering before the LORD.
Ps   48: 2 beautiful in e, is the joy of all

ELEVATION OFFERING[S]
Ex 29:24, 26, 27, 27; Lev 7:30, 34; 8:27, 29; 9:21; 10:15; 14:12, 24; 23:15, 17, 20; Nu 6:20; 8:11, 13, 15, 21; 18:11

ELEVEN
Ge 32:22 his two maids, and his e children,
    37: 9 the moon, and e stars were bowing
Ex 26: 8 the e curtains shall be of the same

Dt   1: 2 way of Mount Seir it takes e days
Mt 28:16 Now the e disciples went to Galilee,
Lk 24: 9 they told all this to the e and to all
    24:33 the e and their companions gathered
Ac   1:26 and he was added to the e apostles.
     2:14 But Peter, standing with the e,

ELI → ELOI
1. High priest in youth of Samuel (1Sa 1-4). Blessed Hannah (1Sa 1:12-18); raised Samuel (1Sa 2:11-26). Prophesied against because of wicked sons (1Sa 2:27-36). Death of Eli and sons (1Sa 4:11-22).
2. "Eli, Eli, lema sabachthani?" (Mt 27:46).

ELIAKIM → =JEHOIAKIM
1. Original name of king Jehoiakim (2Ki 23:34; 2Ch 36:4).
2. Hezekiah's palace administrator (2Ki 18:17-37; 19:2; Isa 36:1-22; 37:2).

ELIASHIB
Ne   3: 1 Then the high priest E set to work

ELIEZER
1. Servant of Abraham (Ge 15:2).
2. Son of Moses (Ex 18:4; 1Ch 23:15-17).

ELIHU
A friend of Job (Job 32-37).

ELIJAH
Prophet; predicted famine in Israel (1Ki 17:1; Jas 5:17). Fed by ravens (1Ki 17:2-6). Raised Sidonian widow's son (1Ki 17:7-24). Defeated prophets of Baal at Carmel (1Ki 18:16-46). Ran from Jezebel (1Ki 19:1-9). Prophesied death of Azariah (2Ki 1). Succeeded by Elishah (1Ki 19:19-21; 2Ki 2:1-18). Taken to heaven in whirlwind (2Ki 2:11-12; Sir 48:1-12; 1Mc 2:58).
Return prophesied (Mal 4:5-6); equated with John the Baptist (Mt 17:9-13; Mk 9:9-13; Lk 1:17). Appeared with Moses in transfiguration of Jesus (Mt 17:1-8; Mk 9:1-8).

ELIM
Ex 15:27 E, where there were twelve springs
Nu 33: 9 at E there were twelve springs of

ELIMELECH
Ru   1: 3 But E, the husband of Naomi, died,
     4: 9 all that belonged to E

ELIPHAZ
1. Firstborn of Esau (Ge 36).
2. A friend of Job (Job 4-5; 15; 22; 42:7, 9).

ELISHA
Prophet; successor of Elijah (1Ki 19:16-21; Sir 48:12-14); inherited his mantle (2Ki 2:1-18). Purified bad water (2Ki 2:19-22). Cursed young men (2Ki 2:23-25). Aided Israel's defeat of Moab (2Ki 3). Provided widow with oil (2Ki 4:1-7). Raised Shunammite woman's son (2Ki 4:8-37). Purified food (2Ki 4:38-41). Fed 100 men (2Ki 4:42-44). Healed Naaman's leprosy (2Ki 5). Made axhead float (2Ki 6:1-7). Captured Arameans (2Ki 6:8-23). Political adviser to Israel (2Ki 6:24-8:6; 9:1-3; 13:14-19), Aram (2Ki 8:7-15). Death (2Ki 13:20).

ELIZABETH*
Mother of John the Baptist (Lk 1:5-58).

ELKANAH
Husband of Hannah, father of Samuel (1Sa 1-2).

ELOI* → ELI
Mk 15:34 "E, E, lema sabachthani?"

ELON
Judge of Israel (Jdg 12:11-12).

ELOQUENT
Ex   4:10 "O my Lord, I have never been e,
Ac 18:24 e man, well-versed in the scriptures.
1Co 1:17 the gospel, and not with e wisdom,

ELSE

Ex   4:13 my Lord, please send someone **e**.”
Nu 12: 3 more so than anyone **e** on the face
Jdg 16: 7 and be like anyone **e**.”
1Ki 4:31 He was wiser than anyone **e**,
Ac   4:12 There is salvation in no one **e**,
Ro   8:39 depth, nor anything **e** in all creation,

ELYMAS* → =BAR-JESUS

Ac 13: 8 But the magician **E** (for that is the

EMBALMED*

Ge 50: 2 So the physicians **e** Israel;
      50:26 **e** and placed in a coffin in Egypt.

EMBARRASSED*

Jdg   3:25 So they waited until they were **e**.
Ezr   9: 6 and **e** to lift my face to you,
Sir 26:24 *a modest daughter will even be e*

EMBERS

Pr 26:21 As charcoal is to hot **e** and wood to

EMBODIMENT*

Ro   2:20 in the law the **e** of knowledge and

EMBRACE → EMBRACED

Pr   4: 8 honor you if you **e** her.
      5:20 **e** the bosom of an adulteress?
Ecc   3: 5 a time to **e**, and a time to refrain

EMBRACED → EMBRACE

Ge 48:10 and he kissed them and **e** them.
Ac 20:37 they **e** Paul and kissed him,

EMBROIDERED

Eze 16:10 I clothed you with **e** cloth
      26:16 and strip off their **e** garments.

EMERALD

Ex 28:17 and **e** shall be the first row;
Rev   4: 3 is a rainbow that looks like an **e**.
      21:19 the third agate, the fourth **e**,
Tob 13:16 will be built with sapphire and **e**,

EMMANUEL* → =IMMANUEL

Mt   1:23 and they shall name him **E**,”

EMMAUS

Lk 24:13 were going to a village called **E**,

EMOTION → EMOTIONS

4Mc 1:14 what reason is and what **e** is,

EMOTIONS → EMOTION

4Mc 1: 1 reason is sovereign over the **e**.

EMPEROR

Mt 22:17 Is it lawful to pay taxes to the **e**, or
Mk 12:17 “Give to the **e** the things that are
            the emperor’s,
Jn 19:12 you are no friend of the **e**.
Ac 17: 7 contrary to the decrees of the **e**,
      25:11 I appeal to the **e**.”
1Pe 2:17 Fear God. Honor the **e**.

EMPTIED → EMPTY

1Ki 17:14 The jar of meal will not be **e**
Ne   5:13 Thus may they be shaken out and **e**.
1Co 1:17 cross of Christ might not be **e** of its
Php 2: 7 but **e** himself, taking the form of

EMPTY → EMPTIED, EMPTY-HANDED

Ru   1:21 the LORD has brought me back **e**;
2Ki 4: 3 **e** vessels and not just a few.
Job 35:16 Job opens his mouth in **e** talk,
Isa 55:11 it shall not return to me **e**,
Mt   6: 7 do not heap up **e** phrases
Lk   1:53 and sent the rich away **e**.
Eph 5: 6 no one deceive you with **e** words,
Col 2: 8 through philosophy and **e** deceit,

EMPTY-HANDED → EMPTY, HAND

Ge 31:42 you would have sent me away **e**.
Ex   3:21 when you go, you will not go **e**;
      23:15 No one shall appear before me **e**.

Dt 15:13 you shall not send him out **e**.
Ru   3:17 not go back to your mother-in-law **e**
Mk 12: 3 and beat him, and sent him away **e**.
Jdt   1:11 they sent back his messengers **e**
Sir 35: 6 Do not appear before the Lord **e**,

EN-GEDI

1Sa 23:29 and lived in the strongholds of **E**.

ENABLE* → ABLE

Ecc   6: 2 yet God does not **e** them to enjoy
Eph   3: 4 a reading of which will **e** you to

ENABLED* → ABLE

2Ch 20:27 LORD had **e** them to rejoice
Ac   7:10 and **e** him to win favor and to show
Col   1:12 has **e** you to share in the inheritance

ENABLES* → ABLE

Ecc   5:19 and whom he **e** to enjoy them,
Php 3:21 **e** him to make all things subject to

ENCAMP → CAMP

Ps 27: 3 an army **e** against me,
Isa 29: 3 And like David I will **e** against you;

ENCAMPS* → CAMP

Ps 34: 7 angel of the LORD **e** around

ENCHANTER → ENCHANTERS, ENCHANTMENT, ENCHANTMENTS

Isa   3: 3 and skillful magician and expert **e**.

ENCHANTERS → ENCHANTER

Da   1:20 better than all the magicians and **e**
      5: 7 king cried aloud to bring in the **e**,

ENCHANTMENT* → ENCHANTER

Nu 23:23 Surely there is no **e** against Jacob,

ENCHANTMENTS → ENCHANTER

Isa 47: 9 and the great power of your **e**.

ENCIRCLE → CIRCLE

Ps 22:12 Many bulls **e** me, strong bulls

ENCLOSE* → CLOSE

SS   8: 9 we will **e** her with boards of cedar.

ENCOMPASSED

2Sa 22: 5 For the waves of death **e** me,
Ps 18: 4 The cords of death **e** me;
   116: 3 The snares of death **e** me;

ENCOURAGE → ENCOURAGED, ENCOURAGEMENT, ENCOURAGES, ENCOURAGING

Dt   1:38 **e** him, for he is the one who will
      3:28 charge Joshua, and **e** and strengthen
2Sa 11:25 and overthrow it.’ And **e** him.”
Job 16: 5 I could **e** you with my mouth,
Ac 15:32 said much to **e** and strengthen the
Eph 6:22 how we are, and to **e** your hearts.
Col 4: 8 and that he may **e** your hearts;
1Th 3: 2 to strengthen and **e** you for the sake
      4:18 **e** one another with these words.
      5:11 Therefore **e** one another and build
      5:14 the idlers, **e** the faint hearted,
2Ti 4: 2 and **e**, with the utmost patience in
Tit 2: 4 that they may **e** the young women
1Pe 5:12 written this short letter to **e** you

ENCOURAGED → ENCOURAGE

2Ch 32: 8 The people were **e** by the words
      35: 2 and **e** them in the service of
Eze 13:22 you have **e** the wicked not to turn
Ac 14:22 the disciples and **e** them to continue
      16:40 they had seen and **e** the brothers
      18:27 the believers **e** him and wrote to the
      27:36 all of them were **e** and took food
Ro   1:12 that we may be mutually **e** by each
1Co 14:31 so that all may learn and all be **e**.
Col 2: 2 I want their hearts to be **e** and united
1Th 3: 7 persecution we have been **e** about
Heb 6:18 taken refuge might be strongly **e**

ENCOURAGEMENT* → ENCOURAGE

Ac   4:36 Barnabas (which means “son of **e**”)
      20: 2 and had given the believers much **e**,
Ro 15: 4 by the **e** of the scriptures we might
      15: 5 God of steadfastness and **e** grant
1Co 14: 3 for their upbuilding and **e** and
Php 2: 1 If then there is any **e** in Christ,
Phm 1: 7 indeed received much joy and **e**
Wis 8: 9 and **e** in cares and grief.
1Mc 10:24 I also will write them words of **e**
      12: 9 we have as **e** the holy books

ENCOURAGES* → ENCOURAGE

Isa 41: 7 The artisan **e** the goldsmith,
      41: 7 **e** the one who strikes the anvil,
Sir 17:24 and he **e** those who are losing hope.

ENCOURAGING* → ENCOURAGE

Ac 20: 1 after **e** them and saying farewell,
1Th 2:12 urging and **e** you and pleading that
Heb 10:25 the habit of some, but **e** one another,
1Mc 5:53 and **e** the people all the way until
2Mc 15: 9 **E** them from the law and the
2Es 10: 3 **e** me to be quiet, I got up in the

ENCROACH

Pr 23:10 or **e** on the fields of orphans,

END → ENDED, ENDLESS, ENDS

Ge   6:13 determined to make an **e** of all flesh,
Ex 12:41 the **e** of four hundred thirty years,
Nu 23:10 and let my **e** be like his!”
Dt   8:16 and in the **e** to do you good.
      31:24 the words of this law to the very **e**,
Ne   9:31 great mercies you did not make an **e**
Ps 119:33 and I will observe it to the **e**.
   119:112 your statutes forever, to the **e**.
Pr   1:19 Such is the **e** of all who are greedy
      5: 4 in the **e** she is bitter as wormwood,
      5:11 at the **e** of your life you will groan,
      14:12 but its **e** is the way to death.
      14:13 and the **e** of joy is grief.
      16:25 but in the **e** it is the way to death.
      20:21 will not be blessed in the **e**.
      25: 8 for what will you do in the **e**,
      29:21 from childhood will come to a bad **e**
Ecc 3:11 from the beginning to the **e**.
      7: 8 Better is the **e** of a thing than its
      12:12 making many books there is no **e**,
Eze 7: 2 The **e** has come upon the four
Da   6:26 and his dominion has no **e**.
      8:17 the vision is for the time of the **e**.”
      9:26 Its **e** shall come with a flood,
      12:13 shall rise for your reward at the **e** of
Mt 10:22 But the one who endures to the **e**
      13:39 the harvest is the **e** of the age,
      24:13 But the one who endures to the **e**
      24:14 and then the **e** will come.
      28:20 always, to the **e** of the age.”
Lk 21: 9 the **e** will not follow immediately.”
Jn 13: 1 he loved them to the **e**.
Ro 6:21 The **e** of those things is death.
     10: 4 For Christ is the **e** of the law so that
1Co 13:10 the partial will come to an **e**.
      15:24 Then comes the **e**, when he hands
Php 3:19 Their **e** is destruction; their god is
Heb 3:14 our first confidence firm to the **e**.
      6: 8 its **e** is to be burned over.
1Pe 4: 7 The **e** of all things is near;
Rev 2:26 to do my works to the **e**,
      21: 6 the beginning and the **e**,
      22:13 the beginning and the **e**.”
Sir 1:13 will have a happy **e**;
      21: 9 and their **e** is a blazing fire.

END OF THE/THIS AGE Mt 13:39, 40, 49;
  24:3; 28:20; Heb 9:26; 2Es 2:34; 6:7, 9; 7:113

END OF THE EARTH Dt 13:7; 28:49, 64;
  Ps 46:9; 61:2; 135:7; Isa 42:10; 43:6; 48:20;
  49:6; 62:11; Jer 25:33; Jdt 11:21; Wis 8:1

MADE/MAKE AN END Ge 6:13; Nu 17:10;
  2Ki 13:17, 19; 2Ch 20:23; Ne 9:31; Ps 119:87;

Jer 30:11, 11; 46:28, 28; Eze 20:13, 17; Na
1:9; Zec 9:6

PUT AN END TO Job 28:3; 32:22; Ps 54:5;
73:27; Isa 13:11; Eze 7:24; 12:23; 23:27, 48;
30:10, 13; Da 9:24; 11:18; Hos 1:4; 2:11; 1Co
13:11; Wis 18:21; 4Mc 4:24

ENDED → END

Rev 15: 1 for with them the wrath of God is e.
       20: 3 until the thousand years were e.

ENDLESS → END

Isa   9: 7 e peace for the throne of David
Na   3:19 has ever escaped your e cruelty?

ENDOR*

1Sa 28: 7 "There is a medium at **E.**"

ENDOWED

Ex   28: 3 whom I have e with skill,
2Ch   2:12 e with discretion and understanding,
Da   1: 4 e with knowledge and insight,

ENDS → END

Ps   2: 8 the e of the earth your possession.
      67: 7 let all the e of the earth revere him.
Pr   30: 4 established all the e of the earth?
Isa 40:28 the Creator of the e of the earth.
Mic   5: 4 shall be great to the e of the earth;
Lk   11:31 she came from the e of the earth to
Ac   13:47 salvation to the e of the earth.'"
Ro   10:18 their words to the e of the world."
1Co 10:11 whom the e of the ages have come.
      13: 8 Love never e. But as for prophecies,
Sir 11:28 he e, a person becomes known.

ENDS OF THE EARTH Dt 33:17; 1Sa
2:10; Job 28:24; Ps 2:8; 22:27; 48:10; 59:13;
65:5; 67:7; 72:8; 98:3; Pr 17:24; 30:4; Isa
5:26; 24:16; 40:28; 41:5, 9; 45:22; 52:10; Jer
10:13; 16:19; 25:31; 51:16; Da 4:22; Mic 5:4;
Zec 9:10; Mt 12:42; Mk 13:27; Lk 11:31; Ac
1:8; 13:47; Tob 13:11; Wis 6:1; Sir 44:21;
1Mc 1:3; 3:9; 8:4; 14:10

ENDURANCE → ENDURE

Lk   8:15 and bear fruit with patient e.
Ro   5: 3 knowing that suffering produces e,
2Co   6: 4 through great e, in afflictions,
1Ti   6:11 godliness, faith, love, e,
Tit   2: 2 and sound in faith, in love, and in e.
Heb 10:36 For you need e, so that when you
Jas   1: 3 the testing of your faith produces e;
2Pe   1: 6 and self-control with e, and e with
Rev   1: 9 and the kingdom and the patient e,
      13:10 Here is a call for the e and faith of
      14:12 Here is a call for the e of the saints,

ENDURE → ENDURANCE, ENDURED,
    ENDURES, ENDURING

Job 20:21 therefore their prosperity will not e.
Ps   72:17 May his name e forever, his fame
      89:29 his throne as long as the heavens e.
     102:26 They will perish, but you e;
     104:31 May the glory of the LORD e forever
Pr   12:19 Truthful lips e forever,
Jer 10:10 the nations cannot e his indignation.
Joel 2:11 terrible indeed—who can e it?
Na   1: 6 Who can e the heat of his anger?
Mal   3: 2 who can e the day of his coming,
Lk   17:25 But first he must e much suffering
Jn   3:36 but must e God's wrath.
1Co   4:12 we bless; when persecuted, we e;
      10:13 out so that you may be able to e it.
2Ti   2:10 I e everything for the sake of the
       2:12 if we e, we will also reign with him;
       4: 5 always be sober, e suffering,
Heb 12: 7 E trials for the sake of discipline.
1Pe   2:19 you e pain while suffering unjustly.

ENDURED → ENDURE

Ps 132: 1 David's favor all the hardships he e;
Mk   5:26 had e much under many physicians,
Ro   9:22 e with much patience the objects of

2Ti   3:11 and Lystra. What persecutions I e!
Heb   6:15 thus Abraham, having patiently e,
      12: 2 that was set before him e the cross,
      12: 3 Consider him who e such hostility

ENDURES → ENDURE

Ge   8:22 As long as the earth e, seedtime and
1Ch 16:41 for his steadfast love e forever.
Ps 102:12 your name e to all generations.
     112: 9 their righteousness e forever;
     136: 1 for his steadfast love e forever.
     145:13 and your dominion e throughout all
La   5:19 your throne e to all generations.
Mt   13:21 but e only for a while,
Jn   6:27 for the food that e for eternal life,
1Co 13: 7 hopes all things, e all things.
2Co   9: 9 his righteousness e forever."
Jas   1:12 Blessed is anyone who e temptation.
1Pe   1:25 but the word of the Lord e forever."
Sir 40:17 and almsgiving e forever.
Bar   4: 1 the law that e forever.
Aza   1:67 he is good, for his mercy e forever.
1Mc 4:24 he is good, for his mercy e forever."

**STEADFAST LOVE ENDURES
FOREVER** 1Ch 16:34, 41; 2Ch 5:13; 7:3, 6;
20:21; Ezr 3:11; Ps 100:5; 106:1; 107:1; 118:1,
2, 3, 4, 29; 136:1, 2, 3, 4, 5, 6, 7, 8, 9, 10, 11,
12, 13, 14, 15, 16, 17, 18, 19, 20, 21, 22, 23,
24, 25, 26; Jer 33:11

HIS MERCY ENDURES FOREVER Sir
51:12 (14x); Aza 1:67, 68; 1Mc 4:24

ENDURING → ENDURE

Ps   19: 9 fear of the LORD is pure, e forever;
     119:86 All your commandments are e;
Da   6:26 For he is the living God, e forever.
2Th   1: 4 and the afflictions that you are e.
1Pe   1:23 the living and e word of God.

ENEMIES → ENEMY

Ex   1:10 join our e and fight against us and
      23:22 be an enemy to your e and a foe to
Dt   6:19 thrusting out all your e from before
Jos 21:44 LORD had given all their e into their
Jdg   2:14 sold them into the power of their e
2Sa   7: 1 had given him rest from all his e
Est   9: 5 the Jews struck down all their e
Ps   23: 5 before me in the presence of my e;
     110: 1 until I make your e your footstool.
Pr   16: 7 causes even their e to be at peace
Isa 59:18 to his adversaries, requital to his e;
Jer 12: 7 of my heart into the hands of her e.
Da   4:19 and its interpretation for your e!
Mic   7: 6 your e are members of your own
Mt   5:44 But I say to you, Love your e and
Mk 12:36 until I put your e under your feet.'"
Lk   6:35 But love your e, do good, and lend,
      20:43 until I make your e your footstool."
Ac   2:35 until I make your e your footstool."
Ro   5:10 For if while we were e,
      11:28 they are e of God for your sake;
      12:20 "if your e are hungry, feed them;
1Co 15:25 must reign until he has put all his e
Eph   6:12 struggle is not against e of blood
Php   3:18 many live as e of the cross of Christ;
Heb   1:13 until I make your e a footstool
      10:13 waiting "until his e would be made
Jdt   8:35 to take vengeance on our e."
AdE   9:22 the Jews got relief from their e.
Sir   6: 9 friends who change into e,
1Mc 4:36 said, "See, our e are crushed;

HIS ENEMIES Nu 32:21; 1Sa 14:47; 2Sa
7:1; 18:19; 22:1; 1Ki 5:3; 1Ch 22:9; 2Ch
32:22; Ps 18:Heading; 68:1, 21; 72:9; 89:42;
127:5; 132:18; Isa 59:18; 66:6, 14; Jer 44:30;
Na 1:2, 8; 1Co 15:25; Heb 10:13; Wis 5:17;
10:12; Sir 30:3, 6; 45:2; 46:16; 47:7; 2Mc
12:28; 4Mc 17:24

MY ENEMIES Nu 23:11; 24:10; 1Sa 2:1;
14:24; 2Sa 5:20; 22:4, 38, 41, 49; 1Ch 14:11;
Ps 3:7; 5:8; 6:10; 7:6; 9:3; 18:3, 37, 40, 48;
23:5; 25:2; 27:6, 11; 31:15; 41:5; 54:5, 7; 56:2,

9; 59:1, 10; 69:4, 14, 18; 71:10; 92:11; 102:8;
119:98; 138:7; 139:22; 143:9, 12; Isa 1:24; La
1:21; 2:22; 3:52

OUR ENEMIES Ex 1:10; Dt 32:31; 1Sa 4:3;
12:10; 2Sa 19:9; Ne 4:11, 15; 5:9; 6:1, 16; Ps
44:10; 80:6; 124:2; La 3:46; Lk 1:71, 74; Jdt
8:11, 15, 19, 33, 35; 13:11, 14, 18; AdE 14:6;
Wis 12:22; 16:8; 18:8; Aza 1:9; 1Mc 4:18, 36;
9:8, 29, 46; 10:26; 12:15, 15; 15:33; 3Mc 2:13;
4Mc 17:20

THEIR ENEMIES Ge 22:17; Ex 32:25; Lev
26:36, 41, 44; Jos 7:8, 12, 12; 10:13; 21:44,
44; 23:1; Jdg 2:14, 14, 18; 8:34; 1Sa 10:1;
14:30; 2Sa 3:18; 1Ki 8:48; 2Ki 21:14, 14; 2Ch
6:28, 34; 20:27; Ne 9:27, 27, 28; Est 8:13; 9:5,
16, 22; Ps 41:2; 78:53; 81:14; 106:42; Pr 16:7;
Isa 9:11; Jer 15:9; 19:7, 9; 20:4, 5; 21:7; 34:20,
21; 49:37; 50:7; Am 9:4; Rev 11:12; Jdt 5:18;
7:19; AdE 13:6; 8:13; 9:16, 22; Wis 10:19;
11:3, 5; 18:2; 12:24; 16:4, 22; 18:1, 4, 7, 10; Sir
6:4; 51:8; Bar 5:6; 1Mc 8:28; 14:31; 2Mc
4:16; 10:21, 26; 3Mc 4:4; 6:6, 15; 7:21; 2Es
1:11

YOUR ENEMIES Ge 14:20; 49:8; Ex 23:22,
27; Lev 26:7, 8, 16, 17, 32, 34, 37, 38, 39; Nu
10:9, 35; 14:42; Dt 1:42; 6:19; 12:10; 20:1, 3,
4, 14; 21:10; 23:9, 14; 25:19; 28:7, 25, 31, 48,
68; 30:7; 33:29; Jos 7:13; 10:19; 22:8; Jdg
3:28; 5:31; 11:36; 1Sa 12:11; 25:26, 29; 2Sa
7:9, 11; 1Ki 3:11; 2Ki 17:39; 1Ch 17:8, 10;
21:12; Ps 21:8; 66:3; 83:2; 89:10, 51; 92:9, 9;
110:1; Pr 24:17; 25:21; Isa 62:8; Jer 15:14;
17:4; La 2:16; Eze 16:27; Da 4:19; Mic 4:10;
5:9; 7:6; Zep 3:15; Mt 5:44; 22:44; Mk 12:36;
Lk 6:27, 35; 19:43; 20:43; Ac 2:35; Ro 12:20;
Heb 1:13; Sir 6:13; 18:31; 42:11; Bar 3:10;
4:6, 18; 2Es 1:16; 3:27, 30

ENEMY → ENEMIES, ENMITY

Ex   15: 6 right hand, O LORD, shattered the e.
      23:22 then I will be an e to your enemies
Dt   33:27 he drove out the e before you,
1Sa 18:29 So Saul was David's e from
2Sa 22:18 He delivered me from my strong e,
Est   3:10 the Agagite, the e of the Jews.
       7: 6 and e, this wicked Haman!"
       9:24 the e of all the Jews,
Ps   8: 2 to silence the e and the avenger.
      18:17 He delivered me from my strong e,
      74:10 Is the e to revile your name forever?
Pr   26:25 when an e speaks graciously,
      27: 6 but profuse are the kisses of an e.
Jer 30:14 I have dealt you the blow of an e,
La   2: 5 The Lord has become like an e;
Mic   2: 8 rise up against my people as an e;
Mt   5:43 love your neighbor and hate your e.'
      13:39 the e who sowed them is the devil;
Lk   10:19 and over all the power of the e;
1Co 15:26 The last e to be destroyed is death.
Jas   4: 4 of the world becomes an e of God.

MY ENEMY 1Sa 19:17; 1Ki 21:20; Job 27:7;
Ps 13:2, 4; 41:11; La 2:22; Mic 7:8, 10; Sir
23:3

THE ENEMY Ge 14:11; Ex 15:6, 9; Dt
28:53, 55, 57; 32:27; 33:27; Jdg 8:24; 1Sa
24:19; 1Ki 8:46; 2Ch 25:8; 26:13; Ezr 8:22,
31; Est 3:10; 8:1; 9:10, 24; Ps 7:5; 8:2; 31:8;
42:9; 43:2; 44:16; 55:3; 61:3; 74:3, 10, 18;
89:22; 106:10; 143:3; Jer 6:25; 18:17; 31:16;
La 1:9, 16; 2:3, 7, 17; Eze 36:2; Hos 8:3; Na
3:11; Hab 1:15; Mt 13:39; Lk 10:19; Jdt 15:4,
5, 5; 16:11, 11; AdE 9:10; Sir 29:13; 36:9;
46:18; Bar 4:21, 26; 1Mc 2:7, 35; 5:13, 27;
6:38; 7:29, 46; 8:26; 9:6, 48; 11:72; 12:26, 28;
14:33, 34; 16:7; 2Mc 8:6, 16, 24, 27, 31;
10:27, 29, 30; 11:12; 12:22; 13:21; 14:17, 22;
15:20, 26; 1Es 4:4; 3Mc 1:5; 6:10, 19; 4Mc
2:14; 3:13; 18:4

YOUR ENEMY 1Sa 24:4; 26:8; 28:16; 2Sa
4:8; Job 13:24; Mt 5:43; Gal 4:16; Sir 12:10;
Bar 4:25; 4Mc 8:10

ENERGY*
Col 1:29 the e that he powerfully inspires

ENGAGED → ENGAGEMENT
Dt 20: 7 Has anyone become e
     28:30 You shall become e to a woman,
Mt   1:18 mother Mary had been e to Joseph,
Lk   1:27 a virgin e to a man whose name was

ENGAGEMENT* → ENGAGED
Tob 6:13 and arrange her e to you.

ENGRAVE → ENGRAVED
Ex 28:11 so you shall e the two stones with
Zec 3: 9 I will e its inscription, says the

ENGRAVED → ENGRAVE
Ex 32:16 writing was the writing of God, e
Jer 17: 1 a diamond point it is e on the tablet

ENJOY → ENJOYMENT
Ge 45:18 and you may e the fat of the land.'
Lev 26:34 land shall e its sabbath years as long
Ps   37: 3 will live in the land, and e security.
Pr   14: 9 but the upright e God's favor.
     28:16 hates unjust gain will e a long life.
Ecc   2: 1 make a test of pleasure; e yourself."
      3:22 that all should e their work, for that
      5:19 and whom he enables to e them,
      6: 2 yet God does not enable them to e
      9: 9 E life with the wife whom you love,
Heb 11:25 than to e the fleeting pleasures

ENJOYMENT → ENJOY
Ecc   2:25 who can eat or who can have e?
      8:15 So I commend e, for there is nothing
1Ti   6:17 with everything for our e.

ENLARGE → LARGE
Ex 34:24 before you, and e your borders;
1Ch 4:10 would bless me and e my border,
Ps 119:32 for you e my understanding.
Isa 54: 2 E the site of your tent, and let the

ENLARGED → LARGE
Isa 26:15 have e all the borders of the land.

ENLARGES → LARGE
Dt 19: 8 the LORD your God e your territory,

ENLIGHTEN* → LIGHT
Sir 45:17 and to e Israel with his law.

ENLIGHTENED* → LIGHT
Ro 10: 2 have a zeal for God, but it is not e.
Eph 1:18 with the eyes of your heart e,
Heb 6: 4 those who have once been e,
     10:32 after you had been e,
2Es 13:53 you alone have been e about this,

ENLIGHTENING* → LIGHT
Ps 19: 8 of the LORD is clear, e the eyes;

ENLIGHTENMENT → LIGHT
Isa 40:14 Whom did he consult for his e,
Da   5:14 and that e, understanding,

ENLIGHTENS* → LIGHT
Jn   1: 9 The true light, which e everyone,

ENMITY → ENEMY
Ge   3:15 put e between you and the woman,
Jas   4: 4 with the world is e with God?

ENOCH
1. Son of Cain (Ge 4:17-18).
2. Descendant of Seth; walked with God and taken by him (Ge 5:18-24; Heb 11:5). Prophet (Jude 14).

ENOUGH
Dt   1: 6 have stayed long e at this mountain.
Pr 30:15 never satisfied; four never say, "E":
Hab 2: 5 like Death they never have e.
Hag 1: 6 you eat, but you never have e;

Mt   6:34 Today's trouble is e for today.
Sir   5: 1 or say, "I have e."
     20: 1 who is wise e to keep silent.
     43:30 for you cannot praise him e.

ENRICH → RICH
Ps 65: 9 earth and water it, you greatly e it;

ENRICHED → RICH
Pr 11:25 A generous person will be e,
     28:25 trusts in the LORD will be e.
1Co 1: 5 every way you have been e in him,
2Co 9:11 be e in every way for your great

ENROLL → ENROLLED
Nu 1: 3 You and Aaron shall e them,

ENROLLED → ENROLL
Nu   1:19 So he e them in the wilderness of
     26:64 had e the Israelites in the wilderness

ENSIGN → ENSIGNS
Isa 62:10 lift up an e over the peoples.

ENSIGNS* → ENSIGN
Nu   2: 2 under e by their ancestral houses;

ENSLAVE* → SLAVE
Ac   7: 6 would e them and mistreat them
1Co 9:27 but I punish my body and e it,
Gal   2: 4 so that they might e us—

ENSLAVED → SLAVE
Ro   6: 6 and we might no longer be e to sin.
Gal   4: 9 want to be e to them again?

ENSNARE → SNARE
Pr   5:22 The iniquities of the wicked e them,

ENSNARED → SNARE
Dt   7:25 because you could be e by it;
Sir 25:21 Do not be e by a woman's beauty,

ENTANGLED
2Pe   2: 2 again e in them and overpowered,

ENTER → ENTERED, ENTERING, ENTERS, ENTRANCE, ENTRY
Ex 40:35 Moses was not able to e the tent
Nu 20:24 not e the land that I have given to
Dt   1:37 saying, "You also shall not e there.
Ps 95:11 I swore, "They shall not e my rest."
   100: 4 E his gates with thanksgiving,
   118:20 the righteous shall e through it.
Pr   4:14 Do not e the path of the wicked,
Isa 26: 2 nation that keeps faith may e in.
Eze 7: 2 will cause breath to e you,
Joel 3: 2 I will e into judgment with them
Mt   5:20 will never e the kingdom of heaven.
     7:13 "E through the narrow gate;
     7:21 'Lord, Lord,' will e the kingdom of
     18: 3 will never e the kingdom of heaven.
     18: 8 to e life maimed or lame than to
     19:17 you wish to e into life, keep the
Mk 10:15 as a little child will never e it."
     10:23 who have wealth to e the kingdom
Lk 13:24 Strive to e through the narrow door;
     13:24 many, I tell you, will try to e and
     24:26 should suffer these things and then e
Jn   3: 5 no one can e the kingdom of God
Ac 14:22 many persecutions that we must e
Heb 3:11 'They will not e my rest.'"
     4: 3 'They shall not e my rest,'"
     4:11 make every effort to e that rest,
     10:19 have confidence to e the sanctuary
Rev 15: 8 and no one could e the temple until
     21:27 But nothing unclean will e it,

ENTERED → ENTER
Ex 24:18 Moses e the cloud, and went up on
2Ch 16:16 e the temple of the LORD to make
Eze 43: 4 the glory of the LORD e the temple
Lk   9:34 were terrified as they e the cloud.
     22: 3 Satan e into Judas called Iscariot,
Jn 13:27 the piece of bread, Satan e into him.

Ac 11: 8 or unclean has ever e my mouth.'
Heb 9: 6 a forerunner on our behalf, has e,
     9:12 he e once for all into the Holy Place,
Rev 11:11 the breath of life from God e them,

ENTERING → ENTER
Lk 11:52 you hindered those who were e."
Heb 4: 1 promise of e his rest is still open,

ENTERS → ENTER
Jn 10: 2 The one who e by the gate
     10: 9 Whoever e by me will be saved,
Heb 6:19 a hope that e the inner shrine

ENTERTAIN → ENTERTAINED
Jdg 16:25 "Call Samson, and let him e us."

ENTERTAINED → ENTERTAIN
Heb 13: 2 have e angels without knowing it.

ENTHRONED → THRONE
1Sa 4: 4 who is e on the cherubim.
2Sa 6: 2 of hosts who is e on the cherubim,
2Ki 19:15 who are e above the cherubim,
1Ch 13: 6 the LORD, who is e on the cherubim,
Ps   9: 7 But the LORD sits e forever,
    22: 3 are holy, e on the praises of Israel.
    29:10 The LORD sits e over the flood;
    29:10 the LORD sits e as king forever.
    33:14 From where he sits e he watches all
    55:19 God, who is e from of old,
    61: 7 May he be e forever before God;
    80: 1 You who are e upon the cherubim,
    99: 1 He sits e upon the cherubim;
   102:12 But you, O LORD, are e forever;
   123: 1 O you who are e in the heavens!
Isa 37:16 who are e above the cherubim,

ENTHUSIASM*
Ac 18:25 and he spoke with burning e
Eph 6: 7 service with e, as to the Lord

ENTICE → ENTICED, ENTICES
2Ch 18:19 LORD said, 'Who will e King Ahab
Pr   1:10 if sinners e you, do not consent.
Ac 20:30 in order to e the disciples to follow
2Pe   2:18 they e people who have just escaped

ENTICED → ENTICE
Job 31: 9 If my heart has been e by a woman,
    31:27 and my heart has been secretly e,
Jer 20: 7 LORD, you have e me, and I was e;
1Co 12: 2 you were e and led astray to idols
Jas   1:14 being lured and e by it;

ENTICES* → ENTICE
Dt 13: 6 If anyone secretly e you—

ENTIRE
Ex 14:28 e army of Pharaoh that had followed
Dt   2:14 the e generation of warriors had
     8: 1 This e commandment that I
Jos   3:17 the e nation finished crossing over
Ac   2: 2 it filled the e house where they were
Gal   5: 3 that he is obliged to obey the e law.

ENTRANCE → ENTER
Ex 26:36 make a screen for the e of the tent,
Mk 16: 3 stone for us from the e to the tomb?

ENTRAP* → TRAP
Mt 22:15 plotted to e him in what he said.

ENTREAT → ENTREATED, ENTREATY
1Ki 13: 6 "E now the favor of the LORD your
Da   9:13 We did not e the favor of the LORD
Zec 8:21 let us go to e the favor of the LORD,
2Co 5:20 we e you on behalf of Christ,

ENTREATED → ENTREAT
Dt   3:23 At that time, too, I e the LORD,
Jdg 13: 8 Then Manoah e the LORD, and said,
1Sa 13:12 I have not e the favor of the LORD';
1Ki 13: 6 So the man of God e the LORD;

ENTREATY → ENTREAT
1Ch 5:20 granted their e because they trusted
2Ch 33:19 prayer, and how God received his e,

ENTRUST → TRUST
Lk 16:11 who will e to you the true riches?
Jn   2:24 Jesus on his part would not e
2Ti   2: 2 from me through many witnesses e
1Pe 4:19 e themselves to a faithful Creator,
Sir 50:24 May he e to us his mercy,

ENTRUSTED → TRUST
Nu 12: 7 he is e with all my house.
Lk 12:48 the one to whom much has been e,
Ro   3: 2 the Jews were e with the oracles
      6:17 of teaching to which you were e,
1Co 9:17 own will, I am e with a commission.
Gal 2: 7 that I had been e with the gospel
1Th 2: 4 have been approved by God to be e
1Ti 1:11 the blessed God, which he e to me.
      6:20 Timothy, guard what has been e to
2Ti 1:12 guard until that day what I have e to
      1:14 Guard the good treasure e to you,
Tit 1: 3 with which I have been e by
1Pe 2:23 he e himself to the one who judges
Jude 1: 3 the faith that was once for all e to

ENTRY → ENTER
2Pe 1:11 e into the eternal kingdom of our

ENVIOUS → ENVY
Ps 37: 1 do not be e of wrongdoers,
1Co 13: 4 love is not e or boastful or arrogant

ENVOY
Pr 13:17 but a faithful e, healing.

ENVY → ENVIOUS, ENVYING
Pr   3:31 Do not e the violent and do not
     23:17 Do not let your heart e sinners,
       24: 1 Do not e the wicked, nor desire to
Ecc 4: 4 in work come from one person's e
Eze 31: 9 the e of all the trees of Eden
Mk   7:22 deceit, licentiousness, e, slander,
Ro   1:29 Full of e, murder, strife, deceit,
Gal 5:21 e, drunkenness, carousing, and
Php 1:15 Some proclaim Christ from e and
1Ti 6: 4 From these come e, dissension,
Tit 3: 3 passing our days in malice and e,
Jas 3:14 But if you have bitter e and selfish
      3:16 For where there is e and selfish
1Pe 2: 1 guile, insincerity, e, and all slander.
Wis 2:24 through the devil's e death entered
Sir 9:11 Do not e the success of sinners,

ENVYING* → ENVY
Gal 5:26 competing against one another, e

EPAPHRAS*
Associate of Paul (Col 1:7; 4:12; Phm 23).

EPAPHRODITUS*
Associate of Paul (Php 2:25; 4:18).

EPHAH
Ex 16:36 An omer is a tenth of an e.
Eze 45:10 have honest balances, an honest e,

EPHESIANS → EPHESUS
Ac 19:28 "Great is Artemis of the E!"

EPHESUS → EPHESIANS
Ac 18:19 When they reached E, he left them
     19: 1 the interior regions and came to E,
     20:17 Miletus he sent a message to E,
1Co 15:32 I fought with wild animals at E,
Eph 1: 1 To the saints who are in E and are
Rev 2: 1 "To the angel of the church in E

EPHOD
Ex 28: 6 They shall make the e of gold,
Lev 8: 7 and put the e on him.
Jdg 8:27 Gideon made an e of it and put it in
     17: 5 and he made an e and teraphim,
1Sa 2:18 a boy wearing a linen e.

1Ch 15:27 and David wore a linen e.
Hos 3: 4 or pillar, without e or teraphim.

EPHPHATHA*
Mk   7:34 "E," that is, "Be opened."

EPHRAIM
1. Second son of Joseph (Ge 41:52; 46:20).
Blessed as firstborn by Jacob (Ge 48). Tribe of
numbered (Nu 1:33; 26:37), blessed (Dt 33:17),
allotted land (Jos 16:4-9; Eze 48:5), failed to fully
possess (Jos 16:10; Jdg 1:29).
2. A term for the Northern Kingdom of Israel
(Isa 7:17; Hos 5).

HILL COUNTRY OF EPHRAIM Jos
17:15; 19:50; 20:7; 21:21; 24:30, 33; Jdg 2:9;
3:27; 4:5; 7:24; 10:1; 17:1, 8; 18:2, 13; 19:1,
16, 18; 1Sa 1:1; 9:4; 14:22, 23; 2Sa 20:21; 1Ki
4:8; 12:25; 2Ki 5:22; 1Ch 6:67; 2Ch 13:4;
15:8; 19:4; Jer 31:6

TRIBE OF EPHRAIM Nu 1:33; 13:8; Jos
21:5, 20; 1Ch 6:66; Ps 78:67

EPHRATH → BETHLEHEM, EPHRATHAH
Ge 35:19 on the way to E (that is, Bethlehem)

EPHRATHAH → EPHRATH
Ru   4:11 May you produce children in E
Mic 5: 2 But you, O Bethlehem of E,

EPHRON
Hittite who sold Abraham a field (Ge 23).

EPICUREAN*
Ac 17:18 E and Stoic philosophers debated

EPILEPTIC* → EPILEPTICS
Mt 17:15 for he is an e and he suffers terribly;

EPILEPTICS* → EPILEPTIC
Mt   4:24 e, and paralytics, and he cured them.

EPIPHANES
1Mc 1:10 a sinful root, Antiochus E,

EQUAL → EQUALITY
Job 28:17 Gold and glass cannot e it,
Ps 55:13 my e, my companion,
Isa 40:25 you compare me, or who is my e?
     46: 5 will you liken me and make me e,
Jn   5:18 thereby making himself e to God.
Sir 2:17 for e to his majesty is his mercy,
      9:10 for new ones cannot e them.

EQUALITY* → EQUAL
Php 2: 6 not regard e with God as something

EQUIP → EQUIPPED
Eph 4:12 to e the saints for the work

EQUIPPED → EQUIP
Eph 4:16 by every ligament with which it is e,
2Ti 3:17 proficient, e for every good work.

EQUITY
2Sa 8:15 David administered justice and e
Ps   9: 8 he judges the peoples with e.
     96:10 He will judge the peoples with e."
     98: 9 and the peoples with e.
     99: 4 of justice, you have established e;
Pr 29:14 If a king judges the poor with e,
Isa 11: 4 with e for the meek of the earth;

ER
Ge 38: 6 Judah took a wife for E his firstborn

ERASING*
Col 2:14 e the record that stood against us

ERASTUS*
Associate(s) of Paul (Ac 19:22; Ro 16:23; 2Ti
4:20).

ERECT → ERECTED
Ex 26:30 Then you shall e the tabernacle
Heb 8: 5 Moses, when he was about to e the

ERECTED → ERECT
1Ki 16:32 He e an altar for Baal
2Ki 21: 3 he e altars for Baal,
1Mc 1:54 e a desolating sacrilege on the altar
      6: 7 abomination that he had e on the

ERR → ERROR, ERRORS
Ps 58: 3 they e from their birth,
Pr 14:22 Do they not e that plan evil?
Sir 28:26 not to e with your tongue,

ERROR → ERR
Lev 5:18 for the e that you committed
Nu 15:25 before the LORD, for their e.
Job 4:18 and his angels he charges with e;
Ro   1:27 the due penalty for their e.
2Pe 2:18 from those who live in e.
      3:17 not carried away with the e of the
1Jn 4: 6 the spirit of truth and the spirit of e,
Jude 1:11 abandon themselves to Balaam's e
Wis 1:12 Do not invite death by the e of your

ERRORS → ERR
Ps 19:12 But who can detect their e?

ESAU → =EDOM
Firstborn of Isaac, twin of Jacob (Ge 25:21-26).
Also called Edom (Ge 25:30). Sold Jacob his
birthright (Ge 25:29-34); lost blessing (Gen 27).
Married Hittites (Ge 26:34), Ishmaelites (Ge
28:6-9). Reconciled to Jacob (Gen 33). Genealogy (Ge 36). The LORD chose Jacob over Esau
(Mal 1:2-3), but gave Esau land (Dt 2:2-12). Descendants eventually obliterated (Ob 1-21; Jer
49:7-22).

ESCAPE → ESCAPED, ESCAPES
Ge   7: 7 went into the ark to e the waters of
1Sa 23:28 that place was called the Rock of E.
2Sa 15:14 will be no e for us from Absalom.
Job 11:20 all way of e will be lost to them,
Ps 68:20 the LORD, belongs e from death.
     89:48 Who can e the power of Sheol?
Pr 12:13 but the righteous e from trouble.
Jer 11:11 upon them that they cannot e;
Eze 6: 9 you who e shall remember me
     17:15 he break the covenant and yet e?
Joel 2:32 there shall be those who e,
Ob   1:17 Zion there shall be those that e,
Mt 23:33 can you e being sentenced to hell?
Ro   2: 3 you will e the judgment of God?
1Th 5: 3 and there will be no e!
2Ti 2:26 may e from the snare of the devil,
Heb 2: 3 how can we e if we neglect so great
     12:25 if they did not e when they refused
     12:25 how much less will we e if we reject
2Pe 1: 4 you may e from the corruption
Sir 16:13 The sinner will not e with plunder,
Sus 1:22 I cannot e your hands.

ESCAPED → ESCAPE
1Sa 19:10 David fled and e that night.
      22: 1 there and e to the cave of Adullam;
Ne   1: 2 those who had e the captivity,
Ps 124: 7 have e like a bird from the snare of
    124: 7 the snare is broken, and we have e.
La   2:22 of the anger of the LORD no one e
Jn 10:39 but he e from their hands.
Heb 11:34 e the edge of the sword,
2Pe 2:20 have e the defilements of the world

ESCAPES → ESCAPE
Joel 2: 3 wilderness, and nothing e them.
Sir 42:20 No thought e him, and nothing is

ESHCOL
Nu 13:23 And they came to the Wadi E,

ESSENTIALS*
Ac 15:28 no further burden than these e:

ESTABLISH → ESTABLISHED,
ESTABLISHES
Ge   6:18 But I will e my covenant with you;

17:21 But my covenant I will e with Isaac,
Dt 28: 9 LORD will e you as his holy people,
1Ki 9: 5 will e your royal throne over Israel
1Ch 28: 7 I will e his kingdom forever
Ps 89: 4 'I will e your descendants forever,
Isa 9: 7 He will e and uphold it with justice
Eze 16:60 e with you an everlasting covenant.
Ro 10: 3 and seeking to e their own,
Heb 8: 8 when I will e a new covenant with
10: 9 He abolishes the first in order to e

ESTABLISHED → ESTABLISH
Ge 9:17 sign of the covenant that I have e
Ex 6: 4 I also e my covenant with them,
Lev 26:46 and laws that the LORD e
2Sa 7:16 your throne shall be e forever.
1Ki 2:46 was e in the hand of Solomon.
Ps 8: 3 moon and the stars that you have e;
9: 7 he has e his throne for judgment.
89: 2 your steadfast love is e forever;
93: 2 your throne is e from of old;
96:10 The world is firmly e; it shall never
103:19 The LORD has e his throne in the
148: 6 He e them forever and ever;
Pr 8:27 When he e the heavens,
16:12 for the throne is e by righteousness.
Isa 2: 2 shall be e as the highest of
54:14 In righteousness you shall be e;
Jer 10:12 who e the world by his wisdom,
33:25 if I had not e my covenant with day
Col 1:23 continue securely e and steadfast
2Pe 1:12 you know them already and are e in
AdE 9:32 Esther e it by a decree forever,

ESTABLISHES → ESTABLISH
Isa 62: 7 him no rest until he e Jerusalem
2Co 1:21 God who e us with you in Christ

ESTATE
Ps 136:23 he who remembered us in our low e,

ESTEEM
Ac 5:13 but the people held them in high e.

ESTHER
Jewess, originally named Hadassah, who lived in Persia; cousin of Mordecai (Est 2:7). Chosen queen of Xerxes (Est 2:8-18). Persuaded by Mordecai to foil Haman's plan to exterminate the Jews (Est 3-4). Revealed Haman's plans to Xerxes, resulting in Haman's death (Est 7), the Jews' preservation (Est 8-9), Mordecai's exaltation (Est 8:15; 9:4; 10). Decreed celebration of Purim (Est 9:18-32). See also the Additions to Esther.

ESTRANGED
Eze 14: 5 e from me through their idols.
Col 1:21 And you who were once e

ETERNAL* → ETERNITY
Ge 49:26 the blessings of the e mountains,
Ecc 12: 5 because all must go to their e home,
Jer 20:11 Their e dishonor will never be
Hab 3: 6 The e mountains were shattered;
Mt 18: 8 and to be thrown into the e fire.
19:16 good deed must I do to have e life?"
19:29 hundredfold, and will inherit e life.
25:41 the e fire prepared for the devil and
25:46 will go away into e punishment, but the righteous into e life."
Mk 3:29 but is guilty of an e sin"—
10:17 what must I do to inherit e life?"
10:30 and in the age to come e life.
16: S [proclamation of e salvation.]
Lk 10:25 "what must I do to inherit e life?"
16: 9 may welcome you into the e homes.
18:18 what must I do to inherit e life?"
18:30 and in the age to come e life."
Jn 3:15 believes in him may have e life.
3:16 may not perish but may have e life.
3:36 believes in the Son has e life;
4:14 spring of water gushing up to e life.
4:36 and is gathering fruit for e life,
5:24 believes him who sent me has e life,

5:39 think that in them you have e life;
6:27 for the food that endures for e life,
6:40 and believe in him may have e life;
6:47 whoever believes has e life.
6:54 and drink my blood have e life,
6:68 You have the words of e life.
10:28 I give them e life, and they will
12:25 in this world will keep it for e life.
12:50 that his commandment is e life.
17: 2 to give e life to all whom you have
17: 3 this is e life, that they may know
Ac 13:46 yourselves to be unworthy of e life,
13:48 destined for e life became believers.
Ro 1:20 creation of the world his e power
2: 7 and immortality, he will give e life;
5:21 e life through Jesus Christ our Lord.
6:22 The end is e life.
6:23 free gift of God is e life in Christ
16:26 to the command of the e God,
2Co 4:17 an e weight of glory beyond all
4:18 but what cannot be seen is e.
5: 1 with hands, e in the heavens.
Gal 6: 8 you will reap e life from the Spirit.
Eph 3:11 in accordance with the e purpose
2Th 1: 9 the punishment of e destruction,
2:16 through grace gave us e comfort
1Ti 1:16 to believe in him for e life.
6:12 take hold of the e life,
6:16 to him be honor and e dominion.
2Ti 2:10 that is in Christ Jesus, with e glory.
Tit 1: 2 of e life that God, who never lies,
3: 7 according to the hope of e life.
Heb 5: 9 the source of e salvation for all who
6: 2 of the dead, and e judgment.
9:12 thus obtaining e redemption.
9:14 the e Spirit offered himself without
9:15 the promised e inheritance,
13:20 by the blood of the e covenant,
1Pe 5:10 called you to his e glory in Christ,
2Pe 1:11 into the e kingdom of our Lord
1Jn 1: 2 declare to you the e life that was
2:25 is what he has promised us, e life.
3:15 murderers do not have e life abiding
5:11 God gave us e life, and this life is in
5:13 may know that you have e life.
5:20 He is the true God and e life.
Jude 1: 6 he has kept in e chains in deepest
1: 7 undergoing a punishment of e fire.
1:21 Lord Jesus Christ that leads to e life.
Rev 14: 6 with an e gospel to proclaim to
Tob 3: 6 release me to go to the e home,
14: 7 they will praise the e God.
14:10 but Nadab went into the e darkness,
Wis 7:26 For she is a reflection of e light,
17: 2 exiles from e providence.
Sir 1:15 made among human beings an e
16:27 he arranged his works in an e order,
17:12 established with them an e covenant
30:17 and e sleep than chronic sickness.
46:19 Before the time of his e sleep,
Sus 1:42 and said, "O e God,
2Mc 1:25 alone are just and almighty and e.
3Mc 6:12 O E One, who have all might and
7:16 ancestors, the e Savior of Israel,
4Mc 10:15 by the e destruction of the tyrant,
12:12 has laid up for you intense and e fire
13:15 of e torment lying before those who
15: 3 that preserves them for e life
17:18 and live the life of e blessedness.

ETERNAL LIFE
Mt 19:16, 29; 25:46; Mk 10:17, 30; Lk 10:25; 18:18, 30; Jn 3:15, 16, 36; 4:14, 36; 5:24, 39; 6:27, 40, 47, 54, 68; 10:28; 12:25, 50; 17:2, 3; Ac 13:46, 48; Ro 2:7; 5:21; 6:22, 23; Gal 6:8; 1Ti 1:16; 6:12; Tit 1:2; 3:7; 1Jn 1:2; 2:25; 3:15; 5:11, 13, 20; Jude 1:21; 4Mc 15:3

ETERNITY* → ETERNAL
Isa 45:17 put to shame or confounded to all e.
57:15 high and lofty one who inhabits e,
2Pe 3:18 glory both now and to the day of e.

Wis 2:23 made us in the image of his own e,
Sir 1: 2 the days of e—who can count them?
1: 4 and prudent understanding from e.
18:10 are a few years among the days of e.
42:21 he is from all e one and the same.
2Es 8:20 "O Lord, you who inhabit e, whose

ETHAN
1Ki 4:31 wiser than E the Ezrahite,
1Ch 15:19 E were to sound bronze cymbals;
Ps 89: T A Maskil of E the Ezrahite.

ETHIOPIA → ETHIOPIAN, ETHIOPIANS
Est 1: 1 provinces from India to E.
Ps 87: 4 Philistia too, and Tyre, with E—
Isa 18: 1 wings beyond the rivers of E,
Eze 30: 4 and anguish shall be in E,
Jdt 1:10 in Egypt as far as the borders of E.

ETHIOPIAN → ETHIOPIA
Jer 38: 7 Ebed-melech the E, a eunuch
Ac 8:27 Now there was an E eunuch,

ETHIOPIANS → ETHIOPIA
Jer 13:23 Can E change their skin
Am 9: 7 Are you not like the E to me,

EUNICE*
Mother of Timothy (2Ti 1:5).

EUNUCH → EUNUCHS
Est 2:14 of Shaashgaz, the king's e,
Isa 56: 3 do not let the e say, "I am just a dry
Jer 38: 7 Ebed-melech the Ethiopian, a e
Ac 8:27 Now there was an Ethiopian e,

EUNUCHS → EUNUCH
2Ki 20:18 be e in the palace of the king of
Isa 56: 4 To the e who keep my sabbaths,
Mt 19:12 are e who have made themselves e for the sake of the kingdom of

EUODIA*
Php 4: 2 I urge E and I urge Syntyche to be

EUPHRATES
Ge 2:14 And the fourth river is the E.
15:18 Egypt to the great river, the river E,
Dt 11:24 the river E, to the Western Sea.
2Ki 24: 7 the Wadi of Egypt to the River E.
Jer 13: 4 and go now to the E,
Rev 9:14 who are bound at the great river E."
16:12 poured his bowl on the great river E

EUTYCHUS*
Ac 20: 9 A young man named E, who was

EVANGELIST* → EVANGELISTS
Ac 21: 8 went into the house of Philip the e,
2Ti 4: 5 do the work of an e, carry out your

EVANGELISTS* → EVANGELIST
Eph 4:11 some e, some pastors and teachers,

EVE*
Ge 3:20 The man named his wife E,
4: 1 Now the man knew his wife E,
2Co 11: 3 afraid that as the serpent deceived E
1Ti 2:13 For Adam was formed first, then E;
Tob 8: 6 his wife E as a helper and support.

EVENING → EVENINGS
Ge 1: 5 there was e and there was morning,
8:11 dove came back to him in the e,
24:11 toward e, the time when women go
Ps 102:11 My days are like an e shadow;
Ecc 11: 6 at e do not let your hands be idle;
Zec 14: 7 for at e time there shall be light.

EVENING ... MORNING
Ge 1:5, 8, 13, 19, 23, 31; Ex 27:21; Lev 24:3; Nu 9:15, 21; Ps 55:17; 2Es 7:40

IN THE EVENING
Ge 8:11; 19:1; 24:63; 29:23; 30:16; Ex 16:6, 8, 13; 29:39, 41; 30:8; Lev 6:20; Dt 16:6; Jos 5:10; 2Sa 11:13; 1Ki

17:6; Est 2:14; Ps 90:6; Pr 7:9; Isa 5:11; Eze 12:7; Mk 13:35; AdE 2:14; 3Mc 5:5

MORNING ... EVENING Ex 18:13, 14; Lev 6:20; 1Sa 17:16; 1Ch 16:40; 2Ch 2:4; 13:11; 31:3; Ezr 3:3; Job 4:20; Ps 65:8; Eze 24:18; Ac 28:23; Sir 18:26; Mc 9:13; 1Es 5:50

UNTIL [THE] EVENING Ex 12:18; 18:13, 14; Lev 11:24, 25, 27, 28, 31, 32, 39, 40, 40; 14:46; 15:5, 6, 7, 8, 10, 10, 11, 16, 17, 18, 19, 21, 22, 23, 27; 17:15; 22:6; Nu 19:7, 8, 10, 21, 22; Jos 7:6; 8:29; 10:26; Jdg 20:23; 20:26; 21:2; Ru 2:17; 1Sa 30:17; 2Sa 1:12; 1Ki 22:35; 2Ch 18:34; Ezr 9:4; Ps 104:23; Eze 46:2; Ac 28:23; 1Mc 9:13; 1Es 8:72; 2Es 10:2

EVENINGS*   → EVENING

Da   8:14 "For two thousand three hundred e
      8:26 vision of the e and the mornings

EVER → EVER-FLOWING, EVERLASTING, FOREVER, FOREVERMORE

Ex   9:18 heaviest hail to fall that has e fallen
     11: 6 as has never been or will e be again.
     15:18 The LORD will reign forever and e."
Dt   4:32 anything so great as this e happened
Job 4: 7 who that was innocent e perished?
Ps   5:11 let them e sing for joy.
     10:16 The LORD is king forever and e;
     25:15 My eyes are e toward the LORD,
     38:17 and my pain is e with me.
     45: 6 O God, endures forever and e.
     45:17 will praise you forever and e.
     48:14 our God forever and e.
     52: 8 steadfast love of God forever and e.
     84: 4 in your house, e singing your praise.
    111: 8 They are established forever and e,
    145: 1 and bless your name forever and e.
    145: 2 and praise your name forever and e.
    145:21 bless his holy name forever and e.
    148: 6 He established them forever and e;
Jer 7: 7 to your ancestors forever and e.
     31:36 If this fixed order were e to cease
Da   7:18 kingdom forever—forever and e."
     12: 3 like the stars forever and e.
Mic 4: 5 of the LORD our God forever and e.
Jn   1:18 No one has e seen God.
Gal 1: 5 to whom be the glory forever and e.
Eph 3:21 to all generations, forever and e.
Php 4:20 and Father be glory forever and e.
1Ti 1:17 be honor and glory forever and e.
     6:16 whom no one has e seen
2Ti 4:18 To him be the glory forever and e.
Heb 1: 8 throne, O God, is forever and e,
     13:21 to whom be the glory forever and e.
1Pe 4:11 glory and the power forever and e.
     5:11 To him be the power forever and e.
1Jn 4:12 No one has e seen God;
Rev 1: 6 glory and dominion forever and e.
     1:18 and see, I am alive forever and e;
     4: 9 the throne, who lives forever and e,
     7:12 might be to our God forever and e!
     10: 6 and e, who created heaven and what
     11:15 and he will reign forever and e."
     14:11 their torment goes up forever and e.
     20:10 day and night forever and e.
     22: 5 and they will reign forever and e.
Tob 13:17 bless the holy name forever and e."

FOREVER AND EVER Ex 15:18; 1Ch 29:10; Ps 9:5; 10:16; 21:4; 45:6, 17; 48:14; 52:8; 111:8; 119:44; 145:1, 2, 21; 148:6; Isa 34:10; Jer 7:7; Da 7:18; 12:3; Mic 4:5; Gal 1:5; Eph 3:21; Php 4:20; 1Ti 1:17; 2Ti 4:18; Heb 1:8; 13:21; 1Pe 4:11; 5:11; Rev 1:6, 18; 4:9, 10; 5:13; 7:12; 10:6; 11:15; 14:11; 15:7; 19:3; 20:10; 22:5; Tob 13:17; 14:15; 1Es 4:38; 4Mc 18:24

EVER-FLOWING → EVER, FLOW

Am   5:24 and righteousness like an e stream.

EVERLASTING → EVER, LAST

Ge   9:16 remember the e covenant between

17: 7 their generations, for an e covenant,
17:13 be in your flesh an e covenant.
17:19 as an e covenant for his offspring
21:33 the name of the LORD, the **E** God.
Dt   33:15 and the abundance of the e hills;
2Sa 23: 5 has made with me an e covenant,
1Ch 16:17 to Israel as an e covenant,
     16:36 the God of Israel, from e to e."
Ne   9: 5 the LORD your God from e to e.
Ps   41:13 the God of Israel, from e to e.
     78:66 he put them to e disgrace.
     90: 2 from e to e you are God.
    103:17 love of the LORD is from e to e on
    105:10 to Israel as an e covenant,
    106:48 the God of Israel, from e to e.
    119:142 righteousness is an e righteousness,
    139:24 and lead me in the way e.
    145:13 Your kingdom is an e kingdom,
Isa 9: 6 God, **E** Father, Prince of Peace.
     24: 5 the statutes, broken the e covenant.
     33:14 among us can live with e flames?"
     35:10 e joy shall be upon their heads;
     40:28 The LORD is the e God,
     45:17 saved by the LORD with e salvation;
     51:11 e joy shall be upon their heads;
     54: 8 with e love I will have compassion
     55: 3 I will make with you an e covenant,
     55:13 an e sign that shall not be cut off.
     56: 5 I will give them an e name that
     60:19 but the LORD will be your e light,
     60:20 for the LORD will be your e light,
     61: 7 possess a double portion; e joy
     61: 8 will make an e covenant with them.
     63:12 to make for himself an e name,
Jer 10:10 he is the living God and the e King.
     23:40 upon you e disgrace and perpetual
     25: 9 and of hissing, and an e disgrace.
     31: 3 I have loved you with an e love;
     32:40 I will make an e covenant with them
     50: 5 to the LORD by an e covenant that
Eze 16:60 establish with you an e covenant.
     37:26 it shall be an e covenant with them;
Da   4: 3 His kingdom is an e kingdom,
     7:14 His dominion is an e dominion that
     7:27 kingdom shall be an e kingdom,
     9:24 to bring in e righteousness,
     12: 2 shall awake, some to e life, and some to shame and e contempt.
Tob 1: 6 for all Israel by an e decree.
Sir 15: 6 and will inherit an e name.
     44:18 **E** covenants were made with him
     45: 7 He made an e covenant with him,
Bar 2:35 an e covenant with them to be their
     4:20 I will cry to the **E** all my days.
1Mc 6:44 and to win for himself an e name.

EVERY → EVERYONE, EVERYONE'S, EVERYTHING, EVERYWHERE

Ge   1:29 I have given you e plant yielding
     1:29 and e tree with seed in its fruit;
     6: 5 and that e inclination of the thoughts
     7: 4 and e living thing that I have made
     7:23 He blotted out e living thing that
Ex   11: 5 **E** firstborn in the land of Egypt
Dt   7:15 will turn away from you e illness;
     8: 3 e word that comes from the mouth
1Ch 28: 9 for the LORD searches e mind,
Ps   7:11 a God who has indignation e day.
     50:10 e wild animal of the forest is mine,
    145: 2 **E** day I will bless you,
Pr   30: 5 **E** word of God proves true;
Ecc 3: 1 a time for e matter under heaven:
     12:14 God will bring e deed into judgment
Isa 40: 4 **E** valley shall be lifted up,
     45:23 "To me e knee shall bow, e tongue shall swear."
Jer 2:20 On e high hill and under e green tree you sprawled and played
La   3:23 they are new e morning; great is
Eze 21: 7 **E** heart will melt and all hands will
Mt   4: 4 e word that comes from the mouth
     7:17 e good tree bears good fruit,

9:35 and curing e disease and e sickness.
12:25 "**E** kingdom divided against itself
Lk   4:13 When the devil had finished e test,
Jn   15: 2 He removes e branch in me that
     21:25 if e one of them were written down,
Ro   3:19 so that e mouth may be silenced,
     14:11 e knee shall bow to me, and e tongue shall give praise to God."
1Co 15:24 after he has destroyed e ruler and e authority
2Co 10: 5 we take e thought captive to obey
Eph 1: 3 with e spiritual blessing in the
     1:21 and above e name that is named,
Php 2:10 at the name of Jesus e knee should
     2:11 e tongue should confess that Jesus
1Th 5:22 abstain from e form of evil.
2Ti 3:17 equipped for e good work.
Heb 3:13 But exhort one another e day,
     12: 1 lay aside e weight and the sin that
1Jn 4: 1 Beloved, do not believe e spirit,
Rev 1: 7 e eye will see him, even those who
     7:17 God will wipe away e tear from
     21: 4 he will wipe e tear from their eyes.
Tob 12:18 Bless him each and e day;
Sir 6:35 to listen to e godly discourse,

EVERY DAY Ex 29:36; Nu 14:34; 1Sa 23:14; 2Ki 25:29, 30; Ne 11:23; Est 2:11; Ps 7:11; 88:9; 109:19; 145:2; Jer 52:33; Lk 16:19; 19:47; 21:37; Ac 5:42; 17:11, 17; 1Co 15:31; Heb 3:13; Tob 10:7; 12:18; AdE 2:11; Sir 45:14; Sus 1:8; Bel 1:3, 4, 6, 32; 1Mc 8:15; 1Es 4:52; 5:51; 2Es 9:44

EVERY GREEN TREE 1Ki 14:23; 2Ki 16:4; 17:10; 2Ch 28:4; Isa 57:5; Jer 2:20; 3:6, 13; 17:2; Eze 6:13; 20:47

EVERY KIND Ge 1:11, 12, 12, 21, 21, 24, 24, 25, 25, 25; 6:19, 20, 21; 7:14, 14, 14; Ex 1:14; 31:3, 5; 35:31, 33, 35; 2Ch 34:13; Ps 144:13; Eze 17:23, 23; 27:18; 39:4, 17; Mt 13:47; Ro 1:29; 1Co 1:5; Eph 4:19; 2Th 2:10; Jas 3:16; Rev 11:6; Tob 4:12; Sir 41:16; 47:25

EVERY MALE Ge 17:10, 12, 23; 34:15, 22, 24; Ex 13:15; Lev 6:18, 29; 7:6; Nu 1:2, 20, 22; 3:15; 18:10; 26:62; 31:7, 17; Jdg 21:11; 1Ki 11:15, 16; 14:10; 21:21; 2Ki 9:8; 2Ch 31:19; 1Mc 5:28, 35, 51

EVERY MAN Ex 11:2; Jdg 5:30; 7:21; 1Sa 25:13; 27:3; 1Ki 22:36, 36; 2Ki 11:11; Ne 4:22; Est 1:22; Jer 30:6; 1Co 11:3; Gal 5:3; Jdt 4:9

EVERY MORNING Ex 30:7; 36:3; Lev 6:12; 1Ch 9:27; 23:30; 2Ch 13:11; Job 7:18; Ps 73:14; Isa 33:2; La 3:23; Am 4:4; Zep 3:5

EVERY NATION 2Ki 17:29, 29; Ac 2:5; 10:35; Rev 7:9; 14:6; Jdt 14:7; AdE 11:7; 13:4, 5; 16:11; Sir 17:17; 2Es 3:8

EVERY ONE Ge 30:33, 35; Lev 25:10, 10, 13; Nu 13:2; 15:12; Jos 22:14; Jdg 6:16; 8:18; 9:49; 20:16; 1Sa 20:15; 22:7; 25:13; 2Sa 2:3; 1Ki 10:25; 2Ki 18:31; 2Ch 9:24; Ps 119:160; Jer 16:12; Eze 20:7; Hag 2:22; Zec 11:6; 13:4; Mt 18:35; Jn 21:25; Ac 2:38; 2Co 1:20; Php 1:4; Jdt 1:12; 2:3; Sir 22:1; 1Mc 2:27; 1Es 1:33; 3Mc 6:25; 2Es 12:49; 4Mc 8:5, 9

EVERY TREE Ge 1:29; 2:9, 16; Ex 9:25; 10:5; Ne 10:35, 37; Isa 44:23; Mt 3:10; 7:19; Lk 3:9; 2Es 16:9

EVERY YEAR Jdg 11:40; 2Sa 14:26; Est 9:27; Lk 2:41; 1Mc 4:59; 8:4; 10:42; 13:52; 2Mc 10:8; 11:3; 1Es 6:30

IN EVERY WAY Ac 17:22; 24:3; Ro 3:2; 1Co 1:5; 2Co 4:8; 6:4; 7:5; 9:11; 11:6; Eph 4:15; Php 1:18; 1Ti 3:4; 4:8; 5:10; Jas 1:7; 1Mc 6:18; 14:35; 2Mc 1:17; 1Es 8:52; 3Mc 3:24; 4Mc 8:3; 18:1

ON EVERY SIDE Nu 2:2; Jos 21:44; Jdg 8:34; 1Sa 12:11; 14:47; 1Ki 5:4; 2Ki 11:11; 1Ch 22:9, 18; 2Ch 14:7; 32:22; Job 1:10; 18:11; 19:10; Ps 12:8; 77:17; 97:3; 118:11; Jer

6:25; Eze 23:24; 28:23; 40:14; 41:10; Lk
19:43; Sir 46:5, 16; 47:7; 51:4, 7; LtJ 6:18;
1Mc 1:37; 13:10; 3Mc 5:7; 2Es 16:39

EVERYONE → EVERY, ONE

Ge   27:29 and blessed be **e** who blesses you!"
Ex   35:21 and whose spirit was willing,
Nu   1: 3 **e** in Israel able to go to war.
     26: 2 **e** in Israel able to go to war."
Ps 128: 1 Happy is **e** who fears the LORD.
Ecc   9: 3 that the same fate comes to **e**.
Jer 31:30 the teeth of **e** who eats sour grapes
Eze 20:11 by whose observance **e** shall live.
Da   12: 1 **e** who is found written in the book.
Joel 2:32 Then **e** who calls on the name of
Mt   7: 8 For **e** who asks receives,
      7:21 "Not **e** who says to me, 'Lord,
     19:11 "Not **e** can accept this teaching,
Lk   11: 4 for we ourselves forgive **e** indebted
Jn   1: 9 The true light, which enlightens **e**,
      3:16 that **e** who believes in him may not
Ac   2:21 Then **e** who calls on the name of
Ro   10:13 "**E** who calls on the name of
1Co 10:33 I try to please **e** in everything I do,
1Ti   2: 4 who desires **e** to be saved
1Pe   2:17 Honor **e**. Love the family of
1Jn   3: 4 **E** who commits sin is guilty of
      4: 7 **e** who loves is born of God and
Rev 13: 8 **e** whose name has not been written
     22:17 And let **e** who hears say, "Come."
Sir 37:28 For not everything is good for **e**,

EVERYONE'S → EVERY, ONE

Ac   1:24 and said, "Lord, you know **e** heart.
Rev 22:12 to repay according to **e** work.

EVERYTHING → EVERY, THING

Ge   1:31 God saw **e** that he had made,
      6:17 **e** that is on the earth shall die.
Ex   19: 8 "**E** that the LORD has spoken we
            will do."
Dt   18:18 speak to them **e** that I command.
     29: 9 you may succeed in **e** that you do.
Ps 150: 6 Let **e** that breathes praise the LORD!
Ecc   3: 1 For **e** there is a season,
      3:11 He has made **e** suitable for its time;
Mt   28:20 obey **e** that I have commanded you.
Mk   7:37 saying, "He has done **e** well;
Lk   1: 3 after investigating **e** carefully
Jn   6:37 **E** that the Father gives me
     14:26 in my name, will teach you **e**,
Ac   4:32 every one owned was held in common.
Ro   14:20 **E** is indeed clean,
1Co   2:10 for the Spirit searches **e**,
     10:31 do **e** for the glory of God.
2Co   5:17 see, **e** has become new!
Gal   6:15 but a new creation is **e**!
Col   3:17 do **e** in the name of the Lord Jesus,
1Th   5:21 but test **e**; hold fast to what is good;
1Ti   4: 4 For **e** created by God is good,
2Pe   1: 3 divine power has given us **e** needed
Sir 15:18 he is mighty in power and sees **e**;
     18:27 One who is wise is cautious in **e**;
     19:15 so do not believe **e** you hear.
     25:11 Fear of the Lord surpasses **e**;

EVERYWHERE → EVERY, WHERE

Lk   9: 6 good news and curing diseases **e**.
Ac   17:30 commands all people **e** to repent.
Sir 50:22 who **e** works great wonders,

EVIDENCE

Nu   35:30 put to death on the **e** of witnesses;
Dt   17: 6 On the **e** of two or three witnesses
     22:15 **e** of the young woman's virginity
Mt   18:16 by the **e** of two or three witnesses.
2Co 13: 1 by the **e** of two or three witnesses."
2Th   1: 5 This is **e** of the righteous judgment
Sus   1:43 men have given false **e** against me.

EVIL → EVILDOER, EVILDOERS,
EVILDOING, EVILS

Ge   2: 9 tree of the knowledge of good and **e**.

      3: 5 be like God, knowing good and **e**."
      6: 5 their hearts was only **e** continually.
     44: 4 'Why have you returned **e** for good?
Ex   32:22 the people, that they are bent on **e**.
Nu   32:13 the generation that had done **e** in
Dt   1:35 not one of this **e** generation—
     13: 5 So you shall purge the **e** from your
     28:20 on account of the **e** of your deeds,
Jdg   2:11 Then the Israelites did what was **e**
      3: 7 The Israelites did what was **e** in the
      3:12 The Israelites again did what was **e**
      3:12 because they had done what was **e**
      4: 1 The Israelites again did what was **e**
      6: 1 The Israelites did what was **e** in the
     10: 6 The Israelites again did what was **e**
     13: 1 The Israelites again did what was **e**
1Sa 12:20 you have done all this **e**,
     16:14 an **e** spirit from the LORD tormented
     18:10 an **e** spirit from God rushed upon
     19: 9 an **e** spirit from the LORD came
1Ki 11: 6 So Solomon did what was **e** in the
     16:25 Omri did what was **e** in the sight of
     16:25 did more **e** than all who were before
2Ki 15:24 He did what was **e** in the sight of
Job   1: 1 feared God and turned away from **e**.
      1: 8 fears God and turns away from **e**."
      2: 3 fears God and turns away from **e**.
     15:35 and bring forth **e** and their heart
     28:28 to depart from **e** is understanding.'"
Ps   5: 4 **e** will not sojourn with you.
     23: 4 the darkest valley, I fear no **e**;
     28: 4 according to the **e** of their deeds;
     34:13 Keep your tongue from **e**,
     34:14 Depart from **e**, and do good;
     37: 8 Do not fret—it leads only to **e**.
     37:27 Depart from **e**, and do good;
     51: 4 and done what is **e** in your sight,
     97:10 The LORD loves those who hate **e**;
    101: 4 I will know nothing of **e**.
    141: 4 Do not turn my heart to any **e**,
Pr   3: 7 fear the LORD, and turn away from **e**
      4:27 turn your foot away from **e**.
      8:13 The fear of the LORD is hatred of **e**.
      8:13 of **e** and perverted speech I hate.
     11:19 but whoever pursues **e** will die.
     11:27 but **e** comes to the one who searches
     14:16 are cautious and turn away from **e**,
     14:22 Do they not err that plan **e**?
     16: 6 the fear of the LORD one avoids **e**.
     17:13 **E** will not depart from the house
     17:13 from the house of one who returns **e**
     20:30 Blows that wound cleanse away **e**;
     24:20 for the **e** have no future;
     26:23 are smooth lips with an **e** heart.
     28: 5 The **e** do not understand justice,
     29: 6 of the **e** there is a snare,
Ecc   4: 3 not seen the **e** deeds that are done
     12:14 secret thing, whether good or **e**.
Isa   5:20 you who call **e** good and good **e**,
     13:11 I will punish the world for its **e**,
Jer   4:14 long shall your **e** schemes lodge
     18: 8 turns from its **e**,
     18:10 but if it does **e** in my sight,
Eze 33:11 turn back from your **e** ways;
Am   5:13 for it is an **e** time.
      5:14 good and not **e**, that you may live;
      5:15 their **e** ways and from the violence
Jnh   3: 8 love the **e**, we tear the skin off my
Mic   3: 2 love have, we tear the skin off my
Hab   1:13 Your eyes are too pure to behold **e**,
Zec   8:17 not devise **e** in your hearts against
Mal   2:17 "All who do **e** are good in the sight
Mt   5:45 he makes his sun rise on the **e** and
      6:13 but rescue us from the **e** one.
      7:11 who are **e**, know how to give good
     12:35 **e** person brings **e** things out of an **e**
            treasure.
     13:38 weeds are the children of the **e** one,
     15:19 out of the heart come **e** intentions,
Mk   7:21 the human heart, that **e** intentions
Lk   11:13 who are **e**, know how to give good
Jn   3:19 because their deeds were **e**.
      3:20 For all who do **e** hate the light and

     17:15 to protect them from the **e** one.
Ro   1:30 haughty, boastful, inventors of **e**,
      2: 9 distress for everyone who does **e**,
      3: 8 do **e** so that good may come"?
      7:19 but the **e** I do not want is what I do.
      7:21 want to do what is good, **e** lies close
     12: 9 hate what is **e**, hold fast to what is
     12:17 Do not repay anyone **e** for **e**,
     12:21 Do not be overcome by **e**, but
            overcome **e** with good.
     14:16 not let your good be spoken of as **e**.
     16:19 good and guileless in what is **e**.
1Co 10: 6 we might not desire **e** as they did.
     14:20 infants in **e**, but in thinking be adults
Eph   5:16 the time, because the days are **e**.
      6:12 the spiritual forces of **e** in the
      6:16 all the flaming arrows of the **e** one.
Col   1:21 and hostile in mind, doing **e** deeds,
      3: 5 impurity, passion, **e** desire,
1Th   5:22 abstain from every form of **e**.
2Th   3: 3 and guard you from the **e** one.
1Ti   6:10 For the love of money is a root of
            all kinds of **e**,
Heb   5:14 practice to distinguish good from **e**.
Jas   1:13 tempted by **e** and he himself tempts
      2: 4 and become judges with **e** thoughts?
      3: 8 a restless **e**, full of deadly poison.
      4:16 arrogance; all such boasting is **e**.
1Pe   2:16 use your freedom as a pretext for **e**.
      3: 9 Do not repay **e** for **e** or abuse for
      3:10 let them keep their tongues from **e**
      3:12 the Lord is against those who do **e**."
      3:17 than to suffer for doing **e**.
1Jn   2:13 you have conquered the **e** one.
      2:14 and you have overcome the **e** one.
      3:12 Cain who was from the **e** one
      5:18 and the **e** one does not touch them.
      5:19 lies under the power of the **e** one.
2Jn   1:11 to welcome is to participate in the **e**
3Jn   1:11 do not imitate what is **e** but imitate
Tob   8: 8 afflicted by a demon or **e** spirit,
     12: 7 Do good and **e** will not overtake
Sir   7: 1 Do no **e**, and **e** will never overtake

EVIL DEED[S] Ezr 9:13; Ecc 4:3; 8:11; Jer
11:18; Mic 2:1; Zec 1:4; Col 1:21; 2Jn 1:11;
1Es 8:86; 2Es 1:5

EVIL ... GOOD Ge 44:4; 1Sa 25:21; Ps
34:14; 35:12; 37:27; 38:20; 52:3; 109:5; Pr
15:3; 17:13; Isa 5:20; 7:15, 16; Jer 18:20;
21:10; 39:16; Am 5:13, 15; Mal 2:17; Mt 5:45;
7:11; Lk 11:13; Ro 3:8; 12:21; 1Pe 3:11; Sir
12:5; LtJ 6:34; 1Mc 16:17; 2Es 2:14; 3:22

EVIL IN THE SIGHT OF THE †LORD
Nu 32:13; Dt 4:25; 17:2; 31:29; Jdg 2:11; 3:7,
12, 12; 4:1; 6:1; 10:6; 13:1; 1Sa 15:19; 1Ki
11:6; 14:22; 15:26, 34; 16:19, 25, 30; 21:20,
25; 22:52; 2Ki 3:2; 8:18, 27; 13:2, 11; 14:24;
15:9, 18, 24, 28; 17:2, 17; 21:2, 6, 16, 20;
23:32, 37; 24:9, 19; 2Ch 21:6; 22:4; 29:6;
33:2, 6, 22; 36:5, 9, 12; Jer 52:2

THE EVIL ONE Mt 5:37; 6:13; 13:19, 38; Jn
17:15; Eph 6:16; 2Th 3:3; 1Jn 2:13, 14; 3:12;
5:18, 19

EVIL SPIRIT[S] Jdg 9:23; 1Sa 16:14, 15, 16,
23, 23; 18:10; 19:9; Lk 7:21; 8:2; Ac 19:12,
13, 15, 16; Tob 6:8

EVIL WAY[S] 1Ki 13:33; 2Ki 17:13; Ps
119:101; Pr 28:10; Jer 18:11; 23:22; 25:5;
26:3; 35:15; 36:3, 7; Eze 20:44; 33:11; 36:31;
Jnh 3:8, 10; Zec 1:4

FROM EVIL 1Sa 25:39; Job 1:1, 8; 2:3;
28:28; Ps 34:13, 14; 37:27; Pr 3:7; 4:27; 13:19;
14:16; Isa 59:15; Jer 9:3; Heb 5:14; 1Pe 3:10,
11

GOOD ... EVIL Ge 2:9, 17; 3:5, 22; 2Sa
14:17; 1Ki 3:9; Job 30:26; Ecc 9:2; 12:14; Isa
5:20, 20; Am 5:14; Mic 3:2; Mt 12:35; Lk
6:45; Ro 7:19, 21; 14:16; 2Co 5:10; Heb 5:14;
Tob 12:7; Sir 11:31; 13:25; 17:7; 33:14; 37:18;
39:4; 2Es 3:22

EVILDOER → DO, EVIL

Ps   52: 6 and will laugh at the **e**, saying,
Mt   5:39 But I say to you, Do not resist an **e**.

EVILDOERS → DO, EVIL

2Sa   7:10 and **e** shall afflict them no more,
Job   8:20 nor take the hand of **e**.
       34: 8 who goes in company with **e**
       34:22 or deep darkness where **e** may hide
Ps   5: 5 before your eyes; you hate all **e**.
       14: 4 all the **e** who eat up my people
       26: 5 I hate the company of **e**,
       34:16 The face of the LORD is against **e**,
       36:12 There the **e** lie prostrate; they are
       53: 4 Have they no knowledge, those **e**,
       64: 2 the wicked, from the scheming of **e**,
       92: 7 sprout like grass and all **e** flourish,
       92: 9 all **e** shall be scattered.
       94: 4 their arrogant words; all the **e** boast.
       94:16 Who stands up for me against **e**?
      119:115 Go away from me, you **e**,
      125: 5 the LORD will lead away with **e**.
      141: 9 and from the snares of **e**.
Pr   4:14 and do not walk in the way of **e**.
       10:29 but destruction for **e**.
       21:15 joy to the righteous, but dismay to **e**.
       24:19 Do not fret because of **e**.
Isa   31: 2 will rise against the house of the **e**,
Jer   23:14 they strengthen the hands of **e**,
Mal   3:15 **e** not only prosper, but when they
Mt   7:23 go away from me, you **e**.'
Lk   13:27 go away from me, all you **e**!'
1Pe   2:12 though they malign you as **e**,

EVILDOING → DO, EVIL

Pr   14:32 wicked are overthrown by their **e**,

EVILS → EVIL

Jer   2:13 my people have committed two **e**:

EWE

2Sa   12: 3 had nothing but one little **e** lamb,

EXACT

Est   4: 7 the **e** sum of money that Haman
Mt   2: 7 from them the **e** time when
Heb   1: 3 the imprint of God's very being,

EXALT → EXALTED, EXALTS

Ex   15: 2 my father's God, and I will **e** him.
Jos   3: 7 "This day I will begin to **e** you in
1Sa   2:10 and **e** the power of his anointed."
1Ch   25: 5 to the promise of God to **e** him;
Ps   34: 3 and let us **e** his name together.
       35:26 those who **e** themselves against me
       37:34 and he will **e** you to inherit the land;
       66: 7 let the rebellious not **e** themselves.
Pr   4: 8 Prize her highly, and she will **e** you;
Isa   25: 1 I will **e** you, I will praise your name;
Eze   29:15 again **e** itself above the nations;
Da   11:36 shall **e** himself and consider himsel
Lk   14:11 who **e** themselves will be humbled,
       18:14 who **e** themselves will be humbled,
Jas   4:10 before the Lord, and he will **e** you.
1Pe   5: 6 so that he may **e** you in due time.
Tob   13: 6 and **e** the King of the ages.
Sir   1:30 not **e** yourself, or you may fall
Aza   1:35 sing praise to him and highly **e** him

EXALTED → EXALT

Nu   24: 7 and his kingdom shall be **e**.
Jos   4:14 the LORD **e** Joshua in the sight of all
2Sa   5:12 he had **e** his kingdom for the sake
       22:47 my rock, and **e** be my God,
       22:49 you **e** me above my adversaries,
       23: 1 the oracle of the man whom God **e**,
1Ki   8:13 I have built you an **e** house,
1Ch   14: 2 that his kingdom was highly **e** for
       29:11 and you are **e** as head above all.
       29:25 The LORD highly **e** Solomon in the
Ne   9: 5 is **e** above all blessing and praise."
Job   24:24 They are **e** a little while, and then
       36:22 See, God is **e** in his power;

Ps   18:46 and **e** be the God of my salvation,
       18:48 you **e** me above my adversaries,
       21:13 Be **e**, O LORD, in your strength!
       46:10 I am **e** among the nations, I am **e** in
              the earth."
       47: 9 belong to God; he is highly **e**.
       57: 5 Be **e**, O God, above the heavens.
       57:11 Be **e**, O God, above the heavens.
       89:19 I have **e** one chosen from the people
       89:24 and in my name his horn shall be **e**.
       89:42 You have **e** the right hand of his
       92:10 But you have **e** my horn like that of
       97: 9 you are **e** far above all gods.
       99: 2 he is **e** over all the peoples.
      108: 5 Be **e**, O God, above the heavens,
      138: 2 have **e** your name and your word
      148:13 for his name alone is **e**;
Pr   11:11 blessing of the upright a city is **e**,
Isa   2:11 the LORD alone will be **e** in that day.
       2:17 LORD alone will be **e** on that day.
       5:16 the LORD of hosts is **e** by justice,
       12: 4 proclaim that his name is **e**.
       33: 5 The LORD is **e**, he dwells on high;
       33:10 I will lift myself up; now I will be **e**.
       52:13 he shall be **e** and lifted up, and shall
Jer   17:12 throne, **e** from the beginning,
La   2:17 and **e** the might of your foes.
Da   5:23 **e** yourself against the Lord of
       11:12 his heart shall be **e**,
Hos   13: 1 he was **e** in Israel;
Mt   23:12 who humble themselves will be **e**.
Lk   14:11 who humble themselves will be **e**."
       18:14 who humble themselves will be **e**."
Ac   2:33 therefore **e** at the right hand of God,
       5:31 God **e** him at his right hand as
Php   1:20 Christ will be **e** now as always in
       2: 9 highly **e** him and gave him the name
Heb   7:26 and **e** above the heavens.
Aza   1:29 to be praised and highly **e** forever;

EXALTS' → EXALT

1Sa   2: 7 he brings low, he also **e**.
Pr   14:29 who has a hasty temper **e** folly.
       14:34 Righteousness **e** a nation,
2Th   2: 4 himself above every so-called god
Sir   7:11 for there is One who humbles and **e**.

EXAMINATION → EXAMINE

Sus   1:48 a daughter of Israel without **e**

EXAMINE → EXAMINATION, EXAMINED, EXAMINES, EXAMINING

La   3:40 Let us test and **e** our ways,
1Co   11:28 **E** yourselves, and only then eat of
2Co   13: 5 **E** yourselves to see whether you
Sir   11: 7 fault before you investigate; **e** first,
       18:20 Before judgment comes, **e** yourself;

EXAMINED → EXAMINE

Lk   23:14 here I have **e** him in your presence
Ac   17:11 the message very eagerly and **e**
       28:18 When they had **e** me, the Romans

EXAMINES → EXAMINE

Ps   11: 4 eyes behold, his gaze **e** humankind.
Pr   5:21 and he **e** all their paths.

EXAMINING → EXAMINE

Ecc   9: 1 All this I laid to heart, **e** it all,

EXAMPLE → EXAMPLES

Jdg   2:17 they did not follow their **e**.
Ecc   9:13 I have also seen this **e** of wisdom
Jn   13:15 For I have set you an **e**,
Ro   4:12 who also follow the **e** of the faith
1Co   10:11 happened to them to serve as an **e**,
Php   3:17 according to the **e** you have in us.
1Ti   1:16 an **e** to those who would come to
       4:12 but set the believers an **e** in speech
Jas   5:10 As an **e** of suffering and patience,
1Pe   2:21 leaving you an **e**,
2Pe   2: 6 made them an **e** of what is coming
Jude   1: 7 an **e** by undergoing a punishment of

Jdt   8:24 let us set an **e** for our kindred,

EXAMPLES → EXAMPLE

1Co   10: 6 these things occurred as **e** for us,
1Pe   5: 3 but be **e** to the flock.

EXCEEDS'

Mt   5:20 unless your righteousness **e** that of

EXCEL' → EXCELLED, EXCELLENCE, EXCELLENT, EXCELLENTLY, EXCELLING, EXCELS

Ge   49: 4 you shall no longer **e** because you
1Co   14:12 strive to **e** in them for building up
2Co   8: 7 Now as you **e** in everything—
       8: 7 **e** also in this generous undertaking.
Sir   33:23 **E** in all that you do;

EXCELLED → EXCEL

2Ch   9:22 Thus King Solomon **e** all the kings

EXCELLENCE → EXCEL

Php   4: 8 if there is any **e** and if there is

EXCELLENT → EXCEL

Isa   28:29 in counsel, and **e** in wisdom.
Da   5:12 because an **e** spirit, knowledge, and
1Co   12:31 I will show you a still more **e** way.
Tit   3: 8 these things are **e** and profitable to
Heb   1: 4 the name he has inherited is more **e**
       8: 6 has now obtained a more **e** ministry,
Jas   2: 7 not they who blaspheme the **e** name

EXCELLENTLY' → EXCEL

Pr   31:29 "Many women have done **e**,

EXCELLING → EXCEL

1Co   15:58 always **e** in the work of the Lord,

EXCELS → EXCEL

Ecc   2:13 wisdom **e** folly as light **e** darkness.

EXCEPT

Nu   14:30 **e** Caleb son of Jephunneh and
2Sa   22:32 And who is a rock, **e** our God?
1Ki   12:20 **e** the tribe of Judah alone.
       15: 5 **e** in the matter of Uriah the Hittite.
Mt   5:32 **e** on the ground of unchastity,
       11:27 no one knows the Son **e** the Father,
       19: 9 divorces his wife, **e** for unchastity,
Lk   11:29 be given to it **e** the sign of Jonah.
Jn   3:13 heaven **e** the one who descended
       6:46 anyone has seen the Father **e** the one
       14: 6 No one comes to the Father **e**
       17:12 lost **e** the one destined to be lost,

EXCESS → EXCESSIVE

Tob   4:15 Do not drink wine to **e**
Sir   31:29 Wine drunk to **e** leads to bitterness

EXCESSIVE' → EXCESS

2Co   2: 7 not be overwhelmed by **e** sorrow.

EXCHANGE → EXCHANGED

Sir   7:18 Do not **e** a friend for money,

EXCHANGED → EXCHANGE

Ps   106:20 They **e** the glory of God for the
Ro   1:23 **e** the glory of the immortal God
       1:25 they **e** the truth about God for a lie
       1:26 Their women **e** natural intercourse

EXCLUDE' → EXCLUDED

Lk   6:22 and when they **e** you, revile you,
Gal   4:17 they want to **e** you, so that you

EXCLUDED → EXCLUDE

2Ch   26:21 was **e** from the house of the LORD.
Ezr   2:62 **e** from the priesthood as unclean;
Ro   3:27 what becomes of boasting? It is **e**.

EXCUSE → EXCUSED

Jn   15:22 but now they have no **e** for their sin.
Ro   1:20 So they are without **e**;
       2: 1 Therefore you have no **e**, whoever

2:15 thoughts will accuse or perhaps e

EXCUSES* → EXCUSE
Lk   14:18 But they all alike began to make e.

EXECUTE → EXECUTED, EXECUTES
Ex   12:12 gods of Egypt I will e judgments;
Ps   110: 6 will e judgment among the nations,
      149: 7 to e vengeance on the nations and
Isa 66:16 by fire will the LORD e judgment,
Eze   5:10 I will e judgments on you,
Hos 11: 9 I will not e my fierce anger;
Jn   5:27 given him authority to e judgment,

EXECUTED → EXECUTE
Nu   33: 4 The LORD e judgments
Ps   9:16 he has e judgment;
Da   2:13 the wise men were about to be e;

EXECUTES → EXECUTE
Dt   10:18 who e justice for the orphan and the
Ps   75: 7 but it is God who e judgment,

EXERCISE → EXERCISED
Ro   6:12 do not let sin e dominion in your
1Co   9:25 Athletes e self-control in all things;
Rev 13: 5 to e authority for forty-two months.

EXERCISED → EXERCISE
Ro   5:14 Yet death e dominion from Adam to

EXHAUST* → EXHAUSTED
Jer 51:58 peoples e themselves for nothing,

EXHAUSTED → EXHAUST
Mic   2: 7 Is the LORD's patience e?

EXHIBITED
1Co   4: 9 God has e us apostles as last of all,
Gal   3: 1 Christ was publicly e as crucified!

EXHORT → EXHORTATION, EXHORTED, EXHORTER
Tit   2:15 e and reprove with all authority.
Heb   3:13 But e one another every day,

EXHORTATION → EXHORT
Ac   13:15 if you have any word of e for the
     15:31 read it, they rejoiced at the e.
Heb 13:22 bear with my word of e,

EXHORTED → EXHORT
Ac   2:40 many other arguments and e them,
     11:23 and he e them all to remain faithful

EXHORTER* → EXHORT
Ro   12: 8 the e, in exhortation;

EXILE → EXILED, EXILES
2Ki 25:11 carried into e the rest of the people
Ezr   6:21 of Israel who had returned from e,
Ps 144:14 there be no breach in the walls, no e,
Isa   5:13 people go into e without knowledge;
Jer 13:19 all Judah is taken into e, wholly
          taken into e.
     48: 7 Chemosh shall go out into e,
     49: 3 For Milcom shall go into e,
La   1: 3 Judah has gone into e with suffering
Tob 13: 6 In the land of my e I acknowledge

EXILED → EXILE
Dt   30: 4 if you are e to the ends of the world,
2Ki 17:23 So Israel was e from their own land
Sir 47:24 until they were e from their land.

EXILES → EXILE
Ezr   6:19 the returned e kept the passover.
Jer 24: 5 regard as good the e from Judah,
Eze 11:25 And I told the e all the things that
1Pe   2:11 I urge you as aliens and e

EXIST → EXISTED, EXISTS
Ro   4:17 existence the things that do not e.
1Co   8: 6 are all things and for whom we e,
Heb   2:10 and through whom all things e,

EXISTED → EXIST
2Pe   3: 5 the word of God heavens e long ago
Rev   4:11 by your will they e and were created

EXISTS → EXIST
Ps 119:89 The LORD e forever;
Heb 11: 6 that he e and that he rewards those

EXODUS*
Heb 11:22 mention of the e of the Israelites

EXORCISTS*
Mt   12:27 whom do your own e cast them out?
Lk   11:19 by whom do your e cast them out?
Ac   19:13 some itinerant Jewish e tried to use

EXPECT → EXPECTANTLY, EXPECTATION, EXPECTED, EXPECTING
Isa 64: 3 awesome deeds that we did not e,
Mt   24:50 come on a day when he does not e

EXPECTANTLY* → EXPECT
Mk   15:43 himself waiting e for the kingdom
Lk   23:51 waiting e for the kingdom of God.

EXPECTATION → EXPECT
Pr   10:28 e of the wicked comes to nothing.
Lk   3:15 As the people were filled with e,

EXPECTED → EXPECT
Isa   5: 7 he e justice, but saw bloodshed;

EXPECTING → EXPECT
Lk   6:35 and lend, e nothing in return.
Php   3:20 that we are e a Savior,

EXPELLED
1Sa 28: 3 Saul had e the mediums and the
Jer 52: 3 that he e them from his presence.

EXPENSIVE*
1Ti   2: 9 or with gold, pearls, or e clothes,

EXPERIENCE
Ac   2:27 or let your Holy One e corruption.
     13:35 not let your Holy One e corruption.'
Gal   3: 4 Did you e so much for nothing?—
Heb 11: 5 so that he did not e death;
Sir 25: 6 Rich e is the crown of the aged,

EXPIATION
Nu   35:33 and no e can be made for the land,

EXPLAIN → EXPLAINED, EXPLAINING
Ge   41:24 was no one who could e it to me."
2Ch   9: 2 Solomon that he could not e to her.
Da   5:12 to interpret dreams, e riddles,
Mt   13:36 "E to us the parable of the weeds of
     15:15 Peter said to him, "E this parable to
Heb   5:11 have much to say that is hard to e,

EXPLAINED → EXPLAIN
Jdg 14:17 Then she e the riddle to her people.
Mk   4:34 but he e everything in private to his
Ac   18:26 and e the Way of God to him more
     28:23 until evening he e the matter

EXPLAINING → EXPLAIN
Ac   17: 3 e and proving that it was necessary
2Ti   2:15 rightly the word of truth.

EXPLOIT
2Pe   2: 3 will e you with deceptive words.

EXPLORE
Dt   1:22 send men ahead of us to e the land
Jdg 18: 2 to spy out the land and to e it;

EXPOSE → EXPOSED
Mt   1:19 unwilling to e her to public disgrace
Eph   5:11 of darkness, but instead e them.

EXPOSED → EXPOSE
Ex   20:26 that your nakedness may not be e
Pr   26:26 enemy's wickedness will be e in
Eze 23:29 of your whorings shall be e.

Jn   3:20 so that their deeds may not be e.
Eph   5:13 everything e by the light becomes
Heb 10:33 sometimes being publicly e to abuse
Rev 16:15 going about naked and e to shame.")

EXPOUND
Dt   1: 5 Moses undertook to e this law as

EXTEND → EXTENDED, EXTENDS
Dt   11:24 territory shall e from the wilderness
Isa 66:12 I will e prosperity to her like a river,
Ro   12:13 e hospitality to strangers.

EXTENDED → EXTEND
1Sa 14:27 he e the staff that was in his hand,
Ezr   7:28 who e to me steadfast love before
AdE   8: 4 king e his golden scepter to Esther,

EXTENDS → EXTEND
Ps   36: 5 O LORD, e to the heavens,
     57:10 your faithfulness e to the clouds.

EXTERNAL
Ro   2:28 is true circumcision something e

EXTOL → EXTOLLED, EXTOLLING
Job 36:24 "Remember to e his work,
Ps   18:49 For this I will e you, O LORD,
     89:16 and e your righteousness.
    117: 1 E him, all you peoples!
SS   1: 4 we will e your love more than wine;

EXTOLLED → EXTOL
Ps   66:17 and he was e with my tongue.
Aza   1:31 to be e and highly glorified forever.

EXTOLLING* → EXTOL
Ac   10:46 speaking in tongues and e God.

EXTORT* → EXTORTED, EXTORTION
Lk   3:14 not e money from anyone by threats

EXTORTED* → EXTORT
Eze 22:29 and have e from the alien

EXTORTION → EXTORT
Ps   62:10 Put no confidence in e,
Eze 22:29 practiced e and committed robbery;

EXTRA
Lk   9: 3 nor money—not even an e tunic.
1Co 16: 2 aside and save whatever e you earn,

EXTRAORDINARY
Ac   19:11 God did e miracles through Paul,
2Co   4: 7 that this e power belongs to God

EXTREME
2Co   8: 2 their e poverty have overflowed in

EXULT → EXULTANT, EXULTATION, EXULTS
Ps   5:11 who love your name may e in you.
     25: 2 do not let my enemies e over me.
     89:16 they e in your name all day long,
     94: 3 how long shall the wicked e?
    149: 5 Let the faithful e in glory;
SS   1: 4 We will e and rejoice in you;
Isa 14: 8 The cypresses e over you,
Hab   3:18 I will e in the God of my salvation.
Rev 19: 7 Let us rejoice and e

EXULTANT → EXULT
Ps   68: 4 name is the LORD—be e before him.

EXULTATION → EXULT
Sir   1:11 The fear of the Lord is glory and e,

EXULTS → EXULT
1Sa   2: 1 "My heart e in the LORD;

EYE → EYED, EYES, EYEWITNESSES
Ex   21:24 e for e, tooth for tooth, hand for
Lev 24:20 e for e, tooth for tooth;
Dt   19:21 life for life, e for e, tooth for tooth,
Ezr   5: 5 e of their God was upon the elders

Ps   17: 8 Guard me as the apple of the **e;**
      94: 9 who formed the **e,** does he not see?
Pr   7: 2 my teachings as the apple of your **e;**
      30:17 The **e** that mocks a father and scorns
Ecc   1: 8 the **e** is not satisfied with seeing,
Isa   64: 4 no **e** has seen any God besides you,
Eze   7: 4 My **e** will not spare you,
Zec   2: 8 touches the apple of my **e.**
      12: 4 of Judah I will keep a watchful **e,**
Mt   5:29 If your right **e** causes you to sin,
       5:38 An **e** for an **e** and a tooth for a tooth.
       6:22 "The **e** is the lamp of the body.
       7: 3 see the speck in your neighbor's **e,**
      18: 9 And if your **e** causes you to stumble,
Mk   10:25 to go through the **e** of a needle
1Co   2: 9 as it is written, "What no **e** has seen,
      12:17 If the whole body were an **e,**
      15:52 in the twinkling of an **e,** at the last
Rev   1: 7 the clouds; every **e** will see him,
Sir   31:13 a greedy **e** is a bad thing.

EYED* → EYE

1Sa   18: 9 So Saul **e** David from that day on.

EYES → EYE

Ge   3: 7 Then the **e** of both were opened,
Nu   15:39 of your own heart and your own **e.**
      22:31 the LORD opened the **e** of Balaam,
      33:55 be as barbs in your **e** and thorns in
Dt   11:12 The **e** of the LORD your God are
      16:19 for a bribe blinds the **e** of the wise
      29: 4 or **e** to see, or ears to hear.
      34: 4 I have let you see it with your **e,**
Jos   23:13 on your sides, and thorns in your **e,**
Jdg   16:28 the Philistines for my two **e."**
1Sa   15:17 Though you are little in your own **e,**
1Ki   10: 7 I came and my own **e** had seen it.
2Ki   6:17 LORD opened the **e** of the servant,
       9:30 she painted her **e,** and adorned her
2Ch   16: 9 **e** of the LORD range throughout the
Job   31: 1 "I have made a covenant with my **e;**
      36: 7 withdraw his **e** from the righteous,
Ps   13: 3 Give light to my **e,** or I will sleep
      19: 8 is clear, enlightening the **e;**
      25:15 My **e** are ever toward the LORD,
      36: 1 no fear of God before their **e.**
      36: 2 flatter themselves in their own **e**
      66: 7 whose **e** keep watch on the nations
     115: 5 **e,** but do not see.
     118:23 it is marvelous in our **e.**
     119:18 Open my **e,** so that I may behold
     119:37 Turn my **e** from looking at vanities;
     121: 1 I lift up my **e** to the hills—
     123: 1 To you I lift up my **e,**
     123: 2 so our **e** look to the LORD our God,
     139:16 Your **e** beheld my unformed
     141: 8 my **e** are turned toward you, O GOD,
Pr   3: 7 Do not be wise in your own **e;**
       4:25 Let your **e** look directly forward,
       6:17 haughty **e,** a lying tongue, and hands
      15: 3 The **e** of the LORD are in every place
      17:24 **e** of a fool to the ends of the earth.
      20: 8 winnows all evil with his **e.**
      22:12 The **e** of the LORD keep watch over
      23:29 Who has redness of **e?**
      26: 5 or they will be wise in their own **e.**
Ecc   2:10 Whatever my **e** desired I did not
SS   4: 1 Your **e** are doves behind your veil.
Isa   1:15 I will hide my **e** from you;
       6: 5 my **e** have seen the King, the LORD
       6:10 that they may not look with their **e,**
      11: 3 He shall not judge by what his **e** see,
      33:17 **e** will see the king in his beauty;
      42: 7 the **e** that are blind,
Jer   9: 1 and my **e** a fountain of tears,
      24: 6 I will set my **e** upon them for good,
La   3:48 My **e** flow with rivers of tears
Eze   1: 8 rims of all four were full of **e** all
      24:16 from you the delight of your **e;**
Da   7: 8 were **e** like human **e** in this horn,
      10: 6 lightning, his **e** like flaming torches,
Am   9: 4 I will fix my **e** on them for harm

Hab   1:13 Your **e** are too pure to behold evil,
Zec   4:10 "These seven are the **e** of the LORD,
Mt   9:30 And their **e** were opened.
      13:15 that they might not look with their **e,**
      21:42 and it is amazing in our **e'?**
Mk   8:25 Jesus laid his hands on his **e** again;
Lk   10:23 "Blessed are the **e** that see what you
      24:31 their **e** were opened, and they
Jn   9:10 "Then how were your **e** opened?"
      10:21 a demon open the **e** of the blind?"
      12:40 that they might not look with their **e,**
Ac   9: 8 and though his **e** were open,
      28:27 that they might not look with their **e,**
Ro   11:10 let their **e** be darkened so that they
Eph   1:18 with the **e** of your heart enlightened,
Heb   4:13 naked and laid bare to the **e** of the
1Pe   3:12 **e** of the Lord are on the righteous,
1Jn   1: 1 what we have seen with our **e,**
       2:16 of the flesh, the desire of the **e,**
Rev   1:14 his **e** were like a flame of fire,
       2:18 who has **e** like a flame of fire,
       4: 6 full of **e** in front and behind;
       5: 6 having seven horns and seven **e,**
       7:17 wipe away every tear from their **e."**
      19:12 His **e** are like a flame of fire,
      21: 4 he will wipe every tear from their **e.**
Tob   2:10 into my **e** and produced white films.
       6: 9 and the **e** will be healed."
Sir   17: 6 Discretion and tongue and **e,**
      23: 4 do not give me haughty **e,**

EYEWITNESSES* → EYE, WITNESS

Lk   1: 2 who from the beginning were **e**
2Pe   1:16 but we had been **e** of his majesty.

EZEKIEL

Priest called to be prophet to the exiles (Eze 1-3; Sir 49:8). Symbolically acted out destruction of Jerusalem (Eze 4-5; 12; 24).

EZION-GEBER

1Ki   9:26 Solomon built a fleet of ships at **E,**
2Ch   20:36 they built the ships in **E.**

EZRA

Priest and teacher of the Law who led a return of exiles to Israel to reestablish temple and worship (Ezr 7-8; 1Es 8-9). Read Law at celebration of Feast of Tabernacles (Ne 8; 1Es 9:37-55). Participated in dedication of Jerusalem's walls (Ne 12).

Deuterocanonical book of 2 Esdras attributed to (2Es 1:1).

F

FACE → FACED, FACES

Ge   1: 2 darkness covered the **f** of the deep,
       7: 4 blot out from the **f** of the ground."
       7:18 ark floated on the **f** of the waters.
      11: 9 abroad over the **f** of all the earth.
      32:30 saying, "For I have seen God **f** to **f,**
Ex   3: 6 Moses hid his **f,** for he was afraid to
      33:11 LORD used to speak to Moses **f** to **f,**
      33:20 But," he said, "you cannot see my **f;**
      34:30 the skin of his **f** was shining,
Lev   20: 6 I will set my **f** against them,
Nu   6:25 LORD make his **f** to shine upon you,
      12: 8 With him I speak **f** to **f**—
      14:14 for you, O LORD, are seen **f** to **f,**
Dt   5: 4 LORD spoke with you **f** to **f** at the
      31:17 I will forsake them and hide my **f**
      34:10 whom the LORD knew **f** to **f.**
Jdg   6:22 seen the angel of the LORD **f** to **f."**
2Ki   14: 8 let us look one another in the **f."**
2Ch   7:14 seek my **f,** and turn from their
      25:17 let us look one another in the **f."**
      30: 9 will not turn away his **f** from you,
Ezr   9: 6 and embarrassed to lift my **f**

Ne   2: 2 king said to me, "Why is your **f** sad,
Est   7: 8 they covered Haman's **f.**
Job   1:11 and he will curse you to your **f."**
Ps   4: 6 Let the light of your **f** shine on us,
      10:11 he has hidden his **f,** he will never
      13: 1 How long will you hide your **f** from
      27: 8 my heart says, "seek his **f!"**
      27: 8 Your **f,** LORD, do I seek.
      31:16 Let your **f** shine upon your servant;
      51: 9 Hide your **f** from my sins,
      67: 1 bless us and make his **f** to shine
      80: 3 your **f** shine, that we may be saved.
     104:29 you hide your **f,** they are dismayed;
     119:135 your **f** shine upon your servant,
Ecc   8: 1 Wisdom makes one's **f** shine,
SS   2:14 voice is sweet, and your **f** is lovely.
Isa   8:17 hiding his **f** from the house of Jacob,
      50: 7 therefore I have set my **f** like flint,
      54: 8 wrath for a moment I hid my **f**
Jer   32: 4 and shall speak with him **f** to **f.**
Eze   1:10 the four had the **f** of a human being,
      10:14 the first **f** was that of the cherub,
      39:23 So I hid my **f** from them and gave
      39:29 I will never again hide my **f** from
Da   10: 6 was like beryl, his **f** like lightning,
Hos   5:15 their guilt and seek my **f.**
Mt   17: 2 and his **f** shone like the sun,
      18:10 their angels continually see the **f**
      26:67 they spat in his **f** and struck him;
Lk   9:29 the appearance of his **f** changed,
Jn   19: 3 and striking him on the **f.**
Ac   6:15 they saw that his **f** was like the **f** of an angel.
1Co   13:12 dimly, but then we will see **f** to **f.**
2Co   3: 7 Israel could not gaze at Moses' **f** because of the glory of his **f,**
       4: 6 of the glory of God in the **f**
      10: 1 am humble when **f** to **f** with you,
1Pe   3:12 the **f** of the Lord is against those
2Jn   1:12 come to you and talk with you **f** to **f,**
3Jn   1:14 and we will talk together **f** to **f.**
Rev   1:16 his **f** was like the sun shining with
       4: 7 creature with a **f** like a human **f,**
      10: 1 his **f** was like the sun,
      22: 4 they will see his **f,** and his name will
Jdt   10:23 marveled at the beauty of her **f.**
Sir   13:26 sign of a happy heart is a cheerful **f,**
      31: 6 their destruction has met them **f** to **f.**
      42: 1 and do not sin to save **f:**

FACE TO FACE Ge 32:30; Ex 33:11; Nu 12:8; 14:14; Dt 5:4; 34:10; Jdg 6:22; Jer 32:4; 34:3; Eze 20:35; Ac 25:16; 1Co 13:12; 2Co 10:1; Col 2:1; 1Th 2:17; 3:10; 2Jn 1:12; 3Jn 1:14; Sir 19:29; 31:6; 45:5; 1Mc 7:28; 11:68

FACE TO ... GROUND Ge 19:1; Ru 2:10; 1Sa 5:3, 4; 20:41; 24:8; 25:41; 28:14; 2Sa 14:4, 22, 33; 18:28; 24:20; 1Ki 1:23, 31; 1Ch 21:21; 2Ch 20:18; Da 8:18; 10:9; Lk 5:12

**HID/HIDDEN/HIDE/HIDES/HIDING ...
FACE** Ex 3:6; Dt 31:17, 18; 32:20; Job 13:24; 34:29; Ps 10:11; 13:1; 22:24; 27:9; 30:7; 44:24; 51:9; 69:17; 88:14; 102:2; 104:29; 143:7; Isa 8:17; 50:6; 54:8; 59:2; 64:7; Jer 33:5; Eze 39:23, 24, 29; Mic 3:4; Tob 13:6; Sir 19:27

SET ... FACE Ge 31:21; Lev 17:10; 20:3, 5, 6; 26:17; Nu 24:1; 2Ki 12:17; Isa 50:7; Jer 21:10; Eze 4:3, 7; 6:2; 13:17; 14:8; 15:7, 7; 20:46; 21:2; 25:2; 28:21; 29:2; 35:2; 38:2; Lk 9:51

FACED → FACE

Ex   37: 9 They **f** one another;

FACES → FACE

Ex   25:20 the **f** of the cherubim shall be turned
1Ch   12: 8 whose **f** were like the **f** of lions,
Ps   34: 5 so your **f** shall never be ashamed.
      83:16 Fill their **f** with shame,
Isa   6: 2 with two they covered their **f,**
Eze   1: 6 Each had four **f,** and each

10:14 Each one had four **f**: the first face
41:18 Each cherub had two **f**:
Mt   6:16 they disfigure their **f** so as to show
2Co   3:18 And all of us, with unveiled **f**,
Rev   9: 7 their **f** were like human **f**,

FACT

Lk   20:37 the **f** that the dead are raised
Heb 11:19 the **f** that God is able to even to raise
2Pe   3: 5 They deliberately ignore this **f**,

FACTIONS*

1Co 11:19 there have to be **f** among you,
Gal   5:20 anger, quarrels, dissensions, **f**,

FADE → FADES

Ps   37: 2 for they will soon **f** like the grass,
Isa 64: 6 We all **f** like a leaf,

FADES → FADE

Isa 40: 7 The grass withers, the flower **f**,
1Pe   5: 4 crown of glory that never **f** away.

FAIL → FAILED, FAILING, FAILINGS, FAILS

Nu   15:22 you unintentionally **f** to observe
Dt   31: 6 he will not **f** you or forsake you."
Jos   1: 5 I will not **f** you or forsake you.
1Ki   2: 4 not **f** you a successor on the throne
1Ch 28:20 He will not **f** you or forsake you,
Isa 58:11 of water, whose waters never **f**.
Eze 47:12 will not wither nor their fruit **f**,
Zep   3: 5 his judgment, each dawn without **f**;
Mk   8:18 Do you have eyes, and **f** to see?
Lk   22:32 that your own faith may not **f**;
Ac   5:38 is of human origin, it will **f**;
2Co 13: 5 indeed, you **f** to meet the test!
Tob 14: 4 None of all their words will **f**,

FAILED → FAIL

Jos 21:45 to the house of Israel had **f**;
     23:14 pass for you, not one of them has **f**.
1Ki   8:56 not one word has **f** of all his good
Ro   9: 6 not as though the word of God had **f**
2Co 13: 6 you will find out that we have not **f**.

FAILING → FAIL

Dt   8:11 by **f** to keep his commandments,
Ne   1: 7 **f** to keep his commandments,

FAILINGS → FAIL

Ro   15: 1 to put up with the **f** of the weak,

FAILS → FAIL

Ps   143: 7 quickly, O Lord; my spirit **f**.
Joel 1:10 the wine dries up, the oil **f**.
Hab   3:17 though the produce of the olive **f**
Jas   2:10 but **f** in one point has become
      4:17 the right thing to do and **f** to do it,

FAINT → FAINTS

Job 23:16 God has made my heart **f**;
Ps   142: 3 When my spirit is **f**, you know my
SS   2: 5 for I am **f** with love.
Isa 40:31 they shall walk and not **f**.
Jer 31:25 and all who are **f** I will replenish.

FAINTS → FAINT

Job 19:27 My heart **f** within me!
Ps   63: 1 my flesh **f** for you,
     84: 2 it **f** for the courts of the Lord;

FAIR → FAIRLY

Ge   6: 2 sons of God saw that they were **f**;
Est   1:11 for she was **f** to behold.
Job 26:13 his wind the heavens were made **f**;
SS   2:10 "Arise, my love, my **f** one,
Hos 10:11 and I spared her **f** neck;
Mt   16: 2 you say, 'It will be **f** weather, for
Mk   7:27 not to take the children's food and

FAIRLY* → FAIR

Ps   58: 1 Do you judge people **f**?
Col   4: 1 treat your slaves justly and **f**,

FAITH* → FAITHFUL, FAITHFULLY,
FAITHFULNESS, FAITHLESS, FAITHLESSLY,
FAITHLESSNESS

Nu   5: 6 breaking **f** with the Lord,
Dt   32:51 broke **f** with me among the Israelites
Jos   2:12 me a sign of good **f**
      7: 1 Israelites broke **f** in regard to the
     22:20 Did not Achan son of Zerah break **f**
     22:22 or in breach of **f** toward the Lord,
Jdg   9:15 'If in good **f** you are anointing me
      9:16 if you acted in good **f** and honor
      9:19 in good **f** and honor with Jerubbaal
Ezr 10: 2 "We have broken **f** with our God
Job 39:12 Do you have **f** in it that it will return
Ps   78:22 because they had no **f** in God,
    106:24 having no **f** in his promise.
    116:10 I kept my **f**, even when I said,
    146: 6 in them; who keeps **f** forever;
Isa   7: 9 If you do not stand firm in **f**,
     26: 2 the righteous nation that keeps **f**
Hab   2: 4 but the righteous live by their **f**.
Mt   6:30 clothe you—you of little **f**?
      8:10 no one in Israel have I found such **f**.
      8:13 done for you according to your **f**."
      8:26 are you afraid, you of little **f**?"
      9: 2 When Jesus saw their **f**, he said to
      9:22 your **f** has made you well."
      9:29 "According to your **f** let it be done
     14:31 You of little **f**, why did you doubt?"
     15:28 "Woman, great is your **f**!
     16: 8 Jesus said, "You of little **f**,
     17:20 to them, "Because of your little **f**.
     17:20 have **f** the size of a mustard seed,
     21:21 if you have **f** and do not doubt,
     21:22 you ask for in prayer with **f**,
     23:23 of the law: justice and mercy and **f**.
Mk   2: 5 When Jesus saw their **f**, he said to
      4:40 Have you still no **f**?'"
      5:34 your **f** has made you well;
     10:52 your **f** has made you well."
     11:22 answered them, "Have **f** in God.
     16:14 he upbraided them for their lack of **f**
Lk   5:20 When he saw their **f**, he said,
      7: 9 even in Israel have I found such **f**."
      7:50 the woman, "Your **f** has saved you;
      8:25 He said to them, "Where is your **f**?"
      8:48 your **f** has made you well;
     12:28 will he clothe you—you of little **f**!
     17: 5 said to the Lord, "Increase our **f**!"
     17: 6 you had **f** the size of a mustard seed,
     17:19 your **f** has made you well."
     18: 8 comes, will he find **f** on earth?"
     18:42 your sight; your **f** has saved you."
     22:32 prayed for you that your own **f** may
Ac   3:16 And by **f** in his name,
      3:16 and the **f** that is through Jesus
      6: 5 a man full of **f** and the Holy Spirit,
      6: 7 the priests became obedient to the **f**.
     11:24 full of the Holy Spirit and of **f**.
     13: 8 turn the proconsul away from the **f**.
     14: 9 intently and seeing that he had **f**
     14:22 encouraged them to continue in the **f**
     14:27 opened a door of **f** for the Gentiles.
     15: 9 by **f** he has made no distinction
     16: 5 churches were strengthened in the **f**
     20:21 about repentance toward God and **f**
     24:24 and heard him speak concerning **f**
     26:18 among those who are sanctified by **f**
     27:25 for I have **f** in God that it will be
Ro   1: 5 to bring about the obedience of **f**
      1: 8 your **f** is proclaimed throughout the
      1:12 encouraged by each other's **f**,
      1:16 for salvation to everyone who has **f**,
      1:17 righteousness of God is revealed
         through **f** for **f**;
      1:17 one who is righteous will live by **f**."
      3:22 through **f** in Jesus Christ for all who
      3:25 by his blood, effective through **f**.
      3:26 justifies the one who has **f** in Jesus.
      3:27 No, but by the law of **f**.
      3:28 that a person is justified by **f** apart

      3:30 circumcised on the ground of **f**
      3:30 uncircumcised through that same **f**.
      3:31 then overthrow the law by this **f**?
      4: 5 such **f** is reckoned as righteousness.
      4: 9 "**F** was reckoned to Abraham as
      4:11 of the righteousness that he had by **f**
      4:12 also follow the example of the **f**
      4:13 but through the righteousness of **f**.
      4:14 **f** is null and the promise is void.
      4:16 For this reason it depends on **f**,
      4:16 who share the **f** of Abraham (for he
      4:19 in **f** when he considered his own
      4:20 grew strong in his **f** as he gave glory
      4:22 his **f** "was reckoned to him as
      5: 1 since we are justified by **f**,
      9:30 that is, righteousness through **f**;
      9:32 did not strive for it on the basis of **f**,
     10: 6 righteousness that comes from **f**
     10: 8 the word of **f** that we proclaim);
     10:17 So **f** comes from what is heard,
     11:20 but you stand only through **f**.
     12: 3 measure of **f** that God has assigned.
     12: 6 prophecy, in proportion to **f**;
     14: 1 Welcome those who are weak in **f**,
     14:22 The **f** that you have, have
     14:23 because they do not act from **f**;
     14:23 does not proceed from **f** is sin.
     16:26 to bring about the obedience of **f**—
1Co   2: 5 that your **f** might rest not on human
     12: 9 to another **f** by the same Spirit,
     13: 2 and if I have all **f**, so as to remove
     13:13 And now **f**, hope, and love abide,
     15:14 in vain and your **f** has been in vain.
     15:17 your **f** is futile and you are still in
     16:13 Keep alert, stand firm in your **f**,
2Co   1:24 to imply that we lord it over your **f**;
      1:24 because you stand firm in the **f**.
      4:13 as we have the same spirit of **f** that
      5: 7 for we walk by **f**, not by sight.
      8: 7 as you excel in everything—in **f**,
     10:15 our hope is that, as your **f** increases,
     13: 5 see whether you are living in the **f**.
Gal   1:23 now proclaiming the **f** he once tried
      2:16 the works of the law but through **f**
      2:16 we might be justified by **f** in Christ,
      2:20 I now live in the flesh I live by **f** in
      3: 8 God would justify the Gentiles by **f**,
      3:11 one who is righteous will live by **f**."
      3:12 But the law does not rest on **f**;
      3:14 the promise of the Spirit through **f**.
      3:22 through **f** in Jesus Christ might be
      3:23 before **f** came, we were imprisoned
         and guarded under the law until **f**
      3:24 so that we might be justified by **f**.
      3:25 But now that **f** has come,
      3:26 are all children of God through **f**.
      5: 5 For through the Spirit, by **f**,
      5: 6 only thing that counts is **f** working
      6:10 for those of the family of **f**.
Eph   1:15 of your **f** in the Lord Jesus and your
      2: 8 you have been saved through **f**,
      3:12 and confidence through **f** in him.
      3:17 may dwell in your hearts through **f**,
      4: 5 one Lord, one **f**, one baptism,
      4:13 of the **f** and of the knowledge of the
      6:16 all of these, take the shield of **f**,
      6:23 whole community, and love with **f**,
Php   1:25 you for your progress and joy in **f**,
      1:27 with one mind for the **f** of
      2:17 of your **f**, I am glad and rejoice
      3: 9 one that comes through **f** in Christ,
      3: 9 righteousness from God based on **f**.
Col   1: 4 we have heard of your **f** in Christ
      1:23 and steadfast in the **f**,
      2: 5 morale and the firmness of your **f**
      2: 7 in him and established in the **f**,
      2:12 also raised with him through **f** in
1Th   1: 3 of **f** and labor of love and
      1: 8 in every place your **f** in God has
      3: 2 you for the sake of your **f**,
      3: 5 I sent to find out about your **f**;
      3: 6 brought us the good news of your **f**

3: 7 about you through your **f**.
3:10 whatever is lacking in your **f**.
5: 8 put on the breastplate of **f** and love,
2Th 1: 3 your **f** is growing abundantly,
1: 4 for your steadfastness and **f**
1:11 every good resolve and work of **f**,
3: 2 and evil people; for not all have **f**.
1Ti 1: 2 my loyal child in the **f**:
1: 4 divine training that is known by **f**.
1: 5 a good conscience, and sincere **f**.
1:14 with the **f** and love that are in Christ
1:19 having **f** and a good conscience.
1:19 have suffered shipwreck in the **f**;
2: 7 a teacher of the Gentiles in **f** and
2:15 provided they continue in **f** and love
3: 9 hold fast to the mystery of the **f**
3:13 and great boldness in the **f** that is in
4: 1 the **f** by paying attention to deceitful
4: 6 the words of the **f** and of the sound
4:12 in speech and conduct, in love, in **f**,
5: 8 has denied the **f** and is worse than
6:10 have wandered away from the **f**
6:11 pursue righteousness, godliness, **f**,
6:12 Fight the good fight of the **f**;
6:21 the mark as regards the **f**.
2Ti 1: 5 I am reminded of your sincere **f**,
1: 5 **f** that lived first in your grandmother
1:13 in the **f** and love that are in Christ
2:18 They are upsetting the **f** of some.
2:22 **f**, love, and peace,
3: 8 of corrupt mind and counterfeit **f**,
3:10 my conduct, my aim in life, my **f**,
3:15 for salvation through **f** in Christ
4: 7 finished the race, I have kept the **f**.
Tit 1: 1 of the **f** of God's elect and the
1: 4 my loyal child in the **f** we share:
1:13 they may become sound in the **f**,
2: 2 sound in **f**, in love, and in endurance
3:15 Greet those who love us in the **f**.
Phm 1: 5 love for all the saints and your **f**
1: 6 the sharing of your **f** may become
Heb 4: 2 not united by **f** with those who
6: 1 from dead works and **f** toward God,
6:12 through **f** and patience inherit the
10:22 a true heart in full assurance of **f**,
10:38 but my righteous one will live by **f**.
10:39 those who have **f** and so are saved.
11: 1 **f** is the assurance of things hoped
11: 2 by **f** our ancestors received approval
11: 3 By **f** we understand that the worlds
11: 4 By **f** Abel offered to God
11: 4 but through his **f** he still speaks.
11: 5 By **f** Enoch was taken so that he did
11: 6 without **f** it is impossible to please
11: 7 By **f** Noah, warned by God about
11: 7 that is in accordance with **f**.
11: 8 By **f** Abraham obeyed when he was
11: 9 By **f** he stayed for a time in
11:11 By **f** he received power of
11:13 All of these died in **f** without having
11:17 By **f** Abraham, when put to the test,
11:20 By **f** Isaac invoked blessings for the
11:21 By **f** Jacob, when dying, blessed
11:22 By **f** Joseph, at the end of his life,
11:23 By **f** Moses was hidden by his
11:24 By **f** Moses, when he was grown up,
11:27 By **f** he left Egypt, unafraid of the
11:28 By **f** he kept the Passover and the
11:29 By **f** the people passed through the
11:30 By **f** the walls of Jericho fell
11:31 By **f** Rahab the prostitute did not
11:33 who through **f** conquered kingdoms,
11:39 they were commended for their **f**,
12: 2 the pioneer and perfecter of our **f**,
13: 7 their way of life, and imitate their **f**.
Jas 1: 3 testing of your **f** produces endurance
1: 6 But ask in **f**, never doubting,
2: 5 to be rich in **f** and to be heirs of the
2:14 if you say you have **f** but do not
have works? Can **f** save you?
2:17 **f** by itself, if it has no works, is dead
2:18 "You have **f** and I have works."

2:18 Show me your **f** apart from your
2:18 by my works will show you my **f**.
2:20 that **f** apart from works is barren?
2:22 You see that **f** was active along
with his works, and **f** was brought
2:24 by works and not by **f** alone.
2:26 so **f** without works is also dead.
5:15 The prayer of **f** will save the sick,
1Pe 1: 5 the power of God through **f** for a
1: 7 that the genuineness of your **f**—
1: 9 are receiving the outcome of your **f**,
1:21 that your **f** and hope are set on God.
5: 9 Resist him, steadfast in your **f**,
2Pe 1: 1 a **f** as precious as ours through the
1: 5 make every effort to support your **f**
1Jn 5: 4 that conquers the world, our **f**.
Jude 1: 3 the **f** that was once for all entrusted
1:20 yourselves up on your most holy **f**;
Rev 2:13 and you did not deny your **f** in me
2:19 your love, **f**, service, and patient
13:10 a call for the endurance and **f** of the
14:12 of God and hold fast to the **f**
Sir 27:17 Love your friend and keep **f** with
40:12 but good **f** will last forever.
1Mc 10:27 Now continue still to keep **f** with us,
2Mc 8: 1 in the Jewish **f**,
2Es 5: 1 and the land shall be barren of **f**.
6: 5 stored up treasures of **f** were sealed
9: 7 on account of the **f** by which they
13:23 who have works and **f** toward the
4Mc 15:24 disregarded all these because of **f** in
16:22 too must have the same **f** in God
17: 2 and showed the courage of your **f**!

BY ... FAITH Hab 2:4; Ac 3:16; 15:9; 26:18;
Ro 1:17; 3:27, 28, 31; 4:11; 5:1; 2Co 5:7; Gal
2:16, 20; 3:8, 11, 24; 5:5; 1Ti 1:4; Heb 4:2;
10:38; 11:2, 3, 4, 5, 7, 8, 9, 11, 17, 20, 21, 22,
23, 24, 27, 28, 29, 30, 31; Jas 2:24

IN ... FAITH Jos 22:22; Jdg 9:15, 16, 19; Isa
7:9; Ac 14:22; 16:5; Ro 4:19, 20; 14:1; 1Co
16:13; 2Co 1:24; 8:7; 13:5; Php 1:25; Col
1:23; 2:7; 1Th 3:10; 1Ti 1:2, 19; 2:7, 15; 3:13;
4:12, 12; 2Ti 1:13; 3:10; Tit 1:4, 13; 2:2; 3:15;
Heb 11:13; Jas 1:6; 2:5; 1Pe 5:9; 2Mc 8:1

LITTLE FAITH Mt 6:30; 8:26; 14:31; 16:8;
17:20; Lk 12:28

THE FAITH Ac 3:16; 6:7; 13:8; 14:22; 16:5;
Ro 4:12, 16; 14:22; 2Co 1:24; 13:5; Gal 1:23;
Eph 4:13; Php 1:27; Col 1:23; 2:7; 1Ti 1:2, 14,
19; 3:9, 13; 4:1, 6; 5:8; 6:10, 12, 21; 2Ti 1:13;
2:18; 4:7; Tit 1:1, 4, 13; 3:15; Jude 1:3; Rev
14:12; 2Es 9:7

THROUGH ... FAITH Ro 1:17; 3:22, 25, 30;
9:30; 11:20; Gal 2:16; 3:14, 22, 26; Eph 2:8;
3:12, 17; Php 3:9; Col 2:12; 1Th 3:7; 2Ti 3:15;
Heb 6:12; 11:4, 33; 1Pe 1:5

FAITHFUL* → FAITH
Dt 7: 9 the **f** God who maintains covenant
32: 4 A **f** God, without deceit, just and
Jdg 5:15 and Issachar **f** to Barak;
1Sa 2: 9 "He will guard the feet of his **f** ones,
2:35 I will raise up for myself a **f** priest,
20:14 show me the **f** love of the LORD;
20:15 never cut off your **f** love from my
22:14 all your servants is so **f** as David?
2Sa 20:19 who are peaceable and **f** in Israel;
2Ch 6:41 let your **f** rejoice in your goodness.
31:18 were **f** in keeping themselves holy.
31:20 did what was good and right and **f**
35:26 of the acts of Josiah and his **f** deeds
Ne 7: 2 he was a **f** man and feared God
9: 8 you found his heart **f** before you,
13:13 for they were considered **f**;
Ps 4: 3 LORD has set apart the **f** for himself;
12: 1 the **f** have disappeared from
16:10 or let your **f** one see the Pit.
30: 4 praises to the LORD, O you his **f**
31: 5 have redeemed me, O LORD, **f** God.
31:23 The LORD preserves the **f**,
32: 6 let all who are **f** offer prayer to you;

37:28 he will not forsake his **f** ones.
50: 5 "Gather to me my **f** ones,
52: 9 In the presence of the **f** I will
69:13 love, answer me. With your **f** help
78: 8 whose spirit was not **f** to God.
79: 2 flesh of your **f** to the wild animals
85: 8 to his **f**, to those who turn to him in
89:19 you spoke in a vision to your **f** one,
97:10 he guards the lives of his **f**;
101: 6 look with favor on the **f** in the land,
111: 7 works of his hands are **f** and just;
116:15 is the death of his **f** ones.
132: 9 and let your **f** shout for joy.
132:16 and its **f** will shout for joy.
141: 5 let the **f** correct me.
145:10 LORD, and all your **f** shall bless you.
145:13 The LORD is **f** in all his words,
148:14 for his people, praise for all his **f**,
149: 1 his praise in the assembly of the **f**.
149: 5 Let the **f** exult in glory;
149: 9 This is glory for all his **f** ones.
Pr 2: 8 preserving the way of his **f** ones.
13:17 brings trouble, but a **f** envoy,
14: 5 A **f** witness does not lie,
25:13 the time of harvest are **f** messengers
28:20 The **f** will abound with blessings,
Isa 1:21 How the **f** city has become a whore!
1:26 the city of righteousness, the **f** city.
25: 1 plans formed of old, **f** and sure.
49: 7 because of the LORD, who is **f**,
Jer 42: 5 a true and **f** witness against us if we
Da 6: 4 because he was **f**,
Hos 11:12 and is **f** to the Holy One.
Mic 7: 2 The **f** have disappeared from the
Zec 8: 3 Jerusalem shall be called the **f** city,
Mt 24:45 "Who then is the **f** and wise slave,
Lk 12:42 "Who then is the **f**
16:10 "Whoever is **f** in a very little is **f**
also in much;
16:11 not been **f** with the dishonest wealth
16:12 And if you have not been **f** with
Ac 11:23 them all to remain **f** to the Lord
16:15 "If you have judged me to be **f**
1Co 1: 9 God is **f**; by him you were called
4:17 who is my beloved and **f** child in
10:13 God is **f**, and he will not let you be
2Co 1:18 As surely as God is **f**,
Eph 1: 1 saints who are in Ephesus and are **f**
6:21 He is a dear brother and a **f** minister
Col 1: 2 To the saints and **f** brothers in
1: 7 He is a **f** minister of Christ on your
4: 7 he is a beloved brother, a **f** minister,
4: 9 the **f** and beloved brother, who is
1Th 5:24 The one who calls you is **f**, and he
2Th 3: 3 But the Lord is **f**; he will strengthen
1Ti 1:12 he judged me **f** and appointed me to
3:11 but temperate, **f** in all things.
2Ti 2: 2 to **f** people who will be able
2:13 he remains **f**—for he cannot deny
Heb 2:17 might be a merciful and **f** high priest
3: 2 was **f** to the one who appointed him,
3: 2 also "was **f** in all God's house."
3: 5 Moses was **f** in all God's house as a
3: 6 was **f** over God's house as a son,
10:23 for he who has promised is **f**.
11:11 considered him **f** who had promised.
1Pe 4:19 to a **f** Creator,
5:12 whom I consider a **f** brother,
1Jn 1: 9 is **f** and just will forgive us our sins
Rev 1: 5 witness, the firstborn of the dead,
2:10 Be **f** until death, and I will give you
2:13 my **f** one, who was killed among
3:14 of the Amen, the **f** and true witness,
17:14 are called and chosen and **f**."
19:11 Its rider is called **F** and True,
Wis 3: 9 the **f** will abide with him in love,
Sir 1:14 is created with the **f** in the womb.
4:16 If they remain **f**, they will inherit
6:14 **F** friends are a sturdy shelter;
6:15 **F** friends are beyond price;
6:16 **F** friends are life-saving medicine;
34: 8 is complete in the mouth of the **f**.

37:13 for no one is more **f** to you than it is.
39:13 Listen to me, my **f** children,
39:24 To the **f** his ways are straight,
44:20 and when he was tested he proved **f**.
1Mc 2:52 Was not Abraham found **f** when
3:13 of **f** soldiers who stayed with him
7: 8 great man in the kingdom and was **f**
7:17 of your **f** ones and their blood they
2Mc 1: 2 and Isaac and Jacob, his **f** servants.
1Es 8:89 O Lord of Israel, you are **f**;
3Mc 2:11 And indeed you are **f** and true.
4Mc 7:15 the **f** seal of death has perfected!

FAITHFULLY* → FAITH

Lev 25:18 and **f** keep my ordinances,
26: 3 commandments and observe them **f**,
Jos 2:14 then we will deal kindly and **f** with
1Sa 12:24 and serve him **f** with all your heart;
2Ch 31:12 **F** they brought in the contributions,
31:15 and Shecaniah were **f** assisting him
34:12 The people did the work **f**.
Ne 9:33 you have dealt **f** and we have acted
Pr 12:22 but those who act **f** are his delight.
Isa 42: 3 he will **f** bring forth justice.
61: 8 I will **f** give them their recompense,
Jer 23:28 who has my word speak my word **f**.
Eze 18: 9 observe my ordinances, acting **f**—
Da 6:16 "May your God, whom you **f** serve,
6:20 has your God whom you **f** serve
3Jn 1: 5 you do **f** whatever you do for the
Tob 14: 8 serve God **f** and do what is pleasing
Sir 1:15 their descendants she will abide **f**.
7:20 Do not abuse slaves who work **f**,
15:15 act **f** is a matter of your own choice.
3Mc 5: 4 proceeded **f** to carry out the orders.
6:25 from their homes those who **f** kept

FAITHFULNESS* → FAITH

Ge 24:27 forsaken his steadfast love and his **f**
32:10 of all the steadfast love and all the **f**
Ex 34: 6 abounding in steadfast love and **f**,
Dt 32:20 children in whom there is no **f**.
Jos 24:14 and serve him in sincerity and in **f**;
1Sa 26:23 for his righteousness and his **f**;
2Sa 2: 6 the LORD show steadfast love and **f**
15:20 the LORD show steadfast love and **f**
1Ki 2: 4 in **f** with all their heart and with all
3: 6 because he walked before you in **f**,
2Ki 20: 3 I have walked before you in **f** with
2Ch 19: 9 in the fear of the LORD, in **f**,
32: 1 these things and these acts of **f**,
Ps 25:10 of the LORD are steadfast love and **f**,
26: 3 and I walk in **f** to you.
30: 9 Will it tell of your **f**?
33: 4 and all his work is done in **f**.
36: 5 to the heavens, your **f** to the clouds.
40:10 I have spoken of your **f** and your
40:10 your steadfast love and your **f**
40:11 and your **f** keep me safe forever.
54: 5 In your **f**, put an end to them.
57: 3 his steadfast love and his **f**.
57:10 your **f** extends to the clouds.
61: 7 appoint steadfast love and **f** to watch
71:22 praise you with the harp for your **f**,
85:10 Steadfast love and **f** will meet;
85:11 **F** will spring up from the ground,
86:15 bounding in steadfast love and **f**.
88:11 in the grave, or your **f** in Abaddon?
89: 1 my mouth I will proclaim your **f**
89: 2 your **f** is as firm as the heavens.
89: 5 your **f** in the assembly of the holy
89: 8 O LORD? Your **f** surrounds you.
89:14 steadfast love and **f** go before you.
89:24 My **f** and steadfast love shall be
89:33 or be false to my **f**.
89:49 by your **f** you swore to David?
91: 4 his **f** is a shield and buckler.
92: 2 in the morning, and your **f** by night,
98: 3 remembered his steadfast love and **f**
100: 5 and his **f** to all generations.
108: 4 and your **f** reaches to the clouds.
111: 8 performed with **f** and uprightness.

115: 1 of your steadfast love and your **f**.
117: 2 the **f** of the LORD endures forever.
119:30 I have chosen the way of **f**;
119:75 and that in **f** you have humbled me.
119:90 Your **f** endures to all generations;
119:138 in righteousness and in all **f**.
138: 2 for your steadfast love and your **f**;
143: 1 ear to my supplications in your **f**;
Pr 3: 3 Do not let loyalty and **f** forsake you;
14:22 who plan good find loyalty and **f**.
16: 6 By loyalty and **f** iniquity is atoned
20:28 Loyalty and **f** preserve the king,
Isa 11: 5 and **f** the belt around his loins.
16: 5 on it shall sit in **f** a ruler who seeks
38: 3 I have walked before you in **f** with
38:18 to the Pit cannot hope for your **f**.
38:19 make known to children your **f**.
65:16 shall bless by the God of **f**,
65:16 shall swear by the God of **f**;
Jer 31: 3 I have continued my **f** to you.
32:41 I will plant them in this land in **f**,
La 3:23 new every morning; great is your **f**.
Hos 2:20 I will take you for my wife in **f**,
4: 1 There is no **f** or loyalty, and no
14: 8 your **f** comes from me.
Mic 7:20 You will show **f** to Jacob and
Zec 8: 8 in **f** and in righteousness.
Ro 3: 3 faithlessness nullify the **f** of God?
Gal 5:22 patience, kindness, generosity, **f**,
3Jn 1: 3 arrived and testified to your **f** to
Wis 3:14 favor will be shown him for his **f**,
Sir 45: 4 his **f** and meekness he consecrated
46:15 By his **f** he was proved to be a
1Mc 14:35 "The people saw Simon's **f** and the
2Es 6:28 **f** shall flourish, and corruption shall
7:34 shall stand, and **f** shall grow strong.

STEADFAST LOVE AND
FAITHFULNESS Ge 24:27; Ex 34:6; 2Sa
2:6; 15:20; Ps 25:10; 40:10, 11; 57:3; 61:7;
85:10; 86:15; 89:14; 98:3; 115:1; 138:2

FAITHLESS → FAITH

Ps 78:57 away and were **f** like their ancestors;
119:158 I look at the **f** with disgust,
Jer 3: 6 what she did, that **f** one, Israel,
3: 8 for all the adulteries of that **f** one,
3:11 **F** Israel has shown herself less
3:12 Return, **f** Israel, says the LORD.
3:14 Return, O **f** children, says the LORD,
3:22 O **f** children, I will heal your
Mal 2:16 and do not be **f**.
Mt 17:17 "You **f** and perverse generation,
Ro 1:31 foolish, **f**, heartless, ruthless.
2Ti 2:13 if we are **f**, he remains faithful—
Rev 21: 8 But as for the cowardly, the **f**,

FAITHLESSLY → FAITH

Eze 15: 8 because they have acted **f**,
Hos 5: 7 They have dealt **f** with the LORD;

FAITHLESSNESS → FAITH

Ezr 10: 6 mourning over the **f** of the exiles.
Jer 3:22 faithless children, I will heal your **f**.
Ro 3: 3 **f** nullify the faithfulness of God?

FALL → DOWNFALL, FALLEN, FALLING,
FALLS, FELL

Ge 2:21 LORD God caused a deep sleep to **f**
Nu 14:29 bodies shall **f** in this very wilderness
1Sa 3:19 none of his words **f** to the ground.
1Ch 21:13 let me **f** into the hand of the LORD.
Ps 35: 8 let them **f** in it—
37:24 shall not **f** headlong, for the LORD
91: 7 A thousand may **f** at your side,
Pr 11:14 and a haughty spirit before a **f**.
26:27 digs a pit will **f** into it,
Ecc 4:10 For if they **f**, one will lift up the
10: 8 Whoever digs a pit will **f** into it;
Isa 40:30 and the young will **f** exhausted;
Jer 6:15 they shall **f** among those who **f**;
Da 11:35 Some of the wise shall **f**,
Hos 10: 8 and to the hills, **F** on us.

Mt 7:25 but it did not **f**,
Mk 4:17 immediately they **f** away.
Lk 10:18 "I watched Satan **f** from heaven like
23:30 'F on us'; and to the hills, 'Cover
Ac 5:15 that Peter's shadow might **f** on some
Ro 3:23 all have sinned and **f** short of the
glory of God;
9:33 a rock that will make them **f**,
11:11 I ask, have they stumbled so as to **f**?
1Co 8:13 I may not cause one of them to **f**.
10:12 watch out that you do not **f**.
1Ti 6: 9 be rich **f** into temptation
Heb 10:31 a fearful thing to **f** into the hands of
1Pe 2: 8 and a rock that makes them **f**."
Rev 6:16 "F on us and hide us from the face
Sir 28:23 Those who forsake the Lord will **f**

FALLEN → FALL

1Sa 5: 3 **f** on his face to the ground before
2Sa 1:19 How the mighty have **f**!
Ps 57: 6 but they have **f** into it
119:56 This blessing has **f** to me,
Isa 14:12 **f** from heaven, O Day Star,
21: 9 he responded, "F, **f** is Babylon;
Am 9:11 the booth of David that is **f**,
Jn 11:11 "Our friend Lazarus has **f** asleep,
Ac 15:16 the dwelling of David, which has **f**;
Gal 5: 4 you have **f** away from grace.
Heb 6: 6 then have **f** away,
Rev 9: 1 I saw a star that had **f** from heaven
14: 8 "F, **f** is Babylon the great!
17:10 of whom five have **f**, one is living,
18: 2 "F, **f** is Babylon the great!
Sir 28:18 have **f** because of the tongue.

FALLING → FALL

Lk 22:44 [like great drops of blood **f** down]
Jude 1:24 him who is able to keep you from **f**,
Sir 34:19 and help against **f**.

FALLOW

Ex 23:11 you shall let it rest and lie **f**,

FALLS → FALL

Pr 11:14 there is no guidance, a nation **f**,
Ecc 4:10 woe to one who is alone and **f** and
Mt 13:21 that person immediately **f** away.
Lk 20:18 it will crush anyone on whom it **f**."
Jn 12:24 unless a grain of wheat **f** into the

FALSE → FALSEHOOD, FALSELY, FALSIFY

Ex 20:16 not bear **f** witness against your
23: 1 You shall not spread a **f** report.
23: 7 Keep far from a **f** charge,
Dt 5:20 Neither shall you bear **f** witness
19:18 If the witness is a **f** witness,
2Ki 17:15 went after **f** idols and became **f**;
Job 36: 4 For truly my words are not **f**;
Ps 40: 4 to those who go astray after **f** gods.
119:29 Put **f** ways far from me;
Pr 12:17 but a **f** witness speaks deceitfully.
14: 5 but a **f** witness breathes out lies.
19: 5 A **f** witness will not go unpunished,
21:28 A **f** witness will perish,
25:18 bears **f** witness against a neighbor.
Mt 7:15 "Beware of **f** prophets, who come to
7:15 fornication, theft, **f** witness, slander.
24:11 many **f** prophets will arise and lead
24:24 For **f** messiahs and **f** prophets will
Mk 10:19 You shall not bear **f** witness;
13:22 **F** messiahs and **f** prophets will
14:57 gave **f** testimony against him,
Lk 6:26 their ancestors did to the **f** prophets.
18:20 You shall not bear **f** witness;
Ac 6:13 They set up **f** witnesses who said,
13: 6 magician, a Jewish **f** prophet,
2Co 11:13 For such boasters are **f** apostles,
11:26 danger from **f** brothers and sisters;
Php 1:18 whether out of **f** motives or true;
2Th 2:11 leading them to believe what is **f**,
Heb 6:18 impossible that God would prove **f**,
2Pe 2: 1 there will be **f** teachers among you,
1Jn 4: 1 many **f** prophets have gone out into

Rev 16:13 and from the mouth of the **f** prophet.
    19:20 the **f** prophet who had performed in
    20:10 where the beast and the **f** prophet
LtJ   6: 8 but they are **f** and cannot speak.
Sus 1:61 convicted them of bearing **f** witness;

FALSE PROPHET[S] Mt 7:15; 24:11, 24;
Mk 13:22; Lk 6:26; Ac 13:6; 2Pe 2:1; 1Jn 4:1;
Rev 16:13; 19:20; 20:10

FALSE WITNESS[ES] Ex 20:16; Dt 5:20;
19:18, 19, 19; Ps 27:12; Pr 12:17; 14:5; 19:5,
9; 21:28; 25:18; Mt 15:19; 18:18; 26:60; Mk
10:19; Lk 18:20; Ac 6:13; Sus 1:61

FALSEHOOD → FALSE
Job 21:34 nothing left of your answers but **f.**"
    31: 5 "If I have walked with **f,**
Ps 119:163 and abhor **f,** but I love your law.
Pr   30: 8 Remove far from me **f** and lying;
Isa 28:15 and in **f** we have taken shelter";
Ro   3: 7 my **f** God's truthfulness abounds to
Eph 4:25 putting away **f,** let all of us speak
Rev 21:27 who practices abomination or **f,**
    22:15 everyone who loves and practices **f.**

FALSELY → FALSE
Lev 19:12 you shall not swear **f** by my name,
Jos 24:27 if you deal **f** with your God."
Jer   5:31 the prophets prophesy **f,**
Zec   5: 3 and everyone who swears **f** shall
Mt   5:11 utter all kinds of evil against you **f**
1Ti   6:20 of what is **f** called knowledge;

FALSIFY* → FALSE
2Co 4: 2 practice cunning or to **f** God's word;

FAME → FAMOUS
Dt   26:19 in praise and in **f** and in honor;
Jos   6:27 and his **f** was in all the land.
1Ch 14:17 The **f** of David went out into all
2Ch 9: 1 of Sheba heard of the **f** of Solomon,
Ps   72:17 his **f** continue as long as the sun.
Isa 66:19 not heard of my **f** or seen my glory;
Mk   1:28 At once his **f** began to spread
1Mc 3:26 His **f** reached the king,

FAMILIAR
Ps   55:13 my companion, my **f** friend,
Isa   8:19 "Consult the ghosts and the **f** spirits

FAMILIES → FAMILY
Ge   8:19 went out of the ark by **f.**
    10: 5 with their own language, by their **f,**
Ex   1:21 feared God, he gave them **f.**
Jos 14: 1 the heads of the **f** of the tribes of
Ps 107:41 and makes their **f** like flocks.
Jer 31: 1 God of all the **f** of Israel,
Am   3: 2 You only have I known of all the **f**
Ac   3:25 all the **f** of the earth shall be blessed.
Tit   1:11 are upsetting whole **f** by teaching

FAMILY → FAMILIES
1Sa 18:18 my kinsfolk, my father's **f** in Israel,
2Ch 22:10 destroy all the royal **f** of the house
Est   4:14 you and your father's **f** will perish.
Pr   6:19 and one who sows discord in a **f.**
Lk   2: 4 was descended from the house and **f**
Ac 16:33 he and his entire **f** were baptized
Gal 6:10 especially for those of the **f** of faith.
Eph 3:15 from whom every **f** in heaven and
1Ti   5: 4 their religious duty to their own **f**
    5: 8 and especially for **f** members,
1Pe 2:17 Love the **f** of believers.

FAMINE → FAMINES
Ge 12:10 Now there was a **f** in the land.
    26: 1 Now there was a **f** in the land,
    41:27 They are seven years of **f.**
    42: 5 **f** had reached the land of Canaan.
    43: 1 Now the **f** was severe in the land,
Ru   1: 1 there was a **f** in the land,
1Ki 18: 2 The **f** was severe in Samaria.
2Ki 4:38 there was a **f** in the land.
    6:25 **f** in Samaria became so great that

2Ch 6:28 "If there is **f** in the land,
Job 5:20 In **f** he will redeem you from death,
Ps 37:19 in the days of **f** they have abundance
Jer 14:15 and **f** shall not come on this land";
Eze 5:16 against you my deadly arrows of **f,**
Am   8:11 not a **f** of bread, or a thirst for water,
Lk   4:25 was a severe **f** over all the land;
Ac 11:28 there would be a severe **f** over all
Ro   8:35 or distress, or persecution, or **f,**
Rev 18: 8 pestilence and mourning and **f**—
Sir 39:29 Fire and hail and **f** and pestilence,
1Mc 6:54 for the **f** proved too much for them.

FAMINES → FAMINE
Lk 21:11 and in various places **f** and plagues;

FAMISHED
Ge 25:29 from the field, and he was **f.**
Mt   4: 2 and afterwards he was **f.**

FAMOUS → FAME
1Ki 1:47 name of Solomon more **f** than yours
Jdt 16:23 She became more and more **f,**
Sir 44: 1 now sing the praises of **f** men,

FAR
Ge 18:25 **F** be that from you!
Nu 16: 3 "You have gone too **f!**
Jos 24:16 **"F** be it from us that we should
1Sa 7:12 "Thus **f** the LORD has helped us."
    12:23 **f** be it from me that I should sin
Job 19:13 "He has put my family **f** from me,
Ps 10: 1 do you stand **f** off?
    22:11 Do not be **f** from me,
 103:12 as **f** as the east is from the west,
 119:155 Salvation is **f** from the wicked,
   139: 2 discern my thoughts from **f** away.
Pr   5: 8 Keep your way **f** from her,
    31:10 She is **f** more precious than jewels.
Isa 29:13 while their hearts are **f** from me,
    57:19 Peace, peace, to the **f** and the near,
Jer 23:23 and not a God **f** off?
Mk   7: 6 but their hearts are **f** from me;
    12:34 are not **f** from the kingdom of God."
1Mc 2:21 **F** be it from us to desert the law

FARMER → FARMERS
2Ti 2: 6 the **f** who does the work who ought
Jas 5: 7 The **f** waits for the precious crop
2Es 8:41 "For just as the **f** sows many seeds

FARMERS → FARMER
Joel 1:11 Be dismayed, you **f,**

FASHION → FASHIONED, FASHIONS
Job 31:15 And did not one **f** us in the womb?
Isa 44:10 Who would **f** a god or cast an image

FASHIONED → FASHION
Job 10: 9 Remember that you **f** me like clay;
Ps 119:73 Your hands have made and **f** me;

FASHIONS → FASHION
Ps 33:15 he who **f** the hearts of them all,
Isa 45: 9 Does the clay say to the one who **f** it

FAST → FASTED, FASTING, FASTS
Dt 10:20 to him you shall hold **f,**
    11:22 and holding **f** to him,
    13: 4 and to him you shall hold **f.**
    30:20 and holding **f** to him;
Jos 22: 5 and to hold **f** to him,
    23: 8 but hold **f** to the LORD your God,
2Ki 18: 6 For he held **f** to the LORD;
2Ch 20: 3 proclaimed a **f** throughout all Judah.
Ezr 8:21 Then I proclaimed a **f** there, at the
Est   4:16 and hold a **f** on my behalf,
Job 23:11 My foot has held **f** to his steps:
Ps 17: 5 My steps have held **f** to your paths;
 139:10 and your right hand shall hold me **f.**
Pr   4: 4 "Let your heart hold **f** my words;
Isa 56: 4 please me and hold **f** my covenant,
    58: 5 Is such the **f** that I choose,
Jer   8: 5 They have held **f** to deceit,

Joel 1:14 Sanctify a **f,** call a solemn assembly.
Jnh 3: 5 they proclaimed a **f,** and everyone,
Zep 1:14 near and hastening **f;**
Mt   6:16 "And whenever you **f,**
    9:14 but your disciples do not **f?"**
Lk 18:12 I **f** twice a week; I give
Ro 12: 9 what is evil, hold **f** to what is good;
Php 2:16 by your holding **f** to the word of life
    3:16 hold **f** to what we have attained.
Col   2:19 and not holding **f** to the head,
1Th 5:21 everything; hold **f** to what is good;
2Th 2:15 hold **f** to the traditions that you
1Ti   3: 9 hold **f** to the mystery of the faith
Heb 4:14 let us hold **f** to our confession.
    10:23 Let us hold **f** to the confession of
1Pe 5:12 the true grace of God. Stand **f** in it.
Rev 3:11 I am coming soon; hold **f** to what
    14:12 hold **f** to the faith of Jesus.
Sir 49: 9 Job who held **f** to all the ways

FASTED → FAST
Jdg 20:26 they **f** that day until evening.
2Sa 12:16 David **f,** and went in and lay all
1Ki 21:27 he **f,** lay in the sackcloth,
Ezr 8:23 So we **f** and petitioned our God for
Zec 7: 5 was it for me that you **f?**
Mt   4: 2 He **f** forty days and forty nights,
Jdt   8: 6 She **f** all the days of her widowhood
1Mc 3:47 They **f** that day, put on sackcloth
2Es 5:20 So I **f** seven days, mourning and

FASTING → FAST
Ps 35:13 I afflicted myself with **f.**
Da   9: 3 supplication with **f** and sackcloth
Mt   6:16 so as to show others that they are **f.**
Ac 13: 2 were worshiping the Lord and **f,**
    14:23 prayer and **f** they entrusted them to
Tob 12: 8 Prayer with **f** is good, but better
Jdt   4: 9 humbled themselves with much **f.**

FASTS* → FAST
Est   9:31 regulations concerning their **f**
Sir 34:31 So if one **f** for his sins,

FAT → FATLING, FATLINGS, FATTED, FATTENED
Ge   4: 4 of his flock, their **f** portions.
Lev 3:16 All **f** is the LORD's.
    7:23 You shall eat no **f**
Jdg   3:17 Now Eglon was a very **f** man.
Eze 34:20 will judge between the **f** sheep and
Bel 1:27 Then Daniel took pitch, **f,**

FATE
Nu 16:29 or if a natural **f** comes on them,
Ps 49:13 Such is the **f** of the foolhardy,
Ecc 2:14 I perceived that the same **f** befalls

FATHER → FATHER'S, FATHER-IN-LAW, FATHERLESS, FATHERS
Ge   2:24 a man leaves his **f** and his mother
    19:32 preserve offspring through our **f."**
    26:24 "I am the God of your **f** Abraham;
    27:38 Bless me, me also, **f!"**
    31: 5 the God of my **f** has been with me.
    46: 3 "I am God, the God of your **f;**
Ex 20:12 Honor your **f** and your mother,
    21:15 Whoever strikes **f** or mother shall
    21:17 Whoever curses **f** or mother shall
    22:17 But if her **f** refuses to give her to
Dt   5:16 Honor your **f** and your mother,
    21:18 son who will not obey his **f**
    32: 6 Is not he your **f,** who created you,
Jdg 17:10 and be to me a **f** and a priest,
    18:19 and be to us a **f** and a priest.
2Sa 7:14 I will be a **f** to him, and he shall be
1Ki 2:12 Solomon sat on the throne of his **f**
1Ch 17:13 I will be a **f** to him, and he shall be
    22:10 a son to me, and I will be a **f** to him,
    28: 6 and I will be a **f** to him.
Job 38:28 "Has the rain a **f,** or who has
Ps 27:10 If my **f** and mother forsake me,
    68: 5 **F** of orphans and protector of

89:26 cry to me, 'You are my **F**, my God,
103:13 As a **f** has compassion for his
Pr   3:12 as a **f** the son in whom he delights.
  10: 1 A wise child makes a glad **f**,
  17:25 Foolish children are a grief to their **f**
  19:26 Those who do violence to their **f**
  20:20 If you curse **f** or mother,
  23:22 Listen to your **f** who begot you,
  23:24 The **f** of the righteous will greatly
  28:24 Anyone who robs **f** or mother and
Isa   8: 4 child knows how to call "My **f**" or
  9: 6 Mighty God, Everlasting **F**, Prince
  45:10 Woe to anyone who says to a **f**,
  63:16 you, O Lᴏʀᴅ, are our **f**;
Jer   2:27 "You are my **f**," and to a stone,
  3:19 I thought you would call me, My **F**,
  31: 9 for I have become a **f** to Israel,
Eze 16: 3 your **f** was an Amorite, and your
  18:19 son suffer for the iniquity of the **f**?"
Mic   7: 6 the **f** with contempt, the daughter
Mal   1: 6 If then I am a **f**, where is the honor
  2:10 Have we not all one **f**?
Mt   5:16 and give glory to your **F** in heaven.
  6: 9 Our **F** in heaven, hallowed be your
  6:14 your heavenly **F** will also forgive
  6:15 neither will your **F** forgive your
  6:26 and yet your heavenly **F** feeds them.
  10:37 Whoever loves **f** or mother more
  11:27 no one knows the Son except the **F**,
  15: 4 For God said, 'Honor your **f** and
  18:10 the face of my **F** in heaven.
  19: 5 a man shall leave his **f** and mother
  19:19 Honor your **f** and mother;
  19:29 or brothers or sisters or **f** or mother
  23: 9 And call no one your **f** on earth, for
       you have one **F**—
  28:19 the name of the **F** and of the Son
       and of the Holy Spirit,
Mk 14:36 "Abba, **F**, for you all things are
       possible;
Lk   6:36 merciful, just as your **F** is merciful.
  9:59 first let me go and bury my **f**."
  11: 2 **F**, hallowed be your name.
  12:30 your **F** knows that you need them.
  12:53 **f** against son and son against **f**,
  14:26 comes to me and does not hate **f**
  15:12 younger of them said to his **f**, '**F**,
  16:24 '**F** Abraham, have mercy on me,
  18:20 Honor your **f** and mother.'"
  23:34 [Then Jesus said, "**F**, forgive them;]
Jn   3:35 The **F** loves the Son and has placed
  4:23 will worship the **F** in spirit and
  5:17 "My **F** is still working,
  5:18 but was also calling God his own **F**,
  5:20 The **F** loves the Son and shows him
  6:44 unless drawn by the **F** who sent me;
  6:46 that anyone has seen the **F** except
  8:19 "You know neither me nor my **F**.
  8:28 but I speak these things as the **F**
  8:41 we have one **f**, God himself."
  8:44 You are from your **f** the devil,
  10:17 For this reason the **F** loves me,
  10:30 The **F** and I are one."
  10:38 the **F** is in me and I am in the **F**."
  12:27 '**F**, save me from this hour'?
  14: 6 comes to the **F** except through me.
  14: 9 has seen me has seen the **F**.
  14:11 that I am in the **F** and the **F** is in me;
  14:21 who love me will be loved by my **F**,
  14:28 because the **F** is greater than I.
  15: 9 As the **F** has loved me, so I have
  15:23 Whoever hates me hates my **F** also.
  20:17 I have not yet ascended to the **F**.
  20:21 As the **F** has sent me, so I send you.
Ac   1: 4 wait there for the promise of the **F**.
Ro   4:16 the faith of Abraham (for he is the **f**
  8:15 When we cry, "Abba! **F**!"
1Co   4:15 in Christ Jesus I became your **f**
2Co   1: 3 the **F** of mercies and the God of all
  6:18 and I will be your **f**,
Gal   4: 6 into our hearts, crying, "Abba! **F**!"
Eph   5:31 a man will leave his **f** and mother

  6: 2 "Honor your **f** and mother"—
Php   2:11 to the glory of God the **F**.
1Th   2:11 like a **f** with his children,
1Ti   5: 1 but speak to him as to a **f**,
Heb   1: 5 be his **F**, and he will be my Son"?
  12: 9 to be subject to the **F** of spirits
Jas   1:17 coming down from the **F** of lights,
1Jn   1: 3 truly our fellowship is with the **F**
  2:15 love of the **F** is not in those who
  2:22 one who denies the **F** and the Son.
  3: 1 See what love the **F** has given us,
2Jn   1: 9 abides in the teaching has both the **F**
Rev   3: 5 confess your name before my **F** and
  3:21 conquered and sat down with my **F**
Wis   2:16 and boasts that God is his **f**.
Sir   3: 3 who honor their **f** atone for sins,
  3:16 forsakes a **f** is like a blasphemer.

BECAME THE FATHER OF Ge 5:3, 4, 6,
9, 12, 15, 18, 21, 25, 28, 32; 10:8, 13, 15, 24,
24, 26; 11:10, 12, 14, 16, 18, 20, 22, 24, 26;
22:23; Ru 4:17, 18; 1Ch 1:10, 11, 13, 18, 18,
20, 34; 2:10, 10, 11, 13, 20, 20, 22, 36, 37, 38,
39, 40, 41, 44, 46; 4:2, 2, 8, 11, 12, 14, 14; 6:4,
11; 7:32; 8:1, 7, 32, 33, 34, 36, 36, 36, 37;
9:38, 39, 40, 42, 42, 43; 14:3; 2Ch 11:21;
13:21; 24:3; Ac 7:8, 8, 29; Tob 1:9

FATHER ABRAHAM Ge 22:7; 26:3, 15,
18, 24; 32:9; Jos 24:3; Lk 16:24, 30; Jn 8:53;
Sir 44:22; 4Mc 16:20; 17:6

FATHER DAVID 1Ki 2:12, 24, 26, 32, 44;
3:3, 6, 7, 14; 5:3, 5; 6:12; 7:51; 8:15, 17, 18,
20, 24, 25, 26; 9:5; 11:4, 6, 12, 27, 33, 43;
15:3, 11, 24; 22:50; 2Ki 22:2; 1Ch 29:23; 2Ch
1:8, 9; 2:3, 7, 14, 17; Ps 27:10; Pr 20:20; 23:25;
16; 7:17, 18; 8:14; 9:31; 21:12

FATHER IN HEAVEN Mt 5:16, 45; 6:1, 9;
7:11, 21; 10:32, 33; 12:50; 16:17; 18:10, 14,
19; Mk 11:25

FATHER ... MOTHER Ge 2:24; 28:7; Ex
20:12; 21:15, 17; Lev 20:9, 9; 21:11; Nu 6:7;
Dt 5:16; 21:13, 18, 19; 27:16; 33:9; Jos 2:13,
18; 6:23; Jdg 14:2, 3, 4, 5, 6, 9, 16; Ru 2:11;
1Sa 22:3; 2Sa 19:37; 1Ki 19:20; 22:52; 2Ki
3:2; Est 2:7, 7; Ps 27:10; Pr 20:20; 23:25;
28:24; Isa 8:4; Eze 22:7; 44:25; Mt 10:37;
15:4, 4, 5; 19:5, 19, 29; Mk 5:40; 7:10, 10, 11,
12; 10:7, 19; Lk 1:59; 2:33; 8:51; 12:53;
14:26; 18:20; Jn 6:42; Eph 5:31; 6:2; 1Ti 1:9;
Heb 7:3; Tob 5:17; 8:21; 9:6; 10:7; 11:17; Sir
23:14; 41:17; 1Mc 13:28; 1Es 4:21, 25

GOD AND FATHER Ro 15:6; 2Co 1:3;
11:31; Gal 1:4; Eph 1:3; 4:6; Php 4:20; 1Th
1:3; 3:11, 13; 1Pe 1:3; Rev 1:6; 3Mc 5:7

GOD OUR FATHER Ro 1:7; 1Co 1:3; 2Co
1:2; Gal 1:3; Eph 1:2; Php 1:2; Col 1:2; 2Th
1:1, 2; 2:16; Phm 1:3

GOD THE FATHER Jn 6:27; 1Co 8:6;
15:24; Gal 1:1; Eph 5:20; 6:23; Php 2:11; Col
1:3; 3:17; 1Th 1:1; 1Ti 1:2; 2Ti 1:2; Tit 1:4;
Jas 1:27; 1Pe 1:2; 2Pe 1:17; 2Jn 1:3; Jude 1:1

HEAVENLY FATHER Mt 5:48; 6:14, 26,
32; 15:13; 18:35; Lk 11:13

FATHER'S → FATHER
Ge   12: 1 your **f** house to the land that I will
  27:34 When Esau heard his **f** words,
  31:19 Rachel stole her **f** household gods.
  49: 4 you went up onto your **f** bed;
Ex   15: 2 my **f** God, and I will exalt him.
Dt   22:30 A man shall not marry his **f** wife,
2Sa 16:21 "Go in to your **f** concubines,
Est   4:14 you and your **f** family will perish.
Pr   4: 1 Listen, children, to a **f** instruction,
Eze 18:17 he shall not die for his **f** iniquity;
Lk   2:49 that I must be in my **F** house?"
Jn   1:14 the glory as of a **f** only son,
  1:18 who is close to the **F** heart,
  2:16 making my **F** house a marketplace!"
  5:43 I have come in my **F** name,
  10:29 can snatch it out of the **F** hand.

  14: 2 **F** house there are many dwelling
Rev 14: 1 and his **F** name written

FATHER'S HOUSE Ge 12:1; 20:13; 24:7,
23, 38, 40; 28:21; 31:14, 30; 38:11, 11; 41:51;
Lev 22:13; Nu 30:3, 16; Dt 22:21, 21; Jdg 9:5,
18; 11:2, 7; 14:15, 19; 19:2, 3; 1Sa 18:2; 22:1,
11, 15, 16, 22; 24:21; 2Sa 3:29; 14:9; 19:28;
24:17; 1Ki 2:31; 18:18; 1Ch 21:17; 28:4; 2Ch
21:13; Ps 45:10; Lk 2:49; 16:27; Jn 2:16; 14:2;
Ac 7:20; Tob 6:16; Sir 42:10; 1Mc 16:2; Pm
151:1; 4Mc 18:7

FATHER-IN-LAW → FATHER
Ex   18: 8 Moses told his **f** all that
Jn   18:13 who was the **f** of Caiaphas,

FATHERLESS* → FATHER
La   5: 3 We have become orphans, **f**;

FATHERS → FATHER
Isa 49:23 Kings shall be your foster **f**,
1Co   4:15 you do not have many **f**.
Eph   6: 4 **f**, do not provoke your children to
Col   3:21 **f**, do not provoke your children,
1Jn   2:13 I am writing to you, **f**,

FATLING* → FAT
2Sa   6:13 he sacrificed an ox and a **f**.
Isa 11: 6 the lion and the **f** together,

FATLINGS → FAT
Ps   66:15 will offer to you burnt offerings of **f**,

FATTED → FAT
Pr   15:17 than a **f** ox and hatred with it.
Lk   15:23 And get the **f** calf and kill it,

FATTENED* → FAT
Jas   5: 5 **f** your hearts in a day of slaughter.

FAULT → FAULTFINDER, FAULTLESS,
     FAULTS
1Sa 29: 3 found no **f** in him to this day."
Mt   18:15 go and point out the **f** when the two
Ro   9:19 "Why then does he still find **f**?
Sir   11: 7 Do not find **f** before you investigate;

FAULTFINDER* → FAULT, FIND
Job 40: 2 a **f** contend with the Almighty?

FAULTLESS* → FAULT
Heb   8: 7 For if that first covenant had been **f**,

FAULTS → FAULT
Ps   19:12 Clear me from hidden **f**.

FAVOR → FAVORABLE, FAVORED,
     FAVORITE, FAVORITISM, FAVORS
Ge   6: 8 Noah found **f** in the sight of the
Ex   33:12 you have also found **f** in my sight.'
  34: 9 "If now I have found **f** in your sight,
Lev 26: 9 I will look with **f** upon you and
Nu   11:15 if I have found **f** in your sight—
Jdg   6:17 "If now I have found **f** with you,
1Sa   2:26 and in **f** with the Lᴏʀᴅ and with
2Ch 33:12 in distress he entreated the **f** of
Est   7: 3 "If I have won your **f**,
Ps   5:12 you cover them with **f**
  30: 5 his **f** is for a lifetime.
  90:17 Let the **f** of the Lord our God be
Pr   3:34 but to the humble he shows **f**.
  8:35 finds me finds life and obtains **f**
  13:15 Good sense wins **f**, but the way of
  18:22 and obtains **f** from the Lᴏʀᴅ.
  19: 6 Many seek the **f** of the generous,
Ecc   9:11 nor **f** to the skillful;
Isa   49: 8 In a time of **f** I have answered you,
  61: 2 of the Lᴏʀᴅ's **f**, and the day of
Da   1: 9 God allowed Daniel to receive **f**
Zec 11: 7 I named **F**, the other I named Unity,
Lk   1:30 for you have found **f** with God.
  2:40 and the **f** of God was upon him.
  2:52 and in divine and human **f**.
  4:19 proclaim the year of the Lord's **f**."

Ac   7:10 and enabled him to win **f**
       7:46 who found **f** with God
2Co 1:15 so that you might have a double **f**;
Sir 32:14 to seek him will find **f.**
      42: 1 and will find **f** with everyone.
1Mc 4:10 to see whether he will **f** us

FAVORABLE → FAVOR

Ps   77: 7 and never again be **f?**
     85: 1 you were **f** to your land;
2Ti   4: 2 be persistent whether the time is **f**

FAVORED → FAVOR

Lk   1:28 and said, "Greetings, **f** one!

FAVORITE → FAVOR

Dt 33: 3 Indeed, O **f** among peoples,
2Sa 23: 1 the **f** of the Strong One of Israel:

FAVORITISM* → FAVOR

Jas   2: 1 with your acts of **f** really believe

FAVORS → FAVOR

Lk   2:14 peace among those whom he **f!**"
Sir 19:25 who abuse **f** to gain a verdict.

FAWNS

Ge 49:21 a doe let loose that bears lovely **f.**
SS   4: 5 Your two breasts are like two **f,**

FEAR → AFRAID, FEARED, FEARFUL, FEARFULLY, FEARING, FEARS, GOD-FEARING

Ge   9: 2 The **f** and dread of you shall rest on
    22:12 for now I know that you **f** God,
    31:42 God of Abraham and the **F** of Isaac.
Ex   9:30 you do not yet **f** the LORD God."
    20:20 to put the **f** of him upon you so that
Dt   2:25 I will begin to put the dread and **f**
    6:13 The LORD your God you shall **f**;
    10:12 Only to **f** the LORD your God,
    31:12 and learn to **f** the LORD your God
Jos   2:24 the inhabitants of the land melt in **f**
    4:24 that you may **f** the LORD your God
1Sa 12:14 If you will **f** the LORD and serve him
    12:24 Only **f** the LORD, and serve him
2Sa 23: 3 over people justly, ruling in the **f**
1Ki   8:43 may know your name and **f** you,
2Ch 19: 7 let the **f** of the LORD be upon you;
    26: 5 who instructed him in the **f** of God;
Est   8:17 the **f** of the Jews had fallen upon
Job   1: 9 "Does Job **f** God for nothing?
    6:14 forsake the **f** of the Almighty.
Ps   2:11 Serve the LORD with **f,** with
    15: 4 who honor those who **f** the LORD;
    19: 9 the **f** of the LORD is pure, enduring
    23: 4 the darkest valley, I **f** no evil;
    27: 1 and my salvation; whom shall I **f?**
    33: 8 Let all the earth **f** the LORD;
    34: 7 encamps around those who **f** him,
    34: 9 O **f** the LORD, you his holy ones,
    34: 9 for those who **f** him have no want.
    34:11 I will teach you the **f** of the LORD.
    46: 2 we will not **f,** though the earth
    55:19 do not change, and do not **f** God.
    90:11 wrath is as great as the **f** that is due
    91: 5 You will not **f** the terror of the night
  111:10 The **f** of the LORD is the beginning
  118: 4 Let those who **f** the LORD say,
  119:63 I am a companion of all who **f** you,
  145:19 fulfills the desire of all who **f** him;
  147:11 takes pleasure in those who **f** him,
Pr   1: 7 **f** of the LORD is the beginning of
    1:29 did not choose the **f** of the LORD,
    2: 5 will understand the **f** of the LORD
    3: 7 **f** the LORD, and turn away from evil.
    8:13 The **f** of the LORD is hatred of evil.
    9:10 The **f** of the LORD is the beginning
    10:27 The **f** of the LORD prolongs life,
    14:27 **f** of the LORD is a fountain of life,
    15:33 The **f** of the LORD is instruction in
    16: 6 by the **f** of the LORD one avoids evil.
    19:23 The **f** of the LORD is life indeed;

    22: 4 **f** of the LORD is riches and honor
    29:25 The **f** of others lays a snare,
Ecc   8:12 well with those who **f** God,
    12:13 **F** God, and keep his commandments
Isa   8:12 do not **f** what it fears, or be in dread.
    11: 3 delight shall be in the **f** of the LORD.
    33: 6 the **f** of the LORD is Zion's treasure.
    35: 4 a fearful heart, "Be strong, do not **f!**
    41:10 do not **f,** for I am with you, do not
    41:13 it is I who say to you, "Do not **f,**
    43: 1 Do not **f,** for I have redeemed you;
    43: 5 Do not **f,** for I am with you;
    51: 7 do not **f** the reproach of others,
    54:14 from oppression, for you shall not **f;**
Jer   5:22 Do you not **f** me?
    17: 8 It shall not **f** when heat comes,
    30:10 have no **f,** my servant Jacob,
Mic   6: 9 (it is sound wisdom to **f** your name):
Zep   3:15 you shall **f** disaster no more.
Mt   10:28 rather **f** him who can destroy both
Mk   5:36 "Do not **f,** only believe."
Lk   12: 5 Yes, I tell you, **f** him!
    18: 4 I have no **f** of God and no respect
Jn   7:13 openly about him for **f** of the Jews.
    12:42 **f** that they would be put out of the
    19:38 because of his **f** of the Jews,
    20:19 disciples had met were locked for **f**
Ac   5:11 And great **f** seized the whole church
Ro   8:15 a spirit of slavery to fall back into **f,**
    13: 3 wish to have no **f** of the authority?
2Co 5:11 knowing the **f** of the Lord,
Php   2:12 work out your own salvation with **f**
Heb 2:15 in slavery by the **f** of death.
1Pe 1:17 live in reverent **f** during the time of
    3:14 Do not **f** what they **f,**
1Jn 4:18 There is no **f** in love, but perfect
         love casts out **f;**
Jude 1:23 have mercy on still others with **f,**
Rev 2:10 not **f** what you are about to suffer.
    14: 7 "**F** God and give him glory,
    15: 4 will not **f** and glorify your name?
Sir   1:11 The **f** of the Lord is glory
    7:29 With all your soul **f** the Lord,
    40:26 but the **f** of the Lord is better
LtJ   6:16 not gods; so do not **f** them.

DO NOT FEAR Nu 14:9, 9; Dt 1:21; 3:2, 29; 31:8; Jos 8:1; 10:8; Jdg 6:23; 2Ch 20:15, 17; Ps 55:19; 118:6; Isa 7:4; 8:12; 35:4; 40:9; 41:10, 13, 14; 43:1, 5; 44:2, 8; 51:7; 54:4; 57:11; 63:17; La 3:57; Eze 3:9; Da 10:12, 19; Hos 10:3; Joel 2:21, 22; Zep 3:16; Hag 2:5; Mal 3:5; Mt 10:28; Mk 5:36; Lk 8:50; 12:4; 1Pe 3:14; Rev 2:10; Tob 5:16, 21; Sir 41:3; LtJ 6:16, 23, 29, 65, 69; 1Mc 2:62; 4:8; 2Mc 7:29; 2Es 2:17; 15:3; 16:75

FEAR AND ... TREMBLING Ps 55:5; Mk 5:33; 1Co 2:3; 2Co 7:15; Eph 6:5; Php 2:12; Jdt 2:28; 2Es 15:33, 37; 4Mc 4:10

FEAR ... GOD Ge 20:11; 22:12; 42:18; Ex 18:21; Lev 19:14, 32; 25:17, 36, 43; Dt 25:18; 2Sa 23:3; 2Ch 20:29; 26:5; Ne 5:9, 15; Job 1:9; 4:6; 15:4; 25:2; Ps 36:1; 55:19; 66:16; Ecc 5:7; 8:12, 13; 12:13; Lk 18:4; 23:40; Ac 13:16, 26; Ro 3:18; 2Co 7:1; 1Pe 2:17; Rev 14:7; Tob 4:21; AdE 2:20; 2Es 7:79; 4Mc 15:8

FEAR OF ... GOD Ge 20:11; 2Sa 23:3; 2Ch 20:29; 26:5; Ne 5:9, 15; Job 4:6; 15:4; Ps 36:1; Lk 18:4; Ro 3:18; 2Co 7:1; 4Mc 15:8

FEAR OF THE *LORD Job 28:28; Ac 9:31; 2Co 5:11; Sir 1:11, 12, 18, 27, 28, 30; 2:10; 9:16; 10:22; 16:2; 19:20; 21:11; 23:27; 25:6, 11; 27:3; 40:26, 26, 27; 45:23; 50:29

FEAR THE *LORD Sir 1:13, 14, 16, 20; 2:7, 8, 9, 15, 16, 17; 6:16, 17; 7:29, 31; 10:19, 20; 21:6; 32:16; 34:14, 16; 2Es 16:70, 71

FEAR OF THE †LORD 2Ch 14:14; 17:10; 19:7, 9; Ps 19:9; 34:11; 111:10; Pr 1:7, 29; 2:5; 8:13; 9:10; 10:27; 14:26, 27; 15:16, 33; 16:6; 19:23; 22:4; 23:17; Isa 11:2, 3; 33:6

FEAR THE †LORD Ex 9:30; Dt 6:2, 24;

10:12, 20; 14:23; 17:19; 31:12, 13; Jos 4:24; 1Sa 12:14, 24; Ps 15:4; 22:23; 25:12; 33:8; 34:9; 112:1; 115:11, 13; 118:4; 135:20; Pr 3:7; 14:2; 24:21; Jer 5:24; 26:19; Hos 10:3

FEARED → FEAR

Ex   1:21 the midwives **f** God, he gave them
    14:31 the people **f** the LORD and believed
1Sa 12:18 greatly **f** the LORD and Samuel.
Job   1: 1 **f** God and turned away from evil.
Ps   89: 7 God **f** in the council of the holy ones
Jnh   1:16 the men **f** the LORD even more,
Hag 1:12 and the people **f** the LORD.
Mk   6:20 for Herod **f** John, knowing that he
Jdt   8: 8 for she **f** God with great devotion.
Sus   1: 2 one who **f** the Lord.

FEARFUL → FEAR

Heb 10:27 but a **f** prospect of judgment,

FEARFULLY* → FEAR

Ps 139:14 I am **f** and wonderfully made.

FEARING → FEAR

Dt   8: 6 walking in his ways and by **f** him.
Col   3:22 but wholeheartedly, **f** the Lord.

FEARS → FEAR

Job   1: 8 upright man who **f** God and turns
    2: 3 upright man who **f** God and turns
Ps   34: 4 and delivered me from all my **f.**
  128: 4 blessed who **f** the LORD.
Pr   31:30 a woman who **f** the LORD is to be
Ecc   7:18 for the one who **f** God shall succeed
2Co 7: 5 disputes without and **f** within.
1Jn 4:18 **f** has not reached perfection in love.
Jdt 16:16 whoever the Lord is great forever.
Sir 15: 1 Whoever **f** the Lord will do this,

FEAST → FEASTING, FEASTS, LOVE-FEASTS

Ps   36: 8 They **f** on the abundance of your
Pr   15:15 a cheerful heart has a continual **f.**
Isa   25: 6 of hosts will make for all peoples a **f**
2Pe   2:13 in their dissipation while they **f** with

FEASTING → FEAST

Est   9:17 made that a day of **f** and gladness.
    9:19 of Adar as a day for gladness and **f,**
Pr   17: 1 than a house full of **f** with strife.
Sir 18:33 not become a beggar by **f** with

FEASTS → FEAST

Job   1: 4 His sons used to go and hold **f** in
Ecc 10:19 **F** are made for laughter; wine
Am   8:10 I will turn your **f** into mourning,
1Mc 1:39 her **f** were turned into mourning,

FEATHERED* → FEATHERS

2Es 11: 1 an eagle that had twelve **f** wings

FEATHERS* → FEATHERED

Da   4:33 as long as eagles' **f** and his nails

FED → FEED

Ex 16:32 with which I **f** you in the wilderness,
Dt   8:16 **f** you in the wilderness with manna
Ps   80: 5 have **f** them with the bread of tears,
Eze 34: 8 but the shepherds have **f** themselves,
Hos 13: 6 When I **f** them, they were satisfied;
1Co   3: 2 I **f** you with milk, not solid food,
Bel   1:27 which he **f** to the dragon.

FEEBLE

1Sa   2: 4 but the **f** gird on strength.
Job   4: 4 and you have made firm the **f** knees.
Isa 35: 3 and make firm the **f** knees.

FEED → FED, FEEDING, FEEDS

1Ki 17: 4 commanded the ravens to **f** you
    17: 9 commanded a widow there to **f** you.
Isa 40:11 He will **f** his flock like a shepherd;
    65:25 wolf and the lamb shall **f** together;
Jer   3:15 who will **f** you with knowledge
Eze 34:14 I will **f** them with good pasture,

FEEDING

Mk 8: 4 "How can one f these people with
Jn 21:15 Jesus said to him, **"F** my lambs."
 21:17 Jesus said to him, **"F** my sheep.
Ro 12:20 "if your enemies are hungry, f them;

FEEDING → FEED

Dt 8: 3 then by f you with manna,
Jer 9:15 I am f this people with wormwood,

FEEDS → FEED

Isa 44:20 He f on ashes; a deluded mind has
Mt 6:26 yet your heavenly Father f them.

FEEL → FELT

Jdg 16:26 "Let me f the pillars on which the
Ps 115: 7 They have hands, but do not f;

FEET → FOOT

Ex 3: 5 Remove the sandals from your f,
 12:11 loins girded, your sandals on your f,
 24:10 Under his f there was something
 30:21 shall wash their hands and their f,
Dt 8: 4 f did not swell these forty years.
Jos 3:15 the f of the priests bearing the ark
Ru 3: 8 and there, lying at his f,
1Sa 2: 9 "He will guard the f of his faithful
2Sa 22:34 He made my f like the f of deer,
Ps 8: 6 you have put all things under their f,
 22:16 My hands and f have shriveled;
 40: 2 and set my f upon a rock,
 56:13 and my f from falling,
 66: 9 and has not let our f slip.
 73: 2 my f had almost stumbled;
 115: 7 f, but do not walk;
 119:105 Your word is a lamp to my f
Pr 1:16 for their f run to evil,
 4:26 Keep straight the path of your f,
 5: 5 Her f go down to death;
 6:18 f that hurry to run to evil,
Isa 6: 2 and with two they covered their f,
 52: 7 are the f of the messenger
Eze 34:18 must you foul the rest with your f?
Da 2:33 its f partly of iron and partly of clay.
Na 1: 3 and the clouds are the dust of his f.
 1:15 f of one who brings good tidings,
Hab 3:19 he makes my f like the f of a deer,
Zec 14: 4 his f shall stand on the Mount of
Mt 10:14 from your f as you leave that house
 22:44 I put your enemies under your f'"?
Lk 1:79 guide our f into the way of peace."
 7:38 to bathe his f with her tears and to
 8:35 sitting at the f of Jesus,
 24:39 Look at my hands and my f;
Jn 13: 5 and began to wash the disciples' f
Ac 4:35 They laid it at the apostles' f,
 5: 2 and laid it at the apostles' f.
Ro 3:15 "Their f are swift to shed blood;
 10:15 the f of those who bring good news!
 16:20 shortly crush Satan under your f.
1Co 12:21 nor again the head to the f,
 15:25 put all his enemies under his f.
Eph 1:22 under his f and has made him the
 6:15 for your f put on whatever will
1Ti 5:10 washed the saints' f, helped the
Heb 1:13 enemies a footstool for your f"?
 2: 8 subjecting all things under their f."
 2:13 and make straight paths for your f,
Rev 1:15 his f were like burnished bronze,
 12: 1 with the moon under her f,

FELIX*

Governor before whom Paul was tried (Ac 23:23-24:27).

FELL → FALL

Ge 7:12 rain f on the earth forty days and
 15:12 a deep sleep f upon Abram,
1Sa 4:18 Eli f over backward from his seat
 31: 4 Saul took his own sword and f upon
1Ki 18:38 fire of the LORD f and consumed
Job 1:16 "The fire of God f from heaven and
Mt 7:25 The rain f, the floods came,
Mk 4: 8 Other seed f into good soil

Jn 18: 6 "I am he," they stepped back and f
Ac 5: 5 these words, he f down and died.
Heb 11:30 of Jericho f after they had been
Rev 1:17 I f at his feet as though dead.
 5:14 the elders f down and worshiped.
 6:13 the stars of the sky f to the earth as
 8:10 and a great star f from heaven,

FELLOW → FELLOWSHIP

Ex 2:13 Why do you strike your f Hebrew?"
Mt 18:31 his f slaves saw what had happened,
Eph 3: 6 the Gentiles have become f heirs,
Rev 22: 9 I am a f servant with you and your

FELLOWSHIP* → FELLOW

Ac 2:42 to the apostles' teaching and f,
1Co 1: 9 were called into the f of his Son,
2Co 6:14 Or what f is there between light and
Gal 2: 9 Barnabas and me the right hand of f,
1Jn 1: 3 so that you also may have f with us;
 1: 3 and truly our f is with the Father and
 1: 6 that we have f with him while we
 1: 7 we have f with one another,

FELT → FEEL

Ex 10:21 a darkness that can be f."
2Co 1: 9 f that we had received the sentence

FEMALE

Ge 1:27 male and f he created them.
 5: 2 Male and f he created them,
 6:19 they shall be male and f.
Dt 4:16 the likeness of male or f,
Mt 19: 4 beginning 'made them male and f,'
Mk 10: 6 'God made them male and f.'
Gal 3:28 there is no longer male and f;

FENCE → FENCED

Job 1:10 Have you not put a f around him

FENCED* → FENCE

Job 3:23 whom God has f in?

FERTILE

Isa 5: 1 had a vineyard on a very f hill.

FERVENTLY

Ac 12: 5 the church prayed f to God for him.
Jas 5:17 he prayed f that it might not rain,
Jdt 4:12 praying f to the God of Israel not

FERVOR* → FERVENT

Jdt 4: 9 Israel cried out to God with great f,

FESTAL → FESTIVAL

Ps 118:27 Bind the f procession with branches,
Zec 3: 4 I will clothe you with f apparel."
Heb 12:22 innumerable angels in f gathering,

FESTIVAL → FESTAL, FESTIVALS

Ex 5: 1 so that they may celebrate a f to me
 23:14 in the year you shall hold a f for me.
1Co 5: 8 Therefore, let us celebrate the f,
AdE 9:26 Mordecai established this f,

FESTIVAL OF BOOTHS Lev 23:34; Dt
 16:13, 16; 31:10; 2Ch 8:13; Ezr 3:4; Zec
 14:16, 18; Jn 7:2; 1Mc 10:21; 2Mc 1:9, 18;
 10:6, 6; 1Es 5:51

FESTIVAL OF UNLEAVENED BREAD
 Ex 12:17; 23:15; 34:18; Lev 23:6; Dt 16:16;
 2Ch 8:13; 30:13, 21; 35:17; Ezr 6:22; Mk
 14:1; Lk 22:1; Ac 12:3; 1Es 1:19; 7:14

FESTIVAL OF WEEKS Ex 34:22; Nu
 28:26; Dt 16:10, 16; 2Ch 8:13; Tob 2:1; 2Mc
 12:31

FESTIVALS → FESTIVAL

Lev 23: 2 are the appointed f of the LORD
Ne 10:33 the new moons, the appointed f,
Isa 1:14 and your appointed f my soul hates;
Hos 2:11 put an end to all her mirth, her f,
Na 1:15 Celebrate your f, O Judah, fulfill
Col 2:16 of food and drink or of observing f,
1Mc 1:45 to profane sabbaths and f,

APPOINTED FESTIVALS Lev 23:2, 2, 4,
 37, 44; Nu 10:10; 15:3; 29:39; 1Ch 23:31; 2Ch
 2:4; 31:3; Ne 10:33; Isa 1:14; 33:20; Eze
 36:38; 44:24; 45:17; 46:9; Hos 2:11

FESTUS*

Governor who sent Paul to Caesar (Ac 25-26).

FEVER

Dt 28:22 will afflict you with consumption, f,
Mk 1:30 mother-in-law was in bed with a f,
Lk 4:39 he stood over her and rebuked the f,
Jn 4:52 one in the afternoon the f left him."
Ac 28: 8 lay sick in bed with f and dysentery.

FEW → FEWEST

Ge 47: 9 f and hard have been the years of
Dt 26: 5 f in number, and there he became a
1Ch 16:19 When they were f in number,
Job 14: 1 f of days and full of trouble,
Ps 105:12 When they were f in number,
Ecc 5: 2 therefore let your words be f.
Mt 7:14 and there are f who find it.
 22:14 many are called, but f are chosen."
 25:21 have been trustworthy in a f things,
Lk 10: 2 is plentiful, but the laborers are f;
 13:23 "Lord, will only a f be saved?"
Sir 32: 8 say much in f words;
1Mc 3:18 between saving by many or by f.

FEWEST* → FEW

Dt 7: 7 for you were the f of all peoples.

FIANCEE

1Co 7:36 not behaving properly toward his f,

FIDELITY

Dt 1:36 his complete f to the LORD."
Tit 2:10 but to show complete and perfect f,
Sir 1:27 f and humility are his delight.

FIELD → FIELDS, GRAINFIELDS

Ge 4: 8 And when they were in the f,
 23:17 So the f of Ephron in Machpelah,
 49:30 f that Abraham bought from Ephron
Lev 19: 9 not reap to the very edges of your f,
Ru 2: 3 gleaned in the f behind the reapers.
 2: 3 the part of the f belonging to Boaz,
Ps 50:11 and all that moves in the f is mine.
 103:15 they flourish like a flower of the f;
Pr 24:30 by the f of one who was lazy,
 31:16 She considers a f and buys it;
Isa 1: 8 like a shelter in a cucumber f,
 5: 8 join house to house, who add f to f,
 40: 6 constancy is like the flower of the f.
Jer 32: 7 "Buy my f that is at Anathoth,
Mt 6:28 Consider the lilies of the f, how
 6:30 if God so clothes the grass of the f,
 13:38 the f is the world, and the good seed
 13:44 is like treasure hidden in a f,
 24:40 Then two will be in the f;
 27: 8 For this reason that f has been
 called the F of Blood
Ac 1:18 (Now this man acquired a f with the
1Co 3: 9 you are God's f, God's building.
2Co 10:13 but will keep within the f that God

FIELDS → FIELD

Ne 5: 3 "We are having to pledge our f,
Ps 144:13 by tens of thousands in our f,
Mic 2: 2 They covet f, and seize them;
Mk 10:30 children, and f with persecutions—
Lk 2: 8 there were shepherds living in the f,
Jn 4:35 see how the f are ripe for harvesting.

FIERCE

Ge 49: 7 Cursed be their anger, for it is f,
Ex 32:12 Turn from your f wrath;
Nu 25: 4 the f anger of the LORD may turn
Jer 30:24 f anger of the LORD will not turn
Hos 11: 9 I will not execute my f anger;
Jnh 3: 9 he may turn from his f anger,

FIERY → FIRE
Ps   21: 9 You will make them like a **f** furnace
Da   7: 9 his throne was **f** flames,
1Pe 4:12 do not be surprised at the **f** ordeal
Aza 1:26 and drove the **f** flame out

FIFTY
Ge 18:24 Suppose there are **f** righteous within
Jn   8:57 "You are not yet **f** years old,

FIG → FIGS
Ge   3: 7 and they sewed **f** leaves together
Jdg   9:10 Then the trees said to the **f** tree,
1Ki   4:25 all of them under their vines and **f**
Pr   27:18 Anyone who tends a **f** tree will eat
Hos   9:10 Like the first fruit on the **f** tree, in its
Mic   4: 4 and under their own **f** trees,
Na   3:12 All your fortresses are like **f** trees
Hab   3:17 Though the **f** tree does not blossom,
Zec   3:10 to come under your vine and **f** tree."
Mt   21:19 And the **f** tree withered at once.
     24:32 "From the **f** tree learn its lesson:
Lk   13: 6 "A man had a **f** tree planted in his
Jn   1:48 "I saw you under the **f** tree before
Jas   3:12 Can a **f** tree, my brothers and sisters,
Rev   6:13 as the **f** tree drops its winter fruit

FIGHT → FIGHTING, FIGHTS, FOUGHT
Ex   14:14 The Lᴏʀᴅ will **f** for you,
     17: 9 for us and go out, **f** with Amalek.
Dt   1:30 is the one who will **f** for you,
Jdg   1: 1 for us against the Canaanites, to **f**
1Sa 17: 9 If he is able to **f** with me and kill me
Ne   4:20 Our God will **f** for us."
Ps   35: 1 **f** against those who **f** against me!
Jer 21: 5 I myself will **f** against you
Zec 14: 3 and **f** against those nations as when
1Ti   1:18 you may **f** the good **f**,
      6:12 **F** the good **f** of the faith;
2Ti   4: 7 I have fought the good **f**,
Sir   4:28 **F** to the death for truth, and the
           Lord God will **f** for you.
1Mc   2:40 and refuse to **f** with the Gentiles

FIGHTING → FIGHT
Ex   2:13 the next day, he saw two Hebrews **f**;
     14:25 the Lᴏʀᴅ is **f** for them against Egypt
Ac   5:39 may even be found **f** against God!"

FIGHTS → FIGHT
Jos 23:10 the Lᴏʀᴅ your God who **f** for you,

FIGS → FIG
2Ki 20: 7 Isaiah said, "Bring a lump of **f**.
Jer 24: 1 Lᴏʀᴅ showed me two baskets of **f**
Na   3:12 like fig trees with first-ripe **f**—
Mk   11:13 for it was not the season for **f**.
Lk   6:44 **F** are not gathered from thorns,
Jas   3:12 yield olives, or a grapevine **f?**

FIGURATIVELY*
Heb 11:19 **f** speaking, he did receive him back.

FIGURE → FIGURES
Dt   4:16 in the form of any **f**—
Eze   8: 2 a **f** that looked like a human being;
Jn   10: 6 Jesus used this **f** of speech with
2Es 13: 3 something like the **f** of a man come

FIGURES → FIGURE
Eze 23:14 she saw male **f** carved on the wall,
Jn   16:25 these things to you in **f** of speech.

FILL → FILLED, FILLS, FULL, FULLNESS,
     FULLY
Ge   1:28 and **f** the earth and subdue it;
      9: 1 fruitful and multiply, and **f** the earth.
Dt   31:20 and they have eaten their **f** and
Ps   72:19 may his glory **f** the whole earth.
     81:10 Open your mouth wide and I will **f**
Isa 27: 6 and the whole world with fruit.
Jer 23:24 Do I not **f** heaven and earth?
Eze 10: 2 **f** your hands with burning coals
Hag   1: 6 drink, but you never have your **f**;

Jn   2: 7 and I will **f** this house with splendor,
      2: 7 Jesus said to them, **"F** the jars with
      6:26 because you ate your **f** of the loaves.
Ro   15:13 **f** you with all joy and peace in
Eph   4:10 so that he might **f** all things.)
Sir 24:19 and eat your **f** of my fruits.

FILLED → FILL
Ge   6:11 and the earth was **f** with violence.
Ex   1: 7 so that the land was **f** with them.
     31: 3 and I have **f** him with divine spirit,
     35:31 he has **f** him with divine spirit,
     40:34 glory of the Lᴏʀᴅ **f** the tabernacle.
Dt   6:11 houses **f** with all sorts of goods that
1Ki   8:11 glory of the Lᴏʀᴅ **f** the house of
2Ki   3:17 but the wadi shall be **f** with water,
2Ch   5:14 the glory of the Lᴏʀᴅ **f** the house of
      7: 1 the glory of the Lᴏʀᴅ **f** the temple.
Ps   71: 8 My mouth is **f** with your praise,
Pr   12:21 but the wicked are **f** with trouble.
Isa   6: 4 and the house **f** with smoke.
Eze 10: 4 the house was **f** with the cloud,
     43: 5 the glory of the Lᴏʀᴅ **f** the temple.
Da   2:35 became a great mountain and **f**
Na   2:12 **f** his caves with prey and his dens
Hab   2:14 earth will be **f** with the knowledge
Mt   5: 6 for righteousness, for they will be **f.**
Lk   1:15 he will be **f** with the Holy Spirit.
      1:41 Elizabeth was **f** with the Holy Spirit
      1:67 Zechariah was **f** with the Holy Spirit
      2:40 and became strong, **f** with wisdom;
Jn   12: 3 house was **f** with the fragrance of
Ac   2: 4 were **f** with the Holy Spirit and
      4: 8 Then Peter, **f** with the Holy Spirit,
      4:31 they were all **f** with the Holy Spirit
      5: 3 "why has Satan **f** your heart to lie to
      7:55 But **f** with the Holy Spirit,
      9:17 may regain your sight and be **f** with
     13: 9 Paul, **f** with the Holy Spirit,
     13:52 And the disciples were **f** with joy
Eph   5:18 but be **f** with the Spirit,
Rev   8: 5 the angel took the censer and **f** it
     15: 8 the temple was **f** with smoke from
Sir 26:10 who love him are **f** with his law.
     39: 6 he will be **f** with the spirit of

FILLS → FILL
Ps 107: 9 the hungry he **f** with good things.
Eph   1:23 the fullness of him who **f** all in all.

FILMS
Tob   2:10 into my eyes and produced white **f.**
     11:13 he peeled off the white **f** from

FILTH → FILTHY
Isa   4: 4 the Lord has washed away the **f** of
Mt   23:27 of the dead and of all kinds of **f.**

FILTHY → FILTH
Dt   29:17 the **f** idols of wood and stone,
Isa 28: 8 All tables are covered with **f** vomit;
     64: 6 righteous deeds are like a **f** cloth.
Zec   3: 3 Joshua was dressed with **f** clothes
Rev 22:11 and the **f** still be **f,**

FINAL
Eze 21:25 the time of **f** punishment,
1Mc   3:42 to cause their **f** destruction.

FIND → FAULTFINDER, FINDING, FINDS,
     FOUND
Ge   18:26 "If I **f** at Sodom fifty righteous in
Ex   33:13 so that I may know you and **f** favor
Nu   32:23 and be sure your sin will **f** you out.
Dt   4:29 you will **f** him if you search after
Job 23: 3 that I knew where I might **f** him,
     37:23 The Almighty—we cannot **f** him;
Ps   61: 4 **f** refuge under the shelter of your
     91: 4 under his wings you will **f** refuge;
    132: 5 until I **f** a place for the Lᴏʀᴅ,
Pr   2: 5 and **f** the knowledge of God.
      4:22 they are life to those who **f** them,
      8:17 those who seek me diligently **f** me.

     14:22 Those who plan good **f** loyalty and
     20: 6 but who can **f** one worthy of trust?
     24:14 if you **f** it, you will **f** a future,
     24:14 if you find it, you will **f** a future,
     31:10 A capable wife who can **f?**
Ecc   2:24 and **f** enjoyment in their toil.
     12:10 Teacher sought to **f** pleasing words,
Jer   6:16 walk in it, and **f** rest for your souls.
     29:13 you search for me, you will **f** me;
Da   6: 4 could **f** no grounds for complaint
Mt   7: 7 be given you; search, and you will **f**;
     11:29 and you will **f** rest for your souls.
     16:25 lose their life for my sake will **f** it.
     22: 9 everyone you **f** to the wedding
Lk   11: 9 search, and you will **f**;
     18: 8 comes, will he **f** faith on earth?"
     23: 4 "I **f** no basis for an accusation
     24: 3 went in, they did not **f** the body.
Jn   10: 9 come in and go out and **f** pasture.
Ac   23: 9 "We **f** nothing wrong with this man.
Ro   9:19 "Why then does he still **f** fault?
Eph   5:10 to **f** out what is pleasing to the Lord.
Sir 11: 7 not **f** fault before you investigate;

FINDING → FIND
Mt   13:46 on **f** one pearl of great value,
Sir 40:18 but better than either is **f** a treasure.

FINDS → FIND
Ps 119:162 like one who **f** great spoil.
Pr   8:35 For whoever **f** me **f** life and obtains
     18:22 He who **f** a wife **f** a good thing,
Ecc   9:10 Whatever your hand **f** to do, do with
Mt   7: 8 and everyone who searches **f,**
Lk   11:10 and everyone who searches **f,**
     12:37 those slaves whom the master **f** alert
     15: 4 after the one that is lost until he **f** it?
     15: 8 and search carefully until she **f** it?
Sir 25:10 How great is the one who **f** wisdom!
     40:19 than either is the one who **f** wisdom.

FINE
Ex   2: 2 when she saw that he was a **f** baby,
Pr   8:19 is better than gold, even **f** gold,
Lk   7:25 those who put on **f** clothing and live
1Pe   3: 3 gold ornaments or **f** clothing;
Rev 19: 8 for the **f** linen is the righteous deeds

FINE GOLD 2Ch 3:5, 8; Job 28:17; 31:24; Ps
19:10; 21:3; 119:127; Pr 8:19; Isa 13:12; La
4:2; Da 2:32

FINE LEATHER Ex 25:5; 26:14; 35:7, 23;
36:19; 39:34; Nu 4:6, 8, 10, 11, 12, 14, 25; Eze
16:10

FINE ... LINEN Ge 41:42; Ex 25:4; 26:1, 31,
36; 27:9, 16, 18; 28:5, 6, 8, 15, 39, 39; 35:6,
23, 25, 35; 36:8, 35, 37; 38:9, 16, 18, 23; 39:2,
3, 5, 8, 24, 27, 28, 28, 28, 29; 1Ch 15:27; 2Ch
2:14; 3:14; 5:12; Est 1:6; 8:15; Pr 31:22; Eze
16:10, 13; 27:7, 16; Lk 16:19; Rev 18:12, 16;
19:8, 8, 14; AdE 1:6; 6:8; 1Es 3:6

FINGER → FINGERS
Ex   8:19 "This is the **f** of God!"
     31:18 of stone, written with the **f** of God.
Dt   9:10 tablets written with the **f** of God;
2Ch 10:10 'My little **f** is thicker than my
Mt   23: 4 themselves are unwilling to lift a **f**
Lk   11:20 if it is by the **f** of God that I cast out
     16:24 send Lazarus to dip the tip of his **f**
Jn   8: 6 [wrote with his **f** on the ground.]
     20:25 and put my **f** in the mark of the nails

FINGERS → FINGER
2Sa 21:20 who had six **f** on each hand,
Ps   8: 3 your heavens, the work of your **f,**
Pr   7: 3 bind them on your **f,** write them on
Da   5: 5 the **f** of a human hand appeared
Mk   7:33 and put his **f** into his ears,

FINISH → FINISHED, FINISHING
Lk   14:30 to build and was not able to **f.'**
Ac   20:24 if only I may **f** my course and the
2Co   8:11 now **f** doing it, so that your

FINISHED → FINISH

Ge   2: 2 on the seventh day God **f** the work
     24:15 Before he had **f** speaking, there was
Ex   40:33 So Moses **f** the work.
Dt   32:45 Moses had **f** reciting all these words
Jos 19:51 So they **f** dividing the land.
1Ki   8:54 Now when Solomon **f** offering all
Ezr   6:14 They **f** their building by command
Ne   6:15 the wall was **f** on the twenty-fifth
Jn   19:30 Jesus had received the wine, he
             said, "It is **f**."
2Ti   4: 7 the good fight, I have **f** the race,
Heb   4: 3 his works were **f** at the foundation
Rev 11: 7 When they have **f** their testimony,
Sir 38: 8 God's works will never be **f**;

FINISHING → FINISH

Jn   17: 4 glorified you on earth by **f** the work

FINS

Dt   14: 9 has **f** and scales you may eat.

FIRE → FIERY, FIREPANS

Ge   15:17 a smoking **f** pot and a flaming torch
     19:24 sulfur and **f** from the LORD
Ex   3: 2 appeared to him in a flame of **f** out
      9:23 and **f** came down on the earth.
     13:21 and in a pillar of **f** by night, to give
     19:18 LORD had descended upon it in **f**;
     40:38 and **f** was in the cloud by night,
Lev   9:24 **F** came out from the LORD and
     10: 2 **f** came out from the presence of the
Nu   11: 1 the **f** of the LORD burned against
     16:35 And **f** came out from the LORD and
Dt   4:12 the LORD spoke to you out of the **f**.
      4:24 the LORD your God is a devouring **f**,
Jdg   6:21 and **f** sprang up from the rock and
1Ki 18:38 Then the **f** of the LORD fell and
     19:12 but the LORD was not in the **f**;
2Ki   1:10 Then **f** came down from heaven,
      2:11 a chariot of **f** and horses of **f**
             separated the two
      6:17 horses and chariots of **f** all around
     16: 3 even made his son pass through **f**,
2Ch   7: 1 **f** came down from heaven and
     28: 3 and made his sons pass through **f**,
     33: 6 He made his son pass through **f**
Ne   1: 3 its gates have been destroyed by **f**."
Ps   11: 6 wicked he will rain coals of **f** and
     50: 3 before him is a devouring **f**,
     89:46 long will your wrath burn like **f**?
Pr   6:27 Can **f** be carried in the bosom
Isa   5:24 as the tongue of **f** devours the
     10:17 The light of Israel will become a **f**,
     30:27 and his tongue is like a devouring **f**;
     66:24 their **f** shall not be quenched,
Jer 23:29 not my word like **f**, says the LORD,
     36:23 entire scroll was consumed in the **f**
Eze   1:13 like burning coals of **f**,
Da   3:25 walking in the middle of the **f**,
      7: 9 and its wheels were burning **f**.
Am   4:11 like a brand snatched from the **f**;
Zec   2: 5 For I will be a wall of **f** all around it,
      3: 2 man a brand plucked from the **f**?"
Mal   3: 2 For he is like a refiner's **f** and like
Mt   3:11 will baptize you with the Holy
             Spirit and **f**.
      5:22 will be liable to the hell of **f**.
     18: 8 and to be thrown into the eternal **f**,
     25:41 the eternal **f** prepared for the devil
Mk   9:43 to go to hell, to the unquenchable **f**.
      9:48 and the **f** is never quenched.
      9:49 "For everyone will be salted with **f**.
Lk   3:16 He will baptize you with the Holy
             Spirit and **f**.
     12:49 "I came to bring **f** to the earth,
Jn   15: 6 are gathered, thrown into the **f**,
Ac   2: 3 Divided tongues, as of **f**, appeared
1Co   3:13 the **f** will test what sort of work each
Heb 10:27 a fury of **f** that will consume the
     12:29 indeed our God is a consuming **f**.
Jas   3: 6 And the tongue is a **f**.

1Pe   1: 7 though perishable, is tested by **f**—
2Pe   3:10 elements will be dissolved with **f**,
Jude 1: 7 a punishment of eternal **f**.
      1:23 by snatching them out of the **f**;
Rev   1:14 his eyes were like a flame of **f**,
      8: 7 came hail and **f**, mixed with blood,
      9:17 **f** and smoke and sulfur came out of
     11: 5 **f** pours from their mouth
     15: 2 to be a sea of glass mixed with **f**,
     19:12 His eyes are like a flame of **f**,
     20:14 the second death, the lake of **f**;
Sir   2: 5 For gold is tested in the **f**,
      7:17 punishment of the ungodly is **f** and
Aza   1: 2 Azariah stood still in the **f** and

DEVOURING FIRE
Ex 24:17; Dt 4:24; 9:3; 2Sa 22:9; Ps 18:8; 50:3; Isa 29:6; 30:27, 30; 33:14

OFFERING BY FIRE
Ex 29:18, 25, 41; 30:20; Lev 1:9, 13, 17; 2:2, 9, 11, 16; 3:3, 5, 9, 11, 14, 16; 7:5, 25, 30; 8:21, 28; 22:27; 23:13, 18, 25, 27; 24:7; Nu 15:3, 10, 13, 14, 25; 18:17; 28:3, 6, 8, 13, 19, 24; 29:6, 13, 36

OFFERINGS BY FIRE
Lev 2:3, 10; 4:35; 5:12; 6:17, 18; 7:35; 10:12, 13, 15; 21:6, 21; 22:22; 23:8, 36, 36, 37; 24:9; Nu 28:2; Jos 13:14; 1Sa 2:28

OUT OF ... FIRE
Dt 4:12, 15, 33, 36; 5:4, 22, 24, 26; 9:10; 10:4; Jude 1:23

PILLAR OF FIRE
Ex 13:21, 22; 14:24; Nu 14:14; Ne 9:12, 19; Wis 18:3; 2Es 1:14

FIREPANS → FIRE

Ex   27: 3 shovels and basins and forks and **f**;
Jer 52:19 the **f**, the basins, the pots,

FIRM → FIRMLY

Ex   14:13 "Do not be afraid, stand **f**,
Ps   33: 9 he commanded, and it stood **f**.
     37:23 Our steps are made **f** by the LORD,
     89: 2 faithfulness is as **f** as the heavens.
Isa   7: 9 If you do not stand **f** in faith,
     22:17 He will seize **f** hold on you,
Da   11:32 to their God shall stand **f** and take
1Co 16:13 Keep alert, stand **f** in your faith,
2Co   1:24 because you stand **f** in the faith.
Gal   5: 1 Stand **f**, therefore, and do not submit
Eph   6:13 having done everything, to stand **f**.
Php   1:27 that you are standing **f** in one spirit,
      4: 1 stand **f** in the Lord in this way,
1Th   3: 8 if you continue to stand **f** in the
2Th   2:15 stand **f** and hold fast to the traditions
2Ti   2:19 But God's **f** foundation stands,
Heb   3: 6 if we hold **f** the confidence
      3:14 our first confidence **f** to the end.
Sir   5:10 Stand **f** for what you know,
1Mc   1:62 But many in Israel stood **f**

FIRMAMENT

Ps   19: 1 and the **f** proclaims his handiwork.
    150: 1 praise him in his mighty **f**!
2Es   6:41 you created the spirit of the **f**,

FIRMLY → FIRM

1Ki   2:12 and his kingdom was **f** established.
1Ch 16:30 world is **f** established; it shall never
Ps 119:89 your word is **f** fixed in heaven.
Ecc 12:11 like nails **f** fixed are the collected
1Co 15: 2 if you hold **f** to the message that I
2Ti   3:14 you have learned and **f** believed,

FIRST → FIRSTBORN, ONE

Ge   1: 5 and there was morning, the **f** day.
      9:20 was the **f** to plant a vineyard.
     13: 4 where he had made an altar at the **f**;
Ex   12: 2 it shall be the **f** month of the year
     23:19 The choicest of the **f** fruits of your
     34:19 All that **f** opens the womb is mine,
     40:17 In the **f** month in the second year,
Nu   18:15 The **f** issue of the womb of all
1Ki 22: 5 Inquire **f** for the word of the LORD."
Pr   3: 9 with the **f** fruits of all your produce;
      8:22 the **f** of his acts of long ago.

     18:17 one who **f** states a case seems right,
Isa 41: 4 I, the LORD, am **f**, and will be with
             the last.
     44: 6 I am the **f** and I am the last;
     48:12 I am the **f**, and I am the last.
Da   7: 4 The **f** was like a lion and had eagles'
Mt   5:24 **f** be reconciled to your brother or
      6:33 But strive **f** for the kingdom of God
      7: 5 **f** take the log out of your own eye,
      8:21 **f** let me go and bury my father."
     19:30 But many who are **f** will be last,
             and the last will be **f**.
     22:38 the greatest and **f** commandment.
Mk   9:11 say that Elijah must come **f**?"
      9:35 **f** must be last of all and servant of
     10:31 But many who are **f** will be last,
             and the last will be **f**."
     10:44 whoever wishes to be **f** among you
     13:10 good news must **f** be proclaimed to
     16: 2 very early on the **f** day of the week,
Lk   11:26 of that person is worse than the **f**."
Jn   2:11 Jesus did this, the **f** of his signs,
      8: 7 who is without sin be the **f** to throw
Ac   11:26 disciples were **f** called "Christians."
Ro   1:16 to the Jew **f** and also to the Greek.
1Co 12:28 appointed in the church **f** apostles,
     15:20 the **f** fruits of those who have died.
     15:45 it is written, "The **f** man, Adam,
2Co   8: 5 they gave themselves **f** to the Lord
Eph   1:12 were the **f** to set our hope on Christ,
      6: 2 the **f** commandment with a promise:
Col   1:18 to have **f** place in everything.
1Th   4:16 and the dead in Christ will rise **f**.
1Ti   2:13 For Adam was formed **f**, then Eve;
Heb   3:14 if only we hold our **f** confidence
      8:13 he has made the **f** one obsolete.
     10: 9 bolishes the **f** in order to establish
Jas   3:17 the wisdom from above is **f** pure,
2Pe   2:20 become worse for them than the **f**.
1Jn   4:19 We love because he **f** loved us.
3Jn   1: 9 who likes to put himself **f**,
Rev   1:17 I am the **f** and the last,
      2: 4 abandoned the love you had at **f**.
      4: 7 the **f** living creature like a lion,
      8: 7 The **f** angel blew his trumpet,
      9:12 The **f** woe has passed.
     13:12 all the authority of the **f** beast
     13:12 its inhabitants worship the **f** beast,
     20: 5 This is the **f** resurrection.
     21: 1 the **f** heaven and the **f** earth had
             passed away,
     22:13 I am the Alpha and the Omega, the
             f and the last,
Sir 11: 7 examine **f**, and then criticize.
2Es   3:21 For the **f** Adam, burdened with an

FIRST DAY
Ge 1:5; 8:5, 13; Ex 12:15, 15, 16; 40:2, 17; Lev 23:7, 24, 35, 39, 40; Nu 1:1, 18; 7:12; 28:18; 29:1; 33:38; Dt 1:3; 16:4; Jdg 20:22; 2Ch 29:17; Ezr 3:6; 7:9, 9; 10:16, 17; Ne 8:2, 18; Eze 26:1; 29:17; 31:1; 32:1; 45:18; Da 10:12; Hag 1:1; Mt 26:17; 28:1; Mk 14:12; 16:2, 9; Lk 24:1; Jn 20:1, 19; Ac 20:7, 18; 1Co 16:2; Php 1:5; AdE 11:2; 2Es 6:38

FIRST FRUITS
Ge 49:3; Ex 23:16, 19; 34:22, 26; Lev 2:14, 14; 23:10, 17, 20; Nu 18:13; 28:26; Dt 18:4; 2Ki 4:42; 2Ch 31:5; Ne 10:35, 35; 12:44; 13:31; Pr 3:9; Jer 2:3; Eze 44:30; Ro 8:23; 11:16; 1Co 15:20, 23; 2Th 2:13; Jas 1:18; Rev 14:4; Tob 1:6; Jdt 11:13; Sir 7:31, 31; 24:25; 35:10; 45:20, 20; 50:8; 1Mc 3:49

FIRST MONTH
Ge 8:13; Ex 12:2, 18; 40:2, 17; Lev 23:5; Nu 9:1, 5; 20:1; 28:16; 33:3, 3; Jos 4:19; 1Ch 12:15; 27:2, 3; 2Ch 29:3, 17, 17; 35:1; Ezr 6:19; 7:9; 8:31; 10:17; Est 3:7, 12; Eze 29:17; 30:20; 32:17; 45:18, 21; Da 10:4; Jdt 2:1; AdE 3:12; 8:9; 1Mc 9:3; 1Es 1:1; 5:6; 7:10; 8:6, 61; 9:17

FIRST YEAR
Ge 8:13; Lev 12:6; 14:10; 2Ch 29:3; 36:22; Ezr 1:1; 5:13; 6:3; Jer 25:1; Da

1:21; 7:1; 9:1, 2; 11:1; 1Mc 13:42; 1Es 2:1;
6:17, 24

FROM FIRST TO LAST 1Ch 29:29; 2Ch
9:29; 12:15; 16:11; 20:34; 25:26; 26:22; 28:26

FIRSTBORN → BEAR, FIRST
Ge 27:19 said to his father, "I am Esau your **f.**
        48:18 Since this one is the **f,**
Ex   4:22 'Thus says the LORD: Israel is my **f**
        11: 5 **f** in the land of Egypt shall die,
        12:29 the LORD struck down all the **f**
        13: 2 Consecrate to me all the **f;**
        34:20 the **f** of your sons you shall redeem.
Nu   3:41 as substitutes for all the **f** among
Dt 21:17 the right of the **f** is his.
Jos   6:26 At the cost of his **f** he shall lay its
1Ki 16:34 at the cost of Abiram his **f,**
Ps 78:51 He struck all the **f** in Egypt,
        89:27 I will make him the **f,**
Eze 20:26 in their offering up all their **f,**
Mic   6: 7 I give my **f** for my transgression,
Zec 12:10 as one weeps over a **f.**
Lk   2: 7 And she gave birth to her **f** son and
Ro   8:29 might be the **f** within a large family.
Col   1:15 invisible God, the **f** of all creation;
        1:18 the beginning, the **f** from the dead,
Heb   1: 6 when he brings the **f** into the world,
        12:23 assembly of the **f** who are enrolled
Rev   1: 5 faithful witness, the **f** of the dead,
Sir 36:17 whom you have named your **f,**
2Es   6:58 whom you have called your **f,**

ALL THE FIRSTBORN Ex 11:5; 12:29, 29;
13:2, 12, 15; 34:20; Nu 3:12, 13, 13, 13, 40,
41, 41, 42, 43, 45; 8:17, 17, 18; Ps 78:51;
105:36

FISH → FISHERMEN, FISHHOOK
Ge   1:26 have dominion over the **f** of the sea,
Ex   7:18 The **f** in the river shall die,
Nu 11: 5 the **f** we used to eat in Egypt
Eze 47: 9 and there will be very many **f,**
Jnh   1:17 a large **f** to swallow up Jonah;
        2: 1 his God from the belly of the **f,**
Mt   7:10 Or if the child asks for a **f,** will give
        14:17 but five loaves and two **f.**"
Mk   8: 7 They had also a few small **f;**
Lk   5: 6 so many **f** that their nets were
Jn   6: 9 has five barley loaves and two **f.**
        21: 5 to them, "Children, you have no **f,**
        21:11 full of large **f,** a hundred fifty-three
Tob   6: 3 Suddenly a large **f** leaped up from
        8: 3 odor of the **f** so repelled the demon
        11: 8 Smear the gall of the **f** on his eyes;

FISHERMEN → FISH, MAN
Mk   1:16 into the sea—for they were **f.**

FISHHOOK → FISH, HOOK
Job 41: 1 you draw out Leviathan with a **f,**

FIT → FITLY, FITNESS, FITTED
Lk   9:62 and looks back is **f** for the kingdom

FITLY → FIT
Pr 25:11 A word **f** spoken is like apples of

FITNESS → FIT
Sir 30:15 Health and **f** are better than any gold

FITTING → FIT
Ps 147: 1 and a song of praise is **f.**
Pr 19:10 It is not **f** for a fool to live in luxury,
        26: 1 so honor is not **f** for a fool.
Col   3:18 be subject to your husbands, as is **f**
Heb   2:10 It was **f** that God, for whom and

FIVE
1Sa   6: 4 "**F** gold tumors and **f** gold mice,
        6:16 When the **f** lords of the Philistines
        17:40 chose **f** smooth stones from the wadi
Isa 30:17 at the threat of **f** you shall flee,
Mt 14:19 Taking the **f** loaves and the two fish,
        16: 9 the **f** loaves for the **f** thousand,

        25: 2 **F** of them were foolish, and **f** were
        25:15 to one he gave **f** talents,
Jn   4:18 for you have had **f** husbands,
1Co 14:19 church I would rather speak **f** words
Rev   9: 5 allowed to torture them for **f** months
        17:10 of whom **f** have fallen, one is living,
1Mc   2: 2 He had **f** sons, John surnamed

FIX → FIXED
Dt 11:18 and **f** them as an emblem on your
Job 14: 3 Do you **f** your eyes on such a one?
Am   9: 4 I will **f** my eyes on them for harm
Wis   6:15 To **f** one's thought on her

FIXED → FIX
2Ki   8:11 He **f** his gaze and stared at him,
Ps 119:89 your word is firmly **f** in heaven.
Lk 16:26 and us a great chasm has been **f,**
Ac 17:31 because he has **f** a day on which he
Sir 17: 2 He gave them a **f** number of days,

FLAME → AFLAME, FLAMES, FLAMING
Ex   3: 2 in a **f** of fire out of a bush;
Jdg 13:20 angel of the LORD ascended in the **f**
Ps 106:18 the **f** burned up the wicked.
Isa 10:17 and his Holy One a **f;**
Ac   7:30 in the **f** of a burning bush.
Rev   1:14 his eyes were like a **f** of fire,
        2:18 who has eyes like a **f** of fire,
        19:12 His eyes are like a **f** of fire,
Aza   1:26 drove the fiery **f** out of the furnace,
1Mc   2:59 believed and were saved from the **f.**

FLAMES → FLAME
Da   3:22 the raging **f** killed the men who
Lk 16:24 for I am in agony in these **f.**'

FLAMING → FLAME
Ge   3:24 and a sword **f** and turning to guard
Da 10: 6 like lightning, his eyes like **f** torches
Eph   6:16 quench all the **f** arrows of the evil

FLASH → FLASHED, FLASHES, FLASHING
Ps 144: 6 Make the lightning **f** and scatter
Eze 21:10 honed to **f** like lightning!

FLASHED → FLASH
Ps 77:17 your arrows **f** on every side.
Ac   9: 3 suddenly a light from heaven **f**

FLASHES → FLASH
Lk 17:24 lightning **f** and lights up the sky
Rev   4: 5 from the throne are **f** of lightning,
        8: 5 of lightning, and an earthquake.
        11:19 there were **f** of lightning, rumblings,
        16:18 came **f** of lightning, rumblings,
2Es   6: 2 and before the **f** of lightning shone,

FLASHING → FLASH
Dt 32:41 when I whet my **f** sword,

FLASK
2Ki   9: 1 take this **f** of oil in your hand,
        9: 3 take the **f** of oil, pour it on his head,

FLATTER → FLATTERED, FLATTERING,
FLATTERS, FLATTERY
Ps   5: 9 they **f** with their tongues.

FLATTERED → FLATTER
Ps 78:36 But they **f** him with their mouths;

FLATTERING → FLATTER
Ps 12: 2 with **f** lips and a double heart they
        12: 3 May the LORD cut off all **f** lips,
Pr 26:28 and a **f** mouth works ruin.
Eze 12:24 or **f** divination within the house of
Jude   1:16 **f** people to their own advantage.

FLATTERS → FLATTER
Pr 29: 5 **f** a neighbor is spreading a net for

FLATTERY → FLATTER
Job 32:21 or use **f** toward anyone.
Eze 33:31 For **f** is on their lips,

Ro 16:18 talk and **f** they deceive the hearts
1Th   2: 5 we never came with words of **f** or

FLAW → FLAWLESS
SS   4: 7 there is no **f** in you.

FLAWLESS → FLAW
SS   6: 9 **f** to her that bore her.

FLAX
Jos   2: 6 and hidden them with the stalks of **f**
Jdg 15:14 became like **f** that has caught fire,
Pr 31:13 She seeks wool and **f,** and works

FLED → FLEE
Ex   2:15 But Moses **f** from Pharaoh.
1Sa 19:18 Now David **f** and escaped;
2Sa   4: 4 His nurse picked him up and **f;**
        19: 9 he has **f** out of the land because of
Ps   3: T when he **f** from his son Absalom.
        57: T when he **f** from Saul, in the cave.
        114: 3 The sea looked and **f;** Jordan turned
Mk 14:50 All of them deserted him and **f.**
Rev 12: 6 the woman **f** into the wilderness,
        16:20 And every island **f** away,
        20:11 and the heaven **f** from his presence,

FLEE → FLED, FLEEING
Ge 19:17 they said, "**F** for your life;
        27:43 **f** at once to my brother Laban in
Lev 26:17 you shall **f** though no one pursues
Nu 35:11 a person without intent may **f** there.
Ps 11: 1 "**F** like a bird to the mountains;
        68: 1 let those who hate him **f** before him.
        139: 7 where can I **f** from your presence?
Isa 30:17 A thousand shall **f** at the threat of
Jer 46: 6 swift cannot **f** away,
        51: 6 **F** from the midst of Babylon, save
Jnh   1: 3 to **f** to Tarshish from the presence
Zec   2: 6 **F** from the land of the north, says
Lk   3: 7 warned you to **f** from the wrath to
1Co 10:14 **f** from the worship of idols.
Jas   4: 7 Resist the devil, and he will **f** from
Rev   9: 6 long to die, but death will **f** from
Tob   6:18 the demon will smell it and **f,**
Sir 21: 2 **F** from sin as from a snake;

FLEECE
Jdg   6:37 if there is dew on the **f** alone,

FLEEING → FLEE
Job 26:13 his hand pierced the **f** serpent.

FLEETING
Ps 39: 4 let me know how **f** my life is.
Pr 21: 6 a lying tongue is a **f** vapor and a
Sir 41:11 The human body is a **f** thing,

FLESH → FLESHPOTS
Ge   2:23 is bone of my bones and **f** of my **f;**
        2:24 and they become one **f.**
        17:13 be in your **f** an everlasting covenant.
Lev 11: 8 Of their **f** you shall not eat,
1Sa 17:44 and I will give your **f** to the birds of
2Ch 32: 8 With him is an arm of **f;**
Job 19:26 then in my **f** I shall see God,
Ps 50:13 Do I eat the **f** of bulls,
        73:26 My **f** and my heart may fail,
Pr   4:22 and healing to all their **f.**
Isa 31: 3 their horses are **f,** and not spirit.
Jer 17: 5 and make mere **f** their strength,
Eze 11:19 the heart of stone from their **f** and
                give them a heart of **f,**
        36:26 of stone and give you a heart of **f.**
        37: 6 and will cause **f** to come upon you,
        44: 7 uncircumcised in heart and **f,**
Joel   2:28 I will pour out my spirit on all **f;**
Mal   2:15 Both **f** and spirit are his.
Mt 16:17 For **f** and blood has not revealed this
        19: 5 and the two shall become one **f**"?
        26:41 but the **f** is weak."
Lk 24:39 a ghost does not have **f** and bones as
Jn   1:14 the Word became **f** and lived among
        3: 6 What is born of the **f** is **f,**

6:51 for the life of the world is my **f.**"
6:63 spirit that gives life; the **f** is useless.
Ac   2:17 I will pour out my Spirit upon all **f,**
Ro   7: 5 While we were living in the **f,**
8: 3 the law, weakened by the **f,**
8: 4 to the **f** but according to the Spirit.
8: 9 But you are not in the **f;**
8:13 live according to the **f,** you will die;
1Co 6:16 it is said, "The two shall be one **f.**"
15:39 Not all **f** is alike,
15:50 **f** and blood cannot inherit the
2Co 12: 7 a thorn was given me in the **f,**
Gal 3: 3 are you now ending with the **f?**
5:17 the **f** desires is opposed to the Spirit,
5:19 Now the works of the **f** are obvious:
Eph 2: 3 following the desires of **f** and senses
5:31 and the two will become one **f.**"
6:12 not against enemies of blood and **f,**
Php 1:22 If I am to live in the **f,**
3: 2 beware of those who mutilate the **f!**
3: 4 have reason for confidence in the **f.**
Col 1:24 in my **f** I am completing what is
1Ti 3:16 revealed in **f,** vindicated in spirit,
Heb 5: 7 In the days of his **f,**
1Pe 1:24 "All **f** is like grass and all its glory
1Jn 2:16 desire of the **f,** the desire of the eyes
4: 2 that Jesus Christ has come in the **f,**
2Jn 1: 7 that Jesus Christ has come in the **f;**
Jude 1: 8 these dreamers also defile the **f,**
Rev 19:18 the **f** of kings, the **f** of captains,
Sir 17:31 So **f** and blood devise evil.
41: 4 This is the Lord's decree for all **f;**
44:20 he certified the covenant in his **f,**

ALL FLESH Ge 6:12, 13, 17, 19; 7:15, 16,
21; 8:17; 9:11, 15, 15, 16, 17; Nu 16:22;
27:16; Dt 5:26; Job 34:15; Ps 65:2; 136:25;
145:21; Isa 49:26; 66:16, 23, 24; Jer 25:31;
32:27; 45:5; Eze 20:48; 21:4, 5; Joel 2:28; Lk
3:6; Ac 2:17; 1Co 15:39; 1Pe 1:24; Sir 41:4;
44:18

ONE FLESH Ge 2:24; Mt 19:5, 6; Mk 10:8,
8; 1Co 6:16; 15:39; Eph 5:31

FLESHPOTS' → FLESH, POT
Ex 16: 3 sat by the **f** and ate our fill of bread;

FLEW → FLY
Ps 18:10 He rode on a cherub, and **f;**
Isa 6: 6 Then one of the seraphs **f** to me,
Rev 8:13 eagle crying with a loud voice as it **f**
2Es 11: 5 Then I saw that the eagle **f** with its
13: 3 this man **f** with the clouds of heaven

FLIES → FLY
Ex   8:21 I will send swarms of **f** on you,
Ps 91: 5 or the arrow that **f** by day,
105:31 and there came swarms of **f,**

FLIGHT → FLY
Dt 32:30 and two put a myriad to **f,**
Mt 24:20 Pray that your **f** may not be in

FLINT
Ex   4:25 Zipporah took a **f** and cut off her
Jos 5: 2 "Make **f** knives and circumcise the
Ps 114: 8 the **f** into a spring of water.
Isa 50: 7 therefore I have set my face like **f,**

FLOAT' → FLOATED
2Ki 6: 6 in there, and made the iron **f.**

FLOATED' → FLOAT
Ge   7:18 the ark **f** on the face of the waters.

FLOCK
Ge   4: 4 brought of the firstlings of his **f,**
Ex   2:17 to their defense and watered their **f.**
3: 1 he led his **f** beyond the wilderness,
Ps 77:20 You led your people like a **f** by the
78:52 in the wilderness like a **f.**
80: 1 you who lead Joseph like a **f!**
SS   4: 1 Your hair is like a **f** of goats,
6: 6 Your teeth are like a **f** of ewes,

Isa 40:11 He will feed his **f** like a shepherd;
Jer 10:21 and all their **f** is scattered.
23: 2 It is you who have scattered my **f,**
31:10 will keep him as a shepherd a **f.**"
Eze 34:22 I will save my **f,** and they shall no
Am   7:15 LORD took me from following the **f,**
Zec 11: 7 of the **f** doomed to slaughter.
Mt 26:31 the sheep of the **f** will be scattered.'
Lk   2: 8 keeping watch over their **f** by night.
12:32 "Do not be afraid, little **f,**
Jn 10:16 So there will be one **f,** one shepherd.
Ac 20:28 over yourselves and over all the **f,**
1Co 9: 7 a **f** and does not get any of its milk?
1Pe 5: 2 the **f** of God that is in your charge,
5: 3 but be examples to the **f.**

FLOG → FLOGGED, FLOGGING,
FLOGGINGS
Mt 10:17 hand you over to councils and **f** you
Mk 10:34 spit upon him, and **f** him, and kill
Ac 22:25 "Is it legal for you to **f** a Roman

FLOGGED → FLOG
Jn 19: 1 Pilate took Jesus and had him **f.**
Ac   5:40 the apostles, they had them **f.**

FLOGGING → FLOG
Pr 18: 6 and a fool's mouth invites a **f.**
Mt 27:26 after **f** Jesus, he handed him over to
Ac 16:23 they had given them a severe **f,**
Heb 11:36 Others suffered mocking and **f,**

FLOGGINGS' → FLOG
2Co 11:23 imprisonments, with countless **f,**

FLOOD → FLOODS
Ge   7: 7 the ark to escape the waters of the **f.**
9:15 waters shall never again become a **f**
Ps 29:10 The LORD sits enthroned over the **f;**
Da   9:26 Its end shall come with a **f,**
Mt 24:38 For as in those days before the **f**
Lk   6:48 a **f** arose, the river burst against that
2Pe 2: 5 a **f** on a world of the ungodly;
Sir 40:10 and on their account the **f** came.

FLOODS → FLOOD
Ex 15: 5 The **f** covered them;
Ps 93: 3 The **f** have lifted up, O LORD,
SS   8: 7 quench love, neither can **f** drown it.
Mt   7:25 The rain fell, the **f** came,

FLOOR → FLOORS
Dt 15:14 threshing **f,** and your wine press,
Jdg 6:37 a fleece of wool on the threshing **f;**
Ru   3: 3 and go down to the threshing **f;**
1Ch 21:15 threshing **f** of Ornan the Jebusite.
2Ch 3: 1 threshing **f** of Ornan the Jebusite.
Mt   3:12 and he will clear his threshing **f**
Bel 1:19 "Look at the **f,**" he said,

FLOORS → FLOOR
Hos 9: 1 a prostitute's pay on all threshing **f.**
Ac 20: 9 he fell to the ground three **f** below

FLOUR
Nu   7:13 both of them full of choice **f** mixed
2Ki 4:41 He said, "Then bring some **f.**"
Lk 13:21 mixed in with three measures of **f**

FLOURISH → FLOURISHES
Ps 72: 7 In his days may righteousness **f**
92: 7 sprout like grass and all evildoers **f,**
92:12 The righteous **f** like the palm tree,
Eze 17:24 green tree and make the dry tree **f.**

FLOURISHES' → FLOURISH
Ps 90: 6 in the morning it **f** and is renewed;
Pr 14:11 but the tent of the upright **f.**

FLOW → EVER-FLOWING, FLOWED,
FLOWING, FLOWS
Lev 12: 7 clean from her **f** of blood.
Ps 78:16 caused waters to **f** down like rivers.
Ecc 1: 7 there they continue to **f.**

Joel 3:18 the hills shall **f** with milk,
Am   9:13 and all the hills shall **f** with it.
Zec 14: 8 waters shall **f** out from Jerusalem,
Jn   7:38 'Out of the believer's heart shall **f**

FLOWED → FLOW
Rev 14:20 and blood **f** from the wine press,

FLOWER → FLOWERS
Job 14: 2 comes up like a **f** and withers,
Ps 103:15 they flourish like a **f** of the field;
Isa 40: 7 The grass withers, the **f** fades,
Jas 1:10 the rich will disappear like a **f** in
1Pe 1:24 The grass withers, and the **f** falls,

FLOWERS → FLOWER
1Ki 6:18 had carvings of gourds and open **f;**

FLOWING → FLOW
Ex   3: 8 a land **f** with milk and honey,
33: 3 up to a land **f** with milk and honey;
Nu 16:14 not brought us into a land **f** with
Jos 5: 6 a land **f** with milk and honey.
2Ki 4: 6 Then the oil stopped **f.**
Jer 32:22 a land **f** with milk and honey;
Eze 20: 6 a land **f** with milk and honey,
32: 6 drench the land with your **f** blood
47: 1 water was **f** from below the
Rev 22: 1 **f** from the throne of God and of the
LAND FLOWING WITH MILK AND
HONEY Ex 3:8, 17; 13:5; 33:3; Lev 20:24;
Nu 16:13, 14; Dt 6:3; 11:9; 26:9, 15; 27:3;
31:20; Jos 5:6; Jer 11:5; 32:22; Eze 20:6, 15;
Sir 46:8; Bar 1:20

FLOWS → FLOW
Ge   2:10 A river **f** out of Eden to water the

FLUTE → FLUTES
1Sa 10: 5 **f,** and lyre playing in front of them;
Mt 11:17 'We played the **f** for you, and you
1Co 14: 7 such as the **f** or the harp.
1Mc 3:45 the **f** and the harp ceased to play.

FLUTES → FLUTE
Ps   5: T To the leader: for the **f.** A Psalm of

FLY → FLEW, FLIES, FLIGHT, FLYING
Ge   1:20 and let birds **f** above the earth
Rev 12:14 she could **f** from the serpent

FLYING → FLY
Zec 5: 1 Again I looked up and saw a **f** scroll
Rev 4: 7 fourth living creature like a **f** eagle.
14: 6 I saw another angel **f** in midheaven,

FOAL'
Ge 49:11 Binding his **f** to the vine
Zec 9: 9 on a colt, the **f** of a donkey.
Mt 21: 5 and on a colt, the **f** of a donkey."

FOAM' → FOAMING, FOAMS
Ps 46: 3 though its waters roar and **f,**
Jude 1:13 casting up the **f** of their own shame;

FOAMING' → FOAM
Ps 75: T there is a cup with **f** wine,
Mk 9:20 and rolled about, **f** at the mouth.

FOAMS → FOAM
Lk   9:39 until he **f** at the mouth;

FOE → FOES
Ex 23:22 and a **f** to your foes.
Ps 60:11 O grant us help against the **f,**
78:42 he redeemed them from the **f;**
La   1: 5 captives before the **f.**
1Mc 2: 9 her youths by the sword of the **f.**

FOES → FOE
Ge 22:60 of the gates of their **f.**"
Ex 23:22 and a foe to your **f.**
Lev 26:17 your **f** shall rule over you,
Ps   3: 1 O LORD, how many are my **f!**
44: 5 Through you we push down our **f;**

110: 2 Rule in the midst of your **f.**
La 1: 5 Her **f** have become the masters,
Rev 11: 5 their mouth and consumes their **f;**

FOILED

Jdt 16: 5 **f** them by the hand of a woman.

FOLD → FOLDING, FOLDS

Ne 5:13 I also shook out the **f** of my garment
Jn 10:16 sheep that do not belong to this **f.**

FOLDING → FOLD

Pr 6:10 a little **f** of the hands to rest,
24:33 a little **f** of the hands to rest,

FOLDS → FOLD

Ps 50: 9 or goats from your **f.**

FOLLOW → FOLLOWED, FOLLOWERS, FOLLOWING, FOLLOWS

Ex 16: 4 whether they will **f** my instruction
23: 2 not **f** a majority in wrongdoing;
Dt 6:14 Do not **f** other gods, any of the gods
Jdg 2:17 they did not **f** their example.
1Sa 8: 3 Yet his sons did not **f** in his ways,
1Ki 11:10 that he should not **f** other gods;
18:21 If the LORD is God, **f** him;
Ps 23: 6 mercy shall **f** me all the days of my
Pr 20: 7 happy are the children who **f** them!
Eze 13: 3 senseless prophets who **f** their own
Mt 4:19 And he said to them, **"F** me,
8:19 "Teacher, I will **f** you wherever you
8:22 But Jesus said to him, **"F** me,
16:24 and take up their cross and **f** me.
Lk 9:23 take up their cross daily and **f** me.
9:61 Another said, "I will **f** you, Lord;
Jn 10: 4 the sheep **f** him because they know
10: 5 They will not **f** a stranger,
10:27 I know them, and they **f** me.
12:26 Whoever serves me must **f** me,
13:36 "Where I am going, you cannot **f** me
21:19 After this he said to him, **"F** me."
1Ti 5:15 have already turned away to **f** Satan.
1Pe 2:21 so that you should **f** in his steps.
2Pe 2:16 we did not **f** cleverly devised myths
Rev 14: 4 these **f** the Lamb wherever he goes.
Sir 5: 2 not **f** your inclination and strength
18:30 SELF-CONTROL Do not **f** your base
1Mc 1:44 to **f** customs strange to the land,

FOLLOWED → FOLLOW

Nu 32:11 they have not unreservedly **f** me—
Jos 14:14 he wholeheartedly **f** the LORD,
Jdg 2:12 they **f** other gods, from among the
Jer 9:14 have stubbornly **f** their own hearts
Mt 9: 9 And he got up and **f** him.
Mk 1:18 they left their nets and **f** him.
14:54 Peter had **f** him at a distance,
Lk 18:28 left our homes and **f** you."
18:43 he regained his sight and **f** him,
Rev 13: 3 the whole earth **f** the beast.

FOLLOWERS → FOLLOW

Mt 16:24 "If any want to become my **f,**

FOLLOWING → FOLLOW

Nu 32:15 If you turn away from **f** him,
Dt 28:14 **f** other gods to serve them.
Mk 14:51 A certain young man was **f** him,
Lk 22:54 But Peter was **f** at a distance.
Eph 2: 2 **f** the course of this world,
1Ti 1:18 by **f** them you may fight the good
2Pe 2:15 **f** the road of Balaam son of Bosor,

FOLLOWS → FOLLOW

Pr 10: 9 but whoever **f** perverse ways
28:18 but whoever **f** crooked ways
Eze 18: 9 **f** my statutes, and is careful
Jn 8:12 **f** me will never walk in darkness

FOLLY → FOOL

1Sa 25:25 Nabal is his name, and **f** is with him
Pr 13:16 but the fool displays **f.**
14:18 The simple are adorned with **f,**

14:24 but **f** is the garland of fools.
14:29 one who has a hasty temper exalts **f.**
15:14 but the mouths of fools feed on **f.**
16:22 but **f** is the punishment of fools.
19: 3 One's own **f** leads to ruin,
22:15 **F** is bound up in the heart of a boy,
26: 4 not answer fools according to their **f**
26: 5 Answer fools according to their **f,**
Ecc 1:17 and to know madness and **f.**
2:13 that wisdom excels **f** as light excels
10: 1 so a little **f** outweighs wisdom and
Mk 7:22 envy, slander, pride, **f.**
2Ti 3: 9 **f** will become plain to everyone.
Sir 20:31 Better are those who hide their **f**

FOOD → FOODS

Ge 1:30 I have given every green plant for **f.**
3: 6 saw that the tree was good for **f,**
9: 3 thing that lives shall be **f** for you;
Nu 21: 5 and we detest this miserable **f."**
Ps 42: 3 My tears have been my **f** day and
78:18 by demanding the **f** they craved.
104:27 to give them their **f** in due season;
111: 5 provides **f** for those who fear him;
136:25 who gives **f** to all flesh,
146: 7 who gives **f** to the hungry.
Pr 12: 9 than to be self-important and lack **f.**
12:11 till their land will have plenty of **f,**
23: 3 delicacies, for they are deceptive **f.**
31:14 she brings her **f** from far away.
31:15 while it is still night and provides **f**
Isa 65:25 but the serpent—its **f** shall be dust!
Da 1: 8 himself with the royal rations of **f**
Mt 3: 4 his **f** was locusts and wild honey.
6:25 Is not life more than **f,**
Jn 4:32 I have **f** to eat that you do not know
4:34 "My **f** is to do the will of him who
6:27 Do not work for the **f** that perishes,
6:55 for my flesh is true **f** and my blood
1Co 3: 2 I fed you with milk, not solid **f,** for
you were not ready for solid **f.**
6:13 **"F** is meant for the stomach and the
stomach for **f,"**
8: 1 concerning **f** sacrificed to idols:
8: 8 **"F** will not bring us close to God."
10: 3 and all ate the same spiritual **f,**
2Co 11:27 hungry and thirsty, often without **f,**
1Ti 6: 8 but if we have **f** and clothing,
Heb 5:14 But solid **f** is for the mature,
Jas 2:15 or sister is naked and lacks daily **f,**
Tob 1:11 from eating the **f** of the Gentiles.
1Mc 1:63 to die rather than to be defiled by **f**

FOODS → FOOD

Mk 7:19 (Thus he declared all **f** clean.)
1Ti 4: 3 and demand abstinence from **f,**
Sir 30:18 CONCERNING **F** Good things poured

FOOL → FOLLY, FOOL'S, FOOLISH, FOOLISHLY, FOOLISHNESS, FOOLS

Ps 49:10 **f** and dolt perish together and leave
Pr 1: 7 **f** and whoever utters slander is a **f**
14:16 but the **f** throws off restraint and is
15: 5 A **f** despises a parent's instruction,
17:12 to confront a **f** immersed in folly.
17:21 The one who begets a **f** gets trouble;
17:21 the parent of a **f** has no joy.
18: 2 **f** takes no pleasure in understanding,
19:10 not fitting for a **f** to live in luxury,
20: 3 but every **f** is quick to quarrel.
23: 9 Do not speak in the hearing of a **f,**
26: 4 or you will be a **f** yourself.
26: 7 does a proverb in the mouth of a **f.**
26:11 to its vomit is a **f** who reverts
27:22 Crush a **f** in a mortar with a pestle
29:11 A **f** gives full vent to anger,
29:20 There is more hope for a **f** than for
Ecc 7:17 and do not be a **f;**
Hos 9: 7 "The prophet is a **f,** the man of the
Mt 5:22 'You **f,'** you will be liable to the
Lk 12:20 But God said to him, 'You **f!**
2Co 11:21 I am speaking as a **f**—I also dare to

Sir 4:27 Do not subject yourself to a **f,**
21:14 The mind of a **f** is like a broken jar;
31:30 increases the anger of a **f**

FOOL'S → FOOL

Pr 18: 6 A **f** lips bring strife, and a **f** mouth
Sir 20:14 A **f** gift will profit you nothing,
21:16 A **f** chatter is like a burden on a

FOOLISH → FOOL

Dt 32: 6 O **f** and senseless people?
Pr 9:13 The **f** woman is loud; she is ignorant
10: 1 but a **f** child is a mother's grief.
14: 1 but the **f** tears it down with her own
15:20 but the **f** despise their mothers.
17:25 **F** children are a grief to their father
Isa 44:25 and makes their knowledge **f;**
Jer 5:21 O **f** and senseless people, who have
Mt 7:26 like a **f** man who built his house
25: 2 Five of them were **f,** and five were
Lk 24:25 he said to them, "Oh, how **f** you are,
Ro 1:14 both to the wise and to the **f**
1Co 1:20 Has not God made **f** the wisdom of
1:27 God chose what is **f** in the world
Gal 3: 1 **f** Galatians! Who has bewitched
Eph 5:17 So do not be **f,** but understand what
Tit 3: 3 For we ourselves were once **f,**
1Pe 2:15 silence the ignorance of the **f.**
Sir 42: 8 ashamed to correct the stupid or **f** or

FOOLISHLY → FOOL

1Sa 13:13 said to Saul, "You have done **f;**
2Sa 24:10 for I have done very **f."**
2Ch 16: 9 You have done **f** in this;
Pr 14:17 One who is quick-tempered acts **f,**

FOOLISHNESS → FOOL

2Sa 15:31 turn the counsel of Ahithophel into **f**
1Co 1:18 cross is **f** to those who are perishing,
1:21 God decided, through the **f** of our
1:23 a stumbling block to Jews and **f** to
1:25 For God's **f** is wiser than human
2:14 for they are **f** to them,
3:19 wisdom of this world is **f** with God.
2Co 11: 1 you would bear with me in a little **f.**

FOOLS → FOOL

Ps 14: 1 **F** say in their hearts, "There is no
God."
53: 1 **F** say in their hearts, "There is no
God."
94: 8 **f,** when will you be wise?
Pr 1: 7 **f** despise wisdom and instruction.
1:32 the complacency of **f** destroys them;
3:35 honor, but stubborn **f,** disgrace.
10:21 but **f** die for lack of sense.
12:15 **F** think their own way is right,
13:19 from evil is an abomination to **f.**
13:20 but the companion of **f** suffers harm.
14: 9 **F** mock at the guilt offering,
14:24 but folly is the garland of **f.**
16:22 but folly is the punishment of **f.**
24: 7 Wisdom is too high for **f;**
26: 4 not answer **f** according to their folly,
26: 5 Answer **f** according to their folly,
Ecc 5: 4 for he has no pleasure in **f.**
7: 4 heart of **f** is in the house of mirth.
7: 5 the wise than to hear the song of **f.**
7: 6 the laughter of **f;** this also is vanity.
Mt 23:17 You blind **f!** For which is greater,
Ro 1:22 Claiming to be wise, they became **f;**
1Co 4:10 We are **f** for the sake of Christ,
2Co 11:19 gladly put up with **f,** being wise
Sir 8:17 Do not consult with **f,** for they

FOOT → BAREFOOT, FEET, FOOTHOLD, FOOTSTOOL, FOUR-FOOTED

Ex 21:24 tooth for tooth, hand for hand, **f** for **f**
32:19 and broke them at the **f** of the
Nu 22:25 scraped Balaam's **f** against the wall;
Dt 11:24 on which you set **f** shall be yours;
Jos 1: 3 the sole of your **f** will tread upon
Ps 26:12 My **f** stands on level ground;

91:12 will not dash your **f** against a stone.
94:18 When I thought, "My **f** is slipping,"
121: 3 He will not let your **f** be moved;
Pr 1:15 keep your **f** from their paths;
3:23 on your way securely and your **f**
4:27 turn your **f** away from evil.
25:17 your **f** be seldom in your neighbor's
Isa 1: 6 From the sole of the **f** even to the
Mt 18: 8 or your **f** causes you to stumble,
Lk 4:11 not dash your **f** against a stone.'"
1Co 12:15 If the **f** would say, "Because I am
Rev 10: 2 his right **f** on the sea and his left **f** on

FOOTHOLD* → FOOT
Ps 69: 2 in deep mire, where there is no **f**;

FOOTSTOOL → FOOT
1Ch 28: 2 for the **f** of our God;
Ps 99: 5 the LORD our God; worship at his **f**.
110: 1 until I make your enemies your **f**."
Isa 66: 1 is my throne and the earth is my **f**;
La 2: 1 not remembered his **f** in the day of
Mt 5:35 for it is his **f**, or by Jerusalem,
Ac 7:49 and the earth is my **f**.
Heb 1:13 hand until I make your enemies a **f**
10:13 until his enemies would be made a **f**

FORBEARANCE
Jer 15:15 In your **f** do not take me away;
Ro 3:25 in his divine **f** he had passed over

FORBID → FORBIDDEN
Ro 2:22 You that **f** adultery, do you commit
1Co 14:39 and do not **f** speaking in tongues;
1Ti 4: 3 They **f** marriage and demand
1Mc 1:45 to **f** burnt offerings and sacrifices

FORBIDDEN → FORBID
Ac 16: 6 been **f** by the Holy Spirit to speak

FORCE → FORCED, FORCES
Ge 34: 2 and lay with her by **f**.
2Sa 13:12 "No, my brother, do not **f** me;
Jn 6:15 to come and take him by **f**
Ac 26:11 I tried to **f** them to blaspheme;

FORCED → FORCE
Ex 1:11 to oppress them with **f** labor.
Jdg 1:28 they put the Canaanites to **f** labor,
1Ki 9:15 the **f** labor that King Solomon
Phm 1:14 be voluntary and not something **f**.

FORCES → FORCE
Mt 5:41 and if anyone **f** you to go one mile,
Eph 6:12 spiritual **f** of evil in the heavenly

FORDS
Jos 2: 7 the way to the Jordan as far as the **f**.

FOREHEAD → FOREHEADS
Ex 13: 9 and as a reminder on your **f**,
28:38 It shall be on Aaron's **f**, and Aaron
Dt 6: 8 fix them as an emblem on your **f**,
11:18 fix them as an emblem on your **f**,
1Sa 17:49 and struck the Philistine on his **f**;
Rev 13:16 marked on the right hand or the **f**,
17: 5 her **f** was written a name, a mystery:

FOREHEADS → FOREHEAD
Eze 9: 4 and put a mark on the **f** of those
Rev 7: 3 of our God with a seal on their **f**."
9: 4 not have the seal of God on their **f**,
14: 1 his Father's name written on their **f**.
20: 4 not received its mark on their **f** or
22: 4 and his name will be on their **f**.

FOREIGN → FOREIGNER, FOREIGNERS
Ge 35: 2 "Put away the **f** gods that are among
Dt 32:12 no **f** god was with him.
Jos 24:23 "Then put away the **f** gods that are
1Ki 11: 1 Solomon loved many **f** women
2Ch 14: 3 He took away the **f** altars and the
33:15 He took away the **f** gods and the
Ps 81: 9 you shall not bow down to a **f** god.
Mal 2:11 married the daughter of a **f** god.

Ac 17:18 to be a proclaimer of **f** divinities."
Tob 4:12 do not marry a **f** woman,

FOREIGN GODS
Ge 35:2, 4; Dt 31:16; Jos 24:20, 23; Jdg 10:16; 1Sa 7:3; 2Ch 33:15; Jer 5:19

FOREIGN WOMEN
1Ki 11:1; Ezr 10:2, 10, 17, 18, 44; Ne 13:26, 27; 1Es 8:92; 9:7, 36

FOREIGNER → FOREIGN
Ex 12:43 no **f** shall eat of it,
Dt 17:15 not permitted to put a **f** over you,
23:20 loans to a **f** you may charge interest,
1Ki 8:41 a **f**, who is not of your people Israel,
Lk 17:18 give praise to God except this **f**?"
1Co 14:11 I will be a **f** to the speaker and the speaker a **f** to me.

FOREIGNERS → FOREIGN
Ge 31:15 Are we not regarded by him as **f**?
Ne 9: 2 separated themselves from all **f**,
Isa 2: 6 and they clasp hands with **f**.
Mt 27: 7 potter's field as a place to bury **f**.
1Co 14:21 by the lips of **f** I will speak to this
Heb 11:13 were strangers and **f** on the earth,

FOREKNEW* → KNOW
Ro 8:29 whom he **f** he also predestined to
11: 2 not rejected his people whom he **f**.

FOREKNOWLEDGE* → KNOW
Ac 2:23 according to the definite plan and **f**
Jdt 9: 6 and your judgment is with **f**.
11:19 For this was told me to give me **f**;
Wis 8: 8 she has **f** of signs and wonders

FOREMOST
1Ti 1:15 sinners—of whom I am the **f**.

FOREORDAINED* → ORDAIN
2Es 7:74 the times that he has **f**."

FORERUNNER* → RUN
Heb 6:20 a **f** on our behalf, has entered,

FORESEEING* → SEE
Ac 2:31 **F** this, David spoke of the
Gal 3: 8 **f** that God would justify the Gentiles

FORESKIN → FORESKINS
Ge 17:14 circumcised in the flesh of his **f**
Ex 4:25 took a flint and cut off her son's **f**,
Dt 10:16 Circumcise, then, the **f** of your heart
Jer 4: 4 remove the **f** of your hearts,

FORESKINS → FORESKIN
Ge 17:11 shall circumcise the flesh of your **f**,
1Sa 18:25 a hundred of **f** of the Philistines,

FOREST
2Sa 18: 8 **f** claimed more victims that day than
1Ki 7: 2 the House of the **F** of the Lebanon
1Ch 16:33 the trees of the **f** sing for joy before
Ps 50:10 every wild animal of the **f** is mine,
Jas 3: 5 How great a **f** is set ablaze by a

FORETOLD → TELL
2Ki 17:23 as he had **f** through all his servants
24:13 all this as the LORD had **f**.
Isa 43: 9 and **f** to us the former things?
Ac 3:18 this way God fulfilled what he had **f**
Sir 49: 6 streets desolate, as Jeremiah had **f**.
2Es 7:26 signs that I have **f** to you will come

FOREVER → EVER
Ge 3:22 the tree of life, and eat, and live **f**"
6: 3 spirit shall not abide in mortals **f**,
Ex 3:15 This is my name **f**, and this my title
31:17 a sign **f** between me and the people
Dt 29:29 belong to us and to our children **f**,
2Sa 7:13 the throne of his kingdom **f**.
7:26 Thus your name will be magnified **f**
1Ki 2:33 on the head of his descendants **f**;
9: 3 and put my name there **f**;
1Ch 16:15 Remember his covenant **f**,
16:41 for his steadfast love endures **f**.

17:24 be established and magnified **f** in
2Ch 5:13 for his steadfast love endures **f**,"
33: 7 I will put my name **f**;
Ezr 3:11 for his steadfast love endures **f**
Ps 9: 7 But the LORD sits enthroned **f**,
19: 9 fear of the LORD is pure, enduring **f**;
28: 9 be their shepherd, and carry them **f**.
29:10 the LORD sits enthroned as king **f**.
33:11 The counsel of the LORD stands **f**,
37:28 The righteous shall be kept safe **f**,
44: 8 we will give thanks to your name **f**.
44:23 Awake, do not cast us off **f**!
61: 4 Let me abide in your tent **f**,
72:19 Blessed be his glorious name **f**;
73:26 of my heart and my portion **f**.
74:10 Is the enemy to revile your name **f**?
77: 8 Has his steadfast love ceased **f**?
79:13 will give thanks to you **f**;
81:15 and their doom would last **f**.
86:12 and I will glorify your name **f**.
89: 1 of your steadfast love, O LORD, **f**;
92: 8 but you, O LORD, are on high **f**.
100: 5 his steadfast love endures **f**,
102:12 But you, O LORD, are enthroned **f**;
104:31 May the glory of the LORD endure **f**;
107: 1 for his steadfast love endures **f**.
110: 4 "You are a priest **f** according to the
111: 3 and his righteousness endures **f**.
112: 6 they will be remembered **f**.
117: 2 faithfulness of the LORD endures **f**.
118: 1 his steadfast love endures **f**!
119:111 Your decrees are my heritage **f**;
119:152 that you have established them **f**.
136: 1 for his steadfast love endures **f**,
146: 6 in them; who keeps faith **f**;
Pr 10:25 but the righteous are established **f**.
27:24 for riches do not last **f**,
Ecc 3:14 that whatever God does endures **f**;
Isa 26: 4 the LORD **f**, for in the LORD GOD
32:17 righteousness, quietness and trust **f**.
40: 8 the word of our God will stand **f**.
51: 6 but my salvation will be **f**,
51: 8 but my deliverance will be **f**,
59:21 says the LORD, from now on and **f**.
Jer 3:12 I will not be angry **f**.
33:11 for his steadfast love endures **f**!"
La 5:19 But you, O LORD, reign **f**;
Da 2:44 to an end, and it shall stand **f**;
6:26 For he is the living God, enduring **f**,
Hos 2:19 And I will take you for my wife **f**;
Jn 6:51 eats of this bread will live **f**;
14:16 another Advocate, to be with you **f**,
Ro 9: 5 who is over all, God blessed **f**.
16:27 Christ, to whom be the glory **f**!
1Th 4:17 and so we will be with the Lord **f**.
Heb 5: 6 "You are a priest **f**, according to the
7:17 "You are a priest **f**, according to the
7:24 because he continues **f**.
13: 8 the same yesterday and today and **f**.
1Pe 1:25 but the word of the Lord endures **f**."
1Jn 2:17 those who do the will of God live **f**.
2Jn 1: 2 abides in us and will be with us **f**.
Rev 1:18 I am alive **f** and ever;
4: 9 who lives **f** and ever,
11:15 and he will reign **f** and ever."
20:10 tormented day and night **f** and ever.
22: 5 and they will reign **f** and ever.
Tob 3:11 Blessed is your name **f**;
Wis 5:15 But the righteous live **f**,
Sir 40:17 and almsgiving endures **f**.
41:13 but a good name lasts **f**.
51:12 *for his mercy endures f;*
Bar 3: 3 For you are enthroned **f**, and we are perishing **f**.
Aza 1:35 praise to him and highly exalt him **f**.
1Mc 4:24 for his mercy endures **f**."
Man 1:13 Do not be angry with me **f**

FOREVER AND EVER
Ex 15:18; 1Ch 29:10; Ps 9:5; 10:16; 21:4; 45:6, 17; 48:14; 52:8; 111:8; 119:44; 145:1, 2, 21; 148:6; Isa 34:10; Jer 7:7; Da 7:18; 12:3; Mic 4:5; Gal 1:5; Eph 3:21; Php 4:20; 1Ti 1:17; 2Ti 4:18;

Heb 1:8; 13:21; 1Pe 4:11; 5:11; Rev 1:6, 18; 4:9, 10; 5:13; 7:12; 10:6; 11:15; 14:11; 15:7; 19:3; 20:10; 22:5; Tob 13:17; 14:15; 1Es 4:38; 4Mc 18:24

HIS MERCY ENDURES FOREVER Sir 51:12, 12, 12, 12, 12, 12, 12, 12, 12, 12, 12, 12, 12, 12; Aza 1:67, 68; 1Mc 4:24

LIVE FOREVER Ge 3:22; Dt 32:40; 1Ki 1:31; Ne 2:3; Job 7:16; Ps 22:26; Da 2:4; 3:9; 5:10; 6:6, 21; Zec 1:5; Jn 6:51, 58; 1Jn 2:17; Wis 5:15; Sir 37:26

STEADFAST LOVE ENDURES FOREVER 1Ch 16:34, 41; 2Ch 5:13; 7:3, 6; 20:21; Ezr 3:11; Ps 100:5; 106:1; 107:1; 118:1, 2, 3, 4, 29; 136:1, 2, 3, 4, 5, 6, 7, 8, 9, 10, 11, 12, 13, 14, 15, 16, 17, 18, 19, 20, 21, 22, 23, 24, 25, 26; Jer 33:11

WHO LIVES FOREVER Da 4:34; 12:7; Rev 4:9, 10; 10:6; 15:7; Tob 13:1; Sir 18:1

FOREVERMORE → EVER

Ps 16:11 in your right hand are pleasures **f.**
125:2 from this time on and **f.**
131:3 in the LORD from this time on and **f.**
Tob 12:17 peace be with you. Bless God **f.**

FOREWARNED → WARN

2Pe 3:17 beloved, since you are **f,**

FORFEIT → FORFEITED, FORFEITS

Mk 8:36 the whole world and **f** their life?
Lk 9:25 but lose or **f** themselves?

FORFEITED → FORFEIT

Hab 2:10 you have **f** your life.

FORFEITS* → FORFEIT

Pr 20:2 provokes him to anger **f** life itself.

FORGAVE* → FORGIVE

Ps 32:5 and you **f** the guilt of my sin.
78:38 compassionate, **f** their iniquity,
85:2 You **f** the iniquity of your people;
Mt 18:27 released him and **f** him the debt.
18:32 I **f** you all that debt because you
Col 2:13 when he **f** us all our trespasses,

FORGET → FORGETFUL, FORGETTING, FORGOT, FORGOTTEN

Ge 41:51 God has made me **f** all my hardship
Dt 4:23 So be careful not to **f** the covenant
6:12 take care that you do not **f** the LORD,
2Ki 17:38 not **f** the covenant that I have made
Job 8:13 Such are the paths of all who **f** God;
Ps 9:17 all the nations that **f** God.
10:12 do not **f** the oppressed.
50:22 "Mark this, then, you who **f** God,
78:7 and not **f** the works of God,
103:2 my soul, and do not **f** all his benefits
119:93 I will never **f** your precepts,
137:5 If I **f** you, O Jerusalem, let my right
Pr 3:1 My child, do not **f** my teaching,
4:5 Get wisdom; get insight: do not **f,**
31:5 else they will drink and **f** what has
Isa 49:15 these may **f,** yet I will not **f** you.
Jer 2:32 Can a girl **f** her ornaments, or a
1Mc 1:49 so that they would **f** the law

FORGETFUL* → FORGET

2Pe 1:9 and is **f** of the cleansing of past sins.

FORGETTING → FORGET

Dt 8:14 **f** the LORD your God, who brought
Php 3:13 **f** what lies behind and straining

FORGIVE* → FORGAVE, FORGIVEN, FORGIVENESS, FORGIVES, FORGIVING

Ge 18:24 and not **f** it for the fifty righteous
18:26 **f** the whole place for their sake."
50:17 **f** the crime of your brothers and
50:17 please **f** the crime of the servants
Ex 10:17 Do **f** my sin just this once,
32:32 But now, if you will only **f** their sin
Nu 14:19 **F** the iniquity of this people
14:20 the LORD said, "I do **f,** just as you
30:5 and the LORD will **f** her,
30:8 and the LORD will **f** her.
30:12 and the LORD will **f** her.
Jos 24:19 he will not **f** your transgressions or
1Sa 25:28 Please **f** the trespass of your servant;
1Ki 8:30 your dwelling place; heed and **f.**
8:34 **f** the sin of your people Israel,
8:36 and **f** the sin of your servants,
8:39 **f,** act, and render
8:50 and **f** your people who have sinned
2Ch 6:21 your dwelling place; hear and **f.**
6:25 and **f** the sin of your people Israel,
6:27 **f** the sin of your servants, your
6:30 **f,** and render to all whose heart you
6:39 and **f** your people who have sinned
7:14 will **f** their sin and heal their land.
Ne 9:17 But you are a God ready to **f,**
Ps 25:18 and my trouble, and **f** all my sins.
65:3 you **f** our transgressions.
79:9 and **f** our sins, for your name's sake.
Isa 2:9 is brought low—do not **f** them!
Jer 18:23 Do not **f** their iniquity, do not blot
31:34 for I will **f** their iniquity,
33:8 and I will **f** all the guilt of their sin
36:3 so that I may **f** their iniquity and
Eze 16:63 when I **f** you all that you have done,
Da 9:19 O Lord, hear; O Lord, **f;**
Hos 1:6 on the house of Israel or **f** them.
Am 7:2 I said, "O Lord GOD, **f,** I beg you!
Mt 6:12 And **f** us our debts, as we
6:14 if you **f** others their trespasses, your heavenly Father will also **f** you;
6:15 but if you do not **f** others, neither will your Father **f** your trespasses.
9:6 has authority on earth to **f** sins"—
18:21 against me, how often should I **f?**
18:35 not **f** your brother or sister from
Mk 2:7 Who can **f** sins but God alone?"
2:10 has authority on earth to **f** sins"—
11:25 "Whenever you stand praying, **f,**
11:25 may also **f** you your trespasses."
Lk 5:21 Who can **f** sins but God alone?"
5:24 has authority on earth to **f** sins"—
6:37 **F,** and you will be forgiven;
11:4 And **f** us our sins, for we ourselves **f** everyone indebted to us.
17:3 if there is repentance, you must **f.**
17:4 and says, 'I repent,' you must **f."**
23:34 [Then Jesus said, "Father, **f** them;]
Jn 20:23 If you **f** the sins of any, they are
2Co 2:7 so now instead you should **f** and
2:10 Anyone whom you **f,** I also **f.**
12:13 not burden you? **F** me this wrong!
Col 3:13 against another, **f** each other;
3:13 forgiven you, so you also must **f.**
1Jn 1:9 is faithful and just will **f** us our sins
Sir 5:6 he will **f** the multitude of my sins,"
16:7 not **f** the ancient giants who revolted
16:11 he is mighty to **f**—but he also pours
28:2 **F** your neighbor the wrong he has
34:23 of sacrifices does he **f** sins.
Man 1:13 **f** me, O Lord, **f** me!

FORGIVEN → FORGIVE

Lev 4:20 for them, and they shall be **f.**
19:22 he committed shall be **f** him.
Nu 15:25 Israelites, and they shall be **f;**
Ps 32:1 are those whose transgression is **f,**
Mt 6:12 as we also have **f** our debtors.
9:5 easier, to say, 'Your sins are **f,'**
12:31 against the Spirit will not be **f.**
Mk 2:9 to the paralytic, 'Your sins are **f,'**
Lk 6:37 Forgive, and you will be **f;**
7:47 one to whom little is **f,** loves little."
Ac 2:38 so that your sins may be **f;**
Ro 4:7 are those whose iniquities are **f,**
Eph 4:32 as God in Christ has **f** you.
Col 3:13 just as the Lord has **f** you,
Jas 5:15 who has committed sins will be **f.**
1Jn 2:12 sins are **f** on account of his name.

FORGIVENESS → FORGIVE

Ps 130:4 there is **f** with you, so that you may
Da 9:9 Lord our God belong mercy and **f,**
Mt 26:28 poured out for many for the **f** of sins
Mk 1:4 a baptism of repentance for the **f**
3:29 against the Holy Spirit can never have **f,**
Lk 1:77 to his people by the **f** of their sins.
3:3 a baptism of repentance for the **f**
24:47 that repentance and **f** of sins is to be
Ac 5:31 might give repentance to Israel and **f**
10:43 who believes in him receives **f**
13:38 this man **f** of sins is proclaimed to
26:18 so that they may receive **f** of sins
Eph 1:7 the **f** of our trespasses,
Col 1:14 we have redemption, the **f** of sins.
Heb 9:22 the shedding of blood there is no **f**
10:18 Where there is **f** of these,
Sir 5:5 not be so confident of **f** that you add
21:1 but ask **f** for your past sins.

FORGIVENESS OF SINS Mt 26:28; Mk 1:4; Lk 1:77; 3:3; 24:47; Ac 5:31; 10:43; 13:38; 26:18; Col 1:14; Heb 9:22

FORGIVES* → FORGIVE

Ps 103:3 who **f** all your iniquity, who heals
Pr 17:9 who **f** an affront fosters friendship,
Lk 7:49 "Who is this who even **f** sins?"
Sir 2:11 **f** sins and saves in time of distress.

FORGIVING* → FORGIVE

Ex 34:7 **f** iniquity and transgression and sin,
Nu 14:18 **f** iniquity and transgression,
Ps 86:5 For you, O Lord, are good and **f,**
99:8 you were a **f** God to them,
Eph 4:32 **f** one another, as God in Christ has

FORGOT → FORGET

Ge 40:23 not remember Joseph, but **f** him.
Dt 32:18 you **f** the God who gave you birth.
1Sa 12:9 But they **f** the LORD their God;
Ps 78:11 They **f** what he had done,
106:13 But they soon **f** his works;
106:21 They **f** God, their Savior,
Jer 23:27 just as their ancestors **f** my name
Hos 2:13 and went after her lovers, and **f** me,
Bar 4:8 You **f** the everlasting God,

FORGOTTEN → FORGET

Ps 9:18 For the needy shall not always be **f,**
10:11 think in their heart, "God has **f,**
44:20 If we had **f** the name of our God,
77:9 Has God **f** to be gracious?
Isa 17:10 have **f** the God of your salvation,
49:14 forsaken me, my Lord has **f** me."
Jer 2:32 Yet my people have **f** me,
Hos 8:14 Israel has **f** his Maker, and built
Mt 16:5 they had **f** to bring any bread.
Lk 12:6 not one of them is **f** in God's sight.
Heb 12:5 And you have **f** the exhortation
Sir 35:9 and it will never be **f.**

FORK

Jer 15:7 winnowed them with a winnowing **f**
Mt 3:12 His winnowing **f** is in his hand,

FORM → FORMED, FORMLESS, FORMS

Ex 20:4 in the **f** of anything that is in heaven
Nu 12:8 and he beholds the **f** of the LORD.
Dt 4:15 Since you saw no **f** when the LORD
Isa 52:14 and his **f** beyond that of mortals—
Eze 1:5 they were of human **f.**
Lk 3:22 descended upon him in bodily **f**
Jn 5:37 never heard his voice or seen his **f,**
Ac 14:11 have come down to us in human **f!"**
1Co 7:31 the present **f** of this world is passing
Php 2:6 though he was in the **f** of God,
1Th 5:22 abstain from every **f** of evil.
2Ti 3:5 outward **f** of godliness but denying

FORMED → FORM

Ge 2:7 the LORD God **f** man from the dust
Job 33:6 I too was **f** from a piece of clay.

Ps   94: 9 He who f the eye, does he not see?
    139:13 you who f my inward parts;
Isa 29:16 or the thing f say of the one who f it,
    43: 1 O Jacob, he who f you,
    43:10 me no god was f, nor shall there
    44: 2 who f you in the womb
    45:18 a chaos, the f it to be inhabited!):
    49: 5 f me in the womb to be his servant,
Jer   1: 5 "Before I f you in the womb I knew
Gal   4:19 until Christ is f in you,
1Ti   2:13 For Adam was f first, then Eve;
2Pe   3: 5 and an earth was f out of water and
Sir 51:12 to him who f all things,

FORMER

Dt   4:32 ask now about f ages, long before
Isa 41:22 Tell us the f things,
    46: 9 remember the f things of old;
Eph 4:22 to put away your f way of life,
1Pe 3:20 who in f times did not obey,
1Mc 4:47 a new altar like the f one.

FORMLESS* → FORM

Ge   1: 2 the earth was a f void and darkness
Wis 11:17 created the world out of f matter,

FORMS → FORM

Am   4:13 For lo, the one who f the mountains,

FORNICATION → FORNICATOR, FORNICATORS

Mk   7:21 that evil intentions come: f,
Ac 15:20 from f and from whatever has been
1Co 6:13 meant not for f but for the Lord,
Gal 5:19 works of the flesh are obvious: f,
Eph 5: 3 But f and impurity of any kind,
Col 3: 5 f, impurity, passion, evil desire,
1Th 4: 3 that you abstain from f;
Rev 14: 8 of the wine of the wrath of her f."
    19: 2 who corrupted the earth with her f,
Tob 4:12 "Beware, my son, of every kind of f.

FORNICATOR* → FORNICATION

1Co 6:18 but the f sins against the body itself.
Eph 5: 5 that no f or impure person,
Sir 23:17 To a f all bread is sweet;

FORNICATORS* → FORNICATION

1Co 6: 9 F, idolaters, adulterers, male
1Ti   1:10 f, sodomites, slave traders, liars,
Heb 13: 4 for God will judge f and adulterers.
Rev 21: 8 the murderers, the f, the sorcerers,
    22:15 and sorcerers and f and murderers

FORSAKE → FORSAKEN, FORSAKES, FORSAKING

Dt 31: 6 he will not fail you or f you."
Jos   1: 5 I will not fail you or f you.
    24:16 For the LORD to serve other gods;
1Ch 28: 9 but if you f him, he will abandon
Ps 27:10 If my father and mother f me,
    94:14 For the LORD will not f his people;
    138: 8 Do not f the work of your hands.
Pr   4: 6 Do not f her, and she will keep you;
    27:10 Do not f your friend or the friend of
Isa   1:28 and those who f the LORD shall be
    55: 7 let the wicked f their way,
Jer 17:13 All who f you shall be put to shame;
Heb 13: 5 "I will never leave you or f you."
Sir 17:25 back to the Lord and f your sins;

FORSAKEN → FORSAKE

Ps   9:10 O LORD, have not f those who seek
    22: 1 my God, why have you f me?
    37:25 righteous f or their children begging
    119:87 but I have not f your precepts.
Isa   1: 4 who have f the LORD,
    49:14 But Zion said, "The LORD has f me,
Mt 27:46 my God, why have you f me?"
2Co 4: 9 persecuted, but not f;
Jdt   9:11 protector of the f,
Bel   1:38 not f those who love you."

FORSAKES → FORSAKE

Pr   2:17 who f the partner of her youth
Sir   3:16 f a father is like a blasphemer,

FORSAKING → FORSAKE

1Sa 8: 8 f me and serving other gods,
Hos 4:12 played the whore, f their God.

FORTH

Ps 19: 2 Day to day pours f speech,
    50: 2 perfection of beauty, God shines f.

FORTIFIED → FORTRESS

Nu 13:28 and the towns are f and very large;
Dt   9: 1 great cities, f to the heavens,

FORTIFIED CITIES Nu 32:36; Jos 14:12;
1Sa 6:18; 2Sa 20:6; 2Ki 18:13; 19:25; 2Ch
8:5; 11:10, 23; 12:4; 14:6; 17:2, 19; 19:5; 21:3;
32:1; 33:14; 34a 36:1; 37:26; Jer 4:5; 5:17;
8:14; 34:7; Hos 8:14; Zep 1:16; 1Mc 1:19

FORTIFIED CITY Jos 19:29; 2Ki 3:19; 10:2;
17:9; 18:8; Ps 60:9; 108:10; Isa 25:2; 27:10;
Jer 1:18

FORTRESS → FORTIFIED, FORTRESSES

2Sa 22: 2 The LORD is my rock, my f, and my
Ps 31: 2 refuge for me, a strong f to save me.
    59: 9 for you, O God, are my f.
    62: 2 my rock and my salvation, my f;
    71: 3 for you are my rock and my f;

FORTRESSES → FORTRESS

Da 11:38 He shall honor the god of f

FORTUNE → FORTUNE-TELLING, FORTUNES

Ge 30:11 "Good f!" so she named him Gad.
Isa 65:11 who set a table for F

FORTUNE-TELLING* → FORTUNE, TELL

Ac 16:16 a great deal of money by f.

FORTUNES → FORTUNE

Dt 30: 3 LORD your God will restore your f
Ps 53: 6 God restores the f of his people,
Jer 32:44 I will restore their f, says the LORD.
Hos 6:11 When I would restore the f of my

FORTY

Ge   7: 4 rain on the earth for f days and f
          nights;
    18:29 "Suppose f are found there."
Ex 16:35 The Israelites ate manna f years,
    24:18 the mountain for f days and f nights.
Nu 14:34 f days, for every day a year,
Dt 25: 3 F lashes may be given but not more;
Jos 14: 7 I was f years old when Moses the
1Sa 4:18 He had judged Israel f years.
2Sa 5: 4 to reign, and he reigned f years.
1Ki 19: 8 f days and f nights to Horeb
2Ch 9:30 in Jerusalem over all Israel f years.
Ne   9:21 F years you sustained them in the
Eze 29:12 cities shall be a desolation f years
Am   2:10 led you f years in the wilderness,
Jnh 3: 4 And he cried out, "F days more,
Mt   4: 2 He fasted f days and f nights,
Lk   4: 2 f days he was tempted by the devil.
2Co 11:24 from the Jews the f lashes minus
Heb 3:17 with whom was he angry f years?
2Es 14:42 They sat f days; they wrote

FORTY DAYS Ge 7:4, 12, 17; 8:6; 50:3; Ex
24:18; 34:28; Nu 13:25; 14:34; Dt 9:9, 11, 18,
25; 10:10; 1Sa 17:16; 1Ki 19:8; Eze 4:6; Jnh
3:4; Mt 4:2; Mk 1:13; Lk 4:2; Ac 1:3; Tob
1:21; 2Mc 5:2; 3Mc 4:15; 6:38; 2Es 14:23, 36,
42, 44, 45

FORTY NIGHTS Ge 7:4, 12; Ex 24:18;
34:28; Dt 9:9, 11, 18, 25; 10:10; 1Ki 19:8; Mt
4:2

FORTY YEARS Ge 5:13; 25:20; 26:34; Ex
16:35; Nu 14:33, 34; 32:13; Dt 2:7; 8:2, 4;

29:5; Jos 5:6; 14:7; Jdg 3:11; 5:31; 8:28; 13:1;
1Sa 4:18; 2Sa 2:10; 5:4; 1Ki 2:11; 11:42; 2Ki
12:1; 1Ch 29:27; 2Ch 9:30; 24:1; Ne 9:21; Job
42:16; Ps 95:10; Eze 29:11, 12, 13; Am 2:10;
5:25; Ac 4:22; 7:23, 30, 36, 42; 13:18, 21; Heb
3:10, 17

FOUGHT → FIGHT

Jos 10:42 the LORD God of Israel f for Israel.
1Co 15:32 If with wild animals
2Ti 4: 7 I have f the good fight, I have
Rev 12: 7 and his angels f against the dragon.

FOUND → FIND

Ge   6: 8 Noah f favor in the sight of the
Ex 12:19 no leaven shall be f in your houses;
    33:12 you have also f favor in my sight.'
2Ki 22: 8 "I have f the book of the law in the
1Ch 28: 9 If you seek him, he will be f by you;
2Ch 15:15 whole desire, and he was f by them,
Pr 10:13 who has understanding wisdom is f,
Ecc 7:27 See, this is what I f,
Isa 55: 6 Seek the LORD while he may be f,
    65: 1 be f by those who did not seek me.
Jer 15:16 Your words were f,
Da   1:19 was f to compare with Daniel,
    5:27 on the scales and f wanting;
    12: 1 who is f written in the book.
Mt   1:18 she was f to be with child from the
          Holy Spirit.
Lk   1:30 for you have f favor with God.
    7: 9 not even in Israel have I f such faith.
    15: 6 for I have f my sheep that was lost.'
    15: 9 for I have f the coin that I had lost.'
    15:24 he was lost and is f!'
Ro 10:20 f by those who did not seek me;
Php 2: 7 And being f in human form,
Rev 5: 4 no one was f worthy to open the
    20:15 not f written in the book of life was
1Mc 1:56 The books of the law that they f

FOUNDATION → FOUNDATIONS, FOUNDED

1Ki 6:37 f of the house of the LORD was laid,
Ezr 3: 6 f of the temple of the LORD was not
Job 38: 4 "Where were you when I laid the f
Ps 97: 2 and justice are the f of his throne.
Isa 28:16 See, I am laying in Zion a f stone,
    28:16 a precious cornerstone, a sure f:
Lk 14:29 when he has laid a f and is not able
Ro 15:20 I do not build on someone else's f,
1Co 3:10 a skilled master builder I laid a f,
    3:11 that f is Jesus Christ.
Eph 2:20 built upon the f of the apostles and
2Ti 2:19 But God's firm f stands, bearing
Heb 6: 1 and not laying again the f:

FOUNDATIONS → FOUNDATION

Ps 82: 5 all the f of the earth are shaken.
    137: 7 Tear it down! Down to its f!"
Pr   8:29 he marked out the f of the earth,
Isa 54:11 and lay your f with sapphires.
Heb 11:10 looked forward to the city that has f,
Rev 21:14 the wall of the city has twelve f,
2Es 6: 2 before the f of paradise were laid,

FOUNDATIONS OF THE EARTH Ps
82:5; Pr 8:29; Isa 24:18; 40:21; 51:13, 16; Jer
31:37; Mic 6:2; Sir 10:16; 16:19; 2Es 6:15;
15:23; 16:15

FOUNDED → FOUNDATION

Ps 78:69 the earth, which he has f forever.
Pr   3:19 The LORD by wisdom f the earth;
Isa 14:32 "The LORD has f Zion,
Mt   7:25 because it had been f on rock.

FOUNTAIN → FOUNTAINS

Ps 36: 9 With you is the f of life;
    68:26 O you who are of Israel's f!"
Pr   5:18 Let your f be blessed, and rejoice in
    10:11 mouth of the righteous is a f of life,
    13:14 teaching of the wise is a f of life,
    14:27 The fear of the LORD is a f of life,

16:22 Wisdom is a **f** of life to one who
18: 4 the **f** of wisdom is a gushing stream.
SS   4:12 bride, a garden locked, a **f** sealed.
Jer   9: 1 and my eyes a **f** of tears,
Joel 3:18 a **f** shall come forth from the house
Zec 13: 1 a **f** shall be opened for the house of
Wis 11: 6 Instead of the **f** of an ever-flowing
Bar   3:12 You have forsaken the **f** of wisdom.
2Es 14:47 the **f** of wisdom, and the river of

FOUNTAINS → FOUNTAIN
Ge   7:11 that day all the **f** of the great deep
Pr   8:28 he established the **f** of the deep,

FOUR → FOURSQUARE, FOURTH
Ge   2:10 divides and becomes **f** branches.
1Ki 18:19 **f** hundred fifty prophets of Baal and
        the **f** hundred prophets of Asherah,
Job 42:16 children's children, **f** generations.
Pr   30:15 **f** never say, "Enough":
     30:18 **f** I do not understand:
     30:21 under **f** it cannot bear up:
     30:24 **F** things on earth are small,
     30:29 **f** are stately in their gait:
Isa 11:12 of Judah from the **f** corners of
Eze   1: 5 something like **f** living creatures.
     10: 9 were **f** wheels beside the cherubim,
     10:14 Each one had **f** faces:
Da   1:17 To these **f** young men God gave
      7: 3 **f** great beasts came up out of the sea
      8: 8 there came up **f** prominent horns
        toward the **f** winds
Zec   1:20 the LORD showed me **f** blacksmiths.
      6: 5 "These are the **f** winds of heaven
Mt   15:38 who had eaten were **f** thousand men,
Mk   8:20 "And the seven for the **f** thousand,
Jn   4:35 Do you not say, '**F** months more,
Rev   4: 6 are **f** living creatures,
      9:14 Release the **f** angels who are bound

FOURSQUARE* → FOUR, SQUARE
Rev 21:16 The city lies **f**, its length

FOURTEEN
Mt   1:17 Abraham to David are **f** generations;
      1:17 to Babylon, **f** generations;
      1:17 to the Messiah, **f** generations.
2Co 12: 2 who **f** years ago was caught up

FOURTH → FOUR
Ge   15:16 come back here in the **f** generation;
Ex   20: 5 the **f** generation of those who reject
Da   3:25 the **f** has the appearance of a god."

FOWLER*
Ps   91: 3 deliver you from the snare of the **f**
Pr   6: 5 like a bird from the hand of the **f**.

FOX* → FOXES
Ne   4: 3 any **f** going up on it would break it
Lk   13:32 to them, "Go and tell that **f** for me,

FOXES → FOX
Jdg 15: 4 went and caught three hundred **f**,
SS   2:15 Catch us the **f**, the little **f**,
Lk   9:58 Jesus said to him, "**F** have holes,

FRACTURE*
Lev 24:20 **f** for **f**, eye for eye, tooth for tooth;

FRAGRANCE → FRAGRANT
SS   4:16 that its **f** may be wafted abroad.
Jn   12: 3 was filled with the **f** of the perfume.
2Co   2:14 spreads in every place the **f**
      2:16 to the other a **f** from life to life.

FRAGRANT → FRAGRANCE
Ex   25: 6 anointing oil and for the **f** incense,
     30: 7 Aaron shall offer **f** incense on it;
Eph   5: 2 a **f** offering and sacrifice to God.
Php   4:18 the gifts you sent, a **f** offering,

FRAME → FRAMES
Ps 139:15 My **f** was not hidden from you,

FRAMES → FRAME
Ex   26:15 You shall make upright **f** of acacia
Nu   3:36 the **f** of the tabernacle, the bars,

FRANKINCENSE → INCENSE
Isa 60: 6 They shall bring gold and **f**,
Mt   2:11 gifts of gold, **f**, and myrrh.

FREE → FREED, FREEDOM, FREELY, FREEWILL
Ex   21: 2 in the seventh he shall go out a **f**
Ps 146: 7 The LORD sets the prisoners **f**;
Lk   13:12 you are set **f** from your ailment."
Jn   8:32 and the truth will make you **f**."
      8:36 if the Son makes you **f**, you will be
        indeed.
Ac   13:39 Jesus everyone who believes is set **f**
Ro   5:15 But the **f** gift is not like the trespass.
      6:18 having been set **f** from sin,
      6:23 but the **f** gift of God is eternal life
      8: 2 Jesus has set you **f** from the law
1Co   9:21 not **f** from God's law but am under
     12:13 Jews or Greeks, slaves or **f**—
Gal   3:28 there is no longer slave or **f**,
      4:22 and the other by a **f** woman.
      5: 1 For freedom Christ has set us **f**.
Eph   6: 8 whether we are slaves or **f**.
Heb 13: 5 your lives **f** from the love of money,
1Pe   2:16 As servants of God, live as **f** people,

FREED → FREE
Ex   6: 7 who has **f** you from the burdens of
Ac   2:24 having **f** him from death,
Ro   6: 7 For whoever has died is **f** from sin.
Rev   1: 5 **f** us from our sins by his blood,

FREEDOM → FREE
Ro   8:21 and will obtain the **f** of the glory
1Co   7:21 Even if you can gain your **f**,
2Co   3:17 the Spirit of the Lord is, there is **f**.
Gal   5: 1 For **f** Christ has set us free.
1Pe   2:16 not use your **f** as a pretext for evil.
2Pe   2:19 They promise them **f**,

FREELY → FREE
Ge   2:16 "You may **f** eat of every tree
Hos 14: 4 I will love them **f**,
Eph   1: 6 glorious grace that he **f** bestowed

FREEWILL → FREE, WILL
Ex   35:29 as a **f** offering to the LORD.
Ezr   1: 4 **f** offerings for the house of God
Ps   54: 6 With a **f** offering I will sacrifice to
FREEWILL OFFERING Ex 35:29; Lev
7:16; 22:18, 21, 23; Nu 15:3; Dt 16:10; 1Ch
29:14; Ezr 3:5; 8:28; Ps 54:6; Eze 46:12, 12
FREEWILL OFFERINGS Ex 36:3, 3; Lev
23:38; Nu 29:39; Dt 12:6, 17; 1Ch 29:6; 2Ch
31:14; Ezr 1:4; 2:68; 7:16; Am 4:5; Jdt 4:14;
16:18

FRENZY
1Sa 10: 5 they will be in a prophetic **f**.
     19:20 the company of the prophets in a **f**,

FRESH
Eze 47: 8 the water will become **f**.
Jas   3:11 both **f** and brackish water?

FRET* → FRETFUL
Ps   37: 1 Do not **f** because of the wicked;
     37: 7 do not **f** over those who prosper in
     37: 8 Do not **f**—it leads only to evil.
Pr   24:19 Do not **f** because of evildoers.
Sir   6:25 and do not **f** under her bonds.

FRETFUL* → FRET
Pr   21:19 than with a contentious and **f** wife.

FRIEND → FRIENDLESS, FRIENDLY, FRIENDS, FRIENDSHIP
Ex   33:11 as one speaks to a **f**.
Dt   13: 6 or your most intimate **f**—

2Sa 16:17 "Is this your loyalty to your **f**?
2Ch 20: 7 the descendants of your **f** Abraham?
Ps   41: 9 Even my bosom **f** in whom I trusted,
Pr   17:17 A **f** loves at all times,
     18:24 but a true **f** sticks closer than one's
     27: 6 Well meant are the wounds a **f**
     27:10 Do not forsake your **f** or the **f** of
SS   5:16 This is my beloved and this is my **f**,
Isa 41: 8 the offspring of Abraham, my **f**;
Mt   11:19 a **f** of tax collectors and sinners!'
Lk   11: 8 anything because he is his **f**,
Jn   3:29 The **f** of the bridegroom,
     19:12 you are no **f** of the emperor.
Jas   2:23 and he was called the **f** of God.
      4: 4 a **f** of the world becomes an enemy
Sir   7:18 Do not exchange a **f** for money,
      9:10 A new **f** is like new wine;
     12: 8 A **f** is not known in prosperity,
     25: 9 Happy is the one who finds a **f**,
     27:17 Love your **f** and keep faith with him

FRIENDLESS* → FRIEND
Pr   19: 4 but the poor are left **f**.

FRIENDLY → FRIEND
Sir 12: 9 One's enemies are **f** when

FRIENDS → FRIEND
Job   2:11 when Job's three **f** heard of all
     42:10 of Job when he had prayed for his **f**;
Pr   16:28 and a whisperer separates close **f**.
La   1: 2 all her **f** have dealt treacherously
Zec 13: 6 I received in the house of my **f**."
Jn   15:13 to lay down one's life for one's **f**.
     15:14 my **f** if you do what I command you
3Jn   1:15 The **f** send you their greetings.
Sir   6: 5 Pleasant speech multiplies **f**,
      6:15 Faithful **f** are beyond price;
     37: 1 but some **f** are **f** only in name.

FRIENDSHIP → FRIEND
Ps   25:14 The **f** of the LORD is for those who
Jas   4: 4 know that **f** with the world is enmity
Wis   7:14 those who get it obtain **f** with God,

FRIGHTEN
Dt   28:26 shall be no one to **f** them away.
Ne   6: 9 for they all wanted to **f** us,

FRINGE → FRINGES
Nu   15:38 a blue cord on the **f** at each corner.
Mt   9:20 and touched the **f** of his cloak,
     14:36 might touch even the **f** of his cloak;

FRINGES* → FRINGE
Nu   15:38 to make **f** on the corners of their
Mt   23: 5 phylacteries broad and their **f** long.

FROGS
Ex   8: 2 plague your whole country with **f**.
Rev 16:13 I saw three foul spirits like **f** coming

FRONT
Ex   14:19 the pillar of cloud moved from in **f**
     32:15 written on the **f** and on the back.
Eze   2:10 writing on the **f** and on the back,
Rev   4: 6 full of eyes in **f** and behind:

FROST
Ex   16:14 as fine as **f** on the ground.
Zec 14: 6 there shall not be either cold or **f**.

FRUIT → FRUITFUL, FRUITLESS, FRUITS
Ge   1:11 and **f** trees of every kind on earth
      3: 3 not eat of the **f** of the tree that is in
      3: 6 she took of its **f** and ate;
Dt   28: 4 Blessed shall be the **f** of your womb,
     28:53 you will eat the **f** of your womb,
Jdg   9:11 and my delicious **f**,
Ps   1: 3 which yield their **f** in its season,
     92:14 In old age they still produce **f**;
Pr   8:19 My **f** is better than gold,
     11:30 **f** of the righteous is a tree of life,
     12:14 the **f** of the mouth one is filled with
     27:18 who tends a fig tree will eat its **f**,

31:31 share in the **f** of her hands,
Isa 27: 6 and fill the whole world with **f.**
Jer 17: 8 and it does not cease to bear **f.**
Eze 47:12 will not wither nor their **f** fail,
Hos 9:10 Like the first **f** on the fig tree, in its
14: 2 and we will offer the **f** of our lips.
Am 8: 1 showed me—a basket of summer **f.**
Mt 3: 8 Bear **f** worthy of repentance.
3:10 not bear good **f** is cut down and
7:17 every good tree bears good **f,**
Lk 6:44 for each tree is known by its own **f.**
13: 6 looking for **f** on it and found none.
Jn 15: 2 every branch in me that bears no **f.**
15: 2 Every branch that bears **f** he prunes
to make it bear more **f.**
15:16 I appointed you to go and bear **f, f**
Ro 7: 4 in order that we may bear **f** for God.
Eph 5: 9 for the **f** of the light is found in all
Col 1:10 as you bear **f** in every good work
Heb 13:15 the **f** of lips that confess his name.
Jude 1:12 autumn trees without **f,** twice dead,
Rev 22: 2 tree of life with its twelve kinds of **f,**

FRUITFUL → FRUIT
Ge 1:22 Be **f** and multiply and fill the waters
9: 1 said to them, "Be **f** and multiply,
17: 6 I will make you exceedingly **f;**
35:11 "I am God Almighty: be **f** and
Ex 1: 7 the Israelites were **f** and prolific;
Ps 105:24 the LORD made his people very **f,**
128: 3 be like a **f** vine within your house;
Php 1:22 that means **f** labor for me;

FRUITS → FRUIT
Ex 23:16 of the first **f** of your labor,
Lev 2:14 grain offering of first **f** to the LORD,
23:17 as first **f** to the LORD.
Nu 28:26 On the day of the first **f,**
Pr 3: 9 with the first **f** of all your produce;
Jer 2: 3 the first **f** of his harvest.
Mt 7:16 You will know them by their **f.**
Lk 3: 8 Bear **f** worthy of repentance.
Ro 8:23 who have the first **f** of the Spirit,
1Co 15:23 in his own order: Christ the first **f,**
Jas 1:18 a kind of first **f** of his creatures.
Rev 14: 4 as first **f** for God and the Lamb,
Sir 35:10 do not stint the first **f** of your hands.
1Mc 3:49 and the first **f** and the tithes,

FIRST FRUITS Ge 49:3; Ex 23:16, 19;
34:22, 26; Lev 2:14, 14; 23:10, 17, 20; Nu
18:13; 28:26; Dt 18:4; 2Ki 4:42; 2Ch 31:5; Ne
10:35, 35; 12:44; 13:31; Pr 3:9; Jer 2:3; Eze
44:30; Ro 8:23; 11:16; 1Co 15:20, 23; 2Th
2:13; Jas 1:18; Rev 14:4; Tob 1:6; Jdt 11:13;
Sir 7:31, 31; 24:25; 35:10; 45:20, 20; 50:8;
1Mc 3:49

FRUSTRATE* → FRUSTRATED, FRUSTRATES, FRUSTRATION
Ezr 4: 5 they bribed officials to **f** their plan

FRUSTRATED → FRUSTRATE
Ne 4:15 and that God had **f** it,

FRUSTRATES* → FRUSTRATE
Job 5:12 He **f** the devices of the crafty,
Ps 33:10 he **f** the plans of the peoples.
Isa 44:25 who **f** the omens of liars,

FRUSTRATION* → FRUSTRATE
Dt 28:20 **f** in everything you attempt to do,

FUEL
Isa 9:19 became like **f** for the fire;
Eze 21:32 You shall be **f** for the fire,

FUGITIVE → FUGITIVES
Ge 4:12 you will be a **f** and a wanderer
Sir 36:30 will become a **f** and a wanderer.

FUGITIVES → FUGITIVE
La 4:15 So they became **f** and wanderers;

FULFILL → FULFILLED, FULFILLING, FULFILLMENT, FULFILLS
Ge 26: 3 and I will **f** the oath that I swore
Nu 23:19 Has he spoken, and will he not **f** it?
2Ch 10:15 so that the LORD might **f** his word,
Ps 20: 5 May the LORD **f** all your petitions.
119:166 and I **f** your commandments.
138: 8 The LORD will **f** his purpose for me;
Ecc 5: 4 **F** what you vow.
Jer 33:14 when I will **f** the promise I made to
Mt 1:22 All this took place to **f** what had
2:15 This was to **f** what had been spoken
3:15 in this way to **f** all righteousness."
5:17 I have come not to abolish but to **f.**
8:17 This was to **f** what had been spoken
12:17 This was to **f** what had been spoken
13:35 This was to **f** what had been spoken
21: 4 to **f** what had been spoken through
Jn 12:38 to **f** the word spoken by the prophet
13:18 But it is to **f** the scripture,
15:25 It was to **f** the word that is written
18: 9 This was to **f** the word that he had
18:32 (This was to **f** what Jesus had said
19:24 This was to **f** what the scripture
19:28 he said (in order to **f** the scripture),
Gal 6: 2 way you will **f** the law of Christ.
2Th 1:11 by his power every good resolve
Jas 2: 8 really **f** the royal law according to

FULFILLED → FULFILL
Jos 23:15 concerning you have been **f** for you,
1Sa 10: 9 and all these signs were **f** that day.
2Ch 6:15 and this day have **f** with your hand.
Pr 13:12 but a desire **f** is a tree of life.
Mt 2:17 Then was **f** what had been spoken
2:23 through the prophets might be **f,**
4:14 the prophet Isaiah might be **f:**
13:14 With them indeed is **f** the prophecy
26:54 how then would the scriptures be **f,**
26:56 scriptures of the prophets may be **f."**
27: 9 Then was **f** what had been spoken
Mk 1:15 "The time is **f,** and the kingdom
14:49 But let the scriptures be **f."**
Lk 1: 1 of the events that have been **f**
4:21 "Today this scripture has been **f**
21:24 until the times of the Gentiles are **f.**
24:44 prophets, and the psalms must be **f."**
Jn 17:12 so that the scripture might be **f.**
19:36 so that the scripture might be **f,**
Ac 1:16 the scripture had to be **f,**
3:18 this way God **f** what he had foretold
Ro 8: 4 requirement of the law might be **f**
13: 8 one who loves another has **f** the law.
Jas 2:23 Thus the scripture was **f** that says,
Rev 10: 7 the mystery of God will be **f,**
17:17 until the words of God will be **f.**
Sir 39:18 commands, his every purpose is **f,**

FULFILLING → FULFILL
Ro 9:31 did not succeed in **f** that law.
13:10 love is the **f** of the law.

FULFILLMENT → FULFILL
2Ch 36:22 in **f** of the word of the LORD spoken
Sir 19:20 there is the **f** of the law.
21:11 **f** of the fear of the Lord is wisdom.

FULFILLS* → FULFILL
Ps 57: 2 to God who **f** his purpose for me.
145:19 He **f** the desire of all who fear him;
Isa 44:26 **f** the prediction of his messengers;

FULL → FILL
Ru 1:21 I went away **f,** but the LORD has
2Ki 4: 6 When the vessels were **f,** she said
2Ch 24:10 into the chest until it was **f.**
Job 14: 1 few of days and **f** of trouble,
Ps 33: 5 the earth is **f** of the steadfast love of
127: 5 man who has his quiver **f** of them.
Pr 19:17 and will be repaid in **f.**
Ecc 1: 7 but the sea is not **f;**
Isa 1:15 your hands are **f** of blood.

6: 3 the whole earth is **f** of his glory."
11: 9 the earth will be **f** of the knowledge
Jer 51:56 of recompense, he will repay in **f.**
La 1: 1 lonely sits the city that once was **f**
Eze 10:12 were **f** of eyes all around.
37: 1 it was **f** of bones.
Mal 3:10 Bring the **f** tithe into the storehouse,
Mt 6:22 your whole body will be **f** of light;
23:25 inside they are **f** of greed
Lk 4: 1 Jesus, **f** of the Holy Spirit,
11:34 your whole body is **f** of light;
11:34 your body is **f** of darkness.
Jn 1:14 **f** of grace and truth,
Ac 6: 3 **f** of the Spirit and of wisdom,
6: 5 a man **f** of faith and the Holy Spirit,
6: 8 Stephen, **f** of grace and power,
11:24 **f** of the Holy Spirit and of faith.
Eph 4:13 of the **f** stature of Christ.
Heb 10:22 in **f** assurance of faith,
Jas 3:17 **f** of mercy and good fruits,
2Jn 1: 8 but may receive a **f** reward.
Rev 4: 6 **f** of eyes in front and behind:
Sir 42:16 work of the Lord is **f** of his glory.

FULLERS'*
Mal 3: 2 refiner's fire and like **f** soap;

FULLNESS → FILL
Dt 33:16 the choice gifts of the earth and its **f,**
Ps 16:11 In your presence there is **f** of joy;
Jn 1:16 From his **f** we have all received,
1Co 10:26 "the earth and its **f** are the Lord's."
Gal 4: 4 But when the **f** of time had come,
Eph 1:23 the **f** of him who fills all in all.
3:19 may be filled with all the **f** of God.
Col 1:19 in him all the **f** of God was pleased
2: 9 in him the whole **f** of deity dwells
2:10 and you have come to **f** in him,
Sir 1:16 To fear the Lord is **f** of wisdom;

FULLY → FILL
Dt 17:11 You must carry out **f** the law
Lk 6:40 but everyone who is **f** qualified will
Ro 4:21 being **f** convinced that God was able
14: 5 be **f** convinced in their own minds.
1Co 13:12 I will know **f,** even as I have been **f**
known.
2Ti 4:17 the message might be **f** proclaimed
2Pe 1:19 prophetic message more **f** confirmed

FURNACE
Ge 19:28 going up like the smoke of a **f.**
Ps 21: 9 You will make them like a fiery **f**
Isa 48:10 have tested you in the **f** of adversity.
Da 3: 6 be thrown into a **f** of blazing fire."
Mt 13:42 will throw them into the **f** of fire,
Rev 1:15 refined as in a **f,**
9: 2 smoke like the smoke of a great **f,**
Sir 31:26 As the **f** tests the work of the smith,
Aza 1:26 of the Lord came down into the **f**

FURNISHED
Mk 14:15 a large room upstairs, **f** and ready.

FURNITURE
Ex 25: 9 the tabernacle and of all its **f,**

FURY
Dt 29:28 in anger, **f,** and great wrath,
Ps 2: 5 and terrify them in his **f,**
Jer 21: 5 in anger, in **f,** and in great wrath.
La 2: 4 he has poured out his **f** like fire.
Hab 3:12 In **f** you trod the earth,
Ro 2: 8 there will be wrath and **f.**
Rev 16:19 the wine-cup of the **f** of his wrath.
19:15 tread the wine press of the **f** of the
Sir 40: 5 and fear of death, and **f** and strife.

FUTILE → FUTILITY
Isa 1:13 bringing offerings is **f;**
Ro 1:21 but they became **f** in their thinking,
1Co 3:20 thoughts of the wise, that they are **f,**
1Pe 1:18 you were ransomed from the **f** ways
Wis 15: 8 these workers form a **f** god

FUTILITY → FUTILE
Ro   8:20 for the creation was subjected to **f,**
Eph 4:17 Gentiles live, in the **f** of their minds.

FUTURE
Ex   13:14 When in the **f** your child asks you,
Ps   22:30 **f** generations will be told about the
Pr   23:18 there is a **f,** and your hope will not
        24:20 for the evil have no **f;**
Jer   29:11 to give you a **f** with hope.
        31:17 hope for your **f,** says the LORD:
1Co   3:22 life or death or the present or the **f—**
1Ti   6:19 of a good foundation for the **f,**

G

GABBATHA·
Jn   19:13 Stone Pavement, or in Hebrew **G.**

GABRIEL·
Angel who interpreted Daniel's visions (Da 8:16-26; 9:20-27); announced births of John (Lk 1:11-20), Jesus (Lk 1:26-38).

GAD
1. Son of Jacob by Zilpah (Ge 30:9-11; 35:26; 1Ch 2:2). Tribe of blessed (Ge 49:19; Dt 33:20-21), numbered (Nu 1:25; 26:18), allotted land east of the Jordan (Nu 32; 34:14; Jos 18:7; 22), west (Eze 48:27-28), 12,000 from (Rev 7:5).
2. Prophet; seer of David (1Sa 22:5; 2Sa 24:11-19; 1Ch 29:29).

GADARENES·
Mt   8:28 to the country of the **G,**

GAIN → GAINED
Ge   24:60 offspring **g** possession of the gates
Ex   14:17 will **g** glory for myself over Pharaoh
1Sa   8: 3 in his ways, but turned aside after **g;**
Ps   90:12 our days that we may **g** a wise heart.
Pr   1: 5 the wise also hear and **g** in learning,
        1:19 the end of all who are greedy for **g;**
        4: 1 be attentive, that you may **g** insight;
       11:18 The wicked earn no real **g,**
       28:16 hates unjust **g** will enjoy a long life.
Ecc   1: 3 What do people **g** from all the toil
Eze   28:22 and I will **g** glory in your midst.
Da   2: 8 you are trying to **g** time,
Mk   8:36 it profit them to **g** the whole world
Lk   9:25 if they **g** the whole world,
       21:19 endurance you will **g** your souls.
Ac   12:24 to advance and **g** adherents.
1Co 13: 3 but do not have love, I **g** nothing.
Php   1:21 living is Christ and dying is **g.**
        3: 8 in order that I may **g** Christ
1Ti   3:13 as deacons **g** a good standing for
        6: 5 that godliness is a means of **g.**
        6: 6 is great **g** in godliness combined
Tit   1: 7 to wine or violent or greedy for **g;**
        1:11 teaching for sordid **g** what it is not
1Pe   5: 2 not for sordid **g** but eagerly.
Jude 1:11 to Balaam's error for the sake of **g,**
Sir   6: 7 When you **g** friends, **g** them
            through testing,
       27: 1 Many have committed sin for **g,**

GAINED → GAIN
Ex   14:18 **g** glory for myself over Pharaoh,
Pr   10: 2 Treasures **g** by wickedness do not
       16:31 it is **g** in a righteous life.
Ecc   2:11 was nothing to be **g** under the sun.

GAIUS
Ro   16:23 **G,** who is host to me and to the
3Jn   1: 1 The elder to the beloved **G,**

GALATIA → GALATIANS
Ac   16: 6 through the region of Phrygia and **G**
       18:23 to place through the region of **G**

1Pe   1: 1 of the Dispersion in Pontus, **G,**

GALATIANS → GALATIA
Gal   3: 1 You foolish **G!** Who has bewitched

GALILEAN· → GALILEE
Mt   26:69 "You also were with Jesus the **G.**"
Mk   14:70 of them; for you are a **G.**"
Lk   22:59 with him; for he is a **G.**"
       23: 6 he asked whether the man was a **G.**
Ac   5:37 After him Judas the **G** rose up at

GALILEANS → GALILEE
Lk   13: 1 **G** whose blood Pilate had mingled
Jn   4:45 came to Galilee, the **G** welcomed
Ac   2: 7 not all these who are speaking **G?**

GALILEE → GALILEAN, GALILEANS
Isa   9: 1 beyond the Jordan, **G** of the nations.
Mt   3:13 Then Jesus came from **G** to John at
        4:15 across the Jordan, **G** of the Gentiles
       21:11 prophet Jesus from Nazareth in **G.**"
       26:32 I will go ahead of you to **G.**"
       28:10 go and tell my brothers to go to **G;**
Lk   23:49 who had followed him from **G,**
Jn   2: 1 there was a wedding in Cana of **G,**
        7:41 the Messiah does not come from **G,**
Tob   1: 5 on all the mountains of **G.**
1Mc   5:15 and all **G** of the Gentiles,

GALL
Job   16:13 he pours out my **g** on the ground.
Mt   27:34 wine to drink, mixed with **g;**
Tob   6: 5 For its **g,** heart, and liver are useful
       11: 8 Smear the **g** of the fish on his eyes;

GALLIO
Proconsul of Achaia, who refused to hear complaints against Paul (Ac 18:12-17).

GALLOWS
Est   7:10 **g** that he had prepared for Mordecai.
        9:13 sons of Haman be hanged on the **g.**"

GAMALIEL
Ac   5:34 a Pharisee in the council named **G,**
       22: 3 in this city at the feet of **G,**

GAME
Ge   25:28 because he was fond of **g;**
       27: 3 out to the field, and hunt **g** for me.
Pr   12:27 The lazy do not roast their **g,**

GAMES·
2Mc   4:18 When the quadrennial **g** were being

GANGRENE·
2Ti   2:17 and their talk will spread like **g.**

GAP· → GAPS
1Ki   11:27 closed up the **g** in the wall of the
Ne   6: 1 the wall and that there was no **g** left

GAPS· → GAP
Ne   4: 7 the **g** were beginning to be closed,

GARDEN → GARDENER, GARDENS
Ge   2: 8 the LORD God planted a **g** in Eden,
        2:15 and put him in the **g** of Eden to till
        3:23 sent him forth from the **g** of Eden,
       13:10 like the **g** of the LORD,
SS   4:12 A **g** locked is my sister, my bride,
Isa   58:11 and you shall be like a watered **g,**
Jer   31:12 life shall become like a watered **g,**
Eze   28:13 You were in Eden, the **g** of God;
       31: 9 of Eden that were in the **g** of God.
Jn   19:41 a **g** in the place where he was
       19:41 and in the **g** there was a new tomb
Sir   40:27 The fear of the Lord is like a **g** of
Sus   1:15 and wished to bathe in the **g,**
2Es   3: 6 And you led him into the **g** that your

GARDENER· → GARDEN
Lk   13: 7 So he said to the **g,** 'See here!
Jn   20:15 Supposing him to be the **g,**

GARDENS → GARDEN
Am   4: 9 I laid waste your **g** and your

GARLAND
Pr   1: 9 for they are a fair **g** for your head,
        4: 9 She will place on your head a fair **g;**

GARMENT → GARMENTS
Ge   9:23 Then Shem and Japheth took a **g,**
       39:12 she caught hold of his **g,**
Dt   22: 5 nor shall a man put on a woman's **g;**
       24:17 not take a widow's **g** in pledge.
Ezr   9: 3 When I heard this, I tore my **g** and
Ne   5:13 I also shook out the fold of my **g**
Ps   102:26 they will all wear out like a **g,**
Isa   50: 9 All of them will wear out like a **g,**
       51: 6 the earth will wear out like a **g,**
Lk   5:36 "No one tears a piece from a new **g**
            and sews it on an old **g;**
Sir   14:17 living beings become old like a **g,**

GARMENTS → GARMENT
Ge   3:21 the LORD God made **g** of skins for
2Sa   13:31 The king rose, tore his **g,**
Pr   31:24 She makes linen **g** and sells them;
Isa   52: 1 your beautiful **g,** O Jerusalem,
       61:10 clothed me with the **g** of salvation,
       63: 1 from Bozrah in **g** stained crimson?
Jdt   10: 3 took off her widow's **g,**
LtJ   6:11 They deck their gods out with **g**

GATE → GATES, GATEWAY
Dt   21:19 to the elders of his town at the **g** of
Jos   2: 5 it was time to close the **g** at dark,
Ru   4:11 all the people who were at the **g,**
Est   2:19 Mordecai was sitting at the king's **g.**
Job   29: 7 When I went out to the **g** of the city,
Ps   69:12 of gossip for those who sit in the **g,**
      118:20 This is the **g** of the LORD;
Mt   7:13 "Enter through the narrow **g;**
Jn   10: 2 who enters by the **g** is the shepherd
       10: 7 I am the **g** for the sheep.
       10: 9 I am the **g.** Whoever enters by me
Ac   3: 2 at the **g** of the temple called the
            Beautiful **G**
       12:13 When he knocked at the outer **g,**
Heb   13:12 Jesus also suffered outside the city **g**

GATES → GATE
Ge   24:60 offspring gain possession of the **g**
Dt   6: 9 of your house and on your **g.**
Ne   1: 3 its **g** have been destroyed by fire."
Ps   24: 7 Lift up your heads, O **g!**
       87: 2 the LORD loves the **g** of Zion more
      100: 4 Enter his **g** with thanksgiving,
      118:19 Open to me the **g** of righteousness,
Isa   60:11 Your **g** shall always be open;
       60:18 walls Salvation, and your **g** Praise.
       62:10 Go through, go through the **g,**
La   4:12 could enter the **g** of Jerusalem.
Eze   48:31 the **g** of the city being named after
Mt   16:18 and the **g** of Hades will not prevail
Rev   21:12 has a great, high wall with twelve **g,**
       21:12 and at the **g** twelve angels;
       21:12 the **g** are inscribed the names of the
       21:21 And the twelve **g** are twelve pearls,
       21:25 Its **g** will never be shut by day—
       22:14 and may enter the city by the **g.**
Tob   13:16 **g** of Jerusalem will be built with
1Mc   4:38 the altar profaned, and the **g** burned.

GATEWAY → GATE, WAY
Ge   19: 1 Lot was sitting in the **g** of Sodom.

GATH
1Sa   5: 8 the ark of the God of Israel to **G.**
       17: 4 Goliath, of **G,** whose height was six
       21:10 he went to King Achish of **G.**
2Sa   1:20 Tell it not in **G,** proclaim it not in
Mic   1:10 Tell it not in **G,** weep not at all;

GATHER → GATHERED, GATHERS, INGATHERING

Ex 16: 4 and **g** enough for that day.
Dt 30: 4 there the LORD your God will **g** you,
Ru   2: 7 and **g** among the sheaves behind
Ne   1: 9 I will **g** them from there and bring
Ps 106:47 and **g** us from among the nations,
Isa 11:12 and **g** the dispersed of Judah from
Jer   3:17 and all nations shall **g** to it,
      23: 3 Then I myself will **g** the remnant of
    31:10 "He who scattered Israel will **g** him,
Joel 3: 2 I will **g** all the nations and bring
Zep 2: 1 G together, **g**, O shameless nation,
     3:20 at the time when I **g** you;
Zec 14: 2 I will **g** all the nations against
Mt 12:30 does not **g** with me scatters.
    13:30 but **g** the wheat into my barn.'"
    23:37 to **g** your children together as
    25:26 and **g** where I did not scatter?
Mk 13:27 and **g** his elect from the four winds,
Lk   3:17 threshing floor and to **g** the wheat
    11:23 does not **g** with me scatters.
    13:34 to **g** your children together as
    17:37 corpse is, there the vultures will **g**."
Jn 11:52 but to **g** into one the dispersed
Eph 1:10 to **g** up all things in him,
Rev 14:18 your sharp sickle and **g** the clusters
    19:17 **g** for the great supper of God,
    20: 8 Gog and Magog, in order to **g** them

GATHERED → GATHER

Ge   1: 9 "Let the waters under the sky be **g**
Ex 16:18 those who **g** much had nothing over,
Nu 11:32 the least anyone **g** was ten homers;
Pr   30: 4 Who has **g** the wind in the hollow
Mt 16: 9 and how many baskets you **g**?
    18:20 two or three are **g** in my name,
    25:32 All the nations will be **g** before him,
2Th 2: 1 Christ and our being **g** together
Rev 14:19 and **g** the vintage of the earth,
    19:19 their armies to make war against
2Es 1:30 I **g** you as a hen gathers her chicks

GATHERS → GATHER

Ps 147: 2 he **g** the outcasts of Israel.
Pr 10: 5 A child who **g** in summer is prudent,
Isa 56: 8 who **g** the outcasts of Israel,
Mt 23:37 as a hen **g** her brood under her
2Es 1:30 as a hen **g** her chicks under her

GAVE → GIVE

Ge   2:20 The man **g** names to all cattle,
     3: 6 and she also **g** some to her husband,
   14:20 And Abram **g** him one tenth of
   28: 4 land that God **g** to Abraham."
   35:12 that I **g** to Abraham and Isaac I will
Ex 31:18 he **g** him the two tablets of the
   34:32 he **g** them in commandment all that
Dt   2:12 the land that the LORD **g** them as a
    2:36 The LORD our God everything to
    3:12 I **g** to the Reubenites and Gadites
    9:10 the LORD **g** me the two stone tablets
   26: 9 into this place and **g** us this land,
   31: 9 **g** it to the priests, the sons of Levi,
Jos 11:23 Joshua **g** it for an inheritance to
   13:14 Levi alone Moses **g** no inheritance;
   15:13 he **g** to Caleb son of Jephunneh
   19:49 the Israelites **g** an inheritance
   21:44 the LORD **g** them rest on every side
   24:13 I **g** you a land on which you had not
Jdg 3: 6 own daughters they **g** to their sons;
1Sa 1: 5 but to Hannah he **g** a double portion,
   27: 6 So that day Achish **g** him Ziklag;
2Sa 8: 6 LORD **g** victory to David wherever
   12: 8 I **g** you your master's house,
   12: 8 and **g** you the house of Israel and
1Ki 4:29 God **g** Solomon very great wisdom,
    5:12 LORD **g** Solomon wisdom, as he
Ezr 2:69 According to their resources they **g**
Ne   9:15 you **g** them bread from heaven,
    9:20 You **g** your good spirit to instruct
    9:20 **g** them water for their thirst.

    9:22 you **g** them kingdoms and peoples,
    9:27 you **g** them into the hands of their
    9:27 you **g** them saviors who saved them
    9:34 and the warnings that you **g** them.
Job 1:21 the LORD **g**, and the LORD has taken
   42:10 LORD **g** Job twice as much as he had
Ps 69:21 and for my thirst they **g** me vinegar
  135:12 and their land as a heritage,
Ecc 12: 7 the breath returns to God who **g** it.
Eze 3: 2 and he **g** me the scroll to eat.
Da   1: 7 palace master **g** them other names:
    1:17 four young men God **g** knowledge
Mt 25:35 for I was hungry and you **g** me food,
   25:35 and you **g** me something to drink,
   25:42 and you **g** me nothing to drink,
   26:26 **g** it to the disciples, and said, "Take,
Mk 6: 7 **g** them authority over the unclean
   11:28 **g** you this authority to do them?"
Jn   1:12 **g** power to become children of God,
    3:16 God so loved the world that he **g**
        his only Son,
   17: 4 by finishing the work that you **g** me
   17: 6 whom you **g** me from the world.
   17: 6 They were yours, and you **g** them
   19:30 bowed his head and **g** up his spirit.
Ac 11:17 If then God **g** them the same gift
        that he **g** us
Ro   1:24 God **g** them up in the lusts
    1:26 **g** them up to degrading passions
    1:28 God **g** them up to a debased mind
    8:32 but **g** him up for all of us,
2Co 8: 3 **g** according to their means,
    8: 5 they **g** themselves first to the Lord
Eph 4: 8 he **g** gifts to his people."
    4:11 The gifts he **g** were that some would
    5: 2 as Christ loved us and **g** himself up
    5:25 as Christ loved the church and **g**
Php 2: 9 highly exalted him and **g** him
2Th 2:16 through grace **g** us eternal comfort
1Ti 2: 6 who **g** himself a ransom
Tit 2:14 He it is who **g** himself for us
1Jn 5:11 God **g** us eternal life,
Rev 11:13 terrified and **g** glory to the God
    13: 2 And the dragon **g** it his power and
    16:19 and **g** her the wine-cup of the fury
    20:13 and Hades **g** up the dead that were

GAZA

Jdg 16: 1 Once Samson went to **G**,
1Sa 6:17 one for Ashdod, one for **G**,
Am   1: 6 For three transgressions of **G**,

GAZE → GAZING

Ps 11: 4 his **g** examines humankind.
Pr   4:25 and your **g** be straight before you.
Isa 47:13 those who **g** at the stars,
2Co 3: 7 Israel could not **g** at Moses' face
Rev 11: 9 nations will **g** at their dead bodies
Sir   9: 8 not **g** at beauty belonging to another

GAZELLE

2Sa 2:18 was as swift of foot as a wild **g**.
SS   2: 9 My beloved is like a **g** or a young
    7: 3 like two fawns, twins of a **g**.

GAZING → GAZE

2Co 3:13 from **g** at the end of the glory
Sir 41:21 and of **g** at another man's wife;

GEDALIAH

Governor of Judah appointed by Nebuchadnezzar (2Ki 25:22-26; Jer 39-41).

GEHAZI*

Servant of Elisha (2Ki 4:12-5:27; 8:4-5).

GEMS

Ex 25: 7 and **g** to be set in the ephod and for

GENEALOGICAL* → GENEALOGY

1Ch 4:33 And they kept a **g** record.
Ezr 2:62 their entries in the **g** records,

GENEALOGIES → GENEALOGY

1Ch 9: 1 So all Israel was enrolled by **g**;
Ne   7:64 among those enrolled in the **g**,
1Ti   1: 4 with myths and endless **g**
Tit   3: 9 But avoid stupid controversies, **g**,

GENEALOGY → GENEALOGICAL, GENEALOGIES

Mt   1: 1 of the **g** of Jesus the Messiah,
Heb 7: 3 father, without mother, without **g**,

GENERATION → GENERATIONS

Ge   7: 1 are righteous before me in this **g**.
   15:16 come back here in the fourth **g**;
Ex   1: 6 all his brothers, and that whole **g**.
   20: 6 steadfast love to the thousandth **g**
   34: 7 to the third and the fourth **g**."
Nu 32:13 until all the **g** that had done evil in
Dt   1:35 not one of this evil **g**—
Jdg 2:10 and another **g** grew up after them,
Ps 48:13 that you may tell the next **g**
   78: 4 to the coming **g** the glorious deeds
  102:18 Let this be recorded for a **g** to come,
  112: 2 the **g** of the upright will be blessed.
  145: 4 One **g** shall laud your works to
Isa 34:17 from **g** to **g** they shall live in it.
Da   4: 3 and his sovereignty is from **g** to **g**.
    4:34 his kingdom endures from **g** to **g**.
Joel 1: 3 and their children another **g**.
Mt 12:39 evil and adulterous **g** asks for a sign,
   17:17 "You faithless and perverse **g**,
   23:36 all this will come upon this **g**.
   24:34 this **g** will not pass away
Mk 9:19 answered them, "You faithless **g**,
   13:30 this **g** will not pass away
Lk   1:50 for those who fear him from **g** to **g**.
    7:31 will I compare the people of this **g**,
   11:29 to say, "This **g** is an evil **g**;
   11:50 **g** may be charged with the blood of
   21:32 this **g** will not pass away
Ac   2:40 Save yourselves from this corrupt **g**.
Php 2:15 midst of a crooked and perverse **g**,
Heb 3:10 Therefore I was angry with that **g**,
Tob 13:11 **G** after **g** will give joyful praise in
1Mc 2:61 "And so observe, from **g** to **g**,

GENERATIONS → GENERATION

Ge   9:12 that is with you, for all future **g**:
    17: 7 after you throughout their **g**,
Ex 12:17 observe this day throughout your **g**
   30:21 his descendants throughout their **g**.
   31:13 me and you throughout your **g**,
   40:15 priesthood throughout all **g** to come.
Dt   7: 9 his commandments, to a thousand **g**,
1Ch 16:15 he commanded, for a thousand **g**,
Job 8: 8 "For inquire now of bygone **g**,
Ps 22:30 future **g** will be told about the Lord,
   33:11 the thoughts of his heart to all **g**.
   45:17 your name to be celebrated in all **g**;
   89: 1 proclaim your faithfulness to all **g**.
   90: 1 our dwelling place in all **g**.
  100: 5 and his faithfulness to all **g**.
  102:12 your name endures to all **g**.
  105: 8 he commanded, for a thousand **g**,
  119:90 Your faithfulness endures to all **g**;
  145:13 dominion endures throughout all **g**.
  146:10 your God, O Zion, for all **g**.
Pr 27:24 nor a crown for all **g**.
Isa 41: 4 calling the **g** from the beginning?
   51: 8 and my salvation to all **g**.
Mt   1:17 Abraham to David are fourteen **g**;
    1:17 deportation to Babylon, fourteen **g**;
    1:17 Babylon to the Messiah, fourteen **g**.
Lk   1:48 now on all **g** will call me blessed;
Eph 3: 5 In former **g** this mystery was not
    3:21 church and in Christ Jesus to all **g**,
Col 1:26 hidden throughout the ages and **g**
Sir 2:10 Consider the **g** of old and see:
    44: 1 our ancestors in their **g**.

ALL GENERATIONS Ge 9:12; Ex 3:15;
40:15; Ps 10:6; 33:11; 45:17; 49:11; 61:6;
71:18; 72:5; 85:5; 89:1, 4; 90:1; 100:5; 102:12,

24; 119:90; 145:13; 146:10; Pr 27:24; Isa
13:20; 51:8; Jer 50:39; La 5:19; Joel 3:20; Mt
1:17; Lk 1:48; Eph 3:21; Tob 1:4; 8:5; 13:10;
Jdt 8:32; Sir 16:27; 24:33; 39:9; 44:16; 45:26

GENEROSITY → GENEROUS

Ro 12: 8 the giver, in **g;**
2Co 8: 2 in a wealth of **g** on their part.
     9:11 in every way for your great **g,**
     9:13 and by the **g** of your sharing
Gal 5:22 joy, peace, patience, kindness, **g,**
Sir 37:11 with a miser about **g** or

GENEROUS → GENEROSITY, GENEROUSLY

Pr 11:25 A **g** person will be enriched,
    22: 9 Those who are **g** are blessed,
Mt 20:15 are you envious because I am **g?'**
Ro 10:12 and is **g** to all who call on him.
2Co 8: 7 excel also in this **g** undertaking.
1Ti 6:18 to be rich in good works, **g,**
Jas 1:17 Every **g** act of giving,
Tob 9: 6 good and noble, upright and **g!**
Sir 14: 5 to whom will he be **g?**
    35:10 Be **g** when you worship the Lord,

GENEROUSLY → GENEROUS

Ps 112: 5 well with those who deal **g** and lend,
Ac 10: 2 he gave alms **g** to the people
Jas 1: 5 ask God, who gives to all **g** and
Sir 35:12 and as **g** as you can afford.

GENTILE → GENTILES

Mt 18:17 as a **G** and a tax collector.
Gal 2:14 live like a **G** and not like a Jew,
1Mc 1:14 according to **G** custom,

GENTILES → GENTILE

Mt 4:15 across the Jordan, Galilee of the **G**
Lk 2:32 the **G** and for glory to your people
   21:24 will be trampled on by the **G,**
   21:24 until the times of the **G** are fulfilled.
   22:25 kings of the **G** lord it over them;
Ac 9:15 to bring my name before **G** and
   10:45 had been poured out even on the **G,**
   11: 1 the **G** had also accepted the word of
   11:18 even to the **G** the repentance that
   13:46 we are now turning to the **G.**
   13:47 have set you to be a light for the **G,**
   14:27 opened a door of faith for the **G.**
   15:19 those **G** who are turning to God,
   18: 6 From now on I will go to the **G."**
   22:21 I will send you far away to the **G.'"**
   26:20 to the **G,** that they should repent
   28:28 of God has been sent to the **G;**
Ro 2:14 **G,** who do not possess the law,
    3:29 Is he not the God of **G** also?
    9:24 the Jews only but also from the **G?**
   11:11 salvation has come to the **G,**
   11:12 if their defeat means riches for **G,**
   11:13 as I am an apostle to the **G,**
   15: 9 **G** might glorify God for his mercy.
   15:27 **G** have come to share in their
1Co 1:23 block to Jews and foolishness to **G,**
2Co 11:26 my own people, danger from **G,**
Gal 1:16 I might proclaim him among the **G,**
    3: 8 God would justify the **G** by faith,
Eph 3: 6 the **G** have become fellow heirs,
    3: 8 to bring to the **G** the news of the
    4:17 must no longer live as the **G** live,
Col 1:27 the **G** are the riches of the glory
1Ti 2: 7 a teacher of the **G** in faith and truth.
2Ti 4:17 be fully proclaimed and all the **G**
Tob 1:11 from eating the food of the **G.**
1Mc 1:11 and make a covenant with the **G**
    2:12 the **G** have profaned them.
    4:54 very day that the **G** had profaned it,
   13:41 the yoke of the **G** was removed
2Es 4:23 Israel has been given over to the **G**

GENTLE → GENTLENESS, GENTLY

Dt 28:54 **g** of men among you will begrudge
    28:56 She who is the most refined and **g**

Pr 15: 4 A **g** tongue is a tree of life,
Jer 11:19 like a **g** lamb led to the slaughter.
Mt 11:29 for I am **g** and humble in heart,
1Th 2: 7 But we were **g** among you,
1Ti 3: 3 not violent but **g,** not quarrelsome,
Tit 3: 2 to be **g,** and to show every courtesy
Jas 3:17 **g,** willing to yield, full of mercy
1Pe 2:18 not only those who are kind and **g**
    3: 4 with the lasting beauty of a **g**

GENTLENESS* → GENTLE

1Co 4:21 or with love in a spirit of **g?**
2Co 10: 1 by the meekness and **g** of Christ—
Gal 5:23 **g,** and self-control. There is no law
    6: 1 restore such a one in a spirit of **g.**
Eph 4: 2 all humility and **g,** with patience,
Php 4: 5 Let your **g** be known to everyone.
1Ti 6:11 godliness, faith, love, endurance, **g.**
2Ti 2:25 correcting opponents with **g.**
Jas 3:13 that your works are done with **g**
1Pe 3:16 yet do it with **g** and reverence.
AdE 15: 8 changed the spirit of the king to **g,**

GENTLY → GENTLE

Job 15:11 or the word that deals **g** with you?
Isa 40:11 and **g** lead the mother sheep.
Heb 5: 2 to deal **g** with the ignorant and

GENUINE* → GENUINENESS

Ro 12: 9 Let love be **g;** hate what is evil,
1Co 11:19 become clear who among you are **g.**
2Co 6: 6 kindness, holiness of spirit, **g** love,
1Pe 1:22 so that you have **g** mutual love,

GENUINENESS* → GENUINE

2Co 8: 8 but I am testing the **g** of your love
1Pe 1: 7 that the **g** of your faith—

GERAR

Ge 20: 2 Abimelech of **G** sent and took Sarah
    26: 6 So Isaac settled in **G.**

GERASENES

Lk 8:26 they arrived at the country of the **G,**

GERIZIM

Dt 27:12 stand on Mount **G** for the blessing
Jos 8:33 in front of Mount **G** and half of

GERSHOM

Ex 2:22 bore a son, and he named him **G;**
1Ch 23:15 The sons of Moses: **G** and Eliezer.

GERSHON → GERSHONITES

Ge 46:11 The children of Levi: **G,** Kohath,
1Ch 23: 6 to the sons of Levi: **G,** Kohath,

GERSHONITES → GERSHON

Nu 3:21 these were the clans of the **G.**
Jos 21: 6 **G** received by lot thirteen towns

GESHEM

Ne 6: 1 **G** the Arab and to the rest of our

GESHUR

2Sa 13:38 Absalom, having fled to **G,**

GET → GETS

Ge 24: 4 and **g** a wife for my son Isaac."
Dt 30:12 **g** it for us so that we may hear it
Pr 4: 5 **G** wisdom; **g** insight: do
    16:16 How much better to **g** wisdom than
    23: 4 Do not wear yourself out to **g** rich;
Eze 18:31 and **g** yourselves a new heart and a
Mt 16:23 said to Peter, **"G** behind me, Satan!
Mk 6: 2 "Where did this man **g** all this?
    13:16 field must not turn back to **g** a coat.
Jn 19:24 cast lots for it to see who will **g** it."

GETHSEMANE*

Mt 26:36 went with them to a place called **G;**
Mk 14:32 They went to a place called **G;**

GETS → GET

Pr 11:16 A gracious woman **g** honor,
    13: 4 of the lazy craves, and **g** nothing,

Sir 36:29 He who acquires a wife **g** his best

GEZER

Jos 16:10 the Canaanites who lived in **G:**
1Ch 14:16 Philistine army from Gibeon to **G.**

GHOST → GHOSTS

Mt 14:26 were terrified, saying, "It is a **g!"**
Lk 24:39 for a **g** does not have flesh and

GHOSTS → GHOST

Dt 18:11 or who consults **g** or spirits,
Isa 8:19 Consult the **g** and the familiar spirits

GIANT* → GIANTS

Sir 47: 4 In his youth did he not kill a **g,**
1Mc 3: 3 Like a **g** he put on his breastplate;

GIANTS → GIANT

1Ch 20: 4 was one of the descendants of the **g;**
Wis 14: 6 when arrogant **g** were perishing,
Sir 16: 7 He did not forgive the ancient **g**
Bar 3:26 The **g** were born there, who were
3Mc 2: 4 even **g** who trusted in their strength

GIBEAH

Jdg 19:12 but we will continue on to **G."**
1Sa 10:26 Saul also went to his home at **G,**
Hos 10: 9 Since the days of **G** you have sinned

GIBEON → GIBEONITES

Jos 10:12 "Sun, stand still at **G,** and Moon, in
2Sa 2:13 and met them at the pool of **G.**
1Ki 3: 5 **G** the LORD appeared to Solomon

GIBEONITES → GIBEON

2Sa 21: 1 because he put the **G** to death."

GIDEON → =JERUBBAAL

Judge, also called Jerubbaal; freed Israel from
Midianites (Jdg 6-8; Heb 11:32). Given sign of
fleece (Jdg 8:36-40).

GIFT → GIFTS

Nu 18: 7 I give your priesthood as a **g;**
Pr 18:16 A **g** opens doors; it gives access to
    21:14 A **g** in secret averts anger;
Ecc 3:13 it is God's **g** that all should eat and
    5:19 this is the **g** of God.
Mt 5:23 So when you are offering your **g** at
    8: 4 offer the **g** that Moses commanded,
Jn 4:10 "If you knew the **g** of God,
Ac 2:38 will receive the **g** of the Holy Spirit.
    8:20 thought you could obtain God's **g**
   11:17 God gave them the same **g** that he
Ro 1:11 some spiritual **g** to strengthen you—
    5:15 the free **g** is not like the trespass.
    5:15 the grace of God and the free **g** in
    6:23 but the free **g** of God is eternal life
1Co 7: 7 each has a particular **g** from God,
2Co 8:12 the **g** is acceptable according to
    9:15 to God for his indescribable **g!**
Eph 2: 8 it is the **g** of God—
    4: 7 to the measure of Christ's **g.**
Php 4:17 Not that I seek the **g,**
1Ti 4:14 Do not neglect the **g** that is in you,
2Ti 1: 6 the **g** of God that is within you
Heb 6: 4 and have tasted the heavenly **g,**
Jas 1:17 with every perfect **g,** is from above,
1Pe 3: 7 also heirs of the gracious **g** of life—
    4:10 whatever **g** each of you has received
Rev 21: 6 the thirsty I will give water as a **g**
    22:17 the water of life as a **g.**
Sir 18:16 So a word is better than a **g.**

GIFTS → GIFT

Nu 18: 8 all the holy **g** of the Israelites;
Dt 12: 6 and your donations, your votive **g,**
Ezr 1: 6 with animals, and with valuable **g,**
Est 9:22 days for sending **g** of food to one
Ps 68:18 in your train and receiving **g**
    76:11 bring **g** to the one who is awesome,
Mt 2:11 offered him **g** of gold, frankincense,
Lk 11:13 how to give good **g** to your children,

21: 1 and saw rich people putting their **g**
21: 5 and **g** dedicated to God,
Ro 11:29 for the **g** and the calling of God are
12: 6 We have a **g** that differ according to
1Co 12: 1 Now concerning spiritual **g**,
12: 4 Now there are varieties of **g**, but the
12:28 deeds of power, then **g** of healing,
12:30 Do all possess **g** of healing?
12:31 But strive for the greater **g**.
14: 1 and strive for the spiritual **g**,
14:12 since you are eager for spiritual **g**,
Eph 4: 8 he gave **g** to his people."
4:11 The **g** he gave were that some
Heb 2: 4 and by **g** of the Holy Spirit,
9: 9 which **g** and sacrifices are offered
Sir 20:29 and **g** blind the eyes of the wise;
32:13 who fills you with his good **g**.

GIHON
Ge 2:13 The name of the second river is **G**;
2Ch 32:30 of **G** and directed them down to the

GILBOA
1Ch 10: 8 Saul and his sons fallen on Mount **G**

GILEAD → GILEADITE
Nu 32:29 you shall give them the land of **G**
Dt 34: 1 the whole land: **G** as far as Dan,
Jdg 11: 1 **G** was the father of Jephthah.
2Sa 2: 9 He made him king over **G**,
1Ch 27:21 for the half-tribe of Manasseh in **G**,
Jer 8:22 Is there no balm in **G**?
46:11 Go up to **G**, and take balm,
Hos 6: 8 **G** is a city of evildoers, tracked
Mic 7:14 let them feed in Bashan and **G** as in
LAND OF GILEAD Nu 32:1, 29; Jos 17:5,
6; 22:9, 13, 15, 32; Jdg 10:4; 20:1; 1Sa 13:7;
2Sa 17:26; 1Ki 4:19; 2Ki 10:33; 1Ch 2:22;
5:9; Zec 10:10; 1Mc 13:22

GILEADITE → GILEAD
Jdg 11: 1 Now Jephthah the **G**, the son of a
2Sa 19:31 Barzillai the **G** had come down

GILGAL
Jos 4:20 of the Jordan, Joshua set up in **G**,
5: 9 so that place is called **G** to this day.
Jdg 2: 1 angel of the LORD went up from **G**
1Sa 7:16 a circuit year by year to Bethel, **G**,

GIRD → GIRDED
1Sa 2: 4 but the feeble **g** on strength.
Ps 45: 3 **G** your sword on your thigh,
65:12 the hills **g** themselves with joy,

GIRDED → GIRD
Ex 12:11 how you shall eat it: your loins **g**,
1Ki 18:46 he **g** up his loins and ran in front of
Ps 18:32 the God who **g** me with strength,
93: 1 he is **g** with strength.

GIRGASHITES
Dt 7: 1 the **G**, the Amorites, the Canaanites,

GIRL → GIRLS
Ge 24:16 The **g** was very fair to look upon,
Ex 1:16 but if it is a **g**, she shall live."
1Ki 1: 4 The **g** was very beautiful.
2Ki 5: 2 raids had taken a young **g** captive
Est 2: 7 the **g** was fair and beautiful,
Am 2: 7 father and son go in to the same **g**,
Mk 5:41 which means, "Little **g**, get up!"
6:22 and the king said to the **g**,
Tob 6:12 the **g** is sensible, brave,

GIRLS → GIRL
Joel 3: 3 sold **g** for wine, and drunk it down.
Zec 8: 5 shall be full of boys and **g** playing

GIVE → GAVE, GIVEN, GIVER, GIVES,
GIVING, GOD-GIVEN, LAWGIVER,
LIFE-GIVING
Ge 9: 3 the green plants, I **g** you everything.
12: 7 your offspring I will **g** this land."

28: 4 May he **g** to you the blessing of
28:22 of all that you **g** me I will surely **g**
one tenth
Ex 13: 5 he swore to your ancestors to **g** you,
17: 2 and said, "**G** us water to drink."
30:15 The rich shall not **g** more,
30:15 and the poor shall not **g** less,
Nu 6:26 upon you, and **g** you peace.
11:13 Where am I to get meat to **g** to all
Dt 15:10 **G** liberally and be ungrudging
Jos 1: 6 I swore to their ancestors to **g** them.
1Sa 1:11 will **g** to your servant a male child,
8: 6 "**G** us a king to govern us."
1Ki 3: 5 said, "Ask what I should **g** you."
11:13 I will **g** one tribe to your son,
2Ch 1:10 **G** me now wisdom and knowledge
Ne 9: 6 To all of them you **g** life,
Job 2: 4 they will **g** to save their lives.
Ps 5: 1 **G** ear to my words, O LORD;
13: 3 **G** light to my eyes, or I will sleep
30:12 I will **g** thanks to you forever.
Pr 21:26 righteous **g** and do not hold back.
23:26 My child, **g** me your heart,
25:21 If your enemies are hungry, **g** them
30: 8 **g** me neither poverty nor riches;
30:15 leech has two daughters; "**G, g,**"
31:31 **G** her a share in the fruit of her
Isa 7:14 the Lord himself will **g** you a sign.
42: 8 my glory I **g** to no other, nor my
Eze 36:26 A new heart I will **g** you,
Hos 9:14 **G** them, O LORD—what will you **g?**
11: 8 How can I **g** you up, Ephraim?
Mt 5:42 **G** to everyone who begs from you,
6: 2 So whenever you **g** alms,
6:11 **G** us this day our daily bread.
7: 6 "Do not **g** what is holy to dogs;
7:11 how to **g** good gifts to your children,
7:11 **g** good things to those who ask him!
10: 8 **g** without payment.
16:19 I will **g** you the keys of the kingdom
22:21 "**G** therefore to the emperor the
Mk 6:23 **g** you, even half of my kingdom."
8:37 can they **g** in return for their life?
10:45 to **g** his life a ransom for many."
Lk 6:38 **g**, and it will be given to you.
6:38 for the measure you **g** will be
11: 3 **G** us each day our daily bread.
11:13 ow to **g** good gifts to your children,
14:33 do not **g** up all your possessions.
Jn 4:14 drink of the water that I will **g** them
6:52 "How can this man **g** us his flesh to
10:28 I **g** them eternal life, and they will
13:34 I **g** you a new commandment,
14:16 and he will **g** you another Advocate,
14:27 leave with you; my peace I **g** to you.
17: 2 to **g** eternal life to all whom you
Ac 3: 6 or gold, but what I have I **g** you;
20:35 more blessed to **g** than to receive.'"
Ro 2: 7 immortality, he will **g** eternal life;
8:32 with him also **g** us everything else?
1Co 13: 3 If I **g** away all my possessions,
2Co 9: 7 **g** as you have made up your mind,
Gal 6: 9 if we do not **g** up.
Heb 13:17 and will **g** an account.
Rev 2: 7 I will **g** permission to eat from the
2:10 and I will **g** you the crown of life.
2:17 and I will **g** a white stone,
2:26 I will **g** authority over the nations;
2:28 the one who conquers I will also **g**
3:21 To the one who conquers I will **g** a
14: 7 "Fear God and **g** him glory,
Tob 4:16 **G** all your surplus as alms,
12: 9 who **g** alms will enjoy a full life,
Sir 7:10 do not neglect to **g** alms.

GIVEN → GIVE
Ge 1:30 I have **g** every green plant for food.
Ex 16:15 the bread that the LORD has **g** you
Nu 8:16 For they are unreservedly **g** to me
Dt 1:21 the LORD your God has **g** the land
26:11 that the LORD your God has **g**
Job 3:23 Why is light **g** to one who cannot

Ps 115:16 the earth he has **g** to human beings.
Isa 9: 6 has been born for us, a son **g** to us;
Da 2:37 God of heaven has **g** the kingdom,
Am 9:15 out of the land that I have **g** them,
Mt 6:33 and all these things will be **g** to you
7: 7 "Ask, and it will be **g** you;
22:30 neither marry nor are **g** in marriage,
25:29 all those who have, more will be **g**,
Mk 4:25 to those who have, more will be **g**;
8:12 no sign will be **g** to this generation."
Lk 6:38 and it will be **g** to you.
8:10 it has been **g** to know the secrets of
11: 9 to you, Ask, and it will be **g** you;
22:19 "This is my body, which is **g** for
Jn 1:17 law indeed was **g** through Moses;
3:27 anything except what has been **g**
6:39 lose nothing of all that he has **g** me,
17:24 those also, whom you have **g** me,
18:11 the cup that the Father has **g** me?"
Ac 5:32 the Holy Spirit whom God has **g**
Ro 5: 5 the Holy Spirit that has been **g** to us.
11:35 "Or who has **g** a gift to him,
1Co 11:24 and when he had **g** thanks,
2Co 5: 5 has **g** us the Spirit as a guarantee.
12: 7 a thorn was **g** me in the flesh,
Eph 4: 7 **g** grace according to the measure
1Ti 4:14 was **g** to you through prophecy with
1Pe 1: 3 great mercy he has **g** us a new birth
2Pe 1: 3 divine power has **g** us everything
1Jn 4:13 because he has **g** us of his Spirit.
5:20 come and has **g** us understanding so
Rev 6: 2 a crown was **g** to him,
20: 4 were **g** authority to judge.
Sir 35:12 Give to the Most High as he has **g**
43:33 and to the godly he has **g** wisdom.

GIVER → GIVE
Ro 12: 8 the **g**, in generosity;
2Co 9: 7 for God loves a cheerful **g**.
Sir 18:18 and the gift of a grudging **g** makes

GIVES → GIVE
Ex 4:11 to him, "Who **g** speech to mortals?
Job 33: 4 the breath of the Almighty **g** me life.
35:10 who **g** strength in the night,
Ps 119:130 The unfolding of your words **g** light;
136:25 who **g** food to all flesh,
Pr 2: 6 For the LORD **g** wisdom;
14:30 A tranquil mind **g** life to the flesh,
28:27 **g** to the poor will lack nothing.
29: 4 By justice a king **g** stability to the
Ecc 2:26 one who pleases him God **g** wisdom
Isa 40:29 He **g** power to the faint,
Mt 10:42 whoever **g** even a cup of cold water
Jn 3:34 for he **g** the Spirit without measure.
5:21 Son **g** life to whomever he wishes.
6:32 my Father who **g** you the true bread
6:37 Everything that the Father **g** me will
6:63 spirit that **g** life; the flesh is useless.
14:27 I do not give to you as the world **g**.
Ro 4:17 who **g** life to the dead
1Co 3: 7 but only God who **g** the growth.
15:57 to God, who **g** us the victory
2Co 3: 6 the letter kills, but the Spirit **g** life.
1Th 4: 8 who also **g** his Holy Spirit to you.
Jas 4: 6 But he **g** all the more grace;
4: 6 but **g** grace to the humble."
1Pe 5: 5 but **g** grace to the humble."
Sir 34:20 he **g** health and life and blessing.
35: 4 **g** alms sacrifices a thank offering.

GIVING → GIVE
Mt 24:38 marrying and **g** in marriage,
Ac 15: 8 to them by **g** them the Holy Spirit,
2Co 1:22 his seal on us and **g** us his Spirit in
Php 4:15 shared with me in the matter of **g**
Jas 1:17 Every generous act of **g**,
Sir 4: 3 or delay **g** to the needy.

GLAD → GLADDEN, GLADDENS,
GLADNESS
Ex 4:14 he sees you his heart will be **g**.

1Ch 16:31 Let the heavens be **g**, and let the
Job 22:19 The righteous see it and are **g**;
Ps   9: 2 I will be **g** and exult in you;
      14: 7 Jacob will rejoice; Israel will be **g**.
      16: 9 Therefore my heart is **g**, and my
      21: 6 you make him **g** with the joy of
      32: 7 you surround me with **g** cries of
      32:11 Be **g** in the LORD and rejoice,
      33:21 Our heart is **g** in him,
      34: 2 let the humble hear and be **g**.
      40: 9 have told the **g** news of deliverance
      40:16 seek you rejoice and be **g** in you;
      45: 8 stringed instruments make you **g**;
      46: 4 river whose streams make **g** the city
      48:11 be **g**, let the towns of Judah rejoice
      53: 6 Jacob will rejoice; Israel will be **g**.
      67: 4 the nations be **g** and sing for joy,
      69:32 Let the oppressed see it and be **g**;
      70: 4 seek you rejoice and be **g** in you.
      90:14 may rejoice and be **g** all our days.
      90:15 Make us **g** as many days as you
      92: 4 have made me **g** by your work;
      96:11 Let the heavens be **g**, and let the
      97: 1 let the many coastlands be **g**!
      97: 8 is **g**, and the towns of Judah rejoice.
     105:38 Egypt was **g** when they departed,
     107:30 they were **g** because they had quiet,
     107:42 The upright see it and are **g**;
     118:24 let us rejoice and be **g** in it.
     149: 2 Let Israel be **g** in its Maker;
Pr   10: 1 A wise child makes a **g** father,
     15:13 A **g** heart makes a cheerful
     15:20 A wise child makes a **g** father,
     17: 5 those who are **g** at calamity will
     23:15 heart is wise, my heart too will be **g**.
     23:24 who begets a wise son will be **g** in
     23:25 Let your father and mother be **g**;
     24:17 not let your heart be **g** when they
     29: 3 loves wisdom makes a parent **g**,
Isa 25: 9 be **g** and rejoice in his salvation.
     35: 1 and the dry land shall be **g**,
     65:18 be **g** and rejoice forever in what I
     66:10 Rejoice with Jerusalem, and be **g**
Jer 20:15 a son," making him very **g**.
     41:13 of the forces with him, they were **g**.
La   4:21 Rejoice and be **g**, O daughter Edom,
Joel 2:21 Do not fear, O soil; be **g** and rejoice,
      2:23 be **g** and rejoice in the LORD your
Zec   8:19 their hearts shall be **g** as with wine.
Mt   5:12 and be **g**, for your reward is great in
Jn   8:56 he saw it and was **g**."
     11:15 For your sake I am **g** I was not there
Ac   2:26 heart was **g**, and my tongue rejoiced
      2:46 ate their food with **g** and generous
     13:48 they were **g** and praised the word of
2Co   2: 2 to make me **g** but the one whom I
Php   2:17 I am **g** and rejoice with all of you—
      2:18 in the same way you also must be **g**
1Pe   4:13 **g** and shout for joy when his glory

GLADDEN* → GLAD

Ps   86: 4 **G** the soul of your servant,
    104:15 and wine to **g** the human heart,
Sir   4:18 back to them again and **g** them,
     40:20 Wine and music **g** the heart,

GLADDENS* → GLAD

Ecc 10:19 wine **g** life, and money meets every

GLADNESS → GLAD

Dt   28:47 with **g** of heart for the abundance
2Ch 29:30 They sang praises with **g**,
Est   8:16 the Jews there was light and **g**, joy
      8:17 there was **g** and joy among the Jews,
      9:22 make them days of feasting and **g**,
Ps   45:15 **g** they are led along as they enter
      51: 8 Let me hear joy and **g**;
     100: 2 Worship the LORD with **g**;
     106: 5 may rejoice in the **g** of your nation,
Pr   10:28 The hope of the righteous ends in **g**,
Isa 16:10 Joy and **g** are taken away from the
     35:10 they shall obtain joy and **g**,

      51: 3 joy and **g** will be found in her,
      51:11 they shall obtain joy and **g**,
      61: 3 the oil of **g** instead of mourning,
Jer   7:34 to an end the sound of mirth and **g**,
     16: 9 voice of mirth and the voice of **g**,
     25:10 sound of mirth and the sound of **g**,
     31:13 and give them **g** for sorrow.
     33:11 of mirth and the voice of **g**,
     48:33 **G** and joy have been taken away
Joel 1:16 and **g** from the house of our God?
Zep   3:17 he will rejoice over you with **g**,
Zec   8:19 shall be seasons of joy and **g**,
Lk   1:14 You will have joy and **g**,
Ac   2:28 full of **g** with your presence.'
Heb   1: 9 has anointed you with the oil of **g**
AdE   8:16 And the Jews had light and **g**
     10:13 with an assembly and joy and **g**
Sir   1:11 and **g** and a crown of rejoicing.
     30:16 and no **g** above joy of heart.

GLASS*

Job 28:17 Gold and **g** cannot equal it,
Rev   4: 6 there is something like a sea of **g**,
     15: 2 saw what appeared to be a sea of **g**
     15: 2 standing beside the sea of **g** who
     21:18 the city is pure gold, clear as **g**.
     21:21 city is pure gold, transparent as **g**.

GLAZE*

Pr   26:23 the **g** covering an earthen vessel are

GLEAM* → GLEAMING

Ps 132:18 but on him, his crown will **g**."
Da   10: 6 legs like the **g** of burnished bronze,
Hab   3:11 at the **g** of your flashing spear.

GLEAMING → GLEAM

Eze   1: 4 of the fire, something like **g** amber.
      8: 2 of brightness, like **g** amber.
     10: 9 of the wheels was like **g** beryl.

GLEAN → GLEANED, GLEANER, GLEANING, GLEANINGS

Dt   24:21 do not **g** what is left;
Ru   2: 2 Let me go to the field and **g** among
Job 24: 6 and they **g** in the vineyard of

GLEANED → GLEAN

Ru   2:17 So she **g** in the field until evening.
Mic   7: 1 after the vintage has been **g**,

GLEANER* → GLEAN

Sir 33:16 like a **g** following the grape-pickers;

GLEANING → GLEAN

Isa 24:13 as at the **g** when the grape harvest

GLEANINGS → GLEAN

Lev 19: 9 or gather the **g** of your harvest.
Isa 17: 6 **G** will be left in it,
Ob   1: 5 would they not leave **g**?

GLIDED* → GLIDING

Job   4:15 A spirit **g** past my face;

GLIDING* → GLIDED

SS   7: 9 goes down smoothly, **g** over lips
Jer 46:22 makes a sound like a snake **g** away;

GLOAT* → GLOATED, GLOATING

Ps   22:17 They stare and **g** over me;
Rev 11:10 inhabitants of the earth will **g** over

GLOATED* → GLOAT

Ob   1:12 should not have **g** over your brother

GLOATING* → GLOAT

Ob   1:13 joined in the **g** over Judah's disaster
Hab   3:14 **g** as if ready to devour the poor

GLOOM

Job   3: 5 Let **g** and deep darkness claim it.
Ps 107:10 Some sat in darkness and in **g**,
Isa   9: 1 there will be no **g** for those who
Joel 2: 2 a day of darkness and **g**,

Am   5:20 not light, and **g** with no brightness
Zep   1:15 a day of darkness and **g**,
Heb 12:18 and darkness, and **g**, and a tempest,
AdE 11: 8 It was a day of darkness and **g**,

GLORIFIED → GLORY

Lev 10: 3 before all the people I will be **g**.'"
1Ch 22: 5 famous and **g** throughout all lands;
Isa 44:23 and will be **g** in Israel.
     60: 9 of Israel, because he has **g** you.
     66: 5 the LORD be **g**, so that we may see
Mt   9: 8 filled with awe, and they **g** God,
Mk   2:12 they were all amazed and **g** God,
Lk   5:26 they **g** God and were filled with awe
      7:16 and they **g** God, saying,
Jn   7:39 because Jesus was not yet **g**.
     11: 4 Son of God may be **g** through it."
     12:16 but when Jesus was **g**,
     12:23 for the Son of Man to be **g**.
     12:28 came from heaven, "I have **g** it,
     13:31 "Now the Son of Man has been **g**,
     13:31 and God has been **g** in him.
     13:32 If God has been **g** in him,
     14:13 that the Father may be **g** in the Son.
     15: 8 My Father is **g** by this,
     17: 4 **g** you on earth by finishing the work
     17:10 and I have been **g** in them.
Ac   3:13 has **g** his servant Jesus,
Ro   8:17 so that we may also be **g** with him.
      8:30 those whom he justified he also **g**.
Gal   1:24 And they **g** God because of me.
2Th   1:10 **g** by his saints and to be marveled
      1:12 name of our Lord Jesus may be **g** in
      3: 1 spread rapidly and be **g** everywhere,
1Pe   4:11 God may be **g** in all things through
Rev 18: 7 she **g** herself and lived luxuriously,
AdE 14: 7 because we **g** their gods.
Sir   3:20 but by the humble he is **g**.
Aza   1:34 and to be sung and **g** forever.

GLORIFIES* → GLORY

Jn   8:54 It is my Father who **g** me,
Wis   8: 3 her noble birth by living with God

GLORIFY → GLORY

Ps   22:23 All you offspring of Jacob, **g** him;
     50:15 deliver you, and you shall **g** me."
     86: 9 O Lord, and shall **g** your name.
     86:12 and I will **g** your name forever.
Isa 25: 3 Therefore strong peoples will **g** you;
     60:13 and I will **g** where my feet rest.
Jn   8:54 Jesus answered, "If I **g** myself,
     12:28 glorified it, and I will **g** it again."
     13:32 God will also **g** him in himself and
                will **g** him at once.
     16:14 He will **g** me, because he will take
     17: 1 **g** your Son so that the Son may **g**
                you,
     17: 5 **g** me in your own presence with the
     21:19 death by which he would **g** God.)
Ro   15: 6 you may with one voice **g** the God
     15: 9 Gentiles might **g** God for his mercy.
1Co   6:20 therefore **g** God in your body.
2Co   9:13 you **g** God by your obedience to
Heb   5: 5 So also Christ did not **g** himself in
1Pe   2:12 see your honorable deeds and **g** God
      4:16 **g** God because you bear this name.
Rev 15: 4 who will not fear and **g** your name?
Sir   3:10 Do not **g** yourself by dishonoring
     43:30 **G** the Lord and exalt him as much

GLORIFYING → GLORY

Lk   2:20 **g** and praising God for all they had
      5:25 and went to his home, **g** God.
     18:43 and followed him, **g** God;

GLORIOUS → GLORY

Ex   15: 6 right hand, O LORD, **g** in power—
     28: 2 **g** adornment of your brother Aaron.
     28:40 make them for their **g** adornment.
Dt   28:58 fearing this **g** and awesome name,
1Ch 29:13 and praise your **g** name.
Ne   9: 5 Blessed be your **g** name, which is

Ps 66: 2 of his name; give to him g praise.
72:19 Blessed be his g name forever;
76: 4 G are you, more majestic than
78: 4 the g deeds of the LORD.
87: 3 G things are spoken of you, O city
90:16 and your g power to their children.
145: 5 On the g splendor of your majesty,
145:12 and the g splendor of your kingdom.
Isa 3: 8 the LORD, defying his g presence.
4: 2 of the LORD shall be beautiful and g,
9: 1 he will make the way of the sea,
11:10 and his dwelling shall be g.
28: 1 the fading flower of its g beauty,
28: 4 the fading flower of its g beauty,
42:21 magnify his teaching and make it g.
60: 7 and I will glorify my g house.
63:12 who caused his g arm to march at
63:14 to make for yourself a g name.
63:15 from your holy and g habitation.
Jer 14:21 do not dishonor your g throne;
17:12 g throne, exalted from the beginning
48:17 scepter is broken, the g staff!"
Eze 20: 6 the most g of all lands.
Ac 2:20 of the Lord's great and g day.
Eph 1: 6 praise of his g grace that he freely
1:18 the riches of his g inheritance
Col 1:11 that comes from his g power,
1Ti 1:11 that conforms to the g gospel of the
Jas 2: 1 in our g Lord Jesus Christ?
1Pe 1: 8 with an indescribable and g joy,
2Pe 2:10 are not afraid to slander the g ones,
Jude 1: 8 and slander the g ones.
Jdt 16:13 O Lord, you are great and g,
Wis 5:16 a g crown and a beautiful diadem
Sir 6:31 You will wear her like a g robe,
Aza 1: 3 and g is your name forever!
1Mc 2: 9 her g vessels have been carried into
14:15 He made the sanctuary g,

GLORIOUS NAME 1Ch 29:13; Ne 9:5; Ps
72:19; Isa 63:14; Jdt 9:8; Aza 1:3, 30; 2Mc
8:15; Man 1:3; 3Mc 2:14

GLORIOUSLY → GLORY

Ex 15: 1 to the LORD, for he has triumphed g;
Isa 12: 5 to the LORD, for he has done g;

GLORY → GLORIFIED, GLORIFIES,
GLORIFY, GLORIFYING, GLORIOUS,
GLORIOUSLY

Ex 14: 4 will gain g for myself over Pharaoh
14:17 will gain g for myself over Pharaoh
14:18 gained g for myself over Pharaoh,
16: 7 you shall see the g of the LORD.
16:10 g of the LORD appeared in the cloud.
24:16 The g of the LORD settled on Mount
24:17 g of the LORD was like a devouring
29:43 and it shall be sanctified by my g;
33:18 Moses said, "Show me your g,
33:22 my g passes by I will put you in a
40:34 g of the LORD filled the tabernacle.
Lev 9:23 the g of the LORD appeared to all
Nu 14:10 Then the g of the LORD appeared at
14:21 the earth shall be filled with the g of
14:22 who have seen my g and the signs
16:19 And the g of the LORD appeared to
16:42 the cloud had covered it and the g of
20: 6 the g of the LORD appeared to them.
Dt 5:24 LORD our God has shown us his g
Jos 7:19 give g to the LORD God of Israel
1Sa 4:21 "The g has departed from Israel,"
15:29 G of Israel will not recant or change
2Sa 1:19 Your g, O Israel, lies slain
1Ki 8:11 g of the LORD filled the house of the
1Ch 16:10 G in his holy name; let the hearts of
16:24 Declare his g among the nations,
16:28 ascribe to the LORD g and strength.
29:11 are the greatness, the power, the g,
2Ch 5:14 the g of the LORD filled the house
7: 1 the g of the LORD filled the temple.
Job 29:20 my g was fresh with me,
Ps 3: 3 are a shield around me, my g,
8: 1 have set your g above the heavens.

8: 5 crowned them with g and honor.
19: 1 heavens are telling the g of God;
24: 7 that the King of g may come in.
26: 8 and the place where your g abides.
29: 1 ascribe to the LORD g and strength.
29: 3 the God of g thunders, the LORD,
29: 9 and in his temple all say, "G!"
57: 5 Let your g be over all the earth.
63: 2 beholding your power and g.
66: 2 sing the g of his name;
72:19 may his g fill the whole earth.
85: 9 that his g may dwell in our land.
89:17 For you are the g of their strength;
96: 3 Declare his g among the nations,
96: 8 Ascribe to the LORD the g due his
97: 6 and all the peoples behold his g.
102:15 and all the kings of the earth your g.
104:31 the g of the LORD endure forever;
106:20 They exchanged the g of God for
108: 5 and let your g be over all the earth.
138: 5 for great is the g of the LORD.
143: 9 This is g for all his faithful ones.
Pr 19:11 it is their g to overlook an offense.
20:29 The g of youths is their strength,
25: 2 It is the g of God to conceal things,
25: 2 the g of kings is to search things out
Isa 2:10 and from the g of his majesty.
4: 5 over all the g there will be a canopy.
6: 3 the whole earth is full of his g."
24:16 of g to the Righteous One.
35: 2 The g of Lebanon shall be given to
35: 2 They shall see the g of the LORD,
40: 5 the g of the LORD shall be revealed,
42: 8 my g I give to no other, nor my
42:12 Let them give g to the LORD,
43: 7 whom I created for my g,
48:11 My g I will not give to another.
60:19 and your God will be your g.
66:18 they shall come and shall see my g,
66:19 declare my g among the nations.
Jer 2:11 But my people have changed their g
Eze 1:28 appearance of the likeness of the g
3:23 and the g of the LORD stood there,
8: 4 the g of the God of Israel was there,
9: 3 g of the God of Israel had gone up
10: 4 the g of the LORD rose up from the
10:18 the g of the LORD went out from the
11:23 g of the LORD ascended from the
43: 2 g of the God of Israel was coming
43: 5 the g of the LORD filled the temple.
44: 4 g of the LORD filled the temple of
Da 2:37 the power, the might, and the g,
7:14 To him was given dominion and g
Hos 4: 7 they changed their g into shame.
Hab 2:14 the knowledge of the g of the LORD,
3: 3 His g covered the heavens,
Zec 2: 5 and I will be the g within it."
12: 7 that the g of the house of David and
Mal 2: 2 not lay it to heart to give g to my
Mt 16:27 his angels in the g of his Father,
24:30 with power and great g.
25:31 the Son of Man comes in his g,
25:31 he will sit on the throne of his g.
Mk 8:38 be ashamed when he comes in the g
10:37 and one at your left, in your g."
13:26 in clouds' with great power and g.
Lk 2: 9 the g of the Lord shone around them
2:14 "G to God in the highest heaven,
2:32 and for g to your people Israel."
9:26 be ashamed when he comes in his g
9:32 had stayed awake, they saw his g
19:38 and g in the highest heaven!"
21:27 in a cloud' with power and great g.
24:26 and then enter into his g?"
Jn 1:14 and we have seen his g,
1:14 the g as of a father's only son,
2:11 Cana of Galilee, and revealed his g;
5:41 I do not accept g from human
7:18 on their own seek their own g;
8:50 Yet I do not seek my own g;
8:54 "If I glorify myself, my g is nothing.
11: 4 rather it is for God's g,

11:40 you would see the g of God?"
12:41 Isaiah said this because he saw his g
17: 5 the g that I had in your presence
17:22 The g that you have given me I have
17:24 be with me where I am, to see my g,
Ac 7: 2 God of g appeared to our ancestor
7:55 the g of God and Jesus standing at
Ro 1:23 the g of the immortal God for
2: 7 by patiently doing good seek for g
2:10 but g and honor and peace
3: 7 to his g, why am I still being
3:23 all have sinned and fall short of the
g of God;
4:20 in his faith as he gave g to God,
5: 2 in our hope of sharing the g of God.
8:18 not worth comparing with the g
9: 4 the g, the covenants, the giving of
9:23 to make known the riches of his g
9:23 he has prepared beforehand for g—
11:36 To him be the g forever.
16:27 Christ, to whom be the g forever!
1Co 2: 7 decreed before the ages for our g.
2: 8 not have crucified the Lord of g.
10:31 do everything for the g of God.
11:15 if a woman has long hair, it is her g?
15:43 sown in dishonor, it is raised in g.
2Co 1:20 that we say the "Amen," to the g
3: 7 not gaze at Moses' face because of
the g of his face, a g now set aside,
3:10 what once had g has lost its g
because of the greater g;
3:11 more has the permanent come in g!
3:18 from one degree of g to another;
4: 4 the light of the gospel of the g
4: 6 of the knowledge of the g of God
4:15 thanksgiving, to the g of God.
4:17 for an eternal weight of g beyond
Eph 1:12 might live for the praise of his g.
1:14 to the praise of his g.
3:13 sufferings for you; they are your g.
3:21 be g in the church and in Christ
Php 1:11 through Jesus Christ for the g and
2:11 to the g of God the Father.
3:19 and their g is in their shame;
4:20 To our God and Father be g forever
Col 1:27 Christ in you, the hope of g.
3: 4 also be revealed with him in g.
1Th 2:12 into his own kingdom and g.
2:20 Yes, you are our g and joy!
2Th 2:14 may obtain the g of our Lord Jesus
1Ti 1:17 God, be honor and g forever and
3:16 throughout the world, taken up in g.
2Ti 2:10 in Christ Jesus, with eternal g.
4:18 To him be the g forever and ever.
Heb 1: 3 reflection of God's g and the exact
2: 7 you have crowned them with g and
2: 9 now crowned with g and honor
2:10 in bringing many children to g,
3: 3 Yet Jesus is worthy of more g than
9: 5 the cherubim of g overshadowing
13:21 to whom be the g forever and ever.
1Pe 1: 7 to result in praise and g and honor
1:24 all its g like the flower of grass.
4:11 To him belong the g and the power
4:13 shout for joy when his g is revealed.
4:14 blessed, because the spirit of g,
5: 1 who shares in the g to be revealed,
5: 4 crown of g that never fades away.
5:10 called you to his eternal g in Christ,
2Pe 1: 3 called us by his own g and goodness
1:17 conveyed to him by the Majestic G,
3:18 g both now and to the day of
Jude 1:25 through Jesus Christ our Lord, be g,
Rev 1: 6 to him be g and dominion forever
4: 9 the living creatures give g and
4:11 to receive g and honor and power,
5:12 and might and honor and g
5:13 be blessing and honor and g and
7:12 and g and wisdom and thanksgiving
11:13 were terrified and gave g to the God
14: 7 "Fear God and give him g,
15: 8 was filled with smoke from the g

16: 9 they did not repent and give him **g.**
19: 1 and **g** and power to our God,
19: 7 rejoice and exult and give him the **g,**
21:11 has the **g** of God and a radiance like
21:23 for the **g** of God is its light,
21:26 People will bring into it the **g** and
Tob 12:15 and enter before the **g** of the Lord."
Jdt 15: 9 "You are the **g** of Jerusalem,
Wis 7:25 emanation of the **g** of the Almighty;
Sir 1:11 The fear of the Lord is **g** and
Bar 5: 4 "Righteous Peace, Godly **G."**
1Mc 1:40 dishonor now grew as great as her **g.**

GAVE/GIVE/GIVING GLORY Jos 7:19;
1Sa 6:5; Ps 115:1; Isa 24:15; 42:12; Jer 13:16;
Mal 2:2; Mt 5:16; Lk 4:6; Jn 9:24; Ac 12:23;
Ro 4:20; 1Pe 1:21; Rev 4:9; 11:13; 14:7; 16:9;
19:7; Sir 51:17; Bar 4:3; 1Es 9:8; 2Es 9:45;
13:57; 4Mc 1:12

GLORY OF ... *GOD Ps 19:1; 106:20; Pr
25:2; Eze 8:4; 9:3; 10:19; 11:22; 43:2; Jn
11:40; Ac 7:55; Ro 3:23; 5:2; 15:7; 1Co 10:31;
2Co 1:20; 4:6, 15; Php 2:11; Rev 15:8; 21:11,
23; AdE 13:14; Bar 4:37; 5:7

GLORY OF THE *LORD Lk 2:9; 2Co
3:18; 8:19; Tob 12:12, 15; 2Mc 2:8

GLORY OF THE †LORD Ex 16:7, 10;
24:16, 17; 40:34, 35; Lev 9:6, 23; Nu 14:10,
21; 16:19, 42; 20:6; 1Ki 8:11; 2Ch 5:14; 7:1,
2, 3; Ps 104:31; 138:5; Isa 35:2; 40:5; 58:8;
60:1; Eze 1:28; 3:12, 23; 10:4, 4, 18; 11:23;
43:4, 5; 44:4; Hab 2:14

HIS GLORY Dt 5:24; 1Ch 16:24; Ps 21:5;
72:19; 78:61; 85:9; 96:3; 97:6; 102:16; 113:4;
148:13; Isa 6:3; 8:7; 10:16; 24:23; 59:19; 60:2;
61:3; Eze 43:2; Da 5:20; Hab 3:3; Zec 2:8; Mt
6:29; 19:28; 25:31, 31; Lk 9:26, 32; 12:27;
24:26; Jn 1:14; 2:11; 12:41; Ro 3:7; 9:23; Eph
1:12, 14; 3:16; Php 3:21; 1Pe 4:13; Jude 1:24;
Sir 42:16, 17, 25; 45:3; 47:8; Bar 5:9; 1Es
5:61; 2Es 16:53, 66

MY GLORY Ex 29:43; 33:22; Nu 14:22; Job
19:9; 29:20; Ps 3:3; Isa 42:8; 43:7; 46:13;
48:11; 66:18, 19, 19; La 3:18; Eze 39:13, 21;
Mic 2:9; Jn 8:54; 17:24; 2Es 7:60

YOUR GLORY Ex 33:18; Jdg 4:9; 2Sa 1:19;
2Ki 14:10; Ps 8:1; 26:8; 45:3; 57:5, 11; 71:8;
102:15; 108:5; Isa 60:19; 62:2; Hab 2:16; Mk
10:37; Eph 3:13; Tob 13:14, 16; AdE 15:13;
Wis 9:10; Sir 9:16; 36:4, 19; Bar 2:18; 4:3;
1Mc 12:12; 14:21; 15:9; 3Mc 2:16; 2Es 2:36;
3:19; 8:30; 15:60

GLUTTON → GLUTTONOUS, GLUTTONS,
GLUTTONY
Pr 23:21 and the **g** will come to poverty,
Mt 11:19 they say, 'Look, a **g** and a drunkard,
Lk 7:34 you say, 'Look, a **g** and a drunkard,
Sir 31:20 nausea and colic are with the **g.**

GLUTTONOUS· → GLUTTON
Pr 23:20 or among **g** eaters of meat;

GLUTTONS· → GLUTTON
Pr 28: 7 of **g** shame their parents.
Tit 1:12 always liars, vicious brutes, lazy **g."**

GLUTTONY → GLUTTON
Sir 23: 6 Let neither **g** nor lust overcome me,

GNASH· → GNASHED, GNASHING
Ps 37:12 and **g** their teeth at them;
112:10 they **g** their teeth and melt away;
La 2:16 hiss, they **g** their teeth, they cry:
Sir 30:10 and in the end you will **g** your teeth.

GNASHED· → GNASH
Job 16: 9 he has **g** his teeth at me;

GNASHING· → GNASH
Ps 35:16 **g** at me with their teeth.
Mt 8:12 will be weeping and **g** of teeth."
13:42 will be weeping and **g** of teeth.
13:50 will be weeping and **g** of teeth.
22:13 will be weeping and **g** of teeth.'
24:51 will be weeping and **g** of teeth.
25:30 will be weeping and **g** of teeth.'
Lk 13:28 **g** of teeth when you see Abraham

GNAT· → GNATS
Mt 23:24 strain out a **g** but swallow a camel!

GNATS → GNAT
Ex 8:16 become **g** throughout the whole land
Ps 105:31 and **g** throughout their country.

GO → GOES, GOING, GONE
Ge 4: 8 "Let us **g** out to the field."
7: 1 LORD said to Noah, "**G** into the ark,
11: 7 **g** down, and confuse their language
18:21 I must **g** down and see whether they
46: 4 will **g** down with you to Egypt,
Ex 3:19 not let you **g** unless compelled by a
5: 1 the God of Israel, 'Let my people **g,**
12:31 "Rise up, **g** away from my people,
12:31 **G,** worship the LORD, as you said.
13:15 stubbornly refused to let us **g,**
32: 1 gods for us, who shall **g** before us;
33: 3 **G** up to a land flowing with milk
33: 3 but I will not **g** up among you,
34: 9 Lord, I pray, let the Lord **g** with us.
Nu 13:30 "Let us **g** up at once and occupy it,
14: 3 be better for us to **g** back to Egypt?"
Dt 1:26 But you were unwilling to **g** up.
Jos 1: 9 God is with you wherever you **g."**
Ru 1:16 Where you **g,** I will **g;**
Ps 122: 1 "Let us **g** to the house of the LORD!"
139: 7 Where can I **g** from your spirit?
Pr 6: 6 **G** to the ant, you lazybones;
31:18 Her lamp does not **g** out at night.
Isa 2: 3 **g** up to the mountain of the LORD,
2: 3 out of Zion shall **g** forth instruction,
55:12 you shall **g** out in joy, and be led
Eze 1:12 wherever the spirit would **g,** they
Mic 4: 2 **g** up to the mountain of the LORD,
4: 2 out of Zion shall **g** forth instruction,
Zec 14: 3 Then the LORD will **g** forth and fight
Mal 4: 2 You shall **g** out leaping like calves
Mt 5:41 forces you to **g** one mile, **g** also
6: 6 **g** into your room and shut the door
28:19 **G** therefore and make disciples of
Mk 10:25 a camel to **g** through the eye of a
Lk 9:57 "I will follow you wherever you **g."**
Jn 6:68 "Lord, to whom can we **g?**
14: 3 if I **g** and prepare a place for you,

GOADS
Ecc 12:11 The sayings of the wise are like **g,**
Ac 26:14 It hurts you to kick against the **g.'**

GOAL
Php 3:14 I press on toward the **g** for the prize

GOAT → GOAT-DEMONS, GOATS, GOATS'
Ge 15: 9 a female **g** three years old, a ram
37:31 took Joseph's robe, slaughtered a **g,**
Lev 16: 9 Aaron shall present the **g** on which
Nu 7:16 one male **g** for a sin offering;
Da 8: 5 The **g** had a horn between its eyes.
8:21 The male **g** is the king of Greece.
Lk 15:29 never given me even a young **g** so
Tob 2:12 also gave her a young **g** for a meal.

GOAT-DEMONS· → DEMON, GOAT
Lev 17: 7 no longer offer their sacrifices for **g,**
2Ch 11:15 and for the **g,** and for the calves
Isa 13:21 and there **g** will dance.
34:14 **g** shall call to each other;

GOATS → GOAT
Nu 7:17 five male **g,** and five male lambs
Ps 50:13 or drink the blood of **g?**
Eze 34:17 and sheep, between rams and **g:**
Mt 25:32 separates the sheep from the **g,**
Heb 9:12 not with the blood of **g** and calves,
10: 4 for the blood of bulls and **g**

GOATS' → GOAT
Ex 26: 7 make curtains of **g** hair for a tent
Nu 31:20 everything made of **g** hair,

*GOD → GOD'S, GOD-FEARING,
GOD-GIVEN, GOD-HATERS, GODDESS,
GODLESS, GODLINESS, GODLY, GODS
Ge 1: 1 In the beginning when **G** created
1: 2 a wind from **G** swept over the face
1: 3 **G** said, "Let there be light"; and
1: 7 So **G** made the dome and separated
1: 9 And **G** said, "Let the waters under
1:11 Then **G** said, "Let the earth put forth
1:21 So **G** created the great sea monsters
1:21 And **G** saw that it was good.
1:22 **G** blessed them, saying, "Be fruitful
1:25 **G** made the wild animals of the
1:25 And **G** saw that it was good.
1:26 **G** said, "Let us make humankind
1:27 So **G** created humankind in his
     image, in the image of **G** he created
1:28 **G** blessed them, and **G** said to them,
1:31 **G** saw everything that he had made,
2: 3 So **G** blessed the seventh day and
2: 4 In the day that the LORD **G** made
2: 7 LORD **G** formed man from the dust
2: 8 LORD **G** planted a garden in Eden,
2:16 the LORD **G** commanded the man,
2:22 LORD **G** had taken from the man he
3: 1 He said to the woman, "Did **G** say,
3: 5 for **G** knows that when you eat
3: 5 be like **G,** knowing good and evil."
3: 8 the sound of the LORD **G** walking
3: 9 But the LORD **G** called to the man,
3:13 the LORD **G** said to the woman,
3:14 The LORD **G** said to the serpent,
3:21 LORD **G** made garments of skins for
3:23 the LORD **G** sent him forth from the
5: 1 When **G** created humankind, he
     made them in the likeness of **G.**
5:24 Enoch walked with **G;**
5:24 was no more, because **G** took him.
6: 2 sons of **G** saw that they were fair;
6: 9 Noah walked with **G.**
6:12 **G** saw that the earth was corrupt;
8: 1 But **G** remembered Noah and all
9: 1 **G** blessed Noah and his sons, and
9: 6 his own image **G** made humankind.
9:16 between **G** and every living creature
14:18 he was priest of **G** Most High.
14:19 Blessed be Abram by **G** Most High,
16:13 I had seen and remained alive
17: 1 and said to him, "I am **G** Almighty;
17: 7 to be **G** to you and to your offspring
19:29 **G** remembered Abraham,
21: 2 the time of which **G** had spoken
21: 6 Sarah said, "**G** has brought laughter
21:17 And **G** heard the voice of the boy;
21:20 **G** was with the boy, and he grew
21:22 "**G** is with you in all that you do;
21:33 of the LORD, the Everlasting **G.**
22: 1 these things **G** tested Abraham.
22: 8 "**G** himself will provide the lamb
22:12 for now I know that you fear **G,**
25:11 of Abraham **G** blessed his son Isaac.
26:24 I am the **G** of your father Abraham;
28:12 angels of **G** were ascending and
28:17 none other than the house of **G,**
30: 2 "Am I in the place of **G,**
31:13 I am the **G** of Bethel,
31:42 **G** saw my affliction and the labor

*GOD distinguishes the words translated "God" and "god" from the compound name "Lord GOD," where GOD represents the proper name *Yahweh*.
For this name see the heading **†GOD**, beginning on page 128.

31:50 remember that G is witness between
32: 1 and the angels of G met him;
32:28 for you have striven with G and
32:30 "For I have seen G face to face,
33:11 because G has dealt graciously with
35: 1 Make an altar there to the G who
35: 5 terror from G fell upon the cities all
35:10 G said to him, "Your name is Jacob;
35:11 G said to him, "I am G Almighty:
41:38 one in whom is the spirit of G?"
41:51 "G has made me forget all my
41:52 "For G has made me fruitful in the
46: 2 G spoke to Israel in visions of the
48:15 the G who has been my shepherd
50:19 Am I in the place of G?
50:20 harm to me, G intended it for good,
50:24 but G will surely come to you,

Ex 1:17 But the midwives feared G;
2:24 G heard their groaning,
2:24 and G remembered his covenant
3: 4 G called to him out of the bush,
3: 6 He said further, "I am the G of your
    father, the G of Abraham, the G of
    Isaac, and the G of Jacob."
3: 6 for he was afraid to look at G.
3:12 shall worship G on this mountain.
3:14 G said to Moses, "I AM WHO I AM."
3:18 the G of the Hebrews, has met with
4:27 he met him at the mountain of G
6: 7 and I will be your G.
7: 1 I have made you like G to Pharaoh,
8:10 there is no one like the LORD our G,
8:19 "This is the finger of G!"
10:16 sinned against the LORD your G,
13:19 "G will surely take notice of you,
14:19 The angel of G who was going
15: 2 this is my G, and I will praise him,
16:12 know that I am the LORD your G.'"
17: 9 with the staff of G in my hand."
18: 4 "The G of my father was my help,
18: 5 at the mountain of G,
19: 3 Then Moses went up to G;
20: 1 Then G spoke all these words:
20: 2 I am the LORD your G, who brought
20: 5 I the LORD your G am a jealous G,
20: 7 of the name of the LORD your G,
20:10 is a sabbath to the LORD your G;
20:12 land that the LORD your G is giving
20:19 not let G speak to us, or we will die.
22:20 Whoever sacrifices to any g,
22:28 You shall not revile G, or curse a
23:19 into the house of the LORD your G.
24:10 and they saw the G of Israel.
29:46 I am the LORD their G.
31:18 stone, written with the finger of G.
34: 6 a G merciful and gracious, slow to
34:14 (for you shall worship no other g,
34:14 name is Jealous, is a jealous G).

Nu 15:40 and you shall be holy to your G.
16:22 O G, the G of the spirits of all flesh,
22: 9 G came to Balaam and said,
22:18 the command of the LORD my G,
22:38 The word G puts in my mouth,
23:19 G is not a human being,
25:13 because he was zealous for his G,
27:16 the G of the spirits of all flesh,

Dt 1:21 the LORD your G has given the land
1:32 have no trust in the LORD your G,
3:22 the LORD your G who fights for you
3:24 what g in heaven or on earth can
4: 7 what other great nation has a g so
    near to it as the LORD our G is
4:24 For the LORD your G is a devouring
    fire, a jealous G.
4:29 you will seek the LORD your G,
4:31 the LORD your G is a merciful G,
4:39 that the LORD is G in heaven
5: 9 I the LORD your G am a jealous G,
5:11 of the name of the LORD your G,
5:12 the LORD your G commanded you.
5:14 a sabbath to the LORD your G;
5:15 the LORD your G brought you out

5:15 the LORD your G commanded you
5:16 the LORD your G commanded you,
5:16 in the land that the LORD your G is
5:24 LORD our G has shown us his glory
5:26 voice of the living G speaking so
6: 2 the LORD your G all the days
6: 4 The LORD is our G, the LORD alone.
6: 5 love the LORD your G with all your
6:13 The LORD your G you shall fear;
6:16 not put the LORD your G to the test,
7: 6 a people holy to the LORD your G;
7: 9 therefore that the LORD your G is G,
7: 9 faithful G who maintains covenant
7:21 is a great and awesome G,
8: 5 so the LORD your G disciplines you.
8:11 do not forget the LORD your G,
8:18 But remember the LORD your G,
9:10 tablets written with the finger of G;
10:12 what does the LORD your G require
10:12 Only to fear the LORD your G,
10:14 heavens belong to the LORD your G,
10:17 LORD your G is G of gods and Lord
10:21 He is your praise; he is your G,
11: 1 You shall love the LORD your G,
11:13 loving the LORD your G,
12:12 rejoice before the LORD your G,
12:28 in the sight of the LORD your G.
13: 3 for the LORD your G is testing you,
14: 1 are children of the LORD your G.
14: 2 a people holy to the LORD your G;
15: 6 When the LORD your G has blessed
15:19 consecrate to the LORD your G;
16:11 Rejoice before the LORD your G—
16:17 to the blessing of the LORD your G
16:22 things that the LORD your G hates.
18:13 loyal to the LORD your G.
18:15 The LORD your G will raise up for
19: 9 by loving the LORD your G and
23: 5 LORD your G turned the curse into
23: 5 because the LORD your G loved you
23:14 the LORD your G travels along with
23:21 make a vow to the LORD your G,
25:16 are abhorrent to the LORD your G.
26: 5 before the LORD your G:
27: 5 an altar there to the LORD your G,
28: 1 only obey the LORD your G,
28:15 will not obey the LORD your G
29:13 and that he may be your G,
29:29 belong to the LORD our G,
30: 2 and return to the LORD your G,
30: 4 there the LORD your G will gather
30: 6 your G will circumcise your heart
30:16 by loving the LORD your G,
30:20 loving the LORD your G, obeying
31: 6 LORD your G who goes with you;
32: 3 ascribe greatness to our G!
32: 4 faithful G, without deceit, just and
32:18 forgot the G who gave you birth.
32:39 there is no g besides me.

Jos 1: 9 LORD your G is with you wherever
1:13 your G is providing you a place of
14: 8 followed the LORD my G.
14:14 the LORD, the G of Israel.
22: 5 to love the LORD your G,
22:22 "The LORD, G of gods! The LORD,
    G of gods!
22:34 between us that the LORD is G."
23: 3 the LORD your G has done to all
23: 3 your G who has fought for you.
23: 8 but hold fast to the LORD your G,
23:11 therefore, to love the LORD your G.
23:14 that the LORD your G promised
23:15 that the LORD your G promised
23:15 that the LORD your G has given you.
24:19 He is a jealous G;

Jdg 1: 7 have done, so G has paid me back."
5: 5 before the LORD, the G of Israel.
6:20 The angel of G said to him,
6:31 If he is a g, let him contend for
8:33 making Baal-berith their g.
13: 6 "A man of G came to me,
13: 6 was like that of an angel of G,

16:23 a great sacrifice to their g Dagon,
16:23 Our g has given Samson our enemy
16:28 strengthen me only this once, O G,
20:27 ark of the covenant of G was there

Ru 1:16 be my people, and your G my G.

1Sa 2: 2 there is no Rock like our G.
2: 3 for the LORD is a G of knowledge,
3: 3 the lamp of G had not yet gone out,
3: 3 where the ark of G was.
4:11 The ark of G was captured;
5:11 The hand of G was very heavy there
10: 9 G gave him another heart;
10:26 whose hearts G had touched.
11: 6 And the spirit of G came upon Saul
12:12 the LORD your G was your king.
16:15 an evil spirit from G is tormenting
17:36 defied the armies of the living G."
17:45 the G of the armies of Israel,
17:46 may know that there is a G in Israel,
19:23 and the spirit of G came upon him.
28:15 and G has turned away from me
30: 6 himself in the LORD his G.

2Sa 6: 7 and G struck him there
7:22 Therefore you are great, O LORD G;
7:22 and there is no G besides you,
7:23 on earth whose G went to redeem it
7:27 O LORD of hosts, the G of Israel,
14:14 But G will not take away a life;
14:17 the king is like the angel of G,
14:17 The LORD your G be with you!"
21:14 G heeded supplications for the land.
22: 3 my G, my rock, in whom
22:31 This G—his way is perfect;
22:32 For who is G, but the LORD?
22:33 The G who has girded me
22:47 my rock, and exalted be my G,

1Ki 2: 3 keep the charge of the LORD your G
4:29 G gave Solomon very great wisdom
5: 5 for the name of the LORD my G,
8:23 He said, "O LORD, G of Israel,
    there is no G like you in heaven
8:27 will G indeed dwell on the earth?
8:60 earth may know that the LORD is G;
8:61 to the LORD our G,
10:24 which G had put into his mind.
11: 4 was not true to the LORD his G,
11:33 Chemosh the g of Moab, and
    Milcom the g of the Ammonites,
15:30 provoked the LORD, the G of Israel.
18:21 If the LORD is G, follow him;
18:24 the g who answers by fire is indeed
    G."
18:36 this day that you are G in Israel,
18:39 "The LORD indeed is G; the LORD
    indeed is G."
20:28 'The LORD is a g of the hills but he
    is not a g

2Ki 1: 2 of Baal-zebub, the g of Ekron,
5:15 there is no G in all the earth except
17: 7 sinned against the LORD their G,
19: 4 to mock the living G,
19:15 "O LORD the G of Israel,
19:19 So now, O LORD our G, save us,

1Ch 12:18 For your G is the one who helps you
13: 2 if it is the will of the LORD our G,
16:35 "Save us, O G of our salvation,
17:20 and there is no G besides you,
17:24 'The LORD of hosts, the G of Israel,
    is Israel's G';
21: 8 David said to G, "I have sinned
21:15 And G sent an angel to Jerusalem
22: 1 the LORD G and here the altar of
22:19 and heart to seek the LORD your G.
28: 2 for the footstool of our G;
28: 9 my son Solomon, know the G of
28:20 for the LORD G, my G, is with you.
29: 1 for mortals but for the LORD G.
29: 2 provided for the house of my G,
29:10 the G of our ancestor Israel, forever
29:13 now, our G, we give thanks to you
29:18 O LORD, the G of Abraham, Isaac,

2Ch 1: 7 That night G appeared to Solomon,

2: 4 for the name of the LORD my **G** and
2: 5 for our **G** is greater than other gods.
5:14 of the LORD filled the house of **G.**
6:14 He said, "O LORD, **G** of Israel,
there is no **G** like you,
6:18 will **G** indeed reside with mortals
10:15 brought about by **G** so that the
13:12 See, **G** is with us at our head,
15: 3 time Israel was without the true **G,**
15:12 the **G** of their ancestors,
18:13 whatever my **G** says,
19: 3 and have set your heart to seek **G."**
19: 7 of justice with the LORD our **G,**
20: 6 **G** of our ancestors, are you not **G** in
20:20 the LORD your **G** and you will be
25: 8 or **G** will fling you down before the
25: 8 has power to help or to overthrow
26: 5 He set himself to seek **G** in the days
30: 9 For the LORD your **G** is gracious
30:19 who set their hearts to seek **G,**
31:21 to seek his **G,** he did with all his
32:15 for no **g** of any nation or kingdom
32:17 contempt on the LORD the **G** of
32:31 **G** left him to himself, in order to
33:12 himself greatly before the **G**
33:19 and how **G** received his entreaty,
34:33 in Israel worship the LORD their **G.**
Ezr 1: 3 may their **G** be with them!—
2:68 for the house of **G,** to erect it
6:16 the dedication of this house of **G**
7: 9 gracious hand of his **G** was upon
7:18 according to the will of your **G.**
7:23 commanded by the **G** of heaven,
8:22 that the hand of our **G** is gracious
8:31 the hand of our **G** was upon us,
9: 6 "O my **G,** I am too ashamed and
9: 9 yet our **G** has not forsaken us in our
9: 9 new life to set up the house of our **G**
10: 3 et us make a covenant with our **G**
Ne 1: 5 I said, "O LORD **G** of heaven,
4:20 Our **G** will fight for us."
5:15 not do so, because of the fear of **G.**
7: 2 a faithful man and feared **G** more
8: 8 from the book, from the law of **G,**
8:18 read from the book of the law of **G.**
9: 5 bless the LORD your **G** from
9:17 But you are a **G** ready to forgive,
9:31 you are a gracious and merciful **G.**
9:32 "Now therefore, our **G**—the great
and mighty and awesome **G,**
10:29 given by Moses the servant of **G,**
10:39 will not neglect the house of our **G.**
12:43 for **G** had made them rejoice with
13: 2 yet our **G** turned the curse into a
13:11 "Why is the house of **G** forsaken?"
13:26 and he was beloved by his **G,**
13:31 Remember me, O my **G,** for good.
Job 1: 1 feared **G** and turned away from evil.
1: 9 "Does Job fear **G** for nothing?
1:22 sin or charge **G** with wrongdoing.
2:10 receive the good at the hand of **G,**
4:17 Can mortals be righteous before **G?**
5:17 happy is the one whom **G** reproves;
8: 3 Does **G** pervert justice?
8:20 **G** will not reject a blameless person,
9: 2 how can a mortal be just before **G?**
11: 7 you find out the deep things of **G?**
12:13 "With **G** are wisdom and strength;
16: 7 Surely now **G** has worn me out;
19:26 then in my flesh I shall see **G,**
20:29 the portion of the wicked from **G,**
21:19 '**G** stores up their iniquity for their
21:22 Will any teach **G** knowledge,
22:12 "Is not **G** high in the heavens?
22:13 you say, 'What does **G** know?
22:21 "Agree with **G,** and be at peace;
25: 2 "Dominion and fear are with **G;**
25: 4 can a mortal be righteous before **G?**
26: 6 Sheol is naked before **G,**
31: 6 and let **G** know my integrity!—
31:14 then shall I do when **G** rises up?
32:13 **G** may vanquish him, not a human.'

33: 6 See, before **G** I am as you are;
33:14 For **G** speaks in one way, and in
33:26 **G** repays him for his righteousness.
34:10 far be it from **G** that he should do
34:23 a time for anyone to go before **G**
36: 5 "Surely **G** is mighty and does not
36:26 Surely **G** is great, and we do not
40: 2 who argues with **G** must respond."
Ps 5: 2 King and my **G,** for to you I pray.
5: 4 not a **G** who delights in wickedness;
7:10 **G** is my shield, who saves the
7:11 **G** is a righteous judge,
14: 5 for **G** is with the company of the
18: 2 **G,** my rock in whom I take refuge,
18:21 not wickedly departed from my **G.**
18:28 LORD, my **G,** lights up my darkness.
18:30 This **G**—his way is perfect;
18:31 For who is **G** except the LORD?
18:32 the **G** who girded me with strength,
18:46 exalted be the **G** of my salvation,
19: 1 heavens are telling the glory of **G;**
22: 1 My **G,** my **G,** why have you
forsaken me?
22:10 bore me you have been my **G.**
27: 9 forsake me, O **G** of my salvation!
29: 3 the **G** of glory thunders, the LORD,
31: 5 redeemed me, O LORD, faithful **G.**
31:14 O LORD; I say, "You are my **G."**
33:12 the nation whose **G** is the LORD,
35:23 for my cause, my **G** and my Lord!
37:31 The law of their **G** is in their hearts;
40: 3 a song of praise to our **G.**
40: 8 I delight to do your will, O my **G;**
42: 1 so my soul longs for you, O **G.**
42: 2 soul thirsts for **G,** for the living **G.**
42: 8 a prayer to the **G** of my life.
42:11 Hope in **G;** for I shall again praise
him, my help and my **G.**
43: 4 with the harp, O **G,** my **G.**
44: 8 In **G** we have boasted continually,
45: 6 Your throne, O **G,** endures forever
45: 7 Therefore **G,** your **G,** has anointed
46: 1 **G** is our refuge and strength,
46: 5 **G** is in the midst of the city;
46:10 "Be still, and know that I am **G!**
47: 1 shout to **G** with loud songs of joy.
47: 6 Sing praises to **G,** sing praises;
47: 7 For **G** is the king of all the earth;
48: 9 O **G,** in the midst of your temple.
48:14 this is **G,** our **G** forever and ever.
49: 7 no price one can give to **G** for it.
50: 2 perfection of beauty, **G** shines forth.
50: 3 Our **G** comes and does not keep
51: 1 Have mercy on me, O **G,**
51:10 Create in me a clean heart, O **G,**
51:17 The sacrifice acceptable to **G** is a
53: 2 **G** looks down from heaven on
54: 4 But surely, **G** is my helper;
55:19 **G,** who is enthroned from of old,
56: 4 In **G,** whose word I praise, in **G** I
trust;
56:13 so that I may walk before **G** in the
57: 3 **G** will send forth his steadfast love
57: 7 O **G,** my heart is steadfast.
59:17 the **G** who shows me steadfast love.
62: 1 **G** alone my soul waits in silence;
62: 7 my mighty rock, my refuge is in **G.**
62: 8 **G** is a refuge for us.
62:11 that power belongs to **G,**
63: 1 O **G,** you are my **G,** I seek you,
65: 5 deliverance, O **G** of our salvation:
66: 1 a joyful noise to **G,** all the earth;
66: 3 Say to **G,** "How awesome are your
66: 5 Come and see what **G** has done:
66:16 and hear, all you who fear **G,**
66:20 be **G,** because he has not rejected
68: 4 Sing to **G,** sing praises to his name;
68: 6 **G** gives the desolate a home to live
68:20 Our **G** is a **G** of salvation,
68:26 "Bless **G** in the great congregation,
68:35 Awesome is **G** in his sanctuary,
69: 5 O **G,** you know my folly;

70: 1 Be pleased, O **G,** to deliver me.
70: 4 say evermore, "**G** is great!"
70: 5 oor and needy; hasten to me, O **G!**
71:17 **G,** from my youth you have taught
71:18 even to old age and gray hairs, O **G,**
71:19 who have done great things, O **G,**
71:22 for your faithfulness, O my **G;**
73:17 until I went into the sanctuary of **G;**
73:26 but **G** is the strength of my heart
76:11 Make vows to the LORD your **G,**
77:13 What **g** is so great as our **G?**
77:14 You are the **G** who works wonders;
78:19 They spoke against **G,** saying,
78:59 When **G** heard, he was full of wrath,
79: 9 Help us, O **G** of our salvation,
81: 1 Sing aloud to **G** our strength;
82: 1 **G** has taken his place in the divine
84: 2 flesh sing for joy to the living **G.**
84:10 doorkeeper in the house of my **G**
84:11 For the LORD **G** is a sun and shield;
86:12 I give thanks to you, O Lord my **G,**
86:15 But you, O Lord, are a **G** merciful
87: 3 are spoken of you, O city of **G.**
89: 7 a **G** feared in the council of the holy
90: 2 everlasting to everlasting you are **G.**
91: 2 "My refuge and my fortress; my **G,**
94: 1 O LORD, you **G** of vengeance, you
G of vengeance,
94:22 and my **G** the rock of my refuge.
95: 3 For the LORD is a great **G,**
95: 7 he is our **G,** and we are the people
99: 8 you were a forgiving **G** to them,
99: 9 for the LORD our **G** is holy.
100: 3 Know that the LORD is **G.**
106:21 They forgot **G,** their Savior,
108: 1 My heart is steadfast, O **G,**
108: 5 Be exalted, O **G,** above the heavens,
113: 5 Who is like the LORD our **G,**
115: 3 Our **G** is in the heavens;
116: 5 and righteous; our **G** is merciful.
123: 2 so our eyes look to the LORD our **G,**
136: 2 O give thanks to the **G** of gods,
136:26 O give thanks to the **G** of heaven,
139:17 to me are your thoughts, O **G!**
139:23 Search me, O **G,** and know my heart
143:10 to do your will, for you are my **G.**
145: 1 I will extol you, my **G** and King,
147: 1 good it is to sing praises to our **G;**
150: 1 Praise **G** in his sanctuary;
Pr 2: 5 and find the knowledge of **G.**
3: 4 good repute in the sight of **G** and of
25: 2 the glory of **G** to conceal things,
30: 5 Every word of **G** proves true;
Ecc 1:13 unhappy business that **G** has given
2:26 who pleases him **G** gives wisdom
3:11 yet they cannot find out what **G** has
3:14 know that whatever **G** does endures
5: 2 for **G** is in heaven, and you upon
5: 4 you make a vow to **G,** do not delay
5:19 this is the gift of **G.**
7:18 fears **G** shall succeed with both.
8:12 will be well with those who fear **G,**
11: 5 so you do not know the work of **G,**
12: 7 the breath returns to **G** who gave it.
12:13 Fear **G,** and keep his
Isa 5:16 the Holy **G** shows himself holy by
7:11 Ask a sign of the LORD your **G;**
9: 6 Wonderful Counselor, Mighty **G,**
12: 2 Surely **G** is my salvation;
17:10 forgotten the **G** of your salvation,
25: 9 said on that day, Lo, this is our **G;**
29:23 will stand in awe of the **G** of Israel.
30:18 For the LORD is a **G** of justice;
35: 4 Here is your **G.** He will come with
37:16 you are **G,** you alone, of all the
40: 1 O comfort my people, says your **G.**
40: 3 in the desert a highway for our **G.**
40: 8 word of our **G** will stand forever.
40:18 To whom then will you liken **G,**
40:28 The LORD is the everlasting
41:10 do not be afraid, for I am your **G;**
41:13 LORD your **G,** hold your right hand;

43:10 Before me no **g** was formed,
44: 6 besides me there is no **g.**
44:15 Then he makes a **g** and worships it,
45:18 who created the heavens (he is **G**!),
48:17 I am the LORD your **G,**
49: 4 and my reward with my **G."**
52: 7 who says to Zion, "Your **G** reigns."
52:12 **G** of Israel will be your rear guard.
53: 4 stricken, struck down by **G,**
55: 7 have mercy on them, and to our **G,**
57:21 no peace, says my **G,** for the wicked
59: 2 between you and your **G,**
60:19 and your **G** will be your glory.
61: 2 and the day of vengeance of our **G;**
61:10 whole being shall exult in my **G;**
62: 5 so shall your **G** rejoice over you.

Jer 3:23 in the LORD our **G** is the salvation
7:23 my voice, and I will be your **G,**
10:10 But the LORD is the true **G;**
23:23 Am I a **G** near by, says the LORD, and not a **G** far off?
23:36 pervert the words of the living **G,**
31:33 I will be their **G,** and they shall be
32:27 **G** of all flesh; is anything too hard
42: 6 obey the voice of the LORD our **G."**
42:13 the voice of the LORD your **G**
51:10 in Zion the work of the LORD our **G.**
51:56 for the LORD is a **G** of recompense,

Eze 1: 1 opened, and I saw visions of **G.**
11:20 be my people, and I will be their **G.**
28: 2 proud and you have said, "I am a **g;**
28:13 You were in Eden, the garden of **G;**
34:31 of my pasture and I am your **G,**
43: 2 glory of the **G** of Israel was coming

Da 2:19 and Daniel blessed the **G** of heaven.
2:28 **G** in heaven who reveals mysteries,
3:17 **G** whom we serve is able to deliver
3:29 the **G** of Shadrach, Meshach,
3:29 no other **g** who is able to deliver
6:16 king said to Daniel, "May your **G,**
9: 4 "Ah, Lord, great and awesome **G,**
10:12 to humble yourself before your **G,**
11:32 to their **G** shall stand firm and take
11:36 consider himself greater than any **g,**
11:36 things against the **G** of gods.

Hos 1: 9 not my people and I am not your **G,**
1:10 to them, "Children of the living **G."**
4: 6 have forgotten the law of your **G,**
6: 6 knowledge of **G** rather than burnt
9: 8 The prophet is a sentinel for my **G**
12: 6 But as for you, return to your **G,**
12: 6 and wait continually for your **G.**
13: 4 you know no **G** but me, and besides

Joel 2:13 Return to the LORD, your **G,**
2:23 and rejoice in the LORD your **G;**

Am 4:12 this to you, prepare to meet your **G,**
4:13 LORD, the **G** of hosts, is his name!

Jnh 1: 6 Perhaps the **g** will spare us a
3: 5 the people of Nineveh believed **G;**
4: 2 I knew that you are a gracious **G**

Mic 3: 7 for there is no answer from **G.**
6: 8 and to walk humbly with your **G?**
7: 7 will wait for the **G** of my salvation;
7:18 Who is a **G** like you,

Na 1: 2 jealous and avenging **G** is the LORD,
Hab 1:11 their own might is their **g!**
3:18 I will exult in the **G** of my salvation.

Zep 3:17 The LORD, your **G,** is in your midst,
Hag 1:14 house of the LORD of hosts, their **G,**
Zec 9:16 that day the LORD their **G** will save
12: 8 the house of David shall be like **G,**
14: 5 Then the LORD my **G** will come,

Mal 2:10 Has not one **G** created us?
2:11 married the daughter of a foreign **g.**
3: 8 Will anyone rob **G?**

Mt 1:23 which means, "**G** is with us."
4: 4 that comes from the mouth of **G.'"**
4: 7 not put the Lord your **G** to the test.'
4:10 written, 'Worship the Lord your **G,**
5: 8 pure in heart, for they will see **G.**
5: 9 for they will be called children of **G.**
6:24 You cannot serve **G** and wealth.

12:28 by the Spirit of **G** that I cast out
16:16 Messiah, the Son of the living **G."**
19: 6 what **G** has joined together, let no
19:26 but for **G** all things are possible."
22:21 and to **G** the things that are God's."
22:32 'I am the **G** of Abraham,
22:37 "'You shall love the Lord your **G**
27:40 If you are the Son of **G,**
27:46 "My **G,** my **G,** why have you forsaken me?"

Mk 1: 1 news of Jesus Christ, the Son of **G.**
1:24 who you are, the Holy One of **G."**
2: 7 Who can forgive sins but **G** alone?"
7:13 word of **G** through your tradition
10: 6 '**G** made them male and female.'
10: 9 what **G** has joined together, let no
10:18 No one is good but **G** alone.
10:24 hard it is to enter the kingdom of **G!**
10:27 for **G** all things are possible.
11:22 answered them, "Have faith in **G.**
12:17 and to **G** the things that are God's."
12:29 the Lord our **G,** the Lord is one;
12:30 the Lord your **G** with all your heart,
15:34 "My **G,** my **G,** why have you forsaken me?"

Lk 1:19 I stand in the presence of **G,**
1:30 for you have found favor with **G.**
1:35 he will be called Son of **G.**
1:37 nothing will be impossible with **G."**
1:47 my spirit rejoices in **G** my Savior,
2:14 "Glory to **G** in the highest heaven,
2:40 and the favor of **G** was upon him.
3:38 son of Seth, son of Adam, son of **G.**
4: 3 to him, "If you are the Son of **G,**
4: 8 written, 'Worship the Lord your **G,**
4:41 shouting, "You are the Son of **G!"**
5:21 Who can forgive sins but **G** alone?"
8:39 how much **G** has done for you."
9:20 answered, "The Messiah of **G."**
10: 9 'The kingdom of **G** has come near
10:27 the Lord your **G** with all your heart,
11:42 neglect justice and the love of **G;**
13:18 "What is the kingdom of **G** like?
18:13 beating his breast and saying, '**G,**
18:19 No one is good but **G** alone.
18:27 for mortals is possible for **G."**
20:25 and to **G** the things that are God's."
20:37 of the Lord as the **G** of Abraham,
22:69 the right hand of the power of **G."**
22:70 "Are you, then, the Son of **G?"**

Jn 1: 1 and the Word was with **G,** and the Word was **G.**
1:12 power to become children of **G,**
1:18 No one has ever seen **G.**
1:18 It is **G** the only Son,
1:29 "Here is the Lamb of **G** who takes
1:49 "Rabbi, you are the Son of **G!**
3: 2 a teacher who has come from **G;**
3:16 **G** so loved the world that he gave his only Son,
3:34 He whom **G** has sent speaks the words of **G,**
4:24 **G** is spirit, and those who worship
5:18 was also calling **G** his own Father, thereby making himself equal to **G.**
5:44 from the one who alone is **G?**
6:29 "This is the work of **G,**
6:33 the bread of **G** is that which comes
6:69 that you are the Holy One of **G."**
7:17 whether the teaching is from **G**
8:42 to them, "If **G** were your Father,
8:47 is from **G** hears the words of **G.**
11:40 you would see the glory of **G?"**
13: 3 that he had come from **G** and was going to **G,**
13:31 and **G** has been glorified in him.
14: 1 Believe in **G,** believe also in me.
17: 3 may know you, the only true **G,**
20:17 to my **G** and your **G."'**
20:28 "My Lord and my **G!"**
20:31 Jesus is the Messiah, the Son of **G,**

Ac 1: 3 speaking about the kingdom of **G.**

2:22 a man attested to you by **G** with
2:24 But **G** raised him up, having freed
2:33 exalted at the right hand of **G,**
2:36 that **G** has made him both Lord
3:15 whom **G** raised from the dead.
3:19 turn to **G** so that your sins may be
4:31 and spoke the word of **G**
5: 4 You did not lie to us but to **G!"**
5:29 "We must obey **G** rather than any
5:31 **G** exalted him at his right hand as
5:32 so is the Holy Spirit whom **G** has
5:39 even be found fighting against **G!"**
6: 7 The word of **G** continued to spread;
7:55 Jesus standing at the right hand of **G**
8:21 for your heart is not right before **G.**
10:46 in tongues and extolling **G.**
11: 9 'What **G** has made clean,
12:24 of **G** continued to advance and gain
13:32 what **G** promised to our ancestors
14:22 we must enter the kingdom of **G."**
15:10 why are you putting **G** to the test
17:23 the inscription, 'To an unknown **g.'**
17:30 **G** has overlooked the times of
20:27 to you the whole purpose of **G.**
20:32 I commend you to **G** and to the
24:16 a clear conscience toward **G** and all
28: 6 and began to say that he was a **g.**

Ro 1: 4 to be Son of **G** with power
1:16 of **G** for salvation to everyone who
1:17 the righteousness of **G** is revealed
1:18 For the wrath of **G** is revealed from
1:24 **G** gave them up in the lusts
1:26 For this reason **G** gave them up
2:11 For **G** shows no partiality.
2:16 according to my gospel, **G,** through
3: 4 is a liar, let **G** be proved true,
3:19 may be held accountable to **G.**
3:23 all have sinned and fall short of the glory of **G;**
3:29 Or is **G** the **G** of Jews only?
3:29 Is he not the **G** of Gentiles also?
4: 3 "Abraham believed **G,** and it was
4: 6 to whom **G** reckons righteousness
4:17 in the presence of the **G** in whom
5: 1 peace with **G** through our Lord
5: 8 But **G** proves his love for us in that
6:22 freed from sin and enslaved to **G,**
6:23 gift of **G** is eternal life in Christ
7: 4 that we may bear fruit for **G.**
8: 7 set on the flesh is hostile to **G;**
8: 8 in the flesh cannot please **G.**
8:17 heirs of **G** and joint heirs with
8:28 for good for those who love **G,**
8:31 If **G** is for us, who is against us?
10: 9 believe in your heart that **G** raised
11: 2 **G** has not rejected his people whom
11:22 the kindness and the severity of **G:**
11:32 For **G** has imprisoned all in
13: 1 there is no authority except from **G,**
14:12 each of us will be accountable to **G.**
16:20 **G** of peace will shortly crush Satan

1Co 1:18 are being saved it is the power of **G.**
1:20 **G** made foolish the wisdom of the
1:24 Christ the power of **G** and the wisdom of **G.**
1:27 But **G** chose what is foolish in the
2: 9 **G** has prepared for those who love
2:11 truly God's except the Spirit of **G.**
3: 6 but **G** gave the growth.
3:17 **G** will destroy that person.
6:20 therefore glorify **G** in your body.
7: 7 each has a particular gift from **G,**
7:15 It is to peace that **G** has called you.
8: 3 but anyone who loves **G** is known
8: 8 "Food will not bring us close to **G."**
10:13 **G** is faithful, and he will not let you
10:31 do everything for the glory of **G.**
12:24 But **G** has so arranged the body,
14:25 declaring, "**G** is really among you."
14:33 for **G** is a **G** not of disorder but of peace.
15:24 the kingdom to **G** the Father.

15:28 so that **G** may be all in all.
15:34 people have no knowledge of **G**.
2Co 1: 9 not on ourselves but on **G** who
2:14 to **G**, who in Christ always leads us
3: 5 our competence is from **G**,
4: 2 of everyone in the sight of **G**.
4: 4 the **g** of this world has blinded the
4: 4 Christ, who is the image of **G**.
4: 7 extraordinary power belongs to **G**
5: 5 prepared us for this very thing is **G**,
5:19 in Christ **G** was reconciling the
5:20 behalf of Christ, be reconciled to **G**.
5:21 become the righteousness of **G**.
6:16 we are the temple of the living **G**;
6:16 among them, and I will be their **G**,
9: 7 for **G** loves a cheerful giver.
10:13 but will keep within the field that **G**
Gal 2: 6 **G** shows no partiality)—
6: 7 not be deceived; **G** is not mocked,
Eph 2: 8 it is the gift of **G**—
2:10 which **G** prepared beforehand to be
2:22 into a dwelling place for **G**.
4: 6 one **G** and Father of all,
4:24 likeness of **G** in true righteousness
5: 1 Therefore be imitators of **G**,
6: 6 doing the will of **G** from the heart.
Php 2: 6 though he was in the form of **G**,
2: 6 did not regard equality with **G** as
2: 9 Therefore **G** also highly exalted him
2:13 for it is **G** who is at work in you,
3:14 the prize of the heavenly call of **G**
3:19 destruction; their **g** is the belly;
4: 7 the peace of **G**, which surpasses all
4:19 my **G** will fully satisfy every need
Col 1:19 fullness of **G** was pleased to dwell,
2:13 **G** made you alive together with him
3: 1 seated at the right hand of **G**.
1Th 2: 4 but to please **G** who tests our hearts.
4: 1 you ought to live and to please **G**
4: 7 For **G** did not call us to impurity
4: 9 yourselves have been taught by **G**
5: 9 For **G** has destined us not for wrath
2Th 1: 8 not know **G** and on those who do
1Ti 1:17 the only **G**, be honor and glory
2: 5 one **G**; there is also one mediator
between **G** and humankind,
4: 4 everything created by **G** is good,
2Ti 1: 6 the gift of **G** that is within you
Tit 1: 2 eternal life that **G**, who never lies,
2:13 of our great **G** and Savior, Jesus
Heb 1: 1 Long ago **G** spoke to our ancestors
3: 4 but the builder of all things is **G**.)
4: 4 **G** rested on the seventh day from
4:12 the word of **G** is living and active,
6:10 For **G** is not unjust; he will
6:18 that **G** would prove false,
7:19 through which we approach **G**.
7:25 to save those who approach **G**
10: 7 **G**, I have come to do your will,
10:31 to fall into the hands of the living **G**.
11: 5 taken away that "he had pleased **G**."
11: 6 And without faith it is impossible to please **G**,
11:16 **G** is not ashamed to be called their **G**;
12: 7 **G** is treating you as children;
12:29 indeed our **G** is a consuming fire.
13:15 offer a sacrifice of praise to **G**,
Jas 1:13 for **G** cannot be tempted by evil
1:27 that is pure and undefiled before **G**,
2:19 believe that **G** is one; you do well.
2:23 "Abraham believed **G**,
2:23 and he was called the friend of **G**.
4: 4 with the world is enmity with **G**?
4: 6 "**G** opposes the proud, but gives
4: 8 Draw near to **G**, and he will draw
1Pe 1:21 you have come to trust in **G**,
1:21 your faith and hope are set on **G**.
1:23 the living and enduring word of **G**.
3:18 in order to bring you to **G**.
4: 2 human desires but by the will of **G**.
4:11 one speaking the very words of **G**;

4:17 to begin with the household of **G**;
5: 5 "**G** opposes the proud, but gives
2Pe 1:21 by the Holy Spirit spoke from **G**.
2: 4 if **G** did not spare the angels when
1Jn 1: 5 **G** is light and in him there is no
2:14 and the word of **G** abides in you,
2:17 who do the will of **G** live forever.
3: 1 we should be called children of **G**;
3: 9 have been born of **G** do not sin,
3:10 The children of **G** and the children
3:20 for **G** is greater than our hearts,
4: 2 By this you know the Spirit of **G**:
4: 7 everyone who loves is born of **G** and knows **G**.
4: 8 Whoever does not love does not know **G**, for **G** is love.
4: 9 **G** sent his only Son into the world
4:11 Beloved, since **G** loved us so much,
4:12 No one has ever seen **G**;
4:15 **G** abides in those who confess that
4:16 believe the love that **G** has for us.
4:16 **G** is love, and those who abide in love abide in **G**, and **G** abides in
4:20 Those who say, "I love **G**,"
5: 2 love **G** and obey his commandments
5: 3 For the love of **G** is this,
5: 4 born of **G** conquers the world.
5:10 Those who believe in the Son of **G**
5:11 **G** gave us eternal life, and this life
5:18 who was born of **G** protects them,
2Jn 1: 9 goes beyond it, does not have **G**;
3Jn 1:11 Whoever does good is from **G**; whoever does evil has not seen **G**.
Jude 1: 4 who pervert the grace of our **G** into
1:21 keep yourselves in the love of **G**;
Rev 2:18 These are the words of the Son of **G**
3: 1 him who has the seven spirits of **G**
4: 5 which are the seven spirits of **G**
4: 8 "Holy, holy, holy, the Lord **G** the Almighty,
6: 9 slaughtered for the word of **G**
7: 2 having the seal of the living **G**,
7:10 "Salvation belongs to our **G** who is
7:12 and might be to our **G** forever
7:17 **G** will wipe away every tear from
11:16 before **G** fell on their faces and worshiped **G**,
12: 5 was snatched away and taken to **G**
13: 6 to utter blasphemies against **G**,
14: 7 "Fear **G** and give him glory,
15: 3 your deeds, Lord **G** the Almighty!
15: 7 golden bowls full of the wrath of **G**,
16:14 for battle on the great day of **G**
17:17 For **G** has put it into their hearts
17:17 the words of **G** will be fulfilled.
18:20 For **G** has given judgment for you
19: 1 and glory and power to our **G**,
19: 6 the Lord our **G** the Almighty reigns.
19: 9 to me, "These are true words of **G**."
19:13 his name is called The Word of **G**.
21: 3 the home of **G** is among mortals. He will dwell with them as their **G**;
21:11 It has the glory of **G** and a radiance
21:23 for the glory of **G** is its light,
22: 5 for the Lord **G** will be their light,
Tob 3:11 "Blessed are you, merciful **G**!
4:19 At all times bless the Lord **G**,
Jdt 3: 8 tribes should call upon him as a **g**.
6: 2 Their **G** will not save them;
8:20 But we know no other **g** but him,
AdE 2:20 she was to fear **G** and keep his laws,
Sir 4:28 and the Lord **G** will fight for you.
32:14 seeks **G** will accept his discipline,
Bar 4: 8 You forgot the everlasting **G**,
Aza 1:22 know that you alone are the Lord **G**,
Sus 1:45 **G** stirred up the holy spirit of
Bel 1: 4 But Daniel worshiped his own **G**.
1: 6 you not think that Bel is a living **g**?
Man 1: 1 Lord Almighty, **G** of our ancestors,
2Es 15:26 **G** knows all who sin against him;
16:67 Indeed, **G** is the judge; fear him!

ANGEL OF *GOD Ge 21:17; 31:11; Ex

14:19; Jdg 6:20; 13:6, 9; 1Sa 29:9; 2Sa 14:17, 20; 19:27; Ac 10:3; 27:23; Gal 4:14; Tob 5:4; 12:22; AdE 15:13; Sus 1:55, 59; Bel 1:39

ARK OF [THE] *GOD 1Sa 3:3; 4:11, 13, 17, 18, 19, 21, 22; 5:1, 2, 7, 8, 8, 10, 10, 10, 11; 6:3; 14:18, 18; 2Sa 6:2, 3, 4, 6, 7, 12, 12; 7:2; 15:24, 25, 29; 1Ch 13:3, 5, 6, 7, 12, 14; 15:1, 2, 15, 24; 16:1; 2Ch 1:4

BEFORE *GOD Ex 18:19, 19; 21:6; 22:8, 9; Jos 24:1; Jdg 21:2; 1Ch 13:8, 10; 16:1; 2Ch 34:27; Job 4:17; 9:2; 15:4; 25:4; 26:6; 33:6; 34:23; 35:2; Ps 56:13; 61:7; 68:2, 3; Ecc 5:2; 8:13; Mic 6:6; Lk 1:6, 8; 24:19; Ac 7:20; 8:21; 10:4, 31; 23:1; Ro 4:2; 14:22; 1Co 14:25; 2Co 7:12; 12:19; Gal 1:20; 3:11; 2Ti 2:14; Jas 1:27; 1Jn 3:21; Rev 8:2, 4; 9:13; 11:16; AdE 10:11, 13; Wis 10:5; LtJ 6:2; 2Es 16:53; 4Mc 13:3; 17:5

CHILDREN OF *GOD Mt 5:9; Lk 20:36; Jn 1:12; 11:52; Ro 8:14, 16, 19, 21; 9:8; Gal 3:26; Php 2:15; 1Jn 3:1, 10; 5:2; Wis 5:5

FEAR ... *GOD Ge 20:11; 22:12; 42:18; Ex 9:30; 18:21; Lev 19:14, 32; 25:17, 36, 43; Dt 6:24; 17:19; 25:18; 2Sa 23:3; 2Ch 20:29; 26:5; Ne 5:9, 15; Job 1:9; 4:6; 15:4; 25:2; Ps 36:1; 55:19; 66:16; Ecc 5:7; 8:12, 13; 12:13; Jer 5:24; Da 6:26; Lk 18:4; 23:40; Ac 13:16, 26; Ro 3:18; 2Co 7:1; 1Pe 2:17; Rev 14:7; Tob 4:21; AdE 2:20; 2Es 7:79; 16:75; 4Mc 15:8

GLORY OF ... *GOD Ps 19:1; 106:20; Pr 25:2; Eze 8:4; 9:3; 10:19; 11:22; 43:2; Jn 11:40; Ac 7:55; Ro 3:23; 5:2; 15:7; 1Co 10:31; 2Co 1:20; 4:6, 15; Php 2:11; Tit 2:13; Rev 15:8; 21:11, 23; AdE 13:14; Bar 4:37; 5:7

*GOD OF ... ANCESTORS Ex 3:13, 15, 16; 4:5; Dt 1:11, 21; 4:1; 6:3; 12:1; 26:7; 27:3; 29:25; Jos 18:3; Jdg 2:12; 2Ki 21:22; 1Ch 5:25; 12:17; 29:20; 2Ch 7:22; 11:16; 13:12, 18; 14:4; 15:12; 19:4; 20:6, 33; 21:10; 24:18, 24; 28:6, 9, 25; 29:5; 30:7, 19, 22; 33:12; 34:32, 33; 36:15; Ezr 7:27; 8:28; 10:11; Da 2:23; Ac 3:13; 5:30; 7:32; 22:14; 24:14; Tob 8:5; Jdt 10:8; Wis 9:1; Aza 1:3, 29; 1Es 1:50; 4:62; 9:8; Man 1:1; 3Mc 7:16; 4Mc 12:17

*GOD ... FATHER Jn 6:27; Ro 1:7; 15:6; 1Co 1:3; 8:6; 15:24; 2Co 1:2, 3; 11:31; Gal 1:1, 3, 4; Eph 1:2, 3; 4:6; 5:20; 6:23; Php 1:2; 2:11; 4:20; Col 1:2, 3; 3:17; 1Th 1:1, 3; 3:11, 13; 2Th 1:1, 2; 2:16; 1Ti 1:2; 2Ti 1:2; Tit 1:4; Phm 1:3; Jas 1:27; 1Pe 1:2, 3; 2Pe 1:17; 2Jn 1:3; Jude 1:1; Rev 1:6; 3Mc 5:7

*GOD MOST HIGH, MOST HIGH *GOD Ge 14:18, 19, 20, 22; Ps 46:4; 57:2; 78:35, 56; Da 3:26; 4:2; 5:18, 21; Mk 5:7; Lk 8:28; Ac 16:17; Heb 7:1; Jdt 13:18; AdE 16:16; Sir 7:9; 24:23; 41:8; 50:17; 1Es 6:31; 8:19, 21; 9:46; 3Mc 6:2; 7:9

*GOD OF HEAVEN Ge 24:3, 7; 2Ch 36:23; Ezr 1:2; 5:11, 12; 6:9, 10; 7:12, 21, 23, 23; Ne 1:4, 5; 2:4, 20; Ps 136:26; Da 2:18, 19, 37, 44; Jnh 1:9; Rev 11:13; 16:11; Tob 7:12; 8:15; Jdt 5:8; 6:19; 11:17; 3Mc 6:28; 7:6

*GOD OF HOSTS 2Sa 5:10; 1Ki 19:10, 14; Ps 59:5; 80:4, 7, 14, 19; 84:8; 89:8; Jer 5:14; 15:16; 35:17; 38:17; 44:7; Hos 12:5; Am 3:13; 4:13; 5:14, 15, 16, 27; 6:8, 14; 1Es 9:46

*GOD OF ISRAEL Ex 5:1; 24:10; 32:27; 34:23; Nu 16:9; Jos 7:13, 19, 20; 8:30; 9:18, 19; 10:40, 42; 13:14, 33; 14:14; 22:16, 24; 24:2, 23; Jdg 4:6; 5:3, 5; 6:8; 11:21, 23; 21:3; Ru 2:12; 1Sa 1:17; 2:30; 5:7, 8, 8, 10, 10, 11; 6:3, 5; 10:18; 14:41, 41; 20:12; 23:10, 11; 25:32, 34; 2Sa 7:27; 12:7; 23:3; 1Ki 1:30, 48; 8:15, 17, 20, 23, 25, 26; 11:9, 31; 14:7, 13; 15:30; 16:13, 26, 33; 17:1, 14; 22:53; 2Ki 9:6; 10:31; 14:25; 18:5; 19:15, 20; 21:12; 22:15, 18; 1Ch 4:10; 5:26; 15:12, 14; 16:4, 36; 17:24; 22:6; 23:25; 24:19; 28:4; 2Ch 2:12; 6:4, 7, 10, 14, 16, 17; 11:16; 13:5; 15:4, 13; 20:19; 29:7,

10; 30:1, 5; 32:17; 33:16, 18; 34:23, 26; 36:13;
Ezr 1:3; 3:2; 4:1, 3; 5:1; 6:14, 21, 22; 7:6, 15;
8:35; 9:4, 15; Ps 41:13; 59:5; 68:8, 35; 69:6;
72:18; 106:48; Isa 17:6; 21:10, 17; 24:15;
29:23; 37:16, 21; 41:17; 45:3, 15; 48:1, 2;
52:12; Jer 7:3, 21; 9:15; 11:3; 13:12; 16:9;
19:3, 15; 21:4; 23:2; 24:5; 25:15, 27; 27:4, 21;
28:2, 14; 29:4, 8, 21, 25; 30:2; 31:23; 32:14,
15, 36; 33:4; 34:2, 13; 35:13, 17, 18, 19; 37:7;
38:17; 39:16; 42:9, 15, 18; 43:10; 44:2, 7, 11,
25; 45:2; 46:25; 48:1; 50:18; 51:33; Eze 8:4;
9:3; 10:19, 20; 11:22; 43:2; 44:2; Zep 2:9; Mal
2:16; Mt 15:31; Lk 1:68; Tob 13:17; Jdt 4:12;
6:21; 10:1; 12:8; 13:7; 14:10; AdE 14:3; Sir
47:18; Bar 2:11; 3:1, 4; 2Mc 9:5; 1Es 1:48;
5:48, 67; 6:1; 7:4, 9; 8:3, 65; 9:39

GRACE OF *GOD Ac 11:23; 13:43; 14:26;
Ro 5:15; 1Co 1:4; 3:10; 15:10, 10; 2Co 1:12;
6:1; 8:1; 9:14; Gal 2:21; Col 1:6; 2Th 1:12; Tit
2:11; Heb 2:9; 12:15; 1Pe 4:10; 5:12; Jude 1:4

HAND OF ... *GOD 1Sa 5:11; 2Ch 30:12;
Ezr 7:9; 8:18, 22, 31; Ne 2:8, 18; Job 2:10;
19:21; 27:11; Ecc 2:24; 9:1; Isa 62:3; Mk
16:19; Ac 2:33; 7:55, 56; Ro 8:34; Col 3:1;
Heb 10:12; 1Pe 3:22; 5:6; Wis 3:1

HOUSE OF *GOD Ge 28:17; Jos 9:23; Jdg
18:31; 2Ki 19:37; 1Ch 6:48; 9:11, 13, 26, 27;
22:1, 2; 23:28; 25:6; 26:20; 28:12, 21; 29:2, 3,
3, 7; 2Ch 3:3; 4:11, 19; 5:1, 14; 7:5; 15:18;
22:12; 23:3, 9; 24:5, 7, 13, 27; 25:24; 28:24,
24; 31:13, 21; 32:21; 33:7; 34:9; 35:8; 36:18,
19; Ezr 1:4; 2:68; 3:8, 9; 4:24; 5:2, 8, 13, 14,
15, 16, 17; 6:3, 5, 5, 7, 7, 8, 12, 16, 17, 22;
7:16, 17, 19, 20, 23, 24; 8:17, 25, 30, 33, 36;
9:9; 10:1, 6, 9; Ne 6:10; 8:16; 10:32, 33, 34,
36, 36, 37, 38, 39; 11:11, 16, 22; 12:40; 13:4,
7, 9, 11, 14; Ps 42:4; 52:8; 55:14; 84:10;
135:2; Ecc 5:1; Isa 2:3; 37:38; Da 1:2; 5:3;
Hos 9:8; Joel 1:13, 16; Am 2:8; Mic 4:2; Mt
12:4; Mk 2:26; Lk 6:4; Heb 10:21; Jdt 3:24; Bar
3:24; 1Es 5:58

KINGDOM OF *GOD Mt 6:33; 12:28;
19:24; 21:31, 43; Mk 1:15; 4:11, 26, 30; 9:1,
47; 10:14, 15, 23, 24, 25; 12:34; 14:25; 15:43;
Lk 4:43; 6:20; 7:28; 8:1, 10; 9:2, 11, 27, 60,
62; 10:9, 11; 11:20; 13:18, 20, 28, 29; 14:15;
16:16; 17:20, 20, 21; 18:16, 17, 24, 25, 29;
19:11; 21:31; 22:16, 18; 23:51; Jn 3:3, 5; Ac
1:3; 8:12; 14:22; 19:8; 28:23, 31; Ro 14:17;
1Co 4:20; 6:9, 10; 15:50; Gal 5:21; Col 4:11;
2Th 1:5; Rev 12:10; Wis 10:10

LAW OF ... *GOD Jos 24:26; 2Ki 17:26, 26,
27; Ezr 7:12, 14, 21, 26; Ne 8:8, 18; 10:28; Ps
37:31; Jer 5:4, 5; Da 6:5; Hos 4:6; Ro 7:22, 25;
Bar 4:12; 1Es 8:21, 23, 24; 3Mc 7:10, 12; 2Es
7:20; 4Mc 13:22

LIVING *GOD Dt 5:26; Jos 3:10; 1Sa 17:26,
36; 2Ki 19:4, 16; Ps 42:2; 84:2; Isa 37:4, 17;
Jer 10:10; 23:36; Da 6:20, 26; Hos 1:10; Mt
16:16; 26:63; Ac 14:15; Ro 9:26; 2Co 3:3;
6:16; 1Ti 3:15; 4:10; Heb 3:12; 9:14; 10:31;
12:22; Rev 7:2; AdE 6:13; 16:16; Bel 1:5, 6,
24, 25; 3Mc 6:28; 4Mc 5:24

*LORD *GOD Da 9:3; Lk 1:32, 68; Rev 1:8;
4:8; 11:17; 15:3; 16:7; 18:8; 21:22; 22:5; Tob
4:19; 14:15; Jdt 6:19; 7:29; 8:35; 9:2; 12:8;
13:4, 7, 18; AdE 13:15; 14:3, 18; Sir 4:28;
47:18; Bar 2:11; Aza 1:22; 2Mc 1:24; 7:6; 1Es
1:27; 5:67; 6:1; 7:4, 9, 15; 9:39, 46; 3Mc 5:35;
2Es 2:3, 48; 15:21; 16:8, 76

†LORD *GOD Ge 2:4, 5, 7, 8, 9, 15, 16, 18,
19, 21, 22; 3:1, 8, 8, 9, 13, 14, 21, 22, 23;
14:22; 24:12; Ex 9:30; 34:23; Jos 7:19, 20;
10:40, 42; 13:14, 33; 22:22, 22; 1Sa 14:41, 41;
2Sa 7:22, 25; 1Ki 8:23, 25; 16:13; 18:36; 1Ch
17:16, 17; 22:1, 19; 24:19; 28:4, 20; 29:1; 2Ch
1:9; 2:12; 6:14, 16, 17, 41, 41, 42; 11:16; 13:5;
20:6; 26:5, 18; 30:7; 33:18; Ezr 9:15; Ne 1:5;

Ps 59:5; 80:4, 19; 84:8, 11; 88:1; 89:8; Isa
17:6; Jer 15:16; 37:7; 44:7; Jnh 4:6

†LORD HIS *GOD Ex 32:11; Lev 4:22; Dt
17:19; 18:7; 1Sa 30:6; 1Ki 5:3; 11:4; 15:3, 4;
2Ki 5:11; 16:2; 2Ch 1:1; 14:2, 11; 15:9; 26:16;
27:6; 28:5; 31:20; 33:12; 34:8; 36:5, 12, 23;
Ezr 7:6; Jnh 2:1; Mic 5:4

†LORD MY *GOD Ge 9:26; Nu 22:18; Dt
4:5; 18:16; 26:14; Jos 14:8, 9; 2Sa 24:24; 1Ki
3:7; 5:4, 5; 8:28; 17:20, 21; 1Ch 21:17; 22:7;
2Ch 2:4; 6:19; Ezr 7:28; 9:5; Ps 7:1, 3; 13:3;
30:2, 12; 38:15; 40:5; 104:1; 109:26; Jer
31:18; Da 9:4, 20; Jnh 2:6; Hab 1:12; Zec
11:4; 14:5

†LORD OUR *GOD Ex 3:18; 5:3; 8:10, 26,
27; 10:25, 26; Dt 1:6, 19, 20, 25, 41; 2:29, 33,
36, 37; 3:3; 4:7; 5:2, 24, 25, 27; 6:20, 24,
25; 29:14, 18, 29; Jos 18:6; 22:19, 29; 24:17,
24; Jdg 11:24; 1Sa 7:8; 1Ki 8:57, 59, 61, 65;
2Ki 18:22; 19:19; 1Ch 13:2; 15:13; 16:14;
29:16; 2Ch 2:4; 13:11; 14:7, 11; 19:7; 29:6;
32:8, 11; Ezr 9:8; Ne 10:34; Ps 20:7; 94:23;
99:5, 8, 9, 9; 105:7; 106:47; 113:5; 122:9;
123:2; Isa 26:13; 36:7; 37:20; Jer 3:22, 23, 25,
25; 5:19, 24; 8:14; 14:22; 16:10; 26:16; 31:6;
37:3; 42:6, 6, 20, 20; 43:2; 50:28; 51:10; Da
9:10, 13, 14; Mic 4:5; 7:17

†LORD THEIR *GOD Ex 10:7; 29:46, 46;
Lev 26:44; Nu 23:21; Jdg 3:7; 8:34; 1Sa 12:9;
1Ki 9:9; 2Ki 17:7, 9, 14, 16, 19; 18:12; 2Ch
31:6; 33:17; 34:33; Ne 9:3, 3, 4; Ps 146:5; Jer
3:21; 7:28; 22:9; 30:9; 43:1, 1; 50:4; Eze
28:26; 34:30; 39:22, 28; Hos 1:7; 3:5; 7:10;
Zep 2:7; Hag 1:12, 12; Zec 9:16; 10:6

†LORD YOUR *GOD Ge 27:20; Ex 6:7;
8:28; 10:8, 16, 17; 15:26; 16:12; 20:2, 5, 7, 10,
12; 23:19, 25; 34:24, 26; Lev 11:44; 18:2, 4,
30; 19:2, 3, 4, 10, 25, 31, 34, 36; 20:7, 24;
23:22, 28, 40, 43; 24:22; 25:17, 38, 55; 26:1,
13; Nu 10:9, 10, 10; 15:41, 41; Dt 1:10, 21, 26,
30, 31, 32; 2:7, 7, 30; 3:18, 20, 21, 22; 4:2, 3,
4, 10, 19, 21, 23, 23, 24, 25, 29, 30, 31, 34, 40;
5:6, 9, 11, 12, 14, 15, 16, 17; 7:1, 2, 6, 6, 9, 12, 16,
18, 19, 19, 20, 21, 22, 23, 25; 8:2, 5, 6, 7, 10,
11, 14, 18, 19, 20; 9:3, 4, 5, 6, 7, 16, 23; 10:9,
12, 12, 13, 14, 17, 20, 22; 11:1, 2, 12, 12,
13, 22, 25, 27, 28, 29, 31; 12:4, 5, 7, 7, 9, 10,
11, 12, 15, 18, 18, 18, 20, 21, 27, 27, 28, 29;
31: 13:3, 3, 4, 5, 5, 10, 12, 16, 18, 18; 14:1, 2,
21, 23, 23, 24, 24, 25, 26, 29; 15:4, 5, 6, 7, 10,
14, 15, 18, 19, 20, 21; 16:1, 1, 2, 5, 6, 7, 8, 10,
10, 11, 11, 15, 15, 16, 17, 18, 20, 21, 22; 17:1,
1, 2, 2, 8, 12, 14, 15; 18:5, 9, 12, 13, 14, 15,
16, 19:1, 1, 2, 3, 8, 9, 10, 14; 20:1, 4, 13, 14,
18, 18, 20, 21, 21, 23; 24:4, 9, 13, 18, 19;
25:15, 16, 19, 19; 26:1, 2, 2, 3, 4, 5, 10, 10, 11,
13, 16, 19; 27:2, 3, 5, 6, 9, 7, 10; 28:1, 1, 2,
8, 9, 13, 15, 45, 47, 52, 53, 58, 62; 29:6, 10,
12, 12; 30:1, 2, 3, 3, 4, 5, 6, 6, 7, 9, 9, 10, 10, 16,
16, 16, 20; 31:3, 6, 11, 12, 13, 26; Jos 1:9, 11,
13, 15, 17; 2:11; 3:3, 9; 4:5, 23, 23, 24; 8:7;
9:9, 24; 10:19; 22:3, 4, 5; 23:3, 3, 5, 5, 8, 10,
11, 13, 13, 14, 15, 15, 16; Jdg 6:10, 26; 1Sa
12:12, 14, 19; 13:13; 15:15, 21, 30; 25:29; 2Sa
14:11, 17; 18:28; 24:3, 23; 1Ki 1:17; 2:3; 10:9;
13:6, 21; 17:12; 18:10; 2Ki 17:39; 19:4, 4;
23:21; 1Ch 11:2; 22:11, 12, 18, 19; 28:8;
29:20; 2Ch 9:8, 8; 16:7; 20:20; 28:10; 30:8, 9;
35:3; Ne 8:9; 9:5; Ps 76:11; 81:10; Isa 7:11;
37:4, 4; 41:13; 43:3; 48:17; 51:15; 55:5; 60:9;
Jer 2:17, 19; 3:13; 13:16; 26:13; 40:2; 42:2, 3,
4, 5, 13, 20, 21; Eze 20:5, 7; Hos 12:9; 13:4;
14:1; Joel 1:14; 2:13, 14, 23, 26; 3:17; Am
9:15; Mic 7:10; Zep 3:17; Zec 6:15

MAN OF *GOD Dt 33:1; Jos 14:6; Jdg 13:6,
8; 1Sa 2:27; 9:6, 7, 8, 10; 1Ki 12:22; 13:1, 4,

5, 6, 6, 7, 8, 11, 12, 14, 14, 19, 21, 23, 26, 29,
31; 17:18, 24; 20:28; 2Ki 1:9, 10, 11, 12, 13;
4:7, 9, 16, 21, 22, 25, 25, 27, 27, 40, 42; 5:8,
14, 15, 20; 6:6, 9, 10, 15; 7:2, 17, 18, 19; 8:2,
4, 7, 8, 11; 13:19; 23:16, 16, 17; 1Ch 23:14;
2Ch 8:14; 11:2; 25:7, 9, 9; 30:16; Ezr 3:2; Ne
12:24, 36; Ps 90:Heading; Jer 35:4; 1Ti 6:11;
1Es 5:49

SON OF ... *GOD Mt 4:3, 6; 8:29; 14:33;
16:16; 26:63; 27:40; Mk 1:1; 3:11; Lk 1:35;
3:38; 4:3, 9, 41; 22:70; Jn 1:34, 49; 3:18; 5:25;
11:4, 27; 19:7; 20:31; Ac 9:20; Ro 1:4; 2Co
1:19; Gal 2:20; Eph 4:13; Heb 4:14; 6:6; 7:3;
10:29; 1Jn 3:8; 4:15; 5:5, 10, 12, 13, 20; Rev
2:18; 2Es 2:47

WORD OF *GOD 1Sa 9:27; 1Ki 12:22; Pr
30:5; Mt 15:6; Mk 7:13; Lk 3:2; 5:1; 8:11, 21;
11:28; Jn 10:35; Ac 4:31; 6:2, 7; 8:14; 11:1;
12:24; 13:5, 7, 46; 17:13; 18:11; Ro 9:6; 1Co
14:36; Eph 6:17; Col 1:25; 1Th 2:13; 2Ti 2:9;
Tit 2:5; Heb 4:12; 6:5; 11:3; 13:7; 1Pe 1:23;
2Pe 3:5; 1Jn 2:14; Rev 1:2, 9; 6:9; 19:13; 20:4;
Tob 14:4

POWER OF *GOD Mt 22:29; Mk 12:24; Lk
22:69; Ac 8:10; 26:18; Ro 1:16; 1Co 1:18, 24;
2:5; 2Co 6:7; 13:4, 4; Col 2:12; 2Ti 1:8; 1Pe
1:5; Jdt 13:19; Wis 7:25; 2Mc 3:24, 28, 34, 38;
9:8, 17; 11:4

SPIRIT OF *GOD Ge 41:38; Nu 24:2; 1Sa
10:10; 11:6; 19:20, 23; 2Ch 15:1; 24:20; Job
27:3; 33:4; Eze 11:24; Mt 3:16; 12:28; Ro 8:9,
14; 15:19; 1Co 2:11; 6:11; 7:40; 12:3; Eph
4:30; Php 3:3; 1Pe 4:14; 1Jn 4:2; 2Es 16:62

*GOD OF JACOB Ex 3:6, 15; 4:5; 2Sa
23:1; Ps 20:1; 24:6; 46:7, 11; 75:9; 76:6; 81:1,
4; 84:8; 94:7; 114:7; 146:5; Isa 2:3; Mic 4:2;
Mt 22:32; Mk 12:26; Lk 20:37; Ac 3:13

WILL OF *GOD Ezr 7:18; Mk 3:35; Jn 7:17;
Ro 8:27; 12:2; 1Co 1:1; 2Co 1:1; 8:5; Gal 1:4;
Eph 1:1; 6:6; Col 1:1; 1Th 4:3; 5:18; 2Ti 1:1;
Heb 10:36; 1Pe 4:2; 1Jn 2:17; Tob 12:18; 2Mc
12:16; 1Es 8:16

†GOD → †LORD

Ge   15: 2   But Abram said, "O Lord G,
Ex   23:17   shall appear before the Lord G.
Jdg   6:22   and Gideon said, "Help me, Lord G!
    16:28   to the LORD and said, "Lord G,
2Sa   7:18   "Who am I, O Lord G,
Ps   71:16   the mighty deeds of the Lord G,
    73:28   I have made the Lord G my refuge.
Isa   25: 8   Lord G will wipe away the tears
    40:10   See, the Lord G comes with might.
    50: 9   It is the Lord G who helps me;
    61: 1   The spirit of the Lord G is upon me,
    61:11   the Lord G will cause righteousness
Jer   32:17   Lord G! It is you who made the
Hab   3:19   G, the Lord, is my strength;
Zep   1: 7   Be silent before the Lord G!

*LORD †GOD OF HOSTS Ps 69:6; Isa
3:15; 10:23, 24; 22:5, 12, 14, 15; 28:22; Jer
2:19; 46:10, 10; 49:5; 50:25, 31; Am 9:5

SAYS THE *LORD †GOD Isa 3:15; Jer
2:19, 22; 49:5; 50:31; Eze 5:11; 11:8, 21;
12:25, 28; 13:8, 16; 14:11, 14, 16, 18, 20, 23;
15:8; 16:8, 14, 19, 23, 30, 43, 48, 63; 17:16;
18:3, 9, 23, 30, 32; 20:3, 31, 33, 36, 40, 44;
21:7, 13; 22:12, 31; 24:14; 26:5, 21; 28:10;
29:20; 30:6; 31:18; 32:8, 14, 16, 31, 32; 33:11;
34:8, 15, 30, 31; 35:6, 11; 36:14, 15, 23, 32;
38:18, 21; 39:5, 8, 10, 13, 20, 29; 43:19, 27;
44:12, 15, 27; 45:9, 15; 47:23; 48:29; Am
3:13; 4:5; 8:3, 9, 11

THUS SAYS THE *LORD †GOD Isa 7:7;
10:24; 22:15; 28:16; 49:22; 52:4; 56:8; 65:13;
Jer 7:20; Eze 2:4; 3:11, 27; 5:5, 7, 8; 6:3, 11;
7:2, 5; 11:7, 16, 17; 12:10, 19, 23, 28; 13:3, 8,
13, 18, 20; 14:4, 6, 21; 15:6; 16:3, 36, 59;

17:3, 9, 19, 22; 20:3, 5, 27, 30, 39, 47; 21:24, 26, 28; 22:3, 19, 28; 23:22, 28, 32, 35, 46; 24:3, 6, 9, 21; 25:3, 6, 8, 12, 13, 15, 16; 26:3, 7, 15, 19; 27:3; 28:2, 6, 12, 22, 25; 29:3, 8, 13, 19; 30:2, 10, 13, 22; 31:10, 15; 32:3, 11; 33:25, 27; 34:2, 10, 11, 17, 20; 35:3, 14; 36:2, 3, 4, 5, 6, 7, 13, 22, 33, 37; 37:5, 9, 12, 19, 21; 38:3, 10, 14, 17; 39:1, 17, 25; 43:18; 44:6, 9; 45:9, 18; 46:1, 16; 47:13; Am 3:11; 5:3; Ob 1:1

GOD'S → *GOD

Ge   6:11 the earth was corrupt in G sight,
Dt 21:23 hung on a tree is under G curse.
2Ch 20:15 for the battle is not yours but **G.**
Mt 27:43 for he said, 'I am G Son.'"
     27:54 "Truly this man was G Son!"
Lk 20:25 and to God the things that are **G."**
Jn   3:36 but must endure G wrath.
     10:36 because I said, 'I am G Son'?
     11: 4 rather it is for G glory,
Ro   2: 4 that G kindness is meant to lead you
     13: 6 for the authorities are G servants,
1Co 2: 7 But we speak G wisdom, secret and
     3: 9 you are G field, G building.
     3:16 that you are G temple and that G
          Spirit dwells in you?
     9:21 (though I am not free from G law
2Co 2:17 For we are not peddlers of G word
2Ti 2:19 But G firm foundation stands,
Tit   1: 7 For a bishop, as G steward, must be
Heb 1: 3 the reflection of G glory and the
          exact imprint of G very being,
     3: 6 was faithful over G house as a son,
     4:10 those who enter G rest also cease
1Pe 2:10 but now you are G people;
     2:15 For it is G will that by doing right
     3: 4 which is very precious in G sight.
1Jn 3: 2 Beloved, we are G children now;
     5:19 We know that we are G children,
Rev 3:14 witness, the origin of G creation:
     11:19 G temple in heaven was opened,
     14:10 will also drink the wine of G wrath,
Wis 2:18 for if the righteous man is G child,
Sir 51:29 May your soul rejoice in G mercy,
GOD'S SON Mt 27:43, 54; Mk 15:39; Jn 10:36
GOD'S WILL Ro 1:10; 15:32; Col 1:9; Heb 10:10; 1Pe 2:15; 3:17; 4:19

GOD-FEARING → FEAR, *GOD

Ac 10:22 a centurion, an upright and G man,
Jdt   8:31 Now since you are a G woman,
Sir 19:24 Better are the G who lack

GOD-GIVEN* → GIVE, *GOD

Ezr 7:25 Ezra, according to the G wisdom
2Mc 6:23 according to the holy G law,

GOD-HATERS* → *GOD, HATE

Ro   1:30 **G,** insolent, haughty, boastful,

GODDESS* → *GOD

1Ki 11: 5 Astarte the g of the Sidonians,
     11:33 Astarte the g of the Sidonians,
Ac 19:27 the temple of the great g Artemis
     19:37 nor blasphemers of our **g.**
2Mc 1:13 by the priests of the g Nanea.

GODLESS → *GOD

2Sa 23: 6 But the g are all like thorns that are
Job 8:13 the hope of the g shall perish.
     13:16 that the g shall not come before him.
     20: 5 the joy of the g is but for a moment?
Ps 119:122 do not let the g oppress me.
Pr 11: 9 the g would destroy their neighbors,
1Ti 1: 9 for the g and sinful,
Heb 12:16 an immoral and g person,
2Pe 3: 7 judgment and destruction of the **g.**
Sir 26:23 *A g wife is given as a portion to*
1Mc 3:15 Once again a strong army of g men

GODLINESS* → *GOD

1Ti 2: 2 peaceable life in all g and dignity.

     4: 7 Train yourself in **g,**
     4: 8 g is valuable in every way,
     6: 3 that is in accordance with **g,**
     6: 5 imagining that g is a means of gain.
     6: 6 in g combined with contentment;
     6:11 pursue righteousness, **g,** faith, love,
2Ti 3: 5 outward form of g but denying its
Tit   1: 1 truth that is in accordance with **g,**
2Pe 1: 3 everything needed for life and **g,**
     1: 6 endurance, and endurance with **g,**
     1: 7 and g with mutual affection,
     3:11 in leading lives of holiness and **g,**
Wis 10:12 g is more powerful than anything
Sir 1:25 but g is an abomination to a sinner.
     49: 3 in lawless times he made g prevail.
2Mc 12:45 for those who fall asleep in **g,**
1Es 1:23 for his heart was full of **g.**
4Mc 7:22 overcome the emotions through **g?**

GODLY* → *GOD

Ps 12: 1 there is no longer anyone who is **g;**
     52: 1 of mischief done against the **g?**
Mal 2:15 the one God desire? G offspring.
2Co 1:12 with frankness and g sincerity,
     7: 9 for you felt a g grief,
     7:10 For g grief produces a repentance
     7:11 this g grief has produced
2Ti 3:12 to live a g life in Christ Jesus will
Tit 2:12 are self-controlled, upright, and **g,**
2Pe 2: 9 how to rescue the g from trial,
Sir 6:35 ready to listen to every g discourse,
     16:13 the patience of the g will not be
     23:12 Such conduct will be far from the **g,**
     27:11 conversation of the g is always wise
     27:29 in the fall of the g will be caught in
     28:22 It has no power over the **g;**
     33:14 so the sinner is the opposite of the **g.**
     37:12 But associate with a g person
     39:27 All these are good for the **g,**
     43:33 and to the g he has given wisdom.
     44:10 But these also were g men,
     44:23 the Lord brought forth a g man,
Bar 5: 4 "Righteous Peace, G Glory."
4Mc 10:10 suffering because of our g training

GODS → *GOD

Ge 31:19 stole her father's household **g.**
     35: 4 they gave to Jacob all the foreign g
Ex 12:12 g of Egypt I will execute judgments:
     15:11 like you, O LORD, among the **g?**
     20: 3 you shall have no other g before me.
     23:13 Do not invoke the names of other **g;**
     32: 4 said, "These are your **g,** O Israel,
Dt   5: 7 you shall have no other g before me.
     7:25 images of their g you shall burn
     13: 2 "Let us follow other **g"** (whom you
Jos 24:14 the g that your ancestors served
Jdg 2:17 they lusted after other g and bowed
Ru   1:15 to her people and to her **g;**
1Sa 4: 7 said, "G have come into the camp."
     17:43 the Philistine cursed David by his **g.**
1Ki 20:23 "Their g are g of the hills,
2Ki 17: 7 They had worshiped other g
1Ch 16:26 For all the g of the peoples are idols,
2Ch 2: 5 for our God is greater than other **g.**
Ps 82: 6 are **g,** children of the Most High,
     97: 7 all g bow down before him.
   135: 5 our Lord is above all **g.**
   136: 2 O give thanks to the God of **g,**
Isa 8:19 should not a people consult their **g,**
Jer 2:11 Has a nation changed its **g,**
     10:11 g who did not make the heavens
     16:20 Can mortals make for themselves
          g? Such are no **g!**
Da   5: 4 and praised the g of gold
Zep 2:11 he will shrivel all the g of the earth,
Jn 10:34 in your law, 'I said, you are **g'?**
Ac 19:26 by saying that g made with hands
          are not **g.**
1Co 8: 5 so-called g in heaven or on earth—
Jdt 3: 8 to destroy all the g of the land,
AdE 14: 7 because we glorified their **g.**

Wis 12:24 accepting as g those animals
LtJ 6: 4 in Babylon you will see g made of
1Mc 5:68 carved images of their g he burned
OTHER GODS Ex 20:3; 23:13; Dt 4:28; 5:7; 6:14; 7:4; 8:19; 11:16, 28; 13:2, 6, 13; 17:3; 18:20; 28:14, 36, 64; 29:26; 30:17; 31:18, 20; Jos 23:16; 24:2, 16; Jdg 2:12, 17, 19; 10:13; 1Sa 8:8; 26:19; 1Ki 9:6, 9; 11:4, 10; 14:9; 2Ki 17:7, 35, 37, 38; 22:17; 2Ch 2:5; 7:19, 22; 28:25; 34:25; Jer 1:16; 7:6, 9, 18; 11:10; 13:10; 16:11, 13; 19:4, 13; 22:9; 25:6; 32:29; 35:15; 44:3, 5, 8, 15; Hos 3:1; Bar 1:22
THEIR GODS Ex 23:24, 32, 33; 34:15, 15, 16, 16; Nu 25:2, 2; 33:4; Dt 7:16, 25; 12:2, 3, 30, 30, 31, 31; 20:18; 32:37; Jos 23:7; Jdg 2:3; 3:6; 2Sa 7:23; 1Ki 11:2, 8; 20:23; 2Ki 19:18; 1Ch 10:10; 14:12; Isa 8:19, 21; 37:19; Jer 48:35; Da 11:8; Jdt 5:8; AdE 14:7; LtJ 6:9, 10, 11, 18, 19, 32, 33, 48, 70, 71; 1Mc 3:48; 5:68

GOES → GO

Nu 5:12 wife g astray and is unfaithful to
Dt 31: 6 the LORD your God who g with you;
Pr 16:18 Pride g before destruction,
     18:12 but humility g before honor.
Isa 42:13 The LORD g forth like a soldier,
Mt 26:24 The Son of Man g as it is written of
2Jn 1: 9 but g beyond it, does not have God;
Rev 14: 4 follow the Lamb wherever he **g.**

GOG

Eze 38: 2 set your face toward **G,** of the land
     38:18 G comes against the land of Israel,
Rev 20: 8 G and Magog, in order to gather

GOING → GO

Ge 6:17 I am g to bring a flood of waters on
Jn   8:21 Where I am **g,** you cannot come."
     13:36 Jesus answered, "Where I am **g,**
     16:10 because I am g to the Father
1Pe 2:25 For you were g astray like sheep.

GOLAN

Dt 4:43 and G in Bashan belonging to the

GOLD → GOLDEN, GOLDSMITH, GOLDSMITHS

Ex   3:22 and of **g,** and clothing, and you shall
     12:35 for jewelry of silver and **g,**
     20:23 make for yourselves gods of **g.**
     25:17 shall make a mercy seat of pure **g;**
     25:31 shall make a lampstand of pure **g.**
     28: 6 They shall make the ephod of **g,** of
     32:31 have made for themselves gods of **g.**
Dt 17:17 and g he must not acquire in great
Jos 7:21 a bar of g weighing fifty shekels,
1Sa 6: 4 "Five g tumors and five g mice,
1Ki 6:21 the inside of the house with pure **g,**
     20: 3 Your silver and g are mine;
2Ch 9:13 weight of g that came to Solomon
Ezr 1: 6 with **g,** with goods, with animals,
Job 22:25 the Almighty is your g and your
     23:10 tested me, I shall come out like **g.**
     28:15 It cannot be gotten for **g,**
     31:24 "If I have made g my trust,
Ps 19:10 More to be desired are they than **g,**
          even much fine **g;**
   115: 4 Their idols are silver and **g,**
  119:127 Truly I love your commandments
          more than **g,** more than fine **g.**
Pr   3:14 and her revenue better than **g,**
     8:19 fruit is better than **g,** even fine **g,**
     22: 1 and favor is better than silver or **g.**
     25:11 word fitly spoken is like apples of g
Isa 60:17 Instead of bronze I will bring **g,**
Da 2:32 head of that statue was of fine **g,**
Hag 2: 8 silver is mine, and the g is mine,
Zec 4: 2 I said, "I see a lampstand all of **g,**
     6:11 the silver and g and make a crown,
Mt   2:11 offered him gifts of **g,** frankincense,
Ac   3: 6 Peter said, "I have no silver or **g,**
1Pe 1: 7 being more precious than g that,
Rev 3:18 I counsel you to buy from me g

9: 7 what looked like crowns of **g**;
21:18 of jasper, while the city is pure **g**,
21:21 and the street of the city is pure **g**,
Tob 12: 8 better to give alms than to lay up **g**.
13:16 of Jerusalem will be built with **g**,
Wis 3: 6 like **g** in the furnace he tried them,
Sir 2: 5 For **g** is tested in the fire,
7:19 for her charm is worth more than **g**.
30:15 and fitness are better than any **g**,
31: 5 who loves **g** will not be justified;
1Mc 1:23 He took the silver and the **g**,
2Es 16:73 like **g** that is tested by fire.

FINE GOLD 2Ch 3:5, 8; Job 28:17; 31:24; Ps
19:10; 21:3; 119:127; Pr 8:19; Isa 13:12; La
4:2; Da 2:32

GOLD ... SILVER Ex 25:3; 31:4; 35:5, 32;
Nu 31:22; 1Ki 10:21, 22; 2Ki 12:13; 14:14;
1Ch 18:10; 22:16; 29:2, 3, 5; 2Ch 2:7, 14;
9:14, 20, 21; 24:14; 25:24; Ezr 1:9, 11; 5:14;
6:5; Est 1:6; Job 28:15; Ps 119:72; Pr 25:11;
SS 1:11; Jer 52:19; Eze 16:13, 17; 28:4; Da
5:2, 3, 4; 11:38, 43; Hab 2:19; Zec 14:14; Mal
3:3; Mt 10:9; Ac 17:29; 1Co 3:12; 2Ti 2:20;
Jas 5:3; Rev 9:20; 18:12; Jdt 2:18; 5:9; 8:7;
AdE 1:6, 6, 7; Wis 13:10; 15:9; Sir 40:25; LtJ
6:8, 10, 39, 50, 55, 58, 70, 71; 1Mc 4:23;
15:32; 2Mc 2:2; 1Es 2:6, 13, 14; 4:18, 19;
6:18, 26; 8:13, 14, 16; 2Es 7:55, 56

PURE GOLD Ex 25:11, 17, 24, 29, 31, 36,
38, 39; 28:14, 22, 36; 30:3; 37:2, 6, 11, 16, 17,
22, 23, 24, 26; 39:15, 25, 30; Lev 24:4, 6; 1Ki
6:20, 21; 7:49, 50; 10:21; 1Ch 28:17; 2Ch 3:4;
4:20, 22; 9:17, 20; 13:11; Job 28:19; La 4:1;
Rev 21:18, 21; Tob 13:16; Bar 3:30

SILVER ... GOLD Ge 13:2; 24:35, 53; 44:8;
Ex 3:22; 11:2; 12:35; Nu 22:18; 24:13; Dt
7:25; 8:13; 17:17; 29:17; Jos 6:19, 24; 7:21;
22:8; 2Sa 8:10, 11; 21:4; 1Ki 7:51; 10:25;
15:15, 18, 19; 20:3, 5, 7; 2Ki 7:8; 16:8; 20:13;
23:33, 35, 35; 1Ch 18:11; 2Ch 1:15; 5:1; 9:24;
15:18; 16:2, 3; 21:3; 32:27; Ezr 1:4, 6; 7:15,
16, 18; 8:25, 28, 30, 33; Ps 105:37; 115:4;
135:15; Pr 22:1; 25:11; Ecc 2:8; SS 3:10; Isa
2:7; 31:7; 39:2; 60:9; Jer 10:4; Eze 7:19;
38:13; Da 2:35, 45; 5:23; 11:8; Hos 2:8; 8:4;
Joel 3:5; Na 2:9; Zep 1:18; Hag 2:8; Zec 6:10,
11; Ac 3:6; 20:33; 1Pe 1:18; Sir 28:24; 51:28;
Bar 3:17; LtJ 6:4, 11, 30, 57; 1Mc 1:23; 2:18;
3:41; 6:1, 12; 8:3; 10:60; 11:24; 15:26; 16:11,
19; 1Es 2:9, 13; 8:55, 58, 60, 62

GOLDEN → GOLD
Ecc 12: 6 and the **g** bowl is broken,
Da 3: 5 fall down and worship the **g** statue
Rev 1:12 turning I saw seven **g** lampstands,
1:13 and with a **g** sash across his chest.
5: 8 a harp and **g** bowls full of incense,
14:14 with a **g** crown on his head,
15: 6 with **g** sashes across their chests.
15: 7 the seven angels seven **g** bowls full
1Mc 1:21 the sanctuary and took the **g** altar,

GOLDSMITH → GOLD
Isa 40:19 and a **g** overlays it with gold,
46: 6 hire a **g**, who makes it into a god;

GOLDSMITHS → GOLD
Jer 10:14 **g** are all put to shame by their idols;
LtJ 6:45 They are made by carpenters and **g**;

GOLGOTHA'
Mt 27:33 **G** (which means Place of a Skull).
Mk 15:22 **G** (which means the place of a skull)
Jn 19:17 which in Hebrew is called **G**.

GOLIATH
Philistine giant killed by David (1Sa 17; 21:9;
Sir 47:4; Pm 151:T).

GOMER
Hos 1: 3 So he went and took **G** daughter of

GOMORRAH
Ge 13:10 Lord had destroyed Sodom and **G**.
18:20 the outcry against Sodom and **G**
19:24 Lord rained on Sodom and **G** sulfur
Dt 29:23 like the destruction of Sodom and **G**
Isa 1: 9 like Sodom, and become like **G**.
Jer 23:14 and its inhabitants like **G**.
Mt 10:15 and **G** on the day of judgment than
Ro 9:29 like Sodom and been made like **G**."
2Pe 2: 6 and **G** to ashes he condemned them
Jude 1: 7 Sodom and **G** and the surrounding

GONE → GO
Nu 16: 7 You Levites have **g** too far!"
Ps 51: T after he had **g** in to Bathsheba.
Isa 53: 6 All we like sheep have **g** astray;
La 1: 3 Judah has **g** into exile with suffering
Mk 5:30 aware that power had **g** forth
1Pe 3:22 has **g** into heaven and is at the right
1Jn 4: 1 many false prophets have **g** out into
2Jn 1: 7 Many deceivers have **g** out into the

GONG'
1Co 13: 1 I am a noisy **g** or a clanging cymbal.

GOOD → BEST, BETTER, GOODNESS,
GOODNESS', GOODS, GOODWILL
Ge 1: 4 And God saw that the light was **g**;
1:10 And God saw that it was **g**.
1:12 And God saw that it was **g**.
1:18 And God saw that it was **g**.
1:21 And God saw that it was **g**.
1:25 And God saw that it was **g**.
1:31 and indeed, it was very **g**.
2: 9 pleasant to the sight and **g** for food,
2: 9 tree of the knowledge of **g** and evil.
2:17 tree of the knowledge of **g** and evil
2:18 not **g** that the man should be alone;
3: 6 saw that the tree was **g** for food,
3:22 become like one of us, knowing **g**
41:26 The seven **g** cows are seven years,
50:20 to me, God intended it for **g**,
Ex 3: 8 ring them up out of that land to a **g**
18: 9 **g** that the Lord had done to Israel,
Nu 10:29 the Lord has promised **g** to Israel."
Dt 6:18 Do what is right and **g** in the sight
Jos 21:45 all the **g** promises that the Lord
23:15 the **g** things that the Lord your God
1Sa 25:21 but he has returned me evil for **g**.
2Sa 14:17 like the angel of God, discerning **g**
1Ki 8:56 not one word has failed of all his **g**
2Ch 7: 3 "For he is **g**, for his steadfast love
31:20 what was **g** and right and faithful
Ne 2:18 themselves to the common **g**.
9:20 gave your **g** spirit to instruct them,
Job 2:10 receive the **g** at the hand of God,
Ps 14: 1 there is no one who does **g**.
34: 8 O taste and see that the Lord is **g**;
34:14 Depart from evil, and do **g**;
37: 3 Trust in the Lord, and do **g**;
37:27 Depart from evil, and do **g**;
52: 9 will proclaim your name, for it is **g**.
73: 1 Truly God is **g** to the upright,
84:11 No **g** thing does the Lord withhold
86: 5 you, O Lord, are **g** and forgiving,
103: 5 who satisfies you with **g** as long as
109: 5 So they reward me evil for **g**,
119:68 You are **g** and do **g**; teach me your
133: 1 How very **g** and pleasant it is
145: 9 The Lord is **g** to all,
147: 1 **g** it is to sing praises to our God;
Pr 3: 4 So you will find favor and **g** repute
3:27 Do not withhold **g** from those to
11:27 diligently seeks **g** seeks favor,
13:22 The **g** leave an inheritance
14:22 Those who plan **g** find loyalty and
15: 3 keeping watch on the evil and the **g**.
15:23 and a word in season, how **g** it is!
15:30 and **g** news refreshes the body.
17:22 A cheerful heart is a **g** medicine,
18:22 He who finds a wife finds a **g** thing,
19: 2 Desire without knowledge is not **g**,

22: 1 A **g** name is to be chosen rather
31:12 She does him **g**, and not harm,
Ecc 12:14 every secret thing, whether **g** or evil.
Isa 5:20 Ah, you who call evil **g** and **g** evil,
40: 9 O Jerusalem, herald of **g** tidings,
52: 7 who brings **g** news, who announces
61: 1 he has sent me to bring **g** news to
Jer 6:16 ancient paths, where the **g** way lies;
13:23 you can do **g** who are accustomed
24: 2 One basket had very **g** figs, the
32:39 own **g** and the **g** of their children
La 3:26 It is **g** that one should wait quietly
Eze 34:14 I will feed them with **g** pasture,
Hos 8: 3 Israel has spurned the **g**;
Am 5:14 Seek **g** and not evil, that you may
Mic 6: 8 has told you, O mortal, what is **g**;
Na 1:15 the feet of one who brings **g** tidings,
Zec 8:15 do **g** to Jerusalem and to the house
Mt 5:13 It is no longer **g** for anything,
5:45 his sun rise on the evil and on the **g**,
7:11 give **g** things to those who ask him!
7:17 every **g** tree bears **g** fruit,
12:35 The **g** person brings **g** things out of
a **g** treasure,
13: 8 Other seeds fell on **g** soil and
13:24 to someone who sowed **g** seed
13:48 put the **g** into baskets but threw out
25:21 'Well done, **g** and trustworthy slave;
Mk 1:15 repent, and believe in the **g** news."
3: 4 do **g** or to do harm on the sabbath.
4: 8 into **g** soil and brought forth grain,
10:18 to him, "Why do you call me **g**?
10:18 No one is **g** but God alone.
Lk 2:10 I am bringing you **g** news of great
3: 9 that does not bear **g** fruit is cut down
6:27 Love your enemies, do **g** to those
6:35 love your enemies, do **g**, and lend,
6:43 "No **g** tree bears bad fruit,
7:22 poor have **g** news brought to them.
8: 8 Some fell into **g** soil, and when it
14:34 "Salt is **g**; but if salt has lost its taste
18:19 No one is **g** but God alone.
19:17 He said to him, 'Well done, **g** slave!
Jn 1:46 anything **g** come out of Nazareth?"
2:10 have kept the **g** wine until now."
10:11 "I am the **g** shepherd.
10:14 I am the **g** shepherd.
Ac 8:12 **g** news about the kingdom of God
Ro 7:12 is holy and just and **g**.
7:16 I agree that the law is **g**.
7:18 that nothing **g** dwells within me,
8:28 that all things work together for **g**
10:15 the feet of those who bring **g** news!"
12: 2 is **g** and acceptable and perfect.
12: 9 what is evil, hold fast to what is **g**;
12:21 but overcome evil with **g**.
13: 4 for it is God's servant for your **g**.
16:19 be wise in what is **g** and guileless in
1Co 15:33 "Bad company ruins **g** morals."
2Co 9: 8 share abundantly in every **g** work.
Gal 6:10 let us work for the **g** of all,
Eph 2:10 created in Christ Jesus for **g** works,
6: 8 that whatever **g** we do,
Php 1: 6 a **g** work among you will bring it to
2:13 will and to work for his **g** pleasure.
Col 1:10 as you bear fruit in every **g** work
1Th 5:21 hold fast to what is **g**;
2Th 2:17 strengthen them in every **g** work
1Ti 1: 5 a **g** conscience, and sincere faith.
1: 8 Now we know that the law is **g**,
1:18 you may fight the **g** fight,
4: 4 For everything created by God is **g**,
6:12 Fight the **g** fight of the faith;
6:18 are to do **g**, to be rich in **g** works,
2Ti 2: 3 Share in suffering like a **g** soldier of
3:17 equipped for every **g** work.
4: 7 I have fought the **g** fight, I have
finished the race,
Tit 2: 3 they are to teach what is **g**,
2: 7 in all respects a model of **g** works,
2:14 who are zealous for **g** deeds.
Heb 5:14 practice to distinguish **g** from evil.

10: 1 the law has only a shadow of the **g**
10:24 one another to love and **g** deeds,
12:10 but he disciplines us for our **g**,
13:16 not neglect to do **g** and to share
1Pe 2: 3 you have tasted that the Lord is **g**.
3:17 For it is better to suffer for doing **g**,
3Jn 1: 2 and that you may be in **g** health,
1:11 Whoever does **g** is from God;
Tob 4: 9 laying up a **g** treasure for yourself
8: 6 not **g** that the man should be alone;
Sir 2: 9 hope for **g** things,
7:19 Do not dismiss a wise and **g** wife,
12: 1 If you do **g**, know to whom you do
26: 3 A **g** wife is a great blessing;
39:27 All these are **g** for the godly,
41:13 but a **g** name lasts forever.
Aza 1:67 to the Lord, for he is **g**,
1Mc 4:24 "For he is **g**,

DO GOOD Ps 34:14; 36:3; 37:3, 27; 51:18;
119:68; 125:4; Ecc 7:20; Isa 1:17; 41:23; Jer
4:22; 10:5; 13:23; Mic 2:7; Zep 1:12; Zec
8:15; Mt 12:12; Mk 3:4; Lk 6:9, 27, 33, 33, 35;
1Th 5:15; 1Ti 6:18; Heb 13:16; 1Pe 3:11;
4:19; Tob 12:7; Sir 12:1, 2, 5; 14:13; LtJ 6:38,
64; 1Mc 11:33; 2Mc 1:2

EVIL ... GOOD Ge 2:9, 17; 3:5, 22; 2Sa
14:17; 1Ki 3:9; Job 30:26; Ecc 9:2; 12:14; Isa
5:20, 20; Am 5:14; Mic 3:2; Mt 12:35; Lk
6:45; Ro 7:19, 21; 14:16; 2Co 5:10; Heb 5:14;
Tob 12:7; Sir 11:31; 13:25; 17:7; 33:14; 37:18;
39:4; 2Es 3:22

GOOD HEALTH Lk 7:10; Ac 4:10; 3Jn 1:2;
Tob 5:16, 16, 17, 21, 21, 21, 22; 7:1, 4, 5; 2Mc
1:10; 11:28; 3Mc 3:12; 7:1

GOOD LAND Nu 14:7; Dt 1:25, 35; 3:25;
4:21, 22; 6:18; 8:7, 10; 9:6; 11:17; Jos 23:13,
15, 16; 1Ki 14:15; 1Ch 28:8; Tob 14:4

GOOD NEWS 1Sa 31:9; 2Sa 4:10; 1Ki 1:42;
2Ki 7:9; 1Ch 10:9; Pr 15:30; 25:25; Isa 52:7;
61:1; Mt 4:23; 9:35; 10:7; 11:5; 24:14; 26:13;
Mk 1:1, 14, 15; 10:29; 13:10; 14:9; 16:15, 20;
Lk 1:19; 2:10; 3:18; 4:18, 43; 7:22; 8:1; 9:6;
16:16; 20:1; Ac 8:12, 25, 35, 40; 13:32; 14:7,
15, 21; 15:7; 16:10; 17:18; 20:24; Ro 10:15,
16; 15:19, 20; 1Co 15:1; 2Co 2:12; 8:18;
10:14, 16; 11:7; 1Th 3:6; 2Th 2:14; Heb 4:2, 6;
1Pe 1:12, 25

GOOD THINGS Ge 45:23; Jos 23:14, 15;
Job 22:18; Ps 104:28; 107:9; Pr 12:14; 13:2;
Ecc 6:3; Jer 2:7; Mt 7:11; 12:34, 35; Lk 1:53;
16:25; Gal 6:6; Heb 9:11; 10:1; Tob 12:6; Jdt
15:8; Wis 2:6; 7:11; 13:1; Sir 2:9; 11:14;
16:29; 30:18; 39:25, 25; 1Mc 14:9; 1Es 8:85;
2Es 7:6; 4Mc 12:11

GOOD WORK[S] Mt 5:16; Jn 10:32, 33; Ac
9:36; 2Co 9:8; Eph 2:10; Php 1:6; Col 1:10;
2Th 2:17; 1Ti 2:10; 5:10, 25; 6:18; 2Ti 2:21;
3:17; Tit 1:16; 2:7; 3:1, 8, 14; 2Es 8:36

NOT GOOD Ge 2:18; Ex 18:17; 1Sa 26:16;
2Sa 17:7; Ne 5:9; Ps 36:4; Pr 16:29; 19:2;
20:23; 24:23; 25:27; 28:21; Isa 65:2; Eze
18:18; 20:25; 36:31; Tob 8:6; Sir 41:16

SEEMS GOOD Jos 9:25; Jdg 10:15; 1Sa
3:18; 11:10; 14:36, 40; 24:4; 2Sa 10:12; 15:26;
19:27, 37, 38; 24:22; 1Ki 21:2; 1Ch 13:2;
19:13; 21:23; Ezr 5:17; 7:18; Est 3:11; Jer
26:14; 1Es 2:21; 8:94

WHAT IS GOOD Dt 12:28; 2Ki 20:3; Job
34:4; Ps 85:12; Ecc 6:12; Isa 38:3; 55:2; Mic
6:8; Mt 19:17; Ro 7:13, 13, 21; 12:2, 9; 13:3;
16:19; 1Th 5:21; Tit 2:3; 1Pe 3:6, 13; 3Jn
1:11; Tob 4:21; Wis 4:12; 14:26; Sir 18:8;
39:4; 3Mc 3:22

GOODNESS → GOOD
Ex 33:19 will make all my **g** pass before you,
2Ch 6:41 let your faithful rejoice in your **g**.
Ps 23: 6 Surely **g** and mercy shall follow me
27:13 that I shall see the **g** of the LORD
Zec 9:17 For what **g** and beauty are his!
Tit 1: 8 lover of **g**, prudent, upright, devout,
3: 4 But when the **g** and loving kindness
Heb 6: 5 tasted the **g** of the word of God and
2Pe 1: 5 to support your faith with **g**, and **g**
Man 1: 7 according to your great **g**

GOODNESS'* → GOOD
Ps 25: 7 for your **g** sake, O LORD!

GOODS → GOOD
Ecc 5:11 When **g** increase, those who eat
Hab 2: 6 yourselves with **g** taken in pledge?
Lk 12:19 'Soul, you have ample **g**
Sir 34:21 If one sacrifices ill-gotten **g**,

GOODWILL → GOOD, WILL
Ac 2:47 having the **g** of all the people.
Php 1:15 nvy and rivalry, but others from **g**.

GORGE → GORGED
Eze 32: 4 wild animals of the whole earth **g**

GORGED → GORGE
Isa 34: 6 it is sated with blood, it is **g** with fat,
Rev 19:21 all the birds were **g** with their flesh.

GORGIAS
1Mc 4: 1 Now **G** took five thousand infantry
5:59 **G** and his men came out of the town

GOSHEN
Ge 45:10 You shall settle in the land of **G**,
Ex 8:22 day I will set apart the land of **G**,

GOSPEL
Mk 8:35 and for the sake of the **g**,
Ro 1: 1 set apart for the **g** of God,
1:16 For I am not ashamed of the **g**;
15:16 the priestly service of the **g** of God,
1Co 1:17 to baptize but to proclaim the **g**,
9:12 obstacle in the way of the **g** of
9:14 who proclaim the **g** should get their
living by the **g**.
9:16 woe to me if I do not proclaim the **g**
2Co 4: 3 And even if our **g** is veiled,
4: 4 from seeing the light of the **g** of
9:13 obedience to the confession of the **g**
11: 4 or a different **g** from the one you
Gal 1: 6 and are turning to a different **g**—
3: 8 the **g** beforehand to Abraham,
Eph 1:13 the **g** of your salvation,
3: 6 in Christ Jesus through the **g**.
6:15 to proclaim the **g** of peace.
Php 1: 7 defense and confirmation of the **g**.
1:27 life in a manner worthy of the **g**
1:27 with one mind for the faith of the **g**,
Col 1:23 from the hope promised by the **g**
1:23 I, Paul, became a servant of this **g**.
1Th 2: 4 entrusted with the message of the **g**,
2Th 1: 8 and on those who do not obey the **g**
2Ti 1: 8 join with me in suffering for the **g**,
Phm 1:13 during my imprisonment for the **g**;
1Pe 4: 6 the reason the **g** was proclaimed
Rev 14: 6 an eternal **g** to proclaim to those

GOSSIP → GOSSIPS
Pr 11:13 A **g** goes about telling secrets,
20:19 A **g** reveals secrets;
2Co 12:20 selfishness, slander, **g**, conceit,
Sir 19: 6 but one who hates **g** has less evil.

GOSSIPS' → GOSSIP
Ro 1:29 strife, deceit, craftiness, they are **g**,
1Ti 5:13 but also **g** and busybodies,
Sir 28:13 Curse the **g** and the double-tongued,

GOURDS'
1Ki 6:18 the house had carvings of **g**
2Ki 4:39 gathered from it a lapful of wild **g**,

GOVERN → GOVERNING, GOVERNMENT,
GOVERNOR, GOVERNORS, GOVERNS
1Sa 8: 5 appoint for us, then, a king to **g** us,
1Ki 3: 9 understanding mind to **g** your
Job 34:17 Shall one who hates justice **g**?

GOVERNING → GOVERN
Ro 13: 1 be subject to the **g** authorities;

GOVERNMENT → GOVERN
Sir 10: 4 The **g** of the earth is in the hand of

GOVERNOR → GOVERN
Ge 42: 6 Now Joseph was **g** over the land;
Ne 5:14 to be their **g** in the land of Judah,
12:26 and in the days of the **g** Nehemiah
Hag 2:21 to Zerubbabel, **g** of Judah, saying,
Mal 1: 8 Try presenting that to your **g**;
Mt 27: 2 and handed him over to Pilate the **g**.
Lk 3: 1 when Pontius Pilate was **g** of Judea,

GOVERNORS → GOVERN
Mk 13: 9 you will stand before **g** and kings

GOVERNS' → GOVERN
Job 36:31 For by these he **g** peoples;
2Es 13:58 and because he **g** the times

GRACE' → GRACIOUS, GRACIOUSLY
Ps 45: 2 **g** is poured upon your lips;
Jer 31: 2 who survived the sword found **g** in
Zec 4: 7 amid shouts of '**G**, **g** to it!'"
Jn 1:14 father's only son, full of **g** and truth.
1:16 we have all received, **g** upon **g**.
1:17 **g** and truth came through Jesus
Ac 4:33 and great **g** was upon them all.
6: 8 Stephen, full of **g** and power,
11:23 he came and saw the **g** of God,
13:43 to continue in the **g** of God.
14: 3 the word of his **g** by granting signs
14:26 been commended to the **g** of God
15:11 that we will be saved through the **g**
15:40 him to the **g** of the Lord.
18:27 through **g** had become believers,
20:24 testify to the good news of God's **g**.
20:32 to God and to the message of his **g**,
Ro 1: 5 through whom we have received **g**
1: 7 **G** to you and peace from God our
3:24 are now justified by his **g** as a gift,
4:16 that the promise may rest on **g** and
5: 2 we have obtained access to this **g**
5:15 the **g** of God and the free gift in the
g of the one man,
5:17 the abundance of **g**
5:20 where sin increased, **g** abounded all
5:21 so **g** might also exercise dominion
6: 1 in sin in order that **g** may abound?
6:14 you are not under law but under **g**.
6:15 we are not under law but under **g**?
11: 5 there is a remnant, chosen by **g**.
11: 6 But if it is by **g**,
11: 6 otherwise **g** would no longer be **g**.
12: 3 the **g** given to me I say to everyone
12: 6 gifts that differ according to the **g**
15:15 because of the **g** given me
16:20 The **g** of our Lord Jesus Christ be
1Co 1: 3 **G** to you and peace from God our
1: 4 because of the **g** of God that has
3:10 According to the **g** of God given to
15:10 But by the **g** of God I am what I am,
15:10 **g** toward me has not been in vain.
15:10 it was not I, but the **g** of God that is
16:23 The **g** of the Lord Jesus be with you.
2Co 1: 2 **G** to you and peace from God our

1:12 not by earthly wisdom but by the **g**
4:15 everything is for your sake, so that **g**
6: 1 you also not to accept the **g** of God
8: 1 about the **g** of God that has been
9:14 the surpassing **g** of God that he has
12: 9 "My **g** is sufficient for you,
13:13 The **g** of the Lord Jesus Christ, the
Gal 1: 3 **G** to you and peace from God our
1: 6 who called you in the **g** of Christ
1:15 and called me through his **g**,
2: 9 recognized the **g** that had been given
2:21 I do not nullify the **g** of God;
5: 4 you have fallen away from **g**.
6:18 the **g** of our Lord Jesus Christ be
Eph 1: 2 **G** to you and peace from God our
1: 6 glorious **g** that he freely bestowed
1: 7 according to the riches of his **g**
2: 5 by **g** you have been saved—
2: 7 of his **g** in kindness toward us
2: 8 For by **g** you have been saved
3: 2 of the commission of God's **g** that
3: 7 of God's **g** that was given me by
3: 8 this **g** was given to me to bring to
4: 7 given **g** according to the measure
4:29 so that your words may give **g** to
6:24 **G** be with all who have an undying
Php 1: 2 **G** to you and peace from God our
1: 7 all of you share in God's **g** with me,
4:23 **g** of the Lord Jesus Christ be with
Col 1: 2 **G** to you and peace from God our
1: 6 truly comprehended the **g** of God.
4:18 **G** be with you.
1Th 1: 1 Jesus Christ: **G** to you and peace.
5:28 The **g** of our Lord Jesus Christ be
2Th 1: 2 **G** to you and peace from God our
1:12 to the **g** of our God and the Lord
2:16 through **g** gave us eternal comfort
3:18 The **g** of our Lord Jesus Christ be
1Ti 1: 2 **G**, mercy, and peace from God the
1:14 the **g** of our Lord overflowed for me
6:21 as regards the faith. **G** be with you.
2Ti 1: 2 **G**, mercy, and peace from God the
1: 9 according to his own purpose and **g**.
1: 9 This **g** was given to us in Christ
2: 1 strong in the **g** that is in Christ Jesus
4:22 be with your spirit. **G** be with you.
Tit 1: 4 **G** and peace from God the Father
2:11 For the **g** of God has appeared,
3: 7 having been justified by his **g**,
3:15 **G** be with all of you.
Phm 1: 3 **G** to you and peace from God our
1:25 **g** of the Lord Jesus Christ be with
Heb 2: 9 the **g** of God he might taste death
4:16 approach the throne of **g** with
4:16 find **g** to help in time of need.
10:29 and outraged the Spirit of **g**?
12:15 no one fails to obtain the **g** of God;
13: 9 the heart to be strengthened by **g**,
13:25 **G** be with all of you.
Jas 4: 6 But he gives all the more **g**;
4: 6 but gives **g** to the humble."
1Pe 1: 2 **g** and peace be yours in abundance.
1:10 the **g** that was to be yours
1:13 on the **g** that Jesus Christ will bring
4:10 good stewards of the manifold **g** of
5: 5 but gives **g** to the humble."
5:10 the God of all **g**,
5:12 testify that this is the true **g** of God.
2Pe 1: 2 **g** and peace be yours in abundance
3:18 grow in the **g** and knowledge of our
2Jn 1: 3 **G**, mercy, and peace will be with us
Jude 1: 4 who pervert the **g** of our God into
Rev 1: 4 **G** to you and peace from him who is
22:21 The **g** of the Lord Jesus be with all
AdE 15:14 and your countenance is full of **g**."
Wis 3: 9 **g** and mercy are upon his holy ones,
4:15 **g** and mercy are with his elect,
Sir 40:22 The eye desires **g** and beauty,
2Es 2:32 and my **g** will not fail."

GRACEFUL* → GRACEFULLY
Ge 29:17 and Rachel was **g** and beautiful.

Pr 5:19 a lovely deer, a **g** doe.
SS 7: 1 **g** are your feet in sandals,
Sir 24:16 and my branches are glorious and **g**.

GRACEFULLY* → GRACEFUL
Na 3: 4 **g** alluring, mistress of sorcery,

GRACIOUS* → GRACE
Ge 43:29 God be **g** to you, my son!"
Ex 33:19 and I will be **g** to whom I will be **g**,
34: 6 the LORD, a God merciful and **g**,
Nu 6:25 to shine upon you, and be **g** to you;
2Sa 12:22 LORD may be **g** to me,
2Ki 13:23 the LORD was **g** to them and had
2Ch 30: 9 LORD your God is **g** and merciful,
Ezr 7: 9 the **g** hand of his God was upon him
8:18 the **g** hand of our God was upon us,
8:22 of our God is **g** to all who seek him,
Ne 2: 8 the **g** hand of my God was upon me.
2:18 hand of my God had been **g** upon
9:17 a God ready to forgive, and
9:31 for you are a **g** and merciful God.
Job 33:24 and he is **g** to that person, and says,
Ps 4: 1 Be **g** to me, and hear my prayer.
6: 2 Be **g** to me, O LORD, for I am
9:13 Be **g** to me, O LORD.
25:16 Turn to me and be **g** to me,
26:11 redeem me, and be **g** to me.
27: 7 when I cry aloud, be **g** to me and
30:10 Hear, O LORD, and be **g** to me!
31: 9 Be **g** to me, O LORD, for I am in
41: 4 I said, "O LORD, be **g** to me;
41:10 But you, O LORD, be **g** to me,
56: 1 Be **g** to me, O God, for people
67: 1 be **g** to us and bless us and make
77: 9 Has God forgotten to be **g**?
86: 3 be **g** to me, O Lord,
86:15 O Lord, are a God merciful and **g**,
86:16 Turn to me and be **g** to me;
103: 8 The LORD is merciful and **g**,
111: 4 the LORD is **g** and merciful.
112: 4 they are **g**, merciful, and righteous.
116: 5 **G** is the LORD, and righteous;
119:58 **g** to me according to your promise.
119:132 Turn to me and be **g** to me,
135: 3 sing to his name, for he is **g**.
145: 8 The LORD is **g** and merciful,
145:13 and **g** in all his deeds.
147: 1 is **g**, and a song of praise is fitting.
Pr 11:16 A **g** woman gets honor,
15:26 to the LORD, but **g** words are pure.
22:11 and are **g** in speech will have the
Isa 30:18 the LORD waits to be **g** to you;
30:19 be **g** to you at the sound of your cry;
33: 2 O LORD, be **g** to us; we wait for you.
63: 7 recount the **g** deeds of the LORD,
Joel 2:13 your God, for he is **g** and merciful,
Am 5:15 will be **g** to the remnant of Joseph.
Jnh 4: 2 for I knew that you are a **g** God and
Zec 1:13 the LORD replied with **g** and
Mal 1: 9 of God, that he may be **g** to us.
Mt 11:26 Father, for such was your **g** will.
Lk 4:22 were amazed at the **g** words that
10:21 Father, for such was your **g** will.
Col 4: 6 Let your speech always be **g**,
1Pe 2: 3 too are also heirs of the **g** gift of life
Sir 6: 5 and a **g** tongue multiplies courtesies.
18:17 Both are to be found in a **g** person.
2Mc 2:22 Lord with great kindness became **g**
10:26 be **g** to them and to be an enemy to
14: 9 nation with the **g** kindness
1Es 8:10 In accordance with my **g** decision,
2Es 7133 and **g**, because he is **g** to those who

GRACIOUSLY* → GRACE
Ge 33:11 because God has dealt **g** with me,
Ps 119:29 and **g** teach me your law.
Sir 7:33 Give **g** to all the living;

GRAFT* → GRAFTED
Ro 11:23 for God has the power to **g** them in

GRAFTED → GRAFT
Ro 11:17 were **g** in their place to share the

GRAIN → GRAINFIELDS, GRAINS, GRANARY
Ge 41: 5 seven ears of **g**, plump and good,
41:57 came to Joseph in Egypt to buy **g**,
Lev 2: 1 presents a **g** offering to the LORD,
Nu 4:16 the regular **g** offering,
Dt 25: 4 an ox while it is treading out the **g**.
Ru 2: 2 and glean among the ears of **g**,
Ps 78:24 and gave them the **g** of heaven.
Joel 2:19 I am sending you **g**, wine, and oil,
Mk 2:23 disciples began to pluck heads of **g**.
1Co 9: 9 an ox while it is treading out the **g**."
1Ti 5:18 An ox while it is treading out the **g**,"

GRAIN OFFERING Ex 29:41; 30:9; 40:29;
Lev 2:1, 3, 4, 6, 8, 9, 10, 11, 14, 14, 15; 5:13;
6:14, 15, 21, 23; 7:9, 10, 37; 9:4, 17; 10:12;
14:10, 20, 21, 31; 23:13, 18; Nu 4:16; 5:15, 15,
18, 18, 25, 25, 26; 6:15, 17; 7:13, 19, 25, 31,
37, 43, 49, 55, 61, 67, 73, 79, 87; 8:8; 15:4, 6,
9, 24; 18:9; 28:5, 8, 9, 12, 12, 13, 20, 26, 28,
31; 29:3, 6, 6, 9, 11, 14, 16, 18, 19, 21, 22, 24,
25, 27, 28, 30, 31, 33, 34, 37, 38; Jos 22:29;
Jdg 13:19, 23; 2Ki 16:13, 15, 15, 15; 1Ch
21:23; 23:29; 2Ch 7:7; Ne 10:33; 13:5, 9; Isa
57:6; 66:3, 20; Jer 14:12; Eze 42:13; 44:29;
45:24; 46:5, 5, 7, 11, 14, 14, 15, 20; Da 2:46;
Joel 1:9, 13; 2:14; Bar 1:10; 2Mc 1:8

GRAIN OFFERINGS Lev 2:13; 23:37; Nu
29:39; Jos 22:23; 1Ki 8:64, 64; Ezr 7:17; Jer
17:26; 33:18; 41:5; Eze 45:15, 17, 17, 25; Am
5:22

GRAINFIELDS → FIELD, GRAIN
Lk 6: 1 Jesus was going through the **g**,

GRAINS* → GRAIN
Isa 48:19 and your descendants like its **g**;
Heb 11:12 as the innumerable **g** of sand

GRANARY → GRAIN
Lk 3:17 and to gather the wheat into his **g**;

GRANDCHILDREN → CHILD
Ex 10: 2 and **g** how I have made fools of the
Pr 17: 6 **G** are the crown of the aged,
1Ti 5: 4 If a widow has children or **g**,

GRANDMOTHER → MOTHER
2Ti 1: 5 a faith that lived first in your **g** Lois

GRANT → GRANTED, GRANTS
Lev 26: 6 And I will **g** peace in the land,
Nu 25:12 hereby **g** him my covenant of peace.
Ps 85: 7 O LORD, and **g** us your salvation.
140: 8 Do not **g**, O LORD, the desires of
Mk 10:40 hand or at my left is not mine to **g**,
Rev 11: 3 I will **g** my two witnesses authority
Sir 45:26 the Lord **g** you wisdom of mind

GRANTED → GRANT
Ge 25:21 and the LORD **g** his prayer.
27:20 the LORD your God **g** me success."
1Sa 1:27 LORD has **g** me the petition that I
Est 7: 2 It shall be **g** you.
Pr 10:24 the desire of the righteous will be **g**.
Jn 6:65 no one can come to me unless it is **g**
Php 1:29 has graciously **g** you the privilege
Sir 6:37 your desire for wisdom will be **g**.

GRANTS → GRANT
Ps 147:14 He **g** peace within your borders;
Sir 17:24 to those who repent he **g** a return,

GRAPE → GRAPES, GRAPEVINE
Nu 6: 3 not drink any **g** juice or eat grapes,

GRAPES → GRAPE
Ge 40:11 I took the **g** and pressed them
Nu 13:23 a branch with a single cluster of **g**,
Dt 32:32 their **g** are **g** of poison,

Isa   5: 2 to yield **g**, but it yielded wild **g**.
Jer 31:29 "The parents have eaten sour **g**,
Eze 18: 2 "The parents have eaten sour **g**,
Mic   6:15 shall tread **g**, but not drink wine.
Mt   7:16 Are **g** gathered from thorns, or figs
Rev 14:18 vine of the earth, for its **g** are ripe."

GRAPEVINE* → GRAPE, VINE

Nu   6: 4 nothing that is produced by the **g**,
Jas   3:12 yield olives, or a **g** figs?

GRASP → GRASPED

1Ki   1:50 to **g** the horns of the altar.
Lk   18:34 and they did not **g** what was said.
Tit   1: 9 **g** of the word that is trustworthy

GRASPED → GRASP

Jdg 16:29 Samson **g** the two middle pillars on
1Ki   2:28 **g** the horns of the altar.

GRASS

Ps   37: 2 for they will soon fade like the **g**,
     103:15 As for mortals, their days are like **g**;
     104:14 cause the **g** to grow for the cattle,
Pr   19:12 but his favor is like dew on the **g**.
Isa 40: 6 All people are **g**, their constancy is
Da   4:25 shall be made to eat **g** like oxen,
Mt   6:30 if God so clothes the **g** of the field,
1Pe   1:24 "All flesh is like **g** and all its glory
Rev   8: 7 and all green **g** was burned up.

GRASSHOPPER → GRASSHOPPERS

Ecc 12: 5 the **g** drags itself along

GRASSHOPPERS → GRASSHOPPER

Nu   13:33 and to ourselves we seemed like **g**,
Isa 40:22 and its inhabitants are like **g**;

GRATIFY*

Ro   13:14 for the flesh, to **g** its desires.
Gal   5:16 do not **g** the desires of the flesh.

GRATITUDE

Col   3:16 with **g** in your hearts sing psalms,

GRAVE → GRAVES

Nu   19:16 or a **g**, shall be unclean seven days.
Ps   49:14 straight to the **g** they descend,
     88:11 steadfast love declared in the **g**,
SS   8: 6 as death, passion fierce as the **g**.
Isa 53: 9 They made his **g** with the wicked

GRAVEL*

Pr   20:17 the mouth will be full of **g**.
La   3:16 He has made my teeth grind on **g**,

GRAVES → GRAVE

Ex   14:11 because there were no **g** in Egypt
Ps   5: 9 their throats are open **g**;
     49:11 Their **g** are their homes forever,
Eze 37:12 and bring you up from your **g**,
Mt   23:29 and decorate the **g** of the righteous,
Lk   11:44 For you are like unmarked **g**,
Jn   5:28 who are in their **g** will hear his voice
Ro   3:13 "Their throats are opened **g**;

GRAVITY*

Tit   2: 7 in your teaching show integrity, **g**,

GRAY

Ps   71:18 even to old age and **g** hairs, O God,
Pr   16:31 **G** hair is a crown of glory;
     20:29 the beauty of the aged is their **g** hair.
Sir   6:18 **g** hair you will still find wisdom.

GREAT → GREATER, GREATEST, GREATLY, GREATNESS

Ge   1:16 God made the two great lights—
      6: 5 wickedness of humankind was **g** in
     12: 2 I will make of you a **g** nation,
     12: 2 and make your name **g**,
     15: 1 your reward shall be very **g**."
     15:18 the river of Egypt to the **g** river,
     21:18 for I will make a **g** nation of him."
     46: 3 I will make of you a **g** nation there.

Ex   32:10 and of you I will make a **g** nation."
     32:11 **g** power and with a mighty hand?
Dt   4:32 anything so **g** as this ever happened
      7:21 is a **g** and awesome God.
     10:17 the **g** God, mighty and awesome,
     29:28 **g** wrath, and cast them into another
Jos   7: 9 what will you do for your **g** name?"
Jdg 16: 5 what makes his strength so **g**,
2Sa   7: 9 make for you a **g** name,
      7:22 Therefore you are **g**, O LORD God;
     22:36 and your help has made me **g**.
     24:14 of the LORD, for his mercy is **g**;
1Ch 16:25 For **g** is the LORD, and greatly to be
     17:19 you have done all these **g** deeds,
Ne   1: 5 the **g** and awesome God who keeps
      8: 6 Ezra blessed the LORD, the **g** God,
Job   5: 9 He does **g** things and unsearchable,
Ps   18:35 your help has made me **g**.
     19:11 in keeping them there is **g** reward.
     25:11 O LORD, pardon my guilt, for it is **g**.
     36: 6 your judgments are like the **g** deep;
     47: 2 a **g** king over all the earth.
     48: 2 the far north, the city of the **g** King.
     68:11 **g** is the company of those who bore
     77:13 What god is so **g** as our God?
     95: 3 the LORD is a **g** God, and a **g** King
     103:11 **g** is his steadfast love toward those
     117: 2 for **g** is his steadfast love toward us,
     119:165 **G** peace have those who love your
     145: 3 **G** is the LORD, and greatly to be
Pr   22: 1 to be chosen rather than **g** riches,
Jer 10: 6 you are **g**, and your name is **g** in
     27: 5 It is I who by my **g** power
     32:19 **g** in counsel and mighty in deed;
La   3:23 is your faithfulness.
Eze 17: 3 A **g** eagle, with **g** wings and long
Da   2:31 there was a **g** statue.
      2:45 The **g** God has informed the king
      7: 3 four **g** beasts came up out of the sea,
      9: 4 "Ah, Lord, **g** and awesome God,
Joel 2:11 Truly the day of the LORD is **g**;
      2:20 Surely he has done **g** things!
Na   1: 3 slow to anger but **g** in power,
Zep   1:14 The **g** day of the LORD is near,
Mal   1:11 for my name is **g** among the nations,
      4: 5 before the **g** and terrible day of the
Mt   4:16 sat in darkness have seen a **g** light,
     13:46 on finding one pearl of **g** value,
     20:26 whoever wishes to be **g** among you
Mk   13:26 coming in clouds' with **g** power
Lk   2:10 bringing you good news of **g** joy
      6:23 surely your reward is **g** in heaven;
      6:35 be **g**, and you will be children of
     21:23 there will be **g** distress on the earth
     21:27 in a cloud' with power and **g** glory.
Eph   1:19 the working of his **g** power.
      2: 4 the **g** love with which he loved us
1Ti   3: 6 the mystery of our religion is **g**:
      6: 6 **g** gain in godliness combined with
Tit   2:13 of the glory of our **g** God and Savior
Heb   2: 3 if we neglect so **g** a salvation?
     10:21 we have a **g** priest over the house of
     12: 1 by so **g** a cloud of witnesses,
     13:20 the **g** shepherd of the sheep,
1Pe   1: 3 By his **g** mercy he has given us a
Jude 1: 6 for the judgment of the **g** Day.
Rev   6:17 the **g** day of their wrath has come,
      7:14 who have come out of the **g** ordeal;
     12: 9 The **g** dragon was thrown down,
     14: 8 "Fallen, fallen is Babylon the **g**!
     16:14 for battle on the **g** day of God
     17: 1 the **g** whore who is seated on many
     18:10 "Alas, alas, the **g** city, Babylon, the
     20:11 I saw a **g** white throne and the one
Tob 11:14 and blessed be his **g** name,
Jdt   2: 5 "Thus says the **G** King,
     16:13 O Lord, you are **g** and glorious,
     16:16 fears the Lord is **g** forever.
Sir   3:18 For **g** is the might of the Lord;
      15:18 For **g** is the wisdom of the Lord;
     17:29 How **g** is the mercy of the Lord,
     26: 3 A good wife is a **g** blessing;

Bel   1:23 there was a **g** dragon,
1Mc   4:25 Israel had a **g** deliverance that day.
Man   1: 7 of **g** compassion, long-suffering,

GREAT CITY Ge 10:12; Jer 22:8; Jnh 1:2; 3:2; 4:11; Rev 11:8; 16:19; 17:18; 18:10, 16, 18, 19, 21; Jdt 1:1

GREAT CROWD[S] Mt 4:25; 8:1, 18; 13:2; 14:14; 15:30; Mk 5:21; 6:34; 8:1; 9:14; Lk 6:17; 8:4; 9:37; Jn 12:9, 12; 1Es 8:91

GREAT DISTRESS Jdg 2:15; 1Sa 28:15; 2Sa 24:14; 1Ch 21:13; Ne 9:37; Lk 21:23; Rev 2:22; 1Mc 9:27; 2Es 10:7

GREAT *GOD Dt 10:17; Ezr 5:8; Ne 8:6; Ps 95:3; Da 2:45; 9:4; 2:31; 3Mc 7:2

GREAT JOY 1Ki 1:40; 1Ch 29:22; 2Ch 30:26; Ne 12:43; Mt 28:8; Lk 2:10; 24:52; Ac 8:8; 15:3; 1Mc 4:58; 14:11; 3Mc 5:44; 2Es 7:91

GREAT KING 2Ki 18:19, 28; Ezr 5:11; Ps 47:2; 48:2; 95:3; Ecc 9:14; Isa 36:4, 13; Hos 5:13; 10:6; Mal 1:14; Mt 5:35; Tob 13:15; Jdt 2:5; 3:2; AdE 13:1; 16:1

GREAT MULTITUDE 1Ki 20:13, 28; 2Ch 13:8; 20:2, 12, 15; Isa 13:4; 16:14; Da 11:11; Mk 3:7; Lk 6:17; Rev 7:9; 19:1, 6; Jdt 7:2; Bar 2:29; 2Mc 8:16; 2Es 2:42; 3:16; 16:68

GREAT POWER Ex 32:11; Dt 4:37; 9:29; Jos 17:17; 2Ki 17:36; Ne 1:10; Ps 66:3; 79:11; 130:7; Isa 47:9; Jer 27:5; 32:17; Mk 13:26; Ac 4:33; Eph 1:19; Rev 11:17; Bar 2:11; 3Mc 6:2; 2Es 15:30, 31

GREAT THINGS 1Sa 12:24; 2Ki 8:4; 1Ch 17:19; Job 5:9; 9:10; 37:5; Ps 71:19; 106:21; 126:2, 3; Jer 45:5; Joel 2:20, 21; Lk 1:49; 1Mc 13:3

GREAT SEA Ge 1:21; Nu 34:6, 7; Jos 1:4; 9:1; 15:47; 23:4; Eze 47:10, 15, 19, 20; 48:28; Da 7:2

GREATER → GREAT

Ge   1:16 the **g** light to rule the day and the
Ex   18:11 that the LORD is **g** than all gods,
2Sa   5:10 And David became **g** and **g**,
2Ch   2: 5 for our God is **g** than other gods.
Mt   11:11 no one has arisen **g** than John
     12: 6 something **g** than the temple is here.
Mk   12:31 no other commandment **g** than these
Lk   11:31 something **g** than Solomon is here!
     11:32 something **g** than Jonah is here!
Jn   1:50 You will see **g** things than these."
     14:12 in fact, will do **g** works than these,
     15:13 No one has **g** love than this,
     15:20 Servants are not **g** than their master.
1Co 12:31 But strive for the **g** gifts.
Heb   2: 1 we must pay **g** attention
     11:26 **g** wealth than the treasures of Egypt,
1Jn   3:20 for God is **g** than our hearts,
      4: 4 for the one who is in you is **g** than
      5: 9 the testimony of God is **g**;

GREATEST → GREAT

Mt   18: 4 humble like this child is the **g**
     22:38 the **g** and first commandment.
     23:11 **g** among you will be your servant.
Lk   9:48 the least among all of you is the **g**."
     22:24 of them was to be regarded as the **g**.
1Co 13:13 and the **g** of these is love.

GREATLY → GREAT

Ge   3:16 "I will **g** increase your pangs in
2Ch 33:12 humbled himself **g** before the God
Ps   96: 4 the LORD, and **g** to be praised;
     145: 3 the LORD, and **g** to be praised;
Isa 61:10 I will **g** rejoice in the LORD,

GREATNESS → GREAT

Ex   15: 7 In the **g** of your majesty you
Dt   3:24 begun to show your servant your **g**
     32: 3 of the LORD; ascribe **g** to our God!
1Ch 29:11 Yours, O LORD, are the **g**, the power
2Ch   9: 6 half of the **g** of your wisdom had

Ps 145: 3 be praised; his **g** is unsearchable.
145: 6 and I will declare your **g**.
150: 2 according to his surpassing **g!**
Eze 38:23 I will display my **g** and my holiness
Da 4:22 Your **g** has increased and reaches to
5:18 Nebuchadnezzar kingship, **g**, glory,
7:27 and the **g** of the kingdoms were
Lk 9:43 all were astounded at the **g** of God.
Eph 1:19 the immeasurable **g** of his power

GREECE → GREEK, GREEKS

Da 8:21 The male goat is the king of **G**,
10:20 the prince of **G** will come.
1Mc 1: 1 had previously become king of **G**.)

GREED → GREEDY

Mt 23:25 but inside they are full of **g**
Lk 12:15 on your guard against all kinds of **g**;
Eph 5: 3 and impurity of any kind, or **g**,
Col 3: 5 evil desire, and **g** (which is idolatry)
2Pe 2: 3 And in their **g** they will exploit you
2:14 They have hearts trained in **g**.

GREEDY → GREED

Pr 15:27 are **g** for unjust gain make trouble
28:25 The **g** person stirs up strife,
1Co 5:11 who is sexually immoral or **g**,
6:10 the **g**, drunkards, revilers, robbers—
Eph 4:19 **g** to practice every kind of impurity.
5: 5 or one who is **g** (that is, an idolater),
1Ti 3: 8 in much wine, not **g** for money;
Tit 1: 7 to wine or violent or **g** for gain;
Sir 14: 9 eye of the **g** person is not satisfied

GREEK → GREECE

Jn 19:20 in Hebrew, in Latin, and in **G**.
Ac 16: 1 but his father was a **G**.
17:12 not a few **G** women and men of
21:37 tribune replied, "Do you know **G?**
Ro 1:16 to the Jew first and also to the **G**,
Gal 3:28 There is no longer Jew or **G**,
Col 3:11 There is no longer **G** and Jew,
2Mc 4:10 over to the **G** way of life.
4Mc 8: 8 by adopting the **G** way of life

GREEKS → GREECE

Jn 12:20 at the festival were some **G**.
Ac 14: 8 would try to convince Jews and **G**.
20:21 as I testified to both Jews and **G**
1Co 1:22 demand signs and **G** desire wisdom,
12:13 Jews or **G**, slaves or free—
1Mc 6: 2 who first reigned over the **G**.

GREEN

Ge 1:30 I have given every **g** plant for food."
9: 3 and just as I gave you the **g** plants,
Ps 23: 2 makes me lie down in **g** pastures;
Jer 17: 8 and its leaves shall stay **g**;
Mk 6:39 to sit down in groups on the **g** grass.

GREET → GREETED, GREETING, GREETINGS

Mt 5:47 And if you **g** only your brothers and
1Co 16:20 **G** one another with a holy kiss.

GREETED → GREET

Mt 23: 7 **g** with respect in the marketplaces,

GREETING → GREET

Lk 1:29 pondered what sort of **g** this might
1Co 16:21 I, Paul, write this **g** with my own
Col 4:18 I, Paul, write this **g** with my own
2Th 3:17 I, Paul, write this **g** with my own

GREETINGS → GREET

Mt 26:49 he came up to Jesus and said, "**G**,
Lk 1:28 to her and said, "**G**, favored one!

GREW → GROW

Ge 21:20 God was with the boy, and he **g** up;
Jdg 13:24 The boy **g**, and the LORD blessed
1Sa 2:21 boy Samuel **g** up in the presence of
3:19 As Samuel **g** up, the LORD was with
2Sa 3: 1 David **g** stronger and stronger,

Isa 53: 2 he **g** up before him like a young
Lk 1:80 child **g** and became strong in spirit,
2:40 child **g** and became strong, filled
13:19 it **g** and became a tree,

GRIEF → GRIEVE, GRIEVED, GRIEVOUS

Ps 10:14 Indeed you note trouble and **g**,
Pr 10: 1 but a foolish child is a mother's **g**.
14:13 and the end of joy is **g**.
Jer 8:18 My joy is gone, **g** is upon me,
La 3:32 causes **g**, he will have compassion
2Co 7: 9 your **g** led to repentance;

GRIEVE → GRIEF

Eph 4:30 do not **g** the Holy Spirit of God,
1Th 4:13 not **g** as others do who have no hope

GRIEVED → GRIEF

Ge 6: 6 and it **g** him to his heart.
Isa 63:10 they rebelled and **g** his holy spirit;
Mt 26:38 "I am deeply **g**, even to death;
2Co 7: 8 I **g** you with that letter,

GRIEVOUS → GRIEF

Ecc 5:13 **g** ill that I have seen under the sun;
6: 2 This is vanity; it is a **g** ill.

GRIND → GRINDING

Job 31:10 then let my wife **g** for another,
La 3:16 He has made my teeth **g** on gravel,

GRINDING → GRIND

Isa 3:15 by **g** the face of the poor?
Lk 17:35 will be two women **g** meal together;

GROAN → GROANED, GROANING, GROANINGS

Pr 29: 2 when the wicked rule, the people **g**.
Ro 8:23 **g** inwardly while we wait for
2Co 5: 2 For in this tent we **g**, longing to be
5: 4 in this tent, we **g** under our burden,
2Es 16:39 and the world will **g**,

GROANED → GROAN

Ex 2:23 Israelites **g** under their slavery,

GROANING → GROAN

Ex 2:24 heard their **g**, and God remembered
6: 5 heard the **g** of the Israelites whom
Jdg 2:18 would be moved to pity by their **g**
Ps 22: 1 from the words of my **g**?
Ro 8:22 whole creation has been **g** in labor

GROANINGS → GROAN

Job 3:24 and my **g** are poured out like water.

GROPE → GROPING

Dt 28:29 you shall **g** about at noon as blind people **g** in darkness,
Isa 59:10 We **g** like the blind along a wall,
Ac 17:27 perhaps **g** for him and find him—

GROPING → GROPE

Ac 13:11 and he went about **g** for someone

GROUND → GROUNDED, GROUNDS

Ge 2: 7 formed man from the dust of the **g**,
3:17 cursed is the **g** because of you;
4:10 is crying out to me from the **g!**
Ex 3: 5 which you are standing is holy **g**."
15:19 walked through the sea on dry **g**.
Jos 3:17 Israel were crossing over on dry **g**,
Jdg 6:37 and it is dry on all the **g**,
1Sa 5: 3 to the **g** before the ark of the LORD.
2Ki 2: 8 the two of them crossed on dry **g**.
Ps 26:12 My foot stands on level **g**;
104:30 and you renew the face of the **g**.
147: 6 he casts the wicked to the **g**.
Isa 53: 2 and like a root out of dry **g**;
Mt 10:29 not one of them will fall to the **g**
13: 5 Other seeds fell on rocky **g**,
25:25 I went and hid your talent in the **g**.
Mk 4:31 which, when sown upon the **g**,
Lk 22:44 [of blood falling down on the **g**.]

Jn 8: 6 wrote with his finger on the **g**.
Sir 33:10 All human beings come from the **g**,
LtJ 6:27 if any of these gods falls to the **g**,

GROUNDED* → GROUND

Eph 3:17 being rooted and **g** in love.

GROUNDS → GROUND

Da 6: 4 they could find no **g** for complaint

GROUP → GROUPS

2Sa 2:13 One **g** sat on one side of the pool,

GROUPS → GROUP

Mk 6:39 to sit down in **g** on the green grass.

GROVES

Dt 6:11 and olive **g** that you did not plant

GROW → GREW, GROWING, GROWN, GROWS, GROWTH, VINEGROWER

Ge 2: 9 the LORD God made to **g** every tree
Nu 6: 5 let the locks of the head **g** long.
Jdg 16:22 the hair of his head began to **g** again
1Sa 2:26 the boy Samuel continued to **g** both
Ps 92:12 and **g** like a cedar in Lebanon.
Isa 9: 7 His authority shall **g** continually,
11: 1 and a branch shall **g** out of his roots.
Eze 47:12 will **g** all kinds of trees for food.
Jnh 4:10 not labor and which you did not **g**;
Mt 6:28 the lilies of the field, how they **g**;
Eph 4:15 we must **g** up in every way into him
Col 1:10 as you **g** in the knowledge of God.
1Pe 2: 2 by it you may **g** into salvation—
2Pe 3:18 But **g** in the grace and knowledge of
Sir 7:10 Do not **g** weary when you pray;
1Mc 2:64 courageous and **g** strong in the law,

GROWING → GROW

Col 1: 6 bearing fruit and **g** in the whole
2Th 1: 3 because your faith is **g** abundantly,

GROWL

Ex 11: 7 But not a dog shall **g** at any of the
Jdt 11:19 and no dog will so much as **g** at you.

GROWN → GROW

Ex 2:11 One day, after Moses had **g** up,
2Ch 10:10 young men who had **g** up with him
Heb 11:24 By faith Moses, when he was **g** up,
Jas 1:15 it is fully **g**, gives birth to death.

GROWS → GROW

Mk 4:32 it **g** up and becomes the greatest
Col 2:19 **g** with a growth that is from God.

GROWTH → GROW

1Co 3: 7 but only God who gives the **g**.
Eph 4:16 promotes the body's **g** in building
Col 2:19 grows with a **g** that is from God.

GRUDGE* → GRUDGING

Ge 50:15 a **g** against us and pays us back in
Lev 19:18 bear a **g** against any of your people,
Mk 6:19 And Herodias had a **g** against him,

GRUDGING → GRUDGE

Sir 14: 6 than one who is **g** to himself;

GRUMBLE* → GRUMBLED, GRUMBLERS, GRUMBLING

Isa 29:24 those who **g** will accept instruction.
Lk 19: 7 All who saw it began to **g** and said,
Jas 5: 9 do not **g** against one another,

GRUMBLED* → GRUMBLE

Dt 1:27 you **g** in your tents and said,
Ps 106:25 They **g** in their tents, and did not
Mt 20:11 they **g** against the landowner.

GRUMBLERS* → GRUMBLE

Jude 1:16 These are **g** and malcontents;

GRUMBLING → GRUMBLE

Lk 15: 2 Pharisees and the scribes were **g**

Sir 46: 7 and stilled their wicked **g.**

GUARANTEE → GUARANTEED

Pr   11:15 To **g** loans for a stranger brings
2Co   5: 5 who has given us the Spirit as a **g.**
Heb   7:22 Jesus has also become the **g** of a

GUARANTEED* → GUARANTEE

Ro   4:16 promise may rest on grace and be **g**
Heb   6:17 he **g** it by an oath,

GUARD → GUARDED, GUARDIAN, GUARDIANS, GUARDING, GUARDS, SAFEGUARD

Ge   3:24 to **g** the way to the tree of life.
1Sa   2: 9 will **g** the feet of his faithful ones,
Ne   4: 9 set a **g** as a protection against them
Ps   17: 8 **G** me as the apple of the eye;
     25:20 O **g** my life, and deliver me;
     91:11 to **g** you in all your ways.
    141: 3 Set a **g** over my mouth, O LORD;
Pr   2:11 and understanding will **g** you.
      4: 6 love her, and she will **g** you.
      4:13 **g** her, for she is your life.
Isa   52:12 the God of Israel will be your rear **g.**
Mt   27:66 the **g** and made the tomb secure by
Lk   12:15 on your **g** against all kinds of greed;
Php   4: 7 will **g** your hearts and your minds
2Th   3: 3 and **g** you from the evil one.
1Ti   6:20 Timothy, **g** what has been entrusted
2Ti   1:12 to **g** until that day what I have
      1:14 **G** the good treasure entrusted to you
2Jn   1: 8 Be on your **g,** so that you do
Sir   6:13 and be on **g** with your friends.
     32:23 **G** yourself in every act, for this is

GUARDED → GUARD

Dt   32:10 **g** him as the apple of his eye.
Jn   17:12 I **g** them, and not one of them was

GUARDIAN → GUARD

Eze 28:14 anointed cherub as **g** I placed you;
1Pe   2:25 to the shepherd and **g** of your souls.
Sir   51:12 *Give thanks to the **g** of Israel,*

GUARDIANS → GUARD

1Co   4:15 might have ten thousand **g** in Christ,
Gal   4: 2 but they remain under **g** and

GUARDING → GUARD

Ps 119: 9 By **g** it according to your word.
Pr   2: 8 **g** the paths of justice

GUARDS → GUARD

Ps   97:10 he **g** the lives of his faithful;
    127: 1 Unless the LORD **g** the city,
Pr   13: 6 Righteousness **g** one whose way is
Mt   28: 4 the **g** shook and became like dead

GUEST → GUESTS

Mk   14:14 Where is my **g** room where I may
Lk   19: 7 to be the **g** of one who is a sinner."

GUESTS → GUEST

Pr   9:18 that her **g** are in the depths of Sheol.
Mt   9:15 "The wedding **g** cannot mourn as
Lk   5:34 "You cannot make wedding **g**
     14: 7 how the **g** chose the places of honor,

GUIDANCE → GUIDE

1Ch 10:13 had consulted a medium, seeking **g,**
Pr   11:14 Where there is no **g,** a nation falls,

GUIDE → GUIDANCE, GUIDED, GUIDES, GUIDING

Ps   31: 3 lead me and **g** me,
     48:14 He will be our **g** forever.
     67: 4 judge the peoples with equity and **g**
     73:24 You **g** me with your counsel,
Isa 58:11 The LORD will **g** you continually,
Lk   1:79 to **g** our feet into the way of peace."
      6:39 Can a blind person **g** a blind person?
Jn   16:13 he will **g** you into all the truth;
Rev   7:17 and he will **g** them to springs of the

GUIDED → GUIDE

Job 31:18 from my mother's womb I **g** the
Ps   78:72 and **g** them with skillful hand.
Gal   5:25 let us also be **g** by the Spirit.

GUIDES → GUIDE

Pr   11: 3 The integrity of the upright **g** them,
Mt   15:14 they are blind **g** of the blind.
     23:16 "Woe to you, blind **g,** who say,
     23:24 You blind **g!** You strain out a gnat
Ac   8:31 unless someone **g** me?"

GUIDING → GUIDE

Ecc   2: 3 my mind still **g** me with wisdom—

GUILT → BLOODGUILT, GUILTLESS, GUILTY

Ge   44:16 God has found out the **g** of your
Lev   4: 3 thus bringing **g** on the people,
      5:15 as your **g** offering to the LORD,
      6: 6 as your **g** offering to the LORD,
1Sa   6: 4 "What is the **g** offering that we shall
Ezr   9:15 **g** has mounted up to the heavens.
Ps   32: 5 and you forgave the **g** of my sin.
     69:27 Add **g** to their **g;**
Pr   14: 9 Fools mock at the **g** offering,
Isa   6: 7 your **g** has departed and your sin is
Jer   2:22 the stain of your **g** is still before me,
Hos   5:15 until they acknowledge their **g** and
     14: 2 say to him, "Take away all **g;**
Zec   3: 9 I will remove the **g** of this land

GUILT OFFERING[S] Lev 5:15, 15, 16, 18,

19; 6:6, 6, 17; 7:1, 2, 5, 7, 37; 14:12, 13, 14,
17, 21, 24, 25, 25, 28; 19:21, 21, 22; 22:16; Nu
6:12; 18:9; 1Sa 6:3, 4, 8, 17; 2Ki 12:16; Ezr
10:19; Pr 14:9; Eze 40:39; 42:13; 44:29;
46:20; Sir 7:31

GUILTLESS → GUILT

Mt   12: 7 would not have condemned the **g.**

GUILTY → GUILT

Ex   23: 7 for I will not acquit the **g.**
     34: 7 yet by no means clearing the **g,**
Nu   14:18 but by no means clearing the **g,**
Ps   51: 5 I was born **g,** a sinner
Pr   21: 8 The way of the **g** is crooked,
Isa   5:23 who acquit the **g** for a bribe,
     50: 9 who will declare me **g?**
Na   1: 3 LORD will by no means clear the **g.**
Mk   3:29 but is **g** of an eternal sin"—
Jn   19:11 is **g** of a greater sin."
1Jn   3: 4 commits sin is **g** of lawlessness,
Sus   1:53 the innocent and acquitting the **g,**

GUSHED → GUSHING

Ps   78:20 struck the rock so that water **g** out
    105:41 opened the rock, and water **g** out;
Isa 48:21 split open the rock and the water **g**
Ac   1:18 and all his bowels **g** out.

GUSHING* → GUSHED

Pr   18: 4 fountain of wisdom is a **g** stream.
Jn   4:14 spring of water **g** up to eternal life."

GYMNASIUM

1Mc   1:14 So they built a **g** in Jerusalem,
2Mc   4: 9 to establish by his authority a **g**
4Mc   4:20 a **g** constructed at the very citadel

ℋ

HABAKKUK

Prophet to Judah (Hab 1:1; 3:1). In deuterocanonical Bel and the Dragon (Bel 1:33-39).

HABIT

Nu   22:30 in the **h** of treating you this way?"
Heb 10:25 the **h** of some, but encouraging one

HAD → HAVE

Ge   4: 4 And the LORD **h** regard for Abel
     11: 1 the whole earth **h** one language
Ex   16:18 who gathered little **h** no shortage;
Nu   11: 4 "If only we **h** meat to eat!
Jdg   1:19 because they **h** chariots of iron.
1Sa   2:12 they **h** no regard for the LORD
Job 42:10 Job twice as much as he **h** before.
Ps   55: 6 "O that I **h** wings like a dove!
Isa   5: 1 My beloved **h** a vineyard on a very
     53: 2 he **h** no form or majesty that we
Eze   1: 6 Each **h** four faces, and each of them
               h four wings.
     10:14 Each one **h** four faces:
     41:18 Each cherub **h** two faces:
Mt   13:46 sold all that he **h** and bought it.
Mk   4: 6 since it **h** no root, it withered away.
     10:22 for he **h** many possessions.
Ac   1:16 the scripture **h** to be fulfilled,
      2:44 and **h** all things in common;
      4:35 distributed to each as any **h** need.
     14: 9 that he **h** faith to be healed,
Ro   4:11 righteousness that he **h** by faith
2Co   8:15 who **h** much did not have too
               much, and the one who **h** little did
Rev 13:11 it **h** two horns like a lamb

HADAD

Edomite adversary of Solomon (1Ki 11:14-25).

HADADEZER

2Sa   8: 3 David also struck down King **H**

HADASSAH* → =ESTHER

Est   2: 7 had brought up **H,** that is Esther,

HADES

Mt   16:18 and the gates of **H** will not prevail
Ac   2:27 not abandon my soul to **H,**
Rev   1:18 I have the keys of Death and of **H.**
      6: 8 and **H** followed with him;
     20:13 Death and **H** gave up the dead that
     20:14 **H** were thrown into the lake of fire.
Wis   1:14 the dominion of **H** is not on earth.
      2: 1 been known to return from **H.**
Sir 17:27 sing praises to the Most High in **H**
     21:10 but at its end is the pit of **H.**
Aza   1:66 For he has rescued us from **H**

HAGAR

Servant of Sarah, wife of Abraham, mother of
Ishmael (Ge 16:1-6; 25:12). Driven away by
Sarah while pregnant (Ge 16:5-16); after birth of
Isaac (Ge 21:9-21; Gal 4:21-31).

HAGGAI*

Post-exilic prophet who encouraged rebuilding
of the temple (Ezr 5:1; 6:14; Hag 1-2; 1Es 6:1;
7:3; 2Es 1:40).

HAIL → HAILSTONES

Ex   9:19 will die when the **h** comes down
      9:26 the Israelites were, there was no **h.**
Ps   78:47 He destroyed their vines with **h,**
    147:17 He hurls down **h** like crumbs—
Jn   19: 3 kept coming up to him, saying, "**H,**
Rev   8: 7 came **h** and fire, mixed with blood,
     16:21 cursed God for the plague of the **h,**
Sir 39:29 Fire and **h** and famine
2Es 15:41 fire and **h** and flying swords

HAILSTONES → HAIL

Jos 10:11 of the **h** than the Israelites killed
Eze 13:11 a deluge of rain, great **h** will fall,
Rev 16:21 and huge **h,** each weighing about

HAIR → HAIRS, HAIRY

Ex   26: 7 make curtains of goats' **h** for a tent
Jdg 16:22 **h** of his head began to grow again
     20:16 sling a stone at a **h,** and not miss.
2Sa 14:26 When he cut the **h** of his head (for
Pr   16:31 Gray **h** is a crown of glory;
     20:29 beauty of the aged is their gray **h.**
Isa   3:24 and instead of well-set **h,** baldness;

Da 4:33 until his **h** grew as long as eagles'
     7: 9 and the **h** of his head like pure wool;
Mt 3: 4 camel's **h** with a leather belt around
Lk 7:44 her tears and dried them with her **h.**
   21:18 But not a **h** of your head will perish.
Jn 11: 2 and wiped his feet with her **h;**
    12: 3 and wiped them with her **h.**
1Co 11: 6 for a woman to have her **h** cut off
   11:14 that if a man wears long **h,**
   11:15 but if a woman has long **h,**
1Ti 2: 9 not with their **h** braided, or with
1Pe 3: 3 outwardly by braiding your **h,**
Rev 1:14 His head and his **h** were white as
    9: 8 their **h** like women's **h,**
Sir 6:18 gray **h** you will still find wisdom.
Bel 1:27 Then Daniel took pitch, fat, and **h,**

HAIRS → HAIR

Ps 40:12 more than the **h** of my head,
Mt 10:30 the **h** of your head are all counted.
Lk 12: 7 the **h** of your head are all counted.

HAIRY → HAIR

Ge 27:11 "Look, my brother Esau is a **h** man,

HAKELDAMA*

Ac 1:19 field was called in their language **H,**

HALAH

2Ki 18:11 settled them in **H,** on the Habor,

HALF → HALF-TRIBE

Ge 15:10 laying each **h** over against the other;
Ex 24: 6 Moses took **h** of the blood and put it
   30:13 **h** a shekel as an offering to the
Jos 8:33 **h** of them in front of Mount Gerizim
2Sa 10: 4 shaved off **h** the beard of each,
1Ki 3:25 give **h** to the one, and **h** to the other.
   10: 7 Not even **h** had been told me;
Ne 4:16 **h** of my servants worked on
   13:24 **h** of their children spoke the
Est 5: 3 even to the **h** of my kingdom."
Isa 44:19 "**H** of it I burned in the fire;
Eze 16:51 Samaria has not committed **h** your
Da 7:25 for a time, two times, and **h** a time.
   12: 7 for a time, two times, and **h** a time,
Mk 6:23 give you, even **h** of my kingdom."
Lk 19: 8 **h** of my possessions, Lord, I will
Rev 8: 1 silence in heaven for about **h** an
   11:11 But after the three and a **h** days,
   12:14 for a time, and times, and **h** a time.

HALF-TRIBE → HALF, TRIBE

Nu 32:33 to the **h** of Manasseh son of Joseph
Jos 4:12 and the **h** of Manasseh crossed over

HALL

1Ki 7: 7 judgment, the **H** of Justice,
Da 5:10 came into the banqueting **h.**
Mt 22:10 wedding **h** was filled with guests.
Ac 19: 9 daily in the lecture **h** of Tyrannus.

HALLELUJAH*

Rev 19: 1 multitude in heaven, saying, "**H!**
   19: 3 Once more they said, "**H!**
   19: 4 on the throne, saying, "Amen. **H!**"
   19: 6 thunderpeals, crying out, "**H!**
Tob 13:17 and all her houses will cry, '**H!**
3Mc 7:13 the whole multitude shouted the **H**

HALLOWED*

Ge 2: 3 blessed the seventh day and **h** it,
Mt 6: 9 Father in heaven, **h** be your name.
Lk 11: 2 Father, **h** be your name.
Sir 33: 9 Some days he exalted and **h,**
2Mc 15: 2 and **h** above other days,"

HAM

Son of Noah (Ge 5:32; 1Ch 1:4), father of
Canaan (Ge 9:18; 10:6-20; 1Ch 1:8-16). Saw
Noah's nakedness (Ge 9:20-27).

HAMAN

Agagite nobleman honored by Xerxes (Est 3:1-
2). Plotted to exterminate the Jews because of

Mordecai (Est 3:3-15). Forced to honor Mordecai
(Est 5-6). Plot exposed by Esther (Est 5:1-8; 7:1-
8). Hanged (Est 7:9-10). See also Additions to
Esther.

HAMATH

2Sa 8: 9 of **H** heard that David had defeated
2Ki 14:28 for Israel Damascus and **H,**
   18:34 Where are the gods of **H** and Arpad

HAMMER → HAMMERED

Jdg 4:21 and took a **h** in her hand,
Jer 10: 4 **h** and nails so that it cannot move.

HAMMERED → HAMMER

Ex 25:18 you shall make them of **h** work,

HAMOR

Ge 34: 2 When Shechem son of **H** the Hivite,

HAMPERED*

Pr 4:12 you walk, your step will not be **h;**

HAMSTRING* → HAMSTRUNG

Jos 11: 6 you shall **h** their horses, and burn

HAMSTRUNG → HAMSTRING

Jos 11: 9 he **h** their horses, and burned their
1Ch 18: 4 David **h** all the chariot horses,

HANAMEL

Jer 32: 7 **H** son of your uncle Shallum is

HANANEL

Ne 3: 1 and as far as the Tower of **H.**
Jer 31:38 for the LORD from the tower of **H** to

HANANI

Ne 7: 2 brother **H** charge over Jerusalem,

HANANIAH → =SHADRACH

1. False prophet; adversary of Jeremiah (Jer 28).
2. Original name of Shadrach (Da 1:6-19; 2:17).

HAND → BAREHANDED, EMPTY-HANDED,
HANDED, HANDFUL, HANDS,
HIGH-HANDEDLY, LEFT-HANDED

Ge 3:22 he might reach out his **h** and take
    4:11 your brother's blood from your **h.**
   16:12 with his **h** against everyone,
   22:12 not lay your **h** on the boy or do
   24: 2 "Put your **h** under my thigh
   25:26 with his **h** gripping Esau's heel;
   37:22 he might rescue him out of their **h**
   47:29 your **h** under my thigh and promise
   48:14 But Israel stretched out his right **h**
Ex 3:19 unless compelled by a mighty **h,**
    4: 6 "Put your **h** inside your cloak."
    6: 1 by a mighty **h** he will let them go;
   13: 3 from there by strength of **h;**
   15: 6 Your right **h,** O LORD, glorious in
   21:24 tooth for tooth, **h** for **h,** foot for foot
   33:22 cover you with my **h** until I have
Dt 4:34 by a mighty **h** and an outstretched
   19:21 tooth for tooth, **h** for **h,** foot for foot
   32:39 and no one can deliver from my **h.**
Jos 8: 7 your God will give it into your **h.**
Jdg 2:15 the **h** of the LORD was against them
1Sa 17:50 there was no sword in David's **h.**
   24:10 how the LORD gave you into my **h**
   26: 9 can raise his **h** against the LORD's
2Sa 1:14 to lift your **h** to destroy the LORD's
   18:12 in my **h** the weight of a thousand
   18:12 not raise my **h** against the king's
1Ki 8:24 have this day fulfilled with your **h.**
    8:42 mighty **h,** and your outstretched arm
   13: 4 Jeroboam stretched out his **h** from
   18:44 cloud no bigger than a person's **h** is
1Ch 21:17 Let your **h,** I pray, O LORD my God,
2Ch 6:15 this day have fulfilled with your **h.**
   32:15 able to save his people from my **h**
   32:22 from the **h** of King Sennacherib
Ezr 7: 9 the gracious **h** of his God was upon
Ne 2: 8 the gracious **h** of my God was upon
    4:17 labored on the work with one **h** and

Job 40: 4 I lay my **h** on my mouth.
Ps 10:12 O LORD; O God, lift up your **h;**
   16: 8 he is at my right **h,** I shall not be
   32: 4 For day and night your **h** was heavy
   37:24 for the LORD holds us by the **h.**
   44: 3 but your right **h,** and your arm,
   45: 9 at your right **h** stands the queen in
   63: 8 your right **h** upholds me.
   74:11 Why do you hold back your **h;**
   75: 8 in the **h** of the LORD there is a cup
   80:17 But let your **h** be upon the one at
         your right **h,**
   91: 7 ten thousand at your right **h,**
   95: 4 In his **h** are the depths of the earth;
   98: 1 right **h** and his holy arm have gotten
 109:31 he stands at the right **h** of the needy,
 110: 1 says to my lord, "Sit at my right **h**
 137: 5 O Jerusalem, let my right **h** wither!
 139:10 even there your **h** shall lead me,
 145:16 You open your **h,** satisfying the
Pr 3:16 Long life is in her right **h;**
   19:24 lazy person buries a **h** in the dish,
   21: 1 heart is a stream of water in the **h** of
   27:16 or to grasp oil in the right **h.**
Ecc 2:24 also, I saw, is from the **h** of God;
    9:10 Whatever your **h** finds to do, do
Isa 1:25 I will turn my **h** against you;
    5:25 and his **h** is stretched out still.
   11: 8 child shall put its **h** on the adder's
   40:12 in the hollow of his **h** and marked
   41:13 LORD your God, hold your right **h;**
   44: 5 will write on the **h,** "The LORD's,"
   48:13 **h** laid the foundation of the earth
   64: 8 we are all the work of your **h.**
Jer 22:24 were the signet ring on my right **h,**
   31:32 by the **h** to bring them out of
   51: 7 was a golden cup in the LORD's **h,**
La 3: 3 against me alone he turns his **h,**
Eze 1: 3 the **h** of the LORD was on him there.
    2: 9 and a **h** was stretched out to me,
Da 3:17 of blazing fire and out of your **h,**
    5: 5 the fingers of a human **h** appeared
   10:10 then a **h** touched me and roused me
Am 7: 7 with a plumb line in his **h.**
Jnh 4:11 not know their right **h**
Hab 2:16 The cup in the LORD's right **h** will
    3: 4 rays came forth from his **h,**
Mt 3:12 His winnowing fork is in his **h,**
    5:30 if your right **h** causes you to sin,
    6: 3 do not let your left **h** know what
         your right **h** is doing,
   12:10 a man was there with a withered **h,**
   18: 8 "If your **h** or your foot causes you
   22:44 "Sit at my right **h,** until I put your
   26:64 seated at the right **h** of Power and
Mk 1:31 took her by the **h** and lifted her up.
    3: 1 was there who had a withered **h.**
    5:41 He took her by the **h** and said to her,
    9:43 If your **h** causes you to stumble, cut
   12:36 "Sit at my right **h,** until I put your
   14:62 seated at the right **h** of the Power,'
Lk 5:13 Then Jesus stretched out his **h,**
    9:62 a **h** to the plow and looks back is fit
   20:42 said to my Lord, "Sit at my right **h,**
   22:69 will be seated at the right **h** of
Jn 10:28 will snatch them out of my **h.**
   20:27 your **h** and put it in my side.
Ac 2:34 said to my Lord, "Sit at my right **h,**
    7:55 and Jesus standing at the right **h**
Ro 8:34 raised, who is at the right **h** of God,
1Co 12:15 would say, "Because I am not a **h,**
Eph 1:20 and seated him at his right **h** in
Col 3: 1 seated at the right **h** of God.
Heb 1:13 "Sit at my right **h** until I make your
    8: 1 one who is seated at the right **h** of
   10:12 "he sat down at the right **h** of God,"
1Pe 3:22 into heaven and is at the right **h**
Rev 1:16 In his right **h** he held seven stars,
    5: 1 saw in the right **h** of the one seated
   13:16 to be marked on the right **h** or the
Jdt 9:10 by the **h** of a woman.
   13:15 struck him down by the **h** of a

AdE 14:14 But save us by your **h,**
Sir   7:32 Stretch out your **h** to the poor,
     33:13 Like clay in the **h** of the potter,
2Es 15:11 bring them out with a mighty **h** and

AT HAND Ge 25:24; Dt 32:35; 1Sa 21:3, 4;
25:8; Job 15:23; Ps 85:9; Isa 13:22; Jer 48:16;
Mic 7:4; Zep 1:7; Mt 26:45, 46; Mk 14:42; Ro
7:21; AdE 16:7; Wis 9:16; Sir 8:16; 1Mc
12:27; 2Mc 12:31; 15:20; 3Mc 5:46; 2Es 2:34;
16:2, 74

FROM ... HAND Ge 4:11; 21:30; 32:11, 11;
33:10; 41:42; 48:22; Dt 7:8; 26:4; 32:39; Jos
22:31; Jdg 2:18; 6:9, 9, 14; 8:34; 9:17; 12:2;
13:5; 17:3; Ru 4:5, 9; 1Sa 7:8, 14; 9:16; 10:1,
18, 18; 12:3, 4; 17:37; 25:35; 2Sa 3:18; 12:7;
13:5, 6, 10; 14:16; 19:9, 9; 22:1, 1; 1Ki 11:31;
2Ki 13:5; 16:7, 7; 17:7; 19:14, 19; 1Ch 29:16;
2Ch 25:15; 30:6; 32:11, 14, 14, 15, 15, 17, 22,
22; Ezr 8:31; Est 3:10; Job 5:15; 6:23, 23;
35:7; Ps 18:Heading, Heading; 31:15; 71:4;
82:4; 88:5; 89:44; 97:10; 106:10, 10; 144:7,
11; Pr 6:5; Ecc 2:24; Isa 1:12; 37:14, 20; 40:2;
43:13; 50:11; 51:22; Jer 21:12; 22:3; 25:15,
17, 28; 34:3; 38:18, 23; 42:11; La 5:8; Eze
13:23; 30:22; 39:3; Mic 5:12; Hab 3:4; Zec
11:6; Mal 1:13; Lk 1:71; Ac 28:4; Rev 5:7;
8:4; 10:10; Wis 2:18; 5:16; 16:15; Sir 27:19;
51:3, 8; Bar 4:18, 21; 3Mc 6:10

HAND OF ... *GOD 1Sa 5:11; 2Ch 30:12;
Ezr 7:9; 8:18, 22, 31; Ne 2:8, 18; Job 2:10;
19:21; 27:11; Ecc 2:24; 9:1; Isa 62:3; Mk
16:19; Ac 2:33; 7:55, 56; Ro 8:34; Col 3:1;
Heb 10:12; 1Pe 3:22; 5:6; Wis 3:1

HAND OF THE *LORD Eze 8:1; Lk 1:66;
Ac 11:21; 13:11; Wis 5:16; Sir 10:4, 5

HAND OF THE †LORD Ex 9:3; 16:3; Jos
4:24; 22:31; Jdg 2:15; Ru 1:13; 1Sa 5:6, 9;
7:13; 12:15; 2Sa 24:14; 1Ki 18:46; 1Ch 21:13;
Ezr 7:6, 28; Job 12:9; Ps 75:8; 118:15, 16, 16;
Pr 21:1; Isa 25:10; 41:20; 51:17; 62:3; 66:14;
Eze 1:3; 3:14, 22; 33:22; 37:1; 40:1

INTO ... HAND Ge 9:2; 14:20; 32:16; Nu
21:34; Dt 20:13; Jos 8:7, 18; 10:19, 30, 32; Jdg
1:2, 4; 3:8, 10, 28; 4:2, 7, 9, 14; 6:1, 13; 7:2, 7,
9, 14, 15; 8:7; 10:7, 7; 11:21, 30, 32; 12:3;
13:1; 16:23, 24; 20:28; 1Sa 12:9, 9, 9; 14:10,
12, 37; 17:46, 47; 23:4, 7, 12, 14, 20; 24:4, 10;
26:8, 23; 2Sa 3:8; 5:19, 19; 16:8; 24:14; 1Ki
20:13, 28; 22:6, 12, 15; 2Ki 12:15; 13:3, 3;
17:20; 18:30; 19:10; 21:14; 22:5, 7, 9; 1Ch
6:15; 14:10, 10; 21:13; 22:18; 2Ch 16:8; 18:5,
11, 14; 24:24; 28:5, 5, 9; 34:17; 36:17; Ezr
5:12; 8:26; Job 9:24; Ps 31:5, 8; 106:41; Isa
19:4; 36:15; 37:10; 47:6; 51:23; 64:7; Jer 20:4,
5; 27:6; 29:21; 32:3, 28, 36; 34:2; 44:30; La
1:7; 2:7; Eze 21:22; 23:31; 30:12, 25; 31:11;
39:23; Da 2:38; Joel 3:8; Zec 11:6, 6

LEFT HAND Ge 13:9; 48:13, 14; Lev 14:15,
16, 26, 27; Jdg 3:21; 16:29; Ne 8:4; Pr 3:16;
SS 2:6; 8:3; Eze 39:3; Da 12:7; Mt 6:3; 25:41;
1Es 4:30

MIGHTY HAND Ex 3:19; 6:1, 1; 32:11; Dt
4:34; 5:15; 6:21; 7:8, 19; 9:26; 11:2; 26:8; 1Ki
8:42; 2Ch 6:32; Eze 20:33, 34; Da 9:15; 1Pe
5:6; Bar 2:11; 1Es 8:47, 61; 2Es 15:11

RIGHT HAND Ge 13:9; 24:49; 48:13, 14, 17,
18; Ex 15:6, 6, 12; Lev 8:23; 14:14, 17, 25, 28;
Nu 20:17; Jos 1:7; Jdg 5:26; 16:29; 2Sa 20:9;
1Ch 12:2; Ne 4:23; 8:4; Job 30:12; 40:14; Ps
16:8, 11; 17:7; 18:35; 20:6; 21:8; 44:3; 45:4, 9;
48:10; 60:5; 63:8; 73:23; 77:10; 78:54; 80:15,
17; 89:13, 25, 42; 91:7; 98:1; 108:6; 109:31;
110:1, 5; 118:15, 16, 16; 121:5; 137:5; 138:7;
139:10; 142:4; Pr 3:16; 27:16; SS 2:6; 8:3; Isa
41:10, 13; 44:20; 45:1; 48:13; 62:8; 63:12; Jer
22:24; La 2:3, 4; Eze 21:22; 39:3; Da 12:7; Jnh
4:11; Hab 2:16; Zec 3:1; Mt 5:30; 6:3; 20:21,
23; 22:44; 25:33, 34; 26:64; 27:29; Mk 10:37,
40; 12:36; 14:62; 16:19; Lk 6:6; 20:42; 22:69;
Ac 2:25, 33, 34; 3:7; 5:31; 7:55, 56; Ro 8:34;

2Co 6:7; Gal 2:9; Eph 1:20; Col 3:1; Heb 1:3,
13; 8:1; 10:12; 12:2; 1Pe 3:22; Rev 1:16, 17,
20; 2:1; 5:1, 7; 10:5; 13:16; Wis 5:16; Sir
12:12; 21:19; 49:11; LtJ 6:15; 1Mc 2:22; 7:47;
2Mc 4:34; 14:33; 15:15; 1Es 4:29; 2Es 3:6;
7:7; 10:30; 15:22; 16:13

HANDED → HAND
Jos 11: 8 And the LORD **h** them over to Israel,
    24:11 and I **h** them over to you.
Jdg 2:23 and had not **h** them over to Joshua.
Mt 26: 2 the Son of Man will be **h** over to be
    27:26 he **h** him over to be crucified.
Ac 2:23 **h** over to you according to
    3:13 whom you **h** over and rejected in
Ro 4:25 **h** over to death for our trespasses
1Co 15: 3 For I **h** on to you as of first

HANDFUL → HAND
Ecc 4: 6 a **h** with quiet than two handfuls

HANDKERCHIEFS*
Ac 19:12 the **h** or aprons that had touched

HANDLE
Col 2:21 "Do not **h,** Do not taste, Do not

HANDS → HAND
Ge 5:29 work and from the toil of our **h."**
    27:22 but the **h** are the **h** of Esau."
Ex 29:10 Aaron and his sons shall lay their **h**
    32:15 two tablets of the covenant in his **h,**
1Sa 5: 4 both his **h** were lying cut off upon
2Sa 24:14 but let me not fall into human **h."**
2Ki 11:12 they clapped their **h** and shouted,
    22:17 to anger with all the work of their **h,**
Ps 18:24 the cleanness of my **h** in his sight.
    22:16 My **h** and feet have shriveled,
    24: 4 who have clean **h** and pure hearts,
    47: 1 Clap your **h,** all you peoples;
    63: 4 lift up my **h** and call on your name.
    90:17 O prosper the work of our **h!**
    115: 7 They have **h,** but do not feel;
    138: 8 Do not forsake the work of your **h.**
Pr 21:25 for lazy **h** refuse to labor.
    24:33 a little folding of the **h** to rest,
    31:13 and works with willing **h.**
    31:20 and reaches out her **h** to the needy.
Ecc 4: 5 Fools fold their **h** and consume
    11: 6 at evening do not let your **h** be idle;
Isa 5:12 or see the work of his **h!**
    35: 3 Strengthen the weak **h,** and make
    37:19 but the work of human **h—**
    45:12 my **h** that stretched out the heavens,
    49:16 inscribed you on the palms of my **h;**
    55:12 trees of the field shall clap their **h.**
    65: 2 I held out my **h** all day long to
Jer 10: 3 worshiped the works of their own **h.**
    20:13 of the needy from the **h** of evildoers.
    26:14 But as for me, here I am in your **h.**
La 3:41 our hearts as well as our **h** to God
Eze 1: 8 their four sides they had human **h.**
Da 2:45 was cut from the mountain not by **h,**
Hos 14: 3 'Our God,' to the work of our **h.**
Mic 7: 3 Their **h** are skilled to do evil;
Zec 8:13 be afraid, but let your **h** be strong.
Mal 1:10 not accept an offering from your **h.**
Mk 7: 5 of the elders, but eat with defiled **h?**
    10:16 in his arms, laid his **h** on them,
    14:41 is betrayed into the **h** of sinners.
Lk 23:46 into your **h** I commend my spirit."
    24:40 he showed them his **h** and his feet.
Jn 3:35 has placed all things in his **h.**
    20:27 "Put your finger here and see my **h.**
Ac 6: 6 prayed and laid their **h** on them,
    8:18 the laying on of the apostles' **h,**
    13: 3 fasting and praying they laid their **h**
    19: 6 When Paul had laid his **h** on them,
    28: 8 and cured him by praying and
            putting his **h**
Ro 10:21 "All day long I have held out my **h**
1Co 15:24 he **h** over the kingdom to God the
1Th 4:11 to work with your **h,** as we directed

1Ti 2: 8 lifting up holy **h** without anger or
    4:14 prophecy with the laying on of **h**
2Ti 1: 6 through the laying on of my **h;**
Heb 6: 2 laying on of **h,** resurrection of the
    10:31 to fall into the **h** of the living God.
1Jn 1: 1 looked at and touched with our **h,**
Rev 20: 4 mark on their foreheads or their **h.**
Jdt 7:25 God has sold us into their **h,**
1Mc 2:48 rescued the law out of the **h** of the

FROM ... HANDS Ex 29:25; 32:19; Lev
8:28; Dt 9:17; Jdg 7:8; 2Ch 30:16; 32:17; Ne
9:27; Ps 140:4; Jer 20:13; 31:11; Eze 13:21;
34:27; Mic 4:10; Mal 1:10; Lk 1:74; Jn 10:39;
Ac 12:11; 2Co 11:33; Jdt 16:2; AdE 14:19; Sir
50:12; 1Mc 5:12; 9:46

HANDS ON Ge 37:27; Ex 22:8, 11; 29:10,
15, 19; Lev 4:15; 8:18, 22; 16:21; 24:14; Nu
8:10, 12; 27:23; Dt 34:9; Jdg 19:27; 1Ki 20:6;
2Ki 11:16; 13:16; 2Ch 23:15; 29:23; Ne 13:21;
Est 3:6; 8:7; 9:2, 16; Job 29:9; 41:8; Ps 55:20;
Jer 2:37; 30:6; Mic 7:16; Mt 19:13, 15; 26:50;
Mk 5:23; 6:5; 8:23, 25; 10:16; 14:46; 16:18;
Lk 4:40; 13:13; 20:19; 22:53; Jn 7:30, 44; Ac
6:6; 8:17; 9:12, 17; 13:3; 19:6; 28:8; AdE
12:2; 6:2; Wis 8:12; Sus 1:34; 1Mc 14:31

HUMAN HANDS Dt 4:28; 2Sa 24:14; 2Ki
19:18; 1Ch 21:13; 2Ch 32:19; Ps 115:4;
135:15; Isa 37:19; Eze 1:8; 10:21; Da 2:34;
8:25; Mt 17:22; Mk 9:31; Lk 9:44; Ac 7:48;
17:24, 25; Eph 2:11; Heb 9:24; Wis 13:10; LtJ
6:51

INTO ... HANDS Lev 26:25; Nu 21:2; Jos
2:24; 21:44; Jdg 7:16; 8:3; 14:9; 15:12, 13, 18;
18:10; 1Sa 24:18; 28:19, 19; 2Sa 21:9; 24:14;
1Ki 15:18; 2Ki 10:24; 12:11; 1Ch 5:20; 21:13;
2Ch 13:16; Ezr 8:33; Ne 9:24, 27; Est 3:9; Job
16:11; Ps 10:14; Jer 12:7; 21:7, 7, 7, 10; 22:25,
25, 25, 25; 26:24; 32:4, 24, 25, 28, 43; 44:30;
Eze 10:7; 16:39; 21:31; 23:9, 9, 28, 28; Mt
17:22; 26:45; Mk 9:31; 14:41; Lk 9:44; 10:30,
36; 23:46; Jn 13:3; Heb 10:31; Jdt 7:25; Wis
12:9; Sir 2:17, 17; 8:1; Sus 1:23; 1Mc 4:30;
5:50; 7:35; 2Mc 12:24, 28; 13:11; 14:42; 1Es
1:53; 6:15; 2Es 6:58; 10:23

HANDSOME
Ge 39: 6 Joseph was **h** and good-looking.
1Sa 16:12 and had beautiful eyes, and was **h,**
    17:42 ruddy and **h** in appearance.
1Ki 1: 6 He was also a very **h** man.
Eze 23: 6 all of them **h** young men,
Da 1: 4 without physical defect and **h,**

HANG → HANGED, HANGING, HUNG
Ge 40:19 and **h** you on a pole;
Est 7: 9 And the king said, "**H** him on that."
Mt 22:40 On these two commandments **h** all
Jdt 14: 1 Take this head and **h** it upon

HANGED → HANG
Ge 40:22 but the chief baker he **h,**
2Sa 17:23 his house in order, and **h** himself;
Est 2:23 both the men were **h** on the gallows.
    7:10 So they **h** Haman on the gallows
Mt 27: 5 and he went and **h** himself.

HANGING → HANG
2Sa 18: 9 left **h** between heaven and earth,
Ac 10:39 put him to death by **h** him on a tree;

HANNAH*
  Wife of Elkanah, mother of Samuel (1Sa 1).
Prayer at dedication of Samuel (1Sa 2:1-10).
Blessed (1Sa 2:18-21).

HAPPEN → HAPPENED, HAPPENING
Ge 49: 1 I may tell you what will **h** to you in
Ex 2: 4 to see what would **h** to him.
Ecc 9:11 but time and chance **h** to them all.
Da 10:14 what is to **h** to your people
Mk 10:32 to tell them what was to **h** to him,
Jn 18: 4 Jesus, knowing all that was to **h** to

HAPPENED → HAPPEN

Dt   4:32 has anything so great as this ever **h**
1Sa   4: 7 For nothing like this has **h** before.
Joel 1: 2 Has such a thing **h** in your days,

HAPPENING → HAPPEN

1Pe   4:12 as though something strange were **h**

HAPPINESS → HAPPY

La   3:17 I have forgotten what **h** is;
Sir   8:19 or you may drive away your **h.**

HAPPY → HAPPINESS

Ge   30:13 And Leah said, "**H** am I!
Dt   33:29 **H** are you, O Israel!
1Ki   4:20 they ate and drank and were **h.**
      10: 8 **H** are your wives! **H** are these your
Est   5: 9 Haman went out that day **h** and in
Job   5:17 **h** is the one whom God reproves;
Ps   1: 1 **H** are those who do not follow the
      2:12 **H** are all who take refuge in him.
      32: 1 **H** are those whose transgression is
      33:12 **H** is the nation whose God is the
           LORD,
      34: 8 **h** are those who take refuge in him.
      40: 4 **H** are those who make the LORD
      41: 1 **H** are those who consider the poor;
      84:12 **h** is everyone who trusts in you.
      112: 1 **H** are those who fear the LORD,
      119: 2 **H** are those who keep his decrees,
      128: 1 **H** is everyone who fears the LORD,
      137: 8 **H** shall they be who pay you back
Pr   3:13 **H** are those who find wisdom,
      8:32 **h** are those who keep my ways.
      8:34 **H** is the one who listens to me,
      31:28 Her children rise up and call her **h;**
Ecc   3:12 nothing better for them than to be **h**
Isa   56: 2 **H** is the mortal who does this,
Jnh   4: 6 so Jonah was very **h** about the bush.
Mal   3:12 Then all nations will count you **h,**
Tob 13:14 **H** are those who love you,
Sir   1:13 who fear the Lord will have a **h** end;
      13:26 sign of a **h** heart is a cheerful face,
      14:20 **H** is the person who meditates on
      25: 9 **H** is the one who finds a friend,
      26: 1 **H** is the husband of a good wife;
      34:17 **H** is the soul that fears the Lord!
Bar   4: 4 **H** are we, O Israel, for we know

HARAN

Ge   11:27 the father of Abram, Nahor, and **H;**
      11:31 but when they came to **H,**

HARASS → HARASSED

Dt   2: 9 "Do not **h** Moab or engage them in
      2:19 do not **h** them or engage them in

HARASSED → HARASS

Mt   9:36 because they were **h** and helpless,

HARBOR → HARBORING, HARBORS

Sir   28: 3 anyone **h** anger against another,

HARBORING* → HARBOR

Pr   26:24 in speaking while **h** deceit within;

HARBORS → HARBOR

Sir   28: 5 If a mere mortal **h** wrath,

HARD → HARD-HEARTED, HARDEN, HARDENED, HARDENING, HARDENS, HARDER, HARDSHIP, HARDSHIPS

Ex   1:14 made their lives bitter with **h** service
      18:26 **h** cases they brought to Moses,
1Ki 10: 1 came to test him with **h** questions.
Job   7: 1 human beings have a **h** service on
Pr   15:15 All the days of the poor are **h,**
Jer 32:17 Nothing is too **h** for you.
Mt   7:14 the road is **h** that leads to life,
      19:23 **h** for a rich person to enter the
Ac   28:27 and their ears are **h** of hearing,
Ro   16:12 who has worked **h** in the Lord.
1Pe   4:18 **h** for the righteous to be saved,

2Pe   3:16 things in them **h** to understand,
Sir 40: 1 **H** work was created for everyone,

HARD-HEARTED* → HARD, HEART

Dt   15: 7 do not be **h** or tight-fisted toward
Pr   28:14 one who is **h** will fall into calamity.
Mt   19: 8 you were so **h** that Moses allowed

HARDEN → HARD

Ex   4:21 but I will **h** his heart,
      14:17 I will **h** the hearts of the Egyptians
1Sa   6: 6 Why should you **h** your hearts as
Ps   95: 8 Do not **h** your hearts, as at Meribah,
Heb   3: 8 not **h** your hearts as in the rebellion,
      4: 7 his voice, do not **h** your hearts."

HARDENED → HARD

Ex   8:32 But Pharaoh **h** his heart this time
      10:20 But the LORD **h** Pharaoh's heart,
Mk   8:17 Are your hearts **h?**
Jn   12:40 and **h** their heart,
Ro   11: 7 elect obtained it, but the rest were **h,**
2Co   3:14 But their minds were **h.**
Heb   3:13 may be **h** by the deceitfulness of sin.
1Es   1:48 he stiffened his neck and **h** his heart

HARDENING* → HARD

Ro   11:25 has come upon part of Israel,

HARDENS → HARD

Ro   9:18 and he **h** the heart of whomever he

HARDER → HARD

Jer   5: 3 have made their faces **h** than rock;
1Co 15:10 I worked **h** than any of them—

HARDSHIP → HARD

Ge   41:51 "God has made me forget all my **h**
Dt   15:18 Do not consider it a **h** when you
Ne   9:32 not treat lightly all the **h** that has
Ro   8:35 Will **h,** or distress, or persecution,

HARDSHIPS → HARD

2Co   6: 4 great endurance, in afflictions, **h,**
      12:10 content with weaknesses, insults, **h,**

HAREM

Est   2: 9 her maids to the best place in the **h.**

HARM → HARMED, HARMFUL

Ge   31: 7 but God did not permit him to **h** me.
      31:52 this heap and this pillar to me, for **h.**
      48:16 who has redeemed me from all **h,**
      50:20 though you intended to do **h** to me,
1Sa 24:11 my son David, for I will never **h**
1Ch 16:22 anointed ones; do my prophets no **h.**
Ne   6: 2 But they intended to do me **h.**
Pr   3:29 Do not plan **h** against your
      12:21 No **h** happens to the righteous,
      13:20 the companion of fools suffers **h.**
      31:12 She does him good, and not **h,**
Jer 29:11 plans for your welfare and not for **h,**
Am   9: 4 I will fix my eyes on them for **h**
Lk   6: 9 or to do **h** on the sabbath,
1Pe   3:13 who will **h** you if you are eager
Rev   9:19 and with them they inflict **h.**
      11: 5 And if anyone wants to **h** them,
Sir   4:22 not show partiality, to your own **h,**

HARMED → HARM

Da   3:27 not singed, their tunics were not **h,**
Rev   2:11 will not be **h** by the second death.

HARMFUL → HARM

2Ki   4:41 And there was nothing **h** in the pot.
1Ti   6: 9 trapped by many senseless and **h**
2Mc 15:39 just as it is **h** to drink wine alone,

HARMONY

Ro   12:16 Live in **h** with one another;
Col   3:14 everything together in perfect **h.**

HARP → HARPISTS, HARPS

1Sa 10: 5 coming down from the shrine with **h**
Ps   33: 2 make melody to him with the **h** of

      108: 2 Awake, O **h** and lyre!
      150: 3 praise him with lute and **h!**
Isa   5:12 whose feasts consist of lyre and **h,**
Da   3: 5 trigon, **h,** drum, and entire musical
Rev   5: 8 each holding a **h** and golden bowls
Pm 151: 2 My hands made a **h;**
2Es 10:22 our **h** has been laid low,

HARPISTS* → HARP

Rev 14: 2 was like the sound of **h** playing
      18:22 the sound of **h** and minstrels and of

HARPS → HARP

1Ch 15:16 on **h** and lyres and cymbals,
      25: 1 who should prophesy with lyres, **h,**
Ne   12:27 with cymbals, **h,** and lyres.
Ps 137: 2 the willows there we hung up our **h.**
Rev 15: 2 with **h** of God in their hands.
Sir 39:15 with songs on your lips, and with **h;**
1Mc   4:54 it was dedicated with songs and **h**

HARSH → HARSHLY

Pr   15: 1 but a **h** word stirs up anger.
Mal   3:13 have spoken **h** words against me,
1Pe   2:18 and gentle but also those who are **h.**
Jude 1:15 the **h** things that ungodly sinners

HARSHLY → HARSH

Ge   42: 7 like strangers and spoke **h**
Dt   26: 6 When the Egyptians treated us **h**
Ru   1:21 the LORD has dealt **h** with me,
2Ch 10:13 The king answered them **h.**
Col   3:19 your wives and never treat them **h.**
1Ti   5: 1 Do not speak **h** to an older man,

HARVEST → HARVESTED, HARVESTING

Ge   8:22 the earth endures, seedtime and **h,**
Ex   23:16 You shall observe the festival of **h,**
Pr   10: 5 child who sleeps in **h** brings shame.
      20: 4 **h** comes, and there is nothing to be
Jer   8:20 "The **h** is past, the summer is ended,
Joel 3:13 Put in the sickle, for the **h** is ripe.
Mt   9:37 to his disciples, "The **h** is plentiful,
      13:39 **h** is the end of the age, and the
Lk   10: 2 He said to them, "The **h** is plentiful,
Jn   4:35 months more, then comes the **h**'?
2Co   9:10 and increase the **h**
Jas   3:18 of righteousness is sown in peace
Rev 14:15 the **h** of the earth is fully ripe."
Sir   6:19 and wait for her good **h.**
2Es   4:28 but the **h** of it has not yet come.

HARVESTED → HARVEST

Hag   1: 6 You have sown much, and **h** little;

HARVESTING* → HARVEST

Jn   4:35 and see how the fields are ripe for **h.**

HAS → HAVE

Ge   1:30 everything that **h** the breath of life,
Dt   21:15 If a man **h** two wives, one of them
2Ch 25: 8 but God **h** power to help or to
Job   1:12 all that he **h** is in your power;
      42: 7 what is right, as my servant Job **h.**
Ps   37:16 a little that the righteous person **h**
Pr   23:29 Who **h** woe? Who **h** sorrow?
Isa 34: 8 For the LORD **h** a day of vengeance,
Jer 23:28 who **h** my word speak my word
Eze   9: 6 but touch no one who **h** the mark.
Mt   8:20 of Man nowhere to lay his head.
       9: 6 **h** authority on earth to forgive sins
Mk   3:30 "He **h** an unclean spirit."
Jn   3:36 believes in the Son **h** eternal life;
       4:44 prophet **h** no honor in the prophet's
      15:13 No one **h** greater love than this,
Ro   6: 9 death no longer **h** dominion over
1Co   7: 7 each **h** a particular gift from God,
       7:13 **h** a husband who is an unbeliever,
      11:15 but if a woman **h** long hair,
Jas   2:17 if it **h** no works, is dead.
1Jn   2:23 who confesses the Son **h** the Father
       5:12 Whoever **h** the Son **h** life;
Rev 20: 6 the second death **h** no power,
Sir 28:22 It **h** no power over the godly;

HASIDEANS*

1Mc 2:42 united with them a company of **H,**
     7:13 **H** were first among the Israelites
2Mc 14: 6 of the Jews who are called **H,**

HASTE → HASTEN, HASTENING, HASTILY, HASTY

Dt 16: 3 out of the land of Egypt in great **h,**
Jos 4:10 The people crossed over in **h.**
Ps 38:22 make **h** to help me, O Lord,

HASTEN → HASTE

Ps 70: 5 But I am poor and needy; **h** to me,

HASTENING* → HASTE

Zep 1:14 day of the LORD is near, near and **h**
2Pe 3:12 and **h** the coming of the day of God,

HASTILY → HASTE

Pr 13:11 Wealth **h** gotten will dwindle,
    25: 8 do not **h** bring into court;
1Ti 5:22 Do not ordain anyone **h,**
2Es 6:34 not act **h** in the last times.'"

HASTY → HASTE

Pr 14:29 who has a **h** temper exalts folly.
Sir 28:11 A **h** quarrel kindles a fire,

HATE → GOD-HATERS, HATED, HATEFUL, HATERS, HATES, HATING, HATRED

Ex 18:21 and **h** dishonest gain;
2Ch 18: 7 but I **h** him,
Ps   5: 5 you **h** all evildoers.
    45: 7 righteousness and **h** wickedness.
    97:10 The LORD loves those who **h** evil;
   119:104 therefore I **h** every false way.
   119:163 I **h** and abhor falsehood, but I love
   129: 5 May all who **h** Zion be put to shame
   139:21 Do I not **h** those who **h** you,
Pr   1:22 scoffing and fools **h** knowledge?
     8:13 of evil and perverted speech I **h.**
     9: 8 who is rebuked will only **h** you;
    13: 5 The righteous **h** falsehood,
    25:17 become weary of you and **h** you.
    29:10 The bloodthirsty **h** the blameless,
Ecc 3: 8 a time to love, and a time to **h;**
Isa 61: 8 I **h** robbery and wrongdoing;
Jer 44: 4 do this abominable thing that I **h!"**
Eze 35: 6 since you did not **h** bloodshed,
Am   5:15 H evil and love good, and establish
Mal 2:16 For I **h** divorce, says the LORD,
Mt   5:43 your neighbor and **h** your enemy.'
Lk   6:22 "Blessed are you when people **h** you
     6:27 do good to those who **h** you,
    14:26 comes to me and does not **h** father
    16:13 slave will either **h** the one and love
Jn   7: 7 The world cannot **h** you, but it hates
Ro   7:15 but I do the very thing I **h.**
    12: 9 **h** what is evil, hold fast to what is
Sir 7:15 Do not **h** hard labor
    33: 2 The wise will not **h** the law,

HATED → HATE

Ge 27:41 Now Esau **h** Jacob because of
    37: 4 they **h** him, and could not speak
Pr   1:29 Because they **h** knowledge
Ecc 2:17 So I **h** life, because what is done
Mal 1: 3 but I have **h** Esau; I have made his
Mt 10:22 be **h** by all because of my name.
Jn 15:18 aware that it **h** me before it **h** you.
Ro   9:13 loved Jacob, but I have **h** Esau."
Heb 1: 9 righteousness and **h** wickedness;

HATEFUL → HATE

Sir 10: 7 Arrogance is **h** to the Lord

HATERS* → HATE

2Ti 3: 3 profligates, brutes, **h** of good,

HATES → HATE

Dt 16:22 things that the LORD your God **h.**
Pr   6:16 six things that the LORD **h,**
    26:28 A lying tongue **h** its victims,

Jn 15:19 therefore the world **h** you.
    15:23 Whoever **h** me **h** my Father also.
Eph 5:29 For no one ever **h** his own body,
Sir 15:11 for he does not do what he **h.**
    15:13 The Lord **h** all abominations;

HATING* → HATE

Tit 3: 3 despicable, **h** one another.
1Jn 2: 9 while **h** a brother or sister, is still in
Jude 1:23 **h** even the tunic defiled by their

HATRED → HATE

Ps 139:22 I hate them with perfect **h;**
Pr 10:12 **H** stirs up strife, but love covers all
    15:17 where love is than a fatted ox and **h**

HAUGHTY

Ps 18:27 but the **h** eyes you bring down.
Pr   6:17 **h** eyes, a lying tongue, and hands
    16:18 and a **h** spirit before a fall.
Zep 3:11 no longer be **h** in my holy mountain.
Ro 12:16 be **h,** but associate with the lowly;
1Ti 6:17 command them not to be **h,**
Sir 23: 4 do not give me **h** eyes,

HAUNT

Isa 35: 7 **h** of jackals shall become a swamp,
Rev 18: 2 a **h** of every foul spirit, a **h** of every

HAVE → HAD, HAS, HAVING

Ge   1:26 and let them **h** dominion over
    18:10 your wife Sarah shall **h** a son.
    27:38 "H you only one blessing,
Ex 16:12 you shall **h** your fill of bread;
    20: 3 you shall **h** no other gods before me.
Dt   5: 7 you shall **h** no other gods before me.
Jos 22:25 you **h** no portion in the LORD.
Ezr 4: 3 shall **h** no part with us in building a
Job 40: 9 H you an arm like God,
Ps 73:25 Whom **h** I in heaven but you?
   115: 5 They **h** mouths, but do not speak;
   119:99 I **h** more understanding than all my
Pr   8:14 I **h** insight, I **h** strength.
Jer 2:28 you **h** as many gods as you **h** towns
    2:28 who **h** eyes, but do not see,
Mal 2:10 H we not all one father?
Mt   3: 9 'We **h** Abraham as our ancestor';
    21:21 if you **h** faith and do not doubt,
Mk 10:21 and you will **h** treasure in heaven;
    14: 7 but you will not always **h** me.
Lk 19:26 those who **h,** more will be given;
          but from those who **h** nothing, even
          what they **h** will be taken away.
Jn   3:16 not perish but may **h** eternal life.
     4:32 I **h** food to eat that you do not know
     8:12 but will **h** the light of life.
    16:12 "I still **h** many things to say to you,
    16:33 in me you may **h** peace.
Ac   3: 6 "I **h** no silver or gold, but what I **h**
Ro   1: we **h** peace with God through our
     8: 9 who does not **h** the Spirit of Christ
    12: 6 We **h** gifts that differ according to
1Co 2:16 But we **h** the mind of Christ.
    13: 1 do not **h** love, I am a noisy gong or
2Co 4: 7 But we **h** this treasure in clay jars,
     8:15 much did not **h** too much, and the
          one who had little did not **h** too little
Eph 1: 7 In him we **h** redemption through his
     2:18 both of us **h** access in one Spirit to
Heb 4:14 Since, then, we **h** a great high priest
     6:19 We **h** this hope, a sure and steadfast
1Jn 2: 1 anyone does sin, we **h** an advocate
     5:12 not **h** the Son of God does not **h** life
Rev 22:14 will **h** the right to the tree of life

HAVEN

Ps 107:30 he brought them to their desired **h.**

HAVILAH

Ge   2:11 land of **H,** where there is gold;

HAVING → HAVE

Mt   7:29 he taught them as one **h** authority,
Ro   2:14 though not **h** the law,

HAVOC*

Ac   9:21 the man who made **h** in Jerusalem

HAY*

1Co 3:12 precious stones, wood, **h,** straw—

HAZAEL

1Ki 19:15 anoint **H** as king over Aram.
2Ki 8: 9 So **H** went to meet him, taking a

HAZOR

Jos 11:11 and he burned **H** with fire.
Jer 49:33 **H** shall become a lair of jackals,

HEAD → BALD-HEAD, BEHEADED, HEADLONG, HEADS, HOTHEAD, HOTHEADS

Ge   3:15 he will strike your **h,** and you will
    28:18 under his **h** and set it up for a pillar
    48:18 put your right hand on his **h."**
Nu   6: 5 no razor shall come upon the **h;**
Dt 28:13 The LORD will make you the **h,** and
Jdg 16:17 A razor has never come upon my **h;**
1Sa 1:11 and no razor shall touch his **h."**
     9: 2 he stood **h** and shoulders above
    17:51 then he cut off his **h** with it.
2Sa 18: 9 His **h** caught fast in the oak,
Ps 23: 5 you anoint my **h** with oil; my cup
   133: 2 It is like the precious oil on the **h,**
Pr   1: 9 they are a fair garland for your **h,**
    10: 6 Blessings are on the **h** of the
Isa 59:17 and a helmet of salvation on his **h;**
Jer 9: 1 O that my **h** were a spring of water,
Eze 8: 3 and took me by a lock of my **h;**
Da   2:32 **h** of that statue was of fine gold,
     7: 9 and the hair of his **h** like pure wool;
Mt   8:20 of Man has nowhere to lay his **h."**
Mk   6:28 brought his **h** on a platter,
Jn 19: 2 crown of thorns and put it on his **h,**
1Co 11: 3 Christ is the **h** of every man, and
          the husband is the **h** of his wife,
          and God is the **h** of Christ.
    11: 4 prophesies with something on his **h**
          disgraces his **h,**
    11: 5 prophesies with her **h** unveiled
          disgraces her **h—**
    12:21 nor again the **h** to the feet,
Eph 1:22 has made him the **h** over all things
     5:23 the husband is the **h** of the wife just
          as Christ is the **h** of the church,
Col 1:18 He is the **h** of the body, the church;
Rev 1:14 His **h** and his hair were white as
    10: 1 a cloud, with a rainbow over his **h;**
    12: 1 on her **h** a crown of twelve stars,
    14:14 with a golden crown on his **h,**
    19:12 and on his **h** are many diadems;
Jdt 13: 8 all her might, and cut off his **h.**
1Mc 7:47 they cut off Nicanor's **h**

HEADLONG → HEAD

Ac   1:18 and falling **h,** he burst open in the

HEADS → HEAD

Ne   4: 4 turn their taunt back on their own **h,**
Ps 22: 7 mouths at me, they shake their **h;**
    24: 7 Lift up your **h,** O gates!
Isa 35:10 everlasting joy shall be upon their **h**
    51:11 everlasting joy shall be upon their **h**
Eze 11:21 bring their deeds upon their own **h,**
Da   7: 6 of a bird on its back and four **h;**
Mt 27:39 derided him, shaking their **h**
Mk   2:23 disciples began to pluck **h** of grain.
Lk 21:28 stand up and raise your **h,**
Ac 18: 6 "Your blood be on your own **h!**
Rev 4: 4 with golden crowns on their **h.**
    12: 3 a great red dragon, with seven **h**
    12: 3 and seven diadems on his **h.**
    17: 9 the seven **h** are seven mountains on
1Mc 3:47 sprinkled ashes on their **h,**

HEAL* → HEALED, HEALER, HEALING, HEALS, HEALTH, HEALTHY

Nu 12:13 to the LORD, "O God, please **h** her."
Dt 32:39 I make alive; I wound and I **h;**

HEALED — HEAR (continued)

2Ki 20: 5 indeed, I will **h** you;
    20: 8 be the sign that the LORD will **h** me,
2Ch 7:14 forgive their sin and **h** their land.
Job 5:18 he strikes, but his hands **h.**
Ps 6: 2 **h** me, for my bones are shaking
    41: 3 you **h** all their infirmities.
    41: 4 **h** me, for I have sinned against you.
Ecc 3: 3 a time to kill, and a time to **h;**
Isa 19:22 listen to their supplications and **h**
    57:18 seen their ways, but I will **h** them;
    57:19 says the LORD; and I will **h** them.
Jer 3:22 I will **h** your faithlessness.
    17:14 **H** me, O LORD, and I shall be
    30:17 wounds I will **h,** says the LORD,
    33: 6 I will **h** them and reveal to them
    51: 9 We tried to **h** Babylon, but she
La 2:13 is your ruin; who can **h** you?
Hos 5:13 not able to cure you or **h** your
    6: 1 he who has torn, and he will **h** us;
    7: 1 I would **h** Israel, the corruption
    14: 4 I will **h** their disloyalty; I will love
Zec 11:16 the wandering, or **h** the maimed,
Mt 13:15 and turn—and I would **h** them.'
Lk 5:17 of the Lord was with him to **h.**
    7: 3 asking him to come and **h** his slave.
    9: 2 the kingdom of God and to **h.**
Jn 4:47 to come down and **h** his son,
    12:40 and turn—and I would **h** them."
Ac 4:30 you stretch out your hand to **h,**
    28:27 and turn—and I would **h** them.'
Tob 3:17 Raphael was sent to **h** both of them:
    5:10 the time is near for God to **h** you;
    12:14 the same time God sent me to **h** you
Sir 38: 9 pray to the Lord, and he will **h** you.

HEALED* → HEAL

Ge 20:17 and God **h** Abimelech, and also **h** his wife
Lev 13:18 skin of one's body a boil that has **h,**
    13:37 hair has grown in it, the itch is **h,**
    14: 3 If the disease is **h** in the leprous
    14:48 the house clean; the disease is **h.**
Dt 28:27 and itch, of which you cannot be **h.**
    28:35 boils of which you cannot be **h,**
Jos 5: 8 in the camp until they were **h.**
1Sa 6: 3 you will be **h** and will be ransomed;
2Ki 8:29 Joram returned to be **h** in Jezreel of
    9:15 Joram had returned to be **h** in
2Ch 22: 6 be **h** in Jezreel of the wounds that
    30:20 The LORD heard Hezekiah, and
Ps 30: 2 to you for help, and you have **h** me.
    107:20 he sent out his word and **h** them,
Isa 6:10 their minds, and turn and be **h."**
    53: 5 and by his bruises we are **h.**
Jer 15:18 wound incurable, refusing to be **h?**
    17:14 Heal me, O LORD, and I shall be **h;**
    51: 8 her wound; perhaps she may be **h.**
    51: 9 Babylon, but she could not be **h.**
Eze 34: 4 you have not **h** the sick,
Hos 11: 3 but they did not know that I **h** them.
Mt 8: 8 the word, and my servant will be **h.**
    8:13 And the servant was **h** in that hour.
    14:36 and all who touched it were **h.**
    15:28 And her daughter was **h** instantly.
Mk 5:29 she felt in her body that she was **h**
    5:34 in peace, and be **h** of your disease."
    6:56 and all who touched it were **h.**
Lk 6:18 and to be **h** of their diseases;
    6:19 power came out from him and **h** all
    7: 7 the word, and let my servant be **h.**
    8:36 possessed by demons had been **h.**
    8:47 how she had been immediately **h,**
    9:11 and **h** those who needed to be cured.
    9:42 Jesus rebuked the unclean spirit, **h**
    14: 4 So Jesus took him and **h** him,
    17:15 of them, when he saw that he was **h,**
    22:51 And he touched his ear and **h** him.
Jn 5:13 man who had been **h** did not know
    7:23 I **h** a man's whole body on the
Ac 4: 9 are asked how this man has been **h,**
    14: 9 and seeing that he had faith to be **h,**
Heb 12:13 be put out of joint, but rather be **h.**

Jas 5:16 one another, so that you may be **h.**
1Pe 2:24 by his wounds you have been **h.**
Rev 13: 3 but its mortal wound had been **h.**
    13:12 whose mortal wound had been **h.**
Tob 2:10 I went to physicians to be **h,**
    6: 9 white films, and the eyes will be **h."**
    12: 3 money back with me, and he **h** you.
Wis 16:10 came to their help and **h** them.
2Es 7:104 or sleep or eat or be **h** in his place,

HEALER* → HEAL

Isa 3: 7 "I will not be a **h;** in my house

HEALING* → HEAL

Pr 3: 8 a **h** for your flesh and a refreshment
    4:22 and **h** to all their flesh.
    12:18 but the tongue of the wise brings **h.**
    13:17 trouble, but a faithful envoy, **h.**
    29: 1 will suddenly be broken beyond **h.**
Isa 19:22 will strike Egypt, striking and **h;**
    58: 8 and your **h** shall spring up quickly;
Jer 8:15 for a time of **h,** but there is terror
    14:19 down so that there is no **h** for us?
    14:19 for a time of **h,** but there is terror
    30:13 no medicine for your wound, no **h**
    33: 6 going to bring it recovery and **h;**
    46:11 there is no **h** for you.
Eze 30:21 it has not been bound up for **h** or
    47:12 for food, and their leaves for **h."**
Mal 4: 2 shall rise, with **h** in its wings.
Ac 4:22 of **h** had been performed was more
    10:38 doing good and **h** all who were
1Co 12: 9 another gifts of **h** by the one Spirit,
    12:28 then deeds of power, then gifts of **h,**
    12:30 Do all possess gifts of **h?**
Rev 22: 2 leaves of the tree are for the **h** of
Wis 16: 9 and no **h** was found for them,
Sir 3:28 befalls the proud, there is no **h,**
    21: 3 no **h** for the wound it inflicts.
    28: 3 and expect **h** from the Lord?
    38: 2 gift of **h** comes from the Most High,
    38:14 success in diagnosis and in **h,**
2Es 7123 and in which are abundance and **h,**

HEALS* → HEAL

Ex 15:26 for I am the LORD who **h** you."
Ps 103: 3 iniquity, who **h** all your diseases,
    147: 3 He **h** the brokenhearted, and binds
Isa 30:26 the wounds inflicted by his blow.
Ac 9:34 to him, "Aeneas, Jesus Christ **h** you;
Wis 16:12 your word, O Lord, that **h** all people
Sir 38: 7 physician **h** and takes away pain;
    43:22 A mist quickly **h** all things;

HEALTH* → HEAL

Ps 38: 3 no **h** in my bones because of my sin.
Pr 16:24 to the soul and **h** to the body.
Isa 38:16 restore me to **h** and make me live!
Jer 8:22 the **h** of my poor people not been
    30:17 For I will restore **h** to you,
Lk 7:10 they found the slave in good **h.**
Ac 3:16 Jesus has given him this perfect **h**
    4:10 good **h** by the name of Jesus Christ
3Jn 1: 2 and that you may be in good **h,**
Tob 5:16 We shall leave in good **h** and return to you in good **h,**
    5:17 and return you in good **h** to me;
    5:21 our child will leave in good **h** and return to us in good **h.**
    5:21 when he returns to you in good **h.**
    5:22 and he will come back in good **h."**
    7: 1 brothers; welcome and good **h!"**
    7: 4 she asked them, "Is he in good **h?"**
    7: 5 replied, "He is alive and in good **h."**
Wis 7:10 I loved her more than **h** and beauty,
    13:18 **h** he appeals to a thing that is weak;
Sir 1:18 peace and perfect **h** to flourish.
    18:19 you fall ill, take care of your **h.**
    30:15 **H** and fitness are better than any
    30:16 no wealth better than **h** of body,
    34:20 he gives **h** and life and blessing.
    38: 8 from him **h** spreads over all the
2Mc 1:10 Greetings and good **h.**

    9:19 wishes for their **h** and prosperity.
    11:28 We also are in good **h.**
3Mc 3:12 its districts, greetings and good **h:**
    7: 1 government, greetings and good **h:**

HEALTHY* → HEAL

Zec 11:16 heal the maimed, or nourish the **h,**
Mt 6:22 if your eye is **h,** your whole body
Lk 11:34 If your eye is **h,** your whole body
    11:34 not **h,** your body is full of darkness.
Sir 30:14 **h,** and fit than rich and afflicted in
    31:20 **H** sleep depends on moderate eating

HEAP → HEAPED

Ge 31:48 "This **h** is a witness between you
Dt 32:23 I will **h** disasters upon them,
Jos 3:13 they shall stand in a single **h."**
1Sa 2: 8 he lifts the needy from the ash **h,**
Pr 25:22 will **h** coals of fire on their heads,
Mt 6: 7 do not **h** up empty phrases
Ro 12:20 doing this you will **h** burning coals
Tob 5:19 Do not **h** money upon money,

HEAPED → HEAP

Rev 18: 5 for her sins are **h** high as heaven,
Sir 37:24 wise person will have praise **h** upon

HEAR → HEARD, HEARERS, HEARING, HEARS

Nu 14:13 "Then the Egyptians will **h** of it,
Dt 1:17 **h** out the small and the great alike;
    1:17 bring to me, and I will **h** it."
    4:36 From heaven he made you **h** his
    5: 1 all Israel, and said to them: **H,**
    6: 3 **H** therefore, O Israel, and observe
    6: 4 **H,** O Israel: The LORD is our God,
    9: 1 **H,** O Israel! You are about to
    13:11 Then all Israel shall **h** and be afraid,
    19:20 The rest shall **h** and be afraid,
    20: 3 and shall say to them: **"H,**
    31:13 may **h** and learn to fear the LORD
Jos 7: 9 all the inhabitants of the land will **h**
1Ki 8:30 **H** the plea of your servant and
    8:30 O **h** in heaven your dwelling place;
    10: 8 attend your **h,** and your wisdom!
2Ki 19:16 Incline your ear, O LORD, and **h;**
    19:16 **h** the words of Sennacherib,
2Ch 6:21 **h** from heaven,
Job 5:27 **H,** and know it for yourself."
    20: 3 I **h** censure that insults me,
    26:14 small a whisper do we **h** of him!
    31:35 that I had one to **h** me!
Ps 30:10 **H,** O LORD, and be gracious to me!
    51: 8 Let me **h** joy and gladness;
    94: 9 who planted the ear, does he not **h?**
    135:17 they have ears, but they do not **h,**
Ecc 7:21 or you may **h** your servant cursing
Isa 1:10 **H** the word of the LORD, you rulers
    21: 3 I am bowed down so that I cannot **h,**
    29:18 On that day the deaf shall **h** the
    30:21 your ears shall **h** a word behind you
    59: 1 nor his ear too dull to **h.**
    65:24 while they are yet speaking I will **h.**
Jer 5:21 who have ears, but do not **h.**
Eze 33: 7 you **h** a word from my mouth,
    37: 4 dry bones, **h** the word of the LORD.
Da 3: 5 when you **h** the sound of the horn,
Mic 6: 2 **H,** you mountains, the controversy
Mt 11: 5 the lepers are cleansed, the deaf **h,**
    13:17 to **h** what you **h,** but did not **h** it.
Mk 12:29 answered, "The first is, **'H,** O Israel:
Lk 7:22 the lepers are cleansed, the deaf **h,**
Jn 5:25 dead will **h** the voice of the Son of
    8:47 The reason you do not **h** them is
Ac 13: 7 and wanted to **h** the word of God.
    13:44 whole city gathered to **h** the word
    17:32 others said, "We will **h** you again
Ro 10:14 to **h** without someone to proclaim
Heb 3: 7 says, "Today, if you **h** his voice,
Rev 1: 3 and blessed are those who **h**
    9:20 which cannot see or **h** or walk.
Sir 5:11 Be quick to **h,** but deliberate in

51:28 **H** but a little of my instruction,
Bar   1: 3 who came to **h** the book,
2Es   9:30 '**H** me, O Israel, and give heed
     14:28 "**H** these words, O Israel.

HEARD → HEAR

Ge   3: 8 They **h** the sound of the LORD God
    21:17 And God **h** the voice of the boy;
Ex   2:24 God **h** their groaning,
     6: 5 also **h** the groaning of the Israelites
    16: 7 he has **h** your complaining against
Nu 12: 2 And the LORD **h** it.
    14:27 **h** the complaints of the Israelites,
Dt   4:32 or has its like ever been **h** of?
Jos 24:27 it has **h** all the words of the LORD
2Sa   7:22 all that we have **h** with our ears.
1Ki   4:34 who had **h** of his wisdom.
    10: 1 of Sheba **h** of the fame of Solomon,
Ne   9:27 to you and you **h** them from heaven,
Job 42: 5 I had **h** of you by the hearing of the
Ps   18: 6 From his temple he **h** my voice,
    62:11 God has spoken; twice have I **h** this:
    78:59 When God **h**, he was full of wrath,
   116: 1 because he has **h** my voice and my
Isa 40:21 not known? Have you not **h?**
    40:28 not known? Have you not **h?**
    66: 8 Who has **h** of such a thing?
Jer 18:13 Who has **h** the like of this?
La   3:56 you **h** my plea, "Do not close your
Eze 10: 5 the wings of the cherubim was **h**
Da 10:12 your words have been **h,**
    12: 8 I **h** but could not understand;
Mt   2: 3 Herod **h** this, he was frightened,
    5:21 "You have **h** that it was said to
    5:27 "You have **h** that it was said,
    5:33 you have **h** that it was said to those
    5:38 "You have **h** that it was said,
    5:43 "You have **h** that it was said,
Mk   6: 2 many who **h** him were astounded.
   14:64 You have **h** his blasphemy!
Lk 12: 3 in the dark will be **h** in the light,
Jn   8:26 I declare to the world what I have **h**
Ac   2: 6 because each one **h** them speaking
    10:44 Spirit fell upon all who **h** the word.
Ro 10:14 in one of whom they have never **h?**
1Co   2: 9 "What no eye has seen, nor ear **h,**
2Co 12: 4 into Paradise and **h** things that are
1Th   2:13 the word of God that you **h** from us,
2Ti   1:13 of sound teaching that you have **h**
Heb   4: 2 the message they **h** did not benefit
2Pe   1:18 **h** this voice come from heaven,
1Jn   1: 3 to you what we have seen and **h** so
    3:11 the message you **h** from the
2Jn   1: 6 commandment just as you have **h** it
Rev   1:10 and I **h** behind me a loud voice like
    22: 8 I, John, am the one who **h** and saw
Sir   3: 5 and when they pray they will be **h.**
Sus   1:44 The Lord **h** her cry.

HEARERS → HEAR

Ro   2:13 For it is not the **h** of the law who
1Ti   4:16 will save both yourself and your **h.**
Jas   1:22 merely **h** who deceive themselves.

HEARING → HEAR

Nu 11: 1 complained in the **h** of the LORD
Dt 31:11 this law before all Israel in their **h.**
2Ch 34:30 in their **h** all the words of the book
Pr 18:13 one gives answer before **h,**
Am   8:11 but of **h** the words of the LORD.
Lk   4:21 has been fulfilled in your **h."**
Jn   7:51 people without first giving them a **h**
1Co 12:17 were an eye, where would the **h** be?
    12:17 If the whole body were **h,**
Sir   4: 8 Give a **h** to the poor,

HEARS → HEAR

Ps 69:33 For the LORD **h** the needy,
Pr 15:29 but he **h** the prayer of the righteous.
Isa 30:19 when he **h** it, he will answer you.
Mt   7:24 then who **h** these words of mine
Lk   6:47 **h** my words, and acts on them.
Jn   5:24 I tell you, anyone who **h** my word

1Jn   5:14 according to his will, he **h** us.
Rev 22:18 I warn everyone who **h** the words
Sir 21:15 intelligent person **h** a wise saying,

HEART → BROKENHEARTED, DISHEARTENED, HARD-HEARTED, HEART'S, HEARTLESS, HEARTS, TENDERHEARTED, WHOLEHEARTEDLY

Ge   6: 6 and it grieved him to his **h.**
    24:45 I had finished speaking in my **h,**
Ex   4:21 but I will harden his **h,**
    7:13 Still Pharaoh's **h** was hardened,
    7:22 so Pharaoh's **h** remained hardened,
    8:15 he hardened his **h,** and would not
    8:19 But Pharaoh's **h** was hardened,
    8:32 Pharaoh hardened his **h** this time
    9: 7 But the **h** of Pharaoh was hardened,
    9:12 LORD hardened the **h** of Pharaoh,
    9:35 So the **h** of Pharaoh was hardened,
   10:20 But the LORD hardened Pharaoh's **h,**
   10:27 But the LORD hardened Pharaoh's **h,**
   11:10 but the LORD hardened Pharaoh's **h,**
   14: 4 I will harden Pharaoh's **h,**
   28:30 on Aaron's **h** when he goes in
   28:30 judgment of the Israelites on his **h**
   35:21 everyone whose **h** was stirred,
Dt   4:29 search after him with all your **h** and
    6: 5 the LORD your God with all your **h,**
   10:12 the LORD your God with all your **h**
   11:13 all your **h** and with all your soul—
   13: 3 the LORD your God with all your **h**
   26:16 diligently with all your **h** and
   29:18 whose **h** is already turning away
   30: 2 children obey him with all your **h**
   30: 6 your God will circumcise your **h**
          and the **h** of your descendants.
   30: 6 the LORD your God with all your **h**
   30:10 the LORD your God with all your **h**
   30:14 in your mouth and in your **h** for you
Jos 22: 5 all your **h** and with all your soul."
1Sa 10: 9 God gave him another **h;**
   12:20 but serve the LORD with all your **h;**
   12:24 serve him faithfully with all your **h;**
   13:14 sought out a man after his own **h;**
   16: 7 but the LORD looks on the **h."**
   17:32 "Let no one's **h** fail because of him;
2Sa   6:16 and she despised him in her **h.**
1Ki   2: 4 in faithfulness with all their **h**
    8:48 if they repent with all their **h** and
    9: 3 my eyes and my **h** will be there for
    9: 4 with integrity of **h** and uprightness,
   11: 4 turned away his **h** after other gods;
   14: 8 and followed me with all his **h,**
   15:14 the **h** of Asa was true to the LORD
2Ki 22:19 because your **h** was penitent,
   23: 3 with all his **h** and all his soul,
1Ch 28: 9 with single mind and willing **h;**
2Ch   6:38 if they repent with all their **h** and
    7:16 my eyes and my **h** will be there for
   15:12 all their **h** and with all their soul.
   15:17 the **h** of Asa was true all his days.
   17: 6 His **h** was courageous in the ways
   22: 9 sought the LORD with all his **h."**
   32:25 done to him, for his **h** was proud.
   34:31 with all his **h** and all his soul,
   36:13 hardened his **h** against turning to
Job 19:27 My **h** faints within me!
   22:22 and lay up his words in your **h.**
   31: 7 and my **h** has followed my eyes,
   37: 1 "At this also my **h** trembles,
Ps   7:10 shield, who saves the upright in **h.**
    9: 1 to the LORD with my whole **h;**
   16: 9 my **h** is glad, and my soul rejoices;
   19:14 meditation of my **h** be acceptable to
   26: 2 and try me; test my **h** and mind.
   28: 7 in him my **h** trusts;
   37: 4 will give you the desires of your **h.**
   44:21 For he knows the secrets of the **h.**
   51:10 Create in me a clean **h,** O God,
   51:17 a broken and contrite **h,** O God,
   66:18 If I had cherished iniquity in my **h,**

   73: 1 to those who are pure in **h.**
   73:26 My flesh and my **h** may fail,
   73:26 strength of my **h** and my portion
   86:11 give me an undivided **h** to revere
   90:12 our days that we may gain a wise **h.**
   97:11 and joy for the upright in **h.**
  104:15 and wine to gladden the human **h,**
  108: 1 My **h** is steadfast, O God, my **h** is
          steadfast;
  109:22 and my **h** is pierced within me.
  111: 1 to the LORD with my whole **h,**
  119: 2 who seek him with their whole **h,**
  119:10 With my whole **h** I seek you;
  119:11 I treasure your word in my **h,**
  119:34 and observe it with my whole **h.**
  119:36 Turn my **h** to your decrees,
  119:58 I implore your favor with all my **h;**
  119:69 my whole **h** I keep your precepts.
  119:111 they are the joy of my **h.**
  119:112 my **h** to perform your statutes
  119:145 With my whole **h** I cry; answer me,
  119:161 my **h** stands in awe of your words.
  138: 1 thanks, O LORD, with my whole **h;**
  139:23 Search me, O God, and know my **h;**
  141: 4 Do not turn my **h** to any evil,
Pr   2: 2 inclining your **h** to understanding;
    3: 1 let your **h** keep my commandments;
    3: 3 write them on the tablet of your **h.**
    3: 5 Trust in the LORD with all your **h,**
    4: 4 "Let your **h** hold fast my words;
    4:21 keep them within your **h.**
    4:23 Keep your **h** with all vigilance,
    6:21 Bind them upon your **h** always;
    6:25 Do not desire her beauty in your **h,**
    7: 3 write them on the tablet of your **h.**
   10: 8 wise of **h** will heed commandments,
   12:25 Anxiety weighs down the human **h,**
   13:12 Hope deferred makes the **h** sick,
   14:13 in laughter the **h** is sad,
   15:13 A glad **h** makes a cheerful
   15:15 a cheerful **h** has a continual feast.
   15:30 The light of the eyes rejoices the **h,**
   17: 3 but the LORD tests the **h.**
   17:22 A cheerful **h** is a good medicine,
   20: 9 can say, "I have made my **h** clean;
   21: 1 The king's **h** is a stream of water in
   21: 2 but the LORD weighs the **h.**
   22:11 a pure **h** and are gracious in speech
   22:15 Folly is bound up in the **h** of a boy,
   23:15 if your **h** is wise, my **h** too will be
          glad.
   23:17 Do not let your **h** envy sinners,
   23:26 My child, give me your **h,**
   24:17 and do not let your **h** be glad when
   27:19 so one human **h** reflects another.
Ecc   2:10 I kept my **h** from no pleasure,
    5: 2 let your **h** be quick to utter a word
    7: 7 and a bribe corrupts the **h.**
    9: 7 and drink your wine with a merry **h;**
SS   4: 9 You have ravished my **h,** my sister,
    5: 2 I slept, but my **h** was awake.
    8: 6 Set me as a seal upon your **h,**
Isa 57:15 and to revive the **h** of the contrite.
   66:14 see, and your **h** shall rejoice;
Jer   3:10 not return to me with her whole **h,**
    3:15 give you shepherds after my own **h,**
    4:14 wash your **h** clean of wickedness so
    9:26 of Israel is uncircumcised in **h.**
   17: 9 The **h** is devious above all else;
   17:10 test the mind and search the **h,**
   24: 7 I will give them a **h** to know that I
   24: 7 return to me with their whole **h.**
   29:13 if you seek me with all your **h,**
   32:39 I will give them one **h** and one way,
   32:41 with all my **h** and all my soul.
Eze 11:19 I will remove the **h** of stone
   11:19 give them a **h** of flesh,
   18:31 get yourselves a new **h** and a new
   28: 2 Because your **h** is proud and you
   36:26 A new **h** I will give you,
   36:26 I will remove from your body the **h**
          of stone and give you a **h** of flesh.

44: 7 uncircumcised in **h** and flesh,
Hos 11: 8 My **h** recoils within me;
Joel 2:12 return to me with all your **h,**
Zep 3:14 Rejoice and exult with all your **h,**
Mal 2: 2 not lay it to **h** to give glory to my
2: 2 because you do not lay it to **h.**
Mt 5: 8 "Blessed are the pure in **h,** for they
5:28 adultery with her in his **h.**
6:21 treasure is, there your **h** will be also.
11:29 for I am gentle and humble in **h,**
12:34 out of the abundance of the **h** the
13:15 For this people's **h** has grown dull,
15:19 out of the **h** come evil intentions,
18:35 your brother or sister from your **h."**
22:37 the Lord your God with all your **h,**
Mk 11:23 and if you do not doubt in your **h,**
12:30 the Lord your God with all your **h,**
Lk 2:19 and pondered them in her **h.**
2:51 treasured all these things in her **h.**
6:45 abundance of the **h** that the mouth
8:15 hold it fast in an honest and good **h,**
10:27 all your **h,** and with all your soul,
12:34 treasure is, there your **h** will be also.
24:25 of **h** to believe all that the prophets
Ac 1:24 "Lord, you know everyone's **h.**
4:32 believed were of one **h** and soul,
5: 3 "why has Satan filled your **h** to lie
8:21 for your **h** is not right before God.
15: 8 And God, who knows the human **h,**
16:14 Lord opened her **h** to listen eagerly
28:27 For this people's **h** has grown dull,
Ro 2:29 circumcision is a matter of the **h—**
10: 8 on your lips and in your **h"** (that is,
10: 9 believe in your **h** that God raised
1Co 14:25 the secrets of the unbeliever's **h** are
2Co 2: 4 anguish of **h** and with many tears,
4: 1 in this ministry, we do not lose **h.**
4:16 So we do not lose **h.**
Eph 1:18 with the eyes of your **h** enlightened,
6: 5 singleness of **h,** as you obey Christ;
6: 6 doing the will of God from the **h.**
Php 1: 7 because you hold me in your **h,**
1Ti 1: 5 that comes from a pure **h,**
2Ti 2:22 who call on the Lord from a pure **h.**
Phm 1:12 sending him, that is, my own **h,**
Heb 3:12 unbelieving **h** that turns away from
4:12 the thoughts and intentions of the **h.**
10:22 let us approach with a true **h** in full
12: 5 or lose **h** when you are punished by
1Pe 1:22 love one another deeply from the **h.**
Rev 18: 7 in her **h** she says, 'I rule as a queen;
Tob 1:12 mindful of God with all my **h.**
Sir 1:12 The fear of the Lord delights the **h,**
2: 2 Set your **h** right and be steadfast,
21: 6 who fear the Lord repent in their **h.**
40:20 Wine and music gladden the **h,**
Bar 2:31 I will give them a **h** that obeys
Aza 1:16 Yet with a contrite **h** and
1Mc 1: 3 and his **h** was lifted up.
2:24 and his **h** was stirred.
Man 1:11 And now I bend the knee of my **h,**

ALL ... HEART Dt 4:29; 6:5; 10:12; 11:13;
13:3; 26:16; 30:2, 6, 10; Jos 22:5; 1Sa 7:3;
12:20, 24; 2Sa 3:21; 1Ki 2:4; 8:23, 48; 14:8;
2Ki 10:30, 31; 23:3, 25; 2Ch 6:14, 30, 38;
15:12, 15; 22:9; 31:21; 34:31; Ps 32:11; 64:10;
94:15; 119:58; Pr 3:5; Ecc 9:1; Jer 29:13;
32:41; Joel 2:12; Zep 3:14; Mt 22:37; Mk
12:30, 33; Lk 10:27; Tob 1:12; 13:6; Sir 7:27;
39:35; 47:8; Aza 1:18; 2Mc 1:3

HARDEN[ED] ... HEART Ex 4:21; 7:3;
8:15, 32; 9:12, 34; 10:1, 20, 27; 11:10; 14:4, 8;
2Ch 36:13; Isa 63:17; Jn 12:40; 1Es 1:48

HUMAN HEART Ge 8:21; 1Ki 8:39; 2Ch
6:30; Ps 64:6; 104:15, 15; Pr 12:25; 25:20;
27:19; Ecc 8:11; Isa 13:7; Mk 7:21; Ac 15:8;
1Co 2:9; Jdt 8:14; Sir 42:18

WHOLE HEART 2Ki 20:3; 2Ch 19:9; Ps
9:1; 86:12; 111:1; 119:2, 10, 34, 69, 145;
138:1; Isa 1:5; 38:3; Jer 3:10; 24:7; Wis 8:21;
4Mc 7:18

HEART'S → HEART
Ps 20: 4 May he grant you your **h** desire,
Eze 24:25 of their eyes and their **h** affection.
Ro 10: 1 my **h** desire and prayer to God for

HEARTLESS· → HEART
Ro 1:31 foolish, faithless, **h,** ruthless.

HEARTS → HEART
Ex 14:17 the **h** of the Egyptians so that they
Jos 5: 1 their **h** melted, and there was no
7: 5 The **h** of the people melted and
11:20 the LORD's doing to harden their **h**
14:23 and incline your **h** to the LORD,
1Sa 6: 6 Why should you harden your **h** as
10:26 warriors whose **h** God had touched.
2Sa 15: 6 Absalom stole the **h** of the people
1Ki 8:39 render to all whose **h** you know—
18:37 that you have turned their **h** back."
1Ch 29:18 and direct their **h** toward you.
2Ch 11:16 Those who had set their **h** to seek
Job 1: 5 and cursed God in their **h."**
Ps 7: 9 test the minds and **h,** O righteous
33:15 he who fashions the **h** of them all,
81:12 I gave them over to their stubborn **h,**
95: 8 not harden your **h,** as at Meribah,
Ecc 9: 3 the **h** of all are full of evil;
9: 3 madness is in their **h** while they live
Isa 29:13 while their **h** are far from me,
51: 7 who have my teaching in your **h;**
Jer 4: 4 remove the foreskin of your **h,**
12: 2 in their mouths yet far from their **h.**
17: 1 on the tablet of their **h,**
31:33 and I will write it on their **h;**
La 5: 17 The joy of our **h** has ceased;
Eze 14: 3 have taken their idols into their **h,**
Mal 4: 6 He will turn the **h** of parents to
their children and the **h** of children
Mt 15: 8 but their **h** are far from me;
Mk 6:52 but their **h** were hardened.
7: 6 but their **h** are far from me;
Lk 1:17 the **h** of parents to their children,
16:15 but God knows your **h;**
24:32 not our **h** burning within us while
Jn 14: 1 "Do not let your **h** be troubled.
14:27 Do not let your **h** be troubled,
Ac 2:46 their food with glad and generous **h,**
15: 9 and in cleansing their **h** by faith
Ro 2:15 law requires is written on their **h,**
5: 5 love has been poured into our **h**
2Co 1:22 and giving us his Spirit in our **h** as
3: 2 are our letter, written on our **h,**
3: 3 of stone but on tablets of human **h.**
4: 6 in our **h** to give the light of the
6:13 to children—open wide your **h** also.
7: 2 Make room in your **h** for us;
Eph 3:17 Christ may dwell in your **h** through
Php 4: 7 guard your **h** and your minds in
Col 3:15 the peace of Christ rule in your **h,**
3:16 gratitude in your **h** sing psalms,
1Th 2: 4 but to please God who tests our **h.**
3:13 so strengthen your **h** in holiness
2Th 2:17 comfort your **h** and strengthen them
Phm 1: 7 **h** of the saints have been refreshed
Heb 3: 8 do not harden your **h** as in the
8:10 write them on their **h,** and I will be
10:16 I will put my laws in their **h,**
10:22 with our **h** sprinkled clean from
Jas 4: 8 purify your **h,** you double-minded.
1Pe 3:15 in your **h** sanctify Christ as Lord.
2Pe 1:19 and the morning star rises in your **h.**
2:14 They have **h** trained in greed.
1Jn 3:20 for God is greater than our **h,**
Rev 2:23 the one who searches minds and **h,**
17:17 into their **h** to carry out his purpose
Sir 14: 2 whose **h** do not condemn them,
48:10 the **h** of parents to their children,
1Mc 1:62 and were resolved in their **h**

HEAT → HEATED
Ge 8:22 cold and **h,** summer and winter,
Ps 19: 6 and nothing is hid from its **h.**

Rev 16: 9 scorched by the fierce **h,**
Aza 1:44 Bless the Lord, fire and **h;**

HEATED → HEAT
Da 3:19 ordered the furnace **h** up seven

HEAVEN → HEAVENLY, HEAVENS
Ge 14:19 by God Most High, maker of **h** and
21:17 angel of God called to Hagar from **h**
22:11 of the LORD called to him from **h,**
24: 3 the God of **h** and earth,
28:12 the top of it reaching to **h;**
Ex 16: 4 "I am going to rain bread from **h**
20:22 that I spoke with you from **h.**
Dt 3:24 god in **h** or on earth can perform
4:26 I call **h** and earth to witness against
26:15 from your holy habitation, from **h,**
30:12 It is not in **h,** that you should say,
30:12 "Who will go up to **h** for us,
31:28 and call **h** and earth to witness
Jos 2:11 LORD your God is indeed God in **h**
1Ki 8:23 like you in **h** above or on earth
8:27 **h** and the highest **h** cannot contain
8:30 O hear in **h** your dwelling place;
22:19 the host of **h** standing beside him to
2Ki 1:10 Then fire came down from **h,**
2: 1 was about to take Elijah up to **h**
19:15 you have made **h** and earth.
2Ch 6:14 no God like you, in **h** or on earth,
7:14 then I will hear from **h,**
Ezr 7:12 scribe of the law of the God of **h:**
Job 16:19 now, in fact, my witness is in **h,**
41:11 —under the whole **h,** who?
Ps 73:25 Whom have I in **h** but you?
121: 2 the LORD, who made **h** and earth.
Pr 30: 4 has ascended to **h** and come down?
Ecc 3: 1 and a time for every matter under **h:**
Isa 14:12 you are fallen from **h,** O Day Star,
66: 1 **H** is my throne and the earth is my
Jer 23:24 Do I not fill **h** and earth?
Da 2:19 and Daniel blessed the God of **h.**
7:13 coming with the clouds of **h.**
Mt 3: 2 "Repent, for the kingdom of **h** has
4:17 "Repent, for the kingdom of **h** has
5:12 glad, for your reward is great in **h,**
5:19 be called least in the kingdom of **h;**
5:19 be called great in the kingdom of **h.**
6: 9 Father in **h,** hallowed be your name.
6:10 will be done, on earth as it is in **h.**
6:20 for yourselves treasures in **h,**
7:21 Lord,' will enter the kingdom of **h,**
7:21 who does the will of my Father in **h.**
16:19 the keys of the kingdom of **h,**
16:19 bind on earth will be bound in **h,**
18: 3 will never enter the kingdom of **h.**
18:18 bind on earth will be bound in **h,**
19:14 that the kingdom of **h** belongs."
19:21 and you will have treasure in **h;**
19:23 person to enter the kingdom of **h.**
23:13 lock people out of the kingdom of **h.**
24:35 **H** and earth will pass away,
26:64 and coming on the clouds of **h."**
28:18 "All authority in **h** and on earth has
Mk 8:11 asking him for a sign from **h,** to test
10:21 and you will have treasure in **h;**
11:30 the baptism of John come from **h,**
13:31 **H** and earth will pass away,
14:62 and 'coming with the clouds of **h.'"**
Lk 3:21 was praying, the **h** was opened,
9:54 to come down from **h** and consume
10:18 "I watched Satan fall from **h** like a
10:20 that your names are written in **h."**
12:33 an unfailing treasure in **h,**
15: 7 in **h** over one sinner who repents
18:22 and you will have treasure in **h;**
19:38 Peace in **h,** and glory in the highest
h!"
21:33 **H** and earth will pass away,
24:51 and was carried up into **h.**
Jn 3:13 No one has ascended into **h** except
the one who descended from **h,**
6:31 gave them bread from **h** to eat.'"

6:38 for I have come down from **h,**
12:28 came from **h,** "I have glorified it,
Ac   1:11 same way as you saw him go into **h.**
7:49 'H is my throne, and the earth is
7:55 he gazed into **h** and saw the glory
9: 3 a light from **h** flashed around him.
11: 5 a large sheet coming down from **h,**
Ro 10: 6 'Who will ascend into **h?'"**
1Co 15:47 the second man is from **h.**
2Co 12: 2 was caught up to the third **h—**
Eph 1:10 things in **h** and things on earth.
Php 2:10 in **h** and on earth and under the
3:20 But our citizenship is in **h,**
Col   1: 5 the hope laid up for you in **h.**
1:16 in **h** and on earth were created,
4: 1 that you also have a Master in **h.**
1Th 1:10 to wait for his Son from **h,**
4:16 God's trumpet, will descend from **h,**
Heb 9:24 but he entered into **h** itself,
12:23 the firstborn who are enrolled in **h,**
1Pe 1: 4 and unfading, kept in **h** for you,
3:22 gone into **h** and is at the right hand
2Pe 1:18 heard this voice come from **h,**
Rev 4: 1 and there in **h** a door stood open!
5:13 Then I heard every creature in **h**
11:19 God's temple in **h** was opened,
12: 1 A great portent appeared in **h:**
12: 7 And war broke out in **h;**
15: 5 the tent of witness in **h** was opened,
19: 1 loud voice of a great multitude in **h,**
19:11 I saw **h** opened, and there was a
19:14 the armies of **h,** wearing fine linen,
21: 1 I saw a new **h** and a new earth;
21: 2 coming down out of **h** from God,
21:10 Jerusalem coming down out of **h**
Jdt   5: 8 and worshiped the God of **h,**
Sir 16:18 Lo, **h** and the highest **h,**
Bel   1: 5 who created **h** and earth and has
1Mc 2:58 was taken up into **h.**
3:50 and they cried aloud to **H,**

DOWN FROM HEAVEN 2Ki 1:10, 10, 12, 12, 14; 2Ch 7:1; Ps 14:2; 33:13; 53:2; 80:14; Isa 55:10; 63:15; La 2:1; Da 4:13, 23; Lk 9:54; Jn 6:33, 38, 41, 42, 50, 51, 58; Ac 11:5; Rev 10:1; 13:13; 18:1; 20:1, 9; 2Mc 2:10

EARTH ... HEAVEN Ge 6:17; Dt 4:32; 1Ki 8:27; 2Ki 19:15; 1Ch 21:16; 2Ch 6:18; Ps 148:13; Isa 37:16; Eze 8:3; Mt 6:10; 16:19, 19; 18:18, 18; Mk 13:27; Col 1:20; Heb 12:26; Rev 20:11; 21:1; 1Es 4:34, 36; 2Es 11:2

FATHER IN HEAVEN Mt 5:16, 45; 6:1, 9; 7:11, 21; 10:32, 33; 12:50; 16:17; 18:10, 14, 19; Mk 11:25

*GOD OF HEAVEN Ge 24:3, 7; 2Ch 36:23; Ezr 1:2; 5:11, 12; 6:9, 10; 7:12, 21, 23, 23; Ne 1:4, 5; 2:4, 20; Ps 136:26; Da 2:18, 19, 37, 44; Jnh 1:9; Rev 11:13; 16:11; Tob 7:12; 8:15; Jdt 5:8; 6:19; 11:17; 3Mc 6:28; 7:6

HEAVEN ... EARTH Ge 14:19, 22; 24:3; Ex 20:11; 31:17; Dt 3:24; 4:26, 39; 30:19; 31:28; Jos 2:11; 2Sa 18:9; 1Ki 8:23; 2Ki 19:15; 2Ch 2:12; 6:14; Ezr 5:11; Ps 69:34; 115:15; 121:2; 124:8; 134:3; 135:6; 146:6; Ecc 5:2; Isa 24:21, 21; 37:16; Jer 23:24; 33:25; La 2:1; Da 6:27; 8:10; Mt 5:18; 11:25; 24:35; 28:18; Mk 13:31; Lk 2:14; 10:21; 16:17; 21:33; Ac 4:24; 14:15; 17:24; 1Co 8:5; Eph 1:10; 3:15; Php 2:10; Col 1:16; Jas 5:12, 18; Rev 5:3, 13; 9:1; 12:4; 13:13; 14:7; 21:1, 1; Tob 10:13; Jdt 7:28; 9:12; AdE 13:10; Wis 18:16; Sir 1:3; LtJ 6:55; Bel 1:5; 1Mc 2:37; 2Mc 7:28; 1Es 6:13; Man 1:2; 2Es 2:14; 6:38

HOST OF HEAVEN Dt 4:19; 17:3; 1Ki 22:19; 2Ki 17:16; 21:3, 5; 23:4; 2Ch 18:18; 33:3, 5; Ne 9:6; Isa 24:21; 34:4; Jer 8:2; 19:13; 33:22; Da 4:35; 8:10; Ac 7:42; Man 1:15

KINGDOM OF HEAVEN Mt 3:2; 4:17; 5:3, 10, 19, 19, 20; 7:21; 8:11; 10:7; 11:11, 12; 13:11, 24, 31, 33, 44, 45, 47, 52; 16:19; 18:1, 3, 4, 23; 19:12, 14, 23; 20:1; 22:2; 23:13; 25:1

*LORD OF HEAVEN Da 5:23; Mt 11:25; Lk 10:21; Ac 17:24; Tob 6:18; 7:11, 16; 10:11, 12, 13; Jdt 9:12

STARS OF HEAVEN Ge 22:17; 26:4; Ex 32:13; Dt 1:10; 1Ch 27:23; Ne 9:23; Heb 11:12; Rev 12:4; Aza 1:13, 41; 2Mc 9:10

UNDER HEAVEN Ge 6:17; Ex 17:14; Dt 2:25; 4:19; 7:24; 9:14; 25:19; 29:20; 2Ki 14:27; Ecc 1:13; 2:3; 3:1; Ac 2:5; 4:12; Col 1:23; AdE 13:10; Bar 5:3; 2Mc 2:18; 2Es 11:6

HEAVENLY → HEAVEN
Job   1: 6 One day the **h** beings came
2: 1 One day the **h** beings came
38: 7 and all the **h** beings shouted for joy?
Ps 89: 6 among the **h** beings is like the LORD
Mt   5:48 as your **h** Father is perfect.
Lk   2:13 the angel a multitude of the **h** host,
2Co 5: 2 longing to be clothed with our **h**
Eph 1: 3 spiritual blessing in the **h** places,
1:20 at his right hand in the **h** places,
6:12 forces of evil in the **h** places.
2Ti   4:18 and save me for his **h** kingdom.
Heb 3: 1 holy partners in a **h** calling,
6: 4 and have tasted the **h** gift,
9:23 **h** things themselves need better
12:22 of the living God, the **h** Jerusalem,

HEAVENLY FATHER Mt 5:48; 6:14, 26, 32; 15:13; 18:35; Lk 11:13

HEAVENS → HEAVEN
Ge   1: 1 when God created the **h** and
2: 1 the **h** and the earth were finished,
7:11 the windows of the **h** were opened.
11: 4 and a tower with its top in the **h,**
Dt 10:14 the heaven of **h** belong to the LORD
28:12 for you his rich storehouse, the **h,**
33:26 rides through the **h** to your help,
2Sa 22:10 He bowed the **h,** and came down;
Ezr 9: 6 our guilt has mounted up to the **h.**
Ne   9: 6 have made heaven, the heaven of **h,**
Job 38:33 you know the ordinances of the **h?**
Ps   8: 3 at your **h,** the work of your fingers,
19: 1 The **h** are telling the glory of God;
33: 6 word of the LORD the **h** were made,
57: 5 Be exalted, O God, above the **h.**
102:25 the **h** are the work of your hands.
103:11 as the **h** are high above the earth,
108: 4 steadfast love is higher than the **h,**
115:16 The **h** are the LORD's heavens,
115:16 The heavens are the LORD's **h,**
136: 5 the **h,** for his steadfast love endures
148: 1 Praise the LORD from the **h;**
Pr   3:19 understanding he established the **h;**
Isa   1: 2 Hear, O **h,** and listen, O earth;
45: 8 Shower, O **h,** from above,
51: 6 Lift up your eyes to the **h,**
51: 6 for the **h** will vanish like smoke,
55: 9 as the **h** are higher than the earth,
65:17 to create new **h** and a new earth;
Jer 10:11 The gods who did not make the **h**
31:37 If the **h** above can be measured,
32:17 **h** and the earth by your great power
Eze   1: 1 **h** were opened, and I saw visions
Joel 2:30 I will show portents in the **h** and on
Mt   3:16 the **h** were opened to him
Ac   2:34 For David did not ascend into the **h,**
7:56 "I see the **h** opened
Eph 4:10 who ascended far above all the **h,**
Heb 4:14 priest who has passed through the **h,**
7:26 and exalted above the **h.**
2Pe 3: 5 the word of God **h** existed long ago
3:10 the **h** will pass away with a loud
Jdt 13:18 who created the **h** and the earth,

HEAVENS ... EARTH Ge 1:1; 2:1, 4; Dt 11:21; 1Ch 16:31; 29:11; Ps 50:4; 78:69; 89:11; 96:11; 103:11; 113:6; 115:16; Pr 25:3; Isa 1:2; 13:13; 49:13; 51:6; 55:9; 65:17; 66:22; Jer 10:11; 32:17; 51:48; Joel 2:30; 3:16; Hab 3:3; Hag 2:6, 21; Zec 12:1; 2Pe 3:7, 13; Jdt 13:18; 2Es 3:18

HEAVIER → HEAVY
Pr 27: 3 a fool's provocation is **h** than both.

HEAVY → HEAVIER
Ex 18:18 task is too **h** for you; you cannot do
1Ki 12: 4 "Your father made our yoke **h.**
Ps 88: 7 Your wrath lies **h** upon me,
Ecc 6: 1 and it lies **h** upon humankind:
Isa 47: 6 you made your yoke exceedingly **h.**
Mt 23: 4 They tie up **h** burdens, hard to bear,
Mk 14:40 for their eyes were very **h;**
Sir 30:13 and make his yoke **h,**

HEBREW → HEBREWS, HEBREWS'
Ge 14:13 came and told Abram the **H,**
41:12 A young **H** was there with us,
Ex   1:19 **H** women are not like the Egyptian
2:11 He saw an Egyptian beating a **H,**
21: 2 When you buy a male **H** slave,
Jer 34: 9 all should set free their **H** slaves,
Jnh   1: 9 "I am a **H,"** he replied.
Jn 19:20 and it was written in **H,** in Latin,
Ac 21:40 addressed them in the **H** language,
Php 3: 5 of Benjamin, a **H** born of Hebrews;
Sir Pr: 2 what was originally expressed in **H**

HEBREWS → HEBREW
Ex   3:18 The LORD, the God of the **H,** has
9: 1 says the LORD, the God of the **H:**
2Co 11:22 Are they **H?** So am I.
Php 3: 5 of Benjamin, a Hebrew born of **H;**
Jdt 10:12 "I am a daughter of the **H,**

HEBREWS' → HEBREW
Ex   2: 6 must be one of the **H** children."

HEBRON → =MAMRE
Ge 13:18 the oaks of Mamre, which are at **H;**
23: 2 **H**) in the land of Canaan.
Jos 14:13 gave **H** to Caleb son of Jephunneh
20: 7 **H**) in the hill country of Judah.
21:13 of Aaron the priest they gave **H,**
Jdg 16: 3 top of the hill that is in front of **H.**
2Sa 2:11 The time that David was king in **H**
3: 2 Sons were born to David at **H:**
1Ch 2:43 sons of **H:** Korah, Tappuah, Rekem,
11: 1 gathered together to David at **H** and

HEDGE'
Isa   5: 5 I will remove its **h,** and it shall be
Hos   2: 6 I will **h** up her way with thorns;
Mic   7: 4 the most upright of them a thorn **h.**

HEED → HEEDED, HEEDS
Ex 22:23 I will surely **h** their cry;
Dt   7:12 If you **h** these ordinances,
18:15 you shall **h** such a prophet.
23: 5 God refused to **h** Balaam;
1Sa 15:22 and to **h** than the fat of rams.
Ps   5: 1 O LORD; give **h** to my sighing.
Pr 10: 8 The wise of heart will **h**
Ecc 7:21 Do not give **h** to everything

HEEDED → HEED
Jos 10:14 when the LORD **h** a human voice;
Ne   9:34 not kept your law or **h**
Jer 26: 5 though you have not **h—**

HEEDS' → HEED
Pr 10:17 **h** instruction is on the path to life,
13:18 but one who **h** reproof is honored.
15: 5 one who **h** admonition is prudent.
15:31 ear that **h** wholesome admonition
Sir 35: 2 who **h** the commandments makes

HEEL → HEELS
Ge   3:15 your head, and you will strike his **h.**
25:26 with his hand gripping Esau's **h;**
Job 18: 9 A trap seizes them by the **h;**
Ps 41: 9 has lifted the **h** against me.
Jn 13:18 has lifted his **h** against me.'
2Es 6: 8 Jacob's hand held Esau's **h**

HEELS → HEEL

Ge   49:17 that bites the horse's **h**

HEIFER

Ge   15: 9 "Bring me a **h** three years old,
Nu   19: 2 to bring you a red **h** without defect,
Jdg 14:18 "If you had not plowed with my **h,**
Heb   9:13 the sprinkling of the ashes of a **h,**

HEIGHT → HIGH

Nu   23: 3 And he went to a bare **h.**
1Sa 16: 7 or on the **h** of his stature,
      17: 4 whose **h** was six cubits and a span.
Ro   8:39 nor **h,** nor depth, nor anything else
Eph   3:18 and length and **h** and depth,
Rev 21:16 its length and width and **h** are equal.
Sir 17:32 marshals the host of the **h** of heaven
2Es   4:21 above the **h** of the heavens."

HEIGHTS → HIGH

Ps   18:33 and set me secure on the **h.**
      95: 4 the **h** of the mountains are his
     148: 1 the heavens; praise him in the **h!**
Hab   3:19 and makes me tread upon the **h.**

HEIR → HEIRS

Ge   15: 4 "This man shall not be your **h;**
Lk   20:14 themselves and said, 'This is the **h;**
Gal   4: 7 then also an **h,** through God.
Heb   1: 2 whom he appointed **h** of all things,
      11: 7 the world and became an **h**

HEIRS → HEIR

Ro   4:14 of the law who are to be the **h,**
      8:17 then **h, h** of God and joint **h** with
              Christ—
Gal   3:29 **h** according to the promise.
Eph   3: 6 the Gentiles have become fellow **h,**
Tit   3: 7 become **h** according to the hope
Heb 11: 9 **h** with him of the same promise.
Jas   2: 5 and to be **h** of the kingdom
1Pe   3: 7 also **h** of the gracious gift of life—

HELD → HOLD

Ex   17:11 Whenever Moses **h** up his hand,
Dt   4: 4 while those of you who **h** fast to
2Ki 18: 6 For he **h** fast to the LORD;
Ps   17: 5 My steps have **h** fast to your paths;
SS   3: 4 I **h** him, and would not let him go
Isa 65: 2 I **h** out my hands all day long to
Ro   10:21 All day long I have **h** out my hands
Col   2:19 and **h** together by its ligaments and
Rev   1:16 In his right hand he **h** seven stars,
      6: 5 Its rider **h** a pair of scales
     10: 2 He **h** a little scroll open in his hand.

HELDAI

Zec   6:14 the crown shall be in the care of **H,**

HELIODORUS

2Mc   3:40 the outcome of the episode of **H**

HELL*

Mt   5:22 you will be liable to the **h** of fire.
      5:29 whole body to be thrown into **h.**
      5:30 for your whole body to go into **h.**
     10:28 both soul and body in **h.**
     18: 9 two eyes and to be thrown into the **h**
     23:15 convert twice as much a child of **h**
     23:33 you escape being sentenced to **h?**
Mk   9:43 to have two hands and to go to **h,**
      9:45 two feet and to be thrown into **h,**
      9:47 two eyes and to be thrown into **h,**
Lk   12: 5 has authority to cast into **h.**
Jas   3: 6 and is itself set on fire by **h.**
2Pe   2: 4 cast them into **h** and committed
2Es   2:29 so that your children may not see **h.**
      7:36 the furnace of **h** shall be disclosed,

HELLENISTS* → HELLENIZATION

Ac   6: 1 **H** complained against the Hebrews
      9:29 He spoke and argued with the **H;**
     11:20 spoke to the **H** also,

HELLENIZATION* → HELLENISTS

2Mc   4:13 such an extreme of **H**

HELMET

Ps 108: 8 Ephraim is my **h;** Judah is my
Isa 59:17 and a **h** of salvation on his head;
Eph   6:17 Take the **h** of salvation, and the
1Th   5: 8 and for a **h** the hope of salvation.
Wis   5:18 and wear impartial justice as a **h;**

HELP → HELPED, HELPER, HELPERS,
   HELPING, HELPLESS, HELPS

Ge   4: 1 "I have produced a man with the **h**
Ex   2:23 Out of the slavery their cry for **h**
     18: 4 "The God of my father was my **h,**
     23: 5 you must **h** to set it free.
Dt   33:26 rides through the heavens to your **h,**
1Ch 12:22 people kept coming to David to **h**
2Ch 16:12 but sought **h** from physicians.
     28:16 to the king of Assyria for **h.**
Ne   6:16 had been accomplished with the **h**
Ps   18: 6 to my God I cried for **h.**
     22:19 O my **h,** come quickly
     30: 2 LORD my God, I cried to you for **h,**
     33:20 he is our **h** and shield.
     40:17 You are my **h** and my deliverer;
     42:11 my **h** and my God.
     46: 1 a very present **h** in trouble.
     79: 9 **H** us, O God of our salvation,
    108:12 O grant us **h** against the foe,
    108:12 for human **h** is worthless.
    115: 9 He is their **h** and their shield.
    121: 1 from where will my **h** come?
    146: 5 Happy are those whose **h** is the God
Ecc   4:10 falls and does not have another to **h.**
Isa 41:10 I will strengthen you, I will **h** you,
La   1: 7 and there was no one to **h** her,
Mk   9:24 "I believe; **h** my unbelief!"
Ac   16: 9 over to Macedonia and **h** us."
     26:22 To this day I have had **h** from God,
1Th   5:14 the faint hearted, **h** the weak,
Heb   2:18 able to **h** those who are being tested.
      4:16 receive mercy and find grace to **h**
Jdt   6:21 called on the God of Israel for **h.**
Sir   2: 6 Trust in him, and he will **h** you;
      3:12 **h** your father in his old age,
     29: 9 **H** the poor for the commandment's

HELPED → HELP

1Sa   7:12 "Thus far the LORD has **h** us."
Ne   8: 7 **h** the people to understand the law,
Ps   86:17 LORD, have **h** me and comforted me
    118:13 I was falling, but the LORD **h** me.
Isa 49: 8 on a day of salvation I have **h** you;
Lk   1:54 He has **h** his servant Israel,
2Co   6: 2 on a day of salvation I have **h** you."

HELPER → HELP

Ge   2:18 I will make him a **h** as his partner."
Ps   10:14 you have been the **h** of the orphan.
     30:10 O LORD, be my **h!"**
Heb 13: 6 Lord is my **h;** I will not be afraid.
Tob   8: 6 Eve as a **h** and support.
AdE 14: 3 and have no **h** but you,
Sir 36:29 **h** fit for him and a pillar of support.

HELPERS → HELP

Sir 40:24 **h** are for a time of trouble.

HELPING → HELP

Ezr   5: 2 were the prophets of God, **h** them.
Ps   22: 1 Why are you so far from **h** me,
Lk   18: 7 Will he delay long in **h** them?

HELPLESS → HELP

Ps   10:14 the **h** commit themselves to you;
Mt   9:36 because they were harassed and **h,**

HELPS → HELP

Ps   37:40 The LORD **h** them and rescues them;
Isa 50: 7 The Lord GOD **h** me;
Ro   8:26 the Spirit **h** us in our weakness;

HEM

1Sa 15:27 Saul caught hold of the **h**
Ps 139: 5 You **h** me in, behind and before,
Isa   6: 1 the **h** of his robe filled the temple.
Lk   19:43 and **h** you in on every side.

HEMAN

1Ch 15:19 The singers **H,** Asaph, and Ethan
Ps   88: T A Maskil of **H** the Ezrahite.

HEMORRHAGE → HEMORRHAGES

Mk   5:29 Immediately her **h** stopped;

HEMORRHAGES → HEMORRHAGE

Lk   8:43 suffering from **h** for twelve years;

HEN

Mt   23:37 as a **h** gathers her brood under her
Lk   13:34 as a **h** gathers her brood under her
2Es   1:30 as a **h** gathers her chicks under her

HERALD

Isa 40: 9 O Zion, **h** of good tidings;
1Ti   2: 7 I was appointed a **h** and an apostle
2Ti   1:11 For this gospel I was appointed a **h**
2Pe   2: 5 Noah, a **h** of righteousness,

HERBS

Ex   12: 8 with unleavened bread and bitter **h.**
Nu   9:11 with unleavened bread and bitter **h.**

HERD → HERDS

2Sa 12: 4 to take one of his own flock or **h**
Jnh   3: 7 No human being or animal, no **h**
Mt   8:31 send us into the **h** of swine."

HERDS → HERD

Dt   8:13 your **h** and flocks have multiplied,
     12: 6 the firstlings of your **h** and flocks.

HERE

Ge   22: 1 And he said, "**H** I am."
Ex   3: 4 And he said, "**H** I am."
1Sa   3: 4 and he said, "**H** I am!"
Ps   40: 7 Then I said, "**H** I am;
Pr   9: 4 that are simple, turn in **h!"**
Isa   6: 8 And I said, "**H** am I; send me!"
     40: 9 lift up your voice, "**H** is your God!"
Mt   12:42 greater than Solomon is **h!**
     24:23 'Look! **H** is the Messiah!'
Mk   16: 6 He has been raised; he is not **h.**
Rev   4: 1 "Come up **h,** and I will show you
     11:12 saying to them, "Come up **h!"**
2Es 14: 2 I answered, "**H** I am, Lord,"

HERITAGE

Ps   61: 5 the **h** of those who fear your name.
    119:111 Your decrees are my **h** forever;
    127: 3 Sons are indeed a **h** from the LORD,
Isa 54:17 is the **h** of the servants of the LORD
Jdt   9:12 God of the **h** of Israel,

HERMON

Dt   3: 8 from the Wadi Arnon to Mount **H**
Ps 133: 3 It is like the dew of **H,**

HEROD → HERODIANS

  1. King of Judea who tried to kill Jesus (Mt 2;
Lk 1:5).
  2. Son of 1. Tetrarch of Galilee who arrested and
beheaded John the Baptist (Mt 14:1-12; Mk 6:14-
29; Lk 3:1, 19-20; 9:7-9); tried Jesus (Lk 23:6-
15).
  3. Grandson of 1. King of Judea who killed
James (Ac 12:2); arrested Peter (Ac 12:3-19).
Death (Ac 12:19-23).

HERODIANS* → HEROD

Mt   22:16 disciples to him, along with the **H,**
Mk   3: 6 immediately conspired with the **H**
     12:13 some **H** to trap him in what he said.

HERODIAS*

Wife of Herod the Tetrarch who persuaded her
daughter to ask for John the Baptist's head (Mt
14:1-12; Mk 6:14-29; Lk 3:19).

HEROES
Ge   6: 4 These were the **h** that were of old,
Isa   5:22 are **h** in drinking wine and valiant

HESHBON
Nu   21:26 For **H** was the city of King Sihon
Dt   3: 6 as we had done to King Sihon of **H,**

HEWN
Ex   20:25 do not build it of **h** stones;
Pr   9: 1 she has **h** her seven pillars.
Isa 51: 1 to the rock from which you were **h,**
Mk   15:46 laid it in a tomb that had been **h**

HEZEKIAH
King of Judah (Sir 48:17-25). Restored the temple and worship (2Ch 29-31). Sought the Lord for help against Assyria (2Ki 18-19; 2Ch 32:1-23; Isa 36-37). Illness healed (2Ki 20:1-11; 2Ch 32:24-26; Isa 38). Judged for showing Babylonians his treasures (2Ki 20:12-21; 2Ch 32:31; Isa 39).

HEZRON
Ru   4:18 Perez became the father of **H,**
Mt   1: 3 and Perez the father of **H,**

HID → HIDE
Ge   3: 8 and his wife **h** themselves from the
Ex   2: 2 a fine baby, she **h** him three months.
       3: 6 Moses **h** his face, for he was afraid
Jos   6:17 live because she **h** the messengers
1Ki 18:13 **h** a hundred of the Lord's prophets
2Ch 22:11 **h** him from Athaliah, so that she
Isa 49: 2 in the shadow of his hand he **h** me;
      49: 2 in his quiver he **h** me away.
      54: 8 wrath for a moment I **h** my face
Eze 39:23 So I **h** my face from them and gave
Mt   13:44 which someone found and **h;**
      25:25 and **h** your talent in the ground.
2Mc   1:19 the fire of the altar and secretly **h** it

HIDDEN → HIDE
Ge   4:14 and I shall be **h** from your face;
Jos   2: 6 up to the roof and **h** them with the
       7:22 **h** in his tent with the silver
1Sa 10:22 has **h** himself among the baggage."
2Ki 11: 3 **h** in the house of the Lord,
Job 28:11 **h** things they bring to light.
Ps   19:12 Clear me from **h** faults.
      69: 5 the wrongs I have done are not **h**
     142: 3 where I walk they have **h** a trap for
Pr   2: 4 and search for it as for **h** treasures—
      27: 5 Better is open rebuke than **h** love.
Isa 40:27 "My way is **h** from the Lord,
      59: 2 your sins have **h** his face from you
Da   2:22 He reveals deep and **h** things;
Mt   13:35 I will proclaim what has been **h**
      13:44 is like treasure **h** in a field.
Mk   4:22 nothing **h,** except to be disclosed;
Lk   10:21 have **h** these things from the wise
      18:34 what he said was **h** from them,
1Co   2: 7 speak God's wisdom, secret and **h,**
       4: 5 now **h** in darkness and will disclose
Eph   3: 9 the plan of the mystery **h** for ages
Col   1:26 that has been **h** throughout the ages
       2: 3 are **h** all the treasures of wisdom
       3: 3 your life is **h** with Christ in God.
Heb   4:13 And before him no creature is **h,**
Rev   2:17 the **h** manna, and I will give a white
Sir 16:17 "I am **h** from the Lord,
      20:30 **H** wisdom and unseen treasure,
      42:20 and nothing is **h** from him.
2Es   5: 1 and the way of truth shall be **h,**

HIDE → HID, HIDDEN, HIDES, HIDING
Ge   18:17 "Shall I **h** from Abraham what I am
Ex   2: 3 she could **h** him no longer she got
Dt   31:17 I will forsake them and **h** my face
Ps   13: 1 How long will you **h** your face
      17: 8 **h** me in the shadow of your wings,
      27: 5 will **h** me in his shelter in the day
      51: 9 **H** your face from my sins,
      89:46 Will you **h** yourself forever?

Isa   1:15 I will **h** my eyes from you;
      53: 3 from whom others **h** their faces
Eze 39:29 I will never again **h** my face from
Rev   6:16 and **h** us from the face of the one
Sir   4:23 and do not **h** your wisdom.
      41:15 Better are those who **h** their folly
             than those who **h** their wisdom.

HIDES → HIDE
Job 42: 3 that **h** counsel without knowledge?'
Isa 45:15 Truly, you are a God who **h** himself,
Lk   8:16 after lighting a lamp **h** it under a jar,

HIDING → HIDE
Ps   32: 7 You are a **h** place for me;
Pr   28:12 wicked prevail, people go into **h.**

HIGH → HEIGHT, HEIGHTS, HIGHER, HIGHEST, HIGHLY, HIGHWAY
Ge   14:18 he was priest of God Most **H.**
      14:22 sworn to the Lord, God Most **H,**
1Ki   3: 2 were sacrificing at the **h** places,
      11: 7 a **h** place for Chemosh the
      12:31 He also made houses on **h** places,
Ps   7: 7 and over it take your seat on **h.**
       7: 7 the steadfast love of the Most **H** he
      46: 4 the holy habitation of the Most **H.**
      82: 6 are gods, children of the Most **H,**
      91: 1 live in the shelter of the Most **H,**
     103:11 as the heavens are **h** above the earth,
     113: 5 Lord our God, who is seated on **h,**
Pr   24: 7 Wisdom is too **h** for fools;
Ecc 10: 6 folly is set in many **h** places,
Isa 14:14 I will make myself like the Most **H.**
Jer   2:20 On every **h** hill and under every
Da   7:18 that the Most **H** is sovereign over
Mic   1: 3 down and tread upon the **h** places
Mt   4: 8 a very **h** mountain and showed him
      17: 1 and led them up a **h** mountain,
Mk   5: 7 Jesus, Son of the Most **H** God?
      14:53 They took Jesus to the **h** priest;
Jn   18:22 that how you answer the **h** priest?"
Ac   23: 4 you dare to insult God's **h** priest?"
Eph   4: 8 "When he ascended on **h** he made
Heb   2:17 a merciful and faithful **h** priest
       7: 1 priest of the Most **H** God,
       7:26 that we should have such a **h** priest,
Wis   5:15 the Most **H** takes care of them.
Sir 12: 6 For the Most **H** also hates sinners
      35:12 Give to the Most **H** as he
Man   1: 7 for you are the Lord Most **H,**

*GOD MOST HIGH Ge 14:18, 19, 20, 22; Ps 57:2; AdE 16:16; Sir 50:17; 1Es 9:46; 3Mc 6:2

HIGH PLACE 1Ki 3:4; 11:7; 2Ki 23:15, 15, 15; 1Ch 16:39; 21:29; 2Ch 1:3, 13; Isa 16:12; Jer 7:31; 48:35; Eze 20:29; Mic 1:5; Sir 22:18; 4Mc 5:1

HIGH PLACES Lev 26:30; Nu 33:52; 2Sa 1:19, 25; 1Ki 3:2, 3; 12:31, 32; 13:2, 32, 33, 33; 14:23; 15:14; 22:43, 43; 2Ki 12:3, 3; 14:4, 4; 15:4, 4, 35, 35; 16:4; 17:9, 11, 29, 32, 32; 18:4, 22; 21:3; 23:5, 8, 8, 9, 13, 19, 20; 2Ch 11:15; 14:3, 5; 15:17; 17:6; 20:33; 21:11; 28:4, 25; 31:1; 32:12; 33:3, 17, 19; 34:3; Ps 78:58; Pr 9:14; Ecc 10:6; Isa 15:2; 36:7; Jer 19:5; 32:35; Eze 6:3, 6; Hos 10:8; Am 7:9; Mic 1:3; Wis 6:5

HIGH PRIEST Nu 35:25, 28, 28, 32; Jos 20:6; 2Ki 12:10; 22:4, 8; 23:4; 2Ch 34:9; Ne 3:1, 20; 13:28; Hag 1:1, 12, 14; 2:2, 4; Zec 3:1, 8; 6:11; Mt 26:3, 51, 57, 58, 62, 63, 65; Mk 2:26; 14:47, 53, 54, 60, 61, 63, 66; Lk 22:50; Jn 11:49, 51; 18:13, 15, 15, 16, 19, 22, 24, 26; Ac 4:6; 5:17, 21, 27; 7:1; 9:1; 19:14; 22:5; 23:2, 4, 5; 24:1; Heb 2:17; 3:1; 4:14, 15; 5:1, 5, 10; 6:20; 7:26; 8:1, 3; 9:7, 11, 25; 13:11; Jdt 4:6, 8, 14; 15:8; Sir 50:1; Bar 1:7; 1Mc 7:5, 9; 10:20, 32, 38, 69; 12:3, 6, 7; 13:36, 42; 14:17, 20, 23, 27, 30, 35, 41, 47; 15:2, 17, 21, 24; 16:12, 24; 2Mc 3:1, 4, 9, 10, 16, 21, 32,

33, 33; 4:13; 14:3, 13; 15:12; 1Es 5:40; 8:2; 3Mc 1:11; 2:1; 4Mc 4:13, 16, 18

MOST HIGH Ge 14:18, 19, 20, 22; Nu 24:16; Dt 32:8; 1Sa 2:10; 2Sa 22:14; Ps 7:17; 9:2; 18:13; 21:7; 46:4; 47:2; 50:14; 56:2; 57:2; 73:11; 77:10; 78:17, 35, 56; 82:6; 83:18; 87:5; 91:1, 9; 92:1; 97:9; 106:7; 107:11; Isa 14:14; La 3:35, 38; Da 3:26; 4:2, 17, 24, 25, 32, 34; 5:18, 21; 7:18, 22, 25, 25, 27; Hos 11:7; Mk 5:7; Lk 1:32, 35, 76; 6:35; 8:28; Ac 7:48; 16:17; Heb 7:1; Tob 1:13; 4:11; Jdt 13:18; AdE 16:16; Wis 5:15; 6:3; Sir 4:10; 7:9, 15; 9:15; 12:2, 6; 17:26, 27; 19:17; 23:18, 23; 24:2, 3, 23; 28:7; 29:11; 33:15; 34:6, 23; 35:8, 12, 21; 37:15; 38:2, 34; 39:5; 41:4, 8; 42:2, 18; 43:2, 12; 44:20; 46:5; 47:5, 8; 48:5; 49:4; 50:7, 14, 15, 16, 17, 19, 21; 2Mc 3:31; 1Es 2:3; 6:31; 8:19, 21; 9:46; Man 1:7; 3Mc 1:20; 6:2; 7:9; 2Es 3:3; 4:2, 11, 34; 5:4, 22, 34; 6:32, 36; 7:19, 23, 33, 37, 42, 50, 70, 74, 77, 78, 79, 81, 83, 87, 88, 89, 102, 122, 132; 8:1, 48, 56, 59; 9:2, 4, 6, 25, 28, 44; 10:24, 38, 50, 52, 54, 57, 59, 59; 11:38, 43, 44; 12:4, 6, 23, 30, 32, 36, 39, 47; 13:13, 26, 29, 44, 47, 56, 57; 14:31, 42, 45

MOST HIGH *GOD Ps 78:35, 56; Da 3:26; 4:2; 5:18, 21; Mk 5:7; Lk 8:28; Ac 16:17; Heb 7:1; Jdt 13:18; Sir 7:9; 24:23; 41:8; 1Es 6:31; 8:19, 21; 3Mc 7:9

ON HIGH Ge 27:39; 2Sa 22:17; 1Ki 12:31; Job 5:11; 16:19; 21:22; 31:2; 39:27; Ps 7:7; 10:5; 18:16; 75:5; 92:8; 93:4; 113:5; 144:7; Isa 32:15; 33:5; 40:26; 58:4; Jer 25:30; La 1:13; Mic 6:6; Hab 2:9; Lk 1:78; 24:49; Eph 4:8; Heb 1:3; Wis 9:17; Sir 16:17; 43:8

HIGHER → HIGH
Dt   28:43 ascend above you **h** and **h,**
Ps   61: 2 Lead me to the rock that is **h** than I;
     108: 4 steadfast love is **h** than the heavens,
Isa 55: 9 so are my ways **h** than your ways

HIGHEST → HIGH
1Ki   8:27 the **h** heaven cannot contain you,
Pr   9: 3 she calls from the **h** places in the
Mt   21: 9 Hosanna in the **h** heaven!"
Lk   2:14 "Glory to God in the **h** heaven,
      19:38 and glory in the **h** heaven!"
Sir 16:18 Lo, heaven and the **h** heaven,

HIGHLY → HIGH
1Ch 29:25 The Lord **h** exalted Solomon in the
Ps   47: 9 to God; he is **h** exalted.
Ro   12: 3 not to think of yourself more **h** than
Aza   1:29 praised and **h** exalted forever;

HIGHWAY → HIGH, WAY
Pr   16:17 The **h** of the upright avoids evil;
Isa 40: 3 make straight in the desert a **h** for

HILKIAH
2Ki 22:10 "The priest **H** has given me a book."
2Ch 34:14 priest **H** found the book of the law

HILL → HILLS
Ex   17: 9 top of the **h** with the staff of God in
1Ki 16:24 He bought the **h** of Samaria
Ps   15: 1 Who may dwell on your holy **h?**
      24: 3 shall ascend the **h** of the Lord?
Isa 40: 4 every mountain and **h** be made low;
Mt   5:14 A city built on a **h** cannot be hid.
Lk   3: 5 mountain and **h** shall be made low,

HILL COUNTRY Ge 10:30; 12:8; 14:6, 10; 31:21, 23, 25, 25, 54; 36:8, 9; Nu 13:17, 29; 14:40, 44, 45; Dt 1:7, 7, 19, 20, 24, 41, 43, 44; 2:3, 37; 3:12, 25; Jos 2:16, 22, 23; 9:1; 10:6, 40; 11:3, 16, 16, 21, 21, 21; 12:8; 13:6; 14:12; 15:48; 16:1; 17:15, 16, 18; 18:12; 19:50; 20:7, 7, 7; 21:11, 21; 24:4, 30, 33; Jdg 1:9, 19, 34; 2:9; 3:27; 4:5; 7:24; Jdt 1:9; 2:15; 4:7; 5:15, 19; 7:4, 7, 10, 18; 10:11; 11:2; 12:15; 17:1, 8; 18:2, 13; 19:1, 16, 18; 1Sa 1:1; 9:4; 13:2; 14:22, 23; 23:14; 2Sa 20:21; 1Ki

4:8; 5:15; 12:25; 2Ki 5:22; 1Ch 6:67; 2Ch 2:2, 18; 13:4; 15:8; 19:4; 21:11; 27:4; Jer 17:26; 31:6; 32:44; 33:13; Mal 1:3; Lk 1:39, 65; Jdt 1:6; 2:22; 5:3, 15, 19; 6:7, 11; 7:1, 18; 10:13; 11:2; 15:2, 5, 7; Sir 46:9; 1Mc 10:70

HILLS → HILL

1Ki 20:23 "Their gods are gods of the **h,**
Ps   50:10 the cattle on a thousand **h.**
     114: 6 that you skip like rams? O **h,**
     121: 1 I lift up my eyes to the **h—**
Pr   8:25 had been shaped, before the **h,**
Isa   2: 2 and shall be raised above the **h;**
Hos 10: 8 Cover us, and to the **h,** Fall on us.
Joel   3:18 the **h** shall flow with milk,
Am   9:13 and all the **h** shall flow with it.
Lk   23:30 'Fall on us'; and to the **h,**

HINDER → HINDERED, HINDRANCE

1Sa 14: 6 nothing can **h** the LORD from saving
Isa 43:13 I work and who can **h** it?
Ac   11:17 who was I that I could **h** God?"
1Pe   3: 7 so that nothing may **h** your prayers.
1Es   2:30 and began to **h** the builders.

HINDERED → HINDER

Lk   11:52 you **h** those who were entering."
Ro   14:13 I have so often been **h** from coming

HINDRANCE* → HINDER

Ac   28:31 with all boldness and without **h.**
Ro   14:13 a stumbling block or **h** in the way

HINGES*

Pr   26:14 a door turns on its **h,** so does a lazy

HINNOM → BEN-HINNOM

2Ch 28: 3 in the valley of the son of **H,**
       33: 6 fire in the valley of the son of **H,**
Jer 32:35 of Baal in the valley of the son of **H,**

HIP

Ge   32:25 Jacob's **h** was put out of joint
Jdg 15: 8 He struck them down **h** and thigh

HIRAM → =HURAM, =HURAM-ABI

King of Tyre; helped David build his palace (2Sa 5:11-12; 1Ch 14:1); helped Solomon build the temple (1Ki 5; 2Ch 2) and his navy (1Ki 9:10-27; 2Ch 8).

HIRE → HIRED, HIRES

Ge   30:18 "God has given me my **h**
Mt   20: 1 early in the morning to **h** laborers

HIRED → HIRE

Dt   23: 4 because they **h** against you Balaam
Ne   6:13 He was **h** for this purpose,
Lk   15:15 **h** himself out to one of the citizens
Jn   10:12 **h** hand, who is not the shepherd
1Mc   5:39 also have **h** Arabs to help them,

HIRES* → HIRE

Pr   26:10 who **h** a passing fool or a drunkard.

HITTITE → HITTITES

Ge   23:10 Ephron the **H** answered Abraham
       27:46 because of the **H** women.
2Sa 11: 3 the wife of Uriah the **H."**
       11:17 Uriah the **H** was killed as well.
Ne   9: 8 the **H,** the Amorite, the Perizzite,
Eze 16: 3 and your mother a **H.**

HITTITES → HITTITE

Ge   25:10 Abraham purchased from the **H.**
Dt   20:17 **H** and the Amorites, the Canaanites
Ezr   9: 1 Canaanites, the **H,** the Perizzites,

HIVITE → HIVITES

Ge   34: 2 Shechem son of Hamor the **H,**

HIVITES → HIVITE

Ex   23:28 which shall drive out the **H,**
Jos   9: 7 But the Israelites said to the **H,**

HOBAB

Nu   10:29 Moses said to **H** son of Reuel
Jdg   4:11 **H** the father-in-law of Moses,

HOLD → HELD, HOLDING, HOLDS

Ex   9: 2 refuse to let them go and still **h**
Dt   13: 4 serve, and to him you shall **h** fast.
Jos 22: 5 commandments, and to **h** fast to him
2Sa   6: 6 to the ark of God and took **h** of it,
Ps   73:23 you **h** my right hand.
       74:11 Why do you **h** back your hand;
     119:101 I **h** back my feet from every evil
     139:10 and your right hand shall **h** me fast.
Pr   3:18 life to those who lay **h** of her;
       4: 4 "Let your heart **h** fast my words;
Isa 22:17 He will seize firm **h** on you,
       41:13 I, the LORD your God, **h** your right
       54: 2 be stretched out; do not **h** back;
Hos 12: 6 **h** fast to love and justice,
Zec   8:23 of every language shall take **h** of
Mk   7: 8 and **h** to human tradition."
Jn   20:17 Jesus said to her, "Do not **h** on to
Ac   7:60 do not **h** this sin against them."
1Co 15: 2 if you **h** firmly to the message that I
Col   1:17 and in him all things **h** together.
1Th   5:21 everything; **h** fast to what is good;
2Th   2:15 and **h** fast to the traditions that you
1Ti   3: 9 **h** fast to the mystery of the faith
       6:12 take **h** of the eternal life,
       6:19 take **h** of the life that really is life.
Heb   3:14 only we **h** our first confidence firm
       4:14 let us **h** fast to our confession.
     10:23 Let us **h** fast to the confession of
Rev 12:17 and **h** the testimony of Jesus.
       19:10 your comrades who **h** the testimony
Sir 21:14 it can **h** no knowledge.
       43:26 by his word all things **h** together.

HOLDING → HOLD

Php   2:16 by your **h** fast to the word of life
Col   2:19 and not **h** fast to the head,
1Ti   4: 8 **h** promise for both the present life
2Ti   3: 5 **h** to the outward form of godliness

HOLDS → HOLD

Ps   37:24 for the LORD **h** us by the hand.
Heb   7:24 but he **h** his priesthood permanently,
Rev   2: 1 who **h** the seven stars in his right
Wis   1: 7 which **h** all things together

HOLE → HOLES

Ps   7:15 fall into the **h** that they have made.
Isa 11: 8 shall play over the **h** of the asp,

HOLES → HOLE

1Sa 13: 6 and in **h** and in rocks and in tombs
Job 30: 6 in **h** in the ground, and in the rocks.
Hag   1: 6 to put them into a bag with **h.**
Mt   8:20 Jesus said to him, "Foxes have **h,**
Heb 11:38 and in caves and **h** in the ground.

HOLIDAY

Est   8:17 among the Jews, a festival and a **h.**
AdE   9:22 from a time of distress to a **h,**

HOLIES* → HOLY

Heb   9: 3 a tent called the Holy of **H.**

HOLINESS → HOLY

Ex   15:11 Who is like you, majestic in **h,**
Nu   20:13 and by which he showed his **h.**
Dt   32:51 by failing to maintain my **h** among
Ps   89:35 and for all I have sworn by my **h;**
       93: 5 **h** befits your house, O LORD,
Eze 20:41 and I will manifest my **h** among you
       36:23 through you I display my **h** before
       38:23 and my **h** and make myself known
Am   4: 2 The Lord GOD has sworn by his **h:**
Lk   1:75 in **h** and righteousness before him
Ro   1: 4 according to the spirit of **h** by
2Co   7: 1 kindness, **h** of spirit, genuine love,
       7: 1 making **h** perfect in the fear of God.
Eph   4:24 of God in true righteousness and **h.**

1Th   4: 7 did not call us to impurity but in **h,**
1Ti   2:15 continue in faith and love and **h,**
Heb 12:10 in order that we may share his **h.**
       12:14 **h** without which no one will see the
2Pe   3:11 leading lives of **h** and godliness,
Wis   9: 3 and rule the world in **h** and

HOLLOW

Ex   27: 8 You shall make it **h,** with boards.
Pr   30: 4 the wind in the **h** of the hand?
Isa 40:12 the waters in the **h** of his hand

HOLOFERNES

Assyrian general (Jdt 2:4). Beguiled and be-headed by Judith (Jdt 10-13).

HOLY → HOLIES, HOLINESS

Ex   3: 5 which you are standing is **h** ground.
       16:23 a **h** sabbath to the LORD;
       19: 6 a priestly kingdom and a **h** nation.
       20: 8 the sabbath day, and keep it **h.**
       26:33 the **h** place from the most **h.**
       28:36 of a signet, "**H** to the LORD."
       29:37 the altar shall be most **h;**
       30:10 It is most **h** to the LORD.
       30:29 so that they may be most **h;**
       40: 9 so that it shall become **h.**
Lev 11:44 and be **h,** for I am **h.**
       19: 2 You shall be **h,** for I the LORD your
           God am **h.**
Nu   4:15 but they must not touch the **h** things,
       6: 5 to the LORD, they shall be **h;**
       16: 7 LORD chooses shall be the **h** one.
Dt   5:12 the sabbath day and keep it **h,**
       23:14 therefore your camp must be **h,**
       26:15 Look down from your **h** habitation,
       33: 2 With him were myriads of **h** ones;
Jos   5:15 for the place where you stand is **h."**
       24:19 serve the LORD, for he is a **h** God.
1Sa   2: 2 "There is no **H** One like the LORD,
       6:20 stand before the LORD, this **h** God?
       21: 5 the vessels of the young men are **h**
2Ki   4: 9 passes our way is a **h** man of God.
1Ch 16:10 Glory in his **h** name; let the hearts
       16:35 we may give thanks to your **h** name,
       29: 3 that I have provided for the **h** house,
2Ch   3: 8 He made the most **h** place;
       30:27 their prayer came to his **h** dwelling
Ezr   9: 2 the **h** seed has mixed itself with the
Ne   11: 1 of ten to live in the **h** city Jerusalem,
Job   6:10 not denied the words of the **H** One.
Ps   2: 6 set my king on Zion, my **h** hill."
       5: 7 bow down toward your **h** temple
       11: 4 The LORD is in his **h** temple;
       22: 3 you are **h,** enthroned on the praises
       24: 3 And who shall stand in his **h** place?
       30: 4 and give thanks to his **h** name.
       33:21 because we trust in his **h** name.
       47: 8 God sits on his **h** throne.
       77:13 Your way, O God, is **h.**
       78:54 And he brought them to his **h** hill,
       89: 5 in the assembly of the **h** ones.
       89:18 our king to the **H** One of Israel.
       99: 3 and awesome name. **H** is he!
       99: 9 for the LORD our God is **h.**
     105: 3 Glory in his **h** name; let the hearts
     111: 9 **H** and awesome is his name.
Pr   9:10 knowledge of the **H** One is insight.
Isa   1: 4 have despised the **H** One of Israel,
       5:16 the **H** God shows himself **h** by
           righteousness.
       6: 3 "**H, h, h** is the LORD of hosts;
       6:13 The **h** seed is its stump.
       8:13 him you shall regard as **h;**
       29:23 will sanctify the **H** One of Jacob,
       40:25 who is my equal? says the **H** One.
       43: 3 your God, the **H** One of Israel,
       52:10 The LORD has bared his **h** arm
       54: 5 **H** One of Israel is your Redeemer,
       57:15 I dwell in the high and **h** place,
       58:13 the day of the LORD honorable;
Jer   2: 3 Israel was **h** to the LORD,
       17:22 but keep the sabbath day **h,**

Eze 22:26 have profaned my **h** things;
    36:20 they profaned my **h** name,
    44:23 the difference between the **h** and
Da   4:13 and there was a **h** watcher,
    8:13 Then I heard a **h** one speaking,
    9:24 and to anoint a most **h** place.
   11:28 shall be set against the **h** covenant.
Jnh 2: 4 I look again upon your **h** temple?'
Hab 2:20 But the LORD is in his **h** temple;
Zec 8: 3 shall be called the **h** mountain.
   14: 5 and all the **h** ones with him.
   14:20 "**H** to the LORD."
Mt 1:18 to be with child from the **H** Spirit.
    3:11 baptize you with the **H** Spirit and
    4: 5 the devil took him to the **h** city and
  24:15 sacrilege standing in the **h** place,
  28:19 and of the Son and of the **H** Spirit,
Mk 1:24 who you are, the **H** One of God."
    3:29 against the **H** Spirit can never have
Lk 1:15 he will be filled with the **H** Spirit.
    1:35 "The **H** Spirit will come upon you,
    1:49 for me, and **h** is his name.
    3:22 the **H** Spirit descended upon him in
    4: 1 Jesus, full of the **H** Spirit,
  10:21 in the **H** Spirit and said, "I thank
  11:13 heavenly Father give the **H** Spirit
Jn 6:69 and know that you are the **H** One
  14:26 But the Advocate, the **H** Spirit,
  20:22 said to them, "Receive the **H** Spirit.
Ac 1: 5 with the **H** Spirit not many days
    2: 4 were filled with the **H** Spirit and
    2:27 your **H** One experience corruption.
    2:38 will receive the gift of the **H** Spirit.
    4:27 against your **h** servant Jesus,
    5: 3 your heart to lie to the **H** Spirit
    8:15 that they might receive the **H** Spirit
  10:44 the **H** Spirit fell upon all who heard
  13:35 your **H** One experience corruption.'
   15: 8 by giving them the **H** Spirit,
   19: 2 even heard that there is a **H** Spirit."
Ro 1: 2 his prophets in the **h** scriptures,
   7:12 law is **h**, and the commandment is
       h and just and good.
  11:16 if the root is **h**, then the branches
       also are **h**.
   12: 1 living sacrifice, **h** and acceptable to
  15:16 sanctified by the **H** Spirit.
  16:16 Greet one another with a **h** kiss.
1Co 7:14 unbelieving husband is made **h**
  16:20 Greet one another with a **h** kiss.
Eph 1: 4 to be **h** and blameless
    2:21 grows into a **h** temple in the Lord;
    3: 5 now been revealed to his **h** apostles
    4:30 do not grieve the **H** Spirit of God,
    5:26 to make her **h** by cleansing her with
Col 1:22 to present you **h** and blameless and
    3:12 God's chosen ones, **h** and beloved,
1Ti 2: 8 lifting up **h** hands without anger or
2Ti 1: 9 and called us with a **h** calling,
Tit 3: 5 rebirth and renewal by the **H** Spirit.
Heb 2: 4 and by gifts of the **H** Spirit,
    6: 4 and have shared in the **H** Spirit,
    7:26 **h**, blameless, undefiled, separated
    9: 2 this is called the **H** Place.
    9:12 entered once for all into the **H** Place
1Pe 1:15 Instead, as he who called you is **h**,
    1:16 "You shall be **h**, for I am **h**."
    2: 5 to be a **h** priesthood,
    2: 9 a royal priesthood, a **h** nation,
    3: 5 that the **h** women who hoped
2Pe 1:21 moved by the **H** Spirit spoke
1Jn 2:20 have been anointed by the **H** One,
Jude 1:14 with ten thousands of his **h** ones,
    1:20 build yourselves up on your most **h**
       faith; pray in the **H** Spirit;
Rev 3: 7 These are the words of the **h** one,
    4: 8 **H, h, h**, the Lord God Almighty
   11: 2 and they will trample over the **h** city
   15: 4 For you alone are **h**.
   20: 6 **h** are those who share in the first
   21: 2 I saw the **h** city, the new Jerusalem,
  21:10 the **h** city Jerusalem coming down

   22:11 and the **h** still be **h**."
   22:19 in the tree of life and in the **h** city,
Tob 11:14 and blessed be all his **h** angels.
Wis 4:15 he watches over his **h** ones.
    6:10 made **h** who observe **h** things
Aza 1:30 blessed is your glorious, **h** name,
1Mc 1:15 and abandoned the **h** covenant.
    4:49 They made new **h** vessels,
2Es 14:22 send the **h** spirit into me,

HOLY CITY Ne 11:1, 18; Isa 48:2; 52:1; Da
9:24; Mt 4:5; 27:53; Rev 11:2; 21:2, 10; 22:19;
Tob 13:9; Aza 1:5; 1Mc 2:7; 2Mc 1:12; 3:1;
9:14; 15:14; 3Mc 6:5

HOLY CONVOCATION Lev 23:3, 7, 8, 21,
24, 27, 35, 36, 37; Nu 28:18, 25, 26; 29:1, 7, 12

HOLY MOUNTAIN Ps 48:1; 99:9; Isa 11:9;
27:13; 56:7; 57:13; 65:11, 25; 66:20; Eze
20:40; 28:14; Da 9:16, 20; 11:45; Joel 2:1;
3:17; Ob 1:16; Zep 3:11; Zec 8:3; 2Pe 1:18;
Wis 9:8; 1Mc 11:37

HOLY NAME Lev 20:3; 22:2, 32; 1Ch 16:10,
35; 29:16; Ps 30:4; 33:21; 97:12; 103:1; 105:3;
106:47; 145:21; Eze 20:39; 36:20, 21, 22;
39:7, 25; 43:7, 8; Am 2:7; Tob 11:14; 13:11,
17; Wis 10:20; Sir 17:10; 47:10; Aza 1:30

HOLY ONE Nu 16:7; 1Sa 2:2; 2Ki 19:22; Job
6:10; Ps 71:22; 78:41; 89:18; 106:16; Pr 9:10;
Isa 1:4; 5:19, 24; 10:17, 20; 12:6; 17:7; 29:19,
23; 30:11, 12, 15; 31:1; 37:23; 40:25; 41:14,
16, 20; 43:3, 14, 15; 45:11; 47:4; 48:17; 49:7,
7; 54:5; 55:5; 60:9, 14; Jer 50:29; 51:5; Eze
39:7; Da 8:13, 13; Hos 11:9, 12; Hab 1:12;
3:3; Mk 1:24; Lk 4:34; Jn 6:69; Ac 2:27;
13:35; 1Jn 2:20; Rev 3:7; 16:5; Sir 4:14; 23:9;
43:10; 47:8; 48:20; Bar 4:22, 37; 5:5; Aza
1:12; 2Mc 14:36

HOLY ONES Dt 33:2, 3; Job 5:1; 15:15; Ps
16:3; 34:9; 89:5, 7; Pr 30:3; Da 4:17; 7:18, 21,
22, 22, 25, 27; 8:24; Zec 14:5; Jude 1:14; Wis
3:9; 4:15; 18:1, 2, 5; Sir 42:17; 45:2; 3Mc 2:2,
21

HOLY PEOPLE Dt 28:9; Isa 62:12; 63:18;
Da 12:7; Wis 10:15, 17; 2Mc 15:24; 3Mc 2:6

HOLY PLACE Ex 26:33, 34; 28:29, 35, 43;
29:30, 31; 31:11; 35:19; 39:1, 41; Lev 6:16,
26, 27, 30; 7:6; 10:13; 14:13; 16:3, 20, 23, 24,
27; 24:9; 1Ki 6:16; 7:50; 8:6, 8, 10; 1Ch 6:49;
2Ch 3:8, 10; 4:22; 5:7, 9, 11; 29:5, 7; 35:5; Ezr
9:8; Ps 24:3; 68:17; 74:4; 134:2; Ecc 8:10; Isa
57:15; Eze 41:4, 21; 42:14; 44:27, 27;
45:3, 4; 48:12; Da 9:24; Mt 24:15; Jn 11:48;
Ac 6:13; 21:28; Heb 9:2, 12, 25; 1Mc 2:12;
2Mc 1:29; 2:18; 3:18; 5:17, 19; 8:17; 10:7;
13:23; 1Es 8:78; 3Mc 1:9, 23; 2:14; 4Mc 4:9,
12

HOLY SPIRIT Ps 51:11; Isa 63:10, 11; Mt
1:18, 20; 3:11; 12:32; 28:19; Mk 1:8; 3:29;
12:36; 13:11; Lk 1:15, 35, 41, 67; 2:25, 26;
3:16, 22; 4:1; 10:21; 11:13; 12:10, 12; Jn 1:33;
14:26; 20:22; Ac 1:2, 5, 8, 16; 2:4, 33, 38; 4:8,
25, 31; 5:3, 32; 6:5; 7:51, 55; 8:15, 17, 19;
9:17, 31; 10:38, 44, 45, 47; 11:15, 16, 24;
13:2, 4, 9, 52; 15:8, 28; 16:6; 19:2, 2, 6; 20:23,
28; 21:11; 28:25; Ro 5:5; 9:1; 14:17; 15:13,
16; 1Co 6:19; 12:3; 2Co 13:13; Eph 1:13;
4:30; 1Th 1:5; 4:8; 2Ti 1:14; Tit 3:5; Heb
2:4; 3:7; 6:4; 9:8; 10:15; 1Pe 1:12; 2Pe 1:21;
Jude 1:20; Wis 9:17; Sus 1:45; 2Es 14:22

HOLY TEMPLE Ps 5:7; 11:4; 65:4; 79:1;
138:2; Jnh 2:4, 7; Mic 1:2; Hab 2:20; Eph
2:21; 2Mc 5:15; 13:10; 14:31; 1Es 1:53

HOLY THINGS Lev 5:15; Nu 4:4, 15, 19,
20; 7:9; 10:21; 18:9; 1Ch 23:13; Eze 22:8, 26;
Wis 6:10; 10:10; Sir 7:31; 1Es 5:40; 2Es 10:22

HOLY VESSELS 1Ki 8:4; 1Ch 22:19; 2Ch
5:5; 1Mc 4:49; 2Mc 4:48; 5:16; 9:16; 1Es
1:41, 45, 54; 2:10; 6:18, 26; 8:17, 55

MOST HOLY Ex 26:33, 34; 29:37; 30:10, 29,
36; 40:10; Lev 2:3, 10; 6:17, 25, 29; 7:1, 6;

10:12, 17; 14:13; 21:22; 24:9; 27:28; Nu 4:4,
19; 18:9, 9, 10; 1Ki 6:16; 7:50; 8:6; 1Ch 6:49;
23:13; 2Ch 3:8, 10; 4:22; 5:7; 31:14; Ezr 2:63;
Ne 7:65; Ps 28:2; Eze 41:4; 42:13, 13; 43:12;
45:3; 48:12; Da 9:24; Jude 1:20; 2Mc 5:15;
6:11; 4Mc 7:4; 14:7

MOST HOLY PLACE Ex 26:34; 1Ki 6:16;
7:50; 8:6; 1Ch 6:49; 2Ch 3:8, 10; 4:22; 5:7;
Eze 41:4; 45:3; 48:12; Da 9:24

HOME → HOMELAND, HOMELESS,
HOMES, HOMETOWN
Dt 6: 7 when you are at **h** and when you
   11:19 when you are at **h** and when you
    24: 5 He shall be free at **h** one year,
1Ch 16:43 David went **h** to bless his household
Ps 68: 6 God gives the desolate a **h**
   84: 3 Even the sparrow finds a **h**,
  113: 9 He gives the barren woman a **h**,
Pr 7:11 her feet do not stay at **h**;
   27: 8 is one who strays from **h**.
Ecc 12: 5 all must go to their eternal **h**,
Eze 36: 8 for they shall soon come **h**.
Hag 1: 9 you brought it **h**, I blew it away.
Mk 2:11 take your mat and go to your **h**."
    5:19 said to him, "Go **h** to your friends,
Lk 10:38 Martha welcomed him into her **h**.
Jn 14:23 to them and make our **h** with them.
   19:27 the disciple took her into his own **h**.
Ac 10:32 staying in the **h** of Simon, a tanner,
   16:15 come and stay at my **h**."
1Co 11:34 If you are hungry, eat at **h**,
2Co 5: 8 the body and at **h** with the Lord.
2Pe 3:13 where righteousness is at **h**.
Sir 11:29 Do not invite everyone into your **h**,

HOMELAND → HOME, LAND
Heb 11:14 that they are seeking a **h**.

HOMELESS· → HOME
Isa 58: 7 the **h** poor into your house;
1Co 4:11 poorly clothed and beaten and **h**,

HOMES → HOME
Nu 32:18 We will not return to our **h** until all
Ne 4:14 your wives, and your **h**."
Ps 49:11 Their graves are their **h** forever,
Hos 11:11 and I will return them to their **h**,
Lk 16: 9 welcome you into the eternal **h**.

HOMETOWN → HOME, TOWN
Mk 6: 4 not without honor, except in their **h**,
Lk 4:24 is accepted in the prophet's **h**.

HOMICIDE
Dt 4:42 to which a **h** could flee,

HONEST → HONESTY
Lev 19:36 You shall have **h** balances, **h**
       weights, an **h** ephah, and an **h** hin:
Dt 25:15 only a full and **h** weight;
Pr 12:17 speaks the truth gives **h** evidence,
   16:11 **H** balances and scales are the
Lk 20:20 sent spies who pretended to be **h**,

HONESTY· → HONEST
Ge 30:33 So my **h** will answer for me later,
Sir 27: 9 so **h** comes home to those

HONEY → HONEYCOMB
Ex 3: 8 a land flowing with milk and **h**,
  16:31 was like wafers made with **h**.
Nu 14: 8 a land that flows with milk and **h**.
Jdg 14: 8 bees in the body of the lion, and **h**.
1Sa 14:26 honeycomb, the **h** was dripping out;
Ps 19:10 sweeter also than **h**, and drippings
 119:103 sweeter than **h** to my mouth!
Pr 5: 3 the lips of a loose woman drip **h**,
  25:16 found **h**, eat only enough for you,
SS 4:11 **h** and milk are under your tongue;
Isa 7:15 and **h** by the time he knows how to
Eze 3: 3 in my mouth it was as sweet as **h**.
Mt 3: 4 and his food was locusts and wild **h**.

Rev 10: 9 but sweet as **h** in your mouth."
2Es 2:19 springs flowing with milk and **h**,

LAND FLOWING WITH MILK AND HONEY Ex 3:8, 17; 13:5; 33:3; Lev 20:24; Nu 16:13, 14; Dt 6:3; 11:9; 26:9, 15; 27:3; 31:20; Jos 5:6; Jer 11:5; 32:22; Eze 20:6, 15; Sir 46:8; Bar 1:20

HONEYCOMB → HONEY

1Sa 14:27 and dipped the tip of it in the **h**,
Pr 16:24 Pleasant words are like a **h**,
SS 5: 1 I eat my **h** with my honey,

HONOR → HONORABLE, HONORABLY, HONORED, HONORING, HONORS

Ex 20:12 **H** your father and your mother,
Dt 5:16 **H** your father and your mother,
1Sa 2: 8 with princes and inherit a seat of **h**.
 2:30 for those who **h** me I will **h**,
1Ch 29:12 Riches and **h** come from you,
2Ch 1:11 wealth, **h**, or the life of those who
 18: 1 Jehoshaphat had great riches and **h**;
Est 6: 6 man whom the king wishes to **h**?"
Ps 8: 5 and crowned them with glory and **h**.
 84:11 and shield; he bestows favor and **h**.
 112: 9 their horn is exalted in **h**.
Pr 3: 9 **H** the LORD with your substance
 3:35 wise will inherit **h**, but stubborn
 11:16 A gracious woman gets **h**,
 15:33 and humility goes before **h**.
 18:12 but humility goes before **h**.
 22: 4 and fear of the LORD is riches and **h**
 25:27 or to seek **h** on top of honor.
 25:27 or to seek honor on top of **h**.
 29:23 who is lowly in spirit will obtain **h**.
Ecc 10: 1 little folly outweighs wisdom and **h**.
Isa 29:13 and **h** me with their lips,
Mal 1: 6 a father, where is the **h** due me?
Mt 13:57 not without **h** except in their own
 15: 4 For God said, '**H** your father and
 19:19 **H** your father and mother;
 23: 6 to have the place of **h** at banquets
Mk 6: 4 "Prophets are not without **h**,
Lk 14: 8 do not sit down at the place of **h**,
Jn 4:44 a prophet has no **h** in the prophet's
 5:23 **h** the Son just as they **h** the Father.
 8:49 I **h** my Father, and you dishonor me.
 12:26 serves me, the Father will **h**.
Ro 12:10 outdo one another in showing **h**.
 13: 7 **h** to whom **h** is due.
1Co 12:23 we clothe with greater **h**,
Eph 6: 2 "**H** your father and mother"—
1Ti 5:17 considered worthy of double **h**,
Heb 2: 7 crowned them with glory and **h**,
 3: 3 the builder of a house has more **h**
1Pe 1: 7 to result in praise and glory and **h**
2Pe 1:17 For he received **h** and glory from
Rev 4: 9 the living creatures give glory and **h**
 4:11 to receive glory and **h** and power,
 5:12 and might and **h** and glory
 7:12 and **h** and power and might be to
 21:26 will bring into it the glory and the **h**
Tob 4: 3 **H** your mother and do not
Sir 3: 3 who **h** their father atone for sins,
 7:31 Fear the Lord and **h** the priest,
 44: 1 HYMN IN **H** OF OUR ANCESTORS

HONORABLE → HONOR

Php 4: 8 whatever is true, whatever is **h**,

HONORABLY → HONOR

Ro 13:13 let us live **h** as in the day,
Heb 13:18 desiring to act **h** in all things.

HONORED → HONOR

Pr 13:18 but one who heeds reproof is **h**.
 27:18 takes care of a master will be **h**.
Isa 49: 5 **h** in the sight of the LORD,
Da 4:34 and **h** the one who lives forever.
Hag 1: 8 I may take pleasure in it and be **h**,
Lk 14:10 you will be **h** in the presence of all
1Co 12:26 if one member is **h**, all rejoice

HONORING → HONOR

Sir 26:26 *A wife **h** her husband will seem wise*

HONORS → HONOR

Mal 1: 6 A son **h** his father, and servants
Mt 15: 8 'This people **h** me with their lips,

HOOF → HOOFS

Ex 10:26 not a **h** shall be left behind,
Dt 14: 6 Any animal that divides the **h**

HOOFS → HOOF

Lev 11: 3 Any animal that has divided **h**

HOOK → FISHHOOK, HOOKS

Isa 37:29 I will put my **h** in your nose and my
Mt 17:27 go to the sea and cast a **h**;

HOOKS → HOOK

Ex 26:37 their **h** shall be of gold,
Isa 2: 4 and their spears into pruning **h**;
Joel 3:10 and your pruning **h** into spears;
Am 4: 2 they shall take you away with **h**,
Mic 4: 3 and their spears into pruning **h**;

HOPE → HOPED, HOPES, HOPING

Ru 1:12 if I thought there was **h** for me,
Ezr 10: 2 there is **h** for Israel in spite of this.
Job 13:15 See, he will kill me; I have no **h**;
 17:15 where then is my **h**?
Ps 9:18 nor the **h** of the poor perish forever.
 33:17 war horse is a vain **h** for victory,
 33:18 on those who **h** in his steadfast love,
 39: 7 My **h** is in you.
 42: 5 disquieted within me? **H** in God;
 62: 5 for my **h** is from him.
 65: 5 the **h** of all the ends of the earth and
 71:14 I will **h** continually, and will praise
 119:43 for my **h** is in your ordinances.
 130: 5 my soul waits, and in his word I **h**;
 130: 7 O Israel, **h** in the LORD!
 146: 5 whose **h** is in the LORD their God,
 147:11 in those who **h** in his steadfast love.
Pr 11: 7 the wicked die, their **h** perishes,
 13:12 **H** deferred makes the heart sick,
 23:18 and your **h** will not be cut off.
 24:14 and your **h** will not be cut off.
 26:12 There is more **h** for fools than for
Ecc 9: 4 is joined with all the living has **h**,
Isa 8:17 and I will **h** in him.
Jer 14: 8 O **h** of Israel, its savior in time of
 29:11 to give you a future with **h**.
La 3:21 and therefore I have **h**:
Eze 37:11 and our **h** is lost; we are cut off
Zec 9:12 your stronghold, O prisoners of **h**;
Mt 12:21 in his name the Gentiles will **h**."
Jn 5:45 on whom you have set your **h**.
Ac 2:26 moreover my flesh will live in **h**.
 23: 6 concerning the **h** of the resurrection
Ro 4:18 against h, he believed that he would
 5: 4 and character produces **h**,
 5: 5 and **h** does not disappoint us,
 8:20 of the one who subjected it, in **h**
 8:24 Now **h** that is seen is not **h**.
 12:12 Rejoice in **h**, be patient in suffering,
 15: 4 of the scriptures we might have **h**.
 15:12 in him the Gentiles shall **h**."
 15:13 the God of **h** fill you with all joy
1Co 13:13 And now faith, **h**, and love abide,
2Co 1:10 on him we have set our **h**
 3:12 Since, then, we have such a **h**,
Eph 1:12 were the first to set our **h** on Christ,
 2:12 no **h** and without God in the world.
 4: 4 called to the one **h** of your calling,
Col 1: 5 of the **h** laid up for you in heaven.
 1:23 from the **h** promised by the gospel
 1:27 Christ in you, the **h** of glory.
1Th 1: 3 labor of love and steadfastness of **h**
 4:13 grieve as others do who have no **h**.
 5: 8 and for a helmet the **h** of salvation.
2Th 2:16 gave us eternal comfort and good **h**,
1Ti 1: 1 our Savior and of Christ Jesus our **h**,
 4:10 we have our **h** set on the living God,

Tit 1: 2 in the **h** of eternal life that God,
 2:13 the blessed **h** and the manifestation
 3: 7 heirs according to the **h** of eternal
Heb 3: 6 and the pride that belong to **h**.
 6:11 to realize the full assurance of **h** to
 6:19 this **h**, a sure and steadfast anchor
 7:19 the introduction of a better **h**,
 10:23 confession of our **h** without
1Pe 1: 3 a living **h** through the resurrection
 1:21 that your faith and **h** are set on God.
 3:15 from you an accounting for the **h**
1Jn 3: 3 all who have this **h** in him purify
Jdt 9:11 savior of those without **h**,
Sir 34:15 their **h** is in him who saves them.
Sus 1:60 who saves those who **h** in him.

HOPED → HOPE

Ps 119:74 because I have **h** in your word.
Heb 11: 1 faith is the assurance of things **h** for,
1Pe 3: 5 the holy women who **h** in God

HOPES → HOPE

Ro 8:24 For who **h** for what is seen?
1Co 13: 7 believes all things, **h** all things,
1Ti 6:17 their **h** on the uncertainty of riches,

HOPHNI*

A wicked priest (1Sa 1:3; 2:34; 4:4-17).

HOPING → HOPE

Ro 4:18 **H** against hope, he believed

HOR

Nu 33:38 Aaron the priest went up Mount **H**
Dt 32:50 brother Aaron died on Mount **H**

HOREB → =SINAI

Ex 3: 1 came to **H**, the mountain of God.
 17: 6 in front of you on the rock at **H**.
Dt 5: 2 God made a covenant with us at **H**.
1Ki 19: 8 forty days and forty nights to **H**
Ps 106:19 a calf at **H** and worshiped a cast
2Es 2:33 command from the Lord on Mount **H**

HORMAH

Nu 14:45 pursuing them as far as **H**.
 21: 3 so the place was called **H**.

HORN → HORNS

1Sa 16: 1 Fill your **h** with oil and set out;
Ps 18: 2 and the **h** of my salvation,
 92:10 exalted my **h** like that of the wild ox
 148:14 He has raised up a **h** for his people,
Da 3: 5 the sound of the **h**,
 7: 8 when another **h** appeared,
 8: 5 The goat had a **h** between its eyes.

HORNET*

Jos 24:12 I sent the **h** ahead of you,

HORNS → HORN

Ge 22:13 caught in a thicket by its **h**.
Ex 27: 2 make **h** for it on its four corners;
Jos 6: 4 trumpets of rams' **h** before the ark.
Da 7: 7 that preceded it, and it had ten **h**.
 7:24 As for the ten **h**, out of this
 8: 3 Both **h** were long, but one
Zec 1:18 And I looked up and saw four **h**.
Rev 5: 6 having seven **h** and seven eyes,
 9:13 from the four **h** of the golden altar
 12: 3 dragon, with seven heads and ten **h**,
 13: 1 rising out of the sea having ten **h**
 13:11 two **h** like a lamb and it spoke like
 17: 3 and it had seven heads and ten **h**.

HORRIBLE* → HORROR

Jer 5:30 **h** thing has happened in the land:
 18:13 The virgin Israel has done a most **h**
Hos 6:10 the house of Israel I have seen a **h**

HORROR → HORRIBLE

Dt 28:25 an object of **h** to all the kingdoms
2Ch 29: 8 he has made them an object of **h**,
Ps 55: 5 upon me, and **h** overwhelms me.
Jer 15: 4 a **h** to all the kingdoms of the earth

HORSE → HORSE'S, HORSEMEN, HORSES

Ex	15: 1	**h** and rider he has thrown into the
Est	6: 8	and a **h** that the king has ridden,
Ps	32: 9	Do not be like a **h** or a mule,
	33:17	The war **h** is a vain hope for victory,
	147:10	delight is not in the strength of the **h**
Pr	26: 3	A whip for the **h,** a bridle for the
Jer	51:21	with you I smash the **h** and its rider;
Zec	1: 8	I saw a man riding on a red **h!**
Rev	6: 2	I looked, and there was a white **h!**
	19:11	and there was a white **h!**

HORSE'S → HORSE

Rev	14:20	as high as a **h** bridle,
2Es	15:35	as high as a **h** belly

HORSEMEN → HORSE, MAN

2Ki	2:12	The chariots of Israel and its **h!"**
	18:24	on Egypt for chariots and for **h?**
Isa	31: 1	in **h** because they are very strong,
Hos	1: 7	or by horses, or by **h."**

HORSES → HORSE

Ge	47:17	food in exchange for the **h,**
Ex	14:23	all of Pharaoh's **h,** chariots, and
Dt	17:16	he must not acquire many **h** for
Jos	11: 6	you shall hamstring their **h,**
1Ki	4:26	have forty thousand stalls of **h** for
	10:26	gathered together chariots and **h;**
2Ki	2:11	a chariot of fire and **h** of fire
	6:17	full of **h** and chariots of fire
Ps	20: 7	pride in chariots, and some in **h,**
Isa	31: 3	their **h** are flesh, and not spirit.
Jer	12: 5	how will you compete with **h?**
Joel	2: 4	They have the appearance of **h,**
Zec	6: 2	The first chariot had red **h,**
	6: 2	the second chariot black **h,**
Rev	9: 7	appearance the locusts were like **h**
	19:14	following him on white **h.**

HOSANNA*

Mt	21: 9	**"H** to the Son of David!
	21: 9	**H** in the highest heaven!"
	21:15	**"H** to the Son of David,"
Mk	11: 9	who followed were shouting, **"H!**
	11:10	**H** in the highest heaven!"
Jn	12:13	went out to meet him, shouting, **"H!**

HOSEA

Prophet whose wife and family pictured the unfaithfulness of Israel (Hos 1-3).

HOSHEA → =JOSHUA

1. Original name of Joshua (Nu 13:8, 16).
2. Last king of Israel (2Ki 15:30; 17:1-6).

HOSPITABLE* → HOSPITABLY, HOSPITALITY

1Ti	3: 2	temperate, sensible, respectable, **h,**
Tit	1: 8	but he must be **h,** a lover
1Pe	4: 9	Be **h** to one another without

HOSPITABLY* → HOSPITABLE

Ac	28: 7	received us and entertained us **h**

HOSPITALITY* → HOSPITABLE

Ro	12:13	of the saints; extend **h** to strangers.
1Ti	5:10	has brought up children, shown **h,**
Heb	13: 2	not neglect to show **h** to strangers,

HOST → HOSTS

Dt	4:19	all the **h** of heaven,
1Ki	22:19	the **h** of heaven standing beside him
2Ki	17:16	worshiped all the **h** of heaven
	23: 5	and all the **h** of the heavens.
Ne	9: 6	and the **h** of heaven worships you.
Isa	34: 4	All the **h** of heaven shall rot away,
	40:26	who brings out their **h** and numbers
Da	8:10	down to the earth some of the **h**
Lk	2:13	angel a multitude of the heavenly **h,**

HOST OF HEAVEN Dt 4:19; 17:3; 1Ki 22:19; 2Ki 17:16; 21:3, 5; 23:4; 2Ch 18:18;

33:3, 5; Ne 9:6; Isa 24:21; 34:4; Jer 8:2; 19:13; 33:22; Da 4:35; 8:10; Ac 7:42; Man 1:15

HOSTILE → HOSTILITY

Lev	26:21	If you continue **h** to me,
Ro	8: 7	that is set on the flesh is **h** to God;
Col	1:21	once estranged and **h** in mind,

HOSTILITY → HOSTILE

Hos	9: 8	and **h** in the house of his God.
Eph	2:14	the dividing wall, that is, the **h**
	2:16	putting to death that **h** through it.
Heb	12: 3	Consider him who endured such **h**

HOSTS → HOST

1Sa	1: 3	and to sacrifice to the LORD of **h**
1Ki	19:10	for the LORD, the God of **h;**
Ps	46: 7	The LORD of **h** is with us;
	59: 5	LORD God of **h,** are God of Israel.
	103:21	Bless the LORD, all his **h,**
Isa	48: 2	the LORD of **h** is his name.
Jer	23:36	the LORD of **h,** our God.
2Es	6: 3	innumerable **h** of angels were

*GOD OF HOSTS 2Sa 5:10; 1Ki 19:10, 14; Ps 59:5; 80:4, 7, 14, 19; 84:8; 89:8; Jer 5:14; 15:16; 35:17; 38:17; 44:7; Hos 12:5; Am 3:13; 4:13; 5:14, 15, 16, 27; 6:8, 14; 1Es 9:46

*LORD †GOD OF HOSTS Ps 69:6; Isa 3:15; 10:23, 24; 22:5, 12, 14, 15; 28:22; Jer 2:19; 46:10, 10; 49:5; 50:25, 31; Am 9:5

†LORD OF HOSTS 1Sa 1:3, 11; 4:4; 15:2; 17:45; 2Sa 6:2, 18; 7:8, 26, 27; 1Ki 18:15; 2Ki 3:14; 19:31; 1Ch 11:9; 17:7, 24; Ps 24:10; 46:7, 11; 48:8; 84:1, 3, 12; Isa 1:9, 24; 2:12; 3:1; 5:7, 9, 16, 24; 6:3, 5; 8:13, 18; 9:7, 13, 19; 10:16, 26, 33; 13:4, 13; 14:22, 23, 24, 27; 17:3; 18:7, 7; 19:4, 12, 16, 17, 18, 20, 25; 21:10; 22:14, 25; 23:9; 24:23; 25:6; 28:5, 29; 29:6; 31:4, 5; 37:16, 32; 39:5; 44:6; 45:13; 47:4; 48:2; 51:15; 54:5; Jer 6:6, 9; 7:3, 21; 8:3; 9:7, 15, 17; 10:16; 11:17, 20, 22; 16:9; 19:3, 11, 15; 20:12; 23:15, 16, 36; 25:8, 27, 28, 29, 32; 26:18; 27:4, 18, 19, 21; 28:2, 14; 29:4, 8, 17, 21, 25; 30:8; 31:23, 35; 32:14, 15, 18; 33:11, 12; 35:13, 18, 19; 39:16; 42:15, 18; 43:10; 44:2, 11, 25; 46:18, 25; 48:1, 15; 49:7, 26, 35; 50:18, 33, 34; 51:5, 14, 19, 33, 57, 58; Mic 4:4; Na 2:13; 3:5; Hab 2:13; Zep 2:9, 10; Hag 1:2, 5, 7, 9, 14; 2:4, 6, 7, 8, 9, 9, 11, 23, 23; Zec 1:3, 3, 3, 4, 6, 12, 14, 16, 17; 2:8, 9, 11; 3:7, 9, 10; 4:6, 9; 5:4; 6:12, 15; 7:3, 4, 9, 12, 12, 13; 8:1, 2, 3, 4, 6, 6, 7, 9, 9, 11, 14, 14, 18, 19, 20, 21, 22, 23; 9:15; 10:3; 12:5; 13:2, 7; 14:16, 17, 21, 21; Mal 1:4, 6, 8, 9, 10, 11, 13, 14; 2:2, 4, 7, 8, 12, 16; 3:1, 5, 7, 10, 11, 12, 14, 17; 4:1, 3

HOT → HOT-TEMPERED, HOTHEAD, HOTHEADS

Ex	11: 8	And in **h** anger he left Pharaoh.
Ps	39: 3	my heart became **h** within me.
	85: 3	you turned from your **h** anger.
Pr	6:28	Or can one walk on **h** coals without
La	4:11	he poured out his **h** anger.
1Ti	4: 2	consciences are seared with a **h** iron
Rev	3:15	you are neither cold nor **h.**

HOT-TEMPERED* → HOT, TEMPER

Jdg	18:25	or else **h** fellows will attack you,
Pr	15:18	Those who are **h** stir up strife,
Sir	28: 8	for the **h** kindle strife,

HOTHEAD* → HEAD, HOT

Pr	29:22	the **h** causes much transgression.

HOTHEADS* → HEAD, HOT

Pr	22:24	and do not associate with **h,**

HOUR

Mt	6:27	by worrying add a single **h** to your
	8:13	the servant was healed in that **h.**
	24:36	about that day and **h** no one knows,
Mk	14:35	if it were possible, the **h** might pass

	14:37	Could you not keep awake one **h?**
Lk	12:40	is coming at an unexpected **h."**
Jn	2: 4	My **h** has not yet come."
	7:30	because his **h** had not yet come.
	8:20	because his **h** had not yet come.
	12:23	**h** has come for the Son of Man to
	12:27	'Father, save me from this **h'?**
	13: 1	Jesus knew that his **h** had come
	17: 1	"Father, the **h** has come;
1Jn	2:18	Children, it is the last **h!**
Rev	3:10	I will keep you from the **h** of trial
	8: 1	silence in heaven for about half an **h**
	14: 7	for the **h** of his judgment has come;
	17:12	receive authority as kings for one **h,**
	18:10	in one **h** your judgment has come."

HOUSE → HOUSEHOLD, HOUSEHOLDS, HOUSES, HOUSETOP, HOUSETOPS, STOREHOUSE, STOREHOUSES

Ge	19: 2	turn aside to your servant's **h** and
	24:23	in your father's **h** for us to spend
	28:17	none other than the **h** of God,
Ex	12:22	shall go outside the door of your **h**
	20:17	shall not covet your neighbor's **h;**
Nu	12: 7	he is entrusted with all my **h.**
Dt	5:21	shall you desire your neighbor's **h,**
Jos	2: 1	the **h** of a prostitute whose name
	6:22	"Go into the prostitute's **h,**
1Sa	1: 7	as she went up to the **h** of the LORD,
2Sa	2:10	But the **h** of Judah followed David.
	3: 1	There was a long war between the **h** of Saul and the **h** of David;
	7: 5	Are you the one to build me a **h** to
	7:11	that the LORD will make you a **h.**
	23: 5	Is not my **h** like this with God?
1Ki	8:43	name has been invoked on this **h**
2Ki	15: 5	and lived in a separate **h.**
1Ch	9:23	in charge of the gates of the **h** of
	17:12	He shall build a **h** for me,
	22: 1	"Here shall be the **h** of the LORD
Ezr	1: 5	rebuild the **h** of the LORD in
	3:11	the foundation of the **h** of the LORD
Ne	10:39	will not neglect the **h** of our God.
Ps	23: 6	in the **h** of the LORD my whole life
	27: 4	in the **h** of the LORD all the days of
	52: 8	a green olive tree in the **h** of God.
	69: 9	zeal for your **h** that has consumed
	84:10	be a doorkeeper in the **h** of my God
	122: 1	"Let us go to the **h** of the LORD!"
	127: 1	Unless the LORD builds the **h,**
Pr	7:27	Her **h** is the way to Sheol,
	9: 1	Wisdom has built her **h,** she has
	14: 1	The wise woman builds her **h,**
	14:11	The **h** of the wicked is destroyed,
	21: 9	iof the housetop than in a **h** shared
Ecc	10:18	and through indolence the **h** leaks.
Isa	5: 8	Ah, you who join **h** to **h,**
	7:13	said: "Hear then, O **h** of David!
	56: 7	my **h** shall be called a **h** of prayer
Jer	3:18	In those days the **h** of Judah shall join the **h** of Israel,
	7:11	this **h,** which is called by my name,
	18: 2	go down to the potter's **h,**
	31:31	a new covenant with the **h** of Israel and the **h** of Judah.
	32:34	set up their abominations in the **h**
Eze	2: 8	rebellious like that rebellious **h;**
	33: 7	made a sentinel for the **h** of Israel;
	39:29	my spirit upon the **h** of Israel,
Joel	3:18	come forth from the **h** of the LORD
Hag	1: 4	while this **h** lies in ruins?
	2: 7	and I will fill this **h** with splendor,
Zec	8: 9	the **h** of the LORD of hosts.
	13: 6	wounds I received in the **h** of my
Mt	7:24	like a wise man who built his **h**
	12:29	a strong man's **h** and plunder his
	13:57	own country and in their own **h."**
	21:13	'My **h** shall be called a **h** of prayer';
Mk	3:25	And if a **h** is divided against itself,
	3:25	that **h** will not be able to stand.
Lk	6:48	That one is like a man building a **h,**
	10: 7	Do not move about from **h** to **h.**

11:17 and **h** falls on **h**.
11:24 return to my **h** from which I came.'
15: 8 does not light a lamp, sweep the **h**,
19: 9 "Today salvation has come to this **h**,
Jn 2:16 my Father's **h** a marketplace!"
2:17 "Zeal for your **h** will consume me."
12: 3 **h** was filled with the fragrance of
14: 2 In my Father's **h** there are many
Ac 20:20 publicly and from **h** to **h**,
Ro 16: 5 Greet also the church in their **h**.
2Co 5: 1 a **h** not made with hands,
Heb 3: 2 also "was faithful in all God's **h**."
8: 8 a new covenant with the **h** of Israel
10:21 a great priest over the **h** of God,
1Pe 2: 5 be built into a spiritual **h**,
2Jn 1:10 into the **h** or welcome anyone who
Jdt 9:13 and against your sacred **h**,
1Mc 7:37 "You chose this **h** to be called by

HOUSE OF DAVID 1Sa 20:16; 2Sa 3:1, 6;
1Ki 12:19, 20, 26; 13:2; 14:8; 2Ki 17:21; 2Ch
10:19; 21:7; Ne 12:37; Ps 122:5; Isa 7:2, 13;
22:22; Jer 21:12; Zec 12:7, 8, 10, 12; 13:1; Lk
1:27; Tob 1:4; Sir 48:15; 1Es 5:5

HOUSE OF ... *GOD Ge 28:17; Jos 9:23;
Jdg 18:31; 2Ki 19:37; 1Ch 6:48; 9:11, 13, 26,
27; 22:1, 2; 23:28; 25:6; 26:20; 28:12, 21;
29:2, 3, 3, 7; 2Ch 3:3; 4:11, 19; 5:1, 14; 7:5;
15:18; 22:12; 23:3, 9; 24:5, 7, 13, 27; 25:24;
28:24, 24; 31:13, 21; 32:21; 33:7; 34:9; 35:8;
36:18, 19; Ezr 1:4; 2:68; 3:8, 9; 4:24; 5:2, 8,
13, 14, 15, 16, 17; 6:3, 5, 5, 7, 8, 12, 16, 17,
22; 7:16, 17, 19, 20, 23, 24; 8:17, 25, 30, 33,
36; 9:9; 10:1, 6, 9; Ne 6:10; 8:16; 10:32, 33,
34, 36, 36, 37, 38, 39; 11:11, 16, 22; 12:40;
13:4, 7, 9, 11, 14; Ps 42:4; 52:8; 55:14; 84:10;
135:2; Ecc 5:1; Isa 2:3; 37:38; Da 1:2; 5:3;
Hos 9:8; Joel 1:13, 16; Am 2:8; Mic 4:2; Mt
12:4; Mk 2:26; Lk 6:4; Heb 10:21; Jdt 9:1; Bar
3:24; 1Es 5:58

HOUSE OF ISRAEL Ex 16:31; 40:38; Lev
10:6; 17:3, 8, 10; 22:18; Nu 20:29; Jos 21:45;
Ru 4:11; 1Sa 7:2, 3; 2Sa 1:12; 6:5, 15; 12:8;
16:3; 1Ki 12:21; 20:31; Ps 98:3; 115:12;
135:19; Isa 5:7; 14:2; 46:3; 63:7; Jer 2:4, 26;
3:18, 20; 5:11, 15; 9:26; 10:1; 11:10, 17;
13:11; 18:6, 6; 23:8; 31:27, 31, 33; 33:14, 17;
48:13; Eze 3:1, 4, 5, 7, 7, 17; 4:3, 4, 5; 5:4;
6:11; 8:6, 10, 11, 12; 9:9; 11:5, 15; 12:6, 9, 10,
24, 27; 13:5, 9; 14:4, 5, 6, 7, 11; 17:2; 18:6,
15, 25, 29, 29, 30, 31; 20:13, 27, 30, 31, 39,
40, 44; 22:18; 24:21; 28:24, 25; 29:6, 16, 21;
33:7, 10, 11, 20; 34:30; 35:15; 36:10, 17, 21,
22, 22, 32, 37; 37:11, 16; 39:12, 22, 23, 25, 29;
40:4; 43:7, 10; 44:6, 6, 12, 22; 45:6, 8, 17, 17;
Hos 1:4, 6; 5:1; 6:10; 11:12; Am 5:1, 4, 25;
6:1, 14; 7:10; 9:9; Mic 1:5; 3:1, 9; Zec 8:13;
Mt 10:6; 15:24; Ac 2:36; 7:42; Heb 8:8, 10;
Jdt 4:15; 6:17; 8:6; 13:14; 14:5, 10; 16:24; Bar
2:26; 3Mc 2:10

HOUSE OF JUDAH 2Sa 2:4, 7, 10, 11; 1Ki
12:21, 23; 2Ki 19:30; 1Ch 28:4; 2Ch 11:1;
19:11; 22:10; Ne 4:16; Isa 22:21; 37:31; Jer
3:18; 5:11; 11:10, 17; 12:14; 13:11; 31:27, 31;
33:14; 36:3; Eze 4:6; 8:17; 25:3, 8, 12; Hos
1:7; 5:12, 14; Zep 2:7; Zec 8:13, 15, 19; 10:3,
6; 12:4; Heb 8:8; Bar 2:26

FATHER'S HOUSE Ge 12:1; 20:13; 24:7,
23, 38, 40; 28:21; 31:14, 30; 38:11, 11; 41:51;
Lev 22:13; Nu 30:3, 16; Dt 22:21, 21; Jdg 9:5,
18; 11:2, 7; 14:15, 19; 19:2, 3; 1Sa 18:2; 22:1,
11, 15, 16, 22; 24:21; 2Sa 3:29; 14:9; 19:28;
24:17; 1Ki 2:31; 18:18; 1Ch 21:17; 28:4; 2Ch
21:13; Ps 45:10; Lk 2:49; 16:27; Jn 2:16; 14:2;
Ac 7:20; Tob 6:16; Sir 42:10; 1Mc 16:2; Pm
151:1; 4Mc 18:7

HOUSE OF JACOB Ge 46:27; Ex 19:3; Ps
114:1; Isa 2:5, 6; 8:17; 10:20; 14:1; 29:22;
46:3; 48:1; 58:1; Jer 2:4; 5:20; Eze 20:5; Am
3:13; 9:8; Ob 1:17, 18; Mic 2:7; 3:9; Lk 1:33;
Ac 7:46; 1Mc 1:28; 2Es 12:46

HOUSE OF SLAVERY Ex 13:3, 14; 20:2;
Dt 5:6; 6:12; 7:8; 8:14; 13:5, 10; Jos 24:17;
Jdg 6:8; Jer 34:13; Mic 6:4

HOUSE OF THE *LORD Bar 1:8, 14; 1Es
1:55; 2:5; 5:62; 6:2, 20, 22, 24, 26, 27, 28, 33;
8:79

HOUSE OF THE †LORD Ex 23:19; 34:26;
Dt 23:18; Jos 6:24; 1Sa 1:7, 24; 3:15; 2Sa
12:20; 1Ki 3:1; 6:1, 37; 7:12, 40, 45, 48, 51,
51; 8:10, 11, 63, 64; 9:1, 10, 15; 10:5, 12;
12:27; 14:26, 28; 15:15, 18; 2Ki 11:3, 4, 4, 7,
10, 13, 15, 18, 19; 12:4, 4, 9, 9, 10, 11, 11, 12,
13, 13, 14, 16, 18; 14:14; 15:35; 16:8, 14, 18;
18:15; 19:1, 14; 20:5, 8; 21:4, 5; 22:3, 4, 5, 5,
8, 9; 23:2, 2, 6, 7, 11, 12, 24; 24:13; 25:9, 13,
13, 16; 1Ch 6:31, 32; 9:23; 22:1, 11, 14; 23:4,
24, 28, 32; 24:19; 25:6; 26:12, 22, 27; 28:12,
13, 13, 20; 29:8; 2Ch 3:1; 4:16; 5:1, 13; 7:2, 7,
11, 11; 8:1, 16, 16; 9:4, 11; 12:9, 11; 15:8;
16:2; 20:5, 28; 23:5, 6, 12, 14, 18, 18, 19, 20;
24:4, 7, 8, 12, 12, 14, 14, 18, 21; 26:19, 21;
27:3; 28:21, 24; 29:3, 5, 15, 16, 16, 17, 18, 20,
25, 31, 35; 30:1, 15; 31:10, 11, 16; 33:4, 5, 15,
15; 34:8, 10, 10, 14, 15, 17, 30, 30; 35:2; 36:7,
10, 14, 18; Ezr 1:3, 5, 7; 2:68; 3:8, 11; 7:27;
8:29; Ne 10:35; Ps 23:6; 27:4; 92:13; 116:19;
118:26; 122:1, 9; 134:1; 135:2; Isa 37:1, 14;
38:20, 22; 66:20; Jer 17:26; 20:1, 2; 26:2, 7, 9,
10, 10; 27:18, 21; 28:1, 5, 6; 29:26; 33:11;
35:2, 4; 36:5, 10; 52:13, 17, 17, 20; La 2:7;
Eze 8:14, 16; 10:19; 11:1; Hos 8:1; 9:4; Joel
1:9, 14; 3:18; Hag 1:14; Zec 7:3; 8:9; 11:13;
14:20, 21

KING'S HOUSE 2Sa 11:2, 8, 9; 15:35; 1Ki
9:1, 10; 10:12; 14:26, 27; 15:18; 16:18, 18;
2Ki 11:5, 16, 19, 20; 12:18; 14:14; 16:8;
18:15; 24:13; 25:9; 2Ch 7:11; 9:11; 12:9, 10;
16:2; 21:17; 23:5, 15, 20; 25:24; Est 9:4; Jer
26:10; 36:12; 38:7, 8; 39:8; 52:13

LORD'S* HOUSE 2Ch 7:2; Isa 2:2; Jer 7:2;
19:14; 26:2; 27:16; 28:3; 36:6, 8, 10; 51:51;
Mic 4:1; Hag 1:2

MY HOUSE Ge 15:2, 3; 41:40; Lev 14:35;
Nu 12:7; Jdg 11:31; 1Sa 20:15; 21:15; 2Sa
7:18; 11:11; 23:5; 1Ki 21:2; 2Ki 20:15; 1Ch
17:14, 16; 28:6; Job 17:13; 19:15; Ps 101:2, 7;
132:3; Pr 7:6; Ecc 2:7; Isa 3:7; 39:4; 56:5, 7, 7;
Jer 11:15; 12:7; 23:11; Eze 8:1; 23:39; Hos
9:15; Hag 1:9; Zec 1:16; 3:7; 9:8; Mal 3:10;
Mt 12:44; 21:13; Mk 11:17; Lk 11:24; 14:23;
19:46; Ac 10:30; Wis 8:16

REBELLIOUS HOUSE Eze 2:5, 6, 7, 8;
3:9, 26, 27; 12:2, 3, 3, 9, 25; 17:12; 24:3; 44:6

THIS HOUSE Ge 39:9; 1Ki 6:12; 8:27, 29,
31, 33, 38, 42, 43; 9:3, 8, 8; 2Ki 21:7; 2Ch
6:18, 20, 22, 24, 29, 32, 33; 7:16, 20, 21, 21;
20:9, 9; 33:7; Ezr 3:12; 5:3, 9, 12, 13, 17; 6:7,
7, 8, 12, 15, 16, 17; 7:24; Jer 7:10, 11; 22:4, 5;
26:6, 9, 12; Hag 1:4; 2:3, 7, 9; Zec 4:9; Lk
10:5; 19:9; 1Mc 7:35, 37; 2Mc 14:36; 1Es 6:4,
11, 17, 27

WHOLE HOUSE Lev 10:6; 2Sa 3:19; 1Ki
6:10, 22, 22; 2Ki 9:8; Ne 4:16; Jer 13:11, 11;
35:3; Eze 11:15; 36:10; 37:11; 39:25; 45:6; Jdt
4:15; Sir 1:17

HOUSEHOLD → HOUSE
Ge 7: 1 "Go into the ark, you and all your **h**,
31:19 and Rachel stole her father's **h** gods.
Ex 12: 3 for each family, a lamb for each **h**.
Jos 24:15 and my **h**, we will serve the LORD."
Pr 31:21 not afraid for her **h** when it snows,
31:27 She looks well to the ways of her **h**,
Mic 7: 6 enemies are members of your own **h**
Mt 10:36 will be members of one's own **h**.
Jn 4:53 believed, along with his whole **h**.
Ac 16:31 you will be saved, you and your **h**."
Eph 2:19 and also members of the **h** of God,
1Ti 3: 4 He must manage his own **h** well,
3:15 how one ought to behave in the **h**

Tit 2: 5 good managers of the **h**, kind,
1Pe 4:17 judgment to begin with the **h** of God

HOUSEHOLDS → HOUSE
Nu 16:32 them up, along with their **h**—
Dt 11: 6 along with their **h**, their tents,

HOUSES → HOUSE
Ex 12: 7 two doorposts and the lintel of the **h**
12:27 passed over the **h** of the Israelites in
Isa 65:21 They shall build **h** and inhabit them;
Jer 29:28 build **h** and live in them,
Eze 11: 3 'The time is not near to build **h**;
Mt 19:29 everyone who has left **h** or brothers
Mk 12:40 devour widows' **h** and for the sake
Ac 4:34 owned lands or **h** sold them and
1Mc 1:31 tore down its **h** and its surrounding

HOUSETOP → HOUSE
Ps 102: 7 I am like a lonely bird on the **h**.
Mt 24:17 the one on the **h** must not go down

HOUSETOPS → HOUSE
Isa 37:27 like grass on the **h**,
Mt 10:27 whispered, proclaim from the **h**.

HOVERING* → HOVERS
Isa 31: 5 Like birds **h** overhead, so the LORD

HOVERS* → HOVERING
Dt 32:11 an eagle stirs up its nest, and **h** over

HOW
Ge 6:15 This is **h** you are to make it:
28:17 and said, "**H** awesome is this place!
Ex 12:11 This is **h** you shall eat it:
Nu 23: 8 **H** can I curse whom God has not
Dt 31:27 **h** much more after my death!
2Sa 1:19 **H** the mighty have fallen!
1Ki 3: 7 I do not know **h** to go out or come
2Ch 6:18 **h** much less this house that I have
Job 25: 4 **H** then can a mortal be righteous
25: 4 **H** can one born of woman be pure?
Ps 6: 3 while you, O LORD—**h** long?
8: 1 **h** majestic is your name in all the
31:19 O **h** abundant is your goodness that
36: 7 **H** precious is your steadfast love,
92: 5 **H** great are your works, O LORD!
119: 9 **H** can young people keep their way
147: 1 **H** good it is to sing praises to our
Pr 15:23 and a word in season, **h** good it is!
Isa 1:21 **H** the faithful city has become a
14:12 **H** you are fallen from heaven,
Jer 1: 6 Truly I do not know **h** to speak,
La 1: 1 **H** lonely sits the city that once was
Eze 33:10 **h** then can we live?"
Hos 11: 8 **H** can I give you up, Ephraim?
Mal 1: 2 you say, "**H** have you loved us?"
Mk 9:50 lost its saltiness, **h** can you season
10:23 "**H** hard it will be for those who
Lk 12:27 Consider the lilies, **h** they grow:
20:44 so **h** can he be his son?"
Jn 3: 4 "**H** can anyone be born after having
7:15 **H** does this man have such learning
Eph 5:15 Be careful then **h** you live,
1Ti 3: 5 not know **h** to manage his own
3: 5 **h** can he take care of God's church?
Heb 2: 3 **h** can we escape if we neglect so
2Pe 2: 9 Lord knows **h** to rescue the godly

HUGE
Jos 10:11 the LORD threw down **h** stones
Rev 16:21 **h** hailstones, each weighing about

HULDAH*
Prophetess inquired by Hilkiah for Josiah (2Ki
22; 2Ch 34:14-28).

HUMAN → HUMANITY, HUMANKIND,
HUMANS
Ge 6: 7 blot out from the earth the **h** beings
Nu 19:16 who has died naturally, or a **h** bone,
1Ki 13: 2 **h** bones shall be burned on you.'"
2Ki 23:14 and covered the sites with **h** bones.

Ps   8: 4 are **h** beings that you are mindful
     22: 6 But I am a worm, and not **h;**
    104:15 and wine to gladden the **h** heart,
Pr   16: 9 The **h** mind plans the way,
Ecc   6: 7 All **h** toil is for the mouth,
      7:29 God made **h** beings straightforward,
Isa 37:19 but the work of **h** hands—
     52:14 beyond **h** semblance, and his form
Da   2:34 a stone was cut out, not by **h** hands,
      5: 5 the fingers of a **h** hand appeared
      8:25 shall be broken, and not by **h** hands.
Hos 11: 4 I led them with cords of **h** kindness,
Mt   9: 8 given such authority to **h** beings.
     15: 9 teaching **h** precepts as doctrines.'"
Mk   7:21 from within, from the **h** heart,
Lk   20: 6 'Of **h** origin,' all the people will
Jn   5:34 Not that I accept such **h** testimony,
      8:15 judge by **h** standards; I judge no one
Ac   5:29 obey God rather than any **h**
      5:38 or this undertaking is of **h** origin,
1Co   1:26 of you were wise by **h** standards,
      2:13 in words not taught by **h** wisdom
2Co   3: 3 but on tablets of **h** hearts.
Php   2: 7 being born in **h** likeness.
Col   2: 8 according to **h** tradition,
      2:22 they are simply **h** commands
1Th   4: 8 rejects not **h** authority but God,
Heb 12: 9 we had **h** parents to discipline us,
Rev   4: 7 with a face like a **h** face,
      9: 7 their faces were like **h** faces,
Jdt   8:16 for God is not like a **h** being,
Sir 17: 1 Lord created **h** beings out of earth,

HUMAN BEING Ex 19:13; Lev 22:5; 24:17,
  21; 27:2; Nu 19:11, 13; 23:19; Job 12:10; 25:6;
  Isa 51:12; 66:3; Eze 1:10; 8:2; 10:14; 29:8; Da
  7:4, 13; Jnh 3:7; Mt 12:12; Jn 10:33; 16:21; Ro
  1:23; 3:20; 9:20; 1Co 2:11; 15:21, 21; Gal
  1:16; Jas 5:17; Jdt 8:16; Wis 13:13; 14:15, 20;
  15:16; 2Es 8:6; 16:27

HUMAN BEINGS Ge 6:7; 7:21, 23; 9:5; Ex
  12:12; 13:2; Lev 27:29; Nu 18:15; Dt 4:32;
  20:19; 2Sa 7:14; 2Ch 19:6; Job 4:17; 5:7; 7:1,
  17; 35:8; Ps 8:4; 115:16; 135:8; 144:3; Ecc
  1:13; 3:18; 6:10; 7:29; Jer 5:26; 7:20; 10:23;
  21:6; 32:43; 33:10, 12; 36:29; 50:3; 51:62; Eze
  14:13, 17; 27:13; 36:11; 38:20; Da 2:38; 4:17;
  Jnh 3:8; Hag 1:11; Mt 9:8; Lk 16:15; Jn 5:41;
  1Co 15:39; 2Co 10:3; Heb 2:6; 6:16; Jdt 11:7;
  AdE 16:24; Wis 7:20; 9:6; Sir 1:15; 10:18;
  17:1; 17:30, 32; 18:7, 8, 13; 31:27; 33:10;
  38:6; LtJ 6:11; 1Es 4:37; 3Mc 2:15; 2Es 13:41;
  16:61; 4Mc 2:21; 14:14

HUMAN HANDS Dt 4:28; 2Sa 24:14; 2Ki
  19:18; 1Ch 21:13; 2Ch 32:19; Ps 115:4;
  135:15; Isa 37:19; Eze 1:8; 10:21; Da 2:34;
  8:25; Mt 17:22; Mk 9:31; Lk 9:44; Ac 7:48;
  17:24, 25; Eph 2:11; Heb 9:24; Wis 13:10; LtJ
  6:51

HUMAN HEART Ge 8:21; 1Ki 8:39; 2Ch
  6:30; Ps 64:6; 104:15, 15; Pr 12:25; 25:20;
  27:19; Ecc 8:11; Isa 13:7; Mk 7:21; Ac 15:8;
  1Co 2:9; Jdt 8:14; Sir 42:18

HUMANITY* → HUMAN
Job   7:20 you watcher of **h?**
Zep   1: 3 I will cut off **h** from the face of the
Eph   2:15 create in himself one new **h**

HUMANKIND → HUMAN
Ge   1:26 "Let us make **h** in our image,
      6: 5 that the wickedness of **h** was great
Ps   33:13 he sees all **h.**
    107: 8 for his wonderful works to **h.**
Mk   2:27 "The sabbath was made for **h,**
1Ti   2: 5 one mediator between God and **h,**
Rev 14: 4 redeemed from **h** as first fruits
Sir 33:10 and **h** was created out of the dust.

HUMANS → HUMAN
Ge   6: 4 went in to the daughters of **h,**
     32:28 striven with God and with **h,**
Ps   36: 6 you save **h** and animals alike,

Ecc   3:19 the fate of **h** and the fate of animals

HUMBLE → HUMBLED, HUMBLY
Ex   10: 3 long will you refuse to **h** yourself
Nu   12: 3 Now the man Moses was very **h,**
Dt   8: 2 to **h** you, testing you to know what
      8:16 to **h** you and to test you,
2Sa 22:28 You deliver a **h** people, but your
2Ch   7:14 by my name **h** themselves,
     33:23 did not **h** himself before the Lᴏʀᴅ,
     36:12 He did not **h** himself before
Job 22:29 for he saves the **h.**
Ps   18:27 For you deliver a **h** people,
     25: 9 He leads the **h** in what is right,
     25: 9 and teaches the **h** his way.
     34: 2 let the **h** hear and be glad.
     55:19 will hear, and will **h** them—
     89:22 the wicked shall not **h** him.
    149: 4 he adorns the **h** with victory.
Pr   3:34 but to the **h** he shows favor.
     11: 2 but wisdom is with the **h.**
Isa 57:15 to revive the spirit of the **h,**
     58: 5 a day to **h** oneself?
     66: 2 to the **h** and contrite in spirit,
Da   10:12 understanding and to **h** yourself
Zep   2: 3 Seek the Lᴏʀᴅ, all you **h** of the land
      3:12 leave in the midst of you a people **h**
Mt   11:29 for I am gentle and **h** in heart,
     21: 5 **h,** and mounted on a donkey,
Lk   14:11 who **h** themselves will be exalted."
2Co 12:21 my God may **h** me before you,
Jas   4: 6 the proud, but gives grace to the **h.**"
      4:10 **H** yourselves before the Lord,
1Pe   3: 8 a tender heart, and a **h** mind.
      5: 5 but gives grace to the **h.**"
      5: 6 **H** yourselves therefore under the
Sir   3:20 but by the **h** he is glorified.
     11: 1 The wisdom of the **h** lifts
     35:21 prayer of the **h** pierces the clouds,
1Mc 14:14 He gave help to all the **h**

HUMBLED → HUMBLE
Lev 26:41 then their uncircumcised heart is **h**
Dt   8: 3 He **h** you by letting you hunger,
1Ki 21:29 "Have you seen how Ahab has **h**
2Ki 22:19 and you **h** yourself before the Lᴏʀᴅ,
2Ch 12: 7 When the Lᴏʀᴅ saw that they **h**
     33:12 and **h** himself greatly before
     34:27 and you **h** yourself before God
Ps   69:10 When I **h** my soul with fasting,
    119:67 I was **h** I went astray,
    119:71 It is good for me that I was **h,**
Isa   2: 9 so people are **h,** and everyone is
      2:11 pride of everyone shall be **h;**
Da   5:22 Belshazzar his son, have not **h** your
Mt   23:12 All who exalt themselves will be **h,**
Lk   14:11 all who exalt themselves will be **h,**
Php   2: 8 he **h** himself and became obedient
Jdt   4: 9 **h** themselves with much fasting.

HUMBLY* → HUMBLE
Mic   6: 8 and to walk **h** with your God?

HUMILIATE* → HUMILIATION, HUMILITY
1Co 11:22 and **h** those who have nothing?

HUMILIATION → HUMILIATE
Pr   29:23 A person's pride will bring **h,**
Ac   8:33 In his **h** justice was denied him.
Php   3:21 He will transform the body of our **h**
Sir   2: 4 and in times of **h** be patient.

HUMILITY* → HUMILIATE
Pr   15:33 and **h** goes before honor.
     18:12 is haughty, but **h** goes before honor.
     22: 4 reward for **h** and fear of the Lᴏʀᴅ
Zep   2: 3 seek righteousness, seek **h;**
Ac   20:19 serving the Lord with all **h** and with
Eph   2: 2 all **h** and gentleness, with patience,
Php   2: 3 but in **h** regard others as better than
Col   2:23 **h,** and severe treatment of the body,
      3:12 with compassion, kindness,
1Pe   5: 5 must clothe yourselves with **h**

Sir   1:27 fidelity and **h** are his delight.
      3:17 perform your tasks with **h;**
     10:28 My child, honor yourself with **h,**
     13:20 **H** is an abomination to the proud;
     36:28 If kindness and **h** mark her speech,

HUNDRED → HUNDREDFOLD
Ge   6: 3 days shall be one **h** twenty years."
     15:13 shall be oppressed for four **h** years;
     17:17 born to a man who is a **h** years old?
1Ki 18:13 I hid a **h** of the Lᴏʀᴅ's prophets
Isa 65:20 one who dies at a **h** years will be
Mt   18:12 If a shepherd has a **h** sheep,
Lk   7:41 owed five **h** denarii, and the other
Ac   1:15 numbered about one **h** twenty
Ro   4:19 (for he was about a **h** years old),
1Co 15: 6 appeared to more than five **h**
Rev   7: 4 one **h** forty-four thousand,
     13:18 Its number is six **h** sixty-six.

HUNDREDFOLD → HUNDRED
Ge   26:12 and in the same year reaped a **h.**
Mt   13: 8 some a **h,** some sixty, some thirty.

HUNG → HANG
Dt   21:23 **h** on a tree is under God's curse.
Jos 10:26 and he **h** them on five trees.
Ps 137: 2 the willows there we **h** up our harps.
Mk   9:42 if a great millstone were **h** around

HUNGER → HUNGRY
Ex   16: 3 to kill this whole assembly with **h.**"
Dt   8: 3 He humbled you by letting you **h,**
Ne   9:15 For their **h** you gave them bread
Pr   19:15 an idle person will suffer **h.**
Isa 49:10 not **h** or thirst,
Mt   5: 6 "Blessed are those who **h** and thirst
2Co   6: 5 riots, labors, sleepless nights, **h;**
Rev   7:16 will **h** no more, and thirst no more;

HUNGRY → HUNGER
Job 24:10 though **h,** they carry the sheaves;
Ps   50:12 "If I were **h,** I would not tell you,
    107: 9 and the **h** he fills with good things.
    146: 7 who gives food to the **h.**
Pr   10: 3 Lᴏʀᴅ does not let the righteous go **h**
     25:21 If your enemies are **h,** give them
Isa 29: 8 as when a **h** person dreams of
                 eating and wakes up still **h,**
     58: 7 to share your bread with the **h,**
Eze 18: 7 gives his bread to the **h** and covers
Mt   12: 1 his disciples were **h,** and they began
     15:32 I do not want to send them away **h,**
     25:35 for I was **h** and you gave me food,
     25:42 I was **h** and you gave me no food,
Mk   11:12 they came from Bethany, he was **h.**
Lk   1:53 he has filled the **h** with good things,
Jn   6:35 comes to me will never be **h,**
Ro   12:20 "if your enemies are **h,** feed them;
1Co   4:11 To the present hour we are **h** and
     11:34 If you are **h,** eat at home,
Php   4:12 of being well-fed and of going **h,**
Tob   4:16 Give some of your food to the **h,**
Sir   4: 2 Do not grieve the **h,**

HUNT → HUNTED, HUNTER
Ge   27: 3 to the field, and **h** game for me.

HUNTED → HUNT
La   3:52 without cause have **h** me like a bird;

HUNTER → HUNT
Ge   10: 9 Nimrod a mighty **h** before the Lᴏʀᴅ
     25:27 boys grew up, Esau was a skillful **h,**

HUR
Ex   17:12 Aaron and **H** held up his hands,

HURAM → =HIRAM
2Ch   4:11 And **H** made the pots, the shovels,

HURAM-ABI → =HIRAM
2Ch   2:13 have dispatched **H,** a skilled artisan,

HURRIED → HURRY

1Sa 25:34 unless you had **h** and come
Da   6:19 and **h** to the den of lions.

HURRIES → HURRY

Ecc 1: 5 and **h** to the place where it rises.

HURRY → HURRIED, HURRIES

Ge 19:22 **H,** escape there, for I can do nothing
Ps 119:60 I **h** and do not delay to keep
Pr   1:16 and they **h** of praise;
     6:18 feet that **h** to run to evil,
Lk 19: 5 "Zacchaeus, **h** and come down;

HURT

Pr   9: 7 whoever rebukes the wicked gets **h.**
Ecc 8: 9 over another to the other's **h.**
Da   6:22 mouths so that they would not **h** me,
Mk 16:18 it will not **h** them;
Jn 21:17 Peter felt **h** because he said to him
Sir 31:30 the anger of a fool to his own **h,**

HUSBAND → HUSBAND'S, HUSBANDS

Ge   3: 6 and she also gave some to her **h,**
     3:16 yet your desire shall be for your **h,**
    16: 3 gave her to her **h** Abram as a wife.
Nu 30: 8 But if, at the time that her **h** hears
Dt 24: 4 her first **h,** who sent her away, is not
Pr   7:19 For my **h** is not at home;
    31:11 The heart of her **h** trusts in her,
    31:23 Her **h** is known in the city gates,
    31:28 her **h** too, and he praises her:
Isa 54: 5 For your Maker is your **h,**
Jer 3:20 as a faithless wife leaves her **h,**
    31:32 they broke, though I was their **h,**
Hos 2:16 the LORD, you will call me, "My **h,"**
Mt   1:19 Her **h** Joseph, being a righteous man
Mk 10:12 if she divorces her **h** and marries
Jn   4:17 answered him, "I have no **h."**
Ro   7: 2 but if her **h** dies, she is discharged
1Co 7: 2 and each woman her own **h.**
     7: 3 The **h** should give to his wife her
              conjugal rights, and likewise the
     7:10 wife should not separate from her **h**
     7:11 or else be reconciled to her **h),**
     7:14 unbelieving **h** is made holy through
     7:39 But if the **h** dies, she is free
2Co 11: 2 I promised you in marriage to one **h,**
Eph 5:23 **h** is the head of the wife just as
     5:33 and a wife should respect her **h.**
Rev 21: 2 as a bride adorned for her **h.**
Sir 26: 1 Happy is the **h** of a good wife;

HUSBAND'S → HUSBAND

Dt 25: 5 Her **h** brother shall go in to her,
Ru   2: 1 Naomi had a kinsman on her **h** side,
Pr   6:34 For jealousy arouses a **h** fury,

HUSBANDS → HUSBAND

Jn   4:18 for you have had five **h,**
1Co 14:35 let them ask their **h** at home.
Eph 5:22 be subject to your **h** as you are to
     5:25 **H,** love your wives, just as Christ
     5:28 In the same way, **h** should love their
Col 3:18 Wives, be subject to your **h,**
     3:19 **H,** love your wives and never treat
Tit 2: 4 the young women to love their **h,**
     2: 5 kind, being submissive to their **h,**
1Pe 3: 1 accept the authority of your **h,**
     3: 7 **H,** in the same way, show
Tob 3: 8 she had been married to seven **h,**

HUSHAI

Wise man of David who frustrated Ahithophel's
advice and foiled Absalom's revolt (2Sa 15:32-
37; 16:15-17:16; 1Ch 27:33).

HUT*

Isa 24:20 like a drunkard, it sways like a **h;**

HYMENAEUS*

A false teacher (1Ti 1:20; 2Ti 2:17).

HYMN* → HYMNS

Mt 26:30 When they had sung the **h,**
Mk 14:26 When they had sung the **h,**
1Co 14:26 come together, each one has a **h,**
Sir 39:14 and sing a **h** of praise;
    44: 1 **H** IN HONOR OF OUR ANCESTORS

HYMNS → HYMN

Ac 16:25 were praying and singing **h** to God,
Eph 5:19 psalms and **h** and spiritual songs
Col 3:16 in your hearts sing psalms, **h,**
Tob 13:17 The gates of Jerusalem will sing **h**
Jdt 15:13 and wearing garlands and singing **h.**
Wis 10:20 sang **h,** O Lord, to your holy name,
Sir 51:11 and will sing **h** of thanksgiving."
Aza 1: 1 singing **h** to God and blessing the
1Mc 4:24 On their return they sang **h** and

HYPOCRISY → HYPOCRITE,
    HYPOCRITES, HYPOCRITICAL

Mt 23:28 but inside you are full of **h** and
Mk 12:15 knowing their **h,** he said to them,
Lk 12: 1 of the Pharisees, that is, their **h.**
1Ti 4: 2 the **h** of liars whose consciences are
Jas 3:17 without a trace of partiality or **h.**

HYPOCRITE* → HYPOCRISY

Mt   7: 5 You **h,** first take the log out of your
Lk   6:42 You **h,** first take the log out of your
Sir 1:29 Do not be a **h** before others,
    32:15 but the **h** will stumble at it.

HYPOCRITES* → HYPOCRISY

Ps 26: 4 nor do I consort with **h;**
Mt   6: 2 as the **h** do in the synagogues and
     6: 5 you pray, do not be like the **h;**
     6:16 fast, do not look dismal, like the **h,**
    15: 7 You **h!** Isaiah prophesied rightly
    22:18 you putting me to the test, you **h?**
    23:13 to you, scribes and Pharisees, **h!**
    23:15 to you, scribes and Pharisees, **h!**
    23:23 to you, scribes and Pharisees, **h!**
    23:25 to you, scribes and Pharisees, **h!**
    23:27 to you, scribes and Pharisees, **h!**
    23:29 to you, scribes and Pharisees, **h!**
    24:51 in pieces and put him with the **h,**
Mk   7: 6 prophesied rightly about you **h,**
Lk 12:56 You **h!** You know how to interpret
    13:15 answered him and said, "You **h!**

HYPOCRITICAL* → HYPOCRISY

Sir 33: 2 one who is **h** about it is like a boat

HYSSOP

Ex 12:22 a bunch of **h,** dip it in the blood that
Nu 19: 6 The priest shall take cedarwood, **h,**
Ps 51: 7 Purge me with **h,** and I shall be
Jn 19:29 full of the wine on a branch of **h**
Heb 9:19 with water and scarlet wool and **h,**

I

I AM See also †LORD; I AM THE †LORD

Ge 15: 1 Abram, **I am** your shield;
    17: 1 "**I am** God Almighty; walk before
Ex   3:14 God said to Moses, "**I** AM WHO I
              AM."
Ps 46:10 "Be still, and know that **I am** God!
Isa 41:10 do not fear, for **I am** with you, do
              not be afraid, for **I am** your God;
    43: 3 For **I am** the LORD your God,
    43:11 I, **I am** the LORD, and besides me
    43:15 **I am** the LORD, your Holy One,
    44: 6 **I am** the first and **I am** the last;
    48:12 **I am** He; **I am** the first, and **I am**
              the last.
Jer 3:14 the LORD, for **I am** your master;
    32:27 **I am** the LORD, the God of all flesh;
Mt 16:15 "But who do you say that **I am?"**

Mk   8:29 "But who do you say that **I am?"**
    14:62 Jesus said, "**I am;** and 'you will see
Jn   6:35 to them, "**I am** the bread of life.
     6:41 "**I am** the bread that came down
     6:51 **I am** the living bread that came
     8:12 "**I am** the light of the world.
     8:24 unless you believe that **I am** he."
     8:28 then you will realize that **I am** he,
     8:58 before Abraham was, **I am.**"
     9: 5 **I am** the light of the world."
    10: 7 **I am** the gate for the sheep.
    10: 9 **I am** the gate. Whoever enters by
    10:11 "**I am** the good shepherd.
    10:36 because I said, 'I **am** God's Son'?
    11:25 "**I am** the resurrection and the life.
    13:19 you may believe that **I am** he.
    14: 6 "**I am** the way, and the truth, and
    14:10 **I am** in the Father and the Father
    15: 1 "**I am** the true vine, and my Father
    15: 5 **I am** the vine, you are the branches.
    18: 5 Jesus replied, "**I am** he."
Ac   9: 5 "**I am** Jesus, whom you are
    18:10 **I am** with you, and no one will lay a
    22: 8 **I am** Jesus of Nazareth whom you
    26:15 'I **am** Jesus whom you are
Rev 1: 8 "**I am** the Alpha and the Omega,"
     1:17 **I am** the first and the last,
     1:18 **I am** alive forever and ever;
     3:11 **I am** coming soon; hold fast to what
    21: 6 **I am** the Alpha and the Omega,
    22: 7 "See, **I am** coming soon!
    22:12 "See, **I am** coming soon;
    22:13 **I am** the Alpha and the Omega,
    22:16 **I am** the root and the descendant of
              David, the bright morning star."
    22:20 "Surely **I am** coming soon."

IBZAN

Judge of Israel (Jdg 12:8-10).

ICE

Job 37:10 By the breath of God **i** is given,

ICHABOD*

1Sa 4:21 She named the child **I,** meaning,

ICONIUM

Ac 14: 1 The same thing occurred in **I,**
2Ti 3:11 that happened to me in Antioch, **I,**

IDDO

2Ch 9:29 the visions of the seer **I** concerning
    12:15 prophet Shemaiah and of the seer **I,**
    13:22 written in the story of the prophet **I.**

IDLE → IDLENESS, IDLER, IDLERS

Pr 19:15 an **i** person will suffer hunger.
Ecc 11: 6 evening do not let your hands be **i;**
2Th 3: 7 were not **i** when we were with you,
1Ti 5:13 Besides that, they learn to be **i,**
     5:13 and they are not merely **i,**
Tit 1:10 **i** talkers and deceivers,
Sir 33:28 in order that he may not be **i,**

IDLENESS → IDLE

Pr 31:27 and does not eat the bread of **i.**
2Th 3: 6 from believers who are living in **i**
Sir 33:29 for **i** teaches much evil.

IDLER → IDLE

Sir 22: 1 The **i** is like a filthy stone,

IDLERS* → IDLE

1Th 5:14 beloved, to admonish the **i,**

IDOL → IDOLATER, IDOLATERS,
    IDOLATROUS, IDOLATRY, IDOLS

Ex 20: 4 shall not make for yourself an **i,**
Dt 27:15 who makes an **i** or casts an image,
Isa 40:19 An **i?**—A workman casts it,
    44:17 rest of it he makes into a god, his **i,**
Hab 2:18 What use is an **i** once its maker has
1Co 8: 4 "no **i** in the world really exists,"

10:19 or that an **i** is anything?
Wis 14: 8 the **i** made with hands is accursed,
Bel 1: 3 Babylonians had an **i** called Bel,

IDOLATER* → IDOL

1Co 5:11 is an **i**, reviler, drunkard, or robber.
Eph 5: 5 or one who is greedy (that is, an **i**),

IDOLATERS* → IDOL

1Co 5:10 or the greedy and robbers, or **i**,
6: 9 **i**, adulterers, male prostitutes,
10: 7 not become **i** as some of them did;
Rev 21: 8 the fornicators, the sorcerers, the **i**,
22:15 and fornicators and murderers and **i**,

IDOLATROUS* → IDOL

2Ki 23: 5 the **i** priests whom the kings
Hos 10: 5 and its **i** priests shall wail over it,
Zep 1: 4 the name of the **i** priests;

IDOLATRY → IDOL

1Sa 15:23 stubbornness is like iniquity and **i**.
Eze 23:49 bear the penalty for your sinful **i**;
Col 3: 5 evil desire, and greed (which is **i**).
1Pe 4: 3 revels, carousing, and lawless **i**.

IDOLS → IDOL

Ex 34:17 You shall not make cast **i**.
Dt 7: 5 and burn their **i** with fire.
1Ki 15:12 removed all the **i** that his ancestors
2Ki 17:15 went after false **i** and became false;
1Ch 16:26 For all the gods of the peoples are **i**,
Ps 31: 6 those who pay regard to worthless **i**,
78:58 moved him to jealousy with their **i**.
115: 4 Their **i** are silver and gold,
Isa 2: 8 Their land is filled with **i**;
42: 8 give to no other, nor my praise to **i**.
44: 9 All who make **i** are nothing,
Jer 10: 5 Their **i** are like scarecrows in a
Eze 14: 3 have taken their **i** into their hearts,
23:37 with their **i** they have committed
23:39 slaughtered their children for their **i**,
Ac 15:20 only from things polluted by **i**
1Co 8: 1 concerning food sacrificed to **i**:
10:14 flee from the worship of **i**.
2Co 6:16 has the temple of God with **i**?
1Th 1: 9 you turned to God from **i**,
1Jn 5:21 children, keep yourselves from **i**.
Rev 2:14 they would eat food sacrificed to **i**
AdE 14: 8 they have covenanted with their **i**
Wis 14:12 For the idea of making **i** was
LtJ 6:44 Whatever is done for these **i** is false.
Bel 1: 5 I do not revere **i** made with hands,
1Mc 1:43 they sacrificed to **i** and profaned the
Pm 151: 6 and he cursed me by his **i**.

IF

Ge 4: 7 **I** you do well, will you not be
Ex 19: 5 **i** you obey my voice and keep my
33:15 "**I** your presence will not go,
Dt 11:27 **i** you obey the commandments of
1Ki 18:21 **I** the Lord is God, follow him;
18:21 but **i** Baal, then follow him."
1Ch 28: 9 **I** you seek him, he will be found by
Jer 18: 8 but **i** that nation, concerning which
Eze 18:21 But **i** the wicked turn away from all
Mt 4: 3 "**I** you are the Son of God,
27:40 **I** you are the Son of God,
Mk 3:24 **I** a kingdom is divided against itself,
5:28 "**I** I but touch his clothes, I will be
Lk 6:32 "**I** you love those who love you,
Jn 13:17 **I** you know these things, you are
blessed **i** you do them.
14:15 "**I** you love me, you will keep my
15:10 **I** you keep my commandments,
Ro 6: 8 But **i** we have died with Christ,
8:31 **I** God is for us, who is against us?
Heb 3: 7 says, "Today, **i** you hear his voice,
Jas 1: 5 **I** any of you is lacking in wisdom,
1Pe 4:16 **i** any of you suffers as a Christian,
1Jn 1: 9 **I** we confess our sins, he who is
Rev 3:20 **I** you hear my voice and open the
Sir 1:26 **I** you desire wisdom,

IGNORANCE → IGNORE

Ac 3:17 friends, I know that you acted in **i**,
17:30 overlooked the times of human **i**,
1Pe 2:15 silence the **i** of the foolish.

IGNORANT → IGNORE

2Co 2:11 for we are not **i** of his designs.
Heb 5: 2 He is able to deal gently with the **i**
2Pe 3:16 the **i** and unstable twist to their own
Sir 20:19 continually on the lips of the **i**.

IGNORANTLY* → IGNORE

1Ti 1:13 because I had acted **i** in unbelief,

IGNORE → IGNORANCE, IGNORANT, IGNORANTLY, IGNORED, IGNORES

Dt 22: 1 or sheep straying away and **i** them;
Pr 12:16 but the prudent **i** an insult.
2Pe 3: 5 They deliberately **i** this fact,

IGNORED → IGNORE

Pr 1:25 because you have **i** all my counsel
2Es 7:23 and they **i** his ways.

IGNORES* → IGNORE

Pr 13:18 are for the one who **i** instruction,

ILL → ILLNESS

Jn 11: 1 Now a certain man was **i**,
1Co 11:30 many of you are weak and **i**,
2Ti 4:20 Trophimus I left **i** in Miletus.

ILLEGITIMATE

Hos 5: 7 for they have borne **i** children.
Jn 8:41 said to him, "We are not **i** children;
Heb 12: 8 then you are **i** and not his children.

ILLICIT

Nu 3: 4 offered **i** fire before the Lord

ILLNESS → ILL

Dt 7:15 will turn away from you every **i**;
2Ki 8: 9 'Shall I recover from this **i**?'"
Ps 41: 3 their **i** you heal all their infirmities.
Jn 11: 4 said, "This **i** does not lead to death;

ILLUSIONS*

Isa 30:10 to us smooth things, prophesy **i**,

IMAGE → IMAGES

Ge 1:26 "Let us make humankind in our **i**,
1:27 in the **i** of God he created them:
9: 6 in his own **i** God made humankind.
Ex 32: 4 and cast an **i** of a calf;
Dt 27:15 who makes an idol or casts an **i**,
Ps 106:20 the glory of God for the **i** of an ox
Ro 8:29 conformed to the **i** of his Son,
1Co 11: 7 he is the **i** and reflection of God;
15:49 the **i** of the man of heaven.
2Co 4: 4 who is the **i** of God.
Col 1:15 He is the **i** of the invisible God,
3:10 according to the **i** of its creator.
Rev 13:14 to make an **i** for the beast that had
14:11 who worship the beast and its **i**
20: 4 not worshiped the beast or its **i** and
Wis 2:23 made us in the **i** of his own eternity,
Sir 17: 3 and made them in his own **i**.

IMAGES → IMAGE

Lev 19: 4 not turn to idols or make cast **i** for
Nu 33:52 destroy all their cast **i**,
Ps 97: 7 All worshipers of **i** are put to shame,
Isa 42:17 those who trust in carved **i**,
Jer 10:14 their **i** are false, and there is no
Ro 1:23 for **i** resembling a mortal human

IMAGINATION* → IMAGINE

Pr 18:11 in their **i** it is like a high wall.
Eze 13: 2 who prophesy out of their own **i**:
13:17 who prophesy out of their own **i**;
Ac 17:29 formed by the art and **i** of mortals.

IMAGINE → IMAGINATION, IMAGINED, IMAGINING

Eph 3:20 far more than all we can ask or **i**,

IMAGINED → IMAGINE

Isa 53: 8 Who could have **i** his future?

IMAGINING → IMAGINE

1Ti 6: 5 **i** that godliness is a means of gain.

IMITATE → IMITATING, IMITATORS

Dt 18: 9 not learn to **i** the abhorrent practices
Heb 13: 7 their way of life, and **i** their faith.
3Jn 1:11 not **i** what is evil but **i** what is good.

IMITATING* → IMITATE

Dt 12:30 that you are not snared into **i** them,
Php 3:17 Brothers and sisters, join in **i** me,

IMITATORS* → IMITATE

1Co 4:16 I appeal to you, then, be **i** of me.
11: 1 Be **i** of me, as I am of Christ.
Eph 5: 1 be **i** of God, as beloved children,
1Th 1: 6 you became **i** of us and of the Lord,
2:14 became **i** of the churches of God in
Heb 6:12 but **i** of those who through faith

IMMANUEL* → =EMMANUEL

Isa 7:14 bear a son, and shall name him **I**.
8: 8 fill the breadth of your land, O **I**.

IMMEASURABLE

Eph 1:19 the **i** greatness of his power for us
Man 1: 6 and unsearchable is your promised

IMMORAL* → IMMORALITY

1Co 5: 9 not to associate with sexually **i**
5:10 the **i** of this world,
5:11 or sister who is sexually **i** or greedy,
Heb 12:16 an **i** and godless person,

IMMORALITY* → IMMORAL

1Co 5: 1 that there is sexual **i** among you,
7: 2 But because of cases of sexual **i**,
10: 8 not indulge in sexual **i** as some of
2Co 12:21 sexual **i**, and licentiousness
Jude 1: 7 indulged in sexual **i** and pursued
Sir 41:17 Be ashamed of sexual **i**,
42: 8 the aged who are guilty of sexual **i**.

IMMORTAL → IMMORTALITY

Ro 1:23 the glory of the **i** God for images
1Ti 1:17 To the King of the ages, **i**, invisible,
Wis 1:15 For righteousness is **i**.
Sir 17:30 since human beings are not **i**.
2Es 2:45 and have put on the **i**,

IMMORTALITY → IMMORTAL

Ro 2: 7 honor and **i**, he will give eternal life;
1Co 15:53 and this mortal body must put on **i**.
15:54 and this mortal body puts on **i**,
1Ti 6:16 It is he alone who has **i** and dwells
2Ti 1:10 brought life and **i** to light through
Wis 8:13 Because of her I shall have **i**,
2Es 7:13 and yield the fruit of **i**.

IMPALE → IMPALED

Nu 25: 4 **i** them in the sun before the Lord,

IMPALED → IMPALE

2Sa 21: 9 they **i** them on the mountain
Ezr 6:11 who then shall be **i** on it.

IMPARTIALLY

1Pe 1:17 the one who judges all people **i**

IMPATIENT

Nu 21: 4 but the people became **i** on the way.

IMPEDIMENT*

Mk 7:32 who had an **i** in his speech;

IMPENITENT*

Ro 2: 5 **i** heart you are storing up wrath

IMPERISHABILITY* → IMPERISHABLE

1Co 15:53 this perishable body must put on i,
     15:54 When this perishable body puts on i,

IMPERISHABLE* → IMPERISHABILITY

Mk 16: S [i proclamation of eternal salvation.]
1Co 9:25 a perishable wreath, but we an i one.
     15:42 is perishable, what is raised is i.
     15:50 nor does the perishable inherit the i.
     15:52 and the dead will be raised i,
1Pe 1: 4 and into an inheritance that is i,
    1:23 not of perishable but of i seed,
Wis 18: 4 through whom the i light of the law

IMPIETY → IMPIOUS

2Ti 2:16 lead people into more and more i,
Tit 1:12 training us to renounce i and

IMPIOUS → IMPIETY

Ps 74:18 and an i people reviles your name.
    74:22 remember how the i scoff at you all

IMPLANTED → PLANT

Jas 1:21 welcome with meekness the i word

IMPLORE → IMPLORED

Ps 119:58 I i your favor with all my heart;
Isa 38: 3 O LORD, I i you, how I have walked
Mal 1: 9 i the favor of God, that he may be
Man 1:13 I earnestly i you, forgive me,
2Es 5:56 I said, "I i you, O Lord,

IMPLORED → IMPLORE

Ex 32:11 But Moses i the LORD his God,

IMPORTANCE* → IMPORTANT

Ex 11: 3 Moses himself was a man of great i
1Co 15: 3 of first i what I in turn had received:

IMPORTANT → IMPORTANCE

Ex 18:22 let them bring every i case to you,
Mk 12:33 much more i than all whole burnt

IMPOSSIBLE

Ge 11: 6 to do will now be i for them.
Zec 8: 6 should it also seem i to me,
Mt 17:20 and nothing will be i for you."
    19:26 and said, "For mortals it is i, but
Mk 10:27 "For mortals it is i, but not for God;
Lk 1:37 For nothing will be i with God."
    18:27 "What is i for mortals is possible
Ac 2:24 i for him to be held in its power.
Heb 6: 4 For it is i to restore again
    6:18 it is i that God would prove false,
    10: 4 is i for the blood of bulls and goats
    11: 6 without faith it is i to please God,

IMPOSTOR* → IMPOSTORS

Mt 27:63 that i said while he was still alive,

IMPOSTORS* → IMPOSTOR

2Co 6: 8 We are treated as i, and yet are true;
2Ti 3:13 and i will go from bad to worse,

IMPRINT*

Heb 1: 3 the exact i of God's very being,

IMPRISONED → PRISON

Jer 37:15 i him in the house of the secretary
Ro 11:32 For God has i all in disobedience
Gal 3:22 i all things under the power of sin,

IMPRISONMENT → PRISON

Ac 23:29 nothing deserving death or i.
    26:31 nothing to deserve death or i."
Heb 11:36 and flogging, and even chains and i.

IMPRISONMENTS* → PRISON

2Co 6: 5 beatings, i, riots, labors, sleepless
    11:23 with far greater labors, far more i,

IMPUDENT

Pr 7:13 and with i face she says to him:
Sir 22: 5 An i daughter disgraces father

IMPURE* → IMPURITIES, IMPURITY

Eph 5: 5 that no fornicator or i person,
1Th 2: 3 not spring from deceit or i motives

IMPURITIES* → IMPURE

Rev 17: 4 and the i of her fornication;

IMPURITY → IMPURE

Zec 13: 1 to cleanse them from sin and i.
Ro 1:24 in the lusts of their hearts to i,
    6:19 as slaves to i and to greater and
2Co 12:21 and have not repented of the i,
Gal 5:19 fornication, i, licentiousness,
Eph 4:19 greedy to practice every kind of i.
    5: 3 But fornication and i of any kind,
Col 3: 5 fornication, i, passion, evil desire,
1Th 4: 7 did not call us to i but in holiness.

IMPUTES*

Ps 32: 2 to whom the LORD i no iniquity,

INCENSE → FRANKINCENSE

Ex 25: 6 anointing oil and for the fragrant i,
    30: 1 make an altar on which to offer i;
    40: 5 the golden altar for i before the ark
Nu 16:17 and put i on it, and each one
2Ch 26:16 to make offering on the altar of i.
Ps 141: 2 Let my prayer be counted as i
Isa 1:13 i is an abomination to me.
Hos 2:13 when she offered i to them and
Lk 1:10 Now at the time of the i offering,
Heb 9: 4 In it stood the golden altar of i and
Rev 5: 8 a harp and golden bowls full of i,
    8: 4 And the smoke of the i,

INCITE* → INCITED

Ac 17:13 to stir up and i the crowds.

INCITED → INCITE

1Ch 21: 1 i David to count the people of Israel.
Ac 13:50 the Jews i the devout women of

INCLINATION → INCLINE

Ge 6: 5 and that every i of the thoughts
    8:21 for the i of the human heart is evil
Ecc 11: 9 Follow the i of your heart and
Sir 5: 2 Do not follow your i and strength

INCLINE → INCLINATION, INCLINED, INCLINES

Jos 24:23 and i your hearts to the LORD,
1Ki 8:58 but i our hearts to him,
Ps 17: 6 i your ear to me, hear my words.
Pr 4:20 i your ear to my sayings.
Isa 37:17 I your ear, O LORD, and hear;
Jer 7:24 Yet they did not obey or i their ear,
Da 9:18 I your ear, O my God, and hear.
Bar 2:16 I your ear, O Lord, and hear;

INCLINED → INCLINE

Ps 40: 1 he i to me and heard my cry.

INCLINES → INCLINE

Ecc 10: 2 The heart of the wise i to the right,

INCREASE → INCREASED, INCREASES, INCREASING

Ge 3:16 greatly i your pangs in childbearing;
Dt 1:11 i you a thousand times more and
Ps 62:10 if riches i, do not set your heart on
Mt 24:12 And because of the i of lawlessness,
Lk 17: 5 said to the Lord, "I our faith!"
Jn 3:30 He must i, but I must decrease."
1Th 3:12 the Lord make you i and abound

INCREASED → INCREASE

Ge 7:17 the waters i, and bore up the ark,
Ac 6: 7 number of the disciples i greatly in
Ro 5:20 but where sin i, grace abounded all

INCREASES → INCREASE

Pr 16:21 pleasant speech i persuasiveness.
    29:16 are in authority, transgression i,

INCREASING → INCREASE

Ac 6: 1 the disciples were i in number,
2Th 1: 3 everyone of you for one another is i.
2Pe 1: 8 are yours and are i among you,

INCREDIBLE

Ac 26: 8 thought i by any of you that God

INCUR → INCURRED

Lev 19:17 or you will i guilt yourself.
Nu 18:22 or else they will i guilt and die.
Ro 13: 2 those who resist will i judgment.
1Ti 5:12 and so they i condemnation

INCURABLE

2Ch 21:18 in his bowels with an i disease.
Jer 15:18 my pain unceasing, my wound i,
    30:12 hurt is i, your wound is grievous.
Mic 1: 9 For her wound is i.

INCURRED → INCUR

Hos 13: 1 but he i guilt through Baal and died.

INDEBTED* → DEBT

Lk 11: 4 forgive everyone i to us.

INDEPENDENT*

1Co 11:11 not i of man or man i of woman.

INDESCRIBABLE

2Co 9:15 Thanks be to God for his i gift!

INDESTRUCTIBLE*

Heb 7:16 but through the power of an i life.

INDIA

Est 1: 1 provinces from I to Ethiopia.

INDICATE → INDICATED

Jn 12:33 He said this to i the kind of death
    21:19 (He said this to i the kind of death

INDICATED → INDICATE

Jn 18:32 he i the kind of death he was to die.)

INDICTMENT

Jer 25:31 LORD has an i against the nations;
Hos 12: 2 The LORD has an i against Judah,

INDIGNANT → INDIGNATION

Mk 10:14 when Jesus saw this, he was i and
Lk 13:14 because Jesus had cured on the

INDIGNATION → INDIGNANT

Ps 7:11 and a God who has i every day.
Jer 10:10 and the nations cannot endure his i.
Na 1: 6 Who can stand before his i?

INDISPENSABLE*

1Co 12:22 body that seem to be weaker are i,

INDULGE → INDULGED, INDULGING, SELF-INDULGENCE, SELF-INDULGENT

Hos 4:18 they i in sexual orgies;
1Co 10: 8 We must not i in sexual immorality
2Pe 2:10 —especially those who i their flesh
Jude 1:16 they i their own lusts;

INDULGED → INDULGE

Jude 1: 7 as they, i in sexual immorality

INDULGING* → INDULGE

1Ti 3: 8 not i in much wine, not greedy for
2Pe 3: 3 scoffing and i their own lusts
Jude 1:18 i their own ungodly lusts."

INEFFECTIVE → INEFFECTUAL

2Pe 1: 8 they keep you from being i and

INEFFECTUAL* → INEFFECTIVE

Heb 7:18 because it was weak and i

INFANT → INFANTS

Isa 65:20 No more shall there be in it an i that
Heb 5:13 who lives on milk, being still an i,

INFANTS → INFANT

Ps	8: 2	Out of the mouths of babes and **i**
Mt	21:16	'Out of the mouths of **i** and nursing
1Co	3: 1	as people of the flesh, as **i** in Christ.
	14:20	**i** in evil, but in thinking be adults.
1Pe	2: 2	Like newborn **i**, long for the pure,

INFERIOR

Job	12: 3	I am not **i** to you.
2Co	12:11	not at all **i** to these super-apostles,
Heb	7: 7	that the **i** is blessed by the superior.

INFIRMITIES*

Ps	41: 3	in their illness you heal all their **i**.
Isa	53: 4	borne our **i** and carried our diseases;
Mt	8:17	took our **i** and bore our diseases."
Lk	8: 2	cured of evil spirits and **i**;
2Es	4:27	this age is full of sadness and **i**.

INFLICT → INFLICTED

Dt	7:15	he will not **i** on you, but will lay

INFLICTED → INFLICT

2Sa	7:14	with blows **i** by human beings.
Isa	30:26	and heals the wounds **i** by his blow.

INGATHERING* → GATHER

Ex	23:16	You shall observe the festival of **i**
	34:22	festival of **i** at the turn of the year.

INHABITANT → INHABITANTS, INHABITED

Isa	6:11	"Until cities lie waste without **i**,
Jer	4: 7	your cities will be ruins without **i**.

INHABITANTS → INHABITANT

Nu	33:55	if you do not drive out the **i** of the
Jos	9:24	to destroy all the **i** of the land before
Rev	6:10	judge and avenge our blood on the **i**
	8:13	Woe, woe, woe to the **i** of the earth,
	13: 8	all the **i** of the earth will worship it,
1Mc	1:28	Even the land trembled for its **i**,

ALL THE INHABITANTS Ge 19:25; Ex 15:15; Nu 33:52; Jos 2:9, 24; 7:9; 8:24, 26; 9:11, 24; 13:6; Jdg 10:18; 11:8; 2Ki 23:2; 2Ch 15:5; Ps 33:8, 14; Jer 1:14; 13:13, 13; 17:20; 25:2, 29, 30; 35:17; 47:2; 51:24; Eze 27:35; 29:6; Da 4:35; Joel 1:14; 2:1; Zep 1:4, 18; Rev 13:8; Jdt 1:12; 5:15, 22

INHABITANTS OF JERUSALEM Jos 15:63; 2Ki 23:2; 2Ch 20:15, 18, 20; 21:11, 13; 22:1; 32:22, 26, 33; 33:9; 34:9, 30, 32; 35:18; Ne 7:3; Isa 5:3; 8:14; 22:21; 30:19; Jer 4:3, 4; 8:1; 11:2, 9, 12; 13:13; 17:20, 25; 18:11; 19:3; 25:2; 32:32; 35:13, 17; 36:31; 42:18; Eze 11:15; 12:19; 15:6; Da 9:7; Zep 1:4; Zec 12:5, 7, 8, 10; 13:1; Bar 1:15

INHABITANTS OF THE EARTH Ps 33:14; Isa 24:6; 26:21; Jer 25:29, 30; Da 4:35, 35; Zep 1:18; Zec 11:6; Rev 3:10; 6:10; 8:13; 11:10, 10; 13:8, 14; 17:2, 8; 2Es 3:35; 6:18

INHABITED → INHABITANT

Isa	45:18	a chaos, he formed it to be **i**!):
Jer	17:25	and this city shall be **i** forever.
Joel	3:20	But Judah shall be **i** forever,
Zec	14:11	it shall be **i**, for never again shall it

INHERIT → INHERITANCE, INHERITED

Lev	20:24	You shall **i** their land,
2Ki	2: 9	me **i** a double share of your spirit."
Ps	37:11	But the meek shall **i** the land,
	37:29	righteous shall **i** the land, and live
Pr	3:35	wise will **i** honor, but stubborn
	11:29	trouble their households will **i** wind,
Zec	2:12	The LORD will **i** Judah as his portion
Mt	5: 5	the meek, for they will **i** the earth.
	19:29	a hundredfold, and will **i** eternal life.
Mk	10:17	what must I do to **i** eternal life?"
Lk	10:25	"what must I do to **i** eternal life?"
	18:18	what must I do to **i** eternal life?"
1Co	6: 9	wrongdoers will not **i** the kingdom
	15:50	blood cannot **i** the kingdom of God,

INHERITANCE → INHERIT

Ex	34: 9	and take us for your **i**."
Dt	10: 9	the LORD is his **i**,
Jos	13: 6	only allot the land to Israel for an **i**,
Pr	13:22	good leave an **i** to their children's
Ecc	7:11	Wisdom is as good as an **i**,
Jer	10:16	and Israel is the tribe of his **i**;
Lk	12:13	to divide the family **i** with me."
Gal	3:18	For if the **i** comes from the law,
	4:30	not share the **i** with the child of the
Eph	1:11	In Christ we have also obtained an **i**,
	1:14	our **i** toward redemption as God's
	5: 5	has any **i** in the kingdom of Christ
Col	1:12	in the **i** of the saints in the light.
	3:24	will receive the **i** as your reward;
Heb	9:15	the promised eternal **i**,
1Pe	1: 4	and into an **i** that is imperishable,

INHERITED → INHERIT

Jer	16:19	Our ancestors have **i** nothing but lies
Heb	1: 4	the name he has **i** is more excellent

INIQUITIES → INIQUITY

Lev	16:22	goat shall bear on itself all their **i**
Ps	51: 9	and blot out all my **i**.
	90: 8	You have set our **i** before you,
	103:10	nor repay us according to our **i**.
Isa	53: 5	transgressions, crushed for our **i**;
	53:11	and he shall bear their **i**.
	59: 2	your **i** have been barriers between
Mic	7:19	he will tread our **i** under foot.
Ro	4: 7	are those whose **i** are forgiven,
Rev	18: 5	and God has remembered her **i**.
Sir	17:20	Their **i** are not hidden from him,

INIQUITY → INIQUITIES

Ex	20: 5	children for the **i** of parents,
	34: 7	forgiving **i** and transgression and sin
Ps	32: 2	to whom the LORD imputes no **i**,
	32: 5	and I did not hide my **i**;
	38:18	confess my **i**; I am sorry for my sin.
	51: 2	Wash me thoroughly from my **i**,
	103: 3	who forgives all your **i**,
Pr	16: 6	and faithfulness **i** is atoned for,
Isa	53: 6	LORD has laid on him the **i** of us all.
Mic	7:18	pardoning **i** and passing over
Tit	2:14	that he might redeem us from all **i**
Sir	17:26	the Most High and turn away from **i**,
2Es	6:19	the doers of **i** the penalty of their **i**,

INJURED → INJURY

Eze	34:16	and I will bind up the **i**,
Ro	14:15	is being **i** by what you eat,

INJURIES* → INJURY

Isa	30:26	LORD binds up the **i** of his people,

INJURY → INJURED, INJURIES

Lev	24:20	the **i** inflicted is the **i** to be suffered.

INJUSTICE

Pr	13:23	but it is swept away through **i**.
	16: 8	than large income with **i**.
Hos	10:13	wickedness, you have reaped **i**,
Ro	9:14	Is there **i** on God's part?
Sir	7: 3	Do not sow in the furrows of **i**,

INK*

Jer	36:18	I wrote them with **i** on the scroll."
2Co	3: 3	not with **i** but with the Spirit of the
2Jn	1:12	I would rather not use paper and **i**;
3Jn	1:13	rather not write with pen and **i**;

INMOST → INNER

Pr	20:27	searching every **i** part.
Ro	7:22	in the law of God in my **i** self,

INN*

Lk	2: 7	there was no place for them in the **i**.
	10:34	brought him to an **i**, and took care

INNER → INMOST, INWARD, INWARDLY

1Ki	6:16	built this within as an **i** sanctuary,
Eze	10: 3	and a cloud filled the **i** court.
Mt	24:26	He is in the **i** rooms,' do not believe
Lk	2:35	**i** thoughts of many will be revealed
	9:47	But Jesus, aware of their **i** thoughts,
2Co	4:16	our **i** nature is being renewed day
Eph	3:16	strengthened in your **i** being with
1Pe	3: 4	let your adornment be the **i** self

INNOCENCE → INNOCENT

Ps	26: 6	I wash my hands in **i**,
Hos	8: 5	long will they be incapable of **i**?

INNOCENT → INNOCENCE

Ex	23: 7	not kill the **i** and those in the right,
Dt	19:10	so that the blood of an **i** person may
Job	34: 5	For Job has said, 'I am **i**,
Ps	19:13	and **i** of great transgression.
Pr	6:17	tongue, and hands that shed **i** blood,
	17:26	impose a fine on the **i** is not right,
Isa	59: 7	and they rush to shed **i** blood;
Mt	10:16	be wise as serpents and **i** as doves.
	27: 4	have sinned by betraying **i** blood."
	27:24	"I am **i** of this man's blood;
Lk	23:47	"Certainly this man was **i**."
Php	2:15	so that you may be blameless and **i**,
Sus	1:53	condemning the **i** and acquitting the
1Mc	1:37	they shed **i** blood;

INQUIRE → INQUIRED

Dt	12:30	do not **i** concerning their gods,
1Sa	28: 7	so that I may go to her and **i** of her."
2Ki	1: 2	**i** of Baal-zebub, the god of Ekron,

INQUIRED → INQUIRE

1Sa	22:10	he **i** of the LORD for him,
	28: 6	When Saul **i** of the LORD,
Zep	1: 6	not sought the LORD or **i** of him.

INSANE*

Ac	26:24	Too much learning is driving you **i**!

INSCRIBE → INSCRIBED, INSCRIPTION

Isa	30: 8	them on a tablet, and **i** it in a book,

INSCRIBED → INSCRIBE

Da	5:25	And this is the writing that was **i**:
	10:21	what is **i** in the book of truth.
Rev	19:12	he has a name **i** that no one

INSCRIPTION → INSCRIBE

Mk	15:26	The **i** of the charge against him read,
Ac	17:23	an altar with the **i**, 'To an unknown
2Ti	2:19	foundation stands, bearing this **i**:

INSCRUTABLE*

Ro	11:33	his judgments and how **i** his ways!

INSECTS

Dt	14:19	all winged **i** are unclean for you;

INSIDE

Ge	6:14	and cover it **i** and out with pitch.
Ex	4: 6	"Put your hand **i** your cloak."
Mt	23:26	First clean the **i** of the cup,
	23:27	but **i** they are full of the bones of
1Co	5:12	are **i** that you are to judge?
Sir	19:12	so is gossip **i** a fool.
Bel	1: 7	only clay **i** and bronze outside,

INSIGHT

Job	34:35	knowledge, his words are without **i**.'
Pr	1: 2	for understanding words of **i**,
	3: 5	and do not rely on your own **i**,
	4: 7	whatever else you get, get **i**.
	9:10	knowledge of the Holy One is **i**.
Da	1:17	Daniel also had **i** into all visions
Eph	1: 8	With all wisdom and **i**
Php	1: 9	and more with knowledge and full **i**
Sir	6:37	It is he who will give **i** to your mind,

INSINCERITY*
1Pe 2: 1 all malice, and all guile, **i**, envy,

INSIST*
1Co 13: 5 It does not **i** on its own way;
Eph 4:17 this I affirm and **i** on in the Lord:
1Ti 4:11 things you must **i** on and teach.
Tit 3: 8 I desire that you **i** on these things,

INSOLENT
Ps 19:13 your servant also from the **i**;
   119:21 You rebuke the **i**, accursed ones,
Ro 1:30 **i**, haughty, boastful, inventors of

INSPIRED → INSPIRES
Ex 35:34 And he has **i** him to teach,
1Th 1: 6 with joy **i** by the Holy Spirit,
2Ti 3:16 All scripture is **i** by God and is
Wis 15:11 one who formed them and **i** them

INSPIRES → INSPIRED
Col 1:29 energy that he powerfully **i** within

INSTALLMENT*
2Co 1:22 Spirit in our hearts as a first **i**.

INSTANT → INSTANTLY
Lk   4: 5 showed him in an **i** all the kingdoms

INSTANTLY → INSTANT
Mt   9:22 And **i** the woman was made well.
   15:28 And her daughter was healed **i**.
   17:18 and the boy was cured **i**.

INSTEAD
Ge 22:13 as a burnt offering **i** of his son.
2Ch 28:20 oppressed him **i** of strengthening
Pr   8:10 Take my instruction **i** of silver,
Isa 60:17 **I** of bronze I will bring gold,
Mk 15:11 release Barabbas for them **i**.
Lk 11:11 will give a snake **i** of a fish?

INSTINCT* → INSTINCTIVELY
2Pe 2:12 mere creatures of **i**, born to be
Jude 1:10 irrational animals, they know by **i**.

INSTINCTIVELY* → INSTINCT
Ro   2:14 do **i** what the law requires,

INSTITUTED → INSTITUTION
Ro 13: 1 that exist have been **i** by God.

INSTITUTION* → INSTITUTED
Nu 10: 8 this shall be a perpetual **i** for you
1Pe 2:13 the authority of every human **i**,

INSTRUCT → INSTRUCTED,
  INSTRUCTION, INSTRUCTIONS,
  INSTRUCTOR, INSTRUCTORS, INSTRUCTS
Dt 17:10 observing everything they **i** you.
Ne 9:20 You gave your good spirit to **i** them,
Ps 32: 8 I will **i** you and teach you the way
   105:22 to **i** his officials at his pleasure,
Ro 15:14 and able to **i** one another.
1Co 2:16 mind of the Lord so as to **i** him?"
  10:11 and they were written down to **i** us,
  14:19 in order to **i** others also,

INSTRUCTED → INSTRUCT
2Ch 26: 5 who **i** him in the fear of God;
Pr 21:11 when the wise are **i**, they increase
Isa 40:13 or as his counselor has **i** him?
Jn 8:28 these things as the Father **i** me.
Ac 7:22 So Moses was **i** in all the wisdom of
  18:25 had been **i** in the Way of the Lord;
2Ti 3: 7 who are always being **i** and can
Wis 6:25 Therefore be **i** by my words,

INSTRUCTION → INSTRUCT
Ex 24:12 which I have written for their **i**."
Pr   1: 2 For learning about wisdom and **i**,
   1: 8 Hear, my child, your father's **i**,
   4: 1 Listen, children, to a father's **i**,
   4:13 Keep hold of **i**; do not let go;
   8:10 Take my **i** instead of silver,

   8:33 Hear **i** and be wise, and do not
  19:20 Listen to advice and accept **i**,
  23:12 Apply your mind to **i** and your ear
Isa 29:24 those who grumble will accept **i**.
Mic 4: 2 For out of Zion shall go forth **i**,
Mal 2: 6 True **i** was in his mouth,
Ro 15: 4 in former days was written for our **i**,
Eph 6: 4 in the discipline and **i** of the Lord.
1Ti 1: 5 But the aim of such **i** is love
Wis 3:11 despise wisdom and **i** are miserable.
Sir 51:26 and let your souls receive **i**;

INSTRUCTIONS → INSTRUCT
Ac 1: 2 giving **i** through the Holy Spirit to
1Ti 3:14 I am writing these **i** to you so that,

INSTRUCTOR → INSTRUCT
Mt 23:10 for you have one **i**, the Messiah.

INSTRUCTORS* → INSTRUCT
Pr 5:13 or incline my ear to my **i**.
Mt 23:10 Nor are you to be called **i**,

INSTRUCTS → INSTRUCT
Ps 16: 7 in the night also my heart **i** me.
  25: 8 therefore he **i** sinners in the way.
Sir 37:23 A wise person **i** his own people,

INSTRUMENT → INSTRUMENTS
Eze 33:32 voice and plays well on an **i**;
Ac 9:15 an **i** whom I have chosen to bring

INSTRUMENTS → INSTRUMENT
1Ch 15:16 as the singers to play on musical **i**,
  23: 5 the LORD with the **i** that I have made
Ro 6:13 to God as **i** of righteousness.
1Mc 13:51 harps and cymbals and stringed **i**,

INSULT → INSULTED, INSULTS
Ps 69: 9 insults of those who **i** you have
Pr 12:16 but the prudent ignore an **i**.
Isa 50: 6 I did not hide my face from **i** and
Mt 5:22 and if you **i** a brother or sister,

INSULTED → INSULT
Lk 18:32 he will be mocked and **i** and spat

INSULTS → INSULT
1Sa 25:14 and he shouted **i** at them.
Ps 69: 9 the **i** of those who insult you have
Eze 34:29 no longer suffer the **i** of the nations.
Lk 22:65 heaping many other **i** on him.
Ro 15: 3 **i** of those who insult you have fallen
2Co 12:10 I am content with weaknesses, **i**,

INTEGRITY*
Ge 20: 5 I did this in the **i** of my heart and
  20: 6 I know that you did this in the **i** of
1Ki 9: 4 with **i** of heart and uprightness,
Job 2: 3 He still persists in his **i**,
  2: 9 "Do you still persist in your **i**?
  4: 6 and the **i** of your ways your hope?
  27: 5 until I die I will not put away my **i**
  31: 6 and let God know my **i**!—
Ps 7: 8 and according to the **i** that is
  25:21 May **i** and uprightness preserve me,
  26: 1 O LORD, for I have walked in my **i**,
  26:11 But as for me, I walk in my **i**;
  41:12 have upheld me because of my **i**,
  101: 2 I will walk with **i** of heart within
Pr 10: 9 Whoever walks in **i** walks securely,
  11: 3 The **i** of the upright guides them,
  14:32 the righteous find a refuge in their **i**.
  17:26 or to flog the noble for their **i**.
  19: 1 Better the poor walking in **i** than
  20: 7 The righteous walk in **i**—happy are
  28: 6 Better to be poor and walk in **i** than
  28:18 One who walks in **i** will be safe,
Mal 2: 6 He walked with me in **i** and
Tit 2: 7 and in your teaching show **i**, gravity,
Sir 7: 6 to the powerful, and so mar your **i**.
2Mc 7:40 So he died in his **i**,

INTELLIGENCE → INTELLIGENT
Ex 31: 3 **i**, and knowledge in every kind of
1Ki 7:14 **i**, and knowledge in working bronze
Pr 8: 5 acquire **i**, you who lack it.
Sir 22:11 fool, for he has left **i** behind.

INTELLIGENT → INTELLIGENCE,
  INTELLIGENTLY
Pr 11:12 but an **i** person remains silent.
  18:15 An **i** mind acquires knowledge,
Ecc 9:11 nor riches to the **i**,
Sir 18:28 Every **i** person knows wisdom,
  19: 2 Wine and women lead **i** men astray,

INTELLIGENTLY* → INTELLIGENT
Pr 13:16 clever do all things **i**,
Sir 14:20 meditates on wisdom and reasons **i**,

INTELLIGIBLE*
1Co 14: 9 tongue you utter speech that is not **i**,

INTEND → INTENDED, INTENT,
  INTENTIONS, INTENTLY
1Ki 5: 5 So I **i** to build a house for the name
Jdt 9: 8 for they **i** to defile your sanctuary,

INTENDED → INTEND
Ge 50:20 Even though you **i** to do harm to
     me, God **i** it for good,
Jer 18:10 the good that I had **i** to do to it.

INTENT → INTEND
Ex 32:12 with evil **i** that he brought them out
Nu 35:11 kills a person without **i** may flee
Bar 1:22 followed the **i** of our own wicked

INTENTIONS → INTEND
Mk 7:21 the human heart, that evil **i** come:
Heb 4:12 judge the thoughts and **i** of the heart.

INTENTLY → INTEND
Ac 6:15 sat in the council looked **i** at him,

INTERCEDE → INTERCEDED,
  INTERCEDES, INTERCESSION,
  INTERCESSIONS
1Sa 2:25 can **i** for the sinner with the LORD;
Jer 7:16 and do not **i** with me,

INTERCEDED → INTERCEDE
Dt 9:20 but I **i** also on behalf of Aaron

INTERCEDES* → INTERCEDE
Ro 8:26 Spirit **i** with sighs too deep for
  8:27 because the Spirit **i** for the saints
  8:34 right hand of God, who indeed **i** for

INTERCESSION* → INTERCEDE
1Sa 2:25 against the LORD, who can make **i**?"
Isa 53:12 and made **i** for the transgressors.
Heb 7:25 he always lives to make **i** for them.

INTERCESSIONS* → INTERCEDE
1Ti 2: 1 **i**, and thanksgivings be made for

INTERCOURSE
Jdg 19:22 so that we may have **i** with him."
Ro 1:26 exchanged natural **i** for unnatural,
Jdt 12:12 go without having **i** with her.

INTEREST → INTERESTS
Ex 22:25 you shall not exact **i** from them.
Dt 23:19 not charge **i** on loans to another
  23:20 to a foreigner you may charge **i**,
Ne 5:10 Let us stop this taking of **i**.
Ps 15: 5 who do not lend money at **i**,
Lk 19:23 I could have collected it with **i**.'

INTERESTS → INTEREST
Isa 58:13 serving your own **i**,
1Co 7:34 and his **i** are divided.
Php 2: 4 to your own **i**, but to the **i** of others.
  2:21 All of them are seeking their own **i**,

INTERMARRY* → MARRY

Dt   7: 3 Do not **i** with them, giving your
Jos 23:12 and **i** with them,
Ezr   9:14 your commandments again and **i**

INTERPRET → INTERPRETATION, INTERPRETATIONS, INTERPRETED, INTERPRETING, INTERPRETS

Ge 41:15 no one who can **i** it.
Mt 16: 3 cannot **i** the signs of the times.
1Co 12:30 Do all speak in tongues? Do all **i**?
    14:13 should pray for the power to **i**.
    14:27 and each in turn; and let one **i**.

INTERPRETATION → INTERPRET

Ge 40:16 baker saw that the **i** was favorable,
Jdg 7:15 the telling of the dream and its **i**,
Da   2: 4 and we will reveal the **i**.”
     5:12 and he will give the **i**.”
     7:16 disclose to me the **i** of the matter:
1Co 12:10 to another the **i** of tongues.
    14:26 a revelation, a tongue, or an **i**.
2Pe 1:20 scripture is a matter of one’s own **i**,
2Es 4:47 show you the **i** of a parable.”
    12:10 “This is the **i** of this vision
    13:15 now show me the **i** of this dream

INTERPRETATIONS* → INTERPRET

Ge 40: 8 to them, “Do not **i** belong to God?
Da 5:16 you can give **i** and solve problems.
2Es 14: 8 and the **i** that you have heard;

INTERPRETED → INTERPRET

Ge 40:22 just as Joseph had **i** to them.
Lk 24:27 he **i** to them the things about himself

INTERPRETING* → INTERPRET

1Co 2:13 **i** spiritual things to those who are

INTERPRETS* → INTERPRET

1Co 14: 5 unless someone **i**,

INTOXICANTS* → INTOXICATED

1Sa 1:11 He shall drink neither wine nor **i**,

INTOXICATED → INTOXICANTS

Pr   5:19 may you be **i** always by her love.

INVADE → INVADED

La   1:10 the nations **i** her sanctuary,
Na   1:15 never again shall the wicked **i** you;

INVADED → INVADE

2Ki 17: 5 the king of Assyria **i** all the land
Joel 1: 6 nation has **i** my land,

INVISIBLE

Ro   1:20 **i** though they are,
Col 1:15 He is the image of the **i** God,
     1:16 and **i**, whether thrones or dominions
1Ti 1:17 To the King of the ages, immortal, **i**,
Heb 11:27 as though he saw him who is **i**.

INVITE → INVITED, INVITES

Mt 22: 9 and **i** everyone you find to
Lk 14:13 when you give a banquet, **i** the poor,
Jdt 12:10 and did not **i** any of his officers.
AdE 5:12 “The queen did not **i** anyone to

INVITED → INVITE

Lk 11:37 a Pharisee **i** him to dine with him;
    14:10 But when you are **i**,
Rev 19: 9 Blessed are those who are **i** to

INVITES → INVITE

Pr 18: 6 and a fool’s mouth **i** a flogging.
1Co 10:27 If an unbeliever **i** you to a meal
Sir 13: 9 When an influential person **i** you,

INVOKE* → INVOKED

Ge 4:26 began to **i** the name of the LORD.
   48:20 “By you Israel will **i** blessings,
Ex 23:13 Do not **i** the names of other gods;
1Ch 16: 4 to **i**, to thank, and to praise the LORD

Isa 48: 1 **i** the God of Israel, but not in truth
Ac   9:14 to bind all who **i** your name.”
1Pe 1:17 If you **i** as Father the one who

INVOKED → INVOKE

Ge 12: 8 and **i** the name of the LORD.

INWARD → INNER

Job 38:36 Who has put wisdom in the **i** parts,
Ps 51: 6 You desire truth in the **i** being;
  139:13 it was you who formed my **i** parts;

INWARDLY → INNER

Ps 62: 4 but **i** they curse.
Mt   7:15 sheep’s clothing but **i** are ravenous
Ro   2:29 a person is a Jew who is one **i**,
    8:23 groan **i** while we wait for adoption,
Sir 19:26 but **i** he is full of deceit.

IRON

Ge 4:22 made all kinds of bronze and **i** tools.
2Ki 6: 6 in there, and made the **i** float.
Ps   2: 9 shall break them with a rod of **i**,
Pr 27:17 **I** sharpens **i**, and one person
Isa 60:17 instead of **i** I will bring silver;
Da 2:33 its legs of **i**, its feet partly of **i**
    7: 7 had great **i** teeth and was devouring,
1Ti 4: 2 consciences are seared with a hot **i**.
Rev 2:27 with an **i** rod, as when clay pots are
    12: 5 to rule all the nations with a rod of **i**.
    19:15 he will rule them with a rod of **i**;

IRRATIONAL

2Pe 2:12 however, are like **i** animals,
Jude 1:10 like **i** animals, they know by instinct
Wis 11:15 to worship **i** serpents and worthless

IRREVOCABLE

Ro 11:29 gifts and the calling of God are **i**.

IRRITABLE* → IRRITATE

1Co 13: 5 it is not **i** or resentful;

IRRITATE* → IRRITABLE

1Sa 1: 6 to provoke her severely, to **i** her,

ISAAC

Son of Abraham by Sarah (Ge 17:19; 21:1-7; 1Ch 1:28). Abrahamic covenant perpetuated with (Ge 17:21; 26:2-5). Offered up by Abraham (Ge 22; Heb 11:17-19). Rebekah taken as wife (Ge 24). Inherited Abraham’s estate (Ge 25:5). Father of Esau and Jacob (Ge 25:19-26; 1Ch 1:34). Nearly lost Rebekah to Abimelech (Ge 26:1-11). Covenant with Abimelech (Ge 26:12-31). Tricked into blessing Jacob (Ge 27). Death (Ge 35:27-29). Father of Israel (Ex 3:6; Dt 29:13; Ro 9:10).

ISAIAH

Prophet to Judah (Isa 1:1). Called by the LORD (Isa 6). Announced judgment to Ahaz (Isa 7), deliverance from Assyria to Hezekiah (2Ki 19; Isa 36-37), deliverance from death to Hezekiah (2Ki 20:1-11; Isa 38). Chronicler of Judah’s history (2Ch 26:22; 32:32).

ISCARIOT

Mt 10: 4 Judas **I**, the one who betrayed him.
Lk 22: 3 Satan entered into Judas called **I**,

ISHBAAL*

Son of Saul who attempted to succeed him as king (2Sa 2:8-4:12).

ISHMAEL → ISHMAELITES

Son of Abraham by Hagar (Ge 16; 1Ch 1:28). Blessed, but not son of covenant (Ge 17:18-21; Gal 4:21-31). Sent away by Sarah (Ge 21:8-21). Children (Ge 25:12-18; 1Ch 1:29-31). Death (Ge 25:17).

ISHMAELITES → ISHMAEL

Ge 37:27 Come, let us sell him to the **I**,

ISLAND

Rev 1: 9 on the **i** called Patmos because of

  16:20 every **i** fled away, and no mountains

ISRAEL → EL-ELOHE-ISRAEL, ISRAEL’S, ISRAELITE, ISRAELITES, =JACOB

1. Name given to Jacob (Ge 32:28; 35:10; see Jacob).
2. Corporate name of Jacob’s descendants; often specifically Northern Kingdom.

Ge 49:24 of the Shepherd, the Rock of **I**,
    49:28 All these are the twelve tribes of **I**,
Ex 28:11 with the names of the sons of **I**;
    28:29 of the sons of **I** in the breastpiece
Nu 19:13 such persons shall be cut off from **I**.
    24:17 and a scepter shall rise out of **I**;
Dt   6: 4 Hear, O **I**: The LORD is our God,
   10:12 **I**, what does the LORD your God
   18: 1 no allotment or inheritance within **I**.
Jos 4:22 ‘I crossed over the Jordan here on
   24:31 I served the LORD all the days of
Jdg 17: 6 In those days there was no king in **I**;
   21: 3 be one tribe lacking in **I**?”
Ru   4:14 and may his name be renowned in **I**!
1Sa 3:20 And all **I** from Dan to Beer-sheba
    4:21 “The glory has departed from **I**,”
  14:23 LORD gave **I** the victory that day.
  15:26 rejected you from being king over **I**.
  17:46 may know that there is a God in **I**,
  18:16 But all **I** and Judah loved David;
2Sa 5: 2 you who shall be ruler over **I**.”
    5: 3 they anointed David king over **I**.
    7:26 ‘The LORD of hosts is God over **I**’;
  14:25 all **I** there was no one to be praised
1Ki 1:35 appointed him to be ruler over **I** and
   8:25 before me to sit on the throne of **I**,
  10: 9 Because the LORD loved **I** forever,
  12:19 So **I** has been in rebellion against
  18:17 “Is it you, you troubler of **I**?”
  19:18 Yet I will leave seven thousand in **I**,
2Ki 5: 8 learn that there is a prophet in **I**.”
  17:20 rejected all the descendants of **I**;
1Ch 17:22 And you made your people **I** to
   21: 1 Satan stood up against **I**,
  29:25 been on any king before him in **I**.
2Ch 9: 8 because your God loved **I**
Ps 22: 3 holy, enthroned on the praises of **I**.
  78:21 his anger mounted against **I**,
  81: 8 O **I**, if you would but listen to me!
  98: 3 and faithfulness to the house of **I**.
  125: 5 with evildoers. Peace be upon **I**!
Isa 1: 3 but **I** does not know, my people do
  11:12 and will assemble the outcasts of **I**,
  27: 6 **I** shall blossom and put forth shoots,
  44:21 **I**, you will not be forgotten by me.
  46:13 salvation in Zion, for **I** my glory.
Jer 2: 3 **I** was holy to the LORD,
  23: 6 Judah will be saved and **I** will live
  31: 2 wilderness; when **I** sought for rest,
  31:10 “He who scattered **I** will gather him,
  31:31 a new covenant with the house of **I**
  33:17 to sit on the throne of the house of **I**,
La   2: 5 like an enemy; he has destroyed **I**;
Eze 32:17 you a sentinel for the house of **I**;
  33: 7 made a sentinel for the house of **I**;
  34: 2 prophesy against the shepherds of **I**:
  36: 1 prophesy to the mountains of **I**,
  37:28 know that I the LORD sanctify **I**,
  39:23 shall know that the house of **I** went
Da 9:20 the sin of my people **I**,
Hos 7: 1 when I would heal **I**, the corruption
  11: 1 When **I** was a child, I loved him,
Am 4:12 Therefore thus I will do to you, O **I**;
   4:12 prepare to meet your God, O **I**!
   7:11 and **I** must go into exile away from
   8: 2 end has come upon my people **I**;
   9:14 restore the fortunes of my people **I**,
Mic 5: 2 for me one who is to rule in **I**,
Zep 3:13 the remnant of **I**; they shall do no
Zec 11:14 the family ties between Judah and **I**.
Mal 1: 5 the LORD beyond the borders of **I**!”
Mt   2: 6 who is to shepherd my people **I**.’”
  10: 6 to the lost sheep of the house of **I**.
  15:24 to the lost sheep of the house of **I**.”

Mk 12:29 answered, "The first is, 'Hear, O **I:**
15:32 Let the Messiah, the King of **I,**
Lk 1:54 He has helped his servant **I,**
2:34 falling and the rising of many in **I,**
22:30 judging the twelve tribes of **I.**
Jn 12:13 of the Lord—the King of **I!"**
Ac 1: 6 you will restore the kingdom to **I?"**
9:15 kings and before the people of **I;**
Ro 9: 6 not all Israelites truly belong to **I,**
9:31 but **I,** who did strive for the
11: 7 **I** failed to obtain what it was
11:26 And so all **I** will be saved;
Eph 2:12 aliens from the commonwealth of **I,**
Heb 8: 8 a new covenant with the house of **I**
Rev 7: 4 out of every tribe of the people of **I:**
Tob 1: 4 from among all the tribes of **I,**
Jdt 8:33 the Lord will deliver **I** by my hand.
15:10 you have done great good to **I,**
Sir 17:17 but **I** is the Lord's own portion.
1Mc 4:25 **I** had a great deliverance that day.
2Es 4:23 why **I** has been given over to the

ALL ISRAEL Ex 18:25; Nu 16:34; Dt 1:1;
5:1; 11:6; 13:11; 21:21; 27:9; 29:2; 31:1, 7, 11,
11; 32:45; 34:12; Jos 3:7, 17; 4:14; 7:24, 25;
8:15, 21, 24, 33; 10:15, 29, 31, 34, 36, 38, 43;
23:2; Jdg 8:27; 20:34; 1Sa 2:22; 3:20; 4:1, 5;
7:5; 11:2; 12:1; 13:4; 14:40; 17:11; 18:16;
19:5; 24:2; 25:1; 28:3, 4; 2Sa 2:9; 3:12, 21, 37;
4:1; 5:5; 8:15; 10:17; 11:1; 12:12; 14:25;
16:21, 22; 17:10, 11, 13; 19:11; 1Ki 1:20;
2:15; 3:28; 4:1, 7; 5:13; 8:62, 65; 11:16, 42;
12:1, 16, 18, 20, 20; 14:13, 18; 15:27, 33;
16:16, 17; 18:19; 22:17; 2Ki 3:6; 9:14; 10:21;
1Ch 9:1; 11:1, 4, 10; 12:38; 13:5, 6, 8; 14:8;
15:3, 28; 17:6; 18:14; 19:17; 21:4, 5; 28:4, 8;
29:21, 23, 25, 26; 2Ch 1:2, 2; 7:6, 8; 9:30;
10:1, 3, 16, 16; 11:3, 13; 12:1; 13:4, 15; 18:16;
24:5; 28:23; 29:24, 24; 30:1, 5, 6; 31:1; 35:3;
Ezr 2:70; 6:17; 8:25, 35; 10:5; Ne 7:73; 12:47;
13:26; Da 9:7, 11; Mal 4:4; Ro 11:26; Tob 1:6;
Jdt 15:14; AdE 13:18; 1Mc 2:70; 5:63; 9:20;
12:52; 13:26; 1Es 5:46, 61; 7:8; 8:7, 55, 65, 96

ASSEMBLY OF ISRAEL Lev 16:17; Dt
31:30; Jos 8:35; 1Ki 8:14, 14, 22, 55; 12:3;
1Ch 13:2; 2Ch 6:3, 3, 12, 13; 1Mc 4:59

CONGREGATION OF ISRAEL Ex 12:3,
6, 19, 47; Lev 4:13; Nu 16:9; 32:4; Jos 22:18,
20; 1Ki 8:5; 2Ch 5:6; 24:6; Sir 50:13

ELDERS OF ISRAEL Ex 3:16, 18; 12:21;
17:5, 6; 18:12; 24:1, 9; Lev 9:1; Nu 11:16, 30;
16:25; Dt 27:1; 31:9; Jos 7:6; 8:10; 1Sa 4:3;
8:4; 2Sa 3:17; 5:3; 17:4, 15; 1Ki 8:1, 3; 1Ch
11:3; 15:25; 2Ch 5:2, 4; Eze 14:1; 20:1, 3; Ac
5:21; 1Mc 11:23

GOD OF ISRAEL Ex 5:1; 24:10; 32:27;
34:23; Nu 16:9; Jos 7:13, 19, 20; 8:30; 9:18,
19; 10:40, 42; 13:14, 33; 14:14; 22:16, 24;
24:2, 23; Jdg 4:6; 5:3, 5; 6:8; 11:21, 23; 21:3;
Ru 2:12; 1Sa 1:17; 2:30; 5:7, 8, 8, 10, 10, 11;
6:3, 5; 10:18; 14:41, 41; 20:12; 23:10, 11;
25:32, 34; 2Sa 7:27; 12:7; 23:3; 1Ki 1:30, 48;
8:15, 17, 20, 23, 25, 26; 11:9, 31; 14:7, 13;
15:30; 16:13, 26, 33; 17:1, 14; 22:53; 2Ki 9:6;
10:31; 14:25; 18:5; 19:15, 20; 21:12; 22:15,
18; 1Ch 4:10; 5:26; 15:12, 14; 16:4, 36; 17:24;
22:6; 23:25; 24:19; 28:4; 2Ch 2:12; 6:4, 7, 10,
14, 16, 17; 11:16; 13:5; 15:4, 13; 20:19; 29:7,
10; 30:1, 5; 32:17; 33:16, 18; 34:23, 26; 36:13;
Ezr 1:3; 3:2; 4:1, 3; 5:1; 6:14, 21, 22; 7:6, 15;
8:35; 9:4, 15; Ps 41:13; 59:5; 68:8, 35; 69:6;
72:18; 106:48; Isa 17:6; 21:10, 17; 24:15;
29:23; 37:16, 21; 41:17; 45:3, 15; 48:1, 2;
52:12; Jer 7:3, 21; 9:15; 11:3; 13:12; 16:9;
19:3, 15; 21:4; 23:2; 24:5; 25:15, 27; 27:4, 21;
28:2, 14; 29:4, 8, 21, 25; 30:2; 31:23; 32:14,
15, 36; 33:4; 34:2, 13; 35:13, 17, 18, 19; 37:7;
38:17; 39:16; 42:9, 15, 18; 43:10; 44:2, 7, 11;
25; 45:2; 46:25; 48:1; 50:18; 51:33; Eze 8:4;
9:3; 10:19, 20; 11:22; 43:2; 44:2; Zep 2:9; Mal
2:16; Mt 15:31; Lk 1:68; Tob 13:17; Jdt 4:12;
6:21; 10:1; 12:8; 13:7; 14:10; AdE 14:3; Sir

47:18; Bar 2:11; 3:1, 4; 2Mc 9:5; 1Es 1:48;
5:48, 67; 6:1; 7:4, 9, 15; 8:3, 65; 9:39

HOUSE OF ISRAEL Ex 16:31; 40:38; Lev
10:6; 17:3, 8, 10; 22:18; Nu 20:29; Jos 21:45;
Ru 4:11; 1Sa 7:2, 3; 2Sa 1:12; 6:5, 15; 12:8;
16:3; 1Ki 12:21; 20:31; Ps 98:3; 115:12;
135:19; Isa 5:7; 14:2; 46:3; 63:7; Jer 2:4, 26;
3:18, 20; 5:11, 15; 9:26; 10:1; 11:10, 17;
13:11; 18:6, 6; 23:8; 31:27, 31, 33; 33:14, 17;
48:13; Eze 3:1, 4, 5, 7, 7, 17; 4:3, 4, 5; 5:4;
6:11; 8:6, 10, 11, 12; 9:9; 11:5, 15; 12:6, 9, 10,
24, 27; 13:5, 9; 14:4, 5, 6, 7, 11; 17:2; 18:6,
15, 25, 29, 29, 30, 31; 20:13, 27, 30, 31, 39,
40, 44; 22:18; 24:21; 28:24, 25; 29:6, 16, 21;
33:7, 10, 11, 20; 34:30; 35:15; 36:10, 17, 21,
22, 22, 32, 37; 37:11, 16; 39:12, 22, 23, 25, 29;
40:4; 43:7, 10; 44:6, 6, 12, 22; 45:6, 8, 17, 17;
Hos 1:4, 6; 5:1; 6:10; 11:12; Am 5:1, 4, 25;
6:1, 14; 7:10; 9:9; Mic 1:5; 3:1, 9; Zec 8:13;
Mt 10:6; 15:24; Ac 2:36; 7:42; Heb 8:8, 10;
Jdt 4:15; 6:17; 8:6; 13:14; 14:5, 10; 16:24; Bar
2:26; 3Mc 2:10

ISRAEL AND JUDAH 1Sa 17:52; 18:16;
2Sa 5:5; 11:11; 21:2; 24:1; 2Ki 17:13; 1Ch
9:1; 2Ch 27:7; 30:1, 6; 31:6; 35:27; 36:8; Jer
30:3, 4; 36:2; 51:5; Eze 9:9; Bar 2:1; 1Es 1:33

JUDAH AND ISRAEL 1Ki 4:20, 25; 2Ch
16:11; 25:26; 28:26; 32:32; 35:18; Zec 11:14

KING OF ISRAEL 1Sa 24:14; 26:20; 2Sa
6:20; 1Ki 20:4, 7, 11, 21, 22, 28, 31, 32, 34,
40, 41, 43; 22:2, 3, 4, 5, 6, 8, 9, 10, 18, 26, 29,
30, 30, 31, 32, 33, 34, 44; 2Ki 3:4, 5, 9, 10, 11,
12, 13, 13; 5:5, 6, 7, 8; 6:9, 10, 11, 12, 21, 26;
7:6; 13:16, 18; 16:7; 2Ch 18:4, 5, 7, 8, 9, 17,
25, 28, 29, 30, 31, 32, 33, 34; 28:5; 35:3;
Ezr 5:11; Pr 1:1; Isa 44:6; Hos 10:15; Zep
3:15; Mt 27:42; Mk 15:32; Jn 1:49; 12:13; 1Es
6:14

KINGS OF ISRAEL 1Ki 14:19; 15:31; 16:5,
14, 20, 27, 33; 22:39; 2Ki 1:18; 8:18; 10:34;
13:8, 12, 13; 14:15, 16, 28, 29; 15:11, 15, 21,
26, 31; 16:3; 17:2, 8; 23:19, 22; 1Ch 9:1; 2Ch
20:34; 21:6, 13; 27:7; 28:2, 27; 33:18; 35:18,
27; 36:8; Mic 1:14; 1Es 1:21, 33

KING OVER [ALL] ISRAEL 1Sa 15:1, 17,
26, 35; 16:1; 23:17; 2Sa 5:3, 12, 17; 12:7;
19:22; 1Ki 1:34; 4:1; 11:37; 12:20; 14:14;
16:16; 19:16; 2Ki 3:1; 9:3, 12; 1Ch 11:3;
12:38; 14:2, 8; 23:1; 28:4, 4; Ne 13:26; Ecc
1:12

LAND OF ISRAEL 1Sa 13:19; 2Ki 5:2, 4;
6:23; 1Ch 13:2; 22:2; 2Ch 2:17; 30:25; 34:7;
Eze 7:2; 11:17; 12:19, 22; 13:9; 18:2; 20:38,
42; 21:2, 3; 25:3, 6; 27:17; 33:24; 36:6; 37:12;
38:18, 19; 40:2; 47:18; Mt 2:20, 21; Tob 1:4;
14:4, 4, 5

MEN OF ISRAEL Dt 29:10; Jdg 7:23;
20:11; 20:31; 1Sa 7:11; 17:19; 26:2; 31:1, 7, 7;
2Sa 2:17; 6:1; 10:9; 17:14, 24; 18:7; 1Ch 10:1,
7; 19:10; 2Ch 13:17; SS 3:7; Jdt 15:13; 1Mc
7:5; 1Es 8:92

MOUNTAINS OF ISRAEL Eze 6:2, 3;
19:9; 33:28; 34:13, 14; 35:12; 36:1, 1, 4, 8;
37:22; 38:8; 39:2, 4, 17

PEOPLE ISRAEL Ex 18:1; Dt 21:8, 8;
26:15; Jdg 11:23; 1Sa 2:29; 9:16; 10:1; 14:41;
15:1; 27:12; 2Sa 3:18; 5:2, 12; 7:7, 8, 10, 11,
24; 1Ki 6:13; 8:16, 16, 30, 33, 34, 36, 38, 41,
43, 52, 56, 59, 66; 14:7; 16:2, 2; 1Ch 11:2, 2;
14:2; 17:7, 9, 10, 21, 22; 2Ch 6:5, 6, 21, 24,
25, 27, 29, 32, 33; 7:10; 20:7; 31:8; 35:3; Ps
135:12; Isa 10:22; Jer 7:12; 12:14; 23:13;
32:21; Eze 14:9; 25:14; 36:8, 12; 38:14, 16;
39:7; Da 9:20; Am 7:8, 15; 8:2; 9:14; Mt 2:6;
Lk 2:32; Ac 13:17; AdE 10:13; Bar 2:35; 1Mc
4:31; 2Mc 1:26; 1Es 1:4; 3Mc 2:6, 16

PEOPLE OF ISRAEL Ex 11:10; 24:5, 11,
17; 31:17; Lev 1:2; 4:2; 7:23, 29, 34, 34, 36,
38; 9:3; 10:11, 14; 11:2; 12:2; 15:2, 31; 16:5,

16, 19, 21, 34; 17:2, 5, 12, 13, 14; 18:2; 19:2;
20:2, 2; 21:24; 22:2, 3, 15, 18, 32; 23:2, 10,
24, 34, 43, 44; 24:2, 8, 10, 15, 23, 23; 25:2, 33,
55; 26:46; 27:2, 34; Nu 20:13; 22:3, 41; 25:8;
Jos 8:33; 22:12; Jdg 11:33; 19:12; 20:3; 1Sa
2:28; 7:6, 7, 7, 8; 8:22; 9:2; 15:6; 2Sa 7:6, 7;
15:6; 19:40, 41, 42, 43, 43; 20:2; 21:2, 2, 2;
24:1, 4; 1Ki 8:2, 63; 9:20; 12:24, 33; 14:24;
16:21; 20:15, 27; 2Ki 8:12; 13:5; 16:3; 17:7, 8,
9, 22, 24; 18:4; 21:2, 9; 1Ch 6:64; 21:1; 27:1;
2Ch 5:2, 10; 6:11; 7:3; 8:2, 8, 9; 10:17, 18;
28:3, 8; 30:6, 21; 31:1, 5, 6; 33:2, 9; 34:33;
35:17; Ezr 6:16, 21; 7:7, 13; 9:1; Ne 1:6, 6;
2:10; 7:73; 8:14, 17; 9:1; 10:39; Ps 103:7;
148:14; Isa 27:12; 31:6; Jer 16:14, 15; 23:7;
32:30, 30, 32; 50:4, 33; Eze 2:3; 4:13; 6:5;
35:5; 37:21; 43:7; 44:9, 15; 48:11; Hos 1:10,
11; 3:1; 4:1; Joel 3:16; Am 2:11; 3:1, 12; 4:5;
9:7; Mic 5:3; Mt 27:9; Lk 1:16; Ac 4:10; 9:15;
10:36; 13:24; 1Co 10:18; 2Co 3:7, 13; Php 3:5;
Rev 2:14; 7:4; Jdt 4:8; 5:1; 6:2; 9:14; 10:8; Bar
2:1, 28; 3:4; 1Mc 5:30; 5:60; 1Es 1:5, 19; 7:6,
10, 13; 8:5, 69; 9:37; Pm 151:7; 2Es 5:35

SONS OF ISRAEL Ge 42:5; 45:21; 46:5;
Ex 1:1; 28:9, 11, 12, 21, 29; 39:6, 7, 14; Dt
23:17; 1Ch 2:1

TRIBES OF ISRAEL Ge 49:16, 28; Ex
24:4; Nu 10:4; 31:4; Dt 29:21; 33:5; Jos 3:12;
12:7; 24:1; Jdg 18:1; 20:2, 10, 12; 21:5, 8, 15;
1Sa 2:28; 9:21; 10:20; 15:17; 2Sa 5:1; 15:10;
19:9; 20:14; 24:2; 1Ki 8:16; 11:32; 14:21; 2Ki
21:7; 1Ch 27:16, 22; 2Ch 6:5; 11:16; 12:13;
33:7; Ezr 6:17; Ps 78:55; Eze 37:19; 47:13, 21,
22; 48:19, 29, 31; Hos 5:9; Zec 9:1; Mt 19:28;
Lk 22:30; Tob 1:4, 4; Sir 45:11; 1Es 7:8

ISRAEL'S → ISRAEL
Hos 5: 5 **I** pride testifies against him;

ISRAELITE → ISRAEL
Ex 35:29 the **I** men and women whose hearts
Ne 9: 2 Then those of **I** descent separated
Jn 1:47 an **I** in whom there is no deceit!"
Ro 11: 1 **I** myself am an **I,** a descendant of

ISRAELITES → ISRAEL
Ex 1: 7 But the **I** were fruitful and prolific;
2:23 The **I** groaned under their slavery,
3: 9 cry of the **I** has now come to me;
12:35 The **I** had done as Moses told them;
14:22 **I** went into the sea on dry ground,
16:12 have heard the complaining of the **I;**
16:35 The **I** ate manna forty years,
28:30 the **I** on his heart before the LORD
29:45 I will dwell among the **I,** and I will
31:16 the **I** shall keep the sabbath,
33: 5 had said to Moses, "Say to the **I,**
39:42 The **I** had done all of the work just
Nu 2:32 the enrollment of the **I** by their
6:23 saying, Thus you shall bless the **I:**
9: 2 Let the **I** keep the passover at its
9:17 then the **I** would set out;
9:17 there the **I** would camp.
14: 2 all the **I** complained against Moses
20:12 my holiness before the eyes of the **I,**
21: 6 bit the people, so that many **I** died.
27:12 the land that I have given to the **I.**
33: 3 after the passover the **I** went out
35:10 Speak to the **I,** and say to them:
Dt 4:44 the law that Moses set before the **I.**
33: 1 blessed the **I** before his death.
Jos 1: 2 that I am giving to them, to the **I.**
5: 6 For the **I** traveled forty years in the
7: 1 the **I** broke faith in regard to the
8:32 And there, in the presence of the **I,**
18: 1 congregation of the **I** assembled at
21: 3 I gave to the Levites the following
22: 9 parting from the **I** at Shiloh,
Jdg 2:11 the **I** did what was evil in the sight
3:12 The **I** again did what was evil in the
4: 1 The **I** again did what was evil in the
6: 1 **I** did what was evil in the sight of

10: 6 The **I** again did what was evil in the
13: 1 The **I** again did what was evil in the
1Sa 17: 2 the **I** gathered and encamped in the
1Ki 9:22 of the **I** Solomon made no slaves;
12:17 over the **I** who were living in the
1Ch 9: 2 possessions in their towns were **I**,
2Co 11:22 they Hebrews? So am I. Are they **I**?

ALL THE ISRAELITES
Ex 10:23; 12:42, 50; 16:6; 34:30, 32; Nu 8:16; 14:2, 10, 39; 17:9; 27:21; 32:18; Dt 27:14; Jos 3:1; 7:23; 10:24; 20:9; Jdg 2:4; 10:8; 19:30; 20:1; 20:26; 1Sa 2:14; 11:15; 13:20; 14:22; 17:24; 2Sa 16:15, 18; 18:17; 19:8; 1Ki 18:20; 2Ch 5:3; Tob 14:7; Sir 46:10; 1Mc 5:45

CONGREGATION OF [THE]
ISRAELITES
Ex 16:1, 2, 9, 10; 17:1; 35:1, 4, 20; Nu 1:2, 53; 8:9, 20; 13:26; 14:5, 7; 15:25, 26; 16:41; 19:9; 25:6; 26:2; 27:20; 31:12; Jos 18:1; Sir 50:20

TRIBES OF THE ISRAELITES
Nu 30:1; 36:9; Jos 4:5, 8; 14:1; 19:51; 21:1; Rev 21:12

ISSACHAR
Son of Jacob by Leah (Ge 30:18; 35:23; 1Ch 2:1). Tribe of blessed (Ge 49:14-15; Dt 33:18-19), numbered (Nu 1:29; 26:25), allotted land (Jos 19:17-23; Eze 48:25), assisted Deborah (Jdg 5:15), 12,000 from (Rev 7:7).

ISSUE
Ge 15: 4 very own **i** shall be your heir."
Nu 18:15 first **i** of the womb of all creatures,

ITALIAN* → ITALY
Ac 10: 1 a centurion of the **I** Cohort,

ITALY → ITALIAN
Ac 27: 1 decided that we were to sail for **I**,
Heb 13:24 Those from **I** send you greetings.

ITCHING
2Ti 4: 3 sound doctrine, but having **i** ears,

ITHAMAR
Son of Aaron (Ex 6:23; 1Ch 6:3). Duties at tabernacle (Ex 38:21; Nu 4:21-33; 7:8).

ITTAI
2Sa 15:19 Then the king said to **I** the Gittite,

IVORY
1Ki 10:22 silver, **i**, apes, and peacocks.
22:39 and the **i** house that he built,
Am 3:15 and the houses of **i** shall perish,
Rev 18:12 all articles of **i**, all articles of costly

IVY* → IVY-LEAF, IVY-WREATHED
2Mc 6: 7 compelled to wear wreathes of **i**

IVY-LEAF* → IVY, LEAF
3Mc 2:29 bodies by fire with the **i** symbol

IVY-WREATHED* → IVY
Jdt 15:12 She took **i** wands in her hands
2Mc 10: 7 carrying **i** wands and beautiful

J

JABBOK
Ge 32:22 and crossed the ford of the **J**.
Dt 3:16 to the **J**, the wadi being boundary of

JABESH
1Sa 11: 1 and all the men of **J** said to Nahash,
31:12 They came to **J** and burned them
1Ch 10:12 of his sons, and brought them to **J**.

JABIN
Jos 11: 1 When King **J** of Hazor heard of this,
Jdg 4:23 God subdued King **J** of Canaan

JACKALS
Ps 63:10 they shall be prey for **j**.
Isa 35: 7 haunt of **j** shall become a swamp,
Mal 1: 3 and his heritage a desert for **j**.

JACOB → =ISRAEL
1. Son of Isaac, younger twin of Esau (Ge 26:21-26; 1Ch 1:34). Bought Esau's birthright (Ge 26:29-34); tricked Isaac into blessing him (Ge 27:1-37). Fled to Haran (Ge 28:1-5). Abrahamic covenant perpetuated through (Ge 28:13-15; Mal 1:2). Vision at Bethel (Ge 28:10-22). Served Laban for Rachel and Leah (Ge 29:1-30). Children (Ge 29:31-30:24; 35:16-26; 1Ch 2-9). Flocks increased (Ge 30:25-43). Returned to Canaan (Ge 31). Wrestled with God; name changed to Israel (Ge 32:22-32). Reconciled to Esau (Ge 33). Returned to Bethel (Ge 35:1-15). Favored Joseph (Ge 37:3). Sent sons to Egypt during famine (Ge 42-43). Settled in Egypt (Ge 46). Blessed Ephraim and Manasseh (Ge 48). Blessed sons (Ge 49:1-28; Heb 11:21). Death (Ge 49:29-33). Burial (Ge 50:1-14).
2. Corporate name of Jacob's descendants; often specifically Northern Kingdom.
Ps 53: 6 **J** will rejoice; Israel will be glad.
59:13 of the earth that God rules over **J**.
135: 4 the LORD has chosen **J** for himself,
Isa 44: 1 But now hear, O **J** my servant,
Jer 30:10 have no fear, my servant **J**,
Eze 39:25 Now I will restore the fortunes of **J**,
Mic 7:20 You will show faithfulness to **J**
Mal 1: 2 Yet I have loved **J**
Ro 9:13 "I have loved **J**,
Sir 36:13 Gather all the tribes of **J**,
1Mc 1:28 house of **J** was clothed with shame.

*GOD OF JACOB
Ex 3:6, 15; 4:5; 2Sa 23:1; Ps 20:1; 24:6; 46:7, 11; 75:9; 76:6; 81:1, 4; 84:8; 94:7; 114:7; 146:5; Isa 2:3; Mic 4:2; Mt 22:32; Mk 12:26; Lk 20:37; Ac 3:13

HOUSE OF JACOB
Ge 46:27; Ex 19:3; Ps 114:1; Isa 2:5, 6; 8:17; 10:20; 14:1; 29:22; 46:3; 48:1; 58:1; Jer 2:4; 5:20; Eze 20:5; Am 3:13; 9:8; Ob 1:17, 18; Mic 2:7; 3:9; Lk 1:33; Ac 7:46; 1Mc 1:28; 2Es 12:46

SERVANT JACOB
Ge 32:4, 18, 20; Isa 45:4; 48:20; Jer 30:10; 46:27, 28; Eze 28:25; 37:25; Bar 3:36

JAEL*
Woman who killed Canaanite general, Sisera (Jdg 4:17-22; 5:6, 24-27).

JAILER
Ge 39:21 favor in the sight of the chief **j**.
Ac 16:27 **j** woke up and saw the prison doors

JAIR
Judge from Gilead (Jdg 10:3-5).

JAIRUS
Synagogue ruler whose daughter Jesus raised (Mk 5:22-43; Lk 8:41-56).

JAMBRES*
2Ti 3: 8 As Jannes and **J** opposed Moses,

JAMES
1. Apostle; brother of John (Mt 4:21-22; 10:2; Mk 3:17; Lk 5:1-10). At transfiguration (Mt 17:1-13; Mk 9:1-13; Lk 9:28-36). Killed by Herod (Ac 12:2).
2. Apostle; son of Alphaeus (Mt 10:3; Mk 3:18; Lk 6:15).
3. Brother of Jesus (Mt 13:55; Mk 6:3; Lk 24:10; Gal 1:19) and Judas (Jude 1). With believers before Pentecost (Ac 1:13). Leader of church at Jerusalem (Ac 12:17; 15; 21:18; Gal 2:9, 12). Author of epistle (Jas 1:1).

JANNES*
2Ti 3: 8 As **J** and Jambres opposed Moses,

JAPHETH
Son of Noah (Ge 5:32; 1Ch 1:4-5). Blessed (Ge 9:18-28). Sons of (Ge 10:2-5).

JAR → JARS
Ge 24:14 offer your **j** that I may drink,'
Ex 16:33 Moses said to Aaron, "Take a **j**,
1Ki 17:14 The **j** of meal will not be emptied
Mk 14: 3 alabaster **j** of very costly ointment
Lk 8:16 lighting a lamp hides it under a **j**,
22:10 man carrying a **j** of water will meet

JARS → JAR
Jdg 7:19 blew the trumpets and smashed the **j**
Jn 2: 6 there were six stone water **j** for
2Co 4: 7 But we have this treasure in clay **j**,

JASHAR*
Jos 10:13 Is this not written in the Book of **J**?
2Sa 1:18 it is written in the Book of **J**.)

JASON
Ac 17: 7 **J** has entertained them as guests.
2Mc 4: 7 **J** the brother of Onias obtained

JASPER
Ex 28:20 a **j**; they shall be set in gold filigree.
Eze 28:13 and moonstone, beryl, onyx, and **j**,
Rev 4: 3 one seated there looks like **j** and
21:19 the first was **j**, the second sapphire,

JAVELIN
1Sa 17:45 to me with sword and spear and **j**;

JAWBONE
Jdg 15:15 Then he found a fresh **j** of a donkey,

JAZER
Nu 21:32 Moses sent to spy out **J**;
32: 1 When they saw that the land of **J**

JEALOUS → JEALOUSLY, JEALOUSY
Ge 37:11 So his brothers were **j** of him,
Ex 20: 5 I the LORD your God am a **j** God,
34:14 whose name is **J**, is a **j** God).
Nu 5:14 and he is **j** of his wife,
11:29 Moses said to him, "Are you **j** for
Dt 4:24 for is a devouring fire, a **j** God.
5: 9 I the LORD your God am a **j** God,
6:15 who is present with you, is a **j** God.
32:16 They made him **j** with strange gods,
32:21 made me **j** with what is no god,
Jos 24:19 He is a **j** God;
Ps 79: 5 Will your **j** wrath burn like fire?
Isa 11:13 Ephraim shall not be **j** of Judah,
Eze 36: 6 I am speaking in my **j** wrath,
39:25 and I will be **j** for my holy name.
Joel 2:18 the LORD became **j** for his land,
Na 1: 2 A **j** and avenging God is the LORD,
Zec 1:14 very **j** for Jerusalem and for Zion.
8: 2 I am **j** for Zion with great jealousy,
Ac 7: 9 patriarchs, **j** of Joseph, sold him
17: 5 Jews became **j**, and with the help
Ro 10:19 "I will make you **j** of those
11:11 so as to make Israel **j**.

JEALOUSLY* → JEALOUS
Jas 4: 5 "God yearns **j** for the spirit

JEALOUSY → JEALOUS
Nu 5:14 if a spirit of **j** comes on him,
1Ki 14:22 provoked him to **j** with their sins
Ps 78:58 they moved him to **j** with their idols.
Pr 6:34 For **j** arouses a husband's fury,
27: 4 but who is able to stand before **j**?
Eze 8: 3 the image of **j**, which provokes to **j**.
Zec 8: 2 I am jealous for Zion with great **j**,
Mk 15:10 out of **j** that the chief priests had
Ac 5:17 the Sadducees), being filled with **j**,
13:45 the crowds, they were filled with **j**;
Ro 13:13 not in quarreling and **j**,
1Co 3: 3 as long as there is **j** and quarreling
10:22 Or are we provoking the Lord to **j**?
2Co 11: 2 I feel a divine **j** for you,
12:20 there may perhaps be quarreling, **j**,

Gal   5:20 enmities, strife, **j**, anger, quarrels,
Sir   30:24 **J** and anger consume life,

JEBUS → =JERUSALEM, JEBUSITE, JEBUSITES

1Ch 11: 4 that is **J**, where the Jebusites were,

JEBUSITE → JEBUS

2Sa 24:18 the threshing floor of Araunah the **J**.
2Ch   3: 1 the threshing floor of Ornan the **J**.

JEBUSITES → JEBUS

Ge   15:21 the Girgashites, and the **J**."
Ex   3: 8 the Perizzites, the Hivites, and the **J**,
Jos 15:63 Judah could not drive out the **J**,
2Sa   5: 6 marched to Jerusalem against the **J**,

JECONIAH → =JEHOIACHIN

A form of Jehoiachin (Jer 24:1).

JEDIDIAH* → =SOLOMON

2Sa 12:25 named him **J**, because of the LORD.

JEDUTHUN

1Ch 16:41 With them were Heman and **J**,
2Ch 35:15 and Heman, and the king's seer **J**.
Ps   39: T the leader: to **J**. A Psalm of David.

JEERED*

2Ki   2:23 boys came out of the city and **j**

JEHOAHAZ

1. Son of Jehu; king of Israel (2Ki 13:1-9).
2. Son of Josiah; king of Judah (2Ki 23:31-34; 2Ch 36:1-4).

JEHOASH → =JOASH

1. Son of Ahaziah, king of Judah (2Ki 12). See Joash, 1.
2. Son of Jehoahaz; king of Israel. Defeat of Aram prophesied by Elisha (2Ki 13:10-25). Defeated Amaziah in Jerusalem (2Ki 14:1-16). See Joash, 2.

JEHOIACHIN → =CONIAH, =JECONIAH

Son of Jehoiakim; king of Judah exiled by Nebuchadnezzar (2Ki 24:8-17; 2Ch 36:8-10; Eze 1:2). Raised from prisoner status (2Ki 25:27-30; Jer 52:31-34).

JEHOIADA

Priest who sheltered Joash from Athaliah (2Ki 11-12; 2Ch 22:11-24:16).

JEHOIAKIM → =ELIAKIM

Son of Josiah; made king of Judah by Nebuchadnezzar (2Ki 23:34-24:6; 2Ch 36:4-8; Jer 22:18-23). Burned scroll of Jeremiah's prophecies (Jer 36).

JEHORAM → =JORAM

1. Son of Jehoshaphat; king of Judah. Prophesied against by Elijah; killed by the LORD (2Ch 21). See Joram, 1.
2. Son of Ahab; king of Israel (2Ch 22:5). With Jehoshaphat fought against Moab (2Ki 3). See Joram, 2.

JEHOSHAPHAT

Son of Asa; king of Judah. Strengthened his kingdom (2Ch 17). Joined with Ahab against Aram (2Ki 22; 2Ch 18). Established judges (2Ch 19). Joined Joram against Moab (2Ki 3; 2Ch 20). Valley of judgment (Joel 3:2, 12).

JEHOZADAK

1Ch   6:15 and **J** went into exile when
Hag   1:12 and Joshua son of **J**, the high priest,

JEHU

1. Prophet against Baasha (2Ki 16:1-7).
2. King of Israel. Anointed by Elijah to obliterate house of Ahab (1Ki 19:16-17); anointed by servant of Elisha (2Ki 9:1-13). Killed Joram and Ahaziah (2Ki 9:14-29; 2Ch 22:7-9). Jezebel (2Ki 9:30-37), relatives of Ahab (2Ki

10:1-17; Hos 1:4), ministers of Baal (2Ki 10:18-29). Death (2Ki 10:30-36).

JEPHTHAH

Judge from Gilead who delivered Israel from Ammon (Jdg 10:6-12:7). Made rash vow concerning his daughter (Jdg 11:30-40).

JEREMIAH

Prophet to Judah (Jer 1:1-3). Called by the LORD (Jer 1). Put in stocks (Jer 20:1-3). Threatened for prophesying (Jer 11:18-23; 26). Opposed by Hananiah (Jer 28). Scroll burned (Jer 36). Imprisoned (Jer 37). Thrown into cistern (Jer 38). Forced to Egypt with those fleeing Babylonians (Jer 43).

JERICHO

Nu   22: 1 of Moab across the Jordan from **J**.
Dt   34: 3 valley of **J**, the city of palm trees—
Jos   3:16 the people crossed over opposite **J**.
      5:10 of the month in the plains of **J**.
      6: 2 "See, I have handed **J** over to you,
      6:26 to build this—this **J**!
1Ki 16:34 In his days Hiel of Bethel built **J**;
2Ki 25: 5 and overtook him in the plains of **J**;
Lk   10:30 going down from Jerusalem to **J**,
     18:35 As he approached **J**, a blind man
     19: 1 He entered **J** and was passing
Heb 11:30 the walls of **J** fell after they had

JEROBOAM

1. Official of Solomon; rebelled to become first king of Israel (1Ki 11:26-40; 12:1-20; 2Ch 10). Idolatry (1Ki 12:25-33; Tob 1:5; Sir 47:23); judgment (1Ki 13-14; 2Ch 13).
2. Son of Jehoash; king of Israel (1Ki 14:23-29).

JERUBBAAL → =GIDEON

Jdg   6:32 on that day Gideon was called **J**,
1Sa 12:11 And the LORD sent **J** and Barak.

JERUSALEM → =JEBUS, JERUSALEM'S, =SALEM

Jos 10: 1 of **J** heard how Joshua had taken Ai,
     15: 8 slope of the Jebusites (that is, **J**);
Jdg   1: 8 people of Judah fought against **J**
1Sa 17:54 of the Philistine and brought it to **J**;
2Sa   5: 5 and at **J** he reigned over all Israel
      9:13 Mephibosheth lived in **J**,
     11: 1 But David remained at **J**.
     15:29 carried the ark of God back to **J**,
     24:16 stretched out his hand toward **J**
1Ki   3: 1 of the LORD and the wall around **J**.
      9:15 the Millo and the wall of **J**, Hazor,
      9:19 Solomon desired to build, in **J**,
     10:26 chariot cities and with the king in **J**.
     10:27 silver as common in **J** as stones,
     11: 7 on the mountain east of **J**
     11:13 servant David and for the sake of **J**,
     11:36 a lamp before me in **J**,
     14:25 Shishak of Egypt came up against **J**;
2Ki 12:17 set his face to go up against **J**,
     14:13 and broke down the wall of **J**
     18:17 They went up and came to **J**.
     18:35 should deliver **J** out of my hand?'"
     19:31 from from **J** a remnant shall go out,
     21: 4 "In **J** I will put my name."
     21:12 upon **J** and Judah such evil that
     23:27 reject this city that I have chosen, **J**,
     24:10 of Babylon came up to **J**,
     24:14 carried away all **J**, all the officials,
     24:20 **J** and Judah so angered the LORD
     25: 1 with all his army against **J**,
     25:10 broke down the walls around **J**.
1Ch   4: 4 David and all Israel marched to **J**,
     21:16 a drawn sword stretched out over **J**.
2Ch   1: 4 for he had pitched a tent for it in **J**.)
      3: 1 house of the LORD in **J** on Mount
      6: 6 chosen **J** in order that my name may
      9: 1 to **J** to test him with hard questions,
     20:15 all Judah and inhabitants of **J**,
     20:27 Then all the people of Judah and **J**,

     29: 8 of the LORD came upon Judah and **J**
     36:19 broke down the wall of **J**,
Ezr   1: 2 to build him a house at **J**
      2: 1 they returned to **J** and Judah,
      3: 1 the people gathered together in **J**.
      4:12 up from you to us have gone to **J**.
      4:24 on the house of God in **J** stopped
      6:12 or to destroy this house of God in **J**,
      7: 8 They came to **J** in the fifth month,
      9: 9 and to give us a wall in Judea and **J**.
     10: 7 that they should assemble at **J**,
Ne   1: 2 the captivity, and about **J**,
      1: 3 the wall of **J** is broken down,
      2:17 Come, let us rebuild the wall of **J**,
      2:20 share or claim or historic right in **J**."
      3: 8 restored **J** as far as the Broad Wall.
      4: 8 and fight against **J** and to cause
     11: 1 out of ten to live in the holy city **J**,
     12:27 at the dedication of the wall of **J**
     12:43 The joy of **J** was heard far away.
Ps   51:18 pleasure; rebuild the walls of **J**,
     79: 1 they have laid **J** in ruins.
    122: 2 are standing within your gates, O **J**!
    122: 6 Pray for the peace of **J**:
    125: 2 As the mountains surround **J**,
    128: 5 May you see the prosperity of **J** all
    137: 5 If I forget you, O **J**, let my right
    147: 2 The LORD builds up **J**;
    147:12 Praise the LORD, O **J**!
Ecc   1:12 Teacher, when king over Israel in **J**,
SS   6: 4 comely as **J**, terrible as an army
Isa   1: 1 concerning Judah and **J** in the days
      2: 1 saw concerning Judah and **J**.
      3: 1 from **J** and from Judah support
      3: 8 For **J** has stumbled and Judah has
      4: 3 who has been recorded for life in **J**,
      8:14 and a snare for the inhabitants of **J**.
     27:13 the LORD on the holy mountain at **J**.
     31: 5 so the LORD of hosts will protect **J**;
     33:20 Your eyes will see **J**, a quiet
     40: 2 Speak tenderly to **J**,
     40: 9 lift up your voice with strength, O **J**,
     52: 1 Put on your beautiful garments, O **J**,
     52: 2 from the dust, rise up, O captive **J**;
     62: 6 O **J**, I have posted sentinels,
     62: 7 establishes **J** and makes it renowned
     65:18 for I am about to create **J** as a joy,
     66:13 you shall be comforted in **J**.
Jer   2: 2 and proclaim in the hearing of **J**,
      3:17 At that time **J** shall be called the
      4: 5 and proclaim in **J**, and say:
      4:14 O **J**, wash your heart clean of
      5: 1 so that I may pardon **J**.
      6: 6 cast up a siege ramp against **J**.
      9:11 I will make **J** a heap of ruins, a lair
     13:27 Woe to you, O **J**! How long will it
     23:14 of **J** I have seen a more shocking
     26:18 **J** shall become a heap of ruins,
     32: 2 king of Babylon was besieging **J**,
     33:10 and the streets of **J** that are desolate,
     39: 1 army came against **J** and besieged
     51:50 and let **J** come into your mind:
     52:14 broke down all the walls around **J**.
La   1: 8 **J** sinned grievously, so she has
Eze   8: 3 brought me in visions of God to **J**,
     14:21 upon **J** my four deadly acts of
     16: 2 make known to **J** her abominations,
     21: 2 toward **J** and preach against the
     23: 4 is Samaria, and Oholibah is **J**.
Da   5: 3 the house of God in **J**,
      6:10 in his upper room open toward **J**,
      9: 2 be fulfilled for the devastation of **J**,
      9:12 what has been done against **J** has
      9:25 went out to restore and rebuild **J**
Joel 3: 1 I restore the fortunes of Judah and **J**,
      3:16 and utters his voice from **J**,
      3:18 shall be holy, and strangers
Am   2: 5 it shall devour the strongholds of **J**.
Mic   1: 5 high place of Judah? Is it not **J**?
      3:12 and the word of the LORD from **J**.
Zep   3:16 On that day it shall be said to **J**:
Zec   1:14 I am very jealous for **J** and for Zion.

1: 17 comfort Zion and again choose **J.**
2: 2 He answered me, "To measure **J,**
2: 4 **J** shall be inhabited like villages
8: 3 and will dwell in the midst of **J;**
8: 3 **J** shall be called the faithful city,
8: 8 and I will bring them to live in **J.**
8: 15 in these days to do good to **J** and
8: 22 to seek the LORD of hosts in **J,**
9: 9 Shout aloud, O daughter **J!**
9: 10 Ehraim and the war horse from **J;**
12: 3 I will make **J** a heavy stone for all
12: 10 of David and the inhabitants of **J,**
14: 2 all the nations against **J** to battle,
14: 8 living waters shall flow out from **J,**
14: 16 nations that have come against **J**
Mt 2: 1 wise men from the East came to **J,**
16: 21 go to **J** and undergo great suffering
20: 18 up to **J,** and the Son of Man will be
21: 10 When he entered **J,** the whole city
23: 37 "**J,** the city that kills the prophets
Mk 10: 33 "See, we are going up to **J,**
15: 41 who had come up with him to **J.**
Lk 2: 22 brought him up to **J** to present him
2: 41 every year his parents went to **J** for
2: 43 the boy Jesus stayed behind in **J,**
4: 9 Then the devil took him to **J,**
9: 31 he was about to accomplish at **J.**
9: 51 he set his face to go to **J.**
18: 31 "See, we are going up to **J,**
21: 20 you see **J** surrounded by armies,
21: 24 **J** will be trampled on by the
23: 28 to them and said, "Daughters of **J,**
24: 47 to all nations, beginning from **J.**
Jn 1: 19 Jews sent priests and Levites from **J**
4: 20 where people must worship is in **J.**"
5: 1 and Jesus went up to **J.**
10: 22 of the Dedication took place in **J.**
Ac 1: 4 he ordered them not to leave **J,**
1: 8 and you will be my witnesses in **J,**
6: 7 the disciples increased greatly in **J;**
9: 13 evil he has done to your saints in **J;**
9: 28 he went in and out among them in **J,**
11: 27 prophets came down from **J**
15: 2 up to **J** to discuss this question with
20: 22 to the Spirit, I am on my way to **J,**
21: 4 they told Paul not to go on to **J.**
23: 11 as you have testified for me in **J,**
Ro 15: 19 so that from **J** and as far around
Gal 4: 25 corresponds to the present **J,**
Heb 12: 22 of the living God, the heavenly **J,**
Rev 3: 12 the new **J** that comes down from
21: 2 And I saw the holy city, the new **J,**
21: 10 showed me the holy city **J** coming
Tob 1: 6 went often to **J** for the festivals,
13: 8 and acknowledge him in **J.**
Jdt 4: 2 alarmed both for **J** and for the
15: 9 "You are the glory of **J,**
1Mc 1: 14 So they built a gymnasium in **J,**
1: 29 and he came to **J** with a large force.
6: 7 that he had erected on the altar in **J;**

DAUGHTER JERUSALEM 2Ki 19:21; Isa
37:22; La 2:13, 15; Mic 4:8; Zep 3:14; Zec 9:9

DAUGHTERS OF JERUSALEM SS 1:5;
2:7; 3:5, 10; 5:8, 16; 8:4; Lk 23:28

INHABITANTS OF JERUSALEM Jos
15:63; 2Ki 23:2; 2Ch 20:15, 18, 20; 21:11, 13;
22:1; 32:22, 26, 33; 33:9; 34:9, 30, 32; 35:18;
Ne 7:3; Isa 5:3; 8:14; 22:21; 30:19; Jer 4:3, 4;
8:1; 11:2, 9, 12; 13:13; 17:20, 25; 18:11; 19:3;
25:2; 32:32; 35:13, 17; 36:31; 42:18; Eze
11:15; 12:19; 15:6; Da 9:7; Zep 1:4; Zec 12:5,
7, 8, 10; 13:1; Bar 1:15

JERUSALEM AND JUDAH 2Ki 21:12;
24:20; Ezr 2:1; Ne 7:6; Isa 3:1; Jer 40:1; 52:3;
Zec 14:21

JUDAH AND JERUSALEM 2Ki 18:22;
23:1, 24; 1Ch 6:15; 2Ch 2:7; 11:14; 20:5, 17,
27; 24:6, 9, 18, 23; 28:10; 29:8; 32:12, 25;
34:3, 5, 29; 35:24; 36:4, 10; Ezr 4:6; 5:1; 7:14;
10:7; Isa 1:1; 2:1; 36:7; Jer 19:7; 27:20; 29:2;

Eze 21:20; Joel 3:1, 6; Mal 3:4; 1Mc 2:6; 1Es
1:35

STREETS OF JERUSALEM Jer 5:1; 7:17,
34; 11:6, 13; 14:16; 33:10; 44:6, 9, 17, 21; Zec
8:4; Tob 13:16

JERUSALEM'S → JERUSALEM
Isa 62: 1 and for **J** sake I will not rest,

JESHUA → =JOSHUA
Ezr 4: 3 **J,** and the rest of the heads of
10: 18 the descendants of **J** son of Jozadak
Ne 12: 1 Zerubbabel son of Shealtiel, and **J:**
Sir 49: 12 so was **J** son of Jozadak;

JESSE
Father of David (Ru 4:17-22; 1Sa 16; 1Ch 2:12-
17).

SON OF JESSE 1Sa 16:18; 20:27, 30, 31;
22:7, 8, 9, 13; 25:10; 2Sa 20:1; 23:1; 1Ki
12:16; 1Ch 10:14; 12:18; 29:26; 2Ch 10:16;
11:18; Ps 72:20; Lk 3:32; Ac 13:22; Sir 45:25

JESUS → JESUS'
1. Jesus the Messiah.
LIFE: Genealogy (Mt 1:1-17; Lk 3:21-37).
Birth announced (Mt 1:18-25; Lk 1:26-45). Birth
(Mt 2:1-12; Lk 2:1-40). Escape to Egypt (Mt
2:13-23). As a boy in the temple (Lk 2:41-52).
Baptism (Mt 3:13-17; Mk 1:9-11; Lk 3:21-22; Jn
1:32-34). Temptation (Mt 4:1-11; Mk 1:12-13;
Lk 4:1-13). Ministry in Galilee (Mt 4:12-18:35;
Mk 1:14-9:50; Lk 4:14-9:50). Transfiguration (Mt 17:1-8; Mk 9:2-8; Lk 9:28-
36), on the way to Jerusalem (Mt 19-20; Mk 10;
Lk 13:10-19:27), in Jerusalem (Mt 21-25; Mk
11-13; Lk 19:28-21:38; Jn 2:12-3:36; 5; 7-12).
Last supper (Mt 26:17-35; Mk 14:12-31; Lk
22:1-38; Jn 13-17). Arrest and trial (Mt 26:36-
27:31; Mk 14:43-15:20; Lk 22:39-23:25; Jn 18:1-
19:16). Crucifixion (Mt 27:32-66; Mk 15:21-47;
Lk 23:26-55; Jn 19:28-42). Resurrection and ap-
pearances (Mt 28; Mk 16; Lk 24; Jn 20-21; Ac
1:1-11; 7:56; 9:3-6; 1Co 15:1-8; Rev 1:1-20).
MIRACLES. *Healings:* official's son (Jn 4:43-
54), demoniac in Capernaum (Mk 1:23-26; Lk
4:33-35), Peter's mother-in-law (Mt 8:14-17; Mk
1:29-31; Lk 4:38-39), leper (Mt 8:2-4; Mk 1:40-
45; Lk 5:12-16), paralytic (Mt 9:1-8; Mk 2:1-12;
Lk 5:17-26), cripple (Jn 5:1-9), shriveled hand
(Mt 12:10-13; Mk 3:1-5; Lk 6:6-11), centurion's
servant (Mt 8:5-13; Lk 7:1-10), widow's son
raised (Lk 7:11-17), demoniac (Mt 12:22-23; Lk
11:14), Gadarene demoniacs (Mt 8:28-34; Mk
5:1-20; Lk 8:26-39), woman's bleeding and
Jairus' daughter (Mt 9:18-26; Mk 5:21-43; Lk
8:40-56), blind man (Mt 9:27-31), mute man (Mt
9:32-33), Canaanite woman's daughter (Mt
15:21-28; Mk 7:24-30), deaf man (Mk 7:31-37),
blind man (Mk 8:22-26), demoniac boy (Mt
17:14-18; Mk 9:14-29; Lk 9:37-43), ten lepers
(Lk 17:11-19), man born blind (Jn 9:1-7),
Lazarus raised (Jn 11), crippled woman (Lk
13:11-17), man with dropsy (Lk 14:1-6), two
blind men (Mt 20:29-34; Mk 10:46-52; Lk 18:35-
43), Malchus' ear (Lk 22:50-51). *Other Miracles:*
water to wine (Jn 2:1-11), catch of fish (Lk 5:1-
11), storm stilled (Mt 8:23-27; Mk 4:37-41; Lk
8:22-25), 5,000 fed (Mt 14:15-21; Mk 6:35-44;
Lk 9:10-17; Jn 6:1-14), walking on water (Mt
14:25-33; Mk 6:48-52; Jn 6:15-21), 4,000 fed
(Mt 15:32-39; Mk 8:1-9), money from fish (Mt
17:24-27), fig tree cursed (Mt 21:18-22; Mk
11:12-14), catch of fish (Jn 21:1-14).
MAJOR TEACHING: Sermon on the Mount
(Mt 5-7; Lk 6:17-49), to Nicodemus (Jn 3), to
Samaritan woman (Jn 4), Bread of Life (Jn 6:22-
59), at Feast of Tabernacles (Jn 7-8), woes to
Pharisees (Mt 23; Lk 11:37-54), Good Shepherd
(Jn 10:1-18), Olivet Discourse (Mt 24-25; Mk 13;
Lk 21:5-36), Upper Room Discourse (Jn 13-16).
PARABLES: Sower (Mt 13:3-23; Mk 4:3-25;

Lk 8:5-18), seed's growth (Mk 4:26-29), wheat
and weeds (Mt 13:24-30, 36-43), mustard seed
(Mt 13:31-32; Mk 4:30-32), yeast (Mt 13:33; Lk
13:20-21), hidden treasure (Mt 13:44), valuable
pearl (Mt 13:45-46), net (Mt 13:47-51), house
owner (Mt 13:52), good Samaritan (Lk 10:25-
37), unmerciful servant (Mt 18:15-35), lost sheep
(Mt 18:10-14; Lk 15:4-7), lost coin (Lk 15:8-10),
prodigal son (Lk 15:11-32), dishonest manager
(Lk 16:1-13), rich man and Lazarus (Lk 16:19-
31), persistent widow (Lk 18:1-8), Pharisee and
tax collector (Lk 18:9-14), payment of workers
(Mt 20:1-16), tenants and the vineyard (Mt
21:28-46; Mt 12:1-12; Lk 20:9-19), wedding
banquet (Mt 22:1-14), faithful servant (Mt 24:45-
51), ten virgins (Mt 25:1-13), talents (Mt 25:1-
30; Lk 19:12-27).
DISCIPLES see APOSTLES. Call (Jn 1:35-51;
Mt 4:18-22; 9:9; Mk 1:16-20; 2:13-14; Lk 5:1-11,
27-28). Named Apostles (Mk 3:13-19; Lk 6:12-
16). Twelve sent out (Mt 10; Mk 6:7-11; Lk 9:1-
5). Seventy sent out (Lk 10:1-24). Defection of
(Jn 6:60-71; Mt 26:56; Mk 14:50-52). Final commission (Mt 28:16-20; Jn 21:15-23; Ac 1:3-8).
Ac 2: 32 This **J** God raised up, and of that all
9: 5 "I am **J,** whom you are persecuting.
9: 34 to him, "Aeneas, **J** Christ heals you;
15: 11 through the grace of the Lord **J,**
16: 31 answered, "Believe on the Lord **J,**
20: 24 that I received from the Lord **J,**
Ro 3: 24 the redemption that is in Christ **J,**
5: 17 life through the one man, **J** Christ.
8: 1 for those who are in Christ **J.**
1Co 1: 7 the revealing of our Lord **J** Christ.
2: 2 nothing among you except **J** Christ,
6: 11 in the name of the Lord **J** Christ
8: 6 and one Lord, **J** Christ,
12: 3 can say "**J** is Lord" except by
2Co 4: 5 we proclaim **J** Christ as Lord and
13: 5 not realize that **J** Christ is in you?—
Eph 1: 5 adoption as his children through **J**
2: 10 created in Christ **J** for good works,
2: 20 Christ **J** himself as the cornerstone.
Php 1: 6 completion by the day of **J** Christ.
2: 5 mind be in you that was in Christ **J,**
2: 10 name of **J** every knee should bend,
Col 3: 17 in the name of the Lord **J,**
1Th 1: 10 **J,** who rescues us from the wrath
4: 14 and rose again, even so, through **J,**
5: 23 at the coming of our Lord **J** Christ.
2Th 1: 7 the Lord **J** is revealed from heaven
2: 1 the coming of our Lord **J** Christ
1Ti 1: 15 **J** came into the world to save
2Ti 1: 10 the appearing of our Savior Christ **J,**
2: 3 like a good soldier of Christ **J.**
3: 12 life in Christ **J** will be persecuted.
Tit 2: 13 our great God and Savior, **J** Christ.
Heb 2: 9 but we do see **J,** who for a little
2: 11 For this reason **J** is not ashamed
3: 1 a heavenly calling, consider that **J,**
3: 3 Yet **J** is worthy of more glory than
4: 14 the heavens, **J,** the Son of God,
6: 20 where **J,** a forerunner on our
7: 22 **J** has also become the guarantee of
8: 6 **J** has now obtained a more excellent
12: 2 to **J** the pioneer and perfecter of our
12: 24 **J,** the mediator of a new covenant,
13: 8 **J** Christ is the same yesterday and
1Pe 1: 3 hope through the resurrection of **J**
2Pe 1: 16 and coming of our Lord **J** Christ,
1Jn 1: 7 the blood of **J** his Son cleanses us
2: 1 advocate with the Father, **J** Christ
4: 15 confess that **J** is the Son of God,
Rev 1: 1 The revelation of **J** Christ,
12: 17 of God and hold the testimony of **J.**
17: 6 and the blood of the witnesses to **J.**
22: 16 **J,** who sent my angel to you with
22: 20 Amen. Come, Lord **J!**
2. Disciple, also called Justus (Col 4:11).
3. Writer of Sirach or Ecclesiasticus (Sir Pr:1;
50:27; 51:1).

CHRIST JESUS Ac 24:24; Ro 3:24; 6:3, 11,

23; 8:1, 2, 34, 39; 15:5, 16, 17; 16:3; 1Co 1:1, 2, 4, 30; 4:15, 17; 15:31; 16:24; 2Co 1:1; Gal 2:4, 16; 3:14, 26, 28; 4:14; 5:6, 24; Eph 1:1, 1; 2:6, 7, 10, 13, 20; 3:1, 6, 11, 21; Php 1:1, 1, 8, 26; 2:5; 3:3, 8, 12, 14; 4:7, 19, 21; Col 1:1, 4; 2:6; 4:12; 1Th 2:14; 5:18; 1Ti 1:1, 1, 2, 12, 14, 15; 2:5; 3:13; 4:6; 5:21; 6:13; 2Ti 1:1, 1, 2, 9, 10, 13; 2:1, 3, 10; 3:12, 15; 4:1; Tit 1:4; Phm 1:1, 9, 23

JESUS CHRIST Mk 1:1; Jn 1:17; 17:3; Ac 2:38; 3:6; 4:10; 8:12; 9:34; 10:36, 48; 11:17; 15:26; 16:18; 28:31; Ro 1:1, 4, 6, 7, 8; 2:16; 3:22; 5:1, 11, 15, 17, 21; 7:25; 13:14; 15:6, 30; 16:20, 25, 27; 1Co 1:2, 3, 7, 8, 9, 10; 2:2; 3:11; 6:11; 8:6; 15:57; 2Co 1:2, 3, 19; 4:5, 6; 8:9; 13:5, 13; Gal 1:1, 3, 12; 2:16; 3:1, 22; 6:14, 18; Eph 1:2, 3, 5, 17; 5:20; 6:23, 24; Php 1:2, 6, 11, 19; 2:11, 21; 3:20; 4:23; Col 1:3; 1Th 1:1, 3; 5:9, 23, 28; 2Th 1:1, 2, 12; 2:1, 14, 16; 3:6, 12, 18; 1Ti 1:16; 6:3, 14; 2Ti 2:8; Tit 1:1; 2:13; 3:6; Phm 1:3, 25; Heb 10:10; 13:8, 21; Jas 1:1; 2:1; 1Pe 1:1, 2, 3, 3, 7, 13; 2:5; 3:21; 4:11; 2Pe 1:1, 1, 8, 11, 14, 16; 2:20; 3:18; 1Jn 1:3; 2:1; 3:23; 4:2; 5:6, 20; 2Jn 1:3, 7; Jude 1:1, 1, 4, 17, 21, 25; Rev 1:1, 2, 5

JESUS OF NAZARETH Mt 26:71; Mk 1:24; 10:47; 16:6; Lk 4:34; 18:37; 24:19; Jn 18:5, 7; 19:19; Ac 2:22; 6:14; 10:38; 22:8; 26:9

LORD JESUS Mk 16:19; Ac 1:21; 4:33; 7:59; 8:16; 9:17; 11:17, 20; 15:11, 26; 16:31; 19:5, 13, 17; 20:21, 24, 35; 21:13; 28:31; Ro 1:7; 5:1, 11; 13:14; 14:14; 15:6, 30; 16:20; 1Co 1:2, 3, 7, 8, 10; 5:4, 4; 6:11; 8:6; 11:23; 15:57; 16:23; 2Co 1:2, 3, 14; 4:14; 8:9; 11:31; 13:13; Gal 1:3; 6:14, 18; Eph 1:2, 3, 15, 17; 5:20; 6:23, 24; Php 1:2; 2:19; 3:20; 4:23; Col 1:3; 3:17; 1Th 1:1, 3; 2:15, 19; 3:11, 13; 4:1, 2; 5:9, 23, 28; 2Th 1:1, 2, 7, 8, 12, 12; 2:1, 8, 14, 16; 3:6, 12, 18; 1Ti 1:14; Phm 1:3, 5, 25; Heb 13:20; Jas 1:1; 2:1; 1Pe 1:3; 2Pe 1:8, 14, 16; Jude 1:4, 17, 21; Rev 22:20, 21

NAME OF JESUS Ac 2:38; 3:6; 4:10, 18; 5:40; 8:12; 9:27; 10:48; 16:18; 26:9; Php 2:10

JESUS' → JESUS

Mk   6:14 for **J** name had become known.
Jn   12: 3 anointed **J** feet, and wiped them
     20: 7 the cloth that had been on **J** head,
2Co   4:11 given up to death for **J** sake,

JETHRO
Father-in-law and adviser of Moses (Ex 3:1; 4:18; 18). Also known as Reuel (Ex 2:18).

JEW → JEWISH, JEWS, JUDAISM

Est   2: 5 Now there was a **J** in the citadel
     10: 3 Mordecai the **J** was next in rank to
Zec   8:23 shall take hold of a **J**,
Jn   4: 9 a **J**, ask a drink of me, a woman of
     18:35 Pilate replied, "I am not a **J**, am I?
Ac   21:39 Paul replied, "I am a **J**, from Tarsus
Ro   1:16 to the **J** first and also to the Greek.
      2: 9 the **J** first and also the Greek,
      2:29 a person is a **J** who is one inwardly,
     10:12 no distinction between **J** and Greek;
1Co   9:20 To the Jews I became as a **J**,
Col   3:11 there is no longer Greek and **J**,
Bel   1:28 saying, "The king has become a **J**;

JEWEL → JEWELS

Pr   20:15 by knowledge are a precious **j**.
SS   4: 9 with one **j** of your necklace.
Rev 21:11 and a radiance like a very rare **j**,
     21:19 of the city are adorned with every **j**;

JEWELS → JEWEL

Job 28:17 it be exchanged for **j** of fine gold.
Pr   3:15 She is more precious than **j**,
      8:11 for wisdom is better than **j**,
Isa 54:12 your gates of **j**, and all your wall
     61:10 as a bride adorns herself with her **j**.
Zec   9:16 for like the **j** of a crown they shall

Rev 17: 4 adorned with gold and **j** and pearls,

JEWISH → JEW

Est   6:13 of the **J** people, you will not prevail
Jn   2: 6 for the **J** rites of purification,
Ac   13: 6 certain magician, a **J** false prophet,
     24:24 his wife Drusilla, who was **J**,
Tit   1:14 not paying attention to **J** myths
1Mc   8:29 Romans make a treaty with the **J**

JEWS → JEW

Ezr   5: 5 was upon the elders of the **J**,
Ne   4: 1 enraged, and he mocked the **J**.
Est   3:13 to kill, and to annihilate all **J**,
      4:14 and deliverance will rise for the **J**
     10: 3 and he was powerful among the **J**
Da   3: 8 came forward and denounced the **J**.
Mt   2: 2 who has been born king of the **J**?
     27:11 "Are you the King of the **J**?"
     27:37 "This is Jesus, the King of the **J**."
Lk   23: 3 "Are you the king of the **J**?"
Jn   4: 9 (**J** do not share things in common
      4:22 for salvation is from the **J**.
      7:13 about him for fear of the **J**.
      9:22 because they were afraid of the **J**;
     19: 3 saying, "Hail, King of the **J**!"
     19:21 This man said, I am King of the **J**.'"
Ac   20:21 both **J** and Greeks about repentance
     21:20 of believers there are among the **J**,
Ro   3:29 Or is God the God of **J** only?
      9:24 not from the **J** only but also from
1Co   1:22 For **J** demand signs and Greeks
      9:20 To the **J** I became as a Jew, in order to win **J**.
     12:13 **J** or Greeks, slaves or free—
1Th   2:14 as they did from the **J**,
Rev   2: 9 those who say that they are **J** and
      3: 9 of Satan who say that they are **J**
AdE   8:17 the **J** had joy and gladness,

ALL [THE] JEWS Est 3:6, 13; 4:13, 16; 9:20, 24, 30; Mk 7:3; Jn 18:20; Ac 18:2; 21:21; 22:12; 24:5; 26:4; Ro 3:9; Tob 11:17; AdE 3:6; 4:13, 16; 8:13; 1Mc 10:29, 34; 1Es 4:49; 3Mc 2:28; 6:18

ELDERS OF THE JEWS Ezr 5:5; 6:7, 8, 14; Ac 25:15; 1Es 6:5, 8, 27; 7:2

KING OF THE JEWS Mt 2:2; 27:11, 29, 37; Mk 15:2, 9, 12, 18, 26; Lk 23:3, 37, 38; Jn 18:33, 39; 19:3, 19, 21, 21

NATION OF THE JEWS 1Mc 8:23, 25, 27; 10:25; 11:30, 33; 13:36; 15:2; 2Mc 10:8

JEZEBEL*
Sidonian wife of Ahab (1Ki 16:31). Promoted Baal worship (1Ki 16:32-33). Killed prophets of the LORD (1Ki 18:4, 13). Opposed Elijah (1Ki 19:1-2). Had Naboth killed (1Ki 21). Death prophesied (1Ki 21:17-24). Killed by Jehu (2Ki 9:30-37). Metaphor of immorality (Rev 2:20).

JEZREEL → JEZREELITE

1Ki 21:23 eat Jezebel within the bounds of **J**.'
2Ki   9:36 the territory of **J** the dogs shall eat
     10: 7 in baskets and sent them to him at **J**.
Hos   1: 4 the LORD said to him, "Name him **J**;
      1: 4 the house of Jehu for the blood of **J**,
      1:11 for great shall be the day of **J**.
      2:22 and the oil, and they shall answer **J**;

JEZREELITE → JEZREEL

1Ki 21: 1 Naboth the **J** had a vineyard in
2Ki   9:25 ground belonging to Naboth the **J**;

JOAB
Nephew of David (1Ch 2:16). Commander of his army (2Sa 8:16). Victorious over Ammon (2Sa 10; 1Ch 19), Rabbah (2Sa 11; 1Ch 20), Jerusalem (1Ch 11:6), Absalom (2Sa 18), Sheba (2Sa 20). Killed Abner (2Sa 3:22-39), Amasa (2Sa 20:1-13). Numbered David's army (2Sa 24; 1Ch 21). Sided with Adonijah (1Ki 1:17, 19). Killed by Benaiah (1Ki 2:5-6, 28-35).

JOANNA*
Lk   8: 3 and **J**, the wife of Herod's steward
     24:10 Now it was Mary Magdalene, **J**,

JOASH → =JEHOASH
1. Son of Ahaziah; king of Judah. Sheltered from Athaliah by Jehoiada (2Ki 11; 2Ch 22:10-23:21). Repaired temple (2Ch 24). See Jehoash, 1.
2. Son of Jehoahaz, king of Israel (2Ki 13; 2Ch 25:17-25). See Jehoash, 2.

JOB
Wealthy man from Uz; feared God (Job 1:1-5). Integrity tested by disaster (Job 1:6-22), personal affliction (Job 2). Maintained innocence in debate with three friends (Job 3-31), Elihu (Job 32-37). Rebuked by the LORD (Job 38-41). Vindicated and restored to greater stature by the LORD (Job 42). Example of righteousness (Eze 14:14, 20; Sir 49:9).

JOCHEBED*
Mother of Moses, Aaron and Miriam (Ex 6:20; Nu 26:59).

JOEL
1. Son of Samuel (1Sa 8:2; 1Ch 6:28).
2. Prophet (Joel 1:1; Ac 2:16).

JOHANAN
1. First high priest in Solomon's temple (1Ch 6:9-10).
2. Jewish leader who tried to save Gedaliah from assassination (Jer 40:13-14); took Jews, including Jeremiah, to Egypt (Jer 40-43).

JOHN → JOHN'S
1. Son of Zechariah and Elizabeth (Lk 1). Called the Baptist (Mt 3:1-12; Mk 1:2-8). Witness to Jesus (Mt 3:11-12; Mk 1:7-8; Lk 3:15-18; Jn 1:6-35; 3:27-30; 5:33-36). Doubts about Jesus (Mt 11:2-6; Lk 7:18-23). Arrest (Mt 4:12; Mk 1:14). Execution (Mt 14:1-12; Mk 6:14-29; Lk 9:7-9). Ministry compared to Elijah (Mt 11:7-19; Mk 9:11-13; Lk 7:24-35).
2. Apostle; brother of James (Mt 4:21-22; 10:2; Mk 3:17; Lk 5:1-10). At transfiguration (Mt 17:1-13; Mk 9:1-13; Lk 9:28-36). Desire to be greatest (Mk 10:35-45). Leader of church at Jerusalem (Ac 4:1-3; Gal 2:9). Elder who wrote epistles (2Jn 1; 3Jn 1). Prophet who wrote Revelation (Rev 1:1; 22:8).
3. Cousin of Barnabas, co-worker with Paul, (Ac 12:12-13:13; 15:37; see Mark).
4. Son of Simon Maccabeus; a high priest (1Mc 13:53; 16).

JOHN'S → JOHN
Lk   7:29 had been baptized with **J** baptism.
Ac   19: 3 They answered, "Into **J** baptism."

JOIN → JOINED
Ex   1:10 **j** our enemies and fight against us
Ne   10:29 with their kin, their nobles,
Jer   3:18 of Judah shall **j** the house of Israel,
Eze 37:17 and **j** them together into one stick,
Da   11:34 and many shall **j** them insincerely.
Ac   5:13 None of the rest dared to **j** them,
      9:26 he attempted to **j** the disciples;
Ro   15:30 to **j** me in earnest prayer to God on
2Ti   1: 8 **j** with me in suffering for the gospel

JOINED → JOIN
Hos   4:17 Ephraim is **j** to idols—let him alone.
Mt   19: 6 what God has **j** together, let no one
Mk   10: 9 what God has **j** together, let no one
Eph   2:21 the whole structure is **j** together and
      4:16 **j** and knit together by every
1Mc   1:15 They **j** with the Gentiles

JOINT → JOINTS
Ge   32:25 and Jacob's hip was put out of **j**
Ps   22:14 and all my bones are out of **j**;

Ro   8:17 heirs of God and **j** heirs with Christ

JOINTS → JOINT
Heb   4:12 soul from spirit, **j** from marrow;

JOKING*
Pr   26:19 a neighbor and says, "I am only **j**!"

JONADAB
2Sa 13: 3 and **J** was a very crafty man.
Jer   35: 8 charge of our ancestor **J** son of

JONAH
  Prophet in days of Jeroboam II (2Ki 14:25). Called to Nineveh; fled to Tarshish (Jnh 1:1-3). Cause of storm; thrown into sea (Jnh 1:4-16). Swallowed by fish (Jnh 1:17). Prayer (Jnh 2). Preached to Nineveh (Jnh 3). Attitude reproved by the LORD (Jnh 4). Sign of (Mt 12:39-41; Lk 11:29-32).

JONATHAN
  1. Son of Saul (1Sa 13:16; 1Ch 8:33). Valiant warrior (1Sa 13-14). Relation to David (1Sa 18:1-4; 19-20; 23:16-18). Killed at Gilboa (1Sa 31). Mourned by David (2Sa 1).
  2. Brother and successor of Judas Maccabeus (1Mc 2:5; 9:28-31).

JOPPA
2Ch   2:16 bring it to you as rafts by sea to **J**;
Ezr   3: 7 trees from Lebanon to the sea, to **J**,
Jnh   1: 3 down to **J** and found a ship going
Ac   9:43 he stayed in **J** for some time with

JORAM → =JEHORAM
  1. Son of Jehoshaphat; king of Judah (2Ki 8:16-24). See Jehoram, 1.
  2. Son of Ahab; king of Israel. Killed with Ahaziah by Jehu (2Ki 8:25-29; 9:14-26; 2Ch 22:5-9). See Jehoram, 2.

JORDAN
Ge   13:10 the plain of the **J** was well watered
Nu   22: 1 of Moab across the **J** from Jericho.
     34:12 the boundary shall go down to the **J**,
Dt   1: 1 spoke to all Israel beyond the **J**—
      3:27 for you shall not cross over this **J**.
Jos   1: 2 Now proceed to cross the **J**,
      3:11 going to pass before you into the **J**.
      3:17 dry ground in the middle of the **J**,
      4: 8 stones out of the middle of the **J**,
      4:22 crossed over the **J** here on dry
     23: 4 the **J** to the Great Sea in the west.
2Ki   2: 7 as they both were standing by the **J**.
      2:13 back and stood on the bank of the **J**.
      5:10 "Go, wash in the **J** seven times,
      6: 4 When they came to the **J**, they cut
Ps   114: 3 sea looked and fled; **J** turned back.
Isa   9: 1 beyond the **J**, Galilee of the nations.
Jer 12: 5 you fare in the thickets of the **J**?
Mt   3: 6 were baptized by him in the river **J**,
      4:15 across the **J**, Galilee of the Gentiles
Mk   1: 9 and was baptized by John in the **J**.
Jn   1:28 took place in Bethany across the **J**

JOSEPH → =BARNABAS, =BARSABBAS
  1. Son of Jacob by Rachel (Ge 30:24; 1Ch 2:2). Favored by Jacob, hated by brothers (Ge 37:3-4). Dreams (Ge 37:5-11). Sold by brothers (Ge 37:12-36). Served Potiphar; imprisoned by false accusation (Ge 39). Interpreted dreams of Pharaoh's servants (Ge 40), of Pharaoh (Ge 41:4-40). Made greatest in Egypt (Ge 41:41-57). Sold grain to brothers (Ge 42-45). Brought Jacob and sons to Egypt (Ge 46-47). Sons Ephraim and Manasseh blessed (Ge 48). Blessed (Ge 49:22-26; Dt 33:13-17). Death (Ge 50:22-26; Ex 13:19; Heb 11:22). 12,000 from (Rev 7:8).
  2. Husband of Mary mother of Jesus (Mt 1:16-24; 2:13-19; Lk 1:27; 2; Jn 1:45).
  3. Disciple from Arimathea; buried Jesus in his tomb (Mt 27:57-61; Mk 15:43-47; Lk 24:50-52).
  4. Original name of Barnabas (Ac 4:36).

JOSHUA → =HOSHEA, =JESHUA
  1. Son of Nun; name changed from Hoshea (Nu 13:8, 16; 1Ch 7:27). Fought Amalekites under Moses (Ex 17:9-14). Servant of Moses on Sinai (Ex 24:13; 32:17). Spied Canaan (Nu 13). With Caleb, allowed to enter land (Nu 14:6, 30). Succeeded Moses (Dt 1:38; 31:1-8; 34:9).
  Charged Israel to conquer Canaan (Jos 1). Crossed Jordan (Jos 3-4). Circumcised sons of wilderness wanderings (Jos 5). Conquered Jericho (Jos 6), Ai (Jos 7-8), five kings at Gibeon (Jos 10:1-28), southern Canaan (Jos 10:29-43), northern Canaan (Jos 11-12). Defeated at Ai (Jos 7). Deceived by Gibeonites (Jos 9). Renewed covenant (Jos 8:30-35; 24:1-27). Divided land among tribes (Jos 13-22). Last words (Jos 23). Death (Jos 24:28-31).
  2. High priest during rebuilding of temple (Hag 1-2; Zec 3:1-9; 6:11). See Jeshua.

JOSIAH
  Son of Amon; king of Judah (2Ki 21:26; 1Ch 3:14). Prophesied (1Ki 13:2). Book of the Law discovered during his reign (2Ki 22; 2Ch 34:14-31). Reforms (2Ki 23:1-25; 2Ch 34:1-13; 35:1-19; Sir 49:1-4). Killed by Pharaoh Neco (2Ki 23:29-30; 2Ch 35:20-27).

JOTHAM
  1. Son of Gideon (Jdg 9).
  2. Son of Azariah (Uzziah); king of Judah (2Ki 15:32-38; 2Ch 26:21-27:9).

JOURNEY
Ge   24:21 the LORD had made his **j** successful.
Ex   3:18 let us now go a three days' **j** into
Ezr   8:21 to seek from him a safe **j** for
Mt   25:14 "For it is as if a man, going on a **j**,
Lk   9: 3 to them, "Take nothing for your **j**,

JOY → JOYFUL, JOYFULLY, JOYOUS, OVERJOYED
1Sa 18: 6 with songs of **j**,
1Ch 12:40 and sheep, for there was **j** in Israel.
     16:27 strength and **j** are in his place.
     16:33 the trees of the forest sing for **j**
     29:22 on that day with great **j**.
2Ch 30:26 There was great **j** in Jerusalem,
Ezr   3:12 though many shouted aloud for **j**,
      6:16 of this house of God with **j**.
      6:22 With **j** they celebrated the festival
Ne   8:10 the **j** of the LORD is your strength."
     12:43 had made them rejoice with great **j**;
     12:43 The **j** of Jerusalem was heard far
Est   8:17 was gladness and **j** among the Jews,
Job   8:21 and your lips with shouts of **j**.
     20: 5 **j** of the godless is but for a moment?
     33:26 he comes into his presence with **j**,
     38: 7 the heavenly beings shouted for **j**?
Ps   5:11 let them ever sing for **j**.
     16:11 your presence there is fullness of **j**;
     20: 5 May we shout for **j** over your
     21: 6 glad with the **j** of your presence.
     27: 6 sacrifices with shouts of **j**;
     30:11 my sackcloth and clothed me with **j**,
     35:27 desire my vindication shout for **j**
     43: 4 altar of God, to God my exceeding **j**
     45:15 With **j** and gladness they are led
     47: 1 shout to God with loud songs of **j**.
     48: 2 is the **j** of all the earth, Mount Zion,
     51: 8 Let me hear **j** and gladness;
     51:12 Restore to me the **j** of your salvation
     65: 8 morning and the evening shout for **j**.
     65:13 they shout and sing together for **j**.
     67: 4 the nations be glad and sing for **j**,
     71:23 My lips will shout for **j** when I sing
     81: 1 shout for **j** to the God of Jacob.
     92: 4 the works of your hands I sing for **j**.
     96:12 all the trees of the forest sing for **j**
     97:11 and **j** for the upright in heart.
     98: 8 let the hills sing together for **j**
    105:43 So he brought his people out with **j**,
    107:22 and tell of his deeds with songs of **j**.

119:111 they are the **j** of my heart.
126: 2 and our tongue with shouts of **j**;
126: 5 in tears reap with shouts of **j**.
126: 6 shall come home with shouts of **j**,
132: 9 and let your faithful shout for **j**.
132:16 and its faithful will shout for **j**.
137: 6 set Jerusalem above my highest **j**.
149: 5 let them sing for **j** on their couches.
Pr   12:20 but those who counsel peace have **j**.
     14:10 and no stranger shares its **j**.
     14:13 and the end of **j** is grief.
     15:23 make an apt answer is a **j** to anyone,
     17:21 the parent of a fool has no **j**.
     21:15 When justice is done, it is a **j** to the
Isa   9: 3 you have increased its **j**;
      9: 3 before you as with **j** at the harvest,
     12: 3 With **j** you will draw water from
     12: 6 aloud and sing for **j**, O royal Zion,
     16:10 **J** and gladness are taken away from
     22:13 but instead there was **j** and festivity,
     24:11 all **j** has reached its eventide;
     24:14 lift up their voices, they sing for **j**;
     26:19 in the dust, awake and sing for **j**!
     35: 2 and rejoice with **j** and singing.
     35: 6 tongue of the speechless sing for **j**.
     35:10 everlasting **j** shall be upon their
     35:10 they shall obtain **j** and gladness,
     42:11 let the inhabitants of Sela sing for **j**,
     48:20 declare this with a shout of **j**,
     49:13 Sing for **j**, O heavens, and exult,
     51: 3 **j** and gladness will be found in her,
     51:11 everlasting **j** shall be upon their
     52: 8 together they sing for **j**;
     55:12 you shall go out in **j**, and be led
     60:15 a **j** from age to age.
     61: 7 everlasting **j** shall be theirs.
     65:18 am about to create Jerusalem as a **j**,
     66: 5 so that we may see your **j**";
Jer 15:16 and your words became to me a **j**
     31:13 I will turn their mourning into **j**,
     33: 9 this city shall be to me a name of **j**,
     48:33 Gladness and **j** have been taken
     48:33 no one treads them with shouts of **j**;
     48:33 the shouting is not the shout of **j**.
     51:48 shall shout for **j** over Babylon;
La   2:15 of beauty, the **j** of all the earth?"
      5:15 The **j** of our hearts has ceased;
Eze 24:25 from them their stronghold, their **j**
Joel 1:12 **j** withers away among the people.
      1:16 **j** and gladness from the house of our
Mt   13:20 and immediately receives it with **j**;
     13:44 in his **j** he goes and sells all that he
     28: 8 tomb quickly with fear and great **j**,
Mk   4:16 they immediately receive it with **j**.
Lk   1:14 You will have **j** and gladness,
      1:44 the child in my womb leaped for **j**.
      2:10 bringing you good news of great **j**
      6:23 Rejoice in that day and leap for **j**,
      8:13 they hear the word, receive it with **j**.
     10:17 The seventy returned with **j**, saying,
     24:41 in their **j** they were disbelieving
     24:52 returned to Jerusalem with great **j**;
Jn   3:29 this reason my **j** has been fulfilled.
     15:11 so that my **j** may be in you, and that your **j** may be complete.
     16:20 pain, but your pain will turn into **j**.
     16:22 no one will take your **j** from you.
     16:24 so that your **j** may be complete.
     17:13 they may have my **j** made complete
Ac   8: 8 So there was great **j** in that city.
     13:52 And the disciples were filled with **j**
     14:17 with food and your hearts with **j**."
Ro   14:17 but righteousness and peace and **j** in
     15:13 fill you with all **j** and peace in
     15:32 I may come to you with **j** and
2Co   1:24 we are workers with you for your **j**,
      2: 3 my **j** would be the **j** of all of you.
Gal   5:22 the fruit of the Spirit is love, **j**,
Php   1: 4 with **j** in every one of my prayers
      1:25 for your progress and **j** in faith,
      2: 2 make my **j** complete:
      4: 1 I love and long for, my **j** and crown,

1Th   1: 6 with **j** inspired by the Holy Spirit,
      2:19 or **j** or crown of boasting before our
      2:20 Yes, you are our glory and **j!**
      3: 9 in return for all the **j** that we feel
2Ti   1: 4 so that I may be filled with **j.**
Phm   1: 7 I have indeed received much **j**
Heb 12: 2 **j** that was set before him endured
     13:17 Let them do this with **j** and not with
Jas   1: 2 consider it nothing but **j,**
      4: 9 and your **j** into dejection.
1Pe   1: 8 with an indescribable and glorious **j,**
1Jn   1: 4 writing these things so that our **j**
2Jn   1:12 so that our **j** may be complete.
3Jn   1: 4 I have no greater **j** than this,
Tob 13:17 Jerusalem will sing hymns of **j,**
AdE   8:17 the Jews had **j** and gladness,
Sir 26: 2 loyal wife brings **j** to her husband,
Bar   5: 9 For God will lead Israel with **j,**
1Mc   3:45 **J** was taken from Jacob;
      4:58 very great **j** among the people,

JOYFUL → JOY

1Ki   8:66 to their tents, **j** and in good spirits
Ezr   6:22 for the LORD had made them **j,**
Ps   68: 3 But let the righteous be **j;**
     95: 1 let us make a **j** noise to the rock
     95: 2 let us make a **j** noise to him
     98: 4 Make a **j** noise to the LORD,
    100: 1 Make a **j** noise to the LORD,
Jdt 14: 9 and made a **j** noise in their town.

JOYFULLY → JOY

Dt   28:47 LORD your God **j** and with gladness
Lk   19:37 the disciples began to praise God **j**
Col   1:11 everything with patience, while **j**
1Mc   4:56 and **j** offered burnt offerings;

JOYOUS → JOY

Ps   98: 4 break forth into **j** song
    113: 9 making her the **j** mother of children.

JUBILANT → JUBILATION

Ps   68: 3 let them be **j** with joy.
Isa 24: 8 the noise of the **j** has ceased,

JUBILATION* → JUBILANT

Pr   11:10 the wicked perish, there is **j.**

JUBILEE

Lev 25:10 It shall be a **j** for you:
Nu   36: 4 when the **j** of the Israelites comes,

JUDAH → JUDEA

1. Son of Jacob by Leah (Ge 29:35; 35:23; 1Ch 2:1). Did not want to kill Joseph (Ge 37:26-27). Among Canaanites, fathered Perez by Tamar (Ge 38). Tribe of blessed as ruling tribe (Ge 49:8-12; Dt 33:7), numbered (Nu 1:27; 26:22), allotted land (Jos 15; Eze 48:7), failed to fully possess (Jos 15:63; Jdg 1:1-20).
2. Name used for people and land of Southern Kingdom.

Ru   1: 7 to go back to the land of **J.**
2Sa   2: 4 Then the people of **J** came,
      2: 4 David king over the house of **J.**
      5: 5 all Israel and **J** thirty-three years.
     24: 1 count the people of Israel and **J.''**
1Ch 28: 4 for he chose **J** as leader,
     28: 4 in the house of **J** my father's house,
Ne   6: 7 'There is a king in **J!'**
Isa   1: 1 he saw concerning **J** and Jerusalem
      3: 8 has stumbled and **J** has fallen,
Jer   2:28 many gods as you have towns, O **J.**
     13:19 all **J** is taken into exile, wholly
     30: 3 Israel and **J,** says the LORD,
     31:31 house of Israel and the house of **J.**
La   1: 3 **J** has gone into exile with suffering
Hos   1: 7 I will have pity on the house of **J,**
Joel 3: 1 when I restore the fortunes of **J** and
Mic   5: 2 who are one of the little clans of **J,**
Zec   1:19 are the horns that have scattered **J,**
      8:15 to Jerusalem and to the house of **J;**
     11:14 the family ties between **J** and Israel.

Mal   2:11 **J** has been faithless,
Mt   2: 6 Bethlehem, in the land of **J,**
      2: 6 least among the rulers of **J;**
Heb   7:14 our Lord was descended from **J,**
      8: 8 of Israel and with the house of **J;**
Rev   5: 5 See, the Lion of the tribe of **J,**
Sir 49: 4 the kings of **J** came to an end.
1Mc   2: 6 blasphemies being committed in **J**
      7:50 the land of **J** had rest for a few days.
      9:57 the land of **J** had rest for two years.

ALL JUDAH 1Ki 15:22; 2Ki 22:13; 2Ch 15:2, 9, 15; 16:6; 17:5, 19; 20:3, 13, 15, 18; 23:8; 25:5; 31:1, 20; 32:33; 34:9; 35:18, 24; Ne 13:12; Jer 13:19; 17:20; 20:4; 26:19; 44:11

CITIES OF JUDAH 2Sa 2:1; 2Ki 18:13; 23:5; 2Ch 10:17; 12:4; 14:5; 17:2, 7, 9, 13; 19:5; 24:5; 25:13; 31:1, 6; Ps 69:35; Isa 36:1; 40:9; 44:26; Jer 1:15; 4:16; 7:34; 10:22; 11:6, 12; 26:2; 32:44; 34:7, 7; Zec 1:12; 1Mc 1:29; 3:8

HOUSE OF JUDAH 2Sa 2:4, 7, 10, 11; 1Ki 12:21, 23; 2Ki 19:30; 1Ch 28:4; 2Ch 11:1; 19:11; 22:10; Ne 4:16; Isa 22:21; 37:31; Jer 3:18; 5:11; 11:10, 17; 12:14; 13:11; 31:27, 31; 33:14; 36:3; Eze 4:6; 8:17; 25:3, 8, 12; Hos 1:7; 5:12, 14; Zep 2:7; Zec 8:13, 15, 19; 10:3, 6; 12:4; Heb 8:8; Bar 2:26

ISRAEL AND JUDAH 1Sa 17:52; 18:16; 2Sa 5:5; 11:11; 21:2; 24:1; 2Ki 17:13; 2Ch 27:7; 30:1, 6; 31:6; 35:27; 36:8; Jer 30:3, 4; 36:2; 51:5; Eze 9:9; Bar 2:1; 1Es 1:33

JERUSALEM AND JUDAH 2Ki 21:12; 24:20; Ezr 2:1; Ne 7:6; Isa 3:1; Jer 40:1; 52:3; Zec 14:21

JUDAH AND BENJAMIN 1Ki 12:23; 2Ch 11:1, 3, 12, 23; 15:2, 8, 9; 25:5; 31:1; 34:9; Ezr 1:5; 4:1; 10:9; 1Es 2:8; 5:66; 9:5

JUDAH AND ISRAEL 1Ki 4:20, 25; 2Ch 16:11; 25:26; 28:26; 32:23; 35:18; Zec 11:14

JUDAH AND JERUSALEM 2Ki 18:22; 23:1, 24; 1Ch 6:15; 2Ch 2:7; 11:14; 20:5, 17, 27; 24:6, 9, 18, 23; 28:10; 29:8; 32:12, 25; 34:3, 5, 29; 35:24; 36:4, 10; Ezr 4:6; 5:1; 7:14; 10:7; Isa 1:1; 2:1; 36:7; Jer 19:7; 27:20; 29:2; Eze 21:20; Joel 3:1, 6; Mal 3:4; 1Mc 2:6; 1Es 1:35

KING OF JUDAH 2Ki 3:9; 22:16, 18; 2Ch 22:1; 34:24, 26; 35:21; Isa 7:1; Jer 21:11; 22:1, 2, 6; 27:18, 21; 32:2; 34:6; 37:7; 38:22; Bar 1:3, 8

KINGS OF JUDAH 1Sa 27:6; 1Ki 14:29; 15:7, 23; 22:45; 2Ki 8:23; 12:18, 19; 14:18; 15:6, 36; 16:19; 18:5; 20:20; 21:17, 25; 23:5, 11, 12, 22, 28; 24:5; 2Ch 16:11; 25:26; 28:26; 32:32; 34:11; Isa 1:1; Jer 1:18; 8:1; 17:19, 20; 19:3, 4, 13; 20:5; 33:4; 44:9; Sir 49:4

LAND OF JUDAH Dt 34:2; Ru 1:7; 1Sa 22:5; 30:16; 1Ki 4:19; 2Ki 23:24; 25:22; 1Ch 6:55; 2Ch 9:11; 15:8; 17:2; Ne 5:14; Isa 19:17; 26:1; Jer 31:23; 37:1; 39:10; 40:12; 43:4, 5; 44:9, 14, 28; Am 7:12; Zec 1:21; Mt 2:6; Bar 1:8; 1Mc 3:39; 5:45, 53, 68; 6:5; 7:10, 22, 50; 9:1, 57, 72; 10:30, 33, 37; 12:4, 46, 52; 13:1, 12

PEOPLE OF JUDAH Nu 2:3; Jos 14:6; 15:1, 12, 13, 20, 21, 63, 63; Jdg 1:8, 9, 16; 2Sa 1:18; 2:4; 19:14, 16, 40, 41, 42, 43, 43; 20:2; 2Ki 14:21; 23:2; 1Ch 9:3; 12:24; 2Ch 13:15, 15, 18; 14:13; 20:27; 25:5, 12; 26:1; 28:10; 32:9; 34:30; Ezr 4:4; 10:9; Ne 11:25; 13:16; Isa 5:3, 7; Jer 4:3, 4; 7:2, 30; 11:2, 9; 17:25; 18:11; 25:1, 2; 26:18; 32:30, 32; 35:13; 36:6, 31; 44:26, 27; 50:4, 33; Da 9:7; Hos 1:11; Joel 3:6, 8, 19; Ob 1:12; Bar 1:15; 1Mc 2:18; 1Es 1:21

TOWNS OF JUDAH 1Ki 12:17; 2Ki 23:8; 2Ch 20:4; 23:2; Ne 11:3, 20; Ps 48:11; 97:8; Jer 7:17; 9:11; 17:26; 25:18; 33:10, 13; 34:22;

36:9; 40:5; 44:2, 6, 17, 21; La 5:11; Bar 2:23; 1Mc 1:44, 51, 54

TRIBE OF JUDAH Ex 31:2; 35:30; 38:22; Nu 1:27; 7:12; 13:6; 34:19; Jos 7:1, 16, 18; 18:11, 14; 19:1, 9; 21:9; 1Ki 12:20; 2Ki 17:18; Ps 78:68; Da 1:6; Rev 5:5; 7:5; Sir 45:25; 1Es 5:5, 66; 9:5

JUDAISM → JEW

Ac   13:43 devout converts to **J** followed Paul
Gal   1:13 no doubt, of my earlier life in **J.**

JUDAS → =BARSABBAS, =THADDAEUS, MACCABEUS

1. Apostle; son of James (Lk 6:16; Jn 14:22; Ac 1:13). Probably also called Thaddaeus (Mt 10:3; Mk 3:18).
2. Brother of James and Jesus (Mt 13:55; Mk 6:3), also called Jude (Jude 1).
3. Christian prophet (Ac 15:22-32).
4. Apostle, also called Iscariot, who betrayed Jesus (Mt 10:4; 26:14-56; Mk 3:19; 14:10-50; Lk 6:16; 22:3-53; Jn 6:71; 12:4; 13:2-30; 18:2-11). Suicide of (Mt 27:3-5; Ac 1:16-25).
5. Leader of the Maccabean revolt (1Mc 2:4, 66). Recaptured Jerusalem and rededicated the temple and altar (1Mc 4:36-61). Death of (1Mc 9).

JUDE* → =JUDAS

Jude   1: 1 **J,** a servant of Jesus Christ and

JUDEA → JUDAH, JUDEAN

Mt   2: 1 Jesus was born in Bethlehem of **J,**
      3: 1 appeared in the wilderness of **J,**
     24:16 in **J** must flee to the mountains;
Mk   3: 8 to him in great numbers from **J,**
Lk   1: 5 In the days of King Herod of **J,**
      3: 1 Pontius Pilate was governor of **J,**
      7:17 about him spread throughout **J** and
Ac   1: 8 my witnesses in Jerusalem, in all **J**
      8: 1 throughout the countryside of **J** and
      9:31 the church throughout **J,** Galilee,
1Th   2:14 of God in Christ Jesus that are in **J,**
Jdt   4: 7 since by them **J** could be invaded;
Bel   1:33 the prophet Habakkuk was in **J;**
1Mc   5:23 led them to **J** with great rejoicing.

JUDEAN → JUDEA

Mk   1: 5 from the whole **J** countryside and

JUDGE → JUDGE'S, JUDGED, JUDGES, JUDGING, JUDGMENT, JUDGMENTS

Ge   16: 5 the LORD **j** between you and me!"
     18:25 Shall not the **J** of all the earth do
     19: 9 and he would play the **j!**
     31:53 of their father—"**j** between us."
Ex   2:14 made you a ruler and **j** over us?
Dt   1:16 and **j** rightly between one person
     17: 9 the levitical priests and the **j** who is
Jdg   2:18 the LORD was with the **j,**
      2:18 their enemies all the days of the **j;**
     11:27 Let the LORD, who is **j,**
1Sa   2:10 LORD will **j** the ends of the earth;
     24:12 the LORD **j** between me and you!
1Ki   8:32 and act, and **j** your servants,
1Ch 16:33 for he comes to **j** the earth.
2Ch   6:23 and act, and **j** your servants,
Ps   7: 8 The LORD judges the peoples; **j** me,
      7:11 God is a righteous **j,** and
     50: 6 righteousness, for God himself is **j.**
     75: 2 that I appoint I will **j** with equity.
     82: 8 Rise up, O God, **j** the earth;
     94: 2 Rise up, O **j** of the earth;
     96:10 He will **j** the peoples with equity."
     96:13 for he is coming to **j** the earth.
     98: 9 will **j** the world with righteousness,
Pr   31: 9 Speak out, **j** righteously,
Isa   2: 4 He shall **j** between the nations,
      3:13 he stands to **j** the peoples.
     11: 3 He shall not **j** by what his eyes see,
     33:22 LORD is our **j,** the LORD is our ruler,

Jer 11:20 O Lord of hosts, who **j** righteously,
Eze   7: 3 I will **j** you according to your ways,
      7:27 their own judgments I will **j** them.
     18:30 I will **j** you, O house of Israel,
     22: 2 you **j**, will you **j** the bloody city?
     33:20 I will **j** all of you according to your
     34:17 I shall **j** between sheep and sheep,
Joel 3:12 sit to **j** all the neighboring nations.
Mic   4: 3 He shall **j** between many peoples,
Mt   7: 1 not **j**, so that you may not be judged.
Lk   6:37 not **j**, and you will not be judged;
     12:14 who set me to be a **j** or arbitrator
     18: 2 a **j** who neither feared God nor had
     19:22 'I will **j** you by your own words,
Jn   5:30 on my own. As I hear, I **j**;
      7:24 Do not **j** by appearances,
      8:15 You **j** by human standards; I **j** no
      8:16 even if I do **j**, my judgment is valid;
     12:47 for I came not to **j** the world,
     12:48 does not receive my word has a **j**;
     18:31 "Take him yourselves and **j** him
Ac   4:19 rather than to God, you must **j**;
      7:27 made you a ruler and a **j** over us?
     10:42 he is the one ordained by God as **j**
Ro   2: 1 whoever you are, when you **j** others;
      2: 1 the **j**, are doing the very same things
      2:16 will **j** the secret thoughts of all.
      3: 6 then how could God **j** the world?
     14: 5 Some **j** one day to be better
1Co   4: 3 I do not even **j** myself.
      5:12 who are inside that you are to **j**?
      6: 2 that the saints will **j** the world?
      6: 3 not know that we are to **j** angels—
2Ti   4: 1 who is to **j** the living and the dead,
      4: 8 righteous **j**, will give me on that day
Heb 10:30 again, "The Lord will **j** his people."
     12:23 and to God the **j** of all,
     13: 4 will **j** fornicators and adulterers.
Jas   4:12 then, are you to **j** your neighbor?
      5: 9 See, the **J** is standing at the doors!
1Pe   4: 5 to him who stands ready to **j**
Rev   6:10 before you **j** and avenge our blood
     20: 4 on them were given authority to **j**.
Tob   3: 2 and truth; you **j** the world.
Sir   7: 6 Do not seek to become a **j**,
     35:15 for the Lord is the **j**,
LtJ   6:54 They cannot **j** their own cause

JUDGE'S → JUDGE
Jn   19:13 Jesus outside and sat on the **j** bench

JUDGED → JUDGE
Ex   18:26 And they **j** the people at all times;
1Sa   7:15 Samuel **j** Israel all the days of his
Ps   9:19 let the nations be **j** before you.
Mt   7: 1 not judge, so that you may not be **j**.
Ro   2:12 have sinned under the law will be **j**
1Co   4: 3 a very small thing that I should be **j**
     11:31 if we **j** ourselves, we would not be **j**.
Jas   2:12 so act as those who are to be **j** by
      3: 1 know that we who teach will be **j**
      5: 9 so that you may not be **j**.
Rev 16: 5 were, for you have **j** these things;
     19: 2 he has **j** the great whore who
     20:12 dead were **j** according to their works

JUDGES → JUDGE
Ex   18:22 Let them sit as **j** for the people all
Jdg   2:16 Then the Lord raised up **j**,
Ru   1: 1 In the days when the **j** ruled,
1Sa   8: 1 he made his sons **j** over Israel.
Job   9:24 he covers the eyes of its **j**—
Ps   7: 8 The Lord **j** the peoples;
     58:11 there is a God who **j** on earth."
Pr   29:14 If a king **j** the poor with equity,
Lk   11:19 Therefore they will be your **j**.
Jn   5:22 The Father **j** no one but has given
1Co   4: 4 It is the Lord who **j** me.
Jas   4:11 evil against the law and **j** the law;
1Pe   1:17 who **j** all people impartially
      2:23 himself to the one who **j** justly.
Rev 18: 8 mighty is the Lord God who **j** her."

19:11 righteousness he **j** and makes war.
Sir 16:12 **j** a person according to one's deeds.

JUDGING → JUDGE
Dt   1:17 You must not be partial in **j**:
Pr   24:23 Partiality in **j** is not good.
Mt   19:28 **j** the twelve tribes of Israel.
Rev 11:18 and the time for **j** the dead,

JUDGMENT → JUDGE
Ex   6: 6 arm and with mighty acts of **j**.
Dt   1:17 by anyone, for the **j** is God's.
     32:41 and my hand takes hold on **j**;
Ps   1: 5 wicked will not stand in the **j**,
      9: 7 he has established his throne for **j**;
     76: 8 From the heavens you uttered **j**;
     82: 1 in the midst of the gods he holds **j**:
    119:66 Teach me good **j** and knowledge,
    122: 5 there the thrones for **j** were set up,
    143: 2 not enter into **j** with your servant,
Pr   18: 1 contempt for all who have sound **j**.
Ecc 11: 9 God will bring you into **j**.
     12:14 God will bring every deed into **j**,
Isa   3:14 into **j** with the elders and princes of
     28: 6 of justice to the one who sits in **j**,
     66:16 For by fire will the Lord execute **j**,
Jer   2:35 I am bringing you to **j** for saying,
     25:31 he is entering into **j** with all flesh,
Eze 20:35 into **j** with you face to face.
Da   7:22 **j** was given for the holy ones of the
Joel 3: 2 I will enter into **j** with them there,
Hab   1:12 Lord, you have marked them for **j**;
Zep   3: 5 Every morning he renders his **j**,
Mal   3: 5 Then I will draw near to you for **j**;
Mt   5:21 murders shall be liable to **j**.'
      5:22 you will be liable to **j**,
     10:15 Gomorrah on the day of **j** than for
     11:24 day of **j** it will be more tolerable for
     12:36 on the day of **j** you will have to give
     12:41 rise up at the **j** with this generation
Jn   5:22 judges no one but has given all **j** to
      5:30 As I hear, I judge; and my **j** is just,
      7:24 appearances, but judge with right **j**."
      9:39 "I came into this world for **j** so that
     12:31 Now is the **j** of this world;
     16: 8 about sin and righteousness and **j**:
     16:11 about **j**, because the ruler
Ac   24:25 self-control, and the coming **j**,
Ro   2: 1 passing **j** on another you condemn
      2: 2 God's **j** on those who do such things
      5:16 **j** following one trespass brought
     12: 3 but to think with sober **j**,
     14:10 Why do you pass **j** on your brother
     14:10 we will all stand before the **j** seat of
     14:13 no longer pass **j** on one another,
1Co   7:40 But in my **j** she is more blessed if
     11:29 eat and drink **j** against themselves.
2Co   5:10 all of us must appear before the **j**
2Th   1: 5 evidence of the righteous **j** of God,
Heb   6: 2 of the dead, and eternal **j**.
      9:27 to die once, and after that the **j**,
     10:27 but a fearful prospect of **j**,
Jas   2:13 mercy triumphs over **j**.
1Pe   4:17 for **j** to begin with the household of
2Pe   2: 4 darkness to be kept until the **j**;
      2: 9 under punishment until the day of **j**
      3: 7 until the day of **j** and destruction of
1Jn   4:17 may have boldness on the day of **j**,
Jude 1: 6 chains in deepest darkness for the **j**
Rev 14: 7 for the hour of his **j** has come;
     17: 1 **j** of the great whore who is seated
     18:10 For in one hour your **j** has come."
Jdt   9: 6 and your **j** is with foreknowledge.
Wis 12:12 Or will resist your **j**?
Sir   6:23 Listen, my child, and accept my **j**;
     18:20 Before **j** comes, examine yourself;
2Es   7:70 he first prepared the **j** and the
              things that pertain to the **j**.

DAY OF JUDGMENT Mt 10:15; 11:22, 24;
12:36; 2Pe 2:9; 3:7; 1Jn 4:17; Jdt 16:17; Wis
3:18; 2Es 7:38, 102, 104, 113; 12:34

JUDGMENTS → JUDGE
1Ch 16:14 his **j** are in all the earth.
Ps 119:75 Lord, that your **j** are right,
Jer   1:16 And I will utter my **j** against them,
Ro   11:33 How unsearchable are his **j** and
Rev 15: 4 for your **j** have been revealed."
     16: 7 your **j** are true and just!"
     19: 2 for his **j** are true and just;
Tob   3: 5 And now your many **j** are true
Wis 17: 1 Great are your **j** and hard to
Sir 32:16 who fear the Lord will form true **j**,
Aza   1: 4 and all your **j** are true.

JUDITH
Virtuous widow and heroine of the deuterocanonical book of Judith (Jdt 8-16).

JUG
1Ki 17:12 and a little oil in a **j**;
Jer 19: 1 buy a potter's earthenware **j**.

JUICE
Nu   6: 3 not drink any grape **j** or eat grapes,

JUMPED → JUMPING
Jn   21: 7 for he was naked, and **j** into the sea.

JUMPING* → JUMPED
Ac   3: 8 **J** up, he stood and began to walk,

JUST → JUSTICE, JUSTIFICATION,
  JUSTIFIED, JUSTIFIES, JUSTIFY, JUSTLY
Ge   18:25 Judge of all the earth do what is **j**?"
Dt   32: 4 and all his ways are **j**.
     32: 4 without deceit, **j** and upright is he;
Ne   9:33 You have been **j** in all that has
Job 35: 2 "Do you think this to be **j**?
Ps   17: 1 Hear a **j** cause, O Lord;
    111: 7 works of his hands are faithful and **j**
    119:121 I have done what is **j** and right;
    145:17 The Lord is **j** in all his ways,
Pr   8:15 and rulers decree what is **j**;
     12: 5 The thoughts of the righteous are **j**;
Isa 26: 7 of the righteous is level; O **J** One,
Eze 33:17 "The way of the Lord is not **j**,"
     45: 9 and do what is **j** and right.
Jn   5:30 I judge; and my judgment is **j**,
Ro   7:12 the commandment is holy and **j** and
2Th   1: 6 For it is indeed **j** of God to repay
Heb   2: 2 or disobedience received a **j** penalty,
1Jn   1: 9 he who is faithful and **j** will forgive
Rev 15: 3 **J** and true are your ways, King of
     16: 5 angel of the waters say, "You are **j**,
     16: 7 your judgments are true and **j**!"
     19: 2 for his judgments are true and **j**;
Tob   3: 2 O Lord, and all your deeds are **j**;
Sir 18: 2 The Lord alone is **j**.

JUSTICE → JUST
Ex   23: 2 with the majority so as to pervert **j**;
     23: 6 not pervert the **j** due to your poor
Dt   16:19 You must not distort **j**; you must
     16:20 **J**, and only **j**, you shall pursue,
     24:17 a resident alien or an orphan of **j**;
     27:19 the orphan, and the widow of **j**."
1Sa   8: 3 they took bribes and perverted **j**.
2Sa 15: 4 and I would give them **j**."
1Ki   3:28 of God was in him, to execute **j**.
      7: 7 pronounce judgment, the Hall of **J**,
     10: 9 he has made you king to execute **j**
2Ch   9: 8 may execute **j** and righteousness."
Job   8: 3 Does God pervert **j**?
      9:19 matter of **j**, who can summon him?
     19: 7 I call aloud, but there is no **j**.
     29:14 my **j** was like a robe and a turban.
     34:12 and the Almighty will not pervert **j**.
     34:17 Shall one who hates **j** govern?
     36:17 judgment **j** and seize you.
     37:23 he is great in power and **j**,
Ps   33: 5 He loves righteousness and **j**;
     37: 6 the **j** of your cause like the noonday.
     72: 1 Give the king your **j**, O God,
     72: 2 righteousness, and your poor with **j**.

82: 3 Give **j** to the weak and the orphan;
89:14 **j** are the foundation of your throne;
99: 4 lover of **j**, you have established
101: 1 I will sing of loyalty and of **j**;
103: 6 The LORD works vindication and **j**
106: 3 Happy are those who observe **j**,
112: 5 who conduct their affairs with **j**.
140:12 and executes **j** for the poor.
Pr 8:20 righteousness, along the paths of **j**,
17:23 bribe to pervert the ways of **j**,
19:28 A worthless witness mocks at **j**,
21:15 **j** is done, it is a joy to the righteous,
28: 5 The evil do not understand **j**,
29: 4 By **j** a king gives stability to the
29:26 it is from the LORD that one gets **j**.
Ecc 3:16 under the sun that in the place of **j**,
5: 8 of the poor and the violation of **j**
Isa 1:17 seek **j**, rescue the oppressed,
1:21 full of **j**, righteousness lodged in her
1:27 Zion shall be redeemed by **j**,
5: 7 he expected **j**, but saw bloodshed;
5:16 the LORD of hosts is exalted by **j**,
9: 7 with **j** and with righteousness
10: 2 to turn aside the needy from **j** and
16: 5 ruler who seeks **j** and is swift to do
28: 6 a spirit of **j** to the one who sits in
28:17 And I will make **j** the line,
29:21 deny **j** to the one in the right.
30:18 For the LORD is a God of **j**;
32: 1 and princes will rule with **j**.
32:16 Then **j** will dwell in the wilderness,
33: 5 filled Zion with **j** and righteousness;
42: 1 he will bring forth **j** to the nations.
42: 3 he will faithfully bring forth **j**.
42: 4 until he has established **j** in the earth
51: 4 and my **j** for a light to the peoples.
56: 1 Thus says the LORD: Maintain **j**,
59: 8 and there is no **j** in their paths.
59: 9 Therefore **j** is far from us,
59:11 We wait for **j**, but there is none;
59:14 **J** is turned back, and righteousness
59:15 it displeased him that there was no **j**.
61: 8 For I the LORD love **j**, I hate robbery
Jer 9:24 I act with steadfast love, **j**,
21:12 the LORD: Execute **j** in the morning,
Eze 34:16 I will feed them with **j**.
Hos 2:19 my wife in righteousness and in **j**,
12: 6 to your God, hold fast to love and **j**,
Am 5: 7 Ah, you that turn **j** to wormwood,
5:15 and establish **j** in the gate;
5:24 But let **j** roll down like waters,
6:12 But you have turned **j** into poison
Mic 3: 1 Should you not know **j**?—
3: 8 of the LORD, and with **j** and might,
3: 9 who abhor **j** and pervert all equity,
Hab 1: 4 slack and **j** never prevails.
Mal 2:17 by asking, "Where is the God of **j**?"
Mt 12:18 he will proclaim **j** to the Gentiles.
12:20 until he brings **j** to victory.
23:23 of the law: **j** and mercy and faith.
Lk 11:42 and neglect **j** and the love of God;
18: 5 I will grant her **j**, so that she may
18: 7 not God grant **j** to his chosen ones
18: 8 he will quickly grant **j** to them.
Ac 8:33 In his humiliation **j** was denied him.
28: 4 **j** has not allowed him to live."
Ro 3: 5 serves to confirm the **j** of God,
Heb 11:33 administered **j**, obtained promises,
Sir 35:22 and does **j** for the righteous,
1Mc 2:29 were seeking righteousness and **j**

JUSTIFICATION* → JUST

Ro 4:25 trespasses and was raised for our **j**.
5:16 following many trespasses brings **j**.
5:18 man's act of righteousness leads to **j**
5:21 also exercise dominion through **j**
2Co 3: 9 more does the ministry of **j** abound
Gal 2:21 for if **j** comes through the law,

JUSTIFIED* → JUST

Job 32: 2 he **j** himself rather than God;
40: 8 you condemn me that you may be **j**?

Ps 51: 4 that you are **j** in your sentence and
Mt 12:37 for by your words you will be **j**,
Lk 18:14 went down to his home **j** rather than
Ac 18:14 be **j** in accepting the complaint of
Ro 2:13 doers of the law who will be **j**.
3: 4 that you may be **j** in your words,
3:20 be **j** in his sight" by deeds
3:24 they are now **j** by his grace as a gift,
3:28 we hold that a person is **j** by faith
4: 2 For if Abraham was **j** by works,
5: 1 Therefore, since we are **j** by faith,
5: 9 now that we have been **j** by his
8:30 and those whom he called he also **j**;
8:30 those whom he **j** he also glorified.
10:10 believes with the heart and so is **j**,
1Co 6:11 were **j** in the name of the Lord Jesus
Gal 2:16 that a person is **j** not by the works
2:16 that we might be **j** by faith in Christ,
2:16 no one will be **j** by the works of the
2:17 But if, in our effort to be **j** in Christ,
3:11 that no one is **j** before God by
3:24 so that we might be **j** by faith.
5: 4 **j** by the law have cut yourselves off
Tit 3: 7 having been **j** by his grace,
Jas 2:21 our ancestor Abraham by works
2:24 is **j** by works and not by faith alone.
2:25 Rahab the prostitute also **j** by works
Sir 1:22 Unjust anger cannot be **j**,
23:11 swears a false oath, he will not be **j**,
31: 5 One who loves gold will not be **j**;

JUSTIFIES* → JUST

Pr 17:15 **j** the wicked and one who condemns
Ro 3:26 and that he **j** the one who has faith
4: 5 who without works trusts him who **j**
8:33 It is God who **j**.

JUSTIFY → JUST

Lk 10:29 wanting to **j** himself, he asked Jesus,
16:15 "You are those who **j** yourselves in
Ro 3:30 and he will **j** the circumcised on the
Gal 3: 8 that God would **j** the Gentiles

JUSTLY → JUST

2Sa 23: 3 One who rules over people **j**,
Jer 7: 5 if you truly act **j** one with another,
Lk 23:41 we indeed have been condemned **j**,
1Pe 2:23 himself to the one who judges **j**,
Wis 9:12 and I shall judge your people **j**,

JUSTUS* → =BARSABBAS, =JESUS

Ac 1:23 Barsabbas, who was also known as **J**
18: 7 named Titius **J**, a worshiper of God;
Col 4:11 Jesus who is called **J** greets you.

𝒦

KADESH → KADESH-BARNEA

Nu 20: 1 and the people stayed in **K**.
Dt 1:46 you had stayed at **K** as many days

KADESH-BARNEA → KADESH

Nu 32: 8 sent them from **K** to see the land.

KEDESH

Jos 12:22 king of **K** one the king of Jokneam
Jdg 4: 6 Barak son of Abinoam from **K**

KEEP → DOORKEEPER, DOORKEEPERS, KEEPER, KEEPING, KEEPS, KEPT

Ge 6:19 to **k** them alive with you;
17: 9 for you, you shall **k** my covenant,
Ex 15:26 and **k** all his statutes,
19: 5 obey my voice and **k** my covenant,
20: 6 love me and **k** my commandments.
Nu 6:24 The LORD bless you and **k** you;
Dt 4: 2 **k** the commandments of the LORD
5:10 love me and **k** my commandments.

6:17 diligently **k** the commandments of
7: 9 and **k** his commandments,
11: 1 and **k** his charge, his decrees, his
13: 4 his commandments you shall **k**,
Jos 22: 5 to **k** his commandments, and to hold
1Ki 8:25 **k** for your servant my father David
8:58 **k** his commandments, his statutes,
2Ki 17:19 also did not **k** the commandments
1Ch 29:18 **k** forever such purposes and
Ne 1: 5 love him and **k** his commandments,
Job 14:16 you would not **k** watch over my sin;
Ps 19:13 **K** back your servant also from the
37:34 Wait for the LORD, and **k** to his way
78:10 They did not **k** God's covenant,
103: 9 nor will he **k** his anger forever.
119: 2 Happy are those who **k** his decrees,
119: 9 can young people **k** their way pure?
121: 7 The LORD will **k** you from all evil;
141: 3 **k** watch over the door of my lips.
Pr 4:21 **k** them within your heart.
7: 2 **k** my commandments and live,
7: 5 may **k** you from the loose woman,
Ecc 3: 6 time to **k**, and a time to throw away;
12:13 Fear God, and **k** his commandments
Isa 26: 3 of steadfast mind you **k** in peace—
Mt 19:17 enter into life, **k** the commandments
Mk 7: 9 in order to **k** your tradition!
Lk 17:33 those who lose their life will **k** it.
Jn 10:24 long will you **k** us in suspense?
12:25 hate their life in this world will **k** it
Ro 16:17 to **k** an eye on those who cause
2Co 12: 7 to **k** me from being too elated.
2Th 3: 6 to **k** away from believers who are
1Ti 5:22 of others; **k** yourself pure.
Heb 13: 5 **k** your lives free from the love of
Jas 3: 2 able to **k** the whole body in check
1Pe 3:10 let them **k** their tongues from evil
2Pe 1: 8 they **k** you from being ineffective
1Jn 5:21 children, **k** yourselves from idols.
Jude 1: 6 angels who did not **k** their own
1:21 **k** yourselves in the love of God;
1:24 Now to him who is able to **k** you
Rev 3:10 I will **k** you from the hour of trial
22: 9 those who **k** the words of this book.
AdE 2:20 to fear God and **k** his laws,
Sir 1:26 wisdom, **k** the commandments,
20: 5 **k** silent and are thought to be wise,

KEEPER → KEEP

Ge 4: 9 am I my brother's **k**?"
Ps 121: 5 The LORD is your **k**;

KEEPING → KEEP

Dt 13:18 God by **k** all his commandments
Ne 9:32 **k** covenant and steadfast love—
Ps 19:11 in **k** them there is great reward.
Pr 15: 3 **k** watch on the evil and the good.
Lk 2: 8 **k** watch over their flock by night.

KEEPS → KEEP

Ne 1: 5 and awesome God who **k** covenant
Ps 34:20 He **k** all their bones; not one
119:167 My soul **k** your decrees;
121: 3 he who **k** you will not slumber.
Pr 11:13 trustworthy in spirit **k** a confidence.
Isa 26: 2 nation that **k** faith may enter in.
56: 2 holds it fast, who **k** the sabbath,
Jn 7:19 Yet none of you **k** the law.
8:51 **k** my word will never see death."
Jas 2:10 whoever **k** the whole law but fails
Rev 22: 7 who **k** the words of the prophecy
Sir 21:11 **k** the law controls his thoughts,

KEILAH

1Sa 23: 5 David rescued the inhabitants of **K**.

KENITE

Jdg 1:16 The descendants of Hobab the **K**,
4:17 Jael wife of Heber the **K**;
4:17 Hazor and the clan of Heber the **K**.

KEPT → KEEP

Ge 37:11 but his father **k** the matter in mind.

Ex   12:42 a vigil to be **k** for the LORD by all
       16:33 be **k** throughout your generations."
Nu   17:10 to be **k** as a warning to rebels,
Dt   7: 8 and **k** the oath that he swore to your
2Sa 22:22 For I have **k** the ways of the LORD,
2Ki 18: 6 but **k** the commandments that
Ps   18:23 and I **k** myself from guilt.
       37:28 righteous shall be **k** safe forever,
Mt   19:20 said to him, "I have **k** all these;
Jn   17: 6 and they have **k** your word.
2Ti   4: 7 finished the race, I have **k** the faith.
Heb 13: 4 let the marriage bed be **k** undefiled;
1Pe   1: 4 and unfading, **k** in heaven for you,
2Pe   3: 7 being **k** until the day of judgment
Rev   3: 8 and yet you have **k** my word
        3:10 **k** my word of patient endurance,
Tob   1:11 I **k** myself from eating the food of

KETTLES*

Mk   7: 4 washing of cups, pots, and bronze **k.**

KETURAH*

Wife of Abraham (Ge 25:1-4; 1Ch 1:32-33).

KEY → KEYS

Isa   22:22 on his shoulder the **k** of the house
Lk   11:52 taken away the **k** of knowledge;
Rev   3: 7 true one, who has the **k** of David,
        9: 1 **k** to the shaft of the bottomless pit;
       20: 1 his hand the **k** to the bottomless pit

KEYS* → KEY

Mt   16:19 you the **k** of the kingdom of heaven,
Rev   1:18 I have the **k** of Death and of Hades.

KICK

Ac   26:14 It hurts you to **k** against the goads.'

KIDNAPER* → KIDNAPS

Dt   24: 7 then that **k** shall die.

KIDNAPS* → KIDNAPER

Ex   21:16 Whoever **k** a person, whether

KIDRON

2Sa 15:23 the king crossed the Wadi **K,**
Jn   18: 1 his disciples across the **K** valley

KILL → KILLED, KILLING, KILLS

Ge   4:14 anyone who meets me may **k** me."
       12:12 will **k** me, but they will let you live.
       20:11 they will **k** me because of my wife.
       26: 7 might **k** me for the sake of Rebekah,
       37:18 they conspired to **k** him.
Ex   2:15 heard of it, he sought to **k** Moses.
        4:23 now I will **k** your firstborn son.'"
1Ki 11:40 sought therefore to **k** Jeroboam;
Ecc   3: 3 a time to **k,** and a time to heal;
Mt   10:28 Do not fear those who **k** the body
              but cannot **k** the soul;
       17:23 will **k** him, and on the third day he
Mk   9:31 human hands, and they will **k** him,
       14: 1 to arrest Jesus by stealth and **k** him;
Jn   7:19 for an opportunity to **k** me?"
       10:10 The thief comes only to steal and **k**
Rev 11: 7 and conquer them and **k** them,

KILLED → KILL

Ge   4: 8 against his brother Abel, and **k** him.
Ex   2:12 seeing no one he **k** the Egyptian
       13:15 LORD **k** all the firstborn in the land
Ne   9:26 their backs and **k** your prophets,
Ps   44:22 we are being **k** all day long,
Hos   6: 5 I have **k** them by the words of my
Mk   8:31 priests, and the scribes, and be **k,**
        9:31 after being **k,** he will rise again."
Lk   11:48 for they **k** them, and you build their
Ac   3:15 and you **k** the Author of life,
       23:12 eat nor drink until they had **k** Paul.
Ro   7:11 deceived me and through it **k** me.
        8:36 your sake we are being **k** all day
       11: 3 "Lord, they have **k** your prophets,
2Co   6: 9 as punished, and yet not **k;**
Rev   9:18 a third of humankind was **k,**

19:21 rest were **k** by the sword of the rider
Bel   1:28 destroyed Bel, and **k** the dragon,
1Mc   2:24 he ran and **k** him on the altar.

KILLING → KILL

1Ki 18: 4 Jezebel was **k** off the prophets of
Ac   8: 1 Saul approved of their **k** him.

KILLS → KILL

Ge   4:15 Whoever **k** Cain will suffer
Nu   35:11 who **k** a person without intent
1Sa   2: 6 The LORD **k** and brings to life;
Pr   1:32 For waywardness **k** the simple,
2Co   3: 6 the letter **k,** but the Spirit gives life.

KIND → KINDLY, KINDNESS, KINDS

Ge   1:11 and fruit trees of every **k** on earth
        1:24 forth living creatures of every **k:**
        6:20 two of every **k** shall come in to you,
2Ch 10: 7 "If you will be **k** to this people and
Ps 145:17 and **k** in all his doings.
Pr   11:17 who are **k** reward themselves,
       14:21 are those who are **k** to the poor.
       14:31 those who are **k** to the needy honor
       19:17 is **k** to the poor lends to the LORD,
Lk   6:35 for he is **k** to the ungrateful and the
Jn   18:32 when he indicated the **k** of death he
       21:19 the **k** of death by which he would
1Co 13: 4 Love is patient; love is **k;**
       15:35 With what **k** of body do they come?
Eph   4:32 and be **k** to one another,
Tit   2: 5 good managers of the household, **k,**

EVERY KIND Ge 1:11, 12, 12, 21, 21, 24,
24, 25, 25, 25; 6:19, 20, 21; 7:14, 14, 14; Ex
1:14; 31:3, 5; 35:31, 33, 35; 2Ch 34:13; Ps
144:13; Eze 17:23, 23; 27:18; 39:4, 17; Mt
13:47; Ro 1:29; 1Co 1:5; Eph 4:19; 2Th 2:10;
Jas 3:7; Rev 11:6; Tob 4:12; Sir 41:16; 47:25

KINDLED

Dt   32:22 For a fire is **k** by my anger,
Lk   12:49 and how I wish it were already **k!**

KINDLY → KIND

Jos   2:12 since I have dealt **k** with you,
Ru   1: 8 May the LORD deal **k** with you,
1Co   4:13 when slandered, we speak **k.**

KINDNESS → KIND

Ru   2:20 whose **k** has not forsaken the living
2Sa   9: 3 of Saul to whom I may show the **k**
Pr   21:21 and **k** will find life and honor.
       31:26 teaching of **k** is on her tongue.
Hos 11: 4 I led them with cords of human **k,**
Ro   2: 4 **k** is meant to lead you to repentance
       11:22 then the **k** and the severity of God:
2Co   6: 6 **k,** holiness of spirit, genuine love,
Gal   5:22 joy, peace, patience, **k,** generosity,
Eph   2: 7 of his grace in **k** toward us
Col   3:12 with compassion, **k,** humility,
Tit   3: 4 loving **k** of God our Savior
Sir   3:14 **k** to a father will not be forgotten,

KINDRED → KINSMAN, NEXT-OF-KIN

Ge   12: 1 "Go from your country and your **k**
       24:40 get a wife for my son from my **k,**
Dt   3:20 When the LORD gives rest to your **k,**
Jos   22: 4 your God has given rest to your **k,**
Est   2:10 Esther did not reveal her people or **k**
        8: 6 to see the destruction of my **k?"**
Ps 133: 1 pleasant it is when **k** live together
Ro   9: 3 my **k** according to the flesh.
Sir 40:24 **K** and helpers are for a time of

KINDS → KIND

Lev 19:19 not sow your field with two **k** of
Dt   25:13 have in your bag two **k** of weights,
Jer 15: 3 over them four **k** of destroyers,
Mt   5:11 utter all **k** of evil against you falsely
1Co 12:10 to another various **k** of tongues,
1Ti   6:10 For the love of money is a root of
              all **k** of evil,
Sir   25: 2 I hate three **k** of people,

KING → KING'S, KINGDOM, KINGDOMS, KINGS, KINGSHIP

Ge   14:18 **K** Melchizedek of Salem brought
       20: 2 **K** Abimelech of Gerar sent and took
       26: 8 **K** Abimelech of the Philistines
Ex   1: 8 Now a new **k** arose over Egypt,
Nu   21:26 Heshbon was the city of **K** Sihon of
       21:33 **K** Og of Bashan came out against
       22:10 "**K** Balak son of Zippor of Moab,
       23:21 acclaimed as a **k** among them.
Dt   17:14 and you say, "I will set a **k** over me,
Jdg   9: 8 trees once went out to anoint a **k**
       17: 6 those days there was no **k** in Israel;
       18: 1 those days there was no **k** in Israel.
       19: 1 days, when there was no **k** in Israel,
       21:25 those days there was no **k** in Israel;
1Sa   8: 5 appoint for us, then, a **k** to govern
        8: 7 rejected me from being **k** over them.
       11:15 they made Saul **k** before the LORD
       12:12 the LORD your God was your **k.**
       15:11 "I regret that I made Saul **k,**
       16: 1 I have rejected him from being **k**
2Sa   2: 4 there they anointed David **k** over
1Ki   1:30 son Solomon shall succeed me as **k,**
Ps   2: 6 set my **k** on Zion, my holy hill."
       10:16 The LORD is **k** forever and ever;
       24: 7 that the **K** of glory may come in.
       33:16 A **k** is not saved by his great army;
       44: 4 You are my **K** and my God;
       47: 7 For God is the **k** of all the earth;
       48: 2 the far north, the city of the great **K.**
Isa   6: 5 have seen the **K,** the LORD of hosts!
       32: 1 See, a **k** will reign in righteousness,
       43:15 the Creator of Israel, your **K.**
Jer 10:10 living God and the everlasting **K.**
       30: 9 LORD their God and David their **k,**
Eze 37:24 My servant David shall be **k** over
Hos   3: 5 LORD their God, and David their **k;**
Mic   2:13 Their **k** will pass on before them,
Zep   3:15 The **k** of Israel, the LORD, is in your
Zec   9: 9 your **k** comes to you; triumphant
       14: 9 the LORD will become **k** over all
Mal   1:14 for I am a great **K,** says the LORD
Mt   2: 2 who has been born **k** of the Jews?
       21: 5 your **k** is coming to you, humble,
       27:11 "Are you the **K** of the Jews?"
       27:37 "This is Jesus, the **K** of the Jews."
Mk   15:32 Let the Messiah, the **K** of Israel,
Lk   19:38 "Blessed is the **k** who comes in the
       23: 3 "Are you the **K** of the Jews?"
Jn   1:49 You are the **K** of Israel!"
       12:13 of the Lord—the **K** of Israel!"
       18:37 Pilate asked him, "So you are a **k?"**
       19:15 "We have no **k** but the emperor."
       19:21 'This man said, I am **K** of the Jews.'
Ac   17: 7 there is another **k** named Jesus."
1Ti   1:17 To the **K** of the ages, immortal,
        6:15 the **K** of kings and Lord of lords.
Heb   7: 1 This "**K** Melchizedek of Salem,
Rev 15: 3 are your ways, **K** of the nations!
       17:14 he is Lord of lords and **K** of kings,
       19:16 "**K** of kings and Lord of lords."
Tob 10:13 Lord of heaven and earth, **K** over all
Jdt   9:12 **K** of all your creation,
Sir   51:12 to the **K** of the kings of kings,

GREAT KING 2Ki 18:19, 28; Ezr 5:11; Ps
47:2; 48:2; 95:3; Ecc 9:14; Isa 36:4, 13; Hos
5:13; 10:6; Mal 1:14; Mt 5:35; Tob 13:15; Jdt
2:5; 3:2; AdE 13:1; 16:1

KING DAVID 2Sa 3:31; 5:3; 6:12, 16; 7:18;
8:8, 10, 11; 9:5; 13:21; 16:5, 6; 17:17, 21;
19:11, 16; 20:21; 1Ki 1:1, 13, 28, 31, 32, 37,
43, 47; 1Ch 15:29; 17:16; 18:10, 11; 21:24;
24:31; 26:26, 32; 27:24; 28:2; 29:1, 9, 24, 29;
2Ch 2:12; 7:6; 8:11; 29:27; 30:26; 35:4; Ezr
3:10; Mt 1:6; 1Es 1:5; 5:60

KING HEZEKIAH 2Ki 18:9, 13, 14, 14, 16,
17; 19:1, 5, 10; 20:14; 1Ch 4:41; 2Ch 29:18,
20, 30; 30:24; 31:13; 32:8, 9, 20, 23; Pr 25:1;
Isa 36:1, 2; 37:1, 5, 10; 38:9; 39:3; Jer 26:18,
19; 2Mc 15:22

KING OF ASSYRIA 2Ki 15:20, 20; 16:8, 9, 9, 18; 17:4, 4, 4, 5, 6, 24, 26, 27; 18:7, 11, 14, 14, 16, 17, 19, 23, 28, 30, 31, 33; 19:4, 6, 8, 10, 32; 20:6; 23:29; 2Ch 28:16, 21; 32:7, 11, 21; 33:11; Ezr 6:22; Isa 7:17, 20; 8:4, 7; 10:12; 20:4, 6; 36:2, 4, 8, 13, 15, 16, 18; 37:4, 6, 8, 10, 33; 38:6; Jer 50:17, 18; Na 3:18

KING OF BABYLON 2Ki 20:18; 24:7, 12, 12, 16, 17, 20; 25:6, 8, 8, 11, 20, 21, 23, 24; Isa 14:4; 39:7; Jer 20:4; 21:4, 10; 25:11, 12; 27:8, 9, 11, 12, 13, 14, 17; 28:2, 4; 29:22; 32:2, 3, 4, 36; 34:2, 3, 7, 21; 36:29; 37:17, 19; 38:3, 17, 18, 22, 23; 39:3, 3, 6, 6, 13; 40:5, 7, 9, 11; 41:2, 18; 42:11; 50:18, 43; 51:31; 52:3, 9, 10, 11, 12, 12, 15, 26, 27, 34; Eze 17:12; 19:9; 21:19, 21; 24:2; 30:24, 25, 25; 32:11; Bar 2:21, 22, 24

KING OF EGYPT Ge 40:1, 1, 5; 41:46; Ex 1:15, 17, 18; 2:23; 3:18, 19; 5:4; 6:11, 13, 27, 29; 14:5, 8; Dt 7:8; 11:3; 1Ki 3:1; 9:16; 11:18; 2Ki 17:7; 18:21; 23:29; 24:7, 7; 2Ch 36:3, 4; Isa 36:6; Jer 25:19; 44:30; 46:2, 17; Eze 29:2, 3; 30:21, 22; 31:2; 32:2; Ac 7:10; Jdt 5:11; 1Mc 10:51; 11:1; 1Es 1:25, 26, 35, 37

KING OF ISRAEL 1Sa 24:14; 26:20; 2Sa 6:20; 1Ki 20:4, 7, 11, 21, 22, 28, 31, 32, 34, 40, 41, 43; 22:2, 3, 4, 5, 6, 8, 9, 10, 18, 26, 29, 30, 30, 31, 32, 33, 34, 44; 2Ki 3:4, 5, 9, 10, 11, 12, 13, 13; 5:5, 6, 7, 8; 6:9, 10, 11, 12, 21, 26; 7:6; 13:16, 18; 16:7; 2Ch 18:4, 5, 7, 8, 9, 17, 25, 28, 29, 29, 30, 31, 32, 33, 34; 28:5; 35:3; Ezr 5:11; Pr 1:1; Isa 44:6; Hos 10:15; Zep 3:15; Mt 27:42; Mk 15:32; Jn 1:49; 12:13; 1Es 6:14

KING OF JUDAH 2Ki 3:9; 22:16, 18; 2Ch 22:1; 34:24, 26; 35:21; Isa 7:1; Jer 21:11; 22:1, 2, 6; 27:18, 21; 32:2; 34:6; 37:7; 38:22; Bar 1:3, 8

KING OF KINGS Ezr 7:12; Eze 26:7; Da 2:37; 1Ti 6:15; Rev 17:14; 19:16; 2Mc 13:4; 3Mc 5:35

KING OF THE JEWS Mt 2:2; 27:11, 29, 37; Mk 15:2, 9, 12, 18, 26; Lk 23:3, 37, 38; Jn 18:33, 39; 19:3, 19, 21, 21

KING OVER [ALL] ISRAEL 1Sa 15:17, 26, 35; 16:1; 23:17; 2Sa 5:3, 12, 17; 12:7; 19:22; 1Ki 1:34; 4:1; 11:37; 12:20; 14:14; 16:16; 19:16; 2Ki 3:1; 9:3, 12; 1Ch 11:3; 12:38; 14:2, 8; 23:1; 28:4, 4; Ne 13:26; Ecc 1:12

KING SOLOMON 1Ki 1:34, 39, 51, 51, 53, 53; 2:17, 19, 22, 23, 25, 29, 45; 4:1, 27; 5:13; 6:2; 7:13, 14, 40, 45, 51; 8:1, 2, 5; 9:11, 15, 26, 28; 10:10, 13, 16, 23; 11:1; 12:2; 2Ki 23:13; 24:13; 1Ch 29:24; 2Ch 4:11, 16; 5:6; 7:5; 8:10, 18; 9:9, 12, 15, 22; 10:2; Ne 13:26; SS 3:9, 11; Jer 52:20; 1Es 1:3

***LORD THE KING** Ge 40:1; 1Sa 24:8; 26:15, 15, 19; 29:8; 2Sa 3:21; 4:8; 9:11; 13:33; 14:9, 12, 15, 17, 17, 18, 19, 19, 22; 15:15, 21, 21; 16:4, 9; 18:28, 31, 32; 19:19, 20, 27, 27, 28, 30, 35, 37; 24:3, 3, 21, 22; 1Ki 1:2, 2, 13, 18, 20, 20, 21, 24, 27, 27, 36, 37; 2:38; 20:9; 1Ch 21:3, 23; Da 1:10; 4:24; 1Es 2:18, 21; 4:46; 6:8, 21, 22

KING'S → KING

Nu 20:17 we will go along the **K** Highway,
2Sa 9:13 for he always ate at the **k** table.
Pr 21: 1 The **k** heart is a stream of water in
Ecc 8: 2 **k** command because of your sacred
Jer 52:33 he dined regularly at the **k** table.
Heb 11:23 they were not afraid of the **k** edict.
1Mc 2:22 We will not obey the **k** words

KING'S COMMAND 1Ki 5:17; 2Ki 18:36; 1Ch 21:6; 2Ch 35:10; Est 1:12; 3:3; 4:3; 8:14, 17; 9:1; Ecc 8:2; Isa 36:21; Da 3:22, 28; AdE 3:3, 4; 8:8; 1Mc 2:23, 31; 3:14; 2Mc 7:30; 1Es 4:5; 3Mc 7:20

KING'S GATE 1Ch 9:18; Est 2:19, 21; 3:2, 3; 4:2, 2, 6; 5:9, 13; 6:10, 12; AdE 4:2

KING'S HOUSE 2Sa 11:2, 8, 9; 15:35; 1Ki 9:1, 10; 10:12; 14:26, 27; 15:18; 16:18, 18; 2Ki 11:5, 16, 19, 20; 12:18; 14:14; 16:8; 18:15; 24:13; 25:9; 2Ch 7:11; 9:11; 12:9, 10; 16:2; 21:17; 23:5, 15, 20; 25:24; Est 9:4; Jer 26:10; 36:12; 38:7, 8; 39:8; 52:13

KING'S SERVANTS 2Sa 11:24; 1Ki 1:47; Est 2:2; 3:2, 3; 4:11; 6:3, 5; Jdt 6:3; AdE 2:2; 6:3, 8; Aza 1:23

KING'S SON 2Sa 18:12, 20; 1Ki 22:26; 2Ki 11:4, 12; 15:5; 2Ch 18:25; 23:3, 11; 28:7; Ps 72:1; Jer 36:26; 38:6; 1Mc 6:17

KING'S SONS 2Sa 9:11; 13:23, 27, 29, 30, 32, 33, 35, 36; 1Ki 1:9; 2Ki 10:6, 7, 8; 1Ch 27:32; Zep 1:8

KINGDOM → KING

Ex 19: 6 you shall be for me a priestly **k** and
Dt 17:18 he has taken the throne of his **k**,
1Sa 13:14 now your **k** will not continue;
    28:17 has torn the **k** out of your hand,
2Sa 7:12 and I will establish his **k**.
1Ki 11:31 "See, I am about to tear the **k**
1Ch 17:11 own sons, and I will establish his **k**.
    29:11 yours is the **k**, O LORD,
Ps 103:19 and his **k** rules over all.
   145:13 Your **k** is an everlasting **k**,
Isa 9: 7 for the throne of David and his **k**.
Jer 18: 7 concerning a nation or a **k**,
Eze 29:14 and there they shall be a lowly **k**.
Da 2:39 After you shall arise another **k**
    2:44 a **k** that shall never be destroyed,
    4: 3 His **k** is an everlasting **k**,
    5:28 your **k** is divided and given to
    7:18 of the Most High shall receive the **k**
    7:27 their **k** shall be an everlasting **k**,
Mt 3: 2 "Repent, for the **k** of heaven has
    4:17 "Repent, for the **k** of heaven has
    4:23 the **k** and curing every disease
    5: 3 for theirs is the **k** of heaven.
    5:10 for theirs is the **k** of heaven.
    5:19 called great in the **k** of heaven.
    5:20 will never enter the **k** of heaven.
    6:10 Your **k** come. Your will be done,
    6:33 strive first for the **k** of God and his
    7:21 'Lord, Lord,' will enter the **k** of
    8:12 of the **k** will be thrown into the
    9:35 proclaiming the good news of the **k**,
   10: 7 'The **k** of heaven has come near.'
   11:11 least in the **k** of heaven is greater
   11:12 of John the Baptist until now the **k**
   12:25 "Every **k** divided against itself is
   12:28 then the **k** of God has come to you.
   13:11 know the secrets of the **k** of heaven,
   13:19 anyone hears the word of the **k** and
   13:24 "The **k** of heaven may be compared
   13:31 "The **k** of heaven is like a mustard
   13:33 "The **k** of heaven is like yeast that a
   13:38 good seed are the children of the **k;**
   13:44 "The **k** of heaven is like treasure
   13:45 the **k** of heaven is like a merchant
   13:47 the **k** of heaven is like a net that
   13:52 the **k** of heaven is like the master of
   16:19 I will give you the keys of the **k** of
   16:28 the Son of Man coming in his **k."**
   18: 1 is the greatest in the **k** of heaven?"
   18: 3 will never enter the **k** of heaven.
   18: 4 is the greatest in the **k** of heaven.
   18:23 For this reason the **k** of heaven may
   19:12 for the sake of the **k** of heaven.
   19:14 these that the **k** of heaven belongs."
   19:23 for a rich person to enter the **k** of
   20: 1 **k** of heaven is like
   20:21 and one at your left, in your **k."**
   21:31 prostitutes are going into the **k** of
   21:43 the **k** of God will be taken away
   22: 2 "The **k** of heaven may be compared
   23:13 lock people out of the **k** of heaven.
   24:14 the **k** will be proclaimed throughout

   25: 1 "Then the **k** of heaven will be like
   25:34 inherit the **k** prepared for you from
   26:29 new with you in my Father's **k."**
Mk 1:15 and the **k** of God has come near;
    3:24 If a **k** is divided against itself, that **k** cannot stand.
    4:11 has been given the secret of the **k**
    4:26 "The **k** of God is as
    6:23 I will give you, even half of my **k."**
    9: 1 until they see that the **k** of God has
    9:47 the **k** of God with one eye than to
   10:14 as these that the **k** of God belongs.
   10:15 the **k** of God as a little child will
   10:23 have wealth to enter the **k** of God!"
   10:24 how hard it is to enter the **k** of God!
   11:10 Blessed is the coming **k** of our
   12:34 You are not far from the **k** of God."
   13: 8 and **k** against **k;**
   14:25 that day when I drink it new in the **k**
   15:43 waiting expectantly for the **k** of God
Lk 1:33 and of his **k** there will be no end."
    4:43 the good news of the **k** of God
    6:20 for yours is the **k** of God.
    7:28 the least in the **k** of God is greater
    8: 1 and bringing the good news of the **k**
    8:10 to know the secrets of the **k** of God;
    9: 2 out to proclaim the **k** of God and
    9:11 spoke to them about the **k** of God,
    9:27 death before they see the **k** of God."
    9:60 you, go and proclaim the **k** of God."
    9:62 plow and looks back is fit for the **k**
   10: 9 **k** of God has come near to you.'
   10:11 the **k** of God has come near.'
   11: 2 be your name. Your **k** come.
   11:20 then the **k** of God has come to you.
   12:31 for his **k**, and these things will be
   12:32 good pleasure to give you the **k**.
   13:18 "What is the **k** of God like?
   13:29 and will eat in the **k** of God.
   14:15 anyone who will eat bread in the **k**
   16:16 then the good news of the **k** of God
   17:20 "The **k** of God is not coming with
   17:21 in fact, the **k** of God is among you."
   18:16 as these that the **k** of God belongs.
   18:24 have wealth to enter the **k** of God!
   18:29 for the sake of the **k** of God,
   19:11 because they supposed that the **k** of
   21:31 you know that the **k** of God is near.
   22:16 not eat it until it is fulfilled in the **k**
   22:18 fruit of the vine until the **k** of God
   22:29 my Father has conferred on me, a **k**,
   22:30 eat and drink at my table in my **k**,
   23:42 when you come into your **k."**
   23:51 waiting expectantly for the **k** of God
Jn 3: 3 no one can see the **k** of God without
    3: 5 no one can enter the **k** of God
   18:36 "My **k** is not from this world.
Ac 1: 3 forty days and speaking about the **k**
    1: 6 you will restore the **k** to Israel?"
    8:12 about the **k** of God and the name of
   14:22 that we must enter the **k** of God."
   19: 8 argued persuasively about the **k** of
   20:25 have gone about proclaiming the **k**,
   28:23 the **k** of God and trying to convince
   28:31 the **k** of God and teaching about
Ro 14:17 the **k** of God is not food and drink
1Co 4:20 the **k** of God depends not on talk but
    6: 9 wrongdoers will not inherit the **k**
   15:24 when he hands over the **k** to God
   15:50 blood cannot inherit the **k** of God,
Eph 5: 5 any inheritance in the **k** of Christ
Col 1:13 transferred us into the **k** of his
    4:11 among my co-workers for the **k**
1Th 2:12 calls you into his own **k** and glory.
2Th 1: 5 make you worthy of the **k** of God,
2Ti 4: 1 in view of his appearing and his **k**,
    4:18 and save me for his heavenly **k**.
Heb 1: 8 scepter is the scepter of your **k**.
   12:28 receiving a **k** that cannot be shaken,
Jas 2: 5 the **k** that he has promised to those
2Pe 1:11 entry into the eternal **k** of our Lord
Rev 1: 6 and made us to be a **k**,

1: 9 the persecution and the **k** and
5:10 a **k** and priests serving our God,
11:15 "The **k** of the world has become the
       k of our Lord and
12:10 the **k** of our God and the authority
16:10 and its **k** was plunged into darkness;
Wis 10:10 she showed him the **k** of God,
2Es 2:13 **k** is already prepared for you;
13:31 against people, and **k** against **k**.

KINGDOM OF *GOD Mt 6:33; 12:28;
19:24; 21:31, 43; Mk 1:15; 4:11, 26, 30; 9:1,
47; 10:14, 15, 23, 24, 25; 12:34; 14:25; 15:43;
Lk 4:43; 6:20; 7:28; 8:1, 10; 9:2, 11, 27, 60,
62; 10:9, 11; 11:20; 13:18, 20, 28, 29; 14:15;
16:16; 17:20, 20, 21; 18:16, 17, 24, 25, 29;
19:11; 21:31; 22:16, 18; 23:51; Jn 3:3, 5; Ac
1:3; 8:12; 14:22; 19:8; 28:23, 31; Ro 14:17;
1Co 4:20; 6:9, 10; 15:50; Gal 5:21; Col 4:11;
2Th 1:5; Rev 12:10; Wis 10:10

KINGDOM OF HEAVEN Mt 3:2; 4:17; 5:3,
10, 19, 19, 20; 7:21; 8:11; 10:7; 11:11, 12;
13:11, 24, 31, 33, 44, 45, 47, 52; 16:19; 18:1,
3, 4, 23; 19:12, 14, 23; 20:1; 22:2; 23:13; 25:1

WHOLE KINGDOM Jos 13:30; 1Ki 11:34;
Est 3:6; Da 1:20; 6:1, 3; 11:17; Jdt 11:8; 1Mc
1:41, 51

KINGDOMS → KING

Dt 3:21 the LORD will do to all the **k** into
1Ki 4:21 over all the **k** from the Euphrates to
2Ki 19:15 you alone, of all the **k** of the earth;
19:19 all the **k** of the earth may know that
2Ch 20: 6 rule over all the **k** of the nations?
Ps 68:32 Sing to God, O **k** of the earth;
Eze 37:22 shall they be divided into two **k**.
Da 2:44 It shall crush all these **k** and bring
Zep 3: 8 is to gather nations, to assemble **k**,
Lk 4: 5 showed him in an instant all the **k** of
Heb 11:33 who through faith conquered **k**,

ALL THE ... KINGDOMS Dt 3:21; 28:25;
1Sa 10:18; 1Ki 4:21; 2Ki 19:15, 19; 1Ch
29:30; 2Ch 17:10; 20:6, 29; 36:23; Ezr 1:2; Ps
135:11; Isa 23:17; 37:16, 20; Jer 15:4; 24:9;
25:26; 29:18; 34:1, 17; Da 7:23; Mt 4:8; Lk
4:5; Bar 2:4; 2Es 12:13

KINGDOMS OF THE EARTH Dt 28:25;
2Ki 19:15, 19; 1Ch 29:30; 2Ch 36:23; Ezr 1:2;
Ps 68:32; Isa 37:16, 20; Jer 15:4; 24:9; 29:18;
34:1, 17

KINGS → KING

Ge 14: 9 of Ellasar, four **k** against five.
17: 6 and **k** shall come from you.
Jos 12: 1 Now these are the **k** of the land,
2Sa 11: 1 the time when **k** go out to battle,
1Ki 10:23 King Solomon excelled all the **k** of
Ps 2: 2 The **k** of the earth set themselves,
68:29 at Jerusalem **k** bear gifts to you.
72:11 May all **k** fall down before him,
89:27 the highest of the **k** of the earth.
110: 5 shatter **k** on the day of his wrath.
138: 4 All the **k** of the earth shall praise
149: 8 bind their **k** with fetters and
Pr 8:15 By me **k** reign, and rulers decree
16:12 It is an abomination to **k** to do evil,
31: 4 it is not for **k** to drink wine,
Isa 24:21 and on earth the **k** of the earth.
52:15 **k** shall shut their mouths because of
60:11 with their **k** led in procession.
Da 2:21 deposes **k** and sets up **k**;
2:47 Lord of **k** and a revealer of
7:24 of this kingdom ten **k** shall arise,
Lk 10:24 I tell you that many prophets and **k**
21:12 you will be brought before **k** and
Ac 4:26 The **k** of the earth took their stand,
1Co 4: 8 I wish that you had become **k**,
1Ti 2: 2 **k** and all who are in high positions,
6:15 the King of **k** and Lord of lords.
Rev 1: 5 and the ruler of the **k** of the earth.
17: 2 the **k** of the earth have committed
17:12 ten **k** who have not yet received a

17:14 he is Lord of lords and King of **k**,
19:16 "King of **k** and Lord of lords."
19:19 the **k** of the earth with their armies
21:24 **k** of the earth will bring their glory
Sir 51:12 to the King of the **k** of **k**,
1Mc 2:48 of the hands of the Gentiles and **k**,

ALL THE KINGS Jos 5:1, 1; 9:1; 10:6; 2Sa
10:19; 1Ki 4:24, 34; 10:15, 23, 29; 16:33; 2Ki
18:5; 2Ch 1:17; 9:14, 22, 23, 26; Ps 102:15;
138:4; Isa 14:18; 62:2; Jer 25:20, 20, 22, 22,
24, 24, 25, 25, 25, 26; 2Es 15:20

BOOK OF THE KINGS 1Ch 9:1; 2Ch
16:11; 20:34; 24:27; 25:26; 27:7; 28:26; 32:32;
35:27; 36:8; 1Es 1:33

KING OF KINGS Ezr 7:12; Eze 26:7; Da
2:37; 1Ti 6:15; Rev 17:14; 19:16; 2Mc 13:4;
3Mc 5:35

KINGS OF ISRAEL 1Ki 14:19; 15:31; 16:5,
14, 20, 27, 33; 22:39; 2Ki 1:18; 8:18; 10:34;
13:8, 12, 13; 14:15, 16, 28, 29; 15:11, 15, 21,
26, 31; 16:3; 17:2, 8; 23:19, 22; 1Ch 9:1; 2Ch
20:34; 21:6, 13; 27:7; 28:2, 27; 33:18; 35:18,
27; 36:8; Mic 1:14; 1Es 1:21, 33

KINGS OF JUDAH 1Sa 27:6; 1Ki 14:29;
15:7, 23; 22:45; 2Ki 8:23; 12:18, 19; 14:18;
15:6, 36; 16:19; 18:5; 20:20; 21:17, 25; 23:5,
11, 12, 22, 28; 24:5; 2Ch 16:11; 25:26; 28:26;
32:32; 34:11; Isa 1:1; Jer 1:18; 8:1; 17:19, 20;
19:3, 4, 13; 20:5; 33:4; 44:9; Sir 49:4

KINGS OF THE EARTH 1Ki 4:34; 10:23;
2Ch 9:22, 23; Ps 2:2; 76:12; 89:27; 102:15;
138:4; 148:11; Isa 24:21; La 4:12; Eze 27:33;
Mt 17:25; Ac 4:26; Rev 1:5; 6:15; 17:2, 18;
18:3, 9; 19:19; 21:24; 1Mc 1:2; 1Es 8:77; 2Es
15:20

KINGSHIP → KING

1Sa 10:25 the rights and duties of the **k**;
Da 7: 14 given dominion and glory and **k**,

KINSMAN → KINDRED

Ge 29:12 that he was her father's **k**,
Ru 3: 2 Now here is our **k** Boaz,
Tob 5: 14 It turns out that you are a **k**,

KISH

1Sa 10:21 Saul the son of **K** was taken by lot.

KISHON

Jdg 5:21 The torrent **K** swept them away,
1Ki 18:40 brought them down to the Wadi **K**,
Ps 83: 9 to Sisera and Jabin at the Wadi **K**,

KISS* → KISSED, KISSES, KISSING

Ge 27:26 "Come near and **k** me, my son."
31:28 why did you not permit me to **k** my
2Sa 15: 5 and take hold of them, and **k** them.
20: 9 with his right hand to **k** him.
1Ki 19:20 Let me **k** my father and my mother,
Ps 2:12 **k** his feet, or he will be angry,
85:10 righteousness and peace will **k** each
Pr 24:26 gives an honest answer gives a **k** on
SS 1: 2 Let him **k** me with the kisses of his
8: 1 If I met you outside, I would **k** you,
Mt 26:48 "The one I will **k** is the man; arrest
Mk 14:44 saying, "The one I,will **k** is the man;
Lk 7:45 You gave me no **k**, but from the
22:47 He approached Jesus to **k** him;
22:48 with a **k** that you are betraying the
Ro 16:16 Greet one another with a holy **k**.
1Co 16:20 Greet one another with a holy **k**.
2Co 13:12 Greet one another with a holy **k**.
1Th 5:26 brothers and sisters with a holy **k**.
1Pe 5:14 Greet one another with a **k** of love.
AdE 13:13 the soles of his feet to save Israel!

KISSED* → KISS

Ge 27:27 So he came near and **k** him;
29:11 Jacob **k** Rachel, and wept aloud.
29:13 he embraced him and **k** him,
31:55 **k** his grandchildren and his
33: 4 and **k** him, and they wept.

45:15 And he **k** all his brothers and wept
48:10 and he **k** them and embraced them.
50: 1 and wept over him and **k** him.
Ex 4:27 at the mountain of God and **k** him.
18: 7 he bowed down and **k** him;
Ru 1: 9 she **k** them, and they wept aloud.
1Sa 10: 1 poured it on his head, and **k** him;
20:41 three times, and they **k** each other,
2Sa 14:33 the king; and the king **k** Absalom.
19:39 king **k** Barzillai and blessed him,
1Ki 19:18 every mouth that has not **k** him."
Job 31:27 and my mouth has **k** my hand;
Mt 26:49 "Greetings, Rabbi!" and **k** him.
Mk 14:45 and said, "Rabbi!" and **k** him.
Lk 15:20 put his arms around him and **k** him.
Ac 20:37 they embraced Paul and **k** him,
Tob 5: 17 he **k** his father and mother.
7: 6 Raguel jumped up and **k** him and
10:12 Then he **k** his daughter Sarah and
10:12 Then she **k** them both and saw them
1Es 4:47 Then King Darius got up and **k** him,
3Mc 5:49 and groans they **k** each other,

KISSES* → KISS

Pr 7:13 She seizes him and **k** him,
27: 6 but profuse are the **k** of an enemy.
SS 1: 2 kiss me with the **k** of his mouth!
7: 9 your **k** like the best wine that goes
Sir 29: 5 One **k** another's hands until he gets

KISSING* → KISS

Hos 13: 2 they say. People are **k** calves!
Lk 7:38 continued **k** his feet and anointing
7:45 she has not stopped **k** my feet.

KNEADING

Dt 28: 5 your basket and your **k** bowl.
28:17 your basket and your **k** bowl.

KNEE* → KNEES

Ge 41:43 in front of him, "Bow the **k!**"
Isa 45:23 "To me every **k** shall bow,
Ro 11: 4 not bowed the **k** to Baal."
14:11 says the Lord, every **k** shall bow to
Php 2:10 at the name of Jesus every **k** should
Man 1:11 And now I bend the **k** of my heart,

KNEEL → KNELT

Ps 95: 6 let us **k** before the LORD, our Maker

KNEES → KNEE

1Ki 19:18 the **k** that have not bowed to Baal,
Isa 35: 3 and make firm the feeble **k**.
Da 6:10 get down on his **k** three times a day
Lk 5: 8 Peter saw it, he fell down at Jesus' **k**
Eph 3:14 I bow my **k** before the Father,
Heb 12:12 and strengthen your weak **k**,

KNELT → KNEEL

2Ch 6:13 he **k** on his knees in the presence of
Mt 8: 2 a leper who came to him and **k**
9:18 of the synagogue came in and **k**
15:25 she came and **k** before him, saying,
17:14 a man came to him, **k** before him,
27:29 a reed in his right hand and **k** before
Lk 22:41 about a stone's throw, **k** down,
Ac 20:36 he **k** down with them all and prayed.
21: 5 There we **k** down on the beach and

KNEW → KNOW

Ge 3: 7 and they **k** that they were naked;
4: 1 Now the man **k** his wife Eve,
Dt 34:10 whom the LORD **k** face to face.
2Ch 33:13 Manasseh **k** that the LORD indeed
Job 23: 3 Oh, that I **k** where I might find him,
Jer 1: 5 I formed you in the womb I **k** you,
Jnh 4: 2 for I **k** that you are a gracious God
Mt 7:23 will declare to them, 'I never **k** you;
12:25 He **k** what they were thinking and
Lk 4:41 they **k** that he was the Messiah.
Jn 2: 4 to them, because he **k** all people
4:10 "If you **k** the gift of God,
8:19 If you **k** me, you would know my
13: 1 Jesus **k** that his hour had come to

13:11 For he **k** who was to betray him;
21:12 because they **k** it was the Lord.
Ro   1:21 they **k** God, they did not honor him

KNIFE → KNIVES

Ge   22:10 and took the **k** to kill his son.
Pr   23: 2 put a **k** to your throat if you have a

KNIT

Job   10:11 and **k** me together with bones and
Ps 139:13 you **k** me together in my mother's
Eph   4:16 and **k** together by every ligament

KNIVES → KNIFE

Jos   5: 2 "Make flint **k** and circumcise the
Pr   30:14 teeth are **k**, to devour the poor

KNOCK* → KNOCKING, KNOCKS

Mt   7: 7 **k**, and the door will be opened for
Lk   11: 9 **k**, and the door will be opened for
      13:25 stand outside and to **k** at the door,

KNOCKING* → KNOCK

SS   5: 2 Listen! my beloved is **k**.
Ac   12:16 Meanwhile Peter continued **k**;
Rev   3:20 I am standing at the door, **k**;

KNOCKS → KNOCK

Mt   7: 8 who **k**, the door will be opened.
Lk   12:36 for him as soon as he comes and **k**.

KNOW → FOREKNEW,
FOREKNOWLEDGE, KNEW, KNOWING,
KNOWLEDGE, KNOWN, KNOWS

Ge   15: 8 how am I to **k** that I shall possess it?
      22:12 for now I **k** that you fear God,
Ex   1: 8 over Egypt, who did not **k** Joseph.
       3:19 I **k**, however, that the king of Egypt
       6: 7 **k** that I am the LORD your God,
       7: 5 shall **k** that I am the LORD.
      14: 4 shall **k** that I am the LORD.
      18:11 Now I **k** that the LORD is greater
      33:12 you have said, 'I **k** you by name,
      33:13 so that I may **k** you and find favor
Nu   16:28 how you shall **k** that the LORD has
Dt   7: 9 **K** therefore that the LORD your God
       8: 2 you to **k** what was in your heart,
Jos   3: 7 they may **k** that I will be with you
       4:24 the peoples of the earth may **k** that
      23:14 and you **k** in your hearts and souls,
1Sa   17:46 the earth may **k** that there is a God
1Ki   8:39 only you **k** what is in every human
Job   11: 6 **K** then that God exacts of you less
      19:25 For I **k** that my Redeemer lives,
      42: 2 "I **k** that you can do all things,
      42: 3 wonderful for me, which I did not **k**.
Ps   9:10 who **k** your name put their trust in
      36:10 who **k** you, and your salvation to
      46:10 "Be still, and **k** that I am God!
     100: 3 **K** that the LORD is God.
     139:23 test me and **k** my thoughts.
Pr   27: 1 you do not **k** what a day may bring.
      30: 4 of the person's child? Surely you **k**!
Ecc   8: 5 wise mind will **k** the time and way.
       8:16 I applied my mind to **k** wisdom,
Isa   1: 3 Israel does not **k**, my people do not
      44: 8 There is no other rock; I **k** not one."
Jer   4:22 but do not **k** how to do good."
       6:15 they did not **k** how to blush.
      22:16 Is not this to **k** me? says the LORD.
      24: 7 a heart to **k** that I am the LORD;
      31:34 "**K** the LORD," for they shall all **k**
Eze   5: 5 shall **k** that there has been a prophet
       6:10 they shall **k** that I am the LORD;
Mt   6: 3 left hand **k** what your right hand is
       7:11 **k** how to give good gifts to your
       9: 6 **k** that the Son of Man has authority
      22:29 you **k** neither the scriptures nor the
      24:42 do not **k** on what day your Lord is
      26:74 swore an oath, "I do not **k** the man!"
Mk   12:24 that you **k** neither the scriptures nor
Lk   1: 4 you may **k** the truth concerning the
      11:13 **k** how to give good gifts to your

12:48 not **k** and did what deserved a
13:25 'I do not **k** where you come from.'
18:20 You **k** the commandments:
21:31 **k** that the kingdom of God is near.
22:34 denied three times that you **k** me."
23:34 [do not **k** what they are doing."]
Jn   1:26 stands one whom you do not **k**,
       3:11 of what we **k** and testify to what we
       4:22 worship what we **k**, for salvation is
       4:42 we **k** that this is truly the Savior of
       6:69 We have come to believe and **k** that
       7:28 **k** me, and you **k** where I am from.
       8:14 because I **k** where I have come from
       8:19 "You **k** neither me nor my Father.
       8:32 and you will **k** the truth,
       8:55 But I do **k** him and I keep his word.
       9:25 thing I do **k**, that though I was blind,
      10: 4 sheep follow him because they **k** his
      10:14 I **k** my own and my own **k** me,
      10:27 I **k** them, and they follow me.
      12:35 you do not **k** where you are going.
      13:17 you **k** these things, you are blessed
      13:35 will **k** that you are my disciples,
      14:17 You **k** him, because he abides with
      15:21 they do not **k** him who sent me.
      16:30 Now we **k** that you **k** all things,
      17: 3 is eternal life, that they may **k** you,
      17:23 that the world may **k** that you have
      21:15 you **k** that I love you."
      21:24 and we **k** that his testimony is true.
Ac   1: 7 **k** the times or periods that the
       1:24 "Lord, you **k** everyone's heart.
Ro   6: 6 We **k** that our old self was crucified
       6:16 not **k** that if you present yourselves
       7:14 For we **k** that the law is spiritual;
       7:18 I **k** that nothing good dwells within
       8:26 do not **k** how to pray as we ought,
       8:28 We **k** that all things work together
1Co   1:21 did not **k** God through wisdom,
       2: 2 **k** nothing among you except Jesus
       3:16 not **k** that you are God's temple and
       5: 6 not **k** that a little yeast leavens the
       6: 2 not **k** that the saints will judge the
       6:15 not **k** that your bodies are members
       6:16 you not **k** that whoever is united to
       6:19 not **k** that your body is a temple of
       8: 2 Anyone who claims to **k** something
       8: 4 we **k** that "no idol in the world
       9:13 not **k** that those who are employed
       9:24 not **k** that in a race the runners all
      12: 2 You **k** that when you were pagans,
      13: 9 we **k** only in part, and we prophesy
      13:12 I **k** only in part; then I will **k** fully,
      14: 9 will anyone **k** what is being said?
      15:58 you **k** that in the Lord your labor is
2Co   4:14 we **k** that the one who raised
       5: 1 we **k** that if the earthly tent we live
       5: 6 we **k** that while we are at home in
       8: 9 you **k** the generous act of our Lord
      12: 2 body or out of the body I do not **k**;
Eph   1:17 revelation as you come to **k** him,
       1:18 you may **k** what is the hope
       3:19 **k** the love of Christ that surpasses
Php   3:10 to **k** Christ and the power of his
       4:12 I **k** what it is to have little,
Col   4: 1 you **k** that you also have a Master in
       4: 6 may **k** how you ought to answer
1Th   3: 3 you yourselves **k** that this is what
       5: 2 yourselves **k** very well that the day
2Th   1: 8 on those who do not **k** God and on
       2: 6 you **k** what is now restraining him,
1Ti   3: 5 not **k** how to manage his own
       3:15 may **k** how one ought to behave in
2Ti   1:12 I **k** the one in whom I have put my
       2:23 you **k** that they breed quarrels.
Tit   1:16 profess to **k** God, but they deny him
Heb   8:11 "**K** the Lord,' for they shall all **k** me,
Jas   1: 3 because you **k** that the testing
       3: 1 **k** that we who teach will be judged
       4: 4 not **k** that friendship with the world
       4:14 even **k** what tomorrow will bring.
1Pe   1:18 You **k** that you were ransomed from

2Pe   1:12 though you **k** them already and are
1Jn   2: 3 by this we may be sure that we **k**
       2: 4 Whoever says, "I have come to **k**
       2:11 and does not **k** the way to go,
       2:18 this we **k** that it is the last hour.
       2:29 If you **k** that he is righteous,
       3: 1 The reason the world does not **k** us
            is that it did not **k** him.
       3: 2 What we do **k** is this:
       3:14 **k** that we have passed from death to
       3:16 **k** love by this, that he laid down his
       3:19 by this we will **k** that we are from
       3:24 by this we **k** that he abides in us,
       4: 8 does not love does not **k** God,
       4:13 By this we **k** that we abide in him
       5: 2 By this we **k** that we love the
       5:13 may **k** that you have eternal life.
       5:15 And if we **k** that he hears us in
       5:18 **k** that those who are born of God
       5:20 so that we may **k** him who is true;
2Jn   1: 1 but also all who **k** the truth,
3Jn   1:12 and you **k** that our testimony is true.
Rev   2: 2 "I **k** your works, your toil
       2: 9 "I **k** your affliction and your poverty
       2:13 "I **k** where you are living,
       2:19 "I **k** your works—your love,
       3: 3 not **k** at what hour I will come to
       3: 8 "I **k** your works. Look, I have set
       3: 8 I **k** that you have but little power,
       3:15 I **k** your works; you are neither cold
AdE   13:12 You **k** all things; you **k**, O Lord,
Sir   5:10 Stand firm for what you **k**,

KNOWING → KNOW

Ge   3: 5 will be like God, **k** good and evil."
       3:22 like one of us, **k** good and evil;
Lev   5:17 If any of you sin without **k** it,
Pr   7:23 not **k** that it will cost him his life.
Jn   13: 3 **k** that the Father had given all
      18: 4 Jesus, **k** all that was to happen to
Php   3: 8 surpassing value of **k** Christ Jesus
Phm   1:21 **k** that you will do even more than I
Heb   13: 2 have entertained angels without **k** it.
2Pe   2:21 than, after **k** it, to turn back

KNOWLEDGE → KNOW

Ge   2: 9 the tree of the **k** of good and evil.
       2:17 but of the tree of the **k** of good and
Nu   24:16 and knows the **k** of the Most High,
2Ch   1:10 Give me now wisdom and **k** to go
Job   21:22 Will any teach God **k**,
      38: 2 darkens counsel by words without **k**
      42: 3 this that hides counsel without **k**?'
Ps   19: 2 and night to night declares **k**.
      73:11 Is there **k** in the Most High?"
      94:10 he who teaches **k** to humankind,
     119:66 Teach me good judgment and **k**,
     139: 6 Such **k** is too wonderful for me;
Pr   1: 4 **k** and prudence to the young—
       1: 7 of the LORD is the beginning of **k**;
       1:29 Because they hated **k** and did not
       2: 5 of the LORD and find the **k** of God.
       2: 6 mouth come **k** and understanding;
       2:10 and **k** will be pleasant to your soul;
       3:20 by his **k** the deeps broke apart,
       8:10 and **k** rather than choice gold;
       8:12 and I attain **k** and discretion.
       9:10 and the **k** of the Holy One is insight.
      10:14 The wise lay up **k**, but the babbling
      11: 9 but by **k** the righteous are delivered.
      12: 1 Whoever loves discipline loves **k**,
      12:23 One who is clever conceals **k**,
      14: 6 **k** is easy for one who understands.
      15: 7 The lips of the wise spread **k**;
      15:14 one who has understanding seeks **k**,
      18:15 An intelligent mind acquires **k**,
      19: 2 Desire without **k** is not good,
      19:25 the intelligent, and they will gain **k**.
      20:15 lips informed by **k** are a precious
      23:12 and your ear to words of **k**.
      24: 4 by **k** the rooms are filled with all
      24: 5 **k** than those who have strength;

Ecc 1:18 who increase **k** increase sorrow.
2:26 him God gives wisdom and **k**
7:12 advantage of **k** is that wisdom gives
Isa 11: 2 spirit of **k** and the fear of the LORD.
11: 9 of the **k** of the LORD as the waters
40:14 Who taught him **k,** and showed him
53:11 shall find satisfaction through his **k.**
Jer 3:15 feed you with **k** and understanding.
10:14 Everyone is stupid and without **k;**
Da 1:17 these four young men God gave **k**
Hos 4: 6 people are destroyed for lack of **k;**
Hab 2:14 earth will be filled with the **k** of the
Mal 2: 7 the lips of a priest should guard **k,**
Lk 1:77 to give **k** of salvation to his people
11:52 you have taken away the key of **k;**
Ro 2:20 in the law the embodiment of **k** and
11:33 riches and wisdom and **k** of God!
15:14 filled with all **k,** and able to instruct
1Co 8: 1 we know that "all of us possess **k."**
8: 1 **K** puffs up, but love builds up.
8:10 if others see you, who possess **k,**
8:11 So by your **k** those weak believers
12: 8 the utterance of **k** according to the
13: 2 understand all mysteries and all **k,**
13: 8 as for **k,** it will come to an end.
2Co 4: 6 to give the light of the **k** of the glory
8: 7 in faith, in speech, in **k,** in utmost
10: 5 obstacle raised up against the **k**
11: 6 untrained in speech, but not in **k;**
Eph 3:19 the love of Christ that surpasses **k,**
4:13 to the unity of the faith and of the **k**
Php 1: 9 and more with **k** and full insight
Col 1:10 good work and as you grow in the **k**
2: 3 the treasures of wisdom and **k.**
3:10 which is being renewed in **k**
1Ti 2: 4 and to come to the **k** of the truth.
6:20 of what is falsely called **k;**
Heb 10:26 in sin after having received the **k** of
2Pe 1: 3 the **k** of him who called us by his
1: 5 goodness, and goodness with **k,**
3:18 and **k** of our Lord and Savior Jesus
1Jn 2:20 and all of you have **k.**
Sir 3:25 without **k** there is no wisdom.
6:33 If you love to listen you will gain **k,**
19:22 The **k** of wickedness is not wisdom,

KNOWN → KNOW

Ex 6: 3 I did not make myself **k** to them.
Dt 13: 2 other gods" (whom you have not **k)**
Ps 9:16 The LORD has made himself **k,**
67: 2 that your way may be **k** upon earth,
98: 2 The LORD has made **k** his victory;
105: 1 make **k** his deeds among the peoples
139: 1 you have searched me and **k** me.
Pr 20:11 make themselves **k** by their acts,
Isa 12: 4 make **k** his deeds among the nations
61: 9 Their descendants shall be **k** among
Jer 7: 9 after other gods that you have not **k,**
Eze 38:23 make myself **k** in the eyes of many
39: 7 My holy name I will make **k**
Zec 14: 7 continuous day (it is **k** to the LORD)
Mt 10:26 secret that will not become **k.**
24:43 if the owner of the house had **k** in
Mk 6:14 for Jesus' name had become **k.**
Lk 6:44 for each tree is **k** by its own fruit.
Jn 1:18 Father's heart, who has made him **k.**
15:15 I have made **k** to you everything
17:26 I made your name **k** to them,
17:26 and I will make it **k,**
Ac 2:28 have made **k** to me the ways of life;
Ro 1:19 what can be **k** about God is plain to
7: 7 I would not have **k** sin.
9:22 his wrath and to make his power,
11:34 who has **k** the mind of the Lord?
16:26 is made **k** to all the Gentiles.
1Co 2:16 For who has **k** the mind of the Lord
8: 3 anyone who loves God is **k** by him.
13:12 fully, even as I have been fully **k.**
2Co 3: 2 on our hearts, to be **k** and read by all
6: 9 as unknown, and yet are well **k;**
Eph 1: 9 made **k** to us the mystery of his will,
3: 3 how the mystery was made **k** to me

6:19 make **k** with boldness the mystery
2Ti 3:15 you have the sacred writings
Heb 3:10 and they have not **k** my ways.'
2Pe 2:21 to have **k** the way of righteousness
Rev 1: 1 he made it **k** by sending his angel
Sir 4:24 wisdom becomes **k** through speech,
12: 8 A friend is not **k** in prosperity,

KNOWS → KNOW

Ge 3: 5 God **k** that when you eat of it your
Est 4:14 Who **k?** Perhaps you have come
Job 23:10 But he **k** the way that I take;
Ps 44:21 For he **k** the secrets of the heart.
94:11 The LORD **k** our thoughts,
103:14 For he **k** how we were made;
Pr 14:10 The heart **k** its own bitterness,
Ecc 2:19 who **k** whether they will be wise or
Joel 2:14 Who **k** whether he will not turn and
Jnh 3: 9 Who **k?** God may relent
Mt 6: 8 your Father **k** what you need before
11:27 no one **k** the Son except the Father,
24:36 about that day and hour no one **k,**
Lk 12:30 your Father **k** that you need them.
16:15 but God **k** your hearts;
Ac 15: 8 And God, who **k** the human heart,
Ro 8:27 **k** what is the mind of the Spirit,
1Co 2:11 what human being **k** what is truly
3:20 The Lord **k** the thoughts of the wise,
2Ti 2:19 "The Lord **k** those who are his,"
Jas 4:17 **k** the right thing to do and fails to
2Pe 2: 9 **k** how to rescue the godly from trial,
1Jn 4: 6 Whoever **k** God listens to us,
4: 7 loves is born of God and **k** God.
Rev 2:17 a new name that no one **k** except
19:12 a name inscribed that no one **k** but
Wis 9:11 she **k** and understands all things,
Sir 15:19 and he **k** every human action.
42:18 Most High **k** all that may be known;
2Es 15:26 For God **k** all who sin against him;

KOHATH → KOHATHITES

Ge 46:11 The children of Levi: Gershon, **K,**
Nu 26:58 Now **K** was the father of Amram.
1Ch 23: 6 to the sons of Levi: Gershon, **K,**

KOHATHITES → KOHATH

Nu 4:15 of meeting that the **K** are to carry.
2Ch 34:12 sons of the **K,** to have oversight.

KORAH → KORAHITES

1. Levite who led rebellion against Moses and
Aaron (Nu 16; Jude 11).
2. Psalms of the sons of Korah: See Korahites.

KORAHITES → KORAH

Psalms of the Korahites: Pss 42; 44-49; 84; 85;
87; 88.

L

LABAN

Brother of Rebekah (Ge 24:29), father of Rachel
and Leah (Ge 29:16). Received Abraham's servant (Ge 24:29-51). Provided daughters as wives
for Jacob in exchange for Jacob's service (Ge
29:1-30). Provided flocks for Jacob's service (Ge
30:25-43). After Jacob's departure, pursued and
covenanted with him (Ge 31).

LABOR → LABORER, LABORERS

Ex 1:11 to oppress them with forced **l.**
20: 9 Six days you shall **l** and do all your
Dt 5:13 Six days you shall **l** and do all your
Jdg 1:28 they put the Canaanites to forced **l,**
Ps 48: 6 pains as of a woman in **l,**
107:12 hearts were bowed down with hard **l**
127: 1 those who build it **l** in vain.
128: 2 eat the fruit of the **l** of your hands;
Pr 12:24 the lazy will be put to forced **l.**

Isa 54: 1 you who have not been in **l!**
55: 2 **l** for that which does not satisfy?
Jer 6:24 pain as of a woman in **l.**
Hab 2:13 that peoples **l** only
Jn 4:38 reap that for which you did not **l.**
4:38 and you have entered into their **l."**
1Co 3: 8 receive wages according to the **l**
15:58 that in the Lord your **l** is not in vain.
Php 2:16 that I did not run in vain or **l** in vain.
1Th 1: 3 your work of faith and **l** of love
Sir 7:15 Do not hate hard **l** or farm work,
2Es 4:42 For just as a woman who is in **l**

WOMAN IN LABOR Ps 48:6; Isa 13:8;
21:3; 42:14; Jer 4:31; 6:24; 13:21; 22:23; 30:6;
48:41; 49:22, 24; 50:43; Mic 4:9, 10; Sir
19:11; 34:5

LABORER → LABOR

Lev 19:13 the wages of a **l** until morning.
Lk 10: 7 for the **l** deserves to be paid.
1Ti 5:18 and, "The **l** deserves to be paid."

LABORERS → LABOR

Dt 24:14 the wages of poor and needy **l,**
Lk 10: 2 harvest is plentiful, but the **l** are few

LACHISH

Jos 10:32 LORD gave **L** into the hand of Israel,
2Ch 25:27 in Jerusalem, and he fled to **L.**

LACK → LACKED, LACKING, LACKS

Dt 8: 9 where you will **l** nothing,
Job 31:19 if I have seen anyone perish for **l** of
clothing,
Ps 34:10 seek the LORD **l** no good thing.
Pr 5:23 They die for **l** of discipline,
10:21 but fools die for **l** of sense.
28:27 gives to the poor will **l** nothing,
Hos 4: 6 are destroyed for **l** of knowledge,
Zec 10: 2 they suffer for **l** of a shepherd.
Mk 16:14 he upbraided them for their **l** of faith
1Co 7: 5 tempt you because of your **l** of
self-control.
Tit 3:13 and see that they **l** nothing.

LACKED → LACK

Dt 2: 7 with you; you have **l** nothing."
Ne 9:21 wilderness so that they **l** nothing;

LACKING → LACK

Ecc 1:15 and what is **l** cannot be counted.
Lk 18:22 "There is still one thing **l.**
Col 1:24 completing what is **l** in Christ's
Jas 1: 4 you may be mature and complete, **l**
1: 5 If any of you is **l** in wisdom, ask
Sir 37:21 since he is **l** in all wisdom.

LACKS → LACK

Pr 11:12 Whoever belittles another **l** sense,
25:28 walls, is one who **l** self-control.
28:16 ruler who **l** understanding is a cruel
2Pe 1: 9 who **l** these things is nearsighted

LADDER

Ge 28:12 that there was a **l** set up on the earth,

LADY*

2Jn 1: 1 elder to the elect **l** and her children,
1: 5 But now, dear **l,** I ask you,

LAID → LAY

Ge 22: 9 his son Isaac, and **l** him on the altar,
Nu 27:23 **l** his hands on him and
Dt 34: 9 because Moses had **l** his hands on
1Ki 6:37 of the house of the LORD was **l,**
Ezr 3:11 of the house of the LORD was **l.**
Job 38: 4 were you when I **l** the foundation of
Ps 18:15 foundations of the world were **l** bare
102:25 Long ago you **l** the foundation of
Isa 14: 8 "Since you were **l** low, no one
44:28 "Your foundation shall be **l."**
53: 6 the LORD has **l** on him the iniquity
Eze 24: 2 The king of Babylon has **l** siege
Zec 4: 9 of Zerubbabel have **l** the foundation

Mk 6:29 took his body, and I it in a tomb.
16: 6 Look, there is the place they I him.
Lk 6:48 and I the foundation on rock;
Jn 19:42 tomb was nearby, they I Jesus there.
Ac 6: 6 prayed and I their hands on them.
7:58 the witnesses I their coats at the feet
1Co 3:11 other than the one that has been I;
Heb 4:13 all are naked and I bare to the eyes
1Jn 3:16 that he I down his life for us—
1Mc 2:12 our glory have been I waste;

LAIR
Jer 9:11 a heap of ruins, a I of jackals;

LAKE
Lk 8:33 down the steep bank into the I
Rev 19:20 were thrown alive into the I of fire
20:10 into the I of fire and sulfur,
20:14 This is the second death, the I of fire

LAMB → LAMB'S, LAMBS
Ge 22: 8 "God himself will provide the I for
30:32 and every black I,
Ex 12:21 and slaughter the passover I.
2Sa 12: 6 he shall restore the I fourfold,
Isa 11: 6 The wolf shall live with the I,
53: 7 like a I that is led to the slaughter,
65:25 wolf and the I shall feed together,
Jer 11:19 like a gentle I led to the slaughter.
Mk 14:12 when the Passover I is sacrificed,
Jn 1:29 L of God who takes away the sin of
Ac 8:32 and like a I silent before its shearer,
1Co 5: 7 For our paschal I, Christ, has been
1Pe 1:19 like that of a I without defect or
Rev 5:12 The L that was slaughtered to
6: 1 I saw the L open one of the seven
7:14 them white in the blood of the L.
12:11 the L and by the word of their
13: 8 in the book of life of the L that was
14: 1 Then I looked, and there was the L,
15: 3 of God, and the song of the L:
17:14 they will make war on the L, and
the L will conquer them,
19: 7 for the marriage of the L has come,
21: 9 the bride, the wife of the L."
21:14 of the twelve apostles of the L.
21:23 and its lamp is the L.
22: 1 from the throne of God and of the L
Sir 13:17 a wolf have in common with a I?

LAMB'S· → LAMB
Rev 21:27 are written in the L book of life.

LAMBS → LAMB
Ex 29:38 two I a year old regularly each day.
Ps 114: 4 skipped like rams, the hills like I.
Isa 40:11 he will gather the I in his arms,
Lk 10: 3 I am sending you out like I into the
Jn 21:15 Jesus said to him, "Feed my I."

LAME
2Sa 4: 4 happened that he fell and became I.
5: 6 blind and the I will turn you back"
Isa 33:23 even the I will fall to plundering.
35: 6 then the I shall leap like a deer,
Mic 4: 6 says the LORD, I will assemble the I
Zep 3:19 And I will save the I and gather the
Mt 11: 5 the I walk, the lepers are cleansed,
15:31 the I walking, and the blind seeing.
Lk 14:13 invite the poor, the crippled, the I,
Jn 5: 3 In these lay many invalids—blind, I,
Ac 3: 2 man I from birth was being carried
8: 7 who were paralyzed or I were cured.

LAMECH
Ge 4:19 L took two wives; the name of the

LAMENT → LAMENTATION, LAMENTS
Jdg 11:40 to I the daughter of Jephthah
2Ch 35:25 Jeremiah also uttered a I for Josiah,
Joel 1: 8 L like a virgin dressed in sackcloth
1Mc 1:27 Every bridegroom took up the I;

LAMENTATION → LAMENT
2Sa 1:17 David intoned this I over Saul
La 2: 5 in daughter Judah mourning and I.
Ac 8: 2 buried Stephen and made loud I

LAMENTS → LAMENT
2Ch 35:25 they are recorded in the L.
Ps 35:14 about as one who I for a mother,

LAMP → LAMPS, LAMPSTAND, LAMPSTANDS
1Sa 3: 3 the I of God had not yet gone out,
2Sa 22:29 Indeed, you are my I, O LORD,
1Ki 11:36 servant David may always have a I
15: 4 his God gave him a I in Jerusalem,
2Ki 8:19 he had promised to give a I to him
Ps 18:28 It is you who light my I;
119:105 Your word is a I to my feet and a
132:17 I have prepared a I for my anointed
Pr 6:23 commandment is a I and the
20:27 human spirit is the I of the LORD,
31:18 Her I does not go out at night.
Mt 5:15 lighting a I puts it under the bushel
6:22 "The eye is the I of the body.
Lk 8:16 after lighting a I hides it under a jar,
Jn 5:35 He was a burning and shining I,
Rev 21:23 and its I is the Lamb.
22: 5 they need no light of I or sun,

LAMPS → LAMP
Ex 25:37 You shall make the seven I for it;
Mt 25: 1 Ten bridesmaids took their I and
Lk 12:35 for action and have your I lit;
1Mc 4:50 and lit the I on the lampstand,
2Mc 1: 8 we lit the I and set out the loaves.

LAMPSTAND → LAMP
Ex 25:31 You shall make a I of pure gold.
Nu 3:31 the table, the I, the altars,
Zec 4: 2 And I said, "I see a I all of gold,
4:11 on the right and the left of the I?"
Heb 9: 2 the first one, in which were the I,
Rev 2: 5 and remove your I from its place,
1Mc 4:50 and lit the lamps on the I,

LAMPSTANDS → LAMP
2Ch 4: 7 He made ten golden I as prescribed,
Rev 1:12 and on turning I saw seven golden I,
1:20 the seven I are the seven churches.
11: 4 the two I that stand before the Lord

LAND → COASTLANDS, HOMELAND, LANDMARK, LANDOWNER, LANDS
Ge 1:10 God called the dry I Earth,
7:22 everything on dry I in whose nostrils
12: 1 and your father's house to the I
12: 7 your offspring I will give this I."
12:10 Now there was a famine in the I.
13:15 for all the I that you see I will give
15:18 "To your descendants I give this I,
17: 8 all the I of Canaan, for a perpetual
24: 7 'To your offspring I will give this I,'
26: 1 Now there was a famine in the I,
28:15 and will bring you back to this I;
31:13 Now leave this I at once and return
40:15 stolen out of the I of the Hebrews;
41:30 the famine will consume the I.
42: 6 Joseph was governor over the I;
50:24 out of this I to the I that he swore to
Ex 1: 7 so that the I was filled with them.
3: 8 a I flowing with milk and honey,
6: 8 into the I that I swore to give to
8:22 know that I the LORD am in this I.
20: 2 brought you out of the I of Egypt,
20:12 in the I that the LORD your God is
34:12 with the inhabitants of the I
Nu 13: 2 to spy out the I of Canaan,
14: 9 and do not fear the people of the I,
14:30 not one of you shall come into the I
26:55 But the I shall be apportioned by lot;
35:33 for blood pollutes the I,
Dt 1: 8 go in and take possession of the I

8: 7 God is bringing you into a good I,
11:10 For the I that you are about to enter
28:21 until it has consumed you off the I
29:24 has the LORD done thus to this I?
34: 1 the LORD showed him the whole I:
Jos 1: 6 in possession of the I that I swore to
2: 1 "Go, view the I, especially Jericho."
5:12 ate the crops of the I of Canaan that
11:23 So Joshua took the whole I,
13: 2 This is the I that still remains:
14: 4 were given to the Levites in the I,
14: 9 the I on which your foot has trodden
Jdg 1:27 Canaanites continued to live in that I
Ru 1: 1 there was a famine in the I,
2Sa 21:14 God heeded supplications for the I.
24:25 answered his supplication for the I,
1Ki 8:34 and bring them again to the I that
17: 7 because there was no rain in the I.
2Ki 17: 5 the king of Assyria invaded all the I
25:21 So Judah went into exile out of its I.
2Ch 7:14 will forgive their sin and heal their I.
7:20 up from the I that I have given you;
32:21 he returned in disgrace to his own I.
36:21 the I had made up for its sabbaths.
Ezr 9:11 I that you are entering to possess is
9:11 a I unclean with the pollutions of
Ne 9:36 slaves in the I that you gave to our
Ps 25:13 their children shall possess the I.
37:11 But the meek shall inherit the I,
37:29 The righteous shall inherit the I,
44: 3 their own sword did they win the I,
136:21 and gave their I as a heritage,
142: 5 my portion in the I of the living."
Pr 2:21 For the upright will abide in the I,
2:11 who till their I will have plenty of
Isa 2: 8 Their I is filled with idols;
9: 2 who lived in a I of deep darkness—
36:18 saved their I out of the hand of
53: 8 was cut off from the I of the living,
Jer 2: 7 when you entered you defiled my I,
22:29 O I, I, I, hear the word of the LORD!
Eze 7:23 For the I is full of bloody crimes;
36:24 and bring you into your own I.
39:28 then gathered them into their own I.
Da 11:41 He shall come into the beautiful I,
Hos 2:23 I will sow him for myself in the I.
Zec 3: 9 remove the guilt of this I in a single
Mal 4: 6 come and strike the I with a curse.
Mk 15:33 darkness came over the whole I
Heb 11: 9 By faith he stayed for a time in the I
Rev 10: 2 on the sea and his left foot on the I,
Tob 14: 7 in safety forever in the I of Abraham
Sir 46: 8 the I flowing with milk and honey.
1Mc 1:44 to follow customs strange to the I,
14:11 He established peace in the I,

ALL THE LAND Ge 13:15; 17:8; 19:28; 41:19, 29, 41, 43, 44, 46, 55, 56; 45:8; 20; 47:13, 20; Ex 9:24, 25; 10:14, 15, 22; Lev 11:2; Dt 11:25; 19:8; 34:2; Jos 1:4; 2:24; 6:27; 9:24; 11:16; 13:4; 21:43; 24:3; Jdg 11:21; 1Sa 13:3, 19; 2Sa 9:7; 24:8; 1Ki 4:10; 9:19; 15:20; 2Ki 10:33; 15:29; 17:5; 1Ch 13:2; 2Ch 8:6; 15:8; 34:7; Job 42:15; Isa 7:24; Jer 44:26; Zec 5:6; Lk 4:25; Jdt 2:6

GOOD LAND Nu 14:7; Dt 1:25, 35; 3:25; 4:21, 22; 6:18; 8:7, 10; 9:6; 11:17; Jos 23:13, 15, 16; 1Ki 14:15; 1Ch 28:8; Tob 14:4

LAND FLOWING WITH MILK AND HONEY Ex 3:8, 17; 13:5; 33:3; Lev 20:24; Nu 16:13, 14; Dt 6:3; 11:9; 26:9, 15; 27:3; 31:20; Jos 5:6; Jer 11:5; 32:22; Eze 20:6, 15; Sir 46:8; Bar 1:20

LAND OF CANAAN Ge 11:31; 12:5, 5; 13:12; 16:3; 17:8; 23:2, 19; 31:18; 33:18; 35:6; 36:5, 6; 37:1; 42:5, 7, 13, 29, 32; 44:8; 45:17, 25; 46:6, 12, 31; 47:1, 4, 13, 14, 15; 48:3, 7; 49:30; 50:5, 13; Ex 6:4; 16:35; Lev 14:34; 18:3; 25:38; Nu 13:2, 17; 26:19; 32:30, 32; 33:40, 51; 34:2, 2, 29; 35:10, 14; Dt 32:49; Jos 5:12; 14:1; 21:2; 22:9, 10, 11, 32; 24:3; Jdg

21:12; 1Ch 16:18; Ps 105:11; Ac 13:19; Jdt 5:9, 10

LAND OF EGYPT Ge 13:10; 21:21; 41:19, 29, 30, 33, 34, 36, 41, 43, 44, 45, 46, 48, 53, 54, 55, 56; 45:8, 18, 19, 20, 26; 46:20; 47:6, 11, 13, 14, 15, 20, 26, 27, 28; 48:5; 50:7; Ex 4:20; 5:12; 6:13, 26, 28; 7:3, 4, 19, 21; 8:5, 6, 7, 16, 17; 9:9, 9, 22, 22, 23, 24, 25; 10:12, 13, 14, 15, 21, 22; 11:3, 5, 6, 9; 12:1, 12, 12, 13, 17, 29, 41, 42, 51; 13:15, 18; 16:1, 3, 6, 32; 19:1; 20:2; *22:21; 23:9; 29:46; 32:1, 4, 7, 8, 11, 23; 33:1; Lev 11:45; 18:3; 19:34, 36; 22:33; 23:43; 25:38, 42, 55; 26:13, 45; Nu 1:1; 3:13; 8:17; 9:1; 14:2; 15:41; 26:4; 33:1, 38; Dt 1:27; 5:6, 15; 6:12; 8:14; 9:7; 10:19; 11:10; 13:5, 10; 15:15; 16:3, 3; 20:1; 24:22; 29:2, 16, 25; 34:11; Jos 24:17; Jdg 2:12; 19:30; 1Sa 12:6; 27:8; 1Ki 6:1; 8:9, 21; 9:9; 12:28; 2Ki 17:7, 36; 2Ch 6:5; 7:22; 20:10; Ps 78:12; 81:5, 10; Isa 11:16; 19:18, 19, 20; 27:13; Jer 2:6; 7:22, 25; 11:4, 7; 16:14; 23:7; 24:8; 31:32; 32:20, 21; 34:13; 42:14, 16; 43:7, 11, 12, 13; 44:1, 8, 12, 12, 13, 14, 15, 24, 26, 26, 27, 28, 28; 46:13; Eze 19:4; 20:5, 6, 8, 9, 10, 36; 23:19, 27; 29:9, 10, 12, 19, 20; 30:13, 13, 25; 32:15; Da 9:15; 11:42; Hos 2:15; 7:16; 11:5; 12:9; 13:4; Am 2:10; 3:1, 9; 9:7; Mic 6:4; 7:15; Zec 10:10; Ac 7:40; 13:17; Heb 8:9; Jude 1:5; Jdt 5:12; AdE 13:16; Bar 1:19, 20; 2:11; 1Mc 1:16, 19, 19; 2Es 1:7; 15:10

LAND OF ISRAEL 1Sa 13:19; 2Ki 5:2, 4; 6:23; 1Ch 13:2; 22:2; 2Ch 2:17; 30:25; 34:7; Eze 7:2; 11:17; 12:19, 22; 13:9; 18:2; 20:38, 42; 21:2, 3; 25:3, 6; 27:17; 33:24; 36:6; 37:12; 38:18, 19; 40:2; 47:18; Mt 2:20, 21; Tob 1:4; 14:4, 4, 5

LAND OF JUDAH Dt 34:2; Ru 1:7; 1Sa 22:5; 30:16; 1Ki 4:19; 2Ki 23:24; 25:22; 1Ch 6:55; 2Ch 9:11; 15:8; 17:2; Ne 5:14; Isa 19:17; 26:1; Jer 31:23; 37:1; 39:10; 40:12; 43:4, 5; 44:9, 14, 28; Am 7:12; Zec 1:21; Mt 2:6; Bar 1:8; 1Mc 3:39; 5:45, 53, 68; 6:5; 7:10, 22, 50; 9:1, 57, 72; 10:30, 33, 37; 12:4, 46, 52; 13:1, 12

LAND OF THE LIVING Job 28:13; Ps 27:13; 52:5; 116:9; 142:5; Isa 38:11; 53:8; Jer 11:19; Eze 26:20; 32:23, 24, 25, 26, 27, 32

PEOPLE OF THE LAND Ge 23:7, 12, 13; 42:6; Ex 5:5; Lev 20:2, 4; Nu 14:9; 2Ki 11:14, 18, 19, 20; 15:5; 16:15; 21:24, 24; 23:30, 35; 24:14; 25:3, 12, 19, 19; 2Ch 23:13, 20, 21; 26:21; 33:25, 25; 36:1; Ezr 4:4; Jer 1:18; 34:19; 37:2; 44:21; 52:6, 16, 25; Eze 7:27; 12:19; 22:29; 33:2; 39:13; 45:16, 22; 46:3, 9; Da 9:6; Hag 2:4; Zec 7:5; Bar 1:9

PEOPLES OF THE LAND 1Ch 5:25; Ezr 10:2, 11; Ne 9:24; 10:30, 31; 1Es 5:50, 50, 72; 7:13; 8:69, 70, 87, 92; 9:9

POSSESS POSSESSED THE LAND Ex 23:30; Jdg 18:9; Ne 9:15, 24; Job 22:8; Ps 25:13; Isa 57:13; 60:21; Eze 33:25, 26; Am 2:10; Ob 1:19

WHOLE LAND Ge 2:11, 13; 13:9; Ex 7:19, 21; 8:16, 17; 9:9, 22; 10:15; 11:6; Dt 34:1; Jos 2:3; 10:40; 11:23; Isa 28:22; Jer 1:18; 4:20, 27; 8:16; 12:11; 15:10; 25:11; 40:4; 45:4; 51:47; Zec 5:3; 13:8; 14:10; Mt 27:45; Mk 15:33; Lk 23:44; Tob 14:4; Jdt 1:9; 5:12; 7:4; Bar 2:23; 2Mc 2:21

LANDMARK → LAND

Pr   22:28 Do not remove the ancient **l** that

LANDOWNER* → LAND, OWN

Mt   20: 1 **l** who went out early in the morning
        20:11 they grumbled against the **l,**
        21:33 was a **l** who planted a vineyard,

LANDS → LAND

Ge   26: 3 descendants I will give all these **l,**
Ezr   9: 2 mixed itself with the peoples of the **l**

Ps 105:44 He gave them the **l** of the nations,
     106:27 scattering them over the **l.**
     107: 3 and gathered in from the **l,**
Eze 20: 6 the most glorious of all **l.**
2Co 10:16 the good news in **l** beyond you,

LANGUAGE → LANGUAGES

Ge   11: 1 whole earth had one **l** and the same
        11: 9 LORD confused the **l** of all the earth;
Dt   28:49 whose **l** you do not understand,
2Ki 18:26 to your servants in the Aramaic **l,**
Ne   13:24 but spoke the **l** of various peoples.
Ps 114: 1 Jacob from a people of strange **l,**
Jer   5:15 a nation whose **l** you do not know,
Ac   2: 6 speaking in the native **l** of each.
        21:40 he addressed them in the Hebrew **l,**
Col   3: 8 and abusive **l** from your mouth.
Rev   5: 9 for God saints from every tribe and **l**
        13: 7 tribe and people and **l** and nation,
        14: 6 to every nation and tribe and **l** and
Bar   4:15 a nation ruthless and of a strange **l,**

LANGUAGES → LANGUAGE

Ac   2: 4 and began to speak in other **l,**
Rev   7: 9 from all tribes and peoples and **l,**
        17:15 and multitudes and nations and **l.**

LANTERNS*

Jn   18: 3 they came there with **l** and torches

LAODICEA

Col   4:16 that you read also the letter from **L.**
Rev   3:14 the angel of the church in **L** write:

LAP

Jdg   7: 5 who **l** the water with their tongues,
Pr   16:33 The lot is cast into the **l,**
Lk   6:38 running over, will be put into your **l;**

LARGE → ENLARGED, ENLARGES, LARGER

Nu   13:28 the towns are fortified and very **l;**
Dt   6:10 a land with fine, **l** cities that you did
        25:13 two kinds of weights, **l** and small.
Jnh   1:17 LORD provided a **l** fish to swallow
Gal   6:11 See what **l** letters I make when

LARGER → LARGE

Dt   11:23 and you will dispossess nations **l**

LASHES

Dt   25: 3 Forty **l** may be given but not more;
        25: 3 if more **l** than these are given,
2Co 11:24 from the Jews the forty **l** minus one.

LAST → EVERLASTING, LASTING, LASTS

Ru   3:10 this **l** instance of your loyalty
2Sa 23: 1 Now these are the **l** words of David:
1Ch 23:27 according to the **l** words of David
Isa   41: 4 I, the LORD, am first, and will be with the **l.**
        44: 6 I am the first and I am the **l;**
        48:12 I am the first, and I am the **l.**
Mt   19:30 But many who are first will be **l,** and the **l** will be first.
        20: 8 beginning with the **l** and then going
        27:64 the **l** deception would be worse than the first."
Mk   9:35 first must be **l** of all and servant of
        15:37 gave a loud cry and breathed his **l.**
Jn   6:40 I will raise them up on the **l** day."
        7:37 On the **l** day of the festival, the great
        11:24 in the resurrection on the **l** day."
        15:16 to go and bear fruit, fruit that will **l,**
Ac   2:17 'In the **l** days it will be,
1Co 15: 8 **L** of all, as to one untimely born,
        15:26 **l** enemy to be destroyed is death.
        15:45 **l** Adam became a life-giving spirit.
        15:52 twinkling of an eye, at the **l** trumpet.
2Ti   3: 1 that in the **l** days distressing times
Heb   1: 2 **l** days he has spoken to us by a Son,
1Pe   1: 5 ready to be revealed in the **l** time.
2Pe   2:20 **l** state has become worse for them
        3: 3 that in the **l** days scoffers will come,

1Jn   2:18 Children, it is the **l** hour!
Jude   1:18 "In the **l** time there will be scoffers,
Rev   1:17 I am the first and the **l,**
        2: 8 are the words of the first and the **l,**
        15: 1 with seven plagues, which are the **l,**
        21: 9 bowls full of the seven **l** plagues
        22:13 the first and the **l,** the beginning and
Sir   2: 3 that your **l** days may be prosperous.
        40:12 but good faith will **l** forever.
2Es   8:50 who inhabit the world in the **l** times,
        14:46 keep the seventy that were written **l,**

LAST DAY Ne 8:18; Jn 6:39, 40, 44, 54; 7:37; 11:24; 12:48

LAST DAYS Ac 2:17; 2Ti 3:1; Heb 1:2; Jas 5:3; 2Pe 3:3; Sir 2:3; 2Es 7:84, 95; 10:59; 12:23, 28; 13:18, 20; 14:22

LAST TIMES 2Es 6:34; 7:73, 77, 87; 8:50, 63; 13:46

LASTING → LAST

Dt   6:24 the LORD our God, for our **l** good,
Heb 10:34 something better and more **l.**

LASTS → LAST

Pr   12:19 but a lying tongue **l** only a moment.
Tob 13: 1 his kingdom **l** throughout all ages.
Sir   41:13 but a good name **l** forever.

LATE → LATER, LATTER

Ps 127: 2 you rise up early and go **l** to rest,
Jas   5: 7 it receives the early and the **l** rains.

LATER → LATE

Joel   2:23 the early and the **l** rain, as before.
Jn   13: 7 but **l** you will understand."
1Ti   4: 1 **l** times some will renounce the faith

LATIN*

Jn   19:20 it was written in Hebrew, in **L,** and

LATTER → LATE

Job 42:12 The LORD blessed the **l** days of Job
Hag   2: 9 The **l** splendor of this house shall

LAUGH → LAUGHED, LAUGHINGSTOCK, LAUGHS, LAUGHTER

Ge   18:13 said to Abraham, "Why did Sarah **l,**
        21: 6 everyone who hears will **l** with me."
Ps   59: 8 But you **l** at them, O LORD;
Ecc   3: 4 a time to weep, and a time to **l;**
Lk   6:21 you who weep now, for you will **l.**

LAUGHED → LAUGH

Ge   17:17 Then Abraham fell on his face and **l,**
        18:12 So Sarah **l** to herself, saying,
Lk   8:53 **l** at him, knowing that she was dead.

LAUGHINGSTOCK → LAUGH

Job 12: 4 a just and blameless man, I am a **l.**
Ps   44:14 the nations, a **l** among the peoples.
La   3:14 have become the **l** of all my people,
Jdt   5:21 become the **l** of the whole world."

LAUGHS → LAUGH

Ps   2: 4 He who sits in the heavens **l;**
        37:13 but the LORD **l** at the wicked,

LAUGHTER → LAUGH

Ge   21: 6 Sarah said, "God has brought **l** for
Ps 126: 2 Then our mouth was filled with **l,**
Pr   14:13 in the heart is sad, and the end of
Ecc   7: 3 Sorrow is better than **l,** for by
        10:19 Feasts are made for **l;** wine gladdens
Jas   4: 9 Let your **l** be turned into mourning

LAVISHED

Eph   1: 8 that he **l** on us.
Sir   1:10 he **l** her upon those who love him.

LAW → LAWFUL, LAWGIVER, LAWLESS, LAWLESSNESS, LAWS, LAWSUIT, LAWSUITS, LAWYER, LAWYERS

Nu   5:29 This is the **l** in cases of jealousy,
        6:13 This is the **l** for the nazirites when

Dt   1: 5 Moses undertook to expound this l
       17:18 have a copy of this l written for him
       27:26 words of this l by observing them."
       31: 9 Then Moses wrote down this l,
       31:11 you shall read this l before all Israel
       31:26 "Take this book of the l and put it
Jos   1: 7 to act in accordance with all the l
        1: 8 book of the l shall not depart out of
        8:32 wrote on the stones a copy of the l
2Ki   22: 8 "I have found the book of the l in
2Ch   6:16 to walk in my l as you have walked
       17: 9 book of the l of the LORD with them
       34:14 of the l of the LORD given through
Ezr   7: 6 a scribe skilled in the l of Moses
Ne   8: 2 priest Ezra brought the l before all
        8: 8 from the book, from the l of God,
Ps   1: 2 their delight is in the l of the LORD,
               and on his l they meditate day and
       19: 7 l of the LORD is perfect, reviving
       37:31 The l of their God is in their hearts;
       40: 8 your l is within my heart."
       89:30 If his children forsake my l and do
      119:18 wondrous things out of your l.
      119:70 but I delight in your l.
      119:72 The l of your mouth is better
      119:77 for your l is my delight.
      119:97 Oh, how I love your l!
     119:142 and your l is the truth.
     119:163 abhor falsehood, but I love your l.
     119:165 peace have those who love your l;
Pr   28: 9 When one will not listen to the l,
       29:18 but happy are those who keep the l.
Jer   2: 8 who handle the l did not know me;
        8: 8 and the l of the LORD is with us,"
       31:33 I will put my l within them,
Da   9:11 "All Israel has transgressed your l
Hos   4: 6 since you have forgotten the l of
Hab   1: 4 the l becomes slack and justice
Zec   7:12 the l and the words that the LORD
Mt   5:17 come to abolish the l or the prophets
        7:12 for this is the l and the prophets.
       22:36 in the l is the greatest?"
       22:40 two commandments hang all the l
       23:23 the weightier matters of the l:
Lk   2:23 (as it is written in the l of the Lord,
        2:39 by the l of the Lord,
       10:26 to him, "What is written in the l?
       16:17 of a letter in the l to be dropped.
       24:44 written about me in the l of Moses,
Jn   1:17 l indeed was given through Moses;
        7:19 Yet none of you keeps the l.
       18:31 and judge him according to your l."
Ac   6:13 against this holy place and the l;
       13:39 you could not be freed by the l
       15: 5 and ordered to keep the l
       28:23 from the l of Moses and from the
Ro   2:12 All who have sinned apart from the
               l will also perish apart from the l,
        2:13 doers of the l who will be justified.
        2:15 that what the l requires is written
        2:20 the l the embodiment of knowledge
        2:25 of value if you obey the l;
        3:19 speaks to those who are under the l,
        3:20 through the l comes the knowledge
        3:21 now, apart from l, the righteousness
        3:28 apart from works prescribed by the l
        3:31 On the contrary, we uphold the l.
        4:13 or to his descendants through the l
        4:15 For the l brings wrath;
        5:13 sin was indeed in the world before
               the l,
        5:20 But l came in, with the result that
        6:14 you are not under l but under grace.
        6:15 sin because we are not under l but
        7: 1 the l is binding on a person only
        7: 4 have died to the l through the body
        7: 5 our sinful passions, aroused by the l,
        7: 6 now we are discharged from the l,
        7: 7 That the l is sin?
        7: 8 Apart from the l sin lies dead.
        7: 9 I was once alive apart from the l,
        7:12 the l is holy, and the commandment

        7:14 For we know that the l is spiritual;
        7:22 delight in the l of God in my inmost
        7:25 mind I am a slave to the l of God,
        8: 2 For the l of the Spirit of life
        8: 3 For God has done what the l,
        8: 4 of the l might be fulfilled in us,
        8: 7 it does not submit to God's l—
        9: 4 the covenants, the giving of the l,
        9:31 did not succeed in fulfilling that l.
       10: 4 For Christ is the end of the l so that
       13: 8 who loves another has fulfilled the l.
       13:10 love is the fulfilling of the l.
1Co   9: 9 For it is written in the l of Moses,
        9:20 that I might win those under the l.
        9:21 that I might win those outside the l.
       15:56 and the power of sin is the l.
Gal   2:19 For through the l I died to the l, so
               that I might live to God.
        3:11 is justified before God by the l;
        3:19 Why then the l?
        4: 4 born of a woman, born under the l,
        5: 4 to be justified by the l have cut
        5:23 There is no l against such things.
        6: 2 way you will fulfill the l of Christ.
Eph   2:15 He has abolished the l with its
Php   3: 5 as to the l, a Pharisee;
        3: 9 of my own that comes from the l,
1Ti   1: 8 Now we know that the l is good,
Tit   3: 9 dissensions, and quarrels about the l
Heb   7:12 necessarily a change in the l as well.
        7:19 (for the l made nothing perfect);
       10: 1 Since the l has only a shadow of the
Jas   1:25 those who look into the perfect l,
        2: 8 if you really fulfill the royal l
        2:10 For whoever keeps the whole l but
        4:11 evil against the l and judges the l;
Sir   2:16 love him are filled with his l.
       33: 2 The wise will not hate the l,
Bar   4: 1 the l that endures forever.
1Mc   1:56 The books of the l that they found
        2:21 Far be it from us to desert the l
        2:48 They rescued the l out of the hands
2Es   14:22 things that were written in your l,

BOOK OF THE/THIS LAW Dt 28:61;
  29:21; 30:10; 31:26; Jos 1:8; 8:31, 34; 23:6;
  24:26; 2Ki 14:6; 22:8, 11; 2Ch 17:9; 34:14,
  15; Ne 8:1, 3, 18; 9:3; Gal 3:10; 1Mc 3:48;
  1Es 9:45

LAW OF ... *GOD Jos 24:26; 2Ki 17:26, 26,
  27; Ezr 7:12, 14, 21, 26; Ne 8:8, 18; 10:28; Ps
  37:31; Jer 5:4, 5; Da 6:5; Hos 4:6; Ro 7:22, 25;
  Bar 4:12; 1Es 8:21, 23, 24; 3Mc 7:10, 12; 2Es
  7:20; 4Mc 13:22

LAW OF MOSES Jos 8:31, 32; 23:6; 1Ki
  2:3; 2Ki 14:6; 23:25; 2Ch 23:18; 30:16; Ezr
  3:2; 7:6; Ne 8:1; Da 9:11, 13; Lk 2:22; 24:44;
  Jn 7:23; Ac 13:39; 15:5; 28:23; 1Co 9:9; Heb
  10:28; Tob 1:8; 7:13; Bar 2:2; Sus 1:3, 62; 1Es
  8:3; 9:39

LAW OF THE †LORD 2Ki 10:31; 1Ch
  16:40; 22:12; 2Ch 12:1; 17:9; 31:3, 4; 34:14;
  35:26; Ezr 7:10; Ne 9:3; Ps 1:2; 19:7; 119:1;
  Jer 8:8; Am 2:4

UNDER [THE] LAW Lk 2:27; Ro 2:12;
  3:19; 6:14, 15; 1Co 9:20, 20, 20, 20; Gal 3:23;
  4:4, 5; Php 3:6; Heb 9:22

WORDS OF THE/THIS LAW Dt 17:19;
  27:3, 8, 26; 28:58; 29:29; 31:12, 24; 32:46; Jos
  8:34; 2Ki 23:24; 2Ch 34:19; Ne 8:9, 13

WORKS OF LAW Gal 2:16, 16, 16; 3:2, 5,
  10, 12

WRITTEN IN ... LAW 1Ki 2:3; 1Ch 16:40;
  2Ch 23:18; 25:4; 31:3; 35:26; Ne 8:14; 10:34,
  36; Da 9:11, 13; Lk 2:23; 10:26; Jn 10:34;
  15:25; 1Co 9:9; Bar 2:2; 2Es 14:22

LAWFUL → LAW
Mt   12:12 So it is l to do good on the sabbath."
       19: 3 "Is it l for a man to divorce his wife
Mk   2:26 not l for any but the priests to eat,

Lk   14: 3 "Is it l to cure people on the sabbath
1Co   6:12 "All things are l for me,"
       10:23 "All things are l," but

LAWGIVER → GIVE, LAW
Jas   4:12 one l and judge who is able to save

LAWLESS → LAW
2Th   2: 8 And then the l one will be revealed,
Heb   10:17 and their l deeds no more."
2Pe   3:17 carried away with the error of the l

LAWLESSNESS → LAW
2Co   6:14 between righteousness and l?
2Th   2: 7 the mystery of l is already at work,
1Jn   3: 4 commits sin is guilty of l; sin is l.
Wis   5:23 L will lay waste the whole earth,
Sir   21: 3 All l is like a two-edged sword;

LAWS → LAW
Ge   26: 5 my statutes, and my l."
Ne   9:13 them right ordinances and true l,
Ps   105:45 keep his statutes and observe his l.
Heb   8:10 I will put my l in their minds,
       10:16 I will put my l in their hearts,
1Mc   3:21 but we fight for our lives and our l.

LAWSUIT → LAW, SUE
Ex   23: 2 when you bear witness in a l,

LAWSUITS → LAW, SUE
1Co   6: 7 to have l at all with one another is

LAWYER → LAW
Lk   10:25 Just then a l stood up to test Jesus.

LAWYERS → LAW
Lk   11:46 And he said, "Woe also to you l!

LAY → LAID, LAYING, LAYS
Ge   22:12 "Do not l your hand on the boy or
Ex   7: 4 I will l my hand upon Egypt
       29:10 shall l their hands on the head of
Nu   8:10 the Israelites shall l their hands on
       27:18 and l your hand upon him;
Dt   9:25 and forty nights that I l prostrate
Job   22:22 and l up his words in your heart.
Ps   139: 5 and l your hand upon me.
Pr   10:14 The wise l up knowledge,
Mt   8:20 of Man has nowhere to l his head."
       28: 6 Come, see the place where he l.
Jn   10:15 And I l down my life for the sheep.
       10:18 but I l it down of my own accord.
       10:18 I have power to l it down,
       13:37 I will l down my life for you."
       15:13 l down one's life for one's friends.
Ac   8:19 that anyone on whom I l my hands
1Co   3:11 no one can l any foundation other
1Jn   3:16 we ought to l down our lives for
Sir   29:11 L up your treasure according to

LAYING → LAY
Isa   28:16 I am l in Zion a foundation stone,
Ac   8:18 the Spirit was given through the l on
2Ti   1: 6 that is within you through the l on
Heb   6: 1 and not l again the foundation:
        6: 2 l on of hands, resurrection of the
1Pe   2: 6 "See, I am l in Zion a stone,
Tob   4: 9 So you will be l up a good treasure

LAYS → LAY
Jn   10:11 The good shepherd l down his life

LAZARUS*
  1. Poor man in Jesus' parable (Lk 16:19-31).
  2. Brother of Mary and Martha whom Jesus
  raised from the dead (Jn 11:1-12:19).

LAZINESS* → LAZY
Pr   19:15 L brings on deep sleep; an idle

LAZY → LAZINESS
Ex   5: 8 do not diminish it, for they are l;
        5:17 He said, "You are l, l;
Pr   12:27 The l do not roast their game,

13: 4 The appetite of the l craves,
24:30 he field of one who was l,
26:15 The l person buries a hand in the
Mt 25:26 replied, 'You wicked and l slave!
Tit 1:12 vicious brutes, l gluttons."

LEAD → LEADER, LEADERS, LEADERSHIP, LEADING, LEADS, LED

Ex 15:10 sank like l in the mighty waters.
   32:34 l the people to the place
Ps 25: 5 L me in your truth,
   27:11 and l me on a level path because of
   61: 2 L me to the rock that is higher than
   139:24 and l me in the way everlasting.
   143:10 Let your good spirit l me on a level
Pr 21: 5 The plans of the diligent l surely to
Ecc 5: 6 Do not let your mouth l you into sin,
Isa 11: 6 and a little child shall l them.
   49:10 he who has pity on them will l them,
Jer 31: 9 with consolations I will l them back,
Da 12: 3 those who l many to righteousness,
Mk 13:22 to l astray, if possible, the elect.
Jn 11: 4 "This illness does not l to death;
Ro 2: 4 meant to l you to repentance?
Sir 19: 2 and women l intelligent men astray,

LEADER → LEAD

Ex 22:28 or curse a l of your people.
1Ch 28: 4 for he chose Judah as l,
Lk 8:41 Jairus, a l of the synagogue.
Jn 3: 1 Nicodemus, a l of the Jews.
Ro 12: 8 the l, in diligence;

LEADERS → LEAD

Nu 1:16 the l of their ancestral tribes,
   7:10 The l also presented offerings for
Isa 3:12 O my people, your l mislead you,
Lk 19:47 the l of the people kept looking for
   23:35 l scoffed at him, saying, "He saved
1Co 3:21 So let no one boast about human l.
Heb 13: 7 Remember your l, those who spoke
   13:17 Obey your l and submit to them,

LEADERSHIP → LEAD

Nu 33: 1 formation under the l of Moses

LEADING → LEAD

Ps 68:18 l captives in your train and receiving
Lk 22:47 one of the twelve, was l them.

LEADS → LEAD

Ps 23: 2 he l me beside still waters;
   25: 9 He l the humble in what is right,
   37: 8 Do not fret—it l only to evil.
   68: 6 he l out the prisoners to prosperity,
Pr 2:18 for her way l down to death,
   12:26 but the way of the wicked l astray.
   14:23 but mere talk l only to poverty.
Mt 7:14 and the road is hard that l to life,
Mk 13: 5 "Beware that no one l you astray.
Jn 10: 3 calls his own sheep by name and l
Ro 6:16 of sin, which l to death,
   6:16 obedience, which l to righteousness
2Co 2:14 in Christ always l us in triumphal
   7:10 a repentance that l to salvation
Sir 20:26 A liar's way l to disgrace,

LEAF → IVY-LEAF, LEAVES

Ge 8:11 beak was a freshly plucked olive l;

LEAH

Wife of Jacob (Ge 29:16-30); bore six sons and
one daughter (Ge 29:31-30:21; 34:1; 35:23; Ru
4:11).

LEAN → LEANED

Ge 41:27 The seven l and ugly cows
Isa 48: 2 and l on the God of Israel;

LEANED → LEAN

Ps 71: 6 Upon you I have l from my birth;

LEAP → LEAPED, LEAPING, LEAPS

2Sa 22:30 and by my God I can l over a wall.

Isa 35: 6 then the lame shall l like a deer,
Lk 6:23 Rejoice in that day and l for joy,

LEAPED → LEAP

Lk 1:41 the child l in her womb.

LEAPING → LEAP

1Ch 15:29 and saw King David l and dancing;
Mal 4: 2 You shall go out l like calves from
Ac 3: 8 walking and l and praising God.

LEAPS → LEAP

Job 37: 1 and l out of its place.

LEARN → LEARNED, LEARNING

Dt 4:10 that they may l to fear me as long as
   5: 1 you shall l them and observe them
   18: 9 must not l to imitate the abhorrent
   31:12 and l to fear the LORD your God and
Ps 119: 7 when I l your righteous ordinances.
Pr 19:25 and the simple will l prudence;
Isa 1:17 l to do good; seek justice,
   26: 9 of the world l righteousness.
Jer 35:13 Can you not l a lesson and obey my
Mt 11:29 my yoke upon you, and l from me;
Mk 13:28 "From the fig tree l its lesson:
1Ti 2:11 Let a woman l in silence with full
   5: 4 should first l their religious duty
Tit 3:14 let people l to devote themselves
Rev 14: 3 No one could l that song except
Sir 8: 8 from them you will l discipline
Bar 3: 9 O Israel; give ear, and l wisdom!

LEARNED → LEARN

Ps 119:152 Long ago I l from your decrees
Jn 6:45 l from the Father comes to me.
Eph 4:20 That is not the way you l Christ!
Php 4: 9 on doing the things that you have l
   4:11 I have l to be content with whatever
2Ti 3:14 you have l and firmly believed,
Heb 5: 8 he l obedience through what he
Rev 2:24 not l what some call 'the deep
           things of Satan,'

LEARNING → LEARN

Pr 1: 5 Let the wise also hear and gain in l,
   9: 9 the righteous and they will gain in l.
Jn 7:15 "How does this man have such l,
Ac 26:24 Too much l is driving you insane!"

LEAST → LESS

1Sa 9:21 from the l of the tribes of Israel,
Isa 60:22 The l of them shall become a clan,
Mt 2: 6 are by no means l among the rulers
   5:19 called l in the kingdom of heaven;
   25:40 of the l of these who are members
Lk 7:28 l in the kingdom of God is greater
   9:48 l among all of you is the greatest."
1Co 15: 9 For I am the l of the apostles,
2Co 11: 5 the l inferior to these super-apostles.
Eph 3: 8 I am the very l of all the saints,

LEATHER

2Ki 1: 8 "A hairy man, with a l belt around
Mt 3: 4 with a l belt around his waist,

LEAVE → LEAVES, LEFT

Ex 11: 8 'L us, you and all the people who
Nu 11:20 'Why did we ever l Egypt?'"
Ru 1:16 to l you or to turn back from
Ps 141: 8 do not l me defenseless.
Pr 14: 7 L the presence of a fool,
Joel 2:14 and l a blessing behind him,
Mt 5:24 l your gift there before the altar and
Mk 10: 7 this reason a man shall l his father
Jn 14:18 not l you orphaned; I am coming to
   14:27 Peace I l with you; my peace I give
Eph 5:31 a man will l his father and mother
Heb 13: 5 said, "I will never l you or forsake

LEAVEN → LEAVENED, LEAVENS

Ex 12:15 on the first day you shall remove l
Dt 16: 4 No l shall be seen with you

LEAVENED → LEAVEN

Ex 12:20 You shall eat nothing l;
Mt 13:33 of flour until all of it was l."

LEAVENS· → LEAVEN

1Co 5: 6 a little yeast l the whole batch of
Gal 5: 9 A little yeast l the whole batch of

LEAVES → LEAF, LEAVE

Ge 3: 7 and they sewed fig l together
Ps 1: 3 and their l do not wither.
Jer 17: 8 and its l shall stay green;
Eze 47:12 Their l will not wither
   47:12 and their l for healing."
Mk 11:13 came to it, he found nothing but l,
Rev 22: 2 l of the tree are for the healing of

LEBANON

Dt 11:24 from the wilderness to the L and
1Ki 4:33 cedar that is in the L to the hyssop
   5: 6 cedars from the L be cut for me.
2Ki 14: 9 thornbush on L sent to a cedar on L,
Ps 29: 5 He makes L skip like a calf,
   92:12 and grow like a cedar in L.
Isa 40:16 L would not provide fuel enough,
Hab 2:17 violence done to L will overwhelm

LECTURE·

Ac 19: 9 daily in the l hall of Tyrannus.

LED → LEAD

Ex 3: 1 he l his flock beyond the wilderness,
Dt 8: 2 your God has l you these forty years
Ne 9:12 l them by day with a pillar of cloud,
Ps 78:52 Then he l out his people like sheep,
   107: 7 he l them by a straight way,
Pr 20: 1 whoever is l astray by it is not wise.
Isa 53: 7 like a lamb that is l to the slaughter,
   55:12 out in joy, and be l back in peace;
Jer 11:19 like a gentle lamb l to the slaughter.
   50: 6 their shepherds have l them astray.
Hos 11: 4 I l them with cords of human
Am 2:10 I l you forty years in the wilderness,
Mt 4: 1 Then Jesus was l up by the Spirit
   27:31 they l him away to crucify him.
Lk 4: 5 Then the devil l him up and showed
   21: 8 "Beware that you are not l astray;
Ac 8:32 "Like a sheep that is l to the
Ro 8:14 For all who are l by the Spirit
2Co 7: 9 because your grief l to repentance;
Tit 3: 3 once foolish, disobedient, l astray,
Wis 2:21 but they were l astray,
Sir 3:24 For their conceit has l many astray,

LEECH·

Pr 30:15 l has two daughters; "Give, give,"

LEEKS·

Nu 11: 5 the cucumbers, the melons, the l,

LEFT → LEAVE, LEFT-HANDED

Ge 7:23 Only Noah was l, and those that
   13: 9 If you take the l hand, then I will go
Nu 26:65 Not one of them was l,
Dt 28:14 either to the right or to the l,
Jos 1: 7 from it to the right hand or to the l,
   23: 6 neither to the right nor to the l,
2Ki 22: 2 not turn aside to the right or to the l.
Pr 4:27 not swerve to the right or to the l;
Isa 30:21 the right or when you turn to the l,
Mt 6: 3 your l hand know what your right
   25:33 his right hand and the goats at the l.
Mk 8: 8 took up the broken pieces l over,
   10:28 we have l everything and followed
   10:40 to sit at my right hand or at my l is
Lk 17:34 one will be taken and the other l.
1Th 4:15 are l until the coming of the Lord,
2Pe 2:15 They have l the straight road
Jude 1: 6 but l their proper dwelling,
Rev 10: 2 the sea and his l foot on
Sir 22:11 for he has l intelligence behind.

LEFT HAND Ge 13:9; 48:13, 14; Lev 14:15,
16, 26, 27; Jdg 3:21; 16:29; Ne 8:4; Pr 3:16;

SS 2:6; 8:3; Eze 39:3; Da 12:7; Mt 6:3; 25:41;
1Es 4:30

LEFT-HANDED* → HAND, LEFT

Jdg 3:15 of Gera, the Benjaminite, a l man.
20:16 hundred picked men who were l;

LEGION → LEGIONS

Lk 8:30 He said, **"L";** for many demons

LEGIONS* → LEGION

Mt 26:53 at once send me more than twelve l

LEGITIMATELY*

1Ti 1: 8 the law is good, if one uses it l.

LEGS

Da 2:33 its l of iron, its feet partly of iron
10: 6 l like the gleam of burnished bronze
Jn 19:33 they did not break his l.
Rev 10: 1 and his l like pillars of fire.

LEMA*

Mt 27:46 "Eli, Eli, l sabachthani?"
Mk 15:34 "Eloi, Eloi, l sabachthani?"

LEMUEL*

Pr 31: 1 The words of King L.
31: 4 It is not for kings, O L,

LEND → LENDER, LENDS

Dt 28:12 You will l to many nations,
28:44 shall l to you but you shall not l
Lk 6:34 sinners l to sinners, to receive
Sir 8:12 Do not l to one who is stronger

LENDER* → LEND

Pr 22: 7 the borrower is the slave of the l.
Isa 24: 2 as with the l, so with the borrower;

LENDS* → LEND

Pr 19:17 is kind to the poor l to the LORD,
Sir 20:15 Today he l and tomorrow he asks it

LENGTH → LONG

Ge 13:17 the l and the breadth of the land,
Dt 30:20 life to you and l of days,
Ps 21: 4 l of days forever and ever.
Pr 3: 2 for l of days and years of life

LEOPARD → LEOPARDS

Isa 11: 6 the l shall lie down with the kid,
Da 7: 6 watched, another appeared, like a l.
Rev 13: 2 And the beast that I saw was like a l,

LEOPARDS → LEOPARD

Jer 13:23 change their skin or l their spots?

LEPER → LEPROSY

Mt 8: 2 and there was a l who came to him
26: 6 in the house of Simon the l,

LEPERS → LEPROSY

Lk 7:22 the lame walk, the l are cleansed,

LEPROSY → LEPER, LEPERS, LEPROUS

2Ki 5: 1 a mighty warrior, suffered from l.
Mt 8: 3 Immediately his l was cleansed.

LEPROUS → LEPROSY

Ex 4: 6 he took it out, his hand was l,
Nu 12:10 Miriam had become l,
2Ki 7: 3 four l men outside the city gate,

LESS → LEAST

Ex 30:15 and the poor shall not give l,
2Ch 6:18 much l this house that I have built!
32:15 How much l will your God save you
Ezr 9:13 punished us l than our iniquities
Heb 12:25 much l will we escape if we reject

LESSON → LESS

Mk 13:28 "From the fig tree learn its l:

LET

Ge 1: 3 God said, **"L** there be light";

1: 6 "L there be a dome in the midst of
1: 9 and l the dry land appear."
1:11 God said, **"L** the earth put forth
1:14 "L there be lights in the dome of
1:20 "L the waters bring forth swarms
1:24 "L the earth bring forth living
1:26 God said, **"L** us make humankind
in our image,
11: 7 l us go down, and confuse their
Ex 5: 1 "L my people go,
5: 2 and I will not l Israel go."
13:17 When Pharaoh l the people go,
Ps 22: 8 to the LORD; l him deliver—
25: 2 do not l me be put to shame;
33: 8 L all the earth fear the LORD;
95: 1 O come, l us sing to the LORD;
118:24 l us rejoice and be glad in it.
Jer 9:24 but l those who boast boast in this,
La 3:40 L us test and examine our ways,
Joel 3:10 l the weakling say, "I am a warrior."
Mt 5:37 L your word be 'Yes, Yes' or 'No,
27:43 l God deliver him now, if he wants
Mk 4: 9 "L anyone with ears to hear listen!"
10: 9 joined together, l no one separate."
Jn 7:37 "L anyone who is thirsty come to
14: 1 "Do not l your hearts be troubled.
Ro 3: 4 a liar, l God be proved true,
1Co 1:31 "L the one who boasts, boast in the
Lord."
2Co 10:17 "L the one who boasts, boast in the
Lord."
Eph 4:26 not l the sun go down on your anger
Php 2: 5 L the same mind be in you
Col 3:15 And l the peace of Christ rule in
3:16 L the word of Christ dwell in you
Heb 10:22 l us approach with a true heart in
Jas 5:12 but l your "Yes" be yes and your
1Jn 4: 7 Beloved, l us love one another,
Rev 2: 7 L anyone who has an ear listen to
22:17 And l everyone who is thirsty come.
Aza 1:52 "L the earth bless the Lord;
1Mc 4:36 l us go up to cleanse the sanctuary

LETTER → LETTERS

Mt 5:18 until heaven and earth pass away,
not one l, not one stroke of a l,
Ac 15:23 with the following l: "The brothers,
2Co 3: 2 are our l, written on our hearts,
3: 6 the l kills, but the Spirit gives life.
2Th 3:14 do not obey what we say in this l;

LETTERS → LETTER

2Ch 32:17 l to throw contempt on the LORD
2Co 3: 7 chiseled in l on stone tablets,
10:10 "His l are weighty and strong,
2Pe 3:16 of this as he does in all his l.

LEVEL

Ps 143:10 your good spirit lead me on a l path.
Isa 26: 7 The way of the righteous is l;
40: 4 the uneven ground shall become l,
45: 2 before you and I the mountains,
Lk 6:17 with them and stood on a l place,

LEVI → LEVITE, LEVITES, LEVITICAL,
=MATTHEW

1. Son of Jacob by Leah (Ge 29:34; 46:11; 1Ch
2:1). With Simeon avenged rape of Dinah (Ge
34). Tribe of blessed (Ge 49:5-7; Dt 33:8-11),
chosen as priests (Nu 3-4), numbered (Nu 3:39;
26:62), given cities, but not land (Nu 18; 35; Dt
10:9; Jos 13:14; 21), land (Eze 48:8-22), 12,000
from (Rev 7:7).
2. See Matthew.

SONS OF LEVI Ex 6:16; 32:26, 28; Nu
3:17; Dt 21:5; 31:9; 1Ch 6:1, 16; 23:6, 24;
24:20; Ne 10:39; Tob 1:7

TRIBE OF LEVI Nu 1:49; 3:6; 18:2; Dt 10:8;
18:1; Jos 13:14, 33; 1Ch 23:14; Rev 7:7; Sir
45:6; 2Es 1:3

LEVIATHAN*

Job 3: 8 those who are skilled to rouse up L.
41: 1 you draw out L with a fishhook,
Ps 74:14 You crushed the heads of L;
104:26 and L that you formed to sport in it.
Isa 27: 1 and strong sword will punish L
27: 1 L the twisting serpent,
2Es 6:49 and the name of the other L.
6:52 to L you gave the seventh part,

LEVITE → LEVI

Ex 4:14 What of your brother Aaron, the L?
Jdg 19: 1 a certain L, residing in the remote
Ac 4:36 There was a L, a native of Cyprus,

LEVITES → LEVI

Nu 1:53 L shall camp around the tabernacle
3:12 The L shall be mine,
8: 6 Take the L from among the
16: 7 You L have gone too far!"
18:21 L I have given every tithe in Israel
35: 7 that you give to the L shall total
Jos 14: 4 no portion was given to the L in the
1Ch 15: 2 but the L were to carry the ark
2Ch 31: 2 his service, the priests and the L,
Ezr 6:18 L in their courses for the service of
Ne 8: 9 L who taught the people said to all

PRIESTS AND ... LEVITES 1Ki 8:4; 1Ch
13:2; 15:14; 23:2; 24:6, 31; 28:13, 21; 2Ch
5:5; 8:15; 11:13; 23:4; 24:5; 29:4; 30:15, 25,
27; 31:2, 2, 4, 9; 34:30; 35:18; Ezr 1:5; 3:8,
12; 6:16, 20; 7:7; 8:29, 30; 9:1; Ne 8:13;
11:20; 12:1, 30, 44; 13:29, 30; Isa 66:21; Jn
1:19; 1Es 1:7, 10, 21; 2:8; 7:9, 10; 8:5, 10, 59,
60, 69, 96; 9:37

LEVITICAL → LEVI

Heb 7:11 attainable through the l priesthood

LEWDNESS

Eze 16:58 You must bear the penalty of your l
23:48 will I put an end to l in the land,
Hos 4:18 they love l more than their glory.

LIABLE

Mt 5:22 you will be l to judgment;

LIAR* → LIE

2Ki 9:12 They said, **"L!** Come on, tell us!"
Job 24:25 If it is not so, who will prove me a l,
34: 6 being right I am counted a l;
Ps 116:11 my consternation, "Everyone is a l."
Pr 17: 4 and a l gives heed to a mischievous
19: 5 and a l will not escape.
19: 9 and the l will perish.
19:22 and it is better to be poor than a l.
30: 6 and you will be found a l.
Jn 8:44 for he is a l and the father of lies.
8:55 I would be a l like you.
Ro 3: 4 Although everyone is a l,
1Jn 1:10 we make him a l, and his word is
2: 4 not obey his commandments, is a l,
2:22 l but the one who denies that Jesus
5:10 have made him a l by not believing
Sir 20:25 A thief is preferable to a habitual l,

LIAR'S* → LIE

Sir 20:26 A l way leads to disgrace,

LIARS → LIE

Ps 63:11 for the mouths of l will be stopped.
Isa 44:25 who frustrates the omens of l, and
1Ti 1:10 sodomites, slave traders, l, perjurers,
4: 2 hypocrisy of l whose consciences
Tit 1:12 who said, "Cretans are always l,
Rev 21: 8 the sorcerers, the idolaters, and all l,
Sir 15: 8 and I will never think of her.
2Es 11:42 the truth, and have loved l;

LIBATION → LIBATIONS

Php 2:17 if I am being poured out as a l over
2Ti 4: 6 I am already being poured out as a l,

LIBATIONS → LIBATION
Jer 19:13 I have been poured out to other gods

LIBERALLY
Dt 15:14 Provide l out of your flock,
Ps 37:26 They are ever giving l and lending,

LIBERTY
Lev 25:10 shall proclaim l throughout the land
Isa 61: 1 to proclaim l to the captives,
1Co 8: 9 this l of yours does not somehow
Jas 2:12 who are to be judged by the law of l.

LICENTIOUS → LICENTIOUSNESS
2Pe 2: 2 many will follow their l ways,

LICENTIOUSNESS* → LICENTIOUS
Mk 7:22 avarice, wickedness, deceit, l, envy,
Ro 13:13 not in debauchery and l,
2Co 12:21 and l that they have practiced.
Gal 5:19 fornication, impurity, l,
Eph 4:19 and have abandoned themselves to l,
1Pe 4: 3 living in l, passions, drunkenness,
2Pe 2: 7 distressed by the l of the lawless
Jude 1: 4 pervert the grace of our God into l

LICK
Ps 72: 9 and his enemies l the dust.
Isa 49:23 and l the dust of your feet.
Mic 7:17 they shall l dust like a snake,

LIE → LIAR, LIAR'S, LIARS, LIES, LYING
Ge 19:32 and we will l with him,
      39: 7 on Joseph and said, "L with me."
Lev 18:22 not l with a male as with a woman;
Nu 23:19 that he should l, or a mortal,
Dt 6: 7 when you l down and when you rise
      11:19 when you l down and when you rise
Ru 3: 4 go and uncover his feet and l down;
Ps 4: 8 O Lord, make me l down in safety.
      23: 2 makes me l down in green pastures;
      89:35 I will not l to David.
Pr 3:24 l down, your sleep will be sweet.
      14: 5 A faithful witness does not l,
Ecc 4:11 if two l together, they keep warm;
Isa 11: 6 leopard shall l down with the kid,
Jer 27:10 For they are prophesying a l to you,
Eze 34:14 shall l down in good grazing land,
Zep 3:13 Then they will pasture and l down,
Ac 5: 3 your heart to l to the Holy Spirit
Ro 1:25 about God for a l and worshiped
Col 3: 9 Do not l to one another,
1Jn 1: 6 we l and do not do what is true;
      2:21 know that no l comes from the truth.
Rev 14: 5 and in their mouth no l was found;
Sir 7:13 Refuse to utter any l,
Sus 1:20 so give your consent, and l with us.

LIES → LIE
Ex 22:19 Whoever l with an animal shall be
Lev 20:13 If a man l with a male as with a
Ps 5: 6 You destroy those who speak l;
      12: 2 They utter l to each other;
      58: 3 they err from their birth, speaking l,
      144: 8 whose mouths speak l,
Isa 59: 3 your lips have spoken l,
Jer 14:14 The prophets are prophesying l in
Hos 11:12 Ephraim has surrounded me with l,
Hab 2:18 a cast image, a teacher of l?
Jn 8:44 for he is a liar and the father of l.
Php 3:13 forgetting what l behind and
            straining forward to what l ahead,

LIFE → LIVE
Ge 1:30 everything that has the breath of l,
      2: 7 into his nostrils the breath of l;
      2: 9 the tree of l also in the midst of the
      6:17 in which is the breath of l;
      9: 5 require a reckoning for human l.
Ex 21: 6 and he shall serve him for l.
      21:23 then you shall give l for l,
Nu 35:31 you shall accept no ransom for the l
Dt 12:23 for the blood is the l,
      19:21 l for l, eye for eye, tooth for tooth,

      30:15 set before you today l and prosperity
      30:19 Choose l so that you and your
      32:47 for you, but rather your very l;
1Sa 19: 5 for he took his l in his hand when
Ne 9: 6 To all of them you give l,
Job 2: 6 in your power; only spare his l."
      10: 1 "I loathe my l; I will give free
      33: 4 breath of the Almighty gives me l.
      33:30 so that they may see the light of l.
Ps 16:11 You show me the path of l.
      17:14 whose portion in l is in this world.
      23: 6 house of the Lord my whole l long.
      27: 1 The Lord is the stronghold of my l;
      34:12 Which of you desires l, and covets
      36: 9 For with you is the fountain of l;
      49: 7 Truly, no ransom avails for one's l,
      49: 8 For the ransom of l is costly,
      63: 3 your steadfast love is better than l,
      91:16 With long l I will satisfy them,
      119:50 that your promise gives me l.
Pr 3: 2 for length of days and years of l
      3:16 Long l is in her right hand;
      3:18 a tree of l to those who lay hold of
      4:23 for from it flow the springs of l.
      6:23 of discipline are the way of l,
      6:26 of another stalks a man's very l.
      7:23 that it will cost him his l.
      8:35 For whoever finds me finds l and
      10:11 of the righteous is a fountain of l,
      10:27 The fear of the Lord prolongs l,
      11:30 fruit of the righteous is a tree of l,
      13:12 but a desire fulfilled is a tree of l.
      13:14 of the wise is a fountain of l,
      14:27 fear of the Lord is a fountain of l,
      15: 4 A gentle tongue is a tree of l,
      16:22 Wisdom is a fountain of l to one
      18:21 Death and l are in the power of the
            tongue,
      19:23 The fear of the Lord is l indeed;
      21:21 and kindness will find l and honor.
Ecc 2:17 So I hated l, because what is done
      7:12 that wisdom gives l to the one who
      9: 9 Enjoy l with the wife whom you
      10:19 wine gladdens l, and money meets
Isa 53:10 you make his l an offering for sin,
La 3:58 O Lord, you have redeemed my l.
Eze 18:27 and right, they shall save their l.
Da 12: 2 shall awake, some to everlasting l,
Jnh 2: 6 you brought up my l from the Pit,
Mal 2: 5 with him was a covenant of l and
Mt 6:25 do not worry about your l,
      7:14 and the road is hard that leads to l,
      10:39 Those who find their l will lose it,
      16:25 want to save their l will lose it,
      19:16 deed must I do to have eternal l?"
      19:29 and will inherit eternal l.
      20:28 to give his l a ransom for many."
      25:46 but the righteous into eternal l."
Mk 3: 4 to save l or to kill?"
      9:43 it is better for you to enter l maimed
      10:30 and in the age to come eternal l.
      10:45 to give his l a ransom for many."
Lk 6: 9 to save l or to destroy it?"
      12:15 l does not consist in the abundance
      12:22 do not worry about your l,
      12:25 a single hour to your span of l?
Jn 1: 4 in him was l, and the l was the light
      3:15 believes in him may have eternal l.
      3:36 believes in the Son has eternal l;
      4:14 of water gushing up to eternal l."
      5:21 raises the dead and gives them l,
      5:24 but has passed from death to l.
      5:39 that in them you have eternal l;
      5:40 you refuse to come to me to have l.
      6:27 the food that endures for eternal l,
      6:35 said to them, "I am the bread of l.
      6:47 whoever believes has eternal l.
      6:48 I am the bread of l.
      6:51 the bread that I will give for the l of
      6:63 the spirit that gives l; the flesh is
      6:68 You have the words of eternal l.
      8:12 darkness but will have the light of l.

      10:10 I came that they may have l,
      10:11 good shepherd lays down his l for
      10:28 I give them eternal l, and they will
      11:25 "I am the resurrection and the l.
      12:25 Those who love their l lose it,
      12:50 that his commandment is eternal l.
      13:37 I will lay down my l for you."
      14: 6 "I am the way, and the truth, and
            the l.
      15:13 lay down one's l for one's friends.
      17: 3 is eternal l, that they may know you,
      20:31 you may have l in his name.
Ac 2:28 made known to me the ways of l;
      3:15 and you killed the Author of l,
      11:18 the repentance that leads to l."
      13:48 for eternal l became believers.
Ro 2: 7 immortality, he will give eternal l;
      5:10 will we be saved by his l.
      5:18 leads to justification and l
      5:21 eternal l through Jesus Christ our
      6: 4 we too might walk in newness of l.
      6:13 have been brought from death to l,
      6:22 The end is eternal l.
      6:23 is eternal l in Christ Jesus our Lord.
      7:10 very commandment that promised l
      8: 2 the law of the Spirit of l in Christ
      8: 6 to set the mind on the Spirit is l and
      8:11 will give l to your mortal bodies
      8:38 convinced that neither death, nor l,
1Co 15:19 If for this l only we have hoped in
      15:36 does not come to l unless it dies.
2Co 2:16 to the other a fragrance from l to l.
      3: 6 the letter kills, but the Spirit gives l.
      4:10 of Jesus may also be made visible
      5: 4 mortal may be swallowed up by l.
Gal 6: 8 will reap eternal l from the Spirit.
Eph 4: 1 to lead a l worthy of the calling
Php 1:20 whether by l or by death.
      2:16 to the word of l that I can boast
      4: 3 whose names are in the book of l.
Col 3: 3 your l is hidden with Christ in God.
1Ti 1:16 to believe in him for eternal l.
      4: 8 holding promise for both the
            present l and the l to come.
      6:12 take hold of the eternal l,
      6:19 they may take hold of the l that
            really is l.
2Ti 1:10 brought l and immortality to light
      3:12 a godly l in Christ Jesus will be
Tit 1: 2 eternal l that God, who never lies,
      3: 7 according to the hope of eternal l.
Heb 7:16 the power of an indestructible l.
Jas 1:12 and will receive the crown of l that
      3:13 Show by your good l that your
1Pe 3: 7 also heirs of the gracious gift of l—
      3:10 who desire l and desire to see good
      4: 2 l no longer by human desires but
2Pe 1: 3 needed for l and godliness,
1Jn 1: 1 concerning the word of l—
      2:25 what he has promised us, eternal l.
      3:14 that we have passed from death to l
      3:16 that he laid down his l for us—
      5:11 God gave us eternal l, and this l is
            in his Son.
      5:20 He is the true God and eternal l.
Jude 1:21 that leads to eternal l.
Rev 2: 7 to eat from the tree of l that is in the
      2: 8 who was dead and came to l:
      2:10 and I will give you the crown of l.
      3: 5 your name out of the book of l;
      11:11 breath of l from God entered them,
      13: 8 the book of l of the Lamb
      17: 8 the book of l from the foundation of
      20: 4 came to l and reigned with Christ
      20:12 book was opened, the book of l.
      20:15 in the book of l was thrown into the
      21: 6 from the spring of the water of l.
      21:27 written in the Lamb's book of l.
      22: 1 the river of the water of l,
      22: 2 the tree of l with its twelve kinds
      22:14 the right to the tree of l and may
      22:17 who wishes take the water of l as

22:19 that person's share in the tree of **l**
Jdt 13:20 because you risked your own **l**
Sir 4:12 Whoever loves her loves **l**,
30:22 A joyful heart is **l** itself,
31:27 Wine is very **l** to human beings if
2Es 8:52 the tree of **l** is planted,

BOOK OF LIFE Php 4:3; Rev 3:5; 13:8;
17:8; 20:12, 15; 21:27

BREATH OF LIFE Ge 1:30; 2:7; 6:17; 7:15,
22; La 4:20; Rev 11:11; 2Es 3:5

DAYS OF ... LIFE Ge 3:14, 17; Dt 4:9; 6:2;
16:3; 17:19; Jos 1:5; 4:14; 1Sa 7:15; 1Ki 4:21;
11:34; 15:5, 6; Job 10:20; Ps 23:6; 27:4; 90:10;
128:5; Pr 31:12; Ecc 2:3; 5:18; 6:12; 8:15; 9:9;
Tob 1:3; 4:3, 5; 10:12, 13; Jdt 16:22; Sir
33:24; 37:25; 41:13; Man 1:15

ETERNAL LIFE Mt 19:16, 29; 25:46; Mk
10:17, 30; Lk 10:25; 18:18, 30; Jn 3:15, 16,
36; 4:14, 36; 5:24, 39; 6:27, 40, 47, 54, 68;
10:28; 12:25, 50; 17:2, 3; Ac 13:46, 48; Ro
2:7; 5:21; 6:22, 23; Gal 6:8; 1Ti 1:16; 6:12; Tit
1:2; 3:7; 1Jn 1:2; 2:25; 3:15; 5:11, 13, 20; Jude
1:21; 4Mc 15:3

LIFE ... DEATH Dt 30:15, 19; 1Sa 28:9; 2Sa
1:23; Jer 21:8; Ro 7:10; 1Co 3:22; Php 1:20;
Rev 12:11; Wis 16:13; Sir 11:14; 15:17; 33:14,
24; 37:18; 2Es 7:92

TREE OF LIFE Ge 2:9; 3:22, 24; Pr 3:18;
11:30; 13:12; 15:4; Rev 2:7; 22:2, 14, 19; 2Es
2:12; 8:52; 4Mc 18:16

WAY OF LIFE Pr 6:23; Jer 21:8; Ac 26:4;
Eph 2:10; 4:22; Heb 13:7; AdE 10:3; Sir
40:29; 2Mc 4:10; 8:17; 3Mc 3:23; 4Mc 2:8;
4:19; 8:8; 17:9

LIFE-GIVING → GIVE, LIVE
1Co 15:45 the last Adam became a **l** spirit.

LIFETIME → LIVE
Ps 30: 5 his favor is for a **l**.
Lk 16:25 during your **l** you received your

LIFT → LIFTED, LIFTING, LIFTS
Dt 32:40 For I **l** up my hand to heaven,
Ps 24: 7 **L** up your heads, O gates!
25: 1 To you, O LORD, I **l** up my soul.
28: 2 as I **l** up my hands toward your
63: 4 I will **l** up my hands and call on
121: 1 I **l** up my eyes to the hills—
123: 1 To you I **l** up my eyes,
134: 2 **L** up your hands to the holy place,
143: 8 for to you I **l** up my soul.
Isa 40: 9 **l** up your voice with strength,
40:26 **L** up your eyes on high and see:
La 2:19 **L** your hands to him for the lives of
3:41 **l** up our hearts as well as our hands
Lk 11:46 do not **l** a finger to ease them.

LIFTED → LIFT
Nu 9:21 when the cloud **l** they would set out.
Ps 41: 9 who ate of my bread, has **l** the heel
93: 3 The floods have **l** up, O LORD,
131: 1 O LORD, my heart is not **l** up,
Isa 52:13 he shall be exalted and **l** up,
63: 9 he **l** them up and carried them all
Eze 3:12 the spirit **l** me up, and as the glory
8: 3 the spirit **l** me up between earth and
11: 1 The spirit **l** me up and brought me to
Mt 21:21 'Be **l** up and thrown into the sea,'
Jn 3:14 so must the Son of Man be **l** up,
8:28 When you have **l** up the Son of Man
12:34 that the Son of Man must be **l** up?
13:18 one who ate my bread has **l** his heel

LIFTING → LIFT
Ps 141: 2 the **l** up of my hands as an evening
Lk 24:50 and, **l** up his hands, he blessed them.
1Ti 2: 8 **l** up holy hands without anger or

LIFTS → LIFT
1Sa 2: 8 he **l** the needy from the ash heap,
Ps 113: 7 and **l** the needy from the ash heap,

Sir 11:12 he **l** them out of their lowly

LIGAMENT* → LIGAMENTS
Eph 4:16 joined and knit together by every **l**

LIGAMENTS → LIGAMENT
Col 2:19 nourished and held together by its **l**

LIGHT → DAYLIGHT, ENLIGHTEN,
ENLIGHTENED, ENLIGHTENING,
ENLIGHTENMENT, ENLIGHTENS, LIGHTEN,
LIGHTENED, LIGHTENS, LIGHTING, LIGHTS
Ge 1: 3 God said, "Let there be **l**"; and
there was **l**.
1: 5 God called the **l** Day,
1:16 the greater **l** to rule the day
Ex 13:21 pillar of fire by night, to give them **l**,
25:37 lamps shall be set up so as to give **l**
Job 3:20 "Why is **l** given to one in misery,
38:19 the way to the dwelling of **l**,
Ps 4: 6 Let the **l** of your face shine on us,
18:28 It is you who **l** my lamp;
27: 1 The LORD is my **l** and my salvation;
36: 9 in your **l** we see light.
36: 9 in your light we see **l**.
56:13 may walk before God in the **l** of life.
89:15 in the **l** of your countenance;
104: 2 wrapped in **l** as with a garment.
119:105 lamp to my feet and a **l** to my path.
119:130 unfolding of your words gives **l**;
139:12 for darkness is as **l** to you.
Pr 4:18 the path of the righteous is like the **l**
13: 9 The **l** of the righteous rejoices,
Ecc 2:13 that wisdom excels folly as **l** excels
Isa 2: 5 let us walk in the **l** of the LORD!
9: 2 in darkness have seen a great **l**;
42: 6 as a covenant to the people, a **l**
45: 7 I form **l** and create darkness,
49: 6 I will give you as a **l** to the nations,
53:11 Out of his anguish he shall see **l**;
58:10 then your **l** shall rise in the darkness
60: 1 Arise, shine; for your **l** has come,
60:19 the LORD will be your everlasting **l**,
Am 5:18 of the LORD? It is darkness, not **l**;
Mic 7: 8 the LORD will be a **l** to me.
Mt 4:16 in darkness have seen a great **l**,
5:14 "You are the **l** of the world.
5:16 let your **l** shine before others,
6:22 your whole body will be full of **l**;
11:30 my yoke is easy, and my burden is **l**.
Mk 13:24 and the moon will not give its **l**,
Lk 2:32 a **l** for revelation to the Gentiles and
8:16 that those who enter may see the **l**.
11:33 that those who enter may see the **l**.
Jn 1: 4 and the life was the **l** of all people.
1: 5 The **l** shines in the darkness,
1: 7 came as a witness to testify to the **l**,
1: 9 true **l**, which enlightens everyone,
3:19 people loved darkness rather than **l**
5:35 willing to rejoice for a while in his **l**.
8:12 saying, "I am the **l** of the world.
8:12 darkness but will have the **l** of life."
9: 5 I am the **l** of the world."
12:35 Walk while you have the **l**,
12:46 I have come as **l** into the world,
Ac 9: 3 suddenly a **l** from heaven flashed
13:47 set you to be a **l** for the Gentiles,
Ro 13:12 and put on the armor of **l**;
2Co 4: 6 "Let **l** shine out of darkness,"
6:14 what fellowship is there between **l**
11:14 Even Satan disguises himself as an
angel of **l**.
Eph 5: 8 but now in the Lord you are **l**. Live
as children of **l**—
5: 9 the fruit of the **l** is found in all that
Col 1:12 the inheritance of the saints in the **l**.
1Th 5: 5 you are all children of **l** and children
1Ti 6:16 and dwells in unapproachable **l**,
1Pe 2: 9 of darkness into his marvelous **l**.
1Jn 1: 5 God is **l** and in him there is no
1: 7 walk in the **l** as he himself is in the
2: 8 and the true **l** is already shining.

2: 9 Whoever says, "I am in the **l**,"
Rev 8:12 a third of their **l** was darkened;
21:23 for the glory of God is its **l**,
22: 5 they need no **l** of lamp or sun, for
the Lord God will be their **l**,
AdE 8:16 And the Jews had **l** and gladness
Wis 7:26 For she is a reflection of eternal **l**,
Bar 5: 9 in the **l** of his glory,
Aza 1:48 Bless the Lord, **l** and darkness;
1Mc 4:50 and these gave **l** in the temple.

LIGHTEN → LIGHT
2Ch 10: 9 'L the yoke that your father put on
Jnh 1: 5 in the ship into the sea, to **l** it

LIGHTENED* → LIGHT
Ac 27:38 **l** the ship by throwing the wheat

LIGHTENS* → LIGHT
2Sa 22:29 the LORD **l** my darkness.

LIGHTING → LIGHT
Lk 8:16 after **l** a lamp hides it under a jar,

LIGHTNING → LIGHTNINGS
Ex 19:16 third day there was thunder and **l**,
20:18 people witnessed the thunder and **l**,
2Sa 22:15 and scattered them—**l**, and routed
Job 37:15 causes the **l** of his cloud to shine?
Eze 1:13 and **l** issued from the fire.
Da 10: 6 body was like beryl, his face like **l**,
Mt 24:27 the **l** comes from the east and
28: 3 His appearance was like **l**,
Lk 10:18 from heaven like a flash of **l**.
Rev 4: 5 from the throne are flashes of **l**,
8: 5 flashes of **l**, and an earthquake.
11:19 there were flashes of **l**, rumblings,
16:18 there came flashes of **l**, rumblings,

LIGHTNINGS → LIGHTNING
Ps 77:18 your **l** lit up the world;
Aza 1:51 Bless the Lord, **l** and clouds;

LIGHTS → LIGHT
Ge 1:14 **l** in the dome of the sky to separate
1:16 God made the two great **l**—
Ps 136: 7 who made the great **l**,
Jas 1:17 coming down from the Father of **l**,

LIKE → ALIKE, LIKENESS
Ge 3: 5 be **l** God, knowing good and evil."
3:22 the man has become **l** one of us,
13:16 will make your offspring **l** the dust
28:14 your offspring shall be **l** the dust of
Ex 7: 1 I have made you **l** God to Pharaoh,
8:10 you may know that there is no one **l**
15:11 "Who is **l** you, O LORD, among the
15:11 Who is **l** you, majestic in holiness,
24:17 of the glory of the LORD was **l**
34: 1 tablets of stone **l** the former ones,
Nu 11: 7 the manna was **l** coriander seed,
13:33 we seemed **l** grasshoppers,
Dt 8:20 **L** the nations that the LORD is
18:15 prophet **l** me from among your own
32:31 Indeed their rock is not **l** our Rock;
33:29 Who is **l** you, a people saved by the
1Sa 2: 2 "There is no Holy One **l** the LORD,
2Sa 7:22 for there is no one **l** you,
1Ki 8:23 no God **l** you in heaven above or
14: 8 have not been **l** my servant David,
21:25 (Indeed, there was no one **l** Ahab,
1Ch 17:21 Who is **l** your people Israel,
Job 1: 8 There is no one **l** him on the earth,
40: 9 Have you an arm **l** God,
Ps 1: 3 **l** trees planted by streams of water,
1: 4 **l** chaff that the wind drives
18:33 He made my feet **l** the feet of a deer,
22:14 I am poured out **l** water,
35:10 "O LORD, who is **l** you?
48:10 Your name, O God, **l** your praise,
86: 8 none **l** you among the gods, O Lord,
90: 4 a thousand years in your sight are **l**
103:15 for mortals, their days are **l** grass;
113: 5 Who is **l** the LORD our God,

114: 4 skipped I rams, the hills I lambs.
144: 4 They are I a breath; their days are I
     a passing shadow.
Pr   7:22 and goes I an ox to the slaughter,
    11:22 L a gold ring in a pig's snout is
    25:11 word fitly spoken is I apples of gold
Ecc 2:16 How can the wise die just I fools?
    12:11 The sayings of the wise are I goads,
Isa   1: 9 we would have been I Sodom,
    1:18 your sins are I scarlet, they shall be
     I snow;
    11: 7 and the lion shall eat straw I the ox.
    40: 6 their constancy is I the flower of the
    46: 9 I am God, and there is no one I me,
    53: 2 and I a root out of dry ground;
    53: 6 All we I sheep have gone astray;
    64: 6 all our righteous deeds are I a filthy
Jer 10: 6 There is none I you, O LORD;
    23:29 Is not my word I fire, says the LORD
La   1:12 if there is any sorrow I my sorrow,
    2: 5 The Lord has become I an enemy;
Eze 1: 4 something I gleaming amber.
    1:26 that seemed I a human form.
    8: 2 a figure that looked I a human being
Da   7: 4 was I a lion and had eagles' wings.
    7:13 one I a human being coming with
    10: 6 body was I beryl, his face I lightning
Hos 1:10 people of Israel shall be I the sand
    6: 4 Your love is I a morning cloud,
    14: 5 I will be I the dew to Israel;
Mic 7:18 Who is a God I you,
Na   1: 6 His wrath is poured out I fire,
Zec 1: 4 Do not be I your ancestors,
Mt 9:36 I sheep without a shepherd.
    10:16 I am sending you out I sheep into
Lk   6:48 That one is I a man building a house
    13:18 "What is the kingdom of God I?
    22:26 and the leader I one who serves.
Ac   3:22 your own people a prophet I me.
Ro   5:15 But the free gift is not I the trespass.
    9:29 we would have fared I Sodom
1Co 13:11 When I was a child, I spoke I a child
Jas 1:24 immediately forget what they were I
1Pe 1:24 "All flesh is I grass
2Pe 3: 8 Lord one day is I a thousand years,
    3:10 day of the Lord will come I a thief,
Rev 1:13 I saw one I the Son of Man,
    2:18 who has eyes I a flame of fire,
    3: 3 not wake up, I will come I a thief,
    4: 7 the first living creature I a lion,
    10: 1 his face was I the sun,
    13: 4 saying, "Who is I the beast,
    16:15 ("So, I am coming I a thief!
    19:12 His eyes are I a flame of fire,
Jdt 8:16 for God is not I a human being,
Sir 9:10 A new friend is I new wine;
    21:14 The mind of a fool is I a broken jar;

LIKENESS → LIKE

Ge 1:26 in our image, according to our I;
    5: 1 he made them in the I of God.
Dt   4:16 the I of male or female,
Ps 17:15 I shall be satisfied, beholding your I.
Eze 1:28 of the I of the glory of the LORD.
Ro 8: 3 his own Son in the I of sinful flesh,
Php 2: 7 of a slave, being born in human I.
Jas 3: 9 curse those who are made in the I of

LILIES → LILY

SS   2:16 he pastures his flock among the I,
Lk 12:27 Consider the I, how they grow:

LILITH*

Isa 34:14 there too L shall repose,

LILY → LILIES

2Ch 4: 5 rim of a cup, like the flower of a I;
SS   2: 1 a rose of Sharon, a I of the valleys.
    2: 2 As a I among brambles,
Hos 14: 5 he shall blossom like the I,

LIMIT → LIMITED, LIMITS

Job 15: 8 And do you I wisdom to yourself?

LIMITED → LIMIT

Nu 11:23 "Is the LORD's power I?

LIMITS → LIMIT

Ex 19:23 saying, 'Set I around the mountain
2Co 10:13 however, will not boast beyond I,

LIMPING*

Ge 32:31 passed Penuel, I because of his hip.
1Ki 18:21 go I with two different opinions?

LINE

Ps 89:29 I will establish his I forever,
Isa 28:10 I upon I, I upon I, here a little,
    28:17 And I will make justice the I,
Am 7: 7 with a plumb I in his hand.

LINEN

Ex 26: 1 with ten curtains of fine twisted I,
    28:39 the checkered tunic of fine I,
Pr 31:22 her clothing is fine I and purple.
    31:24 She makes I garments and sells
Jer 13: 1 "Go and buy yourself a I loincloth,
Eze 2: among them was a man clothed in I,
Da 10: 5 and saw a man clothed in I,
Mk 15:46 wrapped it in the I cloth,
Jn 20: 6 He saw the I wrappings lying there,
Rev 15: 6 robed in pure bright I,
    19: 8 for the fine I is the righteous deeds

LINGER

Pr 23:30 Those who I late over wine,

LION → LION'S, LIONS, LIONS'

Ge 49: 9 he stretches out like a I,
Jdg 14: 6 the I apart barehanded as one might
1Sa 17:34 and whenever a I or a bear came,
Ps 91:13 You will tread on the I and the adder
Ecc 9: 4 a living dog is better than a dead I.
Isa 11: 7 and the I shall eat straw like the ox.
    65:25 the I shall eat straw like the ox;
Jer 4: 7 A I has gone up from its thicket,
    25:38 Like a I he has left his covert;
Eze 1:10 the face of a I on the right side,
    10:14 a human being, the third that of a I,
Da   7: 4 first was like a I and had eagles'
Hos 13: 7 So I will become like a I to them,
1Pe 5: 8 a roaring I your adversary the devil
Rev 4: 7 the first living creature like a I,
    5: 5 See, the L of the tribe of Judah,
Sir 27:28 lies in wait for them like a I.

LION'S → LION

Ge 49: 9 Judah is a I whelp;
2Ti 4:17 So I was rescued from the I mouth.

LIONS → LION

Da   6:20 able to deliver you from the I?"

LIONS' → LION

Joel 1: 6 its teeth are I teeth,
Na   2:11 What became of the I den,
Rev 9: 8 and their teeth like I teeth;
Bel 1:31 They threw Daniel into the I den,

LIPS

Dt 23:23 Whatever your I utter you must
Job 2:10 Job did not sin with his I.
    27: 4 my I will not speak falsehood,
Ps   2: 9 LORD cut off all flattering I,
    40: 9 I have not restrained my I, as you
    63: 3 better than life, my I will praise you.
  119:171 My I will pour forth praise,
    140: 3 under their I is the venom of vipers.
    141: 3 keep watch over the door of my I.
Pr   5: 3 the I of a loose woman drip honey,
    10:13 the I of one who has understanding
    10:18 Lying I conceal hatred,
    10:21 The I of the righteous feed many,
    10:32 The I of the righteous know what is
    12:22 Lying I are an abomination to the
    13: 3 who open wide their I come to ruin.
    15: 7 The I of the wise spread knowledge;
    24:26 honest answer gives a kiss on the I.

26:23 an earthen vessel are smooth I with
    27: 2 a stranger, and not your own I.
Ecc 10:12 but the I of fools consume them.
SS   4:11 Your I distill nectar, my bride;
Isa   6: 5 am lost, for I am a man of unclean I,
    29:13 and honor me with their I,
Hos 14: 2 and we will offer the fruit of our I.
Mal 2: 7 For the I of a priest should guard
Mt 15: 8 with their I, but their hearts are far
Ro   3:13 venom of vipers is under their I."
1Co 14:21 by the I of foreigners I will speak to
Heb 13:15 the fruit of I that confess his name.
1Pe 3:10 and their I from speaking deceit;
Sir 12:16 An enemy speaks sweetly with his I,
    20:20 A proverb from a fool's I will be

LIST

1Ch 27: 1 This is the I of the people of Israel,
1Ti 5: 9 Let a widow be put on the I if

LISTEN → LISTENED, LISTENING,
    LISTENS

Ex   4: 1 they do not believe me or I to me,
    6:30 why would Pharaoh I to me?"
    7:13 and he would not I to them,
    15:26 "If you will I carefully to the voice
    23:22 But if you I attentively to his voice
2Ki 17:40 They would not I, however,
    21: 9 But they did not I; Manasseh misled
Ps   5: 2 L to the sound of my cry, my King
    34:11 Come, O children, I to me;
    81: 8 O Israel, if you would but I to me!
Pr   4: 1 L, children, to a father's instruction,
    13: 1 but a scoffer does not I to rebuke.
Ecc 5: 1 I is better than the sacrifice offered
Isa 1:10 L to the teaching of our God,
Mt 12:42 to I to the wisdom of Solomon,
Mk 4:23 Let anyone with ears to hear I!"
    9: 7 my Son, the Beloved; I to him!"
Lk 16:31 'If they do not I to Moses and the
Jn 10:16 and they will I to my voice.
Ac   3:22 You must I to whatever he tells you.
Jas 1:19 be quick to I, slow to speak,
1Jn 4: 6 is not from God does not I to us.
Rev 2: 7 Let anyone who has an ear I to what
    13: 9 Let anyone who has an ear I:
Sir 6:33 love to I you will gain knowledge,
    11: 8 Do not answer before you I,

LISTENED → LISTEN

Ge 3:17 you have I to the voice of your wife,
Nu 21: 3 The LORD I to the voice of Israel,
Dt 9:19 But the LORD I to me that time also.
    10:10 And once again the LORD I to me.
Da   9: 6 We have not I to your servants the
Lk 10:39 at the Lord's feet and I to what he

LISTENING → LISTEN

1Sa 3:10 said, "Speak, for your servant is I."
2Ti 2:14 but only ruins those who are I.

LISTENS → LISTEN

Pr 8:34 Happy is the one who I to me,
    17: 4 An evildoer I to wicked lips;
Lk 10:16 "Whoever I to you I to me,
Jn 18:37 Everyone who belongs to the truth I
1Jn 4: 6 Whoever knows God I to us,

LITERAL*

Ro 2:29 it is spiritual and not I.

LITTLE

Ex 16:18 who gathered I had no shortage;
    23:30 L by I I will drive them out from
1Ki 17:12 and a I oil in a jug;
Ps   8: 5 have made them a I lower than God,
Pr   6:10 A I sleep, a I slumber,
    13:11 who gather I by I will increase it.
    15:16 Better is a I with the fear of
    16: 8 a I with righteousness than large
Ecc 10: 1 so a I folly outweighs wisdom and
Isa 11: 6 and a I child shall lead them.
Mt 6:30 more clothe you—you of I faith?

8:26 "Why are you afraid, you of l faith?
14:31 "You of l faith, why did you doubt?
16: 8 Jesus said, "You of l faith,
17:20 to them, "Because of your l faith.
19:14 "Let the l children come to me,
Lk 7:47 one to whom l is forgiven, loves l."
18:17 as a l child will never enter it."
1Co 5: 6 a l yeast leavens the whole batch of
2Co 8:15 one who had l did not have too l."
Gal 5: 9 A l yeast leavens the whole batch of
1Ti 5:23 l wine for the sake of your stomach
Heb 2: 7 made them for a l while lower than
1Pe 5:10 after you have suffered for a l while,
1Jn 4: 4 L children, you are from God,
Rev 3: 8 I know that you have but l power,
10: 2 He held a l scroll open in his hand.
Sir 29:23 Be content with l or much,
51:28 Hear but a l of my instruction,

LITTLE CHILD 1Ki 3:7; Isa 11:6; Mk 9:36;
10:15; Lk 9:47; 18:17

LITTLE CHILDREN 2Ch 31:18; Eze 9:6;
Mt 19:13, 14; Mk 10:13, 14; Lk 18:16; Jn
13:33; Gal 4:19; 1Jn 2:1, 12, 28; 3:7, 18; 4:4;
5:21

LITTLE FAITH Mt 6:30; 8:26; 14:31; 16:8;
17:20; Lk 12:28

LIVE → ALIVE, LIFE, LIFE-GIVING,
LIFETIME, LIVED, LIVES, LIVING
Ge 3:22 and eat, and l forever"—
12:12 will kill me, but they will let you l.
Ex 1:16 but if it is a girl, she shall l."
33:20 for no one shall see me and l."
Lev 18: 5 by doing so one shall l:
Nu 21: 8 shall look at it and l."
Dt 4: 1 that you may l to enter and occupy
5:24 and the person may still l.
8: 3 one does not l by bread alone,
30: 6 in order that you may l.
Jdg 1:27 Canaanites continued to l in that
Job 14:14 If mortals die, will they l again?
Ps 24: 1 the world, and those who l in it;
63: 4 So I will bless you as long as I l;
91: 1 l in the shelter of the Most High,
119:175 Let me l that I may praise you,
Pr 4: 4 keep my commandments, and l.
15:27 but those who hate bribes will l.
21: 9 to l in a corner of the housetop
Ecc 3:12 enjoy themselves as long as they l;
Isa 6: 5 I l among a people of unclean lips;
11: 6 The wolf shall l with the lamb,
26:19 Your dead shall l, their corpses shall
55: 3 listen, so that you may l.
Eze 18: 9 he shall surely l, says the Lord GOD.
18:32 the Lord GOD. Turn, then, and l.
20:11 whose observance everyone shall l.
37: 3 "Mortal, can these bones l?"
Am 5: 6 Seek the LORD and l,
Jnh 4: 3 it is better for me to die than to l."
4: 8 "It is better for me to die than to l."
Hab 2: 4 but the righteous l by their faith.
Mt 4: 4 'One does not l by bread alone,
Lk 4: 4 'One does not l by bread alone.'"
10:28 do this, and you will l."
Jn 6:51 eats of this bread will l forever;
11:25 even though they die, will l,
14:19 because I l, you also will l.
Ac 17:24 not l in shrines made by human
17:28 For 'In him we l and move and
Ro 1:17 one who is righteous will l by faith."
6: 8 believe that we will also l with him.
14: 8 If we l, we l to the Lord,
2Co 5:15 those who l might l no longer for
6:16 "I will l in them and walk among
Gal 2:20 and it is no longer I who l,
3:12 works of the law will l
5:25 If we l by the Spirit,
Eph 4:17 must no longer l as the Gentiles l,
5: 8 L as children of light—
1Th 4: 1 learned from us how you ought to l
2Ti 3:12 to l a godly life in Christ Jesus will

Tit 2:12 to l lives that are self-controlled,
Heb 10:38 but my righteous one will l by faith.
1Pe 1:17 l in reverent fear during the time of
1Jn 2:17 who do the will of God l forever.
4: 9 so that we might l through him.
Wis 5:15 But the righteous l forever,
Sir 34:14 those who fear the Lord will l,
37:26 and his name will l forever.
2Es 14:35 when we shall l again;

AS I LIVE Nu 14:21, 28; Dt 32:40; Ps 63:4;
104:33; 116:2; 146:2; Isa 49:18; Jer 22:24;
46:18; Eze 5:11; 14:16, 18, 20; 16:48; 17:16,
19; 18:3; 20:3, 31, 33; 33:11, 27; 34:8; 35:6,
11; Zep 2:9; Ro 14:11; Tob 10:12; Jdt 2:12;
2Es 8:25

LIVE FOREVER Ge 3:22; Dt 32:40; 1Ki
1:31; Ne 2:3; Job 7:16; Ps 22:26; Da 2:4; 3:9;
5:10; 6:6, 21; Zec 1:5; Jn 6:51, 58; 1Jn 2:17;
Wis 5:15; Sir 37:26

LIVE IN THE LAND Ge 34:21; 47:6; Nu
13:28, 29; 35:32; Dt 12:10; 30:20; 31:13; 1Ki
8:40; 2Ki 25:24; 2Ch 6:31; Ps 37:3; Jer 24:8;
35:15; 44:13, 26; La 4:21; Eze 36:28; 37:25

LIVED → LIVE
Ex 12:40 The time that the Israelites had l
Dt 26: 5 into Egypt and l there as an alien,
Jos 24: 2 l beyond the Euphrates and served
24: 7 you l in the wilderness a long time.
Jdg 3: 5 Israelites l among the Canaanites,
Mt 1:18 but before they l together,
Ro 14: 9 to this end Christ died and l again,

LIVES → LIVE
Ge 9: 3 moving thing that l shall be food
Ex 1:14 made their l bitter with hard service
30:16 of the ransom given for your l.
Job 19:25 For I know that my Redeemer l,
Ps 18:46 The LORD l! Blessed be my rock,
Pr 14:25 A truthful witness saves l,
Isa 65:20 an infant that l but a few days,
Da 4:34 and honored the one who l forever.
12: 7 swear by the one who l forever
Jn 11:26 and everyone who l and believes
Ro 6:10 but the life he l, he l to God.
Gal 2:20 but it is Christ who l in me.
Col 1:10 you may lead l worthy of the Lord,
Tit 2:12 to live l that are self-controlled,
Heb 7:25 he always l to make intercession for
13: 5 your l free from the love of money,
1Pe 3: 2 the purity and reverence of your l.
2Pe 3:11 persons ought you to be in leading l
1Jn 2:10 loves a brother or sister l in the light
3:16 to lay down our l for one another.
Rev 4:10 and worship the one who l forever
10: 6 by him who l forever and ever,
15: 7 of God, who l forever and ever;
Tob 13: 1 "Blessed be God who l forever,
Sir 18: 1 He who l forever created the whole

AS THE †LORD LIVES Jdg 8:19; Ru 3:13;
1Sa 14:39, 45; 19:6; 20:3, 21; 25:26; 26:10,
16; 28:10; 29:6; 2Sa 4:9; 12:5; 14:11; 15:21;
1Ki 1:29; 2:24; 22:14; 2Ki 2:2, 4, 6; 4:30;
5:16, 20; 2Ch 18:13; Jer 4:2; 5:2; 12:16; 16:14,
15; 23:7, 8; 38:16; Hos 4:15

WHO LIVES FOREVER Da 4:34; 12:7;
Rev 4:9, 10; 10:6; 15:7; Tob 13:1; Sir 18:1

LIVESTOCK
Ex 34:19 all your male l, the firstborn of cow

LIVING → LIVE
Ge 2: 7 and the man became a l being.
3:20 because she was the mother of all l.
6:19 And of every l thing, of all flesh,
8:21 nor will I ever again destroy every l
Dt 5:26 the voice of the l God speaking out
Jos 3:10 the l God who without fail will
1Sa 17:26 defy the armies of the l God?"
2Ki 19: 4 Assyria has sent to mock the l God,
Ps 84: 2 my flesh sing for joy to the l God.
142: 5 my portion in the land of the l."

Ecc 9: 4 for a l dog is better than a dead lion.
Isa 53: 8 he was cut off from the land of the l,
Jer 2:13 forsaken me, the fountain of l water,
10:10 the l God and the everlasting King.
17:13 forsaken the fountain of l water,
Eze 1: 5 something like four l creatures.
10:17 the spirit of the l creatures was in
Da 6:26 he is the l God, enduring forever.
Hos 1:10 to them, "Children of the l God."
Zec 14: 8 that day l waters shall flow out from
Mt 16:16 the Messiah, the Son of the l God."
22:32 God not of the dead, but of the l."
Jn 4:10 he would have given you l water."
6:51 I am the l bread that came down
7:38 heart shall flow rivers of l water.'"
Ro 9:26 be called children of the l God."
12: 1 present your bodies as a l sacrifice,
14: 9 be Lord of both the dead and the l.
1Co 9:14 should get their l by the gospel.
2Co 6:16 For we are the temple of the l God;
1Ti 4:10 we have our hope set on the l God,
2Ti 4: 1 who is to judge the l and the dead,
Heb 4:12 the word of God is l and active,
10:20 the new and l way that he opened
10:31 to fall into the hands of the l God.
1Pe 1:23 the l and enduring word of God.
2: 4 l stone, though rejected by mortals
Rev 1:18 and the l one. I was dead,
4: 6 are four l creatures,

LAND OF THE LIVING Job 28:13; Ps
27:13; 52:5; 116:9; 142:5; Isa 38:11; 53:8; Jer
11:19; Eze 26:20; 32:23, 24, 25, 26, 27, 32

LIVING BEING Ge 2:7; Dt 11:6; Da 2:30;
1Co 15:45; Tob 13:4; Jdt 11:7; Sir 49:16

LIVING CREATURE Ge 1:21; 2:19; 8:21;
9:10, 12, 15, 16; Lev 11:46, 47, 47; Eze 47:9;
Rev 4:7, 7, 7, 7; 6:3, 5, 7

LIVING CREATURES Ge 1:20, 24; Lev
11:10; Eze 1:5, 13, 13, 14, 15, 15, 19, 19, 20,
21, 22; 3:13; 10:15, 17, 20; Rev 4:6, 8, 9; 5:6,
8, 11, 14; 6:1, 6; 7:11; 8:9; 14:3; 15:7; 19:4;
Bel 1:5; 2Es 6:47, 48, 49

LIVING *GOD Dt 5:26; Jos 3:10; 1Sa 17:26,
36; 2Ki 19:4, 16; Ps 42:2; 84:2; Isa 37:4, 17;
Jer 10:10; 23:36; Da 6:20, 26; Hos 1:10; Mt
16:16; 26:63; Ac 14:15; Ro 9:26; 2Co 3:3;
6:16; 1Ti 3:15; 4:10; Heb 3:12; 9:14; 10:31;
12:22; Rev 7:2; AdE 6:13; 16:16; Bel 1:5, 6,
24, 25; 3Mc 6:28; 4Mc 5:24

LIVING THING Ge 1:28; 6:19; 7:4, 23; 8:17;
Job 12:10; Ps 145:16; Rev 16:3; Sir 18:13

LIVING WATER SS 4:15; Jer 2:13; 17:13; Jn
4:10, 11; 7:38

LOAD → LOADS
Lk 11:46 you l people with burdens hard to

LOADS → LOAD
Gal 6: 5 For all must carry their own l.

LOAF → LOAVES
Pr 6:26 a prostitute's fee is only a l of bread,
Mt 26:26 were eating, Jesus took a l of bread,
Mk 8:14 only one l with them in the boat.
1Co 11:23 he was betrayed took a l of bread,

LOAN → LOANS
Dt 24:10 When you make your neighbor a l
Sir 29: 2 repay your neighbor when a l

LOANS → LOAN
Dt 23:19 interest on l to another Israelite,
Pr 11:15 To guarantee l for a stranger brings

LOAVES → LOAF
Mk 6:41 Taking the five l and the two fish,
6:41 and blessed and broke the l,
8: 6 and he took the seven l,
8:19 the five l for the five thousand,
Lk 11: 5 'Friend, lend me three l of bread;

LOCK → LOCKED, LOCKS

Eze 8: 3 and took me by a l of my head;
Mt 23:13 you l people out of the kingdom of

LOCKED → LOCK

SS   4:12 A garden l is my sister, my bride,
Jn 20:19 were l for fear of the Jews,
Ac   5:23 the prison securely l and the guards
Rev 20: 3 and l and sealed it over him,

LOCKS → LOCK

Nu   6: 5 shall let the l of the head grow long.
Jdg 16:19 shave off the seven l of his head.

LOCUST → LOCUSTS

2Ch 6:28 if there is plague, blight, mildew, l,
Joel 2:25 years that the swarming l has eaten,
Am   4: 9 I devoured your fig trees
Mal 3:11 I will rebuke the l for you,

LOCUSTS → LOCUST

Ex 10: 4 I will bring l into your country.
Mt   3: 4 and his food was l and wild honey.
Rev 9: 3 from the smoke came l on the earth,

LODGE

Ru   1:16 Where you l, I will l;

LOFTY

Isa 26: 5 the l city he lays low.
    57:15 high and l one who inhabits eternity,
Eze 16:24 yourself a l place in every square;

LOG

Mt   7: 3 do not notice the l in your own eye?

LOINS

Ex 12:11 you shall eat it: your l girded,
Heb 7:10 he was still in the l of his ancestor

LOIS·

Godly grandmother of Timothy (2Ti 1:5).

LONELY → ALONE

Ps 25:16 for I am l and afflicted.
La   1: 1 How l sits the city that once was full

LONG → LENGTH, LONGED, LONGER,
LONGING, LONGS

Ex 20:12 that your days may be l in the land
Nu   6: 5 let the locks of the head grow l.
    14:11 "How l will this people despise me?
Dt   6: 2 so that your days may be l.
1Ki 18:21 "How l will you go limping
2Ch 1:11 and have not even asked for l life,
Ps 13: 1 How l, O LORD?
    63: 4 So I will bless you as l as I live;
   116: 2 I will call on him as l as I live.
  119:97 It is my meditation all day l.
 119:174 I l for your salvation, O LORD,
Pr   3:16 L life is in her right hand;
Isa   6:11 Then I said, "How l, O Lord?"
    48: 3 The former things I declared l ago,
Jer 44:14 Although they l to go back to live
Lk 10:13 they would have repented l ago,
1Co 11:14 that if a man wears l hair,
    11:15 but if a woman has l hair,
Php 1: 8 I for all of you with the compassion
Heb 3:13 as l as it is called "today,"
1Pe 1:12 things into which angels l to look!
    2: 2 Like newborn infants, l for the pure,
Rev 6:10 how l will it be before you judge
2Es 1: 9 How l shall I endure them,

LONGED → LONG

Mt 13:17 righteous people l to see what you
2Ti   4: 8 to me but also to all who have l

LONGER → LONG

Ge 17: 5 No l shall your name be Abram,
    32:28 "You shall no l be called Jacob,
Ru   1:20 "Call me no l Naomi, call me Mara,
Isa 29:22 No l shall Jacob be ashamed,

Eze 14:11 house of Israel may no l go astray
Mt   5:13 It is no l good for anything,
Mk 10: 8 So they are no l two, but one flesh.
Jn 13:33 I am with you only a little l.
    15:15 I do not call you servants any l,
Ro   6: 6 we might no l be enslaved to sin.
Gal 2:20 and it is no l I who live,
    3:28 There is no l Jew or Greek,
Eph 2:19 you are no l strangers and aliens,
    4:14 We must no l be children,

LONGING → LONG

Ps 119:20 My soul is consumed with l for
Ro   8:19 the creation waits with eager l for
2Co 5: 2 I to be clothed with our heavenly
    7: 7 told us of your l, your mourning,
    7:11 what alarm, what l, what zeal,

LONGS → LONG

Ps 42: 1 As a deer l for flowing streams, so
            my soul l for you, O God.

LOOK → LOOKED, LOOKING, LOOKS

Ge 15: 5 "L toward heaven and count the
    19:17 do not l back or stop anywhere in
Ex   3: 6 for he was afraid to l at God.
Nu 21: 8 everyone who is bitten shall l at it
Dt   3:27 and l around you to the west,
    3:27 L well, for you shall not cross over
  26:15 L down from your holy habitation,
1Sa 16: 7 "Do not l on his appearance or on
Job 31: 1 how then could I l upon a virgin?
Ps   8: 3 When I l at your heavens,
    34: 5 L to him, and be radiant;
    80:14 l down from heaven, and see;
   123: 2 so our eyes l to the LORD our God,
Pr   4:25 Let your eyes l directly forward,
Isa   3: 9 The l on their faces bears witness
    17: 7 will l to the Holy One of Israel;
    31: 1 do not l to the Holy One of Israel or
    42:18 and you that are blind, l up and see!
Jer   6:16 Stand at the crossroads, and l,
Hab 1:13 and you cannot l on wrongdoing;
Zec 12:10 they l on the one whom they have
            pierced,
Mt   6:26 L at the birds of the air;
    23:27 which on the outside l beautiful,
Mk   8:24 can see people, but they l like trees,
   13:21 'L! Here is the Messiah!'
   16: 6 L, there is the place they laid him.
Lk 24:39 L at my hands and my feet;
Jn   1:36 "L, here is the Lamb of God!"
    4:35 But I tell you, l around you,
  13:33 You will l for me;
  19:37 "They will l on the one whom they
            have pierced."
Php 2: 4 Let each of you l not to your own
            interests,
1Pe 1:12 things into which angels long to l!

LOOKED → LOOK

Ge 19:26 But Lot's wife, behind him, l back,
Ex   2:25 God l upon the Israelites,
Ps 102:19 from heaven the LORD l at the earth,
Eze 10: 1 Then I l, and above the dome that
    37: 8 I l, and there were sinews on them,
Da   7: 9 I l up and saw a ram standing beside
   10: 5 I l up and saw a man clothed in
Hab 3: 6 he l and made the nations tremble.
Zec 1:18 And I l up and saw four horns.
    2: 1 I l up and saw a man with a
    5: 1 Again I l up and saw a flying scroll.
    5: 9 I l up and saw two women coming
    6: 1 again I l up and saw four chariots
Lk   9:16 he l up to heaven, and blessed
  22:61 The Lord turned and l at Peter.
Jn 17: 1 he l up to heaven and said, "Father,
1Jn 1: 1 what we have l at and touched
Rev 4: 1 in heaven a door stood
    5:11 Then I l, and I heard the voice
    6: 2 I l, and there was a white horse!

     7: 9 After this I l, and there was a great
   14: 1 Then I l, and there was the Lamb,
Sir 16:29 Then the Lord l upon the earth,
Sus 1:35 Through her tears she l up toward
2Es 4:48 So I stood and l, and lo,
  11:10 I l again and saw that the voice
  12: 3 When I l again, they were already
  13: 5 After this I l and saw that

LOOKING → LOOK

Mk 16: 6 you are l for Jesus of Nazareth,
Ac   1:11 do you stand l up toward heaven?
Heb 11:26 for he was l ahead to the reward.
  13:14 we are l for the city that is to come.
1Pe 5: 8 l for someone to devour.

LOOKS → LOOK

1Sa 16: 7 but the LORD l on the heart."
Ps 14: 2 The LORD l down from heaven
  33:13 The LORD l down from heaven;
  104:32 who l on the earth and it trembles,
Pr 31:27 She l well to the ways of her
Mt   5:28 who l at a woman with lust
Lk   9:62 to the plow and l back is fit for the
Sir 11: 2 praise individuals for their good l,

LOOSE

Pr   2:16 will be saved from the l woman,
    7: 5 may keep you from the l woman,
Isa 33:23 Your rigging hangs l; it cannot hold
Mt 16:19 and whatever you l on earth will be
  18:18 and whatever you l on earth will be
Sir 9: 3 Do not go near a l woman,

*LORD → *LORD'S, LORDED, LORDS

Ge 18:27 take it upon myself to speak to the L
    45: 8 and l of all his house and ruler over
Ex   4:10 Moses said to the LORD, "O my L,
    34: 9 O Lord, I pray, let the L go with us.
Nu 12:11 Aaron said to Moses, "Oh, my l,
  16:13 that you must also l it over us?
Dt 10:17 God is God of gods and L of lords,
Jos 3:11 L of all the earth is going to pass
1Ki 3:10 It pleased the L that Solomon had
Ne   1:11 O L, let your ear be attentive to the
  10:29 commandment of the LORD our L
Job 28:28 'Truly, the fear of the LORD
Ps 16: 2 I say to the LORD, "You are my L;
    35:23 for my cause, my God and my L!
    38:22 haste to help me, O L, my salvation.
    40:17 but the L takes thought for me.
    54: 4 the L is the upholder of my life.
    57: 9 I will give thanks to you, O L,
    62:12 steadfast love belongs to you, O L.
    68:20 to GOD, the L, belongs escape from
    69: 6 because of me, O L GOD of hosts;
    73:28 I have made the L GOD my refuge,
    86: 5 you, O L, are good and forgiving,
    86: 8 none like you among the gods, O L,
    97: 5 before the L of all the earth.
   110:    The LORD says to my l,
   110: 5 The L is at your right hand;
   130: 3 O LORD, should mark iniquities, L,
   135: 5 our L is above all gods.
   136: 3 O give thanks to the L of lords,
   147: 5 Great is our L, and abundant in
Isa 6: 1 I saw the L sitting on a throne, high
    7:14 the L himself will give you a sign.
    25: 8 L GOD will wipe away the tears
   40:10 See, the L GOD comes with might,
   49:14 my L has forgotten me."
    50: 5 The L GOD has opened my ear,
    61: 1 The spirit of the L GOD is upon me,
Jer 2:19 says the L GOD of hosts.
  46:10 is the day of the L GOD of hosts,
  46:10 the L GOD of hosts holds a sacrifice
La   3:31 For the L will not reject forever.
Eze 4:14 Then I said, "Ah L GOD!
  18:25 say, "The way of the L is unfair."
  36:23 that I am the LORD, says the L GOD,
Da   2:47 God is God of gods and L of kings

---

*LORD distinguishes words translated "Lord" and "lord" from the proper name "LORD," or *Yahweh*. For this name see the heading **†LORD**, on page 183.

5:23 have exalted yourself against the L
9: 3 Then I turned to the L God,
9: 7 Righteousness is on your side, O L,
9: 9 To the L our God belong mercy and
9:19 O L, hear; O L, forgive;
Am 8:11 is surely coming, says the L GOD,
9: 5 The L, GOD of hosts, he who
Mic 1: 2 the L GOD be a witness against you,
1: 2 the L from his holy temple.
Zep 1: 7 Be silent before the L GOD!
Mal 3: 1 the L whom you seek will suddenly
Mt 1:20 of the L appeared to him in a dream
3: 3 'Prepare the way of the L,
4: 7 not put the L your God to the test.'"
4:10 written, 'Worship the L your God,
7:22 many will say to me, 'L, L,
9:38 the L of the harvest to send out
12: 8 the Son of Man is l of the sabbath."
20:25 that the rulers of the Gentiles l it
21: 9 who comes in the name of the L!
22:37 "'You shall love the L your God
22:44 'The L said to my L,
23:39 who comes in the name of the L.'"
Mk 1: 3 'Prepare the way of the L,
5:19 tell them how much the L has done
12:29 The L our God, the L is one;
12:30 the L your God with all your heart,
12:37 David himself calls him L;
Lk 1:11 appeared to him an angel of the L,
1:32 L God will give to him the throne
1:46 said, "My soul magnifies the L,
2: 9 and the glory of the L shone around
2:11 who is the Messiah, the L.
4:18 "The Spirit of the L is upon me,
5:12 "L, if you choose, you can make
5:17 the power of the L was with him to
6: 5 The Son of Man is l of the sabbath."
6:46 "Why do you call me 'L, L,'
10:21 "I thank you, Father, L of heaven
10:27 "You shall love the L your God
19:31 just say this, 'The L needs it.'"
19:38 who comes in the name of the L!
24:34 They were saying, "The L has risen
Jn 1:23 'Make straight the way of the L,'"
9:38 He said, "L, I believe."
13:13 You call me Teacher and L—
20:18 to the disciples, "I have seen the L";
20:28 "My L and my God!"
21:17 to him, "L, you know everything;
Ac 2:21 on the name of the L shall be saved.
2:34 'The L said to my L, "Sit at my
2:36 that God has made him both L
4:26 have gathered together against the L
5:19 the night an angel of the L opened
7:59 Stephen, he prayed, "L Jesus,
8:16 in the name of the L Jesus.
9: 5 He asked, "Who are you, L?"
9:31 Living in the fear of the L and in
10:36 by Jesus Christ—he is L of all.
11:23 to the L with steadfast devotion;
16:31 answered, "Believe on the L Jesus,
22:10 I asked, 'What am I to do, L?'
Ro 4:24 in him who raised Jesus our L
5: 1 God through our L Jesus Christ,
6:23 is eternal life in Christ Jesus our L.
8:39 love of God in Christ Jesus our L.
10: 9 with your lips that Jesus is L
10:12 the same L is L of all and
10:13 who calls on the name of the L shall
12:11 be ardent in spirit, serve the L.
13:14 Instead, put on the L Jesus Christ,
14: 4 the L is able to make them stand.
14: 8 If we live, we live to the L,
14: 9 he might be L of both the dead and
1Co 1:31 the one who boasts, boast in the L."
2: 8 not have crucified the L of glory.
2:16 who has known the mind of the L
3: 5 as the L assigned to each.
4: 4 It is the L who judges me.
6:13 not for fornication but for the L,
6:14 raised the L and will also raise us
7:10 this command—not I but the L—

7:12 To the rest I say—I and not the L—
7:25 I have no command of the L,
7:32 is anxious about the affairs of the
      L, how to please the L;
7:39 anyone she wishes, only in the L.
8: 6 and one L, Jesus Christ,
10:21 cannot drink the cup of the L and
11:23 I received from the L what I also
11:27 for the body and blood of the L.
12: 3 no one can say "Jesus is L" except
15:57 victory through our L Jesus Christ.
15:58 excelling in the work of the L,
16:22 accursed who has no love for the L.
      Our L, come!
2Co 1:24 not mean to imply that we l it over
2:12 a door was opened for me in the L;
3:17 Now the L is the Spirit,
4: 5 we proclaim Jesus Christ as L and
5: 8 the body and at home with the L.
8: 5 they gave themselves first to the L
10:17 the one who boasts, boast in the L."
10:18 but those whom the L commends.
13:10 the L has given me for building up
Gal 6:14 except in the cross of our L Jesus
Eph 2:21 grows into a holy temple in the L;
4: 5 one L, one faith, one baptism,
5: 8 but now in the L you are light.
5:10 to find out what is pleasing to the L.
5:19 melody to the L in your hearts,
5:22 your husbands as you are to the L.
6: 1 Children, obey your parents in the L
6: 8 receive the same again from the L,
6:10 strong in the L and in the strength
Php 2:11 that Jesus Christ is L, to the glory
3: 1 brothers and sisters, rejoice in the L.
3: 8 of knowing Christ Jesus my L.
4: 1 stand firm in the L in this way,
4: 4 Rejoice in the L always;
4: 5 The L is near.
Col 1:10 you may lead lives worthy of the L,
2: 6 have received Christ Jesus the L,
3:13 just as the L has forgiven you,
3:17 do everything in the name of the L,
3:18 as is fitting in the L.
3:20 this is your acceptable duty in the L.
3:24 you serve the L Christ.
4:17 task that you have received in the L.
1Th 1: 6 became imitators of us and of the L,
3: 8 you continue to stand firm in the L.
3:12 And may the L make you increase
4: 1 and urge you in the L Jesus that,
4: 6 because the L is an avenger in all
4:15 are left until the coming of the L,
4:17 to meet the L in the air;
5: 2 day of the L will come like a thief
5:23 at the coming of our L Jesus Christ.
2Th 1: 7 the L Jesus is revealed from heaven
2: 1 the coming of our L Jesus Christ
2: 8 whom the L Jesus will destroy with
3: 3 the L is faithful; he will strengthen
3: 5 the L direct your hearts to the love
1Ti 1:14 grace of our L overflowed for me
6:14 until the manifestation of our L
6:15 the King of kings and L of lords,
2Ti 1: 8 the testimony about our L or of me
2:19 "The L knows those who are his,"
4: 8 which the L, the righteous judge,
4:17 But the L stood by me and gave me
Phm 1:25 grace of the L Jesus Christ be with
Heb 1:10 And, "In the beginning, L,
8: 2 and the true tent that the L,
8:11 'Know the L,' for they shall all
10:30 "The L will judge his people."
12: 6 L disciplines those whom he loves,
12:14 holiness without which no one will
      see the L.
13: 6 "The L is my helper; I will not be
Jas 1: 7 to receive anything from the L.
3: 9 With it we bless the L and Father,
4:10 Humble yourselves before the L,
5:11 you have seen the purpose of the L,
5:15 and the L will raise them up;

1Pe 1:25 the word of the L endures forever."
2: 3 you have tasted that the L is good.
3:12 eyes of the L are on the righteous,
3:15 in your hearts sanctify Christ as L.
2Pe 1:11 into the eternal kingdom of our L
1:16 power and coming of our L Jesus
2: 9 L knows how to rescue the godly
3: 9 The L is not slow about his promise,
3:10 day of the L will come like a thief,
3:18 and knowledge of our L and Savior
Jude 1: 4 and deny our only Master and L,
1:14 L is coming with ten thousands of
Rev 4: 8 "Holy, holy, holy, the L God the
      Almighty,
6:10 "Sovereign L, holy and true,
11: 8 where also their L was crucified.
11:15 has become the kingdom of our L
11:17 L God Almighty, who are and who
14:13 who from now on die in the L."
15: 4 L, who will not fear and glorify
17:14 he is L of lords and King of kings,
19: 6 the L our God the Almighty reigns.
19:16 "King of kings and L of lords."
21:22 temple is the L God the Almighty
22: 5 for the L God will be their light,
22:20 Amen. Come, L Jesus!
Tob 4:19 At all times bless the L God,
Jdt 6: 4 l of the whole earth.
6:19 L God of heaven, see their
Wis 3: 8 the L will reign over them forever.
8: 3 and the L of all loves her.
Sir 1: 1 All wisdom is from the L,
1:12 The fear of the L delights the heart,
4:14 the L loves those who love her.
7:29 With all your soul fear the L,
39:33 All the works of the L are good,
Aza 1:35 Bless the L, all you works of the L;
Sus 1: 2 and one who feared the L.

ANGEL OF THE *LORD Mt 1:20, 24;
2:13, 19; 28:2; Lk 1:11; 2:9; Ac 5:19; 8:26;
12:7, 23; Aza 1:26; Bel 1:34, 36

BEFORE THE *LORD Ex 23:17; Ps 97:5;
Zep 1:7; Lk 1:76; 1Co 4:5; Jas 4:10; Rev 11:4;
Jdt 4:11, 14; 12:4; Sir 7:5; *17:20; 18:26; 35:6;
46:19; Bar 1:5, 17; 2:33; 1Es 7:14; 2Es 2:3;
16:66

BLESS THE *LORD Jas 3:9; Tob 4:19;
13:6; Sir 39:14; 45:26; Aza 1:35, 36, 37, 38,
39, 40, 41, 42, 43, 44, 45, 46, 47, 48, 49, 50,
51, 52, 53, 54, 55, 56, 57, 58, 59, 60, 61, 62,
63, 64, 65, 66

DAY OF *LORD Jer 46:10; 1Co 1:8; 5:5;
2Co 1:14; 1Th 5:2; 2Th 2:2; 2Pe 3:10

FEAR THE *LORD Sir 1:13, 14, 16, 20; 2:7,
8, 9, 15, 16, 17; 6:16, 17; 7:29, 31; 10:19, 20;
21:6; 32:16; 34:14, 16; 2Es 16:70, 71

FEAR OF THE *LORD Job 28:28; Ac 9:31;
2Co 5:11; Sir 1:11, 12, 18, 27, 28, 30; 2:10;
9:16; 10:22; 16:2; 19:20; 21:11; 23:27; 25:6,
11; 27:3; 40:26, 26, 27; 45:23; 50:29

HOUSE OF THE *LORD Bar 1:8, 14; 1Es
1:55; 2:5; 5:62; 6:2, 20, 22, 24, 26, 27, 28, 33;
8:79

*LORD ALMIGHTY 2Co 6:18; Jdt 4:13;
8:13; 16:5, 17; Bar 3:1, 4; Man 1:1; 2Es 1:15,
22, 28, 33; 2:9, 31

*LORD *GOD Da 9:3; Lk 1:32, 68; Rev 1:8;
4:8; 11:17; 15:3; 16:7; 18:8; 21:22; 22:5; Tob
4:19; 14:15; Jdt 6:19; 7:29; 8:35; 9:2; 12:8;
13:4, 7, 18; AdE 13:15; 14:3, 18; Sir 4:28;
47:18; Bar 2:11; Aza 1:22; 2Mc 1:24; 7:6; 1Es
1:27; 5:67; 6:1; 7:4, 9, 15; 9:39, 46; 3Mc 5:35;
2Es 2:3, 48; 15:21; 16:8, 76

*LORD †GOD OF HOSTS Ps 69:6; Isa
3:15; 10:23, 24; 22:5; 12, 14, 15; 28:22; Jer
2:19; 46:10, 10; 49:5; 50:25, 31; Am 9:5

*LORD JESUS Mk 16:19; Ac 1:21; 4:33;
7:59; 8:16; 9:17; 11:17, 20; 15:11, 26; 16:31;
19:5, 13, 17; 20:21, 24, 35; 21:13; 28:31; Ro

1:7; 5:1, 11; 13:14; 14:14; 15:6, 30; 16:20;
1Co 1:2, 3, 7, 8, 10; 5:4, 4; 6:11; 11:23; 15:57;
16:23; 2Co 1:2, 3, 14; 4:14; 8:9; 11:31; 13:13;
Gal 1:3; 6:14, 18; Eph 1:2, 3, 15, 17; 5:20;
6:23, 24; Php 1:2; 2:19; 3:20; 4:23; Col 1:3;
3:17; 1Th 1:1, 3; 2:15, 19; 3:11, 13; 4:1, 2; 5:9,
23, 28; 2Th 1:1, 2, 7, 8, 12, 12; 2:1, 8, 14, 16;
3:6, 12, 18; 1Ti 6:3, 14; Phm 1:3, 5, 25; Heb
13:20; Jas 1:1; 2:1; 1Pe 1:3; 2Pe 1:8, 14, 16;
Jude 1:17, 21; Rev 22:20, 21

*LORD MY/HIS/OUR/THEIR/YOUR
*GOD Ps 86:12; 90:17; Da 9:9, 15; Mt 4:7, 10;
22:37; Mk 12:29, 30; Lk 1:16; 4:8, 12; 10:27;
Ac 2:39; 3:22; Rev 19:6; Tob 4:21; Jdt 4:2;
7:19, 30; 8:14, 16, 23, 25; Bar 1:10, 13, 13, 15,
18, 19, 21, 22; 2:5, 6, 12, 15, 19, 27, 31; 3:4, 6,
8; Bel 1:25; 1Es 1:4; 5:70; 8:27, 79

*LORD OF HEAVEN Da 5:23; Mt 11:25;
Lk 10:21; Ac 17:24; Tob 6:18; 7:11, 16; 10:11,
12, 13; Jdt 9:12

*LORD THE KING Ge 40:1; 1Sa 24:8;
26:15, 15, 19; 29:8; 2Sa 3:21; 4:8; 9:11; 13:33;
14:9, 12, 15, 17, 17, 18, 19, 19, 22; 15:15, 21,
21; 16:4, 9; 18:28, 31, 32; 19:19, 20, 27, 27,
28, 30, 35, 37; 24:3, 3, 21, 22; 1Ki 1:2, 2, 13,
18, 20, 20, 21, 24, 27, 27, 36, 37; 2:38; 20:9;
1Ch 21:3, 23; Da 1:10; 4:24; 1Es 2:18, 21;
4:46; 6:8, 21, 22

NAME OF THE *LORD Mt 21:9; 23:39;
Mk 11:9; Lk 13:35; 19:38; Jn 12:13; Ac 2:21;
8:16; 9:28; 19:5, 13, 17; 21:13; Ro 10:13; 1Co
5:4; 6:11; Col 3:17; 2Ti 2:19; Jas 5:10, 14; Sir
39:35; 47:18; 51:12; 1Es 1:48; 6:1; 2Es 2:47

SAYS THE *LORD *GOD Ac 2:34; 7:49;
Ro 12:19; 14:11; 1Co 14:21; 2Co 6:17, 18;
Heb 8:8, 9, 10; 10:16; Rev 1:8; 2Es 1:14, 21,
27, 32; 2:9, 14, 15, 17, 28, 30, 31; 15:1, 5, 7, 9,
24, 52, 56; 16:48, 74, 76

SAYS THE *LORD †GOD Isa 3:15; 22:14;
Jer 2:19, 22; 49:5; 50:31; Eze 5:11; 11:8, 21;
12:25, 28; 13:8, 16; 14:11, 14, 16, 18, 20, 23;
15:8; 16:8, 14, 19, 23, 30, 43, 48, 63; 17:16;
18:3, 9, 23, 30, 32; 20:3, 31, 33, 36, 40, 44;
21:7, 13; 22:12, 31; 23:34; 24:14; 26:5, 21;
28:10; 29:20; 30:6; 31:18; 32:8, 14, 16, 31, 32;
33:11; 34:8, 15, 30, 31; 35:6, 11; 36:14, 15,
23, 32; 38:18, 21; 39:5, 8, 10, 13, 20, 29;
43:19, 27; 44:12, 15, 27; 45:9, 15; 47:23;
48:29; Am 3:13; 4:5; 8:3, 9, 11

SOVEREIGN *LORD Ac 4:24; Rev 6:10;
2Mc 15:29; 2Es 3:4; 4:38; 5:23, 38; 6:11; 7:17,
45, 58; 12:7; 13:51

TEMPLE OF THE *LORD Jdt 4:2; Wis
3:14; 1Es 1:2, 49; 2:7; 5:58; 6:19; 7:7; 8:60, 67

THUS SAYS THE *LORD †GOD Isa 7:7;
10:24; 22:15; 28:16; 49:22; 52:4; 56:8; 65:13;
Jer 7:20; Eze 2:4; 3:11, 27; 5:5, 7, 8; 6:3, 11;
7:2, 5; 11:7, 16, 17; 12:10, 19, 23, 28; 13:3, 8,
13, 18, 20; 14:4, 6, 21; 15:6; 16:3, 36, 59;
17:3, 9, 19, 22; 20:3, 5, 27, 30, 39, 47; 21:24,
26, 28; 22:3, 19, 28; 23:22, 28, 32, 35, 46;
24:3, 6, 9, 21; 25:3, 6, 8, 12, 13, 15, 16; 26:3,
7, 15, 19; 27:3; 28:2, 6, 12, 22, 25; 29:3, 8, 13,
19; 30:2, 10, 13, 22; 31:10, 15; 32:3, 11;
33:25, 27; 34:2, 10, 11, 17, 20; 35:3, 14; 36:2,
3, 4, 5, 6, 7, 13, 22, 33, 37; 37:5, 9, 12, 19, 21;
38:3, 10, 14, 17; 39:1, 17, 25; 43:18; 44:6, 9;
45:9, 18; 46:1, 16; 47:13; Am 3:11; 5:3; Ob 1:1

WAY OF THE *LORD Eze 18:25, 29;
33:17, 20; Mt 3:3; Mk 1:3; Lk 3:4; Jn 1:23; Ac
18:25; Wis 5:7

WORD OF THE *LORD Eze 6:3; 25:3;
36:4; Lk 22:61; Ac 8:25; 11:16; 13:44, 48, 49;
15:35, 36; 16:32; 19:10, 20; 1Th 1:8; 4:15;
2Th 3:1; 1Pe 1:25; Sir 42:15; 48:3; 1Es 1:57;
2:1; 8:72; 2Es 1:4; 16:36

---

†LORD → †GOD, †LORD'S
Ge 2: 4 that the L God made the earth and
     2: 7 L God formed man from the dust of
     2:16 the L God commanded the man,
     2:22 rib that the L God had taken from
     3: 9 But the L God called to the man,
     3:13 Then the L God said to the woman,
     3:14 The L God said to the serpent,
     3:23 L God sent him forth from the
     4: 4 And the L had regard for Abel and
     4:15 And the L put a mark on Cain,
     4:26 to invoke the name of the L.
     6: 6 the L was sorry that he had made
     6: 8 found favor in the sight of the L.
     8:20 Then Noah built an altar to the L,
    10: 9 was a mighty hunter before the L;
    11: 9 the L confused the language of all
    12: 1 Now the L said to Abram,
    12: 7 So he built there an altar to the L,
    13: 4 Abram called on the name of the L.
    15: 6 and the L reckoned it to him as
              righteousness.
    15:18 the L made a covenant with Abram,
    17: 1 the L appeared to Abram, and said
    18: 1 L appeared to Abraham by the oaks
    18:14 Is anything too wonderful for the L?
    18:19 keep the way of the L by doing
    19:14 the L is about to destroy the city."
    21: 1 and the L did for Sarah as he had
    22:14 that place "The L will provide";
    24: 1 the L had blessed Abraham in all
    25:21 and the L granted his prayer,
    26: 2 The L appeared to Isaac and said,
    26:25 called on the name of the L,
    28:16 "Surely the L is in this place—
    31:49 "The L watch between you and me,
    39: 2 The L was with Joseph,
    39:23 because the L was with him;
Ex 3: 2 There the angel of the L appeared
     3:15 shall say to the Israelites, 'The L,
     4:11 L said to him, "Who gives speech
     4:31 they heard that the L had given heed
     5: 2 But Pharaoh said, "Who is the L,
     6: 2 and said to him: "I am the L.
     6: 7 know that I am the L your God,
     8:10 there is no one like the L our God,
     9:12 the L hardened the heart of Pharaoh,
     9:30 that you do not yet fear the L God."
    10:16 have sinned against the L your God,
    12:27 'It is the passover sacrifice to the L,
    12:29 the L struck down all the firstborn
    13: 9 a strong hand the L brought you out
    13:12 you shall set apart to the L all that
    13:21 L went in front of them in a pillar
    14:13 the deliverance that the L will
    14:30 the L saved Israel that day from the
    15: 3 The L is a warrior; the L is his
              name.
    15:11 is like you, O L, among the gods?
    15:26 for I am the L who heals you."
    16:12 know that I am the L your God.'"
    16:29 The L has given you the sabbath,
    17: 7 saying, "Is the L among us or not?"
    17:15 and called it, The L is my banner.
    18:10 Jethro said, "Blessed be the L,
    19: 8 "Everything that the L has spoken
              we will do."
    19:20 the L descended upon Mount Sinai,
    20: 2 I am the L your God, who brought
    20: 5 I the L your God am a jealous God,
    20: 7 of the name of the L your God,
    20:10 seventh day is a sabbath to the L
    20:11 L blessed the sabbath day and
    23:25 You shall worship the L your God,
    24: 3 the words that the L has spoken we
              will do."
    24:16 The glory of the L settled on Mount
    28:36 a signet, "Holy to the L."
    30:11 The L spoke to Moses:
    32:11 But Moses implored the L his God,

    33: 9 and the L would speak with Moses.
    34: 5 and proclaimed the name, "The L."
    34: 6 and proclaimed, "The L, the L,
    34:14 the L, whose name is Jealous,
    40:34 glory of the L filled the tabernacle.
    40:38 cloud of the L was on the tabernacle
Lev 1: 2 an offering of livestock to the L,
     1: 9 by fire of pleasing odor to the L.
     8:36 the things that the L commanded
     9:23 the glory of the L appeared to all
    10: 2 came out from the presence of the L
    19: 2 for I the L your God am holy.
    20: 8 I am the L; I sanctify you.
    20:26 for I the L am holy,
    23:40 shall rejoice before the L your God
    24:16 who blasphemes the name of the L
Nu   6:24 The L bless you and keep you;
     8: 5 The L spoke to Moses, saying:
    10:29 the L has promised good to Israel."
    11: 1 the fire of the L burned against
    14:14 for you, O L, are seen face to face,
    14:18 'The L is slow to anger,
    14:21 be filled with the glory of the L—
    20:13 of Israel quarreled with the L,
    21: 6 L sent poisonous serpents among
    21:14 in the Book of the Wars of the L,
    22:31 the L opened the eyes of Balaam,
    23:12 what the L puts into my mouth?"
    30: 2 makes a vow to the L,
    32:12 unreservedly followed the L.'
Dt   1:21 the L your God has given the land
     2: 7 Surely the L your God has blessed
     4:29 From there you will seek the L
     4:39 to heart that the L is God in heaven
     5: 6 I am the L your God,
     5: 9 I the L your God am a jealous God,
     5:11 of the name of the L your God;
     5:14 a sabbath to the L your God;
     6: 4 The L is our God, the L alone.
     6: 5 You shall love the L your God with
     6:16 not put the L your God to the test,
     7: 6 people holy to the L your God;
     7: 8 the L loved you and kept the oath
     7: 9 Know therefore that the L your
              God is God,
     8: 5 so the L your God disciplines you.
     9:10 the L gave me the two stone tablets
    10:12 does the L your God require of you?
    10:17 L your God is God of gods
    10:20 You shall fear the L your God;
    11: 1 You shall love the L your God,
    11:13 loving the L your God,
    13: 3 for the L your God is testing you,
    14: 1 You are children of the L your God.
    17:15 a king whom the L your God will
    18: 2 the L is their inheritance
    18:15 The L your God will raise up for
    28: 1 If you will only obey the L your
    28:15 if you will not obey the L your God
    29: 1 words of the covenant that the L
    29:29 The secret things belong to the L
    30: 4 there the L your God will gather
    30: 6 love the L your God with all your
    30:10 when you obey the L your God
    30:16 by loving the L your God, walking
    30:20 loving the L your God, obeying
    31: 6 the L your God who goes with you;
Jos 1:13 L your God is providing you a place
     2:11 The L your God is indeed God in
     7:20 sinned against the L God of Israel.
    10:14 for the L fought for Israel.
    21:44 And the L gave them rest on every
    22: 5 to love the L your God, to walk in
    22:22 "The L, God of gods! The L, God
              of gods!
    22:34 between us that the L is God."
    23:11 to love the L your God.
    24:15 as for me and my household, we
              will serve the L."
    24:18 will serve the L, for he is our God."

Jdg 2:12 and they provoked the **L** to anger.
   3: 9 the **L** raised up a deliverer for the
Ru 1: 8 May the **L** deal kindly with you,
   4:13 the **L** made her conceive,
1Sa 1:11 She made this vow: "O **L** of hosts,
   1:19 and the **L** remembered her.
   1:28 he is given to the **L**."
   2: 2 "There is no Holy One like the **L**,
   2:25 but if someone sins against the **L**,
   2:26 in stature and in favor with the **L**
   3: 1 The word of the **L** was rare in those
   3: 8 Eli perceived that the **L** was calling
   3:19 the **L** was with him and let none
   4: 3 ark of the covenant of the **L** here
   5: 3 the ground before the ark of the **L**.
   7:12 "Thus far the **L** has helped us."
   10: 1 the **L** has anointed you ruler over
   11:15 they made Saul king before the **L**
   12: 5 "The **L** is witness against you,
   12:18 greatly feared the **L** and Samuel.
   12:22 the **L** will not cast away his people,
   12:24 fear the **L**, and serve him faithfully
   13:14 not kept what the **L** commanded
   14: 6 can hinder the **L** from saving
   15:22 "Has the **L** as great delight in burnt
   15:28 "The **L** has torn the kingdom of
   16:13 the spirit of the **L** came mightily
   17:45 to you in the name of the **L** of hosts,
2Sa 6:14 David danced before the **L**
   7:22 Therefore you are great, O **L** God;
   8: 6 The **L** gave victory to David
   12:13 "Now the **L** has put away your sin;
   22: 2 The **L** is my rock, my fortress,
   22:29 you are my lamp, O **L**,
   22:31 the promise of the **L** proves true;
   24:14 let us fall into the hand of the **L**,
1Ki 2: 3 keep the charge of the **L** your God,
   3: 3 Solomon loved the **L**, walking in
   5: 5 build a house for the name of the **L**
   5:12 **L** gave Solomon wisdom, as he
   8:11 glory of the **L** filled the house of
        the **L**.
   8:61 completely to the **L** our God,
   10: 9 Because the **L** loved Israel forever,
   11: 4 his heart was not true to the **L** his
   18:21 If the **L** is God, follow him;
   18:37 Answer me, O **L**, answer me,
   18:39 "The **L** indeed is God; the **L** indeed
        is God."
   19:11 for the **L** is about to pass by."
   22: 5 "Inquire first for the word of the **L**."
2Ki 3:18 is only a trifle in the sight of the **L**,
   13:23 But the **L** was gracious to them
   17:20 The **L** rejected all the descendants
   18: 6 For he held fast to the **L**;
   19:31 The zeal of the **L** of hosts will do
   22: 8 of the law in the house of the **L**."
   23: 3 and made a covenant before the **L**,
   23:25 turned to the **L** with all his heart,
   24: 4 and the **L** was not willing to pardon.
   25: 9 He burned the house of the **L**,
1Ch 10:13 he was unfaithful to the **L**
   11: 9 for the **L** of hosts was with him.
   13: 6 from there the ark of God, the **L**,
   16:11 Seek the **L** and his strength,
   17: 1 ark of the covenant of the **L** is
   17:20 There is no one like you, O **L**,
   21:24 will not take for the **L** what is yours,
   22: 1 "Here shall be the house of the **L**
   22:11 in building the house of the **L** your
   25: 7 were trained in singing to the **L**,
   28: 9 for the **L** searches every mind,
   29:11 yours is the kingdom, O **L**,
2Ch 1: 1 the **L** his God was with him
   2:11 "Because the **L** loves his people he
   5:14 the glory of the **L** filled the house
   6:17 Therefore, O **L**, God of Israel,
   7: 1 the glory of the **L** filled the temple.
   7:12 Then the **L** appeared to Solomon in
   9: 8 Blessed be the **L** your God,
   13:12 Israelites, do not fight against the **L**,
   14: 6 for the **L** gave him peace.

15:15 and the **L** gave them rest all around.
16: 9 eyes of the **L** range throughout the
17: 9 having the book of the law of the **L**
19: 9 in the fear of the **L**, in faithfulness,
20:20 Believe in the **L** your God and you
21: 7 **L** would not destroy the house of
26: 5 and as long as he sought the **L**,
30: 9 For as you return to the **L**,
32: 8 but with us is the **L** our God,
33:13 Manasseh knew that the **L** indeed
36:22 **L** stirred up the spirit of King Cyrus
Ezr 3:10 foundation of the temple of the **L**,
   7: 6 for the hand of the **L** his God was
   7:10 his heart to study the law of the **L**,
Ne 4:14 Remember the **L**, who is great and
   8: 1 which the **L** had given to Israel.
   8:10 the joy of the **L** is your strength."
   9: 6 Ezra said: "You are the **L**, you alone
Job 1: 6 to present themselves before the **L**,
   1:21 the **L** gave, and the **L** has taken
   38: 1 Then the **L** answered Job
   42:12 The **L** blessed the latter days
Ps 1: 2 their delight is in the law of the **L**,
   2: 2 against the **L** and his anointed,
   3: 8 Deliverance belongs to the **L**;
   4: 6 light of your face shine on us, O **L**!"
   5: 3 O **L**, in the morning you hear my
   6: 1 **L**, do not rebuke me in your anger
   7: 1 O **L** my God, in you I take refuge;
   8: 9 O **L**, our Sovereign, how majestic
   9: 9 The **L** is a stronghold for the
   9:19 Rise up, O **L**! Do not let mortals
   10:16 The **L** is king forever and ever;
   11: 5 The **L** tests the righteous and the
   12: 6 of the **L** are promises that are pure,
   13: 1 How long, O **L**? Will you forget me
   14: 6 but the **L** is their refuge.
   15: 4 who honor those who fear the **L**;
   16: 2 I say to the **L**, "You are my Lord;
   16: 8 I keep the **L** always before me;
   17: 1 Hear a just cause, O **L**;
   18: 1 I love you, O **L**, my strength.
   18:31 For who is God except the **L**?
   19: 7 The law of the **L** is perfect, reviving
   19:14 O **L**, my rock and my redeemer.
   20: 5 May the **L** fulfill all your petitions.
   21:13 Be exalted, O **L**, in your strength!
   22: 8 "Commit your cause to the **L**;
   23: 1 The **L** is my shepherd, I shall not
   23: 6 in the house of the **L** my whole life
   24: 3 Who shall ascend the hill of the **L**?
   25: 4 Make me to know your ways, O **L**;
   25:10 All the paths of the **L** are steadfast
   26: 2 Prove me, O **L**, and try me;
   27: 1 The **L** is my light and my salvation;
   27: 4 to behold the beauty of the **L**,
   28: 7 The **L** is my strength and my shield;
   29: 4 The voice of the **L** is powerful;
   30: 4 Sing praises to the **L**, O you his
   31: 5 you have redeemed me, O **L**,
   32: 2 to whom the **L** imputes no iniquity,
   33:12 Happy is the nation whose God is
        the **L**,
   34: 1 I will bless the **L** at all times;
   34: 7 The angel of the **L** encamps around
   34: 8 O taste and see that the **L** is good;
   35:10 shall say, "O **L**, who is like you?
   36: 6 humans and animals alike, O **L**.
   37: 4 Take delight in the **L**, and he will
   37: 5 Commit your way to the **L**;
   38:21 Do not forsake me, O **L**;
   40: 1 I waited patiently for the **L**;
   40:13 Be pleased, O **L**, to deliver me;
   41:10 But you, O **L**, be gracious to me,
   46: 7 The **L** of hosts is with us;
   47: 2 the **L**, the Most High, is awesome,
   48: 1 Great is the **L** and greatly to be
   50: 1 The mighty one, God the **L**,
   55:22 Cast your burden on the **L**,
   59: 8 But you laugh at them, O **L**;
   68: 4 his name is the **L**—be exultant
   69:31 This will please the **L** more than an

70: 5 my help and my deliverer; O **L**,
71: 1 In you, O **L**, I take refuge;
75: 8 in the hand of the **L** there is a cup
78: 4 the glorious deeds of the **L**,
81:10 I am the **L** your God,
83:16 that they may seek your name, O **L**.
84:11 For the **L** God is a sun and shield;
85: 7 Show us your steadfast love, O **L**,
86:11 Teach me your way, O **L**,
87: 2 the **L** loves the gates of Zion more
88: 1 O **L**, God of my salvation,
89: 6 the skies can be compared to the **L**?
91: 9 you have made the **L** your refuge,
92: 1 It is good to give thanks to the **L**,
92: 4 you, O **L**, have made me glad by
93: 1 **L** is king, he is robed in majesty;
94: 1 O **L**, you God of vengeance,
94:12 are those whom you discipline, O **L**,
95: 3 For the **L** is a great God,
96: 1 O sing to the **L** a new song;
96: 5 but the **L** made the heavens.
97: 1 The **L** is king! Let the earth rejoice;
97:10 The **L** loves those who hate evil;
98: 2 The **L** has made known his victory;
99: 1 The **L** is king; let the peoples
100: 2 Worship the **L** with gladness;
101: 1 to you, O **L**, I will sing.
102:12 you, O **L**, are enthroned forever;
103: 1 Bless the **L**, O my soul,
103: 8 The **L** is merciful and gracious,
104:24 O **L**, how manifold are your works!
104:33 I will sing to the **L** as long as I live;
105: 4 Seek the **L** and his strength;
106:47 Save us, O **L** our God,
107: 8 thank the **L** for his steadfast love,
108: 3 I will give thanks to you, O **L**,
109:26 Help me, O **L** my God!
110: 1 The **L** says to my lord,
110: 4 **L** has sworn and will not change
111: 2 Great are the works of the **L**,
111: 4 the **L** is gracious and merciful.
112: 1 Happy are those who fear the **L**,
113: 1 praise the name of the **L**.
113: 5 Who is like the **L** our God,
115: 1 Not to us, O **L**, not to us,
115:18 we will bless the **L** from this time
116: 5 Gracious is the **L**, and righteous;
116:12 What shall I return to the **L** for all
116:15 Precious in the sight of the **L** is the
117: 1 Praise the **L**, all you nations!
118: 7 The **L** is on my side to help me;
118:18 The **L** has punished me severely,
118:24 This is the day that the **L** has made;
118:26 who comes in the name of the **L**.
119: 1 who walk in the law of the **L**.
119:64 earth, O **L**, is full of your steadfast
119:89 The **L** exists forever; your word is
119:126 It is time for the **L** to act,
120: 1 In my distress I cry to the **L**,
121: 2 My help comes from the **L**,
121: 5 The **L** is your keeper; the L<small>ORD</small>
122: 1 "Let us go to the house of the **L**!"
123: 2 so our eyes look to the **L** our God,
124: 1 not been the **L** who was on our side
124: 8 Our help is in the name of the **L**,
125: 2 so the **L** surrounds his people,
126: 3 **L** has done great things for us,
127: 1 Unless the **L** builds the house,
128: 1 Happy is everyone who fears the **L**,
129: 4 The **L** is righteous; he has cut the
130: 5 I wait for the **L**, my soul waits,
131: 3 Israel, hope in the **L** from this time
132: 1 O **L**, remember in David's favor all
132:13 For the **L** has chosen Zion;
133: 3 there the **L** ordained his blessing,
134: 3 the **L**, maker of heaven and earth,
135: 3 Praise the **L**, for the **L** is good;
135: 6 Whatever the **L** pleases he does,
136: 1 give thanks to the **L**, for he is good,
138: 8 steadfast love, O **L**, endures forever.
139: 1 O **L**, you have searched me and
140: 1 Deliver me, O **L**, from evildoers;

3: 6 For I the **L** do not change;
4: 5 and terrible day of the **L** comes.

ANGEL OF THE †LORD Ge 16:7, 9, 10, 11; 22:11, 15; Ex 3:2; Nu 22:22, 23, 24, 25, 26, 27, 31, 32, 34, 35; Jdg 2:1, 4; 5:23; 6:11, 12, 21, 21, 22, 22; 13:3, 13, 15, 16, 16, 17, 18, 20, 21, 21; 2Sa 24:16; 1Ki 19:7; 2Ki 1:3, 15; 19:35; 1Ch 21:12, 15, 16, 18, 30; Ps 34:7; 35:5, 6; Isa 37:36; Zec 1:11, 12; 3:1, 5, 6; 12:8

ARK OF THE †LORD Jos 3:13; 4:5, 11; 6:6, 7, 11, 12, 13, 13; 7:6; 1Sa 4:6; 5:3, 4; 6:1, 2, 8, 11, 15, 18, 19, 21; 7:1, 1; 2Sa 6:9, 10, 11, 13, 15, 16, 17; 1Ki 8:4; 1Ch 15:2, 3, 12, 14; 16:4; 2Ch 8:11

AS THE †LORD LIVES Jdg 8:19; Ru 3:13; 1Sa 14:39, 45; 19:6; 20:3, 21; 25:26; 26:10, 16; 28:10; 29:6; 2Sa 4:9; 12:5; 14:11; 15:21; 1Ki 1:29; 2:24; 22:14; 2Ki 2:2, 4, 6; 4:30; 5:16, 20; 2Ch 18:13; Jer 4:2; 5:2; 12:16; 16:14, 15; 23:7, 8; 38:16; Hos 4:15

BEFORE THE †LORD Ge 10:9, 9; 13:10; 18:22; 19:13, 27; 24:52; 27:7; Ex 16:33; *22:11; 27:21; 28:12, 29, 30, 30, 35, 38; 29:11, 23, 24, 25, 26, 42; 30:8, 16; 34:23, 24, 34; 40:23, 25; Lev 1:3, 5, 11; 3:1, 7, 12; 4:4, 4, 6, 7, 15, 15, 17, 18, 24; 5:19; 6:7, 14, 25; 7:30; 8:26, 27, 29; 9:2, 4, 5, 21; 10:1, 2, 15, 17, 19; 12:7; 14:11, 12, 16, 18, 23, 24, 27, 29, 31; 15:14, 15, 30; 16:1, 7, 10, 12, 13, 18, 30; 19:22; 23:11, 20, 28, 40; 24:3, 4, 8; Nu 3:4, 4; 5:16, 18, 25, 30; 6:16, 20; 7:3; 8:10, 11, 21; 10:9, 10; 14:37; 15:15, 25, 28; 16:7, 16, 17, 38, 40; 17:7, 9; 18:19; 20:3, 9; 25:4; 26:61; 27:5, 21; 31:50, 54; 32:20, 21, 22, 22, 29, 32; Dt 1:45; 4:10; 6:25; 9:18, 25; 10:8; 12:12; 16:11, 16, 16; 18:7; 19:17; 24:13; 26:5, 10, 10, 13; 27:7; 29:10, 14; 31:11; Jos 4:13; 6:8, 26; 7:23; 18:6, 8, 10; 19:51; Jdg 5:5, 5; 11:11; 20:1, 23; *20:26, 26; 1Sa 1:9, 12, 15, 19; 2:18; 6:20; 7:6; 10:19, 25; 11:15, 15; 12:3, 7; 15:33; 16:6; 21:6, 7; 23:18; 26:19; 2Sa 3:28; 5:3; 6:5, 14, 16, 17, 21, 21; 7:18; 21:6, 9; 1Ki 2:45; 8:59, 62, 64, 65; 9:25; 19:11, 11; 22:21; 2Ki 16:14; 19:14, 15; 22:19; 23:3; 1Ch 11:3; 16:33; 17:16; 22:18; 23:13, 31; 29:20, 22; 2Ch 1:6; 7:4; 14:13; 18:20; 19:10; 20:13, 18; 27:6; 31:20; 33:23; 34:31; Job 1:6; 2:1, 1; Ps 37:7; 95:6; 96:13; 97:5; 102:Heading; 109:14, 15; 116:9; Pr 15:11; Isa 37:14; Jer 4:26; 36:7, 9; Eze 41:22; 43:24; 44:3; 46:3, 9; Da 9:20; Mic 6:6; Zec 2:13; 6:5; Mal 3:14

BLESS THE †LORD Dt 8:10; Jdg 5:2, 9; 1Ch 29:20; Ne 9:5; Ps 16:7; 26:12; 34:1; 103:1, 2, 20, 21, 22, 22; 104:1, 35; 115:18; 134:1, 2; 135:19, 19, 20, 20

BLESSED BE THE †LORD Ge 24:27; Ex 18:10; Ru 4:14; 1Sa 25:32, 39; 2Sa 18:28; 1Ki 1:48; 5:7; 8:15, 56; 10:9; 1Ch 16:36; 2Ch 2:12; 6:4; 9:8; Ezr 7:27; Ps 28:6; 31:21; 41:13; 72:18; 89:52; 106:48; 124:6; 135:21; 144:1; Zec 11:5

COVENANT OF THE †LORD Nu 10:33; 14:44; Dt 10:8; 29:12, 25; 31:9, 25, 26; Jos 3:3, 17; 4:7, 18; 6:8; 7:15; 8:33; 23:16; 1Sa 4:3, 4, 5; 1Ki 3:15; 6:19; 8:1, 6, 21; 1Ch 15:25, 26, 28, 29; 16:37; 17:1; 22:19; 28:2, 18; 2Ch 5:2, 7; 6:11; Jer 3:16; 22:9

DAY OF THE †LORD Isa 13:6, 9; 58:13; Eze 13:5; 30:3; Joel 1:15; 2:1, 11, 31; 3:14; Am 5:18, 18, 20; Ob 1:15; Zep 1:7, 14, 14; Mal 4:5

FEAR OF THE †LORD 2Ch 14:14; 17:10; 19:7, 9; Ps 19:9; 34:11; 111:10; Pr 1:7, 29; 2:5; 8:13; 9:10; 10:27; 14:26, 27; 15:16, 33; 16:6; 19:23; 22:4; 23:17; Isa 11:2, 3; 33:6

FEAR THE †LORD Ex 9:30; Dt 6:2, 24; 10:12, 20; 14:23; 17:19; 31:12, 13; Jos 4:24; 1Sa 12:14, 24; Ps 15:4; 22:23; 25:12; 33:8; 34:9; 112:1; 115:11, 13; 118:4; 135:20; Pr 3:7; 14:2; 24:21; Jer 5:24; 26:19; Hos 10:3

GLORY OF THE †LORD Ex 16:7, 10; 24:16, 17; 40:34, 35; Lev 9:6, 23; Nu 14:10, 21; 16:19, 42; 20:6; 1Ki 8:11; 2Ch 5:14; 7:1, 2, 3; Ps 104:31; 138:5; Isa 35:2; 40:5; 58:8; 60:1; Eze 1:28; 3:12, 23; 10:4, 4, 18; 11:23; 43:4, 5; 44:4; Hab 2:14

HAND OF THE †LORD Ex 9:3; 16:3; Jos 4:24; 22:31; Jdg 2:15; Ru 1:13; 1Sa 5:6, 9; 7:13; 12:15; 2Sa 24:14; 1Ki 18:46; 1Ch 21:13; Ezr 7:6, 28; Job 12:9; Ps 75:8; 118:15, 16, 16; Pr 21:1; Isa 25:10; 41:20; 51:17; 62:3; 66:14; Eze 1:3; 3:14, 22; 33:22; 37:1; 40:1

HOUSE OF THE †LORD Ex 23:19; 34:26; Dt 23:18; Jos 6:24; 1Sa 1:7, 24; 3:15; 2Sa 12:20; 1Ki 3:1; 6:1, 37; 7:12, 40, 45, 48, 51, 51; 8:10, 11, 63, 64; 9:1, 10, 15; 10:5, 12; 12:27; 14:26, 28; 15:15, 18; 2Ki 11:3, 4, 4, 7, 10, 13, 15, 18, 19; 12:4, 4, 9, 9, 10, 11, 11, 12, 13, 13, 14, 16, 18; 14:14; 15:35; 16:8, 14, 18; 18:15; 19:1, 14; 20:5, 8; 21:4, 5; 22:3, 4, 5, 5, 8, 9; 23:2, 2, 6, 7, 11, 12, 24; 24:13; 25:9, 13, 13, 16; 1Ch 6:31, 32; 9:23; 22:1, 11, 14; 23:4, 24, 28, 32; 24:19; 25:6; 26:12, 22, 27; 28:12, 13, 13, 20; 29:8; 2Ch 3:1; 4:16; 5:1, 13; 7:2, 7, 11, 11; 8:1, 16, 16; 9:4, 11; 12:9, 11; 15:8; 16:2; 20:5, 28; 23:5, 6, 12, 14, 18, 18, 19, 20; 24:4, 7, 8, 12, 12, 12, 14, 14, 18, 21; 26:19, 21; 27:3; 28:21, 24; 29:3, 5, 15, 16, 16, 17, 18, 20, 25, 31, 35; 30:1, 15; 31:10, 11, 16; 33:4, 5, 15, 15; 34:8, 10, 10, 14, 15, 17, 30, 30; 35:2; 36:7, 10, 14, 18; Ezr 1:3, 5, 7; 2:68; 3:8, 11; 7:27; 8:29; Ne 10:35; Ps 23:6; 27:4; 92:13; 116:19; 118:26; 122:1, 9; 134:1; 135:2; Isa 37:1, 14; 38:20, 22; 66:20; Jer 17:26; 20:1, 2; 26:2, 7, 9, 10, 10; 27:18, 21; 28:1, 5, 6; 29:26; 33:11; 35:2, 4; 36:5, 10; 52:13, 17, 17, 20; La 2:7; Eze 8:14, 16; 10:19; 11:1; Hos 8:1; 9:4; Joel 1:9, 14; 3:18; Hag 1:14; Zec 7:3; 8:9; 11:13; 14:20, 21

I AM THE †LORD Ge 15:7; 28:13; Ex 6:2, 6, 7, 8, 29; 7:5, 17; 10:2; 12:12; 14:4, 18; 15:26; 16:12; 20:2; 29:46, 46; Lev 11:44, 45; 18:2, 4, 5, 6, 21, 30; 19:3, 4, 10, 12, 14, 16, 18, 25, 28, 30, 31, 32, 34, 36, 37; 20:7, 8, 24; 21:12, 15, 23; 22:2, 3, 8, 9, 16, 30, 31, 32, 33; 23:22, 43; 24:22; 25:17, 38, 55; 26:1, 2, 13, 44, 45; Nu 3:13, 41, 45; 10:10; 15:41, 41; Dt 5:6; 29:6; Jdg 6:10; 1Ki 20:13, 28; Ps 81:10; Isa 42:6, 8; 43:3, 11, 15; 44:24; 45:5, 6, 18; 48:17; 49:23, 26; 51:15; 60:22; Jer 9:24; 24:7; 32:27; Eze 6:7, 10, 13, 14; 7:4, 27; 11:10, 12; 12:15, 16, 20; 13:14, 21, 23; 14:8; 15:7; 16:62; 17:24; 20:5, 7, 26, 38, 42, 44; 22:16; 24:27; 25:5, 7, 11, 17; 26:6; 28:22, 23, 26; 29:6, 9, 21; 30:8, 19, 25, 26; 32:15; 33:29; 34:27; 35:4, 9, 15; 36:11, 23, 38; 37:6, 13; 38:23; 39:6, 7, 22, 28; Hos 12:9; Zec 10:6

LAW OF THE †LORD 2Ki 10:31; 1Ch 16:40; 22:12; 2Ch 12:1; 17:9; 31:3, 4; 34:14; 35:26; Ezr 7:10; Ne 9:3; Ps 1:2; 19:7; 119:1; Jer 8:8; Am 2:4

†LORD *GOD Ge 2:4, 5, 7, 8, 9, 15, 16, 18, 19, 21, 22; 3:1, 8, 8, 9, 13, 14, 21, 22, 23; Ex 9:30; 34:23; Jos 7:19, 20; 10:40, 42; 13:14, 33; 1Sa 14:41, 41; 2Sa 7:22, 25; 1Ki 16:13; 1Ch 17:16, 17; 22:1, 19; 24:19; 28:4, 20; 29:1; 2Ch 1:9; 2:12; 6:41, 41, 42; 11:16; 13:5; 26:18; 30:7; 33:18; Ne 1:5; Ps 59:5; 80:4, 19; 84:8, 11; 89:8; Isa 17:6; Jer 44:7; Jnh 4:6

†LORD HIS *GOD Ex 32:11; Lev 4:22; Dt 17:19; 18:7; 1Sa 30:6; 1Ki 5:3; 11:4; 15:3, 4; 2Ki 5:11; 16:2; 2Ch 1:1; 14:2, 11; 15:9; 26:16; 27:6; 28:5; 31:20; 33:12; 34:8; 36:5, 12, 23; Ezr 7:6; Jnh 2:1; Mic 5:4

†LORD MY *GOD Ge 9:26; Nu 22:18; Dt 4:5; 18:16; 26:14; Jos 14:8, 9; 2Sa 24:24; 1Ki 3:7; 5:4, 5; 8:28; 17:20, 21; 1Ch 21:17; 22:7; 2Ch 2:4; 6:19; Ezr 7:28; 9:5; Ps 7:1, 3; 13:3; 30:2, 12; 38:15; 40:5; 104:1; 109:26; Jer

31:18; Da 9:4, 20; Jnh 2:6; Hab 1:12; Zec 11:4; 14:5

†LORD OF HOSTS 1Sa 1:3, 11; 4:4; 15:2; 17:45; 2Sa 6:2, 18; 7:8, 26, 27; 1Ki 18:15; 2Ki 3:14; 19:31; 1Ch 11:9; 17:7, 24; Ps 24:10; 46:7, 11; 48:8; 84:1, 3, 12; Isa 1:9, 24; 2:12; 3:1; 5:7, 9, 16, 24; 6:3, 5; 8:13, 18; 9:7, 13, 19; 10:16, 26, 33; 13:4, 13; 14:22, 23, 24, 27; 17:3; 18:7, 7; 19:4, 12, 16, 17, 18, 20, 25; 21:10; 22:14, 25; 23:9; 24:23; 25:6; 28:5, 29; 29:6; 31:4, 5; 37:16, 32; 39:5; 44:6; 45:13; 47:4; 48:2; 51:15; 54:5; Jer 6:6, 9; 7:3, 21; 8:3; 9:7, 15, 17; 10:16; 11:17, 20, 22; 16:9; 19:3, 11, 15; 20:12; 23:15, 16, 36; 25:8, 27, 28, 29, 32; 26:18; 27:4, 18, 19, 21; 28:2, 14; 29:4, 8, 17, 21, 25; 30:8; 31:23, 35; 32:14, 15, 18; 33:11, 12; 35:13, 18, 19; 39:16; 42:15, 18; 43:10; 44:2, 11, 25; 46:18, 25; 48:1, 15; 49:7, 26, 35; 50:18, 33, 34; 51:5, 14, 19, 33, 57, 58; Mic 4:4; Na 2:13; 3:5; Hab 2:13; Zep 2:9, 10; Hag 1:2, 5, 7, 9, 14; 2:4, 6, 7, 8, 9, 9, 11, 23, 23; Zec 1:3, 3, 3, 4, 6, 12, 14, 16, 17; 2:8, 9, 11; 3:7, 9, 10; 4:6, 9; 5:4; 6:12, 15; 7:3, 4, 9, 12, 12, 13; 8:1, 2, 3, 4, 6, 6, 7, 9, 9, 11, 14, 14, 18, 19, 20, 21, 22, 23; 9:15; 10:3; 12:5; 13:2, 7; 14:16, 17, 21, 21; Mal 1:4, 6, 8, 9, 10, 11, 13, 14; 2:2, 4, 7, 8, 12, 16; 3:1, 5, 7, 10, 11, 12, 14, 17; 4:1, 3

†LORD OUR *GOD Ex 3:18; 5:3; 8:10, 26, 27; 10:25, 26; Dt 1:6, 19, 20, 25, 41; 2:29, 33, 36, 37; 3:3; 4:7; 5:2, 24, 25, 27, 27; 6:20, 24, 25; 29:14, 18, 29; Jos 18:6; 22:19, 29; 24:17, 24; Jdg 11:24; 1Sa 7:8; 1Ki 8:57, 59, 61, 65; 2Ki 18:22; 19:19; 1Ch 13:2; 15:13; 16:14; 29:16; 2Ch 2:4; 13:11; 14:7, 11; 19:7; 29:6; 32:8, 11; Ezr 9:8; Ne 10:34; Ps 20:7; 94:23; 99:5, 8, 9, 9; 105:7; 106:47; 113:5; 122:9; 123:2; Isa 26:13; 36:7; 37:20; Jer 3:22, 23, 25, 25; 5:19, 24; 8:14; 14:22; 16:10; 26:16; 31:6; 37:3; 42:6, 6, 20, 20; 43:2; 50:28; 51:10; Da 9:10, 13, 14; Mic 4:5; 7:17

†LORD THEIR *GOD Ex 10:7; 29:46, 46; Lev 26:44; Nu 23:21; Jdg 3:7; 8:34; 1Sa 12:9; 1Ki 9:9; 2Ki 17:7, 9, 14, 16, 19; 18:12; 2Ch 31:6; 33:17; 34:33; Ne 9:3, 3, 4; Ps 146:5; Jer 3:21; 7:28; 22:9; 30:9; 43:1, 1; 50:4; Eze 28:26; 34:30; 39:22, 28; Hos 1:7; 3:5; 7:10; Zep 2:7; Hag 1:12, 12; Zec 9:16; 10:6

†LORD YOUR *GOD Ge 27:20; Ex 6:7; 8:28; 10:8, 16, 17; 15:26; 16:12; 20:2, 5, 7, 10, 12; 23:19, 25; 34:24, 26; Lev 11:44; 18:2, 4, 30; 19:2, 3, 4, 10, 25, 31, 34, 36; 20:7, 24; 23:22, 28, 40, 43; 24:22; 25:17, 38, 55; 26:1, 13; Nu 10:9, 10, 10; 15:41, 41; Dt 1:10, 21, 26, 30, 31, 32; 2:7, 7, 30; 3:18, 20, 21, 22; 4:2, 3, 4, 10, 19, 21, 23, 23, 24, 25, 29, 30, 34, 34, 40; 5:6, 9, 11, 12, 14, 15, 15, 16, 16, 32, 33; 6:1, 2, 5, 10, 13, 15, 15, 16, 17; 7:1, 2, 6, 6, 9, 12, 16, 18, 19, 19, 20, 21, 22, 23, 25; 8:2, 5, 6, 7, 10, 11, 14, 18, 19, 20; 9:3, 4, 5, 6, 7, 16, 23; 10:9, 12, 12, 12, 13, 14, 17, 20, 22; 11:1, 2, 12, 12, 13, 22, 25, 27, 28, 29, 31; 12:4, 5, 7, 7, 9, 10, 11, 12, 15, 18, 18, 18, 20, 21, 27, 27, 28, 29, 31; 13:3, 3, 4, 5, 5, 10, 12, 16, 18; 14:1, 2, 21, 23, 23, 24, 24, 25, 26, 29; 15:4, 5, 6, 7, 10, 14, 15, 18, 19, 20, 21; 16:1, 1, 2, 5, 6, 7, 8, 10, 10, 11, 11, 15, 15, 16, 16, 17, 18, 20, 21, 22; 17:1, 1, 2, 2, 8, 12, 14, 15; 18:5, 9, 12, 13, 14, 15; 16; 19:1, 1, 2, 3, 8, 9, 10, 14; 20:1, 4, 13, 14, 16, 17, 18; 21:1, 5, 10, 23; 22:5; 23:5, 5, 14, 18, 20, 21, 21, 23; 24:4, 9, 13, 18, 19; 25:15, 16, 19, 19; 26:1, 2, 2, 3, 4, 5, 10, 10, 11, 13, 16, 19; 27:2, 3, 5, 6, 6, 7, 9, 10; 28:1, 1, 2, 8, 9, 13, 15, 45, 47, 52, 53, 58, 62; 29:6, 10, 12, 12; 30:1, 2, 3, 3, 4, 5, 6, 6, 7, 9, 10, 10, 16, 16, 16, 20; 31:3, 6, 11, 12, 13, 26; Jos 1:9, 11, 13, 15, 17; 2:11; 3:3, 9; 4:5, 23, 23, 24; 8:7; 9:9, 24; 10:19; 22:3, 4, 5; 23:3, 3, 5, 5, 8, 10, 11, 13, 13, 14, 15, 15, 16, 16; Jdg 6:10, 26; 1Sa 12:12, 14, 19; 13:13; 15:15, 21, 30; 25:29; 2Sa 14:11, 17; 18:28; 24:3, 23; 1Ki 1:17; 2:3; 10:9;

13:6, 21; 17:12; 18:10; 2Ki 17:39; 19:4, 4; 23:21; 1Ch 11:2; 22:11, 12, 18, 19; 28:8; 29:20; 2Ch 9:8, 8; 16:7; 20:20; 28:10; 30:8, 9; 35:3; Ne 8:9; 9:5; Ps 76:11; 81:10; Isa 7:11; 37:4, 4; 41:13; 43:3; 48:17; 51:15; 55:5; 60:9; Jer 2:17, 19; 3:13; 13:16; 26:13; 40:2; 42:2, 3, 4, 5, 13, 20, 21; Eze 20:5, 7; Hos 12:9; 13:4; 14:1; Joel 1:14; 2:23, 26; 3:17; Am 9:15; Mic 7:10; Zec 6:15

LOVE THE †LORD Dt 6:5; 11:1; 13:3; 30:6; Jos 22:5; 23:11; Ps 31:23; 116:1

NAME OF THE †LORD Ge 4:26; 12:8; 13:4; 21:33; 26:25; Ex 20:7; Lev 24:16; Dt 5:11; 18:5, 7, 22; 21:5; 28:10; 32:3; Jos 9:9; 1Sa 17:45; 20:42; 2Sa 6:2, 18; 1Ki 3:2; 5:3, 5; 8:17, 20; 10:1; 18:24, 32; 22:16; 2Ki 2:24; 5:11; 1Ch 16:2; 21:19; 22:7, 19; 2Ch 2:1, 4; 6:7, 10; 18:15; 33:18; Job 1:21; Ps 7:17; 20:7; 102:15, 21; 113:1, 2, 3; 116:4, 13, 17; 118:10, 11, 12, 26; 122:4; 124:8; 129:8; 135:1; 148:5, 13; Pr 18:10; Isa 18:7; 24:15; 30:27; 48:1; 50:10; 56:6; 59:19; 60:9; Jer 11:21; 26:9, 16, 20; 44:16; Joel 2:26, 32; Am 6:10; Mic 4:5; 5:4; Zep 3:9, 12; Zec 13:3

PRAISE THE †LORD Ge 29:35; 1Ch 16:4; 2Ch 20:19; Ezr 3:10; Ps 22:26; 33:2; 102:18; 104:35; 105:45; 106:1, 48; 111:1; 112:1; 113:1, 9; 115:17, 18; 116:19; 117:1, 2; 135:1, 3, 21; 146:1, 1, 2, 10; 147:1, 12, 20; 148:1, 1, 7, 14; 149:1, 9; 150:1, 6, 6; Isa 62:9; Jer 20:13

SAYS THE †LORD Ge 22:16; Nu 14:28; 2Ki 9:26; 19:33; 20:17; 22:19; 2Ch 34:27; Ps 12:5; Isa 1:11, 18; 14:22, 22, 23; 17:3, 6; 22:25; 30:1; 31:9; 33:10; 37:34; 39:6; 41:14, 21; 43:10, 12; 45:13; 48:22; 49:18; 52:5, 5; 54:1, 8, 10, 17; 55:8; 57:19; 59:20, 21, 21; 65:7, 25; 66:2, 9, 17, 20, 21, 22, 23; Jer 1:8, 15, 19; 2:3, 9, 12, 29; 3:1, 10, 12, 12, 13, 14, 16, 20; 4:1, 9, 17; 5:9, 11, 15, 18, 22, 29; 6:12, 15; 7:11, 13, 19, 30, 32; 8:1, 3, 12, 13, 17; 9:3, 6, 9, 24, 25; 12:17; 13:11, 14, 25; 15:3, 6, 9, 20; 16:5, 11, 14, 16; 17:24; 18:6; 19:6, 12; 21:7, 10, 13, 14; 22:5, 16, 24; 23:1, 2, 4, 5, 7, 11, 12, 23, 24, 24, 28, 29, 30, 31, 31, 32, 32, 33; 25:7, 9, 12, 29, 31; 27:8, 11, 15, 22; 28:4; 29:9, 11, 14, 14, 19, 19, 23, 32; 30:3, 3, 8, 10, 11, 17, 21; 31:1, 14, 16, 17, 20, 27, 28, 31, 32, 33, 34, 36, 37, 38; 32:5, 30, 44; 33:11, 13, 14; 34:5, 17, 22; 35:13; 39:17, 18; 42:11; 44:26, 29; 45:5; 46:5, 23, 26, 28; 48:12, 25, 30, 35, 38, 43, 44, 47; 49:2, 2, 6, 13, 16, 18, 26, 30, 31, 32, 37, 38, 39; 50:4, 10, 20, 21, 30, 35, 40; 51:24, 25, 26, 39, 48, 52, 53; Eze 13:6, 7; 16:58; 37:14; Hos 2:13, 16, 21; 11:11; Joel 2:12; Am 1:5, 15; 2:3, 11, 16; 3:10, 15; 4:3, 6, 8, 9, 10, 11; 5:17, 27; 6:8, 14; 9:7, 8, 12, 13, 15; Ob 1:4, 8; Mic 4:6; 5:10; Na 2:13; 3:5; Zep 1:2, 3, 10; 2:9; 3:8, 20; Hag 1:8, 9, 13; 2:4, 4, 4, 7, 8, 9, 9, 14, 17, 23, 23, 23; Zec 1:3, 3, 4, 16; 2:5, 6, 6, 10; 3:9, 10; 4:6; 5:4; 7:13; 8:6, 11, 14, 17; 10:12; 11:6; 12:4; 13:2, 7, 8; Mal 1:2, 2, 6, 8, 9, 10, 11, 13, 13, 14; 2:2, 4, 8, 16; 16; 3:1, 5, 7, 10, 11, 12, 13, 17; 4:1, 3

SERVANT OF THE †LORD Dt 34:5; Jos 1:1, 13, 15; 8:31, 33; 11:12; 12:6, 6; 13:8; 14:7; 18:7; 22:2, 4, 5; 24:29; Jdg 2:8; 2Ki 18:12; 2Ch 1:3; 24:6; Ps 18:Heading; 36:Heading; Isa 42:19

SPIRIT OF THE †LORD Jdg 3:10; 6:34; 11:29; 13:25; 14:6, 19; 15:14; 1Sa 10:6; 16:13, 14; 2Sa 23:2; 1Ki 18:12; 22:24; 2Ki 2:16; 2Ch 18:23; 20:14; Isa 11:2; 40:13; 63:14; Eze 11:5; 37:1; Mic 3:8

TEMPLE OF THE †LORD 1Sa 1:9; 3:3; 2Ki 18:16; 23:4; 24:13; 2Ch 26:16; 27:2; 29:16; Ezr 3:6, 10; Jer 7:4, 4, 4; 24:1; 38:14; 41:5; Eze 8:16, 16; 44:4, 5; Zec 6:12, 13, 14, 15

THUS SAYS THE †LORD Ex 4:22; 5:1; 7:17; 8:1, 20; 9:1, 13; 10:3; 11:4; 32:27; Jos

7:13; 24:2; Jdg 6:8; 1Sa 10:18; 15:2; 2Sa 7:5, 8; 12:7, 11; 24:12; 1Ki 11:31; 12:24; 13:2, 21; 14:7; 17:14; 20:13, 14, 28, 42; 21:19, 19; 22:11; 2Ki 1:4, 6, 16; 2:21; 3:16, 17; 4:43; 7:1; 9:3, 6, 12; 19:6, 20, 32; 20:1, 5; 21:12; 22:15, 16, 18; 1Ch 17:4, 7; 21:10, 11; 2Ch 11:4; 12:5; 18:10; 20:15; 21:12; 34:23, 24, 26; Isa 29:22; 37:6, 21, 33; 38:1, 5; 43:1, 14, 16; 44:2, 6, 24; 45:1, 11, 14, 18; 48:17; 49:7, 8, 25; 50:1; 52:3; 56:1, 4; 65:8; 66:1, 12; Jer 2:2, 5; 4:3, 27; 5:14; 6:6, 9, 16, 21, 22; 7:3, 21; 8:4; 9:7, 15, 17, 22, 23; 10:2, 18; 11:3, 11, 21, 22; 12:14; 13:9, 12, 13; 14:10, 15; 15:2, 19; 16:3, 5, 9; 17:5, 21; 18:11, 13; 19:3, 11, 15; 20:4; 21:4, 8, 12; 22:1, 3, 6, 11, 18, 30; 23:2, 15, 16, 38; 24:5, 8; 25:8, 27, 28, 32; 26:2, 4, 18; 27:4, 16, 19, 21; 28:2, 11, 13, 14, 16; 29:4, 8, 10, 16, 17, 21, 25, 31, 32; 30:2, 5, 12, 18; 31:2, 7, 15, 16, 23, 35, 37; 32:3, 14, 15, 28, 36, 42; 33:2, 4, 10, 12, 17, 20, 25; 34:2, 4, 13, 17; 35:13, 17, 18, 19; 36:29, 30; 37:7, 9; 38:2, 3, 17; 39:16; 42:9, 15, 18; 43:10; 44:2, 7, 11, 25, 30; 45:2, 4; 47:2; 48:1, 40; 49:1, 7, 12, 28, 35; 50:18, 33; 51:1, 33, 36, 58; Eze 11:5; 21:3; 30:6; Am 1:3, 6, 9, 11, 13; 2:1, 4, 6; 3:12; 5:4, 16; 7:17; Mic 2:3; 3:5; Na 1:12; Hag 1:2, 5, 7; 2:6, 11; Zec 1:3, 4, 14, 16, 17; 3:7; 6:12; 7:9; 8:2, 3, 4, 6, 7, 9, 14, 19, 20, 23; 12:1

VOICE OF THE †LORD Ex 15:26; Dt 5:25; 8:20; 13:18; 18:16; Jos 5:6; 1Sa 12:15; 15:19, 20, 22; 28:18; 1Ki 20:36; 2Ki 18:12; Ps 29:3, 4, 4, 5, 7, 8, 9; 106:25; Isa 30:31; 66:6; Jer 3:25; 7:28; 26:13; 38:20; 42:6, 6, 13, 21; 43:4, 7; 44:23; Da 9:10; Mic 6:9; Hag 1:12; Zec 6:15

WORD OF THE †LORD Ge 15:1, 4; Ex 9:20, 21; Nu 3:16, 51; 15:31; 24:13; 36:5; Jos 8:27; 1Sa 3:1, 7, 21; 15:10, 23, 26; 2Sa 7:4; 12:9; 24:11; 1Ki 2:27; 6:11; 12:24, 24; 13:1, 2, 5, 9, 17, 18, 20, 21, 26, 32; 14:18; 15:29; 16:1, 7, 12, 34; 17:2, 5, 8, 16, 24; 18:1, 31; 19:9; 21:17, 28; 22:5, 19, 38; 2Ki 1:17; 3:12; 4:44; 7:1, 16; 9:26, 36; 10:10, 17; 14:25; 20:4, 16, 19; 23:16; 24:2; 1Ch 11:3, 10; 12:23; 15:15; 17:3; 22:8; 2Ch 11:2, 4; 12:7; 18:4, 18; 30:12; 34:21; 35:6; 36:21, 22; Ezr 1:1; Ps 33:4, 6; 105:19; Isa 1:10; 2:3; 28:13, 14; 38:4; 39:5, 8; 66:5; Jer 1:2, 4, 11, 13; 2:1, 4, 31; 6:10; 7:2; 8:9; 9:20; 13:2, 3, 8; 14:1; 16:1; 17:15, 20; 18:5; 19:3; 20:8; 21:11; 22:2, 29; 23:17; 24:4; 25:3; 27:18; 28:12; 29:20, 30; 31:10; 32:6, 8, 8, 26; 33:1, 19, 23; 34:4, 12; 35:12; 36:27; 37:6; 39:15; 42:7, 15; 43:8; 44:24, 26; 46:1; 47:1; 49:34; Eze 1:3; 3:16; 6:1; 7:1; 11:14; 12:1, 8, 17, 21, 26; 13:1, 2; 14:2, 12; 15:1; 16:1, 35; 17:1, 11; 18:1; 20:2, 45, 47; 21:1, 8, 18; 22:1, 17, 23; 23:1; 24:1, 15, 20; 25:1; 26:1; 27:1; 28:1, 11, 20; 29:1, 17; 30:1, 20; 31:1; 32:1, 17; 33:1, 23; 34:1, 7, 9; 35:1; 36:1, 16; 37:4, 15; 38:1; Da 9:2; Hos 1:1; 4:1; Joel 1:1; Am 7:16; 8:12; Jnh 1:1; 3:1, 3; Mic 1:1; 4:2; Zep 1:1; 2:5; Hag 1:1, 3; 2:1, 10, 20; Zec 1:1, 7; 4:6, 8; 6:9; 7:1, 4, 8; 8:1, 18; 9:1; 11:11; 12:1; Mal 1:1

***LORD'S** → *LORD

Mal 1:12 say that the **L** table is polluted,
Mk 12:11 was the **L** doing, and it is amazing
Lk 4:19 to proclaim the year of the **L** favor."
10:39 who sat at the **L** feet and listened
Ac 21:14 to say, "The **L** will be done."
Ro 14: 8 or whether we die, we are the **L.**"
1Co 10:26 the earth and its fullness are the **L.**"
11:20 it is not really to eat the **L** supper.
11:26 proclaim the **L** death until he comes
Gal 1:19 apostle except James the **L** brother.
2Ti 2:24 **L** servant must not be quarrelsome
1Pe 2:13 For the **L** sake accept the authority
Rev 1:10 I was in the spirit on the **L** day,
Sir 11:17 The **L** gift remains with the devout,
17:17 but Israel is the **L** own portion.

†LORD'S → †LORD

Ex 9:29 know that the earth is the **L.**
32:26 and said, "Who is on the **L** side?
Nu 11:23 "Is the **L** power limited?
32:13 the **L** anger was kindled against
Dt 32: 9 the **L** own portion was his people,
1Sa 17:47 for the battle is the **L**
24:10 for he is the **L** anointed.'
2Sa 1:16 'I have killed the **L** anointed.'"
19:21 because he cursed the **L** anointed?"
1Ki 18:13 I hid a hundred of the **L** prophets
Ps 11: 4 the **L** throne is in heaven.
24: 1 The earth is the **L** and all that is in it
115:16 The heavens are the **L** heavens,
Pr 3:11 do not despise the **L** discipline or
3:33 The **L** curse is on the house of the
16:33 but the decision is the **L** alone.
Isa 2: 2 the mountain of the **L** house
40: 2 that she has received from the **L**
hand double for all her sins.
59: 1 the **L** hand is not too short to save,
61: 2 to proclaim the year of the **L** favor,
Jer 13:17 the **L** flock has been taken captive.
25:17 So I took the cup from the **L** hand,
51: 6 this is the time of the **L** vengeance;
Ob 1:21 and the kingdom shall be the **L.**
Mic 2: 7 Is the **L** patience exhausted?
Hab 2:16 cup in the **L** right hand will come
Zep 2: 3 be hidden on the day of the **L** wrath.

†LORD'S ANOINTED 1Sa 16:6; 24:6,6, 10; 26:9, 11, 16, 23; 2Sa 1:14, 16; 19:21; La 4:20

†LORD'S HOUSE 2Ch 7:2; Isa 2:2; Jer 7:2; 19:14; 26:2; 27:16; 28:3; 36:6, 8, 10; 51:51; Mic 4:1; Hag 1:2

†LORD'S OFFERING Ex 30:14; 35:5, 21, 24; Lev 7:30; 22:27; 23:25, 27; Nu 9:7, 13; 18:28; 31:50

†LORD'S OFFERINGS Lev 6:18; 10:12; 21:6, 21; 23:8, 36, 36

LORDED → *LORD

Ne 5:15 their servants I it over the people.

LORDS → *LORD

Dt 10:17 God is God of gods and Lord of **l,**
Ps 136: 3 O give thanks to the Lord of **l,**
Isa 26:13 other **l** besides you have ruled over
1Co 8: 5 there are many gods and many **l—**
1Ti 6:15 the King of kings and Lord of **l.**
Rev 17:14 he is Lord of **l** and King of kings,
19:16 "King of kings and Lord of **l.**"

LOSE → LOSES, LOSS, LOST

Mk 8:35 who **l** their life for my sake,
Lk 9:25 but **l** or forfeit themselves?
Jn 6:39 I should **l** nothing of all that he has
12:25 Those who love their life will **l**
2Co 4: 1 in this ministry, we do not **l** heart.
4:16 So we do not **l** heart.
Heb 12: 3 you may not grow weary or **l** heart
12: 5 or **l** heart when you are punished by
2Pe 3:17 the lawless and **l** your own stability.
2Jn 1: 8 do not **l** what we have worked for,
Sir 9: 6 or you may **l** your inheritance.

LOSES → LOSE

Lk 15: 8 if she **l** one of them, does not light a

LOSS → LOSE

1Co 3:15 burned up, the builder will suffer **l;**
Php 3: 8 I regard everything as **l** because of
Sir 32:24 who trusts the Lord will not suffer **l.**

LOST → LOSE

Nu 17:12 we are **l,** all of us are **l!**
Ps 119:176 I have gone astray like a **l** sheep;
Jer 50: 6 My people have been **l** sheep;
Eze 34: 4 you have not sought the **l,**
34:16 I will seek the **l,** and I will bring
Mt 10: 6 to the **l** sheep of the house of Israel.
15:24 "I was sent only to the **l** sheep of
18:14 one of these little ones should be **l.**

Lk 15: 4 and go after the one that is **l**
15: 6 I have found my sheep that was **l.'**
15: 9 I have found the coin that I had **l.'**
15:24 he was **l** and is found!'
19:10 came to seek out and to save the **l.'"**
Jn 17:12 not one of them was **l** except the
one destined to be **l,**
2Co 3:10 what once had glory has **l** its glory

LOT → LOT'S, LOTS

Nephew of Abraham (Ge 11:27; 12:5). Chose to live in Sodom (Ge 13). Rescued from four kings (Ge 14). Rescued from Sodom (Ge 19:1-29; 2Pe 2:7). Fathered Moab and Ammon by his daughters (Ge 19:30-38).

Nu 33:54 You shall apportion the land by **l**
1Sa 14:42 "Cast the **l** between me and my son
Est 3: 7 they cast Pur—which means "the **l**"
9:24 and had cast Pur—that is "the **l**"—
Ps 16: 5 and my cup; you hold my **l.**
Pr 16:33 The **l** is cast into the lap,
18:18 Casting the **l** puts an end to disputes
Ecc 3:22 enjoy their work, for that is their **l;**
5:19 to accept their **l** and find enjoyment
Jnh 1: 7 cast lots, and the **l** fell on Jonah.
Ac 1:26 and the **l** fell on Matthias;
Wis 2: 9 our portion, and this our **l.**
Sir 20:25 but the **l** of both is ruin.

LOT'S → LOT

Ge 19:26 **L** wife, behind him, looked back,
Lk 17:32 Remember **L** wife.

LOTS → LOT

Jos 18:10 and Joshua cast **l** for them in Shiloh
1Ch 25: 8 And they cast **l** for their duties,
Ps 22:18 and for my clothing they cast **l.**
Joel 3: 3 and cast **l** for my people,
Mt 27:35 among themselves by casting **l;**
Ac 1:26 they cast **l** for them, and the lot fell
AdE 3: 7 to a decision by casting **l,**
10:10 For this purpose he made two **l,**

LOUD → ALOUD

Ex 12:30 and there was a **l** cry in Egypt,
19:16 a trumpet so **l** that all the people
Ps 47: 1 shout to God with **l** songs of joy.
Pr 9:13 The foolish woman is **l;**
27:14 blesses a neighbor with a **l** voice,
Eze 9: 1 he cried in my hearing with a **l** voice
Mk 15:34 Jesus cried out with a **l** voice,
Jn 11:43 he cried with a **l** voice,
Rev 1:10 behind me a **l** voice like a trumpet
21: 3 I heard a **l** voice from the throne
Jdt 9: 1 Judith cried out to the Lord with a **l**
Sus 1:24 Susanna cried out with a **l** voice,

LOVE* → BELOVED, BELOVED'S, LOVE-FEASTS, LOVE-SONG, LOVED, LOVER, LOVERS, LOVES, LOVING

Ge 22: 2 your only son Isaac, whom you **l,**
24:12 steadfast **l** to my master Abraham.
24:14 have shown steadfast **l** to my master
24:27 not forsaken his steadfast **l** and his
29:20 but a few days because of the **l** he
29:32 surely now my husband will **l** me."
32:10 of the least of all the steadfast **l**
39:21 Joseph and showed him steadfast **l;**
Ex 15:13 "In your steadfast **l** you led
20: 6 but showing steadfast **l** to the
20: 6 of those who **l** me and keep my
21: 5 if the slave declares, "I **l** my master,
34: 6 and abounding in steadfast **l** and
34: 7 steadfast **l** for the thousandth
Lev 19:18 shall **l** your neighbor as yourself:
19:34 you shall **l** the alien as yourself,
Nu 14:18 and abounding in steadfast **l,**
14:19 the greatness of your steadfast **l,**
Dt 5:10 but showing steadfast **l** to the
5:10 those who **l** me and keep my
6: 5 You shall **l** the LORD your God
7: 9 covenant loyalty with those who **l**

7:13 will **l** you, bless you, and multiply
10:12 to walk in all his ways, to **l** him,
10:15 in **l** on your ancestors alone and
10:19 You shall also **l** the stranger,
11: 1 You shall **l** the LORD your God,
13: 3 to know whether you indeed **l**
30: 6 that you will **l** the LORD your God
Jos 22: 5 to **l** the LORD your God,
23:11 therefore, to **l** the LORD your God.
Jdg 14:16 you do not really **l** me.
16: 4 After this he fell in **l** with a woman
16:15 to him, "How can you say, 'I **l** you,'
1Sa 18:22 and all his servants **l** you;
20:14 show me the faithful **l** of the LORD;
20:15 never cut off your faithful **l** from
20:17 made David swear again by his **l**
2Sa 1:26 your **l** to me was wonderful,
1:26 passing the **l** of women.
2: 6 the LORD show steadfast **l** and
7:15 not take my steadfast **l** from him,
13: 1 David's son Amnon fell in **l** with
13: 4 Amnon said to him, "I **l** Tamar,
15:20 the LORD show steadfast **l** and
19: 6 for **l** of those who hate you and for
hatred of those who **l** you.
22:51 shows steadfast **l** to his anointed,
1Ki 3: 6 steadfast **l** to your servant my father
3: 6 for him this great and steadfast **l,**
8:23 and steadfast **l** for your servants
11: 2 Solomon clung to these in **l.**
1Ch 16:34 for his steadfast **l** endures forever.
16:41 for his steadfast **l** endures forever.
17:13 not take my steadfast **l** from him,
2Ch 1: 8 have shown great and steadfast **l**
5:13 for his steadfast **l** endures forever,"
6:14 in steadfast **l** with your servants
6:42 Remember your steadfast **l**
7: 3 for his steadfast **l** endures forever."
7: 6 for his steadfast **l** endures forever—
19: 2 and **l** those who hate the LORD?
20:21 for his steadfast **l** endures forever."
Ezr 3:11 his steadfast **l** endures forever
7:28 and who extended to me steadfast **l**
9: 9 steadfast **l** before the kings of Persia
Ne 1: 5 steadfast **l** with those who **l** him
9:17 and abounding in steadfast **l,**
9:32 keeping covenant and steadfast **l**—
13:22 to the greatness of your steadfast **l.**
Job 10:12 granted me life and steadfast **l,**
37:13 correction, or for his land, or for **l,**
Ps 4: 2 long will you **l** vain words,
5: 7 the abundance of your steadfast **l,**
5:11 who **l** your name may exult in you.
6: 4 for the sake of your steadfast **l.**
13: 5 But I trusted in your steadfast **l;**
17: 7 Wondrously show your steadfast **l,**
18: 1 I **l** you, O LORD, my strength.
18:50 shows steadfast **l** to his anointed,
21: 7 the steadfast **l** of the Most High
25: 6 O LORD, and of your steadfast **l,**
25: 7 to your steadfast **l** remember me,
25:10 LORD are steadfast **l** and faithfulness
26: 3 your steadfast **l** is before my eyes,
26: 8 O LORD, I **l** the house in which you
31: 7 and rejoice in your steadfast **l,**
31:16 save me in your steadfast **l.**
31:21 wondrously shown his steadfast **l**
31:23 **L** the LORD, all you his saints.
32:10 steadfast **l** surrounds those who trust
33: 5 the earth is full of the steadfast **l** of
33:18 on those who hope in his steadfast **l,**
33:22 Let your steadfast **l,** O LORD, be
36: 5 Your steadfast **l,** O LORD,
36: 7 precious is your steadfast **l,** O God!
36:10 O continue your steadfast **l**
40:10 I have not concealed your steadfast **l**
40:11 steadfast **l** and your faithfulness
40:16 may those who **l** your salvation say
42: 8 the LORD commands his steadfast **l,**
44:26 for the sake of your steadfast **l.**
45: T the Korahites. A Maskil. A **l** song.
45: 7 you **l** righteousness and hate

48: 9 We ponder your steadfast **l,**
51: 1 God, according to your steadfast **l;**
52: 3 You **l** evil more than good,
52: 4 You **l** all words that devour,
52: 8 I trust in the steadfast **l** of God
57: 3 God will send forth his steadfast **l**
57:10 steadfast **l** is as high as the heavens;
59:10 God in his steadfast **l** will meet me;
59:16 I will sing aloud of your steadfast **l**
59:17 the God who shows me steadfast **l.**
60: 5 those whom you **l** may be rescued.
61: 7 appoint steadfast **l** and faithfulness
62:12 and steadfast **l** belongs to you,
63: 3 Because your steadfast **l** is better
66:20 or removed his steadfast **l** from me.
69:13 in the abundance of your steadfast **l,**
69:16 LORD, for your steadfast **l** is good;
69:36 those who **l** his name shall live in it.
70: 4 Let those who **l** your salvation say
77: 8 Has his steadfast **l** ceased forever?
85: 7 Show us your steadfast **l,** O LORD,
85:10 Steadfast **l** and faithfulness will
86: 5 abounding in steadfast **l** to all who
86:13 great is your steadfast **l** toward me;
86:15 and abounding in steadfast **l** and
88:11 steadfast **l** declared in the grave,
89: 1 sing of your steadfast **l,** O LORD,
89: 2 that your steadfast **l** is established
89:14 steadfast **l** and faithfulness go
89:24 My faithfulness and steadfast **l** shall
89:28 Forever I will keep my steadfast **l**
89:33 not remove from him my steadfast **l,**
89:49 where is your steadfast **l** of old,
90:14 in the morning with your steadfast **l,**
91:14 Those who **l** me, I will deliver;
92: 2 your steadfast **l** in the morning,
94:18 steadfast **l,** O LORD, held me up.
98: 3 He has remembered his steadfast **l**
100: 5 his steadfast **l** endures forever,
103: 4 who crowns you with steadfast **l** and
103: 8 and abounding in steadfast **l.**
103:11 so great is his steadfast **l**
103:17 the steadfast **l** of the LORD is from
106: 1 for his steadfast **l** endures forever.
106: 7 the abundance of your steadfast **l,**
106:45 the abundance of his steadfast **l.**
107: 1 for his steadfast **l** endures forever.
107: 8 thank the LORD for his steadfast **l,**
107:15 thank the LORD for his steadfast **l,**
107:21 thank the LORD for his steadfast **l,**
107:31 thank the LORD for his steadfast **l,**
107:43 consider the steadfast **l** of the LORD.
108: 4 For your steadfast **l** is higher than
108: 6 those whom you **l** may be rescued.
109: 4 In return for my **l** they accuse me,
109: 5 for good, and hatred for my **l.**
109:21 because your steadfast **l** is good,
109:26 according to your steadfast **l.**
115: 1 steadfast **l** and your faithfulness.
116: 1 I **l** the LORD, because he has heard
117: 2 For great is his steadfast **l** toward us,
118: 1 his steadfast **l** endures forever!
118: 2 "His steadfast **l** endures forever."
118: 3 "His steadfast **l** endures forever."
118: 4 "His steadfast **l** endures forever."
118:29 for his steadfast **l** endures forever.
119:41 Let your steadfast **l** come to me,
119:47 commandments, because I **l** them.
119:48 your commandments, which I **l,**
119:64 O LORD, is full of your steadfast **l;**
119:76 your steadfast **l** become my comfort
119:88 In your steadfast **l** spare my life,
119:97 Oh, how I **l** your law!
119:113 the double-minded, but I **l** your law.
119:119 therefore I **l** your decrees.
119:124 servant according to your steadfast **l**
119:127 I **l** your commandments more than
119:132 your custom toward those who **l**
119:149 In your steadfast **l** hear my voice;
119:159 Consider how I **l** your precepts;
119:159 according to your steadfast **l.**
119:163 abhor falsehood, but I **l** your law.

119:165 peace have those who I your law;
119:167 soul keeps your decrees; I I them
122: 6 "May they prosper who I you.
130: 7 with the LORD there is steadfast I,
136: 1 for his steadfast I endures forever.
136: 2 for his steadfast I endures forever;
136: 3 for his steadfast I endures forever;
136: 4 for his steadfast I endures forever;
136: 5 for his steadfast I endures forever;
136: 6 for his steadfast I endures forever;
136: 7 for his steadfast I endures forever;
136: 8 for his steadfast I endures forever;
136: 9 for his steadfast I endures forever;
136:10 for his steadfast I endures forever;
136:11 for his steadfast I endures forever;
136:12 for his steadfast I endures forever;
136:13 for his steadfast I endures forever;
136:14 for his steadfast I endures forever;
136:15 for his steadfast I endures forever;
136:16 for his steadfast I endures forever;
136:17 for his steadfast I endures forever;
136:18 for his steadfast I endures forever;
136:19 for his steadfast I endures forever;
136:20 for his steadfast I endures forever;
136:21 for his steadfast I endures forever;
136:22 for his steadfast I endures forever;
136:23 for his steadfast I endures forever;
136:24 for his steadfast I endures forever;
136:25 for his steadfast I endures forever;
136:26 for his steadfast I endures forever.
138: 2 steadfast I and your faithfulness;
138: 8 your steadfast I, O LORD, endures
143: 8 Let me hear of your steadfast I in
143:12 In your steadfast I cut off my
145: 8 and abounding in steadfast I.
145:20 LORD watches over all who I him,
147:11 in those who hope in his steadfast I.
Pr   1:22 will you I being simple?
    4: 6 I her, and she will guard you.
    5:19 you be intoxicated always by her I.
    7:18 let us take our fill of I until morning;
    7:18 let us delight ourselves with I.
    8:17 I I those who I me,
    8:21 endowing with wealth those who I
    8:36 all who hate me I death."
    9: 8 the wise, when rebuked, will I you.
 10:12 but I covers all offenses.
 13:24 who I them are diligent to discipline
 15:17 dinner of vegetables where I is than
 18:21 and those who I it will eat its fruits.
 19: 8 To get wisdom is to I oneself;
 20:13 Do not I sleep, or else you will
 22:11 who I a pure heart and are gracious
 27: 5 Better is open rebuke than hidden I.
Ecc 3: 8 a time to I, and a time to hate;
    9: 1 it is I or hate one does not know.
    9: 6 Their I and their hate
    9: 9 Enjoy life with the wife whom you I
SS   1: 2 For your I is better than wine,
    1: 3 therefore the maidens I you.
    1: 4 we will extol your I more than
         wine; rightly do they I you.
    1: 9 my I, to a mare among Pharaoh's
    1:15 Ah, you are beautiful, my I;
    2: 2 so is my I among maidens.
    2: 4 and his intention toward me was I.
    2: 5 for I am faint with I.
    2: 7 stir up or awaken I until it is ready!
    2:10 my I, my fair one, and come away;
    2:13 my I, my fair one, and come away.
    3: 5 stir up or awaken I until it is ready!
    3:10 its interior was inlaid with I.
    4: 1 beautiful you are, my I, how very
    4: 7 You are altogether beautiful, my I;
    4:10 How sweet is your I,
    4:10 how much better is your I than wine,
    5: 1 friends, drink, and be drunk with I.
    5: 2 "Open to me, my sister, my I,
    5: 8 tell him this: I am faint with I.
    6: 4 You are beautiful as Tirzah, my I,
    7:12 There I will give you my I.
    8: 4 stir up or awaken I until it is ready!

    8: 6 for I is strong as death, passion
    8: 7 Many waters cannot quench I,
    8: 7 If one offered for I all the wealth of
Isa 16: 5 in steadfast I in the tent of David,
 43: 4 and I I you, I give people in return
 54: 8 but with everlasting I I will have
 54:10 but my steadfast I shall not depart
 55: 3 my steadfast, sure I for David.
 56: 6 to I the name of the LORD,
 61: 8 For I the LORD I justice,
 63: 7 to the abundance of his steadfast I.
 63: 9 in his I and in his pity he redeemed
 66:10 be glad for her, all you who I her;
Jer 2: 2 the devotion of your youth, your I
   5:31 my people I to have it so,
   9:24 I act with steadfast I, justice,
  16: 5 the LORD, my steadfast I and mercy.
  31: 3 loved you with an everlasting I;
  32:18 show steadfast I to the thousandth
  33:11 for his steadfast I endures forever!"
La 3:22 steadfast I of the LORD never ceases,
   3:32 to the abundance of his steadfast I;
Eze 16: 8 you were at the age for I.
  23:17 came to her into the bed of I,
  33:32 you are like a singer of I songs,
Da 9: 4 steadfast I with those who I you
Hos 2:19 in steadfast I, and in mercy.
   3: 1 I a woman who has a lover and is
   3: 1 turn to other gods and I raisin cakes.
   4:18 I lewdness more than their glory.
   6: 4 Your I is like a morning cloud,
   6: 6 I desire steadfast I and not sacrifice,
   9:15 I will I them no more; all their
  10:12 righteousness; reap steadfast I;
  11: 4 of human kindness, with bands of I.
  12: 6 return to your God, hold fast to I
  14: 4 heal their disloyalty; I will I them
Joel 2:13 and abounding in steadfast I,
Am 4: 5 so you I to do, O people of Israel!
   5:15 Hate evil and I good, and establish
Jnh 4: 2 and abounding in steadfast I,
Mic 3: 2 and I the evil, who tear the skin off
   6: 8 but to do justice, and to I kindness,
Zep 3:17 he will renew you in his I;
Zec 8:17 and I no false oath;
   8:19 therefore I truth and peace.
Mt 5:43 'You shall I your neighbor
   5:44 L your enemies and pray
   5:46 For if you I those who I you,
   6: 5 for they I to stand and pray in the
   6:24 either hate the one and I the other,
  19:19 shall I your neighbor as yourself."
  22:37 "'You shall I the Lord your God
  22:39 shall I your neighbor as yourself.'
  23: 6 They I to have the place of honor at
  24:12 the I of many will grow cold.
Mk 12:30 you shall I the Lord your God
  12:31 shall I your neighbor as yourself.'
  12:33 and 'to I him with all the heart, and
  12:33 'to I one's neighbor as oneself,'—
Lk 6:27 to you that listen, L your enemies,
   6:32 "If you I those who I you,
   6:32 For even sinners I those who I them.
   6:35 But I your enemies, do good,
   7:42 which of them will I him more?"
   7:47 hence she has shown great I.
  10:27 "You shall I the Lord your God
  11:42 and neglect justice and the I of God;
  11:43 For you I to have the seat of honor
  16:13 either hate the one and I the other,
  20:46 I to be greeted with respect in the
Jn 5:42 you do not have the I of God in you.
   8:42 were your Father, you would I me,
  11: 3 "Lord, he whom you I is ill."
  12:25 Those who I their life lose it,
  13:34 new commandment, that you I one
  13:34 you also should I one another.
  13:35 if you have I for one another."
  14:15 "If you I me, you will keep my
  14:21 and keep them are those who I me;
  14:21 me will be loved by my Father,
  14:21 I them and reveal myself to them."

  14:23 who I me will keep my word,
  14:23 and my Father will I them
  14:24 not I me does not keep my words;
  14:31 world may know that I I the Father.
  15: 9 so I have loved you; abide in my I.
  15:10 you will abide in my I,
  15:10 and abide in his I.
  15:12 you I one another as I have loved
  15:13 No one has greater I than this,
  15:17 so that you may I one another.
  15:19 the world would I you as its own.
  17:26 the I with which you have loved me
  21:15 do you I me more than these?"
  21:15 you know that I I you."
  21:16 "Simon son of John, do you I me?"
  21:16 you know that I I you."
  21:17 "Simon son of John, do you I me?"
  21:17 him the third time, "Do you I me?"
  21:17 you know that I I you.
Ro 5: 5 God's I has been poured into our
   5: 8 But God proves his I for us in that
   8:28 for good for those who I God,
   8:35 will separate us from the I of Christ?
   8:39 able to separate us from the I of God
  12: 9 Let I be genuine; hate what is evil,
  12:10 I one another with mutual affection;
  13: 8 anything, except to I one another;
  13: 9 "L your neighbor as yourself."
  13:10 L does no wrong to a neighbor;
  13:10 I is the fulfilling of the law.
  14:15 you are no longer walking in I.
  15:30 our Lord Jesus Christ and by the I of
1Co 2: 9 God has prepared for those who I
   4:21 or with I in a spirit of gentleness?
   8: 1 Knowledge puffs up, but I builds up.
  13: 1 and of angels, but do not have I,
  13: 2 remove mountains, but do not have I
  13: 3 but do not have I, I gain nothing.
  13: 4 L is patient; I is kind; I is not
         envious or boastful or arrogant
  13: 8 L never ends. But as for prophecies,
  13:13 faith, hope, and I abide, these three;
         and the greatest of these is I.
  14: 1 Pursue I and strive for the spiritual
  16:14 Let all that you do be done in I.
  16:22 anyone be accursed who has no I for
  16:24 My I be with all of you in Christ
2Co 2: 4 but to let you know the abundant I
   2: 8 urge you to reaffirm your I for him.
   5:14 For the I of Christ urges us on,
   6: 6 holiness of spirit, genuine I,
   8: 7 eagerness, and in our I for you—
   8: 8 of your I against the earnestness of
   8:24 show them the proof of your I and
  11:11 Because I do not I you?
  12:15 If I I you more, am I to be loved
  13:11 the God of I and peace will be with
  13:13 the Lord Jesus Christ, the I of God,
Gal 5: 6 is faith working through I.
   5:13 but through I become slaves to one
   5:14 shall I your neighbor as yourself."
   5:22 the fruit of the Spirit is I, joy,
Eph 1: 4 holy and blameless before him in I.
   1:15 and your I toward all the saints,
   2: 4 out of the great I with which he
   3:17 are being rooted and grounded in I.
   3:19 I of Christ that surpasses knowledge
   4: 2 bearing with one another in I,
   4:15 But speaking the truth in I,
   4:16 growth in building itself up in I.
   5: 2 in I, as Christ loved us and gave
   5:25 Husbands, I your wives,
   5:28 husbands should I their wives
   5:33 should I his wife as himself,
   6:23 whole community, and I with faith,
   6:24 with all who have an undying I
Php 1: 9 that your I may overflow more and
   1:16 These proclaim Christ out of I,
   2: 1 any consolation from I, any sharing
   2: 2 the same mind, having the same I,
   4: 1 whom I I and long for,
Col 1: 4 and of the I that you have for all

1: 8 known to us your l in the Spirit.
2: 2 to be encouraged and united in l,
3:14 Above all, clothe yourselves with l,
3:19 l your wives and never treat them
1Th 1: 3 labor of l and steadfastness of hope
3: 6 the good news of your faith and l.
3:12 abound in l for one another
3:12 just as we abound in l for you.
4: 9 concerning l of the brothers and
4: 9 by God to l one another;
4:10 you do l all the brothers and sisters
5: 8 put on the breastplate of faith and l,
5:13 esteem them very highly in l
2Th 1: 3 and the l of everyone of you
2:10 refused to l the truth and so be saved
3: 5 direct your hearts to the l of God
1Ti 1: 5 the aim of such instruction is l that
1:14 the faith and l that are in Christ
2:15 provided they continue in faith and l
4:12 example in speech and conduct, in l,
6:10 For the l of money is a root of all
    kinds of evil,
6:11 righteousness, godliness, faith, l,
2Ti 1: 7 and of l and of self-discipline.
1:13 in the faith and l that are in Christ
2:22 and pursue righteousness, faith, l,
3:10 my patience, my l, my steadfastness,
4:10 in l with this present world,
Tit 2: 2 in faith, in l, and in endurance.
2: 4 the young women to l their
    husbands, to l their children,
3:15 Greet those who l us in the faith.
Phm 1: 5 of your l for all the saints and your
1: 7 and encouragement from your l,
1: 9 appeal to you on the basis of l—
Heb 6:10 the l that you showed for his sake
10:24 provoke one another to l and good
13: 1 Let mutual l continue.
13: 5 your lives free from the l of money,
Jas 1:12 has promised to those who l him.
2: 5 he has promised to those who l him?
2: 8 shall l your neighbor as yourself."
1Pe 1: 8 you have not seen him, you l him;
1:22 so that you have genuine mutual l, l
    one another deeply from the heart.
2:17 L the family of believers.
3: 8 of spirit, sympathy, l for one another
4: 8 maintain constant l for one another,
    for l covers a multitude of sins.
5:14 Greet one another with a kiss of l.
2Pe 1: 7 and mutual affection with l.
1Jn 2: 5 the l of God has reached perfection.
2:15 not l the world or the things in the
2:15 The l of the Father is not in those
    who l the world;
3: 1 See what the l the Father has given us,
3:10 do not l their brothers and sisters.
3:11 that we should l one another.
3:14 from death to life because we l one
3:14 Whoever does not l abides in death.
3:16 We know l by this, that he laid
3:17 How does God's l abide in anyone
3:18 Little children, let us l, not in word
3:23 Son Jesus Christ and l one another,
4: 7 Beloved, let us l one another,
    because l is from God;
4: 8 Whoever does not l does not know
    God, for God is l.
4: 9 God's l was revealed among us in
4:10 In this is l, not that we loved God
4:11 we also ought to l one another.
4:12 if we l one another, God lives in us,
    and his l is perfected in us.
4:16 believe the l that God has for us.
4:16 God is l, and those who abide in l
    abide in God,
4:17 L has been perfected among us in
4:18 There is no fear in l, but perfect l
    casts out fear;
4:18 fears has not reached perfection in l.
4:19 We l because he first loved us.
4:20 Those who say, "I l God,"

4:20 for those who do not l a brother
4:20 cannot l God whom they have not
4:21 who l God must l their brothers and
5: 2 we l the children of God, when we l
    God and obey his commandments.
5: 3 For the l of God is this,
2Jn 1: 1 whom I l in the truth,
1: 3 the Father's Son, in truth and l.
1: 5 the beginning, let us l one another.
1: 6 And this is l, that we walk according
3Jn 1: 1 beloved Gaius, whom I l in truth.
1: 6 they have testified to your l before
Jude 1: 2 May mercy, peace, and l be yours
1:21 keep yourselves in the l of God;
Rev 2: 4 abandoned the l you had at first.
2:19 your l, faith, service, and patient
3:19 and discipline those whom I l.
Tob 4:13 So now, my son, l your kindred,
13:10 and l all those within you who are
13:14 Happy are those who l you,
14: 7 who sincerely l God will rejoice,
AdE 13:12 not in insolence or pride or for any l
Wis 1: 1 L righteousness, you rulers of the
3: 9 the faithful will abide with him in l,
6:12 easily discerned by those who l her,
6:17 concern for instruction is l of her,
6:18 l of her is the keeping of her laws,
11:24 For you l all things that exist,
11:26 O Lord, you who l the living.
Sir Pr: 1 those who l learning might make
1:10 lavished her upon those who l him.
2:15 and those who l him walk his ways.
2:16 who l him are filled with his law.
4:10 will l you more than does your
4:14 the Lord loves those who l her.
6:33 If you l to listen you will gain
7:21 Let your soul l intelligent slaves;
7:30 With all your might l your Maker.
27:17 L your friend and keep faith with
34:19 of the Lord are on those who l him,
40:20 the l of friends is better than either.
48:11 and were adorned with your l!
Bel 1:38 have not forsaken those who l you."
1Mc 4:33 with the sword of those who l you,
2Mc 6:20 even for the natural l of life.
3Mc 2:10 because you l the house of Israel,
2Es 5:33 do you l him more than his Maker
5:40 of the l that I have promised to my
8:30 but l those who have always put
8:47 short of being able to l my creation
    more than I l it.
4Mc 2:11 It is superior to l for one's wife,
2:12 precedence over l for children,
13:26 make their brotherly l more fervent
14: 1 mastered the emotions of brotherly l
14:13 is a mother's l for her children,
14:14 a sympathy and parental l for their
14:17 around them in the anguish of l,
15: 4 of parents who l their children?
15: 6 in herself tender l toward them,
15:11 with them out of l for her children,
15:13 nature and affection of parental l,
15:23 for the time, her parental l.
15:25 nature, family, parental l,
16: 3 as was her innate parental l,

LOVE OF *GOD Ps 52:8; Lk 11:42; Jn 5:42;
Ro 8:39; 2Co 13:13; 2Th 3:5; 1Jn 2:5; 5:3;
Jude 1:21

LOVE ONE ANOTHER Jn 13:34, 34;
15:12, 17; Ro 12:10; 13:8; 1Th 4:9; 1Pe 1:22;
1Jn 3:11, 14, 23; 4:7, 11, 12; 2Jn 1:5

LOVE ONE'S/YOUR NEIGHBOR Lev
19:18; Mt 5:43; 19:19; 22:39; Mk 12:31, 33;
Ro 13:9; Gal 5:14; Jas 2:8

LOVE THE *LORD Mt 22:37; Mk 12:30; Lk
10:27

LOVE THE †LORD Dt 6:5; 11:1; 13:3;
30:6; Jos 22:5; 23:11; Ps 31:23; 116:1

STEADFAST LOVE Ge 24:12, 14, 27;
32:10; 39:21; Ex 15:13; 20:6; 34:6, 7; Nu
14:18, 19; Dt 5:10; 2Sa 2:6; 7:15; 15:20;

22:51; 1Ki 3:6, 6; 8:23; 1Ch 16:34, 41; 17:13;
2Ch 1:8; 5:13; 6:14, 42; 7:3, 6; 20:21; Ezr
3:11; 7:28; 9:9; Ne 1:5; 9:17, 32; 13:22; Job
10:12; Ps 5:7; 6:4; 13:5; 17:7; 18:50; 21:7;
25:6, 7, 10; 26:3; 31:7, 16, 21; 32:10; 33:5, 18,
22; 36:5, 7, 10; 40:10, 11; 42:8; 44:26; 48:9;
51:1; 52:8; 57:3, 10; 59:10, 16, 17; 61:7;
62:12; 63:3; 66:20; 69:13, 16; 77:8; 85:7, 10;
86:5, 13, 15; 88:11; 89:1, 2, 14, 24, 28, 33, 49;
90:14; 92:2; 94:18; 98:3; 100:5; 103:4, 8, 11,
17; 106:1, 7, 45; 107:1, 8, 15, 21, 31, 43;
108:4; 109:21, 26; 115:1; 117:2; 118:1, 2, 3, 4,
29; 119:41, 64, 76, 88, 124, 149, 159; 130:7;
136:1, 2, 3, 4, 5, 6, 7, 8, 9, 10, 11, 12, 13, 14,
15, 16, 17, 18, 19, 20, 21, 22, 23, 24, 25, 26;
138:2, 8; 143:8, 12; 145:8; 147:11; Isa 16:5;
54:10; 63:7; Jer 9:24; 16:5; 32:18; 33:11; La
3:22, 32; Da 9:4; Hos 2:19; 6:6; 10:12; Joel
2:13; Jnh 4:2

LOVE-FEASTS* → FEAST, LOVE
Jude 1:12 These are blemishes on your l,

LOVE-SONG* → LOVE, SING
Isa 5: 1 my l concerning his vineyard:

LOVED* → LOVE
Ge 24:67 she became his wife; and he l her.
25:28 Isaac l Esau, because he was fond
    of game; but Rebekah l Jacob.
27:14 savory food, such as his father l.
29:18 Jacob l Rachel; so he said,
29:30 and he l Rachel more than Leah.
34: 3 he l the girl, and spoke tenderly to
37: 3 Israel l Joseph more than any other
37: 4 their father l him more than all his
Dt 4:37 And because he l your ancestors,
7: 8 the LORD l you and kept the oath
21:15 one of them l and the other disliked,
21:15 the l and the disliked have borne
21:16 the l as the firstborn in preference
23: 5 because the LORD your God l you.)
1Sa 1: 5 because he l her,
16:21 Saul l him greatly,
18: 1 and Jonathan l him as his own soul.
18: 3 because he l him as his own soul.
18:16 But all Israel and Judah l David;
18:20 Saul's daughter Michal l David.
18:28 that Saul's daughter Michal l him,
20:17 for he l him as he l his own life.
2Sa 12:24 Solomon. The LORD l him,
13:21 he l him, for he was his firstborn.
1Ki 3: 3 Solomon l the LORD, walking in the
10: 9 Because the LORD l Israel forever,
11: 1 Solomon l many foreign women
2Ch 9: 8 Because your God l Israel
11:21 Rehoboam l Maacah daughter
26:10 in the fertile lands, for he l the soil.
Est 2:17 the king l Esther more than all the
Job 19:19 whom I l have turned against me.
Ps 109:17 He l to curse; let curses come on
SS 7: 6 fair and pleasant you are, O l one,
Isa 57: 8 with them, you have l their bed,
Jer 2:25 It is hopeless, for I have l strangers,
8: 2 which they have l and served,
14:10 Truly they have l to wander,
31: 3 have l you with an everlasting love;
Eze 16:37 those you l and all those you hated;
Hos 9: 1 You have l a prostitute's pay
9:10 detestable like the thing they l.
10:11 was a trained heifer that l to thresh,
11: 1 When Israel was a child, I l him,
Mic 7: 5 have no confidence in a l one;
Mal 1: 2 I have l you, says the LORD.
1: 2 But you say, "How have you l us?"
1: 2 Yet I have l Jacob
Mk 10:21 Jesus, looking at him, l him and
Jn 3:16 God so l the world that he gave his
    only Son,
3:19 people l darkness rather than light
11: 5 Jesus l Martha and her sister and
11:36 the Jews said, "See how he l him!"

12:43 I human glory more than the glory
13: 1 Having I his own who were in the
world, he I them to the end.
13:23 One of his disciples—the one
whom Jesus I—
13:34 Just as I have I you,
14:21 who love me will be I by my Father,
14:28 If you I me, you would rejoice that
15: 9 the Father has I me, so I have I you;
15:12 love one another as I have I you.
16:27 you have I me and have believed
17:23 have I them even as you have I me.
17:24 have given me because you I me
17:26 love with which you have I me may
19:26 disciple whom he I standing beside
20: 2 the one whom Jesus I, and said to
21: 7 disciple whom Jesus I said to Peter,
21:20 disciple whom Jesus I following
Ro 8:37 conquerors through him who I us.
9:13 I Jacob, but I have hated Esau."
2Co 12:15 If I love you more, am I to be I less?
Gal 2:20 who I me and gave himself for me.
Eph 2: 4 the great love with which he I us
5: 2 Christ I us and gave himself up for
5:25 just as Christ I the church and gave
2Th 2:16 who I us and through grace gave us
Heb 1: 9 You have I righteousness and hated
2Pe 2:15 who I the wages of doing wrong,
1Jn 4:10 not that we I God but that he I us
4:11 Beloved, since God I us so much,
4:19 We love because he first I us.
Rev 3: 9 and they will learn that I have I you.
Tob 6:18 father's lineage, he I her very much,
AdE 2:17 king I Esther and she found favor
14: 2 every part that she I to adorn she
Wis 4:10 some who pleased God and were I
7:10 I I her more than health and beauty,
8: 2 I I her and sought her from my
16:26 whom you I, O Lord, might learn
Sir 3:17 you will be I by those whom God
7:35 for such deeds you will be I.
15:13 are not I by those who fear him.
47: 8 all his heart, and he I his Maker.
47:16 you were I for your peaceful reign.
47:22 destroy the family line of him who I
Bar 3:36 Jacob and to Israel, whom he I.
2Mc 14:37 a man who I his compatriots
2Es 3:14 you I him, and to him alone you
4:23 people whom you I has been given
5:27 to this people, whom you have I,
11:42 the truth, and have I liars;
4Mc 13:24 they I one another all the more.
15: 3 She I religion more, the religion
15: 6 than any other mother, I her children
15:10 and I their brothers and their mother

LOVELIEST* → LOVELY

Jer 6: 2 daughter Zion to the I pasture.

LOVELINESS* → LOVELY

2Es 10:50 and the I of her beauty.

LOVELY* → LOVELIEST, LOVELINESS

Ge 29:17 Leah's eyes were I, and Rachel was
49:21 a doe let loose that bears I fawns.
2Sa 1:23 Saul and Jonathan, beloved and I!
Ps 84: 1 I is your dwelling place, O LORD of
Pr 5:19 a I deer, a graceful doe.
SS 1:16 are beautiful, my beloved, truly I.
2:14 voice is sweet, and your face is I.
4: 3 crimson thread, and your mouth is I.
Hos 9:13 young palm planted in a I meadow,
Jdt 8: 7 and was very I to behold.
1Es 4:18 woman I in appearance and beauty,

LOVER* → LOVE

Ps 11: 5 and his soul hates the I of violence.
99: 4 Mighty King, I of justice,
Ecc 5:10 I of money will not be satisfied with
5:10 nor the I of wealth, with gain.
Isa 47: 8 hear this, you I of pleasures,
Hos 3: 1 love a woman who has a I and is an
1Ti 3: 3 quarrelsome, and not a I of money.

Tit 1: 8 a I of goodness, prudent, upright,
4Mc 2: 8 even though a I of money,

LOVERS* → LOVE

Jer 2:33 you direct your course to seek I!
3: 1 have played the whore with many I;
3: 2 waysides you have sat waiting for I,
4:30 Your I despise you; they seek your
22:20 for all your I are crushed.
22:22 and your I shall go into captivity;
30:14 All your I have forgotten you;
La 1: 2 all her I she has no one to comfort
1:19 I called to my I but they deceived
Eze 16:33 but you gave your gifts to all your I,
16:36 in your whoring with your I,
16:37 I will gather all your I,
23: 5 she lusted after her I the Assyrians,
23: 9 delivered her into the hands of her I,
23:22 your I from whom you turned
Hos 2: 5 For she said, "I will go after my I;
2: 7 She shall pursue her I, but not
2:10 her shame in the sight of her I,
2:12 my pay, which my I have given me.
2:13 and went after her I, and forgot me,
8: 9 Ephraim has bargained for I.
Lk 16:14 Pharisees, who were I of money,
2Ti 3: 2 For people will be I of themselves,
I of money,
3: 4 I of pleasure rather than I of God,
Wis 15: 9 L of evil things and fit for such
Sir Pr: 1 also as I of learning to be able through
26:22 as a tower of death to her I.
2Es 15:47 to please and glory in your I,
15:51 you cannot receive your mighty I.

LOVES* → LOVE

Ge 44:20 children, and his father I him.'
Dt 10:18 and who I the strangers,
15:16 he I you and your household,
Ru 4:15 for your daughter-in-law who I you,
2Ch 2:11 the LORD I his people he has made
Ps 11: 7 he I righteous deeds; the upright
33: 5 He I righteousness and justice;
37:28 For the LORD I justice;
47: 4 the pride of Jacob whom he I.
78:68 Mount Zion, which he I.
87: 2 the LORD I the gates of Zion more
97:10 The LORD I those who hate evil;
119:140 well tried, and your servant I it.
146: 8 the LORD I the righteous.
Pr 3:12 for the LORD reproves the one he I,
12: 1 Whoever I discipline I knowledge,
13: 1 A wise child I discipline,
15: 9 but he I the one who pursues
16:13 he I those who speak what is right.
17:17 A friend I at all times,
17:19 One who I transgression I strife;
21:17 Whoever I pleasure will suffer want;
21:17 I wine and oil will not be rich.
29: 3 who I wisdom makes a parent glad,
SS 1: 7 Tell me, you whom my soul I,
3: 1 night I sought him whom my soul I;
3: 2 I will seek him whom my soul I."
3: 3 you seen him whom my soul I?"
3: 4 when I found him whom my soul I.
Isa 1:23 I a bribe and runs after gifts.
48:14 The LORD I him; he shall perform
Hos 3: 1 as the LORD I the people of Israel,
3: 1 false balances, he I to oppress.
Mal 2:11 sanctuary of the LORD, which he I,
Mt 10:37 Whoever I father or mother more
10:37 whoever I son or daughter more
Lk 7: 5 for he I our people, and it is he who
7:47 to whom little is forgiven, I little."
Jn 3:35 The Father I the Son and has placed
5:20 The Father I the Son and shows him
10:17 For this reason the Father I me,
16:27 for the Father himself I you,
Ro 13: 8 who I another has fulfilled the law.
1Co 8: 3 anyone who I God is known by him.
2Co 9: 7 for God I a cheerful giver.
Eph 5:28 He who I his wife I himself.

Heb 12: 6 Lord disciplines those whom he I,
1Jn 2:10 Whoever I a brother or sister lives in
4: 7 who I is born of God and knows
5: 1 who I the parent I the child.
Rev 1: 5 who I us and freed us from our sins
22:15 who I and practices falsehood.
AdE 6: 9 the person whom the king I and
Wis 7:28 for God I nothing so much as
8: 3 and the Lord of all I her.
8: 7 if anyone I righteousness, her labors
Sir 3:26 whoever I danger will perish in it.
4:12 Whoever I her I life,
4:14 the Lord I those who love her.
13:15 Every creature I its like,
30: 1 who I his son will whip him often,
31: 5 One who I gold will not be justified;
LtJ 6: 9 might for a girl who I ornaments.
2Mc 15:14 a man who I the family of Israel
1Es 4:24 he brings it back to the woman he I.
4:25 man I his wife more than his father

LOVING* → LOVE

Dt 11:13 I the LORD your God, and serving
11:22 I the LORD your God, walking in all
19: 9 I the LORD your God and walking
30:16 by I the LORD your God, walking in
30:20 I the LORD your God, obeying him,
Isa 56:10 dreaming, lying down, I to slumber.
Tit 3: 4 and I kindness of God our Savior
Wis 7:22 distinct, invulnerable, I the good,

LOW → LOWER, LOWERED, LOWEST, LOWING, LOWLY

Ps 116: 6 when I was brought I,
136:23 who remembered us in our I estate,
Isa 2:11 eyes of people shall be brought I,
40: 4 every mountain and hill be made I;
Lk 3: 5 mountain and hill shall be made I,
Jas 1:10 and the rich in being brought I,

LOWER → LOW

Dt 28:43 while you shall descend I and I.
Ps 8: 5 have made them a little I than God,
Eph 4: 9 had also descended into the I parts
Heb 2: 7 made them for a little while I than

LOWERED → LOW

Ex 17:11 he I his hand, Amalek prevailed.
Ac 10:11 being I to the ground by its four

LOWEST → LOW

Ge 9:25 I of slaves shall he be to his brothers
Lk 14:10 go and sit down at the I place,

LOWING → LOW

1Sa 15:14 and the I of cattle that I hear?"

LOWLY → LOW

Job 5:11 he sets on high those who are I,
Ps 138: 6 the LORD is high, he regards the I;
Pr 16:19 It is better to be of a I spirit
29:23 who is I in spirit will obtain honor.
Lk 1:52 their thrones, and lifted up the I;
Ro 12:16 but associate with the I;
Jdt 9:11 But you are the God of the I,

LOYAL → LOYALTY

2Sa 22:26 With the I you show yourself I;
Da 11:32 who are I to their God
Sir 26: 2 A I wife brings joy to her husband,

LOYALTY → LOYAL

Dt 7: 9 God who maintains covenant I
Ru 3:10 this last instance of your I
Ps 101: 1 I will sing of I and of justice;
Pr 16: 6 I and faithfulness iniquity is atoned
19:22 What is desirable in a person is I,
Hos 4: 1 There is no faithfulness or I,

LUKE*

Associate of Paul (Col 4:14; 2Ti 4:11; Phm 24).

LUKEWARM* → WARM

Rev 3:16 because you are I, and neither cold

LUMP
Ro   9:21 of the same l one object for special

LURE
Mt 13:22 and the l of wealth choke the word,

LURK
Ps   56: 6 they l, they watch my steps.
Hos 13: 7 like a leopard I will l beside the way

LUST → LUSTED, LUSTFUL, LUSTS
Isa 57: 5 you that burn with l among the oaks,
Eze 23:17 and they defiled her with their l;
Mt   5:28 looks at a woman with l has already
2Pe   1: 4 that is in the world because of l,
Sir   23: 6 neither gluttony nor l overcome me,
Sus   1: 8 and they began to l for her.

LUSTED → LUST
Eze 23: 5 she l after her lovers the Assyrians,

LUSTFUL → LUST
Eze 16:26 your l neighbors, multiplying your
1Th 4: 5 not with l passion, like the Gentiles

LUSTS → LUST
Ro   1:24 gave them up in the l of their hearts
Eph 4:22 old self, corrupt and deluded by its l
2Pe   3: 3 scoffing and indulging their own l

LUTE* → LUTES
Ps   92: 3 to the music of the l and the harp,
   150: 3 praise him with l and harp!

LUTES* → LUTE
1Mc 4:54 with songs and harps and l

LUXURIOUSLY* → LUXURY
Rev 18: 7 As she glorified herself and lived l,

LUXURY → LUXURIOUSLY
Pr   19:10 It is not fitting for a fool to live in l,
Jas   5: 5 You have lived on the earth in l and
Rev 18: 9 and lived in l with her,
Sir 18:32 Do not revel in great l,

LUZ → =BETHEL
Ge 28:19 name of the city was L at the first.
     48: 3 God Almighty appeared to me at L

LYDDA
Ac   9:32 also to the saints living in L.

LYDIA → LYDIA'S
Ac 16:14 named L, a worshiper of God,

LYDIA'S* → LYDIA
Ac 16:40 the prison they went to L home;

LYING → LIE
Ru   3: 8 turned over, and there, l at his feet,
1Sa 3: 3 Samuel was l down in the temple of
     5: 4 were l cut off upon the threshold;
   26: 5 Saul was l within the encampment,
1Ki 22:23 a l spirit in the mouth of all these
Ps 31:18 the l lips be stilled that speak
   120: 2 from l lips, from a deceitful tongue.
Pr   6:17 a l tongue, and hands that shed
  12:19 but a l tongue lasts only a moment.
  12:22 L lips are an abomination to the
  21: 6 getting of treasures by a l tongue
  26:28 A l tongue hates its victims,
Eze 13: 9 false visions and utter l divinations;
Hos 4: 2 Swearing, l, and murder,
Mt   8:14 mother-in-law l in bed with a fever;
Mk 7:30 home, found the child l on the bed,
Lk   2:12 wrapped in bands of cloth and l in
Jn   5: 6 When Jesus saw him l there and
  20: 6 He saw the linen wrappings l there,
Ro   9: 1 the truth in Christ—I am not l;
Wis 1:11 and a l mouth destroys the soul.

LYRE → LYRES
Ge   4:21 ancestor of all those who play the l
1Sa 18:10 while David was playing the l,
Ps 33: 2 Praise the LORD with the l;

    57: 8 Awake, O harp and l! I will awake
Da   3: 5 pipe, l, trigon, harp, drum,
Pm 151: 2 my fingers fashioned a l.

LYRES → LYRE
1Ch 15:16 on harps and l and cymbals,
   25: 6 l for the service of the house of God
Ne 12:27 with cymbals, harps, and l.

LYSIAS
Ac 23:26 "Claudius L to his Excellency
1Mc 3:32 He left L, a distinguished man

LYSTRA
Ac 14: 8 In L there was a man sitting who
2Ti 3:11 to me in Antioch, Iconium, and L.

M

MACCABEUS → JUDAS
1Mc 2: 4 Judas called M,
   2:66 Judas M has been a mighty warrior

MACEDONIA
Ac 16: 9 a man of M pleading with him and
  18: 5 Silas and Timothy arrived from M,
  20: 3 so he decided to return through M.

MACHPELAH
Ge 23: 9 he may give me the cave of M,
  49:30 in the field at M,
  50:13 in the cave of the field at M,

MAD → MADMEN, MADNESS
Dt 28:34 driven m by the sight that your eyes
Jer 51: 7 and so the nations went m.

MADE → MAKE
Ge   1: 7 So God m the dome and separated
   1:16 God m the two great lights—
   1:25 God m the wild animals of the earth
   1:31 God saw everything that he had m,
   2:22 he m into a woman and brought her
   3:21 the LORD God m garments of skins
   6: 6 was sorry that he had m humankind
   9: 6 his own image God m humankind.
  15:18 the LORD m a covenant with Abram,
  24:21 LORD had m his journey successful.
  45: 9 God has m me lord of all Egypt;
Ex   1:14 m their lives bitter with hard service
   2:14 "Who m you a ruler and judge over
   7: 1 I have m you like God to Pharaoh,
  15:25 the LORD m for them a statute and
  20:11 For in six days the LORD m heaven
  24: 8 of the covenant that the LORD has m
  36: 8 the workers m the tabernacle with
  37: 1 Bezalel m the ark of acacia wood;
  37:10 He also m the table of acacia wood,
  37:17 also m the lampstand of pure gold.
  37:25 He m the altar of incense of acacia
  37:29 He m the holy anointing oil also,
  38: 9 He m the court; for the south side
  39: 1 m the sacred vestments for Aaron;
Nu 14:36 m all the congregation complain
  21: 2 Then Israel m a vow to the LORD
  21: 9 So Moses m a serpent of bronze,
Dt   1:28 Our kindred have m our hearts melt
   5: 2 LORD our God m a covenant with us
  32: 6 who m you and established you?
  32:21 m me jealous with what is no god,
Jos 24:25 So Joshua m a covenant with the
Jdg 11:30 Jephthah m a vow to the LORD,
1Sa 1:11 She m this vow: "O LORD of hosts,
  15:11 "I regret that I m Saul king,
  20:16 Thus Jonathan m a covenant with
2Sa 23: 5 he has m with me an everlasting
1Ki 12:28 and m two calves of gold.
2Ki 17:38 forget the covenant that I have m
  18: 4 bronze serpent that Moses had m,
  19:15 you have m heaven and earth.

2Ch 2:12 LORD God of Israel, who m heaven
   3:10 he m two carved cherubim
   4:19 So Solomon m all the things that
Ne   9: 6 you have m heaven, the heaven of
   9:10 You m a name for yourself,
Job 7:20 Why have you m me your target?
  31: 1 "I have m a covenant with my eyes;
  33: 4 The spirit of God has m me,
Ps   8: 5 have m them a little lower than God
  33: 6 of the LORD the heavens were m,
  73:28 I have m the Lord GOD my refuge,
  95: 5 The sea is his, for he m it, and the
  96: 5 but the LORD m the heavens.
  98: 2 The LORD has m known his victory;
  100: 3 It is he that m us, and we are his;
  118:24 This is the day that the LORD has m;
  136: 7 who m the great lights,
  139:14 I am fearfully and wonderfully m.
Pr   8:26 he had not yet m earth and fields,
Ecc 3:11 m everything suitable for its time;
   7:13 straight what he has m crooked?
Isa 43: 7 whom I formed and m."
  45:12 I m the earth, and created
  53:12 m intercession for the transgressors.
  66: 2 All these things my hand has m,
Jer 10:12 he who m the earth by his power,
  27: 5 outstretched arm have m the earth,
  31:32 that I m with their ancestors when I
  33: 2 says the LORD who m the earth,
  51:15 he who m the earth by his power,
Eze 3:17 have m you a sentinel for the house
  33: 7 have m a sentinel for the house of
Da   3: 1 Nebuchadnezzar m a golden statue
Am   5: 8 one who m the Pleiades and Orion,
Jnh 1: 9 who m the sea and the dry land."
Mt   5:33 carry out the vows you have m to
Mk   2:27 "The sabbath was m for humankind,
  15: 5 But Jesus m no further reply,
Lk 17:19 your faith has m you well."
  19:46 but you have m it a den of robbers."
Jn   1:18 who has m him known.
   9: 6 and m mud with the saliva and
Ac   2:36 that God has m him both Lord and
  10:15 time, "What God has m clean,
  17:24 The God who m the world and
1Co 1:20 Has not God m foolish the wisdom
  15:22 so all will be m alive in Christ.
2Co 3: 6 has m us competent to be ministers
   5:21 For our sake he m him to be sin
  12: 9 for power is m perfect in weakness.
Eph 2: 5 m us alive together with Christ—
   2:14 in his flesh he has m both groups
Heb 2: 7 You have m them for a little while
   8: 9 not like the covenant that I m with
Jas   3: 9 we curse those who are m in the
Rev 5:10 you have m them to be a kingdom
  14: 7 and worship him who m heaven
  19: 7 and his bride has m herself ready;
Tob 8: 6 You m Adam, and for him you m
        his wife Eve as a helper and support
Wis 14: 8 the idol m with hands is accursed,
Sir 43:33 For the Lord has m all things,
1Mc 4:49 They m new holy vessels,

MADMEN → MAD, MAN
1Sa 21:15 Do I lack m, that you have brought

MADNESS → MAD
Dt 28:28 The LORD will afflict you with m,
Ecc 7:25 is folly and that foolishness is m,
   9: 3 m is in their hearts while they live,
2Pe 2:16 and restrained the prophet's m.

MAGDALENE
Mt 27:56 Among them were Mary M,
Mk 16: 1 the sabbath was over, Mary M,
Lk   8: 2 Mary, called M, from whom seven
Jn 20: 1 Mary M came to the tomb and saw

MAGIC → MAGICIAN, MAGICIANS
Ac   8:11 he had amazed them with his m.

MAGICIAN → MAGIC
Da 2:10 asked such a thing of any **m** or
Ac 13: 6 a certain **m**, a Jewish false prophet,

MAGICIANS → MAGIC
Ge 41: 8 and called for all the **m** of Egypt
Ex 7:11 and they also, the **m** of Egypt,
7:22 the **m** of Egypt did the same by their
8: 7 **m** did the same by their secret arts,
8:18 The **m** tried to produce gnats by
9:11 The **m** could not stand before Moses
9:11 boils afflicted the **m** as well as all
Da 2: 2 So the king commanded that the **m**,
5:11 him chief of the **m**, enchanters,

MAGNIFIED → MAGNIFY
2Sa 7:26 Thus your name will be **m** forever

MAGNIFIES* → MAGNIFY
Lk 1:46 Mary said, "My soul **m** the Lord,

MAGNIFY → MAGNIFIED, MAGNIFIES
Ps 34: 3 O **m** the LORD with me,

MAGOG
Eze 38: 2 face toward Gog, of the land of **M**,
39: 6 **M** and on those who live securely
Rev 20: 8 Gog and **M**, in order to gather them

MAHANAIM
Ge 32: 2 So he called that place **M**.
2Sa 17:24 Then David came to **M**,

MAHER-SHALAL-HASH-BAZ
Isa 8: 3 the LORD said to me, Name him **M**;

MAHLON
Ru 1: 5 both **M** and Chilion also died,

MAID → MAIDS
Ps 123: 2 as the eyes of a **m** to the hand of
Isa 24: 2 as with the **m**, so with her mistress;

MAIDENS
SS 1: 3 therefore the **m** love you.
2: 2 so is my love among **m**.

MAIDS → MAID
Ge 24:61 Then Rebekah and her **m** rose up,
1Sa 25:42 her five **m** attended her.
Est 2: 9 advanced her and her **m** to the best

MAIMED
Mk 9:43 better for you to enter life **m** than

MAINTAIN → MAINTAINS
Lev 26: 9 and I will **m** my covenant with you.
Ru 4: 5 to **m** the dead man's name on his
Ps 82: 3 the right of the lowly and the
Isa 56: 1 Thus says the LORD: **M** justice,
Eph 4: 3 to **m** the unity of the Spirit in

MAINTAINS → MAINTAIN
Dt 7: 9 the faithful God who **m** covenant
Ps 140:12 the cause of the needy,

MAJESTIC → MAJESTY
Ex 15:11 Who is like you, **m** in holiness,
Job 37: 4 he thunders with his **m** voice and
Ps 8: 1 how **m** is your name in all the earth!
8: 9 how **m** is your name in all the earth!
76: 4 **m** than the everlasting mountains.
93: 4 **m** on high is the LORD!
Isa 30:30 the LORD will cause his **m** voice to
2Pe 1:17 conveyed to him by the **M** Glory,

MAJESTY → MAJESTIC
Ex 15: 7 In the greatness of your **m** you
1Ch 16:27 Honor and **m** are before him;
29:11 the glory, the victory, and the **m**;
Est 1: 4 the splendor and pomp of his **m** for
Job 37:22 around God is awesome **m**,
40:10 "Deck yourself with **m** and dignity;
Ps 21: 5 splendor and **m** you bestow on him.
45: 3 O mighty one, in your glory and **m**.
45: 4 In your **m** ride on victoriously for

68:34 to God, whose **m** is over Israel;
93: 1 The LORD is king, he is robed in **m**;
96: 6 Honor and **m** are before him;
104: 1 You are clothed with honor and **m**,
145: 5 On the glorious splendor of your **m**,
Isa 2:10 and from the glory of his **m**.
2:19 and from the glory of his **m**,
2:21 and from the glory of his **m**,
24:14 the west over the **m** of the LORD.
26:10 and do not see the **m** of the LORD.
35: 2 of the LORD, the **m** of our God.
53: 2 or **m** that we should look at him,
Da 4:30 power and for my glorious **m**?"
Mic 5: 4 in the **m** of the name of the LORD
Ac 19:27 be deprived of her **m** that brought
Heb 1: 3 sat down at the right hand of the **M**
8: 1 right hand of the throne of the **M** in
2Pe 1:16 we had been eyewitnesses of his **m**.
Jude 1:25 Jesus Christ our Lord, be glory, **m**,

MAJORITY
Ex 23: 2 shall not follow a **m** in wrongdoing;

MAKE → MADE, MAKER, MAKERS, MAKES, MAKING, MERRYMAKERS, MERRYMAKING, MISCHIEF-MAKER, MONEY-MAKING, TENTMAKERS
Ge 1:26 "Let us **m** humankind in our image,
2:18 will **m** him a helper as his partner."
6:14 **M** yourself an ark of cypress wood;
11: 4 and let us **m** a name for ourselves;
12: 2 I will **m** of you a great nation,
13:16 I will **m** your offspring like the dust
17: 6 I will **m** you exceedingly fruitful;
17: 6 and I will **m** nations of you,
21:18 for I will **m** a great nation of him."
22:17 will **m** your offspring as numerous
24:40 and **m** your way successful.
26: 4 will **m** your offspring as numerous
28: 3 bless you and **m** you fruitful
46: 3 for I will **m** of you a great nation
48: 4 to **m** you fruitful and increase your
Ex 6: 3 I did not **m** myself known to them.
9: 4 But the LORD will **m** a distinction
20: 4 You shall not **m** for yourself an idol,
20:23 You shall not **m** gods of silver
25: 9 of all its furniture, so you shall **m** it.
25:10 They shall **m** an ark of acacia wood;
25:23 You shall **m** a table of acacia wood,
25:31 shall **m** a lampstand of pure gold.
25:40 see that you **m** them according to
28: 2 You shall **m** sacred vestments for
32: 1 "Come, **m** gods for us, who shall go
32:10 and of you I will **m** a great nation."
Nu 6:25 LORD **m** his face to shine upon you,
21: 8 to Moses, "**M** a poisonous serpent,
Dt 7: 2 **M** no covenant with them
30: 9 your God will **m** you abundantly
Jos 9: 7 how can we **m** a treaty with you?"
2Sa 7: 9 and I will **m** for you a great name,
Ezr 10: 3 let us **m** a covenant with our God
10:11 **m** confession to the LORD the God
Job 7:17 that you **m** so much of them,
Ps 4: 8 O LORD, **m** me lie down in safety,
27: 6 sing and **m** melody to the LORD.
108: 1 I will sing and **m** melody.
110: 1 I **m** your enemies your footstool."
115: 8 Those who **m** them are like them;
119:165 nothing can **m** them stumble.
Pr 3: 6 and he will **m** straight your paths.
Ecc 5: 4 you **m** a vow to God, do not delay
Isa 6:10 **M** the mind of this people dull,
14:14 I will **m** myself like the Most High."
29:16 of its maker, "He did not **m** me";
40: 3 **m** straight in the desert a highway
44: 9 All who **m** idols are nothing,
55: 3 I will **m** with you an everlasting
61: 8 I will **m** an everlasting covenant
66:22 and the new earth, which I will **m**,
Jer 10:11 not **m** the heavens and the earth
16:20 Can mortals **m** for themselves gods?
30:10 and no one shall **m** him afraid.

31:31 when I will **m** a new covenant with
32:40 I will **m** an everlasting covenant
Eze 34:25 **m** with them a covenant of peace
37:26 I will **m** a covenant of peace with
39: 7 My holy name I will **m** known
Hos 2:18 I will **m** for you a covenant on that
Mt 3: 3 of the Lord, **m** his paths straight.'"
27:65 go, **m** it as secure as you can."
28:19 and **m** disciples of all nations,
Mk 1:17 and I will **m** you fish for people."
Lk 1:17 to **m** ready a people prepared for
Jn 1:23 '**M** straight the way of the Lord,'"
Ac 2:35 I **m** your enemies your footstool."'
Ro 14: 4 for the Lord is able to **m** them stand.
2Co 5: 9 we **m** it our aim to please him.
Heb 1:13 until I **m** your enemies a footstool
2:17 to **m** a sacrifice of atonement for
4:11 **m** every effort to enter that rest,
2Pe 1: 5 you must **m** every effort to support
1Jn 1:10 have not sinned, we **m** him a liar,
Rev 17:14 they will **m** war on the Lamb,
19:19 with their armies gathered to **m** war
Sir 2: 6 **m** your ways straight, and hope in
1Mc 1:11 and a covenant with the Gentiles

MAKER → MAKE
Ge 14:19 God Most High, **m** of heaven and
Job 4:17 beings be pure before their **M**?
32:22 my **M** would soon put an end to me!
35:10 no one says, 'Where is God my **M**,
36: 3 and ascribe righteousness to my **M**.
40:19 **M** can approach it with the sword.
Ps 95: 6 kneel before the LORD, our **M**!
134: 3 May the LORD, **m** of heaven and
149: 2 Let Israel be glad in its **M**;
Pr 14:31 who oppress the poor insult their **M**,
17: 5 who mock the poor insult their **M**;
22: 2 the LORD is the **m** of them all.
Isa 17: 7 that day people will regard their **M**,
29:16 Shall the thing made say of its **m**,
45: 9 Woe to you who strive with your **M**,
45:11 the Holy One of Israel, and its **M**:
51:13 have forgotten the LORD, your **M**,
54: 5 For your **M** is your husband,
Hos 8:14 Israel has forgotten his **M**, and buil
Hab 2:18 its **m** trusts in what has been made,
Sir 7:30 With all your might love your **M**,
32:13 But above all bless your **M**,
38:15 He who sins against his **M**,

MAKERS* → MAKE
Isa 45:16 the **m** of idols go in confusion

MAKES → MAKE
Ex 4:11 Who **m** them mute or deaf, seeing
11: 7 the LORD **m** a distinction between
Ps 23: 2 He **m** me lie down in green pastures
Pr 13:12 Hope deferred **m** the heart sick,
15:13 glad heart **m** a cheerful countenance
Mk 7:37 **m** the deaf to hear and the mute to
Jn 8:36 So if the Son **m** you free,
1Pe 2: 8 "A stone that **m** them stumble,

MAKING → MAKE
Ps 19: 7 are sure, **m** wise the simple;
Ecc 12:12 Of **m** many books there is no end,
Mt 21:13 but you are **m** it a den of robbers."
Jn 5:18 thereby **m** himself equal to God
Eph 2:15 in place of the two, thus **m** peace,
5:16 the most of the time, because the
Col 1:20 by **m** peace through the blood of
Rev 21: 5 "See, I am **m** all things new."

MALACHI*
Mal 1: 1 word of the LORD to Israel by **M**.
2Es 1:40 Haggai, Zechariah and **M**,

MALE → MALES
Ge 1:27 **m** and female he created them.
5: 2 **M** and female he created them,
6:19 they shall be **m** and female.
17:10 **m** among you shall be circumcised.
Lev 20:13 If a man lies with a **m** as with a

MALES

2Ki 23: 7 houses of the **m** temple prostitutes
Mt 19: 4 'made them **m** and female,'
Lk 2:23 firstborn **m** shall be designated as
1Co 6: 9 idolaters, adulterers, **m** prostitutes,
Rev 12: 5 she gave birth to a son, a **m** child,

MALES → MALE

Ex 12:48 all his **m** shall be circumcised;

MALICE → MALICIOUS

Ro 1:29 wickedness, evil, covetousness, **m.**
1Co 5: 8 the old yeast, the yeast of **m** and
Eph 4:31 and slander, together with all **m,**
Col 3: 8 anger, wrath, **m,** slander, and
Tit 3: 3 passing our days in **m** and envy,
1Pe 2: 1 Rid yourselves, therefore, of all **m,**

MALICIOUS → MALICE

Ex 23: 1 the wicked to act as a **m** witness.
Dt 19:16 If a **m** witness comes forward to
Ps 35:11 **M** witnesses rise up; they ask me

MALIGN → MALIGNED

1Pe 2:12 though they **m** you as evildoers,

MALIGNED* → MALIGN

1Pe 3:16 so that, when you are **m,**
2Pe 2: 2 the way of truth will be **m.**

MAMRE → =HEBRON

Ge 13:18 came and settled by the oaks of **M,**
25: 9 son of Zohar the Hittite, east of **M,**

MAN → FISHERMEN, HORSEMEN, KINSMAN, MADMEN, MAN'S, MEN

Ge 2: 7 LORD God formed **m** from the dust
2:15 the **m** and put him in the garden of
2:18 not good that the **m** should be alone;
2:20 the **m** there was not found a helper
2:23 for out of **M** this one was taken."
2:25 the **m** and his wife were both naked,
3: 9 But the LORD God called to the **m,**
3:22 the **m** has become like one of us,
4: 1 "I have produced a **m** with the help
32:24 **m** wrestled with him until daybreak.
Lev 20:10 **m** commits adultery with the wife of
20:13 If a **m** lies with a male as
Dt 22: 5 a **m** put on a woman's garment;
Jdg 8:21 for as the **m** is, so is his strength."
1Sa 13:14 sought out a **m** after his own heart;
Est 6: 7 "For the **m** whom the king wishes
Job 38: 3 Gird up your loins like a **m,**
40: 7 "Gird up your loins like a **m;**
Ps 90: T A Prayer of Moses, the **m** of God.
127: 5 Happy is the **m** who has his quiver
Pr 30:19 and the way of a **m** with a girl.
Isa 53: 3 a **m** of suffering and acquainted
Jer 30: 6 can a **m** bear a child?
Zec 6:12 Here is a **m** whose name is Branch;
Mt 9: 6 Son of **M** has authority on earth to
19: 5 'For this reason a **m** shall leave his
Mk 9:12 is it written about the Son of **M,**
Lk 6: 5 The Son of **M** is lord of the sabbath.
Jn 3:14 so must the Son of **M** be lifted up,
9:35 "Do you believe in the Son of **M?"**
Ac 7:56 and the Son of **M** standing at
16: 9 a **m** of Macedonia pleading with
Ro 5:12 came into the world through one **m,**
1Co 7: 1 well for a **m** not to touch a woman."
7: 2 each **m** should have his own wife
11: 3 that Christ is the head of every **m,**
11: 7 **m** ought not to have his head veiled,
11: 7 but woman is the reflection of **m.**
11:14 that if a **m** wears long hair,
15:47 The first **m** was from the earth, a **m** of dust;
15:49 borne the image of the **m** of dust,
Eph 5:31 a **m** will leave his father and mother
Rev 1:13 I saw one like the Son of **M,**
14:14 cloud was one like the Son of **M,**
Sir 25: 8 the **m** who lives with a sensible wife

EVERY MAN Ex 11:2; Jdg 5:30; 7:21; 1Sa 25:13; 27:3; 1Ki 22:36, 36; 2Ki 11:11; Ne

4:22; Est 1:22; Jer 30:6; 1Co 11:3; Gal 5:3; Jdt 4:9

MAN OF *GOD Dt 33:1; Jos 14:6; Jdg 13:6, 8; 1Sa 2:27; 9:6, 7, 8, 10; 1Ki 12:22; 13:1, 4, 5, 6, 6, 7, 8, 11, 12, 14, 14, 19, 21, 23, 26, 29, 31; 17:18, 24; 20:28; 2Ki 1:9, 10, 11, 12, 13; 4:7, 9, 16, 21, 22, 25, 25, 27, 27, 40, 42; 5:8, 14, 15, 20; 6:6, 9, 10, 15; 7:2, 17, 18, 19; 8:2, 4, 7, 8, 11; 13:19; 23:16, 16, 17; 1Ch 23:14; 2Ch 8:14; 11:2; 25:7, 9, 9; 30:16; Ezr 3:2; Ne 12:24, 36; Ps 90:Heading; Jer 35:4; 1Ti 6:11; 1Es 5:49

OLD MAN Ge 25:8; 43:27; 44:20; Jdg 19:16, 17, 20, 22; 1Sa 4:18; 28:14; Jer 51:22; Lk 1:18; Phm 1:9; 1Es 1:53; 4Mc 5:6; 6:2, 10; 7:13; 8:5

RIGHTEOUS MAN Ge 6:9; 2Sa 4:11; Mt 1:19; Lk 23:50; 2Pe 2:7, 8; Wis 2:12, 18; 10:4, 5, 6, 10, 13; 19:17

SON OF MAN 2Sa 17:25; Mt 8:20; 9:6; 10:23; 11:19; 12:8, 32, 40; 13:37, 41; 16:13, 27, 28; 17:9, 12, 22; 19:28; 20:18, 28; 24:27, 30, 30, 37, 39, 44; 25:31; 26:2, 24, 24, 45, 64; Mk 2:10, 28; 8:31, 38; 9:9, 12, 31; 10:33, 45; 13:26; 14:21, 21, 41, 62; Lk 5:24; 6:5, 22; 7:34; 9:22, 26, 44, 58; 11:30; 12:8, 10, 40; 17:22, 24, 26, 30; 18:8, 31; 19:10; 21:27, 36; 22:22, 48, 69; 24:7; Jn 1:51; 3:13, 14; 5:27; 6:27, 53, 62; 8:28; 9:35; 12:23, 34, 34; 13:31; Ac 7:56; Rev 1:13; 14:14

YOUNG MAN Ge 4:23; 34:19; Nu 11:27; Dt 32:25; Jdg 8:14; 9:54, 54; 17:7, 11, 12; 19:19; 1Sa 9:2; 14:1, 6; 17:55, 58; 20:22; 30:13; 2Sa 1:5, 6, 13; 13:17, 34; 14:21; 18:5, 12, 29, 32, 32; 1Ki 11:28; 2Ki 9:4, 6; 2Ch 36:17; Pr 7:7; Ecc 11:9; Isa 62:5; Jer 51:22; Zec 2:4; Mt 19:20, 22; Mk 14:51; 16:5; Lk 7:14; Ac 7:58; 20:9; 23:17, 18, 22; Tob 1:4; 5:5, 7, 10, 10; 2Mc 7:25, 30; 1Es 1:53; 4:58; 2Es 2:43, 46

MAN'S → MAN

Nu 17: 2 Write each **m** name on his staff,
Ecc 9:16 yet the poor **m** wisdom is despised,
Ro 5:18 so one **m** act of righteousness leads
Sir 41:21 and of gazing at another **m** wife;

MANAGE* → MANAGER, MANAGERS

1Ti 3: 4 He must **m** his own household well,
3: 5 know how to **m** his own household,
3:12 and let them **m** their children
5:14 children, and **m** their households,

MANAGER → MANAGE

Mt 20: 8 owner of the vineyard said to his **m,**
Lk 12:42 then is the faithful and prudent **m**
16: 1 There was a rich man who had a **m,**

MANAGERS* → MANAGE

Tit 2: 5 chaste, good **m** of the household,

MANASSEH

1. Firstborn of Joseph (Ge 41:51; 46:20). Blessed by Jacob but not as firstborn (Ge 48). Tribe of blessed (Dt 33:17), numbered (Nu 1:35; 26:34), half allotted land east of Jordan (Nu 32; Jos 13:8-33), half west (Jos 16; Eze 48:4), failed to fully possess (Jos 17:12-13; Jdg 1:27), 12,000 from (Rev 7:6).

2. Son of Hezekiah; king of Judah (2Ki 21:1-18; 2Ch 33:1-20). Judah exiled for his detestable sins (2Ki 21:10-15). Repentance (2Ch 33:12-19).

TRIBE OF MANASSEH Nu 1:35; 2:20; 10:23; 13:11; Jos 17:1, 2; 20:8; 22:7; Rev 7:6

MANDRAKES

Ge 30:14 give me some of your son's **m.**"
SS 7:13 The **m** give forth fragrance,

MANGER

Lk 2:12 in bands of cloth and lying in a **m.**"

MANIFESTATION

1Co 12: 7 the **m** of the Spirit for the common
2Th 2: 8 annihilating him by the **m** of his
1Ti 6:14 until the **m** of our Lord Jesus Christ,
Tit 2:13 the **m** of the glory of our great God

MANIFOLD

Ps 104:24 O LORD, how **m** are your works!
1Pe 4:10 Like good stewards of the **m** grace

MANNA

Ex 16:31 The house of Israel called it **m;**
Nu 11: 6 nothing at all but this **m** to look at."
Dt 8:16 in the wilderness with **m** that your
Jos 5:12 The **m** ceased on the day they ate
Ps 78:24 he rained down on them **m** to eat,
Jn 6:49 ate the **m** in the wilderness,
Heb 9: 4 were a golden urn holding the **m,**
Rev 2:17 I will give some of the hidden **m,**

MANNER

1Co 11:27 cup of the Lord in an unworthy **m**
Php 1:27 life in a **m** worthy of the gospel

MANOAH*

Father of Samson (Jdg 13:2-21; 16:31).

MANTLE

Ge 25:25 all his body like a hairy **m;**
Jos 7:21 a beautiful **m** from Shinar,
1Ki 19:19 and threw his **m** over him.
2Ki 2: 8 Elijah took his **m** and rolled it up,
2:13 He picked up the **m** of Elijah that
Zec 13: 4 they will not put on a hairy **m**

MANY

Dt 15: 6 you will lend to **m** nations,
17:17 And he must not acquire **m** wives
1Ki 8: 5 sacrificing so **m** sheep and oxen
11: 1 Solomon loved **m** foreign women
Ps 32:10 **M** are the torments of the wicked,
34:12 and covets **m** days to enjoy good?
106:43 **M** times he delivered them,
Pr 10:19 When words are **m,** transgression is
15:22 but with **m** advisers they succeed.
31:29 "**M** women have done excellently,
Ecc 5: 3 For dreams come with **m** cares,
12:12 Of making **m** books there is no end,
SS 8: 7 **M** waters cannot quench love,
Isa 52:15 so he shall startle **m** nations;
53:11 shall make **m** righteous,
53:12 yet he bore the sin of **m,**
Jer 11:13 your gods have become as **m** as
Da 9:27 covenant with **m** for one week,
12: 3 those who lead **m** to righteousness,
Mt 6: 7 heard because of their **m** words.
10:31 are of more value than **m** sparrows.
18:21 As **m** as seven times?"
22:14 **m** are called, but few are chosen."
24: 5 and they will lead **m** astray.
26:28 poured out for **m** for the forgiveness
Mk 10:31 But **m** who are first will be last,
10:45 and to give his life a ransom for **m.**"
Lk 2:34 for the falling and the rising of **m** in
10:41 worried and distracted by **m** things;
Jn 2:23 **m** believed in his name because
20:30 Now Jesus did **m** other signs in the
21:25 also **m** other things that Jesus did;
Ac 1: 3 to them by **m** convincing proofs,
5:12 Now **m** signs and wonders were
14:22 **m** persecutions that we must enter
Ro 5:19 the **m** will be made righteous,
12: 5 who are **m,** are one body in Christ,
1Co 1:26 not of you were wise by human
12:12 just as the body is one and has **m**
Heb 2:10 in bringing **m** children to glory,
9:28 offered once to bear the sins of **m,**
Jas 3: 1 Not **m** of you should become teachers,
1Jn 2:18 so now **m** antichrists have come.
2Jn 1: 7 **M** deceivers have gone out into the
Rev 5:11 of **m** angels surrounding the throne
19:12 and on his head are **m** diadems;
Sir 27: 1 **M** have committed sin for gain,

1Mc 1:62 But **m** in Israel stood firm and were

MAON
1Sa 23:24 his men were in the wilderness of **M**

MARA* → =NAOMI
Ru 1:20 no longer Naomi, call me **M**,

MARAH
Ex 15:23 That is why it was called **M**.

MARCH → MARCHING
Jos 6: 4 the seventh day you shall **m** around
Pr 30:27 yet all of them **m** in rank;

MARCHING → MARCH
2Sa 5:24 of **m** in the tops of the balsam trees,

MARITAL* → MARRY
Ex 21:10 or **m** rights of the first wife.
Mt 1:25 but had no **m** relations with her

MARK → MARKED, MARKS
Cousin of Barnabas (Ac 12:12; 15:37-39; Col 4:10; 2Ti 4:11; Phm 24; 1Pe 5:13), see John.
Ge 4:15 And the LORD put a **m** on Cain,
Eze 9: 6 but touch no one who has the **m**.
Rev 14: 9 receive a **m** on their foreheads or
16: 2 sore came on those who had the **m**
19:20 who had received the **m** of the beast
20: 4 its image and had not received its **m**

MARKED → MARK
Hab 1:12 you have **m** them for judgment;
Eph 1:13 **m** with the seal of the promised
4:30 with which you were **m** with a seal
Rev 7: 3 we have **m** the servants of our God
13:16 **m** on the right hand or the forehead

MARKET → MARKETPLACE, MARKETPLACES
Mk 7: 4 not eat anything from the **m** unless
1Co 10:25 Eat whatever is sold in the meat **m**

MARKETPLACE → MARKET
Lk 7:32 like children sitting in the **m** and
Jn 2:16 Stop making my Father's house a **m**

MARKETPLACES → MARKET
Mt 23: 7 to be greeted with respect in the **m**,

MARKS → MARK
1Co 7:18 to remove the **m** of circumcision.
Gal 6:17 I carry the **m** of Jesus branded on
1Mc 1:15 and removed the **m** of circumcision,

MARRED*
Isa 52:14 so **m** was his appearance,

MARRIAGE → MARRY
Dt 24: 1 Suppose a man enters into **m**
Mt 22:30 are given in **m**, but are like angels
24:38 marrying and giving in **m**,
1Co 7:38 who refrains from **m** will do better.
Heb 13: 4 Let **m** be held in honor by all,
13: 4 and let the **m** bed be kept undefiled;
Rev 19: 7 for the **m** of the Lamb has come,
Sir 23:18 one who sins against his **m** bed

MARRIED → MARRY
Ge 20: 3 for she is a **m** woman."
Dt 24: 5 When a man is newly **m**,
Ezr 10:10 trespassed and **m** foreign women,
Isa 62: 4 and your land shall be **m**.
Mal 2:11 has **m** the daughter of a foreign god.
Mk 12:23 For the seven had **m** her."
Ro 7: 2 a woman is bound by the law to
1Co 7:10 To the **m** I give this command—
7:33 **m** man is anxious about the affairs
Gal 4:27 the children of the one who is **m**."
1Ti 3: 2 be above reproach, **m** only once,
3:12 Let deacons be **m** only once,
5: 9 and has been **m** only once;
Tit 1: 6 **m** only once, whose children are

MARRIES → MARRY
Mt 5:32 whoever **m** a divorced woman commits adultery.
19: 9 and **m** another commits adultery."
Mk 10:11 and **m** another commits adultery
Lk 16:18 and **m** another commits adultery,
16:18 and whoever **m** a woman divorced
Ro 7: 3 if she **m** another man, she is not an
1Co 7:28 and if a virgin **m**, she does not sin.
7:38 he who **m** his fiancee does well;

MARROW
Heb 4:12 soul from spirit, joints from **m**;

MARRY → INTERMARRY, MARITAL, MARRIAGE, MARRIED, MARRIES, MARRYING
Mt 19:10 it is better not to **m**."
22:30 in the resurrection they neither **m**
Mk 12:19 the man shall **m** the widow and
1Co 7: 9 it is better to **m** than to be aflame
7:28 But if you **m**, you do not sin,
1Ti 5:14 I would have younger widows **m**,

MARRYING → MARRY
Ne 13:27 treacherously against our God by **m** foreign women?"
Mt 24:38 **m** and giving in marriage,
Lk 17:27 and **m** and being given in marriage,

MARTHA*
Sister of Mary and Lazarus (Lk 10:38-42; Jn 11; 12:2).

MARVELED → MARVEL
2Th 1:10 be **m** at on that day among all who
Jdt 10:19 They **m** at her beauty and admired
11:20 They **m** at her wisdom and said,

MARVELOUS → MARVELED, MARVELS
1Ch 16:24 his **m** works among all the peoples.
Job 5: 9 **m** things without number.
Ps 96: 3 his **m** works among all the peoples.
98: 1 for he has done **m** things.
118:23 LORD's doing; it is **m** in our eyes.
131: 1 things too great and too **m** for me.
Sir 39:20 and nothing is too **m** for him.

MARVELS → MARVELOUS
Ex 34:10 all your people I will perform **m**,
Ps 78:12 sight of their ancestors he worked **m**

MARY
1. Mother of Jesus (Mt 1:16-25; Lk 1:27-56; 2:1-40). With Jesus at temple (Lk 2:41-52), at the wedding in Cana (Jn 2:1-5), questioning his sanity (Mk 3:21), at the cross (Jn 19:25-27). Among disciples after Ascension (Ac 1:14).
2. Magdalene; former demoniac (Lk 8:2). Helped support Jesus' ministry (Lk 8:1-3). At the cross (Mt 27:56; Mk 15:40; Jn 19:25), burial (Mt 27:61; Mk 15:47). Saw angel after resurrection (Mt 28:1-10; Mk 16:1-9; Lk 24:1-12); also Jesus (Jn 20:1-18).
3. Sister of Martha and Lazarus (Jn 11). Washed Jesus' feet (Jn 12:1-8).
4. Mother of James and Joses; witnessed crucifixion (Mt 27:56; Mk 15:40) and empty tomb (Mk 16:1; Lk 24:10).

MASONS
1Ch 22:15 stonecutters, **m**, carpenters,
2Ch 24:12 and they hired **m** and carpenters to
Ezr 3: 7 So they gave money to the **m** and

MASSAH
Ex 17: 7 He called the place **M** and Meribah,
Dt 33: 8 whom you tested at **M**, with whom
Ps 95: 8 on the day at **M** in the wilderness,

MASTER → MASTER'S, MASTERS, TASKMASTERS
Ge 4: 7 desire is for you, but you must **m** it.
24:12 steadfast love to my **m** Abraham.

Ex 21: 5 if the slave declares, "I love my **m**,
Ps 12: 4 are our own—who is our **m**?"
Mal 1: 6 if I am a **m**, where is the respect due
Mt 10:24 nor a slave above the **m**;
24:46 Blessed is that slave whom his **m**
25:21 enter into the joy of your **m**.'
25:23 His **m** said to him, 'Well done,
25:23 enter into the joy of your **m**.'
Jn 13:16 servants are not greater than their **m**
15:20 Servants are not greater than their **m**
Eph 6: 9 that both of you have the same **M**
Col 4: 1 that you also have a **M** in heaven.
2Pe 2: 1 deny the **M** who bought them—
Sir 23: 1 O Lord, Father and **M** of my life,

MASTER'S → MASTER
Ge 39: 7 **m** wife cast her eyes on Joseph

MASTERS → MASTER
Pr 25:13 they refresh the spirit of their **m**.
Mt 6:24 "No one can serve two **m**;
Lk 16:13 No slave can serve two **m**;
Eph 6: 5 obey your earthly **m** with fear and
6: 9 And, **m**, do the same to them.
Col 3:22 obey your earthly **m** in everything,
4: 1 **M**, treat your slaves justly and fairly
1Ti 6: 1 their **m** as worthy of all honor,
6: 2 Those who have believing **m** must
Tit 2: 9 be submissive to their **m** and to
1Pe 2:18 accept the authority of your **m** with

MAT → MATS
Mk 2: 9 and take your **m** and walk'?
Jn 5: 8 "Stand up, take your **m** and walk."

MATCH → MATCHED
Lk 5:36 the new will not **m** the old.
2Co 11:15 Their end will **m** their deeds.

MATCHED* → MATCH
2Co 8:11 eagerness may be **m** by completing

MATERIAL
Ro 15:27 to be of service to them in **m** things.
1Co 9:11 much if we reap your **m** benefits?

MATS* → MAT
Mk 6:55 began to bring the sick on **m**
Ac 5:15 and laid them on cots and **m**,

MATTANIAH → =ZEDEKIAH
Original name of King Zedekiah (2Ki 24:17).

MATTATHIAS
Priest who started the Maccabean revolt (1Mc 2).

MATTER → MATTERS
Ecc 3: 1 a time for every **m** under heaven:
12:13 end of the **m**; all has been heard.
Sir 31:15 and in every **m** be thoughtful.

MATTERS → MATTER
Mt 23:23 neglected the weightier **m** of the law
Sir 3:23 Do not meddle in **m** that

MATTHEW* → =LEVI
Apostle; former tax collector (Mt 9:9-13; 10:3; Mk 3:18; Lk 6:15; Ac 1:13). Also called Levi (Mk 2:14-17; Lk 5:27-32).

MATTHIAS
Disciple chosen to replace Judas (Ac 1:23-26).

MATURE* → MATURITY
Lk 8:14 and the fruit does not **m**.
1Co 2: 6 among the **m** we do speak wisdom,
Php 3:15 who are **m** be of the same mind;
Col 1:28 may present everyone in Christ.
4:12 you may stand **m** and fully assured
Heb 5:14 But solid food is for the **m**,
Jas 1: 4 so that you may be **m** and complete,
1Mc 16: 3 by Heaven's mercy are **m** in years.

MATURITY → MATURE
Eph 4:13 to **m**, to the measure of the full

MEAL

1Ki 17:14 The jar of **m** will not be emptied
Mt 24:41 Two women will be grinding **m**
1Co 10:27 If an unbeliever invites you to a **m**
Heb 12:16 sold his birthright for a single **m**.

MEAN → MEANING, MEANINGLESS, MEANS, MEANT

Ex 12:26 What do you **m** by this observance?
Jos 4: 6 'What do those stones **m** to you?'
Mk 9:10 this rising from the dead could **m**.

MEANING → MEAN

Ge 40: 5 and each dream with its own **m**.
Dt 6:20 "What is the **m** of the decrees
2Es 10:40 This therefore is the **m** of the vision.

MEANINGLESS* → MEAN

1Ti 1: 6 from these and turned to **m** talk,

MEANS → MEAN

Ex 34: 7 yet by no **m** clearing the guilty,
Nu 14:18 but by no **m** clearing the guilty,
Mt 9:13 learn what this **m**, 'I desire mercy,
1Co 9:22 that I might by all **m** save some.
Sir 8:13 Do not give surety beyond your **m**;

MEANT → MEAN

Lk 8: 9 asked him what this parable **m**.
1Co 6:13 body is **m** not for fornication

MEASURE → MEASURED, MEASURES, MEASURING

Dt 25:15 have only a full and honest **m**,
Ps 147: 5 his understanding is beyond **m**.
Eze 45: 3 the holy district you shall **m** off
Zec 2: 2 He answered me, "To **m** Jerusalem,
Mk 4:24 **m** you give will be the **m** you get,
Lk 6:38 A good **m**, pressed down, shaken
Jn 3:34 for he gives the Spirit without **m**.
Eph 4:13 the **m** of the full stature of Christ.
Rev 11: 1 "Come and **m** the temple of God

MEASURED → MEASURE

Isa 40:12 Who has **m** the waters in the hollow
Jer 31:37 If the heavens above can be **m**,

MEASURES → MEASURE

Dt 25:14 have in your house two kinds of **m**,
Pr 20:10 Diverse weights and diverse **m** are

MEASURING → MEASURE

Eze 40: 3 and a **m** reed in his hand;
Zec 2: 1 a man with a **m** line in his hand.
Rev 11: 1 I was given a **m** rod like a staff,
21:15 talked to me had a **m** rod of gold

MEAT

Ex 16:12 'At twilight you shall eat **m**,
Nu 11:13 Where am I to get **m** to give to all
Pr 23:20 or among gluttonous eaters of **m**;
Eze 11: 3 this city is the pot, and we are the **m**
Ro 14:21 not to eat **m** or drink wine or do
1Co 8:13 of their falling, I will never eat **m**,
10:25 in the **m** market without raising any

MEDAD

Nu 11:27 "Eldad and **M** are prophesying in

MEDDLES*

Pr 26:17 who **m** in the quarrel of another.

MEDE → MEDIA

Da 5:31 Darius the **M** received the kingdom,

MEDES → MEDIA

Da 5:28 is divided and given to the **M**
6: 8 according to the law of the **M** and
Ac 2: 9 **M**, Elamites, and residents of

MEDIA → MEDE, MEDES

Ezr 6: 2 the capital in the province of **M**,
Da 8:20 these are the kings of **M** and Persia.
Tob 1:14 Until his death I used to go into **M**,

MEDIATOR

Job 33:23 for one of them an angel, a **m**,
Gal 3:19 ordained through angels by a **m**.
1Ti 2: 5 **m** between God and humankind,
Heb 8: 6 he is the **m** of a better covenant,
9:15 he is the **m** of a new covenant,
12:24 the **m** of a new covenant,

MEDICINE

Pr 17:22 A cheerful heart is a good **m**,
Jer 30:13 no **m** for your wound,
Tob 11:11 he applied the **m** on his eyes,
Sir 6:16 Faithful friends are life-saving **m**;

MEDITATE* → MEDITATES, MEDITATING, MEDITATION

Jos 1: 8 you shall **m** on it day and night,
Ps 1: 2 on his law they **m** day and night.
38:12 and **m** treachery all day long.
63: 6 **m** on you in the watches of the night
77: 3 I think of God, and I moan; I **m**,
77: 6 I **m** and search my spirit:
77:12 I will **m** on all your work,
119:15 I will **m** on your precepts,
119:23 servant will **m** on your statutes.
119:27 I will **m** on your wondrous works.
119:48 and I will **m** on your statutes.
119:78 as for me, I will **m** on your precepts.
119:148 that I may **m** on your promise.
143: 5 I **m** on the works of your hands.
145: 5 on your wondrous works, I will **m**.
Wis 12:22 we may **m** upon your goodness,
Sir 6:37 and **m** at all times on his

MEDITATES* → MEDITATE

Sir 14:20 Happy is the person who **m** on
39: 7 as he **m** on his mysteries.

MEDITATING* → MEDITATE

1Ki 18:27 either he is **m**, or he has wandered

MEDITATION* → MEDITATE

Job 15: 4 and hindering **m** before God.
Ps 19:14 of my mouth and the **m** of my heart
49: 3 the **m** of my heart shall be
104:34 May my **m** be pleasing to him,
119:97 It is my **m** all day long.
119:99 for your decrees are my **m**.

MEDIUM* → MEDIUMS

Lev 20:27 A man or a woman who is a **m**
1Sa 28: 7 for me a woman who is a **m**,
28: 7 to him, "There is a **m** at Endor."
1Ch 10:13 moreover, he had consulted a **m**,

MEDIUMS → MEDIUM

Lev 19:31 Do not turn to **m** or wizards;
1Sa 28: 3 Saul had expelled the **m**
2Ki 21: 6 and dealt with **m** and with wizards.
23:24 Josiah put away the **m**, wizards,

MEEK* → MEEKNESS

Ps 10:17 you will hear the desire of the **m**;
37:11 But the **m** shall inherit the land,
Isa 11: 4 with equity for the **m** of the earth;
29:19 The **m** shall obtain fresh joy in the
Mt 5: 5 "Blessed are the **m**, for they will
2Es 11:42 for you have oppressed the **m** and

MEEKNESS* → MEEK

2Co 10: 1 by the **m** and gentleness of Christ—
Col 3:12 kindness, humility, **m**, and patience.
Jas 1:21 with **m** the implanted word
Sir 45: 4 faithfulness and **m** he consecrated

MEET → MEETING, MEETS, MET

Ex 19:17 people out of the camp to **m** God.
30:36 tent of meeting where I shall **m** with
Ps 79: 8 compassion come speedily to **m** us,
85:10 love and faithfulness will **m**;
Am 4:12 prepare to **m** your God,
1Th 4:17 together with them to **m** the Lord

MEETING → MEET

Ex 27:21 In the tent of **m**, outside the curtain
29:44 I will consecrate the tent of **m** and
33: 7 he called it the tent of **m**.
40:34 the cloud covered the tent of **m**,
Jos 18: 1 and set up the tent of **m** there.

TENT OF MEETING
Ex 27:21; 28:43; 29:4,
10, 11, 30, 32, 42, 44; 30:16, 18, 20, 26, 36;
31:7; 33:7, 7; 35:21; 38:8, 30; 39:32, 40; 40:2,
6, 7, 12, 22, 24, 26, 29, 30, 32, 34, 35; Lev 1:1,
3, 5; 3:2, 8, 13; 4:4, 5, 7, 7, 14, 16, 18, 18;
6:16, 26, 30; 8:3, 4, 31, 33, 35; 9:5, 23; 10:7,
9; 12:6; 14:11, 23; 15:14, 29; 16:7, 16, 17, 20,
23, 33; 17:4, 5, 6, 9; 19:21; 24:3; Nu 1:1; 2:2,
17; 3:7, 8, 25, 38; 4:3, 4, 15, 23, 25, 28, 31,
30, 31, 33, 35, 37, 39, 41, 43, 47; 6:10, 13, 18;
7:5, 89; 8:9, 15, 19, 22, 24, 26; 10:3; 11:16;
12:4; 14:10; 16:18, 19, 42, 43, 50; 17:4; 18:4,
6, 21, 22, 23, 31; 19:4; 20:6; 25:6; 27:2; 31:54;
Dt 31:14, 14; Jos 18:1; 19:51; 1Sa 2:22; 1Ki
8:4; 1Ch 6:32; 9:21; 23:32; 2Ch 1:3, 6, 13; 5:5

MEETS → MEET

Ge 4:14 anyone who **m** me may kill me."
Ecc 10:19 and money **m** every need.

MEGIDDO

Jos 12:21 of Taanach one the king of **M** one
Jdg 1:27 the inhabitants of **M** and its villages;

MELCHIZEDEK

Ge 14:18 King **M** of Salem brought out bread
Ps 110: 4 a priest forever according to the
order of **M**."
Heb 5:10 priest according to the order of **M**.
6:20 forever according to the order of **M**.
7: 1 This "King **M** of Salem, priest of
7:11 according to the order of **M**,

MELODY

Jdg 5: 3 I will make **m** to the LORD, the God
Ps 57: 7 I will sing and make **m**.

MELONS*

Nu 11: 5 the cucumbers, the **m**, the leeks,

MELT → MELTED, MELTS

Dt 1:28 made our hearts **m** by reporting,
Jos 14: 8 made the heart of the people **m**;
Ps 97: 5 The mountains **m** like wax before
Mic 1: 4 Then the mountains will **m** under
Na 1: 5 quake before him, and the hills **m**;
2Pe 3:12 and the elements will **m** with fire?

MELTED → MELT

Jos 2:11 soon as we heard it, our hearts **m**,
Ps 22:14 it is **m** within my breast;
Eze 22:22 As silver is **m** in a smelter,

MELTS → MELT

Ps 147:18 He sends out his word, and **m** them;
Am 9: 5 he who touches the earth and it **m**,

MEMBER → MEMBERS

Mt 18:15 the **m** of the church sins against you,
Mk 15:43 a respected **m** of the council,
1Co 12:14 not consist of one **m** but of many.

MEMBERS → MEMBER

Mic 7: 6 are **m** of your own household.
Mt 10:36 will be **m** of one's own household.
Ro 7:23 I see in my **m** another law at war
12: 4 as in one body we have many **m**,
1Co 6:15 that your bodies are **m** of Christ?
12:18 God arranged the **m** in the body,
12:24 our more respectable **m** do not need
Eph 2:19 citizens with the saints and also are
3: 6 **m** of the same body,
4:25 for we are **m** of one another.
5:30 because we are **m** of his body.

MEMORIAL → MEMORY

Lev 5:12 a handful of it as its **m** portion,
6:15 and they shall turn its **m** portion

Jos   4: 7 stones shall be to the Israelites a **m**
Isa 55:13 and it shall be to the LORD for a **m,**

MEMORY → MEMORIAL
Dt   32:26 and blot out the **m** of them
Job 18:17 Their **m** perishes from the earth,
Pr   10: 7 The **m** of the righteous is a blessing,
Sir 10:17 erases the **m** of them from the earth.

MEN → MAN
Ge 18: 2 and saw three **m** standing near him.
Nu   1:44 twelve **m,** each representing his
      13: 2 "Send **m** to spy out the land of
Jdg 15:15 and with it he killed a thousand **m.**
1Ki 12:10 young **m** who had grown up with
Ps 148:12 Young **m** and women alike,
Da   1:17 four young **m** God gave knowledge
      3:25 "But I see four **m** unbound,
Mt   2: 1 wise **m** from the East came to
Mk   6:44 loaves numbered five thousand **m.**
Lk   9:30 they saw two **m,** Moses and Elijah,
Ac   4:13 were uneducated and ordinary **m,**
Ro   1:27 **M** committed shameless acts with **m**
1Ti   2: 8 in every place the **m** should pray,
Tit   2: 2 Tell the older **m** to be temperate,
      2: 6 the younger **m** to be self-controlled.
2Pe   1:21 but **m** and women moved by
Tob   7:11 I have given her to seven **m**
Sir 19: 2 and women lead intelligent **m** astray
      44: 1 now sing the praises of famous **m,**
2Es 14:42 gave understanding to the five **m,**

ALL THE MEN Ge 17:27; Dt 21:21; 29:10;
  Jdg 7:21, 24; 9:51; 12:4; 20:11; 1Sa 11:1;
  17:19; 2Sa 1:11; 17:14, 24; 2Ki 24:16; 1Ch
  10:7; Ezr 10:17; Jer 44:15; Jdt 7:12; 10:4;
  15:13; 1Mc 11:70

MEN AND WOMEN Ex 35:22, 29; Jos 6:21;
  8:25; Jdg 9:49, 51; 16:27, 27; 1Sa 22:19; 2Sa
  6:19; Ne 8:2; Est 7:4; Ps 148:12; Ecc 2:8; Jer
  44:20; Lk 12:45; Ac 2:18; 5:14; 8:3, 12; 22:4;
  Eph 6:7; 2Pe 1:21; Jdt 6:16; 8:7; Bel 1:20; 1Es
  8:91; 9:40, 41

MEN OF ISRAEL Dt 29:10; Jdg 7:23;
  20:11; 20:31; 1Sa 7:11; 17:19; 26:2; 31:1, 7, 7;
  2Sa 2:17; 6:1; 10:9; 17:14, 24; 18:7; 1Ch 10:1,
  7; 19:10; 2Ch 13:17; SS 3:7; Jdt 15:13; 1Mc
  7:5; 1Es 8:92

OLD MEN La 5:14; Eze 9:6; Joel 2:28; Zec
  8:4; Ac 2:17; 1Mc 14:9; 1Es 5:63; 3Mc 1:23;
  4:5

WISE MEN Ge 41:8; Ex 7:11; Job 34:2; Da
  2:12, 13, 14, 18, 24, 24, 27, 48; 4:6, 18; 5:7, 8,
  15; Mt 2:1, 7, 16, 16

YOUNG MEN Ge 14:24; 22:3, 5, 19; Ex
  24:5; Jos 6:23; Jdg 14:10; Ru 2:9, 9, 15; 3:10;
  1Sa 2:17; 16:18; 21:2, 4, 5; 25:5, 5, 8, 8, 9, 12,
  14, 19, 25, 27; 26:22; 30:17; 2Sa 1:15; 2:14,
  21; 4:12; 13:32; 16:2; 18:15; 1Ki 12:8, 10, 14;
  20:14, 15, 17, 19; 2Ki 8:12; 2Ch 10:8, 10, 14;
  Job 29:8; Ps 78:63; 148:12; SS 2:3; Isa 13:18;
  23:4; 31:8; Jer 6:11; 9:21; 11:22; 31:13; 48:15;
  49:26; 50:30; 51:3; La 1:15, 18; 2:21; 5:13, 14;
  Eze 9:6; 23:6, 12, 23; 30:17; Da 1:4, 10, 13,
  15, 17; Joel 2:28; Am 4:10; 8:13; Zec 9:17; Ac
  2:17; 5:6, 10; Jdt 2:27; 6:16; 7:22, 23; 10:9;
  16:4, 6; 1Mc 1:26; 2Mc 3:26, 33; 4:12; 10:35;
  12:27; 13:15; 1Es 1:53; 3:4, 16; 8:50; 2Es
  10:22; 4Mc 8:5; 9:6; 14:9, 12, 20; 16:17

MENAHEM*
King of Israel (2Ki 15:14-23).

MENE*
Da   5:25 inscribed: M, M, TEKEL, and PARSIN.
      5:26 S, God has numbered the days

MENTION → MENTIONED
Am   6:10 not the name of the LORD."
Eph 5:12 to **m** what such people do secretly;

MENTIONED → MENTION
Eph 5: 3 must not even be **m** among you,

MEPHIBOSHETH
Son of Jonathan shown kindness by David (2Sa
4:4; 9; 21:7). Accused of siding with Absalom
(2Sa 16:1-4; 19:24-30).

MERAB*
Daughter of Saul (1Sa 14:49; 18:17-19; 2Sa
21:8).

MERARI
Ge 46:11 of Levi: Gershon, Kohath, and **M.**
1Ch 6:19 The sons of **M:** Mahli and Mushi.
2Ch 34:12 and Obadiah, of the sons of **M,**

MERCHANDISE → MERCHANT
Ne 10:31 in **m** or any grain on the sabbath

MERCHANT → MERCHANDISE,
MERCHANTS
Pr 31:14 She is like the ships of the **m,**
Mt 13:45 is like a **m** in search of fine pearls;

MERCHANTS → MERCHANT
Na   3:16 increased your **m** more than the
Rev 18:11 the **m** of the earth weep and mourn

MERCIES → MERCY
Ne   9:19 great **m** did not forsake them in
La   3:22 his **m** never come to an end;
2Co 1: 3 the Father of **m** and the God of all
Sir 18: 5 And who can fully recount his **m?**

MERCIFUL → MERCY
Ge 19:16 the LORD being **m** to him,
Dt   4:31 the LORD your God is a **m** God,
1Ki 20:31 of the house of Israel are **m** kings;
Ne   9:31 for you are a gracious and **m** God.
Ps   57: 1 Be **m** to me, O God, be **m** to me,
     111: 4 the LORD is gracious and **m.**
     145: 8 The LORD is gracious and **m,**
Jer   3:12 not look on you in anger, for I am **m**
Mt   5: 7 "Blessed are the **m,** for they will
Lk   6:36 Be **m,** just as your Father is **m.**
     18:13 'God, be **m** to me, a sinner!'
Ro 11:32 so that he may be **m** to all.
Heb 2:17 be a **m** and faithful high priest
Sir   2:11 the Lord is compassionate and **m;**
     29: 1 The **m** lend to their neighbors;

MERCILESS → MERCY
Sir 37:11 or with the **m** about kindness,

MERCY → MERCIES, MERCIFUL,
MERCILESS
Ge 43:14 God Almighty grant you **m** before
Ex 25:17 make a **m** seat of pure gold;
     33:19 show **m** on whom I will show **m.**
Dt   7: 2 with them and show them no **m.**
Jos 11:20 receive no **m,** but be exterminated,
1Ch 21:13 of the LORD, for his **m** is very great;
Job   9:15 I must appeal for **m** to my accuser.
Ps   25: 6 Be mindful of your **m,** O LORD,
     40:11 Do not, O LORD, withhold your **m**
     51: 1 Have **m** on me, O God,
     69:16 according to your abundant **m,** turn
    119:156 Great is your **m,** O LORD;
     123: 2 until he has **m** upon us.
     123: 3 Have **m** upon us, O LORD, have **m**
Pr 12:10 but the **m** of the wicked is cruel.
     21:10 neighbors find no **m** in their eyes.
     28:13 and forsakes them will obtain **m.**
Isa 13:18 have no **m** on the fruit of the womb;
     47: 6 your hand, you showed them no **m;**
     55: 7 that he may have **m** on them,
Jer   6:23 they are cruel and have no **m,**
     50:42 they are cruel and have no **m.**
Da   2:18 to seek **m** from the God of heaven
     9: 9 To the Lord our God belong **m**
Hab 1:17 and destroying nations without **m?**
     3: 2 in wrath may you remember **m.**
Zec 1:12 will you withhold **m** from Jerusalem
     7: 9 kindness and **m** to one another;
Mt   5: 7 merciful, for they will receive **m.**

     9:13 learn what this means, 'I desire **m,**
     9:27 "Have **m** on us, Son of David!"
    12: 7 'I desire **m** and not sacrifice,'
    15:22 "Have **m** on me, Lord, Son of David
    17:15 "Lord, have **m** on my son,
    18:33 as I had **m** on you?'
    20:30 "Lord, have **m** on us, Son of David!
    20:31 even more loudly, "Have **m** on us,
    23:23 of the law: justice and **m** and faith.
Mk   5:19 and what he has shown you."
    10:47 Jesus, Son of David, have **m** on me!
    10:48 "Son of David, have **m** on me!"
Lk   1:50 His **m** is for those who fear him
     1:58 Lord had shown his great **m** to her,
     1:72 Thus he has shown the **m** promised
     1:78 By the tender **m** of our God,
    10:37 "The one who showed him **m."**
    18:38 Jesus, Son of David, have **m** on me!
    18:39 "Son of David, have **m** on me!"
Ro   9:15 "I will have **m** on whom I have **m,**
     9:18 he has **m** on whomever he chooses,
     9:23 of his glory for the objects of **m,**
    11:30 now received **m** because of their
    11:31 by the **m** shown to you, they too
        may now receive **m.**
    15: 9 might glorify God for his **m.**
1Co 7:25 who by the Lord's **m** is trustworthy.
2Co 4: 1 by God's **m** that we are engaged in
Eph 2: 4 But God, who is rich in **m,**
Php 2:27 But God had **m** on him,
1Ti 1: 2 Grace, **m,** and peace from God the
     1:13 **m** because I had acted ignorantly
     1:16 for that very reason I received **m,**
2Ti   1: 2 Grace, **m,** and peace from God the
     1:16 the Lord grant **m** to the household
     1:18 the Lord grant that he will find **m**
Tit   3: 5 had done, but according to his **m,**
Heb 4:16 so that we may receive **m** and find
    10:28 dies without **m** "on the testimony of
Jas   2:13 judgment will be without **m** to
        anyone who has shown no **m; m**
        triumphs over judgment.
     3:17 full of **m** and good fruits,
1Pe 1: 3 great **m** he has given us a new birth
     2:10 but now you have received **m.**
2Jn 1: 3 **m,** and peace will be with us from
Jude 1:21 look forward to the **m** of our Lord
     1:23 and have **m** on still others with fear,
Tob 3: 2 all your ways are **m** and truth;
Jdt 13:14 not withdrawn his **m** from the house
Wis 4:15 grace and **m** are with his elect,
Sir   2: 7 who fear the Lord, wait for his **m;**
     2:17 for equal to his majesty is his **m,**
    17:29 How great is the **m** of the Lord,
    51:12 *for his **m** endures forever;*

MERELY
Jas   1:22 and not **m** hearers who deceive

MERIBAH
Ex 17: 7 He called the place Massah and **M,**
Nu 20:13 These are the waters of **M,**
Dt 33: 8 you contended at the waters of **M;**
Ps 95: 8 Do not harden your hearts, as at **M,**
    106:32 the LORD at the waters of **M,**

MERRY
Ecc   9: 7 and drink your wine with a **m** heart;
Lk 12:19 relax, eat, drink, be **m.'**

MESHACH → =MISHAEL
Hebrew exiled to Babylon; name changed from
Mishael (Da 1:6-7). Refused defilement by food
(Da 1:8-20). Refused to worship idol (Da 3:1-
18); saved from furnace (Da 3:19-30).

MESHECH
Ge 10: 2 Madai, Javan, Tubal, **M,**
Ps 120: 5 that I am an alien in **M,**
Eze 38: 3 Gog, chief prince of **M** and Tubal;
     39: 1 Gog, chief prince of **M** and Tubal!

MESOPOTAMIA
Ac   2: 9 Elamites, and residents of **M,**

7: 2 Abraham when he was in **M**,

MESSAGE → MESSENGER, MESSENGERS

Jdg 3:20 "I have a **m** from God for you."
Pr 26: 6 to send a **m** by a fool.
Isa 28: 9 and to whom will he explain the **m**?
Jn 12:38 "Lord, who has believed our **m**,
Ac 2:41 who welcomed his **m** were baptized,
5:20 tell the people the whole **m** about
10:36 the **m** he sent to the people of Israel,
17:11 they welcomed the **m** very eagerly
Ro 10:16 "Lord, who has believed our **m**?"
1Co 1:18 the **m** about the cross is foolishness
2Co 5:19 entrusting the **m** of reconciliation to
Heb 4: 2 but the **m** they heard did not benefit
1Jn 1: 5 the **m** we have heard from him and
3:11 the **m** you have heard from the

MESSENGER → MESSAGE

Isa 42:19 or deaf like my **m** whom I send?
Hag 1:13 Then Haggai, the **m** of the LORD,
Mal 2: 7 for he is the **m** of the LORD of hosts.
3: 1 sending my **m** to prepare the way
Mt 11:10 I am sending my **m** ahead of you,
2Co 12: 7 a **m** of Satan to torment me,

MESSENGERS → MESSAGE

2Sa 15:10 Absalom sent secret **m** throughout
2Ch 36:15 sent persistently to them by his **m**,
Ps 104: 4 you make the winds your **m**,
Isa 44:26 and fulfills the prediction of his **m**;

MESSIAH → CHRIST, MESSIAHS

Mt 1: 1 the genealogy of Jesus the **M**,
1:18 the birth of Jesus the **M**
16:16 Peter answered, "You are the **M**,
26:63 tell us if you are the **M**,
Mk 13:21 at that time, 'Look! Here is the **M**!'
Lk 2:11 a Savior, who is the **M**, the Lord.
23:35 save himself if he is the **M** of God,
Jn 1:20 but confessed, "I am not the **M**."
1:41 **M**" (which is translated Anointed).
4:25 "I know that **M** is coming"
10:24 If you are the **M**, tell us plainly."
Ac 2:36 God has made him both Lord and **M**
3:20 may send the **M** appointed for you,
Ro 9: 5 according to the flesh, comes the **M**,
Rev 11:15 kingdom of our Lord and of his **M**,
2Es 7:28 For my son the **M** shall be revealed
7:29 my son the **M** shall die,
12:32 this is the **M** whom the Most High

MESSIAHS* → MESSIAH

Mt 24:24 For false **m** and false prophets will
Mk 13:22 False **m** and false prophets will

MET → MEET

Ge 32: 1 and the angels of God **m** him;
Ex 3:18 God of the Hebrews, has **m** with us;
Mt 28: 9 Suddenly Jesus **m** them and said,
Jn 18: 2 Jesus often **m** there with his

METHUSELAH

Ge 5:27 of **M** were nine hundred sixty-nine

MICAH

1. Idolater from Ephraim (Jdg 17-18).
2. Prophet from Moresheth (Jer 26:18-19; Mic 1:1).

MICAIAH

Prophet of the LORD who spoke against Ahab (1Ki 22:1-28; 2Ch 18:1-27).

MICHAEL

Archangel (Jude 9); warrior in angelic realm, protector of Israel (Da 10:13, 21; 12:1; Rev 12:7).

MICHAL*

Daughter of Saul, wife of David (1Sa 14:49; 18:20-28). Warned David of Saul's plot (1Sa 19). Saul gave her to Paltiel (1Sa 25:44); David retrieved her (2Sa 3:13-16). Criticized David for dancing before the ark (2Sa 6:16-23; 1Ch 15:29).

MIDDLE → MIDST

Ge 3: 3 tree that is in the **m** of the garden,
Jos 3:17 stood on dry ground in the **m** of
4: 3 stones from here out of the **m** of
Eze 1: 4 and in the **m** of the fire,
Ac 1:18 he burst open in the **m**
Rev 22: 2 the **m** of the street of the city.

MIDIAN → MIDIANITE, MIDIANITES

Ex 2:15 He settled in the land of **M**,
18: 1 Jethro, the priest of **M**, Moses'
Ps 83: 9 Do to them as you did to **M**,

MIDIANITE → MIDIAN

Ge 37:28 When some **M** traders passed by,
Nu 25: 6 brought a **M** woman into his family,

MIDIANITES → MIDIAN

Ge 37:36 the **M** had sold him in Egypt to
Nu 31: 2 "Avenge the Israelites on the **M**;
Jdg 6:16 and you shall strike down the **M**,

MIDNIGHT → NIGHT

Ex 11: 4 **m** I will go out through Egypt.
12:29 At **m** the LORD struck down all the
Ps 119:62 At **m** I rise to praise you,
Ac 16:25 **m** Paul and Silas were praying

MIDST → MIDDLE

Dt 13: 5 purge the evil from your **m**.
Ps 135: 9 sent signs and wonders into your **m**,
136:14 made Israel pass through the **m** of it,
Mt 10:16 like sheep into the **m** of wolves;
Aza 1: 1 around in the **m** of the flames,

MIDWIVES

Ex 1:17 But the **m** feared God; they did not

MIGHT → ALMIGHTY, MIGHTY

Dt 5:29 so that it **m** go well with them and
Jdg 16:30 He strained with all his **m**;
2Sa 6: 5 before the LORD with all their **m**,
6:14 before the LORD with all his **m**;
2Ch 6:41 you and the ark of your **m**.
20: 6 In your hand are power and **m**,
Ps 54: 1 and vindicate me by your **m**.
80: 2 Stir up your **m**, and come to save
119:71 so that I **m** learn your statutes.
Ecc 9:10 hand finds to do, do with your **m**;
Isa 63:15 Where are your zeal and your **m**?
Jer 16:21 to teach them my power and my **m**,
Mic 3: 8 of the LORD, and with justice and **m**,
Zec 4: 6 **m**, nor by power, but by my spirit,
Mt 13:15 that they **m** not look with their eyes,
Mk 14:35 if it were possible, the hour **m** pass
Lk 22: 4 about how he **m** betray him
Jn 1: 7 so that all **m** believe through him.
Ac 28:27 that they **m** not look with their eyes,
1Co 9:22 that I **m** by all means save some.
2Co 8: 9 by his poverty you **m** become rich.
1Pe 2:24 we **m** live for righteousness;
1Jn 4: 9 that we **m** live through him.
Sir 3:20 For great is the **m** of the Lord;
7:30 With all your **m** love your Maker,

MIGHTY → MIGHT

Ge 10: 9 Nimrod a **m** hunter before the LORD
49:24 by the hands of the **M** One of Jacob,
Ex 6: 1 by a **m** hand he will let them go;
Dt 3:24 deeds and **m** acts like yours!
5:15 a **m** hand and an outstretched arm;
7: 8 has brought you out with a **m** hand,
10:17 the great God, **m** and awesome,
34:12 the **m** deeds and all the terrifying
2Sa 1:19 How the **m** have fallen!
2Ch 14:11 helping the **m** and the weak.
Ne 9:32 the great and **m** and awesome God,
Job 36: 5 "Surely God is **m** and does not
36: 5 is **m** in strength of understanding.
Ps 24: 8 strong and **m**, the LORD, **m** in battle.
45: 3 your sword on your thigh, O **m** one,
50: 1 The **m** one, God the LORD,
62: 7 my **m** rock, my refuge is in God.

68:33 he sends out his voice, his **m** voice.
71:16 I will come praising the **m** deeds of
77:12 and muse on your **m** deeds.
89: 8 LORD God of hosts, who is as **m** as
93: 4 than the thunders of **m** waters,
99: 4 **M** King, lover of justice, you have
106: 2 can utter the **m** doings of the LORD,
110: 2 sends out from Zion your **m** scepter.
145: 4 and shall declare your **m** acts.
145:12 known to all people your **m** deeds,
150: 1 praise him in his **m** firmament!
Isa 9: 6 Wonderful Counselor, **M** God,
49:26 Redeemer, the **M** One of Jacob.
60:16 Redeemer, the **M** One of Jacob.
63: 1 announcing vindication, **m** to save."
Jer 32:19 great in counsel and **m** in deed;
Eze 20:33 a **m** hand and an outstretched arm,
Da 4: 3 are his signs, how **m** his wonders!
Lk 1:49 the **M** One has done great things
1Pe 5: 6 therefore under the **m** hand
Rev 18: 8 for **m** is the Lord God who judges
Sir 15:18 is **m** in power and sees everything;
Bar 2:11 Egypt with a **m** hand and with signs

MIGHTY HAND

Ex 3:19; 6:1, 1; 32:11; Dt 4:34; 5:15; 6:21; 7:8, 19; 9:26; 11:2; 26:8; 1Ki 8:42; 2Ch 6:32; Eze 20:33, 34; Da 9:15; 1Pe 5:6; Bar 2:11; 1Es 8:47, 61; 2Es 15:11

MIGHTY ONE

Ge 49:24; 1Ch 1:10; Ps 45:3; 50:1; 52:1; 132:2, 5; Isa 1:24; 49:26; 60:16; Lk 1:49; Jdt 16:6; Sir 46:5, 6, 16; 2Es 6:32; 9:45; 10:24; 11:43; 12:47

MIGHTY WARRIOR

Ge 10:8; Jdg 6:12; 11:1; 2Ki 5:1; 2Ch 17:17; 28:7; Jer 14:9; Sir 47:5; 1Mc 2:66; 4:30; 10:19

MIGHTY WARRIORS

Jos 10:7; 1Ch 5:24; 7:2, 5, 7, 9, 11, 40; 8:40; 11:11; 12:1, 25, 30; 28:1; 29:24; 2Ch 13:3; 14:8; 17:13, 14, 16; 25:6; 26:12; 32:21; Jer 5:16; 48:14; Eze 27:10; 1Mc 2:42

MIGHTY WATERS

Ex 15:10; 2Sa 22:17; Ne 9:11; Ps 18:16; 29:3; 32:6; 77:19; 93:4; 107:23; 144:7; Isa 17:12; 23:3; 43:16; Jer 51:13, 55; Eze 1:24; 31:15; 43:2; Hab 3:15; 2Es 6:17

MILCAH

Ge 11:29 the name of Nahor's wife was **M**.

MILCOM → =MOLECH

1Ki 11:33 and **M** the god of the Ammonites,
Jer 49: 3 For **M** shall go into exile,
Zep 1: 5 to the LORD, but also swear by **M**;

MILDEW

Dt 28:22 and drought, and with blight and **m**;
2Ch 6:28 if there is plague, blight, **m**, locust,
Am 4: 9 I struck you with blight and **m**;

MILE

Mt 5:41 if anyone forces you to go one **m**,
go also the second **m**.

MILETUS

2Ti 4:20 Trophimus I left ill in **M**.

MILK

Ex 3: 8 a land flowing with **m** and honey,
23:19 not boil a kid in its mother's **m**.
Pr 30:33 For as pressing **m** produces curds,
SS 4:11 honey and **m** are under your tongue;
Isa 55: 1 buy wine and **m** without money
Joel 3:18 the hills shall flow with **m**,
1Co 3: 2 I fed you with **m**, not solid food,
Heb 5:12 You need **m**, not solid food;
1Pe 2: 2 long for the pure, spiritual **m**,

LAND FLOWING WITH MILK AND HONEY

Ex 3:8, 17; 13:5; 33:3; Lev 20:24; Nu 16:13, 14; Dt 6:3; 11:9; 26:9, 15; 27:3; 31:20; Jos 5:6; Jer 11:5; 32:22; Eze 20:6, 15; Sir 46:8; Bar 1:20

MILLSTONE → STONE

Jdg 9:53 a certain woman threw an upper **m**

Lk 17: 2 be better for you if a **m** were hung

MIND → DOUBLE-MINDED, MINDFUL, MINDS

Ge 37:11 but his father kept the matter in **m**.
Nu 23:19 mortal, that he should change his **m**.
Dt 29: 4 the LORD has not given you a **m** to
1Sa 15:29 will not recant or change his **m**;
1Ch 28: 9 for the LORD searches every **m**,
Ps 26: 2 and try me; test my heart and **m**.
    110: 4 sworn and will not change his **m**,
Ecc 2: 3 my **m** still guiding me with wisdom
Isa 26: 3 of steadfast **m** you keep in peace—
Jer 17:10 I the LORD test the **m** and search
La 3:21 call to **m**, and therefore I have hope:
Eze 28: 2 you compare your **m** with the **m** of
            a god.
Da 4:16 Let his **m** be changed from that of a
Jnh 3: 9 God may relent and change his **m**;
Mt 22:37 all your soul, and with all your **m**.'
Mk 3:21 "He has gone out of his **m**."
    5:15 clothed and in his right **m**,
    12:30 your **m**, and with all your strength.'
Lk 10:27 your strength, and with all your **m**;
Ro 1:28 God gave them up to a debased **m**
    7:25 with my **m** I am a slave to the law
    8: 6 but to set the **m** on the Spirit is life
    8: 7 **m** that is set on the flesh is hostile
    11:34 who has known the **m** of the Lord?
1Co 1:10 united in the same **m** and the same
    2:16 who has known the **m** of the Lord
    2:16 But we have the **m** of Christ.
    14:14 prays but my **m** is unproductive.
2Co 5:13 if we are in our right **m**, it is for you
Php 2: 5 same **m** be in you that was in Christ
1Th 4:11 live quietly, to **m** your own affairs,
2Ti 3: 8 of corrupt **m** and counterfeit faith,
Heb 7:21 sworn and will not change his **m**,
Rev 17: 9 "This calls for a **m** that has wisdom:
Sir 21:14 The **m** of a fool is like a broken jar;
    37:17 The **m** is the root of all conduct;

MINDFUL → MIND

Ps 8: 4 beings that you are **m** of them,
    111: 5 he is ever **m** of his covenant.
Heb 2: 6 beings that you are **m** of them,

MINDS → MIND

Ps 7: 9 you who test the **m** and hearts,
Ecc 3:11 past and future into their **m**,
Jer 23:16 They speak visions of their own **m**,
Lk 24:45 **m** to understand the scriptures,
Ro 8: 5 their **m** on the things of the Spirit.
2Co 3:14 But their **m** were hardened.
    4: 4 blinded the **m** of the unbelievers,
Eph 4:23 be renewed in the spirit of your **m**,
Php 4: 7 guard your hearts and your **m** in
Col 3: 2 Set your **m** on things that are above,
Heb 8:10 I will put my laws in their **m**,
    10:16 and I will write them on their **m**,"
1Pe 1:13 prepare your **m** for action;
Rev 2:23 the one who searches **m** and hearts,

MINGLED

Ps 106:35 they **m** with the nations and learned

MINISTER → MINISTERED, MINISTERING, MINISTERS, MINISTRY

Ex 28:43 to **m** in the holy place;
Dt 10: 8 stand before the LORD to **m** to him,
1Ch 15: 2 the LORD and to **m** to him forever.
Ps 101: 2 that is blameless shall **m** to me.
Ro 15:16 a **m** of Christ Jesus to the Gentiles

MINISTERED → MINISTER

1Ch 6:32 **m** with song before the tabernacle

MINISTERING → MINISTER

1Sa 2:18 Samuel was **m** before the LORD,
    3: 1 the boy Samuel was **m** to the LORD

MINISTERS → MINISTER

Ps 103:21 his **m** that do his will.

MINISTRY → MINISTER

Ac 1:17 was allotted his share in this **m**."
Ro 11:13 to the Gentiles, I glorify my **m** in
    12: 7 **m**, in ministering;
2Co 3: 7 Now if the **m** of death,
    4: 1 mercy that we are engaged in this **m**
    5:18 has given us the **m** of reconciliation;
    6: 3 no fault may be found with our **m**,
Eph 4:12 equip the saints for the work of **m**,
2Ti 4: 5 evangelist, carry out your **m** fully.
Heb 8: 6 now obtained a more excellent **m**,

MIRACLES*

1Ch 16:12 his **m**, and the judgments he uttered,
Ps 78:11 and the **m** that he had shown them.
    78:43 and his **m** in the fields of Zoan.
    105: 5 his **m**, and the judgments he uttered,
    105:27 and in the land of Ham.
Ac 8:13 the signs and great **m**
    19:11 did extraordinary **m** through Paul,
1Co 12:10 to another the working of **m**,
    12:29 Are all teachers? Do all work **m**?
Gal 3: 5 work **m** among you by your doing
Heb 2: 4 signs and wonders and various **m**,
Sir 45: 3 By his words he performed swift **m**;

MIRE

Ps 69:14 rescue me from sinking in the **m**;
Isa 57:20 its waters toss up **m** and mud.

MIRIAM

Sister of Moses and Aaron (Nu 26:59). Led dancing at Red Sea (Ex 15:20-21). Struck with leprosy for criticizing Moses (Nu 12). Death (Nu 20:1).

MIRROR

Job 37:18 the skies, hard as a molten **m**?
1Co 13:12 For now we see in a **m**, dimly,
2Co 3:18 as though reflected in a **m**,
Jas 1:23 who look at themselves in a **m**;

MISCARRIAGE → MISCARRY

Ex 21:22 pregnant woman so that there is a **m**

MISCARRY* → MISCARRIAGE

Ex 23:26 No one shall **m** or be barren in your

MISERY

Ex 3: 7 I have observed the **m** of my people
Ps 119:92 I would have perished in my **m**.
Ro 3:16 ruin and **m** are in their paths,

MISFORTUNE → MISFORTUNES

Nu 23:21 No **m** is beheld **m** in Jacob;
Jdg 2:15 was against them to bring **m**,
Pr 13:21 **M** pursues sinners, but prosperity

MISFORTUNES → MISFORTUNE

Ge 41:52 fruitful in the land of my **m**."
Nu 11: 1 hearing of the LORD about their **m**,

MISHAEL → =MESHACH

Original name of Meshach (Da 1:6-19; 2:17; Aza 1:66).

MISLEAD → MISLEADS, MISLED

Pr 28:10 Those who **m** the upright into evil
Isa 3:12 O my people, your leaders **m** you,

MISLEADS → MISLEAD

Dt 27:18 "Cursed be anyone who **m** a blind
Pr 14: 8 but the folly of fools **m**.

MISLED → MISLEAD

2Ki 21: 9 Manasseh **m** them to do more evil
1Mc 1:11 from Israel and **m** many,

MISS → MISSED, MISSING

Jdg 20:16 sling a stone at a hair, and not **m**.

MISSED → MISS

1Ti 6:21 **m** the mark as regards the faith.

MISSING → MISS

Isa 40:26 mighty in power, not one is **m**.

MISSION

Ac 12:25 after completing their **m**

MIST → MISTS

Isa 44:22 like a cloud, and your sins like **m**;
Hos 13: 3 they shall be like the morning **m** or
Ac 13:11 Immediately **m** and darkness came
Jas 4:14 you are a **m** that appears for a little

MISTAKE → MISTAKES

Jos 20: 3 kills a person without intent or by **m**
Ecc 5: 6 the messenger that it was a **m**;

MISTAKES → MISTAKE

Jas 3: 2 For all of us make many **m**.
Sir 23: 3 Otherwise my **m** may be multiplied,

MISTRESS

Ge 16: 4 she looked with contempt on her **m**.
Ps 123: 2 eyes of a maid to the hand of her **m**,
Isa 47: 7 You said, "I shall be **m** forever,"
Na 3: 4 gracefully alluring, **m** of sorcery,

MISTS* → MIST

2Pe 2:17 These are waterless springs and **m**

MISUSES*

Ex 20: 7 not acquit anyone who **m** his name.
Dt 5:11 not acquit anyone who **m** his name.

MIX → MIXED, MIXES, MIXING

Rev 18: 6 **m** a double draught for her in the

MIXED → MIX

Ex 29: 2 unleavened cakes **m** with oil,
Ezr 9: 2 Thus the holy seed has **m** itself
Ps 75: 8 a cup with foaming wine, well **m**;
Pr 9: 5 and drink of the wine I have **m**.
Da 2:41 as you saw the iron **m** with the clay.
Mk 15:23 offered him wine **m** with myrrh;
Rev 8: 7 hail and fire, **m** with blood,
    15: 2 what appeared to be a sea of glass **m**

MIXES* → MIX

Hos 7: 8 Ephraim **m** himself with the peoples

MIXING → MIX

Isa 5:22 wine and valiant at **m** drink,

MIZPAH

Ge 31:49 and the pillar **M**, for he said,
1Sa 7: 6 judged the people of Israel at **M**.
Jer 41: 1 they ate bread together there at **M**,
1Mc 3:46 formerly had a place of prayer in **M**.

MOAB → MOABITE, MOABITES

Ge 19:37 bore a son, and named him **M**;
Nu 22: 3 **M** was in great dread of the people,
Dt 34: 5 died there in the land of **M**,
Jdg 3:12 strengthened King Eglon of **M**
Ru 1: 1 went to live in the country of **M**,
1Sa 22: 4 He left them with the king of **M**,
2Ki 1: 1 of Ahab, **M** rebelled against Israel.
    23:13 for Chemosh the abomination of **M**,
Isa 15: 1 An oracle concerning **M**.
Jer 48: 1 Concerning **M**. Thus says the LORD
    48:16 The calamity of **M** is near at hand
Eze 25:11 I will execute judgments upon **M**.
Am 2: 1 For three transgressions of **M**, and
Zep 2: 9 **M** shall become like Sodom and

MOABITE → MOAB

Dt 23: 3 **M** shall be admitted to the assembly
Ru 1:22 returned together with Ruth the **M**,
    4:10 I have also acquired Ruth the **M**,
Ne 13: 1 **M** should ever enter the assembly

MOABITES → MOAB

Ge 19:37 the ancestor of the **M** to this day.

MOAN → MOANING
Ps   77: 3 I think of God, and I **m**;
Isa 59:11 like doves we **m** mournfully.

MOANING → MOAN
Ps   6: 6 I am weary with my **m**;

MOCK → MOCKED, MOCKER, MOCKING, MOCKS
2Ki 19: 4 has sent to **m** the living God,
Ps 22: 7 All who see me **m** at me;
Pr   1:26 I will **m** when panic strikes you,
      14: 9 Fools **m** at the guilt offering,
Mk 10:34 they will **m** him, and spit upon him,

MOCKED → MOCK
1Ki 18:27 At noon Elijah **m** them, saying,
Ne   2:19 they **m** and ridiculed us, saying,
Mt 27:29 and knelt before him and **m** him,
Lk 23:11 with contempt and **m** him;
Gal   6: 7 God is not **m**, for you reap

MOCKER* → MOCK
Pr 20: 1 Wine is a **m**, strong drink a brawler,

MOCKING → MOCK
Mt 27:31 After **m** him, they stripped
     27:41 the scribes and elders, were **m** him,
Heb 11:36 Others suffered **m** and flogging,

MOCKS → MOCK
Pr 19:28 A worthless witness **m** at justice,
    30:17 that **m** a father and scorns to obey a

MODEIN
1Mc 2:23 to offer sacrifice on the altar in **M**,

MODEL
Tit   2: 7 in all respects a **m** of good works,

MODERATE → MODERATION
Sir 31:22 In everything you do be **m**,

MODERATION → MODERATE
Sir 31:27 life to human beings if taken in **m**.
    31:28 drunk at the proper time and in **m** is

MODEST → MODESTLY, MODESTY
Sir 26:15 A **m** wife adds charm to charm,
    32:10 approval goes before one who is **m**.

MODESTLY* → MODEST
1Ti   2: 9 women should dress themselves **m**

MODESTY* → MODEST
1Ti   2:15 faith and love and holiness, with **m**.
3Mc 1:19 and, neglecting proper **m**,

MOLDED* → MOLDS
Ro   9:20 Will what is **m** say to the one who
Wis 7: 1 of a mother I was **m** into flesh,
Sir 33:13 to be **m** as he pleases,

MOLDS → MOLDED
Ro   9:20 molded say to the one who **m** it,

MOLDY
Jos   9: 5 all their provisions were dry and **m**.

MOLECH → =MILCOM
Lev 18:21 to sacrifice them to **M**,
2Ki 23:10 through fire as an offering to **M**.
Jer 32:35 their sons and daughters to **M**,

MOMENT → MOMENTARY
Ex 33: 5 single **m** I should go up among you.
Nu   4:20 on the holy things even for a **m**;
Job 20: 5 joy of the godless is but for a **m**?
Ps 30: 5 For his anger is but for a **m**;
Pr 12:19 but a lying tongue lasts only a **m**.
Isa 54: 7 For a brief **m** I abandoned you,
    66: 8 a nation be delivered in one **m**?
Jn 18:27 and at that **m** the cock crowed.
1Co 15:52 in a **m**, in the twinkling of an eye,
Sir 20: 7 wise remain silent until the right **m**,

MOMENTARY* → MOMENT
2Co 4:17 this slight **m** affliction is preparing

MONEY
Ex 22:25 If you lend **m** to my people,
    30:16 You shall take the atonement **m**
2Ki 12: 4 the **m** offered as sacred donations
Ps 15: 5 who do not lend **m** at interest,
Ecc 5:10 The lover of **m** will not be satisfied
           with **m**;
     7:12 wisdom is like the protection of **m**,
   10:19 and **m** meets every need.
Isa 55: 1 buy wine and milk without **m** and
Mic 3:11 its prophets give oracles for **m**;
Mk 11:15 the tables of the **m** changers
Lk   3:14 not extort **m** from anyone by threats
     9: 3 nor bag, nor bread, nor **m**—not even
Jn   2:14 **m** changers seated at their tables.
1Ti   3: 3 quarrelsome, and not a lover of **m**.
     6: 8 In much wine, not greedy for **m**;
     6:10 For the love of **m** is a root of all
           kinds of evil,
2Ti   3: 2 lovers of themselves, lovers of **m**,
Heb 13: 5 your lives free from the love of **m**,
Tob 5:19 Do not heap **m** upon **m**,
Sir   7:18 Do not exchange a friend for **m**,
    18:33 by feasting with borrowed **m**,

MONSTER → MONSTERS
Jer 51:34 he has swallowed me like a **m**;
Mt 12:40 nights in the belly of the sea **m**,

MONSTERS* → MONSTER
Ge   1:21 So God created the great sea **m**
Ps 148: 7 you sea **m** and all deeps,
2Es 5: 8 women shall bring forth **m**.

MONTH → MONTHS
Ex 12: 2 be the first **m** of the year for you.
    40: 2 **m** you shall set up the tabernacle of
Nu   3:15 shall enroll every male from a **m** old
    11:21 that they may eat for a whole **m**'!
Ezr 6:19 the first **m** the returned exiles kept
Ne   8: 2 on the first day of the seventh **m**.
Est 9:21 the fourteenth day of the **m** Adar
Eze 47:12 they will bear fresh fruit every **m**,
Rev 9:15 the **m**, and the year, to kill a third
    22: 2 producing its fruit each **m**;
1Mc 1:59 On the twenty-fifth day of the **m**
     4:59 twenty-fifth day of the **m** of Chislev

FIRST MONTH Ge 8:13; Ex 12:2, 18; 40:2,
17; Lev 23:5; Nu 9:1, 5; 20:1; 28:16; 33:3, 3;
Jos 4:19; 1Ch 12:15; 27:2, 3; 2Ch 29:3, 17, 17;
35:1; Ezr 6:19; 7:9; 8:31; 10:17; Est 3:7, 12;
Eze 29:17; 30:20; 32:17; 45:18, 21; Da 10:4;
Jdt 2:1; AdE 3:12; 8:9; 1Mc 9:3; 1Es 1:1; 5:6;
7:10; 8:6, 61; 9:17

SEVENTH MONTH Ge 8:4; Lev 16:29;
23:24, 27, 34, 39, 41; 25:9; Nu 29:1, 7, 12; 1Ki
8:2; 2Ki 25:25; 1Ch 27:10; 2Ch 5:3; 7:10;
31:7; Ezr 3:1, 6; Ne 7:73; 8:2, 14; Jer 28:17;
41:1; Eze 45:25; Hag 2:1; 1Mc 10:21; 1Es
5:47, 53; 9:37, 40

MONTHS → MONTH
Ex   2: 2 a fine baby, she hid him three **m**.
Jdg 11:37 Grant me two **m**, so that I may go
1Sa 6: 1 country of the Philistines seven **m**.
1Ch 13:14 of Obed-edom in his house three **m**,
Jn   4:35 Do you not say, 'Four **m** more,
Rev 9: 5 allowed to torture them for five **m**,
    11: 2 over the holy city for forty-two **m**.
    13: 5 exercise authority for forty-two **m**.

MOON → MOONS
Ge 37: 9 the sun, the **m**, and eleven stars
Dt 17: 3 the sun or the **m** or any of the host
Jos 10:13 sun stood still, and the **m** stopped,
Ps   8: 3 the **m** and the stars that you have
    72: 7 until the **m** is no more.
    89:37 established forever like the **m**,
  104:19 made the **m** to mark the seasons;

  121: 6 not strike you by day, nor the **m**
  136: 9 **m** and stars to rule over the night,
  148: 3 sun and **m**; praise him, all you
SS   6:10 fair as the **m**, bright as the sun,
Isa 13:10 and the **m** will not shed its light.
Jer 31:35 **m** and the stars for light by night,
Eze 32: 7 and the **m** shall not give its light.
Joel 2:31 to darkness, and the **m** to blood,
Hab 3:11 the **m** stood still in its exalted place,
Mt 24:29 and the **m** will not give its light;
Ac   2:20 to darkness and the **m** to blood,
1Co 15:41 and another glory of the **m**,
Rev 6:12 the full **m** became like blood,
     8:12 and a third of the **m**, and a third of
    12: 1 with the **m** under her feet,
    21:23 no need of sun or **m** to shine on it,
Sir 27:11 but the fool changes like the **m**.
Aza 1:40 Bless the Lord, sun and **m**;
2Es 7:39 a day that has no sun or **m** or stars,

NEW MOON Ex 19:1; Nu 29:6; 1Sa 20:5, 18,
24, 27; 2Ki 4:23; Ezr 3:5; Ps 81:3; Isa 1:13;
47:13; 66:23, 23; Eze 46:1, 6; Hos 5:7; Am
8:5; Jdt 8:6, 6; Sir 43:8; 1Es 5:53, 57; 8:6, 6;
9:16, 17, 37, 40

MOONS → MOON
2Ch 8:13 the new **m**, and the three annual
    31: 3 the new **m**, and the appointed
Col 2:16 or of observing festivals, new **m**,

MORALS*
1Co 15:33 "Bad company ruins good **m**."

MORDECAI
Benjamite exile who raised Esther (Est 2:5-15).
Exposed plot to kill Xerxes (Est 2:19-23).
Refused to honor Haman (Est 3:1-6; 5:9-14).
Charged Esther to foil Haman's plot against the
Jews (Est 4). Xerxes forced Haman to honor
Mordecai (Est 6). Mordecai exalted (Est 8-10).
Established Purim (Est 9:18-32). See also Addi-
tions to Esther.

MORE → MOST
Ge   3: 1 serpent was **m** crafty than any other
     5:24 was no, because God took him.
    37: 3 Israel loved Joseph **m** than any
Ex   1:12 But the **m** they were oppressed,
     1:12 the **m** they multiplied and spread,
Nu 12: 3 **m** so than anyone else on the face
Jos 10:11 there were **m** who died because of
Jdg 16:30 were **m** than those he had killed
2Sa 18: 8 forest claimed **m** victims that day
1Ki 16:33 Ahab did **m** to provoke the anger of
Job 42:12 blessed the latter days of Job **m** than
Ps 19:10 **M** to be desired are they than gold,
    37:10 while, and the wicked will be no **m**;
    69:31 will please the LORD **m** than an ox
    71:14 and will praise you yet **m** and **m**.
  119:127 Truly I love your commandments
           m than gold, **m** than fine gold.
  130: 6 soul waits for the Lord **m** than
Pr 21: 3 and justice is **m** acceptable to
    31:10 She is far **m** precious than jewels.
Ecc 6:11 The **m** words, the **m** vanity,
Isa 54: 1 will be **m** than the children of
Jer 31:34 and remember their sin no **m**.
La   5: 7 no **m**, and we bear their iniquities.
Jnh 3: 4 And he cried out, "Forty days **m**,
Mt   2:18 consoled, because they are no **m**."
Mk   4:25 to those who have, **m** will be given;
    12:43 this poor widow has put in **m** than
Lk   3:16 who is **m** powerful than I is coming;
    12:23 For life is **m** than food, and the
           body **m** than clothing.
Jn   4:35 Do you not say, 'Four months **m**,
    21:15 do you love me **m** than these?"
Ac 17:11 These Jews were **m** receptive than
Ro   5: 9 Much **m** surely then,
     8:37 things we are **m** than conquerors
1Co 12:31 a still **m** excellent way.
2Co 3: 9 **m** does the ministry of justification
Heb 8:12 I will remember their sins no **m**."

Jas   10:17 and their lawless deeds no **m.**"
Jas   4: 6 But he gives all the **m** grace;
2Pe   1:19 message **m** fully confirmed.
Rev   7:16 will hunger no **m**, and thirst no **m**;
         10: 6 "There will be no **m** delay,
         21: 4 Death will be no **m**; mourning and
                    crying and pain will be no **m**,
         22: 5 And there will be no **m** night;

MORIAH·

Ge   22: 2 you love, and go to the land of **M**,
2Ch   3: 1 the LORD in Jerusalem on Mount **M**,

MORNING → MORNINGS

Ge   1: 5 and there was **m**, the first day.
Ex   12:10 let none of it remain until the **m**;
         16:12 in the **m** you shall have your fill of
         29:39 One lamb you shall offer in the **m**,
Dt   28:67 you shall say, "If only it were **m!**"
2Sa   23: 4 is like the light of **m**,
Ezr   3: 3 upon it to the LORD, **m** and evening.
Job   38: 7 when the **m** stars sang together and
Ps   5: 3 LORD, in the **m** you hear my voice;
         30: 5 but joy comes with the **m**.
        130: 6 than those who watch for the **m.**
Pr   27:14 early in the **m**, will be counted as
Ecc   11: 6 In the **m** sow your seed, and at
Isa   50: 4 **M** by **m** he wakens—
La   3:23 every **m**; great is your faithfulness.
Hos   6: 4 Your love is like a **m** cloud,
         13: 3 the **m** mist or like the dew that goes
Zep   3: 5 Every **m** he renders his judgment,
Lk   24:22 They were at the tomb early this **m**,
Ac   2:15 for it is only nine o'clock in the **m**.
2Pe   1:19 the day dawns and the **m** star rises
Rev   2:28 conquers I will also give the **m** star.
         22:16 of David, the bright **m** star."

EVENING ... MORNING Ge 1:5, 8, 13, 19, 23, 31; Ex 27:21; Lev 24:3; Nu 9:15, 21; Ps 55:17; 2Es 7:40

EVERY MORNING Ex 30:7; 36:3; Lev 6:12; 1Ch 9:27; 23:30; 2Ch 13:11; Job 7:18; Ps 73:14; Isa 33:2; La 3:23; Am 4:4; Zep 3:5

IN THE MORNING Ge 19:27; 20:8; 21:14; 22:3; 24:54; 26:31; 28:18; 31:55; 40:6; 41:8; 49:27; Ex 7:15; 8:20; 9:13; 16:7, 8, 12, 13; 24:4; 29:39, 41; 34:2, 2, 4; Lev 6:20; Nu 9:21; 14:40; 16:5; 22:13, 21; 28:4, 8; Dt 28:67; Jos 3:1; 6:12; 7:14, 16; 8:10, 14; Jdg 6:28; 9:33; 19:5, 8, 9, 27; 20:19; Ru 3:13; 1Sa 1:19; 9:19; 15:12; 17:20; 19:11; 20:35; 25:37; 29:10, 10, 11; 2Sa 11:14; 24:11; 1Ki 3:21, 21; 17:6; 2Ki 3:22; 6:15; 10:9; 2Ch 20:20; Est 2:14; 5:14; Job 1:5; Ps 5:3; 59:16; 88:13; 90:5, 6, 14; 92:2; 143:8; Pr 27:14; Ecc 10:16; 11:6; Isa 5:11; 17:11; Jer 20:16; 21:12; Eze 12:8; 24:18; 33:22; Hos 7:6; Mt 14:25; 16:3; 20:1; 21:18; Mk 1:35; 6:48; 11:20; 15:25; Lk 21:38; Jn 8:2; 18:28; Ac 2:15; 23:12; 27:39; Tob 9:6; AdE 2:14; 5:14; Bel 1:12, 16; 1Mc 3:58; 4:52; 6:33; 11:67; 16:5; 1Es 1:11; 3Mc 5:10

MORNING ... EVENING Ex 18:13, 14; Lev 6:20; 1Sa 17:16; 1Ch 16:40; 2Ch 2:4; 13:11; 31:3; Ezr 3:3; Job 4:20; Ps 65:8; Eze 24:18; Ac 28:23; Sir 18:26; 1Mc 9:13; 1Es 5:50

UNTIL [THE] MORNING Ex 12:10, 10, 22; 16:19, 20, 23, 24; 23:18; 29:34; 34:25; Lev 6:9; 7:15; 19:13; 22:30; Nu 9:12, 15, 21; Dt 16:4; Jdg 19:25; Ru 3:13, 14; 1Sa 3:15; 14:36; 25:36; 2Sa 2:27; 2Ki 7:9; 10:8; Pr 7:18; Isa 38:13; Zep 3:3; 1Mc 12:29

MORNINGS· → MORNING

Da   8:14 "For two thousand three hundred
                    evenings and **m**;
         8:26 vision of the evenings and the **m**

MORTAL → MORTALS

Nu   23:19 **m**, that he should change his mind.
1Sa   15:29 **m**, that he should change his mind."
Job   9: 2 how can a **m** be just before God?
         22: 2 "Can a **m** be of use to God?

Ps   56:11 What can a mere **m** do to me?
Isa   51:12 afraid of a mere **m** who must die,
Ro   1:23 for images resembling a **m** human
         6:12 exercise dominion in your **m** bodies,
         8:11 will give life to your **m** bodies also
1Co   15:53 **m** body must put on immortality.
2Co   5: 4 is **m** may be swallowed up by life.
1Jn   5:16 There is sin that is **m**;
Rev   13: 3 but its **m** wound had been healed.

MORTALS → MORTAL

Ge   6: 3 spirit shall not abide in **m** forever,
Ex   4:11 "Who gives speech to **m?**
Job   28:13 **M** do not know the way to it,
Ps   8: 4 **m** that you care for them?
        118: 6 What can **m** do to me?
Isa   52:14 his form beyond that of **m—**
Mk   10:27 **m** it is impossible, but not for God;
1Co   13: 1 If I speak in the tongues of **m** and
Heb   2: 6 or **m**, that you care for them?
Sir   35:24 repays **m** according to their deeds,

MOSES

Levite; brother of Aaron (Ex 6:20; 1Ch 6:3). Put in basket along Nile; discovered and raised by Pharaoh's daughter (Ex 2:1-10). Fled to Midian after killing Egyptian (Ex 2:11-15). Married to Zipporah, fathered Gershom (Ex 2:16-22).
Called by the LORD to deliver Israel (Ex 3-4). Pharaoh's resistance (Ex 5). Ten plagues (Ex 7-11). Passover and Exodus (Ex 12-13). Led Israel through Red Sea (Ex 14). Song of deliverance (Ex 15:1-21). Brought water from rock (Ex 17:1-7). Raised hands to defeat Amalekites (Ex 17:8-16). Delegated judges (Ex 18; Dt 1:9-18).
Received Law at Sinai (Ex 19-23; 25-31; Jn 1:17). Announced Law to Israel (Ex 19:7-8; 24; 35). Broke tablets because of golden calf (Ex 32; Dt 9). Saw glory of the LORD (Ex 33-34). Supervised building of tabernacle (Ex 36-40). Set apart Aaron and priests (Lev 8-9). Numbered tribes (Nu 1-4; 26). Opposed by Aaron and Miriam (Nu 12). Sent spies into Canaan (Nu 13). Announced forty years of wandering for failure to enter land (Nu 14). Opposed by Korah (Nu 16). Forbidden to enter land for striking rock (Nu 20:1-13; Dt 1:37). Lifted bronze snake for healing (Nu 21:4-9; Jn 3:14). Final address to Israel (Dt 1-33). Succeeded by Joshua (Nu 27:12-23; Dt 34). Death and burial by God (Dt 34:5-12). Praise of (Sir 45).
"Law of Moses" (1Ki 2:3; Ezr 3:2; Mk 12:26; Lk 24:44). "Book of Moses" (2Ch 25:12; Ne 13:1). "Song of Moses" (Ex 15:1-21; Rev 15:3). "Prayer of Moses" (Ps 90).

BOOK OF MOSES 2Ch 25:4; 35:12; Ezr 6:18; Ne 13:1; Mk 12:26; Tob 6:13; 7:11, 12; 1Es 1:11; 5:49; 7:6, 9

LAW OF MOSES Jos 8:31, 32; 23:6; 1Ki 2:3; 2Ki 14:6; 23:25; 2Ch 23:18; 30:16; Ezr 3:2; 7:6; Ne 8:1; Da 9:11, 13; Lk 2:22; 24:44; Jn 7:23; Ac 13:39; 15:5; 28:23; 1Co 9:9; Heb 10:28; Tob 1:8; 7:13; Bar 2:2; Sus 1:3, 62; 1Es 8:3; 9:39

MOSES THE SERVANT Jos 1:1, 13, 15; 8:31, 33; 11:12; 12:6; 13:8; 14:7; 18:7; 22:2, 4, 5; 2Ki 18:12; 1Ch 6:49; 2Ch 1:3; 24:9; Ne 10:29

SERVANT MOSES Ex 14:31; Nu 12:7, 8; Jos 1:2, 7; 9:24; 11:15; 1Ki 8:56; 2Ki 21:8; Ne 1:7, 8; 9:14; Ps 105:26; Mal 4:4; Bar 1:20; 2:28

MOST → MORE

Ge   14:18 he was priest of God **M** High.
Ex   26:33 the holy place from the **m** holy.
Nu   4: 4 concerns the **m** holy things.
         24:16 the knowledge of the **M** High,
Jdg   5:24 "**M** blessed of women be Jael,
Ps   46: 4 the holy habitation of the **M** High.
         78:35 the **M** High God their redeemer.
         91: 1 live in the shelter of the **M** High,
Isa   14:14 I will make myself like the **M** High.

Jer   3:19 the **m** beautiful heritage of all the
Eze   20: 6 the **m** glorious of all lands.
Da   4:17 that the **M** High is sovereign over
         7:25 speak words against the **M** High,
Mk   5: 7 Jesus, Son of the **M** High God?
Lk   1:32 be called the Son of the **M** High,
         1:76 be called the prophet of the **M** High;
1Co   10: 5 God was not pleased with **m** of
Eph   5:16 making the **m** of the time,
Col   4: 5 making the **m** of the time.
Jude   1:20 yourselves up on your **m** holy faith;
Wis   5:15 the **M** High takes care of them.
Sir   12: 6 For the **M** High also hates sinners
2Es   12:32 the Messiah whom the **M** High has

*GOD MOST HIGH Ge 14:18, 19, 20, 22; Ps 57:2; Sir 50:17; 1Es 9:46; 3Mc 6:2

MOST HIGH Nu 24:16; Dt 32:8; 1Sa 2:10; 2Sa 22:14; Ps 7:17; 9:2; 18:13; 21:7; 46:4; 47:2; 50:14; 56:2; 73:11; 77:10; 78:17, 35, 56; 82:6; 83:18; 87:5; 91:1, 9; 92:1; 97:9; 106:7; 107:11; Isa 14:14; La 3:35, 38; Da 3:26; 4:2, 17, 24, 25, 32, 34; 5:18, 21; 7:18, 22, 25, 25, 27; Hos 11:7; Mk 5:7; Lk 1:32, 35, 76; 6:35; 8:28; Ac 7:48; 16:17; Heb 7:1; Tob 1:13; 4:11; Jdt 13:18; Wis 5:15; 6:3; Sir 4:10; 7:9, 15; 9:15; 12:2, 6; 17:26, 27; 19:17; 23:18, 23; 24:2, 3, 23; 28:7; 29:11; 33:15; 34:6, 23; 35:8, 12, 21; 37:15; 38:2, 34; 39:5; 41:4, 8; 42:2, 18; 43:2, 12; 44:20; 46:5; 47:5, 8; 48:5; 49:4; 50:7, 14, 15, 16, 19, 21; 2Mc 3:31; 1Es 2:3; 6:31; 8:19, 21; Man 1:7; 3Mc 1:20; 7:9; 2Es 3:3; 4:2, 11, 34; 5:4, 22, 34; 6:32, 36; 7:19, 23, 33, 37, 42, 50, 70, 74, 77, 78, 79, 81, 83, 87, 88, 89, 102, 122, 132; 8:1, 48, 56, 59; 9:2, 4, 6, 25, 28, 44; 10:24, 38, 50, 52, 54, 57, 59, 59; 11:38, 43, 44; 12:4, 6, 23, 30, 32, 36, 39, 47; 13:13, 26, 29, 44, 47, 56, 57; 14:31, 42, 45

MOST HIGH *GOD Ps 78:35, 56; Da 3:26; 4:2; 5:18, 21; Mk 5:7; Lk 8:28; Ac 16:17; Heb 7:1; Jdt 13:18; Sir 7:9; 24:23; 41:8; 1Es 6:31; 8:19, 21; 3Mc 7:9

MOST HOLY Ex 26:33, 34; 29:37; 30:10, 29, 36; 40:10; Lev 2:3, 10; 6:17, 25, 29; 7:1, 6; 10:12, 17; 14:13; 21:22; 24:9; 27:28; Nu 4:4, 19; 18:9, 9, 10; 1Ki 6:16; 7:50; 8:6; 1Ch 6:49; 23:13; 2Ch 3:8, 10; 4:22; 5:7; 31:14; Ezr 2:63; Ne 7:65; Ps 28:2; Eze 41:4; 42:13, 13; 43:12; 45:3; 48:12; Da 9:24; Jude 1:20; 2Mc 5:15; 6:11; 4Mc 7:4; 14:7

MOST HOLY PLACE Ex 26:34; 1Ki 6:16; 7:50; 8:6; 1Ch 6:49; 2Ch 3:8, 10; 4:22; 5:7; Eze 41:4; 45:3; 48:12; Da 9:24

MOTH

Ps   39:11 consuming like a **m** what is dear to
Isa   51: 8 **m** will eat them up like a garment,
Mt   6:19 where **m** and rust consume and

MOTHER → GRANDMOTHER, MOTHER'S, MOTHER-IN-LAW, MOTHERS

Ge   2:24 a man leaves his father and his **m**
         3:20 because she was the **m** of all living.
Ex   20:12 Honor your father and your **m**,
         21:15 strikes father or **m** shall be put to
         21:17 curses father or **m** shall be put to
Dt   5:16 Honor your father and your **m**,
         21:18 not obey his father and **m**,
         22: 6 shall not take the **m** with the young.
         27:16 anyone who dishonors father or **m.**"
Jdg   5: 7 Deborah, arose as a **m** in Israel.
1Sa   2:19 **m** used to make for him a little robe
2Sa   20:19 to destroy a city that is a **m** in Israel;
1Ki   19:20 "Let me kiss my father and my **m**,
Ps   27:10 If my father and **m** forsake me,
         51: 5 a sinner when my **m** conceived me.
        113: 9 her the joyous **m** of children.
Pr   20:20 If you curse father or **m**,
         23:22 not despise your **m** when she is old.
         23:25 Let your father and **m** be glad;
         29:15 **m** is disgraced by a neglected child.
         30:17 scorns to obey a **m** will be pecked

31: 1 An oracle that his **m** taught him:
SS   6: 9 the darling of her **m**, flawless to her
Isa   8: 4 how to call "My father" or "My **m**,"
      66:13 As a **m** comforts her child, so I will
Jer 20:17 my **m** would have been my grave,
Hos   2: 2 Plead with your **m**, plead—
Mic   7: 6 the daughter rises up against her **m**,
Mt   2:11 they saw the child with Mary his **m**;
      10:35 and a daughter against her **m**,
      10:37 loves father or **m** more than me is
      12:48 "Who is my **m**, and who are my
      19: 5 a man shall leave his father and **m**
      19:19 Honor your father and **m**;
Mk   7:10 'Honor your father and your **m**';
      7:10 speaks evil of father or **m** must
      10:19 Honor your father and **m**.'"
Lk   12:53 **m** against daughter and daughter
            against **m**,
      14:26 and does not hate father and **m**,
      18:20 Honor your father and **m**.'"
Jn   19:27 to the disciple, "Here is your **m**."
Eph   5:31 a man will leave his father and **m**
      6: 2 "Honor your father and **m**"—
2Ti   1: 5 Lois and your **m** Eunice
Heb   7: 3 Without father, without **m**, without
Rev 17: 5 **m** of whores and of earth's
Tob   3: 3 Honor your **m** and do not abandon
Sir   3: 6 who honor their **m** obey the Lord;
2Es 10: 7 For Zion, the **m** of us all,

FATHER ... MOTHER Ge 2:24; 28:7; Ex
20:12; 21:15, 17; Lev 20:9, 9, 17; 21:11; Nu
6:7; Dt 5:16; 21:13, 18, 19; 27:16; 33:9; Jos
2:13, 18; 6:23; Jdg 14:2, 3, 4, 5, 6, 9, 16; Ru
2:11; 1Sa 22:3; 2Sa 19:37; 1Ki 19:20; 22:52;
2Ki 3:2; Est 2:7, 7; Ps 27:10; Pr 19:26; 20:20;
23:25; 28:24; Isa 8:4; Eze 22:7; 44:25; Mt
10:37; 15:4, 4, 5; 19:5, 19, 29; Mk 5:40; 7:10,
10, 11, 12; 10:7, 19; Lk 1:59; 2:33; 8:51;
12:53; 14:26; 18:20; Jn 6:42; Eph 5:31; 6:2;
1Ti 1:9; Heb 7:3; Tob 5:17; 8:21; 9:6; 10:7;
11:17; Sir 23:14; 41:17; 1Mc 13:28; 1Es 4:21,
25

MOTHER'S → MOTHER
Ex   23:19 shall not boil a kid in its **m** milk.
Job   1:21 "Naked I came from my **m** womb,
Pr   1: 8 and do not reject your **m** teaching,
      6:20 and do not forsake your **m** teaching.
Ecc   5:15 As they came from their **m** womb,
      11: 5 comes to the bones in the **m** womb,
Isa 50: 1 Where is your **m** bill of divorce
Jn   3: 4 a second time into the **m** womb and

MOTHER-IN-LAW → MOTHER
Dt   27:23 anyone who lies with his **m**."
Ru   2:11 "All that you have done for your **m**
Mic   7: 6 the daughter-in-law against her **m**;
Mt   10:35 a daughter-in-law against her **m**;
Mk   1:30 Simon's **m** was in bed with a fever,
Tob 10:12 your father-in-law and your **m**,

MOTHERS → MOTHER
Pr   15:20 but the foolish despise their **m**.
      30:11 and do not bless their **m**.
Hos 10:14 when **m** were dashed in pieces
Mk   10:30 brothers and sisters, **m** and children,
1Ti   5: 2 to older women as **m**, to younger

MOTIONED
Jn   13:24 therefore **m** to him to ask Jesus
Ac   12:17 He **m** to them with his hand to be
      19:33 Alexander **m** for silence and tried to

MOTIVES
Php   1:18 whether out of false **m** or true;
1Th   2: 3 not spring from deceit or impure **m**

MOUNT → MOUNTAIN, MOUNTAINS,
MOUNTED
Ge   22:14 "On the **m** of the LORD it shall be
Ex   19:20 the LORD descended upon **M** Sinai,
      34:29 Moses came down from **M** Sinai.
Nu   33:39 when he died on **M** Hor.

Dt   11:29 the blessing on **M** Gerizim and the
            curse on **M** Ebal.
      34: 1 from the plains of Moab to **M** Nebo
Jos   8:30 Joshua built on **M** Ebal an altar to
1Ch 10: 8 and his sons fallen on **M** Gilboa.
2Ch   3: 1 LORD in Jerusalem on **M** Moriah,
Ps   74: 2 Remember **M** Zion, where you
      78:68 **M** Zion, which he loves.
Isa 14:13 I will sit on the **m** of assembly
Mic   4: 7 will reign over them in **M** Zion
Zec 14: 4 the **M** of Olives shall be split in two
Mk   13: 3 he was sitting on the **M** of Olives
Heb 12:22 But you have come to **M** Zion and
Rev 14: 1 the Lamb, standing on **M** Zion!

MOUNT OF OLIVES 2Sa 15:30; Zec 14:4,
4; Mt 21:1; 24:3; 26:30; Mk 11:1; 13:3; 14:26;
Lk 19:29, 37; 21:37; 22:39; Jn 8:1

MOUNT SINAI Ex 19:11, 18, 20, 23; 24:16;
31:18; 34:2, 4, 29, 32; Lev 7:38; 25:1; 26:46;
27:34; Nu 3:1; 28:6; Ne 9:13; Ac 7:30, 38; Gal
4:24, 25; 2Es 3:17; 14:4

MOUNT ZION 2Ki 19:31; Ps 48:2, 11; 74:2;
78:68; 125:1; Isa 4:5; 8:18; 10:12; 18:7; 24:23;
29:8; 31:4; 37:32; La 5:18; Joel 2:32; Ob 1:17,
21; Mic 4:7; Heb 12:22; Rev 14:1; Jdt 9:13;
14:27; 2Es 2:42; 13:35

MOUNTAIN → MOUNT
Ex   3: 1 and came to Horeb, the **m** of God.
      19: 2 camped there in front of the **m**.
      19:20 Moses to the top of the **m**,
      24:18 on the **m** for forty days and forty
      32:19 and broke them at the foot of the **m**.
Dt   5: 4 with you face to face at the **m**,
Job 14:18 "But the **m** falls and crumbles away,
Ps   48: 1 in the city of our God. His holy **m**,
      68:16 look with envy, O many-peaked **m**
Isa   2: 2 the **m** of the LORD's house shall be
      11: 9 not hurt or destroy on all my holy **m**
      40: 4 and every **m** and hill be made low;
      65:25 not hurt or destroy on all my holy **m**
Da   2:45 saw that a stone was cut from the **m**
Mic   4: 1 the **m** of the LORD's house shall be
Mt   4: 8 a very high **m** and showed him all
      17:20 you will say to this **m**, 'Move from
Mk   9: 2 and led them up a high **m** apart,
Lk   3: 5 every **m** and hill shall be made low,
Jn   4:21 neither on this **m** nor in Jerusalem.
2Pe   1:18 we were with him on the holy **m**.
Rev   6:14 every **m** and island was removed
       8: 8 something like a great **m**, burning
      21:10 carried me away to a great, high **m**

HOLY MOUNTAIN Ps 48:1; 99:9; Isa 11:9;
27:13; 56:7; 57:13; 65:11, 25; 66:20; Eze
20:40; 28:14; Da 9:16, 20; 11:45; Joel 2:1;
3:17; Ob 1:16; Zep 3:11; Zec 8:3; 2Pe 1:18;
Wis 9:8; 1Mc 11:37

MOUNTAINS → MOUNT
Ge   7:20 the waters swelled above the **m**,
      8: 4 ark came to rest on the **m** of Ararat.
Ps   36: 6 righteousness is like the mighty **m**,
      46: 2 the **m** shake in the heart of the sea;
      90: 2 Before the **m** were brought forth,
      97: 5 **m** melt like wax before the LORD,
      125: 2 As the **m** surround Jerusalem,
Isa   2: 2 established as the highest of the **m**,
      52: 7 beautiful upon the **m** are the feet of
      54:10 For the **m** may depart and the hills
      55:12 and the hills before you shall
Eze 34: 6 over all the **m** and on every high
      39: 4 You shall fall upon the **m** of Israel,
Hos 10: 8 They shall say to the **m**, Cover us,
Mic   4: 1 established as the highest of the **m**,
Na   1:15 On the **m** the feet of one who brings
Mk   13:14 those in Judea must flee to the **m**,
Lk   23:30 begin to say to the **m**, 'Fall on us';
1Co 13: 2 have all faith, so as to remove **m**,
Rev   6:16 to the **m** and rocks, "Fall on us and
      16:20 and no **m** were to be found;

Sir 43:16 when he appears, the **m** shake.
Aza   1:53 Bless the Lord, **m** and hills;

MOUNTED → MOUNT
Ps   78:21 his anger **m** against Israel,
Mt   21: 5 humble, and **m** on a donkey,

MOURN → MOURNED, MOURNFUL,
MOURNING, MOURNS
Ge   23: 2 Abraham went in to **m** for Sarah
Ne   8: 9 do not **m** or weep."
Ecc   3: 4 a time to **m**, and a time to dance;
Isa 61: 2 of our God; to comfort all who **m**;
Zec 12:10 they shall **m** for him,
Mt   5: 4 "Blessed are those who **m**,
      9:15 wedding guests cannot **m** as long as
Lk   6:25 for you will **m** and weep.
1Co   7:30 who **m** as though they were not
Sir   7:34 but **m** with those who **m**.

MOURNED → MOURN
Nu   14:39 the Israelites, the people **m** greatly.
Ne   1: 4 and wept, and for days,
1Co   5: 2 Should you not rather have **m**,

MOURNING → MOURN
Est   4: 3 there was great **m** among the Jews,
      9:22 and from **m** into a holiday;
Ps   30:11 You have turned my **m** into dancing
Ecc   7: 2 It is better to go to the house of **m**
Isa 61: 3 the oil of gladness instead of **m**,
Jer   6:26 make **m** as for an only child,
      31:13 turn their **m** into joy, I will comfort
La   5:15 our dancing has been turned to **m**.
Rev 21: 4 and crying and pain will be no
Sir 22:12 **M** for the dead lasts seven days,
1Mc   1:39 her feasts were turned into **m**,

MOURNS → MOURN
Zec 12:10 as one **m** for an only child,

MOUTH → MOUTHS
Ex   4:12 Now go, and I will be with your **m**
      4:15 will be with your **m** and with his **m**,
Nu   16:30 ground opens its **m** and swallows
      22:38 word God puts in my **m**, that is
Dt   8: 3 that comes from the **m** of the LORD.
      18:18 my words in the **m** of the prophet,
      30:14 in your **m** and in your heart for you
Jos   1: 8 law shall not depart out of your **m**;
2Ki   4:34 putting his **m** upon his **m**,
Job 23:12 in my bosom the words of his **m**.
      40: 4 I lay my hand on my **m**.
Ps   17: 3 my **m** does not transgress.
      19:14 Let the words of my **m** and
      40: 3 He put a new song in my **m**,
      71: 8 My **m** is filled with your praise,
      78: 2 I will open my **m** in a parable;
      119:103 sweeter than honey to my **m**!
      141: 3 Set a guard over my **m**, O LORD;
Pr   2: 6 from his **m** come knowledge and
      8: 7 for my **m** will utter truth;
      10:11 The **m** of the righteous is a fountain
      10:31 The **m** of the righteous brings forth
      26:28 and a flattering **m** works ruin.
      27: 2 praise you, and not your own **m**—
Ecc   5: 2 Never be rash with your **m**,
      6: 7 All human toil is for the **m**,
SS   1: 2 kiss me with the kisses of his **m**!
Isa 40: 5 for the **m** of the LORD has spoken."
      45:23 **m** has gone forth in righteousness
      48: 3 my **m** and I made them known;
      49: 2 He made my **m** like a sharp sword,
      51:16 I have put my words in your **m**,
      53: 7 so he did not open his **m**.
      55:11 word be that goes out from my **m**;
      59:21 my words that I have put in your **m**,
      59:21 shall not depart out of your **m**,
Jer   1: 9 I have put my words in your **m**,
Eze   3: 2 I opened my **m**, and he gave me
Da   7: 8 and a **m** speaking arrogantly.
Hos   6: 5 killed them by the words of my **m**,
Mal   2: 7 should seek instruction from his **m**,

Mt   4: 4 every word that comes from the **m**
     12:34 abundance of the heart the **m** speaks
     15:11 it is not what goes into the **m**
Lk   6:45 of the heart that the **m** speaks.
Ac   8:32 so he does not open his **m.**
2Th   2: 8 with the breath of his **m,**
Jas   3:10 From the same **m** come blessing and
1Pe   2:22 and no deceit was found in his **m.**"
Rev   1:16 **m** came a sharp, two-edged sword,
      2:16 with the sword of my **m.**
      3:16 I am about to spit you out of my **m.**
     10:10 it was sweet as honey in my **m,**
     13: 6 It opened its **m** to utter blasphemies
     19:15 From his **m** comes a sharp sword
Wis   1:11 and a lying **m** destroys the soul.
Sir 21:26 The mind of fools is in their **m,**
     28:25 and a bolt for your **m.**

MOUTHS → MOUTH

Ps   73: 9 They set their **m** against heaven,
     78:36 But they flattered him with their **m;**
    115: 5 They have **m,** but do not speak;
    135:17 and there is no breath in their **m.**
Pr   15: 2 but the **m** of fools pour out folly.
Isa 52:15 shall shut their **m** because of him;
Da   6:22 sent his angel and shut the lions' **m**
Ro   3:14 "Their **m** are full of cursing and
Eph   4:29 Let no evil talk come out of your **m,**
Heb 11:33 promises, shut the **m** of lions,
Jas   3: 3 If we put bits into the **m** of horses
Rev   9:17 and sulfur came out of their **m.**

MOVE → MOVED, MOVES

Dt   19:14 not **m** your neighbor's boundary
Isa 46: 7 it cannot **m** from its place.
Mt   17:20 'M from here to there,' and it will
                m;
Ac   17:28 For 'In him we live and **m** and have
2Es   5:44 "The creation cannot **m** faster than

MOVED → MOVE

Ge   7:21 all flesh died that **m** on the earth,
1Sa   1:13 only her lips **m,** but her voice
1Ch 16:30 established; it shall never be **m.**
Ps   93: 1 the world; it shall never be **m;**
Eze   1:19 When the living creatures **m,**
Jn   11:33 disturbed in spirit and deeply **m.**

MOVES → MOVE

Dt   27:17 **m** a neighbor's boundary marker."
Ps   50:11 and all that **m** in the field is mine.

MUCH

Ex   16:18 who gathered **m** had nothing over,
Dt   28:38 You shall carry **m** seed into the field
1Ki   8:27 **m** less this house that I have built!
Job   7:17 that you make so **m** of them,
     42:10 Lord gave Job twice as **m** as he had
Ps   19:10 they than gold, even **m** fine gold;
Pr   16:16 **m** better to get wisdom than gold!
Ecc   1:18 For in **m** wisdom is **m** vexation,
      9:18 but one bungler destroys **m** good.
     12:12 **m** study is a weariness of the flesh.
Hag   1: 9 You have looked for **m,** and, lo,
Mt   12:12 **m** more valuable is a human
     23:15 convert twice as **m** a child of hell
Lk   12:48 to whom **m** has been given, **m** will
                be required;
     16:10 in a very little is faithful also in **m;**
Jn   8:26 I have **m** to say about you and **m** to
                condemn;
     12:24 but if it dies, it bears **m** fruit.
     15: 5 in me and I in them bear **m** fruit,
2Co   3:11 **m** more has the permanent come in
      8:15 who had **m** did not have too **m,**
1Ti   3: 8 not indulging in **m** wine, not greedy
Heb   1: 4 become as **m** superior to angels as
      9:14 **m** more will the blood of Christ,
1Jn   4:11 since God loved us so **m,**

MUD → MUDDIED

Isa 57:20 its waters toss up mire and **m.**
Jer 38: 6 Jeremiah sank in the **m.**

Jn   9: 6 and spread the **m** on the man's eyes,
2Pe   2:22 washed only to wallow in the **m."**

MUDDIED* → MUD

Pr   25:26 Like a **m** spring or a polluted

MULBERRY

Lk   17: 6 you could say to this **m** tree,

MULE

2Sa 18: 9 Absalom was riding on his **m,**
1Ki   1:38 Solomon ride on King David's **m,**
Ps   32: 9 Do not be like a horse or a **m,**

MULTIPLIED → MULTIPLY

Ex   1: 7 they **m** and grew exceedingly strong
     11: 9 my wonders may be **m** in the land
Ro   5:20 the result that the trespass **m;**

MULTIPLIES → MULTIPLY

Job 34:37 and **m** his words against God."
Sir   6: 5 Pleasant speech **m** friends,

MULTIPLY → MULTIPLIED, MULTIPLIES

Ge   1:28 to them, "Be fruitful and **m,**
      9: 7 And you, be fruitful and **m,**
Ex   7: 3 I will **m** my signs and wonders in
Dt   6: 3 that you may **m** greatly in a land

MULTITUDE → MULTITUDES

Da   10: 6 of his words like the roar of a **m.**
Mk   3: 7 great **m** from Galilee followed him;
Jas   5:20 and will cover a **m** of sins.
1Pe   4: 8 for love covers a **m** of sins.
Rev   7: 9 a great **m** that no one could count,
     19: 6 seemed to be the voice of a great **m,**
Sir   5: 6 he will forgive the **m** of my sins,"

MULTITUDES → MULTITUDE

Joel 3:14 **M, m,** in the valley of decision!
Rev 17:15 are peoples and **m** and nations

MURDER → MURDERED, MURDERER,
   MURDERERS, MURDERS

Ex   20:13 You shall not **m.**
Dt   5:17 You shall not **m.**
Hos   4: 2 lying, and **m,** and stealing and
Mt   5:21 of ancient times, 'You shall not **m';**
     15:19 of the heart come evil intentions, **m,**
Mk   10:19 commandments: 'You shall not **m,**
Lk   23:25 in prison for insurrection and **m,**
Ro   1:29 Full of envy, **m,** strife, deceit,
     13: 9 commit adultery; You shall not **m,**
Jas   2:11 also said, "You shall not **m."**
1Jn   3:12 And why did he **m** him?

MURDERED → MURDER

Mt   23:31 of those who **m** the prophets.
1Jn   3:12 from the evil one and **m** his brother.

MURDERER → MURDER

Nu   35:16 the **m** shall be put to death.
     35:31 accept no ransom for the life of a **m**
Jn   8:44 He was a **m** from the beginning
Ac   3:14 asked to have a **m** given to you,

MURDERERS → MURDER

1Ti   1: 9 kill their father or mother, for **m,**
1Jn   3:15 who hate a brother or sister are **m,**
Rev 21: 8 the faithless, the polluted, the **m,**
     22:15 and sorcerers and fornicators and **m**

MURDERS → MURDER

Mt   5:21 **m** shall be liable to judgment.'
Rev   9:21 of their **m** or their sorceries or their

MURMURING*

Php   2:14 all things without **m** and arguing,

MUSIC → MUSICAL, MUSICIAN,
   MUSICIANS

1Sa 19: 9 while David was playing **m.**
1Ch 25: 6 direction of their father for the **m**
Ps   92: 3 to the **m** of the lute and the harp,
La   5:14 city gate, the young men their **m.**

Eze 26:13 I will silence the **m** of your songs;
Lk   15:25 he heard **m** and dancing.
Sir 40:20 Wine and **m** gladden the heart,

MUSICAL → MUSIC

1Ch 15:16 singers to play on **m** instruments,
2Ch 23:13 singers with their **m** instruments
Ne   12:36 with the **m** instruments of David
Da   3: 5 harp, drum, and entire **m** ensemble,

MUSICIAN → MUSIC

2Ki   3:15 But get me a **m."**

MUSICIANS → MUSIC

Ps   68:25 the singers in front, the **m** last,

MUST

Ge   4: 7 desire is for you, but you **m** master
Dt   7: 2 then you **m** utterly destroy them.
     18:13 You **m** remain completely loyal to
Ps 119:84 How long **m** your servant endure?
Mt   16:21 that he **m** go to Jerusalem
     17:10 say that Elijah **m** come first?"
Mk   10:17 what **m** I do to inherit eternal life?"
     13: 7 this **m** take place, but the end is still
Lk   9:22 of Man **m** undergo great suffering,
Jn   3: 7 'You **m** be born from above.'
      3:14 so **m** the Son of Man be lifted up,
      3:30 He **m** increase, but I **m** decrease."
      4:24 worship him **m** worship in spirit
     20: 9 that he **m** rise from the dead.
1Co 10: 9 We **m** not put Christ to the test,
2Co   5:10 of us **m** appear before the judgment
Gal   6: 4 All **m** test their own work;
      6: 5 For all **m** carry their own loads.
1Ti   3: 2 Now a bishop **m** be above reproach,
      3: 8 Deacons likewise **m** be serious,
Heb 11: 6 **m** believe that he exists and that he
Rev   4: 1 I will show you what **m** take place
     22: 6 servants what **m** soon take place."

MUSTARD*

Mt   13:31 kingdom of heaven is like a **m** seed
     17:20 have faith the size of a **m** seed,
Mk   4:31 It is like a **m** seed, which,
Lk   13:19 It is like a **m** seed that someone took
     17: 6 If you had faith the size of a **m** seed

MUTE

Ex   4:11 Who makes them **m** or deaf,
Mt   9:33 the one who had been **m** spoke;
Mk   7:37 to hear and the **m** to speak."

MUTILATE*

Php   3: 2 beware of those who **m** the flesh!

MUTTER*

Isa   8:19 the familiar spirits that chirp and **m;**

MUTUAL → MUTUALLY

Ro   12:10 love one another with **m** affection;
     14:19 for peace and for **m** upbuilding.
Heb 13: 1 Let **m** love continue.
2Pe   1: 7 and godliness with **m** affection, and
                m affection with love.

MUTUALLY* → MUTUAL

Ro   1:12 that we may be **m** encouraged

MUZZLE

Dt   25: 4 not **m** an ox while it is treading out
Ps   39: 1 a **m** on my mouth as long as the
1Co   9: 9 not **m** an ox while it is treading out
1Ti   5:18 not **m** an ox while it is treading out

MYRIAD → MYRIADS

Dt   32:30 and two put a **m** to flight,

MYRIADS → MYRIAD

Dt   33: 2 With him were **m** of holy ones;
Rev   5:11 they numbered **m** of **m**

MYRRH

Ps   45: 8 your robes are all fragrant with **m**
SS   1:13 My beloved is to me a bag of **m**

Mt 2:11 gifts of gold, frankincense, and **m.**
Mk 15:23 offered him wine mixed with **m;**
Jn 19:39 bringing a mixture of **m** and aloes,
Rev 18:13 spice, incense, **m,** frankincense,

MYRTLE
Isa 55:13 of the brier shall come up the **m;**
Zec 1: 8 He was standing among the **m** trees

MYSTERIES → MYSTERY
Da 2:28 is a God in heaven who reveals **m,**
2:29 the revealer of **m** disclosed to you
2:47 Lord of kings and a revealer of **m,**
1Co 13: 2 understand all **m** and all knowledge,
14: 2 they are speaking **m** in the Spirit.
Wis 14:23 or celebrate secret **m,**
Sir 39: 7 as he meditates on his **m.**
3Mc 2:30 who have been initiated into the **m,**

MYSTERY → MYSTERIES
Da 2:18 God of heaven concerning this **m,**
2:19 **m** was revealed to Daniel in a vision
2:27 can show to the king the **m** that
2:30 this **m** has not been revealed to me
2:47 have been able to reveal this **m!"**
4: 9 and that no **m** is too difficult
Ro 11:25 I want you to understand this **m:**
16:25 of the **m** that was kept secret
1Co 2: 1 not come proclaiming the **m** of God
15:51 Listen, I will tell you a **m!**
Eph 1: 9 made known to us the **m** of his will,
3: 3 how the **m** was made known to me
3: 4 my understanding of the **m** of Christ
3: 9 the plan of the **m** hidden for ages
5:32 a great **m,** and I am applying it to
6:19 with boldness the **m** of the gospel,
Col 1:26 **m** that has been hidden throughout
1:27 are the riches of the glory of this **m,**
2: 2 have the knowledge of God's **m,**
4: 3 that we may declare the **m** of Christ,
2Th 2: 7 the **m** of lawlessness is already at
1Ti 3: 9 must hold fast to the **m** of the faith
3:16 the **m** of our religion is great:
Rev 1:20 As for the **m** of the seven stars that
10: 7 the **m** of God will be fulfilled,
17: 5 a name, a **m:** "Babylon the great,
17: 7 I will tell you the **m** of the woman,

MYTHS
1Ti 1: 4 not to occupy themselves with **m**
4: 7 with profane **m** and old wives' tales.
2Ti 4: 4 to the truth and wander away to **m.**
Tit 1:14 not paying attention to Jewish **m** or
2Pe 1:16 did not follow cleverly devised **m**

NAAMAN
Aramean general whose leprosy was cleansed
by Elisha (2Ki 5; Lk 4:27).

NABAL
Wealthy Carmelite the LORD killed for refusing
to help David (1Sa 25). David married Abigail,
his widow (1Sa 25:39-42).

NABOTH
Jezreelite killed by Jezebel for his vineyard (1Ki
21). Ahab's family destroyed for this (1Ki 21:17-
24; 2Ki 9:21-37).

NADAB
1. Firstborn of Aaron (Ex 6:23); killed with
Abihu for offering unauthorized fire (Lev 10; Nu
3:4).
2. Son of Jeroboam I; king of Israel (1Ki 15:25-
32).

NAHASH
1Sa 11: 1 **N** the Ammonite went up

NAHOR
Ge 11:26 the father of Abram, **N,** and Haran.
22:23 These eight Milcah bore to **N,**
24:15 the wife of **N,** Abraham's brother,

NAHUM
Prophet against Nineveh (Na 1:1; Tob 14:4; 2Es
1:40).

NAILING* → NAILS
Col 2:14 He set this aside, **n** it to the cross.

NAILS → NAILING
Ecc 12:11 like **n** firmly fixed are the collected
Isa 41: 7 fasten it with **n** so that it cannot be
Jn 20:25 put my finger in the mark of the **n**

NAIOTH
1Sa 19:18 and Samuel went and settled at **N.**

NAKED → NAKEDNESS
Ge 2:25 the man and his wife were both **n,**
Job 1:21 "**N** I came from my mother's
womb, and **n** I shall I return there;
Ecc 5:15 they shall go again, **n** as they came;
Isa 58: 7 when you see the **n,** to cover them,
Mk 14:52 he left the linen cloth and ran off **n.**
2Co 5: 3 taken it off we will not be found **n.**
11:27 often without food, cold and **n.**
Rev 3:17 pitiable, poor, blind, and **n.**

NAKEDNESS → NAKED
Ge 9:22 of Canaan, saw the **n** of his father,
Ex 20:26 so that your **n** may not be exposed
Eze 16: 8 cloak over you, and covered your **n:**
Ro 8:35 or persecution, or famine, or **n,**
Rev 3:18 shame of your **n** from being seen;

NAME → NAME'S, NAMED, NAMES
Ge 2:19 every living creature, that was its **n.**
4:26 people began to invoke the **n** of
11: 4 and let us make a **n** for ourselves;
12: 2 bless you, and make your **n** great,
12: 8 and invoked the **n** of the LORD.
13: 4 Abram called on the **n** of the LORD.
17: 5 but your **n** shall be Abraham;
21:33 called there on the **n** of the LORD,
26:25 called on the **n** of the LORD,
32:29 asked him, "Please tell me your **n.**"
Ex 3:15 my **n** forever, and this my title
6: 3 but by my **n** 'The LORD' I did not
20: 7 wrongful use of the **n** of the LORD
20: 7 acquit anyone who misuses his **n.**
33:17 in my sight, and I know you by **n.**"
33:19 and will proclaim before you the **n,**
34: 5 and proclaimed the **n,** "The LORD."
34:14 the LORD, whose **n** is Jealous,
Nu 17: 2 Write each man's **n** on his staff,
Dt 5:11 wrongful use of the **n** of the LORD
5:11 acquit anyone who misuses his **n.**
10: 8 and to bless in his **n,** to this day.
12:11 as a dwelling for his **n:**
18: 5 and minister in the **n** of the LORD,
25: 6 so that his **n** may not be blotted out
28:58 this glorious and awesome **n,**
Jos 7: 9 and cut off our **n** from the earth.
Jdg 13:17 angel of the LORD, "What is your **n,**
Ru 4: 5 to maintain the dead man's **n** on his
1Sa 17:45 to you in the **n** of the LORD of hosts,
25:25 for as his is, so is he; Nabal is his
n, and folly is with him;
2Sa 6: 2 called by the **n** of the LORD of hosts
7: 9 and I will make for you a great **n,**
1Ki 5: 5 house for the **n** of the LORD my God
8:29 'My **n** shall be there,'
18:24 Then you call on the **n** of your god
and I will call on the **n** of the LORD;
1Ch 17: 8 and I will make for you a **n,**
2Ch 7:14 called by my **n** humble themselves,
Ezr 6:12 who has established his **n** there
Ne 9:10 You made a **n** for yourself,
Ps 5:11 who love your **n** may exult in you.
8: 1 majestic is your **n** in all the earth!

9: 5 you have blotted out their **n** forever
9:10 know your **n** put their trust in you,
20: 7 our pride is in the **n** of the LORD
29: 2 to the LORD the glory of his **n;**
34: 3 and let us exalt his **n** together.
44:20 If we had forgotten the **n** of our God
54: 1 Save me, O God, by your **n,**
66: 2 sing the glory of his **n;**
68: 4 Sing to God, sing praises to his **n;**
74:10 the enemy to revile your **n** forever?
74:21 let the poor and needy praise your **n.**
79: 9 salvation, for the glory of your **n;**
96: 8 to the LORD the glory due his **n;**
103: 1 that is within me, bless his holy **n.**
113: 1 praise the **n** of the LORD.
115: 1 not to us, but to your **n** give glory,
124: 8 Our help is in the **n** of the LORD,
138: 2 and give thanks to your **n** for your
145: 1 and bless your **n** forever and ever.
149: 3 Let them praise his **n** with dancing,
Pr 10: 7 but the **n** of the wicked will rot.
18:10 The **n** of the LORD is a strong tower;
22: 1 A good **n** is to be chosen rather
30: 4 What is the person's **n?**
Ecc 7: 1 A good **n** is better than precious
SS 1: 3 your **n** is perfume poured out;
Isa 12: 4 thanks to the LORD, call on his **n;**
12: 4 proclaim that his **n** is exalted.
26: 8 your **n** and your renown are the
40:26 numbers them, calling them all by **n**
42: 8 I am the LORD, that is my **n;**
50:10 the **n** of the LORD and relies upon
56: 5 I will give them an everlasting **n**
57:15 inhabits eternity, whose **n** is Holy:
63:14 to make for yourself a glorious **n.**
Jer 7:11 this house, which is called by my **n,**
10: 6 great, and your **n** is great in might.
15:16 I am called by your **n,** O LORD,
27:15 are prophesying falsely in my **n,**
Eze 20: 9 But I acted for the sake of my **n,**
20:14 But I acted for the sake of my **n,**
20:22 and acted for the sake of my **n,**
36:22 but for the sake of my holy **n,**
48:35 the **n** of the city from that time on
Da 2:20 "Blessed be the **n** of God from age
Hos 12: 5 the God of hosts, the LORD is his **n!**
Joel 2:32 on the **n** of the LORD shall be saved;
Am 9:12 the nations who are called by my **n,**
Mic 5: 4 in the majesty of the **n** of the LORD
6: 9 (it is sound wisdom to fear your **n):**
Zep 3: 9 may call on the **n** of the LORD
Zec 6:12 Here is a man whose **n** is Branch:
13: 9 will call on my **n,** and I will answer
14: 9 the LORD will be one and his **n** one.
Mal 1: 6 "How have we despised your **n?**"
4: 2 But for you who revere my **n**
Mt 1:21 a son, and you are to **n** him Jesus,
6: 9 Our Father in heaven, hallowed be
your **n.**
7:22 Lord, did we not prophesy in your **n**
12:21 in his **n** the Gentiles will hope."
18:20 two or three are gathered in my **n,**
24: 5 many will come in my **n,** saying,
28:19 baptizing them in the **n** of the Father
Mk 9:41 you bear the **n** of Christ
11: 9 the one who comes in the **n** of the
Lk 1:31 and you will **n** him Jesus.
11: 2 Father, hallowed be your **n.**
19:38 the king who comes in the **n** of the
Jn 1:12 received him, who believed in his **n,**
5:43 I have come in my Father's **n,**
5:43 another comes in his own **n,**
10: 3 He calls his own sheep by **n** and
12:28 Father, glorify your **n.**"
14:13 I will do whatever you ask in my **n,**
15:16 whatever you ask him in my **n.**
16:23 ask anything of the Father in my **n,**
16:24 not asked for anything in my **n.**
17:11 protect them in your **n** that you
20:31 believing you may have life in his **n.**
Ac 2:21 Then everyone who calls on the **n** of
3:16 And by faith in his **n,**

4:12 for there is no other **n** under heaven
4:17 speak no more to anyone in this **n.**"
5:40 them not to speak in the **n** of Jesus,
15:17 Gentiles over whom my **n** has been
Ro 10:13 who calls on the **n** of the Lord shall
1Co 6:11 in the **n** of the Lord Jesus Christ
Eph 3:15 in heaven and on earth takes its **n.**
Php 2: 9 gave him the **n** that is above every **n**
2:10 so that at the **n** of Jesus every knee
Col 3:17 do everything in the **n** of the Lord
2Ti 2:19 the **n** of the Lord turn away from
Heb 1: 4 **n** he has inherited is more excellent
13:15 the fruit of lips that confess his **n.**
Jas 5:14 anointing them with oil in the **n** of
1Pe 4:16 glorify God because you bear this **n.**
1Jn 2:12 are forgiven on account of his **n.**
3:23 in the **n** of his Son Jesus Christ
5:13 things to you who believe in the **n**
Rev 2: 3 and bearing up for the sake of my **n,**
2:13 Yet you are holding fast to my **n,**
2:17 the white stone is written a new **n**
3: 5 confess your **n** before my Father
3: 8 and have not denied my **n.**
3:12 I will write on you the **n** of my God,
11:18 and saints and all who fear your **n,**
13:17 the **n** of the beast or the number of
its **n.**
14: 1 one hundred forty-four thousand
who had his **n** and his Father's **n**
16: 9 but they cursed the **n** of God,
19:12 a **n** inscribed that no one knows but
19:13 his **n** is called The Word of God.
19:16 on his thigh he has a **n** inscribed,
20:15 whose **n** was not found written in
22: 4 and his **n** will be on their foreheads.
Tob 11:14 and blessed be his great **n,**
Jdt 16: 1 exalt him, and call upon his **n.**
Sir 2:17 and equal to his **n** are his works.
41:13 but a good **n** lasts forever.

GLORIOUS NAME 1Ch 29:13; Ne 9:5; Ps
72:19; Isa 63:14; Jdt 9:8; 2Mc 8:15; Man 1:3;
3Mc 2:14

HOLY NAME Lev 20:3; 22:2, 32; 1Ch 16:10,
35; 29:16; Ps 30:4; 33:21; 97:12; 103:1; 105:3;
106:47; 145:21; Eze 20:39; 36:20, 21, 22;
39:7, 7, 25; 43:7, 8; Am 2:7; Tob 11:14; 13:11,
17; Wis 10:20; Sir 17:10; 47:10; Aza 1:30

NAME OF *GOD Lev 18:21; 19:12; 21:6;
1Ki 18:24, 25; 2Ch 33:18; Ezr 5:1; Ne 13:25;
Ps 20:1, 5; 44:20; 69:30; Pr 30:9; Da 2:20; 4:8;
Mic 4:5; Ro 2:24; 1Ti 6:1; 1Jn 5:13; Rev 3:12;
16:9; Sir 47:18; 1Es 6:1; 2Es 2:45

NAME OF JESUS Ac 2:38; 3:6; 4:10, 18;
5:40; 8:12; 9:27; 10:48; 16:18; 26:9; Php 2:10

NAME OF THE *LORD Mt 21:9; 23:39;
Mk 11:9; Lk 13:35; 19:38; Jn 12:13; Ac 2:21;
8:16; 9:28; 19:5, 13, 17; 21:13; Ro 10:13; 1Co
5:4; 6:11; Col 3:17; 2Ti 2:19; Jas 5:10, 14; Sir
39:35; 47:18; 51:12; 1Es 1:48; 6:1; 2Es 2:47

NAME OF THE †LORD Ge 4:26; 12:8;
13:4; 21:33; 26:25; Ex 20:7; Lev 24:16; Dt
5:11; 18:5, 7, 22; 21:5; 28:10; 32:3; Jos 9:9;
1Sa 17:45; 20:42; 2Sa 6:2, 18; 1Ki 3:2; 5:3, 5;
8:17, 20; 10:1; 18:24, 32; 22:16; 2Ki 2:24;
5:11; 1Ch 16:2; 21:19; 22:7, 19; 2Ch 2:1, 4;
6:7, 10; 18:15; 33:18; Job 1:21; Ps 7:17; 20:7;
102:15, 21; 113:1, 2, 3; 116:4, 13, 17; 118:10,
11, 12, 26; 122:4; 124:8; 129:8; 135:1; 148:5,
13; Pr 18:10; Isa 18:7; 24:15; 30:27; 48:1;
50:10; 56:6; 59:19; 60:9; Jer 11:21; 26:9, 16,
20; 44:16; Joel 2:26, 32; Am 6:10; Mic 4:5;
5:4; Zep 3:9, 12; Zec 13:3

NAME'S → NAME
Ps 23: 3 in right paths for his **n** sake.
79: 9 forgive our sins, for your **n** sake.
106: 8 Yet he saved them for his **n** sake,
Eze 20:44 when I deal with you for my **n** sake,

NAMED → NAME
Ge 3:20 The man **n** his wife Eve,

5:29 he **n** him Noah, saying, "Out of the
27:36 said, "Is he not rightly **n** Jacob?
Ex 2:10 She **n** him Moses, "because,"
1Sa 4:21 She **n** the child Ichabod, meaning,
7:12 and Jeshanah, and **n** it Ebenezer;

NAMES → NAME
Ge 2:20 The man gave **n** to all cattle,
Ex 28: 9 engrave on them the **n** of the sons
Hos 2:17 I will remove the **n** of the Baals
Mt 10: 2 are the **n** of the twelve apostles:
Lk 10:20 but rejoice that your **n** are written
Php 4: 3 whose **n** are in the book of life.
Rev 17: 3 beast that was full of blasphemous **n**
17: 8 whose **n** have not been written in
21:12 inscribed the **n** of the twelve tribes
21:14 the twelve **n** of the twelve apostles

NAOMI → =MARA
Wife of Elimelech, mother-in-law of Ruth (Ru
1:2, 4). Left Bethlehem for Moab during famine
(Ru 1:1). Returned a widow, with Ruth (Ru 1:6-
22). Advised Ruth to seek marriage with Boaz
(Ru 2:17-3:4). Cared for Ruth's son Obed (Ru
4:13-17).

NAPHTALI
Son of Jacob by Bilhah (Ge 30:8; 35:25; 1Ch
2:2). Tribe of blessed (Ge 49:21; Dt 33:23), numbered (Nu 1:43; 26:50), allotted land (Jos 19:32-
39; Eze 48:3), failed to fully possess (Jdg 1:33),
supported Deborah (Jdg 4:10; 5:18), David (1Ch
12:34), 12,000 from (Rev 7:6).

TRIBE OF NAPHTALI Nu 1:43; 2:29;
10:27; 13:14; Jos 19:32, 32, 39; 21:6, 32; Jdg
4:6; 1Ki 7:14; 1Ch 6:76; Rev 7:6; Tob 1:1

NARD
Jn 12: 3 of pure **n,** anointed Jesus' feet,

NARROW
Nu 22:24 angel of the LORD stood in a **n** path
Mt 7:13 "Enter through the **n** gate;
Lk 13:24 "Strive to enter through the **n** door;

NATHAN
Prophet and chronicler of Israel's history (1Ch
29:29; 2Ch 9:29). Announced the Davidic covenant (2Sa 7; 1Ch 17). Denounced David's sin
with Bathsheba (2Sa 12). Supported Solomon
(1Ki 1).

NATHANAEL → =BARTHOLOMEW?
Apostle (Jn 1:45-49; 21:2). Probably also called
Bartholomew (Mt 10:3).

NATION → NATIONS
Ge 12: 2 I will make of you a great **n,** and
15:14 judgment on the **n** that they serve,
35:11 **n** and a company of nations shall
Ex 19: 6 a priestly kingdom and a holy **n.**
32:10 and of you I will make a great **n.**"
Nu 14:12 of you a **n** greater and mightier than
Dt 4: 7 other great **n** has a god so near to it
Jos 4: 1 entire **n** had finished crossing over
5: 8 circumcising of all the **n** was done,
2Sa 7:23 another **n** on earth whose God went
1Ch 16:20 wandering from **n** to **n,**
Ps 33:12 Happy is the **n** whose God is the
LORD,
147:20 has not dealt thus with any other **n;**
Pr 11:14 there is no guidance, a **n** falls,
14:34 Righteousness exalts a **n,**
Isa 2: 4 **n** shall not lift up sword against **n,**
9: 3 You have multiplied the **n,**
26: 2 righteous **n** that keeps faith may
60:12 For the **n** and kingdom that will
65: 1 to a **n** that did not call on my name.
66: 8 a **n** be delivered in one moment?
Jer 2:11 Has a **n** changed its gods,
18: 8 if that **n,** concerning which I have
Eze 37:22 I will make them one **n** in the land,
Mic 4: 3 **n** shall not lift up sword against **n,**
Mal 3: 9 robbing me—the whole **n** of you!

Mt 24: 7 For **n** will rise against **n,**
Jn 11:50 than to have the whole **n** destroyed.
1Pe 2: 9 a holy **n,** God's own people,
Rev 5: 9 and language and people and **n;**
7: 9 from every **n,**
14: 6 to every **n** and tribe and language
2Es 15:15 and **n** shall rise up to fight against **n,**

EVERY NATION 2Ki 17:29, 29; Ac 2:5;
10:35; Rev 7:9; 14:6; Jdt 14:7; AdE 11:7; 13:4,
5; 16:11; Sir 17:17; 2Es 3:8

NATION OF THE JEWS 1Mc 8:23, 25, 27;
10:25; 11:30, 33; 13:36; 15:2; 2Mc 10:8

WHOLE NATION Mal 3:9; Jn 11:50; Jdt
9:14; AdE 16:13; 10:3; 2Mc 7:38; 10:8; 14:8;
1Es 1:32; 3Mc 5:5

NATIONS → NATION
Ge 17: 4 the ancestor of a multitude of **n.**
18:18 the **n** of the earth shall be blessed in
22:18 all the **n** of the earth gain blessing
25:23 "Two **n** are in your womb,
Ex 34:24 For I will cast out **n** before you,
Dt 7: 1 seven **n** mightier and more
15: 6 you will rule over many **n,**
Jos 23: 7 not be mixed with these **n** left here
Jdg 3: 1 the **n** that the LORD left to test all
1Sa 8:20 so that we also may be like other **n,**
1Ki 4:34 from all the **n** to hear the wisdom
2Ki 17:15 followed the **n** that were around
2Ch 20: 6 rule over all the kingdoms of the **n?**
Ps 2: 1 Why do the **n** conspire, and the
2: 8 and I will make the **n** your heritage,
9: 5 You have rebuked the **n,** you have
22:28 and he rules over the **n.**
33:10 the counsel of the **n** to nothing;
46:10 I am exalted among the **n,**
47: 8 God is king over the **n;**
66: 7 whose eyes keep watch on the **n**—
67: 2 your saving power among all **n.**
72:17 May all **n** be blessed in him;
106:35 mingled with the **n** and learned to
110: 6 will execute judgment among the **n,**
113: 4 The LORD is high above all **n,**
Isa 2: 2 all the **n** shall stream to it.
11:10 the **n** shall inquire of him,
12: 4 make known his deeds among the **n;**
40:15 the **n** are like a drop from a bucket,
42: 1 he will bring forth justice to the **n.**
52:15 so he shall startle many **n;**
60: 3 **N** shall come to your light,
66:18 I am coming to gather all **n** and
Jer 1: 5 I appointed you a prophet to the **n.**"
3:17 and all **n** shall gather to it,
31:10 Hear the word of the LORD, O **n,**
33: 9 before all the **n** of the earth who
46:28 I will make an end of all the **n**
La 1: 1 she that was great among the **n!**
Eze 22: 4 made you a disgrace before the **n,**
36:23 the **n** shall know that I am the LORD,
37:22 Never again shall they be two **n,**
39:21 will display my glory among the **n;**
Joel 2:17 a mockery, a byword among the **n.**
3: 2 I will gather all the **n** and bring
Am 9:12 and all the **n** who are called
Zep 3: 8 For my decision is to gather **n,**
Hag 2: 7 that the treasure of all **n** shall come,
Zec 8:13 have been a cursing among the **n,**
8:23 from **n** of every language shall take
9:10 he shall command peace to the **n;**
14: 2 gather all the **n** against Jerusalem to
Mal 1:11 for my name is great among the **n,**
3:12 Then all **n** will count you happy,
Mt 24: 9 hated by all **n** because of my name.
24:14 as a testimony to all the **n;**
25:32 All the **n** will be gathered before
28:19 and make disciples of all **n,**
Mk 11:17 a house of prayer for all the **n**'?
Ro 4:18 become "the father of many **n,**"
Rev 2:26 I will give authority over the **n,**
12: 5 to rule all the **n** with a rod of iron.
15: 4 All **n** will come and worship before

18:23 all **n** were deceived by your sorcery.
19:15 to strike down the **n,**
20: 8 to deceive the **n** at the four corners
21:24 The **n** will walk by its light,
22: 2 the tree are for the healing of the **n.**
Sir 44:21 that the **n** would be blessed through

ALL ... NATIONS Ge 18:18; 22:18; 26:4; Dt
11:23; 17:14; 26:19; 28:1; 29:24; 30:1; Jos
23:3, 4; 2Sa 8:11; 1Ki 4:34; 1Ch 14:17; 18:11;
2Ch 32:23; Ne 6:16; Ps 9:17; 59:5, 8; 67:2;
72:11, 17; 82:8; 86:9; 113:4; 117:1; 118:10;
Isa 2:2; 14:26; 25:7; 29:7, 8; 34:2; 37:18;
40:17; 43:9; 52:10; 61:11; 66:18, 20; Jer 3:17,
19; 9:26; 25:9, 13, 15, 17; 26:6; 27:7; 28:11,
14; 29:14, 18; 30:11; 33:9; 36:2; 43:5; 44:8;
46:28; Eze 25:8; 31:6; 39:21; Da 3:7; 4:1;
5:19; 6:25; 7:14; Joel 3:2, 11; Am 9:9, 12; Ob
1:15, 16; Hab 2:5; Hag 2:7, 7; Zec 7:14; 12:3,
9; 14:2, 19; Mal 3:12; Mt 24:9, 14; 25:32;
28:19; Mk 11:17; 13:10; Lk 21:24; 24:47; Ac
14:16; 17:26; Rev 12:5; 14:8; 15:4; 18:3, 23;
Tob 3:4; 13:5; Jdt 3:8; AdE 13:4; 3:14; 4:11;
14:5; 10:10, 11; Sir 36:2; LtJ 6:51; 1Mc 2:19;
12:53; 13:6; 2Mc 8:9; 1Es 1:49; 3Mc 3:19, 20;
6:26; 7:4; 2Es 1:11; 13:33, 33

OTHER NATIONS 1Sa 8:5, 20; Ne 5:8; Eze
25:8; Hos 9:1; AdE 3:8; 2Mc 4:35; 6:14; 11:3;
2Es 1:24; 6:56

NATIVE
Ex 12:49 one law for the **n** and for the alien
Ac 2: 8 each of us, in our own **n** language?

NATURAL → NATURE
Nu 16:29 If these people die a **n** death,
Ro 1:26 women exchanged **n** intercourse
6:19 because of your **n** limitations.
11:21 if God did not spare the **n** branches,

NATURE → NATURAL
Ro 1:20 his eternal power and divine **n,**
1Co 11:14 Does not **n** itself teach you that if
Eph 2: 3 and we were by **n** children of wrath,
2Pe 1: 4 become participants of the divine **n.**

NAZARETH
Mt 2:23 made his home in a town called **N,**
Mk 1:24 have you to do with us, Jesus of **N?**
Lk 1:26 to a town in Galilee called **N,**
4:16 When he came to **N,** where he had
Jn 1:46 Can anything good come out of **N?**
19:19 "Jesus of **N,** the King of the Jews."
Ac 2:22 of **N,** a man attested to you by God
10:38 Jesus of **N** with the Holy Spirit

JESUS OF NAZARETH Mt 26:71; Mk
1:24; 10:47; 16:6; Lk 4:34; 18:37; 24:19; Jn
18:5, 7; 19:19; Ac 2:22; 6:14; 10:38; 22:8; 26:9

NAZIRITE → NAZIRITES
Nu 6: 2 make a special vow, the vow of a **n,**
Jdg 13: 5 boy shall be a **n** to God from birth.

NAZIRITES → NAZIRITE
Am 2:12 But you made the **n** drink wine,

NAZOREAN*
Mt 2:23 "He will be called a **N.**"

NEAR → NEARER, NEARSIGHTED
Dt 4: 7 has a god so **n** to it as the LORD
30:14 No, the word is very **n** to you;
Ps 69:18 Draw **n** to me, redeem me,
73:28 But for me it is good to be **n** God;
145:18 LORD is **n** to all who call on him,
Isa 55: 6 call upon him while he is **n;**
Eze 7: 7 The time has come, the day is **n**—
Joel 1:15 For the day of the LORD is **n,**
Zep 1:14 The great day of the LORD is **n, n**
and hastening fast;
Mal 3: 5 I will draw **n** to you for judgment;
Mk 1:15 the kingdom of God has come **n;**
Lk 10: 9 'The kingdom of God has come **n**
21:28 your redemption is drawing **n.**"

Ro 10: 8 "The word is **n** you, on your lips
Php 4: 5 The Lord is **n.**
Jas 4: 8 Draw **n** to God, and he will draw **n**
to you.
1Pe 4: 7 The end of all things is **n;**
Rev 1: 3 is written in it; for the time is **n.**
22:10 of this book, for the time is **n.**

NEARER → NEAR
Ro 13:11 For salvation is **n** to us now than

NEARSIGHTED* → NEAR, SEE
2Pe 1: 9 lacks these things is **n** and blind,

NEBO
Dt 34: 1 from the plains of Moab to Mount **N**
Isa 46: 1 Bel bows down, **N** stoops,

NEBUCHADNEZZAR
Babylonian king, also spelled Nebuchadrezzar.
Subdued and exiled Judah (2Ki 24-25; 2Ch 36;
Jer 39). Dreams interpreted by Daniel (Da 2; 4).
Worshiped God (Da 3:28-29; 4:34-37).

NEBUZARADAN
2Ki 25: 8 **N,** the captain of the bodyguard,
Jer 52:12 **N** the captain of the bodyguard who

NECESSARY
Lk 24:26 **n** that the Messiah should suffer
Ac 15: 5 "It is **n** for them to be circumcised
2Co 9: 5 I thought it **n** to urge the brothers to
Php 1:24 to remain in the flesh is more **n** for
Heb 9:23 Thus it was **n** for the sketches of

NECK → NECKS, STIFF-NECKED
Ge 27:16 and on the smooth part of his **n.**
Ps 75: 5 on high, or speak with insolent **n."**
Pr 1: 9 your head, and pendants for your **n.**
3:22 your soul and adornment for your **n.**
6:21 always; tie them around your **n.**
SS 7: 4 Your **n** is like an ivory tower.
Jer 28:10 from the **n** of the prophet Jeremiah,
Hos 10:11 and I spared her fair **n;**
Mt 18: 6 were fastened around your **n**
Sir 51:26 Put your **n** under her yoke,

NECKS → NECK
Jos 10:24 on the **n** of these kings."
Isa 3:16 and walk with outstretched **n,**
Jer 7:26 but they stiffened their **n.**

NECO
Pharaoh who killed Josiah (2Ki 23:29-30; 2Ch
35:20-22), deposed Jehoahaz (2Ki 23:33-35; 2Ch
36:3-4).

NEED → NEEDED, NEEDS, NEEDY
Mt 3:14 saying, "I **n** to be baptized by you,
6: 8 for your Father knows what you **n**
Mk 2:17 are well have no **n** of a physician,
Lk 12:30 your Father knows that you **n** them.
15:14 and he began to be in **n.**
Ac 2:45 the proceeds to all, as any had **n.**
4:35 distributed to each as any had **n.**
1Co 12:21 to the hand, "I have no **n** of you,"
2Co 8:14 your present abundance and their **n,**
1Th 5: 1 do not **n** to have anything written to
2Ti 2:15 worker who has no **n** to be ashamed,
Heb 4:16 and find grace to help in time of **n.**
1Jn 2:27 you do not **n** anyone to teach you;
3:17 and sees a brother or sister in **n**
Rev 21:23 no **n** of sun or moon to shine on it,
22: 5 they **n** no light of lamp or sun,

NEEDED → NEED
Ex 16:18 gathered as much as each of them **n.**
Ac 17:25 as though he **n** anything,
2Pe 1: 3 everything **n** for life and godliness,

NEEDLE
Lk 18:25 a camel to go through the eye of a **n**

NEEDS → NEED
Ex 16:16 as much of it as each of you **n,**

Pr 12:10 The righteous know the **n** of their
Isa 58:11 and satisfy your **n** in parched places,
Mt 21: 3 just say this, 'The Lord **n** them.'
Jas 2:16 yet you do not supply their bodily **n,**

NEEDY → NEED
Dt 15:11 hand to the poor and **n** neighbor
1Sa 2: 8 he lifts the **n** from the ash heap,
Job 29:16 I was a father to the **n,**
Ps 9:18 the **n** shall not always be forgotten,
35:10 and **n** from those who despoil them.
69:33 For the LORD hears the **n,**
70: 5 But I am poor and **n;** hasten to me,
72:12 For he delivers the **n** when they call,
74:21 let the poor and **n** praise your name.
113: 7 and lifts the **n** from the ash heap,
140:12 LORD maintains the cause of the **n,**
Pr 14:31 who are kind to the **n** honor him.
31: 9 defend the rights of the poor and **n.**
31:20 and reaches out her hands to the **n.**
Am 8: 4 Hear this, you that trample on the **n,**
Sir 4: 3 or delay giving to the **n.**

NEGEB
Ge 13: 1 and Lot with him, into the **N.**
24:62 and was settled in the **N.**
Jos 11:16 the hill country and all the **N**
Ps 126: 4 like the watercourses in the **N.**

NEGLECT → NEGLECTED, NEGLECTING
Dt 12:19 not **n** the Levite as long as you live
14:27 in your towns, do not **n** them,
Ne 10:39 We will not **n** the house of our God.
Lk 11:42 and in justice and the love of God;
Ac 6: 2 that we should **n** the word of God
1Ti 4:14 Do not **n** the gift that is in you,
Heb 2: 3 escape if we **n** so great a salvation?
Sir 7:10 do not **n** to give alms.

NEGLECTED → NEGLECT
Mt 23:23 **n** the weightier matters of the law:

NEGLECTING → NEGLECT
Lk 11:42 have practiced, without **n** the others.

NEHEMIAH
Cupbearer of Artaxerxes (Ne 2:1); governor of
Israel (Ne 8:9). Returned to Jerusalem to rebuild
walls (Ne 2-6). With Ezra, reestablished worship
(Ne 8). Prayer confessing nation's sin (Ne 9).
Dedicated wall (Ne 12). Story of the miraculous
fire (2Mc 1).

NEHUSHTAN*
2Ki 18: 4 made offerings to it; it was called **N.**

NEIGHBOR → NEIGHBOR'S, NEIGHBORS
Ex 3:22 each woman shall ask her **n**
20:16 bear false witness against your **n.**
20:17 or anything that belongs to your **n.**
Dt 5:20 bear false witness against your **n.**
Pr 3:29 not plan harm against your **n** who
24:28 a witness against your **n** without
25:18 who bears false witness against a **n.**
27:10 a **n** who is nearby than kindred who
27:14 blesses a **n** with a loud voice,
29: 5 a **n** is spreading a net for the
Isa 19: 2 one against the other, **n** against **n,**
Mt 5:43 love your **n** and hate your enemy.'
19:19 You shall love your **n** as yourself.
Mk 12:31 'You shall love your **n** as yourself.'
Lk 10:27 your mind; and your **n** as yourself.'
10:29 asked Jesus, "And who is my **n?**"
Ro 13: 9 "Love your **n** as yourself."
13:10 Love does no wrong to a **n;**
15: 2 must please our **n** for the good
purpose of building up the **n.**
Jas 2: 8 "You shall love your **n** as yourself."
Sir 29:20 Assist your **n** to the best of your
ability,

LOVE ONE'S/YOUR NEIGHBOR Lev
19:18; Mt 5:43; 19:19; 22:39; Mk 12:31, 33;
Ro 13:9; Gal 5:14; Jas 2:8

NEIGHBOR'S → NEIGHBOR

Ex 20:17 You shall not covet your **n** house;
22:26 If you take your **n** cloak in pawn,
Dt 5:21 Neither shall you covet your **n** wife.
19:14 not move your **n** boundary marker,
27:17 who moves a **n** boundary marker."
Pr 25:17 your foot be seldom in your **n** house
Mt 7: 3 the speck in your **n** eye,

NEIGHBORS → NEIGHBOR

2Ki 4: 3 borrow vessels from all your **n,**
Ezr 1: 6 All their **n** aided them with silver
Ps 79: 4 We have become a taunt to our **n,**
80: 6 You make us the scorn of our **n;**
Sir 29: 1 The merciful lend to their **n;**

NEPHEW

Ge 14:14 Abram heard that his **n** had been
Tob 1:22 He was my **n** and so a close relative.

NEPHILIM

Ge 6: 4 The **N** were on the earth in those
Nu 13:33 There we saw the **N** (the Anakites

NEST → NESTED, NESTS

Dt 22: 6 If you come on a bird's **n,**
Ob 1: 4 though your **n** is set among the stars
Hab 2: 9 setting your **n** on high to be safe

NESTED → NEST

Da 4:12 the birds of the air **n** in its branches,

NESTS → NEST

Mt 8:20 and birds of the air have **n;**
Lk 13:19 made **n** in its branches."

NET → NETS

Ps 35: 8 let the **n** that they hid ensnare them;
Pr 1:17 **n** baited while the bird is looking
La 1:13 he spread a **n** for my feet;
Hab 1:15 he drags them out with his **n,**
Mt 13:47 like a **n** that was thrown into the sea
Mk 1:16 and his brother Andrew casting a **n**
Jn 21: 6 "Cast the **n** to the right side of the

NETS → NET

Ps 141:10 Let the wicked fall into their own **n,**
Mt 4:20 they left their **n** and followed him.
Lk 5: 4 let down your **n** for a catch."

NEVER

Ge 8:21 "I will **n** again curse the ground
Dt 32:17 to deities they had **n** known,
34:10 **N** since has there arisen a prophet
1Ki 8:25 'There shall **n** fail you a successor
2Ch 18: 7 he **n** prophesies anything favorable
Ps 15: 5 do these things shall **n** be moved.
30: 6 "I shall **n** be moved."
119:93 I will **n** forget your precepts,
Pr 10:30 The righteous will **n** be removed,
27:20 and human eyes are **n** satisfied.
30:15 Three things are **n** satisfied;
Isa 51: 6 and my deliverance will **n** be ended.
Jer 33:17 David shall **n** lack a man to sit on
La 3:22 steadfast love of the LORD **n** ceases,
his mercies **n** come to an end;
Da 2:44 will set up a kingdom that shall **n**
6:26 His kingdom shall **n** be destroyed,
Joel 2:26 shall **n** again be put to shame.
Mt 7:23 will declare to them, 'I **n** knew you;
Mk 3:29 against the Holy Spirit can **n** have
Jn 4:14 I will give them will **n** be thirsty.
6:35 comes to me will **n** be hungry,
8:51 keeps my word will **n** see death."
10:28 eternal life, and they will **n** perish.
11:26 lives and believes in me will **n** die.
1Co 13: 8 Love **n** ends. But as for prophecies,
Heb 13: 5 he has said, "I will **n** leave you or
1Pe 5: 4 crown of glory that **n** fades away.
2Pe 1:10 if you do this, you will **n** stumble.
Sir 4:25 **N** speak against the truth,
38: 8 God's works will **n** be finished;

NEW → ANEW, NEWBORN, NEWNESS

Ex 1: 8 Now a **n** king arose over Egypt,
Jdg 5: 8 **n** gods were chosen, then war was
Ezr 9: 9 n life to set up the house of our God
Ps 33: 3 Sing to him a **n** song;
40: 3 He put a **n** song in my mouth,
98: 1 O sing to the LORD a **n** song,
Ecc 1: 9 there is nothing **n** under the sun.
Isa 42: 9 and **n** things I now declare;
42:10 Sing to the LORD a **n** song,
43:19 I am about to do a **n** thing;
62: 2 **n** name that the mouth of the LORD
65:17 I am about to create **n** heavens and
a **n** earth;
66:22 as the **n** heavens and the **n** earth,
Jer 31:31 I will make a **n** covenant with the
La 3:23 they are **n** every morning;
Eze 11:19 and put a **n** spirit within them;
18:31 yourselves a **n** heart and a **n** spirit!
36:26 A **n** heart I will give you,
Mt 9:17 is **n** wine put into old wineskins;
13:52 out of his treasure what is **n**
Mk 1:27 A **n** teaching—with authority!
Lk 5:39 drinking old wine desires **n** wine,
22:20 is the **n** covenant in my blood.
Jn 13:34 I give you a **n** commandment,
Ac 17:19 May we know what this **n** teaching
1Co 5: 7 so that you may be a **n** batch,
11:25 saying, "This cup is the **n** covenant
2Co 3: 6 to be ministers of a **n** covenant,
5:17 is in Christ, there is a **n** creation:
Gal 6:15 but a **n** creation is everything!
Eph 2:15 create in himself one **n** humanity
4:24 to clothe yourselves with the **n** self,
Col 3:10 clothed yourselves with the **n** self,
Heb 8: 8 when I will establish a **n** covenant
9:15 he is the mediator of a **n** covenant,
10:20 the **n** and living way that he opened
12:24 the mediator of a **n** covenant,
1Pe 1: 3 mercy he has given us a **n** birth into
2Pe 3:13 we wait for **n** heavens and a **n** earth,
1Jn 2: 7 writing you no **n** commandment,
2Jn 1: 5 writing you a **n** commandment,
Rev 2:17 the white stone is written a **n** name
3:12 the **n** Jerusalem that comes down
3:12 of heaven, and my own **n** name.
5: 9 sing a **n** song: "You are worthy to
14: 3 they sing a **n** song before the throne
21: 1 I saw a **n** heaven and a **n** earth;
21: 2 I saw the holy city, the **n** Jerusalem,
21: 5 "See, I am making all things **n.**"
Jdt 16: 1 Raise to him a **n** psalm;
Sir 9:10 for **n** ones cannot equal them.
1Mc 4:47 built a **n** altar like the former one.

NEW COVENANT Jer 31:31; Lk 22:20; 1Co 11:25; 2Co 3:6; Heb 8:8, 13; 9:15; 12:24

NEW MOON Ex 19:1; Nu 29:6; 1Sa 20:5, 18, 24, 27; 2Ki 4:23; Ezr 3:5; Ps 81:3; Isa 1:13; 47:13; 66:23, 23; Eze 46:1, 6; Hos 5:7; Am 8:5; Jdt 8:6, 6; Sir 43:8; 1Es 5:53, 57; 8:6, 6; 9:16, 17, 37, 40

NEW MOONS 1Ch 23:31; 2Ch 2:4; 8:13; 31:3; Ne 10:33; Isa 1:14; Eze 45:17; 46:3; Hos 2:11; Col 2:16; 1Mc 10:34; 1Es 5:52; 2Es 1:31

NEW SONG Ps 33:3; 40:3; 96:1; 98:1; 144:9; 149:1; Isa 42:10; Rev 5:9; 14:3; Jdt 16:13

NEW WINE Hos 4:11; 9:2; Hag 1:11; Zec 9:17; Mt 9:17, 17; Mk 2:22, 22; Lk 5:37, 37, 38, 39; Ac 2:13; Sir 9:10

NEWBORN → BEAR, NEW

1Pe 2: 2 Like **n** infants, long for the pure,

NEWNESS* → NEW

Ro 6: 4 so we too might walk in **n** of life.

NEWS

2Ki 7: 9 This is a day of good **n;**
Pr 15:30 and good **n** refreshes the body.
25:25 so is good **n** from a far country.

Isa 52: 7 who brings good **n**, who announces
61: 1 to bring good **n** to the oppressed,
Mt 4:23 the good **n** of the kingdom
9:35 the good **n** of the kingdom,
11: 5 the poor have good **n** brought to
Mk 1:15 repent, and believe in the good **n.**"
Lk 1:19 and to bring you this good **n.**
2:10 bringing you good **n** of great joy
3:18 the good **n** to the people.
4:43 proclaim the good **n** of the kingdom
8: 1 bringing the good **n** of the kingdom
16:16 the good **n** of the kingdom of God
Ac 14: 7 continued proclaiming the good **n.**
14:21 proclaimed the good **n** to that city
17:18 was telling the good **n** about Jesus
Ro 10:15 the feet of those who bring good **n!**"

GOOD NEWS 1Sa 31:9; 2Sa 4:10; 1Ki 1:42; 2Ki 7:9; 1Ch 10:9; Pr 15:30; 25:25; Isa 52:7; 61:1; Mt 4:23; 9:35; 10:7; 11:5; 24:14; 26:13; Mk 1:1, 14, 15; 10:29; 13:10; 14:9; 16:15, 20; Lk 1:19; 2:10; 3:18; 4:18, 43; 7:22; 8:1; 9:6; 16:16; 20:1; Ac 8:12, 25, 35, 40; 13:32; 14:7, 15, 21; 15:7; 16:10; 17:18; 20:24; Ro 10:15, 16; 15:19, 20; 1Co 15:1; 2Co 2:12; 8:18; 10:14, 16; 11:7; 1Th 3:6; 2Th 2:14; Heb 4:2, 6; 1Pe 1:12, 25

NEXT-OF-KIN → KINDRED

Ru 3: 9 for you are **n.**"
4:14 not left you this day without **n;**

NICANOR

1Mc 7:43 The army of **N** was crushed,
2Mc 15:37 how matters turned out with **N,**

NICODEMUS

Pharisee who visted Jesus at night (Jn 3). Argued for fair treatment of Jesus (Jn 7:50-52). With Joseph, prepared Jesus for burial (Jn 19:38-42).

NICOLAITANS*

Rev 2: 6 you hate the works of the **N,** which
2:15 to the teaching of the **N.**

NIGER*

Ac 13: 1 Barnabas, Simeon who was called **N**

NIGHT → MIDNIGHT, NIGHTS

Ge 1: 5 and the darkness he called **N.**
1:16 and the lesser light to rule the **n—**
8:22 day and **n,** shall not cease."
Ex 13:21 a pillar of fire by **n,** to give them
40:38 and fire was in the cloud by **n,**
Dt 28:66 **n** and day you shall be in dread,
Jos 1: 8 you shall meditate on it day and **n,**
Job 35:10 who gives strength in the **n,**
Ps 1: 2 on his law they meditate day and **n.**
16: 7 in the **n** also my heart instructs me.
19: 2 and **n** to **n** declares knowledge.
42: 8 and at **n** his song is with me,
63: 6 on you in the watches of the **n;**
74:16 Yours is the day, yours also the **n;**
77: 6 I commune with my heart in the **n;**
90: 4 or like a watch in the **n.**
91: 5 You will not fear the terror of the **n,**
119:55 I remember your name in the **n,**
121: 6 by day, nor the moon by **n.**
136: 9 over the **n,** for his steadfast love
Pr 31:18 Her lamp does not go out at **n.**
Ecc 2:23 even at **n** their minds do not rest.
Isa 21:11 "Sentinel, what of the **n?**
Jer 33:20 and my covenant with the **n,**
Mt 24:43 part of the **n** the thief was coming,
Lk 2: 8 keeping watch over their flock by **n,**
6:12 and he spent the **n** in prayer to God.
Jn 3: 2 He came to Jesus by **n** and said to
9: 4 is coming when no one can work.
11:10 But those who walk at **n** stumble,
1Co 11:23 on the **n** when he was betrayed
1Th 5: 2 Lord will come like a thief in the **n.**
5: 5 we are not of the **n** or of darkness.
Rev 8:12 from shining, and likewise the **n.**

20:10 will be tormented day and **n** forever
21:25 and there will be no **n** there.
22: 5 And there will be no more **n**;
2Es 14:42 and ate their bread at **n.**

NIGHTS → NIGHT

Ge 7:12 on the earth forty days and forty **n.**
Ex 24:18 mountain for forty days and forty **n.**
1Ki 19: 8 of that food forty days and forty **n**
Jnh 1:17 of the fish three days and three **n.**
Mt 4: 2 He fasted forty days and forty **n,**
12:40 for three days and three **n** the Son
2Co 6: 5 riots, labors, sleepless **n,** hunger;
Aza 1:47 Bless the Lord, **n** and days;

FORTY NIGHTS Ge 7:4, 12; Ex 24:18;
34:28; Dt 9:9, 11, 18, 25; 10:10; 1Ki 19:8; Mt
4:2

NILE

Ge 41: 2 of the **N** seven sleek and fat cows,
Ex 1:22 Hebrews you shall throw into the **N,**
7:17 will strike the water that is in the **N,**

NIMROD

Ge 10: 9 **N** a mighty hunter before the LORD.

NINE

Nu 34:13 to the **n** tribes and to the half-tribe;
Jos 13: 7 to the **n** tribes and the half-tribe of
Mk 15:25 It was **n** o'clock in the morning
Ac 2:15 it is only **n** o'clock in the morning.

NINETY

Ge 17:17 Can Sarah, who is **n** years old, bear

NINETY-NINE

Ge 17: 1 When Abram was **n** years old,
Lk 15: 4 leave the **n** in the wilderness and go

NINEVEH

Jnh 1: 2 "Go at once to **N,** that great city,
Na 1: 1 An oracle concerning **N.**
Mt 12:41 The people of **N** will rise up at the
Tob 1:10 and came as a captive to **N,**

NOAH

Righteous man (Eze 14:14, 20) called to build
ark (Ge 6-8; Heb 11:7; 1Pe 3:20; 2Pe 2:5). God's
covenant with (Ge 9:1-17). Drunkenness of (Ge
9:18-23). Blessed sons, cursed Canaan (Ge 9:24-
27). Praised (Sir 44:17-18).

NOB

1Sa 21: 1 David came to **N** to the priest

NOBLE → NOBLES

Isa 32: 8 But those who are **n** plan **n** things,
1Co 1:26 not many were of **n** birth.
1Ti 3: 1 the office of bishop desires a **n** task.

NOBLES → NOBLE

Job 34:19 who shows no partiality to **n,**
Pr 8:16 and **n,** all who govern rightly.

NOISE → NOISY

Ex 32:17 "There is a **n** of war in the camp."
Ps 66: 1 Make a joyful **n** to God, all the earth
Isa 29: 6 thunder and earthquake and great **n,**
2Pe 3:10 will pass away with a loud **n,**
Jdt 14: 9 made a joyful **n** in their town.

NOISY* → NOISE

1Co 13: 1 I am a **n** gong or a clanging cymbal.

NONE

Nu 14:23 **n** of those who despised me
Dt 33:26 There is **n** like God,
1Sa 3:19 let **n** of his words fall to the ground.
Ps 86: 8 **n** like you among the gods, O Lord,
Jer 10: 6 There is **n** like you, O LORD;
Jn 19:36 "**N** of his bones shall be broken."
Sir 39:18 and **n** can limit his saving power.

NOON → AFTERNOON

Am 8: 9 I will make the sun go down at **n,**
Mk 15:33 When it was **n,** darkness came over

NORTH

Ps 89:12 The **n** and the south—you created
Isa 41:25 I stirred up one from the **n,**
Jer 4: 6 I am bringing evil from the **n,**
Eze 1: 4 a stormy wind came out of the **n:**
Da 11: 6 come to the king of the **n** to ratify
Zec 2: 6 Flee from the land of the **n,**

NOSE → NOSES

2Ki 19:28 I will put my hook in your **n**

NOSES* → NOSE

Ps 115: 6 They have ears, but do not hear; **n,**

NOSTRILS

Ge 2: 7 breathed into his **n** the breath of life;
7:22 in whose **n** was the breath of life
Ex 15: 8 the blast of your **n** the waters piled
Ps 18:15 at the blast of the breath of your **n.**
Isa 2:22 who have only breath in their **n,**

NOTE

1Sa 2:21 And the LORD took **n** of Hannah;
1Ch 21:15 the LORD took **n** and relented

NOTHING

2Sa 24:24 to the LORD my God that cost me **n.**
2Ch 9: 2 there was **n** hidden from Solomon
Ne 9:21 the wilderness so that they lacked **n;**
Job 1: 9 "Does Job fear God for **n?**
Ps 73:25 **n** on earth that I desire other than
Pr 10:28 of the wicked comes to **n.**
13: 4 of the lazy craves, and gets **n,**
28:27 gives to the poor will lack **n,**
Ecc 1: 9 there is **n** new under the sun.
3:22 So I saw that there is **n** better than
8:15 **n** better for people under the sun
Isa 44: 9 All who make idols are **n,**
53: 2 **n** in his appearance that we should
Jer 32:17 **N** is too hard for you.
Da 9:26 shall be cut off and shall have **n,**
Mt 17:20 and **n** will be impossible for you."
Lk 1:37 For **n** will be impossible with God."
8:17 For **n** is hidden that will not be
12: 2 **N** is covered up that will not be
23:15 he has done **n** to deserve death.
Jn 5:30 "I can do **n** on my own.
15: 5 apart from me you can do **n.**
Ro 7:18 know that **n** good dwells within me,
1Co 2: 2 to know **n** among you except Jesus
13: 2 but do not have love, I am **n.**
1Ti 6: 7 for we brought **n** into the world, so
that we can take **n** out of it;
Heb 7:19 (for the law made **n** perfect);
1Pe 3: 7 so that **n** may hinder your prayers.
Sir 32:19 Do **n** without deliberation,
39:20 and **n** is too marvelous for him.
42:24 and he has made **n** incomplete.

NOTICE

Ex 2:25 and God took **n** of them.
Ps 142: 4 no one who takes **n** of me;
Isa 58: 3 but you do not **n?**"

NOTORIOUS

Mt 27:16 At that time they had a **n** prisoner,

NOW

Ge 22:12 for **n** I know that you fear God,
Ezr 9: 8 But **n** for a brief moment favor has
Ps 20: 6 **N** I know that the LORD will help
Lk 1:48 from **n** on all generations will call
me blessed;
Jn 2:10 have kept the good wine until **n.**"
5:25 the hour is coming, and is **n** here,
9:25 that though I was blind, **n** I see."
13:19 I tell you this **n,** before it occurs,
13:36 I am going, you cannot follow me **n**
16:12 but you cannot bear them **n.**
Ro 3:21 **n,** apart from law, the righteousness
5: 9 **n** that we have been justified by his
8: 1 therefore **n** no condemnation for
13:11 For salvation is nearer to us **n**
1Co 13:13 And **n** faith, hope, and love abide,

2Co 6: 2 see, **n** is the day of salvation!
Eph 2: 2 the spirit that is **n** at work
3: 5 **n** been revealed to his holy apostles
Col 1:26 has **n** been revealed to his saints.
1Pe 1: 8 even though you do not see him **n,**
2:10 but **n** you have received mercy.
1Jn 2:18 so **n** many antichrists have come.
Rev 1:19 **N** write what you have seen, what is

NOWHERE → WHERE

Lk 9:58 Son of Man has **n** to lay his head."

NULLIFY

Ro 3: 3 **n** the faithfulness of God?
Gal 2:21 I do not **n** the grace of God;

NUMBER → NUMBERED, NUMBERS, NUMEROUS

Ge 32:12 counted because of their **n.'**"
Nu 1:45 So the whole **n** of the Israelites,
26:51 the **n** of the Israelites enrolled.
Dt 32: 8 of the peoples according to the **n**
Ps 105:12 When they were few in **n,**
147: 4 He determines the **n** of the stars;
Ac 2:47 their **n** those who were being saved.
6: 1 the disciples were increasing in **n,**
11:21 great **n** became believers and turned
Ro 11:25 until the full **n** of the Gentiles has
Rev 6:11 until the **n** would be complete both
7: 4 the **n** of those who were sealed,
13:18 Its **n** is six hundred sixty-six.
Sir 37:25 but the days of Israel are without **n.**

NUMBERED → NUMBER

2Sa 24:10 because he had **n** the people.
Da 5:26 MENE, God has **n** the days
Sir 41:13 The days of a good life are **n,**

NUMBERS → NUMBER

Ge 48: 4 fruitful and increase your **n;**
Ac 9:31 it increased in **n.**
16: 5 and increased in **n** daily.

NUMEROUS → NUMBER

Ge 17: 2 and will make you exceedingly **n.**"
22:17 as **n** as the stars of heaven
Ex 1: 9 the Israelite people are more **n**
Dt 28:63 in making you prosperous and **n,**
Zec 10: 8 shall be as **n** as they were before.

NURSE → NURSED, NURSING

Ge 21: 7 that Sarah would **n** children?
Ex 2: 7 a **n** from the Hebrew women
Ru 4:16 in her bosom, and became his **n.**
Isa 66:11 that you may **n** and be satisfied

NURSED → NURSE

Ex 2: 9 the woman took the child and **n** it.
Lk 11:27 and the breasts that **n** you!"
23:29 and the breasts that never **n.'**

NURSING → NURSE

Isa 11: 8 The **n** child shall play over the hole
of the asp,
49:15 Can a woman forget her **n** child,
Lk 21:23 who are **n** infants in those days!

O

OAK → OAKS

Ge 35: 4 Jacob hid them under the **o** that was
2Sa 18:10 "I saw Absalom hanging in an **o.**"
Eze 6:13 green tree, and under every leafy **o,**

OAKS → OAK

Ps 29: 9 voice of the LORD causes the **o** to
Isa 57: 5 with lust among the **o,** under every

OATH

Ge 21:31 there both of them swore an **o.**

26: 3 the **o** that I swore to your father
Nu 30: 2 or swears an **o** to bind himself by a
Dt 7: 8 and kept the **o** that he swore to your
29:12 by an **o,** which the LORD your God
Jos 2:17 from this **o** that you have made us
1Sa 14:24 He had laid an **o** on the troops,
Ne 13:25 them take an **o** in the name of God,
Ps 15: 4 stand by their **o** even to their hurt;
119106 I have sworn an **o** and confirmed it,
132:11 a sure **o** from which he will not turn
Ecc 8: 2 command because of your sacred **o.**
Mt 26:72 Again he denied it with an **o,**
Heb 7:20 This was confirmed with an **o;**
Sir 41:19 Be ashamed of breaking an **o**

OBADIAH
1. Believer who sheltered 100 prophets from Jezebel (1Ki 18:1-16).
2. Prophet against Edom (Ob 1; 2Es 1:39).

OBED
Ru 4:22 **O** of Jesse, and Jesse of David.
Lk 3:32 son of **O,** son of Boaz, son of Sala,

OBED-EDOM
2Sa 6:12 ark of God from the house of **O**
1Ch 13:13 to the house of **O** the Gittite.

OBEDIENCE → OBEY
Ge 49:10 and the **o** of the peoples is his.
Ro 1: 5 the **o** of faith among all
5:19 so by the one man's **o** the many will
6:16 which leads to death, or of **o,**
15:18 to win **o** from the Gentiles.
16:19 For while your **o** is known to all,
16:26 to bring about the **o** of faith—
2Co 7:15 as he remembers the **o** of all of you,
9:13 you glorify God by your **o** to
10: 6 when your **o** is complete.
Phm 1:21 Confident of your **o,** I am writing to
Heb 5: 8 learned **o** through what he suffered;
1Pe 1:22 have purified your souls by your **o**
4Mc 5:16 more powerful than our **o** to the law.
9: 2 should practice ready **o** to the law

OBEDIENT* → OBEY
Ex 24: 7 spoken we will do, and we will be **o.**
Ps 103:20 his bidding, **o** to his spoken word.
Isa 1:19 If you are willing and **o,** you shall
Lk 2:51 came to Nazareth, and was **o**
Ac 6: 7 of the priests became **o** to the faith.
Ro 6:16 yourselves to anyone as **o** slaves,
6:17 become **o** from the heart to the form
2Co 2: 9 whether you are **o** in everything.
Php 2: 8 and became **o** to the point of death
Tit 3: 1 to be **o,** to be ready for every good
1Pe 1: 2 by the Spirit to be **o** to Jesus Christ
1:14 **o** children, do not be conformed to
Sir 7:23 and make them **o** from their youth.
LtJ 6:60 sent to do a service, they are **o.**
2Es 7:22 were not **o,** and spoke against him;

OBEY → OBEDIENCE, OBEDIENT, OBEYED, OBEYING, OBEYS
Ex 19: 5 if you **o** my voice and keep my
Dt 11:27 if you **o** the commandments of
12:28 Be careful to **o** all these words that
13: 4 his voice you shall **o,** him you shall
21:18 and rebellious son who will not **o**
28: 1 If you will only **o** the LORD your
28:15 if you will not **o** the LORD your God
30: 2 your children **o** him with all your
30:10 when you **o** the LORD your God
Jos 24:24 we will serve, and him we will **o."**
Jdg 3: 4 to know whether Israel would **o**
1Sa 15:22 Surely, to **o** is better than sacrifice.
Ezr 7:26 All who will not **o** the law
Jer 7:23 I gave them, **"O** my voice,
11: 7 to this day, saying, **O** my voice.
42: 6 we will **o** the voice of the LORD our
42: 6 go well with us when we **o** the voice
Mt 8:27 even the winds and the sea **o** him?"
28:20 **o** everything that I have commanded

Lk 11:28 the word of God and **o** it!"
Ac 5:29 "We must **o** God rather than any
5:32 God has given to those who **o** him."
Ro 6:12 to make you **o** their passions.
6:16 are slaves of the one whom you **o,**
2Co 10: 5 every thought captive to **o** Christ.
Gal 3:10 all the things written in the book
Eph 6: 1 Children, **o** your parents in the Lord,
6: 5 **o** your earthly masters with fear and
6: 5 singleness of heart, as you **o** Christ;
Col 3:20 Children, **o** your parents in
3:22 Slaves, **o** your earthly masters in
2Th 3:14 do not **o** what we say in this letter;
Heb 5: 9 eternal salvation for all who **o** him,
13:17 **O** your leaders and submit to them,
1Pe 4:17 not for those who do not **o** the
1Jn 2: 3 if we **o** his commandments.
3:24 All who **o** his commandments abide
5: 3 love of God is this, that we **o** his
Sir 3: 6 honor their mother **o** the Lord;
1Mc 2:22 We will not **o** the king's words by

OBEYED → OBEY
Ge 22:18 because you have **o** my voice."
26: 5 Abraham **o** my voice and kept my
Jos 1:17 Just as we **o** Moses in all things,
2Ki 18:12 they neither listened nor **o.**
Jer 3:13 have not **o** my voice, says the LORD.
Da 9:10 have not **o** the voice of the LORD
Php 2:12 just as you have always **o** me,
Heb 11: 8 By faith Abraham **o** when he was
1Pe 3: 6 Sarah **o** Abraham and called him
Bar 2:10 Yet we have not **o** his voice,
Aza 1: 7 We have not **o** your commandments
2Es 1: 8 for they have not **o** my law—

OBEYING → OBEY
1Sa 15:22 as in **o** the voice of the LORD?
1Co 7:19 but **o** the commandments of God is

OBEYS → OBEY
1Jn 2: 5 but whoever **o** his word, truly
Sir 24:22 **o** me will not be put to shame,

OBJECT → OBJECTS
Ro 9:21 the same lump one **o** for special use

OBJECTS → OBJECT
Ro 9:23 of his glory for the **o** of mercy,

OBSCENE*
Eph 5: 4 Entirely out of place is **o,** silly,

OBSERVANCE → OBSERVE
Ex 12:26 'What do you mean by this **o?'**
Eze 20:11 by whose **o** everyone shall live.

OBSERVE → OBSERVANCE, OBSERVED, OBSERVES, OBSERVING
Ex 12:14 **o** it as a perpetual ordinance.
23:15 **o** the festival of unleavened bread;
23:16 You shall **o** the festival of harvest,
23:16 shall **o** the festival of ingathering at
34:22 You shall **o** the festival of weeks,
Lev 20: 8 Keep my statutes, and **o** them;
Dt 4: 6 You must **o** them diligently,
5:12 **O** the sabbath day and keep it holy,
11:22 **o** this entire commandment
26:16 so **o** them diligently with all your
Ps 119: 8 I will **o** your statutes;
1Mc 2:67 rally around you all who **o** the law,

OBSERVED → OBSERVE
Dt 33: 9 For they **o** your word, and kept
Jos 22: 2 "You have **o** all that Moses

OBSERVES → OBSERVE
Ps 33:15 and **o** all their deeds.

OBSERVING → OBSERVE
Dt 30: 8 **o** all his commandments
Mk 7: 3 thus **o** the tradition of the elders;
Gal 4:10 You are **o** special days, and months,
Col 2:16 of food and drink or of **o** festivals,

OBSOLETE
Heb 8:13 he has made the first one **o.**

OBSTACLE
1Co 9:12 **o** in the way of the gospel of Christ.
2Co 6: 3 are putting no **o** in anyone's way,

OBTAIN → OBTAINED, OBTAINING
Ro 11: 7 Israel failed to **o** what it was seeking
2Ti 2:10 that they may also **o** the salvation
Sir 15: 1 holds to the law will **o** wisdom.

OBTAINED → OBTAIN
Eph 1:11 we have also **o** an inheritance,
Php 3:12 Not that I have already **o** this
Heb 8: 6 Jesus has now **o** a more excellent

OBTAINING → OBTAIN
1Th 5: 9 for **o** salvation through our Lord
Heb 9:12 thus **o** eternal redemption.

OBVIOUS
Gal 5:19 Now the works of the flesh are **o:**

OCCUPY
Dt 11:31 and when you **o** it and live in it,
Ne 2: 8 and for the house that I shall **o."**
Ps 131: 1 not **o** myself with things too great

ODED
2Ch 28: 9 was there, whose name was **O;**

ODOR → ODORS
Ge 8:21 the LORD smelled the pleasing **o,**
Ex 29:18 it is a pleasing **o,** an offering
Lev 1: 9 of pleasing **o** to the LORD.
Tob 8: 3 of the fish so repelled the demon

ODORS → ODOR
Lev 26:31 and I will not smell your pleasing **o.**

OFFEND* → OFFENDED, OFFENDER, OFFENSE, OFFENSES
Job 34:31 I will not **o** any more;
Jn 6:61 said to them, "Does this **o** you?

OFFENDED → OFFEND
Pr 18:19 An ally **o** is stronger than a city;

OFFENDER* → OFFEND
Mt 18:17 and if the **o** refuses to listen
Lk 17: 3 you must rebuke the **o,**

OFFENSE → OFFEND
Dt 19:15 in connection with any **o**
Pr 19:11 their glory to overlook an **o.**
Mt 11: 6 blessed is anyone who takes no **o** at
Mk 6: 3 And they took **o** at him.
Gal 5:11 **o** of the cross has been removed.

OFFENSES → OFFEND
Pr 10:12 but love covers all **o.**

OFFER → OFFERED, OFFERING, OFFERINGS
Ge 22: 2 and **o** him there as a burnt offering
Ex 29:38 this is what you shall **o** on the altar:
Dt 12:14 you shall **o** your burnt offerings
Ps 4: 5 **O** right sacrifices, and put your trust
Hos 14: 2 and we will **o** the fruit of our lips.
Mt 5:24 and then come and **o** your gift.
Heb 9:25 Nor was it to **o** himself again and
13:15 continually **o** a sacrifice of praise to
Sir 38:11 **O** a sweet-smelling sacrifice,
1Mc 2:23 to **o** sacrifice on the altar in Modein,

OFFERED → OFFER
Ge 22:13 **o** it up as a burnt offering instead of
Ex 40:27 and **o** fragrant incense on it;
40:29 it the burnt offering
1Sa 13: 9 And he **o** the burnt offering.
Ps 106:28 and ate sacrifices **o** to the dead;
Ecc 5: 1 better than the sacrifice **o** by fools;
Mt 27:34 they **o** him wine to drink, mixed
1Co 8: 4 eating of food **o** to idols,

OFFERING → OFFER

Heb 5: 7 Jesus o up prayers and
7:27 did once for all when he o himself.
9:14 o himself without blemish to God,
11: 4 By faith Abel o to God
11:17 when put to the test, o up Isaac.
1Mc 1:59 they o sacrifice on the altar that was
4:53 they rose and o sacrifice,

OFFERING → OFFER

Ge 4: 4 LORD had regard for Abel and his o,
22: 2 and offer him there as a burnt o
22: 8 will provide the lamb for a burnt o,
Ex 29:14 fire outside the camp; it is a sin o.
29:18 it is a burnt o to the LORD;
29:18 odor, an o by fire to the LORD.
29:24 raise them as an elevation o before
29:40 of a hin of wine for a drink o.
1Sa 13: 9 Saul said, "Bring the burnt o here
1Ch 21:26 from heaven on the altar of burnt o.
2Ch 7: 1 heaven and consumed the burnt o
Ezr 6:17 as a sin o for all Israel,
Ps 40: 6 Sacrifice and o you do not desire,
51:16 if I were to give a burnt o,
Isa 53:10 When you make his life an o for sin,
Da 8:11 it took the regular burnt o away
9:27 he shall make sacrifice and o cease;
11:31 shall abolish the regular burnt o
12:11 the regular burnt o is taken away
Mt 5:23 when you are o your gift at the altar,
Eph 5: 2 a fragrant o and sacrifice to God.
Php 2:17 the o of your faith,
4:18 the gifts you sent, a fragrant o,
Heb 10:14 For by a single o he has perfected
Sir 35: 2 makes an o of well-being.
35: 4 gives alms sacrifices a thank o.
1Mc 4:44 what to do about the altar of burnt o,

BURNT OFFERING
Ge 22:2, 3, 6, 7, 8, 13;
Ex 18:12; 29:18, 25, 42; 30:9, 28; 31:9; 35:16;
38:1; 40:6, 10, 29, 29; Lev 1:3, 4, 6, 9, 10, 13,
14, 17; 3:5; 4:7, 10, 18, 24, 25, 25, 29, 30, 33,
34; 5:7, 10; 6:9, 9, 10, 12, 25; 7:2, 8, 8, 37;
8:18, 21, 28; 9:2, 3, 7, 12, 13, 14, 16, 17, 22,
24; 10:19; 12:6, 8; 14:13, 19, 20, 22, 31;
15:15, 30; 16:3, 5, 24, 24; 17:8; 22:18; 23:12,
18; Nu 6:11, 14, 16; 7:15, 21, 27, 33, 39, 45,
51, 57, 63, 69, 75, 81, 87; 8:12; 15:3, 5, 8, 24;
28:6, 10, 10, 11, 13, 14, 15, 19, 23, 23, 24, 27,
31; 29:2, 6, 6, 8, 11, 13, 16, 19, 22, 25, 28, 31,
34, 36, 38; Dt 13:16; Jos 22:26, 29; Jdg 6:26;
11:31; 13:16, 23; 1Sa 6:14; 7:9, 10; 13:9, 9,
10, 12; 2Sa 24:22; 1Ki 18:33, 38; 2Ki 3:27;
5:17; 10:25; 16:13, 15, 15, 15, 15; 1Ch 6:49;
16:40; 21:26, 29; 22:1; 2Ch 4:6; 7:1, 7; 29:18,
24, 27, 27, 28, 32; Ezr 8:35; Ne 10:33; Job
42:8; Ps 40:6; 51:16; Isa 19:21; 40:16; Jer
14:12; Eze 40:38, 39, 42; 43:24; 44:11; 45:23;
46:2, 4, 12, 12, 13, 15; Da 8:11, 12, 13; 11:31;
12:11; Wis 3:6; Aza 1:15; 1Mc 1:54, 59; 4:44,
53; 7:33; 4Mc 18:11

DRINK OFFERING Ge 35:14; Ex 29:40, 41;
30:9; Lev 23:13; Nu 4:7; 6:17; 15:5, 7, 10, 24;
28:7, 7, 8, 9, 10, 15, 24, 31; 29:16, 22, 25, 28,
34, 38; 2Ki 16:13, 15; Isa 57:6; Joel 1:9, 13;
2:14; Sir 50:15

ELEVATION OFFERING Ex 29:24, 26, 27,
27; Lev 7:30, 34; 8:27, 29; 9:21; 10:15; 14:12,
24; 23:15, 17, 20; Nu 6:20; 8:11, 13, 15, 21

FREEWILL OFFERING Ex 35:29; Lev
7:16; 22:18, 21, 23; Nu 15:3; Dt 16:10; 1Ch
29:14; Ezr 3:5; 8:28; Ps 54:6; Eze 46:12, 12

GRAIN OFFERING Ex 29:41; 30:9; 40:29;
Lev 2:1, 3, 4, 6, 8, 9, 10, 11, 14, 14, 15; 5:13;
6:14, 15, 21, 23; 7:9, 10, 37; 9:4, 17; 10:12;
14:10, 20, 21, 31; 23:13, 18; Nu 4:16; 5:15, 15,
18, 18, 25, 25, 26; 6:15, 17; 7:13, 19, 25, 31,
37, 43, 49, 55, 61, 67, 73, 79, 87; 8:8; 15:4, 6,
9, 24; 18:9; 28:5, 8, 9, 12, 12, 13, 20, 26, 28,
31; 29:3, 6, 6, 9, 11, 14, 16, 18, 19, 21, 22, 24,
25, 27, 28, 30, 31, 33, 34, 37, 38; Jos 22:29;
Jdg 13:19, 23; 2Ki 16:13, 15, 15, 15; 1Ch
21:23; 23:29; 2Ch 7:7; Ne 13:5, 9; Isa

57:6; 66:3, 20; Jer 14:12; Eze 42:13; 44:29;
45:24; 46:5, 5, 7, 11, 14, 14, 15, 20; Da 2:46;
Joel 1:9, 13; 2:14; Bar 1:10; 2Mc 1:8

GUILT OFFERING Lev 5:15, 15, 16, 18,
19; 6:6, 6, 17; 7:1, 2, 5, 7, 37; 14:12, 13, 14,
17, 21, 24, 25, 25, 28; 19:21, 21, 22; 22:16; Nu
6:12; 18:9; 1Sa 6:3, 4, 8, 17; Ezr 10:19; Pr
14:9; Eze 40:39; 42:13; 44:29; 46:20; Sir 7:31

†LORD'S OFFERING Ex 30:14; 35:5, 21,
24; Lev 7:30; 22:27; 23:25, 27; Nu 9:7, 13;
18:28; 31:50

OFFERING BY FIRE Ex 29:18, 25, 41;
30:20; Lev 1:9, 13, 17; 2:2, 9, 11, 16; 3:3, 5, 9,
11, 14, 16; 7:5, 25, 30; 8:21, 28; 22:27; 23:13,
18, 25, 27; 24:7; Nu 15:3, 10, 13, 14, 25;
18:17; 28:3, 6, 8, 13, 19, 24; 29:6, 13, 36

OFFERING OF WELL-BEING Lev 4:31;
7:11, 14, 33; 9:4, 22; Nu 6:14; 15:8; Sir 35:2;
47:2

SIN OFFERING Ex 29:14, 36, 36; 30:10;
Lev 4:3, 8, 14, 20, 21, 24, 25, 29, 29, 32, 33,
33, 34; 5:6, 7, 8, 9, 9, 11, 11, 12; 6:17, 25, 25,
26, 30; 7:7, 37; 8:2, 14, 14; 9:2, 3, 7, 8, 10, 15,
15, 22; 10:16, 17, 19, 19; 12:6, 8; 14:13, 13,
19, 22, 31; 15:15, 30; 16:3, 5, 6, 9, 11, 11, 15,
25, 27, 27; 23:19; Nu 6:11, 14, 16; 7:16, 22,
28, 34, 40, 46, 52, 58, 64, 70, 76, 82, 87; 8:8,
12; 15:24, 25, 27; 18:9; 28:15, 22; 29:5, 11,
11, 16, 19, 22, 25, 28, 31, 34, 38; 2Ch 29:21,
23, 24; Ezr 6:17; 8:35; Ps 40:6; Eze 40:39;
42:13; 43:19, 21, 22, 25; 44:27, 29; 45:19, 22,
23; 46:20; 2Mc 2:11; 12:43

OFFERINGS → OFFER
Ge 8:20 and offered burnt o on the altar.
1Sa 15:22 the LORD as great delight in burnt o
Ps 119:108 Accept my o of praise, O LORD,
Isa 1:13 bringing o is futile;
Jer 6:20 Your burnt o are not acceptable,
Hos 6: 6 of God rather than burnt o.
Mal 3: 8 In your tithes and o!
Mk 12:33 important than all whole burnt o
Heb 10: 6 in burnt o and sin o you have taken
no pleasure.
Sir 14:11 and present worthy o to the Lord.
35: 1 keeps the law makes many o;
1Mc 1:45 to forbid burnt o and sacrifices
4:56 and joyfully offered burnt o;

BURNT OFFERINGS Ge 8:20; Ex 10:25;
20:24; 24:5; 32:6; Lev 23:37; Nu 10:10; 23:15,
6, 15, 17; 29:39; Dt 12:6, 11, 13, 14, 27; 27:6;
33:10; Jos 8:31; 22:23, 27, 28; Jdg 20:26;
21:4; 1Sa 6:15; 10:8; 15:22; 2Sa 6:17, 18;
24:24, 25; 1Ki 3:4, 15; 8:64, 64; 9:25; 10:5;
2Ki 10:24; 1Ch 16:1, 2, 40; 21:23, 24, 26;
23:31; 29:21; 2Ch 1:6; 2:4; 7:7; 8:12; 9:4;
13:11; 23:18; 24:14, 14; 29:7, 31, 32, 34, 35,
35; 30:15; 31:2, 3, 3, 3; 35:12, 14, 16; Ezr 3:2,
3, 4, 5, 6; 6:3, 9; 8:35; Job 1:5; Ps 50:8; 51:19,
19; 66:13, 15; Isa 1:11; 43:23; 56:7; Jer 6:20;
7:21, 22; 17:26; 19:5; 33:18; Eze 40:42; 43:18,
27; 45:15, 17, 17, 25; Hos 6:6; Am 5:22; Mic
6:6; Mk 12:33; Heb 10:6, 8; Jdt 4:14; 16:16,
18; Bar 1:10; Aza 1:17; 1Mc 1:45; 4:56; 5:54;
2Mc 2:10; 1Es 4:52; 5:49, 50

DRINK OFFERINGS Ex 25:29; 37:16; Lev
23:18, 37; Nu 6:15; 28:14; 29:6, 11, 18, 19, 21,
24, 27, 30, 31, 33, 37, 39; 2Ch 29:35; Ezr
7:17; Ps 16:4; Jer 7:18; Eze 20:28; 45:17; Hos
9:4; 1Mc 1:22, 45

FREEWILL OFFERINGS Ex 36:3, 3; Lev
23:38; Nu 29:39; Dt 12:6, 17; 1Ch 29:6; 2Ch
31:14; Ezr 1:4; 2:68; 7:16; Am 4:5; Jdt 4:14;
16:18

GRAIN OFFERINGS Lev 2:13; 23:37; Nu
29:39; Jos 22:23; 1Ki 8:64, 64; Ezr 7:17; Jer
17:26; 33:18; 41:5; Eze 45:15, 17, 17, 25; Am
5:22

†LORD'S OFFERINGS Lev 6:18; 10:12;
21:6, 21; 23:8, 36, 36

OFFERINGS BY FIRE Lev 2:3, 10; 4:35;
5:12; 6:17, 18; 10:12, 13, 15; 21:6, 21; 22:22;
23:8, 36, 36, 37; 24:9; Nu 28:2; Jos 13:14; 1Sa
2:28

OFFERINGS OF WELL-BEING Ex
20:24; 24:5; 29:28; Lev 6:12; 10:14; Nu 29:39;
Jos 8:31; 22:23, 27; 1Sa 11:15; 13:9; 2Sa 6:17,
18; 24:25; 1Ki 3:15; 2Ki 16:13; 1Ch 16:1, 2;
21:26; 2Ch 7:7; 29:35; 30:22; 31:2; Eze 43:27;
45:15, 17; 46:2, 12, 12; Am 5:22

SIN OFFERINGS 2Ki 12:16; Ne 10:33; Eze
45:17, 25; Heb 10:6, 8; Bar 1:10

OFFICER → OFFICERS
2Ti 2: 4 aim is to please the enlisting o.

OFFICERS → OFFICER
Ex 15: 4 picked o were sunk in the Red Sea.

OFFICIALS
Ex 5:21 bad odor with Pharaoh and his o,
9:20 Those o of Pharaoh who feared the
Pr 29:12 all his o will be wicked.

OFFSPRING
Ge 3:15 and between your o and hers;
12: 7 "To your o I will give this land."
13:16 I will make your o like the dust of
26: 4 will give to your o all these lands;
28:14 be blessed in you and in your o.
2Sa 7:12 I will raise up your o after you,
Isa 44: 3 and my blessing on your o.
53:10 he shall see his o, and shall prolong
Mal 2:15 does the one God desire? Godly o.
Ac 17:29 Since we are God's o, we ought not
Gal 3:16 made to Abraham and to his o;
Sus 1:56 "You o of Canaan and not of Judah,
2Es 12:32 who will arise from the o of David,

OFTEN
Lk 13:34 How o have I desired
Jn 18: 2 Jesus o met there with his disciples.

OG
Nu 21:33 King O of Bashan came out against
Dt 31: 4 do to them as he did to Sihon and O,
Ps 136:20 and O, king of Bashan,

OHOLIAB
Craftsman who worked on the tabernacle (Ex
31:6; 35:34; 36:1-2; 38:23).

OIL
Ge 28:18 for a pillar and poured o on the top
35:14 offering on it, and poured o on it.
Ex 25: 6 o for the lamps, spices for the
anointing o
29: 7 You shall take the anointing o,
30:25 it shall be a holy anointing o.
Dt 14:23 your wine, and your o, as well
1Sa 10: 1 vial of o and poured it on his head,
16:13 Then Samuel took the horn of o,
1Ki 17:16 neither did the jug of o fail,
2Ki 4: 6 Then the o stopped flowing.
Ps 23: 5 you anoint my head with o
45: 7 anointed you with the o of gladness
104:15 o to make the face shine,
133: 2 It is like the precious o on the head,
Pr 5: 3 and her speech is smoother than o;
21:17 loves wine and o will not be rich.
Isa 1: 6 or bound up, or softened with o.
61: 3 o of gladness instead of mourning,
Joel 2:24 vats shall overflow with wine and o.
Mt 25: 3 they took no o with them;
Heb 1: 9 with the o of gladness beyond your
Jas 5:14 anointing them with o in the name

OINTMENT
Mk 14: 4 "Why was the o wasted in this way?

OLD → OLDER
Ge 17:12 when he is eight days o,
17:17 Sarah, who is ninety years o, bear a
21: 7 I have borne him a son in his o age."

Nu   1: 3 from twenty years o and upward,
        14:29 from twenty years o and upward,
Dt   32: 7 Remember the days of o,
Ps   71: 9 not cast me off in the time of o age;
        74:12 Yet God my King is from of o,
Pr   22: 6 when o, they will not stray.
La   5:21 renew our days as of o—
Joel   2:28 your o men shall dream dreams,
Mic   5: 2 origin is from of o, from ancient
Mk   2:22 puts new wine into o wineskins;
Jn   3: 4 be born after having grown o?
Ac   2:17 and your o men shall dream dreams.
Ro   4:19 he was about a hundred years o,
1Co   5: 7 o yeast so that you may be a new
2Co   5:17 everything o has passed away;
Eph   4:22 your o self, corrupt and deluded by
1Jn   2: 7 but an o commandment that you
        2: 7 o commandment is the word that
Sir   8: 6 Do not disdain one who is o,
        9:10 Do not abandon o friends,

DAYS OF OLD Dt 32:7; 2Ki 19:25; Ps 44:1;
77:5; 143:5; Isa 23:7; 37:26; 51:9; 63:9, 11; Jer
46:26; La 1:7; Am 9:11; Mic 7:14, 20; Mal
3:4; Sir 50:23

FROM OF OLD Job 20:4; Ps 25:6; 55:19;
74:12; 78:2; 93:2; 119:52; Isa 44:7, 8; 48:8;
63:16; Jer 25:5; Joel 2:2; Mic 5:2; Hab 1:12;
Lk 1:70; Sir 14:17; 42:18; 51:8; 1Es 2:23, 26

OLD AGE Ge 15:15; 21:2, 7; 25:8; 37:3;
44:20; Jdg 8:32; Ru 4:15; 1Sa 2:31, 32; 1Ki
15:23; 1Ch 29:28; Job 5:26; 21:7; Ps 71:9, 18;
92:14; Isa 46:4; Lk 1:36; Tob 3:10; 14:13; Wis
3:17; 4:8, 9, 16; Sir 3:12; 25:3; 30:24; 46:9;
2Mc 6:23, 25, 27; 3Mc 6:1; 2Es 5:50, 53;
14:17; 4Mc 5:12, 33, 36; 6:12, 18

OLD MAN Ge 25:8; 43:27; 44:20; Jdg 19:16,
17, 20, 22; 1Sa 4:18; 28:14; Jer 51:22; Lk
1:18; Phm 1:9; 1Es 1:53; 4Mc 5:6; 6:2, 10;
7:13; 8:5

OLD MEN La 5:14; Eze 9:6; Joel 2:28; Zec
8:4; Ac 2:17; 1Mc 14:9; 1Es 5:63; 3Mc 1:23;
4:5

OLDER → OLD

1Ti   5: 1 Do not speak harshly to an o man,
        5: 2 to o women as mothers, to younger
Tit   2: 2 Tell the o men to be temperate,
        2: 3 tell the o women to be reverent in

OLIVE → OLIVES

Ge   8:11 beak was a freshly plucked o leaf;
Jdg   9: 8 to the o tree, 'Reign over us.'
Ps   52: 8 But I am like a green o tree
Jer   11:16 once called you, "A green o tree,
Hab   3:17 o fails and the fields yield no food;
Zec   4: 3 And by it there are two o trees,
Ro   11:17 and you, a wild o shoot,
       11:24 grafted back into their own o tree.
Rev   11: 4 two o trees and the two lampstands

OLIVES → OLIVE

Zec   14: 4 Mount of O shall be split in two
Mt   24: 3 he was sitting on the Mount of O,
Jas   3:12 my brothers and sisters, yield o,

OMEGA*

Rev   1: 8 "I am the Alpha and the O,"
        21: 6 I am the Alpha and the O,
        22:13 I am the Alpha and the O, the first

OMENS

Dt   13: 1 among you and promise you o
Mt   24:24 and produce great signs and o,
Sir   34: 5 o and dreams are unreal,

OMRI
King of Israel (1Ki 16:21-26).

ONAN

Ge   38: 8 Judah said to O, "Go in to
       46:12 (but Er and O died in the land of

ONCE → ONE

Ge   18:32 Lord be angry if I speak just o more.
Ex   30:10 O a year Aaron shall perform the
Job   40: 5 I have spoken o, and I will not
La   1: 1 How lonely sits the city that o was
Ro   6:10 he died, he died to sin, o for all;
        7: 9 I was o alive apart from the law,
Eph   5: 8 For o you were darkness,
Heb   7:27 this he did o for all when he offered
        9:12 entered o for all into the Holy Place,
        9:27 it is appointed for mortals to die o,
1Pe   2:10 o you had not received mercy,
        3:18 Christ also suffered for sins o for all

ONE → EVERYONE, EVERYONE'S, FIRST,
ONCE, ONES

Ge   2:24 and they become o flesh.
Jos   23:10 O of you puts to flight a thousand,
Ps   14: 3 no o who does good, no, not o.
Ecc   4: 9 Two are better than o, because they
Isa   30:17 thousand shall flee at the threat of o,
Eze   34:23 I will set up over them o shepherd,
       37:22 will make them o nation in the land,
Zec   14: 9 the LORD will be o and his name o.
Mal   2:10 Has not o God created us?
Mk   10: 8 no longer two, but o flesh.
       10:21 and said, "You lack o thing;
       12:29 the Lord our God, the Lord is o;
Lk   10:42 there is need of only o thing.
Jn   1:18 No o has ever seen God.
       10:16 So there will be o flock, o shepherd.
       10:30 The Father and I are o."
       17:22 so that they may be o, as we are o,
Ro   3:10 no o who is righteous, not even o;
        5:15 the grace of the o man, Jesus Christ,
1Co   6:16 prostitute becomes o body with her?
        8: 4 and that "there is no God but o."
       10:17 we who are many are o body,
       12:13 For in the o Spirit we were all
                baptized into o body—
Eph   4: 5 o Lord, o faith, o baptism,
1Ti   2: 5 o God; there is also o mediator
                between God and humankind,
2Pe   3: 8 Lord o day is like a thousand years,
                and a thousand years are like o day.
Sir   1: 8 There is but o who is wise,

EVIL ONE Mt 5:37; 6:13; 13:19, 38; Jn
17:15; Eph 6:16; 2Th 3:3; 1Jn 2:13, 14; 3:12;
5:18, 19

HOLY ONE Nu 16:7; 1Sa 2:2; 2Ki 19:22; Job
6:10; Ps 71:22; 78:41; 89:18; 106:16; Pr 9:10;
Isa 1:4; 5:19, 24; 10:17, 20; 12:6; 17:7; 29:19,
23; 30:11, 12, 15; 31:1; 37:23; 40:25; 41:14,
16, 20; 43:3, 14, 15; 45:11; 47:4; 48:17; 49:7,
7; 54:5; 55:5; 60:9, 14; Jer 50:29; 51:5; Eze
39:7; Da 8:13, 13; Hos 11:9, 12; Hab 1:12;
3:3; Mk 1:24; Lk 4:34; Jn 6:69; Ac 2:27;
13:35; 1Jn 2:20; Rev 3:7; 16:5; Sir 4:14; 23:9;
43:10; 47:8; 48:20; Bar 4:22, 37; 5:5; Aza
1:12; 2Mc 14:36

LOVE ONE ANOTHER Jn 13:34, 34;
15:12, 17; Ro 12:10; 13:8; 1Th 4:9; 1Pe 1:22;
1Jn 3:11, 14, 23; 4:7, 11, 12; 2Jn 1:5

MIGHTY ONE Ge 49:24; 1Ch 1:10; Ps 45:3;
50:1; 52:1; 132:2, 5; Isa 1:24; 49:26; 60:16; Lk
1:49; Jdt 16:6; Sir 46:5, 6, 16; 2Es 6:32; 9:45;
10:24; 11:43; 12:47

ONE ANOTHER Ge 11:3; 37:19; 42:1, 21,
28; 43:33; Ex 10:23; 16:15; 26:3, 3, 5, 6;
36:10, 10, 12; 37:9; Lev 19:11; 25:14, 17;
26:37; Nu 14:4; Dt 25:11; Jdg 6:29; 10:18; 1Sa
10:11; 18:7; 21:11; 29:5; 2Sa 14:6; 1Ki 20:29;
2Ki 3:23; 7:3, 6, 9; 14:8, 11; 2Ch 20:23; 25:17,
21; Ne 4:19; Est 9:19, 22; Isa 13:8; 41:6; Jer
23:27, 30, 35; 31:34; 34:15; 36:16; Eze 1:9;
3:13; 4:17; 24:23; 33:30; Da 2:43; 7:3; Joel
2:8; Jnh 1:7; Zec 7:9, 10; 8:16, 17; 11:9; Mal
2:10; 3:16; Mt 11:16; 16:7; 21:25; 24:10, 10;
Mk 1:27; 4:41; 8:16; 9:34, 50; 10:26; 11:31;
12:7, 28; 14:4; 16:3; Lk 2:15; 4:36; 6:11; 7:32;

8:25; 12:1; 20:5; 22:23; Jn 4:33; 5:44; 7:35;
11:56; 12:19; 13:22, 34, 34, 35; 15:12, 17;
16:17; 19:24; Ac 2:12; 4:15; 19:38; 21:6;
26:31; 28:4; Ro 1:27; 12:10, 10, 16; 13:8;
14:13; 15:5, 7, 14; 16:16; 1Co 6:7; 7:5; 11:33;
12:25; 16:20; 2Co 10:12, 12; 13:11, 12; Gal
5:13, 15, 15, 26, 26; Eph 4:2, 25, 32, 32; 5:21;
Col 3:9, 13, 16; 1Th 3:12; 4:9, 18; 5:11, 15;
2Th 1:3; Tit 3:3; Heb 3:13; 8:11; 10:24, 25;
Jas 4:11; 5:9, 16, 16; 1Pe 1:22; 3:8; 4:8, 9, 10;
5:5, 14; 1Jn 1:7; 3:11, 14, 16, 23; 4:7, 11, 12;
2Jn 1:5; Rev 6:4; Jdt 7:4; 10:19; 15:2; AdE
9:19, 19; Wis 5:3; 14:24, 24; 18:23; 19:18; Sir
16:28; 1Mc 3:43; 7:29; 10:54, 56; 11:6; 12:50;
13:28; 2Mc 7:5; 14:26; 1Es 3:4; 4:4, 6, 33; 2Es
5:9; 13:31, 33; 15:16, 35; 4Mc 13:8, 13, 23,
24, 25

ONE BODY Jdg 20:1; Ro 12:4, 5; 1Co 6:16;
10:17; 12:12, 13, 20; Eph 2:16; 4:4; Col 3:15

ONE FLESH Ge 2:24; Mt 19:5, 6; Mk 10:8,
8; 1Co 6:16; 15:39; Eph 5:31

ONES → ONE

Dt   33: 3 all his holy o were in your charge;
1Ch   16:13 children of Jacob, his chosen o.
Ps   37:28 he will not forsake his faithful o.
       105:15 "Do not touch my anointed o;
Mt   18: 6 of these little o who believe in me,
Jude   1:14 with ten thousands of his holy o,
Wis   4:15 he watches over his holy o.

HOLY ONES Dt 33:2, 3; Job 5:1; 15:15; Ps
16:3; 34:9; 89:5, 7; Pr 30:3; Da 4:17; 7:18, 21,
22, 25, 27; 8:24; Zec 14:5; Jude 1:14; Wis 3:9;
4:15; 18:1, 2, 5; Sir 42:17; 45:2; 3Mc 2:2, 21

ONESIMUS*

Col   4: 9 he is coming with O, the faithful
Phm   1:10 appealing to you for my child, O,

ONIAS

1Mc   12: 7 a letter was sent to the high priest O
2Mc   3: 1 the piety of the high priest O
        4:36 the unreasonable murder of O,

ONIONS*

Nu   11: 5 the melons, the leeks, the o,

ONLY

Ge   6: 5 their hearts was o evil continually.
        7:23 O Noah was left, and those that
       22: 2 "Take your son, your o son Isaac,
Nu   11: 4 and said, "If o we had meat to eat!
Dt   15: 5 if o you will obey the LORD your
1Ki   18:22 "I, even I o, am left a prophet
Ps   37: 8 Do not fret—it leads o to evil.
Mt   4:10 Lord your God, and serve o him.'"
Mk   13:32 nor the Son, but o the Father.
Jn   1:14 the glory as of a father's o son,
        1:18 It is God the o Son,
        3:16 that he gave his o Son,
Ro   3:29 Or is God the God of Jews o?
1Ti   1:17 the o God, be honor and glory
1Jn   4: 9 God sent his o Son into the world so

ONLY SON Ge 22:2, 12, 16; Am 8:10; Lk
7:12; Jn 1:14, 18; 3:16, 18; Heb 11:17; 1Jn
4:9; Tob 6:15

ONYX

Ex   28: 9 You shall take two o stones,
Rev   21:20 the fifth o, the sixth carnelian,

OPEN → OPENED, OPENING, OPENLY,
OPENS

Dt   28:12 will o for you his rich storehouse,
Ps   51:15 O Lord, o my lips,
       78: 2 I will o my mouth in a parable;
       118:19 O to me the gates of righteousness,
       145:16 You o your hand, satisfying the
Pr   15:11 and Abaddon lie o before the LORD,
       27: 5 Better is o rebuke than hidden love.
SS   5: 2 "O to me, my sister, my love,
Isa   42: 7 to o the eyes that are blind,
       53: 7 so he did not o his mouth.

OPENED

Mal 3:10 o the windows of heaven for you
Mt 13:35 o my mouth to speak in parables;
17:27 o its mouth, you will find a coin;
Rev 3: 8 I have set before you an o door,
4: 1 there in heaven a door stood o!
5: 2 "Who is worthy to o the scroll
Bel 1:27 The dragon ate them, and burst o.

OPENED → OPEN

Ge 3: 7 Then the eyes of both were o,
Nu 16:32 earth o its mouth and swallowed
Ne 8: 5 Ezra o the book in the sight of all
Ps 105:41 He o the rock, and water gushed out
Isa 35: 5 the eyes of the blind shall be o,
50: 5 The Lord GOD has o my ear,
Da 7:10 in judgment, and the books were o.
Zec 13: 1 a fountain shall be o for the house
Mt 3:16 heavens were o to him and he saw
Lk 11: 9 knock, and the door will be o for
24:45 he o their minds to understand the
Ac 10:11 He saw the heaven o and something
Heb 10:20 new and living way that he o for us
Rev 11:19 Then God's temple in heaven was o,
20:12 book was o, the book of life.
1Mc 3:48 And they o the book of the law

OPENING → OPEN

Lk 24:32 while he was o the scriptures to us?"

OPENLY → OPEN

Jn 7:26 And here he is, speaking o,
18:20 Jesus answered, "I have spoken o to
Sir 51:13 I sought wisdom o in my prayer.

OPENS → OPEN

Ps 146: 8 the LORD o the eyes of the blind.
Rev 3: 7 who o and no one will shut,

OPHIR

1Ki 10:11 which carried gold from O,
Isa 13:12 and humans than the gold of O.

OPINIONS

1Ki 18:21 go limping with two different o?

OPPONENTS

Lk 13:17 all his o were put to shame;
21:15 of your o will be able to withstand
2Ti 2:25 correcting o with gentleness.

OPPORTUNE → OPPORTUNITY

Lk 4:13 departed from him until an o time.

OPPORTUNITY → OPPORTUNE

Mt 26:16 began to look for an o to betray him.
Ro 7: 8 seizing an o in the commandment,
2Co 5:12 giving you an o to boast about us,
Gal 5:13 not use your freedom as an o for
Php 4:10 but had no o to show it.
Heb 11:15 they would have had o to return.

OPPOSE → OPPOSED, OPPOSES

1Th 2:15 they displease God and o everyone
2Ti 3: 8 counterfeit faith, also o the truth.

OPPOSED → OPPOSE

Gal 3:21 law then o to the promises of God?
5:17 the flesh desires is o to the Spirit,
2Ti 3: 8 As Jannes and Jambres o Moses,

OPPOSES → OPPOSE

2Th 2: 4 He o and exalts himself above every
Jas 4: 6 "God o the proud, but gives grace
1Pe 5: 5 "God o the proud, but gives grace

OPPRESS → OPPRESSED, OPPRESSES,
OPPRESSING, OPPRESSION, OPPRESSOR

Ex 1:11 to o them with forced labor.
22:21 You shall not wrong or o a resident
Ps 105:14 he allowed no one to o them;
Zec 7:10 do not o the widow, the orphan,
Mal 3: 5 those who o the hired workers
Jas 2: 6 Is it not the rich who o you?

OPPRESSED → OPPRESS

Ge 15:13 shall be o for four hundred years;
Ex 1:12 But the more they were o,
Jdg 2:18 those who persecuted and o them.
Ps 9: 9 The LORD is a stronghold for the o,
103: 6 and justice for all who are o.
146: 7 who executes justice for the o;
Isa 1:17 seek justice, rescue the o,
53: 7 He was o, and he was afflicted,
Lk 4:18 to let the o go free,
Jdt 9:11 God of the lowly, helper of the o,
Sir 4: 9 Rescue the o from the oppressor;

OPPRESSES → OPPRESS

Pr 28: 3 who o the poor is a beating rain
Eze 18:12 o the poor and needy, commits

OPPRESSING → OPPRESS

Ps 37:35 I have seen the wicked o,
Pr 22:16 O the poor in order to enrich oneself

OPPRESSION → OPPRESS

Dt 26: 7 our affliction, our toil, and our o.
Ps 72:14 From o and violence he redeems
119:134 Redeem me from human o,
Jer 9: 6 O upon o, deceit upon deceit!
Eze 45: 9 Put away violence and o,

OPPRESSOR → OPPRESS

Ps 72: 4 to the needy, and crush the o.
Isa 51:13 But where is the fury of the o?
Jer 22: 3 the o anyone who has been robbed.

ORACLE → ORACLES

Nu 23: 7 Then Balaam uttered his o, saying:
2Sa 23: 1 The o of David, son of Jesse,
Pr 31: 1 An o that his mother taught him:

ORACLES → ORACLE

Dt 18:11 or who seeks o from the dead.
La 2:14 have seen o for you that are false
Mic 3:11 its prophets give o for money;
Ro 3: 2 entrusted with the o of God.

ORDAIN → FOREORDAINED, ORDAINED,
ORDINANCE, ORDINANCES, ORDINATION

Ex 29: 9 shall then o Aaron and his sons.
1Ti 5:22 Do not o anyone hastily,

ORDAINED → ORDAIN

Nu 3: 3 whom he o to minister as priests.
Ps 133: 3 there the LORD o his blessing,

ORDER → ORDERED, ORDERLY, ORDERS

Dt 8: 2 in o to humble you, testing you
Ps 110: 4 according to the o of Melchizedek."
Mk 7: 9 in o to keep your tradition!
Jn 10:17 I lay down my life in o to take it up
Ro 7: 4 in o that we may bear fruit for God.
Heb 5:10 according to the o of Melchizedek.
7:11 one according to the o of Aaron?
1Pe 3:18 in o to bring you to God.

ORDERED → ORDER

Pr 20:24 All our steps are o by the LORD;

ORDERLY → ORDER

Lk 1: 3 to write an o account for you,

ORDERS → ORDER

Ac 5:28 strict o not to teach in this name,

ORDINANCE → ORDAIN

Ex 12:17 your generations as a perpetual o.
29: 9 shall be theirs by a perpetual o.

ORDINANCES → ORDAIN

Ps 19: 9 o of the LORD are true and righteous
119:43 for my hope is in your o.
1Mc 2:21 from us to desert the law and the o.

ORDINARY

Ac 4:13 they were uneducated and o men,

ORDINATION → ORDAIN

Ex 29:22 the right thigh (for it is a ram of o),

OREB

Jdg 7:25 captains of Midian, O and Zeeb;
Ps 83:11 Make their nobles like O and Zeeb,

ORIGIN → ORIGINATE

Mt 21:26 But if we say, 'Of human o,'
Ac 5:38 or this undertaking is of human o,
Rev 3:14 the o of God's creation:

ORIGINATE* → ORIGIN

1Co 14:36 Or did the word of God o with you?

ORNAMENT → ORNAMENTS

Pr 25:12 or an o of gold is a wise rebuke to a
Tit 2:10 they may be an o to the doctrine
Sir 6:30 Her yoke is a golden o,

ORNAMENTS → ORNAMENT

Ex 33: 6 stripped themselves of their o,
1Pe 3: 3 by wearing gold o or fine clothing;

ORNAN → =ARAUNAH

1Ch 21:15 by the threshing floor of O
2Ch 3: 1 threshing floor of O the Jebusite.

ORPAH

Ru 1: 4 wives; the name of the one was O

ORPHAN → ORPHANED, ORPHANS

Ex 22:22 You shall not abuse any widow or o.
Ps 82: 3 Give justice to the weak and the o;
Isa 1:17 defend the o, plead for the widow.
Hos 14: 3 In you the o finds mercy."

ORPHANED → ORPHAN

Jn 14:18 will not leave you o; I am coming

ORPHANS → ORPHAN

Ps 68: 5 Father of o and protector of widows
Jas 1:27 to care for o and widows in their
Sir 4:10 Be a father to o, and be like a

OTHER → OTHERS

Ge 28:17 none o than the house of God,
Ex 20: 3 you shall have no o gods before me.
23:13 Do not invoke the names of o gods;
Dt 4:35 there is no o besides him.
Jdg 2:19 following o gods,
1Sa 8:20 that we also may be like o nations,
1Ki 11: 4 turned away his heart after o gods;
2Ki 17: 7 They had worshiped o gods
2Ch 2: 5 for our God is greater than o gods.
Ps 147:20 has not dealt thus with any o nation;
Isa 44: 8 There is no o rock; I know not one.
45: 5 I am the LORD, and there is no o;
Jer 7: 6 go after o gods to your own hurt,
Da 3:29 is no o god who is able to deliver
Mt 6:24 to the one and despise the o.
Lk 17:34 one will be taken and the o left.
Jn 20:30 Now Jesus did many o signs in the
21:25 also many o things that Jesus did;
1Co 3:11 For no one can lay any foundation o
2Pe 3:16 as they do the o scriptures.
Sir 1: 4 Wisdom was created before all o

OTHER GODS
Ex 20:3; 23:13; Dt 4:28; 5:7;
6:14; 7:4; 8:19; 11:16, 28; 13:2, 6, 13; 17:3;
18:20; 28:14, 36, 64; 29:26; 30:17; 31:18, 20;
Jos 23:16; 24:2, 16; Jdg 2:12, 17, 19; 10:13;
1Sa 8:8; 26:19; 1Ki 9:6, 9; 11:4, 10; 14:9; 2Ki
17:7, 35, 37, 38; 22:17; 2Ch 2:5; 7:19, 22;
28:25; 34:25; Jer 1:16; 7:6, 9, 18; 11:10;
13:10; 16:11, 13; 19:4, 13; 22:9; 25:6; 32:29;
35:15; 44:3, 5, 8, 15; Hos 3:1; Bar 1:22

NO OTHER
Ex 20:3; 30:32; 34:14; Dt 4:35,
39; 5:7; Jdg 7:14; 1Ki 3:13; 8:60; 22:7; 1Ch
23:17; 2Ch 18:6; Isa 42:8; 44:8; 45:5, 6, 14,
18, 21, 22; 46:9; Da 3:29; Joel 2:27; Mk 12:31,
32; Ac 4:12; Tob 3:15; 6:15; Jdt 8:20; 9:14;
11:21; Bar 3:35; Bel 1:41; 1Mc 10:38

OTHERS → OTHER

Mt   7:12 do to **o** as you would have them do
Lk   6:31 Do to **o** as you would have them do
Php 2: 3 but in humility regard **o** as better

OTHNIEL

Nephew of Caleb (Jos 15:15-19; Jdg 1:12-15).
Judge who freed Israel from Aram (Jdg 3:7-11).

OUGHT

Ro   8:26 do not know how to pray as we **o**,
     12: 3 of yourself more highly than you **o**,
2Pe 3:11 what sort of persons **o** you to be
1Jn 3:16 we **o** to lay down our lives for one
3Jn 1: 8 we **o** to support such people,

OUTCOME → COME

Isa 41:22 and that we may know their **o**;
Da 12: 8 what shall be the **o** of these things?"
Heb 13: 7 consider the **o** of their way of life,
1Pe 1: 9 you are receiving the **o** of your faith,

OUTER → OUTSIDE

Mt 22:13 and throw him into the **o** darkness,
    25:30 throw him into the **o** darkness,

OUTSIDE → OUTER, OUTSIDERS

Pr 22:13 lazy person says, "There is a lion **o!**
Lk 11:39 Pharisees clean the **o** of the cup and
    13:33 prophet to be killed **o** of Jerusalem.'
1Co 5:13 God will judge those **o**.
Heb 13:12 Jesus also suffered **o** the city gate in
Rev 22:15 **O** are the dogs and sorcerers and
Bel 1: 7 only clay inside and bronze **o**,
Pm 151: 1 (though it is **o** the number),

OUTSIDERS → OUTSIDE

1Co 14:23 and **o** or unbelievers enter,
Col 4: 5 Conduct yourselves wisely toward **o**
1Th 4:12 you may behave properly toward **o**
1Ti 3: 7 he must be well thought of by **o**,

OUTSTRETCHED → STRETCH

Ex   6: 6 I will redeem you with an **o** arm
Dt   4:34 by a mighty hand and an **o** arm,
1Ki 8:42 your mighty hand, and your **o** arm
Ps 136:12 an **o** arm, for his steadfast love
Isa 3:16 are haughty and walk with **o** necks,
Jer 27: 5 by my great power and my **o** arm
    32:17 great power and by your **o** arm!
Eze 20:33 with a mighty hand and an **o** arm,

OUTWARD → OUTWARDLY

1Sa 16: 7 they look on the **o** appearance,
2Co 5:12 those who boast in **o** appearance
2Ti 3: 5 the **o** form of godliness but denying

OUTWARDLY* → OUTWARD

Ro 2:28 a person is not a Jew who is one **o**,
1Pe 3: 3 not adorn yourselves **o** by braiding

OUTWEIGHS* → WEIGH

Ecc 10: 1 so a little folly **o** wisdom and honor.

OUTWITTED

2Co 2:11 that we may not be **o** by Satan;

OVER

Ex 12:13 I see the blood, I will pass **o** you,
    12:23 two doorposts, the LORD will pass **o**
Ps   1: 6 watches **o** the way of the righteous,
     8: 6 given them dominion **o** the works
  145:20 LORD watches **o** all who love him,
Mk 15:15 he handed him **o** to be crucified.

OVERCOME

Jn   1: 5 and the darkness did not **o** it.
Ro 12:21 Do not be **o** by evil, but **o** evil with
1Jn 2:14 and you have **o** the evil one.
Sir 23: 6 Let neither gluttony nor lust **o** me,

OVERFLOW → OVERFLOWS

Ps 65:11 your wagon tracks **o** with richness.
Joel 2:24 the vats shall **o** with wine and oil.
Php 1: 9 that your love may **o** more and more

OVERFLOWS → OVERFLOW

Ps 23: 5 anoint my head with oil; my cup **o**.

OVERJOYED → JOY

Ac 12:14 Peter's voice, she was so **o** that,

OVERLOOK → OVERLOOKED

Pr 19:11 and it is their glory to **o** an offense.
Heb 6:10 he will not **o** your work
Sir 32:18 not **o** a thoughtful suggestion;

OVERLOOKED → OVERLOOK

Ac 17:30 has **o** the times of human ignorance,

OVERSEERS

Ac 20:28 the Holy Spirit has made you **o**,

OVERSHADOW* → OVERSHADOWED, OVERSHADOWING

Lk 1:35 power of the Most High will **o** you;

OVERSHADOWED → OVERSHADOW

Lk 9:34 a cloud came and **o** them;

OVERSHADOWING → OVERSHADOW

Ex 25:20 **o** the mercy seat with their wings.
Heb 9: 5 cherubim of glory **o** the mercy seat.

OVERSIGHT → OVERSEE

1Pe 5: 2 the **o**, not under compulsion but

OVERTAKE → OVERTAKEN

Jn 12:35 so that the darkness may not **o** you.
Tob 12: 7 Do good and evil will not **o** you.
Sir 7: 1 no evil, and evil will never **o** you.

OVERTAKEN → OVERTAKE

1Co 10:13 No testing has **o** you that

OVERTHREW → OVERTHROW

Ge 19:25 he **o** those cities, and all the Plain,
Jer 50:40 God **o** Sodom and Gomorrah and

OVERTHROW → OVERTHREW, OVERTHROWS

Ac   5:39 you will not be able to **o** them—
Ro   3:31 Do we then **o** the law by this faith?

OVERTHROWS → OVERTHROW

Pr 13: 6 but sin **o** the wicked.
    22:12 but he **o** the words of the faithless.

OVERTURNED

Mk 11:15 **o** the tables of the money changers

OVERWHELM → OVERWHELMED, OVERWHELMING

Dt 28:59 the LORD will **o** both you and your
Ps 88: 7 and you **o** me with all your waves.

OVERWHELMED → OVERWHELM

Ps 90: 7 by your wrath we are **o**.
2Co 2: 7 may not be **o** by excessive sorrow.

OVERWHELMING → OVERWHELM

Pr 27: 4 Wrath is cruel, anger is **o**,
Isa 28:15 **o** scourge passes through it will not

OWE → OWES

Mt 18:28 he said, 'Pay what you **o**.'
Ro 13: 8 **O** no one anything, except to love

OWES* → OWE

Dt 15: 3 member of your community **o** you.
Phm 1:18 or **o** you anything, charge that to my

OWN → LANDOWNER, OWNER

Ge 15: 4 your very **o** issue shall be your heir.
Ex 32:13 you swore to them by your **o** self,
Dt 18:15 prophet like me from among your **o**
    24:16 for their **o** crimes may persons be
1Sa 13:14 sought out a man after his **o** heart;
Ps 141:10 Let the wicked fall into their **o** nets,
Pr   3: 7 Do not be wise in your **o** eyes;
    26:12 see persons wise in their **o** eyes?

Isa 48:11 For my **o** sake, for my **o** sake, I do it
     53: 6 we have all turned to our **o** way,
Jer 31:30 But all shall die for their **o** sins;
Eze 33: 4 blood shall be upon their **o** heads.
Lk   6:42 not see the log in your **o** eye?
Jn   1:11 He came to what was his **o**, and his
       o people did not accept him.
    10:18 but I lay it down of my **o** accord.
Ro   8:32 He who did not withhold his **o** Son,
1Co 6:19 and that you are not your **o**?
Php 2: 4 Let each of you look not to your **o**
Sir 17:17 but Israel is the Lord's **o** portion.

OWNER → OWN

Mt 21:40 when the **o** of the vineyard comes,
    24:43 if the **o** of the house had known

OX → OXEN

Ex 20:17 or male or female slave, or **o**,
Dt 22:10 not plow with an **o** and a donkey
    25: 4 not muzzle an **o** while it is treading
Pr   7:22 and goes like an **o** to the slaughter,
Isa 11: 7 the lion shall eat straw like the **o**.
    65:25 the lion shall eat straw like the **o**;
Eze 1:10 the face of an **o** on the left side,
Lk 13:15 of you on the sabbath untie his **o**
1Co 9: 9 not muzzle an **o** while it is treading
1Ti 5:18 not muzzle an **o** while it is treading
Rev 4: 7 the second living creature like an **o**,

OXEN → OX

1Ki 19:20 He left the **o**, ran after Elijah,
Lk 14:19 said, 'I have bought five yoke of **o**,
1Co 9: 9 Is it for **o** that God is concerned?

𝒫

PAGANS*

1Co 5: 1 that is not found even among **p**;
    10:20 No, I imply that what **p** sacrifice,
    12: 2 You know that when you were **p**,
4Mc 18: 5 to compel the Israelites to become **p**

PAID → PAY

Jdg 1: 7 so God has **p** me back."
Isa 40: 2 her term, that her penalty is **p**,
Mt 26:15 They **p** him thirty pieces of silver.
Col 3:25 For the wrongdoer will be **p** back

PAIN → PAINFUL, PAINS

Ge 3:16 in **p** shall bring forth children,
Job 6:10 I would even exult in unrelenting **p**;
    33:19 chastened with **p** upon their beds,
Jer 4:19 my anguish! I writhe in **p!**
    15:18 Why is my **p** unceasing, my wound
Jn 16:21 a woman is in labor, she has **p**,
1Pe 2:19 endure **p** while suffering unjustly.
Rev 21: 4 and crying and **p** will be no more,

PAINFUL → PAIN

2Co 2: 1 not to make you another **p** visit.
Heb 12:11 discipline always seems **p** rather

PAINS → PAIN

Ro 8:22 creation has been groaning in labor **p**
1Th 5: 3 as labor **p** come upon a pregnant

PAIRS

Ge 7: 2 seven **p** of all clean animals,
Sir 42:24 All things come in **p**,

PALACES

2Ch 36:19 burned all its **p** with fire,
Hos 8:14 forgotten his Maker, and built **p**;
Lk   7:25 and live in luxury are in royal **p**.

PALE

Isa 29:22 no longer shall his face grow **p**.
Jer 30: 6 Why has every face turned **p?**
Da 10: 8 and my complexion grew deathly **p**,

PALM → PALMS

Rev 6: 8 and there was a **p** green horse!

PALM → PALMS

Ex 15:27 of water and seventy **p** trees;
Jdg 4: 5 the **p** of Deborah between Ramah
1Ki 6:29 **p** trees, and open flowers,
Ps 92:12 righteous flourish like the **p** tree,
Jn 12:13 So they took branches of **p** trees
Rev 7: 9 robed in white, with **p** branches in

PALMS → PALM

Isa 49:16 I have inscribed you on the **p** of my

PANELED

Hag 1: 4 yourselves to live in your **p** houses,

PANGS

Ge 3:16 increase your **p** in childbearing;
Ps 116: 3 the **p** of Sheol laid hold on me;
Isa 13: 8 **P** and agony will seize them;
Mk 13: 8 but the beginning of the birth **p.**
Rev 12: 2 and was crying out in birth **p,**

PANIC

Dt 20: 3 Do not lose heart, or be afraid, or **p,**
1Sa 14:15 There was a **p** in the camp,
Zec 14:13 a great **p** from the LORD shall fall
Jdt 14: 3 Then **p** will come over them,

PAPER*

2Jn 1:12 I would rather not use **p** and ink;
3Mc 4:20 both the **p** and the pens they used
2Es 15: 2 and cause them to be written on **p;**

PAPYRUS

Ex 2: 3 a **p** basket for him, and plastered it

PARABLE → PARABLES

Ps 78: 2 I will open my mouth in a **p;**
Mt 13:18 "Hear then the **p** of the sower.
15:15 said to him, "Explain this **p** to us."
21:33 "Listen to another **p.** There was a
Lk 20:19 had told this **p** against them,
2Es 4:47 show you the interpretation of a **p.**"

PARABLES → PARABLE; See also
JESUS: PARABLES

Mt 13:35 I will open my mouth to speak in **p;**
Lk 8:10 but to others I speak in **p,**
Sir 39: 2 penetrates the subtleties of **p;**

PARADISE

Lk 23:43 today you will be with me in **P.**"
2Co 12: 4 was caught up into **P** and heard
Rev 2: 7 tree of life that is in the **p** of God.
2Es 4: 7 or which are the entrances of **p?**'
8:52 for you that **p** is opened,

PARALYTIC → PARALYZED

Mt 9: 2 saw their faith, he said to the **p,**

PARALYZED → PARALYTIC

Jn 5: 3 many invalids—blind, lame, and **p.**
Ac 8: 7 who were **p** or lame were cured.

PARAN

Ge 21:21 He lived in the wilderness of **P;**
Nu 10:12 settled down in the wilderness of **P.**
Hab 3: 3 the Holy One from Mount **P.**

PARCHED

Ps 143: 6 my soul thirsts for you like a **p** land.

PARCHMENTS*

2Ti 4:13 also the books, and above all the **p.**

PARDON → PARDONED

Ex 34: 9 **p** our iniquity and our sin,
Dt 29:20 LORD will be unwilling to **p** them,
2Ch 30:18 saying, "The good LORD **p** all
Job 7:21 Why do you not **p** my transgression
Isa 55: 7 our God, for he will abundantly **p.**

PARDONED → PARDON

Nu 14:19 just as you have **p** this people,
Sir 28: 2 your sins will be **p** when you pray.

PARENT → PARENTS

Dt 8: 5 that as a **p** disciplines a child
Eze 18:20 nor a **p** suffer for the iniquity of a

PARENTS → PARENT

Ex 34: 7 iniquity of the **p** upon the children
Pr 17: 6 and the glory of children is their **p.**
19:14 and wealth are inherited from **p,**
Mal 4: 6 turn the hearts of **p** to their children
Mk 13:12 against **p** and have them put to
Lk 1:17 turn the hearts of **p** to their children,
2:27 the **p** brought in the child Jesus,
18:29 or wife or brothers or **p** or children,
21:16 You will be betrayed even by **p** and
Jn 9: 3 "Neither this man nor his **p** sinned;
Ro 1:30 of evil, rebellious toward **p,**
2Co 12:14 but **p** for their children.
Eph 6: 1 Children, obey your **p** in the Lord,
Col 3:20 Children, obey your **p** in everything,
1Ti 5: 4 make some repayment to their **p;**
2Ti 3: 2 disobedient to their **p,** ungrateful,
Sir 48:10 turn the hearts of **p** to their children,

PARSIN* → PERES

Da 5:25 MENE, MENE, TEKEL, and **P.**

PART → APART, PARTED, PARTIAL,
PARTLY, PARTS

Nu 18:29 the best of all of them is the **p** to be
Ezr 4: 3 no **p** with us in building a house
Ac 8:21 You have no **p** or share in this,
1Co 13: 9 For we know only in **p,** and we
prophesy only in **p;**

PARTAKE

1Co 10:17 for we all **p** of the one bread.

PARTED → PART

Ac 15:39 so sharp that they **p** company;

PARTIAL → PART

Pr 18: 5 It is not right to be **p** to the guilty,
1Co 13:10 the **p** will come to an end.
Sir 7: 6 you may be **p** to the powerful,

PARTIALITY

Dt 16:19 distort justice; you must not show **p;**
2Ch 19: 7 or **p,** or taking of bribes."
Job 13: 8 Will you show **p** toward him,
13:10 rebuke you if in secret you show **p.**
Ps 82: 2 and show **p** to the wicked?
Pr 24:23 **P** in judging is not good.
28:21 To show **p** is not good—
Mal 2: 9 have shown **p** in your instruction.
Mt 22:16 for you do not regard people with **p.**
Ro 2:11 For God shows no **p.**
Gal 2: 6 God shows no **p)—**
Eph 6: 9 and with him there is no **p.**
1Ti 5:21 doing nothing on the basis of **p.**
Jas 3:17 without a trace of **p** or hypocrisy.
Sir 35:15 and with him there is no **p.**

PARTICIPANTS → PARTICIPATE

2Pe 1: 4 may become **p** of the divine nature.

PARTICIPATE* → PARTICIPANTS

1Ti 5:22 and do not **p** in the sins of others;
2Jn 1:11 for to welcome is to **p** in the evil

PARTLY → PART

Da 2:33 its feet **p** of iron and **p** of clay.

PARTNER → PARTNERS, PARTNERSHIP

Pr 2:17 who forsakes the **p** of her youth
1Co 7:15 But if the unbelieving **p** separates,

PARTNERS → PARTNER

1Co 10:20 not want you to be **p** with demons.
Heb 3: 1 holy **p** in a heavenly calling,

PARTNERSHIP* → PARTNER

2Co 6:14 **p** is there between righteousness

PARTS → PART

Pr 18: 8 down into the inner **p** of the body.

PASHHUR

Priest; opponent of Jeremiah (Jer 20:1-6).

PASS → PASSED, PASSING

Ex 12:13 when I see the blood, I will **p** over
12:23 two doorposts, the LORD will **p** over
33:19 make all my goodness **p** before you,
Nu 20:17 Now let us **p** through your land.
21:22 "Let me **p** through your land;
1Ki 19:11 for the LORD is about to **p** by."
Ps 105:19 until what he had said came to **p,**
Isa 43: 2 **p** through the waters, I will be with
Jer 22: 8 many nations will **p** by this city,
La 1:12 nothing to you, all you who **p** by?
Da 7:14 dominion that shall not **p** away,
Am 5:17 I will **p** through the midst of you,
Mt 24:35 Heaven and earth will **p** away, but
my words will not **p** away.
Mk 14:35 if it were possible, the hour might **p**
2Pe 3:10 then the heavens will **p** away

PASSED → PASS

Ge 15:17 torch **p** between these pieces.
Ex 12:27 he **p** over the houses of the Israelites
33:22 with my hand until I have **p** by;
34: 6 LORD **p** before him, and proclaimed,
Nu 33: 8 **p** through the sea into the
Ps 37:36 I **p** by, and they were no more;
Lk 10:32 **p** by on the other side.
1Co 10: 1 and all **p** through the sea,
2Co 5:17 everything old has **p** away;
Heb 11:29 By faith the people **p** through the
1Jn 3:14 that we have **p** from death to life
Rev 21: 1 and the first earth had **p** away,
21: 4 for the first things have **p** away."
2Es 8:54 sorrows have **p** away,

PASSING → PASS

1Co 7:31 present form of this world is **p** away
1Jn 2: 8 because the darkness is **p** away and
2:17 the world and its desire are **p** away,
Wis 2: 5 allotted time is the **p** of a shadow,

PASSION → PASSIONS

SS 8: 6 **p** fierce as the grave.
1Co 7: 9 to marry than to be aflame with **p.**
Col 3: 5 fornication, impurity, **p,** evil desire,
Sir 6: 4 Evil **p** destroys those who have it,

PASSIONS → PASSION

Ro 7: 5 were living in the flesh, our sinful **p,**
Gal 5:24 have crucified the flesh with its **p**
2Ti 2:22 Shun youthful **p** and pursue
Tit 3: 3 led astray, slaves to various **p** and

PASSOVER

Ex 12:11 It is the **p** of the LORD.
Nu 9: 2 Let the Israelites keep the **p** at its
Dt 16: 1 the month of Abib by keeping the **p**
Jos 5:10 **p** in the evening on the fourteenth
2Ki 23:21 the **p** to the LORD your God as
2Ch 30: 1 to keep the **p** to the LORD the God
Ezr 6:19 the returned exiles kept the **p.**
Mk 14:12 when the **P** lamb is sacrificed,
Lk 22: 8 the **P** meal for us that we may eat it.
Heb 11:28 By faith he kept the **P** and the

PAST

Ac 14:16 In **p** generations he allowed all the
2Pe 1: 9 forgetful of the cleansing of **p** sins.

PASTORS*

Eph 4:11 evangelists, some **p** and teachers,

PASTURE → PASTURES

Ps 79:13 we your people, the flock of your **p,**
95: 7 God, and we are the people of his **p,**
100: 3 his people, and the sheep of his **p.**
Jer 23: 1 and scatter the sheep of my **p!**
50: 7 the LORD, the true **p,** the LORD,
Jn 10: 9 will come in and go out and find **p.**

PASTURES → PASTURE

Ps 23: 2 He makes me lie down in green **p;**

PATCH

Mk 2:21 otherwise, the **p** pulls away from it,

PATH → PATHS

Nu 22:24 of the LORD stood in a narrow **p**
Ps 16:11 You show me the **p** of life.
27:11 and lead me on a level **p** because of
119:105 lamp to my feet and a light to my **p.**
Pr 2: 9 justice and equity, every good **p;**
12:28 the **p** of righteousness there is life,
15:19 **p** of the upright is a level highway.
15:24 For the wise the **p** of life leads
Isa 26: 7 make smooth the **p** of the righteous.
Jer 31: 9 a straight **p** in which they shall not
Mt 13: 4 he sowed, some seeds fell on the **p,**
Jdt 13:20 straight **p** before our God."
Sir 50:29 for the fear of the Lord is their **p.**

PATHS → PATH

Job 8:13 the **p** of all who forget God;
Ps 17: 5 My steps have held fast to your **p;**
23: 3 in right **p** for his name's sake.
25: 4 O LORD; teach me your **p.**
Pr 2:13 who forsake the **p** of uprightness to
2:18 and her **p** to the shades;
3: 6 and he will make straight your **p.**
4:11 have led you in the **p** of uprightness.
5:21 he examines all their **p.**
8:20 righteousness, along the **p** of justice,
Isa 2: 3 and that we may walk in his **p.**"
Jer 6:16 and look, and ask for the ancient **p,**
Mic 4: 2 and that we may walk in his **p.**"
Mt 3: 3 of the Lord, make his **p** straight.'"
Heb 12:13 and make straight **p** for your feet,

PATIENCE → PATIENT

Pr 25:15 With **p** a ruler may be persuaded,
Mic 2: 7 Is the LORD's **p** exhausted?
Ro 2: 4 his kindness and forbearance and **p?**
9:22 endured with much **p** the objects of
2Co 6: 6 **p,** kindness, holiness of spirit,
Col 1:11 to endure everything with **p,**
3:12 humility, meekness, and **p.**
1Ti 1:16 Christ might display the utmost **p,**
2Ti 3:10 my aim in life, my faith, my **p,**
4: 2 with the utmost **p** in teaching.
Heb 6:12 faith and **p** inherit the promises.
Jas 5:10 As an example of suffering and **p,**
2Pe 3:15 regard the **p** of our Lord as salvation

PATIENT → PATIENCE, PATIENTLY

Ne 9:30 Many years you were **p** with them,
Job 6:11 what is my end, that I should be **p?**
Ecc 7: 8 the **p** in spirit are better than
Lk 8:15 and bear fruit with **p** endurance.
Ro 12:12 Rejoice in hope, be **p** in suffering,
1Co 13: 4 Love is **p;** love is kind; love is
1Th 5:14 help the weak, be **p** with all of them.
2Ti 2:24 to everyone, an apt teacher, **p,**
Jas 5: 7 Be **p,** therefore, beloved,
5: 8 You also must be **p.**
2Pe 3: 9 as some think of slowness, but is **p**
Rev 1: 9 the kingdom and the **p** endurance,
2: 2 your toil and your **p** endurance.
2:19 faith, service, and **p** endurance.
3:10 have kept my word of **p** endurance,
Wis 15: 1 you, our God, are kind and true, **p,**
Sir 1:23 Those who are **p** stay calm until
2Es 7:74 How long the Most High has been **p**

PATIENTLY → PATIENT

Ps 37: 7 Be still before the LORD, and wait **p**
40: 1 I waited **p** for the LORD;
Ac 26: 3 I beg of you to listen to me **p.**
Heb 6:15 thus Abraham, having **p** endured,
1Pe 3:20 God waited **p** in the days of Noah,
Rev 2: 3 also know that you are enduring **p**
2Mc 6:14 nations the Lord waits **p** to punish

PATMOS·

Rev 1: 9 island called **P** because of the word

PATRIARCH· → PATRIARCHS

Heb 7: 4 Abraham the **p** gave him a tenth of

PATRIARCHS → PATRIARCH

Jn 7:22 not from Moses, but from the **p),**
Ac 7: 9 "The **p,** jealous of Joseph,
Ro 9: 5 to them belong the **p,** and from them
15: 8 the promises given to the **p,**

PATTERN

Ex 25:40 make them according to the **p** for
Nu 8: 4 **p** that the LORD had shown Moses,
Heb 8: 5 make everything according to the **p**

PAUL → =SAUL

Also called Saul (Ac 13:9). Pharisee from Tarsus (Ac 9:11; Php 3:5). Apostle (Gal 1). At stoning of Stephen (Ac 8:1). Persecuted Church (Ac 9:1-2; Gal 1:13). Vision of Jesus on road to Damascus (Ac 9:4-9; 26:12-18). In Arabia (Gal 1:17). Preached in Damascus; escaped death through the wall in a basket (Ac 9:19-25). In Jerusalem; sent back to Tarsus (Ac 9:26-30).
Brought to Antioch by Barnabas (Ac 11:22-26). First missionary journey to Cyprus and Galatia (Ac 13-14). Stoned at Lystra (Ac 14:19-20). At Jerusalem council (Ac 15). Split with Barnabas over Mark (Ac 15:36-41).
Second missionary journey with Silas (Ac 16-20). Called to Macedonia (Ac 16:6-10). Freed from prison in Philippi (Ac 16:16-40). In Thessalonica (Ac 17:1-9). Speech in Athens (Ac 17:16-33). In Corinth (Ac 18). In Ephesus (Ac 19). Return to Jerusalem (Ac 20). Farewell to Ephesian elders (Ac 20:13-38). Arrival in Jerusalem (Ac 21:1-26). Arrested (Ac 21:27-36). Addressed crowds (Ac 22), Sanhedrin (Ac 23:1-11). Sent to Caesarea (Ac 23:12-35). Trial before Felix (Ac 24), Festus (Ac 25:1-12). Before Agrippa (Ac 25:13-26:32). Voyage to Rome; shipwreck (Ac 27). Arrival in Rome (Ac 28).
Letters: Romans, 1 and 2 Corinthians, Galatians, Ephesians, Philippians, Colossians, 1 and 2 Thessalonians, 1 and 2 Timothy, Titus, Philemon.

PAVEMENT

Ex 24:10 his feet there was something like a **p**
Jn 19:13 bench at a place called The Stone **P,**

PAY → PAID, PAYING, PAYMENT, REPAID, REPAY, REPAYING, REPAYS

Ex 22: 4 the thief shall **p** double.
Dt 24:15 You shall **p** them their wages daily
Pr 6:31 are caught, they will **p** sevenfold;
19:19 person will **p** the penalty;
24:29 I will **p** them back for what they
Mt 20: 4 and I will **p** you whatever is right.'
22:17 lawful to **p** taxes to the emperor, or
Lk 19: 8 I will **p** back four times as much."
Ro 13: 6 the same reason you also **p** taxes,
13: 7 **P** to all what is due them—
1Mc 2:68 **P** back the Gentiles in full,

PAYING → PAY

Ge 42:21 we are **p** the penalty for what we did

PAYMENT → PAY

Isa 65: 7 I will measure into their laps full **p**
Mt 10: 8 received without **p;** give without **p.**

PEACE → PEACEABLE, PEACEFUL, PEACEMAKERS

Lev 26: 6 And I will grant **p** in the land,
Nu 6:26 upon you, and give you **p.**
25:12 hereby grant him my covenant of **p.**
Dt 20:10 to fight against it, offer it terms of **p.**
Jos 9:15 And Joshua made **p** with them,
11:19 made **p** with the Israelites, except
Jdg 6:24 and called it, The LORD is **p.**
1Sa 1:17 Then Eli answered, "Go in **p;**
7:14 There was **p** also between Israel and
20:42 Jonathan said to David, "Go in **p,**
2Sa 10:19 made **p** with Israel, and became

1Ki 2:33 be **p** from the LORD forevermore."
2Ki 9:17 and let him say, 'Is it **p?**'"
1Ch 19:19 they made **p** with David,
22: 9 he shall be a man of **p.**
Job 22:21 "Agree with God, and be at **p;**
Ps 29:11 the LORD bless his people with **p!**
34:14 from evil, and do good; seek **p,**
85: 8 for he will speak **p** to his people,
85:10 righteousness and **p** will kiss each
119:165 **p** have those who love your law;
120: 7 I am for **p;** but when I speak, they
122: 6 Pray for the **p** of Jerusalem:
147:14 He grants **p** within your borders;
Pr 3:17 and all her paths are **p.**
12:20 but those who counsel **p** have joy.
16: 7 their enemies to be at **p** with them.
Ecc 3: 8 a time for war, and a time for **p.**
Isa 9: 6 Everlasting Father, Prince of **P.**
26: 3 of steadfast mind you keep in **p**—
in **p** because they trust in you.
32:17 effect of righteousness will be **p,**
48:22 "There is no **p,**" says the LORD.
52: 7 of the messenger who announces **p,**
54:10 covenant of **p** shall not be removed,
55:12 go out in joy, and be led back in **p;**
57: 2 they enter into **p;** those who walk
57:19 **P, p,** to the far and the near,
57:21 no **p,** says my God, for the wicked.
59: 8 The way of **p** they do not know,
59: 8 no one who walks in them knows **p.**
Jer 6:14 saying, "**P, p,**" when there is no **p.**
8:11 saying, "**P, p,**" when there is no **p.**
La 3:17 my soul is bereft of **p;**
Eze 13:10 saying, "**P,**" when there is no **p;**
34:25 a covenant of **p** and banish wild
37:26 I will make a covenant of **p** with
Mic 5: 5 and he shall be the one of **p.**
Na 1:15 good tidings, who proclaims **p!**
Zec 8:19 therefore love truth and **p.**
9:10 he shall command **p** to the nations;
Mt 10:13 house is worthy, let your **p** come
10:34 not come to bring **p,** but a sword.
Mk 9:50 and be at **p** with one another."
Lk 1:79 to guide our feet into the way of **p.**"
2:14 on earth **p** among those whom he
7:50 "Your faith has saved you; go in **p.**"
19:38 **P** in heaven, and glory in the highest
19:42 this day the things that make for **p!**
Jn 14:27 **P** I leave with you; my **p** I give to
16:33 so that in me you may have **p.**
Ac 10:36 preaching **p** by Jesus Christ—
Ro 2:10 and **p** for everyone who does good,
3:17 the way of **p** they have not known."
5: 1 we have **p** with God through our
8: 6 the mind on the Spirit is life and **p.**
14:19 then pursue what makes for **p** and
16:20 God of **p** will shortly crush Satan
1Co 7:15 It is to **p** that God has called you.
14:33 is a God not of disorder but of **p.**
2Co 13:11 God of love and **p** will be with you.
Gal 5:22 the fruit of the Spirit is love, joy, **p,**
Eph 2:14 for he is our **p;** in his
2:15 in place of the two, thus making **p,**
2:17 proclaimed **p** to you who were far
off and **p** to those who were near;
4: 3 unity of the Spirit in the bond of **p.**
6:15 to proclaim the gospel of **p.**
Php 4: 7 the **p** of God, which surpasses all
Col 1:20 by making **p** through the blood of
3:15 the **p** of Christ rule in your hearts,
1Th 5: 3 they say, "There is **p** and security,"
5:13 Be at **p** among yourselves.
5:23 May the God of **p** himself sanctify
2Th 3:16 the Lord of **p** himself give you **p** at
2Ti 2:22 righteousness, faith, love, and **p,**
Heb 7: 2 king of Salem, that is, "king of **p.**"
12:14 Pursue **p** with everyone, and the
13:20 Now may the God of **p,**
Jas 3:18 a harvest of righteousness is sown
in **p** for those who make **p.**
1Pe 3:11 let them seek **p** and pursue it.
2Pe 3:14 strive to be found by him at **p,**

Rev 6: 4 rider was permitted to take **p** from
1Mc 14:11 He established **p** in the land,

PEACEABLE → PEACE

2Sa 20:19 who are **p** and faithful in Israel;
1Ti 2: 2 a quiet and **p** life in all godliness
Jas 3:17 from above is first pure, then **p,**

PEACEFUL → PEACE

Heb 12:11 it yields the **p** fruit of righteousness

PEACEMAKERS* → PEACE

Mt 5: 9 "Blessed are the **p,** for they will be

PEARL* → PEARLS

Mt 13:46 on finding one **p** of great value,
Rev 21:21 each of the gates is a single **p,**

PEARLS → PEARL

Job 28:18 the price of wisdom is above **p.**
Mt 7: 6 do not throw your **p** before swine,
    13:45 like a merchant in search of fine **p;**
1Ti 2: 9 their hair braided, or with gold, **p,**
Rev 21:21 And the twelve gates are twelve **p,**

PEBBLE

Am 9: 9 but no **p** shall fall to the ground.

PEDDLERS*

2Co 2:17 not **p** of God's word like so many;

PEG

Jdg 4:21 drove the **p** into his temple,
Isa 22:23 fasten him like a **p** in a secure place,
Zec 10: 4 out of them the tent **p,**

PEKAH*

King of Israel (2Ki 15:25-31; 2Ch 28:6; Isa 7:1).

PEKAHIAH*

Son of Menahem; king of Israel (2Ki 15:22-26).

PELETHITES

2Sa 20: 7 along with the Cherethites, the **P,**
1Ch 18:17 over the Cherethites and the **P;**

PEN

Ps 45: 1 my tongue is like the **p** of a ready
Jer 17: 1 of Judah is written with an iron **p;**
3Jn 1:13 but I would rather not write with **p**

PENALTY

Ge 42:21 the **p** for what we did to our brother;
Pr 19:19 tempered person will pay the **p;**
Eze 23:49 bear the **p** for your sinful idolatry;
Ro 1:27 in their own persons the due **p**
2Pe 2:13 suffering the **p** for doing wrong.
Wis 14:31 but the just **p** for those who sin,

PENIEL*

Ge 32:30 So Jacob called the place **P,**

PENINNAH

1Sa 1: 2 **P** had children, but Hannah had no

PENNIES* → PENNY

Lk 12: 6 not five sparrows sold for two **p?**

PENNY* → PENNIES

Mt 5:26 until you have paid the last **p.**
    10:29 Are not two sparrows sold for a **p?**
Mk 12:42 in two small copper coins, which
        are worth a **p.**
Lk 12:59 until you have paid the very last **p."**

PENTECOST*

Ac 2: 1 When the day of **P** had come,
    20:16 if possible, on the day of **P.**
1Co 16: 8 But I will stay in Ephesus until **P,**
Tob 2: 1 At our festival of **P,**
2Mc 12:32 After the festival called **P,**

PEOPLE → PEOPLE'S, PEOPLES

Ge 11: 6 LORD said, "Look, they are one **p,**
Ex 3:10 send you to Pharaoh to bring my **p,**
    5: 1 the God of Israel, 'Let my **p** go,
    6: 7 as my **p,** and I will be your God.

8:23 I will make a distinction between
      my **p** and your **p.**
13:17 When Pharaoh let the **p** go,
15:13 the **p** whom you redeemed;
15:24 the **p** complained against Moses,
19: 8 The **p** all answered as one:
24: 3 all the **p** answered with one voice,
32: 1 the **p** gathered around Aaron,
32: 9 said to Moses, "I have seen this **p,**
32:12 and do not bring disaster on your **p.**
33:13 too that this nation is your **p."**
Nu 11:11 lay the burden of all this **p** on me?
    14:11 "How long will this **p** despise me?
    14:19 just as you have pardoned this **p,**
    21: 7 So Moses prayed for the **p.**
    22: 5 saying, "A **p** has come out of Egypt;
Dt 4: 6 nation is a wise and discerning **p!"**
    4:20 a **p** of his very own possession,
    5:28 "I have heard the words of this **p,**
    7: 6 for you are a **p** holy to the LORD
    26:18 his treasured **p,** as he promised you,
    31: 7 will go with this **p** into the land that
    31:16 Then this **p** will begin to prostitute
    32: 9 the LORD's own portion was his **p,**
    32:43 O heavens, his **p,** worship him,
    33:29 like you, a **p** saved by the LORD,
Jos 1: 6 you shall put this **p** in possession of
    3:16 the **p** crossed over opposite Jericho.
    24:25 Joshua made a covenant with the **p**
Jdg 2: 7 **p** worshiped the LORD all the days
Ru 1:16 your **p** shall be my **p,**
1Sa 8: 7 "Listen to the voice of the **p** in all
    10:24 no one like him among all the **p."**
    12:22 the LORD will not cast away his **p,**
2Sa 5: 2 shall be shepherd of my **p** Israel,
    7:10 place for my **p** Israel and will plant
    7:23 Who is like your **p,** like Israel?
    24:17 the angel who was destroying the **p,**
1Ki 3: 8 of the **p** whom you have chosen,
    8:30 of your servant and of your **p** Israel
    8:56 who has given rest to his **p** Israel
    18:39 When all the **p** saw it, they fell on
2Ki 23: 3 All the **p** joined in the covenant.
    25:11 the rest of the **p** who were left in
1Ch 29:17 and now I have seen your **p,**
2Ch 2:11 the LORD loves his **p** he has made
    7: 5 the **p** dedicated the house of God.
    7:14 if my **p** who are called by my name
    30: 6 "O **p** of Israel, return to the LORD,
    36:16 the wrath of the LORD against his **p**
Ezr 2: 1 the **p** of the province who came
    3: 1 **p** gathered together in Jerusalem.
Ne 4: 1 They are your servants and your **p,**
    4: 6 for the **p** had a mind to work.
    8: 1 all the **p** gathered together into the
Est 3: 6 been told who Mordecai's **p** were,
    7: 3 lives of my **p**—that is my request.
Job 12: 2 "No doubt you are the **p,**
Ps 3: 8 may your blessing be on your **p!**
    29:11 the LORD give strength to his **p!**
    29:11 the LORD bless his **p** with peace!
    33:12 the **p** whom he has chosen as his
    50: 4 that he may judge his **p:**
    53: 6 God restores the fortunes of his **p,**
    81:13 O that my **p** would listen to me,
    94:14 For the LORD will not forsake his **p;**
    95: 7 and we are the **p** of his pasture,
    95:10 They are a **p** whose hearts go astray,
    125: 2 so the LORD surrounds his **p,**
    135:14 For the LORD will vindicate his **p,**
    144:15 happy are the **p** whose God is the
          LORD.
    149: 4 the LORD takes pleasure in his **p;**
Pr 14:34 but sin is a reproach to any **p.**
    29: 2 when the wicked rule, the **p** groan.
    29:18 no prophecy, the **p** cast off restraint,
Isa 1: 3 not know, my **p** do not understand.
    1: 4 sinful nation, **p** laden with iniquity,
    5:13 **p** go into exile without knowledge;
    6:10 Make the mind of this **p** dull,
    9: 2 **p** who walked in darkness have seen
    19:25 saying, "Blessed be Egypt my **p,**

25: 8 disgrace of his **p** he will take away
29:13 these **p** draw near with their mouths
40: 1 Comfort, O comfort my **p,** says
40: 7 surely the **p** are grass.
42: 6 given you as a covenant to the **p,**
49: 8 given you as a covenant to the **p,**
49:13 For the LORD has comforted his **p,**
51: 4 Listen to me, my **p,** and give heed
52: 6 my **p** shall know my name;
53: 8 for the transgression of my **p.**
60:21 Your **p** shall all be righteous;
62:12 They shall be called, "The Holy **P,**
65: 2 a rebellious **p,** who walk in a way
Jer 2:11 But my **p** have changed their glory
    2:13 for my **p** have committed two evils:
    2:32 my **p** have forgotten me, days
    4:22 "For my **p** are foolish, they do not
    5:14 and this **p** wood, and the fire shall
    5:31 my **p** love to have it so, but what
    6:27 and a refiner among my **p** so that
    7:16 As for you, do not pray for this **p,**
    7:23 your God, and you shall be my **p;**
    18:15 But my **p** have forgotten me,
    23: 2 the shepherds who shepherd my **p:**
    30: 3 I will restore the fortunes of my **p,**
    31:33 their God, and they shall be my **p.**
    50: 6 My **p** have been lost sheep;
La 1: 1 sits the city that once was full of **p!**
Eze 13:23 I will save my **p** from your hand.
    36: 8 and yield your fruit to my **p** Israel;
    36:28 be my **p,** and I will be your God.
    36:38 towns be filled with flocks of **p.**
    37:13 you up from your graves, O my **p,**
    38:14 when my **p** Israel are living securely
    39: 7 make known among my **p** Israel;
Da 7:27 shall be given to the **p** of the holy
    8:24 shall destroy the powerful and the **p**
    9:19 city and your **p** bear your name!"
    9:24 "Seventy weeks are decreed for
          your **p**
    10:14 happen to your **p** at the end of days.
    11:32 the **p** who are loyal to their God
    12: 1 great prince, the protector of your **p,**
Hos 1:10 "You are not my **p,**" it shall be said
    2:23 say to Lo-ammi, "You are my **p";**
    4:14 a **p** without understanding comes to
Joel 2:18 and had pity on his **p.**
    3:16 But the LORD is a refuge for his **p,**
Am 9:14 restore the fortunes of my **p** Israel,
Mic 3: 5 the prophets who lead my **p** astray,
    6: 2 LORD has a controversy with his **p,**
    7:14 Shepherd your **p** with your staff,
Zep 2: 9 The remnant of my **p** shall plunder
Hag 1:12 and the **p** feared the LORD.
Zec 2:11 on that day, and shall be my **p;**
    8: 7 I will save my **p** from the east
    13: 9 I will say, "They are my **p";**
Mt 1:21 he will save his **p** from their sins."
    2: 6 who is to shepherd my **p** Israel.'"
    4:16 the **p** who sat in darkness have seen
Mk 7: 6 'This **p** honors me with their lips,
    8:27 "Who do **p** say that I am?"
Lk 1:17 ready a **p** prepared for the Lord."
    1:68 for he has looked favorably on his **p**
    2:10 of great joy for all the **p:**
    21:23 the earth and wrath against this **p;**
Jn 11:50 the **p** than to have the whole nation
    18:14 to have one person die for the **p.**
Ac 2:47 and having the goodwill of all the **p.**
    3:22 from your own **p** a prophet like me.
    5:13 but the **p** held them in high esteem.
    15:14 from among them a **p** for his name.
    18:10 many in this city who are my **p."**
Ro 9:25 "Those who were not my **p** I will
          call 'my **p,'**
    11: 1 I ask, then, has God rejected his **p?**
    15:10 "Rejoice, O Gentiles, with his **p";**
2Co 6:16 their God, and they shall be my **p.**
1Ti 6: 9 and harmful desires that plunge **p**
Tit 1:10 There are also many rebellious **p,**
    2:14 a **p** of his own who are zealous
Heb 2:17 of atonement for the sins of the **p.**

4: 9 rest still remains for the **p** of God;
5: 3 sins as well as for those of the **p.**
8:10 their God, and they shall be my **p.**
10:30 again, "The Lord will judge his **p."**
13:12 to sanctify the **p** by his own blood.
1Pe 2: 9 a holy nation, God's own **p,**
2:10 Once you were not a **p,** but now
you are God's **p;**
2Pe 2: 1 prophets also arose among the **p,**
Rev 18: 4 "Come out of her, my **p,** so that
Jdt 13:17 humiliated the enemies of your **p."**
Aza 1:60 "Bless the Lord, all **p** on earth;
1Mc 3:43 "Let us restore the ruins of our **p,**

ALL ... PEOPLE Ge 19:4; 25:18; 26:11;
29:22; 35:6; 41:40; 42:6; Ex 1:22; 5:23; 11:8;
18:14, 21, 23; 19:11, 16; 20:18; 23:27; 24:3;
32:3; 33:8, 10, 10; 34:10, 10; Lev 9:23, 24;
10:3; 16:21, 33; 17:2; 19:2; 21:24; 22:18; Nu
11:11, 12, 13, 14, 29; 13:32; 14:39; 21:23, 33,
34, 35; 25:4; 31:11; 32:15; Dt 2:32, 33; 3:1, 3;
13:9; 17:7, 13; 20:11; 27:1, 15, 16, 17, 18, 19,
20, 21, 22, 23, 24, 25, 26; Jos 1:2; 4:11; 5:4, 5,
5; 6:5, 5; 7:3; 8:5, 14, 16, 25; 10:21; 11:14;
24:2, 27; Jdg 2:4; 7:12; 8:10; 9:49, 57; 11:20,
21; 14:3; 16:30; 17:6; 20:2, 8; 21:25; Ru 3:11;
4:9, 11; 1Sa 2:23; 8:21; 10:24, 24, 24, 25;
11:4, 15; 12:18, 19; 13:7; 14:15, 20, 38, 39;
15:6, 8; 18:5; 23:8; 30:6; 2Sa 2:28, 30; 3:31,
32, 34, 35, 36, 36, 37; 6:2, 19, 19; 7:7; 8:15;
12:29, 31; 15:17, 23, 23, 30; 16:6, 14; 17:2, 3,
3, 16, 22; 18:5; 19:9, 14, 39, 40, 41, 42; 20:2,
12, 13, 22; 1Ki 1:39, 40; 4:30; 8:2, 38, 63;
9:20; 12:12, 31; 13:33; 18:21, 24, 30, 30, 39;
20:8, 8, 15; 2Ki 10:9, 18; 11:14, 18, 19, 20;
14:21; 16:15; 17:32; 23:2, 2, 3, 21; 25:26; 1Ch
13:4; 16:36, 43; 18:14; 20:3; 28:21; 2Ch 6:29;
7:3, 4, 5; 8:7; 10:12; 20:27; 23:5, 6, 10, 13, 16,
17, 20, 21; 24:10, 10, 23; 26:1; 29:36; 31:1, 1;
32:9; 34:30, 30; 35:13; 36:23; Ezr 3:11; 7:25;
10:9, 9; Ne 8:1, 3, 5, 5, 5, 6, 9, 9, 11, 12, 13;
9:10, 10, 32; 11:24; Est 1:5; 3:6; Job 1:3; 2:4;
36:25; Ps 36:7; 62:8; 106:48; 116:14, 18;
145:12; Ecc 1:2; 4:16; Isa 5:14; 8:12; 9:9;
13:14; 40:5, 6; 64:9; Jer 7:2; 19:14; 25:1, 2,
19, 20; 26:7, 8, 8, 9, 11, 12, 16, 17, 18; 27:16;
28:1, 5, 7, 11; 29:1, 16, 25; 32:32; 34:8, 10,
19; 36:6, 9, 9, 10; 38:1, 4; 41:10, 10, 13, 14,
16; 42:1, 8, 17; 43:1, 4; 44:15, 20, 20, 24, 27;
48:31; La 1:11; 3:14; Eze 39:13; 45:16, 22; Da
6:26; 9:6; Am 9:1, 10; Hag 1:12, 14; 2:4; Zec
2:13; 7:5; Mal 2:9; Mk 1:5; Lk 2:10;
3:21; 7:29; 8:37, 47; 9:13; 18:43; 19:48; 20:6,
45; 21:38; 24:19; Jn 1:4; 2:24; 8:2; 12:32;
17:2; Ac 2:47; 3:9, 11; 4:10, 10; 5:34; 10:41;
12:11; 13:24; 17:30; 24:16; 1Co 9:22, 22;
15:19, 29; Php 2:29; 1Ti 4:10; Heb 9:19, 19;
1Pe 1:17; Jude 1:5; Tob 12:6; 13:8, 14; 14:15;
Jdt 1:6; 2:28; 4:3; 5:14, 22; 6:16; 7:13, 23;
8:29; 13:17, 20; 15:10, 11, 13, 14, 14; AdE
1:11; 13:2; Wis 12:13; 13:1; 16:12; Sir 44:22;
48:15, 15; 50:17; Bar 1:3, 4, 7; Aza 1:60; Sus
1:47, 50; 1Mc 1:41, 51; 2:18; 4:55; 5:27; 6:19;
7:18, 22; 10:7; 11:51; 12:44; 14:12, 14, 46;
2Mc 1:26; 2:17; 3:34; 4:5; 11:6; 1Es 1:13;
4:10, 41; 5:62; 9:53; 3Mc 7:6, 8; 2Es 6:54;
8:62; 12:40; 13:36; 14:27; 15:57; 4Mc 1:11;
4:12

ELDERS OF MY/THE PEOPLE Ex 19:7;
Nu 11:16, 24; Ru 4:4; 1Sa 15:30; Jer 19:1; Mt
21:23; 26:3, 47; 27:1; Lk 22:66; Sus 1:41; 1Mc
7:33; 12:35

HOLY PEOPLE Dt 28:9; Isa 62:12; 63:18;
Da 12:7; Wis 10:15, 17; 2Mc 15:24; 3Mc 2:6

PEOPLE ISRAEL Ex 18:1; Dt 21:8, 8;
26:15; Jdg 11:23; 1Sa 2:29; 9:16; 10:1; 14:41;
15:1; 27:12; 2Sa 3:18; 5:2, 12; 7:7, 8, 10, 11,
24; 1Ki 6:13; 8:16, 16, 30, 33, 34, 36, 38, 41,
43, 52, 56, 59, 66; 14:7; 16:2, 2; 1Ch 11:2, 2;
14:2; 17:7, 9, 10, 21, 22; 2Ch 6:5, 6, 21, 24,
25, 27, 29, 32, 33; 7:10; 20:7; 31:8; 35:3; Ps
135:12; Isa 10:22; Jer 7:12; 12:14; 23:13;

32:21; Eze 14:9; 25:14; 36:8, 12; 38:14, 16;
39:7; Da 9:20; Am 7:8, 15; 8:2; 9:14; Mt 2:6;
Lk 2:32; Ac 13:17; AdE 10:13; Bar 2:35; 1Mc
4:31; 2Mc 1:26; 1Es 1:4; 3Mc 2:6, 16

PEOPLE OF ISRAEL Ex 11:10; 24:5, 11,
17; 31:17; Lev 1:2; 4:2; 7:23, 29, 34, 34, 36,
38; 9:3; 10:11, 14; 11:2; 12:2; 15:2, 31; 16:5,
16, 19, 21, 34; 17:2, 5, 12, 13, 14; 18:2; 19:2;
20:2, 2; 21:24; 22:2, 3, 15, 18, 32; 23:2, 10,
24, 34, 43, 44; 24:2, 8, 10, 15, 23, 23; 25:2, 33,
55; 26:46; 27:2, 34; Nu 20:13; 22:3, 41; 25:8;
Jos 8:33; 22:12; Jdg 11:33; 19:12; 20:3; 1Sa
2:28; 7:6, 7, 7, 8; 8:22; 9:2; 15:6; 2Sa 7:6, 7;
15:6; 19:40, 41, 42, 43, 43; 20:2; 21:2, 2, 2;
24:1, 4; 1Ki 8:2, 63; 9:20; 12:24, 33; 14:24;
16:21; 20:15, 27; 2Ki 8:12; 13:5; 16:3; 17:7, 8,
9, 22, 24; 18:4; 21:2, 9; 1Ch 6:64; 21:1; 27:1;
2Ch 5:2, 10; 6:11; 7:3; 8:2, 8, 9; 10:17, 18;
28:3, 8; 30:6, 21; 31:1, 5, 6; 33:2, 9; 34:33;
35:17; Ezr 6:16, 21; 7:7, 13; 9:1; Ne 1:6, 6;
2:10; 7:73; 8:14, 17; 9:1; 10:39; Ps 103:7;
148:14; Isa 27:12; 31:6; Jer 16:14, 15; 23:7;
32:30, 30, 32; 50:4, 33; Eze 2:3; 4:13; 6:5;
35:5; 37:21; 43:7; 44:9, 15; 48:11; Hos 1:10,
11; 3:1; 4:1; Joel 3:16; Am 2:11; 3:1, 12; 4:5;
9:7; Mic 5:3; Mt 27:9; Lk 1:16; Ac 4:10; 9:15;
10:36; 13:24; 1Co 10:18; 2Co 3:7, 13; Php 3:5;
Rev 2:14; 7:4; Jdt 4:8; 5:1; 6:2; 9:14; 10:8; Bar
2:1, 28; 3:4; 1Mc 1:30; 5:60; 1Es 1:5, 19; 7:6,
10, 13; 8:5, 69; 9:37; Pm 151:7; 2Es 5:35

PEOPLE OF JUDAH Nu 2:3; Jos 14:6;
15:1, 12, 13, 20, 21, 63, 63; Jdg 1:8, 9, 16; 2Sa
1:18; 2:4; 19:14, 16, 40, 41, 42, 43, 43; 20:2;
2Ki 14:21; 23:2; 1Ch 9:3; 12:24; 2Ch 13:15,
15, 18; 14:13; 20:27; 25:5, 12; 26:1; 28:10;
32:9; 34:30; Ezr 4:4; 10:9; Ne 11:25; 13:16;
Isa 5:3, 7; Jer 4:3, 4; 7:2, 30; 11:2, 9; 17:25;
18:11; 25:1, 2; 26:18; 32:30, 32; 35:13; 36:6,
31; 44:26, 27; 50:4, 33; Da 9:7; Hos 1:11; Joel
3:6, 8, 19; Ob 1:12; Bar 1:15; 1Mc 2:18; 1Es
1:21

PEOPLE OF THE LAND Ge 23:7, 12, 13;
42:6; Ex 5:5; Lev 20:2, 4; Nu 14:9; 2Ki 11:14,
18, 19, 20; 15:5; 16:15; 21:24, 24; 23:30, 35;
24:14; 25:3, 12, 19, 19; 2Ch 23:13, 20, 21;
26:21; 33:25, 25; 36:1; Ezr 4:4; Jer 1:18;
34:19; 37:2; 44:21; 52:6, 16, 25, 25; Eze 7:27;
12:19; 22:29; 33:2; 39:13; 45:16, 22; 46:3, 9;
Da 9:6; Hag 2:4; Zec 7:5; Bar 1:9

PEOPLE OF THE †LORD Nu 16:41; Dt
27:9; Jdg 5:11, 13; 1Sa 2:24; 10:1; 2Sa 6:21;
2Ki 9:6; Eze 36:20; Zep 2:10

PEOPLE'S → PEOPLE
2Ch 25:15 **p** gods who could not deliver their
Mt 13:15 For this **p** heart has grown dull,
Ac 28:27 For this **p** heart has grown dull,

PEOPLES → PEOPLE
Ge 17:16 kings of **p** shall come from her."
25:23 two **p** born of you shall be divided;
27:29 Let **p** serve you, and nations bow
28: 3 you may become a company of **p.**
48: 4 I will make of you a company of **p,**
Dt 4:27 LORD will scatter you among the **p;**
7: 7 for you were the fewest of all **p.**
14: 2 LORD has chosen out of all the **p** on
28:10 All the **p** of the earth shall see that
Jos 4:24 that all the **p** of the earth may know
that the hand
Jdg 2:12 of the **p** who were all around them,
1Ki 8:43 that all the **p** of the earth may know
2Ch 7:20 proverb and a byword among all **p.**
Ezr 3: 3 were in dread of the neighboring **p,**
10: 2 married foreign women from the **p**
Ne 10:30 not give our daughters to the **p** of
Ps 2: 1 and the **p** plot in vain?
9: 8 he judges the **p** with equity.
67: 3 Let the **p** praise you, O God;
87: 6 LORD records, as he registers the **p,**
96:10 He will judge the **p** with equity."

117: 1 Extol him, all you **p!**
Isa 2: 4 and shall arbitrate for many **p;**
11:10 shall stand as a signal to the **p;**
17:12 Ah, the thunder of many **p,**
25: 6 make for all **p** a feast of rich food,
34: 1 O nations, to hear; O **p,** give heed!
49:22 and raise my signal to the **p;**
55: 4 See, I made him a witness to the **p,**
Jer 10: 3 For the customs of the **p** are false:
Da 7:14 that all **p,** nations,
Mic 4: 1 above the hills. **P** shall stream to it,
5: 7 of Jacob, surrounded by many **p,**
Zep 3: 9 I will change the speech of the **p** to
3:20 praised among all the **p** of the earth,
Zec 8:20 **P** shall yet come, the inhabitants of
12: 2 of reeling for all the surrounding **p;**
Ac 4:25 and the **p** imagine vain things?
Rev 10:11 must prophesy again about many **p**
21: 3 they will be his **p,** and God himself

ALL ... PEOPLES Ge 19:5; Dt 4:19; 7:6, 7,
16, 19; 10:15; 14:2; 28:10, 37, 64; 30:3; Jos
4:24; 24:17, 18; 1Ki 8:43, 53, 60; 9:7; 1Ch
16:24, 26; 2Ch 6:33; 7:20; 32:13; Est 1:16;
3:12, 14; 8:13; 9:2; Ps 47:1; 49:1; 67:2, 3, 5;
96:3, 5; 97:6; 99:2; 117:1; 148:11; Isa 25:6, 7;
56:7; Jer 25:24; 34:1; La 1:18; Eze 28:19;
31:12; 38:6, 9; 39:4; Da 3:7, 7; 4:1; 5:19; 6:25;
7:14; Mic 4:5; Hab 2:5, 8; Zep 3:20; Zec
11:10; 12:2, 3, 6; 14:12; Lk 2:31; Ac 15:17;
Ro 15:11; Rev 7:9; Bar 2:4; 1Es 5:50; 2Es 5:27

PEOPLES OF THE EARTH Dt 28:10; Jos
4:24; 1Ki 8:43, 53, 60; 2Ch 6:33; 32:19; Eze
31:12; Zep 3:20

PEOPLES OF THE LAND 1Ch 5:25; Ezr
10:2, 11; Ne 9:24; 10:30, 31; 1Es 5:50, 50, 72;
7:13; 8:69, 70, 87, 92; 9:9

PEOR
Nu 25: 3 Israel yoked itself to the Baal of **P,**
Dt 4: 3 did with regard to the Baal of **P—**
Jos 22:17 not had enough of the sin at **P**

PERCEIVE → PERCEIVED
Pr 24:12 not he who weighs the heart **p** it?
Lk 8:10 so that 'looking they may not **p,**
9:45 so that they could not **p** it.

PERCEIVED → PERCEIVE
Isa 64: 4 no one has heard, no ear has **p,**
Sir 6:22 she is not readily **p** by many.

PERES → PARSIN
Da 5:28 **P,** your kingdom is divided and

PEREZ
Ge 38:29 Therefore he was named **P.**
Ru 4:12 your house be like the house of **P,**
Mt 1: 3 Judah the father of **P** and Zerah by

PERFECT → PERFECTED, PERFECTER,
PERFECTION
Lev 22:21 to be acceptable it must be **p;**
Dt 32: 4 work is **p,** and all his ways are just.
2Sa 22:31 This God—his way is **p;**
1Ki 6:22 that the whole house might be **p;**
Job 36: 4 who is **p** in knowledge is with you.
37:16 of the one whose knowledge is **p,**
Ps 18:30 This God—his way is **p;**
19: 7 The law of the LORD is **p,** reviving
SS 6: 9 My dove, my **p** one, is the only one,
Eze 16:14 for it was **p** because of my splendor
27: 3 you have said, "I am **p** in beauty."
28:12 full of wisdom and **p** in beauty.
Mt 5:48 Be **p,** therefore, as your heavenly
Father is **p.**
19:21 said to him, "If you wish to be **p,**
Ro 12: 2 what is good and acceptable and **p.**
2Co 7: 1 holiness **p** in the fear of God.
12: 9 for power is made **p** in weakness."
Col 3:14 everything together in **p** harmony.
Tit 2:10 but to show complete and **p** fidelity,
Heb 2:10 the pioneer of their salvation **p**
5: 9 and having been made **p,**

7:19 (for the law made nothing **p**);
7:28 a Son who has been made **p** forever.
9: 9 that cannot **p** the conscience of the
9:11 and **p** tent (not made with hands,
10: 1 make **p** those who approach.
11:40 apart from us, be made **p**.
12:23 the spirits of the righteous made **p**,
Jas 1:17 act of giving, with every **p** gift,
1:25 But those who look into the **p** law,
3: 2 makes no mistakes in speaking is **p**,
1Jn 4:18 in love, but **p** love casts out fear;
Rev 3: 2 not found your works **p** in the sight
Wis 6:15 thought on her is **p** understanding,

PERFECTED → PERFECT

Heb 10:14 For by a single offering he has **p**
1Jn 4:12 God lives in us, and his love is **p** in
2Es 8:52 and wisdom **p** beforehand.

PERFECTER* → PERFECT

Heb 12: 2 Jesus the pioneer and **p** of our faith,

PERFECTION* → PERFECT

Ps 50: 2 Out of Zion, the **p** of beauty, God
119:96 I have seen a limit to all **p**,
La 2:15 city that was called the **p** of beauty,
Eze 28:12 You were the signet of **p**,
Heb 6: 1 Therefore let us go on toward **p**,
7:11 if **p** had been attainable through
1Jn 2: 5 the love of God has reached **p**.
4:18 fears has not reached **p** in love.

PERFORM → PERFORMED,
PERFORMING

Ex 3:20 all my wonders that I will **p** in it;
Ps 119:112 to **p** your statutes forever,
Jer 21: 2 the LORD will **p** a wonderful deed

PERFORMED → PERFORM

Ex 4:30 **p** the signs in the sight of the people
Ne 9:17 mindful of the wonders that you **p**
Jn 10:41 they were saying, "John **p** no sign,
Rev 19:20 the false prophet who had **p** in its

PERFORMING → PERFORM

Rev 16:14 These are demonic spirits, **p** signs,

PERFUME

SS 1: 3 your name is **p** poured out;
Jn 12: 5 "Why was this **p** not sold

PERGAMUM*

Rev 1:11 to **P**, to Thyatira, to Sardis, to
2:12 to the angel of the church in **P** write:

PERIL

Ro 8:35 or famine, or nakedness, or **p**,
2Co 1:10 who rescued us from so deadly a **p**

PERISH → PERISHABLE, PERISHED,
PERISHES, PERISHING

Lev 26:38 You shall **p** among the nations,
Jos 23:13 until you **p** from this good land that
Est 4:16 against the way; and if I **p**, I **p**."
Ps 1: 6 but the way of the wicked will **p**.
37:20 the wicked **p**, and the enemies of
73:27 those who are far from you will **p**;
102:26 They will **p**, but you endure;
Pr 11:10 the wicked **p**, there is jubilation.
19: 9 go unpunished, and the liar will **p**.
21:28 A false witness will **p**, but
28:28 when they **p**, the righteous increase.
Isa 29:14 The wisdom of their wise shall **p**,
60:12 that will not serve you shall **p**;
Jer 51:18 of their punishment they shall **p**.
Jnh 1: 6 a thought so that we do not **p**."
3: 9 fierce anger, so that we do not **p**."
Lk 13: 3 unless you repent, you will all **p** as
21:18 But not a hair of your head will **p**.
Jn 3:16 who believes in him may not **p**
10:28 eternal life, and they will never **p**
Ac 8:20 "May your silver **p** with you,
Ro 2:12 will also **p** apart from the law,
Col 2:22 regulations refer to things that **p**

Heb 1:11 they will **p**, but you remain;
2Pe 3: 9 with you, not wanting any to **p**,

PERISHABLE → PERISH

1Co 9:25 they do it to receive a **p** wreath,
15:42 What is sown is **p**, what is raised is
1Pe 1:18 not with **p** things like silver or gold,
1:23 not of **p** but of imperishable seed,

PERISHED → PERISH

Dt 2:14 of warriors had **p** from the camp,
Job 4: 7 who that was innocent ever **p**?
Ps 119:92 I would have **p** in my misery.
Jer 7:28 truth has **p**; it is cut off from their

PERISHES → PERISH

Jn 6:27 Do not work for the food that **p**,
Jas 1:11 its flower falls, and its beauty **p**.

PERISHING → PERISH

1Co 1:18 is foolishness to those who are **p**,
2Co 2:15 and among those who are **p**;
4: 3 it is veiled to those who are **p**.

PERIZZITES

Ge 13: 7 the Canaanites and the **P** lived in
Ex 3: 8 the Hittites, the Amorites, the **P**,
Jos 24:11 the Amorites, the **P**, the Canaanites,

PERJURERS*

1Ti 1:10 sodomites, slave traders, liars, **p**,

PERMANENT → PERMANENTLY

Jn 8:35 slave does not have a **p** place in the
2Co 3:11 much more has the **p** come in glory!

PERMANENTLY* → PERMANENT

Heb 7:24 but he holds his priesthood **p**,

PERMISSION → PERMIT

Jn 19:38 Pilate gave him **p**;
Sir 15:20 has not given anyone **p** to sin.

PERMIT → PERMISSION, PERMITTED

Hos 5: 4 not **p** them to return to their God.
1Ti 2:12 I **p** no woman to teach or to have

PERMITTED → PERMIT

1Co 14:34 For they are not **p** to speak,
2Co 12: 4 that no mortal is **p** to repeat.

PERPETUAL

Ge 48: 4 offspring after you for a **p** holding.'
Ex 29: 9 shall be theirs by a **p** ordinance.
Lev 6:13 A **p** fire shall be kept burning

PERPLEXED

2Co 4: 8 **p**, but not driven to despair;

PERSECUTE → PERSECUTED,
PERSECUTING, PERSECUTION,
PERSECUTIONS, PERSECUTOR,
PERSECUTORS

Ps 119:84 you judge those who **p** me?
Mt 5:11 when people revile you and **p** you
5:44 and pray for those who **p** you,
Lk 11:49 some of whom they will kill and **p**,'
21:12 they will arrest you and **p** you;
Jn 15:20 they persecuted me, they will **p** you;
Ac 9: 4 "Saul, Saul, why do you **p** me?"
Ro 12:14 Bless those who **p** you; bless

PERSECUTED → PERSECUTE

Ps 119:86 I am **p** without cause; help me!
Mt 5:10 "Blessed are those who are **p**
5:12 in the same way they **p** the prophets
Jn 15:20 they **p** me, they will persecute you;
Ac 22: 4 I **p** this Way up to the point of death
1Co 4:12 we bless; when **p**, we endure;
15: 9 because I **p** the church of God.
2Co 4: 9 **p**, but not forsaken; struck down,
2Ti 3:12 godly life in Christ Jesus will be **p**.
Heb 11:37 destitute, **p**, tormented—

PERSECUTING → PERSECUTE

Ac 9: 5 "I am Jesus, whom you are **p**.
22: 8 Jesus of Nazareth whom you are **p**.'
26:15 'I am Jesus whom you are **p**.
Gal 1:13 I was violently **p** the church of God

PERSECUTION → PERSECUTE

Mt 13:21 or **p** arises on account of the word,
Ac 8: 1 a severe **p** began against the church
Ro 8:35 Will hardship, or distress, or **p**, or
Heb 10:33 publicly exposed to abuse and **p**,

PERSECUTIONS → PERSECUTE

Mk 10:30 and children, and fields with **p**—
2Co 12:10 **p**, and calamities for the sake of
2Th 1: 4 and faith during all your **p**
2Ti 3:11 What **p** I endured!

PERSECUTOR* → PERSECUTE

Php 3: 6 as to zeal, a **p** of the church;

PERSECUTORS → PERSECUTE

Ps 142: 6 Save me from my **p**,
Jer 15:15 down retribution for me on my **p**.

PERSEVERANCE* → PERSEVERE

Heb 12: 1 let us run with **p** the race that is set

PERSEVERE → PERSEVERANCE,
PERSEVERED

Da 12:12 Happy are those who **p**
Ro 12:12 be patient in suffering, **p** in prayer.

PERSEVERED* → PERSEVERE

Heb 11:27 for he **p** as though he saw him who
Sir 2:10 anyone **p** in the fear of the Lord

PERSIA → PERSIANS

Ezr 1: 1 the spirit of King Cyrus of **P**
Da 8:20 these are the kings of Media and **P**.
10:20 to fight against the prince of **P**,

PERSIANS → PERSIA

Da 6:15 a law of the Medes and **P** that
Jdt 16:10 The **P** trembled at her boldness,

PERSIST* → PERSISTENCE, PERSISTENT

Job 2: 9 "Do you still **p** in your integrity?
Ro 11:23 if they do not **p** in unbelief,
1Ti 4:16 As for those who **p** in sin,
Heb 10:26 For if we willfully **p** in sin after

PERSISTENCE* → PERSIST

Lk 11: 8 at least because of his **p** he will

PERSISTENT* → PERSIST

2Ti 4: 2 be **p** whether the time is favorable

PERSUADE → PERSUADED,
PERSUADING, PERSUASIVELY,
PERSUASIVENESS

2Co 5:11 we try to **p** others;

PERSUADED → PERSUADE

Pr 25:15 With patience a ruler may be **p**,
Mt 27:20 priests and the elders **p** the crowds

PERSUADING → PERSUADE

Ac 26:28 quickly **p** me to become a Christian

PERSUASIVELY* → PERSUADE

Ac 19: 8 argued **p** about the kingdom of God.

PERSUASIVENESS* → PERSUADE

Pr 16:21 and pleasant speech increases **p**.
16:23 and adds **p** to their lips.

PERVERSE → PERVERSION, PERVERT,
PERVERTED

Dt 32:20 for they are a **p** generation,
Pr 3:32 **p** are an abomination to the LORD,
17:20 the **p** of tongue fall into calamity.
Lk 9:41 "You faithless and **p** generation,
Wis 1: 3 **p** thoughts separate people from
Sir 36:25 A **p** mind will cause grief,

PERVERSION → PERVERSE
Lev 18:23 sexual relations with it: it is **p.**
2Ch 19: 7 no **p** of justice with the LORD our
Wis 14:26 sexual **p,** disorder in marriages,

PERVERT → PERVERSE
Ex 23: 2 with the majority so as to **p** justice;
Job 8: 3 Does God **p** justice? Or does the
              Almighty **p** the right?
      34:12 and the Almighty will not **p** justice.
Pr 17:23 bribe to **p** the ways of justice.
Gal 1: 7 and want to **p** the gospel of Christ.

PERVERTED → PERVERSE
1Sa 8: 3 they took bribes and **p** justice.
Jer 3:21 because they have **p** their way,

PESTILENCE
Dt 32:24 burning consumption, bitter **p.**
Ps 91: 6 or the **p** that stalks in darkness,
Rev 18: 8 **p** and mourning and famine—
2Es 15:49 poverty, famine, sword, and **p,**

PETER → =CEPHAS, =SIMON
    Apostle, brother of Andrew, also called Simon
(Mt 10:2; Mk 3:16; Lk 6:14; Ac 1:13), and Cephas (Jn 1:42). Confession of Christ (Mt 16:13-
20; Mk 8:27-30; Lk 9:18-27). At transfiguration
(Mt 17:1-8; Mk 9:2-8; Lk 9:28-36; 2Pe 1:16-18).
Caught fish with coin (Mt 17:24-27). Denial of
Jesus predicted (Mt 26:31-35; Mk 14:27-31; Lk
22:31-34; Jn 13:31-38). Denied Jesus (Mt 26:69-
75; Mk 14:66-72; Lk 22:54-62; Jn 18:15-27).
Commissioned by Jesus to shepherd his flock (Jn
21:15-23).
    Speech at Pentecost (Ac 2). Healed beggar (Ac
3:1-10). Speech at temple (Ac 3:11-26), before
Sanhedrin (Ac 4:1-22). In Samaria (Ac 8:14-25).
Sent by vision to Cornelius (Ac 10). Announced
salvation of Gentiles in Jerusalem (Ac 11; 15).
Freed from prison (Ac 12). Inconsistency at Antioch (Gal 2:11-21). At Jerusalem Council (Ac
15).
    Letters: 1 and 2 Peter.

PETITION → PETITIONED, PETITIONS
Est 7: 2 to Esther, "What is your **p,**

PETITIONED → PETITION
Ezr 8:23 So we fasted and **p** our God for this,

PETITIONS' → PETITION
Ps 20: 5 May the LORD fulfill all your **p.**

PHARAOH → PHARAOH'S
Ge 12:15 they praised her to **P.**
      41:14 Then **P** sent for Joseph,
      47:10 Then Jacob blessed **P,**
Ex 1:22 Then **P** commanded all his people,
      2:15 But Moses fled from **P.**
      3:11 "Who am I that I should go to **P,**
      5: 2 But **P** said, "Who is the LORD,
      11: 1 will bring one more plague upon **P**
      14:17 I will gain glory for myself over **P**
Dt 7: 8 from the hand of **P** king of Egypt.
Isa 36: 6 Such is **P** king of Egypt to all who
Ro 9:17 For the scripture says to **P,**

PHARAOH'S → PHARAOH
Ex 7: 3 But I will harden **P** heart,
      7:13 Still **P** heart was hardened,
      7:22 so **P** heart remained hardened,
      8:19 But **P** heart was hardened,
      10:20 But the LORD hardened **P** heart,
      10:27 But the LORD hardened **P** heart,
      11:10 but the LORD hardened **P** heart,
      14: 4 I will harden **P** heart,
Heb 11:24 refused to be called a son of **P**

PHARISEE → PHARISEES
Lk 11:37 a **P** invited him to dine with him;
Jn 3: 1 a **P** named Nicodemus,
Ac 5:34 a **P** in the council named Gamaliel,
      23: 6 in the council, "Brothers, I am a **P,**

Php 3: 5 as to the law, a **P;**

PHARISEES → PHARISEE
Mt 5:20 that of the scribes and **P,**
      16: 6 beware of the yeast of the **P** and
      23:13 "But woe to you, scribes and **P,**
Mk 2:18 and the disciples of the **P** fast,
Lk 11:42 "But woe to you **P!**
Ac 23: 7 a dissension began between the **P**

PHILADELPHIA'
Rev 1:11 to Sardis, to **P,** and to Laodicea."
      3: 7 to the angel of the church in **P** write:

PHILEMON'
Phm 1: 1 To **P** our dear friend and co-worker,

PHILIP
    1. Apostle (Mt 10:3; Mk 3:18; Lk 6:14; Jn 1:43-
48; 14:8; Ac 1:13).
    2. Deacon (Ac 6:1-7); evangelist in Samaria (Ac
8:4-25), to Ethiopian (Ac 8:26-40).
    3. Herod Philip I (Mt 14:3; Mk 6:17).
    4. Herod Philip II (Lk 3:1).

PHILIPPI
Mt 16:13 came into the district of Caesarea **P,**
Ac 16:12 to **P,** which is a leading city of
Php 1: 1 saints in Christ Jesus who are in **P,**

PHILISTIA → PHILISTINE, PHILISTINES
Ex 15:14 pangs seized the inhabitants of **P.**
Ps 60: 8 over **P** I shout in triumph."
Zec 9: 6 I will make an end of the pride of **P.**

PHILISTINE → PHILISTIA
1Sa 14: 1 to the **P** garrison on the other side."
      17:23 champion, the **P** of Gath, Goliath
      17:37 save me from the hand of this **P.**"
Pm 151: 6 I went out to meet the **P,**

PHILISTINES → PHILISTIA
Ge 21:34 alien many days in the land of the **P.**
      26: 1 Gerar, to King Abimelech of the **P.**
Ex 23:31 from the Red Sea to the sea of the **P,**
Jdg 10: 7 sold them into the hand of the **P**
      13: 1 into the hand of the **P** forty years.
      16: 5 The lords of the **P** came to her and
      16:30 said, "Let me die with the **P.**"
1Sa 4: 1 **P** mustered for war against Israel,
      5: 1 the **P** captured the ark of God,
      13:20 the **P** to sharpen their plowshare,
      17: 1 the **P** gathered their armies for battle
      17:51 **P** saw that their champion was dead,
      23: 1 "The **P** are fighting against Keilah,
      27: 1 than to escape to the land of the **P;**
      31: 1 Now the **P** fought against Israel;
2Sa 5:17 all the **P** went up in search of David;
      8: 1 David attacked the **P** and subdued
      21:15 The **P** went to war again with Israel,
2Ki 18: 8 He attacked the **P** as far as Gaza
Jer 47: 4 For the LORD is destroying the **P,**
Eze 25:16 stretch out my hand against the **P,**
Am 1: 8 the remnant of the **P** shall perish,

PHILOSOPHERS' → PHILOSOPHY
Ac 17:18 Epicurean and Stoic **p** debated with

PHILOSOPHY → PHILOSOPHERS
Col 2: 8 no one takes you captive through **p**

PHINEHAS
    1. Grandson of Aaron (Ex 6:25; Jos 22:30-32).
Zeal for the LORD stopped plague (Nu 25:7-13;
Ps 106:30).
    2. Son of Eli; a wicked priest (1Sa 1:3; 2:12-17;
4:1-19).

PHOEBE'
Ro 16: 1 I commend to you our sister **P,**

PHRASES
Mt 6: 7 not heap up empty **p** as the Gentiles

PHYLACTERIES'
Mt 23: 5 make their **p** broad and their fringes

PHYSICAL
Da 1: 4 without **p** defect and handsome,
Ro 2:28 something external and **p.**
1Co 15:44 It is sown a **p** body, it is raised a
1Ti 4: 8 while **p** training is of some value,

PHYSICIAN → PHYSICIANS
Jer 8:22 Is there no **p** there?
Mt 9:12 who are well have no need of a **p,**
Col 4:14 Luke, the beloved **p,** and Demas

PHYSICIANS → PHYSICIAN
Job 13: 4 all of you are worthless **p.**
Mk 5:26 had endured much under many **p,**
Tob 2:10 I went to **p** to be healed,
Sir 38: 1 Honor **p** for their services,

PIECE → BREASTPIECE, PIECES
Ex 15:25 the LORD showed him a **p** of wood,
Mk 2:21 "No one sews a **p** of unshrunk cloth
Jn 13:26 when he had dipped the **p** of bread,
      19:23 woven in one **p** from the top.

PIECES → PIECE
Ge 15:17 torch passed between these **p.**
Jdg 20: 6 my concubine and cut her into **p,**
1Ki 11:30 and tore it into twelve **p.**
2Ki 18: 4 in the bronze serpent that Moses
Ps 2: 9 dash them in **p** like a potter's vessel.
Mic 1: 7 All her images shall be beaten to **p,**
Mt 14:20 what was left over of the broken **p,**
      15:37 they took up the broken **p** left over,
Lk 20:18 on that stone will be broken to **p;**
1Mc 1:56 law that they found they tore to **p**

PIERCE → PIERCED
Ex 21: 6 master shall **p** his ear with an awl;
Lk 2:35 and a sword will **p** your own soul

PIERCED → PIERCE
Nu 25: 8 and **p** the two of them,
Zec 12:10 look on the one whom they have **p,**
Jn 19:37 look on the one whom they have **p.**"
1Ti 6:10 **p** themselves with many pains.
Rev 1: 7 even those who **p** him;

PIETY → PIOUS, PIOUSLY
Mt 6: 1 Beware of practicing your **p** before
Ac 3:12 or **p** we had made him walk?

PIG → PIG'S, PIGS
Dt 14: 8 the **p,** because it divides the hoof

PIG'S' → PIG
Pr 11:22 gold ring in a **p** snout is a beautiful

PIGEON → PIGEONS
Lev 12: 6 a **p** or a turtledove for a sin offering.

PIGEONS → PIGEON
Lk 2:24 pair of turtledoves or two young **p.**"

PIGS → PIG
Isa 66:17 eating the flesh of **p,** vermin, and
Lk 15:16 with the pods that the **p** were eating;

PILATE
    Governor of Judea. Questioned Jesus (Mt 27:1-
26; Mk 15:15; Lk 22:66-23:25; Jn 18:28-19:16);
sent him to Herod (Lk 23:6-12); consented to his
crucifixion when crowds chose Barabbas (Mt
27:15-26; Mk 15:6-15; Lk 23:13-25; Jn 19:1-10).

PILLAR → PILLARS
Ge 19:26 back, and she became a **p** of salt.
      28:18 set it up for a **p** and poured oil
      31:52 and the **p** is a witness,
Ex 13:21 and in a **p** of fire by night,
Nu 14:14 in a **p** of cloud by day and in a **p** of
              fire by night.
1Ti 3:15 the **p** and bulwark of the truth.
Rev 3:12 you a **p** in the temple of my God;

Wis 10: 7 a **p** of salt standing as a monument
Sir 36:29 helper fit for him and a **p** of support.

PILLAR OF CLOUD
Ex 13:21, 22; 14:19; 33:9, 10; Nu 12:5; 14:14; Dt 31:15, 15; Ne 9:12, 19; Ps 99:7; Sir 24:4

PILLAR OF FIRE
Ex 13:21, 22; 14:24; Nu 14:14; Ne 9:12, 19; Wis 18:3; 2Es 1:14

PILLARS → PILLAR
Ex 24: 4 the mountain, and set up twelve **p**,
Jdg 16:29 Samson grasped the two middle **p**
1Ki 7:15 He cast two **p** of bronze.
2Ki 25:13 bronze **p** that were in the house of
Ps 75: 3 it is I who keep its **p** steady.
144:12 our daughters like corner **p**,
Pr 9: 1 she has hewn her seven **p**.
Rev 10: 1 and his legs like **p** of fire.

PINE
Isa 24:16 But I say, I **p** away, I **p** away.
60:13 the **p**, to beautify the place of my

PINIONS
Dt 32:11 and bears them aloft on its **p**,
Ps 91: 4 he will cover you with his **p**,
Eze 17: 3 with great wings and long **p**,

PIONEER*
Heb 2:10 make the **p** of their salvation perfect
12: 2 Jesus the **p** and perfecter of our faith

PIOUS
Sir 26:23 *but a p wife is given to the man who*
2Mc 1:19 the **p** priests of that time took some

PIPE
Ps 150: 4 praise him with strings and **p**!
Da 3: 5 **p**, lyre, trigon, harp, drum,

PISGAH
Dt 3:27 Go up to the top of **P** and look

PIT
Ex 21:33 If someone leaves a **p** open,
Ps 7:15 They make a **p**, digging it out,
40: 2 He drew me up from the desolate **p**,
103: 4 who redeems your life from the **P**,
Pr 23:27 For a prostitute is a deep **p**;
26:27 Whoever digs a **p** will fall into it,
Isa 24:17 Terror, and the **p**, and the snare are
38:17 have held back my life from the **p**
Eze 19: 4 he was caught in their **p**;
Jnh 2: 6 you brought up my life from the **P**,
Mt 15:14 both will fall into a **p**."
Rev 9: 1 key to the shaft of the bottomless **p**;
20: 3 into the **p**, and locked and sealed it
Sir 21:10 but at its end is the **p** of Hades.
2Es 7:36 The **p** of torment shall appear,

PITCH
Ge 6:14 and cover it inside and out with **p**.
Ex 2: 3 and plastered it with bitumen and **p**;
Bel 1:27 Then Daniel took **p**, fat, and hair,

PITIED → PITY
Ps 106:46 be **p** by all who held them captive.
1Co 15:19 we are of all people most to be **p**.

PITY → PITIED
Dt 7:16 showing them no **p**;
Job 19:21 Have **p** on me, have **p** on me,
Ps 72:13 has **p** on the weak and the needy,
Eze 7: 4 will not spare you, I will have no **p**.
Hos 1: 6 for I will no longer have **p**
2:23 And I will have **p** on Lo-ruhamah,
Joel 2:18 and had **p** on his people.
Lk 10:33 he saw him, he was moved with **p**.

PLACE → PLACES
Ge 22:14 that **p** "The LORD will provide";
28:16 "Surely the LORD is in this **p**—
50:19 Am I in the place of God?
Ex 3: 5 the **p** on which you are standing is
26:33 shall separate for you the holy **p**
32:34 to the **p** about which I have spoken

Dt 12: 5 the **p** that the LORD your God will
Jos 5:15 for the **p** where you stand is holy."
1Ki 8:13 a **p** for you to dwell in forever."
2Ch 6:21 hear from heaven your dwelling **p**;
Ezr 9: 8 and given us a stake in his holy **p**
Ps 24: 3 And who shall stand in his holy **p**?
26: 8 and the **p** where your glory abides.
32: 7 You are a hiding **p** for me;
84: 1 lovely is your dwelling **p**, O LORD
132:14 "This is my resting **p** forever;
Ecc 6: 6 do not all go to one **p**?
Eze 37:27 My dwelling **p** shall be with them;
Da 7: 9 thrones were set in **p**, and an
Hag 2: 9 and in this **p** I will give prosperity,
Mt 27:33 Golgotha (which means **P** of
Jn 14: 3 And if I go and prepare a **p** for you,
2Pe 1:19 as to a lamp shining in a dark **p**,
Rev 1: 1 his servants what must soon take **p**;
20:11 and no **p** was found for them.
22: 6 servants what must soon take **p**."

HIGH PLACE
1Ki 3:4; 11:7; 2Ki 23:15, 15, 15; 1Ch 16:39; 21:29; 2Ch 1:3, 13; Isa 16:12; Jer 7:31; 48:35; Eze 20:29; Mic 1:5; Sir 22:18; 4Mc 5:1

HOLY PLACE
Ex 26:33, 34; 28:29, 35, 43; 29:30, 31; 31:11; 35:19; 39:1, 41; Lev 6:16, 26, 27, 30; 7:6; 10:13; 14:13; 16:3, 20, 23, 24, 27; 24:9; 1Ki 6:16; 7:50; 8:6, 8, 10; 1Ch 6:49; 2Ch 3:8, 10; 4:22; 5:7, 9, 11; 29:5, 7; 35:5; Ezr 9:8; Ps 24:3; 68:17; 74:4; 134:2; Ecc 8:10; Isa 57:15; Eze 41:4, 21, 23; 42:14; 44:27, 27; 45:3, 4; 48:12; Da 9:24; Mt 24:15; Jn 11:48; Ac 6:13; 21:28; Heb 9:2, 12, 25; 1Mc 2:12; 2Mc 1:29; 2:18; 3:18; 5:17, 19; 8:17; 10:7; 13:23; 1Es 8:78; 3Mc 1:9, 23; 2:14; 4Mc 4:9, 12

MOST HOLY PLACE
Ex 26:34; 1Ki 6:16; 7:50; 8:6; 1Ch 6:49; 2Ch 3:8, 10; 4:22; 5:7; Eze 41:4; 45:3; 48:12; Da 9:24

PLACES → PLACE
Lev 26:30 I will destroy your high **p**
1Sa 7:16 and he judged Israel in all these **p**.
1Ki 3: 2 people were sacrificing at the high **p**
2Ki 18: 4 He removed the high **p**, broke down
Ps 78:58 him to anger with their high **p**;
Jer 19: 5 high **p** of Baal to burn their children
Jn 14: 2 house there are many dwelling **p**.

HIGH PLACES
Lev 26:30; Nu 33:52; 2Sa 1:19, 25; 1Ki 3:2, 3; 12:31, 32; 13:2, 32, 33, 33; 14:23; 15:14; 22:43, 43; 2Ki 12:3, 3; 14:4, 4; 15:4, 4, 35, 35; 16:4; 17:9, 11, 29, 32, 32; 18:4, 22; 21:3; 23:5, 8, 8, 9, 13, 19, 20; 2Ch 11:15; 14:3, 5; 15:17; 17:6; 20:33; 21:11; 28:4, 25; 31:1; 32:12; 33:3, 17, 19; 34:3; Ps 78:58; Pr 9:14; Ecc 10:6; Isa 15:2; 36:7; Jer 19:5; 32:35; Eze 6:3, 6; Hos 10:8; Am 7:9; Mic 1:3; Wis 6:5

PLAGUE → PLAGUED, PLAGUES
Ex 11: 1 will bring one more **p** upon Pharaoh
32:35 the LORD sent a **p** on the people,
Nu 11:33 the people with a very great **p**.
14:37 report about the land died by a **p**
16:48 and the **p** was stopped.
25: 8 So the **p** was stopped among the
2Ch 6:28 famine in the land, if there is **p**,
Zec 14:12 the **p** with which the LORD will
Rev 11: 6 strike the earth with every kind of **p**,
16:21 they cursed God for the **p** of the hail
2Es 16:19 Famine and, **p**, tribulation and

PLAGUED → PLAGUE
Ps 73: 5 they are not **p** like other people.
73:14 For all day long I have been **p**,

PLAGUES → PLAGUE
Hos 13:14 O Death, where are your **p**?
Rev 9:18 three **p** a third of humankind was
15: 1 seven angels with seven **p**, which
21: 9 seven bowls full of the seven last **p**
22:18 God will add to that person the **p**

PLAIN
Ge 13:12 among the cities of the **P** and
19:29 God destroyed the cities of the **P**,
Isa 40: 4 and the rough places a **p**.
Ro 1:19 be known about God is **p** to them,

PLAN → PLANNED, PLANS
Ex 26:30 the tabernacle according to the **p**
Pr 14:22 Do they not err that **p** evil?

PLANNED → PLAN
Ex 32:14 his mind about the disaster that he **p**
Isa 14:24 as I have **p**, so shall it come to pass:
23: 9 The LORD of hosts has **p** it—
46:11 I have **p**, and I will do it.
Sus 1:61 wickedly **p** to do to their neighbor.

PLANS → PLAN
Ps 20: 4 heart's desire, and fulfill all your **p**.
Pr 15:22 Without counsel, **p** go wrong,
16: 3 and your **p** will be established.
19:21 human mind may devise many **p**,
20:18 **P** are established by taking advice;
Jer 29:11 **p** for your welfare and not for harm,
2Co 1:17 Do I make my **p** according
Tob 4:19 all your paths and **p** may prosper.

PLANT → IMPLANTED, PLANTED, PLANTING, PLANTS, REPLANTED
Ge 1:29 I have given you every **p** yielding
9:20 was the first to **p** a vineyard.
Ecc 3: 2 time to **p**, and a time to pluck up
Am 9:15 I will **p** them upon their land,
Mt 15:13 "Every **p** that my heavenly Father

PLANTED → PLANT
Ge 2: 8 the LORD God **p** a garden in Eden,
Ps 1: 3 like trees **p** by streams of water,
92:13 are **p** in the house of the LORD;
Isa 60:21 They are the shoot that I **p**,
Jer 17: 8 They shall be like a tree **p** by water,
Mt 15:13 that my heavenly Father has not **p**
21:33 a landowner who **p** a vineyard,
Lk 13: 6 had a fig tree **p** in his vineyard;
1Co 3: 6 I **p**, Apollos watered, but God gave

PLANTING → PLANT
Isa 61: 3 **p** of the LORD, to display his glory.

PLANTS → PLANT
Ge 1:11 **p** yielding seed, and fruit trees of
9: 3 and just as I gave you the green **p**,
Ps 144:12 in their youth be like **p** full grown,
Pr 31:16 fruit of her hands she **p** a vineyard.
1Co 3: 7 So neither the one who **p** nor
9: 7 Who **p** a vineyard and does not eat
Sir 10:15 and **p** the humble in their place.

PLASTER
Dt 27: 2 large stones and cover them with **p**.
Da 5: 5 began writing on the **p** of the wall

PLATE → BREASTPLATE, BREASTPLATES, PLATES
Mt 23:25 the outside of the cup and of the **p**,

PLATES → PLATE
Ex 25:29 make its **p** and dishes for incense,

PLATFORM
2Ch 6:13 Solomon had made a bronze **p** five
Ne 8: 4 scribe Ezra stood on a wooden **p**

PLATTER
Mk 6:25 the head of John the Baptist on a **p**."

PLAY → PLAYED, PLAYING
Ge 19: 9 and he would **p** the judge!
Ps 33: 3 **p** skillfully on the strings, with loud
Isa 11: 8 child shall **p** over the hole of the asp

PLAYED → PLAY
Mt 11:17 'We **p** the flute for you, and you did
1Co 14: 7 will anyone know what is being **p**?

PLAYING → PLAY

1Sa 18:10 while David was **p** the lyre,
     19: 9 while David was **p** music.
Zec 8: 5 city shall be full of boys and girls **p**
Rev 14: 2 was like the sound of harpists **p**

PLEA → PLEAS

1Ki 8:28 your servant's prayer and his **p,**
      9: 3 I have heard your prayer and your **p,**
La   3:56 heard my **p,** "Do not close your ear

PLEAD → PLEADED

2Ch 6:37 and **p** with you in the land of their
Ps 119:154 **P** my cause and redeem me;
Isa 1:17 defend the orphan, **p** for the widow.
Mic 6: 1 **p** your case before the mountains,

PLEADED → PLEAD

2Sa 12:16 David therefore **p** with God for the

PLEAS → PLEA

2Ch 6:39 their prayer and their **p,**

PLEASANT

Ge 49:15 and that the land was **p;**
Ps 16: 6 have fallen for me in **p** places;
    106:24 Then they despised the **p** land,
    133: 1 **p** it is when kindred live together in
Pr   2:10 knowledge will be **p** to your soul;
    16:21 **p** speech increases persuasiveness.
    16:24 **P** words are like a honeycomb,
Heb 12:11 always seems painful rather than **p**
Sir 6: 5 **P** speech multiplies friends,

PLEASE → PLEASED, PLEASES,
PLEASING, PLEASURE, PLEASURES

Ex 21: 8 If she does not **p** her master,
Ps 69:31 will **p** the LORD more than an ox
Jer 27: 5 and I give it to whomever I **p.**
Ro   8: 8 who are in the flesh cannot **p** God.
    15: 1 and not to **p** ourselves.
    15: 3 For Christ did not **p** himself;
1Co 7:32 of the Lord, how to **p** the Lord;
     7:33 of the world, how to **p** his wife,
    10:33 as I try to **p** everyone in everything
2Co 5: 9 we make it our aim to **p** him.
1Th 2: 4 even so we speak, not to **p** mortals,
     2: 4 but to **p** God who tests our hearts.
     4: 1 how you ought to live and to **p** God
2Ti 2: 4 soldier's aim is to **p** the enlisting
Heb 11: 6 without faith it is impossible to **p**
            God,
Sir 2:16 Those who fear the Lord seek to **p**

PLEASED → PLEASE

Nu 14: 8 If the LORD is **p** with us,
    24: 1 Balaam saw that it **p** the LORD to
1Sa 12:22 it has **p** the LORD to make you
1Ki 3:10 **p** the Lord that Solomon had asked
Ps 40:13 Be **p,** O LORD, to deliver me;
Isa 42:21 The LORD was **p,** for the sake
Da   8: 4 it did as it **p** and became strong.
Mic 6: 7 Will the LORD be **p** with thousands
Mt   3:17 Beloved, with whom I am well **p."**
    17: 5 him I am well **p;** listen to him!"
Mk   1:11 with you I am well **p."**
Lk   3:22 with you I am well **p."**
1Co 10: 5 God was not **p** with most of them,
Col 1:19 the fullness of God was **p** to dwell,
Heb 11: 5 taken away that "he had **p** God."
2Pe 1:17 Beloved, with whom I am well **p."**
Sir 44:16 Enoch **p** the Lord and was taken up,

PLEASES → PLEASE

Ps 115: 3 the heavens; he does whatever he **p.**
    135: 6 Whatever the LORD **p** he does,
Ecc 2:26 one who **p** him God gives wisdom
     7:26 one who **p** God escapes her,
Da 11: 3 dominion and take action as he **p.**
    11:36 "The king shall act as he **p.**
1Jn 3:22 commandments and do what **p** him.

PLEASING → PLEASE

Ge   8:21 when the LORD smelled the **p** odor,
Ex 29:18 it is a **p** odor, an offering by fire to
Ezr 6:10 may offer **p** sacrifices to the God of
Ps 104:34 May my meditation be **p** to him,
Eph 5:10 to find out what is **p** to the Lord.
Php 4:18 a sacrifice acceptable and **p** to God.
1Ti 5: 4 for this is **p** in God's sight,
Heb 13:21 that which is **p** in his sight,

PLEASURE → PLEASE

Ge 18:12 my husband is old, shall I have **p?"**
Ps 147:10 nor his **p** in the speed of a runner;
Pr 10:23 wise conduct is **p** to a person of
    18: 2 A fool takes no **p** in understanding,
    21:17 Whoever loves **p** will suffer want;
Ecc 2: 2 of laughter, "It is mad," and of **p,**
Jer 6:10 they take no **p** in it.
Eze 18:32 I have no **p** in the death of anyone,
    33:11 no **p** in the death of the wicked,
Hag 1: 8 I may take **p** in it and be honored,
Eph 1: 5 according to the good **p** of his will,
     1: 9 according to his good **p** that he set
1Ti 5: 6 the widow who lives for **p** is dead
2Ti 3: 4 lovers of **p** rather than lovers of God
2Pe 2:13 count it a **p** to revel in the daytime.
Sir 25: 1 I take **p** in three things,

PLEASURES → PLEASE

Ps 16:11 your right hand are **p** forevermore.
Lk   8:14 by the cares and riches and **p**
Tit 3: 3 slaves to various passions and **p,**
Heb 11:25 of God than to enjoy the fleeting **p**
Jas 4: 3 to spend what you get on your **p.**

PLEDGE

Ge 38:17 she said, "Only if you give me a **p,**
Nu 30: 2 an oath to bind himself by a **p,**
Dt 24: 6 for that would be taking a life in **p.**
    24:17 not take a widow's garment in **p.**
Pr   6: 1 if you have given your **p** to your
Eze 18: 7 but restores to the debtor his **p,**

PLENTIFUL → PLENTY

Mt   9:37 to his disciples, "The harvest is **p,**
Lk 10: 2 He said to them, "The harvest is **p,**

PLENTY → PLENTIFUL

Pr 12:11 their land will have **p** of food,
Php 4:12 and I know what it is to have **p.**

PLOT → PLOTS, PLOTTED

Ne   4:15 our enemies heard that their **p** was
Ps   2: 1 and the peoples **p** in vain?
    64: 6 a cunningly conceived **p."**
Na   1: 9 Why do you **p** against the LORD?

PLOTS → PLOT

Na   1:11 who **p** evil against the LORD,

PLOTTED → PLOT

Est 9:24 **p** against the Jews to destroy them,

PLOW → PLOWED, PLOWSHARES

Dt 22:10 not **p** with an ox and a donkey
Pr 20: 4 lazy person does not **p** in season;
Lk   9:62 a hand to the **p** and looks back

PLOWED → PLOW

Jdg 14:18 "If you had not **p** with my heifer,
Ps 129: 3 The plowers **p** on my back;

PLOWSHARES → PLOW

Isa 2: 4 they shall beat their swords into **p,**
Joel 3:10 Beat your **p** into swords, and your
Mic 4: 3 they shall beat their swords into **p,**

PLUCK

Dt 23:25 you may **p** the ears with your hand,
Mk   2:23 disciples began to **p** heads of grain.

PLUMB

Am   7: 8 "See, I am setting a **p** line in

PLUNDER → PLUNDERED

Ex   3:22 and so you shall **p** the Egyptians."
Est 3:13 month of Adar, and to **p** their goods.
     8:11 and women, and to **p** their goods
     9:10 but they did not touch the **p.**
Jer 30:16 those who **p** you shall be plundered,
Eze 39:10 and **p** those who plundered them,
Hab 2: 8 that survive of the peoples shall **p**
Zep 2: 9 The remnant of my people shall **p**

PLUNDERED → PLUNDER

Ex 12:36 And so they **p** the Egyptians.
Jdg 2:14 over to plunderers who **p** them,
Mk   3:27 then indeed the house can be **p.**

PLUNGE

1Ti 6: 9 and harmful desires that **p** people

PODS*

Lk 15:16 with the **p** that the pigs were eating;

POETS*

Ac 17:28 even some of your own **p** have said,

POINT

Heb 12: 4 not yet resisted to the **p** of shedding
Jas 2:10 in one **p** has become accountable

POISON → POISONOUS

Dt 32:32 their grapes are grapes of **p,**
Ps 69:21 They gave me **p** for food,
Am   6:12 But you have turned justice into **p**
Jas 3: 8 a restless evil, full of deadly **p.**

POISONOUS → POISON

Nu 21: 6 sent **p** serpents among the people,

POLE → POLES

Nu 21: 8 poisonous serpent, and set it on a **p;**
Dt 16:21 not plant any tree as a sacred **p**
Jdg 6:25 cut down the sacred **p** that is beside
1Ki 16:33 Ahab also made a sacred **p.**

POLES → POLE

Ex 25:13 You shall make **p** of acacia wood,
Dt 12: 3 their pillars, burn their sacred **p**
2Ki 17:10 for themselves pillars and sacred **p**

POLISHED

Isa 49: 2 he made me a **p** arrow,
Eze 21:11 It is sharpened, the sword is **p,**

POLLUTE → POLLUTED, POLLUTES

Nu 35:33 not **p** the land in which you live;

POLLUTED → POLLUTE

Pr 25:26 a **p** fountain are the righteous who
Ac 15:20 from things **p** by idols and from
Rev 21: 8 the cowardly, the faithless, the **p,**

POLLUTES* → POLLUTE

Nu 35:33 blood **p** the land, and no expiation

POMEGRANATES

Ex 28:33 On its lower hem you shall make **p**
Dt   8: 8 of vines and fig trees and **p,**
1Ki 7:18 the capitals that were above the **p;**
SS   8: 2 to drink, the juice of my **p.**

PONDER → PONDERED

Ps 48: 9 We **p** your steadfast love,
    64: 9 and **p** what he has done.

PONDERED → PONDER

Lk   2:19 treasured all these words and **p** them

PONTIUS

Lk   3: 1 **P** Pilate was governor of Judea,

POOL → POOLS

2Sa 2:13 met them at the **p** of Gibeon.
1Ki 22:38 They washed the chariot by the **p** of
Ps 114: 8 who turns the rock into a **p** of water,
Jn   5: 2 by the Sheep Gate there is a **p,**
     9: 7 wash in the **p** of Siloam" (which

POOLS → POOL

Ps 107:35 He turns a desert into **p** of water,

POOR → POOREST, POVERTY

Ex 23: 3 be partial to the **p** in a lawsuit.
23: 6 not pervert the justice due to your **p**
Dt 15:11 Open your hand to the **p** and needy
24:12 If the person is **p,** you shall not
24:14 not withhold the wages of **p** and
1Sa 2: 8 He raises up the **p** from the dust;
2Sa 12: 1 the one rich and the other **p.**
Job 5:16 So the **p** have hope, and injustice
24: 4 **p** of the earth all hide themselves.
30:25 Was not my soul grieved for the **p?**
Ps 14: 6 would confound the plans of the **p,**
34: 6 This **p** soul cried, and was heard by
40:17 As for me, I am **p** and needy,
112: 9 they have given to the **p;**
113: 7 He raises the **p** from the dust,
140:12 and executes justice for the **p.**
Pr 13: 7 pretend to be **p,** yet have great
14:20 The **p** are disliked even by their
14:31 oppress the **p** insult their Maker,
17: 5 who mock the **p** insult their Maker;
19: 1 the **p** walking in integrity than one
19:17 is kind to the **p** lends to the LORD,
19:22 and it is better to be **p** than a liar.
21:13 close your ear to the cry of the **p,**
22: 2 rich and the **p** have this in common:
22: 9 for they share their bread with the **p.**
22:22 not rob the **p** because they are **p,**
28: 6 to be **p** and walk in integrity than to
28:27 gives to the **p** will lack nothing,
29: 7 righteous know the rights of the **p;**
31: 9 defend the rights of the **p** and needy.
31:20 She opens her hand to the **p,**
Ecc 4:13 a **p** but wise youth than an old but
Isa 3:14 the spoil of the **p** is in your houses.
10: 2 rob the **p** of my people of their right
14:30 The firstborn of the **p** will graze,
25: 4 For you have been a refuge to the **p,**
32: 7 to ruin the **p** with lying words,
Jer 22:16 judged the cause of the **p** and needy;
Eze 18:12 oppresses the **p** and needy,
Am 2: 7 the head of the **p** into the dust
4: 1 oppress the **p,** who crush the needy,
5:11 because you trample on the **p** and
Zec 7:10 the orphan, the alien, or the **p;**
Mt 5: 3 "Blessed are the **p** in spirit,
11: 5 and the **p** have good news brought
Mk 10:21 own, and give the money to the **p,**
12:42 **p** widow came and put in two small
14: 7 For you always have the **p** with you,
Lk 4:18 to bring good news to the **p.**
6:20 "Blessed are you who are **p,**
14:13 you give a banquet, invite the **p,**
19: 8 Lord, I will give to the **p;**
21: 2 a **p** widow put in two small copper
Jn 13:29 you always have the **p** with you,
Ro 15:26 to share their resources with the **p.**
2Co 6:10 as **p,** yet making many rich;
8: 9 for your sakes he became **p,**
9: 9 scatters abroad, he gives to the **p;**
Jas 2: 2 and if a **p** person in dirty clothes
2: 5 Has not God chosen the **p** in the
Rev 3:17 pitiable, **p,** blind, and naked.
Sir 4: 8 Give a hearing to the **p,**
7:32 Stretch out your hand to the **p,**

POOREST → POOR

2Ki 24:14 except the **p** people of the land.
Jer 52:16 left some of the **p** people of the land

PORCIUS*

Ac 24:27 Felix was succeeded by **P** Festus;

PORTENT → PORTENTS

Ps 71: 7 I have been like a **p** to many,
Isa 20: 3 as a sign and a **p** against Egypt
Rev 12: 1 A great **p** appeared in heaven:
15: 1 I saw another **p** in heaven,

PORTENTS → PORTENT

Dt 13: 1 and promise you omens or **p,**
Lk 21:11 will be dreadful **p** and great signs

PORTION → APPORTION, APPORTIONED

Dt 32: 9 the LORD's own **p** was his people,
Jos 18: 7 The Levites have no **p** among you,
1Sa 1: 5 but to Hannah he gave a double **p,**
Ps 16: 5 LORD is my chosen **p** and my cup;
73:26 the strength of my heart and my **p**
119:57 LORD is my **p;** I promise to keep
142: 5 my **p** in the land of the living."
Isa 53:12 I will allot him a **p** with the great,
61: 7 they shall possess a double **p;**
Jer 10:16 is the LORD, the **p** of Jacob,
La 3:24 "The LORD is my **p,**" says my soul,
Zec 2:12 LORD will inherit Judah as his **p** in
Sir 17:17 Israel is the Lord's own **p.**
26:23 *A godless wife is given as a **p** to*

POSITION

Jude 1: 6 angels who did not keep their own **p**

POSSESS → POSSESSED, POSSESSING, POSSESSION, POSSESSIONS

Nu 33:53 for I have given you the land to **p.**
Dt 28:21 the land that you are entering to **p.**
1Sa 10: 6 the spirit of the LORD will **p** you,
Ezr 9:11 that you are entering to **p** is a land
Ps 25:13 and their children shall **p** the land.
Isa 14: 2 house of Israel will **p** the nations as
60:21 they shall **p** the land forever.
Da 7:18 shall receive the kingdom and **p**
Ro 2:14 who do not **p** the law,

POSSESSED → POSSESS

Mt 8:16 many who were **p** with demons;
Heb 10:34 you yourselves **p** something better

POSSESSING → POSSESS

2Co 6:10 nothing, and yet **p** everything.
1Mc 1:57 found **p** the book of the covenant,

POSSESSION → POSSESS

Ex 6: 8 I will give it to you for a **p.**
19: 5 treasured **p** out of all the peoples.
Dt 7: 6 and take **p** of the land that I swore
7: 6 to be his people, his treasured **p**
Jos 1:11 to go in to take **p** of the land that
21:43 having taken **p** of it, they settled
Ps 2: 8 and the ends of the earth your **p.**
135: 4 for himself, Israel as his own **p.**
Mal 3:17 my special **p** on the day when I act,
Sir 36:29 acquires a wife gets his best **p,**

POSSESSIONS → POSSESS

Ge 15:14 they shall come out with great **p.**
Ecc 5:19 to whom God gives wealth and **p**
Mt 19:21 sell your **p,** and give the money to
Lk 12:15 not consist in the abundance of **p."**
19: 8 half of my **p,** Lord, I will give to
Ac 4:32 claimed private ownership of any **p,**
1Co 13: 3 If I give away all my **p,**
Heb 10:34 accepted the plundering of your **p,**

POSSIBLE

Mt 19:26 but for God all things are **p."**
26:39 if it is **p,** let this cup pass from me;
Mk 10:27 for God all things are **p."**
14:35 if it were **p,** the hour might pass
Lk 18:27 impossible for mortals is **p** for God.

POSTERITY

Ps 37:37 for there is **p** for the peaceable.
Tob 4:12 and their **p** will inherit the land.

POSTS

Jdg 16: 3 doors of the city gate and the two **p,**

POT → FLESHPOTS, POTSHERD, POTTER, POTTER'S

2Ki 4:40 there is death in the **p!"**
Jer 1:13 And I said, "I see a boiling **p,**

Eze 11: 3 city is the **p,** and we are the meat.'

POTIPHAR*

Egyptian who bought Joseph (Ge 37:36), set him over his house (Ge 39:1-6), sent him to prison (Ge 39:7-30).

POTSHERD → POT

Job 2: 8 Job took a **p** with which to scrape
Ps 22:15 my mouth is dried up like a **p,**

POTTER → POT

Isa 29:16 Shall the **p** be regarded as the clay?
45: 9 earthen vessels with the **p!**
64: 8 we are the clay, and you are our **p;**
Jer 18: 6 of Israel, just as this **p** has done?
Ro 9:21 Has the **p** no right over the clay,
Sir 33:13 Like clay in the hand of the **p,**

POTTER'S → POT

Jer 18: 2 go down to the **p** house,
Mt 27: 7 to buy the **p** field as a place to bury

POUR → POURED, POURING, POURS

Dt 12:16 **p** it out on the ground like water.
Ps 62: 8 **p** out your heart before him;
79: 6 **P** out your anger on the nations that
Isa 44: 3 I will **p** my spirit upon your
Eze 20: 8 I thought I would **p** out my wrath
39:29 I **p** out my spirit upon the house of
Joel 2:28 I will **p** out my spirit on all flesh;
Zec 12:10 I will **p** out a spirit of compassion
Mal 3:10 windows of heaven for you and **p**
Ac 2:17 I will **p** out my Spirit upon all flesh,
Rev 16: 1 **p** out on the earth the seven bowls

POURED → POUR

Ge 28:18 for a pillar and **p** oil on the top of it.
35:14 and he **p** out a drink offering on it,
2Sa 23:16 he **p** it out to the LORD,
2Ch 34:25 my wrath will be **p** out on this place
Ps 22:14 I am **p** out like water, and all my
SS 1: 3 your name is perfume **p** out;
Isa 19:14 **p** into them a spirit of confusion;
32:15 until a spirit from on high is **p** out
La 4:11 he **p** out his hot anger,
Mt 26:28 is **p** out for many for the forgiveness
Mk 14: 3 open the jar and **p** the ointment
Lk 22:20 is **p** out for you is the new covenant
Ac 2:33 he has **p** out this that you both see
10:45 of the Holy Spirit had been **p** out
Ro 5: 5 love has been **p** into our hearts
Php 2:17 if I am being **p** out as a libation
2Ti 4: 6 am already being **p** out as a libation,
Tit 3: 6 This Spirit he **p** out on us richly
Rev 14:10 **p** unmixed into the cup of his anger,
16: 2 the first angel went and **p** his bowl

POURING → POUR

1Sa 1:15 **p** out my soul before the LORD.
2Ki 4: 5 vessels to her, and she kept **p.**

POURS → POUR

Ps 19: 2 Day to day **p** forth speech,
Rev 11: 5 fire **p** from their mouth

POVERTY → POOR

Pr 6:11 **p** will come upon you like a robber,
10:15 the **p** of the poor is their ruin.
13:18 **P** and disgrace are for the one who
14:23 but mere talk leads only to **p.**
24:34 **p** will come upon you like a robber,
28:19 pursuits will have plenty of **p.**
30: 8 give me neither **p** nor riches;
31: 7 let them drink and forget their **p,**
Mk 12:44 out of her **p** has put in everything
Lk 21: 4 out of her **p** has put in all she had to
2Co 8: 2 their extreme **p** have overflowed in
8: 9 by his **p** you might become rich.
Rev 2: 9 "I know your affliction and your **p,**
Sir 10:31 One who is honored in **p,**
11:14 **p** and wealth, come from the Lord.

POWDER

Ex 32:20 ground it to **p**, scattered it on the

POWER → POWERFUL, POWERS

Ex   9:16 show you my **p**, and to make
     15: 6 right hand, O LORD, glorious in **p**—
     32:11 great **p** and with a mighty hand?
Dt   8:17 not say to yourself, "My **p** and the
     34:12 terrifying displays of **p** that Moses
1Sa 11: 6 in **p** when he heard these words,
1Ch 29:11 O LORD, are the greatness, the **p**,
2Ch 20: 6 In your hand are **p** and might,
Job 36:22 See, God is exalted in his **p**;
     37:23 he is great in **p** and justice,
Ps 63: 2 beholding your **p** and glory.
     66: 3 your great **p**, your enemies cringe
     68:34 Ascribe **p** to God, whose majesty is
    130: 7 and with him is great **p** to redeem.
    147: 5 Great is our Lord, and abundant in **p**
Pr   3:27 when it is in your **p** to do it.
     18:21 and life are in the **p** of the tongue,
Ecc 8: 8 or **p** over the day of death;
Isa 40:26 he is great in strength, mighty in **p**,
     40:29 He gives **p** to the faint,
Jer 10:12 It is he who made the earth by his **p**,
     27: 5 It is I who by my great **p**
     32:17 great **p** and by your outstretched
Da   2:20 for wisdom and **p** are his.
      6:27 saved Daniel from the **p** of the lions.
Hos 13:14 I ransom them from the **p** of Sheol?
Mic 3: 8 But as for me, I am filled with **p**,
Na   1: 3 LORD is slow to anger but great in **p**,
Zec 4: 6 by might, nor by **p**, but by my spirit,
Mt 22:29 the scriptures nor the **p** of God.
     24:30 on the clouds of heaven' with **p** and
Mk   9: 1 kingdom of God has come with **p**."
     13:26 coming in clouds' with great **p** and
Lk   1:17 the spirit and **p** of Elijah he will go
      1:35 **p** of the Most High will overshadow
      4:14 Jesus, filled with the **p** of the Spirit,
      6:19 for **p** came out from him and healed
      8:46 for I noticed that **p** had gone out
      9: 1 **p** and authority over all demons
     10:19 and over all the **p** of the enemy;
     21:27 of Man coming in a cloud' with **p**
     24:49 until you have been clothed with **p**
Jn 19:11 "You would have no **p** over me
Ac   1: 8 But you will receive **p** when
      4:33 With great **p** the apostles gave their
      8:10 "This man is the **p** of God that is
     10:38 with the Holy Spirit and with **p**;
     26:18 to light and from the **p** of Satan
Ro   1:16 it is the **p** of God for salvation
      1:20 creation of the world his eternal **p**
      9:17 purpose of showing my **p** in you,
     15:13 you may abound in hope by the **p** of
     15:19 by the **p** of signs and wonders,
     15:19 by the **p** of the Spirit of God,
1Co 1:17 might not be emptied of its **p**.
      1:18 are being saved it is the **p** of God.
      1:24 Christ the **p** of God and the wisdom
      2: 4 demonstration of the Spirit and of **p**,
      6:14 Lord and will also raise us by his **p**.
     15:24 and every authority and **p**.
     15:56 and the **p** of sin is the law.
2Co 4: 7 this extraordinary **p** belongs to God
      6: 7 truthful speech, and the **p** of God;
     10: 4 divine **p** to destroy strongholds.
     12: 9 for **p** is made perfect in weakness."
     13: 4 but lives by the **p** of God.
Gal 3:22 all things under the **p** of sin,
Eph 1:19 the immeasurable greatness of his **p**
      1:19 to the working of his great **p**.
      1:21 above all rule and authority and **p**
      3:16 with **p** through his Spirit,
      3:20 the **p** at work within us is able
      6:10 the Lord and in the strength of his **p**.
Php 3:10 Christ and the **p** of his resurrection
      3:21 by the **p** that also enables him
Col 1:11 that comes from his glorious **p**,
1Th 1: 5 but also in **p** and in the Holy Spirit
2Ti 1: 7 a spirit of **p** and of love and

      3: 5 form of godliness but denying its **p**.
Heb 2:14 the one who has the **p** of death,
      7:16 the **p** of an indestructible life.
1Pe 1: 5 the **p** of God through faith for a
2Pe 1: 3 divine **p** has given us everything
      1:16 to you the **p** and coming
Jude 1:25 be glory, majesty, **p**, and authority,
Rev 4:11 to receive glory and honor and **p**,
      5:12 to receive **p** and wealth and wisdom
      7: 2 four angels who had been given **p**
     11:17 you have taken your great **p** and
     12:10 have come the salvation and the **p**
     13: 2 dragon gave it his **p** and his throne
     19: 1 and glory and **p** to our God,
     20: 6 these the second death has no **p**,
Jdt 9:14 the God of all **p** and might,
Sir 28:22 It has no **p** over the godly;
     39:18 and none can limit his saving **p**.

DEEDS OF POWER Mt 7:22; 11:20, 21,
23; 13:54, 58; Mk 6:2; Lk 10:13; 19:37; Ac
2:11, 22; 1Co 12:28

GREAT POWER Ex 32:11; Dt 4:37; 9:29;
Jos 17:17; 2Ki 17:36; Ne 1:10; Ps 66:3; 79:11;
130:7; Isa 47:9; Jer 27:5; 32:17; Mk 13:26; Ac
4:33; Eph 1:19; Rev 11:17; Bar 2:11; 3Mc 6:2;
2Es 15:30, 31

POWER OF *GOD Mt 22:29; Mk 12:24; Lk
22:69; Ac 8:10; Ro 1:16; 1Co 1:18, 24; 2:5;
2Co 6:7; 13:4, 4; Col 2:12; 2Ti 1:8; 1Pe 1:5;
Jdt 13:19; Wis 7:25; 2Mc 3:24, 28, 34, 38; 9:8,
17; 11:4

POWERFUL → POWER

Ex   1: 9 more numerous and more **p** than we
Est 9: 4 Mordecai was **p** in the king's house,
Ps 29: 4 The voice of the LORD is **p**;
Mk   1: 7 one who is more **p** than I is coming
Ac   9:22 Saul became increasingly more **p**
1Co 1:26 not many were **p**,
Heb 1: 3 he sustains all things by his **p** word.
Jas 5:16 The prayer of the righteous is **p** and
Sir 7: 6 you may be partial to the **p**,
      8: 1 Do not contend with the **p**,

POWERS → POWER

Mt 14: 2 reason these **p** are at work in him."
Ro   8:38 present, nor things to come, nor **p**,
Eph 6:12 against the cosmic **p** of this present
Col 1:16 thrones or dominions or rulers or **p**
Heb 6: 5 of God and the **p** of the age to come,
1Pe 3:22 and **p** made subject to him.

PRACTICE → PRACTICED, PRACTICES, PRACTICING

Eze 13:23 see false visions or **p** divination;
Mt 23: 3 for they do not **p** what they teach.
Tob 4: 6 To all those who **p** righteousness
Sir 50:29 For if they put them into **p**,

PRACTICED → PRACTICE

Mt 23:23 ought to have **p** without neglecting
Ac   8: 9 Simon had previously **p** magic
     19:19 who **p** magic collected their books

PRACTICES → PRACTICE

Ex 23:24 or worship them, or follow their **p**,
Jdg 2:19 not drop any of their **p** or their
Ps 101: 7 No one who **p** deceit shall remain
Col 3: 9 stripped off the old self with its **p**
Rev 22:15 who loves and **p** falsehood.
2Es 15: 8 neither will I tolerate their wicked **p**

PRACTICING → PRACTICE

Mt   6: 1 "Beware of **p** your piety before
1Co 7: 9 if they are not **p** self-control,

PRAISE → PRAISED, PRAISES, PRAISING

Ex 15: 2 this is my God, and I will **p** him,
Dt 10:21 He is your **p**; he is your God,
     26:19 in **p** and in fame and in honor;
1Ch 23: 5 instruments that I have made for **p**."
2Ch 5:13 in unison in **p** and thanksgiving

     20:21 LORD and **p** him in holy splendor,
Ezr 3:10 were stationed to **p** the LORD
Ne   9: 5 is exalted above all blessing and **p**."
Ps 22:23 You who fear the LORD, **p** him!
     33: 1 **P** befits the upright.
     34: 1 **p** shall continually be in my mouth.
     40: 3 a song of **p** to our God.
     42: 5 Hope in God; for I shall again **p** him
     43: 5 for I shall again **p** him, my help and
     45:17 the peoples will **p** you forever and
     51:15 and my mouth will declare your **p**.
     56: 4 whose word I **p**, in God I trust;
     65: 1 **P** is due to you, O God, in Zion;
     66: 2 of his name; give to him glorious **p**.
     66: 8 let the sound of his **p** be heard,
     69:30 will **p** the name of God with a song;
     69:34 Let heaven and earth **p** him,
     71: 8 My mouth is filled with your **p**,
     71:14 and will **p** you yet more and more.
     71:22 also **p** you with the harp for your
     74:21 let the poor and needy **p** your name.
     89: 5 Let the heavens **p** your wonders,
    100: 4 thanksgiving, and his courts with **p**.
    102:18 people yet unborn may **p** the LORD:
    106: 2 of the LORD, or declare all his **p**?
    111:10 His **p** endures forever.
    113: 1 **p** the name of the LORD.
    117: 1 **P** the LORD, all you nations!
    119:175 Let me live that I may **p** you,
    135: 1 **P** the LORD! **P** the name of the
    138: 1 before the gods I sing your **p**;
    139:14 I **p** you, for I am fearfully and
    145:21 mouth will speak the **p** of the LORD,
    146: 1 **P** the LORD! **P** the LORD, O my soul
    147: 1 **P** the LORD! How good it is to sing
    147: 1 gracious, and a song of **p** is fitting.
    148: 1 **P** the LORD! **P** the LORD from the
    148:13 Let them **p** the name of the LORD,
    149: 1 his **p** in the assembly of the faithful.
    150: 2 **P** him for his mighty deeds;
    150: 6 that breathes the LORD!
Pr 27: 2 Let another **p** you, and not your own
     31:31 let her works **p** her in the city gates.
Isa 38:18 thank you, death cannot **p** you;
     42:10 his **p** from the end of the earth!
     61: 3 mantle of **p** instead of a faint spirit.
Jer 33: 9 **p** and a glory before all the nations
Da   4:37 **p** and extol and honor the King of
Hab 3: 3 and the earth was full of his **p**.
Mt 21:16 nursing babies you have prepared **p**
Lk 19:37 disciples began to **p** God joyfully
Ro   2:29 Such a person receives **p** not from
     15:11 let all the peoples **p** him";
1Co 14:15 but I will sing **p** with the mind also.
Eph 1: 6 to the **p** of his glorious grace
      1:12 might live for the **p** of his glory.
      1:14 to the **p** of his glory.
1Th 2: 6 nor did we seek **p** from mortals,
Heb 13:15 continually offer a sacrifice of **p** to
Jas 5:13 They should sing songs of **p**.
Rev 19: 5 "**P** our God, all you his servants,
Tob 12: 6 Bless and sing **p** to his name.
Jdt 15:14 people loudly sang this song of **p**.
Sir 11: 2 not **p** individuals for their good
     24: 1 THE **P** OF WISDOM Wisdom praises
Aza 1:35 sing **p** to him and highly exalt him

PRAISE THE †LORD Ge 29:35; 1Ch 16:4;
2Ch 20:19; Ezr 3:10; Ps 22:26; 33:2; 102:18;
104:35; 105:45; 106:1, 48; 111:1; 112:1;
113:1, 9; 115:17, 18; 116:19; 117:1, 2; 135:1,
3, 21; 146:1, 1, 2, 10; 147:1, 12, 20; 148:1, 1,
7, 14; 149:1, 9; 150:1, 6, 6; Isa 62:9; Jer 20:13

SING PRAISE Ps 7:17; 9:2; 104:33; 1Co
14:15, 15; Tob 12:6; AdE 13:17; Sir 39:35;
Aza 1:35, 36, 37, 38, 39, 40, 41, 42, 43, 44, 45,
46, 47, 48, 49, 50, 51, 52, 53, 54, 55, 56, 57,
58, 59, 60, 61, 62, 63, 64, 65, 66, 68

PRAISED → PRAISE

Ge 12:15 saw her, they **p** her to Pharaoh.
Jdg 16:24 saw him, they **p** their god;
2Sa 14:25 **p** so much for his beauty as

Ps   18: 3 the LORD, who is worthy to be **p,**
     48: 1 is the LORD and greatly to be **p**
Pr   31:30 who fears the LORD is to be **p.**
Da   4:34 **p** and honored the one who lives
      5: 4 They drank the wine and **p** the gods
Lk   18:43 the people, when they saw it, **p** God.
     23:47 what had taken place, he **p** God and
Aza   1:28 **p** and glorified and blessed God

PRAISES → PRAISE

2Sa 22:50 nations, and sing **p** to your name.
2Ch 29:30 They sang **p** with gladness,
Ps   9:11 Sing **p** to the LORD, who dwells in
      9:14 so that I may recount all your **p,**
     18:49 nations, and sing **p** to your name.
     47: 6 Sing **p** to God, sing **p;**
    147: 1 How good it is to sing **p** to our God;
Pr   31:28 her husband too, and he **p** her:
Sir 44: 1 now sing the **p** of famous men,

PRAISING → PRAISE

Lk   2:13 of the heavenly host, **p** God
      2:20 glorifying and **p** God for all they
Ac   2:47 **p** God and having the goodwill of
      3: 8 walking and leaping and **p** God.

PRAY → PRAYED, PRAYER, PRAYERS, PRAYING, PRAYS

Ex   8: 9 to **p** for you and for your officials
Nu   21: 7 **p** to the LORD to take away the
1Sa 12:23 against the LORD by ceasing to **p**
1Ki   8:30 of your people Israel when they **p**
2Ch   6:38 and **p** toward their land, which you
      7:14 humble themselves, **p,** seek my face
Ezr   6:10 and **p** for the life of the king and his
Job 42: 8 and my servant Job shall **p** for you,
Ps   5: 2 King and my God, for to you I **p.**
    122: 6 **P** for the peace of Jerusalem:
Jer   7:16 As for you, do not **p** for this people,
     29: 7 and **p** to the LORD on its behalf,
     29:12 call upon me and come and **p** to me,
Mt   5:44 and **p** for those who persecute you,
      6: 5 you **p,** do not be like the hypocrites;
      6: 9 "**P** then in this way: Our Father in
     14:23 up the mountain by himself to **p.**
     19:13 might lay his hands on them and **p.**
     26:36 here while I go over there and **p.**"
Lk   5:33 frequently fast and **p,**
      6:28 **p** for those who abuse you.
     11: 1 teach us to **p,** as John taught his
     18: 1 to **p** always and not to lose heart.
     18:10 men went up to the temple to **p,**
     22:40 "**P** that you may not come into the
Ro   8:26 do not know how to **p** as we ought,
1Co 11:13 for a woman to **p** to God with her
           head unveiled?
     14:13 should **p** for the power to interpret.
     14:15 I will **p** with the spirit, but I will **p**
           with the mind also;
Eph   3:16 I **p** that, according to the riches of
      6:18 **P** in the Spirit at all times in every
1Th   5:17 **p** without ceasing,
2Th   1:11 To this end we always **p** for you,
Jas   5:13 suffering? They should **p.**
      5:16 and **p** for one another, so that you
1Jn   5:16 not say that you should **p** about that.
Jude 1:20 most holy faith; **p** in the Holy Spirit;
Sir   3: 5 and when they **p** they will be heard.
     37:15 But above all **p** to the Most High

PRAYED → PRAY

Ge   20:17 Then Abraham **p** to God;
     25:21 Isaac **p** to the LORD for his wife,
Nu   11: 2 Moses **p** to the LORD, and the fire
     21: 7 So Moses **p** for the people.
1Sa   1:27 For this child I **p;** and the LORD has
2Ki   6:17 Then Elisha **p:** "O LORD,
2Ch 30:18 But Hezekiah **p** for them, saying,
Ne   4: 9 So we **p** to our God,
Job 42:10 Job when he had **p** for his friends;
Da   9: 4 I **p** to the LORD my God and made
Jnh   2: 1 Then Jonah **p** to the LORD his God

Mt   26:39 threw himself on the ground and **p,**
Mk   1:35 to a deserted place, and there he **p.**
     14:35 threw himself on the ground and **p**
Lk   22:41 a stone's throw, knelt down, and **p,**
Ac   4:31 When they had **p,** the place
      6: 6 who **p** and laid their hands on them.
      8:15 **p** for them that they might receive
Jas   5:17 he **p** fervently that it might not rain,
Aza   1: 2 Azariah stood still in the fire and **p**

PRAYER → PRAY

Ge   25:21 and the LORD granted his **p,**
1Ki   8:49 heaven your dwelling place their **p**
2Ch   7:12 have heard your **p,** and have chosen
     30:27 their **p** came to his holy dwelling in
     33:19 His **p,** and how God received his
Job 42: 8 for I will accept his **p** not to deal
Ps   4: 1 Be gracious to me, and hear my **p.**
      6: 9 the LORD accepts my **p.**
     17: 1 give ear to my **p** from lips free of
     55: 1 Give ear to my **p,** O God;
     65: 2 O you who answer **p!** To you
     66:20 not rejected my **p** or removed his
Pr   15: 8 the **p** of the upright is his delight.
     15:29 but he hears the **p** of the righteous.
Isa 56: 7 house shall be called a house of **p**
Hab   3: 1 A **p** of the prophet Habakkuk
Mt   21:13 house shall be called a house of **p';**
     21:22 Whatever you ask for in **p** with faith
Mk   9:29 kind can come out only through **p.**"
     11:24 I tell you, whatever you ask for in **p,**
Ac   1:14 constantly devoting themselves to **p,**
      6: 4 will devote ourselves to **p** and to
     10:31 'Cornelius, your **p** has been heard
     16:13 we supposed there was a place of **p;**
Ro   10: 1 and **p** to God for them is that they
     12:12 patient in suffering, persevere in **p.**
1Co   7: 5 to devote yourselves to **p,**
Php   1: 9 my **p,** that your love may overflow
      4: 6 in everything by **p** and supplication
Col   4: 2 Devote yourselves to **p,** keeping
1Ti   4: 5 sanctified by God's word and by **p.**
Jas   5:15 The **p** of faith will save the sick,
      5:16 The **p** of the righteous is powerful
1Pe   3:12 and his ears are open to their **p.**
Sir   4: 6 their Creator will hear their **p.**
     51: 1 **P** OF JESUS SON OF SIRACH
1Mc   3:46 formerly had a place of **p** in Mizpah

PRAYERS → PRAY

Isa   1:15 even though you make many **p,**
Mk   12:40 the sake of appearance say long **p.**
Ac   2:42 to the breaking of bread and the **p.**
2Co   1:11 also join in helping us by your **p,**
1Ti   2: 1 then, I urge that supplications, **p,**
Heb   5: 7 Jesus offered up **p** and supplications
1Pe   3: 7 so that nothing may hinder your **p.**
Rev   5: 8 which are the **p** of the saints.
      8: 3 to offer with the **p** of all the saints
Jdt   4:13 The Lord heard their **p** and had

PRAYING → PRAY

1Sa   1:13 Hannah was **p** silently; only her lips
Da   6:11 and found Daniel **p** and seeking
Mk   11:25 "Whenever you stand **p,** forgive,
Lk   3:21 also had been baptized and was **p,**
      9:29 And while he was **p,** the appearance
Ac   16:25 At this moment he is **p,**
     16:25 were **p** and singing hymns to God,

PRAYS → PRAY

Da   6: 7 whoever **p** to anyone, divine or
1Co 11: 4 Any man who **p** or prophesies with
     14:14 spirit **p** but my mind is unproductive
Sir 34:29 When one **p** and another curses,

PREACH → PREACHING

Mic   2:11 "I will **p** to you of wine and strong
Tit   1: 9 able both to **p** with sound doctrine

PREACHING → PREACH

1Ti   5:17 those who labor in **p** and teaching;

PRECEDE

1Th   4:15 by no means **p** those who have died.

PRECEPT* → PRECEPTS

Isa 28:10 For it is **p** upon **p, p** upon **p,**
     28:13 "**P** upon **p, p** upon **p,**

PRECEPTS* → PRECEPT

Ps   19: 8 the **p** of the LORD are right,
    111: 7 and just; all his **p** are trustworthy.
    119: 4 You have commanded your **p** to
    119:15 I will meditate on your **p,**
    119:27 understand the way of your **p,**
    119:40 See, I have longed for your **p;**
    119:45 at liberty, for I have sought your **p.**
    119:56 for I have kept your **p.**
    119:63 of those who keep your **p.**
    119:69 with my whole heart I keep your **p.**
    119:78 as for me, I will meditate on your **p,**
    119:87 but I have not forsaken your **p.**
    119:93 I will never forget your **p,**
    119:94 save me, for I have sought your **p.**
    119:100 the aged, for I keep your **p.**
    119:104 Through your **p** I get understanding;
    119:110 but I do not stray from your **p.**
    119:128 Truly I direct my steps by all your **p**
    119:134 that I may keep your **p.**
    119:141 yet I do not forget your **p.**
    119:159 Consider how I love your **p;**
    119:168 I keep your **p** and decrees,
    119:173 for I have chosen your **p.**
Pr   4: 2 for I give you good **p:**
Jer 35:18 ancestor Jonadab, and kept all his **p,**
Mt   15: 9 teaching human **p** as doctrines.'"
Mk   7: 7 teaching human **p** as doctrines.'
Sir 18:14 and who are eager for his **p.**
2Es 16:76 who keep my commandments and **p**

PRECIOUS

1Sa 26:21 my life was **p** in your sight today;
2Ch   3: 6 the house with settings of **p** stones.
Ps   72:14 and **p** is their blood in his sight.
    116:15 **P** in the sight of the LORD is the
Pr   3:15 She is more **p** than jewels,
Isa 28:16 a tested stone, a **p** cornerstone,
Eze 28:13 every **p** stone was your covering,
1Pe   1:19 but with the **p** blood of Christ,
      2: 4 rejected by mortals yet chosen and **p**
      2: 6 a cornerstone chosen and **p;**
2Pe   1: 1 received a faith as **p** as ours
      1: 4 his **p** and very great promises,

PREDESTINED*

Ac   4:28 your plan had **p** to take place.
Ro   8:29 also **p** to be conformed to the image
      8:30 those whom he **p** he also called;

PREDICTED → PREDICTION

2Ki 23:16 who had **p** these things.
Ac   3:24 those after him, also **p** these days.
     11:28 **p** by the Spirit that there would be

PREDICTION* → PREDICTED, PREDICTIONS

Isa 44:26 and fulfills the **p** of his messengers;

PREDICTIONS* → PREDICT

Jude 1:17 the **p** of the apostles of our Lord

PREGNANT

Ge   19:36 of Lot became **p** by their father.
Ex   21:22 who are fighting injure a **p** woman
Ps   7:14 are **p** with mischief, and bring forth
Mt   24:19 Woe to those who are **p** and
1Th   5: 3 labor pains come upon a **p** woman,
Rev 12: 2 She was **p** and was crying out in

PREPARATION → PREPARE

Mt   27:62 next day, that is, after the day of **P,**
Jn   19:14 it was the day of **P** for the Passover;

PREPARATIONS → PREPARE

Mk   14:12 the **p** for you to eat the Passover?"

PREPARE → PREPARATION, PREPARATIONS, PREPARED

Ps   23: 5 You **p** a table before me in the
Isa 40: 3 wilderness **p** the way of the LORD,
Am 4:12 do this to you, **p** to meet your God,
Mal 3: 1 sending my messenger to **p** the way
Mt   3: 3 '**P** the way of the Lord, make his
      11:10 who will **p** your way before you.'
Jn 14: 2 I have told you that I go to **p** a place
1Pe 1:13 Therefore **p** your minds for action;

PREPARED → PREPARE

Ex 23:20 bring you to the place that I have **p.**
1Ch 15: 1 and he **p** a place for the ark of God
2Ch 1: 4 to the place that David had **p**
Mt 20:23 whom it has been **p** by my Father."
      25:34 the kingdom **p** for you from the
Lk 1:17 make ready a people **p** for the Lord.
Ro 9:23 which he has **p** beforehand for glory
1Co 2: 9 God has **p** for those who love him"
Eph 2:10 God **p** beforehand to be our way of
Heb 10: 5 but a body you have **p** for me;
      11:16 indeed, he has **p** a city for them.
Rev 12: 6 where she has a place **p** by God,
      21: 2 **p** as a bride adorned for her husband
Jdt 9: 6 For all your ways are **p** in advance,
2Es 7:70 he first **p** the judgment and

PRESCRIBED

2Ki 23:21 passover to the LORD your God as **p**
Ezr 3: 4 kept the festival of booths, as **p,**
Ro 3:20 justified in his sight" by deeds **p** by

PRESENCE → PRESENT

Ex 18:12 with Moses' father-in-law in the **p**
      25:30 the bread of the **P** on the table
      33:14 He said, "My **p** will go with you,
Nu 4: 7 the **P** they shall spread a blue cloth,
Dt 4:37 out of Egypt with his own **p,**
1Sa 2:21 boy Samuel grew up in the **p** of the
      21: 6 bread of the **P,** which is removed
2Ki 24:20 that he expelled them from his **p.**
Job 1:12 Satan went out from the **p** of the
      2: 7 Satan went out from the **p** of the
Ps 16:11 In your **p** there is fullness of joy;
      21: 6 glad with the joy of your **p.**
      23: 5 before me in the **p** of my enemies;
      31:20 your **p** you hide them from human
      41:12 and set me in your **p** forever.
      51:11 Do not cast me away from your **p,**
      52: 9 In the **p** of the faithful I will
     114: 7 Tremble, O earth, at the **p** of the
     139: 7 Or where can I flee from your **p?**
Isa 63: 9 no messenger or angel but his **p**
Eze 38:20 shall quake at my **p,** and
Jn 8:38 what I have seen in the Father's **p;**
      17: 5 glorify me in your own **p** with the
             glory that I had in your **p**
Ac 2:28 full of gladness with your **p.'**
2Th 1: 9 the **p** of the Lord and from the glory
Heb 9:24 now to appear in the **p** of God on
Jude 1:24 stand without blemish in the **p**
Rev 20:11 earth and the heaven fled from his **p**

PRESENT → PRESENCE, PRESENTED

Nu 16:17 each one of you **p** his censer before
Job 1: 6 the heavenly beings came to **p**
      2: 1 Satan also came among them to **p**
Isa 45:21 Declare and **p** your case;
Lk 2:22 up to Jerusalem to **p** him to
Ro 6:13 but **p** yourselves to God as
      8:18 that the sufferings of this **p** time are
      8:38 nor things **p,** nor things to come,
1Co 3:22 or death or the **p** or the future—
      7:31 the **p** form of this world is passing
2Co 11: 2 to **p** you as a chaste virgin to Christ.
Eph 5:27 **p** the church to himself in splendor,
Col 1:22 to **p** you holy and blameless and
1Ti 4: 8 promise for both the **p** life and the
2Ti 2:15 **p** yourself to God as one approved
Tit 2:12 in the **p** age to live lives that are
2Pe 3: 7 the **p** heavens and earth have been

PRESENTED → PRESENT

Ac 1: 3 After his suffering he **p** himself

PRESERVE → PRESERVES

Ge 19:32 so that we may **p** offspring through
Ps 32: 7 you **p** me from trouble;
Pr 14: 3 but the lips of the wise **p** them.

PRESERVES → PRESERVE

Ps 31:23 The LORD **p** the faithful,
Sir 32:24 one who keeps the law **p** himself,

PRESS → PRESSED, PRESSURE

Php 3:12 but I **p** on to make it my own,
      3:14 I **p** on toward the goal for the prize
Rev 14:20 and blood flowed from the wine **p,**
      19:15 the wine **p** of the fury of the wrath

PRESSED → PRESS

Lk 6:38 A good measure, **p** down, shaken
Php 1:23 I am hard **p** between the two:

PRESSURE → PRESS

2Co 11:28 I am under daily **p** because of my

PRESUMES → PRESUMPTUOUSLY

Dt 18:20 who **p** to speak in my name a word

PRESUMPTUOUSLY → PRESUMES

Dt 17:13 and will not act **p** again.
     18:22 The prophet has spoken it **p;**
Ne 9:16 they and our ancestors acted **p**

PRETENDED

1Sa 21:13 **p** to be mad when in their presence.
Lk 20:20 sent spies who **p** to be honest,

PRETEXT

1Th 2: 5 or with a **p** for greed;
1Pe 2:16 not use your freedom as a **p** for evil.

PREVAIL → PREVAILED, PREVAILING, PREVAILS

Ge 32:25 that he did not **p** against Jacob,
1Sa 2: 9 for not by might does one **p.**
2Ch 14:11 let no mortal **p** against you."
Ro 3: 4 and **p** in your judging."
Jdt 11:10 nor can the sword **p** against them,
Wis 7:30 but against wisdom evil does not **p.**

PREVAILED → PREVAIL

Ge 32:28 God and with humans, and have **p.''**
Ex 17:11 Moses held up his hand, Israel **p;**
Hos 12: 4 He strove with the angel and **p,**

PREVAILS → PREVAIL

Hab 1: 4 becomes slack and justice never **p.**

PREY

Ge 15:11 when birds of **p** came down on the
Na 2:13 I will cut off your **p** from the earth,

PRICE → BRIDE-PRICE

Ge 23: 9 the full **p** let him give it to me in
1Ch 21:22 give it to me at its full **p—**
Job 28:18 the **p** of wisdom is above pearls.
Zec 11:13 this lordly **p** at which I was valued
Mt 27: 9 the **p** of the one on whom a **p** had
             been set,
Ac 5: 8 And she said, "Yes, that was the **p.''**
1Co 6:20 For you were bought with a **p;**
      7:23 You were bought with a **p;**
Sir 6:15 Faithful friends are beyond **p;**

PRIDE → PROUD

2Ch 32:26 Hezekiah humbled himself for the **p**
Ps 20: 7 our **p** is in the name of the LORD
      47: 4 the **p** of Jacob whom he loves.
Pr 8:13 **P** and arrogance and the way of evil
      11: 2 When **p** comes, then comes disgrace
      16:18 **P** goes before destruction,
      29:23 A person's **p** will bring humiliation,
Isa 2:11 the **p** of everyone shall be humbled;
      25:11 their **p** will be laid low despite the
Da 4:37 to bring low those who walk in **p.**

Am 8: 7 LORD has sworn by the **p** of Jacob:
Mk 7:22 licentiousness, envy, slander, **p,**
2Co 7: 4 about you; I have great **p** in you;
1Jn 2:16 the desire of the eyes, the **p** in riches
Sir 10:13 For the beginning of **p** is sin,

PRIEST → PRIESTHOOD, PRIESTLY, PRIESTS

Ge 14:18 he was **p** of God Most High.
Ex 2:16 **p** of Midian had seven daughters.
      18: 1 Jethro, the **p** of Midian, Moses'
Nu 5:10 anyone gives to the **p** shall be his.
Jdg 17:10 and be to me a father and a **p,**
1Sa 2:11 in the presence of the **p** Eli.
      2:35 I will raise up for myself a faithful **p**
      21: 6 So the **p** gave him the holy bread;
2Ch 13: 9 becomes a **p** of what are no gods.
Ne 8: 9 and Ezra the **p** and scribe,
Ps 110: 4 "You are a **p** forever according to
Jer 23:11 Both prophet and **p** are ungodly;
Eze 1: 3 came to the **p** Ezekiel son of Buzi,
Zec 6:13 There shall be a **p** by his throne,
Mk 14:63 Then the high **p** tore his clothes and
Heb 2:17 a merciful and faithful high **p**
      3: 1 apostle and high **p** of our confession
      4:14 great high **p** who has passed through
      4:15 not have a high **p** who is unable to
      5: 6 "You are a **p** forever, according to
      6:20 having become a high **p** forever
      7: 3 the Son of God, he remains a **p**
      7:15 obvious when another **p** arises,
      7:26 that we should have such a high **p,**
      8: 1 we have such a high **p,**
      9:11 Christ came as a high **p** of the good
     10:21 since we have a great **p** over the
     13:11 into the sanctuary by the high **p** as
Sir 7:31 Fear the Lord and honor the **p,**

CHIEF PRIEST 2Ki 25:18; 2Ch 19:11;
24:11; 26:20; 31:10; Ezr 7:5; Jer 52:24; 1Es
9:39, 40, 49

HIGH PRIEST Nu 35:25, 28, 32; Jos
20:6; 2Ki 12:10; 22:4, 8; 23:4; 2Ch 34:9; Ne
3:1, 20; 13:28; Hag 1:1, 12, 14; 2:2, 4; Zec 3:1,
8; 6:11; Mt 26:3, 51, 57, 58, 62, 63, 65; Mk
2:26; 14:47, 53, 54, 60, 61, 63, 66; Lk 22:50;
Jn 11:49, 51; 18:13, 15, 15, 16, 19, 22, 24, 26;
Ac 4:6; 5:17, 21, 27; 7:1; 9:1; 19:14; 22:5;
23:2, 4, 5; 24:1; Heb 2:17; 3:1; 4:14, 15; 5:1,
5, 10; 6:20; 7:26; 8:1, 3; 9:7, 11, 25; 13:11; Jdt
4:6, 8, 14; 15:8; Sir 50:1; Bar 1:7; 1Mc 7:5, 9;
10:20, 32, 38, 69; 12:3, 6, 7, 20; 13:36, 42;
14:17, 20, 23, 27, 30, 35, 41, 47; 15:2, 17, 21,
24; 16:12, 24; 2Mc 3:1, 4, 9, 10, 16, 21, 32,
33, 33; 4:13; 14:3, 13; 15:12; 1Es 5:40; 8:2;
3Mc 1:11; 2:1; 4Mc 4:13, 16, 18

PRIESTHOOD → PRIEST

Ex 29: 9 the **p** shall be theirs by a perpetual
Nu 16:10 yet you seek the **p** as well!
      25:13 after him a covenant of perpetual **p,**
Ezr 2:62 so they were excluded from the **p**
Heb 7:24 but he holds his **p** permanently,
1Pe 2: 5 a holy **p,** to offer spiritual sacrifices
      2: 9 But you are a chosen race, a royal **p,**
2Mc 11: 3 the high **p** for sale every year.

PRIESTLY → PRIEST

Ex 19: 6 a **p** kingdom and a holy nation.

PRIESTS → PRIEST

Ex 28: 1 the Israelites, to serve me as **p—**
      40:15 that they may serve me as **p:**
Dt 31: 9 this law, and gave it to the **p,**
Jos 3:15 and the feet of the **p** bearing the ark
      6: 4 with seven **p** bearing seven trumpets
1Sa 22:17 "Turn and kill the **p** of the LORD,
2Ch 5: 7 **p** brought the ark of the covenant
      31: 2 appointed the divisions of the **p** and
      34: 5 burned the bones of the **p** on their
Ezr 6:20 the **p** and the Levites had purified
      10: 5 stood up and made the leading **p,**
Ne 3:28 the Horse Gate the **p** made repairs,

13:30 I established the duties of the **p** and
Ps 99: 6 Moses and Aaron were among his **p**
Jer 5:31 and the **p** rule as the prophets direct;
Eze 22:26 Its **p** have done violence to my
Mic 3:11 its **p** teach for a price, its prophets
Mal 1: 6 says the LORD of hosts to you, O **p,**
Mt 20:18 will be handed over to the chief **p**
27: 3 thirty pieces of silver to the chief **p**
Mk 2:26 not lawful for any but the **p** to eat,
15: 3 the chief **p** accused him of many
Jn 19:15 chief **p** answered, "We have no king
Ac 6: 7 many of the **p** became obedient to
Heb 7:27 Unlike the other high **p,** he has no
Rev 1: 6 **p** serving his God and Father,
5:10 a kingdom and **p** serving our God,
20: 6 they will be **p** of God and of Christ,
Bel 1:28 the dragon, and slaughtered the **p.**"
1Mc 4:42 blameless **p** devoted to the law,

CHIEF PRIESTS Ezr 8:29; Mt 2:4; 16:21;
20:18; 21:15, 23, 45; 26:3, 14, 47, 59; 27:1, 3,
6, 12, 20, 41, 62; 28:11; Mk 8:31; 10:33;
11:18, 27; 14:1, 10, 43, 53, 55; 15:1, 3, 10, 11,
31; Lk 9:22; 19:47; 20:1, 19; 22:2, 4, 52, 66;
23:4, 10, 13; 24:20; Jn 7:32, 45; 11:47, 57;
12:10; 18:3, 35; 19:6, 15, 21; Ac 4:23; 5:24;
9:14, 21; 22:30; 23:14; 25:2, 15; 26:10, 12

LEVITICAL PRIESTS Dt 17:9, 18; 18:1;
24:8; 27:9; Jos 3:3; 8:33; 2Ch 23:18; Jer
33:18; Eze 43:19; 44:15; 1Es 5:56, 63

PRIESTS AND ... LEVITES 1Ki 8:4; 1Ch
13:2; 15:14; 23:2; 24:6, 31; 28:13, 21; 2Ch
5:5; 8:15; 11:13; 23:4, 6; 24:5; 29:4; 30:15, 25,
27; 31:2, 2, 4, 9; 34:30; 35:18; Ezr 1:5; 3:8,
12; 6:16, 20; 7:7; 8:29, 30; Ne 8:13; 11:20;
12:1, 30, 44, 44; 13:29, 30; Isa 66:21; Jn 1:19;
1Es 1:7, 10, 21; 2:8; 7:9, 10; 8:5, 10, 59, 60,
69, 96; 9:37

PRINCE → PRINCES, PRINCESS
Dt 33:16 brow of the **p** among his brothers.
Isa 9: 6 Everlasting Father, **P** of Peace.
Eze 34:24 my servant David shall be among
37:25 David shall be their **p** forever.
45:17 the obligation of the **p** regarding
46: 8 the **p** enters, he shall come in by the
Da 8:11 against the **p** of the host it acted
8:25 even rise up against the **P** of princes
10:20 to fight against the **p** of Persia,
10:20 the **p** of Greece will come.
10:21 princes except Michael, your **p.**
11:22 and the **p** of the covenant as well.
12: 1 "At that time Michael, the great **p,**

PRINCES → PRINCE
1Sa 2: 8 to make them sit with **p** and inherit
Ps 113: 8 to make them sit with **p,**
118: 9 LORD than to put confidence in **p.**
146: 3 not put your trust in **p,** in mortals,
148:11 **p** and all rulers of the earth!
Isa 40:23 brings **p** to naught, and makes the
Eze 19: 1 a lamentation for the **p** of Israel,
Da 8:25 even rise up against the Prince of **p.**
10:13 Michael, one of the chief **p,** came to

PRINCESS → PRINCE
Ps 45:13 The **p** is decked in her chamber

PRISCA See PRISCILLA

PRISCILLA[*] → =PRISCA
Wife of Aquila, also called Prisca; co-worker
with Paul (Ac 18; Ro 16:3; 1Co 16:19; 2Ti 4:19);
instructor of Apollos (Ac 18:24-28).

PRISON → IMPRISONED,
IMPRISONMENT, IMPRISONMENTS,
PRISONER, PRISONERS
Ge 39:20 he remained there in **p.**
Jdg 16:25 So they called Samson out of the **p,**
2Ki 25:29 Jehoiachin put aside his **p** clothes.
Ps 142: 7 Bring me out of **p,** so that I may
Isa 42: 7 from the **p** those who sit in darkness

Mt 14:10 and had John beheaded in the **p.**
25:36 I was in **p** and you visited me.'
Lk 22:33 I am ready to go with you to **p** and
Ac 8: 3 he committed them to **p.**
12: 5 While Peter was kept in **p,**
16:26 foundations of the **p** were shaken;
Heb 13: 3 Remember those who are in **p,**
13: 3 as though you were in **p** with them;
1Pe 3:19 a proclamation to the spirits in **p,**
Rev 2:10 about to throw some of you into **p**
20: 7 Satan will be released from his **p**

PRISONER → PRISON
2Ki 24:12 took him **p** in the eighth year
Mk 15: 6 at the festival he used to release a **p**
Eph 3: 1 that I Paul am a **p** for Christ Jesus

PRISONERS → PRISON
Ps 68: 6 he leads out the **p** to prosperity,
79:11 Let the groans of the **p** come before
107:10 **p** in misery and in irons,
146: 7 The LORD sets the **p** free;
Isa 61: 1 to the captives, and release to the **p;**
Zec 9:12 to your stronghold, O **p** of hope;

PRIVATE → PRIVATELY
Mk 4:34 everything in **p** to his disciples.

PRIVATELY → PRIVATE
Mk 9:28 his disciples asked him **p,**
13: 3 John, and Andrew asked him **p,**

PRIVILEGE
2Co 8: 4 the **p** of sharing in this ministry to

PRIZE
1Co 9:24 but only one receives the **p?**
Php 3:14 the **p** of the heavenly call of God in

PROBLEMS[*]
Da 5:12 solve **p** were found in this Daniel,
5:16 can give interpretations and solve **p.**
2Es 4: 3 and to put before you three **p.**

PROCESSION → PROCEED
Ps 42: 4 led them in **p** to the house of God,
118:27 Bind the festal **p** with branches,
Isa 60:11 with their kings led in **p.**
2Co 2:14 always leads us in triumphal **p,**

PROCLAIM → PROCLAIMED,
PROCLAIMING, PROCLAIMS,
PROCLAMATION
Ex 33:19 **p** before you the name, 'The LORD';
Dt 32: 3 For I will **p** the name of the LORD;
2Sa 1:20 **p** it not in the streets of Ashkelon;
Ne 8:15 publish and **p** in all their towns
Ps 22:31 and **p** his deliverance to a people
97: 6 The heavens **p** his righteousness;
Isa 12: 4 **p** that his name is exalted.
61: 1 to **p** liberty to the captives,
Jer 7: 2 and **p** there this word, and say,
50: 2 set up a banner and **p,**
Jnh 3: 2 **p** to it the message that I tell you."
Mt 10:27 whispered, **p** from the housetops.
12:18 and he will **p** justice to the Gentiles.
Lk 4:19 to **p** the year of the Lord's favor."
9:60 you, go and **p** the kingdom of God."
Ac 17:23 you worship as unknown, this I **p**
Ro 10: 8 the word of faith that we **p);**
10:14 to hear without someone to **p** him?
1Co 11:26 **p** the Lord's death until he comes.
Gal 1: 8 heaven should **p** to you a gospel
Php 1:15 Some **p** Christ from envy and
Col 1:28 It is he whom we **p,**
Rev 14: 6 with an eternal gospel to **p** to those

PROCLAIMED → PROCLAIM
Ex 34: 5 and **p** the name, "The LORD."
Isa 43:12 I declared and saved and **p,**
Mk 13:10 the good news must first be **p** to all
Lk 16:16 news of the kingdom of God is **p,**
Ro 9:17 my name may be **p** in all the earth."
15:19 I have fully **p** the good news

Col 1:23 which has been **p** to every creature
2Ti 4:17 the message might be fully **p** and all

PROCLAIMING → PROCLAIM
Mk 1:14 Jesus came to Galilee, **p** the good
Ac 4: 2 were teaching the people and **p** that
17: 3 Messiah, Jesus whom I am **p** to you.

PROCLAIMS → PROCLAIM
Ps 19: 1 and the firmament **p** his handiwork.
Na 1:15 brings good tidings, who **p** peace!

PROCLAMATION → PROCLAIM
Ro 16:25 my gospel and the **p** of Jesus Christ,
1Pe 3:19 made a **p** to the spirits in prison,

PROCONSUL
Ac 13:12 the **p** saw what had happened, he

PRODUCE → PRODUCED, PRODUCES
Nu 18:12 choice **p** that they give to the LORD,
Jos 5:11 they ate the **p** of the land,
Pr 3: 9 with the first fruits of all your **p;**

PRODUCED → PRODUCE
Nu 17: 8 It put forth buds, **p** blossoms,
Ro 7: 8 **p** in me all kinds of covetousness.

PRODUCES → PRODUCE
Pr 30:33 so pressing anger **p** strife.
Lk 6:45 good treasure of the heart **p** good,
Ro 5: 3 knowing that suffering **p** endurance,
2Co 7:10 For godly grief **p** a repentance that
Heb 6: 8 But if it **p** thorns and thistles,
Jas 1: 3 testing of your faith **p** endurance;

PROFANE → PROFANED, PROFANES
Lev 22:32 You shall not **p** my holy name,
Eze 20:39 my holy name you shall no more **p**
1Mc 1:45 to **p** sabbaths and festivals,

PROFANED → PROFANE
Jer 34:16 you turned around and **p** my name
Eze 20: 9 not be **p** in the sight of the nations
36:20 they **p** my holy name, in that it was
39: 7 not let my holy name be **p** any more
Jdt 4:12 and the sanctuary to be **p**
1Mc 1:43 sacrificed to idols and **p** the sabbath.
4:54 very day that the Gentiles had **p** it,

PROFANES → PROFANE
Ex 31:14 who **p** it shall be put to death;

PROFESS[*] → PROFESSED,
PROFESSES, PROFESSING
1Ti 2:10 proper for women who **p** reverence
Tit 1:16 They **p** to know God, but

PROFESSES[*] → PROFESS
Wis 2:13 He **p** to have knowledge of God,

PROFESSING[*] → PROFESS
1Ti 6:21 by **p** it some have missed the mark

PROFIT → PROFITED
Ps 30: 9 "What **p** is there in my death,
Pr 14:23 In all toil there is **p,**
Mt 16:26 For what will it **p** them if they gain
Sir 29:11 and it will **p** you more than gold.

PROFITABLE[*] → PROFIT
Pr 31:18 perceives that her merchandise is **p.**
Tit 3: 8 are excellent and **p** to everyone.
Wis 8: 7 nothing in life is more **p**
Sir 7:22 if they are **p** to you, keep them.

PROGRESS
Php 1:25 with all of you for your **p** and joy
1Ti 4:15 so that all may see your **p.**

PROLONG
Ps 85: 5 you **p** your anger to all generations?
Isa 53:10 and shall **p** his days;

PROMINENT
Da 8: 8 four **p** horns toward the four winds

PROMISE → PROMISED, PROMISES

1Ki   6:12   then I will establish my **p** with you,
      8:20   Now the LORD has upheld the **p**
Ne   5:13   who does not perform this **p.**
       9: 8   your **p,** for you are righteous.
Ps 105:42   For he remembered his holy **p,**
   106:24   having no faith in his **p.**
   119:41   your salvation according to your **p.**
   119:50   that your **p** gives me life.
   119:58   gracious to me according to your **p.**
  119:172   My tongue will sing of your **p,**
Ac   2:39   the **p** is for you, for your children,
     26: 7   a **p** that our twelve tribes hope to
Ro   4:13   the **p** that he would inherit the world
     4:20   made him waver concerning the **p**
      9: 8   the children of the **p** are counted as
Gal   3:18   it no longer comes from the **p;**
     4:28   are children of the **p,** like Isaac.
Eph   2:12   and strangers to the covenants of **p,**
      6: 2   the first commandment with a **p:**
1Ti   4: 8   holding **p** for both the present life
2Ti   1: 1   the **p** of life that is in Christ Jesus,
Heb   4: 1   the **p** of entering his rest is still open
     6:13   When God made a **p** to Abraham,
2Pe   2:19   They **p** them freedom,
      3: 9   The Lord is not slow about his **p,**
     3:13   But, in accordance with his **p,**

PROMISED → PROMISE

Ge   18:19   for Abraham what he has **p** him."
     21: 1   the LORD did for Sarah as he had **p.**
     28:15   until I have done what I have **p** you.
Ex   32:13   **p** I will give to your descendants,
Nu   10:29   for the LORD has **p** good to Israel."
Dt   1:11   and bless you, as he has **p** you!
     15: 6   God has blessed you, as he **p** you,
    26:18   his treasured people, as he **p** you,
Jos   23: 5   as the LORD your God **p** you.
2Sa   7:28   **p** this good thing to your servant,
1Ki   8:15   with his hand has fulfilled what he **p**
      9: 5   as I **p** your father David, saying,
2Ch   6:15   my father David, what you **p** to him.
Lk   24:49   sending upon you what my Father **p**
Ac   13:23   to Israel a Savior, Jesus, as he **p;**
   13:32   the good news that what God **p** to
Ro   4:21   God was able to do what he had **p.**
2Co   1: 1   I **p** you in marriage to one husband,
Eph   1:13   with the seal of the **p** Holy Spirit;
Tit   1: 2   who never lies, **p** before the ages
Heb   10:23   for he who has **p** is faithful.
   10:36   you may receive what was **p.**
Jas   1:12   Lord has **p** to those who love him.
      2: 5   heirs of the kingdom that he has **p**
1Jn   2:25   this is what he has **p** us, eternal life.

PROMISES → PROMISE

Jos   21:45   the good **p** that the LORD had made
Ps   12: 6   **p** of the LORD are **p** that are pure,
Ro   9: 4   of the law, the worship, and the **p;**
     15: 8   that he might confirm the **p** given
2Co   1:20   every one of God's **p** is a "Yes."
      7: 1   Since we have these **p,** beloved,
Gal   3:21   law then opposed to the **p** of God?
Heb   8: 6   has been enacted through better **p.**
2Pe   1: 4   his precious and very great **p,**
Wis 12:21   and covenants full of good **p!**

PROMPT* → PROMPTED

Ex   25: 2   from all whose hearts **p** them

PROMPTED* → PROMPT

Mt   14: 8   **P** by her mother, she said,

PRONOUNCE

Jdg   12: 6   "Sibboleth," for he could not **p** it
1Ch 23:13   and **p** blessings in his name forever;

PROOF → PROVE

2Co   8:24   the **p** of your love and of our reason

PROOFS* → PROVE

Isa   41:21   bring your **p,** says the King of Jacob
Ac   1: 3   to them by many convincing **p,**

PROPER

Mt   3:15   for it is **p** for us in this way
1Co 11:13   is it **p** for a woman to pray to God
Jude   1: 6   but left their **p** dwelling,
Sir   31:28   Wine drunk at the **p** time and in

PROPERTY

Ge   23: 4   **p** among you for a burying place,
Lev   25:10   of you, return to your **p**
Mt   12:29   man's house and plunder his **p,**
Lk   15:12   'Father, give me the share of the **p**
Ac   5: 1   his wife Sapphira, sold a piece of **p;**

PROPHECIES → PROPHESY

1Co 13: 8   as for **p,** they will come to an end;
Tob 14: 4   not a single word of the **p** will fail.
Sir   Pr: 2   but even the Law itself, the **P,**

PROPHECY → PROPHESY

Pr   29:18   Where there is no **p,** the people
Ac   21: 9   daughters who had the gift of **p.**
1Co 12:10   to another **p,** to another
     14: 6   some revelation or knowledge or **p**
     14:22   while **p** is not for unbelievers but
2Pe   1:20   that no **p** of scripture is a matter
Rev   1: 3   who reads aloud the words of the **p,**
   19:10   testimony of Jesus is the spirit of **p.**
   22: 7   one who keeps the words of the **p**
   22:18   who hears the words of the **p**
Tob   2: 6   Then I remembered the **p** of Amos,

PROPHESIED → PROPHESY

Nu   11:25   the spirit rested upon them, they **p.**
Jer   2: 8   the prophets **p** by Baal,
   26:11   because he has **p** against this city,
Mt   11:13   prophets and the law **p** until John
Mk   7: 6   "Isaiah **p** rightly about you
Jn   11:51   high priest that year he **p** that Jesus
Ac   19: 6   and they spoke in tongues and **p—**
Jude   1:14   seventh generation from Adam, **p,**

PROPHESIES → PROPHESY

2Ch 18: 7   for he never **p** anything favorable
Jer   28: 9   As for the prophet who **p** peace,
Eze 12:27   years ahead; he **p** for distant times."
1Co 11: 4   Any man who prays or **p** with
     14: 5   One who **p** is greater than one

PROPHESY → PROPHECIES,
PROPHECY, PROPHESIED, PROPHESIES,
PROPHESYING, PROPHET, PROPHET'S,
PROPHETESS, PROPHETIC, PROPHETS

Isa   30:10   "Do not **p** to us what is right;
Jer   5:31   the prophets **p** falsely,
Eze   13: 2   **p** against the prophets of Israel
   13:17   who **p** out of their own imagination;
    34: 2   **p** against the shepherds of Israel:
    37: 4   he said to me, "**P** to these bones,
Joel   2:28   sons and your daughters shall **p,**
Am   2:12   saying, "You shall not **p.**"
     7:16   You say, 'Do not **p** against Israel,
Mt   7:22   Lord, did we not **p** in your name,
Lk   22:64   him and kept asking him, "**P!**
Ac   2:17   sons and your daughters shall **p,**
1Co 13: 9   only in part, and we **p** only in part;
     14: 5   in tongues, but even more to **p.**
     14: 39   So, my friends, be eager to **p,**
Rev 11: 3   my two witnesses authority to **p**

PROPHESYING → PROPHESY

Nu   11:27   Eldad and Medad are **p** in the camp.
Jer   14:14   They are **p** to you a lying vision,
Rev 11: 6   may fall during the days of their **p,**

PROPHET → PROPHESY

Ex   7: 1   your brother Aaron shall be your **p.**
Dt   18:18   a **p** like you from among their own
   18:18   put my words in the mouth of the **p,**
   18:22   a **p** speaks in the name of the LORD
   34:10   arisen a **p** in Israel like Moses,
1Sa   3:20   Samuel was a trustworthy **p** of the
      9: 9   a **p** was formerly called a seer.)
1Ki   1: 8   son of Jehoiada, and the **p** Nathan,

   18:36   the **p** Elijah came near and said,
   22: 7   Is there no other **p** of the LORD here
2Ki   5: 8   may learn that there is a **p** in Israel."
     6:12   It is Elisha, the **p** in Israel,
     20: 1   The **p** Isaiah son of Amoz came to
2Ch 35:18   since the days of the **p** Samuel;
   36:12   before the **p** Jeremiah who spoke
Ezr   6:14   of the **p** Haggai and Zechariah
Jer   1: 5   I appointed you a **p** to the nations."
   23:11   Both **p** and priest are ungodly;
     28: 1   the **p** Hananiah son of Azzur,
Eze   2: 5   shall know that there has been a **p**
   33:33   know that a **p** has been among them.
Da   9: 2   word of the LORD to the **p** Jeremiah,
Hos   9: 7   The **p** is a fool, the man of the spirit
Am   7:14   answered Amaziah, "I am no **p,**
Hab   1: 1   oracle that the **p** Habakkuk saw.
Hag   1: 1   of the LORD came by the **p** Haggai
Zec   1: 1   to the **p** Zechariah son of Berechiah
Mal   4: 5   the **p** Elijah before the great and
Mt   10:41   welcomes a **p** in the name of a **p**
     11: 9   Yes, I tell you, and more than a **p.**
   12:39   to it except the sign of the **p** Jonah.
Lk   1:76   be called the **p** of the Most High;
     4:24   no **p** is accepted in the prophet's
     7:16   "A great **p** has risen among us!"
     20: 6   are convinced that John was a **p.**"
   24:19   a **p** mighty in deed and word before
Jn   1:21   "Are you the **p?**"
     7:40   crowd said, "This is really the **p.**"
Ac   7:37   a **p** for you from your own people
     13: 6   a certain magician, a Jewish false **p,**
   21:10   a **p** named Agabus came down
1Co 14:37   Anyone who claims to be a **p,**
Rev 16:13   and from the mouth of the false **p.**
   19:20   the false **p** who had performed in
   20:10   where the beast and the false **p** were
Aza   1:15   In our day we have no ruler, or **p,**
1Mc   4:46   until a **p** should come to tell what
   14:41   until a trustworthy **p** should arise,
2Es   1: 1   The book of the **p** Ezra

PROPHET'S → PROPHESY

Am   7:14   "I am no prophet, nor a **p** son;
Mt   10:41   will receive a **p** reward;
Lk   4:24   is accepted in the **p** hometown.

PROPHETESS* → PROPHESY

Jdg   4: 4   Deborah, a **p,** wife of Lappidoth,
2Ki 22:14   the **p** Huldah the wife of Shallum
Ne   6:14   also the **p** Noadiah and the rest of
Isa   8: 3   And I went to the **p,**

PROPHETIC → PROPHESY

1Sa 10:10   and he fell into a **p** frenzy,
   19:23   he fell into a **p** frenzy,
1Co 13: 2   And if I have **p** powers,
2Pe   1:19   **p** message more fully confirmed.

PROPHETS → PROPHESY

Nu   11:29   that all the LORD's people were **p,**
1Sa 10:11   Is Saul also among the **p?**"
   19:24   said, "Is Saul also among the **p?**"
     28: 6   not by dreams, or by Urim, or by **p.**
1Ki 18: 4   Jezebel was killing off the **p** of the
   18:40   said to them, "Seize the **p** of Baal;
   19:10   and killed your **p** with the sword.
2Ki 17:23   through all his servants the **p.**
1Ch 16:22   anointed ones; do my **p** no harm."
2Ch 18:22   spirit in the mouth of these your **p;**
Ne   9:30   them by your spirit through your **p;**
Ps 105:15   anointed ones; do my **p** no harm."
Jer   5:13   The **p** are nothing but wind,
   14:14   **p** are prophesying lies in my name;
     23: 9   Concerning the **p:** My heart is
   23:30   See, therefore, I am against the **p,**
La   2: 9   **p** obtain no vision from the LORD.
Eze 13: 2   the **p** of Israel who are prophesying;
Hos   6: 5   I have hewn them by the **p,**
Mic   3: 6   The sun shall go down upon the **p,**
Zep   3: 4   Its **p** are reckless, faithless persons;
Zec   1: 5   And the **p,** do they live forever?
Mt   5:17   come to abolish the law or the **p;**

7:12 for this is the law and the **p.**
7:15 false **p,** who come to you in sheep's
22:40 hang all the law and the **p."**
24:24 false **p** will appear and produce
Lk   6:23 is what their ancestors did to the **p.**
10:24 that many **p** and kings desired
11:49 'I will send them **p** and apostles,
16:29 'They have Moses and the **p;**
24:25 believe all that the **p** have declared!
24:44 **p,** and the psalms must be fulfilled."
Ac   3:24 all the **p,** as many as have spoken,
10:43 All the **p** testify about him
13: 1 Antioch there were **p** and teachers:
26:22 but what the **p** and Moses said
28:23 the law of Moses and from the **p,**
Ro   1: 2 promised beforehand through his **p**
3:21 and is attested by the law and the **p,**
11: 3 "Lord, they have killed your **p,**
1Co 12:28 the church first apostles, second **p,**
12:29 Are all apostles? Are all **p?**
14:32 the spirits of **p** are subject to the **p,**
Eph   2:20 the foundation of the apostles and **p,**
3: 5 revealed to his holy apostles and **p**
4:11 some **p,** some evangelists,
1Th   2:15 both the Lord Jesus and the **p,**
Heb   1: 1 in many and various ways by the **p,**
1Pe   1:10 the **p** who prophesied of the grace
2Pe   2: 1 false **p** also arose among the people,
3: 2 spoken in the past by the holy **p,**
1Jn   4: 1 for many false **p** have gone out into
Rev 11:10 these two **p** had been a torment to
16: 6 they shed the blood of saints and **p,**
18:20 you saints and apostles and **p!**
22: 6 Lord, the God of the spirits of the **p,**
1Mc 9:27 that **p** ceased to appear among them.
2Es 12:42 of all the **p** you alone are left to us,

COMPANY OF PROPHETS 1Sa 19:20;
1Ki 20:35; 2Ki 2:3, 5, 7, 15; 4:1, 38, 38; 5:22;
6:1; 9:1

FALSE PROPHETS Mt 7:15; 24:11, 24;
Mk 13:22; Lk 6:26; 2Pe 2:1; 1Jn 4:1

SERVANTS THE PROPHETS 2Ki 9:7;
17:13, 23; 21:10; 24:2; Ezr 9:11; Jer 7:25;
25:4; 26:5; 29:19; 35:15; 44:4; Eze 38:17; Da
9:6, 10; Am 3:7; Zec 1:6; Rev 10:7; 11:18; Bar
2:20, 24; 1Es 8:82; 2Es 1:32; 2:1

PROPORTION
Dt   16:10 in **p** to the blessing that you have
Ro   12: 6 prophecy, in **p** to faith;
Sir 28:10 In **p** to the fuel, so will the fire burn,

PROPOSED
Ac   1:23 they **p** two, Joseph called Barsabbas

PROSPER → PROSPERED,
PROSPERING, PROSPERITY, PROSPEROUS
Ge   39: 3 LORD caused all that he did to **p**
39:23 he did, the LORD made it **p.**
1Ki   2: 3 so that you may **p** in all that you do
Ps   1: 3 In all that they do, they **p.**
Pr   17:20 The crooked mind do not **p,**
28:13 who conceals transgressions will **p,**
Isa 53:10 the will of the LORD shall **p.**
Jer 12: 1 Why does the way of the guilty **p?**
Tob   4: 6 act in accordance with truth will **p**
Sir 15:10 and the Lord will make it **p.**

PROSPERED → PROSPER
1Ch 29:23 he **p,** and all Israel obeyed him.
2Ch 14: 7 So they built and **p.**
31:21 with all his heart; and he **p.**
Da   6:28 So this Daniel **p** during the reign of
1Mc 4:55 blessed Heaven, who had **p** them.

PROSPERING → PROSPER
Dt   30: 9 will again take delight in **p** you,

PROSPERITY → PROSPER
Dt   28:11 LORD will make you abound in **p,**
30:15 have set before you today life and **p,**
Job 21:16 **p** indeed their own achievement?
36:11 they complete their days in **p,**

Ps   25:13 in **p,** and their children shall possess
73: 3 I saw the **p** of the wicked.
Pr   8:18 are with me, enduring wealth and **p.**
13:21 but **p** rewards the righteous.
Isa 48:18 your **p** would have been like a river,
Sir 12: 8 A friend is not known in **p,**

PROSPEROUS → PROSPER
Dt   30: 9 God will make you abundantly **p**
Jos   1: 8 For then you shall make your way **p**

PROSTITUTE → PROSTITUTED,
PROSTITUTES
Ge   38:15 he thought her to be a **p,**
Ex   34:15 they **p** themselves to their gods
Dt   23:17 sons of Israel shall be a temple **p.**
23:18 not bring the fee of a **p**
Jos   2: 1 a **p** whose name was Rahab,
6:25 the **p,** with her family and all who
Pr   7:10 toward him, decked out like a **p,**
23:27 a **p** is a deep pit; an adulteress is a
1Co   6:15 and make them members of a **p?**
6:16 is united to a **p** becomes one body
Heb 11:31 By faith Rahab the **p** did not perish
Jas   2:25 the **p** also justified by works when

PROSTITUTED → PROSTITUTE
Ps 106:39 and **p** themselves in their doings.

PROSTITUTES → PROSTITUTE
1Ki   3:16 two women who were **p** came to
14:24 also male temple **p** in the land.
15:12 He put away the male temple **p** out
Pr   29: 3 **p** is to squander one's substance.
Joel   3: 3 traded boys for **p,** and sold girls for
Mt   21:31 the **p** are going into the kingdom of
Lk   15:30 has devoured your property with **p,**
1Co   6: 9 idolaters, adulterers, male **p,**
Sir   9: 6 Do not give yourself to **p,**

PROSTRATE
Dt   9:18 I lay **p** before the LORD as before,
Eze   9: 8 I fell **p** on my face and cried out,
Da   8:17 I became frightened and fell **p.**

PROTECT → PROTECTED,
PROTECTION, PROTECTOR, PROTECTS
Ps   12: 7 You, O LORD, will **p** us;
20: 1 name of the God of Jacob **p** you!
91:14 I will **p** those who know my name.
140: 1 **p** me from those who are violent,
Jn   17:11 **p** them in your name that you have
17:15 ask you to **p** them from the evil one.

PROTECTED → PROTECT
Jos 24:17 He **p** us along all the way that we
Mk   6:20 and holy man, and he **p** him.
Jn   17:12 I **p** them in your name that you

PROTECTION → PROTECT
Ps   5:11 Spread your **p** over them,
Ecc   7:12 **p** of wisdom is like the **p** of money,

PROTECTOR → PROTECT
Ps   68: 5 and **p** of widows is God in his holy
Da   12: 1 great prince, the **p** of your people,
Sir 51: 2 for you have been my **p** and helper

PROTECTS → PROTECT
Ps 116: 6 The LORD **p** the simple;
Jdt   9:14 no other who **p** the people of Israel

PROTEST*
Lk   10:11 we wipe off in **p** against you.
Ac   13:51 shook the dust off their feet in **p**
18: 6 in **p** he shook the dust from his

PROUD → PRIDE
2Ch 32:25 done to him, for his heart was **p.**
Ps   94: 2 give to the **p** what they deserve!
Pr   16:19 than to divide the spoil with the **p.**
21: 4 Haughty eyes and a **p** heart—
Isa   2:12 has a day against all that is **p**
Eze 28:17 heart was **p** because of your beauty;

Hos 13: 6 satisfied, and their heart was **p;**
Ob   1: 3 Your **p** heart has deceived you,
Ro   11:20 do not become **p,** but stand in awe.
Jas   4: 6 God opposes the **p,** but gives grace
1Pe   5: 5 God opposes the **p,** but gives grace
Sir 10: 9 How can dust and ashes be **p?**

PROVE → PROOF, PROOFS, PROVED,
PROVING
Ezr   2:59 not **p** their families or their descent,
Ps   26: 2 **P** me, O LORD, and try me;
Heb   6:18 impossible that God would **p** false,

PROVED → PROVE
Dt   17: 4 and the charge is **p** true that such
Ro   3: 4 let God be **p** true,

PROVERB → PROVERBS
Ps   49: 4 I will incline my ear to a **p;**
Pr   26: 7 so does a **p** in the mouth of a fool.
26: 9 is a **p** in the mouth of a fool.
Eze 18: 3 this **p** shall no more be used by you
Lk   4:23 you will quote to me this **p,** 'Doctor,
Sir 20:20 **p** from a fool's lips will be rejected,

PROVERBS → PROVERB
1Ki   4:32 He composed three thousand **p,**
Job 13:12 Your maxims are **p** of ashes,
Pr   1: 1 The **p** of Solomon son of David,
10: 1 The **p** of Solomon.
25: 1 These are other **p** of Solomon that
Ecc 12: 9 and studying and arranging many **p.**
Sir 39: 3 seeks out the hidden meanings of **p**

PROVIDE → PROVIDED, PROVIDES,
PROVISION, PROVISIONED, PROVISIONS
Ge   22: 8 "God himself will **p** the lamb for
22:14 called that place "The LORD will **p"**
Isa 61: 3 to **p** for those who mourn in Zion—
1Co 10:13 testing he will also **p** the way out so
1Ti   5: 8 whoever does not **p** for relatives,

PROVIDED → PROVIDE
Ge   22:14 mount of the LORD it shall be **p."**
1Ki   8:21 There I have a place for the ark,
1Ch 29: 2 I have **p** for the house of my God,
Ps   68:10 O God, you **p** for the needy.
Jnh   1:17 the LORD **p** a large fish to swallow
Ro   11:22 **p** you continue in his kindness,
Heb 11:40 since God had **p** something better so

PROVIDES → PROVIDE
Ps 111: 5 He **p** food for those who fear him;
Pr   31:15 night and **p** food for her household
1Ti   6:17 who richly **p** us with everything

PROVING* → PROVE
Ac   9:22 by **p** that Jesus was the Messiah.
17: 3 and **p** that it was necessary for the

PROVISION → PROVIDE
Ro   13:14 and make no **p** for the flesh,

PROVISIONS → PROVIDE
Ps 132:15 I will abundantly bless its **p;**

PROVOCATION → PROVOKE
Pr   27: 3 but a fool's **p** is heavier than both.

PROVOKE → PROVOCATION,
PROVOKED, PROVOKES
Dt   32:21 **p** them with a foolish nation.
1Ki 16:33 Ahab did more to **p** the anger of the
Jer 25: 6 not **p** me to anger with the work of
Eze   8:17 and **p** my anger still further?
Heb 10:24 how to **p** one another to love

PROVOKED → PROVOKE
Dt   9: 7 you **p** the LORD your God to wrath
Jdg   2:12 and they **p** the LORD to anger.
Ps   78:41 and **p** the Holy One of Israel.
Jer   8:19 ("Why have they **p** me to anger
Bar   4: 7 For you **p** the one who made you
Man   1:10 for I have **p** your wrath

PROVOKES → PROVOKE
Eze   8: 3 of jealousy, which **p** to jealousy.

PROWLS*
1Pe   5: 8 your adversary the devil **p** around,

PRUDENCE → PRUDENT
Pr   1: 4 knowledge and **p** to the young—
       8: 5 learn **p**; acquire intelligence,
       8:12 live with **p**, and I attain knowledge
      19:25 and the simple will learn **p**;
Wis   8: 7 for she teaches self-control and **p**,

PRUDENT → PRUDENCE
Pr   12:16 but the **p** ignore an insult.
      19:14 but a **p** wife is from the LORD.
Jer   49: 7 Has counsel perished from the **p?**
Am   5:13 the **p** will keep silent in such a time;
Tit   1: 8 a lover of goodness, **p**, upright,
       2: 2 men to be temperate, serious, **p**,

PRUNES → PRUNING
Jn   15: 2 he **p** to make it bear more fruit.

PRUNING → PRUNES
Isa   2: 4 and their spears into **p** hooks;
Joel   3:10 and your **p** hooks into spears;
Mic   4: 3 and their spears into **p** hooks;

PSALM → PSALMS
Ps   47: 7 sing praises with a **p**.
Ac   13:33 in the second **p**, 'You are my Son';
Jdt   16: 1 Raise to him a new **p**;
Pm 151: T This **p** is ascribed to David

PSALMS → PSALM
Lk   20:42 David himself says in the book of **P**,
      24:44 and the **p** must be fulfilled."
Ac   1:20 "For it is written in the book of **P**,
Eph   5:19 you sing **p** and hymns and spiritual
Col   3:16 with gratitude in your hearts sing **p**,

PTOLEMY
1Mc   1:18 engaged King **P** of Egypt in battle,
      10:51 ambassadors to **P** king of Egypt
      11:16 and King **P** was triumphant.

PUBLIC → PUBLICLY
Mt   1:19 to expose her to **p** disgrace,
Col   2:15 and made a **p** example of them,
1Ti   4:13 to the **p** reading of scripture.

PUBLICLY → PUBLIC
Lk   1:80 the day he appeared **p** to Israel.
Ac   20:20 teaching you **p** and from house to
Gal   3: 1 Christ was **p** exhibited as crucified!
Heb   10:33 sometimes being **p** exposed to abuse

PUFFED → PUFFS
Col   2:18 **p** up without cause by a human way
1Ti   3: 6 or he may be **p** up with conceit

PUFFS* → PUFFED
1Co   8: 1 Knowledge **p** up, but love builds up.

PUL → =TIGLATH-PILESER
2Ki   15:19 **P** of Assyria came against the land;

PULL → PULLED, PULLS
Ru   2:16 You must also **p** out some handfuls
Jer   38:10 and **p** the prophet Jeremiah up

PULLED → PULL
Jdg   6:32 because he **p** down his altar.
2Ki   23:15 he **p** down that altar along with the
Ezr   9: 3 and **p** hair from my head and beard,
Ne   13:25 beat some of them and **p** out their

PULLS → PULL
Mt   9:16 for the patch **p** away from the cloak,

PUNISH → PUNISHED, PUNISHING,
PUNISHMENT
Ex   32:34 I will **p** them for their sin."

2Sa   7:14 I will **p** him with a rod such as
Isa   13:11 I will **p** the world for its evil,
Jer   2:19 Your wickedness will **p** you,
      21:14 I will **p** you according to the fruit of
Hos   10:10 the wayward people to **p** them;
Zep   1:12 **p** the people who rest complacently
Ac   4:21 finding no way to **p** them because
1Pe   2:14 by him to **p** those who do wrong
Sir   5: 3 for the Lord will surely **p** you.

PUNISHED → PUNISH
Lev   18:25 and I **p** it for its iniquity,
Ezr   9:13 have **p** us less than our iniquities
Jer   6: 6 This is the city that must be **p**;

PUNISHING* → PUNISH
Ex   20: 5 **p** children for the iniquity of parents
Dt   5: 9 **p** children for the iniquity of parents
Joel   2:13 in steadfast love, and relents from **p**.
Jnh   4: 2 and ready to relent from **p**.
Ac   26:11 **p** them often in all the synagogues

PUNISHMENT → PUNISH
Ge   4:13 "My **p** is greater than I can bear!
Ps   91: 8 look with your eyes and see the **p**
Pr   16:22 but folly is the **p** of fools.
Isa   53: 5 was the **p** that made us whole,
La   4: 6 greater than the **p** of Sodom,
Hos   9: 7 The days of **p** have come,
Mt   25:46 these will go away into eternal **p**,
2Pe   2: 9 under **p** until the day of judgment
1Jn   4:18 for fear has to do with **p**,
Jude   1: 7 by undergoing a **p** of eternal fire.
Sir   5: 7 and at the time of **p** you will perish.

PUR → PURIM
Est   3: 7 they cast **P**—which means "the lot"

PURE → PURIFICATION, PURIFIED,
PURIFY, PURITY
Ex   25:11 You shall overlay it with **p** gold,
      25:31 shall make a lampstand of **p** gold.
      37: 6 He made a mercy seat of **p** gold;
2Sa   22:27 with the **p** you show yourself **p**,
1Ki   6:21 the inside of the house with **p** gold,
Job   4:17 beings be **p** before their Maker?
Ps   19: 9 the fear of the LORD is **p**, enduring
      24: 4 who have clean hands and **p** hearts,
     119: 9 can young people keep their way **p?**
Pr   15:26 but gracious words are **p**.
      20: 9 I am **p** from my sin"?
      20:11 whether what they do is **p** and right.
Hab   1:13 Your eyes are too **p** to behold evil,
Mt   5: 8 "Blessed are the **p** in heart, for they
Php   1:10 in the day of Christ you may be **p**
       4: 8 whatever is **p**, whatever is pleasing,
1Ti   1: 5 that comes from a **p** heart,
       5:22 of others; keep yourself **p**.
2Ti   2:22 who call on the Lord from a **p** heart.
Tit   1:15 To the **p** all things are **p**,
       1:15 corrupt and unbelieving nothing is **p**
Heb   10:22 our bodies washed with **p** water.
Jas   1:27 Religion that is **p** and undefiled
       3:17 the wisdom from above is first **p**,
1Jn   3: 3 purify themselves, just as he is **p**.
Rev   21:18 of jasper, while the city is **p** gold,
Tob   8:15 O God, with every **p** blessing;
Wis   7:25 and a **p** emanation of the glory

PURE GOLD Ex 25:11, 17, 24, 29, 31, 36,
38, 39; 28:14, 22, 36; 30:3; 37:2, 6, 11, 16, 17,
22, 23, 24, 26; 39:15, 25, 30; Lev 24:4, 6; 1Ki
6:20, 21; 7:49, 50; 10:21; 1Ch 28:17; 2Ch 3:4;
4:20, 22; 9:17, 20; 13:11; Job 28:19; La 4:1;
Rev 21:18, 21; Tob 13:16; Bar 3:30

PURGE → PURGES
Dt   13: 5 you shall **p** the evil from your midst.
      19:19 you shall **p** the evil from your midst.
Ps   51: 7 **P** me with hyssop, and I shall be

PURGES* → PURGE
Tob   12: 9 and **p** away every sin.

PURIFICATION → PURE
Lk   2:22 the time came for their **p** according
Jn   2: 6 water jars for the Jewish rites of **p**,
Ac   21:24 go through the rite of **p** with them,
Heb   1: 3 When he had made **p** for sins,
2Mc   1:18 shall celebrate the **p** of the temple,

PURIFIED → PURE
Ezr   6:20 the priests and the Levites had **p**
Ne   12:30 And the priests and the Levites
Ps   12: 6 on the ground, **p** seven times.
Da   12:10 Many shall be **p**, cleansed, and
1Pe   1:22 **p** your souls by your obedience to

PURIFY → PURE
Nu   19:12 shall **p** themselves with the water on
Mal   3: 3 he will **p** the descendants of Levi
Tit   2:14 **p** for himself a people of his own
Heb   9:14 **p** our conscience from dead works
Jas   4: 8 **p** your hearts, you double-minded.
1Jn   3: 3 all who have this hope in him **p**

PURIM → PUR
Est   9:26 are called **P**, from the word Pur.

PURITY → PURE
2Co   6: 6 by **p**, knowledge, patience, kindness
1Ti   4:12 and conduct, in love, in faith, in **p**.
       5: 2 as sisters—with absolute **p**.
1Pe   3: 2 the **p** and reverence of your lives.
Sir   51:20 my soul to her, and in **p** I found her.

PURPLE
Ex   25: 4 **p**, and crimson yarns and fine linen,
Pr   31:22 her clothing is fine linen and **p**.
Da   5:29 and Daniel was clothed in **p**,
Mk   15:17 And they clothed him in a **p** cloak;
Rev   17: 4 woman was clothed in **p** and scarlet,
      18:16 in **p** and scarlet, adorned with gold,

PURPOSE → PURPOSED, PURPOSES
Ps   57: 2 to God who fulfills his **p** for me.
     138: 8 The LORD will fulfil his **p** for me;
Pr   19:21 it is the **p** of the LORD that will be
Isa   46:10 saying, "My **p** shall stand,
      55:11 it shall accomplish that which I **p**,
Ro   8:28 who are called according to his **p**.
       9:11 God's **p** of election might continue,
       9:17 the very **p** of showing my power in
1Co   3: 8 one who waters have a common **p**,
Eph   1:11 to the **p** of him who accomplishes
       3:11 was in accordance with the eternal **p**
2Ti   1: 9 works but according to his own **p**
Heb   6:17 the unchangeable character of his **p**,
Rev   17:17 hearts to carry out his **p** by agreeing

PURPOSED → PURPOSE
La   2:17 The LORD has done what he **p**,
Zec   8:15 I have **p** in these days to do good

PURPOSES → PURPOSE
Pr   20: 5 The **p** in the human mind are like

PURSE → PURSES
Lk   10: 4 Carry no **p**, no bag, no sandals;
      22:36 the one who has a **p** must take it,
Jn   13:29 because Judas had the common **p**,

PURSES* → PURSE
Lk   12:33 Make **p** for yourselves that do not

PURSUE → PURSUED, PURSUES
Dt   19: 6 of blood in hot anger might **p**
Ps   34:14 and do good; seek peace, and **p** it.
Isa   51: 1 to me, you that **p** righteousness,
Ro   14:19 Let us then **p** what makes for peace
1Co   14: 1 **P** love and strive for the spiritual
1Ti   6:11 **p** righteousness, godliness, faith,
2Ti   2:22 passions and **p** righteousness,
Heb   12:14 **P** peace with everyone, and the
1Pe   3:11 let them seek peace and **p** it.
Sir   27: 8 If you **p** justice, you will attain it

PURSUED → PURSUE

Ex 14:23 Egyptians **p,** and went into the sea
Ps 18:37 I **p** my enemies and overtook them;

PURSUES → PURSUE

Lev 26:17 you shall flee though no one **p** you.
Pr 11:19 but whoever **p** evil will die.
    13:21 Misfortune **p** sinners, but prosperity
    21:21 Whoever **p** righteousness
    28: 1 The wicked flee when no one **p,**
Sir 31: 5 **p** money will be led astray by it.

PUT → PUTS, PUTTING

Ge   2:15 and **p** him in the garden of Eden to
    3:15 I will **p** enmity between you and
    4:15 And the LORD **p** a mark on Cain.
    24: 2 "**P** your hand under my thigh
    47:29 **p** your hand under my thigh and
Ex   4: 6 "**P** your hand inside your cloak."
    4: 6 He **p** his hand into his cloak;
Nu 17:10 "**P** back the staff of Aaron before
1Sa   5: 3 So they took Dagon and **p** him back
    7: 4 So Israel **p** away the Baals and the
1Ki 11:36 where I have chosen to **p** my name.
2Ch 33: 7 I will **p** my name forever;
Ps 25: 2 do not let me be **p** to shame;
    40: 3 He **p** a new song in my mouth,
Isa 11: 8 shall **p** its hand on the adder's den.
    42: 1 I have **p** my spirit upon him;
    59:17 He **p** on righteousness like a
Jer   1: 9 I have **p** my words in your mouth.
    32:14 and **p** them in an earthenware jar,
Eze 36:27 I will **p** my spirit within you,
    37:14 I will **p** my spirit within you,
Mt   4: 7 not **p** the Lord your God to the test.'
    12:18 I will **p** my Spirit upon him,
Mk 12:44 has **p** in everything she had,
Jn 20:25 **p** my finger in the mark of the nails
Ro   8:13 the Spirit you **p** to death the deeds
    9:33 in him will not be **p** to shame."
    10:11 believes in him will be **p** to shame."
1Co 13:11 adult, I **p** an end to childish ways.
    15:25 reign until he has **p** all his enemies
Eph   6:11 **P** on the whole armor of God,
Heb   8:10 I will **p** my laws in their minds,
1Pe   3:18 He was **p** to death in the flesh,
Sir 24:22 obeys me will not be **p** to shame,
    51:26 **P** your neck under her yoke,
2Es 12:37 **p** it in a hidden place;

PUTS → PUT

Nu 23:12 what the LORD **p** into my mouth?"
Lk   9:62 "No one who **p** a hand to the plow

PUTTING → PUT

Eph   4:25 So then, **p** away falsehood,
Col   2:11 by **p** off the body of the flesh

Q

QUAILS

Ex 16:13 In the evening **q** came up
Nu 11:31 and it brought **q** from the sea and
Ps 105:40 They asked, and he brought **q,**
Wis 16: 2 and you prepared **q** to eat,
2Es   1:15 The **q** were a sign to you;

QUAKE → EARTHQUAKE,
EARTHQUAKES, QUAKED, QUAKES

Ps 60: 2 You have caused the land to **q;**
Na   1: 5 The mountains **q** before him,

QUAKED → QUAKE

Jdg   5: 5 The mountains **q** before the LORD,
2Sa 22: 8 of the heavens trembled and **q,**
Isa 64: 3 the mountains **q** at your presence.

QUAKES → QUAKE

Joel 2:10 earth **q** before them, the heavens

QUARREL → QUARRELED,
QUARRELING, QUARRELS, QUARRELSOME

Pr 17:14 so stop before the **q** breaks out.
    20: 3 but every fool is quick to **q.**
    26:17 who meddles in the **q** of another.
Sir 28:11 A hasty **q** kindles a fire,

QUARRELED → QUARREL

Ex 17: 7 the Israelites **q** and tested the LORD,
Nu 20: 3 The people **q** with Moses and said,

QUARRELING → QUARREL

Ro 13:13 not in **q** and jealousy.
1Co   3: 3 there is jealousy and **q** among you,
2Co 12:20 I fear that there may perhaps be **q,**

QUARRELS → QUARREL

2Ti   2:23 you know that they breed **q.**
Tit   3: 9 dissensions, and **q** about the law,

QUARRELSOME* → QUARREL

Pr 26:21 so is a **q** person for kindling strife.
1Ti   3: 3 not **q,** and not a lover of money.
2Ti   2:24 the Lord's servant must not be **q**

QUEEN

1Ki 10: 1 the **q** of Sheba heard of the fame of
2Ch 15:16 from being **q** mother because she
Est   1:12 But **Q** Vashti refused to come at
    2:17 and made her **q** instead of Vashti.
Jer   7:18 to make cakes for the **q** of heaven;
Eze 16:13 exceedingly beautiful, fit to be a **q.**
Mt 12:42 The **q** of the South will rise up at
Ac   8:27 of the Candace, **q** of the Ethiopians,
Rev 18: 7 in her heart she says, 'I rule as a **q;**

QUENCH → QUENCHED

SS   8: 7 Many waters cannot **q** love,
Isa   1:31 with no one to **q** them.
Jer   4: 4 and burn with no one to **q** it,

QUENCHED → QUENCH

2Ki 22:17 and it will not be **q.**
Isa 66:24 their fire shall not be **q,**
Jer   7:20 it will burn and not be **q,**
Mk   9:48 and the fire is never **q.**
Heb 11:34 **q** raging fire, escaped the edge of

QUESTION → QUESTIONS

Job 38: 3 like a man, I will **q** you,
    40: 7 I will **q** you, and you declare to me.
Mt 22:35 a lawyer, asked him a **q** to test him.
Mk 11:29 said to them, "I will ask you one **q;**
Sir 19:15 **Q** a friend, for often it is slander;

QUESTIONS → QUESTION

2Ch   9: 1 to Jerusalem to test him with hard **q,**
Mt 22:46 anyone dare to ask him any more **q.**

QUICK → QUICK-TEMPERED, QUICKLY

Pr 20: 3 but every fool is **q** to quarrel.
Ecc   5: 2 nor let your heart be **q** to utter a
    7: 9 Do not be **q** to anger,
Jas   1:19 be **q** to listen, slow to speak,
Sir   5:11 Be **q** to hear, but deliberate

QUICK-TEMPERED* → QUICK,
TEMPER

Pr 14:17 One who is **q** acts foolishly,
Tit   1: 7 he must not be arrogant or **q**
Sir   8:16 Do not pick a fight with the **q,**

QUICKLY → QUICK

Jos 23:16 shall perish **q** from the good land
Ps 22:19 O my help, come **q** to my aid!
Ecc   4:12 A threefold cord is not **q** broken.
Mt 28: 7 Then go **q** and tell his disciples,
Jn 13:27 "Do **q** what you are going to do."
Ro   9:28 execute his sentence on the earth **q**
Gal   1: 6 so **q** deserting the one who called
Sir 19: 4 One who trusts others too **q**

QUIET → QUIETED, QUIETLY, QUIETNESS

Pr 17: 1 Better is a dry morsel with **q** than

Ecc   9:17 The **q** words of the wise are more to
1Ti   2: 2 **q** and peaceable life in all godliness
1Pe   3: 4 beauty of a gentle and **q** spirit,

QUIETED → QUIET

Ps 131: 2 But I have calmed and **q** my soul,

QUIETLY → QUIET

La   3:26 wait **q** for the salvation of the LORD.
Mt   1:19 planned to dismiss her **q.**
1Th   4:11 to live **q,** to mind your own affairs,
Sir 21:20 but the wise smile **q.**

QUIETNESS* → QUIET

Isa 30:15 **q** and in trust shall be your strength.
    32:17 result of righteousness, **q** and trust

QUIRINIUS*

Lk   2: 2 while **Q** was governor of Syria.

QUIVER

Ps 127: 5 Happy is the man who has his **q**
           full of them.
Isa 49: 2 in his **q** he hid me away.

QUOTE*

Lk   4:23 you will **q** to me this proverb,

R

RABBI → RABBOUNI

Mt 23: 8 But you are not to be called **r,**
    26:49 to Jesus and said, "Greetings, **R!**"
Jn   1:38 "**R**" (which translated means
           Teacher),

RABBOUNI* → RABBI

Jn 20:16 "**R!**" (which means Teacher).

RACE

Ecc   9:11 the sun the **r** is not to the swift,
1Co   9:24 that in a **r** the runners all compete,
2Ti   4: 7 finished the **r,** I have kept the faith.
Heb 12: 1 let us run with perseverance the **r**
1Pe   2: 9 But you are a chosen **r,** a royal

RACHEL

Daughter of Laban (Ge 29:16); wife of Jacob
(Ge 29:28); bore two sons (Ge 30:22-24; 35:16-
24; 46:19). Stole Laban's gods (Ge 31:19, 32-35).
Death (Ge 35:19-20).

RADIANCE* → RADIANT

Rev 21:11 and a **r** like a very rare jewel,
Wis   7:10 because her **r** never ceases.

RADIANT → RADIANCE

Ps 34: 5 and be **r;** so your faces shall never
SS   5:10 My beloved is all **r** and ruddy,
Isa 60: 5 Then you shall see and be **r;**
Wis   6:12 Wisdom is **r** and unfading,

RAGE → RAGING

Ps 78:21 the LORD heard, he was full of **r;**
Ac   4:25 'Why did the Gentiles **r,** and the

RAGING → RAGE

Jnh   1:15 and the sea ceased from its **r.**
Lk   8:24 rebuked the wind and the **r** waves;

RAGS

Jer 38:12 "Just put the **r** and clothes between

RAGUEL

Tob   3:17 and Sarah, daughter of **R,**
    14:13 of **R** and that of his father Tobit.

RAHAB

Prostitute of Jericho who hid Israelite spies (Jos
2; 6:22-25; Heb 11:31; Jas 2:25). Mother of Boaz
(Mt 1:5).

RAIN → RAINBOW, RAINED, RAINS

Ge   2: 5 the LORD God had not caused it to **r**
       7: 4 For in seven days I will send **r** on
Ex 16: 4 "I am going to **r** bread from heaven
Dt 11:14 the early **r** and the later **r**,
1Ki 17: 1 neither dew nor **r** these years,
     18: 1 I will send **r** on the earth."
2Ch 6:26 no **r** because they have sinned
Job 38:28 the **r** a father, or who has begotten
Ps 147: 8 with clouds, prepares **r** for the earth,
Isa 45: 8 let the skies **r** down righteousness;
Jer 14:22 any idols of the nations bring **r?**
Zec 14:17 there will be no **r** upon them.
Mt   5:45 sends **r** on the righteous and on the
     7:25 The **r** fell, the floods came,
Jas   5:17 prayed fervently that it might not **r**,
Rev 11: 6 so that no **r** may fall during the days
Aza 1:42 "Bless the Lord, all **r** and dew;

RAINBOW → RAIN

Rev 4: 3 the throne is a **r** that looks like an
    10: 1 in a cloud, with a **r** over his head;

RAINED → RAIN

Ge 19:24 **r** on Sodom and Gomorrah sulfur
Ex   9:23 LORD **r** hail on the land of Egypt;
Ps 78:24 he **r** down on them manna to eat,
    78:27 he **r** flesh upon them like dust,
Lk 17:29 it **r** fire and sulfur from heaven and

RAINS → RAIN

Lev 26: 4 I will give you your **r** in their season
Jas   5: 7 receives the early and the late **r**.

RAISE → RISE

Dt 18:15 God will **r** up for you a prophet
1Sa 2:35 will **r** up for myself a faithful priest,
Pr   8: 1 does not understanding **r** her voice?
Isa 11:12 He will **r** a signal for the nations,
    14:13 **r** my throne above the stars of God;
Mt   3: 9 God is able from these stones to **r**
Jn   2:19 and in three days I will **r** it up."
    6:39 but **r** it up on the last day.
Ac   3:22 Lord your God will **r** up for you
1Co 6:14 raised the Lord and will also **r** us
2Co 4:14 who raised the Lord Jesus will **r** us
Heb 11:19 that God is able even to **r** someone

RAISED → RISE

Jdg 2:18 the LORD **r** up judges for them,
Mt 17:23 and on the third day he will be **r**."
Lk   7:22 the deaf hear, the dead are **r**,
Ac   2:24 God **r** him up, having freed him
    10:40 but God **r** him on the third day and
    13:30 But God **r** him from the dead;
Ro   4:25 and was **r** for our justification.
    6: 4 just as Christ was **r** from the dead
    8:11 who **r** Jesus from the dead dwells
    8:11 he who **r** Christ from the dead will
    9:17 I have **r** you up for the very purpose
    10: 9 believe in your heart that God **r** him
1Co 15: 4 **r** on the third day in accordance
    15:20 Christ has been **r** from the dead,
2Co 5:15 him who died and was **r** for them.
Eph 2: 6 and **r** us up with him and seated us
Col 2:12 who **r** him from the dead.

RAISES → RISE

1Sa 2: 8 He **r** up the poor from the dust;
Ps 113: 7 He **r** the poor from the dust,
Jn   5:21 just as the Father **r** the dead and

RAM → RAMS, RAMS'

Ge 22:13 and took the **r** and offered it up as
Ex 29:22 (for it is a **r** of ordination),
Da   8: 3 saw a **r** standing beside the river.

RAMAH

Jer 31:15 A voice is heard in **R,** lamentation
Mt   2:18 "A voice was heard in **R,** wailing

RAMESES

Ex   1:11 built supply cities, Pithom and **R,**

RAMPARTS

Ps 48:13 consider well its **r;**
Lk 19:43 when your enemies will set up **r**

RAMS → RAM

1Sa 15:22 and to heed than the fat of **r**.
Ps 114: 4 mountains skipped like **r**, the hills
Mic 6: 7 be pleased with thousands of **r**,

RAMS' → RAM

Ex 25: 5 tanned **r** skins, fine leather, acacia
Jos   6: 4 bearing seven trumpets of **r** horns

RAN → RUN

Ge 39:12 in her hand, and fled and **r** outside.
1Ki 18:46 his loins and **r** in front of Ahab
Lk 24:12 But Peter got up and **r** to the tomb;

RANGE

2Ch 16: 9 LORD **r** throughout the entire earth,
Zec 4:10 which **r** through the whole earth."

RANK → RANKS

Est 10: 3 Mordecai the Jew was next in **r** to

RANKS → RANK

1Sa 17:10 said, "Today I defy the **r** of Israel!
Jn   1:15 who comes after me **r** ahead of me

RANSOM → RANSOMED

Nu 35:31 you shall accept no **r** for the life of
Ps 49: 8 For the **r** of life is costly, and can
Hos 13:14 I **r** them from the power of Sheol?
Mt 20:28 and to give his life a **r** for many."
Mk 10:45 and to give his life a **r** for many."
1Ti 2: 6 who gave himself a **r** for all

RANSOMED → RANSOM

Isa 35:10 And the **r** of the LORD shall return,
    51:11 So the **r** of the LORD shall return,
Rev 5: 9 by your blood you **r** for God saints

RAPHAEL

Tob 3:17 So **R** was sent to heal both of them:
    5: 4 the angel **R** standing in front of him;
   12:15 I am **R,** one of the seven angels

RARE

1Sa 3: 1 word of the LORD was **r** in those

RASH → RASHLY

Ps 106:33 and he spoke words that were **r**.
Ecc 5: 2 Never be **r** with your mouth,

RASHLY' → RASH

Pr 20:25 for one to say **r**, "It is holy,"

RATHER

Job 32: 2 he justified himself **r** than God;
Mt 10: 6 go **r** to the lost sheep of the house
Jn 11: 4 **r** it is for God's glory,
Ac   5:29 "We must obey God **r** than any
1Co 9:12 we endure anything **r** than put an
    14:19 church I would **r** speak five words

RAVEN → RAVENS

Ge   8: 7 sent out the **r;** and it went to and
Job 38:41 Who provides for the **r** its prey,

RAVENS → RAVEN

1Ki 17: 6 **r** brought him bread and meat in
Ps 147: 9 and to the young **r** when they cry.
Lk 12:24 Consider the **r:** they neither sow

RAW

Ex 12: 9 not eat any of it **r** or boiled in water,
1Sa 2:15 boiled meat from you, but only **r**."

RAZOR

Nu   6: 5 of their nazirite vow no **r** shall come
Jdg 16:17 "A **r** has never come upon my head;
1Sa 1:11 and no **r** shall touch his head."

REACH → REACHED, REACHES

Ex   4: 4 said to Moses, "**R** out your hand,
Jn 20:27 **R** out your hand and put it in my

Sir 35:20 and his prayer will **r** to the clouds.

REACHED → REACH

Ps 18:16 He **r** down from on high, he took
Jn 20: 4 outran Peter and **r** the tomb first.
Php 3:12 or have already **r** the goal;

REACHES → REACH

Ps 108: 4 your faithfulness **r** to the clouds.
Pr 31:20 and **r** out her hands to the needy.

READ → READER, READING, READS

Ex 24: 7 and **r** it in the hearing of the people;
Dt 17:19 with him and he shall **r** in it all
Jos   8:34 he **r** all the words of the law,
2Ki 23: 2 he **r** in their hearing all the words
Ne   8: 8 they **r** from the book, from the law
Isa 34:16 and **r** from the book of the LORD:
Jer 36: 6 You shall **r** them also in the hearing
    36:23 As Jehudi **r** three or four columns,
Da   5:16 to **r** the writing and tell me its
Mk 12:10 Have you not **r** this scripture:
Lk   4:16 as was his custom. He stood up to **r**,
2Co 3: 2 our hearts, to be known and **r** by all;
    3:15 this very day whenever Moses is **r**,

READER → READ

Mt 24:15 Daniel (let the **r** understand),
Mk 13:14 not to be (let the **r** understand),

READING → READ

Ne   8: 8 so that the people understood the **r**.
Ac   8:30 you understand what you are **r?**"
1Ti 4:13 attention to the public **r** of scripture,

READS' → READ

Rev 1: 3 Blessed is the one who **r** aloud the

READY

Ps 119:173 Let your hand be **r** to help me,
Mt 24:44 Therefore you also must be **r**,
    25:10 those who were **r** went with him
Lk   1:17 **r** a people prepared for the Lord."
1Pe 1: 5 a salvation **r** to be revealed in
    3:15 Always be **r** to make your defense
Rev 9:15 who had been held **r** for the hour,
   19: 7 and his bride has made herself **r;**

REAFFIRM'

2Co 2: 8 So I urge you to **r** your love for him.

REALITIES'

Heb 10: 1 and not the true form of these **r**,

REALIZED

Jdg 13:21 Manoah **r** that it was the angel of
1Sa 18:28 when Saul **r** that the LORD was with

REAP → REAPER, REAPERS, REAPS

Lev 19: 9 you shall not **r** to the very edges
Job 4: 8 who plow iniquity and sow trouble **r**
Ps 126: 5 sow in tears **r** with shouts of joy.
Hos 8: 7 and they shall **r** the whirlwind.
    10:12 righteousness; **r** steadfast love;
Lk 12:24 the ravens: they neither sow nor **r**,
Jn   4:38 to **r** that for which you did not labor
1Co 9:11 much if we **r** your material benefits?
2Co 9: 6 sows sparingly will also **r** sparingly,
Gal 6: 7 for you **r** whatever you sow.
Rev 14:15 for the hour to **r** has come,

REAPER → REAP

Jn   4:36 The **r** is already receiving wages

REAPERS → REAP

Mt 13:39 and the **r** are angels.

REAPS' → REAP

Am 9:13 plows shall overtake the one who **r**,
Jn   4:37 'One sows and another **r**.'

REAR

Nu 10:25 as the **r** guard of all the camps,
Jos   6: 9 the **r** guard came after the ark,
Isa 52:12 God of Israel will be your **r** guard.

REASON → REASONED
Mt 19: 5 this **r** a man shall leave his father
Jn 12:27 this **r** that I have come to this hour.
Ro   4:16 For this **r** it depends on faith,
Heb 9:15 For this **r** he is the mediator of a
2Pe 1: 5 For this very **r**, you must make

REASONED → REASON
1Co 13:11 thought like a child, I **r** like a child;

REBEKAH
Sister of Laban, secured as bride for Isaac (Ge 24). Mother of Esau and Jacob (Ge 25:19-26). Taken by Abimelech as sister of Isaac; returned (Ge 26:1-11). Encouraged Jacob to trick Isaac out of blessing (Ge 27:1-17).

REBEL → REBELLED, REBELLION, REBELLIOUS, REBELS
Ex 23:21 do not **r** against him, for he will
Nu 14: 9 Only, do not **r** against the LORD;
Jos 22:18 If you **r** against the LORD today,
1Sa 12:14 not **r** against the commandment

REBELLED → REBEL
Nu 20:24 because you **r** against my command
Dt   1:26 You **r** against the command of
Ne   9:26 they were disobedient and **r**
Ps 78:56 tested the Most High God, and **r**
Isa 63:10 they **r** and grieved his holy spirit;

REBELLION → REBEL
Jos 22:16 an altar today in **r** against the LORD?
1Sa 15:23 For **r** is no less a sin than divination,
2Th 2: 3 the **r** comes first and the lawless one
Heb 3: 8 not harden your hearts as in the **r,**

REBELLIOUS → REBEL
Dt 21:18 **r** son who will not obey his father
Ps 78: 8 a stubborn and **r** generation,
Eze 2: 5 to hear (for they are a **r** house),
REBELLIOUS HOUSE Eze 2:5, 6, 7, 8; 3:9, 26, 27; 12:2, 3, 3, 9, 25; 17:12; 24:3; 44:6

REBELS → REBEL
Jos 1:18 Whoever **r** against your orders

REBIRTH → BEAR
Tit 3: 5 the water of **r** and renewal by the

REBUILD → BUILD
Ezr 1: 3 and **r** the house of the LORD,
     5: 2 set out to **r** the house of God
Ne   2:17 let us **r** the wall of Jerusalem,
Da   9:25 went out to restore and **r** Jerusalem
Am   9:14 they shall **r** the ruined cities and
Ac 15:16 and I will **r** the dwelling of David,
Tob 14: 5 and they will **r** the temple of God,

REBUILT → BUILD
Ezr 6: 3 at Jerusalem, let the house be **r,**
Eze 36:36 the LORD, have **r** the ruined places,
1Mc 4:48 They also **r** the sanctuary

REBUKE → REBUKED, REBUKES
Ps   6: 1 O LORD, do not **r** me in your anger,
    50: 8 Not for your sacrifices do I **r** you;
   119:21 You **r** the insolent, accursed ones,
Pr 17:10 A **r** strikes deeper into a discerning
    25:12 of gold is a wise **r** to a listening ear.
    27: 5 Better is open **r** than hidden love.
    30: 6 to his words, or else he will **r** you,
Ecc 7: 5 It is better to hear the **r** of the wise
Isa 54: 9 angry with you and will not **r** you.
Zec 3: 2 said to Satan, "The LORD **r** you,
Mk   8:32 Peter took him aside and began to **r**
Lk 17: 3 sins, you must **r** the offender.
2Ti 4: 2 convince, **r**, and encourage,
Tit 1:13 For this reason **r** them sharply,
Jude 1: 9 but said, "The Lord **r** you!"
Sir 20: 1 There is a **r** that is untimely,

REBUKED → REBUKE
Ps 106: 9 He **r** the Red Sea, and it became dry

Mt   8:26 got up and **r** the winds and the sea;
    17:18 Jesus **r** the demon, and it came out
Lk   3:19 been **r** by him because of Herodias,
     4:39 and **r** the fever, and it left her.
2Pe 2:16 but was **r** for his own transgression;

REBUKES → REBUKE
Pr   9: 7 whoever **r** the wicked gets hurt.
    28:23 Whoever **r** a person will afterward

RECEDED*
Ge   8: 3 waters gradually **r** from the earth.

RECEIVE → RECEIVED, RECEIVES, RECEIVING
Ge   4:11 to **r** your brother's blood from your
Dt   9: 9 the mountain to **r** the stone tablets,
Ps 24: 5 They will **r** blessing from the LORD,
Mt 10:41 will **r** a prophet's reward;
Mk 10:15 does not **r** the kingdom of God as
    10:30 who will not **r** a hundredfold now
Lk   7:22 blind **r** their sight, the lame walk,
Jn 16:24 Ask and you will **r**, so that your joy
    20:22 said to them, **"R** the Holy Spirit.
Ac   1: 8 But you will **r** power when
     2:38 you will **r** the gift of the Holy Spirit.
    19: 2 "Did you **r** the Holy Spirit
    20:35 'It is more blessed to give than to **r.'**
Ro 11:31 they too may now **r** mercy.
1Co 4: 5 one will **r** commendation from God.
Heb 4:16 may **r** mercy and find grace to help
Jas 1: 7 must not expect to **r** anything from
     1:12 the test and will **r** the crown
1Jn 3:22 we **r** from him whatever we ask,
Rev 4:11 to **r** glory and honor and power,
     5:12 to **r** power and wealth and wisdom

RECEIVED → RECEIVE
Nu 23:20 See, I **r** a command to bless;
Jos 14: 1 inheritances that the Israelites **r** in
Mt   6: 2 I tell you, they have **r** their reward.
    10: 8 You **r** without payment; give
Mk 11:24 believe that you have **r** it, and it
Jn   1:12 But to all who **r** him, who believed
     1:16 From his fullness we have all **r,**
Ac   8:17 and they **r** the Holy Spirit.
    10:47 baptizing these people who have **r**
Ro   8:15 but you have **r** a spirit of adoption.
    11:30 now **r** mercy because of their
1Co 2:12 have **r** not the spirit of the world,
    11:23 I **r** from the Lord what I also handed
Col 2: 6 therefore have **r** Christ Jesus the
     4:17 complete the task that you have **r**
1Ti 4: 4 provided it is **r** with thanksgiving;
Heb 11: 2 by faith our ancestors **r** approval.
1Pe 2:10 once you had not **r** mercy,
     2:10 but now you have **r** mercy.
     4:10 whatever gift each of you has **r.**
2Pe 1: 1 who have **r** a faith as precious as
     1:17 he **r** honor and glory from God the
Rev 19:20 which he deceived those who had **r**
    20: 4 not **r** its mark on their foreheads or

RECEIVES → RECEIVE
Lk 11:10 For everyone who asks **r,**
Jn 13:20 whoever **r** one whom I send **r** me;
Ac 10:43 who believes in him **r** forgiveness
1Co 9:24 but only one **r** the prize?
Rev 14:11 and its image and for anyone who **r**

RECEIVING → RECEIVE
Ps 68:18 and **r** gifts from people,
1Pe 1: 9 you are **r** the outcome of your faith,

RECENT*
1Ti 3: 6 He must not be a **r** convert,

RECHABITES
Jer 35: 5 before the **R** pitchers full of wine,

RECITE → RECITED, RECITING
Ex 17:14 and **r** it in the hearing of Joshua:
Dt 31:28 I may **r** these words in their hearing

RECITED → RECITE
Dt 31:30 Moses **r** the words of this song,

RECITING* → RECITE
Dt 32:45 Moses had finished **r** all these

RECKLESS
2Ti 3: 4 **r**, swollen with conceit, lovers of
Sir 4:29 Do not be **r** in your speech,

RECKONED → RECKONING
Ge 15: 6 LORD **r** it to him as righteousness.
Ro   4: 3 it was **r** to him as righteousness."
Gal 3: 6 it was **r** to him as righteousness,
Jas 2:23 it was **r** to him as righteousness,"
1Mc 2:52 it was **r** to him as righteousness?

RECKONING → RECKONED, RECKONS
Ge   9: 5 I will require a **r** for human life.
Sir 2:14 you do when the Lord's **r** comes?

RECKONS* → RECKONING
Ro   4: 6 **r** righteousness apart from works:

RECLINING
Est 7: 8 on the couch where Esther was **r;**
Jn 13:23 whom Jesus loved—was **r** next to

RECOGNITION* → RECOGNIZE
1Co 16:18 So give **r** to such persons.

RECOGNIZE → RECOGNITION, RECOGNIZED, RECOGNIZING
Ge 42: 8 his brothers, they did not **r** him.
Job 2:12 from a distance, they did not **r** him,
Lk 19:44 did not **r** the time of your visitation

RECOGNIZED → RECOGNIZE
Ge 42: 8 Although Joseph had **r** his brothers,
Lk 24:31 eyes were opened, and they **r** him;

RECOGNIZING → RECOGNIZE
Lk 24:16 but their eyes were kept from **r** him.

RECOMMENDATION*
2Co 3: 1 letters of **r** to you or from you,

RECOMPENSE → RECOMPENSED
Dt 32:35 Vengeance is mine, and **r,**
Isa 40:10 reward is with him, and his **r** before
    62:11 reward is with him, and his **r** before

RECOMPENSED → RECOMPENSE
Ps 18:20 the cleanness of my hands he **r** me.

RECONCILE → RECONCILED, RECONCILIATION, RECONCILING
Ac   7:26 were quarreling and tried to **r** them,
Eph 2:16 might **r** both groups to God in one
Col 1:20 God was pleased to **r** to himself all

RECONCILED → RECONCILE
Mt   5:24 first be **r** to your brother or sister,
Ro   5:10 we were **r** to God through the death
     5:10 having been **r**, will we be saved by
1Co 7:11 let her remain unmarried or else be **r**
2Co 5:18 who **r** us to himself through Christ,
     5:20 on behalf of Christ, be **r** to God.
Col 1:22 now **r** in his fleshly body through

RECONCILIATION → RECONCILE
Ro   5:11 whom we have now received **r.**
    11:15 if their rejection is the **r** of the world
2Co 5:18 and has given us the ministry of **r;**
     5:19 entrusting the message of **r** to us.

RECONCILING* → RECONCILE
2Co 5:19 God was **r** the world to himself,

RECORD → RECORDED, RECORDS
Ps 56: 8 Are they not in your **r?**
Col 2:14 erasing the **r** that stood against us

RECORDED → RECORD
Est 9:20 Mordecai **r** these things, and sent

Rev 20:12 their works, as **r** in the books.

RECORDS → RECORD
1Ch 4:22 to Lehem (now the **r** are ancient).
Ezr 2:62 their entries in the genealogical **r,**

RECOUNT
Ps 9:14 so that I may **r** all your praises,
    79:13 to generation we will **r** your praise.
Isa 63: 7 **r** the gracious deeds of the LORD,
Sir 18: 5 And who can fully **r** his mercies?

RECOVER
Isa 38: 1 for you shall die; you shall not **r."**
Jn 4:52 the hour when he began to **r,**

RED
Ge 25:25 came out **r,** all his body like a hairy
Ex 15: 4 officers were sunk in the **R** Sea.
Nu 19: 2 the Israelites to bring you a **r** heifer
2Ki 3:22 water opposite them as **r** as blood.
Ps 106: 9 rebuked the **R** Sea, and it became
Pr 23:31 Do not look at wine when it is **r,**
Isa 1:18 though they are **r** like crimson,
Zec 1: 8 I saw a man riding on a **r** horse!
    6: 2 The first chariot had **r** horses,
Mt 16: 3 for the sky is **r** and threatening.'
Heb 11:29 people passed through the **R** Sea as
Rev 6: 4 out came another horse, bright **r;**
    12: 3 a great **r** dragon, with seven heads
1Mc 4: 9 ancestors were saved at the **R** Sea,

RED SEA Ex 10:19; 13:18; 15:4, 22; 23:31;
Nu 14:25; 21:4; 33:10, 11; Dt 1:40; 2:1; 11:4;
Jos 2:10; 4:23; 24:6; Jdg 11:16; 1Ki 9:26; Ne
9:9; Ps 106:7, 9, 22; 136:13, 15; Jer 49:21; Ac
7:36; Heb 11:29; Jdt 5:13; Wis 10:18; 19:7;
1Mc 4:9

REDEEM → REDEEMED, REDEEMER, REDEEMS, REDEMPTION
Ex 6: 6 I will **r** you with an outstretched
    13:13 among your children you shall **r.**
Lev 25:25 **r** what the relative has sold.
Ru 4: 6 "I cannot **r** it for myself
2Sa 7:23 whose God went to **r** it as a people,
Ps 26:11 **r** me, and be gracious to me.
    44:26 **R** us for the sake of your steadfast
    130: 8 will **r** Israel from all its iniquities.
Hos 13:14 Shall I **r** them from Death?
Lk 24:21 hoped that he was the one to **r** Israel
Gal 4: 5 to **r** those who were under the law,
Tit 2:14 that he might **r** us from all iniquity

REDEEMED → REDEEM
Ex 15:13 you led the people whom you **r;**
Dt 15:15 and the LORD your God **r** you;
Ne 1:10 whom you **r** by your great power
Job 33:28 He has **r** my soul from going down
Ps 107: 2 Let the **r** of the LORD say so,
    107: 2 of the LORD say so, those he **r**
Isa 1:27 Zion shall be **r** by justice,
    35: 9 but the **r** shall walk there.
    44:22 return to me, for I have **r** you.
    63: 9 in his love and in his pity he **r** them;
Lk 1:68 on his people and **r** them.
Rev 14: 3 one hundred forty-four thousand
           who have been **r**

REDEEMER → REDEEM
Job 19:25 For I know that my **R** lives,
Ps 19:14 O LORD, my rock and my **r.**
    78:35 the Most High God their **r.**
Isa 44: 6 and his **R,** the LORD of hosts:
    48:17 Thus says the LORD, your **R,**
    59:20 And he will come to Zion as **R,**
Sir 51:12 *Give thanks to the r of Israel.*

REDEEMS → REDEEM
Ps 34:22 The LORD **r** the life of his servants;
    103: 4 who **r** your life from the Pit,
1Mc 4:11 who **r** and saves Israel."

REDEMPTION → REDEEM
Lev 25:24 provide for the **r** of the land.

Ps 111: 9 He sent **r** to his people;
Lk 2:38 to all who were looking for the **r**
    21:28 because your **r** is drawing near."
Ro 3:24 through the **r** that is in Christ Jesus,
    8:23 for adoption, the **r** of our bodies.
1Co 1:30 and sanctification and **r,**
Eph 1: 7 In him we have **r** through his blood,
    1:14 our inheritance toward **r** as God's
    4:30 with a seal for the day of **r.**
Col 1:14 in whom we have **r,** the forgiveness
Heb 9:12 own blood, thus obtaining eternal **r.**

REDUCED
Eze 16:27 against you, **r** your rations,

REED → REEDS
2Ki 18:21 that broken **r** of a staff,
Isa 42: 3 a bruised **r** he will not break,
Mt 12:20 He will not break a bruised **r**
Lk 7:24 A **r** shaken by the wind?

REEDS → REED
Ex 2: 3 child in it and placed it among the **r**

REEL → REELED, REELING
Ps 60: 3 wine to drink that made us **r.**
Isa 28: 7 the prophet **r** with strong drink,

REELED → REEL
Ps 107:27 they **r** and staggered like drunkards,

REELING* → REEL
Zec 12: 2 to make Jerusalem a cup of **r** for all

REFINE* → REFINED, REFINER
Jer 9: 7 I will now **r** and test them,
Zec 13: 9 **r** them as one refines silver,
Mal 3: 3 of Levi and **r** them like gold

REFINED → REFINE
Job 28: 1 and a place for gold to be **r.**
Ps 12: 6 silver **r** in a furnace on the ground,
Isa 48:10 See, I have **r** you, but not like silver;
Da 12:10 shall be purified, cleansed, and **r,**

REFINER → REFINE
Mal 3: 3 will sit as a **r** and purifier of silver,

REFLECT → REFLECTED, REFLECTION, REFLECTS
Sir 6:37 **R** on the statutes of the Lord,

REFLECTED → REFLECT
2Co 3:18 though **r** in a mirror,

REFLECTION → REFLECT
1Co 11: 7 since he is the image and **r** of God;
Heb 1: 3 He is the **r** of God's glory
Wis 7:26 For she is a **r** of eternal light,

REFLECTS* → REFLECT
Pr 27:19 Just as water **r** the face,
    27:19 so one human heart **r** another.
Sir 14:21 who **r** in his heart on her ways

REFRAIN
Ps 37: 8 **R** from anger, and forsake wrath.
Ecc 3: 5 time to embrace, and a time to **r**

REFRESH → REFRESHES, REFRESHING
Phm 1:20 **R** my heart in Christ.

REFRESHES* → REFRESH
Pr 15:30 and good news **r** the body.

REFRESHING* → REFRESH
Ac 3:20 so that times of **r** may come

REFUGE
Nu 35:11 select cities to be cities of **r** for you,
Jos 20: 2 'Appoint the cities of **r,** of which I
Ru 2:12 whose wings you have come for **r!"**
2Sa 22: 3 my rock, in whom I take **r,**
    22: 3 my stronghold and my **r,** my savior;
    22:31 a shield for all who take **r** in him.
Ps 2:12 Happy are all who take **r** in him.

    5:11 But let all who take **r** in you rejoice;
    11: 1 In the LORD I take **r;**
    16: 1 O God, for in you I take **r.**
    17: 7 who seek **r** from their adversaries
    31: 2 a rock of **r** for me, a strong fortress
    34: 8 happy are those who take **r** in him.
    36: 7 All people may take **r** in the shadow
    46: 1 God is our **r** and strength,
    59:16 have been a fortress for me and a **r**
    62: 8 God is a **r** for us.
    71: 1 In you, O LORD, I take **r;**
    91: 2 to the LORD, "My **r** and my fortress;
    118: 8 to take **r** in the LORD than to put
    144: 2 my shield, in whom I take **r,**
Pr 14:26 and one's children will have a **r.**
    14:32 righteous find a **r** in their integrity.
    30: 5 a shield to those who take **r** in him.
Isa 25: 4 For you have been a **r** to the poor,
    25: 4 a **r** to the needy in their distress,
Jer 16:19 my **r** in the day of trouble,
Na 1: 7 he protects those who take **r** in him,

CITIES OF REFUGE Nu 35:6, 11, 13, 14;
Jos 20:2; 1Ch 6:57, 67

CITY OF REFUGE Nu 35:25, 26, 27, 28,
32; Jos 21:13, 21, 27, 32, 38

REFUSE → REFUSED
Ex 8: 2 If you **r** to let them go,
Nu 14:11 And how long will they **r** to believe
Eze 3:27 and let those who **r** to hear, **r;**
Jn 5:40 you **r** to come to me to have life.
Heb 12:25 do not **r** the one who is speaking;

REFUSED → REFUSE
Ex 13:15 Pharaoh stubbornly **r** to let us go,
Jer 5: 3 but they **r** to take correction.
2Th 2:10 because they **r** to love the truth and
Heb 12:25 not escape when they **r** the one who

REFUTE* → REFUTED
Tit 1: 9 and to **r** those who contradict it.

REFUTED* → REFUTE
Ac 18:28 he powerfully **r** the Jews in public,

REGAIN → REGAINED
Ac 9:17 so that you may **r** your sight

REGAINED → REGAIN
Lk 18:43 Immediately he **r** his sight
Ac 22:13 In that very hour I **r** my sight

REGARD → REGARDED, REGARDING
Ge 4: 4 And the LORD had **r** for Abel
1Sa 2:12 they had no **r** for the LORD
Ps 74:20 Have **r** for your covenant,
Isa 8:13 of hosts, him you shall **r** as holy;
Php 2: 6 did not **r** equality with God as
    3: 7 these I have come to **r** as los
Heb 12: 5 not **r** lightly the discipline of the
2Pe 3:15 and **r** the patience of our Lord as

REGARDED → REGARD
Mk 11:32 for all **r** John as truly a prophet.

REGISTERED
Lk 2: 5 He went to be **r** with Mary,

REGRET
1Sa 15:11 "I **r** that I made Saul king,
2Co 7:10 leads to salvation and brings no **r,**

REGULAR
Nu 28: 3 daily, as a **r** offering.
2Ki 25:30 a **r** allowance was given him by the

REGULATIONS
Col 2:20 Why do you submit to **r,**
Heb 9:10 **r** for the body imposed until the

REHOBOAM
Son of Solomon (1Ki 11:43; 1Ch 3:10). Harsh treatment of subjects caused divided kingdom (1Ki 12:1-24; 14:21-31; 2Ch 10-12).

REIGN → REIGNED, REIGNS

Ex 15:18 The LORD will **r** forever and ever."
Dt 17:20 his descendants may **r** long over his
1Sa 8:11 be the ways of the king who will **r**
Ps 146:10 The LORD will **r** forever,
Pr 8:15 By me kings **r**, and rulers decree
Isa 24:23 LORD of hosts will **r** on Mount Zion
    32: 1 See, a king will **r** in righteousness,
Jer 23: 5 he shall **r** as king and deal wisely,
La 5:19 But you, O LORD, **r** forever;
Mic 4: 7 LORD will **r** over them in Mount
Lk 1:33 **r** over the house of Jacob forever,
1Co 15:25 **r** until he has put all his enemies
2Ti 2:12 we will also **r** with him;
Rev 5:10 and they will **r** on earth."
    11:15 and he will **r** forever and ever."
    11:17 your great power and begun to **r**.
    20: 6 will **r** with him a thousand years.
    22: 5 and they will **r** forever and ever.

REIGNED → REIGN

Rev 20: 4 and **r** with Christ a thousand years.

REIGNS → REIGN

Isa 52: 7 who says to Zion, "Your God **r**."
Rev 19: 6 the Lord our God the Almighty **r**.

REJECT → REJECTED, REJECTION, REJECTS

Ex 20: 5 generation of those who **r** me,
Isa 30:12 Because you **r** this word,
Hos 4: 6 I **r** you from being a priest to me.

REJECTED → REJECT

Nu 11:20 have **r** the LORD who is among you,
1Sa 8: 7 but they have **r** me from being king
    15:23 he has also **r** you from being king."
2Ki 17:20 LORD **r** all the descendants of Israel;
Ps 60: 1 O God, you have **r** us, broken our
    66:20 not **r** my prayer or removed his
    118:22 The stone that the builders **r**
Isa 5:24 have **r** the instruction of the LORD
    53: 3 He was despised and **r** by others;
Jer 8: 9 they have **r** the word of the LORD,
    14:19 Have you completely **r** Judah?
Zec 10: 6 shall be as though I had not **r** them;
Mt 21:42 'The stone that the builders **r**
Ac 4:11 This Jesus is 'the stone that was **r**
1Ti 4: 4 and nothing is to be **r**, provided
1Pe 2: 4 though **r** by mortals yet chosen and
    2: 7 "The stone that the builders **r**

REJECTION* → REJECT

Ro 11:15 if their **r** is the reconciliation of the

REJECTS → REJECT

Lk 10:16 and whoever **r** you **r** me,
Jn 12:48 The one who **r** me and does
1Th 4: 8 whoever **r** this **r** not human

REJOICE → REJOICED, REJOICES, REJOICING

Lev 23:40 shall **r** before the LORD your God
1Ch 16:10 of those who seek the LORD **r**.
    16:31 heavens be glad, and let the earth **r**,
2Ch 6:41 let your faithful **r** in your goodness.
Ne 12:43 had made them **r** with great joy;
Ps 5:11 But let all who take refuge in you **r**;
    9:14 Zion, **r** in your deliverance.
    14: 7 Jacob will **r**; Israel will be glad.
    31: 7 exult and **r** in your steadfast love,
    51: 8 the bones that you have crushed **r**.
    63:11 But the king shall **r** in God;
    64:10 Let the righteous **r** in the LORD and
    97: 1 Let the earth **r**; let the many
    104:31 may the LORD **r** in his works—
    105: 3 of those who seek the LORD **r**.
    118:24 let us **r** and be glad in it.
    119:162 I **r** at your word like one who finds
    149: 2 the children of Zion **r** in their King.
Pr 5:18 and **r** in the wife of your youth,
    23:25 let her who bore you **r**.
    24:17 Do not **r** when your enemies fall,

    29: 2 are in authority, the people **r**;
Isa 9: 3 they **r** before you as with joy at the
    35: 1 the desert shall **r** and blossom;
    62: 5 so shall your God **r** over you.
Hab 3:18 yet I will **r** in the LORD;
Zep 3:17 he will **r** over you with gladness,
Zec 9: 9 **R** greatly, O daughter Zion!
Lk 6:23 **R** in that day and leap for joy,
    10:20 Nevertheless, do not **r** at this,
    10:20 but **r** that your names are written in
    15: 6 saying to them, '**R** with me,
    15: 9 '**R** with me, for I have found
Ro 12:15 **R** with those who **r**,
Php 2:17 I am glad and **r** with all of you—
    3: 1 brothers and sisters, **r** in the Lord.
    4: 4 **R** in the Lord always; again I will
            say, **R**.
1Th 5:16 **R** always,
1Pe 4:13 **r** insofar as you are sharing Christ's
Rev 18:20 **R** over her, O heaven, you saints
    19: 7 Let us **r** and exult and give him the
Sir 8: 7 Do not **r** over any one's death;

REJOICED → REJOICE

Ex 18: 9 Jethro **r** for all the good that
1Ch 29: 9 King David also **r** greatly.
Job 31:25 **r** because my wealth was great,
Jn 8:56 Your ancestor Abraham **r** that

REJOICES → REJOICE

Ps 16: 9 my heart is glad, and my soul **r**;
Pr 11:10 well with the righteous, the city **r**;
Isa 62: 5 as the bridegroom **r** over the bride,
Lk 1:47 and my spirit **r** in God my Savior,
1Co 13: 6 in wrongdoing, but **r** in the truth.

REJOICING → REJOICE

2Sa 6:12 to the city of David with **r**;
Ne 8:17 And there was very great **r**.
Pr 8:30 his delight, **r** before him always,
2Co 6:10 as sorrowful, yet always **r**;
Sir 30:22 **r** lengthens one's life span.

REKINDLE*

2Ti 1: 6 I remind you to **r** the gift of God

RELATIONS → RELATIVE

Lev 18:20 sexual **r** with your kinsman's wife,
    20:15 has sexual **r** with an animal,
Mt 1:25 but had no marital **r** with her until

RELATIVE → RELATIONS, RELATIVES

Ru 2:20 said to her, "The man is a **r** of ours,

RELATIVES → RELATIVE

Lk 21:16 by parents and brothers, by **r** and
1Ti 5: 8 whoever does not provide for **r**,

RELEASE → RELEASED

Isa 61: 1 liberty to the captives, and **r** to
Mt 27:15 the governor was accustomed to **r**
Lk 4:18 sent me to proclaim **r** to the captives
Rev 9:14 "**R** the four angels who are bound at

RELEASED → RELEASE

2Ki 25:27 **r** King Jehoiachin of Judah from
Mk 15:15 to satisfy the crowd, **r** Barabbas for
Rev 20: 7 Satan will be **r** from his prison

RELENT* → RELENTED, RELENTS

Eze 24:14 I will not spare, I will not **r**.
Joel 2:14 whether he will not turn and **r**,
Jnh 3: 9 God may **r** and change his mind;
    4: 2 and ready to **r** from punishing.
Zec 8:14 I did not **r**, says the LORD of hosts,
Man 1: 7 and you **r** at human suffering.

RELENTED* → RELENT

2Sa 24:16 the LORD **r** concerning the evil,
1Ch 21:15 LORD took note and **r** concerning
Jer 4:28 I have not **r** nor will I turn back.
Am 7: 3 The LORD **r** concerning this;
    7: 6 The LORD **r** concerning this;

RELENTS* → RELENT

Joel 2:13 steadfast love, and **r** from punishing

RELIED → RELY

2Ch 13:18 because they **r** on the LORD,
    16: 8 Yet because you **r** on the LORD,

RELIEF

Est 4:14 **r** and deliverance will rise for the
    9:22 Jews gained **r** from their enemies,
La 3:56 to my cry for help, but give me **r**!"
2Th 1: 7 to give **r** to the afflicted as well as
AdE 9:16 and got **r** from their enemies.

RELIGION → RELIGIOUS

Ac 25:19 with him about their own **r** and
    26: 5 sect of our **r** and lived as a Pharisee,
Jas 1:26 their hearts, their **r** is worthless.
    1:27 **R** that is pure and undefiled before
1Mc 1:43 from Israel gladly adopted his **r**;
    2:19 abandoning the **r** of their ancestors,

RELIGIOUS → RELIGION

Ac 17:22 extremely **r** you are in every way.
1Ti 5: 4 they should first learn their **r** duty
Jas 1:26 If any think they are **r**,

RELY → RELIED

2Ki 18:20 On whom do you now **r**,
2Ch 14:11 O LORD our God, for we **r** on you,
Pr 3: 5 and do not **r** on your own insight.
Ro 2:17 and **r** on the law and boast of your
2Co 1: 9 so that we would **r** not on ourselves
Gal 3:10 all who **r** on the works of the law
Sir 5: 1 Do not **r** on your wealth,

REMAIN → REMAINDER, REMAINED, REMAINS

Nu 33:55 whom you let **r** shall be as barbs
Mk 14:34 **r** here, and keep awake."
1Co 7:20 Let each of you **r** in the condition
Heb 11:1 they will perish, but you **r**;
Sir 20: 7 wise **r** silent until the right moment,

REMAINDER → REMAIN

Ex 29:34 then you shall burn the **r** with fire;

REMAINED → REMAIN

2Sa 11: 1 But David **r** at Jerusalem.
Mt 2:15 and **r** there until the death of Herod.
1Jn 2:19 they would have **r** with us.

REMAINS → REMAIN

Jos 13: 2 This is the land that still **r**:
2Ti 2:13 he **r** faithful—for he cannot deny
Heb 4: 9 a sabbath rest still **r** for the people
    7: 3 Son of God, he **r** a priest forever.
    10:26 there no longer **r** a sacrifice for sins,

REMEDY

2Ch 36:16 so great that there was no **r**.

REMEMBER → REMEMBERED, REMEMBERS, REMEMBRANCE

Ge 9:15 I will **r** my covenant that is between
Ex 20: 8 **R** the sabbath day, and keep it holy.
Dt 5:15 **R** that you were a slave in the land
    8:18 But **r** the LORD your God,
Jos 1:13 "**R** the word that Moses the servant
1Ch 16:12 **R** the wonderful works he has done,
Ne 5:19 **R** for my good, O my God,
    13:31 **R** me, O my God, for good.
Job 10: 9 **R** that you fashioned me like clay;
    36:24 "**R** to extol his work, of which
Ps 74: 2 **R** your congregation, which you
    74: 2 **R** Mount Zion, where you came to
    77:11 I will **r** your wonders of old.
Ecc 12: 1 **R** your creator in the days of your
Isa 46: 8 **R** this and consider, recall it to mind
    64: 9 LORD, and do not **r** iniquity forever.
Jer 31:34 and **r** their sin no more.
La 5: 1 **R**, O LORD, what has befallen us;
Eze 36:31 Then you shall **r** your evil ways,
Hos 7: 2 that I **r** all their wickedness.

Hab 3: 2 in wrath may you **r** mercy.
Mk   8:18 And do you not **r?**
Lk 17:32 **R** Lot's wife.
    23:42 **r** me when you come into your
Php 1: 3 I thank my God every time I **r** you,
2Ti 2: 8 **R** Jesus Christ, raised from the dead
Heb 8:12 and I will **r** their sins no more."
Jude 1:17 **r** the predictions of the apostles
Rev 3: 3 **R** then what you received and heard
Sir 23:18 The Most High will not **r** sins."
    28: 7 **r** the covenant of the Most High,
1Mc 4:10 **r** his covenant with our ancestors

REMEMBERED → REMEMBER

Ge   8: 1 God **r** Noah and all the wild animals
    19:29 of the Plain, God **r** Abraham,
    30:22 God **r** Rachel, and God heeded her
Ex   2:24 God **r** his covenant with Abraham,
     6: 5 and I have **r** my covenant.
1Sa 1:19 Hannah, and the LORD **r** her.
Ps 78:35 They **r** that God was their rock,
    98: 3 He has **r** his steadfast love and
   106:45 For their sake he **r** his covenant,
   136:23 It is he who **r** us in our low estate,
Isa 17:10 have not **r** the Rock of your refuge;
    65:17 the former things shall not be **r** or
Eze 18:22 committed shall be **r** against them;
    33:13 of their righteous deeds shall be **r;**
Mt 26:75 Then Peter **r** what Jesus had said:
Jn   2:17 His disciples **r** that it was written,
Rev 16:19 God **r** great Babylon and gave her
    18: 5 and God has **r** her iniquities.

REMEMBERS → REMEMBER

Ps 103:14 he **r** that we are dust.

REMEMBRANCE → REMEMBER

Lk 22:19 Do this in **r** of me."
1Co 11:24 Do this in **r** of me."

REMIND → REMINDER

Jn 14:26 **r** you of all that I have said to you.

REMINDER → REMIND

Ex 13: 9 and as a **r** on your forehead,
Heb 10: 3 in these sacrifices there is a **r** of sin

REMISSION

Dt 15: 1 you shall grant a **r** of debts.

REMNANT

Ge 45: 7 before you to preserve for you a **r**
2Ki 19:31 for from Jerusalem a **r** shall go out,
Ezr 9: 8 who has left us a **r,**
Isa 10:21 A **r** will return, the **r** of Jacob,
    11:11 a second time to recover the **r** that
Jer 23: 3 myself will gather the **r** of my flock
    50:20 will pardon the **r** that I have spared.
Zep 3:13 **r** of Israel; they shall do no wrong
Zec 8:12 the **r** of this people to possess all
Ro   9:27 only a **r** of them will be saved;
    11: 5 too at the present time there is a **r,**

REMOVAL → REMOVE

Isa 27: 9 the full fruit of the **r** of his sin:
1Pe 3:21 not as a **r** of dirt from the body,

REMOVE → REMOVAL, REMOVED, REMOVES

Ex 12:15 the first day you shall **r** leaven from
Ps 39:10 **R** your stroke from me; I am worn
Isa 1:25 as with lye and **r** all your alloy.
Eze 36:26 **r** from your body the heart of stone
Zec 3: 9 I will **r** the guilt of this land in a
Lk 22:42 if you are willing, **r** this cup from

REMOVED → REMOVE

2Ki 17:18 Israel and **r** them out of his sight;
Pr 10:30 The righteous will never be **r,**
Jn 20: 1 the stone had been **r** from the tomb.
Rev 6:14 mountain and island was **r** from its
1Mc 1:15 and **r** the marks of circumcision,

REMOVES → REMOVE

Ps 103:12 far he **r** our transgressions from us.
Jn 15: 2 He **r** every branch in me that bears

REND*

Joel 2:13 **r** your hearts and not your clothing.

RENDER

Ps 28: 4 **r** them their due reward.
Eph 6: 7 **R** service with enthusiasm,
Rev 18: 6 **R** to her as she herself has rendered,

RENEW → RENEWAL, RENEWED, RENEWING

Isa 40:31 for the LORD shall **r** their strength,
La   5:21 or days as of old—
Zep 3:17 he will **r** you in his love;

RENEWAL → RENEW

Mt 19:28 I tell you, at the **r** of all things,
Col 3:11 In that **r** there is no longer Greek
Tit 3: 5 of rebirth and **r** by the Holy Spirit.

RENEWED → RENEW

Ps 103: 5 your youth is **r** like the eagle's.
2Co 4:16 inner nature is being **r** day by day.
Eph 4:23 to be **r** in the spirit of your minds,
Col 3:10 being **r** in knowledge according to

RENEWING* → RENEW

Ro 12: 2 transformed by the **r** of your minds,

RENOUNCE → RENOUNCED

Ps 10:13 Why do the wicked **r** God,
1Ti 4: 1 in later times some will **r** the faith
Tit 2:12 training us to **r** impiety and worldly

RENOUNCED* → RENOUNCE

Ps 89:39 **r** the covenant with your servant;
2Co 4: 2 We have **r** the shameful things that

RENOWN

Ge   6: 4 that were of old, warriors of **r.**
Ps 135:13 O LORD, endures forever, your **r,**
Isa 26: 8 and your **r** are the soul's desire.

REPAID → PAY

Pr 11:31 If the righteous are **r** on earth,
Lk 14:14 you will be **r** at the resurrection of

REPAIR → REPAIRED, REPAIRER, REPAIRING

2Ch 24: 5 money from all Israel to **r** the house
Ezr 9: 9 he house of our God, to **r** its ruins,
Am   9:11 and **r** its breaches, and raise up its

REPAIRED → REPAIR

2Ch 15: 8 He **r** the altar of the LORD that was
    29: 3 the house of the LORD and **r** them.

REPAIRER* → REPAIR

Isa 58:12 shall be called the **r** of the breach,

REPAIRING → REPAIR

2Ki 12: 7 "Why are you not **r** the house?
Ezr 4:12 the walls and **r** the foundations.

REPAY → PAY

Dt 32: 6 Do you thus **r** the LORD,
Ps 28: 4 **R** them according to their work,
    35:12 They **r** me evil for good; my soul is
   103:10 nor **r** us according to our iniquities.
Isa 59:18 to their deeds, so will he **r;**
Jer 25:14 will **r** them according to their deeds
    51:56 of recompense, he will **r** in full.
Joel 2:25 I will **r** you for the years that
Ro 12:17 Do not **r** anyone evil for evil,
    12:19 "Vengeance is mine, I will **r,**
Heb 10:30 "Vengeance is mine, I will **r."**
1Pe 3: 9 not **r** evil for evil or abuse for abuse
     3: 9 on the contrary, **r** with a blessing.
Rev 18: 6 and **r** her double for her deeds;

REPAYING* → PAY

2Ch 6:23 **r** the guilty by bringing their

Jer 51: 6 he is **r** her what is due.

REPAYS → PAY

1Th 5:15 none of you **r** evil for evil,
Sir 35:13 For the Lord is the one who **r,**

REPENT → REPENTANCE, REPENTED, REPENTS

1Ki 8:47 **r,** and plead with you in the land
Job 42: 6 and **r** in dust and ashes."
Mt   3: 2 **"R,** for the kingdom of heaven has
     4:17 time Jesus began to proclaim, **"R,**
Mk   6:12 and proclaimed that all should **r.**
Lk 13: 3 but unless you **r,** you will all perish
Ac   2:38 **"R,** and be baptized every one of
     3:19 **R** therefore, and turn to God so
    17:30 all people everywhere to **r,**
    26:20 that they should **r** and turn to God
Rev 2: 5 **r,** and do the works you did at first.
     2: 5 from its place, unless you **r.**
     2:21 I gave her time to **r,**
     2:21 she refuses to **r** of her fornication.
     9:20 not **r** of the works of their hands or
    16: 9 they did not **r** and give him glory.
Sir 18:21 and when you have sinned,
Man 1:13 O Lord, are the God of those who **r,**

REPENTANCE → REPENT

Mt   3: 8 Bear fruit worthy of **r.**
Mk   1: 4 a baptism of **r** for the forgiveness
Lk   3: 8 Bear fruits worthy of **r.**
     5:32 not the righteous but sinners to **r."**
    24:47 that **r** and forgiveness of sins is to
Ac   5:31 give **r** to Israel and forgiveness
    11:18 has given even to the Gentiles the **r**
    20:21 to both Jews and Greeks about **r**
    26:20 God and do deeds consistent with **r.**
Ro   2: 4 kindness is meant to lead you to **r?**
2Co 7:10 **r** that leads to salvation and brings
Heb 6: 1 **r** from dead works and faith toward
2Pe 3: 9 any to perish, but all to come to **r.**

REPENTED → REPENT

Zec 1: 6 So they **r** and said, "The LORD
Mt 11:21 would have **r** long ago in sackcloth
Lk 11:32 they **r** at the proclamation of Jonah,

REPENTS* → REPENT

Jer 8: 6 no one **r** of wickedness, saying,
Lk 15: 7 in heaven over one sinner who **r**
    15:10 of God over one sinner who **r."**

REPHAIM

Ge 15:20 the Hittites, the Perizzites, the **R,**
Jos 12: 4 one of the last of the **R,**

REPLANTED* → PLANT

Eze 36:36 and **r** that which was desolate;

REPLY

Mk 15: 5 But Jesus made no further **r,**

REPORT → REPORTS

Ge 37: 2 Joseph brought a bad **r** of them to
Nu 13:32 to the Israelites an unfavorable **r**
1Ki 10: 7 prosperity far surpass the **r** that I

REPORTS → REPORT

2Ch 9: 6 I did not believe the **r** until I came
Mt 14: 1 Herod the ruler heard **r** about Jesus;

REPRESENT

Ex 18:19 should **r** the people before God,

REPROACH

Job 27: 6 my heart does not **r** me for any of
Pr 14:34 but sin is a **r** to any people.
Isa 51: 7 do not fear the **r** of others,
Jer 20: 8 of the LORD has become for me a **r**
1Ti 3: 2 Now a bishop must be above **r,**
     5: 7 so that they may be above **r.**

REPROOF → REPROVE

Pr   3:11 discipline or be weary of his **r,**
    13:18 but one who heeds **r** is honored.

Sir 32:17 The sinner will shun **r**,

REPROVE → REPROOF, REPROVES

Pr 19:25 **r** the intelligent, and they will gain
Tit 2:15 exhort and **r** with all authority.
Rev 3:19 **r** and discipline those whom I love.

REPROVES → REPROVE

Job 5:17 How happy is the one whom God **r**;
Pr 3:12 for the LORD **r** the one he loves,

REQUEST → REQUESTS

Est 7: 3 of my people—that is my **r**.
Ps 21: 2 have not withheld the **r** of his lips.

REQUESTS → REQUEST

Php 4: 6 let your **r** be made known to God.

REQUIRE → REQUIRED

Ge 9: 5 lifeblood I will surely **r** a reckoning:
Dt 10:12 does the LORD your God **r** of you?
Mic 6: 8 the LORD **r** of you but to do justice,

REQUIRED → REQUIRE

Ps 40: 6 sin offering you have not **r**.
1Co 4: 2 it is **r** of stewards that they be found

RESCUE → RESCUED, RESCUES

2Ch 32:17 in other lands did not **r** their people
Ps 22: 8 him **r** the one in whom he delights!"
31: 2 Incline your ear to me; **r** me
69:14 **r** me from sinking in the mire;
82: 4 **R** the weak and the needy;
Isa 1:17 seek justice, **r** the oppressed,
31: 5 and deliver it, he will spare and **r** it.
Eze 34:10 I will **r** my sheep from their mouths,
Mt 6:13 but **r** us from the evil one.
Ro 7:24 will **r** me from this body of death?
2Co 1:10 that he will **r** us again,
2Pe 2: 9 the Lord knows how to **r** the godly
Sir 29:12 it will **r** you from every disaster;

RESCUED → RESCUE

Ne 9:28 and many times you **r** them
Ps 60: 5 whom you love may be **r**.
71:23 my soul also, which you have **r**.
81: 7 In distress you called, and I **r** you;
Ac 12:11 and **r** me from the hands of Herod
Col 1:13 has **r** us from the power of darkness
2Pe 2: 7 if he **r** Lot, a righteous man
Wis 10: 6 Wisdom **r** a righteous man when
Sir 51:12 and **r** me in time of trouble.
Aza 1:66 For he has **r** us from Hades
1Mc 2:48 They **r** the law out of the hands of

RESCUES → RESCUE

Ps 34:19 but the LORD **r** them from them all.
37:40 The LORD helps them and **r** them;
Da 6:27 and **r**, he works signs and wonders
1Th 1:10 Jesus, who **r** us from the wrath that
Sir 40:24 but almsgiving **r** better than either.

RESERVED

Ge 27:36 he said, "Have you not **r** a blessing
2Pe 2:17 the deepest darkness has been **r**.
3: 7 and earth have been **r** for fire,

RESIST → RESISTED, RESISTS

Mt 5:39 I say to you, Do not **r** an evildoer.
Ro 9:19 For who can **r** his will?"
Jas 4: 7 **R** the devil, and he will flee from
1Pe 5: 9 **R** him, steadfast in your faith,
Wis 12:12 Or will **r** your judgment?

RESISTED → RESIST

Job 9: 4 mighty in strength—who has **r** him,
Heb 12: 4 against sin you have not yet **r** to

RESISTS* → RESIST

Ro 13: 2 whoever **r** authority **r** what God has appointed,

RESOLVED

Da 1: 8 Daniel **r** that he would not defile
1Mc 1:62 **r** in their hearts not to eat unclean

RESPECT → RESPECTABLE, RESPECTED, RESPECTFUL

Mal 1: 6 if I am a master, where is the **r** due
Mk 12: 6 saying, 'They will **r** my son.'
Ro 13: 7 **r** to whom **r** is due,
Eph 5:33 and a wife should **r** her husband.
1Th 5:12 to **r** those who labor among you,
Heb 2:17 his brothers and sisters in every **r**,
4:15 who in every **r** has been tested

RESPECTABLE → RESPECT

1Co 12:23 our less **r** members are treated
1Ti 3: 2 temperate, sensible, **r**, hospitable,

RESPECTED → RESPECT

Mk 15:43 a **r** member of the council,
Ac 5:34 of the law, **r** by all the people,
Heb 12: 9 to discipline us, and we **r** them.

RESPECTFUL* → RESPECT

1Ti 3: 4 his children submissive and **r**

RESPOND

2Ch 32:25 not **r** according to the benefit done
Hos 2:15 shall **r** as in the days of her youth,

REST → RESTED, RESTING, RESTS

Ge 8: 4 the ark came to **r** on the mountains
Ex 16:23 'Tomorrow is a day of solemn **r**,
31:15 seventh day is a sabbath of solemn **r**
33:14 and I will give you **r**."
Lev 25: 4 a sabbath of complete **r** for the land,
Nu 10:36 whenever it came to **r**, he would say
Dt 12:10 he gives you **r** from your enemies
Jos 1:13 God is providing you a place of **r**,
11:23 And the land had **r** from war.
14:15 And the land had **r** from war.
21:44 the LORD gave them **r** on every side
2Sa 7:11 give you **r** from all your enemies.
1Ki 5: 4 LORD my God has given me **r** on
1Ch 28: 2 of **r** for the ark of the covenant of
Job 3:17 and there the weary are at **r**.
Ps 95:11 swore, "They shall not enter my **r**."
Pr 6:10 a little folding of the hands to **r**,
Isa 11: 2 spirit of the LORD shall **r** on him,
30:15 returning and you shall be saved;
44:17 The **r** of it he makes into a god,
Jer 6:16 walk in it, and find **r** for your souls.
47: 6 into your scabbard, **r** and be still!"
Mt 11:28 and I will give you **r**.
Mk 6:31 all by yourselves and **r** a while."
1Co 2: 5 faith might **r** not on human wisdom
Gal 3:12 But the law does not **r** on faith;
Heb 3:11 I swore, 'They will not enter my **r**.'
4: 3 we who have believed enter that **r**,
4: 3 'They shall not enter my **r**,'"
4:10 those who enter God's **r** also cease
Rev 14:11 There is no **r** day or night for those
14:13 Spirit, "they will **r** from their labors,

RESTED → REST

Ge 2: 2 he **r** on the seventh day from all the
Ex 16:30 So the people **r** on the seventh day.
20:11 all that is in them, but **r** the seventh
Nu 11:25 when the spirit **r** upon them,
Heb 4: 4 God **r** on the seventh day from all

RESTING → REST

Dt 28:65 no **r** place for the sole of your foot.
Ps 132:14 "This is my **r** place forever;
La 1: 3 the nations, and finds no **r** place;

RESTITUTION

Ex 22: 1 The thief shall make **r**,
Nu 5: 7 shall make full **r** for the wrong,

RESTLESS*

Jas 3: 8 a **r** evil, full of deadly poison.

RESTORE → RESTORED, RESTORES

Dt 30: 3 LORD your God will **r** your fortunes
2Ch 24: 4 time afterward Joash decided to **r**
Ne 4: 2 Jews doing? Will they **r** things?
Ps 51:12 **R** to me the joy of your salvation,
80: 3 **R** us, O God; let your face shine,
126: 4 **R** our fortunes, O LORD,
Isa 49: 6 of Jacob and to **r** the survivors
La 5:21 **R** us to yourself, O LORD,
Da 9:25 the word went out to **r** and rebuild
Zec 9:12 I declare that I will **r** to you double.
Mt 17:11 "Elijah is indeed coming and will **r**
Ac 1: 6 you will **r** the kingdom to Israel?"
1Pe 5:10 will himself **r**, support, strengthen,
1Mc 3:43 "Let us **r** the ruins of our people,

RESTORED → RESTORE

Ex 4: 7 it was **r** like the rest of his body—
2Ki 5:10 and your flesh shall be **r** and you
Ps 85: 1 you **r** the fortunes of Jacob.
Mk 3: 5 stretched it out, and his hand was **r**.
8:25 looked intently and his sight was **r**,
1Mc 4:57 they **r** the gates and

RESTORES → RESTORE

Ps 14: 7 LORD **r** the fortunes of his people,
23: 3 he **r** my soul. He leads me in right
53: 6 God **r** the fortunes of his people,

RESTRAINED → RESTRAINT

Ps 78:38 often he **r** his anger, and did not stir
2Pe 2:16 a human voice and **r** the prophet's

RESTRAINING → RESTRAINT

2Th 2: 6 And you know what is now **r** him,

RESTRAINT → RESTRAINED, RESTRAINING

Pr 14:16 but the fool throws off **r**
29:18 no prophecy, the people cast off **r**,

RESTS → REST

Dt 33:12 beloved of the LORD **r** in safety—
Ps 16: 9 my body also **r** secure.
Pr 19:23 one **r** secure and suffers no harm.
Isa 9: 6 authority **r** upon his shoulders;

RESULT

1Pe 1: 7 may be found to **r** in praise and

RESURRECTION*

Mt 22:23 to him, saying there is no **r**;
22:28 In the **r**, then, whose wife of
22:30 For in the **r** they neither marry nor
22:31 And as for the **r** of the dead,
27:53 After his **r** they came out of the
Mk 12:18 Sadducees, who say there is no **r**,
12:23 In the **r** whose wife will she be?
Lk 14:14 be repaid at the **r** of the righteous."
20:27 those who say there is no **r**,
20:33 In the **r**, therefore, whose wife will
20:35 in the **r** from the dead neither marry
20:36 of God, being children of the **r**.
Jn 5:29 done good, to the **r** of life,
5:29 to the **r** of condemnation.
11:24 rise again in the **r** on the last day."
11:25 said to her, "I am the **r** and the life.
Ac 1:22 become a witness with us to his **r**."
2:31 David spoke of the **r** of the Messiah
4: 2 that in Jesus there is the **r** of
4:33 gave their testimony to the **r** of
17:18 good news about Jesus and the **r**.)
17:32 they heard of the **r** of the dead,
23: 6 concerning the hope of the **r** of
23: 8 Sadducees say that there is no **r**, or
24:15 a **r** of both the righteous and the
24:21 'It is about the **r** of the dead that
Ro 1: 4 to the spirit of holiness by **r** from
6: 5 certainly be united with him in a **r**
1Co 15:12 you say there is no **r** of the dead?
15:13 If there is no **r** of the dead,
15:21 the **r** of the dead has also come
15:42 So it is with the **r** of the dead.
Php 3:10 know Christ and the power of his **r**
3:11 I may attain the **r** from the dead.
2Ti 2:18 that the **r** has already taken place.
Heb 6: 2 **r** of the dead, and eternal judgment.
11:35 Women received their dead by **r**.

11:35 in order to obtain a better **r.**
1Pe 1: 3 a living hope through the **r** of Jesus
3:21 through the **r** of Jesus Christ,
Rev 20: 5 This is the first **r.**
20: 6 are those who share in the first **r.**
2Mc 7:14 for you there will be no **r** to life!"
12:43 honorably, taking account of the **r.**
2Es 2:23 will give you the first place in my **r.**

RETAIN
Nu 36: 7 all Israelites shall **r** the inheritance
Mic 7:18 He does not **r** his anger forever,
Jn 20:23 if you **r** the sins of any,

RETIRE
Nu 8:25 the age of fifty years they shall **r**

RETRIBUTION
Isa 66: 6 dealing **r** to his enemies!
Jer 5: 9 bring **r** on a nation such as this?
Ro 11: 9 a stumbling block and a **r** for them;

RETURN → RETURNED, RETURNS
Ge 3:19 you are dust, and to dust you shall **r.**
18:10 "I will surely **r** to you in due season,
Nu 10:36 it came to rest, he would say, **"R,**
Dt 30: 2 and **r** to the LORD your God,
2Sa 12:23 I shall go to him, but he will not **r**
2Ch 30: 9 his face from you, if you **r** to him."
Ne 1: 9 but if you **r** to me and keep my
Job 10:21 never to **r,** to the land of gloom
16:22 go the way from which I shall not **r.**
22:23 If you **r** to the Almighty, you will
Ps 51:13 and sinners will **r** to you.
104:29 they die and **r** to their dust.
116:12 What shall I **r** to the LORD
Isa 10:21 remnant will **r,** the remnant of Jacob
35:10 the ransomed of the LORD shall **r,**
44:22 **r** to me, for I have redeemed you.
55:11 it shall not **r** to me empty,
Jer 3:12 **R,** faithless Israel, says the LORD.
4: 1 If you **r,** O Israel, says the LORD,
24: 7 shall **r** to me with their whole heart.
31: 8 a great company, they shall **r** here.
La 3:40 our ways, and **r** to the LORD.
Hos 5: 4 Their deeds do not permit them to **r**
6: 1 let us **r** to the LORD;
12: 6 But as for you, **r** to your God,
14: 1 **R,** O Israel, to the LORD your God,
Joel 2:12 **r** to me with all your heart,
Am 4: 6 yet you did not **r** to me,
Zec 1: 3 **R** to me, says the LORD of hosts,
and I will **r** to you, says the LORD
10: 9 they shall rear their children and **r.**
Mal 3: 7 **R** to me, and I will **r** to you,
Ro 9: 9 "About this time I will **r** and Sarah

RETURNED → RETURN
Ge 8: 9 and it **r** to him to the ark,
Nu 13:25 of forty days they **r** from spying out
Ezr 2: 1 they **r** to Jerusalem and Judah,
Ne 7: 6 they **r** to Jerusalem and Judah,
1Pe 2:25 but now you have **r** to the shepherd
Jdt 4: 3 only recently **r** from exile,

RETURNS → RETURN
Pr 26:11 dog that **r** to its vomit is a fool who
Ecc 12: 7 and the breath **r** to God who gave it.
Sir 40:11 All that is of earth **r** to earth,

REUBEN → REUBENITES
Firstborn of Jacob by Leah (Ge 29:32; 46:8;
1Ch 2:1). Attempted to rescue Joseph (Ge 37:21-
30). Lost birthright for sleeping with Bilhah (Ge
35:22; 49:4). Tribe of blessed (Ge 49:3-4; Dt
33:6), numbered (Nu 1:21; 26:7), allotted land
east of Jordan (Nu 32; 34:14; Jos 13:15), west
(Eze 48:6), failed to help Deborah (Jdg 5:15-16),
supported David (1Ch 12:37), 12,000 from (Rev
7:5).

TRIBE OF REUBEN Nu 1:21; 13:4; Jos
20:8; 21:7, 36; 1Ch 6:78; Rev 7:5

REUBENITES → REUBEN
Nu 32: 1 the **R** and the Gadites owned a very
Dt 29: 8 gave it as an inheritance to the **R,**
Jos 13: 8 the **R** and the Gadites received their

REVEAL → REVEALED, REVEALS, REVELATION, REVELATIONS
Est 2:10 Esther did not **r** her people or
Da 2:11 no one can **r** it to the king except
Mt 11:27 to whom the Son chooses to **r** him.
Sir 1:30 The Lord will **r** your secrets

REVEALED → REVEAL
Dt 29:29 **r** things belong to us and to our
Isa 40: 5 the glory of the LORD shall be **r,**
53: 1 has the arm of the LORD been **r?**
Da 2:19 mystery was **r** to Daniel in a vision
Mt 11:25 and the intelligent and have **r** them
16:17 flesh and blood has not **r** this to you
Lk 17:30 on the day that the Son of Man is **r.**
Jn 2:11 and **r** his glory; and his disciples
12:38 has the arm of the Lord been **r?"**
Ro 1:17 in it the righteousness of God is **r**
8:18 with the glory about to be **r**
1Co 2:10 God has **r** to us through the Spirit;
3:13 because it will be **r** with fire,
Eph 3: 5 now been **r** to his holy apostles and
2Th 1: 7 the Lord Jesus is **r** from heaven
2: 3 and the lawless one is **r,**
1Pe 1: 7 and honor when Jesus Christ is **r.**
1:20 but was **r** at the end of the ages for
4:13 shout for joy when his glory is **r.**
1Jn 3: 2 we do know is this: when he is **r,**
Rev 15: 4 for your judgments have been **r."**

REVEALS → REVEAL
Da 2:22 He **r** deep and hidden things;
2:28 a God in heaven who **r** mysteries,
Am 4:13 the wind, **r** his thoughts to mortals,

REVELATION* → REVEAL
2Sa 7:27 have made this **r** to your servant,
Mic 3: 6 and darkness to you, without **r.**
Lk 2:32 a light for **r** to the Gentiles and for
Ro 16:25 the **r** of the mystery that was kept
1Co 14: 6 some **r** or knowledge or prophecy
14:26 each one has a hymn, a lesson, a **r,**
14:30 If a **r** is made to someone else
Gal 1:12 I received it through a **r** of Jesus
2: 2 I went up in response to a **r.**
Eph 1:17 and **r** as you come to know him,
3: 3 was made known to me by **r,**
Rev 1: 1 The **r** of Jesus Christ, which God

REVELATIONS* → REVEAL
2Co 12: 1 but I will go on to visions and **r** of
12: 7 the exceptional character of the **r.**

REVELING
2Pe 2:13 **r** in their dissipation while they

REVENGE → VENGEANCE
Jdg 16:28 this one act of **r** I may pay back

REVENUE
Ro 13: 7 **r** to whom **r** is due,

REVERE → REVERED, REVERENCE, REVERENT, REVERING
Jos 24:14 "Now therefore **r** the LORD,
Ps 119:48 I **r** your commandments,
Mal 4: 2 But for you who **r** my name the sun
Tob 4: 5 **"R** the Lord all your days,
Bel 1: 5 not **r** idols made with hands,

REVERED → REVERE
1Ki 18: 3 (Now Obadiah **r** the LORD greatly;
Mal 2: 5 **r** me and stood in awe of my name.

REVERENCE → REVERE
Eph 5:21 subject to one another out of **r** for
1Pe 3: 2 see the purity and **r** of your lives.

REVERENT* → REVERE
Tit 2: 3 older women to be **r** in behavior,
Heb 5: 7 heard because of his **r** submission.
1Pe 1:17 live in **r** fear during the time of

REVERING* → REVERE
Ne 1:11 who delight in **r** your name.

REVILE → REVILED
Ex 22:28 You shall not **r** God, or curse
Ps 74:10 the enemy to **r** your name forever?
Mt 5:11 people **r** you and persecute you

REVILED → REVILE
1Co 4:12 When **r,** we bless;
1Pe 4:14 If you are **r** for the name of Christ,

REVIVE → REVIVING
Ps 85: 6 Will you not **r** us again,
Isa 57:15 to **r** the spirit of the humble,
Hos 6: 2 After two days he will **r** us;

REVIVING → REVIVE
Ps 19: 7 of the LORD is perfect, **r** the soul;

REVOKED
Est 8: 8 with the king's ring cannot be **r."**
Da 6: 8 the Persians, which cannot be **r."**

REWARD → REWARDED, REWARDING, REWARDS
Ge 15: 1 your **r** shall be very great."
1Sa 24:19 So may the LORD **r** you with good
Ps 19:11 in keeping them there is great **r.**
127: 3 the fruit of the womb a **r.**
Pr 11:18 who sow righteousness get a true **r.**
25:22 and the LORD will **r** you.
Isa 40:10 **r** is with him, and his recompense
49: 4 and my **r** with my God."
62:11 **r** is with him, and his recompense
Mt 5:12 glad, for your **r** is great in heaven,
6: 1 you have no **r** from your Father in
6: 5 I tell you, they have received their **r.**
10:41 a prophet will receive a prophet's **r;**
10:41 a righteous person will receive the **r**
Lk 6:23 for surely your **r** is great in heaven;
6:35 Your **r** will be great, and you will
1Co 3:14 the builder will receive a **r.**
9:17 I do this of my own will, I have a **r;**
Col 3:24 the inheritance as your **r;**
Heb 11:26 for he was looking ahead to the **r.**
2Jn 1: 8 but may receive a full **r.**
Rev 22:12 I am coming soon; my **r** is with me,
Sir 11:22 of the Lord is the **r** of the pious,

REWARDED → REWARD
2Sa 22:21 The LORD **r** me according to my
2Ch 15: 7 for your work shall be **r."**
Pr 13:13 respect the commandment will be **r.**

REWARDING → REWARD
1Ki 8:32 and vindicating the righteous by **r**
Rev 11:18 for **r** your servants,

REWARDS → REWARD
1Sa 26:23 The LORD **r** everyone for his
Heb 11: 6 and that he **r** those who seek him.
2Es 2:35 Be ready for the **r** of the kingdom,

REZIN
Isa 7: 1 King **R** of Aram and King Pekah

RHODA*
Ac 12:13 a maid named **R** came to answer.

RIB → RIBS
Ge 2:22 **r** that the LORD God had taken from

RIBLAH
2Ki 25: 6 him up to the king of Babylon at **R,**

RIBS → RIB
Ge 2:21 then he took one of his **r** and closed

RICH → ENRICH, ENRICHED, RICHES, RICHLY

Ge 26:13 the man became **r**; he prospered
2Sa 12: 1 the one **r** and the other poor.
Job 34:19 nor regards the **r** more than the poor
Ps 21: 3 For you meet him with **r** blessings;
   49:16 not be afraid when some become **r**,
Pr 13: 7 pretend to be **r**, yet have nothing;
   21:17 loves wine and oil will not be **r**.
   22: 2 The **r** and the poor have this in
   23: 4 Do not wear yourself out to get **r**;
   28:20 to be **r** will not go unpunished.
   28:22 to get **r** and does not know that loss
Ecc 5:12 of the **r** will not let them sleep.
Isa 53: 9 and his tomb with the **r**,
Eze 34:14 and they shall feed on **r** pasture on
Mt 19:23 hard for a **r** person to enter the
Lk 1:53 and sent the **r** away empty.
   6:24 "But woe to you who are **r**,
   12:21 but are not **r** toward God."
   16: 1 a **r** man who had a manager,
   16:19 a **r** man who was dressed in purple
   21: 1 and saw **r** people putting their gifts
2Co 6:10 as poor, yet making many **r**;
   8: 9 by his poverty you might become **r**.
Eph 2: 4 But God, who is **r** in mercy,
1Ti 6: 9 be **r** fall into temptation
   6:17 those who in the present age are **r**,
   6:18 to do good, to be **r** in good works,
Jas 1:10 and the **r** in being brought low,
   1:10 the **r** will disappear like a flower in
   2: 5 the poor in the world to be **r** in faith
   5: 1 Come now, you **r** people,
Rev 2: 9 poverty, even though you are **r**.
   3:17 you say, 'I am **r**, I have prospered,
   3:18 by fire so that you may be **r**;
Sir 8: 2 Do not quarrel with the **r**,

RICHES → RICH

1Ki 3:13 both **r** and honor all your life;
   10:23 of the earth in **r** and in wisdom.
Ps 49: 6 boast of the abundance of their **r**?
   62:10 if **r** increase, do not set your heart
  119:14 of your decrees as much as in all **r**.
Pr 3:16 in her left hand are **r** and honor.
   11:28 who trust in their **r** will wither,
   22: 1 is to be chosen rather than great **r**,
   27:24 for **r** do not last forever,
   30: 8 give me neither poverty nor **r**;
Lk 8:14 they are choked by the cares and **r**
Ro 9:23 to make known the **r** of his glory
   11:12 their defeat means **r** for Gentiles,
   11:33 O the depth of the **r** and wisdom
Eph 2: 7 the immeasurable **r** of his grace in
   3: 8 Gentiles the news of the boundless **r**
Col 1:27 the Gentiles are the **r** of the glory
   2: 2 the **r** of assured understanding and
1Jn 2:16 the desire of the eyes, the pride in **r**
Sir 13:24 **R** are good if they are free from sin;

RICHLY → RICH

Col 3:16 the word of Christ dwell in you **r**;
1Ti 6:17 who **r** provides us with everything
Tit 3: 6 This Spirit he poured out on us **r**

RID

Col 3: 8 But now you must get **r** of all such
Jas 1:21 **r** yourselves of all sordidness and
1Pe 2: 1 **R** yourselves, therefore, of all

RIDDLE → RIDDLES

Jdg 14:12 "Let me now put a **r** to you.
Ps 49: 4 solve my **r** to the music of the harp.
Eze 17: 2 propound a **r**, and speak an allegory

RIDDLES → RIDDLE

Nu 12: 8 face to face—clearly, not in **r**;
Pr 1: 6 the words of the wise and their **r**.
Da 5:12 to interpret dreams, explain **r**,

RIDE → RIDER, RIDERS, RIDES, RIDING

Ps 45: 4 In your majesty **r** on victoriously

RIDER → RIDE

Ex 15: 1 and **r** he has thrown into the sea.
Rev 6: 2 Its **r** had a bow;
   19:11 Its **r** is called Faithful and True,

RIDERS → RIDE

Rev 9:17 the **r** wore breastplates the color of

RIDES → RIDE

Dt 33:26 **r** through the heavens to your help,
Ps 68: 4 a song to him who **r** upon the clouds

RIDING → RIDE

Zec 9: 9 humble and **r** on a donkey,

RIGGING*

Isa 33:23 Your **r** hangs loose; it cannot hold

RIGHT → BIRTHRIGHT, RIGHTLY, RIGHTS

Ge 13: 9 the left hand, then I will go to the **r**;
   48:13 Ephraim in his **r** hand toward
Ex 14:22 forming a wall for them on their **r**
   15: 6 Your **r** hand, O LORD, glorious in
   15:26 and do what is **r** in his sight,
Dt 5:32 shall not turn to the **r** or to the left.
   6:18 Do what is **r** and good in the sight
   13:18 doing what is **r** in the sight of
   28:14 either to the **r** or to the left,
Jos 1: 7 do not turn from it to the **r** hand or
1Sa 12:23 in the good and the **r** way.
1Ki 15: 5 David did what was **r** in the sight
Ne 9:13 them **r** ordinances and true laws,
Job 40:14 own **r** hand can give you victory.
   42: 7 have not spoken of me what is **r**,
Ps 4: 5 Offer **r** sacrifices, and put your trust
   16: 8 he is at my **r** hand, I shall not be
   16:11 in your **r** hand are pleasures
   17: 7 their adversaries at your **r** hand.
   18:35 and your **r** hand has supported me;
   19: 8 precepts of the LORD are **r**, rejoicing
   25: 9 He leads the humble in what is **r**,
   44: 3 but your **r** hand, and your arm,
   45: 4 cause of truth and to defend the **r**;
   63: 8 your **r** hand upholds me.
   73:23 with you; you hold my **r** hand.
   80:17 be upon the one at your **r** hand,
   89:13 your hand, high your **r** hand.
   91: 7 ten thousand at your **r** hand,
  110: 1 says to my lord, "Sit at my **r** hand
  110: 5 The Lord is at your **r** hand;
  118:15 **r** hand of the LORD does valiantly;
  137: 5 O Jerusalem, let my **r** hand wither!
  139:10 and your **r** hand shall hold me fast.
Pr 3:16 Long life is in her **r** hand;
   4:27 Do not swerve to the **r** or to the left;
   12:15 Fools think their own way is **r**,
   14:12 a way that seems **r** to a person,
   16:25 there is a way that seems to be **r**,
   18:17 who first states a case seems **r**,
   21: 2 deeds are **r** in the sight of the doer,
Isa 30:10 "Do not prophesy to us what is **r**;
   30:21 to the **r** or when you turn to the left,
   41:10 with my victorious **r** hand.
   41:13 LORD your God, hold your **r** hand;
   48:13 my **r** hand spread out the heavens,
   64: 5 You meet those who gladly do **r**,
Eze 1:10 the face of a lion on the **r** side,
   18: 5 and does what is lawful and **r**—
   18:21 and do what is lawful and **r**,
   33:14 and do what is lawful and **r**—
Hos 14: 9 For the ways of the LORD are **r**,
Am 3:10 They do not know how to do **r**,
Jnh 4:11 not know their **r** hand
Zec 3: 1 standing at his **r** hand to accuse him.
Mt 5:29 If your **r** eye causes you to sin,
   6: 3 know what your **r** hand is doing,
  22:44 "Sit at my **r** hand, until I put your
  25:33 sheep at his **r** hand and the goats at
Mk 14:62 seated at the **r** hand of the Power,'
Jn 7:24 but judge with **r** judgment."
Ac 2:34 said to my Lord, "Sit at my **r** hand,
   7:55 and Jesus standing at the **r** hand
Ro 8:34 raised, who is at the **r** hand of God,

   9:21 Has the potter no **r** over the clay,
1Co 9: 4 Do we not have the **r** to our food
2Co 8:21 is **r** not only in the Lord's sight but
Eph 1:20 and seated him at his **r** hand in
   6: 1 parents in the Lord, for this is **r**.
Col 3: 1 where Christ is, seated at the **r** hand
2Th 3:13 do not be weary in doing what is **r**.
Heb 1: 3 he sat down at the **r** hand of the
   1:13 "Sit at my **r** hand until I make your
   10:12 "he sat down at the **r** hand of God,"
1Pe 3:14 if you do suffer for doing what is **r**,
   3:22 into heaven and is at the **r** hand
1Jn 2:29 who does **r** has been born of him.
   3: 7 who does what is **r** is righteous,
Rev 1:16 In his **r** hand he held seven stars,
  22:11 and the righteous still do **r**,
  22:14 have to the tree of life and may
Sir 20: 7 remain silent until the **r** moment,
Bar 1:15 The Lord our God is in the **r**,

DO WHAT IS ... RIGHT
Ex 15:26; Dt 6:18; 12:25; 21:9; 1Ki 11:38; Ps 15:2; Isa 16:5; 56:1; Eze 18:21, 27; 33:14, 19; 45:9; 2Co 8:21; 13:7; 1Jn 3:10; Tob 13:6; 14:8

IN THE RIGHT
Ge 38:26; Ex 9:27; 23:7, 8; Dt 6:25; 16:19; 25:1; 2Ch 6:23; 12:6; Job 35:2; Pr 22:6; 27:16; Isa 29:21; Jer 12:1; La 1:18; Eze 16:52; Rev 5:1; Bar 1:15; 2:6

NOT RIGHT
2Ki 17:9; Job 33:12; Pr 17:26; 18:5; Jer 23:10; Hab 2:4; Jn 8:48; Ac 6:2; 8:21; Tit 1:11; Jdt 8:11; Sir 10:23; 2Mc 6:20

RIGHT HAND
Ge 13:9; 24:49; 48:13, 14, 17, 18; Ex 15:6, 6, 12; Lev 8:23; 14:14, 17, 25, 28; Nu 20:17; Jos 1:7; Jdg 5:26; 16:29; 2Sa 20:9; 1Ch 12:2; Ne 4:23; 8:4; Job 30:12; 40:14; Ps 16:8, 11; 17:7; 18:35; 20:6; 21:8; 44:3; 45:4, 9; 48:10; 60:5; 63:8; 73:23; 77:10; 78:54; 80:15, 17; 89:13, 25, 42; 91:7; 98:1; 108:6; 109:31; 110:1, 5; 118:15, 16, 16; 121:5; 137:5; 138:7; 139:10; 142:4; Pr 3:16; 27:16; SS 2:6; 8:3; Isa 41:10, 13; 44:20; 45:1; 48:13; 62:8; 63:12; Jer 22:24; La 2:3, 4; Eze 21:22; 39:3; Da 12:7; Jnh 4:11; Hab 2:16; Zec 3:1; Mt 5:30; 6:3; 20:21, 23; 22:44; 25:33, 34; 26:64; 27:29; Mk 10:37, 40; 12:36; 14:62; 16:19; Lk 6:6; 20:42; 22:69; Ac 2:25, 33, 34; 3:7; 5:31; 7:55, 56; Ro 8:34; 2Co 6:7; Gal 2:9; Eph 1:20; Col 3:1; Heb 1:3, 13; 8:1; 10:12; 12:2; 1Pe 3:22; Rev 1:16, 17, 20; 2:1; 5:1, 7; 10:5; 13:16; Wis 5:16; Sir 12:12; 21:19; 49:11; LtJ 6:15; 1Mc 2:22; 7:47; 2Mc 4:34; 14:33; 15:15; 1Es 4:29; 2Es 3:6; 7:7; 10:30; 15:22; 16:13

RIGHTEOUS → RIGHTEOUSLY, RIGHTEOUSNESS, RIGHTEOUSNESS'

Ge 6: 9 Noah was a **r** man, blameless in his
   18:23 will indeed sweep away the **r**
1Sa 24:17 to David, "You are more **r** than I.
Ne 9: 8 fulfilled your promise, for you are **r**.
Job 4:17 'Can mortals be **r** before God?
   36: 7 not withdraw his eyes from the **r**,
Ps 1: 5 sinners in the congregation of the **r**;
   5:12 For you bless the **r**, O LORD;
   7:11 God is a **r** judge, and a God who
   11: 7 For the LORD is **r**; he loves **r** deeds;
  34:15 The eyes of the LORD are on the **r**,
  37:16 a little that the **r** person has than the
  37:21 the **r** are generous and keep giving;
  37:25 the **r** forsaken or their children
  37:30 The mouths of the **r** utter wisdom,
  55:22 never permit the **r** to be moved.
  64:10 Let the **r** rejoice in the LORD and
  68: 3 But let the **r** be joyful;
  112: 4 they are gracious, merciful, and **r**.
  116: 5 Gracious is the LORD, and **r**;
  118:20 the **r** enter through it.
  119: 7 when I learn your **r** ordinances.
  119:137 You are **r**, O LORD,
  140:13 **r** shall give thanks to your name;
  143: 2 for no one living is **r** before you.
  146: 8 bowed down; the LORD loves the **r**.
Pr 3:33 but he blesses the abode of the **r**.

4: 18 But the path of the **r** is like the light
10: 6 Blessings are on the head of the **r**,
10: 7 The memory of the **r** is a blessing,
10: 11 mouth of the **r** is a fountain of life,
10: 16 The wage of the **r** leads to life,
10: 20 The tongue of the **r** is choice silver;
10: 24 the desire of the **r** will be granted.
10: 28 The hope of the **r** ends in gladness,
11: 9 by knowledge the **r** are delivered.
11: 23 desire of the **r** ends only in good;
11: 30 The fruit of the **r** is a tree of life,
12: 10 The **r** know the needs of their
12: 21 No harm happens to the **r**,
13: 5 The **r** hate falsehood,
13: 9 The light of the **r** rejoices,
14: 32 the **r** find a refuge in their integrity.
15: 28 of the **r** ponders how to answer,
15: 29 but he hears the prayer of the **r**.
16: 31 it is gained in a **r** life.
18: 10 the **r** run into it and are safe.
20: 7 The **r** walk in integrity—
21: 15 justice is done, it is a joy to the **r**,
23: 24 father of the **r** will greatly rejoice;
28: 1 but the **r** are as bold as a lion.
29: 2 When the **r** are in authority, the
29: 6 but the **r** sing and rejoice.
29: 7 The **r** know the rights of the poor;
29: 27 unjust are an abomination to the **r**,
Ecc   7: 15 there are **r** people who perish
7: 20 no one on earth so **r** as to do good
8: 14 **r** people who are treated according
Isa 26: 7 The way of the **r** is level;
26: 7 you make smooth the path of the **r**.
45: 21 a **r** God and a Savior; there is no
53: 11 The **r** one, my servant, shall make
many **r**,
64: 6 all our **r** deeds are like a filthy cloth.
Jer 23: 5 I will raise up for David a **r** Branch,
33: 15 I will cause a **r** Branch to spring
Eze   3: 20 if the **r** turn from their righteousness
18: 5 If a man is **r** and does what is lawful
18: 20 the righteousness of the **r** shall be
33: 12 of the **r** shall not save them when
Hab   2: 4 but the **r** live by their faith.
Zep   3: 5 The LORD within it is **r**; he does no
Mal   3: 18 between the **r** and the wicked,
Mt   5: 45 rain on the **r** and on the unrighteous.
13: 43 Then the **r** will shine like the sun in
13: 49 and separate the evil from the **r**
25: 37 Then the **r** will answer him, 'Lord,
25: 46 but the **r** into eternal life."
Mk   2: 17 come to call not the **r** but sinners."
Ac   3: 14 you rejected the Holy and **R** One
24: 15 a resurrection of both the **r** and
Ro   1: 17 one who is **r** will live by faith."
2: 5 God's **r** judgment will be revealed.
2: 13 the hearers of the law who are **r** in
3: 10 no one who is **r**, not even one;
5: 19 the many will be made **r**.
2Ti   4: 8 the **r** judge, will give me on that day
Heb 10: 38 but my **r** one will live by faith.
Jas   5: 16 The prayer of the **r** is powerful and
1Pe   3: 12 the eyes of the Lord are on the **r**,
3: 18 the **r** for the unrighteous,
4: 18 "If it is hard for the **r** to be saved,
2Pe   2: 7 and if he rescued Lot, a **r** man
1Jn   2: 1 with the Father, Jesus Christ the **r**;
3: 7 Everyone who does what is right is
r, just as he is is.
Rev 19: 8 the fine linen is the **r** deeds of the
Tob   3: 2 "You are **r**, O Lord,
Wis   5: 15 **r** live forever, and their reward
Sir 35: 22 and does justice for the **r**,
1Mc   2: 24 He gave vent to **r** anger;
2Es 14: 32 And since he is a **r** judge,

RIGHTEOUS DEEDS Ps 11:7; Isa 64:6;
Eze 3:20; 18:24; 33:13; Rev 19:8; Tob 2:14;
Sir 32:16; 44:10; Bar 2:19; 2Es 7:35

RIGHTEOUS MAN Ge 6:9; 2Sa 4:11; Mt
1:19; Lk 23:50; 2Pe 2:7, 8; Wis 2:12, 18; 10:4,
5, 6, 10, 13; 19:17

RIGHTEOUS ONE Pr 21:12; Isa 24:16;
53:11; Ac 3:14; 7:52; 22:14; Heb 10:38; Jas 5:6

RIGHTEOUSLY → RIGHTEOUS
Isa 33: 15 who walk **r** and speak uprightly,
Jer 11: 20 O LORD of hosts, who judge **r**,

RIGHTEOUSNESS → RIGHTEOUS
Ge   15: 6 the LORD reckoned it to him as **r**.
Dt   9: 4 because of my **r** that the LORD has
1Sa 26: 23 LORD rewards everyone for his **r**
1Ki 10: 9 king to execute justice and **r**."
Job 27: 6 I hold fast my **r**, and will not let it
37: 23 and abundant **r** he will not violate.
Ps   7: 17 to the LORD the thanks due to his **r**,
9: 8 He judges the world with **r**;
17: 15 I shall behold your face in **r**;
18: 20 rewarded me according to my **r**;
33: 5 He loves **r** and justice; the earth is
35: 24 LORD, my God, according to your **r**,
35: 28 of your **r** and of your praise all day
36: 6 Your **r** is like the mighty mountains,
45: 7 you love **r** and hate wickedness.
50: 6 heavens declare his **r**, for God
71: 2 In your **r** deliver me and rescue me;
71: 19 and your **r**, O God, reach
72: 2 May he judge your people with **r**,
85: 10 **r** and peace will kiss each other.
89: 14 **R** and justice are the foundation of
96: 13 He will judge the world with **r**,
98: 9 He will judge the world with **r**,
103: 17 and his **r** to children's children,
106: 31 as **r** from generation to generation
111: 3 and his **r** endures forever.
118: 19 Open to me the gates of **r**,
132: 9 Let your priests be clothed with **r**,
145: 7 and shall sing aloud of your **r**.
Pr   8: 20 I walk in the way of **r**, along the
10: 2 but **r** delivers from death.
11: 5 The **r** of the blameless keeps their
11: 6 The **r** of the upright saves them,
11: 18 those who sow **r** get a true reward.
12: 28 In the path of **r** there is life,
13: 6 **R** guards one whose way is upright,
14: 34 **R** exalts a nation, but sin is a
15: 9 but he loves the one who pursues **r**.
16: 12 for the throne is established by **r**.
21: 21 pursues **r** and kindness will find life
Ecc   7: 15 people who perish in their **r**,
Isa   1: 26 you shall be called the city of **r**,
5: 16 Holy God shows himself holy by **r**.
9: 7 justice and with **r** from this time
11: 4 but with **r** he shall judge the poor,
11: 5 **R** shall be the belt around his waist,
26: 9 the inhabitants of the world learn **r**.
28: 17 justice the line, and **r** the plummet;
32: 1 See, a king will reign in **r**,
32: 17 The effect of **r** will be peace, and
result of **r**, quietness and trust
33: 5 he filled Zion with justice and **r**;
42: 6 in **r**, I have taken you by the hand
42: 21 was pleased, for the sake of his **r**,
45: 8 and let the skies rain down **r**;
45: 24 said of me, are **r** and strength;
59: 17 He put on **r** like a breastplate,
61: 10 has covered me with the robe of **r**,
Jer   9: 24 and **r** in the earth, for in these
23: 6 be called: "The LORD is our **r**."
33: 16 be called: "The LORD is our **r**."
Eze   3: 20 righteous turn from their **r** and
14: 20 save only their own lives by their **r**.
18: 20 the **r** of the righteous shall be his
33: 12 The **r** of the righteous shall not save
Da   9: 24 to bring in everlasting **r**,
12: 3 and those who lead many to **r**,
Hos   2: 19 I will take you for my wife in **r** and
10: 12 Sow for yourselves **r**; reap steadfast
Am   5: 24 and **r** like an ever-flowing stream.
Zep   2: 3 seek **r**, seek humility; perhaps you
Mal   4: 2 my name the sun of **r** shall rise,
Mt   3: 15 for us in this way to fulfill all **r**."
5: 6 those who hunger and thirst for **r**,

5: 20 your **r** exceeds that of the scribes
6: 33 for the kingdom of God and his **r**,
Jn   16: 8 about sin and **r** and judgment:
Ro   1: 17 the **r** of God is revealed through
3: 22 the **r** of God through faith in Jesus
4: 3 and it was reckoned to him as **r**."
4: 5 such faith is reckoned as **r**.
4: 6 God reckons **r** apart from works:
4: 9 was reckoned to Abraham as **r**."
4: 13 the law but through the **r** of faith.
4: 22 faith "was reckoned to him as **r**."
5: 18 act of **r** leads to justification
6: 13 to God as instruments of **r**.
6: 16 or of obedience, which leads to **r**?
6: 18 have become slaves of **r**.
6: 19 present your members as slaves to **r**
8: 10 the Spirit is life because of **r**.
9: 30 who did not strive for **r**, have
attained it, that is, **r** through faith;
10: 3 ignorant of the **r** that comes from
10: 4 be **r** for everyone who believes.
14: 17 of God is not food and drink but **r**
1Co   1: 30 **r** and sanctification and redemption,
2Co   5: 21 we might become the **r** of God.
6: 7 the weapons of **r** for the right hand
6: 14 what partnership is there between **r**
9: 9 to the poor; his **r** endures forever."
9: 10 and increase the harvest of your **r**.
11: 15 themselves as ministers of **r**.
Gal   3: 6 and it was reckoned to him as **r**,"
Eph   4: 24 to the likeness of God in true **r**
6: 14 and put on the breastplate of **r**.
Php   1: 11 of **r** that comes through Jesus Christ
3: 6 as to **r** under the law, blameless.
3: 9 the **r** from God based on faith.
1Ti   6: 11 pursue **r**, godliness, faith, love,
2Ti   2: 22 Shun youthful passions and pursue **r**
3: 16 for correction, and for training in **r**,
4: 8 reserved for me the crown of **r**,
Heb   5: 13 is unskilled in the word of **r**.
7: 2 in the first place, means "king of **r**";
11: 7 became an heir to the **r** that is in
12: 11 of **r** to those who have been trained
Jas   2: 23 and it was reckoned to him as **r**,"
3: 18 of **r** is sown in peace for those who
1Pe   2: 24 free from sins, we might live for **r**;
2Pe   2: 21 never to have known the way of **r**
3: 13 heavens and a new earth, where **r** is
Rev 19: 11 and in **r** he judges and makes war.
Tob 12: 8 than both is almsgiving with **r**.
Wis   1: 15 For **r** is immortal.
2Es 16: 52 and **r** will reign over us.

RIGHTEOUSNESS' → RIGHTEOUS
Mt   5: 10 those who are persecuted for **r** sake,

RIGHTLY → RIGHT
Mk   7: 6 prophesied **r** about you hypocrites,
Lk   7: 43 said to him, "You have judged **r**."
2Ti   2: 15 **r** explaining the word of truth.

RIGHTS → RIGHT
Ex   21: 10 or marital **r** of the first wife.
Pr   31: 8 for the **r** of all the destitute.
Jer   5: 28 do not defend the **r** of the needy.
La   3: 35 when human **r** are perverted in the
1Co   9: 15 have made no use of any of these **r**,

RING → EARRINGS
Ge   41: 42 Removing his signet **r** from his
Est   3: 12 and sealed with the king's **r**,
8: 10 sealed them with the king's **r**,
Pr   11: 22 a gold **r** in a pig's snout is a
Jer 22: 24 of Judah were the signet **r** on my
Hag   2: 23 and make you like a signet **r**;
Lk   15: 22 put a **r** on his finger and sandals on

RIOT → RIOTS
Mk   14: 2 there may be a **r** among the people."

RIOTS' → RIOT
2Co   6: 5 imprisonments, **r**, labors, sleepless

RIPE

Joel   3:13 Put in the sickle, for the harvest is **r.**
Mk   4:29 But when the grain is **r,**
Jn   4:35 how the fields are **r** for harvesting.
Rev 14:15 the harvest of the earth is fully **r."**

RISE → ARISE, ARISEN, AROSE, RAISE,
RAISED, RAISES, RISEN, RISES, RISING,
ROSE

Nu 24:17 and a scepter shall **r** out of Israel;
Ps   3: 7 **R** up, O LORD! Deliver me,
      7: 6 **R** up, O LORD, in your anger;
   74:22 **R** up, O God, plead your cause;
   94: 2 **R** up, O judge of the earth;
Isa 26:19 dead shall live, their corpses shall **r.**
Da 12:13 shall **r** for your reward at the end of
Am   8:14 they shall fall, and never **r** again.
Mal   4: 2 the sun of righteousness shall **r,**
Mt   5:45 he makes his sun **r** on the evil and
   27:63 'After three days I will **r** again.'
Mk   8:31 killed, and after three days **r** again.
   13: 8 For nation will **r** against nation,
Lk 18:33 on the third day he will **r** again."
Jn 20: 9 that he must **r** from the dead.
Ac 17: 3 the Messiah to suffer and to **r** from
Eph 5:14 **R** from the dead, and Christ will
1Th 4:16 and the dead in Christ will **r** first.

RISEN → RISE

Isa 60: 1 glory of the LORD has **r** upon you.
Lk 24:34 saying, "The Lord has **r** indeed,

RISES → RISE

Ecc   1: 5 The sun **r** and the sun goes down,
Isa   2:19 when he **r** to terrify the earth.
Lk 16:31 even if someone **r** from the dead.'"
2Pe 1:19 day dawns and the morning star **r**

RISING → RISE

Ps 113: 3 From the **r** of the sun to its setting
Mt   2: 2 For we observed his star at its **r,**
Mk   9:10 questioning what this **r** from
Lk   2:34 destined for the falling and the **r** of
Rev 13: 1 a beast **r** out of the sea

RIVALRY

Php 1:15 proclaim Christ from envy and **r,**

RIVER → RIVERS

Ge   2:10 A **r** flows out of Eden to water the
   15:18 from the **r** of Egypt to the great **r,**
Dt   1: 7 as far as the great **r,** the **r** Euphrates.
   11:24 the **r** Euphrates, to the Western Sea.
Ps 46: 4 a **r** whose streams make glad the
Isa 48:18 prosperity would have been like a **r,**
   66:12 extend prosperity to her like a **r,**
Eze 47:12 On the banks, on both sides of the **r,**
Mt   3: 6 baptized by him in the **r** Jordan,
Rev 16: 1 the serpent poured water like a **r**
   22: 1 showed me the **r** of the water of life,
2Es 14:47 wisdom, and the **r** of knowledge."

RIVERS → RIVER

Ps 78:16 caused waters to flow down like **r.**
   78:44 He turned their **r** to blood,
  137: 1 By the **r** of Babylon—there we sat
Rev 8:10 it fell on a third of the **r** and on the
   16: 4 angel poured his bowl into the **r** and
Aza 1:55 Bless the Lord, seas and **r;**

ROAD → CROSSROADS

Nu 22:22 of the LORD took his stand in the **r**
Mt   7:13 and the **r** is easy that leads to
Mk 11: 8 people spread their cloaks on the **r,**

ROAR → ROARED, ROARING, ROARS

Ps 46: 3 though its waters **r** and foam,
Isa 17:13 The nations **r** like the roaring of
Jer 25:30 The LORD will **r** from on high,

ROARING → ROAR

Ps 65: 7 You silence the **r** of the seas,
1Pe 5: 8 a **r** lion your adversary the devil

ROARS → ROAR

Hos 11:10 the LORD, who **r** like a lion;
Joel 3:16 The LORD **r** from Zion,
Am   1: 2 The LORD **r** from Zion,

ROASTED

Ex 12: 8 they shall eat it **r** over the fire

ROB → ROBBER, ROBBERS, ROBBERY,
ROBS

Mal   3: 8 anyone **r** God? Yet you are robbing
Ro   2:22 abhor idols, do you **r** temples?

ROBBER → ROB

1Co 5:11 an idolater, reviler, drunkard, or **r.**

ROBBERS → ROB

Jer   7:11 become a den of **r** in your sight?
Mt 21:13 but you are making it a den of **r."**
Lk 10:30 and fell into the hands of **r,** who
   19:46 but you have made it a den of **r."**
1Co 6:10 **r**—none of these will inherit the

ROBBERY → ROB

Ps 62:10 and set no vain hopes on **r;**
Isa 61: 8 I hate **r** and wrongdoing;
Eze 22:29 extortion and committed **r;**

ROBE → ROBED, ROBES

Ge 37: 3 had made him a long **r** with sleeves.
Ex 28: 4 a breastpiece, an ephod, a **r,**
1Sa 2:19 little **r** and take it to him each year,
   15:27 Saul caught hold of the hem of his **r**
2Sa 13:18 was wearing a long **r** with sleeves;
Isa   6: 1 the hem of his **r** filled the temple.
   61:10 with the **r** of righteousness,
Lk 15:22 to his slaves, 'Quickly, bring out a **r**
Jn 19: 5 crown of thorns and the purple **r.**
Rev 1:13 a long **r** and with a golden sash
   6:11 They were each given a white **r** and
   19:13 He is clothed in a **r** dipped in blood,
Bar 5: 2 Put on the **r** of the righteousness

ROBED → ROBE

Est 6:11 and **r** Mordecai and led him riding
Ps 93: 1 LORD is king, he is **r** in majesty;
Isa 63: 1 Who is this so splendidly **r,**
Rev 7: 9 **r** in white, with palm branches
   15: 6 **r** in pure bright linen,

ROBES → ROBE

Ps 45: 8 your **r** are all fragrant with myrrh
Mk 12:38 who like to walk around in long **r,**
Rev 22:14 Blessed are those who wash their **r,**

ROBS → ROB

Pr 28:24 Anyone who **r** father or mother and

ROCK → ROCKS, ROCKY

Ge 49:24 of the Shepherd, the **R** of Israel,
Ex 17: 6 there in front of you on the **r**
   17: 6 Strike the **r,** and water will come
   33:22 of the **r,** and I will cover you with
Nu 20: 8 you shall bring water out of the **r**
Dt 32: 4 The **R,** his work is perfect, and all
   32:13 the crags, with oil from flinty **r;**
   32:15 and scoffed at the **R** of his salvation.
   32:31 Indeed their **r** is not like our **R;**
1Sa 2: 2 there is no **R** like our God.
2Sa 22: 2 The LORD is my **r,** my fortress,
Ps 18: 2 The LORD is my **r,** my fortress,
   19:14 O LORD, my **r** and my redeemer.
   27: 5 he will set me high on a **r.**
   40: 2 miry bog, and set my feet upon a **r,**
   61: 2 Lead me to the **r** that is higher than
   62: 2 He alone is my **r** and my salvation,
   92:15 he is my **r,** and there is no
Isa 26: 4 GOD you have an everlasting **r.**
   44: 8 There is no other **r;** I know not one.
   48:21 water flow for them from the **r;**
   51: 1 to the **r** from which you were hewn,
Mt   7:24 wise man who built his house on **r.**
   16:18 and on this **r** I will build my church,
Mk 15:46 that had been hewn out of the **r.**

ROARS → ROAR

Ro   9:33 a **r** that will make them fall,
1Co 10: 4 followed them, and the **r** was Christ.
1Pe 2: 8 and a **r** that makes them fall."
Wis 11: 4 water was given them out of flinty **r**
Sir 51:12 *Give thanks to the **r** of Isaac,*

ROCKS → ROCK

Ps 78:15 He split **r** open in the wilderness,
Isa   2:19 the caves of the **r** and the holes of
Na   1: 6 by him the **r** are broken in pieces.
Mt 27:51 earth shook, and the **r** were split.
Rev 6:15 in the caves and among the **r** of the

ROCKY → ROCK

Mk   4: 5 Other seed fell on **r** ground,

ROD → RODS

2Sa 7:14 I will punish him with a **r** such as
Ps   2: 9 shall break them with a **r** of iron,
   23: 4 your **r** and your staff—they comfort
Pr 13:24 who spare the **r** hate their children,
   14: 3 talk of fools is a **r** for their backs,
   22:15 but the **r** of discipline drives it far
   23:13 if you beat them with a **r,** they will
   29:15 The **r** and reproof give wisdom,
Isa 11: 4 the earth with the **r** of his mouth,
Heb 9: 4 and Aaron's **r** that budded,
Rev 2:27 to rule them with an iron **r,**
   19:15 rule them with a **r** of iron;

RODS → ROD

2Co 11:25 Three times I was beaten with **r.**

ROLL → ROLLED, ROLLING

Am   5:24 But let justice **r** down like waters,
Mk 16: 3 "Who will **r** away the stone for us
Heb 1:12 like a cloak you will **r** them up,

ROLLED → ROLL

Jos   5: 9 I have **r** away from you the disgrace
Lk 24: 2 They found the stone **r** away from

ROLLING* → ROLL

Pr 26:27 back on the one who starts it **r.**
Rev 6:14 sky vanished like a scroll **r** itself up,

ROMAN → ROME

Ac 16:37 men who are **R** citizens,
   22:25 for you to flog a **R** citizen who is

ROMANS → ROME

Jn 11:48 the **R** will come and destroy both
1Mc 8: 1 Judas heard of the fame of the **R,**
   14:24 to confirm the alliance with the **R.**

ROME → ROMAN, ROMANS

Ac 18: 2 had ordered all Jews to leave **R.**
   28:14 And so we came to **R.**
Ro   1:15 the gospel to you also who are in **R.**

ROOF

Ge 19: 8 come under the shelter of my **r."**
Jos   2: 6 to the **r** and hidden them
2Sa 11: 2 he saw from the **r** a woman bathing;
Mt   8: 8 to have you come under my **r;**
Mk   2: 4 they removed the **r** above him;
Ac 10: 9 Peter went up on the **r** to pray.

ROOM → ROOMS

Mt   6: 6 your **r** and shut the door and pray
Mk 14:15 He will show you a large **r** upstairs.
Ro 12:19 but leave **r** for the wrath of God;
2Co 7: 2 Make **r** in your hearts for us;
Eph 4:27 and do not make **r** for the devil.

ROOMS → ROOM

Mt 24:26 in the inner **r,'** do not believe it.

ROOT → ROOTED, ROOTS

Pr 12:12 but the **r** of the righteous bears fruit.
Isa 11:10 On that day the **r** of Jesse
   53: 2 and like a **r** out of dry ground;
Mt   3:10 the ax is lying at the **r** of the trees;
   13:21 a person has no **r,**
Ro 11:18 but the **r** that supports you.

15:12 "The **r** of Jesse shall come,
1Ti   6:10 For the love of money is a **r** of all
           kinds of evil,
Rev   5: 5 the tribe of Judah, the **R** of David,
      22:16 I am the **r** and the descendant of
Sir   1:20 To fear the Lord is the **r** of wisdom,
      47:22 to David a **r** from his own family.
1Mc   1:10 From them came forth a sinful **r**,

ROOTED → ROOT

Eph   3:17 are being **r** and grounded in love.
Col   2: 7 **r** and built up in him and

ROOTS → ROOT

Isa   11: 1 and a branch shall grow out of his **r**.
Jer   17: 8 sending out its **r** by the stream.
Eze   17: 9 Will he not pull up its **r**,

ROSE → RISE

SS   2: 1 I am a **r** of Sharon, a lily
Eze   1:19 living creatures **r** from the earth,
           the wheels **r**.
Ac   10:41 with him after he **r** from the dead.
1Th   4:14 believe that Jesus died and **r** again,

ROT → ROTTED

Pr   10: 7 but the name of the wicked will **r**.
Zec   14:12 their flesh shall **r** while they

ROTTED → ROT

Jas   5: 2 Your riches have **r**, and your clothes

ROUGH*

Isa   40: 4 and the **r** places a plain.
      42:16 the **r** places into level ground.
Lk   3: 5 and the **r** ways made smooth;
Jn   6:18 The sea became **r** because
Bar   4:26 children have traveled **r** roads;

ROUND

Ecc   1: 6 **r** and **r** goes the wind,

ROUSE → AROUSED, AROUSES

Job   3: 8 who are skilled to **r** up Leviathan.
Ps   59: 4 **R** yourself, come to my help
Hab   2:19 to silent stone, "**R** yourself!"

ROUTED

Dt   32:30 How could one have **r** a thousand,
Ps   18:14 flashed forth lightnings, and **r** them.

ROYAL

1Ki   9: 5 your **r** throne over Israel forever,
2Ch   22:10 to destroy all the **r** family of the
Est   4:14 to **r** dignity for just such a time as
Isa   62: 3 a **r** diadem in the hand of your God.
Da   1: 8 not defile himself with the **r** rations
Jas   2: 8 if you really fulfill the **r** law
1Pe   2: 9 are a chosen race, a **r** priesthood,

RUBBISH

1Co   4:13 have become like the **r** of the world,
Php   3: 8 and I regard them as **r**,

RUDDER

Jas   3: 4 they are guided by a very small **r**

RUDDY

1Sa   16:12 he was **r**, and had beautiful eyes,
SS   5:10 My beloved is all radiant and **r**,

RUDE

1Co   13: 5 or **r**. It does not insist on its own

RUIN → RUINED, RUINS

Pr   10: 8 but a babbling fool will come to **r**.
      10:14 the babbling of a fool brings **r** near.
      19:13 A stupid child is **r** to a father,
      26:28 and a flattering mouth works **r**.
SS   2:15 little foxes, that **r** the vineyards—
Isa   25: 2 the city a heap, the fortified city a **r;**
Eze   21:27 A **r**, a **r**, a **r**—I will make it!
Hos   4:14 without understanding comes to **r**.
Zep   1:15 a day of **r** and devastation,
1Ti   6: 9 desires that plunge people into **r**
Sir   20:25 but the lot of both is **r**.

RUINED → RUIN

Ex   10: 7 not yet understand that Egypt is **r?**"
Eze   36:36 the LORD, have rebuilt the **r** places,
Sir   8: 2 for gold has **r** many,

RUINS → RUIN

Ezr   9: 9 the house of our God, to repair its **r**,
Ne   2:17 Jerusalem lies in **r** with its gates
Jer   9:11 I will make Jerusalem a heap of **r**,
Am   9:11 repair its breaches, and raise up its **r**
Mic   3:12 Jerusalem shall become a heap of **r**,
Ac   15:16 from its **r** I will rebuild it,
1Co   15:33 "Bad company **r** good morals."
2Ti   2:14 but only **r** those who are listening.
1Mc   3:43 "Let us restore the **r** of our people,

RULE → RULER, RULER'S, RULERS, RULES

Ge   3:16 husband, and he shall **r** over you."
Dt   15: 6 you will **r** over many nations,
Jdg   8:22 Israelites said to Gideon, "**R** over us
Ps   110: 2 **R** in the midst of your foes.
Pr   12:24 The hand of the diligent will **r**,
      17: 2 slave who deals wisely will **r** over
Isa   3: 4 and babes shall **r** over them.
      32: 1 and princes will **r** with justice.
Zec   6:13 and shall sit and **r** on his throne.
Ro   15:12 the one who rises to **r** the Gentiles;
1Co   7:17 This is my **r** in all the churches.
Eph   1:21 far above all **r** and authority and
Col   3:15 the peace of Christ **r** in your hearts,
Rev   2:27 to **r** them with an iron rod,
      12: 5 to **r** all the nations with a rod of iron
      19:15 he will **r** them with a rod of iron;

RULER → RULE

Ex   2:14 made you a **r** and judge over us?
Pr   23: 1 When you sit down to eat with a **r**,
      25:15 With patience a **r** may be persuaded
      29:12 If a **r** listens to falsehood,
      29:26 Many seek the favor of a **r**,
Ecc   9:17 the shouting of a **r** among fools.
Mt   2: 6 a **r** who is to shepherd my people
Ac   7:27 made you a **r** and a judge over us?
1Co   15:24 after he has destroyed every **r**
Eph   2: 2 the **r** of the power of the air,
Col   2:10 head of every **r** and authority.
Rev   1: 5 and the **r** of the kings of the earth.
Sir   4:27 or show partiality to a **r**.
Aza   1:15 In our day we have no **r**,

RULER'S → RULE

Ge   49:10 the **r** staff from between his feet,

RULERS → RULE

Ps   2: 2 and the **r** take counsel together,
Pr   8:15 and **r** decree what is just;
      31: 4 or for **r** to desire strong drink;
Isa   1:10 word of the LORD, you **r** of Sodom!
      40:23 makes the **r** of the earth as nothing.
Mt   2: 6 least among the **r** of Judah;
      20:25 that the **r** of the Gentiles lord it
Ac   4:26 the **r** have gathered together against
Ro   13: 3 **r** are not a terror to good conduct,
1Co   2: 6 not a wisdom of this age or of the **r**
Eph   3:10 now be made known to the **r**
      6:12 against the **r**, against the authorities,
Col   1:16 whether thrones or dominions or **r**

RULES → RULE

2Sa   23: 3 One who **r** over people justly,
Ps   22:28 and he **r** over the nations.
      66: 7 who **r** by his might forever,
      103:19 and his kingdom **r** over all.
Isa   40:10 and his arm **r** for him;
2Ti   2: 5 competing according to the **r**.
Rev   17:18 you saw is the great city that **r** over

RUMOR → RUMORS

Eze   7:26 comes upon disaster, **r** follows **r**;
Jn   21:23 So the **r** spread in the community

RUMORS → RUMOR

Jer   51:46 or fearful at the **r** heard in the land
Mt   24: 6 you will hear of wars and **r** of wars;

RUN → FORERUNNER, RAN, RUNNERS, RUNNING, RUNS

Ps   119:32 I **r** the way of your commandments,
Pr   4:12 and if you **r**, you will not stumble.
      18:10 the righteous **r** into it and are safe.
Isa   40:31 they shall **r** and not be weary,
1Co   9:24 **R** in such a way that you may win
Gal   2: 2 or had not **r**, in vain.
Php   2:16 of Christ that I did not **r**
Heb   12: 1 let us **r** with perseverance the race

RUNNERS* → RUN

1Co   9:24 that in a race the **r** all compete,

RUNNING → RUN

Ps   133: 2 **r** down upon the beard, on the beard
      133: 2 **r** down over the collar of his robes.
Gal   5: 7 You were **r** well; who prevented

RUNS → RUN

Jn   10:12 and leaves the sheep and **r** away—

RUSH

Isa   59: 7 and they **r** to shed innocent blood;
Ac   2: 2 a sound like the **r** of a violent wind,

RUST → RUSTED

Mt   6:19 where moth and **r** consume
LtJ   6:12 cannot save themselves from **r**

RUSTED* → RUST

Jas   5: 3 Your gold and silver have **r**,

RUTH

   Moabitess; widow who went to Bethlehem with
mother-in-law Naomi (Ru 1). Gleaned in field of
Boaz; shown favor (Ru 2). Proposed marriage to
Boaz (Ru 3). Married (Ru 4:1-12); bore Obed,
ancestor of David (Ru 4:13-22), Jesus (Mt 1:5).

RUTHLESS

Ex   1:13 **r** in imposing tasks on the Israelites.
Ro   1:31 foolish, faithless, heartless, **r**.

S

SABACHTHANI*

Mt   27:46 a loud voice, "Eli, Eli, lema **s?**"
Mk   15:34 a loud voice, "Eloi, Eloi, lema **s?**"

SABBATH → SABBATHS

Ex   16:23 a day of solemn rest, a holy **s** to
      20: 8 Remember the **s** day, and keep it
           holy.
      31:14 keep the **s**, because it is holy for you
Nu   15:32 a man gathering sticks on the **s** day.
Dt   5:12 Observe the **s** day and keep it holy,
2Ch   36:21 the days that it lay desolate it kept **s**,
Ne   13:17 you are doing, profaning the **s** day?
Isa   56: 2 who holds it fast, who keeps the **s**,
      58:13 If you refrain from trampling the **s**,
Jer   17:21 the **s** day or bring it in by the gates
Mt   12: 1 through the grainfields on the **s**;
Mk   2:28 Son of Man is lord even of the **s**."
Lk   6: 9 to do good or to do harm on the **s**,
      13:10 in one of the synagogues on the **s**,
      14: 3 "Is it lawful to cure people on the **s**,
1Mc   1:43 to idols and profaned the **s**.
      2:38 on the **s**, and they died,

SABBATHS → SABBATH

Ex   31:13 "You shall keep my **s**, for this is a
Eze   20:12 Moreover I gave them my **s**,
1Mc   1:45 to profane **s** and festivals,
1Es   1:58 "Until the land has enjoyed its **s**,

SACKCLOTH → CLOTH

1Ch 21:16 David and the elders, clothed in **s**,
Ps   30:11 you have taken off my **s** and
            clothed me with joy,
Da   9: 3 supplication with fasting and **s** and
Joel 1:13 Put on **s** and lament, you priests;
Jnh   3: 5 everyone, great and small, put on **s**.
Mt   11:21 would have repented long ago in **s**
Rev   6:12 the sun became black as **s**,
Jdt   4:10 they all put **s** around their waists.
      8: 5 She put **s** around her waist
1Mc 2:14 put on **s**, and mourned greatly.

SACRED

Ex   28: 2 You shall make **s** vestments for
     34:13 and cut down their **s** poles
La   4: 1 The **s** stones lie scattered
1Mc 1:47 **s** precincts and shrines for idols,

SACRIFICE → SACRIFICED, SACRIFICES

Ex   5:17 'Let us go and **s** to the LORD.'
     12:27 'It is the passover **s** to the LORD,
Lev   3: 1 If the offering is a **s** of well-being,
1Sa   2:13 When anyone offered a **s**,
     15:22 Surely, to obey is better than **s**,
Ps   40: 6 **S** and offering you do not desire,
     50:14 Offer to God a **s** of thanksgiving,
     51:16 For you have no delight in **s**;
     54: 6 With a freewill offering I will **s** to
    141: 2 of my hands as an evening **s**.
Pr   15: 8 **s** of the wicked is an abomination
     21: 3 and justice is more acceptable to
            the LORD than **s**.
     21:27 **s** of the wicked is an abomination;
Da   9:27 he shall make **s** and offering cease;
Hos   6: 6 For I desire steadfast love and not **s**,
Zep   1: 7 the LORD has prepared a **s**,
Mt   9:13 this means, 'I desire mercy, not **s**.'
Ro   3:25 put forward as a **s** of atonement
1Co 10:20 they **s** to demons and not to God.
Eph   5: 2 a fragrant offering and **s** to God.
Php   2:17 poured out as a libation over the **s**
      4:18 a **s** acceptable and pleasing to God.
Heb   9:26 of the age to remove sin by the **s**
     11: 4 a more acceptable **s** than Cain's.
     13:15 let us continually offer a **s** of praise
1Jn   2: 2 and he is the atoning **s** for our sins,
      4:10 Son to be the atoning **s** for our sins.
Sir 30:19 Of what use to an idol is a **s**?
1Mc 1:47 swine and other unclean animals,
      4:53 and offered **s**, as the law directs,

SACRIFICED → SACRIFICE

Dt   32:17 They **s** to demons, not God,
Lk   22: 7 the Passover lamb had to be **s**.
Ac   15:29 from what has been **s** to idols and
1Co   5: 7 our paschal lamb, Christ, has been **s**.
      8: 1 Now concerning food **s** to idols:
Rev   2:14 so that they would eat food **s**
      2:20 practice fornication or to eat food **s**

SACRIFICES → SACRIFICE

Ex   22:20 Whoever **s** to any god, other than
2Ch   7: 1 the burnt offering and the **s**;
Ezr   6: 3 rebuilt, the place where **s** are offered
Ps   4: 5 Offer right **s**, and put your trust in
     50: 8 Not for your **s** do I rebuke you;
Isa   1:11 to me is the multitude of your **s**?
     56: 7 and their **s** will be accepted
Jer   6:20 nor are your **s** pleasing to me.
Am   5:25 to me **s** and offerings the forty years
Mk   12:33 this is much more important than
            all whole burnt offerings and **s**."
Heb   7:27 has no need to offer **s** day after day,
      9:23 heavenly things themselves need
            better **s** than these.
     13:16 for such **s** are pleasing to God.
1Pe   2: 5 to offer spiritual **s** acceptable to God
Sir 35: 4 who gives alms **s** a thank offering.

SAD

1Sa   1: 8 Why is your heart **s**?
Ne   2: 1 never been **s** in his presence before.

Lk   18:23 he became **s**; for he was very rich.
2Es   5:16 And why is your face **s**?

SADDUCEES

Mt   16: 1 The Pharisees and **S** came,
     16: 6 beware of the yeast of the Pharisees
            and **S**."
     22:34 heard that he had silenced the **S**,
Mk   12:18 **S**, who say there is no resurrection,
Ac   23: 7 between the Pharisees and the **S**,

SAFE → SAFEGUARD, SAFELY, SAFETY

Ezr   8:21 to seek from him a **s** journey for
Ps   37:28 righteous shall be kept **s** forever,
Pr   18:10 the righteous run into it and are **s**.
     28:18 who walks in integrity will be **s**,
Jer 12: 5 And if in a **s** land you fall down,

SAFEGUARD* → GUARD, SAFE

Php   3: 1 and for you it is a **s**.

SAFELY → SAFE

Pr   28:26 walk in wisdom come through **s**.

SAFETY → SAFE

Dt   12:10 around so that you live in **s**,
Ps   4: 8 O LORD, make me lie down in **s**.
Isa 14:30 and the needy lie down in **s**;
Jer 33:16 saved and Jerusalem will live in **s**.
Eze 34:28 they shall live in **s**,
Hos   2:18 and I will make you lie down in **s**.

SAGES

Isa 19:12 Where now are your **s**?
Mt   23:34 I send you prophets, **s**, and scribes,
Sir   8: 8 Do not slight the discourse of the **s**,

SAINT* → SAINTS, SAINTS'

Php   4:21 Greet every **s** in Christ Jesus.

SAINTS → SAINT

Ps   31:23 Love the LORD, all you his **s**.
Ac   9:13 much evil he has done to your **s** in
Ro   8:27 the Spirit intercedes for the **s**
1Co   6: 1 will judge the world?
Eph   1:15 and your love toward all the **s**,
      1:18 glorious inheritance among the **s**,
      3: 8 the very least of all the **s**,
      4:12 equip the **s** for the work of ministry,
      6:18 and always persevere in
            supplication for all the **s**.
Col   1:12 to share in the inheritance of the **s**
      1:26 but has now been revealed to his **s**.
1Th   3:13 of our Lord Jesus with all his **s**.
Phm   1: 7 hearts of the **s** have been refreshed
Jude 1: 3 the faith that was once for all
            entrusted to the **s**.
Rev   5: 8 which are the prayers of the **s**.
      5: 9 and by your blood you ransomed
            for God **s**
      8: 3 to offer with the prayers of all the **s**
     13: 7 allowed to make war on the **s** and
     14:12 a call for the endurance of the **s**,
     16: 6 shed the blood of **s** and prophets,
     17: 6 was drunk with the blood of the **s**
     18:20 you **s** and apostles and prophets!
     19: 8 for the fine linen is the righteous
            deeds of the **s**.

SAINTS'* → SAINT

1Ti   5:10 washed the **s'** feet, helped the

SAKE → SAKES

Ge   12:16 for her **s** he dealt well with Abram;
Jos 23: 3 to all these nations for your **s**,
1Sa 12:22 not cast away his people, for his
            great name's **s**,
1Ki 11:12 the **s** of your father David I will not
Ps   23: 3 He leads me in right paths for his
            name's **s**.
     25:11 For your name's **s**, O LORD, pardon
     69: 7 for your **s** that I have borne reproach
    106: 8 Yet he saved them for his name's **s**,
    109:21 act on my behalf for your name's **s**;

    132:10 your servant David's **s** do not turn
Isa 42:21 for the **s** of his righteousness,
     43:25 for my own **s**, and I will
     48: 9 For my name's **s** I defer my anger,
     48:11 For my own **s**, for my own **s**, I do it,
     62: 1 For Zion's **s** I will not keep silent,
Jer 14: 7 act, O LORD, for your name's **s**;
     14:21 Do not spurn us, for your name's **s**;
Eze 20: 9 But I acted for the **s** of my name,
     20:14 But I acted for the **s** of my name,
     20:22 and acted for the **s** of my name,
     36:32 It is not for your **s** that I will act,
Da   9:17 and for your own **s**, Lord,
Mt   10:39 who lose their life for my **s** will find
     19:29 for my name's **s**, will receive a
Mk   13:20 but for the **s** of the elect,
Ro   8:36 "For your **s** we are being killed all
      9: 3 from Christ for the **s** of my own
     14:20 Do not, for the **s** of food,
1Co   9:23 I do it all for the **s** of the gospel,
2Co   4:11 up to death for Jesus' **s**,
     12:10 and calamities for the **s** of Christ;
1Pe   2:13 For the Lord's **s** accept the authority
3Jn   1: 7 their journey for the **s** of Christ,
Bar   2:14 and for your own **s** deliver us,
Aza   1:11 For your name's **s** do not give us up
2Es   8: 1 made this world for the **s** of many,

SAKES → SAKE

2Co   8: 9 yet for your **s** he became poor,

SALE → SELL

Dt   28:68 for **s** to your enemies as male and

SALEM → =JERUSALEM

Ge   14:18 King Melchizedek of **S** brought out
Heb   7: 2 king of **S**, that is, "king of peace."

SALIVA

Jn   9: 6 mud with the **s** and spread the mud

SALT → SALTED, SALTINESS

Ge   19:26 back, and she became a pillar of **s**.
Nu   18:19 a covenant of **s** forever before the
2Ki   2:20 a new bowl, and put **s** in it."
Mt   5:13 "You are the **s** of the earth;
Mk   9:50 **S** is good; but if **s** has lost its
            saltiness, how can you season it?
Col   4: 6 always be gracious, seasoned with **s**,

SALTED → SALT

Mk   9:49 "For everyone will be **s** with fire.

SALTINESS → SALT

Lk   14:34 how can its **s** be restored?

SALVATION* → SAVE

Ge   49:18 I wait for your **s**, O LORD.
Ex   15: 2 and he has become my **s**;
Dt   32:15 and scoffed at the Rock of his **s**.
2Sa 22: 3 my shield and the horn of my **s**,
     22:36 have given me the shield of your **s**,
     22:47 my God, the rock of my **s**,
     22:51 He is a tower of **s** for his king,
1Ch 16:23 Tell of his **s** from day to day.
     16:35 Say also: "Save us, O God of our **s**,
2Ch   6:41 O LORD God, be clothed with **s**,
Job 13:16 This will be my **s**, that the godless
Ps   13: 5 my heart shall rejoice in your **s**.
     18: 2 my shield, and the horn of my **s**,
     18:35 have given me the shield of your **s**,
     18:46 and exalted be the God of my **s**,
     24: 5 vindication from the God of their **s**.
     25: 5 for you are the God of my **s**;
     27: 1 The LORD is my light and my **s**;
     27: 9 do not forsake me, O God of my **s**!
     35: 3 say to my soul, "I am your **s**."
     36:10 and your **s** to the upright of heart!
     37:39 **s** of the righteous is from the LORD;
     38:22 haste to help me, O Lord, my **s**.
     40:10 of your faithfulness and your **s**;
     40:16 may those who love your **s** say
     50:23 go the right way I will show the **s**
     51:12 Restore to me the joy of your **s**,

51:14 O God, O God of my **s,**
62: 1 in silence; from him comes my **s.**
62: 2 He alone is my rock and my **s,**
62: 6 He alone is my rock and my **s,**
65: 5 with deliverance, O God of our **s;**
68:19 who daily bears us up; God is our **s.**
68:20 Our God is a God of **s,**
69:29 let your **s,** O God, protect me.
70: 4 Let those who love your **s** say
71:15 of your deeds of **s** all day long,
74:12 my King is from of old, working **s**
79: 9 Help us, O God of our **s,**
85: 4 Restore us again, O God of our **s,**
85: 7 O LORD, and grant us your **s.**
85: 9 his **s** is at hand for those who fear
88: 1 O LORD, God of my **s,** when,
89:26 my God, and the Rock of my **s!'**
91:16 satisfy them, and show them my **s.**
95: 1 a joyful noise to the rock of our **s!**
96: 2 tell of his **s** from day to day.
116:13 the cup of **s** and call on the name of
118:14 and my might; he has become my **s.**
118:21 and have become my **s.**
119:41 your **s** according to your promise.
119:81 My soul languishes for your **s;**
119:123 eyes fail from watching for your **s,**
119:155 **S** is far from the wicked,
119:166 I hope for your **s,** O LORD,
119:174 I long for your **s,** O LORD,
132:16 Its priests I will clothe with **s,**
Isa 12: 2 Surely God is my **s;** I will trust,
12: 2 and my might; he has become my **s.**
12: 3 With joy you will draw water from
      the wells of **s.**
17:10 have forgotten the God of your **s,**
25: 9 let us be glad and rejoice in his **s.**
33: 2 our **s** in the time of trouble.
33: 6 of **s,** wisdom, and knowledge;
45: 8 the earth open, that **s** may spring up,
45:17 Israel is saved by the LORD with
      everlasting **s;**
46:13 not far off, and my **s** will not tarry;
46:13 put **s** in Zion, for Israel my glory.
49: 6 that my **s** may reach to the end of
      the earth."
49: 8 on a day of **s** I have helped you;
51: 5 my **s** has gone out and my arms
51: 6 but my **s** will be forever, and my
51: 8 and my **s** to all generations.
52: 7 brings good news, who announces **s,**
52:10 the earth shall see the **s** of our God.
56: 1 for soon my **s** will come, and my
59:11 for **s,** but it is far from us.
59:17 and a helmet of **s** on his head;
60:18 you shall call your walls **S,**
61:10 clothed me with the garments of **s,**
62: 1 and her **s** like a burning torch.
62:11 daughter Zion, "See, your **s** comes;
Jer 3:23 the LORD our God is the **s** of Israel.
La   3:26 one should wait quietly for the **s** of
Mic 7: 7 I will wait for the God of my **s;**
Hab 3:18 I will exult in the God of my **s.**
Mk 16: S [proclamation of eternal **s.**]
Lk   1:77 of **s** to his people by the forgiveness
     2:30 for my eyes have seen your **s,**
     3: 6 all flesh shall see the **s** of God.'"
     ... "Today **s** has come to this house,
     ...orship what we know, for **s** is
     ...no one else,
     ...**s** has been sent.
     ...the ends of
     ...

Eph 1:13 gospel of your **s,** and had believed
     6:17 Take the helmet of **s,** and the sword
Php 1:28 of their destruction, but of your **s.**
     2:12 work out your own **s** with fear and
      trembling;
1Th 5: 8 and for a helmet the hope of **s.**
     5: 9 for obtaining **s** through our Lord
2Th 2:13 as the first fruits for **s** through
2Ti 2:10 obtain the **s** that is in Christ Jesus,
     3:15 to instruct you for **s** through faith
Tit 2:11 has appeared, bringing **s** to all,
Heb 1:14 of those who are to inherit **s?**
     2: 3 escape if we neglect so great a **s?**
     2:10 of their **s** perfect through sufferings.
     5: 9 source of eternal **s** for all who obey
     6: 9 in your case, things that belong to **s.**
1Pe 1: 5 power of God through faith for a **s**
     1: 9 the outcome of your faith, the **s** of
      your souls.
     1:10 Concerning this **s,** the prophets who
     2: 2 so that by it you may grow into **s**—
2Pe 3:15 regard the patience of our Lord as **s.**
Jude 5 to write to you about the **s** we share,
Rev 7:10 "S belongs to our God who is seated
     12:10 **s** and the power and the kingdom of
     19: 1 S and glory and power to our God,
Wis 5: 2 at the unexpected **s** of the righteous.
     6:24 of the wise is the **s** of the world,
Bar 4:24 so they soon will see your **s** by God,
     4:29 everlasting joy with your **s.**
2Es 6:25 shall be saved and shall see my **s**
     7:66 or **s** promised to them after death.
     7:131 joy over those to whom **s** is assured.
     8:39 **s,** and their receiving their reward.
     9: 8 see my **s** in my land and within my

SALVE*

Rev 3:18 and **s** to anoint your eyes so

SAMARIA → SAMARITAN, SAMARITANS, SHEMER

1Ki 16:24 and called the city that he built, **S,**
     16:32 house of Baal, which he built in **S.**
     20:43 resentful and sullen, and came to **S.**
2Ki 17: 5 the king of Assyria captured **S;**
Isa 7: 9 The head of Ephraim is **S,**
     36:19 they delivered **S** out of my hand?
Eze 23: 4 As for their names, Oholah is **S,**
Hos 8: 5 Your calf is rejected, O **S.**
Am   6: 1 those who feel secure on Mount **S,**
Mic 1: 6 I will make **S** a heap in the open
Jn   4: 4 But he had to go through **S.**
Ac   1: 8 in all Judea and **S,** and to the ends
     8: 1 the countryside of Judea and **S.**
     8:14 heard that **S** had accepted the word

SAMARITAN → SAMARIA

Lk 10:33 But a **S** while traveling came near
    17:16 And he was a **S.**
Jn   4: 7 A **S** woman came to draw water,
     8:48 that you are a **S** and have a demon?"

SAMARITANS → SAMARIA

Jn   4: 9 (Jews do not share things in
      common with **S.**)
Ac   8:25 good news to many villages of the **S**

SAME

Ex   5: 8 shall require of them the **s** quantity
     7:11 did the **s** by their secret arts.
     7:22 magicians of Egypt did the **s** by
     8: 7 But the magicians did the **s** by their
Dt   7:19 the **s** to all the peoples of whom
1Sa 2:34 both of them shall die on the **s** day.
Ps 102:27 but you are the **s,** and your years
Ecc 2:14 I perceived that the **s** fate befalls all
     9: 3 that the **s** fate comes to everyone.
Mt   5:12 **s** way they persecuted the prophets
Ac   1:11 in the **s** way as you saw him go into
     11:17 If then God gave them the **s** gift
Ro   2: 1 judge, are doing the very **s** things.
     10:12 the **s** Lord is Lord of all and

12: 4 and not all the members have the **s**
      function,
1Co 10: 3 and all ate the **s** spiritual food,
     12: 4 varieties of gifts, but the **s** Spirit;
     12: 5 varieties of services, but the **s** Lord;
Php 2: 5 Let the **s** mind be in you that was in
      Christ Jesus,
Heb 1:12 you are the **s,** and your years will
     13: 8 Jesus Christ is the **s** yesterday and
Wis 15: 8 form a futile god from the **s** clay—
Sir 42:21 he is from all eternity one and the **s.**

SAMSON*

Danite judge. Birth promised (Jdg 13). Married
to Philistine, but wife given away (Jdg 14).
Vengeance on the Philistines (Jdg 15). Betrayed
by Delilah (Jdg 16:1-22). Death (Jdg 16:23-31).
Feats of strength: killed lion (Jdg 14:6), 30 Philistines (Jdg 14:19), 1, 000 Philistines with jawbone
(Jdg 15:13-17), carried off gates of Gaza (Jdg
16:3), pushed down temple of Dagon (Jdg 16:25-
30; Heb 11:32).

SAMUEL

Ephraimite judge and prophet (Heb 11:32).
Birth prayed for (1Sa 1:10-18). Dedicated to
temple by Hannah (1Sa 1:21-28). Raised by Eli
(1Sa 2:11, 18-26). Called as prophet (1Sa 3). Led
Israel to victory over Philistines (1Sa 7). Asked
by Israel for a king (1Sa 8). Anointed Saul as king
(1Sa 9-10). Farewell speech (1Sa 12). Rebuked
Saul for sacrifice (1Sa 13). Announced rejection
of Saul (1Sa 15). Anointed David as king (1Sa
16). Protected David from Saul (1Sa 19:18-24).
Death (1Sa 25:1). Returned from dead to condemn Saul (1Sa 28).

SANBALLAT

Led opposition to Nehemiah's rebuilding of Jerusalem (Ne 2:10, 19; 4: 6).

SANCTIFICATION* → SANCTIFY

Ro   6:19 as slaves to righteousness for **s.**
     6:22 the advantage you get is **s.**
1Co 1:30 righteousness and **s** and redemption,
1Th 4: 3 For this is the will of God, your **s:**
2Th 2:13 for salvation through **s** by the Spirit
Sir 7:31 the sacrifice of **s,** and the first fruits

SANCTIFIED → SANCTIFY

Ex 29:43 and it shall be **s** by my glory;
Lev 22:32 be **s** among the people of Israel:
1Ch 15:14 the priests and the Levites **s**
Jn 17:19 so that they also may be **s** in truth.
Ac 20:32 the inheritance among all who are **s.**
    26:18 those who are **s** by faith in me.'
Ro 15:16 acceptable, **s** by the Holy Spirit.
1Co 1: 2 to those who are **s** in Christ Jesus,
     6:11 But you were washed, you were **s,**
Heb 2:11 those who are **s** all have one Father.
     10:29 the covenant by which they were **s,**
1Pe 1: 2 and **s** by the Spirit to be obedient to

SANCTIFY → SANCTIFICATION, SANCTIFIED

Lev 11:44 **s** yourselves therefore, and be holy,
    20: 8 I am the LORD; I **s** you.
Jn 17:17 **S** them in the truth; your word is
      truth.
    17:19 And for their sakes I **s** myself,
1Th 5:23 the God of peace himself **s** you
Heb 13:12 to **s** the people by his own blood.
1Pe 3:15 but in your hearts **s** Christ as Lord.

SANCTUARIES → SANCTUARY

Lev 26:31 will make your **s** desolate,
Am   7: 9 the **s** of Israel shall be laid waste,

SANCTUARY → SANCTUARIES

Ex 15:17 that you made your abode, the **s,**
    25: 8 And have them make me a **s,**
Nu   3:28 attending to the duties of the **s.**
    18: 1 for offenses connected with the **s,**
1Ki 6:19 inner **s** he prepared in the innermost

1Ch 22:19 and build the s of the LORD God so
Ps 20: 2 May he send you help from the s,
     60: 6 God has promised in his s:
     63: 2 So I have looked upon you in the s,
     68:24 of my God, my King, into the s—
     68:35 Awesome is God in his s, the God
     73:17 until I went into the s of God;
     74: 7 They set your s on fire;
    114: 2 Judah became God's s, Israel his
    150: 1 Praise God in his s; praise him in
Isa   8:14 He will become a s, a stone one
La   1:10 even seen the nations invade her s,
Eze   5:11 because you have defiled my s
     37:26 and will set my s among them
Da   8:11 and overthrew the place of his s.
      9:26 shall destroy the city and the s.
Heb   8: 2 a minister in the s and the true tent
      8: 5 offer worship in a s that is a sketch
      9:24 Christ did not enter a s made by
             human hands,
1Mc   1:21 He arrogantly entered the s
      4:36 cleanse the s and dedicate it."

SAND
Ge 22:17 as the stars of heaven and as the s
    32:12 your offspring as the s of the sea,
    41:49 like the s of the sea—
Ex   2:12 the Egyptian and hid him in the s.
1Ki 4:20 as numerous as the s by the sea;
Hos 1:10 Israel shall be like the s of the sea,
Mt   7:26 be like foolish man who built his
            house on s.
Ro   9:27 of Israel were like the s of the sea,
Heb 11:12 and as the innumerable grains of s

SANDAL → SANDALS
Dt   25: 9 pull his s off his foot,
Ru   4: 7 took off a s and gave it to the other;
Jn   1:27 worthy to untie the thong of his s."

SANDALS → SANDAL
Ex   3: 5 Remove the s from your feet,
     12:11 loins girded, your s on your feet,
Dt   29: 5 the s on your feet have not worn out
Jos   5:15 "Remove the s from your feet,
Mt   3:11 I am not worthy to carry his s.

SANG → SING
Ex   15: 1 Moses and the Israelites s this song
     15:21 And Miriam s to them: "Sing to the
Nu   21:17 Then Israel s this song: "Spring up,
Jdg   5: 1 Barak son of Abinoam s on that day
1Sa 18: 7 the women s to one another as they
2Ch 29:30 They s praises with gladness,
Ezr   3:11 and they s responsively, praising
Ne   12:42 And the singers s with Jezrahiah as
Job 38: 7 when the morning stars s together
Ps 106:12 believed his words; they s his praise
1Mc 4:24 On their return they s hymns and

SANK → SINK
1Sa 17:49 the stone s into his forehead,
Jer 38: 6 and Jeremiah s in the mud.

SAPPHIRA*
Ac   5: 1 with the consent of his wife S,

SAPPHIRE
Ex   24:10 like a pavement of s stone,
     28:18 the second row a turquoise, a s and
Eze   1:26 like a throne, in appearance like s;
     10: 1 above them something like a s,
Rev 21:19 the first was jasper, the second s,
Tob 13:16 of Jerusalem will be built with s

SARAH → =SARAI
Wife of Abraham, originally named Sarai; bar-
ren (Ge 11:29-31; 1Pe 3:6). Taken by Pharaoh as
Abraham's sister; returned (Ge 12:10-20). Gave
Hagar to Abraham; sent her away in pregnancy
(Ge 16). Name changed; Isaac promised (Ge
17:15-21; 18:10-15; Heb 11:11). Taken by Abi-
melech as Abraham's sister; returned (Ge 20).

Isaac born; Hagar and Ishmael sent away (Ge
21:1-21; Gal 4:21-31). Death (Ge 23).

SARAI → =SARAH
Ge   17:15 you shall not call her S,

SARDIS
Rev   3: 1 to the angel of the church in S write:

SASH → SASHES
Ex   28: 4 a checkered tunic, a turban, and a s.
Rev   1:13 a long robe and with a golden s

SASHES → SASH
Rev 15: 6 with golden s across their chests.

SAT → SIT
Ge   48: 2 he summoned his strength and s up
Ex   2:15 and s down by a well.
Jdg 19:15 and s down in the open square of
Ru   4: 1 to the gate and s down there
1Ki 19: 4 s down under a solitary broom tree.
Ne   1: 4 these words I s down and wept,
Ps 137: 1 there we s down and there we wept
Mt   5: 1 and after he s down, his disciples
     13: 2 that he got into a boat and s there,
     28: 2 and rolled back the stone and s on it.
Lk   7:15 The dead man s up and began to
     10:39 who s at the Lord's feet and listened
Jn   12:14 found a young donkey and s on it;
Heb   1: 3 he s down at the right hand of the
     10:12 "he s down at the right hand of God,
Rev 20:11 and s down with my Father
     20:11 throne and the one who s on it;

SATAN
1Ch 21: 1 S stood up against Israel,
Job   1: 6 and S also came among them.
      2: 1 S also came among them to present
Zec   3: 2 And the LORD said to S,
      3: 2 "The LORD rebuke you, O S!
Mt   4:10 Jesus said to him, "Away with you,
             S!
     12:26 If S casts out S, he is divided
     16:23 said to Peter, "Get behind me, S!
Mk   4:15 S immediately comes and takes
Lk   10:18 "I watched S fall from heaven like
     22: 3 S entered into Judas called Iscariot,
Jn   13:27 piece of bread, S entered into him.
Ac   5: 3 "why has S filled your heart to lie to
     26:18 and from the power of S to God,
Ro   16:20 The God of peace will shortly crush
             S under your feet.
1Co   5: 5 to hand this man over to S for the
      7: 5 that S may not tempt you because
2Co   2:11 that we may not be outwitted by S;
     11:14 Even S disguises himself as an
             angel of light.
     12: 7 a messenger of S to torment me,
2Th   2: 9 is apparent in the working of S,
1Ti   1:20 whom I have turned over to S,
      5:15 already turned away to follow S.
Rev   2: 9 but are a synagogue of S.
      2:13 killed among you, where S lives.
      2:24 some call 'the deep things of S,'
      3: 9 those of the synagogue of S
     12: 9 who is called the Devil and S,
     20: 2 that ancient serpent, who is the
             Devil and S,
     20: 7 S will be released from his prison

SATISFACTION* → SATISFY
Pr   18:20 the yield of the lips brings s.
Isa 53:11 shall find s through his knowledge.
Tit   2: 9 to give s in every respect;

SATISFIED → SATISFY
Lev 26:26 though you eat, you shall not be s.
Ru   2:14 She ate until she was s,
Ps   17:15 I shall be s, beholding your likeness.
     22:26 The poor shall eat and be s;
     63: 5 My soul is s as with a rich feast,
Pr   18:20 of the mouth one's stomach is s;
     27:20 Sheol and Abaddon are never s,

     30:15 Three things are never s;
Ecc   5:10 The lover of money will not be s
             with money;
Hos 13: 6 When I fed them, they were s;
Joel 2:26 You shall eat in plenty and be s,
Mic   6:14 You shall eat, but not be s,
Jn   14: 8 the Father, and we will be s."
Sir 14: 9 eye of the greedy person is not s

SATISFIES* → SATISFY
Ps 103: 5 who s you with good as long as you
    107: 9 For he s the thirsty, and the hungry

SATISFY → SATISFACTION, SATISFIED, SATISFIES
Ps   90:14 S us in the morning with your
             steadfast love,
     91:16 With long life I will s them,
    132:15 I will s its poor with bread.
Pr   5:19 May her breasts s you at all times;
      6:30 not despised who steal only to s
             their appetite
Isa 55: 2 labor for that which does not s?
     58:10 and s the needs of the afflicted,
Jer 31:25 I will s the weary, and all who are
Mk   15:15 So Pilate, wishing to s the crowd,

SATRAPS
Est   3:12 to the king's s and to the governors
Da   6: 1 the kingdom one hundred twenty s,

SAUL → =PAUL
1. Benjamite; anointed by Samuel as first king
of Israel (1Sa 9-10). Defeated Ammonites (1Sa
11). Rebuked for offering sacrifice (1Sa 13:1-15).
Defeated Philistines (1Sa 14). Rejected as king
for failing to annihilate Amalekites (1Sa 15).
Soothed from evil spirit by David (1Sa 16:14-
23). Sent David against Goliath (1Sa 17).
Jealousy and attempted murder of David (1Sa
18:1-11). Gave David Michal as wife (1Sa 18:12-
30). Second attempt to kill David (1Sa 19). Anger
at Jonathan (1Sa 20:26-34). Pursued David:
killed priests at Nob (1Sa 22), went to Keilah and
Ziph (1Sa 23), life spared by David at En Gedi
(1Sa 24) and in his tent (1Sa 26). Rebuked by
Samuel's spirit for consulting witch at Endor
(1Sa 28). Wounded by Philistines; took his own
life (1Sa 31; 1Ch 10). Lamented by David (2Sa
1:17-27). Children (1Sa 14:49-51; 1Ch 8).
2. See Paul.

SAVAGE
Ac   20:29 s wolves will come in among you,

SAVE → SALVATION, SAVED, SAVES, SAVING, SAVIOR, SAVIORS
2Sa 22: 3 my savior; you s me from violence.
1Ch 16:35 "S us, O God of our salvation,
Ps   6: 4 Turn, O LORD, s my life;
     28: 9 O s your people, and bless your
     31:16 s me in your steadfast love.
     54: 1 S me, O God, by your name,
     69:35 God will s Zion and rebuild the
     71: 2 incline your ear to me and s me.
     86: 2 s your servant who trusts in you.
    109:31 to s them from those who would
    119:94 I am yours; s me,
Pr   2:12 It will s you from the way of evil,
      6: 3 my child, and s yourself,
Isa 33:22 the LORD is our king; he will s ᵘ
     35: 4 He will come and s you."
     36:20 LORD should s Jerusalem ou
     38:20 LORD will s me, and we w⁻
     45:20 praying to a god that car⁻
     46: 7 it does not answer or s⁻
     59: 1 LORD's hand is not tᵘ
     63: 1 announcing vindic⁻
Jer 15:20 for I am with yoⁱ
     17:14 s me, and I shaⁱ
La   4:17 for a nation thⁱ
Eze   3:18 in order to sⁱ
      7:19 gold canⁱⁱ

14:14 they would **s** only their own lives
33:12 not **s** them when they transgress;
34:22 I will **s** my flock, and they shall no
Hos 1: 7 I will **s** them by the LORD their God;
1: 7 not **s** them by bow, or by sword,
Zep 1:18 nor their gold will be able to **s** them
Zec 8: 7 I will **s** my people from the east
Mt 1:21 he will **s** his people from their sins."
16:25 For those who want to **s** their life will lose it,
27:42 saved others; he cannot **s** himself.
Lk 6: 9 to **s** life or to destroy it?"
19:10 Son of Man came to seek out and to **s** the lost."
23:37 "If you are the King of the Jews, **s** yourself!"
Jn 12:27 'Father, **s** me from this hour'?
12:47 came not to judge the world, but to **s**
Ac 2:40 "**S** yourselves from this corrupt
Ro 11:14 and thus **s** some of them.
1Co 7:16 you might **s** your husband.
9:22 that I might by all means **s** some.
1Ti 1:15 Christ Jesus came into the world to **s** sinners—
Heb 7:25 to **s** those who approach God
Jas 2:14 not have works? Can faith **s** you?
5:20 will **s** the sinner's soul from death
Jude 1:23 **s** others by snatching them out of
Jdt 6: 2 Their God will not **s** them;
Sir 42: 1 and do not sin to **s** face:
51: 8 and **s** them from the hand

SAVED → SAVE

Ex 14:30 the LORD **s** Israel that day from the Egyptians;
Dt 33:29 like you, a people **s** by the LORD,
2Ch 32:22 So the LORD **s** Hezekiah and the
Ps 18: 3 so I shall be **s** from my enemies.
22: 5 To you they cried, and were **s**;
33:16 A king is not **s** by his great army;
34: 6 and was **s** from every trouble.
106: 8 Yet he **s** them for his name's sake,
116: 6 when I was brought low, he **s** me.
Isa 45:17 But Israel is **s** by the LORD
45:22 Turn to me and be **s**, all the ends of
Jer 4:14 of wickedness so that you may be **s**.
8:20 summer is ended, and we are not **s**."
17:14 save me, and I shall be **s**;
Eze 3:19 but you will have **s** your life.
33: 5 they would have **s** their lives.
Joel 2:32 on the name of the LORD shall be **s**;
Mt 10:22 who endures to the end will be **s**.
19:25 and said, "Then who can be **s**?"
24:13 who endures to the end will be **s**.
Mk 15:31 He **s** others; he cannot save himself.
Lk 7:50 the woman, "Your faith has **s** you;
13:23 "Lord, will only a few be **s**?"
Jn 10: 9 Whoever enters by me will be **s**,
Ac 2:21 on the name of the Lord shall be **s**.'
2:47 number those who were being **s**.
4:12 by which we must be **s**."
15:11 that we will be **s** through the grace
16:30 "Sirs, what must I do to be **s**?"
Ro 5: 9 we be **s** through him from the wrath
8:24 For in hope we were **s**.
9:27 only a remnant of them will be **s**;

Tit 3: 5 he **s** us, not because of any works
Heb 10:39 those who have faith and so are **s**.
1Pe 4:18 If it is hard for the righteous to be **s**,
AdE 10: 9 The Lord has **s** his people;
Aza 1:66 **s** us from the power of death,
1Mc 2:59 and were **s** from the flame.
Man 1: 7 so that they may be **s**.

SAVES → SAVE

Ps 7:10 God is my shield, who **s** the upright
34:18 and **s** the crushed in spirit.
145:19 he also hears their cry, and **s** them.
Pr 14:25 A truthful witness **s** lives,
1Pe 3:21 baptism, which this prefigured, now **s** you—
Sir 2:11 and **s** in time of distress.
Sus 1:60 who **s** those who hope in him.

SAVING → SAVE

1Sa 14: 6 nothing can hinder the LORD from **s**
Ps 40:10 I have not hidden your **s** help
78:22 and did not trust his **s** power.
Sir 39:18 and none can limit his **s** power.

SAVIOR* → SAVE

2Sa 22: 3 my stronghold and my refuge, my **s**;
2Ki 13: 5 Therefore the LORD gave Israel a **s**,
Ps 17: 7 O **s** of those who seek refuge
106:21 They forgot God, their **S**,
Isa 19:20 of oppressors, he will send them a **s**,
43: 3 the Holy One of Israel, your **S**.
43:11 I, I am the LORD, and besides me there is no **s**.
45:15 O God of Israel, the **S**.
45:21 a righteous God and a **S**;
49:26 know that I am the LORD your **S**,
60:16 am your **S** and your Redeemer,
63: 8 and he became their **s**
Jer 14: 8 of Israel, its **s** in time of trouble,
Hos 13: 4 and besides me there is no **s**.
Lk 1:47 and my spirit rejoices in God my **S**,
1:69 He has raised up a mighty **s** for us
2:11 this day in the city of David a **S**,
Jn 4:42 that this is truly the **S** of the world."
Ac 5:31 that he might give repentance
13:23 to Israel a **S**, Jesus, as he promised;
Eph 5:23 the body of which he is the **S**.
Php 3:20 there that we are expecting a **S**,
1Ti 1: 1 by the command of God our **S**
2: 3 acceptable in the sight of God our **S**,
4:10 who is the **S** of all people,
2Ti 1:10 the appearing of our **S** Christ Jesus,
Tit 1: 3 by the command of God our **S**,
1: 4 the Father and Christ Jesus our **S**.
2:10 to the doctrine of God our **S**.
2:13 of the glory of our great God and **S**,
3: 4 kindness of God our **S** appeared,
3: 6 richly through Jesus Christ our **S**,
2Pe 1: 1 of our God and **S** Jesus Christ:
1:11 and **S** Jesus Christ will be richly
2:20 knowledge of our Lord and **S** Jesus
3: 2 commandment of the Lord and **S**
3:18 knowledge of our Lord and **S** Jesus
1Jn 4:14 sent his Son as the **S** of the world.
Jude 1:25 to the only God our **S**,
Jdt 9:11 **s** of those without hope.
AdE 15: 2 the aid of the all-seeing God and **S**,
16:13 our **s** and perpetual benefactor,
Wis 16: 7 but by you, the **S** of all.
Sir 46: 1 implies, a great **s** of God's elect,
51: 1 King, and praise you, O God my **S**.
Bar 4:22 to you from your everlasting **s**.
1Mc 4:30 "Blessed are you, O **S** of Israel,
9:21 the mighty fallen, the **s** of Israel!"
2Mc 3:35 and made very great vows to the **S**
3Mc 6:29 praised their holy God and **S**,
6:32 praising God, their **S** and worker of
7:16 God of their ancestors, the eternal **S**
2Es 2:36 I publicly call on my **s** to witness.

SAVIORS* → SAVE

Ne 9:27 you gave them **s** who saved them

SAW → SEE

Ge 1: 4 And God **s** that the light was good;
1:31 God **s** everything that he had made,
3: 6 the woman **s** that the tree was good
6: 2 sons of God **s** that they were fair;
6:12 God **s** that the earth was corrupt;
22:13 Abraham looked up and **s** a ram,
Ex 2: 2 when she **s** that he was a fine baby,
2: 5 She **s** the basket among the reeds
2:11 He **s** an Egyptian beating a Hebrew,
24:10 and they **s** the God of Israel.
Nu 22:23 The donkey **s** the angel of the LORD
Dt 4:15 you **s** no form when the LORD spoke
32:19 The LORD **s** it, and was jealous he
2Sa 11: 2 he **s** from the roof a woman bathing;
Ps 73: 3 I **s** the prosperity of the wicked.
Ecc 2:13 Then I **s** that wisdom excels folly
8:17 then I **s** all the work of God,
Isa 6: 1 I **s** the Lord sitting on a throne, high
Eze 1: 1 the heavens were opened, and I **s** visions of God.
Da 4:10 Upon my bed this is what I **s**;
8: 2 I was looking and **s** myself in Susa
10: 7 I, Daniel, alone **s** the vision;
Am 9: 1 I **s** the LORD standing beside the
Mt 3:16 he **s** the Spirit of God descending like a dove
9: 2 When Jesus **s** their faith, he said to
Mk 1:10 he **s** the heavens torn apart and
3:11 Whenever the unclean spirits **s** him,
Lk 9:32 had stayed awake, they **s** his glory
Jn 1:29 next day he **s** Jesus coming toward
19:35 (He who has testified so that
20: 1 **s** that the stone had been removed
20: 8 also went in, and he **s** and believed;
Ac 7:55 and **s** the glory of God and Jesus
10:11 He **s** the heaven opened and
Heb 11:27 as though he **s** him who is invisible.
Rev 1: 2 even to all that he **s**
1:12 turning I **s** seven golden lampstands,
5: 6 Then I **s** between the throne and
21: 1 I **s** a new heaven and a new earth;
21:22 I **s** no temple in the city,
22: 8 And when I heard and **s** them,
1Mc 4:38 There they **s** the sanctuary desolate,
2Es 10:32 I **s**, and can still see,
11: 1 I **s** rising from the sea an eagle
12:35 This is the dream that you **s**,

SAWN*

Heb 11:37 they were **s** in two,

SAY → SAYING, SAYINGS, SAYS

Ge 3: 1 He said to the woman, "Did God **s**,
12:19 Why did you **s**, 'She is my sister,'
18:13 and **s**, 'Shall I indeed bear a child,
26: 9 did you **s**, 'She is my sister'?"
Mt 10:19 are to speak or what you are to **s**;
16:15 "But who do you **s** that I am?"
Mk 2: 9 Which is easier, to **s** to the paralytic,
8:27 "Who do people **s** that I am?"
Lk 11:54 catch him in something he might **s**.
Jn 8:26 I have much to **s** about you
8:43 do you not understand what I **s**?
12:49 commandment about what to **s** and
16:12 "I still have many things to **s** to you,
1Co 15:12 of you **s** there is no resurrection of
Rev 22:17 The Spirit and the bride **s**, "Come."
Sir 11:23 Do not **s**, "What do I need,

SAYING → SAY

1Ti 1:15 The **s** is sure and worthy of full
3: 1 The **s** is sure: whoever aspires to the
4: 9 The **s** is sure and worthy of full
2Ti 2:11 The **s** is sure: If we have died with
Tit 3: 8 The **s** is sure.
Rev 2: 7 what the Spirit is **s** to the churches.

SAYINGS → SAY

Job 32:11 I listened for your wise **s**,
Ps 78: 2 I will utter dark **s** from of old,
Ecc 12:11 The **s** of the wise are like goads,

(partial text visible in lower-left margin, rotated)
filled in
Jesus had
at the Messiah
annulled—
fulfilled,
e **s** that he was reading
o the public reading of **s**,
inspired by God and is

...s."
...wer
...day
...e **s**.
...be **s**.
...d
...ng,
...oly

Sir   1:25 the treasuries of wisdom are wise **s,**

SAYS → SAY

1Sa   9: 6 Whatever he **s** always comes true.
Ps 110: 1 The LORD **s** to my lord,
Ecc   1: 2 Vanity of vanities, **s** the Teacher,
        12: 8 Vanity of vanities, **s** the Teacher;
Ro   3:19 we know that whatever the law **s,**
1Ti   4: 1 Now the Spirit expressly **s** that

SAYS THE *LORD *GOD Ac 2:34; 7:49;
Ro 12:19; 14:11; 1Co 14:21; 2Co 6:17, 18;
Heb 8:8, 9, 10; 10:16; Rev 1:8; 2Es 1:14, 21,
27, 32; 2:9, 14, 15, 17, 28, 30, 31; 15:1, 5, 7, 9,
24, 52, 56; 16:48, 74, 76

SAYS THE *LORD †GOD Isa 3:15; 22:14;
Jer 2:19, 22; 49:5; 50:31; Eze 5:11; 11:8, 21;
12:25, 28; 13:8, 16; 14:11, 14, 16, 18, 20, 23;
15:8; 16:8, 14, 19, 23, 30, 43, 48, 63; 17:16;
18:3, 9, 23, 30, 32; 20:3, 31, 33, 36, 40, 44;
21:7, 13; 22:12, 31; 23:34; 24:14; 26:5, 21;
28:10; 29:20; 30:6; 31:18; 32:8, 14, 16, 31, 32;
33:11; 34:8, 15, 30, 31; 35:6, 11; 36:14, 15,
23, 32; 38:18, 21; 39:5, 8, 10, 13, 20, 29;
43:19, 27; 44:12, 15, 27; 45:9, 15; 47:23;
48:29; Am 3:13; 4:5; 8:3, 9, 11

SAYS THE †LORD Ge 22:16; Nu 14:28;
2Ki 9:26; 19:33; 20:17; 22:19; 2Ch 34:27; Ps
12:5; Isa 1:11, 18; 14:22, 23; 17:3, 6;
22:25; 30:1; 31:9; 33:10; 37:34; 39:6; 41:14,
21; 43:10, 12; 45:13; 48:22; 49:18; 52:5, 5;
54:1, 8, 10, 17; 55:8; 57:19; 59:20, 21, 21;
65:7, 25; 66:2, 9, 17, 20, 21, 22, 23; Jer 1:8,
15, 19; 2:3, 9, 12, 29; 3:1, 10, 12, 12, 13, 14,
16, 20; 4:1, 9, 17; 5:9, 11, 15, 18, 22, 29; 6:12,
15; 7:11, 13, 19, 30, 32; 8:1, 3, 12, 13, 17; 9:3,
6, 9, 24, 25; 12:17; 13:11, 14, 25; 15:3, 6, 9,
20; 16:5, 11, 14, 16; 17:24; 18:6; 19:6, 12;
21:7, 10, 13, 14; 22:5, 16, 24; 23:1, 2, 4, 5, 7,
11, 12, 23, 24, 24, 28, 29, 30, 31, 31, 32, 32,
33; 25:7, 9, 12, 29, 31; 27:8, 11, 15, 22; 28:4;
29:9, 11, 14, 14, 19, 19, 23, 32; 30:3, 3, 8, 10,
11, 17, 21; 31:1, 14, 16, 17, 20, 27, 28, 31, 32,
33, 34, 36, 37, 38; 32:5, 30, 44; 33:11, 13, 14;
34:5, 17, 22; 35:13; 39:17, 18; 42:11; 44:26,
29; 45:5; 46:5, 23, 26, 28; 48:12, 25, 30, 35,
38, 43, 44, 47; 49:2, 2, 6, 13, 16, 18, 26, 30,
31, 32, 37, 38, 39; 50:4, 10, 20, 21, 30, 35, 40;
51:24, 25, 26, 39, 48, 52, 53; Eze 13:6, 7;
16:58; 37:14; Hos 2:13, 16, 21; 11:11; Joel
2:12; Am 1:5, 15; 2:3, 11, 16; 3:10, 15; 4:3, 6,
8, 9, 10, 11; 5:17, 27; 6:8, 14; 9:7, 8, 12, 13,
15; Ob 1:4, 8; Mic 4:6; 5:10; Na 2:13; 3:5; Zep
1:2, 3, 10; 2:9; 3:8, 20; Hag 1:8, 9, 13; 2:4, 4,
4, 7, 8, 9, 9, 14, 17, 23, 23, 23; Zec 1:3, 3, 4,
16; 2:5, 6, 6, 10; 3:9, 10; 4:6; 5:4; 7:13; 8:6,
11, 14, 17; 10:12; 11:6; 12:4; 13:2, 7, 8; Mal
1:2, 2, 6, 8, 9, 10, 11, 13, 13, 14; 2:2, 4, 8, 16,
16; 3:1, 5, 7, 10, 11, 12, 13, 17; 4:1, 3

THUS SAYS THE *LORD †GOD Isa 7:7;
10:24; 22:15; 28:16; 49:22; 52:4; 56:8; 65:13;
Jer 7:20; Eze 2:4; 3:11, 27; 5:5, 7, 8; 6:3, 11;
7:2, 5; 11:7, 16, 17; 12:10, 19, 23, 28; 13:3, 8,
13, 18, 20; 14:4, 6, 21; 15:6; 16:3, 36, 59;
17:3, 9, 19, 22; 20:3, 5, 27, 30, 39, 47; 21:24,
26, 28; 22:3, 19, 28; 23:22, 28, 32, 35, 46;
24:3, 6, 9, 21; 25:3, 6, 8, 12, 13, 15, 16; 26:3,
7, 15, 19; 27:3; 28:2, 6, 12, 22, 25; 29:3, 8, 13,
19; 30:2, 10, 13, 22; 31:10, 15; 32:3, 11;
33:25, 27; 34:2, 10, 11, 17, 20; 35:3, 14; 36:2,
3, 4, 5, 6, 7, 13, 22, 33, 37; 37:5, 9, 12, 19, 21;
38:3, 10, 14, 17; 39:1, 17, 25; 43:18; 44:6, 9;
45:9, 18; 46:1, 16; 47:13; Am 3:11; 5:3; Ob 1:1

THUS SAYS THE †LORD Ex 4:22; 5:1;
7:17; 8:1, 20; 9:1, 13; 10:3; 11:4; 32:27; Jos
7:13; 24:2; Jdg 6:8; 1Sa 10:18; 15:2; 2Sa 7:5,
8; 12:7, 11; 24:12; 1Ki 11:31; 12:24; 13:2, 21;
14:7; 17:14; 20:13, 14, 28, 42; 21:19, 19;
22:11; 2Ki 1:4, 6, 16; 2:21; 3:16, 17; 4:43; 7:1;
9:3, 6, 12; 19:6, 20, 32; 20:1, 5; 21:12; 22:15,
16, 18; 1Ch 17:4, 7; 21:10, 11; 2Ch 11:4; 12:5;
18:10; 20:15; 21:12; 34:23, 24, 26; Isa 29:22;

37:6, 21, 33; 38:1, 5; 43:1, 14, 16; 44:2, 6, 24;
45:1, 11, 14, 18; 48:17; 49:7, 8, 25; 50:1; 52:3;
56:1, 4; 65:8; 66:1, 12; Jer 2:2, 5; 4:3, 27;
5:14; 6:6, 9, 16, 21, 22; 7:3, 21; 8:4; 9:7, 15,
17, 22, 23; 10:2, 18; 11:3, 11, 21, 22; 12:14;
13:9, 12, 13; 14:10, 15; 15:2, 19; 16:3, 5, 9;
17:5, 21; 18:11, 13; 19:3, 11, 15; 20:4; 21:4, 8,
12; 21:3, 6, 11, 18, 30; 23:2, 15, 16, 38;
24:5, 8; 25:8, 27, 28, 32; 26:2, 4, 18; 27:4, 16,
19, 21; 28:2, 11, 13, 14, 16; 29:4, 8, 10, 16, 17,
21, 25, 31, 32; 30:2, 5, 12, 18; 31:2, 7, 15, 16,
23, 35, 37; 32:3, 14, 15, 28, 36, 42; 33:2, 4, 10,
12, 17, 20, 25; 34:2, 2, 4, 13, 17; 35:13, 17, 18,
19; 36:29, 30; 37:7, 9; 38:2, 3, 17; 39:16; 42:9,
15, 18; 43:10; 44:2, 7, 11, 25, 30; 45:2, 4;
47:2; 48:1, 40; 49:1, 7, 12, 28, 35; 50:18, 33;
51:1, 33, 36, 58; Eze 11:5; 21:3; 30:6; Am 1:3,
6, 9, 11, 13; 2:1, 4, 6; 3:12; 5:4, 16; 7:17; Mic
2:3; 3:5; Na 1:12; Hag 1:2, 5, 7; 2:6, 11; Zec
1:3, 4, 14, 16, 17; 3:7; 6:12; 7:9; 8:2, 3, 4, 6, 7,
9, 14, 19, 20, 23; 12:1

SCABBARD*

Jer   47: 6 into your **s,** rest and be still!

SCALES

Pr   16:11 Honest balances and **s** are the
                   LORD's;
Da   5:27 you have been weighed on the **s**
Ac   9:18 something like **s** fell from his eyes,
Rev   6: 5 Its rider held a pair of **s** in his hand,

SCARLET

Isa   1:18 your sins are like **s,** they shall be
                   like snow;
Mt   27:28 stripped him and put a **s** robe on him
Heb   9:19 with water and **s** wool and hyssop,
Rev 17: 3 I saw a woman sitting on a **s** beast

SCATTER → SCATTERED, SCATTERS

Dt   4:27 LORD will **s** you among the peoples;
Ne   1: 8 I will **s** you among the peoples;
Jer   9:16 I will **s** them among nations that
Bar   2:29 the nations, where I will **s** them.

SCATTERED → SCATTER

Ge   11: 4 we shall be **s** abroad upon the face
Nu 10:35 O LORD, let your enemies be **s,**
Dt   30: 3 the LORD your God has **s** you.
2Ch 18:16 "I saw all Israel **s** on the mountains,
Ps   89:10 your enemies with your mighty
Jer   31:10 "He who **s** Israel will gather him,
La   4:16 The LORD himself has **s** them,
Eze 34:12 when they are among their **s** sheep,
Zec   1:19 the horns that have **s** Judah, Israel,
        13: 7 Strike the shepherd, that the sheep
                   may be **s;**
Mk 14:27 'I will strike the shepherd, and the
                   sheep will be **s.'**
Ac   8: 1 the apostles were **s** throughout the
          8: 4 were **s** went from place to place,
Tob 13: 5 among whom you have been **s.**

SCATTERS → SCATTER

Mt   12:30 whoever does not gather with me **s.**
Jn   10:12 the wolf snatches them and **s** them.

SCEPTER

Ge   49:10 The **s** shall not depart from Judah,
Nu   24:17 and a **s** shall rise out of Israel;
Est   4:11 if the king holds out the golden **s** to
Ps   45: 6 Your royal **s** is a **s** of equity;
        125: 3 the **s** of wickedness shall not rest on
Heb   1: 8 righteous **s** is the **s** of your kingdom.

SCHEME → SCHEMES, SCHEMING

Ps   31:13 as they **s** together against me,

SCHEMES → SCHEME

Job 18: 7 their own **s** throw them down.
Ps   10: 2 caught in the **s** they have devised.

SCHEMING* → SCHEME

Ps   64: 2 from the **s** of evildoers,

Eph   4:14 by their craftiness in deceitful **s.**

SCOFF → SCOFFED, SCOFFER, SCOFFERS

Ps   74:10 How long, O God, is the foe to **s?**

SCOFFED → SCOFF

Dt   32:15 and **s** at the Rock of his salvation.
Zep   2:10 because they **s** and boasted
Lk   23:35 but the leaders **s** at him, saying,

SCOFFER → SCOFF

Pr   9: 7 Whoever corrects a **s** wins abuse;
        14: 6 A **s** seeks wisdom in vain,
Isa   29:20 and the **s** shall cease to be;

SCOFFERS → SCOFF

Ps   1: 1 or sit in the seat of **s;**
Pr   19:29 Condemnation is ready for **s,**
Isa   28:14 **s** who rule this people in Jerusalem.
2Pe   3: 3 that in the last days **s** will come,

SCORCH* → SCORCHED, SCORCHING

Rev 16: 8 it was allowed to **s** them with fire;

SCORCHED → SCORCH

Mk   4: 6 And when the sun rose, it was **s;**

SCORCHING → SCORCH

Jas   1:11 its **s** heat and withers the field;

SCORN → SCORNED, SCORNERS

Ps   39: 8 Do not make me the **s** of the fool.
        89:41 has become the **s** of his neighbors.
        109:25 I am an object of **s** to my accusers;
        119:22 take away from me their **s** and
Mic   6:16 so you shall bear the **s** of my people.

SCORNED → SCORN

Ps   22: 6 **s** by others, and despised by the
SS   8: 7 of his house, it would be utterly **s.**
2Es   7:81 have **s** the law of the Most High.

SCORNERS* → SCORN

Pr   3:34 Toward the **s** he is scornful,

SCORPION → SCORPIONS

Lk   11:12 child asks for an egg, will give a **s?**
Rev   9: 5 like the torture of a **s** when it stings

SCORPIONS → SCORPION

1Ki 12:11 but I will discipline you with **s.'"**
Rev   9:10 They have tails like **s,** with stingers,

SCOUNDRELS

1Sa   2:12 Now the sons of Eli were **s;**
1Ki   21:10 seat two **s** opposite him, and have
Sir   11:33 Beware of **s,** for they devise evil,

SCOURGE

Ps   91:10 no **s** come near your tent.
Isa   28:18 the overwhelming **s** passes through

SCRIBE → SCRIBES

Ne   8: 1 the **s** Ezra to bring the book of the
        12:36 and the **s** Ezra went in front of them.
Mk   12:32 the **s** said to him, "You are right,
Sir   38:24 The wisdom of the **s** depends on

SCRIBES → SCRIBE

Mt   7:29 having authority, and not as their **s.**
        23:13 "But woe to you, **s** and Pharisees,
Mk   12:38 he taught, he said, "Beware of the **s**
Ac   4: 5 elders, and **s** assembled in Jerusal

SCRIPTURE → SCRIPTURES

Mk   12:10 Have you not read this **s:**
Lk   4:21 "Today this **s** has been
Jn   2:22 the **s** and the word th
        7:42 Has not the **s** said
        10:35 and the **s** cann
Ac   1:16 the **s** had to b
        8:32 passage of
1Ti   4:13 attentio
2Ti   3:16 All **s**
                   use

2Pe 1:20 no prophecy of **s** is a matter of one's own interpretation,

SCRIPTURES → SCRIPTURE
Mt   22:29 you know neither the **s** nor the power of God.
Mk   14:49 But let the **s** be fulfilled."
Lk   24:27 the things about himself in all the **s**,
     24:45 their minds to understand the **s**,
Jn   5:39 "You search the **s** because you think
Ac   17:11 and examined the **s** every day
     18:28 showing by the **s** that the Messiah
1Co 15: 3 our sins in accordance with the **s**,
     15: 4 third day in accordance with the **s**,
2Pe   3:16 as they do the other **s**.
Sir Pr: 1 Now, those who read the **s** must

SCROLL
Ps   40: 7 the **s** of the book it is written of me.
Isa   34: 4 and the skies roll up like a **s**.
Jer   36: 4 Baruch wrote on a **s** at Jeremiah's
      45: 1 a **s** at the dictation of Jeremiah,
Eze   3: 1 eat this **s**, and go, speak to the
Zec   5: 1 I looked up and saw a flying **s**.
Lk   4:17 the **s** of the prophet Isaiah was given
Heb   10: 7 (in the **s** of the book it is written of
Rev   5: 2 to open the **s** and break its seals?"
       6:14 The sky vanished like a **s** rolling
      10: 8 take the **s** that is open in the hand of
Bar   1:14 And you shall read aloud this **s**

SEA → SEAS, SEASHORE
Ge   1:26 have dominion over the fish of the **s**,
      32:12 your offspring as the sand of the **s**,
      41:49 like the sand of the **s—**
Ex   14:16 Israelites may go into the **s** on dry
      14:27 tossed the Egyptians into the **s**.
      15: 1 and rider he has thrown into the **s**.
Nu   11:31 and it brought quails from the **s** and
      34: 6 shall have the Great **S** and its coast;
Dt   11:24 river Euphrates, to the Western **S**.
      30:13 Neither is it beyond the **s**, that you
1Ki   7:23 Then he made the molten **s**;
2Ki   25:13 the stands and the bronze **s** that
Ne   9:11 passed through the **s** on dry land,
Job   11: 9 the earth, and broader than the **s**.
Ps   46: 2 mountains shake in the heart of the **s**
      74:13 You divided the **s** by your might;
      93: 4 majestic than the waves of the **s**,
      95: 5 The **s** is his, for he made it,
     106: 7 against the Most High at the Red **S**.
     139: 9 settle at the farthest limits of the **s**,
Ecc   1: 7 All streams run to the **s**, but the **s** is not full;
Isa   10:22 Israel were like the sand of the **s**,
      48:18 your success like the waves of the **s**;
      57:20 the tossing **s** that cannot keep still;
Da   7: 3 great beasts came up out of the **s**,
Jnh   1: 4 LORD hurled a great wind upon the **s**
Mic   7:19 all our sins into the depths of the **s**.
Hab   2:14 as the waters cover the **s**.
Zec   9:10 his dominion shall be from **s** to **s**,
Mt   18: 6 were drowned in the depth of the **s**.
Mk   11:23 'Be taken up and thrown into the **s**, '
1Co   10: 1 and all passed through the **s**,
Heb   11:29 By faith the people passed through the Red **S**
Jas   1: 6 who doubts is like a wave of the **s**,
Jude   1:13 of the **s**, casting up the foam of
Rev   4: 6 there is something like a **s** of glass,
       8: 8 with fire, was thrown into the **s**.
      10: 2 Setting his right foot on the **s** and
      13: 1 a beast rising out of the **s** having
      15: 2 a **s** of glass mixed with fire,
      20:13 the **s** gave up the dead that were in it
      21: 1 and the **s** was no more.
Bar   3:30 Who has gone over the **s**,
DEAD SEA Ge 14:3; Nu 34:3, 12; Dt 3:17; Jos 3:16; 12:3; 15:2, 5; 18:19; 2Es 5:7
GREAT SEA Ge 1:21; Nu 34:6, 7; Jos 1:4; 9:1; 15:47; 23:4; Eze 47:10, 15, 19, 20; 48:28; Da 7:2

RED SEA Ex 10:19; 13:18; 15:4, 22; 23:31; Nu 14:25; 21:4; 33:10, 11; Dt 1:40; 2:1; 11:4; Jos 2:10; 4:23; 24:6; Jdg 11:16; 1Ki 9:26; Ne 9:9; Ps 106:7, 9, 22; 136:13, 15; Jer 49:21; Ac 7:36; Heb 11:29; Jdt 5:13; Wis 10:18; 19:7; 1Mc 4:9

SEAL → SEALED, SEALING, SEALS
Est   8: 8 and **s** it with the king's ring;
SS   8: 6 Set me as a **s** upon your heart,
Isa   8:16 **s** the teaching among my disciples.
Da   8:26 As for you, **s** up the vision,
       9:24 to **s** both vision and prophet,
Jn   6:27 that God the Father has set his **s**."
1Co   9: 2 for you are the **s** of my apostleship
2Co   1:22 by putting his **s** on us and giving us
Eph   1:13 the **s** of the promised Holy Spirit;
Rev   6: 3 When he opened the second **s**,
       6: 5 When he opened the third **s**,
       6: 7 When he opened the fourth **s**,
       6: 9 When he opened the fifth **s**,
       6:12 When he opened the sixth **s**,
       7: 2 having the **s** of the living God,
       7: 3 our God with a **s** on their foreheads.
       8: 1 the Lamb opened the seventh **s**,
       9: 4 those people who do not have the **s**
      10: 4 "**S** up what the seven thunders have
      22:10 not **s** up the words of the prophecy
Sir   22:27 and an effective **s** upon my lips,
Bel   1:11 the door and **s** it with your signet.

SEALED → SEAL
Isa   29:11 they say, "We cannot, for it is **s**."
Da   6:17 the king **s** it with his own signet
      12: 9 to remain secret and **s** until the time
Rev   5: 1 and on the back, **s** with seven seals;
       7: 4 the number of those who were **s**,
      20: 3 and locked and **s** it over him,

SEALING* → SEAL
Mt   27:66 the tomb secure by **s** the stone.

SEALS → SEAL
Rev   5: 2 to open the scroll and break its **s**?"
       6: 1 the Lamb open one of the seven **s**,

SEAMLESS*
Jn   19:23 the tunic was **s**, woven in one piece

SEARCH → SEARCHED, SEARCHES, SEARCHING
Dt   4:29 if you **s** after him with all your heart
Ezr   5:17 a **s** made in the royal archives there
Ps   139:23 **S** me, O God, and know my heart;
Pr   2: 4 and **s** for it as for hidden treasures—
      25: 2 the glory of kings is to **s** things out.
Jer   17:10 LORD test the mind and **s** the heart,
Eze   34:11 I myself will **s** for my sheep,
Mt   2: 8 "Go and **s** diligently for the child;
Lk   15: 8 and **s** carefully until she finds it?

SEARCHED → SEARCH
Job   5:27 See, we have **s** this out; it is true.
Ps   139: 1 you have **s** me and known me.

SEARCHES → SEARCH
1Ch   28: 9 for the LORD **s** every mind,
Pr   11:27 evil comes to the one who **s** for it.
Ro   8:27 And God, who **s** the heart,
1Co   2:10 the Spirit **s** everything, even the depths of God.
Rev   2:23 I am the one who **s** minds and hearts

SEARCHING → SEARCH
Mk   1:37 said to him, "Everyone is **s** for you."
Lk   2:49 to them, "Why were you **s** for me?"

SEARED*
1Ti   4: 2 consciences are **s** with a hot iron.

SEAS → SEA
Ge   1:10 were gathered together he called **S**.
Ps   65: 7 You silence the roaring of the **s**,
Jnh   2: 3 into the deep, into the heart of the **s**,

Aza   1:55 Bless the Lord, **s** and rivers;

SEASHORE → SEA, SHORE
Ge   22:17 and as the sand that is on the **s**.
Jos   11: 4 in number like the sand on the **s**,
1Ki   4:29 understanding as vast as the sand on the **s**,
Heb   11:12 innumerable grains of sand by the **s**.
Rev   12:18 the dragon took his stand on the sand of the **s**.

SEASON → SEASONED, SEASONS
Ge   17:21 bear to you at this **s** next year."
Dt   28:12 the rain of your land in its **s**
2Ki   4:16 He said, "At this **s**, in due time,
Ps   1: 3 which yield their fruit in its **s**,
Pr   20: 4 The lazy person does not plow in **s**;
Ecc   3: 1 For everything there is a **s**,
Mk   11:13 for it was not the **s** for figs.

SEASONED → SEASON
Ex   30:35 **s** with salt, pure and holy;
Col   4: 6 always be gracious, **s** with salt,

SEASONS → SEASON
Ge   1:14 let them be for signs and for **s** and
Ps   104:19 have made the moon to mark the **s**;
Gal   4:10 and months, and **s**, and years.
1Th   5: 1 Now concerning the times and the **s**,

SEAT → SEATED
Ex   25:17 make a mercy **s** of pure gold;
      40:20 and set the mercy **s** above the ark;
Lev   16: 2 the curtain before the mercy **s** that
2Ki   25:28 a **s** above the other seats of the kings
Ps   1: 1 or sit in the **s** of scoffers;
Pr   31:23 his **s** among the elders of the land.
Mt   23: 2 "The scribes and the Pharisees sit on Moses' **s**;
Ro   14:10 stand before the judgment **s** of God.
2Co   5:10 must appear before the judgment **s**
Heb   9: 5 of glory overshadowing the mercy **s**.

SEATED → SEAT
Ps   113: 5 the LORD our God, who is **s** on high,
Lk   22:69 the Son of Man will be **s** at the right
Eph   1:20 and is **s** at his right hand
       2: 6 and raised us up with him and **s** us
Col   3: 1 where Christ is, **s** at the right hand
Rev   4: 4 **s** on the thrones were twenty-four elders,
      14:14 and **s** on the cloud was one like the Son of Man,
      19: 4 and worshiped God who is **s** on
      20: 4 **s** on them were given authority to
      21: 5 one who was **s** on the throne said,

SECLUSION*
Lk   1:24 for five months she remained in **s**.

SECOND → TWO
Ge   22:15 LORD called to Abraham a **s** time
      41: 5 he fell asleep and dreamed a **s** time;
Ex   4: 8 they may believe the **s** sign.
Nu   9:11 In the **s** month on the fourteenth day
1Ki   9: 2 LORD appeared to Solomon a **s** time,
Eze   10:14 the **s** face was that of a human being
Da   7: 5 Another beast appeared, a **s** one,
Jnh   3: 1 of the LORD came to Jonah a **s** time,
Hag   2:20 the LORD came a **s** time to Haggai
Zec   11:14 Then I broke my **s** staff Unity,
Mt   22:39 And a **s** is like it:
Jn   3: 4 a **s** time into the mother's womb
1Co   12:28 **s** prophets, third teachers;
      15:47 the **s** man is from heaven.
Tit   3:10 After a first and a **s** admonition,
Heb   9:28 appear a **s** time, not to deal with sin,
Rev   2:11 not be harmed by the **s** death.
       4: 7 the **s** living creature like an ox,
       6: 3 When he opened the **s** seal,
       8: 8 The **s** angel blew his trumpet,
      11:14 The **s** woe has passed.
      16: 3 The **s** angel poured his bowl into
      20: 6 Over these the **s** death has no power,

20:14 This is the s death, the lake of fire;
21: 8 and sulfur, which is the s death."
2Es 11: 1 On the s night I had a dream:

SECRET → SECRETLY, SECRETS
Ex 7:11 did the same by their s arts.
7:22 did the same by their s arts,
8: 7 did the same by their s arts,
8:18 tried to produce gnats by their s arts,
Dt 29:29 The s things belong to the LORD
Ps 90: 8 our s sins in the light of your
139:15 when I was being made in s,
Pr 9:17 and bread eaten in s is pleasant."
21:14 A gift in s averts anger;
Ecc 12:14 including every s thing,
Jer 23:24 s places so that I cannot see them?
Mt 6: 4 so that your alms may be done in s;
6: 6 and pray to your Father who is in s;
6: 18 but by your Father who is in s;
Mk 4:11 "To you has been given the s of the kingdom
Jn 18:20 I have said nothing in s.
Ro 2:16 will judge the s thoughts of all.
1Co 2: 7 But we speak God's wisdom, s and
Php 4:12 circumstances I have learned the s
Sir 8:17 for they cannot keep a s.

SECRETLY → SECRET
Dt 13: 6 If anyone s entices you—
2Ki 17: 9 of Israel s did things that were not
Mt 2: 7 Herod s called for the wise men and
2Pe 2: 1 will s bring in destructive opinions.

SECRETS → SECRET
Ps 44:21 For he knows the s of the heart.
Pr 11:13 A gossip goes about telling s,
Mt 13:11 it has been given to know the s of
1Co 14:25 After the s of the unbeliever's heart
Sir 27:16 betrays s destroys confidence,
2Es 10:38 has revealed many s to you.

SECT
Ac 24: 5 ringleader of the s of the Nazarenes.
26: 5 the strictest s of our religion and

SECURE → SECURELY, SECURITY
Ps 16: 9 soul rejoices; my body also rests s.
Am 6: 1 those who feel s on Mount Samaria.
Mt 27:64 command the tomb to be made s
Sir 4:15 and all who listen to her will live s.

SECURELY → SECURE
Pr 10: 9 Whoever walks in integrity walks s,
Col 1:23 that you continue s established

SECURITY → SECURE
Ps 122: 7 and s within your towers."
Pr 12: 3 No one finds s by wickedness,
1Th 5: 3 they say, "There is peace and s,"

SEDUCES·
Ex 22:16 man s a virgin who is not engaged

SEE → FORESEEING, NEAR-SIGHTED, SAW, SEEING, SEEN, SEER, SEERS, SEES, SIGHT
Ge 2:19 to s what he would call them;
8: 8 to s if the waters had subsided from
9:16 I will s it and remember the
13:15 land that you s I will give to you
Ex 12:13 when I s the blood, I will pass over
14:13 and s the deliverance that
33:20 for no one shall s me and live."
Nu 14:23 shall s the land that I swore to give
Dt 34: 4 I have let you s it with your eyes,
Job 19:26 then in my flesh I shall s God,
Ps 16:10 or let your faithful one s the Pit.
34: 8 O taste and s that the LORD is good;
115: 5 eyes, but do not s.
Isa 40: 5 and all people shall s it together,
53:10 he shall s his offspring;
53:11 Out of his anguish he shall s light;
Eze 8:12 they say, 'The LORD does not s us,

Da 3:25 replied, "But I s four men unbound,
Joel 2:28 and your young men shall s visions.
Mic 7: 9 to the light; I shall s his vindication.
Mt 5: 8 pure in heart, for they will s God.
7: 5 will s clearly to take the speck out
13:16 blessed are your eyes, for they s,
Mk 8:18 Do you have eyes, and fail to s?
14:62 'you will s the Son of Man seated at
Lk 3: 6 all flesh shall s the salvation of God.
Jn 9:25 that though I was blind, now I s."
14:19 In a little while the world will no longer s me, but you will s me;
16:16 a little while, and you will s me."
Ac 2:17 and your young men shall s visions,
1Co 13:12 For now we s in a mirror, dimly, but then we will s face to face.
2Co 13: 5 Examine yourselves to s whether
Heb 12:14 holiness without which no one will s the Lord.
1Jn 3: 2 for we will s him as he is.
Rev 1: 7 the clouds; every eye will s him,
22: 4 they will s his face,
Tob 2:10 four years I remained unable to s.
11: 8 regain his sight and s the light."

SEED → SEEDS, SEEDTIME
Ge 1:11 plants yielding s, and fruit trees
Ecc 11: 6 In the morning sow your s,
Isa 6:13 The holy s is its stump.
55:10 giving s to the sower and bread to
Mt 13:31 like a mustard s that someone took
17:20 have faith the size of a mustard s,
Mk 4:31 It is like a mustard s, which,
Lk 8:11 The s is the word of God.
2Co 9:10 supplies s to the sower and bread
1Pe 1:23 of perishable but of imperishable s,
1Jn 3: 9 because God's s abides in them;
2Es 4:31 a grain of evil s has produced.

SEEDS → SEED
Mt 13: 8 Other s fell on good soil
Mk 4:31 is the smallest of all the s on earth;

SEEDTIME· → SEED
Ge 8:22 as the earth endures, s and harvest,

SEEING → SEE
Ge 16:13 and remained alive after s him?"
Mt 15:31 the lame walking, and the blind s.
2Co 3:18 s the glory of the Lord as though
Sir 42:25 Who could ever tire of s his glory?

SEEK → SEEKERS, SEEKING, SEEKS, SELF-SEEKING, SOUGHT
Dt 4:29 From there you will s the LORD
1Ch 10:14 not s guidance from the LORD.
28: 9 If you s him, he will be found by
2Ch 7:14 pray, s my face, and turn from their
15: 2 If you s him, he will be found by
Ezr 9:12 never s their peace or prosperity.
Ps 4: 2 love vain words, and s after lies?
9:10 have not forsaken those who s you.
24: 6 the company of those who s him,
34:10 those who s the LORD lack no good
63: 1 O God, you are my God, I s you,
105: 3 of those who s the LORD rejoice.
105: 4 S the LORD and his strength;
105: 4 s his presence continually.
119: 2 who s him with their whole heart,
119:10 With my whole heart I s you;
119:176 s out your servant, for I do
Pr 8:17 those who s me diligently find me.
25:27 or to s honor on top of honor.
28: 5 those who s the LORD understand it
Isa 1:17 s justice, rescue the oppressed,
55: 6 S the LORD while he may be found,
65: 1 found by those who did not s me.
Jer 29:13 if you s me with all your heart,
Hos 10:12 for it is time to s the LORD,
Am 5: 6 S the LORD and live, or he will
Zep 2: 3 S the LORD, all you humble of the
Lk 19:10 Son of Man came to s out and to save the lost."

Jn 5:30 because I s to do not my own will
Ac 15:17 that all other peoples may s the Lord
Ro 10:20 found by those who did not s me;
1Co 7:18 Let him not s circumcision.
7:27 Do not s to be free.
10:24 Do not s your own advantage,
Heb 11: 6 that he rewards those who s him.
1Pe 3:11 let them s peace and pursue it.
Sir 2:16 who fear the Lord s to please him,
24:34 but for all who s wisdom.

SEEKING → SEEK
1Co 10:33 not s my own advantage, but that of

SEEKS → SEEK
Pr 11:27 Whoever diligently s good s favor,
14: 6 A scoffer s wisdom in vain,
15:14 who has understanding s knowledge
Jn 4:23 s such as these to worship him.
Ro 3:11 there is no one who s God.
Sir 32:15 The one who s the law
39: 1 He s out the wisdom of all the

SEEM → SEEMED, SEEMS
Zec 8: 6 should it also s impossible to me,

SEEMED → SEEM
Ge 29:20 and they s to him but a few days
Nu 13:33 we s like grasshoppers,
Lk 24:11 these words s to them an idle tale,
Rev 13: 3 One of its heads s to have received

SEEMS → SEEM
Pr 14:12 a way that s right to a person,
16:25 there is a way that s to be right,
Heb 12:11 discipline always s painful rather

SEEN → SEE
Ge 16:13 I really s God and remained alive
Ex 33:23 but my face shall not be s."
Nu 14:14 for you, O LORD, are s face to face,
Dt 4: 9 the things that your eyes have s nor
Jos 23: 3 and you have s all that
Jdg 6:22 I have s the angel of the LORD face
13:22 shall surely die, for we have s God."
Ezr 3:12 old people who had s the first house
Ps 37:25 I have not s the righteous forsaken
37:35 I have s the wicked oppressing,
98: 3 ends of the earth have s the victory
Isa 6: 5 have s the King, the LORD of hosts!"
9: 2 in darkness have s a great light;
64: 4 no eye has s any God besides you,
Mt 2: 9 the star that they had s at its rising,
4:16 sat in darkness have s a great light,
Lk 2:30 for my eyes have s your salvation,
Jn 1:14 and we have s his glory,
1:18 No one has ever s God.
6:46 Not that anyone has s the Father
6:46 he has s the Father.
14: 9 Whoever has s me has s the Father.
20:25 told him, "We have s the Lord."
20:29 Blessed are those who have not s
Ro 8:24 Now hope that is s is not hope.
1Co 2: 9 as it is written, "What no eye has s,
Php 4: 9 and received and heard and s in me,
1Ti 3:16 s by angels, proclaimed among
1Pe 1: 8 you have not s him, you love him;
1Jn 1: 3 we declare to you what we have s
4:12 No one has ever s God;
3Jn 1:11 whoever does evil has not s God.
Rev 1:19 Now write what you have s, what is,
2Es 10:32 and lo, what I have s I saw,
14: 8 the dreams that you have s,

SEER → SEE
1Sa 9: 9 a prophet was formerly called a s.)
2Sa 24:11 came to the prophet Gad, David's s,
1Ch 29:25 in the records of the s Samuel,
29:29 and in the records of the s Gad,
2Ch 9:29 of the s Iddo concerning Jeroboam
29:30 words of David and of the s Asaph.
Am 7:12 Amaziah said to Amos, "O s, go,

SEERS → SEE
2Ch 33:19 written in the records of the **s**.
Mic 3: 7 the **s** shall be disgraced,

SEES → SEE
Ps 33:13 from heaven; he **s** all humankind.
Isa 47:10 you said, "No one **s** me."
Mt   6: 4 Father who **s** in secret will reward
       6: 6 Father who **s** in secret will reward
     6:18 Father who **s** in secret will reward
Jn   5:19 but only what he **s** the Father doing;
1Jn 3:17 and **s** a brother or sister in need

SEIR
Ge 32: 3 to his brother Esau in the land of **S**,
Dt   2: 4 descendants of Esau, who live in **S**.
Eze 35: 2 set your face against Mount **S**,

SELECT
Ex 12:21 "Go, **s** lambs for your families,
Ac   6: 3 **s** from among yourselves seven

SELF → SELFISH, SELFISHNESS
Ro   6: 6 our old **s** was crucified with him
Eph 4:22 your old **s**, corrupt and deluded by
Col 3:10 clothed yourselves with the new **s**,
1Pe 3: 4 let your adornment be the inner **s**

SELF-ABASEMENT*
Col 2:18 insisting on **s** and worship of angels,

SELF-CONDEMNED* → CONDEMN
Gal 2:11 to his face, because he stood **s**;
Tit   3:11 is perverted and sinful, being **s**.

SELF-CONTROL → CONTROL
Pr 25:28 without walls, is one who lacks **s**.
Ac 24:25 And as he discussed justice, **s**,
1Co 7: 5 tempt you because of your lack of **s**.
2Pe 1: 6 and knowledge with **s**, and **s** with
      endurance,
Sir 18:30 **s** Do not follow your base desires,

SELF-CONTROLLED* → CONTROL
Tit   1: 8 prudent, upright, devout, and **s**.
     2: 5 to be **s**, chaste, good managers of
     2: 6 urge the younger men to be **s**.
     2:12 present age to live lives that are **s**,
4Mc 15:10 they were righteous and **s** and brave

SELF-DENIAL* → DENY
Lev 23:29 who does not practice **s** during
Sir 11:18 rich through diligence and **s**,

SELF-DISCIPLINE* → DISCIPLINE
2Ti   1: 7 spirit of power and of love and of **s**.
Sir 26:14 and nothing is so precious as her **s**.

SELF-INDULGENCE* → INDULGE
Mt 23:25 inside they are full of greed and **s**.
Gal 5:13 freedom as an opportunity for **s**,
Col 2:23 they are of no value in checking **s**.

SELF-INDULGENT* → INDULGE
Pr 18: 1 The one who lives alone is **s**,

SELF-SEEKING* → SEEK
Ro   2: 8 those who are **s** and who obey not

SELFISH* → SELF
Ps 119:36 to your decrees, and not to **s** gain.
Php 1:17 proclaim Christ out of **s** ambition,
     2: 3 Do nothing from **s** ambition or
Jas   3:14 if you have bitter envy and **s**
     3:16 where there is envy and **s** ambition,

SELFISHNESS* → SELF
2Co 12:20 anger, **s**, slander, gossip, conceit,

SELL → SALE, SELLING, SELLS, SOLD
Ge 25:31 said, "First **s** me your birthright."
Pr 23:23 Buy truth, and do not **s** it;
Mk 10:21 **s** what you own, and give the money
Ac   2:45 they would **s** their possessions
Rev 13:17 or **s** who does not have the mark,

SELLING → SELL
Mk 11:15 began to drive out those who were **s**
Lk 17:28 eating and drinking, buying and **s**,
Jn   2:14 the temple he found people **s** cattle,

SELLS → SELL
Pr 31:24 makes linen garments and **s** them;
Mt 13:44 **s** all that he has and buys that field.

SEND → SENDING, SENDS, SENT
Ge   7: 4 For in seven days I will **s** rain on
Ex 23:27 I will **s** my terror in front of you,
     33: 2 I will **s** an angel before you,
Dt 28:20 The LORD will **s** upon you disaster,
1Sa 5:11 "**S** away the ark of the God of Israel
Ps 43: 3 O **s** out your light and your truth;
     57: 3 He will **s** from heaven and save me,
  104:30 When you **s** forth your spirit,
Ecc 11: 1 **S** out your bread upon the waters,
Isa   6: 8 And I said, "Here am I; **s** me!"
Mal   4: 5 I will **s** you the prophet Elijah
Mt   9:38 to **s** out laborers into his harvest."
   24:31 he will **s** out his angels with a loud
Lk 11:49 'I will **s** them prophets and apostles,
   20:13 I will **s** my beloved son;
Jn   3:17 God did not **s** the Son into the
      world to condemn the world,
   14:26 whom the Father will **s** in my name,
   15:26 I will **s** to you from the Father,
   16: 7 but if I go, I will **s** him to you.
Ac   3:20 may **s** the Messiah appointed for
1Co 1:17 For Christ did not **s** me to baptize

SENDING → SEND
Mt 10:16 I am **s** you out like sheep into the
Ro   8: 3 by **s** his own Son in the likeness of
Rev 1: 1 by **s** his angel to his servant John,

SENDS → SEND
Ps 68:33 listen, he **s** out his voice,
Mt   5:45 **s** rain on the righteous and on the

SENNACHERIB
Assyrian king whose siege of Jerusalem was overthrown by the LORD following prayer of Hezekiah and Isaiah (2Ki 18:13-19:37; 2Ch 32:1-21; Isa 36-37).

SENSE → SENSELESS, SENSES, SENSIBLE
Dt 32:28 They are a nation void of **s**;
Ecc 10: 3 fools walk on the road, they lack **s**,

SENSELESS → SENSE
Ro   1:21 their **s** minds were darkened.

SENSES → SENSE
Eph 2: 3 following the desires of flesh and **s**,

SENSIBLE → SENSE
1Ti   3: 2 married only once, temperate, **s**,
Tob 6:12 girl is **s**, brave, and very beautiful,
Sir 25: 8 who lives with a **s** wife,
   33: 3 The **s** person will trust in the law;
   40:23 but a **s** wife is better than either.

SENSITIVITY*
Eph 4:19 They have lost all **s** and have

SENSUAL*
1Ti   5:11 **s** desires alienate them from Christ,

SENT → SEND
Ge   8: 8 Then he **s** out the dove from him,
   45: 5 God **s** me before you to preserve life
Ex   3:14 'I AM has **s** me to you.'"
Nu 13:17 Moses **s** them to spy out the land of
   16:29 then the LORD has not **s** me.
   21: 6 LORD **s** poisonous serpents among
Jos   2: 1 **s** two men secretly from Shittim as
   24:12 I **s** the hornet ahead of you,
2Sa 24:15 So the LORD **s** a pestilence on Israel
2Ki 14: 9 thornbush on Lebanon **s** to a cedar
Ps 107:20 he **s** out his word and healed them,
Isa 55:11 succeed in the thing for which I **s** it.
   61: 1 he has **s** me to bring good news to
Jer   3: 8 I had **s** her away with a decree of
   28: 9 be known that the LORD has truly **s**
   44: 4 persistently **s** to you all my servants
Eze 39:28 because I **s** them into exile
Da   3:28 and Abednego, who has **s** his angel
   6:22 God **s** his angel and shut the lions'
Mt 10:40 and whoever welcomes me
      welcomes the one who **s** me.
Lk   1:26 the angel Gabriel was **s** by God
   4:18 He has **s** me to proclaim release to
   9: 2 **s** them out to proclaim the kingdom
  10:16 rejects me rejects the one who **s** me.
  13:34 and stones those who are **s**
Jn   1: 6 There was a man **s** from God,
   3:28 but I have been **s** ahead of him.'
   4:34 is to do the will of him who **s** me
   5:24 believes him who **s** me has eternal
   8:16 but I and the Father who **s** me.
   9: 4 of him who **s** me while it is day;
  16: 5 now I am going to him who **s** me;
  17: 3 and Jesus Christ whom you have **s**.
  17:18 As you have **s** me into the world,
  17:18 so I have **s** them into the world.
  20:21 the Father has **s** me, so I send you."
Ro 10:15 to proclaim him unless they are **s**?
Gal 4: 4 of time had come, God **s** his Son,
   4: 6 God has **s** the Spirit of his Son into
      our hearts,
1Jn 4:10 and **s** his Son to be the atoning
Rev 22:16 who **s** my angel to you with this
2Es 4: 1 angel that had been **s** to me,
   7: 1 the angel who had been **s** to me

SENTENCE → SENTENCED
Ecc 8:11 Because **s** against an evil deed is not
Ac 13:28 they found no cause for a **s** of death,
2Co 1: 9 that we had received the **s** of death

SENTENCED → SENTENCE
Mt 23:33 How can you escape being **s** to hell?
1Co 4: 9 as though **s** to death,

SENTINEL → SENTINELS
Eze 3:17 made you a **s** for the house of Israel;
   33: 3 and if the **s** sees the sword coming

SENTINELS → SENTINEL
Isa 56:10 Israel's **s** are blind,
Jer   6:17 Also I raised up **s** for you:

SEPARATE → SEPARATED, SEPARATES
Ex 26:33 the curtain shall **s** for you the holy
Mt 19: 6 what God has joined together, let
      no one **s**."
Ro   8:35 will **s** us from the love of Christ?
1Co 7:10 wife should not **s** from her husband
2Co 6:17 out from them, and be **s** from them,

SEPARATED → SEPARATE
Ge   1: 4 God **s** the light from the darkness.
   1: 7 and **s** the waters that were under the
Lev 20:24 I have **s** you from the peoples.
Ne 13: 3 **s** from Israel all those of foreign
Heb 7:26 **s** from sinners, and exalted above

SEPARATES* → SEPARATE
Pr 16:28 and a whisperer **s** close friends.
Mt 25:32 as a shepherd **s** the sheep from
1Co 7:15 But if the unbelieving partner **s**,

SERAPHS*
Isa   6: 2 **S** were in attendance above him;
   6: 6 Then one of the **s** flew to me,

SERIOUS
1Ti   3: 8 Deacons likewise must be **s**,
   3:11 Women likewise must be **s**,
Tit   2: 2 the older men to be temperate, **s**,
1Pe 4: 7 be **s** and discipline yourselves for

SERPENT → SERPENTS
Ge   3: 1 the **s** was more crafty than any other

3:13 The woman said, "The s tricked me,
3:14 The LORD God said to the s,
Nu 21: 9 Moses made a s of bronze,
2Ki 18: 4 the bronze s that Moses had made,
Isa 27: 1 punish Leviathan the fleeing s,
65:25 but the s—its food shall be dust!
2Co 11: 3 the s deceived Eve by its cunning,
Rev 12: 9 great dragon was thrown down, that ancient s,
20: 2 He seized the dragon, that ancient s,

SERPENTS → SERPENT

Nu 21: 6 the LORD sent poisonous s among
Mt 10:16 wise as s and innocent as doves.
1Co 10: 9 and were destroyed by s.
Rev 9:19 their tails are like s, having heads;

SERVANT → SERVANT'S, SERVANTS

Ex 14:31 believed in the LORD and in his s Moses.
Nu 12: 7 Not so with my s Moses;
1Sa 3:10 "Speak, for your s is listening."
1Ki 3: 7 you have made your s king in place
8:56 he spoke through his s Moses.
8:66 the LORD had shown to his s David
20:40 your s was busy here and there,
Job 1: 8 "Have you considered my s Job?
2: 3 "Have you considered my s Job?
42: 8 and my s Job shall pray for you,
Ps 19:11 Moreover by them is your s warned;
19:13 Keep back your s also from the
31:16 Let your face shine upon your s;
78:70 He chose his s David, and took him
89: 3 I have sworn to my s David:
105:26 He sent his s Moses, and Aaron
119:135 Make your face shine upon your s,
136:22 a heritage to his s Israel,
Pr 11:29 and the fool will be s to the wise.
14:35 A s who deals wisely has the king's
Isa 41: 8 But you, Israel, my s, Jacob,
42: 1 Here is my s, whom I uphold,
43:10 and my s whom I have chosen,
44: 1 O Jacob my s, Israel whom I have
45: 4 For the sake of my s Jacob,
48:20 The LORD has redeemed his s Jacob
49: 3 "You are my s, Israel,
52:13 my s shall prosper; he shall be
53:11 my s, shall make many righteous,
Jer 30:10 as for you, have no fear, my s Jacob,
33:21 could my covenant with my s David
Eze 34:24 my s David shall be prince among
Zec 3: 8 going to bring my s the Branch.
Mt 8:13 And the s was healed in that hour.
20:26 be great among you must be your s,
Lk 1:38 Then Mary said, "Here am I, the s of the Lord;
1:54 He has helped his s Israel,
1:69 for us in the house of his s David,
Jn 12:26 where I am, there will my s be also.
Ac 3:13 has glorified his s Jesus,
Ro 1: 1 Paul, a s of Jesus Christ, called to
13: 4 for it is God's s for your good.
Gal 2:17 is Christ then a s of sin?
Col 1:23 I, Paul, became a s of this gospel.
1Ti 4: 6 a good s of Christ Jesus,
2Ti 2:24 Lord's s must not be quarrelsome
Heb 3: 5 faithful in all God's house as a s,
Rev 15: 3 sing the song of Moses, the s of God
19:10 a fellow s with you and your

MOSES THE SERVANT Dt 34:5; Jos 1:1,
13, 15; 8:31, 33; 11:12; 12:6, 6; 13:8; 14:7;
18:7; 22:2, 4, 5; 2Ki 18:12; 1Ch 6:49; 2Ch 1:3;
24:6, 9; Ne 10:29; Da 9:11; Rev 15:3

SERVANT DAVID 1Sa 19:4; 2Sa 3:18; 7:5,
8, 26; 1Ki 8:66; 11:13, 32, 34, 36; 14:8; 2Ki
8:19; 19:34; 1Ch 17:4, 7, 24; 2Ch 6:17, 42; Ps
78:70; 89:3, 20; 144:10; Isa 37:35; Jer 33:21,
22, 26; Eze 34:23, 24; 37:24, 25; Lk 1:69; 1Mc
4:30

SERVANT JACOB Ge 32:4, 18, 20; Isa
45:4; 48:20; Jer 30:10; 46:27, 28; Eze 28:25;
37:35; Bar 3:36

SERVANT MOSES Ex 14:31; Nu 12:7, 8;
Jos 1:2, 7; 9:24; 11:15; 1Ki 8:56; 2Ki 21:8; Ne
1:7, 8; 9:14; Ps 105:26; Mal 4:4; Bar 1:20; 2:28

SERVANT OF *GOD 1Ch 6:49; 2Ch 24:9;
Ne 10:29; Da 9:11; Ro 13:4; Tit 1:1; Jas 1:1;
Rev 15:3

SERVANT OF THE †LORD Dt 34:5; Jos
1:1, 13, 15; 8:31, 33; 11:12; 12:6, 6; 13:8;
14:7; 18:7; 22:2, 4, 5; 24:29; Jdg 2:8; 2Ki
18:12; 2Ch 1:3; 24:6; Ps 18:Heading;
36:Heading; Isa 42:19

SERVANT'S → SERVANT

2Ch 6:19 Regard your s prayer and his plea,
Ps 119:122 Guarantee your s well-being;

SERVANTS → SERVANT

Dt 32:36 have compassion on his s,
2Ki 17:23 as he had foretold through all his s
Ezr 5:11 'We are the s of the God of heaven
Job 4:18 Even in his s he puts no trust,
Ps 34:22 The LORD redeems the life of his s;
90:13 Have compassion on your s!
113: 1 Praise, O s of the LORD;
Isa 65: 8 so I will do for my s' sake,
65:14 my s shall sing for gladness of heart,
Jer 7:25 sent all my s the prophets
Da 9: 6 not listened to your s the prophets,
Jn 15:15 I do not call you s any longer,
15:20 'S are not greater than their master.'
Ac 4:29 to your s to speak your word with
Ro 13: 6 for the authorities are God's s,
1Co 3: 5 S through whom you came to
Heb 1: 7 and his s flames of fire."
1Pe 2:16 As s of God, live as free people,
Rev 7: 3 marked the s of our God with a seal
19: 2 avenged on her the blood of his s."
22: 3 and his s will worship him;
Aza 1:10 we, your s who worship you,
2Es 1:32 I sent you my s the prophets,

ALL SERVANTS Ge 20:8; 27:37; 40:20;
41:37; 50:7; Dt 29:2; 34:11; Isa 18:5, 22, 30;
19:1; 22:6, 14; 2Sa 10:19; 11:9; 13:31, 36;
16:6, 11; 19:14; 1Ki 3:15; 2Ki 9:7; 17:23; 1Ch
21:3; 2Ch 32:9; Ezr 2:58; Ne 5:16; 7:60; 9:10;
Est 3:2; 4:11; Ps 119:91; 134:1; 135:9; Jer
7:25; 25:4; 35:15; 44:4; Rev 19:5; Jdt 10:20;
11:20; AdE 15:16; Aza 1:21; 1Es 5:35

KING'S SERVANTS 2Sa 11:24; 1Ki 1:47;
Est 2:2; 3:2, 3; 4:11; 6:3, 5; Jdt 6:3; AdE 2:2;
6:3, 8; Aza 1:23

SERVANTS THE PROPHETS 2Ki 9:7;
17:13, 23; 21:10; 24:2; Ezr 9:11; Jer 7:25;
25:4; 26:5; 29:19; 35:15; 44:4; Eze 38:17; Da
9:6, 10; Am 3:7; Zec 1:6; Rev 10:7; 11:18; Bar
2:20, 24; 1Es 8:82; 2Es 1:32; 2:1

TEMPLE SERVANTS 1Ch 9:2; Ezr 2:43,
58, 70; 7:7, 24; 8:17, 20; Ne 3:26, 31; 7:46, 60,
73; 10:28; 11:3, 21, 21; 1Es 1:3; 5:29, 35; 8:5,
22, 49, 49

SERVE → SERVED, SERVES, SERVICE, SERVING

Ge 15:14 judgment on the nation that they s,
25:23 the elder shall s the younger."
Ex 28: 1 the Israelites, to s me as priests—
Dt 6:13 you shall s, and by his name alone
10:12 s the LORD your God with all your
13: 4 him you shall s, and to him you
28:47 not s the LORD your God joyfully
Jos 22: 5 and to s him with all your heart and
24:14 s him in sincerity and in faithfulness
24:15 if you are unwilling to s the LORD,
choose this day whom you will s,
24:15 as for me and my household, we
will s the LORD."
24:18 will s the LORD, for he is our God."
1Sa 7: 3 heart to the LORD, and s him only,
12:20 but s the LORD with all your heart;
12:24 s him faithfully with all your heart;
2Ki 17:35 bow yourselves to them or s them

Ne 9:35 they did not s you and did not turn
Job 36:11 and s him, they complete their days
Ps 2:11 S the LORD with fear, with
Isa 60:12 that will not s you shall perish;
Jer 2:20 and you said, "I will not s!"
25: 6 do not go after other gods to s and
Da 3:17 God whom we s is able to deliver
Mt 4:10 Lord your God, and s only him.'"
6:24 You cannot s God and wealth.
Mk 10:45 the Son of Man came not to be served but to s,
Lk 16:13 No slave can s two masters;
16:13 You cannot s God and wealth."
Ro 12:11 be ardent in spirit, s the Lord.
1Th 1: 9 to s a living and true God,
1Ti 6: 2 rather they must s them all the more,
1Pe 4:10 s one another with whatever gift

SERVED → SERVE

Ge 29:20 So Jacob s seven years for Rachel,
Jos 24:15 gods your ancestors s in the region
Jer 5:19 have forsaken me and s foreign gods
Mt 20:28 as the Son of Man came not to be s but to serve,
Jn 12: 2 Martha s, and Lazarus was one of
Ac 17:25 nor is he s by human hands,
Ro 1:25 worshiped and s the creature rather

SERVES → SERVE

Lk 22:26 and the leader like one who s.
Jn 12:26 Whoever s me must follow me,
Ro 14:18 thus s Christ is acceptable to God
1Pe 4:11 whoever s must do so with the

SERVICE → SERVE

Nu 3: 8 as they do s at the tabernacle.
8:25 shall retire from the duty of the s
Job 7: 1 human beings have a hard s on earth
Mk 14: 6 She has performed a good s for me.
1Co 16:15 themselves to the s of the saints;
Rev 2:19 love, faith, s, and patient endurance.

SERVING → SERVE

1Sa 8: 8 forsaking me and s other gods,
1Ki 9: 9 worshiping them and s them;
2Ch 12: 8 know the difference between s me
2Ti 2: 4 No one s in the army gets entangled
1Pe 1:12 they were s not themselves but you,
Rev 1: 6 priests s his God and Father,

SET → SETS, SETTING, SUNSET

Ge 9:13 I have s my bow in the clouds,
28:18 and s it up for a pillar
31:45 took a stone, and s it up as a pillar.
35:14 Jacob s up a pillar in the place
Ex 24: 4 mountain, and s up twelve pillars,
40:18 Moses s up the tabernacle;
Nu 9:23 of the LORD they would s out.
Dt 10:15 yet the LORD s his heart in love
27: 2 you shall s up large stones and
28: 1 the LORD your God will s you high
30:15 I have s before you today life and
Jos 4: 9 (Joshua s up twelve stones in the
Ps 3: 3 but the LORD has s apart the faithful
8: 1 s your glory above the heavens.
Isa 41:21 S forth your case, says the LORD;
50: 7 therefore I have s my face like flint,
Da 11:28 s against the holy covenant.
Ac 1: 7 or periods that the Father has s
Ro 1: 1 s apart for the gospel of God,
6:18 having been s free from sin,
8: 2 s you free from the law of sin
2Co 3:14 since only in Christ is it s aside.
Col 2:14 s this aside, nailing it to the cross.
1Pe 1:13 s all your hope on the grace

SETH

Ge 4:25 she bore a son and named him S,
1Ch 1: 1 Adam, S, Enosh;

SETS → SET

Job 5:11 he s on high those who are lowly,
Ps 146: 7 The LORD s the prisoners free;

Da   2:21 deposes kings and **s** up kings;
Heb   4: 7 again he **s** a certain day—

SETTING → SET

Dt   11:26 I am **s** before you today a blessing
            and a curse;
Jer 21: 8 I am **s** before you the way of life

SETTLE → SETTLED

Ge   26: 2 **s** in the land that I shall show you.
     47: 4 servants **s** in the land of Goshen."
Nu   33:53 possession of the land and **s** in it,
Dt   26: 1 and you possess it, and **s** in it,

SETTLED → SETTLE

Ex   24:16 The glory of the LORD **s** on Mount
     40:35 because the cloud **s** upon it,
Dt   19: 1 **s** in their towns and in their houses,
2Ki 18:11 **s** them in Halah, on the Habor,
Ne   7:73 and all Israel **s** in their towns.

SEVEN → SEVENFOLD, SEVENTH

Ge   7: 2 Take with you **s** pairs of all clean
            animals,
     21:28 Abraham set apart **s** ewe lambs of
     29:18 so he said, "I will serve you **s** years
     41: 2 came up out of the Nile **s** sleek and
     41: 5 **s** ears of grain, plump and good,
Ex   2:16 priest of Midian had **s** daughters.
     12:15 **S** days you shall eat unleavened
     25:37 You shall make the **s** lamps for it;
     29:35 **s** days you shall ordain them.
Nu   23: 1 Balaam said to Balak, "Build me **s**
            altars here,
Dt   7: 1 **s** nations mightier and more
Jos   6: 4 march around the city **s** times,
Jdg 16:13 If you weave the **s** locks of my head
1Sa   2: 5 The barren has borne **s**, but she
1Ki 19:18 Yet I will leave **s** thousand in Israel,
2Ki   5:10 "Go, wash in the Jordan **s** times,
Ps 119:164 **S** times a day I praise you
Pr   6:16 **s** that are an abomination to him:
      9: 1 she has hewn her **s** pillars.
     24:16 they fall **s** times, they will rise again
     26:25 there are **s** abominations concealed
Isa   4: 1 **S** women shall take hold of one man
Da   3:19 the furnace heated up **s** times more
      4:16 And let **s** times pass over him.
      9:25 prince, there shall be **s** weeks;
Zec   3: 9 on a single stone with **s** facets,
      4: 2 there are **s** lamps on it,
Mt   18:22 Jesus said to him, "Not **s** times, but,
            I tell you, seventy-seven times.
Mk   12:20 were **s** brothers; the first married
     16: 9 whom he had cast out **s** demons.
Lk   11:26 brings **s** other spirits more evil than
Ro   11: 4 "I have kept for myself **s** thousand
Rev   1: 4 John to the **s** churches that are in
            Asia:
      1:12 turning I saw **s** golden lampstands,
      1:16 In his right hand he held **s** stars,
      3: 1 the **s** spirits of God and the **s** stars:
      4: 5 which are the **s** spirits of God;
      5: 1 and on the back, sealed with **s** seals;
      6: 1 the Lamb open one of the **s** seals,
      8: 2 I saw the **s** angels who stand before
     10: 4 when the **s** thunders had sounded,
     12: 3 a great red dragon, with **s** heads and
     12: 3 and **s** diadems on his heads.
     15: 1 **s** angels with **s** plagues.
     15: 7 the **s** angels **s** golden bowls full of
            the wrath of God,
     16: 1 the **s** bowls of the wrath of God."
     17: 9 the **s** heads ae **s** mountains
Tob   3: 8 she had been married to **s** husbands,
Sir 20:12 but pay for it **s** times over.
     40: 8 but to sinners **s** times more,
2Es   5:20 So I fasted **s** days, mourning and
      7:30 back to primeval silence for **s** days,
     13: 1 After **s** days I dreamed a dream in

SEVEN DAYS Ge 7:4, 10; 8:10, 12; 31:23;
     50:10; Ex 7:25; 12:15, 19; 13:6, 7; 22:30;

23:15; 29:30, 35, 37; 34:18; Lev 8:33, 33, 35;
12:2; 13:4, 5, 21, 26, 31, 33, 50, 54; 14:8, 38;
15:13, 19, 24, 28; 22:27; 23:6, 8, 34, 36, 39,
40, 41, 42; Nu 12:14, 14, 15; 19:11, 14, 16;
28:17, 24; 29:12; 31:19; Dt 16:3, 4, 13, 15; Jdg
14:12, 17; 1Sa 10:8; 13:8; 31:13; 1Ki 8:65;
16:15; 20:29; 2Ki 3:9; 1Ch 9:25; 10:12; 2Ch
7:8, 9, 9; 30:21, 22, 23, 23; 35:17; Ezr 6:22;
Ne 8:18; Est 1:5; Job 2:13; Isa 30:26; Eze
3:15, 16; 43:25, 26; 44:26; 45:21, 23, 23, 25;
Ac 20:6; 21:4, 27; 28:14; Heb 11:30; Tob
11:18; Jdt 16:24; AdE 2:18; Sir 22:12; 1Es
1:19; 4:63; 7:14; 3Mc 6:30; 7:17; 2Es 5:13, 19,
20, 21; 6:31, 35; 7:30, 31, 101, 101; 9:23, 27;
12:39, 40, 51; 13:1; 4Mc 14:7

SEVEN TIMES Ge 33:3; Lev 4:6, 17; 8:11;
14:7, 16, 27, 51; 16:14, 19; 25:8; Nu 19:4; Jos
6:4, 15, 15; 1Ki 18:43; 2Ki 4:35; 5:10, 14; Ps
12:6; 119:164; Pr 24:16; Da 3:19; 4:16, 23, 25,
32; Mt 18:21, 22; Lk 17:4, 4; Sir 20:12; 40:8

SEVEN YEARS Ge 5:7; 11:21; 29:18, 20,
27, 30; 41:26, 26, 27, 27, 29, 30, 36, 48, 53,
54; Lev 25:8; Nu 13:22; Jdg 6:1, 25; 12:9; 2Sa
2:11; 5:5; 1Ki 2:11; 6:38; 2Ki 8:1, 2, 3; 11:21;
1Ch 3:4; 29:27; 2Ch 24:1; Eze 39:9; Lk 2:36

SEVENFOLD → SEVEN

Ge   4:15 kills Cain will suffer a **s** vengeance.
      4:24 If Cain is avenged **s**, truly Lamech
            seventy-sevenfold."
Lev 26:18 to punish you **s** for your sins.
Pr   6:31 if they are caught, they will pay **s**;

SEVENTH → SEVEN

Ge   2: 2 on the **s** day God finished the work
Ex   16:30 So the people rested on the **s** day.
     20:10 the **s** day is a sabbath to the LORD
     23:11 but the **s** year you shall let it rest
     23:12 but on the **s** day you shall rest,
Dt   31:10 "Every **s** year, in the scheduled
Jos   6:16 And at the **s** time, when the priests
Heb   4: 4 God rested on the **s** day from all his
Jude 1:14 in the **s** generation from Adam,
Rev   8: 1 When the Lamb opened the **s** seal,
     11:15 Then the **s** angel blew his trumpet,
     16:17 The **s** angel poured his bowl into
1Mc   6:53 because it was the **s** year;

SEVENTH DAY Ge 2:2, 2, 3; Ex 12:15, 16;
13:6; 16:26, 27, 29, 30; 20:10, 11; 23:12;
24:16; 31:15, 17; 34:21; 35:2; Lev 13:5, 6, 27,
32, 34, 51; 14:9, 39; 23:3, 8; Nu 6:9; 7:48;
19:12, 12, 19, 19; 28:25; 29:32; 31:19, 24; Dt
5:14; 16:8; Jos 6:4, 15; Jdg 14:17, 18; 2Sa
12:18; 1Ki 20:29; 2Ki 25:8; Est 1:10; Eze
30:20; 45:20; Heb 4:4, 4; AdE 1:10; Bar 1:2;
Bel 1:40; 2Mc 6:11; 12:38; 15:4

SEVENTH MONTH Ge 8:4; Lev 16:29;
23:24, 27, 34, 39, 41; 25:9; Nu 29:1, 7, 12; 1Ki
8:2; 2Ki 25:25; 1Ch 27:10; 2Ch 5:3; 7:10;
31:7; Ezr 3:1, 6; Ne 7:73; 8:2, 14; Jer 28:17;
41:1; Hag 2:1; 1Mc 10:21; 1Es
5:47, 53; 9:37, 40

SEVENTH YEAR Ex 23:11; Lev 25:4, 20;
Dt 15:1, 9, 12; 31:10; 2Ki 11:4; 12:1; 18:9;
2Ch 23:1; Ezr 7:7, 8; Ne 10:31; Est 2:16; Jer
34:14; 52:28; Eze 20:1; AdE 2:16; 1Mc 6:53;
1Es 8:6, 6; 4Mc 2:8

SEVENTY → SEVENTY-SEVEN

Ge   46:27 who came into Egypt were **s**.
Ex   24: 1 Abihu, and **s** of the elders of Israel,
Nu   11:25 on him and put it on the **s** elders;
2Ch 36:21 it kept sabbath, to fulfill **s** years.
Ps   90:10 The days of our life are **s** years,
Jer 25:12 Then after **s** years are completed,
Da   9: 2 of Jerusalem, namely, **s** years.
      9:24 **S** weeks are decreed for your people

SEVENTY-SEVEN → SEVENTY

Mt   18:22 Jesus said to him, "Not seven
            times, but, I tell you, **s** times.

SEVERE

Ge   12:10 for the famine was **s** in the land.
     41:57 the famine became **s** throughout the
1Ki 18: 2 The famine was **s** in Samaria.
2Ki 25: 3 the famine became so **s** in
Lk   4:25 a **s** famine over all the land;
     15:14 a **s** famine took place throughout
Ac   11:28 there would be a **s** famine over all
2Co   8: 2 for during a **s** ordeal of affliction,

SEWED* → SEWS

Ge   3: 7 and they **s** fig leaves together
Job 16:15 I have **s** sackcloth upon my skin,

SEWS → SEWED

Mt   9:16 No one **s** a piece of unshrunk cloth

SEX* → SEXUAL, SEXUALLY

1Pe   3: 7 paying honor to the woman as the
            weaker **s**,
4Mc 15: 5 that mothers are the weaker **s**

SEXUAL → SEX

Nu   25: 1 **s** relations with the women of Moab
1Co   5: 1 reported that there is **s** immorality
     10: 8 not indulge in **s** immorality as some
2Co 12:21 **s** immorality, and licentiousness
Jude 1: 7 indulged in **s** immorality and
Sir 41:17 Be ashamed of **s** immorality,

SEXUALLY* → SEX

1Ki   1: 4 but the king did not know her **s**.
1Co   5: 9 not to associate with **s** immoral
      5:11 who is **s** immoral or greedy,

SHADE

Ps 121: 5 LORD is your **s** at your right hand.
Isa 25: 4 the rainstorm and a **s** from the heat.
Eze 31: 6 and in its **s** all great nations lived.
Jnh   4: 6 to give **s** over his head,
Mk   4:32 the birds of the air can make nests
            in its **s**."

SHADOW

2Ki 20:11 brought the **s** back the ten intervals,
1Ch 29:15 our days on the earth are like a **s**,
Job 14: 2 flees like a **s** and does not last.
Ps   17: 8 hide me in the **s** of your wings,
     36: 7 All people may take refuge in the **s**
     57: 1 **s** of your wings I will take refuge,
     63: 7 in the **s** of your wings I sing for joy.
     91: 1 who abide in the **s** of the Almighty,
Isa 49: 2 in the **s** of his hand he hid me;
     51:16 and hidden you in the **s** of my hand,
Mt   4:16 and **s** of death light has dawned."
Lk   1:79 sit in darkness and in the **s** of death,
Ac   5:15 Peter's **s** might fall on some of them
Col   2:17 are only a **s** of what is to come,
Heb   8: 5 a sketch and **s** of the heavenly one;
     10: 1 the law has only a **s** of the good
2Es   2:36 Flee from the **s** of this age,

SHADRACH → =HANANIAH

Hebrew exiled to Babylon; name changed from
Hananiah (Da 1:6-7). Refused defilement by food
(Da 1:8-20). Refused to worship idol (Da 3:1-
18); saved from furnace (Da 3:19-30).

SHAKE → SHAKEN, SHAKES, SHAKING,
SHOOK

Ps   64: 8 all who see them will **s** with horror.
Hag   2: 6 in a little while, I will **s** the heavens
      2:21 saying, I am about to **s** the heavens
Mk   6:11 **s** off the dust that is on your feet as
Heb 12:26 promised, "Yet once more I will **s**

SHAKEN → SHAKE

Ps   62: 2 my fortress; I shall never be **s**.
Mt   24:29 and the powers of heaven will be **s**.
Lk   6:38 measure, pressed down, **s** together,
Ac   2:25 my right hand so that I will not be **s**;
Heb 12:28 a kingdom that cannot be **s**,

SHAKES → SHAKE

Ps 29: 8 voice of the LORD **s** the wilderness;

SHAKING → SHAKE

Mt 27:39 passed by derided him, **s** their heads
Mk 15:29 **s** their heads and saying, "Aha!

SHALLUM

King of Israel (2Ki 15:10-16).

SHALMANESER

King of Assyria; conquered and deported Israel (2Ki 17:3-4; 18:9; Tob 1:2).

SHAME → ASHAMED, SHAMEFUL, SHAMELESS

Ps   4: 2 you people, shall my honor suffer **s**?
    25: 3 those who wait for you be put to **s**;
    69: 6 who hope in you be put to **s** because
    97: 7 worshipers of images are put to **s**,
Pr 18:13 one gives answer before hearing, it
            is folly and **s.**
Isa 30: 5 brings neither help nor profit, but **s**
    45:17 not be put to **s** or confounded to all
    61: 7 Because their **s** was double,
Jer   8: 9 The wise shall be put to **s**,
Eze 39:26 They shall forget their **s**, and all
Da   9: 7 but open **s**, as at this day, falls on us,
    12: 2 some to **s** and everlasting contempt.
Hos   4: 7 they changed their glory into **s**.
Joel 2:26 shall never again be put to **s**.
Ro   9:33 believes in him will not be put to **s**."
    10:11 believes in him will not be put to **s.**"
1Co   1:27 foolish in the world to **s** the wise;
Php   3:19 and their glory is in their **s**;
Heb 12: 2 endured the cross, disregarding its **s**,
1Pe   2: 6 believes in him will not be put to **s.**"
1Jn   2:28 be put to **s** before him at his coming.
Aza   1:19 Do not put us to **s**,

SHAMEFUL → SHAME

Jer   3:24 "But from our youth the **s** thing has
2Co   4: 2 We have renounced the **s** things
Eph   5:12 For it is **s** even to mention

SHAMELESS → SHAME

Jer 13:27 your **s** prostitutions on the hills of
Zep   2: 1 Gather together, gather, O **s** nation,
Ro   1:27 Men committed **s** acts with men
Sir 23: 6 do not give me over to **s** passion.

SHAMGAR*

Judge; killed 600 Philistines (Jdg 3:31; 5:6).

SHAPED

Pr   8:25 Before the mountains had been **s**,
Hab   2:18 an idol once its maker has **s** it—

SHAPHAN

2Ki 22: 8 When Hilkiah gave the book to **S**,

SHARE → SHARED, SHARERS, SHARING

Nu 18:20 I am your **s** and your possession
2Sa 20: 1 no **s** in the son of Jesse!
2Ch 10:16 "What **s** do we have in David?
Ne   2:20 but you have no **s** or claim or
Pr   31:31 Give her a **s** in the fruit of her hands
Lk   3:11 "Whoever has two coats must **s**
    15:12 give me the **s** of the property that
Ac   8:21 You have no part or **s** in this,
Ro   1:11 may **s** with you some spiritual gift
    15:27 for if the Gentiles have come to **s**
2Co   1: 7 so also you **s** in our consolation.
Eph   4:28 have something to **s** with the needy.
Col   1:12 to **s** in the inheritance of the saints
1Ti   6:18 works, generous, and ready to **s**,
2Ti   2: 6 who ought to have the first **s** of
Heb 12:10 in order that we may **s** his holiness.
    13:16 not neglect to do good and to **s**
Jude 1: 3 to you about the salvation we **s**,
Rev 18: 4 so that you do not **s** in her plagues;
    22:19 God will take away that person's **s**
            in the tree of life

SHARED → SHARE

Heb   2:14 himself likewise **s** the same things,
     6: 4 and have **s** in the Holy Spirit,

SHARERS* → SHARE

Eph   3: 6 and **s** in the promise in Christ Jesus

SHARING → SHARE

Ro   5: 2 our hope of **s** the glory of God.
2Co   9:13 and by the generosity of your **s** with
Php   3:10 the **s** of his sufferings by becoming
Phm   1: 6 the **s** of your faith may become
1Pe   4:13 as you are **s** Christ's sufferings,

SHARON

SS   2: 1 I am a rose of **S**, a lily

SHARP → SHARPENED, SHARPENS, SHARPER

Pr   5: 4 **s** as a two-edged sword.
Isa   5:28 arrows are **s**, all their bows bent,
Ac   15:39 The disagreement became so **s**
Rev   1:16 mouth came a **s**, two-edged sword,
     2:12 him who has the **s** two-edged sword:
    14:14 and a **s** sickle in his hand!
    19:15 a **s** sword with which to strike down

SHARPENED → SHARP

Eze 21: 9 a sword is **s**, it is also polished;

SHARPENS → SHARP

Pr   27:17 Iron is iron, and one person **s** the
            wits of another.

SHARPER* → SHARP

Heb   4:12 **s** than any two-edged sword,

SHATTER → SHATTERED, SHATTERS

Ps 110: 5 he will **s** kings on the day
Da   2:40 it shall crush and **s** all these.

SHATTERED → SHATTER

Ex   15: 6 right hand, O LORD, **s** the enemy.
1Sa   2:10 His adversaries shall be **s**;
Isa   7: 8 sixty-five years Ephraim will be **s**,

SHATTERS → SHATTER

Ps   46: 9 he breaks the bow, and **s** the spear;

SHAVE → SHAVED

Nu   6:18 the nazirites shall **s** the consecrated
Dt   14: 1 or **s** your forelocks for the dead.
Jdg 16:19 him **s** off the seven locks of his head

SHAVED → SHAVE

Nu   6:19 they have **s** the consecrated head.
Jdg 16:17 If my head were **s**,
1Co 11: 5 the same thing as having her head **s**.

SHEAF → SHEAVES

Ge   37: 7 and bowed down to my **s**."
Lev 23:11 He shall raise the **s** before the LORD,
Dt   24:19 and forget a **s** in the field,

SHEAR → SHEARER, SHEARERS

Dt   15:19 nor **s** the firstling of your flock.

SHEARER* → SHEAR

Ac   8:32 and like a lamb silent before its **s**,

SHEARERS → SHEAR

Isa 53: 7 like a sheep that before its **s** is silent

SHEAVES → SHEAF

Ge   37: 7 then your **s** gathered around it,
Ru   2:15 glean even among the standing **s**,
Ps 126: 6 with shouts of joy, carrying their **s**.

SHEBA

1. Benjamite; rebelled against David (2Sa 20).
2. Queen of Sheba (1Ki 10; 2Ch 9). Queen of the South (Mt 12:42; Lk 11:31).

SHECHEM

1. Raped Jacob's daughter Dinah; killed by Simeon and Levi (Ge 34).

2. City where Joshua renewed the covenant (Jos 24). Abimelech as king (Jdg 9).

SHED → BLOODSHED, SHEDDING, SHEDS

Ge   9: 6 by a human shall that person's
            blood be **s**;
Nu   35:33 for the blood that is **s** in it,
    35:33 by the blood of the one who **s** it.
Dt   19:10 of an innocent person may not be **s**
2Ki 21:16 Manasseh **s** very much innocent
Pr   6:17 and hands that **s** innocent blood,
Isa 59: 7 and they rush to **s** innocent blood;
Eze 22:12 In you, they take bribes to **s** blood;
Mt   23:35 may come all the righteous blood **s**
Ro   3:15 "Their feet are swift to **s** blood;
Rev 16: 6 **s** the blood of saints and prophets,
1Mc   1:24 He **s** much blood, and spoke

SHEDDING → SHED

Eze 22: 3 **S** blood within itself;
Heb   9:22 and without the **s** of blood there is
            no forgiveness
    12: 4 not yet resisted to the point of **s**
            your blood.

SHEDS → SHED

Ge   9: 6 Whoever **s** the blood of a human,
Sir 28:11 and a hasty dispute **s** blood.

SHEEP → SHEEP'S

Ge   4: 2 Now Abel was a keeper of **s**,
Nu   27:17 not be like **s** without a shepherd."
Dt   17: 1 or a **s** that has a defect,
1Sa 15:14 "What then is this bleating of **s** in
1Ki 22:17 like **s** that have no shepherd;
Ps   44:22 and accounted as **s** for the slaughter.
    74: 1 your anger smoke against the **s**
    78:52 Then he led out his people like **s**,
   100: 3 his people, and the **s** of his pasture.
   119:176 I have gone astray like a lost **s**;
Isa 13:14 or like **s** with no one to gather them,
    53: 6 All we like **s** have gone astray;
    53: 7 a **s** that before its shearers is silent,
Jer 23: 1 who destroy and scatter the **s**
    50: 6 My people have been lost **s**;
Eze 34:15 myself will be the shepherd of my **s**,
Zec 13: 7 Strike the shepherd, that the **s** may
            be scattered;
Mt   9:36 like **s** without a shepherd.
    10: 6 to the lost **s** of the house of Israel.
    10:16 I am sending you out like **s** into the
    12:11 "Suppose one of you has only one **s**
    25:32 as a shepherd separates the **s** from
Lk   15: 4 a hundred **s** and losing one of them,
Jn   10: 3 and the **s** hear his voice.
    10: 3 He calls his own **s** by name and
    10: 7 I am the gate for the **s**.
    10:11 The good shepherd lays down his
            life for the **s**.
    10:15 And I lay down my life for the **s**.
    10:27 My **s** hear my voice.
    21:17 Jesus said to him, "Feed my **s**.
Ac   8:32 Like a **s** he was led to the slaughter.
Ro   8:36 accounted as **s** to be slaughtered."
Heb 13:20 the great shepherd of the **s**,
1Pe   2:25 For you were going astray like **s**,
Pm 151: 1 I tended my father's **s**.

SHEEP'S* → SHEEP

Mt   7:15 come to you in **s** clothing but
            inwardly are ravenous wolves.

SHEET*

Isa 25: 7 the **s** that is spread over all nations;
Ac   10:11 like a large **s** coming down,
    11: 5 like a large **s** coming down

SHEKEL → SHEKELS

Ex   30:13 half a **s** as an offering to the LORD.

SHEKELS → SHEKEL

1Ch 21:25 David paid Ornan six hundred **s** of
Hos   3: 2 I bought her for fifteen **s** of silver
Zec 11:12 as my wages thirty **s** of silver.

SHELAH

Ge 38:11 until my son S grows up"—
    46:12 The children of Judah: Er, Onan, S,

SHELTER

Ps 27: 5 hide me in his s in the day of trouble
    31:20 In the s of your presence you hide
    31:20 your s from contentious tongues.
    55: 8 a s for myself from the raging wind
    61: 4 refuge under the s of your wings.
    91: 1 who live in the s of the Most High,
Isa 1: 8 like a s in a cucumber field,
     4: 6 and a refuge and a s from the storm
    25: 4 a s from the rainstorm and a shade
Rev 7:15 is seated on the throne will s them.
Sir 6:14 Faithful friends are a sturdy s:

SHEM

  Son of Noah (Ge 5:32; 6:10). Blessed (Ge 9:26).
  Descendants (Ge 10:21-31; 11:10-32; Lk 3:36).

SHEMAIAH

1Ki 12:22 of God came to S the man of God:
2Ch 12: 5 the prophet S came to Rehoboam
Jer 29:31 Because S has prophesied to you,

SHEMER → SAMARIA

1Ki 16:24 bought the hill of Samaria from S

SHEOL

Ge 37:35 down to S to my son, mourning."
Nu 16:30 and they go down alive into S,
Dt 32:22 burns to the depths of S;
Job 17:13 If I look for S as my house,
    26: 6 S is naked before God,
Ps   6: 5 in S who can give you praise?
    16:10 For you do not give me up to S,
    55:15 let them go down alive to S;
   139: 8 if I make my bed in S, you are there.
Pr   7:27 Her house is the way to S,
    23:14 you will save their lives from S.
    27:20 S and Abaddon are never satisfied,
Isa 7:11 let it be deep as S or high as heaven.
    28:15 and with S we have an agreement;
Hos 13:14 O S, where is your destruction?
Jnh 2: 2 out of the belly of S I cried,

SHEPHERD → SHEPHERDS

Ge 48:15 God who has been my s all my life
    49:24 name of the S, the Rock of Israel,
Nu 27:17 may not be like sheep without a s."
2Sa 7: 7 whom I commanded to s my people
1Ki 22:17 like sheep that have no s;
1Ch 11: 2 who shall be s of my people Israel,
Ps 23: 1 The LORD is my s, I shall not want.
    28: 9 be their s, and carry them forever.
    78:71 he brought him to be the s
    80: 1 O S of Israel, you who lead Joseph
Ecc 12:11 sayings that are given by one s.
Isa 40:11 He will feed his flock like a s;
Jer 31:10 and will keep him as a s a flock."
Eze 34: 5 scattered, because there was no s;
Zec 10: 2 they suffer for lack of a s.
    11: 9 So I said, "I will not be your s.
    11:17 worthless s, who deserts the flock!
    13: 7 "Awake, O sword, against my s,
    13: 7 Strike the s, that the sheep may be
           scattered;
Mt   2: 6 ruler who is to s my people Israel.'"
    25:32 as a s separates the sheep from
    26:31 'I will strike the s, and the sheep of
           the flock will be scattered.'
Mk   6:34 they were like sheep without a s;
Jn 10:11 "I am the good s.
    10:14 I am the good s.
    10:16 So there will be one flock, one s.
Heb 13:20 the great s of the sheep,
1Pe 2:25 have returned to the s and guardian
     5: 4 And when the chief s appears,
Rev 7:17 the Lamb at the center of the throne
           will be their s,
2Es 5:18 like a s who leaves the flock

SHEPHERDS → SHEPHERD

Ge 46:34 all s are abhorrent to the Egyptians."
Ex   2:19 An Egyptian helped us against the s;
Nu 14:33 children shall be s in the wilderness
Isa 56:11 The s also have no understanding;
Jer 3:15 I will give you s after my own heart,
    23: 1 Woe to the s who destroy and
    50: 6 their s have led them astray,
Eze 34: 2 prophesy against the s of Israel:
Zec 10: 3 My anger is hot against the s,
Lk   2: 8 there were s living in the fields,

SHESHBAZZAR

Ezr 1: 8 to S the prince of Judah.
     5:16 S came and laid the foundations

SHIBBOLETH* → SIBBOLETH

Jdg 12: 6 say S," and he said, "Sibboleth,"

SHIELD → SHIELDED, SHIELDS

Ge 15: 1 I am your s; your reward shall be
Dt 33:29 the s of your help, and the sword of
2Sa 22:36 given me the s of your salvation,
Ps   3: 3 LORD, are a s around me, my glory,
     5:12 cover them with favor as with a s.
     7:10 God is my s, who saves the upright
    18: 2 rock in whom I take refuge, my s,
    28: 7 The LORD is my strength and my s;
    33:20 he is our help and s.
    84:11 For the LORD God is a sun and s;
    91: 4 his faithfulness is a s and buckler.
   115: 9 He is their help and their s.
   119:114 You are my hiding place and my s;
   144: 2 stronghold and my deliverer, my s,
Pr   2: 7 a s to those who walk blamelessly,
    30: 5 a s to those who take refuge in him.
Zec 12: 8 the LORD will s the inhabitants
Eph 6:16 With all of these, take the s of faith,

SHIELDED* → SHIELD

Dt 32:10 he s him, cared for him, guarded

SHIELDS → SHIELD

Ps 47: 9 s of the earth belong to God;

SHIFTING*

Col 1:23 without s from the hope promised

SHILOH

Jos 18: 1 of the Israelites assembled at S,
1Sa 1:24 to the house of the LORD at S;
     3:21 The LORD continued to appear at S,
Ps 78:60 He abandoned his dwelling at S,

SHIMEI

  Cursed David (2Sa 16:5-14); spared (2Sa 19:16-
  23). Killed by Solomon (1Ki 2:8-9, 36-46).

SHINAR

Ge 11: 2 in the land of S and settled there.
Jos 7:21 a beautiful mantle from S,
Da   1: 2 These he brought to the land of S,

SHINE → SHINES, SHINING, SHONE, SUNSHINE

Nu   6:25 LORD make his face to s upon you,
Ps   4: 6 light of your face s on us, O LORD!"
    37: 6 your vindication s like the light,
    67: 1 and make his face to s upon us,
    80: 1 upon the cherubim, s forth
    94: 1 you God of vengeance, s forth!
Isa 60: 1 s; for your light has come,
Da 12: 3 Those who are wise shall s like the
Mt   5:16 let your light s before others,
    13:43 the righteous will s like the sun in
2Co 4: 6 "Let light s out of darkness,"
Eph 5:14 the dead, and Christ will s on you."
Php 2:15 which you s like stars in the world.
Rev 21:23 no need of sun or moon to s on it,

SHINES → SHINE

Ps 50: 2 perfection of beauty, God s forth.
Pr   4:18 which s brighter and brighter until
Isa 62: 1 her vindication s out like the dawn,

Jn   1: 5 The light s in the darkness,

SHINING → SHINE

Ex 34:30 the skin of his face was s,
Jn   5:35 He was a burning and s lamp,
2Pe 1:19 to this as to a lamp s in a dark place,
1Jn 2: 8 and the true light is already s.
Rev 1:16 his face was like the sun s with full

SHIP → SHIPS, SHIPWRECK, SHIPWRECKED

Jnh 1: 4 that the s threatened to break up.
Ac 27:22 of life among you, but only of the s.

SHIPS → SHIP

1Ki 9:26 built a fleet of s at Ezion-geber,
    22:48 the s were wrecked at Ezion-geber.
Ps 107:23 Some went down to the sea in s,
Pr 31:14 She is like the s of the merchant,
Jas 3: 4 Or look at s: though they are
Rev 8: 9 and a third of the s were destroyed.

SHIPWRECK* → SHIP

1Ti 1:19 persons have suffered s in the faith;

SHIPWRECKED* → SHIP

2Co 11:25 Three times I was s;

SHISHAK

2Ch 12: 2 King S of Egypt came up

SHONE → SHINE

Mt 17: 2 and his face s like the sun,
Lk   2: 9 the glory of the Lord s around them,
2Co 4: 6 who has s in our hearts to give

SHOOK → SHAKE

Ex 19:18 the whole mountain s violently.
Isa 6: 4 the thresholds s at the voices of
Mt 27:51 The earth s, and the rocks were split
Ac 13:51 So they s the dust off their feet in
    18: 6 protest he s the dust from his clothes
Heb 12:26 At that time his voice s the earth;

SHOOT → SHOOTS

Isa 11: 1 A s shall come out from the stump
           of Jesse,
    60:21 They are the s that I planted,
Ro 11:17 you, a wild olive s, were grafted in

SHOOTS → SHOOT

Ps 128: 3 be like olive s around your table.
Hos 14: 6 His s shall spread out; his beauty

SHORE → SEASHORE

Lk   5: 3 to put out a little way from the s.

SHORT

Isa 59: 1 the LORD's hand is not too s to save,
Mt 24:22 if those days had not been cut s,
Lk 19: 3 because he was s in stature.
Ro   3:23 all have sinned and fall s of the
           glory of God;
1Co 7:29 the appointed time has grown s;
Rev 12:12 because he knows that his time is s!

SHOULDER → SHOULDERS

Isa 22:22 I will place on his s the key of the

SHOULDERS → SHOULDER

Ex 28:12 before the LORD on his two s for
Dt 33:12 the beloved rests between his s.
Isa 9: 4 burden, and the bar across their s,
     9: 6 authority rests upon his s;
Mt 23: 4 and lay them on the s of others;
Lk 15: 5 he lays it on his s and rejoices.

SHOUT → SHOUTED, SHOUTS

Jos 6:16 Joshua said to the people, "S!
Ezr 3:11 great s when they praised the LORD,
Ps 20: 5 May we s for joy over your victory,
    35:27 who desire my vindication s for joy
    47: 1 s to God with loud songs of joy.
Isa 12: 6 S aloud and sing for joy,
    44:23 s, O depths of the earth;

54: 1 burst into song and **s**, you who have
Zec   9: 9 **S** aloud, O daughter Jerusalem!
Lk   19:40 were silent, the stones would **s** out."
Rev 10: 3 he gave a great **s**, like a lion roaring.
Sus   1:60 raised a great **s** and blessed God,

SHOUTED → SHOUT
1Sa 17: 8 He stood and **s** to the ranks of Israel,
Job 38: 7 all the heavenly beings **s** for joy?
Mk   15:13 They **s** back, "Crucify him!"

SHOUTS → SHOUT
Ps   27: 6 in his tent sacrifices with **s** of joy;
    126: 5 sow in tears reap with **s** of joy.
Zec   4: 7 the top stone amid **s** of 'Grace,

SHOW → SHOWED, SHOWING, SHOWN, SHOWS
Ge   12: 1 to the land that I will **s** you.
    24:12 and **s** steadfast love to my master
Ex   9:16 **s** you my power, and to make
    25: 9 In accordance with all that I **s** you
    33:18 Moses said, "**S** me your glory,
Dt   4: 6 for this will **s** your wisdom and
     7: 2 with them and **s** them no mercy.
1Sa 20:14 **s** me the faithful love of the LORD;
2Sa   9: 1 may **s** kindness for Jonathan's sake?
    22:26 With the loyal you **s** yourself loyal;
         with the blameless you **s** yourself
         blameless;
Ps   17: 7 Wondrously **s** your steadfast love,
    18:26 with the pure you **s** yourself pure;
         and with the crooked you **s** yourself
         perverse.
    85: 7 **S** us your steadfast love, O LORD,
Pr   12:16 Fools **s** their anger at once,
    28:21 To **s** partiality is not good—
Isa 30:18 he will rise up to **s** mercy to you.
Jer 32:18 **s** steadfast love to the thousandth
Joel 2:30 I will **s** portents in the heavens and
Mic   7:20 You will **s** faithfulness to Jacob
Zec   7: 9 **s** kindness and mercy to one another
Mt   22:19 **S** me the coin used for the tax."
Jn   2:18 sign can you **s** us for doing this?"
    14: 8 said to him, "Lord, **s** us the Father,
Ac   2:19 I will **s** portents in the heaven above
1Co 12:31 will **s** you a still more excellent way
2Co 11:30 I will boast of the things that **s** my
         weakness.
Eph   2: 7 he might **s** the immeasurable riches
Tit   2: 7 **S** yourself in all respects a model of
         good works,
     3: 2 and to **s** every courtesy to everyone.
Jas   2:18 **S** me your faith apart from your
         works, and I by my works will **s**
         you my faith.
Rev   1: 1 to **s** his servants what must soon
     4: 1 I will **s** you what must take place
    17: 1 I will **s** you the judgment of
    21: 9 I will **s** you the bride, the wife of
Sir   4:27 or **s** partiality to a ruler.
    35:16 He will not **s** partiality to the poor;
2Es   4: 3 sent to **s** you three ways,

SHOWED → SHOW
Ge   39:21 with Joseph and **s** him steadfast love
Dt   34: 1 and the LORD **s** him the whole land:
Mt   4: 8 and **s** him all the kingdoms
Lk   24:40 he **s** them his hands and his feet.
Jn   20:20 he **s** them his hands and his side.
Rev 21:10 and **s** me the holy city Jerusalem
    22: 1 **s** me the river of the water of life,

SHOWERS
Dt   32: 2 rain on grass, like **s** on new growth.
Jer   3: 3 Therefore the **s** have been withheld,
Eze 34:26 will send down the **s** in their season;
    34:26 they shall be **s** of blessing.

SHOWING → SHOW
Ex   20: 6 **s** steadfast love to the thousandth
Dt   5:10 **s** steadfast love to the thousandth

SHOWN → SHOW
Ex   25:40 is being **s** you on the mountain.
Dt   4:35 To you it was **s** so that you would
1Ki   3: 6 "You have **s** great and steadfast love
Ps   78:11 and the miracles that he had **s** them.
Jn   10:32 "I have **s** you many good works
Ro   1:19 because God has **s** it to them.

SHOWS → SHOW
Pr   3:34 but to the humble he **s** favor.
Ro   2:11 For God **s** no partiality.
     9:16 but on God who **s** mercy.
Tob   3: 2 For he afflicts, and he **s** mercy;

SHREWDLY*
Ex   1:10 Come, let us deal **s** with them,
Lk   16: 8 manager because he had acted **s**;

SHRINK → SHRINKS
Heb 10:39 we are not among those who **s** back

SHRINKS* → SHRINK
Heb 10:38 no pleasure in anyone who **s** back."

SHUDDER
Eze 32:10 their kings shall **s** because of you.
Jas   2:19 Even the demons believe—and **s**.

SHUHITE
Job   2:11 Eliphaz the Temanite, Bildad the **S**,

SHULAMMITE
SS   6:13 Return, return, O **S**!

SHUN → SHUNNED
1Co   6:18 **S** fornication! Every sin
1Ti   6:11 you, man of God, **s** all this;
2Ti   2:22 **S** youthful passions and pursue
Sir 32:17 The sinner will **s** reproof,

SHUNAMMITE
1Ki   1: 3 and found Abishag the **S**,
2Ki   4:12 Gehazi, "Call the **S** woman."

SHUNNED* → SHUN
Pr   19: 7 more are they **s** by their friends!

SHUT
Ge   7:16 and the LORD **s** him in.
    19: 6 to the men, the door after him,
Dt   11:17 and he will **s** up the heavens, so that
Jos   6: 1 Now Jericho was **s** up inside and out
2Ch   6:26 "When heaven is **s** up and there is
Isa 22:22 he shall open, and no one shall **s**;
    52:15 kings shall **s** their mouths because
    60:11 day and night they shall not be **s**,
Da   6:22 God sent his angel and **s** the lions'
Heb 11:33 promises, **s** the mouths of lions,
Rev   3: 7 who opens and no one will **s**,
    11: 6 They have authority to **s** the sky,
    21:25 Its gates will never be **s** by day—

SIBBOLETH* → SHIBBOLETH
Jdg 12: 6 say Shibboleth," and he said, "**S**,"

SICK → SICKBED, SICKNESS
Pr   13:12 Hope deferred makes the heart **s**,
Eze 34: 4 you have not healed the **s**,
Mt   8:16 and cured all who were **s**.
     9:12 of a physician, but those who are **s**.
    10: 8 Cure the **s**, raise the dead, cleanse
    25:36 I was **s** and you took care of me,
Ac   19:12 were brought to the **s**,
Jas   5:14 Are any among you **s**?
Sir   7:35 Do not hesitate to visit the **s**,

SICKBED* → BED, SICK
Ps   41: 3 The LORD sustains them on their **s**;

SICKLE
Joel 3:13 Put in the **s**, for the harvest is ripe.
Mk   4:29 at once he goes in with his **s**,
Rev 14:14 and a sharp **s** in his hand!

SICKNESS → SICK
Ex   23:25 I will take **s** away from among you.

Mt   4:23 and curing every disease and every **s**

SIDE → ASIDE, SIDES
1Ch 22: 9 from all his enemies on every **s**;
Ps   91: 7 A thousand may fall at your **s**,
    124: 1 the LORD who was on our **s**
Eze   1:10 the face of a lion on the right **s**,
     1:10 the face of an ox on the left **s**,
     4: 4 Then lie on your left **s**, and place
Jn   19:18 one on either **s**, with Jesus between
    19:34 soldiers pierced his **s** with a spear,
    20:20 he showed them his hands and his **s**.
Rev 22: 2 either **s** of the river is the tree of life

SIDES → SIDE
Ex   29:16 its blood and dash it against all **s** of
Nu   33:55 in your eyes and thorns in your **s**;
Jos 23:13 a scourge on your **s**,

SIDON
Jdg   1:31 or the inhabitants of **S**, or of Ahlab,
1Ki 17: 9 which belongs to **S**, and live there;
Eze 28:21 your face toward **S**, and prophesy
Mt   11:21 in you had been done in Tyre and **S**,
Mk   7:31 way of **S** towards the Sea of Galilee.
Lk   4:26 except to a widow at Zarephath in **S**.

SIEGE → BESIEGED
2Ki   6:25 the **s** continued, famine in Samaria
    25: 1 against Jerusalem, and laid **s** to it;
Eze   4: 2 and build a **s** wall against it,

SIEVE*
Isa 30:28 the nations with the **s** of destruction,
Am   9: 9 one shakes with a **s**, but no pebble
Sir 27: 4 a **s** is shaken, the refuse appears;

SIFT*
Jdg   7: 4 to the water and I will **s** them out
Isa 30:28 to **s** the nations with the sieve of
Lk   22:31 Satan has demanded to **s** all of you

SIGHED → SIGHING
Mk   8:12 he **s** deeply in his spirit and said,

SIGHING → SIGHED
Ps   5: 1 O LORD; give heed to my **s**.
Isa 35:10 and sorrow and **s** shall flee away.

SIGHT → SEE
Ge   6:11 the earth was corrupt in God's **s**,
Ex   3: 3 turn aside and look at this great **s**,
Ps   51: 4 and done what is evil in your **s**,
    72:14 and precious is their blood in his **s**.
    90: 4 For a thousand years in your **s** are
         like yesterday
    116:15 Precious in the **s** of the LORD is the
Pr   3: 4 find favor and good repute in the **s**
Jer 18:10 but if it does evil in my **s**,
Mt   11: 5 blind receive their **s**, the lame walk,
Ac   1: 9 and a cloud took him out of their **s**.
     4:19 right in God's **s** to listen to you
         rather than to God,
2Co   5: 7 for we walk by faith, not by **s**.
1Pe   3: 4 which is very precious in God's **s**.

EVIL IN THE SIGHT OF THE †LORD
Nu 32:13; Dt 4:25; 17:2; 31:29; Jdg 2:11; 3:7, 12, 12; 4:1; 6:1; 10:6; 13:1; 1Sa 15:19; 1Ki 11:6; 14:22; 15:26, 34; 16:19, 25, 30; 21:20, 25; 22:52; 2Ki 3:2; 8:18, 27; 13:2, 11; 14:24; 15:9, 18, 24, 28; 17:2, 17; 21:2, 6, 16, 20; 23:32, 37; 24:9, 19; 2Ch 21:6; 22:4; 29:6; 33:2, 6, 22; 36:5, 9, 12; Jer 7:30; 52:2; Mal 2:17

FAVOR IN ... SIGHT Ge 6:8; 32:5; 39:4, 21; Ex 11:3; 12:36; 33:12, 13, 13, 16, 17; 34:9; Nu 11:11, 15; 32:5; Ru 2:10, 13; 1Sa 1:18; 16:22; 20:29; 25:8; 27:5; 2Sa 14:22; 16:4; 1Ki 11:19; AdE 5:8; Sir 3:18; 44:23; Bar 1:12; 2:14; 2Es 4:44; 5:56; 6:11; 7:75, 102, 104; 8:42; 12:7

RIGHT IN THE SIGHT OF THE †LORD
Dt 12:25, 28; 13:18; 21:9; 1Ki 15:5, 11; 22:43;

2Ki 12:2; 14:3; 15:3, 34; 16:2; 18:3; 22:2; 2Ch 14:2; 20:32; 24:2; 25:2; 26:4; 27:2; 28:1; 29:2; 34:2

SIGN → SIGNS

Ge   9:12 the **s** of the covenant that I make
     17:11 a **s** of the covenant between me
Ex   3:12 the **s** for you that it is I who sent you
     12:13 The blood shall be a **s** for you on
     13:16 It shall serve as a **s** on your hand
Nu 16:38 they shall be a **s** to the Israelites.
Jdg   6:17 show me a **s** that it is you who speak
1Ki 13: 3 "This is the **s** that the LORD has
Isa   7:14 the Lord himself will give you a **s**.
     55:13 an everlasting **s** that shall not be cut
Eze 20:12 as a **s** between me and them,
     24:24 Thus Ezekiel shall be a **s** to you;
Mt 12:38 we wish to see a **s** from you."
     16: 1 and to test Jesus they asked him to show them a **s**
     24: 3 the **s** of your coming and of the end
     24:30 the **s** of the Son of Man will appear
Mk   8:12 does this generation ask for a **s**?
Lk   2:12 This will be a **s** for you:
     11:29 no **s** will be given to it except the **s** of Jonah.
Jn   2:18 "What **s** can you show us for doing
Ro   4:11 He received the **s** of circumcision
1Co 14:22 then, are a **s** not for believers but

SIGNET

Ge 41:42 Removing his **s** ring from his hand,
Est   3:10 the king took his **s** ring from his
      8: 2 Then the king took off his **s** ring,
Jer 22:24 the **s** ring on my right hand,
Da   6:17 king sealed it with his own **s** and with the **s** of his lords,
Hag 2:23 and make you like a **s** ring;
Sir 17:22 is like a **s** ring with the Lord,
Bel   1:11 shut the door and seal it with your **s**.

SIGNS → SIGN

Ge   1:14 be for **s** and for seasons and for days
Ex   4: 9 not believe even these two **s** or heed
      7: 3 I will multiply my **s** and wonders in
Ps 78:43 when he displayed his **s** in Egypt,
  105:27 They performed his **s** among them,
Isa   8:18 whom the LORD has given me are **s**
Da   6:27 he works **s** and wonders in heaven
Mt 16: 3 cannot interpret the **s** of the times.
     24:24 and produce great **s** and omens,
Mk 13:22 prophets will appear and produce **s**
Jn   3: 2 for no one can do these **s** that you
      7:31 do more **s** than this man has done?"
      9:16 who is a sinner perform such **s**?"
     20:30 Jesus did many other **s** in the
Ac   2:19 above and **s** on the earth below,
      5:12 many **s** and wonders were done
1Co 1:22 Jews demand **s** and Greeks desire
2Co 12:12 **s** of a true apostle were performed
     12:12 **s** and wonders and mighty works.
2Th 2: 9 uses all power, **s**, lying wonders,
Heb 2: 4 God added his testimony by **s** and
Rev 13:13 It performs great **s**, even making fire
     16:14 demonic spirits, performing **s**,
     19:20 in its presence the **s**
2Es 4:52 the **s** about which you ask me,
      5:13 the **s** that I am permitted to tell you,

SIHON

Nu 21:21 Israel sent messengers to King **S** of
Dt 31: 4 do to them as he did to **S** and Og,
Ps 136:19 **S**, king of the Amorites,

SILAS

Prophet (Ac 15:22-32); co-worker with Paul on second missionary journey (Ac 16-18; 2Co 1:19). Co-writer with Paul (1Th 1:1; 2Th 1:1); Peter (1Pe 5:12).

SILENCE → SILENCED, SILENT

Ps   8: 2 to **s** the enemy and the avenger.
1Pe 2:15 right you should **s** the ignorance of
Rev 8: 1 **s** in heaven for about half an hour.

SILENCED → SILENCE

Mt 22:34 the Pharisees heard that he had **s** the Sadducees,
Ro   3:19 so that every mouth may be **s**,
Tit   1:11 be **s**, since they are upsetting whole families

SILENT → SILENCE

Ps 30:12 soul may praise you and not be **s**.
     39: 2 I was **s** and still; I held my peace to
Pr 17:28 who keep **s** are considered wise;
Isa 53: 7 a sheep that before its shearers is **s**,
     62: 1 For Zion's sake I will not keep **s**,
Jer   4:19 is beating wildly; I cannot keep **s**;
Zep 1: 7 Be **s** before the Lord GOD!
Mk 14:61 But he was **s** and did not answer.
Ac   8:32 and like a lamb **s** before its shearer,
1Co 14:34 women should be **s** in the churches.
1Ti 2:12 over a man; she is to keep **s**.

SILOAM

Jn   9: 7 "Go, wash in the pool of **S**"

SILVER → SILVERSMITH

Ge 37:28 Ishmaelites for twenty pieces of **s**.
Ex 11: 2 to ask her neighbor for objects of **s**
     20:23 not make gods of **s** alongside me,
     25: 3 you shall receive from them: gold, **s**,
Dt 17:17 also **s** and gold he must not acquire
Jos   7:21 and two hundred shekels of **s**,
2Ch 1:15 king made **s** and gold as common
Ps 12: 6 **s** refined in a furnace on the ground,
     66:10 you have tried us as **s** is tried.
    115: 4 Their idols are **s** and gold,
Pr   2: 4 like **s**, and search for it as for hidden
      3:14 for her income is better than **s**,
      8:10 Take my instruction instead of **s**,
     22: 1 and favor is better than **s** or gold.
     25: 4 Take away the dross from the **s**,
     25:11 like apples of gold in a setting of **s**.
Isa 48:10 I have refined you, but not like **s**;
Eze 22:18 all of them, **s**, bronze, tin, iron, and
Da   2:32 its chest and arms of **s**,
      5: 4 and praised the gods of gold and **s**,
Hag 2: 8 The **s** is mine, and the gold is mine,
Zec 11:12 as my wages thirty shekels of **s**.
     13: 9 refine them as one refines **s**,
Mal 3: 3 refine them like gold and **s**,
Mt 26:15 They paid him thirty pieces of **s**.
Ac   3: 6 But Peter said, "I have no **s** or gold,
1Co 3:12 on the foundation with gold, **s**,
2Ti 2:20 not only of gold and **s** but also of
1Pe 1:18 not with perishable things like **s** or
1Mc 1:23 He took the **s** and the gold,

SILVER ... GOLD Ge 13:2; 24:35, 53; 44:8; Ex 3:22; 11:2; 12:35; Nu 22:18; 24:13; Dt 7:25; 8:13; 17:17; 29:17; Jos 6:19, 24; 7:21; 22:8; 2Sa 8:10, 11; 21:4; 1Ki 7:51; 10:25; 15:15, 18, 19; 20:3, 5, 7; 2Ki 7:8; 16:8; 18:14; 20:13; 23:33, 35, 35; 1Ch 18:11; 2Ch 1:15; 5:1; 9:24; 15:18; 16:2, 3; 21:3; 32:27; 36:3; Ezr 1:4, 6; 7:15, 16, 18; 8:25, 28, 30, 33; Job 28:1; Ps 105:37; 115:4; 135:15; Pr 22:1; 25:11; Ecc 2:8; SS 3:10; Isa 2:7, 20; 31:7; 39:2; 60:9; Jer 10:4; Eze 7:19; 38:13; Da 2:35, 45; 5:23; 11:8; Hos 2:8; 8:4; Joel 3:5; Na 2:9; Zep 1:18; Hag 2:8; Zec 6:10, 11; 9:3; 13:9; Ac 3:6; 20:33; 1Pe 1:18; Sir 28:24; 51:28; Bar 3:17; LtJ 6:4, 11, 30, 57; 1Mc 1:23; 2:18; 3:41; 6:1, 12; 8:3; 10:60; 11:24; 15:26; 16:11, 19; 2Mc 3:11; 1Es 1:36; 2:9, 13; 8:55, 58, 60, 62; 2Es 7:56

GOLD ... SILVER Ex 25:3; 31:4; 35:5, 32; Nu 31:22; 1Ki 10:21, 22; 2Ki 12:13; 14:14; 25:15; 1Ch 18:10; 22:14, 16; 29:2, 3, 5; 2Ch 2:7, 14; 9:14, 20, 21; 24:14; 25:24; Ezr 1:9, 10, 11; 2:69; 5:14; 6:5; Ne 7:72; Est 1:6; Job 22:25; 28:15; Ps 119:72; Pr 25:11; SS 1:11; Isa 40:19; Jer 52:19; Eze 16:13, 17; 28:4; Da 2:32; 5:2, 3, 4; 11:38, 43; Hab 2:19; Zec 14:14; Mal 3:3; Mt 10:9; Ac 17:29; 1Co 3:12; 2Ti 2:20; Jas 5:3; Rev 9:20; 18:12; Jdt 2:18; 5:9; 8:7;

AdE 1:6, 6, 7; Wis 13:10; 15:9; Sir 40:25; LtJ 6:8, 10, 39, 50, 55, 58, 70, 71; 1Mc 4:23; 15:32; 2Mc 2:2; 1Es 2:6, 13, 14; 4:18, 19; 5:45; 6:18, 26; 8:13, 14, 16; 2Es 7:55, 56

SILVERSMITH → SILVER

Ac 19:24 a **s** who made silver shrines of

SIMEON → =SIMON

1. Son of Jacob by Leah (Ge 29:33; 35:23; 1Ch 2:1). With Levi killed Shechem for rape of Dinah (Ge 34:25-29). Held hostage by Joseph in Egypt (Ge 42:24-43:23). Tribe of blessed (Ge 49:5-7), numbered (Nu 1:23; 26:14), allotted land (Jos 19:1-9; Eze 48:24), 12, 000 from (Rev 7:7).
2. Godly Jew who blessed the infant Jesus (2:25-35).
3. See Peter (Ac 15:14; 2Pe 1:1).

TRIBE OF SIMEON Nu 1:23; 2:12; 10:19; 13:5; Jos 19:1, 8, 9, 9; 21:9; Rev 7:7; Jdt 6:15

SIMON → =PETER, =SIMEON

1. See Peter.
2. Apostle, called the Zealot (Mt 10:4; Mk 3:18; Lk 6:15; Ac 1:13).
3. Samaritan sorcerer (Ac 8:9-24).

SIMPLE → SIMPLY

Ps 19: 7 are sure, making wise the **s**;
  119:130 it imparts understanding to the **s**.
Pr   1:22 O **s** ones, will you love being **s**?
      8: 5 O **s** ones, learn prudence;
     14:15 The **s** believe everything,

SIN → SINFUL, SINNED, SINNER, SINNER'S, SINNERS, SINNING, SINS

Ge   4: 7 if you do not do well, **s** is lurking at the door;
Ex 32:32 if you will only forgive their **s**—
     34: 7 forgiving iniquity and transgression and **s**,
Nu   5: 7 the **s** that has been committed.
     32:23 and be sure your **s** will find you out.
1Sa 12:23 that I should **s** against the LORD
     15:23 For rebellion is no less a **s** than divination,
1Ki 8:46 "If they **s** against you—
      8:46 for there is no one who does not **s**—
     13:34 became **s** to the house of Jeroboam,
2Ch 7:14 forgive their **s** and heal their land.
Ne 13:26 Did not King Solomon of Israel **s**
Job 1:22 In all this Job did not **s** or charge
      2:10 In all this Job did not **s** with his lips.
Ps   4: 4 When you are disturbed, do not **s**;
     32: 5 and you forgave the guilt of my **s**.
     38:18 my iniquity; I am sorry for my **s**.
     39: 1 will guard my ways that I may not **s**
     51: 2 and cleanse me from my **s**.
  119:11 so that I may not **s** against you.
Pr   5:22 they are caught in the toils of their **s**.
     20: 9 I am pure from my **s**"?
Ecc 5: 6 not let your mouth lead you into **s**,
Isa   3: 9 they proclaim their **s** like Sodom,
      6: 7 departed and your **s** is blotted out."
     53:12 yet he bore the **s** of many,
Jer 16:18 repay their iniquity and their **s**,
Da   9:20 confessing my **s** and the **s** of my
Mic 6: 7 of my body for the **s** of my soul?"
Mt   5:29 If your right eye causes you to **s**,
Mk   3:29 but is guilty of an eternal **s**"—
Jn   1:29 the Lamb of God who takes away the **s** of the world!
      8: 7 [without **s** be the first to throw]
      8:34 everyone who commits **s** is a slave to **s**.
      8:46 Which of you convicts me of **s**?
     16: 9 about **s**, because they do not believe
Ac   7:60 Lord, do not hold this **s** against them
Ro   4: 8 whom the Lord will not reckon **s**."
      5:12 and death came through **s**,
      5:20 but where **s** increased,
      6: 2 who died to **s** go on living in it?

6:11 consider yourselves dead to **s** and
6:14 **s** will have no dominion over you,
6:23 For the wages of **s** is death,
7: 7 That the law is **s**?
7:25 I am a slave to the law of **s**.
8: 2 has set you free from the law of **s**
14:23 does not proceed from faith is **s**.
1Co 8:12 it is weak, you **s** against Christ.
15:56 The sting of death is **s**, and the power of **s** is the law.
2Co 5:21 For our sake he made him to be **s** who knew no **s**,
Eph 4:26 Be angry but do not **s**;
1Ti 5:20 As for those who persist in **s**,
Heb 4:15 tested as we are, yet without **s**.
9:26 remove **s** by the sacrifice of himself.
10:18 there is no longer any offering for **s**.
11:25 to enjoy the fleeting pleasures of **s**.
12: 1 every weight and the **s** that clings
Jas 1:15 it gives birth to **s**,
1Pe 2:22 "He committed no **s**, and no deceit
1Jn 1: 7 Jesus his Son cleanses us from all **s**.
1: 8 If we say that we have no **s**,
2: 1 to you so that you may not **s**.
2: 1 anyone does **s**, we have an advocate
3: 4 Everyone who commits **s** is guilty of lawlessness; **s** is lawlessness.
3: 5 and in him there is no **s**.
3: 9 have been born of God do not **s**,
5:16 There is **s** that is mortal;
5:17 All wrongdoing is **s**, but there is **s** that is not mortal.
Tob 12:10 but those who commit **s**
Wis 10:13 but delivered him from **s**.
Sir 3:30 so almsgiving atones for **s**.
7: 8 Do not commit a **s** twice;
42: 1 and do not **s** to save face:

SIN OFFERING Ex 29:14, 36, 36; 30:10;
Lev 4:3, 8, 14, 20, 21, 24, 25, 29, 29, 32, 33, 33, 34; 5:6, 7, 8, 9, 9, 11, 11, 12; 6:17, 25, 25, 26, 30; 7:7, 37; 8:2, 14, 14; 9:2, 3, 7, 8, 10, 15, 15, 22; 10:16, 17, 19, 19; 12:6, 8; 14:13, 13, 19, 22, 31; 15:15, 30; 16:3, 5, 6, 9, 11, 11, 15, 25, 27, 27; 23:19; Nu 6:11, 14, 16; 7:16, 22, 28, 34, 40, 46, 52, 58, 64, 70, 76, 82, 87; 8:8, 12; 15:24, 25, 27; 18:9; 28:15, 22; 29:5, 11, 11, 16, 19, 22, 25, 28, 31, 34, 38; 2Ch 29:21, 23, 24, 24; Ezr 6:17; 8:35; Ps 40:6; Eze 40:39; 42:13; 43:19, 21, 22, 25; 44:27, 29; 45:19, 22, 23; 46:20; 2Mc 2:11; 12:43

SIN OFFERINGS 2Ki 12:16; Ne 10:33; Eze 45:17, 25; Heb 10:6, 8; Bar 1:10

SINAI → =HOREB
Ex 19: 1 they came into the wilderness of **S**.
19:20 the Lord descended upon Mount **S**,
31:18 speaking with Moses on Mount **S**,
Nu 1:19 enrolled them in the wilderness of **S**
Ps 68:17 the Lord came from **S** into the holy
Gal 4:25 Now Hagar is Mount **S** in Arabia

MOUNT SINAI Ex 19:11, 18, 20, 23; 24:16; 31:18; 34:2, 4, 29, 32; Lev 7:38; 25:1; 26:46; 27:34; Nu 3:1; 28:6; Ne 9:13; Ac 7:30, 38; Gal 4:24, 25; 2Es 3:17; 14:4

SINCERE → SINCERELY, SINCERITY
Mk 12:14 "Teacher, we know that you are **s**,
2Co 11: 3 will be led astray from a **s**
1Ti 1: 5 a good conscience, and **s** faith.
2Ti 1: 5 I am reminded of your **s** faith,

SINCERELY → SINCERE
Job 33: 3 what my lips know they speak **s**.

SINCERITY → SINCERE
1Co 5: 8 the unleavened bread of **s** and truth.
2Co 1:12 with frankness and godly **s**,
2:17 in Christ we speak as persons of **s**,

SINEWS
Eze 37: 6 I will lay **s** on you,
Col 2:19 held together by its ligaments and **s**,

SINFUL → SIN
Isa 1: 4 **s** nation, people laden with iniquity,
Lk 5: 8 from me, Lord, for I am a **s** man!"
Ro 7: 5 living in the flesh, our **s** passions,
8: 3 Son in the likeness of **s** flesh,
1Mc 1:10 From them came forth a **s** root,

SING → LOVE-SONG, SANG, SINGER, SINGERS, SINGING, SONG, SONGS, SUNG
Ex 15: 1 "I will **s** to the Lord,
1Sa 21:11 Did they not **s** to one another of him
Ps 5:11 let them ever **s** for joy.
13: 6 I will **s** to the Lord,
30: 4 **S** praises to the Lord, O you his
33: 3 **S** to him a new song;
47: 6 **S** praises to God, **s** praises;
57: 7 I will **s** and make melody.
59:16 But I will **s** of your might;
63: 7 shadow of your wings I **s** for joy.
66: 2 **s** the glory of his name;
68: 4 **S** to God, **s** praises to his name;
89: 1 I will **s** of your steadfast love,
95: 1 O come, let us **s** to the Lord;
96: 1 O **s** to the Lord a new song;
98: 1 O **s** to the Lord a new song,
101: 1 I will **s** of loyalty and of justice;
108: 1 I will **s** and make melody.
119:172 My tongue will **s** of your promise,
137: 3 "**S** us one of the songs of Zion!"
147: 1 good it is to **s** praises to our God;
149: 1 **S** to the Lord a new song.
Isa 5: 1 **s** for my beloved my love-song
27: 2 A pleasant vineyard, **s** about it!
54: 1 **S**, O barren one who did not bear;
Jer 31: 7 **S** aloud with gladness for Jacob,
1Co 14:15 I will **s** praise with the spirit, but I will **s** praise with the mind also.
Eph 5:19 as you **s** psalms and hymns and
Col 3:16 gratitude in your hearts **s** psalms,
Jas 5:13 They should **s** songs of praise.
Rev 5: 9 They **s** a new song:
15: 3 And they **s** the song of Moses,
Jdt 16:13 I will **s** to my God a new song;
Aza 1:35 **s** praise to him and highly exalt him

SING PRAISE Ps 7:17; 9:2; 104:33; 1Co 14:15, 15; Tob 12:6; AdE 13:17; Sir 39:35; Aza 1:35, 36, 37, 38, 39, 40, 41, 42, 43, 44, 45, 46, 47, 48, 49, 50, 51, 52, 53, 54, 55, 56, 57, 58, 59, 60, 61, 62, 63, 64, 65, 66, 68

SING PRAISES 2Sa 22:50; 1Ch 16:9; 2Ch 29:30; Ps 9:11; 18:49; 30:4; 47:6, 6, 6, 6, 7; 57:9; 59:17; 61:8; 66:4, 4; 68:4, 32; 71:22, 23; 75:9; 92:1; 98:4, 5; 105:2; 108:3; 146:2; 147:1; Isa 12:5; Ro 15:9; Sir 17:27

SING TO THE †LORD Ex 15:1, 21; 1Ch 16:23; 2Ch 20:21; Ps 13:6; 95:1; 96:1, 1, 2; 98:1; 104:33; 147:7; 149:1; Isa 42:10; Jer 20:13

SINGED*
Da 3:27 the hair of their heads was not **s**,

SINGER* → SING
1Ch 6:33 Heman, the **s**, son of Joel,
Eze 33:32 you are like a **s** of love songs;

SINGERS → SING
1Ch 15:16 to appoint their kindred as the **s**
Ezr 2:70 and the **s**, the gatekeepers,
Ps 68:25 the **s** in front, the musicians last,

SINGING → SING
1Ch 16: 7 David first appointed the **s** of praises
SS 2:12 the time of **s** has come,
Isa 35:10 and come to Zion with **s**;
51:11 and come to Zion with **s**;
Zep 3:17 exult over you with loud **s**
Ac 16:25 and Silas were praying and **s** hymns
Rev 5:13 and all that is in them, **s**,
Aza 1: 1 **s** hymns to God and blessing the

SINGLE
Nu 13:23 a branch with a **s** cluster of grapes,

Zec 3: 9 on a **s** stone with seven facets,
Mt 6:27 worrying add a **s** hour to your span
Jn 12:24 it remains just a **s** grain;
Heb 12:16 who sold his birthright for a **s** meal.
Rev 21:21 each of the gates is a **s** pearl,

SINK → SANK
Ps 69: 2 I **s** in deep mire, where there is no
Jer 51:64 shall Babylon **s**, to rise no more,

SINNED → SIN
Nu 14:40 Lord has promised, for we have **s**."
1Sa 15:24 Saul said to Samuel, "I have **s**;
2Sa 12:13 "I have **s** against the Lord."
24:10 I have **s** greatly in what I have done.
2Ch 6:37 'We have **s**, and have done wrong;
Job 1: 5 "It may be that my children have **s**,
33:27 sings to others and says, 'I **s**,
Ps 51: 4 Against you, you alone, have I **s**,
Jer 2:35 judgment for saying, "I have not **s**."
14:20 for we have **s** against you.
La 5: 7 Our ancestors **s**; they are no more,
Da 9: 5 we have **s** and done wrong,
Mic 7: 9 because I have **s** against him,
Mt 27: 4 have **s** by betraying innocent blood.
Lk 15:18 "Father, I have **s** against heaven
Jn 9: 2 disciples asked him, "Rabbi, who **s**,
Ro 3:23 since all have **s** and fall short of the glory of God;
5:12 and so death spread to all because all have **s**—
2Pe 2: 4 not spare the angels when they **s**,
1Jn 1:10 If we say that we have not **s**,
Sir 18:21 and when you have **s**, repent.
Man 1:12 I have **s**, O Lord, I have **s**,
2Es 7:46 is there that has not **s**,

SINNER → SIN
Ps 51: 5 a **s** when my mother conceived me.
Lk 15: 7 over one **s** who repents than
18:13 'God, be merciful to me, a **s**!'
Jn 9:16 who is a **s** perform such signs?"
Jas 5:20 that whoever brings back a **s**
Sir 3:27 and the **s** adds sin to sins.

SINNER'S → SIN
Pr 13:22 but the **s** wealth is laid up for the
Jas 5:20 will save the **s** soul from death

SINNERS → SIN
Ge 13:13 great **s** against the Lord.
Ps 1: 1 or take the path that **s** tread,
25: 8 therefore he instructs **s** in the way.
51:13 and **s** will return to you.
Pr 1:10 if **s** entice you, do not consent.
23:17 Do not let your heart envy **s**,
Ecc 9: 2 As are the good, so are the **s**;
Isa 1:28 But rebels and **s** shall be destroyed
Mt 9:13 to call not the righteous but **s**."
Mk 14:41 the Son of Man is betrayed into the hands of **s**.
Lk 6:33 For even **s** do the same.
15: 2 "This fellow welcomes **s** and eats
Ro 5: 8 we still were **s** Christ died for us.
1Ti 1:15 Jesus came into the world to save **s**
Heb 7:26 separated from **s**, and exalted above
12: 3 hostility against himself from **s**,
1Mc 2:62 Do not fear the words of **s**,

SINNING → SIN
Ecc 7:20 as to do good without ever **s**.
1Jn 3: 8 devil has been **s** from the beginning.

SINS → SIN
1Sa 2:25 but if someone **s** against the Lord,
2Ki 14: 6 be put to death for their own **s**."
17:22 of Israel continued in all the **s**
Ps 51: 9 Hide your face from my **s**,
79: 9 deliver us, and forgive our **s**,
103:10 not deal with us according to our **s**,
Isa 1:18 your **s** are like scarlet, they shall be like snow;
38:17 cast all my **s** behind your back.

40: 2 LORD's hand double for all her **s.**
43:25 and I will not remember your **s.**
59: 2 your **s** have hidden his face from
La   3:39 about the punishment of their **s?**
Eze 18: 4 only the person who **s** that shall die.
33:10 and our **s** weigh upon us,
Mic 7:19 cast all our **s** into the depths of the
Mt   1:21 he will save his people from their **s.**
9: 6 the Son of Man has authority on
      earth to forgive **s"**—
18:15 member of the church **s** against you,
26:28 for many for the forgiveness of **s.**
Mk   1: 5 the river Jordan, confessing their **s.**
Lk   5:24 the Son of Man has authority on
      earth to forgive **s"**—
11: 4 forgive us our **s,** for we ourselves
17: 3 another disciple **s,** you must rebuke
Jn   8:24 that you would die in your **s,**
20:23 you forgive the **s** of any,
Ac   2:38 so that your **s** may be forgiven;
3:19 to God so that your **s** may be wiped
10:43 in him receives forgiveness of **s**
22:16 baptized, and have your **s** washed
26:18 they may receive forgiveness of **s**
Ro   4: 7 and whose **s** are covered;
1Co 6:18 fornicator **s** against the body itself.
15: 3 Christ died for our **s** in accordance
Eph 2: 1 dead through the trespasses and **s**
1Ti 5:22 do not participate in the **s** of others;
Heb 1: 3 he had made purification for **s,**
2:17 a sacrifice of atonement for the **s** of
7:27 first for his own **s,**
8:12 I will remember their **s** no more."
9:28 offered once to bear the **s** of many,
10: 4 of bulls and goats to take away **s.**
10:12 for all time a single sacrifice for **s,**
10:26 no longer remains a sacrifice for **s,**
Jas 5:16 confess your **s** to one another,
5:20 and will cover a multitude of **s.**
1Pe 2:24 bore our **s** in his body on the cross,
3:18 also suffered for **s** once for all.
4: 8 for love covers a multitude of **s.**
1Jn 1: 9 If we confess our **s,** he who is
      faithful and just will forgive us our **s**
2: 2 he is the atoning sacrifice for our **s,**
3: 5 that he was revealed to take away **s,**
4:10 to be the atoning sacrifice for our **s.**
Rev 1: 5 loves us and freed us from our **s**
Sir 2:11 he forgives **s** and saves
3: 3 honor their father atone for **s,**
4:26 not be ashamed to confess your **s,**
34:31 So if one fasts for his **s,**

ISERA
4: 2 the commander of his army was **S,**
5:26 she struck **S** a blow,

R → SISTERS
Say you are my **s,** so that it may go
of his wife Sarah, "She is my **s."**
is wife, he said, "She is my **s";**
v to wisdom, "You are my **s,"**
hed my heart, my **s,** my bride,
r false **s** Judah saw it.
der **s** is Samaria, who lived
does the will of God is
and **s** and mother."
me to do all the work
artha and her **s** and
ou our **s** Phoebe,
elect **s** send you
6:7; 2Sa 13:4;
Mt 5:22, 22, 23,
10, 10, 15,
15; 1Jn 2:9,

BROTHERS ... SISTERS Jos 2:13; Job
42:11; Ps 22:22; Mt 5:47; 19:29; Mk 3:32;
10:29, 30; Lk 14:26; Ac 16:40; Ro 1:13; 7:1;
8:12; 10:1; 11:25; 12:1; 15:14, 30; 16:14, 17;
1Co 1:10, 11, 26; 2:1; 3:1; 4:6; 7:24, 29; 10:1;
11:33; 12:1; 14:6, 20; 15:1, 6, 31, 50; 16:15,
20; 2Co 1:8; 8:1; 11:26; 13:11; Gal 1:11; 3:15;
5:13; 6:18; Php 1:14; 3:1, 17; 4:1; Col 1:2;
4:15; 1Th 1:4; 2:1, 9, 14, 17; 3:7; 4:1, 9, 10,
13; 5:1, 12, 26; 2Th 1:3; 2:1, 13, 15; 3:1, 13;
1Ti 4:6; 2Ti 4:21; Heb 2:11, 12, 17; 3:1, 12;
13:22; Jas 1:2; 2:1, 5, 14; 3:1, 10, 12; 4:11;
5:19; 1Pe 5:9; 2Pe 1:10; 1Jn 3:10, 13; 4:20, 21;
Rev 6:11; Jdt 7:30; Sir 25:1; 2Mc 15:18

SIT → SAT, SITS, SITTING
Ex   18:14 Why do you **s** alone, while all the
1Ki 8:25 to **s** on the throne of Israel,
Ps   1: 1 or **s** in the seat of scoffers;
26: 5 and will not **s** with the wicked.
110: 1 says to my lord, **"S** at my right hand
139: 2 You know when I **s** down and when
Isa 14:13 I will **s** on the mount of assembly
16: 5 and on it shall **s** in faithfulness
Jer 33:17 never lack a man to **s** on the throne
Eze 28: 2 I **s** in the seat of the gods,
Mic 4: 4 shall all **s** under their own vines and
Mal 3: 3 he will **s** as a refiner and purifier of
Mt   20:23 to **s** at my right hand and at my left,
22:44 **"S** at my right hand, until I put your
23: 2 "The scribes and the Pharisees **s** on
      Moses' seat;
Mk   14:32 his disciples, **"S** here while I pray."
Lk   22:30 and you will **s** on thrones judging
Jn   6:10 "Make the people **s** down."
Ac   2:34 to my Lord, **"S** at my right hand,
Heb 1:13 **s** at my right hand until I make

SITS → SIT
Ps   2: 4 He who **s** in the heavens laughs;
29:10 LORD **s** enthroned as king forever.
99: 1 He **s** enthroned upon the cherubim;
Isa 28: 6 to the one who **s** in judgment,
40:22 who **s** above the circle of the earth,
La   1: 1 lonely the city that once was full
      of people!

SITTING → SIT
2Ch 18:18 I saw the LORD **s** on his throne,
Est 2:19 Mordecai was **s** at the king's gate.
Isa 6: 1 I saw the Lord **s** on a throne,
Lk   8:35 **s** at the feet of Jesus, clothed and
Rev 17: 3 a woman **s** on a scarlet beast that

SIX → SIXTH
Ex   20: 9 **S** days you shall labor and do all
1Ch 20: 6 who had **s** fingers on each hand,
Pr   6:16 are **s** things that the LORD hates,
Isa 6: 2 above him; each had **s** wings:
Rev 4: 8 each of them with **s** wings,
13:18 Its number is **s** hundred sixty-six.

SIXTH → SIX
Rev 6:12 he opened the **s** seal, I looked,
16:12 The **s** angel poured his bowl on

SIXTY
Mt   13: 8 some a hundredfold, some **s,** some

SIXTY-SIX
Rev 13:18 Its number is six hundred **s.**

SIZE
Mt   17:20 have faith the **s** of a mustard seed,

SKIES → SKY
Ps   89: 6 For who in the **s** can be compared
      to the LORD?
89:37 an enduring witness in the **s."**
Jer 51: 9 and has been lifted up even to the **s.**

SKILL → SKILLED, SKILLFUL, SKILLFULLY
Ex   28: 3 whom I have endowed with **s,**
1Ki 7:14 he was full of **s,** intelligence,

Pr   1: 5 and the discerning acquire **s,**
Da   1:17 God gave knowledge and **s** in every

SKILLED → SKILL
Jer 4:22 They are **s** in doing evil,
Mic 7: 3 Their hands are **s** to do evil;
1Co 3:10 **s** master builder I laid a foundation,

SKILLFUL → SKILL
Ex   31: 6 and I have given skill to all the **s,**
Ps   78:72 and guided them with **s** hand.
Ecc 9:11 nor favor to the **s;**

SKILLFULLY → SKILL
Ps   33: 3 play **s** on the strings, with loud

SKIN → SKINS, WINESKINS
Ex   34:30 the **s** of his face was shining,
Job 2: 4 Satan answered the LORD, **"S** for **s!**
19:20 My bones cling to my **s** and to my
19:26 after my **s** has been thus destroyed,
Jer 13:23 Can Ethiopians change their **s**
Eze 37: 6 with **s,** and put breath in you,

SKINS → SKIN
Ex   25: 5 tanned rams' **s,** fine leather, acacia
Lk   5:37 the new wine will burst the **s** and

SKIP*
Ps   29: 6 He makes Lebanon **s** like a calf,
114: 6 O mountains, that you **s** like rams?

SKIRTS
La   1: 9 Her uncleanness was in her **s;**

SKULL
2Ki 9:35 they found no more of her than the **s**
Mt   27:33 Golgotha (which means Place of a **S)**

SKY → SKIES
Ge   1: 8 God called the dome **S.**
Dt   28:23 **s** over your head shall be bronze,
Pr   30:19 the way of an eagle in the **s,**
Mt   16: 3 to interpret the appearance of the **s,**
Rev 6:13 the stars of the **s** fell to the earth as
6:14 The **s** vanished like a scroll rolling
11: 6 They have authority to shut the **s,**

SLACK
Pr   18: 9 **s** in work is close kin to a vandal.
Hab 1: 4 So the law becomes **s**
Sir 2:12 Woe to timid hearts and to **s** hands,

SLAIN → SLAYER
1Ch 10: 1 and fell **s** on Mount Gilboa.
Eze 37: 9 and breathe upon these **s,**

SLANDER → SLANDERED, SLANDERER,
           SLANDERERS, SLANDEROUS, SLANDERS
Ps   15: 3 who do not **s** with their tongue,
Pr   10:18 and whoever utters **s** is a fool.
Mt   15:19 fornication, theft, false witness, **s.**
2Co 12:20 jealousy, anger, selfishness, **s,**
Eph 4:31 and anger and wrangling and **s,**
Col 3: 8 **s,** and abusive language from your
1Pe 2: 1 all guile, insincerity, envy, and all **s.**
2Pe 2:10 are not afraid to **s** the glorious ones,
Jude 1: 8 authority, and **s** the glorious ones.
Sir 28:15 **S** has driven virtuous women from

SLANDERED → SLANDER
1Co 4:13 when **s,** we speak kindly.

SLANDERER → SLANDER
Jer 9: 4 every neighbor goes around like a **s.**

SLANDERERS* → SLANDER
Ro   1:30 **s,** God-haters, insolent, haughty,
1Ti 3:11 likewise must be serious, not **s,**
2Ti 3: 3 implacable, **s,** profligates, brutes,
Tit 2: 3 not to be **s** or slaves to drink;

SLANDEROUS → SLANDER
2Pe 2:11 not bring against them a **s** judgment

SLANDERS → SLANDER
Ps 101: 5 secretly s a neighbor I will destroy.

SLAPPED
2Ch 18:23 s him on the cheek, and said,
Mt 26:67 and struck him; and some s him,

SLAUGHTER → SLAUGHTERED
Ex 12: 6 of Israel shall s it at twilight.
29:11 you shall s the bull before the LORD,
Dt 12:15 whenever you desire you may s and
Pr 7:22 and goes like an ox to the s,
Isa 53: 7 like a lamb that is led to the s,
Jer 11:19 I was like a gentle lamb led to the s.
Zec 11: 4 a shepherd of the flock doomed to s.
Ac 8:32 "Like a sheep he was led to the s,

SLAUGHTERED → SLAUGHTER
Nu 14:16 that he has s them in the wilderness.
Ro 8:36 we are accounted as sheep to be s."
Rev 5: 6 a Lamb standing as if it had been s,
6: 9 who had been s for the word of God
13: 8 book of life of the Lamb that was s.

SLAVE → ENSLAVE, ENSLAVED, SLAVERY, SLAVES
Ge 9:26 and let Canaan be his s.
21:10 Cast out this s woman with her son;
Mk 10:44 first among you must be s of all.
Jn 8:34 who commits sin is a s to sin.
Ro 7:25 I am a s to the law of God,
1Co 7:21 Were you a s when called?
9:19 I have made myself a s to all,
Gal 3:28 there is no longer s or free,
4:30 "Drive out the s and her child;
Php 2: 7 taking the form of a s,
Col 3:11 s and free; but Christ is all and in all
1Ti 1:10 sodomites, s traders, liars, perjurers,
Phm 1:16 as a s but more than a s, a beloved brother—
Rev 13:16 both rich and poor, both free and s,

SLAVERY → SLAVE
Ex 2:23 Israelites groaned under their s,
20: 2 out of the house of s;
Dt 7: 8 redeemed you from the house of s,
Ezr 9: 9 God has not forsaken us in our s,
Ro 7:14 of the flesh, sold into s under sin.
Gal 5: 1 do not submit again to a yoke of s.
1Ti 6: 1 s regard their masters as worthy

HOUSE OF SLAVERY Ex 13:3, 14; 20:2;
Dt 5:6; 6:12; 7:8; 8:14; 13:5, 10; Jos 24:17;
Jdg 6:8; Jer 34:13; Mic 6:4

SLAVES → SLAVE
Ge 9:25 of s shall he be to his brothers."
1Ki 9:22 of the Israelites Solomon made no s;
Ecc 10: 7 I have seen s on horseback,
Jer 34: 9 all should set free their Hebrew s,
Jn 8:33 and have never been s to anyone.
Ro 6:16 are s of the one whom you obey,
1Co 7:23 do not become s of human masters.
12:13 Jews or Greeks, s or free—
Eph 6: 5 S, obey your earthly masters with
Col 3:22 S, obey your earthly masters in
4: 1 Masters, treat your s justly and
Tit 2: 9 Tell s to be submissive to their
2Pe 2:19 people are s to whatever masters

SLAYER → SLAYS, SLAIN
Nu 35: 6 where you shall permit a s to flee,
Jos 20: 5 they shall not give up the s,

SLAYS* → SLAYER
Job 5: 2 and jealousy s the simple.

SLEEK
Ge 41: 4 thin cows ate up the seven s and fat

SLEEP → ASLEEP, SLEEPER, SLEEPING, SLEEPLESS, SLEEPS, SLEPT
Ge 2:21 God caused a deep s to fall upon
15:12 a deep s fell upon Abram,

Ex 22:27 in what else shall that person s?
Dt 24:13 your neighbor may s in the cloak
1Sa 26:12 a deep s from the LORD had fallen
Ps 4: 8 I will both lie down and s in peace;
13: 3 or I will s the s of death,
76: 5 of their spoil; they sank into s;
78:65 Then the Lord awoke as from s,
121: 4 He who keeps Israel will neither slumber nor s.
127: 2 for he gives s to his beloved.
132: 4 not give s to my eyes or slumber to
Pr 6: 9 When will you rise from your s?
6:10 A little s, a little slumber,
Ecc 5:12 Sweet is the s of laborers,
Isa 29:10 upon you a spirit of deep s;
Da 12: 2 Many of those who s in the dust of
Ac 20: 9 into a deep s while Paul talked still
1Th 5: 7 for those who s s at night,

SLEEPER → SLEEP
Eph 5:14 "S, awake! Rise from the dead,

SLEEPING → SLEEP
Mt 9:24 for the girl is not dead but s."
26:40 to the disciples and found them s;

SLEEPLESS* → SLEEP
2Co 6: 5 riots, labors, s nights, hunger;
11:27 many a s night, hungry and thirsty,

SLEEPS → SLEEP
Pr 6:29 he who s with his neighbor's wife;
10: 5 child who s in harvest brings shame.

SLEPT → SLEEP
SS 5: 2 I s, but my heart was awake.
Mt 25: 5 all of them became drowsy and s.

SLING
Jdg 20:16 every one could s a stone at a hair,
1Sa 17:50 with a s and a stone,
1Ch 12: 2 s stones with either the right hand
Pr 26: 8 like binding a stone in a s to give

SLIP → SLIPPED, SLIPPERY, SLIPPING, SLIPS
Dt 4: 9 nor to let them s from your mind all
32:35 for the time when their foot shall s;
Ps 37:31 their steps do not s.
Sir 20:18 A s on the pavement is better than a s of the tongue;

SLIPPED → SLIP
Ps 17: 5 to your paths; my feet have not s.
73: 2 my steps had nearly s.

SLIPPERY* → SLIP
Ps 35: 6 Let their way be dark and s,
73:18 Truly you set them in s places;
Jer 23:12 like s paths in the darkness,

SLIPPING → SLIP
Ps 94:18 When I thought, "My foot is s,"

SLOW* → SLOWNESS
Ex 4:10 but I am s of speech and s of tongue.
34: 6 merciful and gracious, s to anger,
Nu 14:18 'The LORD is s to anger,
Jdg 18: 9 Do not be s to go,
Ne 9:17 s to anger and abounding in
Ps 86:15 s to anger and abounding in
103: 8 s to anger and abounding in
145: 8 s to anger and abounding in
Pr 14:29 s to anger has great understanding,
15:18 who are s to anger calm contention.
16:32 One who is s to anger is better than
19:11 with good sense are s to anger,
Joel 2:13 s to anger, and abounding in
Jnh 4: 2 s to anger, and abounding in
Na 1: 3 The LORD is s to anger but great in
Lk 24:25 and how s of heart to believe all that
Jas 1:19 be quick to listen, s to speak, s to anger;
2Pe 3: 9 The Lord is not s about his promise,

Tob 12: 6 Do not be s to acknowledge him.
Sir 5: 4 for the Lord is s to anger,
11:12 who are s and need help,

SLOWNESS → SLOW
2Pe 3: 9 think of s, but is patient with you,

SLUGGISH
Ro 11: 8 "God gave them a s spirit,
Heb 6:12 so that you may not become s,

SLUMBER
Ps 121: 3 he who keeps you will not s.
121: 4 He who keeps Israel will neither s nor sleep.
Pr 6:10 a little s, a little folding of the hands

SMALL → SMALLEST
Nu 26:54 and to a s tribe you shall give a s inheritance;
Mk 12:42 poor widow came and put in two s copper coins,
Lk 19:17 been trustworthy in a very s thing,
Jas 3: 5 So also the tongue is a s member,
Pm 151: 1 I was s among my brothers,

SMALLEST → SMALL
Mk 4:31 is the s of all the seeds on earth;

SMASH
Dt 12: 3 down their altars, s their pillars,

SMEAR
Ps 119:69 The arrogant s me with lies,
Eze 13:10 these prophets s whitewash on it.

SMELL → SWEET-SMELLING
Dt 4:28 neither see, nor hear, nor eat, nor s.
Ps 115: 6 not hear; noses, but do not s.
Da 3:27 not even the s of fire came from
Tob 6:18 the demon will s it and flee,

SMOKE → SMOKING
Ex 19:18 Now Mount Sinai was wrapped in s,
Ps 68: 2 As s is driven away, so drive them
104:32 touches the mountains and they s.
Isa 6: 4 and the house filled with s.
Joel 2:30 blood and fire and columns of s.
Rev 8: 4 And the s of the incense,
9: 2 darkened with the s from the shaft.
15: 8 with s from the glory of God and

SMOKING → SMOKE
Ge 15:17 s fire pot and a flaming torch passed
Ex 20:18 of the trumpet, and the mountain s,

SMOLDERING
Mt 12:20 a bruised reed or quench a s wick

SMOOTH → SMOOTHER
1Sa 17:40 chose five s stones from the wadi,
Pr 6:24 from the s tongue of the adulteress
7:21 with her s talk she compels him.
Lk 3: 5 and the rough ways made s;

SMOOTHER* → SMOOTH
Ps 55:21 with speech s than butter,
Pr 5: 3 and her speech is s than oil;

SMYRNA
Rev 2: 8 to the angel of the church in

SNAKE → SNAKES
Ex 4: 3 and it became a s; and Mo
7:10 and his officials, and it be
Mic 7:17 they shall lick dust like a
Lk 11:11 will give a s instead of a

SNAKES → SNAKE
Lk 10:19 authority to tread on s

SNARE → ENSNARE, ENSNA/ SNARES
Ex 23:33 it will surely be a s
Dt 7:16 for that would be a
Jdg 2: 3 and their gods sha

Ps 69:22 a trap for them, a **s** for their allies.
    91: 3 deliver you from the **s** of the fowler
Pr 29:25 The fear of others lays a **s,**
Ro 11: 9 their table become a **s** and a trap,

SNARES → SNARE
Ps 18: 5 the **s** of death confronted me.
Pr 13:14 so that one may avoid the **s** of death.

SNATCH → SNATCHED, SNATCHES
Jn 10:28 No one will **s** them out of my hand.

SNATCHED → SNATCH
Am 4:11 were like a brand **s** from the fire;
Ac 8:39 the Spirit of the Lord **s** Philip away;
Rev 12: 5 But her child was **s** away

SNATCHES → SNATCH
Mt 13:19 the evil one comes and **s** away what

SNEEZED*
2Ki 4:35 the child **s** seven times,

SNIFF*
Mal 1:13 you **s** at me, says the LORD of hosts.

SNOUT*
Pr 11:22 Like a gold ring in a pig's **s**

SNOW → SNOWS
Ex 4: 6 his hand was leprous, as white as **s.**
Nu 12:10 Miriam had become leprous, as
         white as **s.**
2Ki 5:27 his presence leprous, as white as **s.**
Ps 51: 7 and I shall be whiter than **s.**
Isa 1:18 your sins are like scarlet, they shall
         be like **s;**
Da 7: 9 his clothing was white as **s,**
Mt 28: 3 and his clothing white as **s.**
Rev 1:14 as white wool, white as **s;**

SNOWS* → SNOW
Pr 31:21 for her household when it **s,**
Aza 1:50 Bless the Lord, frosts and **s;**

SO-CALLED → CALL
1Co 8: 5 **s** gods in heaven or on earth—
2Th 2: 4 exalts himself above every **s** god

SOAP*
Job 9:30 If I wash myself with **s** and cleanse
Jer 2:22 yourself with lye and use much **s,**
Mal 3: 2 a refiner's fire and like fullers' **s;**

SOBER
Ro 12: 3 but to think with **s** judgment,
1Th 5: 6 but let us keep awake and be **s;**
2Ti 4: 5 always be **s,** endure suffering,

SOCKET
Ge 32:25 he struck him on the hip **s;**

SODOM → SODOMITES
Ge 13:12 and moved his tent as far as **S.**
    13:13 Now the people of **S** were wicked,
    18:20 the outcry against **S** and Gomorrah
    19:24 rained on **S** and Gomorrah sulfur
Isa 1: 9 we would have been like **S,**
Eze 16:49 This was the guilt of your sister **S:**
Lk 10:12 it will be more tolerable for **S** than
Ro 9:29 we would have fared like **S** and
Jude 1: 7 **S** and Gomorrah and the
Rev 11: 8 city that is prophetically called **S**

SODOMITES* → SODOM
1Co 6: 9 adulterers, male prostitutes, **s,**
1Ti 1:10 **s,** slave traders, liars, perjurers,

SOFT
Pr 15: 1 A **s** answer turns away wrath,
    25:15 a **s** tongue can break bones.

SOIL → SOILED
Ge 9:20 Noah, a man of the **s,**
Mt 13:23 as for what was sown on good **s,**

SOILED* → SOIL
Zep 3: 1 Ah, **s,** defiled, oppressing city!
Rev 3: 4 who have not **s** their clothes;

SOLD → SELL
Ge 37:28 **s** him to the Ishmaelites for twenty
Dt 32:30 unless their Rock had **s** them,
Jdg 4: 2 So the LORD **s** them into the hand
    10: 7 he **s** them into the hand of the
1Ki 21:25 who **s** himself to do what was evil
Mt 10:29 Are not two sparrows **s** for a penny?
    13:46 and **s** all that he had and bought it.
Ac 5: 1 of his wife Sapphira, **s** a piece
Ro 7:14 of the flesh, **s** into slavery under sin.
1Co 10:25 Eat whatever is **s** in the meat market
Heb 12:16 **s** his birthright for a single meal.
1Mc 1:15 and **s** themselves to do evil.

SOLDIER → SOLDIERS
2Ti 2: 3 Share in suffering like a good **s** of
    Christ Jesus.

SOLDIERS → SOLDIER
Mt 27:27 the **s** of the governor took Jesus into
    28:12 give a large sum of money to the **s,**
Jn 19:23 When the **s** had crucified Jesus,
    19:34 the **s** pierced his side with a spear,

SOLE
Dt 28:65 resting place for the **s** of your foot.
Isa 1: 6 the **s** of the foot even to the head,

SOLEMN
Isa 1:13 I cannot endure **s** assemblies with
    iniquity.
Joel 2:15 sanctify a fast; call a **s** assembly;
Am 5:21 no delight in your **s** assemblies.

SOLID
1Co 3: 2 I fed you with milk, not **s** food,
Heb 5:14 But **s** food is for the mature,

SOLOMON → =JEDIDIAH
  Son of David by Bathsheba; king of Judah (2Sa
12:24; 1Ch 3:5, 10). Appointed king by David
(1Ki 1); adversaries Adonijah, Joab, Shimei
killed by Benaiah (1Ki 2). Asked for wisdom
(1Ki 3; 2Ch 1). Judged between two prostitutes
(1Ki 3:16-28). Built temple (1Ki 5-7; 2Ch 2-5);
prayer of dedication (1Ki 8; 2Ch 6). Visited by
Queen of Sheba (1Ki 10; 2Ch 9). Wives turned
his heart from God (1Ki 11:1-13). Jeroboam
rebelled against (1Ki 11:26-40). Death (1Ki
11:41-43; 2Ch 9:29-31).
  Proverbs of (1Ki 4:32; Pr 1:1; 10:1; 25:1);
psalms of (Ps 72; 127); song of (SS 1:1).

SOLVE
Da 5:16 give interpretations and **s** problems.
2Es 4: 4 If you can **s** one of them for me,

SOME
Ge 3: 6 and she also gave **s** to her husband,
1Co 9:22 that I might by all means save **s.**
Eph 4:11 The gifts he gave were that **s** would
    be apostles, **s** prophets, **s**
    evangelists, **s** pastors and teachers,
Php 1:15 **S** proclaim Christ from envy and
1Ti 4: 1 later times **s** will renounce the faith
2Ti 2:20 **s** for special use, **s** for ordinary.
2Pe 3:16 **s** things in them hard to understand,

SOMEONE
Ex 4:13 "O my Lord, please send **s** else."
    12:30 was not a house without **s** dead.
Lk 16:31 even if **s** rises from the dead.'"
Ro 10:14 to hear without **s** to proclaim him?

SOMETHING
Ex 24:10 Under his feet there was **s** like a
    pavement
Nu 16:30 But if the LORD creates **s** new,
Mt 25:35 thirsty and you gave me **s** to drink,
Ac 3: 5 expecting to receive **s** from them.
    9:18 **s** like scales fell from his eyes,

Php 2: 6 not regard equality with God as **s** to
    be exploited,
Rev 8: 8 and **s** like a great mountain, burning

SON → SONS
Ge 5: 3 the father of a **s** in his likeness,
    17:19 your wife Sarah shall bear you a **s,**
    21: 2 conceived and bore Abraham a **s**
    21:10 this slave woman with her **s;**
    22: 2 "Take your **s,** your only **s** Isaac,
    22:12 since you have not withheld your **s,**
    your only **s,** from me."
    25:11 God blessed his **s** Isaac.
Ex 4:23 now I will kill your firstborn **s.'"**
Dt 18:10 a **s** or daughter pass through fire,
    21:18 rebellious **s** who will not obey his
2Sa 7:14 and he shall be a **s** to me.
1Ki 3:23 Your **s** is dead, and my **s** is the
    living one.'"
    8:19 but your **s** who shall be born to you
2Ki 6:29 So we cooked my **s** and ate him.
1Ch 22:10 He shall be a **s** to me,
Ps 2: 7 He said to me, "You are my **s;**
Pr 3:12 a father the **s** in whom he delights.
Isa 7:14 is with child and shall bear a **s,**
    8: 3 and she conceived and bore a **s.**
    9: 6 has been born for us, a **s** given to us;
Jer 31:20 Is Ephraim my dear **s?**
Hos 11: 1 and out of Egypt I called my **s.**
Am 7:14 "I am no prophet, nor a prophet's **s;**
Mal 1: 6 A **s** honors his father, and servants
Mt 1: 1 the **s** of David, the **s** of Abraham.
    1:23 virgin shall conceive and bear a **s,**
    2:15 "Out of Egypt I have called my **s."**
    3:17 from heaven said, "This is my **S,**
    4: 3 "If you are the **S** of God,
    8:20 but the **S** of Man has nowhere to
    lay his head."
    11:27 and no one knows the **S** except the
    Father,
    12: 8 the **S** of Man is lord of the sabbath."
    12:32 a word against the **S** of Man will be
    forgiven,
    12:40 and three nights the **S** of Man will
    13:55 Is not this the carpenter's **s?**
    14:33 "Truly you are the **S** of God."
    16:16 "You are the Messiah, the **S** of the
    living God."
    16:27 "For the **S** of Man is to come with
    17: 5 cloud a voice said, "This is my **S,**
    19:28 the **S** of Man is seated on the throne
    20:18 the **S** of Man will be handed over to
    20:28 the **S** of Man came not to be served
    but to serve,
    21: 9 "Hosanna to the **S** of David!
    22:42 of the Messiah? Whose **s** is he?"
    24:27 will be the coming of the **S** of Man.
    24:30 'the **S** of Man coming on the clouds
    24:44 the **S** of Man is coming at an
    unexpected hour.
    25:31 the **S** of Man comes in his glory,
    26:63 tell us if you are the Messiah, the **S**
    of God."
    27:54 "Truly this man was God's **S!"**
    28:19 in the name of the Father and of the
    S and of the Holy Spirit,
Mk 1:11 came from heaven, "You are my **S,**
    2:28 **S** of Man is lord even of the sabbath
    8:38 the **S** of Man will also be ashamed
    9: 7 my **S,** the Beloved; listen to him!"
    10:45 the **S** of Man came not to be served
    but to serve,
    13:32 the angels in heaven, nor the **S,**
    14:62 'you will see the **S** of Man seated at
    15:39 "Truly this man was God's **S!"**
Lk 1:32 be called the **S** of the Most High,
    1:35 he will be called **S** of God.
    2: 7 her firstborn **s** and wrapped him in
    3:22 came from heaven, "You are my **S,**
    9:35 my **S,** my Chosen; listen to him!"
    9:58 but the **S** of Man has nowhere to
    lay his head."

12: 8 the S of Man also will acknowledge
15:21 longer worthy to be called your s.'
18: 8 S of Man comes, will he find faith
18:31 that is written about the S of Man
19:10 S of Man came to seek out and to
       save the lost."
20:44 so how can he be his s?"
Jn   1:34 testified that this is the S of God.'
      1:49 "Rabbi, you are the S of God!
      3:14 so must the S of Man be lifted up,
      3:16 God so loved the world that he
             gave his only S,
      3:36 believes in the S has eternal life;
      5:19 the S can do nothing on his own,
      6:40 the S and believe in him may have
             eternal life;
      11: 4 that the S of God may be glorified
      12:34 Who is this S of Man?"
      13:31 the S of Man has been glorified,
      17: 1 glorify your S so that the S may
             glorify you,
Ac   7:56 heavens opened and the S of Man
      13:33 my S; today I have begotten you.'
Ro   1: 4 be S of God with power according
      5:10 to God through the death of his S,
      8: 3 by sending his own S in the likeness
      8:29 be conformed to the image of his S,
      8:32 He who did not withhold his own S,
1Co 15:28 the S himself will also be subjected
Col   1:13 into the kingdom of his beloved S,
1Th   1:10 to wait for his S from heaven,
Heb   1: 2 last days he has spoken to us by a S,
      1: 5 my S; today I have begotten you"?
      4:14 the S of God, let us hold fast to our
      5: 5 my S, today I have begotten you";
      7:28 a S who has been made perfect
      10:29 by those who have spurned the S
Jas   2:21 when he offered his s Isaac on
2Pe   1:17 saying, "This is my S, my Beloved,
1Jn   1: 3 with the Father and with his S Jesus
      1: 7 the blood of Jesus his S cleanses us
      2:23 who denies the S has the Father;
      3: 8 The S of God was revealed for this
      4: 9 God sent his only S into the world
      4:14 that the Father has sent his S as
      5: 5 believes that Jesus is the S of God?
      5:11 eternal life, and this life is in his S.
Rev   1:13 the lampstands I saw one like the S
      2:18 are the words of the S of God,
      12: 5 she gave birth to a s, a male child,
      14:14 the cloud was one like the S of Man,
Sir   4:10 be like a s of the Most High,
2Es 13:32 then my S will be revealed,
      14: 9 henceforth you shall live with my S

BELOVED SON; SON, THE BELOVED
Mt 3:17; 17:5; Mk 1:11; 9:7; 12:6; Lk 3:22;
20:13; Col 1:13; 2Pe 1:17

KING'S SON 2Sa 18:12, 20; 1Ki 22:26; 2Ki
11:4, 12; 15:5; 2Ch 18:25; 23:3, 11; 28:7; Ps
72:1; Jer 36:26; 38:6; 1Mc 6:17

ONLY SON Ge 22:2, 12, 16; Am 8:10; Lk
7:12; Jn 1:14, 18; 3:16, 18; Heb 11:17; 1Jn
4:9; Tob 6:15

SON OF AARON Nu 3:32; 4:16, 28, 33;
7:8; 16:37; 25:7, 11; 26:1; Jos 24:33; Jdg
20:28; 1Es 5:5; 8:2; 2Es 1:3

SON OF DAVID 2Ch 1:1; 11:18; 13:6; 35:3;
Pr 1:1; Ecc 1:1; Mt 1:1, 20; 9:27; 12:23; 15:22;
20:30, 31; 21:9, 15; 22:42; Mk 10:47, 48;
12:35; Lk 3:31; 18:38, 39; 1Es 1:3

SON OF *GOD Mt 4:3, 6; 8:29; 14:33;
26:63; 27:40; Mk 1:1; 3:11; Lk 1:35; 3:38; 4:3,
9, 41; 22:70; Jn 1:34, 49; 3:18; 5:25; 11:4, 27;
19:7; 20:31; Ac 9:20; Ro 1:4; 2Co 1:19; Gal
2:20; Eph 4:13; Heb 4:14; 6:6; 7:3; 10:29; 1Jn
3:8; 4:15; 5:5, 10, 12, 13, 20; Rev 2:18; 2Es
2:47

SON OF JESSE 1Sa 16:18; 20:27, 30, 31;
22:7, 8, 9, 13; 25:10; 2Sa 20:1; 23:1; 1Ki

12:16; 1Ch 10:14; 12:18; 29:26; 2Ch 10:16;
11:18; Ps 72:20; Lk 3:32; Ac 13:22; Sir 45:25

SON OF MAN 2Sa 17:25; Mt 8:20; 9:6;
10:23; 11:19; 12:8, 32, 40; 13:37, 41; 16:13,
27, 28; 17:9, 12, 22; 19:28; 20:18, 28; 24:27,
30, 30, 37, 39, 44; 25:31; 26:2, 24, 24, 45, 64;
Mk 2:10, 28; 8:31, 38; 9:9, 12, 31; 10:33, 45;
13:26; 14:21, 21, 41, 62; Lk 5:24; 6:5, 22;
7:34; 9:22, 26, 44, 58; 11:30; 12:8, 10, 40;
17:22, 24, 26, 30; 18:8, 31; 19:10; 21:27, 36;
22:22, 48, 69; 24:7; Jn 1:51; 3:13, 14; 5:27;
6:27, 53, 62; 8:28; 9:35; 12:23, 34, 34; 13:31;
Ac 7:56; Rev 1:13; 14:14

SONG → SING

Ex   15: 1 sang this s to the LORD:
Dt   31:21 s will confront them as a witness,
     32:44 and recited all the words of this s in
Ps   33: 3 Sing to him a new s;
     40: 3 He put a new s in my mouth,
     69:30 praise the name of God with a s;
     96: 1 O sing to the LORD a new s;
     98: 4 break forth into joyous s and sing
     149: 1 Sing to the LORD a new s,
Isa 54: 1 burst into s and shout,
     55:12 hills before you shall burst into s,
Rev   5: 9 They sing a new s: "You are worthy
      14: 3 No one could learn that s except
      15: 3 and the s of the Lamb:
Jdt 16:13 I will sing to my God a new s:

NEW SONG Ps 33:3; 40:3; 96:1; 98:1;
144:9; 149:1; Isa 42:10; Rev 5:9; 14:3; Jdt
16:13

SONGS → SING

1Ki   4:32 his s is numbered a thousand and five.
Ne   12:46 were s of praise and thanksgiving
Ps   42: 4 glad shouts and s of thanksgiving,
     47: 1 shout to God with loud s of joy.
     137: 3 "Sing us one of the s of Zion!"
Eph   5:19 psalms and hymns and spiritual s
Col   3:16 hymns, and spiritual s to God.
Jas   5:13 They should sing s of praise.
1Mc   4:54 it was dedicated with s and harps

SONS → SON

Ge   6: 2 the s of God saw that they were fair;
      9: 1 God blessed Noah and his s,
     10:32 These are the families of Noah's s,
     35:22 Now the s of Jacob were twelve.
Ex   13:15 every firstborn of my s I redeem.'
     28: 9 on them the names of the s of Israel,
Nu   18: 8 and your s as a priestly portion due
Dt   7: 3 giving your daughters to their s or
             taking their daughters for your s,
Ru   4:15 who is more to you than seven s,
1Sa   1: 8 Am I not more to you than ten s?"
Ps 127: 3 S are indeed a heritage from the
             LORD.
     132:12 If your s keep my covenant and my
Joel 2:28 s and your daughters shall prophesy,
Ac   2:17 s and your daughters shall prophesy,
2Co   6:18 you shall be my s and daughters,
1Mc   1:48 and to leave their s uncircumcised.
      2: 2 He had five s, John surnamed

AARON'S SONS Ex 28:1, 40; Lev 1:5, 8,
11; 2:2; 3:2, 5, 8; 8:13, 24; 9:12, 18; 10:1; Nu
3:38

KING'S SONS 2Sa 9:11; 13:23, 27, 29, 30,
32, 33, 35, 36; 1Ki 1:9; 2Ki 10:6, 7, 8; 1Ch
27:32; Zep 1:8

SONS ... DAUGHTERS Ge 5:4, 7, 10, 13,
16, 19, 22, 26, 30; 6:4; 11:11, 13, 15, 17, 19,
21, 23, 25; 19:12; 31:28; 36:6; 37:35; 46:7, 15;
Ex 3:22; 10:9; 21:4; 32:2; 34:16; Lev 10:14;
Nu 18:11, 19; 21:29; 26:33; Dt 7:3; 12:12, 31;
16:11, 14; 28:32, 41, 53; 32:19; Jos 7:24; 17:3;
Jdg 12:9; 1Sa 1:4; 2:21; 30:3, 6, 19; 2Sa 5:13;
19:5; 2Ki 17:17; 1Ch 2:34; 4:27; 14:3; 23:22;
25:5; 2Ch 11:21; 13:21; 24:3; 28:8; 29:9;
31:18; Ezr 9:12; Ne 4:14; 5:2, 5; 10:28; 13:25;

Job 1:2, 13, 18; 42:13; Ps 106:37, 38; Isa 56:5;
Jer 3:24; 5:17; 7:31; 11:22; 14:16; 16:2, 3;
19:9; 29:6, 6, 6; 32:35; 35:8; Eze 14:16, 18,
22; 16:20; 23:4, 10, 25, 47; 24:21, 25; Joel
2:28; 3:8; Am 7:17; Ac 2:17; 2Co 6:18; Tob
4:13; Wis 9:7; Bar 4:10, 14; 1Es 5:1; 2Es 1:28

SONS OF AARON Lev 3:13; 6:14; 7:10,
33; 9:9; 16:1; 21:1; Nu 3:2, 3; 10:8; 1Ch 6:3,
50, 54, 57; 24:1; Tob 1:7; Sir 50:13, 16; 1Es
1:13, 14

SONS OF ISRAEL Ge 42:5; 45:21; 46:5;
Ex 1:1; 28:9, 11, 12, 21, 29; 39:6, 7, 14; Dt
23:17; 1Ch 2:1

SOON

Ps   37: 2 for they will s fade like the grass,
     106:13 But they s forgot his works;
Isa 56: 1 for s my salvation will come,
Rev   1: 1 to show his servants what must s
             take place;
      3:11 I am coming s; hold fast to what
      22: 7 "See, I am coming s!
      22:12 I am coming s; my reward is with
      22:20 says, "Surely I am coming s."

SOOTHSAYER* → SOOTHSAYERS

Dt 18:10 who practices divination, or is a s,

SOOTHSAYERS → SOOTHSAYER

Isa   2: 6 and of s like the Philistines,
Mic   5:12 and you shall have no more s;

SORCERERS → SORCERY

Ex   7:11 summoned the wise men and the s;
Jer 27: 9 your soothsayers, or your s,
Da   2: 2 s, and the Chaldeans be summoned
Rev 21: 8 murderers, the fornicators, the s,
      22:15 Outside are the dogs and s and

SORCERIES → SORCERY

Isa 47: 9 in spite of your many s and the
Rev   9:21 not repent of their murders or their s

SORCERY → SORCERERS, SORCERIES

Gal   5:20 s, enmities, strife, jealousy, anger,
Rev 18:23 all nations were deceived by your s.

SORDID*

Tit   1:11 by teaching for s gain what it is not
1Pe   5: 2 not for s gain but eagerly.

SOREK*

Jdg 16: 4 with a woman in the valley of S,

SORES

Job   2: 7 and inflicted loathsome s on Job
Isa   1: 6 bruises and s and bleeding wounds;
Lk   16:20 named Lazarus, covered with s,

SORROW → SORROWFUL, SORROWS

Est   9:22 turned for them from s into gladness
Ps 119:28 My soul melts away for s;
Pr   23:29 Who has woe? Who has s?
Ecc   1:18 who increase knowledge increase s.
Isa 35:10 and s and sighing shall flee away.
     51:11 and s and sighing shall flee away.
Ro   9: 2 great s and unceasing anguish in

SORROWFUL → SORROW

2Co   6:10 as s, yet always rejoicing;

SORROWS → SORROW

Ps   16: 4 choose another god multiply their s;
2Es   8:54 s have passed away,

SOUGHT → SEEK

1Sa 13:14 has s out a man after his own heart;
2Ch 26: 5 long as he s the LORD, God made
Ps   34: 4 I s the LORD, and he answered me,
     119:45 for I have s your precepts.
Sir 51:13 I s wisdom openly in my prayer.

SOUL → SOULS

Dt   6: 5 all your s, and with all your might.
     10:12 all your heart and with all your s,

30: 6 all your heart and with all your **s**,
Jos 22: 5 all your heart and with all your **s."**
2Ki 23:25 with all his **s**, and with all his might,
Ps 16: 9 heart is glad, and my **s** rejoices;
19: 7 The law of the LORD is perfect,
reviving the **s**;
23: 3 he restores my **s**.
25: 1 To you, O LORD, I lift up my **s**.
33:20 Our **s** waits for the LORD;
34: 2 My **s** makes its boast in the LORD;
42: 1 so my **s** longs for you, O God.
42:11 Why are you cast down, O my **s**,
62: 5 For God alone my **s** waits in silence,
63: 8 My **s** clings to you; your right hand
94:19 your consolations cheer my **s**.
103: 1 Bless the LORD, O my **s**,
108: 1 and make melody. Awake, my **s!**
116: 7 Return, O my **s**, to your rest,
130: 5 I wait for the LORD, my **s** waits,
Pr 13:19 A desire realized is sweet to the **s**,
16:24 sweetness to the **s** and health to the
24:14 that wisdom is such to your **s**;
La 3:20 My **s** continually thinks of it and
Mic 6: 7 the fruit of my body for the sin of
my **s?"**
Mt 10:28 but cannot kill the **s**; rather fear him
who can destroy both **s** and body
22:37 all your **s**, and with all your mind.'
Lk 1:46 Mary said, "My **s** magnifies the
Lord,
2:35 a sword will pierce your own **s** too."
1Th 5:23 and **s** and body be kept sound
Heb 4:12 piercing until it divides **s** from spirit
6:19 a sure and steadfast anchor of the **s**,
Jas 5:20 will save the sinner's **s** from death
1Pe 2:11 flesh that wage war against the **s**.
3Jn 1: 2 just as it is well with your **s**.
Sir 6:26 Come to her with all your **s**,
7:29 With all your **s** fear the Lord,

SOULS → SOUL

Jer 6:16 walk in it, and find rest for your **s**.
Mt 11:29 and you will find rest for your **s**.
1Pe 1: 9 of your faith, the salvation of your **s**.
2:25 the shepherd and guardian of your **s**.
2Pe 2:14 They entice unsteady **s**.
Rev 6: 9 **s** of those who had been slaughtered
20: 4 **s** of those who had been beheaded
Sir 51:26 and let your **s** receive instruction;

SOUND

Ge 3: 8 the **s** of the LORD God walking in
Ex 32:18 it is the **s** of revelers that I hear."
Dt 4:12 the **s** of words but saw no form;
Ps 66: 8 let the **s** of his praise be heard,
115: 7 they make no **s** in their throats.
Pr 3:21 keep **s** wisdom and prudence,
8:14 I have good advice and **s** wisdom;
Eze 1:24 like the **s** of mighty waters,
3:12 behind me the **s** of loud rumbling;
Joel 2: 1 **s** the alarm on my holy mountain!
Jn 3: 8 and you hear the **s** of it,
Ac 2: 2 from heaven there came a **s** like
1Co 14: 8 if the bugle gives an indistinct **s**,
15:52 For the trumpet will **s**, and the dead
1Ti 1:10 else is contrary to the **s** teaching
6: 3 the **s** words of our Lord Jesus Christ
2Ti 1:13 the standard of **s** teaching that you
4: 3 will not put up with **s** doctrine,
Tit 1: 9 able both to preach with **s** doctrine
2: 1 what is consistent with **s** doctrine.
Rev 1:15 voice was like the **s** of many waters.
19: 6 like the **s** of many waters
2Es 6:17 its **s** was like the **s** of mighty waters.

SOUR

Jer 31:29 "The parents have eaten **s** grapes,
Eze 18: 2 "The parents have eaten **s** grapes,
Mk 15:36 filled a sponge with **s** wine,

SOURCE

Heb 5: 9 the **s** of eternal salvation for all who

SOUTH

Ps 89:12 north and the **s**—you created them;
Da 11: 5 the king of the **s** shall grow strong,
Mt 12:42 The queen of the **S** will rise up at

SOVEREIGN → SOVEREIGNTY

1Ki 4:21 Solomon was **s** over all the
Ps 8: 1 O LORD, our **S**, how majestic
Ac 4:24 **"S** Lord, who made the heaven
Rev 6:10 **"S** Lord, holy and true, how long
SOVEREIGN *LORD Ac 4:24; Rev 6:10;
2Mc 13:4; 4:38; 5:23, 38; 6:11; 7:17,
45, 58; 12:7; 13:51

SOVEREIGNTY → SOVEREIGN

Da 4: 3 his **s** is from generation to generation.
4:34 For his **s** is an everlasting **s**,

SOW → SOWED, SOWER, SOWING,
SOWN, SOWS

Ex 23:10 For six years you shall **s** your land
Job 4: 8 who plow iniquity and **s** trouble
Ps 126: 5 **s** in tears reap with shouts of joy.
Ecc 11: 6 In the morning **s** your seed,
Hos 8: 7 they **s** the wind, and they shall reap
10:12 **S** for yourselves righteousness;
Mt 6:26 they neither **s** nor reap nor gather
13: 3 A sower went out to **s**.
1Co 15:36 What you **s** does not come to life
unless it dies.
2Pe 2:22 "The **s** is washed only to wallow in
the mud."
2Es 9:31 For I **s** my law in you,

SOWED → SOW

Mt 13:24 to someone who **s** good seed
Lk 13:19 took and **s** in the garden;

SOWER → SOW

Isa 55:10 seed to the **s** and bread to the eater,
Mt 13:18 "Hear then the parable of the **s**.
Jn 4:36 **s** and reaper may rejoice together.
2Co 9:10 supplies seed to the **s**

SOWING → SOW

Zec 8:12 For there shall be a **s** of peace;
2Co 9:10 multiply your seed for **s**

SOWN → SOW

Mk 4:15 away the word that is **s** in them.
1Co 9:11 If we have **s** spiritual good among
15:42 What is **s** is perishable,
2Es 4:28 about which you ask me has been **s**,
8:41 all that have been **s** will come up in

SOWS → SOW

Pr 22: 8 **s** injustice will reap calamity,
Mk 4:14 The sower **s** the word.
Jn 4:37 'One **s** and another reaps.'
2Co 9: 6 who **s** sparingly will also reap

SPACIOUS

Ps 66:12 brought us out to a **s** place.

SPAN

Ps 90:10 then their **s** is only toil and trouble;
Isa 40:12 marked off the heavens with a **s**,
Mt 6:27 add a single hour to your **s** of life?

SPARE → SPARED, SPARINGLY

Ps 78:50 he did not **s** them from death,
119:88 In your steadfast love **s** my life,
Eze 6: 8 But I will **s** some.
Ro 11:21 perhaps he will not **s** you.
2Pe 2: 4 if God did not **s** the angels when
2Es 8:45 But **s** your people and have mercy

SPARED → SPARE

Ge 12:13 my life may be **s** on your account."
Jos 6:25 all who belonged to her, Joshua **s**.

SPARINGLY* → SPARE

2Co 9: 6 who sows **s** will also reap **s**,

SPARROW → SPARROWS

Ps 84: 3 Even the **s** finds a home,

SPARROWS → SPARROW

Mt 10:29 Are not two **s** sold for a penny?
Lk 12: 7 you are of more value than many **s**.

SPAT → SPIT

Lk 18:32 mocked and insulted and **s** upon.
Jn 9: 6 he **s** on the ground and made mud

SPEAK → SPEAKER, SPEAKING, SPEAKS,
SPEECH, SPEECHLESS, SPOKE, SPOKEN

Ge 18:27 take it upon myself to **s** to the Lord,
37: 4 and could not **s** peaceably to him.
Ex 4:12 and teach you what you are to **s**."
33:11 Thus the LORD used to **s** to Moses
face to face,
Nu 12: 8 With him I **s** face to face—
22:35 but only what I tell you to **s**."
Dt 18:20 presumes to **s** in my name a word
1Sa 3: 9 calls you, you shall say, **'S**, LORD,
2Ki 18:26 **s** to your servants in the Aramaic
Job 13: 3 But I would **s** to the Almighty,
Ps 49: 3 My mouth shall **s** wisdom;
135:16 They have mouths, but they do not **s**
Pr 23: 9 Do not **s** in the hearing of a fool,
31: 8 **S** out for those who cannot **s**,
Ecc 3: 7 time to keep silence, and a time to **s**;
Isa 28:11 with alien tongue he will **s** to this
40: 2 **S** tenderly to Jerusalem, and cry to
Jer 10: 5 a cucumber field, and they cannot **s**;
Eze 3:18 or **s** to warn the wicked from their
Da 7:25 shall **s** words against the Most High,
Mt 13:13 The reason I **s** to them in parables is
Mk 7:37 the deaf to hear and the mute to **s**."
Jn 12:49 about what to say and what to **s**.
Ac 2: 4 began to **s** in other languages,
4:18 and ordered them not to **s**
1Co 12:30 Do all **s** in tongues?
13: 1 If I **s** in the tongues of mortals and
14: 2 For those who **s** in a tongue do not
s to other people but to God;
14:19 church I would rather **s** five words
Eph 4:25 **s** the truth to our neighbors,
Jas 1:19 be quick to listen, slow to **s**,
Sir 4:25 Never **s** against the truth,

SPEAKER → SPEAK

Ex 6:30 "Since I am a poor **s**,
1Co 14:11 I will be a foreigner to the **s** and the
s a foreigner to me.

SPEAKING → SPEAK

Dt 5:26 heard the voice of the living God **s**
Mt 10:20 the Spirit of your Father **s** through
Ac 2: 6 **s** in the native language of each.
10:46 they heard them **s** in tongues and
1Co 14:39 and do not forbid **s** in tongues;
Eph 4:15 But **s** the truth in love,

SPEAKS → SPEAK

Ex 33:11 as one **s** to a friend.
Mt 12:32 whoever **s** against the Holy Spirit
Lk 6:45 of the abundance of the heart that
the mouth **s**.
1Co 14: 5 greater than one who **s** in tongues,
Heb 11: 4 died, but through his faith he still **s**.

SPEAR → SPEARS

1Sa 17: 7 of his **s** was like a weaver's beam,
19:10 to pin David to the wall with the **s**;
20:33 But Saul threw his **s** at him to strike
Ps 46: 9 breaks the bow, and shatters the **s**;
Jn 19:34 the soldiers pierced his side with a **s**,

SPEARS → SPEAR

Isa 2: 4 and their **s** into pruning hooks;
Joel 3:10 and your pruning hooks into **s**;
Mic 4: 3 and their **s** into pruning hooks;

SPECIAL

Nu 6: 2 men or women make a **s** vow,

Ro 9:21 the same lump one object for **s** use
Gal 4:10 You are observing **s** days, and

SPECK
Mt 7: 4 'Let me take the **s** out of your eye, '

SPECTACLE
1Co 4: 9 we have become a **s** to the world,

SPEECH → SPEAK
Ex 4:10 I am slow of **s** and slow of tongue."
Ps 19: 2 Day to day pours forth **s**,
19: 3 There is no **s**, nor are there words;
Pr 4:24 Put away from you crooked **s**,
5: 3 and her **s** is smoother than oil;
29:20 you see someone who is hasty in **s**?
Jn 10: 6 Jesus used this figure of **s** with
2Co 8: 7 in faith, in **s**, in knowledge,
1Ti 4:12 set the believers an example in **s**
1Jn 3:18 let us love, not in word or **s**,
Sir 4:29 Do not be reckless in your **s**,

SPEECHLESS → SPEAK
Isa 35: 6 and the tongue of the **s** sing for joy.
2Pe 2:16 **s** donkey spoke with a human voice

SPEEDILY
Ps 31: 2 Incline your ear to me; rescue me **s**.
79: 8 your compassion come **s** to meet us,

SPELLS·
Dt 18:11 who casts **s**, or who consults ghosts

SPEND → SPENT
Ge 19: 2 we will **s** the night in the square."
Jdg 19:20 do not **s** the night in the square."
Isa 55: 2 Why do you **s** your money for that
2Co 12:15 I will most gladly **s** and be spent for you.

SPENT → SPEND
Mk 5:26 and had **s** all that she had;
Lk 6:12 and he **s** the night in prayer to God.
15:14 When he had **s** everything,

SPICES
Ex 25: 6 **s** for the anointing oil and for
1Ki 10:10 never again did **s** come in such
Jn 19:40 wrapped it with the **s** in linen cloths,

SPIED → SPY
Jos 6:22 said to the two men who had **s** out

SPIES → SPY
Ge 42: 9 He said to them, "You are **s**;
Nu 13:32 we have gone through as **s**
Jos 2: 1 two men secretly from Shittim as **s**,
Heb 11:31 she had received the **s** in peace.

SPIN
Mt 6:28 they grow; they neither toil nor **s**,

SPIRIT → SPIRITS, SPIRITUAL,
   SPIRITUALLY
Ge 6: 3 "My **s** shall not abide in mortals forever,
Ex 31: 3 and I have filled him with divine **s**,
Nu 11:25 **s** rested upon them, they prophesied.
24: 2 Then the **s** of God came upon him,
Dt 34: 9 Joshua son of Nun was full of the **s** of wisdom,
Jdg 6:34 the **s** of the LORD took possession of Gideon;
11:29 **s** of the LORD came upon Jephthah,
13:25 The **s** of the LORD began to stir him
14: 6 The **s** of the LORD rushed on him,
15:14 the **s** of the LORD rushed on him,
1Sa 10: 6 Then the **s** of the LORD will possess
16:13 the **s** of the LORD came mightily upon David
16:14 **s** of the LORD departed from Saul,
16:15 evil **s** from God is tormenting you.
28: 8 And he said, "Consult a **s** for me,
2Sa 23: 2 **s** of the LORD speaks through me,
2Ki 2: 9 inherit a double share of your **s**."

2:15 "The **s** of Elijah rests on Elisha."
2Ch 18:21 and be a lying **s** in the mouth of all his prophets.'
Ne 9:20 You gave your good **s** to instruct
Job 33: 4 The **s** of God has made me,
Ps 31: 5 Into your hand I commit my **s**;
34:18 and saves the crushed in **s**.
51:10 and put a new and right **s** within me.
51:11 do not take your holy **s** from me.
51:17 acceptable to God is a broken **s**;
106:33 for they made his **s** bitter,
139: 7 Where can I go from your **s**?
143:10 your good **s** lead me on a level path.
Pr 16:18 and a haughty **s** before a fall.
20:27 human **s** is the lamp of the LORD,
29:23 who is lowly in **s** will obtain honor.
Isa 11: 2 The **s** of the LORD shall rest on him,
32:15 until a **s** from on high is poured out
42: 1 I have put my **s** upon him;
44: 3 pour my **s** upon your descendants,
48:16 the Lord GOD has sent me and his **s**.
57:15 who are contrite and humble in **s**,
59:21 my **s** that is upon you,
61: 1 The **s** of the Lord GOD is upon me,
63:10 they rebelled and grieved his holy **s**;
Eze 3:12 the **s** lifted me up, and as the glory
11:19 and put a new **s** within them;
13: 3 prophets who follow their own **s**,
36:26 and a new **s** I will put within you;
Da 4: 8 endowed with a **s** of the holy gods
Joel 2:28 I will pour out my **s** on all flesh;
Zec 4: 6 Not by might, nor by power, but by my **s**,
Mt 1:18 to be with child from the Holy **S**.
3:11 baptize you with the Holy **S** and fire
3:16 he saw the **S** of God descending like a dove
4: 1 led up by the **S** into the wilderness
5: 3 "Blessed are the poor in **s**,
10:20 but the **S** of your Father speaking through you.
12:31 but blasphemy against the **S** will not be forgiven.
26:41 the **s** indeed is willing, but the flesh is weak."
28:19 name of the Father and of the Son and of the Holy **S**,
Mk 1: 8 will baptize you with the Holy **S**."
Lk 1:15 he will be filled with the Holy **S**.
1:35 "The Holy **S** will come upon you,
1:80 child grew and became strong in **s**,
3:16 He will baptize you with the Holy **S** and fire.
4: 1 Jesus, full of the Holy **S**,
4:18 "The **S** of the Lord is upon me,
11:13 the heavenly Father give the Holy **S**
23:46 into your hands I commend my **s**."
Jn 1:33 one who baptizes with the Holy **S**.'
3: 5 without being born of water and **S**.
3: 6 and what is born of the **S** is **s**.
3:34 for he gives the **S** without measure.
4:24 God is **s**, and those who worship him must worship in **s** and truth."
6:63 It is the **s** that gives life; the flesh is useless.
7:39 Now he said this about the **S**,
14:17 This is the **S** of truth,
14:26 But the Advocate, the Holy **S**,
15:26 the **S** of truth who comes from the Father,
16:13 When the **S** of truth comes,
20:22 said to them, "Receive the Holy **S**.
Ac 1: 5 Holy **S** not many days from now."
1: 8 the Holy **S** has come upon you;
2: 4 of them were filled with the Holy **S**
2:17 I will pour out my **S** upon all flesh,
2:38 will receive the gift of the Holy **S**.
4:31 filled with the Holy **S** and spoke the
5: 3 filled your heart to lie to the Holy **S**
6: 3 full of the **S** and of wisdom,
7:51 are forever opposing the Holy **S**,
8:15 that they might receive the Holy **S**

9:17 and be filled with the Holy **S**."
11:16 will be baptized with the Holy **S**.'
13: 2 and fasting, the Holy **S** said,
19: 2 not even heard that there is a Holy **S**
Ro 7: 6 the old written code but in the new life of the **S**.
8: 4 not according to the flesh but according to the **S**.
8: 5 their minds on the things of the **S**.
8: 9 not in the flesh; you are in the **S**,
8: 9 since the **S** of God dwells in you.
8: 9 not have the **S** of Christ does not belong to him.
8:13 by the **S** you put to death the deeds of the body,
8:15 you have received a **s** of adoption.
8:16 it is that very **S** bearing witness with our **s**
8:23 who have the first fruits of the **S**,
8:26 the **S** helps us in our weakness;
8:26 **S** intercedes with sighs too deep for
1Co 2:10 has revealed to us through the **S**;
2:14 not receive the gifts of God's **S**,
5: 3 absent in body, I am present in **s**,
6:17 united to the Lord becomes one **s**
6:19 your body is a temple of the Holy **S**
12: 4 are varieties of gifts, but the same **S**;
12:13 the one **S** we were all baptized into one body—
2Co 1:22 his seal on us and giving us his **S**
3: 3 not with ink but with the **S** of the
3: 6 the letter kills, but the **S** gives life.
3:17 the Lord is the **S**, and where the **S** of the Lord is, there is freedom.
5: 5 has given us the **S** as a guarantee.
7: 1 every defilement of body and of **s**,
Gal 3: 2 receive the **S** by doing the works of
3:14 might receive the promise of the **S**
5:16 Live by the **S**, I say, and do not
5:22 the fruit of the **S** is love, joy, peace,
5:25 let us also be guided by the **S**.
6: 8 but if you sow to the **S**,
Eph 1:13 the seal of the promised Holy **S**;
2:18 both of us have access in one **S**
4: 3 maintain the unity of the **S** in the
4: 4 There is one body and one **S**,
4:30 do not grieve the Holy **S** of God,
5:18 be filled with the **S**,
6:17 and the sword of the **S**,
Col 2: 5 in body, yet I am with you in **s**,
1Th 5:19 Do not quench the **S**.
5:23 may your **s** and soul and body be
2Th 2:13 through sanctification by the **S** and
1Ti 3:16 revealed in flesh, vindicated in **s**,
2Ti 1: 7 did not give us a **s** of cowardice,
1: 7 a **s** of power and of love and of
4:22 The Lord be with your **s**.
Heb 2: 4 and by gifts of the Holy **S**,
4:12 piercing until it divides soul from **s**,
6: 4 and have shared in the Holy **S**,
10:29 and outraged the **S** of grace?
1Pe 1: 2 sanctified by the **S** to be obedient
3: 4 lasting beauty of a gentle and quiet **s**
2Pe 1:21 moved by the Holy **S** spoke
1Jn 3:24 by the **S** that he has given us.
4: 1 Beloved, do not believe every **s**,
4:13 because he has given us of his **S**.
Jude 1:20 most holy faith; pray in the Holy **S**;
Rev 1:10 I was in the **s** on the Lord's day,
2: 7 what the **S** is saying to the churches.
4: 2 At once I was in the **s**,
Wis 1: 6 For wisdom is a kindly **s**,

EVIL SPIRIT Jdg 9:23; 1Sa 16:14, 15, 16, 23, 23; 18:10; 19:9; Ac 19:15, 16; Tob 6:8

HOLY SPIRIT Ps 51:11; Isa 63:10, 11; Mt 1:18, 20; 3:11; 12:32; 28:19; Mk 1:8; 3:29; 12:36; 13:11; Lk 1:15, 35, 41, 67; 2:25, 26; 3:16, 22; 4:1; 10:21; 11:13; 12:10, 12; Jn 1:33; 14:26; 20:22; Ac 1:2, 5, 8, 16; 2:4, 33, 38; 4:8, 25, 31; 5:3, 32; 6:5; 7:51, 55; 8:15, 17, 19; 9:17, 31; 10:38, 44, 45, 47; 11:15, 16, 24;

13:2, 4, 9, 52; 15:8, 28; 16:6; 19:2, 2, 6; 20:23,
28; 21:11; 28:25; Ro 5:5; 9:1; 14:17; 15:13,
16; 1Co 6:19; 12:3; 2Co 13:13; Eph 1:13;
4:30; 1Th 1:5, 6; 4:8; 2Ti 1:14; Tit 3:5; Heb
2:4; 3:7; 6:4; 9:8; 10:15; 1Pe 1:12; 2Pe 1:21;
Jude 1:20; Wis 9:17; Sus 1:45; 2Es 14:22

SPIRIT OF *GOD Ge 41:38; Nu 24:2; 1Sa
10:10; 11:6; 19:20, 23; 2Ch 15:1; 24:20; Job
27:3; 33:4; Eze 11:24; Mt 3:16; 12:28; Ro 8:9,
14; 15:19; 1Co 2:11; 7:40; 12:3; Eph 4:30; Php
3:3; 1Pe 4:14; 1Jn 4:2

SPIRIT OF THE *LORD Isa 61:1; Lk 4:18;
Ac 5:9; 8:39; 2Co 3:17; Wis 1:7

SPIRIT OF THE †LORD Jdg 3:10; 6:34;
11:29; 13:25; 14:6, 19; 15:14; 1Sa 10:6; 16:13,
14; 2Sa 23:2; 1Ki 18:12; 22:24; 2Ki 2:16; 2Ch
18:23; 20:14; Isa 11:2; 40:13; 63:14; Eze 11:5;
37:1; Mic 3:8

UNCLEAN SPIRIT Zec 13:2; Mt 12:43; Mk
1:23, 26; 3:30; 5:2, 8; 7:25; 9:25; Lk 8:29;
9:42; 11:24

SPIRITS → SPIRIT

Nu 16:22 the God of the s of all flesh,
    27:16 the God of the s of all flesh,
Dt 18:11 or who consults ghosts or s,
Mt 12:45 seven other s more evil than itself,
Lk 4:36 power he commands the unclean s,
Ac 8: 7 unclean s, crying with loud shrieks,
1Co 12:10 to another the discernment of s,
    14:32 the s of prophets are subject to the
            prophets,
Gal 4: 3 we were enslaved to the elemental s
Col 2:20 you died to the elemental s of
Heb 12: 9 to be subject to the Father of s
1Pe 3:19 a proclamation to the s in prison,
1Jn 4: 1 but test the s to see whether they
            are from God;
Rev 1: 4 seven s who are before his throne,
    16:13 I saw three foul s like frogs coming
    22: 6 the God of the s of the prophets,

UNCLEAN SPIRITS Mt 10:1; Mk 1:27;
3:11; 5:12, 13; 6:7; Lk 4:36; 6:18; Ac 5:16; 8:7

SPIRITUAL → SPIRIT

Ro 1:11 some s gift to strengthen you—
    7:14 For we know that the law is s;
    12: 1 to God, which is your s worship.
    15:27 Gentiles have come to share in their
            s blessings.
1Co 2:13 interpreting s things to those who
            are s.
    3: 1 I could not speak to you as s people,
    9:11 If we have sown s good among you,
    10: 3 and all ate the same s food,
    12: 1 Now concerning s gifts, brothers
    14: 1 Pursue love and strive for the s gifts,
    15:44 physical body, it is raised a s body.
    15:46 the s that is first, but the physical,
Eph 1: 3 every s blessing in the heavenly
    5:19 sing psalms and hymns and s songs
    6:12 against the s forces of evil in the
Col 1: 9 of God's will in all s wisdom
    3:16 hymns, and s songs to God.
1Pe 2: 2 infants, long for the pure, s milk,
    2: 5 yourselves be built into a s house,

SPIRITUALLY → SPIRIT

1Co 2:14 because they are s discerned.

SPIT → SPAT

Dt 25: 9 his sandal off his foot, s in his face,
Mk 14:65 began to s on him, to blindfold him,
Rev 3:16 am about to s you out of my mouth.

SPLENDOR

Ex 15:11 majestic in holiness, awesome in s,
1Ch 16:29 Worship the LORD in holy s;
Job 37:22 Out of the north comes golden s;
Ps 21: 5 s and majesty you bestow on him.
    29: 2 worship the LORD in holy s.
    96: 9 Worship the LORD in holy s;

145: 5 On the glorious s of your majesty,
145:12 and the glorious s of your kingdom.
Eph 5:27 to present the church to himself in s,

SPLIT

Nu 16:31 the ground under them was s apart.
Zec 14: 4 Mount of Olives shall be s in two
Mt 27:51 earth shook, and the rocks were s.
Rev 16:19 The great city was s into three parts,

SPOIL

Ex 15: 9 I will overtake, I will divide the s,
Ps 119:162 rejoice like one who finds great s.

SPOKE → SPEAK

Ge 16:13 she named the LORD who s to her,
    39:10 she s to Joseph day after day,
Ex 20: 1 Then God s all these words:
Dt 4:12 the LORD s to you out of the fire.
    5: 4 LORD s with you face to face at the
Ps 99: 7 He s to them in the pillar of cloud;
Mt 9:33 the one who had been mute s;
Mk 4:33 many such parables he s the word
1Co 13:11 When I was a child, I s like a child,
2Co 4:13 "I believed, and so I s"—
Heb 1: 1 Long ago God s to our ancestors in
    13: 7 those who s the word of God to you;
2Pe 1:21 moved by the Holy Spirit s from
1Mc 1:24 and s with great arrogance.

SPOKEN → SPEAK

Nu 12: 2 the LORD s only through Moses?
Dt 18:22 prophet has s it presumptuously;
Job 42: 7 you have not s of me what is right,
Pr 25:11 A word fitly is like apples of gold
Jer 29:23 have s in my name lying words that
Heb 1: 2 last days he has s to us by a Son,

SPONGE

Jn 19:29 a s full of the wine on a branch

SPOT → SPOTS, SPOTTED

Eph 5:27 without a s or wrinkle or anything
1Ti 6:14 keep the commandment without s or
2Pe 3:14 at peace, without s or blemish;

SPOTS → SPOT

Jer 13:23 their skin or leopards their s?

SPOTTED → SPOT

Ge 30:32 from it every speckled and s sheep

SPRANG → SPRING

Mt 13: 5 and they s up quickly,
Mk 4: 5 it s up quickly, since it had no depth

SPREAD → SPREADING, SPREADS

Ge 10:32 from these the nations s abroad on
Ex 23: 1 You shall not s a false report.
    37: 9 cherubim s out their wings above,
Ps 5:11 S your protection over them,
    78:19 "Can God s a table in the wilderness
Pr 15: 7 The lips of the wise s knowledge;
Isa 48:13 my right hand s out the heavens;
Eze 1:11 Their wings were s out above;
Mk 11: 8 people s their cloaks on the road,
Jn 21:23 So the rumor s in the community
Ac 6: 7 The word of God continued to s;
    13:49 the word of the Lord s throughout
Ro 5:12 and so death s to all
2Th 3: 1 the word of the Lord may s rapidly
2Ti 2:17 and their talk will s like gangrene.

SPREADING → SPREAD

1Sa 2:24 that I hear the people of the LORD s
Pr 29: 5 is a s net for the neighbor's feet.

SPREADS → SPREAD

2Co 2:14 s in every place the fragrance

SPRING → SPRANG, SPRINGS

Ge 16: 7 found her by a s of water in
Ps 85:11 Faithfulness will s up from the
Isa 45: 8 earth open, that salvation may s up,
    58:11 like a s of water, whose waters

Jer 9: 1 O that my head were a s of water,
Jn 4:14 a s of water gushing up to eternal
            life."
Rev 21: 6 from the s of the water of life.

SPRINGS → SPRING

Pr 5:16 Should your s be scattered abroad,
Isa 49:10 and by s of water will guide them.
2Pe 2:17 waterless s and mists driven by
Rev 7:17 guide them to s of the water of life,

SPRINKLE → SPRINKLED, SPRINKLING

Nu 8: 7 s the water of purification on them,
Eze 36:25 I will s clean water upon you,
2Mc 1:21 priests to s the liquid on the wood

SPRINKLED → SPRINKLE

Lev 8:11 He s some of it on the altar seven
Heb 10:22 with our hearts s clean from an evil
1Pe 1: 2 and to be s with his blood:

SPRINKLING → SPRINKLE

Heb 11:28 kept the Passover and the s of blood,

SPROUT → SPROUTED

Nu 17: 5 the staff of the man whom I choose
            shall s;

SPURN → SPURNED

Ps 77: 7 "Will the Lord s forever,
Jer 14:21 Do not s us, for your name's sake;

SPURNED → SPURN

La 2: 6 indignation has s king and priest.
Hos 8: 3 Israel has s the good;

SPY → SPIED, SPIES, SPYING

Nu 13: 2 men to s out the land of Canaan,
Jos 6:25 whom Joshua sent to s out Jericho.

SPYING· → SPY

Ge 42:30 and charged us with s on the land.
Nu 13:25 they returned from s out the land.

SQUANDERED·

Lk 15:13 he s his property in dissolute living.

SQUARE → FOURSQUARE, SQUARES

Ge 19: 2 we will spend the night in the s."
Ex 27: 1 altar shall be s, and it shall be three
    28:16 It shall be s and doubled,
    30: 2 it shall be s, and shall be two cubits
Jdg 19:20 do not spend the night in the s."
Ne 8: 1 people gathered together into the s

SQUARES → SQUARE

Pr 1:20 in the s she raises her voice.

STABILITY

Pr 29: 4 By justice a king gives s to the land,

STAFF → STAFFS

Ge 38:25 the signet and the cord and the s."
    49:10 the ruler's s from between his feet,
Ex 4: 4 and it became a s in his hand—
    7:12 but Aaron's s swallowed up theirs.
    14:16 But you lift up your s,
Nu 17: 6 the s of Aaron was among theirs.
    20:11 struck the rock twice with his s;
Ps 23: 4 your rod and your s—they comfort
            me.
Mic 7:14 Shepherd your people with your s,
Zec 11:10 I took my s Favor and broke it,

STAFFS → STAFF

Nu 17: 7 Moses placed the s before the LORD

STAGES

Nu 33: 1 the s by which the Israelites went

STAGGER → STAGGERED

Isa 28: 7 with wine, they s with strong drink;
    29: 9 s, but not from strong drink!
Jer 25:16 and s and go out of their minds

STAGGERED' → STAGGER
Ps 107:27 they reeled and **s** like drunkards,

STAIN → STAINED
Jer 2:22 the **s** of your guilt is still before me,

STAINED → STAIN
Isa 63: 1 from Bozrah in garments **s** crimson?

STAKES
Isa 54: 2 your cords and strengthen your **s**.

STALK → STALKS
Ge 41: 5 and good, were growing on one **s**.

STALKS → STALK
Jos 2: 6 hidden them with the **s** of flax that
Ps 91: 6 or the pestilence that **s** in darkness,

STALL → STALLS
Mal 4: 2 leaping like calves from the **s**.

STALLS → STALL
1Ki 4:26 Solomon also had forty thousand **s**
Hab 3:17 the fold and there is no herd in the **s,**

STAND → STANDING, STANDS, STOOD
Ex 9:11 magicians could not **s** before Moses
14:13 "Do not be afraid, **s** firm,
Nu 30: 4 then all her vows shall **s,**
30: 4 which she has bound herself shall **s.**
Dt 10: 8 to **s** before the LORD to minister to
11:25 No one will be able to **s** against you;
Jos 3: 8 you shall be still in the Jordan.'"
10:12 "Sun, **s** still at Gibeon, and Moon,
2Ch 20:17 take your position, **s** still,
Job 19:25 at the last he will **s** upon the earth;
Ps 1: 5 wicked will not **s** in the judgment,
10: 1 O LORD, do you **s** far off?
24: 3 And who shall **s** in his holy place?
76: 7 can **s** before you when once your
130: 3 mark iniquities, Lord, who could **s?**
Isa 7: 9 If you do not **s** firm in faith, you
shall not **s** at all.
11:10 the root of Jesse shall **s** as a signal
29:23 will **s** in awe of the God of Israel.
Eze 22:30 and **s** in the breach before me
Mic 5: 4 he shall **s** and feed his flock in
Hab 3: 2 of your renown, and I **s** in awe,
Zec 14: 4 shall **s** on the Mount of Olives,
Mal 3: 2 and who can **s** when he appears?
Mt 12:25 house divided against itself will **s.**
Ro 5: 2 to this grace in which we **s;**
14: 4 for the Lord is able to make them **s.**
14:10 we will all **s** before the judgment
seat of God.
1Co 16:13 Keep alert, **s** firm in your faith,
2Co 1:24 because you **s** firm in the faith.
Eph 6:11 may be able to **s** against the wiles of
Col 4:12 you may **s** mature and fully assured
2Th 2:15 **s** firm and hold fast to the traditions
Rev 6:17 and who is able to **s?"**
Sir 5:10 **S** firm for what you know,

STANDARD → STANDARDS
2Ti 1:13 Hold to the **s** of sound teaching

STANDARDS → STANDARD
Jn 8:15 You judge by human **s;** I judge no
1Co 1:26 of you were wise by human **s,**
2Co 10: 3 not wage war according to human **s;**

STANDING → STAND
Ge 18:22 remained **s** before the LORD.
Ex 3: 5 on which you are **s** is holy ground."
Nu 22:23 donkey saw the angel of the LORD **s**
Jos 4:10 the ark remained **s** in the middle of
the Jordan,
2Ch 18:18 all the host of heaven **s** to the right
Am 7: 7 Lord was **s** beside a wall built with
9: 1 I saw the LORD **s** beside the altar,
Zec 1: 8 He was **s** among the myrtle trees in
3: 1 showed me the high priest Joshua **s**
3: 1 Satan **s** at his right hand to accuse

Ac 7:55 saw the glory of God and Jesus **s**
1Co 10:12 So if you think you are **s,**
1Ti 3:13 serve well as deacons gain a good **s**
Jas 5: 9 See, the Judge is **s** at the doors!
Rev 3:20 I am **s** at the door, knocking;
7: 9 **s** before the throne and before the
Lamb,
20:12 **s** before the throne, and books were
opened.

STANDS → STAND
1Ki 7:27 He also made the ten **s** of bronze;
2Ki 25:13 the **s** and the bronze sea that were
Ps 26:12 My foot **s** on level ground;
Isa 3:13 he **s** to judge the peoples.
Jn 1:26 **s** one whom you do not know,
2Ti 2:19 God's firm foundation **s,** bearing

STAR → STARS
Nu 24:17 a **s** shall come out of Jacob,
Isa 14:12 are fallen from heaven, O Day **S,**
Mt 2: 2 For we observed his **s** at its rising,
2Pe 1:19 day dawns and the morning **s** rises
Rev 2:28 I will also give the morning **s.**
8:11 The name of the **s** is Wormwood.
9: 1 saw a **s** that had fallen from heaven
22:16 the descendant of David, the bright
morning **s."**
Sir 50: 6 Like the morning **s** among the

STARS → STAR
Ge 1:16 to rule the night—and the **s.**
15: 5 toward heaven and count the **s,**
37: 9 eleven **s** were bowing down to me."
Dt 1:10 you are as numerous as the **s** of
Job 38: 7 when the morning **s** sang together
Ps 148: 3 praise him, all you shining **s!**
Isa 14:13 raise my throne above the **s** of God;
Da 12: 3 like the **s** forever and ever.
Joel 2:10 and the **s** withdraw their shining.
Mk 13:25 the **s** will be falling from heaven,
Php 2:15 you shine like **s** in the world.
Rev 1:16 In his right hand he held seven **s,**
6:13 and the **s** of the sky fell to the earth
8:12 of the moon, and a third of the **s,**
12: 1 on her head a crown of twelve **s.**
12: 4 a third of the **s** of heaven and threw
Aza 1:41 Bless the Lord, **s** of heaven;
2Es 7:39 a day that has no sun or moon or **s,**

STATUE
Da 2:31 there was a great **s.**
3: 1 a golden **s** whose height was sixty
Ac 19:35 and of the **s** that fell from heaven?

STATURE
1Sa 2:26 Samuel continued to grow both in **s**

STATUTE → STATUTES
Lev 16:29 This shall be a **s** to you forever:
Nu 19:21 It shall be a perpetual **s** for them.
Ps 81: 4 For it is a **s** for Israel,

STATUTES → STATUTE
Ge 26: 5 commandments, my **s,** and my laws.
Ex 15:26 commandments and keep all his **s,**
Dt 4: 1 give heed to the **s** and ordinances
1Ki 3: 3 walking in the **s** of his father David;
11:33 keeping my **s** and my ordinances,
Ne 9:13 good **s** and commandments,
Ps 119: 8 I will observe your **s;**
Isa 24: 5 transgressed laws, violated the **s,**
Sir 6:37 Reflect on the **s** of the Lord,
2Es 7:11 and when Adam transgressed my **s,**

STAY → STAYED
Ex 16:29 each of you **s** where you are;
Pr 7:11 her feet do not **s** at home;

STAYED → STAY
Lk 2:43 the boy Jesus **s** behind in Jerusalem,

STEADFAST
Ex 15:13 "In your **s** love you led

34: 6 abounding in **s** love and faithfulness
Nu 14:18 and abounding in **s** love,
2Sa 7:15 I will not take my **s** love from him,
Ne 9:32 keeping covenant and **s** love—
Ps 13: 5 But I trusted in your **s** love;
57: 7 My heart is **s,** O God, my heart is **s.**
108: 1 My heart is **s,** O God, my heart is **s;**
119: 5 that my ways may be **s** in keeping
136: 1 for his **s** love endures forever.
Isa 26: 3 Those of **s** mind you keep in peace
Joel 2:13 to anger, and abounding in **s** love,
Jnh 4: 2 to anger, and abounding in **s** love,
Heb 6:19 a sure and **s** anchor of the soul,
1Pe 5: 9 Resist him, **s** in your faith,

STEADFAST LOVE Ge 24:12, 14, 27;
32:10; 39:21; Ex 15:13; 20:6; 34:6, 7; Nu
14:18, 19; Dt 5:10; 2Sa 2:6; 7:15; 15:20;
22:51; 1Ki 3:6, 6; 8:23; 1Ch 16:34, 41; 17:13;
2Ch 1:8; 5:13; 6:14, 42; 7:3, 6; 20:21; Ezr
3:11; 7:28; 9:9; Ne 1:5; 9:17, 32; 13:22; Job
10:12; Ps 5:7; 6:4; 13:5; 17:7; 18:50; 21:7;
25:6, 7, 10; 26:3; 31:7, 16, 21; 32:10; 33:5, 18,
22; 36:5, 7, 10; 40:10, 11; 42:8; 44:26; 48:9;
51:1; 52:8; 57:3, 10; 59:10, 16, 17; 61:7;
62:12; 63:3; 66:20; 69:13, 16; 77:8; 85:7, 10;
86:5, 13, 15; 88:11; 89:1, 2, 14, 24, 28, 33, 49;
90:14; 92:2; 94:18; 98:3; 100:5; 103:4, 8, 11,
17; 106:1, 7, 45; 107:1, 8, 15, 21, 31, 43;
108:4; 109:21, 26; 115:1; 117:2; 118:1, 2, 3, 4,
29; 119:41, 64, 76, 88, 124, 149, 159; 130:7;
136:1, 2, 3, 4, 5, 6, 7, 8, 9, 10, 11, 12, 13, 14,
15, 16, 17, 18, 19, 20, 21, 22, 23, 24, 25, 26;
138:2, 8; 143:8, 12; 145:8; 147:11; Isa 16:5;
54:10; 63:7; Jer 9:24; 16:5; 32:18; 33:11; La
3:22, 32; Da 9:4; Hos 2:19; 6:6; 10:12; Joel
2:13; Jnh 4:2

STEADY
Ex 17:12 so his hands were **s** until the sun set.

STEAL → STEALING, STOLE, STOLEN
Ge 31:30 why did you **s** my gods?'"
Ex 20:15 You shall not **s**.
Dt 5:19 Neither shall you **s**.
Jer 23:30 who **s** my words from one another.
Mt 6:19 and where thieves break in and **s;**
19:18 not commit adultery; You shall not **s**
Jn 10:10 The thief comes only to **s** and kill
Ro 2:21 preach against stealing, do you **s?**
13: 9 shall not murder; You shall not **s;**

STEALING → STEAL
Ro 2:21 you preach against **s,** do you steal?

STEPHEN'
Early church leader (Ac 6:5). Arrested (Ac 6:8-
15). Speech to Sanhedrin (Ac 7). Stoned (Ac
7:54-60; 8:2; 11:19; 22:20).

STEPS
Ex 20:26 You shall not go up by **s** to my altar,
Ps 37:23 Our **s** are made firm by the LORD,
Pr 5: 5 her **s** follow the path to Sheol.
14:15 but the clever consider their **s**.
16: 9 but the LORD directs the **s**.
20:24 All our **s** are ordered by the LORD;
Jer 10:23 as they walk cannot direct their **s**.
1Pe 2:21 so that you should follow in his **s**.

STEW
Ge 25:29 Once when Jacob was cooking a **s,**
2Ki 4:39 and cut them up into the pot of **s,**

STEWARD → STEWARDS
Jn 2: 9 the **s** tasted the water that
Tit 1: 7 a bishop, as God's **s,** must be
blameless.

STEWARDS → STEWARD
1Co 4: 2 it is required of **s** that they be found
trustworthy.
1Pe 4:10 good **s** of the manifold grace of God

STICK → STICKS

2Ki 6: 6 showed him the place, he cut off a **s**,
Eze 37:16 take a **s** and write on it, "For Judah,
    37:16 then take another **s** and write on it,
    37:16 "For Joseph (the **s** of Ephraim) and
Mt 27:48 on a **s**, and gave it to him to drink.

STICKS → STICK

Pr 18:24 a true friend **s** closer than one's
           nearest kin.

STIFF-NECKED → NECK, STIFFENED

Ex 32: 9 "I have seen this people, how **s** they
    34: 9 Although this is a **s** people,
Ac   7:51 "You **s** people, uncircumcised in
Bar 2:30 for they are a **s** people.

STIFFENED → STIFF-NECKED

2Ch 36:13 he **s** his neck and hardened their heart
Jer 19:15 because they have **s** their necks,

STILL → STILLBORN

Ex 14:14 and you have only to keep **s**."
Jos 10:13 sun stood **s**, and the moon stopped,
Ps   37: 7 Be **s** before the Lord, and wait
    46:10 "Be **s**, and know that I am God!
    83: 1 not hold your peace or be **s**, O God!
    89: 9 when its waves rise, you **s** them.
Ecc   2: 3 mind **s** guiding me with wisdom—
Da 11:35 there is **s** an interval until the time
Hab 3:11 moon stood **s** in its exalted place,
Mk 4:39 and said to the sea, "Peace! Be **s**!"
    8:17 you **s** not perceive or understand?
Ro   5: 8 while we **s** were sinners Christ died
          for us.
Heb 11: 4 but through his faith he **s** speaks.
Rev 22:11 and the righteous **s** do right,

STILLBORN* → BEAR, STILL

Nu 12:12 Do not let her be like one **s**,
Job 3:16 why was I not buried like a **s** child,
Ecc   6: 3 I say that a **s** child is better off than

STING

1Co 15:55 Where, O death, is your **s**?"

STINGY

Pr 23: 6 Do not eat the bread of the **s**;

STIR → STIRRED, STIRS

Ps 78:38 and did not **s** up all his wrath.
    80: 2 **S** up your might, and come to save
SS   2: 7 do not **s** up or awaken love

STIRRED → STIR

Hag 1:14 Lord **s** up the spirit of Zerubbabel
Ac 13:50 and **s** up persecution against Paul
Sir 51:21 My heart was **s** to seek her;

STIRS → STIR

Pr 10:12 Hatred **s** up strife, but love covers
    15: 1 but a harsh word **s** up anger.
    28:25 The greedy person **s** up strife,
    29:22 One given to anger **s** up strife,
Lk 23: 5 "He **s** up the people by teaching

STOIC*

Ac 17:18 Epicurean and **S** philosophers

STOLE → STEAL

Ge 31:19 **s** her father's household gods.
2Sa 15: 6 Absalom **s** the hearts of the people
Mt 28:13 **s** him away while we were asleep.'

STOLEN → STEAL

Pr   9:17 "**S** water is sweet, and bread eaten

STOMACH

Eze 3: 3 ethat I give you and fill your **s**
Mk   7:19 not the heart but the **s**,
1Co 6:13 "Food is meant for the **s** and the **s**
1Ti 5:23 a little wine for the sake of your **s**
Rev 10: 9 it will be bitter to your **s**,

STONE → CORNERSTONE, MILLSTONE, STONED, STONES, STONING

Ge 28:18 the **s** that he had put under his head
    31:45 So Jacob took a **s**, and set it up as a
    35:14 had spoken with him, a pillar of **s**;
Ex 17: 4 They are almost ready to **s** me."
    28:10 six of their names on the one **s**,
    28:10 of the remaining six on the other **s**,
    31:18 tablets of **s**, written with the finger
          of God.
    34: 1 "Cut two tablets of **s** like the former
Dt   4:13 and he wrote them on two **s** tablets.
    16:22 nor shall you set up a **s** pillar—
    28:36 serve other gods, of wood and **s**.
1Sa 7:12 a **s** and set it up between Mizpah
    17:50 the Philistine with a sling and a **s**,
Ps   91:12 will not dash your foot against a **s**.
  118:22 The **s** that the builders rejected has
Isa   8:14 a sanctuary, a **s** one strikes against;
    28:16 in Zion a foundation **s**, a tested **s**,
Jer   3: 9 committing adultery with **s** and tree.
Eze 11:19 the heart of **s** from their flesh and
    36:26 from your body the heart of **s**
Zec   3: 9 on a single **s** with seven facets,
Mt   4: 6 will not dash your foot against a **s**.'"
    7: 9 child asks for bread, will give a **s**?
    24: 2 not one **s** will be left here upon
          another;
Mk 12:10 'The **s** that the builders rejected has
    16: 3 "Who will roll away the **s** for us
Lk   4: 3 command this **s** to become a loaf of
          bread."
    20:18 who falls on that **s** will be broken
Jn   8: 7 [without sin be the first to throw a **s**
          at her."]
    10:32 of these are you going to **s** me?"
    19:13 at a place called The **S** Pavement,
Ac   4:11 This Jesus is 'the **s** that was rejected
Ro   9:32 have stumbled over the stumbling **s**,
2Co 3: 3 not on tablets of **s** but on tablets of
          human hearts.
1Pe 2: 4 living **s**, though rejected by mortals
    2: 6 "See, I am laying in Zion a **s**,
Rev 2:17 and I will give a white **s**,

STONED → STONE

Nu 15:36 the camp and **s** him to death,
Jos   7:25 And all Israel **s** him to death;
1Ki 21:13 took him outside the city, and **s** him
2Ch 24:21 by command of the king they **s** him
Ac 14:19 Then they **s** Paul and dragged him
Heb 11:37 **s** to death, they were sawn in two,

STONES → STONE

Ex 28: 9 You shall take two onyx **s**,
    28:21 twelve **s** with names corresponding
Dt 27: 2 shall set up large **s** and cover them
Jos   4: 3 'Take twelve **s** from here out of the
1Sa 17:40 chose five smooth **s** from the wadi,
1Ki 18:31 Elijah took twelve **s**, according to
Ps 102:14 For your servants hold its **s** dear,
Ecc 3: 5 a time to throw away **s**, and a time
          to gather **s** together;
Mt   3: 9 God is able from these **s** to raise
    4: 3 command these **s** to become loaves
          of bread."
Mk 13: 1 large **s** and what large buildings!"
Lk 19:40 were silent, the **s** would shout out."
1Co 3:12 precious **s**, wood, hay, straw—
1Pe 2: 5 like living **s**, let yourselves be built
Sir 21:10 of sinners is paved with smooth **s**,

STONING* → STONE

1Sa 30: 6 for the people spoke of **s** him,
Ac   7:59 they were **s** Stephen, he prayed,
2Co 11:25 Once I received a **s**.

STOOD → STAND

Ge 28:13 the Lord **s** beside him and said,
Ex 15: 8 the floods **s** up in a heap;
Jos   3:17 **s** on dry ground in the middle of
    10:13 the sun **s** still, and the moon stopped

STICK

Lk 10:25 Just then a lawyer **s** up to test Jesus.
    22:28 who have **s** by me in my trials;
Jn 20:19 Jesus came and **s** among them and
2Ti   4:17 Lord **s** by me and gave me strength,
Jas   1:12 **s** the test and will receive the crown
1Mc 1:62 But many in Israel **s** firm

STOOP

Mk 1: 7 not worthy to **s** down and untie the

STOP → STOPPED

Ge 19:17 look back or **s** anywhere in the Plain
Job 37:14 **s** and consider the wondrous works
Mk   9:39 But Jesus said, "Do not **s** him;

STOPPED → STOP

Nu 16:48 and the living; and the plague was **s**.
Jos 10:13 The sun **s** in midheaven,
2Ki 4: 6 Then the oil **s** flowing.
Eze 1:21 when they **s**, the others **s**;
Mk 5:29 Immediately her hemorrhage **s**;

STORE → SHOREHOUSE, STOREHOUSES, STORING

Pr   7: 1 and **s** up my commandments
Mt   6:19 Do not **s** up for yourselves treasures
Lk 12:17 for I have no place to **s** my crops?'
Sir 29:12 **S** up almsgiving in your treasury,

STOREHOUSE → HOUSE, STORE

Dt 28:12 Lord will open for you his rich **s**,
Mal 3:10 Bring the full tithe into the **s**,

STOREHOUSES → HOUSE, STORE

Job 38:22 Have you entered the **s** of the snow,
Ps   33: 7 he put the deeps in **s**.
   135: 7 and brings out the wind from his **s**.
Isa 39: 2 armory, all that was found in his **s**.

STORING* → STORE

Ro   2: 5 you are **s** up wrath for yourself
1Ti 6:19 **s** up for themselves the treasure of

STORM

Ps 107:29 he made the **s** be still,
Jer 30:23 Look, the **s** of the Lord!
Jnh 1:12 this great **s** has come upon you."
Na   1: 3 His way is in whirlwind and **s**,

STRAIGHT → STRAIGHTFORWARD

Ps 107: 7 he led them by a **s** way,
Pr   3: 6 and he will make **s** your paths.
    4:25 and your gaze be **s** before you.
    11: 5 of the blameless keeps their ways **s**,
    15:21 of understanding walks **s** ahead.
Isa 40: 3 make **s** in the desert a highway for
          our God.
Mt   3: 3 'Prepare the way of the Lord, make
          his paths **s**.'"
Lk   3: 5 and the crooked shall be made **s**,
Jn   1:23 'Make **s** the way of the Lord, '"
Ac   9:11 Get up and go to the street called **S**,
2Pe 2:15 They have left the **s** road and have
Wis 10:10 she guided him on **s** paths;
Sir   2: 6 make your ways **s**, and hope in him.

STRAIGHTFORWARD* → STRAIGHT

Ecc 7:29 that God made human beings **s**,

STRAIN → STRAINING

Mt 23:24 **s** out a gnat but swallow a camel!

STRAINING → STRAIN

Php 3:13 what lies behind and **s** forward

STRANGE → STRANGER, STRANGERS

Dt 32:16 They made him jealous with **s** gods,
1Co 14:21 "By people of **s** tongues and by the
Heb 13: 9 away by all kinds of **s** teachings;
1Pe 4:12 something **s** were happening to you.

STRANGER → STRANGE

Ge 23: 4 a **s** and an alien residing among you;
Dt 10:19 You shall also love the **s**,
Mt 25:35 I was a **s** and you welcomed me,

Jn 10: 5 They will not follow a **s**,

STRANGERS → STRANGE

Dt 10:19 for you were **s** in the land of Egypt.
1Ch 16:19 of little account, and **s** in the land,
Pr 5:17 and not for sharing with **s**.
Ro 12:13 extend hospitality to **s**.
Eph 2:12 and **s** to the covenants of promise,
Heb 11:13 They confessed that they were **s**
13: 2 not neglect to show hospitality to **s**,
3Jn 1: 5 even though they are **s** to you;
1Mc 1:38 she became a dwelling of **s**;

STRAW

Ex 5:10 says Pharaoh, 'I will not give you **s**.
Isa 11: 7 and the lion shall eat **s** like the ox.
1Co 3:12 precious stones, wood, hay, **s**—

STRAY → ASTRAY, STRAYED

Ps 119:10 do not let me **s** from your
commandments.
Pr 7:25 do not **s** into her paths.
22: 6 and when old, they will not **s**.

STRAYED → STRAY

Hos 7:13 Woe to them, for they have **s** from
Wis 5: 6 we who **s** from the way of truth,

STREAM → STREAMS

Isa 2: 2 all the nations shall **s** to it.
Am 5:24 righteousness like an ever-flowing **s**
Mic 4: 1 above the hills. Peoples shall **s** to it,

STREAMS → STREAM

Dt 10: 7 to Jotbathah, a land with flowing **s**.
Ps 1: 3 like trees planted by **s** of water,
42: 1 As a deer longs for flowing **s**,
46: 4 a river whose **s** make glad the city
Ecc 1: 7 All **s** run to the sea,
Isa 35: 6 the wilderness, and **s** in the desert;
44: 4 like willows by flowing **s**.

STREET → STREETS

Pr 1:20 Wisdom cries out in the **s**;
Mt 6: 5 the synagogues and at the **s** corners,
Ac 9:11 and go to the **s** called Straight,
Rev 21:21 and the **s** of the city is pure gold,
22: 2 the middle of the **s** of the city.

STREETS → STREET

Ps 144:14 and no cry of distress in our **s**.
Zec 8: 5 of boys and girls playing in its **s**.
Mt 12:19 will anyone hear his voice in the **s**.

STRENGTH → STRONG

Ex 15: 2 The LORD is my **s** and my might,
Dt 33:25 and as your days, so is your **s**.
Jdg 16:15 have not told me what makes your **s**
1Sa 2: 1 my **s** is exalted in my God.
2Sa 22:33 with **s** has opened wide my path.
1Ch 16:11 Seek the LORD and his **s**,
16:28 ascribe to the LORD glory and **s**.
29:12 to make great and to give **s**
Ne 8:10 for the joy of the LORD is your **s**."
Job 12:13 "With God are wisdom and **s**;
Ps 18: 1 I love you, O LORD, my **s**.
21:13 Be exalted, O LORD, in your **s**!
28: 7 The LORD is my **s** and my shield;
29:11 May the LORD give **s** to his people!
46: 1 God is our refuge and **s**,
59: 9 O my **s**, I will watch for you;
59:17 O my **s**, I will sing praises to you,
65: 6 By your **s** you established the
mountains;
73:26 God is the **s** of my heart and
84: 5 Happy are those whose **s** is in you,
84: 7 They go from **s** to **s**;
96: 7 ascribe to the LORD glory and **s**.
105: 4 Seek the LORD and his **s**;
118:14 The LORD is my **s** and my might;
147:10 delight is not in the **s** of the horse,
Pr 24: 5 knowledge than those who have **s**;
30:25 a people without **s**, yet they provide
31:25 **S** and dignity are her clothing.

Isa 12: 2 LORD GOD is my **s** and my might;
40:26 he is great in **s**, mighty in power,
40:31 for the LORD shall renew their **s**,
Mic 5: 4 stand and feed his flock in the **s** of
Hab 3:19 GOD, the Lord, is my **s**;
Mk 12:30 all your mind, and with all your **s**.'
Lk 1:51 He has shown **s** with his arm;
10:27 and with all your **s**,
1Co 1:25 and God's weakness is stronger
than human **s**.
2Ti 4:17 Lord stood by me and gave me **s**,
Heb 11:34 won **s** out of weakness,
1Pe 4:11 serves must do so with the **s**
Jdt 9:11 your **s** does not depend on numbers,
1Mc 3:19 but **s** comes from Heaven.

STRENGTHEN → STRONG

Jdg 16:28 and **s** me only this once, O God,
2Ch 16: 9 to **s** those whose heart is true to him.
Ps 89:21 my arm also shall **s** him.
119:28 **s** me according to your word.
Isa 35: 3 **S** the weak hands, and make firm
41:10 I will **s** you, I will help you,
Eze 34:16 and I will **s** the weak,
Lk 22:32 have turned back, **s** your brothers."
Ac 15:32 to encourage and **s** the believers.
1Th 3:13 so **s** your hearts in holiness that you
2Th 2:17 and **s** them in every good work and
Heb 12:12 hands and **s** your weak knees,
1Pe 5:10 support, **s**, and establish you.

STRENGTHENED → STRONG

Job 4: 3 you have **s** the weak hands.
Eze 34: 4 You have not **s** the weak,
Ac 16: 5 So the churches were **s** in the faith
Heb 13: 9 well for the heart to be **s** by grace,

STRENGTHENS → STRONG

Isa 40:29 to the faint, and **s** the powerless.
Php 4:13 I can do all things through him who
s me.

STRETCH → OUTSTRETCHED, STRETCHED

Ex 3:20 will **s** out my hand and strike Egypt
14:16 and **s** out your hand over the sea
Ps 138: 7 you **s** out your hand, and your right
Zep 1: 4 I will **s** out my hand against Judah,
Mk 3: 5 said to the man, "**S** out your hand."
Ac 4:30 while you **s** out your hand to heal,
Sir 7:32 **S** out your hand to the poor,

STRETCHED → STRETCH

Ex 14:21 Moses **s** out his hand over the sea.
2Sa 24:16 the angel **s** out his hand toward
Jerusalem
1Ki 13: 4 that he **s** out against him withered
Isa 5:25 and his hand is **s** out still.
45:12 my hands that **s** out the heavens,
Jer 10:12 **s** out the heavens.
Mt 12:13 He **s** it out, and it was restored,

STRICKEN → STRIKE

Isa 53: 4 yet we accounted him **s**,
53: 8 **s** for the transgression of my people.

STRICT → STRICTEST, STRICTNESS

Ac 5:28 "We gave you **s** orders not to teach

STRICTEST* → STRICT

Ac 26: 5 the **s** sect of our religion and lived

STRICTNESS → STRICT

Jas 3: 1 teach will be judged with greater **s**.

STRIFE → STRIVE

Pr 17: 1 than a house full of feasting with **s**.
18: 6 A fool's lips bring **s**, and a fool's
20: 3 It is honorable to refrain from **s**,
22:10 Drive out a scoffer, and **s** goes out;
23:29 Who has sorrow? Who has **s**?
30:33 so pressing anger produces **s**.
Ro 1:29 Full of envy, murder, **s**, deceit,
Gal 5:20 enmities, **s**, jealousy, anger,

STRIKE → STRICKEN, STRIKES, STRUCK

Ge 3:15 he will **s** your head, and you will **s**
his heel."
Ex 3:20 stretch out my hand and **s** Egypt
12:12 I will **s** down every firstborn in the
17: 6 **S** the rock, and water will come out
Isa 11: 4 he shall **s** the earth with the rod of
Zec 13: 7 **S** the shepherd, that the sheep may
be scattered;
Mal 4: 6 come and **s** the land with a curse.
Mk 14:27 'I will **s** the shepherd, and the sheep
will be scattered.'
Rev 11: 6 to **s** the earth with every kind of
19:15 to **s** down the nations,

STRIKES → STRIKE

Ex 21:12 Whoever **s** a person mortally shall
Mt 5:39 **s** you on the right cheek,

STRIPPED

Ge 37:23 they **s** him of his robe, the long robe
Ex 33: 6 **s** themselves of their ornaments,
Mt 27:28 They **s** him and put a scarlet robe
Ac 16:22 the magistrates had them **s** of their

STRIPS

Jn 11:44 hands and feet bound with **s** of cloth

STRIVE → STRIFE, STRIVING

Isa 45: 9 Woe to you who **s** with your Maker,
Mt 6:33 But **s** first for the kingdom of God
Ro 9:30 who did not **s** for righteousness,
1Co 12:31 But **s** for the greater gifts.
2Pe 3:14 **s** to be found by him at peace,

STRIVING* → STRIVE

Lk 12:29 do not keep **s** for what you are to eat
Php 1:27 **s** side by side with one mind for the

STROKE

Mt 5:18 not one letter, not one **s** of a letter,
Lk 16:17 than for one **s** of a letter in the law

STRONG → STRENGTH, STRENGTHEN, STRENGTHENED, STRENGTHENS, STRONGER, STRONGHOLD, STRONGHOLDS

Dt 31: 6 Be **s** and bold; have no fear
Jos 1: 6 Be **s** and courageous; for you shall
10:25 be a strong and courageous for
2Sa 10:12 Be **s**, and let us be courageous for
1Ki 2: 2 to go the way of all the earth. Be **s**,
1Ch 22:13 Be **s** and of good courage.
28:20 "Be **s** and of good courage, and act.
2Ch 32: 7 "Be **s** and of good courage.
Ps 24: 8 The LORD, **s** and mighty,
31: 2 a **s** fortress to save me.
35:10 deliver the weak from those too **s**
140: 7 O LORD, my Lord, my **s** deliverer,
Pr 18:10 The name of the LORD is a **s** tower;
31:17 with strength, and makes her arms **s**
Ecc 9:11 nor the battle to the **s**, nor bread to
SS 8: 6 for love is as **s** as death, passion fierce
Isa 35: 4 who are of a fearful heart, "Be **s**,
53:12 he shall divide the spoil with the **s**;
Jer 50:34 Their Redeemer is **s**; the LORD of
Eze 3:14 hand of the LORD being **s** upon me.
Da 2:40 shall be a fourth kingdom, **s** as iron;
Zec 8:13 Let your hands be **s**—
Mt 12:29 a **s** man's house and plunder his
Lk 1:80 child grew and became **s** in spirit,
2:40 child grew and became **s**, filled
Ro 15: 1 We who are **s** ought to put up with
1Co 1:27 in the world to shame the **s**;
16:13 in your faith, be courageous, be **s**.
2Co 12:10 whenever I am weak, then I am **s**.
Eph 6:10 be **s** in the Lord and in the strength
Col 1:11 be made **s** with all the strength
2Ti 2: 1 be **s** in the grace that is in Christ

STRONG DRINK Lev 10:9; Nu 6:3; 28:7; Dt 14:26; 29:6; Jdg 13:4, 7, 14; 1Sa 1:15; Pr 20:1; 31:4, 6; Isa 5:11; 24:9; 28:7, 7, 7; 29:9; 56:12; Mic 2:11; Lk 1:15

STRONGER → STRONG

2Sa 3: 1 David grew s and s,
1Co 1:25 God's weakness is s than human
strength.

STRONGHOLD → STRONG

1Sa 22: 4 all the time that David was in the s.
Ps 9: 9 The LORD is a s for the oppressed,
9: 9 a s in times of trouble.
18: 2 and the horn of my salvation, my s.
27: 1 The LORD is the s of my life;
144: 2 my s and my deliverer, my shield,
Na 1: 7 a s in a day of trouble;

STRONGHOLDS → STRONG

Am 6: 8 the pride of Jacob and hate his s;
2Co 10: 4 they have divine power to destroy s.

STRUCK → STRIKE

Ge 32:25 he s him on the hip socket;
Ex 12:29 At midnight the LORD s down all
Nu 20:11 and s the rock twice with his staff;
22:23 and Balaam s the donkey,
1Sa 17:49 and s the Philistine on his forehead;
Ps 78:20 he s the rock so that water gushed
Da 2:34 it s the statue on its feet of iron and
Ac 23: 3 yet in violation of the law you order
me to be s?"

STRUCTURE

Ezr 5: 3 this house and to finish this s?"

STRUGGLE → STRUGGLED

Eph 6:12 our s is not against enemies of
blood and flesh,
Heb 12: 4 In your s against sin you have not
yet resisted to to the point of

STRUGGLED → STRUGGLE

Ge 25:22 The children s together within her;

STUBBLE

Ex 15: 7 it consumed them like s.
Isa 33:11 conceive chaff, you bring forth s;
Mal 4: 1 arrogant and all evildoers will be s;

STUBBORN → STUBBORNLY,
STUBBORNNESS

Dt 9: 6 for you are a s people.
Ps 78: 8 a s and rebellious generation,
Hos 4:16 Like a s heifer, Israel is s;

STUBBORNLY → STUBBORN

Ex 13:15 When Pharaoh s refused to let us go,
Ac 19: 9 When some s refused to believe

STUBBORNNESS → STUBBORN

Dt 9:27 pay no attention to the s of this
Mk 16:14 for their lack of faith and s,

STUDENTS* → STUDY

Mt 23: 8 one teacher, and you are all s.

STUDIED* → STUDY

Ps 111: 2 s by all who delight in them.

STUDY → STUDENTS, STUDIED,
STUDYING

Ezr 7:10 Ezra had set his heart to s the law
Ecc 12:12 much s is a weariness of the flesh.

STUDYING* → STUDY

Ecc 12: 9 and s and arranging many proverbs.

STUMBLE → STUMBLED, STUMBLING

Ps 37:24 we s, we shall not fall headlong,
119:165 nothing can make them s.
Pr 3:23 securely and your foot will not s.
4:12 and if you run, you will not s.
Jer 13:16 before your feet s on the mountains
31: 9 path in which they shall not s;
Hos 14: 9 but transgressors s in them.
Mal 2: 8 you have caused many to s by your
instruction;
Mt 18: 9 And if your eye causes you to s,

Jn 11: 9 who walk during the day do not s,
Ro 9:33 a stone that will make people s,
1Pe 2: 8 "A stone that makes them s,
2: 8 s because they disobey the word,

STUMBLED → STUMBLE

Ro 9:32 have s over the stumbling stone,

STUMBLING → STUMBLE

Eze 14: 3 placed their iniquity as a s block
Mt 16:23 You are a s block to me;
18: 7 one by whom the s block comes!
Ro 9:32 have stumbled over the s stone,
11: 9 a s block and a retribution for them;
14:13 a s block or hindrance in the way of
1Co 1:23 a s block to Jews and foolishness to
8: 9 not somehow become a s block to
Sir 31:29 bitterness of spirit, to quarrels and s.

STUMP

Isa 6:13 The holy seed is its s.
11: 1 A shoot shall come out from the s
of Jesse,

STUPID

Pr 12: 1 those who hate to be rebuked are s.
2Ti 2:23 Have nothing to do with s and
Tit 3: 9 avoid s controversies, genealogies,

SUBDUE → SUBDUED

Ge 1:28 and fill the earth and s it;
1Ch 17:10 and I will s all your enemies.

SUBDUED → SUBDUE

Ps 47: 3 He s peoples under us, and nations

SUBJECT → SUBJECTED

Jdg 1:30 and became s to forced labor.
Ro 13: 1 be s to the governing authorities;
1Co 14:32 the spirits of prophets are s to the
prophets,
Gal 4:21 who desire to be s to the law,
5:18 you are not s to the law.
Eph 5:21 Be s to one another out of
reverence for Christ.
Tit 3: 1 Remind them to be s to rulers and
Sir 4:27 Do not s yourself to a fool,

SUBJECTED → SUBJECT

Ro 8:20 for the creation was s to futility,
1Co 15:28 When all things are s to him,

SUBMISSION* → SUBMIT

1Ti 2:11 a woman learn in silence with full s.
Heb 5: 7 was heard because of his reverent s.

SUBMISSIVE → SUBMIT

1Ti 3: 4 keeping his children s and respectful
Tit 2: 5 kind, being s to their husbands,

SUBMIT → SUBMISSION, SUBMISSIVE

Ps 81:11 Israel would not s to me.
Lk 10:17 your name even the demons s to us!
Ro 8: 7 it does not s to God's law—
Gal 5: 1 do not s again to a yoke of slavery.
Col 2:20 Why do you s to regulations,
Heb 13:17 Obey your leaders and s to them,
Jas 4: 7 S yourselves therefore to God.

SUCCEED → SUCCESS, SUCCESSFUL

1Ki 22:22 are to entice him, and you shall s;
Pr 15:22 but with many advisers they s.
Ecc 10:10 but wisdom helps one to s.
Ro 9:31 did not s in fulfilling that law.

SUCCESS → SUCCEED

Ge 24:12 please grant me s today and show
1Sa 18:14 David had s in all his undertakings;
Ne 2:20 is the one who will give us s,
Ps 118:25 O LORD, we beseech you, give us s!
Sir 9:11 Do not envy the s of sinners,
10: 5 Human s is in the hand of the Lord,

SUCCESSFUL → SUCCEED

Ge 24:56 the LORD has made my journey s;

Jos 1: 7 that you may be s wherever you go.

SUCCOTH

Ge 33:17 But Jacob journeyed to S,
Jdg 8:16 he trampled the people of S.

SUCH

Ps 139: 6 S knowledge is too wonderful for
144:15 people to whom s blessings fall;
Jer 5: 9 retribution on a nation s as this?
Mt 8:10 no one in Israel have I found s faith.
Jn 9:16 who is a sinner perform s signs?"
1Co 9:24 Run in s a way that you may win it.
2Co 3: 4 S is the confidence that we have
Gal 5:23 There is no law against s things.
Heb 7:26 that we should have a s high priest,
12: 3 Consider him who endured s
hostility
2Jn 1: 7 any s person is the deceiver and the
antichrist!
3Jn 1: 8 we ought to support s people,

SUDDEN → SUDDENLY

Pr 3:25 Do not be afraid of s panic,
1Th 5: 3 s destruction will come upon them,

SUDDENLY → SUDDEN

Mal 3: 1 Lord whom you seek will s come to
his temple.
Mt 28: 9 S Jesus met them and said,
Mk 13:36 find you asleep when he comes s.
Ac 9: 3 s a light from heaven flashed around

SUE → LAWSUIT, LAWSUITS

Mt 5:40 if anyone wants to s you and take

SUFFER → SUFFERED, SUFFERING,
SUFFERINGS, SUFFERS

Zec 10: 2 they s for lack of a shepherd.
Lk 22:15 this Passover with you before I s;
24:26 the Messiah should s these things
24:46 the Messiah is to s and to rise from
Ac 3:18 that his Messiah would s.
1Co 3:15 is burned up, the builder will s loss;
Heb 9:26 then he would have had to s again
1Pe 3:17 For it is better to s for doing good,
Rev 2:10 Do not fear what you are about to s.

SUFFERED → SUFFER

Php 3: 8 For his sake I have s the loss of all
Heb 2:18 he himself was tested by what he s,
5: 8 obedience through what he s;
1Pe 2:21 because Christ also s for you,
4: 1 Since therefore Christ s in the flesh,

SUFFERING → SUFFER

Job 2:13 they saw that his s was very great.
Isa 53: 3 a man of s and acquainted with
infirmity;
Mk 8:31 Son of Man must undergo great s,
Ro 5: 3 knowing that s produces endurance,
12:12 Rejoice in hope, be patient in s,
Php 1:29 but of s for him as well—
2Ti 1: 8 but join with me in s for the gospel,
Jas 5:10 As an example of s and patience,
1Pe 3:17 if s should be God's will,
Man 1: 7 and you relent at human s.

SUFFERINGS → SUFFER

Ro 5: 3 but we also boast in our s,
8:18 the s of this present time are not
worth comparing
2Co 1: 5 as the s of Christ are abundant for us
1: 7 we know that as you share in our s,
Php 3:10 sharing of his s by becoming like
1Pe 1:11 it testified in advance to the s
4:13 insofar as you are sharing Christ's s,

SUFFERS → SUFFER

Pr 13:20 but the companion of fools s harm.
1Co 12:26 If one member s, all suffer together
1Pe 4:16 Yet if any of you s as a Christian,

SUFFICIENT
2Co 12: 9 "My grace is **s** for you,

SUITABLE
Ge 49:28 each one of them with a **s** blessing.
Ecc 3:11 has made everything **s** for its time;

SULFUR
Ge 19:24 rained on Sodom and Gomorrah **s**
Ps 11: 6 On the wicked he will rain coals of fire and **s**;
Lk 17:29 it rained fire and **s** from heaven and
Rev 9:17 and **s** came out of their mouths.
14:10 with fire and **s** in the presence of the holy angels
19:20 the lake of fire that burns with **s**.
20:10 into the lake of fire and **s**,
21: 8 in the lake that burns with fire and **s**,

SUM → SUMMED
Ps 119:160 The **s** of your word is truth;
Ecc 7:25 wisdom and the **s** of things,

SUMMED* → SUM
Ro 13: 9 commandment, are **s** up in this word
Gal 5:14 the whole law is **s** up in a single commandment,

SUMMER
Pr 6: 8 it prepares its food in **s**,
Mk 13:28 its leaves, you know that **s** is near.

SUMMON → SUMMONS
Ps 68:28 **S** your might, O God; show your

SUMMONS → SUMMON
Ps 50: 1 and **s** the earth from the rising of

SUN → SUNSET
Jos 10:13 And the **s** stood still,
Jdg 5:31 your friends be like the **s** as it rises
Ps 72: 5 May he live while the **s** endures,
84:11 For the LORD God is a **s** and shield;
113: 3 the **s** to its setting the name of the
121: 6 The **s** shall not strike you by day,
136: 8 the **s** to rule over the day,
148: 3 and moon; praise him, all you
Ecc 1: 9 there is nothing new under the **s**.
SS 6:10 bright as the **s**, terrible as an army
Isa 60:19 The **s** shall no longer be your light
Joel 2:31 The **s** shall be turned to darkness,
3:15 The **s** and the moon are darkened,
Mic 3: 6 The **s** shall go down upon the
Mal 4: 2 for you who revere my name the **s**
Mt 5:45 he makes his **s** rise on the evil and
13:43 righteous will shine like the **s** in the
17: 2 and his face shone like the **s**,
Mk 13:24 **s** will be darkened, and the moon
Ac 2:20 The **s** shall be turned to darkness
Eph 4:26 not let the **s** go down on your anger,
Rev 1:16 his face was like the **s** shining with
8:12 and a third of the **s** was struck,
9: 2 the **s** and the air were darkened
10: 1 his face was like the **s**,
12: 1 a woman clothed with the **s**,
19:17 I saw an angel standing in the **s**,
21:23 no need of **s** or moon to shine on it,
22: 5 they need no light of lamp or **s**,
Aza 1:40 Bless the Lord, **s** and moon;

SUNG → SING
Mt 26:30 When they had **s** the hymn,
Aza 1:34 and to be **s** and glorified forever.

SUNSET → SET, SUN
Dt 24:15 pay them their wages daily before **s**,

SUPER-APOSTLES* → APOSTLE
2Co 11: 5 not in the least inferior to these **s**.
12:11 for I am not at all inferior to these **s**,

SUPERIOR
Heb 1: 4 having become as much **s** to angels
7: 7 that the inferior is blessed by the **s**.

SUPPER
Lk 22:20 he did the same with the cup after **s**,
1Co 11:25 way he took the cup also, after **s**,
Rev 19: 9 to the marriage **s** of the Lamb."

SUPPLICATION → SUPPLICATIONS
2Sa 24:25 LORD answered his **s** for the land,
Ps 6: 9 The LORD has heard my **s**;
Zec 12:10 a spirit of compassion and **s**
Eph 6:18 at all times in every prayer and **s**.

SUPPLICATIONS → SUPPLICATION
2Sa 21:14 God heeded **s** for the land.
Ps 143: 1 to my **s** in your faithfulness;
1Ti 2: 1 then, I urge that **s**, prayers,
Heb 5: 7 Jesus offered up prayers and **s**,

SUPPLIES
2Co 9:10 who **s** seed to the sower and bread

SUPPORT → SUPPORTED, SUPPORTS
Ps 18:18 but the LORD was my **s**.
Mk 7:11 'Whatever **s** you might have had
Ro 11:18 remember that it is not you that **s** the root,
3Jn 1: 7 accepting no **s** from non-believers.

SUPPORTED → SUPPORT
Ps 18:35 and your right hand has **s** me;

SUPPORTS → SUPPORT
Ro 11:18 but the root that **s** you.

SUPPRESS*
Ro 1:18 who by their wickedness **s** the truth.

SURE → SURELY, SURETY
Nu 32:23 and be **s** your sin will find you out.
Ps 19: 7 the decrees of the LORD are **s**,
132:11 a **s** oath from which he will not turn
Pr 4:26 and all your ways will be **s**
Isa 28:16 a **s** foundation: "One who trusts
Eph 5: 5 Be **s** of this, that no fornicator or
Heb 6:19 a **s** and steadfast anchor of the soul,
1Jn 2: 3 we may be **s** that we know him,
2: 5 we may be **s** that we are in him:

SURELY → SURE
Ge 28:16 "**S** the LORD is in this place—
50:24 but God will **s** come to you,
Ex 13:19 "God will **s** take notice of you,
Ps 23: 6 **S** goodness and mercy shall follow
54: 4 But **s**, God is my helper;
85: 9 **S** his salvation is at hand for those
Pr 23:18 **S** there is a future, and your hope
Isa 12: 2 **S** God is my salvation; I will trust,
53: 4 **S** he has borne our infirmities
Eze 33:15 they shall **s** live, they shall not die.
Mk 14:19 one after another, "**S**, not I?"
2Co 1:18 As **s** as God is faithful,

SURETY → SURE
Ge 43: 9 I myself will be **s** for him;
Pr 17:18 to become **s** for a neighbor.
Sir 8:13 Do not give **s** beyond your means;

SURPASS → SURPASSES, SURPASSING
Pr 31:29 "Many women have done excellently, but you **s** them all."

SURPASSES → SURPASS
Eph 3:19 the love of Christ that **s** knowledge,
Php 4: 7 the peace of God, which **s** all understanding,
Sir 25:11 Fear of the Lord **s** everything;

SURPASSING → SURPASS
Ps 150: 2 according to his **s** greatness!
2Co 9:14 pray for you because of the **s** grace
Php 3: 8 I regard everything as loss because of the **s** value

SURPRISE → SURPRISED
1Th 5: 4 for that day to **s** you like a thief;

SURPRISED → SURPRISE
1Pe 4:12 do not be **s** at the fiery ordeal that is

SURROUND → SURROUNDED, SURROUNDS
Ps 22:12 strong bulls of Bashan **s** me;
32: 7 **s** me with glad cries of deliverance.
125: 2 As the mountains **s** Jerusalem,
Hab 1: 4 The wicked **s** the righteous—

SURROUNDED → SURROUND
Ge 19: 4 people to the last man, **s** the house;
Jdg 19:22 the city, a perverse lot, **s** the house,
Ps 118:11 They **s** me, **s** me on every side;
Lk 21:20 you see Jerusalem **s** by armies,
Heb 12: 1 **s** by so great a cloud of witnesses,
Rev 20: 9 of the earth and **s** the camp of

SURROUNDS → SURROUND
Ps 32:10 love **s** those who trust in the LORD.
89: 8 Your faithfulness **s** you.
125: 2 so the LORD **s** his people,

SURVIVED → SURVIVES, SURVIVORS
Ne 1: 2 I asked them about the Jews that **s**,

SURVIVES → SURVIVED
1Co 3:14 has been built on the foundation **s**,

SURVIVORS → SURVIVED
Isa 1: 9 If the LORD of hosts had not left us a few **s**,
Eze 14:22 Yet, **s** shall be left in it,
Ro 9:29 "If the Lord of hosts had not left **s** to us,

SUSA
Ezr 4: 9 the Babylonians, the people of **S**,
Ne 1: 1 while I was in **S** the capital,
Est 1: 2 his royal throne in the citadel of **S**,

SUSANNA
Righteous woman wrongly accused of immorality (Sus 1:1-44); vindicated by Daniel (Sus 1:45-64).

SUSPENSE
Jn 10:24 "How long will you keep us in **s**?

SUSPICIONS*
1Ti 6: 4 dissension, slander, base **s**,

SUSTAIN → SUSTAINED, SUSTAINS
Ps 51:12 and **s** in me a willing spirit.
55:22 on the LORD, and he will **s** you;

SUSTAINED → SUSTAIN
Dt 32:10 He **s** him in a desert land,
Ne 9:21 Forty years you **s** them in the wilderness

SUSTAINS → SUSTAIN
Ps 3: 5 for the LORD **s** me.
Heb 1: 3 he **s** all things by his powerful word.

SWALLOW → SWALLOWED
Nu 16:34 they said, "The earth will **s** us too!"
Ps 21: 9 LORD will **s** them up in his wrath,
84: 3 a home, and the **s** a nest for herself,
Jnh 1:17 provided a large fish to **s** up Jonah;
Mt 23:24 You strain out a gnat but **s** a camel!

SWALLOWED → SWALLOW
Ge 41: 7 The thin ears **s** up the seven plump
Nu 16:32 earth opened its mouth and **s** them
Ps 106:17 The earth opened and **s** up Dathan,
1Co 15:54 "Death has been **s** up in victory."
2Co 5: 4 what is mortal may be **s** up by life.

SWAYED
2Ti 3: 6 and **s** by all kinds of desires,

SWEAR → SWEARING, SWEARS, SWORE, SWORN
Dt 10:20 and by his name you shall **s**.

32:40 I lift up my hand to heaven, and **s:**
Jos 2:12 **s** to me by the LORD that you
23: 7 or **s** by them, or serve them,
Ps 24: 4 and do not **s** deceitfully.
Isa 45:23 "To me every knee shall bow,
          every tongue shall **s.**"
Mt   5:34 Do not **s** at all, either by heaven,
Heb 6:13 had no one greater by whom to **s,**
Jas 5:12 Above all, my beloved, do not **s,**

SWEARING → SWEAR

Hos 4: 2 **S,** lying, and murder, and stealing

SWEARS → SWEAR

Zec 5: 3 and everyone who **s** falsely shall
Mt 23:20 So whoever **s** by the altar,
Sir 23:11 who **s** many oaths is full of iniquity,

SWEAT

Ge   3:19 By the **s** of your face you shall eat
Lk 22:44 [his **s** became like great drops of
          blood falling on the ground.]

SWEEP → SWEPT

Ge 18:23 indeed **s** away the righteous with
Ps 90: 5 You **s** them away; they are like a
Lk 15: 8 does not light a lamp, **s** the house,

SWEET → SWEETER

Ex 15:25 the water, and the water became **s.**
Job 20:12 wickedness is **s** in their mouth,
Ps 119:103 How **s** are your words to my taste,
Pr   9:17 "Stolen water is **s,** and bread eaten
    13:19 A desire realized is **s** to the soul,
    20:17 Bread gained by deceit is **s,**
Ecc 5:12 **S** is the sleep of laborers,
Isa 5:20 who put bitter for **s** and **s** for bitter!
Eze 3: 3 I ate it; and in my mouth it was as **s**
          as honey.
Joel 3:18 the mountains shall drip **s** wine,
Am   9:13 the mountains shall drip **s** wine,
Rev 10:10 it was **s** as honey in my mouth,

SWEETER → SWEET

Jdg 14:18 "What is **s** than honey?
Ps 19:10 **s** also than honey, and drippings of
   119:103 **s** than honey to my mouth!

SWELL

Dt   8: 4 your feet did not **s** these forty years.
Ne   9:21 not wear out and their feet did not **s.**

SWEPT → SWEEP

Ps 88:16 Your wrath has **s** over me;
Mt 12:44 it finds it empty, **s,** and put in order.
Rev 12: 4 His tail is **s** down a third of the stars

SWERVE → SWERVED

Pr   4:27 Do not **s** to the right or to the left;

SWERVED* → SWERVE

2Ti 2: ? have **s** from the truth by claiming

SWIFT → SWIFTLY

Ecc 9:11 the race is not to the **s,** nor the battle
Jer 46: 6 The **s** cannot flee away, nor can the
Ro   3:15 "Their feet are **s** to shed blood;
2Pe 2: 1 bringing **s** destruction on themselves

SWIFTLY → SWIFT

Dt 32:35 is at hand, their doom comes **s.**
Ps 147:15 to the earth; his word runs **s.**

SWINE

Mt   7: 6 do not throw your pearls before **s,**
Mk   5:12 "Send us into the **s;**
1Mc 1:47 to sacrifice **s** and other unclean
          animals,

SWORD → SWORDS

Ge   3:24 and a **s** flaming and turning to guard
Ex 18: 4 delivered me from the **s** of Pharaoh"
Nu 14: 3 into this land to fall by the **s?**
Dt 32:41 when I whet my flashing **s,**
Jos 5:13 standing before him with a drawn **s**

1Sa 17:45 "You come to me with **s** and spear
    17:47 LORD does not save by **s** and spear;
    31: 4 Saul took his own **s** and fell upon it.
2Sa 12:10 the **s** shall never depart from your
          house,
1Ch 21:30 he was afraid of the **s** of the angel
Ne   4:18 the builders had his **s** strapped at
Ps 22:20 Deliver my soul from the **s,**
    44: 3 for not by their own **s** did they win
          the land,
    44: 6 not in my bow do I trust, nor can
          my **s** save me.
    45: 3 Gird your **s** on your thigh, O mighty
Pr   5: 4 wormwood, sharp as a two-edged **s.**
    12:18 Rash words are like **s** thrusts,
Isa 2: 4 shall not lift up **s** against nation,
    49: 2 He made my mouth like a sharp **s,**
Jer 15: 2 and those destined for the **s,** to the **s;**
La   1:20 In the street the **s** bereaves;
Eze 5: 2 I will unsheathe the **s** after them.
Hos 2:18 and I will abolish the bow, the **s,**
Mic 4: 3 shall not lift up **s** against nation,
Mt 10:34 not come to bring peace, but a **s.**
    26:52 who take the **s** will perish by the **s.**
Lk   2:35 a **s** will pierce your own soul too."
Ac 12: 2 brother of John, killed with the **s.**
Ro 13: 4 authority does not bear the **s** in vain!
Eph 6:17 and the **s** of the Spirit, which is the
          word of God.
Heb 4:12 sharper than any two-edged **s,**
    11:34 escaped the edge of the **s,**
    11:37 in two, they were killed by the **s;**
Rev 1:16 mouth came a sharp, two-edged **s,**
     6: 4 and has given a great **s.**
    13:14 that had been wounded by the **s** and
    19:15 a sharp **s** with which to strike down
Sir 21: 3 All lawlessness is like a two-edged **s**
Pm 151: 7 But I drew his own **s;**

SWORDS → SWORD

Ps 57: 4 their tongues sharp **s.**
    64: 3 who whet their tongues like **s,**
Isa 2: 4 shall beat their **s** into plowshares,
Joel 3:10 Beat your plowshares into **s,**
Mic 4: 3 shall beat their **s** into plowshares,
Mk 14:48 come out with **s** and clubs to arrest

SWORE → SWEAR

Ge 26: 3 oath that I **s** to your father Abraham.
Ex   6: 8 the land that I **s** to give to Abraham,
    32:13 how you **s** to them by your own self,
Nu 14:30 shall come into the land in which I **s**
Dt   6:10 he **s** to your ancestors, to Abraham,
Ps 89:49 by your faithfulness you **s** to David?
   132:11 The LORD **s** to David a sure oath
Lk   1:73 that he **s** to our ancestor Abraham,
Heb 3:11 in my anger I **s,** 'They will not
          enter my rest.'"
     6:13 by whom to swear, he **s** by himself,
Rev 10: 6 and **s** by him who lives forever and

SWORN → SWEAR

Ge 22:16 "By myself I have **s,** says the LORD:
Ps 89:35 and for all I have **s** by my holiness;
   110: 4 The LORD has **s** and will not change
          his mind,
Am   4: 2 The Lord GOD has **s** by his holiness:
Heb 7:21 "The Lord has **s** and will not
          change his mind,

SYCAMORE

Lk 19: 4 and climbed a **s** tree to see him,

SYCHAR*

Jn   4: 5 came to a Samaritan city called **S,**

SYMBOL

1Co 11:10 a woman ought to have a **s** of
          authority on her head,

SYMPATHIZE*

Heb 4:15 do not have a high priest who is
          unable to **s** with our weaknesses,

SYMPATHY → SYMPATHETIC, SYMPATHIZE

Php 2: 1 any compassion and **s,**
1Pe 3: 8 all of you, have unity of spirit, **s,**

SYNAGOGUE → SYNAGOGUES

Mt 13:54 began to teach the people in their **s,**
Lk   4:16 he went to the **s** on the sabbath day,
     8:41 man named Jairus, a leader of the **s.**
Ac 13:14 the sabbath day they went into the **s**
    14: 1 and Barnabas went into the Jewish **s**
    18: 4 he would argue the **s** and would try
    18:26 He began to speak boldly in the **s;**
Rev 2: 9 and the **s** of Satan,
     3: 9 the **s** of Satan who say that they are

SYNAGOGUES → SYNAGOGUE

Mt   4:23 teaching in their **s** and proclaiming
     6: 2 as the hypocrites do in the **s** and
    10:17 to councils and flog you in their **s;**
Lk 12:11 When they bring you before the **s,**
Jn 18:20 always taught in **s** and in the temple,
Ac 13: 5 proclaimed the word of God in the **s**

SYNTYCHE*

Php 4: 2 and I urge **S** to be of the same mind

SYRIA → SYRIAN, SYROPHOENICIAN

Mt   4:24 So his fame spread throughout all **S,**

SYRIAN → SYRIA

Lk   4:27 none of them was cleansed except
          Naaman the **S.**"

SYROPHOENICIAN* → SYRIA

Mk   7:26 woman was a Gentile, of **S** origin.

T

TABERNACLE

Ex 25: 9 concerning the pattern of the **t**
    38:21 These are the records of the **t,** the **t**
          of the covenant,
    40:18 Moses set up the **t;** he laid its bases,
    40:34 the glory of the LORD filled the **t.**
Lev 8:10 the anointing oil and anointed the **t**
Nu   1:50 shall appoint the Levites over the **t**
1Ch 6:48 for all the service of the **t** of the
          house of God.

TABITHA* → =DORCAS

Disciple, also known as Dorcas, whom Peter
raised from the dead (Ac 9:36-42).

TABLE → TABLES

Ex 25:23 You shall make a **t** of acacia wood,
Nu   3:31 Their responsibility was to be the
          ark, the **t,**
Ps 23: 5 a **t** before me in the presence of my
          enemies;
    78:19 God spread a **t** in the wilderness?
1Co 10:21 You cannot partake of the **t** of the
          Lord and the **t** of demons.

TABLES → TABLE

Mk 11:15 he overturned the **t** of the money
          changers
Jn   2:15 the money changers and overturned
          their **t.**
Ac   6: 2 neglect the word of God in order to
          wait on **t.**

TABLET → TABLETS

Pr   3: 3 write them on the **t** of your heart.
     7: 3 write them on the **t** of your heart.
Isa 30: 8 Go now, write it before them on a **t,**
Lk   1:63 He asked for a writing **t** and wrote,

TABLETS → TABLET

Ex 31:18 gave him the two **t** of the covenant,

32:19 and he threw the **t** from his hands
Dt   10: 5 put the **t** in the ark that I had made;
2Co 3: 3 not on **t** of stone but on **t** of human
hearts.

TAIL → TAILS

Dt   28:13 make you the head, and not the **t;**
Jdg 15: 4 and he turned the foxes **t** to **t,**
Rev 12: 4 His **t** swept down a third of the
stars of heaven

TAILS → TAIL

Rev   9:10 have **t** like scorpions, with stingers,
9:19 their **t** are like serpents,

TAKE → TAKEN, TAKES, TAKING, TOOK

Ge   22: 2 "**T** your son, your only son Isaac,
Ex   6: 7 I will **t** you as my people,
34: 9 and **t** us for your inheritance."
Nu   1: 2 **T** a census of the whole
congregation
Dt   1: 8 go in and **t** possession of the land
12:32 do not add to it or **t** anything from
31:26 "**T** this book of the law and put it
1Sa   8:11 he will **t** your sons and appoint them
1Ki 11:34 not **t** the whole kingdom away from
19: 4 now, O LORD, **t** away my life,
1Ch 17:13 I will not **t** my steadfast love from
Job 23:10 But he knows the way that I **t;**
Ps   2:12 Happy are all who **t** refuge in him.
27:14 and let your heart **t** courage;
31:24 and let your heart **t** courage,
51:11 do not **t** your holy spirit from me.
118: 8 to **t** refuge in the LORD than to put
Hos   1: 2 **t** for yourself a wife of whoredom
14: 2 **T** words with you and return to the
LORD; say to him, "**T** away all guilt;
Mt   1:20 not be afraid to **t** Mary as your wife,
2:13 **t** the child and his mother, and flee
2:20 the child and his mother,
7: 5 first **t** the log out of your own eye,
7: 5 you will see clearly to **t** the speck
11:29 **T** my yoke upon you, and learn
16:24 deny themselves and **t** up their cross
17:27 **t** the first fish that comes up;
26:26 and said, "**T,** eat; this is my body."
Mk   2: 9 'Stand up and **t** your mat and walk'?
8:34 deny themselves and **t** up their cross
Lk   21: 7 sign that this is about to **t** place?"
Ac   1:20 another **t** his position of overseer.'
Eph   6:13 **t** up the whole armor of God,
1Ti   3: 5 how can he **t** care of God's church?
6:12 **t** hold of the eternal life,
Rev   1: 1 his servants what must soon **t** place;
4: 1 you what must **t** place after this."
5: 9 "You are worthy to **t** the scroll and
22:17 who wishes **t** the water of life as

TAKEN → TAKE

Ge   2:23 for out of Man this one was **t.**"
27:36 now he has **t** away my blessing."
Nu   8:16 I have **t** them for myself,
19: 3 **t** outside the camp and slaughtered
Jos   7:11 have **t** some of the devoted things;
Ecc   3:14 nothing can be added to it, nor
anything **t** from it;
Jer   13:17 the LORD's flock has been **t** captive.
38:28 until the day that Jerusalem was **t.**
Da   5: 2 his father Nebuchadnezzar had **t**
Zec   3: 4 I have **t** your guilt away from you,
Mt   13:12 even what they have will be **t** away.
24:40 one will be **t** and one will be left.
Jn   20:13 "They have **t** away my Lord,
1Ti   3:16 believed in throughout the world, **t**
up in glory.
Heb 11: 5 By faith Enoch was **t** so that he did
Rev   5: 8 When he had **t** the scroll,
Sir   44:16 Enoch pleased the Lord and was **t**

TAKES → TAKE

1Ki 20:11 not brag like one who **t** it off."
Ps   149: 4 the LORD **t** pleasure in his people;
Na   1: 2 LORD **t** vengeance on his adversaries

Mk   4:15 Satan immediately comes and **t**
away the word
Lk   6:30 and if anyone **t** away your goods,
Jn   1:29 "Here is the Lamb of God who **t**
away the sin of the world!
10:18 No one **t** it from me,
Rev 22:19 if anyone **t** away from the words of
Wis   5:15 the Most High **t** care of them.

TAKING → TAKE

Php   2: 7 **t** the form of a slave,

TALENT → TALENTS

Mt   25:25 and hid your **t** in the ground.

TALENTS → TALENT

Mt   25:15 to one he gave five **t,**

TALES*

1Ti   4: 7 profane myths and old wives' **t.**

TALITHA*

Mk   5:41 "**T** cum," which means, "Little girl,
get up!"

TALK → TALKING

Dt   6: 7 **t** about them when you are at home
1Co   4:20 depends not on **t** but on power.
Eph   4:29 no evil **t** come out of your mouths,

TALKING → TALK

Lk   9:30 Moses and Elijah, **t** to him.
24:32 burning within us while he was **t**

TALL → TALLER

1Ch 11:23 a man of great stature, five cubits **t.**

TALLER → TALL

Dt   1:28 'The people are stronger and **t** than
1Sa 10:23 was head and shoulders **t** than any

TAMAR

1. Wife of Judah's sons Er and Onan (Ge 38:1-
10). Tricked Judah into fathering children when
he refused her his third son (Ge 38:11-30; Mt
1:3).
2. Daughter of David, raped by Amnon (2Sa
13).

TAMARISK

Ge   21:33 Abraham planted a **t** tree in
Beer-sheba,

TAMBOURINE → TAMBOURINES

Ex   15:20 Aaron's sister, took a **t** in her hand;
Ps   150: 4 Praise him with **t** and dance;

TAMBOURINES → TAMBOURINE

Jer   31: 4 Again you shall take your **t,**
Jdt   16: 1 Begin a song to my God with **t,**

TAME

Jas   3: 8 but no one can **t** the tongue—

TANNER

Ac   9:43 some time with a certain Simon, a **t.**

TARGET

Job 16:12 he set me up as his **t;**

TARSHISH

Ps   48: 7 an east wind shatters the ships of **T.**
Isa   60: 9 wait for me, the ships of **T** first,
Jnh   1: 3 But Jonah set out to flee to **T**
4: 2 why I fled to **T** at the beginning;

TARSUS

Ac   9:11 look for a man of **T** named Saul.
11:25 Barnabas went to **T** to look for Saul,

TASK → TASKMASTERS, TASKS

Ex   18:18 **t** is too heavy for you;
Ac   6: 3 whom we may appoint to this **t,**
1Ti   3: 1 the office of bishop desires a noble **t**

TASKMASTERS → MASTER, TASK

Ex   1:11 they set **t** over them to oppress them

TASKS → TASK

Lk   10:40 Martha was distracted by her many **t**
Sir   3:17 perform your **t** with humility;

TASSELS*

Dt   22:12 make **t** on the four corners of the

TASTE → TASTED

Ex   16:31 and the **t** of it was like wafers made
Ps   34: 8 O **t** and see that the LORD is good;
119:103 How sweet are your words to my **t,**
Pr   24:13 the honeycomb are sweet to your **t.**
SS   2: 3 and his fruit was sweet to my **t,**
Mt   16:28 not **t** death before they see the Son
Col   2:21 not handle, Do not **t,** Do not "touch"?
Heb   2: 9 he might **t** death for everyone.

TASTED → TASTE

Heb   6: 4 and have **t** the heavenly gift,
1Pe   2: 3 you have **t** that the Lord is good.

TATTOO*

Lev 19:28 or **t** any marks upon you:

TAUGHT → TEACH

Dt   31:22 Moses wrote this song and **t** it to
2Ki 17:28 him how they should worship
2Ch 17: 9 They **t** in Judah, having the book of
Ps 119:102 your ordinances, for you have **t** me.
Pr   4: 4 he **t** me, and said to me,
31: 1 An oracle that his mother **t** him:
Isa   40:14 Who **t** him knowledge,
50: 4 my ear to listen as those who are **t.**
54:13 children shall be **t** by the LORD,
Hos 11: 3 Yet it was I who **t** Ephraim to walk,
Mt   7:29 he **t** them as one having authority,
Jn   6:45 'And they shall all be **t** by God.'
1Co   2:13 in words not **t** by human wisdom
but by the Spirit,
Gal   6: 6 who are **t** the word must share
1Jn   2:27 just as it has **t** you, abide in him.

TAUNT → TAUNTS

Ps   102: 8 All day long my enemies **t** me;
Jer   24: 9 a disgrace, a byword, a **t,**

TAUNTS → TAUNT

La   3:61 You have heard their **t,** O LORD,

TAX → TAXES

2Ch 24: 6 Judah and Jerusalem the **t** levied
Mt   5:46 even the **t** collectors do the same?
11:19 a friend of **t** collectors and sinners!'
17:24 your teacher not pay the temple **t?"**
Lk   18:10 Pharisee and the other a **t** collector.

TAXES → TAX

Mt   22:17 Is it lawful to pay **t** to the emperor,
Ro   13: 7 **t** to whom **t** are due,

TEACH → TAUGHT, TEACHER,
TEACHERS, TEACHES, TEACHING,
TEACHINGS

Ex   4:12 be with your mouth and **t** you what
18:20 **t** them the statutes and instructions
Dt   1: 3 to **t** you to observe in the land that
11:19 **T** them to your children, talking
1Ki   8:36 when you **t** them the good way
Job   6:24 "**T** me, and I will be silent;
21:22 Will any **t** God knowledge,
Ps   25: 4 O LORD; **t** me your paths.
32: 8 and **t** you the way you should go;
34:11 I will **t** you the fear of the LORD.
51:13 I will **t** transgressors your ways,
78: 5 he commanded our ancestors to **t**
90:12 So **t** us to count our days that we
143:10 **T** me to do your will, for you are
my God.
Pr   9: 9 **t** the righteous and they will gain in
Jer   31:34 No longer shall they **t** one another,
Mic   4: 2 that he may **t** us his ways and that
Lk   11: 1 "Lord, **t** us to pray, as John taught
his disciples."

Jn   12:12 for the Holy Spirit will **t** you at
      14:26 will **t** you everything,
Ac   5:28 strict orders not to **t** in this name,
Ro   2:21 that **t** others, will you not **t** yourself?
1Co 11:14 Does not nature itself **t** you
Col   3:16 **t** and admonish one another in all
             wisdom;
1Ti   1: 3 not to **t** any different doctrine,
      2:12 I permit no woman to **t** or to have
             authority over a man;
2Ti   2: 2 people who will be able to **t** others
Tit   2: 1 **t** what is consistent with sound
             doctrine.
Heb 5:12 to **t** you again the basic elements of
      8:11 they shall not **t** one another or say
Jas   3: 1 that we who **t** will be judged
1Jn 2:27 so you do not need anyone to **t** you.

TEACHER → TEACH
Ecc 1: 1 words of the **T**, the son of David,
      12: 9 **T** also taught the people knowledge,
Mt 10:24 "A disciple is not above the **t**,
    22:36 "**T**, which commandment in the law
Lk   6:40 A disciple is not above the **t**,
     6:40 fully qualified will be like the **t**.
Jn   1:38 "Rabbi" (which translated means **T**)
     3: 2 you are a **t** who has come from God;
   13:14 Lord and **T**, have washed your feet,
Ro 12: 7 the **t**, in teaching;
1Ti   3: 2 respectable, hospitable, an apt **t**,
2Ti   1:11 a herald and an apostle and a **t**,

TEACHERS → TEACH
Ps 119:99 more understanding than all my **t**,
Pr   5:13 not listen to the voice of my **t** or
1Co 12:28 second prophets, third **t**;
Eph 4:11 evangelists, some pastors and **t**,
2Ti   4: 3 **t** to suit their own desires,
Heb 5:12 by this time you ought to be **t**,
Jas   3: 1 Not many of you should become **t**,
2Pe 2: 1 as there will be false **t** among you,

TEACHES → TEACH
Ps 25: 9 and **t** the humble his way.
    94:10 he who **t** knowledge to humankind,
Isa 48:17 who **t** you for your own good,
Mt   5:19 and **t** them will be called great in
             the kingdom
1Ti   6: 3 Whoever **t** otherwise and does not
1Jn 2:27 his anointing **t** you about all things,
Sir 33:29 for idleness **t** much evil.

TEACHING → TEACH
Ps 78: 1 Give ear, O my people, to my **t**;
Pr   1: 8 and do not reject your mother's **t**;
     3: 1 My child, do not forget my **t**,
     6:23 is a lamp and the **t** a light,
   13:14 The **t** of the wise is a fountain of life
Mt 28:20 and **t** them to obey everything
Mk   1:27 A new **t**—with authority!
    11:18 crowd was spellbound by his **t**.
Lk 19:47 Every day he was **t** in the temple.
Jn   7:17 will know whether the **t** is
Ac   2:42 devoted themselves to the apostles' **t**
Ro 12: 7 in ministering; the teacher, in **t**;
Col   1:28 and **t** everyone in all wisdom,
1Ti   4:13 of scripture, to exhorting, to **t**.
     5:17 those who labor in preaching and **t**;
     6: 3 and the **t** that is in accordance
2Ti   3:16 by God and is useful for **t**,
Tit   1:11 by **t** for sordid gain what it is not
             right to teach.
     2: 7 in your **t** show integrity, gravity,
2Jn 1: 9 Everyone who does not abide in the
             t of Christ,
     1: 9 abides in the **t** has both the Father
    1:10 to you and does not bring this **t**;
Rev 2:20 and is **t** and beguiling my servants

TEACHINGS → TEACH
Pr   7: 2 keep my **t** as the apple of your eye;
Col 2:22 are simply human commands and **t**.
Heb 13: 9 away by all kinds of strange **t**;

TEAR → TEARS, TORE, TORN
1Ki 11:13 however, **t** away the entire kingdom
Mk 2:21 from the old, and a worse **t** is made.
Rev 7:17 God will wipe away every **t** from
    21: 4 he will wipe every **t** from their eyes.

TEARS → TEAR
Job 12:14 If he **t** down, no one can rebuild;
Ps 42: 3 My **t** have been my food day and
   126: 5 sow in **t** reap with shouts of joy.
Pr 15:25 The Lord **t** down the house of the
             proud,
Isa 25: 8 Lord GOD will wipe away the **t**
             from all faces,
Jer   9: 1 and my eyes a fountain of **t**,
   31:16 weeping, and your eyes from **t**;
La   1:16 I weep; my eyes flow with **t**;
Lk   7:38 bathe his feet with her **t** and to dry
2Co 2: 4 anguish of heart and with many **t**,
Php 3:18 and now I tell you even with **t**.
Heb 5: 7 with loud cries and **t**,
Sus 1:35 Through her **t** she looked up toward
             Heaven,

TEETH → TOOTH
Nu 11:33 the meat was still between their **t**,
Job 19:20 I have escaped by the skin of my **t**.
Ps   3: 7 you break the **t** of the wicked.
    35:16 gnashing at me with their **t**.
Jer 31:29 and the children's **t** are set on edge."
Da   7: 7 had great iron **t** and was devouring,
Joel 1: 6 its **t** are lions' **t**,
Mt   8:12 will be weeping and gnashing of **t**."
Ac   7:54 became enraged and ground their **t**
Rev 9: 8 and their **t** like lions' **t**;
Sir 21: 2 Its **t** are lion's **t**,

TEKEL*
Da   5:25 MENE, MENE, **T**, and PARSIN.
     5:27 **T**, you have been weighed on the
             scales

TEKOA
2Sa 14: 4 the woman of **T** came to the king,
Am 1: 1 who was among the shepherds of **T**,

TELL → FORETOLD, FORTUNE-TELLING,
TELLING, TELLS, TOLD
Ex   6:11 "Go and **t** Pharaoh king of Egypt to
Nu 22:35 speak only what I **t** you to speak."
Ru   3: 4 and he will **t** you what to do."
1Sa 3:15 Samuel was afraid to **t** the vision to
2Ch 18:15 to **t** me nothing but the truth in the
Ps 50:12 "If I were hungry, I would not **t** you,
    66:16 I will **t** what he has done for me.
    78: 4 we will **t** to the coming generation
   105: 2 **t** of all his wonderful works.
Isa 41:23 **T** us what is to come hereafter,
Da   2: 4 **T** your servants the dream,
Jn 20:15 **t** me where you have laid him,
1Co 15:51 Listen, I will **t** you a mystery!
2Es 5:13 signs that I am permitted to **t** you,
     8: 2 But I **t** you a parable, Ezra.

TELLING → TELL
Ps 19: 1 The heavens are **t** the glory of God;
    26: 7 and **t** all your wondrous deeds.

TELLS → TELL
Jn 19:35 and he knows that he **t** the truth.)

TEMANITE
Job 2:11 Eliphaz the **T**, Bildad the Shuhite,

TEMPER → HOT-TEMPERED,
QUICK-TEMPERED, TEMPERATE
Pr 14:29 has a hasty **t** exalts folly.
    16:32 one whose **t** is controlled

TEMPERATE → TEMPER
1Ti   3: 2 married only once, **t**, sensible,
     3:11 not slanderers, but **t**, faithful in all
Tit   2: 2 Tell the older men to be **t**, serious,

TEMPEST
Ps 50: 3 and a mighty **t** all around him.
    55: 8 a shelter for myself from the raging
             wind and **t**."

TEMPLE → TEMPLES
Jdg 4:21 to him and drove the peg into his **t**,
1Sa 3: 3 Samuel was lying down in the **t** of
             the LORD,
1Ki 6: 7 any tool of iron was heard in the **t**
2Ch 2:12 who will build a **t** for the LORD,
Ezr 3:10 the foundation of the **t** of the LORD,
Ps 11: 4 The LORD is in his holy **t**;
    27: 4 of the LORD, and to inquire in his **t**.
    30: T A Song at the dedication of the **t**.
Isa 6: 1 and the hem of his robe filled the **t**.
Jer 7: 4 "This is the **t** of the LORD, the **t** of
             the LORD, the **t** of the LORD."
Eze 8:16 at the entrance of the **t** of the LORD,
    43: 4 the glory of the LORD entered the **t**
Da   5: 2 of the **t** in Jerusalem,
Mic 1: 2 the Lord from his holy **t**.
Hab 2:20 But the LORD is in his holy **t**;
Mt   4: 5 placed him on the pinnacle of the **t**,
    12: 6 something greater than the **t** is here.
    26:61 to destroy the **t** of God and to build
    27:51 the curtain of the **t** was torn in two,
Mk 15:38 the curtain of the **t** was torn in two,
Lk 21: 5 some were speaking about the **t**,
Jn 2:14 the **t** he found people selling cattle,
     2:21 was speaking of the **t** of his body.
Ac 2:46 spent much time together in the **t**,
     5:42 in the **t** and at home they did not
             cease to teach
1Co 3:16 that you are God's **t** and that God's
             Spirit dwells in you?
     6:19 your body is a **t** of the Holy Spirit
2Co 6:16 has the **t** of God with idols?
     6:16 For we are the **t** of the living God;
Eph 2:21 and grows into a holy **t** in the Lord;
2Th 2: 4 that he takes his seat in the **t** of God
Rev 3:12 make you a pillar in the **t** of my God
   11:19 Then God's **t** in heaven was opened,
   11:19 the ark of his covenant was seen
             within his **t**;
   21:22 I saw no **t** in the city,
   21:22 its **t** is the Lord God the Almighty
             and the Lamb.
Tob 14: 5 and they will rebuild the **t** of God,
1Mc 2: 8 Her **t** has become like a person
             without honor;
     4:48 sanctuary and the interior of the **t**,

HOLY TEMPLE Ps 5:7; 11:4; 65:4; 79:1;
138:2; Jnh 2:4, 7; Mic 1:2; Hab 2:20; Eph
2:21; 2Mc 5:15; 13:10; 14:31; 1Es 1:53

TEMPLE OF ... *GOD Jdg 9:27; Mt 26:61;
2Co 6:16; 2Th 2:4; Rev 3:12; 11:1; Tob 14:4,
5, 5; Jdt 5:18; 1Es 5:44, 53, 56, 57; 8:17, 18

TEMPLE OF THE *LORD Jdt 4:2; Wis
3:14; 1Es 1:2, 49; 2:7; 5:58; 6:19; 7:7; 8:60, 67

TEMPLE OF THE †LORD 1Sa 1:9; 3:3;
2Ki 18:16; 23:4; 24:13; 2Ch 26:16; 27:2;
29:16; Ezr 3:6, 10; Jer 7:4, 4, 4; 24:1; 38:14;
41:5; Eze 8:16, 16; 44:4, 5; Zec 6:12, 13, 14,
15

TEMPLE SERVANTS 1Ch 9:2; Ezr 2:43,
58, 70; 7:7, 24; 8:17, 20; Ne 3:26, 31; 7:46, 60,
73; 10:28; 11:3, 21, 21; 1Es 1:3; 5:29, 35; 8:5,
22, 49, 49

TEMPLES → TEMPLE
Ro 2:22 You that abhor idols, do you rob **t**?

TEMPORARY
2Co 4:18 for what can be seen is **t**,

TEMPT* → TEMPTATION, TEMPTED,
TEMPTER, TEMPTS
1Co 7: 5 so that Satan may not **t** you because

TEMPTATION* → TEMPT
1Ti   6: 9 who want to be rich into **t** and

Jas 1:12 Blessed is anyone who endures **t**.

TEMPTED* → TEMPT
Mt   4: 1 the wilderness he be **t** by the devil.
Mk 1:13 wilderness forty days, **t** by Satan;
Lk   4: 2 for forty days he was **t** by the devil.
Gal 6: 1 care that you yourselves are not **t**.
1Th 3: 5 that somehow the tempter had **t** you
Jas 1:13 No one, when **t**, should say, "I am
             being **t** by God"; for God cannot be
             t by evil
      1:14 But one is **t** by one's own desire,

TEMPTER* → TEMPT
Mt   4: 3 The **t** came and said to him,
1Th 3: 5 that somehow the **t** had tempted you

TEMPTS* → TEMPT
Jas 1:13 by evil and he himself **t** no one.

TEN → TENTH
Ge 18:32 Suppose **t** are found there."
Ex 34:28 the covenant, the **t** commandments.
Dt   4:13 that is, the **t** commandments;
      10: the **t** commandments that
1Sa 1: 8 Am I not more to you than **t** sons?"
2Ki 20: 9 shall it retreat **t** intervals?"
Ps 91: 7 **t** thousand at your right hand,
Da   1:12 "Please test your servants for **t** days.
      7:24 for the **t** horns, out of this kingdom
             t kings shall arise,
Mt 25: 1 **T** bridesmaids took their lamps and
      25:28 give it to the one with the **t** talents.
Lk 15: 8 what woman having **t** silver coins,
Rev 12: 3 with seven heads and **t** horns,
      17:12 the **t** horns that you saw are **t** kings

TENANTS
Mt 21:34 he sent his slaves to the **t** to collect

TEND → TENDED
Jn 21:16 Jesus said to him, **"T** my sheep."

TENDED* → TEND
Ps 78:72 With upright heart he **t** them,
Zec 11: 7 and I **t** the sheep.
Pm 151: 1 I **t** my father's sheep.

TENDER → TENDERHEARTED, TENDERLY
Hos 11: 8 my compassion grows warm and **t**.
Lk   1:78 By the **t** mercy of our God,
1Pe 3: 8 love for one another, a **t** heart,

TENDERHEARTED* → HEART, TENDER
Eph 4:32 **t**, forgiving one another,

TENDERLY → TENDER
Ge 34: 3 he loved the girl, and spoke **t** to her.
Isa 40: 2 Speak **t** to Jerusalem, and cry to her
Hos 2:14 her into the wilderness, and speak **t**

TENT → TENTMAKERS, TENTS
Ex 27:21 the **t** of meeting, outside the curtain
      33: 7 he called it the **t** of meeting.
      40: 2 the tabernacle of the **t** of meeting.
2Sa 7: 2 but the ark of God stays in a **t**."
Ps 61: 4 Let me abide in your **t** forever,
Isa 33:20 a quiet habitation, an immovable **t**,
      54: 2 Enlarge the site of your **t**,
2Co 5: 1 the earthly **t** we live in is destroyed,
Heb 9:11 the greater and perfect **t** (not made
             with hands,

TENT OF MEETING Ex 27:21; 28:43; 29:4,
10, 11, 30, 32, 42, 44; 30:16, 18, 20, 26, 36;
31:7; 33:7, 7; 35:21; 38:8, 30; 39:32, 40; 40:2,
6, 7, 12, 22, 24, 26, 29, 30, 32, 34, 35; Lev 1:1,
3, 5; 3:2, 8, 13; 4:4, 5, 7, 7, 14, 16, 18, 18;
6:16, 26, 30; 8:3, 4, 31, 33, 35; 9:5, 23; 10:7,
9; 12:6; 14:11, 23; 15:14, 29; 16:7, 16, 17, 20,
23, 33; 17:4, 5, 6, 9; 19:21; 24:3; Nu 1:1; 2:2,
17; 3:7, 8, 25, 25, 38; 4:3, 4, 15, 23, 25, 28,
30, 31, 33, 35, 37, 39, 41, 43, 47; 6:10, 13, 18;

7:5, 89; 8:9, 15, 19, 22, 24, 26; 10:3; 11:16;
12:4; 14:10; 16:18, 19, 42, 43, 50; 17:4; 18:4,
6, 21, 22, 23, 31; 19:4; 20:6; 25:6; 27:2; 31:54;
Dt 31:14, 14; Jos 18:1; 19:51; 1Sa 2:22; 1Ki
8:4; 1Ch 6:32; 9:21; 23:32; 2Ch 1:3, 6, 13; 5:5

TENTH → TEN
Ge 14:20 Abram gave him one **t** of everything
Isa 6:13 Even if a **t** part remain in it,
Lk 18:12 I fast twice a week; I give a **t** of all
Heb 7: 4 Abraham the patriarch gave him a **t**

TENTMAKERS* → MAKE, TENT
Ac 18: 3 together—by trade they were **t**.

TENTS → TENT
Ps 84:10 than live in the **t** of wickedness.

TERAH
Ge 11:27 **T** was the father of Abram, Nahor,

TERAPHIM
Jdg 17: 5 and he made an ephod and **t**,
2Ki 23:24 put away the mediums, wizards, **t**,

TEREBINTH
Isa 6:13 a **t** or an oak whose stump remains

TERRIFIED → TERROR
Est 7: 6 Haman was **t** before the king and
Mt 14:26 they were **t**, saying, "It is a ghost!"
      27:54 and what took place, they were **t**
Rev 11:13 were **t** and gave glory to the God

TERRIFY → TERROR
Ps   2: 5 and **t** them in his fury, saying,
Isa 2:19 when he rises to **t** the earth.

TERRIFYING → TERROR
Ge 15:12 a deep and **t** darkness descended
Heb 12:21 so **t** was the sight that Moses said,

TERRITORY
Jos 1: 4 Sea in the west shall be your **t**.

TERROR → TERRIFIED, TERRIFY,
TERRIFYING, TERRORS
Ex 23:27 I will send my **t** in front of you,
Ps 31:13 **t** all around!—
      91: 5 You will not fear the **t** of the night,
Isa 2:19 from the **t** of the LORD,
      24:17 **T**, and the pit, and the snare are
      54:14 from **t**, for it shall not come near
Jer 20:10 many whispering: **"T** is all around!
Ro   3: 3 rulers are not a **t** to good conduct,

TERRORS → TERROR
Job 6: 4 the **t** of God are arrayed against me.
Ps 55: 4 the **t** of death have fallen upon me.

TERTIUS*
Ro 16:22 I **T**, the writer of this letter,

TEST → TESTED, TESTER, TESTING,
TESTS
Ex 16: 4 In that way I will **t** them,
Dt   6:16 not put the LORD your God to the **t**,
1Ki 10: 1 came to **t** him with hard questions.
Ps 26: 2 and try me; **t** my heart and mind.
      106:14 and put God to the **t** in the desert;
      139:23 **t** me and know my thoughts.
Jer 9: 7 I will now refine and **t** them,
Mal 3:10 and thus put me to the **t**,
Lk   4:12 not put the Lord your God to the **t**.'
      10:25 then a lawyer stood up to **t** Jesus.
Ac   5: 9 to put the Spirit of the Lord to the **t**?
1Co 3:13 the fire will **t** what sort of work
      10: We must not put Christ to the **t**,
2Co 13: 5 **T** yourselves.
      13: indeed, you fail to meet the **t**!
Gal 6: 4 All must **t** their own work;
1Th 5:21 but **t** everything; hold fast to what
Heb 3: 9 your ancestors put me to the **t**,
      11:17 Abraham, when put to the **t**,
Jas 1:12 has stood the **t** and will receive

1Jn 4: 1 **t** the spirits to see whether they are
             from God;
Rev 3:10 the whole world to **t** the inhabitants
Jdt 8:12 Who are you to put God to the **t**
Sir 37:27 My child, **t** yourself while you live;

TESTED → TEST
Ge 22: 1 After these things God **t** Abraham.
Ex 17: 7 Israelites quarreled and **t** the LORD,
Nu 14:22 and yet have **t** me these ten times
Job 23:10 when he has **t** me, I shall come out
Ps 66:10 For you, O God, have **t** us;
      78:41 They **t** God again and again,
Pr 27:21 so a person is **t** by being praised.
Ecc 7:23 All this I have **t** by wisdom;
Isa 28:16 in Zion a foundation stone, a **t** stone,
      48:10 **t** you in the furnace of adversity.
Da   1:14 agreed to this proposal and **t** them
1Ti 3:10 And let them first be **t**;
Heb 2:18 to help those who are being **t**.
      4:15 been **t** as we are, yet without sin.
Sir 44:20 when he was **t** he proved faithful.
1Mc 2:52 Abraham found faithful when **t**,

TESTER* → TEST
Jer 6:27 a **t** and a refiner among my people

TESTIFIED → TESTIFY
Jn   1:15 (John **t** to him and cried out,
      5:37 has himself **t** on my behalf.
1Pe 1:11 it **t** in advance to the sufferings

TESTIFIES → TESTIFY
Jn   5:32 There is another who **t** on my behalf
1Jn 5: 6 Spirit is the one that **t**,
Rev 22:20 The one who **t** to these things says,

TESTIFY → TESTIFIED, TESTIFIES,
TESTIMONY
Isa 59:12 and our sins **t** against us.
Jer 14: 7 Although our iniquities **t** against us,
Jn   1: 7 came as a witness to **t** to the light,
      5:39 and it is they that **t** on my behalf.
      7: 7 I **t** against it that its works are evil.
      15:26 he will **t** on my behalf.
Ac 10:43 All the prophets **t** about him
1Jn 4:14 do **t** that the Father has sent his Son
      5: 7 There are three that **t**:

TESTIMONY → TESTIFY
Nu 35:30 put to death on the **t** of a single
Mt 24:14 as a **t** to all the nations;
Mk 14:59 on this point their **t** did not agree.
Lk 22:71 said, "What further **t** do we need?
Jn   8:17 that the **t** of two witnesses is valid.
      21:24 and we know that his **t** is true.
Heb 2: 4 while God added his **t** by signs and
1Jn 5: 9 If we receive human **t**, the **t** of God
             is greater;
Rev 1: 9 the word of God and the **t** of Jesus.
      12:11 and by the word of their **t**,
      19:10 **t** of Jesus is the spirit of prophecy."

TESTING → TEST
Dt 13: 3 for the LORD your God is **t** you,
Lk   8:13 a while and in a time of **t** fall away.
1Co 10:13 No **t** has overtaken you that is not
             common
Heb 3: 8 as on the day of **t** in the wilderness,
Jas 1: 3 **t** of your faith produces endurance;

TESTS → TEST
Pr 17: 3 but the LORD **t** the heart.
1Th 2: 4 but to please God who **t** our hearts.

THADDAEUS* → =JUDAS
Apostle (Mt 10:3; Mk 3:18); probably also
known as Judas son of James (Lk 6:16; Ac 1:13).

THANK → THANKFULNESS, THANKS,
THANKSGIVING
2Ch 29:31 bring sacrifices and **t** offerings to
      29:31 brought sacrifices and **t** offerings;
Ps 52: 9 I will **t** you forever,

56:12　I will render **t** offerings to you.
107:　8　**t** the LORD for his steadfast love,
Isa　38:18　For Sheol cannot **t** you,
　　　38:19　living, the living, they **t** you,
Lk　18:11　I **t** you that I am not like other
Jn　11:41　I **t** you for having heard me.
Php　1:　3　I **t** my God every time I remember
1Th　3:　9　can we **t** God enough for you in
Sir　35:　4　gives alms sacrifices a **t** offering.

THANKFULNESS → THANK

1Co　10:30　If I partake with **t**, why should I be

THANKS → THANK

1Ch　16:　8　give **t** to the LORD, call on his name,
Ezr　3:11　praising and giving **t** to the LORD,
Ne　12:31　two great companies that gave **t**
Ps　7:17　LORD the **t** due to his righteousness,
　　　28:　7　and with my song I give **t** to him.
　　　30:12　my God, I will give **t** to you forever.
　　　75:　1　We give **t** to you, O God; we give **t**;
　　　107:　1　O give **t** to the LORD, for he is good;
　　　118:28　my God, and I will give **t** to you;
　　　136:　2　O give **t** to the God of gods,
Ro　1:21　not honor him as God or give **t** to
　　　14:　6　since they give **t** to God;
1Co　11:24　and when he had given **t**,
　　　15:57　But **t** be to God, who gives us the
　　　　　　victory
2Co　2:14　But **t** be to God, who in Christ
　　　9:15　**T** be to God for his indescribable
1Th　5:18　give **t** in all circumstances;
Rev　4:　9　give glory and honor and **t** to
　　　11:17　We give you **t**, Lord God Almighty,
Sir　51:　1　I give **t** to your name,
　　　51:12　*Give* **t** *to the* LORD,
Aza　1:67　Give **t** to the Lord, for he is good,

THANKSGIVING → THANK

Lev　7:12　If you offer it for **t**,
Ps　50:14　Offer to God a sacrifice of **t**,
　　　95:　2　Let us come into his presence with **t**
　　　100:　T　A Psalm of **t**.
　　　100:　4　Enter his gates with **t**, and his courts
　　　147:　7　Sing to the LORD with **t**;
Jnh　2:　9　I with the voice of **t** will sacrifice to
2Co　9:11　will produce **t** to God through us;
Php　4:　6　with **t** let your requests be made
　　　　　　known to God.
1Ti　4:　3　with **t** by those who believe and
Rev　7:12　glory and wisdom and **t** and honor
Jdt　15:14　Judith began this **t** before all Israel,
1Mc　4:56　of well-being and a **t** offering.

THEFT → THIEF

Mt　15:19　fornication, **t**, false witness, slander.
Mk　7:21　evil intentions come: fornication, **t**,

THEFTS* → THIEF

Rev　9:21　or their fornication or their **t**.

THEME*

Ps　45:　1　My heart overflows with a goodly **t**;

THEOPHILUS*

Lk　1:　3　account for you, most excellent **T**,
Ac　1:　1　**T**, I wrote about all that Jesus did

THESSALONICA

Ac　17:　1　they came to **T**,
Php　4:16　For even when I was in **T**,

THICK

Ex　19:16　as well as a **t** cloud on the mountain,
Ps　97:　2　Clouds and **t** darkness are all around
Joel　2:　2　a day of clouds and **t** darkness!
Zep　1:15　a day of clouds and **t** darkness,

THICKET

Ge　22:13　caught in a **t** by its horns.

THIEF → THEFT, THEFTS, THIEVES

Ex　22:　1　The **t** shall make restitution,
Lk　12:39　at what hour the **t** was coming,
Jn　10:10　The **t** comes only to steal and kill

1Th　5:　2　day of the Lord will come like a **t** in
1Pe　4:15　none of you suffer as a murderer, a **t**
Rev　16:15　("See, I am coming like a **t**!

THIEVES → THIEF

Mt　6:19　and where **t** break in and steal;
Jn　10:　8　All who came before me are **t** and
1Co　6:10　**t**, the greedy, drunkards, revilers,
Eph　4:28　**T** must give up stealing;

THIGH → THIGHS

Ge　24:　2　"Put your hand under my **t**
　　　47:29　your hand under my **t** and promise
Jdg　15:　8　He struck them down hip and **t**
Rev　19:16　on his **t** he has a name inscribed,

THIGHS → THIGH

Da　2:32　its middle and **t** of bronze,

THIN

Ge　41:　7　The **t** ears swallowed up the seven

THING → ANYTHING, EVERYTHING, THINGS

Ge　18:25　Far be it from you to do such a **t**,
Jdg　19:24　this man do not do such a vile **t**."
2Sa　13:12　for such a **t** is not done in Israel;
Ps　27:　4　One **t** I asked of the LORD,
　　　84:11　No good **t** does the LORD withhold
Isa　43:19　I am about to do a new **t**;
Jer　31:22　the LORD has created a new **t** on the
Mk　10:21　land said, "You lack one **t**;
Lk　10:42　there is need of only one **t**.
Jn　9:25　One **t** I do know, that though I was
　　　　　　blind, now I see."
Ro　7:15　but I do the very **t** I hate.
Php　3:13　but this one **t** I do:

LIVING THING Ge 1:28; 6:19; 7:4, 23; 8:17;
　　Job 12:10; Ps 145:16; Rev 16:3; Sir 18:13

SUCH A THING Ge 18:25; 34:7; 44:7; Lev
　　15:10; Jdg 19:24, 30; 2Sa 11:11; 13:12; 14:13;
　　1Ki 9:8; 22:8; 2Ki 7:2, 19; 2Ch 7:21; 18:7; Ezr
　　7:27; Isa 66:8; Jer 2:10; 40:16; Da 2:10; Joel
　　1:2; 1Co 5:4; Wis 4:15; 1Mc 9:10

THINGS → THING

Job　11:　7　Can you find out the deep **t** of God?
Ps　15:　5　do these **t** shall never be moved.
　　　71:19　You who have done great **t**, O God,
　　　87:　3　Glorious **t** are spoken of you,
Pr　6:16　There are six **t** that the LORD hates,
Ecc　1:　8　All **t** are wearisome; more than
Isa　42:　9　and new **t** I now declare;
　　　66:　2　All these **t** my hand has made,
Jer　10:　6　for he is the one who formed all **t**,
Joel　2:21　for the LORD has done great **t**!
Mt　19:26　but for God all **t** are possible."
Mk　11:33　what authority I am doing these **t**."
Jn　1:　3　All **t** came into being through him,
　　　1:50　You will see greater **t** than these."
　　　21:25　are also many other **t** that Jesus did;
1Co　2:10　these **t** God has revealed to us
　　　　　　through the Spirit;
Gal　5:23　There is no law against such **t**.
Eph　1:22　And he has put all **t** under his feet
Col　1:17　He himself is before all **t**,
　　　1:17　and in him all **t** hold together.
　　　3:　1　seek the **t** that are above,
Heb　1:　3　sustains all **t** by his powerful word.
1Pe　4:　7　The end of all **t** is near;
Rev　4:11　you created all **t**, and by your will
　　　21:　4　for the first **t** have passed away."

ALL THESE THINGS Ge 20:8; 29:13; Lev
　　20:23; Dt 4:30; 30:1; Jdg 13:23; 1Sa 19:7; 2Sa
　　13:21; 1Ki 18:36; 1Ch 29:17; 2Ch 4:18; Job
　　33:29; Ecc 11:9; Isa 45:7; 66:2, 2; Jer 2:34;
　　5:19; 7:13; Eze 16:30, 43; 17:18; Da 2:40; Zec
　　8:12, 17; Mt 6:32, 32, 33; 13:34; 24:33, 34;
　　26:1; Mk 13:4, 30; Lk 1:65; 2:51; 7:18; 12:30;
　　18:34; 21:36; 24:14; Jn 15:21; Ac 7:50; Ro
　　8:37; 1Th 4:6; 2Pe 3:11; Tob 12:20; 14:4; Jdt

8:14; AdE 4:9; Sir 42:23; 1Mc 6:59; 11:29;
14:35; 2Es 6:33; 12:37

ALL THINGS Ge 24:1; Jos 1:17; 2Sa 14:20;
23:5; 2Ki 14:3; 1Ch 29:14; Job 42:2; Ps 8:6;
119:91; Pr 13:16; Ecc 1:8; 5:9; 1sa 44:24; Jer
10:16; 51:19; Mt 11:27; 17:11; 19:26, 28; Mk
9:12, 23; 10:27; 14:36; Lk 10:22; 21:32; Jn
1:3; 3:35; 4:25; 13:3; 16:30; Ac 2:44; 17:25;
Ro 8:28; 11:36; 1Co 2:15; 3:21; 4:13; 6:12, 12,
12; 8:6, 6; 9:22, 25; 10:23, 23, 23; 11:12;
13:7, 7, 7, 7; 14:26, 40; 15:27, 27, 27, 28, 28;
2Co 11:6; Gal 3:22; Eph 1:10, 11, 22, 22; 3:9;
4:10; Php 2:14; 3:8, 21; 4:13; Col 1:16, 16, 17,
17, 20; 1Ti 3:11; 6:13; 2Ti 2:7; Tit 1:15; Heb
1:2, 3; 2:8, 8, 10; 3:4; 13:18; 1Pe 4:7, 11; 2Pe
3:4; 1Jn 2:27; Rev 4:11; 21:5; AdE 13:9, 12;
14:15; 16:18, 21; Wis 1:7, 10, 14; 7:22, 24, 27,
27; 8:1, 5; 9:1, 11; 10:2; 11:20, 23, 24, 26;
12:1, 15; 15:1; 16:17; 18:14, 16; Sir 18:26;
24:8; 42:24; 43:22, 26, 33; Bar 3:32; Sus 1:42;
2Mc 1:24; 7:23; 12:22; 15:2; 1Es 3:12; 4:35;
8:21; Man 1:4; 3Mc 2:3, 21; 5:28; 7:18; 2Es
8:44; 11:6; 16:62; 4Mc 11:5

GOOD THINGS Ge 45:23; Jos 23:14, 15;
Job 22:18; Ps 104:28; 107:9; Pr 12:14; 13:2;
Ecc 6:3; Jer 2:7; Mt 7:11; 12:34, 35; Lk 1:53;
16:25; Gal 6:6; Heb 9:11; 10:1; Tob 12:6; Jdt
15:8; Wis 2:6; 7:11; 13:1; Sir 2:9; 11:14;
16:29; 30:18; 39:25, 25; 1Mc 14:9; 1Es 8:85;
2Es 7:6; 4Mc 12:11

GREAT THINGS 1Sa 12:24; 2Ki 8:4; 1Ch
17:19; Job 5:9; 9:10; 37:5; Ps 71:19; 106:21;
126:2, 3; Jer 45:5; Joel 2:20, 21; Lk 1:49; 1Mc
13:3

HOLY THINGS Lev 5:15; Nu 4:4, 15, 19,
20; 7:9; 10:21; 18:9; 1Ch 23:13; Eze 22:8, 26;
Wis 6:10; 10:10; Sir 7:31; 1Es 5:40; 2Es 10:22

THINGS TO COME Isa 41:22; 44:7; Zec
3:8; Ro 8:38; Heb 10:1; Wis 8:8

THINK → THINKING, THOUGHT, THOUGHTS

Ps　63:　6　when I **t** of you on my bed,
　　　144:　3　or mortals that you **t** of them?
Mt　22:42　"What do you **t** of the Messiah?
Jn　5:39　because you **t** that in them you have
　　　　　　eternal life;
Ro　12:　3　not to **t** of yourself more highly than
1Co　10:12　So if you **t** you are standing,
Php　4:　8　anything worthy of praise, **t** about

THINKING → THINK

Mt　12:25　He knew what they were **t**
Ro　1:21　but they became futile in their **t**,
1Co　14:20　infants in evil, but in **t** be adults.

THIRD → THREE

Eze　5:12　One **t** of you shall die of pestilence
　　　10:14　a human being, the **t** that of a lion,
Da　5:　7　and rank it in the kingdom."
Hos　6:　2　on the **t** day he will raise us up,
Mt　26:44　and prayed for the **t** time,
Mk　14:41　He came a **t** time and said to them,
Lk　18:33　and on the **t** day he will rise again."
Jn　21:17　He said to him the **t** time, "Simon
2Co　12:　2　was caught up to the **t** heaven—
Rev　4:　7　**t** living creature with a face like a
　　　6:　5　When he opened the **t** seal,
　　　8:10　The **t** angel blew his trumpet,
　　　12:　4　down a **t** of the stars of heaven
2Es　11:18　Then the **t** wing raised itself up,

THIRD DAY Ge 1:13; 22:4; 31:22; 34:25;
40:20; 42:18; Ex 19:11, 11, 15, 16; Lev 7:17,
18; 19:6, 7; Nu 7:24; 19:12, 12, 19; 29:20; Jos
9:17; Jdg 20:30; 1Sa 20:12; 30:1; 2Sa 1:2; 1Ki
3:18; 12:12, 12; 2Ki 20:5, 8; 2Ch 10:12, 12;
Ezr 6:15; Est 5:1; Hos 6:2; Mt 16:21; 17:23;
20:19; 27:64; Lk 9:22; 13:32; 18:33; 24:7, 21,
46; Jn 2:1; Ac 10:40; 27:19; 1Co 15:4; AdE
15:1; 2Es 6:42, 44, 51; 14:1

THIRST → THIRSTS, THIRSTY

Ex 17: 3 our children and livestock with t?"
Dt 28:48 in hunger and t, in nakedness
Ps 69:21 and for my t they gave me vinegar
Mt 5: 6 "Blessed are those who hunger and t for righteousness,
Rev 7:16 will hunger no more, and t no more;
Sir 24:21 who drink of me will t for more.

THIRSTS* → THIRST

Ps 42: 2 soul t for God, for the living God.
63: 1 I seek you, my soul t for you;
143: 6 soul t for you like a parched land.
Isa 55: 1 who t, come to the waters;

THIRSTY → THIRST

Ps 107: 9 he satisfies the t, and the hungry he
Pr 25:21 if they are t, give them water to
Mt 25:35 I was t and you gave me something
Jn 4:14 I will give them will never be t.
6:35 believes in me will never be t.
7:37 "Let anyone who is t come to me,
19:28 to fulfill the scripture), "I am t."
Ro 12:20 if they are t, give them something
2Co 11:27 many a sleepless night, hungry and t
Rev 21: 6 the t I will give water as a gift from
22:17 And let everyone who is t come.

THIRTY

Ge 41:46 Joseph was t years old when he
2Sa 23:24 Among the T were Asahel brother
Pr 22:20 for you t sayings of admonition and
Mt 13: 8 a hundredfold, some sixty, some t.
Mk 4:20 t and sixty and a hundredfold."
Lk 3:23 Jesus was about t years old when he began his work.

THISTLE* → THISTLES

Hos 10: 8 Thorn and t shall grow up on their

THISTLES → THISTLE

Ge 3:18 and t it shall bring forth for you;
Heb 6: 8 But if it produces thorns and t,

THOMAS*

Apostle (Mt 10:3; Mk 3:18; Lk 6:15; Jn 11:16; 14:5; 21:2; Ac 1:13). Doubted resurrection (Jn 20:24-28).

THONG

Lk 3:16 I am not worthy to untie the t of his sandals.
Ac 13:25 I am not worthy to untie the t of the sandals.

THORN → THORNBUSH, THORNS

Isa 55:13 the t shall come up the cypress;
Mic 7: 4 the most upright of them a t hedge.
2Co 12: 7 a t was given me in the flesh,

THORNBUSH → BUSH, THORN

2Ki 14: 9 "A t on Lebanon sent to a cedar on

THORNS → THORN

Ge 3:18 t and thistles it shall bring forth for
Nu 33:55 in your eyes and t in your sides;
Jer 12:13 have sown wheat and have reaped t,
Mt 13: 7 Other seeds fell among t,
Jn 19: 2 the soldiers wove a crown of t and
Heb 6: 8 But if it produces t and thistles,

THOUGH

Ps 37:24 t we stumble, we shall not fall
Isa 1:18 t your sins are like scarlet,
Hab 3:17 T the fig tree does not blossom,
Jn 11:25 who believe in me, even t they die,
Ro 9: 6 not as t the word of God had failed.

THOUGHT → THINK

1Sa 1:13 therefore Eli t she was drunk.
Pr 21:29 but the upright give t to their ways.
1Co 13:11 I spoke like a child, I t like a child,
2Co 10: 5 take every t captive to obey Christ.

THOUGHTS → THINK

Ge 6: 5 of the t of their hearts was only evil
Ps 92: 5 Your t are very deep!
94:11 The LORD knows our t,
139:23 test me and know my t.
Isa 55: 8 For my t are not your t,
Mt 9: 4 But Jesus, perceiving their t, said,
Ro 2:15 and their conflicting t will accuse
1Co 3:20 "The Lord knows the t of the wise,
Heb 4:12 to judge the t and intentions of the heart.
Sir 21:11 keeps the law controls his t,

THOUSAND → TEN-THOUSANDTH, THOUSANDS

Dt 7: 9 and keep his commandments, to a t generations,
32:30 How could one have routed a t,
Jos 23:10 One of you puts to flight a t,
Jdg 15:16 the jawbone of a donkey I have slain a t men."
Ps 50:10 the cattle on a t hills.
84:10 is better than a t elsewhere.
90: 4 For a t years in your sight are like yesterday
91: 7 A t may fall at your side,
105: 8 he commanded, for a t generations,
SS 5:10 distinguished among ten t.
Mt 14:21 who ate were about five t men,
15:38 who had eaten were four t men,
2Pe 3: 8 with the Lord one day is like a t years, and a t years are like one day.
Rev 20: 4 and reigned with Christ a t years.

THOUSANDS → THOUSAND

1Sa 18: 7 "Saul has killed his t, and David his ten t."
Ps 68:17 twice ten thousand, t upon t,
Da 7:10 A thousand t served him,
Mic 6: 7 the LORD be pleased with t of rams,
Jude 1:14 the Lord is coming with ten t of his holy ones,
Rev 5:11 myriads of myriads and t of t,

THREAT → THREATEN, THREATS

Isa 30:17 A thousand shall flee at the t of one,
La 2:17 he has carried out his t;

THREATEN → THREAT

1Pe 2:23 when he suffered, he did not t;

THREATS → THREAT

Ac 9: 1 still breathing t and murder against the disciples
Bar 2:24 and you have carried out your t,

THREE → THIRD

Ge 6:10 Noah had t sons, Shem, Ham, and Japheth.
18: 2 and saw t men standing near him.
Ex 23:14 T times in the year you shall hold a festival
Dt 19:15 of two or t witnesses shall a charge be sustained.
1Sa 31: 8 Saul and his t sons fallen on Mount
2Sa 23: 9 among the t warriors was Eleazar
Job 2:11 when Job's t friends heard of all
Pr 30:15 T things are never satisfied:
30:18 T things are too wonderful for me;
30:21 Under t things the earth trembles;
30:29 T things are stately in their stride;
Da 3:24 t men that we threw bound into the
7: 5 had t tusks in its mouth among its
Am 1: 3 For t transgressions of Damascus,
Jnh 1:17 in the belly of the fish t days and t nights.
Zec 11: 8 month I disposed of the t shepherds,
Mt 12:40 so for t days and t nights the Son of Man will be in the heart of the earth.
17: 4 I will make t dwellings here,
18:20 two or t are gathered in my name,
26:34 you will deny me t times."
26:75 crows, you will deny me t times."

27:63 'After t days I will rise again.'
Mk 8:31 be killed, and after t days rise again.
14:30 you will deny me t times."
Jn 2:19 and in t days I will raise it up."
1Co 13:13 faith, hope, and love abide, these t;
14:27 let there be only two or at most t,
2Co 12: 8 T times I appealed to the Lord
13: 1 the evidence of two or t witnesses."
1Jn 5: 7 There are t that testify:
Sir 25: 1 I take pleasure in t things,
25: 2 I hate t kinds of people,

THREE DAYS

Ge 40:12, 13, 18, 19; 42:17; Ex 10:22, 23; 15:22; Jos 1:11; 2:16, 22; 3:2; 9:16; Jdg 14:14; 19:4; 15:8; 9:20; 30:12, 13; 2Sa 20:4; 1Ki 12:5; 2Ki 2:17; 1Ch 12:39; 21:12; 2Ch 10:5; 20:25; Ezr 8:15, 32; 10:8, 9; Ne 2:11; Est 4:16; Am 4:4; Jnh 1:17; Mt 12:40, 40; 15:32; 26:61; 27:40, 63; Mk 8:2, 31; 9:31; 10:34; 14:58; 15:29; Lk 2:46; Jn 2:19, 20; Ac 9:9; 25:1; 28:7, 12, 17; Jdt 2:21; 12:7; AdE 4:16; 1Mc 10:34; 11:18; 2Mc 5:14; 13:12; 1Es 8:41, 62; 9:4, 5; 3Mc 6:38; 2Es 13:58

THREE DAYS'

Ge 30:36; Ex 3:18; 5:3; 8:27; Nu 10:33, 33; 33:8; 2Sa 24:13; Jnh 3:3; 1Mc 5:24

THREE MONTHS

Ge 38:24; Ex 2:2; 2Sa 6:11; 24:13; 2Ki 23:31; 24:8; 1Ch 13:14; 21:12; 2Ch 36:2, 9; Am 4:7; Lk 1:56; Ac 7:20; 19:8; 20:3; 28:11; Heb 11:23; Jdt 16:20; 1Es 1:35, 44

THREE TIMES

Ex 23:14, 17; 34:23, 24; Nu 22:28, 32, 33; 24:10; Dt 16:16; Jdg 16:15; 1Sa 20:41; 1Ki 9:25; 17:21; 2Ki 13:18, 19, 25; Job 33:29; Da 6:10, 13; Mt 26:34, 75; Mk 14:30, 72; Lk 22:34, 61; Jn 13:38; Ac 10:16; 11:10; 2Co 11:25, 25; 12:8; Sir 13:7; 43:4; 48:3

THREE YEARS

Ge 11:13, 15; 15:9, 9, 9; Lev 19:23; 25:21; Jdg 9:22; 2Sa 13:38; 21:1; 24:13; 1Ki 2:39; 10:22; 15:2; 22:1; 2Ki 17:5; 18:10; 24:1; 1Ch 21:12; 2Ch 9:21; 11:17, 17; 13:2; 31:16; Isa 16:14; 20:3; Da 1:5; Lk 4:25; 13:7; Ac 20:31; Gal 1:18; Jas 5:17; Jdt 8:4; 2Mc 4:23; 7:27; 14:1

THRESH → THRESHING

Mic 4:13 Arise and t, O daughter Zion,

THRESHING → THRESH

Ru 3: 3 and go down to the t floor;
2Sa 24:18 the t floor of Araunah the Jebusite."
2Ch 3: 1 on the t floor of Ornan the Jebusite.
Hos 9: 1 a prostitute's pay on all t floors.
Lk 3:17 to clear his t floor and to gather the

THRESHOLD

1Sa 5: 4 hands were lying cut off upon the t;
Eze 10:18 went out from the t of the house
47: 1 water was flowing from below the t

THREW → THROW

Ex 7:10 Aaron t down his staff before
15:25 he t it into the water,
32:19 and he t the tablets from his hands
2Ki 6: 6 t it in there, and made the iron float.
Da 6:24 men that we t bound into the fire?"
Jnh 1:15 So they picked Jonah up and t him into the sea;
Rev 20: 3 and t him into the pit,
Bel 1:31 They t Daniel into the lions' den,

THROATS

Ps 5: 9 their t are open graves;
115: 7 they make no sound in their t.
Ro 3:13 "Their t are opened graves;

THRONE → ENTHRONED, THRONES

2Sa 7:13 the t of his kingdom forever.
1Ch 17:12 and I will establish his t forever.
Ps 11: 4 the LORD's t is in heaven.
45: 6 Your t, O God, endures forever and
47: 8 God sits on his holy t.
89:14 justice are the foundation of your t;

Pr 20:28 and his **t** is upheld by righteousness.
Isa 6: 1 I saw the Lord sitting on a **t,** high
66: 1 Heaven is my **t** and the earth is my
Jer 33:21 not have a son to reign on his **t,**
Eze 1:26 there was something like a **t,**
Da 7: 9 and an Ancient One took his **t,**
7: 9 his **t** was fiery flames, and its
Mt 5:34 by heaven, for it is the **t** of God,
19:28 the Son of Man is seated on the **t** of his glory,
Lk 1:32 the Lord God will give to him the **t**
Ac 7:49 'Heaven is my **t,** and the earth is
Heb 1: 8 of the Son he says, "Your **t,** O God,
4:16 therefore approach the **t** of grace with boldness,
12: 2 his seat at the right hand of the **t**
Rev 2:13 you are living, where Satan's **t** is.
3:21 sat down with my Father on his **t.**
4: 2 and there in heaven stood a **t,**
4:10 they cast their crowns before the **t,**
5:13 on the **t** and to the Lamb be blessing
20:11 I saw a great white **t** and the one
22: 1 flowing from the **t** of God and of
22: 3 But the **t** of God and of the Lamb

THRONES → THRONE

Ps 122: 5 the **t** of the house of David.
Da 7: 9 **t** were set in place,
Mt 19:28 twelve **t,** judging the twelve tribes
Col 1:16 whether **t** or dominions or rulers or
Rev 4: 4 Around the throne are twenty-four **t,**
20: 4 Then I saw **t,** and those seated

THRONG

Ps 35:18 in the mighty **t** I will praise you.
42: 1 how I went with the **t,**

THROUGH

Ge 21:12 **t** Isaac that offspring shall be named
Ex 15:19 Israelites walked **t** the sea on dry
Isa 43: 2 When you pass **t** the waters, I will
Jn 14: 6 No one comes to the Father except **t** me.
Ro 5: 1 peace with God **t** our Lord Jesus
1Co 8: 6 and one Lord, Jesus Christ, **t** whom are all things and **t** whom we exist.
Gal 2:19 For **t** the law I died to the law,
Eph 2: 8 For by grace you have been saved **t** faith,
Col 1:16 all things have been created **t** him
Heb 1: 2 **t** whom he also created the worlds.

THROW → THREW, THROWN

Ex 1:22 Hebrews you shall **t** into the Nile,
4: 3 And he said, "**T** it on the ground."
Zec 11:13 said to me, "**T** it into the treasury"
Mt 5:30 cut it off and **t** it away;
7: 6 do not **t** your pearls before swine,
Jn 8: 7 [who is without sin be the first to **t**]

THROWN → THROW

Ex 15: 1 horse and rider he has **t** into the sea.
Da 3:21 **t** into the furnace of blazing fire.
6:12 shall be **t** into a den of lions?"
Mk 11:23 'Be taken up and **t** into the sea,'
Rev 12: 9 The great dragon was **t** down,
19:20 were **t** alive into the lake of fire
20:10 **t** into the lake of fire and sulfur,
20:14 Hades were **t** into the lake of fire.

THUMMIM

Ex 28:30 you shall put the Urim and the **T,**
Ezr 2:63 be a priest to consult Urim and **T.**

THUNDER → THUNDERED, THUNDERS

Ex 9:23 and the LORD sent **t** and hail,
20:18 witnessed the **t** and lightning,
Job 40: 9 and can you **t** with a voice like his?
Mk 3:17 name Boanerges, that is, Sons of **T**);
Rev 4: 5 and rumblings and peals of **t,**
6: 1 as with a voice of **t,** "Come!"
16:18 peals of **t,** and a violent earthquake,

THUNDERED → THUNDER

Ps 18:13 The LORD also **t** in the heavens,

THUNDERS → THUNDER

Job 37: 5 God **t** wondrously with his voice;
Ps 29: 3 God of glory **t,** the LORD, over
Rev 10: 3 he shouted, the seven **t** sounded.
10: 4 "Seal up what the seven **t** have said,

THUS

THUS SAYS THE *LORD Eze 21:9; Ac 15:17; Bar 2:21; 2Es 1:12, 15, 22, 28, 33; 2:1, 10; 15:21

THUS SAYS THE *LORD †GOD Isa 7:7; 10:24; 22:15; 28:16; 49:22; 52:4; 56:8; 65:13; Jer 7:20; Eze 2:4; 3:11, 27; 5:5, 7, 8; 6:3, 11; 7:2, 5; 11:7, 16, 17; 12:10, 19, 23, 28; 13:3, 8, 13, 18, 20; 14:4, 6, 21; 15:6; 16:3, 36, 59; 17:3, 9, 19, 22; 20:3, 5, 27, 30, 39, 47; 21:24, 26, 28; 22:3, 19, 28; 23:22, 28, 32, 35, 46; 24:3, 6, 9, 21; 25:3, 6, 8, 12, 13, 15, 16; 26:3, 7, 15, 19; 27:3; 28:2, 6, 12, 22, 25; 29:3, 8, 13, 19; 30:2, 10, 13, 22; 31:10, 15; 32:3, 11; 33:25, 27; 34:2, 10, 11, 17, 20; 35:3, 14; 36:2, 3, 4, 5, 6, 7, 13, 22, 33, 37; 37:5, 9, 12, 19, 21; 38:3, 10, 14, 17; 39:1, 17, 25; 43:18; 44:6, 9; 45:9, 18; 46:1, 16; 47:13; Am 3:11; 5:3; Ob 1:1

THUS SAYS THE †LORD Ex 4:22; 5:1; 7:17; 8:1, 20; 9:1, 13; 10:3; 11:4; 32:27; Jos 7:13; 24:2; Jdg 6:8; 1Sa 10:18; 15:2; 2Sa 7:5, 8; 12:7, 11; 24:12; 1Ki 11:31; 12:24; 13:2, 21; 14:7; 17:14; 20:13, 14, 28, 42; 21:19, 19; 22:11; 2Ki 1:4, 6, 16; 2:21; 3:16, 17; 4:43; 7:1; 9:3, 6, 12; 19:6, 20, 32; 20:1, 5; 21:12; 22:15, 16, 18; 1Ch 17:4, 7; 21:10, 11; 2Ch 11:4; 12:5; 18:10; 20:15; 21:12; 34:23, 24, 26; Isa 29:22; 37:6, 21, 33; 38:1, 5; 43:1, 14, 16; 44:2, 6, 24; 45:1, 11, 14, 18; 48:17; 49:7, 8, 25; 50:1; 52:3; 56:1, 4; 65:8; 66:1, 12; Jer 2:2, 5; 4:3, 27; 5:14; 6:6, 9, 16, 21, 22; 7:3, 21; 8:4; 9:7, 15, 17, 22, 23; 10:2, 18; 11:3, 11, 21, 22; 12:14; 13:9, 12, 13; 14:10, 15; 15:2, 19; 16:3, 5, 9; 17:5, 21; 18:11, 13; 19:3, 11, 15; 20:4; 21:4, 8, 12; 22:1, 3, 6, 11, 18, 30; 23:2, 15, 16, 38; 24:5, 8; 25:8, 27, 28, 32; 26:2, 4, 18; 27:4, 16, 19, 21; 28:2, 11, 13, 14, 16; 29:4, 8, 10, 16, 17, 21, 25, 31, 32; 30:2, 5, 12, 18; 31:2, 7, 15, 16, 23, 35, 37; 32:3, 14, 15, 28, 36, 42; 33:2, 4, 10, 12, 17, 20, 25; 34:2, 4, 13, 17; 35:13, 17, 18, 19; 36:29, 30; 37:7, 9; 38:2, 3, 17; 39:16; 42:9, 15, 18; 43:10; 44:2, 7, 11, 25, 30; 45:2, 4; 47:2; 48:1, 40; 49:1, 7, 12, 28, 35; 50:18, 33; 51:1, 33, 36, 58; Eze 11:5; 21:3; 30:6; Am 1:3, 6, 9, 11, 13; 2:1, 4, 6; 3:12; 5:4, 16; 7:17; Mic 2:3; 3:5; Na 1:12; Hag 1:2, 5, 7; 2:6, 11; Zec 1:3, 4, 14, 16, 17; 3:7; 6:12; 7:9; 8:2, 3, 4, 6, 7, 9, 14, 19, 20, 23; 12:1

THWARTED

Job 42: 2 that no purpose of yours can be **t.**

THYATIRA

Ac 16:14 of **T** and a dealer in purple cloth.
Rev 2:18 the angel of the church in **T** write:

TIBERIAS

Jn 6: 1 also called the Sea of **T.**

TIBERIUS·

Lk 3: 1 year of the reign of Emperor **T,**

TIBNI·

King of Israel (1Ki 16:21-22).

TIDINGS

Isa 40: 9 O Zion, herald of good **t;**
41:27 to Jerusalem a herald of good **t.**
Na 1:15 the feet of one who brings good **t,**

TIE → TIED

Pr 6:21 **t** them around your neck.
Mt 23: 4 **t** up heavy burdens, hard to bear,

TIED → TIE

Jos 2:21 **t** the crimson cord in the window.
Lk 19:30 enter it you will find **t** there a colt
Jn 13: 4 and **t** a towel around himself.

TIGHT-FISTED·

Dt 15: 7 or **t** toward your needy neighbor.

TIGLATH-PILESER → =PUL

2Ki 16: 7 messengers to King **T** of Assyria,

TIGRIS

Ge 2:14 The name of the third river is **T,**
Da 10: 4 of the great river (that is, the **T),**

TILES·

Lk 5:19 with his bed through the **t** into

TILL

Ge 2:15 put him in the garden of Eden to **t** it
4:12 you **t** the ground, it will no longer

TIMBER

1Ki 5:10 supplied Solomon's every need for **t**

TIME → TIMES

Ge 4:26 At that **t** people began to invoke the name of the LORD.
Dt 32:35 for the **t** when their foot shall slip;
Est 4:14 dignity for just such a **t** as this."
Ps 119:126 It is **t** for the LORD to act,
Ecc 3: 1 a **t** for every matter under heaven:
3:11 made everything suitable for its **t;**
8: 5 wise mind will know the **t** and way.
Da 7:25 for a **t,** two times, and half a **t.**
12: 1 There shall be a **t** of anguish,
12: 7 for a **t,** two times, and half a **t,**
Hos 10:12 for it is **t** to seek the LORD,
Lk 21: 8 and, 'The **t** is near!'
Ro 5: 6 at the right **t** Christ died for the ungodly.
1Co 4: 5 not pronounce judgment before the **t**
7:29 the appointed **t** has grown short;
2Co 6: 2 "At an acceptable **t** I have listened
6: 2 See, now is the acceptable **t;**
Gal 4: 4 when the fullness of **t** had come,
Eph 5:16 making the most of the **t,**
Col 4: 5 making the most of the **t.**
Heb 9:28 a second **t,** not to deal with sin,
10:12 But when Christ had offered for all **t**
1Pe 4:17 **t** has come for judgment to begin
Rev 1: 3 written in it, for the **t** is near.
2:21 I gave her **t** to repent,
12:14 for a **t,** and times, and half a **t.**
22:10 of this book, for the **t** is near.

APPOINTED TIME Ezr 23:15; Nu 9:2, 3, 7, 13; 28:2; 1Sa 9:24; 2Sa 24:15; Job 34:23; Ps 102:13; Ecc 3:17; Jer 33:20; Eze 22:4; Da 8:19; Hab 2:3; 1Co 7:29; Sir 36:10; 39:16, 17, 34; 48:10

FOR ALL TIME Lev 25:34; Dt 4:40; 18:5; 1Sa 1:22; 1Ki 9:3; 2Ch 7:16; Ps 77:8; Jer 32:39; 33:18; 35:19; Eze 46:14; Heb 7:25; 10:12, 14; AdE 16:24; 9:28; Bar 3:32; 1Mc 10:30; 15:8; 3Mc 3:29

TIME APPOINTED Ex 34:18; Lev 23:4; 1Sa 13:8; Est 9:27; Da 11:27, 29, 35; 1Es 9:12

TIME IS [SURELY] COMING 1Sa 2:31; Jer 48:12; 49:2; 51:52; Eze 24:14; Am 4:2; 8:11; 9:13; 2Ti 4:3

TIME OF ... DISTRESS Jdg 10:14; 2Ch 28:22; Ps 32:6; Jer 15:11; 30:7; AdE 9:22; Sir 2:11; 22:23; 35:26; 1Mc 2:53; 13:5

TIME TO COME Dt 4:30; 6:20; 31:29; Jos 4:6, 21; 22:24, 27, 28; Pr 31:25; Isa 30:8; 42:23

TIMES → TIME

Ex 23:14 Three **t** in the year you shall hold a festival
Jos 6: 4 march around the city seven **t,**
Ps 9: 9 a stronghold in **t** of trouble,
31:15 My **t** are in your hand;

62: 8 Trust in him at all **t**, O people;
Pr 17:17 A friend loves at all **t**,
24:16 they fall seven **t**, they will rise again
Isa 46:10 from ancient **t** things not yet done.
Da 7:25 for a time, two **t**, and half a time.
Mt 16: 3 cannot interpret the signs of the **t**.
18:22 Jesus said to him, "Not seven **t**, but,
I tell you, seventy-seven **t**.
Mk 14:30 you will deny me three **t**."
Lk 17: 4 sins against you seven **t** a day, and
turns back to you seven **t** and says,
Ac 1: 7 to know the **t** or periods that the
1Ti 4: 1 later **t** some will renounce the faith
2Ti 3: 1 in the last days distressing **t** will
Rev 12:14 for a time, and **t**, and half a time.
Sir 20:12 but pay for it seven **t** over.
2Es 3:14 you revealed the end of the **t**,

APPOINTED TIMES Ezr 10:14; Ne 10:34;
13:31; Tob 14:4; 2Es 4:27

AT ALL TIMES Ex 18:22, 26; Job 27:10; Ps
10:5; 34:1; 62:8; 106:3; 119:20; Pr 5:19;
17:17; Lk 21:36; Gal 4:18; Eph 5:20; 6:18;
2Th 3:16; Tob 4:19; 14:8; Wis 19:22; Sir 6:37;
22:6; 26:4; 1Mc 1:36

LAST TIMES 2Es 6:34; 7:73, 77, 87; 8:50,
63; 13:46

SEVEN TIMES Ge 33:3; Lev 4:6, 17; 8:11;
14:7, 16, 27, 51; 16:14, 19; 25:8; Nu 19:4; Jos
6:4, 15, 15; 1Ki 18:43; 2Ki 4:35; 5:10, 14; Ps
12:6; 119:164; Pr 24:16; Da 3:19; 4:16, 23, 25,
32; Mt 18:21, 22; Lk 17:4, 4; Sir 20:12; 40:8

THREE TIMES Ex 23:14, 17; 34:23, 24; Nu
22:28, 32, 33; 24:10; Dt 16:16; Jdg 16:15; 1Sa
20:41; 1Ki 9:25; 17:21; 2Ki 13:18, 19, 25; Job
33:29; Da 6:10, 13; Mt 26:34, 75; Mk 14:30,
72; Lk 22:34, 61; Jn 13:38; Ac 10:16; 11:10;
2Co 11:25, 25; 12:8; Sir 13:7; 43:4; 48:3

TIMOTHY
Believer from Lystra (Ac 16:1). Joined Paul on
second missionary journey (Ac 16-20). Sent to
settle problems at Corinth (1Co 4:17; 16:10). Led
church at Ephesus (1Ti 1:3). Co-writer with Paul
(1Th 1:1; 2Th 1:1; Phm 1).

TIP
Jdg 6:21 angel of the LORD reached out the **t**
of the staff
1Sa 14:27 dipped the **t** of it in the honeycomb,

TIRED
Jn 4: 6 **t** out by his journey, was sitting by

TIRZAH
1Ki 15:33 began to reign over all Israel at **T**;

TISHBITE
1Ki 17: 1 Elijah the **T**, of Tishbe in Gilead,
2Ki 1: 8 He said, "It is Elijah the **T**."

TITHE → TITHES
Nu 18:26 from it to the LORD, a **t** of the **t**.
Dt 12:17 the **t** of your grain, your wine, and
Mal 3:10 Bring the full **t** into the storehouse,
Mt 23:23 For you **t** mint, dill, and cummin,

TITHES → TITHE
Ne 10:37 to the Levites the **t** from our soil,
Mal 3: 8 In your **t** and offerings!

TITUS
Gentile co-worker of Paul (Gal 2:1-3; 2Ti 4:10);
sent to Corinth (2Co 2:13; 7-8; 12:18), Crete (Tit
1:4-5).

TOBIAH
Enemy of Nehemiah and the exiles (Ne 2:10-19;
4; 6; 13:4-9).

TOBIAS
Tob 1: 9 the father of a son whom I named **T**.
3:17 in marriage to **T** son of Tobit,

TOBIJAH
Zec 6:14 And the crown shall be in the care
of Heldai, **T**,

TOBIT
Tob 1: 1 This book tells the story of **T**
1: 3 I, **T**, walked in the ways of truth
3:17 **T**, by removing the white films
7: 4 "Do you know our kinsman **T**?"
11:16 Then **T**, rejoicing and praising God,

TODAY → TODAY'S
Ex 14:13 Egyptians whom you see **t** you
shall never see again.
34:11 Observe what I command you **t**.
Dt 5: 3 who are all of us here alive **t**.
30:15 set before you **t** life and prosperity,
Ps 2: 7 are my son; **t** I have begotten you.
95: 7 that **t** you would listen to his voice!
Mt 6:34 Today's trouble is enough for **t**.
Lk 4:21 "**T** this scripture has been fulfilled
19: 9 "**T** salvation has come to this house,
23:43 **t** you will be with me in Paradise."
Ac 13:33 are my Son; **t** I have begotten you.'
Heb 1: 5 are my Son; **t** I have begotten you"?
3: 7 as the Holy Spirit says, "**T**,
3:13 as long as it is called "**t**,"
4: 7 in the words already quoted, "**T**,
13: 8 Jesus Christ is the same yesterday
and **t** and forever.

TODAY'S → TODAY
Mt 6:34 **T** trouble is enough for today.

TOES
Da 2:42 As the **t** of the feet were part iron

TOGETHER
Ge 3: 7 they sewed fig leaves **t** and made
Dt 22:10 with an ox and a donkey yoked **t**.
Ps 2: 2 and the rulers take counsel **t**,
34: 3 and let us exalt his name **t**.
133: 1 when kindred live **t** in unity!
139:13 knit me **t** in my mother's womb.
Isa 11: 6 calf and the lion and the fatling **t**,
65:25 The wolf and the lamb shall feed **t**,
Eze 37: 7 the bones came **t**, bone to its bone.
Mt 19: 6 what God has joined **t**, let no one
separate."
Ac 2:44 All who believed were **t** and had all
4:26 have gathered **t** against the Lord
5:12 were all **t** in Solomon's Portico.
Eph 2: 5 made us alive **t** with Christ—

TOIL
Ge 3:17 in **t** you shall eat of it all the days
5:29 from our work and from the **t**
Ecc 3:13 drink and take pleasure in all their **t**.

TOLA
A judge of Israel (Jdg 10:1-2).

TOLD → TELL
Ge 3:11 "Who **t** you that you were naked?
Jdg 16:17 So he **t** her his whole secret, and
1Ki 10: 7 Not even half had been **t** me;
Ps 44: 1 O God, our ancestors have **t** us,
Lk 2:20 as it had been **t** them.
Jn 14:29 I have **t** you this before it occurs,

TOLERABLE → TOLERATE
Lk 10:12 it will be more **t** for Sodom than for
10:14 judgment will be more **t** for Tyre

TOLERATE → TOLERABLE
Ps 101: 5 an arrogant heart I will not **t**.
Rev 2: 2 I know that you cannot **t** evildoers;

TOMB → TOMBS
Mk 15:46 laid it in a **t** that had been hewn out
Lk 24: 2 the stone rolled away from the **t**,

TOMBS → TOMB
Mt 23:29 For you build the **t** of the prophets
27:52 The **t** also were opened, and many

TOMORROW
Pr 27: 1 boast about **t**, for you do not know
Isa 22:13 "Let us eat and drink, for **t** we die."
Mt 6:34 "So do not worry about **t**,
6:34 for **t** will bring worries of its own.
1Co 15:32 "Let us eat and drink, for **t** we die."
Jas 4:14 do not even know what **t** will bring.

TONGUE → DOUBLE-TONGUED, TONGUES
Ex 4:10 I am slow of speech and slow of **t**."
Job 33: 2 the **t** in my mouth speaks.
Ps 34:13 Keep your **t** from evil, and your lips
39: 1 that I may not sin with my **t**;
51:14 and my **t** will sing aloud of your
deliverance.
52: 4 You love all words that devour, O
deceitful **t**.
71:24 All day long my **t** will talk
119:172 My **t** will sing of your promise,
137: 6 Let my **t** cling to the roof of my
mouth,
139: 4 before a word is on my **t**, O LORD,
Pr 6:17 a lying **t**, and hands that shed
12:18 but the **t** of the wise brings healing.
15: 4 A gentle **t** is a tree of life,
18:21 Death and life are in the power of
the **t**,
25:15 and a soft **t** can break bones.
26:28 A lying **t** hates its victims,
28:23 than one who flatters with the **t**.
31:26 the teaching of kindness is on her **t**.
SS 4:11 honey and milk are under your **t**;
Isa 45:23 shall bow, every **t** shall swear."
50: 4 GOD has given me the **t** of a teacher,
59: 3 your **t** mutters wickedness.
Mk 7:33 and he spat and touched his **t**.
Lk 16:24 his finger in water and cool my **t**;
Ro 14:11 every **t** shall give praise to God."
1Co 14: 2 those who speak in a **t** do not speak
to other people but to God;
14: 4 speak in a **t** build up themselves,
14: 9 if in a **t** you utter speech that is not
14:13 one who speaks in a **t** should pray
for the power to interpret.
14:19 than ten thousand words in a **t**.
14:26 a hymn, a lesson, a revelation, a
14:27 in a **t**, let there be only two or
Php 2:11 every **t** should confess that Jesus
Christ is Lord,
Jas 3: 5 So also the **t** is a small member,
3: 8 but no one can tame the **t**—
Sir 5:14 and do not lay traps with your **t**,
19:16 Who has not sinned with his **t**?
20:18 is better than a slip of the **t**;
23: 7 DISCIPLINE OF THE **T**

TONGUES → TONGUE
Jdg 7: 5 those who lap the water with their **t**,
Ps 12: 4 "With our **t** we will prevail;
Isa 66:18 coming to gather all nations and **t**;
Jer 23:31 who use their own **t** and say, "Says
the LORD."
Ac 2: 3 Divided **t**, as of fire, appeared
10:46 speaking in **t** and extolling God.
19: 6 and they spoke in **t** and prophesied
Ro 3:13 they use their **t** to deceive."
1Co 12:10 to another various kinds of **t**, to
another the interpretation of **t**.
12:28 of leadership, various kinds of **t**.
12:30 Do all speak in **t**?
13: 1 If I speak in the **t** of mortals and of
13: 8 as for **t**, they will cease;
14: 5 would like all of you to speak in **t**,
14: 5 in **t**, unless someone interprets,
14:18 I thank God that I speak in **t** more
14:21 "By people of strange **t** and by the
14:22 **T**, then, are a sign not for believers
14:39 and do not forbid speaking in **t**;

TOOK → TAKE
Ge 2:21 he **t** one of his ribs and closed up its

3: 6 she **t** of its fruit and ate;
5:24 he was no more, because God **t** him.
Jos 11:16 So Joshua **t** all that land:
Ps 78:70 and **t** him from the sheepfolds;
Da 7: 9 and an Ancient One **t** his throne,
Mt 4: 5 the devil **t** him to the holy city and
4: 8 devil **t** him to a very high mountain
8:17 "He **t** our infirmities and bore our
26:26 were eating, Jesus **t** a loaf of bread,
26:27 Then he **t** a cup,
1Co 11:23 he was betrayed **t** a loaf of bread,
11:25 In the same way he **t** the cup also,
1Mc 1:23 He **t** the silver and the gold,
4:47 they **t** unhewn stones, as the law

TOOTH → TEETH
Ex 21:24 **t** for **t**, hand for hand, foot for foot,
Mt 5:38 'An eye for an eye and a **t** for a **t**.'

TOP → TOPS
Ge 28:12 the **t** of it reaching to heaven;
Ex 19:20 LORD summoned Moses to the **t** of
Dt 28:13 you shall be only at the **t**,
Mt 27:51 the curtain of the temple was torn
     in two, from **t** to bottom.
Jn 19:23 woven in one piece from the **t**.

TOPHETH
2Ki 23:10 He defiled **T**, which is in the valley
Jer 19:12 making this city like **T**.

TOPPLE·
Isa 40:20 to set up an image that will not **t**.

TOPS → TOP
Ge 8: 5 the **t** of the mountains appeared.

TORCH → TORCHES
Ge 15:17 a flaming **t** passed between these
Isa 62: 1 and her salvation like a burning **t**.
Rev 8:10 blazing like a **t**,

TORCHES → TORCH
Eze 1:13 like moving to and fro among
Da 10: 6 lightning, his eyes like flaming **t**,
Rev 4: 5 of the throne burn seven flaming **t**,

TORE → TEAR
Ge 37:34 Then Jacob **t** his garments,
Jos 7: 6 Then Joshua **t** his clothes,
1Ki 14: 8 and **t** the kingdom away from the
     house of David
Mt 26:65 Then the high priest **t** his clothes
1Mc 1:56 they **t** to pieces and burned with fire
4:45 So they **t** down the altar,

TORMENT → TORMENTED, TORMENTORS, TORMENTS
Lk 16:28 not also come into this place of **t**.'
2Co 12: 7 a messenger of Satan to **t** me,

TORMENTED → TORMENT
1Sa 16:14 an evil spirit from the LORD **t** him.
Rev 20:10 they will be **t** day and night forever

TORMENTORS· → TORMENT
Ps 137: 3 and our **t** asked for mirth, saying,
Isa 51:23 I will put it into the hand of your **t**,

TORMENTS → TORMENT
Ps 32:10 Many are the **t** of the wicked,

TORN → TEAR
Ge 37:33 Joseph is without doubt **t** to pieces."
1Sa 28:17 has **t** the kingdom out of your hand,
Mk 1:10 the heavens **t** apart and the Spirit
Lk 23:45 curtain of the temple was **t** in two.
Gal 4:15 you would have **t** out your eyes

TORTURED
Mt 18:34 handed him over to be **t** until
Heb 11:35 were **t**, refusing to accept release,
13: 3 those who are being **t**, as

TOSSED → TOSSING
Eph 4:14 **t** to and fro and blown about by
     every wind of doctrine,
Jas 1: 6 driven and **t** by the wind;

TOSSING → TOSSED
Isa 57:20 wicked are like the **t** sea that cannot

TOUCH → TOUCHED, TOUCHES
Ge 3: 3 nor shall you **t** it, or you shall die.'"
Ex 19:12 Any who **t** the mountain shall be
     put to death.
Nu 4:15 but they must not **t** the holy things,
Ps 105:15 "Do not **t** my anointed ones;
Isa 52:11 from there! **T** no unclean thing;
Eze 9: 6 but **t** no one who has the mark.
Mt 9:21 only **t** his cloak, I will be made well.
Lk 18:15 infants to him that he might **t** them;
24:39 **T** me and see;
2Co 6:17 and **t** nothing unclean; then I will
Col 2:21 not handle, Do not taste, Do not **t**"?
Heb 11:28 destroyer of the firstborn would not
     t the firstborn of Israel.
Wis 3: 1 and no torment will ever **t** them.

TOUCHED → TOUCH
Ex 4:25 and **t** Moses' feet with it, and said,
1Sa 10:26 warriors whose hearts God had **t**.
Isa 6: 7 The seraph **t** my mouth with it and
Jer 1: 9 the LORD put out his hand and **t** my
     mouth;
Da 10:16 Then one in human form **t** my lips,
Mt 8: 3 stretched out his hand and **t** him,
14:36 and all who **t** it were healed.
Mk 5:30 and said, "Who **t** my clothes?"
Ac 19:12 or aprons that had **t** his skin were
1Jn 1: 1 have looked at and **t** with our hands,

TOUCHES → TOUCH
Ps 104:32 **t** the mountains and they smoke.
Am 9: 5 he who **t** the earth and it melts,
Zec 2: 8 who **t** you **t** the apple of my eye.
Heb 12:20 "If even an animal **t** the mountain,

TOWER → TOWERS, WATCHTOWER
Ge 11: 4 and a **t** with its top in the heavens,
Ps 61: 3 a strong **t** against the enemy.
Pr 18:10 The name of the LORD is a strong **t**;
Lk 14:28 which of you, intending to build a **t**,

TOWERS → TOWER
Ps 48:12 go all around it, count its **t**,
122: 7 and security within your **t**."
Tob 13:16 The **t** of Jerusalem will be built
     with gold,

TOWN → HOMETOWN, TOWNS
Ne 7: 6 Jerusalem and Judah, each to his **t**.
Mt 2:23 his home in a **t** called Nazareth,
10:11 Whatever **t** or village you enter,

TOWNS → TOWN
Nu 35: 2 **t** for the Levites to live in;
Jos 14: 4 in the land, but only **t** to live in,
Jer 11:13 For your gods have become as
     many as your **t**,
Lk 2: 3 went to their own **t** to be registered.

TRADE → TRADED, TRADERS
Ge 42:34 and you may **t** in the land.'"
Isa 23:17 and she will return to her **t**,
Rev 18:22 any **t** will be found in you no more;

TRADED → TRADE
Joel 3: 3 and **t** boys for prostitutes,

TRADERS → TRADE
Zec 14:21 no longer be **t** in the house of the
     LORD
1Ti 1:10 sodomites, slave **t**, liars, perjurers,

TRADITION
Mt 15: 2 disciples break the **t** of the elders?
Mk 7:13 your **t** that you have handed on.

Col 2: 8 empty deceit, according to human **t**,

TRAIN → TRAINED, TRAINING, TRAINS
Ps 68:18 leading captives in your **t** and
Pr 22: 6 **T** children in the right way, and
1Ti 4: 7 **T** yourself in godliness,

TRAINED → TRAIN
Heb 5:14 faculties have been **t** by practice
12:11 to those who have been **t** by it.

TRAINING → TRAIN
1Ti 4: 8 while physical **t** is of some value,
2Ti 3:16 and for **t** in righteousness,
Tit 2:12 **t** us to renounce impiety and

TRAINS → TRAIN
2Sa 22:35 He **t** my hands for war,
Ps 18:34 He **t** my hands for war,
144: 1 my rock, who **t** my hands for war,

TRAITOR → TREASON
Lk 6:16 and Judas Iscariot, who became a **t**.

TRAMPLE → TRAMPLED
Ps 91:13 the serpent you will **t** under foot.
Am 2: 7 **t** the head of the poor into the dust
5:11 because you **t** on the poor and take
8: 4 Hear this, you that **t** on the needy,
Mt 7: 6 swine, or they will **t** them under foot
Rev 11: 2 and they will **t** over the holy city

TRAMPLED → TRAMPLE
2Ki 9:33 and on the horses, which **t** on her.
Isa 63: 6 I **t** down peoples in my anger,
Da 8: 7 the ram down to the ground and **t**
8:10 some of the stars, and **t** on them.
Mt 5:13 but is thrown out and **t** under foot.
Lk 21:24 and Jerusalem will be **t** on by the
     Gentiles,
1Mc 3:45 The sanctuary was **t** down,

TRANCE·
Da 8:18 was speaking to me, I fell into a **t**,
10: 9 sound of his words, I fell into a **t**,
Ac 10:10 was being prepared, he fell into a **t**.
11: 5 and in a **t** I saw a vision.
22:17 praying in the temple, I fell into a **t**

TRANSFER
2Sa 3:10 to **t** the kingdom from the house of
     Saul,

TRANSFIGURED·
Mt 17: 2 And he was **t** before them,
Mk 9: 2 And he was **t** before them,

TRANSFORM· → TRANSFORMED
Php 3:21 will **t** the body of our humiliation

TRANSFORMED → TRANSFORM
Ro 12: 2 be **t** by the renewing of your minds,
2Co 3:18 are being **t** into the same image

TRANSGRESS → TRANSGRESSED, TRANSGRESSION, TRANSGRESSIONS, TRANSGRESSOR, TRANSGRESSORS
Nu 14:41 continue to **t** the command of
Jos 23:16 If you **t** the covenant of the LORD
Wis 6: 9 you may learn wisdom and not **t**.

TRANSGRESSED → TRANSGRESS
Dt 26:13 I have neither **t** nor forgotten any
Da 9:11 "All Israel has **t** your law and turned

TRANSGRESSION → TRANSGRESS
Ex 23:21 for he will not pardon your **t**;
34: 7 forgiving iniquity and **t** and sin,
Ps 19:13 blameless, and innocent of great **t**.
Isa 53: 8 stricken for the **t** of my people.
Da 9:24 to finish the **t**, to put an end to sin,
Mic 1: 5 All this is for the **t** of Jacob
3: 8 to declare to Jacob his **t** and
6: 7 Shall I give my firstborn for my **t**,
Gal 6: 1 if anyone is detected in a **t**,

2Pe 2:16 but was rebuked for his own t;

TRANSGRESSIONS → TRANSGRESS
Ps 32: 5 "I will confess my t to the LORD,"
39: 8 Deliver me from all my t.
51: 1 according to your abundant mercy blot out my t.
51: 3 For I know my t, and my sin is ever
65: 3 overwhelm us, you forgive our t.
103:12 so far he removes our t from us.
Isa 43:25 I, I am He who blots out your t for
50: 1 your t your mother was put away.
53: 5 But he was wounded for our t,
Mic 1:13 for in you were found the t of Israel.
Gal 3:19 It was added because of t,
Man 1:12 sinned, and I acknowledge my t.

TRANSGRESSOR* → TRANSGRESS
Gal 2:18 then I demonstrate that I am a t.
1Ti 2:14 but the woman was deceived and became a t.
Jas 2:11 you have become a t of the law.

TRANSGRESSORS → TRANSGRESS
Ps 51:13 Then I will teach t your ways,
Isa 53:12 and was numbered with the t;
53:12 and made intercession for the t.

TRANSPARENT*
Rev 21:21 of the city is pure gold, t as glass.

TRAP → ENTRAP, TRAPPED
Jos 23:13 they shall be a snare and a t for you,
Ps 69:22 Let their table be a t for them,
Isa 8:14 a t and a snare for the inhabitants of Jerusalem.
Lk 20:20 in order to t him by what he said,
Ro 11: 9 their table become a snare and a t,

TRAPPED → TRAP
Ps 59:12 let them be t in their pride.
1Ti 6: 9 and are t by many senseless and harmful desires

TRAVEL → TRAVELER
Ex 13:21 they might t by day and by night.

TRAVELER → TRAVEL
Job 31:32 I have opened my doors to the t—
Jer 14: 8 like a t turning aside for the night?

TREACHEROUS → TREASON
Ps 25: 3 be ashamed who are wantonly t.
Isa 24:16 For the t deal treacherously,
Hab 1:13 why do you look on the t,
2Ti 3: 4 t, reckless, swollen with conceit,

TREAD → DOWNTRODDEN, TREADING, TREAD
Dt 33:29 and you shall t on their backs.
Ps 91:13 You will t on the lion and the adder,
Mic 7:19 he will t our iniquities under foot.
Lk 10:19 to t on snakes and scorpions,
Rev 19:15 he will t the wine press of the fury

TREADING → TREAD
Dt 25: 4 not muzzle an ox while it is t out
1Co 9: 9 not muzzle an ox while it is t out
1Ti 5:18 not muzzle an ox while it is t out

TREADS → TREAD
Am 4:13 and t on the heights of the earth—

TREASON → TRAITOR, TREACHEROUS
2Ki 11:14 Athaliah tore her clothes and cried, "T! T!"

TREASURE → TREASURED, TREASURER, TREASURERS, TREASURES, TREASURIES, TREASURY
Ps 119:11 I t your word in my heart,
Isa 33: 6 the fear of the LORD is Zion's t.
Mt 6:21 where your t is, there your heart
13:44 kingdom of heaven is like t hidden

19:21 and you will have t in heaven;
Lk 12:33 an unfailing t in heaven,
2Co 4: 7 But we have this t in clay jars,
1Ti 6:19 the t of a good foundation for
2Ti 1:14 Guard the good t entrusted to you,
Sir 41:14 hidden wisdom and unseen t—

TREASURED* → TREASURE
Ex 19: 5 be my t possession out of all the
Dt 7: 6 to be his people, his t possession.
14: 2 to be his people, his t possession.
26:18 to be his t people, as he promised
Job 23:12 I have t in my bosom the words of his mouth.
Eze 7:22 so that they may profane my t place;
Lk 2:19 But Mary t all these words and
2:51 His mother t all these things in her heart.

TREASURES → TREASURE
Dt 33:19 and the hidden t of the sand.
2Ki 24:13 He carried off all the t of the house
Pr 10: 2 T gained by wickedness do not profit,
Isa 45: 3 the t of darkness and riches hidden
Mt 6:19 "Do t store up for yourselves t on earth,
Col 2: 3 are hidden all the t of wisdom
Heb 11:26 to be greater wealth than the t

TREASURIES → TREASURE
Pr 8:21 who love me, and filling their t.
Sir 1:25 In the t of wisdom are wise sayings,

TREASURY → TREASURE
Mt 27: 6 not lawful to put them into the t,
Mk 12:43 those who are contributing to the t.
Sir 29:12 Store up almsgiving in your t,

TREATING → TREATMENT
Heb 12: 7 God is t you as children;

TREATMENT → TREATING
Col 2:23 humility, and severe t of the body,

TREATY
Jos 9: 6 so now make a t with us."

TREE → TREES
Ge 1:29 and every t with seed in its fruit;
2: 9 the t of life also in the midst of the garden, and the t of the knowledge of good and evil.
3: 1 'You shall not eat from any t in the
3:24 to guard the way to the t of life.
Dt 21:23 hung on a t is under God's curse.
1Ki 14:23 high hill and under every green t;
19: 4 sat down under a solitary broom t.
Ps 52: 8 But I am like a green olive t in the house of God.
92:12 righteous flourish like the palm t,
Pr 3:18 She is a t of life to those who lay hold of her;
11:30 fruit of the righteous is a t of life,
27:18 who tends a fig t will eat its fruit,
Isa 65:22 like the days of a t shall the days of my people
Jer 17: 8 shall be like a t planted by water,
Eze 17:24 I bring low the high t, I make high the low t;
Da 4:10 a t at the center of the earth,
Hos 9:10 Like the first fruit on the fig t,
14: 6 his beauty shall be like the olive t,
Hab 3:17 Though the fig t does not blossom,
Zec 3:10 to come under your vine and fig t."
Mt 3:10 every t therefore that does
12:33 for the t is known by its fruit.
Mk 11:13 Seeing in the distance a fig t in leaf,
Lk 19: 4 climbed a sycamore t to see him,
Ac 5:30 had killed by hanging him on a t.
Ro 11:24 grafted back into their own olive t.
Jas 3:12 Can a fig t, my brothers and sisters,
Rev 2: 7 from the t of life that is in the paradise of God.

22: 2 the t of life with its twelve kinds
22:14 have the right to the t of life and
22:19 take away that person's share in the t

EVERY GREEN TREE 1Ki 14:23; 2Ki 16:4; 17:10; 2Ch 28:4; Isa 57:5; Jer 2:20; 3:6, 13; 17:2; Eze 6:13; 20:47

EVERY TREE Ge 1:29; 2:9; Ex 9:25; 10:5; Ne 10:35, 37; Isa 44:23; Mt 3:10; 7:19; Lk 3:9; 2Es 16:29

TREE OF LIFE Ge 2:9; 3:22, 24; Pr 3:18; 11:30; 13:12; 15:4; Rev 2:7; 22:2, 14, 19; 2Es 2:12; 8:52; 4Mc 18:16

TREES → TREE
Ge 1:11 and fruit t of every kind on earth
3: 2 "We may eat of the fruit of the t in the garden,
Dt 20:19 Are t in the field human beings
Jdg 9: 8 t once went out to anoint a king
1Ch 14:15 marching in the tops of the balsam t,
Ps 96:12 all the t of the forest sing for joy
Isa 55:12 all the t of the field shall clap their
Eze 47:12 will grow all kinds of t for food.
Zec 4:11 "What are these two olive t on the
Mt 3:10 the ax is lying at the root of the t;
Mk 8:24 "I can see people, but they look like t, walking."
Jude 1:12 autumn t without fruit, twice dead,
Rev 8: 7 and a third of the t were burned up,
11: 4 two olive t and the two lampstands

TREMBLE → TREMBLED, TREMBLES, TREMBLING
1Ch 16:30 t before him, all the earth.
Ps 99: 1 The LORD is king; let the peoples t!
114: 7 T, O earth, at the presence of the LORD,
Jer 5:22 the LORD; Do you not t before me?
Joel 2: 1 Let all the inhabitants of the land t,
Hab 3: 6 he looked and made the nations t.

TREMBLED → TREMBLE
Ex 19:16 the people who were in the camp t.
20:18 they were afraid and t and stood at
2Sa 22: 8 the foundations of the heavens t

TREMBLES → TREMBLE
Ps 97: 4 up the world; the earth sees and t.
104:32 who looks on the earth and it t,
Isa 66: 2 humble and contrite in spirit, who t

TREMBLING → TREMBLE
Ps 2:11 Serve the LORD with fear, with t
Php 2:12 work out your own salvation with fear and t;

FEAR AND ... TREMBLING Ps 55:5; Mk 5:33; 1Co 2:3; 2Co 7:15; Eph 6:5; Php 2:12; Jdt 15:2; 2Es 15:33, 37; 4Mc 4:10

TRENCH
1Ki 18:38 licked up the water that was in the t.

TRESPASS → TRESPASSES
Ro 5:15 But the free gift is not like the t.
5:17 If, because of the one man's t,
5:18 as one man's t led to condemnation
5:20 with the result that the t multiplied;

TRESPASSES → TRESPASS
Mt 6:14 For if you forgive others their t,
Ro 5:16 free gift following many t brings justification.
2Co 5:19 not counting their t against them,
Eph 2: 1 were dead through the t and sins
Col 2:13 when he forgave us all our t,

TRIAL → TRIALS
Nu 35:12 not die until there is a t before the
Ps 37:33 when they are brought to t.
Mk 13:11 When they bring you to t and hand
Lk 11: 4 do not bring us to the time of t."
22:40 may not come into the time of t."

2Pe 2: 9 knows how to rescue the godly
from **t,**
Rev 3:10 I will keep you from the hour of **t**

TRIALS → TRIAL

Dt 7:19 the great **t** that your eyes saw,
29: 3 the great **t** that your eyes saw,
Lk 22:28 who have stood by me in my **t;**
Jas 1: 2 whenever you face **t** of any kind,
1Pe 1: 6 you have had to suffer various **t,**

TRIBAL → TRIBE

Jos 11:23 according to their **t** allotments.

TRIBE → HALF-TRIBE, TRIBAL, TRIBES

Nu 1: 4 A man from each **t** shall be with you
36: 9 No inheritance shall be transferred
from one **t**
Jos 13:14 the **t** of Levi alone Moses gave no
inheritance;
Jdg 21: 6 One **t** is cut off from Israel this day.
1Ki 11:13 I will give one **t** to your son,
Ps 78:68 but he chose the **t** of Judah,
Heb 7:13 belonged to another **t,**
Rev 5: 5 See, the Lion of the **t** of Judah,
5: 9 saints from every **t** and language
14: 6 to every nation and **t** and language

TRIBE OF ASHER Nu 1:41; 2:27; 10:26;
13:13; Jos 19:24, 31; 21:6, 30; 1Ch 6:74; Lk
2:36; Rev 7:6

TRIBE OF BENJAMIN Nu 1:37; 2:22;
10:24; 13:9; 34:21; Jos 18:11, 20, 21, 28;
21:17; Jdg 20:12; 1Sa 9:21; 10:20, 21; 1Ki
12:21; 1Ch 6:60; Ac 13:21; Ro 11:1; Php 3:5;
Rev 7:8; AdE 11:2; 2:5; 2Mc 3:4

TRIBE OF EPHRAIM Nu 1:33; 13:8; Jos
21:5, 20; 1Ch 6:66; Ps 78:67

TRIBE OF DAN Ex 31:6; 35:34; 38:23; Lev
24:11; Nu 1:39; 13:12; Jos 19:40, 48; 21:5, 23

TRIBE OF GAD Nu 1:25; 2:14; 10:20;
13:15; Jos 20:8; 21:7, 38; 1Ch 6:80; Rev 7:5

TRIBE OF ISSACHAR Nu 1:29; 2:5;
10:15; 13:7; Jos 19:17, 23; 21:6, 28; 1Ch 6:72;
Rev 7:7

TRIBE OF JOSEPH Nu 13:11; 36:5; Jos
17:14, 16; 18:11; Rev 7:8

TRIBE OF JUDAH Ex 31:2; 35:30; 38:22;
Nu 1:27; 7:12; 13:6; 34:19; Jos 7:1, 16, 18;
18:11, 14; 19:1, 9; 21:9; 1Ki 12:20; 2Ki 17:18;
Ps 78:68; Da 1:6; Rev 5:5; 7:5; Sir 45:25; 1Es
5:5, 66; 9:5

TRIBE OF LEVI Nu 1:49; 3:6; 18:2; Dt 10:8;
18:1; Jos 13:14, 33; 1Ch 23:14; Rev 7:7; Sir
45:6; 2Es 1:3

TRIBE OF MANASSEH Nu 1:35; 2:20;
10:23; 13:11; Jos 17:1, 2; 20:8; 22:7; Rev 7:6

TRIBE OF NAPHTALI Nu 1:43; 2:29;
10:27; 13:14; Jos 19:32, 32, 39; 21:6, 32; Jdg
4:6; 1Ki 7:14; 1Ch 6:76; Rev 7:6; Tob 1:1

TRIBE OF REUBEN Nu 1:21; 13:4; Jos
20:8; 21:7, 36; 1Ch 6:78; Rev 7:5

TRIBE OF SIMEON Nu 1:23; 2:12; 10:19;
13:5; Jos 19:1, 8, 9, 9; 21:9; Rev 7:7; Jdt 6:15

TRIBE OF ZEBULUN Nu 1:31; 2:7; 10:16;
13:10; Jos 19:10, 16; 21:7, 34; Jdg 4:6; 1Ch
6:77; Rev 7:8

TRIBES → TRIBE

Ge 49:28 All these are the twelve **t** of Israel,
Ex 24: 4 to the twelve **t** of Israel.
39:14 with its name, for the twelve **t.**
1Ki 11:31 of Solomon, and will give you ten **t.**
18:31 of the sons of Jacob,
Ps 122: 4 To it the **t** go up, the **t** of the LORD,
Isa 49: 6 be my servant to raise up the **t**
Mt 19:28 judging the twelve **t** of Israel.
Jas 1: 1 To the twelve **t** in the Dispersion:
Rev 21:12 inscribed the names of the twelve **t**

ALL THE TRIBES Dt 29:21; Jos 24:1; Jdg
20:2, 10; 21:5; 1Sa 2:28; 10:20; 2Sa 5:1;

15:10; 19:9; 20:14; 24:2; 1Ki 11:32; 14:21;
2Ki 21:7; 2Ch 11:16; 12:13; 33:7; Jer 1:15;
25:9; Eze 48:19; Zec 9:1; Mt 24:30; Rev 1:7;
Tob 1:4, 4; Sir 36:13

TRIBES OF ISRAEL Ge 49:16, 28; Ex
24:4; Nu 10:4; 31:4; Dt 29:21; 33:5; Jos 3:12;
12:7; 24:1; Jdg 18:1; 20:2, 10, 12; 21:5, 8, 15;
1Sa 2:28; 9:21; 10:20; 15:17; 2Sa 5:1; 15:10;
19:9; 20:14; 24:2; 1Ki 8:16; 11:32; 14:21; 2Ki
21:7; 1Ch 27:16, 22; 2Ch 6:5; 11:16; 12:13;
33:7; Ezr 6:17; Ps 78:55; Eze 37:19; 47:13, 21,
22; 48:19, 29, 31; Hos 5:9; Zec 9:1; Mt 19:28;
Lk 22:30; Tob 1:4; Sir 45:11; 1Es 7:8

TRIBES OF THE ISRAELITES Nu 30:1;
36:9; Jos 4:5, 8; 14:1; 19:51; 21:1; Rev 21:12

TWELVE TRIBES Ge 49:28; Ex 24:4;
28:21; 39:14; Eze 47:13; Mt 19:28; Lk 22:30;
Ac 26:7; Jas 1:1; Rev 21:12; Sir 44:23

TRIBUTE

Nu 31:28 set aside as **t** for the LORD,
1Ki 4:21 they brought **t** and served Solomon

TRIED → TRY

Ex 8:18 magicians **t** to produce gnats by
Jn 19:12 From then on Pilate **t** to release him,
Gal 1:23 the faith he once **t** to destroy."

TRIMMED

Mt 25: 7 bridesmaids got up and **t** their lamps

TRIUMPH → TRIUMPHAL, TRIUMPHING, TRIUMPHS

Ps 54: 7 has looked in **t** on my enemies.
112: 8 they will look in **t** on their foes.
118: 7 look in **t** on those who hate me.
Pr 28:12 the righteous **t,** there is great glory,

TRIUMPHAL* → TRIUMPH

2Co 2:14 who in Christ always leads us in **t**
procession,

TRIUMPHING* → TRIUMPH

Col 2:15 public example of them, **t** over them

TRIUMPHS → TRIUMPH

Jas 2:13 mercy **t** over judgment.

TRIVIAL*

1Co 6: 2 are you incompetent to try **t** cases?

TROPHIMUS

2Ti 4:20 **T** I left ill in Miletus.

TROUBLE → TROUBLED, TROUBLER, TROUBLES

Jos 7:25 "Why did you bring **t** on us?
Job 5: 7 but human beings are born to **t** just
14: 1 few of days and full of **t,**
Ps 9: 9 a stronghold in times of **t.**
10:14 Indeed you note **t** and grief,
22:11 for **t** is near and there is no one to
27: 5 hide me in his shelter in the day of **t**
32: 7 you preserve me from **t;**
37:39 he is their refuge in the time of **t.**
41: 1 LORD delivers them in the day of **t.**
46: 1 a very present help in **t.**
50:15 Call on me in the day of **t;**
66:14 mouth promised when I was in **t.**
86: 7 In the day of my **t** I call on you,
90:10 then their span is only toil and **t;**
91:15 I will be with them in **t,**
107: 6 they cried to the LORD in their **t,**
119:143 **T** and anguish have come upon me,
138: 7 Though I walk in the midst of **t,**
143:11 In your righteousness bring me out
of **t.**
Pr 11: 8 The righteous are delivered from **t,**
11:29 Those who **t** their households will
inherit wind,
12:13 but the righteous escape from **t.**
12:21 but the wicked are filled with **t.**
15:27 are greedy for unjust gain make **t**

25:19 in a faithless person in time of **t.**
Ecc 12: 1 before the days of **t** come,
Isa 33: 2 our salvation in the time of **t.**
Jer 14: 8 hope of Israel, its savior in time of **t,**
Na 1: 7 is good, a stronghold in a day of **t;**
Mt 6:34 Today's **t** is enough for today.
13:21 **t** or persecution arises on account
of the word,
Sir 51:10 do not forsake me in the days of **t,**

DAY OF ... TROUBLE Ps 20:1; 27:5; 41:1;
50:15; 77:2; 86:7; Pr 16:4; Jer 16:19; 51:2; Na
1:7

TROUBLED → TROUBLE

Jn 14: 1 "Do not let your hearts be **t.**
14:27 Do not let your hearts be **t,**

TROUBLER → TROUBLE

1Ki 18:17 to him, "Is it you, you **t** of Israel?"

TROUBLES → TROUBLE

Job 5:19 He will deliver you from six **t;**
Ps 25:17 Relieve the **t** of my heart,
34:17 and rescues them from all their **t.**

TRUE → TRUTH

Nu 11:23 see whether my word will come **t**
Dt 18:22 does not take place or prove **t,**
1Sa 9: 6 Whatever he says always comes **t.**
1Ki 10: 6 "The report was that I heard in my
2Ch 15: 3 time Israel was without the **t** God,
Ps 119:151 and all your commandments are **t.**
Pr 22:21 to show you what is right and **t,**
Jer 10:10 But the LORD is the **t** God;
28: 9 the word of that prophet comes **t,**
50: 7 the **t** pasture, the LORD,
Lk 16:11 who will entrust to you the **t** riches?
Jn 1: 9 The **t** light, which enlightens
4:23 the **t** worshipers will worship the
Father in spirit and truth,
6:32 Father who gives you the **t** bread
7:28 who sent me is **t,** and you do not
15: 1 "I am the **t** vine, and my Father is
17: 3 they may know you, the only **t** God,
19:35 His testimony is **t,** and he knows
21:24 and we know that his testimony is **t.**
Ro 3: 4 Although everyone is a liar, let God
be proved **t,**
Eph 4:24 likeness of God in **t** righteousness
Php 4: 8 Finally, beloved, whatever is **t,**
1Th 1: 9 to serve a living and **t** God,
1Jn 2: 8 a new commandment that is **t** in him
2: 8 and the **t** light is already shining.
5:20 so that we may know him who is **t;**
5:20 He is the **t** God and eternal life.
3Jn 1:12 you know that our testimony is **t.**
Rev 3: 7 the words of the holy one, the **t** one,
3:14 the Amen, the faithful and **t** witness,
6:10 "Sovereign Lord, holy and **t,**
15: 3 Just and **t** are your ways, King of
16: 7 your judgments are **t** and just!"
19: 2 for his judgments are **t** and just;
19: 9 to me, "These are **t** words of God."
19:11 Its rider is called Faithful and **T,**
21: 5 these words are trustworthy and **t."**
22: 6 "These words are trustworthy and **t,**

TRUMPET → TRUMPETERS, TRUMPETS

Ex 19:16 a blast of a **t** so loud that all the
Isa 27:13 on that day a great **t** will be blown,
Eze 33: 5 of the **t** and did not take warning;
Joel 2:15 Blow the **t** in Zion; sanctify a fast;
Zec 9:14 GOD will sound the **t** and march
Mt 24:31 his angels with a loud **t** call,
1Co 15:52 twinkling of an eye, at the last **t.**
1Th 4:16 and with the sound of God's **t,**
Rev 1:10 behind me a loud voice like a **t**
8: 7 The first angel blew his **t,**

TRUMPETERS → TRUMPET

2Ch 5:13 It was the duty of the **t** and singers

TRUMPETS → TRUMPET

Nu 10: 2 Make two silver t; you shall make
    29: 1 It is a day for you to blow the t,
Jos 6: 8 blowing the t,
Jdg 7:19 they blew the t and smashed the jars
Rev 8: 2 and seven t were given to them.

TRUST → ENTRUST, ENTRUSTED, TRUSTED, TRUSTEES, TRUSTING, TRUSTS, TRUSTWORTHY

Ex 19: 9 when I speak with you and so t you
Nu 20:12 "Because you did not t in me,
Dt   1:32 you have no t in the LORD your God
Jdg 11:20 not t Israel to pass through his
1Ch 9:22 established them in their office of t.
Job 4:18 Even in his servants he puts no t,
    15:15 God puts no t even in his holy ones,
    15:31 Let them not t in emptiness,
    31:24 "If I have made gold my t,
Ps   4: 5 and put your t in the LORD.
     9:10 know your name put their t in you,
    25: 2 O my God, in you I t;
    31: 6 but I t in the LORD.
    31:14 I t in you, O LORD; I say, "You are my God."
    32:10 love surrounds those who t in
    33:21 because we t in his holy name.
    37: 3 T in the LORD, and do good;
    37: 5 t in him, and he will act.
    40: 3 and put their t in the LORD.
    40: 4 Happy are those who make the LORD their t,
    44: 6 in my bow do I t, nor can my sword
    49: 6 those who t in their wealth and
    52: 8 I t in the steadfast love of God
    55:23 But I will t in you.
    56: 3 when I am afraid, I put my t in you.
    56: 4 whose word I praise, in God I t;
    56:11 in God I t; I am
    62: 8 T in him at all times, O people;
    71: 5 Lord, are my hope, my t, O LORD,
    78:22 and did not t his saving power.
    91: 2 my God, in whom I t."
   115: 8 so are all who t in them.
   115: 9 O Israel, t in the LORD!
   115:10 O house of Aaron, t in the LORD!
   115:11 who fear the LORD, t in the LORD!
   119:42 for I t in your word.
   125: 1 Those who t in the LORD are like
   135:18 who t them shall become like them,
   143: 8 for in you I put my t.
   146: 3 Do not put your t in princes,
Pr   3: 5 T in the LORD with all your heart,
    16:20 happy are those who t in the LORD.
    22:19 So that your t may be in the LORD,
Isa 12: 2 Surely God is my salvation; I will t,
    26: 4 T in the LORD forever,
    30:15 and in it shall be your strength.
    31: 1 t in chariots because they are many
    42:17 those who t in carved images,
Jer 2:37 has rejected those in whom you t,
     5:17 your fortified cities in which you t.
     7: 4 Do not t in these deceptive words:
     7:14 in which you t, and to
     9: 4 and put no t in any of your kin;
    17: 7 Blessed are those who t in the LORD, whose t is the LORD.
    28:15 and you made this people t in a lie.
    49:11 and let your widows t in me.
Mic 7: 5 Put no t in a friend, have no
Heb 2:13 And again, "I will put my t in him."
Sir 2: 6 T in him, and he will help you;

TRUSTED → TRUST

1Sa 27:12 Achish t David, thinking,
2Ki 18: 5 He t in the LORD the God of Israel;
1Ch 5:20 their entreaty because they t in him.
Job 12:20 deprives of speech those who are t,
Ps 22: 4 In you our ancestors t; they trusted,
    22: 5 they t, and you delivered them.

    22: 5 in you they t, and were not put to shame.
    26: 1 t in the LORD without wavering.
    41: 9 Even my bosom friend in whom I t,
    52: 7 but t in abundant riches, and sought
Jer 13:25 you have forgotten me and t in lies.
    38:22 'Your t friends have seduced you
Eze 16:15 But you t in your beauty,
Da   3:28 delivered his servants who t in him.
     6:23 because he had t in his God.
Zep 3: 2 It has not t in the LORD;
Lk 11:22 takes away his armor in which he t
Sir 2:10 has anyone t in the Lord
Sus 1:35 for her heart t in the Lord.

TRUSTEES* → TRUST

Gal 4: 2 they remain under guardians and t

TRUSTING → TRUST

Jer 7: 8 Here you are, t in deceptive words

TRUSTS → TRUST

Ps 21: 7 For the king t in the LORD,
    28: 7 in him my heart t;
    84:12 happy is everyone who t in you.
    86: 2 save your servant who t in you.
Pr 28:25 t in the LORD will be enriched.
    29:25 but one who t in the LORD is secure.
Isa 28:16 "One who t will not panic."
Hab 2:18 its maker t in what has been made,
Mt 27:43 He t in God; let God deliver him
Ro   4: 5 t him who justifies the ungodly,

TRUSTWORTHY* → TRUST

Ex 18:21 are t, and hate dishonest gain;
1Sa 3:20 knew that Samuel was a t prophet
Ps 111: 7 and just; all his precepts are t.
Pr 11:13 who is t in spirit keeps a confidence.
Da   2:45 is certain, and its interpretation t."
Mt 25:21 'Well done, good and t slave;
    25:23 'Well done, good and t slave;
Lk 19:17 have been t in a very small thing,
1Co 4: 2 of stewards that they be found t.
     7:25 as one who by the Lord's mercy is t.
Tit 1: 9 a firm grasp of the word that is t in
Rev 21: 5 for these words are t and true."
    22: 6 "These words are t and true,
Tob 5: 3 find yourself a t man to go with you
     5: 9 he is t enough to go with you."
    10: 6 The man who went with him is t
Sir 31:23 testimony to his generosity is t.
    36:21 and let your prophets be found t.
    46:15 words he became known as a t seer.
    48:22 who was great and t in his visions.
1Mc 14:41 until a t prophet should arise,
2Es 15: 2 for they are t and true.

TRUTH → TRUE, TRUTHFUL, TRUTHFULNESS

Ge 42:16 whether there is t in you;
1Ki 17:24 the word of the LORD in your mouth is t."
    22:16 to tell me nothing but the t in the
2Ch 18:15 to tell me nothing but the t in the
Ps 15: 2 and speak the t from their heart;
    25: 5 Lead me in your t, and teach me,
    43: 3 O send out your light and your t;
    45: 4 victoriously for the cause of t
    51: 6 You desire t in the inward being;
    52: 3 and lying more than speaking the t.
    86:11 O LORD, that I may walk in your t;
    96:13 and the peoples with his t.
   119:43 not take the word of t utterly out of
   119:142 and your law is the t.
   119:160 The sum of your word is t;
   145:18 to all who call on him in t.
Pr 23:23 Buy t, and do not sell it;
Isa 45:19 I the LORD speak the t, I declare
    48: 1 invoke the God of Israel, but not in t
    59:14 for t stumbles in the public square,
    59:15 T is lacking, and whoever turns
Jer 5: 1 who acts justly and seeks t—
     5: 3 LORD, do your eyes not look for t?

     7:28 t has perished; it is cut off from
     9: 3 land for falsehood, and not for t;
     9: 5 and no one speaks the t;
    26:15 for in t the LORD sent me to you
Da   8:12 it cast t to the ground,
    10:21 what is inscribed in the book of t.
Am   5:10 they abhor the one who speaks the t.
Zec 8:16 Speak the t to one another,
     8:19 therefore love t and peace.
Mk   5:33 and told him the whole t.
Lk 20:21 but teach the way of God in accordance with t.
Jn   1:14 father's only son, full of grace and t.
     1:17 grace and t came through Jesus Christ.
     4:23 worship the Father in spirit and t,
     4:24 must worship in spirit and t."
     5:33 and he testified to the t.
     8:32 and you will know the t,
     8:32 and the t will make you free."
     8:40 who has told you the t that I heard
     8:44 because there is no t in him.
     8:45 I tell the t, you do not believe me.
    14: 6 Jesus said to him, "I am the way, and the t, and the life.
    14:17 This is the Spirit of t,
    15:26 the Spirit of t who comes from the Father,
    16:13 When the Spirit of t comes, he will guide you into all the t;
    17:17 Sanctify them in the t; your word is t.
    18:37 I came into the world, to testify to the t.
    18:38 Pilate asked him, "What is t?"
    19:35 and he knows that he tells the t.)
Ac 20:30 will come distorting the t
Ro   1:18 by their wickedness suppress the t.
     1:25 the t about God for a lie
     2: 2 such things is in accordance with t."
     2: 8 who obey not the t but wickedness,
     2:20 in the law the embodiment of knowledge and t,
     9: 1 I am speaking the t in Christ—
    15: 8 of the circumcised on behalf of the t
1Co 5: 8 unleavened bread of sincerity and t.
    13: 6 in wrongdoing, but rejoices in the t.
2Co 4: 2 of the t we commend ourselves to
    11:10 As the t of Christ is in me,
    12: 6 for I will be speaking the t,
    13: 8 we cannot do anything against the t, but only for the t.
Gal 5: 7 prevented you from obeying the t?
Eph 1:13 when you had heard the word of t,
     4:15 But speaking the t in love,
     4:21 and were taught in him, as t is
     6:14 the belt of t around your waist,
Col 1: 5 before in the word of the t,
2Th 2:10 refused to love the t and so be saved
     2:13 and through belief in the t.
1Ti 2: 4 to come to the knowledge of the t.
     2: 7 teacher of the Gentiles in faith and t.
     3:15 the pillar and bulwark of the t.
     4: 3 those who believe and know the t.
     6: 5 in mind and bereft of the t,
2Ti 2:15 rightly explaining the word of t.
     2:18 swerved from the t by claiming that
     2:25 repent and come to know the t,
     3: 7 never arrive at a knowledge of the t.
     3: 8 counterfeit faith, also oppose the t.
     4: 4 turn away from listening to the t
Tit 1: 1 and the knowledge of the t that is
     1:14 of those who reject the t.
Heb 10:26 received the knowledge of the t,
Jas 1:18 the word of t,
     3:14 do not be boastful and false to the t.
     5:19 among you wanders from the t
1Pe 1:22 to the t so that you have genuine
2Pe 1:12 established in the t that has come to
     2: 2 the way of t will be maligned.
1Jn 1: 8 and the t is not in us.
     2: 4 in such a person the t does not exist;

2:21 not because you do not know the **t,**
2:21 know that no lie comes from the **t.**
3:18 word or speech, but in **t** and action.
3:19 we will know that we are from the **t**
4: 6 we know the spirit of **t** and the spirit
5: 6 for the Spirit is the **t.**
2Jn 1: 1 whom I love in the **t,**
1: 2 because of the **t** that abides in us
1: 3 the Father's Son, in **t** and love.
1: 4 of your children walking in the **t.**
3Jn 1: 1 the beloved Gaius, whom I love in **t.**
1: 3 testified to your faithfulness to the **t,**
1: 4 my children are walking in the **t.**
1: 8 may become co-workers with the **t.**
1:12 and so has the **t** itself.
Tob 3: 2 all your ways are mercy and **t;**
Sir 4:25 Never speak against the **t,**
2Es 5: 1 and the way of **t** shall be hidden,

TRUTHFUL* → TRUTH
Pr 12:19 **T** lips endure forever,
14:25 A **t** witness saves lives,
2Co 6: 7 **t** speech, and the power of God;

TRUTHFULNESS* → TRUTH
Ro 3: 7 God's **t** abounds to his glory,

TRY → TRIED
Ps 26: 2 Prove me, O LORD, and **t** me;
Lk 13:24 will **t** to enter and will not be able.
1Co 10:33 I **t** to please everyone in everything
2Co 5:11 we **t** to persuade others;
Eph 5:10 **T** to find out what is pleasing to the Lord.

TRYPHO
1Mc 11:39 A certain **T** had formerly been one
13:31 **T** dealt treacherously with

TUMORS
1Sa 5: 6 he terrified and struck them with **t,**
6: 4 "Five gold **t** and five gold mice,

TUNIC → TUNICS
Ex 28: 4 an ephod, a robe, a checkered **t,**
Lk 9: 3 nor money—not even an extra **t.**
Jn 19:23 **t** was seamless, woven in one piece

TUNICS → TUNIC
Ex 28:40 For Aaron's sons you shall make **t**
Da 3:27 their **t** were not harmed,
Mt 10:10 or two **t,** or sandals, or a staff;

TURBAN
Ex 28: 4 a checkered tunic, a **t,** and a sash.
Zec 3: 5 So they put a clean **t** on his head

TURN → TURNED, TURNING, TURNS
Ex 23:27 I will make all your enemies **t** their
32:12 **T** from your fierce wrath;
Nu 32:15 If you **t** away from following him,
Dt 5:32 shall not **t** to the right or to the left.
28:14 if you do not **t** aside from any of
30:10 because you **t** to the LORD your God
Jos 1: 7 do not **t** from it to the right hand or
2Ch 7:14 and **t** from their wicked ways,
30: 9 will not **t** away his face from you,
Ps 6: 4 **T,** O LORD, save my life;
25:16 **T** to me and be gracious to me,
119:36 **T** my heart to your decrees,
119:132 **T** to me and be gracious to me,
Pr 7:25 Do not let your hearts **t** aside to her ways;
Isa 6:10 and **t** and be healed."
28: 6 to those who **t** back the battle at
29:16 You **t** things upside down!
30:21 you **t** to the right or when you **t** to the left,
45:22 **T** to me and be saved, all the ends of the earth!
Jer 18:11 **T** now, all of you from your evil
31:13 I will **t** their mourning into joy,
Eze 33: 9 But if you warn the wicked to **t** from their ways,

33:11 **t** back, **t** back from your evil ways;
Joel 2:14 whether he will not **t** and relent,
Jnh 3: 9 he may **t** from his fierce anger,
Mal 4: 6 He will **t** the hearts of parents to their children
Mt 5:39 But if anyone strikes you on the right cheek, **t** the other also.
Lk 1:17 to **t** the hearts of parents to their children,
Jn 12:40 understand with their heart and **t—**
16:20 but your pain will **t** into joy.
Ac 3:19 and **t** to God so that your sins may be wiped out,
26:18 they may **t** from darkness to light
Gal 4: 9 how can you **t** back again
2Ti 4: 4 **t** away from listening to the truth
1Pe 3:11 **t** away from evil and do good;

TURNED → TURN
Dt 23: 5 your God **t** the curse into a blessing
1Ki 11: 4 his wives **t** away his heart after
2Ch 15: 4 in their distress they **t** to the LORD,
Est 9:22 had been **t** for them from sorrow
Ps 30:11 have **t** my mourning into dancing;
66: 6 He **t** the sea into dry land;
114: 3 sea looked and fled; Jordan **t** back.
Ecc 2:12 I **t** to consider wisdom and madness
Isa 9:12 For all this his anger has not **t** away;
53: 6 we have all **t** to our own way,
Hos 7:11 Ephraim is a cake not **t.**
Joel 2:31 The sun shall be **t** to darkness,
Jnh 3:10 how they **t** from their evil ways,
Zec 7:11 to listen, and **t** a stubborn shoulder,
Lk 22:32 when once you have **t** back,
Ro 3:12 All have **t** aside, together they have

TURNING → TURN
Ge 3:24 and a sword flaming and **t** to guard
2Ki 21:13 wiping it and **t** it upside down.
Ac 13:46 we are now **t** to the Gentiles.

TURNS → TURN
Dt 30:17 if your heart **t** away and you do not
Pr 15: 1 A soft answer **t** away wrath,
21: 1 he **t** it wherever he will.
Isa 44:25 who **t** back the wise,
2Co 3:16 but when one **t** to the Lord, the veil is removed.
2Pe 2:22 "The dog **t** back to its own vomit,"

TURTLEDOVES
Lev 5: 7 two **t** or two pigeons,
12: 8 she shall take two **t** or two pigeons,
Lk 2:24 "a pair of **t** or two young pigeons."

TWELVE
Ge 35:22 Now the sons of Jacob were **t.**
49:28 All these are the **t** tribes of Israel,
Ex 24: 4 the mountain, and set up **t** pillars,
28:21 **t** stones with names corresponding
Jos 4: 3 'Take **t** stones from here out of the
1Ki 11:30 and tore it into **t** pieces.
18:31 Elijah took **t** stones, according to
Mt 10: 1 Jesus summoned his **t** disciples
Lk 9:17 **t** baskets of broken pieces.
Jas 1: 1 To the **t** tribes in the Dispersion:
Rev 12: 1 and on her head a crown of **t** stars.
21:12 It has a great, high wall with **t** gates,
21:12 inscribed the names of the **t** tribes
21:14 wall of the city has **t** foundations,
21:14 the **t** names of the **t** apostles of
21:21 And the **t** gates are **t** pearls,
22: 2 tree of life with **t** kinds of fruit,

TWELVE TRIBES Ge 49:28; Ex 24:4;
28:21; 39:14; Eze 47:13; Mt 19:28; Lk 22:30;
Ac 26:7; Jas 1:1; Rev 21:12; Sir 44:23

TWENTY
Nu 1: 3 from **t** years and upward,

TWICE → TWO
Ex 16: 5 **t** as much as they gather on other days."

Nu 20:11 and struck the rock **t** with his staff;
1Sa 18:11 But David eluded him **t.**
1Ki 11: 9 who had appeared to him **t,**
Job 42:10 the LORD gave Job **t** as much as he had before.
Mk 14:30 very night, before the cock crows **t,**
Sir 7: 8 Do not commit a sin **t;**

TWILIGHT
Ex 12: 6 of Israel shall slaughter it at **t.**
16:12 to them, 'At **t** you shall eat meat,

TWIN → TWINS
Jn 20:24 But Thomas (who was called the **T),**

TWINKLING*
1Co 15:52 in the **t** of an eye, at the last trumpet

TWINS → TWIN
Ge 25:24 there were **t** in her womb.

TWISTED → TWISTING
Ex 26: 1 with ten curtains of fine **t** linen,

TWISTING → TWISTED
Mt 27:29 after **t** some thorns into a crown,

TWO → SECOND, TWICE, TWO-EDGED
Ge 1:16 God made the **t** great lights—
4:19 Lamech took **t** wives; the name of
6:19 bring **t** of every kind into the ark,
Ex 31:18 the **t** tablets of the covenant,
34: 1 "Cut **t** tablets of stone like the
Dt 4:13 he wrote them on **t** stone tablets.
17: 6 of **t** or three witnesses the death
25:13 not have in your bag **t** kinds of weights,
1Ki 3:16 **t** women who were prostitutes came to the king
Pr 30: 7 **T** things I ask of you;
30:15 leech has **t** daughters; "Give, give,"
Ecc 4: 9 **T** are better than one, because they
Isa 6: 2 with **t** they covered their faces,
Eze 1:11 each creature had **t** wings,
Da 8: 3 beside the river. It had **t** horns.
Zec 4:11 "What are these **t** olive trees on the
14: 4 Mount of Olives shall be split in **t**
Mt 6:24 "No one can serve **t** masters;
18:16 by the evidence of **t** or three witnesses.
19: 5 and the **t** shall become one flesh'?
Mk 6: 7 and began to send them out **t** by **t,**
12:42 and put in **t** small copper coins,
15:27 with him they crucified **t** bandits,
Lk 9:30 they saw **t** men, Moses and Elijah,
17:35 be **t** women grinding meal together;
18:10 "**T** men went up to the temple to pray,
1Co 6:16 "The **t** shall be one flesh."
Gal 4:24 these women are **t** covenants.
Eph 5:31 and the **t** will become one flesh."
Rev 11: 3 I will grant my **t** witnesses authority
19:20 These **t** were thrown alive into the lake of fire

TWO-EDGED → EDGE, TWO
Heb 4:12 sharper than any **t** sword,
Rev 1:16 his mouth came a sharp, **t** sword,
2:12 of him who has the sharp **t** sword;
Sir 21: 3 All lawlessness is like a **t** sword;

TYCHICUS*
Companion of Paul (Ac 20:4; Eph 6:21; Col 4:7; 2Ti 4:12; Tit 3:12).

TYPE
Ro 5:14 a **t** of the one who was to come.

TYRANNUS*
Ac 19: 9 argued daily in the lecture hall of **T.**

TYRE
1Ki 5: 1 King Hiram of **T** sent his servants to Solomon,
Ps 45:12 the people of **T** will seek your favor

Isa 23: 1 The oracle concerning **T**.
Eze 27: 2 raise a lamentation over **T**,
28:12 a lamentation over the king of **T**,
Mt 11:22 be more tolerable for **T** and Sidon

$\mathcal{U}$

UGLY

Ge 41: 3 Then seven other cows, **u** and thin,

UNAPPROACHABLE

1Ti 6:16 and dwells in **u** light, whom no one
has ever seen

UNBELIEF → UNBELIEVER,
UNBELIEVER'S, UNBELIEVERS,
UNBELIEVING

Mk 6: 6 And he was amazed at their **u**.
9:24 cried out, "I believe; help my **u**!"
Ro 11:20 were broken off because of their **u**,
11:23 of Israel, if they do not persist in **u**,
1Ti 1:13 because I had acted ignorantly in **u**,
Heb 3:19 were unable to enter because of **u**.
2Es 15: 4 all unbelievers shall die in their **u**.

UNBELIEVER* → UNBELIEF

1Co 7:12 believer has a wife who is an **u**,
7:13 woman has a husband who is an **u**,
10:27 If an **u** invites you to a meal and
14:24 an **u** or outsider who enters is
reproved by all
2Co 6:15 does a believer share with an **u**?
1Ti 5: 8 has denied the faith and is worse
than an **u**.

UNBELIEVER'S* → UNBELIEF

1Co 14:25 secrets of the **u** heart are disclosed,

UNBELIEVERS* → UNBELIEF

Ro 15:31 may be rescued from the **u** in Judea,
1Co 6: 6 goes to court against a believer—
and before **u** at that?
14:22 a sign not for believers but for **u**,
while prophecy is not for **u** but for
14:23 in tongues, and outsiders or **u** enter,
2Co 4: 4 has blinded the minds of the **u**,
6:14 Do not be mismatched with **u**.
2Es 15: 4 For all **u** shall die in their unbelief.

UNBELIEVING* → UNBELIEF

Ac 14: 2 the **u** Jews stirred up the Gentiles
1Co 7:14 For the **u** husband is made holy
through his wife, and the **u** wife is
7:15 if the **u** partner separates, let it be
Tit 1:15 to the corrupt and **u** nothing is pure.
Heb 3:12 **u** heart that turns away from the
living God.
Wis 10: 7 as a monument to an **u** soul.

UNCEASING

Ro 9: 2 I have great sorrow and **u** anguish

UNCHANGEABLE

Heb 6:18 so that through two **u** things,

UNCHASTITY*

Mt 5:32 except on the ground of **u**,
19: 9 divorces his wife, except for **u**,

UNCIRCUMCISED
→ UNCIRCUMCISION

Ex 12:48 But no **u** person shall eat of it;
1Sa 17:26 For who is this **u** Philistine that he
Jer 9:26 For all these nations are **u**, and all
the house of Israel is **u** in heart.
Ac 7:51 people, **u** in heart and ears,
Ro 3:30 and the **u** through that same faith.
4:11 he had by faith while he was still **u**.
1Co 7:18 anyone at the time of his call **u**?
Gal 2: 7 entrusted with the gospel for the **u**,

Col 3:11 circumcised and **u**, barbarian,
1Mc 1:48 and to leave their sons **u**.

UNCIRCUMCISION
→ UNCIRCUMCISED

Ro 2:25 your circumcision has become **u**.
1Co 7:19 Circumcision is nothing, and **u** is
nothing;
Gal 5: 6 in Christ Jesus neither circumcision
nor **u** counts
6:15 circumcision nor **u** is anything;
Col 2:13 dead in trespasses and the **u**

UNCLEAN → UNCLEANNESS

Lev 5: 2 when any of you touch any **u** thing
Ps 106:39 Thus they became **u** by their acts,
Isa 6: 5 I am lost, for I am a man of **u** lips,
52:11 from there! Touch no **u** thing;
Mk 3:11 Whenever the **u** spirits saw him,
6: 7 them authority over the **u** spirits.
Ac 10:14 eaten anything that is profane or **u**."
Ro 14:14 in the Lord Jesus that nothing is **u**
2Co 6:17 and touch nothing **u**; then I will
Rev 21:27 But nothing **u** will enter it,
1Mc 1:47 sacrifice swine and other **u** animals,

UNCLEAN SPIRIT Zec 13:2; Mt 12:43; Mk
1:23, 26; 3:30; 5:2, 8; 7:25; 9:25; Lk 8:29;
9:42; 11:24

UNCLEAN SPIRITS Mt 10:1; Mk 1:27;
3:11; 5:12, 13; 6:7; Lk 4:36; 6:18; Ac 5:16; 8:7

UNCLEANNESS → UNCLEAN

Lev 5: 3 Or when you touch human **u**—
1Mc 13:48 He removed all **u** from it,

UNCLOTHED*

2Co 5: 4 not to be **u** but to be further clothed,

UNCOVER → UNCOVERED

Ru 3: 4 then, go and **u** his feet and lie down;

UNCOVERED → UNCOVER

Ge 9:21 and he lay **u** in his tent.
Ru 3: 7 and **u** his feet, and lay down.
Lk 12: 2 Nothing is covered up that will not
be **u**,

UNDER

Ge 24: 2 "Put your hand **u** my thigh
47:29 your hand **u** my thigh and promise
1Ki 4:25 all of them **u** their vines and fig
Ps 8: 6 you have put all things **u** their feet,
91: 4 and **u** his wings you will find refuge
Jer 3:13 among strangers **u** every green tree,
Mic 4: 4 they shall all sit **u** their own vines
4: 4 under their own vines and **u**
Mt 5:15 lighting a lamp puts it **u** the bushel
22:44 until I put your enemies **u** your feet"
Lk 13:34 hen gathers her brood **u** her wings,
Ac 4:12 for there is no other name **u** heaven
Ro 6:14 since you are not **u** law but **u** grace.
1Co 9:21 not free from God's law but am **u**
Christ's law)
15:27 all things in subjection **u** his feet."
Gal 3:10 of the law are **u** a curse;
4: 4 born of a woman, born **u** the law,
Eph 1:22 And he has put all things **u** his feet
Rev 6: 9 I saw **u** the altar the souls

UNDER [THE] LAW Lk 2:27; Ro 2:12;
3:19; 6:14, 15; 1Co 9:20, 20, 20; Gal 3:23;
4:4, 5; Php 3:6; Heb 9:22

UNDERGOING

1Pe 5: 9 are **u** the same kinds of suffering.

UNDERSTAND → UNDERSTANDING,
UNDERSTANDS, UNDERSTOOD

Ge 11: 7 will not **u** one another's speech."
Job 42: 3 I have uttered what I did not **u**,
Ps 73:16 But when I thought how to **u** this,
119:27 Make me **u** the way of your
precepts
Pr 2: 5 then you will **u** the fear of the LORD

2: 9 you will **u** righteousness and justice
30:18 for me; four I do not **u**:
Isa 1: 3 does not know, my people do not **u**.
44:18 minds as well, so that they cannot **u**.
Jer 17: 9 it is perverse—who can **u** it?
Da 9:25 Know therefore and **u**: from the
Hos 14: 9 Those who are wise **u** these things;
Mt 13:15 and **u** with their heart and turn—
24:15 the prophet Daniel (let the reader **u**),
Mk 4:13 to them, "Do you not **u** this parable?
Lk 24:45 he opened their minds to **u** the
scriptures,
Jn 13: 7 but later you will **u**."
Ac 8:30 "Do you **u** what you are reading?"
Ro 7:15 I do not **u** my own actions.
15:21 have never heard of him shall **u**."
1Co 2:12 **u** the gifts bestowed on us by God.
2:14 **u** them because they are spiritually
discerned.
Eph 5:17 but **u** what the will of the Lord is.
Heb 11: 3 By faith we **u** that the worlds were
prepared by the word of God,
2Pe 1:20 First of all you must **u** this,
3: 3 First of all you must **u** this,
3:16 some things in them hard to **u**,

UNDERSTANDING → UNDERSTAND

Ex 36: 1 has given skill and **u** to know how
Dt 32:28 there is no **u** in them.
1Ki 4:29 breadth of **u** as vast as the sand on
Job 12:12 the aged, and **u** in length of days?
28:12 And where is the place of **u**?
28:28 and to depart from evil is **u**.'"
32: 8 of the Almighty, that makes for **u**.
Ps 111:10 those who practice it have a good **u**.
119:34 Give me **u**, that I may keep your law
119:104 Through your precepts I get **u**;
119:130 it imparts **u** to the simple.
136: 5 who by **u** made the heavens,
147: 5 in power; his **u** is beyond measure.
Pr 2: 2 and inclining your heart to **u**;
2: 6 from his mouth come knowledge
and **u**;
3:13 find wisdom, and those who get **u**,
10:23 but wise conduct is pleasure to a
person of **u**.
14:29 slow to anger has great **u**,
15:21 a person of **u** walks straight ahead.
15:32 those who heed admonition gain **u**.
16:16 To get **u** is to be chosen rather than
17:27 one who is cool in spirit has **u**.
18: 2 A fool takes no pleasure in **u**,
19: 8 to keep **u** is to prosper.
23:23 buy wisdom, instruction, and **u**.
Isa 11: 2 the spirit of wisdom and **u**,
40:14 and showed him the way of **u**?
40:28 grow weary; his **u** is unsearchable.
56:11 The shepherds also have no **u**;
Jer 3:15 feed you with knowledge and **u**.
10:12 by his **u** stretched out the heavens.
Da 5:12 and **u** to interpret dreams, explain
10:12 that you set your mind to gain **u** and
Hos 4:11 and new wine take away the **u**.
Mk 12:33 all the **u**, and with all the strength,'
Lk 2:47 heard him were amazed at his **u**
Ro 3:11 there is no one who has **u**,
Php 4: 7 peace of God, which surpasses all **u**,
Col 1: 9 in all spiritual wisdom and **u**,
2: 2 may have all the riches of assured **u**
2Ti 2: 7 Lord will give you **u** in all things.
Jas 3:13 Who is wise and **u** among you?
1Jn 5:20 that the Son of God has come and
has given us **u**
Tob 4:19 For none of the nations has **u**,

UNDERSTANDS → UNDERSTAND

1Ch 28: 9 and every plan and thought.
Job 28:23 "God **u** the way to it, and he knows
Mt 13:23 the one who hears the word and **u** it,

UNDERSTOOD → UNDERSTAND

Ne 8:12 had **u** the words that were declared

Isa　40:21　**u** from the foundations of the earth?
Ro　　1:20　have been **u** and seen through
1Co　2:　8　None of the rulers of this age **u** this;

UNDERTAKEN
Lk　　1:　1　Since many have **u** to set down
1Mc　4:51　finished all the work they had **u.**

UNDIVIDED·
Ps　86:11　an **u** heart to revere your name.

UNDYING·
Eph　6:24　Grace be with all who have an **u**
　　　　　love for our Lord

UNEXPECTED
Mt　24:44　Son of Man is coming at an **u** hour.

UNFAILING
Lk　12:33　an **u** treasure in heaven,

UNFAIR
Eze　18:25　"The way of the Lord is **u."**

UNFAITHFUL　→ UNFAITHFULNESS
Nu　　5:12　man's wife goes astray and is **u** to
1Ch　10:13　he was **u** to the LORD in that he did
Ro　　3:　3　What if some were **u?**

UNFAITHFULNESS　→ UNFAITHFUL
1Ch　9:　1　exile in Babylon because of their **u.**

UNFIT
1Co　15:　9　**u** to be called an apostle,
Tit　　1:16　disobedient, **u** for any good work.

UNFOLDING·
Ps　119:130　The **u** of your words gives light;

UNFORMED·
Ps　139:16　Your eyes beheld my **u** substance.

UNGODLINESS　→ UNGODLY
Isa　32:　6　practice **u,** to utter error concerning
　　　　　the LORD,
Jer　23:15　**u** has spread throughout the land."
Jude　1:15　everyone of all the deeds of **u**
2Es　13:37　the assembled nations for their **u**

UNGODLY　→ UNGODLINESS
Jer　23:11　Both prophet and priest are **u;**
Ro　　5:　6　the right time Christ died for the **u.**
2Pe　　2:　6　example of what is coming to the **u;**
Jude　1:15　have committed in such an **u** way,
　　　　1:15　all the harsh things that **u** sinners
Sir　12:　5　but do not give to the **u;**

UNGRATEFUL
Lk　　6:35　he is kind to the **u** and the wicked.
2Ti　　3:　2　disobedient to their parents, **u,**

UNGRUDGING·
Dt　15:10　Give liberally and be **u** when you

UNHOLY
1Ti　　1:　9　and sinful, for the **u** and profane,
2Ti　　3:　2　to their parents, ungrateful, **u,**

UNINTENTIONALLY
Lev　　4:　2　When anyone sins **u** in any of
Nu　15:22　if you **u** fail to observe all these
Dt　　4:42　someone who **u** kills another person

UNITED　→ UNITY
Ro　　6:　5　**u** with him in a resurrection like his.
1Co　1:10　be **u** in the same mind and the same
　　　　6:16　**u** to a prostitute becomes one body
　　　　6:17　**u** to the Lord becomes one spirit
Col　　2:　2　their hearts to be encouraged and **u**

UNITY　→ UNITED
Ps　133:　1　when kindred live together in **u!**
Eph　4:　3　to maintain the **u** of the Spirit in the
　　　　4:13　**u** of the faith and of the knowledge
1Pe　　3:　8　Finally, all of you, have **u** of spirit,

UNIVERSE
Col　　2:　8　to the elemental spirits of the **u,**
　　　　2:20　to the elemental spirits of the **u,**

UNJUST
Lev　19:15　You shall not render an **u** judgment;
Lk　18:　6　"Listen to what the **u** judge says.
Ro　　3:　5　That God is **u** to inflict wrath on us?
Heb　6:10　For God is not **u;** he will

UNKNOWN
Ac　17:23　with the inscription, 'To an **u** god.'
2Co　　6:　9　as **u,** and yet are well known;

UNLEAVENED
Ex　12:17　shall observe the festival of **u** bread,
Dt　16:16　of **u** bread, at the festival of weeks,
Mt　26:17　first day of U Bread the disciples

FESTIVAL OF UNLEAVENED BREAD
Ex　12:17; 23:15; 34:18; Lev 23:6; Dt 16:16;
　　2Ch 8:13; 30:13, 21; 35:17; Ezr 6:22; Mk
　　14:1; Lk 22:1; Ac 12:3; 1Es 1:19; 7:14

UNLEAVENED BREAD　Ge 19:3; Ex 12:8,
　　15, 17, 18, 20; 13:6, 7; 23:15, 15; 29:2, 23;
　　34:18, 18; Lev 8:2, 26, 26; 23:6, 6; Nu 6:15,
　　17; 9:11; 28:17; Dt 16:3, 8, 16; 2Ki 23:9; 1Ch
　　23:29; 2Ch 8:13; 30:13, 21; 35:17; Ezr 6:22;
　　Eze 45:21; Mt 26:17; Mk 14:1, 12; Lk 22:1, 7;
　　Ac 12:3; 20:6; 1Co 5:8; 1Es 1:10, 19; 7:14

UNLESS
Ps　127:　1　U the LORD builds the house,
La　　5:22　**u** you have utterly rejected us,
Lk　13:　3　but **u** you repent, you will all perish
Jn　　4:48　"U you see signs and wonders you
　　　12:24　**u** a grain of wheat falls into the
　　　　　earth and dies,
Ac　　8:31　How can I, **u** someone guides me?

UNLIKE
Heb　7:27　U the other high priests, he has no

UNLOVED
Pr　30:23　**u** woman when she gets a husband,

UNMARRIED
1Co　7:　8　well for them to remain **u** as I am.
　　　　7:32　**u** man is anxious about the affairs
　　　　　of the Lord,

UNNATURAL·
Ro　　1:26　exchanged natural intercourse for **u,**
Jude　1:　7　immorality and pursued **u** lust,

UNPRODUCTIVE·
1Co　14:14　my spirit prays but my mind is **u.**
Tit　　3:14　so that they may not be **u.**

UNPROFITABLE
Tit　　3:　9　for they are **u** and worthless.

UNPUNISHED
Pr　　6:29　no one who touches her will go **u.**
　　　11:21　Be assured, the wicked will not go **u**
　　　19:　5　A false witness will not go **u,**
　　　28:20　in a hurry to be rich will not go **u.**

UNQUENCHABLE
Lk　　3:17　the chaff he will burn with **u** fire."

UNRIGHTEOUS
　　→ UNRIGHTEOUSNESS
Mt　　5:45　rain on the righteous and on the **u.**
1Pe　　3:18　the righteous for the **u,** in order to
2Pe　　2:　9　**u** under punishment until the day

UNRIGHTEOUSNESS
　　→ UNRIGHTEOUS
Ps　92:15　and there is no **u** in him.
1Jn　　1:　9　and cleanse us from all **u.**

UNSEARCHABLE
Isa　40:28　his understanding is **u.**
Ro　11:33　How **u** are his judgments and

UNSHRUNK
Mt　　9:16　No one sews a piece of **u** cloth on
　　　　　an old cloak,

UNSPIRITUAL·
1Co　　2:14　who are **u** do not receive the gifts
Jas　　3:15　but is earthly, **u,** devilish.

UNSTABLE
2Pe　　3:16　and **u** twist to their own destruction,

UNTIE
Mk　　1:　7　and **u** the thong of his sandals.
Lk　13:15　each of you on the sabbath **u** his ox
　　　19:30　U it and bring it here.

UNVEILED
1Co　11:　5　with her head **u** disgraces her head
2Co　　3:18　And all of us, with **u** faces,
Sus　　1:32　the scoundrels ordered her to be **u,**

UNWASHED·
Mt　15:20　to eat with **u** hands does not defile."

UNWILLING
Dt　10:10　The LORD was **u** to destroy you.
　　　29:20　the LORD will be **u** to pardon them,
Jos　24:15　Now if you are **u** to serve the LORD,
Mt　23:　4　**u** to lift a finger to move them.
2Th　3:10　Anyone **u** to work should not eat.

UNWISE
Eph　5:15　not as **u** people but as wise,

UNWORTHY
1Co　11:27　drinks the cup of the Lord in an **u**
　　　　　manner

UPHELD　→ UPHOLD
Isa　59:16　and his righteousness **u** him.
Ro　14:　4　And they will be **u,**

UPHOLD　→ UPHELD, UPHOLDS
Isa　41:10　I will **u** you with my victorious
　　　　　right hand.
　　　42:　1　my servant, whom I **u,** my chosen,
Ro　　3:31　On the contrary, we **u** the law.

UPHOLDS　→ UPHOLD
Ps　37:17　but the LORD **u** the righteous.
　　　63:　8　clings to you; your right hand **u** me.
　　145:14　The LORD **u** all who are falling,

UPRIGHT　→ UPRIGHTLY, UPRIGHTNESS
Ge　37:　7　Suddenly my sheaf rose and stood **u**
Dt　32:　4　without deceit, just and **u** is he;
Job　1:　1　That man was blameless and **u,**
　　　　1:　8　and a man who fears God and turns
　　　　2:　3　and **u** man who fears God and turns
Ps　　7:10　God is my shield, who saves the **u**
　　　11:　7　the **u** shall behold his face.
　　　25:　8　Good and **u** is the LORD;
　　　33:　1　O you righteous. Praise befits the **u.**
　　　64:10　Let all the **u** in heart glory.
　　　92:15　showing that the LORD is **u;**
　　　97:11　and joy for the **u** in heart.
　　　112:　4　in the darkness as a light for the **u;**
　　　119:　7　I will praise you with an **u** heart,
Pr　　2:　7　stores up sound wisdom for the **u;**
　　　　2:21　For the **u** will abide in the land,
　　　　3:32　but the **u** are in his confidence.
　　　11:　3　The integrity of the **u** guides them,
　　　15:　8　but the prayer of the **u** is his delight.
　　　21:29　but the **u** give thought to their ways.
Tit　　1:　8　a lover of goodness, prudent, **u,**
　　　　2:12　live lives that are self-controlled, **u,**

UPRIGHTLY　→ UPRIGHT
Ps　84:11　withhold from those who walk **u.**
Pr　14:　2　who walk **u** fear the LORD,

UPRIGHTNESS　→ UPRIGHT
Ps　25:21　May integrity and **u** preserve me,
　　　111:　8　performed with faithfulness and **u.**
Pr　　4:11　I have led you in the paths of **u.**

UPROOTED

Jer 31:40 never again be **u** or overthrown.
Lk 17: 6 'Be **u** and planted in the sea,'
Jude 1:12 trees without fruit, twice dead, **u;**

UPWARD

Ex 30:14 from twenty years old and **u,**
Nu 1: 3 from twenty years old and **u,**
Ezr 3: 8 from twenty years old and **u,**

UR

Ge 15: 7 LORD who brought you from **U** of
Ne 9: 7 him out of **U** of the Chaldeans

URGED → URGING

Ge 19:15 morning dawned, the angels **u** Lot,
Ex 12:33 The Egyptians **u** the people

URGES → URGING

2Co 5:14 For the love of Christ **u** us on,

URGING → URGED, URGES

1Th 2:12 **u** and encouraging you and pleading

URIAH

Hittite husband of Bathsheba, killed at David's order (2Sa 11).

URIM

Ex 28:30 of judgment you shall put the **U**
1Sa 28: 6 by dreams, or by **U,** or by prophets.
Ezr 2:63 should be a priest to consult **U**

USE → USED, USEFUL, USELESS, USES

Ex 20: 7 not make wrongful **u** of the name of
Dt 5:11 not make wrongful **u** of the name of
Ro 9:21 one object for special **u** and another
for ordinary **u?**
Gal 5:13 only do not **u** your freedom as an
2Ti 2:20 for special **u,** some for ordinary.
1Pe 2:16 yet do not **u** your freedom as a
pretext for evil.
Sir 14: 3 and of what **u** is wealth to a miser?
30:19 Of what **u** to an idol is a sacrifice?

USED → USE

Mt 22:19 Show me the coin **u** for the tax."
Jn 10: 6 Jesus **u** this figure of speech with
1Co 6:11 this is what some of you **u** to be.

USEFUL → USE

Eph 4:29 but only what is **u** for building up,
2Ti 2:21 dedicated and **u** to the owner of the
3:16 All scripture is inspired by God and
is **u**
Phm 1:11 but now he is indeed **u** both to you
Heb 6: 7 and that produces a crop **u** to those

USELESS → USE

1Sa 12:21 not turn aside after **u** things that
Jn 6:63 gives life; the flesh is **u.**
Phm 1:11 Formerly he was **u** to you,

USES → USE

1Ti 1: 8 that the law is good, if one **u** it
legitimately.

UTTER → UTTERANCE, UTTERED, UTTERING, UTTERLY, UTTERS

Lev 5: 4 whatever people **u** in an oath,
Dt 23:23 Whatever your lips **u** you must
diligently perform,
Ps 78: 2 I will **u** dark sayings from of old,
Mt 5:11 **u** all kinds of evil against you
falsely
Rev 13: 6 its mouth to **u** blasphemies

UTTERANCE → UTTER

Pr 6: 2 you are snared by the **u** of your lips,
Lk 4:36 "What kind of **u** is this?
1Co 12: 8 through the Spirit the **u** of wisdom,

UTTERED → UTTER

Nu 23: 7 Then Balaam **u** his oracle, saying:
2Sa 22:14 the Most High **u** his voice.

Ps 76: 8 From the heavens you **u** judgment;

UTTERING → UTTER

Rev 13: 5 mouth **u** haughty and blasphemous

UTTERLY → UTTER

Ps 119: 8 do not **u** forsake me.
SS 8: 7 it would be **u** scorned.

UTTERS → UTTER

Ps 46: 6 he **u** his voice, the earth melts.
Joel 3:16 and **u** his voice from Jerusalem,
Am 1: 2 and **u** his voice from Jerusalem;

UZ

Job 1: 1 the land of **U** whose name was Job.

UZZAH

2Sa 6: 6 **U** reached out his hand to the ark of
1Ch 13: 9 **U** put out his hand to hold the ark,

UZZIAH → =AZARIAH

Son of Amaziah; king of Judah also known as Azariah (2Ki 15:1-7; 1Ch 6:24; 2Ch 26). Struck with leprosy because of pride (2Ch 26:16-23).

𝒱

VAIN → VANITIES, VANITY

Lev 26:16 You shall sow your seed in **v,**
Ps 2: 1 and the peoples plot in **v?**
33:17 war horse is a **v** hope for victory,
73:13 All in **v** I have kept my heart clean
127: 1 those who build it labor in **v.**
Isa 65:23 They shall not labor in **v,**
Eze 6:10 I did not threaten in **v** to bring this
disaster
Mt 15: 9 in **v** do they worship me,
Ac 4:25 and the peoples imagine **v** things?
1Co 15: 2 unless you have come to believe in
v.
15:58 in the Lord your labor is not in **v.**
2Co 6: 1 not to accept the grace of God in **v.**
Gal 2: 2 or had not run, in **v.**
Php 2:16 that I did not run in **v** or labor in **v.**

VALIANT → VALIANTLY

1Sa 31:12 all the **v** men set out,

VALIANTLY → VALIANT

Ps 60:12 With God we shall do **v;**
118:15 "The right hand of the LORD does **v;**

VALID

Jn 8:14 my testimony is **v** because I know
Heb 2: 2 if the message declared through
angels was **v,**

VALLEY → VALLEYS

Jos 7:26 to this day is called the **V** of Achor.
10:12 and Moon, in the **v** of Aijalon."
Jdg 16: 4 fell in love with a woman in the **v**
1Sa 17: 3 mountain on the other side, with a **v**
2Ki 23:10 which is in the **v** of Ben-hinnom,
2Ch 33: 6 his son pass through fire in the **v** of
Ps 23: 4 through the darkest **v,** I fear no evil;
Isa 22: 1 oracle concerning the **v** of vision.
40: 4 Every **v** shall be lifted up,
Eze 37: 2 there were very many lying in the **v,**
Hos 2:15 the **V** of Achor a door of hope.
Joel 3:14 multitudes, in the **v** of decision!
Lk 3: 5 Every **v** shall be filled, and every
mountain

VALLEYS → VALLEY

Dt 8: 7 underground waters welling up in **v**
SS 2: 1 I am a rose of Sharon, a lily of the **v.**

VALUE

Mt 13:46 on finding one pearl of great **v,**
Ro 3: 1 Or what is the **v** of circumcision?

1Ti 4: 8 while physical training is of some **v,**

VANISH → VANISHED, VANISHES

Ps 37:20 they **v**—like smoke they **v** away.

VANISHED → VANISH

Lk 24:31 they **v** from their sight.
Rev 6:14 sky **v** like a scroll rolling itself up,

VANISHES → VANISH

Jas 4:14 a mist that appears for a little while
and then **v.**

VANITIES → VAIN

Ecc 1: 2 Vanity of **v,** says the Teacher,
vanity of **v!**
12: 8 Vanity of **v!** says the Teacher;

VANITY → VAIN

Ecc 1: 2 **V** of vanities, says the Teacher, **v** of
vanities! All is **v.**
12: 8 **V** of vanities, says the Teacher; all
is **v.**

VARIOUS

Mk 1:34 he cured many who were sick with
v diseases,
Heb 1: 1 in many and **v** ways by the prophets,
1Pe 1: 6 while you have had to suffer **v** trials,

VASHTI

Queen of Persia replaced by Esther (Est 1-2; AdE 1-2).

VAST

Ps 139:17 How **v** is the sum of them!

VATS

Pr 3:10 your **v** will be bursting with wine.
Joel 2:24 the **v** shall overflow with wine and

VEGETABLES

Pr 15:17 Better is a dinner of **v** where love is
Da 1:12 Let us be given **v** to eat and water
Ro 14: 2 while the weak eat only **v.**

VEGETATION

Ge 1:11 God said, "Let the earth put forth **v:**

VEIL → VEILED

Ex 34:33 he put a **v** on his face;
2Co 3:13 a **v** over his face to keep the people
3:15 a **v** lies over their minds;

VEILED → VEIL

1Co 11: 7 a man ought not to have his head **v,**
2Co 4: 3 And even if our gospel is **v,** it is **v**
to those who are perishing.

VENGEANCE → AVENGE, AVENGED, AVENGER, AVENGES, AVENGING, REVENGE

Ge 4:15 kills Cain will suffer a sevenfold **v."**
Nu 31: 3 to execute the LORD's **v** on Midian.
Ps 94: 1 O LORD, you God of **v,**
Isa 35: 4 For the LORD has a day of **v,**
61: 2 and the day of **v** of our God;
Jer 50:15 For this is the **v** of the LORD:
Na 1: 2 the LORD takes **v** on his adversaries
Sir 28: 1 The vengeful will face the Lord's **v,**

VENOM

Dt 32:33 of serpents, the cruel **v** of asps.
Ps 58: 4 They have **v** like the **v** of a serpent,

VENT

Pr 29:11 A fool gives full **v** to anger,
La 4:11 The LORD gave full **v** to his wrath;

VERDICT

Da 2: 9 there is but one **v** for you.
Lk 23:24 Pilate gave his **v** that their demand
Sir 4: 9 and do not be hesitant in giving a **v.**
19:25 who abuse favors to gain a **v.**

VERY

Ge 1:31 and indeed, it was **v** good.
15: 1 your reward shall be **v** great."

Dt   30:14 No, the word is **v** near to you;
Jos   23:11 Be **v** careful, therefore, to love
1Ki   19:10 "I have been **v** zealous for the LORD
Ps   104: 1 O LORD my God, you are **v** great.
Mt   4: 8 a **v** high mountain and showed him
Sir   43:29 Awesome is the Lord and **v** great,

VICTIMS
Pr   7:26 and numerous are her **v**.

VICTORIES → VICTORY
Ps   44: 4 you command **v** for Jacob.

VICTORIOUS → VICTORY
Isa   41:10 uphold you with my **v** right hand.
Zec   9: 9 triumphant and **v** is he,

VICTORIOUSLY* → VICTORY
Ps   45: 4 In your majesty ride on **v** for the

VICTORY → VICTORIES, VICTORIOUS, VICTORIOUSLY
1Sa   2: 1 because I rejoice in my **v**.
        14:23 the LORD gave Israel the **v** that day.
2Sa   8: 6 LORD gave **v** to David wherever he
Ps   33:17 The war horse is a vain hope for **v**,
        48:10 Your right hand is filled with **v**.
Pr   21:31 but the **v** belongs to the LORD.
        24: 6 abundance of counselors there is **v**.
Zep   3:17 your midst, a warrior who gives **v**;
1Co   15:54 Death has been swallowed up in **v**."
        15:57 the **v** through our Lord Jesus Christ.
1Jn   5: 4 this is the **v** that conquers the
                world, our faith.

VIEW
Dt   32:49 and **v** the land of Canaan,
2Ti   4: 1 and in **v** of his appearing and his

VILE
Jdg   19:23 do not do this **v** thing.
2Sa   13:12 do not do anything so **v**!

VILLAGE
Mt   10:11 Whatever town or **v** you enter,

VINDICATE → VINDICATED, VINDICATION
Ps   26: 1 **V** me, O LORD, for I have walked
        35:24 **V** me, O LORD, my God,
        54: 1 and **v** me by your might.
       135:14 For the LORD will **v** his people,

VINDICATED → VINDICATE
Job   13:18 I know that I shall be **v**.
Mt   11:19 Yet wisdom is **v** by her deeds."
1Ti   3:16 He was revealed in flesh, **v** in spirit,

VINDICATION → VINDICATE
Ps   24: 5 **v** from the God of their salvation.
       103: 6 The LORD works **v** and justice
Isa   54:17 of the LORD and their **v** from me,

VINE → GRAPEVINE, VINEGROWER, VINES, VINEYARD, VINEYARDS
Dt   32:32 Their **v** comes from the vinestock
                of Sodom,
Ps   80: 8 You brought a **v** out of Egypt;
       128: 3 like a fruitful **v** within your house;
Isa   36:16 of you will eat from your own **v**
Jer   2:21 Yet I planted you as a choice **v**,
Eze   17: 6 and became a **v** spreading out,
Hos   10: 1 Israel is a luxuriant **v** that yields its
Mk   14:25 again drink of the fruit of the **v** until
Jn   15: 1 "I am the true **v**, and my Father is
Rev   14:18 gather the clusters of the **v** of the

VINEGAR*
Nu   6: 3 shall drink no wine **v** or other **v**,
Ps   69:21 my thirst they gave me **v** to drink.
Pr   10:26 Like **v** to the teeth, and smoke to
        25:20 Like **v** on a wound is one who

VINEGROWER* → GROW, VINE
Jn   15: 1 the true vine, and my Father is the **v**.

VINES → VINE
Hab   3:17 and no fruit is on the **v**;

VINEYARD → VINE
Ge   9:20 was the first to plant a **v**.
Dt   22: 9 not sow your **v** with a second kind
1Ki   21: 1 Naboth the Jezreelite had a **v** in
Pr   31:16 the fruit of her hands she plants a **v**.
SS   1: 6 but my own **v** I have not kept!
Isa   5: 1 my love-song concerning his **v**:
         5: 1 had a **v** on a very fertile hill.
        27: 2 A pleasant **v**, sing about it!
Mt   21:33 a landowner who planted a **v**,
1Co   9: 7 Who plants a **v** and does not eat any

VINEYARDS → VINE
Nu   22:24 in a narrow path between the **v**,
Dt   6:11 **v** and olive groves that you did not
SS   2:15 for our **v** are in blossom."

VIOLATE → VIOLATED
Ps   89:31 if they **v** my statutes and do

VIOLATED → VIOLATE
Ps   55:20 and **v** a covenant with me

VIOLENCE → VIOLENT, VIOLENTLY
Ge   6:11 and the earth was filled with **v**.
Job   19: 7 Even when I cry out, '**V**!'
Ps   7:16 on their own heads their **v** descends.
        73: 6 **v** covers them like a garment.
Isa   53: 9 although he had done no **v**,
        60:18 **V** shall no more be heard in your
                land,
Eze   22:26 priests have done **v** to my teaching
        45: 9 Put away **v** and oppression,
Joel   3:19 the **v** done to the people of Judah,
Jnh   3: 8 from the **v** that is in their hands.
Hab   2:17 **v** done to Lebanon will overwhelm
         2:17 because of human bloodshed and **v**
Zep   3: 4 they have done **v** to the law.
Mal   2:16 and covering one's garment with **v**,
1Ti   1:13 a persecutor, and a man of **v**.

VIOLENT → VIOLENCE
Pr   3:31 Do not envy the **v** and
Eze   18:10 a son who is **v**, a shedder of blood,
Mt   11:12 and the **v** take it by force.
1Ti   3: 3 not **v** but gentle, not quarrelsome,
Tit   1: 7 or addicted to wine or **v** or greedy

VIOLENTLY → VIOLENCE
Ex   19:18 while the whole mountain shook **v**.
Gal   1:13 was **v** persecuting the church of God

VIPER → VIPERS
Ac   28: 3 when a **v**, driven out by the heat,

VIPERS → VIPER
Ps   140: 3 under their lips is the venom of **v**.
Mt   12:34 You brood of **v**! How can you
        23:33 You snakes, you brood of **v**!
Lk   3: 7 baptized by him, "You brood of **v**!
Ro   3:13 venom of **v** is under their lips."

VIRGIN → VIRGINITY, VIRGINS
1Ki   1: 2 "Let a young **v** be sought for my
                lord the king,
Jer   31:21 Return, O **v** Israel, return to these
La   2:13 comfort you, O **v** daughter Zion?
Mt   1:23 the **v** shall conceive and bear a son,
Lk   1:34 "How can this be, since I am a **v**?"
1Co   7:28 and if a **v** marries, she does not sin.
2Co   11: 2 present you as a chaste **v** to Christ.
Sir   9: 5 Do not look intently at a **v**,

VIRGINITY → VIRGIN
Dt   22:14 I did not find evidence of her **v**."

VIRGINS → VIRGIN
Est   2: 2 "Let beautiful young **v** be sought
1Co   7:25 concerning **v**, I have no command
                of the Lord,

VISIBLE
Eph   5:13 but everything exposed by the light
                becomes **v**,
Col   1:16 things **v** and invisible, whether
Heb   11: 3 from things that are not **v**.

VISION → VISIONS
Ge   15: 1 of the LORD came to Abram in a **v**,
Nu   24: 4 who sees the **v** of the Almighty,
1Sa   3:15 Samuel was afraid to tell the **v** to
Ps   89:19 you spoke in a **v** to your faithful one
Isa   22: 1 oracle concerning the valley of **v**.
Da   7: 2 saw in my **v** by night the four winds
         8: 1 Belshazzar a **v** appeared to me,
         8:26 As for you, seal up the **v**,
         9:24 to seal both **v** and prophet,
        10: 7 I, Daniel, alone saw the **v**;
Lk   1:22 they realized that he had seen a **v** in
Ac   9:10 Lord said to him in a **v**, "Ananias."
        10:17 to make of the **v** that he had seen,
        16: 9 During the night Paul had a **v**:
        26:19 not disobedient to the heavenly **v**,
Rev   9:17 was how I saw the horses in my **v**,
2Es   10:40 therefore is the meaning of the **v**.

VISIONS → VISION
Ge   46: 2 God spoke to Israel in **v** of the
Nu   12: 6 make myself known to them in **v**;
1Sa   3: 1 those days; **v** were not widespread.
Jer   23:16 They speak **v** of their own minds,
La   2:14 seen for you false and deceptive **v**;
Eze   1: 1 were opened, and I saw **v** of God.
Da   1:17 Daniel also had insight into all **v**
Joel   2:28 and your young men shall see **v**.
Ac   2:17 and your young men shall see **v**,

VOICE → VOICES
Ge   3:17 listened to the **v** of your wife,
Dt   4:33 the **v** of a god speaking out of a fire,
1Sa   15:22 as in obeying the **v** of the LORD?
Job   40: 9 can you thunder with a **v** like his?
Ps   19: 4 their **v** goes out through all the earth
        29: 3 The **v** of the LORD is over the waters
        95: 7 hat today you would listen to his **v**!
Pr   1:20 in the squares she raises her **v**.
         8: 1 does not understanding raise her **v**?
Isa   40: 3 A **v** cries out: "In the wilderness
Jer   31:15 A **v** is heard in Ramah, lamentation
Da   9:14 for we have disobeyed his **v**.
Mt   2:18 "A **v** was heard in Ramah, wailing
         3:17 And a **v** from heaven said, "This is
                my Son,
Mk   1: 3 **v** of one crying out in the wilderness
Jn   1:23 **v** of one crying out in the wilderness
         5:25 the dead will hear the **v** of the Son
        10: 3 and the sheep hear his **v**.
        12:28 Then a **v** came from heaven, "I
                have glorified it,
Ro   10:18 Their **v** has gone out to all the earth,
Heb   3: 7 today, if you hear his **v**,
2Pe   1:17 from God the Father when that **v**
                was conveyed
Rev   3:20 if you hear my **v** and open the door,

VOICE OF THE *LORD Isa 6:8; Ac 7:31;
Bar 1:18, 21; 2:22; 3:4

VOICE OF THE †LORD Ex 15:26; Dt
5:25; 8:20; 13:18; 18:16; Jos 5:6; 1Sa 12:15;
15:19, 20, 22; 28:18; 1Ki 20:36; 2Ki 18:12; Ne
29:3, 4, 5, 7, 8, 9; 106:25; Isa 30:31; 66:6;
Jer 3:25; 7:28; 26:13; 38:20; 42:6, 6, 13, 21;
43:4, 7; 44:23; Da 9:10; Mic 6:9; Hag 1:12;
Zec 6:15

VOICES → VOICE
Rev   11:15 and there were loud **v** in heaven,

VOID
Ge   1: 2 the earth was a formless **v**
Dt   32:28 They are a nation **v** of sense;
Mt   15: 6 you make **v** the word of God.
Ro   4:14 faith is null and the promise is **v**.

VOMIT

Lev 18:28 land will **v** you out for defiling it,
Pr 26:11 Like a dog that returns to its **v** is
Isa 28: 8 All tables are covered with filthy **v**;
2Pe 2:22 "The dog turns back to its own **v**,"

VOTIVE

Lev 7:16 if the sacrifice you offer is a **v** offering
Dt 12: 6 and your donations, your **v** gifts,

VOW → VOWED, VOWS

Ge 28:20 Then Jacob made a **v**, saying,
Nu 6: 2 a special **v**, the **v** of the nazirite,
21: 2 Then Israel made a **v** to the LORD
30: 2 When a man makes a **v** to the LORD,
Dt 23:21 If you make a **v** to the LORD your
Jdg 11:30 Jephthah made a **v** to the LORD, and
1Sa 1:11 She made this **v**: "O LORD of hosts,
Ecc 5: 4 Fulfill what you **v**.
Ac 18:18 for he was under a **v**.
Sir 18:23 Before making a **v**, prepare yourself

VOWED → VOW

Jnh 2: 9 what I have **v** I will pay.

VOWS → VOW

Nu 30: 4 then all her **v** shall stand,
Ps 22:25 my **v** I will pay before those who fear him.
50:14 and pay your **v** to the Most High.
116:14 I will pay my **v** to the LORD in the
Jnh 1:16 a sacrifice to the LORD and made **v**.

VULTURE → VULTURES

Hos 8: 1 a **v** is over the house of the LORD,

VULTURES → VULTURE

Mt 24:28 corpse is, there the **v** will gather.

W

WADI

Nu 34: 5 from Azmon to the **W** of Egypt,
2Ki 24: 7 from the **W** of Egypt to the River

WAFERS

Ex 16:31 was like **w** made with honey.

WAGE → WAGES

2Co 10: 3 we do not **w** war according to human standards;

WAGES → WAGE

Mic 1: 7 for as the **w** of a prostitute she gathered them, and as the **w** of a
Mal 3: 5 the hired workers in their **w**,
Jn 6: 7 "Six months' **w** would not buy
Ro 4: 4 **w** are not reckoned as a gift but as
6:23 For the **w** of sin is death,
2Pe 2:15 who loved the **w** of doing wrong.

WAIL → WAILED

Isa 13: 6 **W**, for the day of the LORD is near;
Mic 1: 8 For this I will lament and **w**;

WAILED → WAIL

Nu 11:18 have **w** in the hearing of the LORD,

WAIST

2Ki 1: 8 with a leather belt around his **w**."
Isa 11: 5 Righteousness shall be the belt around his **w**,
Mt 3: 4 with a leather belt around his **w**,
Eph 6:14 the belt of truth around your **w**,
Jdt 8: 5 She put sackcloth around her **w**

WAIT → WAITED, WAITING, WAITS

Ps 27:14 **W** for the LORD; be strong,
27:14 heart take courage; **w** for the LORD!
37:34 **W** for the LORD, and keep to his

130: 5 I **w** for the LORD, my soul waits,
Pr 1:18 yet they lie in **w**—to kill
Isa 30:18 blessed are all those who **w** for him.
La 3:26 should **w** quietly for the salvation of
Hab 2: 3 If it seems to tarry, **w** for it;
3:16 I **w** quietly for the day of calamity
Ac 1: 4 to **w** there for the promise of the
Ro 8:23 while we **w** for adoption,
Gal 5: 5 **w** for the hope of righteousness.
1Th 1:10 to **w** for his Son from heaven,
Tit 2:13 while we **w** for the blessed hope and
Sir 2: 7 fear the Lord, **w** for his mercy;
6:19 and **w** for her good harvest.

WAITED → WAIT

Ps 40: 1 I **w** patiently for the LORD;

WAITING → WAIT

Heb 9:28 to save those who are eagerly **w** for

WAITS → WAIT

Ps 130: 6 my soul **w** for the Lord more than
Ro 8:19 the creation w with eager longing

WAKE → AWAKE, AWAKEN, AWAKENED, AWOKE, WAKENS

Ro 13:11 the moment for you to **w** from sleep.
Rev 3: 2 **W** up, and strengthen what remains

WAKENS* → WAKE

Isa 50: 4 Morning by morning he **w**—
50: 4 w my ear to listen as those who are

WALK → WALKED, WALKING, WALKS

Ge 17: 1 **w** before me, and be blameless.
Dt 10:12 to **w** in all his ways, to love him,
26:17 and for you to **w** in his ways,
28: 9 LORD your God and **w** in his ways.
Jos 22: 5 to **w** in all his ways, to keep his
Ps 15: 2 who **w** blamelessly, and do what is
23: 4 I **w** through the darkest valley, I fear no evil;
84:11 from those who **w** uprightly.
89:15 who **w**, O LORD, in the light of
115: 7 not feel; feet, but do not **w**;
119:45 I shall **w** at liberty, for I have sought
Pr 4:12 When you **w**, your step will not be
6:22 When you **w**, they will lead you;
9: 6 and **w** in the way of insight."
Isa 2: 3 his ways and that we may **w**
2: 5 let us **w** in the light of the LORD!
30:21 "This is the way; **w** in it."
40:31 they shall **w** and not faint.
43: 2 when you **w** through fire you shall not be burned,
57: 2 those who **w** uprightly will rest on
Jer 6:16 **w** in it, and find rest for your souls.
6:16 But they said, "We will not **w** in it."
Da 4:37 to bring low those who **w** in pride.
Am 3: 3 Do two **w** together unless they have
Mic 4: 5 we will **w** in the name of the LORD
6: 8 and to **w** humbly with your God?
Zec 10:12 shall **w** in his name, says the LORD.
Mk 2: 9 Stand up and take your mat and **w**'?
Jn 8:12 follows me will never **w** in darkness
Ac 3: 8 he stood and began to **w**,
2Co 5: 7 for we **w** by faith, not by sight.
1Jn 1: 7 if we **w** in the light as he himself is
2Jn 1: 6 **w** according to his commandments;
3Jn 1: 3 namely how you **w** in the truth.
Rev 9:20 which cannot see or hear or **w**.
21:24 The nations will **w** by its light,

WALKED → WALK

Ge 5:24 Enoch **w** with God; then he was no more,

WALKING → WALK

Dt 8: 6 in his ways and by fearing him.
1Ki 3: 3 **w** in the statutes of his father David;
Da 3:25 **w** in the middle of the fire, and they are not hurt;
Mt 14:26 the disciples saw him **w** on the sea,

Ac 3: 8 **w** and leaping and praising God.
2Jn 1: 4 some of your children **w** in the truth,
3Jn 1: 4 that my children are **w** in the truth.

WALKS → WALK

Pr 10: 9 Whoever **w** in integrity **w** securely,
13:20 **w** with the wise becomes wise,

WALL → WALLS

Ex 14:22 the waters forming a **w** for them on
Jos 2:15 she resided within the **w** itself.
6:20 shout, and the **w** fell down flat;
2Ki 25: 4 a breach was made in the city **w**;
Ne 1: 3 the **w** of Jerusalem is broken down,
2:17 let us rebuild the **w** of Jerusalem,
12:27 the dedication of the **w** of Jerusalem
Da 5: 5 writing on the plaster of the **w** of
Zec 2: 5 I will be a **w** of fire all around it,
Ac 9:25 down through an opening in the **w**,
2Co 11:33 a basket through a window in the **w**,
Eph 2:14 has broken down the dividing **w**,
Rev 21:12 a great, high **w** with twelve gates,

WALLOW

2Pe 2:22 sow is washed only to **w** in the mud.

WALLS → WALL

Ne 2:13 **w** of Jerusalem that had been broken
Ps 51:18 rebuild the **w** of Jerusalem,
122: 7 Peace be within your **w**, and
Pr 25:28 Like a city breached, without **w**,
Isa 26: 1 sets up victory like **w** and bulwarks.
60:18 you shall call your **w** Salvation,
Jer 52:14 broke down all the **w** around
Heb 11:30 the **w** of Jericho fell after they had

WANDER → WANDERED, WANDERER, WANDERING

Nu 32:13 he made them **w** in the wilderness for forty years,

WANDERED → WANDER

Ps 107: 4 Some **w** in desert wastes, finding
Eze 34: 6 they **w** over all the mountains and
1Ti 6:10 to be rich some have **w** away

WANDERER → WANDER

Ge 4:12 a fugitive and a **w** on the earth."

WANDERING → WANDER

Dt 26: 5 "A **w** Aramean was my ancestor;

WANT → WANTED, WANTING, WANTS

Ps 23: 1 LORD is my shepherd, I shall not **w**.
Lk 18:41 "What do you **w** me to do for you?"
19:14 'We do not **w** this man to rule over
Ro 7:15 For I do not do what I **w**,
2Co 12:14 I do not **w** what is yours but you;
Php 3:10 I **w** to know Christ and the power

WANTED → WANT

Mt 14: 5 Though Herod **w** to put him to death

WANTING → WANT

Da 5:27 on the scales and found **w**;
2Pe 3: 9 not **w** any to perish, but all to come to repentance.

WANTS → WANT

Mt 5:42 not refuse anyone who **w** to borrow
27:43 let God deliver him now, if he **w** to;

WAR → WARRIOR, WARRIORS, WARS

Ex 17:16 The LORD will have **w** with Amalek
32:17 "There is a noise of **w** in the camp."
Jos 11:23 And the land had rest from **w**.
Ps 68:30 scatter the peoples who delight in **w**.
120: 7 I am for peace; but when I speak, they are for **w**.
144: 1 my rock, who trains my hands for **w**
Ecc 3: 8 a time for **w**, and a time for peace.
9:18 Wisdom is better than weapons of **w**
Isa 2: 4 neither shall they learn **w** any more.
Da 7:21 this horn made **w** with the holy ones
9:26 and to the end there shall be **w**.

Ro   7:23 in my members another law at **w**
2Co 10: 3 we do not wage **w** according to
                  human standards;
1Pe   2:11 the desires of the flesh that wage **w**
Rev 12: 7 And **w** broke out in heaven;
        17:14 they will make **w** on the Lamb,
        19:11 in righteousness he judges and
                  makes **w.**

WARM → LUKEWARM, WARMING, WARMS

Ecc   4:11 if two lie together, they keep **w;**
Hag   1: 6 clothe yourselves, but no one is **w;**
Jas   2:16 keep **w** and eat your fill,"

WARMING → WARM

Mk   14:67 When she saw Peter **w** himself,

WARMS → WARM

Isa   44:15 Part of it he takes and **w** himself;

WARN → FOREWARNED, WARNED, WARNING, WARNINGS, WARNS

Ex   19:21 **w** the people not to break through
1Sa   8: 9 you shall solemnly **w** them,
Eze   3:18 to **w** the wicked from their wicked
        3:19 you **w** the wicked, and they do not
        3:21 If, however, you **w** the righteous
        33: 9 if you **w** the wicked to turn from
Lk   16:28 that he may **w** them, so that they
Ac   4:17 let us **w** them to speak no more to
2Th   3:15 not regard them as enemies, but **w**
2Ti   2:14 and **w** them before God that they are
Rev 22:18 I **w** everyone who hears the words

WARNED → WARN

2Ki   17:13 the LORD **w** Israel and Judah by
                  every prophet
Ne   9:29 you **w** them in order to turn them
Ps   2:10 be wise; be **w,** O rulers of the earth.
        19:11 Moreover by them is your servant **w**
Mt   2:12 been **w** in a dream not to return to
                  Herod,
        2:22 And after being **w** in a dream,
        3: 7 Who **w** you to flee from the wrath
                  to come?
1Th   4: 6 beforehand and solemnly **w** you.
Heb 11: 7 **w** by God about events as yet
                  unseen,
        12:25 they refused the one who **w** them
                  on earth,

WARNING → WARN

Jer   6: 8 Take **w,** O Jerusalem, or I shall turn
Eze   33: 5 But if they had taken **w,**

WARNS → WARN

Heb 12:25 reject the one who **w** from heaven!

WARRIOR → WAR

Ex   15: 3 LORD is a **w;** the LORD is his name.
1Ch 28: 3 you are a **w** and have shed blood.'
Jer   20:11 the LORD is with me like a dread **w;**
1Mc   2:66 Judas Maccabeus has been a
                  mighty **w** from his youth;
MIGHTY WARRIOR Ge 10:8; Jdg 6:12;
        11:1; 2Ki 5:1; 2Ch 17:17; 28:7; Jer 14:9; Sir
        47:5; 1Mc 2:66; 4:30; 10:19

WARRIORS → WAR

Ge   6: 4 that were of old, **w** of renown.
2Sa 23:22 and won a name beside the three **w.**
MIGHTY WARRIORS Jos 10:7; 1Ch 5:24;
        7:2, 5, 7, 9, 11, 40; 8:40; 11:11; 12:1, 25, 30;
        28:1; 29:24; 2Ch 13:3; 14:8; 17:13, 14, 16;
        25:6; 26:12; 32:21; Jer 5:16; 48:14; Eze 27:10;
        1Mc 2:42

WARS → WAR

Nu   21:14 it is said in the Book of the **W** of
Ps   46: 9 **w** cease to the end of the earth;
Mt   24: 6 you will hear of **w** and rumors of **w;**

WASH → WASHED, WASHING

2Ki   5:10 "Go, **w** in the Jordan seven times,

Ps   51: 7 **w** me, and I shall be whiter than
                  snow.
Jer   4:14 **w** your heart clean of wickedness
Lk   11:38 that he did not first **w** before dinner.
Jn   9: 7 **w** in the pool of Siloam"
        13: 5 and began to **w** the disciples' feet
Rev   22:14 Blessed are those who **w** their robes,

WASHED → WASH

Ps   73:13 and **w** my hands in innocence.
Jn   9:11 and **w** and received my sight."
1Co   6:11 you were **w,** you were sanctified,
Heb 10:22 our bodies **w** with pure water.
2Pe   2:22 sow is **w** only to wallow in the mud.
Rev   7:14 they have **w** their robes and

WASHING → WASH

Ex   30:18 basin with a bronze stand for **w.**
Mk   7: 2 defiled hands, that is, without **w**
Eph   5:26 by cleansing her with the **w** of
                  water by the word,

WASTE → WASTES, WASTING

Lev   26:31 I will lay your cities **w,**
Isa   6:11 Until cities lie **w** without inhabitant,
Jer   2:15 They have made his land a **w;**
Eze   4:17 and **w** away under their punishment.
1Mc   2:12 and our glory have been laid **w;**

WASTES → WASTE

Ps   31: 9 my eye **w** away from grief,
        107: 4 Some wandered in desert **w,**

WASTING → WASTE

2Co   4:16 though our outer nature is **w** away,

WATCH → WATCHER, WATCHES, WATCHING, WATCHTOWER

Ge   31:49 "The LORD **w** between you and me,
Dt   4:15 take care and **w** yourselves closely,
Ps   59: 9 O my strength, I will **w** for you;
        90: 4 or like a **w** in the night.
        141: 3 keep **w** over the door of my lips.
Pr   6:22 you lie down, they will **w** over you;
Lk   2: 8 keeping **w** over their flock by night.
Heb 13:17 they are keeping **w** over your souls

WATCHER → WATCH

Job   7:20 I do to you, you **w** of humanity?
Da   4:13 and there was a holy **w,**

WATCHES → WATCH

Ps   1: 6 for the LORD **w** over the way of the
                  righteous,
        33:14 where he sits enthroned he **w** all
        63: 6 meditate on you in the **w** of the
        145:20 The LORD **w** over all who love him,
        146: 9 The LORD **w** over the strangers;
La   2:19 the night, at the beginning of the **w!**
Wis   3: 9 and he **w** over his elect.
        4:15 and that he **w** over his holy ones.

WATCHING → WATCH

Ps   119:82 **w** for your promise;
        119:123 **w** for your salvation,
Jer   1:12 I am **w** over my word to perform it."

WATCHTOWER → TOWER, WATCH

Isa   5: 2 he built a **w** in the midst of it,
Mt   21:33 dug a wine press in it, and built a **w.**

WATER → WATERCOURSES, WATERED, WATERLESS, WATERS

Ex   7:20 all the **w** in the river was turned
                  into blood,
        15:25 he threw it into the **w,** and the **w**
                  became sweet.
        17: 1 no **w** for the people to drink.
Nu   5:19 be immune to this **w** of bitterness
        20: 2 there was no **w** for the congregation;
        21: 5 For there is no food and no **w,**
2Ki   2: 8 the **w** was parted to the one side
        6: 5 his ax head fell into the **w;**
Ps   1: 3 like trees planted by streams of **w,**

        22:14 I am poured out like **w,** and all my
107:35 He turns a desert into pools of **w,**
Pr   5:15 Drink **w** from your own cistern,
        5:15 flowing **w** from your own well.
        9:17 "Stolen **w** is sweet, and bread eaten
        25:21 if they are thirsty, give them **w** to
Isa   12: 3 With joy you will draw **w** from the
        30:20 of adversity and the **w** of affliction,
        32: 2 like streams of **w** in a dry place,
        49:10 and by springs of **w** will guide them.
Jer   2:13 the fountain of living **w,**
        17: 8 shall be like a tree planted by **w,**
        31: 9 I will let them walk by brooks of **w,**
Eze   36:25 I will sprinkle clean **w** upon you,
Mt   14:29 walking on the **w,** and came
Mk   1: 8 I have baptized you with **w;**
        9:41 cup of **w** to drink because you bear
Lk   5: 4 "Put out into the deep **w** and let
                  down
Jn   2: 9 tasted the **w** that had become wine,
        3: 5 without being born of **w** and Spirit.
        4:10 he would have given you living **w."**
        7:38 heart shall flow rivers of living **w.'"**
        19:34 and at once blood and **w** came out.
Eph   5:26 by cleansing her with the washing
                  of **w** by the word,
Heb 10:22 and our bodies washed with pure **w.**
Jas   3:11 opening both fresh and brackish **w?**
1Jn   5: 6 the one who came by **w** and blood,
Rev   7:17 to springs of the **w** of life,
        21: 6 the thirsty I will give **w** as a gift
                  from the spring of the **w** of life.
        22: 1 showed me the river of the **w** of life,
        22:17 who wishes take the **w** of life as
Sir   15: 3 give him the **w** of wisdom to drink.

LIVING WATER SS 4:15; Jer 2:13; 17:13; Jn
        4:10, 11; 7:38

WATERCOURSES → COURSE, WATER

Ps   126: 4 O LORD, like the **w** in the Negeb.

WATERED → WATER

Ps   104:16 trees of the LORD are **w** abundantly,
1Co   3: 6 I planted, Apollos **w,** but God gave
                  the growth.

WATERLESS → WATER

Lk   11:24 through **w** regions looking for a
2Pe   2:17 are **w** springs and mists driven by a
Jude   1:12 are **w** clouds carried along by the

WATERS → WATER

Ge   1: 2 swept over the face of the **w.**
        1:10 that were gathered together
                  he called Seas.
        7: 7 the ark to escape the **w** of the flood.
Ex   14:21 dry land; and the **w** were divided.
Jos   4: 7 the **w** of the Jordan were cut off.
Ps   18:16 he drew me out of mighty **w;**
        23: 2 he leads me beside still **w;**
        106:32 They angered the LORD at the **w** of
                  Meribah,
Ecc   11: 1 Send out your bread upon the **w,**
SS   8: 7 Many **w** cannot quench love,
Isa   11: 9 of the LORD as the **w** cover
        43: 2 through the **w,** I will be with you;
        55: 1 who thirsts, come to the **w;**
        58:11 spring of water, whose **w** never fail.
Hab   2:14 as the **w** cover the sea.
1Co   3: 7 nor the one who **w** is anything,
Rev   8:11 A third of the **w** became wormwood
        11: 6 and they have authority over the **w**
MIGHTY WATERS Ex 15:10; 2Sa 22:17;
        Ne 9:11; Ps 18:16; 29:3; 32:6; 77:19; 93:4;
        107:23; 144:7; Isa 17:12; 23:3; 43:16; Jer
        51:13, 55; Eze 1:24; 31:15; 43:2; Hab 3:15;
        2Es 6:17

WAVE → WAVES

Jas   1: 6 who doubts is like a **w** of the sea,

WAVER → WAVERING

Ro   4:20 No distrust made him **w** concerning

WAVERING → WAVER

Heb 10:23 confession of our hope without **w**,
Jude 1:22 have mercy on some who are **w**;

WAVES → WAVE

2Sa 22: 5 For the **w** of death encompassed me,
Ps 89: 9 when its **w** rise, you still them.
Jude 1:13 **w** of the sea, casting up the foam

WAX

Ps 22:14 my heart is like **w**; it is melted
    97: 5 The mountains melt like **w** before
         the LORD,

WAY → GATEWAY, HIGHWAY, WAYS, WAYWARDNESS

Ge 3:24 to guard the **w** to the tree of life.
Ex 13:21 to lead them along the **w**,
    18:20 known to them the **w** they are to go
Dt 1:33 who goes before you on the **w** to
1Sa 12:23 in the good and the right **w**.
2Sa 22:31 This God—his **w** is perfect;
1Ki 8:36 good **w** in which they should walk;
2Ch 6:27 good **w** in which they should walk;
Job 23:10 But he knows the **w** that I take;
Ps   1: 6 the LORD watches over the **w** of the
         righteous, but the **w** of the wicked
         will perish.
    18:30 This God—his **w** is perfect;
    32: 8 and teach you the **w** you should go;
    37: 5 Commit your **w** to the LORD;
    86:11 Teach me your **w**, O LORD,
   119: 9 How can young people keep their
         w pure?
   139:24 and lead me in the **w** everlasting.
Pr   4:11 I have taught you the **w** of wisdom;
    12:15 Fools think their own **w** is right,
    14:12 There is a **w** that seems right to a
         person, but its end is the **w** to death.
    16:17 guard their **w** preserve their lives.
    19: 2 moves too hurriedly misses the **w**.
    22: 6 Train children in the right **w**,
    30:19 the **w** of an eagle in the sky,
Isa 30:21 saying, "This is the **w**; walk in it."
    35: 8 and it shall be called the Holy **W**;
    40: 3 "In the wilderness prepare the **w** of
         the LORD.
    48:17 leads you in the **w** you should go.
    53: 6 we have all turned to our own **w**,
    55: 7 let the wicked forsake their **w**, and
Jer 21: 8 I am setting before you the **w** of life
        and the **w** of death.
Mal 3: 1 I am sending my messenger to
        prepare the **w**
Mt   3: 3 'Prepare the **w** of the Lord,
     5:12 for in the same **w** they persecuted
Lk   7:27 will prepare your **w** before you.'
Jn 14: 6 Jesus said to him, "I am the **w**, and
       the truth, and the life.
Ac   1:11 in the same **w** as you saw him go
       into heaven."
     9: 2 found any who belonged to the **W**,
    19: 9 spoke evil of the **W** before the
       congregation,
    22: 4 I persecuted this **W** up to the point
       of death
    24:14 that according to the **W**,
1Co 9:24 Run in such a **w** that you may win
    10:13 but with the testing he will also
       provide the **w** out
    12:31 show you a still more excellent **w**.
Eph 4:20 not the **w** you learned Christ!
Heb 9: 8 the Holy Spirit indicates that the **w**
    10:20 the new and living **w** that he opened
2Pe 2:21 known the **w** of righteousness than,
2Es 5: 1 and the **w** of truth shall be hidden.

EVIL WAY 1Ki 13:33; Ps 119:101; Jer 18:11;
23:22; 25:5; 26:3; 35:15

IN EVERY WAY Ac 17:22; 24:3; Ro 3:2;
1Co 1:5; 2Co 4:8; 6:4; 7:5; 9:11; 11:6; Eph
4:15; Php 1:18; 1Ti 3:4; 4:8; 5:10; Jas 1:7;

1Mc 6:18; 14:35; 2Mc 1:17; 1Es 8:52; 3Mc
3:24; 4Mc 8:3; 18:1

WAY OF LIFE Pr 6:23; Jer 21:8; Ac 26:4;
Eph 2:10; 4:22; Heb 13:7; AdE 10:3; Sir
40:29; 2Mc 4:10; 8:17; 3Mc 3:23; 4Mc 2:8;
4:19; 8:8; 17:9

WAY OF THE *LORD Eze 18:25, 29;
33:17, 20; Mt 3:3; Mk 1:3; Lk 3:4; Jn 1:23; Ac
18:25; Wis 5:7

WAY OF THE †LORD Ge 18:19; Jdg 2:22;
2Ki 21:22; Pr 10:29; Isa 40:3; Jer 5:4, 5

WAYS → WAY

Ge   6:12 for all flesh had corrupted its **w**
       upon the earth.
Ex 33:13 show me your **w**,
Dt 10:12 to walk in all his **w**, to love him,
    26:17 and for you to walk in his **w**,
    30:16 LORD your God, walking in his **w**,
    32: 4 is perfect, and all his **w** are just.
Jos 22: 5 to walk in all his **w**, to keep his
1Ki 8:58 to walk in all his **w**,
2Ki 17:13 "Turn from your evil **w** and keep
Job 34:21 his eyes are upon the **w** of mortals,
Ps 25: 4 Make me to know your **w**, O LORD;
    51:13 I will teach transgressors your **w**,
  119:59 I think of your **w**, I turn my feet to
  139: 3 and are acquainted with all my **w**.
  145:17 The LORD is just in all his **w**,
Pr   3: 6 In all your **w** acknowledge him,
     3:17 Her **w** are ways of pleasantness,
     3:17 Her ways are **w** of pleasantness,
     4:26 and all your **w** will be sure.
     5:21 For human **w** are under the eyes of
     6: 6 consider its **w**, and be wise.
     7:25 Do not let your hearts turn aside to
       her **w**;
    16: 2 All one's **w** may be pure in one's
       own eyes,
    16: 7 the **w** of people please the LORD,
Isa   2: 3 that he may teach us his **w** and that
    42:24 in whose **w** they would not walk,
    55: 8 nor are your **w** my **w**, says the LORD
Jer 18:11 and amend your **w** and your doings.
Eze 16:47 You not only followed their **w**,
    28:15 in your **w** from the day that you
    33: 8 the wicked to turn from their **w**,
Da   4:37 are truth, and his **w** are justice;
Hos 14: 9 For the **w** of the LORD are right,
Jnh 3:10 how they turned from their evil **w**,
Lk   3: 5 and the rough **w** made smooth;
1Co 13:11 an adult, I put an end to childish **w**.
Col   3: 7 the **w** you also once followed,
Rev 15: 3 Just and true are your **w**, King of
Sir 2:15 who love him keep his **w**.
2Es 4: 3 have been sent to show you three **w**,

EVIL WAYS 2Ki 17:13; Pr 28:10; Jer 36:3, 7;
Eze 20:44; 33:11; 36:31; Jnh 3:8, 10; Zec 1:4

WAYWARDNESS* → WAY

Pr 1:32 For **w** kills the simple, and the

WEAK → WEAKENED, WEAKER, WEAKLING, WEAKNESS, WEAKNESSES

Jdg 16: 7 then I shall become **w**, and be like
Ps 72:13 He has pity on the **w** and the needy,
    82: 3 Give justice to the **w** and the orphan
    82: 4 Rescue the **w** and the needy;
Eze 34: 4 You have not strengthened the **w**,
Mt 26:41 the spirit indeed is willing, but the
       flesh is **w**."
Ac 20:35 such work we must support the **w**,
Ro 15: 1 Welcome those who are **w** in faith,
    15: 1 to put up with the failings of the **w**,
1Co 1:27 God chose what is **w** in the world
     8: 9 become a stumbling block to the **w**.
     9:22 To the **w** I became **w**, so that I
       might win the **w**.
    11:30 For this reason many of you are **w**
2Co 12:10 whenever I am **w**, then I am strong.
Gal 4: 9 **w** and beggarly elemental spirits?

1Th 5:14 the faint hearted, help the **w**,
Heb 7:18 commandment because it was **w**
    12:12 and strengthen your **w** knees,

WEAKENED → WEAK

Ro   8: 3 done what the law, **w** by the flesh,

WEAKER → WEAK

2Sa 3: 1 the house of Saul became **w** and **w**.
1Co 12:22 that seem to be **w** are indispensable,
1Pe 3: 7 honor to the woman as the **w** sex,
4Mc 15: 5 that mothers are the **w** sex

WEAKLING* → WEAK

Joel 3:10 let the **w** say, "I am a warrior."

WEAKNESS → WEAK

Ro 8:26 the Spirit helps us in our **w**;
1Co 1:25 God's **w** is stronger than human
       strength.
     2: 3 **w** and in fear and in much trembling
   15:43 It is sown in **w**, it is raised in power.
2Co 11:30 boast of the things that show my **w**.
    12: 9 for power is made perfect in **w**."
    13: 4 For he was crucified in **w**,
Heb 5: 2 since he himself is subject to **w**;
     7:28 priests those who are subject to **w**,
   11:34 won strength out of **w**, became

WEAKNESSES* → WEAK

2Co 12: 5 not boast, except of my **w**.
    12: 9 boast all the more gladly of my **w**,
    12:10 I am content with **w**, insults,
Heb 4:15 to sympathize with our **w**,

WEALTH

Dt   8:18 he who gives you power to get **w**,
2Ch 1:11 **w**, honor, or the life of those who
Ps 49: 6 those who trust in their **w** and boast
    49:10 perish together and leave their **w**
   112: 3 **W** and riches are in their houses,
Pr 13: 7 pretend to be poor, yet have great **w**.
    13:11 **W** hastily gotten will dwindle,
    13:22 the sinner's **w** is laid up for the
       righteous.
    19: 4 **W** brings many friends,
Ecc 5:10 nor the lover of **w**, with gain.
SS   8: 7 If one offered for love all the **w** of
Mt 13:22 but the cares of the world and the
       lure of **w** choke
Lk 16:11 faithful with the dishonest **w**,
Rev 5:12 receive power and **w** and wisdom
Sir 5: 1 Do not rely on your **w**,
    5: 8 Do not depend on dishonest **w**,
   11:14 poverty and **w**, come from the Lord.

WEANED

Ge 21: 8 The child grew, and was **w**;
1Sa 1:22 as the child is **w**, I will bring him,
Ps 131: 2 like a **w** child with its mother;

WEAPON → WEAPONS

Ne 4:17 hand and with the other held a **w**.
Isa 54:17 No **w** that is fashioned against you

WEAPONS → WEAPON

Ecc 9:18 Wisdom is better than **w** of war,
Isa 13: 5 LORD and the **w** of his indignation,
Jn 18: 3 with lanterns and torches and **w**.
2Co 6: 7 the **w** of righteousness for the right
    10: 4 for the **w** of our warfare are not
       merely human,

WEAR → WEARING

Dt   8: 4 clothes on your back did not **w** out
    22: 5 woman shall not **w** a man's apparel,
Ps 102:26 they will all **w** out like a garment,
Pr 23: 4 Do not **w** yourself out to get rich;
Isa 51: 6 the earth will **w** out like a garment,
Mt 6:31 or 'What will we **w**?'
Heb 1:11 they will all **w** out like clothing;

WEARIED → WEARY

Isa 43:24 you have **w** me with your iniquities.

Mal 2:17 have **w** the LORD with your words.

WEARING → WEAR
1Sa 18: 4 of the robe that he was **w,**
2Sa 13:18 she was **w** a long robe with sleeves;
1Ki 11:30 new garment he was **w** and tore it
Jn   19: 5 came out, **w** the crown of thorns
Jas   2: 3 notice of the one **w** the fine clothes
1Pe   3: 3 and by **w** gold ornaments or fine

WEARY → WEARIED
Isa   1:14 become a burden to me, I am **w**
     40:28 He does not faint or grow **w;**
     40:31 they shall run and not be **w,**
     50: 4 how to sustain the **w** with a word.
Jer   9: 5 iniquity and are too **w** to repent.
Mt   11:28 all you that are **w** and are carrying
Heb 12: 3 you may not grow **w** or lose heart.
Rev   2: 3 and that you have not grown **w.**

WEDDING
Mt   22: 2 to a king who gave a **w** banquet
     22:11 who was not wearing a **w** robe,
Jn   2: 1 there was a **w** in Cana of Galilee,

WEEDS
Mt   13:25 and sowed **w** among the wheat,

WEEK → WEEKS
Mt   28: 1 the first day of the **w** was dawning,
Lk   18:12 I fast twice a **w;** I give a tenth of all
1Co 16: 2 On the first day of every **w,**

WEEKS → WEEK
Ex   34:22 You shall observe the festival of **w,**
Lev 23:15 you shall count off seven **w**
     25: 8 shall count off seven **w** of years,
Da   9:24 "Seventy **w** are decreed for your

WEEP → WEEPING, WEPT
Ecc   3: 4 a time to **w,** and a time to laugh;
La   1:16 For these things I **w;** my eyes flow
Lk   6:21 "Blessed are you who **w** now, for
               you will laugh.
     23:28 "Daughters of Jerusalem, do not **w**
               for me, but **w** for yourselves and
Ro   12:15 **w** with those who **w.**

WEEPING → WEEP
Ps   6: 8 LORD has heard the sound of my **w.**
     30: 5 **W** may linger for the night,
    126: 6 who go out **w,** bearing the seed for
Jer 31:15 Rachel is **w** for her children;
Mt   2:18 Rachel **w** for her children;
      8:12 will be **w** and gnashing of teeth."
     13:42 will be **w** and gnashing of teeth.
     22:13 will be **w** and gnashing of teeth.'
     24:51 will be **w** and gnashing of teeth.
     25:30 will be **w** and gnashing of teeth.'

WEIGH → OUTWEIGHS, WEIGHED, WEIGHS, WEIGHTS
1Co 14:29 and let the others **w** what is said.

WEIGHED → WEIGH
1Sa   2: 3 and by him actions are **w.**
Job 28:15 silver cannot be **w** out as its price.
Da   5:27 you have been **w** on the scales
Lk   1:34 not **w** down with dissipation and

WEIGHS → WEIGH
Pr   12:25 Anxiety **w** down the human heart,
     21: 2 but the LORD **w** the heart.
     24:12 he who **w** the heart perceive it?

WEIGHTS → WEIGH
Dt   25:13 not have in your bag two kinds of **w**
Pr   20:23 Differing **w** are an abomination to
               the LORD,

WELCOME → WELCOMES
Mt   10:14 not **w** you or listen to your words,
2Jn   1:10 or **w** anyone who comes to you
3Jn   1:10 he refuses to **w** the friends,

WELCOMES → WELCOME
Mt   18: 5 Whoever **w** one such child in my
               name **w** me.

WELL → WELLS
Ge   4: 7 If you do **w,** will you not be
               accepted?
     12:16 for her sake he dealt **w** with Abram;
Dt   5:16 it may go **w** with you in the land
      6: 3 so that it may go **w** with you,
     12:28 that it may go **w** with you and with
2Ch   6: 8 did **w** to consider building a house
Pr   5:15 flowing water from your own **w.**
     23:27 an adulteress is a narrow **w.**
Mt   3:17 with whom I am **w** pleased."
     17: 5 I am **w** pleased; listen to him!"
     25:21 His master said to him, 'W done,
Lk   14: 5 or an ox that has fallen into a **w,**
     17:19 your faith has made you **w."**
Jn   4: 6 Jacob's **w** was there, and Jesus,
Ac   15:29 from these, you will do **w.**
Eph   6: 3 that it may be **w** with you and
2Pe   1:17 with whom I am **w** pleased."
3Jn   1: 2 just as it is **w** with your soul.

WELL-BEING
Lev   3: 1 If the offering is a sacrifice of **w,**
Ps 119:122 Guarantee your servant's **w;**

WELLS → WELL
Isa 12: 3 water from the **w** of salvation.

WEPT → WEEP
Nu   14: 1 and the people **w** that night.
Ezr   3:12 **w** with a loud voice when they saw
               this house,
Ps 137: 1 we **w** when we remembered Zion.
Isa 38: 3 And Hezekiah **w** bitterly.
Lk   19:41 and saw the city, he **w** over it,
     22:62 And he went out and **w** bitterly.

WEST → WESTERN
Ps 103:12 as far as the east is from the **w,**
    107: 3 from the east and from the **w,**
Isa 43: 5 and from the **w** I will gather you;
Zec 14: 4 split in two from east to **w** by

WESTERN → WEST
Nu   34: 6 this shall be your **w** boundary.
Dt   11:24 the river Euphrates, to the **W** Sea.
Zec 14: 8 and half of them to the **w** sea;

WHATEVER
Ps 135: 6 **W** the LORD pleases he does,
Mt   16:19 **w** you bind on earth will be bound
     18:18 **w** you bind on earth will be bound
Mk   11:24 I tell you, **w** you ask for in prayer,
Jn   14:13 I will do **w** you ask in my name,
     15:16 Father will give you **w** you ask him
Gal   6: 7 for you reap **w** you sow.
Php   4: 8 beloved, **w** is true, **w** is honorable,
      4:11 learned to be content with **w** I have.
1Jn   5:15 know that he hears us in **w** we ask,
LtJ   6:44 **W** is done for these idols is false.

WHEAT
Ex   34:22 the first fruits of **w** harvest,
Mt   3:12 will gather his **w** into the granary;
     13:25 and sowed weeds among the **w,**
Lk   22:31 Satan has demanded to sift all of
               you like **w,**
Jn   12:24 unless a grain of **w** falls into the
               earth and dies,

WHEEL → WHEELS
Eze   1:16 something like a **w** within a **w.**

WHEELS → WHEEL
Ex   14:25 He clogged their chariot **w** so that
Eze   1:16 the appearance of the **w** and their
Da   7: 9 and its **w** were burning fire.

WHENEVER
Dt   4: 7 LORD our God is **w** we call to him?

Jas   1: 2 **w** you face trials of any kind,
1Jn   3:20 **w** our hearts condemn us;

WHERE → EVERYWHERE, NOWHERE, WHEREVER
Dt   32:37 Then he will say: **W** are their gods,
Job 28:12 "But **w** shall wisdom be found?
Ps   26: 8 and the place **w** your glory abides.
     42: 3 continually "**W** is your God?"
    121: 1 from **w** will my help come?
    139: 7 **W** can I go from your spirit?
Hos 13:14 O Death, **w** are your plagues?
     13:14 O Sheol, **w** is your destruction?
Mal   1: 6 If then I am a father, **w** is the honor
Mt   6:21 **w** your treasure is, there your heart
     28: 6 Come, see the place **w** he lay.
Jn   3: 8 The wind blows **w** it chooses,
     13:33 'W I am going, you cannot come.'
1Co 15:55 "W, O death, is your victory?
Col   3: 1 **w** Christ is, seated at the right hand
2Pe   3: 4 "W is the promise of his coming?

WHEREVER → WHERE
Jos   1: 7 you may be successful **w** you go.
Mk   14: 9 the good news is proclaimed in
Lk   9:57 "I will follow you **w** you go."
Rev 14: 4 these follow the Lamb **w** he goes.

WHETHER
Ro   14: 8 **w** we live or **w** we die, we are the
               Lord's.
1Jn   4: 1 but test the spirits to see **w** they are
               from God;

WHILE
Isa 55: 6 Seek the LORD **w** he may be found,
               call upon him **w** he is near;
     65:24 **w** they are yet speaking I will hear.
Da   9:21 **w** I was speaking in prayer,
Jn   12:35 Walk **w** you have the light,
     16:16 a little **w,** and you will see me."
Ro   5: 8 in that **w** we still were sinners
               Christ died for us.
2Co   5: 4 For **w** we are still in this tent,
Tit   2:13 **w** we wait for the blessed hope and
1Pe   5:10 after you have suffered for a little **w,**

WHIP
Jn   2:15 Making a **w** of cords, he drove all

WHIRLWIND → WIND
2Ki   2:11 Elijah ascended in a **w** into heaven.
Ps   77:18 crash of your thunder was in the **w;**
Hos   8: 7 For they sow the wind, and they
               shall reap the **w.**
Na   1: 3 His way is in **w** and storm,
Sir 48:12 Elijah was enveloped in the **w,**

WHISPER → WHISPERED, WHISPERER
Job 26:14 how small a **w** do we hear of him!

WHISPERED → WHISPER
Mt   10:27 what you hear **w,** proclaim from the
               housetops.

WHISPERER → WHISPER
Pr   16:28 and a **w** separates close friends.
Sir 21:28 A **w** degrades himself

WHITE → WHITER, WHITEWASH, WHITEWASHED
Da   7: 9 his clothing was **w** as snow,
Zec   1: 8 were red, sorrel, and **w** horses.
      6: 3 the third chariot **w** horses,
Mt   5:36 cannot make one hair **w** or black.
     28: 3 and his clothing **w** as snow.
Ac   1:10 two men in **w** robes stood by them.
Rev   1:14 His head and his hair were **w** as **w**
               wool, **w** as snow;
      2:17 the **w** stone is written a new name
      3: 4 will walk with me, dressed in **w,**
      6: 2 I looked, and there was a **w** horse!
      7:13 "Who are these, robed in **w,**
     14:14 I looked, and there was a **w** cloud,

19:11 and there was a **w** horse!
20:11 I saw a great **w** throne and the one who sat on it;

WHITER → WHITE

Ps 51: 7 wash me, and I shall be **w** than snow.

WHITEWASH → WHITE

Eze 13:10 a wall, these prophets smear **w** on it.
22:28 Its prophets have smeared **w** on their behalf,

WHITEWASHED* → WHITE

Mt 23:27 For you are like **w** tombs,
Ac 23: 3 "God will strike you, you **w** wall!

WHOEVER

Mt 12:50 For **w** does the will of my Father
Mk   3:29 **w** blasphemes against the Holy Spirit
     9:40 **W** is not against us is for us.
Jn   3:36 **W** believes in the Son has eternal life;

WHOLE → WHOLEHEARTEDLY, WHOLE

Ge 11: 1 **w** earth had one language and the
    18:28 destroy the **w** city for lack of five?"
Ex 12:47 The **w** congregation of Israel shall celebrate it.
    19: 5 Indeed, the **w** earth is mine,
Dt 13:16 as a **w** burnt offering to the LORD
Jos 2: 3 come only to search out the **w** land."
1Ki 10:24 The **w** earth sought the presence of Solomon
Ps 72:19 may his glory fill the **w** earth.
   119:10 With my **w** heart I seek you;
Ecc 12:13 for that is the **w** duty of everyone.
Isa 1: 5 The **w** head is sick, and the **w** heart faint.
     6: 3 the **w** earth is full of his glory."
    14:26 planned concerning the **w** earth;
Eze 37:11 bones are the **w** house of Israel.
Da   2:35 mountain and filled the **w** earth.
Zep 1:18 the **w** earth shall be consumed;
Mt   5:29 your **w** body to be thrown into hell.
     6:22 your **w** body will be full of light;
    16:26 if they gain the **w** world but forfeit their life?
Mk 15:33 darkness came over the **w** land until
Lk 21:35 who live on the face of the **w** earth.
Ac 17:26 to inhabit the **w** earth,
    20:27 from declaring to you the **w** purpose
Ro   3:19 **w** world may be held accountable
     8:22 the **w** creation has been groaning
1Co 5: 6 a little yeast leavens the **w** batch of
    12:17 **w** body were an eye, where would the hearing be?
Gal 5: 9 A little yeast leavens the **w** batch of
     5:14 **w** law is summed up in a single commandment,
Eph 2:21 the **w** structure is joined together
Tit 1:11 upsetting **w** families by teaching
Jas 2:10 whoever keeps the **w** law but fails
1Jn 2: 2 but also for the sins of the **w** world.
     5:19 the **w** world lies under the power of the evil one.
Rev 3:10 the **w** world to test the inhabitants of
    12: 9 the deceiver of the **w** world—
    13: 3 In amazement the **w** earth followed the beast.

WHOLE ARMY Jdg 20:26; 2Sa 8:9; 1Ch 18:9; Jer 37:10; Jdt 1:13; 2:19, 22; 7:1; 11:18; 1Mc 5:43; 2Mc 9:9; 4Mc 3:8

WHOLE ASSEMBLY Ex 16:3; Dt 5:22; 31:30; Jos 22:12; 1Ch 13:2, 4; 29:1, 20; 2Ch 1:3; 6:12, 13; 23:3; 29:28; 30:23, 25, 25; Ezr 2:64; 10:14; Ne 7:66; Lk 1:10; Ac 15:12; Sus 1:60

WHOLE BODY Lev 15:16; Nu 8:7; Mt 5:29, 30; 6:22, 23; Lk 11:34, 36; Jn 7:23; Ac 5:21;

1Co 12:17, 17; Eph 4:16; Col 2:19; Jas 3:2, 6; 2Mc 15:12; 2Es 12:3

WHOLE CONGREGATION Ex 12:3, 47; 16:1, 2, 9, 10; 17:1; Lev 4:13; 8:3; 9:5; 24:14, 16; Nu 1:2, 18; 3:7; 8:9, 20; 10:3; 14:2, 10; 15:24, 33, 36; 16:19, 19, 22, 41; 20:1, 22, 27; 25:6; 26:2; 27:21, 22; Jos 18:1; 22:16, 18; Jdg 21:13; Sir 1:30; 50:13, 20

WHOLE EARTH Ge 8:9; 9:19; 11:1, 4; Ex 19:5; 1Ki 10:24; Ps 72:19; Isa 6:3; 13:5; 14:7, 26; 54:5; Jer 50:23; 51:25, 41; Eze 32:4; 35:14; Da 2:35, 39; 4:11, 20; 7:23; 8:5; Mic 4:13; Zep 1:18; Zec 1:11; 4:10, 14; Lk 21:35; Ac 17:26; Rev 13:3; Jdt 2:5, 9; 6:4; 11:7; Wis 5:23; 1Es 4:36; 3Mc 1:29; 2Es 11:2, 32, 46; 15:27

WHOLE HEART 2Ki 20:3; 2Ch 19:9; Ps 9:1; 86:12; 111:1; 119:2, 10, 34, 69, 145; 138:1; Isa 1:5; 38:3; Jer 3:10; 24:7; Wis 8:21; 4Mc 7:18

WHOLE HOUSE Lev 10:6; 2Sa 3:19; 1Ki 6:10, 22, 22; 2Ki 9:8; Ne 4:16; Jer 13:11, 11; 35:3; Eze 11:15; 36:10; 37:11; 39:25; 45:6; Jdt 4:15; Sir 1:17

WHOLE KINGDOM Jos 13:30; 1Ki 11:34; Est 3:6; Da 1:20; 6:1, 3; 11:17; Jdt 11:8; 1Mc 1:41, 51

WHOLE LAND Ge 2:11, 13; 13:9; Ex 7:19, 21; 8:16, 17; 9:9, 22; 10:15; 11:6; Dt 34:1; Jos 2:3; 10:40; 11:23; Isa 28:22; Jer 1:18; 4:20, 27; 8:16; 12:11; 15:10; 25:11; 40:4; 45:4; 51:47; Zec 5:3; 13:8; 14:10; Mt 27:45; Mk 15:33; Lk 23:44; Tob 14:4; Jdt 1:9; 5:12; 7:4; Bar 2:23; 2Mc 2:21

WHOLE NATION Mal 3:9; Jn 11:50; Jdt 9:14; AdE 16:13; 10:3; 2Mc 7:38; 10:8; 14:8; 1Es 1:32; 3Mc 5:5

WHOLE WORLD Job 34:13; Isa 27:6; Da 6:25; Mt 16:26; 26:13; Mk 8:36; 14:9; Lk 9:25; Ro 3:19; Col 1:6; 1Jn 2:2; 5:19; Rev 3:10; 12:9; 16:14; Tob 14:6; Jdt 5:21; 10:19; 11:8, 16, 23; AdE 13:2; Wis 11:22; 17:20; 18:24; LtJ 6:62; Aza 1:22; 2Mc 3:12; 8:18; 3Mc 6:5; 2Es 10:8

WHOLEHEARTEDLY → HEART, WHOLE

Nu 14:24 he has a different spirit and has followed me **w**,
Jos 14: 8 yet I **w** followed the LORD my God.
    14: 9 have **w** followed the LORD my God.
    14:14 because he **w** followed the LORD,
Tob 2: 2 who is **w** mindful of God,

WHOLESOME → WHOLE

2Ki 2:22 So the water has been **w** to this day,

WHORE → WHOREDOM, WHORING

Ge 34:31 our sister be treated like a **w**?"
    38:24 Tamar has played the **w**;
Isa 1:21 the faithful city has become a **w**!
Eze 16:17 and with them played the **w**;
Hos 2: 5 For their mother has played the **w**;
Rev 17: 1 the judgment of the great **w**
    19: 2 judged the great **w** who corrupted

WHOREDOM → WHORE

Hos 1: 2 to Hosea, "Go, take for yourself a wife of **w** and have children of **w**,
     2: 4 because they are children of **w**.

WHORING → WHORE

Jer 3: 2 polluted the land with your **w**

WHY

Ge   4: 6 said to Cain, "**W** are you angry,
    12:19 **W** did you say, 'She is my sister,'
    32:29 "**W** is it that you ask my name?"
Jdg 13:18 "**W** do you ask my name?
Job 24: 1 "**W** are times not kept by the Almighty,

Ps   2: 1 **W** do the nations conspire,
    10: 1 **W**, O LORD, do you stand far off?
    22: 1 My God, my God, **w** have you forsaken me?
    42: 5 **W** are you cast down, O my soul,
    79:10 **W** should the nations say, "Where is their God?"
Isa 1: 5 **W** do you continue to rebel?
    40:27 **W** do you say, O Jacob, and speak,
La   5:20 **W** have you forgotten us completely?
Am   5:18 **W** do you want the day of the LORD?
Mt   9:11 "**W** does your teacher eat with tax collectors
    17:19 "**W** could we not cast it out?"
    27:46 "My God, my God, **w** have you forsaken me?"
Mk 10:18 Jesus said to him, "**W** do you call me good?
Ac   9: 4 Saul, **w** do you persecute me?"

WICK

Isa 42: 3 dimly burning **w** he will not quench;
Mt 12:20 or quench a smoldering **w** until

WICKED → WICKEDLY, WICKEDNESS

Ge 13:13 Now the people of Sodom were **w**,
    18:23 the righteous with the **w**?
Ex 23: 1 You shall not join hands with the **w**
Nu 14:35 to all this **w** congregation gathered
2Ki 17:11 did **w** things, provoking the LORD
2Ch 7:14 and turn from their **w** ways,
    19: 2 "Should you help the **w** and love
Job 15:20 The **w** writhe in pain all their days,
    20:29 the portion of the **w** from God,
    27:13 the portion of the **w** with God,
Ps   1: 1 do not follow the advice of the **w**,
     1: 5 the **w** will not stand in the judgment,
     7: 9 let the evil of the **w** come to an end,
    10:13 Why do the **w** renounce God,
    11: 6 On the **w** he will rain coals of fire
    12: 8 On every side the **w** prowl,
    26: 5 and will not sit with the **w**.
    32:10 Many are the torments of the **w**,
    36: 1 Transgression speaks to the **w** deep
    37:13 but the LORD laughs at the **w**,
    37:40 he rescues them from the **w**,
    50:16 to the **w** God says:
    58: 3 The **w** go astray from the womb;
    73: 3 I saw the prosperity of the **w**.
    82: 2 and show partiality to the **w**?
   112:10 desire of the **w** comes to nothing.
   119:61 the cords of the **w** ensnare me,
   119:155 Salvation is far from the **w**,
   140: 8 Do not grant, O LORD, the desires of the **w**;
   141:10 Let the **w** fall into their own nets,
   146: 9 the way of the **w** he brings to ruin.
Pr   4:14 Do not enter the path of the **w**,
     5:22 The iniquities of the **w** ensnare them
     6:18 a heart that devises **w** plans,
     9: 7 whoever rebukes the **w** gets hurt.
    10:20 the mind of the **w** is of little worth.
    10:28 the expectation of the **w** comes to nothing.
    11: 5 the **w** fall by their own wickedness.
    11:10 the **w** perish, there is jubilation.
    11:21 the **w** will not go unpunished,
    12: 5 the advice of the **w** is treacherous.
    12:10 but the mercy of the **w** is cruel.
    14:19 the **w** at the gates of the righteous.
    21:10 The souls of the **w** desire evil;
    21:29 The **w** put on a bold face,
    24: 1 Do not envy the **w**, nor desire to be
    28: 1 The **w** flee when no one pursues,
    28: 4 who forsake the law praise the **w**,
    29: 7 the **w** have no such understanding.
    29:16 When the **w** are in authority,
    29:27 upright are an abomination to the **w**.
Ecc 7:15 are **w** people who prolong their life
     8:14 according to the conduct of the **w**,

Isa 11: 4 and with the breath of his lips he
            shall kill the **w.**
   13:11 and the **w** for their iniquity;
   26:10 If favor is shown to the **w,**
   48:22 "There is no peace," says the LORD,
            "for the **w."**
   53: 9 They made his grave with the **w**
   55: 7 let the **w** forsake their way,
   57:20 **w** are like the tossing sea that
            cannot keep still;
Eze 3:18 to the **w,** "You shall surely die,"
   13:22 encouraged the **w** not to turn from
            their **w** way and save their lives;
   18:21 if the **w** turn away from all their sins
   18:23 any pleasure in the death of the **w,**
   21:25 As for you, vile, **w** prince of Israel,
   33: 8 If I say to the **w,** "O **w** ones,
   33:11 no pleasure in the death of the **w,**
            but that the **w** turn from their ways
   33:19 the **w** turn from their wickedness,
Da 12:10 the **w** shall continue to act wickedly.
   12:10 None of the **w** shall understand,
Na   1:15 never again shall the **w** invade you;
Lk   6:35 kind to the ungrateful and the **w.**
1Co 5:13 Drive out the **w** person from among
Sir 15:20 not commanded anyone to be **w,**

WICKEDLY → WICKED

Ge 19: 7 my brothers, do not act so **w.**
Jdg 19:23 my brothers, do not act so **w.**
2Ch 6:37 done wrong; we have acted **w';**
Da 12:10 the wicked shall continue to act **w.**

WICKEDNESS → WICKED

Ge   6: 5 The LORD saw that the **w** of
Dt   9: 4 because of the **w** of these nations
Ps   5: 4 not a God who delights in **w;**
    45: 7 you love righteousness and hate **w.**
Pr 11: 5 but the wicked fall by their own **w.**
Ecc 3:16 place of righteousness, **w** was there
Jer 3: 2 the land with your whoring and **w.**
     8: 6 no one repents of **w,** saying,
    14:20 We acknowledge our **w,** O LORD,
Eze 18:20 **w** of the wicked shall be his own.
    33:19 when the wicked turn from their **w,**
Jnh 1: 2 for their **w** has come up before me."
Lk 11:39 inside you are full of greed and **w.**
Ac   1:18 a field with the reward of his **w;**
Ro   1:18 and **w** of those who by their **w**
            suppress the truth.
2Ti 2:19 of the Lord turn away from **w."**
Heb 1: 9 loved righteousness and hated **w;**
Wis 2:21 for their **w** blinded them,
Sir 19:22 The knowledge of **w** is not wisdom,

WIDE

Ps 81:10 Open your mouth **w** and I will fill it.
Mt   7:13 the gate is **w** and the road is easy
2Co 6:13 —open **w** your hearts also.

WIDOW → WIDOW'S, WIDOWHOOD, WIDOWS

Ex 22:22 shall not abuse any **w** or orphan.
Dt 10:18 justice for the orphan and the **w,**
Ru   4: 5 the **w** of the dead man,
Ps 146: 9 he upholds the orphan and the **w,**
Isa 1:17 defend the orphan, plead for the **w.**
La   1: 1 How like a **w** she has become,
Mk 12:19 marry the **w** and raise up children
Lk   2:37 as a **w** to the age of eighty-four.
    18: 3 a **w** who kept coming to him
    21: 3 this poor **w** has put in more than all
1Ti 5: 4 If a **w** has children or grandchildren,
Rev 18: 7 I am no **w,** and I will never see grief
Jdt 8: 4 Judith remained as a **w** for three

WIDOW'S → WIDOW

Ge 38:14 she put off her **w** garments,
Job 29:13 I caused the **w** heart to sing for joy.
Pr 15:25 but maintains the **w** boundaries.
Jdt 8: 5 and dressed in **w** clothing.

WIDOWHOOD → WIDOW

Isa 54: 4 disgrace of your **w** you will
            remember no more.

WIDOWS → WIDOW

Dt 14:29 orphans, and the **w** in your towns,
Ps 68: 5 protector of **w** is God in his holy
Lk   4:25 **w** in Israel in the time of Elijah,
Ac   6: 1 their **w** were being neglected in
1Co 7: 8 To the unmarried and the **w** I say
1Ti 5: 3 Honor **w** who are really **w.**
Jas 1:27 to care for orphans and **w** in their

WIFE → WIVES

Ge   2:24 and his mother and clings to his **w,**
     3:20 The man named his **w** Eve,
    12:18 not tell me that was your **w?**
    19:26 Lot's **w,** behind him, looked back,
    20:11 they will kill me because of my **w.**
    24:67 Rebekah, and she became his **w;**
Ex 20:17 shall not covet your neighbor's **w,**
Nu   5:12 **w** goes astray and is unfaithful to
Dt   5:21 shall you covet your neighbor's **w.**
    24: 5 to be happy with the **w** whom he
            has married.
Ru   4:13 took Ruth and she became his **w.**
2Sa 12:10 taken the **w** of Uriah the Hittite to
            be your **w.**
Ps 128: 3 Your **w** will be like a fruitful vine
Pr   5:18 and rejoice in the **w** of your youth,
     6:24 preserve you from the **w** of another,
    12: 4 good **w** is the crown of her husband,
    18:22 who finds a **w** finds a good thing,
    19:14 but a prudent **w** is from the LORD.
    31:10 A capable **w** who can find?
Ecc 9: 9 Enjoy life with the **w** whom you
            love,
Hos 1: 2 a **w** of whoredom and have children
Mal 2:14 companion and your **w** by covenant.
Mt   1:20 not be afraid to take Mary as your **w**
     5:32 that anyone who divorces his **w,**
    19: 3 to divorce his **w** for any cause?"
Mk   6:18 for you to have your brother's **w."**
    10: 2 lawful for a man to divorce his **w?"**
    12:23 In the resurrection whose **w** will
            she be?
Lk 17:32 Remember Lot's **w.**
    18:29 no one who has left house or **w**
1Co 7: 2 each man should have his own **w**
     7:11 husband should not divorce his **w.**
     7:33 of the world, how to please his **w,**
Eph 5:23 husband is the head of the **w** just as
     5:28 He who loves his **w** loves himself.
     5:33 should love his **w** as himself,
     5:33 and a **w** should respect her husband.
Rev 21: 9 the bride, the **w** of the Lamb."
Tob 8: 6 his **w** Eve as a helper and support.
Sir 7:19 Do not dismiss a wise and good **w,**
    26: 1 Happy is the husband of a good **w;**
    26: 3 A good **w** is a great blessing;

WILD

Ge   1:25 the **w** animals of the earth of every
     8: 1 But God remembered Noah and all
            the **w** animals
Ex 32:25 saw that the people were running **w**
Mk   1: 6 and he ate locusts and **w** honey.
     1:13 and he was with the **w** beasts;
Ro 11:17 a **w** olive shoot,
1Co 15:32 with **w** animals at Ephesus,
Jude 1:13 **w** waves of the sea, casting up the

WILDERNESS

Ex   4:27 "Go into the **w** to meet Moses."
Isa 40: 3 the **w** prepare the way of the LORD,
Mt   3: 3 voice of one crying out in the **w:**
    24:26 He is in the **w,'** do not go out.

WILL* → FREEWILL, GOODWILL, WILLING, WILLINGLY, WILLS

Nu 24:13 do either good or bad of my own **w;**
1Sa 2:25 the **w** of the LORD to kill them.
1Ch 13: 2 if it is the **w** of the LORD our God,

Ezr 7:18 according to the **w** of your God.
    10:11 God of your ancestors, and do his **w**
Ps 27:12 Do not give me up to the **w** of my
            adversaries,
    40: 8 I delight to do your **w,** O my God;
    41: 2 You do not give them up to the **w**
            of their enemies.
   103:21 his ministers that do his **w.**
   143:10 Teach me to do your **w,**
Isa 30: 1 make an alliance, but against my **w,**
    53:10 it was the **w** of the LORD to crush
            him with pain.
    53:10 through him the **w** of the LORD
            shall prosper.
Jer 3:17 stubbornly follow their own evil **w.**
     7:24 in the stubbornness of their evil **w,**
    11: 8 in the stubbornness of an evil **w.**
    13:10 who stubbornly follow their own **w**
    16:12 following your stubborn evil **w,**
    18:12 the stubbornness of our evil **w."**
Eze 16:27 you up to the **w** of your enemies,
Dan 11:28 He shall work his **w,** and return to
Mt   6:10 Your **w** be done, on earth as it is in
            heaven.
     7:21 does the **w** of my Father in heaven.
    11:26 for such was your gracious **w.**
    12:50 does the **w** of my Father in heaven
    18:14 not the **w** of your Father in heaven
    21:31 of the two did the **w** of his father?"
    26:42 unless I drink it, your **w** be done."
Mk   3:35 does the **w** of God is my brother and
Lk 10:21 for such was your gracious **w.**
    22:42 yet, not my **w** but yours be done."
Jn   1:13 born, not of blood or of the **w** of the
            flesh or of the **w** of man, but of God
     4:34 "My food is to do the **w** of him who
     5:30 not my own **w** but the **w** of him
            who sent me.
     6:38 not to do my own **w,** but the **w** of
            him who sent me
     6:39 this is the **w** of him who sent me,
     6:40 This is indeed the **w** of my Father,
     7:17 who resolves to do the **w** of God
     9:31 who worships him and obeys his **w.**
    21:22 "If it is my **w** that he remain until I
    21:23 "If it is my **w** that he remain until I
Ac 21:14 to say, "The Lord's **w** be done."
    22:14 has chosen you to know his **w**
Ro   2:18 know his **w** and determine what is
     8:20 not of its own **w** but by the **w** of the
            one who subjected it,
     8:27 the Spirit intercedes for the saints
            according to the **w** of God.
     9:16 not on human **w** or exertion,
     9:19 For who can resist his **w?"**
    12: 2 the **w** of God—what is good and
    15:32 that by God's **w** I may come to you
1Co 1: 1 an apostle of Christ Jesus by the **w**
            of God,
     9:17 For if I do this of my own **w,** I have
            a reward; but if not of my own **w,**
2Co 1: 1 Paul, an apostle of Christ Jesus by
            the **w** of God,
Gal 1: 4 according to the **w** of our God and
            Father,
     3:15 once a person's **w** has been ratified,
Eph 1: 5 according to the good pleasure of
            his **w,**
     1: 9 known to us the mystery of his **w,**
     1:11 all things according to his counsel
            and **w.**
     5:17 understand what the **w** of the Lord
     6: 6 doing the **w** of God from the heart.
Php 2:13 both to **w** and to work for his good
Col 1: 9 with the knowledge of God's **w**
1Th 4: 3 For this is the **w** of God, your
            sanctification;
     5:18 give thanks in all circumstances;
            for this is the **w** of God
2Ti 2:26 held captive by him to do his **w.**
Heb 2: 4 gifts of the Holy Spirit, distributed
            according to his **w.**

9:16 Where a **w** is involved, the death of
9:17 For a **w** takes effect only at death,
10: 7 'I have come to do your **w**, O God'
10: 9 "See, I have come to do your **w**."
10:10 it is by God's **w** that we have been sanctified
10:36 when you have done the **w** of God,
13:21 so that you may do his **w**,
Jas 3: 4 wherever the **w** of the pilot directs.
1Pe 2:15 God's **w** that by doing right
3:17 if suffering should be God's **w**,
4: 2 human desires but by the **w** of God.
4:19 suffering in accordance with God's **w**
2Pe 1:21 no prophecy ever came by human **w**
1Jo 2:17 who do the **w** of God live forever.
5:14 if we ask anything according to his **w**, he hears us.
Rev 4:11 and by your **w** they existed and
Tob 12:18 not acting on my own **w**, but by the **w** of God.
AdE 13: 9 when it is your **w** to save
Wis 14: 5 your **w** that works of your wisdom
Sir 41: 4 you reject the **w** of the Most High?
42:15 and all his creatures do his **w**.
43:16 At his **w** the south wind blows;
1Mc 3: 60 But as his **w** in heaven may be, so shall he do."
2Mc 1: 3 to worship him and to do his **w**
12:16 took the town by the **w** of God,
1Es 7:15 he had changed the **w** of the king of
8:16 accordance with the **w** of your God;
9: 9 do his **w**; separate yourselves from
3Mc 2:26 themselves also followed his **w**.
2Es 3: 8 every nation walked after its own **w**;
8: 5 and against your **w** you depart,
4Mc 11:12 splendid favors that you grant us against your **w**,
18:16 tree of life for those who do his **w**.'

WILL OF ... *GOD 1Ch 13:2; Ezr 7:18; Mk 3:35; Jn 1:13; 7:17; Ro 8:27; 12:2; 1Co 1:1; 2Co 1:1; 8:5; Gal 1:4; Eph 1:1; 6:6; Col 1:1; 1Th 4:3; 5:18; 2Ti 1:1; Heb 10:36; 1Pe 4:2; 1Jn 2:17; Tob 12:18; 2Mc 12:16; 1Es 8:16

***GOD'S WILL** Ro 1:10; 15:32; Col 1:9; Heb 10:10; 1Pe 2:15; 3:17; 4:19

WILLING → WILL
2Ki 24: 4 and the LORD was not **w** to pardon,
1Ch 28: 9 with single mind and **w** heart;
Ps 51:12 and sustain in me a **w** spirit.
Mt 23:37 and you were not **w**!
26:41 the spirit indeed is **w**, but the flesh is weak."
Lk 22:42 if you are **w**, remove this cup from

WILLINGLY → WILL
Jdg 5: 2 when the people offer themselves **w**
La 3:33 does not **w** afflict or grieve anyone.
1Mc 2:42 offered themselves **w** for the law.

WILLS → WILL
Col 4:12 assured in everything that God **w**.
Wis 9:13 who can discern what the Lord **w**?

WIN → WINS, WON
1Co 9:19 so that I might **w** more of them.
1Pe 5: 4 you will **w** the crown of glory

WIND → WHIRLWIND, WINDS
Ge 1: 2 a **w** from God swept over
1Ki 19:11 but the LORD was not in the **w**;
Ps 1: 4 like chaff that the **w** drives away.
18:10 swiftly upon the wings of the **w**,
104: 3 you ride on the wings of the **w**,
Pr 11:29 Those who trouble their households will inherit **w**,
30: 4 Who has gathered the **w** in the
Ecc 1:14 all is vanity and a chasing after **w**.
8: 8 No one has power over the **w** to restrain the **w**,
Eze 5: 2 one third you shall scatter to the **w**,
Hos 8: 7 they sow the **w**, and they shall reap

Jnh 1: 4 LORD hurled a great **w** upon the sea,
4: 8 God prepared a sultry east **w**,
Mk 4:41 even the **w** and the sea obey him?"
Jn 3: 8 The **w** blows where it chooses,
Ac 2: 2 a sound like the rush of a violent **w**,
Eph 4:14 blown about by every **w** of doctrine,
Jas 1: 6 driven and tossed by the **w**;

WINDOW → WINDOWS
Jos 2:21 she tied the crimson cord in the **w**.
1Sa 19:12 let David down through the **w**;
Ac 20: 9 who was sitting in the **w**,
2Co 11:33 let down in a basket through a **w** in

WINDOWS → WINDOW
Ge 7:11 the **w** of the heavens were opened.
2Ki 7: 2 "Even if the LORD were to make **w** in the sky,
Mal 3:10 open the **w** of heaven for you and

WINDS → WIND
Ps 104: 4 you make the **w** your messengers,
Mt 7:25 the **w** blew and beat on that house,
8:27 even the **w** and the sea obey him?"
24:31 will gather his elect from the four **w**,
Heb 1: 7 "He makes his angels **w**, and his
Aza 1:43 Bless the Lord, all you **w**;

WINE → WINESKINS
Ge 9:21 He drank some of the **w** and became drunk,
19:32 let us make our father drink **w**,
Nu 6: 3 shall separate themselves from **w**
Dt 7:13 your grain and your **w** and your oil,
Jdg 13: 4 not to drink **w** or strong drink,
1Sa 1:14 drunk neither **w** nor strong drink,
Ne 13:12 brought the tithe of the grain, **w**,
Ps 4: 7 when their grain and **w** abound.
75: 8 there is a cup with foaming **w**,
104:15 and **w** to gladden the human heart,
Pr 3:10 your vats will be bursting with **w**.
9: 2 she has mixed her **w**, she has also
20: 1 **W** is a mocker, strong drink a
23:31 Do not look at **w** when it is red,
31: 4 it is not for kings to drink **w**,
31: 6 and **w** to those in bitter distress;
Ecc 2: 3 how to cheer my body with **w**—
9: 7 drink your **w** with a merry heart;
10:19 **w** gladdens life, and money meets every need.
SS 1: 2 For your love is better than **w**,
7: 9 the best **w** that goes down smoothly,
Isa 5:22 are heroes in drinking **w** and valiant
28: 7 they are confused with **w**,
29: 9 Be drunk, but not from **w**;
51:21 who are drunk, but not with **w**:
55: 1 buy **w** and milk without money and
Da 1: 8 with the royal rations of food and **w**
Joel 2:24 vats shall overflow with **w** and oil.
3:18 the mountains shall drip sweet **w**,
Am 2:12 But you made the nazirites drink **w**,
Mic 2:11 "I will preach to you of **w** and
Mt 9:17 is new **w** put into old wineskins;
9:17 new **w** is put into fresh wineskins;
27:34 him **w** to drink, mixed with gall;
Lk 23:36 coming up and offering him sour **w**,
Jn 2: 3 said to him, "They have no **w**."
2: 9 tasted the water that had become **w**,
Ac 2:13 "They are filled with new **w**."
Ro 14:21 drink **w** or do anything that makes
Eph 5:18 Do not get drunk with **w**, for that is debauchery;
1Ti 3: 8 not indulging in much **w**, not greedy
5:23 little **w** for the sake of your stomach
Rev 14: 8 made all nations drink of the **w** of
14:10 also drink the **w** of God's wrath,
18: 3 have drunk of the **w** of the wrath
Sir 9:10 A new friend is like new **w**;
31:28 **W** drunk at the proper time and
31:29 **W** drunk to excess leads to bitterness of spirit,
40:20 **W** and music gladden the heart,

NEW WINE Hos 4:11; 9:2; Hag 1:11; Zec 9:17; Mt 9:17, 17; Mk 2:22, 22; Lk 5:37, 37, 38, 39; Ac 2:13; Sir 9:10

WINESKINS → SKIN, WINE
Job 32:19 like new **w**, it is ready to burst.
Mt 9:17 Neither is new wine put into old **w**;

WING → WINGED, WINGS
2Ch 3:11 touched the **w** of the other cherub;
Eze 1:11 of which touched the **w** of another,

WINGED → WING
Ge 1:21 and every **w** bird of every kind.

WINGS → WING
Ex 19: 4 and how I bore you on eagles' **w**
37: 9 cherubim spread out their **w** above,
Ru 2:12 under whose **w** you have come for refuge!"
1Ki 8: 7 the cherubim spread out their **w**
Ps 17: 8 hide me in the shadow of your **w**,
91: 4 under his **w** you will find refuge;
Isa 6: 2 above him; each had six **w**:
40:31 shall mount up with **w** like eagles,
Eze 1: 6 and each of them had four **w**,
10:21 Each had four faces, each four **w**,
Zec 5: 9 The wind was in their **w**;
Mal 4: 2 shall rise, with healing in its **w**.
Lk 13:34 hen gathers her brood under her **w**,
Rev 4: 8 creatures, each of them with six **w**,
2Es 11: 1 an eagle that had twelve feathered **w**
12:16 the interpretation of the twelve **w**

WINNOW → WINNOWED, WINNOWERS, WINNOWING, WINNOWS
Isa 41:16 shall **w** them and the wind shall

WINNOWING → WINNOW
Mt 3:12 His **w** fork is in his hand,

WINNOWS' → WINNOW
Pr 20: 8 on the throne of judgment **w** all evil
20:26 A wise king **w** the wicked,

WINS → WIN
Pr 13:15 Good sense **w** favor, but the way of

WINTER
Ge 8:22 summer and **w**, day and night,
Ps 74:17 you made summer and **w**.
Mk 13:18 Pray that it may not be in **w**.

WIPE → WIPED
Isa 25: 8 Lord GOD will **w** away the tears from all faces,
Rev 7:17 and God will **w** away every tear from their eyes."
21: 4 he will **w** every tear from their eyes.

WIPED → WIPE
Ac 3:19 so that your sins may be **w** out,

WISDOM → WISE
Dt 4: 6 will show your **w** and discernment
1Ki 4:29 God gave Solomon very great **w**,
10: 6 accomplishments and of your **w**,
2Ch 1:10 **w** and knowledge to go out and
Job 11: 6 tell you the secrets of **w**! For **w** is many-sided.
12:13 "With God are **w** and strength;
28:12 "But where shall **w** be found?
28:28 the fear of the Lord, that is **w**;
Ps 37:30 The mouths of the righteous utter **w**,
51: 6 teach me **w** in my secret heart.
111:10 The fear of the LORD is the beginning of **w**;
Pr 1: 7 fools despise **w** and instruction.
1:20 **W** cries out in the street;
2: 6 For the LORD gives **w**; from his
3:13 Happy are those who find **w**,
4: 5 Get **w**; get insight: do
4: 7 The beginning of **w** is this:
8:11 for **w** is better than jewels,

9: 1 **W** has built her house, she has hewn
9:10 The fear of the LORD is the beginning of **w,**
11: 2 but **w** is with the humble.
13:10 but **w** is with those who take advice.
15:33 fear of the LORD is instruction in **w,**
19: 8 To get **w** is to love oneself;
23:23 buy **w,** instruction, and understanding.
29: 3 A child who loves **w** makes a parent glad,
29:15 The rod and reproof give **w,**
31:26 She opens her mouth with **w,**
Ecc 1:13 to search out by **w** all that is done
2: 3 my mind still guiding me with **w**—
2:13 I saw that **w** excels folly as light
7:12 protection of **w** is like the protection of money,
9:18 **W** is better than weapons of war,
10: 1 a little folly outweighs **w** and honor.
Isa 11: 2 the spirit of **w** and understanding,
28:29 in counsel, and excellent in **w.**
Jer 9:23 Do not let the wise boast in their **w,**
10:12 who established the world by his **w,**
Eze 28:12 full of **w** and perfect in beauty.
Da 5:14 and excellent **w** are found in you.
Mic 6: 9 LORD cries to the city (it is sound **w**
Mt 11:19 Yet **w** is vindicated by her deeds."
12:42 to listen to the **w** of Solomon,
13:54 this man get this **w** and these deeds
Lk 2:40 and became strong, filled with **w;**
2:52 Jesus increased in **w** and in years,
Ac 6: 3 full of the Spirit and of **w,**
Ro 11:33 the depth of the riches and **w** and
1Co 1:17 the gospel, and not with eloquent **w,**
1:19 "I will destroy the **w** of the wise,
1:20 made foolish the **w** of the world?
1:30 who became for us **w** from God,
2: 7 But we speak God's **w,** secret and
3:19 the **w** of this world is foolishness with God.
12: 8 through the Spirit the utterance of **w**
Eph 1:17 of **w** and revelation as you come to know him,
Col 1: 9 in all spiritual **w** and understanding,
1:28 and teaching everyone in all **w,**
2: 3 in whom are hidden all the treasures of **w**
2:23 have indeed an appearance of **w**
Jas 1: 5 any of you is lacking in **w,** ask God,
3:13 with gentleness born of **w.**
3:17 But the **w** from above is first pure,
Rev 5:12 wealth and **w** and might and honor
7:12 and **w** and thanksgiving and honor
13:18 This calls for **w:** let anyone with
17: 9 "This calls for a mind that has **w:**
Wis 6:12 **W** is radiant and unfading,
7: 7 the spirit of **w** came to me.
Sir 1: 1 All **w** is from the Lord,
1:16 To fear the Lord is fullness of **w;**
19:20 The whole of **w** is fear of the Lord,
24: 1 THE PRAISE OF **W**
Bar 3:12 You have forsaken the fountain of **w**
2Es 8: 4 O my soul, and drink **w,**
14:47 the fountain of **w,** and the river of

WISE → WISDOM, WISELY, WISER

Ge 41:39 no one so discerning and **w** as you.
Ex 7:11 Pharaoh summoned the **w** men and
Dt 4: 6 great nation is a **w** and discerning
16:19 of the **w** and subverts the cause of
1Ki 3:12 I give you a **w** and discerning mind;
Job 5:13 takes the **w** in their own craftiness;
32: 9 It is not the old that are **w,**
Ps 2:10 O kings, be **w;** be warned, O rulers
19: 7 are sure, making the simple;
94: 8 fools, when will you be **w?**
107:43 Let those who are **w** give heed to
Pr 3: 7 Do not be **w** in your own eyes;
6: 6 consider its ways, and be **w.**
9: 9 Give instruction to the **w,**
10: 1 A **w** child makes a glad father,

13: 1 A **w** child loves discipline,
13:20 walks with the **w** becomes **w,**
16:23 The mind of the **w** makes their speech judicious,
17:28 Even fools who keep silent are considered **w;**
23:15 My child, if your heart is **w,**
24: 5 **W** warriors are mightier than strong
26: 5 or they will be **w** in their own eyes.
29:11 but the **w** quietly holds it back.
Ecc 2:14 The **w** have eyes in their head,
7:19 to the **w** more than ten rulers that
9:17 the **w** are more to be heeded than
12:11 The sayings of the **w** are like goads,
Isa 29:14 The wisdom of their **w** shall perish,
Jer 8: 9 The **w** shall be put to shame,
9:23 not let the **w** boast in their wisdom,
Da 2:21 he gives wisdom to the **w** and
11:35 Some of the **w** shall fall,
12: 3 are **w** shall shine like the brightness
Mt 11:25 have hidden these things from the **w**
25: 2 were foolish, and five were **w.**
Ro 1:22 Claiming to be **w,** they became fools;
16:27 to the only **w** God, through Jesus
1Co 1:19 "I will destroy the wisdom of the **w,**
1:26 not many of you were **w** by human
3:18 If you think that you are **w** in this
3:19 He catches the **w** in their craftiness;
Eph 5:15 not as unwise people but as **w,**
Jas 3:13 is **w** and understanding among you?
Sir 7:19 Do not dismiss a **w** and good wife,
33: 2 The **w** will not hate the law,

WISE MEN Ge 41:8; Ex 7:11; Job 34:2; Da 2:12, 13, 14, 18, 24, 24, 27, 48; 4:6, 18; 5:7, 8, 15; Mt 2:1, 7, 16, 16

WISELY → WISE

Jer 23: 5 he shall reign as king and deal **w,**
Col 4: 5 Conduct yourselves **w** toward outsiders,

WISER → WISE

1Ki 4:31 He was **w** than anyone else,
Pr 9: 9 and they will become **w** still;
26:16 The lazy person is **w** in self-esteem
Ro 12:16 do not claim to be **w** than you are.
1Co 1:25 For God's foolishness is **w** than human wisdom,

WISH → WISHES

Jn 15: 7 ask for whatever you **w,** and it will be done
Ro 9: 3 could **w** that I myself were accursed
Rev 3:15 I **w** that you were either cold or hot.

WISHES → WISH

Est 6: 6 man whom the king **w** to honor?"
Rev 22:17 Let anyone who **w** take the water of life as a gift.

WITHER → WITHERED, WITHERS

Ps 1: 3 and their leaves do not **w.**
Eze 47:12 Their leaves will not **w** nor their

WITHERED → WITHER

Ge 41:23 **w,** thin, and blighted by the east
Zec 11:17 Let his arm be completely **w,**
Mt 13: 6 since they had no root, they **w** away.
21:19 And the fig tree **w** at once.

WITHERS → WITHER

Ps 129: 6 the grass on the housetops that **w**
Isa 40: 7 The grass **w,** the flower fades,
Jn 15: 6 is thrown away like a branch and **w;**
1Pe 1:24 The grass **w,** and the flower falls,

WITHHELD → WITHHOLD

Ge 22:12 not **w** your son, your only son,
Am 4: 7 And I also **w** the rain from you
Hag 1:10 and the earth has **w** its produce.

WITHHOLD → WITHHELD, WITHHOLDS

Ne 9:20 and did not **w** your manna from their mouths,
Ps 40:11 Do not, O LORD, **w** your mercy
84:11 No good thing does the LORD **w** from those who walk uprightly.
Pr 23:13 Do not **w** discipline from your children;
Ro 8:32 He who did not **w** his own Son,

WITHHOLDS → WITHHOLD

Eze 18:17 **w** his hand from iniquity, takes no

WITHIN

Ps 40: 8 your law is **w** my heart."
42: 5 and why are you disquieted **w** me?
51:10 and put a new and right spirit **w** me.
122: 7 Peace be **w** your walls, and security **w** your towers."
Pr 2: 1 treasure up my commandments **w**
4:21 keep them **w** your heart.
Jer 31:33 I will put my law **w** them,
Zep 3: 5 The LORD **w** it is righteous; he does no wrong.
Zec 2: 5 LORD, and I will be the glory **w** it."
12: 1 and formed the human spirit **w:**
Mk 7:21 from **w,** from the human heart,
1Co 2:11 the human spirit that is **w?**
Rev 11:19 the ark of his covenant was seen **w** his temple:

WITHOUT

Nu 27:17 may not be like sheep **w** a shepherd.
2Ch 15: 3 For a long time Israel was **w** the true God, and **w** a teaching priest, and **w** law;
18:16 like sheep **w** a shepherd;
Ps 26: 1 trusted in the LORD **w** wavering.
69: 4 those who hate me **w** cause;
Pr 6:27 **w** burning one's clothes?
19: 2 Desire **w** knowledge is not good,
Isa 52: 3 you shall be redeemed **w** money.
55: 1 buy wine and milk **w** money and **w** price.
Mt 9:36 helpless, like sheep **w** a shepherd.
23:23 practiced **w** neglecting the others.
Jn 3:34 for he gives the Spirit **w** measure.
8: 7 [who is **w** sin be the first to throw]
Eph 2:12 at that time **w** Christ,
2:12 no hope and **w** God in the world.
Php 2:14 Do all things **w** murmuring and
Heb 4:15 tested as we are, yet **w** sin.
9:22 and **w** the shedding of blood there is no forgiveness of sins.
1Pe 1:19 that of a lamb **w** defect or blemish.

WITHSTAND → WITHSTOOD

Jos 23: 9 no one has been able to **w** you to
2Ch 20: 6 so that no one is able to **w** you.
Est 9: 2 and no one could **w** them,
Eph 6:13 able to **w** on that evil day,

WITHSTOOD → WITHSTAND

Jos 21:44 not one of all their enemies had **w**

WITNESS → EYEWITNESSES, WITNESSED, WITNESSES

Ge 31:44 let it be a **w** between you and me."
Nu 35:30 on the testimony of a single **w.**
Dt 19:15 single **w** shall not suffice to convict
Jos 22:27 to be a **w** between us and you,
Jdg 11:10 "The LORD will be **w** between us;
1Sa 12: 5 "The LORD is **w** against you,
12: 5 and his anointed is **w** this day,
12: 5 And they said, "He is **w.**"
Job 16:19 in fact, my **w** is in heaven,
Pr 12:17 but a false **w** speaks deceitfully.
14:25 A truthful **w** saves lives,
19: 9 A false **w** will not go unpunished,
21:28 A false **w** will perish, but a good
Ro 2:15 their own conscience also bears **w;**
1Pe 5: 1 and a **w** of the sufferings of Christ,
Rev 1: 5 faithful **w,** the firstborn of the dead,

2:13 even in the days of Antipas my **w,**
3:14 of the Amen, the faithful and true **w,**

FALSE WITNESS
Ex 20:16; Dt 5:20;
19:18, 19, 19; Pr 12:17; 14:5; 19:5, 9; 21:28;
25:18; Mt 15:19; 19:18; Mk 10:19; Lk 18:20;
Sus 1:61

WITNESSES → WITNESS
Dt 17: 6 or three **w** the death sentence shall be executed;
19:15 on the evidence of two or three **w**
Jos 24:22 "You are **w** against yourselves
24:22 And they said, "We are **w."**
Ru 4:10 his native place; today you are **w."**
Ps 27:12 for false **w** have risen against me,
Isa 43:10 You are my **w,** says the LORD,
Mt 18:16 by the evidence of two or three **w**
26:60 though many false **w** came forward.
Mk 14:63 "Why do we still need **w?**
Ac 1: 8 and you will be my **w** in Jerusalem,
2:32 and of that all of us are **w.**
6:13 They set up false **w** who said,
Heb 12: 1 surrounded by so great a cloud of **w,**
Rev 11: 3 my two **w** authority to prophesy

WIVES → WIFE
Ge 6:18 your wife, and your sons' **w** with
Dt 17:17 not acquire many **w** for himself,
21:15 If a man has two **w,**
1Ki 11: 3 Among his **w** were seven hundred
11: 3 and his **w** turned away his heart.
1Ch 14: 3 David took more **w** in Jerusalem,
Ezr 10:11 of the land and from the foreign **w."**
Mt 19: 8 allowed you to divorce your **w,**
Eph 5:22 **W,** be subject to your husbands as
5:25 love your **w,** just as Christ loved the church
Col 3:18 **W,** be subject to your husbands,
1Pe 3: 1 **W,** in the same way, accept the

WIZARDS
Lev 19:31 Do not turn to mediums or **w;**
1Sa 28: 3 expelled the mediums and the **w**
2Ki 23:24 Josiah put away the mediums, **w,**

WOE → WOES
Job 10:15 If I am wicked, **w** to me!
Pr 23:29 Who has **w?** Who has sorrow?
Isa 3:11 **W** to the guilty! How unfortunate
6: 5 And I said: "**W** is me!
Jer 13:27 **W** to you, O Jerusalem! How long
23: 1 **W** to the shepherds who destroy
La 5:16 **w** to us, for we have sinned!
Hos 9:12 **W** to them indeed when I depart
Mt 18: 7 **W** to the world because of stumbling blocks!
23:13 "But **w** to you, scribes and Pharisees
23:16 "**W** to you, blind guides, who say,
Mk 14:21 but **w** to that one by whom the Son
Lk 6:24 "But **w** to you who are rich,
11:42 "But **w** to you Pharisees!
11:52 **W** to you lawyers! For you have
1Co 9:16 and **w** to me if I do not proclaim the gospel!
Jude 1:11 **W** to them! For they go the way of Cain,
Rev 8:13 "**W, w, w** to the inhabitants of the earth,

WOES* → WOE
Rev 9:12 There are still two **w** to come.

WOLF → WOLVES
Isa 11: 6 The **w** shall live with the lamb,
65:25 **w** and the lamb shall feed together,
Jn 10:12 sees the **w** coming and leaves the sheep

WOLVES → WOLF
Eze 22:27 Its officials within it are like **w** tearing the prey,
Zep 3: 3 its judges are evening **w** that leave nothing until the morning.

Mt 7:15 in sheep's clothing but inwardly are ravenous **w.**
10:16 like sheep into the midst of **w;**
Ac 20:29 savage **w** will come in among you,

WOMAN → WOMAN'S, WOMEN, WOMEN'S
Ge 2:22 he made into a **w** and brought her to
2:23 this one shall be called **W,**
3: 6 when the **w** saw that the tree was good for food,
3:12 man said, "The **w** whom you gave
3:15 enmity between you and the **w,**
3:16 To the **w** he said, "I will greatly increase your pangs in childbearing;
12:11 you are a **w** beautiful in appearance;
20: 3 for she is a married **w."**
21:10 "Cast out this slave **w** with her son;
Ex 3:22 each **w** shall ask her neighbor
21:22 injure a pregnant **w** so that there is a miscarriage,
Nu 30: 3 When a **w** makes a vow to the LORD
Dt 20: 7 Has anyone become engaged to a **w**
21:11 a beautiful **w** whom you desire
22: 5 A **w** shall not wear a man's apparel,
24: 1 a man enters into marriage with a **w,**
Jdg 4: 9 will sell Sisera into the hand of a **w.**
9:54 say about me, 'A **w** killed him.'"
14: 2 "I saw a Philistine **w** at Timnah;
16: 4 he fell in love with a **w** in the valley
Ru 3:11 know that you are a worthy **w.**
1Sa 1:15 my lord, I am a **w** deeply troubled;
25: 3 The **w** was clever and beautiful,
28: 7 for me a **w** who is a medium,
2Sa 11: 2 he saw from the roof a **w** bathing;
13:17 "Put this **w** out of my presence,
14: 2 brought from there a wise **w.**
20:16 Then a wise **w** called from the city,
1Ki 17:24 So the **w** said to Elijah,
2Ki 4: 8 where a wealthy **w** lived,
8: 1 **w** whose son he had restored to life,
9:34 "See to that cursed **w** and bury her;
Job 2:10 "You speak as any foolish **w** would
14: 1 born of **w,** few of days and full of
Ps 113: 9 He gives the barren **w** a home,
Pr 9:13 The foolish **w** is loud;
11:16 A gracious **w** gets honor,
11:22 a beautiful **w** without good sense.
14: 1 The wise **w** builds her house,
30:23 an unloved **w** when she gets a husband,
31:30 but a **w** who fears the LORD is to be praised.
Isa 54: 1 of the desolate **w** will be more than
Mt 5:28 everyone who looks at a **w** with lust
9:20 a **w** who had been suffering from hemorrhages
15:22 Just then a Canaanite **w** from that
26: 7 **w** came to him with an alabaster jar
Mk 7:25 but a **w** whose little daughter had
Lk 7:37 a **w** in the city, who was a sinner,
10:38 a **w** named Martha welcomed him
13:12 he called her over and said, "**W,**
15: 8 "Or what **w** having ten silver coins,
Jn 2: 4 And Jesus said to her, "**W,**
4: 7 A Samaritan **w** came to draw water,
8: 4 this **w** was caught in the very act
19:26 his mother, "**W,** here is your son."
20:15 to her, "**W,** why are you weeping?
Ac 16:14 certain **w** named Lydia, a worshiper
17:34 and a **w** named Damaris,
Ro 7: 2 a married **w** is bound by the law to
1Co 7: 2 and each **w** her own husband.
7:34 the unmarried **w** and the virgin are
7:34 but the married **w** is anxious about
11: 6 For if a **w** will not veil herself,
11: 7 but **w** is the reflection of man.
11:12 For just as **w** came from man, so man comes through **w;**
Gal 4: 4 born of a **w,** born under the law,
1Ti 2:11 Let a **w** learn in silence with full submission.

5:16 any believing **w** has relatives who are really widows,
Rev 2:20 you tolerate that **w** Jezebel,
12: 1 a **w** clothed with the sun,
12: 4 the dragon stood before the **w** who
12:13 the **w** who had given birth to the male child.
17: 3 a **w** sitting on a scarlet beast that
17:18 The **w** you saw is the great city that
Jdt 8:31 a God-fearing **w,** pray for us,
16: 5 foiled them by the hand of a **w.**
Sir 9: 3 Do not go near a loose **w,**
Sus 1: 2 a very beautiful **w** and one who feared the Lord.
2Es 10:44 The **w** whom you saw is Zion,

WOMAN IN LABOR
Ps 48:6; Isa 13:8;
21:3; 42:14; Jer 4:31; 6:24; 13:21; 22:23; 30:6;
48:41; 49:22, 24; 50:43; Mic 4:9, 10; Sir
19:11; 34:5

YOUNG WOMAN
Ge 24:43; Dt 22:15, 16,
21, 23, 24, 26, 26; Ru 2:5; 4:12; 2Ch 36:17;
Isa 7:14; 62:5; 1Es 1:53

WOMAN'S → WOMAN
Dt 22: 5 nor shall a man put on a **w** garment,
Sus 1:46 no part in shedding this **w** blood!"

WOMB
Ge 25:23 to her, "Two nations are in your **w,**
29:31 Leah was unloved, he opened her **w**
30:22 God heeded her and opened her **w.**
Ex 13: 2 the first to open the **w** among the
Dt 7:13 he will bless the fruit of your **w**
1Sa 1: 5 though the LORD had closed her **w.**
Job 1:21 Naked I came from my mother's **w;**
Ps 22: 9 it was you who took me from the **w,**
139:13 knit me together in my mother's **w.**
Pr 31: 2 No, son of my **w!**
Ecc 11: 5 the breath comes to the bones in the mother's **w,**
Jer 1: 5 "Before I formed you in the **w** I knew you,
Lk 1:44 the child in my **w** leaped for joy.
Jn 3: 4 into the mother's **w** and be born?"
Ro 4:19 when he considered the barrenness of Sarah's **w.**

WOMEN → WOMAN
Nu 25: 1 sexual relations with the **w** of Moab.
Jdg 5:24 "Most blessed of **w** be Jael,
Ezr 10: 2 married foreign **w** from the peoples
Ne 13:26 foreign **w** made even him to sin.
SS 1: 8 O fairest among **w,**
Isa 3:12 and **w** rule over them.
Zec 5: 9 and saw two **w** coming forward.
Mt 11:11 born of **w** no one has arisen greater than John
24:41 Two **w** will be grinding meal
28: 5 But the angel said to the **w,** "Do not be afraid;
Mk 15:41 and there were many other **w** who
Lk 1:42 "Blessed are you among **w,**
8: 2 **w** who had been cured of evil spirits
23:27 **w** who were beating their breasts
23:55 **w** who had come with him from
Ac 1:14 with certain **w,** including Mary
2:18 upon my slaves, both men and **w,**
8:12 were baptized, both men and **w.**
16:13 spoke to the **w** who had gathered
17: 4 and not a few of the leading **w.**
Ro 1:26 exchanged natural intercourse
1Co 14:34 **w** should be silent in the churches.
Php 4: 3 my loyal companion, help these **w,**
1Ti 2: 9 that the **w** should dress themselves modestly
5: 2 to older **w** as mothers, to younger **w** as sisters—with absolute purity.
2Ti 3: 6 households and captivate silly **w,**
Tit 2: 3 older **w** to be reverent in behavior,
2: 4 they may encourage the young **w**
Heb 11:35 **W** received their dead by resurrection.

1Pe 3: 5 that the holy **w** who hoped in God
Jdt 15:13 in the dance, leading all the **w,**
Sir 19: 2 Wine and **w** lead intelligent men
            astray,

FOREIGN WOMEN 1Ki 11:1; Ezr 10:2, 10,
17, 18, 44; Ne 13:26, 27; 1Es 8:92; 9:7, 36

MEN AND WOMEN Ex 35:22, 29; Jos 6:21;
8:25; Jdg 9:49, 51; 16:27, 27; 1Sa 22:19; 2Sa
6:19; Ne 8:2; Est 7:4; Ps 148:12; Ecc 2:8; Jer
44:20; Lk 12:45; Ac 2:18; 5:14; 8:3, 12; 22:4;
Eph 6:7; 2Pe 1:21; Jdt 6:16; 8:7; Bel 1:20; 1Es
8:91; 9:40, 41

WOMEN AND CHILDREN Ge 33:5; Dt
2:34; 3:6; 31:12; Ezr 10:1; Ne 12:43; Est 3:13;
Jer 40:7; Mt 14:21; 15:38; Jdt 4:11; 7:32; Bel
1:20; 1Mc 1:32; 2Mc 5:13; 4Mc 4:9

YOUNG WOMEN Jdg 12:9; 21:21, 21; Ru
2:8, 22, 23; 3:2; Est 2:8; Isa 23:4; Jer 31:13;
La 1:18; 2:21; 3:51; Eze 9:6; Am 8:13; Zec
9:17; Tit 2:4; 1Mc 1:26; 2Mc 3:19; 3Mc 1:18;
4:6

WOMEN'S → WOMAN

Rev 9: 8 their hair like **w** hair, and their teeth

WON → WIN

2Sa 8:13 David **w** a name for himself.
      23:18 and **w** a name beside the Three.
Est 2: 9 girl pleased him and **w** his favor,
1Pe 3: 1 they may be **w** over without a word

WONDER → WONDERFUL,
WONDERFULLY, WONDERS, WONDROUS

Ex 7: 9 'Perform a **w,**' then you shall say to

WONDERFUL → WONDER

Ge 18:14 Is anything too **w** for the LORD?
Jdg 13:18 do you ask my name? It is too **w."**
2Sa 1:26 your love to me was **w,**
1Ch 16: 9 tell of all his **w** works.
Job 42: 3 too **w** for me, which I did not know.
Ps 105: 2 tell of all his **w** works.
     107: 8 for his **w** works to humankind.
    107:15 for his **w** works to humankind.
    107:21 for his **w** works to humankind.
    107:31 for his **w** works to humankind.
    119:129 Your decrees are **w;**
    139: 6 Such knowledge is too **w** for me;
    139:14 **W** are your works; that I know very
           well.
Isa 9: 6 named **W** Counselor, Mighty God,
    28:29 he is **w** in counsel, and excellent in
           wisdom.
Lk 13:17 was rejoicing at all the **w** things
Sir 11: 4 for the works of the Lord are **w,**

WONDERFULLY* → WONDER

Ps 139:14 for I am fearfully and **w** made.

WONDERS → WONDER

Ex 3:20 and strike Egypt with all my **w** that
    11:10 all these **w** before Pharaoh;
    15:11 awesome in splendor, doing **w?**
Ps 78:32 they did not believe in his **w.**
    89: 5 Let the heavens praise your **w,**
   136: 4 who alone does great **w,**
Da 4: 3 are his signs, how mighty his **w!**
Jn 4:48 signs and **w** you will not believe."
2Co 12:12 signs and **w** and mighty works.
2Th 2: 9 who uses all power, signs, lying **w,**
Heb 2: 4 added his testimony by signs and **w**
Sir 18: 6 to fathom the **w** of the Lord.

WONDROUS → WONDER

Ps 26: 7 and telling all your **w** deeds.
    72:18 who alone does **w** things.
2Es 14: 5 I told him many **w** things,

WOOD → CEDARWOOD, WOODEN,
WOODS

Ge 6:14 Make yourself an ark of cypress **w;**
    22: 9 and laid the **w** in order.

Ex 15:25 the LORD showed him a piece of **w;**
    25:10 They shall make an ark of acacia **w;**
    25:13 You shall make poles of acacia **w,**
    25:23 You shall make a table of acacia **w,**
    26:15 make upright frames of acacia **w** for
    27: 1 shall make the altar of acacia **w,**
Dt 28:64 serve other gods, of **w** and stone,
1Ki 18:23 lay it on the **w,** but put no fire to it;
Isa 44:19 I fall down before a block of **w?"**
    60:17 instead of **w,** bronze, instead of
Eze 20:32 and worship **w** and stone."
Hos 4:12 My people consult a piece of **w,**
Hab 2:19 who say to the **w,** "Wake up!"
1Co 3:12 silver, precious stones, **w,** hay,

WOODEN → WOOD

Ne 8: 4 a **w** platform that had been made
         for the purpose;

WOODS → WOOD

2Ki 2:24 two she-bears came out of the **w**

WOOL

Dt 22:11 shall not wear clothes made of **w**
Pr 31:13 She seeks **w** and flax, and works
Isa 1:18 they shall become like **w.**
Da 7: 9 and the hair of his head like pure **w;**
Rev 1:14 and his hair were white as white **w,**

WORD → BYWORD, WORDS

Ge 15: 1 the **w** of the LORD came to Abram
Nu 30: 2 he shall not break his **w;**
Dt 8: 3 but by every **w** that comes from the
         mouth of the LORD.
    30:14 No, the **w** is very near to you;
1Sa 3: 1 The **w** of the LORD was rare in
         those days;
1Ki 8:56 not one **w** has failed of all his good
         promise,
    17: 2 The **w** of the LORD came to him,
1Ch 17: 3 the **w** of the LORD came to Nathan,
2Ch 36:22 in fulfillment of the **w** of the LORD
Ps 33: 4 For the **w** of the LORD is upright,
    56: 4 In God, whose **w** I praise,
    56:10 In God, whose **w** I praise,
    56:10 in the LORD, whose **w** I praise,
   107:20 he sent out his **w** and healed them,
   119: 9 By guarding it according to your **w.**
   119:11 I treasure your **w** in my heart,
   119:42 for I trust in your **w.**
   119:74 because I have hoped in your **w.**
   119:89 your **w** is firmly fixed in heaven.
   119:105 Your **w** is a lamp to my feet and
   139: 4 Even before a **w** is on my tongue,
Pr 12:25 but a good **w** cheers it up.
    15: 1 but a harsh **w** stirs up anger.
    15:23 and a **w** in season, how good it is!
    25:11 A **w** fitly spoken is like apples of
    30: 5 Every **w** of God proves true;
Isa 1:10 Hear the **w** of the LORD, you rulers
    40: 8 the **w** of our God will stand forever.
    55:11 so shall my **w** be that goes out from
         my mouth;
Jer 5:13 for the **w** is not in them.
    23:29 Is not my **w** like fire, says the LORD,
Da 9: 2 to the **w** of the LORD to the prophet
         Jeremiah,
Mt 4: 4 but by every **w** that comes from the
         mouth of God.'"
    5:37 Let your **w** be 'Yes, Yes' or 'No,
         No';
    12:36 an account for every careless **w** you
    15: 6 you make void the **w** of God.
Mk 4:14 The sower sows the **w.**
Lk 1: 2 eyewitnesses and servants of the **w,**
Jn 1: 1 In the beginning was the **W,** and
         the **W** was with God, and the **W**
         was God.
    1:14 And the **W** became flesh and lived
         among us,
    8:37 there is no place in you for my **w.**
    17:17 Sanctify them in the truth; your **w**
         is truth.

Ac 4:31 and spoke the **w** of God
    6: 4 to prayer and to serving the **w."**
Ro 9: 6 as though the **w** of God had failed.
    10: 8 "The **w** is near you, on your lips
    10: 8 the **w** of faith that we proclaim);
2Co 2:17 For we are not peddlers of God's **w**
         like so many;
    4: 2 cunning or to falsify God's **w;**
Gal 6: 6 Those who are taught the **w**
Eph 6:17 which is the **w** of God.
Php 2:16 the **w** of life that I can boast on the
Col 3:16 Let the **w** of Christ dwell in you
         richly;
2Ti 2:15 rightly explaining the **w** of truth.
Heb 1: 3 and he sustains all things by his
         powerful **w.**
    4:12 the **w** of God is living and active,
    6: 5 tasted the goodness of the **w** of God
Jas 1:21 with meekness the implanted **w**
    1:22 But be doers of the **w,**
1Pe 1:23 the living and enduring **w** of God.
2Pe 3: 5 by the **w** of God heavens existed
1Jn 1: 1 concerning the **w** of life—
    2: 5 but whoever obeys his **w,**
Rev 3: 8 and yet you have kept my **w** and
    12:11 and by the **w** of their testimony,
    19:13 his name is called The **W** of God.
    20: 4 testimony to Jesus and for the **w**
Sir 3: 8 Honor your father by **w** and deed,
    18:16 So a **w** is better than a gift.
2Es 1: 4 The **w** of the Lord came to me,

WORD OF *GOD 1Sa 9:27; 1Ki 12:22; Pr
30:5; Mt 15:6; Mk 7:13; Lk 3:2; 5:1; 8:11, 21;
11:28; Jn 10:35; Ac 4:31; 6:2, 7; 8:14; 11:1;
12:24; 13:5, 7, 46; 17:13; 18:11; Ro 9:6; 1Co
14:36; Eph 6:17; Col 1:25; 1Th 2:13; 2Ti 2:9;
Tit 2:5; Heb 4:12; 6:5; 11:3; 13:7; 1Pe 1:23;
2Pe 3:5; 1Jn 2:14; Rev 1:2, 9; 6:9; 19:13; 20:4;
Tob 14:4

WORD OF THE *LORD Eze 6:3; 25:3;
36:4; Lk 22:61; Ac 8:25; 11:16; 13:44, 48, 49;
15:35, 36; 16:32; 19:10, 20; 1Th 1:8; 4:15;
2Th 3:1; 1Pe 1:25; Sir 42:15; 48:3; 1Es 1:57;
2:1; 8:72; 2Es 1:4; 16:36

WORD OF THE †LORD Ge 15:1, 4; Ex
9:20, 21; Nu 3:16, 51; 15:31; 24:13; 36:5; Jos
8:27; 1Sa 3:1, 7, 21; 15:10, 23, 26; 2Sa 7:4;
12:9; 24:11; 1Ki 2:27; 6:11; 12:24, 24; 13:1, 2,
5, 9, 17, 18, 20, 21, 26, 32; 14:18; 15:29; 16:1,
7, 12, 34; 17:2, 5, 8, 16, 24; 18:1, 31; 19:9;
21:17, 28; 22:5, 19, 38; 2Ki 1:17; 3:12; 4:44;
7:1, 16; 9:26, 36; 10:10, 17; 14:25; 20:4, 16,
19; 23:16; 24:2; 1Ch 11:3, 10; 12:23; 15:15;
17:3; 22:8; 2Ch 11:2, 4; 12:7; 18:4, 18; 30:12;
34:21; 35:6; 36:21, 22; Ezr 1:1; Ps 33:4, 6;
105:19; Isa 1:10; 2:3; 28:13, 14; 38:4; 39:5, 8;
66:5; Jer 1:2, 4, 11, 13; 2:1, 4, 31; 6:10; 7:2;
8:9; 9:20; 13:2, 3, 8; 14:1; 16:1; 17:15, 20;
18:5; 19:3; 20:8; 21:11; 22:2, 29; 23:17; 24:4;
25:3; 27:18; 28:12; 29:20, 30; 31:10; 32:6, 8,
8, 26; 33:1, 19, 23; 34:4, 12; 35:3; 36:27;
37:6; 39:15; 42:7, 15; 43:8; 44:24, 26; 46:1;
47:1; 49:34; Eze 1:3; 3:16; 6:1; 7:1; 11:14;
12:1, 8, 17, 21, 26; 13:1, 2; 14:2, 12; 15:1;
16:1, 35; 17:1, 11; 18:1; 20:2, 45, 47; 21:1, 8,
18; 22:1, 17, 23; 23:1; 24:1, 15, 20; 25:1; 26:1;
27:1; 28:1, 11, 20; 29:1, 17; 30:1, 20; 31:1;
32:1, 17; 33:1, 23; 34:1, 7, 9; 35:1; 36:1, 16;
37:4, 15; 38:1; Da 9:2; Hos 1:1; 4:1; Joel 1:1;
Am 7:16; 8:12; Jnh 1:1; 3:1; Mic 1:1; 4:2;
Zep 1:1; 2:5; Hag 1:1, 3; 2:1, 10, 20; Zec 1:1,
7; 4:6, 8; 6:9; 7:1, 4, 8; 8:1, 18; 9:1; 11:11;
12:1; Mal 1:1

WORDS → WORD

Ex 20: 1 Then God spoke all these **w:**
    24: 3 "All the **w** that the LORD has
         spoken we will do."
    34:28 on the tablets the **w** of the covenant,
Dt 11:18 put these **w** of mine in your heart
    13: 3 not heed the **w** of those prophets or

18:19 the **w** that the prophet shall speak in my name,
31:24 in a book the **w** of this law
32:45 had finished reciting all these **w**
Jos 8:34 he read all the **w** of the law,
2Sa 7:28 you are God, and your **w** are true,
23: 1 Now these are the last **w** of David:
Ps 5: 1 Give ear to my **w**, O LORD;
19: 4 and their **w** to the end of the world.
19:14 Let the **w** of my mouth and the
64: 3 who aim bitter **w** like arrows,
119:103 How sweet are your **w** to my taste,
119:130 The unfolding of your **w** gives light;
Pr 2: 1 if you accept my **w** and treasure
2:16 the adulteress with her smooth **w,**
10:19 When **w** are many, transgression is not lacking,
12:18 Rash **w** are like sword thrusts,
16:24 Pleasant **w** are like a honeycomb,
26:22 The **w** of a whisperer are like delicious morsels:
30: 6 Do not add to his **w**, or else he will rebuke you,
Ecc 5: 2 therefore let your **w** be few.
Jer 15:16 Your **w** were found, and I ate them,
15:16 and your **w** became to me a joy and
Da 9:12 He has confirmed his **w,**
Hos 6: 5 killed them by the **w** of my mouth,
Zec 1: 6 But my **w** and my statutes,
Mt 7:24 then who hears these **w** of mine
12:37 by your **w** you will be justified, and by your **w** you will be condemned."
24:35 but my **w** will not pass away.
Lk 6:47 hears my **w**, and acts on them.
Jn 6:68 You have the **w** of eternal life.
15: 7 abide in me, and my **w** abide in you,
Ro 8:26 that very Spirit intercedes with sighs too deep for **w.**
1Co 2:13 in **w** not taught by human wisdom
14:19 than ten thousand **w** in a tongue.
Rev 1: 3 reads aloud the **w** of the prophecy,
19: 9 to me, "These are true **w** of God."
22: 6 "These **w** are trustworthy and true,
22:19 takes away from the **w** of the book
Tob 14: 4 None of all their **w** will fail,
Sir 32: 8 Be brief; say much in few **w;**

ALL THE WORDS Ge 45:27; Ex 4:28, 30; 24:3, 3, 4; Dt 9:10; 17:19; 27:3, 8; 28:58; 29:29; 31:12; 32:44, 46, 46; Jos 8:34; 24:27; 1Sa 8:10, 21; 2Ki 19:4; 22:16; 23:2; 2Ch 34:30; Pr 8:8; Isa 37:17; Jer 11:8; 25:13; 26:2, 12; 30:2; 36:2, 4, 11, 13, 16, 20, 32; Bar 1:21

WORDS OF *GOD Nu 24:4, 16; Ezr 9:4; Ps 107:11; Jn 3:34; 8:47; 1Pe 4:11; Rev 17:17; 19:9

WORDS OF THE/THIS LAW Dt 17:19; 27:3, 8, 26; 28:58; 29:29; 31:12, 24; 32:46; Jos 8:34; 2Ki 23:24; 2Ch 34:19; Ne 8:9, 13

WORDS OF THE †LORD Ex 4:28; 24:3, 4; Nu 11:24; Dt 5:5; Jos 3:9; 24:27; 1Sa 8:10; 15:1; 2Ch 29:15; Jer 36:4, 6, 8, 11; 37:2; 43:1; Am 8:11; Zec 7:12

WORK → CO-WORKER, CO-WORKERS, WORKED, WORKER, WORKING, WORKS
Ge 2: 2 the seventh day God finished the **w**
Ex 20:10 you shall not do any **w—**
23:12 Six days you shall do your **w,**
32:16 The tablets were the **w** of God,
40:33 So Moses finished the **w.**
Dt 5:14 you shall not do any **w—**
27:15 the **w** of an artisan, and sets it up in
1Ch 22:16 Now begin the **w,** and the LORD be with you."
2Ch 2: 7 an artisan skilled to **w** in gold,
8:16 Thus all the **w** of Solomon was accomplished
Ezr 4:24 the **w** on the house of God in Jerusalem stopped
6: 7 let the **w** on this house of God alone
Job 1:10 You have blessed the **w** of his hands

Ps 8: 3 heavens, the **w** of your fingers,
77:12 I will meditate on all your **w,**
90:17 O prosper the **w** of our hands!
Ecc 11: 5 so you do not know the **w** of God,
Isa 2: 8 bow down to the **w** of their hands,
64: 8 we are all the **w** of your hand.
Jer 48:10 Accursed is the one who is slack in doing the **w**
Lk 13:14 "There are six days on which **w** ought to be done;
Jn 6:27 Do not **w** for the food that perishes,
6:29 "This is the **w** of God,
9: 4 We must **w** the works of him who
9: 4 night is coming when no one can **w.**
17: 4 by finishing the **w** that you gave me
Ac 13: 2 the **w** to which I have called them."
Ro 14:20 sake of food, destroy the **w** of God.
1Co 3:13 the **w** of each builder will become visible,
3:13 the fire will test what sort of **w** each
4:12 we grow weary from the **w** of our
Gal 6: 4 All must test their own **w;**
6:10 let us **w** for the good of all,
Eph 3:20 the power at **w** within us is able
Php 1: 6 who began a good **w** among you will bring it to completion
2:12 **w** out your own salvation with fear
1Th 4:11 to **w** with your hands, as we directed
2Th 2: 7 For the mystery of lawlessness is already at **w,**
3:10 unwilling to **w** should not eat.
2Ti 2:21 ready for every good **w.**
3:17 equipped for every good **w.**
Heb 6:10 not overlook your **w** and the love

WORKED → WORK
1Co 15:10 I **w** harder than any of them—
2Th 3: 8 toil and labor we **w** night and day,
2Jn 1: 8 you do not lose what we have **w** for,

WORKER → WORK
2Ti 2:15 a **w** who has no need to be ashamed,

WORKING → WORK
Jn 5:17 "My Father is still **w,** and I also am **w.**"
Gal 5: 6 that counts is faith **w** through love.

WORKS → WORK
Ps 8: 6 given them dominion over the **w**
46: 8 behold the **w** of the LORD;
92: 5 How great are your **w,** O LORD!
103: 6 The LORD **w** vindication and justice
Pr 31:31 let her **w** praise her in the city gates.
Ro 4: 6 whom God reckons righteous apart from **w:**
Gal 2:16 and not by doing the **w** of the law,
5:19 the **w** of the flesh are obvious:
Eph 2: 9 not the result of **w,** so that no one may boast.
2:10 created in Christ Jesus for good **w,**
1Ti 6:18 to do good, to be rich in good **w,**

GOOD WORKS Mt 5:16; Jn 10:32; Ac 9:36; Eph 2:10; 1Ti 2:10; 5:10, 25; 6:18; Tit 2:7; 3:8, 14; 2Es 8:36

WONDERFUL WORKS 1Ch 16:9, 12; Ps 105:2, 5; 106:7; 107:8, 15, 21, 31; 139:14

WORKS OF THE LAW Gal 2:16, 16, 16; 3:2, 5, 10, 12

WORLD → WORLDLY, WORLDS
1Ch 16:30 The **w** is firmly established; it shall never be moved.
Ps 9: 8 He judges the **w** with righteousness;
19: 4 and their words to the end of the **w.**
50:12 for the **w** and all that is in it is mine.
96:13 will judge the **w** with righteousness,
Isa 13:11 I will punish the **w** for its evil,
Mt 4: 8 all the kingdoms of the **w**
5:14 "You are the light of the **w.**
16:26 if they gain the whole **w** but forfeit their life?

Jn 1:10 yet the **w** did not know him.
1:29 the Lamb of God who takes away the sin of the **w!**
3:16 God so loved the **w** that he gave his only Son,
3:17 God did not send the Son into the **w** to condemn the **w,**
8:12 saying, "I am the light of the **w.**
9: 5 As long as I am in the **w,** I am the light of the **w.**"
15:19 therefore the **w** hates you.
16:33 courage; I have conquered the **w!**"
17:18 so I have sent them into the **w.**
18:36 "My kingdom is not from this **w.**
Ac 17:31 on which he will have the **w** judged
Ro 3:19 and the whole **w** may be held accountable to God.
5:12 just as sin came into the **w** through one man,
10:18 their words to the ends of the **w.**"
1Co 1:27 But God chose what is foolish in the **w** to shame the wise;
3:19 the wisdom of this **w** is foolishness with God.
6: 2 that the saints will judge the **w?**
2Co 5:19 in Christ God was reconciling the **w** to himself,
Gal 6:14 the **w** has been crucified to me, and I to the **w.**
1Ti 1:15 Christ Jesus came into the **w** to save sinners—
6: 7 we brought nothing into the **w,**
Heb 1: 6 he brings the firstborn into the **w,**
11: 7 by this he condemned the **w** and
11:38 of whom the **w** was not worthy.
Jas 1:27 to keep oneself unstained by the **w.**
4: 4 that friendship with the **w** is enmity with God?
4: 4 friend of the **w** becomes an enemy of God.
1Pe 1:20 before the foundation of the **w,**
1Jn 2: 2 but also for the sins of the whole **w.**
2:15 Do not love the **w** or the things in the **w.**
5: 4 that conquers the **w,** our faith.
Rev 11:15 "The kingdom of the **w** has become the kingdom of our Lord
13: 8 written from the foundation of the **w**

ALL THE WORLD Ge 19:31; 41:57; Mk 16:15; Lk 2:1; Ac 11:28; 22:15; 1Pe 5:9; Aza 1:9, 14; 2Mc 5:15

WHOLE WORLD Job 34:13; Isa 27:6; Da 6:25; Mt 16:26; 26:13; Mk 8:36; 14:9; Lk 9:25; Ro 3:19; Col 1:6; 1Jn 2:2; 5:19; Rev 3:10; 12:9; 16:14; Tob 14:6; Jdt 5:21; 10:19; 11:8, 16, 23; AdE 13:2; Wis 11:22; 17:20; 18:24; LtJ 6:62; Aza 1:22; 2Mc 3:12; 8:18; 3Mc 6:5; 2Es 10:8

WORLDLY → WORLD
Tit 2:12 to renounce impiety and **w** passions,

WORLDS* → WORLD
Heb 1: 2 through whom he also created the **w**
11: 3 the **w** were prepared by the word of God,

WORM → WORMS
Ps 22: 6 But I am a **w,** and not human;
Isa 41:14 Do not fear, you **w** Jacob,
Mk 9:48 where their **w** never dies,

WORMS → WORM
Ac 12:23 and he was eaten by **w** and died.

WORMWOOD
Am 5: 7 Ah, you that turn justice to **w,**
Rev 8:11 The name of the star is **W.**

WORRIED* → WORRY
Lk 10:41 Martha, you are **w** and distracted by many things;

Sir   6:30 Her **y** is a golden ornament,
      28:20 For its **y** is a **y** of iron,

YOKED → YOKE
Dt   22:10 not plow with an ox and a donkey **y**
             together.

YOUNG → YOUNGER, YOUNGEST,
YOUTH, YOUTHFUL, YOUTHS
Dt   22: 6 shall not take the mother with the **y**.
      32:25 for **y** man and woman alike,
Ru   2: 5 whom does this **y** woman belong?"
1Sa   2:17 the sin of the **y** men was very great
2Ch   10:14 with advice of the **y** men,
      36:17 had no compassion on **y** man or **y**
             woman,
Ps   37:25 I have been **y**, and now am old,
      78:63 Fire devoured their **y** men,
      119: 9 can **y** people keep their way pure?
Pr   7: 7 the youths, a **y** man without sense,
Ecc   11: 9 Rejoice, **y** man, while you are **y**,
La   1:18 my **y** women and **y** men have gone
             into captivity.
Da   1: 4 **y** men without physical defect and
       1:17 To these four **y** men God gave
             knowledge
Joel   2:28 and your **y** men shall see visions,
Mk   14:51 A certain **y** man was following him,
      16: 5 entered the tomb, they saw a **y** man,
Lk   2:24 of turtledoves or two **y** pigeons."
Ac   2:17 and your **y** men shall see visions,
       7:58 at the feet of a **y** man named Saul.
      20: 9 A **y** man named Eutychus,
1Jn   2:13 I am writing to you, **y** people,

YOUNG MAN Ge 4:23; 34:19; Nu 11:27; Dt
32:25; Jdg 8:14; 9:54, 54; 17:7, 11, 12; 19:19;
1Sa 9:2; 14:1, 6; 17:55, 58; 20:22; 30:13; 2Sa
1:5, 6, 13; 13:17, 34; 14:21; 18:5, 12, 29, 32,
32; 1Ki 11:28; 2Ki 9:4, 6; 2Ch 36:17; Pr 7:7;
Ecc 11:9; Isa 62:5; Jer 51:22; Zec 2:4; Mt
19:20, 22; Mk 14:51; 16:5; Lk 7:14; Ac 7:58;
20:9; 23:17, 18, 22; Tob 1:4; 5:5, 7, 10, 10;
6:1, 3, 4, 4, 6, 7, 11; 7:2; 8:1; Sus 1:21, 37, 40;
2Mc 7:25, 30; 1Es 1:53; 4:58; 2Es 2:43, 46

YOUNG MEN Ge 14:24; 22:3, 5, 19; Ex
24:5; Jos 6:23; Jdg 14:10; Ru 2:9, 9, 15; 3:10;
1Sa 2:17; 16:18; 21:2, 4, 5; 25:5, 5, 8, 8, 9, 12,
14, 19, 25, 27; 26:22; 30:17; 2Sa 1:15; 2:14,
21; 4:12; 13:32; 16:2; 18:15; 1Ki 12:8, 10, 14;
20:14, 15, 17, 19; 2Ki 8:12; 2Ch 10:8, 10, 14;
Job 29:8; Ps 78:63; 148:12; SS 2:3; Isa 13:18;
23:4; 31:8; Jer 6:11; 9:21; 11:22; 31:13; 48:15;
49:26; 50:30; 51:3; La 1:15, 18; 2:21; 5:13, 14;
Eze 9:6; 23:6, 12, 23; 30:17; Da 1:4, 10, 13,
15, 17; Joel 2:28; Am 4:10; 8:13; Zec 9:17; Ac
2:17; 5:6, 10; Jdt 2:27; 6:16; 7:22, 23; 10:9;
16:4, 6; 1Mc 1:26; 2Mc 3:26, 33; 4:12; 10:35;
12:27; 13:15; 1Es 1:53; 3:4, 16; 8:50; 2Es
10:22; 4Mc 8:5; 9:6; 14:9, 12, 20; 16:17

YOUNG WOMAN Ge 24:43; Dt 22:15, 16,
21, 23, 24, 26, 26; Ru 2:5; 4:12; 2Ch 36:17;
Isa 7:14; 62:5; 1Es 1:53

YOUNG WOMEN Jdg 12:9; 21:21, 21; Ru
2:8, 22, 23; 3:2; Est 2:8; Isa 23:4; Jer 31:13;
La 1:18; 2:21; 3:51; Eze 9:6; Am 8:13; Zec
9:17; Tit 2:4; 1Mc 1:26; 2Mc 3:19; 3Mc 1:18;
4:6

YOUNGER → YOUNG
Ge   19:35 and the **y** rose, and lay with him;
      25:23 the elder shall serve the **y**."
Ro   9:12 "The elder shall serve the **y**."
1Ti   5: 1 to **y** men as brothers,
       5: 2 to **y** women as sisters—with
             absolute purity.
       5:14 So I would have **y** widows marry,
             bear children,
1Pe   5: 5 **y** must accept the authority of the
             elders.

YOUNGEST → YOUNG
Ge   9:24 knew what his **y** son had done

      42:20 and bring your **y** brother to me.
Jos   6:26 and at the cost of his **y** he shall set
             up its gates!"
1Sa   17:14 David was the **y**; the three eldest
             followed Saul,
1Ki   16:34 and set up its gates at the cost of his
             y son Segub,
Lk   22:26 greatest among you must become
             like the **y**,

YOUTH → YOUNG
Ge   8:21 of the human heart is evil from **y**;
1Sa   17:33 he has been a warrior from his **y**."
Ps   71: 5 my trust, O LORD, from my **y**.
      103: 5 so that your **y** is renewed like
      144:12 May our sons in their **y** be like
             plants full grown,
Pr   2:17 who forsakes the partner of her **y**
       5:18 and rejoice in the wife of your **y**,
Ecc   4:13 a poor but wise **y** than an old but
             foolish king,
      11:10 for **y** and the dawn of life are vanity.
      12: 1 Remember your creator in the days
             of your **y**,
Isa   65:20 who dies at a hundred years will be
             considered a **y**,
Eze   16:60 with you in the days of your **y**,
Mal   2:14 a witness between you and the wife
             of your **y**,

YOUTHFUL → YOUNG
2Ti   2:22 Shun **y** passions and pursue
             righteousness,

YOUTHS → YOUNG
Pr   20:29 The glory of **y** is their strength,
Isa   40:30 Even **y** will faint and be weary,

Z

ZACCHAEUS
Lk   19: 2 A man was there named **Z**;

ZADOK
2Sa   15:27 The king also said to the priest **Z**,
1Ki   1:26 and the priest **Z**, and Benaiah
Ne   13:13 the scribe **Z**, and Pedaiah

ZALMON
Jdg   9:48 So Abimelech went up to Mount **Z**,
Ps   68:14 Almighty scattered kings there,
             snow fell on **Z**.

ZALMUNNA
Jdg   8: 5 and I am pursuing Zebah and **Z**,
Ps   83:11 all their princes like Zebah and **Z**,

ZAPHON
Jos   13:27 Beth-nimrah, Succoth, and **Z**,

ZAREPHATH
1Ki   17: 9 now to **Z**, which belongs to Sidon,
Lk   4:26 except to a widow at **Z** in Sidon.

ZEAL → ZEALOT, ZEALOUS
Nu   25:11 by manifesting such **z** among them
2Ki   10:16 and see my **z** for the LORD."
      19:31 The **z** of the LORD of hosts will do
             this.
Ps   69: 9 It is **z** for your house that has
             consumed me;
      119:139 My **z** consumes me
Isa   37:32 The **z** of the LORD of hosts will do
             this.
Jn   2:17 "**Z** for your house will consume me.
Ro   10: 2 testify that they have a **z** for God,
      12:11 Do not lag in **z**, be ardent in spirit,
2Co   7:11 what longing, what **z**,
Php   3: 6 as to **z**, a persecutor of the church;
1Mc   2:26 Thus he burned with **z** for the law,

ZEALOT·→ ZEAL
Lk   6:15 and Simon, who was called the **Z**,
Ac   1:13 and Simon the **Z**, and Judas son of
2Mc   4: 2 and a **z** for the laws.

ZEALOUS → ZEAL
Nu   25:13 because he was **z** for his God,
1Ki   19:10 "I have been very **z** for the LORD,
      19:14 "I have been very **z** for the LORD,
Ac   21:20 and they are all **z** for the law.
Gal   1:14 I was far more **z** for the traditions
1Mc   2:27 "Let every one who is **z** for the law

ZEBAH
Jdg   8: 5 and I am pursuing **Z** and Zalmunna,
Ps   83:11 their princes like **Z** and Zalmunna,

ZEBEDEE
Mt   4:21 in the boat with their father **Z**,
      26:37 Peter and the two sons of **Z**,
Mk   1:20 they left their father **Z** in the boat
      10:35 James and John, the sons of **Z**,
Lk   5:10 sons of **Z**, who were partners with
             Simon.

ZEBOIIM
Dt   29:23 Admah and **Z**,
Hos   11: 8 How can I treat you like **Z**?

ZEBUL
Jdg   9:30 When **Z** the ruler of the city heard

ZEBULUN
Son of Jacob by Leah (Ge 30:20; 35:23; 1Ch
2:1). Tribe of blessed (Ge 49:13; Dt 33:18-19),
numbered (Nu 1:31; 26:27), allotted land (Jos
19:10-16; Eze 48:26), failed to fully possess (Jdg
1:30), supported Deborah (Jdg 4:6-10; 5:14, 18),
David (1Ch 12:33), 12,000 from (Rev 7:8).
TRIBE OF ZEBULUN Nu 1:31; 2:7; 10:16;
13:10; Jos 19:10, 16; 21:7, 34; Jdg 4:6; 1Ch
6:77; Rev 7:8

ZECHARIAH
1. Son of Jeroboam II; king of Israel (2Ki 15:8-
12).
2. Post-exilic prophet who encouraged rebuilding of temple (Ezr 5:1; 6:14; Zec 1:1).

ZEDEKIAH → =MATTANIAH
1. False prophet (1Ki 22:11-24; 2Ch 18:10-23).
2. Mattaniah, son of Josiah (1Ch 3:15), made
king of Judah by Nebuchadnezzar (2Ki 24:17-
25:7; 2Ch 36:10-14; Jer 37-39; 52:1-11).

ZEEB
Jdg   7:25 captains of Midian, Oreb and **Z**;
Ps   83:11 Make their nobles like Oreb and **Z**,

ZELOPHEHAD
Nu   26:33 Now **Z** son of Hepher had no sons,
             but daughters:
Jos   17: 3 **Z** son of Hepher son of Gilead

ZEPHANIAH
Prophet; descendant of Hezekiah (Zep 1:1).

ZERUBBABEL
Descendant of David (1Ch 3:19; Mt 1:3). Led
return from exile (Ezr 2:2; Ne 7:7). Governor of
Israel; helped rebuild altar and temple (Ezr 3;
Hag 1-2; Zec 4).

ZERUIAH
2Sa   2:18 The three sons of **Z** were there,
             Joab, Abishai, and Asahel.

ZEUS
Ac   14:12 Barnabas they called **Z**,
2Mc   6: 2 to call it the temple of Olympian **Z**,

ZIBA
2Sa   9: 2 servant of the house of Saul whose
             name was **Z**,
      16: 1 **Z** the servant of Mephibosheth met
             him,

ZIKLAG

1Sa 27: 6 So that day Achish gave him **Z;**
    30: 1 They had attacked **Z,** burned it down,
    30:26 When David came to **Z,** he sent part

ZILPAH

Servant of Leah, mother of Jacob's sons Gad and Asher (Ge 30:9-12; 35:26, 46:16-18).

ZIMRI

King of Israel (1Ki 16:9-20).

ZIN

Nu 13:21 and spied out the land from the wilderness of **Z**

ZION

2Sa 5: 7 David took the stronghold of **Z,**
2Ki 19:31 from Mount **Z** a band of survivors.
Ps 2: 6 "I have set my king on **Z,** my holy hill."
    9:11 Sing praises to the LORD, who dwells in **Z.**
    14: 7 O that deliverance for Israel would come from **Z!**
    48: 2 is the joy of all the earth, Mount **Z,**
    50: 2 Out of **Z,** the perfection of beauty,
    65: 1 Praise is due to you, O God, in **Z;**
    74: 2 Remember Mount **Z,** where you came to dwell.
    78:68 Mount **Z,** which he loves.
    87: 2 the LORD loves the gates of **Z** more
    102:13 rise up and have compassion on **Z,**
    137: 3 "Sing us one of the songs of **Z!**"
SS 3:11 Look, O daughters of **Z,** at King Solomon,
Isa 1:27 **Z** shall be redeemed by justice,
    2: 3 For out of **Z** shall go forth instruction,

    14:32 "The LORD has founded **Z,**
    28:16 I am laying in **Z** a foundation stone,
    40: 9 Get you up to a high mountain, O **Z,**
    51: 3 For the LORD will comfort **Z;**
    51:11 and come to **Z** with singing;
    52: 1 awake, put on your strength, O **Z!**
    52: 8 the return of the LORD to **Z.**
Jer 50: 5 They shall ask the way to **Z,**
La 2:13 that I may comfort you, O virgin daughter **Z?**
Joel 2: 1 Blow the trumpet in **Z;**
    3:16 The LORD roars from **Z,**
    3:21 for the LORD dwells in **Z.**
Am 1: 2 The LORD roars from **Z,**
    6: 1 Alas for those who are at ease in **Z,**
Mic 3:12 because of you **Z** shall be plowed as a field;
    4: 2 For out of **Z** shall go forth instruction,
Zec 1:17 the LORD will again comfort **Z**
    9: 9 Rejoice greatly, O daughter **Z!**
Mt 21: 5 "Tell the daughter of **Z,** Look, your king is coming to you, humble,
Ro 9:33 in **Z** a stone that will make people stumble,
    11:26 "Out of **Z** will come the Deliverer;
Heb 12:22 But you have come to Mount **Z** and
1Pe 2: 6 "See, I am laying in **Z** a stone,
Rev 14: 1 the Lamb, standing on Mount **Z!**
Sir 24:10 and so I was established in **Z.**
2Es 10:44 The woman whom you saw is **Z,**

DAUGHTER ZION 2Ki 19:21; Ps 9:14; Isa 1:8; 10:32; 16:1; 37:22; 52:2; 62:11; Jer 4:31; 6:2, 23; La 1:6; 2:1, 4, 8, 10, 13, 18; 4:22; Mic 1:13; 4:8, 10, 13; Zep 3:14; Zec 2:10; 9:9; Mt 21:5; Jn 12:15

MOUNT ZION 2Ki 19:31; Ps 48:2, 11; 74:2; 78:68; 125:1; Isa 4:5; 8:18; 10:12; 18:7; 24:23; 29:8; 31:4; 37:32; La 5:18; Joel 2:32; Ob 1:17,

21; Mic 4:7; Heb 12:22; Rev 14:1; Jdt 9:13; 1Mc 4:37, 60; 5:54; 6:48, 62; 7:33; 10:11; 14:27; 2Es 2:42; 13:35

ZIPH → ZIPHITES

1Sa 23:14 hill country of the Wilderness of **Z.**

ZIPHITES → ZIPH

1Sa 23:19 some **Z** went up to Saul at Gibeah
    26: 1 Then the **Z** came to Saul at Gibeah,

ZIPPOR

Nu 22: 4 Balak son of **Z** was king of Moab at that time.

ZIPPORAH*

Daughter of Reuel; wife of Moses (Ex 2:21-22; 4:20-26; 18:1-6).

ZIV

1Ki 6: 1 in the month of **Z,** which is the second month,

ZOAN

Ps 78:43 and his miracles in the fields of **Z.**

ZOAR

Ge 19:22 Therefore the city was called **Z.**
    19:30 Now Lot went up out of **Z**

ZOBAH

1Sa 14:47 against the kings of **Z,** and against the Philistines;
1Ch 18: 3 David also struck down King Hadadezer of **Z,**

ZOPHAR*

One of Job's friends (Job 2:11; 11; 20; 42:9).

ZORAH

Jdg 13: 2 There was a certain man of **Z,**